THE EUROPEAN FOOTBALL YEARBOOK 2015/16

General Editor
Mike Hammond

The only authoritative annual on the European game

**Further copies of The European Football Yearbook 2015/16
are available from:
www.carltonbooks.co.uk
hotline number +44 (0) 141 306 3100**

The European Football Yearbook 2015/16

First published by Carlton Books Ltd, England in 2015

Printed by mpress ltd, England

ISBN 978-1 78097 692 1

UEFA – the Union of European Football Associations – is the governing body of football on the continent of Europe. UEFA's core mission is to promote, protect and develop European football at every level of the game, to promote the principles of unity and solidarity, and to deal with all questions relating to European football.

UEFA is an association of associations based on representative democracy, and is the governing body of European football.

UEFA
Route de Genève 46
Case postale
CH-1260 Nyon 2
Switzerland

Tel: +41 (0) 848 00 2727
Web: UEFA.com

Media Desk
Tel: +41 (0) 848 04 2727

All views expressed in the European Football Yearbook do not necessarily reflect those of UEFA. Every effort has been made to ensure the accuracy of the data in the European Football Yearbook, official and unofficial.

Front cover image: Gerard Piqué is watched by celebrating FC Barcelona team-mates as he lifts the UEFA Champions League trophy in Berlin

**The European Football Yearbook 2012/13, 2013/14 and 2014/15
are available from:
www.calmproductions.com
orders@calmproductions.com
UK hotline 0845 408 2606**

THE EUROPEAN FOOTBALL YEARBOOK 2015 16

General Editor
Mike Hammond

Assistant Editor
Jesper Krogshede Sørensen

Nation-by-nation
Correspondents and Researchers
Nikolai Belov (Russia), Sílvia Casals (Andorra), José Del Olmo (Spain), Sean DeLoughry (Republic of Ireland), Tamás Dénes (Hungary), Mike Farrugia (Malta), Arno Funck (Luxembourg), Stoyan Georgiev (Bulgaria), GFT (Julian Fortuna, Aaron Payas, Sean Mascarenhas, Ryan Gonzalez) (Gibraltar), Marshall Gillespie (Northern Ireland), Clas Glenning (France, Sweden), Miron Goihman (Moldova), Elia Gorini (San Marino), Marcel Haisma (Netherlands), Michael Hansen (Denmark), Romeo Ionescu (Romania), Mikael Kirakosyan (Armenia), Jesper Krogshede Sørensen (Faroe Islands, Italy), Fuad & Fedja Krvavac (Bosnia & Herzegovina), Zdeněk Kučera (Czech Republic), Ambrosius Kutschera (Austria), Almantas Laužadis (Lithuania), Tarmo Lehiste (Estonia), Dag Lindholm (Norway), Ewan Macdonald (Scotland), Ivica Madžarović (Montenegro), Erlan Manashev (Kazakhstan), Goran Mancevski (FYR Macedonia), Rasim Mövsümov (Azerbaijan), Giovanni Nappi (Albania), Kazimierz Oleszek (Poland), Olexandr Pauk (Belarus, Ukraine), Luca Pelliccioni (San Marino), Humberto Pereira Silva (Portugal), Dmitri Portnov (Latvia), Ivan Reić (Croatia), Mike Ritter & Silvia Schäfer (Germany), Grega Sever (Slovenia), Revaz Shengelia (Georgia), Vídir Sigurdsson (Iceland), Erdinç Sivritepe (Turkey), Dušan Stamenković (Serbia), Edouard Stutz (Switzerland), Matej Széher (Slovakia), Mel Thomas (Wales), Vesa Tikander (Finland), Serge Van Hoof (Belgium), Victor Vassallo (Malta), Georgios J Vassalos (Greece), Jacob Zelazo (Cyprus, Israel); additional assistance Charlie Hammond and Gabriel Mantz

Photography
Getty Images, Sportsfile, Getty Images/AFP, Getty Images/Bongarts, Action Images; additional assistance Domenic Aquilina, Agencja Gazeta, Rustam Hajiyev, Alex Klein, N. KUSTURA/www.avaz.ba, LSA Photo, Dobrilo Malidzan, Pruccoli/FSGC, Rafał Rusek/Pressfocus, Smiles 'n' More Photography, Tonči Vlašić

UEFA
Project management
David Farrelly
Editorial
John Atkin, Richard Binks, Sam Crompton, Wayne Harrison, Michael Harrold, Patrick Hart, Andrew Haslam, Tom Kell, Paul Saffer, James Wirth
Data
Andy Lockwood, Rob Esteva, Jim Agnew

Production
Print
m press ltd, England; Cliff Moulder
Distribution
Carlton Books Ltd; Martin Corteel, Jim Greenhough
Design
Keith Jackson
Graphics
Mikhail Sipovich
Data extraction
deltatre (Antonio Bellissimo, Stefano Strignano, Carlo Bruno, Marco Aimone Chiorat)

Foreword
Luis Enrique

National three-letter codes

There are many instances throughout the European Football Yearbook where country names are abbreviated using three-letter codes. These codes are shown below, listed alphabetically by nation and divided into Europe and the Rest of the World.

Europe

ALB	Alb	Albania
AND	And	Andorra
ARM	Arm	Armenia
AUT	Aut	Austria
AZE	Aze	Azerbaijan
BLR	Blr	Belarus
BEL	Bel	Belgium
BIH	Bih	Bosnia & Herzegovina
BUL	Bul	Bulgaria
CRO	Cro	Croatia
CYP	Cyp	Cyprus
CZE	Cze	Czech Republic
DEN	Den	Denmark
ENG	Eng	England
EST	Est	Estonia
FRO	Fro	Faroe Islands
FIN	Fin	Finland
FRA	Fra	France
GEO	Geo	Georgia
GER	Ger	Germany
GIB	Gib	Gibraltar
GRE	Gre	Greece
HUN	Hun	Hungary
ISL	Isl	Iceland
ISR	Isr	Israel
ITA	Ita	Italy
KAZ	Kaz	Kazakhstan
LVA	Lva	Latvia
LIE	Lie	Liechtenstein
LTU	Ltu	Lithuania
LUX	Lux	Luxembourg
MKD	Mkd	Former Yugoslav Republic of Macedonia
MLT	Mlt	Malta
MDA	Mda	Moldova
MNE	Mne	Montenegro
NED	Ned	Netherlands
NIR	Nir	Northern Ireland
NOR	Nor	Norway
POL	Pol	Poland
POR	Por	Portugal
IRL	Irl	Republic of Ireland
ROU	Rou	Romania
RUS	Rus	Russia
SMR	Smr	San Marino
SCO	Sco	Scotland
SRB	Srb	Serbia
SVK	Svk	Slovakia
SVN	Svn	Slovenia
ESP	Esp	Spain
SWE	Swe	Sweden
SUI	Sui	Switzerland
TUR	Tur	Turkey
UKR	Ukr	Ukraine
WAL	Wal	Wales

Rest of the World

AFG	Afg	Afghanistan
ALG	Alg	Algeria
ANG	Ang	Angola
ATG	Atg	Antigua & Barbuda
ARG	Arg	Argentina
AUS	Aus	Australia
BAH	Bah	Bahamas
BHR	Bhr	Bahrain
BAN	Ban	Bangladesh
BRB	Brb	Barbados
BEN	Ben	Benin
BER	Ber	Bermuda
BOL	Bol	Bolivia
BOT	Bot	Botswana
BRA	Bra	Brazil
BFA	Bfa	Burkina Faso
BDI	Bdi	Burundi
CMR	Cmr	Cameroon
CAN	Can	Canada
CPV	Cpv	Cape Verde Islands
CAY	Cay	Cayman Islands
CTA	Cta	Central African Republic
CHA	Cha	Chad
CHI	Chi	Chile
CHN	Chn	China
COL	Col	Colombia
COM	Com	Comoros
CGO	Cgo	Congo
COD	Cod	Congo DR
CRC	Crc	Costa Rica
CUB	Cub	Cuba
CUW	Cuw	Curacao
DJI	Dji	Djibouti
DOM	Dom	Dominican Republic
ECU	Ecu	Ecuador
EGY	Egy	Egypt
SLV	Slv	El Salvador
EQG	Eqg	Equatorial Guinea
ETH	Eth	Ethiopia
FIJ	Fij	Fiji
GAB	Gab	Gabon
GAM	Gam	Gambia
GHA	Gha	Ghana
GRN	Grn	Grenada
GUM	Gum	Guam
GUA	Gua	Guatemala
GUI	Gui	Guinea
GNB	Gnb	Guinea-Bissau
GUY	Guy	Guyana
HAI	Hai	Haiti
HON	Hon	Honduras
HKG	Hkg	Hong Kong
IND	Ind	India
IDN	Idn	Indonesia
IRN	Irn	Iran
IRQ	Irq	Iraq
CIV	Civ	Ivory Coast
JAM	Jam	Jamaica
JPN	Jpn	Japan
JOR	Jor	Jordan
KEN	Ken	Kenya
KUW	Kuw	Kuwait
KGZ	Kgz	Kyrgyzstan

LIB	Lib	Lebanon
LBR	Lbr	Liberia
LBY	Lby	Libya
MAD	Mad	Madagascar
MWI	Mwi	Malawi
MAS	Mas	Malaysia
MLI	Mli	Mali
MTQ	Mtq	Martinique
MTN	Mtn	Mauritania
MRI	Mri	Mauritius
MEX	Mex	Mexico
MSR	Msr	Montserrat
MAR	Mar	Morocco
MOZ	Moz	Mozambique
NAM	Nam	Namibia
ANT	Ant	Netherlands Antilles
NCL	Ncl	New Caledonia
NZL	Nzl	New Zealand
NIG	Nig	Niger
NGA	Nga	Nigeria
PRK	Prk	North Korea
OMA	Oma	Oman
PAK	Pak	Pakistan
PLE	Ple	Palestine
PAN	Pan	Panama
PAR	Par	Paraguay
PER	Per	Peru
PHI	Phi	Philippines
PUR	Pur	Puerto Rico
QAT	Qat	Qatar
RWA	Rwa	Rwanda
STP	Stp	Sao Tome & Principe
KSA	Ksa	Saudi Arabia
SEN	Sen	Senegal
SLE	Sle	Sierra Leone
SIN	Sin	Singapore
SOL	Sol	Solomon Islands
SOM	Som	Somalia
RSA	Rsa	South Africa
KOR	Kor	South Korea
SKN	Skn	St Kitts & Nevis
VIN	Vin	St Vincent & Grenadines
SDN	Sdn	Sudan
SUR	Sur	Surinam
SYR	Syr	Syria
TAH	Tah	Tahiti
TJK	Tjk	Tajikistan
TAN	Tan	Tanzania
THA	Tha	Thailand
TOG	Tog	Togo
TRI	Tri	Trinidad & Tobago
TUN	Tun	Tunisia
TKM	Tkm	Turkmenistan
UGA	Uga	Uganda
UAE	Uae	United Arab Emirates
USA	Usa	United States
URU	Uru	Uruguay
UZB	Uzb	Uzbekistan
VEN	Ven	Venezuela
VIE	Vie	Vietnam
YEM	Yem	Yemen
ZAM	Zam	Zambia
ZIM	Zim	Zimbabwe

Contents

THE EUROPEAN FOOTBALL YEARBOOK 2015 2016

Foreword

It gives me great pleasure to write the foreword for this edition of the European Football Yearbook. I know that to do so is a tradition for the coach of the UEFA Champions League winners, and I am delighted to follow in the footsteps of those outstanding coaches and managers who have preceded me over the years.

The 2014/15 season, my first as the head coach of FC Barcelona, could hardly have reached a more fulfilling conclusion. We set ourselves several goals at the start of the season and thanks to a mixture of endeavour, commitment and skill from everyone involved, we were able to achieve all of our objectives. The statistics show that this was one of Barcelona's best seasons.

Winning the Liga and Copa del Rey was a source of great satisfaction for me and everyone associated with this magnificent club, but even those extraordinary achievements were eclipsed for many by our success in the UEFA Champions League.

The night of triumph in Berlin's Olympiastadion is one I shall treasure for as long as I live, and I am sure the same goes for all the players, the coaching staff, the club's administrators and, of course, all the Barça fans – not only the thousands present in the Olympiastadion but also the millions spread across the world.

Winning the treble is a rare feat, and for Barcelona to become the first club to do it twice in the entire 60-year history of Europe's premier club competition is an accomplishment of which the club is extremely proud. It goes without saying that I am overjoyed to have replicated what Pep Guardiola achieved in 2008/09.

In the last ten years FC Barcelona has been the most successful football club in the world; these players are so hungry for more. I feel honoured and privileged to have been given the opportunity to work with some of the most talented and dedicated footballers in the world, and I look forward very much to continuing our collaboration and pursuing new goals in

2015/16. Becoming the first team to make a successful defence of the UEFA Champions League is of course high on our list of priorities.

For now, though, the wonderful memories of our 2014/15 campaign are still fresh, and it is a pleasure to see the happy faces of my players celebrating with club football's most coveted trophy on the front cover of this book.

As ever, the European Football Yearbook is the complete archive of the past season, and the stories and statistics contained in these pages will last forever – just like the happy memories of a successful football club.

Luis Enrique
Head coach
FC Barcelona
UEFA Champions League winners
2014/15

Introduction

From the General Editor

To readers old and new - a warm welcome to the 2015/16 edition of the European Football Yearbook.

This is the 28th year that I have worked on the publication – more than half of my life – but the pride and satisfaction I get from putting it together is still considerable, especially when the response from those of you who purchase, read and refer to it is so positive and encouraging.

The months of June and, especially, July may have become something of an annual blur as the race intensifies and the pressure increases to have everything written, laid out, checked, double-checked and triple-checked before the printer gets to work in early August, but the summer overtime is worth every minute when, firstly, I see the finished product and, secondly, the emails of appreciation and congratulation begin to flow into my inbox.

As my own biggest critic, and someone who has always believed in, and been guided by, the pursuit of perfection, it is very gratifying to be told that I have 'nailed it'. That was how one long-standing reader in Sweden succinctly passed his verdict on last year's edition.

I'm not sure whether it was Mr Bergström's use of a contemporary English-language colloquialism to express his thoughts that was so impressive, but his comment stayed with me – to the extent that I am quoting it here.

My reason for bringing it up is that his viewpoint was reflective of many others that I received in response to the 2014/15 Yearbook and, as a consequence, I am pleased to report that this latest edition is virtually unchanged from last year's in terms of its content structure, layout and style.

As you read these words you will notice that the object in your hands is, once again, a satisfyingly weighty tome of 752 glossy pages, all of them in full colour. It is designed to feel good and look good, but above all we hope that the content within, which seeks to provide an in-depth, all-bases-covered review of the past European football season – and one you won't find in such detail anywhere else – does its job and gives you many hours of pleasure as you dip in and out of the various chapters or, as I know some aficionados do, read it systematically from cover to cover.

This being a UEFA.com-backed publication, you will find comprehensive coverage of all the competitions organised by European football's governing body, with particular focus of course on the UEFA Champions League, UEFA Europa League and the European Qualifiers for next summer's main event in France, UEFA EURO 2016.

The various youth and futsal competitions are also included, while this year we have added a chapter on the UEFA Regions' Cup, the biennial tournament for amateur teams, and also expanded our coverage of women's football with squads, appearances and goals for their Under-19 and Under-17 final tournaments.

The Top 100 Players of the Season chapter, one of the most thumbed-through sections of the Yearbook, has a slight design modification this year but stays otherwise as it was, albeit of course with a different selection of players – some familiar, others included for the first time.

The nation-by-nation section, made up of separate chapters on all 54 UEFA member associations, is the midfield engine-room of the Yearbook, its meticulously-researched, at-a-glance, all-in-one-place statistical content saving you endless hours of internet-surfing, while its narrative reviews provide concise summaries of all the main points of interest and achievements in each country.

The Yearbook closes by looking forward to the new season with a handy dates-for-your-diary guide to all the major UEFA events scheduled for 2015/16. Also listed here are the groups for the 2018 FIFA World Cup European Qualifiers, as drawn at the end of July in the Russian city of St Petersburg, plus the qualifying fixtures for the Women's EURO 2017 in the Netherlands.

I look forward very much to hearing your views and comments on this 2015/16 edition. Have we 'nailed it' again? Please let me know on mike.hammond@uefa.ch.

＊ ＊ ＊ ＊ ＊

I would like to thank everyone who has contributed to this edition of the European Football Yearbook. A full list of acknowledgements appears on page five.

Special gratitude goes to UEFA, and particularly David Farrelly, for lending their generous and indispensable support to this long-running project, while it is safe to say that the Yearbook would not be what it is without the beyond-the-call-of-duty efforts of my two faithful associates – eagle-eyed assistant editor Jesper and ever-dependable designer Keith.

On an additional personal note, and at the risk of repeating myself from last year, thank you to my beloved Leicester City. Being a football fan brings a roller-coaster of emotions, generally with more troughs than peaks, but sometimes, as with that amazing Great Escape in the final two months of the 2014/15 season, it can be an unforgettable joyride.

And finally, my loving thanks, as always, to Sue, Rebecca and Charlie.

Mike Hammond
1 August, 2015

2014/15 season summary

The contrasting fortunes of Germany and Spain at the 2014 FIFA World Cup finals were put forward by some as an indication that the power balance of European football was shifting. But if the 2014/15 season was anything to go by, talk of all-conquering Spain being on the wane was a little premature.

When the UEFA Champions League final was played in Berlin's Olympiastadion on 6 June, there was only one German player involved – FC Barcelona goalkeeper Marc-André ter Stegen – and the way the Catalan club's celebrated South American attacking trident of Luis Suárez, Lionel Messi and Neymar tore into Juventus in that glorious 3-1 victory provided persuasive evidence that Spanish clubs remain the teams to beat in Europe.

That had already been strongly suggested when Sevilla FC defeated FC Dnipro Dnipropetrovsk 3-2 in the final of the UEFA Europa League in Warsaw, becoming in the process the first side to win the competition back-to-back, the first to win the trophy for a fourth time (UEFA Cup included) and – perhaps more significantly – the first club to qualify directly for the UEFA Champions League group stage as UEFA Europa League winners.

Consolation of a kind for Germany came as 1. FFC Frankfurt overcame Paris Saint-Germain in the final of the UEFA Women's Champions League, although that success was perhaps overshadowed by subsequent disappointments. Star striker Célia Šašić announced her retirement – at the age of just 27 – after the national team were eliminated in the semi-finals of the FIFA Women's World Cup in Canada, and a Germany side featuring Ter Stegen were demolished 5-0 by Portugal in the semi-finals of the UEFA European Under-21 Championship in the Czech Republic.

Spain's continuing strength was demonstrated as they claimed European titles at women's Under-17 and men's Under-19 levels but, conversely, they failed to reach the Under-21 finals, a tournament they had won in 2011 and 2013, while Barcelona were relieved of the UEFA Futsal Cup at the final tournament in Lisbon when Kazakhstan's Kairat Almaty overcame the holders 3-2 to reclaim the title they had won two years earlier.

England boasts one of the most powerful domestic leagues in Europe, but its most tangible continental achievement in 2014/15 was arguably Chelsea FC's success in the UEFA Youth League – the competition for European clubs' elite development sides. Portugal, meanwhile, were expected to run away with the U21 final, but it didn't work out that way, Sweden defeating them on penalties to claim the trophy for the first time. Further success for Sweden followed in Israel as they became European champions at women's Under-19 level, defeating Spain in the final.

The qualifying campaign for the first 24-team UEFA European Championship, to be staged in France in the summer of 2016, provided an intriguing, if surprising, snapshot of the state of the European international game. Of the teams topping their respective qualifying groups at the summer break - Iceland, Wales, Slovakia, Poland, England, Romania, Austria, Croatia and Portugal – only two represented top-ten ranked associations in terms of UEFA coefficients.

While the world knows the names of the game's top stars, the unpredictability of football may be part of what keeps fans coming back. An estimated global TV audience of 180 million in over 200 territories tuned in to the UEFA Champions League final, and UEFA.com attracted 104 million visits in 2014/15, including two million on the day of the final in Berlin – both significant increases on the previous season.

The interest in European and international football has never been greater, and the following 113 pages provide comprehensive narrative, statistical and pictorial round-ups of all the UEFA competitions played in 2014/15, kicking off overleaf with the story of how Barcelona reclaimed their crown as kings of the European club game.

Barcelona triumph in Berlin

For the fourth time in ten seasons, the UEFA Champions League was won by FC Barcelona, the Catalan club claiming their fifth European Cup triumph overall at the expense of Juventus, who thus became the first club to lose six finals.

Champions of Europe for the first time in 1992, Barcelona joined FC Bayern München and Liverpool FC on five titles with a 3-1 success at the Berlin Olympiastadion. Goals from Ivan Rakitić and – after Álvaro Morata had equalised – Luis Suárez and Neymar secured a victory that gave Barcelona their second treble of Liga, Copa del Rey and UEFA Champions League as coach Luis Enrique emulated Josep Guardiola's feat of six years previously by capturing all three trophies during his first season in charge.

Barça's journey to the German capital began slowly as a narrow home win against APOEL FC preceded a defeat at Paris Saint-Germain, but that loss was the catalyst for a run of nine straight victories. The sequence included three against the French champions and, for the second campaign running, two against Manchester City FC in the round of 16. Guardiola returned to his spiritual

home with his Bayern team for the semi-final, but unanswered goals in the last 13 minutes at the Camp Nou from Lionel Messi (two) and Neymar effectively settled the tie.

Barcelona's Berlin opponents were a Juve side making their first final appearance since 2003 and also seeking a treble, having added a first Coppa Italia since 1995 to their fourth consecutive Serie A triumph. Massimiliano Allegri's men had ousted Borussia Dortmund, AS Monaco FC and holders Real Madrid CF en route, with Morata getting the decisive semi-final goal against his former club, but Barcelona proved a bridge too far.

Madrid were irresistible in the autumn, winning all six group games and equalling Bayern's competition record with a tenth straight success, at FC Schalke 04 in the round of 16 first leg. While a 4-3 home defeat in the return did not halt the progress of Carlo Ancelotti's troops, they won just one of four matches thereafter, edging past 2014 runners-up Club Atlético de Madrid in the last eight before losing 3-2 on aggregate to Juventus. There was also semi-final heartache for Bayern, who had put seven goals past both AS Roma

and FC Shakhtar Donetsk before overturning a 3-1 quarter-final first-leg deficit against FC Porto with a 6-1 masterclass in Munich.

Paris knocked Chelsea FC out in the round of 16 thanks to an impressive second-leg effort in London with ten men but fell in the quarter-finals for the third year in a row, while Arsenal FC suffered a fourth straight last-16 exit and Manchester City's elimination by Barcelona at the same stage meant that, for the second time in three years, no English representatives were present in the last eight.

Group stage highlights included Shakhtar's Luiz Adriano scoring eight goals against FC BATE Borisov, Francesco Totti becoming the competition's oldest marksman, and Xavi Hernández overtaking Raúl González as its leading appearance maker. The long-serving Barça midfielder then beat Madrid's Iker Casillas to become the first man to play 150 UEFA Champions League games before enjoying the perfect finale to his Azulgrana career as he lifted club football's most coveted trophy in Berlin.

Qualifying rounds

The honour of scoring the first goal of the 2014/15 UEFA Champions League went to Andorran international Marc Pujol, whose fifth-minute strike on 1 July 2014 gave FC Santa Coloma a home victory against FC Banants, which set up a dramatic away goals win after a 3-3 aggregate draw. FC Levadia Tallinn and HB Tórshavn were the other two sides to progress from the first qualifying round, the latter seeing off Gibraltar's inaugural participants, Lincoln FC.

Among the entries for the second qualifying round were AC Sparta Praha, Celtic FC, FK Partizan, FC Steaua București and GNK Dinamo Zagreb, all of whom made comfortable progress, whereas FC BATE Borisov needed away goals to beat Albania's KF Skënderbeu. In the next round, however, Partizan were derailed by Bulgarian champions PFC Ludogorets Razgrad, while Aalborg BK ousted Dinamo Zagreb and Sparta were defeated by Malmö FF.

Celtic were given a lucky reprieve against Legia Warsawa, who fielded an ineligible player late in a second leg that they initially won 2-0 to complete a 6-1 aggregate success; instead the Scottish champions were awarded a 3-0 win and therefore progressed thanks to Callum McGregor's first-leg goal in Poland. Respite was brief, however, as NK Maribor earned a shock 2-1 play-off win over the Glasgow club to reach the group stage for the first time in 15 years.

Malmö had never previously made it that far, but two Markus Rosenberg goals secured an aggregate win against FC Salzburg, making them the first Swedish group stage qualifiers since 2000. A debut appearance was also claimed by Ludogorets, for whom defender Cosmin Moți went in goal after regular keeper Vladislav Stoyanov's red card and promptly saved two Steaua penalties in the shoot-out.

Athletic Club returned for the first time since 1998 by scoring three times in the last half-hour at home to SSC Napoli, while Arsenal FC edged out Beşiktaş JK 1-0 with a goal from new signing Alexis Sánchez. In contrast, APOEL FC, BATE, FC Zenit, Bayer 04 Leverkusen and FC Porto all enjoyed relatively serene progress.

6

Madrid became just the sixth team to win all six group stage fixtures and the first club to do it twice. The other four sides with perfect group records are Milan (1992/93), Paris (1994/95), Spartak Moskva (1995/96) and Barcelona (2002/03). None of these clubs – nor indeed Madrid on either occasion – went on to lift the trophy.

Group stage

Malmö were drawn in **Group A**, alongside Club Atlético de Madrid, Juventus and Olympiacos FC, and although they beat Olympiacos 2-0 in their first home game, those would be the Swedish champions' only points. Indeed, all three teams were level after matchday two, with Olympiacos surprisingly beating Atlético prior to their defeat in Sweden and Diego Simeone's side bouncing back by overcoming Juventus, themselves victors against Malmö on opening night thanks to two goals from Carlos Tévez, the Argentinian striker's first in the competition for five years.

Atlético, however, soon pulled away at the top. Arda Turan's 75th-minute half-volley against Juve secured the first of four straight victories – including a 5-0 home demolition of Malmö in which Koke provided four assists – and a goalless draw in Turin on matchday six confirmed the Spanish side as the winners of the section.

The identity of the second qualifiers was not settled until matchday six. Olympiacos, with Roberto enjoying an inspired evening in goal, beat Juventus 1-0 in Piraeus but lost 3-2 in Turin two weeks later, Paul Pogba scoring the crucial winner for the Bianconeri before Roberto saved a late Arturo Vidal penalty to give his team a head-to-head advantage. Massimiliano Allegri's side took control of their own destiny, however, with a 2-0 win at Malmö while Olympiacos were losing 4-0 in Madrid – where Mario Mandžukić scored a hat-trick – and the stalemate at home to Atlético proved enough to secure second place, with Olympiacos having to settle for third.

Malmö striker Markus Rosenberg (centre) holds off Salzburg's André Ramalho in the clubs' play-off tie

Goalmouth action in the Group C encounter between Monaco and Benfica

Group B was dominated by Real Madrid, who started with a 5-1 home win against FC Basel 1893 and never let up. Cristiano Ronaldo had scored a record nine goals in the 2013/14 group stage, and he struck again in five of Madrid's six games, the exception being a 1-0 home win over Liverpool FC on matchday four that was decided by Karim Benzema.

Madrid's perfect record left Basel, Liverpool and debutants Ludogorets playing for second place. Although Liverpool opened with a 2-1 home win over the Bulgarian champions, they only sneaked victory thanks to Steven Gerrard's penalty three minutes into added time, and on matchday two they were beaten 1-0 in Basel, the Swiss side bouncing back from their loss in Madrid thanks to a goal from skipper Marco Streller.

Liverpool's hopes were further dented by home and away defeats to Madrid, the first at Anfield proving particularly painful as a superb strike by Ronaldo and two more from Benzema settled the outcome by half-time, while the points in the other double-header were shared as Basel lost 1-0 at Ludogorets – Yordan Minev's 92nd-minute winner giving Bulgaria its first group stage points – before thrashing them 4-0 at home. A subsequent 2-2 draw between Ludogorets and Liverpool meant elimination for the Bulgarian club and a must-win final-day fixture at Anfield for Brendan Rodgers' side. Fabian Frei gave Basel a deserved 25-minute lead, and Lazar Marković's red card early in the second period left Liverpool with a mountain to climb. They gave it their best shot, with Gerrard equalising from a free-kick on what would turn out to be his final appearance in the competition, but Basel, so often the slayers of Premier League giants, survived a late siege and went through.

Group C was closely contested, with AS Monaco FC, in their first European campaign since 2004/05, taking first place thanks to their excellent defence, which conceded just once in their six fixtures. Leonardo Jardim's side managed only four goals of their own, but that proved enough for them to finish above Bayer 04 Leverkusen, FC Zenit and SL Benfica. The Ligue 1 side collected five points from their first three

games without conceding and, despite a 1-0 loss at Benfica – the Portuguese champions' sole win – a second 1-0 victory against Bayer 04 Leverkusen and a 2-0 home win over FC Zenit completed the job.

Leverkusen responded to their opening 1-0 loss at Monaco with three wins in a row, beating Benfica 3-1 and Zenit 2-0 at home and 2-1 away. That proved sufficient to take the German club into the next round prior to kick-off at home to Monaco on matchday five, with Zenit having completed the double over Benfica earlier in the evening. André Villas-Boas's side needed to win their final game, in the Stade Louis II, to get through at their hosts' expense, but second-half strikes from Monaco defenders Aymen Abdennour and Fabinho sent the Russian club into the UEFA Europa League, while Leverkusen surrendered group leadership to Monaco with a goalless draw at Benfica, whose fate as the group's bottom club had already been sealed.

Borussia Dortmund and Arsenal were drawn together in **Group D**. It was the second season running, and the third time in four years, that the pair had faced each other in the group stage. That experience proved invaluable as they cruised through at the expense of RSC Anderlecht, who finished third, and a Galatasaray AŞ team that garnered just a single point. That came from a 1-1 draw against Anderlecht on matchday one before Cesare Prandelli's side subsequently conceded four goals in each of their next three matches, against Arsenal in London – where new recruit Danny Welbeck scored the first hat-trick of his career – and home and away to Dortmund.

The 2-0 loss at Anderlecht on matchday five signalled the end for Prandelli and confirmed Galatasaray's fourth place in the standings. The Belgian champions also managed three draws to finish on six points, their undoubted highlight a remarkable recovery from 3-0 down to rescue a point at Arsenal. Two weeks earlier, in Brussels, Anderlecht had conceded twice late on to the same opponents to lose a game they should have won, so revenge was especially sweet as defender Anthony Vanden Borre scored twice in the final 30 minutes before Aleksandar Mitrović headed in a 90th-minute equaliser.

That result ultimately cost Arsenal first place, Arsène Wenger's side finishing level on 13 points with a Dortmund side going through a disastrous run in the Bundesliga. In contrast to the previous season, when Dortmund had won in London and Arsenal triumphed in Germany, this time each side won their home game 2-0 as well as defeating Galatasaray twice and collecting four points from Anderlecht. A 1-1 draw in Brussels on matchday six, while Arsenal were again beating Galatasaray 4-1 in a match embellished by an astonishing long-range strike from Aaron Ramsey, was enough for Dortmund to finish top on goal difference.

FC Bayern München, Manchester City FC and PFC CSKA Moskva were also drawn together for the second year in a row, alongside AS Roma in **Group E**. The German champions would win it at a canter, Josep Guardiola's side claiming victories in five of their six games and clinching first place with two matches to spare.

Bayern began slowly, beating City 1-0 with a late deflected goal from the English club's former defender Jérôme Boateng, then CSKA by the same scoreline in Russia, before hitting form spectacularly with a 7-1 win at Roma, five of their goals coming in a scintillating first-half performance.

KEY FACT

77

The first of Lionel Messi's three goals for Barcelona – his fifth hat-trick in the competition, also a record – against APOEL on matchday five made him the UEFA Champions League's all-time top scorer, eclipsing the record of 71 strikes he shared with Raúl González. The Argentinian international ended the campaign on 77, level with Cristiano Ronaldo.

The Giallorossi had started well, dismantling CSKA 5-1 before earning a 1-1 draw at City, in which Francesco Totti – three days after his 38th birthday – replaced Ryan Giggs as the UEFA Champions League's oldest scorer. However, two defeats by Bayern placed Rudi Garcia's team in peril, and their cause was further dented by Vasili Berezutski's last-gasp equaliser for CSKA on matchday five.

That set up a win-or-bust meeting on matchday six with City, who had taken just one point from their two games with CSKA – losing with nine men in Manchester after allowing a two-goal lead to slip in Khimki – but came from behind to beat Bayern 3-2 thanks to a majestic hat-trick from Sergio Agüero. Despite the absence through injury of their star striker for the visit to Rome, City's confidence was sufficiently buoyed for them to stun the large crowd in the Stadio Olimpico and claim a famous 2-0 win, Samir Nasri's sublime opener being supplemented late on by Pablo Zabaleta as CSKA's 3-0 defeat in Munich enabled Manuel Pellegrini's side to go through as group runners-up with eight points.

The matchday six showdown in **Group F** came at the Camp Nou as FC Barcelona hosted Paris Saint-Germain to determine which team would finish first, both clubs having already booked their places in the round of 16. The French champions held the edge having beaten Barça 3-2 in an epic matchday two contest, but Luis Enrique's charges ultimately proved too strong, running out 3-1 winners on home turf despite an opener for the visitors from ex-Barça striker Zlatan Ibrahimović, who had missed the first meeting through injury. For the first time, Barcelona's three forwards Lionel Messi, Neymar and Luis Suárez all found the net in the same match; it would not be the last.

Suárez had opened his Barcelona account with the first goal in a 4-0 win at APOEL on matchday five, a game more notable for a Messi hat-trick – with all three goals, unusually, coming from his right foot – that took him on to 74 UEFA Champions League goals, surpassing Raúl González's competition record. Messi scored in each of the last five group games, registering eight in total, with defender Gerard Piqué having grabbed the only goal against APOEL (from a Messi assist) on matchday one.

Paris finished with 13 points, two behind Barcelona but eight ahead of AFC Ajax, with whom they drew 1-1 in Amsterdam on matchday one. The Dutch champions finished third in their group for the fifth year in a row, while APOEL's sole point came via a 1-1 home draw with Ajax in their second fixture, three of their five defeats coming by a 1-0 margin.

Group G looked set to be tightly contested when both matchday one fixtures, between Chelsea FC and FC Schalke 04 at Stamford Bridge and Maribor and Sporting Clube de Portugal at the Stadion Ljudski vrt, ended 1-1, but early appearances proved deceptive. Instead Chelsea ran away with it, dropping points again only at Maribor on

Lionel Messi (centre) is joined in celebration by Pedro after completing his hat-trick against APOEL

matchday four to win the group by six points, scoring 17 goals in the process – the most of any of the 32 teams.

José Mourinho's side were joined in the knockout phase by Schalke, who collected just two points from their first two fixtures and then traded high-scoring home wins with Sporting. A 5-0 humbling by Chelsea in Gelsenkirchen – on a particularly painful evening for new coach Roberto Di Matteo against the team he led to victory in 2012 – meant that Sporting went into the final round of fixtures with a two-point advantage over Schalke. However, while Sporting were losing 3-1 at Stamford Bridge, Max Meyer's second-half strike brought Schalke the victory they needed at Maribor. The Slovenian side's first home defeat enabled the German club to leapfrog Sporting and bring the Lisbon club's first UEFA Champions League campaign since 2007 to an early end.

FC Porto set the tone for **Group H** early on, opening with a pulsating 6-0 home win against FC BATE Borisov, in which Algerian midfielder Yacine Brahimi became the seventh player to mark his UEFA Champions League debut with a hat-trick. The Portuguese side, who had won only one group game in 2013/14, confirmed their resurgence when Jackson Martínez scored two late goals to rescue a 2-2 draw at FC Shakhtar Donetsk.

Two wins against Athletic, and a 3-0 victory at BATE, confirmed first place for Julen Lopetegui's side before they closed their group campaign with a 1-1 draw at home to second-placed Shakhtar. The Ukrainian champions had also bowed out early the previous year, but Luiz Adriano's record-equalling nine group stage goals were the foundation of their campaign, the Brazilian scoring five in the 7-0 victory at BATE on matchday three and another three in a 5-0 home

Shakhtar's Luiz Adriano scores his fifth, and his team's seventh, goal from the penalty spot away to BATE

win two weeks later. That made him the first player to score hat-tricks in consecutive UEFA Champions League games and only the second – after Messi – to register five goals in one game.

BATE ended up conceding 24 goals, a group stage record, with their sole highlight a 2-1 home win against Athletic. The Bilbao club had held Shakhtar 0-0 on matchday one but their next points did not arrive until their fifth outing, when they posted a 2-0 victory in Ukraine. That was followed by a 2-0 home win against BATE, which secured the consolation prize of a UEFA Europa League berth.

Round of 16

The round of 16 draw threw up three ties that had been played in the previous season's knockout phase, with Barcelona taking on Manchester City and Real Madrid meeting Schalke – both repeats of last-16 ties – and Chelsea renewing acquaintance with a Paris side they had beaten in the quarter-finals. While Barcelona and Madrid would repeat their 2014 victories, there was to be a significant change of script for Chelsea and Paris.

The English club had retrieved a two-goal first-leg deficit to win on away goals the previous season, and they looked set for an encore against Laurent Blanc's side

when the first leg, again staged at the Parc des Princes, finished 1-1. Branislav Ivanović and Edinson Cavani traded headed goals in a match that the home side dominated, yet the advantage was Chelsea's as the tie resumed across the Channel three weeks later.

The balance further tipped against the Ligue 1 champions at Stamford Bridge when Ibrahimović was dismissed on 31 minutes, and Chelsea looked to be heading through when Gary Cahill gave them an 81st-minute lead. Five minutes later, however, their former defender David Luiz – who had moved to Paris the previous summer – headed home to take the game into extra time. Chelsea regained the upper hand when Thiago Silva was penalised for handball and Eden Hazard slotted in the penalty, but Paris were not finished. With six minutes remaining, Silva's towering header from another corner made it 3-3 on aggregate, and this time the away goals rule favoured Paris.

Madrid looked on course for a straightforward qualification as a goal in each half from Cristiano Ronaldo and Marcelo gave them a 2-0 first-leg victory away to Schalke, where they had won 6-1 a year earlier. Ronaldo added two more to his tally at the Santiago Bernabéu, but both were equalisers after Christian Fuchs and former Madrid striker Klaas-Jan

Huntelaar had twice given Schalke the lead. Benzema's 53rd-minute strike might have finished them off, but further goals from 19-year-old debutant Leroy Sané (57) and Huntelaar (84) put Schalke within one more goal of dumping the holders out. Madrid just managed to hang on, but the Bernabéu crowd showed their dissatisfaction at the final whistle by jeering the team from the field.

Barcelona, meanwhile, had Suárez to thank for a repeat of their first-leg victory at the City of Manchester Stadium, the former Liverpool striker scoring twice in the first half to put the visitors in command. Agüero's second-half effort coupled with Joe Hart's last-minute penalty save from Messi gave City a glimmer of hope heading to the Camp Nou, but Ivan Rakitić's 31st-minute strike was to settle the outcome on a night notable above all else for a magnificently defiant goalkeeping display from Hart. City's only hope came and went when Agüero missed a 78th-minute penalty.

England's third surviving representatives, Arsenal, were aiming to reach a first quarter-final since 2009/10 but fell behind at home to Monaco through Geoffrey Kondogbia's deflected 38th-minute strike in the visitors' first meaningful attack. Former Tottenham Hotspur FC striker Dimitar Berbatov marked his return to north London with Monaco's second eight minutes into the second half, and although Alex Oxlade-Chamberlain pulled one back a minute into added time, the Gunners' desperation for an equaliser allowed Monaco to grab a third goal in the last play of the game, Yannick Ferreira Carrasco racing clear on the counter to leave Arsène Wenger's side staring at another last-16 elimination.

Arsenal travelled to the Stade Louis II, Wenger's former place of employment, looking to make UEFA Champions League history by becoming the first side to overturn a home first-leg defeat of more than one goal, but despite dominating throughout they were to fall fractionally short. Olivier Giroud and Aaron Ramsey both struck to leave Arsenal needing one more goal, but they failed to find it, and a relieved Monaco edged through to the quarter-finals for the first time since finishing runners-up in 2004.

Juventus also produced a stirring second-leg showing away from home, winning 3-0 at Dortmund thanks to two goals from Tévez – his first a brilliant

KEY FACT

19

Real Madrid featured in the knockout phase for a record 19th time. They have never failed to progress from the group stage and in 2014/15 stretched their record run to 18 consecutive knockout phase appearances. The next best-placed clubs in that category are Arsenal (12) and Barcelona (11), both of whose sequences are also ongoing.

long-range effort – and an assist for Álvaro Morata. The margin of defeat was Dortmund's heaviest in the UEFA Champions League, while Tévez's two goals gave him six in eight appearances for the season – the same number he had managed in his previous 33. Furthermore, it catapulted Juve into the last eight for the second time in three years, Tévez and Morata having also scored in a 2-1 first-leg win.

The Atlético-Leverkusen tie proved to be considerably closer, Hakan Çalhanoğlu scoring a fine goal to decide a tight first leg in Germany. In the Vicente Calderón return, the defences were again on top, but Mario Suárez's deflected first-half effort took the tie to extra time and,

ultimately, penalties. Leverkusen had never won a round of 16 tie – their progress to the 2002 final had come via two group stages – and shoot-out misses from Hakan, Ömer Toprak and Stefan Kiessling extended that miserable run despite Raúl García and Koke also failing from the spot for Atlético.

It looked as if the ties between Shakhtar and Bayern and Basel and Porto might be equally tight after each of the first legs ended in a draw, but they would be anything but. Shakhtar held Bayern 0-0 at the Arena Lviv, but their hopes of a similar result in Munich were effectively ended when Olexandr Kucher collected the fastest red card in UEFA Champions League history in conceding the penalty from which Thomas Müller gave Bayern a fourth-minute lead. Müller got his second goal of the night seven minutes after the interval, by which time Bayern were already 3-0 up, Boateng and Franck Ribéry having added to that early breakthrough. Bayern, however, refused to let up and piled on further misery through Holger Badstuber, Robert Lewandowski and Mario Götze, thus equalling the record for the biggest knockout win in the competition, Bayern's own 7-0 success against Basel in 2012.

Basel were bidding to reach the quarter-finals for the first time, and

Atlético keeper Jan Oblak makes a save in the penalty shoot-out against Leverkusen

Paulo Sousa's side made a promising start against Porto when Derlis González fired them into an early lead at St Jakob-Park, but Porto, who themselves had not figured in the last eight since 2009, levelled through Danilo's penalty in the 79th minute. In the return, Brahimi's 14th-minute effort put Porto ahead in the tie and Basel were to be undone by three more top-quality goals after the interval, Héctor Herrera making it 3-1 on aggregate in the 47th minute before spectacular long-range strikes from Casemiro and Vincent Aboubakar crowned an impressive home display.

Quarter-finals

Paired with Bayern in the last eight, Porto again delivered the goods at home, recording a richly deserved 3-1 victory in the first leg. Bayern, eyeing a fourth straight appearance in the semi-finals, had not lost in 11 previous fixtures in Portugal, but with their defence, especially goalkeeper Manuel Neuer, looking uncharacteristically shaky all evening, they were on the back foot throughout at the Estádio do Dragão. Ricardo Quaresma profited from defensive errors to score twice in the first ten minutes before Thiago Alcántara gave the visitors a foothold with his first UEFA Champions League strike. Jackson Martínez, though, skilfully restored Porto's two-goal cushion to leave Bayern – shorn of several key players including Arjen Robben, David Alaba, Bastian Schweinsteiger and Ribéry – facing an uphill struggle.

Having never previously overturned a two-goal first-leg away defeat in UEFA competition, Bayern's hopes of a fourth successive semi-final appearance were in serious jeopardy, but Guardiola's charges bristled with intent from the outset in Munich. They were level on aggregate before a quarter of the match had elapsed, Thiago and Boateng heading them into a two-goal lead on the night. Lewandowski added two more either side of Müller's deflected effort to make it 5-0 at half-time, and although Martínez scored for Porto and then almost grabbed a second shortly afterwards to induce some alarm, Bayern eventually cruised through, Xabi Alonso making the final score 6-1 with a late free-kick.

Barcelona's winning run continued, their prospects of a seventh semi-final in eight

Real Madrid's Javier Hernández celebrates his late quarter-final winner in the Bernabéu against Atlético

years receiving a notable boost in the first leg of their quarter-final tie as they ended PSG's nine-year, 33-match unbeaten home run in Europe with a 3-1 victory. Neymar gave Barça an early lead before Suárez stole the Brazilian's thunder with two glorious goals in 13 second-half minutes. The first came from the right as he cut into the box, nutmegging David Luiz and outmuscling Maxwell before firing inside the near post. With 11 minutes to go he scored again, playing a one-two with Javier Mascherano, then once more slipping the ball between Luiz's legs before curling a sumptuous finish into the top corner.

Jérémy Mathieu's own goal did little to take the gloss off Barcelona's first-leg triumph, and Luis Enrique's side picked up where they had left off at the Camp

Nou. While Paris were hurried whenever they had possession, the Catalan club looked to have all the time in the world to run the visitors' back line ragged. Two goals from Neymar – the first a gem set up by Andrés Iniesta's brilliant slalom run from the halfway line – meant the job was done by the 34th minute, inflicting a third straight last-eight elimination on their opponents.

The remaining two quarter-finals were both settled by a single goal. Neither Atlético nor Real Madrid, the two finalists from the previous season, were able to force a breakthrough in a lively first leg at the Vicente Calderón, although it took a fine display from Jan Oblak in the Atlético goal to deny the visitors, who had not beaten their city rivals in the teams' previous six meetings of the season.

It was a similar story a week later at the Santiago Bernabéu, where, with the clock ticking down, the tie looked set to become just the third in UEFA Champions League history to finish goalless after 180 minutes. Madrid were without Bale and Benzema through injury in addition to long-term absentee Luka Modrić, but the contest swung their way when Atlético midfielder Arda Turan collected his second yellow card 14 minutes from time. With two minutes remaining, the holders finally made the

breakthrough, Javier Hernández turning a loose ball into the empty net following Cristiano Ronaldo's burst into the penalty area to fire Madrid into a fifth straight semi-final.

The Juventus-Monaco tie also finished 1-0, the only goal coming in the first leg in Turin where Monaco's winless run in Italy stretched to seven games. Arturo Vidal scored it, confidently converting a penalty 12 minutes into the second half after Morata had been clumsily floored by Ricardo Carvalho. Juve duly held out for a goalless draw at the Stade Louis II to reach their first semi-final since 2003.

Semi-finals

The semi-final draw, featuring four of Europe's most prestigious and successful clubs, kept Barcelona and Real Madrid apart, but intriguingly it put Bayern boss Guardiola up against ex-club Barça for the first time as an opposition coach. Juventus, meanwhile, were set the task of ousting the holders in a battle between the record champions of Italy and Spain.

In a pulsating first half at the Camp Nou, Guardiola appeared to have got his tactics wrong as Barcelona bossed the game, with Bayern having cause to be grateful to goalkeeper Neuer, who saved one-on-ones with Suárez and Neymar to keep the scoreline blank at the break. Lewandowski had spurned an equally presentable opening for the visitors, yet just when it was starting to look as if Bayern would escape unscathed in an increasingly fractious encounter, up stepped the brilliant Messi – on his 100th European appearance – to change the game and the tie. The Argentinian maestro put Barcelona ahead 13 minutes from time, beating Neuer at his near post with a crisp left-foot shot. Not long afterwards he made it 2-0, his sublime control and body movement putting Boateng on the floor before his deft right-footed chip left Neuer helpless again. As Bayern pressed to reduce the arrears in the closing seconds, Messi hit them again, his pass releasing Neymar to roll in a third.

Barça's late salvo gave Bayern only a minimal chance of turning the tie around in Munich, and although they made the perfect start when Medhi Benatia headed them into a seventh-minute lead, home hopes were effectively extinguished by two clinical goals from

Álvaro Morata (right) beats Iker Casillas to score a crucial away goal for Juventus in Madrid

Neymar, both set up by the unselfish Suárez. Lewandowski made it 2-2 on the night with a brilliant equaliser, and Müller's 74th-minute strike halted Barça's 18-game unbeaten streak in all competitions, but the Blaugrana had already booked their place in Berlin – for their eighth European Cup final – with something to spare.

The other semi-final was more delicately poised after the first leg, Tévez's second-half penalty giving Juventus the edge in Turin. Juve, who had beaten Madrid on their last semi-final appearance 12 years before, delighted the home fans with a vibrant start that brought early reward as Morata struck from close range against the club he left in 2014, but Madrid levelled before the half-hour with Cristiano Ronaldo's ninth UEFA Champions League goal of the season and 76th overall as the Portuguese superstar headed in James

Rodríguez's perfectly-flighted cross. Juve, however, regained the initiative through Tévez's spot kick two minutes before the hour, the Argentinian picking himself up after a clumsy trip by Daniel Carvajal to beat Iker Casillas from the spot.

Madrid, bidding to become the first side to make a successful defence of the trophy in the UEFA Champions League era, were on top from the outset at the Santiago Bernabéu, and they gained due reward midway through the first half as James won a penalty, conceded by Giorgio Chiellini, that Ronaldo slotted in. Carlo Ancelotti's side continued to look the likelier scorers throughout the opening period, but Juve responded strongly after half-time and Morata again reminded Madrid of the talent they had let go, firing the visitors level shortly before the hour. Madrid failed to clear Andrea Pirlo's free-kick and Paul Pogba's powerful leap knocked the ball on to Morata, who shot down and in past Casillas. Thereafter some typically determined defending from the newly re-crowned Italian champions carried them through to their eighth European Cup final – and first since 2003.

Final

After an epic and engrossing season, hopes were high for the final showdown at the Berlin Olympiastadion – and Barcelona and Juventus did not disappoint.

The game began at breakneck speed and Juve, pressing their opponents hard and deep from the first whistle, might have scored twice inside the first ten minutes, Pogba falling to connect with a header and Vidal firing over. By then, however, the Bianconeri were behind, undone by a typical Barcelona move. Messi's sweeping crossfield pass to Jordi Alba wrong-footed the Juve defence before Neymar turned the ball inside to Andrés Iniesta. The Barça skipper then touched it into the path of Ivan Rakitić, and the Croatian's left-foot strike did the rest.

One-nil down already and things could have got even worse for Juve soon afterwards, with Neymar shooting just too high before an astounding reaction save from Gianluigi Buffon. The 37-year-old looked to have been sent the wrong way by Dani Alves's shot, but he stuck out a left hand to parry and then had a touch of fortune as Messi's follow-up header landed on the roof of the net.

A Juve defence lacking the injured Chiellini was being worked overtime by Barcelona's inventive attack, but Allegri's men did finally gain a foothold in the game. Pogba, an increasingly prominent presence, would have picked out Morata but for a crucial Javier Mascherano interception, while Morata curled an effort past the post as Juve pressed high. Barça, however, were equally adept at pressuring the Juventus defence, and they came within a whisker of extending their lead before half-time as Suárez's shot flicked the outside of Buffon's post.

Four minutes after the interval, Buffon was called on again, after Barcelona had broken at lightning speed. Rakitić slid in Suárez, but the Juve keeper stood tall and blocked at the near post. Suárez and Messi then both fired just too high as Barça threatened to take command. Instead, to considerable surprise, the next goal came from the team in black and white. Claudio Marchisio was the architect, his clever back-heel playing in Stephan Lichtsteiner down the right. The full-back's cross allowed Tévez to turn Piqué, and although Marc-André ter Stegen blocked the shot, the ball fell for Morata, who made no mistake.

Now it was Barcelona having to defend, with Tévez shooting just too high and Pogba straight at Ter Stegen, but once again the pendulum swung back the other way – and in decisive fashion. Sixty-eight minutes had elapsed when Messi picked up the ball on the halfway

5

Berlin was a fifth UEFA Champions League final for both Barça and Juventus, matching the feat of Bayern. The record number of participations still belongs to Milan, with six. Juve became the first side to lose six European Cup finals having previously been level with Bayern and Benfica on five losses.

line, drove forward and worked enough space for his left foot to unleash a shot that Buffon could only parry. With the Juve defenders caught off balance, Suárez pounced to lash the loose ball into the roof of the net and put Barça back in front.

Neymar then had an effort chalked off as his header past Buffon was diverted in off his hand, before Piqué just cleared the bar with a fierce effort after great work from Rakitić. At 2-1 the door remained ajar for Juve, but Roberto Pereyra lost his footing at the crucial moment and Marchisio's effort was turned behind by Ter Stegen.

With Juve piling forward in the closing minutes, Barcelona found openings on the counter-attack and finally clinched the title with the final kick of the evening. Pedro Rodríguez, who had just come on as a substitute, unselfishly played in Neymar on the left, and the Brazilian's unerring finish – which placed him as the season's joint top scorer, alongside Messi and Ronaldo, on ten goals – supplied the final coat of gloss to a gleaming and glorious UEFA Champions League final.

With the last kick of the game Neymar prepares to strike Barcelona's third goal in the final against Juventus

First qualifying round

01/07/14, Estadi Comunal, Andorra la Vella
FC Santa Coloma 1-0 FC Banants
08/07/14, FFA Academy Stadium, Yerevan
FC Banants 3-2 FC Santa Coloma
Aggregate: 3-3; FC Santa Coloma qualify on away goals.

01/07/14, San Marino Stadium, Serravalle
SP La Fiorita 0-1 FC Levadia Tallinn
08/07/14, Kadriorg, Tallinn
FC Levadia Tallinn 7-0 SP La Fiorita
Aggregate: 8-0; FC Levadia Tallinn qualify.

02/07/14, Victoria Stadium, Gibraltar
Lincoln FC 1-1 HB Tórshavn
08/07/14, Tórsvøllur, Torshavn
HB Tórshavn 5-2 Lincoln FC
Aggregate: 6-3; HB Tórshavn qualify.

Second qualifying round

15/07/14, Ta' Qali National Stadium, Ta' Qali
Valletta FC 0-1 Qarabağ FK
22/07/14, Tofiq Bährramov Republican stadium, Baku
Qarabağ FK 4-0 Valletta FC
Aggregate: 5-0; Qarabağ FK qualify.

15/07/14, Štadión Pasienky, Bratislava
ŠK Slovan Bratislava 1-0 The New Saints FC
22/07/14, Belle Vue, Rhyl
The New Saints FC 0-2 ŠK Slovan Bratislava
Aggregate: 0-3; ŠK Slovan Bratislava qualify.

15/07/14, KR-völlur, Reykjavik
KR Reykjavík 0-1 Celtic FC
22/07/14, Murrayfield, Edinburgh
Celtic FC 4-0 KR Reykjavík
Aggregate: 5-0; Celtic FC qualify.

15/07/14, NK Zrinjski, Mostar
HŠK Zrinjski 0-0 NK Maribor
23/07/14, Stadion Ljudski vrt, Maribor
NK Maribor 2-0 HŠK Zrinjski
Aggregate: 2-0; NK Maribor qualify.

15/07/14, Solitude, Belfast
Cliftonville FC 0-0 Debreceni VSC
22/07/14, Debrecen Stadion, Debrecen
Debreceni VSC 2-0 Cliftonville FC
Aggregate: 2-0; Debreceni VSC qualify.

15/07/14, Borisov Arena, Borisov
FC BATE Borisov 0-0 KF Skënderbeu
22/07/14, Skënderbeu, Korca
KF Skënderbeu 1-1 FC BATE Borisov
Aggregate: 1-1; FC BATE Borisov qualify on away goal.

15/07/14, Estadi Comunal, Andorra la Vella
FC Santa Coloma 0-1 Maccabi Tel-Aviv FC
22/07/14, Antonis Papadopoulos, Larnaca
Maccabi Tel-Aviv FC 2-0 Santa Coloma
Aggregate: 3-0; Maccabi Tel-Aviv FC qualify.

15/07/14, Stadionul Sheriff, Tiraspol
FC Sheriff 2-0 FK Sutjeska
22/07/14, Gradski, Niksic
FK Sutjeska 0-3 FC Sheriff
Aggregate: 0-5; FC Sheriff qualify.

15/07/14, Nacionalna Arena Filip II Makedonski, Skopje
FK Rabotnicki 0-0 HJK Helsinki
23/07/14, Helsinki Football Stadium, Helsinki
HJK Helsinki 2-1 FK Rabotnicki
Aggregate: 2-1; HJK Helsinki qualify.

Maccabi Tel-Aviv's Gal Alberman is stalked by FC Santa Coloma's Joel Martínez (right)

15/07/14, Stadion Letná, Prague
AC Sparta Praha 7-0 FC Levadia Tallinn
22/07/14, Kadriorg, Tallinn
FC Levadia Tallinn 1-1 AC Sparta Praha
Aggregate: 1-8; AC Sparta Praha qualify.

15/07/14, Stadion FK Partizan, Belgrade
FK Partizan 3-0 HB Tórshavn
22/07/14, Tórsvøllur, Torshavn
HB Tórshavn 1-3 FK Partizan
Aggregate: 1-6; FK Partizan qualify.

15/07/14, Stadion Maksimir, Zagreb
GNK Dinamo Zagreb 2-0 VMFD Žalgiris
22/07/14, LFF, Vilnius
VMFD Žalgiris 0-2 GNK Dinamo Zagreb
Aggregate: 0-4; GNK Dinamo Zagreb qualify.

16/07/14, Malmö New Stadium, Malmo
Malmö FF 0-0 FK Ventspils
23/07/14, Ventspils Olimpiskais Centrs, Ventspils
FK Ventspils 0-1 Malmö FF
Aggregate: 0-1; Malmö FF qualify.

16/07/14, Marienlyst, Drammen
Strømsgodset IF 0-1 FC Steaua Bucureşti
23/07/14, Arena Naţională, Bucharest
FC Steaua Bucureşti 2-0 Strømsgodset IF
Aggregate: 3-0; FC Steaua Bucureşti qualify.

16/07/14, Ludogorets Arena, Razgrad
PFC Ludogorets Razgrad 4-0 F91 Dudelange
22/07/14, Jos Nosbaum, Dudelange
F91 Dudelange 1-1 PFC Ludogorets Razgrad
Aggregate: 1-5; PFC Ludogorets Razgrad qualify.

16/07/14, Stadion Wojska Polskiego, Warsaw
Legia Warszawa 1-1 Saint Patrick's Athletic FC
23/07/14, Tallaght Stadium, Dublin
Saint Patrick's Athletic FC 0-5 Legia Warszawa
Aggregate: 1-6; Legia Warszawa qualify.

16/07/14, Boris Paichadze Erovnuli Stadioni, Tbilisi
FC Dinamo Tbilisi 0-1 FC Aktobe
23/07/14, Tsentralniy, Aktobe
FC Aktobe 3-0 FC Dinamo Tbilisi
Aggregate: 4-0; FC Aktobe qualify.

Third qualifying round

29/07/14, Stadion Letná, Prague
AC Sparta Praha 4-2 Malmö FF
06/08/14, Malmö New Stadium, Malmo
Malmö FF 2-0 AC Sparta Praha
Aggregate: 4-4; Malmö FF qualify on away goals.

29/07/14, Štadión Pasienky, Bratislava
ŠK Slovan Bratislava 2-1 FC Sheriff
06/08/14, Stadionul Sheriff, Tiraspol
FC Sheriff 0-0 ŠK Slovan Bratislava
Aggregate: 1-2; ŠK Slovan Bratislava qualify.

29/07/14, Debrecen Stadion, Debrecen
Debreceni VSC 1-0 FC BATE Borisov
05/08/14, Borisov Arena, Borisov
FC BATE Borisov 3-1 Debreceni VSC
Aggregate: 3-2; FC BATE Borisov qualify.

30/07/14, Helsinki Football Stadium, Helsinki
HJK Helsinki 2-2 APOEL FC
06/08/14, GSP Stadium, Nicosia
APOEL FC 2-0 HJK Helsinki
Aggregate: 4-2; APOEL FC qualify.

30/07/14, Antonis Papadopoulos, Larnaca
AEL Limassol FC 1-0 FC Zenit
06/08/14, Stadion Petrovski, St Petersburg
FC Zenit 3-0 AEL Limassol FC
Aggregate: 3-1; FC Zenit qualify.

30/07/14, NSK Olimpiyskyi, Kyiv
FC Dnipro Dnipropetrovsk 0-0 FC København
06/08/14, FC København Stadium, Copenhagen
FC København 2-0 FC Dnipro Dnipropetrovsk
Aggregate: 2-0; FC København qualify.

30/07/14, Stadion Letzigrund, Zurich
Grasshopper Club Zürich 0-2 LOSC Lille
05/08/14, Grand Stade Lille Métropole, Villeneuve d'Ascq
LOSC Lille 1-1 Grasshopper Club Zürich
Aggregate: 3-1; LOSC Lille qualify.

30/07/14, Tsentralniy, Aktobe
FC Aktobe 2-2 FC Steaua Bucureşti
06/08/14, Arena Naţională, Bucharest
FC Steaua Bucureşti 2-1 FC Aktobe
Aggregate: 4-3; FC Steaua Bucureşti qualify.

30/07/14, Feijenoord Stadion, Rotterdam
Feyenoord 1-2 Beşiktaş JK
06/08/14, Atatürk Olimpiyat Stadium, Istanbul
Beşiktaş JK 3-1 Feyenoord
Aggregate: 5-2; Beşiktaş JK qualify.

30/07/14, Stade Maurice Dufrasne, Liege
R. Standard de Liège 0-0 Panathinaikos FC
05/08/14, Apostolos Nikolaidis, Athens
Panathinaikos FC 1-2 R. Standard de Liège
Aggregate: 1-2; R. Standard de Liège qualify.

30/07/14, Aalborg Stadion, Aalborg
Aalborg BK 0-1 GNK Dinamo Zagreb
06/08/14, Stadion Maksimir, Zagreb
GNK Dinamo Zagreb 0-2 Aalborg BK
Aggregate: 1-2; Aalborg BK qualify.

30/07/14, Tofiq Bährramov Republican stadium, Baku
Qarabağ FK 2-1 FC Salzburg
06/08/14, Stadion Salzburg, Salzburg
FC Salzburg 2-0 Qarabağ FK
Aggregate: 3-2; FC Salzburg qualify.

30/07/14, Stadion Ljudski vrt, Maribor
NK Maribor 1-0 Maccabi Tel-Aviv FC
05/08/14, Antonis Papadopoulos, Larnaca
Maccabi Tel-Aviv FC 2-2 NK Maribor
Aggregate: 2-3; NK Maribor qualify.

30/07/14, Stadion Wojska Polskiego, Warsaw
Legia Warszawa 4-1 Celtic FC
06/08/14, Murrayfield, Edinburgh
Celtic FC 3-0(f) Legia Warszawa
Aggregate: 4-4; Celtic FC qualify on away goal.

30/07/14, Ludogorets Arena, Razgrad
PFC Ludogorets Razgrad 0-0 FK Partizan
06/08/14, Stadion FK Partizan, Belgrade
FK Partizan 2-2 PFC Ludogorets Razgrad
Aggregate: 2-2; PFC Ludogorets Razgrad qualify on away goals.

Play-offs

19/08/14, Stadion Salzburg, Salzburg
FC Salzburg 2-1 Malmö FF
Goals: 1-0 Schiemer 16, 2-0 Jonatan Soriano 54, 2-1 Forsberg 90
27/08/14, Malmö New Stadium, Malmo
Malmö FF 3-0 FC Salzburg
Goals: 1-0 Rosenberg 11(p), 2-0 Eriksson 19, 3-0 Rosenberg 84
Aggregate: 4-2; Malmö FF qualify.

19/08/14, FC København Stadium, Copenhagen
FC København 2-3 Bayer 04 Leverkusen
Goals: 0-1 Kiessling 5, 1-1 M Jørgensen 9, 2-1 Amartey 13, 2-2 Bellarabi 31, 2-3 Son 42
27/08/14, BayArena, Leverkusen
Bayer 04 Leverkusen 4-0 FC København
Goals: 1-0 Son 2, 2-0 Hakan Çalhanoğlu 7, 3-0 Kiessling 31(p), 4-0 Kiessling 65
Aggregate: 7-2; Bayer 04 Leverkusen qualify.

19/08/14, Stadio San Paolo, Naples
SSC Napoli 1-1 Athletic Club
Goals: 0-1 Muniain 41, 1-1 Higuaín 68
27/08/14, Estadio de San Mamés, Bilbao
Athletic Club 3-1 SSC Napoli
Goals: 0-1 Hamšík 47, 1-1 Aduriz 61, 2-1 Aduriz 69, 3-1 Ibai Gómez 74
Aggregate: 4-2; Athletic Club qualify.

19/08/14, Arena Naţională, Bucharest
FC Steaua Bucureşti 1-0 PFC Ludogorets Razgrad
Goal: 1-0 Chipciu 88
27/08/14, Natsionalen Stadion Vasil Levski, Sofia
PFC Ludogorets Razgrad 1-0 FC Steaua Bucureşti (aet)
Goal: 1-0 Wanderson 90
Aggregate: 1-1; PFC Ludogorets Razgrad qualify 6-5 on penalties.

19/08/14, Atatürk Olimpiyat Stadium, Istanbul
Beşiktaş JK 0-0 Arsenal FC
27/08/14, Arsenal Stadium, London
Arsenal FC 1-0 Beşiktaş JK
Goal: 1-0 Alexis Sánchez 45+1
Aggregate: 1-0, Arsenal FC qualify.

20/08/14, Stadion Ljudski vrt, Maribor
NK Maribor 1-1 Celtic FC
Goals: 0-1 McGregor 6, 1-1 Bohar 14
26/08/14, Celtic Park, Glasgow
Celtic FC 0-1 NK Maribor
Goal: 0-1 Marcos Tavares 75
Aggregate: 1-2; NK Maribor qualify.

20/08/14, Aalborg Stadion, Aalborg
Aalborg BK 1-1 APOEL FC
Goals: 1-0 Thomsen 16, 1-1 Vinícius 54
26/08/14, GSP Stadium, Nicosia
APOEL FC 4-0 Aalborg BK
Goals: 1-0 Vinícius 29, 2-0 De Vincenti 44, 3-0 Aloneftis 64, 4-0 Sheridan 75
Aggregate: 5-1; APOEL FC qualify.

20/08/14, Štadión Pasienky, Bratislava
ŠK Slovan Bratislava 1-1 FC BATE Borisov
Goals: 0-1 Jablonský 44(og), 1-1 Vittek 80
26/08/14, Borisov Arena, Borisov
FC BATE Borisov 3-0 ŠK Slovan Bratislava
Goals: 1-0 Gordeichuk 41, 2-0 Krivets 84, 3-0 Rodionov 85
Aggregate: 4-1; FC BATE Borisov qualify.

20/08/14, Stade Maurice Dufrasne, Liège
R. Standard de Liège 0-1 FC Zenit
Goal: 0-1 Shatov 16
26/08/14, Stadion Petrovski, St Petersburg
FC Zenit 3-0 R. Standard de Liège
Goals: 1-0 Rondón 30, 2-0 Hulk 54(p), 3-0 Hulk 58
Aggregate: 4-0; FC Zenit qualify.

20/08/14, Grand Stade Lille Métropole, Villeneuve d'Ascq
LOSC Lille 0-1 FC Porto
Goal: 0-1 Herrera 61
26/08/14, Estádio do Dragão, Porto
FC Porto 2-0 LOSC Lille
Goals: 1-0 Brahimi 49, 2-0 Martínez 69
Aggregate: 3-0; FC Porto qualify.

Group stage

Group A

16/09/14, Juventus Stadium, Turin (att: 31,218)
Juventus 2-0 Malmö FF
Goals: 1-0 Tévez 59, 2-0 Tévez 90
Referee: Marciniak (POL)

16/09/14, Stadio Georgios Karaiskakis, Piraeus (att: 31,946)
Olympiacos FC 3-2 Club Atlético de Madrid
Goals: 1-0 Masuaku 13, 2-0 Afellay 31, 2-1 Mandžukic 38, 3-1 Mitroglou 73, 3-2 Griezmann 86
Referee: Proença (POR)

01/10/14, Malmö New Stadium, Malmo (att: 20,500)
Malmö FF 2-0 Olympiacos FC
Goals: 1-0 Rosenberg 42, 2-0 Rosenberg 82
Referee: Karasev (RUS)

01/10/14, Estadio Vicente Calderón, Madrid (att: 44,322)
Club Atlético de Madrid 1-0 Juventus
Goal: 1-0 Arda Turan 75
Referee: Brych (GER)

22/10/14, Estadio Vicente Calderón, Madrid (att: 34,502)
Club Atlético de Madrid 5-0 Malmö FF
Goals: 1-0 Koke 48, 2-0 Mandžukic 61, 3-0 Griezmann 63, 4-0 Godín 87, 5-0 Cerci 90+3
Referee: Jug (SVN)

22/10/14, Stadio Georgios Karaiskakis, Piraeus (att: 31,411)
Olympiacos FC 1-0 Juventus
Goal: 1-0 Kasami 36
Referee: Mažic (SRB)

04/11/14, Malmö New Stadium, Malmo (att: 20,500)
Malmö FF 0-2 Club Atlético de Madrid
Goals: 0-1 Koke 30, 0-2 Raúl García 78
Referee: Clattenburg (ENG)

04/11/14, Juventus Stadium, Turin (att: 39,091)
Juventus 3-2 Olympiacos FC
Goals: 1-0 Pirlo 21, 1-1 Botía 24, 1-2 N'Dinga 61, 2-2 Roberto 65(og), 3-2 Pogba 66
Referee: Atkinson (ENG)

26/11/14, Estadio Vicente Calderón, Madrid (att: 40,121)
Club Atlético de Madrid 4-0 Olympiacos FC
Goals: 1-0 Raúl García 9, 2-0 Mandžukic 38, 3-0 Mandžukic 62, 4-0 Mandžukic 65
Referee: Stark (GER)

26/11/14, Malmö New Stadium, Malmo (att: 20,500)
Malmö FF 0-2 Juventus
Goals: 0-1 Llorente 49, 0-2 Tévez 88
Referee: Proença (POR)

09/12/14, Juventus Stadium, Turin (att: 39,219)
Juventus 0-0 Club Atlético de Madrid
Referee: Collum (SCO)

09/12/14, Stadio Georgios Karaiskakis, Piraeus (att: 27,562)
Olympiacos FC 4-2 Malmö FF
Goals: 1-0 David Fuster 22, 1-1 Kroon 59, 2-1 Domínguez 63, 2-2 Rosenberg 81, 3-2 Mitroglou 87, 4-2 Afellay 90
Referee: Lannoy (FRA)

Stefan Kiessling (in red) opens the scoring for Leverkusen at FC København

Group B

16/09/14, Anfield, Liverpool (att: 43,307)
Liverpool FC 2-1 PFC Ludogorets Razgrad
Goals: 1-0 Balotelli 82, 1-1 Dani Abalo 90+1, 2-1 Gerrard 90+3(p)
Referee: Jug (SVN)

16/09/14, Estadio Santiago Bernabéu, Madrid (att: 65,364)
Real Madrid CF 5-1 FC Basel 1893
Goals: 1-0 Suchý 14(og), 2-0 Bale 30, 3-0 Cristiano Ronaldo 31, 4-0 James Rodríguez 37, 4-1 González 38, 5-1 Benzema 79
Referee: Skomina (SVN)

01/10/14, St Jakob-Park, Basel (att: 36,000)
FC Basel 1893 1-0 Liverpool FC
Goal: 1-0 Streller 52
Referee: Eriksson (SWE)

01/10/14, Natsionalen Stadion Vasil Levski, Sofia (att: 41,484)
PFC Ludogorets Razgrad 1-2 Real Madrid CF
Goals: 1-0 Marcelinho 6, 1-1 Cristiano Ronaldo 24(p), 1-2 Benzema 77
Referee: Thomson (SCO)

22/10/14, Anfield, Liverpool (att: 43,521)
Liverpool FC 0-3 Real Madrid CF
Goals: 0-1 Cristiano Ronaldo 23, 0-2 Benzema 30, 0-3 Benzema 41
Referee: Rizzoli (ITA)

22/10/14, Natsionalen Stadion Vasil Levski, Sofia (att: 29,150)
PFC Ludogorets Razgrad 1-0 FC Basel 1893
Goal: 1-0 Minev 90+2
Referee: Aytekin (GER)

04/11/14, St Jakob-Park, Basel (att: 35,272)
FC Basel 1893 4-0 PFC Ludogorets Razgrad
Goals: 1-0 Embolo 34, 2-0 González 41, 3-0 Gashi 59, 4-0 Suchý 65
Referee: Lannoy (FRA)

04/11/14, Estadio Santiago Bernabéu, Madrid (att: 79,283)
Real Madrid CF 1-0 Liverpool FC
Goal: 1-0 Benzema 27
Referee: Kassai (HUN)

Karim Benzema scored three goals for Real Madrid against Liverpool

26/11/14, St Jakob-Park, Basel (att: 36,000)
FC Basel 1893 0-1 Real Madrid CF
Goal: 0-1 Cristiano Ronaldo 35
Referee: Mažic (SRB)

26/11/14, Natsionalen Stadion Vasil Levski, Sofia (att: 37,143)
PFC Ludogorets Razgrad 2-2 Liverpool FC
Goals: 1-0 Dani Abalo 3, 1-1 Lambert 8, 1-2 Henderson 37, 2-2 Terziev 88
Referee: Mateu Lahoz (ESP)

09/12/14, Anfield, Liverpool (att: 43,290)
Liverpool FC 1-1 FC Basel 1893
Goals: 0-1 Frei 25, 1-1 Gerrard 81
Referee: Kuipers (NED)

09/12/14, Estadio Santiago Bernabéu, Madrid (att: 58,393)
Real Madrid CF 4-0 PFC Ludogorets Razgrad
Goals: 1-0 Cristiano Ronaldo 20(p), 2-0 Bale 38, 3-0 Arbeloa 80, 4-0 Medrán 88
Referee: Turpin (FRA)

Group C

16/09/14, Estádio do Sport Lisboa e Benfica, Lisbon (att: 35,294)
SL Benfica 0-2 FC Zenit
Goals: 0-1 Hulk 5, 0-2 Witsel 22
Referee: Moen (NOR)

16/09/14, Stade Louis II, Monaco (att: 8,130)
AS Monaco FC 1-0 Bayer 04 Leverkusen
Goal: 1-0 João Moutinho 61
Referee: Královec (CZE)

01/10/14, Stadion Petrovski, St Petersburg (att: 13,817)
FC Zenit 0-0 AS Monaco FC
Referee: Clattenburg (ENG)

01/10/14, BayArena, Leverkusen (att: 25,202)
Bayer 04 Leverkusen 3-1 SL Benfica
Goals: 1-0 Kiessling 25, 2-0 Son 34, 2-1 Salvio 62, 3-1 Hakan Çalhanoglu 64(p)
Referee: Atkinson (ENG)

22/10/14, BayArena, Leverkusen (att: 27,254)
Bayer 04 Leverkusen 2-0 FC Zenit
Goals: 1-0 Donati 58, 2-0 Papadopoulos 63
Referee: Kuipers (NED)

22/10/14, Stade Louis II, Monaco (att: 12,776)
AS Monaco FC 0-0 SL Benfica
Referee: Marciniak (POL)

04/11/14, Estádio do Sport Lisboa e Benfica, Lisbon (att: 32,565)
SL Benfica 1-0 AS Monaco FC
Goal: 1-0 Talisca 82
Referee: Fernández Borbalán (ESP)

04/11/14, Stadion Petrovski, St Petersburg (att: 17,010)
FC Zenit 1-2 Bayer 04 Leverkusen
Goals: 0-1 Son 68, 0-2 Son 73, 1-2 Rondón 89
Referee: Undiano Mallenco (ESP)

26/11/14, Stadion Petrovski, St Petersburg (att: 14,123)
FC Zenit 1-0 SL Benfica
Goal: 1-0 Danny 79
Referee: Rizzoli (ITA)

26/11/14, BayArena, Leverkusen (att: 26,230)
Bayer 04 Leverkusen 0-1 AS Monaco FC
Goal: 0-1 Ocampos 72
Referee: Tagliavento (ITA)

09/12/14, Estádio do Sport Lisboa e Benfica, Lisbon (att: 17,564)
SL Benfica 0-0 Bayer 04 Leverkusen
Referee: Kulbakov (BLR)

09/12/14, Stade Louis II, Monaco (att: 11,319)
AS Monaco FC 2-0 FC Zenit
Goals: 1-0 Abdennour 63, 2-0 Fabinho 89
Referee: Skomina (SVN)

Group D

16/09/14, BVB Stadion Dortmund, Dortmund (att: 65,851)
Borussia Dortmund 2-0 Arsenal FC
Goals: 1-0 Immobile 45, 2-0 Aubameyang 48
Referee: Olegário Benquerença (POR)

16/09/14, Ali Sami Yen Spor Kompleksi, Istanbul (att: 28,553)
Galatasaray AŞ 1-1 RSC Anderlecht
Goals: 0-1 Praet 52, 1-1 Burak Yilmaz 90+1
Referee: Vad (HUN)

01/10/14, Arsenal Stadium, London (att: 59,803)
Arsenal FC 4-1 Galatasaray AŞ
Goals: 1-0 Welbeck 22, 2-0 Welbeck 30, 3-0 Alexis Sánchez 41, 4-0 Welbeck 52, 4-1 Burak Yilmaz 63(p)
Referee: Rocchi (ITA)

01/10/14, Constant Vanden Stock Stadium, Brussels (att: 18,649)
RSC Anderlecht 0-3 Borussia Dortmund
Goals: 0-1 Immobile 3, 0-2 Ramos 69, 0-3 Ramos 79
Referee: Tagliavento (ITA)

22/10/14, Constant Vanden Stock Stadium, Brussels (att: 19,881)
RSC Anderlecht 1-2 Arsenal FC
Goals: 1-0 Najar 71, 1-1 Gibbs 89, 1-2 Podolski 90+1
Referee: Velasco Carballo (ESP)

22/10/14, Ali Sami Yen Spor Kompleksi, Istanbul (att: 36,324)
Galatasaray AŞ 0-4 Borussia Dortmund
Goals: 0-1 Aubameyang 6, 0-2 Aubameyang 18, 0-3 Reus 41, 0-4 Ramos 83
Referee: Mateu Lahoz (ESP)

04/11/14, Arsenal Stadium, London (att: 59,872)
Arsenal FC 3-3 RSC Anderlecht
Goals: 1-0 Arteta 25(p), 2-0 Alexis Sánchez 29, 3-0 Oxlade-Chamberlain 58, 3-1 Vanden Borre 61, 3-2 Vanden Borre 73(p), 3-3 Mitrović 90
Referee: Turpin (FRA)

04/11/14, BVB Stadion Dortmund, Dortmund (att: 65,851)
Borussia Dortmund 4-1 Galatasaray AŞ
Goals: 1-0 Reus 39, 2-0 Papastathopoulos 56, 2-1 Hakan Balta 70, 3-1 Immobile 74, 4-1 Semih Kaya 85(og)
Referee: Královec (CZE)

26/11/14, Arsenal Stadium, London (att: 59,902)
Arsenal FC 2-0 Borussia Dortmund
Goals: 1-0 Sanogo 2, 2-0 Alexis Sánchez 57
Referee: Kassai (HUN)

26/11/14, Constant Vanden Stock Stadium, Brussels (att: 19,857)
RSC Anderlecht 2-0 Galatasaray AŞ
Goals: 1-0 Mbemba 44, 2-0 Mbemba 86
Referee: Bebek (CRO)

09/12/14, BVB Stadion Dortmund, Dortmund (att: 65,851)
Borussia Dortmund 1-1 RSC Anderlecht
Goals: 1-0 Immobile 58, 1-1 Mitrović 84
Referee: Undiano Mallenco (ESP)

09/12/14, Ali Sami Yen Spor Kompleksi, Istanbul (att: 20,590)
Galatasaray AŞ 1-4 Arsenal FC
Goals: 0-1 Podolski 3, 0-2 Ramsey 11, 0-3 Ramsey 29, 1-3 Sneijder 88, 1-4 Podolski 90+2
Referee: Fernández Borbalán (ESP)

Group E

17/09/14, Stadio Olimpico, Rome (att: 40,888)
AS Roma 5-1 PFC CSKA Moskva
Goals: 1-0 Iturbe 6, 2-0 Gervinho 10, 3-0 Maicon 20, 4-0 Gervinho 31, 5-0 Ignashevich 50(og), 5-1 Musa 82
Referee: Fernández Borbalán (ESP)

17/09/14, Fußball Arena München, Munich (att: 68,000)
FC Bayern München 1-0 Manchester City FC
Goal: 1-0 Boateng 90
Referee: Undiano Mallenco (ESP)

30/09/14, City of Manchester Stadium, Manchester (att: 37,509)
Manchester City FC 1-1 AS Roma
Goals: 1-0 Agüero 4(p), 1-1 Totti 23
Referee: Kuipers (NED)

30/09/14, Arena Khimki, Khimki
PFC CSKA Moskva 0-1 FC Bayern München
Goal: 0-1 Müller 22(p)
Referee: Collum (SCO)

21/10/14, Arena Khimki, Khimki
PFC CSKA Moskva 2-2 Manchester City FC
Goals: 0-1 Agüero 29, 0-2 Milner 38, 1-2 Doumbia 65, 2-2 Natcho 86(p)
Referee: Vad (HUN)

21/10/14, Stadio Olimpico, Rome (att: 70,544)
AS Roma 1-7 FC Bayern München
Goals: 0-1 Robben 9, 0-2 Götze 23, 0-3 Lewandowski 25, 0-4 Robben 30, 0-5 Müller 36(p), 1-5 Gervinho 66, 1-6 Ribéry 78, 1-7 Shaqiri 80
Referee: Eriksson (SWE)

05/11/14, City of Manchester Stadium, Manchester (att: 45,143)
Manchester City FC 1-2 PFC CSKA Moskva
Goals: 0-1 Doumbia 2, 1-1 Touré 8, 1-2 Doumbia 34
Referee: Sidiropoulos (GRE)

05/11/14, Fußball Arena München, Munich (att: 68,000)
FC Bayern München 2-0 AS Roma
Goals: 1-0 Ribéry 38, 2-0 Götze 64
Referee: Çakir (TUR)

25/11/14, City of Manchester Stadium, Manchester (att: 44,510)
Manchester City FC 3-2 FC Bayern München
Goals: 1-0 Agüero 22(p), 1-1 Xabi Alonso 40, 1-2 Lewandowski 45, 2-2 Agüero 85, 3-2 Agüero 90+1
Referee: Královec (CZE)

25/11/14, Arena Khimki, Khimki
PFC CSKA Moskva 1-1 AS Roma
Goals: 0-1 Totti 43, 1-1 V Berezutski 90+3
Referee: Brych (GER)

10/12/14, Stadio Olimpico, Rome (att: 54,119)
AS Roma 0-2 Manchester City FC
Goals: 0-1 Nasri 60, 0-2 Zabaleta 86
Referee: Mažic (SRB)

10/12/14, Fußball Arena München, Munich (att: 68,000)
FC Bayern München 3-0 PFC CSKA Moskva
Goals: 1-0 Müller 18(p), 2-0 Rode 84, 3-0 Götze 90
Referee: Olegário Benquerença (POR)

Group F

17/09/14, Camp Nou, Barcelona (att: 62,832)
FC Barcelona 1-0 APOEL FC
Goal: 1-0 Piqué 28
Referee: Aytekin (GER)

Sergio Agüero puts Manchester City 1-0 up at home to Roma

17/09/14, Amsterdam ArenA, Amsterdam (att: 50,430)
AFC Ajax 1-1 Paris Saint-Germain
Goals: 0-1 Cavani 14, 1-1 Schöne 74
Referee: Stark (GER)

30/09/14, Parc des Princes, Paris (att: 46,400)
Paris Saint-Germain 3-2 FC Barcelona
Goals: 1-0 David Luiz 10, 1-1 Messi 12, 2-1 Verratti 26, 3-1 Matuidi 54, 3-2 Neymar 56
Referee: Rizzoli (ITA)

30/09/14, GSP Stadium, Nicosia (att: 17,190)
APOEL FC 1-1 AFC Ajax
Goals: 0-1 Andersen 28, 1-1 Manduca 31(p)
Referee: Mažic (SRB)

21/10/14, Camp Nou, Barcelona (att: 79,357)
FC Barcelona 3-1 AFC Ajax
Goals: 1-0 Neymar 7, 2-0 Messi 24, 2-1 El Ghazi 88, 3-1 Sandro Ramírez 90+4
Referee: Collum (SCO)

21/10/14, GSP Stadium, Nicosia (att: 18,659)
APOEL FC 0-1 Paris Saint-Germain
Goal: 0-1 Cavani 87
Referee: Hategan (ROU)

05/11/14, Parc des Princes, Paris (att: 45,816)
Paris Saint-Germain 1-0 APOEL FC
Goal: 1-0 Cavani 1
Referee: Olegário Benquerença (POR)

05/11/14, Amsterdam ArenA, Amsterdam (att: 52,117)
AFC Ajax 0-2 FC Barcelona
Goals: 0-1 Messi 36, 0-2 Messi 76
Referee: Proença (POR)

25/11/14, Parc des Princes, Paris (att: 46,130)
Paris Saint-Germain 3-1 AFC Ajax
Goals: 1-0 Cavani 33, 1-1 Klaassen 67, 2-1 Ibrahimović 78, 3-1 Cavani 83
Referee: Jug (SVN)

25/11/14, GSP Stadium, Nicosia (att: 20,626)
APOEL FC 0-4 FC Barcelona
Goals: 0-1 Suárez 27, 0-2 Messi 38, 0-3 Messi 58, 0-4 Messi 87
Referee: Rocchi (ITA)

10/12/14, Camp Nou, Barcelona (att: 82,570)
FC Barcelona 3-1 Paris Saint-Germain
Goals: 0-1 Ibrahimović 15, 1-1 Messi 19, 2-1 Neymar 42, 3-1 Suárez 77
Referee: Atkinson (ENG)

10/12/14, Amsterdam ArenA, Amsterdam (att: 51,796)
AFC Ajax 4-0 APOEL FC
Goals: 1-0 Schöne 45+1(p), 2-0 Schöne 50, 3-0 Klaassen 53, 4-0 Milik 74
Referee: Velasco Carballo (ESP)

Group G

17/09/14, Stamford Bridge, London (att: 40,648)
Chelsea FC 1-1 FC Schalke 04
Goals: 1-0 Fàbregas 11, 1-1 Huntelaar 62
Referee: Bebek (CRO)

17/09/14, Stadion Ljudski vrt, Maribor (att: 12,211)
NK Maribor 1-1 Sporting Clube de Portugal
Goals: 0-1 Nani 80, 1-1 Zahovič 90+2
Referee: Turpin (FRA)

30/09/14, José Alvalade, Lisbon (att: 40,734)
Sporting Clube de Portugal 0-1 Chelsea FC
Goal: 0-1 Matić 34
Referee: Mateu Lahoz (ESP)

30/09/14, Stadion Gelsenkirchen, Gelsenkirchen (att: 47,997)
FC Schalke 04 1-1 NK Maribor
Goals: 0-1 Bohar 37, 1-1 Huntelaar 56
Referee: Velasco Carballo (ESP)

21/10/14, Stamford Bridge, London (att: 41,126)
Chelsea FC 6-0 NK Maribor
Goals: 1-0 Rémy 13, 2-0 Drogba 23(p), 3-0 Terry 31, 4-0 Viler 54(og), 5-0 Hazard 77(p), 6-0 Hazard 90
Referee: Makkelie (NED)

21/10/14, Stadion Gelsenkirchen, Gelsenkirchen (att: 49,943)
FC Schalke 04 4-3 Sporting Clube de Portugal
Goals: 0-1 Nani 16, 1-1 Obasi 34, 2-1 Huntelaar 51, 3-1 Höwedes 60, 3-2 Adrien Silva 64(p), 3-3 Adrien Silva 78, 4-3 Choupo-Moting 90+3(p)
Referee: Karasev (RUS)

05/11/14, José Alvalade, Lisbon (att: 35,473)
Sporting Clube de Portugal 4-2 FC Schalke 04
Goals: 0-1 Slimani 17(og), 1-1 Sarr 26, 2-1 Jefferson 52, 3-1 Nani 72, 3-2 Aogo 88, 4-2 Slimani 90+1
Referee: Tagliavento (ITA)

05/11/14, Stadion Ljudski vrt, Maribor (att: 12,646)
NK Maribor 1-1 Chelsea FC
Goals: 1-0 Ibraimi 50, 1-1 Matić 73
Referee: Orsato (ITA)

25/11/14, José Alvalade, Lisbon (att: 32,739)
Sporting Clube de Portugal 3-1 NK Maribor
Goals: 1-0 Carlos Mané 10, 2-0 Nani 35, 2-1 Jefferson 42(og), 3-1 Slimani 65
Referee: Thomson (SCO)

25/11/14, Stadion Gelsenkirchen, Gelsenkirchen (att: 54,442)
FC Schalke 04 0-5 Chelsea FC
Goals: 0-1 Terry 2, 0-2 Willian 29, 0-3 Kirchhoff 44(og), 0-4 Drogba 76, 0-5 Ramires 78
Referee: Eriksson (SWE)

10/12/14, Stamford Bridge, London (att: 41,089)
Chelsea FC 3-1 Sporting Clube de Portugal
Goals: 1-0 Fàbregas 8(p), 2-0 Schürrle 16, 2-1 Silva 50, 3-1 Mikel 56
Referee: Moen (NOR)

10/12/14, Stadion Ljudski vrt, Maribor (att: 12,540)
NK Maribor 0-1 FC Schalke 04
Goal: 0-1 Meyer 62
Referee: Marciniak (POL)

Group H

17/09/14, Estádio do Dragão, Porto (att: 35,108)
FC Porto 6-0 FC BATE Borisov
Goals: 1-0 Brahimi 5, 2-0 Brahimi 32, 3-0 Martínez 37, 4-0 Brahimi 57, 5-0 Adrián López 61, 6-0 Aboubakar 76
Referee: Nijhuis (NED)

17/09/14, Estadio de San Mamés, Bilbao (att: 48,351)
Athletic Club 0-0 FC Shakhtar Donetsk
Referee: Sidiropoulos (GRE)

30/09/14, Arena Lviv, Lviv (att: 33,217)
FC Shakhtar Donetsk 2-2 FC Porto
Goals: 1-0 Alex Teixeira 52, 2-0 Luiz Adriano 85, 2-1 Martínez 89(p), 2-2 Martínez 90+4
Referee: Çakir (TUR)

30/09/14, Borisov Arena, Borisov (att: 11,886)
FC BATE Borisov 2-1 Athletic Club
Goals: 1-0 Polyakov 19, 2-0 Karnitski 41, 2-1 Aduriz 45
Referee: Lannoy (FRA)

21/10/14, Estádio do Dragão, Porto (att: 38,116)
FC Porto 2-1 Athletic Club
Goals: 1-0 Herrera 45, 1-1 Guillermo Fernández 58, 2-1 Ricardo Quaresma 75
Referee: Skomina (SVN)

21/10/14, Borisov Arena, Borisov (att: 12,113)
FC BATE Borisov 0-7 FC Shakhtar Donetsk
Goals: 0-1 Alex Teixeira 11, 0-2 Luiz Adriano 28(p), 0-3 Douglas Costa 35, 0-4 Luiz Adriano 36, 0-5 Luiz Adriano 40, 0-6 Luiz Adriano 44, 0-7 Luiz Adriano 82(p)
Referee: Bebek (CRO)

05/11/14, Estadio de San Mamés, Bilbao (att: 47,243)
Athletic Club 0-2 FC Porto
Goals: 0-1 Martínez 56, 0-2 Brahimi 73
Referee: Brych (GER)

05/11/14, Arena Lviv, Lviv (att: 29,173)
FC Shakhtar Donetsk 5-0 FC BATE Borisov
Goals: 1-0 Srna 19, 2-0 Alex Teixeira 48, 3-0 Luiz Adriano 58(p), 4-0 Luiz Adriano 83, 5-0 Luiz Adriano 90+3
Referee: Stark (GER)

25/11/14, Borisov Arena, Borisov (att: 10,147)
FC BATE Borisov 0-3 FC Porto
Goals: 0-1 Herrera 56, 0-2 Martínez 65, 0-3 Tello 89
Referee: Hategan (ROU)

25/11/14, Arena Lviv, Lviv (att: 33,485)
FC Shakhtar Donetsk 0-1 Athletic Club
Goal: 0-1 San José 68
Referee: Clattenburg (ENG)

10/12/14, Estádio do Dragão, Porto (att: 28,010)
FC Porto 1-1 FC Shakhtar Donetsk
Goals: 0-1 Stepanenko 50, 1-1 Aboubakar 87
Referee: Buquet (FRA)

10/12/14, Estadio de San Mamés, Bilbao (att: 42,852)
Athletic Club 2-0 FC BATE Borisov
Goals: 1-0 San José 47, 2-0 Susaeta 88
Referee: Orsato (ITA)

Final group tables

Group A

		Pld	Home W	D	L	F	A	Away W	D	L	F	A	Total W	D	L	F	A	Pts
1	Club Atlético de Madrid	6	3	0	0	10	0	1	1	1	4	3	4	1	1	14	3	13
2	Juventus	6	2	1	0	5	2	1	0	2	2	2	3	1	2	7	4	10
3	Olympiacos FC	6	3	0	0	8	4	0	0	3	2	9	3	0	3	10	13	9
4	Malmö FF	6	1	0	2	2	4	0	0	3	2	11	1	0	5	4	15	3

Group B

		Pld	Home W	D	L	F	A	Away W	D	L	F	A	Total W	D	L	F	A	Pts
1	Real Madrid CF	6	3	0	0	10	1	3	0	0	6	1	6	0	0	16	2	18
2	FC Basel 1893	6	2	0	1	5	1	0	1	2	2	7	2	1	3	7	8	7
3	Liverpool FC	6	1	1	1	3	5	0	1	2	2	4	1	2	3	5	9	5
4	PFC Ludogorets Razgrad	6	1	1	1	4	4	0	0	3	1	10	1	1	4	5	14	4

Group C

		Pld	Home W	D	L	F	A	Away W	D	L	F	A	Total W	D	L	F	A	Pts
1	AS Monaco FC	6	2	1	0	3	0	1	1	1	1	1	3	2	1	4	1	11
2	Bayer 04 Leverkusen	6	2	0	1	5	2	1	1	1	2	2	3	1	2	7	4	10
3	FC Zenit	6	1	1	1	2	2	1	0	2	2	4	2	1	3	4	6	7
4	SL Benfica	6	1	1	1	1	2	0	1	2	1	4	1	2	3	2	6	5

Group D

		Pld	Home W	D	L	F	A	Away W	D	L	F	A	Total W	D	L	F	A	Pts
1	Borussia Dortmund	6	2	1	0	7	2	2	0	1	7	2	4	1	1	14	4	13
2	Arsenal FC	6	2	1	0	9	4	2	0	1	6	4	4	1	1	15	8	13
3	RSC Anderlecht	6	1	0	2	3	5	0	3	0	5	5	1	3	2	8	10	6
4	Galatasaray AŞ	6	0	1	2	2	9	0	0	3	2	10	0	1	5	4	19	1

Group E

		Pld	Home W	D	L	F	A	Away W	D	L	F	A	Total W	D	L	F	A	Pts
1	FC Bayern München	6	3	0	0	6	0	2	0	1	10	4	5	0	1	16	4	15
2	Manchester City FC	6	1	1	1	5	5	1	1	1	4	3	2	2	2	9	8	8
3	AS Roma	6	1	0	2	6	10	0	2	1	2	4	1	2	3	8	14	5
4	PFC CSKA Moskva	6	0	2	1	3	4	1	0	2	3	9	1	2	3	6	13	5

Group F

		Pld	Home W	D	L	F	A	Away W	D	L	F	A	Total W	D	L	F	A	Pts
1	FC Barcelona	6	3	0	0	7	2	2	0	1	8	3	5	0	1	15	5	15
2	Paris Saint-Germain	6	3	0	0	7	3	1	1	1	3	4	4	1	1	10	7	13
3	AFC Ajax	6	1	1	1	5	3	0	1	2	3	7	1	2	3	8	10	5
4	APOEL FC	6	0	1	2	1	6	0	0	3	0	6	0	1	5	1	12	1

Group G

		Pld	Home W	D	L	F	A	Away W	D	L	F	A	Total W	D	L	F	A	Pts
1	Chelsea FC	6	2	1	0	10	2	2	1	0	7	1	4	2	0	17	3	14
2	FC Schalke 04	6	1	1	1	5	9	1	1	1	4	5	2	2	2	9	14	8
3	Sporting Clube de Portugal	6	2	0	1	7	4	0	1	2	5	8	2	1	3	12	12	7
4	NK Maribor	6	0	2	1	2	3	0	1	2	2	10	0	3	3	4	13	3

Group H

		Pld	Home W	D	L	F	A	Away W	D	L	F	A	Total W	D	L	F	A	Pts
1	FC Porto	6	2	1	0	9	2	2	1	0	7	2	4	2	0	16	4	14
2	FC Shakhtar Donetsk	6	1	1	1	7	3	1	2	0	8	1	2	3	1	15	4	9
3	Athletic Club	6	1	1	1	2	2	1	0	2	3	4	2	1	3	5	6	7
4	FC BATE Borisov	6	1	0	2	2	11	0	0	3	0	13	1	0	5	2	24	3

Round of 16

17/02/15, Parc des Princes, Paris (att: 46,146)
Paris Saint-Germain 1-1 Chelsea FC
Goals: 0-1 Ivanović 36, 1-1 Cavani 54
Referee: Çakır (TUR)
11/03/15, Stamford Bridge, London (att: 37,692)
Chelsea FC 2-2 Paris Saint-Germain (aet)
Goals: 1-0 Cahill 81, 1-1 David Luiz 86, 2-1 Hazard 96(p), 2-2 Thiago Silva 114
Referee: Kuipers (NED)
Aggregate: 3-3; Paris Saint-Germain qualify on away goals.

17/02/15, Arena Lviv, Lviv (att: 34,187)
FC Shakhtar Donetsk 0-0 FC Bayern München
Referee: Undiano Mallenco (ESP)
11/03/15, Fußball Arena München, Munich (att: 70,000)
FC Bayern München 7-0 FC Shakhtar Donetsk
Goals: 1-0 Müller 4(p), 2-0 Boateng 34, 3-0 Ribéry 49, 4-0 Müller 52, 5-0 Badstuber 63, 6-0 Lewandowski 75, 7-0 Götze 87
Referee: Collum (SCO)
Aggregate: 7-0; FC Bayern München qualify.

18/02/15, St Jakob-Park, Basel (att: 34,464)
FC Basel 1893 1-1 FC Porto
Goals: 1-0 González 11, 1-1 Danilo 79(p)
Referee: Clattenburg (ENG)
10/03/15, Estádio do Dragão, Porto (att: 43,108)
FC Porto 4-0 FC Basel 1893
Goals: 1-0 Brahimi 14, 2-0 Herrera 47, 3-0 Casemiro 56, 4-0 Aboubakar 76
Referee: Eriksson (SWE)
Aggregate: 5-1; FC Porto qualify.

18/02/15, Arena AufSchalke, Gelsenkirchen (att: 54,442)
FC Schalke 04 0-2 Real Madrid CF
Goals: 0-1 Cristiano Ronaldo 26, 0-2 Marcelo 79
Referee: Atkinson (ENG)
10/03/15, Estadio Santiago Bernabéu, Madrid (att: 69,986)
Real Madrid CF 3-4 FC Schalke 04
Goals: 0-1 Fuchs 20, 1-1 Cristiano Ronaldo 25, 1-2 Huntelaar 40, 2-2 Cristiano Ronaldo 45, 3-2 Benzema 53, 3-3 Sané 57, 3-4 Huntelaar 84
Referee: Skomina (SVN)
Aggregate: 5-4; Real Madrid CF qualify.

24/02/15, City of Manchester Stadium, Manchester (att: 45,081)
Manchester City FC 1-2 FC Barcelona
Goals: 0-1 Suárez 16, 0-2 Suárez 30, 1-2 Agüero 69
Referee: Brych (GER)
18/03/15, Camp Nou, Barcelona (att: 92,551)
FC Barcelona 1-0 Manchester City FC
Goal: 1-0 Rakitić 31
Referee: Rocchi (ITA)
Aggregate: 3-1; FC Barcelona qualify.

24/02/15, Juventus Stadium, Turin (att: 41,182)
Juventus 2-1 Borussia Dortmund
Goals: 1-0 Tévez 13, 1-1 Reus 18, 2-1 Morata 43
Referee: Mateu Lahoz (ESP)
18/03/15, BVB Stadion Dortmund, Dortmund (att: 65,851)
Borussia Dortmund 0-3 Juventus
Goals: 0-1 Tévez 3, 0-2 Morata 70, 0-3 Tévez 79
Referee: Mažić (SRB)
Aggregate: 1-5; Juventus qualify.

25/02/15, Arsenal Stadium, London (att: 59,868)
Arsenal FC 1-3 AS Monaco FC
Goals: 0-1 Kondogbia 38, 0-2 Berbatov 53, 1-2 Oxlade-Chamberlain 90+1, 1-3 Ferreira Carrasco 90+4
Referee: Aytekin (GER)
17/03/15, Stade Louis II, Monaco (att: 18,123)
AS Monaco FC 0-2 Arsenal FC
Goals: 0-1 Giroud 36, 0-2 Ramsey 79
Referee: Moen (NOR)
Aggregate: 3-3; AS Monaco FC qualify on away goals.

25/02/15, BayArena, Leverkusen (att: 29,079)
Bayer 04 Leverkusen 1-0 Club Atlético de Madrid
Goal: 1-0 Hakan Çalhanoğlu 57
Referee: Královec (CZE)
17/03/15, Estadio Vicente Calderón, Madrid (att: 48,273)
Club Atlético de Madrid 1-0 Bayer 04 Leverkusen (aet)
Goal: 1-0 Mario Suárez 27
Referee: Rizzoli (ITA)
Aggregate: 1-1; Club Atlético de Madrid qualify 3-2 on penalties.

Xabi Alonso is congratulated by Bayern team-mates after completing the scoring in the 6-1 win against Porto

Quarter-finals

14/04/15, Estadio Vicente Calderón, Madrid (att: 52,553)
Club Atlético de Madrid 0-0 Real Madrid CF
Referee: Mažić (SRB)
22/04/15, Estadio Santiago Bernabéu, Madrid (att: 78,300)
Real Madrid CF 1-0 Club Atlético de Madrid
Goal: 1-0 Hernández 88
Referee: Brych (GER)
Aggregate: 1-0; Real Madrid CF qualify.

14/04/15, Juventus Stadium, Turin (att: 40,801)
Juventus 1-0 AS Monaco FC
Goal: 1-0 Vidal 57(p)
Referee: Královec (CZE)
22/04/15, Stade Louis II, Monaco (att: 16,889)
AS Monaco FC 0-0 Juventus
Referee: Collum (SCO)
Aggregate: 0-1; Juventus qualify.

15/04/15, Estádio do Dragão, Porto (att: 50,092)
FC Porto 3-1 FC Bayern München
Goals: 1-0 Ricardo Quaresma 3(p), 2-0 Ricardo Quaresma 10, 2-1 Thiago 28, 3-1 Martínez 65
Referee: Velasco Carballo (ESP)
21/04/15, Fußball Arena München, Munich (att: 70,000)
FC Bayern München 6-1 FC Porto
Goals: 1-0 Thiago 14, 2-0 Boateng 22, 3-0 Lewandowski 27, 4-0 Müller 36, 5-0 Lewandowski 40, 5-1 Martínez 73, 6-1 Xabi Alonso 88
Referee: Atkinson (ENG)
Aggregate: 7-4; FC Bayern München qualify.

15/04/15, Parc des Princes, Paris (att: 45,893)
Paris Saint-Germain 1-3 FC Barcelona
Goals: 0-1 Neymar 18, 0-2 Suárez 67, 0-3 Suárez 79, 1-3 Mathieu 82(og)
Referee: Clattenburg (ENG)
21/04/15, Camp Nou, Barcelona (att: 84,477)
FC Barcelona 2-0 Paris Saint-Germain
Goals: 1-0 Neymar 14, 2-0 Neymar 34
Referee: Moen (NOR)
Aggregate: 5-1; FC Barcelona qualify.

Chelsea keeper Thibaut Courtois stretches in vain to keep out an equalising header from Paris skipper Thiago Silva (No2) in the round of 16 second leg at Stamford Bridge

UEFA Champions League

Semi-finals

05/05/15, Juventus Stadium, Turin (att: 41,011)
Juventus 2-1 Real Madrid CF
Goals: 1-0 Morata 8, 1-1 Cristiano Ronaldo 27, 2-1 Tévez 58(p)
Referee: Atkinson (ENG)
13/05/15, Estadio Santiago Bernabéu, Madrid (att: 78,153)
Real Madrid CF 1-1 Juventus
Goals: 1-0 Cristiano Ronaldo 23(p), 1-1 Morata 57
Referee: Eriksson (SWE)
Aggregate: 2-3; Juventus qualify.

06/05/15, Camp Nou, Barcelona (att: 95,639)
FC Barcelona 3-0 FC Bayern München
Goals: 1-0 Messi 77, 2-0 Messi 80, 3-0 Neymar 90+4
Referee: Rizzoli (ITA)
12/05/15, Fußball Arena München, Munich (att: 70,000)
FC Bayern München 3-2 FC Barcelona
Goals: 1-0 Benatia 7, 1-1 Neymar 15, 1-2 Neymar 29, 2-2 Lewandowski 59, 3-2 Müller 74
Referee: Clattenburg (ENG)
Aggregate: 3-5; FC Barcelona qualify.

Final

06/06/15, Olympiastadion, Berlin (att: 70,442)
Juventus 1-3 FC Barcelona
Goals: 0-1 Rakitić 4, 1-1 Morata 55, 1-2 Suárez 68, 1-3 Neymar 90+7
Referee: Çakır (TUR)
Juventus: Buffon, Pogba, Marchisio, Morata (Llorente 85), Tévez, Barzagli, Bonucci, Pirlo, Vidal (Pereyra 79), Lichtsteiner, Evra (Coman 89). Coach: Massimiliano Allegri (ITA)
Barcelona: Ter Stegen, Piqué, Rakitić (Mathieu 90+1), Busquets, Iniesta (Xavi 78), Suárez (Pedro 90+6), Messi, Neymar, Mascherano, Jordi Alba, Dani Alves. Coach: Luis Enrique (ESP)
Yellow cards: Vidal 11 (Juventus), Pogba 41 (Juventus), Suárez 70 (Barcelona)

Carlos Tévez gestures to the Juventus fans after giving his team the lead against Real Madrid in Turin

Top goalscorers

10	Lionel Messi (Barcelona)
	Cristiano Ronaldo (Real Madrid)
	Neymar (Barcelona)
9	Luiz Adriano (Shakhtar)
7	Jackson Martínez (Porto)
	Luis Suárez (Barcelona)
	Carlos Tévez (Juventus)
	Thomas Müller (Bayern)
6	Edinson Cavani (Paris)
	Sergio Agüero (Man. City)
	Robert Lewandowski (Bayern)
	Karim Benzema (Real Madrid)

Squads/Appearances/Goals

AFC Ajax

No	Name	Nat	DoB	Aps	(s)	Gls
Goalkeepers						
22	Jasper Cillessen		22/04/89	6		
Defenders						
5	Nicolai Boilesen	DEN	16/02/92	4		
24	Stefano Denswil		07/05/93	1	(1)	
4	Niklas Moisander	FIN	29/09/85	5		
12	Jaïro Riedewald		09/09/96		(3)	
6	Mike van der Hoorn		15/10/92	1		
2	Ricardo van Rhijn		13/06/91	6		
3	Joël Veltman		15/01/92	5		
26	Nick Viergever		03/08/89	4	(1)	
Midfielders						
10	Davy Klaassen		21/02/93	6		2
20	Lasse Schöne	DEN	27/05/86	6		3
25	Thulani Serero	RSA	11/04/90	5		
32	Niki Zimling	DEN	19/04/85	1	(2)	
Forwards						
16	Lucas Andersen	DEN	13/09/94	6		1
21	Anwar El Ghazi		03/05/95	1	(4)	1
11	Ricardo Kishna		04/01/95	3	(1)	
19	Arkadiusz Milik	POL	28/02/94	2	(3)	1
9	Kolbeinn Sigthórsson	ISL	14/03/90	4		
30	Richairo Zivkovic		05/09/96		(1)	

RSC Anderlecht

No	Name	Nat	DoB	Aps	(s)	Gls
Goalkeepers						
1	Silvio Proto		23/05/83	5		
33	Davy Roef		06/02/94	1		
Defenders						
3	Olivier Deschacht		16/02/81	6		
24	Michaël Heylen		03/01/94		(1)	
22	Chancel Mbemba	COD	08/08/94	6		2
2	Fabrice N'Sakala	COD	21/07/90	1		
14	Bram Nuytinck	NED	04/05/90	2		
39	Anthony Vanden Borre		24/10/87	4		2
Midfielders						
18	Frank Acheampong	GHA	16/10/93	5	(1)	
20	Ibrahima Conté	GUI	03/04/91	6		
16	Steven Defour		15/04/88	4		
32	Leander Dendoncker		15/04/95	1	(3)	
19	Sacha Kljestan	USA	09/09/85	2	(2)	
7	Andy Najar	HON	16/03/93	5		1
10	Dennis Praet		14/05/94	6		1
31	Youri Tielemans		07/05/97	5	(1)	
Forwards						
45	Aleksandar Mitrović	SRB	16/09/94	4	(1)	2
15	Cyriac	CIV	15/08/90	2	(3)	
42	Nathan Kabasele		14/01/94		(1)	
38	Andy Kawaya		23/08/96		(2)	
9	Matías Suárez	ARG	09/05/88	1	(2)	

Luis Suárez (centre) pounces to restore Barcelona's lead against Juventus in the UEFA Champions League final

APOEL FC

No	Name	Nat	DoB	Aps	(s)	Gls
Goalkeepers						
78	Urko Pardo	ESP	28/01/83	6		
Defenders						
15	Marios Antoniades		14/05/90	5		
5	Carlão	BRA	19/01/86	6		
44	Nicholas Ioannou		10/11/95	1		
3	João Guilherme	BRA	21/04/86	5		
28	Mário Sérgio	POR	28/07/81	6		
23	Anatasios Papazoglou	GRE	24/09/88	1		
6	John Arne Riise	NOR	24/09/80		(1)	
Midfielders						
11	Nektarios Alexandrou		19/12/83	1		
46	Efstathios Aloneftis		29/03/83	3	(2)	
4	Kostakis Artymatas		15/04/93		(1)	
10	Kostas Charalambides		25/07/81		(1)	
30	Tomás De Vincenti	ARG	09/02/89	1	(4)	
7	Georgios Efrem		05/07/89	3	(2)	
21	Gustavo Manduca	BRA	08/06/80	4	(1)	1
26	Nuno Morais	POR	29/01/84	6		
8	Tiago Gomes	POR	19/08/85	6		
16	Vinícius	BRA	16/05/86	6		
Forwards						
79	Rafik Djebbour	ALG	08/03/84	1	(4)	
9	Cillian Sheridan	IRL	23/02/89	5	(1)	
20	Pieros Sotiriou		13/01/93		(1)	

Athletic Club

No	Name	Nat	DoB	Aps	(s)	Gls
Goalkeepers						
1	Gorka Iraizoz		06/03/81	6		
Defenders						
24	Mikel Balenziaga		29/02/88	6		
16	Xabier Etxeita		31/10/87	2		
18	Carlos Gurpegui		19/08/80	2	(2)	
15	Andoni Iraola		22/06/82	2	(1)	
4	Aymeric Laporte	FRA	27/05/94	5		
6	Mikel San José		30/05/89	5		2
Midfielders						
23	Ager Aketxe		30/12/93		(1)	
7	Beñat Etxebarria		19/02/87	4	(1)	
10	Óscar De Marcos		14/04/89	5	(1)	
11	Ibai Gómez		11/11/89	4		
8	Ander Iturraspe		08/03/89	5		
17	Mikel Rico		04/11/84	6		
19	Iker Muniain		19/12/92	3	(2)	
14	Markel Susaeta		14/12/87	4	(2)	1
2	Gaizka Toquero		09/08/84		(1)	
29	Unai López		30/10/95		(2)	
Forwards						
20	Aritz Aduriz		11/02/81	3	(2)	1
22	Guillermo Fernández		23/05/93	3	(1)	1
21	Borja Viguera		26/03/87	1	(2)	

FC Barcelona

No	Name	Nat	DoB	Aps	(s)	Gls
Goalkeepers						
1	Marc-André ter Stegen	GER	30/04/92	13		
Defenders						
21	Adriano	BRA	26/10/84	1	(6)	
15	Marc Bartra		15/01/91	5	(1)	
22	Dani Alves	BRA	06/05/83	11		
18	Jordi Alba		21/03/89	11		
14	Javier Mascherano	ARG	08/06/84	12		
24	Jérémy Mathieu	FRA	29/10/83	3	(4)	
2	Martín Montoya		14/04/91	1		
3	Gerard Piqué		02/02/87	11		1
Midfielders						
5	Sergio Busquets		16/07/88	9	(1)	
8	Andrés Iniesta		11/05/84	10	(1)	
12	Rafinha	BRA	12/02/93	1	(5)	
4	Ivan Rakitić	CRO	10/03/88	11	(1)	2
26	Sergi Samper		20/01/95	1		
20	Sergi Roberto		07/02/92	1	(1)	
6	Xavi Hernández		25/01/80	2	(8)	
Forwards						
10	Lionel Messi	ARG	24/06/87	13		10
31	Munir El Haddadi		01/09/95	1	(2)	
11	Neymar	BRA	05/02/92	12		10
7	Pedro Rodríguez		28/07/87	4	(5)	
29	Sandro Ramírez		09/07/95		(3)	1
9	Luis Suárez	URU	24/01/87	10		7

Arsenal FC

No	Name	Nat	DoB	Aps	(s)	Gls
Goalkeepers						
26	Emiliano Martínez	ARG	02/09/92	2		
13	David Ospina	COL	31/08/88	2	(1)	
1	Wojciech Szczęsny	POL	18/04/90	4		
Defenders						
39	Héctor Bellerín	ESP	19/03/95	4		
21	Calum Chambers		20/01/95	5		
2	Mathieu Debuchy	FRA	28/07/85	1		
3	Kieran Gibbs		26/09/89	6	(1)	1
6	Laurent Koscielny	FRA	10/09/85	4		
4	Per Mertesacker	GER	29/09/84	8		
18	Nacho Monreal	ESP	26/02/86	4		
73	Stefan O'Connor		23/01/97		(1)	
Midfielders						
8	Mikel Arteta	ESP	26/03/82	3		1
28	Joel Campbell	CRC	26/06/92	1	(2)	
34	Francis Coquelin	FRA	13/05/91	2		
20	Mathieu Flamini	FRA	07/03/84	3	(2)	
70	Ainsley Maitland-Niles		29/08/97		(1)	
11	Mesut Özil	GER	15/10/88	4		
16	Aaron Ramsey	WAL	26/12/90	5	(1)	3
7	Tomáš Rosický	CZE	04/10/80		(3)	
22	Yaya Sanogo	FRA	27/01/93	2	(1)	1
19	Santi Cazorla	ESP	13/12/84	6	(1)	
10	Jack Wilshere		01/01/92	2	(1)	
35	Gedion Zelalem	USA	26/01/97		(1)	
Forwards						
17	Alexis Sánchez	CHI	19/12/88	7		3
12	Olivier Giroud	FRA	30/09/86	2		1
15	Alex Oxlade-Chamberlain		15/08/93	4	(3)	2
9	Lukas Podolski	GER	04/06/85	1	(4)	3
14	Theo Walcott		16/03/89		(2)	
23	Danny Welbeck		26/11/90	6		3

Club Atlético de Madrid

No	Name	Nat	DoB	Aps	(s)	Gls
Goalkeepers						
1	Miguel Ángel Moyá		02/04/84	7		
13	Jan Oblak	SVN	07/01/93	3	(1)	
Defenders						
15	Cristian Ansaldi	ARG	20/09/86	3		
24	José María Giménez	URU	20/01/95	3	(1)	
2	Diego Godín	URU	16/02/86	9		1
18	Jesús Gámez		10/04/85	2	(1)	
20	Juanfran		09/01/85	10		
23	Miranda	BRA	07/09/84	8		
3	Guilherme Siqueira	BRA	28/04/86	5	(1)	
Midfielders						
10	Arda Turan	TUR	30/01/87	10		1
22	Cani		03/08/81	1		
14	Gabi		10/07/83	6	(1)	
7	Antoine Griezmann	FRA	21/03/91	5	(4)	2
6	Koke		08/01/92	9		2
4	Mario Suárez		24/02/87	6	(2)	1
8	Raúl García		11/07/86	5	(5)	2
21	Cristian Rodríguez	URU	30/09/85		(2)	
17	Saúl Ñíguez		21/11/94	4	(1)	
5	Tiago	POR	02/05/81	4		
Forwards						
22	Alessio Cerci	ITA	23/07/87		(2)	1
11	Raúl Jiménez	MEX	05/05/91		(1)	
9	Mario Mandžukić	CRO	21/05/86	10		5
19	Fernando Torres		20/03/84		(3)	

FC Basel 1893

No	Name	Nat	DoB	Aps	(s)	Gls
Goalkeepers						
1	Tomáš Vaclík	CZE	29/03/89	8		
Defenders						
5	Arlind Ajeti	ALB	25/09/93		(1)	
27	Naser Aliji	ALB	27/12/93	1		
4	Philipp Degen		15/02/83	1		
19	Behrang Safari	SWE	09/02/85	7		
6	Walter Samuel	ARG	23/03/78	3	(1)	
16	Fabian Schär		20/12/91	7		
17	Marek Suchý	CZE	29/03/88	7		1
34	Taulant Xhaka	ALB	28/03/91	7		
Midfielders						
39	Davide Callà		06/10/84	1	(4)	
10	Matías Delgado	ARG	15/12/82		(2)	
21	Marcelo Díaz	CHI	30/12/86		(3)	
33	Mohamed Elneny	EGY	11/07/92	8		
20	Fabian Frei		08/01/89	8		1
24	Ahmed Hamoudi	EGY	30/07/90	1	(3)	
8	Serey Die	CIV	07/11/84	2		
7	Luca Zuffi		27/03/90	6	(1)	
Forwards						
36	Breel Embolo		14/02/97	4	(4)	1
11	Shkëlzen Gashi	ALB	15/07/88	5		1
25	Derlis González	PAR	20/03/94	7	(1)	3
14	Yōichirō Kakitani	JPN	03/01/90		(3)	
30	Giovanni Sio	CIV	31/03/89		(1)	
9	Marco Streller		18/06/81	5		1

⊕ UEFA Champions League

FC BATE Borisov

No	Name	Nat	DoB	Aps	(s)	Gls
Goalkeepers						
16	Sergei Chernik		20/07/88	5		
34	Artem Soroko		01/04/92	1		
Defenders						
21	Yegor Filipenko		10/04/88	3		
3	Vitali Gaiduchik		12/07/89	2	(1)	
14	Anri Khagush	RUS	23/09/86	5		
22	Filip Mladenović	SRB	15/08/91	5		
33	Denis Polyakov		17/04/91	4		1
55	Nemanja Tubić	SRB	08/04/84	3		
Midfielders						
9	Ilya Aleksiyevich		10/02/91	1	(2)	
25	Dmitri Baga		04/01/90		(3)	
7	Aleksandr Karnitski		14/02/89	5	(1)	1
2	Dmitri Likhtarovich		01/03/78	2	(1)	
23	Edgar Olekhnovich		17/05/87	3	(2)	
8	Aleksandr Volodko		18/06/86	5		
42	Maksim Volodko		10/11/92	4	(1)	
5	Evgeni Yablonski		10/05/95	5		
77	Andriy Yakovlev	UKR	20/02/89	1	(2)	
Forwards						
62	Mikhail Gordeichuk		23/10/89	6		
20	Vitali Rodionov		11/12/83	3	(2)	
13	Nikolai Signevich		20/02/92	3	(3)	

FC Bayern München

No	Name	Nat	DoB	Aps	(s)	Gls
Goalkeepers						
1	Manuel Neuer		27/03/86	12		
Defenders						
27	David Alaba	AUT	24/06/92	6		
28	Holger Badstuber		13/03/89	2	(2)	1
5	Medhi Benatia	MAR	17/04/87	7		1
18	Juan Bernat	ESP	01/03/93	11	(1)	
17	Jérôme Boateng		03/09/88	11		3
4	Dante	BRA	18/10/83	3	(4)	
21	Philipp Lahm		11/11/83	8		
13	Rafinha	BRA	07/09/85	9	(2)	
Midfielders						
16	Gianluca Gaudino		11/11/96	1		
19	Mario Götze		03/06/92	9	(2)	4
34	Pierre Hojbjerg	DEN	05/08/95	2	(1)	
8	Javi Martínez	ESP	02/09/88		(1)	
7	Franck Ribéry	FRA	07/04/83	5	(1)	3
20	Sebastian Rode		11/10/90	2	(5)	1
31	Bastian Schweinsteiger		01/08/84	5	(1)	
11	Xherdan Shaqiri	SUI	10/10/91		(4)	1
6	Thiago Alcántara	ESP	11/04/91	4		2
30	Mitchell Weiser		21/04/94		(2)	
3	Xabi Alonso	ESP	25/11/81	10		2
Forwards						
9	Robert Lewandowski	POL	21/08/88	10	(2)	6
25	Thomas Müller		13/09/89	10		7
14	Claudio Pizarro	PER	03/10/78		(2)	
10	Arjen Robben	NED	23/01/84	5	(2)	2

Borussia Dortmund

No	Name	Nat	DoB	Aps	(s)	Gls
Goalkeepers						
22	Mitchell Langerak	AUS	22/08/88	1		
1	Roman Weidenfeller		06/08/80	7		
Defenders						
37	Erik Durm		12/05/92	3	(1)	
28	Matthias Ginter		19/01/94	2	(3)	
15	Mats Hummels		16/12/88	3	(1)	
25	Sokratis Papastathopoulos	GRE	09/06/88	6		1
26	Łukasz Piszczek	POL	03/06/85	5		
29	Marcel Schmelzer		22/01/88	6		
4	Neven Subotić	SRB	10/12/88	7		
Midfielders						
6	Sven Bender		27/04/89	6		
16	Jakub Błaszczykowski	POL	14/12/85		(3)	
19	Kevin Grosskreutz		19/07/88	4		
8	Ilkay Gündoğan		24/10/90	4	(2)	
14	Miloš Jojić	SRB	19/03/92		(2)	
7	Shinji Kagawa	JPN	17/03/89	4	(1)	
23	Kevin Kampl	SVN	09/10/90	1		
5	Sebastian Kehl		13/02/80	4		
21	Oliver Kirch		21/08/82		(3)	
18	Nuri Şahin	TUR	05/09/88	2		
11	Marco Reus		31/05/89	4		3
Forwards						
17	Pierre-Emerick Aubameyang	GAB	18/06/89	7	(1)	3
9	Ciro Immobile	ITA	20/02/90	5	(1)	4
10	Henrikh Mkhitaryan	ARM	21/01/89	7		
20	Adrián Ramos	COL	22/01/86		(6)	3

Bayer 04 Leverkusen

No	Name	Nat	DoB	Aps	(s)	Gls
Goalkeepers						
1	Bernd Leno		04/03/92	8		
Defenders						
17	Sebastian Boenisch	POL	01/02/87	2	(1)	
26	Giulio Donati	ITA	05/02/90	3	(2)	1
13	Roberto Hilbert		16/10/84	4		
16	Tin Jedvaj	CRO	28/11/95	2	(1)	
21	Ömer Toprak	TUR	21/07/89	7		
14	Kyriakos Papadopoulos	GRE	23/02/92	1	(2)	1
5	Emir Spahić	BIH	18/08/80	8		
18	Wendell	BRA	20/07/93	5		
Midfielders						
38	Karim Bellarabi		08/04/90	8		
8	Lars Bender		27/04/89	7		
27	Gonzalo Castro		11/06/87	5		
10	Hakan Çalhanoğlu	TUR	08/02/94	8		2
15	Levin Öztunali		15/03/96		(1)	
3	Stefan Reinartz		01/01/89	2	(1)	
6	Simon Rolfes		21/01/82	1	(3)	
Forwards						
19	Julian Brandt		02/05/96	1	(4)	
9	Josip Drmic	SUI	08/08/92	3	(4)	
11	Stefan Kiessling		25/01/84	5	(3)	1
23	Robbie Kruse	AUS	05/10/88	1	(1)	
7	Son Heung-min	KOR	08/07/92	7	(1)	3

SL Benfica

No	Name	Nat	DoB	Aps	(s)	Gls
Goalkeepers						
1	Artur	BRA	25/01/81	3		
20	Júlio César	BRA	03/09/79	3		
13	Paulo Lopes		29/06/78		(1)	
Defenders						
34	André Almeida		10/09/90	5	(1)	
23	Loris Benito	SUI	07/01/92	1		
37	César	BRA	28/12/92	1	(1)	
19	Eliseu		01/10/83	3		
33	Jardel	BRA	29/08/86	4		
2	Lisandro López	ARG	01/09/89	2		
4	Luisão	BRA	13/02/81	5		
14	Maxi Pereira	URU	08/06/84	4	(1)	
Midfielders						
24	Bryan Cristante	ITA	03/03/95	2	(1)	
9	Nicolás Gaitán	ARG	23/02/88	5		
97	João Teixeira		06/02/94		(1)	
35	Enzo Pérez	ARG	22/02/86	5		
21	Pizzi		06/10/89	1		
18	Eduardo Salvio	ARG	13/07/90	5		1
7	Andreas Samaris	GRE	13/06/89	3	(2)	
30	Talisca	BRA	01/02/94	5	(1)	1
Forwards						
9	Derley	BRA	29/12/87	3	(2)	
15	Ola John	NED	19/05/92	1	(1)	
9	Lima	BRA	11/08/83	4	(2)	
16	Nélson Oliveira		08/08/91		(1)	
32	Tiago		12/07/90	1	(2)	

Chelsea FC

No	Name	Nat	DoB	Aps	(s)	Gls
Goalkeepers						
1	Petr Čech	CZE	20/05/82	3		
13	Thibaut Courtois	BEL	11/05/92	5		
Defenders						
6	Nathan Aké	NED	18/02/95		(1)	
28	César Azpilicueta	ESP	28/08/89	4		
24	Gary Cahill		19/12/85	6		1
3	Filipe Luís	BRA	09/08/85	5		
2	Branislav Ivanović	SRB	22/02/84	7		1
26	John Terry		07/12/80	7		2
5	Kurt Zouma	FRA	27/10/94	3	(1)	
Midfielders						
23	Juan Cuadrado	COL	26/05/88		(1)	
4	Cesc Fàbregas	ESP	04/05/87	8		2
10	Eden Hazard	BEL	07/01/91	7		3
36	Ruben Loftus-Cheek		23/01/96		(1)	
21	Nemanja Matić	SRB	01/08/88	8		2
12	John Obi Mikel	NGA	22/04/87	1	(1)	1
8	Oscar	BRA	09/09/91	4	(3)	
7	Ramires	BRA	24/03/87	3	(3)	1
17	Mohamed Salah	EGY	15/06/92	1	(1)	
14	André Schürrle	GER	06/11/90	3	(1)	1
22	Willian	BRA	09/08/88	5	(2)	1
Forwards						
19	Diego Costa	ESP	07/10/88	5	(2)	
11	Didier Drogba	CIV	11/03/78	2	(3)	2
18	Loïc Rémy	FRA	02/01/87	1	(3)	1
35	Dominic Solanke		14/09/97		(1)	

PFC CSKA Moskva

No	Name	Nat	DoB	Aps	(s)	Gls
Goalkeepers						
35	Igor Akinfeev		08/04/86	6		
Defenders						
6	Aleksei Berezutski		20/06/82	2		
24	Vasili Berezutski		20/06/82	6		1
4	Sergei Ignashevich		14/07/79	6		
2	Mário Fernandes	BRA	19/09/90	6		
14	Kirill Nababkin		08/09/86	2		
42	Georgi Schennikov		27/04/91	4	(1)	
Midfielders						
19	Aleksandrs Cauņa	LVA	19/01/88	1	(1)	
10	Alan Dzagoev		17/06/90	3		
15	Dmitri Efremov		01/04/95		(5)	
25	Roman Eremenko	FIN	19/03/87	6		
23	Georgi Milanov	BUL	19/02/92	3	(3)	
66	Bebras Natcho	ISR	18/02/88	6		1
7	Zoran Tošić	SRB	28/04/87	3	(2)	
3	Pontus Wernbloom	SWE	25/06/86	2		
Forwards						
88	Seydou Doumbia	CIV	31/12/87	4	(2)	3
18	Ahmed Musa	NGA	14/10/92	6		1
8	Kirill Panchenko		16/10/89		(1)	

Juventus

No	Name	Nat	DoB	Aps	(s)	Gls
Goalkeepers						
1	Gianluigi Buffon		28/01/78	13		
Defenders						
15	Andrea Barzagli		08/05/81	2	(4)	
19	Leonardo Bonucci		01/05/87	13		
4	Martín Cáceres	URU	07/04/87	2		
3	Giorgio Chiellini		14/08/84	12		
33	Patrice Evra	FRA	15/05/81	10		
26	Stephan Lichtsteiner	SUI	16/01/84	13		
5	Angelo Ogbonna		23/05/88	1		
Midfielders						
22	Kwadwo Asamoah	GHA	09/12/88	3		
8	Claudio Marchisio		19/01/86	11	(1)	
20	Simone Padoin		18/03/84	1	(3)	
7	Simone Pepe		30/08/83		(1)	
37	Roberto Pereyra	ARG	07/01/91	3	(9)	
21	Andrea Pirlo		19/05/79	10		1
6	Paul Pogba	FRA	15/03/93	10		1
2	Rômulo		22/05/87		(1)	
27	Stefano Sturaro		09/03/93	1	(1)	
23	Arturo Vidal	CHI	22/05/87	12		1
Forwards						
11	Kingsley Coman	FRA	13/06/96		(2)	
12	Sebastian Giovinco		26/01/87		(3)	
14	Fernando Llorente	ESP	26/02/85	4	(5)	1
32	Alessandro Matri		19/08/84		(2)	
9	Álvaro Morata	ESP	23/10/92	9	(3)	5
10	Carlos Tévez	ARG	05/02/84	13		7

PFC Ludogorets Razgrad

No	Name	Nat	DoB	Aps	(s)	Gls
Goalkeepers						
26	Milan Borjan	CAN	23/10/87	1		
21	Vladislav Stoyanov		08/06/87	5		
Defenders						
15	Alexander Alexandrov		13/04/86	2	(1)	
6	Brayan Angulo	COL	02/11/89	1		
80	Júnior Caiçara	BRA	27/04/89	6		
25	Yordan Minev		14/10/80	5		1
27	Cosmin Moți	ROU	03/12/84	6		
55	Georgi Terziev		18/04/92	4		1
Midfielders						
7	Mihail Alexandrov		11/06/89	6		
12	Anicet Abel	MAD	16/03/90	1	(3)	
17	Dani Abalo	ESP	29/09/87	5	(1)	2
18	Svetoslav Dyakov		31/05/84	6		
8	Fábio Espinho	POR	18/08/85	5	(1)	
84	Marcelinho	BRA	24/08/84	6		1
93	Virgil Misidjan	NED	24/07/93	3	(2)	
88	Wanderson	BRA	02/01/88		(4)	
Forwards						
9	Roman Bezjak	SVN	21/02/89	4		
11	Júnior Quixadá	BRA	12/12/85		(2)	
99	Hamza Younés	TUN	16/04/86		(4)	

Galatasaray AŞ

No	Name	Nat	DoB	Aps	(s)	Gls
Goalkeepers						
1	Fernando Muslera	URU	16/06/86	5		
38	Sinan Bolat		03/09/88	1		
Defenders						
13	Alex Telles	BRA	15/12/92	5		
21	Aurélien Chedjou	CMR	20/06/85	5		
22	Hakan Balta		23/03/83	2		1
26	Semih Kaya		24/02/91	6		
77	Tarık Çamdal		24/03/91	4	(1)	
88	Veysel Sarı		25/07/88	2		
Midfielders						
11	Bruma	POR	24/10/94	2	(2)	
6	Blerim Dzemaili	SUI	12/04/86	3	(1)	
52	Emre Çolak		20/05/91	1	(1)	
3	Felipe Melo	BRA	26/06/83	6		
20	Furkan Özçal		03/09/90		(1)	
4	Hamit Altıntop		08/12/82	3	(2)	
29	Olcan Adın		30/09/85		(1)	
8	Selçuk İnan		10/02/85	4		
10	Wesley Sneijder	NED	09/06/84	6		1
23	Yasin Öztekin		19/03/87		(3)	
35	Yekta Kurtuluş		11/12/85	1		
Forwards						
17	Burak Yılmaz		15/07/85	5	(1)	2
19	Goran Pandev	MKD	27/07/83	3		
9	Umut Bulut		15/03/83	2	(3)	

Liverpool FC

No	Name	Nat	DoB	Aps	(s)	Gls
Goalkeepers						
22	Simon Mignolet	BEL	06/08/88	6		
Defenders						
19	Javi Manquillo	ESP	05/05/94	4		
2	Glen Johnson		23/08/84	3		
3	José Enrique	ESP	23/01/86	2		
6	Dejan Lovren	CRO	05/07/89	4		
18	Alberto Moreno	ESP	05/07/92	3	(2)	
17	Mamadou Sakho	FRA	13/02/90	1		
37	Martin Škrtel	SVK	15/12/84	5		
4	Kolo Touré	CIV	19/03/81	2		
Midfielders						
24	Joe Allen	WAL	14/03/90	4		
23	Emre Can	GER	12/01/94	1	(1)	
10	Philippe Coutinho	BRA	12/06/92	3	(2)	
8	Steven Gerrard		30/05/80	5	(1)	2
14	Jordan Henderson		17/06/90	5		1
20	Adam Lallana		10/05/88	2	(2)	
21	Lucas Leiva	BRA	09/01/87	3	(1)	
50	Lazar Marković	SRB	02/03/94	2	(2)	
Forwards						
45	Mario Balotelli	ITA	12/08/90	3		1
29	Fabio Borini	ITA	29/03/91	1	(1)	
9	Rickie Lambert		16/02/82	2	(1)	1
31	Raheem Sterling		08/12/94	5	(1)	

Malmö FF

No	Name	Nat	DoB	Aps	(s)	Gls
Goalkeepers						
25	Robin Olsen		08/01/90	6		
Defenders						
4	Filip Helander		22/04/93	6		
21	Erik Johansson		30/12/88	5		
32	Pa Konate		25/04/94	2	(1)	
20	Ricardinho	BRA	09/09/84	5		
3	Anton Tinnerholm		26/02/91	6		
Midfielders						
8	Enoch Adu	GHA	14/09/90	6		
15	Paweł Cibicki		09/01/94		(3)	
7	Magnus Eriksson		08/04/90	6		
33	Emil Forsberg		23/10/91	6		
6	Markus Halsti	FIN	19/03/84	6		
14	Simon Kroon		16/06/93		(4)	1
31	Erdal Rakip		13/02/96		(3)	
11	Simon Thern		18/09/92		(3)	
Forwards						
24	Isaac Kiese Thelin		24/06/92	6		
26	Agon Mehmeti	ALB	20/11/89		(1)	
9	Markus Rosenberg		27/09/82	6		3

Manchester City FC

No	Name	Nat	DoB	Aps	(s)	Gls
Goalkeepers						
1	Joe Hart		19/04/87	8		
Defenders						
22	Gaël Clichy	FRA	26/07/85	6		
26	Martín Demichelis	ARG	20/12/80	6	(1)	
11	Aleksandar Kolarov	SRB	10/11/85	2	(2)	
4	Vincent Kompany	BEL	10/04/86	7		
20	Eliaquim Mangala	FRA	13/02/91	3		
3	Bacary Sagna	FRA	14/02/83	3	(1)	
5	Pablo Zabaleta	ARG	16/01/85	5	(1)	1
Midfielders						
25	Fernandinho	BRA	04/05/85	4	(3)	
6	Fernando	BRA	25/07/87	5		
15	Jesús Navas	ESP	21/11/85	5	(2)	
18	Frank Lampard		20/06/78	1	(2)	
7	James Milner		04/01/86	6	(2)	1
8	Samir Nasri	FRA	26/06/87	5	(1)	1
21	David Silva	ESP	08/01/86	5	(1)	
42	Yaya Touré	CIV	13/05/83	5		1
Forwards						
16	Sergio Agüero	ARG	02/06/88	6	(1)	6
14	Wilfried Bony	CIV	10/12/88		(2)	
10	Edin Džeko	BIH	17/03/86	5	(1)	
35	Stevan Jovetić	MNE	02/11/89	1	(4)	

AS Monaco FC

No	Name	Nat	DoB	Aps	(s)	Gls
Goalkeepers						
1	Danijel Subašić	CRO	27/10/84	10		
Defenders						
5	Aymen Abdennour	TUN	06/08/89	6		1
21	Elderson Echijile	NGA	20/01/88	2	(1)	
2	Fabinho	BRA	23/10/93	9	(1)	1
3	Layvin Kurzawa		04/09/92	7	(1)	
24	Andrea Raggi	ITA	24/06/84	8		
6	Ricardo Carvalho	POR	18/05/78	6		
38	Almany Touré	MLI	28/04/96	1		
13	Wallace	BRA	14/10/94	3	(1)	
Midfielders						
14	Tiémoué Bakayoko		17/08/94	2	(1)	
15	Bernardo Silva	POR	10/08/94	1	(6)	
7	Nabil Dirar	MAR	25/02/86	7	(2)	
17	Yannick Ferreira Carrasco	BEL	04/09/93	6	(4)	
8	João Moutinho	POR	08/09/86	10		1
22	Geoffrey Kondogbia		15/02/93	8		1
12	Matheus Carvalho	BRA	11/03/92		(2)	
11	Lucas Ocampos	ARG	11/07/94	4	(2)	1
28	Jérémy Toulalan		10/09/83	8		
Forwards						
9	Dimitar Berbatov	BUL	30/01/81	7	(2)	1
18	Valère Germain		17/04/90		(3)	
23	Anthony Martial		05/12/95	4	(3)	
19	Lacina Traoré	CIV	20/08/90	1	(1)	

Paris Saint-Germain

No	Name	Nat	DoB	Aps	(s)	Gls
Goalkeepers						
30	Salvatore Sirigu	ITA	12/01/87	10		
Defenders						
32	David Luiz	BRA	22/04/87	9	(1)	2
21	Lucas Digne		20/07/93		(1)	
5	Marquinhos	BRA	14/05/94	7		
17	Maxwell	BRA	27/08/81	10		
2	Thiago Silva	BRA	22/09/84	6		1
23	Gregory van der Wiel	NED	03/02/88	9	(1)	
Midfielders						
4	Yohan Cabaye		14/01/86	2	(3)	
20	Clément Chantôme		11/09/87	2	(3)	
7	Lucas Moura	BRA	13/08/92	5	(3)	
14	Blaise Matuidi		09/04/87	10		1
27	Javier Pastore	ARG	20/06/89	7	(3)	
25	Adrien Rabiot		03/04/95	2	(2)	
8	Thiago Motta	ITA	28/08/82	6		
24	Marco Verratti	ITA	05/11/92	7		1
Forwards						
15	Jean-Christophe Bahebeck		01/05/93		(3)	
9	Edinson Cavani	URU	14/02/87	10		6
10	Zlatan Ibrahimović	SWE	03/10/81	6		2
22	Ezequiel Lavezzi	ARG	03/05/85	4	(4)	

NK Maribor

No	Name	Nat	DoB	Aps	(s)	Gls
Goalkeepers						
33	Jasmin Handanovič		28/01/78	6		
Defenders						
44	Arghus	BRA	19/01/88	4		
7	Aleš Mejač		18/03/83	3		
26	Aleksander Rajčević		17/11/86	6		
30	Petar Stojanovič		07/10/95	5		
4	Marko Šuler		09/03/83	2		
28	Mitja Viler		01/09/86	5		
Midfielders						
39	Damjan Bohar		18/10/91	3	(3)	1
5	Željko Filipovič		03/10/88	6		
10	Agim Ibraimi	MKD	29/08/88	5	(1)	1
70	Aleš Mertelj		22/03/87	6		
6	Welle N'Diaye	SEN	05/04/90		(2)	
8	Sintayehu Sallalich	ISR	20/06/91	4	(1)	
22	Dare Vršič		26/09/84	3	(2)	
Forwards						
9	Marcos Tavares	BRA	30/03/84	6		
14	Jean-Philippe Mendy	FRA	04/03/87		(6)	
11	Luka Zahovič		15/11/95	2	(3)	1

Olympiacos FC

No	Name	Nat	DoB	Aps	(s)	Gls
Goalkeepers						
16	Roberto	ESP	10/02/86	6		
Defenders						
22	Éric Abidal	FRA	11/09/79	6		
3	Alberto Botía	ESP	27/01/89	6		1
14	Omar Elabdellaoui	NOR	05/12/91	6		
20	Konstantinos Giannoulis		09/12/87		(2)	
26	Arthur Masuaku	FRA	07/11/93	6		1
23	Dimitrios Siovas		16/09/88		(1)	
Midfielders						
6	Ibrahim Afellay	NED	02/04/86	4	(2)	2
18	Andreas Bouhalakis		05/04/93		(1)	
19	David Fuster	ESP	03/02/82	1	(4)	1
10	Alejandro Domínguez	ARG	10/06/81	5	(1)	1
9	Jimmy Durmaz	SWE	22/03/89		(1)	
11	Pajtim Kasami	SUI	02/06/92	4	(2)	1
2	Ioannis Maniatis		12/10/86	6		
5	Luka Milivojević	SRB	07/04/91	5		
8	Delvin N'Dinga	CGO	14/03/88	5	(1)	1
Forwards						
27	Jorge Benítez	PAR	02/09/92		(1)	
17	Dimitrios Diamantakos		05/03/93		(2)	
7	Kostas Mitroglou		12/03/88	6		2

FC Porto

No	Name	Nat	DoB	Aps	(s)	Gls
Goalkeepers						
25	Andrés Fernández	ESP	16/12/86	1		
12	Fabiano	BRA	29/02/88	9		
Defenders						
26	Alex Sandro	BRA	26/01/91	8		
2	Danilo	BRA	15/07/91	8		1
4	Maicon	BRA	14/09/88	9		
5	Iván Marcano	ESP	23/06/87	6		
3	Bruno Martins Indi	NED	08/02/92	7	(2)	
13	Diego Reyes	MEX	19/09/92	1		
Midfielders						
8	Yacine Brahimi	ALG	08/02/90	9		5
6	Casemiro	BRA	23/02/92	8		1
15	Evandro	BRA	23/08/86	2	(3)	
16	Héctor Herrera	MEX	19/04/90	9		3
30	Óliver Torres	ESP	10/11/94	6	(2)	
10	Juan Quintero	COL	18/01/93	2	(3)	
36	Rúben Neves		13/03/97	1	(6)	
Forwards						
99	Vincent Aboubakar	CMR	22/01/92	3	(1)	3
18	Adrián López	ESP	08/01/88	2	(3)	1
17	Hernâni		20/08/91		(1)	
28	Kelvin	BRA	01/06/93		(1)	
9	Jackson Martínez	COL	03/10/86	7	(1)	7
21	Ricardo		06/10/93	1	(1)	
7	Ricardo Quaresma		26/09/83	5	(4)	3
11	Cristian Tello	ESP	11/08/91	5	(2)	1

Real Madrid CF

No	Name	Nat	DoB	Aps	(s)	Gls
Goalkeepers						
1	Iker Casillas		20/05/81	10		
13	Keylor Navas	CRC	15/12/86	2		
Defenders						
17	Álvaro Arbeloa		17/01/83	6	(3)	1
15	Daniel Carvajal		11/01/92	5		
5	Fábio Coentrão	POR	11/03/88	4		
12	Marcelo	BRA	12/05/88	8	(3)	1
18	Nacho		18/01/90	2	(4)	
3	Pepe	POR	26/02/83	6		
4	Sergio Ramos		30/03/86	8		
2	Raphaël Varane	FRA	25/04/93	11	(1)	
Midfielders						
24	Asier Illarramendi		08/03/90	2	(5)	
23	Isco		21/04/92	10	(1)	
10	James Rodríguez	COL	12/07/91	8	(1)	1
6	Sami Khedira	GER	04/04/87	1	(1)	
8	Toni Kroos	GER	04/01/90	11	(1)	
16	Lucas Silva	BRA	16/02/93	1		
26	Álvaro Medrán		15/03/94		(1)	1
19	Luka Modrić	CRO	09/09/85	5	(1)	
Forwards						
11	Gareth Bale	WAL	16/07/89	9	(1)	2
9	Karim Benzema	FRA	19/12/87	8	(1)	6
7	Cristiano Ronaldo	POR	05/02/85	12		10
14	Javier Hernández	MEX	01/06/88	3	(5)	1
20	Jesé		26/02/93		(3)	

FC Schalke 04

No	Name	Nat	DoB	Aps	(s)	Gls
Goalkeepers						
1	Ralf Fährmann		27/09/88	6		
40	Timon Wellenreuther		03/12/95	2		
Defenders						
15	Dennis Aogo		14/01/87	7		1
5	Felipe Santana	BRA	17/03/86	1		
2	Marvin Friedrich		13/12/95		(1)	
23	Christian Fuchs	AUT	07/04/86	5		1
4	Benedikt Höwedes		29/02/88	6		1
24	Kaan Ayhan	TUR	10/11/94	3	(1)	
3	Jan Kirchhoff		01/10/90	2	(2)	
32	Joël Matip	CMR	08/08/91	3		
33	Matija Nastasić	SRB	28/03/93	2		
22	Atsuto Uchida	JPN	27/03/88	5	(2)	
Midfielders						
27	Tranquillo Barnetta	SUI	22/05/85	3	(1)	
9	Kevin-Prince Boateng	GHA	06/03/87	5	(1)	
11	Christian Clemens		04/08/91		(1)	
10	Julian Draxler		20/09/93	3		
8	Leon Goretzka		06/02/95		(1)	
12	Marco Höger		16/09/89	7		
7	Max Meyer		18/09/95	3	(5)	1
33	Roman Neustädter		18/02/88	8		
18	Sidney Sam		31/01/88	1	(2)	
19	Leroy Sané		11/01/96		(1)	1
Forwards						
13	Eric Maxim Choupo-Moting	CMR	23/03/89	6	(2)	1
25	Klaas-Jan Huntelaar	NED	12/08/83	8		5
20	Chinedu Obasi	NGA	01/06/86	2	(2)	1
36	Felix Platte		11/02/96		(1)	

Sporting Clube de Portugal

No	Name	Nat	DoB	Aps	(s)	Gls
Goalkeepers						
1	Rui Patrício		15/02/88	6		
Defenders						
41	Cédric		31/08/91	5		
4	Jefferson	BRA	05/07/88	3		1
3	Maurício	BRA	20/09/88	5		
26	Paulo Oliveira		08/01/92	4	(1)	
29	Naby Sarr	FRA	13/08/93	3	(1)	1
33	Jonathan Silva	ARG	29/06/94	3		1
Midfielders						
23	Adrien Silva		15/03/89	6		2
8	André Martins		21/01/90	1	(2)	
11	Diego Capel	ESP	16/02/88	1	(3)	
17	João Mário		19/01/93	5	(1)	
24	Oriol Rosell	ESP	07/07/92		(1)	
47	Ricardo Esgaio		16/05/93	1		
14	William Carvalho		07/04/92	6		
Forwards						
36	Carlos Mané		11/03/94	2	(2)	1
18	André Carrillo	PER	14/06/91	4	(2)	
10	Fredy Montero	COL	26/07/87		(5)	
77	Nani		17/11/86	5		4
9	Islam Slimani	ALG	18/06/88	6		2

AS Roma FC

No	Name	Nat	DoB	Aps	(s)	Gls
Goalkeepers						
26	Morgan De Sanctis		26/03/77	4		
28	Łukasz Skorupski	POL	05/05/91	2		
Defenders						
23	Davide Astori		07/01/87	2		
3	Ashley Cole	ENG	20/12/80	2	(1)	
25	José Holebas	GRE	27/06/84	3	(2)	
13	Maicon	BRA	26/07/81	3		1
44	Kostas Manolas	GRE	14/06/91	6		
35	Vasilios Torosidis	GRE	10/06/85	3	(1)	
2	Mapou Yanga-Mbiwa	FRA	15/05/89	4	(1)	
Midfielders						
16	Daniele De Rossi		24/07/83	3		
24	Alessandro Florenzi		11/03/91	3	(3)	
20	Seydou Keita	MLI	16/01/80	5		
8	Adem Ljajić	SRB	29/09/91	2	(2)	
4	Radja Nainggolan	BEL	04/05/88	6		
15	Miralem Pjanić	BIH	02/04/90	4	(2)	
6	Kevin Strootman	NED	13/02/90		(1)	
Forwards						
22	Mattia Destro		20/03/91	1	(1)	
27	Gervinho	CIV	27/05/87	5	(1)	3
7	Juan Manuel Iturbe	ARG	04/06/93	3	(3)	1
10	Francesco Totti		27/09/76	5		2

FC Shakhtar Donetsk

No	Name	Nat	DoB	Aps	(s)	Gls
Goalkeepers						
30	Andriy Pyatov		28/06/84	8		
Defenders						
38	Serhiy Kryvtsov		15/03/91	1	(1)	
5	Olexandr Kucher		22/10/82	6		
66	Márcio Azevedo	BRA	05/02/86	2		
18	Ivan Ordets		08/07/92	1		
44	Yaroslav Rakitskiy		03/08/89	8		
13	Vyacheslav Shevchuk		13/05/79	6		
33	Darijo Srna	CRO	01/05/82	7		1
Midfielders						
29	Alex Teixeira	BRA	06/01/90	8		3
10	Bernard	BRA	08/09/92	1	(4)	
20	Douglas Costa	BRA	14/09/90	8		1
17	Fernando	BRA	03/03/92	6	(1)	
8	Fred	BRA	05/03/93	3	(4)	
77	Ilsinho	BRA	12/10/85	1	(2)	
11	Marlos	BRA	07/06/88		(6)	
6	Taras Stepanenko		08/08/89	7		1
Forwards						
21	Olexandr Gladkiy		24/08/87	1	(2)	
9	Luiz Adriano	BRA	12/04/87	7		9
28	Taison	BRA	13/01/88	7	(1)	
7	Wellington Nem	BRA	06/02/92		(2)	

FC Zenit

No	Name	Nat	DoB	Aps	(s)	Gls
Goalkeepers						
1	Yuri Lodygin		26/05/90	6		
Defenders						
2	Aleksandr Anyukov		28/09/82	4	(1)	
4	Domenico Criscito	ITA	30/12/86	6		
24	Ezequiel Garay	ARG	10/10/86	6		
6	Nicolas Lombaerts	BEL	20/03/85	6		
13	Luís Neto	POR	26/05/88		(1)	
19	Igor Smolnikov		08/08/88	2	(1)	
Midfielders						
35	Danny	POR	07/08/83	6		1
20	Viktor Fayzulin		22/04/86	3	(1)	
21	Javi García	ESP	08/02/87	6		
8	Pavel Mogilevets		25/01/93		(1)	
5	Aleksandr Ryazantsev		05/09/86	1	(2)	
17	Oleg Shatov		29/07/90	3	(3)	
28	Axel Witsel	BEL	12/01/89	6		1
Forwards						
10	Andrey Arshavin		29/05/81		(3)	
7	Hulk	BRA	25/07/86	6		
11	Aleksandr Kerzhakov		27/11/82	1	(2)	
23	José Salomón Rondón	VEN	16/09/89	5	(1)	1

Successful trophy defence
for Unai Emery's side

Unprecedented fourth
triumph for Andalusian club

Dogged Dnipro defeated 3-2
in epic Warsaw final

Sevilla scale new heights

Sevilla FC broke new ground in 2014/15 as they became the first club to win the UEFA Cup/UEFA Europa League on four occasions. In so doing, the Andalusian outfit elevated themselves above an esteemed trio of three-time winners in Juventus, Liverpool FC and FC Internazionale Milano. Even more remarkably, their record fourth triumph came less than a decade after their first.

That the holders retained the trophy tells only half the story, however, of a fascinating competition in which fresh records were set and new landmarks reached on virtually every matchday.

FC Dnipro Dnipropetrovsk may have been vanquished in the final, going down 3-2 in Warsaw's National Stadium, but Myron Markevych and his valiant team won the hearts of many during a 19-game European odyssey in which even their home games were played nearly 400km away in Kyiv.

Although the Ukrainian capital soon warmed to Dnipro, it was to watch and support the more traditional NSK Olimpiyskyi stadium inhabitants, FC Dynamo Kyiv, that a competition record crowd of 67,553 turned out for the round

of 16 second-leg success over Everton FC. Indeed six of the all-time top ten UEFA Europa League attendances were set during the campaign.

Not one of those, however, witnessed a goal quite like the one scored at White Hart Lane on matchday three. Picking up a loose ball on the edge of the box, Tottenham Hotspur FC's Erik Lamela brought his left foot behind his right to power in an outrageous 'rabona' finish.

There was no shortage of alacrity as well as quality. FC Steaua Bucureşti's Claudiu Keşerü set a new competition mark as he registered the fastest ever hat-trick (11 minutes) against Aalborg BK on matchday one, while Sevilla midfielder Vitolo struck the quickest UEFA Europa League goal in history, opening the scoring after just 13.21 seconds in the round of 16 first-leg victory against Villarreal CF.

It was far from a stroll for Unai Emery's team, who had needed to avoid defeat on matchday six to extend their involvement into the new year. They edged a 1-0 win over HNK Rijeka but certainly did not head into the knockout phase as the form team. That honour went instead to FC Dinamo Moskva,

only the sixth side ever to navigate the UEFA Europa League group stage with a 100% record.

Dinamo made it through to the round of 16 but were undone there by SSC Napoli, one of five Serie A participants to make it that far – another first to add to the competition's book of records. One entry that Italy no longer hold on their own, however, is that of the country with most UEFA Cup/UEFA Europa League wins, Spain drawing level with them on nine thanks to Sevilla's feat.

Alhough the Spanish side headed into the final as overwhelming favourites, it was Dnipro who went in front through Nikola Kalinić after just seven minutes. Sevilla were ahead themselves soon enough, Poland midfielder Grzegorz Krychowiak equalising back in his homeland before Carlos Bacca added a second, but Ruslan Rotan's perfectly executed free-kick drew a defiant Dnipro level. Bacca was to have the last word, though, striking the decisive blow 17 minutes from time. It was so near, so far for Dnipro, who missed out not only on silverware but also the new bonus prize of a place in the group stage of the 2015/16 UEFA Champions League.

Group stage

In a group stage packed with pedigree – including seven former UEFA Cup/UEFA Europa League winners – the spotlight was stolen by FC Dinamo Moskva as the Russian club became the sixth team to win all six group stage games. There were no frills from Stanislav Cherchesov's men, however. Each of their **Group E** victories came courtesy of a single-goal margin and a rock-solid defence that was breached just three times. With Panathinaikos FC enduring a miserable campaign that yielded just two draws, the second qualification place came down to a showdown between Estoril Praia and PSV and hinged on a protracted matchday five meeting. With the Portuguese hosts leading 3-2 at half-time and needing a win, the heavens opened, which forced a suspension of 19 hours. Refreshed after a night's sleep, PSV grabbed the equaliser they needed, through Dutch international Georginio Wijnaldum, to secure progress.

Fellow Eredivisie outfit Feyenoord went one better by topping **Group G** ahead of holders Sevilla, though Croatian outsiders HNK Rijeka were also in the mix throughout. Fuelled by the goals of Andrej Kramarić – including a 14-minute hat-trick in a 3-1 win against Feyenoord – they sat just a point behind Sevilla after three games. However, defeats in the Netherlands and Spain ended Rijeka's hopes, and after Feyenoord and Sevilla had exchanged 2-0 victories, it was the Dutch side who came out on top. Both were flawless at home, but Unai Emery's men failed to secure a win on their travels, and a final day 3-0 triumph at R. Standard de Liège put the 1974 and 2002 winners through as section winners.

With the prospect of a final in their home city, Legia Warszawa impressed as they swept through **Group L**, winning five of their six games. Inspired by 19-year-old Slovakian schemer Ondrej Duda – dubbed Dudinho – the Polish champions set the pace thanks to a trio of 1-0 wins. Miroslav Radović set them on their way on matchday one against KSC Lokeren OV, before they repeated the trick away to Trabzonspor AŞ and FC Metalist Kharkiv. Lokeren made a gallant late charge, concluding with a draw and two wins to end on ten points, level with the Turkish side, but they missed out on the head-to-head rule, a 2-0 defeat in Trabzon ultimately proving decisive.

Matching Legia's impressive 15-point haul were FC Dynamo Kyiv in **Group J**, captain Andriy Yarmolenko leading from the front with three goals and four assists. The Ukrainian side's only slip came at an erratic Aalborg BK. The Danish club's chances of advancing seemed non-existent after a 6-0 opening loss at FC Steaua Bucureşti, which included a UEFA Europa League record 11-minute hat-trick from Claudiu Keşerü. Kent Nielsen's side lost all three away games without scoring but were a different beast on home soil. Three wins at the Aalborg Stadion proved enough to pip Steaua to qualification.

After cruising through the group stage with a perfect record in 2013/14, FC Salzburg could not quite repeat the feat, blotting their copybook with an opening **Group D** draw at home to Celtic FC (2-2). However, it was plain sailing from then on for the Austrian champions, who proved prolific in front of goal by scoring a record 21 times. The previous season's top scorer, Jonatan Soriano, weighed in with five goals, including a hat-trick in the 5-1 win at GNK Dinamo Zagreb, but Salzburg's Spanish skipper was outshone by Brazilian team-mate Alan, who struck eight times in just five appearances. He signed off with a double in the closing 5-1 win over Romanian debutants FC Astra Giurgiu before departing for Chinese club Guangzhou Evergrande FC ahead of the knockout phase.

VfL Borussia Mönchengladbach were the group stage's other great entertainers as they battled for supremacy in **Group A**, going undefeated to advance ahead of Villarreal CF. The top two shared a pair of draws, the second of which was secured by Granit Xhaka's thunderbolt free-kick for the Bundesliga outfit. Strikes from distance were a trademark of Lucien Favre's side, further underlined by Håvard Nordtveit's screamer at FC Zürich and Branimir Hrgota's delicious lob at home to the same opposition on matchday six. Zürich pushed Villarreal close for second, beating the Spanish side in a remarkable match in Switzerland when all five goals came in 11 first-half minutes, but the Swiss club's campaign floundered with a final-day defeat away to Gladbach.

Mönchengladbach midfielder Håvard Nordtveit lets fly to score against Zürich

Four Italian clubs entered the group stage and they all advanced, with SSC Napoli perhaps the most impressive of the quartet. A trio of home wins provided the backbone to their **Group I** supremacy, with three goals scored in each. Rafael Benítez's team were joined in the next round by BSC Young Boys, who inflicted the only loss on the Italian side with a 2-0 win in Berne on matchday three. It was not until the final matchday that the Swiss side confirmed their progress, however. Trailing AC Sparta Praha by a point going into the sides' showdown at the Stade de Suisse, Guillaume Hoarau's 75th-minute penalty and Renato Steffen's late effort secured progression for Young Boys. ŠK Slovan Bratislava propped up the group having conceded a record 20 goals – and scored just one – in their six defeats.

ACF Fiorentina matched their Serie A rivals' tally of 13 points in **Group K**, but in contrast it was away from home where they made hay, collecting the full nine points. The last of their three wins came at EA Guingamp, which secured progress with a game to spare – an explanation perhaps of their shock final-day lapse as they lost 2-1 at home to bottom side FC Dinamo Minsk. While the Belarusian outfit bowed out on a high, PAOK FC and Guingamp contested a matchday six showdown in Salonika. Locked together on seven points beforehand, it was the French group stage first-timers who prevailed. After beating PAOK 2-0 in France, they repeated the dose with a 2-1 win in Greece thanks to two goals from Claudio Beauvue.

Another debutant, Qarabağ FK, came within a whisker of a famous scalp and progress from **Group F**. The first Azerbaijani side to win a UEFA group stage game thanks to a shock 1-0 victory at Dnipro on matchday three, their destiny was in their own hands on the final day. However, they failed to get the win they needed in front of a huge crowd at home to section winners FC Internazionale Milano only because a last-minute goal was heartbreakingly ruled out during a frantic finish. That allowed Dnipro to jump from fourth to second with a 1-0 win against AS Saint-Étienne, who had drawn their first five games, while Inter strode through undefeated despite scoring just six times.

Torino FC completed the Italian clean sweep, finishing a point behind Club

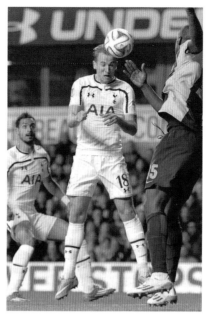

Tottenham striker Harry Kane heads home to complete his hat-trick against Asteras Tripolis

Brugge KV in **Group B** on their return to European competition after two decades away. The Granata were in pole position at the halfway stage after victories over FC København and HJK Helsinki but a loss in Finland opened the door for Club Brugge, who seized the initiative thanks to a 4-0 win in Copenhagen, with Lior Refaelov scoring a first-half hat-trick. The Belgian side clinched first place thanks to Refaelov's late winner in a closing 2-1 triumph over HJK.

For the third season running Tottenham Hotspur FC made it to the round of 32, but they were forced to play second fiddle to Beşiktaş JK in **Group C** as both advanced in businesslike manner. They each started with a pair of draws but really showed their muscle on matchday three, Spurs powering past Asteras Tripolis FC 5-1 in a memorable display that included a stunning Erik Lamela 'rabona' as well as a Harry Kane hat-trick. The Black Eagles, meanwhile, soared to a 4-0 victory in Belgrade at FK Partizan, and 2-1 wins in the return encounters left the two pacesetters dead level with two to play. A Beşiktaş slip-up in a 2-2 draw at Asteras looked to have let Tottenham in, but Cenk Tosun grabbed the only goal as the sides met on the final day to pinch top spot by a point from the north London side.

Spurs' domestic rivals Everton FC struck an early blow in **Group H** to ensure they cruised into the last 32,

laying down a resounding marker with an opening 4-1 win against VfL Wolfsburg. Two away draws followed before a 3-0 home success against a disappointing and ultimately winless LOSC Lille. An impressive 2-0 victory at Wolfsburg then secured top spot for Roberto Martínez's men with a game to spare. Barring the two defeats by the Toffees, the Bundesliga side impressed enough to follow them through, 4-2 and 5-1 wins against FC Krasnodar doing enough to wrest control of second spot, which was confirmed on the last day with a dominant 3-0 win at LOSC.

Round of 32

There were seven domestic title holders in the UEFA Europa League round of 32, as many as lined up for the UEFA Champions League knockout phase. They did not fare well, however, and by the end of the action just one was still standing.

AFC Ajax were the only national champions to advance, defeating Polish counterparts Legia, whose dream of a final in their home city was chiefly scuppered by three goals in the tie from one of their own, Poland striker Arkadiusz Milik. RSC Anderlecht (Belgium), Olympiacos FC (Greece), Aalborg (Denmark), Celtic (Scotland) and Salzburg (Austria) also bowed out.

The round of 32 also threw up a couple of ties with history. Liverpool FC had thrashed Beşiktaş by a record 8-0 margin in the 2007/08 UEFA Champions League group stage. Seven years on, though, revenge was duly meted out by the Turkish club. A 1-0 home win at Anfield made that a slightly more distant possibility but, cheered on by a bumper crowd of 63,324, the force was with Beşiktaş a week later as the Reds returned to the Atatürk Olimpiyat Stadium, scene of their 2005 UEFA Champions League final triumph. A beautiful strike from Tolgay Arslan 18 minutes from time forced the game into an additional half an hour, and then came the inevitable penalty shoot-out. Unlike AC Milan a decade earlier, the Turkish side did not flinch, and it was Liverpool's Dejan Lovren who blazed the decisive penalty over. Beşiktaş's victory was presided over by Slaven Bilić, a former Everton defender. Worse still for Liverpool, by the end of the night their city rivals, who routed Young Boys 7-2 on aggregate, were the last British side standing.

Tottenham lost to Fiorentina, victims of poor defending in Tuscany, while Celtic were edged out by Inter in a thriller fitting of the fixture's rich history, most notably when Jock Stein's Scots beat Helenio Herrera's Inter 2-1 in the 1967 European Cup final. An added-time strike from John Guidetti earned Celtic a 3-3 draw in a pulsating encounter at Celtic Park, and although Virgil van Dijk was sent off before half-time in the San Siro return, the tie was in the balance until Fredy Guarín smashed home a beauty two minutes from time.

Further successes for AS Roma, Torino and Napoli made it a clean sweep for Italy, with a record five teams from Serie A making it through to the last 16, all of them after second-leg victories. Roma, who overcame Feyenoord, were one of only three latecomers from the UEFA Champions League to advance, along with Ajax and an out-of-season FC Zenit side whose clinical evisceration of PSV, 4-0 on aggregate, caught the eye. So too did Dnipro's victory over Olympiacos, the Ukrainian side showing their mettle by twice coming from behind to earn a second-leg draw following a 2-0 home win.

Round of 16

If Dnipro had attracted attention the previous round, Europe really began to sit up and take notice when they ended Ajax's ambitions. The Ukrainian club won the first leg 1-0, but with five first-choice players absent through injury or suspension, and coach Myron Markevych laid up with a virus, the odds were against them in Amsterdam. Not for the first time (nor the last) they were to come through. Riechedly Bazoer evened up the tie but the Dutch champions were unable to press home their advantage and Yevhen Konoplyanka silenced the Amsterdam ArenA with a typically stylish finish seven minutes into extra time. Mike van der Hoorn restored Ajax's lead on the night but that away goal ended both Ajax and Dutch interest in European competiton for 2014/15. Dnipro, by contrast, made it an unlikely Ukrainian double in the last eight, with Dynamo Kyiv having overturned a first-leg deficit for the second successive round.

A mixture of fortune and wonderful long-range finishing from Yarmolenko and Antunes saw Dynamo through against Everton, 6-4 on aggregate. It

Club Brugge's Boli Bolingoli-Mbombo celebrates a decisive goal against Beşiktaş in Istanbul

meant that for the first time since 1992/93 the European quarter-finals were devoid of English representation. For Club Brugge (after 20 years) and Napoli (26), however, there was a welcome return to the last eight of a continental competition.

Boli Bolingoli-Mbombo's late double sent Club Brugge through as Michel Preud'homme's side came from behind home and away against Beşiktaş. Napoli, meanwhile, did the damage in their first meeting with Dinamo Moskva, Gonzalo Higuaín scoring a hat-trick as the Italian side recovered from Kevin Kuranyi's early opener before sealing the deal with a siege-resisting 0-0 draw in Moscow. The storm Sevilla had to weather was more meteorological than metaphorical as they successfully dampened Liga rivals Villarreal's initial ardour to convert their 3-1 first-leg win into a 5-2 aggregate success. Wolfsburg saw off Inter in identical fashion, with Kevin De Bruyne scoring two goals and setting up another in Germany before

the Bundesliga high fliers nicked a late win in Milan.

Zenit also had a two-goal cushion from their first encounter with Torino, but they were given a belated scare as Kamil Glik halved the deficit with a 90th-minute header in Turin. The Russian side hung on but yellow cards (and consequent bans) for Domenico Criscito, Hulk, Danny and Igor Smolnikov would seriously undermine their quarter-final challenge. Of the five Italian sides who started the round, only two survived, with Fiorentina joining Napoli thanks to a 4-1 aggregate win over Roma. Second in Serie A, the Giallorossi went into the tie against a Viola side led by their former striker Vincenzo Montella as favourites, even more so after a 1-1 away draw, but they were blown away inside 22 minutes of the return at the Stadio Olimpico by three goals from Fiorentina defenders.

Quarter-finals

"It's probably the hardest draw we could get," acknowledged André Villas-Boas after his Zenit side were paired with Sevilla in the last eight. The holders were by now firm favourites to defend their crown. Not only were they hitting form at just the right time, but on each of their previous three quarter-final appearances they had gone on to lift the trophy. Their credentials, however, were to be given a stern examination by the Russian league leaders.

With 17 minutes remaining of the first leg in Spain, Zenit led, only for Carlos Bacca's header to make it 1-1 before

8

For the second successive season, a Salzburg player took the UEFA Europa League top scorer prize, Alan following in Jonatan Soriano's footsteps despite leaving for China during the winter. That allowed Everton's Romelu Lukaku to match him, the Belgian's eight goals coming from nine games; Alan did it in five.

Denis Suárez crashed in a remarkable volleyed winner. When Bacca drew first blood a week later, that looked to be that, but after José Salomón Rondón had equalised, Hulk brought the tie level with an astonishing long-range strike that crashed in off the underside of the bar. Enter Sevilla supersub Kevin Gameiro, who, with extra time looming, ended a lethal counterattack with a sublime finish to end Zenit's flawless UEFA Europa League home record and snatch qualification for his team.

The Club Brugge-Dnipro tie also went to the wire. The Belgian side were the last unbeaten team in the competition, 14 games and counting (qualifying included), and they came into the contest fresh from a first major trophy triumph in eight years following a 2-1 win over Anderlecht in a thrilling Belgian Cup final. They had goalkeeper Matthew Ryan to thank for a first-leg draw, and the tie was still scoreless after 172 minutes when substitute Yevhen Shakhov struck, his deflected shot finding the net after he had been played through by skipper Ruslan Rotan's measured through ball. It put Dnipro into the uncharted territory of a first European semi-final.

Napoli took on Wolfsburg in a mouth-watering clash that seemed too close to call. After 23 minutes, though, the tie seemed all but over as Gonzalo Higuaín recovered his shooting boots, scoring and then setting up Marek Hamšík. Napoli went on to win 4-1, inflicting on Wolfsburg their heaviest home defeat in Europe and also providing a nice 55th birthday present for coach Rafael Benítez. A 2-2 draw in Italy seven days later completed the job.

Fiorentina ensured that half the semi-final lineup was Italian as they defeated Dynamo Kyiv. The tie hinged on a red card five minutes before half-time in the second leg for Dynamo's Dutch forward Jeremain Lens. At the time the teams were still locked at 1-1 from the first instalment, when Khouma Babacar's last-gasp goal had cancelled out Lens' deflected strike. Mario Gomez swiftly made the one-man advantage count with a somewhat fortuitous finish from Joaquín's cross, but a dominant Fiorentina could not kill off their doughty opponents until Manuel Vargas converted their 25th shot of the game in added time.

Semi-finals

Based purely on European pedigree, the tie between 1989 UEFA Cup winners Napoli and first-time semi-finalists Dnipro looked tilted firmly in the Italian club's favour, but by now no one was underestimating the Ukrainian side, masters of winning by doing just enough. Yevhen Seleznyov, a gangly 29-year-old forward, proved to be their hero, though as ever the plaudits had to be shared with his parsimonious back line, superbly marshalled by Brazilian defender Douglas in front of imperious goalkeeper Denys Boyko.

Seleznyov climbed off the bench to earn the Ukrainian side a share of the spoils in Italy, albeit from an offside position that escaped the notice of the officials. His close-range strike cancelled out the goal that David López had headed home for the hosts shortly after half-time. Boyko repeatedly denied Higuaín in both legs, and as Dnipro's defence held firm in Kyiv, Seleznyov's 58th-minute winner – a fine header from an equally fine Konoplyanka cross – decided the contest against the odds in front of 62,344 mostly ecstatic fans in the rain-drenched Ukrainian capital.

But while there would be a new team in the UEFA Europa League final, the other side to make it to Warsaw would be instantly recognisable. Sevilla's run to glory in 2013/14 had been marked by regular dices with death, including two penalty shoot-outs and a last-minute winner. Their narrow quarter-final success had hinted at a return to that template, but their last-four meeting with Fiorentina could not have been more straightforward.

Emery pulled off a masterstroke for the first leg, handing Aleix Vidal a free-ranging role at right-back. The 25-year-old, normally a midfielder, responded with two goals and a decisive pass for Gameiro to make it 3-0 and inflict a first UEFA Europa League away defeat on Fiorentina in 12 matches. The Viola's chances of turning the tie around in Florence went from improbable to nigh-on impossible thanks to two Sevilla goals in the opening 27 minutes, the first from Bacca, the second from the competition's most frequent participant, Portuguese defender Daniel Carriço. Josip Iličič's second-half penalty miss compounded Fiorentina's misery as the Andalusian side cantered through to their second successive UEFA Europa League final.

Dnipro's Jaba Kankava (left) tussles for possession with Napoli's Gökhan Inler in the semi-final second leg

Final

The 2014/15 UEFA Europa League concluded with the most exciting of the competition's six finals. Few gave outsiders Dnipro much of a chance against the holders in Warsaw, yet the Ukrainian side never flinched against superior opponents and gave everything they had to cause an upset, taking the lead and then drawing level as Sevilla appeared to be striding to victory. Ultimately, though, it was the finishing skill of Colombian striker Carlos Bacca that proved to be the difference between the two sides, his second goal of the game midway through the second half giving Sevilla the trophy for the second year in succession and an unprecedented fourth time in all.

The Spanish side had looked set to remain level with Liverpool FC, Juventus and FC Internazionale Milano on three wins when Nikola Kalinić gave Dnipro a seventh-minute lead. The Croatian, selected ahead of semi-final hero Seleznyov, flicked on a long ball forward before meeting Matheus's precise first-time cross with an emphatic header. Unai Emery's team were level soon enough, however, Poland midfielder Grzegorz Krychowiak giving the Warsaw locals particular reason to cheer by finishing adroitly following a corner.

Bacca, who had laid on Krychowiak's equaliser with a deft touch inside a crowded penalty area, then put Sevilla ahead, latching on to captain José Antonio Reyes's brilliant defence-splitting pass and rounding Boyko to stroke the ball accurately into the net at the near post. Although Dnipro showed admirable defiance to draw level through skipper Rotan's delicate

KEY FACT

92

Experience counts. While much was made of Napoli boss Rafael Benítez's nous, the final ultimately involved the two coaches with the most appearances in the competition, group stage to final. Sevilla's Unai Emery oversaw his 50th match in Warsaw while Dnipro's Myron Markevych was involved for the 42nd time.

free-kick on the stroke of half-time, it was to be Sevilla's – and Bacca's – evening. As the holders turned up the heat in the second half, the Colombian international provided a calm, instinctive finish 17 minutes from time after Vitolo had brushed off a series of defensive ricochets to play him in with a clever outside-of-the-boot pass.

Bacca came close to a hat-trick a few minutes later, only to be denied by a brilliant Boyko save, but it proved inconsequential as Dnipro were unable to muster a decent chance of their own in the closing stages. Indeed the only other major incident of note came three minutes from time when Matheus suddenly collapsed, causing widespread alarm both on the pitch and in the stands. Fortunately, his condition was not as serious as first thought but, with all three substitutes used, it left Dnipro having to chase the remainder of the game with just ten men. They could not find another equaliser, leaving Sevilla to celebrate another memorable and historic European triumph.

Carlos Bacca rifles in Sevilla's winning goal against Dnipro in Warsaw

First qualifying round

01/07/14, Ta' Qali National Stadium, Ta' Qali
Sliema Wanderers FC 1-1 Ferencvárosi TC
10/07/14, Ferenc Puskás, Budapest
Ferencvárosi TC 2-1 Sliema Wanderers FC
Aggregate: 3-2; Ferencvárosi TC qualify.

01/07/14, La Frontière, Esch-sur-Alzette
AS Jeunesse Esch 0-2 Dundalk FC
10/07/14, Oriel Park, Dundalk
Dundalk FC 3-1 AS Jeunesse Esch
Aggregate: 5-1; Dundalk FC qualify.

01/07/14, Nacionalna Arena Filip II Makedonski, Skopje
FK Shkëndija 2-1 FC Zimbru Chisinau
10/07/14, Stadionul Zimbru, Chisinau
FC Zimbru Chisinau 2-0 FK Shkëndija
Aggregate: 3-2; FC Zimbru Chisinau qualify.

03/07/14, Gradski, Niksic
FK Čelik Nikšić 0-5 FC Koper
10/07/14, ŠRC Bonifika, Koper
FC Koper 4-0 FK Čelik Nikšić
Aggregate: 9-0; FC Koper qualify.

03/07/14, District Sport Complex, Orhei
FC Veris 0-0 PFC Litex Lovech
11/07/14, Natsionalen Stadion Vasil Levski, Sofia
PFC Litex Lovech 3-0 FC Veris
Aggregate: 3-0; PFC Litex Lovech qualify.

03/07/14, Nacionalna Arena Filip II Makedonski, Skopje
FK Turnovo 0-1 FC Chikhura Sachkhere
10/07/14, Mikheil Meskhi, Tbilisi
FC Chikhura Sachkhere 3-1 FK Turnovo
Aggregate: 4-1; FC Chikhura Sachkhere qualify.

03/07/14, Gyumri City, Gyumri
FC Shirak 1-2 FC Shakhter Karagandy
10/07/14, Shakhter, Karagandy
FC Shakhter Karagandy 4-0 FC Shirak
Aggregate: 6-1; FC Shakhter Karagandy qualify.

03/07/14, Estadi Comunal, Andorra la Vella
UE Santa Coloma 0-3 FK Metalurg Skopje
10/07/14, Nacionalna Arena Filip II Makedonski, Skopje
FK Metalurg Skopje 2-0 UE Santa Coloma
Aggregate: 5-0; FK Metalurg Skopje qualify.

03/07/14, FFA Academy Stadium, Yerevan
FC Pyunik 1-4 FC Astana
10/07/14, Astana Arena, Astana
FC Astana 2-0 FC Pyunik
Aggregate: 6-1; FC Astana qualify.

03/07/14, Tartu Tamme, Tartu
FC Santos Tartu 0-7 Tromsø IL
10/07/14, Alfheim, Tromso
Tromsø IL 6-1 FC Santos Tartu
Aggregate: 13-1; Tromsø IL qualify.

03/07/14, Gargždai Stadium, Gargzdai
FK Banga 0-0 Sligo Rovers FC
10/07/14, The Showgrounds, Sligo
Sligo Rovers FC 4-0 FK Banga
Aggregate: 4-0; Sligo Rovers FC qualify.

03/07/14, Saviniemi Football Stadium, Kouvola
Myllykosken Pallo -47 1-0 ÍF Fuglafjørdur
10/07/14, Tórsvøllur, Torshavn
ÍF Fuglafjørdur 0-0 Myllykosken Pallo -47
Aggregate: 0-1; Myllykosken Pallo -47 qualify.

03/07/14, Rakvere, Rakvere
JK Sillamäe Kalev 2-1 FC Honka Espoo
10/07/14, ISS, Vantaa
FC Honka Espoo 3-2 JK Sillamäe Kalev (aet)
Aggregate: 4-4; JK Sillamäe Kalev qualify on away goals.

03/07/14, Nantporth, Bangor
AUK Broughton FC 1-1 FK Haugesund
10/07/14, Haugesund, Haugesund
FK Haugesund 2-1 AUK Broughton FC
Aggregate: 3-2; FK Haugesund qualify.

03/07/14, Rhcinpark, Vaduz
FC Vaduz 3-0 College Europa FC
10/07/14, Victoria Stadium, Gibraltar
College Europa FC 0-1 FC Vaduz
Aggregate: 0-4; FC Vaduz qualify.

03/07/14, Tehtaan Kenttä, Valkeakoski
VPS Vaasa 2-1 IF Brommapojkarna
10/07/14, Stockholms, Stockholm
IF Brommapojkarna 2-0 VPS Vaasa
Aggregate: 3-2; IF Brommapojkarna qualify.

03/07/14, Tórsvøllur, Torshavn
B36 Tórshavn 1-2 Linfield FC
08/07/14, Mourneview Park, Lurgan
Linfield FC 1-1 B36 Tórshavn
Aggregate: 3-2; Linfield FC qualify.

03/07/14, Lerkendal Stadion, Trondheim
Rosenborg BK 4-0 FK Jelgava
10/07/14, Zemgales Olympic Centre, Jelgava
FK Jelgava 0-2 Rosenborg BK
Aggregate: 0-6; Rosenborg BK qualify.

03/07/14, Toftir, Toftir
Víkingur 2-1 FC Daugava Daugavpils
10/07/14, Sloka, Jurmala
FC Daugava Daugavpils 1-1 Víkingur
Aggregate: 2-3; Víkingur qualify.

03/07/14, Gamla Ullevi, Gothenburg
IFK Göteborg 0-0 CS Fola Esch
10/07/14, Stade Josy Barthel, Luxembourg
CS Fola Esch 0-2 IFK Göteborg
Aggregate: 0-2; IFK Göteborg qualify.

03/07/14, Laugardalsvöllur, Reykjavik
Fram Reykjavík 0-1 Nõmme Kalju FC
10/07/14, Kadriorg, Tallinn
Nõmme Kalju FC 2-2 Fram Reykjavík
Aggregate: 3-2; Nõmme Kalju FC qualify.

03/07/14, Stjörnuvöllur, Gardabaer
Stjarnan 4-0 Bangor City FC
10/07/14, Nantporth, Bangor
Bangor City FC 0-4 Stjarnan
Aggregate: 0-8; Stjarnan qualify.

03/07/14, Kaplakrikavöllur, Hafnarfjördur
FH Hafnarfjördur 3-0 Glenavon FC
10/07/14, Mourneview Park, Lurgan
Glenavon FC 2-3 FH Hafnarfjördur
Aggregate: 2-6; FH Hafnarfjördur qualify.

03/07/14, Stade Municipal de Differdange, Differdange
FC Differdange 03 1-0 FK Atlantas
10/07/14, Klaipédosmiesto Centrinis, Klaipeda
FK Atlantas 3-1 FC Differdange 03
Aggregate: 3-2; FK Atlantas qualify.

03/07/14, Lazur, Burgas
PFC Botev Plovdiv 4-0 AC Libertas
10/07/14, San Marino Stadium, Serravalle
AC Libertas 0-2 PFC Botev Plovdiv
Aggregate: 0-6; PFC Botev Plovdiv qualify.

03/07/14, Brandywell, Derry
Derry City FC 4-0 Aberystwyth Town FC
10/07/14, Park Avenue, Aberystwyth
Aberystwyth Town FC 0-5 Derry City FC
Aggregate: 0-9; Derry City FC qualify.

Action from the first qualifying round as Sliema's Marko Potezica (left) challenges Stjepan Kukuruzović of Ferencváros

03/07/14, Pittodrie, Aberdeen
Aberdeen FC 5-0 FC Daugava Riga
10/07/14, Daugava, Riga
FC Daugava Riga 0-3 Aberdeen FC
Aggregate: 0-8; Aberdeen FC qualify.

03/07/14, Seaview, Belfast
Crusaders FC 3-1 FK Ekranas
10/07/14, Aukštaitija, Panevezys
FK Ekranas 1-2 Crusaders FC
Aggregate: 2-5; Crusaders FC qualify.

03/07/14, Sheriff small Arena, Tiraspol
FC Tiraspol 2-3 İnter Bakı PİK
10/07/14, Shafa, Baku
İnter Bakı PİK 3-1 FC Tiraspol
Aggregate: 6-3; İnter Bakı PİK qualify.

03/07/14, Ta' Qali National Stadium, Ta' Qali
Hibernians FC 2-4 FC Spartak Trnava
10/07/14, Štadión FC ViOn, Zlate Moravce
FC Spartak Trnava 5-0 Hibernians FC
Aggregate: 9-2; FC Spartak Trnava qualify.

03/07/14, FK Cukaricki, Belgrade
FK Čukarički 4-0 UE Sant Julià
10/07/14, Estadi Comunal, Andorra la Vella
UE Sant Julià 0-0 FK Čukarički
Aggregate: 0-4; FK Čukarički qualify.

03/07/14, Qäbälä Şähär Stadionu, Qäbälä
Qäbälä FK 0-2 NK Široki Brijeg
10/07/14, Pecara, Siroki Brijeg
NK Široki Brijeg 3-0 Qäbälä FK
Aggregate: 5-0; NK Široki Brijeg qualify.

03/07/14, Tsentralniy, Almaty
FC Kairat Almaty 1-0 FK Kükësi
10/07/14, Stadiumi Kombëtar Qemal Stafa, Tirana
FK Kükësi 0-0 FC Kairat Almaty
Aggregate: 0-1; FC Kairat Almaty qualify.

03/07/14, Park Mladezi, Split
RNK Split 2-0 FC Mika
10/07/14, MIKA Sport Complex, Yerevan
FC Mika 1-1 RNK Split
Aggregate: 1-3; RNK Split qualify.

03/07/14, Arena Petrol, Celje
NK Rudar Velenje 1-1 KF Laçi
10/07/14, Laçi, Lac
KF Laçi 1-1 NK Rudar Velenje (aet)
Aggregate: 2-2; KF Laçi qualify 3-2 on penalties.

03/07/14, Debrecen Stadion, Debrecen
Diósgyőri VTK 2-1 Birkirkara FC
10/07/14, Ta' Qali National Stadium, Ta' Qali
Birkirkara FC 1-4 Diósgyőri VTK
Aggregate: 2-6; Diósgyőri VTK qualify.

03/07/14, San Marino Stadium, Serravalle
SS Folgore 1-2 FK Budućnost Podgorica
10/07/14, Gradski, Niksic
FK Budućnost Podgorica 3-0 SS Folgore
Aggregate: 5-1; FK Budućnost Podgorica qualify.

03/07/14, Mikheil Meskhi, Tbilisi
FC Sioni Bolnisi 2-3 KS Flamurtari
10/07/14, Flamurtari, Vlora
KS Flamurtari 1-2 FC Sioni Bolnisi
Aggregate: 4-4; KS Flamurtari qualify on away goals.

03/07/14, Asim Ferhatović Hase Stadion, Sarajevo
FK Željezničar 0-0 FK Lovćen
10/07/14, Pod Malim Brdom, Petrovac
FK Lovćen 0-1 FK Željezničar
Aggregate: 0-1; FK Željezničar qualify.

Second qualifying round

17/07/14, Lokomotiva Košice, Kosice
MFK Košice 0-1 FC Slovan Liberec
24/07/14, U Nisy, Liberec
FC Slovan Liberec 3-0 MFK Košice
Aggregate: 4-0; FC Slovan Liberec qualify.

17/07/14, Laçi, Lac
KF Laçi 0-3 FC Zorya Luhansk
24/07/14, Obolon, Kyiv
FC Zorya Luhansk 2-1 KF Laçi
Aggregate: 5-1; FC Zorya Luhansk qualify.

17/07/14, Gradski, Niksic
FK Budućnost Podgorica 0-2 AC Omonia
24/07/14, GSP Stadium, Nicosia
AC Omonia 0-0 FK Budućnost Podgorica
Aggregate: 2-0; AC Omonia qualify.

17/07/14, Štadión MFK Dubnica, Dubnica nad Vahom
FK AS Trenčín 4-0 FK Vojvodina
24/07/14, Karadjordje, Novi Sad
FK Vojvodina 3-0 FK AS Trenčín
Aggregate: 3-4; FK AS Trenčín qualify.

17/07/14, Piast, Gliwice
Ruch Chorzów 3-2 FC Vaduz
24/07/14, Rheinpark, Vaduz
FC Vaduz 0-0 Ruch Chorzów
Aggregate: 2-3; Ruch Chorzów qualify.

17/07/14, Borås Arena, Boras
IF Elfsborg 0-1 İnter Bakı PİK
24/07/14, Şäfa, Baku
İnter Bakı PİK 0-1 IF Elfsborg (aet)
Aggregate: 1-1; IF Elfsborg qualify 4-3 on penalties.

17/07/14, Traktor, Minsk
FC Dinamo Minsk 3-0 Myllykosken Pallo -47
24/07/14, Saviniemi Football Stadium, Kouvola
Myllykosken Pallo -47 0-0 FC Dinamo Minsk
Aggregate: 0-3; FC Dinamo Minsk qualify.

17/07/14, Kadriorg, Tallinn
Nõmme Kalju FC 1-0 KKS Lech Poznań
24/07/14, Municipal Stadium Poznan, Poznan
KKS Lech Poznań 3-0 Nõmme Kalju FC
Aggregate: 3-1; KKS Lech Poznań qualify.

17/07/14, Toftir, Toftir
Víkingur 0-0 Tromsø IL
24/07/14, Alfheim, Tromso
Tromsø IL 1-2 Víkingur
Aggregate: 1-2; Víkingur qualify.

17/07/14, Stockholms, Stockholm
IF Brommapojkarna 4-0 Crusaders FC
24/07/14, Seaview, Belfast
Crusaders FC 1-1 IF Brommapojkarna
Aggregate: 1-5; IF Brommapojkarna qualify.

UEFA Europa League

17/07/14, Mestský, Mlada Boleslav
FK Mladá Boleslav 2-1 NK Široki Brijeg
24/07/14, Pecara, Siroki Brijeg
NK Široki Brijeg 0-4 FK Mladá Boleslav
Aggregate: 1-6; FK Mladá Boleslav qualify.

17/07/14, Lerkendal Stadion, Trondheim
Rosenborg BK 1-2 Sligo Rovers FC
24/07/14, The Showgrounds, Sligo
Sligo Rovers FC 1-3 Rosenborg BK
Aggregate: 3-4; Rosenborg BK qualify.

17/07/14, Klaipédosmiesto Centrinis, Klaipeda
FK Atlantas 0-0 FC Shakhter Karagandy
24/07/14, Shakhter, Karagandy
FC Shakhter Karagandy 3-0 FK Atlantas
Aggregate: 3-0; FC Shakhter Karagandy qualify.

17/07/14, Astana Arena, Astana
FC Astana 3-0 Hapoel Tel-Aviv FC
24/07/14, Antonis Papadopoulos, Larnaca
Hapoel Tel-Aviv FC 1-0 FC Astana
Aggregate: 1-3; FC Astana qualify.

17/07/14, Raatti, Oulu
RoPS Rovaniemi 1-1 Asteras Tripolis FC
24/07/14, Theodoros Kolokotronis Stadium, Tripoli Arkadia
Asteras Tripolis FC 4-2 RoPS Rovaniemi
Aggregate: 5-3; Asteras Tripolis FC qualify.

17/07/14, Ilie Oană, Ploiesti
FC Petrolul Ploieşti 2-0 KS Flamurtari
24/07/14, Flamurtari, Vlora
KS Flamurtari 1-3 FC Petrolul Ploieşti
Aggregate: 1-5; FC Petrolul Ploieşti qualify.

17/07/14, Swissporarena, Lucerne
FC Luzern 1-1 Saint Johnstone FC
24/07/14, McDiarmid Park, Perth
Saint Johnstone FC 1-1 FC Luzern (aet)
Aggregate: 2-2; Saint Johnstone FC qualify 5-4 on penalties.

17/07/14, Fir Park, Motherwell
Motherwell FC 2-2 Stjarnan
24/07/14, Stjörnuvöllur, Gardabaer
Stjarnan 3-2 Motherwell FC (aet)
Aggregate: 5-4; Stjarnan qualify.

17/07/14, Pittodrie, Aberdeen
Aberdeen FC 0-0 FC Groningen
24/07/14, Euroborg, Groningen
FC Groningen 1-2 Aberdeen FC
Aggregate: 1-2; Aberdeen FC qualify.

17/07/14, Mourneview Park, Lurgan
Linfield FC 1-0 AIK Solna
24/07/14, Friends Arena, Solna
AIK Solna 2-0 Linfield FC
Aggregate: 2-1; AIK Solna qualify.

17/07/14, Brandywell, Derry
Derry City FC 0-1 FC Shakhtyor Soligorsk
24/07/14, Stroitel, Soligorsk
FC Shakhtyor Soligorsk 5-1 Derry City FC
Aggregate: 6-1; FC Shakhtyor Soligorsk qualify.

17/07/14, Lazur, Burgas
PFC Botev Plovdiv 2-1 SKN St Pölten
24/07/14, NV Arena, St Polten
SKN St Pölten 2-0 PFC Botev Plovdiv
Aggregate: 3-2; SKN St Pölten qualify.

17/07/14, Oriel Park, Dundalk
Dundalk FC 0-2 HNK Hajduk Split
24/07/14, Stadion Poljud, Split
HNK Hajduk Split 1-2 Dundalk FC
Aggregate: 3-2; HNK Hajduk Split qualify.

17/07/14, ETO Park, Gyor
Győri ETO FC 0-3 IFK Göteborg
24/07/14, Gamla Ullevi, Gothenburg
IFK Göteborg 0-1 Győri ETO FC
Aggregate: 3-1; IFK Göteborg qualify.

17/07/14, Neman, Grodno
FC Neman Grodno 1-1 FH Hafnarfjördur
24/07/14, Kaplakrikavöllur, Hafnarfjördur
FH Hafnarfjördur 2-0 FC Neman Grodno
Aggregate: 3-1; FH Hafnarfjördur qualify.

17/07/14, David Abashidze, Zestaponi
FC Zestafoni 0-0 FC Spartak Trnava
24/07/14, Štadión FC ViOn, Zlate Moravce
FC Spartak Trnava 3-0 FC Zestafoni
Aggregate: 3-0; FC Spartak Trnava qualify.

17/07/14, Bakcell Arena, Baku
Neftçi PFK 1-2 FC Koper
24/07/14, ŠRC Bonifika, Koper
FC Koper 0-2 Neftçi PFK
Aggregate: 2-3; Neftçi PFK qualify.

17/07/14, Regenboogstadion, Waregem
SV Zulte Waregem 2-1 Zawisza Bydgoszcz
24/07/14, The Krzyszkowiak, Bydgoszcz
Zawisza Bydgoszcz 1-3 SV Zulte Waregem
Aggregate: 2-5; SV Zulte Waregem qualify.

17/07/14, Tsentralniy, Almaty
FC Kairat Almaty 1-1 Esbjerg fB
24/07/14, Esbjerg Arena, Esbjerg
Esbjerg fB 1-0 FC Kairat Almaty
Aggregate: 2-1; Esbjerg fB qualify.

17/07/14, Molde Stadion, Molde
Molde FK 4-1 ND Gorica
24/07/14, Športni Park, Nova Gorica
ND Gorica 1-1 Molde FK
Aggregate: 2-5; Molde FK qualify.

17/07/14, Nacionalna Arena Filip II Makedonski, Skopje
FK Metalurg Skopje 0-0 FK Željezničar
22/07/14, Asim Ferhatović Hase Stadion, Sarajevo
FK Željezničar 2-2 FK Metalurg Skopje
Aggregate: 2-2; FK Metalurg Skopje qualify on away goals.

Aleksei Yanushkevich of Shakhtyor Soligorsk (left) holds off Derry's Nathan Boyle

17/07/14, Park Mladezi, Split
RNK Split 2-1 Hapoel Beer Sheva FC
24/07/14, GSZ, Larnaca
Hapoel Beer Sheva FC 0-0 RNK Split
Aggregate: 1-2; RNK Split qualify.

17/07/14, Stadionul Dr Constantin Rădulescu, Cluj-Napoca
CFR 1907 Cluj 0-0 FK Jagodina
24/07/14, Gradski, Jagodina
FK Jagodina 0-1 CFR 1907 Cluj
Aggregate: 0-1; CFR 1907 Cluj qualify.

17/07/14, Kantrida, Rijeka
HNK Rijeka 1-0 Ferencvárosi TC
24/07/14, Ferenc Puskás, Budapest
Ferencvárosi TC 1-2 HNK Rijeka
Aggregate: 1-3; HNK Rijeka qualify.

17/07/14, Natsionalen Stadion Vasil Levski, Sofia
PFC CSKA Sofia 1-1 FC Zimbru Chisinau
24/07/14, Stadionul Zimbru, Chisinau
FC Zimbru Chisinau 0-0 PFC CSKA Sofia
Aggregate: 1-1; FC Zimbru Chisinau qualify on away goal.

17/07/14, Lovech Stadion, Lovech
PFC Litex Lovech 0-2 Diósgyőri VTK
24/07/14, Sóstói út, Nyiregyhaza
Diósgyőri VTK 1-2 PFC Litex Lovech
Aggregate: 3-2; Diósgyőri VTK qualify.

17/07/14, Asim Ferhatović Hase Stadion, Sarajevo
FK Sarajevo 0-1 FK Haugesund
24/07/14, Haugesund, Haugesund
FK Haugesund 1-3 FK Sarajevo
Aggregate: 2-3; FK Sarajevo qualify.

17/07/14, FK Čukarički, Belgrade
FK Čukarički 0-4 SV Grödig
24/07/14, Stadion Salzburg, Salzburg
SV Grödig 1-2 FK Čukarički
Aggregate: 5-2; SV Grödig qualify.

17/07/14, Bursa Atatürk, Bursa
Bursaspor 0-0 FC Chikhura Sachkhere
24/07/14, Mikheil Meskhi, Tbilisi
FC Chikhura Sachkhere 0-0 Bursaspor (aet)
Aggregate: 0-0; FC Chikhura Sachkhere qualify 4-1 on penalties.

17/07/14, A. Le Coq Arena, Tallinn
JK Sillamäe Kalev 0-4 FC Krasnodar
24/07/14, Kuban, Krasnodar
FC Krasnodar 5-0 JK Sillamäe Kalev
Aggregate: 9-0; FC Krasnodar qualify.

Third qualifying round

31/07/14, Piast, Gliwice
Ruch Chorzów 0-0 Esbjerg fB
07/08/14, Esbjerg Arena, Esbjerg
Esbjerg fB 2-2 Ruch Chorzów
Aggregate: 2-2; Ruch Chorzów qualify on away goals.

31/07/14, Borås Arena, Boras
IF Elfsborg 4-1 FH Hafnarfjördur
07/08/14, Kaplakrikavöllur, Hafnarfjördur
FH Hafnarfjördur 2-1 IF Elfsborg
Aggregate: 3-5; IF Elfsborg qualify.

31/07/14, Stjörnuvöllur, Gardabaer
Stjarnan 1-0 KKS Lech Poznań
07/08/14, Municipal Stadium Poznan, Poznan
KKS Lech Poznań 0-0 Stjarnan
Aggregate: 0-1; Stjarnan qualify.

31/07/14, Shakhter, Karagandy
FC Shakhter Karagandy 4-2 HNK Hajduk Split
07/08/14, Stadion Poljud, Split
HNK Hajduk Split 3-0 FC Shakhter Karagandy
Aggregate: 5-4; HNK Hajduk Split qualify.

31/07/14, Mestský, Mlada Boleslav
FK Mladá Boleslav 1-4 Olympique Lyonnais
07/08/14, Stade de Gerland, Lyon
Olympique Lyonnais 2-1 FK Mladá Boleslav
Aggregate: 6-2; Olympique Lyonnais qualify.

31/07/14, Štadión MŠK Žilina, Zilina
FK AS Trenčín 0-0 Hull City AFC
07/08/14, KC Stadium, Hull
Hull City AFC 2-1 FK AS Trenčín
Aggregate: 2-1; Hull City AFC qualify.

31/07/14, GSP Stadium, Nicosia
AC Omonia 3-0 FK Metalurg Skopje
07/08/14, Nacionalna Arena Filip II Makedonski, Skopje
FK Metalurg Skopje 0-1 AC Omonia
Aggregate: 0-4; AC Omonia qualify.

31/07/14, Stockholms, Stockholm
IF Brommapojkarna 0-3 Torino FC
07/08/14, Stadio Olimpico, Turin
Torino FC 4-0 IF Brommapojkarna
Aggregate: 7-0; Torino FC qualify.

31/07/14, PSV Stadion, Eindhoven
PSV Eindhoven 1-0 SKN St Pölten
07/08/14, NV Arena, St Polten
SKN St Pölten 2-3 PSV Eindhoven
Aggregate: 2-4; PSV Eindhoven qualify.

31/07/14, Marin Anastasovici, Giurgiu
FC Astra Giurgiu 3-0 FC Slovan Liberec
07/08/14, U Nisy, Liberec
FC Slovan Liberec 2-3 FC Astra Giurgiu
Aggregate: 2-6; FC Astra Giurgiu qualify.

31/07/14, Tórsvøllur, Torshavn
Víkingur 1-5 HNK Rijeka
07/08/14, Kantrida, Rijeka
HNK Rijeka 4-0 Víkingur
Aggregate: 9-1; HNK Rijeka qualify.

31/07/14, Gamla Ullevi, Gothenburg
IFK Göteborg 0-1 Rio Ave FC
07/08/14, Rio Ave, Vila do Conde
Rio Ave FC 0-0 IFK Göteborg
Aggregate: 1-0; Rio Ave FC qualify.

31/07/14, Stade de Suisse, Berne
BSC Young Boys 1-0 Ermis Aradippou FC
07/08/14, Antonis Papadopoulos, Larnaca
Ermis Aradippou FC 0-2 BSC Young Boys
Aggregate: 0-3; BSC Young Boys qualify.

31/07/14, McDiarmid Park, Perth
Saint Johnstone FC 1-2 FC Spartak Trnava
07/08/14, Štadión FC ViOn, Zlate Moravce
FC Spartak Trnava 1-1 Saint Johnstone FC
Aggregate: 3-2; FC Spartak Trnava qualify.

31/07/14, Dr Necmettin Şeyhoğlu Stadium, Karabuk
Kardemir Karabükspor 0-0 Rosenborg BK
07/08/14, Lerkendal Stadion, Trondheim
Rosenborg BK 1-1 Kardemir Karabükspor
Aggregate: 1-1; Kardemir Karabükspor qualify on away goal.

31/07/14, Park Mladezi, Split
RNK Split 2-0 FC Chornomorets Odesa
07/08/14, Chornomorets, Odessa
FC Chornomorets Odesa 0-0 RNK Split
Aggregate: 0-2; RNK Split qualify.

31/07/14, Astana Arena, Astana
FC Astana 1-1 AIK Solna
07/08/14, Friends Arena, Solna
AIK Solna 0-3 FC Astana
Aggregate: 1-4; FC Astana qualify.

Real Sociedad's Alberto de la Bella is shadowed by Aberdeen's Barry Robson

31/07/14, Regenboogstadion, Waregem
SV Zulte Waregem 2-5 FC Shakhtyor Soligorsk
07/08/14, Borisov Arena, Borisov
FC Shakhtyor Soligorsk 2-2 SV Zulte Waregem
Aggregate: 7-4; FC Shakhtyor Soligorsk qualify.

31/07/14, Arena Khimki, Khimki
FC Dinamo Moskva 1-1 Hapoel Kiryat Shmona FC
07/08/14, GSP Stadium, Nicosia
Hapoel Kiryat Shmona FC 1-2 FC Dinamo Moskva
Aggregate: 2-3; FC Dinamo Moskva qualify.

31/07/14, Borisov Arena, Borisov
FC Dinamo Minsk 1-0 CFR 1907 Cluj
07/08/14, Stadionul Dr Constantin Rădulescu, Cluj-Napoca
CFR 1907 Cluj 0-2 FC Dinamo Minsk
Aggregate: 0-3; FC Dinamo Minsk qualify.

31/07/14, Bakcell Arena, Baku
Neftçi PFK 0-0 FC Chikhura Sachkhere
07/08/14, Mikheil Meskhi, Tbilisi
FC Chikhura Sachkhere 2-3 Neftçi PFK
Aggregate: 2-3; Neftçi PFK qualify.

31/07/14, Coface Arena, Mainz
1. FSV Mainz 05 1-0 Asteras Tripolis FC
07/08/14, Theodoros Kolokotronis Stadium, Tripoli Arkadia
Asteras Tripolis FC 3-1 1. FSV Mainz 05
Aggregate: 3-2; Asteras Tripolis FC qualify.

31/07/14, Debrecen Stadion, Debrecen
Diósgyőri VTK 1-5 FC Krasnodar
07/08/14, Kuban, Krasnodar
FC Krasnodar 3-0 Diósgyőri VTK
Aggregate: 8-1; FC Krasnodar qualify.

31/07/14, Stadion Dynamo im. Valeriy Lobanovskiy, Kyiv
FC Zorya Luhansk 1-1 Molde FK
07/08/14, Molde Stadion, Molde
Molde FK 1-2 FC Zorya Luhansk
Aggregate: 2-3; FC Zorya Luhansk qualify.

31/07/14, Asim Ferhatović Hase Stadion, Sarajevo
FK Sarajevo 1-2 Atromitos FC
07/08/14, Peristeri, Athens
Atromitos FC 1-3 FK Sarajevo (aet)
Aggregate: 3-4; FK Sarajevo qualify.

31/07/14, Anoeta, San Sebastian
Real Sociedad de Fútbol 2-0 Aberdeen FC
07/08/14, Pittodrie, Aberdeen
Aberdeen FC 2-3 Real Sociedad de Fútbol
Aggregate: 2-5; Real Sociedad de Fútbol qualify.

31/07/14, Jan Breydelstadion, Bruges
Club Brugge KV 3-0 Brøndby IF
07/08/14, Brøndby, Brondby
Brøndby IF 0-2 Club Brugge KV
Aggregate: 0-5; Club Brugge KV qualify.

31/07/14, Ilie Oană, Ploiesti
FC Petrolul Ploieşti 1-1 FC Viktoria Plzeň
07/08/14, Doosan Arena, Plzen
FC Viktoria Plzeň 1-4 FC Petrolul Ploieşti
Aggregate: 2-5; FC Petrolul Ploieşti qualify.

31/07/14, Stadion Salzburg, Salzburg
SV Grödig 1-2 FC Zimbru Chisinau
07/08/14, Stadionul Zimbru, Chisinau
FC Zimbru Chisinau 0-1 SV Grödig
Aggregate: 2-2; FC Zimbru Chisinau qualify on away goals.

Play-offs

20/08/14, NSK Olimpiyskyi, Kyiv
FC Dnipro Dnipropetrovsk 2-1 HNK Hajduk Split
28/08/14, Stadion Poljud, Split
HNK Hajduk Split 0-0 FC Dnipro Dnipropetrovsk
Aggregate: 1-2; FC Dnipro Dnipropetrovsk qualify.

20/08/14, Laugardalsvöllur, Reykjavik
Stjarnan 0-3 FC Internazionale Milano
28/08/14, Stadio Giuseppe Meazza, Milan
FC Internazionale Milano 6-0 Stjarnan
Aggregate: 9-0; FC Internazionale Milano qualify.

21/08/14, Piast, Gliwice
Ruch Chorzów 0-0 FC Metalist Kharkiv
28/08/14, NSK Olimpiyskyi, Kyiv
FC Metalist Kharkiv 1-0 Ruch Chorzów (aet)
Aggregate: 1-0; FC Metalist Kharkiv qualify.

21/08/14, PSV Stadion, Eindhoven
PSV Eindhoven 1-0 FC Shakhtyor Soligorsk
28/08/14, Borisov Arena, Borisov
FC Shakhtyor Soligorsk 0-2 PSV Eindhoven
Aggregate: 0-3; PSV Eindhoven qualify.

21/08/14, Antonis Papadopoulos, Larnaca
AEL Limassol FC 1-2 Tottenham Hotspur FC
28/08/14, White Hart Lane, London
Tottenham Hotspur FC 3-0 AEL Limassol FC
Aggregate: 5-1; Tottenham Hotspur FC qualify.

21/08/14, Helsinki Football Stadium, Helsinki
HJK Helsinki 2-1 SK Rapid Wien
28/08/14, Ernst-Happel-Stadion, Vienna
SK Rapid Wien 3-3 HJK Helsinki
Aggregate: 4-5; HJK Helsinki qualify.

21/08/14, Borås Arena, Boras
IF Elfsborg 2-1 Rio Ave FC
28/08/14, Rio Ave, Vila do Conde
Rio Ave FC 1-0 IF Elfsborg
Aggregate: 2-2; Rio Ave FC qualify on away goal.

21/08/14, Stade de Suisse, Berne
BSC Young Boys 3-1 Debreceni VSC
28/08/14, Debrecen Stadion, Debrecen
Debreceni VSC 0-0 BSC Young Boys
Aggregate: 1-3; BSC Young Boys qualify.

21/08/14, Arena Khimki, Khimki
FC Dinamo Moskva 2-2 AC Omonia
28/08/14, GSP Stadium, Nicosia
AC Omonia 1-2 FC Dinamo Moskva
Aggregate: 3-4; FC Dinamo Moskva qualify.

21/08/14, IJsseldeltastadion, Zwolle
PEC Zwolle 1-1 AC Sparta Praha
28/08/14, Stadion Letná, Prague
AC Sparta Praha 3-1 PEC Zwolle
Aggregate: 4-2; AC Sparta Praha qualify.

21/08/14, Borisov Arena, Borisov
FC Dinamo Minsk 2-0 CD Nacional
28/08/14, Estádio da Madeira, Funchal
CD Nacional 2-3 FC Dinamo Minsk
Aggregate: 2-5; FC Dinamo Minsk qualify.

21/08/14, Tsentralniy, Aktobe
FC Aktobe 0-1 Legia Warszawa
28/08/14, Stadion Wojska Polskiego, Warsaw
Legia Warszawa 2-0 FC Aktobe
Aggregate: 3-0; Legia Warszawa qualify.

21/08/14, Dr Necmettin Şeyhoğlu Stadium, Karabuk
Kardemir Karabükspor 1-0 AS Saint-Étienne
28/08/14, Geoffroy-Guichard, Saint-Etienne
AS Saint-Étienne 1-0 Kardemir Karabükspor (aet)
Aggregate: 1-1; AS Saint-Étienne qualify 4-3 on penalties.

21/08/14, Štadión FC ViOn, Zlate Moravce
FC Spartak Trnava 1-3 FC Zürich
28/08/14, AFG Arena, St Gallen
FC Zürich 1-1 FC Spartak Trnava
Aggregate: 4-2; FC Zürich qualify.

21/08/14, Ilie Oană, Ploiesti
FC Petrolul Ploieşti 1-3 GNK Dinamo Zagreb
28/08/14, Stadion Maksimir, Zagreb
GNK Dinamo Zagreb 2-1 FC Petrolul Ploieşti
Aggregate: 5-2; GNK Dinamo Zagreb qualify.

21/08/14, Stadion FK Partizan, Belgrade
FK Partizan 3-2 Neftçi PFK
28/08/14, Tofiq Bähramov Republican stadium, Baku
Neftçi PFK 1-2 FK Partizan
Aggregate: 3-5; FK Partizan qualify.

21/08/14, AFG Arena, St Gallen
Grasshopper Club Zürich 1-2 Club Brugge KV
28/08/14, Jan Breydelstadion, Bruges
Club Brugge KV 1-0 Grasshopper Club Zürich
Aggregate: 3-1; Club Brugge KV qualify.

21/08/14, GSP Stadium, Nicosia
Apollon Limassol FC 1-1 FC Lokomotiv Moskva
28/08/14, Stadion Lokomotiv, Moscow
FC Lokomotiv Moskva 1-4 Apollon Limassol FC
Aggregate: 2-5; Apollon Limassol FC qualify.

21/08/14, SC Hrvatskih vitezova, Dugopolje
RNK Split 0-0 Torino FC
28/08/14, Stadio Olimpico, Turin
Torino FC 1-0 RNK Split
Aggregate: 1-0; Torino FC qualify.

21/08/14, Stade de Gerland, Lyon
Olympique Lyonnais 1-2 FC Astra Giurgiu
28/08/14, Marin Anastasovici, Giurgiu
FC Astra Giurgiu 0-1 Olympique Lyonnais
Aggregate: 2-2; FC Astra Giurgiu qualify on away goals.

21/08/14, Daknam, Lokeren
KSC Lokeren OV 1-0 Hull City AFC
28/08/14, KC Stadium, Hull
Hull City AFC 2-1 KSC Lokeren OV
Aggregate: 2-2; KSC Lokeren OV qualify on away goal.

Karabükspor's Tanju Kayhan (left) is challenged by Kévin Monnet-Paquet of St-Étienne

21/08/14, Anoeta, San Sebastian
Real Sociedad de Fútbol 1-0 FC Krasnodar
28/08/14, Kuban, Krasnodar
FC Krasnodar 3-0 Real Sociedad de Fútbol
Aggregate: 3-1; FC Krasnodar qualify.

21/08/14, Asim Ferhatović Hase Stadion, Sarajevo
FK Sarajevo 2-3 VfL Borussia Mönchengladbach
28/08/14, Borussia-Park, Monchengladbach
VfL Borussia Mönchengladbach 7-0 FK Sarajevo
Aggregate: 10-2; VfL Borussia Mönchengladbach qualify.

21/08/14, Stadion Dynamo im. Valeriy Lobanovskiy, Kyiv
FC Zorya Luhansk 1-1 Feyenoord
28/08/14, Feijenoord Stadion, Rotterdam
Feyenoord 4-3 FC Zorya Luhansk
Aggregate: 5-4; Feyenoord qualify.

21/08/14, Astana Arena, Astana
FC Astana 0-3 Villarreal CF
28/08/14, Estadio El Madrigal, Villarreal
Villarreal CF 4-0 FC Astana
Aggregate: 7-0; Villarreal CF qualify.

21/08/14, Tofiq Bähramov Republican stadium, Baku
Qarabağ FK 0-0 FC Twente
28/08/14, FC Twente Stadion, Enschede
FC Twente 1-1 Qarabağ FK
Aggregate: 1-1; Qarabağ FK qualify on away goal.

21/08/14, Hüseyin Avni Aker Stadyumu, Trabzon
Trabzonspor AŞ 2-0 FC Rostov
28/08/14, Olimp 2, Rostov-na-Donu
FC Rostov 0-0 Trabzonspor AŞ
Aggregate: 0-2; Trabzonspor AŞ qualify.

21/08/14, Apostolos Nikolaidis, Athens
Panathinaikos FC 4-1 FC Midtjylland
28/08/14, Herning Stadion, Herning
FC Midtjylland 1-2 Panathinaikos FC
Aggregate: 2-6; Panathinaikos FC qualify.

21/08/14, Stadionul Zimbru, Chisinau
FC Zimbru Chisinau 1-0 PAOK FC
28/08/14, Stadio Toumba, Salonika
PAOK FC 4-0 FC Zimbru Chisinau
Aggregate: 4-1; PAOK FC qualify.

21/08/14, Theodoros Kolokotronis Stadium, Tripoli Arkadia
Asteras Tripolis FC 2-0 Maccabi Tel-Aviv FC
28/08/14, Antonis Papadopoulos, Larnaca
Maccabi Tel-Aviv FC 3-1 Asteras Tripolis FC
Aggregate: 3-3; Asteras Tripolis FC qualify on away goal.

21/08/14, Kantrida, Rijeka
HNK Rijeka 1-0 FC Sheriff
28/08/14, Stadionul Sheriff, Tiraspol
FC Sheriff 0-3 HNK Rijeka
Aggregate: 0-4; HNK Rijeka qualify.

Group stage

Group A

18/09/14, Borussia-Park, Monchengladbach
VfL Borussia Mönchengladbach 1-1 Villarreal CF
Goals: 1-0 Herrmann 21, 1-1 Uche 68

18/09/14, GSP Stadium, Nicosia
Apollon Limassol FC 3-2 FC Zürich
Goals: 1-0 Papoulis 9, 2-0 Marcos Gullón 40, 2-1 Rikan 50, 2-2 Yapi Yapo 53, 3-2 Koch 87(og)

02/10/14, Stadion Letzigrund, Zurich
FC Zürich 1-1 VfL Borussia Mönchengladbach
Goals: 1-0 Etoundi 23, 1-1 Nordtveit 25

02/10/14, Estadio El Madrigal, Villarreal
Villarreal CF 4-0 Apollon Limassol FC
Goals: 1-0 Gerard Moreno 9, 2-0 Espinosa 44, 3-0 Espinosa 51, 4-0 Gerard Moreno 82

23/10/14, Estadio El Madrigal, Villarreal
Villarreal CF 4-1 FC Zürich
Goals: 1-0 Cani 6, 1-1 Schönbächler 43, 2-1 Vietto 57, 3-1 Bruno Soriano 60, 4-1 Giovani dos Santos 78

23/10/14, Borussia-Park, Monchengladbach
VfL Borussia Mönchengladbach 5-0 Apollon Limassol FC
Goals: 1-0 Traoré 11, 2-0 Hrgota 56, 3-0 Traoré 67, 4-0 Herrmann 83, 5-0 Angeli 90+1(og)

06/11/14, Stadion Letzigrund, Zurich
FC Zürich 3-2 Villarreal CF
Goals: 0-1 Pina 19, 1-1 Etoundi 21, 1-2 Moreno 23, 2-2 Buff 26, 3-2 Chikhaoui 29

06/11/14, GSP Stadium, Nicosia
Apollon Limassol FC 0-2 VfL Borussia Mönchengladbach
Goals: 0-1 Raffael 56, 0-2 Herrmann 90+5

27/11/14, Estadio El Madrigal, Villarreal
Villarreal CF 2-2 VfL Borussia Mönchengladbach
Goals: 1-0 Vietto 26, 1-1 Raffael 55, 2-1 Cheryshev 63, 2-2 Xhaka 67

27/11/14, Stadion Letzigrund, Zurich
FC Zürich 3-1 Apollon Limassol FC
Goals: 0-1 Farley 23, 1-1 Djimsiti 32, 2-1 Chikhaoui 39(p), 3-1 Chikhaoui 59(p)

11/12/14, Borussia-Park, Monchengladbach
VfL Borussia Mönchengladbach 3-0 FC Zürich
Goals: 1-0 Herrmann 31, 2-0 Hrgota 59, 3-0 Hrgota 64

11/12/14, GSP Stadium, Nicosia
Apollon Limassol FC 0-2 Villarreal CF
Goals: 0-1 Gerard Moreno 35, 0-2 Vietto 40

Group B

18/09/14, Jan Breydelstadion, Bruges
Club Brugge KV 0-0 Torino FC

18/09/14, FC København Stadium, Copenhagen
FC København 2-0 HJK Helsinki
Goals: 1-0 N Jørgensen 68, 2-0 N Jørgensen 81

02/10/14, Stadio Olimpico, Turin
Torino FC 1-0 FC København
Goal: 1-0 Quagliarella 90+4(p)

02/10/14, Helsinki Football Stadium, Helsinki
HJK Helsinki 0-3 Club Brugge KV
Goals: 0-1 Heikkinen 19(og), 0-2 De Sutter 70, 0-3 De Bock 78

23/10/14, Stadio Olimpico, Turin
Torino FC 2-0 HJK Helsinki
Goals: 1-0 Molinaro 35, 2-0 Amauri 58

23/10/14, Jan Breydelstadion, Bruges
Club Brugge KV 1-1 FC København
Goals: 0-1 Amartey 89, 1-1 Víctor Vázquez 90+2

06/11/14, FC København Stadium, Copenhagen
FC København 0-4 Club Brugge KV
Goals: 0-1 Refaelov 7, 0-2 Refaelov 30, 0-3 Refaelov 36, 0-4 Vormer 60

06/11/14, Helsinki Football Stadium, Helsinki
HJK Helsinki 2-1 Torino FC
Goals: 1-0 Baah 60, 2-0 Moren 81, 2-1 Quagliarella 90

27/11/14, Stadio Olimpico, Turin
Torino FC 0-0 Club Brugge KV

27/11/14, Helsinki Football Stadium, Helsinki
HJK Helsinki 2-1 FC København
Goals: 1-0 Baah 29, 1-1 Nilsson 90, 2-1 Kandji 90+3

11/12/14, Jan Breydelstadion, Bruges
Club Brugge KV 2-1 HJK Helsinki
Goals: 1-0 Felipe Gedoz 28(p), 1-1 Kandji 51, 2-1 Refaelov 88

11/12/14, FC København Stadium, Copenhagen
FC København 1-5 Torino FC
Goals: 1-0 Amartey 6, 1-1 Martínez 15, 1-2 Amauri 42(p), 1-3 Martínez 47, 1-4 Darmian 49, 1-5 Silva 53

Group C

18/09/14, Stadion FK Partizan, Belgrade
FK Partizan 0-0 Tottenham Hotspur FC

18/09/14, Atatürk Olimpiyat Stadium, Istanbul
Beşiktaş JK 1-1 Asteras Tripolis FC
Goals: 1-0 Gökhan Töre 33, 1-1 Parra 88

02/10/14, White Hart Lane, London
Tottenham Hotspur FC 1-1 Beşiktaş JK
Goals: 1-0 Kane 27, 1-1 Ba 89(p)

02/10/14, Theodoros Kolokotronis Stadium, Tripoli Arkadia
Asteras Tripolis FC 2-0 FK Partizan
Goals: 1-0 Usero 22, 2-0 Parra 52

23/10/14, White Hart Lane, London
Tottenham Hotspur FC 5-1 Asteras Tripolis FC
Goals: 1-0 Kane 13, 2-0 Lamela 30, 3-0 Lamela 66, 4-0 Kane 74, 5-0 Kane 81, 5-1 Barrales 89

23/10/14, Stadion FK Partizan, Belgrade
FK Partizan 0-4 Beşiktaş JK
Goals: 0-1 Kavlak 18, 0-2 Ba 45, 0-3 Oguzhan Özyakup 52, 0-4 Gökhan Töre 54

06/11/14, Theodoros Kolokotronis Stadium, Tripoli Arkadia
Asteras Tripolis FC 1-2 Tottenham Hotspur FC
Goals: 0-1 Townsend 36(p), 0-2 Kane 42, 1-2 Barrales 90(p)

06/11/14, Atatürk Olimpiyat Stadium, Istanbul
Beşiktaş JK 2-1 FK Partizan
Goals: 1-0 Ba 57(p), 2-0 Ba 62, 2-1 Marković 78

27/11/14, White Hart Lane, London
Tottenham Hotspur FC 1-0 FK Partizan
Goal: 1-0 Stambouli 49

27/11/14, Theodoros Kolokotronis Stadium, Tripoli Arkadia
Asteras Tripolis FC 2-2 Beşiktaş JK
Goals: 0-1 Ba 15, 0-2 Gökhan Töre 61(p), 1-2 Barrales 72, 2-2 Parra 83

11/12/14, Stadion FK Partizan, Belgrade
FK Partizan 0-0 Asteras Tripolis FC

11/12/14, Atatürk Olimpiyat Stadium, Istanbul
Beşiktaş JK 1-0 Tottenham Hotspur FC
Goal: 1-0 Cenk Tosun 59

Group D

18/09/14, Stadion Salzburg, Salzburg
FC Salzburg 2-2 Celtic FC
Goals: 0-1 Wakaso 14, 1-1 Alan 36, 1-2 Brown 60, 2-2 Jonatan Soriano 78

18/09/14, Stadion Maksimir, Zagreb
GNK Dinamo Zagreb 5-1 FC Astra Giurgiu
Goals: 1-0 Soudani 17, 2-0 Soudani 24, 3-0 Soudani 45+1, 4-0 Henríquez 70, 4-1 Chitu 82, 5-1 Ćorić 90+2

02/10/14, Celtic Park, Glasgow
Celtic FC 1-0 GNK Dinamo Zagreb
Goal: 1-0 Commons 6

02/10/14, Marin Anastasovici, Giurgiu
FC Astra Giurgiu 1-2 FC Salzburg
Goals: 1-0 Seto 15, 1-1 Kampl 36, 1-2 Jonatan Soriano 42

23/10/14, Celtic Park, Glasgow
Celtic FC 2-1 FC Astra Giurgiu
Goals: 1-0 Ścepović 73, 2-0 Johansen 79, 2-1 Enache 81

Salzburg striker Alan scores the first of his two goals against Celtic in Glasgow

23/10/14, Stadion Salzburg, Salzburg
FC Salzburg 4-2 GNK Dinamo Zagreb
Goals: 1-0 Alan 14, 2-0 Alan 45, 3-0 André Ramalho 49, 4-0 Alan 52, 4-1 Ademi 81, 4-2 Henríquez 89

06/11/14, Stadion Maksimir, Zagreb
GNK Dinamo Zagreb 1-5 FC Salzburg
Goals: 0-1 Jonatan Soriano 40, 0-2 Kampl 59, 1-2 Henríquez 60, 1-3 Jonatan Soriano 64, 1-4 Bruno 72, 1-5 Jonatan Soriano 85

06/11/14, Marin Anastasovici, Giurgiu
FC Astra Giurgiu 1-1 Celtic FC
Goals: 0-1 Johansen 32, 1-1 William 79

27/11/14, Celtic Park, Glasgow
Celtic FC 1-3 FC Salzburg
Goals: 0-1 Alan 8, 0-2 Alan 13, 1-2 Johansen 30, 1-3 Keita 90+2

27/11/14, Marin Anastasovici, Giurgiu
FC Astra Giurgiu 1-0 GNK Dinamo Zagreb
Goal: 1-0 Bukari 50

11/12/14, Stadion Salzburg, Salzburg
FC Salzburg 5-1 FC Astra Giurgiu
Goals: 1-0 Sabitzer 9, 2-0 Kampl 34, 3-0 Alan 46, 3-1 Florescu 51, 4-1 Alan 70, 5-1 Kampl 90+2

11/12/14, Stadion Maksimir, Zagreb
GNK Dinamo Zagreb 4-3 Celtic FC
Goals: 1-0 Pjaca 14, 1-1 Commons 23, 1-2 Šćepović 30, 2-2 Pjaca 40, 3-2 Brozović 48, 4-2 Pjaca 50, 4-3 Pivarić 82(og)

Group E

18/09/14, PSV Stadion, Eindhoven
PSV Eindhoven 1-0 Estoril Praia
Goal: 1-0 De Jong 26(p)

18/09/14, Apostolos Nikolaidis, Athens
Panathinaikos FC 1-2 FC Dinamo Moskva
Goals: 0-1 Kokorin 40, 0-2 Ionov 49, 1-2 Dinas 63

02/10/14, Arena Khimki, Khimki
FC Dinamo Moskva 1-0 PSV Eindhoven
Goal: 1-0 Zhirkov 90+3

02/10/14, António Coimbra da Mota, Estoril
Estoril Praia 2-0 Panathinaikos FC
Goals: 1-0 Kléber 52, 2-0 Diogo Amado 66

23/10/14, António Coimbra da Mota, Estoril
Estoril Praia 1-2 FC Dinamo Moskva
Goals: 0-1 Kokorin 52, 0-2 Zhirkov 80, 1-2 Yohan Tavares 90+5

23/10/14, PSV Stadion, Eindhoven
PSV Eindhoven 1-1 Panathinaikos FC
Goals: 1-0 Depay 44, 1-1 Karelis 87

06/11/14, Arena Khimki, Khimki
FC Dinamo Moskva 1-0 Estoril Praia
Goal: 1-0 Kuranyi 77

06/11/14, Apostolos Nikolaidis, Athens
Panathinaikos FC 2-3 PSV Eindhoven
Goals: 1-0 Ajagun 11, 1-1 Depay 27, 2-1 Petrić 43, 2-2 De Jong 65, 2-3 Wijnaldum 78

27/11/14, Arena Khimki, Khimki
FC Dinamo Moskva 2-1 Panathinaikos FC
Goals: 1-0 Berg 14, 1-1 Triantafyllopoulos 55(og), 2-1 Ionov 61

27 & 28/11/14, António Coimbra da Mota, Estoril
Estoril Praia 3-3 PSV Eindhoven
Goals: 0-1 Depay 6, 1-1 Tozé 12, 1-2 Narsingh 14, 2-2 Kuca 30, 3-2 Diogo Amado 39, 3-3 Wijnaldum 82

11/12/14, PSV Stadion, Eindhoven
PSV Eindhoven 0-1 FC Dinamo Moskva
Goal: 0-1 Ionov 90

11/12/14, Apostolos Nikolaidis, Athens
Panathinaikos FC 1-1 Estoril Praia
Goals: 1-0 Karelis 55, 1-1 Kléber 87

Group F

18/09/14, NSK Olimpiyskyi, Kyiv
FC Dnipro Dnipropetrovsk 0-1 FC Internazionale Milano
Goal: 0-1 D'Ambrosio 71

18/09/14, Tofiq Bähramov Republican stadium, Baku
Qarabağ FK 0-0 AS Saint-Étienne

02/10/14, Geoffroy-Guichard, Saint-Etienne
AS Saint-Étienne 0-0 FC Dnipro Dnipropetrovsk

02/10/14, Stadio Giuseppe Meazza, Milan
FC Internazionale Milano 2-0 Qarabağ FK
Goals: 1-0 D'Ambrosio 18, 2-0 Icardi 85

23/10/14, Stadio Giuseppe Meazza, Milan
FC Internazionale Milano 0-0 AS Saint-Étienne

23/10/14, NSK Olimpiyskyi, Kyiv
FC Dnipro Dnipropetrovsk 0-1 Qarabağ FK
Goal: 0-1 Muarem 21

06/11/14, Geoffroy-Guichard, Saint-Etienne
AS Saint-Étienne 1-1 FC Internazionale Milano
Goals: 0-1 Dodô 33, 1-1 Bayal Sall 50

06/11/14, Tofiq Bähramov Republican stadium, Baku
Qarabağ FK 1-2 FC Dnipro Dnipropetrovsk
Goals: 0-1 Kalinić 15, 1-1 George 36, 1-2 Kalinić 73

27/11/14, Stadio Giuseppe Meazza, Milan
FC Internazionale Milano 2-1 FC Dnipro Dnipropetrovsk
Goals: 0-1 Rotan 16, 1-1 Kuzmanović 30, 2-1 Osvaldo 50

27/11/14, Geoffroy-Guichard, Saint-Etienne
AS Saint-Étienne 1-1 Qarabağ FK
Goals: 0-1 Nadirov 15, 1-1 Van Wolfswinkel 21

11/12/14, NSK Olimpiyskyi, Kyiv
FC Dnipro Dnipropetrovsk 1-0 AS Saint-Étienne
Goal: 1-0 Fedetskiy 66

11/12/14, Tofiq Bähramov Republican stadium, Baku
Qarabağ FK 0-0 FC Internazionale Milano

Group G

Group G
18/09/14, Stade Maurice Dufrasne, Liege
R. Standard de Liège 2-0 HNK Rijeka
Goals: 1-0 Ciman 74, 2-0 Vinícius Araújo 87

18/09/14, Estadio Ramón Sánchez Pizjuán, Seville
Sevilla FC 2-0 Feyenoord
Goals: 1-0 Krychowiak 8, 2-0 Mbia 31

02/10/14, Feijenoord Stadion, Rotterdam
Feyenoord 2-1 R. Standard de Liège
Goals: 1-0 Van Beek 47, 1-1 Jonathan Viera 65, 2-1 Manu 84

Kevin Mirallas (right) celebrates scoring Everton's fourth goal at home to Wolfsburg

02/10/14, Kantrida, Rijeka
HNK Rijeka 2-2 Sevilla FC
Goals: 0-1 Iago Aspas 26, 1-1 Kramarić 53(p), 2-1 Kvržić 68, 2-2 Mbia 90+1

23/10/14, Kantrida, Rijeka
HNK Rijeka 3-1 Feyenoord
Goals: 1-0 Kramarić 63, 1-1 Toornstra 66, 2-1 Kramarić 71, 3-1 Kramarić 76(p)

23/10/14, Stade Maurice Dufrasne, Liege
R. Standard de Liège 0-0 Sevilla FC

06/11/14, Feijenoord Stadion, Rotterdam
Feyenoord 2-0 HNK Rijeka
Goals: 1-0 El Ahmadi 8, 2-0 Immers 20

06/11/14, Estadio Ramón Sánchez Pizjuán, Seville
Sevilla FC 3-1 R. Standard de Liège
Goals: 1-0 Gameiro 19, 1-1 M'Poku 32, 2-1 Reyes 41, 3-1 Bacca 90

27/11/14, Kantrida, Rijeka
HNK Rijeka 2-0 R. Standard de Liège
Goals: 1-0 Moisés 26, 2-0 Kramarić 34(p)

27/11/14, Feijenoord Stadion, Rotterdam
Feyenoord 2-0 Sevilla FC
Goals: 1-0 Toornstra 56, 2-0 El Ahmadi 83

11/12/14, Stade Maurice Dufrasne, Liege
R. Standard de Liège 0-3 Feyenoord
Goals: 0-1 Toornstra 16, 0-2 Boëtius 60, 0-3 Manu 88

11/12/14, Estadio Ramón Sánchez Pizjuán, Seville
Sevilla FC 1-0 HNK Rijeka
Goal: 1-0 Denis Suárez 20

Group H

18/09/14, Goodison Park, Liverpool
Everton FC 4-1 VfL Wolfsburg
Goals: 1-0 Rodriguez 15(og), 2-0 Coleman 45+1, 3-0 Baines 47(p), 4-0 Mirallas 89, 4-1 Rodriguez 90+4

18/09/14, Grand Stade Lille Métropole, Villeneuve d'Ascq
LOSC Lille 1-1 FC Krasnodar
Goals: 0-1 Laborde 35, 1-1 Kjær 63

02/10/14, VfL Wolfsburg Arena, Wolfsburg
VfL Wolfsburg 1-1 LOSC Lille
Goals: 0-1 Origi 77(p), 1-1 De Bruyne 82

02/10/14, Kuban, Krasnodar
FC Krasnodar 1-1 Everton FC
Goals: 1-0 Ari 43, 1-1 Eto'o 82

23/10/14, Grand Stade Lille Métropole, Villeneuve d'Ascq
LOSC Lille 0-0 Everton FC

23/10/14, Kuban, Krasnodar
FC Krasnodar 2-4 VfL Wolfsburg
Goals: 0-1 Granqvist 37(og), 0-2 De Bruyne 46, 1-2 Granqvist 51(p), 1-3 Luiz Gustavo 64, 1-4 De Bruyne 80, 2-4 Wanderson 86

06/11/14, Goodison Park, Liverpool
Everton FC 3-0 LOSC Lille
Goals: 1-0 Osman 27, 2-0 Jagielka 42, 3-0 Naismith 61

06/11/14, VfL Wolfsburg Arena, Wolfsburg
VfL Wolfsburg 5-1 FC Krasnodar
Goals: 1-0 Hunt 47, 2-0 Hunt 57, 2-1 Wanderson 72, 3-1 Guilavogui 73, 4-1 Bendtner 89(p), 5-1 Bendtner 90+1

27/11/14, VfL Wolfsburg Arena, Wolfsburg
VfL Wolfsburg 0-2 Everton FC
Goals: 0-1 Lukaku 43, 0-2 Mirallas 75

27/11/14, Kuban, Krasnodar
FC Krasnodar 1-1 LOSC Lille
Goals: 1-0 Ari 35, 1-1 Roux 79

11/12/14, Goodison Park, Liverpool
Everton FC 0-1 FC Krasnodar
Goal: 0-1 Laborde 30

11/12/14, Grand Stade Lille Métropole, Villeneuve d'Ascq
LOSC Lille 0-3 VfL Wolfsburg
Goals: 0-1 Vieirinha 45+1, 0-2 Rodriguez 65, 0-3 Rodriguez 89(p)

Group I

18/09/14, Stade de Suisse, Berne
BSC Young Boys 5-0 ŠK Slovan Bratislava
Goals: 1-0 Lecjaks 5, 2-0 Steffen 29, 3-0 Nuzzolo 63, 4-0 Nikci 80, 5-0 Hoarau 90+2

18/09/14, Stadio San Paolo, Naples
SSC Napoli 3-1 AC Sparta Praha
Goals: 0-1 Hušbauer 14, 1-1 Higuaín 23(p), 2-1
Mertens 51, 3-1 Mertens 81

02/10/14, Stadion Letná, Prague
AC Sparta Praha 3-1 BSC Young Boys
Goals: 1-0 Vácha 27, 2-0 Lafata 28, 2-1 Hoarau
52, 3-1 Lafata 85

02/10/14, Štadión Pasienky, Bratislava
ŠK Slovan Bratislava 0-2 SSC Napoli
Goals: 0-1 Hamšík 35, 0-2 Higuaín 74

23/10/14, Štadión Pasienky, Bratislava
ŠK Slovan Bratislava 0-3 AC Sparta Praha
Goals: 0-1 Lafata 56, 0-2 Konaté 61, 0-3 Krejčí 81

23/10/14, Stade de Suisse, Berne
BSC Young Boys 2-0 SSC Napoli
Goals: 1-0 Hoarau 52, 2-0 Bertone 90+2

06/11/14, Stadion Letná, Prague
AC Sparta Praha 4-0 ŠK Slovan Bratislava
Goals: 1-0 Lafata 29, 2-0 Krejčí 32, 3-0
Nhamoinesu 74, 4-0 Lafata 83

06/11/14, Stadio San Paolo, Naples
SSC Napoli 3-0 BSC Young Boys
Goals: 1-0 De Guzmán 45+2, 2-0 De Guzmán 65,
3-0 De Guzmán 83

27/11/14, Štadión Pasienky, Bratislava
ŠK Slovan Bratislava 1-3 BSC Young Boys
Goals: 0-1 Hoarau 9(p), 1-1 Soumah 11, 1-2 Kubo
18, 1-3 Kubo 63

27/11/14, Stadion Letná, Prague
AC Sparta Praha 0-0 SSC Napoli

11/12/14, Stade de Suisse, Berne
BSC Young Boys 2-0 AC Sparta Praha
Goals: 1-0 Hoarau 75(p), 2-0 Steffen 90+4

11/12/14, Stadio San Paolo, Naples
SSC Napoli 3-0 ŠK Slovan Bratislava
Goals: 1-0 Mertens 6, 2-0 Hamšík 16, 3-0 Zapata 75

Group J

18/09/14, Rio Ave, Vila do Conde
Rio Ave FC 0-3 FC Dynamo Kyiv
Goals: 0-1 Yarmolenko 20, 0-2 Belhanda 25, 0-3
Kravets 70

18/09/14, Arena Naţională, Bucharest
FC Steaua Bucureşti 6-0 Aalborg BK
Goals: 1-0 Sânmărtean 51, 2-0 Rusescu 59(p),
3-0 Keşerü 61, 4-0 Keşerü 65, 5-0 Keşerü 72,
6-0 Rusescu 73

02/10/14, Aalborg Stadion, Aalborg
Aalborg BK 1-0 Rio Ave FC
Goal: 1-0 Helenius 46

02/10/14, NSK Olimpiyskyi, Kyiv
FC Dynamo Kyiv 3-1 FC Steaua Bucureşti
Goals: 1-0 Yarmolenko 40, 2-0 Kravets 66, 2-1
Rusescu 89, 3-1 Teodorczyk 90+1

23/10/14, Aalborg Stadion, Aalborg
Aalborg BK 3-0 FC Dynamo Kyiv
Goals: 1-0 Enevoldsen 11, 2-0 Thomsen 39, 3-0
Thomsen 90+1

23/10/14, Arena Naţională, Bucharest
FC Steaua Bucureşti 2-1 Rio Ave FC
Goals: 1-0 Rusescu 17, 2-0 Rusescu 45, 2-1 Del
Valle 48

06/11/14, Rio Ave, Vila do Conde
Rio Ave FC 2-2 FC Steaua Bucureşti
Goals: 1-0 Diego Lopes 35, 1-1 Keşeruu 61, 2-1
Diego Lopes 77p, 2-2 Filip 90+4

06/11/14, NSK Olimpiyskyi, Kyiv
FC Dynamo Kyiv 2-0 Aalborg BK
Goals: 1-0 Vida 70, 2-0 Gusev 90+3

27/11/14, Aalborg Stadion, Aalborg
Aalborg BK 1-0 FC Steaua Bucureşti
Goal: 1-0 Enevoldsen 72

27/11/14, NSK Olimpiyskyi, Kyiv
FC Dynamo Kyiv 2-0 Rio Ave FC
Goals: 1-0 Lens 53, 2-0 Miguel Veloso 78

11/12/14, Rio Ave, Vila do Conde
Rio Ave FC 2-0 Aalborg BK
Goals: 1-0 Del Valle 59, 2-0 Del Valle 79

11/12/14, Arena Naţională, Bucharest
FC Steaua Bucureşti 0-2 FC Dynamo Kyiv
Goals: 0-1 Yarmolenko 71, 0-2 Lens 90+4

Group K

18/09/14, Stadio Artemio Franchi, Florence
ACF Fiorentina 3-0 EA Guingamp
Goals: 1-0 Vargas 34, 2-0 Cuadrado 67, 3-0
Bernardeschi 88

18/09/14, Stadio Toumba, Salonika
PAOK FC 6-1 FC Dinamo Minsk
Goals: 1-0 Nikolić 3(og), 2-0 Athanasiadis 11,
3-0 Athanasiadis 16, 4-0 Athanasiadis 28,
5-0 Papadopoulos 50, 5-1 Nikolić 80, 6-1
Tzandaris 90

02/10/14, Roudourou, Guingamp
EA Guingamp 2-0 PAOK FC
Goals: 1-0 Marveaux 47, 2-0 Marveaux 50

02/10/14, Borisov Arena, Borisov
FC Dinamo Minsk 0-3 ACF Fiorentina
Goals: 0-1 Aquilani 33, 0-2 Ilićič 62, 0-3
Bernardeschi 67

23/10/14, Borisov Arena, Borisov
FC Dinamo Minsk 0-0 EA Guingamp

23/10/14, Stadio Toumba, Salonika
PAOK FC 0-1 ACF Fiorentina
Goal: 0-1 Vargas 38

Skipper Andriy Yarmolenko led by example as
Dynamo Kyiv topped Group J

06/11/14, Roudourou, Guingamp
EA Guingamp 2-0 FC Dinamo Minsk
Goals: 1-0 Beauvue 44, 2-0 Mandanne 86

06/11/14, Stadio Artemio Franchi, Florence
ACF Fiorentina 1-1 PAOK FC
Goals: 0-1 Martens 81, 1-1 Pasqual 88

27/11/14, Roudourou, Guingamp
EA Guingamp 1-2 ACF Fiorentina
Goals: 0-1 Marin 6, 0-2 Babacar 13, 1-2 Beauvue
45(p)

27/11/14, Borisov Arena, Borisov
FC Dinamo Minsk 0-2 PAOK FC
Goals: 0-1 Athanasiadis 82, 0-2 Athanasiadis 88

11/12/14, Stadio Artemio Franchi, Florence
ACF Fiorentina 1-2 FC Dinamo Minsk
Goals: 0-1 Kontsevoi 39, 0-2 Nikolić 55, 1-2
Marin 88

11/12/14, Stadio Toumba, Salonika
PAOK FC 1-2 EA Guingamp
Goals: 0-1 Beauvue 7, 1-1 Athanasiadis 22(p), 1-2
Beauvue 83

Group L

18/09/14, Stadion Wojska Polskiego, Warsaw
Legia Warszawa 1-0 KSC Lokeren OV
Goal: 1-0 Radović 58

18/09/14, Arena Lviv, Lviv
FC Metalist Kharkiv 1-2 Trabzonspor AŞ
Goals: 0-1 Constant 25, 1-1 Homenyuk 61, 1-2
Papadopoulos 90+4

02/10/14, Daknam, Lokeren
KSC Lokeren OV 1-0 FC Metalist Kharkiv
Goal: 1-0 De Pauw 74

02/10/14, Hüseyin Avni Aker Stadyumu, Trabzon
Trabzonspor AŞ 0-1 Legia Warszawa
Goal: 0-1 Kucharczyk 16

*22/10/14, Stadion Dynamo im. Valeriy
Lobanovskiy, Kyiv*
FC Metalist Kharkiv 0-1 Legia Warszawa
Goal: 0-1 Duda 28

23/10/14, Hüseyin Avni Aker Stadyumu, Trabzon
Trabzonspor AŞ 2-0 KSC Lokeren OV
Goals: 1-0 Yatabaré 54, 2-0 Constant 87

06/11/14, Daknam, Lokeren
KSC Lokeren OV 1-1 Trabzonspor AŞ
Goals: 1-0 Patosi 5, 1-1 Waris 45+2

06/11/14, Stadion Wojska Polskiego, Warsaw
Legia Warszawa 2-1 FC Metalist Kharkiv
Goals: 0-1 Kobin 22, 1-1 Saganowski 29, 2-1
Duda 84

27/11/14, Daknam, Lokeren
KSC Lokeren OV 1-0 Legia Warszawa
Goal: 1-0 Vanaken 7

27/11/14, Hüseyin Avni Aker Stadyumu, Trabzon
Trabzonspor AŞ 3-1 FC Metalist Kharkiv
Goals: 1-0 Belkalem 36, 1-1 Homenyuk 68,
2-1 Mehmet Ekici 86, 3-1 Goryainov 90+5(og)

11/12/14, Stadion Wojska Polskiego, Warsaw
Legia Warszawa 2-0 Trabzonspor AŞ
Goals: 1-0 Fatih Öztürk 22(og), 2-0 Orlando Sá 56

11/12/14, Arena Lviv, Lviv
FC Metalist Kharkiv 0-1 KSC Lokeren OV
Goal: 0-1 Leye 16

Final group tables

Group A

	Pld	Home W D L F A	Away W D L F A	Total W D L F A	Pts
1 VfL Borussia Mönchengladbach	6	2 1 0 9 1	1 2 0 5 3	3 3 0 14 4	12
2 Villarreal CF	6	2 1 0 10 3	1 1 1 5 4	3 2 1 15 7	11
3 FC Zürich	6	2 1 0 7 4	0 0 3 3 10	2 1 3 10 14	7
4 Apollon Limassol FC	6	1 0 2 3 6	0 0 3 1 12	1 0 5 4 18	3

Group B

	Pld	Home W D L F A	Away W D L F A	Total W D L F A	Pts
1 Club Brugge KV	6	1 2 0 3 2	2 1 0 7 0	3 3 0 10 2	12
2 Torino FC	6	2 1 0 3 0	1 1 1 6 3	3 2 1 9 3	11
3 HJK Helsinki	6	2 0 1 4 5	0 0 3 1 6	2 0 4 5 11	6
4 FC København	6	1 0 2 3 9	0 1 2 2 4	1 1 4 5 13	4

Group C

	Pld	Home W D L F A	Away W D L F A	Total W D L F A	Pts
1 Beşiktaş JK	6	2 1 0 4 2	1 2 0 7 3	3 3 0 11 5	12
2 Tottenham Hotspur FC	6	2 1 0 7 2	1 1 1 2 2	3 2 1 9 4	11
3 Asteras Tripolis FC	6	1 1 1 5 4	0 2 1 2 6	1 3 2 7 10	6
4 FK Partizan	6	0 2 1 0 4	0 0 3 1 5	0 2 4 1 9	2

Group D

	Pld	Home W D L F A	Away W D L F A	Total W D L F A	Pts
1 FC Salzburg	6	2 1 0 11 5	3 0 0 10 3	5 1 0 21 8	16
2 Celtic FC	6	2 0 1 4 4	0 2 1 6 7	2 2 2 10 11	8
3 GNK Dinamo Zagreb	6	2 0 1 10 9	0 0 3 2 6	2 0 4 12 15	6
4 FC Astra Giurgiu	6	1 1 1 3 3	0 0 3 3 12	1 1 4 6 15	4

Group E

	Pld	Home W D L F A	Away W D L F A	Total W D L F A	Pts
1 FC Dinamo Moskva	6	3 0 0 4 1	3 0 0 5 2	6 0 0 9 3	18
2 PSV Eindhoven	6	1 1 1 2 2	1 1 1 6 6	2 2 2 8 8	8
3 Estoril Praia	6	1 1 1 6 5	0 1 2 1 3	1 2 3 7 8	5
4 Panathinaikos FC	6	0 1 2 4 6	0 1 2 2 5	0 2 4 6 11	2

Group F

	Pld	Home W D L F A	Away W D L F A	Total W D L F A	Pts
1 FC Internazionale Milano	6	2 1 0 4 1	1 2 0 2 1	3 3 0 6 2	12
2 FC Dnipro Dnipropetrovsk	6	1 0 2 1 2	1 1 1 3 3	2 1 3 4 5	7
3 Qarabağ FK	6	0 2 1 1 2	1 1 1 2 3	1 3 2 3 5	6
4 AS Saint-Étienne	6	0 3 0 2 2	0 2 1 0 1	0 5 1 2 3	5

Group G

	Pld	Home W D L F A	Away W D L F A	Total W D L F A	Pts
1 Feyenoord	6	3 0 0 6 1	1 0 2 4 5	4 0 2 10 6	12
2 Sevilla FC	6	3 0 0 6 1	0 2 1 2 4	3 2 1 8 5	11
3 HNK Rijeka	6	2 1 0 7 3	0 0 3 0 5	2 1 3 7 8	7
4 R. Standard de Liège	6	1 1 1 2 3	0 0 3 2 7	1 1 4 4 10	4

Group H

	Pld	Home W D L F A	Away W D L F A	Total W D L F A	Pts
1 Everton FC	6	2 0 1 7 2	1 2 0 3 1	3 2 1 10 3	11
2 VfL Wolfsburg	6	1 1 1 6 4	2 0 1 8 6	3 1 2 14 10	10
3 FC Krasnodar	6	0 2 1 6 6	1 1 1 3 6	1 3 2 7 12	6
4 LOSC Lille	6	0 2 1 1 4	0 2 1 2 5	0 4 2 3 9	4

Group I

	Pld	Home W D L F A	Away W D L F A	Total W D L F A	Pts
1 SSC Napoli	6	3 0 0 9 1	1 1 1 2 2	4 1 1 11 3	13
2 BSC Young Boys	6	3 0 0 9 0	1 0 2 4 7	4 0 2 13 7	12
3 AC Sparta Praha	6	2 1 0 7 1	1 0 2 4 5	3 1 2 11 6	10
4 ŠK Slovan Bratislava	6	0 0 3 1 8	0 0 3 0 12	0 0 6 1 20	0

Group J

	Pld	Home W D L F A	Away W D L F A	Total W D L F A	Pts
1 FC Dynamo Kyiv	6	3 0 0 7 1	2 0 1 5 3	5 0 1 12 4	15
2 Aalborg BK	6	3 0 0 5 0	0 3 0 10	3 0 3 5 10	9
3 FC Steaua Bucureşti	6	2 0 1 8 3	0 1 2 3 6	2 1 3 11 9	7
4 Rio Ave FC	6	1 1 1 4 5	0 0 3 1 5	1 1 4 5 10	4

Group K

	Pld	Home W D L F A	Away W D L F A	Total W D L F A	Pts
1 ACF Fiorentina	6	1 1 1 5 3	3 0 0 6 1	4 1 1 11 4	13
2 EA Guingamp	6	2 0 1 5 2	1 1 1 3 2	3 1 2 8 4	10
3 PAOK FC	6	1 0 2 7 4	1 1 1 3 3	2 1 3 10 7	7
4 FC Dinamo Minsk	6	0 1 2 0 5	1 0 2 3 9	1 1 4 3 14	4

Group L

	Pld	Home W D L F A	Away W D L F A	Total W D L F A	Pts
1 Legia Warszawa	6	3 0 0 5 1	2 0 1 2 1	5 0 1 7 2	15
2 Trabzonspor AŞ	6	2 0 1 5 2	1 1 1 3 4	3 1 2 8 6	10
3 KSC Lokeren OV	6	2 1 0 3 1	1 0 2 1 3	3 1 2 4 4	10
4 FC Metalist Kharkiv	6	0 0 3 1 4	0 0 3 2 6	0 0 6 3 10	0

Round of 32

19/02/15, Stade de Suisse, Berne (att: 20,835)
BSC Young Boys 1-4 Everton FC
Goals: 1-0 Hoarau 10, 1-1 Lukaku 24, 1-2 Coleman 28, 1-3 Lukaku 39, 1-4 Lukaku 58
Referee: Manuel De Sousa (POR)
26/02/15, Goodison Park, Liverpool (att: 25,058)
Everton FC 3-1 BSC Young Boys
Goals: 0-1 Sanogo 13, 1-1 Lukaku 25(p), 2-1 Lukaku 30, 3-1 Mirallas 42
Referee: Johannesson (SWE)
Aggregate: 7-2; Everton FC qualify.

19/02/15, Stadio Olimpico, Turin (att: 25,725)
Torino FC 2-2 Athletic Club
Goals: 0-1 Iñaki Williams 9, 1-1 Maxi López 18, 2-1 Maxi López 42, 2-2 Gurpegui 73
Referee: Koukoulakis (GRE)

26/02/15, Estadio de San Mamés, Bilbao (att: 44,180)
Athletic Club 2-3 Torino FC
Goals: 0-1 Quagliarella 16(p), 1-1 Iraola 44, 1-2 Maxi López 45+2, 2-2 De Marcos 61, 2-3 Darmian 68
Referee: Liany (ISR)
Aggregate: 4-5; Torino FC qualify.

19/02/15, VfL Wolfsburg Arena, Wolfsburg (att: 19,207)
VfL Wolfsburg 2-0 Sporting Clube de Portugal
Goals: 1-0 Dost 46, 2-0 Dost 63
Referee: Yefet (ISR)
26/02/15, José Alvalade, Lisbon (att: 23,097)
Sporting Clube de Portugal 0-0 VfL Wolfsburg
Referee: Buquet (FRA)
Aggregate: 0-2; VfL Wolfsburg qualify.

19/02/15, Aalborg Stadion, Aalborg (att: 8,102)
Aalborg BK 1-3 Club Brugge KV
Goals: 0-1 Oularé 25, 0-2 Refaelov 29, 0-3 Petersen 61(og), 1-3 Helenius 71(p)
Referee: Hagen (NOR)
26/02/15, Jan Breydelstadion, Bruges (att: 11,804)
Club Brugge KV 3-0 Aalborg BK
Goals: 1-0 Víctor Vázquez 11, 2-0 Oularé 64, 3-0 Bolingoli-Mbombo 74
Referee: Sidiropoulos (GRE)
Aggregate: 6-1; Club Brugge KV qualify.

19/02/15, Stadio Olimpico, Rome (att: 29,292)
AS Roma 1-1 Feyenoord
Goals: 1-0 Gervinho 22, 1-1 Kazım-Richards 55
Referee: Haţegan (ROU)
26/02/15, Feijenoord Stadion, Rotterdam (att: 45,000)
Feyenoord 1-2 AS Roma
Goals: 0-1 Ljajić 45+2, 1-1 Manu 57, 1-2 Gervinho 60
Referee: Turpin (FRA)
Aggregate: 2-3; AS Roma qualify.

19/02/15, PSV Stadion, Eindhoven (att: 21,000)
PSV Eindhoven 0-1 FC Zenit
Goal: 0-1 Hulk 64
Referee: Tagliavento (ITA)
26/02/15, Stadion Petrovski, St Petersburg (att: 17,194)
FC Zenit 3-0 PSV Eindhoven
Goals: 1-0 Rondón 28, 2-0 Hulk 48, 3-0 Rondón 67
Referee: Çakır (TUR)
Aggregate: 4-0; FC Zenit qualify.

19/02/15, NSK Olimpiyskyi, Kyiv (att: 5,837)
FC Dnipro Dnipropetrovsk 2-0 Olympiacos FC
Goals: 1-0 Kankava 50, 2-0 Rotan 54
Referee: Schörgenhofer (AUT)
26/02/15, Stadio Georgios Karaiskakis, Piraeus (att: 24,854)
Olympiacos FC 2-2 FC Dnipro Dnipropetrovsk
Goals: 1-0 Mitroglou 14, 1-1 Fedetskiy 22, 2-1 Domínguez 90(p), 2-2 Kalinić 90+2
Referee: Makkelie (NED)
Aggregate: 2-4; FC Dnipro Dnipropetrovsk qualify.

19/02/15, Hüseyin Avni Aker Stadyumu, Trabzon (att: 21,096)
Trabzonspor AŞ 0-4 SSC Napoli
Goals: 0-1 Henrique 6, 0-2 Higuaín 20, 0-3 Gabbiadini 27, 0-4 Zapata 90+2
Referee: Bezborodov (RUS)
26/02/15, Stadio San Paolo, Naples (att: 14,410)
SSC Napoli 1-0 Trabzonspor AŞ
Goal: 1-0 De Guzmán 19
Referee: Bebek (CRO)
Aggregate: 5-0; SSC Napoli qualify.

19/02/15, Anfield, Liverpool (att: 43,353)
Liverpool FC 1-0 Beşiktaş JK
Goal: 1-0 Balotelli 85(p)
Referee: Marciniak (POL)
26/02/15, Atatürk Olimpiyat Stadium, Istanbul (att: 63,324)
Beşiktaş JK 1-0 Liverpool FC (aet)
Goal: 1-0 Arslan 72
Referee: Skomina (SVN)
Aggregate: 1-1; Beşiktaş JK qualify 5-4 on penalties.

19/02/15, White Hart Lane, London (att: 34,235)
Tottenham Hotspur FC 1-1 ACF Fiorentina
Goals: 1-0 Soldado 6, 1-1 Basanta 36
Referee: Velasco Carballo (ESP)
26/02/15, Stadio Artemio Franchi, Florence (att: 29,886)
ACF Fiorentina 2-0 Tottenham Hotspur FC
Goals: 1-0 Gomez 54, 2-0 Salah 71
Referee: Göçek (TUR)
Aggregate: 3-1; ACF Fiorentina qualify.

19/02/15, Celtic Park, Glasgow (att: 58,500)
Celtic FC 3-3 FC Internazionale Milano
Goals: 0-1 Shaqiri 4, 0-2 Palacio 13, 1-2 Armstrong 24, 2-2 Campagnaro 26(og), 2-3 Palacio 45, 3-3 Guidetti 90+3
Referee: Vad (HUN)
26/02/15, Stadio Giuseppe Meazza, Milan (att: 37,133)
FC Internazionale Milano 1-0 Celtic FC
Goal: 1-0 Guarín 88
Referee: Kružliak (SVK)
Aggregate: 4-3; FC Internazionale Milano qualify.

19/02/15, Estadio Ramón Sánchez Pizjuán, Seville (att: 26,850)
Sevilla FC 1-0 VfL Borussia Mönchengladbach
Goal: 1-0 Iborra 70
Referee: Stavrev (MKD)

Ajax's Polish striker Arkadiusz Milik scores the winner at home to Legia

26/02/15, Borussia-Park, Monchengladbach (att: 45,337)
VfL Borussia Mönchengladbach 2-3 Sevilla FC
Goals: 0-1 Bacca 8, 1-1 Xhaka 19, 1-2 Vitolo 26, 2-2 Hazard 29, 2-3 Vitolo 79
Referee: Strahonja (CRO)
Aggregate: 2-4; Sevilla FC qualify.

19/02/15, Amsterdam ArenA, Amsterdam (att: 46,761)
AFC Ajax 1-0 Legia Warszawa
Goal: 1-0 Milik 35
Referee: Eriksson (SWE)
26/02/15, Stadion Wojska Polskiego, Warsaw
Legia Warszawa 0-3 AFC Ajax
Goals: 0-1 Milik 11, 0-2 Viergever 13, 0-3 Milik 43
Referee: Fernández Borbalán (ESP)
Aggregate: 0-4; AFC Ajax qualify.

19/02/15, Constant Vanden Stock Stadium, Brussels (att: 17,317)
RSC Anderlecht 0-0 FC Dinamo Moskva
Referee: Zwayer (GER)
26/02/15, Arena Khimki, Khimki (att: 12,316)
FC Dinamo Moskva 3-1 RSC Anderlecht
Goals: 0-1 Mitrović 29, 1-1 Kozlov 47, 2-1 Yusupov 64, 3-1 Kuranyi 90+5
Referee: Moen (NOR)
Aggregate: 3-1; FC Dinamo Moskva qualify.

19/02/15, Roudourou, Guingamp (att: 16,191)
EA Guingamp 2-1 FC Dynamo Kyiv
Goals: 0-1 Miguel Veloso 19, 1-1 Beauvue 72, 2-1 Diallo 75
Referee: Vinčić (SVN)
26/02/15, NSK Olimpiyskyi, Kyiv (att: 54,308)
FC Dynamo Kyiv 3-1 EA Guingamp
Goals: 1-0 Teodorczyk 31, 2-0 Buyalskiy 46, 2-1 Mandanne 66, 3-1 Gusev 75(p)
Referee: Strömbergsson (SWE)
Aggregate: 4-3; FC Dynamo Kyiv qualify.

19/02/15, Estadio El Madrigal, Villarreal (att: 12,532)
Villarreal CF 2-1 FC Salzburg
Goals: 1-0 Uche 32, 1-1 Jonatan Soriano 48(p), 2-1 Cheryshev 54
Referee: Madden (SCO)
26/02/15, Stadion Salzburg, Salzburg (att: 26,020)
FC Salzburg 1-3 Villarreal CF
Goals: 1-0 Djuricin 18, 1-1 Vietto 33, 1-2 Vietto 76, 1-3 Giovani dos Santos 79
Referee: Hansen (DEN)
Aggregate: 2-5; Villarreal CF qualify.

12/03/15, VfL Wolfsburg Arena, Wolfsburg (att: 25,374)
VfL Wolfsburg 3-1 FC Internazionale Milano
Goals: 0-1 Palacio 6, 1-1 Naldo 28, 2-1 De Bruyne 63, 3-1 De Bruyne 76
Referee: Marciniak (POL)
19/03/15, Stadio Giuseppe Meazza, Milan (att: 38,800)
FC Internazionale Milano 1-2 VfL Wolfsburg
Goals: 0-1 Caligiuri 24, 1-1 Palacio 71, 1-2 Bendtner 89
Referee: Clattenburg (ENG)
Aggregate: 2-5; VfL Wolfsburg qualify.

12/03/15, Jan Breydelstadion, Bruges (att: 12,977)
Club Brugge KV 2-1 Beşiktaş JK
Goals: 0-1 Gökhan Töre 46, 1-1 De Sutter 62, 2-1 Refaelov 79(p)
Referee: Thomson (SCO)
19/03/15, Atatürk Olimpiyat Stadium, Istanbul (att: 65,110)
Beşiktaş JK 1-3 Club Brugge KV
Goals: 1-0 Ramon 48, 1-1 De Sutter 61, 1-2 Bolingoli-Mbombo 80, 1-3 Bolingoli-Mbombo 90
Referee: Karasev (RUS)
Aggregate: 2-5; Club Brugge KV qualify.

12/03/15, NSK Olimpiyskyi, Kyiv (att: 10,581)
FC Dnipro Dnipropetrovsk 1-0 AFC Ajax
Goal: 1-0 Zozulya 30
Referee: Bebek (CRO)
19/03/15, Amsterdam ArenA, Amsterdam (att: 51,756)
AFC Ajax 2-1 FC Dnipro Dnipropetrovsk (aet)
Goals: 1-0 Bazoer 60, 1-1 Konoplyanka 97, 2-1 Van der Hoorn 117
Referee: Kulbakov (BLR)
Aggregate: 2-2; FC Dnipro Dnipropetrovsk qualify on away goal.

12/03/15, Stadion Petrovski, St Petersburg (att: 17,271)
FC Zenit 2-0 Torino FC
Goals: 1-0 Witsel 38, 2-0 Criscito 53
Referee: Manuel De Sousa (POR)
19/03/15, Stadio Olimpico, Turin (att: 24,736)
Torino FC 1-0 FC Zenit
Goal: 1-0 Glik 90
Referee: Jug (SVN)
Aggregate: 1-2; FC Zenit qualify.

12/03/15, Goodison Park, Liverpool (att: 26,150)
Everton FC 2-1 FC Dynamo Kyiv
Goals: 0-1 Gusev 14, 1-1 Naismith 39, 2-1 Lukaku 82(p)
Referee: Velasco Carballo (ESP)
19/03/15, NSK Olimpiyskyi, Kyiv (att: 67,553)
FC Dynamo Kyiv 5-2 Everton FC
Goals: 1-0 Yarmolenko 21, 1-1 Lukaku 29, 2-1 Teodorczyk 35, 3-1 Miguel Veloso 37, 4-1 Gusev 56, 5-1 Antunes 76, 5-2 Jagielka 82
Referee: Aytekin (GER)
Aggregate: 6-4; FC Dynamo Kyiv qualify.

12/03/15, Estadio El Madrigal, Villarreal (att: 19,930)
Villarreal CF 1-3 Sevilla FC
Goals: 0-1 Vitolo 1, 0-2 Mbia 26, 1-2 Vietto 48, 1-3 Gameiro 50
Referee: Orsato (ITA)
19/03/15, Estadio Ramón Sánchez Pizjuán, Seville (att: 28,784)
Sevilla FC 2-1 Villarreal CF
Goals: 1-0 Iborra 69, 1-1 Giovani dos Santos 73, 2-1 Suárez 83
Referee: Atkinson (ENG)
Aggregate: 5-2; Sevilla FC qualify.

UEFA Europa League

12/03/15, Stadio San Paolo, Naples (att: 17,727)
SSC Napoli 3-1 FC Dinamo Moskva
Goals: 0-1 Kuranyi 2, 1-1 Higuaín 25, 2-1 Higuaín 31(p), 3-1 Higuaín 55
Referee: Sidiropoulos (GRE)
19/03/15, Arena Khimki, Khimki (att: 17,356)
FC Dinamo Moskva 0-0 SSC Napoli
Referee: Nijhuis (NED)
Aggregate: 1-3; SSC Napoli qualify.

12/03/15, Stadio Artemio Franchi, Florence (att: 23,557)
ACF Fiorentina 1-1 AS Roma
Goals: 1-0 Iličič 17, 1-1 Keita 77
Referee: Mateu Lahoz (ESP)
19/03/15, Stadio Olimpico, Rome (att: 30,591)
AS Roma 0-3 ACF Fiorentina
Goals: 0-1 Gonzalo Rodríguez 10(p), 0-2 Alonso 18, 0-3 Basanta 22
Referee: Çakır (TUR)
Aggregate: 1-4; ACF Fiorentina qualify.

Quarter-finals

16/04/15, Estadio Ramón Sánchez Pizjuán, Seville (att: 28,450)
Sevilla FC 2-1 FC Zenit
Goals: 0-1 Ryazantsev 29, 1-1 Bacca 73, 2-1 Denis Suárez 88
Referee: Nijhuis (NED)
23/04/15, Stadion Petrovski, St Petersburg (att: 18,121)
FC Zenit 2-2 Sevilla FC
Goals: 0-1 Bacca 6(p), 1-1 Rondón 48, 2-1 Hulk 72, 2-2 Gameiro 85
Referee: Rizzoli (ITA)
Aggregate: 3-4; Sevilla FC qualify.

16/04/15, Jan Breydelstadion, Bruges (att: 26,600)
Club Brugge KV 0-0 FC Dnipro Dnipropetrovsk
Referee: Skomina (SVN)
23/04/15, NSK Olimpiyskyi, Kyiv (att: 16,234)
FC Dnipropetrovsk 1-0 Club Brugge KV
Goal: 1-0 Shakhov 82
Referee: Undiano Mallenco (ESP)
Aggregate: 1-0; FC Dnipro Dnipropetrovsk qualify.

16/04/15, VfL Wolfsburg Arena, Wolfsburg (att: 25,112)
VfL Wolfsburg 1-4 SSC Napoli
Goals: 0-1 Higuaín 15, 0-2 Hamšík 23, 0-3 Hamšík 64, 0-4 Gabbiadini 77, 1-4 Bendtner 80
Referee: Mateu Lahoz (ESP)
23/04/15, Stadio San Paolo, Naples (att: 27,262)
SSC Napoli 2-2 VfL Wolfsburg
Goals: 1-0 Callejón 50, 2-0 Mertens 65, 2-1 Klose 71, 2-2 Perišić 73
Referee: Çakır (TUR)
Aggregate: 6-3; SSC Napoli qualify.

16/04/15, NSK Olimpiyskyi, Kyiv (att: 65,535)
FC Dynamo Kyiv 1-1 ACF Fiorentina
Goals: 1-0 Lens 36, 1-1 Babacar 90+2
Referee: Marciniak (POL)
23/04/15, Stadio Artemio Franchi, Florence (att: 28,058)
ACF Fiorentina 2-0 FC Dynamo Kyiv
Goals: 1-0 Gomez 43, 2-0 Vargas 90+4
Referee: Eriksson (SWE)
Aggregate: 3-1; ACF Fiorentina qualify.

Semi-finals

07/05/15, Stadio San Paolo, Naples (att: 41,095)
SSC Napoli 1-1 FC Dnipro Dnipropetrovsk
Goals: 1-0 David López 50, 1-1 Seleznyov 81
Referee: Moen (NOR)
14/05/15, NSK Olimpiyskyi, Kyiv (att: 62,344)
FC Dnipro Dnipropetrovsk 1-0 SSC Napoli
Goal: 1-0 Seleznyov 58
Referee: Mažić (SRB)
Aggregate: 2-1; FC Dnipro Dnipropetrovsk qualify.

07/05/15, Estadio Ramón Sánchez Pizjuán, Seville (att: 35,840)
Sevilla FC 3-0 ACF Fiorentina
Goals: 1-0 Aleix Vidal 17, 2-0 Aleix Vidal 52, 3-0 Gameiro 75
Referee: Brych (GER)
14/05/15, Stadio Artemio Franchi, Florence (att: 32,466)
ACF Fiorentina 0-2 Sevilla FC
Goals: 0-1 Bacca 22, 0-2 Daniel Carriço 27
Referee: Skomina (SVN)
Aggregate: 0-5; Sevilla FC qualify.

Final

27/05/15, National Stadium Warsaw, Warsaw (att: 45,000)
FC Dnipro Dnipropetrovsk 2-3 Sevilla FC
Goals: 1-0 Kalinić 7, 1-1 Krychowiak 28, 1-2 Bacca 31, 2-2 Rotan 44, 2-3 Bacca 73
Referee: Atkinson (ENG)
Dnipro: Boyko, Kankava (Shakhov 85), Kalinić (Seleznyov 78), Konoplyanka, Léo Matos, Cheberyachko, Douglas, Fedorchuk (Bezus 68), Rotan, Fedetskiy, Matheus. Coach: Myron Markevych (UKR)
Sevilla: Sergio Rico, Trémoulinas, Krychowiak, Daniel Carriço, Bacca (Gameiro 82), Reyes (Coke 58), Kolodziejczak, Éver Banega (Iborra 89), Vitolo, Aleix Vidal, Mbia. Coach: Unai Emery (ESP)
Yellow cards: Kankava 17 (Dnipro), Kalinić 45+2 (Dnipro), Krychowiak 45+2 (Sevilla), Daniel Carriço 62 (Sevilla), Bezus 70 (Dnipro), Bacca 74 (Sevilla), Rotan 75 (Dnipro), Léo Matos 83 (Dnipro)

Squads/Appearances/Goals

Aalborg BK

No	Name	Nat	DoB	Aps	(s)	Gls
Goalkeepers						
22	Carsten Christensen		28/08/86	1	(1)	
1	Nicolai Larsen		09/03/91	7		
Defenders						
31	Jakob Blåbjerg		11/01/95	1	(1)	
20	Henrik Dalsgaard		27/07/89	8		
6	Donny Gorter	NED	15/06/88	6		
2	Patrick Kristensen		28/04/87	1	(1)	
5	Kenneth Emil Petersen		15/01/85	8		
26	Rasmus Thelander		09/07/91	8		
Midfielders						
9	Thomas Augustinussen		20/03/81		(6)	
30	Andreas Bruhn		17/02/94	6	(1)	
25	Frederik Børsting		13/02/95	2		
7	Thomas Enevoldsen		27/07/87	6	(2)	2
21	Kasper Risgård		04/01/83	7		
23	Nicolaj Thomsen		08/05/93	8		2
16	Mathias Thrane		04/09/93		(1)	
14	Mathias Wichmann		06/08/91	1	(1)	
8	Rasmus Würtz		18/09/83	8		
Forwards						
28	Viktor Ahlmann		03/01/95		(1)	
19	Søren Frederiksen		08/07/89		(4)	
11	Nicklas Helenius		08/05/91	7	(1)	2
18	Anders Jacobsen		27/10/89	3	(4)	

AFC Ajax

No	Name	Nat	DoB	Aps	(s)	Gls
Goalkeepers						
22	Jasper Cillessen		22/04/89	4		
Defenders						
5	Nicolai Boilesen	DEN	16/02/92	4		
12	Jaïro Riedewald		09/09/96		(1)	
6	Mike van der Hoorn		15/10/92	1	(2)	1
2	Ricardo van Rhijn		13/06/91	4		
3	Joël Veltman		15/01/92	3		
26	Nick Viergever		03/08/89	4		1
Midfielders						
27	Riechedly Bazoer		12/10/96	4		1
10	Davy Klaassen		21/02/93	4		
20	Lasse Schöne	DEN	27/05/86	1	(1)	
25	Thulani Serero	RSA	11/04/90	3	(1)	
8	Daley Sinkgraven		04/07/95	1	(3)	
Forwards						
16	Lucas Andersen	DEN	13/09/94		(1)	
21	Anwar El Ghazi		03/05/95	4		
11	Ricardo Kishna		04/01/95	3	(1)	
19	Arkadiusz Milik	POL	28/02/94	4		3
9	Kolbeinn Sigthórsson	ISL	14/03/90		(1)	
30	Richairo Zivkovic		05/09/96		(1)	

Top goalscorers

8	Alan (Salzburg)
	Romelu Lukaku (Everton)
7	Gonzalo Higuaín (Napoli)
	Carlos Bacca (Sevilla)
6	Guillaume Hoarau (Young Boys)
	Stefanos Athanasiadis (PAOK)
	Jonatan Soriano (Salzburg)
	Lior Refaelov (Club Brugge)
	Luciano Vietto (Villarreal)

Alan   Romelu Lukaku

RSC Anderlecht

No	Name	Nat	DoB	Aps	(s)	Gls
Goalkeepers						
1	Silvio Proto		23/05/83	2		
Defenders						
12	Maxime Colin	FRA	15/11/91		(1)	
3	Olivier Deschacht		16/02/81	2		
2	Fabrice N'Sakala	COD	21/07/90	2		
13	Rolando	POR	31/08/85	2		
39	Anthony Vanden Borre		24/10/87	2		
Midfielders						
18	Frank Acheampong	GHA	16/10/93	2		
20	Ibrahima Conté	GUI	03/04/91	1		
16	Steven Defour		15/04/88	2		
32	Leander Dendoncker		15/04/95	2		
7	Andy Najar	HON	16/03/93	1	(1)	
31	Youri Tielemans		07/05/97	2		
Forwards						
45	Aleksandar Mitrović	SRB	16/09/94	2		1
15	Cyriac	CIV	15/08/90		(1)	
42	Nathan Kabasele		14/01/94		(1)	
35	Aaron Leya Iseka		15/11/97		(2)	

Asteras Tripolis FC

No	Name	Nat	DoB	Aps	(s)	Gls
Goalkeepers						
1	Tomás Košický	SVK	11/03/86	5		
21	Konstantinos Theodoropoulos		27/03/90	1		
Defenders						
30	Dorin Goian	ROU	12/12/80	3		
27	Braian Lluy	ARG	25/04/89	6		
3	Athanasios Panteliadis		06/09/87	6		
15	Khalifa Sankaré	SEN	15/08/84	6		
Midfielders						
11	Nicolás Fernández	ARG	17/11/86	1	(2)	
17	Ritchie Kitoko	BEL	11/06/88		(1)	
25	Dimitrios Kourbelis		02/11/93	1		
5	Juan Munafo	ARG	20/03/88	3	(2)	
10	Martín Rolle	ARG	02/02/85	4		
4	Éric Tié Bi	CIV	20/07/90	1		
19	Anastasios Tsokanis		02/05/91	3		
8	Fernando Usero	ESP	27/03/84	4	(1)	1
13	Georgios Zisopoulos		23/05/84	6		
Forwards						
39	Ziguy Badibanga	BEL	26/11/91	1	(2)	
14	Anastasios Bakasetas		28/06/93	1	(2)	
9	Jerónimo Barrales	ARG	28/01/87	2	(4)	3
70	Ioannis Gianniotas		29/04/93	3	(2)	
7	Pablo Mazza	ARG	21/12/87	5	(1)	
23	Facundo Parra	ARG	15/06/85	4	(1)	3

Athletic Club

No	Name	Nat	DoB	Aps	(s)	Gls
Goalkeepers						
13	Iago Herrerín		25/01/88	2		
Defenders						
3	Jon Aurtenetxe		03/01/92	1		
16	Xabier Etxeita		31/10/87	2		
18	Carlos Gurpegui		19/08/80	1	(1)	1
15	Andoni Iraola		22/06/82	1	(1)	1
4	Aymeric Laporte	FRA	27/05/94	2		
6	Mikel San José		30/05/89	2		
Midfielders						
7	Beñat Etxebarria		19/02/87	2		
10	Óscar De Marcos		14/04/89	2		1
17	Mikel Rico		04/11/84	2		
19	Iker Muniain		19/12/92	2		
14	Markel Susaeta		14/12/87		(1)	
29	Unai López		30/10/95		(1)	
Forwards						
20	Aritz Aduriz		11/02/81	1		
30	Iñaki Williams		15/06/94	1	(1)	1
9	Kike Sola		25/02/86		(1)	
21	Borja Viguera		26/03/87	1		

Apollon Limassol FC

No	Name	Nat	DoB	Aps	(s)	Gls
Goalkeepers						
83	Bruno Vale	POR	08/04/83	5		
23	Isli Hidi	ALB	15/10/80	1		
Defenders						
27	Angelis Angeli		31/05/89	4	(1)	
50	João Paulo	POR	06/06/81	3	(1)	
16	Georgios Merkis		30/07/84	5		
2	Dustley Mulder	CUW	27/01/85	3		
28	Marios Stylianou		23/09/93	2	(1)	
88	Georgios Vasiliou		12/06/84	2		
42	Christos Wheeler		29/06/97	1		
Midfielders						
70	Farley	BRA	14/01/94	3		1
8	Nicolae Grigore	ROU	19/07/83		(1)	
56	Rachid Hamdani	MAR	08/04/85	6		
17	Hugo López	ESP	15/05/88	3	(2)	
48	Charalambous Kyriakou		09/02/95		(1)	
6	Marcos Gullón	ESP	20/02/89	3	(1)	1
14	Camel Meriem	FRA	18/10/79	4	(1)	
26	Fotios Papoulis	GRE	22/01/85	4	(1)	1
20	Bertrand Robert	FRA	16/11/83	5		
Forwards						
19	Abraham Gneki Gulé	CIV	25/07/86	3	(1)	
77	Fabrice Olinga	CMR	12/05/96	1	(1)	
11	Jan Rezek	CZE	05/05/82	2	(2)	
10	Gastón Sangoy	ARG	05/10/84	3	(2)	
9	Thuram	BRA	01/02/91	3	(2)	

FC Astra Giurgiu

No	Name	Nat	DoB	Aps	(s)	Gls
Goalkeepers						
1	Silviu Lung		04/06/89	6		
Defenders						
5	Syam Ben Youssef	TUN	31/03/89	6		
23	Joãozinho	POR	02/07/89	1		
13	Júnior Morais	BRA	22/07/86	6		
15	Cristian Oros		15/10/84	6		
26	Laurențiu Rus		07/05/85	2	(1)	
Midfielders						
9	Gabriel Enache		18/08/90	5		1
4	George Florescu		21/05/84	2	(4)	1
16	Elliot Grandin	FRA	17/10/87		(1)	
14	Vincent Laban	CYP	09/09/84	4		
22	Vasilios Pliatsikas	GRE	14/04/88	5		
8	Takayuki Seto	JPN	05/02/86	4	(1)	1
91	William	BRA	15/12/91	4	(2)	1
6	Seidu Yahaya	GHA	31/12/89	4	(1)	
Forwards						
10	Constantin Budescu		19/02/89	6		
19	Sadat Bukari	GHA	12/04/89	3	(1)	1
20	Aurelian Chițu		25/03/91	1	(2)	1
21	Kehinde Fatai	NGA	19/02/90	1	(2)	

Beşiktaş JK

No	Name	Nat	DoB	Aps	(s)	Gls
Goalkeepers						
1	Cenk Gönen		21/02/88	5		
29	Tolga Zengin		10/10/83	5		
Defenders						
33	Atınç Nukan		20/07/93		(1)	
22	Ersan Gülüm		17/05/87	4		
19	Pedro Franco	COL	23/04/91	9		
3	İsmail Köybaşı		10/07/89	1	(2)	
44	Daniel Opare	GHA	18/10/90	3		
31	Ramon	BRA	06/05/88	8		1
2	Serdar Kurtuluş		23/07/87	8		
6	Tomáš Sivok	CZE	15/09/83	4		
Midfielders						
7	Gökhan Töre		20/01/92	10		4
13	Atiba Hutchinson	CAN	08/02/83	7		
21	Kerim Koyunlu		19/11/93	1	(8)	
20	Necip Uysal		24/01/91	6	(2)	
15	Oğuzhan Özyakup		23/09/92	4	(3)	1
5	José Sosa	ARG	19/06/85	5	(2)	
18	Tolgay Arslan	GER	16/08/90	2	(1)	1
8	Veli Kavlak	AUT	03/11/88	9		1
Forwards						
9	Demba Ba	SEN	25/05/85	8		5
23	Cenk Tosun		07/06/91	1	(3)	1
14	Furkan Yaman		08/01/96		(1)	
11	Mustafa Pektemek		11/08/88	2	(3)	
10	Olcay Şahan		26/05/87	10		

VfL Borussia Mönchengladbach

No	Name	Nat	DoB	Aps	(s)	Gls
Goalkeepers						
1	Yann Sommer	SUI	17/12/88	8		
Defenders						
15	Álvaro Domínguez	ESP	16/05/89	6		
4	Roel Brouwers	NED	28/11/81	2	(1)	
24	Tony Jantschke		07/04/90	8		
19	Fabian Johnson		11/12/87	3	(2)	
39	Martin Stranzl	AUT	16/06/80	6		
17	Oscar Wendt	SWE	24/10/85	6	(1)	
Midfielders						
6	Mahmoud Dahoud		01/01/96		(1)	
28	André Hahn		13/08/90	1	(2)	
26	Thorgan Hazard	BEL	29/03/93	6	(1)	1
7	Patrick Herrmann		12/02/91	3	(5)	4
27	Julian Korb		21/03/92	3		
23	Christoph Kramer		19/02/91	5		
16	Håvard Nordtveit	NOR	21/06/90	4		1
8	Ibrahima Traoré	GUI	21/04/88	4	(3)	2
34	Granit Xhaka	SUI	27/09/92	7		2
Forwards						
31	Branimir Hrgota	SWE	12/01/93	7	(1)	3
10	Max Kruse		19/03/88	4	(3)	
11	Raffael	BRA	28/03/85	5	(2)	2

Club Brugge KV

No	Name	Nat	DoB	Aps	(s)	Gls
Goalkeepers						
1	Mathew Ryan	AUS	08/04/92	12		
Defenders						
28	Laurens De Bock		07/11/92	7	(2)	1
2	Davy De Fauw		08/07/81	9		
4	Óscar Duarte	CRC	03/06/89	11		
44	Brandon Mechele		28/01/93	12		
19	Thomas Meunier		12/09/91	8		
Midfielders						
63	Boli Bolingoli-Mbombo		01/07/95	4	(1)	3
43	Sander Coopman		12/03/95	1	(1)	
18	Felipe Gedoz	BRA	12/07/93	7	(2)	1
6	Fernando	BRA	03/05/81	4	(1)	
8	Lior Refaelov	ISR	26/04/86	8	(3)	6
5	Francisco Silva	CHI	11/02/86	5	(2)	
3	Timmy Simons		11/12/76	11	(1)	
7	Víctor Vázquez	ESP	20/01/87	7	(3)	2
25	Ruud Vormer	NED	11/05/88	8	(2)	1
Forwards						
30	Nicolás Castillo	CHI	14/02/93	2	(1)	
9	Tom De Sutter		03/07/85	5	(5)	3
55	Tuur Dierckx		09/05/95		(4)	
22	José Izquierdo	COL	07/07/92	4	(2)	
58	Obbi Oularé		08/01/96	4	(4)	2
17	Waldemar Sobota	POL	19/05/87	1	(1)	
42	Nikola Storm		30/09/94	2	(1)	

FC Dinamo Moskva

No	Name	Nat	DoB	Aps	(s)	Gls
Goalkeepers						
30	Vladimir Gabulov		19/10/83	9		
1	Anton Shunin		27/01/87	1		
Defenders						
3	Alexander Büttner	NED	11/02/89	7	(1)	
5	Douglas	NED	12/01/88	6	(1)	
13	Vladimir Granat		22/05/87		(1)	
15	Tomáš Hubočan	SVK	17/09/85	7	(1)	
25	Aleksei Kozlov		25/12/86	6		1
23	Stanislav Manolev	BUL	16/12/85	2		
28	Boris Rotenberg	FIN	19/05/86	1	(1)	
4	Christopher Samba	CGO	28/03/84	9		
Midfielders						
27	Igor Denisov		17/05/84	3	(1)	
7	Balázs Dzsudzsák	HUN	23/12/86	8	(1)	
11	Aleksei Ionov		18/02/89	5	(5)	3
16	Christian Noboa	ECU	08/04/85	5		
88	Aleksandr Tashaev		23/06/94		(2)	
6	William Vainqueur	FRA	19/11/88	9		
14	Mathieu Valbuena	FRA	28/09/84	8	(1)	
8	Artur Yusupov		01/09/89	5	(2)	1
18	Yuri Zhirkov		20/08/83	4	(4)	2
47	Roman Zobnin		11/02/94	1		
Forwards						
9	Aleksandr Kokorin		19/03/91	8		2
22	Kevin Kuranyi	GER	02/03/82	6	(4)	3
99	Aleksandr Prudnikov		26/02/89		(3)	

Celtic FC

No	Name	Nat	DoB	Aps	(s)	Gls
Goalkeepers						
26	Craig Gordon		31/12/82	8		
Defenders						
4	Efe Ambrose	NGA	18/10/88	4	(2)	
22	Jason Denayer	BEL	28/06/95	6		
41	Darnell Fisher	ENG	04/04/94		(1)	
3	Emilio Izaguirre	HON	10/05/86	8		
23	Mikael Lustig	SWE	13/12/86	2		
2	Adam Matthews	WAL	13/01/92	4	(2)	
21	Charlie Mulgrew		06/03/86	3		
5	Virgil van Dijk	NED	08/07/91	8		
Midfielders						
14	Stuart Armstrong		30/03/92	2		1
16	Jo Inge Berget	NOR	11/09/90		(1)	
6	Nir Biton	ISR	30/10/91	3		
8	Scott Brown		25/06/85	7		1
15	Kris Commons		30/08/83	3	(2)	2
49	James Forrest		07/07/91		(2)	
53	Liam Henderson		25/04/96		(2)	
25	Stefan Johansen	NOR	08/01/91	8		3
33	Beram Kayal	ISR	02/05/88		(3)	
16	Gary Mackay-Steven		31/08/90	2		
42	Callum McGregor		14/06/93	5		
27	Alexandar Tonev	BUL	03/02/90	1	(3)	
32	Wakaso Mubarak	GHA	25/07/90	4	(1)	1
Forwards						
28	Leigh Griffiths		20/08/90	2	(2)	
9	John Guidetti	SWE	15/04/92	1	(1)	1
12	Stefan Šćepović	SRB	10/01/90	4		2
10	Anthony Stokes	IRL	25/07/88	3	(1)	

FC Dinamo Minsk

No	Name	Nat	DoB	Aps	(s)	Gls
Goalkeepers						
30	Aleksandr Gutor		18/04/89	3		
35	Sergei Ignatovich		29/06/92	3		
Defenders						
17	Umaru Bangura	SLE	07/10/87	2		
16	Sergei Karpovich		29/03/94	3	(1)	
26	Sergei Kontsevoi		21/06/86	5		1
3	Dmitri Molosh		10/12/81	3		
6	Sergei Politevich		09/04/90	5		
20	Oleg Veretilo		10/07/88	6		
Midfielders						
88	Nenad Adamović	SRB	12/01/89	4	(2)	
7	Artem Bykov		19/10/92		(1)	
21	Hernán Figueredo	URU	15/05/85	2	(2)	
18	Nikita Korzun		06/03/95		(1)	
9	Nemanja Nikolić	MNE	01/01/88	6		2
4	Slobodan Simović	SRB	22/05/89	4	(1)	
22	Igor Stasevich		21/10/85	5	(1)	
15	Chigozie Udoji	NGA	16/09/86	3	(1)	
2	Ihor Voronkov	UKR	24/04/81	5		
23	Yaroslav Yarotski		28/03/96		(2)	
Forwards						
11	Adama Diomandé	NOR	14/02/90	2	(1)	
9	Franck Dja Djédjé	CIV	02/06/86	5	(1)	
8	Hleb Rassadkin		05/04/95		(2)	

GNK Dinamo Zagreb

No	Name	Nat	DoB	Aps	(s)	Gls
Goalkeepers						
34	Eduardo	POR	19/09/82	6		
Defenders						
3	Luis Ibáñez	ARG	15/07/88	1		
6	Ivo Pinto	POR	07/01/90	6		
19	Josip Pivarić		30/01/89	5		
22	Leonardo Sigali	ARG	29/05/87	4		
4	Josip Šimunić		18/02/78	3		
5	Jozo Šimunović		04/08/94	2	(2)	
87	Jérémy Taravel	FRA	17/04/87	3		
Midfielders						
16	Arijan Ademi	MKD	29/05/91	5		1
7	Franko Andrijašević		22/06/91		(1)	
8	Domagoj Antolić		30/06/90	6		
77	Marcelo Brozović		16/11/92	6		1
24	Ante Ćorić		14/04/97		(2)	1
10	Paulo Machado	POR	31/03/86	1	(2)	
20	Marko Pjaca		06/05/95	1	(2)	3
55	Ognjen Vukojević		20/12/83	1	(1)	
Forwards						
90	Duje Čop		01/02/90	3	(2)	
11	Júnior Fernandes	CHI	10/04/88		(3)	
9	Ángelo Henríquez	CHI	13/04/94	4	(2)	3
2	El Arbi Hillel Soudani	ALG	25/11/87	6		3
28	Wilson Eduardo	POR	08/07/90	3		

UEFA Europa League

FC Dnipro Dnipropetrovsk

No	Name	Nat	DoB	Aps	(s)	Gls
Goalkeepers
71	Denys Boyko		29/01/88	15		
Defenders
14	Yevhen Cheberyachko		19/06/83	12		
23	Douglas	BRA	04/04/90	15		
6	Egídio	BRA	18/06/86	4		
44	Artem Fedetskiy		26/04/85	13		2
12	Léo Matos	BRA	02/04/86	6		
24	Valeriy Luchkevych		11/01/96	7	(1)	
3	Ondřej Mazuch	CZE	15/03/89	5		
17	Ivan Strinić	CRO	17/07/87	4		
2	Alexandru Vlad	ROU	06/12/89	2		
Midfielders
9	Roman Bezus		26/09/90	4	(4)	
20	Bruno Gama	POR	15/11/87	4	(10)	
25	Valeriy Fedorchuk		05/10/88	7	(1)	
7	Jaba Kankava	GEO	18/03/86	10	(1)	1
10	Yevhen Konoplyanka		29/09/89	14	(1)	1
4	Serhiy Kravchenko		24/04/83	5	(1)	
89	Serhiy Politylo		09/01/89	1	(1)	
29	Ruslan Rotan		29/10/81	13		3
28	Yevhen Shakhov		30/11/90	2	(7)	1
Forwards
99	Matheus	BRA	15/01/83	3	(3)	
9	Nikola Kalinić	CRO	05/01/88	9	(6)	4
11	Yevhen Seleznyov		20/07/85	3	(7)	2
18	Roman Zozulya		17/11/89	7		1

Estoril Praia

No	Name	Nat	DoB	Aps	(s)	Gls
Goalkeepers
31	Paweł Kieszek	POL	16/04/84	3		
1	Vagner	BRA	06/06/86	3		
Defenders
5	Anderson Luiz	BRA	31/07/88	4		
55	Babanco	CPV	27/07/85	1	(1)	
4	Bruno Miguel		24/09/82	2		
30	Bruno Nascimento	BRA	30/05/91	2		
22	Emídio Rafael		24/01/86	5		
12	Mano		09/04/87	2		
26	Rúben Fernandes		06/05/86	3		
2	Yohan Tavares		02/03/88	6		1
Midfielders
16	Matías Cabrera	URU	16/05/86	2	(1)	
25	Diogo Amado		21/01/90	5	(1)	2
15	Anderson Esiti	NGA	24/05/94	5		
8	Filipe Gonçalves		12/08/84	1	(2)	
70	Tozé		14/01/93	5		1
Forwards
11	Arthuro	BRA	27/08/82	1	(3)	
7	Javier Balboa	EQG	13/05/85		(1)	
9	Bruno Lopes	BRA	19/08/86	2	(1)	
13	Kléber	BRA	02/05/90	3	(2)	2
20	Kuca	CPV	02/08/89	5	(1)	1
32	Ricardo Vaz		26/11/94		(3)	
19	Sebá	BRA	08/06/92	6		

Feyenoord

No	Name	Nat	DoB	Aps	(s)	Gls
Goalkeepers
16	Kenneth Vermeer		10/01/86	8		
Defenders
23	Khalid Boulahrouz		28/12/81	4	(1)	
5	Terence Kongolo		14/02/94	7		
4	Joris Mathijsen		05/04/80	1		
18	Miguel Nelom		22/09/90	7		
22	Sven van Beek		28/07/94	6		1
2	Luke Wilkshire	AUS	02/10/81	5	(1)	
25	Lucas Woudenberg		25/04/94	1		
Midfielders
6	Jordy Clasie		27/06/91	8		
8	Karim El Ahmadi	MAR	27/01/85	7		2
10	Lex Immers		08/06/86	6		1
26	Rick Karsdorp		11/02/95	1	(2)	
24	Matthew Steenvoorden		09/01/93	1		
28	Jens Toornstra		04/04/89	8		3
21	Tonny Trindade de Vilhena		03/01/95	4	(1)	
Forwards
29	Anass Achahbar		13/01/94		(1)	
14	Bilal Başaçıkoğlu	TUR	26/03/95		(2)	
7	Jean-Paul Boëtius		22/03/94	2	(3)	1
31	Wessel Dammers		01/03/95		(1)	
15	Colin Kazım-Richards	TUR	26/08/86	7		1
17	Elvis Manu		13/08/93	4	(2)	3
27	Ruben Schaken		03/04/82	1		
19	Mitchell te Vrede		07/08/91		(3)	

FC Dynamo Kyiv

No	Name	Nat	DoB	Aps	(s)	Gls
Goalkeepers
23	Olexandr Rybka		10/04/87	3		
1	Olexandr Shovkovskiy		02/01/75	9		
Defenders
5	Antunes	POR	01/04/87	6		1
26	Mykyta Burda		24/03/95	5	(1)	
2	Danilo Silva	BRA	24/11/86	10		
6	Aleksandar Dragovic	AUT	06/03/91	10		
34	Yevhen Khacheridi		28/07/87	6	(1)	
27	Yevhen Makarenko		21/05/91	1		
3	Yevhen Selin		09/05/88		(1)	
24	Domagoj Vida	CRO	29/04/89	9	(1)	1
Midfielders
90	Younes Belhanda	MAR	25/02/90	7	(2)	1
29	Vitaliy Buyalskiy		06/01/93	4	(3)	1
28	Yevhen Chumak		25/08/95		(3)	
19	Denys Garmash		19/04/90		(1)	
20	Oleh Gusev		25/04/83	4	(5)	4
45	Vladyslav Kalitvintsev		04/01/93		(5)	
4	Miguel Veloso	POR	11/05/86	5	(4)	3
17	Serhiy Rybalka		01/04/90	11		
16	Serhiy Sydorchuk		02/05/91	9	(2)	
10	Andriy Yarmolenko		23/10/89	11		4
Forwards
22	Artem Kravets		03/06/89	8	(2)	2
7	Jeremain Lens	NED	24/11/87	10		3
85	Dieumerci Mbokani	COD	22/11/85	1	(2)	
91	Łukasz Teodorczyk	POL	03/06/91	3	(3)	3

Everton FC

No	Name	Nat	DoB	Aps	(s)	Gls
Goalkeepers
24	Tim Howard	USA	06/03/79	9		
1	Joel Robles	ESP	17/06/90	1		
Defenders
30	Antolín Alcaraz	PAR	30/07/82	4	(1)	
3	Leighton Baines		11/12/84	5		1
27	Tyias Browning		27/05/94	1		
23	Séamus Coleman	IRL	11/10/88	5		2
15	Sylvain Distin	FRA	16/12/77	3		
29	Luke Garbutt		21/05/93	4		
2	Tony Hibbert		20/02/81	4		
6	Phil Jagielka		17/08/82	9		2
50	Gethin Jones	WAL	13/10/95		(1)	
8	Bryan Oviedo	CRC	18/02/90	2		
26	John Stones		28/05/94	3		
Midfielders
19	Christian Atsu	GHA	10/01/92	3	(4)	
20	Ross Barkley		05/12/93	4	(1)	
18	Gareth Barry		23/02/81	9		
17	Muhamed Bešić	BIH	10/09/92	2	(3)	
51	Kieran Dowell		10/10/97		(1)	
4	Darron Gibson	IRL	25/10/87	2	(2)	
42	Ryan Ledson		19/08/97	1		
16	James McCarthy	IRL	12/11/90	7	(1)	
7	Aiden McGeady	IRL	04/04/86	5		
11	Kevin Mirallas	BEL	05/10/87	5		3
21	Leon Osman		17/05/81	2	(5)	1
22	Steven Pienaar	RSA	17/03/82	2		
Forwards
5	Samuel Eto'o	CMR	10/03/81	3	(1)	1
9	Arouna Koné	CIV	11/11/83	1	(3)	
41	Christopher Long		25/02/92		(1)	
10	Romelu Lukaku	BEL	13/05/93	7	(2)	8
35	Conor McAleny		12/08/92	1		
14	Steven Naismith	SCO	14/09/86	6		2

ACF Fiorentina

No	Name	Nat	DoB	Aps	(s)	Gls
Goalkeepers
1	Neto	BRA	19/07/89	7		
12	Ciprian Tătăruşanu	ROU	09/02/86	7		
Defenders
28	Marcos Alonso	ESP	28/12/90	7	(3)	1
19	José María Basanta	ARG	03/04/84	10		2
2	Gonzalo Rodríguez	ARG	10/04/84	9	(1)	1
23	Manuel Pasqual		13/03/82	5	(2)	1
4	Micah Richards	ENG	24/06/88	5	(2)	
15	Stefan Savić	MNE	08/01/91	8	(1)	
40	Nenad Tomović	SRB	30/08/87	10	(1)	
Midfielders
10	Alberto Aquilani		07/07/84	2	(5)	1
5	Milan Badelj	CRO	25/02/89	9	(4)	
20	Borja Valero	ESP	12/01/85	10	(1)	
11	Juan Cuadrado	COL	26/05/88	3	(2)	1
14	Matías Fernández	CHI	15/05/86	7	(1)	
72	Josip Iličić	SVN	29/01/88	4	(3)	2
17	Joaquín	ESP	21/07/81	8		
16	Jasmin Kurtić	SVN	10/01/89	5		
32	Andrea Lazzari		03/12/84	3	(3)	
8	Marko Marin	GER	13/03/89	2	(2)	2
7	David Pizarro	CHI	11/09/79	7	(3)	
74	Mohamed Salah	EGY	15/06/92	8		1
6	Juan Manuel Vargas	PER	05/10/83	6	(3)	3
Forwards
30	Khouma Babacar	SEN	17/03/93	2	(3)	2
29	Federico Bernardeschi		16/02/94	2	(1)	2
33	Mario Gomez	GER	10/07/85	8		2
43	Simone Minelli		08/01/97		(1)	

UEFA Europa League

EA Guingamp

No	Name	Nat	DoB	Aps	(s)	Gls
Goalkeepers						
1	Jonas Lössl	DEN	01/02/89	7		
30	Mamadou Samassa	MLI	16/02/90	1		
Defenders						
3	Benjamin Angoua	CIV	28/11/86	5		
6	Maxime Baca		02/06/83		(1)	
2	Lars Jacobsen	DEN	20/09/79	6		
29	Christophe Kerbrat		02/08/86	5	(1)	
4	Baïssama Sankoh	GUI	20/03/92	3		
15	Jérémy Sorbon		05/08/83	6		
Midfielders						
12	Claudio Beauvue		16/04/88	8		5
5	Moustapha Diallo	SEN	14/05/86	3	(3)	1
20	Laurent Dos Santos		21/03/93	2	(1)	
26	Thibault Giresse		25/05/81	2	(4)	
7	Dorian Lévêque		22/11/89	5		
18	Lionel Mathis		04/10/81	8		
23	Jérémy Pied		23/02/89	5	(2)	
10	Younousse Sankharé		10/09/89	5	(1)	
24	Sambou Yatabaré	MLI	02/03/89	5	(3)	
Forwards						
17	Rachid Alioui	MAR	18/06/92	1		
14	Ladislas Douniama	CGO	24/05/86		(1)	
13	Christophe Mandanne		07/02/85	5	(2)	2
21	Sylvain Marveaux		15/04/86	5	(1)	2
8	Ronnie Schwartz	DEN	29/08/89	1	(1)	

FC Internazionale Milano

No	Name	Nat	DoB	Aps	(s)	Gls
Goalkeepers						
30	Juan Pablo Carrizo	ARG	06/05/84	8		
1	Samir Handanovič	SVN	14/07/84	2		
Defenders						
6	Marco Andreolli		10/06/86	4	(1)	
14	Hugo Campagnaro	ARG	27/06/80	4	(2)	
33	Danilo D'Ambrosio		09/09/88	5	(1)	2
93	Federico Dimarco		10/11/97		(1)	
22	Dodô	BRA	06/02/92	4	(1)	1
54	Isaac Donkor	GHA	15/08/95	1		
2	Jonathan	BRA	27/02/86		(1)	
5	Juan	BRA	10/06/91	9		
25	Ibrahima Mbaye	SEN	19/11/94	3		
55	Yuto Nagatomo	JPN	12/09/86	2		
23	Andrea Ranocchia		16/02/88	6		
21	Davide Santon		02/01/91	4		
15	Nemanja Vidić	SRB	21/10/81	3	(1)	
Midfielders						
92	Enrico Baldini		13/11/96		(1)	
13	Fredy Guarín	COL	30/06/86	8		1
88	Hernanes	BRA	29/05/85	6	(1)	
10	Mateo Kovačić	CRO	06/05/94	3	(3)	
44	René Krhin	SVN	21/05/90	1	(1)	
17	Zdravko Kuzmanović	SRB	22/09/87	6	(2)	1
90	Yann M'Vila	FRA	29/06/90	4		
18	Gary Medel	CHI	03/08/87	6	(1)	
20	Joel Obi	NGA	22/05/91	1	(3)	
96	Andrea Palazzi		24/02/96		(1)	
91	Xherdan Shaqiri	SUI	10/10/91	3	(1)	1
Forwards						
97	Federico Bonazzoli		21/05/97	2		
9	Mauro Icardi	ARG	19/02/93	8		1
7	Pablo Osvaldo		12/01/86	2	(3)	1
8	Rodrigo Palacio	ARG	05/02/82	5	(1)	4
28	George Pușcaș	ROU	08/04/96		(1)	

FC Krasnodar

No	Name	Nat	DoB	Aps	(s)	Gls
Goalkeepers						
31	Andriy Dykan	UKR	16/07/77	5		
88	Andrei Sinitsin		23/06/88	1		
Defenders						
6	Andreas Granqvist	SWE	16/04/85	5		1
5	Sergei Petrov	POL	04/11/87	5		
17	Vitali Kaleshin		03/10/80	6		
4	Aleksandr Martynovich	BLR	26/08/87		(1)	
98	Sergei Petrov		02/01/91	2	(3)	
27	Ragnar Sigurdsson	ISL	19/06/86	6		
Midfielders						
20	Ruslan Adzhindzhal		22/06/74		(1)	
76	Aleksandr Ageev		22/05/96		(1)	
10	Odil Ahmedov	UZB	25/11/87	4		
18	Vladimir Bystrov		31/01/84		(1)	
8	Yuri Gazinski		20/07/89	6		
11	Marat Izmailov		21/09/82	4	(1)	
22	Joãozinho	BRA	25/12/88	2		
21	Ricardo Laborde	COL	16/02/88	5	(1)	2
7	Pavel Mamaev		17/09/88	2	(2)	
33	Mauricio Pereyra	URU	15/03/90	6		
Forwards						
9	Ari	BRA	11/12/85	5		2
19	Nikita Burmistrov		06/07/89		(2)	
14	Wanderson	BRA	18/02/86	2	(4)	2

HJK Helsinki

No	Name	Nat	DoB	Aps	(s)	Gls
Goalkeepers						
12	Toni Doblas	ESP	05/08/80	6		
13	Carljohan Eriksson		25/04/95		(1)	
Defenders						
3	Gideon Baah	GHA	01/10/91	5		2
5	Tapio Heikkilä		08/04/90		(2)	
6	Markus Heikkinen		13/10/78	5		
11	Veli Lampi		18/07/84	4		
16	Valtteri Moren		15/06/91	4		1
27	Sebastian Sorsa		25/01/84	6		
Midfielders						
32	Anthony Annan	GHA	21/07/86	5		
99	Macoumba Kandji	SEN	02/08/85	4	(2)	2
31	Robin Lod		17/04/93	6		
24	Joel Perovuo		11/08/85		(3)	
28	Rasmus Schüller		18/06/91	1	(1)	
10	Teemu Tainio		27/11/79	4		
4	Mika Väyrynen		28/12/81	4	(1)	
80	Erfan Zeneli		28/12/86	4	(2)	
Forwards						
17	Nikolai Alho		12/03/93	1	(2)	
30	Aristide Bancé	BFA	19/09/84	2		
33	Roni Porokara		12/12/83	1	(2)	
8	Demba Savage	GAM	17/06/88	4		

FC København

No	Name	Nat	DoB	Aps	(s)	Gls
Goalkeepers						
1	Stephan Andersen		26/11/81	6		
Defenders						
15	Mikael Antonsson	SWE	31/05/81	5	(1)	
3	Pierre Bengtsson	SWE	12/04/88	5		
2	Tom Høgli	NOR	24/02/84	5		
37	Lasse Lindbjerg		15/04/92		(1)	
25	Mathias "Zanka" Jørgensen		23/04/90	5		
4	Per Nilsson	SWE	15/09/82	2		1
Midfielders						
18	Daniel Amartey	GHA	21/12/94	6		2
6	Claudemir	BRA	27/03/88	4	(1)	
8	Thomas Delaney		03/09/91	3	(2)	
19	Rúrik Gíslason	ISL	25/02/88	4	(1)	
10	Nicolai Jørgensen		15/01/91	3	(3)	2
9	Bashkim Kadrii		09/07/91	2		
36	Brandur Olsen	FRO	19/12/95		(1)	
Forwards						
32	Danny Amankwaa		30/01/94	2	(3)	
11	Andreas Cornelius		16/03/93	4		
22	Steve De Ridder	BEL	25/02/87	3	(1)	
33	Yones Felfel		24/11/95		(1)	
17	Alex Kacaniklic	SWE	13/08/91	4	(1)	
24	Youssef Toutouh		06/10/92	3	(2)	

Legia Warszawa

No	Name	Nat	DoB	Aps	(s)	Gls
Goalkeepers						
12	Dušan Kuciak	SVK	21/05/85	8		
Defenders						
28	Łukasz Broź		17/12/85	8		
17	Tomasz Brzyski		10/01/82	2		
2	Dossa Júnior	CYP	28/07/86	4		
15	Iñaki Astiz	ESP	05/11/83	4		
3	Tomasz Jodłowiec		08/09/85	8		
4	Igor Lewczuk		30/05/85	1		
25	Jakub Rzeźniczak		26/10/86	7		
Midfielders						
31	Krystian Bielik		04/01/98		(1)	
8	Ondrej Duda	SVK	05/12/94	6		2
6	Guilherme	BRA	21/05/91	6		
23	Hélio Pinto	POR	29/02/84		(1)	
16	Michał Masłowski		19/12/89	2		
32	Miroslav Radović	SRB	16/01/84	2		1
21	Ivica Vrdoljak	CRO	19/09/83	8		
33	Michał Żyro		20/09/92	6	(1)	
Forwards						
20	Jakub Kosecki		29/08/90	2	(4)	
18	Michał Kucharczyk		20/03/91	8		1
70	Orlando Sá	POR	26/05/88	5	(1)	1
9	Marek Saganowski		31/10/78	1	(6)	1

LOSC Lille

No	Name	Nat	DoB	Aps	(s)	Gls
Goalkeepers						
1	Vincent Enyeama	NGA	29/08/82	6		
Defenders						
25	Marko Baša	MNE	29/12/82	6		
18	Franck Béria		23/05/83	3	(1)	
2	Sébastien Corchia		01/11/90	6		
14	Simon Kjær	DEN	26/03/89	5		1
22	David Rozehnal	CZE	05/07/80	2		
15	Djibril Sidibé		29/07/92	1	(1)	
23	Pape Souaré	SEN	06/06/90	5		
Midfielders						
4	Florent Balmont		02/02/80	6		
6	Jonathan Delaplace		20/03/86	1	(1)	
5	Idrissa Gueye	SEN	26/09/89	6		
17	Marcos Lopes	POR	28/12/95	1		
10	Marvin Martin		10/01/88	1	(1)	
24	Rio Mavuba		08/03/84	4	(1)	
12	Soualiho Meïté		17/03/94		(1)	
Forwards						
11	Michael Frey	SUI	19/07/94	2	(1)	
27	Divock Origi	BEL	18/04/95	5		1
9	Ronny Rodelin		18/11/89	1	(4)	
26	Nolan Roux		01/03/88	2	(3)	1
20	Ryan Mendes	CPV	08/01/90	3	(3)	

KSC Lokeren OV

No	Name	Nat	DoB	Aps	(s)	Gls
Goalkeepers						
1	Boubacar Barry	CIV	30/12/79	6		
Defenders						
25	Alexander Corryn		03/01/94	1		
13	Georgios Galitsios	GRE	06/07/86	5		
5	Mijat Maric	SUI	30/04/84	6		
4	Grégory Mertens		21/02/91	1	(1)	
3	Denis Odoi		27/05/88	6		
2	Alexander Scholz	DEN	24/10/92	5	(1)	
Midfielders						
28	Evariste Ngolok		15/11/88	1	(2)	
7	Killian Overmeire		06/12/85	6		
8	Koen Persoons		12/07/83	5	(1)	
14	Jordan Remacle		14/02/87	2	(3)	
20	Hans Vanaken		24/08/92	4		1
Forwards						
18	Besart Abdurahimi	MKD	31/07/90	2	(2)	
23	Eugene Ansah	GHA	16/12/94		(1)	
29	Nill De Pauw		06/01/90	6		1
17	Cyriel Dessers		08/12/94	1	(2)	
19	Júnior Dutra	BRA	25/04/88	2	(2)	
9	Mbaye Leye	SEN	01/12/82	5	(1)	1
10	Ayanda Patosi	RSA	31/10/92	2	(1)	1

SSC Napoli

No	Name	Nat	DoB	Aps	(s)	Gls
Goalkeepers						
45	Mariano Andújar	ARG	30/07/83	8		
1	Rafael Cabral	BRA	20/05/90	6		
Defenders						
33	Raúl Albiol	ESP	04/09/85	9	(1)	
5	Miguel Britos	URU	17/07/85	12		
31	Faouzi Ghoulam	ALG	01/02/91	11	(2)	
4	Henrique	BRA	14/10/86	6	(3)	1
26	Kalidou Koulibaly	FRA	20/06/91	7		
11	Christian Maggio		11/02/82	7		
18	Juan Camilo Zúñiga	COL	14/12/85		(3)	
Midfielders						
7	José Callejón	ESP	11/02/87	10	(4)	1
19	David López	ESP	09/10/89	7	(2)	1
6	Jonathan de Guzmán	NED	13/09/87	6	(2)	4
77	Walter Gargano	URU	23/07/84	5	(1)	
17	Marek Hamšík	SVK	27/07/87	7	(5)	4
88	Gökhan Inler	SUI	27/06/84	11		
8	Jorginho		20/12/91	6		
14	Dries Mertens	BEL	06/05/87	11	(2)	4
16	Giandomenico Mesto		25/05/82	4	(2)	
Forwards						
23	Manolo Gabbiadini		26/11/91	3	(3)	2
9	Gonzalo Higuaín	ARG	10/12/87	10	(4)	7
24	Lorenzo Insigne		04/06/91	3	(2)	
21	Michu	ESP	21/03/86	1	(1)	
91	Duván Zapata	COL	01/04/91	4	(4)	2

Liverpool FC

No	Name	Nat	DoB	Aps	(s)	Gls
Goalkeepers						
22	Simon Mignolet	BEL	06/08/88	2		
Defenders						
19	Javi Manquillo	ESP	05/05/94		(1)	
6	Dejan Lovren	CRO	05/07/89	1	(1)	
18	Alberto Moreno	ESP	05/07/92	2		
17	Mamadou Sakho	FRA	13/02/90	1		
37	Martin Škrtel	SVK	15/12/84	2		
4	Kolo Touré	CIV	19/03/81	1		
Midfielders						
24	Joe Allen	WAL	14/03/90	2		
23	Emre Can	GER	12/01/94	2		
10	Philippe Coutinho	BRA	12/06/92	1		
14	Jordan Henderson		17/06/90	1		
33	Jordon Ibe		08/12/95	2		
20	Adam Lallana		10/05/88	1	(1)	
Forwards						
45	Mario Balotelli	ITA	12/08/90	1	(1)	1
9	Rickie Lambert		16/02/82		(1)	
31	Raheem Sterling		08/12/94	1	(1)	
15	Daniel Sturridge		01/09/89	2		

FC Metalist Kharkiv

No	Name	Nat	DoB	Aps	(s)	Gls
Goalkeepers						
81	Vladimir Dišljenković	SRB	02/07/81	2		
29	Olexandr Goryainov		29/06/75	4		
Defenders						
4	Andriy Berezovchuk		16/04/81	2	(2)	
30	Papa Gueye	SEN	07/06/84	3		
45	Olexandr Osman		18/04/94	1	(1)	
17	Serhiy Pshenychnykh		19/11/81	5		
6	Marco Torsiglieri	ARG	12/01/88	4		
3	Cristian Villagra	ARG	27/12/85	5		
24	Ayila Yussuf	NGA	04/11/84	2		
Midfielders						
7	Serhiy Bolbat		13/06/93	4	(1)	
19	Chaco Torres	ARG	20/06/85	2		
10	Cleiton Xavier	BRA	23/03/83	3		
8	Edmar		16/06/80	2	(1)	
77	Vasyl Kobin		24/05/85	5	(1)	1
16	Serhiy Kostyuk		05/03/86		(1)	
32	Oleh Krasnopyorov		25/07/80	6		
22	Denys Kulakov		01/05/86		(5)	
46	Artem Radchenko		02/01/95	2	(2)	
82	Pavlo Rebenok		23/07/85	3	(1)	
43	Yuriy Tkachuk		18/04/95	2		
Forwards						
14	Volodymyr Homenyuk		19/07/85	5	(1)	2
50	Jajá	BRA	28/02/86	4		

Olympiacos FC

No	Name	Nat	DoB	Aps	(s)	Gls
Goalkeepers						
16	Roberto	ESP	10/02/86	2		
Defenders						
14	Omar Elabdellaoui	NOR	05/12/91	2		
45	Felipe Santana	BRA	17/03/86	2		
26	Arthur Masuaku	FRA	07/11/93	2		
23	Dimitrios Siovas		16/09/88	2		
Midfielders						
6	Ibrahim Afellay	NED	02/04/86	2		
10	Alejandro Domínguez	ARG	10/06/81	2		1
77	Mathieu Dossevi	TOG	12/02/88	1	(1)	
9	Jimmy Durmaz	SWE	22/03/89	1	(1)	
11	Pajtim Kasami	SUI	02/06/92	2		
2	Ioannis Maniatis		12/10/86	1		
5	Luka Milivojević	SRB	07/04/91	1	(1)	
Forwards						
25	Kostas Fortounis		16/10/92		(2)	
7	Kostas Mitroglou		12/03/88	2		1

UEFA Europa League

Panathinaikos FC

No	Name	Nat	DoB	Aps	(s)	Gls
Goalkeepers						
1	Stefanos Kotsolis		05/06/79	3		
15	Luke Steele	ENG	24/09/84	3		
Defenders						
31	Christos Bourbos		01/06/83	3		
3	Adamantios Chouchoumis		17/07/94	1		
4	Georgios Koutroumbis		10/02/91	2	(2)	
21	Nano	ESP	27/10/84	5		
24	Spiridon Risvanis		03/01/94	1		
23	Gordon Schildenfeld	CRO	18/03/85	5		
5	Konstantinos Triantafyllopoulos		03/04/93	5	(1)	
Midfielders						
14	Abdul Ajagun	NGA	10/02/93	3	(1)	1
11	Emir Bajrami	SWE	07/03/88	2		
22	Ouasim Bouy	NED	11/06/93	2	(1)	
18	Christos Donis		09/10/94	3	(3)	
7	Viktor Klonaridis	BEL	28/07/92	2	(1)	
8	Anastasios Lagos		12/04/92	4	(1)	
6	David Mendes da Silva	NED	04/08/82	3		
32	Danijel Pranjić	CRO	02/12/81	4	(2)	
10	Zeca	POR	31/08/88	4		
Forwards						
9	Marcus Berg	SWE	17/08/86	1	(2)	1
26	Athanasios Dinas		12/11/89	4		1
19	Nikolaos Karelis		24/02/92	3	(2)	2
33	Mladen Petrić	CRO	01/01/81	3	(2)	1

FK Partizan

No	Name	Nat	DoB	Aps	(s)	Gls
Goalkeepers						
25	Milan Lukač		04/10/85	6		
Defenders						
13	Lazar Ćirković		22/08/92	5		
30	Branko Ilić	SVN	06/02/83	5		
5	Nemanja Petrović		17/04/92	1	(1)	
6	Vojislav Stanković		22/09/87	6		
35	Miladin Stevanović		11/02/96	2		
3	Vladimir Volkov	MNE	06/06/86	6		
4	Miroslav Vulićević		29/05/85	2		
Midfielders						
18	Nikola Drinčić	MNE	07/09/84	4		
14	Petar Grbić	MNE	07/08/88	5	(1)	
22	Saša Ilić		30/12/77	3	(2)	
7	Predrag Luka		11/05/88		(2)	
21	Saša Marković		13/03/91	3	(2)	1
11	Nikola Ninković		19/12/94	3	(2)	
55	Danilo Pantić		26/10/96	4		
17	Andrija Živković		11/07/96	3	(2)	
Forwards						
10	Ismaël Fofana	CIV	08/09/88		(1)	
9	Nemanja Kojić		03/02/90		(3)	
27	Danko Lazović		17/05/83	4	(1)	
29	Nenad Marinković		28/09/88		(1)	
32	Petar Škuletić		29/06/90	4		

Qarabağ FK

No	Name	Nat	DoB	Aps	(s)	Gls
Goalkeepers						
13	Ibrahim Šehić	BIH	02/09/88	6		
Defenders						
25	Ansi Agolli	ALB	11/10/82	6		
55	Bädavi Hüseynov		11/07/91	6		
5	Maksim Medvedev		29/09/89	5		
14	Räşad F Sadıqov		16/06/82	5	(1)	
24	Admir Teli	ALB	02/06/81	1	(2)	
Midfielders						
99	Namiq Äläsgärov		03/02/95	l	(3)	
70	Chumbinho	BRA	21/09/86	1		
11	Danilo Dias	BRA	06/11/85	1		
41	Leroy George	NED	21/04/87	5		1
10	Muarem Muarem	MKD	22/10/88	6		1
17	Vüqar Nadirov		15/06/87	3	(3)	1
2	Qara Qarayev		12/10/92	6		
18	İlqar Qurbanov		25/04/86	1	(2)	
20	Richard	BRA	20/03/89	6		
77	Cavid Tağiyev		22/07/92		(3)	
7	Namiq Yusifov		14/08/86	4	(1)	
Forwards						
9	Reynaldo	BRA	24/08/89	4		

PAOK FC

No	Name	Nat	DoB	Aps	(s)	Gls
Goalkeepers						
71	Panagiotis Glykos		10/10/86	6		
Defenders						
4	Georgios Katsikas		14/06/90	5		
70	Stilianos Kitsiou		28/09/93	1	(1)	
15	Miguel Vítor	POR	30/06/89	6		
5	Răzvan Raţ	ROU	26/05/81	5		
2	Ioannis Skondras		21/02/90	5		
21	Nikolaos Spyropoulos		10/10/83	1	(1)	
3	Georgios Tzavellas		26/11/87	1	(2)	
Midfielders						
7	Eyal Golasa	ISR	07/10/91	2	(4)	
26	Ergys Kaçe	ALB	08/07/93	5		
8	Hedwiges Maduro	NED	13/02/85		(2)	
40	Maarten Martens	BEL	02/07/84		(3)	1
32	Theofanis Tzandaris		13/06/93	6		1
6	Alexandros Tziolis		13/02/85	5		
Forwards						
33	Stefanos Athanasiadis		24/12/88	6		6
9	Dimitrios Papadopoulos		20/10/81		(5)	1
11	Róbert Mak	SVK	08/03/91	2		
10	Facundo Pereyra	ARG	03/09/87	4		
14	Dimitrios Salpingidis		18/08/81	6		

PSV Eindhoven

No	Name	Nat	DoB	Aps	(s)	Gls
Goalkeepers						
22	Remko Pasveer		08/11/83	2		
1	Jeroen Zoet		06/01/91	6		
Defenders						
4	Santiago Arias	COL	13/01/92	4		
20	Joshua Brenet		20/03/94	4	(1)	
5	Jeffrey Bruma		13/11/91	6		
2	Nicolas Isimat-Mirin	FRA	15/11/91	4	(2)	
3	Karim Rekik		02/12/94	6		
28	Abel Tamata	COD	05/12/90		(1)	
15	Jetro Willems		30/03/94	8		
Midfielders						
18	Andrés Guardado	MEX	28/09/86	6		
29	Jorrit Hendrix		06/02/95	4	(3)	
27	Oscar Hiljemark	SWE	28/06/92	1		
6	Adam Maher		20/07/93	7	(1)	
24	Marcel Ritzmaier	AUT	22/04/93		(4)	
23	Rai Vloet		08/05/95		(1)	
10	Georginio Wijnaldum		11/11/90	6	(1)	2
Forwards						
9	Luuk de Jong		27/08/90	6	(1)	2
7	Memphis Depay		13/02/94	6		3
14	Florian Jozefzoon		09/02/91	2	(3)	
17	Jürgen Locadia		07/11/93	3	(3)	
11	Luciano Narsingh		13/09/90	7		1

HNK Rijeka

No	Name	Nat	DoB	Aps	(s)	Gls
Goalkeepers						
25	Ivan Vargić		15/03/87	6		
Defenders						
22	Marin Leovac		07/08/88	4		
13	Marko Lešković		27/04/91	5		
15	Matej Mitrović		10/11/93	4		
19	Miral Samardžić	SVN	17/02/87	3	(1)	
11	Ivan Tomečak		07/12/89	6		
29	Marko Vešović	MNE	28/08/91	2	(3)	
Midfielders						
14	Goran Cvijanović	SVN	09/09/86	4	(2)	
8	Mato Jajalo		25/05/88	6		
89	Vedran Jugović		31/07/89	5	(1)	
20	Zoran Kvržić	BIH	07/08/88	3	(3)	1
16	Ivan Močinić		30/04/93	2		
88	Moisés	BRA	17/03/88	5	(1)	1
21	Damir Zlomislić	BIH	20/07/91		(1)	
Forwards						
28	Josip Ivančić		29/03/91		(2)	
91	Andrej Kramarić		19/06/91	6		5
99	Ivan Krstanović		05/01/83	1	(4)	
10	Anas Sharbini		21/02/87	4		

Rio Ave FC

No	Name	Nat	DoB	Aps	(s)	Gls
Goalkeepers						
1	Cássio	BRA	12/08/80	4		
93	Ederson	BRA	17/08/93	2		
Defenders						
3	Prince-Désir Gouano	FRA	24/12/93	4		
12	Lionn	BRA	29/01/89	3		
46	Marcelo	BRA	27/07/89	4	(1)	
16	Nuno Lopes		19/12/86	3		
25	Roderick		30/03/91	2		
15	Tiago Pinto		01/02/88	6		
Midfielders						
14	André Vilas Boas		04/06/83	2	(2)	
10	Diego Lopes	BRA	03/05/94	4	(1)	2
6	Luís Gustavo		28/09/92	2		
20	Pedro Moreira		15/03/89	4		
11	Renan Bressan	BLR	03/11/88	3	(3)	
8	Tarantini		07/10/83	4	(1)	
30	Alhassan Wakaso	GHA	07/01/92	3	(2)	
Forwards						
13	Emmanuel Boateng	GHA	23/05/96	4	(1)	
28	Yonathan Del Valle	VEN	28/05/90	4		3
77	Esmaël Gonçalves		25/06/91	2	(1)	
9	Ahmed Hassan	EGY	05/03/93	2	(3)	
33	William Jebor	LBR	10/11/91		(1)	
17	Ukra		16/03/88	4	(2)	

AS Saint-Étienne

No	Name	Nat	DoB	Aps	(s)	Gls
Goalkeepers						
16	Stéphane Ruffier		27/09/86	6		
Defenders						
26	Moustapha Bayal Sall	SEN	30/11/85	5		1
23	Paul Baysse		18/05/88	1	(1)	
20	Jonathan Brison		07/02/83	3		
29	François Clerc		18/04/83	1		
24	Loïc Perrin		07/08/85	5		
19	Florentin Pogba	GUI	19/08/90	4	(1)	
2	Kévin Théophile-Catherine		28/10/89	4		
Midfielders						
6	Jérémy Clément		26/08/84	5		
10	Renaud Cohade		29/09/84	3	(2)	
8	Benjamin Corgnet		06/04/87	1	(1)	
28	Ismaël Diomandé	CIV	28/08/92	2	(2)	
7	Max-Alain Gradel	CIV	30/11/87	5		
18	Fabien Lemoine		16/03/87	5	(1)	
27	Franck Tabanou		30/01/89	3	(1)	
Forwards						
21	Romain Hamouma		29/03/87	3	(1)	
9	Mevlüt Erdinç	TUR	25/02/87	2		
11	Yohan Mollo		18/07/89	1	(1)	
22	Kévin Monnet-Paquet		19/08/88	3	(2)	
12	Allan Saint-Maximin		12/03/97		(1)	
13	Ricky van Wolfswinkel	NED	27/01/89	4	(1)	1

Sevilla FC

No	Name	Nat	DoB	Aps	(s)	Gls
Goalkeepers						
13	Beto	POR	01/05/82	5		
29	Sergio Rico		01/09/93	10	(1)	
Defenders						
24	Alejandro Arribas		01/05/89	2	(1)	
23	Coke		26/04/87	6	(2)	
6	Daniel Carriço	POR	04/08/88	14		1
5	Diogo Figueiras	POR	07/01/91	6	(2)	
3	Fernando Navarro		25/06/82	5	(1)	
15	Timothée Kolodziejczak	FRA	01/10/91	9		
21	Nicolás Pareja	ARG	19/01/84	7		
2	Benoît Trémoulinas	FRA	28/12/85	9	(1)	
Midfielders						
22	Aleix Vidal		21/08/89	11		2
17	Denis Suárez		06/01/94	3	(6)	3
18	Gerard Deulofeu		13/03/94	2	(3)	
19	Éver Banega	ARG	29/06/88	11	(1)	
12	Vicente Iborra		16/01/88	7	(4)	2
4	Grzegorz Krychowiak	POL	29/01/90	13		2
25	Stéphane Mbia	CMR	20/05/86	10	(3)	3
10	José Antonio Reyes		01/09/83	10	(3)	1
20	Vitolo		02/11/89	9	(2)	3
Forwards						
9	Carlos Bacca	COL	08/09/86	8	(7)	7
7	Kevin Gameiro	FRA	09/05/87	6	(6)	4
14	Iago Aspas		01/08/87	2	(1)	1

AS Roma

No	Name	Nat	DoB	Aps	(s)	Gls
Goalkeepers						
28	Łukasz Skorupski	POL	05/05/91	4		
Defenders						
23	Davide Astori		07/01/87		(2)	
25	José Holebas	GRE	27/06/84	4		
44	Kostas Manolas	GRE	14/06/91	4		
35	Vasilios Torosidis	GRE	10/06/85	4		
2	Mapou Yanga-Mbiwa	FRA	15/05/89	4		
Midfielders						
16	Daniele De Rossi		24/07/83	4		
24	Alessandro Florenzi		11/03/91	2	(1)	
20	Seydou Keita	MLI	16/01/80	3	(1)	1
8	Adem Ljajić	SRB	29/09/91	3		1
4	Radja Nainggolan	BEL	04/05/88	2	(1)	
32	Leandro Paredes	ARG	29/06/94		(1)	
15	Miralem Pjanić	BIH	02/04/90	3	(1)	
Forwards						
88	Seydou Doumbia	CIV	31/12/87		(1)	
27	Gervinho	CIV	27/05/87	3	(1)	2
7	Juan Manuel Iturbe	ARG	04/06/93	1	(2)	
10	Francesco Totti		27/09/76			
53	Daniele Verde		20/06/96	1	(1)	

FC Salzburg

No	Name	Nat	DoB	Aps	(s)	Gls
Goalkeepers						
31	Péter Gulácsi	HUN	06/05/90	7		
33	Alexander Walke	GER	06/06/83	1		
Defenders						
5	André Ramalho	BRA	16/02/92	7		1
4	Peter Ankersen	DEN	22/09/90	4	(1)	
45	Duje Ćaleta-Car	CRO	17/09/96	1		
36	Martin Hinteregger		07/09/92	8		
15	Franz Schiemer		21/03/86		(2)	
2	Benno Schmitz	GER	17/11/94	2		
6	Christian Schwegler	SUI	06/06/84	3	(2)	
17	Andreas Ulmer		30/10/85	6		
Midfielders						
14	Valon Berisha	NOR	07/02/93		(2)	
77	Massimo Bruno	BEL	17/09/93	4	(3)	1
11	Felipe Pires	BRA	18/04/95		(2)	
3	Stefan Ilsanker		18/05/89	6		
44	Kevin Kampl	SVN	09/10/90	6		4
8	Naby Keïta	GUI	10/02/95	3	(3)	1
41	Konrad Laimer		27/05/97	2	(1)	
37	Valentino Lazaro		24/03/96	1	(1)	
24	Christoph Leitgeb		14/04/85	6		
18	Takumi Minamino	JPN	16/01/95	1		
Forwards						
27	Alan	BRA	10/07/89	5		8
9	Marco Djuricin		12/12/92	2		1
26	Jonatan Soriano	ESP	24/09/85	7	(1)	6
42	Nils Quaschner	GER	22/04/94		(1)	
7	Marcel Sabitzer		17/03/94	6	(2)	1

ŠK Slovan Bratislava

No	Name	Nat	DoB	Aps	(s)	Gls
Goalkeepers						
1	Dušan Perniš		28/11/84	6		
Defenders						
18	Mamadou Bagayoko	CIV	31/12/89	2		
4	Erik Čikoš		31/07/88	6		
16	Nicolás Gorosito	ARG	17/08/88	5		
26	Benoît Hudák		21/03/93	3	(1)	
14	Tomáš Jablonský	CZE	21/06/87	3		
21	Kristián Kolčák		30/01/90	5	(1)	
3	Branislav Niňaj		17/05/94	2		
Midfielders						
23	Lukáš Gašparovič		17/02/93		(1)	
8	Erik Grendel		13/10/88	5		
29	Matej Jakúbek		19/01/95		(1)	
81	Richard Lásik		18/08/92	4		
12	Karol Mészáros		25/07/93	1		
11	Marko Milinković	SRB	16/04/88	2	(3)	
20	Seydouba Soumah	GUI	11/06/91	3	(1)	1
17	Samuel Štefánik		16/11/91	2	(1)	
7	Igor Žofčák		10/04/83	3	(3)	
Forwards						
27	Filip Ďuriš		28/03/95		(1)	
6	Pavel Fořt	CZE	26/06/83		(1)	
9	Juraj Halenár		28/06/83	4	(1)	
7	František Kubík		14/03/89	5	(1)	
77	Lester Peltier	TRI	13/09/88	5		
33	Róbert Vittek		01/04/82		(1)	

AC Sparta Praha

No	Name	Nat	DoB	Aps	(s)	Gls
Goalkeepers						
35	David Bičík		06/04/81	4		
1	Marek Štěch		28/01/90	2		
Defenders						
5	Jakub Brabec		06/08/92	6		
25	Mario Holek		28/10/86	5		
16	Pavel Kadeřábek		25/04/92	6		
15	Radoslav Kováč		27/11/79	1	(1)	
26	Costa Nhamoinesu	ZIM	06/01/86	6		1
Midfielders						
9	Bořek Dočkal		30/09/88	6		
22	Josef Hušbauer		16/03/90	3		1
18	Tiémoko Konaté	CIV	03/03/90	3	(2)	1
23	Ladislav Krejčí		05/07/92	6		2
11	Lukáš Mareček		17/04/90	3	(3)	
8	Marek Matějovský		20/12/81	6		
7	Tomáš Přikryl		04/07/92	1	(2)	
17	Kamil Vacek		18/05/87		(4)	
6	Lukáš Vácha		13/05/89	3		1
Forwards						
29	Roman Bednář		26/03/83		(3)	
21	David Lafata		18/09/81	5		5
49	Patrik Schick		24/01/96		(2)	

R. Standard de Liège

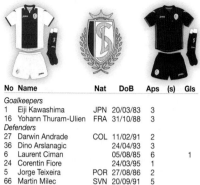

No	Name	Nat	DoB	Aps	(s)	Gls
Goalkeepers						
1	Eiji Kawashima	JPN	20/03/83	3		
16	Yohann Thuram-Ulien	FRA	31/10/88	3		
Defenders						
27	Darwin Andrade	COL	11/02/91	2		
36	Dino Arslanagic		24/04/93	3		
6	Laurent Ciman		05/08/85	6		1
24	Corentin Fiore		24/03/95	1		
5	Jorge Teixeira	POR	27/08/86	2		
66	Martin Milec	SVN	20/09/91	5		
8	Ronnie Stam	NED	18/06/84	1		
37	Jelle Van Damme		10/10/83	5		
Midfielders						
33	Mehdi Carcela-González	MAR	01/07/89	1		
15	Julien De Sart		23/12/94	2	(1)	
21	Eyong Enoh	CMR	23/03/86	2		
4	Ricardo Faty	SEN	04/08/86	3		
25	Jeff Louis	HAI	08/08/92	4	(1)	
67	Tortol Lumanza		13/04/94	1	(2)	
17	Deni Milosevic		09/03/95		(1)	
40	Paul-José M'Poku	COD	19/04/92	4	(1)	1
63	Geoffrey Mujangi Bia		12/08/89	4	(1)	
14	Yuji Ono	JPN	22/12/92	1	(2)	
23	Adrien Trebel	FRA	03/03/91	5		
Forwards						
10	Igor De Camargo		12/05/83	4	(2)	
11	Jonathan Viera	ESP	21/10/89	1	(2)	1
9	Vinícius Araújo	BRA	22/02/93	2	(2)	1
32	Tony Watt	SCO	29/12/93	1	(3)	

Torino FC

No	Name	Nat	DoB	Aps	(s)	Gls
Goalkeepers						
1	Jean-François Gillet	BEL	31/05/79	2		
30	Daniele Padelli		25/10/85	8		
Defenders						
5	Cesare Bovo		14/01/83	2	(1)	
36	Matteo Darmian		02/12/89	10		2
25	Kamil Glik	POL	03/02/88	7		1
18	Pontus Jansson	SWE	13/02/91	4	(1)	
19	Nikola Maksimović	SRB	25/11/91	8		
32	Salvatore Masiello		31/01/82	1		
3	Cristian Molinaro		30/07/83	8	(1)	1
24	Emiliano Moretti		11/06/81	7		
21	Gastón Silva	URU	05/03/94	4		1
Midfielders						
94	Marco Benassi		08/09/94	7		
7	Omar El Kaddouri	MAR	21/08/90	7	(3)	
8	Alexander Farnerud	SWE	01/05/84	1	(3)	
14	Alessandro Gazzi		28/01/83	9		
91	Giovanni Graziano		07/11/95		(1)	
23	Antonio Nocerino		09/04/85		(2)	
28	Juan Sánchez Miño	ARG	01/01/90	3		
20	Giuseppe Vives		14/07/80	2	(2)	
Forwards						
22	Amauri		03/06/80	5	(2)	2
10	Barreto	BRA	12/07/85		(1)	
9	Marcelo Larrondo	ARG	16/08/88		(3)	
17	Josef Martínez	VEN	19/05/93	7	(3)	2
11	Maxi López		03/04/84	3	(1)	3
27	Fabio Quagliarella		31/01/83	5	(4)	3

Sporting Clube de Portugal

No	Name	Nat	DoB	Aps	(s)	Gls
Goalkeepers						
1	Rui Patrício		15/02/88	2		
Defenders						
41	Cédric		31/08/91	2		
4	Jefferson	BRA	05/07/88	1		
26	Paulo Oliveira		08/01/92	2		
33	Jonathan Silva	ARG	29/06/94	1		
55	Tobias Figueiredo		02/02/94	1		
Midfielders						
23	Adrien Silva		15/03/89	2		
8	André Martins		21/01/90		(1)	
17	João Mário		19/01/93	2		
24	Oriol Rosell	ESP	07/07/92	1		
14	William Carvalho		07/04/92	1		
Forwards						
36	Carlos Mané		11/03/94		(2)	
18	André Carrillo	PER	14/06/91	2		
10	Fredy Montero	COL	26/07/87	1	(1)	
77	Nani		17/11/86	2		
9	Islam Slimani	ALG	18/06/88		(1)	
19	Junya Tanaka	JPN	15/07/87	1	(1)	

FC Steaua Bucureşti

No	Name	Nat	DoB	Aps	(s)	Gls
Goalkeepers						
24	Giedrius Arlauskis	LTU	01/12/87	6		
Defenders						
8	Lucian Filip		25/09/90	3	(1)	1
14	Iasmin Latovlevici		11/05/86	3	(1)	
5	Srdjan Luchin		04/03/86	1		
6	Paul Papp		11/11/89	5	(1)	
2	Cornel Râpă		16/01/90	2		
4	Łukasz Szukała	POL	26/05/84	5		
33	Fernando Varela	CPV	26/11/87	5		
Midfielders						
55	Alexandru Bourceanu		24/04/85	2	(1)	
21	Nicandro Breeveld	NED	07/07/86	1	(2)	
7	Alexandru Chipciu		18/05/89	5		
77	Adrian Popa		24/07/88	4	(1)	
11	Andrei Prepeliţă		08/12/85	5		
18	Lucian Sânmărtean		13/03/80	6		1
12	Nicolae Stanciu		07/05/93		(3)	
10	Cristian Tănase		18/02/87	5		
Forwards						
9	Gabriel Iancu		15/04/94	1	(1)	
28	Claudiu Keşerü		02/12/86	6		4
25	Raul Rusescu		09/07/88	1	(3)	5

Tottenham Hotspur FC

No	Name	Nat	DoB	Aps	(s)	Gls
Goalkeepers						
1	Hugo Lloris	FRA	26/12/86	6		
13	Michel Vorm	NED	20/10/83	2		
Defenders						
6	Vlad Chiricheş	ROU	14/11/89	4		
33	Ben Davies	WAL	24/04/93	7		
15	Eric Dier		15/01/94	3		
21	Federico Fazio	ARG	17/03/87	6		
4	Younès Kaboul	FRA	04/01/86	1		
16	Kyle Naughton		17/11/88	2		
3	Danny Rose		02/07/90	1		
5	Jan Vertonghen	BEL	24/04/87	6		
2	Kyle Walker		28/05/90	2	(1)	
Midfielders						
42	Nabil Bentaleb	ALG	24/11/94	4	(1)	
29	Étienne Capoue	FRA	11/07/88	1	(2)	
22	Nacer Chadli	BEL	02/08/89	3	(1)	
19	Mousa Dembélé	BEL	16/07/87	4	(1)	
23	Christian Eriksen	DEN	14/02/92	3	(1)	
11	Erik Lamela	ARG	04/03/92	4	(3)	2
7	Aaron Lennon		16/04/87	2	(3)	
38	Ryan Mason		13/06/91		(2)	
8	Paulinho	BRA	25/07/88	5	(1)	
25	Benjamin Stambouli	FRA	13/08/90	6		1
17	Andros Townsend		16/07/91	6	(1)	1
44	Harry Winks		02/02/96		(1)	
Forwards						
10	Emmanuel Adebayor	TOG	26/02/84	1	(1)	
18	Harry Kane		28/07/93	4	(3)	5
9	Roberto Soldado	ESP	27/05/85	5	(2)	1

Trabzonspor AŞ

No	Name	Nat	DoB	Aps	(s)	Gls
Goalkeepers						
26	Fatih Öztürk		22/12/86	4	(1)	
12	Hakan Arıkan		17/08/82	2		
1	Onur Kıvrak		01/01/88	2		
Defenders						
4	Aykut Demir		22/10/88	3		
21	Essaïd Belkalem	ALG	01/01/89	6		1
3	José Bosingwa	POR	24/08/82	7		
68	İshak Doğan		09/08/90	2	(1)	
77	Musa Nizam		08/09/90	4	(2)	
30	Avraam Papadopoulos	GRE	03/12/84	5		1
61	Zeki Yavru		05/09/91	2	(2)	
Midfielders						
11	Kévin Constant	GUI	10/05/87	5		2
66	Fatih Atik		25/06/84	4	(2)	
6	Carl Medjani	ALG	15/05/85	7		
5	Mehmet Ekici		25/03/90	6	(1)	1
10	Özer Hurmacı		20/11/86	2		
38	Salih Dursun		12/07/91	3	(3)	
9	Sefa Yılmaz		14/02/90	3	(5)	
8	Soner Aydoğdu		05/01/91	2	(2)	
32	Yusuf Erdoğan		07/08/92	1	(1)	
99	Erkan Zengin	SWE	05/08/85	2		
Forwards						
7	Óscar Cardozo	PAR	20/05/83	7	(1)	
28	Majeed Waris	GHA	19/09/91	5		1
86	Mustapha Yatabaré	MLI	26/01/86	4	(2)	1

VfL Wolfsburg

No	Name	Nat	DoB	Aps	(s)	Gls
Goalkeepers						
1	Diego Benaglio	SUI	08/09/83	12		
Defenders						
24	Sebastian Jung		22/06/90	5	(1)	
5	Timm Klose	SUI	09/05/88	2	(1)	1
31	Robin Knoche		22/05/92	11		
25	Naldo	BRA	10/09/82	11		1
34	Ricardo Rodríguez	SUI	25/08/92	9		3
4	Marcel Schäfer		07/06/84	3	(3)	
15	Christian Träsch		01/09/87	5	(1)	
8	Vieirinha	POR	24/01/86	8	(2)	1
Midfielders						
27	Maximilian Arnold		27/05/94	2	(6)	
7	Daniel Caligiuri	ITA	15/01/88	6	(5)	1
14	Kevin De Bruyne	BEL	28/06/91	11		5
23	Josuha Guilavogui	FRA	19/09/90	9	(1)	1
10	Aaron Hunt		04/09/86	3	(2)	2
22	Luiz Gustavo	BRA	23/07/87	11		1
19	Junior Malanda	BEL	28/08/94	2	(1)	
9	Ivan Perišić	CRO	02/02/89	6	(3)	1
17	André Schürrle		06/11/90	4		
Forwards						
3	Nicklas Bendtner	DEN	16/01/88	2	(6)	4
12	Bas Dost	NED	31/05/89	6	(3)	2
11	Ivica Olić	CRO	14/09/79	4	(1)	

FC Zenit

No	Name	Nat	DoB	Aps	(s)	Gls
Goalkeepers						
1	Yuri Lodygin		26/05/90	6		
Defenders						
2	Aleksandr Anyukov		28/09/82	2		
4	Domenico Criscito	ITA	30/12/86	4		1
24	Ezequiel Garay	ARG	10/10/86	5		
57	Dzhamaldin Khodzhaniyazov		18/07/96		(1)	
6	Nicolas Lombaerts	BEL	20/03/85	2	(1)	
33	Luís Neto	POR	26/05/88	6		
33	Milan Rodić	SRB	02/04/91	1		
19	Igor Smolnikov		08/08/88	5		
Midfielders						
35	Danny	POR	07/08/83	5		
21	Javi García	ESP	08/02/87	5		
8	Pavel Mogilevets		25/01/93		(2)	
5	Aleksandr Ryazantsev		05/09/86	1	(4)	1
17	Oleg Shatov		29/07/90	6		
44	Anatoliy Tymoshchuk	UKR	30/03/79	1	(4)	
28	Axel Witsel	BEL	12/01/89	6		1
Forwards						
10	Andrey Arshavin		29/05/81		(1)	
7	Hulk	BRA	25/07/86	5		3
11	Aleksandr Kerzhakov		27/11/82		(1)	
23	José Salomón Rondón	VEN	16/09/89	6		3

Villarreal CF

No	Name	Nat	DoB	Aps	(s)	Gls
Goalkeepers						
1	Sergio Asenjo		28/06/89	7		
25	Juan Carlos		27/07/87	3		
Defenders						
28	Adrián Marín		09/01/97	3		
94	Eric Bailly	CIV	12/04/94	2		
16	José Antonio Dorado		10/07/82	1	(2)	
20	Gabriel	BRA	26/11/90	6		
18	Jaume Costa		18/03/88	5		
2	Mario Gaspar		24/11/90	8	(1)	
5	Matéo Musacchio	ARG	26/08/90	5		
22	Antonio Rukavina	SRB	26/01/84	4		
15	Víctor Ruiz		25/01/89	7		
Midfielders						
21	Bruno Soriano		12/06/84	5	(1)	1
92	Joel Campbell	CRC	26/06/92	1	(3)	
10	Cani		03/08/81	4		1
17	Denis Cheryshev	RUS	26/12/90	5	(2)	2
24	Javier Espinosa		19/09/92	3	(2)	2
6	Jonathan dos Santos	MEX	26/04/90	7	(2)	
19	Moi Gómez		23/06/94	4	(1)	
4	Tomás Pina		14/10/87	6	(2)	1
4	Manu Trigueros		17/10/91	5	(3)	
Forwards						
23	Gerard Moreno		07/04/92	4	(2)	4
9	Giovani dos Santos	MEX	11/05/89	1	(5)	3
8	Ikechukwu Uche	NGA	05/01/84	5	(2)	2
7	Luciano Vietto	ARG	05/12/93	9	(1)	6

BSC Young Boys

No	Name	Nat	DoB	Aps	(s)	Gls
Goalkeepers						
18	Yvon Mvogo		06/06/94	7		
1	Marco Wölfli		22/08/82	1		
Defenders						
93	Marco Bürki		10/07/93		(1)	
3	Florent Hadergjonaj		31/07/94	4	(2)	
8	Jan Lecjaks	CZE	09/08/90	7		1
21	Alain Rochat		02/02/83	4	(2)	
23	Scott Sutter		13/05/86	4		
5	Milan Vilotić	SRB	21/10/86	6		
5	Steve von Bergen		10/06/83	7		
22	Gregory Wüthrich		04/12/94	1		
Midfielders						
6	Leonardo Bertone		14/03/94	4	(3)	1
10	Moreno Costanzo		20/02/88	1		
14	Milan Gajić	SRB	17/11/86	5		
30	Adrian Nikci		10/11/89		(4)	1
29	Raphael Nuzzolo		05/07/83	7	(1)	1
35	Sekou Sanogo	CIV	05/05/89	8		1
11	Renato Steffen		03/11/91	7		2
16	Tauljant Sulejmanov	MKD	15/11/96		(1)	
Forwards						
7	Samuel Afum	GHA	24/12/90	1	(4)	
9	Alexander Gerndt	SWE	14/07/86		(2)	
99	Guillaume Hoarau	FRA	05/03/84	7	(1)	6
31	Yuya Kubo	JPN	24/12/93	5	(2)	2
19	Gonzalo Zárate	ARG	06/08/84	2	(1)	

FC Zürich

No	Name	Nat	DoB	Aps	(s)	Gls
Goalkeepers						
1	David Da Costa		19/04/86	6		
Defenders						
5	Berat Djimsiti		19/02/93	5		1
30	Nico Elvedi		30/09/96	2	(2)	
25	Ivan Kecojević	MNE	10/04/88	4		
13	Alain Nef		06/02/82	4		
16	Philippe Koch		08/02/91	3	(2)	
Midfielders						
26	Cédric Brunner		17/02/94		(1)	
24	Maurice Brunner		29/01/91		(2)	
15	Oliver Buff		03/08/92	4	(1)	1
17	Yassine Chikhaoui	TUN	22/09/86	5		3
10	Davide Chiumiento		22/11/84	5		
22	Asmir Kajević	MNE	15/02/90	1		
20	Burim Kukeli	ALB	16/01/84	5		
18	Avi Rikan	ISR	10/09/88	2		1
34	Francisco Rodríguez		14/09/95	3	(2)	
27	Marco Schönbächler		11/01/90	6		1
37	Gilles Yapi Yapo	CIV	30/01/82	4		1
Forwards						
9	Amine Chermiti	TUN	26/12/87	3	(3)	
14	Franck Etoundi	CMR	30/08/90	4	(2)	2
23	Patrick Rossini		02/04/88		(3)	

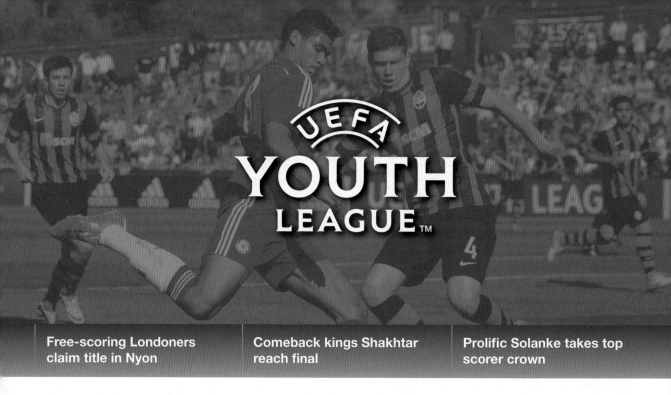

Chelsea sparkle in the sunshine

The second season of the UEFA Youth League's two-year trial proved just as popular and successful as the inaugural campaign, the consequence of which is a permanent place for the competition in UEFA's annual calendar. Furthermore, it has been expanded from 32 to 64 teams with a remodelled two-stream format and a new age-limit structure.

The 2014/15 competition, again run in tandem with the UEFA Champions League, had UEFA Youth League regulars such as Chelsea FC's Ruben Loftus-Cheek and FC Schalke 04's Leroy Sané appearing for the seniors, with the latter becoming the first player to score in both competitions during the same campaign.

The group stage offered up plenty of excitement, with 358 goals scored in 96 games – a healthy average of 3.73. The previous season's semi-final quartet of FC Barcelona, SL Benfica, Real Madrid CF and Schalke progressed en bloc to the knockout phase – along with all four English teams, including Manchester City FC, the only side to claim six wins out of six.

Defending champions Barcelona, who finished second in their section to AFC Ajax, relinquished their crown in the round of 16 away to RSC Anderlecht, losing the single-legged tie 1-0 in Brussels. The Belgian club set a UEFA Youth League attendance record in that game, with 12,871 fans present inside the Constant Vanden Stock Stadium, and would break it in the next round (13,162) as they subjected FC Porto to a 5-0 demolition.

Anderlecht were joined in the semi-finals by Chelsea, AS Roma and FC Shakhtar Donetsk, the four teams congregating at the Colovray Sports Centre in Nyon, located just across the road from UEFA headquarters, in unseasonably high mid-spring temperatures.

Chelsea players pose with the UEFA Youth League trophy

Three entertaining, high-scoring encounters took place on the sun-baked banks of Lake Geneva, and when the final whistle sounded at the end of the two semi-finals, it was Shakhtar, the tournament's only unbeaten team, and Chelsea, the competition's highest scorers, who were celebrating.

Shakhtar, who had come from behind in both previous knockout rounds (before prevailing on penalties) repeated the trick against Anderlecht, shrugging off a one-goal deficit to win 3-1 with three late goals, substitute Viktor Kovalenko making the difference by scoring two of them and setting up the other. In the second semi-final Dominic Solanke netted twice as Chelsea cruised past Roma 4-0, all of their goals coming in a stunning second-half blitz.

Solanke was to find the net again in the final as Chelsea dominated and defeated a valiant Shakhtar 3-2, his goal sandwiched between two Isaiah Brown strikes as the London club followed Barcelona on to the competition's roll of honour. Solanke's three goals in Nyon took him past Munir El Haddadi's winning total of the previous campaign as he finished with an impressive haul of 12 goals in nine appearances.

Group stage

Group A

16/09/14, Stadio Silvio Piola, Vercelli
Juventus 2-0 Malmö FF

16/09/14, Olympiacos FC Training Centre, Piraeus
Olympiacos FC 1-2 Club Atlético de Madrid

01/10/14, Ciudad Deportiva Cerro Del Espino, Majadahonda
Club Atlético de Madrid 1-0 Juventus

01/10/14, Malmö Idrottsplats, Malmo
Malmö FF 1-3 Olympiacos FC

22/10/14, Ciudad Deportiva Cerro Del Espino, Majadahonda
Club Atlético de Madrid 3-1 Malmö FF

22/10/14, Olympiacos FC Training Centre, Piraeus
Olympiacos FC 1-1 Juventus

04/11/14, Stadio Silvio Piola, Vercelli
Juventus 0-3 Olympiacos FC

04/11/14, Malmö Idrottsplats, Malmo
Malmö FF 1-2 Club Atlético de Madrid

26/11/14, Ciudad Deportiva Cerro Del Espino, Majadahonda
Club Atlético de Madrid 0-2 Olympiacos FC

26/11/14, Malmö Idrottsplats, Malmo
Malmö FF 2-2 Juventus

09/12/14, Stadio Silvio Piola, Vercelli
Juventus 0-3 Club Atlético de Madrid

09/12/14, Olympiacos FC Training Centre, Piraeus
Olympiacos FC 2-0 Malmö FF

	Pld	W	D	L	F	A	Pts
1 Club Atlético de Madrid	6	5	0	1	11	5	15
2 Olympiacos FC	6	4	1	1	12	4	13
3 Juventus	6	1	2	3	5	10	5
4 Malmö FF	6	0	1	5	5	14	1

Group B

16/09/14, Langtree Park, St Helens
Liverpool FC 4-0 PFC Ludogorets Razgrad

16/09/14, Estadio Alfredo Di Stéfano, Madrid
Real Madrid CF 2-0 FC Basel 1893

01/10/14, Campus FC Basel 1893, Basel
FC Basel 1893 3-2 Liverpool FC

01/10/14, Georgi Asparuhov Stadion, Sofia
PFC Ludogorets Razgrad 0-3 Real Madrid CF

22/10/14, Langtree Park, St Helens
Liverpool FC 3-2 Real Madrid CF

22/10/14, Georgi Asparuhov Stadion, Sofia
PFC Ludogorets Razgrad 0-5 FC Basel 1893

04/11/14, Campus FC Basel 1893, Basel
FC Basel 1893 6-0 PFC Ludogorets Razgrad

04/11/14, Estadio Alfredo Di Stéfano, Madrid
Real Madrid CF 4-1 Liverpool FC

26/11/14, Campus FC Basel 1893, Basel
FC Basel 1893 3-2 Real Madrid CF

26/11/14, Georgi Asparuhov Stadion, Sofia
PFC Ludogorets Razgrad 2-3 Liverpool FC

09/12/14, Langtree Park, St Helens
Liverpool FC 3-0 FC Basel 1893

09/12/14, Estadio Alfredo Di Stéfano, Madrid
Real Madrid CF 6-0 PFC Ludogorets Razgrad

	Pld	W	D	L	F	A	Pts
1 Real Madrid CF	6	4	0	2	19	7	12
2 Liverpool FC	6	4	0	2	16	9	12
3 FC Basel 1893	6	4	0	2	17	9	12
4 PFC Ludogorets Razgrad	6	0	0	6	0	27	0

Borja Mayoral, the leading marksman of Group B winners Real Madrid

Group C

16/09/14, Stade de formation AS Monaco 1, La Turbie
AS Monaco FC 3-1 Bayer 04 Leverkusen

16/09/14, Caixa Futebol Campus, Seixal
SL Benfica 0-0 FC Zenit

01/10/14, Minor Sport Arena Petrovski, St Petersburg
FC Zenit 0-3 AS Monaco FC

01/10/14, Ulrich Haberland Stadion, Leverkusen
Bayer 04 Leverkusen 2-3 SL Benfica

22/10/14, Ulrich Haberland Stadion, Leverkusen
Bayer 04 Leverkusen 1-4 FC Zenit

22/10/14, Stade de formation AS Monaco 1, La Turbie
AS Monaco FC 0-1 SL Benfica

04/11/14, Minor Sport Arena Petrovski, St Petersburg
FC Zenit 0-3 Bayer 04 Leverkusen

04/11/14, Caixa Futebol Campus, Seixal
SL Benfica 3-0 AS Monaco FC

26/11/14, Minor Sport Arena Petrovski, St Petersburg
FC Zenit 5-1 SL Benfica

26/11/14, Ulrich Haberland Stadion, Leverkusen
Bayer 04 Leverkusen 4-0 AS Monaco FC

09/12/14, Stade de formation AS Monaco 1, La Turbie
AS Monaco FC 1-3 FC Zenit

09/12/14, Caixa Futebol Campus, Seixal
SL Benfica 4-1 Bayer 04 Leverkusen

	Pld	W	D	L	F	A	Pts
1 SL Benfica	6	4	1	1	12	8	13
2 FC Zenit	6	3	1	2	12	9	10
3 Bayer 04 Leverkusen	6	2	0	4	12	14	6
4 AS Monaco FC	6	2	0	4	7	12	6

Group D

16/09/14, Esenyurt Necmi Kadioglu Stadyumu, Istanbul
Galatasaray AŞ 3-0 RSC Anderlecht

17/09/14, Montanhydraulik-Stadion, Holzwickede
Borussia Dortmund 0-2 Arsenal FC

01/10/14, Meadow Park, Borehamwood
Arsenal FC 5-1 Galatasaray AŞ

02/10/14, Van Roy Stadium, Denderleeuw
RSC Anderlecht 5-0 Borussia Dortmund

21/10/14, Van Roy Stadium, Denderleeuw
RSC Anderlecht 4-3 Arsenal FC

22/10/14, Esenyurt Necmi Kadioglu Stadyumu, Istanbul
Galatasaray AŞ 3-2 Borussia Dortmund

04/11/14, Meadow Park, Borehamwood
Arsenal FC 1-2 RSC Anderlecht

04/11/14, Montanhydraulik-Stadion, Holzwickede
Borussia Dortmund 5-2 Galatasaray AŞ

25/11/14, Van Roy Stadium, Denderleeuw
RSC Anderlecht 2-0 Galatasaray AŞ

26/11/14, Meadow Park, Borehamwood
Arsenal FC 1-0 Borussia Dortmund

09/12/14, Esenyurt Necmi Kadioglu Stadyumu, Istanbul
Galatasaray AŞ 1-3 Arsenal FC

10/12/14, Montanhydraulik-Stadion, Holzwickede
Borussia Dortmund 1-1 RSC Anderlecht

	Pld	W	D	L	F	A	Pts
1 RSC Anderlecht	6	4	1	1	15	8	13
2 Arsenal FC	6	4	0	2	15	8	12
3 Galatasaray AŞ	6	2	0	4	10	18	6
4 Borussia Dortmund	6	1	1	4	8	14	4

Group E

17/09/14, Centro d'Italia, Rieti
AS Roma 3-1 PFC CSKA Moskva

17/09/14, An der Grünwalderstrasse, Munich
FC Bayern München 1-4 Manchester City FC

30/09/14, Stadium Oktyabr, Moscow
PFC CSKA Moskva 3-1 FC Bayern München

30/09/14, Ewen Fields, Hyde
Manchester City FC 2-1 AS Roma

21/10/14, Stadio Agostino Di Bartolomei, Rome
AS Roma 1-0 FC Bayern München

21/10/14, Stadium Oktyabr, Moscow
PFC CSKA Moskva 0-2 Manchester City FC

05/11/14, Ewen Fields, Hyde
Manchester City FC 4-2 PFC CSKA Moskva

05/11/14, An der Grünwalderstrasse, Munich
FC Bayern München 3-2 AS Roma

25/11/14, Stadium Oktyabr, Moscow
PFC CSKA Moskva 0-2 AS Roma

25/11/14, Ewen Fields, Hyde
Manchester City FC 6-0 FC Bayern München

10/12/14, Campo Agostino Di Bartolomei, Rome
AS Roma 0-4 Manchester City FC

10/12/14, An der Grünwalderstrasse, Munich
FC Bayern München 3-2 PFC CSKA Moskva

	Pld	W	D	L	F	A	Pts
1 Manchester City FC	6	6	0	0	22	4	18
2 AS Roma	6	3	0	3	9	10	9
3 FC Bayern München	6	2	0	4	8	18	6
4 PFC CSKA Moskva	6	1	0	5	8	15	3

Group F

16/09/14, Mini Estadi, Barcelona
FC Barcelona 3-0 APOEL FC

18/09/14, De Toekomst, Duivendrecht
AFC Ajax 6-1 Paris Saint-Germain

30/09/14, Charlety, Paris
Paris Saint-Germain 2-2 FC Barcelona

30/09/14, GSZ, Larnaca
APOEL FC 0-0 AFC Ajax

21/10/14, Mini Estadi, Barcelona
FC Barcelona 2-2 AFC Ajax

22/10/14, GSZ, Larnaca
APOEL FC 0-3 Paris Saint-Germain

04/11/14, De Toekomst, Duivendrecht
AFC Ajax 1-0 FC Barcelona

05/11/14, Stade Georges-Lefèvre, Saint-Germain-en-Laye
Paris Saint-Germain 6-0 APOEL FC

25/11/14, GSZ, Larnaca
APOEL FC 2-3 FC Barcelona

26/11/14, Charlety, Paris
Paris Saint-Germain 3-6 AFC Ajax

09/12/14, De Toekomst, Duivendrecht
AFC Ajax 4-1 APOEL FC

09/12/14, Mini Estadi, Barcelona
FC Barcelona 0-0 Paris Saint-Germain

		Pld	W	D	L	F	A	Pts
1	AFC Ajax	6	4	2	0	19	7	14
2	FC Barcelona	6	2	3	1	10	7	9
3	Paris Saint-Germain	6	2	2	2	15	14	8
4	APOEL FC	6	0	1	5	3	19	1

Group G

17/09/14, Chelsea FC Training Ground, Surrey
Chelsea FC 4-1 FC Schalke 04

17/09/14, Mestni Stadion Ptuj, Ptuj
NK Maribor 1-3 Sporting Clube de Portugal

30/09/14, Stimberg-Stadion, Erkenschwick
FC Schalke 04 5-0 NK Maribor

30/09/14, CGD Stadium Aurelio Pereira, Alcochete
Sporting Clube de Portugal 0-5 Chelsea FC

21/10/14, Chelsea FC Training Ground, Surrey
Chelsea FC 2-0 NK Maribor

21/10/14, Stimberg-Stadion, Erkenschwick
FC Schalke 04 3-0 Sporting Clube de Portugal

05/11/14, Športni park, Lendava
NK Maribor 0-7 Chelsea FC

05/11/14, CGD Stadium Aurelio Pereira, Alcochete
Sporting Clube de Portugal 2-3 FC Schalke 04

25/11/14, CGD Stadium Aurelio Pereira, Alcochete
Sporting Clube de Portugal 3-2 NK Maribor

25/11/14, Stimberg-Stadion, Erkenschwick
FC Schalke 04 2-0 Chelsea FC

10/12/14, Športni park, Lendava
NK Maribor 1-5 FC Schalke 04

10/12/14, Chelsea FC Training Ground, Surrey
Chelsea FC 6-0 Sporting Clube de Portugal

		Pld	W	D	L	F	A	Pts
1	Chelsea FC	6	5	0	1	24	3	15
2	FC Schalke 04	6	5	0	1	19	7	15
3	Sporting Clube de Portugal	6	2	0	4	8	20	6
4	NK Maribor	6	0	0	6	4	25	0

Group H

17/09/14, Centro de Treinos e Formação Desportiva, Vila Nova de Gaia
FC Porto 2-1 FC BATE Borisov

17/09/14, Estadio de Lezama, Lezama
Athletic Club 0-2 FC Shakhtar Donetsk

30/09/14, Medyk, Morshyn
FC Shakhtar Donetsk 1-1 FC Porto

30/09/14, Gorodskoi Stadion, Borisov
FC BATE Borisov 1-2 Athletic Club

21/10/14, Centro de Treinos e Formação Desportiva, Vila Nova de Gaia
FC Porto 2-0 Athletic Club

21/10/14, Gorodskoi Stadion, Borisov
FC BATE Borisov 1-4 FC Shakhtar Donetsk

05/11/14, Lasesarre, Baracaldo
Athletic Club 3-1 FC Porto

Aaron Leya Iseka of Anderlecht (left) in round of 16 action against Barcelona

05/11/14, Medyk, Morshyn
FC Shakhtar Donetsk 1-0 FC BATE Borisov

25/11/14, Medyk, Morshyn
FC Shakhtar Donetsk 6-0 Athletic Club

25/11/14, Gorodskoi Stadion, Borisov
FC BATE Borisov 0-0 FC Porto

10/12/14, Centro de Treinos e Formação Desportiva, Vila Nova de Gaia
FC Porto 1-1 FC Shakhtar Donetsk

10/12/14, Lasesarre, Baracaldo
Athletic Club 4-0 FC BATE Borisov

		Pld	W	D	L	F	A	Pts
1	FC Shakhtar Donetsk	6	4	2	0	15	3	14
2	FC Porto	6	2	3	1	7	5	9
3	Athletic Club	6	3	0	3	9	12	9
4	FC BATE Borisov	6	0	1	5	2	13	1

Round of 16

27/01/15, Ciudad Deportiva Cerro Del Espino, Majadahonda (att: 902)
Club Atlético de Madrid 1-0 Arsenal FC
Goal: 1-0 Diedhiou 1

17/02/15, Estadio Alfredo Di Stéfano, Madrid (att: 660)
Real Madrid CF 1-1 FC Porto (aet)
Goals: 1-0 Mayoral 60, 1-1 Leonardo 81(p)
FC Porto qualify 3-1 on penalties.

23/02/15, FFU Training complex, Kyiv (att: 918)
FC Shakhtar Donetsk 1-1 Olympiacos FC (aet)
Goals: 0-1 Vergos 12, 1-1 Vachiberadze 27(p)
FC Shakhtar Donetsk qualify 5-4 on penalties.

23/02/15, Constant Vanden Stock Stadium, Brussels (att: 12,871)
RSC Anderlecht 1-0 FC Barcelona
Goal: 1-0 Leya Iseka 53

24/02/15, Caixa Futebol Campus, Seixal (att: 1,230)
SL Benfica 2-1 Liverpool FC
Goals: 1-0 Hildeberto Pereira 6, 1-1 Canós 9, 2-1 Diogo Gonçalves 75

24/02/15, Mini-Stadium, Manchester (att: 1,545)
Manchester City FC 1-1 FC Schalke 04 (aet)
Goals: 1-0 Byrne 33, 1-1 Sivodedov 90+1
Manchester City FC qualify 3-1 on penalties.

24/02/15, De Toekomst, Duivendrecht (att: 4,433)
AFC Ajax 0-0 AS Roma (aet)
AS Roma qualify 6-5 on penalties.

25/02/15, EBB Stadium, Aldershot (att: 387)
Chelsea FC 3-1 FC Zenit
Goals: 0-1 Kubyshkin 13, 1-1 Solanke 21, 2-1 Palmer 49, 3-1 Colkett 72(p)

Quarter-finals

10/03/15, Chelsea FC Training Ground, Surrey (att: 628)
Chelsea FC 2-0 Club Atlético de Madrid
Goals: 1-0 Manzanara 38(og), 2-0 Solanke 89

17/03/15, Caixa Futebol Campus, Seixal (att: 1,320)
SL Benfica 1-1 FC Shakhtar Donetsk (aet)
Goals: 1-0 João Carvalho 42, 1-1 Shtander 64
FC Shakhtar Donetsk qualify 5-4 on penalties.

17/03/15, Stadio Comunale Domenico Francioni, Latina (att: 4,200)
AS Roma 2-1 Manchester City FC
Goals: 1-0 Vestenický 62, 2-0 Pellegrini 86, 2-1 Ambrose 90+1(p)

18/03/15, Constant Vanden Stock Stadium, Brussels (att: 13,162)
RSC Anderlecht 5-0 FC Porto
Goals: 1-0 Leya Iseka 4, 2-0 Leya Iseka 16(p), 3-0 Bourard 25, 4-0 Leya Iseka 55(p), 5-0 Lumor 62(og)

Semi-finals

10/04/15, Colovray Sports Centre, Nyon (att: 3,000)
RSC Anderlecht 1-3 FC Shakhtar Donetsk
Goals: 1-0 Bourard 55, 1-1 Kovalenko 76, 1-2 Arendaruk 80, 1-3 Kovalenko 87

10/04/15, Colovray Sports Centre, Nyon (att: 4,000)
AS Roma 0-4 Chelsea FC
Goals: 0-1 Colkett 47, 0-2 Solanke 49, 0-3 Solanke 56, 0-4 Abraham 83

Final

13/04/15, Colovray Sports Centre, Nyon (att: 4,000)
FC Shakhtar Donetsk 2-3 Chelsea FC
Goals: 0-1 Brown 7, 1-1 Christensen 37(og), 1-2 Solanke 47, 1-3 Brown 55, 2-3 Kovalenko 90+2
Referee: Gözübüyük (NED)
Shakhtar Donetsk: Kudryk, Kyryukhantsev, Sahutkin, Matviyenko, Hladchenko, Vachiberadze, Arendaruk (Merkushov 78), Pikhalonok, Boryachuk, Zubkov, Shtander (Kovalenko 71). Coach: Valeriy Kryventsov (UKR)
Chelsea: Collins, Aina, Christensen, Clarke-Salter, Dasilva, Colkett, Brown, Loftus-Cheek, Solanke, Musonda (Abraham 85), Boga (Palmer 71). Coach: Adi Viveash (ENG)
Yellow cards: Vachiberadze 80 (Shakhtar Donetsk), Kovalenko 85 (Shakhtar Donetsk)

Top goalscorers

12	Dominic Solanke (Chelsea FC)
8	Aaron Leya Iseka (RSC Anderlecht)
7	Borja Mayoral (Real Madrid CF)
6	Zakaria El Azzouzi (AFC Ajax)
	Jerome Sinclair (Liverpool FC)
	Jack Byrne (Manchester City FC)
5	Nikos Vergos (Olympiacos FC)
	Leonardo (FC Porto)
	Marc Brasnic (Bayer 04 Leverkusen)
	Daniel Crowley (Arsenal FC)
	Charlie Colkett (Chelsea FC)

Portuguese superstar scores twice to defeat Sevilla 2-0

Ancelotti claims record-equalling third Super Cup

All-Spanish encounter attracts big crowd in Cardiff

Ronaldo at the double for Madrid

Real Madrid CF began the new season as they ended the old one – with their hands on a European trophy – as Cristiano Ronaldo's two goals earned the UEFA Champions League winners a 2-0 victory against Sevilla FC in front of a one-off UEFA Super Cup record crowd of 30,854 in the Cardiff City Stadium.

Madrid went into the mid-August fixture, staged for the first time in the Welsh capital, with a powerful lineup. Coach Carlo Ancelotti, who was bidding to move alongside Pep Guardiola with a record-equalling third victory in the competition (following his successes with AC Milan in 2003 and 2007), fielded Gareth Bale and Ronaldo either side of Karim Benzema in attack, with new signings James Rodríguez and Toni Kroos, who had both played starring roles at the FIFA World Cup earlier in the summer, stationed in midfield.

With so much quality in their ranks, it was no surprise that Madrid quickly took control of the contest. Bale, back in his home city, came close to the opening goal after 18 minutes when he stretched to meet a James cross at the far post, but Denis Suárez denied him with a decisive block. Then, after Federico

Fazio had headed a deflected Fábio Coentrão cross off his goal line, Ronaldo broke clear only for Beto to save.

The soon-to-be-crowned UEFA Best Player in Europe for 2013/14 had scored more Liga goals against Sevilla than any other side, and once again the Andalusian outfit would be powerless in their attempts to contain him. Ronaldo began the move that broke the deadlock after half an hour, playing a crossfield ball to James, who in turn fed Bale on the left; the Welshman's measured cross begged for a connection, and Ronaldo provided it at the far post with a cool volleyed finish.

Real Madrid savour their UEFA Super Cup success in Cardiff

After Daniel Carriço had failed to beat Iker Casillas from close range, Ronaldo's second goal soon after the restart effectively killed the contest. Benzema fed the Portugal forward on the left, and he advanced into the area before shooting powerfully across Beto, whose fingertip contact was insufficient to keep the ball out of the net.

Unai Emery's UEFA Europa League holders spared their noisy fans further dismay as Beto denied James with a brilliant one-handed stop, but the trophy belonged to Madrid, victorious in the competition for only the second time – 12 years after the first.

Final

12/08/14, Cardiff City Stadium, Cardiff (att: 30,854)
Real Madrid CF 2-0 Sevilla FC
Goals: 1-0 Cristiano Ronaldo 30, 2-0 Cristiano Ronaldo 49
Referee: Clattenburg (ENG)
Real Madrid: Casillas, Pepe, Sergio Ramos, Fábio Coentrão (Marcelo 84), Cristiano Ronaldo, Kroos, Benzema, James Rodríguez (Isco 72), Bale, Carvajal, Modrić (Illarramendi 86). Coach: Carlo Ancelotti (ITA)
Sevilla: Beto, Fazio, Fernando Navarro, Krychowiak, Daniel Carriço, Bacca, Suárez (Reyes 78), Vitolo, Pareja, Aleix Vidal (Aspas 66), Coke (Figueiras 84). Coach: Unai Emery (ESP)
Yellow cards: Vitolo 42 (Sevilla), Carvajal 45 (Real Madrid), Kroos 53 (Real Madrid), Fernando Navarro 66 (Sevilla)

Holders Spain will be hoping to defend the Henri Delaunay Cup in France in 2016

Lille

Lens

Saint-Denis

Paris

Lyon

Saint-Étienne

Bordeaux

Toulouse

Nice

Marseille

0	150	300 km
0		150 miles

MATCH SCHEDULE / CALENDRIER DES MATCHES

Venues:
- BORDEAUX — Stade de Bordeaux — 42,000
- LENS AGGLO — Stade Bollaert-Delelis — 35,000
- LILLE MÉTROPOLE — Stade Pierre Mauroy — 50,100
- LYON — Stade de Lyon — 58,000
- MARSEILLE — Stade Vélodrome — 67,000
- NICE — Stade de Nice — 35,000
- PARIS — Parc des Princes — 45,000
- SAINT-DENIS — Stade de France — 80,000
- SAINT-ÉTIENNE — Stade Geoffroy Guichard — 41,500
- TOULOUSE — Stadium de Toulouse — 33,000

Group matches / Matches de groupe

Matchday 1 / 1ère journée de matches

Date	Bordeaux	Lens Agglo	Lille Métropole	Lyon	Marseille	Nice	Paris	Saint-Denis	Saint-Étienne	Toulouse
10.06								(1) FRA-A2 21:00		
11.06	(3) B3-B4 18:00	(2) A3-A4 15:00			(4) B1-B2 21:00					
12.06			(7) C1-C2 21:00			(6) C3-C4 18:00	(5) D3-D4 15:00			
13.06				(10) E1-E2 21:00				(9) E3-E4 18:00		(8) D1-D2 15:00
14.06	(11) F3-F4 18:00								(12) F1-F2 21:00	

Matchday 2 / 2ème journée de matches

Date	Bordeaux	Lens Agglo	Lille Métropole	Lyon	Marseille	Nice	Paris	Saint-Denis	Saint-Étienne	Toulouse
15.06			(13) B2-B4 15:00		(15) FRA-A3 21:00		(14) A2-A4 18:00			
16.06		(16) B1-B3 15:00		(17) C2-C4 18:00				(18) C1-C3 21:00		
17.06						(21) D1-D3 21:00			(20) D2-D4 18:00	(19) E2-E4 15:00
18.06	(22) E1-E3 15:00				(23) F2-F4 18:00		(24) F1-F3 21:00			

Matchday 3 / 3ème journée de matches

Date	Bordeaux	Lens Agglo	Lille Métropole	Lyon	Marseille	Nice	Paris	Saint-Denis	Saint-Étienne	Toulouse
19.06			(26) A4-FRA 21:00	(25) A2-A3 21:00						
20.06									(28) B4-B1 21:00	(27) B2-B3 21:00
21.06	(32) D4-D1 21:00	(31) D2-D3 21:00			(29) C2-C3 18:00		(30) C4-C1 18:00			
22.06			(35) E2-E3 21:00	(34) F4-F1 18:00		(36) E4-E1 21:00		(33) F2-F3 18:00		

23.06 – 24.06 — Rest days / Jours de repos

Round of 16 / Huitièmes de finale

Date	Bordeaux	Lens Agglo	Lille Métropole	Lyon	Marseille	Nice	Paris	Saint-Denis	Saint-Étienne	Toulouse
25.06		(39) WD-3B/E/F 21:00					(38) WB-3A/C/D 18:00		(37) RA-RC 15:00	
26.06			(41) WC-3A/B/F 18:00	(40) WA-3C/D/E 15:00						(42) WF-RE 21:00
27.06						(44) RB-RF 21:00		(43) WE-RD 18:00		

28.06 – 29.06 — Rest days / Jours de repos

Quarter-finals / Quarts de finale

Date	Bordeaux	Lens Agglo	Lille Métropole	Lyon	Marseille	Nice	Paris	Saint-Denis	Saint-Étienne	Toulouse
30.06					(45) W37 v W39 21:00					
01.07			(46) W38 v W42 21:00							
02.07	(47) W41 v W43 21:00									
03.07								(48) W40 v W44 21:00		

04.07 – 05.07 — Rest days / Jours de repos

Semi-finals / Demi-finales

Date	Lyon	Marseille
06.07	(49) W45 v W46 21:00	
07.07		(50) W47 v W48 21:00

08.07 – 09.07 — Rest days / Jours de repos

Final / Finale

Date	Saint-Denis
10.07	(51) W49 v W50 21:00

W = Winner, R = Runner-up, 3 = Third-placed
The UEFA EURO 2016 final tournament takes place from Friday 10 June to Sunday 10 July 2016.
Kick-off times are CET.
UEFA will publish the final match schedule after the draw on 12 December 2015.

W = Vainqueur, R = Deuxième, 3 = Troisième
La phase finale de l'UEFA EURO 2016 se déroulera du vendredi 10 juin au dimanche 10 juillet 2016.
Les heures de coup d'envoi sont indiquées en HEC.
L'UEFA publiera la version finale du calendrier après le tirage au sort du 12 décembre 2015.

EUROPEAN QUALIFIERS

Upsets abound on road to France

The final tournament of UEFA EURO 2016, newly enlarged to incorporate 24 teams and 51 matches, will be staged at ten stadiums in France, with the opening game taking place on 10 June at the Stade de France and the final a month to the day later at the same venue in the northern suburbs of Paris.

While the impact of the increased number of participating nations on the final tournament itself remains to be seen, there is no doubt that the expansion from 16 to 24 finalists has re-energised the qualifying competition. From day one of the newly branded and formally structured European Qualifiers, in September 2014, it was clear that the lure of two automatic qualifying places per group plus a guaranteed play-off spot for the third-placed teams – the best of which qualifies directly – would raise hopes and therefore bring out the best in a number of national sides whose previous qualifying ambitions were invariably restricted to making up the numbers.

After six of the ten matchdays had elapsed, with two double-header Weeks of Football in September and October to come, the standings of the nine qualifying groups provided conclusive evidence of the tournament's increased competitiveness. While several sections

were headed by nations that had never previously qualified for the UEFA European Championship – Iceland in Group A, Wales in Group B, Slovakia in Group C and Austria in Group G – only two of the seeded teams – England and Portugal – stood at the summit of their respective groups.

Even reigning world champions Germany and holders Spain had to take second billing in their respective pools, while the Netherlands, qualifiers for each of the past seven final tournaments, were struggling to finish in the top two. There was even worse news

for 2004 European champions Greece, winless, rock bottom of Group F and seemingly out for the count after shock home and away defeats against the Faroe Islands.

With four matchdays remaining, no team had yet secured their qualification, but for some, such as England and Slovakia, with six wins out of six, it was almost within reach. For others, there was the promise of much more tension and excitement to come before the qualifying tournament reached its conclusion and the names of the 23 teams to join hosts France at the finals would be decided.

Faroe Islands players greet the final whistle with jubilation after their second Group F victory over Greece

Group A

Placed in pot five at the UEFA EURO 2016 qualifying draw, outsiders Iceland looked to be en route to France as they topped Group A with 15 points from a possible 18. Having shown considerable promise in reaching the 2014 FIFA World Cup qualifying play-offs, where they lost to Croatia, the fulfilment of a first appearance at a major international tournament appeared to be theirs for the taking with four games to go, albeit with visits to the Netherlands and Turkey bookending their closing fixture schedule.

Iceland, led by former long-serving Sweden coach Lars Lagerbäck, gave notice of their intentions on matchday one with a thumping 3-0 home win against Turkey, and they proved that was no flash in the pan by later taking all three points in the Laugardalsvöllur against both the Netherlands (2-0) – thanks to a Gylfi Sigurdsson double – and the Czech Republic (2-1). With their sublime home form supplemented by a pair of convincing 3-0 wins in Latvia and Kazakhstan, Iceland could even afford to lose away to the Czechs – despite taking the lead – and enter the summer recess with a two-point cushion at the top of the table.

That 2-1 win in Plzen in November enabled Pavel Vrba's Czech team to set the early pace with four wins out of four, the first of them a last-gasp victory in Prague against 2014 World Cup semi-finalists the Netherlands, but a surprise 1-1 draw at home to Latvia – when, as against the Dutch, a late Václav Pilař goal proved crucial – and the June defeat in Iceland set them back, enabling Guus Hiddink's struggling Oranje to close the gap between second and third place to three points.

With home games to come against both of the teams above them, there was still reason for Dutch fans to believe that their side could recover, without the departed Hiddink, and seize automatic qualification – a feeling buoyed by their 2-0 win in Latvia on matchday six. Less optimistic, perhaps, were the supporters of fourth-placed Turkey, whose dismal start to the campaign, which yielded a solitary point from their first three games, was alleviated by a hard-fought 1-0 win at bottom-placed Kazakhstan in June.

Gareth Bale strikes against Belgium in Cardiff to send Wales to the top of Group B

Group B

Wales, commanded by an inspired Gareth Bale, surprisingly led the way in Group B, with a three-point advantage over section favourites Belgium, as they chased down a first major tournament qualification in 58 years.

Chris Coleman's side did not get off to the most impressive of starts as a Bale double was required to rescue them after going a goal behind in their opening fixture away to Andorra, but those three points provided a platform for improvement, and after four points were culled from the visits to the Cardiff City Stadium of Bosnia & Herzegovina (0-0) and Cyprus (2-1), a stirring defensive performance in Brussels enabled Wales to protect their unbeaten record by holding the 2014 World Cup quarter-finalists to a goalless draw. It was then that Bale lifted his team to a higher plane, scoring two memorable goals in a superb 3-0 win in Haifa against Israel, who at the time had not dropped a point, and then, in June, grabbing the winner in front of an ecstatic capacity crowd in the top-of-the-table showdown against Belgium, then second in the FIFA world rankings, in Cardiff.

Marc Wilmots' star-studded Red Devils were expected to sweep all before them but victories in only half of their first six matches, two of them at home to Andorra and Cyprus, amounted to a disappointing return – as did their failure to score in 180 minutes against Wales. Their only performance of real substance came in the postponed matchday one fixture away to Israel, which they won 1-0 with an early Marouane Fellaini goal.

Eli Gutman's side were the early pacesetters with wins in their opening three games, but they followed that up with the same number of defeats to remain two points adrift of Belgium, and level with Cyprus. Georgios Efrem scored the first hat-trick for a Cypriot international in the home win against Andorra, and Nestoras Mytidis added the second in the return fixture eight months later, but with Bosnia & Herzegovina, the group seeds, having recovered from a terrible start, the fight for third place promised to be gripping to the last.

Group C

Slovakia supplied a number of famous names to the Czechoslovakia side that were crowned champions of Europe in 1976, but the country has never qualified independently for the UEFA European Championship, so it was an astonishing achievement for Ján Kozák's unsung side to be perched at the top of the Group C table after six matches with a maximum haul of 18 points. Thanks to their 14-point cushion over Belarus, the section's fourth-placed team, Slovakia were already guaranteed a play-off spot at the very least, but the presence in their slipstream of Spain, the holders, and a dangerous Ukraine side suggested that they still had a bit of work to do to secure their automatic ticket to France.

Ukraine were the first to feel the force of Kozák's vibrant new outfit as Slovakia headed to Kyiv on the opening night and returned with a 1-0 win thanks to midfielder Róbert Mak's first-half strike. If that result was impressive, it was eclipsed a month later when Spain visited Zilina and were sent packing with a 2-1 defeat – their first qualifying loss for eight years.

A rousing display by the home side was rewarded with Miroslav Štoch's late winning header, and from that moment

on Slovakia never looked back. Potentially tricky trips to Borisov and Skopje were dealt with in confident fashion, and the team's flawless record was maintained in the spring with home wins against Luxembourg and FYR Macedonia. Three goals from captain Marek Hamšík, three assists from Vladimír Weiss and telling contributions from several other regulars had left the side within touching distance of a historic first EURO qualification.

Spain, the 2008 and 2012 winners, also looked set to be present in France to defend their title and bid for an unprecedented hat-trick of Henri Delaunay Cup wins. Memories of a miserable World Cup defence in Brazil were quickly dispelled with an opening 5-1 win against FYR Macedonia, and they duly recovered from that shock defeat in Zilina by hitting a combined seven goals past Luxembourg and Belarus without conceding. Potentially more important than those two successes, however, was the 1-0 victory against Ukraine in Seville on matchday five, which wrested control of second place for Vicente del Bosque's men. That position was preserved with another 1-0 win in Belarus, courtesy of the influential David Silva's solitary strike, but with 12 points to their credit and the same number still to play for, Ukraine were far from out of the hunt for a top-two placing.

Group D

Group D presented a major challenge to all of its six participants, and that included freshly anointed world champions Germany, whose global triumph in Brazil had been followed by the international retirements of several leading players, among them captain Philipp Lahm and record marksman Miroslav Klose. With the Republic of Ireland, Poland and Scotland to keep them company, alongside Georgia and competition debutants Gibraltar, the road to France promised to be a bumpy one for Joachim Löw's side, and so it proved.

Heading Germany at the top of the standings with four matchdays remaining were Poland, who not only boasted an unbeaten record but were also the top-scoring team across all nine qualifying groups, with 20 goals, and possessed the competition's leading individual marksman in seven-goal Robert Lewandowski, who

signed off for the summer by scoring a 'perfect' four-minute hat-trick against Georgia in Warsaw.

Lewandowski was not alone in making a decisive contribution towards Poland's position of supremacy, with two of his team-mates, striker Arkadiusz Milik and defender Kamil Glik, both producing colossal performances in the section-defining 2-0 win over Germany in Warsaw on matchday two. Poland's first victory over their neighbours in 19 attempts was wildly celebrated by the locals, and although points were subsequently surrendered in draws against Scotland (2-2 at home) and the Republic of Ireland (1-1 away), a pair of 4-0 wins against Georgia gave Adam Nawałka's side a narrow lead at the top of the group.

Despite failing to reproduce their scintillating World Cup form, Germany sat just a point behind. Scotland pushed Löw's men all the way in a 2-1 defeat in Dortmund, while Ireland came away from Gelsenkirchen with a point thanks to a last-ditch equaliser from defender John O'Shea on his 100th appearance. While the two teams from the British Isles still harboured hopes of qualifying for France, it was Gordon Strachan's Scotland who looked better placed to do so, having beaten their Celtic cousins 1-0 in Glasgow and taken a point from their June trip to Dublin.

Group E

England's painful early exit from the 2014 World Cup was put behind them as they took advantage of a favourable UEFA EURO 2016 qualifying group to run up six successive victories and take a giant stride towards the final tournament across the Channel. Switzerland, unsurprisingly, were the best of the rest in a section dominated by Roy Hodgson's new-look side, who scored 18 goals and conceded just three.

England's perfect record was almost brought to a halt on matchday six when two of those three goals were scored against them by Slovenia in Ljubljana, but two magnificent long-range strikes from Jack Wilshere – his first international goals – and a late winner from captain Wayne Rooney – his fifth of this qualifying competition and 48th in all – secured a dramatic 3-2 win to keep the wagon rolling. The winning run had started nine months earlier in what was widely seen as the Three Lions' most testing outing, against Switzerland in Basel, where two Danny Welbeck goals sealed an impressive 2-0 win. Thereafter it was relatively plain sailing as England picked off each of their other adversaries one by one, with Welbeck adding four further goals to his tally.

Switzerland, who reached the round of 16 at the 2014 World Cup, took time to

Arkadiusz Milik rises to head Poland into the lead against Germany in Warsaw

get their campaign up and running. The opening defeat to England was followed by another one, 1-0 against Slovenia in Maribor, but then came four successive wins, with Vladimir Petković's men showing particularly impressive spirit to come from behind in Lithuania on matchday six and claim a 2-1 win that left them healthily placed in second with a three-point advantage over Slovenia.

While automatic qualification looked certain for England and likely for Switzerland, the section's play-off place remained up for grabs, with Slovenia, Estonia and Lithuania having all consistently taken points off each other. Srečko Katanec's Slovenia looked best placed to prevail with nine points in the bag, despite an opening loss in Estonia, who had seven, while Lithuania were a point further back, their highlight a 1-0 win over Magnus Pehrsson's men in Vilnius on matchday two. With four rounds remaining only San Marino, without a goal but with a rare and precious point gained in a 0-0 draw at home to Estonia, had nothing left to play for.

Group F

With section seeds Greece enduring a catastrophic campaign, and Finland also failing to rise to the challenge, Group F appeared to have evolved into a three-way battle for the two automatic qualifying places, with Romania leading the way after six matches, closely followed by two nations that have not qualified for a major tournament since the 1986 World Cup – Northern Ireland and Hungary.

Romania closed the season by holding on to top spot – and preserving their unbeaten record – thanks to a goalless draw against Northern Ireland in Belfast. They led despite a mid-campaign change of coach, with Victor Pițurcă stepping aside after three matches – which produced two wins and a draw – and being replaced by the man who led the country to the quarter-finals of the 1994 World Cup, Anghel Iordănescu. His first match brought a 2-0 win at home to Northern Ireland, in which right-back Paul Papp became the team's unlikely hero with two goals in five second-half minutes.

Romania's watertight defence was breached only once in six games, when Hungary captain Balázs Dzsudzsák fired in a free-kick to earn a 1-1 draw in

Danny Welbeck is congratulated by Rickie Lambert (No19) as England seal a 2-0 victory in Switzerland

Bucharest on matchday two. His team certainly needed that point as they were surprisingly defeated 2-1 at home by Northern Ireland the previous month – a result that cost coach Attila Pintér his job. Under new boss Pál Dárdai, Hungary's fortunes changed for the better, and two 1-0 wins over Finland, the second, in Helsinki, secured by a blockbuster strike from Zoltán Stieber, looked like taking them into the play-offs at least.

Kyle Lafferty was the main man for Northern Ireland as they sought to end a 30-year spell in the international wilderness, the strapping striker scoring five of their eight goals, including the late winner in Budapest, a brilliant counter-attacking goal to seal a 2-0 win in Greece and a match-winning double against Finland at Windsor Park. For all his efforts, though, the big story of the group was written by the Faroe Islands, who beat Greece 1-0 in Piraeus and then repeated the trick with a 2-1 win over the hapless 2004 European champions, whose appointment of Uruguayan Sergio Markarián seemed to have made no difference after their atrocious start under Italian Claudio Ranieri, leaving them winless with just two points and effectively out of contention.

Group G

Austria's only previous participation at the UEFA European Championship was in 2008, when they co-hosted the tournament, but a historic first ever qualification looked on the cards as

Marcel Koller's side went into the summer break undefeated and on top of Group G with a four-point lead over Sweden – who were also yet to lose – and an eight-point advantage over third-placed Russia.

A youthful, dynamic and well-drilled unit, Austria kicked off with a disappointing 1-1 draw against Sweden in Vienna, but those would be the only points they dropped all season. Their most impressive, and potentially significant, results were the two 1-0 wins against Russia, the first in a sold-out Ernst-Happel-Stadion in November, the second seven months later in Moscow, where a spectacular overhead kick from striker Marc Janko rewarded a dominant and disciplined team display.

Later that evening Sweden also posted an important win, 3-1 at home to Montenegro, and as ever it was their inspirational skipper, Zlatan Ibrahimović, with his fourth and fifth goals of the competition, who kept the Blågult on track for France. He had been absent through injury for the previous two qualifiers at the Friends Arena, against Russia and Liechtenstein, but had returned to score all three goals as Sweden drew 1-1 in Montenegro and won 2-0 in Moldova.

The struggles of Russia, encapsulated by that home defeat against Austria, suggested that Fabio Capello's team had made little progress since their woeful World Cup in Brazil. They started decently enough, with a 4-0 win against Liechtenstein and a 1-1 draw in Sweden, but thereafter their only success came with a 3-0 forfeit win over Montenegro after their matchday five encounter in Podgorica had been abandoned in the 67th minute because of repeated crowd disorder. For that reason only, the 2018 World Cup hosts still seemed best-placed to take the play-off spot.

Group H

Having shared a pair of 1-1 draws and remained unbeaten in their other four fixtures, Croatia and Italy appeared to have a firm grip on the two automatic qualifying places in Group H, with Norway and Bulgaria seemingly locked in a direct duel for the play-off spot.

Croatia preserved their two-point lead over the Azzurri at the top of the table in June when the two front-runners shared

the spoils in Split. It was a strange, low-key encounter, played in an empty stadium as punishment for crowd disturbances in Croatia's previous home qualifier, when they hammered Norway 5-1 in Zagreb. Croatia striker Mario Mandžukić was at the centre of almost everything meaningful that happened, missing an early penalty, heading his team in front, then handling in his own area to concede the spot-kick from which Antonio Candreva, with a Panenka-type chip, converted Italy's equaliser. Candreva had also scored Italy's goal in the first meeting, in Milan, putting the Azzurri ahead with a crisp low drive before Ivan Perišić equalised soon afterwards – albeit with the aid of an uncharacteristic error from veteran Italy keeper Gianluigi Buffon.

Both teams went into that first meeting with a maximum return of nine points from their opening three games, Italy having opened up with a fine 2-0 win in Oslo and Croatia, with Ivan Rakitić and Luka Modrić skillfully pulling the strings in midfield, running in nine goals without reply against Malta, Bulgaria and Azerbaijan. While Croatia won 1-0 in Sofia, Italy would go on to drop points in the Bulgarian capital in March. Indeed, only a late equaliser from substitute Éder, on his international debut, rescued a point after the hosts had led 2-1 for most of the game.

Bulgaria went into that match with a new coach, Ivaylo Petev having replaced Luboslav Penev after an embarrassing home draw against Malta in November. A vital 1-0 win in the return fixture at Ta' Qali put Bulgaria back in the qualifying frame, and its value doubled when on the same evening Norway were held 0-0 at home by Azerbaijan. Having won three successive qualifiers after their opening defeat by Italy, including a 2-1 success at home to Bulgaria, Per-Mathias Høgmo's team appeared to be on the slide as they looked ahead towards a potentially crucial matchday seven showdown in Sofia.

Group I

As the UEFA EURO 2016 qualifying competition entered its summer break, a clear picture emerged in the only five-team section, with Portugal, already assured of a play-off place, topping the table ahead of outsiders Albania, handily placed having played one game fewer than the other four teams, and

Denmark. The landscape looked decidedly grim for both Armenia and Serbia, however, with the latter punished twice over – with a 3-0 forfeit defeat and an additional three-point penalty – for the abandonment of their home fixture against Albania in October

The group kicked off with a huge shock as Albania beat Portugal – albeit without injured skipper Cristiano Ronaldo – in Aveiro, a stunning volley from Bekim Balaj snatching all three points for Gianni De Biasi's team and bringing Portugal boss Paulo Bento the sack. His replacement, Fernando Santos, would lead the 2004 runners-up from the foot of the table to its summit, however, as they won each of their next four matches. Unsurprisingly, it was Ronaldo who inspired the revival.

First of all he snatched a late, late winner in Copenhagen against Denmark as he leapt high to head in Ricardo Quaresma's pinpoint cross. Then, a month later, he was on hand to score another winner at home to Armenia, becoming the competition's all-time scorer in the process. And after firing blanks for once in a 2-1 home win over Serbia, he closed the season with a brilliant hat-trick in a closely contested 3-2 victory against Armenia in Yerevan. His third goal – a 30-metre howitzer into

the top corner was arguably the very best of his record 26 UEFA European Championship goals.

Denmark recovered from their home defeat to Portugal by racking up six points from their back-to-back matches against a Serbia side that went into the competition with high hopes of challenging for automatic qualification. Nicklas Bendtner scored twice in the 3-1 win in Belgrade before a pair of Poulsens – Yussuf and Jakob – earned a 2-0 home win in the return fixture seven months later.

Albania added to their opening win in Portugal by drawing with Denmark and beating Armenia at home. In fact, De Biasi's side were unbeaten after four games. The original 3-0 forfeit defeat handed to them after their fixture in Belgrade was abandoned amidst chaotic scenes of player and crowd disorder was later reversed by the Court of Arbitration for Sport, leaving Albania with ten points rather than seven and in second place, ahead of Denmark on goal difference, rather than third. With half of their fixture programme still to be completed, and a June win over France to encourage them, Albania looked on course for their best ever finish to a qualifying campaign – and one that might lead them all the way to the UEFA EURO 2016 finals.

Albania's Bekim Balaj modestly celebrates his spectacular winning goal against Portugal

European Qualifiers

Qualifying round

Group A

09/09/14, Stadion Letná, Prague (att: 17,946)
Czech Republic 2-1 Netherlands
Goals: 1-0 Dočkal 22, 1-1 De Vrij 55,
2-1 Pilař 90+1
Referee: Rocchi (ITA)
Czech Republic: Čech, Kadeřábek, M Kadlec,
Procházka, Krejčí (Pilař 66), Limberský, Dočkal,
Rosický, Vácha (Kolář 81), Lafata (Vydra 72),
Darida. Coach: Pavel Vrba (CZE)
Netherlands: Cillessen, Janmaat, Veltman
(Narsingh 39), De Vrij, Martins Indi, De Jong,
Wijnaldum, Blind, Van Persie, Sneijder, Depay.
Coach: Guus Hiddink (NED)

09/09/14, Laugardalsvöllur, Reykjavik (att: 8,811)
Iceland 3-0 Turkey
Goals: 1-0 Bödvarsson 19, 2-0 G Sigurdsson 76,
3-0 Sigthórsson 77
Referee: Bebek (CRO)
Iceland: Halldórsson, R Sigurdsson, B Bjarnason
(Gíslason 70), Sigthórsson, G Sigurdsson
(Ó Skúlason 89), K Árnason, Gunnarsson,
E Bjarnason, Hallfredsson, Bödvarsson
(Kjartansson 90+2), A Skúlason. Coach: Lars
Lagerbäck (SWE) & Heimir Hallgrímsson (ISL)
Turkey: Onur Kıvrak, Emre Belözoğlu, Gökhan
Gönül, Selçuk İnan (Ozan Tufan 65), Arda
Turan, Mehmet Topal (Hakan Çalhanoğlu 76),
Burak Yılmaz, Caner Erkin, Olcan Adın (Mustafa
Pektemek 65), Ömer Toprak, Ersan Gülüm.
Coach: Fatih Terim (TUR)
Red card: Ömer Toprak 59 (Turkey)

09/09/14, Astana Arena, Astana (att: 10,200)
Kazakhstan 0-0 Latvia
Referee: Kružliak (SVK)
Kazakhstan: Sidelnikov, Vorotnikov,
Abdulin, Smakov, Islamkhan (Nurgaliyev 82),
Miroshnichenko, Nuserbayev (Dzholchiev 73),
Shomko, Bogdanov, Khizhnichenko, Logvinenko.
Coach: Yuri Krasnozhan (RUS)
Latvia: Koliņko, Maksimenko, Bulvītis, Laizāns,
Gabovs, Kovaļovs, Šabala, Gorkšs, Lazdiņš
(Fertovs 27), Rudņevs (E Višņakovs 79), Zjuzins.
Coach: Marians Pahars (LVA)

10/10/14, Skonto Stadions, Riga (att: 6,354)
Latvia 0-3 Iceland
Goals: 0-1 G Sigurdsson 66, 0-2 A Gunnarsson
77, 0-3 Gíslason 90
Referee: Schörgenhofer (AUT)
Latvia: Koliņko, Morozs, Bulvītis, Dubra, Gabovs,
Kovaļovs (A Višņakovs 81), Šabala (E Višņakovs
81), Gorkšs, Rugins (Freimanis 63), Rudņevs,
Fertovs. Coach: Marians Pahars (LVA)
Iceland: Halldórsson, R Sigurdsson, B
Bjarnason, Sigthórsson, G Sigurdsson (Ó
Skúlason 80), K Árnason, Gunnarsson,
E Bjarnason, Hallfredsson (Gíslason 87),
Bödvarsson (Finnbogason 77), A Skúlason.
Coach: Lars Lagerbäck (SWE) & Heimir
Hallgrímsson (ISL)
Red card: Rudņevs 55 (Latvia)

*10/10/14, Amsterdam ArenA, Amsterdam
(att: 47,500)*
Netherlands 3-1 Kazakhstan
Goals: 0-1 Abdulin 17, 1-1 Huntelaar 62, 2-1
Afellay 82, 3-1 Van Persie 89(p)
Referee: Jug (SVN)
Netherlands: Cillessen, Van der Wiel, De Vrij,
Martins Indi (Fer 81), Blind, De Jong (Huntelaar
56), Lens, Afellay, Van Persie, Sneijder, Robben.
Coach: Guus Hiddink (NED)
Kazakhstan: Mokin, Vorotnikov, Abdulin,
Karpovich (Korobkin 79), Dmitrenko (Gurman
72), Dzholchiev, Miroshnichenko, Suyumbayev,
Shomko, Bogdanov, Khizhnichenko (Nurgaliyev
90). Coach: Yuri Krasnozhan (RUS)
Red card: Dzholchiev 64 (Kazakhstan)

Kolbeinn Sigthórsson – on target for Iceland against
Turkey in Reykjavik

10/10/14, Şükrü Saracoğlu, Istanbul (att: 24,007)
Turkey 1-2 Czech Republic
Goals: 1-0 Umut Bulut 8, 1-1 Sivok 15, 1-2
Dočkal 58
Referee: Eriksson (SWE)
Turkey: Tolga Zengin, Semih Kaya, Gökhan
Gönül, Selçuk İnan (Oğuzhan Özyakup 79),
Umut Bulut, Arda Turan, Gökhan Töre (Olcan
Adın 68), Mehmet Topal, Ozan Tufan, Caner
Erkin, Olcay Şahan (Muhammet Demir 66).
Coach: Fatih Terim (TUR)
Czech Republic: Čech, Kadeřábek, M Kadlec,
Sivok, Limberský, Dočkal (Plašil 90+2), Rosický,
Vácha, Krejčí (Pilař 68), Lafata (Vydra 84), Darida.
Coach: Pavel Vrba (CZE)

13/10/14, Laugardalsvöllur, Reykjavik (att: 9,760)
Iceland 2-0 Netherlands
Goals: 1-0 G Sigurdsson 10(p),
2-0 G Sigurdsson 42
Referee: Velasco Carballo (ESP)
Iceland: Halldórsson, R Sigurdsson, B
Bjarnason, Sigthórsson, G Sigurdsson,
K Árnason, Gunnarsson, E Bjarnason,
Hallfredsson, Bödvarsson (Gíslason 89),
A Skúlason (Sævarsson 46). Coach: Lars
Lagerbäck (SWE) & Heimir Hallgrímsson (ISL)
Netherlands: Cillessen, Van der Wiel, De Vrij,
Martins Indi, Blind, De Jong, Lens (Promes 68),
Afellay (Fer 78), Van Persie, Sneijder (Huntelaar
46), Robben. Coach: Guus Hiddink (NED)

13/10/14, Astana Arena, Astana (att: 13,752)
Kazakhstan 2-4 Czech Republic
Goals: 0-1 Dočkal 13, 0-2 Lafata 44, 0-3 Krejčí
56, 1-3 Logvinenko 84, 1-4 Necid 88, 2-4
Logvinenko 90+1
Referee: Gestranius (FIN)
Kazakhstan: Sidelnikov, Vorotnikov, Abdulin,
Karpovich (Konysbayev 58), Islamkhan,
Tagybergen, Miroshnichenko (Beysebekov 83),

Nuserbayev, Shomko, Khizhnichenko (Nurgaliyev
70), Logvinenko. Coach: Yuri Krasnozhan (RUS)
Czech Republic: Čech, Kadeřábek, M Kadlec,
Sivok (Procházka 81), Limberský, Dočkal, Kolář,
Vácha, Krejčí (Pilař 69), Lafata (Necid 79), Darida.
Coach: Pavel Vrba (CZE)

13/10/14, Skonto Stadions, Riga (att: 6,442)
Latvia 1-1 Turkey
Goals: 0-1 Bilal Kisa 47, 1-1 Šabala 54(p)
Referee: Madden (SCO)
Latvia: Koliņko, Dubra, A Višņakovs, Gabovs
(Freimanis 38), Ikaunieks, Šabala, E Višņakovs
(Rakels 80), Gorkšs, Zjuzins (Morozs 83), Fertovs,
Kurakins. Coach: Marians Pahars (LVA)
Turkey: Volkan Babacan, Semih Kaya, Gökhan
Gönül, Umut Bulut, Arda Turan, Gökhan Töre
(Hamit Altıntop 70), Oğuzhan Özyakup (Bilal Kisa
40), Mehmet Topal, Ozan Tufan, Caner Erkin,
Olcay Şahan (Adem Büyük 59). Coach: Fatih
Terim (TUR)
Red card: Freimanis 90+1 (Latvia)

16/11/14, Doosan Arena, Plzen (att: 11,533)
Czech Republic 2-1 Iceland
Goals: 0-1 Sigurdsson 9, 1-1 Kadeřábek 45+1,
2-1 Bödvarsson 61(og)
Referee: Stark (GER)
Czech Republic: Čech, Kadeřábek, M Kadlec,
Sivok, Dočkal, Rosický (Procházka 90+2), Pudil,
Plašil, Krejčí (Pilař 65), Lafata (Necid 82), Darida.
Coach: Pavel Vrba (CZE)
Iceland: Halldórsson, R Sigurdsson, B Bjarnason
(Gudmundsson 77), Sigthórsson, G Sigurdsson,
K Árnason, Gunnarsson, E Bjarnason
(Sævarsson 62), Hallfredsson (Gíslason 62),
Bödvarsson, A Skúlason. Coach: Lars Lagerbäck
(SWE) & Heimir Hallgrímsson (ISL)

*16/11/14, Amsterdam ArenA, Amsterdam
(att: 47,500)*
Netherlands 6-0 Latvia
Goals: 1-0 Van Persie 6, 2-0 Robben 35, 3-0
Huntelaar 42, 4-0 Bruma 78, 5-0 Robben 82, 6-0
Huntelaar 89
Referee: Liany (ISR)
Netherlands: Cillessen, Van der Wiel, Bruma, De
Vrij, Willems, Blind (Clasie 20), Afellay (Depay 69),
Sneijder, Lens, Van Persie (Wijnaldum 79),
Robben. Coach: Guus Hiddink (NED)
Latvia: Koliņko, Dubra, Gabovs, Šabala, E
Višņakovs (Rudņevs 70), Gorkšs, Ikaunieks
(Laizāns 46), Zjuzins (Cauņa 54), Fertovs, Kurakins,
A Višņakovs. Coach: Marians Pahars (LVA)

*16/11/14, Ali Sami Yen Spor Kompleksi, Istanbul
(att: 27,549)*
Turkey 3-1 Kazakhstan
Goals: 1-0 Burak Yılmaz 26(p), 2-0 Burak Yılmaz
29, 3-0 Serdar Aziz 83, 3-1 Smakov 87(p)
Referee: Eskov (RUS)
Turkey: Volkan Babacan, Semih Kaya, Serdar
Aziz, Selçuk İnan, Umut Bulut (Mehmet Topal 74),
Arda Turan, Ozan Tufan, Burak Yılmaz, Caner
Erkin, Volkan Şen (Gökhan Töre 81), Olcay Şahan
(Mehmet Ekici 85). Coach: Fatih Terim (TUR)
Kazakhstan: Mokin, Gurman, Abdulin (Maliy 76),
Konysbayev, Smakov, Islamkhan, Tagybergen,
Shomko, Lunin (Shchetkin 73), Khizhnichenko
(Nurgaliyev 82), Logvinenko. Coach: Yuri
Krasnozhan (RUS)

28/03/15, Stadion Eden, Prague (att: 13,722)
Czech Republic 1-1 Latvia
Goals: 0-1 A Višņakovs 30, 1-1 Pilař 90
Referee: Estrada (ESP)
Czech Republic: Čech, Gebre Selassie, M
Kadlec, Procházka, Limberský, Dočkal, Rosický,
Plašil (Pilař 46), Krejčí (Necid 57), Lafata (V
Kadlec 81), Darida. Coach: Pavel Vrba (CZE)
Latvia: Vaņins, Maksimenko, Dubra, Laizāns
(Ikaunieks 66), A Višņakovs (Fertovs 82), Šabala,
Gorkšs, Rakels, Tarasovs, Zjuzins (Žigajevs 87),
Freimanis. Coach: Marians Pahars (LVA)

Turkey's Burak Yılmaz works himself into space to score against the Netherlands

28/03/15, Astana Arena, Astana (att: 13,182)
Kazakhstan 0-3 Iceland
Goals: 0-1 Gudjohnsen 20, 0-2 B Bjarnason 32, 0-3 B Bjarnason 90+1
Referee: Sidiropoulos (GRE)
Kazakhstan: Sidelnikov, Gurman (Kuantayev 67), Vorotnikov, Abdulin (Shchetkin 80), Smakov, Islamkhan, Tagybergen, Nurgaliyev (Konysbayev 56), Suyumbayev, Tazhimbetov, Logvinenko. Coach: Yuri Krasnozhan (RUS)
Iceland: Halldórsson, Sævarsson, R Sigurdsson, Gudmundsson, B Bjarnason, Sigthórsson (Bödvarsson 70), G Sigurdsson, K Árnason, Gunnarsson (Hallfredsson 72), Gudjohnsen (Finnbogason 83), A Skúlason. Coach: Lars Lagerbäck (SWE) & Heimir Hallgrímsson (ISL)

28/03/15, Amsterdam ArenA, Amsterdam (att: 49,500)
Netherlands 1-1 Turkey
Goals: 0-1 Burak Yılmaz 37, 1-1 Huntelaar 90+2
Referee: Brych (GER)
Netherlands: Cillessen, Van der Wiel, De Vrij, Martins Indi (Willems 77), Blind, De Jong (Dost 63), Afellay, Wijnaldum (Narsingh 46), Huntelaar, Sneijder, Depay. Coach: Guus Hiddink (NED)
Turkey: Volkan Babacan, Hakan Balta, Serdar Aziz (Ersan Gülüm 69), Gökhan Gönül, Selçuk İnan, Gökhan Töre, Volkan Şen (Hakan Çalhanoğlu 61), Mehmet Topal, Ozan Tufan, Burak Yılmaz (Kazim-Richards 79), Caner Erkin. Coach: Fatih Terim (TUR)

12/06/15, Laugardalsvöllur, Reykjavik (att: 9,767)
Iceland 2-1 Czech Republic
Goals: 0-1 Dočkal 55, 1-1 Gunnarsson 60, 2-1 Sigthórsson 76
Referee: Collum (SCO)
Iceland: Halldórsson, Sævarsson, R Sigurdsson, Gudmundsson, B Bjarnason, Sigthórsson (Gíslason 90+3), G Sigurdsson, K Árnason, Gunnarsson, Hallfredsson (Bödvarsson 63), A Skúlason. Coach: Lars Lagerbäck (SWE) & Heimir Hallgrímsson (ISL)
Czech Republic: Čech, Kadeřábek, Procházka, Sivok, Necid, Limberský, Dočkal (Darida 84), Rosický, Pilař (Krejčí 67), Plašil, Vácha (Škoda 79). Coach: Pavel Vrba (CZE)

12/06/15, Almaty Ortalyk Stadion, Almaty (att: 25,125)
Kazakhstan 0-1 Turkey
Goal: 0-1 Arda Turan 83
Referee: Oliver (ENG)
Kazakhstan: Pokatilov, Maliy, Gurman (Tagybergen 78), Abdulin, Konysbayev, Smakov (Beysebekov 67), Islamkhan (Kukeyev 85), Schmidtgal, Shomko, Khizhnichenko, Logvinenko. Coach: Yuri Krasnozhan (RUS)
Turkey: Volkan Babacan, Semih Kaya (Emre Taşdemir 75), Hakan Balta, Serdar Aziz, Hakan Çalhanoğlu, Gökhan Gönül, Selçuk İnan, Arda Turan, Mehmet Topal (Volkan Şen 46), Ozan Tufan (Umut Bulut 64), Burak Yılmaz. Coach: Fatih Terim (TUR)

12/06/15, Skonto Stadions, Riga (att: 8,087)
Latvia 0-2 Netherlands
Goals: 0-1 Wijnaldum 67, 0-2 Narsingh 71
Referee: Moen (NOR)
Latvia: Vaņins, Maksimenko, A Višņakovs (Karašausks 75), Šabala (E Višņakovs 62), Gorkšs, Ikaunieks, Rakels, Tarasovs, Zjuzins, Jagodinskis, Freimanis (Gabovs 37). Coach: Marians Pahars (LVA)
Netherlands: Cillessen, Van der Wiel, De Vrij, Martins Indi, Willems (Janmaat 77), Blind, Narsingh, Sneijder, Huntelaar, Van Persie (Wijnaldum 63), Depay (Lens 87). Coach: Guus Hiddink (NED)

Remaining fixtures

03/09/15
Czech Republic –
Kazakhstan
Netherlands – Iceland
Turkey – Latvia

06/09/15
Iceland – Kazakhstan
Latvia – Czech
Republic
Turkey – Netherlands

10/10/15
Czech Republic –
Turkey
Iceland – Latvia
Kazakhstan –
Netherlands

13/10/15
Latvia – Kazakhstan
Netherlands – Czech
Republic
Turkey – Iceland

Group B

09/09/14, Estadi Nacional, Andorra la Vella (att: 3,150)
Andorra 1-2 Wales
Goals: 1-0 Lima 6(p), 1-1 Bale 22, 1-2 Bale 81
Referee: Vinčič (SVN)
Andorra: Pol, C Martínez (Sonejee 83), Vales, E García, Lima, Riera, Peppe (Vieira 53), Ayala (Sánchez 86), Lorenzo, Maneiro, Rubio. Coach: Koldo Alvarez (AND)
Wales: Hennessey, Gunter, N Taylor, Chester, Davies, A Williams, Allen, King (G Williams 77), Church (Ledley 62), Ramsey (Huws 90+4), Bale. Coach: Chris Coleman (WAL)

09/09/14, Bilino Polje, Zenica (att: 12,100)
Bosnia & Herzegovina 1-2 Cyprus
Goals: 1-0 Ibišević 6, 1-1 Christofi 45, 1-2 Christofi 73
Referee: Aranovskiy (UKR)
Bosnia & Herzegovina: Begović, Vršajević, Bičakčić, Bešić, Ibišević, Pjanić, Džeko, Sušić (Medunjanin 62), Šunjić, Lulić, Prcić (Hajrović 62). Coach: Safet Sušić (BIH)
Cyprus: Georgallides, Dossa Júnior, Merkis, Aloneftis (Charalambides 46), Kyriakou, Christofi, Makrides (Sielis 83), Laban, Antoniades, Efrem (Alexandrou 71), Nicolaou. Coach: Pambos Christodoulou (CYP)

10/10/14, King Baudouin Stadium, Brussels (att: 45,459)
Belgium 6-0 Andorra
Goals: 1-0 De Bruyne 31(p), 2-0 De Bruyne 34, 3-0 Chadli 37, 4-0 Origi 59, 5-0 Mertens 65, 6-0 Mertens 68
Referee: Boiko (UKR)
Belgium: Courtois, Alderweireld, Lombaerts, Kompany (Pocognoli 56), Vertonghen, Nainggolan, De Bruyne, Mertens, Defour, Origi (Lukaku 66), Chadli (Fellaini 61). Coach: Marc Wilmots (BEL)
Andorra: Pol, C Martínez (Moreno 78), Vales, E García, Lima, Vieira, Riera (M García 72), San Nicolás, Ayala, Maneiro, Rubio (Lorenzo 61). Coach: Koldo Alvarez (AND)

10/10/14, GSP Stadium, Nicosia (att: 19,164)
Cyprus 1-2 Israel
Goals: 0-1 Damari 38, 0-2 Ben Haim II 45, 1-2 Makrides 67
Referee: Orsato (ITA)
Cyprus: Georgallides, Dossa Júnior, Merkis, Christofi, Charalambides (Sotiriou 46), Makrides, Laban, Antoniades, Stylianou (Kyriakou 46), Makris (Alexandrou 70), Nicolaou. Coach: Pambos Christodoulou (CYP)
Israel: Marciano, Meshumar, Ben Haim I, Natcho, Zahavi, Ben Haim II (Refaelov 73), Yeini, Vermouth (Biton 82), Ben Harush, Tibi, Damari (Shechter 70). Coach: Eli Gutman (ISR)

10/10/14, Cardiff City Stadium, Cardiff (att: 30,741)
Wales 0-0 Bosnia & Herzegovina
Referee: Bezborodov (RUS)
Wales: Hennessey, Gunter, N Taylor, Chester, Davies, A Williams, King, Church (Robson-Kanu 65), Bale, Ledley, J Williams (G Williams 83). Coach: Chris Coleman (WAL)
Bosnia & Herzegovina: Begović, Bešić, Medunjanin, Ibišević (Hajrović 83), Pjanić, Džeko, Mujdža, Sušić, Šunjić, Lulić, Hadžić. Coach: Safet Sušić (BIH)

13/10/14, Estadi Nacional, Andorra la Vella (att: 2,032)
Andorra 1-4 Israel
Goals: 0-1 Damari 3, 1-1 Lima 15(p), 1-2 Damari 41, 1-3 Damari 82, 1-4 Hemed 90+6(p)
Referee: Balaj (ROU)
Andorra: Pol, C Martínez, Vales, E García, Lima (Ayala 40), Vieira, Riera, Peppe (Toscano 83), Lorenzo, Maneiro, Rubio (Pujol 70). Coach: Koldo Alvarez (AND)
Israel: Marciano, Meshumar, Ben Haim I, Biton, Natcho, Zahavi (Refaelov 70), Ben Haim II, Vermouth (Shechter 65), Tawatha, Tibi, Damari (Hemed 84). Coach: Eli Gutman (ISR)

13/10/14, Bilino Polje, Zenica (att: 12,070)
Bosnia & Herzegovina 1-1 Belgium
Goals: 1-0 Džeko 28, 1-1 Nainggolan 51
Referee: Banti (ITA)
Bosnia & Herzegovina: Begović, Bešić,
Medunjanin, Ibišević, Pjanić, Džeko, Mujdža,
Sušić (Višća 71), Šunjić, Lulić, Hadžić. Coach:
Safet Sušić (BIH)
Belgium: Courtois, Alderweireld, Lombaerts,
Kompany, Vertonghen, Nainggolan, De Bruyne,
Lukaku (Mertens 57), Hazard, Defour (Fellaini 78),
Origi. Coach: Marc Wilmots (BEL)

13/10/14, Cardiff City Stadium, Cardiff (att: 21,273)
Wales 2-1 Cyprus
Goals: 1-0 Cotterill 13, 2-0 Robson-Kanu 23, 2-1
Laban 36
Referee: Gräfe (GER)
Wales: Hennessey, Gunter, N Taylor, Chester, A
Williams, King, Church (Cotterill 6), Robson-Kanu
(J Taylor 84), Bale, Ledley, G Williams (Edwards
58). Coach: Chris Coleman (WAL)
Cyprus: Kissas, Dossa Júnior (Angeli 29;
Papathanasiou 85), Merkis, Kyriakou, Christofi,
Makrides, Laban, Antoniades, Efrem, Sotiriou,
Nicolaou (Alexandrou 68). Coach: Pambos
Christodoulou (CYP)
Red card: King 47 (Wales)

*16/11/14, King Baudouin Stadium, Brussels
(att: 41,535)*
Belgium 0-0 Wales
Referee: Královec (CZE)
Belgium: Courtois, Alderweireld, Lombaerts,
Vertonghen, Witsel, De Bruyne, Fellaini, Hazard,
Origi (Mertens 73; Januzaj 89), Vanden Borre,
Chadli (Benteke 62). Coach: Marc Wilmots (BEL)
Wales: Hennessey, Gunter, N Taylor, Chester, A
Williams, Allen, Cotterill (G Williams 46), Robson-
Kanu (Huws 90+5), Ramsey, Bale, Ledley. Coach:
Chris Coleman (WAL)

16/11/14, GSP Stadium, Nicosia (att: 6,078)
Cyprus 5-0 Andorra
Goals: 1-0 Merkis 9, 2-0 Efrem 31, 3-0 Efrem 42,
4-0 Efrem 60, 5-0 Christofi 87(p)
Referee: Clattenburg (ENG)
Cyprus: Georgallides, Demetriou, Merkis,
Angeli, Aloneftis (Makris 46), Christofi,
Mytidis (Kolokoudias 63), Laban, Antoniades,
Efrem (Laifis 78), Nicolaou. Coach: Pambos
Christodoulou (CYP)
Andorra: Pol, C Martínez, Vales, E García, Lima
(Rodríguez 49), Pujol, Vieira (Ayala 46), Riera,
Lorenzo, M García, Rubio (Rodrigues 73). Coach:
Koldo Alvarez (AND)

16/11/14, Itztadion Sammy Ofer, Haifa (att: 28,300)
Israel 3-0 Bosnia & Herzegovina
Goals: 1-0 Vermouth 36, 2-0 Damari 45, 3-0
Zahavi 70
Referee: Mateu Lahoz (ESP)
Israel: Marciano, Meshumar, Ben Haim I, Natcho
(Biton 74), Zahavi, Ben Haim II, Yeini, Vermouth
(Refaelov 70), Ben Harush (Davidzada 78), Tibi,
Damari. Coach: Eli Gutman (ISR)
Bosnia & Herzegovina: Begović, Spahić, Kvržić,
Bešić (Prcić 46), Medunjanin, Pjanić (Cimirot 61),
Mujdža (Višća 46), Šunjić, Lulić, Hajrović, Hadžić.
Coach: Safet Sušić (BIH)
Red card: Šunjić 47 (Bosnia & Herzegovina)

28/03/15, Estadi Nacional, Andorra la Vella (att: 2,498)
Andorra 0-3 Bosnia & Herzegovina
Goals: 0-1 Džeko 13, 0-2 Džeko 49, 0-3 Džeko 62
Referee: Vad (HUN)
Andorra: Pol, Vales, Sonejee, Lima, Clemente (C
Martínez 54), Vieira, San Nicolás, Lorenzo (Rubio
85), Gómez (Riera 59), M García, Rodríguez.
Coach: Koldo Alvarez (AND)
Bosnia & Herzegovina: Begović, Spahić, Vranješ
(Cocalić 73), Bešić, Ibišević (Djuric 67), Pjanić,
Džeko, Mujdža, Lulić (Medunjanin 77), Zukanović,
Višća. Coach: Mehmed Baždarević (BIH)

*28/03/15, King Baudouin Stadium, Brussels
(att: 45,213)*
Belgium 5-0 Cyprus
Goals: 1-0 Fellaini 21, 2-0 Benteke 35, 3-0
Fellaini 66, 4-0 Hazard 67, 5-0 Batshuayi 80
Referee: Haţegan (ROU)
Belgium: Courtois, Alderweireld, Lombaerts,
Kompany, Vertonghen, Witsel, De Bruyne, Fellaini
(Ferreira Carrasco 69), Benteke (Batshuayi 77),
Hazard (Mertens 69), Nainggolan. Coach: Marc
Wilmots (BEL)
Cyprus: Kissas, Merkis, Kyriakou, Sotiriou,
Mytidis, Makrides (Kastanos 84), Laban
(Oikonomidis 57), Antoniades, Laifis, Makris
(Eleftheriou 71), Nicolaou. Coach: Pambos
Christodoulou (CYP)

28/03/15, Itztadion Sammy Ofer, Haifa (att: 30,200)
Israel 0-3 Wales
Goals: 0-1 Ramsey 45+1, 0-2 Bale 50, 0-3 Bale 77
Referee: Mažić (SRB)
Israel: Marciano, Ben Haim I, Natcho, Zahavi
(Sahar 70), Refaelov, Ben Haim II (Biton 60), Yeini,
Dgani, Ben Harush, Tibi, Damari (Hemed 43).
Coach: Eli Gutman (ISR)
Wales: Hennessey, Gunter, N Taylor, Davies,
A Williams, Allen, Robson-Kanu (Vokes 68),
Ramsey (MacDonald 85), Bale, Ledley (Vaughan
47), Collins. Coach: Chris Coleman (WAL)
Red card: Tibi 51 (Israel)

31/03/15, Itztstadion Teddy, Jerusalem (att: 29,750)
Israel 0-1 Belgium
Goal: 0-1 Fellaini 9
Referee: Clattenburg (ENG)
Israel: Marciano, Ben Haim I, Biton, Gershon,
Natcho, Zahavi, Hemed (Ben Haim II 46), Yeini
(Refaelov 66), Sahar, Ben Harush (Barda 84),
Dgani. Coach: Eli Gutman (ISR)
Belgium: Courtois, Alderweireld, Lombaerts,
Kompany, Vertonghen, Witsel, De Bruyne, Fellaini,
Benteke (Denayer 66), Hazard (Chadli 63),
Nainggolan (Origi 86). Coach: Marc Wilmots (BEL)
Red card: Kompany 64 (Belgium)

George Efrem became Cyprus's first ever hat-trick
scorer in his team's 5-0 home win against Andorra

12/06/15, Estadi Nacional, Andorra la Vella (att: 1,054)
Andorra 1-3 Cyprus
Goals: 1-0 Dossa Júnior 2(og), 1-1 Mytidis 13,
1-2 Mytidis 45, 1-3 Mytidis 53
Referee: Welz (GER)
Andorra: Pol, C Martínez, Vales, Rebés (Peppe
79), Moreno (Lima 67), Rodrigues, A Sánchez,
Ayala (Sonejee 60), Rodríguez, M García, Rubio.
Coach: Koldo Alvarez (AND)
Cyprus: Georgallides, Dossa Júnior, Demetriou,
Sielis, Christofi (Alexandrou 82), Mytidis,
Makridis (Kastanos 88), Laban (Oikonomidis 76),
Antoniades, Efrem, Nicolaou. Coach: Pambos
Christodoulou (CYP)

12/06/15, Stadion Bilino polje, Zenica (att: 12,100)
Bosnia & Herzegovina 3-1 Israel
Goals: 0-1 Ben Haim II 41, 1-1 Višća 42,
2-1 Džeko 45+2(p), 3-1 Višća 75
Referee: Buquet (FRA)
Bosnia & Herzegovina: Begović, Spahić,
Kolašinac, Vranješ, Bešić, Medunjanin, Pjanić
(Ibišević 88), Džeko, Mujdža, Lulić (Hadžić 85), Višća
(Hajrović 80). Coach: Mehmed Baždarević (BIH)
Israel: Marciano, Ben Haim I, Biton (Kehat 80),
Gershon, Natcho, Zahavi, Ben Haim II, Yeini
(Damari 46), Sahar (Buzaglo 62), Dgani, Ben
Harush. Coach: Eli Gutman (ISR)

12/06/15, Cardiff City Stadium, Cardiff (att: 33,280)
Wales 1-0 Belgium
Goal: 1-0 Bale 25
Referee: Brych (GER)
Wales: Hennessey, Gunter, N Taylor, Richards,
Chester, A Williams, Allen, Robson-Kanu (King
90+3), Ramsey, Bale (Vokes 87), Ledley. Coach:
Chris Coleman (WAL)
Belgium: Courtois, Alderweireld (Ferreira Carrasco
77), Lombaerts, Nainggolan, Vertonghen, Witsel,
De Bruyne, Benteke, Hazard, Mertens (Lukaku 46),
Denayer. Coach: Marc Wilmots (BEL)

Remaining fixtures

03/09/15
**Belgium – Bosnia &
Herzegovina**
Cyprus – Wales
Israel – Andorra

10/10/15
Andorra – Belgium
**Bosnia & Herzegovina
– Wales**
Israel – Cyprus

06/09/15
**Bosnia & Herzegovina –
Andorra**
Cyprus – Belgium
Wales – Israel

13/10/15
Belgium – Israel
**Cyprus – Bosnia &
Herzegovina**
Wales – Andorra

Group C

*08/09/14, Stade Josy Barthel, Luxembourg
(att: 3,265)*
Luxembourg 1-1 Belarus
Goals: 1-0 Gerson 42, 1-1 Dragun 78
Referee: Mažeika (LTU)
Luxembourg: Joubert, Jänisch, Schnell,
Philippe, Gerson, Da Mota (Laterza 67), Dersi,
Martins, Jans, Holter (Payal 77), Turpel (Luisi 63).
Coach: Luc Holtz (LUX)
Belarus: Gutor, Dragun, Martynovich, Shitov,
Veretilo (Stasevich 62), Krivets, Kislyak (Kornilenko
73), Balanovich, Olekhnovich (Aleksiyevich 77),
Filipenko, Kalachev. Coach: Georgi Kondratiev (BLR)

*08/09/14, Estadi Ciutat de València, Valencia
(att: 18,553)*
Spain 5-1 FYR Macedonia
Goals: 1-0 Sergio Ramos 16(p), 2-0 Paco Alcácer
17, 2-1 Ibraimi 28(p), 3-1 Busquets 45+3, 4-1 Silva
50, 5-1 Pedro 90+1
Referee: Sidiropoulos (GRE)
Spain: Casillas, Albiol, Juanfran, Koke (El
Haddadi 77), Paco Alcácer (Isco 57), Fàbregas,
Pedro, Sergio Ramos (Bartra 68), Busquets, Jordi
Alba, Silva. Coach: Vicente del Bosque (ESP)
FYR Macedonia: Pacovski, Cuculi, Mojsov, Sikov,
Trajkovski, Jahovic, Ibraimi, Ristovski, Alioski
(Demiri 46), Abdurahimi (Velkoski 74), Spirovski
(Radeski 64). Coach: Bosko Djurovski (MKD)

08/09/14, NSK Olimpiyskyi, Kyiv (att: 38,454)
Ukraine 0-1 Slovakia
Goal: 0-1 Mak 17
Referee: Thomson (SCO)
Ukraine: Pyatov, Kovalchuk (Bezus 66), Kucher, Stepanenko, Yarmolenko, Zozulya, Gusev (Gromov 81), Shevchuk, Fedetskiy, Rakitskiy, Edmar. Coach: Mykhailo Fomenko (UKR)
Slovakia: Kozáčik, Pekarík, Ďurica, Gyömbér, Weiss (Stoch 67), Nemec (Kiss 63), Hubočan, Hamšík, Kucka, Mak (Ďuriš 90+2), Pečovský. Coach: Ján Kozák (SVK)

09/10/14, Borisov Arena, Borisov (att: 10,512)
Belarus 0-2 Ukraine
Goals: 0-1 Martynovich 82(og), 0-2 Sydorchuk 90+3
Referee: Van Boekel (NED)
Belarus: Zhevnov, Dragun, Martynovich (Savitski 87), Polyakov, Stasevich (Kislyak 46), Gordeichuk (Kornilenko 79), Krivets, Balanovich, Verkhovtsov, Filipenko, Kalachev. Coach: Georgi Kondratiev (BLR)
Ukraine: Pyatov, Khacheridi, Kucher, Stepanenko, Yarmolenko, Zozulya (Tymoshchuk 90+1), Konoplyanka, Shevchuk, Rotan (Sydorchuk 64), Fedetskiy, Edmar (Budkivskiy 79). Coach: Mykhailo Fomenko (UKR)

09/10/14, Nacionalna Arena Filip II Makedonski, Skopje (att: 11,500)
FYR Macedonia 3-2 Luxembourg
Goals: 1-0 Trajkovski 20, 1-1 Bensi 39, 1-2 Turpel 44, 2-2 Jahovic 66(p), 3-2 Abdurahimi 90+2
Referee: Mazzoleni (ITA)
FYR Macedonia: Pacovski, Cuculi (Alioski 46), Mojsov, Sikov, Trajkovski, Demiri, Ibraimi (Abdurahimi 46), Ristovski, Muarem (Jahovic 60), Ademi, Kostovski. Coach: Bosko Djurovski (MKD)
Luxembourg: Joubert, Chanot, Jänisch, Philipps, Gerson, Martins, Da Mota (Holter 63), Bensi (Laterza 75), Mutsch, Jans, Turpel (Deville 70). Coach: Luc Holtz (LUX)

09/10/14, Štadión MŠK Žilina, Zilina (att: 9,478)
Slovakia 2-1 Spain
Goals: 1-0 Kucka 17, 1-1 Paco Alcácer 82, 2-1 Stoch 87
Referee: Kuipers (NED)
Slovakia: Kozáčik, Pekarík, Škrtel, Ďurica, Gyömbér, Weiss (Ďuriš 54), Hubočan, Hamšík, Kucka (Kiss 83), Mak (Stoch 61), Pečovský. Coach: Ján Kozák (SVK)
Spain: Casillas, Albiol (Pedro 58), Piqué, Busquets, Iniesta, Koke, Fàbregas, Juanfran (Santi Cazorla 81), Jordi Alba, Diego Costa, Silva (Paco Alcácer 71). Coach: Vicente del Bosque (ESP)

12/10/14, Borisov Arena, Borisov (att: 3,684)
Belarus 1-3 Slovakia
Goals: 0-1 Hamšík 65, 1-1 Kalachev 79, 1-2 Hamšík 84, 1-3 Šesták 90+1
Referee: Gumienny (BEL)
Belarus: Zhevnov, Dragun, Martynovich, Shitov (Stasevich 76), Renan Bressan (Gordeichuk 46), Krivets, Balanovich, Verkhovtsov, Bordachev, Filipenko (Polyakov 55), Kalachev. Coach: Georgi Kondratiev (BLR)
Slovakia: Kozáčik, Pekarík, Škrtel, Ďurica, Gyömbér, Weiss (Stoch 80), Nemec, Hamšík, Kucka (Kiss 86), Mak (Šesták 62), Pečovský. Coach: Ján Kozák (SVK)

12/10/14, Stade Josy Barthel, Luxembourg (att: 8,125)
Luxembourg 0-4 Spain
Goals: 0-1 Silva 27, 0-2 Paco Alcácer 42, 0-3 Diego Costa 69, 0-4 Bernat 88
Referee: Gil (POL)
Luxembourg: Joubert, Chanot, Jänisch, Philipps, Gerson, Martins (Turpel 61), Da Mota (Payal 75), Bensi, Mutsch (Deville 86), Jans, Holter. Coach: Luc Holtz (LUX)
Spain: De Gea, Piqué, Busquets, Iniesta (Bernat 70), Koke, Paco Alcácer, Bartra, Jordi Alba, Diego Costa (Rodrigo 82), Silva (Pedro 70), Carvajal. Coach: Vicente del Bosque (ESP)

12/10/14, Arena Lviv, Lviv (att: 33,978)
Ukraine 1-0 FYR Macedonia
Goal: 1-0 Sydorchuk 45+2
Referee: Delferiere (BEL)
Ukraine: Pyatov, Khacheridi, Kucher, Stepanenko, Yarmolenko, Zozulya (Budkivskiy 77), Konoplyanka, Shevchuk, Rotan (Tymoshchuk 90+2), Fedetskiy, Sydorchuk (Edmar 90+5). Coach: Mykhailo Fomenko (UKR)
FYR Macedonia: Pacovski, Alioski, Damcevski, Sikov, Trajkovski, Jahovic (Velkoski 62), Ristovski, Ademi, Gligorov (Stojkov 86), Abdurahimi, Ivanovski (Kostovski 70). Coach: Bosko Djurovski (MKD)

15/11/14, Nacionalna Arena Filip II Makedonski, Skopje (att: 11,322)
FYR Macedonia 0-2 Slovakia
Goals: 0-1 Kucka 25, 0-2 Nemec 38
Referee: Proença (POR)
FYR Macedonia: Pacovski, Alioski, Mojsov, Sikov, Trajkovski, Demiri (Babunski 74), Stojkov (Kostovski 46), Velkoski (Ivanovski 70), Ristovski, Ademi, Abdurahimi. Coach: Bosko Djurovski (MKD)
Slovakia: Kozáčik, Pekarík (Švento 46), Škrtel, Ďurica, Weiss (Ďuriš 78), Stoch, Nemec, Hubočan, Hamšík, Kucka (Kiss 55), Pečovský. Coach: Ján Kozák (SVK)

15/11/14, Stade Josy Barthel, Luxembourg (att: 4,379)
Luxembourg 0-3 Ukraine
Goals: 0-1 Yarmolenko 33, 0-2 Yarmolenko 53, 0-3 Yarmolenko 56
Referee: Jakobsson (ISL)
Luxembourg: Joubert, Chanot, Jänisch, Schnell, Gerson, Martins (Da Mota 53), Bensi (Joachim 63), Mutsch, Jans, Holter, Turpel (Deville 76). Coach: Luc Holtz (LUX)
Ukraine: Pyatov, Khacheridi, Tymoshchuk, Yarmolenko, Zozulya (Budkivskiy 72), Konoplyanka (Morozyuk 76), Oliynyk (Kovalchuk 85), Shevchuk, Fedetskiy, Rakitskiy, Sydorchuk. Coach: Mykhailo Fomenko (UKR)

15/11/14, Estadio Nuevo Colombino, Huelva (att: 19,249)
Spain 3-0 Belarus
Goals: 1-0 Isco 18, 2-0 Busquets 19, 3-0 Pedro 55
Referee: Hansen (DEN)
Spain: Casillas, Piqué, Busquets (Bruno Soriano 46), Koke, Paco Alcácer, Pedro, Sergio Ramos, Juanfran, Jordi Alba, Santi Cazorla (Callejón 69), Isco (Morata 80). Coach: Vicente del Bosque (ESP)

Belarus: Zhevnov, Dragun, Martynovich (Bordachev 31), Kornilenko (Signevich 67), Krivets (Kislyak 80), Matveichik, Balanovich, Nekhaichik, Politevich, Yanushkevich, Kalachev. Coach: Andrei Zygmantovich (BLR)

27/03/15, Nacionalna Arena Filip II Makedonski, Skopje (att: 3,447)
FYR Macedonia 1-2 Belarus
Goals: 1-0 Trajkovski 9, 1-1 Kalachev 44, 1-2 Kornilenko 82
Referee: Taylor (ENG)
FYR Macedonia: Pacovski, Georgievski, Polozani (Bardi 31), Markoski, Sikov, Trajkovski, Velkoski (B Todorovski 63), Ibraimi, Hasani, Ristovski, Abdurahimi (Blazevski 75). Coach: Bosko Djurovski (MKD)
Belarus: Zhevnov, Martynovich, Shitov, Kornilenko, Stasevich (Nekhaichik 90+3), Hleb (Dragun 87), Kislyak, Mayevski (Putilo 80), Bordachev, Filipenko, Kalachev. Coach: Aleksandr Khatskevich (BLR)

27/03/15, Štadión MŠK Žilina, Zilina (att: 9,524)
Slovakia 3-0 Luxembourg
Goals: 1-0 Nemec 10, 2-0 Weiss 21, 3-0 Pekarík 40
Referee: Studer (SUI)
Slovakia: Kozáčik, Pekarík, Škrtel, Ďurica, Weiss (Mak 71), Stoch (Šesták 85), Nemec, Hubočan, Hamšík, Kucka (Hrošovský 59), Pečovský. Coach: Ján Kozák (SVK)
Luxembourg: Joubert, Chanot, Schnell, Philipps, Gerson, Bensi (Laterza 78), Joachim, Mutsch, Jans, Holter (Da Mota 51), Deville (Payal 64). Coach: Luc Holtz (LUX)

27/03/15, Estadio Ramón Sánchez Pizjuán, Seville (att: 33,775)
Spain 1-0 Ukraine
Goal: 1-0 Morata 28
Referee: Çakır (TUR)
Spain: Casillas, Piqué, Busquets, Iniesta (Santi Cazorla 74), Morata (Pedro 65), Koke, Sergio Ramos, Juanfran, Jordi Alba (Bernat 78), Silva, Isco. Coach: Vicente del Bosque (ESP)
Ukraine: Pyatov, Khacheridi, Tymoshchuk, Kucher, Stepanenko (Garmash 76), Yarmolenko, Zozulya (Kravets 32; Budkivskiy 91), Konoplyanka, Shevchuk, Rotan, Fedetskiy. Coach: Mykhailo Fomenko (UKR)

Slovakia captain Marek Hamšík takes on Belarus skipper Timofei Kalachev in Borisov

14/06/15, Borisov Arena, Borisov (att: 13,121)
Belarus 0-1 Spain
Goal: 0-1 Silva 45
Referee: Schörgenhofer (AUT)
Belarus: Gorbunov, Martynovich, Shitov, Kornilenko, Hleb (Putilo 89), M Volodko (Stasevich 81), Kiolyak (Draguń 78), Nekhaichik, Mayevski, Bordachev, Filipenko. Coach: Aleksandr Khatskevich (BLR)
Spain: Casillas, Piqué, Busquets, Morata, Fàbregas (Isco 75), Pedro (Vitolo 65), Sergio Ramos, Juanfran, Jordi Alba, Santi Cazorla, Silva (Bernat 85). Coach: Vicente del Bosque (ESP)

14/06/15, Štadión MŠK Žilina, Zilina (att: 10,765)
Slovakia 2-1 FYR Macedonia
Goals: 1-0 Saláta 8, 2-0 Hamšík 38, 2-1 Ademi 69
Referee: Hansen (DEN)
Slovakia: Kozáčik, Pekarík, Škrtel, Weiss, Nemec (Hološko 84), Hubočan, Saláta, Hamšík (Duda 80), Kucka (Hrošovský 73), Mak, Pečovský. Coach: Ján Kozák (SVK)
FYR Macedonia: Pacovski, A Todorovski, Dimitrovski, Mojsov, Trajkovski (Ivanovski 56), Muarem (Velkoski 82), Ibraimi (Abdurahimi 89), Hasani, Trajcevski, Ademi, Zuta. Coach: Ljubinko Drulović (SRB)
Red card: Hasani 84 (FYR Macedonia)

14/06/15, Arena Lviv, Lviv (att: 21,635)
Ukraine 3-0 Luxembourg
Goals: 1-0 Kravets 49, 2-0 Garmash 57, 3-0 Konoplyanka 86
Referee: Hunter (NIR)
Ukraine: Pyatov, Morozyuk, Khacheridi, Stepanenko, Yarmolenko, Konoplyanka, Shevchuk, Rotan (Garmash 46), Sydorchuk, Rakitskiy (Kucher 77), Kravets (Seleznyov 69). Coach: Mykhailo Fomenko (UKR)
Luxembourg: Joubert, Chanot, Schnell, Gerson, Da Mota (Deville 71), Payal, Malget, Mutsch, Jans, Holter (Philipps 77), Turpel (Bensi 52). Coach: Luc Holtz (LUX)

Remaining fixtures

<table>
<tr><td>05/09/15</td><td>09/10/15</td></tr>
<tr><td>Luxembourg – FYR Macedonia</td><td>FYR Macedonia – Ukraine</td></tr>
<tr><td>Spain – Slovakia</td><td>Slovakia – Belarus</td></tr>
<tr><td>Ukraine – Belarus</td><td>Spain – Luxembourg</td></tr>
<tr><td>08/09/15</td><td>12/10/15</td></tr>
<tr><td>Belarus – Luxembourg</td><td>Belarus – FYR Macedonia</td></tr>
<tr><td>FYR Macedonia – Spain</td><td></td></tr>
<tr><td>Slovakia – Ukraine</td><td>Luxembourg – Slovakia</td></tr>
<tr><td></td><td>Ukraine – Spain</td></tr>
</table>

Group D

07/09/14, Boris Paichadze Erovnuli Stadioni Dinamo Arena, Tbilisi (att: 22,000)
Georgia 1-2 Republic of Ireland
Goals: 0-1 McGeady 24, 1-1 Okriashvili 38, 1-2 McGeady 90
Referee: Blom (NED)
Georgia: Loria (Kvaskhvadze 46), Lobjanidze, Kverkvelia, Kashia, Khubutia, Kankava, Daushvili, Gelashvili, Ananidze (Targamadze 63), Okriashvili (Mchedlidze 88), Kvirkvelia. Coach: Temur Ketsbaia (GEO)
Republic of Ireland: Forde, Coleman, Wilson, O'Shea, Whelan, McGeady, McCarthy (Meyler 90+1), Keane (Long 76), Walters, Ward, Quinn (Brady 76). Coach: Martin O'Neill (NIR)

07/09/14, BVB Stadion Dortmund, Dortmund (att: 60,209)
Germany 2-1 Scotland
Goals: 1-0 Müller 18, 1-1 Anya 66, 2-1 Müller 70
Referee: Moen (NOR)
Germany: Neuer, Höwedes, Rudy, Schürrle (Podolski 84), Müller, Durm, Boateng, Kroos, Götze, Kramer, Reus (Ginter 90+2). Coach: Joachim Löw (GER)

Thomas Müller (13) punches the air after scoring his second goal for Germany against Scotland

Scotland: Marshall, Hutton, Whittaker, R Martin, Hanley, Morrison, D Fletcher (McArthur 58), Mulgrew, Naismith (Maloney 82), Bannan (S Fletcher 58), Anya. Coach: Gordon Strachan (SCO)
Red card: Mulgrew 90+4 (Scotland)

07/09/14, Estádio Algarve, Faro (att: 1,620)
Gibraltar 0-7 Poland
Goals: 0-1 Grosicki 11, 0-2 Grosicki 48, 0-3 Lewandowski 50, 0-4 Lewandowski 53, 0-5 Szukała 58, 0-6 Lewandowski 86, 0-7 Lewandowski 90+2
Referee: Johannesson (SWE)
Gibraltar: J Perez, Wiseman, J Chipolina, Artell (Payas 88), R Casciaro, R Chipolina, L Casciaro, Bado (Gosling 46), K Casciaro (Priestley 63), Walker, B Perez. Coach: Allen Bula (GIB)
Poland: Szczęsny, Szukała, Milik (Sobota 71), Krychowiak, Lewandowski, Klich (Mączyński 71), Grosicki (Starzyński 78), Rybus, Wawrzyniak, Glik, Olkowski. Coach: Adam Nawałka (POL)

11/10/14, Stadion Narodowy, Warsaw (att: 56,934)
Poland 2-0 Germany
Goals: 1-0 Milik 51, 2-0 Mila 88
Referee: Proença (POR)
Poland: Szczęsny, Szukała, Jodłowiec, Milik (Mila 77), Krychowiak, Lewandowski, Grosicki (Sobota 71), Rybus, Wawrzyniak (Jędrzejczyk 84), Glik, Piszczek. Coach: Adam Nawałka (POL)
Germany: Neuer, Hummels, Schürrle (Podolski 77), Bellarabi, Müller, Durm, Rüdiger (Kruse 83), Boateng, Kroos, Götze, Kramer (Draxler 71). Coach: Joachim Löw (GER)

11/10/14, Dublin Arena, Dublin (att: 35,123)
Republic of Ireland 7-0 Gibraltar
Goals: 1-0 Keane 6, 2-0 Keane 14, 3-0 Keane 18(p), 4-0 McClean 46, 5-0 J Perez 52(og), 6-0 McClean 53, 7-0 Hoolahan 56
Referee: Trattou (CYP)
Republic of Ireland: Forde, Ward (Brady 70), Wilson, O'Shea, McGeady, Hendrick, Keane (Murphy 63), McClean, Meyler, Gibson, Hoolahan (Doyle 63). Coach: Martin O'Neill (NIR)
Gibraltar: J Perez (Robba 60), Wiseman, J Chipolina, R Casciaro, R Chipolina (Santos 57), L Casciaro, Bado (Gosling 46), Walker, Gosling, B Perez, Payas. Coach: Allen Bula (GIB)

11/10/14, Ibrox Stadium, Glasgow (att: 34,719)
Scotland 1-0 Georgia
Goal: 1-0 Khubutia 28(og)
Referee: Zelinka (CZE)
Scotland: Marshall, Hutton, Robertson, R Martin, Hanley, Maloney, Morrison, Brown, S Fletcher (C Martin 90), Naismith (McArthur 80), Anya. Coach: Gordon Strachan (SCO)

Georgia: Loria, Lobjanidze, Kverkvelia, Grigalava, Khubutia, Kankava, Daushvili, Gelashvili, Kvirkvelia (Okriashvili 46), Papava (Dzaria 70), Kazaishvili (Chanturia 80). Coach: Temur Ketsbaia (GEO)

14/10/14, Arena AufSchalke, Gelsenkirchen (att: 51,204)
Germany 1-1 Republic of Ireland
Goals: 1-0 Kroos 71, 1-1 O'Shea 90+4
Referee: Skomina (SVN)
Germany: Neuer, Ginter (Podolski 46), Hummels, Bellarabi (Rudy 86), Müller, Draxler (Kruse 70), Durm, Rüdiger, Boateng, Kroos, Götze. Coach: Joachim Löw (GER)
Republic of Ireland: Forde, Ward, Wilson, O'Shea, Whelan (Hendrick 53), McGeady, Keane (Gibson 76), McClean, Meyler, Quinn (Hoolahan 76), Walters. Coach: Martin O'Neill (NIR)

14/10/14, Estádio Algarve, Faro (att: 281)
Gibraltar 0-3 Georgia
Goals: 0-1 Gelashvili 9, 0-2 Okriashvili 19, 0-3 Kankava 69
Referee: Lechner (AUT)
Gibraltar: Robba, Wiseman, J Chipolina, R Casciaro, L Casciaro, K Casciaro (Priestley 46), Walker, B Perez, Santos (R Chipolina 76), Garcia, Guiling (Gosling 75). Coach: Allen Bula (GIB)
Georgia: Loria, Lobjanidze, Kverkvelia, Grigalava, Khubutia, Kankava, Gelashvili (Papunashvili 67), Ananidze (Ebralidze 80), Chanturia (Dvalishvili 76), Okriashvili, Dzaria. Coach: Temur Ketsbaia (GEO)

14/10/14, Stadion Narodowy, Warsaw (att: 55,197)
Poland 2-2 Scotland
Goals: 1-0 Mączyński 11, 1-1 Maloney 18, 1-2 Naismith 57, 2-2 Milik 76
Referee: Undiano Mallenco (ESP)
Poland: Szczęsny, Jędrzejczyk, Szukała, Sobota (Mila 63), Milik, Krychowiak, Lewandowski, Grosicki (Żyro 89), Glik, Mączyński, Piszczek. Coach: Adam Nawałka (POL)
Scotland: Marshall, Hutton, Whittaker, R Martin, Greer, Maloney, Morrison, Brown, S Fletcher (D Fletcher 71), Naismith (C Martin 71), Anya. Coach: Gordon Strachan (SCO)

14/11/14, Boris Paichadze Erovnuli Stadioni Dinamo Arena, Tbilisi (att: 25,635)
Georgia 0-4 Poland
Goals: 0-1 Glik 51, 0-2 Krychowiak 71, 0-3 Mila 73, 0-4 Milik 90+2
Referee: Tagliavento (ITA)
Georgia: Loria, Lobjanidze, Kverkvelia, Kashia, Grigalava, Khubutia, Kankava, Daushvili, Ananidze (Okriashvili 59), Kobakhidze (Dzalamidze 88), Mchedlidze (Chanturia 68). Coach: Temur Ketsbaia (GEO)
Poland: Szczęsny, Jędrzejczyk, Szukała, Milik, Krychowiak, Lewandowski, Grosicki (Rybus 69), Glik, Mączyński (Jodłowiec 66), Mila (Linetty 86), Piszczek. Coach: Adam Nawałka (POL)

14/11/14, Grundig Stadion, Nuremberg (att: 43,520)
Germany 4-0 Gibraltar
Goals: 1-0 Müller 12, 2-0 Müller 29, 3-0 Götze 38, 4-0 Santos 67(og)
Referee: Tudor (ROU)
Germany: Neuer, Mustafi, Khedira (Volland 60), Podolski, Bellarabi, Müller, Durm (Hector 72), Boateng, Kroos (L Bender 79), Götze, Kruse. Coach: Joachim Löw (GER)
Gibraltar: Robba, Wiseman, J Chipolina, Artell, R Casciaro, R Chipolina, L Casciaro (K Casciaro 71), Walker, Sergeant (Santos 58), B Perez (Priestley 90+1), Garcia. Coach: Allen Bula (GIB)

14/11/14, Celtic Park, Glasgow (att: 59,239)
Scotland 1-0 Republic of Ireland
Goal: 1-0 Maloney 75
Referee: Mažić (SRB)
Scotland: Marshall, Whittaker, Mulgrew, R Martin, Hanley, Maloney, Brown, S Fletcher (C Martin 56), Naismith, Anya (D Fletcher 88), Robertson. Coach: Gordon Strachan (SCO)
Republic of Ireland: Forde, Coleman, Ward, O'Shea, McGeady, Hendrick (Keane 78), Long (Brady 68), McClean, Gibson (Quinn 68), Walters, Keogh. Coach: Martin O'Neill (NIR)

29/03/15, Boris Paichadze Erovnuli Stadioni Dinamo Arena, Tbilisi (att: 51,000)
Georgia 0-2 Germany
Goals: 0-1 Reus 39, 0-2 Müller 44
Referee: Turpin (FRA)
Georgia: Loria, Lobjanidze, Kverkvelia, Kashia, Amisulashvili (Dvali 4), Makharadze (Kenia 63), Kankava, Okriashvili (Chanturia 46), Kobakhidze, Navalovski, Mchedlidze. Coach: Kakhaber Tskhadadze (GEO)
Germany: Neuer, Hector, Hummels, Schweinsteiger, Özil, Reus, Müller (Schürrle 86), Rudy, Boateng, Kroos, Götze (Podolski 87). Coach: Joachim Löw (GER)

29/03/15, Dublin Arena, Dublin (att: 50,500)
Republic of Ireland 1-1 Poland
Goals: 0-1 Peszko 26, 1-1 Long 90+1
Referee: Eriksson (SWE)
Republic of Ireland: Given, Coleman, Wilson, O'Shea, Whelan (Long 84), McGeady (McClean 68), McCarthy, Keane, Walters, Brady, Hoolahan. Coach: Martin O'Neill (NIR)
Poland: Fabiański, Szukała, Jodłowiec, Milik (Mila 84), Krychowiak, Lewandowski, Rybus, Wawrzyniak, Glik, Olkowski, Peszko (Kucharczyk 88). Coach: Adam Nawałka (POL)

29/03/15, Hampden Park, Glasgow (att: 34,255)
Scotland 6-1 Gibraltar
Goals: 1-0 Maloney 18(p), 1-1 L Casciaro 19, 2-1 S Fletcher 29, 3-1 Maloney 34(p), 4-1 Naismith 39, 5-1 S Fletcher 77, 6-1 S Fletcher 90
Referee: Gestranius (FIN)
Scotland: Marshall, Hutton, Robertson, Ritchie (Greer 46), R Martin, Maloney, Morrison, Brown, S Fletcher, Naismith (Rhodes 67), Anya (Bannan 74). Coach: Gordon Strachan (SCO)
Gibraltar: Robba, Wiseman, J Chipolina, Artell (Garcia 53), R Casciaro, R Chipolina (Gosling 74), L Casciaro, Payas, Walker, Priestley, Bardon (Duarte 82). Coach: David Wilson (SCO)

13/06/15, Estádio Algarve, Faro-Loule (att: 7,467)
Gibraltar 0-7 Germany
Goals: 0-1 Schürrle 28, 0-2 Kruse 47, 0-3 Gündoğan 51, 0-4 Bellarabi 57, 0-5 Schürrle 65, 0-6 Schürrle 71, 0-7 Kruse 81
Referee: Pisani (MLT)
Gibraltar: J Perez, J Chipolina, R Casciaro, R Chipolina, L Casciaro, Payas (Sergeant 82), K Casciaro (Bosio 78), Walker, Gosling, Priestley (Coombes 61), Garcia. Coach: David Wilson (SCO)
Germany: Weidenfeller, Hector, Rudy, Schweinsteiger, Özil, Schürrle, Bellarabi, Herrmann (Podolski 56), Boateng, Götze (Kruse 36), Gündoğan (Khedira 67). Coach: Joachim Löw (GER)

Shaun Maloney strokes home a penalty in Scotland's 6-1 home win against Gibraltar

13/06/15, Stadion Narodowy, Warsaw (att: 56,512)
Poland 4-0 Georgia
Goals: 1-0 Milik 62, 2-0 Lewandowski 89, 3-0 Lewandowski 90+2, 4-0 Lewandowski 90+3
Referee: Kulbakov (BLR)
Poland: Fabiański, Szukała, Mączyński, Milik, Krychowiak, Lewandowski, Grosicki (Jodłowiec 80), Rybus, Pazdan (Komorowski 90), Peszko (Błaszczykowski 64), Piszczek. Coach: Adam Nawałka (POL)
Georgia: Loria, Lobjanidze, Kashia, Amisulashvili, Kazaishvili, Okriashvili (Daushvili 46), Ananidze, Vatsadze (Chanturia 63), Kobakhidze (Tskhadadze 76), Dvali, Navalovski. Coach: Kakhaber Tskhadadze (GEO)

13/06/15, Aviva Stadium, Dublin (att: 49,063)
Republic of Ireland 1-1 Scotland
Goals: 1-0 Walters 38, 1-1 O'Shea 47(og)
Referee: Rizzoli (ITA)
Republic of Ireland: Given, Coleman, Wilson, O'Shea, Whelan (McClean 68), McCarthy, Hendrick, Walters, Brady, Hoolahan (Keane 73), Murphy (Long 80). Coach: Martin O'Neill (NIR)
Scotland: Marshall, Hutton, Forsyth, R Martin, Mulgrew, Maloney, Morrison, Brown (McArthur 85), S Fletcher, Naismith (Berra 90+2), Ritchie (Anya 46). Coach: Gordon Strachan (SCO)

Remaining fixtures

04/09/15
Georgia – Scotland
Germany – Poland
Gibraltar – Republic of Ireland

07/09/15
Poland – Gibraltar
Republic of Ireland – Georgia
Scotland – Germany

08/10/15
Georgia – Gibraltar
Republic of Ireland – Germany
Scotland – Poland

11/10/15
Germany – Georgia
Gibraltar – Scotland
Poland – Republic of Ireland

Group E

08/09/14, A. Le Coq Arena, Tallinn (att: 6,561)
Estonia 1-0 Slovenia
Goal: 1-0 Purje 86
Referee: Marciniak (POL)
Estonia: Pareiko, Lindpere (Purje 85), Morozov, Kallaste, Henri Anier, Zenjov, Vunk, Klavan, Antonov (Kams 67), Mets, Teniste (Jääger 71). Coach: Magnus Pehrsson (SWE)
Slovenia: Handanovič, Brečko, Samardžić, Cesar, Iličič (Birsa 62), Kurtić, Novakovič, Struna, Rotman (Lazarevič 89), Kampl, Stevanovič. Coach: Srečko Katanec (SVN)
Red card: Stevanovič 79 (Slovenia)

08/09/14, San Marino Stadium, Serravalle (att: 986)
San Marino 0-2 Lithuania
Goals: 0-1 Matulevičius 5, 0-2 Novikovas 36
Referee: Kovařík (CZE)
San Marino: A Simoncini, Battistini, Hirsch (Stefanelli 75), Brolli, D Simoncini, M Vitaioli, Bonini (Buscarini 87), Selva, Tosi (Cervellini 55), A Gasperoni, F Vitaioli. Coach: Pierangelo Manzaroli (SMR)
Lithuania: Arlauskis, Freidgeimas, Kijanskas, Slavickas, Žaliūkas, Matulevičius (Stankevičius 86), Kalonas, Novikovas, Chvedukas, Panka (Vičius 66), Černych (Kuklys 90). Coach: Igoris Pankratjevas (LTU)

08/09/14, St Jakob-Park, Basel (att: 35,500)
Switzerland 0-2 England
Goals: 0-1 Welbeck 58, 0-2 Welbeck 90+4
Referee: Çakır (TUR)
Switzerland: Sommer, Lichtsteiner, Von Bergen, Inler, Seferovic, Xhaka (Dzemaili 74), Behrami, Rodriguez, Mehmedi (Drmic 64), Djourou, Shaqiri. Coach: Vladimir Petković (SUI)
England: Hart, Stones, Baines, Henderson, Cahill, Jones (Jagielka 77), Wilshere (Milner 73), Delph, Welbeck, Rooney (Lambert 90), Sterling. Coach: Roy Hodgson (ENG)

09/10/14, Wembley Stadium, London (att: 55,990)
England 5-0 San Marino
Goals: 1-0 Jagielka 25, 2-0 Rooney 43(p), 3-0 Welbeck 49, 4-0 Townsend 72, 5-0 Della Valle 78(og)
Referee: Borski (POL)
England: Hart, Chambers, Gibbs, Henderson (Oxlade-Chamberlain 46), Cahill, Jagielka, Milner, Wilshere, Welbeck (Townsend 66), Rooney, Sterling (Lallana 46). Coach: Roy Hodgson (ENG)
San Marino: A Simoncini, Palazzi (Buscarini 74), Battistini, F Vitaioli, Brolli, Della Valle, Hirsch, Chiaruzzi, Tosi (L Gasperoni 63), Selva (Rinaldi 87), M Vitaioli. Coach: Pierangelo Manzaroli (SMR)

09/10/14, LFF, Vilnius (att: 4,780)
Lithuania 1-0 Estonia
Goal: 1-0 Mikoliūnas 76
Referee: Gómez (ESP)
Lithuania: Arlauskis, Vičius, Freidgeimas, Kijanskas, Vaitkūnas (Beniušis 90), Kalonas (Mikoliūnas 63), Novikovas, Panka, Černych, Andriuškevičius. Coach: Igoris Pankratjevas (LTU)
Estonia: Pareiko, Lindpere (Vassiljev 76), Bärengrub, Henri Anier, Zenjov (Ojamaa 64), Vunk (Purje 80), Klavan, Antonov, Jääger, Mets, Kallaste. Coach: Magnus Pehrsson (SWE)
Red card: Kallaste 86 (Estonia)

09/10/14, Stadion Ljudski vrt, Maribor (att: 8,500)
Slovenia 1-0 Switzerland
Goal: 1-0 Novakovič 79(p)
Referee: Stark (GER)
Slovenia: Handanovič, Brečko, Cesar, Ilič, Ljubijankič (Kurtič 46), Birsa (Lazarevič 55), Novakovič, Struna, Kirm (Pečnik 72), Kampl, Mertelj. Coach: Srečko Katanec (SVN)
Switzerland: Sommer, Lichtsteiner, Senderos (Von Bergen 70), Inler (Kasami 82), Seferovic, Xhaka, Behrami, Rodriguez, Drmic (Mehmedi 74), Djourou, Shaqiri. Coach: Vladimir Petković (SUI)

12/10/14, A. Le Coq Arena, Tallinn (att: 10,195)
Estonia 0-1 England
Goal: 0-1 Rooney 74
Referee: Strahonja (CRO)
Estonia: Pareiko, Morozov, Henri Anier, Zenjov (Ojamaa 80), Vunk (Kruglov 83), Vassiljev (Lindpere 46), Klavan, Antonov, Jääger, Mets, Pikk. Coach: Magnus Pehrsson (SWE)
England: Hart, Chambers, Baines, Henderson (Sterling 64), Cahill, Jagielka, Wilshere, Delph (Oxlade-Chamberlain 61), Welbeck (Lambert 80), Rooney, Lallana. Coach: Roy Hodgson (ENG)
Red card: Klavan 48 (Estonia)

12/10/14, LFF, Vilnius (att: 4,250)
Lithuania 0-2 Slovenia
Goals: 0-1 Novakovič 33, 0-2 Novakovič 37
Referee: Koukoulakis (GRE)
Lithuania: Arlauskis, Freidgeimas, Kijanskas, Žulpa, Vaitkūnas, Matulevičius, Novikovas, Chvedukas (Mikoliūnas 75), Panka (Vičius 32), Černych, Andriuškevičius. Coach: Igoris Pankratjevas (LTU)
Slovenia: Handanovič, Brečko, Stevanovič (Mertelj 46), Cesar, Ilič, Pečnik (Birsa 66), Kurtič, Novakovič, Struna, Kirm (Lazarevič 86), Kampl. Coach: Srečko Katanec (SVN)

14/10/14, San Marino Stadium, Serravalle (att: 2,289)
San Marino 0-4 Switzerland
Goals: 0-1 Seferovic 10, 0-2 Seferovic 23, 0-3 Dzemaili 30, 0-4 Shaqiri 79
Referee: Chapron (FRA)
San Marino: A Simoncini, Bonini, Battistini, F Vitaioli (Cervellini 17), Brolli, Della Valle, Palazzi, Chiaruzzi, Stefanelli, A Gasperoni (L Gasperoni 69), M Vitaioli (Hirsch 61). Coach: Pierangelo Manzaroli (SMR)
Switzerland: Sommer, Lichtsteiner (Widmer 59), Von Bergen, Seferovic, Xhaka, Rodriguez, Dzemaili, Kasami (Barnetta 71), Drmic (Mehmedi 46), Djourou, Shaqiri. Coach: Vladimir Petković (SUI)

15/11/14, Wembley Stadium, London (att: 82,309)
England 3-1 Slovenia
Goals: 0-1 Henderson 58(og), 1-1 Rooney 59(p), 2-1 Welbeck 66, 3-1 Welbeck 72
Referee: Olegário Benquerença (POR)
England: Hart, Clyne, Gibbs, Henderson, Cahill, Jagielka (Smalling 89), Wilshere, Lallana (Milner 80), Welbeck, Rooney, Sterling (Oxlade-Chamberlain 85). Coach: Roy Hodgson (ENG)
Slovenia: Handanovič, Brečko, Cesar, Ilič, Kurtič (Rotman 75), Birsa (Lazarevič 63), Novakovič, Struna, Kirm (Ljubijankič 78), Kampl, Mertelj. Coach: Srečko Katanec (SVN)

15/11/14, San Marino Stadium, Serravalle (att: 759)
San Marino 0-0 Estonia
Referee: Brych (GER)
San Marino: A Simoncini, Bonini, Palazzi, F Vitaioli, D Simoncini, Brolli, Hirsch (Battistini 60), Chiaruzzi, Tosi, Selva (Rinaldi 83), M Vitaioli (F Golinucci 77). Coach: Pierangelo Manzaroli (SMR)
Estonia: Aksalu, Morozov, Kruglov, Aleksandr Dmitrijev (Lindpere 46), Zenjov, Ojamaa (Henri Anier 62), Vassiljev, Antonov, Mets, Artjunin (Teever 74), Teniste. Coach: Magnus Pehrsson (SWE)

15/11/14, AFG Arena, St Gallen (att: 17,300)
Switzerland 4-0 Lithuania
Goals: 1-0 Arlauskis 66(og), 2-0 Schär 68, 3-0 Shaqiri 80, 4-0 Shaqiri 90
Referee: Moen (NOR)
Switzerland: Sommer, Lichtsteiner, Moubandje (Fernandes 75), Inler, Seferovic (Schönbächler 83), Behrami, Dzemaili, Mehmedi (Drmic 63), Djourou, Schär, Shaqiri. Coach: Vladimir Petković (SUI)
Lithuania: Arlauskis, Vičius (Eliošius 82), Freidgeimas, Kijanskas, Žulpa, Vaitkūnas (Borovskij 64), Matulevičius, Novikovas (Kazlauskas 87), Chvedukas, Černych, Andriuškevičius. Coach: Igoris Pankratjevas (LTU)

27/03/15, Wembley Stadium, London (att: 83,671)
England 4-0 Lithuania
Goals: 1-0 Rooney 6, 2-0 Welbeck 45, 3-0 Sterling 58, 4-0 Kane 73
Referee: Královec (CZE)
England: Hart, Clyne, Baines, Henderson (Barkley 71), Cahill, Jones, Sterling, Carrick, Welbeck (Walcott 77), Rooney (Kane 71), Delph. Coach: Roy Hodgson (ENG)
Lithuania: Arlauskis, Freidgeimas, Kijanskas, Mikuckis (Stankevičius 66), Žaliūkas, Žulpa, Matulevičius, Mikoliūnas (Kazlauskas 88), Chvedukas, Černych, Andriuškevičius (Slavickas 83). Coach: Igoris Pankratjevas (LTU)

27/03/15, ŠRC Stožice, Ljubljana (att: 8,325)
Slovenia 6-0 San Marino
Goals: 1-0 Iličič 10, 2-0 Kampl 49, 3-0 Andraž Struna 50, 4-0 Novakovič 52, 5-0 Lazarevič 73, 6-0 Ilič 88
Referee: Drachta (AUT)
Slovenia: Handanovič, Brečko (Stojanovič 76), Cesar, Ilič, Iličič (Berič 72), Kurtič, Birsa, Novakovič, Struna, Kirm (Lazarevič 60), Kampl. Coach: Srečko Katanec (SVN)
San Marino: Benedettini, Bonini, Palazzi, Brolli, D Simoncini, Della Valle (F Vitaioli 78), Hirsch (A Golinucci 84), Mazza, Tosi (Battistini 56), Selva, M Vitaioli. Coach: Pierangelo Manzaroli (SMR)

27/03/15, Swissporarena, Lucerne (att: 14,500)
Switzerland 3-0 Estonia
Goals: 1-0 Schär 17, 2-0 Xhaka 27, 3-0 Seferovic 80
Referee: Makkelie (NED)
Switzerland: Sommer, Lichtsteiner (Widmer 78), Inler, Seferovic, Xhaka (Frei 87), Behrami, Rodriguez, Drmic (Stocker 62), Djourou, Schär, Shaqiri. Coach: Vladimir Petković (SUI)
Estonia: Pareiko, Aleksandr Dmitrijev (Kruglov 63), Henri Anier (Ojamaa 56), Zenjov (Alliku 87), Vassiljev, Klavan, Antonov, Jääger, Mets, Kallaste, Teniste. Coach: Magnus Pehrsson (SWE)

14/06/15, A. Le Coq Arena, Tallinn (att: 6,131)
Estonia 2-0 San Marino
Goals: 1-0 Zenjov 35, 2-0 Zenjov 63
Referee: Kružliak (SVK)
Estonia: Aksalu, Lindpere (Kruglov 84), Aleksandr Dmitrijev, Alliku, Purje, Zenjov (Teever 89), Vassiljev (Antonov 79), Klavan, Mets, Kallaste, Teniste. Coach: Magnus Pehrsson (SWE)
San Marino: A Simoncini, Bonini, Battistini, Brolli, Della Valle, Palazzi, Hirsch, Tosi (Cervellini 71), L Gasperoni, Rinaldi (Stefanelli 79), M Vitaioli (Bianchi 89). Coach: Pierangelo Manzaroli (SMR)

14/06/15, LFF stadionas, Vilnius (att: 4,786)
Lithuania 1-2 Switzerland
Goals: 1-0 Černych 64, 1-1 Drmic 69, 1-2 Shaqiri 84
Referee: Thomson (SCO)
Lithuania: Zubas, Mikuckis, D Česnauskis (Lukša 86), Vaitkūnas, Matulevičius, Žulpa (Chvedukas 61), Klimavičius, Slivka (Vičius 76), Panka, Černych, Andriuškevičius. Coach: Igoris Pankratjevas (LTU)
Switzerland: Sommer, Lichtsteiner, Inler (Dzemaili 57), Seferovic (Mehmedi 57), Xhaka, Behrami, Rodriguez, Drmic (Embolo 81), Djourou, Schär, Shaqiri. Coach: Vladimir Petković (SUI)

14/06/15, Stadion Stožice, Ljubljana (att: 15,796)
Slovenia 2-3 England
Goals: 1-0 Novakovič 37, 1-1 Wilshere 57, 1-2 Wilshere 73, 2-2 Pečnik 84, 2-3 Rooney 86
Referee: Undiano Mallenco (ESP)
Slovenia: Handanovič, Brečko, Cesar, Ilič, Iličič (Birsa 61), Kurtič (Lazarevič 79), Novakovič, Jokič, Kirm (Pečnik 72), Kampl, Mertelj. Coach: Srečko Katanec (SVN)
England: Hart, Jones (Lallana 46), Gibbs, Henderson, Cahill, Smalling, Wilshere, Delph (Clyne 85), Sterling, Rooney, Townsend (Walcott 74). Coach: Roy Hodgson (ENG)

Remaining fixtures

05/09/15
Estonia – Lithuania
San Marino – England
Switzerland – Slovenia

08/09/15
England – Switzerland
Lithuania – San Marino
Slovenia – Estonia

09/10/15
England – Estonia
Slovenia – Lithuania
Switzerland – San Marino

12/10/15
Estonia – Switzerland
Lithuania – England
San Marino – Slovenia

Swiss striker Haris Seferovic (No9) heads goalwards watched by Lithuania's Georgas Freidgeimas

European Qualifiers

Group F

07/09/14, Tórsvøllur, Torshavn (att: 3,300)
Faroe Islands 1-3 Finland
Goals: 1-0 Holst 41, 1-1 Riku Riski 53, 1-2 Riku Riski 78, 1-3 Eremenko 82
Referee: Evans (WAL)
Faroe Islands: Nielsen, Næs, V Davidsen, Færø, Nattestad, Hansson, Benjaminsen, Jacobsen (Baldvinsson 55), Sørensen (Jónsson 76), Holst, Klettskard (Edmundsson 46). Coach: Lars Olsen (DEN)
Finland: Mäenpää, N Moisander, Toivio, Eremenko, Hetemaj, Pukki (Pohjanpalo 88), Riku Riski, Arkivuo, Sparv, Uronen (Markkanen 75), Ring. Coach: Mixu Paatelainen (FIN)

07/09/14, Stadio Georgios Karaiskakis, Piraeus
Greece 0-1 Romania
Goal: 0-1 Marica 10(p)
Referee: Clattenburg (ENG)
Greece: Karnezis, Mantalos (Christodoulopoulos 65), Manolas, Mitroglou, Samaras (Diamantakos 46), Salpingidis, Torosidis, Papastathopoulos, Holebas, Samaris (Kone 65), Tachtsidis. Coach: Claudio Ranieri (ITA)
Romania: Tătărușanu, Raț, Tamaş, Hoban (Prepeliță 84), Chiricheş, Chipciu (Torje 90), Pintilii, Marica, Maxim (Enache 68), Stancu, Grigore. Coach: Victor Pițurcă (ROU)
Red card: Marica 53 (Romania)

07/09/14, Groupama Aréna, Budapest (att: 20,672)
Hungary 1-2 Northern Ireland
Goals: 1-0 Priskin 75, 1-1 McGinn 81, 1-2 K Lafferty 88
Referee: Aytekin (GER)
Hungary: Gulácsi, Vanczák, Lipták, Dzsudzsák, Varga, Rudolf (Kovács 70), Tőzsér, Balogh, Gyurcsó (Lovrencsics 58), Nikolić (Priskin 46), Juhász. Coach: Attila Pintér (HUN)
Northern Ireland: Carroll, C McLaughlin, McAuley (Cathcart 9), Baird, Davis, K Lafferty, Brunt, C Evans, Norwood (McKay 79), Hughes, Ward (McGinn 66). Coach: Michael O'Neill (NIR)

11/10/14, Helsingin Olympiastadion, Helsinki (att: 26,548)
Finland 1-1 Greece
Goals: 0-1 Karelis 24, 1-1 Hurme 55
Referee: Fernández Borbalán (ESP)
Finland: Mäenpää, N Moisander, Toivio, Eremenko, Hetemaj (Hämäläinen 46), Pukki (Pohjanpalo 64), Riku Riski (Tainio 88), Arkivuo, Sparv, Ring, Hurme. Coach: Mixu Paatelainen (FIN)
Greece: Karnezis, Maniatis, Manolas, Vyntra, Torosidis, Mavrias (Moras 70), Athanasiadis (Mitroglou 84), Karelis (Samaras 81), Papastathopoulos, Samaris, Tachtsidis. Coach: Claudio Ranieri (ITA)

11/10/14, Windsor Park, Belfast (att: 10,049)
Northern Ireland 2-0 Faroe Islands
Goals: 1-0 McAuley 6, 2-0 K Lafferty 20
Referee: Yefet (ISR)
Northern Ireland: Carroll, C McLaughlin, McAuley (McCullough 56), Baird, McGinn (McCourt 67), Davis, K Lafferty (Magennis 84), Norwood, Ferguson, Hughes, Ward. Coach: Michael O'Neill (NIR)
Faroe Islands: Nielsen, Næs, V Davidsen, Gregersen, Nattestad, Hansson, Benjaminsen, Holst (B Olsen 82), Klettskard (Hansen 75), Justinussen (Bartalsstovu 90+1), Edmundsson. Coach: Lars Olsen (DEN)

11/10/14, Arena Naţională, Bucharest (att: 52,000)
Romania 1-1 Hungary
Goals: 1-0 Rusescu 45, 1-1 Dzsudzsák 82
Referee: Collum (SCO)
Romania: Tătărușanu, Raț, Hoban, Chiricheş, Chipciu, Pintilii, Rusescu, Goian (Gardoș 5), Sânmărtean (Tănase 67), Maxim (Stancu 84), Grigore. Coach: Victor Pițurcă (ROU)

Romania's Paul Papp (right) shares his joy with Vlad Chiricheş after scoring his second goal against Northern Ireland in Bucharest

Hungary: Király, Kádár, Elek, Dzsudzsák, Varga, Gera (Tőzsér 77), Szalai, Lovrencsics (K Simon 63), Stieber (Nikolić 46), Korcsmár, Juhász. Coach: Pál Dárdai (HUN)

14/10/14, Tórsvøllur, Torshavn (att: 2,000)
Faroe Islands 0-1 Hungary
Goal: 0-1 Szalai 21
Referee: Kulbakov (BLR)
Faroe Islands: Nielsen, Næs, V Davidsen, Gregersen, Nattestad, Hansson, Benjaminsen, Holst (Bartalsstovu 69), Edmundsson (Hansen 76), Vatnhamar (Sørensen 81), B Olsen. Coach: Lars Olsen (DEN)
Hungary: Dibusz, K Simon, Korhut, Kádár, Dzsudzsák, Varga, Tőzsér (Kalmár 73), Gera, Szalai (Priskin 84), Nikolić (Fiola 46), Juhász. Coach: Pál Dárdai (HUN)

14/10/14, Helsingin Olympiastadion, Helsinki (att: 19,408)
Finland 0-2 Romania
Goals: 0-1 Stancu 54, 0-2 Stancu 83
Referee: Tagliavento (ITA)
Finland: Mäenpää, N Moisander, Toivio, Eremenko, Hetemaj (Pohjanpalo 64), Pukki (Riku Riski 46), Arkivuo, Sparv, Ring, Hämäläinen (Markkanen 74), Hurme. Coach: Mixu Paatelainen (FIN)
Romania: Tătărușanu, Raț, Luchin, Hoban, Chiricheş, Chipciu (Sânmărtean 49), Pintilii, Tănase (Enache 84), Torje, Stancu (Rusescu 86), Grigore. Coach: Victor Pițurcă (ROU)
Red card: Ring 56 (Finland)

14/10/14, Stadio Georgios Karaiskakis, Piraeus (att: 18,726)
Greece 0-2 Northern Ireland
Goals: 0-1 Ward 9, 0-2 K Lafferty 51
Referee: Lannoy (FRA)
Greece: Karnezis, Maniatis, Manolas, Samaras (Salpingidis 67), Mitroglou, Vyntra (Stafylidis 16), Torosidis, Athanasiadis (Samaris 46), Karelis, Papastathopoulos, Tachtsidis. Coach: Claudio Ranieri (ITA)
Northern Ireland: Carroll, C McLaughlin, McAuley, Baird, Davis, K Lafferty (Magennis 72), Ferguson (Reeves 78), C Evans, Norwood, Hughes, Ward (McGivern 59). Coach: Michael O'Neill (NIR)

14/11/14, Stadio Georgios Karaiskakis, Piraeus (att: 16,821)
Greece 0-1 Faroe Islands
Goal: 0-1 Edmundsson 61
Referee: Rizzoli (ITA)
Greece: Karnezis, Maniatis, Karabelas (Mantalos 78), Manolas, Moras, Kone, Christodoulopoulos, Torosidis, Gekas (Athanasiadis 46), Karelis (Mavrias 62), Samaris. Coach: Claudio Ranieri (ITA)
Faroe Islands: Nielsen, Næs, V Davidsen, Gregersen, Nattestad, Hansson, Benjaminsen, B Olsen (K Olsen 88), Holst (Justinussen 76), Edmundsson (Færø 86), Vatnhamar. Coach: Lars Olsen (DEN)

14/11/14, Groupama Aréna, Budapest (att: 19,600)
Hungary 1-0 Finland
Goal: 1-0 Gera 84
Referee: Turpin (FRA)
Hungary: Király, Lang, Kádár, Fiola, Elek, Dzsudzsák, Tőzsér, Gera, Szalai (Nikolić 63), K Simon (Lovrencsics 77), Juhász (Forró 57). Coach: Pál Dárdai (HUN)
Finland: Hradecky, N Moisander, Toivio, Eremenko, Hetemaj, Pukki (Pohjanpalo 65), Sparv, Halsti (Markkanen 85), Uronen, Hämäläinen (Riku Riski 82), Hurme. Coach: Mixu Paatelainen (FIN)

14/11/14, Arena Naţională, Bucharest (att: 28,892)
Romania 2-0 Northern Ireland
Goals: 1-0 Papp 74, 2-0 Papp 79
Referee: Eriksson (SWE)
Romania: Tătărușanu, Papp, Raț, Chiricheş, Chipciu, Pintilii, Stancu (Keşerü 46), Tănase (Maxim 58), Torje (Hoban 80), Sânmărtean, Grigore. Coach: Anghel Iordănescu (ROU)
Northern Ireland: Carroll, C McLaughlin, McGivern, McAuley, Baird, McGinn (Clingan 63), K Lafferty, Brunt, C Evans (McKay 78), Norwood, Hughes. Coach: Michael O'Neill (NIR)

29/03/15, Groupama Aréna, Budapest (att: 22,000)
Hungary 0-0 Greece
Referee: Karasev (RUS)
Hungary: Király, Kádár, Leandro, Elek (Pintér 70), Dzsudzsák, Tőzsér, Gera, Szalai (Nikolić 68), Fiola, Stieber, Juhász. Coach: Pál Dárdai (HUN)
Greece: Karnezis, Stafylidis, Manolas, K Papadopoulos, Kone (Katsouranis 77), Christodoulopoulos (Fortounis 69), Fetfatzidis (Gianniotas 77), Torosidis, Athanasiadis, Papastathopoulos, Samaris. Coach: Sergio Markarián (URU)

29/03/15, Windsor Park, Belfast (att: 10,264)
Northern Ireland 2-1 Finland
Goals: 1-0 K Lafferty 33, 2-0 K Lafferty 38, 2-1 Sadik 90+1
Referee: Marciniak (POL)
Northern Ireland: Carroll, C McLaughlin, McAuley, J Evans, Baird, McGinn (Dallas 64), Davis (C Evans 46), K Lafferty (Magennis 79), Brunt, Norwood, Ward. Coach: Michael O'Neill (NIR)
Finland: Hradecky, Sorsa, N Moisander, Toivio (Arajuuri 46), Eremenko, Pukki (Sadik 70), Sparv, Mattila, Uronen, Ring, Hämäläinen (Pohjanpalo 43). Coach: Mixu Paatelainen (FIN)

29/03/15, Ilie Oană, Ploiesti (att: 13,898)
Romania 1-0 Faroe Islands
Goal: 1-0 Keşerü 21
Referee: Artur Dias (POR)
Romania: Pantilimon, Papp, Raț, Chiricheş, Pintilii, Rusescu (Tănase 60), Keşerü, Sânmărtean (Prepeliță 86), Maxim, Grigore, Popa (Torje 71). Coach: Anghel Iordănescu (ROU)
Faroe Islands: Nielsen, V Davidsen, Gregersen, Nattestad, Vatnhamar, B Olsen (Sørensen 80), Holst, Edmundsson, Jacobsen (Joensen 80), Færø (A Olsen 74), J Davidsen. Coach: Lars Olsen (DEN)

13/06/15, Tórsvøllur, Torshavn (att: 4,731)
Faroe Islands 2-1 Greece
Goals: 1-0 Hansson 32, 2-0 B Olsen 70, 2-1 Papastathopoulos 84
Referee: Hagen (NOR)
Faroe Islands: Nielsen, Gregersen, Nattestad, Hansson, Benjaminsen, B Olsen, Sørensen (J Davidsen 13), Holst (Færø 74), Edmundsson (Joensen 90+2), Vatnhamar, B Hansen. Coach: Lars Olsen (DEN)
Greece: Karnezis, Stafylidis, Manolas, Kone (Fountas 81), Mitroglou, Christodoulopoulos (Ninis 46), Karelis, Torosidis, Fetfatzidis (Kolovos 71), Papastathopoulos, Samaris. Coach: Sergio Markarián (URU)

13/06/15, Helsingin Olympiastadion, Helsinki (att: 20,434)
Finland 0-1 Hungary
Goal: 0-1 Stieber 82
Referee: Jug (SVN)
Finland: Hradecky, N Moisander, Eremenko, Hetemaj, Pukki (Riku Riski 46), Arkivuo, Sparv, Halsti, Mattila (Pohjanpalo 85), Hämäläinen, Raitala. Coach: Mixu Paatelainen (FIN)
Hungary: Király, Lang, Kádár, Dzsudzsák (A Simon 88), Tőzsér, Gera, Szalai (Nikolić 77), Fiola, Stieber, Priskin (Németh 46), Juhász. Coach: Pál Dárdai (HUN)

13/06/15, Windsor Park, Belfast (att: 10,000)
Northern Ireland 0-0 Romania
Referee: Velasco Carballo (ESP)
Northern Ireland: McGovern, C McLaughlin, McAuley, J Evans (Cathcart 79), Baird, Davis, K Lafferty, Brunt, Dallas, Norwood, Ward (C Evans 79). Coach: Michael O'Neill (NIR)
Romania: Tătărușanu, Papp, Sepsi, Chiricheș, Chipciu (Stancu 61), Pintilii, Maxim (Tamaş 90), Torje, Keşerü (Andone 72), Prepeliţă, Grigore. Coach: Anghel Iordanescu (ROU)

Remaining fixtures

04/09/15
Faroe Islands –
Northern Ireland
Greece – Finland
Hungary – Romania

07/09/15
Finland – Faroe Islands
Northern Ireland –
Hungary
Romania – Greece

08/10/15
Hungary – Faroe
Islands
Northern Ireland –
Greece
Romania – Finland

11/10/15
Faroe Islands –
Romania
Finland – Northern
Ireland
Greece – Hungary

Group G

08/09/14, Ernst-Happel-Stadion, Vienna (att: 48,500)
Austria 1-1 Sweden
Goals: 1-0 Alaba 7(p), 1-1 Zengin 12
Referee: Královec (CZE)
Austria: Almer, Dragovic, Hinteregger, Fuchs, Arnautovic, Alaba, Junuzovic (Leitgeb 76), Harnik (Lazaro 86), Baumgartlinger, Klein, Janko (Okotie 68). Coach: Marcel Koller (SUI)
Sweden: Isaksson, Antonsson, M Olsson, Granqvist, S Larsson, Ekdal, Källström (Wernbloom 85), Ibrahimović, Bengtsson, Durmaz (Elmander 72), Zengin. Coach: Erik Hamrén (SWE)

08/09/14, Gradski Stadion Podgorica, Podgorica (att: 8,759)
Montenegro 2-0 Moldova
Goals: 1-0 Vučinić 45+2, 2-0 Tomašević 73
Referee: Kulbakov (BLR)
Montenegro: Poleksić, Volkov (Balić 46), Tomašević, Vučinić, Bećiraj (Jovović 66), Damjanović (N Vukčević 81), Savić, Zverotić, V Božović, Nikolić, Simić. Coach: Branko Brnović (MNE)
Moldova: Cebanu, Armas, Golovatenco, Racu, Epureanu, Ionita, A Antoniuc (M Antoniuc 54), Dedov, Alexeev, Gheorghiev (Cebotari 81), Sidorenco (Posmac 68). Coach: Ion Caras (MDA)

08/09/14, Arena Khimki, Khimki (att: 11,236)
Russia 4-0 Liechtenstein
Goals: 1-0 M Büchel 4(og), 2-0 Burgmeier 50(og), 3-0 Kombarov 54(p), 4-0 Dzyuba 65
Referee: Delferiere (BEL)
Russia: Akinfeev, Logdygin 72), Smolnikov, Ignashevich, Glushakov, Kokorin, Dzagoev (Ozdoev 64), Kerzhakov (Dzyuba 46), V Berezutski, Cheryshev, Samedov, Kombarov. Coach: Fabio Capello (ITA)
Liechtenstein: Jehle, Quintans (Wolfinger 87), A Christen (Brändle 64), Wieser, Frick, Burgmeier, M Büchel, Yildiz, N Hasler, Salanovic, Polverino (Gubser 73). Coach: René Pauritsch (AUT)

09/10/14, Rheinpark, Vaduz (att: 2,790)
Liechtenstein 0-0 Montenegro
Referee: Evans (WAL)
Liechtenstein: Jehle (Biçer 62), Kaufmann, Quintans (Kühne 80), Wieser (A Christen 44), Frick, Burgmeier, M Büchel, Yildiz, N Hasler, Salanovic, Polverino. Coach: René Pauritsch (AUT)
Montenegro: Poleksić, Pavićević, Jovanović, Tomašević, S Vukčević (Nikolić 57), Jovetić (Grbić 74), Bećiraj (Vučinić 46), Damjanović, Jovović, Zverotić, Simić. Coach: Branko Brnović (MNE)

09/10/14, Stadionul Zimbru, Chisinau (att: 9,381)
Moldova 1-2 Austria
Goals: 0-1 Alaba 12(p), 1-1 Dedov 27(p), 1-2 Janko 51
Referee: Manuel De Sousa (POR)
Moldova: Cebanu, Armas, Epureanu, Golovatenco, Jardan, Erhan (Patras 87), Cojocari (A Antoniuc 65), Gatcan, Ionita, Dedov, Picusciac (Sidorenco 46). Coach: Alexandru Curteian (MDA)
Austria: Almer, Dragovic, Fuchs, Arnautovic (Leitgeb 79), Alaba, Junuzovic (Ilsanker 86), Baumgartlinger, Prödl, Klein, Sabitzer (Harnik 46), Janko. Coach: Marcel Koller (SUI)
Red card: Janko 82 (Austria)

09/10/14, Friends Arena, Solna (att: 49,023)
Sweden 1-1 Russia
Goals: 0-1 Kokorin 10, 1-1 Toivonen 49
Referee: Rizzoli (ITA)
Sweden: Isaksson, Antonsson, Granqvist, M Olsson, Bahoui (Kacaniklic 79), S Larsson, Källström (Wernbloom 86), Bengtsson, Toivonen (Elmander 57), Durmaz, Zengin. Coach: Erik Hamrén (SWE)
Russia: Akinfeev, Smolnikov, Ignashevich, Glushakov, Kokorin, V Berezutski, Shatov, Samedov (Grigoryev 73), Fayzulin (Dzagoev 87), Dzyuba, Kombarov (Granat 88). Coach: Fabio Capello (ITA)

12/10/14, Ernst-Happel-Stadion, Vienna (att: 44,200)
Austria 1-0 Montenegro
Goal: 1-0 Okotie 24
Referee: Nijhuis (NED)
Austria: Almer, Dragovic, Hinteregger, Fuchs, Arnautovic (Hinterseer 62), Alaba, Okotie (Lazaro 83), Junuzovic (Ilsanker 77), Harnik, Baumgartlinger, Klein. Coach: Marcel Koller (SUI)
Montenegro: Poleksić, Volkov, V Berezutski, Jovetić (Jovetić 46), Vučinić, Bećiraj, Savić, Zverotić (Jovović 70), V Božović (Damjanović 76), Nikolić, Simić. Coach: Branko Brnović (MNE)

12/10/14, Otkrytie Arena, Moscow (att: 30,017)
Russia 1-1 Moldova
Goals: 1-0 Dzyuba 73(p), 1-1 Epureanu 74
Referee: Jakobsson (ISL)
Russia: Akinfeev, Parshivlyuk, Ignashevich, Glushakov, Dzagoev, Kerzhakov (Ozdoev 46), Granat, V Berezutski, Cheryshev (Poloz 62), Ionov (Schennikov 75), Dzyuba. Coach: Fabio Capello (ITA)
Moldova: Cebanu, Armas, Epureanu, Golovatenco, Jardan, Erhan, Cojocari (Racu 73), Gatcan, Ionita, Dedov (Sidorenco 82), Picusciac (Patras 46). Coach: Alexandru Curteian (MDA)

Jimmy Durmaz (centre) scores for Sweden in their 2-0 win at home to Liechtenstein

Austria's Martin Harnik fires past Liechtenstein skipper Mario Frick to put his team 1-0 up in Vaduz

12/10/14, Friends Arena, Solna (att: 22,528)
Sweden 2-0 Liechtenstein
Goals: 1-0 Zengin 34, 2-0 Durmaz 46
Referee: Mažeika (LTU)
Sweden: Isaksson, Antonsson, Granqvist, M Olsson, Ekdal (Bahoui 74), Källström, Elmander (Wernbloom 79), Bengtsson, Forsberg (Hrgota 66), Durmaz, Zengin. Coach: Erik Hamrén (SWE)
Liechtenstein: Biçer, Kaufmann, Quintans, A Christen (Kühne 78), Frick, Burgmeier, M Büchel (Wolfinger 83), Yildiz (Brändle 27), N Hasler, Salanovic, Polverino. Coach: René Pauritsch (AUT)

15/11/14, Ernst-Happel-Stadion, Vienna (att: 47,500)
Austria 1-0 Russia
Goal: 1-0 Okotie 73
Referee: Atkinson (ENG)
Austria: Almer, Dragovic (Prödl 86), Hinteregger, Fuchs, Ilsanker, Arnautovic (Sabitzer 90+1), Junuzovic, Harnik, Klein, Leitgeb, Janko (Okotie 59). Coach: Marcel Koller (SUI)
Russia: Akinfeev, Parshivlyuk, Ignashevich, Glushakov, Kokorin, V Berezutski, Shirokov, Shatov (Dzagoev 81), Cheryshev (Ionov 56), Fayzulin (Dzyuba 75), Kombarov. Coach: Fabio Capello (ITA)

15/11/14, Stadionul Zimbru, Chisinau (att: 6,843)
Moldova 0-1 Liechtenstein
Goal: 0-1 Burgmeier 74
Referee: Gestranius (FIN)
Moldova: Cebanu, Armas, Epureanu, Golovatenco, Racu, Patras (Suvorov 75), Ionita, Gatcan, Cojocari (Spataru 56), Dedov, Ginsari. Coach: Alexandru Curteian (MDA)
Liechtenstein: B Büchel, Brändle (Kühne 63), Kaufmann, Quintans (Kieber 90), A Christen, Wieser, Burgmeier, M Büchel (Gubser 88), N Hasler, Salanovic, Polverino. Coach: René Pauritsch (AUT)

15/11/14, Gradski Stadion Podgorica, Podgorica (att: 10,538)
Montenegro 1-1 Sweden
Goals: 0-1 Ibrahimović 9, 1-1 Jovetić 80(p)
Referee: Collum (SCO)
Montenegro: M Božović, Volkov, N Vukčević, Baša, Tomašević (Janković 77), Jovetić, Damjanović (Bećiraj 67), Savić, Jovović, Zverotić, V Božović (Bakić 46). Coach: Branko Brnović (MNE)

Sweden: Isaksson, Lustig (Wendt 46), Antonsson, Granqvist, Bengtsson, Ekdal, Källström, Ibrahimović, Forsberg (S Larsson 63), Durmaz, Zengin (Kiese Thelin 86). Coach: Erik Hamrén (SWE)

27/03/15, Rheinpark, Vaduz (att: 5,864)
Liechtenstein 0-5 Austria
Goals: 0-1 Harnik 14, 0-2 Janko 16, 0-3 Alaba 59, 0-4 Junuzovic 74, 0-5 Arnautovic 90+3
Referee: Zwayer (GER)
Liechtenstein: Jehle, Kaufmann, Quintans (Salanovic 55), A Christen (Kühne 83), Wieser, Frick, Burgmeier, M Büchel (Gubser 88), Oehri, N Hasler, Polverino. Coach: René Pauritsch (AUT)
Austria: Almer, Dragovic, Hinteregger, Fuchs, Arnautovic, Alaba, Junuzovic (Hinterseer 82), Harnik (Sabitzer 72), Baumgartlinger, Klein, Janko (Djuricin 77). Coach: Marcel Koller (SUI)

27/03/15, Stadionul Zimbru, Chisinau (att: 10,375)
Moldova 0-2 Sweden
Goals: 0-1 Ibrahimović 46, 0-2 Ibrahimović 84(p)
Referee: Bebek (CRO)
Moldova: Cebanu, Armas, Epureanu, Golovatenco, Racu, Bolohan, Ionita (Cojocari 36), Gatcan, G Andronic (Frunza 70), Dedov, Boghiu (Gheorghiev 86). Coach: Alexandru Curteian (MDA)
Sweden: Isaksson, Bengtsson, Granqvist, M Olsson, S Larsson (Forsberg 80), Ekdal, Källström, Ibrahimović, E Johansson, Kiese Thelin (Berg 70), Zengin (Wernbloom 85). Coach: Erik Hamrén (SWE)
Red card: Granqvist 90+3 (Sweden)

27/03/15, Gradski Stadion Podgorica, Podgorica
Montenegro 0-3 (w/o) Russia
Referee: Aytekin (GER)
Montenegro: Poleksić, Volkov, N Vukčević, Baša, Jovetić, Vučinić, Kašćelan, Zverotić, Marušić, Balić (Bakić 46), Simić. Coach: Branko Brnović (MNE)
Russia: Akinfeev (Lodygin 2), Smolnikov, Ignashevich, Denisov, Kokorin, Dzagoev (Torbinski 46), V Berezutski, Shirokov, Shatov, Zhirkov, Kombarov. Coach: Fabio Capello (ITA)

14/06/15, Rheinpark Stadion, Vaduz (att: 2,080)
Liechtenstein 1-1 Moldova
Goals: 1-0 Wieser 20, 1-1 Boghiu 43
Referee: Kovařík (CZE)
Liechtenstein: Jehle, Kaufmann, A Christen, Erne (Brändle 83), Wieser, Frick, Burgmeier, M Büchel (Gubser 69), Oehri (Kühne 42), Yildiz, Polverino. Coach: René Pauritsch (AUT)
Moldova: Cebanu, Armas, Epureanu (Carp 46), Erhan, Racu, Cojocari, Gatcan, Patras (M Antoniuc 89), Dedov, Boghiu, Cheptine (Milinceanu 37). Coach: Alexandru Curteian (MDA)

14/06/15, Otkrytie Arena, Moscow (att: 33,750)
Russia 0-1 Austria
Goal: 0-1 Janko 33
Referee: Mažić (SRB)
Russia: Akinfeev, Novoseltsev, Smolnikov, Glushakov, Kokorin, V Berezutski (Chernov 12), Shirokov, Shatov, Zhirkov, Ivanov (Miranchuk 46), Kombarov (Kerzhakov 71). Coach: Fabio Capello (ITA)
Austria: Almer, Dragovic, Hinteregger, Fuchs, Ilsanker, Arnautovic, Junuzovic (Prödl 86), Harnik (Sabitzer 65), Baumgartlinger, Klein, Janko (Okotie 75). Coach: Marcel Koller (SUI)

14/06/15, Friends Arena, Solna (att: 32,224)
Sweden 3-1 Montenegro
Goals: 1-0 Berg 37, 2-0 Ibrahimović 40, 3-0 Ibrahimović 44, 3-1 Damjanović 64(p)
Referee: Göçek (TUR)
Sweden: Isaksson, Bengtsson, E Johansson, S Larsson, Ekdal, Källström (Wernbloom 72), Ibrahimović (Toivonen 90), Milosevic, Wendt, Berg, Zengin (Forsberg 64). Coach: Erik Hamrén (SWE)
Montenegro: Poleksić, N Vukčević, Tomašević, Mugoša, Damjanović, Bećiraj, Savić, Kašćelan (Boljević 46), Zverotić (Saveljić 58), Marušić, Simić (Balić 74). Coach: Branko Brnović (MNE)

Remaining fixtures

05/09/15
Austria – Moldova
Montenegro – Liechtenstein
Russia – Sweden

08/09/15
Liechtenstein – Russia
Moldova – Montenegro
Sweden – Austria

09/10/15
Liechtenstein – Sweden
Moldova – Russia
Montenegro – Austria

12/10/15
Austria – Liechtenstein
Sweden – Moldova
Russia – Montenegro

Group H

09/09/14, Bakcell Arena, Baku (att: 11,000)
Azerbaijan 1-2 Bulgaria
Goals: 0-1 Micanski 14, 1-1 Nazarov 54, 1-2 Hristov 87
Referee: Yefet (ISR)
Azerbaijan: K Ağayev, Qarayev, Şükürov, B Hüseynov, Cavadov (Abdullayev 46), Dadaşov, Äliyev, Nazarov, R F Sadıqov, Abışov (Quliyev 74), Budak (Nadirov 90). Coach: Berti Vogts (GER)
Bulgaria: Stoyanov, A Popov, Bodurov, M Alexandrov (Hristov 83), Manolev, V Minev, Milanov, Gadzhev, Micanski (Galabinov 58), Dyakov, G Iliev (Nedelev 74). Coach: Luboslav Penev (BUL)

09/09/14, Stadion Maksimir, Zagreb (att: 8,333)
Croatia 2-0 Malta
Goals: 1-0 Modrić 46, 2-0 Kramarić 81
Referee: Bezborodov (RUS)
Croatia: Subašić, Milić, Ćorluka, Lovren, Rakitić, Halilović (Kramarić 67), Modrić, Srna, Brozović, Mandžukić (Olić 79), Kovačić (Jelavić 46). Coach: Niko Kovač (CRO)
Malta: Hogg, Borg, Agius, R Fenech, Failla, P Fenech (Scicluna 87), Mifsud (Bezzina 33), Schembri, R Muscat (Kristensen 76), Camilleri, Z Muscat. Coach: Pietro Ghedin (ITA)
Red card: Borg 31 (Malta)

09/09/14, Ullevaal Stadion, Oslo (att: 26,265)
Norway 0-2 Italy
Goals: 0-1 Zaza 16, 0-2 Bonucci 62
Referee: Mažić (SRB)
Norway: Nyland, Nordtveit, King, Johansen, Elabdellaoui, Skjelbred (Gamst Pedersen 75), Flo, Nielsen (T Elyounoussi 50), Jønsson (Tettey 70), Dæhli, Forren. Coach: Per-Mathias Høgmo (NOR)
Italy: Buffon, Darmian (Pasqual 61), Astori, Zaza (Destro 83), Florenzi (Poli 87), Immobile, Ranocchia, De Rossi, Bonucci, De Sciglio, Giaccherini. Coach: Antonio Conte (ITA)

10/10/14, Natsionalen Stadion Vasil Levski, Sofia (att: 29,733)
Bulgaria 0-1 Croatia
Goal: 0-1 Bodurov 36(og)
Referee: Mateu Lahoz (ESP)
Bulgaria: Stoyanov, A Popov, Zanev (G Iliev 46), Bodurov, Y Minev, I Popov, Manolev, Milanov, Gadzhev (Tonev 68), Micanski (Galabinov 46), Dyakov. Coach: Luboslav Penev (BUL)
Croatia: Subašić, Pranjić, Perišić, Ćorluka, Rakitić (Kovačić 80), Modrić, Srna, Brozović, Mandžukić, Olić, Vida. Coach: Niko Kovač (CRO)

10/10/14, Renzo Barbera, Palermo (att: 33,000)
Italy 2-1 Azerbaijan
Goals: 1-0 Chiellini 44, 1-1 Chiellini 76(og), 2-1 Chiellini 82
Referee: Göçek (TUR)
Italy: Buffon, De Sciglio, Chiellini, Zaza, Marchisio, Immobile, Ranocchia, Florenzi (Giovinco 77), Bonucci, Darmian (Candreva 81), Pirlo (Aquilani 73). Coach: Antonio Conte (ITA)
Azerbaijan: K Ağayev, Qarayev, Allahverdiyev, B Hüseynov, Abdullayev, Qırtımov (Ramaldanov 46), Daşaşov (C Hüseynov 59), Äliyev, Nazarov, R F Sadıqov, Ämirquliyev (Nadirov 86). Coach: Berti Vogts (GER)

10/10/14, Ta' Qali National Stadium, Ta' Qali (att: 8,076)
Malta 0-3 Norway
Goals: 0-1 Dæhli 22, 0-2 King 26, 0-3 King 49
Referee: Gautier (FRA)
Malta: Hogg, Z Muscat, P Fenech, Agius, R Fenech (Kristensen 72), Failla, Briffa (Grioli 72), Mifsud, R Muscat, Schembri (Vella 85), Camilleri. Coach: Pietro Ghedin (ITA)
Norway: Nyland, Tettey (Singh 78), Nordtveit, King (Nielsen 75), Johansen, T Elyounoussi, Elabdellaoui, Skjelbred (Samuelsen 62), Linnes, Dæhli, Forren. Coach: Per-Mathias Høgmo (NOR)

13/10/14, Gradski vrt, Osijek (att: 16,021)
Croatia 6-0 Azerbaijan
Goals: 1-0 Kramarić 11, 2-0 Perišić 34, 3-0 Perišić 45, 4-0 Brozović 45+1, 5-0 Modrić 57(p), 6-0 R F Sadıqov 61(og)
Referee: Studer (SUI)
Croatia: Subašić, Pranjić, Ćorluka, Rakitić, Modrić (Halilović 60), Srna, Brozović, Mandžukić, Kovačić (Perišić 24), Vida, Kramarić (Olić 76). Coach: Niko Kovač (CRO)
Azerbaijan: K Ağayev, Qarayev (Ramazanov 30; C Hüseynov 41), Ramaldanov, Allahverdiyev (Quliyev 66), B Hüseynov, Abdullayev, Äliyev, Nazarov, R F Sadıqov, Medvedev, Ämirquliyev. Coach: Berti Vogts (GER)

13/10/14, Ta' Qali National Stadium, Ta' Qali (att: 16,942)
Malta 0-1 Italy
Goal: 0-1 Pellè 24
Referee: Haţegan (ROU)
Malta: Hogg, Z Muscat, P Fenech, Agius, Failla (Bezzina 90+3), Briffa, Mifsud, R Muscat, Schembri (Cohen 85), Mintoff (Baldacchino 72), Camilleri. Coach: Pietro Ghedin (ITA)
Italy: Buffon, Chiellini, Verratti, Candreva, Marchisio, Immobile (Giovinco 65), Florenzi (Aquilani 59), Pellè (Ogbonna 75), Bonucci, Darmian, Pasqual. Coach: Antonio Conte (ITA)
Red cards: Mifsud 28 (Malta), Bonucci 73 (Italy)

13/10/14, Ullevaal Stadion, Oslo (att: 18,990)
Norway 2-1 Bulgaria
Goals: 1-0 T Elyounoussi 13, 1-1 Bodurov 43, 2-1 Nielsen 72
Referee: Olegário Benquerença (POR)
Norway: Nyland, Tettey, Nordtveit, King (Nielsen 58), Johansen, T Elyounoussi (Samuelsen 83), Elabdellaoui, Skjelbred, Linnes, Dæhli (Ødegaard 63), Forren. Coach: Per-Mathias Høgmo (NOR)
Bulgaria: Mihaylov, A Popov, Bodurov, I Popov, Manolev (Y Minev 69), V Minev, Hristov (Galabinov 56), Milanov, Tonev, Dyakov, G Iliev (M Alexandrov 76). Coach: Luboslav Penev (BUL)

16/11/14, Bakcell Arena, Baku (att: 9,200)
Azerbaijan 0-1 Norway
Goal: 0-1 Nordtveit 25
Referee: Aranovskiy (UKR)
Azerbaijan: S Ağayev, Şükürov, Medvedev, Cavadov, Abdullayev, Äliyev, R F Sadıqov, Abışov (Qarayev 65), Ämirquliyev, İmamverdiyev (Nazarov 69), Yunuszadä. Coach: Mahmud Qurbanov (AZE)
Norway: Nyland, Høgli, Tettey, Nordtveit, Johansen, T Elyounoussi (Gulbrandsen 90+1), Elabdellaoui, Skjelbred, Nielsen (Søderlund 72), Dæhli (Samuelsen 57), Forren. Coach: Per-Mathias Høgmo (NOR)

16/11/14, Natsionalen Stadion Vasil Levski, Sofia (att: 3,300)
Bulgaria 1-1 Malta
Goals: 1-0 Galabinov 6, 1-1 Failla 49(p)
Referee: Strömbergsson (SWE)
Bulgaria: Stoyanov, Terziev, Bodurov, M Alexandrov, I Popov, Manolev, V Minev, Galabinov (Micanski 58), Milanov (Marquinhos 58), Dyakov, G Iliev (Tonev 71). Coach: Luboslav Penev (BUL)
Malta: Hogg, Caruana, P Fenech, Agius, Failla (Bezzina 81), Briffa, Farrugia (Vella 90+3), R Muscat, Schembri (R Fenech 78), Camilleri, Z Muscat. Coach: Pietro Ghedin (ITA)

Croatia's Ivan Perišić holds off Norway's Alexander Tettey in a Group H encounter

16/11/14, Stadio Giuseppe Meazza, Milan (att: 63,222)
Italy 1-1 Croatia
Goals: 1-0 Candreva 11, 1-1 Perišić 15
Referee: Kuipers (NED)
Italy: Buffon, De Sciglio, Chiellini, Candreva, Zaza (Pellè 63), Marchisio, Immobile (El Shaarawy 52), Ranocchia, De Rossi, Darmian, Pasqual (Soriano 28). Coach: Antonio Conte (ITA)
Croatia: Subašić, Pranjić, Perišić, Ćorluka, Rakitić, Modrić (Kovačić 83), Srna, Brozović (Badelj 83), Mandžukić, Olić (Kramarić 68), Vida. Coach: Niko Kovač (CRO)

28/03/15, Tofiq Bährämov Republican stadium, Baku (att: 14,600)
Azerbaijan 2-0 Malta
Goals: 1-0 C Hüseynov 4, 2-0 Nazarov 90+2
Referee: Özkahya (TUR)
Azerbaijan: K Ağayev, Qarayev, Medvedev, B Hüseynov, R F Sadıqov, C Hüseynov, Nadirov (İsrafilov 81), Ämirquliyev, Äläsgärov (R Qurbanov 22), Daşdämirov, İsmayılov (Nazarov 70). Coach: Robert Prosinečki (CRO)
Malta: Hogg, Caruana, Bezzina (Pisani 46), Borg, Agius, Briffa, R Muscat, Schembri (R Fenech 81), P Fenech, Camilleri (Z Muscat 36), Effiong. Coach: Pietro Ghedin (ITA)

28/03/15, Natsionalen Stadion Vasil Levski, Sofia (att: 6,000)
Bulgaria 2-2 Italy
Goals: 0-1 Y Minev 4(og), 1-1 Popov 11, 2-1 Micanski 17, 2-2 Éder 84
Referee: Skomina (SVN)
Bulgaria: Mihaylov, Bodurov, Y Minev, M Alexandrov, I Popov (Slavchev 85), Manolev, Milanov (V Vasilev 88), Gadzhev, Micanski (Bozhinov 73), Dyakov, A Alexandrov. Coach: Ivaylo Petev (BUL)
Italy: Sirigu, Chiellini, Darmian, Antonelli (Gabbiadini 77), Candreva, Zaza (Éder 58), Immobile, Verratti, Barzagli, Bonucci, Bertolacci (Soriano 72). Coach: Antonio Conte (ITA)

28/03/15, Stadion Maksimir, Zagreb (att: 23,920)
Croatia 5-1 Norway
Goals: 1-0 Brozović 30, 2-0 Perišić 53, 3-0 Olić 65, 3-1 Tettey 80, 4-1 Schildenfeld 87, 5-1 Pranjić 90+4
Referee: Velasco Carballo (ESP)
Croatia: Subašić, Pranjić, Perišić, Ćorluka, Rakitić (Schildenfeld 75), Modrić, Srna, Brozović, Mandžukić (Badelj 87), Olić (Kramarić 70), Vida. Coach: Niko Kovač (CRO)
Norway: Nyland, Høgli, Tettey, Nordtveit, Johansen, T Elyounoussi (Abdellaoue 79), Ødegaard, Skjelbred (Samuelsen 19), Linnes, Dæhli (Nielsen 61), Forren. Coach: Per-Mathias Høgmo (NOR)
Red card: Ćorluka 74 (Croatia)

12/06/15, Stadion Poljud, Split
Croatia 1-1 Italy
Goals: 1-0 Mandžukić 11, 1-1 Candreva 36(p)
Referee: Atkinson (ENG)
Croatia: Subašić, Pranjić (Vrsaljko 72), Perišić, Rakitić, Srna, Schildenfeld, Brozović, Mandžukić, Olić (Rebić 46), Kovačić (Leovac 90+2), Vida. Coach: Niko Kovač (CRO)
Italy: Buffon (Sirigu 46), Darmian, Astori, Candreva, Marchisio, El Shaarawy (Ranocchia 80), De Silvestri (De Sciglio 27), Parolo, Bonucci, Pellè, Pirlo. Coach: Antonio Conte (ITA)
Red card: Srna 90 (Croatia)

12/06/15, National Stadium, Ta' Qali (att: 3,924)
Malta 0-1 Bulgaria
Goal: 0-1 I Popov 56
Referee: Stavrev (MKD)
Malta: Haber, A Muscat (Herrera 63), Agius, P Fenech, Failla, Briffa (Schembri 76), Mifsud (Cohen 84), R Muscat, Camilleri, Effiong, Z Muscat. Coach: Pietro Ghedin (ITA)
Bulgaria: Mitrev, Bandalovski, Bodurov, Y Minev, M Alexandrov (Milanov 75), I Popov (Chochev 81), Manolev, Gadzhev, Micanski (R Vasilev 90), Dyakov, A Aleksandrov. Coach: Ivaylo Petev (BUL)

12/06/15, Ullevaal Stadion, Oslo (att: 21,228)
Norway 0-0 Azerbaijan
Referee: Gil (POL)
Norway: Nyland, Høgli, Hovland, Nordtveit, King (Diomandé 79), Johansen, Søderlund (Eikrem 68), Ødegaard, Elabdellaoui, Skjelbred (Helland 52), Forren. Coach: Per-Mathias Høgmo (NOR)
Azerbaijan: K Ağayev, Qarayev, Medvedev, B Hüseynov, R Qurbanov (Nadirov 81), Nazarov (M Qurbanov 90+3), R F Sadıqov, C Hüseynov, Ämirquliyev, Daşdämirov, İsmayılov. Coach: Robert Prosinečki (CRO)

Remaining fixtures

03/09/15
Azerbaijan – Croatia
Bulgaria – Norway
Italy – Malta

10/10/15
Azerbaijan – Italy
Croatia – Bulgaria
Norway – Malta

06/09/15
Italy – Bulgaria
Malta – Azerbaijan
Norway – Croatia

13/10/15
Bulgaria – Azerbaijan
Italy – Norway
Malta – Croatia

Group I

07/09/14, Parken Stadium, Copenhagen (att: 20,141)
Denmark 2-1 Armenia
Goals: 0-1 Mkhitaryan 50, 1-1 Højbjerg 65, 2-1 Kahlenberg 80
Referee: Tudor (ROU)
Denmark: Schmeichel, Ankersen, Kjær (Okore 57), Boilesen, Kvist (Kahlenberg 74), Krohn-Dehli, Eriksen, Bendtner, Bjelland, Schöne (Vibe 56), Højbjerg. Coach: Morten Olsen (DEN)
Armenia: Berezovski, Haroyan, Arzumanyan (Voskanyan 66), Artur Yedigaryan, Hovsepyan, Ghazaryan, Hovhannisyan, Mkoyan, Mkhitaryan (Pizzelli 71), Hayrapetyan, Manucharyan (Dashyan 84). Coach: Bernard Challandes (SUI)

07/09/14, Municipal, Aveiro (att: 23,205)
Portugal 0-1 Albania
Goal: 0-1 Balaj 52
Referee: Buquet (FRA)
Portugal: Rui Patrício, Pepe, Fábio Coentrão, William Carvalho (Ricardo Horta 56), João Moutinho, Éder, Vieirinha (Ivan Cavaleiro 46), Ricardo Costa (Miguel Veloso 73), André Gomes, Nani, João Pereira. Coach: Paulo Bento (POR)
Albania: Berisha, Lenjani (Lila 75), Hysaj, Cana, Agolli, Kukeli (Kaçe 66), Xhaka, Mavraj, Balaj (Çikalleshi 82), Roshi, Abrashi. Coach: Gianni De Biasi (ITA)

11/10/14, Elbasan Arena, Elbasan (att: 11,330)
Albania 1-1 Denmark
Goals: 1-0 Lenjani 38, 1-1 Vibe 81
Referee: Kassai (HUN)
Albania: Berisha, Lila (Curri 87), Lenjani, Hysaj, Cana, Agolli, Kukeli, Xhaka (Rama 82), Mavraj, Balaj (Çikalleshi 69), Abrashi. Coach: Gianni De Biasi (ITA)
Denmark: Schmeichel, Ankersen (Bech 71), Kjær, Boilesen, Kvist, Krohn-Dehli, Eriksen, Bendtner, Bjelland, Y Poulsen (Vibe 46), Højbjerg (Kahlenberg 79). Coach: Morten Olsen (DEN)

Cristiano Ronaldo lets fly from distance in Portugal's 3-2 victory against Armenia in Yerevan

11/10/14, Vazgen Sargsyan anvan Hanrapetakan Marzadasht, Yerevan (att: 14,527)
Armenia 1-1 Serbia
Goals: 1-0 Arzumanyan 73, 1-1 Z Tošić 89
Referee: Hagen (NOR)
Armenia: Berezovski, Haroyan, Voskanyan, Arzumanyan, Mkrtchyan (Hovsepyan 52), Artur Yedigaryan, Pizzelli (Karapetyan 84), Sarkisov, Hovhannisyan, Hayrapetyan, Manucharyan (Dashyan 66). Coach: Bernard Challandes (SUI)
Serbia: Stojković, Nastasić, Ivanović, Z Tošić, Gudelj (A Mitrović 74), Djordjević (Lazović 69), Tadić, Kolarov, S Mitrović, Matić, Marković (Kuzmanović 26). Coach: Dick Advocaat (NED)

14/10/14, Parken Stadium, Copenhagen (att: 36,562)
Denmark 0-1 Portugal
Goal: 0-1 Cristiano Ronaldo 90+5
Referee: Brych (GER)
Denmark: Schmeichel, Kjær, Agger, Boilesen (S Poulsen 58), Jacobsen, Kvist, Krohn-Dehli, Eriksen, Bendtner, Vibe (Bech 46), Højbjerg. Coach: Morten Olsen (DEN)
Portugal: Rui Patrício, Pepe, Eliseu, Ricardo Carvalho, Cristiano Ronaldo, João Moutinho, Danny (Éder 77), William Carvalho, Nani (João Mário 68), Tiago (Ricardo Quaresma 84), Cédric. Coach: Fernando Santos (POR)

14/10/14, Stadion FK Partizan, Belgrade (att: 25,550)
Serbia 0-3 (w/o) Albania
Referee: Atkinson (ENG)
Serbia: Stojković, Nastasić, Ivanović, Z Tošić, Gudelj, Tadić, Kolarov, S Mitrović, Matić, Lazović, Djuričić. Coach: Dick Advocaat (NED)
Albania: Berisha, Lila, Lenjani, Hysaj, Cana, Agolli, Kukeli, Xhaka, Mavraj, Balaj, Abrashi. Coach: Gianni De Biasi (ITA)

14/11/14, Estádio Algarve, Faro (att: 21,042)
Portugal 1-0 Armenia
Goal: 1-0 Cristiano Ronaldo 72
Referee: Sidiropoulos (GRE)
Portugal: Rui Patrício, Pepe, Bosingwa, Ricardo Carvalho, Cristiano Ronaldo, João Moutinho, Danny (Ricardo Quaresma 70), Raphael Guerreiro, Nani (William Carvalho 88), Tiago, Hélder Postiga (Éder 56). Coach: Fernando Santos (POR)
Armenia: Berezovski, Haroyan, Voskanyan, Arzumanyan, Mkrtchyan (Pizzelli 84), Artur Yedigaryan (Sarkisov 77), Ghazaryan (Manucharyan 84), Hovhannisyan, Movsisyan, Mkhitaryan, Hayrapetyan. Coach: Bernard Challandes (SUI)

14/11/14, Stadion FK Partizan, Belgrade (att: 150)
Serbia 1-3 Denmark
Goals: 1-0 Z Tošić 4, 1-1 Bendtner 60, 1-2 Kjær 62, 1-3 Bendtner 85
Referee: Çakır (TUR)
Serbia: Stojković, D Tošić, Biševac, Ivanović, Z Tošić, Gudelj (A Mitrović 66), Tadić (Marković 71), S Mitrović, Matić, Lazović, Djuričić (Kuzmanović 46). Coach: Dick Advocaat (NED)
Denmark: Schmeichel, Ankersen (Jacobsen 70), Kjær, Boilesen, Kvist, Krohn-Dehli, Eriksen, Bendtner (Y Poulsen 88), Bjelland, Kahlenberg (Würtz 88), Vibe. Coach: Morten Olsen (DEN)

29/03/15, Elbasan Arena, Elbasan (att: 12,300)
Albania 2-1 Armenia
Goals: 0-1 Mavraj 76(og), 1-1 Mavraj 77, 2-1 Gashi 81
Referee: Fernández Borbalán (ESP)
Albania: Berisha, Hysaj, Cana, Agolli, Memushaj (Gashi 46), Kukeli, Xhaka, Mavraj, Çikalleshi, Roshi (Salihi 69), Abrashi (Lenjani 46). Coach: Gianni De Biasi (ITA)
Armenia: Berezovski, Andonyan, Arzumanyan, Artur Yedigaryan (Koryan 84), Pizzelli, Ghazaryan, Movsisyan, Mkhitaryan, Hambardzumyan, Hayrapetyan, Manucharyan (Hovhannisyan 67). Coach: Bernard Challandes (SUI)
Red card: Hambardzumyan 70 (Armenia)

29/03/15, Estádio do Sport Lisboa e Benfica, Lisbon (att: 58,430)
Portugal 2-1 Serbia
Goals: 1-0 Ricardo Carvalho 10, 1-1 Matić 61, 2-1 Fábio Coentrão 63
Referee: Rocchi (ITA)
Portugal: Rui Patrício, Bruno Alves, Fábio Coentrão (Ricardo Quaresma 78), Ricardo Carvalho (José Fonte 17), Cristiano Ronaldo, João Moutinho, Danny (William Carvalho 86), Bosingwa, Nani, Eliseu, Tiago. Coach: Ilídio Vale (POR)
Serbia: Stojković, Nastasić, Ivanović, Petrović, A Mitrović, Tadić (Z Tošić 78), Kolarov, Matić, Basta, Marković (Djuričić 65), Ljajić (Škuletić 85). Coach: Radovan Ćurčić (SRB)

13/06/15, Vazgen Sargsyan anvan Hanrapetakan Marzadasht, Yerevan (att: 14,527)
Armenia 2-3 Portugal
Goals: 1-0 Pizzelli 14, 1-1 Cristiano Ronaldo 29(p), 1-2 Cristiano Ronaldo 55, 1-3 Cristiano Ronaldo 58, 2-3 Mkoyan 72
Referee: Gumienny (BEL)
Armenia: Berezovski, Andonyan, Arzumanyan, Mkrtchyan (Hovsepyan 29), Pizzelli, Ghazaryan, Sarkisov (Koryan 72), Hovhannisyan (Özbiliz 61), Mkoyan, Mkhitaryan, Hayrapetyan. Coach: Sargis Hovsepyan (ARM)
Portugal: Rui Patrício, Bruno Alves, Fábio Coentrão (Adrien Silva 72), Ricardo Carvalho (José Fonte 78), Cristiano Ronaldo, João Moutinho, Danny (William Carvalho 63), Vieirinha, Nani, Tiago, Eliseu. Coach: Ilídio Vale (POR)
Red card: Tiago 62 (Portugal)

13/06/15, Parken Stadium, Copenhagen (att: 30,887)
Denmark 2-0 Serbia
Goals: 1-0 Y Poulsen 13, 2-0 J Poulsen 87
Referee: Kuipers (NED)
Denmark: Schmeichel, Kjær, Agger, Jacobsen, Kvist (Christensen 77), Krohn-Dehli (J Poulsen 61), Eriksen, Bendtner, S Poulsen, Y Poulsen (Vibe 73), Højbjerg. Coach: Morten Olsen (DEN)
Serbia: Stojković, Nastasić, Ivanović, Z Tošić (Kostić 65), A Mitrović (Škuletić 90), Kolarov, Maksimović, Matić, Fejsa, Marković, Ljajić (Djuričić 81). Coach: Radovan Ćurčić (SRB)

Remaining fixtures

04/09/15
Denmark – Albania
Serbia – Armenia

08/10/15
Albania – Serbia
Portugal – Denmark

07/09/15
Albania – Portugal
Armenia – Denmark

11/10/15
Armenia – Albania
Serbia – Portugal

Tables (after matchday six)

Group A

	Pld	Home W D L F A	Away W D L F A	Total W D L F A	Pts
1 Iceland	6	3 0 0 7 1	2 0 1 7 2	5 0 1 14 3	15
2 Czech Republic	6	2 1 0 5 3	2 0 1 7 5	4 1 1 12 8	13
3 Netherlands	6	2 1 0 10 2	1 0 2 3 4	3 1 2 13 6	10
4 Turkey	6	1 0 1 4 3	1 2 1 3 5	2 2 2 7 8	8
5 Latvia	6	0 1 2 1 6	0 2 1 1 7	0 3 3 2 13	3
6 Kazakhstan	6	0 1 3 2 8	0 0 2 2 6	0 1 5 4 14	1

Group B

	Pld	Home W D L F A	Away W D L F A	Total W D L F A	Pts
1 Wales	6	2 1 0 3 1	2 1 0 5 1	4 2 0 8 2	14
2 Belgium	6	2 1 0 11 0	1 1 1 2 2	3 2 1 13 2	11
3 Israel	6	1 0 2 3 4	2 0 1 7 5	3 0 3 10 9	9
4 Cyprus	6	1 0 1 6 2	2 0 2 6 9	3 0 3 12 11	9
5 Bosnia & Herzegovina	6	1 1 1 5 4	1 1 1 3 3	2 2 2 8 7	8
6 Andorra	6	0 0 4 3 12	0 0 2 0 11	0 0 6 3 23	0

Group C

	Pld	Home W D L F A	Away W D L F A	Total W D L F A	Pts
1 Slovakia	6	3 0 0 7 2	3 0 0 6 1	6 0 0 13 3	18
2 Spain	6	3 0 0 9 1	2 0 1 6 2	5 0 1 15 3	15
3 Ukraine	6	2 0 1 4 1	2 0 1 5 1	4 0 2 9 2	12
4 Belarus	6	0 0 3 1 6	1 1 1 3 5	1 1 4 4 11	4
5 FYR Macedonia	6	1 0 2 4 6	0 0 3 2 8	1 0 5 6 14	3
6 Luxembourg	6	0 1 2 1 8	0 0 3 2 9	0 1 5 3 17	1

Group D

	Pld	Home W D L F A	Away W D L F A	Total W D L F A	Pts
1 Poland	6	2 1 0 8 2	2 1 0 12 1	4 2 0 20 3	14
2 Germany	6	2 1 0 7 2	2 0 1 9 2	4 1 1 16 4	13
3 Scotland	6	3 0 0 8 1	0 2 1 4 5	3 2 1 12 6	11
4 Republic of Ireland	6	1 2 0 9 2	1 1 1 3 3	2 3 1 12 5	9
5 Georgia	6	0 0 3 1 8	1 0 2 3 5	1 0 5 4 13	3
6 Gibraltar	6	0 0 3 0 17	0 0 3 1 17	0 0 6 1 34	0

Group E

	Pld	Home W D L F A	Away W D L F A	Total W D L F A	Pts
1 England	6	3 0 0 12 1	3 0 0 6 2	6 0 0 18 3	18
2 Switzerland	6	2 0 1 7 2	2 0 1 6 2	4 0 2 13 4	12
3 Slovenia	6	2 0 1 9 3	1 0 2 3 4	3 0 3 12 7	9
4 Estonia	6	2 0 1 3 1	0 1 2 0 4	2 1 3 3 5	7
5 Lithuania	6	1 0 2 2 4	1 0 2 2 8	2 0 4 4 12	6
6 San Marino	6	0 1 2 0 6	0 0 3 0 13	0 1 5 0 19	1

Group F

	Pld	Home W D L F A	Away W D L F A	Total W D L F A	Pts
1 Romania	6	2 1 0 4 1	2 1 0 3 0	4 2 0 7 1	14
2 Northern Ireland	6	2 1 0 4 1	2 0 1 4 3	4 1 1 8 4	13
3 Hungary	6	1 1 1 2 2	2 1 0 3 1	3 2 1 5 3	11
4 Faroe Islands	6	1 0 2 3 5	1 0 2 1 3	2 0 4 4 8	6
5 Finland	6	0 1 2 1 4	1 0 2 4 4	1 1 4 5 8	4
6 Greece	6	0 0 3 0 4	0 2 1 2 3	0 2 4 2 7	2

Group G

	Pld	Home W D L F A	Away W D L F A	Total W D L F A	Pts
1 Austria	6	2 1 0 3 1	3 0 0 8 1	5 1 0 11 2	16
2 Sweden	6	2 1 0 6 2	1 2 0 4 2	3 3 0 10 4	12
3 Russia	6	1 1 1 5 2	1 1 1 4 2	2 2 2 9 4	8
4 Montenegro	6	1 1 1 3 4	0 1 2 1 4	1 2 3 4 8	5
5 Liechtenstein	6	0 2 1 1 6	1 0 2 1 6	1 2 3 2 12	5
6 Moldova	6	0 0 3 1 5	0 2 1 2 4	0 2 4 3 9	2

Group H

	Pld	Home W D L F A	Away W D L F A	Total W D L F A	Pts
1 Croatia	6	3 1 0 14 2	1 1 0 2 1	4 2 0 16 3	13
2 Italy	6	1 1 0 3 2	2 2 0 6 3	3 3 0 9 5	12
3 Norway	6	1 1 1 2 3	2 0 1 5 5	3 1 2 7 8	10
4 Bulgaria	6	0 2 1 3 4	2 0 1 4 3	2 2 2 7 7	8
5 Azerbaijan	6	1 0 2 3 3	0 1 2 1 8	1 1 4 4 11	4
6 Malta	6	0 0 3 0 5	0 1 2 1 5	0 1 5 1 10	1

NB Croatia – 1 pt deducted.

Group I

	Pld	Home W D L F A	Away W D L F A	Total W D L F A	Pts
1 Portugal	5	2 0 1 3 2	2 0 0 4 2	4 0 1 7 4	12
2 Albania	4	1 1 0 3 2	2 0 0 4 0	3 1 0 7 2	10
3 Denmark	5	2 0 1 4 2	1 1 0 4 2	3 1 1 8 4	10
4 Armenia	5	0 1 1 3 4	0 0 3 2 5	0 1 4 5 9	1
5 Serbia	5	0 0 2 1 6	0 1 2 2 5	0 1 4 3 11	-2

NB Serbia – 3 pts deducted.

Top goalscorers (after matchday six)

7	Robert Lewandowski (Poland)
6	Danny Welbeck (England)
5	Omer Damari (Israel)
	Zlatan Ibrahimović (Sweden)
	Cristiano Ronaldo (Portugal)
	Thomas Müller (Germany)
	Edin Džeko (Bosnia & Herzegovina)
	Kyle Lafferty (Northern Ireland)
	Wayne Rooney (England)
	Gareth Bale (Wales)
	Milivoje Novaković (Slovenia)
4	Klaas-Jan Huntelaar (Netherlands)
	Ivan Perišić (Croatia)
	Shaun Maloney (Scotland)
	Arkadiusz Milik (Poland)
	Gylfi Thór Sigurdsson (Iceland)
	Bořek Dočkal (Czech Republic)
	Xherdan Shaqiri (Switzerland)

Sweden stick to their task

Comeback kings Sweden were crowned UEFA European Under-21 champions for the first time in 2015 as Håkan Ericson's never-say-die side, backed in the Czech Republic by legions of their fans, overcame much-fancied Portugal 4-3 on penalties after a goalless draw in the Prague final.

While Sweden captured the main prize, there was widespread sympathy for Rui Jorge's Portugal, the only team to qualify for the final tournament with a 100% success rate. A gifted squad featuring top-class talents such as midfield anchorman William Carvalho and playmaker Bernardo Silva, they topped their group, ahead of Sweden, and routed Germany 5-0 in the semi-finals but were unable to deliver the coup de grace in the decider against their dogged opponents from Scandinavia.

Two penalty saves from Patrik Carlgren in a shoot-out that took place in front of the Blågult's boisterous supporters carried Sweden to glory, prompting wild celebrations from the goalkeeper, his team-mates and the yellow-clad hordes amassed at that end of the Eden Arena.

Ericson's side had already shown their mettle by qualifying for the finals in dramatic fashion, overturning a 2-0 first-leg defeat by France in the play-offs thanks to a last-gasp strike from midfielder Oscar Lewicki. Prior to that they had only managed to squeeze their way to the top of their qualifying group thanks to captain Oscar Hiljemark's 92nd-minute winner against Turkey.

While Sweden's presence in the Czech Republic was a surprise, the big shock was the absence of the team that had lifted the trophy in the previous two tournaments, Spain, who were eliminated by Serbia in the play-offs, a 2-1 home defeat in Cadiz ending the country's 35-match unbeaten run at U21 level.

At the finals, Sweden found themselves a goal and a man down against Italy in their opening game, but the Group B outsiders struck twice in the second half to secure an unlikely triumph that would ultimately prove decisive as they edged out the Azzurrini on the head-to-head rule. They went through to the semi-finals as runners-up behind Portugal, with whom they shared a 1-1 draw on matchday three as England trooped home at the end of the group stage for the third competition running.

In Group B, there was agony for the tournament hosts as they too exited early, their 4-0 win over Serbia, which featured a hat-trick from the competition's top marksman, Jan Kliment, proving insufficient when set alongside a defeat by Denmark and a draw against Germany. Although they lost heavily to Germany, Jess Thorup's Denmark topped the group to book an all-Nordic last-four date with Sweden.

Qualification for the semi-finals carried the added bonus of a place at the 2016 Olympics in Rio de Janeiro, and the two matches were to bring goals galore. Five different players found the net as an inspired Portugal condemned Germany to their heaviest ever reverse in the competition, qualifying included, while Sweden, for once not requiring any backs-to-the-wall heroics, impressively downed Denmark 4-1 at the Letná.

So, just six days after their Group A encounter, Sweden and Portugal met once more in the final. Again there was nothing to separate the sides, and after 120 largely uneventful minutes, the competition's first final shoot-out since 2002 was required to determine the new champions. Carlgren proved to be the hero, saving spot kicks from Ricardo Esgaio and player of the tournament William Carvalho to secure Sweden's first men's UEFA trophy.

UEFA European Under-21 Championship

Final tournament

The final tournament began well for the hosts when Pavel Kadeřábek fired them ahead against Denmark, but by the end of matchday one the Czech Republic were propping up Group A. They were eventually defeated by Danish substitute Pione Sisto's late winner at the Eden Arena before Germany and Serbia shared a 1-1 draw in the Letná, Emre Can cancelling out Filip Djuričić's early opener for the play-off conquerors of Spain.

In Group B, Italy and England – two of only three surviving participants from the 2013 finals – both kicked off with a defeat. The Azzurrini succumbed 2-1 to Sweden thanks to Isaac Kiese Thelin's late penalty, while Gareth Southgate's highly-rated side registered 22 shots against Portugal but still lost 1-0.

There was hope for England on matchday two, however, when Jesse Lingard's splendid 85th-minute strike secured a 1-0 win in Olomouc to give last-gasp specialists Sweden a taste of their own medicine. Italy and Portugal then drew 0-0 in Uherske Hradiste, a result in stark contrast to the avalanche of goals the previous evening in Group A. The Czech Republic thrashed Serbia 4-0, while Germany ran out 3-0 victors over Denmark thanks to two goals from Kevin Volland and one from Matthias Ginter.

Horst Hrubesch – coach of Germany's 2009-winning side – was still forced to sweat on matchday three, however, as his team survived a late Czech barrage to cling on to a 1-1 draw that qualified them as Group A runners-up. Denmark, fielding eight senior internationals, simultaneously beat Serbia 2-0 to top of the group.

Luigi Di Biagio's Italy headed into the final round of group games knowing that only a victory against England coupled with defeat for Sweden against Portugal would book their progress. Two goals from Marco Benassi helped the Azzurrini to fulfil their half of the bargain in a 3-1 win, but Sweden and Portugal were also aware that a point apiece would take both teams through if England lost. Italian hopes were raised when Portugal took the lead with eight minutes left, but Simon Tibbling's 89th-minute equaliser served to eliminate Italy and set up a Scandinavian derby at the Letná.

That match-up came just a fortnight after Denmark and Sweden had drawn 2-2 in a pre-tournament friendly. It would be nowhere near as tight when it mattered, though, as goals from John Guidetti, Tibbling, Robin Quaison and Oscar Hiljemark carried Sweden to a 4-1 triumph and only a second appearance in an U21 final. Already there were fellow one-time runners-up Portugal, Rui Jorge's

team having produced the performance of the finals in Olomouc as they ripped Germany to shreds with a masterful 5-0 win, the goals coming from Bernardo Silva, Ricardo, Ivan Cavaleiro, João Mário and Ricardo Horta. Absent from the scoresheet was William Carvalho, but the Sporting Clube de Portugal midfielder put in a display of great authority that helped him to win the official player of the tournament vote.

There may have been goals aplenty in the semis, but the pressure of the occasion led to a much more cautious approach from Sweden and Portugal in the final. The result was a disappointing stalemate that failed to spark significantly into life until the two hours of regular play were over and the penalty shoot-out had begun.

The first five spot kicks were all converted before Sweden keeper Patrik Carlgren denied Ricardo Esgaio. Then it was Abdul Khalil's turn to miss for Sweden, but after Victor Nilsson-Lindelöf had made it 4-3, William Carvalho, of all people, became Portugal's fall guy, allowing Carlgren to save again and his country to claim the UEFA European Under-21 Championship trophy for the first time. "It's like a fairy tale and it's incredible," said Sweden coach Håkan Ericson, succinctly summing up his team's history-making achievement.

Patrik Carlgren makes a decisive save in the penalty shoot-out of the final against Portugal to deliver the trophy to Sweden for the first time

Qualifying round

Group 1

Wales 1-0 Moldova
Lithuania 2-1 San Marino
Finland 2-2 Lithuania
San Marino 0-3 Moldova
Wales 1-5 Finland
San Marino 0-1 Lithuania
Lithuania 0-1 Finland
England 1-0 Moldova
San Marino 1-0 Wales
Finland 1-1 England
Moldova 0-0 Wales
San Marino 0-4 England
Wales 2-0 Lithuania
Wales 4-0 San Marino
England 5-0 Lithuania
Moldova 1-0 Finland
England 3-0 Finland
Moldova 2-0 San Marino
England 9-0 San Marino
Moldova 3-0 Lithuania
England 1-0 Wales
San Marino 0-0 Finland
Wales 1-3 England
Finland 1-0 Moldova
Lithuania 0-3 Moldova

05/09/14, Dariaus ir Giréno stadionas, Kaunas
Lithuania 0-1 England
Goal: 0-1 Kane 81

05/09/14, Turku Stadium, Turku
Finland 2-2 Wales
Goals: 1-0 Lod 19, 1-1 Burns 65, 1-2 Evans 69, 2-2 Väyrynen 87

09/09/14, Wiklöf Holding Arena, Mariehamn
Finland 5-0 San Marino
Goals: 1-0 Väyrynen 8, 2-0 Väisänen 26, 3-0 D O'Shaughnessy 57, 4-0 Hovi 64, 5-0 Lam 79

09/09/14, Stadionul Sheriff, Tiraspol
Moldova 0-3 England
Goals: 0-1 Berahino 16, 0-2 Berahino 51, 0-3 Kane 84

09/09/14, SRC Alytus, Alytus
Lithuania 1-1 Wales
Goals: 1-0 Tamulevičius 81, 1-1 Evans 90

Group 2

Andorra 0-3 Russia
Bulgaria 3-0 Andorra
Andorra 0-3 Bulgaria
Estonia 0-1 Denmark
Estonia 1-1 Andorra
Slovenia 0-1 Estonia
Russia 2-1 Slovenia
Denmark 6-0 Andorra
Bulgaria 1-1 Estonia
Slovenia 2-2 Denmark
Russia 3-1 Bulgaria
Bulgaria 3-3 Russia
Denmark 2-2 Slovenia
Slovenia 2-1 Bulgaria
Russia 0-2 Denmark
Slovenia 0-1 Russia
Andorra 0-2 Estonia
Bulgaria 2-3 Denmark
Bulgaria 1-5 Slovenia
Andorra 0-2 Denmark
Russia 1-0 Estonia
Denmark 8-0 Estonia
Andorra 0-5 Slovenia
Estonia 1-2 Russia

Harry Kane of England (right) in qualifying action against Moldova

03/09/14, Mestni, Ajdovscina
Slovenia 5-0 Andorra
Goals: 1-0 Vučkič 18, 2-0 Bratanovič 55, 3-0 Stojanovič 60, 4-0 Lotrič 82, 5-0 Lotrič 88

03/09/14, Aalborg Stadion, Aalborg
Denmark 4-2 Russia
Goals: 1-0 L Christensen 5, 1-1 Koryan 33, 2-1 L Christensen 44, 3-1 Vestergaard 56, 4-1 A Christensen 73, 4-2 Davydov 89

03/09/14, A. Le Coq Arena, Tallinn
Estonia 2-2 Bulgaria
Goals: 0-1 Kolev 8, 1-1 Vihmann 49, 2-1 Hannes Anier 65(p), 2-2 Chunchukov 79

08/09/14, Rakvere, Rakvere
Estonia 1-7 Slovenia
Goals: 0-1 Mitrovič 16, 0-2 Šporar 18(p), 0-3 Vrhovec 27, 0-4 Verbič 32, 0-5 Krajnc 63, 0-6 Hotič 80, 1-6 Liivak 83(p), 1-7 Hotič 89

09/09/14, Aalborg Stadion, Aalborg
Denmark 7-1 Bulgaria
Goals: 1-0 L Andersen 18, 2-0 L Andersen 32, 3-0 Durmisi 36, 4-0 Vestergaard 42, 4-1 Karachanakov 49, 5-1 Berggreen 65, 6-1 Bech 67, 7-1 Zohore 78

09/09/14, Luzhniki Sports Complex, Moscow
Russia 5-0 Andorra
Goals: 1-0 Serderov 2, 2-0 Davydov 34, 3-0 Davydov 44, 4-0 Khodzhaniyazov 75, 5-0 Mogilevets 90+2

Group 3

Scotland 3-0 Luxembourg
Luxembourg 1-7 Slovakia
Luxembourg 0-3 Georgia
Netherlands 4-0 Scotland
Luxembourg 0-1 Netherlands
Slovakia 1-0 Georgia
Georgia 0-6 Netherlands
Scotland 2-1 Slovakia
Georgia 2-1 Scotland
Slovakia 3-0 Luxembourg
Scotland 1-1 Georgia

Slovakia 2-2 Netherlands
Georgia 1-3 Slovakia
Georgia 0-3(w/o) Luxembourg
Scotland 1-6 Netherlands
Netherlands 3-1 Luxembourg

04/09/14, De Adelaarshorst, Deventer
Netherlands 0-1 Georgia
Goal: 0-1 Jigauri 71

04/09/14, National Training Centre, Senec
Slovakia 1-1 Scotland
Goals: 0-1 Fraser 67, 1-1 Duda 90

08/09/14, Stade Municipal de Differdange, Differdange
Luxembourg 0-3 Scotland
Goals: 0-1 Gauld 32, 0-2 MacLeod 36, 0-3 Gauld 63

08/09/14, Willem II, Tilburg
Netherlands 0-1 Slovakia
Goal: 0-1 Zreläk 72

Group 4

Albania 1-2 Hungary
Bosnia & Herzegovina 4-1 Albania
Albania 0-1 Austria
Hungary 4-1 Bosnia & Herzegovina
Austria 2-6 Spain
Bosnia & Herzegovina 0-2 Austria
Spain 4-0 Albania
Hungary 0-2 Austria
Spain 3-2 Bosnia & Herzegovina
Spain 1-0 Hungary
Albania 0-1 Bosnia & Herzegovina
Hungary 0-2 Albania
Bosnia & Herzegovina 1-6 Spain
Albania 0-2 Spain
Austria 4-2 Hungary
Austria 1-3 Albania

04/09/14, Pancho stadium, Felcsut
Hungary 0-1 Spain
Goal: 0-1 Saúl Ñíguez 66

05/09/14, NV Arena, St Polten
Austria 2-0 Bosnia & Herzegovina
Goals: 1-0 Stöger 11, 2-0 Djuricin 33

08/09/14, Asim Ferhatović Hase Stadion, Sarajevo
Bosnia & Herzegovina 1-4 Hungary
Goals: 0-1 Vécsei 1, 0-2 Kleinheisler 18, 0-3 Bacsa 51, 0-4 Bese 53, 1-4 Zolotić 87

09/09/14, Estadio Municipal Ciudadde Puertollano, Puertollano
Spain 1-1 Austria
Goals: 1-0 Sarabia 50, 1-1 Gregoritsch 90+5

Group 5

Latvia 4-0 Liechtenstein
Liechtenstein 0-5 Croatia
Latvia 0-2 Switzerland
Liechtenstein 0-6 Switzerland
Ukraine 0-2 Croatia
Croatia 4-0 Liechtenstein
Latvia 1-5 Ukraine
Switzerland 0-2 Croatia
Croatia 0-2 Switzerland
Liechtenstein 0-2 Latvia
Switzerland 1-2 Ukraine
Croatia 3-1 Latvia
Switzerland 5-1 Liechtenstein
Croatia 1-1 Ukraine
Liechtenstein 2-5 Ukraine
Ukraine 2-1 Latvia

UEFA European Under-21 Championship

03/09/14, Zemgales Olympic Centre, Jelgava
Latvia 1-3 Croatia
Goals: 0-1 Bagarić 48, 0-2 Rebić 52(p), 1-2 Gutkovskis 55, 1-3 Županić 70

04/09/14, KP Tcentralnyi, Cherkassy
Ukraine 2-0 Switzerland
Goals: 1-0 Ryzhuk 7, 2-0 Memeshev 77

08/09/14, Cornaredo, Lugano
Switzerland 7-1 Latvia
Goals: 1-0 Jevtic 5(p), 2-0 Brahimi 14, 3-0 Tarashaj 27, 4-0 Rodriguez 47, 5-0 Jevtic 60(p), 5-1 Klimaševičs 64, 6-1 Tabakovic 69, 7-1 Tabakovic 72

08/09/14, KP Tcentralnyi, Cherkassy
Ukraine 3-0 Liechtenstein
Goals: 1-0 Kulach 23, 2-0 Kulach 58, 3-0 Zahn 62(og)

Group 6

Faroe Islands 2-2 Romania
Montenegro 3-0 Faroe Islands
Faroe Islands 1-4 Republic of Ireland
Faroe Islands 0-3 Germany
Republic of Ireland 0-4 Germany
Montenegro 3-2 Romania
Germany 2-0 Montenegro
Romania 0-0 Republic of Ireland
Republic of Ireland 0-1 Romania
Germany 3-2 Faroe Islands
Republic of Ireland 5-2 Faroe Islands
Montenegro 1-1 Germany
Montenegro 0-0 Republic of Ireland
Romania 2-2 Germany
Romania 3-1 Faroe Islands
Republic of Ireland 1-2 Montenegro

04/09/14, Dinamo, Bucharest
Romania 4-3 Montenegro
Goals: 1-0 Boldor 10, 1-1 Djordjević 15, 1-2 Djordjević 33, 1-3 Djordjević 35, 2-3 Puşcaş 67, 3-3 Bumba 79(p), 4-3 F Tănase 82

05/09/14, Erdgas Sportpark, Halle
Germany 2-0 Republic of Ireland
Goals: 1-0 P Hofmann 47, 2-0 J Hofmann 50

09/09/14, Toftir, Toftir
Faroe Islands 1-0 Montenegro
Goal: 1-0 Jonsson 31

09/09/14, Magdeburg Stadium, Magdeburg
Germany 8-0 Romania
Goals: 1-0 Malli 1, 2-0 P Hofmann 12, 3-0 Younes 16, 4-0 J Hofmann 44, 5-0 Schulz 63, 6-0 Da Costa 80, 7-0 Stark 86, 8-0 J Hofmann 89

Group 7

Poland 2-0 Malta
Poland 3-1 Turkey
Turkey 4-0 Malta
Sweden 3-1 Poland
Greece 5-0 Malta
Turkey 2-2 Sweden
Turkey 1-0 Greece
Poland 2-0 Sweden
Malta 0-4 Greece
Turkey 1-0 Poland
Greece 5-1 Sweden
Malta 1-5 Poland
Poland 3-1 Greece
Sweden 5-0 Malta
Malta 1-2 Sweden
Greece 2-1 Turkey

05/09/14, Örjans vall, Halmstad
Sweden 3-0 Greece
Goals: 1-0 Guidetti 52, 2-0 Kiese Thelin 73, 3-0 Kiese Thelin 90+1

05/09/14, Ta' Qali National Stadium, Ta' Qali
Malta 0-3 Turkey
Goals: 0-1 Emrah Başsan 11, 0-2 Emrah Başsan 48, 0-3 Muhammet Demir 83

09/09/14, Örjans vall, Halmstad
Sweden 4-3 Turkey
Goals: 0-1 Emrah Başsan 29, 1-1 Olsson 34, 2-1 Olsson 58, 3-1 Olsson 71, 3-2 Kerim Koyunlu 84, 3-3 Enes Ünal 86, 4-3 Hiljemark 90+2

09/09/14, FC Katerini, Katerini
Greece 3-1 Poland
Goals: 1-0 Karelis 12, 1-1 Przybyłko 24, 2-1 Gianniotas 88(p), 3-1 Gianniotas 90+3

Group 8

Azerbaijan 0-0 FYR Macedonia
Portugal 5-1 Norway
Israel 7-2 Azerbaijan
Norway 2-1 FYR Macedonia
Norway 1-3 Azerbaijan
Portugal 3-0 Israel
Azerbaijan 0-2 Portugal
Norway 1-3 Israel
Israel 4-1 Norway
FYR Macedonia 1-0 Azerbaijan
Israel 3-4 Portugal
FYR Macedonia 1-3 Norway
Portugal 2-0 FYR Macedonia
FYR Macedonia 0-1 Portugal
Azerbaijan 0-1 Norway

13/08/14, Nacionalna Arena Filip II Makedonski, Skopje
FYR Macedonia 0-3 Israel
Goals: 0-1 Mizrahi 33, 0-2 Mizrahi 41, 0-3 Gozlan 81

03/09/14, Dalga Stadium, Baku
Azerbaijan 0-3 Israel
Goals: 1-0 Ramazanov 22, 2-0 Hacıyev 31, 3-0 Hacıyev 87

04/09/14, Marienlyst, Drammen
Norway 1-2 Portugal
Goals: 0-1 Carlos Mané 22, 0-2 Ricardo 62, 1-2 Bakenga 66

09/09/14, Municipal, Rio Maior
Portugal 3-1 Azerbaijan
Goals: 1-0 Rafa Silva 13, 1-1 Abatsiyev 55, 2-1 Edgar Ié 82, 3-1 Ricardo Esgaio 90+1(p)

09/09/14, Antonis Papadopoulos, Larnaca
Israel 2-1 FYR Macedonia
Goals: 1-0 Mikha 25, 1-1 Sulejmanov 48, 2-1 Dabbur 54(p)

Group 9

Belgium 2-0 Cyprus
Cyprus 3-0 Northern Ireland
Serbia 2-1 Cyprus
Italy 1-3 Belgium
Cyprus 0-2 Italy
Belgium 1-0 Northern Ireland
Northern Ireland 0-1 Belgium
Cyprus 2-1 Serbia
Belgium 0-1 Italy
Serbia 3-1 Northern Ireland
Italy 3-0 Northern Ireland
Serbia 2-2 Belgium
Serbia 1-0 Italy
Northern Ireland 1-0 Cyprus
Northern Ireland 0-2 Italy
Belgium 0-3 Serbia

05/09/14, Ammochostos, Larnaca
Cyprus 0-6 Belgium
Goals: 0-1 Tielemans 13, 0-2 Denayer 57, 0-3 M'Poku 63, 0-4 Batshuayi 74, 0-5 Batshuayi 83, 0-6 Kabasele 90+2

Germany players gather together to celebrate the final goal of their 8-0 victory against Romania in Magdeburg

05/09/14, Adriatico, Pescara
Italy 3-2 Serbia
Goals: 0-1 Pešić 8, 0-2 Pešić 13, 1-2 Belotti 23, 2-2 Belotti 45+4(p), 3-2 Berardi 75

09/09/14, Shamrock Park, Portadown
Northern Ireland 1 4 Serbia
Goals: 0-1 Pešić 34, 0-2 Srnić 36, 0-3 Srnić 56, 0-4 Kostić 58, 1-4 Brobbell 67

09/09/14, Teofilo Patini, Castel Di Sangro
Italy 7-1 Cyprus
Goals: 0-1 Sotiriou 29, 1-1 Bernardeschi 42, 2-1 A Panayiotou 45+2(og), 3-1 Sturaro 56, 4-1 Belotti 62, 5-1 Dezi 70, 6-1 Longo 76, 7-1 Rugani 80

Group 10

Belarus 1-2 Iceland
Armenia 1-2 Iceland
Belarus 0-1 Kazakhstan
Kazakhstan 0-1 Armenia
Iceland 4-1 Belarus
France 5-0 Kazakhstan
Belarus 1-2 France
Iceland 2-0 Kazakhstan
Kazakhstan 1-2 Belarus
Armenia 1-4 France
Armenia 1-2 Kazakhstan
Iceland 3-4 France
France 6-0 Armenia
Belarus 0-1 Armenia
France 1-0 Belarus
Kazakhstan 3-2 Iceland

03/09/14, Fylkisvöllur, Reykjavik
Iceland 4-0 Armenia
Goals: 1-0 Fridjonsson 24, 2-0 Fridjonsson 57(p), 3-0 Atlason 68, 4-0 Finsen 90

04/09/14, Astana Arena, Astana
Kazakhstan 1-5 France
Goals: 0-1 Sanson 17, 0-2 Kurzawa 31, 1-2 Murtazayev 36, 1-3 Kurzawa 42, 1-4 Sanogo 50, 1-5 Sanogo 53

08/09/14, Stade Abbé-Deschamps, Auxerre
France 1-1 Iceland
Goals: 1-0 Sanogo 63, 1-1 Emilsson 80

09/09/14, Hrazdan Central Stadium, Yerevan
Armenia 2-1 Belarus
Goals: 1-0 Papikyan 61, 1-1 Saroka 71, 2-1 Hakobyan 90

Final tables

Group 1

		Pld	Home W D L F A	Away W D L F A	Total W D L F A	Pts
1	England	10	5 0 0 19 0	4 1 0 12 2	9 1 0 31 2	28
2	Finland	10	2 3 0 11 5	2 1 2 6 5	4 4 2 17 10	16
3	Moldova	10	3 1 1 6 3	2 0 3 6 3	5 1 4 12 6	16
4	Wales	10	3 0 2 9 8	0 3 2 3 5	3 3 4 12 13	12
5	Lithuania	10	1 1 3 3 7	1 1 3 3 12	2 2 6 6 19	8
6	San Marino	10	1 1 3 1 8	0 0 5 1 22	1 1 8 2 30	4

Group 2

		Pld	Home W D L F A	Away W D L F A	Total W D L F A	Pts
1	Denmark	10	4 1 0 27 5	4 1 0 10 4	8 2 0 37 9	26
2	Russia	10	4 0 1 11 4	3 1 1 11 8	7 1 2 22 12	22
3	Slovenia	10	2 1 2 9 5	3 1 1 20 6	5 2 3 29 11	17
4	Bulgaria	10	1 2 2 10 12	1 1 3 8 14	2 3 5 18 26	9
5	Estonia	10	0 2 3 5 13	2 1 2 4 10	2 3 5 9 23	9
6	Andorra	10	0 0 5 0 15	0 1 4 1 20	0 1 9 1 35	1

Group 3

		Pld	Home W D L F A	Away W D L F A	Total W D L F A	Pts
1	Slovakia	8	2 2 0 7 3	3 0 1 12 4	5 2 1 19 7	17
2	Netherlands	8	2 0 2 7 3	3 1 0 15 3	5 1 2 22 6	16
3	Scotland	8	2 1 1 7 8	1 1 2 5 7	3 2 3 12 15	11
4	Georgia	8	1 0 3 3 13	2 1 1 5 2	3 1 4 8 15	10
5	Luxembourg	8	0 0 4 1 14	1 0 3 4 9	1 0 7 5 23	3

Group 4

		Pld	Home W D L F A	Away W D L F A	Total W D L F A	Pts
1	Spain	8	3 1 0 9 3	4 0 0 15 3	7 1 0 24 6	22
2	Austria	8	2 0 2 9 11	3 1 0 6 1	5 1 2 15 12	16
3	Hungary	8	1 0 3 4 6	2 0 2 8 7	3 0 5 12 13	9
4	Bosnia & Herzegovina	8	1 0 3 6 13	1 0 3 4 9	2 0 6 10 22	6
5	Albania	8	0 0 4 1 6	2 0 2 6 9	2 0 6 7 15	6

Group 5

		Pld	Home W D L F A	Away W D L F A	Total W D L F A	Pts
1	Croatia	8	2 1 1 8 4	4 0 0 12 1	6 1 1 20 5	19
2	Ukraine	8	3 0 1 7 3	3 1 0 13 5	6 1 1 20 8	19
3	Switzerland	8	2 0 2 13 6	3 0 1 10 2	5 0 3 23 8	15
4	Latvia	8	1 0 3 6 10	1 0 3 5 12	2 0 6 11 22	6
5	Liechtenstein	8	0 0 4 2 18	0 0 4 1 16	0 0 8 3 34	0

Group 6

		Pld	Home W D L F A	Away W D L F A	Total W D L F A	Pts
1	Germany	8	4 0 0 15 2	2 2 0 10 3	6 2 0 25 5	20
2	Romania	8	2 2 0 9 6	1 1 2 5 13	3 3 2 14 19	12
3	Montenegro	8	2 2 0 7 3	1 0 3 5 8	3 2 3 12 11	11
4	Republic of Ireland	8	1 0 3 6 9	1 2 1 4 3	2 2 4 10 12	8
5	Faroe Islands	8	1 1 2 4 9	0 0 4 5 14	1 1 6 9 23	4

Group 7

		Pld	Home W D L F A	Away W D L F A	Total W D L F A	Pts
1	Sweden	8	4 0 0 15 4	1 1 2 5 10	5 1 2 20 14	16
2	Greece	8	4 0 0 15 3	1 0 3 5 7	5 0 3 20 10	15
3	Poland	8	4 0 0 10 2	1 0 3 7 8	5 0 3 17 10	15
4	Turkey	8	3 1 0 8 2	1 0 3 8 9	4 1 3 16 11	13
5	Malta	8	0 0 4 2 14	0 0 4 0 16	0 0 8 2 30	0

Group 8

		Pld	Home W D L F A	Away W D L F A	Total W D L F A	Pts
1	Portugal	8	4 0 0 13 2	4 0 0 9 4	8 0 0 22 6	24
2	Israel	8	3 0 1 16 8	2 0 2 6 7	5 0 3 22 15	15
3	Norway	8	1 0 3 5 9	2 0 2 6 10	3 0 5 11 19	9
4	Azerbaijan	8	1 1 2 3 3	1 0 3 6 12	2 1 5 9 15	7
5	FYR Macedonia	8	1 0 3 2 7	0 1 3 2 6	1 1 6 4 13	4

Group 9

		Pld	Home W D L F A	Away W D L F A	Total W D L F A	Pts
1	Italy	8	3 0 1 14 6	3 0 1 5 1	6 0 2 19 7	18
2	Serbia	8	3 1 0 8 4	2 0 2 10 6	5 1 2 18 10	16
3	Belgium	8	2 0 2 3 4	3 1 0 12 3	5 1 2 15 7	16
4	Cyprus	8	2 0 2 5 9	0 0 4 2 12	2 0 6 7 21	6
5	Northern Ireland	8	1 0 3 2 7	0 0 4 1 10	1 0 7 3 17	3

Group 10

		Pld	Home W D L F A	Away W D L F A	Total W D L F A	Pts
1	France	8	3 1 0 13 1	4 0 0 15 6	7 1 0 28 7	22
2	Iceland	8	3 0 1 13 5	2 1 1 7 6	5 1 2 20 11	16
3	Kazakhstan	8	1 0 3 5 10	2 0 2 3 8	3 0 5 8 18	9
4	Armenia	8	1 0 3 5 9	2 0 2 2 10	3 0 5 7 19	9
5	Belarus	8	0 0 4 2 6	1 0 3 4 8	1 0 7 6 14	3

UEFA European Under-21 Championship

Play-offs

09/10/14, AZ Stadion, Alkmaar (att: 11,659)
Netherlands 0-2 Portugal
Goals: 0-1 Sérgio Oliveira 45+1(p), 0-2 Carlos Mané 82
Referee: Sidiropoulos (GRE)
Netherlands: Hahn, Ligeon (Brenet 46), Van Beek, Rekik, Willems (Sinkgraven 79), Aké, El Ghazi (John 68), Ebecilio, Castaignos, Maher, Manu. Coach: Adrie Koster (NED)
Portugal: José Sá, Ricardo Esgaio, Paulo Oliveira, Raphael Guerreiro, Rúben Neves, Rafa Silva (Iuri Medeiros 73), Ivan Cavaleiro (Carlos Mané 61), Rúben Vezo, Sérgio Oliveira, Ricardo (Ricardo Horta 78), Bernardo Silva. Coach: Rui Jorge (POR)
14/10/14, A Mata Real, Pacos de Ferreira (att: 4,480)
Portugal 5-4 Netherlands
Goals: 1-0 Rúben Vezo 13, 1-1 Weghorst 15, 2-1 Rúben Neves 20, 2-2 Kongolo 45+2, 3-2 Ricardo 50, 3-3 Aké 64, 4-3 Ricardo 66, 5-3 Bernardo Silva 87, 5-4 Aké 89(p)
Referee: Oliver (ENG)
Portugal: José Sá, Ricardo Esgaio, Paulo Oliveira, Raphael Guerreiro, Rúben Neves, Tozé (Iuri Medeiros 73), Ivan Cavaleiro (Carlos Mané 46), Rúben Vezo, Sérgio Oliveira, Ricardo (Ricardo Horta 81), Bernardo Silva. Coach: Rui Jorge (POR)
Netherlands: Hahn, Rekik, Willems, Aké, Weghorst, Maher (Drost 72), Kongolo, Hupperts (El Ghazi 69), John, Manu, Brenet (Ligeon 71). Coach: Adrie Koster (NED)
Aggregate: 7-4; Portugal qualify.

10/10/14, Štadión FC ViOn, Zlate Moravce (att: 3,847)
Slovakia 1-1 Italy
Goals: 0-1 Belotti 54, 1-1 Zrelák 69
Referee: Artur Dias (POR)
Slovakia: Rusov, Niňaj, Pauschek, Dionatan, Mihalík (Lobotka 56), Paur, Schranz (Malec 66), Mazáň, Zrelák, Hrošovský, Lásik. Coach: Ivan Galád (SVK)
Italy: Bardi, Zappacosta, Biraghi, Baselli (Crisetig 70), Bianchetti, Rugani, Battocchio, Viviani, Belotti (Longo 88), Berardi, Bernardeschi (Molina 60). Coach: Luigi Di Biagio (ITA)
14/10/14, Giglio, Reggio Emilia (att: 5,149)
Italy 3-1 Slovakia
Goals: 1-0 Bernardeschi 5, 2-0 Belotti 15(p), 2-1 Lobotka 63, 3-1 Longo 90
Referee: McLean (SCO)
Italy: Bardi, Zappacosta, Biraghi, Crisetig, Bianchetti, Rugani, Battocchio, Viviani (Benassi 54), Belotti (Longo 77), Berardi (Baselli 86), Bernardeschi. Coach: Luigi Di Biagio (ITA)
Slovakia: Rusov, Niňaj (Škriniar 21), Pauschek, Dionatan, Paur (Lobotka 46), Schranz (Malec 83), Mazáň, Zrelák, Hrošovský, Lásik, Duda. Coach: Ivan Galád (SVK)
Red cards: Duda 34 (Slovakia), Zrelák 78 (Slovakia), Rusov 90+6 (Slovakia)
Aggregate: 4-2; Italy qualify.

10/10/14, Gradski, Jagodina (att: 7,500)
Serbia 0-0 Spain
Referee: Karasev (RUS)
Serbia: Dmitrović, Kovačević (Mijailović 82), Petković, Veljković, Pantić, Radoja, Pešić (Djurdjević 87), Čaušić, Kostić, Petrović, Srnić (Čavrić 67). Coach: Radovan Čurčić (SRB)
Spain: Arrizabalaga, Javi Manquillo, Moreno, Sergi Gómez, Marc Muniesa, Saúl Ñíguez, Muniain (Óliver Torres 77), Sergi Roberto, Morata, Isco, Deulofeu (Sarabia 70). Coach: Albert Celades (ESP)

Sweden's Oscar Lewicki (No8) puts his country through to the finals at the expense of France

14/10/14, Ramón de Carranza, Cadiz (att: 17,200)
Spain 1-2 Serbia
Goals: 0-1 Saúl Ñíguez 31(og), 1-1 Sergi Roberto 90+2, 1-2 Kostić 90+3
Referee: Zwayer (GER)
Spain: Arrizabalaga, Javi Manquillo, Gaya, Sergi Gómez, Marc Muniesa (Óliver Torres 69), Saúl Ñíguez, Muniain (Sandro Ramírez 55), Sergi Roberto, El Haddadi, Isco, Deulofeu (Sarabia 62). Coach: Albert Celades (ESP)
Serbia: Dmitrović, Kovačević, Veljković, Radoja (Mijailović 85), Pešić (Čavrić 71), Čaušić, Kostić, Petrović, Ćirković, Srnić, Stojković (Filipović 64). Coach: Radovan Čurčić (SRB)
Aggregate: 1-2; Serbia qualify.

10/10/14, Molineux, Wolverhampton (att: 23,107)
England 2-1 Croatia
Goals: 0-1 Livaja 13, 1-1 Kane 58, 2-1 Berahino 85(p)
Referee: Estrada (ESP)
England: Butland, Keane (Dier 46), Shaw, Hughes (Ince 56), Gibson, Moore, Berahino, Caskey, Kane, Carroll, Redmond. Coach: Gareth Southgate (ENG)
Croatia: Livaković, Župarić, Milić (Miloš 90+1), Bradarić, Datković, Mitrović, Pjaca, Pavičić, Rebić, Livaja (Bagarić 70), Ćorić (Pašalić 63). Coach: Nenad Gračan (CRO)
14/10/14, Cibalia Vinkovci, Vinkovci (att: 6,352)
Croatia 1-2 England
Goals: 0-1 Moore 9, 1-1 Livaja 38, 1-2 Hughes 73
Referee: Turpin (FRA)
Croatia: Livaković, Milić, Bradarić, Datković, Mitrović, Pjaca, Pašalić (Caktaš 67), Rebić (Bagarić 34), Miloš, Livaja, Halilović (Mišić 79). Coach: Nenad Gračan (CRO)
England: Butland, Dier, Shaw, Hughes, Gibson, Moore, Berahino, Caskey, Kane, Carroll, Redmond (Ince 85). Coach: Gareth Southgate (ENG)
Aggregate: 2-4; England qualify.

10/10/14, Aalborg Stadion, Aalborg (att: 6,125)
Denmark 0-0 Iceland
Referee: Liany (ISR)
Denmark: Busk, Scholz, Sørensen, Vestergaard, Knudsen, A Christensen, Amankwaa, L Christensen, Cornelius, L Andersen (Toutouh 67), Thomsen. Coach: Jess Thorup (DEN)
Iceland: R Rúnarsson, Ingason, Gudjónsson, O Ómarsson, Magnússon, Thórarinsson, Yeoman, Traustason, Finsen, Atlason, Fridjónsson. Coach: Eyjólfur Sverrisson (ISL)

14/10/14, Laugardalsvöllur, Reykjavik (att: 2,503)
Iceland 1-1 Denmark
Goals: 0-1 Thomsen 90, 1-1 Fridjonsson 90+3(p)
Referee: Vad (HUN)
Iceland: Schram, Ingason, Gudjónsson, O Ómarsson, Hermannsson, Thórarinsson, Yeoman, Traustason (Vilhjálmsson 90+3), Finsen (Atlason 90+3), T Rúnarsson, Fridjónsson. Coach: Eyjólfur Sverrisson (ISL)
Denmark: Busk, Scholz, Okore, Vestergaard, Knudsen, Christensen, Amankwaa (Sørensen 90+3), L Christensen, Cornelius, Toutouh, Thomsen. Coach: Jess Thorup (DEN)
Aggregate: 1-1; Denmark qualify on away goal.

10/10/14, KP Tcentralnyi, Cherkassy (att: 9,442)
Ukraine 0-3 Germany
Goals: 0-1 P Hofmann 35, 0-2 Volland 61, 0-3 J Hofmann 79
Referee: Özkahya (TUR)
Ukraine: Koval, Pysko (Noyok 46), Karavayev (Memeshev 60), Ryzhuk, Kalitvintsev, Babenko, Nasonov, Malinovskiy (Buyalskiy 65), Malyshev, Neplyakh, Kulach. Coach: Serhiy Kovalets (UKR)
Germany: Ter Stegen, Heintz, Günter, Geis, Malli (Meyer 46), Volland, Leitner, Korb, Knoche, P Hofmann (Kimmich 64), J Hofmann (Bittencourt 84). Coach: Horst Hrubesch (GER)
14/10/14, Georg-Meiches, Essen (att: 5,128)
Germany 2-0 Ukraine
Goals: 1-0 Volland 89, 2-0 Bittencourt 90+1
Referee: Makkelie (NED)
Germany: Ter Stegen, Heintz, Da Costa, Geis, Volland, Leitner (Kimmich 58), Knoche, P Hofmann (Stark 77), Schulz, Meyer, J Hofmann (Bittencourt 46). Coach: Horst Hrubesch (GER)
Ukraine: Shevchenko, Kostevych (Neplyakh 71), Ordets, Karavayev, Ryzhuk, Bolbat (Kalitvintsev 53), Yurchenko, Budkivskiy, Nasonov, Buyalskiy (Malinovskiy 58), Malyshev. Coach: Serhiy Kovalets (UKR)
Red card: Karavayev 90+3 (Ukraine)
Aggregate: 5-0; Germany qualify.

10/10/14, MMArena, Le Mans (att: 8,896)
France 2-0 Sweden
Goals: 1-0 Thauvin 44(p), 2-0 Kondogbia 81
Referee: Hansen (DEN)
France: Areola, Kurzawa, Zouma (Foulquier 38), Umtiti, Ntep, Sanson (Bahebeck 80), Martial (Coman 61), Thauvin, Imbula, Kondogbia, Laporte. Coach: Pierre Mankowski (FRA)
Sweden: Carlgren, Baffo, Milosevic, Helander, Augustinsson, Ssewankambo (Hallberg 73), Khalili (Ishak 85), Lewicki, Tibbling (Olsson 76), Guidetti, Kiese Thelin. Coach: Håkan Ericson (SWE)

14/10/14, Örjans vall, Halmstad (att: 2,863)
Sweden 4-1 France
Goals: 1-0 Kiese Thelin 3, 2-0 Kiese Thelin 35, 3-0 Lewicki 71, 3-1 Kurzawa 87, 4-1 Lewicki 88
Referee: Krużliak (SVK)
Sweden: Carlgren, Krafth, Milosevic, Baffo, Konate, Olsson (Ishak 87), Khalili, Lewicki, Hallberg (Tibbling 69), Guidetti (Nilsson-Lindelöf 90+1), Kiese Thelin. Coach: Håkan Ericson (SWE)
France: Areola, Foulquier, Kurzawa, Umtiti, Tolisso (Fekir 75), Ntep, Thauvin, Bahebeck (Coman 65), Imbula, Kondogbia, Laporte. Coach: Pierre Mankowski (FRA)
Aggregate: 4-3; Sweden qualify.

Top goalscorers
(Qualifying round/Play-offs)

10	Saido Berahino (England)
9	Arkadiusz Milik (Poland)
8	Álvaro Morata (Spain)
	Emil Atlason (Iceland)
	Munas Dabbur (Israel)
7	Marcelo Brozović (Croatia)
	Quincy Promes (Netherlands)
	Philipp Hofmann (Germany)
6	Harry Kane (England)
	Kevin Volland (Germany)
	Nikolaos Karelis (Greece)
	Florian Thauvin (France)
	Andrea Belotti (Italy)
	Luc Castaignos (Netherlands)
	Tim Väyrynen (Finland)

Final tournament

Group A

17/06/15, Eden Arena, Prague (att: 15,987)
Czech Republic 1-2 Denmark
Goals: 1-0 Kadeřábek 35, 1-1 Vestergaard 56, 1-2 Sisto 84
Referee: Marciniak (POL)
Czech Republic: Koubek, Kadeřábek, Brabec, Petrák, Zmrhal, Kliment, Frýdek, Krejčí (Skalák 76), Baránek (Jánoš 82), Přikryl (Trávník 62), Hybš. Coach: Jakub Dovalil (CZE)
Denmark: Busk, Scholz, Sørensen (L Christensen 25), Vestergaard, Knudsen, A Christensen, Fischer (Sisto 57), Poulsen, Højbjerg, Thomsen, Falk (Berggreen 89). Coach: Jess Thorup (DEN)
Yellow cards: Knudsen 3 (Denmark), Vestergaard 31 (Denmark)

17/06/15, Stadion Letná, Prague (att: 5,490)
Germany 1-1 Serbia
Goals: 0-1 Djuričić 8, 1-1 Can 17
Referee: Estrada (ESP)
Germany: Ter Stegen, Korb, Günter, Ginter, Vulland, Leitner (Kimmich 46), Can, Hofmann (Schulz 71), Knoche, Younes, Meyer (Bittencourt 77). Coach: Horst Hrubesch (GER)
Serbia: Dmitrović, Pantić, Čausić, Pešić (Trujić 90+3), Djuričić, Petrović, Brašanac, Spajić, Jojić (Milunović 90), Srnić (Čavrić 77), Stojković. Coach: Mladen Dodić (SRB)
Red card: Günter 69 (Germany)
Yellow cards: Leitner 43 (Germany), Günter 48 (Germany), Čausić 52 (Serbia), Brašanac 54 (Serbia), Günter 69 (Germany), Pantić 75 (Serbia)

20/06/15, Stadion Letná, Prague (att: 16,253)
Serbia 0-4 Czech Republic
Goals: 0-1 Kliment 7, 0-2 Kliment 21, 0-3 Kliment 56, 0-4 Frýdek 59
Referee: Turpin (FRA)
Serbia: Dmitrović, Pantić, Čausić (Kovačević 63), Pešić, Djuričić, Petrović, Brašanac, Spajić, Jojić (Milunović 85), Srnić, Stojković (Petković 46). Coach: Mladen Dodić (SRB)
Czech Republic: Koubek, Kadeřábek, Kadlec (Trávník 29), Brabec, Petrák, Zmrhal, Kliment (Přikryl 82), Skalák (Masopust 75), Frýdek, Hybš, Kalas. Coach: Jakub Dovalil (CZE)
Yellow cards: Brašanac 11 (Serbia), Djuričić 68 (Serbia), Masopust 84 (Czech Republic)

20/06/15, Eden Arena, Prague (att: 13,268)
Germany 3-0 Denmark
Goals: 1-0 Volland 32, 2-0 Volland 48, 3-0 Ginter 53
Referee: Karasev (RUS)
Germany: Ter Stegen, Korb, Ginter, Schulz, Bittencourt (Gnabry 79), Volland (Klaus 82), Can (Geis 77), Kimmich, Younes, Meyer, Heintz. Coach: Horst Hrubesch (GER)
Denmark: Busk, Scholz, Vestergaard, Knudsen, A Christensen, L Christensen, Poulsen (Bech 61), Thomsen, Jønsson (Nørgaard 77), Brock-Madsen, Sisto (Fischer 72). Coach: Jess Thorup (DEN)
Yellow cards: Knudsen 17 (Denmark), Poulsen 51 (Denmark)

23/06/15, Eden Arena, Prague (att: 18,068)
Czech Republic 1-1 Germany
Goals: 0-1 Schulz 55, 1-1 Krejčí 66
Referee: Makkelie (NED)
Czech Republic: Koubek, Kadeřábek, Brabec, Petrák, Zmrhal, Kliment, Skalák (Masopust 61), Frýdek (Přikryl 79), Trávník (Krejčí 59), Hybš, Kalas. Coach: Jakub Dovalil (CZE)
Germany: Ter Stegen, Korb, Günter, Ginter, Schulz (Hofmann 90+2), Volland, Can, Kimmich, Younes (Bittencourt 64), Meyer (Malli 82), Heintz. Coach: Horst Hrubesch (GER)
Yellow cards: Younes 23 (Germany), Frýdek 32 (Czech Republic), Korb 65 (Germany), Kimmich 88 (Germany), Can 90+4 (Germany)

23/06/15, Stadion Letná, Prague (att: 4,297)
Denmark 2-0 Serbia
Goals: 1-0 Falk 21, 2-0 Fischer 47
Referee: Sidiropoulos (GRE)
Denmark: Busk, Scholz, Vestergaard, A Christensen, Fischer (L Christensen 66), Poulsen, Højbjerg (Nørgaard 89), Durmisi, Thomsen, Falk (Bech 85), Jønsson. Coach: Jess Thorup (DEN)
Serbia: Dmitrović, Kovačević, Petković, Čausić, Pešić, Djuričić, Čavrić (Milunović 59), Petrović, Spajić, Jojić (Trujić 66), Ćirković (Pantić 81). Coach: Mladen Dodić (SRB)
Yellow cards: Ćirković 41 (Serbia), A Christensen 54 (Denmark), Petrović 62 (Serbia), Petković 63 (Serbia)

		Pld	W	D	L	F	A	Pts
1	Denmark	3	2	0	1	4	4	6
2	Germany	3	1	2	0	5	2	5
3	Czech Republic	3	1	1	1	6	3	4
4	Serbia	3	0	1	2	1	7	1

Group B

18/06/15, Andrův stadion, Olomouc (att: 6,719)
Italy 1-2 Sweden
Goals: 1-0 Berardi 29(p), 1-1 Guidetti 56, 1-2 Kiese Thelin 86(p)
Referee: Sidiropoulos (GRE)
Italy: Bardi, Sabelli, Rugani, Viviani, Sturaro, Belotti (Trotta 78), Berardi, Bianchetti, Baselli (Cataldi 69), Battocchio (Verdi 61), Zappacosta. Coach: Luigi Di Biagio (ITA)
Sweden: Carlgren, Milosevic, Helander, Augustinsson, Lewicki, Hiljemark, Khalili, Guidetti (Ishak 76), Kiese Thelin, Baffo, Larsson (Nilsson-Lindelöf 46). Coach: Håkan Ericson (SWE)
Red cards: Milosevic 28 (Sweden), Sturaro 80 (Italy)
Yellow cards: Helander 24 (Sweden), Viviani 43 (Italy), Bianchetti 48 (Italy), Guidetti 64 (Sweden), Hiljemark 71 (Sweden), Bardi 85 (Italy)

18/06/15, City Stadium, Uherske Hradiste (att: 7,167)
England 0-1 Portugal
Goal: 0-1 João Mário 57
Referee: Makkelie (NED)
England: Butland, Jenkinson, Garbutt, Gibson, Ward-Prowse (Hughes 54), Kane, Carroll (Pritchard 79), Redmond, Chalobah, Lingard (Ings 74), Moore. Coach: Gareth Southgate (ENG)
Portugal: José Sá, Ricardo Esgaio, Tiago Ilori, Paulo Oliveira, Raphael Guerreiro, William Carvalho, Sérgio Oliveira, Bernardo Silva, Ivan Cavaleiro (Iuri Medeiros 73), Ricardo (Carlos Mané 79), João Mário (Rúben Neves 85). Coach: Rui Jorge (POR)
Yellow cards: Gibson 48 (England), Bernardo Silva 49 (Portugal), Jenkinson 62 (England), João Mário 83 (Portugal)

Bernardo Silva had an excellent final tournament for Portugal

UEFA European Under-21 Championship

21/06/15, Andrův stadion, Olomouc (att: 11,257)
Sweden 0-1 England
Goal: 0-1 Lingard 85
Referee: Estrada (ESP)
Sweden: Carlgren, Nilsson-Lindelöf, Helander, Augustinsson, Lewicki, Hiljemark, Khalili (Quaison 87), Guidetti (Ishak 81), Kiese Thelin, Tibbling (Larsson 78), Baffo. Coach: Håkan Ericson (SWE)
England: Butland, Jenkinson, Garbutt, Gibson, Pritchard (Lingard 55), Kane, Carroll (Loftus-Cheek 73), Redmond, Chalobah, Hughes (Ings 46), Moore. Coach: Gareth Southgate (ENG)
Yellow cards: Khalili 70 (Sweden), Baffo 79 (Sweden)

21/06/15, City Stadium, Uherske Hradiste (att: 7,085)
Italy 0-0 Portugal
Referee: Marciniak (POL)
Italy: Bardi, Biraghi, Crisetig (Trotta 76), Rugani, Romagnoli, Belotti (Viviani 85), Berardi, Benassi, Battocchio (Bernardeschi 62), Cataldi, Zappacosta. Coach: Luigi Di Biagio (ITA)
Portugal: José Sá, Ricardo Esgaio, Tiago Ilori, Paulo Oliveira, Raphael Guerreiro, William Carvalho, Rafa Silva (Gonçalo Paciência 54), Sérgio Oliveira, Bernardo Silva (Iuri Medeiros 78), Carlos Mané, João Mário (Tozé 81). Coach: Rui Jorge (POR)
Yellow cards: Bernardeschi 65 (Italy), Biraghi 69 (Italy), Romagnoli 87 (Italy), Gonçalo Paciência 90+1 (Portugal)

24/06/15, Andrův stadion, Olomouc (att: 11,563)
England 1-3 Italy
Goals: 0-1 Belotti 25, 0-2 Benassi 27, 0-3 Benassi 72, 1-3 Redmond 90+3
Referee: Karasev (RUS)
England: Butland, Jenkinson, Garbutt, Forster-Caskey (Loftus-Cheek 63), Stones, Gibson, Kane, Redmond, Chalobah, Lingard, Ings. Coach: Gareth Southgate (ENG)
Italy: Bardi, Biraghi, Crisetig, Rugani, Romagnoli, Belotti, Berardi (Sabelli 63), Benassi, Trotta (Verdi 75), Cataldi, Zappacosta (Viviani 83). Coach: Luigi Di Biagio (ITA)
Yellow cards: Zappacosta 57 (Italy), Loftus-Cheek 67 (England)

24/06/15, City Stadium, Uherske Hradiste (att: 7,263)
Portugal 1-1 Sweden
Goals: 1-0 Gonçalo Paciência 82, 1-1 Tibbling 89
Referee: Turpin (FRA)
Portugal: José Sá, Ricardo Esgaio, Tiago Ilori (Tobias Figueiredo 29), Paulo Oliveira, Raphael Guerreiro, William Carvalho, Sérgio Oliveira, Bernardo Silva, Ivan Cavaleiro (Gonçalo Paciência 58), Ricardo (Iuri Medeiros 74), João Mário. Coach: Rui Jorge (POR)
Sweden: Carlgren, Nilsson-Lindelöf, Milosevic, Augustinsson, Lewicki, Hiljemark, Khalili (Quaison 83), Hrgota (Tibbling 52), Guidetti, Kiese Thelin, Baffo (Helander 80). Coach: Håkan Ericson (SWE)
Yellow cards: Lewicki 18 (Sweden), Sérgio Oliveira 65 (Portugal)

	Pld	W	D	L	F	A	Pts
1 Portugal	3	1	2	0	2	1	5
2 Sweden	3	1	1	1	3	3	4
3 Italy	3	1	1	1	4	3	4
4 England	3	1	0	2	2	4	3

Semi-finals

27/06/15, Andrův stadion, Olomouc (att: 9,876)
Portugal 5-0 Germany
Goals: 1-0 Bernardo Silva 25, 2-0 Ricardo 33, 3-0 Ivan Cavaleiro 45+1, 4-0 João Mário 46, 5-0 Ricardo Horta 71
Referee: Sidiropoulos (GRE)

Portugal: José Sá, Ricardo Esgaio, Paulo Oliveira, Raphael Guerreiro (João Cancelo 64), William Carvalho, Sérgio Oliveira, Bernardo Silva (Rafa Silva 50), Tobias Figueiredo, Ivan Cavaleiro (Ricardo Horta 46), Ricardo, João Mário. Coach: Rui Jorge (POR)
Germany: Ter Stegen, Korb (Klaus 87), Günter, Ginter, Schulz (Bittencourt 50), Geis (Meyer 46), Volland, Can, Kimmich, Younes, Heintz. Coach: Horst Hrubesch (GER)
Red card: Bittencourt 75 (Germany)
Yellow cards: Ricardo Esgaio 18 (Portugal), Kimmich 23 (Germany), Bittencourt 63 (Germany), Bittencourt 75 (Germany)

27/06/15, Stadion Letná, Prague (att: 9,834)
Denmark 1-4 Sweden
Goals: 0-1 Guidetti 23(p), 0-2 Tibbling 26, 1-2 Bech 63, 1-3 Quaison 83, 1-4 Hiljemark 90+5
Referee: Karasev (RUS)
Denmark: Busk, Scholz, Vestergaard, Knudsen, A Christensen, Poulsen, Højbjerg, Bech (Fischer 90+2), Thomsen, Falk (Sisto 65), Jønsson (L Christensen 57). Coach: Jess Thorup (DEN)
Sweden: Carlgren, Nilsson-Lindelöf, Milosevic, Helander, Augustinsson, Lewicki, Hiljemark, Khalili, Guidetti (Ishak 59), Kiese Thelin (Larsson 90+3), Tibbling (Quaison 72). Coach: Håkan Ericson (SWE)
Yellow card: Vestergaard 59 (Denmark)

Final

30/06/15, Eden Arena, Prague (att: 18,867)
Sweden 0-0 Portugal (aet; 4-3 on pens)
Referee: Marciniak (POL)
Sweden: Carlgren, Nilsson-Lindelöf, Milosevic, Helander (Baffo 46), Augustinsson, Lewicki, Hiljemark, Khalili, Kiese Thelin, Tibbling (Quaison 66). Coach: Håkan Ericson (SWE)
Portugal: José Sá, Ricardo Esgaio, Tiago Ilori, Paulo Oliveira, Raphael Guerreiro, William Carvalho, Sérgio Oliveira (Tozé 54), Bernardo Silva, Ivan Cavaleiro (Iuri Medeiros 61), Ricardo (Gonçalo Paciência 70), João Mário. Coach: Rui Jorge (POR)
Yellow cards: Baffo 110 (Sweden), Nilsson-Lindelöf 112 (Sweden)

Top goalscorers *(Final tournament)*

3 Jan Kliment (Czech Republic)

2 Kevin Volland (Germany)
Marco Benassi (Italy)
João Mário (Portugal)
John Guidetti (Sweden)
Simon Tibbling (Sweden)

Squads/Appearances/Goals

Czech Republic

No	Name	DoB	Aps	(s)	Gls	Club
Goalkeepers						
1	Tomáš Koubek	26/08/92	3			Hradec Králové
16	Jiří Pavlenka	14/04/92				Baník
Defenders						
15	Jan Baránek	26/06/93	1			Plzeň
5	Jakub Brabec	06/08/92	3			Sparta Praha
21	Matěj Hanousek	02/06/93				Dukla Praha
19	Matěj Hybš	03/01/93	3			Jihlava
20	Jakub Jugas	05/05/92				Brno
2	Pavel Kadeřábek	25/04/92	3		1	Sparta Praha
22	Tomáš Kalas	15/05/93	2			Chelsea (ENG)
14	Ladislav Takács	15/07/96				Teplice
Midfielders						
11	Martin Frýdek	24/03/92	3		1	Liberec
7	David Houska	29/06/93				Sigma
4	Adam Jánoš	20/07/92		(1)		Jihlava
13	Ladislav Krejčí	05/07/92	1	(1)	1	Sparta Praha
18	Lukáš Masopust	12/02/93		(2)		Jablonec
6	Ondřej Petrák	11/03/92	3			Nürnberg (GER)
17	Tomáš Přikryl	04/07/92	1	(2)		Dukla Praha
10	Jiří Skalák	12/03/92	2	(1)		Mladá Boleslav
12	Michal Trávník	17/05/94	1	(2)		Slovácko
8	Jaromír Zmrhal	02/08/93	3			Slavia Praha
Forwards						
3	Václav Kadlec	20/05/92	1			Sparta Praha
9	Jan Kliment	01/09/93	3		3	Jihlava

Denmark

No	Name	DoB	Aps	(s)	Gls	Club
Goalkeepers						
1	Jakob Busk	12/09/93	4			Sandefjord (NOR)
22	David Jensen	25/03/92				Nordsjælland
16	Frederik Rønnow	04/08/92				Horsens
Defenders						
12	Patrick Banggaard	04/04/94				Midtjylland
6	Andreas Christensen	10/04/96	4			Chelsea (ENG)
13	Riza Durmisi	08/01/94	1			Brøndby
5	Jonas Knudsen	16/09/92	3			Esbjerg
14	Christoffer Remmer	16/01/93				København
2	Alexander Scholz	24/10/92	4			Standard Liège (BEL)
3	Frederik Sørensen	14/04/92	1			Verona (ITA)
4	Jannik Vestergaard	03/08/92	4		1	Bremen (GER)
Midfielders						
8	Lasse Vigen Christensen	15/08/94	1	(3)		Fulham (ENG)
18	Rasmus Falk	15/01/92	3		1	OB
10	Pierre Højbjerg	05/08/95	3			Augsburg (GER)
19	Jens Jønsson	10/01/93	3			AGF
17	Christian Nørgaard	10/03/94		(2)		Brøndby
23	Pione Sisto	04/02/95	1	(2)	1	Midtjylland
15	Nicolaj Thomsen	08/05/93	4			AaB
Forwards						
11	Uffe Bech	13/01/93	1	(2)	1	Nordsjælland
21	Emil Berggreen	10/05/93		(1)		Braunschweig (GER)
20	Nicolai Brock-Madsen	09/01/93	1			Randers
7	Viktor Fischer	09/06/94	2	(2)	1	Ajax (NED)
9	Yussuf Poulsen	15/06/94	4			RB Leipzig (GER)

England

No	Name	DoB	Aps	(s)	Gls	Club
Goalkeepers						
13	Marcus Bettinelli	24/05/92				Fulham
12	Jonathan Bond	19/05/93				Watford
1	Jack Butland	10/03/93	3			Stoke
Defenders						
21	Calum Chambers	20/01/95				Arsenal
3	Luke Garbutt	21/05/93	3			Everton
6	Ben Gibson	15/01/93	3			Middlesbrough
2	Carl Jenkinson	08/02/92	3			Arsenal
15	Michael Keane	11/01/93				Burnley
20	Liam Moore	31/01/93	2			Leicester
5	John Stones	28/05/94	1			Everton
22	Matt Targett	18/09/95				Southampton
Midfielders						
10	Tom Carroll	28/05/92	2			Tottenham
14	Nathaniel Chalobah	12/12/94	3			Chelsea
4	Jake Forster-Caskey	25/04/94	1			Brighton
19	Will Hughes	17/04/95	1	(1)		Derby
16	Jesse Lingard	15/12/92	2	(1)	1	Man. United
23	Ruben Loftus-Cheek	23/01/96		(2)		Chelsea
7	Alex Pritchard	03/05/93	1	(1)		Tottenham
11	Nathan Redmond	06/03/94	3		1	Norwich
8	James Ward-Prowse	01/11/94	1			Southampton
Forwards						
18	Benik Afobe	12/02/93				Wolves
17	Danny Ings	23/07/92	1	(2)		Burnley
9	Harry Kane	28/07/93	3			Tottenham

Italy

No	Name	DoB	Aps	(s)	Gls	Club
Goalkeepers						
1	Francesco Bardi	18/01/92	3			Chievo
20	Nicola Leali	17/02/93				Cesena
14	Marco Sportiello	10/05/92				Atalanta
Defenders						
12	Federico Barba	01/09/93				Empoli
13	Matteo Bianchetti	17/03/93	1			Spezia
3	Cristiano Biraghi	01/09/92	2			Chievo
17	Armando Izzo	02/03/92				Genoa
6	Alessio Romagnoli	12/01/95	2			Sampdoria
5	Daniele Rugani	29/07/94	3			Empoli
2	Stefano Sabelli	13/01/93	1	(1)		Bari
22	Davide Zappacosta	11/06/92	3			Atalanta
Midfielders						
16	Daniele Baselli	12/03/92	1			Atalanta
15	Marco Benassi	08/09/94	2		2	Torino
21	Danilo Cataldi	06/08/94	2	(1)		Lazio
4	Lorenzo Crisetig	20/01/93	2			Cagliari
8	Stefano Sturaro	09/03/93	1			Juventus
7	Federico Viviani	24/03/92	1	(2)		Latina
Forwards						
18	Christian Battocchio	10/02/92	2			Virtus Entella
9	Andrea Belotti	20/12/93	3		1	Palermo
10	Domenico Berardi	01/08/94	3		1	Sassuolo
11	Federico Bernardeschi	16/02/94		(1)		Fiorentina
19	Marcello Trotta	29/09/92	1	(2)		Avellino
23	Simone Verdi	12/07/92		(2)		Empoli

Serbia

No	Name	DoB	Aps	(s)	Gls	Club
Goalkeepers						
1	Marko Dmitrović	24/01/92	3			Charlton (ENG)
12	Nikola Perić	04/02/92				Jagodina
23	Nemanja Stevanović	08/05/92				Čukarički
Defenders						
20	Lazar Ćirković	22/08/92	1			Partizan
5	Uroš Ćosić	24/10/92				Pescara (ITA)
17	Aleksandar Filipović	20/12/94				Jagodina
6	Aleksandar Pantić	11/04/92	2	(1)		Córdoba (ESP)
3	Marko Petković	03/09/92	1	(1)		Crvena zvezda
13	Nemanja Petrović	17/04/92	3			Partizan
15	Uroš Spajić	13/02/93	3			Toulouse (FRA)
22	Filip Stojković	22/01/93	2			Čukarički
Midfielders						
14	Darko Brašanac	12/02/92	2			Partizan
7	Goran Čaušić	05/05/92	3			Eskişehirspor (TUR)
10	Filip Djuričić	30/01/92	3		1	Southampton (ENG)
8	Mirko Ivanić	13/09/93				Vojvodina
18	Miloš Jojić	19/03/92	3			Dortmund (GER)
2	Aleksandar Kovačević	09/01/92	1	(1)		Crvena zvezda
4	Srdjan Mijailović	10/11/93				Kayserispor (TUR)
21	Slavoljub Srnić	12/01/92	2			Čukarički
Forwards						
11	Aleksandar Čavrić	18/05/94	1	(1)		Genk (BEL)
16	Luka Milunović	21/12/92		(3)		Platanias (GRE)
9	Aleksandar Pešić	21/05/92	3			Toulouse (FRA)
19	Nikola Trujić	14/04/92		(2)		Napredak

Germany

No	Name	DoB	Aps	(s)	Gls	Club
Goalkeepers						
23	Timo Horn	12/05/93				Köln
1	Bernd Leno	04/03/92				Leverkusen
12	Marc-André ter Stegen	30/04/92	4			Barcelona (ESP)
Defenders						
4	Matthias Ginter	19/01/94	4		1	Dortmund
3	Christian Günter	28/02/93	3			Freiburg
22	Dominique Heintz	15/08/93	3			Kaiserslautern
16	Robin Knoche	22/05/92	1			Wolfsburg
2	Julian Korb	21/03/92	4			M'gladbach
5	Nico Schulz	01/04/93	3	(1)	1	Hertha
Midfielders						
18	Maximilian Arnold	27/05/94				Wolfsburg
7	Leonardo Bittencourt	19/12/93	1	(3)		Hannover
11	Emre Can	12/01/94	4		1	Liverpool (ENG)
14	Kerem Demirbay	03/07/93				Kaiserslautern
6	Johannes Geis	17/08/93	1	(1)		Mainz
17	Joshua Kimmich	08/02/95	3	(1)		RB Leipzig
21	Felix Klaus	13/09/92		(2)		Freiburg
10	Moritz Leitner	08/12/92	1			Stuttgart
8	Yunus Malli	24/02/92		(1)		Mainz
20	Max Meyer	18/09/95	3	(1)		Schalke
19	Amin Younes	06/08/93	4			Kaiserslautern
Forwards						
15	Serge Gnabry	14/07/95		(1)		Arsenal (ENG)
13	Philipp Hofmann	30/03/93	1	(1)		Kaiserslautern
9	Kevin Volland	30/07/92	4		2	Hoffenheim

Portugal

No	Name	DoB	Aps	(s)	Gls	Club
Goalkeepers						
22	Bruno Varela	04/11/94				Benfica
12	Daniel Fernandes	13/11/92				Osnabrück (GER)
1	José Sá	17/01/93	5			Marítimo
Defenders						
15	Frederico Venâncio	04/02/93				Setúbal
13	João Cancelo	27/05/94		(1)		Valencia (ESP)
4	Paulo Oliveira	08/01/92	5			Sporting
5	Raphael Guerreiro	22/12/93	5			Lorient (FRA)
2	Ricardo Esgaio	16/05/93	5			Académica
3	Tiago Ilori	26/02/93	4			Bordeaux (FRA)
14	Tobias Figueiredo	02/02/94	1	(1)		Sporting
Midfielders						
10	Bernardo Silva	10/08/94	5		1	Monaco (FRA)
23	João Mário	19/01/93	5		2	Sporting
7	Rafa Silva	17/05/93	1	(1)		Braga
16	Rúben Neves	13/03/97		(1)		Porto
8	Sérgio Oliveira	02/06/92	5			Paços Ferreira
20	Tozé	14/01/93		(2)		Estoril
6	William Carvalho	07/04/92	5			Sporting
Forwards						
17	Carlos Mané	11/03/94	1	(1)		Sporting
9	Gonçalo Paciência	01/08/94		(3)	1	Porto
11	Iuri Medeiros	10/07/94		(4)		Arouca
18	Ivan Cavaleiro	18/10/93	4		1	Deportivo (ESP)
21	Ricardo	06/10/93	4		1	Porto
19	Ricardo Horta	15/09/94		(1)	1	Málaga (ESP)

Sweden

No	Name	DoB	Aps	(s)	Gls	Club
Goalkeepers						
1	Patrik Carlgren	08/01/92	5			AIK
23	Andreas Linde	24/07/93				Molde (NOR)
3	Jacob Rinne	20/06/93				Örebro
Defenders						
5	Ludwig Augustinsson	21/04/94	5			København (DEN)
17	Joseph Baffo	07/11/92	3	(1)		Halmstad
4	Filip Helander	22/04/93	4	(1)		Malmo
18	Sebastian Holmén	29/04/92				Elfsborg
21	Pa Konate	25/04/94				Malmö
2	Victor Nilsson-Lindelöf	17/07/94	4	(1)		Benfica (POR)
3	Alexander Milosevic	30/01/92	4			Beşiktaş (TUR)
Midfielders						
22	Simon Gustafsson	11/01/95				Häcken
7	Oscar Hiljemark	28/06/92	5		1	PSV (NED)
8	Abdul Khalili	07/06/92	5			Mersin (TUR)
19	Sam Larsson	10/04/93	1	(2)		Heerenveen (NED)
6	Oscar Lewicki	14/07/92	5			Malmö
15	Kristoffer Olsson	30/06/95				Midtjylland (DEN)
20	Robin Quaison	09/10/93		(4)		Palermo (ITA)
16	Simon Tibbling	07/09/94	3	(1)	2	Groningen (NED)
13	Arber Zeneli	25/02/95				Elfsborg
Forwards						
10	John Guidetti	15/04/92	5		2	Man. City (ENG)
4	Branimir Hrgota	12/01/93	1			M'gladbach (GER)
14	Mikael Ishak	31/03/93		(3)		Randers (DEN)
11	Isaac Kiese Thelin	24/06/92	5		1	Bordeaux (FRA)

Victory sealed with 2-0 win against Russia

France and hosts Greece exit in semi-finals

All four teams finish level on points in Group B

Record seventh title for Spain

Spain, historically the UEFA European Under-19 Championship's dominant force, travelled to Greece having gone two years without success, but they ended that mini-drought by defeating Russia 2-0 in Katerini to claim the trophy for the seventh time in the 14 years of the competition.

As usual, with just eight teams at the finals, a number of big names failed to qualify, among them 2013 champions Serbia, 2014 runners-up Portugal and England. The latter were knocked out in dramatic circumstances by France, who started their finals campaign with a 1-0 win against Austria and slowly gained momentum thereafter, confirming a semi-final place with a game to spare thanks to a 3-1 win against Ukraine. A subsequent 2-0 victory over Greece sealed their position as Group A winners, but despite that defeat the hosts accompanied France through courtesy of a 2-0 win against Ukraine and a goalless draw with Austria.

Group B was extremely tight, with all four teams finishing level on points – a first for the U19 finals. Spain and the Netherlands seized the early initiative with wins against holders Germany (3-0) and Russia (1-0) respectively, but both relinquished their advantage next time

out, Russia running out 3-1 victors against Spain and Gianluca Rizzo's last-gasp goal reviving German hopes at the expense of the Dutch. A superior goal difference enabled Russia to progress as group winners after a 2-2 draw against Germany, while Spain withstood a second-half Netherlands fightback to claim a 1-1 draw that carried them through as runners-up, behind Russia on the head-to-head rule.

Both semi-finals were closely-contested – at least initially. In front of almost 15,000 spectators in Larissa, Greece twice went close against Russia in the first 45 minutes only to fall apart after Nikita Chernov had headed Dmitri

Spain – Under-19 champions of Europe for the seventh time

Khomukha's side into a 50th-minute lead. Aleksei Gasilin added a second goal shortly afterwards and Ramil Sheydaev's penalty – his record-breaking 12th goal of the campaign – made it 3-0. Greece then lost Timos Tselepidis to a red card before Chernov completed their misery with a late fourth to send Russia into their first U19 final.

France and Spain were drawn together in a U19 semi-final for the fourth time, the previous three meetings having all gone to extra time, two to penalties. The encounter in Katerini looked to be heading the same way until Marco Asensio's solo strike gave Spain an 88th-minute lead. The same player added a second deep into added time to send his team into their eighth final.

Russia and Spain were thus re-united nine days after their group encounter, but a repeat result never looked likely, with only four excellent saves from goalkeeper Anton Mitryushkin inside the first half-hour preventing Spain from running away with it. Luis de la Fuente's side finally broke through on 39 minutes with a third goal of the tournament from top scorer Borja Mayoral before substitute Matías Nahuel clinched victory – and that record-extending seventh title – 12 minutes from time.

Qualifying round

Group 1

10-15/10/14 Grevenmacher, Differdange, Beggen
England 3-0 Belarus, Belgium 4-0 Luxembourg, Luxembourg 0-8 England, Belgium 3-2 Belarus, England 4-2 Belgium, Belarus 2-2 Luxembourg

		Pld	W	D	L	F	A	Pts
1	England	3	3	0	0	15	2	9
2	Belgium	3	2	0	1	9	6	6
3	Belarus	3	0	1	2	4	8	1
4	Luxembourg	3	0	1	2	2	14	1

Group 2

09-14/10/14 Jelgava, Jurmala
Germany 6-0 Kazakhstan, Austria 1-0 Latvia, Austria 1-0 Kazakhstan, Latvia 0-3 Germany, Germany 1-5 Austria, Kazakhstan 0-3 Latvia

		Pld	W	D	L	F	A	Pts
1	Austria	3	3	0	0	7	1	9
2	Germany	3	2	0	1	10	5	6
3	Latvia	3	1	0	2	3	4	3
4	Kazakhstan	3	0	0	3	0	10	0

Group 3

07-12/10/14 Dugopolje, Sinj, Sibenik
Turkey 7-3 Iceland, Croatia 1-0 Estonia, Turkey 0-0 Estonia, Iceland 1-4 Croatia, Croatia 0-0 Turkey, Estonia 3-0 Iceland

		Pld	W	D	L	F	A	Pts
1	Croatia	3	2	1	0	5	1	7
2	Turkey	3	1	2	0	7	3	5
3	Estonia	3	1	1	1	3	1	4
4	Iceland	3	0	0	3	4	14	0

Group 4

10-15/11/14 Tatabanya, Dunaujvaros
Slovakia 2-1 Slovenia, Hungary 1-1 Azerbaijan, Slovakia 4-1 Azerbaijan, Slovenia 1-1 Hungary, Hungary 0-3 Slovakia, Azerbaijan 3-2 Slovenia

		Pld	W	D	L	F	A	Pts
1	Slovakia	3	3	0	0	9	2	9
2	Azerbaijan	3	1	1	1	5	7	4
3	Hungary	3	0	2	1	2	5	2
4	Slovenia	3	0	1	2	4	6	1

Group 5

09-14/10/14 Dungannon, Portadown, Belfast
Czech Republic 2-0 Northern Ireland, Russia 7-0 Faroe Islands, Russia 5-2 Northern Ireland, Faroe Islands 0-2 Czech Republic, Czech Republic 0-3 Russia, Northern Ireland 3-0 Faroe Islands

		Pld	W	D	L	F	A	Pts
1	Russia	3	3	0	0	15	2	9
2	Czech Republic	3	2	0	1	4	3	6
3	Northern Ireland	3	1	0	2	5	7	3
4	Faroe Islands	3	0	0	3	0	12	0

Group 6

13-18/11/14 Wexford, Waterford, Tramore
Switzerland 8-0 Gibraltar, Republic of Ireland 1-0 Malta, Republic of Ireland 4-1 Gibraltar, Malta 1-7 Switzerland, Switzerland 1-1 Republic of Ireland, Gibraltar 1-3 Malta

		Pld	W	D	L	F	A	Pts
1	Switzerland	3	2	1	0	16	2	7
2	Republic of Ireland	3	2	1	0	6	2	7
3	Malta	3	1	0	2	4	9	3
4	Gibraltar	3	0	0	3	2	15	0

Group 7

12-17/11/14 Lagos, Ferreira, Albufeira, Parchal
Denmark 1-0 Albania, Portugal 2-1 Wales, Denmark 4-0 Wales, Albania 1-4 Portugal, Portugal 2-1 Denmark, Wales 2-1 Albania

		Pld	W	D	L	F	A	Pts
1	Portugal	3	3	0	0	8	3	9
2	Denmark	3	2	0	1	6	2	6
3	Wales	3	1	0	2	3	7	3
4	Albania	3	0	0	3	2	7	0

Group 8

12-17/11/14 Shefayim, Netanya
Ukraine 2-2 Sweden, Israel 2-1 Bulgaria, Sweden 1-0 Israel, Ukraine 5-1 Bulgaria, Israel 0-5 Ukraine, Bulgaria 1-5 Sweden

		Pld	W	D	L	F	A	Pts
1	Ukraine	3	2	1	0	12	3	7
2	Sweden	3	2	1	0	8	3	7
3	Israel	3	1	0	2	2	7	3
4	Bulgaria	3	0	0	3	3	12	0

Group 9

10-15/10/14 Novi Sad, Stara Pazova
Italy 3-0 Armenia, Serbia 4-0 San Marino, Italy 6-0 San Marino, Armenia 0-1 Serbia, Serbia 1-3 Italy, San Marino 0-2 Armenia

		Pld	W	D	L	F	A	Pts
1	Italy	3	3	0	0	12	1	9
2	Serbia	3	2	0	1	6	3	6
3	Armenia	3	1	0	2	2	4	3
4	San Marino	3	0	0	3	0	12	0

Group 10

09-14/10/14 Grudziadz, Inowroclaw, Tuchola
Netherlands 7-0 Andorra, Netherlands 3-0 Moldova, Andorra 0-3 Poland, Poland 1-2 Netherlands, Moldova 2-1 Andorra

		Pld	W	D	L	F	A	Pts
1	Netherlands	3	3	0	0	12	1	9
2	Poland	3	2	0	1	8	3	6
3	Moldova	3	1	0	2	3	8	3
4	Andorra	3	0	0	3	1	12	0

Group 11

08-13/10/14 Tbilisi
Romania 0-1 Cyprus, Georgia 0-2 Montenegro, Romania 0-1 Montenegro, Cyprus 1-3 Georgia, Georgia 3-1 Romania, Montenegro 6-3 Cyprus

		Pld	W	D	L	F	A	Pts
1	Montenegro	3	3	0	0	9	3	9
2	Georgia	3	2	0	1	6	4	6
3	Cyprus	3	1	0	2	5	9	3
4	Romania	3	0	0	3	1	5	0

Group 12

08-13/10/14 Skopje
Bosnia & Herzegovina 5-0 Liechtenstein, Liechtenstein 0-6 France, France 0-0 Bosnia & Herzegovina

		Pld	W	D	L	F	A	Pts
1	France	3	2	1	0	8	1	7
2	Bosnia & Herzegovina	3	1	2	0	6	1	5
3	FYR Macedonia	3	1	1	1	7	4	4
4	Liechtenstein	3	0	0	3	1	16	0

Group 13

07-12/10/14 Kaunas, Alytus
Scotland 2-2 Finland, Norway 2-0 Lithuania, Norway 0-0 Finland, Lithuania 0-0 Scotland, Scotland 1-1 Norway, Finland 0-3 Lithuania

		Pld	W	D	L	F	A	Pts
1	Norway	3	1	2	0	3	1	5
2	Lithuania	3	1	1	1	3	2	4
3	Scotland	3	0	3	0	3	3	3
4	Finland	3	0	2	1	2	5	2

Elite round

Group 1

29/05-03/06/15 Tbilisi
Portugal 6-1 Turkey, Spain 4-1 Georgia, Spain 5-0 Turkey, Georgia 2-3 Portugal, Portugal 0-4 Spain, Turkey 1-2 Georgia

		Pld	W	D	L	F	A	Pts
1	Spain	3	3	0	0	13	1	9
2	Portugal	3	2	0	1	9	7	6
3	Georgia	3	1	0	2	5	8	3
4	Turkey	3	0	0	3	2	13	0

Group 2

26-31/03/15 Mannheim, Sandhausen, Walldorf
Slovakia 1-1 Germany, Republic of Ireland 0-1 Czech Republic, Germany 3-2 Republic of Ireland, Slovakia 3-0 Czech Republic, Republic of Ireland 2-2 Slovakia, Czech Republic 0-6 Germany

		Pld	W	D	L	F	A	Pts
1	Germany	3	2	1	0	10	3	7
2	Slovakia	3	1	2	0	6	3	5
3	Czech Republic	3	1	0	2	1	9	3
4	Republic of Ireland	3	0	1	2	4	6	1

Group 3

26-31/03/15 Norrkoping, Atvidaberg
Sweden 1-1 Lithuania, Russia 1-0 Belgium, Russia 6-0 Lithuania, Belgium 2-0 Sweden, Sweden 1-3 Russia, Lithuania 2-2 Belgium

		Pld	W	D	L	F	A	Pts
1	Russia	3	3	0	0	10	1	9
2	Belgium	3	1	1	1	4	3	4
3	Lithuania	3	0	2	1	3	9	2
4	Sweden	3	0	1	2	2	6	1

Group 4

26-31/03/15 Assen, Harkema
Switzerland 0-1 Norway, Netherlands 1-0 Serbia, Serbia 3-1 Switzerland, Netherlands 1-1 Norway, Switzerland 0-4 Netherlands, Norway 2-4 Serbia

		Pld	W	D	L	F	A	Pts
1	Netherlands	3	2	1	0	6	1	7
2	Serbia	3	2	0	1	7	4	6
3	Norway	3	1	1	1	4	5	4
4	Switzerland	3	0	0	3	1	8	0

Group 5

14-19/05/15 Siroki Brijeg, Mostar
Montenegro 2-1 Poland, Ukraine 1-1 Bosnia & Herzegovina, Montenegro 1-0 Bosnia & Herzegovina, Poland 2-4 Ukraine, Ukraine 2-0 Montenegro, Bosnia & Herzegovina 2-0 Poland

		Pld	W	D	L	F	A	Pts
1	Ukraine	3	2	1	0	7	3	7
2	Montenegro	3	2	0	1	3	3	6
3	Bosnia & Herzegovina	3	1	1	1	3	2	4
4	Poland	3	0	0	3	3	8	0

UEFA European Under-19 Championship

Group 6

26-31/03/15 Lindabrunn, Schwechat-Rannersdorf, Wiener Neustadt
Italy 2-2 Croatia, Austria 1-2 Scotland, Italy 0-0 Scotland, Croatia 0-2 Austria, Austria 2-1 Italy, Scotland 1-1 Croatia

		Pld	W	D	L	F	A	Pts
1	Austria	3	2	0	1	5	3	6
2	Scotland	3	1	2	0	3	2	5
3	Italy	3	0	2	1	3	4	2
4	Croatia	3	0	2	1	3	5	2

Group 7

26-31/03/15 Bayeux, Saint-Lo, Flers
England 3-2 Denmark, France 2-0 Azerbaijan, Denmark 0-2 France, England 1-0 Azerbaijan, France 2-1 England, Azerbaijan 0-3 Denmark

		Pld	W	D	L	F	A	Pts
1	France	3	3	0	0	6	1	9
2	England	3	2	0	1	5	4	6
3	Denmark	3	1	0	2	5	5	3
4	Azerbaijan	3	0	0	3	0	6	0

Top goalscorers (Qualifying/Elite rounds)

10 Ramil Sheydaev (Russia)

5 Nicolas Hunziker (Switzerland)
Federico Bonazzoli (Italy)
Marko Kvasina (Austria)
Tomáš Vestenický (Slovakia)
Abdelhak Nouri (Netherlands)
Patrick Roberts (England)

Final tournament

Group A

06/07/15, Veria, Veria
Greece 2-0 Ukraine
Goals: 1-0 Orfanidis 20, 2-0 Karachalios 76
Referee: Taylor (ENG)

06/07/15, FC Katerini, Katerini
Austria 0-1 France
Goal: 0-1 Blin 34
Referee: Kabakov (BUL)

09/07/15, AEL FC Arena, Larissa
Ukraine 1-3 France
Goals: 0-1 Guirassy 31, 1-1 Zubkov 55, 1-2 Dembélé 62, 1-3 Lukyanchuk 90+2(og)
Referee: Treimanis (LVA)

09/07/15, AEL FC Arena, Larissa
Greece 0-0 Austria
Referee: Ekberg (SWE)

12/07/15, FC Katerini, Katerini
France 2-0 Greece
Goals: 1-0 Diakhaby 5, 2-0 Dembélé 64
Referee: Guida (ITA)

12/07/15, Veria, Veria
Ukraine 2-2 Austria
Goals: 1-0 Zubkov 14, 1-1 Kvasina 47, 2-1 Luchkevych 63, 2-2 Kvasina 87
Referee: Bognar (HUN)

		Pld	W	D	L	F	A	Pts
1	France	3	3	0	0	6	1	9
2	Greece	3	1	1	1	2	2	4
3	Austria	3	0	2	1	2	3	2
4	Ukraine	3	0	1	2	3	7	1

Group B

07/07/15, AEL FC Arena, Larissa
Netherlands 1-0 Russia
Goal: 1-0 Van Amersfoort 44
Referee: Bognar (HUN)

07/07/15, AEL FC Arena, Larissa
Germany 0-3 Spain
Goals: 0-1 Merino 8, 0-2 Mayoral 72(p), 0-3 Matías Nahuel 90+3
Referee: Guida (ITA)

10/07/15, Veria, Veria
Spain 1-3 Russia
Goals: 1-0 Mayoral 13, 1-1 Barinov 37, 1-2 Gasilin 48, 1-3 Sheydaev 54
Referee: Kabakov (BUL)

10/07/15, FC Katerini, Katerini
Germany 1-0 Netherlands
Goal: 1-0 Rizzo 89
Referee: Taylor (ENG)

13/07/15, FC Katerini, Katerini
Russia 2-2 Germany
Goals: 0-1 Kehrer 12, 1-1 Kehrer 32(og), 2-1 Bezdenezhnykh 45+2, 2-2 Werner 65
Referee: Ekberg (SWE)

13/07/15, Veria, Veria
Spain 1-1 Netherlands
Goals: 1-0 Mirani 8(og), 1-1 Van Amersfoort 54(p)
Referee: Treimanis (LVA)

		Pld	W	D	L	F	A	Pts
1	Russia	3	1	1	1	5	4	4
2	Spain	3	1	1	1	5	4	4
3	Netherlands	3	1	1	1	2	2	4
4	Germany	3	1	1	1	3	5	4

Semi-finals

16/07/15, AEL FC Arena, Larissa
Russia 4-0 Greece
Goals: 1-0 Chernov 50, 2-0 Gasilin 52, 3-0 Sheydaev 64(p), 4-0 Chernov 79
Referee: Bognar (HUN)

16/07/15, FC Katerini, Katerini
France 0-2 Spain
Goals: 0-1 Asensio 88, 0-2 Asensio 90+5
Referee: Ekberg (SWE)

Final

19/07/15, FC Katerini, Katerini (att: 4,149)
Spain 2-0 Russia
Goals: 1-0 Mayoral 39, 2-0 Matías Nahuel 78
Referee: Taylor (ENG)
Spain: Sivera, Caricol, Meré, Merino, Dani Ceballos, Mayoral (Carlos Fernández 90), Asensio, Hernández, Vallejo, Pedraza (Matías Nahuel 74), Borja (Marín 81). Coach: Luis de la Fuente (ESP)
Russia: Mitryushkin, Makarov, Chernov, Khodzhaniyazov, Yakuba, Guliev, Barinov, Sheydaev, Golovin (Zuev 46), Melkadze (Bezdenezhnykh 62), Gasilin (Zhemaletdinov 70). Coach: Dmitri Khomukha (RUS)
Yellow cards: Golovin 34 (Russia), Khodzhaniyazov 45+1 (Russia), Guliev 83 (Russia), Matías Nahuel 90+1 (Spain)

Top goalscorers (Final tournament)

3 Borja Mayoral (Spain)

2 Marko Kvasina (Austria)
Moussa Dembele (France)
Pelle van Amersfoort (Netherlands)
Nikita Chernov (Russia)
Aleksei Gasilin (Russia)
Ramil Sheydaev (Russia)
Marco Asensio (Spain)
Matías Nahuel (Spain)
Olexandr Zubkov (Ukraine)

Squads/Appearances/Goals

Austria

No	Name	DoB	Aps	(s)	Gls	Club
Goalkeepers						
1	Osman Hadzikic	12/03/96	1			Austria Wien
21	Alexander Schlager	01/02/96	2			Grödig
Defenders						
15	David Domej	08/01/96	3			Hajduk Split (CRO)
11	Petar Gluhakovic	25/03/96	2			Austria Wien
5	David Gugganig	10/02/97	3			Liefering
16	Manuel Haas	07/05/96	2			Kapfenberg
3	Stefan Peric	13/02/97	3			Stuttgart (GER)
4	Maximilian Ullmann	17/06/96	1			LASK
Midfielders						
8	Sascha Horvath	22/08/96	3	(1)		Sturm
12	Philipp Malicsek	03/06/97	1	(1)		Admira
18	Dominik Prokop	02/06/97	2	(1)		Austria Wien
10	Xaver Schlager	28/09/97	3			Liefering
6	Lukas Tursch	29/03/96	3			Austria Lustenau
Forwards						
17	Felipe Dorta	17/06/96	1			LASK
7	Adrian Grbic	04/08/96	1	(2)		Stuttgart (GER)
9	Marko Kvasina	20/12/96	3		2	Austria Wien
20	Tobias Pellegrini	03/04/96		(3)		LASK
19	Daniel Ripic	14/03/96	3			Stuttgart (GER)

France

No	Name	DoB	Aps	(s)	Gls	Club
Goalkeepers						
1	Florian Escales	03/02/96	3			Marseille
16	Bingourou Kamara	21/10/96	1			Tours
Defenders						
4	Mouctar Diakhaby	19/12/96	4		1	Lyon
5	Abdou Diallo	04/05/96	3			Monaco
2	Angelo Fulgini	20/08/96	4			Valenciennes
14	Lucas Hernández	14/02/96	3			Atlético (ESP)
15	Benjamin Pavard	28/03/96	1	(1)		LOSC
3	Nicolas Senzemba	25/03/96	1			Sochaux
Midfielders						
13	Alexis Blin	16/09/96	3		1	Toulouse
6	Olivier Kemen	20/07/96	3			Newcastle (ENG)
8	Samed Kilic	28/01/96	3	(1)		Auxerre
11	Neal Maupay	14/08/96	2			Nice
18	Marcus Thuram	06/08/97	1	(2)		Sochaux
17	Lucas Tousart	29/04/97	2	(1)		Valenciennes
Forwards						
7	Maxwell Cornet	27/09/96	3			Lyon
10	Kingsley Coman	13/06/96	3	(1)		Juventus (ITA)
12	Moussa Dembélé	12/07/96	1	(3)	2	Fulham (ENG)
9	Sehrou Guirassy	12/03/96	3	(1)	1	Laval

Germany

No	Name	DoB	Aps	(s)	Gls	Club
Goalkeepers						
1	Marius Funk	01/01/96	3			Stuttgart
12	Raif Husic	05/02/96				Bremen
Defenders						
20	Jannik Dehm	02/05/96				Karlsruhe
18	Jonas Föhrenbach	26/01/96	3			Freiburg
19	Niko Kijewski	28/03/96				Braunschweig
2	Lukas Klostermann	03/06/96	3			RB Leipzig
3	Lukas Klünter	26/05/96	3			Köln
5	Jonathan Tah	11/02/96	3			Hamburg
Midfielders						
7	Nadiem Amiri	27/10/96	3			Hoffenheim
15	Boubacar Barry	15/04/96	1			Karlsruhe
13	Max Christiansen	25/09/96	2			Ingolstadt
10	Lucas Cueto	24/03/96	1	(2)		Köln
16	Erdal Öztürk	07/02/96		(3)		Hoffenheim
6	Thilo Kehrer	21/09/96	3		1	Schalke
Forwards						
14	Gianluca Rizzo	06/11/96		(3)	1	M'gladbach
11	Leroy Sané	11/01/96	3			Schalke
8	Luca Waldschmidt	19/05/96	2	(1)		Frankfurt
9	Timo Werner	06/03/96	3		1	Stuttgart

Netherlands

No	Name	DoB	Aps	(s)	Gls	Club
Goalkeepers						
1	Joël Drommel	16/11/96	3			Twente
16	Yanick van Osch	24/03/97				PSV
Defenders						
3	Terry Lartey Sanniez	10/08/96	3			Ajax
13	Julian Lelieveld	24/11/97	1			Vitesse
15	Augustine Loof	01/01/96	1	(2)		PSV
4	Damon Mirani	13/05/96	3			Ajax
2	Leeroy Owusu	13/08/96	2			Ajax
5	Kenneth Paal	24/06/97	2			PSV
Midfielders						
10	Frenkie de Jong	12/05/97	3			Willem II
6	Laros Duarte	28/02/97	2			PSV
8	Abdelhak Nouri	02/04/97	3			Ajax
17	Thomas Ouwejan	30/09/96	1	(2)		AZ
18	Michel Vlap	02/06/97		(1)		Heerenveen
Forwards						
14	Tarik Kada	26/05/96	1	(1)		Heerenveen
7	Issa Kallon	03/01/96	2	(1)		Utrecht
12	Gervane Kastaneer	09/06/96		(2)		Den Haag
11	Bilal Ould-Chikh	28/07/97	3			Twente
9	Pelle van Amersfoort	01/04/96	3		2	Heerenveen

Spain

No	Name	DoB	Aps	(s)	Gls	Club
Goalkeepers						
1	Antonio Sivera	11/08/96	5			Valencia
13	Unai Simón	11/06/97				Athletic
Defenders						
18	Borja	16/03/97	4			Racing Club
3	Aaron Caricol	22/04/97	5			Espanyol
2	Antonio Marín	17/06/96	1	(1)		Almería
4	Jorge Meré	17/04/97	5			Sporting Gijón
5	José Carlos Ramírez	10/05/96				Betis
15	Jesús Vallejo	05/01/97	5			Zaragoza
Midfielders						
16	Pape Cheikh	08/08/97		(4)		Celta
8	Dani Ceballos	07/08/96	5			Betis
14	Rodrigo Hernández	22/06/96	5			Villarreal
11	Matías Nahuel	22/11/96		(5)	2	Villarreal
6	Mikel Merino	22/06/96	5		1	Osasuna
Forwards						
10	Marco Asensio	21/01/96	5		2	Mallorca
19	Carlos Fernández	22/05/96		(5)		Sevilla
7	David Concha	20/11/96	1			Racing Club
9	Borja Mayoral	05/04/97	5		3	Real Madrid
17	Alfonso Pedraza	09/04/96	4			Villarreal

Greece

No	Name	DoB	Aps	(s)	Gls	Club
Goalkeepers						
1	Konstantinos Kotsaris	25/07/96	4			Panathinaikos
13	Christos Theodorakis	17/09/96		(1)		Atromitos
Defenders						
14	Alkis Markopouliotis	13/08/96	2	(1)		AEK Athens
4	Albert Roussos	22/02/96	4			Juventus (ITA)
2	Manolis Saliakas	12/09/96	3	(1)		Olympiacos
5	Timos Tselepidis	02/02/96	4			PAOK
3	Kostas Tsimikas	12/05/96	3	(1)		Olympiacos
Midfielders						
6	Zisis Karachalios	10/01/96	4		1	Olympiacos
16	Giorgos Kiriakopoulos	05/02/96	4			Asteras
23	Vasilis Miliotis	29/02/96		(1)		Asteras
10	Petros Orfanidis	23/03/96	2	(2)	1	Xanthi
20	Stilianos Pozoglou	22/01/96	1	(1)		PAOK
8	Paschalis Staikos	08/02/96	4			Panathinaikos
15	Nikos Vasaitis	14/04/96		(1)		PAOK
Forwards						
9	Efthimios Koulouris	06/03/96	3			PAOK
11	Panagiotis Kynigopoulos	24/09/96	3			Aiginiakos
17	Dimitris Mavrias	03/10/96	1	(1)		Anagennisi Karditsas
19	Nikolas Vergos	13/01/96	2	(2)		Olympiacos

Russia

No	Name	DoB	Aps	(s)	Gls	Club
Goalkeepers						
1	Anton Mitryushkin	08/02/96	5			Spartak Moskva
12	Maksim Rudakov	22/01/96				Zenit
Defenders						
3	Nikita Chernov	14/01/96	5		2	CSKA Moskva
23	Vasily Cherov	13/01/96		(1)		Krasnodar
4	Dzhamaldin Khodzhaniyazov	18/07/96	3			Zenit
14	Aleksandr Likhachev	22/07/96	1			Spartak Moskva
2	Sergei Makarov	03/10/96	5			Lokomotiv Moskva
5	Denis Yakuba	26/05/96	5			Kuban
Midfielders						
8	Dmitri Barinov	11/09/96	5		1	Lokomotiv Moskva
17	Igor Bezdenezhnykh	08/08/96	2	(2)	1	Ufa
10	Aleksandr Golovin	30/05/96	5			CSKA Moskva
16	Georgi Melkadze	04/04/97	4	(1)		Spartak Moskva
15	Ilmir Nurisov	05/08/96		(3)		Kuban
Forwards						
19	Aleksei Gasilin	01/03/96	4	(1)	2	Zenit
7	Ayaz Guliev	27/11/96	5			Spartak Moskva
9	Ramil Sheydaev	15/03/96	5		2	Zenit
21	Rifat Zhemaletdinov	20/09/96		(4)		Lokomotiv Moskva
11	Aleksandr Zuev	26/06/96	1	(3)		Spartak Moskva

Ukraine

No	Name	DoB	Aps	(s)	Gls	Club
Goalkeepers						
12	Oleh Mozil	07/04/96				Karpaty
1	Vadym Soldatenko	28/05/96	3			Dynamo Kyiv
Defenders						
6	Ihor Kyryukhantsev	29/01/96	3			Shakhtar Donetsk
16	Pavlo Lukyanchuk	19/05/96	3			Dynamo Kyiv
4	Mykola Matviyenko	02/05/96	3			Shakhtar Donetsk
21	Bohdan Mykhaylichenko	21/03/97	2	(1)		Dynamo Kyiv
2	Olexandr Osman	18/04/96	1			Metalist
13	Ivan Zotko	09/07/96				Metalist
Midfielders						
18	Dmytro Klots	15/04/96	2			Karpaty
10	Viktor Kovalenko	14/02/96	2			Shakhtar Donetsk
14	Valeriy Luchkevych	11/01/96	2	(1)	1	Dnipro
20	Viktor Tsygankov	15/11/97	1	(2)		Dynamo Kyiv
8	Beka Vachiberadze	05/03/96	2			Shakhtar Donetsk
17	Olexandr Zinchenko	15/12/96	3			Ufa (RUS)
Forwards						
7	Denys Arendaruk	16/04/96	1	(1)		Shakhtar Donctsk
11	Artem Besedin	31/03/96	1	(2)		Metalist
9	Andriy Boryachuk	23/04/96	2	(1)		Shakhtar Donetsk
22	Olexandr Zubkov	03/08/96	2	(1)	2	Shakhtar Donetsk

Expanded event favours France

The first 16-team UEFA European Under-17 Championship finals for 13 years turned out to be France's tournament as they impressively swept all before them in Bulgaria.

Not since a squad containing Karim Benzema, Hatem Ben Arfa, Jérémy Menez and Samir Nasri prevailed in 2004 had Les Petits Bleus experienced U17 success. That changed in Burgas, where Jean-Claude Giuntini's side overcame four-time finalists Germany 4-1 to secure France's second title at this level. As he had been throughout the competition, ace marksman Odsonne Edouard was France's inspiration, scoring the first hat-trick in an Under-17 final.

Giuntini's team delivered a statement of intent in their opening match, putting five without reply past Group C opponents Scotland. Edouard supplied the third goal – the first of eight he would chalk up in Bulgaria, a finals record – as France raced into a 4-0 lead with just 35 minutes on the clock. Germany, meanwhile, got their Group B campaign up and running with a 2-0 win against Belgium.

The second biggest crowd of the tournament turned up for the hosts' Group A opener. Most of the 10,640 fans – a record for a U17 fixture other than a final –

who had made their way to Stara Zagora's Beroe Stadium went home disappointed, however, as Croatia ran out 2-0 victors. Germany and France's next successes were less emphatic, 1-0 against Slovenia and Russia respectively, while Belgium revived their hopes by seeing off the Czech Republic 3-0 in Sozopol and Croatia became the first team to qualify for the last eight after overcoming Austria 1-0.

France and Germany then made it a perfect group stage of maximum points and no goals conceded. The former overcame Greece, whose defeat enabled Russia, 2-0 winners against Scotland, to finish runners-up in Group C. Felix Passlack struck twice in a 4-0 stroll as Germany made short work of the Czechs.

The first two quarter-finals went to penalties, Belgium eliminating Croatia and

Germany ousting Spain. Russia rode their luck as they ended the reign of holders and Group D winners England, with Aleksei Tataev heading the only goal four minutes after Aleksandr Maksimenko had saved Nathan Holland's penalty, while Edouard scored a back-heeled double in France's comprehensive 3-0 defeat of Italy.

Both semi-finals were closely contested. France conceded their first goal, a header from Belgium's Rubin Seigers, but they survived a shoot-out in which seven of the ten spot kicks were either missed or saved. Luca Zidane, son of the great Zinédine, stopped three of them, with Edouard converting the decisive penalty. Janni Serra's 68th-minute header against Russia smoothed Germany's passage to the final on the back of a fifth straight clean sheet.

Edouard shone even brighter in the denouement at Lazur Stadium in front of 14,680 spectators. Germany's previously impenetrable defence had no answer to the forward's power and finishing as he plundered a trophy-winning treble. Not surprisingly, coach Giuntini was full of high praise for his match winner, claiming that he can "afford to have very big ambitions". As a prelude to his career, the tournament could not have gone much better for the Paris Saint-Germain youngster – nor, indeed, for his triumphant team.

France – 2015 European U17 champions

UEFA European Under-17 Championship

Qualifying round

Group 1

22-27/09/14 Galway, Athlone, Longford
Scotland 4-0 Faroe Islands, Republic of Ireland 5-0 Gibraltar, Scotland 4-0 Gibraltar, Faroe Islands 2-4 Republic of Ireland, Republic of Ireland 0-0 Scotland, Gibraltar 0-0 Faroe Islands

	Pld	W	D	L	F	A	Pts
1 Scotland	3	2	1	0	8	0	7
2 Republic of Ireland	3	2	1	0	9	2	7
3 Faroe Islands	3	0	1	2	2	8	1
4 Gibraltar	3	0	1	2	0	9	1

Group 2

26-31/10/14 Tbilisi
Poland 4-0 Estonia, Georgia 3-0 Liechtenstein, Poland 4-0 Liechtenstein, Estonia 1-2 Georgia, Georgia 0-1 Poland, Liechtenstein 0-2 Estonia

	Pld	W	D	L	F	A	Pts
1 Poland	3	3	0	0	9	0	9
2 Georgia	3	2	0	1	5	2	6
3 Estonia	3	1	0	2	3	6	3
4 Liechtenstein	3	0	0	3	0	9	0

Group 3

15-20/10/14 Vadul lui Voda, Chisinau, Orhei
Iceland 0-0 Moldova, Italy 3-0 Armenia, Iceland 2-0 Armenia, Moldova 0-3 Italy, Italy 1-1 Iceland, Armenia 0-4 Moldova

	Pld	W	D	L	F	A	Pts
1 Italy	3	2	1	0	7	1	7
2 Iceland	3	1	2	0	3	1	5
3 Moldova	3	1	1	1	4	3	4
4 Armenia	3	0	0	3	0	9	0

Group 4

25-30/10/14 Paphos
England 4-1 Cyprus, France 3-0 FYR Macedonia, England 1-0 FYR Macedonia, Cyprus 0-4 France, France 1-3 England, FYR Macedonia 1-2 Cyprus

	Pld	W	D	L	F	A	Pts
1 England	3	3	0	0	8	2	9
2 France	3	2	0	1	8	3	6
3 Cyprus	3	1	0	2	3	9	3
4 FYR Macedonia	3	0	0	3	1	6	0

Group 5

25-30/09/14 Jelgava, Riga
Ukraine 0-0 Greece, Sweden 2-1 Latvia, Greece 0-0 Sweden, Ukraine 0-0 Latvia, Sweden 0-0 Ukraine, Latvia 0-1 Greece

	Pld	W	D	L	F	A	Pts
1 Sweden	3	1	2	0	2	1	5
2 Greece	3	1	2	0	1	0	5
3 Ukraine	3	0	3	0	0	0	3
4 Latvia	3	0	1	2	1	3	1

Group 6

19-24/09/14 Kidricevo, Bakovci, Radenci
Turkey 0-5 Slovenia, Portugal 3-0 Northern Ireland, Turkey 3-4 Northern Ireland, Slovenia 0-1 Portugal, Portugal 1-0 Turkey, Northern Ireland 0-0 Slovenia

	Pld	W	D	L	F	A	Pts
1 Portugal	3	3	0	0	5	0	9
2 Slovenia	3	1	1	1	5	1	4
3 Northern Ireland	3	1	1	1	4	6	4
4 Turkey	3	0	0	3	3	10	0

Kiril Ristovski (left) and Layton Ndukwu in action during the Group 4 qualifier between FYR Macedonia and England

Group 7

21-26/10/14 Tatabanya, Telki
Croatia 8-1 Kazakhstan, Hungary 1-0 Israel, Croatia 0-0 Israel, Kazakhstan 0-1 Hungary, Hungary 1-2 Croatia, Israel 6-0 Kazakhstan

	Pld	W	D	L	F	A	Pts
1 Croatia	3	2	1	0	10	2	7
2 Hungary	3	2	0	1	2	3	6
3 Israel	3	1	1	1	6	1	4
4 Kazakhstan	3	0	0	3	1	15	0

Group 8

17-22/10/14 Stara Pazova, Jakovo
Serbia 1-0 Malta, Netherlands 2-0 Finland, Serbia 1-0 Finland, Malta 0-1 Netherlands, Netherlands 1-0 Serbia, Finland 2-1 Malta

	Pld	W	D	L	F	A	Pts
1 Netherlands	3	3	0	0	4	0	9
2 Serbia	3	2	0	1	2	1	6
3 Finland	3	1	0	2	2	4	3
4 Malta	3	0	0	3	1	4	0

Group 9

08-13/10/14 Pogradec, Korca
Austria 2-0 San Marino, Norway 3-0 Albania, San Marino 0-4 Norway, Austria 2-0 Albania, Norway 0-2 Austria, Albania 5-1 San Marino

	Pld	W	D	L	F	A	Pts
1 Austria	3	3	0	0	6	0	9
2 Norway	3	2	0	1	7	2	6
3 Albania	3	1	0	2	5	6	3
4 San Marino	3	0	0	3	1	11	0

Group 10

23-28/10/14 Tessenderlo, Eisden, Beringen
Switzerland 0-1 Bosnia & Herzegovina, Belgium 3-0 Azerbaijan, Belgium 4-1 Bosnia & Herzegovina, Azerbaijan 2-1 Switzerland, Switzerland 1-0 Belgium, Bosnia & Herzegovina 1-1 Azerbaijan

	Pld	W	D	L	F	A	Pts
1 Belgium	3	2	0	1	7	2	6
2= Azerbaijan	3	1	1	1	3	5	4
Bosnia & Herzegovina	3	1	1	1	3	5	4
4 Switzerland	3	1	0	2	2	3	3

Group 11

24-29/10/14 Senec, Velky Biel
Slovakia 1-0 Luxembourg, Spain 2-1 Lithuania, Slovakia 2-0 Lithuania, Luxembourg 0-3 Spain, Spain 3-1 Slovakia, Lithuania 0-3 Luxembourg

	Pld	W	D	L	F	A	Pts
1 Spain	3	3	0	0	8	2	9
2 Slovakia	3	2	0	1	4	3	6
3 Luxembourg	3	1	0	2	3	4	3
4 Lithuania	3	0	0	3	1	7	0

Group 12

25-30/09/14 Andorra la Vella
Czech Republic 2-1 Romania, Denmark 3-1 Andorra, Romania 6-1 Denmark, Czech Republic 1-0 Andorra, Denmark 0-1 Czech Republic, Andorra 0-1 Romania

	Pld	W	D	L	F	A	Pts
1 Czech Republic	3	3	0	0	4	1	9
2 Romania	3	2	0	1	8	3	6
3 Denmark	3	1	0	2	4	8	3
4 Andorra	3	0	0	3	1	5	0

Group 13

19-24/10/14 Minsk, Molodechno
Russia 0-0 Wales, Belarus 1-0 Montenegro, Russia 2-0 Montenegro, Wales 1-2 Belarus, Belarus 1-2 Russia, Montenegro 1-2 Wales

	Pld	W	D	L	F	A	Pts
1 Russia	3	2	1	0	4	1	7
2 Belarus	3	2	0	1	4	3	6
3 Wales	3	1	1	1	3	3	4
4 Montenegro	3	0	0	3	1	5	0

Elite round

Group 1

20-25/03/15 Benidorm, Alcoy
France 1-0 Israel, Spain 2-0 Sweden, Sweden 1-7 France, Spain 0-0 Israel, France 1-1 Spain, Israel 2-0 Sweden

	Pld	W	D	L	F	A	Pts
1 France	3	2	1	0	9	2	7
2 Spain	3	1	2	0	3	1	5
3 Israel	3	1	1	1	2	1	4
4 Sweden	3	0	0	3	1	11	0

Group 2

17-22/03/15 Baku
Portugal 0-0 Serbia, Croatia 4-0 Azerbaijan, Serbia 0-3 Croatia, Portugal 3-0 Azerbaijan, Croatia 1-0 Portugal, Azerbaijan 0-4 Serbia

	Pld	W	D	L	F	A	Pts
1 Croatia	3	3	0	0	8	0	9
2 Portugal	3	1	1	1	3	1	4
3 Serbia	3	1	1	1	4	3	4
4 Azerbaijan	3	0	0	3	0	11	0

Group 3

12-17/03/15 Gendt, Schijndel
Belgium 4-0 Northern Ireland, Netherlands 2-0 Georgia, Georgia 0-4 Belgium, Netherlands 1-1 Northern Ireland, Belgium 0-0 Netherlands, Northern Ireland 2-4 Georgia

	Pld	W	D	L	F	A	Pts
1 Belgium	3	2	1	0	8	0	7
2 Netherlands	3	1	2	0	3	1	5
3 Georgia	3	1	0	2	4	8	3
4 Northern Ireland	3	0	1	2	3	9	1

Group 4

21-26/03/15 Wronki, Grodzisk Wielkopolski
**Republic of Ireland 2-2 Greece, Poland 0-2
Belarus, Belarus 1-3 Republic of Ireland, Poland
0-1 Greece, Republic of Ireland 0-1 Poland,
Greece 0-0 Belarus**

		Pld	W	D	L	F	A	Pts
1	Greece	3	1	2	0	3	2	5
2	Republic of Ireland	3	1	1	1	5	4	4
3	Belarus	3	1	1	1	3	3	4
4	Poland	3	1	0	2	1	3	3

Group 5

21-26/03/15 Krasnodar
**Austria 1-0 Iceland, Russia 0-0 Wales, Austria
3-2 Wales, Iceland 0-4 Russia, Russia 1-1
Austria, Wales 1-0 Iceland**

		Pld	W	D	L	F	A	Pts
1	Austria	3	2	1	0	5	3	7
2	Russia	3	1	2	0	5	1	5
3	Wales	3	1	1	1	3	3	4
4	Iceland	3	0	0	3	0	6	0

Group 6

*21-26/03/15 Burton-on-Trent, Nuneaton,
Chesterfield*
**England 3-1 Norway, Romania 0-3 Slovenia,
Norway 2-0 Romania, England 3-1 Slovenia,
Romania 1-2 England, Slovenia 1-0 Norway**

		Pld	W	D	L	F	A	Pts
1	England	3	3	0	0	8	3	9
2	Slovenia	3	2	0	1	5	3	6
3	Norway	3	1	0	2	3	4	3
4	Romania	3	0	0	3	1	7	0

Group 7

20-25/03/15 Tatabanya, Telki, Felcsut
**Scotland 2-0 Bosnia & Herzegovina, Czech
Republic 1-0 Hungary, Czech Republic 2-2
Bosnia & Herzegovina, Hungary 0-0 Scotland,
Scotland 0-1 Czech Republic, Bosnia &
Herzegovina 2-1 Hungary**

		Pld	W	D	L	F	A	Pts
1	Czech Republic	3	2	1	0	4	2	7
2	Scotland	3	1	1	1	2	1	4
3	Bosnia & Herzegovina	3	1	1	1	4	5	4
4	Hungary	3	0	1	2	1	3	1

Group 8

21-26/03/15 Wetzlar, Marburg
**Germany 3-0 Slovakia, Italy 1-0 Ukraine,
Germany 3-0 Ukraine, Slovakia 0-2 Italy, Italy
2-2 Germany, Ukraine 1-2 Slovakia**

		Pld	W	D	L	F	A	Pts
1	Germany	3	2	1	0	8	2	7
2	Italy	3	2	1	0	5	2	7
3	Slovakia	3	1	0	2	2	6	3
4	Ukraine	3	0	0	3	1	6	0

Top goalscorers (Qualifying/Elite rounds)

8	Jan Mlakar (Slovenia)
7	Patrick Cutrone (Italy)
5	Odsonne Edouard (France)
	José Luis Zalazar (Spain)
	Dennis Van Vaerenbergh (Belgium)
4	Florinel Coman (Romania)
	José Gomes (Portugal)
	Layton Ndukwu (England)
	Giorgi Arabidze (Georgia)
	Trevor Clarke (Republic of Ireland)

Final tournament

Group A

06/05/15, Lazur, Burgas
Spain 1-1 Austria
Goals: 1-0 Aleñá 46(p), 1-1 Lovric 62
Referee: Kristoffersen (DEN)

06/05/15, Beroe, Stara Zagora
Bulgaria 0-2 Croatia
Goals: 0-1 Babić 24, 0-2 Blečić 80+3
Referee: Raczkowski (POL)

09/05/15, Sozopol Stadium, Sozopol
Croatia 1-0 Austria
Goal: 1-0 Lovren 52
Referee: Muntean (MDA)

09/05/15, Lazur, Burgas
Bulgaria 1-2 Spain
Goals: 0-1 Kuki 11, 1-1 Yordanov 35, 1-2 Fran
Villalba 47
Referee: Avram (ROU)

12/05/15, Sozopol Stadium, Sozopol
Austria 1-1 Bulgaria
Goals: 1-0 Filip 34, 1-1 Yordanov 43
Referee: Grujić (SRB)

12/05/15, Hadzhi Dimitar, Sliven
Croatia 0-0 Spain
Referee: Lambrechts (BEL)

		Pld	W	D	L	F	A	Pts
1	Croatia	3	2	1	0	3	0	7
2	Spain	3	1	2	0	3	2	5
3	Austria	3	0	2	1	2	3	2
4	Bulgaria	3	0	1	2	2	5	1

Group B

06/05/15, Hadzhi Dimitar, Sliven
Czech Republic 1-0 Slovenia
Goal: 1-0 Lingr 44
Referee: Avram (ROU)

06/05/15, Sozopol Stadium, Sozopol
Belgium 0-2 Germany
Goals: 0-1 Passlack 43, 0-2 Schmidt 46
Referee: Grujić (SRB)

09/05/15, Sozopol Stadium, Sozopol
Czech Republic 0-3 Belgium
Goals: 0-1 Azzaoui 29, 0-2 Azzaoui 75(p), 0-3 Van
Vaerenbergh 78
Referee: Kristoffersen (DEN)

09/05/15, Lazur, Burgas
Slovenia 0-1 Germany
Goal: 0-1 Eggestein 8
Referee: Jaccottet (SUI)

12/05/15, Beroe, Stara Zagora
Germany 4-0 Czech Republic
Goals: 1-0 Passlack 10, 2-0 Karakas 33, 3-0
Passlack 40+2, 4-0 Saglam 53
Referee: Sant (MLT)

12/05/15, Lazur, Burgas
Slovenia 0-1 Belgium
Goal: 0-1 Van Vaerenbergh 80+3
Referee: Reinshreiber (ISR)

		Pld	W	D	L	F	A	Pts
1	Germany	3	3	0	0	7	0	9
2	Belgium	3	2	0	1	4	2	6
3	Czech Republic	3	1	0	2	1	7	3
4	Slovenia	3	0	0	3	0	3	0

Group C

07/05/15, Sozopol Stadium, Sozopol
Greece 2-2 Russia
Goals: 1-0 Kirtzialidis 37, 1-1 Pletnev 59, 2-1
Pavlidis 64, 2-2 Denisov 72
Referee: Lambrechts (BEL)

07/05/15, Beroe, Stara Zagora
Scotland 0-5 France
Goals: 0-1 Ikone 18, 0-2 Ikone 20, 0-3 Edouard
25, 0-4 Boutobba 35, 0-5 Doucoure 47
Referee: Sant (MLT)

France's Odsonne Edouard was the eight-goal star of
the finals in Bulgaria

10/05/15, Hadzhi Dimitar, Sliven
Russia 0-1 France
Goal: 0-1 Edouard 50
Referee: Grujić (SRB)

10/05/15, Sozopol Stadium, Sozopol
Greece 1-0 Scotland
Goal: 1-0 Pavlidis 39
Referee: Raczkowski (POL)

13/05/15, Sozopol Stadium, Sozopol
France 1-0 Greece
Goal: 1-0 Rambaud 80+4
Referee: Jaccottet (SUI)

13/05/15, Hadzhi Dimitar, Sliven
Russia 2-0 Scotland
Goals: 1-0 Denisov 52, 2-0 Pletnev 65
Referee: Muntean (MDA)

		Pld	W	D	L	F	A	Pts
1	France	3	3	0	0	7	0	9
2	Russia	3	1	1	1	4	3	4
3	Greece	3	1	1	1	3	3	4
4	Scotland	3	0	0	3	0	8	0

Group D

07/05/15, Sozopol Stadium, Sozopol
Republic of Ireland 0-0 Netherlands
Referee: Muntean (MDA)

07/05/15, Lazur, Burgas
Italy 0-1 England
Goal: 0-1 Edwards 47
Referee: Jaccottet (SUI)

10/05/15, Beroe, Stara Zagora
Republic of Ireland 0-2 Italy
Goals: 0-1 Lo Faso 9, 0-2 Mazzocchi 56
Referee: Reinshreiber (ISR)

10/05/15, Beroe, Stara Zagora
Netherlands 1-1 England
Goals: 0-1 Fosu-Mensah 18(og), 1-1 Boultam 56(p)
Referee: Lambrechts (BEL)

13/05/15, Beroe, Stara Zagora
England 1-0 Republic of Ireland
Goal: 1-0 Edwards 71
Referee: Raczkowski (POL)

13/05/15, Lazur, Burgas
Netherlands 1-1 Italy
Goals: 0-1 Cutrone 6, 1-1 Giraudo 63(og)
Referee: Kristoffersen (DEN)

		Pld	W	D	L	F	A	Pts
1	England	3	2	1	0	3	1	7
2	Italy	3	1	1	1	3	2	4
3	Netherlands	3	0	3	0	2	2	3
4	Republic of Ireland	3	0	1	2	0	3	1

Quarter-finals

15/05/15, Lazur, Burgas
Croatia 1-1 Belgium (aet)
Goals: 1-0 Majić 34, 1-1 Azzaoui 53
Referee: Avram (ROU)
Belgium qualify 5-3 on penalties.

15/05/15, Beroe, Stara Zagora
Germany 0-0 Spain (aet)
Referee: Reinshreiber (ISR)
Germany qualify 4-2 on penalties.

16/05/15, Lazur, Burgas
England 0-1 Russia
Goal: 0-1 Tataev 29
Referee: Sant (MLT)

16/05/15, Beroe, Stara Zagora
France 3-0 Italy
Goals: 1-0 Edouard 5, 2-0 Ikone 53, 3-0
Edouard 72
Referee: Grujić (SRB)

FIFA U-17 World Cup qualifying play-offs

19/05/15, Sozopol Stadium, Sozopol
Croatia 1-0 Italy
Goal: 1-0 Moro 15
Referee: Kristoffersen (DEN)

19/05/15, Hadzhi Dimitar, Sliven
Spain 0-0 England (aet)
Referee: Muntean (MDA)
England qualify 5-3 on penalties.

Semi-finals

19/05/15, Lazur, Burgas
Belgium 1-1 France (aet)
Goals: 0-1 Edouard 23, 1-1 Seigers 52
Referee: Jaccottet (SUI)
France qualify 2-1 on penalties.

19/05/15, Beroe, Stara Zagora
Germany 1-0 Russia
Goal: 1-0 Serra 68
Referee: Avram (ROU)

Final

22/05/15, Lazur, Burgas (att: 14,680)
France 4-1 Germany
Goals: 1-0 Edouard 40, 2-0 Edouard 47, 2-1
Karakas 50, 3-1 Edouard 70, 4-1 Gül 80+3(og)
Referee: Raczkowski (POL)
France: Zidane, Georgen, Maouassa, Upamecano,
Doucoure, Makengo, Edouard (Samba 80+1), Cognat
(Callegari 69), Boutobba, Ikone, Reine Adélaïde
(Pelican 61). Coach: Jean-Claude Giuntini (FRA)
Germany: Frommann, Passlack, Gül, Karakas,
Abu Hanna, Eggestein, Schmidt (Serra 51), Köhlert
(Saglam 69), Nesseler (Özcan 48), Busam, Janelt.
Coach: Christian Wück (GER)
Yellow cards: Reine Adélaïde 49 (France), Cognat
66 (France), Upamecano 74 (France), Passlack 76
(Germany), Özcan 80+4 (Germany)

Top goalscorers *(Final tournament)*

8	Odsonne Edouard (France)
3	Ismail Azzaoui (Belgium)
	Felix Passlack (Germany)
	Nanitamo Ikone (France)
2	Vangelis Pavlidis (Greece)
	Tonislav Yordanov (Bulgaria)
	Dmitri Pletnev (Russia)
	Yegor Denisov (Russia)
	Marcus Edwards (England)
	Erdinc Karakas (Germany)
	Dennis Van Vaerenbergh (Belgium)

Squads/Appearances/Goals

Austria

No	Name	DoB	Aps	(s)	Gls
Goalkeepers					
1	Fabian Ehmann	28/08/98	3		
21	Dominik Krischke	21/05/98			
Defenders					
4	Boris Basara	22/02/98		(1)	
16	Jan Heilmann	16/03/98	3		
17	Niklas Kölbl	03/04/98		(1)	
18	Florian Prirsch	11/09/98	3		
15	Paul Sahanek	08/09/98	3		
6	Aleksandar Skrbic	29/10/98			
14	Maximilian Wöber	04/02/98	3		
Midfielders					
8	Kevin Danso	19/09/98	2	(1)	
11	Daniel Hautzinger	12/05/98		(2)	
20	Sandi Lovric	28/03/98	3		1
13	Anes Omerovic	20/05/98	3		
10	Samuel Oppong	12/05/98		(2)	
7	Albin Ramadani	15/01/98	3		
Forwards					
12	Oliver Filip	15/01/98	3		1
9	Arnel Jakupovic	29/05/98	3		
19	Patrick Schmidt	22/07/98	1	(2)	

Belgium

No	Name	DoB	Aps	(s)	Gls
Goalkeepers					
12	Gaetan Coucke	03/11/98			
1	Jens Teunckens	30/01/98	5		
Defenders					
13	Dries Caignau	08/01/98	1	(2)	
2	Kino Delorge	05/01/98	5		
4	Wout Faes	03/04/98	4		
14	Siebe Horemans	02/06/98			
5	Christophe Janssens	09/03/98	5		
3	Rubin Seigers	11/01/98	5		
Midfielders					
8	Alper Ademoglu	10/04/98	5		
7	Ismail Azzaoui	06/01/98	5		3
11	Lennerd Daneels	10/04/98	3	(2)	
10	Orel Mangala	18/03/98	3	(1)	
15	Dante Rigo	11/12/98	2	(2)	
6	Matisse Thuys	24/01/98	5		
18	Matthias Verreth	20/02/98	2	(2)	
Forwards					
16	Nelson Azevedo-Janelas	12/02/98		(1)	
9	Dennis Van Vaerenbergh	26/06/98	5		2
17	Jorn Vancamp	28/10/98		(3)	

Bulgaria

No	Name	DoB	Aps	(s)	Gls
Goalkeepers					
1	Daniel Naumov	29/03/98	2		
12	Dimitar Sheytanov	15/03/99	1		
Defenders					
15	Petko Hristov	01/03/99	3		
3	Danail Ivanov	07/08/98			
2	Dimitar Savov	29/01/98	3		
5	Kristiyan Slavov	23/05/98	3		
14	Mateo Stamatov	22/03/99	3		
Midfielders					
7	Aleks Borimirov	13/05/98		(1)	
13	Asen Chandarov	13/11/98	2	(1)	
16	Georgi Chukalov	25/02/98			
4	Radoslav Dimitrov	03/07/98	2	(1)	
17	Pavel Golovodov	28/06/98	3		
11	Svetoslav Kovachev	14/03/98	1	(2)	
10	Iliyan Stefanov	20/09/98	2	(1)	
8	Georgi Yanev	04/01/98	1	(2)	
Forwards					
6	Georgi Rusev	02/07/98	3		
18	Tonislav Yordanov	27/11/98	3		2
9	Valentin Yoskov	05/06/98	1	(2)	

Croatia

No	Name	DoB	Aps	(s)	Gls
Goalkeepers					
12	Ivan Nevistić	31/07/98	1		
1	Adrian Šemper	12/01/98	4		
Defenders					
13	Mihael Briški	02/01/99	1		
4	Martin Erlić	24/01/98	2		
2	Matej Hudećek	27/12/98	4		
5	Branimir Kalaica	01/06/98	5		
6	Vinko Soldo	15/02/98	4	(1)	
3	Borna Sosa	21/01/98	5		
Midfielders					
7	Josip Brekalo	23/06/98	4	(1)	
8	Neven Djurasek	15/08/98	4		
16	Marko Gjira	05/05/99	3	(1)	
14	Dino Halilović	08/02/98	1	(3)	
11	Davor Lovren	03/10/98	4	(1)	1
10	Nikola Moro	12/03/98	4		1
15	Saša Urošević	26/01/99	1		
19	Adrian Zenko	04/04/98	1	(2)	
Forwards					
17	Matko Babić	28/07/98	2	(3)	1
18	Adrian Blečić	08/03/98	2	(2)	1
9	Karlo Majić	03/03/98	3	(1)	1

UEFA European Under-17 Championship

Czech Republic

No	Name	DoB	Aps	(s)	Gls
Goalkeepers					
16	Martin Jedlička	24/01/98	2		
1	Filip Truksa	03/07/98	1	(1)	
Defenders					
17	Tomáš Balvín	13/05/98			
20	Matěj Chaluš	02/02/98	3		
2	Denis Granečný	07/09/98	3		
3	Libor Holík	12/05/98	3		
4	Marek Richter	23/05/98	3		
15	Daniel Souček	18/07/98			
Midfielders					
11	Dominik Breda	27/02/98		(3)	
9	Marcel Čermák	25/11/98	2	(1)	
13	Alex Král	19/05/98	3		
5	Daniel Köstl	23/05/98	1		
6	Michal Sadílek	31/05/99	3		
18	Ondřej Žežulka	25/09/98	3		
Forwards					
8	Ondřej Lingr	07/10/98	2	(1)	1
10	Ondřej Šašinka	21/03/98	3		
19	Daniel Turyna	26/02/98	1	(1)	
7	Antonín Vaníček	22/04/98		(2)	

France

No	Name	DoB	Aps	(s)	Gls
Goalkeepers					
16	Nicolas Kocik	04/08/98			
1	Luca Zidane	13/05/98	6		
Defenders					
15	Bradlay Danger	29/01/98	1		
5	Mamadou Doucoure	21/05/98	6		1
2	Alec Georgen	17/09/98	5		
3	Christ-Emmanuel Maouassa	06/07/98	6		
14	Issa Samba	29/01/98	2	(1)	
4	Dayot Upamecano	27/10/98	5	(1)	
Midfielders					
10	Bilal Boutobba	29/08/98	5	(1)	1
18	Lorenzo Callegari	27/02/98		(1)	
8	Timothé Cognat	25/01/98	5		
17	Nicolas Janvier	11/08/98	1	(4)	
6	Jean-Victor Makengo	12/06/98	3	(2)	
12	Jeff Reine Adélaïde	17/01/98	4	(1)	
99	Jean Ruiz	06/04/98	4		
Forwards					
7	Odsonne Edouard	16/01/98	5		8
11	Nanitamo Ikone	02/05/98	6		3
9	Maxime Pelican	12/05/98	2	(4)	
13	Jordan Rambaud	16/03/98		(2)	1

Greece

No	Name	DoB	Aps	(s)	Gls
Goalkeepers					
1	Chrysostomos Iakovidis	30/07/98			
12	Marios Siampanis	28/09/99	3		
Defenders					
18	Stergios Dodontsakis	23/11/98		(3)	
4	Stefanos Evangelou	12/05/98	3		
17	Antonios Fouasis	13/06/98		(1)	
3	Alexandros Katranis	04/05/98	3		
2	Polykarpos Liaptsis	12/03/98			
5	Dimitris Nikolaou	13/08/98	3		
16	Panagiotis Retsos	09/08/98	3		
Midfielders					
19	Kostas Chatzidimpas	12/05/99	1	(2)	
14	Nikos Karamitos	14/07/98		(1)	
8	Stathis Lamprou	20/09/98	1	(1)	
10	Theodoros Mingos	06/02/98	3		
6	Spyros Natsos	09/06/98	2		
15	Vangelis Pavlidis	21/11/98	3		2
Forwards					
11	Kostas Kirtzialidis	23/03/98	2	(1)	1
7	Dimitris Limnios	27/05/98	3		
9	Ioannis Tsingos	18/05/99	3		

England

No	Name	DoB	Aps	(s)	Gls
Goalkeepers					
13	Will Huffer	30/10/98		(1)	
1	Paul Woolston	14/08/98	5		
Defenders					
6	Danny Collinge	09/04/98	4		
3	Jay DaSilva	22/04/98	5		
5	Reece Oxford	16/12/98	5		
15	Easah Suliman	26/01/98	1	(2)	
2	James Yates	03/04/98	5		
Midfielders					
14	Trent Arnold	07/10/98	2	(1)	
4	Tom Davies	30/06/98	3		
10	Marcus Edwards	03/12/98	4	(1)	2
12	Tayo Edun	14/05/98	1	(1)	
7	Nathan Holland	19/06/98	3		
18	Herbie Kane	23/11/98	5		
17	Layton Ndukwu	07/09/98	3	(1)	
8	Daniel Wright	04/01/98	1	(2)	
Forwards					
16	Stephy Mavididi	31/05/98	3	(1)	
9	Ike Ugbo	21/09/98	1	(4)	
11	Chris Willock	31/01/98	4	(1)	

Germany

No	Name	DoB	Aps	(s)	Gls
Goalkeepers					
1	Constantin Frommann	27/05/98	6		
12	Markus Schubert	12/06/98			
Defenders					
6	Joel Abu Hanna	22/01/98	4	(2)	
17	Enes Akyol	16/02/98	2	(2)	
18	Jonas Busam	03/05/98	6		
5	Erdinc Karakas	23/03/98	5	(1)	2
13	Daniel Nesseler	15/03/98	5	(1)	
Midfielders					
3	Dzenis Burnic	22/05/98	2	(2)	
8	Niklas Dorsch	15/01/98	1		
7	Dennis Geiger	10/06/98		(2)	
4	Gökhan Gül	17/07/98	5		
20	Vitaly Janelt	10/05/98	4		
15	Salih Özcan	11/01/98	3	(3)	
2	Felix Passlack	29/05/98	6		3
14	Görkem Saglam	11/04/98	3	(1)	1
10	Niklas Schmidt	01/03/98	4	(1)	1
Forwards					
9	Johannes Eggestein	08/05/98	4		1
11	Mats Köhlert	02/05/98	4		
16	Janni Serra	13/03/98	2	(3)	1

Italy

No	Name	DoB	Aps	(s)	Gls
Goalkeepers					
12	Tommaso Cucchietti	24/01/98			
1	Gianluigi Donnarumma	25/02/99	5		
Defenders					
7	Luca Coccolo	23/02/98		(2)	
8	Edoardo Degl'Innocenti	07/08/98		(5)	
3	Federico Giraudo	11/08/98	5		
6	Andres Llamas	05/04/98	5		
5	Andrea Malberti	10/04/98		(1)	
4	Alessandro Mattioli	13/02/98	5		
2	Giuseppe Scalera	26/01/98	5		
Midfielders					
11	Mattia El Hilali	20/01/98	5		
14	Alessandro Eleuteri	08/06/98	1		
15	Simone Lo Faso	18/02/98	4	(1)	1
10	Manuel Locatelli	08/01/98	5		
13	Luca Matarese	16/04/98	2	(2)	
9	Filippo Melegoni	18/02/99	4		
Forwards					
16	Patrick Cutrone	03/01/98	5		1
18	Simone Mazzocchi	17/08/98	3	(1)	1
17	Gianluca Scamacca	01/01/99	1	(3)	

UEFA European Under-17 Championship

Netherlands

No	Name	DoB	Aps	(s)	Gls
Goalkeepers					
1	Justin Bijlow	22/01/98	3		
16	Thijmen Nijhuis	25/07/98			
Defenders					
14	Matthijs de Ligt	12/08/99	1	(1)	
13	Sherel Floranus	23/08/98		(2)	
3	Timothy Fosu-Mensah	02/01/98	3		
4	Mats Knoester	19/11/98	2		
2	Giovanni Troupée	20/03/98	3		
5	Rick van Drongelen	20/12/98	3		
Midfielders					
10	Teun Bijleveld	27/05/98	2	(1)	
6	Reda Boultam	03/03/98	2		1
12	Dani De Wit	28/01/98	3		
8	Carel Eiting	11/02/98	2		
15	Mink Peeters	28/05/98	1		
Forwards					
11	Javairo Dilrosun	22/06/98	3		
7	Rashaan Fernandes	29/07/98	2	(1)	
17	Jay-Roy Grot	13/03/98	2	(1)	
18	Donyell Malen	19/01/99		(3)	
9	Nigel Robertha	13/02/98	1		

Russia

No	Name	DoB	Aps	(s)	Gls
Goalkeepers					
1	Denis Adamov	20/02/98			
12	Aleksandr Maksimenko	19/03/98	5		
Defenders					
18	Amir Gavrilov	13/06/98	5		
4	Nikita Kalugin	12/03/98	5		
3	Konstantin Kotov	25/06/98	5		
7	Danil Krugovoi	28/05/98		(1)	
5	Aleksei Tataev	08/10/98	5		1
Midfielders					
6	Ivan Galanin	05/06/98	3	(1)	
2	Andrei Kudryavtsev	06/11/98	1	(1)	
11	Aleksandr Lomovitski	27/01/98	4		
17	Mikhail Lysov	29/01/98	2	(3)	
8	Georgi Makhatadze	26/03/98	5		
16	Dmitri Pletnev	16/01/98	4	(1)	2
14	Artem Selyukov	16/03/98	3	(1)	
10	Boris Tsygankov	17/04/98	3	(1)	
Forwards					
15	Vladislav Bragin	25/01/98		(4)	
13	Yegor Denisov	06/02/98	4	(1)	2
9	Artem Galadzhan	22/05/98	1		
19	Aleksandr Scherbakov	26/06/98		(1)	

Slovenia

No	Name	DoB	Aps	(s)	Gls
Goalkeepers					
12	Igor Vekič	06/05/98			
1	Rok Vodišek	05/12/98	3		
Defenders					
18	Rok Bužinel	28/03/98		(1)	
2	Sandi Čoralič	12/02/98	2	(1)	
5	Oskar Cvjetičanin	26/04/98	3		
6	Luka Guček	29/01/99	3		
3	Sven Karič	07/03/98	1		
17	Matija Rom	01/11/98	3		
Midfielders					
7	Jakob Novak	04/03/98	2	(1)	
4	Sandi Ogrinec	05/06/98	3		
8	Dejan Petrovič	12/01/98	1	(1)	
16	Janez Pišek	04/05/98	1	(2)	
10	Vitja Valenčič	12/03/99	3		
Forwards					
11	Timi Elšnik	29/04/98	3		
9	Jan Mlakar	23/10/98	3		
13	Gaber Petric	11/05/98		(1)	
14	Kristjan Sredojević	21/06/98	2	(1)	
20	Kevin Žižek	21/06/98		(1)	

Republic of Ireland

No	Name	DoB	Aps	(s)	Gls
Goalkeepers					
16	David Craddock	30/01/98			
1	Caoimhin Kelleher	23/11/98	3		
Defenders					
14	Shane Hanney	19/02/98	1		
5	Darragh Leahy	15/04/98	3		
3	Jonathan Lunney	02/02/98	3		
4	Conor Masterson	08/09/98	3		
15	Robert McCourt	06/04/98	1		
2	Corey O'Keeffe	05/06/98	2		
Midfielders					
6	Marcus Agyei-Tabi	02/02/99	3		
7	Zachary Elbouzedi	05/04/98	2	(1)	
8	Conor Levingston	21/01/98	3		
10	Connor Ronan	06/03/98	3		
18	Anthony Scully	19/04/99		(3)	
12	Luke Wade-Slater	02/03/98	1	(1)	
Forwards					
17	Jamie Aherne	08/07/98	1	(2)	
9	Joshua Barrett	21/06/98	2	(1)	
11	Trevor Clarke	26/03/98	2		
13	Jamie Gray	13/04/98			

Scotland

No	Name	DoB	Aps	(s)	Gls
Goalkeepers					
12	Ross Doohan	29/03/98	1		
1	Robby McCrorie	18/03/98	2		
Defenders					
2	Mark Finlayson	30/05/98	2	(1)	
5	Daniel Harvie	14/07/98	3		
18	Daniel Higgins	08/04/98	1		
4	Tom McIntyre	06/11/98	3		
3	Ross McCrorie	18/03/98	3		
Midfielders					
6	Liam Burt	01/02/99	2		
14	Regan Hendry	21/01/98	3		
8	Mark Hill	10/07/98	3		
17	Glenn Middleton	01/01/00	2	(1)	
15	Lewis Morrison	12/03/99		(2)	
10	Frank Ross	18/02/98	2		
16	Harry Souttar	22/10/98	1	(1)	
13	Iain Wilson	15/12/98	2		
Forwards					
7	Jack Aitchison	05/03/00		(2)	
9	Calvin Miller	09/01/98	3		
11	Zak Rudden	06/02/00		(2)	

Spain

No	Name	DoB	Aps	(s)	Gls
Goalkeepers					
13	Iñaki	02/03/99	3		
1	Alejandro Santomé	14/04/98	2		
Defenders					
4	Alex Martín	25/01/98	5		
2	José María Amo	09/04/98	4		
3	Cucu	22/07/98	5		
16	Dani Morer	05/02/98	4		
5	Isma	07/02/98	1		
12	Jon	24/05/98	1		
Midfielders					
6	Carles Aleñá	05/01/98	5		1
8	Fran Villalba	11/05/98	4	(1)	1
11	Óscar	28/06/98		(4)	
14	Pepelu	11/08/98	4		
15	Toni Moya	20/03/98	1	(1)	
Forwards					
10	Carles Pérez	16/02/98	3	(2)	
7	Dani Olmo	07/05/98	5		
17	Ferni	07/04/98	2	(2)	
19	Fran Navarro	03/02/98	1	(3)	
9	Kuki	05/05/98	5		1

UEFA REGIONS' CUP ™

Home joy for Irish amateurs

Widely regarded as the world's most prestigious competition for amateur sides, the UEFA Regions' Cup gives its participants the opportunity to compete at a European level, and there was a new name on the trophy in 2015 as Eastern Region IRL, the runners-up to Braga in 2011 (while competing as Leinster & Munster), triumphed on home soil after defeating Croatian opponents Zagreb Region 1-0 in the Dublin final. Gerry Smith's side thus became the fifth host team – and third in a row, after Braga and 2013 champions Veneto – to win the final tournament, which has been staged every other year since 1999.

Described by UEFA Youth and Amateur Football Committee chairman Jim Boyce as "the Champions League for amateur players", the ninth edition of the competition was played in the traditional amateur spirit, but the football on view during the nine days of competition in the capital city of the Republic of Ireland was never less than fully committed as teams from Turkey, Northern Ireland, Croatia, Germany, the Czech Republic, Bosnia & Herzegovina and Poland – who had all successfully come through the qualifying phase – congregated in Dublin to do battle with the hosts.

Smith's team, drawn in Group A, secured their place in the final after just two of their three games as they followed up an opening 2-0 success against Ankara with another 2-0 victory against South Moravia, who had also kicked off with a win, 1-0 against Tuzla. The hosts could afford to rotate their squad and rest some key players for their final game, in which they went on

Eastern Region IRL captain Kenneth Hoey lifts the UEFA Regions' Cup

to defeat Tuzla 2-1, knowing that their final opponents on 4 July still had plenty of work to do.

Sreten Čuk's Zagreb side emerged as early favourites to top Group B, mauling Dolnośląski 4-0 on the opening day and then beating Eastern Region NIR 3-1 on day two. However, with Württembergischer FV taking four points from their opening two games, both sides went into their final group fixture, at Home Farm FC's Whitehall Stadium, with qualification still in their hands. The German team, who needed all three points to progress, took an early lead, but Zagreb, marshalled by classy playmaker Božidar Karamatić, recovered to win 2-1.

The final, staged in front of 1,172 spectators at Shamrock Rovers FC's Tallaght Stadium, turned out to be a bridge too far, however, for the tiring Croatian side. The injured Karamatić was not risked from the start, and Čuk's side could muster little response to David Lacey's early opener, which ultimately proved decisive. "It's probably the best day of my life, it's unbelievable," said Lacey after the final whistle. "We've tried for so long to win this trophy. We got the silver medal in 2011, and now we got gold."

Preliminary round

Group A

23-27/07/14 Rakvere, Tallinn
Dostyk 0-3 Västergötland, North Wales 3-1 Northern Estonia, North Wales 3-0 Dostyk, Västergötland 8-0 Northern Estonia, Västergötland 2-1 North Wales, Northern Estonia 3-0 Dostyk

		Pld	W	D	L	F	A	Pts
1	Västergötland	3	3	0	0	13	1	9
2	North Wales	3	2	0	1	7	3	6
3	Northern Estonia	3	1	0	2	4	11	3
4	Dostyk	3	0	0	3	0	9	0

Group B

15-19/06/14 Bakovci, Radenci
MNZ Murska Sobota 2-1 Evia Region, San Marino 0-0 East, West and Central Scotland, MNZ Murska Sobota 1-1 San Marino, East, West and Central Scotland 1-2 Evia Region, East, West and Central Scotland 3-1 MNZ Murska Sobota, Evia Region 1-1 San Marino

		Pld	W	D	L	F	A	Pts
1	East, West and Central Scotland	3	1	1	1	4	3	4
2	Evia Region	3	1	1	1	4	4	4
3	MNZ Murska Sobota	3	1	1	1	4	5	4
4	San Marino	3	0	3	0	2	2	3

Intermediary round

Group 1

20-24/10/14 Porec, Novigrad
Çagirgan 1-7 Zagreb Region, RTU Futbola Centrs 2-1 Västergötland, Çagirgan 0-1 RTU Futbola Centrs, Västergötland 0-0 Zagreb Region, Västergötland 8-4 Çağırğan, Zagreb Region 4-0 RTU Futbola Centrs

		Pld	W	D	L	F	A	Pts
1	Zagreb Region	3	2	1	0	11	1	7
2	RTU Futbola Centrs	3	2	0	1	3	5	6
3	Västergötland	3	1	1	1	9	6	4
4	Çağırğan	3	0	0	3	5	16	0

Group 2

23-27/09/14 Poprad
Württembergischer FV 2-1 Eastern Slovakia, Isle of Man League 2-0 East, West and Central Scotland, Württembergischer FV 7-0 Isle of Man League, East, West and Central Scotland 0-2 Eastern Slovakia, East, West and Central Scotland 0-1 Württembergischer FV, Eastern Slovakia 1-0 Isle of Man League

		Pld	W	D	L	F	A	Pts
1	Württembergischer FV	3	3	0	0	10	1	9
2	Eastern Slovakia	3	2	0	1	4	2	6
3	Isle of Man League	3	1	0	2	2	8	3
4	East, West and Central Scotland	3	0	0	3	0	5	0

Group 3

25-29/09/14 Stara Pazova, Jakovo
FA of Vojvodina 3-0 South-West Bulgaria, Association Cantonale Vaudoise de Football 0-0 South Moravia, FA of Vojvodina 2-2 Association Cantonale Vaudoise de Football, South Moravia 2-1 South-West Bulgaria, South Moravia 3-0 FA of Vojvodina, South-West Bulgaria 2-1 Association Cantonale Vaudoise de Football

		Pld	W	D	L	F	A	Pts
1	South Moravia	3	2	1	0	5	1	7
2	FA of Vojvodina	3	1	1	1	5	5	4
3	South-West Bulgaria	3	1	0	2	3	6	3
4	Association Cantonale Vaudoise de Football	3	0	2	1	3	4	2

Group 4

20-24/10/14 Mórahalom, Hodmezovasarhely
FK Nevežis 1-2 FC Karmiel Tzfat, Eastern Region IRL 4-1 East Hungary, Eastern Region IRL 6-1 FK Nevežis, FC Karmiel Tzfat 0-2 East Hungary, FC Karmiel Tzfat 0-1 Eastern Region IRL, East Hungary 3-1 FK Nevežis

		Pld	W	D	L	F	A	Pts
1	Eastern Region IRL	3	3	0	0	11	2	9
2	East Hungary	3	2	0	1	6	5	6
3	FC Karmiel Tzfat	3	1	0	2	2	4	3
4	FK Nevežis	3	0	0	3	3	11	0

Group 5

23-27/09/14 Chisinau, Vadul lui Voda, Orhei, Ternovca
AF Piatykhatska 0-4 Selección Catalana de Fútbol, Eastern Region NIR 5-1 ARF Telenești, AF Piatykhatska 0-4 Eastern Region NIR, ARF Telenești 0-10 Selección Catalana de Fútbol, ARF Telenești 0-5 AF Piatykhatska, Selección Catalana de Fútbol 0-1 Eastern Region NIR

		Pld	W	D	L	F	A	Pts
1	Eastern Region NIR	3	3	0	0	10	1	9
2	Selección Catalana de Fútbol	3	2	0	1	14	1	6
3	AF Piatykhatska	3	1	0	2	5	8	3
4	ARF Telenești	3	0	0	3	1	20	0

Group 6

01-05/10/14 Gozo
Ankara 2-1 South Region Russia, Gozo Amateur 2-0 Region of Vaasa, Ankara 2-1 Gozo Amateur, Region of Vaasa 0-1 South Region Russia, South Region Russia 3-1 Gozo Amateur, Region of Vaasa 0-1 Ankara

		Pld	W	D	L	F	A	Pts
1	Ankara	3	3	0	0	5	2	9
2	South Region Russia	3	2	0	1	5	3	6
3	Gozo Amateur	3	1	0	2	4	5	3
4	Region of Vaasa	3	0	0	3	0	4	0

Group 7

25-29/09/14 Tuzla, Banovici
Lazio 1-0 Leiria Regional Association, Tuzla Canton 2-1 ALF-2007 (Minsk), ALF-2007 (Minsk) 0-4 Leiria Regional Association, Lazio 1-2 Tuzla Canton, ALF-2007 (Minsk) 0-2 Lazio, Leiria Regional Association 1-3 Tuzla Canton

		Pld	W	D	L	F	A	Pts
1	Tuzla Canton	3	3	0	0	7	3	9
2	Lazio	3	2	0	1	4	2	6
3	Leiria Regional Association	3	1	0	2	5	4	3
4	ALF-2007 (Minsk)	3	0	0	3	1	8	0

Group 8

13-17/09/14 Polkowice, Legnica, Lubin
Ligue de Paris Île-de-France 1-0 News Amateurs Macedonia, Brașov 2-5 Dolnośląski Region, Brașov 0-4 Ligue de Paris Île-de-France, News Amateurs Macedonia 1-5 Dolnośląski Region, News Amateurs Macedonia 2-2 Brașov, Dolnośląski Region 1-1 Ligue de Paris Île-de-France

		Pld	W	D	L	F	A	Pts
1	Dolnośląski Region	3	2	1	0	11	4	7
2	Ligue de Paris Île-de-France	3	2	1	0	6	1	7
3	News Amateurs Macedonia	3	0	1	2	3	8	1
4	Brașov	3	0	1	2	4	11	1

Final tournament

Group A

26/06/15, Belfield Bowl, UCD, Dublin
South Moravia 1-0 Tuzla Canton
Goal: 1-0 Žoček 10

26/06/15, Tallaght Stadium, Dublin
Eastern Region IRL 2-0 Ankara
Goals: 1-0 Moorhouse 27, 2-0 D Dunne 45+1(p)

28/06/15, Tallaght Stadium, Dublin
Eastern Region IRL 2-0 South Moravia
Goals: 1-0 D Dunne 22, 2-0 Breen 61

28/06/15, Belfield Bowl, UCD, Dublin
Ankara 2-1 Tuzla Canton
Goals: 0-1 Šako 16, 1-1 Salim Uzun 75(p), 2-1 Salim Uzun 79

01/07/15, Tallaght Stadium, Dublin
Tuzla Canton 1-2 Eastern Region IRL
Goals: 1-0 Rock 29, 1-1 M Mešanović 35, 1-2 Gibbons 74

01/07/15, Carlisle Grounds, Dublin
Ankara 4-2 South Moravia
Goals: 1-0 Salim Uzun 22, 2-0 Volkan Solak 26, 2-1 Ullmann 28, 3-1 Salim Uzun 32, 3-2 Ullmann 62, 4-2 Muzaffer İlhan 74

		Pld	W	D	L	F	A	Pts
1	Eastern Region IRL	3	3	0	0	6	1	9
2	Ankara	3	2	0	1	6	5	6
3	South Moravia	3	1	0	2	3	6	3
4	Tuzla Canton	3	0	0	3	2	5	0

Group B

26/06/15, Carlisle Grounds, Dublin
Zagreb Region 4-0 Dolnośląski Region
Goals: 1-0 Brujić 13, 2-0 Rexhepi 75, 3-0 Rexhepi 88, 4-0 Špišić 90+1

26/06/15, Whitehall, Dublin
Eastern Region NIR 2-2 Württembergischer FV
Goals: 1-0 Thompson 12, 2-0 Thompson 14, 2-1 Pflumm 79(p), 2-2 Marinić 81

28/06/15, Richmond Park, Dublin
Zagreb Region 3-1 Eastern Region NIR
Goals: 1-0 Štulec 8, 2-0 Rexhepi 67, 2-1 Murray 77(p), 3-1 Karamatić 83

28/06/15, Whitehall, Dublin
Dolnośląski Region 0-1 Württembergischer FV
Goal: 0-1 Asch 82

01/07/15, Whitehall, Dublin
Württembergischer FV 1-2 Zagreb Region
Goals: 1-0 Kleinschrodt 4, 1-1 Strjački 31, 1-2 Štulec 76

01/07/15, Tolka Park, Dublin
Dolnośląski Region 1-2 Eastern Region NIR
Goals: 1-0 Niedojad 5, 1-1 O'Riordan 55, 1-2 O'Riordan 85

		Pld	W	D	L	F	A	Pts
1	Zagreb Region	3	3	0	0	9	2	9
2	Württembergischer FV	3	1	1	1	4	4	4
3	Eastern Region NIR	3	1	1	1	5	6	4
4	Dolnośląski Region	3	0	0	3	1	7	0

Final

04/07/15, Tallaght Stadium, Dublin (att: 1,172)
Eastern Region IRL 1-0 Zagreb Region
Goal: 1-0 Lacey 10
Referee: Hänni (SUI)
Eastern Region IRL: O'Connell, Murray, Sule (Carr 68), Moorhouse (Rock 84), Lynch, Breen, Hoey, D Dunne, Lacey (T Dunne 60), L Dunne, Lee. Coach: Gerry Smith (IRL)
Zagreb: Nevistić, Janjiš, Rexhepi (Čibarić 82), Vrbat, Rihtar, Ivkovčić, Perić (Mohač 49), Puretić (Karamatić 57), Brujić, Štulec, Ćunčić. Coach: Sreten Ćuk (CRO)
Yellow cards: Rexhepi 16 (Zagreb), Brujić 26 (Zagreb), Ćunčić 84 (Zagreb), Rock 86 (Eastern Region IRL)

Top goalscorers (Final tournament)

4	Salim Uzun (Ankara)
3	Arjan Rexhepi (Zagreb Region)

**Record winners end
seven-year wait for trophy**

**First-time finalists Paris
defeated by late goal**

**Wolfsburg's hat-trick dream
dies in semi-finals**

Fourth title for Frankfurt

**A seven-year wait ended for 1. FFC
Frankfurt as they became European club
champions for the fourth time with a
dramatic 2-1 victory over Paris Saint-
Germain in Berlin.**

Inaugural UEFA Women's Cup winners in
2002, Frankfurt added two more triumphs in
2006 and 2008 but then found themselves
eclipsed first by German rivals FCR 2001
Duisburg and 1. FFC Turbine Potsdam, then
by the two clubs that monopolised the
trophy between 2011 and 2014 - Olympique
Lyonnais and VfL Wolfsburg. None of those
teams managed to claim more than two
titles, though, so Frankfurt moved two clear
of Umeå IK, Potsdam, Lyon and Wolfsburg in
the competition's all-time roll of honour
following their record sixth final appearance.

On the surface Frankfurt's run to the final
was more impressive than that of Paris. The
German club managed 40 goals in their eight
games, keeping seven straight clean sheets
after conceding twice away to Kazakhstan's
FC BIIK-Kazygurt in the round of 32 first leg.
Paris, meanwhile, struck just 15 goals and
conceded four.

By their own admission Frankfurt had the
better of the draw, easing past BIIK, Italy's
ASD Torres Femminile Sassari, Bristol
Academy WFC and Brøndby IF. Paris,
meanwhile, edged FC Twente to earn a
round of 16 showdown with Lyon, in which
the capital side avenged their regular
domestic defeats by drawing 1-1 at home

before winning 1-0 at Stade de Gerland. The
first Scottish quarter-finalists, Glasgow City
FC, were duly swept aside before Paris
made history by becoming the first team to
beat Wolfsburg in Europe, ending the
holders' two-year continental reign with a 2-0
away win that provided sufficient protection
ahead of a 2-1 second-leg home defeat.

In front of a sell-out 18,700 crowd at the
Friedrich-Ludwig-Jahn-Sportpark in eastern
Berlin, Frankfurt dominated the early stages
of the final and took the lead in the 32nd
minute with a far-post header from Célia
Šašić, who thus equalled the competition
single-season goal record of 14 in her debut
European campaign. Half of that tally had
come in the semi-final demolition of Brøndby.

Paris levelled against the run of play eight
minutes later when Kenza Dali set up
Marie-Laure Delie. In the second half Paris

brought on Laura Georges and another
German in Josephine Henning - a pair with
five European club titles between them – and
their physical presence helped to quell
Frankfurt's previously potent attacking trio of
Šašić, Boquete and Dzsenifer Marozsán.

Extra-time loomed, especially after influential
Frankfurt midfielder Simone Laudehr
succumbed to injury, but two minutes into
added time substitute Mandy Islacker
became the unlikely Frankfurt hero, brilliantly
swivelling to loop in a half-volley and make
the final score 2-1

Frankfurt's fourth triumph increased
Germany's cumulative tally to nine in the 14
editions of the competition, and in Colin Bell,
whose sweeper system was key to stifling
Paris, they boasted the first Englishman to
coach a winning UEFA Champions League
team for either men or women.

Frankfurt's Mandy Islacker (No17) scores the late winning goal in the final against Paris

UEFA Women's Champions League

Qualifying round

Group 1

09-14/08/14 Riga

FC Zürich Frauen 1-1 FC Minsk, Konak Belediyespor 11-0 Rīgas Futbola skola, FC Minsk 1-2 Konak Belediyespor, FC Zürich Frauen 2-0 Rīgas Futbola skola, Konak Belediyespor 0-4 FC Zürich Frauen, Rīgas Futbola skola 0-7 FC Minsk

	Pld	W	D	L	F	A	Pts
1 FC Zürich Frauen	3	2	1	0	7	1	7
2 Konak Belediyespor	3	2	0	1	13	5	6
3 FC Minsk	3	1	1	1	9	3	4
4 Rīgas Futbola skola	3	0	0	3	0	20	0

Group 2

09-14/08/14 Cluj-Napoca

FC NSA Sofia 5-0 Hibernians FC, Olimpia Cluj Napoca 1-2 Raheny United FC, Raheny United FC 2-0 FC NSA Sofia, Olimpia Cluj Napoca 5-0 Hibernians FC, FC NSA Sofia 1-4 Olimpia Cluj Napoca, Hibernians FC 1-2 Raheny United FC

	Pld	W	D	L	F	A	Pts
1 Raheny United FC	3	3	0	0	6	2	9
2 Olimpia Cluj Napoca	3	2	0	1	10	3	6
3 FC NSA Sofia	3	1	0	2	6	6	3
4 Hibernians FC	3	0	0	3	1	12	0

Group 3

09-14/08/14 Petrovac, Niksic

MTK Hungária FC 3-0 Pärnu Jalgpalliklubi, ŽNK Pomurje 4-0 Ekonomist, MTK Hungária FC 1-0 Ekonomist, Pärnu Jalgpalliklubi 0-4 ŽNK Pomurje, ŽNK Pomurje 1-2 MTK Hungária FC, Ekonomist 1-2 Pärnu Jalgpalliklubi

	Pld	W	D	L	F	A	Pts
1 MTK Hungária FC	3	3	0	0	6	1	9
2 ŽNK Pomurje	3	2	0	1	9	2	6
3 Pärnu Jalgpalliklubi	3	1	0	2	2	8	3
4 Ekonomist	3	0	0	3	1	7	0

Group 4

09-14/08/14 Falkirk, Airdrie, Cumbernauld

WFC Kharkiv 5-0 Glentoran Belfast United, Glasgow City FC 5-0 FC Union Nové Zámky, FC Union Nové Zámky 1-3 WFC Kharkiv, Glasgow City FC 1-0 Glentoran Belfast United, WFC Kharkiv 0-4 Glasgow City FC, Glentoran Belfast United 5-2 FC Union Nové Zámky

	Pld	W	D	L	F	A	Pts
1 Glasgow City FC	3	3	0	0	10	0	9
2 WFC Kharkiv	3	2	0	1	8	5	6
3 Glentoran Belfast United	3	1	0	2	5	8	3
4 FC Union Nové Zámky	3	0	0	3	3	13	0

Lara Dickenmann of Lyon (all black) is challenged by Paris's Jessica Houara-D'Hommeaux in the all-French round of 16 tie

Group 5

09-14/08/14 Vinkovci, Osijek

ZFK Spartak Subotica 3-0 Amazones Dramas AS, ŽNK Osijek 12-0 SS-11 Goliador-Real, ZFK Spartak Subotica 19-0 SS-11 Goliador-Real, Amazones Dramas AS 1-3 ŽNK Osijek, ŽNK Osijek 1-0 ZFK Spartak Subotica, SS-11 Goliador-Real 0-11 Amazones Dramas AS

	Pld	W	D	L	F	A	Pts
1 ŽNK Osijek	3	3	0	0	16	1	9
2 ZFK Spartak Subotica	3	2	0	1	22	1	6
3 Amazones Dramas AS	3	1	0	2	12	6	3
4 SS-11 Goliador-Real	3	0	0	3	0	42	0

Group 6

09-14/08/14 Šiauliai, Pakruojis

Klaksvíkar Ítrottarfelag 1-2 Vllaznia, Apollon Ladies FC 3-1 Gintra Universitetas, Apollon Ladies FC 0-0 Vllaznia, Gintra Universitetas 2-0 Klaksvíkar Ítrottarfelag, Klaksvíkar Ítrottarfelag 1-3 Apollon Ladies FC, Vllaznia 0-5 Gintra Universitetas

	Pld	W	D	L	F	A	Pts
1 Apollon Ladies FC	3	2	1	0	6	2	7
2 Gintra Universitetas	3	2	0	1	8	3	6
3 Vllaznia	3	1	1	1	2	6	4
4 Klaksvíkar Ítrottarfelag	3	0	0	3	2	7	0

Group 7

09-14/08/14 Sarajevo

WFC SFK 2000 Sarajevo 0-3 KKPK Medyk Konin, Åland United 4-0 ZFK Kocani, WFC SFK 2000 Sarajevo 7-0 ZFK Kocani, KKPK Medyk Konin 7-0 Åland United, Åland United 0-1 WFC SFK 2000 Sarajevo, ZFK Kocani 1-11 KKPK Medyk Konin

	Pld	W	D	L	F	A	Pts
1 KKPK Medyk Konin	3	3	0	0	21	1	9
2 WFC SFK 2000 Sarajevo	3	2	0	1	8	36	6
3 Åland United	3	1	0	2	4	8	3
4 ZFK Kocani	3	0	0	3	1	22	0

Group 8

09-14/08/14 Fatima, Leiria

Standard de Liège 0-1 Clube Atlético Ouriense, ASA Tel-Aviv University SC 2-0 Cardiff Met Ladies FC, Standard de Liège 10-0 Cardiff Met Ladies FC, Clube Atlético Ouriense 2-1 ASA Tel-Aviv University SC, ASA Tel-Aviv University SC 0-1 Standard de Liège, Cardiff Met Ladies FC 2-1 Clube Atlético Ouriense

	Pld	W	D	L	F	A	Pts
1 Clube Atlético Ouriense	3	2	0	1	4	3	6
2 Standard de Liège	3	2	0	1	11	1	6
3 ASA Tel-Aviv University SC	3	1	0	2	3	3	3
4 Cardiff Met Ladies FC	3	1	0	2	2	13	3

Round of 32

08/10/14, BIIK Stadium, Shymkent
FC BIIK-Kazygurt 2-2 1. FFC Frankfurt
16/10/14, Am Brentano Bad, Frankfurt am Main
1. FFC Frankfurt 4-0 FC BIIK-Kazygurt
Aggregate: 6-2; 1. FFC Frankfurt qualify.

08/10/14, CSK YSC Stadium, Ryazan
Ryazan-VDV 1-3 FC Rosengård
15/10/14, Malmö Idrottsplats, Malmo
FC Rosengård 2-0 Ryazan-VDV
Aggregate: 5-1; FC Rosengård qualify.

08/10/14, Miejski Im. Zkotej Jedenastki, Konin
KKPK Medyk Konin 2-0 Glasgow City FC
15/10/14, Excelsior Stadium, Airdrie
Glasgow City FC 3-0 KKPK Medyk Konin (aet)
Aggregate: 3-2; Glasgow City FC qualify.

08/10/14, Tsirion Stadium, Limassol
Apollon Ladies FC 1-0 Brøndby IF
16/10/14, Brøndby, Brondby
Brøndby IF 3-1 Apollon Ladies FC (aet)
Aggregate: 3-2; Brøndby IF qualify.

08/10/14, Siauliai central stadium, Siauliai
Gintra Universitetas 1-1 AC Sparta Praha
15/10/14, Stadion Letná, Prague
AC Sparta Praha 1-1 Gintra Universitetas (aet)
Aggregate: 2-2; Gintra Universitetas qualify 5-4 on penalties.

08/10/14, Nadderud, Bekkestua
Stabæk Fotball 0-1 VfL Wolfsburg
16/10/14, VfL-Stadion, Wolfsburg
VfL Wolfsburg 2-1 Stabæk Fotball
Aggregate: 3-1; VfL Wolfsburg qualify.

08/10/14, Pancho stadium, Felcsut
MTK Hungária FC 1-2 NÖSV Neulengbach
15/10/14, Wienerwaldstadion, Neulengbach
NÖSV Neulengbach 2-2 MTK Hungária FC (aet)
Aggregate: 4-3; NÖSV Neulengbach qualify.

08/10/14, Gradski vrt, Osijek
ŽNK Osijek 2-5 FC Zürich Frauen
15/10/14, Stadion Letzigrund, Zurich
FC Zürich Frauen 2-0 ŽNK Osijek
Aggregate: 7-2; FC Zürich Frauen qualify.

08/10/14, Stadion Eden, Prague
SK Slavia Praha 0-1 FC Barcelona
15/10/14, Mini Estadi, Barcelona
FC Barcelona 3-0 SK Slavia Praha
Aggregate: 4-0; FC Barcelona qualify.

08/10/14, Stobart Halton, Widnes
Liverpool Ladies FC 2-1 Linköpings FC
16/10/14, Linköping Arena, Linkoping
Linköpings FC 3-0 Liverpool Ladies FC
Aggregate: 4-2; Linköpings FC qualify.

08/10/14, Športni park, Lendava
ŽNK Pomurje 2-4 ASD Torres Femminile Sassari
15/10/14, Vanni Sanna, Sassari
ASD Torres Femminile Sassari 3-1 ŽNK Pomurje
Aggregate: 7-3; ASD Torres Femminile Sassari qualify.

08/10/14, FC Twente Stadion, Enschede
FC Twente 1-2 Paris Saint-Germain
15/10/14, Charlety, Paris
Paris Saint-Germain 1-0 FC Twente
Aggregate: 3-1; Paris Saint-Germain qualify.

08/10/14, Municipal, Fatima
Clube Atlético Ouriense 0-3 Fortuna Hjørring
15/10/14, Frederikshavn Stadium, Frederikshavn
Fortuna Hjørring 6-0 Clube Atlético Ouriense
Aggregate: 9-0; Fortuna Hjørring qualify.

08/10/14, Stjörnuvöllur, Gardabaer
Stjarnan 2-5 WFC Zvezda 2005
16/10/14, Zvezda, Perm
WFC Zvezda 2005 3-1 Stjarnan
Aggregate: 8-3; WFC Zvezda 2005 qualify.

09/10/14, Richmond Park, Dublin
Raheny United FC 0-4 Bristol Academy WFC
16/10/14, Ashton Gate, Bristol
Bristol Academy WFC 2-1 Raheny United FC
Aggregate: 6-1; Bristol Academy WFC qualify.

09/10/14, Mario Rigamonti, Brescia
ACF Brescia Femminile 0-5 Olympique Lyonnais
15/10/14, Stade de Gerland, Lyon
Olympique Lyonnais 9-0 ACF Brescia Femminile
Aggregate: 14-0; Olympique Lyonnais qualify.

Round of 16

08/11/14, Malmö Idrottsplats, Malmo
FC Rosengård 2-1 Fortuna Hjørring
Goals: 1-0 Mittag 12, 1-1 Podersen 50, 2-1 Schmidt 66
Referee: Gaál (HUN)
13/11/14, Aalborg Stadion, Aalborg
Fortuna Hjørring 0-2 FC Rosengård
Goals: 0-1 Marta 44(p), 0-2 Schmidt 77
Referee: Mularczyk (POL)
Aggregate: 1-4; FC Rosengård qualify.

08/11/14, Linköping Arena, Linkoping
Linköpings FC 5-0 WFC Zvezda 2005
Goals: 1-0 Rohlin 11, 2-0 Harder 26, 3-0 Rolfö 37, 4-0 Ericsson 39, 5-0 Knudsen 75
Referee: Zadinová (CZE)
13/11/14, Zvezda, Perm
WFC Zvezda 2005 3-0 Linköpings FC
Goals: 1-0 Pantyukhina 1, 2-0 Nahi 58, 3-0 Andrushchak 86
Referee: Bastos (POR)
Aggregate: 3-5; Linköpings FC qualify.

08/11/14, Charlety, Paris
Paris Saint-Germain 1-1 Olympique Lyonnais
Goals: 0-1 Petit 20, 1-1 Alushi 49
Referee: Monzul (UKR)
12/11/14, Stade de Gerland, Lyon
Olympique Lyonnais 0-1 Paris Saint-Germain
Goal: 0-1 Alushi 80
Referee: Kulcsár (HUN)
Aggregate: 1-2; Paris Saint-Germain qualify.

08/11/14, Mini Estadi, Barcelona
FC Barcelona 0-1 Bristol Academy WFC
Goal: 0-1 Corredera 26(og)
Referee: Dorcioman (ROU)
13/11/14, Ashton Gate, Bristol
Bristol Academy WFC 1-1 FC Barcelona
Goals: 0-1 Losada 40, 1-1 Watts 83(p)
Referee: Pustovoitova (RUS)
Aggregate: 2-1; Bristol Academy WFC qualify.

09/11/14, Am Brentano Bad, Frankfurt am Main
1. FFC Frankfurt 5-0 ASD Torres Femminile Sassari
Goals: 1-0 Šašic 7, 2-0 Garefrekes 15, 3-0 Verónica Boquete 19, 4-0 Šašic 31, 5-0 Laudehr 45+1(p)
Heteree: Persson (SWE)
12/11/14, Vanni Sanna, Sassari
ASD Torres Femminile Sassari 0-4 1. FFC Frankfurt
Goals: 0-1 Marozsán 33, 0-2 Piacezzi 41(og), 0-3 Šašic 45, 0-4 Šašic 88
Referee: Adámková (CZE)
Aggregate: 0-9; 1. FFC Frankfurt qualify.

09/11/14, Brøndby, Brondby
Brøndby IF 5-0 Gintra Universitetas
Goals: 1-0 Lahmti 6, 2-0 Madsen 16, 3-0 Madsen 21, 4-0 Ali Abu Alful 47, 5-0 Nielsen 89
Referee: Azzopardi (MLT)
12/11/14, Šiauliai central stadium, Siauliai
Gintra Universitetas 2-0 Brøndby IF
Goals: 1-0 Vanagaite 11, 2-0 Alekperova 42
Referee: Hussein (GER)
Aggregate: 2-5; Brøndby IF qualify.

09/11/14, Wienerwaldstadion, Neulengbach
NÖSV Neulengbach 0-4 VfL Wolfsburg
Goals: 0-1 Müller 16, 0-2 Vojteková 63(og), 0-3 Müller 79, 0-4 Popp 81
Referee: Mitsi (GRE)
12/11/14, VfL-Stadion, Wolfsburg
VfL Wolfsburg 7-0 NÖSV Neulengbach
Goals: 1-0 Magull 3, 2-0 Popp 24, 3-0 Magull 32, 4-0 Wagner 63, 5-0 Wagner 65, 6-0 Fischer 89, 7-0 Bernauer 90+1
Referee: Albon (ROU)
Aggregate: 11-0; VfL Wolfsburg qualify.

09/11/14, Stadion Letzigrund, Zurich
FC Zürich Frauen 2-1 Glasgow City FC
Goals: 1-0 Humm 10, 1-1 Brown 52, 2-1 Stierli 59
Referee: Frappart (FRA)
12/11/14, Excelsior Stadium, Airdrie
Glasgow City FC 4-2 FC Zürich Frauen
Goals: 0-1 Zehnder 45+9, 1-1 Grant 55, 2-1 Ross 64(p), 2-2 Humm 66, 3-2 Love 81, 4-2 Lappin 87
Referee: Larsson (SWE)
Aggregate: 5-4; Glasgow City FC qualify.

Bristol players greet the final whistle with jubilation as they knock out Barcelona

Glasgow's Nicola Doherty is pursued by Paris duo Marie-Laure Delie (left) and Kosovare Asllani in the quarter-final tie

Quarter-finals

21/03/15, Ashton Gate, Bristol
Bristol Academy WFC 0-5 1. FFC Frankfurt
Goals: 0-1 Verónica Boquete 36, 0-2 Schmidt 45, 0-3 Marozsán 66, 0-4 Islacker 78, 0-5 Garefrekes 81
Referee: Larsson (SWE)
29/03/15, Am Brentano Bad, Frankfurt am Main
1. FFC Frankfurt 7-0 Bristol Academy WFC
Goals: 1-0 Ando 8, 2-0 Marozsán 38, 3-0 Islacker 58, 4-0 Islacker 68, 5-0 Islacker 75, 6-0 Störzel 87, 7-0 Löber 90+3(p)
Referee: Bastos (POR)
Aggregate: 12-0; 1. FFC Frankfurt qualify.

22/03/15, Linköping Arena, Linkoping
Linköpings FC 0-1 Brøndby IF
Goal: 0-1 Rohlin 14(og)
Referee: Mularczyk (POL)
28/03/15, Brøndby, Brondby
Brøndby IF 1-1 Linköpings FC
Goals: 1-0 Madsen 6, 1-1 Knudsen 44
Referee: Steinhaus (GER)
Aggregate: 2-1; Brøndby IF qualify.

22/03/15, Excelsior Stadium, Airdrie
Glasgow City FC 0-2 Paris Saint-Germain
Goals: 0-1 Lahmari 19, 0-2 Hamraoui 53
Referee: Hussein (GER)

28/03/15, Parc des Princes, Paris
Paris Saint-Germain 5-0 Glasgow City FC
Goals: 1-0 Lappin 26(og), 2-0 Delie 54, 3-0 Delannoy 65(p), 4-0 Delie 68, 5-0 Dali 87(p)
Referee: Gaál (HUN)
Aggregate: 7-0; Paris Saint-Germain qualify.

22/03/15, AOK stadium, Wolfsburg
VfL Wolfsburg 1-1 FC Rosengård
Goals: 0-1 Marta 56, 1-1 Faisst 66
Referee: Frappart (FRA)
28/03/15, Malmö Idrottsplats, Malmo
FC Rosengård 3-3 VfL Wolfsburg
Goals: 0-1 Popp 4, 1-1 Marta 24, 2-1 Mittag 42, 2-2 Peter 55, 2-3 Popp 81, 3-3 Gunnarsdóttir 90+3
Referee: Staubli (SUI)
Aggregate: 4-4; VfL Wolfsburg qualify on away goals.

Semi-finals

18/04/15, AOK stadium, Wolfsburg
VfL Wolfsburg 0-2 Paris Saint-Germain
Goals: 0-1 Delannoy 12(p), 0-2 Cruz Traña 26
Referee: Larsson (SWE)
26/04/15, Charlety, Paris
Paris Saint-Germain 1-2 VfL Wolfsburg
Goals: 1-0 Kaci 6, 1-1 Müller 71, 1-2 Jakabfi 74
Referee: Monzul (UKR)
Aggregate: 3-2; Paris Saint-Germain qualify.

19/04/15, Am Brentano Bad, Frankfurt am Main
1. FFC Frankfurt 7-0 Brøndby IF
Goals: 1-0 Šašić 10(p), 2-0 Sevecke 28(og), 3-0 Šašić 32, 4-0 Marozsán 41, 5-0 Laudehr 46, 6-0 Šašić 62, 7-0 Šašić 69
Referee: Kulcsár (HUN)
25/04/15, Brøndby, Brondby
Brøndby IF 0-6 1. FFC Frankfurt
Goals: 0-1 Verónica Boquete 7, 0-2 Šašić 14, 0-3 Šašić 25, 0-4 Verónica Boquete 32, 0-5 Šašić 39, 0-6 Verónica Boquete 84
Referee: Mitsi (GRE)
Aggregate: 0-13; 1. FFC Frankfurt qualify.

Final

14/05/15, Friedrich-Ludwig-Jahn-Sportpark, Berlin (att: 18,300)
1. FFC Frankfurt 2-1 Paris Saint-Germain
Goals: 1-0 Šašić 32, 1-1 Delie 40, 2-1 Islacker 90+2
Referee: Staubli (SUI)
Frankfurt: Schumann, Hendrich, Verónica Boquete, Šašić, Marozsán, Laudehr (Ando 87), Priessen, Garefrekes, Crnogorčević (Islacker 66), Schmidt (Huth 79), Kuznik. Coach: Colin Bell (ENG)
Paris: Kiedrzynek, Dali, Boulleau (Henning 60), Delannoy, Asllani (Sarr 90+5), Houara-D'Hommeaux, Krahn, Kaci, Delie, Alushi (Georges 58), Cruz Traña. Coach: Farid Benstiti (FRA)
Yellow cards: Laudehr 44 (Frankfurt), Delannoy 74 (Paris), Krahn 84 (Paris)

Top goalscorers

14	Célia Šašić (Frankfurt)
6	Fabienne Humm (Zürich)
	Verónica Boquete (Frankfurt)
	Dzsenifer Marozsán (Frankfurt)
5	Mandy Islacker (Frankfurt)
	José Nahi (Zvezda 2005)
	Eugénie Le Sommer (Lyon)
	Anja Mittag (Rosengård)

Road to Netherlands 2017 takes shape

Preliminary round results

Group 1

04/04/15, District Sport Complex, Orhei
Luxembourg 4-3 Latvia

04/04/15, CPSM, Vadul lui Voda
Moldova 2-0 Lithuania

06/04/15, District Sport Complex, Orhei
Lithuania 2-0 Luxembourg

06/04/15, CPSM, Vadul lui Voda
Moldova 0-1 Latvia

09/04/15, CPSM, Vadul lui Voda
Luxembourg 0-3 Moldova

09/04/15, District Sport Complex, Orhei
Latvia 1-1 Lithuania

		Pld	W	D	L	F	A	Pts
1	Moldova	3	2	0	1	5	1	6
2	Latvia	3	1	1	1	5	5	4
3	Lithuania	3	1	1	1	3	3	4
4	Luxembourg	3	1	0	2	4	8	3

Group 2

04/04/15, Victor Tedesco, Hamrun
Georgia 2-0 Faroe Islands

04/04/15, Victor Tedesco, Hamrun
Andorra 3-5 Malta

06/04/15, Victor Tedesco, Hamrun
Faroe Islands 8-0 Andorra

06/04/15, Victor Tedesco, Hamrun
Georgia 1-2 Malta

09/04/15, Victor Tedesco, Hamrun
Malta 2-4 Faroe Islands

09/04/15, Ta' Qali National Stadium, Ta' Qali
Andorra 0-7 Georgia

Action from the preliminary round encounter in Malta between Group 2 winners Georgia (all red) and the Faroe Islands

		Pld	W	D	L	F	A	Pts
1	Georgia	3	2	0	1	10	2	6
2	Faroe Islands	3	2	0	1	12	4	6
3	Malta	3	2	0	1	9	8	6
4	Andorra	3	0	0	3	3	20	0

Qualifying groups

Group 1

Iceland, Scotland, Belarus, Slovenia, FYR Macedonia

Group 2

Spain, Finland, Republic of Ireland, Portugal, Montenegro

Group 3

France, Ukraine, Romania, Greece, Albania

Group 4

Sweden, Denmark, Poland, Slovakia, Moldova

Group 5

Germany, Russia, Hungary, Turkey, Croatia

Group 6

Italy, Switzerland, Czech Republic, Northern Ireland, Georgia

Group 7

England, Belgium, Serbia, Bosnia & Herzegovina, Estonia

Group 8

Norway, Austria, Wales, Israel, Kazakhstan

NB Qualifying fixtures appear on page 752.

Goals galore for ace striker Stina Blackstenius

Second title sealed with 3-1 win against Spain

Record crowd attend eventful final in Netanya

Sweden surge to victory

Twelve months on from a Vivianne Miedema-inspired first victory at the UEFA European Women's Under-19 Championship for the Netherlands, another tall, blonde No9 hogged the headlines as Sweden triumphed for the second time, defeating Spain 3-1 in the final. Stina Blackstenius had already established new goalscoring records before she showcased her devastating pace and power to a wider audience in the televised final, staged in the Israeli town of Netanya.

Spain appeared to be in control when Blackstenius announced her presence on 24 minutes with a barnstorming move that left the final record crowd of 7,230 collectively nodding in approval. The Linköpings FC forward was rampant. Spain could not get near her, with red shirts strewn across the turf as she ran amok. Two goals before the interval lifted her tally to an astonishing 20 from ten appearances in the 2014/15 competition.

"It's very difficult to deal with a player like that," admitted Spain boss Jorge Vilda, whose father Ángel had been in charge three years earlier when Spain lost 1-0 to Sweden in the final. "It's like playing against a team with Cristiano Ronaldo or Lionel Messi. When they are

that much better than the rest, it's hard to get hold of them." His side managed it for a while, and halved the deficit nine minutes from time through Sandra Hernández, but Blackstenius would not be denied. With a minute left she surged to the byline and pulled the ball back for Filippa Angeldal to drive in and seal victory for Calle Barling's team.

It was fitting that the final hung in the balance until the end. Both semis had gone to extra time and penalties, Spain edging out France while Sweden got the

Jubilant Sweden players celebrate their triumph in Israel

better of Germany after a thrilling 3-3 draw, with Blackstenius scoring an 88th-minute equaliser. Germany should perhaps have seen it coming as Sweden had required another last-gasp goal on the final day of their elite round qualifying section to qualify for Israel at Italy's expense.

England's passage to the final tournament was even more dramatic as they benefited from an unprecedented decision to retake a 94th-minute penalty against Norway five days after it was awarded, as a result of a refereeing error. Leah Williamson held her nerve to take England through alongside their opponents, who qualified as the best runners-up. The sides were paired again at the finals in Group B, but both failed to get out of the group, with Spain and Germany going through despite the latter's shock 2-0 defeat to Norway.

The progress of France and Sweden from Group A was confirmed after two of the three games, but there was a nice sub-plot in the last round as hosts Israel, making their debut at the finals, scored their first goal. Blackstenius would score six times as many on her own, though, as the superstar-in-the-making blasted Sweden all the way to victory.

UEFA European Women's Under-19 Championship

Qualifying round

Group 1

13-10/09/14 Marijampolc, Kaunao
Spain 7-0 Croatia, Iceland 8-0 Lithuania, Spain 14-0 Lithuania, Croatia 0-1 Iceland, Iceland 1-2 Spain, Lithuania 2-3 Croatia

		Pld	W	D	L	F	A	Pts
1	Spain	3	3	0	0	23	1	9
2	Iceland	3	2	0	1	10	2	6
3	Croatia	3	1	0	2	3	10	3
4	Lithuania	3	0	0	3	2	25	0

Group 2

13-18/09/14 Baku
Ukraine 1-0 Azerbaijan, Denmark 3-0 Cyprus, Cyprus 1-3 Ukraine, Denmark 3-0 Azerbaijan, Ukraine 1-4 Denmark, Azerbaijan 0-0 Cyprus

		Pld	W	D	L	F	A	Pts
1	Denmark	3	3	0	0	10	1	9
2	Ukraine	3	2	0	1	5	5	6
3	Azerbaijan	3	0	1	2	0	4	1
4	Cyprus	3	0	1	2	1	6	1

Group 3

13-18/09/14 Fier, Vlora
Norway 3-0 Poland, Scotland 8-0 Albania, Poland 1-3 Scotland, Norway 11-0 Albania, Scotland 0-0 Norway, Albania 0-5 Poland

		Pld	W	D	L	F	A	Pts
1	Norway	3	2	1	0	14	0	7
2	Scotland	3	2	1	0	11	1	7
3	Poland	3	1	0	2	6	6	3
4	Albania	3	0	0	3	0	24	0

Group 4

13-18/09/14 Bursa, Inegol
Wales 3-1 Kazakhstan, Italy 1-0 Turkey, Italy 8-0 Kazakhstan, Turkey 1-1 Wales, Wales 0-3 Italy, Kazakhstan 1-6 Turkey

		Pld	W	D	L	F	A	Pts
1	Italy	3	3	0	0	12	0	9
2	Turkey	3	1	1	1	7	3	4
3	Wales	3	1	1	1	4	5	4
4	Kazakhstan	3	0	0	3	2	17	0

Group 5

13-18/09/14 Jakovo, Stara Pazova, Pecinci
Netherlands 9-0 Faroe Islands, Serbia 5-1 Latvia, Netherlands 10-0 Latvia, Faroe Islands 2-5 Serbia, Serbia 1-2 Netherlands, Latvia 0-3 Faroe Islands

		Pld	W	D	L	F	A	Pts
1	Netherlands	3	3	0	0	21	1	9
2	Serbia	3	2	0	1	11	5	6
3	Faroe Islands	3	1	0	2	5	14	3
4	Latvia	3	0	0	3	1	18	0

Group 6

13-18/09/14 Kristianstad, Staffanstorp, Trelleborg
Sweden 3-0 Moldova, Republic of Ireland 3-0 Montenegro, Moldova 1-1 Republic of Ireland, Sweden 12-0 Montenegro, Republic of Ireland 1-5 Sweden, Montenegro 2-3 Moldova

Sweden's Stina Blackstenius - the star of the whole competition with 20 goals

		Pld	W	D	L	F	A	Pts
1	Sweden	3	3	0	0	20	1	9
2	Republic of Ireland	3	1	1	1	5	6	4
3	Moldova	3	1	1	1	4	6	4
4	Montenegro	3	0	0	3	2	18	0

Group 7

13-18/09/14 Sarajevo
Czech Republic 2-0 Bosnia & Herzegovina, Romania 0-0 Malta, Czech Republic 6-0 Malta, Bosnia & Herzegovina 1-1 Romania, Romania 1-0 Czech Republic, Malta 1-4 Bosnia & Herzegovina

		Pld	W	D	L	F	A	Pts
1	Czech Republic	3	2	0	1	8	1	6
2	Romania	3	1	2	0	2	1	5
3	Bosnia & Herzegovina	3	1	1	1	5	4	4
4	Malta	3	0	1	2	1	10	1

Group 8

13-18/09/14 Viseu, Tondela, Santa Comba Dao, Penalva Castelo, Nelas, Mangualde
Russia 9-0 Belarus, Portugal 9-0 FYR Macedonia, FYR Macedonia 0-4 Russia, Portugal 6-0 Belarus, Russia 1-0 Portugal, Belarus 2-2 FYR Macedonia

		Pld	W	D	L	F	A	Pts
1	Russia	3	3	0	0	14	0	9
2	Portugal	3	2	0	1	15	1	6
3	FYR Macedonia	3	0	1	2	2	15	1
4	Belarus	3	0	1	2	2	17	1

Group 9

13-18/09/14 Buk, Papa
Belgium 4-0 Slovenia, Hungary 4-0 Estonia, Belgium 1-0 Estonia, Slovenia 1-0 Hungary, Hungary 1-2 Belgium, Estonia 2-4 Slovenia

		Pld	W	D	L	F	A	Pts
1	Belgium	3	3	0	0	7	1	9
2	Slovenia	3	2	0	1	5	6	6
3	Hungary	3	1	0	2	5	3	3
4	Estonia	3	0	0	3	2	9	0

Group 10

13-18/09/14 Tammela, Kaarina
Finland 4-0 Greece, Northern Ireland 8-0 Georgia, Greece 0-1 Northern Ireland, Finland 7-0 Georgia, Northern Ireland 0-3 Finland, Georgia 0-8 Greece

		Pld	W	D	L	F	A	Pts
1	Finland	3	3	0	0	14	0	9
2	Northern Ireland	3	2	0	1	9	3	6
3	Greece	3	1	0	2	8	5	3
4	Georgia	3	0	0	3	0	23	0

Group 11

13-18/09/14 Albena, Kavarna
Switzerland 5-0 Slovakia, Austria 8-0 Bulgaria, Switzerland 9-0 Bulgaria, Slovakia 0-3 Austria, Austria 0-2 Switzerland, Bulgaria 2-7 Slovakia

		Pld	W	D	L	F	A	Pts
1	Switzerland	3	3	0	0	16	0	9
2	Austria	3	2	0	1	11	2	6
3	Slovakia	3	1	0	2	7	10	3
4	Bulgaria	3	0	0	3	2	24	0

Elite round

Group 1

04-09/04/15 Lagos, Ferreiras, Faro-Loule, Parchal
Finland 2-2 Turkey, Spain 2-0 Portugal, Spain 5-0 Turkey, Portugal 1-1 Finland, Finland 0-6 Spain, Turkey 0-1 Portugal

		Pld	W	D	L	F	A	Pts
1	Spain	3	3	0	0	13	0	9
2	Portugal	3	1	1	1	2	3	4
3	Finland	3	0	2	1	3	9	2
4	Turkey	3	0	1	2	2	8	1

Group 2

04-09/04/15 Jakovo, Stara Pazova, Pecinci
Sweden 0-0 Austria, Italy 4-2 Serbia, Sweden 4-2 Serbia, Austria 2-3 Italy, Italy 1-2 Sweden, Serbia 1-5 Austria

		Pld	W	D	L	F	A	Pts
1	Sweden	3	2	1	0	6	3	7
2	Italy	3	2	0	1	8	6	6
3	Austria	3	1	1	1	7	4	4
4	Serbia	3	0	0	3	5	13	0

Group 3

04-09/04/15 Melun, Ozoir La Ferriere
France 5-0 Iceland, Russia 2-0 Romania, France 2-0 Romania, Iceland 1-4 Russia, Russia 0-1 France, Romania 0-3 Iceland

		Pld	W	D	L	F	A	Pts
1	France	3	3	0	0	8	0	9
2	Russia	3	2	0	1	6	2	6
3	Iceland	3	1	0	2	4	9	3
4	Romania	3	0	0	3	0	7	0

Group 4

04-09/04/15 Belfast
England 2-2 Norway, Switzerland 1-0 Northern Ireland, Norway 2-0 Switzerland, England 9-1 Northern Ireland, Switzerland 1-3 England, Northern Ireland 1-8 Norway

		Pld	W	D	L	F	A	Pts
1	England	3	2	1	0	14	4	7
2	Norway	3	2	1	0	12	3	7
3	Switzerland	3	1	0	2	2	5	3
4	Northern Ireland	3	0	0	3	2	18	0

UEFA European Women's Under-19 Championship

Group 5

04-09/04/15 Forst, Schwetzingen
**Belgium 1-0 Ukraine, Germany 6-0 Scotland,
Scotland 2-2 Belgium, Germany 9-0 Ukraine,
Belgium 1-3 Germany, Ukraine 0-3 Scotland**

		Pld	W	D	L	F	A	Pts
1	Germany	3	3	0	0	18	1	9
2	Belgium	3	1	1	1	4	5	4
3	Scotland	3	1	1	1	5	8	4
4	Ukraine	3	0	0	3	0	13	0

Group 6

04-09/04/15 Meerssen, Landgraaf
**Netherlands 6-0 Czech Republic, Denmark
4-0 Slovenia, Netherlands 3-0 Slovenia,
Czech Republic 1-2 Denmark, Denmark 1-0
Netherlands, Slovenia 0-2 Czech Republic**

		Pld	W	D	L	F	A	Pts
1	Denmark	3	3	0	0	7	1	9
2	Netherlands	3	2	0	1	9	1	6
3	Czech Republic	3	1	0	2	3	8	3
4	Slovenia	3	0	0	3	0	9	0

Top goalscorers (Qualifying/Elite rounds)

14	Stina Blackstenius (Sweden)
9	Jill Roord (Netherlands)
8	Andrea Sánchez (Spain)
7	Mariona Caldentey (Spain)
	Nahikari García (Spain)
6	Julia Glaser (Switzerland)
	Valentina Bergamaschi (Italy)
	Margarita Chernomyrdina (Russia)

Final tournament

Group A

15/07/15, Netanya Municipal Stadium, Netanya
France 1-0 Denmark
Goal: 1-0 Léger 49

15/07/15, Lod Municipal, Lod
Israel 0-3 Sweden
Goals: 0-1 Björn 22, 0-2 Blackstenius 28, 0-3
Blackstenius 72

18/07/15, Haberfeld Stadium, Rishon Le-zion
Sweden 1-0 Denmark
Goal: 1-0 Angeldal 35(p)

18/07/15, Netanya Municipal Stadium, Netanya
Israel 0-4 France
Goals: 0-1 Mateo 10, 0-2 Carage 26, 0-3 Gathrat
63, 0-4 Léger 90

21/07/15, Lod Municipal, Lod
Denmark 2-1 Israel
Goals: 0-1 Avital 22, 1-1 Sørensen 33, 2-1
Sørensen 60

21/07/15, Netanya Municipal Stadium, Netanya
Sweden 0-1 France
Goal: 0-1 E Andersson 5(og)

		Pld	W	D	L	F	A	Pts
1	France	3	3	0	0	6	0	9
2	Sweden	3	2	0	1	4	1	6
3	Denmark	3	1	0	2	2	3	3
4	Israel	3	0	0	3	1	9	0

Group B

15/07/15, Haberfeld Stadium, Rishon Le-zion
England 1-2 Germany
Goals: 0-1 Ehegötz 25, 1-1 George 30,
1-2 Knaak 87

15/07/15, Ramla Municipal Stadium, Ramla
Spain 4-0 Norway
Goals: 1-0 Redondo 22, 2-0 García 26, 3-0 Pilar
38, 4-0 Redondo 83

18/07/15, Ramla Municipal Stadium, Ramla
England 1-3 Spain
Goals: 1-0 Flint 9, 1-1 Pilar 54, 1-2 Redondo 82,
1-3 Gálvez 90

18/07/15, Lod Municipal, Lod
Germany 0-2 Norway
Goals: 0-1 Fjelldal 5, 0-2 Knaak 33(og)

21/07/15, Ramla Municipal Stadium, Ramla
Norway 0-0 England

21/07/15, Haberfeld Stadium, Rishon Le-zion
Germany 1-0 Spain
Goal: 1-0 Gálvez 39(og)

		Pld	W	D	L	F	A	Pts
1	Germany	3	2	0	1	3	3	6
2	Spain	3	2	0	1	7	2	6
3	Norway	3	1	1	1	2	4	4
4	England	3	0	1	2	2	5	1

Semi-finals

24/07/15, Netanya Municipal Stadium, Netanya
Germany 3-3 Sweden (aet)
Goals: 1-0 Knaak 12, 1-1 Almqvist 21, 1-2
Blackstenius 44, 2-2 Ehegötz 58, 3-2 Gier 78, 3-3
Blackstenius 88
Sweden qualify 4-2 on penalties.

24/07/15, Lod Municipal, Lod
France 1-1 Spain (aet)
Goals: 1-0 Léger 36, 1-1 Sánchez 42
Spain qualify 5-4 on penalties.

Final

27/07/15, Netanya Municipal Stadium, Netanya
(att: 7,230)
Spain 1-3 Sweden
Goals: 0-1 Blackstenius 28, 0-2 Blackstenius 36,
1-2 Hernández 81, 1-3 Angeldal 89
Referee: Lehtovaara (FIN)
Spain: De Toro, Nuria, Turmo (Baños 88), Gálvez,
Pilar, García, Ortega (Domínguez 60), Sánchez
(Mañoso 79), Hernández, Beltrán, Redondo. Coach:
Jorge Vilda (ESP)
Sweden: Holmgren, Aronsson, Ekholm, Björn
(Göthberg 88), Ökvist, Löfqvist, Almqvist (E
Andersson 79), Blackstenius, Hallin (Angeldal 68),
Oskarsson, De Jongh. Coach: Calle Barrling (SWE)
Yellow card: Aronsson 90+3 (Sweden)

Top goalscorers (Final tournament)

6	Stina Blackstenius (Sweden)
3	Marie-Charlotte Léger (France)
3	Alba Redondo (Spain)
2	Filippa Angeldal (Sweden)
	Nicoline Sørensen (Denmark)
	Pilar Garrote (Spain)
	Nina Ehegötz (Germany)
	Rebecca Knaak (Germany)

Squads/Appearances/Goals

Denmark

No	Name	DoB	Aps	(s)	Gls
Goalkeepers					
1	Naja Bahrenscheer	03/09/96	3		
16	Thora Hansen	13/01/96			
Defenders					
7	Emilie Henriksen	15/03/97	3		
4	Maja Kildemoes	15/08/96	3		
11	Stine Larsen	24/01/96	3		
2	Sofie Obel	13/06/97	1		
5	Louise Ringsing	20/08/96	1	(1)	
6	Rikke Sevecke	15/06/96	3		
Midfielders					
8	Sara Thrige Andersen	15/05/96	3		
17	Sofie Broch-Lips	22/11/96		(2)	
3	Ida Guldager	25/10/96	1	(1)	
9	Sarah Hansen	14/09/96	3		
19	Signe Schioldan	04/01/97	2		
10	Nicoline Sørensen	15/08/97	3		2
Forwards					
14	Signe Bruun	06/04/98	1	(2)	
12	Marie Maj Madsen	16/05/96	2		
15	Rikke Madsen	09/08/97		(1)	
13	Amalie Vangsgaard	29/11/96	1	(1)	

England

No	Name	DoB	Aps	(s)	Gls
Goalkeepers					
13	Sophie Baggaley	29/11/96			
1	Caitlin Leach	16/11/96	3		
Defenders					
6	Molly Bartrip	01/06/96	3		
16	Ashlee Brown	04/08/96			
3	Gabrielle George	02/02/97	3		1
15	Elisha N'Dow	13/10/96			
5	Ellie Stewart	02/11/96	3		
2	Eloise Wilson	11/05/97	3		
Midfielders					
4	Jodie Brett	09/03/96	3		
8	Jenna Dear	29/05/96	3		
14	Millie Turner	07/07/96		(2)	
10	Katie Zelem	20/01/96	3		
Forwards					
11	Rosella Ayane	16/03/96	3		
9	Natasha Flint	02/08/96	3		1
18	Mollie Green	04/08/97		(2)	
17	Jenna Legg	23/06/97		(1)	
12	Taome Oliver	11/05/96			
7	Claudia Walker	10/06/96	3		

France

No	Name	DoB	Aps	(s)	Gls
Goalkeepers					
16	Romane Bruneau	27/08/96		(1)	
1	Cindy Perrault	26/01/96	4		
Defenders					
5	Noémie Carage	09/09/96	2	(1)	1
13	Estelle Cascarino	05/02/97	2		
4	Hawa Cissoko	10/04/97	3		
12	Pauline Dhaeyer	27/03/96	3		
3	Théa Greboval	05/04/97	3		
2	Marion Romanelli	24/07/96	3		
Midfielders					
6	Laura Condon	18/03/97	2	(2)	
10	Maëlle Garbino	09/08/96	3	(1)	
8	Juliane Gathrat	24/08/96	3	(1)	1
14	Grace Geyoro	02/07/97	2		
19	Anissa Lahmari	17/02/97		(3)	
17	Clara Mateo	28/11/97	3	(1)	1
15	Laurie Teinturier	20/02/96	1		
Forwards					
7	Delphine Cascarino	05/02/97	1		
11	Sakina Karchaoui	26/01/96	4		
9	Marie-Charlotte Léger	13/03/96	3	(1)	3
18	Anaïs Pugnetti	08/03/97	2	(1)	

Israel

No	Name	DoB	Aps	(s)	Gls
Goalkeepers					
18	Hannah Elizabeth Boshari	22/02/97	2		
1	Fortuna Rubin	04/06/96	1		
Defenders					
8	Keren Goor	28/07/98	2	(1)	
7	Noam Kedem	14/02/98	3		
20	Shayna Rebecca Levi	06/04/97	2		
5	Shai Pearl	01/03/97	3		
Midfielders					
16	Maia Nedara Cabrera	17/07/99		(1)	
11	Gina Eide	20/08/98		(2)	
4	Anna Manevich	15/07/96	2		
15	Alina Metkalov	17/03/98	3		
9	Shahar Nakav	12/04/97	1		
12	Opal Sofer	20/05/97	2	(1)	
6	Summer Galya Sofer	09/01/96	1	(1)	
3	Sarit Winstok	05/01/99	1	(1)	
Forwards					
10	Eden Avital	25/03/97	3		1
17	Marian Awad	29/10/96	3		
13	Dalia Dakwar	09/10/96	2	(1)	
14	Lauren Justine Leah Goetzman	11/02/97	2	(1)	

Spain

No	Name	DoB	Aps	(s)	Gls
Goalkeepers					
1	Paula Canals	20/06/96			
13	Elena De Toro	31/01/97	5		
Defenders					
16	Beatriz Beltrán	10/12/97	5		
5	Rocío Gálvez	15/04/97	5		1
9	Lucía Gómez	11/10/96	3		
2	Nuria Garrote	10/06/97	4		
12	Jennifer Santiago	18/10/96			
18	Paola Soldevila	07/12/96	1	(1)	
3	Marta Turmo	27/06/96	5		
Midfielders					
14	Leire Baños	29/11/96	1	(4)	
15	Sandra Hernández	25/05/97	5		1
8	Laura Ortega	10/11/97	2	(2)	
6	Pilar Garrote	10/06/97	4	(1)	2
17	Alba Redondo	27/08/96	5		3
Forwards					
4	Laura Domínguez	12/08/97		(5)	
7	Nahikari García	10/03/97	5		1
11	Paula Mañoso	29/01/97		(2)	
10	Andrea Sánchez	28/02/97	5		1

Germany

No	Name	DoB	Aps	(s)	Gls
Goalkeepers					
1	Lena Pauels	02/02/98	2		
12	Carina Schlüter	08/11/96	2		
Defenders					
2	Michaela Brandenburg	17/12/97	4		
13	Isabella Hartig	12/08/97	3		
15	Franziska Jaser	20/01/96			
5	Rebecca Knaak	23/06/96	4		2
3	Felicitas Rauch	30/04/96	4		
14	Johanna Tietge	16/04/96			
4	Joelle Wedemeyer	12/08/96	4		
Midfielders					
6	Rieke Dieckmann	16/08/96	4		
8	Jenny Gaugigl	22/08/96	2	(1)	
16	Saskia Matheis	06/06/97	2	(1)	
11	Lea Schüller	12/11/97	3	(1)	
17	Pia-Sophie Wolter	13/11/97	1	(3)	
Forwards					
9	Nina Ehegötz	22/02/97	4		2
10	Laura Freigang	01/02/98	4		
18	Madeline Gier	28/04/96		(3)	1
7	Jasmin Sehan	16/06/97	1	(3)	

Norway

No	Name	DoB	Aps	(s)	Gls
Goalkeepers					
1	Cecilie Fiskerstrand	20/03/96	2		
12	Aurora Mikalsen	21/03/96	1		
Defenders					
3	Marit Clausen	25/06/96	3		
13	Ingrid Elvebakken	28/04/97			
2	Tuva Hansen	04/08/97	3		
4	Kristine Leine	06/08/96	3		
5	Marit B Lund	07/11/97	3		
Midfielders					
7	Cecilie Dekkerhus	14/08/97	3		
14	Sara Eriksen	20/03/96			
9	Johanne Fridlund	24/07/96	3		
16	Karoline Haugland	23/02/98	1	(1)	
6	Karina Sævik	24/03/96	3		
Forwards					
11	Vilde Fjelldal	23/09/97	3		1
17	Vilde Hasund	27/06/97		(2)	
15	Maria Hiim	06/10/97	2		
8	Nora Eide Lie	22/04/97	3		
10	Marie Markussen	15/02/97		(3)	
18	Pernille Velta	20/06/96		(1)	

Sweden

No	Name	DoB	Aps	(s)	Gls
Goalkeepers					
1	Matilda Haglund	05/12/96	1		
12	Emma Holmgren	13/05/97	4		
Defenders					
13	Emelie Andersson	13/09/96	2	(2)	
2	Ronja Aronsson	20/12/96	5		
4	Nathalie Björn	04/05/97	3		1
3	Julia Ekholm	17/06/96	5		
15	Maja Göthberg	16/07/97	1	(2)	
5	Lotta Ökvist	17/02/97	4	(1)	
Midfielders					
7	Tove Almqvist	05/01/96	4		1
8	Filippa Angeldal	14/07/97	2	(3)	2
18	Michelle De Jongh	19/05/97	5		
6	Ellen Löfqvist	08/10/97	4	(1)	
11	Julia Zigiotti Olme	24/12/97	1	(1)	
14	Anna Oskarsson	23/06/96	4	(1)	
Forwards					
9	Stina Blackstenius	05/02/96	4		6
16	Rebecka Blomqvist	24/07/97	2	(2)	
10	Linda Hallin	14/03/96	2	(1)	
17	Emma Jansson	09/05/96	2		

Third title claimed with 5-2 win over Switzerland

Holders Germany suffer shock semi-final exit

Iceland hosts first eight-team summer finals

Spain blow hot in Iceland

The eighth UEFA European Women's Under-17 Championship, played at six venues in and around the Icelandic capital of Reykyavik, was the competition's first eight-team summer final tournament. Included among the participants were three of the previous season's semi-finalists in holders and four-time champions Germany, twice-victorious Spain and England. Also present were frequent qualifiers France and four countries appearing for the second time - Norway, the Republic of Ireland, Switzerland and hosts Iceland.

The draw was tough on the home nation, pitting them with Germany, England and Spain, but although Ulfar Hinriksson's inexperienced team predictably lost all three of their Group A fixtures, they improved as the competition progressed. As for the holders, they dispatched Iceland 5-0 on matchday one, only to yield to Spain's impressive pressing and transitional play in a humbling 4-0 defeat that was a repeat of the sides' group stage result in England 18 months previously. Anouschka Bernhard's team recovered on that occasion to beat the Iberians on penalties in the final, and here their revival was again emphatic – a Stefanie Sanders-fuelled 5-0 demolition of

England, which lifted them above their opponents into second place.

Matchday three brought drama in Group B. France had become the first qualified side with narrow wins over Ireland and Norway, and they were set to complete a procession into the semi-finals when they led Switzerland 1-0 at half-time. However, the Alpine outfit improved as the game went on, their equaliser pipping Norway to second spot before Jolanda Stampfli's last-gasp winner unseated France from the top of the group.

The reward for Monica Di Fonzo's outsiders was a last-four shot at

Spain's players enjoy their victory

Germany, but first up in the Valsvöllur double-header were Spain and France. It was the toughest test yet for Pedro López's Group A winners and, sure enough, Sandrine Soubreyrand's France led through Sarah Galera's 63rd-minute strike until 60 seconds from time, when Natalia Montilla lobbed a brilliant equaliser. In the ensuing shoot-out, Lucía García converted Spain's decisive penalty for a 4-3 success. The conclusion to the second semi-final was no less exciting, Switzerland successfully shutting out six-goal top scorer Sanders before substitute Amira Arfaoui finished a fine move to eliminate the champions at the death.

Three days later, at the same Reykjavik venue, first-time finalists Switzerland were punished for another circumspect start. García's fifth goal of the finals and a Luisa Felder own goal made it 2-0 to Spain inside 13 minutes, and a second own goal soon after half-time left the Swiss with too big a mountain to climb. The subsequent trading of goals between Géraldine Reuteler and Arfaoui, and Carmen Menayo and Lorena Navarro, added to the entertainment, but the outcome was already settled as Spain's fifth final appearance delivered their third UEFA European Women's Under-17 Championship crown.

Qualifying round

Group 1

20-31/10/14 Albena, Kavarna

England 9-0 Moldova, Russia 1-0 Bulgaria, England 5-0 Bulgaria, Moldova 1-7 Russia, Russia 1-4 England, Bulgaria 2-0 Moldova

		Pld	W	D	L	F	A	Pts
1	England	3	3	0	0	18	1	9
2	Russia	3	2	0	1	9	5	6
3	Bulgaria	3	1	0	2	2	6	3
4	Moldova	3	0	0	3	1	18	0

Group 2

17-22/10/14 Tallinn, Rakvere

Poland 5-0 Estonia, Finland 9-0 Bosnia & Herzegovina, Poland 4-0 Bosnia & Herzegovina, Estonia 0-8 Finland, Finland 2-0 Poland, Bosnia & Herzegovina 1-0 Estonia

		Pld	W	D	L	F	A	Pts
1	Finland	3	3	0	0	19	0	9
2	Poland	3	2	0	1	9	2	6
3	Bosnia & Herzegovina	3	1	0	2	1	13	3
4	Estonia	3	0	0	3	0	14	0

Group 3

11-16/10/14 Buk, Szombathely

Switzerland 5-0 Azerbaijan, Hungary 2-0 Portugal, Switzerland 2-1 Portugal, Azerbaijan 1-3 Hungary, Hungary 0-3 Switzerland, Portugal 2-0 Azerbaijan

		Pld	W	D	L	F	A	Pts
1	Switzerland	3	3	0	0	10	1	9
2	Hungary	3	2	0	1	5	4	6
3	Portugal	3	1	0	2	3	4	3
4	Azerbaijan	3	0	0	3	1	10	0

Group 4

17-22/10/14 Subotica

Republic of Ireland 2-0 Lithuania, Serbia 1-1 Romania, Republic of Ireland 2-0 Romania, Lithuania 1-4 Serbia, Romania 3-3 Lithuania, Serbia 1-1 Republic of Ireland

		Pld	W	D	L	F	A	Pts
1	Republic of Ireland	3	2	1	0	5	1	7
2	Serbia	3	1	2	0	6	3	5
3	Romania	3	0	2	1	4	6	2
4	Lithuania	3	0	1	2	4	9	1

Group 5

18-23/10/14 Trumau, Lindabrunn, Traiskirchen

Czech Republic 4-2 Ukraine, Austria 6-0 Northern Ireland, Czech Republic 2-0 Northern Ireland, Ukraine 2-6 Austria, Austria 1-0 Czech Republic, Northern Ireland 3-2 Ukraine

		Pld	W	D	L	F	A	Pts
1	Austria	3	3	0	0	13	2	9
2	Czech Republic	3	2	0	1	6	3	6
3	Northern Ireland	3	1	0	2	3	10	3
4	Ukraine	3	0	0	3	6	13	0

Group 6

09-14/10/14 Porec, Novigrad

Sweden 5-1 Croatia, Scotland 9-0 Montenegro, Sweden 6-0 Montenegro, Croatia 0-3 Scotland, Montenegro 0-2 Croatia, Scotland 3-1 Sweden

		Pld	W	D	L	F	A	Pts
1	Scotland	3	3	0	0	15	1	9
2	Sweden	3	2	0	1	12	4	6
3	Croatia	3	1	0	2	3	8	3
4	Montenegro	3	0	0	3	0	17	0

Group 7

06-11/10/14 Riga, Olaine

Wales 0-2 Belarus, Belgium 3-0 Latvia, Belgium 2-0 Belarus, Latvia 0-3 Wales, Wales 0-5 Belgium, Belarus 8-0 Latvia

		Pld	W	D	L	F	A	Pts
1	Belgium	3	3	0	0	10	0	9
2	Belarus	3	2	0	1	8	2	6
3	Wales	3	1	0	2	3	7	3
4	Latvia	3	0	0	3	0	12	0

Group 8

16-21/10/14 Skopje

Denmark 10-0 FYR Macedonia, Turkey 5-0 Kazakhstan, Denmark 11-0 Kazakhstan, FYR Macedonia 0-5 Turkey, Turkey 0-2 Denmark, Kazakhstan 0-1 FYR Macedonia

		Pld	W	D	L	F	A	Pts
1	Denmark	3	3	0	0	23	0	9
2	Turkey	3	2	0	1	10	2	6
3	FYR Macedonia	3	1	0	2	1	15	3
4	Kazakhstan	3	0	0	3	0	17	0

Group 9

25-30/09/14 Torshavn, Toftir

Italy 4-0 Faroe Islands, Norway 1-0 Greece, Norway 4-0 Faroe Islands, Greece 0-1 Italy, Italy 2-0 Norway, Faroe Islands 0-3 Greece

		Pld	W	D	L	F	A	Pts
1	Italy	3	3	0	0	7	0	9
2	Norway	3	2	0	1	5	2	6
3	Greece	3	1	0	2	3	2	3
4	Faroe Islands	3	0	0	3	0	11	0

Group 10

22-27/10/14 Bakovci, Beltinci

Netherlands 3-0 Israel, Slovenia 1-2 Slovakia, Netherlands 2-1 Slovakia, Israel 2-0 Slovenia, Slovenia 2-2 Netherlands, Slovakia 1-0 Israel

		Pld	W	D	L	F	A	Pts
1	Netherlands	3	2	1	0	7	3	7
2	Slovakia	3	2	0	1	4	3	6
3	Israel	3	1	0	2	2	4	3
4	Slovenia	3	0	1	2	3	6	1

Elite round

Group 1

11-16/04/15 Mersin, Adana

Finland 1-2 Turkey, Switzerland 8-1 Serbia, Finland 2-1 Serbia, Turkey 0-4 Switzerland, Switzerland 4-0 Finland, Serbia 2-0 Turkey

		Pld	W	D	L	F	A	Pts
1	Switzerland	3	3	0	0	16	1	9
2	Serbia	3	1	0	2	4	10	3
3	Finland	3	1	0	2	3	7	3
4	Turkey	3	1	0	2	2	7	3

Group 2

09-14/04/15 Cobh, Cork

Netherlands 5-1 Hungary, England 0-2 Republic of Ireland, Republic of Ireland 0-0 Netherlands, England 4-1 Hungary, Netherlands 0-2 England, Hungary 0-0 Republic of Ireland

		Pld	W	D	L	F	A	Pts
1	England	3	2	0	1	6	3	6
2	Republic of Ireland	3	1	2	0	2	0	5
3	Netherlands	3	1	1	1	5	3	4
4	Hungary	3	0	1	2	2	9	1

Group 3

09-14/04/15 Siena, Montepulciano

Germany 6-0 Belarus, Italy 0-1 Czech Republic, Germany 5-1 Czech Republic, Belarus 0-2 Italy, Italy 0-5 Germany, Czech Republic 1-1 Belarus

		Pld	W	D	L	F	A	Pts
1	Germany	3	3	0	0	16	1	9
2	Czech Republic	3	2	0	1	6	6	6
3	Italy	3	1	0	2	2	6	3
4	Belarus	3	0	0	3	1	12	0

Group 4

22-27/03/15 Sochi

Belgium 5-0 Romania, Spain 3-0 Russia, Spain 5-0 Romania, Russia 0-1 Belgium, Belgium 0-4 Spain, Romania 5-2 Russia

		Pld	W	D	L	F	A	Pts
1	Spain	3	3	0	0	12	0	9
2	Belgium	3	2	0	1	6	4	6
3	Romania	3	1	0	2	5	12	3
4	Russia	3	0	0	3	2	9	0

Group 5

11-16/04/15 Lindabrunn, St Polten

Denmark 1-1 Sweden, Austria 2-3 Norway, Denmark 0-1 Norway, Sweden 1-0 Austria, Austria 1-0 Denmark, Norway 1-1 Sweden

		Pld	W	D	L	F	A	Pts
1	Norway	3	2	1	0	5	3	7
2	Sweden	3	1	2	0	3	2	5
3	Austria	3	1	0	2	3	4	3
4	Denmark	3	0	1	2	1	3	1

Group 6

23-28/03/15 Koszalin, Kolobrzeg

Scotland 2-0 Slovakia, France 2-0 Poland, Poland 0-1 Scotland, France 1-0 Slovakia, Scotland 1-3 France, Slovakia 0-2 Poland

		Pld	W	D	L	F	A	Pts
1	France	3	3	0	0	6	1	9
2	Scotland	3	2	0	1	4	3	6
3	Poland	3	1	0	2	2	3	3
4	Slovakia	3	0	0	3	0	5	0

Top goalscorers (Qualifying/Elite rounds)

10	Signe Bruun (Denmark)
9	Camille Surdez (Switzerland)
7	Georgia Stanway (England)
6	Viktoria Pinther (Austria)
5	Emilia Ukkonen (Finland)
	Annamaria Serturini (Italy)
	Kader Hançar (Turkey)

UEFA European Women's Under-17 Championship

Carmen Menayo of Spain scores her side's fourth goal in the final

Final tournament

Group A

22/06/15, Grindavíkurvöllur, Grindavik
England 1-1 Spain
Goals: 1-0 Cross 51, 1-1 García 54

22/06/15, Grindavíkurvöllur, Grindavik
Iceland 0-5 Germany
Goals: 0-1 Krug 5, 0-2 Sanders 35, 0-3 Sanders 43,
0-4 Dallmann 70, 0-5 Orschmann 73

25/06/15, Akranesvöllur, Akranes
Germany 0-4 Spain
Goals: 0-1 García 9, 0-2 García 21, 0-3 García 36,
0-4 Bonmati 80+4

25/06/15, Akranesvöllur, Akranes
Iceland 1-3 England
Goals: 0-1 Plumptre 28, 0-2 Devlin 44, 1-2 Pálsdóttir
66, 1-3 Allen 78

28/06/15, Kópavogsvöllur, Kopavogur
Spain 2-0 Iceland
Goals: 1-0 Guijarro 17, 2-0 Sierra 63

28/06/15, Fylkisvöllur, Reykjavik
Germany 5-0 England
Goals: 1-0 Pawollek 2, 2-0 Sanders 37, 3-0 Sanders
46, 4-0 Sanders 72, 5-0 Sanders 80

		Pld	W	D	L	F	A	Pts
1	Spain	3	2	1	0	7	1	7
2	Germany	3	2	0	1	10	4	6
3	England	3	1	1	1	4	7	4
4	Iceland	3	0	0	3	1	10	0

Group B

22/06/15, Kópavogsvöllur, Kopavogur
Republic of Ireland 0-1 France
Goal: 0-1 Laurent 65

22/06/15, Kópavogsvöllur, Kopavogur
Switzerland 2-2 Norway
Goals: 0-1 Kvernvolden 10, 1-1 Reuteler 36,
2-1 Jenzer 48, 2-2 Wilmann 51

25/06/15, Laugardalsvöllur, Reykjavik
Republic of Ireland 0-1 Switzerland
Goal: 0-1 Lehmann 55

25/06/15, Laugardalsvöllur, Reykjavik
France 2-0 Norway
Goals: 1-0 Katoto 20, 2-0 Fercocq 36

28/06/15, Kópavogsvöllur, Kopavogur
Norway 2-0 Republic of Ireland
Goals: 1-0 Norem 19, 2-0 Kvernvolden 40

28/06/15, Fylkisvöllur, Reykjavik
France 1-2 Switzerland
Goals: 1-0 De Almeida 9, 1-1 Reuteler 66,
1-2 Stampfli 80+2

		Pld	W	D	L	F	A	Pts
1	Switzerland	3	2	1	0	5	3	7
2	France	3	2	0	1	4	2	6
3	Norway	3	1	1	1	4	4	4
4	Republic of Ireland	3	0	0	3	0	4	0

Semi-finals

01/07/15, Valsvöllur, Reykjavik
Spain 1-1 France
Goals: 0-1 Galera 63, 1-1 Montilla 79
Spain qualify 4-3 on penalties.

01/07/15, Valsvöllur, Reykjavik
Switzerland 1-0 Germany
Goal: 1-0 Arfaoui 80

Final

04/07/15, Valsvöllur, Reykjavik (att: 757)
Spain 5-2 Switzerland
Goals: 1-0 García 6, 2-0 Felder 13(og), 3-0 Mégroz
50(og), 3-1 Reuteler 55, 4-1 Menayo 64, 4-2 Arfaoui 78,
5-2 Navarro 80+2
Referee: Bollenberg (AUT)
Spain: Peña, Batlle, Pujadas (Sierra 76), Aleixandri,
Guijarro, Oroz (Fernández 16), Menayo, Rodríguez,
Bonmati, Montilla (Navarro 61), García. Coach: Pedro
López (ESP)
Switzerland: Furrer, Dubs (Staffoni 73), Felder,
Hofmann, Hurni, Jenzer, Kaufmann, Lehmann (Stampfli
58), Lienhard (Arfaoui 37), Mégroz, Reuteler. Coach:
Monica Di Fonzo (SUI)

Top goalscorers *(Final tournament)*

6	Stefanie Sanders (Germany)
5	Lucía García (Spain)
3	Géraldine Reuteler (Switzerland)
2	Amira Arfaoui (Switzerland)
	Ingrid Kvernvolden (Norway)

Squads/Appearances/Goals

England

No	Name	DoB	Aps	(s)	Gls
Goalkeepers					
13	Sandy MacIver	18/06/98	2		
1	Sian Rogers	28/06/98	1		
Defenders					
12	Danielle Brown	06/10/98	2		
6	Megan Finnigan	02/04/98	3		
5	Grace Fisk	05/01/98	2		
2	Serena Fletcher	06/12/98	1	(1)	
3	Mayumi Pacheco	25/08/98	3		
15	Lucy Parker	18/11/98	1		
Midfielders					
10	Georgia Allen	16/06/98	3		1
16	Zoe Cross	06/02/98	2		1
7	Charlotte Devlin	23/02/98	1	(2)	1
8	Rachel Hardy	09/02/98		(1)	
4	Chloe Peplow	03/12/98	3		
14	Mollie Rouse	27/11/98	1		
11	Megan Tinsley	03/01/98		(2)	
Forwards					
18	Rianna Dean	21/10/98	2	(1)	
9	Chloe Kelly	15/01/98	3		
17	Ashleigh Plumptre	08/05/98	3		1

France

No	Name	DoB	Aps	(s)	Gls
Goalkeepers					
16	Mylène Chavas	07/01/98			
1	Jade Lebastard	03/05/98	4		
19	Camille Pecharman	07/10/98			
Defenders					
2	Elisa De Almeida	11/01/98	1	(1)	1
12	Pauline Dechilly	07/04/98	2		
4	Sarah Galera	03/01/98	3		1
14	Tess Laplacette	22/05/99	3		
3	Agathe Ollivier	02/04/98	3		
5	Julie Piga	12/01/98	4		
Midfielders					
8	Cloe Bodain	02/02/98	3	(1)	
10	Inès Boutaleb	08/11/98	3	(1)	
13	Hélène Fercocq	27/08/98	2	(2)	1
15	Christy Gavory	05/05/98	3		
11	Emelyne Laurent	04/11/98	3	(1)	1
6	Amira Ould Braham	17/02/98	2	(1)	
Forwards					
7	Catherine Karadjov	19/06/98	1	(1)	
9	Marie-Antoinette Katoto	01/11/98	3		1
17	Estelle Laurier	16/01/98	3	(1)	
18	Océane Ringenbach	07/11/98	1	(2)	

Germany

No	Name	DoB	Aps	(s)	Gls
Goalkeepers					
1	Vanessa Fischer	18/04/98	3		
12	Nadine Winckler	30/11/98	1		
Defenders					
13	Emma Dörr	25/06/98	1	(1)	
14	Katja Friedl	07/02/98		(3)	
3	Anna Gerhardt	17/04/98	4		
5	Luisa Guttenberger	01/12/98	3		
2	Vildan Kardesler	24/02/98	4		
4	Victoria Krug	12/01/98	4		1
Midfielders					
15	Jule Dallmann	18/02/98		(1)	1
6	Jana Feldkamp	15/03/98	4		
7	Giulia Gwinn	02/07/99	4		
10	Jenny Hipp	06/02/98	4		
8	Janina Minge	11/06/99	4		
11	Isabella Möller	04/02/98	2	(2)	
16	Tanja Pawollek	18/01/99	2	(1)	1
17	Aline Reinkober	02/01/98		(1)	
Forwards					
18	Dina Orschmann	08/01/98		(3)	1
9	Stefanie Sanders	12/06/98	4		6

Norway

No	Name	DoB	Aps	(s)	Gls
Goalkeepers					
12	Benedicte Håland	10/02/98			
1	Hildegunn Sævik	09/01/98	3		
Defenders					
5	Heidi Ellingsen	28/07/98	2		
13	Susanne Haaland	15/01/98	2		
3	Julie Hansen	23/06/98	2		
18	Tanja Løfshus	14/04/98		(2)	
14	Nora Nilsen	15/04/98	1		
2	Svanhild Sand	20/10/98	2	(1)	
4	Sarah Suphellen	10/07/98	1	(1)	
Midfielders					
7	Siw Dovle	28/04/98	2	(1)	
15	Gabrielle Lie	08/02/98	1		
8	Frida Maanum	16/07/99	3		
16	Jenny Norem	29/09/98	1		1
6	Ingrid Syrstad Engen	29/04/98	3		
11	Andrea Wilmann	31/12/98	2		1
Forwards					
17	Synnøve Hafnor	27/01/98	2	(1)	
9	Ingrid Kvernvolden	01/05/98	3		2
10	Andrea Norheim	30/01/99	3		

Spain

No	Name	DoB	Aps	(s)	Gls
Goalkeepers					
13	Amaia Peña	22/11/98	4		
1	Noelia Ramos	10/02/99	1		
Defenders					
4	Laia Aleixandri	25/08/00	4		
2	Ona Batlle	10/06/99	4	(1)	
9	Cintia Montagut	16/04/98	2		
3	Berta Pujadas	09/04/00	4	(1)	
12	Lucía Rodríguez	24/05/99	4	(1)	
5	Andrea Sierra	15/05/98	1	(1)	1
Midfielders					
14	Aitana Bonmati	18/01/98	4		1
6	Paula Fernández	01/07/99	1	(2)	
8	Patricia Guijarro	17/05/98	5		1
10	Maite Oroz	25/03/98	5		
Forwards					
17	Lucía García	14/07/98	5		5
11	Carmen Menayo	14/04/98	5		1
18	Leyre Monente	15/02/00	1	(2)	
15	Natalia Montilla	18/10/98	4		1
16	Lorena Navarro	11/11/00		(4)	1
7	Paula Sancho	12/06/98	1	(1)	

Iceland

No	Name	DoB	Aps	(s)	Gls
Goalkeepers					
12	Anita Dögg Gudmundsdóttir	24/10/00			
1	Ingibjörg Valgeirsdóttir	14/01/98	3		
Defenders					
2	Gudný Árnadóttir	04/08/00	3		
13	Kristín Dis Árnadóttir	19/08/99	1		
17	Kristín Thóra Birgisdóttir	19/11/98		(2)	
15	Una Margrét Einarsdóttir	11/12/98	1	(1)	
14	Alexandra Jóhannsdóttir	19/03/00	1	(2)	
3	Eyvör Halla Jónsdóttir	02/07/99	3		
5	Selma Sól Magnúsdóttir	23/04/98	3		
4	Ingibjörg Rún Óladóttir	08/02/98		(1)	
Midfielders					
10	Jasmín Erla Ingadóttir	12/08/98	3		
8	Andrea Mist Pálsdóttir	25/10/98	3		1
6	Anna Rakel Pétursdóttir	24/08/98	3		
Forwards					
11	Agla Maria Albertsdottir	05/08/99	3		
18	Elena Brynjarsdóttir	18/01/98		(1)	
16	Gudrún Gyda Haralz	24/06/99		(2)	
9	Kim Olafsson	27/08/98	3		
7	Andrea Celeste Thorisson	14/03/98	3		

Republic of Ireland

No	Name	DoB	Aps	(s)	Gls
Goalkeepers					
16	Nadine Maher	02/02/98		(1)	
1	Amanda McQuillan	24/03/98	3		
Defenders					
2	Fiona Donnolly	15/08/98	3		
4	Jamie Finn	21/04/98	3		
3	Courtney Higgins	24/09/98	1		
5	Chloe Moloney	19/05/98	3		
11	Jessica Nolan	20/07/98	3		
17	Niamh Prior	24/03/98		(2)	
Midfielders					
6	Evelyn Daly	31/12/98	3		
14	Lucy McCartan	23/12/98		(2)	
8	Roma McLaughlin	06/03/98	2		
4	Aislinn Meaney	24/10/98	2		
10	Saoirse Noonan	13/07/99	2		
13	Sophie Watters	08/12/98			
Forwards					
18	Dearbhaile Beirne	05/08/98		(2)	
7	Sarah McKevitt	14/06/98	2	(1)	
12	Heather Payne	26/01/00	2	(1)	
9	Eleanor Ryan-Doyle	14/05/98	3		

Switzerland

No	Name	DoB	Aps	(s)	Gls
Goalkeepers					
1	Melanie Egli	23/06/98			
12	Nadja Furrer	30/04/98	5		
19	Noemi Stadelmann	15/02/98			
Defenders					
2	Elisa Barth	13/06/98		(2)	
4	Luisa Felder	18/09/98	5		
7	Thais Hurni	22/07/98	5		
9	Sarah Kaufmann	05/02/98	5		
13	Naomi Mégroz	06/08/98	5		
15	Nathalia Spälti	19/02/98			
6	Flavia von Känel	05/10/98			
Midfielders					
5	Yara Hofmann	29/09/98	5		
8	Lara Jenzer	05/08/98	5		1
11	Nathalie Lienhard	20/08/98	5		
17	Mathilde Staffoni	16/07/98		(3)	
Forwards					
18	Amira Arfaoui	08/08/99	1	(3)	2
3	Kim Dubs	22/09/98	3	(1)	
10	Alisha Lehmann	21/01/99	5		1
14	Géraldine Reuteler	21/04/99	5		3
16	Jolanda Stampfli	01/04/98	1	(4)	1

Six teams secure qualification with 100% records

Holders Italy and six-time winners Spain lead the way

Play-offs to decide final four qualifiers in September

Seven join hosts Serbia in finals

The identities of seven of the 12 UEFA Futsal EURO 2016 finalists were revealed by the outcome of the competition's main qualifying round, and as a result a familiar look to the lineup at the final tournament in Belgrade began to take shape.

With Serbia assured of their place as hosts, a record 45 teams entered qualifying for the remaining 11 berths. Scotland took part for the first time, one of 24 nations who kicked off in the preliminary round in January. It proved a tough debut for the Scots, though, as they lost their opener 6-1 against Israel and went on to suffer further heavy defeats against Sweden (13-0) and Armenia (also 6-1).

Denmark and Switzerland, who edged England for the best runners-up spot on goals scored, fared much better as they made it through to the next qualifying phase for the first time, progressing alongside group winners Finland, Georgia, France, Latvia and Armenia. However, with the big guns entering in the main round, all seven preliminary round qualifiers fell away in March, with only Finland and France registering a win. The teams who came to the fore were holders Italy, six-time winners Spain, former champions Russia, Ukraine, Croatia and

Slovenia, all of whom topped their groups with ease, winning every game.

Group 7, on the other hand, was tighter. There were no surprises on the opening day as 2012 runners-up Portugal beat Georgia 7-0 and hosts Romania overcame Kazakhstan 6-4. But the next day Kazakhstan, who had never qualified for the finals, saw off Portugal 3-1, leaving Jorge Braz's side in real peril, with Romania on top after defeating Georgia 4-1. To open the final day's

Ukraine won all three of their main round qualifying matches in Baku

games, Kazakhstan defeated Georgia 4-0, which meant that Portugal needed to beat Romania by a three-goal margin to top the group. They did just that, triumphing 4-1 with Tiago Brito scoring the clinching goal just 72 seconds from the end.

That goal pushed Romania down from first to third in the group, but fortunately their six-point tally made them the best third-placed side across the seven groups and they joined Kazakhstan and other runners-up Bosnia & Herzegovina, Hungary, Belarus, Azerbaijan, the Czech Republic and Slovakia in the play-off draw.

In those two-legged ties on 15 and 22 September, one first-time finalist is assured as Bosnia & Herzegovina meet Kazakhstan. There will be a reunion for Hungary coach Sito Rivera with the nation he left on the eve of the 2014 play-offs, Romania, while the Czech Republic, who have not missed a major finals since the 2000 FIFA Futsal World Cup, are up against Belarus. Azerbaijan will bid to reach a fourth straight final tournament against another team seeking a debut appearance, Slovakia.

The four play-off winners will join the other eight teams in the final tournament that runs from 2 to 13 February, 2016.

Preliminary round

Group A

14-17/01/15 Blagoevgrad

Greece 3-0 Gibraltar, Bulgaria 2-2 Denmark, Denmark 4-0 Greece, Bulgaria 3-1 Gibraltar, Gibraltar 1-9 Denmark, Greece 2-3 Bulgaria

		Pld	W	D	L	F	A	Pts
1	Denmark	3	2	1	0	15	3	7
2	Bulgaria	3	2	1	0	8	5	7
3	Greece	3	1	0	2	5	7	3
4	Gibraltar	3	0	0	3	2	15	0

Group B

14-17/01/15 Podgorica

Finland 3-0 Wales, Montenegro 4-0 Cyprus, Cyprus 0-5 Finland, Montenegro 2-1 Wales, Wales 2-1 Cyprus, Finland 2-0 Montenegro

		Pld	W	D	L	F	A	Pts
1	Finland	3	3	0	0	10	0	9
2	Montenegro	3	2	0	1	6	3	6
3	Wales	3	1	0	2	3	6	3
4	Cyprus	3	0	0	3	1	11	0

Group C

14-17/01/15 Kaunas

Georgia 6-3 Estonia, Lithuania 3-5 Switzerland, Switzerland 1-1 Georgia, Lithuania 5-2 Estonia, Estonia 5-7 Switzerland, Georgia 8-2 Lithuania

		Pld	W	D	L	F	A	Pts
1	Georgia	3	2	1	0	15	6	7
2	Switzerland	3	2	1	0	13	9	7
3	Lithuania	3	1	0	2	10	15	3
4	Estonia	3	0	0	3	10	18	0

Group D

14-17/01/15 Ciorescu

France 5-1 San Marino, Moldova 4-2 Albania, Albania 2-5 France, Moldova 7-0 San Marino, San Marino 0-11 Albania, France 4-2 Moldova

		Pld	W	D	L	F	A	Pts
1	France	3	3	0	0	14	5	9
2	Moldova	3	2	0	1	13	6	6
3	Albania	3	1	0	2	15	9	3
4	San Marino	3	0	0	3	1	23	0

Group E

14-17/01/15 Paola

Latvia 3-2 Andorra, Malta 0-3 England, England 2-2 Latvia, Malta 0-4 Andorra, Andorra 2-3 England, Latvia 8-0 Malta

		Pld	W	D	L	F	A	Pts
1	Latvia	3	2	1	0	13	4	7
2	England	3	2	1	0	8	4	7
3	Andorra	3	1	0	2	8	6	3
4	Malta	3	0	0	3	0	15	0

Group F

14-17/01/15 Skovde

Israel 6-1 Scotland, Sweden 3-4 Armenia, Armenia 2-2 Israel, Sweden 13-0 Scotland, Scotland 1-6 Armenia, Israel 0-4 Sweden

		Pld	W	D	L	F	A	Pts
1	Armenia	3	2	1	0	12	6	7
2	Sweden	3	2	0	1	20	4	6
3	Israel	3	1	1	1	8	7	4
4	Scotland	3	0	0	3	2	25	0

Main round

Group 1

18-21/03/15 Sarajevo

Bosnia & Herzegovina 2-1 Netherlands, Russia 5-0 Latvia, Bosnia & Herzegovina 7-3 Latvia, Netherlands 0-3 Russia, Latvia 3-3 Netherlands, Russia 2-1 Bosnia & Herzegovina

		Pld	W	D	L	F	A	Pts
1	Russia	3	3	0	0	10	1	9
2	Bosnia & Herzegovina	3	2	0	1	10	6	6
3	Netherlands	3	0	1	2	4	8	1
4	Latvia	3	0	1	2	6	15	1

Group 2

18-21/03/15 Skopje

Spain 9-1 Switzerland, FYR Macedonia 3-3 Hungary, Hungary 0-5 Spain, FYR Macedonia 7-6 Switzerland, Switzerland 2-8 Hungary, Spain 7-1 FYR Macedonia

		Pld	W	D	L	F	A	Pts
1	Spain	3	3	0	0	21	2	9
2	Hungary	3	1	1	1	11	10	4
3	FYR Macedonia	3	1	1	1	11	16	4
4	Switzerland	3	0	0	3	9	24	0

Group 3

18-21/03/15 Krosno

Italy 4-0 Finland, Poland 0-0 Belarus, Belarus 1-2 Italy, Poland 2-3 Finland, Finland 0-2 Belarus, Italy 6-3 Poland

		Pld	W	D	L	F	A	Pts
1	Italy	3	3	0	0	12	4	9
2	Belarus	3	1	1	1	3	2	4
3	Finland	3	1	0	2	3	8	3
4	Poland	3	0	1	2	5	9	1

Group 4

18-21/03/15 Baku

Ukraine 5-2 Denmark, Azerbaijan 3-1 Belgium, Belgium 2-9 Ukraine, Azerbaijan 11-2 Denmark, Denmark 3-5 Belgium, Ukraine 3-2 Azerbaijan

		Pld	W	D	L	F	A	Pts
1	Ukraine	3	3	0	0	17	6	9
2	Azerbaijan	3	2	0	1	16	6	6
3	Belgium	3	1	0	2	8	15	3
4	Denmark	3	0	0	3	7	21	0

Croatia's Dario Marinović on the ball in the main round Group 6 decider against Slovakia

Latvia edged out England in winning preliminary round Group E

Group 5

18-21/03/15 Lasko

Slovenia 4-0 Norway, Czech Republic 5-3 France, Norway 0-4 Czech Republic, Slovenia 11-2 France, France 3-1 Norway, Czech Republic 1-3 Slovenia

		Pld	W	D	L	F	A	Pts
1	Slovenia	3	3	0	0	18	3	9
2	Czech Republic	3	2	0	1	10	6	6
3	France	3	1	0	2	8	17	3
4	Norway	3	0	0	3	1	11	0

Group 6

18-21/03/15 Dubrovnik

Slovakia 7-1 Armenia, Croatia 10-0 Turkey, Turkey 1-5 Slovakia, Croatia 8-0 Armenia, Armenia 3-7 Turkey, Slovakia 2-3 Croatia

		Pld	W	D	L	F	A	Pts
1	Croatia	3	3	0	0	21	2	9
2	Slovakia	3	2	0	1	14	5	6
3	Turkey	3	1	0	2	8	18	3
4	Armenia	3	0	0	3	4	22	0

Group 7

18-21/03/15 Calarasi

Portugal 7-0 Georgia, Romania 6-4 Kazakhstan, Kazakhstan 3-1 Portugal, Romania 4-1 Georgia, Georgia 0-4 Kazakhstan, Portugal 4-1 Romania

		Pld	W	D	L	F	A	Pts
1	Portugal	3	2	0	1	12	4	6
2	Kazakhstan	3	2	0	1	11	7	6
3	Romania	3	2	0	1	11	9	6
4	Georgia	3	0	0	3	1	15	0

Play-off draw

15 & 22 September, 2015

**Romania v Hungary
Bosnia & Herzegovina v Kazakhstan
Czech Republic v Belarus
Azerbaijan v Slovakia**

Kairat recapture their crown

In front of bumper crowds in Lisbon, Kairat Almaty regained the UEFA Futsal Cup they had won in Tbilisi two years earlier, holders FC Barcelona falling 3-2 to the team from Kazakhstan in an entertaining and closely contested final.

Comparing the two triumphs, goalkeeper Higuita claimed that the second one meant more. "When we became champions the first time, there were people who said it was just dumb luck. Today we proved it wasn't".

What he meant was that when, in 2013, Kairat became Kazakhstan's first UEFA champions in any discipline, critics claimed that coach Cacau had just caught Barcelona and Moscow's MFK Dinamo by surprise with their use of Higuita as part-keeper/part-outfield player. That tactic was deployed again in Lisbon as Kairat overcame ISK Dina Moskva and Barcelona at the Meo Arena. This time, however, no one had the excuse of being confounded by how Cacau had set up his team.

Kairat stormed into the finals with 28 goals in three elite round games, twice as many as any other qualifier. In the semis they took on Dina, the dominant Russian and European side of the 1990s who were participating in this 14-year-old UEFA competition for the first time. Dina valiantly

scored twice in the last two minutes to force extra time but Kairat eventually romped clear to win 7-4, four of the goals coming from star man Leo.

Up against them in the final were Barcelona, the winners of the previous year's tournament in Baku, who won their semi thanks to two last-gasp goals against hosts Sporting Clube de Portugal. The home team were urged on by a

UEFA Futsal Cup winners Kairat show off their medals

competition-record 12,076 fans, the first five-figure crowd registered for a UEFA club futsal fixture. Ultimately their vibrant support proved in vain as Barcelona won 5-3, but they were consoled two days later as Sporting claimed third place, Alex scoring four times in a one-sided 8-3 win over Dina.

Barcelona, who stood poised to equal two UEFA Futsal Cup records by claiming a third title and a second in a row, were most observers' favourites to win the final. But Kairat were the only team ever to have beaten Barcelona in Europe, in the 2013 semis, and they led 2-0 at half-time, the second goal coming from Divanei, the former Sporting player whose presence ensured that his team gained the Portuguese fans' backing. Barcelona twice pulled a goal back, but Kairat stood firm to prevail 3-2, Higuita's passing in attack proving just as important as his goalkeeping.

Cacau, the fourth coach to win the UEFA Futsal Cup for a second time, was understandably proud of his champions: "We played a complete match," he said, "and this final was a great show." He could have been speaking for the finals as a whole, an unprecedented aggregate attendance of almost 30,000 having watched the four games, which had sold out in a fortnight.

Preliminary round

Group A

26-29/08/14 Dublin

Hovocubo 8-0 Wrexham Futsal Club, Eden Futsal 4-2 Istanbul Üniversitesi SK, Istanbul Üniversitesi SK 1-2 Hovocubo, Eden Futsal 9-2 Wrexham Futsal Club, Wrexham Futsal Club 2-8 Istanbul Üniversitesi SK, Hovocubo 3-2 Eden Futsal

		Pld	W	D	L	F	A	Pts
1	Hovocubo	3	3	0	0	13	3	9
2	Eden Futsal	3	2	0	1	15	7	6
3	Istanbul Üniversitesi SK	3	1	0	2	11	8	3
4	Wrexham Futsal Club	3	0	0	3	4	25	0

Group B

27-30/08/14 Sarajevo

MNK Centar Sarajevo 7-1 Malmö City FC, Baku United FC 10-0 Gibraltar Scorpions FC, MNK Centar Sarajevo 10-7 Gibraltar Scorpions FC, Malmö City FC 0-10 Baku United FC, Gibraltar Scorpions FC 4-4 Malmö City FC, Baku United FC 6-3 MNK Centar Sarajevo

		Pld	W	D	L	F	A	Pts
1	Baku United FC	3	3	0	0	26	3	9
2	MNK Centar Sarajevo	3	2	0	1	20	14	6
3	Gibraltar Scorpions FC	3	0	1	2	11	24	1
4	Malmö City FC	3	0	1	2	5	21	1

Group C

27-30/08/14 Bielsko Biala

FS Ilves Tampere 5-0 FK Lokomotyvas Radviliškis, Rekord Bielsko-Biała 10-0 Perth Saltires, Perth Saltires 0-12 FS Ilves Tampere, Rekord Bielsko-Biała 5-2 FK Lokomotyvas Radviliškis, FK Lokomotyvas Radviliškis 10-2 Perth Saltires, FS Ilves Tampere 1-2 Rekord Bielsko-Biała

		Pld	W	D	L	F	A	Pts
1	Rekord Bielsko-Biała	3	3	0	0	17	3	9
2	FS Ilves Tampere	3	2	0	1	18	2	6
3	FK Lokomotyvas Radviliškis	3	1	0	2	12	12	3
4	Perth Saltires	3	0	0	3	2	32	0

Group D

27-30/08/14 Nicosia

NAFI Stuttgart 3-4 KF Flamurtari Vlorë, FC APOEL Nicosia 5-3 FC Anzhi Tallinn, FC Anzhi Tallinn 6-2 NAFI Stuttgart, FC APOEL Nicosia 9-1 KF Flamurtari Vlorë, KF Flamurtari Vlorë 3-3 FC Anzhi Tallinn, NAFI Stuttgart 1-10 FC APOEL Nicosia

		Pld	W	D	L	F	A	Pts
1	FC APOEL Nicosia	3	3	0	0	24	5	9
2	FC Anzhi Tallinn	3	1	1	1	12	10	4
2	KF Flamurtari Vlorë	3	1	1	1	8	15	4
4	NAFI Stuttgart	3	0	0	3	6	20	0

Group E

27-30/08/14 Schwaz

FC Stalitsa Minsk 2-1 Talgrig Yerevan, Futsal Schwaz 3-4 FC Encamp, FC Encamp 1-7 FC Stalitsa Minsk, Futsal Schwaz 4-10 Talgrig Yerevan, Talgrig Yerevan 9-1 FC Encamp, FC Stalitsa Minsk 12-3 Futsal Schwaz

Dmitri Prudnikov of Dina Moskva

		Pld	W	D	L	F	A	Pts
1	FC Stalitsa Minsk	3	3	0	0	21	5	9
2	Talgrig Yerevan	3	2	0	1	20	7	6
3	FC Encamp	3	1	0	2	6	19	3
4	Futsal Schwaz	3	0	0	3	10	26	0

Group F

27-29/08/14 Zagreb

MNK Alumnus Zagreb 7-2 Balzan Youths FC, Balzan Youths FC 5-3 København, København 2-7 MNK Alumnus Zagreb

		Pld	W	D	L	F	A	Pts
1	MNK Alumnus Zagreb	2	2	0	0	14	4	6
2	Balzan Youths FC	2	1	0	1	7	10	3
3	København	2	0	0	2	5	12	0

Group G

28-30/08/14 Podgorica

FC Agama Podgorica 4-1 ASA Ben Gurion, ASA Ben Gurion 4-9 KMF Zelezarec Skopje, KMF Zelezarec Skopje 4-1 FC Agama Podgorica

		Pld	W	D	L	F	A	Pts
1	KMF Zelezarec Skopje	2	2	0	0	13	5	6
2	FC Agama Podgorica	2	1	0	1	5	5	3
3	ASA Ben Gurion	2	0	0	2	5	13	0

Group H

29-31/08/14 Varna

FC Grand Pro Varna 2-2 FC Progress Chisinau, FC Progress Chisinau 4-1 Uni Futsal Bulle, Uni Futsal Bulle 1-8 FC Grand Pro Varna

		Pld	W	D	L	F	A	Pts
1	FC Grand Pro Varna	2	1	1	0	10	3	4
2	FC Progress Chisinau	2	1	1	0	6	3	4
3	Uni Futsal Bulle	2	0	0	2	2	12	0

Main round

Group 1

30/09-03/10/14 Chrudim

Sporting Club de Paris 6-3 KMF Zelezarec Skopje, FK EP Chrudim 3-2 FC Stalitsa Minsk, FC Stalitsa Minsk 7-10 Sporting Club de Paris, FK EP Chrudim 4-2 KMF Zelezarec Skopje, KMF Zelezarec Skopje 3-6 FC Stalitsa Minsk, Sporting Club de Paris 6-4 FK EP Chrudim

		Pld	W	D	L	F	A	Pts
1	Sporting Club de Paris	3	3	0	0	22	14	9
2	FK EP Chrudim	3	2	0	1	11	10	6
3	FC Stalitsa Minsk	3	1	0	2	15	16	3
4	KMF Zelezarec Skopje	3	0	0	3	8	16	0

Group 2

02-05/10/14 Riga

Iberia Star Tbilisi 0-4 Rekord Bielsko-Biała, FK Nikars Riga 4-1 FC Grand Pro Varna, FC Grand Pro Varna 4-0 Iberia Star Tbilisi, FK Nikars Riga 3-1 Rekord Bielsko-Biała, Rekord Bielsko-Biała 0-2 FC Grand Pro Varna, Iberia Star Tbilisi 1-0 FK Nikars Riga

		Pld	W	D	L	F	A	Pts
1	FK Nikars Riga	3	2	0	1	7	3	6
2	FC Grand Pro Varna	3	2	0	1	7	4	6
3	Rekord Bielsko-Biała	3	1	0	2	5	5	3
4	Iberia Star Tbilisi	3	1	0	2	1	8	3

Group 3

02-05/10/14 Troitsk

Futsal Team Charleroi 4-2 MNK Alumnus Zagreb, ISK Dina Moskva 4-2 FC Deva, FC Deva 2-3 Futsal Team Charleroi, ISK Dina Moskva 8-3 MNK Alumnus Zagreb, MNK Alumnus Zagreb 2-4 FC Deva, Futsal Team Charleroi 1-5 ISK Dina Moskva

		Pld	W	D	L	F	A	Pts
1	ISK Dina Moskva	3	3	0	0	17	6	9
2	Futsal Team Charleroi	3	2	0	1	8	9	6
3	FC Deva	3	1	0	2	8	9	3
4	MNK Alumnus Zagreb	3	0	0	3	7	16	0

Group 4

02-05/10/14 Nova Gorica

Inter FS 5-0 Hovocubo, KMN Kobarid 1-6 Lokomotiv Kharkiv, Lokomotiv Kharkiv 2-5 Inter FS, KMN Kobarid 5-0 Hovocubo, Hovocubo 0-5 Lokomotiv Kharkiv, Inter FS 6-2 KMN Kobarid

		Pld	W	D	L	F	A	Pts
1	Inter FS	3	3	0	0	16	4	9
2	Lokomotiv Kharkiv	3	2	0	1	13	6	6
3	KMN Kobarid	3	1	0	2	8	12	3
4	Hovocubo	3	0	0	3	0	15	0

Group 5

01-04/10/14 Kragujevac

Luparense C/5 2-6 Baku United FC, KMF Ekonomac Kragujevac 3-1 Athina '90, Athina '90 0-3 Luparense C/5, KMF Ekonomac Kragujevac 1-4 Baku United FC, Baku United FC 2-0 Athina '90, Luparense C/5 2-3 KMF Ekonomac Kragujevac

		Pld	W	D	L	F	A	Pts
1	Baku United FC	3	3	0	0	12	3	9
2	KMF Ekonomac Kragujevac	3	2	0	1	7	7	6
3	Luparense C/5	3	1	0	2	7	9	3
4	Athina '90	3	0	0	3	1	8	0

UEFA Futsal Cup

Group 6

02-05/10/14 Berettyóújfalu

Slov-Matic Bratislava 5-1 FC APOEL Nicosia, MVFC Berettyóújfalu 3-2 Vegakameratene, Vegakameratene 0-3 Slov-Matic Bratislava, MVFC Berettyóújfalu 2-3 FC APOEL Nicosia, FC APOEL Nicosia 3-3 Vegakameratene, Slov-Matic Bratislava 1-5 MVFC Berettyóújfalu

	Pld	W	D	L	F	A	Pts
1 MVFC Berettyóújfalu	3	2	0	1	10	6	6
2 Slov-Matic Bratislava	3	2	0	1	9	6	6
3 FC APOEL Nicosia	3	1	1	1	7	10	4
4 Vegakameratene	3	0	1	2	5	9	1

Elite round

Group A

20-23/11/14 Odivelas

Inter FS 6-0 FC Grand Pro Varna, Sporting Clube de Portugal 5-3 Futsal Team Charleroi, Futsal Team Charleroi 0-4 Inter FS, Sporting Clube de Portugal 8-2 FC Grand Pro Varna, FC Grand Pro Varna 0-3 Futsal Team Charleroi, Inter FS 0-1 Sporting Clube de Portugal

	Pld	W	D	L	F	A	Pts
1 Sporting Clube de Portugal	3	3	0	0	14	5	9
2 Inter FS	3	2	0	1	10	1	6
3 Futsal Team Charleroi	3	1	0	2	6	9	3
4 FC Grand Pro Varna	3	0	0	3	2	17	0

Group B

18-21/11/14 Pardubice

Araz Naxçivan 3-4 Slov-Matic Bratislava, FK EP Chrudim 0-3 ISK Dina Moskva, ISK Dina Moskva 5-4 Araz Naxçivan, FK EP Chrudim 2-1 Slov-Matic Bratislava, Slov-Matic Bratislava 1-4 ISK Dina Moskva, Araz Naxçivan 0-6 FK EP Chrudim

	Pld	W	D	L	F	A	Pts
1 ISK Dina Moskva	3	3	0	0	12	5	9
2 FK EP Chrudim	3	2	0	1	8	4	6
3 Slov-Matic Bratislava	3	1	0	2	6	9	3
4 Araz Naxçivan	3	0	0	3	7	15	0

Group C

20-23/11/14 Almaty

KMF Ekonomac Kragujevac 1-4 Sporting Club de Paris, Kairat Almaty 11-2 FK Nikars Riga, FK Nikars Riga 5-5 KMF Ekonomac Kragujevac, Kairat Almaty 11-7 Sporting Club de Paris, Sporting Club de Paris 5-4 FK Nikars Riga, KMF Ekonomac Kragujevac 3-6 Kairat Almaty

Divanei hooks in Kairat's second goal in the final against Barcelona

	Pld	W	D	L	F	A	Pts
1 Kairat Almaty	3	3	0	0	28	12	9
2 Sporting Club de Paris	3	2	0	1	16	16	6
3 KMF Ekonomac Kragujevac	3	0	1	2	9	15	1
4 FK Nikars Riga	3	0	1	2	11	21	1

Group D

19-22/11/14 Barcelona

Lokomotiv Kharkiv 2-1 Baku United FC, FC Barcelona 4-1 MVFC Berettyóújfalu, MVFC Berettyóújfalu 1-4 Lokomotiv Kharkiv, FC Barcelona 5-1 Baku United FC, Baku United FC 6-0 MVFC Berettyóújfalu, Lokomotiv Kharkiv 0-5 FC Barcelona

	Pld	W	D	L	F	A	Pts
1 FC Barcelona	3	3	0	0	14	2	9
2 Lokomotiv Kharkiv	3	2	0	1	6	7	6
3 Baku United FC	3	1	0	2	8	7	3
4 MVFC Berettyóújfalu	3	0	0	3	2	14	0

Semi-finals

24/04/15, Meo Arena, Lisbon

ISK Dina Moskva 4-7 Kairat Almaty (aet)
Goals: 0-1 Leo 10, 1-1 Esquerdinha 23, 1-2 Leo 35, 1-3 Leo 38, 2-3 Esquerdinha 39, 3-3 Prudnikov 39, 3-4 Divanei 41, 3-5 Douglas 45, 3-6 Lukaian 46, 4-6 Prudnikov 47, 4-7 Leo 49

24/04/15, Meo Arena, Lisbon

FC Barcelona 5-3 Sporting Clube de Portugal
Goals: 0-1 Diogo 15, 1-1 Wilde 25, 3-1 Wilde 27, 3-2 João Matos 32, 3-3 Caio 36, 4-3 Bateria 39, 5-3 Paco Sedano 39

Third place play-off

26/04/15, Meo Arena, Lisbon

ISK Dina Moskva 3-8 Sporting Clube de Portugal
Goals: 1-0 Esquerdinha 11, 1-1 Alex 16, 1-2 Alex 17, 1-3 João Matos 23, 1-4 Marcelinho 26, 1-5 Alex 29, 1-6 Diogo 29, 2-6 Esquerdinha 32, 2-7 Cristiano 35, 3-7 Kuzenok 36, 3-8 Alex 37

Final

26/04/15, Meo Arena, Lisbon (att: 5,110)

Kairat Almaty 3-2 FC Barcelona
Goals: 1-0 Humberto 16, 2-0 Divanei 18, 2-1 Saad 29, 3-1 Igor 31, 3-2 Lin 31
Referees: Kovács (HUN) & Malfer (ITA)
Kairat: Higuita, Marcão, Igor, Lukaian, Douglas, Divanei, Humberto, Zhamankulov, Joan, Suleimenov, Leo, Pershin. Coach: Cacau (KAZ)
Barcelona: Cristian, Paco Sedano, Mendiola, Gabriel, Lin, Bateria, Wilde, Aicardo, Ari, Dyego, Lozano, Saad. Coach: Marc Carmona (ESP)
Red card: Lozano 30 (Barcelona)
Yellow card: Leo 30 (Kairat)

Top goalscorers (Final tournament)

4 Alex (Sporting)
Esquerdinha (Dina Moskva)
Leo (Kairat)

2 Dmitri Prudnikov (Dina Moskva)
Wilde (Barcelona)
João Matos (Sporting)
Diogo (Sporting)
Divanei (Kairat)

Alex   Esquerdinha   Leo

THE EUROPEAN FOOTBALL YEARBOOK 2015 2016

TOP 100 PLAYERS

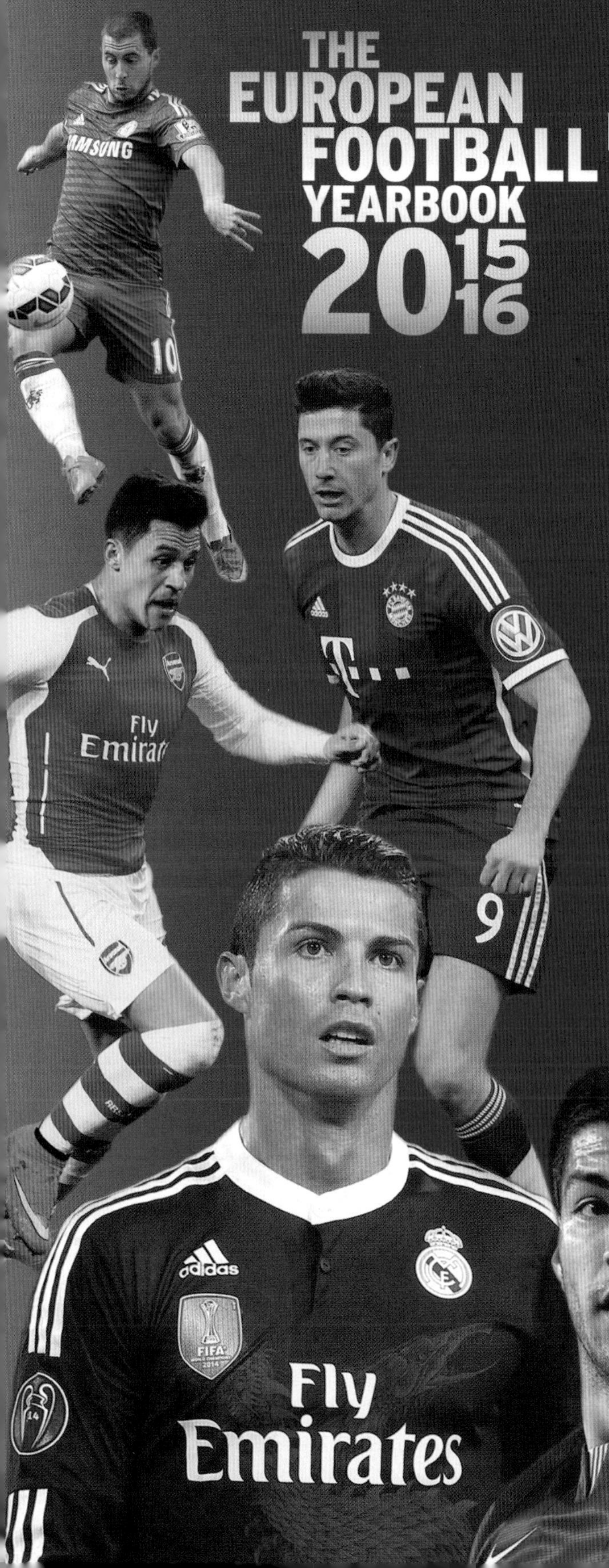

Welcome to the Top 100 Players of the Season chapter.

Turn the page and you will find an alphabetical list of those players who have made it into this year's European Football Yearbook Top 100.

Following on from that index are individual profiles of each of the chosen players, incorporating a narrative description of achievements and successes during the season, plus historical career statistics and all the relevant facts and figures for 2014/15.

It should be pointed out that the selection has no official UEFA stamp of approval, but the Top 100 does have a proud history of its own within this publication. Indeed, this is the 11th year that it has been run – and yes, Cristiano Ronaldo and Lionel Messi are the two players who have featured most often.

The selection has been compiled with careful consideration by a panel of European Football Yearbook and UEFA.com contributors – with some fine-tuning by myself – and aims to recognise those high-performers who have achieved the most significant feats during the 2014/15 season.

Value judgement rankings such as these inevitably trigger debate, so if you wish to have your say on who should be in or out, and indeed why that should be so, please feel free to contact me at the email address below.

Please note that the statistical data in the profiles is up to date as of 1 August 2015.

Mike Hammond
General Editor
mike.hammond@uefa.ch

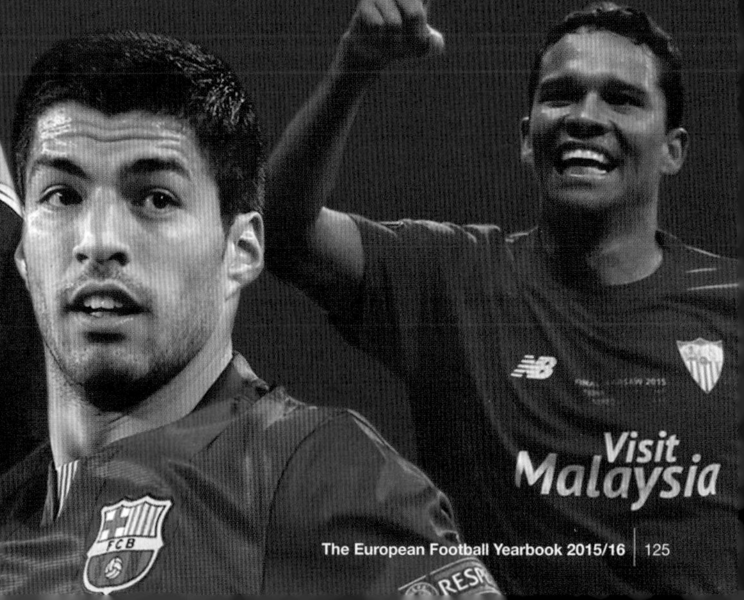

Top 100 players

Sergio Agüero (Manchester City FC, Argentina)
Alexis Sánchez (Arsenal FC, Chile)
Pierre-Emerick Aubameyang (Borussia Dortmund, Gabon)
Charlie Austin (Queens Park Rangers FC, England)
Carlos Bacca (Sevilla FC, Colombia)
Gareth Bale (Real Madrid CF, Wales)
Claudio Beauvue (EA Guingamp, France)
Karim Bellarabi (Bayer 04 Leverkusen, Germany)
Bernardo Silva (AS Monaco FC, Portugal)
Leonardo Bonucci (Juventus, Italy)
Denys Boyko (FC Dnipro Dnipropetrovsk, Ukraine)
Yacine Brahimi (FC Porto, Algeria)
Claudio Bravo (FC Barcelona, Chile)
Gianluigi Buffon (Juventus, Italy)
Sergio Busquets (FC Barcelona, Spain)
Gary Cahill (Chelsea FC, England)
Antonio Candreva (SS Lazio, Italy)
Giorgio Chiellini (Juventus, Italy)
Thibaut Courtois (Chelsea FC, Belgium)
Philippe Coutinho (Liverpool FC, Brazil)
Cristiano Ronaldo (Real Madrid CF, Portugal)
Dani Alves (FC Barcelona, Brazil)
Kevin De Bruyne (VfL Wolfsburg, Belgium)
David de Gea (Manchester United FC, Spain)
Stefan de Vrij (SS Lazio, Netherlands)
Memphis Depay (PSV Eindhoven, Netherlands)
Diego Costa (Chelsea FC, Spain)
Bořek Dočkal (AC Sparta Praha, Czech Republic)
Alejandro Domínguez (Olympiacos FC, Argentina)
Bas Dost (VfL Wolfsburg, Netherlands)
Paulo Dybala (US Città di Palermo, Argentina)
Roman Eremenko (PFC CSKA Moskva, Finland)
Cesc Fàbregas (Chelsea FC, Spain)
Nabil Fekir (Olympique Lyonnais, France)
Felipe Anderson (SS Lazio, Brazil)
Ezequiel Garay (FC Zenit, Argentina)
André-Pierre Gignac (Olympique de Marseille, France)
Kamil Glik (Torino FC, Poland)
Antoine Griezmann (Club Atlético de Madrid, France)
Hakan Çalhanoğlu (Bayer 04 Leverkusen, Turkey)
Joe Hart (Manchester City FC, England)
Eden Hazard (Chelsea FC, Belgium)
Patrick Herrmann (VfL Borussia Mönchengladbach, Germany)
Gonzalo Higuaín (SSC Napoli, Argentina)
Hulk (FC Zenit, Brazil)
Zlatan Ibrahimović (Paris Saint-Germain, Sweden)
Mauro Icardi (FC Internazionale Milano, Argentina)
Branislav Ivanović (Chelsea FC, Serbia)
James Rodríguez (Real Madrid CF, Colombia)
Jonas (SL Benfica, Brazil)
Jonatan Soriano (FC Salzburg, Spain)
Zlatko Junuzovic (SV Werder Bremen, Austria)
Harry Kane (Tottenham Hotspur FC, England)
Yevhen Konoplyanka (FC Dnipro Dnipropetrovsk, Ukraine)

Andrej Kramarić (HNK Rijeka/Leicester City FC, Croatia)
Grzegorz Krychowiak (Sevilla FC, Poland)
Alexandre Lacazette (Olympique Lyonnais, France)
Robert Lewandowski (FC Bayern München, Poland)
Claudio Marchisio (Juventus, Italy)
Jackson Martínez (FC Porto, Colombia)
Nemanja Matić (Chelsea FC, Serbia)
Blaise Matuidi (Paris Saint-Germain, France)
Alexander Meier (Eintracht Frankfurt, Germany)
Lionel Messi (FC Barcelona, Argentina)
Arkadiusz Milik (AFC Ajax, Poland)
Aleksandar Mitrović (RSC Anderlecht, Serbia)
Luka Modrić (Real Madrid CF, Croatia)
Álvaro Morata (Juventus, Spain)
Thomas Müller (FC Bayern München, Germany)
Radja Nainggolan (AS Roma, Belgium)
Manuel Neuer (FC Bayern München, Germany)
Neymar (FC Barcelona, Brazil)
Nicolás Otamendi (Valencia CF, Argentina)
Javier Pastore (Paris Saint-Germain, Argentina)
Dimitri Payet (Olympique de Marseille, France)
Gerard Piqué (FC Barcelona, Spain)
Paul Pogba (Juventus, France)
Ivan Rakitić (FC Barcelona, Croatia)
Lior Refaelov (Club Brugge KV, Israel)
Arjen Robben (FC Bayern München, Netherlands)
Roberto Firmino (TSG 1899 Hoffenheim, Brazil)
Ricardo Rodriguez (VfL Wolfsburg, Switzerland)
Santi Cazorla (Arsenal FC, Spain)
Gylfi Sigurdsson (Swansea City AFC, Iceland)
David Silva (Manchester City FC, Spain)
Wesley Sneijder (Galatasaray AŞ, Netherlands)
Luis Suárez (FC Barcelona, Uruguay)
John Terry (Chelsea FC, England)
Carlos Tévez (Juventus, Argentina)
Thiago Silva (Paris Saint-Germain, Brazil)
Luca Toni (Hellas Verona FC, Italy)
Raphaël Varane (Real Madrid CF, France)
Marco Verratti (Paris Saint-Germain, Italy)
Arturo Vidal (Juventus, Chile)
Vitolo (Sevilla FC, Spain)
Georginio Wijnaldum (PSV Eindhoven, Netherlands)
William Carvalho (Sporting Clube de Portugal, Portugal)
Willian (Chelsea FC, Brazil)
Granit Xhaka (VfL Borussia Mönchengladbach, Switzerland)
Andriy Yarmolenko (FC Dynamo Kyiv, Ukraine)

NB Clubs indicated are those the players belonged to in the 2014/15 season.

Key to competitions:

WCF	=	FIFA World Cup final tournament
WCQ	=	FIFA World Cup qualifying round
ECF	=	UEFA EURO final tournament
ECQ	=	UEFA EURO qualifying round
CC	=	FIFA Confederations Cup
CA	=	Copa América
ANF	=	Africa Cup of Nations final tournament
ANQ	=	Africa Cup of Nations qualifying round
CGC	=	CONCACAF Gold Cup

Sergio Agüero

Striker, Height 172cm
Born 02/06/88, Quilmes, Argentina

Although the 2014/15 season brought no silverware for Manchester City FC, it furthered the reputation of their brilliant Argentinian striker. Agüero won the Premier League's golden boot with 26 goals – the highest tally of his four seasons at City – and also struck six more in the UEFA Champions League, including a magnificent hat-trick to keep his team's hopes alive in a vital group game at home to FC Bayern München. Sharp, skilful and an exquisite finisher, the 27-year-old ended his season in Chile at the 2015 Copa América, scoring three goals as Argentina finished runners-up to the hosts.

International career

ARGENTINA
Debut 03/09/06 v Brazil (n, London, friendly), lost 0-3
First goal 17/11/07 v Bolivia (h, Buenos Aires, WCQ), won 3-0
Caps 66 **Goals** 29
Major tournaments FIFA World Cup 2010; Copa América 2011; FIFA World Cup 2014; Copa América 2015

Club career

Major honours UEFA Europa League (2010); UEFA Super Cup (2010); English League (2012, 2014); English League Cup (2014)
Clubs 02-06 CA Independiente; 06-11 Club Atlético de Madrid (ESP); 11- Manchester City FC (ENG)

2014/15 appearances/goals

Domestic league English Premier League 30(3)/26
Europe UEFA Champions League 6(1)/6
National team Copa América 2015 5/3; Friendlies 5/5

Alexis Sánchez

Winger/Attacking midfielder,
Height 169cm
Born 19/12/88, Tocopilla, Chile

An exceptionally good debut season in the Premier League with Arsenal FC ended on a career high as Alexis helped Chile to a first ever victory in the Copa América, his Panenka-style penalty deciding the outcome of the shoot-out in the Santiago final against Argentina. Prior to becoming a national hero, the 26-year-old received widespread praise in England for the energy, skill and all-round excellence that he brought to Arsenal, helping the Gunners to retain the FA Cup with three goals at Wembley – two in the semi-final, one in the final – and top-scoring for the club with 16 in the Premier League.

International career

CHILE
Major honours Copa América (2015)
Debut 27/04/06 v New Zealand (h, La Calera, friendly), won 1-0
First goal 07/09/07 v Switzerland (n, Vienna, friendly), lost 1-2
Caps 86 **Goals** 27
Major tournaments FIFA World Cup 2010; Copa América 2011; FIFA World Cup 2014; Copa América 2015

Club career

Major honours UEFA Super Cup (2011); FIFA Club World Cup (2011); Chilean League (clausura 2006, apertura 2007); Argentinian League (clausura 2008); Spanish League (2013); Spanish Cup (2012); English FA Cup (2015)
Clubs 05-06 CD Cobreloa; 06-11 Udinese Calcio (ITA); 06-07 CSD Colo-Colo (loan); 07-08 CA River Plate (ARG) (loan); 11-14 FC Barcelona (ESP); 14- Arsenal FC (ENG)

2014/15 appearances/goals

Domestic league English Premier League 34(1)/16
Europe UEFA Champions League 7/3; UEFA Champions League play-offs 2/1
National team Copa América 2015 6/1; Friendlies 8(1)/2

Pierre-Emerick Aubameyang

Striker, Height 187cm
Born 18/06/89, Laval, France

With Robert Lewandowski sold to FC Bayern München, Borussia Dortmund acquired two new strikers, Ciro Immobile and Adrián Ramos, to fill the void. But while that pair struggled to bear the weight of expectation, Aubameyang, in his second season at the club, rose impressively to the challenge. The tall, pacy Gabon international notched 26 goals and ten assists for Jürgen Klopp's side, his 16-goal haul in the Bundesliga placing him third in the division's scoring charts. He also found the net in both the semi-final and final of the German Cup as Dortmund finished runners-up for the second year in a row.

International career

GABON
Debut 28/03/09 v Morocco (a, Casablanca, WCQ), won 2-1
First goal 28/03/09 v Morocco (a, Casablanca, WCQ), won 2-1
Caps 42 **Goals** 17
Major tournaments Africa Cup of Nations 2010; Africa Cup of Nations 2012; Africa Cup of Nations 2015

Club career

Major honours French League Cup (2013)
Clubs 08-11 AC Milan (ITA); 08-09 Dijon FCO (FRA) (loan); 09-10 LOSC Lille (FRA) (loan); 10-11 AS Monaco FC (FRA) (loan); 11-13 AS Saint-Étienne (FRA); 13- Borussia Dortmund (GER)

2014/15 appearances/goals

Domestic league German Bundesliga 31(2)/16
Europe UEFA Champions League 7(1)/3
National team African Cup of Nations 2015 3/1; African Cup of Nations 2015 qualifying 4/2; African Cup of Nations 2017 qualifying 1/-; Friendlies 3/-

Charlie Austin

Striker, Height 188cm
Born 05/07/09, Hungerford, England

Newly-promoted Queens Park Rangers FC finished bottom of the 2014/15 Premier League table but they scored more goals than six of the teams above them, and the reason for that was the marksmanship of their prolific No9. Austin, a former non-league journeyman who had scored in abundance at Championship level in each of the previous three seasons (the first two with Burnley FC), enjoyed an equally productive debut top-flight campaign, his poaching instincts in the penalty box bringing him 18 league goals – the fourth highest tally in the division – and an end-of-season call-up to the England squad.

International career

ENGLAND
Uncapped

Club career

Clubs 06-07 Kintbury Rangers FC; 07-08 Hungerford Town FC; 08-09 Poole Town FC; 09-11 Swindon Town FC; 11-13 Burnley FC; 13- Queens Park Rangers FC

2014/15 appearances/goals

Domestic league English Premier League 35/18

Carlos Bacca

Striker, Height 181cm
Born 08/09/86, Barranquilla, Colombia

Bacca's second season in Spain with Sevilla FC ended like the first, with victory in the UEFA Europa League. The Colombian striker may have been overlooked as man of the match for the final against FC Dnipro Dnipropetrovsk in favour of team-mate Éver Banega, but it was his two fine goals in Warsaw, including the second-half winner, that secured the Andalusian club's back-to-back triumph. The 28-year-old was on song all season, scoring 20 goals in the Spanish Liga and seven in Europe – consistent productivity that attracted the eye of AC Milan, who bought him for €30m in July.

International career

COLOMBIA
Debut 11/08/10 v Bolivia (a, La Paz, friendly), drew 1-1
First goal 11/08/10 v Bolivia (a, La Paz, friendly), drew 1-1
Caps 20 **Goals** 7
Major tournaments FIFA World Cup 2014; Copa América 2015

Club career

Major honours *UEFA Europa League (2014, 2015)*
Clubs 07-12 Atlético Junior; 07 & 08 Barranquilla FC (loan); 07-08 AC Minervén FC (VEN); 12-13 Club Brugge KV (BEL); 13-15 Sevilla FC (ESP); 15- AC Milan (ITA)

2014/15 appearances/goals

Domestic league Spanish Liga 31(6)/20
Europe UEFA Europa League 8(7)/7
National team Copa América 2015 1(1)/-; Friendlies 4(2)/4

Gareth Bale

Attacking midfielder/Winger,
Height 183cm
Born 16/07/89, Cardiff, Wales

Bale's second season at Real Madrid CF did not go as well as his first, with the world's most expensive player occasionally being singled out for criticism by the Madrid media and supporters as the team's fortunes declined in the spring after an excellent autumn. Whenever the 26-year-old donned the red shirt of his country, though, he was universally revered. His form in the opening six games of Wales's UEFA EURO 2016 qualifying campaign was nothing short of sensational, five goals capping a succession of mesmerising individual displays that fired Chris Coleman's team to the top of their group.

International career

WALES
Debut 27/05/06 v Trinidad & Tobago (n, Graz, friendly), won 2-1
First goal 07/10/06 v Slovakia (h, Cardiff, ECQ), lost 1-5
Caps 50 **Goals** 17

Club career

Major honours *UEFA Champions League (2014); UEFA Super Cup (2014); FIFA Club World Cup (2014); Spanish Cup (2014)*
Clubs 06-07 Southampton FC (ENG); 07-13 Tottenham Hotspur FC (ENG); 13- Real Madrid CF (ESP)

2014/15 appearances/goals

Domestic league Spanish Liga 30(1)/13
Europe UEFA Champions League 9(1)/2
National team UEFA EURO 2016 qualifying 6/5

Claudio Beauvue

Striker, Height 174cm
Born 16/04/88, Saint-Claude, Guadeloupe

EA Guingamp went further than ever before in European competition, reaching the 2014/15 UEFA Europa League round of 32, and it was largely down to the efficiency of their Guadeloupe-born forward that they got so far. Beauvue struck five goals in the competition, including the two in the final group game at PAOK FC that sent the Brittany club into the knockout phase. The 27-year-old also scored 17 times in Ligue 1 – the fifth-best total in the division – to help his team into a top-ten finish. It would be his last season at Guingamp as Olympique Lyonnais swooped to sign him in the summer.

International career

FRANCE
Uncapped

Club career

Major honours *French Cup (2014)*
Clubs 07-11 ES Troyes AC; 11-13 LB Châteauroux; 13 SC Bastia (loan); 13-15 EA Guingamp; 15- Olympique Lyonnais

2014/15 appearances/goals

Domestic league French Ligue 1 34(2)/17
Europe UEFA Europa League 8/5

Karim Bellarabi

Winger, Height 183cm
Born 08/04/90, Berlin, Germnay

Back at parent club Bayer 04 Leverkusen after a year on loan at Eintracht Braunschweig, Bellarabi could hardly have returned with a bigger bang, scoring after just nine seconds of the opening game of the season away to Borussia Dortmund – the fastest Bundesliga goal of all time. That lit the fuse for a sparkling season that would bring the tricky winger a top-scoring 12 league goals for Leverkusen, regular call-ups to the German national team – for whom he opted in preference to Morocco, his father's country of origin – and a first international goal in the June UEFA EURO 2016 qualifier against Gibraltar.

International career

GERMANY
Debut 11/10/14 v Poland (a, Warsaw, ECQ), lost 0-2
First goal 13/06/15 v Gibraltar (a, Faro, ECQ), won 7-0
Caps 7 **Goals** 1

Club career

Clubs 07-08 FC Oberneuland; 08-11 Eintracht Braunschweig; 11- Bayer 04 Leverkusen; 13-14 Eintracht Braunschweig (loan)

2014/15 appearances/goals

Domestic league German Bundesliga 32(1)/12
Europe UEFA Champions League 8/-; UEFA Champions League play-offs 2/1
National team UEFA EURO 2016 qualifying 4/1; Friendlies 1(2)/-

Bernardo Silva

Attacking midfielder, Height 173cm
Born 10/08/94, Lisbon, Portugal

Unable to make the first-team breakthrough at SL Benfica, the club he joined as a schoolboy, Bernardo Silva jumped at the chance to spend the 2014/15 season on loan at AS Monaco FC. In fact, the young left-footer performed so well that he was offered a permanent contract by the Principality club in January and played even better in the second half of the campaign, scoring freely in the final few weeks as Monaco grabbed third place in Ligue 1. The Portuguese schemer carried that fine form into the UEFA European Under-21 Championship finals, where he was one of the classiest players on view.

International career

PORTUGAL
Debut 31/03/15 v Cape Verde (h, Estoril, friendly), lost 0-2
Caps 1 **Goals** 0

Club career

Major honours *Portuguese League (2014); Portuguese Cup (2014)*
Clubs 13-14 SL Benfica; 14 AS Monaco FC (FRA) (loan); 15- AS Monaco FC (FRA)

2014/15 appearances/goals

Domestic league French Ligue 1 25(7)/9
Europe UEFA Champions League 1(6)/-
National team Friendlies 1/-

Leonardo Bonucci

Centre-back, Height 190cm
Born 01/05/87, Viterbo, Italy

The 2014/15 season might have taken a lot out of Bonucci, with a total of 52 outings for his club plus another nine for Italy, but the Juventus defender certainly put in the same amount. His fifth season with the Bianconeri was his best, with a unique treble of Serie A, Coppa Italia and UEFA Champions League being ruined only by FC Barcelona in Berlin, where Bonucci was without regular central defensive partner Giorgio Chiellini. A goalscorer for the Azzurri in their opening UEFA EURO 2016 qualifier against Norway, he also struck important Serie A goals against AS Roma, AC Milan and SS Lazio.

International career

ITALY
Debut 03/03/10 v Cameroon (n, Monaco, friendly), drew 0-0
First goal 03/06/10 v Mexico (n, Brussels, friendly), lost 1-2
Caps 47 **Goals** 3
Major tournaments FIFA World Cup 2010; UEFA EURO 2012; FIFA Confederations Cup 2013; FIFA World Cup 2014

Club career

Major honours *Italian League (2006, 2012, 2013, 2014, 2015); Italian Cup (2015)*
Clubs 05-07 FC Internazionale Milano; 07-09 FC Treviso; 09 AC Pisa (loan); 09-10 AS Bari; 10- Juventus

2014/15 appearances/goals

Domestic league Italian Serie A 33(1)/3
Europe UEFA Champions League 13/-
National team UEFA EURO 2016 qualifying 5/1; Friendlies 4/-

Denys Boyko

Goalkeeper, Height 194cm
Born 29/01/88, Kyiv, Ukraine

FC Dnipro Dnipropetrovsk played 19 European matches in 2014/15. Keeping goal from start to finish in every one was Boyko. More remarkable still were his performances, which included five clean sheets in successive home fixtures at the business end of the UEFA Europa League. The 27-year-old did not concede more than two goals in a match until the final, which Sevilla FC won 3-2, and in the previous round he was the difference between Dnipro and SSC Napoli, denying the Italian club, and especially Gonzalo Higuaín, with a string of brilliant saves. He also kept his goal intact on his senior Ukraine debut in a friendly against Lithuania.

International career

UKRAINE
Debut 18/11/14 v Lithuania (h, Kyiv, friendly), drew 0-0
Caps 3 **Goals** 0

Club career

Clubs 05-10 FC Dynamo-2 Kyiv; 10-14 FC Dynamo Kyiv; 08 FC CSKA Kyiv (loan); 09 FC Obolon Kyiv (loan); 11-12 FC Kryvbas Kryvyi Rih (loan); 13-14 FC Dnipro Dnipropetrovsk (loan); 14- FC Dnipro Dnipropetrovsk

2014/15 appearances/goals

Domestic league Ukrainian Premier League 21/-
Europe UEFA Champions League qualifying 2/-; UEFA Europa League 15/-; UEFA Europa League play-offs 2/-
National team Friendlies 3/-

Yacine Brahimi

Attacking midfielder, Height 175cm
Born 08/02/90, Paris, France

An excellent FIFA World Cup for Algeria in Brazil persuaded FC Porto to lure Brahimi away from Granada CF on a five-year contract. The Portuguese club got an early return on their investment when he marked his UEFA Champions League debut with a hat-trick – the first of his career – in the opening group game at home to FC BATE Borisov. The technically gifted 25-year-old would go on to enjoy an outstanding debut campaign for Julen Lopetegui's side, both in Europe, where Porto were quarter-finalists, and on the domestic front, while also starring mid-season for Algeria at the Africa Cup of Nations.

International career

ALGERIA
Debut 26/03/13 v Benin (h, Blida, WCQ), won 3-1
First goal 22/06/14 v South Korea (n, Porto Alegre, WCF), won 4-1
Caps 22 **Goals** 4
Major tournaments FIFA World Cup 2014; Africa Cup of Nations 2015

Club career

Clubs 09-13 Stade Rennais FC (FRA); 09-10 Clermont Foot (FRA) (loan); 12-13 Granada CF (ESP) (loan); 13-14 Granada CF (ESP); 14- FC Porto (POR)

2014/15 appearances/goals

Domestic league Portuguese Liga 25(3)/7
Europe UEFA Champions League 9/5; UEFA Champions League play-offs 2/1
National team African Cup of Nations 2015 qualifying 5(1)/3; Africa Cup of Nations 2015 4/-; Friendlies 2/-

Claudio Bravo

Goalkeeper, Height 187cm
Born 13/04/83, Viluco, Chile

After six years with Real Sociedad de Fútbol, Bravo was rewarded, aged 31, with a four-year contract at FC Barcelona. One of two new goalkeepers at the Camp Nou, along with Marc-André ter Stegen, the Chilean was handed Liga duties by coach Luis Enrique while the young German donned the gloves in the other competitions. Bravo could not have made a better start, setting a new Liga record by keeping his goal unbreached for 754 minutes. His season ended on a massive high, too, as he skippered Chile to victory on home soil at the 2015 Copa América, featuring for every minute of their historic triumph.

International career

CHILE
Major honours Copa América (2015)
Debut 11/07/04 v Paraguay (n, Arequipa, CA), drew 1-1
Caps 95 **Goals** 0
Major tournaments Copa América 2004; Copa América 2007; FIFA World Cup 2010; Copa América 2011; FIFA World Cup 2014; Copa América 2015

Club career

Major honours UEFA Champions League (2015); Chilean League (apertura 2006); Spanish League (2015); Spanish Cup (2015)
Clubs 02-06 CSD Colo-Colo; 06-14 Real Sociedad de Fútbol (ESP); 14- FC Barcelona (ESP)

2014/15 appearances/goals

Domestic league Spanish Liga 37/-
National team Copa América 2015 6/-; Friendlies 6/-

Gianluigi Buffon

Goalkeeper, Height 191cm
Born 28/01/78, Carrara, Italy

At 37 years of age, Buffon proved that he is still one of the world's best goalkeepers, winning his sixth Serie A title with Juventus – and fourth in a row – and playing a pivotal role in skippering the club to the UEFA Champions League final. It was his second appearance in European club football's flagship fixture, but, as in 2003 against AC Milan in Manchester, he ended up on the losing side as FC Barcelona triumphed 3-1 in Berlin, leaving his long and illustrious career still unadorned with the ultimate club prize. His place in the official UEFA Champions League squad of the season may have softened the blow.

International career

ITALY
Major honours FIFA World Cup (2006)
Debut 29/10/97 v Russia (a, Moscow, WCQ), drew 1-1
Caps 148 **Goals** 0
Major tournaments FIFA World Cup 1998; FIFA World Cup 2002; UEFA EURO 2004; FIFA World Cup 2006; UEFA EURO 2008; FIFA Confederations Cup 2009; FIFA World Cup 2010; UEFA EURO 2012; FIFA Confederations Cup 2013; FIFA World Cup 2014

Club career

Major honours UEFA Cup (1999); Italian League (2002, 2003, 2012, 2013, 2014, 2015); Italian Cup (1999, 2015)
Clubs 95-01 Parma FC; 01- Juventus

2014/15 appearances/goals

Domestic league Italian Serie A 33/-
Europe UEFA Champions League 13/-
National team UEFA EURO 2016 qualifying 5/-; Friendlies 1/-

Sergio Busquets

Midfielder, Height 189cm
Born 16/07/88, Sabadell, Spain

Having inherited the No5 shirt from retired FC Barcelona icon Carles Puyol, Busquets did it justice with a season of maximum endeavour that was rewarded with victories in the Liga, Copa del Rey and UEFA Champions League. A veteran of the 2008/09 season, his first as a Barça first-XI regular, the indefatigable midfield linchpin therefore claimed a second career treble. He scored just one goal all season for his club – a vital winner at Valencia CF – but managed two for Spain as he opened his international scoring account on his 70th appearance, against FYR Macedonia, and added a second, against Belarus, three matches later.

International career

SPAIN
Major honours FIFA World Cup (2010); UEFA European Championship (2012)
Debut 01/04/09 v Turkey (a, Istanbul, WCQ), won 2-1
First goal 08/09/14 v FYR Macedonia (h, Valencia, ECQ), won 5-1
Caps 77 **Goals** 2
Major tournaments FIFA Confederations Cup 2009; FIFA World Cup 2010; UEFA EURO 2012; FIFA Confederations Cup 2013; FIFA World Cup 2014

Club career

Major honours UEFA Champions League (2009, 2011, 2015); UEFA Super Cup (2009, 2011); FIFA World Club Cup (2009, 2011); Spanish League (2009, 2010, 2011, 2013, 2015); Spanish Cup (2009, 2012, 2015)
Clubs 08- FC Barcelona

2014/15 appearances/goals

Domestic league Spanish Liga 29(4)/1
Europe UEFA Champions League 9(1)/-
National team UEFA EURO 2016 qualifying 6/2; Friendlies 2(1)/-

Gary Cahill

Centre-back, Height 193cm
Born 19/12/85, Dronfield, England

A Chelsea FC player since January 2012, it took Cahill less than three and a half years to complete a clean sweep of major club trophies, his double success of Premier League and League Cup in 2014/15 following on from previous FA Cup, UEFA Champions League and UEFA Europa League triumphs. The only current England international in José Mourinho's side, he continued to form a solid line of resistance alongside compatriot skipper John Terry in the centre of defence. He was also the only outfield player to feature for every minute of England's opening six UEFA EURO 2016 qualifiers, all of which they won.

International career

ENGLAND
Debut 03/09/10 v Bulgaria (h, London, ECQ), won 4-0
First goal 02/09/11 v Bulgaria (a, Sofia, ECQ), won 3-0
Caps 36 **Goals** 3
Major tournaments FIFA World Cup 2014

Club career

Major honours UEFA Champions League (2012); UEFA Europa League (2013); English League (2015); English FA Cup (2012); English League Cup (2015)
Clubs 04-08 Aston Villa FC; 04-05 Burnley FC (loan); 07-08 Sheffield United FC (loan); 08-12 Bolton Wanderers FC; 12- Chelsea FC

2014/15 appearances/goals

Domestic league English Premier League 33(3)/1
Europe UEFA Champions League 6/1
National team UEFA EURO 2016 qualifying 6/-; Friendlies 3/-

Antonio Candreva

Winger, Height 181cm
Born 28/02/87, Rome, Italy

Having made his reputation as one of the finest crossers of the ball in the game, Candreva has now added to his attacking armoury a sharp eye for goal. The 28-year-old found the net on ten of his 34 league appearances for SS Lazio in 2014/15, thus reaching double figures for the second Serie A campaign in succession as the Rome side claimed third place. Furthermore, the versatile right winger broke his duck for Italy, scoring his first goal in the Azzurri's UEFA EURO 2016 qualifier at home to Croatia and then repeating the trick against the same opponents with an audacious chipped penalty in the return.

International career

ITALY
Debut 14/11/09 v Netherlands (h, Pescara, friendly), drew 0-0
First goal 16/11/14 v Croatia (h, Milan, ECQ), drew 1-1
Caps 29 **Goals** 2
Major tournaments FIFA Confederations Cup 2013; FIFA World Cup 2014

Club career

Major honours Italian Cup (2013)
Clubs 04-07 Ternana Calcio; 07-12 Udinese Calcio; 08-10 AS Livorno Calcio (loan); 10 Juventus (loan); 10-11 Parma FC (loan); 11-12 AC Cesena (loan); 12- SS Lazio

2014/15 appearances/goals

Domestic league Italian Serie A 31(3)/10
National team UEFA EURO 2016 qualifying 4(1)/2; Friendlies 1(1)/-

Giorgio Chiellini

Centre-back, Height 186cm
Born 14/08/84, Pisa, Italy

A decisive figure in Juventus's fourth straight scudetto success, Chiellini also captained the Bianconeri to victory in the Coppa Italia, leading by example in the final against SS Lazio with the team's equalising goal in a 2-1 win. Sadly, however, the powerful Italian international centre-back was ruled out of the UEFA Champions League final with a calf injury. He had started and finished every one of Juve's 12 matches en route to Berlin and proved to be a huge loss as FC Barcelona won 3-1, with Luis Suárez, the man who infamously bit him at the 2014 FIFA World Cup, rubbing salt into his wounds by scoring the second goal.

International career

ITALY
Debut 17/11/04 v Finland (h, Messina, friendly), won 1-0
First goal 21/11/07 v Faroe Islands (h, Modena, ECQ), won 3-1
Caps 76 **Goals** 6
Major tournaments UEFA EURO 2008; FIFA Confederations Cup 2009; FIFA World Cup 2010; UEFA EURO 2012; FIFA Confederations Cup 2013; FIFA World Cup 2014

Club career

Major honours Italian League (2012, 2013, 2014, 2015); Italian Cup (2015)
Clubs 00-04 AS Livorno Calcio; 04-05 AFC Fiorentina; 05- Juventus

2014/15 appearances/goals

Domestic league Italian Serie A 27(1)/-
Europe UEFA Champions League 12/-
National team UEFA EURO 2016 qualifying 4/2; Friendlies 1/-

Thibaut Courtois

Goalkeeper, Height 198cm
Born 11/05/92, Bree, Belgium

Three years after being bought by Chelsea FC from KRC Genk, Courtois finally made his debut for the west London club. The giant goalkeeper had become a global star in the interim, both for Club Atlético de Madrid, where he spent all that time on loan, and the Belgian national side, and he reinforced his standing with an excellent debut campaign at Stamford Bridge. Selected by José Mourinho as first-choice keeper ahead of long-serving Petr Čech, he helped the Blues to their first Premier League title in five years. Brave, commanding and practically error-free, he is a master of his trade already at 23.

International career

BELGIUM
Debut 15/11/11 v France (a, Paris, friendly), drew 0-0
Caps 31 **Goals** 0
Major tournaments FIFA World Cup 2014

Club career

Major honours UEFA Europa League (2012); UEFA Super Cup (2012); Belgian League (2011); Spanish League (2014); English League (2015); Spanish Cup (2013); English League Cup (2015)
Clubs 09-11 KRC Genk; 11- Chelsea FC (ENG); 11-14 Club Atlético de Madrid (ESP) (loan)

2014/15 appearances/goals

Domestic league English Premier League 32/-
Europe UEFA Champions League 5/-
National team UEFA EURO 2016 qualifying 6/-; Friendlies 3/-

Philippe Coutinho

Attacking midfielder, Height 171cm
Born 12/06/92, Rio de Janeiro, Brazil

Liverpool FC crashed back to earth in 2014/15 as they dropped from second to sixth in the Premier League and suffered two early exits in Europe. With Luis Suárez departed, Daniel Sturridge injured, Steven Gerrard on his way out and Raheem Sterling falling out of favour, the Kop needed a new star. Fortunately, Coutinho stepped up to the plate. The clever, elusive midfielder was the Merseysiders' outstanding performer on all fronts, not least in the team's lengthy FA Cup run, to which he contributed three fine goals. Selection in the Premier League Team in the Year and a place in Brazil's Copa América squad were appropriate rewards.

International career

BRAZIL
Debut 07/10/10 v Iran (n, Abu Dhabi, friendly), won 3-0
First goal 07/06/15 v Mexico (h, Sao Paulo, friendly), won 2-0
Caps 11 **Goals** 1
Major tournaments Copa América 2015

Club career

Clubs 09-10 CR Vasco da Gama; 10-13 FC Internazionale Milano (ITA); 12 RCD Espanyol (ESP) (loan); 13- Liverpool FC (ENG)

2014/15 appearances/goals

Domestic league English Premier League 32(3)/5
Europe UEFA Champions League 3(2)/-; UEFA Europa League 1/-
National team Copa América 2015 2(1)/-; Friendlies 3(4)/1

Cristiano Ronaldo

Striker/Winger, Height 184cm
Born 05/02/85, Funchal, Madeira, Portugal

The great Cristiano Ronaldo turned 30 in February 2015, shortly after collecting a second successive FIFA Ballon d'Or, but there was not the remotest indication during the months that followed of any erosion of the Portuguese megastar's extraordinary talent. On the contrary, he ended the season with more goals than ever before for Real Madrid CF – 61 in all competitions including a Pichichi-retaining 48 in the Liga – and also struck five in four UEFA European Championship qualifiers for Portugal to become that competition's all-time leading marksman. Victories in the UEFA Super Cup and the FIFA Club World Cup also helped to swell his copious collection of winner's medals.

International career

PORTUGAL
Debut 20/08/03 v Kazakhstan (h, Chaves, friendly), won 1-0
First goal 12/06/04 v Greece (h, Porto, ECF), lost 1-2
Caps 120 **Goals** 55
Major tournaments UEFA EURO 2004; FIFA World Cup 2006; UEFA EURO 2008; FIFA World Cup 2010; UEFA EURO 2012; FIFA World Cup 2014

Club career

Major honours UEFA Champions League (2008, 2014); UEFA Super Cup (2014); FIFA Club World Cup (2008, 2014); English League (2007, 2008, 2009); Spanish League (2012); English FA Cup (2004); Spanish Cup (2011, 2014); English League Cup (2006, 2009)
Clubs 02-03 Sporting Clube de Portugal; 03-09 Manchester United FC (ENG); 09- Real Madrid CF (ESP)

2014/15 appearances/goals

Domestic league Spanish Liga 35/48
Europe UEFA Champions League 12/10
National team UEFA EURO 2016 qualifying 4/5; Friendlies 2/-

Dani Alves

Right-back, Height 171cm
Born 06/05/83, Juazeiro, Brazil

Dani Alves lifted his haul of major trophies during a seven-year spell at FC Barcelona to 15 as he helped the Catalan club to a historic second treble of championship, cup and UEFA Champions League. A treble-winner also in his first season at the Camp Nou, the 32-year-old Brazilian looked set to end his Barcelona career the way he had started it as the club stalled on offering him a new contract, but to widespread surprise, especially after another pacy right-back, Aleix Vidal, had just been recruited from Sevilla FC, he signed on in June for two more seasons. Barça fans will hope that he performs as well in those as he did in 2014/15.

International career

BRAZIL
Major honours Copa América (2007); FIFA Confederations Cup (2009, 2013)
Debut 10/10/06 v Ecuador (n, Solna, friendly), won 2-1
First goal 15/07/07 v Argentina (n, Maracaibo, CA), won 3-0
Caps 83 **Goals** 6
Major Tournaments Copa América 2007; FIFA Confederations Cup 2009; FIFA World Cup 2010; Copa América 2011; FIFA Confederations Cup 2013; FIFA World Cup 2014; Copa América 2015

Club career

Major honours UEFA Champions League (2009, 2011, 2015); UEFA Cup (2006, 2007); UEFA Super Cup (2006, 2009, 2011); FIFA Club World Cup (2009, 2011); Spanish League (2009, 2010, 2011, 2013, 2015); Spanish Cup (2007, 2009, 2012, 2015)
Clubs 01-02 EC Bahia; 02-08 Sevilla FC (ESP); 08- FC Barcelona (ESP)

2014/15 appearances/goals

Domestic league Spanish Liga 29(1)/-
Europe UEFA Champions League 11/-
National team Copa América 2015 4/-

Kevin De Bruyne

Attacking midfielder, Height 181cm
Born 28/06/91, Drongen, Belgium

A landslide winner of the 2015 German Footballer of the Year poll with 367 votes – 273 more than runner-up Arjen Robben – as well as the Bundesliga's player of the year, De Bruyne's first full season at VfL Wolfsburg was an unqualified triumph. Handed a roving attacking role by coach Dieter Hecking, the Belgian international caused havoc to opposition defences all season long. As a creator of goals he had no equal, setting a new single-season Bundesliga record of 21 assists. He also scored plenty, too, including a majestic double at home to FC Bayern München and a crucial strike in the German Cup final.

International career

BELGIUM
Debut 11/08/10 v Finland (a, Turku, friendly), lost 0-1
First goal 12/10/12 v Serbia (a, Belgrade, WCQ), won 3-0
Caps 33 **Goals** 8
Major tournaments FIFA World Cup 2014

Club career

Major honours *Belgian League (2011); German Cup (2015)*
Clubs 08-12 KRC Genk; 12-14 Chelsea FC (ENG); 12 KRC Genk (loan); 12-13 SV Werder Bremen (GER) (loan); 14- VfL Wolfsburg (GER)

2014/15 appearances/goals

Domestic league German Bundesliga 34/10
Europe UEFA Europa League 11/5
National team UEFA EURO 2016 qualifying 6/2; Friendlies 1/-

David de Gea

Goalkeeper, Height 190cm
Born 07/11/90, Madrid, Spain

Manchester United FC underwent a turbulent transition under Louis van Gaal in 2014/15, with lots of new players and injuries making stability of selection virtually impossible. The one constant, however, was De Gea, who enjoyed the most impressive of his four seasons at Old Trafford, coming to his team's rescue on countless occasions to help United return to the Premier League's top four. One particularly brilliant performance, in a 3-0 win at home to Liverpool FC, was the stuff of legends. Already the heir apparent to Iker Casillas for Spain, the talk of the summer was that he would also soon be replacing the legendary keeper at Real Madrid CF.

International career

SPAIN
Debut 07/06/14 v El Salvador (n, Landover, USA, friendly), won 2-0
Caps 5 **Goals** 0
Major tournaments FIFA World Cup 2014

Club career

Major honours *UEFA Europa League (2010); UEFA Super Cup (2010); English League (2013)*
Clubs 09-11 Club Atlético de Madrid; 11- Manchester United FC (ENG)

2014/15 appearances/goals

Domestic league English Premier League 37/-
National team UEFA EURO 2016 qualifying 1/-; Friendlies 3/-

Stefan de Vrij

Centre-back, Height 189cm
Born 05/02/92, Ouderkerk aan der IJssel, Netherlands

An excellent 2013/14 Eredivisie campaign for Feyenoord and an impressive 2014 FIFA World Cup with the Netherlands prompted SS Lazio to bring De Vrij to Rome. The 23-year-old defender turned out to be one of the club's finest acquisitions of recent years, bringing strength, authority and athleticism to the Lazio back line and making a significant contribution to the team's third-place finish in Serie A and qualification for the Coppa Italia final. He was also an ever-present in the Oranje's first six UEFA EURO 2016 qualifiers, scoring in their opening fixture against the Czech Republic and again in a 2-0 friendly win over Spain.

International career

NETHERLANDS
Debut 15/08/12 v Belgium (a, Brussels, friendly), lost 2-4
First goal 13/06/14 v Spain (n, Salvador, WCF), won 5-1
Caps 28 **Goals** 3
Major tournaments FIFA World Cup 2014

Club career

Clubs 09-14 Feyenoord; 14- SS Lazio (ITA)

2014/15 appearances/goals

Domestic league Italian Serie A 29(1)/-
National team UEFA EURO 2016 qualifying 6/1; Friendlies 2(1)/1

Memphis Depay

Winger, Height 176cm
Born 13/02/94, Moordrccht,
Netherlands

Depay was expected to leave PSV
Eindhoven in the summer of 2014 after a
successful FIFA World Cup in Brazil, but
instead he opted to stay on and help the
club he had joined as a schoolboy to end
AFC Ajax's four-year reign as Dutch
champions. It was a mission the skilful
winger accomplished in style, netting 22
goals to top the Eredivisie scoring charts
as PSV cruised to their first title in seven
years. His profile duly enhanced, he left
Eindhoven to rejoin former Netherlands
boss Louis van Gaal at Manchester
United FC, the Premier League club
pouncing early to secure his services on
a four-year contract

International career

NETHERLANDS
Debut 15/10/13 v Turkey (a, Istanbul, WCQ),
won 2-0
First goal 18/06/14 v Australia (n, Porto Alegre,
WCF), won 3-2
Caps 17 **Goals** 3
Major tournaments FIFA World Cup 2014

Club career

Major honours Dutch League (2015); Dutch Cup
(2012)
Clubs 11-15 PSV Eindhoven; 15- Manchester
United FC (ENG)

2014/15 appearances/goals

Domestic league Dutch Eredivisie 30/22
Europe UEFA Europa League 6/3; UEFA Europa
League qualifying/play-offs 2(1)/3
National team UEFA EURO 2016 qualifying 3(1)/-;
Friendlies 3/1

Diego Costa

Striker, Height 188cm
Born 07/10/88, Lagarto, Brazil

Diego Costa's late-blooming career took
on added impetus as he made an
explosive start to life at Chelsea FC,
scoring seven goals in his opening four
Premier League outings, including a
hat-trick at home to Swansea City AFC.
Although his debut season at Stamford
Bridge was interrupted periodically with
muscular injuries, the robust,
confrontational Spanish international
striker made a massive difference to the
potency of the Chelsea front line.
Although he remained surprisingly
goal-free in Europe, he struck 20 times in
Chelsea's Premier League triumph and
was also credited with the team's second
goal in the League Cup final.

International career

BRAZIL
Debut 21/03/13 v Italy (n, Geneva, friendly), drew
2-2
Caps 2 **Goals** 0
SPAIN
Debut 05/03/14 v Italy (h, Madrid, friendly), won 1-0
First goal 12/10/14 v Luxembourg (a,
Luxembourg, ECQ), won 4-0
Caps 7 **Goals** 1
Major tournaments FIFA World Cup 2014

Club career

Major honours UEFA Super Cup (2010, 2012);
Spanish League (2014); English League (2015);
Spanish Cup (2013); English League Cup (2015)
Clubs 06-07 SC Braga (POR); 06 FC Penafiel (POR)
(loan); 07-09 Club Atlético de Madrid; 07 SC Braga
(POR) (loan); 07-08 RC Celta de Vigo (loan); 08-09
Albacete Balompié (loan); 09-10 Real Valladolid CF;
10-14 Club Atlético de Madrid; 12 Rayo Vallecano
de Madrid (loan); 14- Chelsea FC (ENG)

2014/15 appearances/goals

Domestic league English Premier League 24(2)/20
Europe UEFA Champions League 5(2)/-
National team UEFA EURO 2016 qualifying 2/1;
Friendlies 1/-

Bořek Dočkal

Midfielder, Height 181cm
Born 30/09/88, Mestec Kralove,
Czech Republic

The man most responsible for making the
Czech Republic the early leaders of their
UEFA EURO 2016 qualifying group with
goals in each of their first three fixtures,
the first a beauty against the
Netherlands, Dočkal made it four in the
competition when he struck again in
June against Iceland in Reykjavik. It was
an impressive return for a midfielder
renowned more for his measured passing
and crossing, but the 26-year-old did not
restrict his goalscoring to the
international arena, racking up another
ten strikes for AC Sparta Praha in the
Czech 1. Liga, where they finished
runners-up to FC Viktoria Plzeň.

International career

CZECH REPUBLIC
Debut 14/11/12 v Slovakia (h, Olomouc, friendly),
won 3-0
First goal 14/11/12 v Slovakia (h, Olomouc,
friendly), won 3-0
Caps 17 **Goals** 6

Club career

Major honours Czech League (2014); Czech Cup
(2014)
Clubs 06-08 SK Slavia Praha; 06-07 SK Kladno
(loan); 08-11 FC Slovan Liberec; 10-11 Konyaspor
(TUR) (loan); 11-13 Rosenborg BK (NOR); 13- AC
Sparta Praha

2014/15 appearances/goals

Domestic league Czech 1. Liga 27(2)/10
Europe UEFA Champions League qualifying 4/-;
UEFA Europa League 6/-; UEFA Europa League
play-offs 2/1
National team UEFA EURO 2016 qualifying 6/4;
Friendlies (2)/-

Alejandro Domínguez

Attacking midfielder, Height 176cm
Born 10/06/81, Lanus, Argentina

Outstanding all season for Olympiacos FC in 2014/15, Domínguez saved his best for last with a magnificent solo goal in the Greek Cup final against Xanthi FC, running with the ball from his own half before curling it into the far corner and extending his team's lead in a match they eventually won 3-1 to complete the domestic double. The wily Argentinian schemer registered 15 goals and 11 assists in the Piraeus club's Superleague triumph, and although there were offers for him to return to his homeland, the 34-year-old chose to make the locals happy by tying himself to Olympiacos for another two years.

International career

ARGENTINA
Uncapped

Club career

Major honours UEFA Cup (2008); UEFA Super Cup (2008); Argentinian League (clausura 2002, clausura 2003); Russian League (2007, 2009); Greek League (2014, 2015); Greek Cup (2015)
Clubs 00-01 Quilmes AC; 01-04 CA River Plate; 04-07 FC Rubin Kazan (RUS); 07-09 FC Zenit (RUS); 09-10 FC Rubin Kazan (RUS); 10-12 Valencia CF (ESP); 11-12 CA River Plate (loan); 12-13 Rayo Vallecano de Madrid (ESP); 13-Olympiacos FC (GRE)

2014/15 appearances/goals

Domestic league Greek Superleague 26(4)/15
Europe UEFA Champions League 5(1)/1; UEFA Europa League 2/1

Bas Dost

Striker, Height 196cm
Born 31/05/89, Deventer, Netherlands

A mere third choice in the VfL Wolfsburg attack at the start of the 2014/15 season, Dost looked set to leave at the winter break, but coach Dieter Hecking selected him for the first game of the spring campaign, at home to unbeaten runaway Bundesliga leaders FC Bayern München, and the tall Dutch striker responded by scoring twice in a fabulous 4-1 win. His confidence restored, he suddenly went goal-crazy, scoring 11 in six league games, including four in a remarkable 5-4 win at Bayer 04 Leverkusen, plus two more in the UEFA Europa League. A first cap for the Netherlands was an inevitable consequence.

International career

NETHERLANDS
Debut 28/03/15 v Turkey (h, Amsterdam, ECQ), drew 1-1
Caps 2 **Goals** 0

Club career

Major honours German Cup (2015)
Clubs 07-08 Emmen; 08-10 Heracles Almelo; 10-12 sc Heerenveen; 12- VfL Wolfsburg (GER)

2014/15 appearances/goals

Domestic league German Bundesliga 17(4)/16
Europe UEFA Europa League 6(3)/2
National team UEFA EURO 2016 qualifying (1)/-; Friendlies (1)/-

Paulo Dybala

Striker, Height 179cm
Born 15/11/93, Cordoba, Argentina

Although he played his part in US Città di Palermo's runaway 2013/14 Serie B title triumph, no one was quite prepared for the impact that Dybala would have on his return to Italy's top division. In tandem with his fellow Argentinian-Italian Franco Vázquez he terrorised Serie A defences all season long with his speed, precision and fabulous technique. He provided 13 goals and ten assists as the Sicilian club avoided relegation with ease, prompting interest from some of European football's top clubs. Among those were Juventus, who duly signed up the 21-year-old on a five-year contract for a reported €32m fee.

International career

ARGENTINA
Uncapped

Club career

Clubs 11-12 Instituto de Córdoba; 12-15 US Città di Palermo (ITA); 15- Juventus (ITA)

2014/15 appearances/goals

Domestic league Italian Serie A 34/13

Roman Eremenko

Midfielder, Height 180cm
Born 19/03/87, Moscow, Russia

Signed by PFC CSKA Moskva from FC Rubin Kazan in August 2014, Eremenko thus returned to his place of birth, and it became a happy homecoming for the Finland international as he imposed himself straight away alongside ex-Rubin team-mate Bebras Natcho as the team's creator-in-chief. Three Premier-Liga player of the month awards ended up in his possession before he scooped the end-of-season MVP trophy as well. The 28-year-old also closed the campaign as the 13-goal top scorer of a CSKA side that won five and drew one of their last six matches to finish runners-up behind champions FC Zenit.

International career

FINLAND
Debut 06/06/07 v Belgium (h, Helsinki, ECQ), won 2-0
First goal 03/03/10 v Malta (a, Ta'Qali, friendly), won 2-1
Caps 68 **Goals** 5

Club career

Major honours Ukrainian League (2009); Russian Cup (2012)
Clubs 04-05 FF Jaro; 05-09 Udinese Calcio (ITA); 07 AC Siena (ITA) (loan); 08-09 FC Dynamo Kyiv (UKR) (loan); 09-11 FC Dynamo Kyiv (UKR); 11-14 FC Rubin Kazan (RUS); 14- PFC CSKA Moskva (RUS)

2014/15 appearances/goals

Domestic league Russian Premier-Liga 25/13
Europe UEFA Champions League 6/-
National team UEFA EURO 2016 qualifying 6/1; Friendlies 2/-

Cesc Fàbregas

Midfielder, Height 177cm
Born 04/05/87, Vilassar de Mar, Spain

Eight seasons at Arsenal FC, during which he established himself as one of the game's finest midfield talents, failed to provide Fàbregas with the Premier League winner's medal he craved, but on returning to London after a three-year spell with FC Barcelona, the Spanish international hit the jackpot at the first attempt with Chelsea FC. He slotted perfectly into José Mourinho's team, forming an excellent little-and-large midfield liaison with Nemanja Matić and going on to top the Premier League assists chart with 18 – two shy of former Arsenal team-mate Thierry Henry's 2002/03 record.

International career

SPAIN
Major honours FIFA World Cup (2010); UEFA European Championship (2008, 2012)
Debut 01/03/06 v Ivory Coast (h, Valladolid, friendly), won 3-2
First goal 10/06/08 v Russia (n, Innsbruck, ECF), won 4-1
Caps 97 **Goals** 14
Major tournaments FIFA World Cup 2006; UEFA EURO 2008; FIFA Confederations Cup 2009; FIFA World Cup 2010; UEFA EURO 2012; FIFA Confederations Cup 2013; FIFA World Cup 2014

Club career

Major honours UEFA Super Cup (2011); FIFA Club World Cup (2011); Spanish League (2013); English League (2015); English FA Cup (2005); Spanish Cup (2012); English League Cup (2015)
Clubs 03-11 Arsenal FC (ENG); 11-14 FC Barcelona; 14- Chelsea FC (ENG)

2014/15 appearances/goals

Domestic league English Premier League 33(1)/3
Europe UEFA Champions League 8/2
National team UEFA EURO 2016 qualifying 3/-; Friendlies 3/1

Nabil Fekir

Attacking midfielder, Height 173cm
Born 18/07/93, Lyon, France

A handful of uneventful appearances in the Olympique Lyonnais first team during the previous season did not prepare the club's fans, nor the wider-watching public, for the impact that Fekir would have on the French championship in 2014/15. The effervescent young attacking midfielder became not just a regular in coach Hubert Fournier's team but also one of their chief assets. Lively, inventive and always looking to run at defenders, the diminutive left-footer ended the season with the honour of being voted Ligue 1 Young Player of the Year. He also became a senior French international and a potential star of UEFA EURO 2016.

International career

FRANCE
Debut 26/03/15 v Brazil (h, Saint-Denis, friendly), lost 1-3
First goal 07/06/15 v Belgium (h, Saint-Denis, friendly), lost 3-4
Caps 4 **Goals** 1

Club career

Clubs 13- Olympique Lyonnais

2014/15 appearances/goals

Domestic league French Ligue 1 34/13
Europe UEFA Europa League qualifying 1(1)/-
National team Friendlies (4)/1

Felipe Anderson

Attacking midfielder, Height 178cm
Born 15/04/93, Santa Maria, Brazil

Serie A discovered a new star in the second half of the 2014/15 season as Brazilian midfielder Felipe Anderson, who had struggled to make any headway in his first 18 months at SS Lazio following a high-profile move from Santos FC, came thrillingly to the fore in Stefano Pioli's resurgent team. The 22-year-old began his love affair with the local tifosi by scoring five goals in as many games around the turn of the year, the last of them a brilliant long-range strike in the Rome derby. By the end of term the gifted left-footer had inspired Lazio to a third-place finish in Serie A and a return to the UEFA Champions League.

International career

BRAZIL
Debut 07/06/15 v Mexico (h, Sao Paulo, friendly), won 2-0
Caps 1 **Goals** 0

Club career

Major honours Copa Libertadores (2012); Recopa Sudamericana (2012)
Clubs 10-13 Santos FC; 13- SS Lazio (ITA)

2014/15 appearances/goals

Domestic league Italian Serie A 23(9)/10
National team Friendlies (1)/-

Ezequiel Garay

Centre-back, Height 189cm
Born 10/10/86, Rosario, Argentina

A frustrated runner-up with Argentina at both the 2014 FIFA World Cup and 2015 Copa América, Garay had better fortune on the club front as he followed a domestic treble with SL Benfica by landing the Russian Pemier-Liga title in his debut season with FC Zenit. An expensive addition to the St Petersburg club's ranks at €15m, the 28-year-old centre-back justified the fee with a succession of high-quality performances, his experience and solidity proving crucial as Zenit conceded just 17 goals in their 30 league games. For the second year running, however, Garay's hopes of UEFA Europa League success were ended by Sevilla FC.

International career

ARGENTINA
Debut 22/08/07 v Norway (a, Oslo, friendly), lost 1-2
Caps 31 **Goals** 0
Major tournaments Copa América 2011; FIFA World Cup 2014; Copa América 2015

Club career

Major honours Argentinian League (clausura 2004); Portuguese League (2014); Russian League (2015); Spanish Cup (2011); Portuguese Cup (2014)
Clubs 04-05 CA Newell's Old Boys; 05-08 Real Racing Club (ESP); 08-11 Real Madrid CF (ESP); 08-09 Real Racing Club (ESP) (loan); 11-14 SL Benfica (POR); 14- FC Zenit (RUS)

2014/15 appearances/goals

Domestic league Russian Premier-Liga 25(1)/1
Europe UEFA Champions League 6/-;
UEFA Champions League qualifying/play-offs 4/-;
UEFA Europa League 5/-
National team Copa América 2015 4/-;
Friendlies 2/-

André-Pierre Gignac

Striker, Height 187cm
Born 05/12/85, Martigues, France

Gignac's fifth and final season as an Olympique de Marseille player was his most productive as he chalked up 21 Ligue 1 goals to end the campaign as the division's second highest scorer. The 2014/15 campaign promised more than it eventually delivered for Marseille, but Gignac responded positively to the idiosyncratic methods of new coach Marcelo Bielsa and had ten goals on the board by mid-October. A return to the international fold brought his first goal for France in exactly five years, but his UEFA EURO 2016 ambitions appeared to be shelved in the summer when he opted to pursue his career in Mexico.

International career

FRANCE
Debut 01/04/09 v Lithuania (h, Saint-Denis, WCQ), won 1-0
First goal 12/08/09 v Faroe Islands (a, Torshavn, WCQ), won 1-0
Caps 21 **Goals** 5
Major tournaments FIFA World Cup 2010

Club career

Major honours French League Cup (2011, 2012)
Clubs 04-07 FC Lorient; 05-06 Pau FC (loan); 07-10 Toulouse FC; 10-15 Olympique de Marseille; 15- Tigres UANL (MEX)

2014/15 appearances/goals

Domestic league French Ligue 1 36(2)/21
National team Friendlies 2(2)/1

Kamil Glik

Centre-back, Height 190cm
Born 03/02/88, Jastrzebie Zdroj, Poland

An excellent season in Serie A with Torino FC, for whom Glik scored seven goals – the most in the division by a defender – was supplemented by some towering performances for the Polish national team as they went unbeaten through the first six games of the UEFA EURO 2016 campaign. On top of the pile was his magnificent display in the historic 2-0 victory over Germany in Warsaw, where he headed, blocked and tackled as if his life depended on it to thwart the world champions. The big centre-back also got his name on the scoresheet for his country the following month in a 4-0 away win in Georgia.

International career

POLAND
Debut 20/01/10 v Thailand (a, Nakhon Ratchasima, friendly), won 3-1
First goal 20/01/10 v Thailand (a, Nakhon Ratchasima, friendly), won 3-1
Caps 31 **Goals** 3

Club career

Clubs 06 UD Horadada (ESP); 07-08 Real Madrid CF C (ESP); 08-10 GKS Piast Gliwice; 10-11 US Città di Palermo (ITA); 11 AS Bari (ITA) (loan); 11- Torino FC (ITA)

2014/15 appearances/goals

Domestic league Italian Serie A 31(1)/7
Europe UEFA Europa League 7/1; UEFA Europa League qualifying/play-offs 4/-
National team UEFA EURO 2016 qualifying 5/1; Friendlies 2/-

Antoine Griezmann

Winger/Striker, Height 176cm
Born 21/03/91, Macon, France

Armed with a lucrative six-year contract, Griezmann made his first season at Club Atlético de Madrid one to remember, scoring 22 goals in the Liga – the highest single-campaign tally ever recorded by a Frenchman in Spain's top division and behind only Cristiano Ronaldo and Lionel Messi in the final Pichichi listings. Although the sole tangible reward for the 24-year-old's excellent season was the Spanish Super Cup, the ex-Real Sociedad de Fútbol forward doubled his number of French international caps to 18, scoring twice, and all but cemented his place in Didier Deschamps' UEFA EURO 2016 side.

International career

FRANCE
Debut 05/03/14 v Netherlands (h, Paris, friendly), won 2-0
First goal 01/06/14 v Paraguay (h, Nice, friendly), drew 1-1
Caps 18 **Goals** 5
Major tournaments FIFA World Cup 2014

Club career

Clubs 09-14 Real Sociedad de Fútbol (ESP); 14- Club Atlético de Madrid (ESP)

2014/15 appearances/goals

Domestic league Spanish Liga 29(8)/22
Europe UEFA Champions League 5(4)/2
National team Friendlies 7(2)/2

Hakan Çalhanoğlu

Attacking midfielder, Height 176cm
Born 08/02/94, Mannheim, Germany

Recruited on a five-year contract from Hamburger SV, German-born Turkish international Hakan enjoyed a fabulous first season at Bayer 04 Leverkusen, enhancing his reputation as one of the most inventive set-piece experts in Europe. A free-kick from almost on the halfway line had adorned his final season at Hamburg, and although there was nothing quite to match that for his new club, a superb strike in a 2-0 win against FC Bayern München was acclaimed with similar fervour by the BayArena faithful. His excellent club form was transported into the international arena with Turkey, for whom he scored three goals in two friendlies.

International career

TURKEY
Debut 06/09/13 v Andorra (h, Kayseri, WCQ), won 5-0
First goal 31/03/15 v Luxembourg (a, Luxembourg, friendly), won 2-1
Caps 9 **Goals** 3

Club career

Clubs 11-12 Karlsruher SC (GER); 12-14 Hamburger SV (GER); 12-13 Karlsruher SC (GER) (loan); 14- Bayer 04 Leverkusen (GER)

2014/15 appearances/goals

Domestic league German Bundesliga 31(2)/8
Europe UEFA Champions League 8/2; UEFA Champions League play-offs 2/1
National team UEFA EURO 2016 qualifying 1(2)/-; Friendlies 2/3

Joe Hart

Goalkeeper, Height 191cm
Born 19/04/87, Shrewsbury, England

Back to his very best in 2014/15, Hart shone repeatedly for club and country. He also earned the appreciation of Lionel Messi, who described the Manchester City FC goalkeeper as a "phenomenon" after a magnificent display against FC Barcelona at the Camp Nou in the UEFA Champions League during which he made a succession of world-class saves. He had also kept out a last-minute Messi penalty in the first leg of the round of 16 tie. The winner of the Premier League Golden Glove – awarded to the keeper with the most clean sheets – for the fourth time in six seasons, he also collected his 50th England cap in March.

International career

ENGLAND
Debut 01/06/08 v Trinidad & Tobago (a, Port of Spain, friendly), won 3-0
Caps 52 **Goals** 0
Major tournaments FIFA World Cup 2010; UEFA EURO 2012; FIFA World Cup 2014

Club career

Major honours *English League (2012, 2014); English FA Cup (2011); English League Cup (2014)*
Clubs 03-06 Shrewsbury Town FC; 06- Manchester City FC; 07 Tranmere Rovers FC (loan); 07 Blackpool FC (loan); 09-10 Birmingham City FC (loan)

2014/15 appearances/goals

Domestic league English Premier League 36/-
Europe UEFA Champions League 8/-
National team UEFA EURO 2016 qualifying 6/-; Friendlies 3/-

Eden Hazard

Winger/Attacking midfielder, Height 170cm
Born 07/01/91, La Louviere, Belgium

A logical winner of the two prestigious 2014/15 player of the year awards in England, Hazard was the most consistently dazzling performer in Chelsea FC's Premier League-winning team, starting all 38 games and starring in almost all of them. He scored 14 goals, set up nine more and thrilled neutrals and partisans alike with his deft close control, sudden burst of pace and sharp, incisive passing. In June he captained Belgium to a 4-3 win over France, scoring his eighth international goal in the process. A return to the Stade de France with his country on 10 July next year will be high on his list of priorities for 2015/16.

International career

BELGIUM
Debut 19/11/08 v Luxembourg (a, Luxembourg, friendly), drew 1-1
First goal 07/10/11 v Kazakhstan (h, Brussels, ECQ), won 4-1
Caps 58 **Goals** 8
Major tournaments FIFA World Cup 2014

Club career

Major honours *UEFA Europa League (2013); French League (2011); English League (2015); French Cup (2011); English League Cup (2015)*
Clubs 07-12 LOSC Lille (FRA); 12- Chelsea FC (ENG)

2014/15 appearances/goals

Domestic league English Premier League 38/14
Europe UEFA Champions League 7/3
National team UEFA EURO 2016 qualifying 5/1; Friendlies 2/1

Patrick Herrmann

Attacking midfielder, Height 179cm
Born 12/02/91, Saarbrucken, Germany

A German youth international at every age group from Under-16 upwards, Herrmann finally completed the set in June 2015 when he made his debut for the senior Nationalmannschaft – over two years after he had received his first call-up. The pressure on coach Joachim Löw to include the gifted, in-form 24-year-old was considerable after an outstanding campaign for VfL Borussia Mönchengladbach, in which he played a major role in steering the club to third place in the Bundesliga and into the UEFA Champions League group stage for the first time. His goal tally in all competitions was 16 – nine more than in any previous season.

International career

GERMANY
Debut 10/06/15 v United States (h, Cologne, friendly), lost 1-2
Caps 2 **Goals** 0

Club career

Clubs 09- VfL Borussia Mönchengladbach

2014/15 appearances/goals

Domestic league German Bundesliga 26(6)/11
Europe UEFA Europa League 3(5)/4; UEFA Europa League play-offs (2)/-
National team UEFA EURO 2016 qualifying 1/-; Friendlies 1/-

Gonzalo Higuaín

Striker, Height 184cm
Born 10/12/87, Brest, France

With 18 goals in Serie A, another eight in European competition, one in the Coppa Italia and two vital equalisers in SSC Napoli's Italian Super Cup victory (on penalties) against Juventus three days before Christmas in Doha, Higuaín was entitled to feel proud of his 2014/15 achievements. But after scoring from the spot against Juve in Qatar, he would later rue two crucial missed spot kicks – the first in Napoli's final league game, which they lost 4-2 at home against SS Lazio to miss out on UEFA Champions League qualification, the second for Argentina in the shoot-out at the end of the Copa América final against Chile.

International career

ARGENTINA
Debut 10/10/09 v Peru (h, Buenos Aires, WCQ), won 2-1
First goal 10/10/09 v Peru (h, Buenos Aires, WCQ), won 2-1
Caps 52 **Goals** 25
Major tournaments FIFA World Cup 2010; Copa América 2011; FIFA World Cup 2014; Copa América 2015

Club career

Major honours Spanish League (2007, 2008, 2012); Spanish Cup (2011); Italian Cup (2014)
Clubs 04-06 CA River Plate; 07-13 Real Madrid CF (ESP); 13- SSC Napoli (ITA)

2014/15 appearances/goals

Domestic league Italian Serie A 31(6)/18
Europe UEFA Champions League play-offs 2/1; UEFA Europa League 10(4)/7
National team Copa América 2015 1(3)/2; Friendlies 3(2)/2

Hulk

Winger/Striker, Height 180cm
Born 25/07/86, Campina Grande, Brazil

Occasionally accused of self-indulgence in the past, Hulk became a valuable and reliable team player under coach André Villas-Boas as FC Zenit won the Russian Premier-Liga title. Indeed, the barrel-chested Brazilian international with the explosive left foot was very much Zenit's go-to man throughout a season that not only brought success on the domestic front but also a lengthy run in continental competition. The ex-FC Porto forward was the Premier-Liga's top scorer, with 15 goals, most of them as spectacular as they were significant, and his six strikes in Europe included an outrageous long-distance lob against eventual winners Sevilla FC.

International career

BRAZIL
Major honours FIFA Confederations Cup (2013)
Debut 14/11/09 v England (n, Doha, friendly), won 1-0
First goal 26/05/12 v Denmark (n, Hamburg, friendly), won 3-1
Caps 41 **Goals** 9
Major tournaments FIFA Confederations Cup 2013; FIFA World Cup 2014

Club career

Major honours UEFA Europa League (2011); Portuguese League (2009, 2011, 2012); Russian League (2015); Portuguese Cup (2009, 2010, 2011)
Clubs 04 SC Vitória; 05-08 Kawasaki Frontale (JPN); 06 Consadole Sapporo (JPN) (loan); 07 Tokyo Verdy (JPN) (loan); 08 Tokyo Verdy (JPN); 08-12 FC Porto (POR); 12- FC Zenit (RUS)

2014/15 appearances/goals

Domestic league Russian Premier-Liga 27(1)/15
Europe UEFA Champions League 6/1; UEFA Champions League qualifying/play-offs 4/2; UEFA Europa League 5/3

Zlatan Ibrahimović

Striker, Height 192cm
Born 03/10/81, Malmo, Sweden

Although injuries and suspensions restricted his availability in 2014/15, Ibrahimović more than made up for it when he did take the field. The maverick Swede's astonishing collection of domestic championship winner's medals reached double figures as he completed a hat-trick of Ligue 1 titles with Paris Saint-Germain, contributing 19 goals, and he also scored a hat-trick in the club's League Cup final victory over SC Bastia. Furthermore, he reached the double milestone of 50 goals and 100 caps for Sweden and went on to score eight times for his country during the course of the season, including five in four European Qualifiers.

International career

SWEDEN
Debut 31/01/01 v Faroe Islands (h, Vaxjo, friendly), drew 0-0
First goal 07/10/01 v Azerbaijan (h, Solna, WCQ), won 3-0
Caps 105 **Goals** 56
Major tournaments FIFA World Cup 2002; UEFA EURO 2004; FIFA World Cup 2006; UEFA EURO 2008; UEFA EURO 2012

Club career

Major honours UEFA Super Cup (2009); FIFA Club World Cup (2009); Dutch League (2002, 2004); Italian League (2007, 2008, 2009, 2011); Spanish League (2010); French League (2013, 2014, 2015); Dutch Cup (2002); French Cup (2015); French League Cup (2014, 2015)
Clubs 99-01 Malmö FF; 01-04 AFC Ajax (NED); 04-06 Juventus (ITA); 06-09 FC Internazionale Milano (ITA); 09-11 FC Barcelona (ESP); 10-11 AC Milan (ITA) (loan); 11-12 AC Milan (ITA); 12- Paris Saint-Germain (FRA)

2014/15 appearances/goals

Domestic league French Ligue 1 23(1)/19
Europe UEFA Champions League 6/2
National team UEFA EURO 2016 qualifying 4/5; Friendlies 3/3

Mauro Icardi

Striker, Height 181cm
Born 19/02/93, Rosario, Argentina

An injury-curtailed first season with FC Internazionale Milano was followed by a blistering second as Icardi fired 22 goals to share the Serie A capocannoniere crown with Hellas Verona FC veteran Luca Toni. Although Inter failed to qualify for Europe for the second time in three seasons, the powerful 22-year-old striker elected to stay on with the Nerazzurri, signing a new four-year contract. Having opened his 2014/15 Serie A goal account with a hat-trick against US Sassuolo Calcio, the former FC Barcelona trainee found the net consistently, ending the campaign with a last-day double in a 4-3 win at home to Empoli FC.

International career

ARGENTINA
Debut 15/10/13 v Uruguay (a, Montevideo, WCQ), lost 2-3
Caps 1 **Goals** 0

Club career

Clubs 11-13 UC Sampdoria (ITA); 13- FC Internazionale Milano (ITA)

2014/15 appearances/goals

Domestic league Italian Serie A 33(3)/22
Europe UEFA Europa League 8/1; UEFA Europa League play-offs 1(1)/3

Branislav Ivanović

Right-back/Centre-back,
Height 188cm
Born 22/02/84, Sremska Mitrovica, Serbia

A little over seven years after his arrival at Chelsea FC, Ivanović completed a clean sweep of trophies with the west London club as they beat Tottenham Hotspur FC to win the League Cup. It was in the Premier League, however, that the 31-year-old made his biggest mark. An ever-present contributor to the Blues' triumphant campaign – barring the last few seconds of a 1-1 draw at Manchester United FC after receiving a 93rd-minute red card – he impressed both as an attacker and defender at right-back. It was not a happy season internationally, however, for the captain of Serbia as his country tumbled out of UEFA EURO 2016 qualifying contention.

International career

SERBIA
Debut 08/06/05 v Italy (n, Toronto, friendly), drew 1-1
First goal 12/09/07 v Portugal (a, Lisbon, ECQ), drew 1-1
Caps 79 **Goals** 10
Major tournaments FIFA World Cup 2010

Club career

Major honours UEFA Champions League (2012); UEFA Europa League (2013); English League (2010, 2015); Russian Cup (2007); English FA Cup (2009, 2010, 2012); English League Cup (2015)
Clubs 02-03 FK Srem; 03-05 OFK Beograd; 06-07 FC Lokomotiv Moskva (RUS); 08- Chelsea FC (ENG)

2014/15 appearances/goals

Domestic league English Premier League 38/4
Europe UEFA Champions League 7/1
National team UEFA EURO 2016 qualifying 5/-; Friendlies 3/2

James Rodríguez

Attacking midfielder, Height 180cm
Born 12/07/91, Cucuta, Colombia

James joined Real Madrid CF on the crest of a wave in the summer of 2014. The top scorer at the FIFA World Cup in Brazil, where he struck six goals for Colombia, he arrived in the Spanish capital as a newly-anointed global superstar, so the pressure was on him to give the Bernabéu faithful what they wanted and justify his reported €80m fee. Nine months later the general consensus was that he had done just that. Although his season was interrupted from February to April with a fractured toe, he scored 17 goals in all competitions and confirmed his galáctico status with many moments of exquisite skill and flair.

International career

COLOMBIA
Debut 11/10/11 v Bolivia (a, La Paz, WCQ), won 2-1
First goal 03/06/12 v Peru (a, Lima, WCQ), won 1-0
Caps 37 **Goals** 12
Major tournaments FIFA World Cup 2014; Copa América 2015

Club career

Major honours UEFA Europa League (2011); UEFA Super Cup (2014); FIFA Club World Cup (2014); Argentinian Championship (apertura 2009); Portuguese Championship (2011, 2012, 2013); Portuguese Cup (2011)
Clubs 07-08 Envigado FC; 08-10 CA Banfield (ARG); 10-13 FC Porto (POR); 13-14 AS Monaco FC (FRA); 14- Real Madrid CF (ESP)

2014/15 appearances/goals

Domestic league Spanish Liga 29/13
Europe UEFA Champions League 8(1)/1
National team Copa América 2015 4/0; Friendlies 6/1

Jonas

Striker, Height 181cm
Born 01/04/84, Sao Paulo, Brazil

After leaving Valencia CF, Brazilian striker Jonas opted to pursue his career at the age of 30 with SL Benfica. Unfortunately he signed too late to be included in the Lisbon club's UEFA Champions League squad, and when he went on to inspire the Eagles to a successful Primeira Liga title defence, becoming Portugal's player of the year in the process, it begged the question whether Benfica might have fared rather better in Europe – they finished bottom of their group – had he been available to help. With a final all-competitions total of 31 goals in 35 games, his first season in Portuguese domestic football could hardly have gone better.

International career

BRAZIL
Debut 27/03/11 v Scotland (n, London, friendly), won 2-0
First goal 14/11/11 v Egypt (n, Al-Rayyan, friendly), won 2-0
Caps 8 **Goals** 2

Club career

Major honours Portuguese League (2015); Portuguese Cup (2015)
Clubs 05-06 Guarani FC; 06-07 Santos FC; 07-11 Grêmio FBPA; 08-09 Portuguesa (loan); 11-14 Valencia CF (ESP); 14- SL Benfica (POR)

2014/15 appearances/goals

Domestic league Portugese Liga 25(2)/20

Jonatan Soriano

Striker, Height 180cm
Born 24/09/85, El Pont de Vilomara, Spain

The goals continued to flow for the captain of FC Salzburg in 2014/15 as Jonatan Soriano bagged 46 in 49 games to help his team win the double of Bundesliga and ÖFB-Cup for the second straight year and race through their UEFA Europa League group with five wins and a draw. The Catalan striker's 31-goal league haul matched his figure of the previous campaign, earning him a second successive golden boot. Little wonder, then, that Salzburg extended the 29-year-old's contract midway through the season, rebuffing foreign clubs' increasing interest in a player who was once a free-scoring striker for the FC Barcelona B team.

International career

SPAIN
Uncapped

Club career

Major honours Austrian League (2012, 2014, 2015); Austrian Cup (2012, 2014, 2015)
Clubs 02-09 RCD Espanyol; 06 UD Almería (loan); 07 Polideportivo Ejido (loan); 09 Albacete Balompié (loan); 09-12 FC Barcelona B; 12- FC Salzburg (AUT)

2014/15 appearances/goals

Domestic league Austrian Bundesliga 29(3)/31
Europe UEFA Champions League qualifying/play-offs 4/2; UEFA Europa League 7(1)/6

Zlatko Junuzovic

Midfielder, Height 171cm
Born 26/09/87, Loznica, Serbia

A former Austrian Bundesliga footballer of the year, Junuzovic has lifted his game to another level since joining SV Werder Bremen, and in 2014/15, his third season with the north German side, the classy 27-year-old midfielder hit peak form for both club and country. His composure on the ball and set-piece expertise helped to lift Bremen from the relegation zone to mid-table of the Bundesliga – while earning him a new contract in the process – and he was also a prominent figure in Austria's excellent UEFA EURO 2016 qualifying run, starting all six matches as the central playmaker in Marcel Koller's ever-improving side.

International career

AUSTRIA
Debut 01/03/06 v Canada (h, Vienna, friendly), lost 0-2
First goal 07/10/11 v Azerbaijan (a, Baku, ECQ), won 4-1
Caps 40 **Goals** 5

Club career

Clubs 05-07 Grazer AK; 07-09 SK Austria Kärnten; 09-12 FK Austria Wien; 12- SV Werder Bremen (GER)

2014/15 appearances/goals

Domestic league German Bundesliga 32(1)/6
National team UEFA EURO 2016 qualifying 6/1; Friendlies 2/-

Harry Kane

Striker, Height 188cm
Born 28/07/93, London, England

Six players were shortlisted for the PFA Premier League Young Player of the Year award, but there was never any likelihood that it would be won by anyone other than Kane. Having worked his way into the Tottenham Hotspur FC first team by popular demand, the powerful young striker took the Premier League by storm with a barrage of goals. He ended the season with 31, of which 21 came in the Premier League, making him the second-highest scorer in the division. A first senior cap for England, in a UEFA EURO 2016 qualifier against Lithuania, was almost inevitably marked with another goal – just 79 seconds after his introduction.

International career

ENGLAND
Debut 27/03/15 v Lithuania (h, London, ECQ), won 4-0
First goal 27/03/15 v Lithuania (h, London, ECQ), won 4-0
Caps 2 **Goals** 1

Club career

Clubs 09- Tottenham Hotspur FC; 11 Leyton Orient FC (loan); 12 Millwall FC (loan); 12-13 Norwich City FC (loan); 13 Leicester City FC (loan)

2014/15 appearances/goals

Domestic league English Premier League 28(6)/21
Europe UEFA Europa League 4(3)/5; UEFA Europa League play-offs 2/2
National team UEFA EURO 2016 qualifying (1)/1; Friendlies 1/-

Yevhen Konoplyanka

Winger, Height 176cm
Born 29/09/89, Kirovohrad, Ukraine

Three years after making a name for himself at UEFA EURO 2012, Konoplyanka finally got his big-money move to a foreign club when he left FC Dnipro Dnipropetrovsk in July for Sevilla FC. A few weeks earlier the gifted winger had been playing against the Andalusian side in the UEFA Europa League final, only to end up on the losing side in Warsaw. A standout figure throughout Dnipro's marathon European campaign with his clever footwork, elegant movement and endless creativity, he also enjoyed a productive season for Ukraine, taking his goal tally into double figures in the last fixture of the campaign, against Luxembourg in Lviv.

International career

UKRAINE
Debut 25/05/10 v Lithuania (h, Kharkiv, friendly), won 4-0
First goal 29/05/10 v Romania (h, Lviv, friendly), won 3-2
Caps 45 **Goals** 10
Major tournaments UEFA EURO 2012

Club career

Clubs 07-15 FC Dnipro Dnipropetrovsk; 15- Sevilla FC (ESP)

2014/15 appearances/goals

Domestic league Ukrainian Premier League 14(7)/7
Europe UEFA Champions League qualifying 2/-; UEFA Europa League 14(1)/1
National team UEFA EURO 2016 qualifying 5/1; Friendlies 1(2)/1

Andrej Kramarić

Striker, Height 177cm
Born 19/06/91, Zagreb, Croatia

Kramarić showed former club GNK Dinamo Zagreb what they were missing with a phenomenal run of goalscoring for HNK Rijeka during the first half of the season, scoring 21 goals in 18 domestic league fixtures plus another seven in the UEFA Europa League, including a hat-trick against Feyenoord. His league tally would keep him on top of the 1. HNL scorer charts right through to the end of the season despite a January move to Leicester City FC. The skilful, two-footed 23-year-old helped his new club to avoid relegation from the Premier League and also scored three goals in his first six internationals for Croatia.

International career

CROATIA
Debut 04/09/14 v Cyprus (h, Pula, friendly), won 2-0
First goal 09/09/14 v Malta (h, Zagreb, ECQ), won 2-0
Caps 6 **Goals** 3

Club career

Major honours Croatian League (2010, 2011); Croatian Cup (2011, 2014)
Clubs 09-13 GNK Dinamo Zagreb; 12-13 NK Lokomotiva Zagreb (loan); 13-15 HNK Rijeka; 15- Leicester City FC (ENG)

2014/15 appearances/goals

Domestic league Croatian 1. HNL 18/21; English Premier League 6(7)/2
Europe UEFA Europa League 6/5; UEFA Europa League qualifying/play-offs 4(2)/2
National team UEFA EURO 2016 qualifying 1(3)/2; Friendlies 1(1)/1

Grzegorz Krychowiak

Midfielder, Height 186cm
Born 29/01/90, Gryfice, Poland

A move from Stade de Reims to Sevilla FC in the summer of 2014 worked wonders for Krychowiak's career. The gritty midfielder went on to enjoy a fabulous season both for his new club and the Polish national team, helping the former to a successful defence of the UEFA Europa League, not least with a goal in the final on native soil in Warsaw, and the latter to the top of their UEFA EURO 2016 qualifying group. An ever-present for his country on the road to France, starting and finishing all six matches, the 24-year-old also won himself a place in the Spanish Liga's official team of the season.

International career

POLAND
Debut 14/12/08 v Serbia (n, Antalya, friendly), won 1-0
First goal 14/11/14 v Georgia (a, Tbilisi, ECQ), won 4-0
Caps 26 **Goals** 1

Club career

Major honours UEFA Europa League (2015)
Clubs 08-12 FC Girondins de Bordeaux (FRA); 09-11 Stade de Reims (FRA) (loan); 11-12 FC Nantes (FRA) (loan); 12-14 Stade de Reims (FRA); 14- Sevilla FC (ESP)

2014/15 appearances/goals

Domestic league Spanish Liga 31(1)/2
Europe UEFA Europa League 13/2
National team UEFA EURO 2016 qualifying 6/1; Friendlies 1/-

Alexandre Lacazette

Striker, Height 175cm
Born 28/05/91, Lyon, France

Lacazette ended the 2014/15 season with a double helping of individual recognition, winning the Ligue 1 golden boot and player of the season gong. Formidable in front of goal all season, he seldom went more than two games without scoring. But for a thigh muscle strain that kept him out of action for most of February, including a 1-1 draw at home to Paris Saint-Germain, he might well have ended up with a Ligue 1 winner's medal too. As it was, Lyon finished second, with the France international subsequently making encouraging noises to the locals that he would stay on and help the club in the UEFA Champions League.

International career

FRANCE
Debut 05/06/13 v Uruguay (a, Montevideo, friendly), lost 0-1
First goal 29/03/15 v Denmark (h, Saint-Etienne, friendly), won 2-0
Caps 8 **Goals** 1

Club career

Major honours French Cup (2012)
Clubs 10- Olympique Lyonnais

2014/15 appearances/goals

Domestic league French Ligue 1 33/27
Europe UEFA Europa League qualifying/play-offs 4/1
National team Friendlies 3(3)/1

Robert Lewandowski

Striker, Height 184cm
Born 21/08/88, Warsaw, Poland

Lewandowski scored fewer goals in his first season for FC Bayern München than in any of his previous three with Borussia Dortmund, but the Polish striker's powerful presence at the apex of the Bayern attack, where he replaced Mario Mandžukić, still served to make the best team in Germany a little bit better. His 17 league strikes included a magnificent goal-of-the-season contender against Eintracht Frankfurt, but he arguably saved his best performance of the campaign until last, scoring a 'perfect' hat-trick between the 89th and 93rd minutes of Poland's UEFA EURO 2016 qualifier at home to Georgia to become the competition's leading marksman with seven goals.

International career

POLAND
Debut 10/09/08 v San Marino (a, Serravalle, WCQ), won 2-0
First goal 10/09/08 v San Marino (a, Serravalle, WCQ), won 2-0
Caps 68 **Goals** 26
Major tournaments UEFA EURO 2012

Club career

Major honours Polish League (2010); German League (2011, 2012, 2015); Polish Cup (2009); German Cup (2012)
Clubs 06-08 Znicz Pruszków; 08-10 KKS Lech Poznań; 10-14 Borussia Dortmund (GER); 14- FC Bayern München (GER)

2014/15 appearances/goals

Domestic league German Bundesliga 28(3)/17
Europe UEFA Champions League 10(2)/6
National team UEFA EURO 2016 qualifying 6/7; Friendlies 1/-

Claudio Marchisio

Midfielder, Height 179cm
Born 19/01/86, Turin, Italy

A loyal servant to Juventus since the 2006/07 season, which the Bianconeri spent in Serie B, Marchisio had another excellent campaign in 2014/15, reaching the milestone of 300 appearances for the club in April. His consistency of performance alongside Andrea Pirlo in the Juve midfield helped the team to a first domestic double in 20 years. Although he was suspended for the Coppa Italia final against SS Lazio, he impressed in the UEFA Champions League decider against FC Barcelona, skillfully starting the move that led to his team's equaliser. His loyalty to Juventus will now extend to 2020 after he penned a new five-year contract in June.

International career

ITALY
Debut 12/08/09 v Switzerland (a, Basel, friendly), drew 0-0
First goal 07/10/11 v Serbia (a, Belgrade, ECQ), drew 1-1
Caps 52 **Goals** 4
Major tournaments FIFA World Cup 2010; UEFA EURO 2012; FIFA Confederations Cup 2013; FIFA World Cup 2014

Club career

Major honours *Italian League (2012, 2013, 2014, 2015); Italian Cup (2015)*
Clubs 06- Juventus; 07-08 Empoli FC (loan)

2014/15 appearances/goals

Domestic league Italian Serie A 33(2)/3
Europe UEFA Champions League 11(1)/-
National team UEFA EURO 2016 qualifying 4/-; Friendlies 1/-

Jackson Martínez

Striker, Height 185cm
Born 03/10/86, Quibdo, Colombia

The first man to top the Portuguese Primeira Liga goal charts three seasons running since Mário Jardel in 1998/99, Martínez completed the hat-trick with 21 goals for FC Porto, making it 67 in total during his three-year spell at the Estádio do Dragão. There will be no matching Jardel's four-in-a-row feat, however, as the Colombian striker left Porto at the end of the season for Club Atlético de Madrid, costing the Spanish club a cool €35m. He also enjoyed a fertile final season for Porto in Europe, scoring eight goals in the UEFA Champions League, including one in each leg of the quarter-final against FC Bayern München.

International career

COLOMBIA
Debut 05/09/09 v Ecuador (h, Medellin, WCQ), won 2-0
First goal 05/09/09 v Ecuador (h, Medellin, WCQ), won 2-0
Caps 39 **Goals** 10
Major tournaments Copa América 2011; FIFA World Cup 2014; Copa América 2015

Club career

Major honours *Colombian League (finalización 2009); Portuguese League (2013)*
Clubs 06-10 Independiente Medellín; 10-12 Chiapas FC (MEX); 12-15 FC Porto (POR); 15- Club Atlético de Madrid (ESP)

2014/15 appearances/goals

Domestic league Portuguese Liga 29(1)/21
Europe UEFA Champions League 7(1)/7; UEFA Champions League play-offs 2/1
National team Copa América 2015 1(2)/-; Friendlies 3(3)/-

Nemanja Matić

Midfielder, Height 194cm
Born 01/08/88, Ub, Serbia

There is a saying in football that a player, or indeed a coach, should never go back to a former club, but that didn't ring true at Chelsea FC in 2014/15 as José Mourinho, in his second spell at Stamford Bridge, led the Blues to the Premier League title while Matić, in his first full season back after three years at SL Benfica, was widely acclaimed as the league's best defensive midfielder. Named 2014 Serbian Player of the Year, the tall, muscular left-footer won a place in the Premier League Team of the Year and was also a consistent performer in Europe, scoring the winner on his return to Lisbon against Sporting Clube de Portugal.

International career

SERBIA
Debut 14/12/08 v Poland (n, Antalya, friendly), lost 0-1
First goal 29/03/15 v Portugal (a, Lisbon, ECQ), lost 1-2
Caps 21 **Goals** 1

Club career

Major honours *English League (2010, 2015); Portuguese League (2014); Slovakian Cup (2009); English FA Cup (2010); Portuguese Cup (2014); English League Cup (2015)*
Clubs 05-07 FK Kolubara; 07-09 MFK Košice (SVK); 09-11 Chelsea FC (ENG); 10-11 Vitesse (NED) (loan); 11-14 SL Benfica (POR); 14- Chelsea FC (ENG)

2014/15 appearances/goals

Domestic league English Premier League 35(1)/1
Europe UEFA Champions League 8/2
National team UEFA EURO 2016 qualifying 5/1; Friendlies 3/-

Blaise Matuidi

Midfielder, Height 175cm
Born 09/04/87, Toulouse, France

One of the most dependable members of the Paris Saint-Germain team that won all four domestic prizes available to them in 2014/15, Matuidi is also now firmly established as a mainstay for Didier Deschamps' France. Although generally categorised as a defensive midfielder, the 28-year-old has constructive as well as destructive qualities, his leggy athleticism and eye for a goal, especially with his favoured left foot, providing a useful auxiliary asset in attack. A 90-minute performer in both the League Cup and Coupe de France final wins, he also scored the winning goal for Paris against FC Barcelona in a UEFA Champions League group game.

International career

FRANCE
Debut 07/09/10 v Bosnia & Herzegovina (a, Sarajevo, ECQ), won 2-0
First goal 05/03/14 v Netherlands (h, Paris, friendly), won 2-0
Caps 35 **Goals** 4
Major tournaments UEFA EURO 2012; FIFA World Cup 2014

Club career

Major honours French League (2013, 2014, 2015); French Cup (2015); French League Cup (2014, 2015)
Clubs 04-07 ES Troyes AC; 07-11 AS Saint-Étienne; 11- Paris Saint-Germain

2014/15 appearances/goals

Domestic league French Ligue 1 25(9)/4
Europe UEFA Champions League 10/1
National team Friendlies 5(2)/-

Alexander Meier

Attacking midfielder/Striker, Height 196cm
Born 17/01/83, Buchholz, Germany

A stalwart figure for Eintracht Frankfurt since 2004, Meier's only major achievement of note prior to the 2014/15 season had been topping the German second division goal charts when the club won promotion in 2011/12. The strapping 32-year-old, who can operate both up front or in midfield, rediscovered that scoring form three seasons later and claimed the Bundesliga's Torschützenkönig prize, although he had an anxious wait to see whether his 19-goal tally would be enough to make him Frankfurt's first winner since Anthony Yeboah in 1993/94 as he sat out the final few weeks of the campaign with a knee injury.

International career

GERMANY
Uncapped

Club career

Clubs 01-03 FC St Pauli; 03-04 Hamburger SV; 04- Eintracht Frankfurt

2014/15 appearances/goals

Domestic league German Bundesliga 24(2)/19

Lionel Messi

Striker, Height 170cm
Born 24/06/87, Rosario, Argentina

The incomparable genius of Messi was on near-permanent display during a 2014/15 season that, even by his extraordinarily high standards, ranked as one of his very best. The treble of Liga, Copa del Rey and UEFA Champions League was won by FC Barcelona in scintillating style, and the Argentinian, as ever, contributed to the team's success with performances of consistent beauty and splendour, setting astonishing new goalscoring records along the way. Argentina's agonising Copa América final defeat on penalties by Chile kept his international trophy cupboard bare, but with Barcelona there appears to be no limit to what the extraordinary 28-year-old can achieve.

International career

ARGENTINA
Debut 17/08/05 v Hungary (a, Budapest, friendly), won 2-1
First goal 01/03/06 v Croatia (n, Basel, friendly), lost 2-3
Caps 103 **Goals** 46
Major tournaments FIFA World Cup 2006; Copa América 2007; FIFA World Cup 2010; Copa América 2011; FIFA World Cup 2014; Copa América 2015

Club career

Major honours UEFA Champions League (2006, 2009, 2011, 2015); UEFA Super Cup (2009, 2011); FIFA Club World Cup (2009, 2011); Spanish League (2005, 2006, 2009, 2010, 2011, 2013, 2015); Spanish Cup (2009, 2012, 2015)
Clubs 04- FC Barcelona (ESP)

2014/15 appearances/goals

Domestic league Spanish Liga 37(1)/43
Europe UEFA Champions League 13/10
National team Copa América 6/1; Friendlies 3(1)/3

Arkadiusz Milik

Striker, Height 186cm
Born 28/02/94, Tychy, Poland

An elegant 21-year-old forward with a velvet touch as well as a ferocious left-foot shot, Milik thoroughly enjoyed himself on loan at AFC Ajax in 2014/15, scoring 23 goals, including four in Europe, and consequently earning himself a permanent transfer to Amsterdam from Bayer 04 Leverkusen. Above all, though, it was his brilliant displays for Poland that caught the eye. A nine-goal marksman for his country in the 2015 UEFA European Under-21 Championship campaign, he scored four fabulous goals for the senior side in the UEFA EURO 2016 qualifiers, the first of them with a header in a momentous 2-0 win against world champions Germany.

International career

POLAND
Debut 12/10/12 v South Africa (h, Warsaw, friendly), won 1-0
First goal 14/12/12 v FYR Macedonia (n, Antalya, friendly), won 4-1
Caps 17 **Goals** 7

Club career

Clubs 10-11 Rozwój Katowice; 11-12 Górnik Zabrze; 13-15 Bayer 04 Leverkusen (GER); 13-14 FC Augsburg (GER) (loan); 14-15 AFC Ajax (NED) (loan); 15- AFC Ajax (NED)

2014/15 appearances/goals

Domestic league Dutch Eredivisie 14(7)/11
Europe UEFA Champions League 2(3)/1; UEFA Europa League 4/3
National team UEFA EURO 2016 qualifying 6/4; Friendlies 1(1)/1

Aleksandar Mitrović

Striker, Height 189cm
Born 16/09/94, Smederevo, Serbia

Named player of the tournament at the 2013 UEFA European Under-19 Championship, Mitrović has kicked on impressively since then. The capricious young Serbian striker left FK Partizan for RSC Anderlecht after that tournament and followed up a fine first season in Belgium with an outstanding second in 2014/15, which, although it delivered no club silverware, brought the 20-year-old individual recognition as the Pro League's leading scorer, with 20 goals. Tough and powerful, he crossed the North Sea in the summer to join Newcastle United FC, challenging himself with the arduous task of becoming the 'new Alan Shearer'.

International career

SERBIA
Debut 07/06/13 v Belgium (a, Brussels, WCQ), lost 1-2
First goal 06/09/13 v Croatia (h, Belgrade, WCQ), drew 1-1
Caps 13 **Goals** 1

Club career

Major honours Serbian League (2013); Belgian League (2014)
Clubs 11-12 FK Teleoptik; 12-13 FK Partizan; 13-15 RSC Anderlecht (BEL); 15- Newcastle United FC (ENG)

2014/15 appearances/goals

Domestic league Belgian Pro League 36(1)/20
Europe UEFA Champions League 4(1)/2; UEFA Europa League 2/1
National team UEFA EURO 2016 qualifying 2(2)/-; Friendlies 2(1)/-

Luka Modrić

Midfielder, Height 174cm
Born 09/09/85, Zadar, Croatia

With Modrić making the play in midfield alongside new signing Toni Kroos during the first few months of the 2014/15 season, Real Madrid CF were a sight to behold. Everything was running with smooth precision in Carlo Ancelotti's side as they rattled off the victories at home and in Europe. But then the Croatian international schemer picked up a thigh injury in a UEFA EURO 2016 qualifier against Italy that would sideline him for the next four months. Just when he appeared to have rediscovered full fitness and form, another injury, to his knee, finished off his season, and all the main prizes ended up at FC Barcelona.

International career

CROATIA
Debut 01/03/06 v Argentina (n, Basel, friendly), won 3-2
First goal 16/08/06 v Italy (a, Livorno, friendly), won 2-0
Caps 84 **Goals** 10
Major tournaments FIFA World Cup 2006; UEFA EURO 2008; UEFA EURO 2012; FIFA World Cup 2014

Club career

Major honours UEFA Champions League (2014); UEFA Super Cup (2014); Croatian League (2006, 2007, 2008); Croatian Cup (2007, 2008); Spanish Cup (2014)
Clubs 02-08 GNK Dinamo Zagreb; 03-04 HŠK Zrinjski (BIH) (loan); 04-05 NK Inter Zaprešić (loan); 08-12 Tottenham Hotspur FC (ENG); 12- Real Madrid CF (ESP)

2014/15 appearances/goals

Domestic league Spanish Liga 16/1
Europe UEFA Champions League 5(1)/-
National team UEFA EURO 2016 qualifying 5/2; Friendlies 1/-

Álvaro Morata

Striker, Height 187cm
Born 23/10/92, Madrid, Spain

The 'law of the ex', a favoured idiom of the Italian football media, came into force in the semi-final of the UEFA Champions League as Morata, bought by Juventus from Real Madrid CF for €20m the previous summer, scored in both legs to eliminate his old club and send his new one through to the final. The 22-year-old, a double scorer also in the round of 16 against Borussia Dortmund, registered again, albeit in vain, against FC Barcelona in Berlin. A European Under-21 champion in 2013, he was handed a first senior call-up for Spain, and, rising again to the big occasion, scored a vital winner on his first competitive start in a UEFA EURO 2016 qualifier against Ukraine.

International career

SPAIN
Debut 15/11/14 v Belarus (h, Huelva, ECQ), won 3-0
First goal 27/03/15 v Ukraine (h, Seville, ECQ), won 1-0
Caps 5 **Goals** 1

Club career

Major honours UEFA Champions League (2014); Spanish League (2012); Italian League (2015); Spanish Cup (2011, 2014); Italian Cup (2015)
Clubs 10-14 Real Madrid CF; 14- Juventus (ITA)

2014/15 appearances/goals

Domestic league Spanish Liga 11(18)/8
Europe UEFA Champions League 9(3)/5
National team UEFA EURO 2016 qualifying 2(1)/1; Friendlies 1(1)/-

Thomas Müller

Attacking midfielder/Striker, Height 186cm
Born 13/09/89, Weilheim, Germany

With seven goals in the 2014/15 UEFA Champions League, the most in the season by an FC Bayern München player, Müller became the all-time highest-scoring German in the competition, overtaking former team-mate Mario Gomez and ending the campaign with a cumulative tally of 28. The 25-year-old showed no sign of post-FIFA World Cup fatigue as he claimed his fourth Bundesliga winner's medal in six years, scoring 13 goals in the competition for the third season in a row. He also found the net five times in as many UEFA EURO 2016 qualifiers for Germany, including a match-winning double in a difficult opener at home to Scotland.

International career

GERMANY
Major honours FIFA World Cup (2014)
Debut 03/03/10 v Argentina (h, Munich, friendly), lost 0-1
First goal 13/06/10 v Australia (n, Durban, WCF), won 4-0
Caps 63 **Goals** 27
Major tournaments FIFA World Cup 2010; UEFA EURO 2012; FIFA World Cup 2014

Club career

Major honours UEFA Champions League (2013); UEFA Super Cup (2013); FIFA Club World Cup (2013); German League (2010, 2013, 2014, 2015); German Cup (2010, 2013, 2014)
Clubs 08- FC Bayern München

2014/15 appearances/goals

Domestic league German Bundesliga 28(4)/13
Europe UEFA Champions League 10/7
National team UEFA EURO 2016 qualifying 5/5; Friendlies 1(1)/-

Radja Nainggolan

Midfielder, Height 175cm
Born 04/05/88, Antwerp, Belgium

A Belgian international who has spent his entire career in Italy, Nainggolan was a dynamic presence in midfield for AS Roma in 2014/15 – his first full season with the Giallorossi. The extravagantly-coiffured 27-year-old regularly outshone all others in Rudi Garcia's side, his all-action style driving the team to second place in Serie A. A spectacular winning goal at Genoa CFC was the highlight of an excellent season that also earned him a regular spot in the Belgian national side, for whom he scored memorable goals against Bosnia & Herzegovina and France but made a costly defensive error in the big European Qualifier away to Wales.

International career

BELGIUM
Debut 29/05/09 v Chile (n, Chiba, Kirin Cup), drew 1-1
First goal 05/03/14 v Ivory Coast (h, Brussels, friendly), drew 2-2
Caps 12 **Goals** 3

Club career

Clubs 06-10 Piacenza Calcio (ITA); 10 Cagliari Calcio (ITA) (loan); 10-14 Cagliari Calcio (ITA); 14 AS Roma (ITA) (loan); 14- AS Roma (ITA)

2014/15 appearances/goals

Domestic league Italian Serie A 30(5)/5
Europe UEFA Champions League 6/-; UEFA Europa League 2(1)/-
National team UEFA EURO 2016 qualifying 5/1; Friendlies 1(1)/1

Manuel Neuer

Goalkeeper, Height 193cm
Born 27/03/86, Gelsenkirchen, Germany

FC Bayern München have broken several Bundesliga records in recent years, and Germany's 2014 FIFA World Cup-winning goalkeeper Neuer set another new one in 2014/15 as he chalked up 20 clean sheets, bettering the 19 of another famous Bayern custodian, Oliver Kahn. Fresh from his sweeper/keeper heroics in Brazil, the 29-year-old enjoyed another exemplary season, strengthening his reputation as the world's best in his position with a succession of high-quality performances and vital saves. The occasional off-day, as at FC Porto in the UEFA Champions League quarter-final first leg, stood out only because of its rarity.

International career

GERMANY
Major honours FIFA World Cup (2014)
Debut 02/06/09 v United Arab Emirates (a, Dubai, friendly), won 7-2
Caps 58 **Goals** 0
Major tournaments FIFA World Cup 2010; UEFA EURO 2012; FIFA World Cup 2014

Club career

Major honours UEFA Champions League (2013); UEFA Super Cup (2013); FIFA Club World Cup (2013); German League (2013, 2014, 2015); German Cup (2011, 2013, 2014)
Clubs 05-11 FC Schalke 04; 11- FC Bayern München

2014/15 appearances/goals

Domestic league German Bundesliga 31(1)/-
Europe UEFA Champions League 12/-
National team UEFA EURO 2016 qualifying 5/-; Friendlies 1/-

Neymar

Striker, Height 174cm
Born 05/02/92, Mogi das Cruzes, Brazil

A disappointing debut season with FC Barcelona was erased from memory as Neymar paraded his world-class talent in Luis Enrique's all-conquering team on an ever more consistent basis, his form peaking spectacularly in the latter stages of the club's UEFA Champions League triumph as he scored seven goals in five games, making it ten for the season – the same number as Lionel Messi and Cristiano Ronaldo – with his trophy-clinching 97th-minute strike against Juventus in Berlin. The brilliant Brazilian forward also struck 22 goals in Barça's Liga triumph and seven in the Copa del Rey, including one in the final, a 3-1 win against Athletic Club.

International career

BRAZIL
Major honours FIFA Confederations Cup (2013)
Debut 10/08/10 v United States (a, East Rutherford, friendly), won 2-0
First goal 10/08/10 v United States (a, East Rutherford, friendly), won 2-0
Caps 65 **Goals** 44
Major tournaments Copa América 2011; FIFA Confederations Cup 2013; FIFA World Cup 2014; Copa América 2015

Club career

Major honours UEFA Champions League (2015); Copa Libertadores (2011); Recopa Sudamericana (2012); Spanish Championship (2015); Brazilian Cup (2010); Spanish Cup (2015)
Clubs 09-13 Santos FC; 13- FC Barcelona (ESP)

2014/15 appearances/goals

Domestic league Spanish Liga 29(4)/22
Europe UEFA Champions League 12/10
National team Copa América 2015 2/1; Friendlies 8(1)/8

Nicolás Otamendi

Centre-back, Height 183cm
Born 12/02/88, Buenos Aires, Argentina

A place in the Spanish Liga's official team of the season was just recognition for Otamendi after an outstanding debut campaign in the division with Valencia CF. A pillar of the club's defence, the ex-FC Porto centre-back made his rugged presence felt with one commanding performance after another. He also scored six goals, the most significant of them coming in the early-January home win against Real Madrid CF, which helped to end an all-competitions 22-match winning run for the visitors that had lasted since mid-September. He carried his Valencia form into the Copa América, where he was one of the leading men for runners-up Argentina.

International career

ARGENTINA
Debut 20/05/09 v Panama (h, Santa Fe, friendly), won 3-1
First goal 02/09/11 v Venezuela (n, Kolkata, friendly), won 1-0
Caps 25 **Goals** 1
Major tournaments FIFA World Cup 2010; Copa América 2015

Club career

Major honours UEFA Europa League (2011); Argentinian League (clausura 2009); Portuguese League (2011, 2012, 2013); Portuguese Cup (2011)
Clubs 07-10 CA Vélez Sarsfield; 10-14 FC Porto (POR); 14- Valencia CF (ESP); 14 Clube Atlético Mineiro (BRA) (loan)

2014/15 appearances/goals

Domestic league Spanish Liga 35/6
National team Copa América 2015 5/-; Friendlies 4/-

Javier Pastore

Attacking midfielder, Height 187cm
Born 20/06/89, Cordoba, Argentina

Pastore's fourth season as a Paris Saint-Germain player was his best by some distance – a fact acknowledged by the club when, in June, they extended his contract to 2019 with vastly improved terms. The Argentinian playmaker made a telling contribution to PSG's domestic trophy clean sweep, adding consistency to his craft and creativity. He registered five goals and ten assists in the Ligue 1 triumph and also caught the eye with some graceful performances in the UEFA Champions League. For Argentina he was an ever-present at the 2015 Copa América, reproducing his fine club form in Chile to help his country reach the final.

International career

ARGENTINA
Debut 24/05/10 v Canada (h, Buenos Aires, friendly), won 5-0
First goal 31/03/15 v Ecuador (n, East Rutherford, friendly), won 2-1
Caps 25 **Goals** 2
Major tournaments FIFA World Cup 2010; Copa América 2011; Copa América 2015

Club career

Major honours French League (2013, 2014, 2015); French Cup (2015); French League Cup (2014, 2015)
Clubs 07-08 CA Talleres; 08-09 CA Huracán; 09-11 US Città di Palermo (ITA); 11- Paris Saint-Germain (FRA)

2014/15 appearances/goals

Domestic league French Ligue 1 31(3)/5
Europe UEFA Champions League 7(3)/-
National team Copa América 2015 6/1; Friendlies 4(2)/1

Dimitri Payet

Winger/Attacking midfielder, Height 175cm
Born 29/03/87, Saint-Pierre, Reunion

A creative tour de force for Olympique de Marseille in 2014/15, Payet was officially credited with the highest number of assists in Ligue 1 (16) as well as the most successful crosses (93). He also scored seven goals himself, the last of them in a 3-0 win against SC Bastia on what would be his swansong appearance. A few weeks later the 28-year-old ended his two-year stay at the Stade Vélodrome by signing for West Ham United FC. He moved to east London as a France regular, having played in seven successive games for Didier Deschamps' developing side and, in June against Belgium, scored his first international goal.

International career

FRANCE
Debut 09/10/10 v Romania (h, Saint-Denis, ECQ), won 2-0
First goal 07/06/15 v Belgium (h, Saint-Denis, friendly), lost 3-4
Caps 15 **Goals** 1

Club career

Clubs 05-07 FC Nantes; 07-11 AS Saint-Étienne; 11-13 LOSC Lille; 13-15 Olympique de Marseille; 15- West Ham United FC (ENG)

2014/15 appearances/goals

Domestic league French Ligue 1 35(1)/7
National team Friendlies 4(4)/1

Gerard Piqué

Centre-back, Height 190cm
Born 02/02/87, Barcelona, Spain

Rumours circulated in the Spanish media during the 2014/15 season that Piqué and his new head coach at FC Barcelona, Luis Enrique, did not get on. But there was no evidence of any disharmony on the pitch, where the tall, strapping Spanish international centre-back marshalled the Barça rearguard with customary authority and composure. In fact, his consistency of performance during the second half of the season was comparable to that of the three South American superstars up front as the Catalan club charged towards their celebrated treble – the second in the 28-year-old's seven-year sojourn back at the Camp Nou.

International career

SPAIN
Major honours FIFA World Cup (2010); UEFA European Championship (2012)
Debut 11/02/09 v England (h, Seville, friendly), won 2-0
First goal 28/03/09 v Turkey (h, Madrid, WCQ), won 1-0
Caps 69 **Goals** 4
Major tournaments FIFA Confederations Cup 2009; FIFA World Cup 2010; UEFA EURO 2012; FIFA Confederations Cup 2013; FIFA World Cup 2014

Club career

Major honours UEFA Champions League (2008, 2009, 2011, 2015); UEFA Super Cup (2009, 2011); FIFA Club World Cup (2009, 2011); English League (2008); Spanish Championship (2009, 2010, 2011, 2013, 2015); Spanish Cup (2009, 2012, 2015); English League Cup (2006)
Clubs 04-08 Manchester United FC (ENG); 06-07 Real Zaragoza (loan); 08- FC Barcelona

2014/15 appearances/goals

Domestic league Spanish Liga 26(1)/5
Europe UEFA Champions League 11/1
National team UEFA EURO 2016 qualifying 5/-; Friendlies 2(1)/-

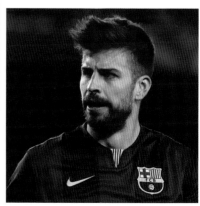

Paul Pogba

Midfielder, Height 186cm
Born 15/03/93, Lagny-sur-Marne, France

Officially recognised as the Best Young Player at the 2014 FIFA World Cup, Pogba added further lustre to his growing reputation with a catalogue of stellar displays for Juventus in 2014/15. The 22-year-old French midfielder, who allies physical strength and athleticism with refined technique and touch, missed two months of action during the spring with a hamstring injury, but he was back in May as Massimiliano Allegri's side clinched the domestic double and knocked out holders Real Madrid CF to reach the UEFA Champions League final. Coveted by Europe's biggest clubs, his future was the subject of intense speculation during the summer.

International career

FRANCE
Debut 22/03/13 v Georgia (h, Paris, WCQ), won 3-1
First goal 10/09/13 v Belarus (a, Gomel, WCQ), won 4-2
Caps 23 **Goals** 5
Major tournaments FIFA World Cup 2014

Club career

Major honours *Italian League (2013, 2014, 2015); Italian Cup (2015)*
Clubs 11-12 Manchester United FC (ENG); 12- Juventus (ITA)

2014/15 appearances/goals

Domestic league Italian Serie A 24(2)/8
Europe UEFA Champions League 10/1
National team Friendlies 5(2)/2

Ivan Rakitić

Midfielder, Height 184cm
Born 10/03/88, Mohlin, Switzerland

A superb 2013/14 season for Sevilla FC was followed by a dazzling debut campaign for FC Barcelona as Rakitić helped his new club to victories in the Spanish Liga, Copa del Rey and UEFA Champions League. Brought to the Camp Nou ostensibly to replace Xavi Hernández as the team's central creative hub, the versatile Croatian international not only rose to that challenge but added a more direct and penetrative approach to the team's play. He scored vital goals, too, opening his UEFA Champions League account with the winner at home to Manchester City FC and giving Barça a fourth-minute lead in the final against Juventus.

International career

CROATIA
Debut 08/09/07 v Estonia (h, Zagreb, ECQ), won 2-0
First goal 12/09/07 v Andorra (a, Andorra la Vella, ECQ), won 6-0
Caps 71 **Goals** 9
Major tournaments UEFA EURO 2008; UEFA EURO 2012; FIFA World Cup 2014

Club career

Major honours *UEFA Champions League (2015); UEFA Europa League (2014); Spanish Championship (2015); Swiss Cup (2007); Spanish Cup (2015)*
Clubs 05-07 FC Basel 1893 (SUI); 07-11 FC Schalke 04 (GER); 11-14 Sevilla FC (ESP); 14- FC Barcelona (ESP)

2014/15 appearances/goals

Domestic league Spanish Liga 23(9)/5
Europe UEFA Champions League 11(1)/2
National team UEFA EURO 2016 qualifying 6/-

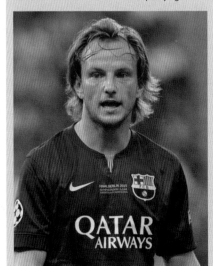

Lior Refaelov

Attacking midfielder, Height 176cm
Born 26/04/86, Or Akiva, Israel

A three-time Israeli champion with Maccabi Haifa FC, Refaelov finally tasted success with Club Brugge KV in his fourth season, and he was the man who ended the team's eight-year wait for silverware by scoring the stunning stoppage-time volley that won the Belgian Cup final against RSC Anderlecht. The Israeli international impressed also in the Pro League, contributing ten goals to his team's title challenge, which ended disappointingly with a runners-up spot behind KAA Gent, and in the UEFA Europa League, scoring six times in the competition proper, including a hat-trick at FC København, to help steer the team unbeaten into the quarter-finals.

International career

ISRAEL
Debut 22/08/07 v Belarus (a, Minsk, friendly), lost 1-2
First goal 26/05/10 v Uruguay (a, Montevideo, friendly), lost 1-4
Caps 35 **Goals** 5

Club career

Major honours *Israeli League (2006, 2009, 2011); Belgian Cup (2015)*
Clubs 04-11 Maccabi Haifa FC; 11- Club Brugge KV (BEL)

2014/15 appearances/goals

Domestic league Belgian Pro League 26(3)/10
Europe UEFA Europa League 8(3)/6; UEFA Europa League qualifying/play-offs 1(2)/-
National team UEFA EURO 2016 qualifying 1(4)/-

Arjen Robben

Winger, Height 180cm
Born 23/01/84, Bcdum, Netherlands

Not for the first time in his illustrious career Robben was cruelly cut down in his prime through injury, a calf problem bringing a premature end to his brilliant 2014/15 season in March – though he did make a failed attempt at a comeback in FC Bayern München's German Cup semi-final defeat by Borussia Dortmund. The Dutch flier's sixth season in Munich was one of his finest with any club as he repeatedly tore defences to ribbons with his pace, skill and devastating left foot. He scored 17 goals in the Bundesliga – a personal-best tally – and also bagged a brace in Bayern's wonderful 7-1 win at AS Roma.

International career

NETHERLANDS
Debut 30/04/03 v Portugal (h, Eindhoven, friendly), drew 1-1
First goal 11/10/03 v Moldova (h, Eindhoven, ECQ), won 5-0
Caps 86 **Goals** 28
Major tournaments UEFA EURO 2004; FIFA World Cup 2006; UEFA EURO 2008; FIFA World Cup 2010; UEFA EURO 2012; FIFA World Cup 2014

Club career

Major honours UEFA Champions League (2013); UEFA Super Cup (2013); FIFA Club World Cup (2013); Dutch League (2003); English League (2005, 2006); Spanish League (2008); German League (2010, 2013, 2014, 2015); English FA Cup (2007); German Cup (2010, 2013, 2014); English League (2005, 2007)
Clubs 00-02 FC Groningen; 02-04 PSV Eindhoven; 04-07 Chelsea FC (ENG); 07-09 Real Madrid CF (ESP); 09- FC Bayern München (GER)

2014/15 appearances/goals

Domestic league German Bundesliga 20(1)/17
Europe UEFA Champions League 5(2)/2
National team UEFA EURO 2016 qualifying 3/2; Friendlies 1/-

Roberto Firmino

Attacking midfielder, Height 181cm
Born 02/10/91, Maceio, Brazil

Having delighted supporters of TSG 1899 Hoffenheim with his skills for four seasons, Roberto Firmino will now be eager to develop his game further with Liverpool FC. The 23-year-old penned a five-year deal with the Merseysiders in June while he was playing for Brazil at the 2015 Copa América, where he scored his first competitive international goal in a group stage win against Venezuela. German crowds will miss his fancy footwork, dribbles and powerful shooting, which were all on resplendent display in 2014/15, helping the provincial outfit to an eighth-place finish – the second-highest in the club's brief Bundesliga history.

International career

BRAZIL
Debut 12/11/14 v Turkey (a, Istanbul, friendly), won 4-0
First goal 18/11/14 v Austria (a, Vienna, friendly), won 2-1
Caps 10 **Goals** 4
Major tournaments Copa América 2015

Club career

Clubs 09-10 Figueirense FC; 11-15 TSG 1899 Hoffenheim (GER); 15- Liverpool FC (ENG)

2014/15 appearances/goals

Domestic league German Bundesliga 33/7
National team Copa América 2015 3(1)/1; Friendlies 2(4)/3

Ricardo Rodriguez

Left-back, Height 180cm
Born 25/08/92, Zurich, Switzerland

Rodriguez built on the strong impression he had made for Switzerland at the FIFA World Cup in Brazil with an exceptional season at club level for VfL Wolfsburg. The versatile left-back stood out as much for his attacking prowess as his defending, notably with his finely-judged crosses and accuracy and efficiency from set pieces. He scored several important goals, including two at LOSC Lille to take Wolfsburg through to the knockout phase of the UEFA Europa League and a winning penalty in the quarter-final of the German Cup, which his team went on to win, giving the ex-FC Zürich man the first major honour of his career.

International career

SWITZERLAND
Debut 07/10/11 v Wales (a, Swansea, ECQ), lost 0-2
Caps 30 **Goals** 0
Major tournaments FIFA World Cup 2014

Club career

Major honours German Cup (2015)
Clubs 10-12 FC Zürich; 12- VfL Wolfsburg (GER)

2014/15 appearances/goals

Domestic league German Bundesliga 26/6
Europe UEFA Europa League 9/3
National team UEFA EURO 2016 qualifying 5/-

Santi Cazorla

Attacking midfielder, Height 169cm
Born 13/12/84, Llanera, Spain

Operating in a deeper midfield role than usual for much of the 2014/15 season, Santi Cazorla was a hugely influential figure for Arsenal FC. He started the campaign by opening the scoring in the Gunners' 3-0 win against Manchester City FC in the FA Community Shield at Wembley and ended it in the same stadium with a man-of-the-match display in the FA Cup final rout of Aston Villa FC. In the Premier League the Spanish international schemer registered seven goals and ten assists, excelling against City again with a vintage display in a 2-0 victory away to the defending champions in January.

International career

SPAIN
Major honours UEFA European Championship (2008, 2012)
Debut 31/05/08 v Peru (h, Huelva, friendly), won 2-1
First goal 19/11/08 v Chile (h, Villarreal, friendly), won 3-0
Caps 73 **Goals** 11
Major tournaments UEFA EURO 2008; FIFA Confederations Cup 2009; UEFA EURO 2012; FIFA Confederations Cup 2013; FIFA World Cup 2014

Club career

Major honours English FA Cup (2014, 2015)
Clubs 03-06 Villarreal CF; 06-07 RC Recreativo de Huelva; 07-11 Villarreal CF; 11-12 Málaga CF; 12- Arsenal FC (ENG)

2014/15 appearances/goals

Domestic league English Premier League 33(4)/7
Europe UEFA Champions League 6(1)/-
National team UEFA EURO 2016 qualifying 2(2)/-; Friendlies 2(1)/-

Gylfi Sigurdsson

Midfielder, Height 186cm
Born 08/09/89, Reykjavik, Iceland

After two seasons at Tottenham Hotspur FC, Sigurdsson returned to Swansea City AFC, where he had enjoyed a fabulous spell on loan in 2012, and duly won back the affection of the locals with an abundance of goals and assists, his first strike coming on the opening day of the season to give his club a historic first victory over Manchester United FC at Old Trafford. Having helped Iceland to reach the 2014 FIFA World Cup qualifying play-offs, he did his best to steer his country towards the UEFA EURO 2016 finals, scoring four goals, including both in a famous 2-0 win against the Netherlands in Reykjavik.

International career

ICELAND
Debut 29/05/10 v Andorra (h, Reykjavik, friendly), won 4-0
First goal 07/10/11 v Portugal (a, Porto, ECQ), lost 3-5
Caps 30 **Goals** 9

Club career

Clubs 08-10 Reading FC (ENG); 08 Shrewsbury Town FC (ENG) (loan); 09 Crewe Alexandra FC (ENG) (loan); 10-12 TSG 1899 Hoffenheim (GER); 12 Swansea City AFC (ENG) (loan); 12-14 Tottenham Hotspur FC (ENG); 14- Swansea City AFC (ENG)

2014/15 appearances/goals

Domestic league English Premier League 32/7
National team UEFA EURO 2016 qualifying 6/4

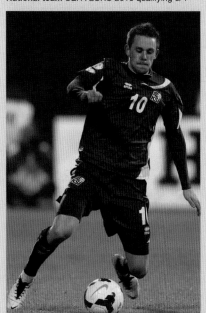

David Silva

Attacking midfielder, Height 170cm
Born 08/01/86, Arguinegin, Gran Canaria, Spain

Unlike in 2011/12 and 2013/14, Silva did not have a Premier League winner's medal to show for his efforts, but while some Manchester City FC stalwarts went off the boil in 2014/15 as they surrendered the title to Chelsea FC, the Spanish midfield wizard was as effervescent as ever. When he was not setting up goals for Sergio Agüero and co, he was scoring them himself, registering double figures in a league campaign for the first time in his career. The 29-year-old also excelled for Spain, scoring three fine goals in the UEFA EURO 2016 qualifiers for the defending champions, including an acrobatic winner in June against Belarus.

International career

SPAIN
Major honours FIFA World Cup (2010); UEFA European Championship (2008, 2012)
Debut 15/11/06 v Romania (h, Cadiz, friendly), lost 0-1
First goal 22/08/07 v Greece (a, Thessaloniki, friendly), won 3-2
Caps 91 **Goals** 23
Major tournaments UEFA EURO 2008; FIFA Confederations Cup 2009; FIFA World Cup 2010; UEFA EURO 2012; FIFA Confederations Cup 2013; FIFA World Cup 2014

Club career

Major honours English League (2012, 2014); Spanish Cup (2008); English FA Cup (2011); English League Cup (2014)
Clubs 03-04 Valencia CF B; 04-05 SD Eibar (loan); 05-06 RC Celta de Vigo (loan); 06-10 Valencia CF; 10- Manchester City FC (ENG)

2014/15 appearances/goals

Domestic league English Premier League 32/12
Europe UEFA Champions League 5(1)/-
National team UEFA EURO 2016 qualifying 5/3; Friendlies (3)/-

Wesley Sneijder

Attacking midfielder, Height 170cm
Born 09/06/84, Utrecht, Netherlands

Sneijder added a couple of new entries to his lengthy roll of honour as he inspired Galatasaray AŞ to the Turkish league and cup double. The experienced midfielder was a major influence as Galatasaray beat eternal rivals Fenerbahçe SK in the race to become the first club to win 20 Turkish league titles and, therefore, embellish their badge with a fourth star. It was two late long-range screamers from the Dutchman that won the home derby in October, and he also struck two crucial goals in the Süper Lig run-in. A 2014/15 ever-present for the Netherlands, he won his 115th cap – just 15 shy of Edwin van der Sar's Oranje record – three days after his 31st birthday in June.

International career

NETHERLANDS
Debut 30/04/03 v Portugal (h, Eindhoven, friendly), drew 1-1
First goal 11/10/03 v Moldova (h, Eindhoven, ECQ), won 5-0
Caps 115 **Goals** 28
Major tournaments UEFA EURO 2004; FIFA World Cup 2006; UEFA EURO 2008; FIFA World Cup 2010; UEFA EURO 2012; FIFA World Cup 2014

Club career

Major honours UEFA Champions League (2010); FIFA Club World Cup (2010); Dutch League (2004); Spanish League (2008); Italian League (2010); Turkish League (2013, 2015); Dutch Cup (2006, 2007); Italian Cup (2010, 2011); Turkish Cup (2013, 2015)
Clubs 02-07 AFC Ajax; 07-09 Real Madrid CF (ESP); 09-13 FC Internazionale Milano (ITA); 13- Galatasaray AŞ (TUR)

2014/15 appearances/goals

Domestic league Turkish Süper Lig 29(2)/10
Europe UEFA Champions League 6/1
National team UEFA EURO 2016 qualifying 6/-; Friendlies 3(1)/1

Luis Suárez

Striker, Height 181cm
Born 24/01/87, Salto, Uruguay

An €81m summer signing from Liverpool FC, Suárez had a two-month wait before he could make his debut for FC Barcelona, but once his post-FIFA World Cup ban had been lifted, the striker would become as much of an idol at the Camp Nou as he had been at Anfield. His brilliant post-Christmas form galvanised the team as they powered their way to a magnificent treble. The Uruguayan's highlights reel was extensive, including European doubles away to Manchester City FC and Paris Saint-Germain, the winner at home to Real Madrid CF and, to cap the lot, the all-important second goal in the UEFA Champions League final against Juventus.

International career

URUGUAY
Major honours Copa América (2011)
Debut 07/02/07 v Colombia (a, Cucuta, friendly), won 3-1
First goal 13/10/07 v Bolivia (h, Montevideo, WCQ), won 5-0
Caps 82 **Goals** 43
Major tournaments FIFA World Cup 2010; Copa América 2011; FIFA Confederations Cup 2013; FIFA World Cup 2014

Club career

Major honours UEFA Champions League (2015); Uruguayan League (2006); Dutch League (2011); Spanish League (2015); Dutch Cup (2010); Spanish Cup (2015); English League Cup (2012)
Clubs 05-06 Club Nacional; 06-07 FC Groningen (NED); 07-11 AFC Ajax (NED); 11-14 Liverpool FC (ENG); 14- FC Barcelona (ESP)

2014/15 appearances/goals

Domestic league Spanish Liga 25(2)/16
Europe UEFA Champions League 10/7
National team Friendlies 3/3

John Terry

Centre-back, Height 182cm
Born 07/12/80, Barking, England

Those England fans who bemoaned the absence of the country's former captain from the 2014 FIFA World Cup were provided with fresh evidence to support their view that his international retirement had come far too soon as Terry skippered Chelsea FC to the Premier League title in imperious fashion. The 34-year-old played from first whistle to last in all 38 league games and was also voted man of the match in the League Cup final win against Tottenham Hotspur FC, in which he scored Chelsea's first goal. Five strikes in the Premier League made him the competition's all-time top-scoring defender, his grand total of 39 including at least one in 15 consecutive campaigns.

International career

ENGLAND
Debut 03/06/03 v Serbia & Montenegro (h, Leicester, friendly), won 2-1
First goal 30/05/06 v Hungary (h, Manchester, friendly), won 3-1
Caps 78 **Goals** 6
Major tournaments UEFA EURO 2004; FIFA World Cup 2006; FIFA World Cup 2010; UEFA EURO 2012

Club career

Major honours UEFA Champions League (2012); UEFA Europa League (2013); English League (2005, 2006, 2010, 2015); English FA Cup (2007, 2009, 2010, 2012); English League Cup (2005, 2007, 2015)
Clubs 98- Chelsea FC; 00 Nottingham Forest FC (loan)

2014/15 appearances/goals

Domestic league English Premier League 38/5
Europe UEFA Champions League 7/2

Carlos Tévez

Striker, Height 173cm
Born 05/02/84, Buenos Aires, Argentina

Tévez spent just two seasons with Juventus before fulfilling a personal ambition by re-signing for his boyhood club CA Boca Juniors, but the 31-year-old striker left behind a bundle of happy memories in Turin. His second season with the Bianconeri, which included a recall to the Argentina squad after a three-year absence, outdid even his first as he spearheaded Massimiliano Allegri's side to a Serie A/Coppa Italia double and also rediscovered his eye for goal in Europe, ending a five-year barren spell in the UEFA Champions League by scoring seven times to usher Juve into their first final for 12 years.

International career

ARGENTINA
Debut 30/03/04 v Ecuador (h, Buenos Aires, WCQ), won 1-0
First goal 17/07/04 v Peru (a, Chiclayo, CA), won 1-0
Caps 72 **Goals** 13
Major tournaments Copa América 2004; FIFA Confederations Cup 2005; FIFA World Cup 2006; Copa América 2007; FIFA World Cup 2010; Copa América 2011; Copa América 2015

Club career

Major honours UEFA Champions League (2008); Copa Libertadores (2003); FIFA Club World Cup (2008); European/South American Cup (2003); Argentinian League (apertura 2003); Brazilian League (2005); English League (2008, 2009, 2012); Italian League (2014, 2015); English FA Cup (2011); Italian Cup (2015); English League Cup (2009)
Clubs 01-04 CA Boca Juniors; 05-06 SC Corinthians (BRA); 06-07 West Ham United FC (ENG); 07-09 Manchester United FC (ENG); 09-13 Manchester City FC (ENG); 13-15 Juventus (ITA); 15- CA Boca Juniors

2014/15 appearances/goals

Domestic league Italian Serie A 29(3)/20
Europe UEFA Champions League 13/7
National team Copa América 2015 (4)/-;
Friendlies 1(3)/-

Thiago Silva

Centre-back, Height 183cm
Born 22/09/84, Rio de Janeiro, Brazil

As the captain of Paris Saint-Germain, Thiago Silva had a lot of trophy-lifting to do in 2014/15. Every domestic prize available ended up in the hands of the Brazilian defender, who recovered from a bout of post-FIFA World Cup blues to lead by example as Paris added the Coupe de la Ligue, Ligue 1 title and Coupe de France to the pre-season Trophée des Champions (French Super Cup). Domestic man-of-the-match awards were commonplace for the 30-year-old in the spring, but it was his brilliant tie-clinching header in the UEFA Champions League round of 16 meeting with Chelsea FC that did most to upgrade his international profile.

International career

BRAZIL
Major honours FIFA Confederations Cup (2013)
Debut 12/10/08 v Venezuela (a, San Cristobal, WCQ), won 4-0
First goal 30/05/12 v United States (a, Landover, friendly), won 4-1
Caps 59 **Goals** 4
Major tournaments FIFA World Cup 2010; Copa América 2011; FIFA Confederations Cup 2013; FIFA World Cup 2014; Copa América 2015

Club career

Major honours Italian League (2011); French League (2013, 2014, 2015); Brazilian Cup (2007); French Cup (2015); French League Cup (2014, 2015)
Clubs 01-03 RS Futebol Clube; 04 EC Juventude; 04 FC Porto (POR); 05 FC Dinamo Moskva (RUS); 06-09 Fluminense FC; 09-12 AC Milan (ITA); 12- Paris Saint-Germain (FRA)

2014/15 appearances/goals

Domestic league French Ligue 1 26/1
Europe UEFA Champions League 6/1
National team Copa América 2015 3/1;
Friendlies 2(2)/-

Luca Toni

Striker, Height 193cm
Born 26/05/77, Pavullo nel Frignano, Italy

Four days after celebrating his 38th birthday, Toni scored his 22nd league goal of the 2014/15 season for Hellas Verona FC in a 2-2 draw against Juventus. The following day a double from FC Internazionale Milano's Mauro Icardi left the two players level at the top of the Serie A goal charts, enabling the veteran striker to become the oldest capocannoniere in history – nine years after he had claimed the prize alone as an ACF Fiorentina player with 31 goals, the highest winning total for 47 years. It was a formidable feat at the end of a season in which the 2006 FIFA World Cup winner registered his 300th career goal.

International career

ITALY
Major honours FIFA World Cup (2006)
Debut 18/08/04 v Iceland (a, Reykjavik, friendly), lost 0-2
First goal 04/09/04 v Norway (h, Palermo, WCQ), won 2-1
Caps 47 **Goals** 16
Major tournaments FIFA World Cup 2006; UEFA EURO 2008; FIFA Confederations Cup 2009

Club career

Major honours German League (2008, 2010); German Cup (2008, 2010)
Clubs 94-96 Modena FC; 96-97 Empoli FC; 97-98 US Fiorenzuola 1922; 98-99 AS Cisco Lodigiani; 99-00 Treviso FC; 00-01 Vicenza Calcio; 02-03 Brescia Calcio; 03-05 US Città di Palermo; 05-07 ACF Fiorentina; 07-10 FC Bayern München (GER); 10 AS Roma (loan); 10-11 Genoa CFC; 11-12 Juventus; 12 Al Nasr SC (UAE); 12-13 ACF Fiorentina; 13- Hellas Verona FC

2014/15 appearances/goals

Domestic league Italian Serie A 36(2)/22

Raphaël Varane

Centre-back, Height 191cm
Born 25/04/93, Lille, France

There are many options available to France boss Didier Deschamps as he strives to construct a team that will do the country proud at UEFA EURO 2016, but one player already appears to be inked on to his teamsheet. Although there were only friendlies, centralised or otherwise, on Les Bleus' fixture list in 2014/15, Varane, the pacy, elegant 22-year-old Real Madrid CF defender, was not given a moment's rest. The only player to start all ten games, he was also there at the finish of every one, and added further to his value with his first two international goals, in successive games against Sweden and Brazil.

International career

FRANCE
Debut 22/03/13 v Georgia (h, Paris, WCQ), won 3-1
First goal 18/11/14 v Sweden (h, Marseille, friendly), won 1-0
Caps 21 **Goals** 2
Major tournaments FIFA World Cup 2014

Club career

Major honours UEFA Champions League (2014); UEFA Super Cup (2014); FIFA Club World Cup (2014); Spanish League (2012); Spanish Cup (2014)
Clubs 10-11 RC Lens; 11- Real Madrid CF (ESP)

2014/15 appearances/goals

Domestic league Spanish Liga 21(6)/-
Europe UEFA Champions League 11(1)/-
National team Friendlies 10/2

Marco Verratti

Midfielder, Height 165cm
Born 05/11/92, Pescara, Italy

Enticed to the French capital from Pescara Calcio while still a teenager, Verratti has become part of the Paris Saint-Germain furniture, and the diminutive defensive midfielder was at his grittiest and most tenacious in 2014/15 as Laurent Blanc's side claimed a historic clean sweep of domestic silverware. The Italian international had not scored in his first two seasons at the club, but he opened his account in style with a header in the UEFA Champions League group game against FC Barcelona at the Parc des Princes, which Paris won 3-2. Two further goals followed in Ligue 1, which the 22-year-old won for the third time in three attempts.

International career

ITALY
Debut 15/08/12 v England (n, Berne, friendly), lost 1-2
First goal 06/02/13 v Netherlands (a, Amsterdam, friendly), drew 1-1
Caps 12 **Goals** 1
Major tournaments FIFA World Cup 2014

Club career

Major honours French League (2013, 2014, 2015); French Cup (2015); French League Cup (2014, 2015)
Clubs 08-12 Pescara Calcio; 12- Paris Saint-Germain (FRA)

2014/15 appearances/goals

Domestic league French Ligue 1 28(4)/2
Europe UEFA Champions League 7/1
National team UEFA EURO 2016 qualifying 2/-; Friendlies (2)/-

Arturo Vidal

Midfielder, Height 181cm
Born 22/05/87, Santiago, Chile

Vidal was not at his absolute best for Juventus in 2014/15, but the Chilean midfield powerhouse scored a couple of momentous goals towards the end of the campaign – an unstoppable penalty to decide the team's UEFA Champions League quarter-final against AS Monaco FC and the winner at UC Sampdoria that clinched the scudetto. That was the prelude for a busy summer that brought disappointment in Berlin against FC Barcelona then joy on home soil in the Copa América – where he scored three goals and was named man of the match in the final against Argentina – and, at the end of July, a €35m move to FC Bayern München.

International career

CHILE
Major honours Copa América (2015)
Debut 07/02/07 v Venezuela (a, Maracaibo, friendly), won 1-0
First goal 05/09/09 v Venezuela (h, Santiago, WCQ), drew 2-2
Caps 64 **Goals** 12
Major tournaments FIFA World Cup 2010; Copa América 2011; FIFA World Cup 2014; Copa América 2015

Club career

Major honours Chilean League (apertura 2006, clausura 2006, apertura 2007); Italian League (2012, 2013, 2014, 2015); Italian Cup (2015)
Clubs 05-07 CSD Colo-Colo; 07-11 Bayer 04 Leverkusen (GER); 11-15 Juventus (ITA); 15- FC Bayern München (GER)

2014/15 appearances/goals

Domestic league Italian Serie A 23(5)/7
Europe UEFA Champions League 12/1
National team Copa América 2015 6/3; Friendlies 6/1

Vitolo

Winger/Attacking midfielder,
Height 183cm
Born 02/11/89, Las Palmas, Canary
Islands, Spain

The Canary Islands have produced a
number of top-class Spanish footballers,
among them David Silva, Juan Carlos
Valerón and Pedro Rodríguez. The latest
to have emerged is Víctor Machín Pérez,
otherwise known as Vitolo. Brought to
the mainland by Sevilla FC in 2013, the
attacking midfielder's excellent second
season in Andalusia was rewarded with a
first senior cap for Spain. He was
particularly prominent in the club's UEFA
Europa League triumph, scoring the
competition's fastest ever goal in the
round of 16 tie against Villarreal CF and
supplying a clever assist for Carlos
Bacca's winner in the 3-2 final victory
over FC Dnipro Dnipropetrovsk.

International career

SPAIN
Debut 31/03/15 v Netherlands (a, Amsterdam,
friendly), lost 0-2
Caps 3 **Goals** 0

Club career

Major honours *UEFA Europa League (2014, 2015)*
Clubs 10-13 UD Las Palmas; 13- Sevilla FC

2014/15 appearances/goals

Domestic league Spanish Liga 25(3)/6
Europe UEFA Europa League 9(2)/3
National team UEFA EURO 2016 qualifying (1)/-;
Friendlies (2)/-

Georginio Wijnaldum

Midfielder, Height 175cm
Born 11/11/90, Rotterdam,
Netherlands

A Dutch Cup winner in his first season at
PSV Eindhoven, Wijnaldum had to wait
until his fourth before he became an
Eredivisie champion. The 24-year-old
was the captain and creative heartbeat of
Phillip Cocu's side, propelling them to
victory with a series of top-notch
performances. He could not quite match
the penalty-box productivity of team-
mates Memphis Depay and Luuk de
Jong, but his final tally of 14 goals
amounted to an impressive output
nonetheless. He also scored an
important UEFA EURO 2016 qualifying
goal for the Netherlands in Latvia in June
before leaving PSV for Newcastle United
FC on a five-year contract.

International career

NETHERLANDS
Debut 02/09/11 v San Marino (h, Eindhoven,
ECQ), won 11-0
First goal 02/09/11 v San Marino (h, Eindhoven,
ECQ), won 11-0
Caps 20 **Goals** 3
Major tournaments FIFA World Cup 2014

Club career

Major honours *Dutch League (2015); Dutch Cup
(2008, 2012)*
Clubs 07-11 Feyenoord; 11-15 PSV Eindhoven;
15- Newcastle United FC (ENG)

2014/15 appearances/goals

Domestic league Dutch Eredivisie 32(1)/14
Europe UEFA Europa League 6(1)/2; UEFA Europa
League play-offs 1/-
National team UEFA EURO 2016 qualifying 2(2)/1;
Friendlies 2(2)/-

William Carvalho

Midfielder, Height 187cm
Born 07/04/92, Luanda, Angola

A hugely impressive 2014/15 season had
a cruel ending for William Carvalho when,
on the last day of June, he missed his
penalty in the shoot-out at the end of the
goalless UEFA European Under-21
Championship final, enabling Sweden to
take the trophy at the expense of his
Portugal side. Compensation came in the
form of the official Player of the
Tournament award, recognition for his
colossal display in the 5-0 semi-final rout
of Germany. The 23-year-old midfield
anchorman had enjoyed better shoot-out
fortune with his club as Sporting Clube
de Portugal came from behind to defeat
SC Braga on penalties in the Portuguese
Cup final.

International career

PORTUGAL
Debut 19/11/13 v Sweden (a, Solna, WCQ),
won 3-2
Caps 13 **Goals** 0
Major tournaments FIFA World Cup 2014

Club career

Major honours *Portuguese Cup (2015)*
Clubs 11- Sporting Clube de Portugal;
11 CD Fátima (loan); 12-13 Cercle Brugge KSV
(BEL) (loan)

2014/15 appearances/goals

Domestic league Portuguese Liga 28(2)/1
Europe UEFA Champions League 6/-;
UEFA Europa League 1/-
National team UEFA EURO 2016 qualifying 2(3)/-;
Friendlies (2)/-

Willian

Winger, Height 174cm
Born 09/08/88, Ribeirao Pires, Brazil

Chelsea FC manager José Mourinho demands of his wide midfielders-cum-wingers that they help out in defence when the opposition are in possession, and Brazilian international Willian followed those orders so well that he commanded a regular place in the Blues' Premier League-winning side, outshining his compatriot Oscar and even ensuring that expensive mid-season recruit Juan Cuadrado barely got a look-in. There was also vibrancy and potency in attack from the former FC Shakhtar Donetsk player, his pace and trickery unsettling many defences and setting up a succession of chances for his team-mates. His end-of-season reward was a place in Brazil's 2015 Copa América side.

International career

BRAZIL
Debut 10/11/11 v Gabon (a, Libreville, friendly), won 2-0
First goal 16/11/13 v Honduras (n, Miami, friendly), won 5-0
Caps 26 **Goals** 4
Major tournaments FIFA World Cup 2014; Copa América 2015

Club career

Major honours UEFA Cup (2009); Ukrainian League (2008, 2010, 2011, 2012, 2013); English League (2015); Ukrainian Cup (2008, 2011, 2012, 2013); English League Cup (2015)
Clubs 06-07 SC Corinthians; 07-13 FC Shakhtar Donetsk (UKR); 13 FC Anji Makhachkala (RUS); 13- Chelsea FC (ENG)

2014/15 appearances/goals

Domestic league English Premier League 28(8)/2
Europe UEFA Champions League 5(2)/1
National team Copa América 2015 4/-; Friendlies 9(1)/2

Granit Xhaka

Midfielder, Height 185cm
Born 27/09/92, Basel, Switzerland

The midfield conductor-in-chief of a VfL Borussia Mönchengladbach side that finished third in the 2014/15 Bundesliga to guarantee a first group stage involvement in the UEFA Champions League, Xhaka received widespread praise for his efforts, not least from his compatriot coach Lucien Favre. An elegant left-footer with that much-treasured ability to dictate the tempo of a game, the 22-year-old is a rising star of Swiss football and will hope to back up his 2014 FIFA World Cup appearance with an impressive showing at UEFA EURO 2016. His most prominent contribution towards taking his country to those finals was a splendid long-range goal in a 3-0 qualifying win over Estonia.

International career

SWITZERLAND
Debut 04/06/11 v England (a, London, ECQ), drew 2-2
First goal 15/11/11 v Luxembourg (a, Luxembourg, friendly), won 1-0
Caps 36 **Goals** 6
Major tournaments FIFA World Cup 2014

Club career

Major honours Swiss League (2011, 2012); Swiss Cup (2012)
Clubs 10-12 FC Basel 1893; 12- VfL Borussia Mönchengladbach (GER)

2014/15 appearances/goals

Domestic league German Bundesliga 30/2
Europe UEFA Europa League 7/2; UEFA Europa League play-offs 2/1
National team UEFA EURO 2016 qualifying 5/1; Friendlies (1)/-

Andriy Yarmolenko

Winger, Height 187cm
Born 23/10/89, St Petersburg, Russia

A dynamic and decisive figure in FC Dynamo Kyiv's Ukrainian double-winning campaign, Yarmolenko was a menace to defences all season long, his strength, balance and formidable shooting power sourcing many of Dynamo's goals as the country's most decorated club finally got the better of FC Shakhtar Donetsk in the league while also denying them on penalties to retain the Ukrainian Cup. Serhiy Rebrov's side also made good progress in the UEFA Europa League, with their statuesque No10 registering six assists – the joint-highest figure in the competition alongside Villarreal CF's Luciano Vietto – and four goals, including an absolute belter against Everton FC in the round of 16.

International career

UKRAINE
Debut 05/09/09 v Andorra (h, Kyiv, WCQ), won 5-0
First goal 05/09/09 v Andorra (h, Kyiv, WCQ), won 5-0
Caps 49 **Goals** 19
Major tournaments UEFA EURO 2012

Club career

Major honours Ukrainian League (2009, 2015); Ukrainian Cup (2014, 2015)
Clubs 06 FC Desna Chernihiv; 07-08 FC Dynamo-2 Kyiv; 08- FC Dynamo Kyiv

2014/15 appearances/goals

Domestic league Ukrainian Premier League 24(2)/14
Europe UEFA Europa League 11/4
National team UEFA EURO 2016 qualifying 6/3; Friendlies 2(1)/1

Nation-by-nation

Welcome to the Nation-by-nation section of the European Football Yearbook.

Here you will find separate chapters, alphabetically arranged, on each of the 54 UEFA member associations containing the following information.

Association directory

The member association's official logo, name, address, contact details, senior officials, year of formation and, where applicable, national stadium as of July 2015.

Map/Club index

A map of the country illustrating the locations of its top-division clubs, which are listed in alphabetical order, plus any clubs promoted to the top division at the end of the 2014/15 (2014) season. Teams qualified for the 2015/16 UEFA Champions League and UEFA Europa League are indicated as such with colour coding, as are relegated teams. Official logos are set beside all clubs.

NB Locations are those where the club played all or the majority of their home matches during the 2014/15 (2014) season.

Review

A narrative review of the season, headed by an appropriate photo, is divided into four sections – Domestic league, Domestic cup, Europe and National team.

DOMESTIC SEASON AT A GLANCE

Domestic league final table

The final standings of the member association's top division including home, away and total records. The champions are indicated in bold type.

Key: Pld = matches played, W = matches won, D = matches drawn, L = matches lost, F = goals for (scored), A = goals against (conceded), Pts = points

················· = play-off line

– – – – – – – – – = relegation line

Any peculiarities, such as the deduction of points, clubs withdrawn or relegation issues, are indicated as *NB* at the foot of the table.

European qualification

The clubs qualified for the 2015/16 UEFA Champions League and UEFA Europa League are indicated, together with (in brackets) the round for which they have qualified. Champions and Cup winners are highlighted.

The league's top scorer(s), promoted club(s), relegated club(s) and the result of the domestic cup final(s) are listed in summary.

Player of the season

Newcomer of the season

Team of the season

These are either official selections or personal choices of the correspondents.

NATIONAL TEAM

Home (left) and away (right) playing kits, international honours and major international tournament appearances head this section. Also included are the member association's top five all-time international cap-holders and goalscorers. Players active in 2014/15 are highlighted in bold.

Results 2014/15

Details on all senior international matches played between August 2014 and June 2015 with date, opponent, venue, result, scorer(s) and goal time(s).

Key: H = home, A = away, N = neutral, W = won, D = drawn, L = lost, *og* = own goal, *p* = penalty, *(aet)* = after extra time, (ECQ) = UEFA EURO 2016 qualification

Appearances 2014/15

Details on all participants in the aforementioned matches (coaches and players), including name, date of birth and, for each player, club(s), match-by-match appearances and all-time international caps and goals scored.

Opponents are ranged across the top and abbreviated with the appropriate three-letter country code – capital letters identify a competitive match (i.e. UEFA EURO 2016 qualification round).

Changes of national team coach are indicated with the appropriate appointment dates; temporary coaches are indicated in brackets.

Non-native coaches and clubs are indicated with the appropriate three-letter country code.

Key: G = goalkeeper, D = defender, M = midfielder, A = attacker, s = substitute, * = red card.

The number appearing after the letter indicates the minute in which a substitution took place. The number preceding an asterisk indicates the minute in which a red card occurred.

EUROPE

Details including opponent, result, scorers, goaltimes, lineups and red cards of all matches played by the member association's clubs in the 2014/15 UEFA Champions League and UEFA Europa League, including qualifying rounds and play-offs. Each team's entry is headed by home and away playing kits (those used in 2014/15) and the club logo. The home kit is on the left.

Key: *(aet)* = after extra time

DOMESTIC LEAGUE CLUB-BY-CLUB

Information on each top-division club, displayed in alphabetical order, is provided in six parts:

1) Club name and a circular swatch indicating shirt and short colours.

2) The year in which the club was founded, the home stadium(s) used during the season (with capacity) and, where applicable, the official club website.

3) Major honours, including European, international and domestic competitions. National 'super cups', secondary leagues and minor or age-restricted knockout competitions are not included.

4) The coach(es)/manager(s) used during the season and, in the case of new appointments, the dates on which they took place. Non-native coaches/ managers are indicated with the appropriate three-letter country code.

5) League fixtures chronologically listed, including dates, opponents, results and goalscorers.

Key: h = home, a = away, W = won, D = drawn, L = lost, og = own goal, (p) = penalty, (w/o) = walkover/forfeit

6) A list of all players used in the league campaign, including name, nationality (where non-native), date of birth, principal playing position, appearances and goals. Where applicable, squad numbers are also included.

Key: No = squad (shirt) number, Name = first name and family name, or, in some instances, 'football name', Nat = nationality (native unless listed with three-letter country code), DoB = date of birth, Pos = playing position, Aps = number of appearances in the starting lineup, (s) = number of appearances as a substitute, Gls = number of goals scored, G = goalkeeper, D = defender, M = midfielder, A = attacker.

Top goalscorers

A list of the top ten (and equal) goalscorers in the member association's top division. The figures refer to league goals only.

Promoted club(s)

Information on each promoted club is provided in four parts:

1) Club name and a circular swatch indicating shirt and short colours.

2) The year in which the club was founded, the home stadium(s) used during the season (with capacity) and, where applicable, the official club website.

3) Major honours, including European, international and domestic competitions. National 'super cups', secondary leagues and minor or age-restricted knockout competitions are not included.

4) The coach(es)/manager(s) used during the season and, in the case of new appointments, the dates on which they took place. Non-native coaches/ managers are indicated with the appropriate three-letter country code.

Second level final table

The final classification of the member association's second level (i.e. feeder league to the top division) table(s). Play-off details, where applicable, are also indicated.

Key: Pld = matches played, W = matches won, D = matches drawn, L = matches lost, F = goals for (scored), A = goals against (conceded), Pts = points.

- - - - - - - - - = promotion line (at the top)

················· = play-off line

- - - - - - - - - = relegation line (at the bottom)

Any peculiarities, such as the deduction of points, clubs withdrawn or promotion issues, are indicated as NB at the foot of the final league table.

DOMESTIC CUP(S)

Results from the member association's principal domestic knockout competition, beginning at the round in which the top-division clubs (or some of them) enter.

Goalscorers and goaltimes are indicated from the quarter-final stage, with complete lineups, referees and red cards added for the final.

Details of the latter stages of significant secondary knockout competitions are also included for some member associations.

Key: (aet) = after extra time, (w/o) = walkover/forfeit

NB A complete key to all three-letter country codes can be found on page 6.

ALBANIA
Federata Shqiptarë e Futbollit (FShF)

Address	Rruga e Elbasanit
	AL-1000 Tiranë
Tel	+355 42 346 605
Fax	+355 42 346 609
E-mail	fshf@fshf.org.al
Website	fshf.org

President	Armand Duka
General secretary	Ilir Shulku
Media officer	Tritan Kokona
Year of formation	1930
National stadium	Elbasani Arena,
	Elbasan (15,000)

KATEGORIA SUPERIORE CLUBS

 ① **KF Apolonia**

 ② **KF Elbasani**

 ③ **KS Flamurtari**

 ④ **FK Kukësi**

 ⑤ **KF Laçi**

 ⑥ **FK Partizani**

 ⑦ **KF Skënderbeu**

 ⑧ **KF Teuta**

 ⑨ **KF Tirana**

 ⑩ **KF Vllaznia**

PROMOTED CLUBS

 ⑪ **KF Tërbuni**

 ⑫ **FK Bylis**

KEY:

● – UEFA Champions League

◐ – UEFA Europa League

● – Promoted

○ – Relegated

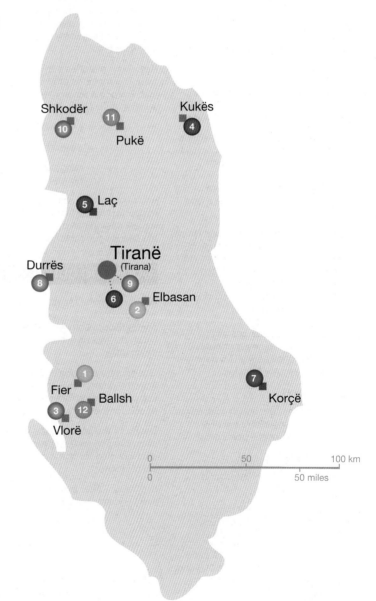

Skënderbeu still in charge

A gripping four-club contest for the Kategoria Superiore title ended with a familiar outcome as KF Skënderbeu, champions in each of the previous four seasons, came through to triumph again, leaving FK Kukësi, FK Partizani and KF Tirana in their wake.

Kukës, who boasted the league's runaway top scorer in 31-goal Pero Pejić, finished second to Skënderbeu for the third year running, and their determined bid for a first major trophy brought further disappointment in the Albanian Cup as they lost the final for the second straight year, going down 2-1 to KF Laçi.

Record fifth successive league title for Korce club	**Second cup win in three years for Laç**	**Free-scoring Kukës fail to land first trophy**

Domestic league

No team had ever previously won the Albanian championship five years running, and for much of the 2014/15 campaign – lengthened to 36 matches – it seemed that Skënderbeu, led once again by Mirel Josa, might also fall short.

With the prolific Pejić sold to Kukës, there was a noticeable shortage of firepower as the team made a stodgy start, scoring just six goals in their first eight matches, of which they won only three.

With Kukës and the two Tirana clubs all beginning well, Josa's men had a lot of catching-up to do, but by the winter break they had hauled themselves back into contention, sitting second behind leaders Kukës with the top four separated by just three points. It was not until the spring, however, that Skënderbeu finally managed to move to the front of the title race for the first time.

While the other three contenders had all been uneasy pacesetters, Skënderbeu dug in during the run-in, relinquishing the lead briefly after a 1-0 defeat at Laç but reclaiming it in style with a 5-2 win over Partizani and cementing it with a vital 1-0 win at Kukës, Albanian international Sabien Lilaj scoring the 65th-minute winner that gained revenge for his team's domestic cup elimination by the same opponents four days earlier. Although that away win

was pivotal, it was Skënderbeu's consistent form in Korce, where they were unbeaten all season and scored 43 of their 58 goals, that underpinned their historic triumph. Fittingly they sealed the title in their last home game with a 2-0 win over KS Flamurtari.

As Kukës reflected on another title that had got away – three seasons in the Kategoria Superiore had all brought runners-up placings – Partizani joined them in the UEFA Europa League after taking third place ahead of Tirana. Having collected eight points from the four meetings with their city rivals, it was no more than Shpëtim Duro's side deserved.

Domestic cup

Despite knocking Skënderbeu out of the cup, Kukës were unable to shed their bridesmaid tag in the final, against Laç. Following their home defeat by the champions, for which coach Artim Sakiri paid the price with the sack, they had been in good form, but at the Qemal Stafa stadium it was Laç, the 2012/13 winners, who reclaimed the trophy with a 2-1 win, the decisive goal coming from their leading marksman, Nigerian forward Segun Adeniyi.

Europe

A year after Skënderbeu and Kukës had reached the UEFA Europa League

play-offs, there was major disappointment for both clubs as their 2014/15 European adventure ended after just two matches. It was a forgettable season for Albanian clubs all round, with the only successes coming on away goals – Flamurtari against FC Sioni Bolinisi – and penalties – Laç against NK Rudar Velenje, with Adeniyi scoring in each leg.

National team

In contrast to the clubs, the Albanian national team enjoyed a fabulous season. Gianni De Biasi's team of expatriate talents made excellent progress in their UEFA EURO 2016 qualifying campaign, and their season got even better in the summer when the Court of Arbitration for Sport ruled that the 3-0 forfeit defeat initially imposed on them for the abandonment of their October fixture against Serbia in Belgrade had been reversed. Their other three qualifiers yielded seven points, starting with a magnificent 1-0 win in Portugal, and although half of their fixture schedule remained, there was no denying that Albania had a team fit to grace the finals – as hosts France could readily testify after De Biasi's men got the better of them in their two centralised friendlies, drawing 1-1 in Rennes and defeating them, with a goal from promising PAOK FC midfielder Ergys Kaçe, 1-0 in Elbasan.

DOMESTIC SEASON AT A GLANCE

Kategoria Superiore 2014/15 final table

		Pld	Home					Away					Total					Pts
			W	D	L	F	A	W	D	L	F	A	W	D	L	F	A	
1	**KF Skënderbeu**	36	15	3	0	43	9	9	4	5	15	9	24	7	5	58	18	79
2	FK Kukësi	36	14	2	2	33	7	9	4	5	26	20	23	6	7	59	27	75
3	FK Partizani	36	13	4	1	25	7	9	3	6	17	17	22	7	7	42	24	73
4	KF Tirana	36	14	3	1	28	7	7	5	6	19	20	21	8	7	47	27	71
5	KF Laçi	36	13	4	1	29	8	7	5	6	17	11	20	9	7	46	19	69
6	KS Flamurtari	36	8	4	6	20	14	2	4	12	9	23	10	8	18	29	37	38
7	KF Vllaznia	36	7	3	8	15	15	4	2	12	12	26	11	5	20	27	41	35
8	KF Teuta	36	7	2	9	12	17	2	0	16	19	37	9	2	25	31	54	29
9	KF Apolonia	36	6	3	9	16	23	1	1	16	3	33	7	4	25	19	56	25
10	KF Elbasani	36	2	1	15	10	39	2	1	15	9	35	4	2	30	19	74	14

NB KF Vllaznia – 3 pts deducted.

European qualification 2015/16

Champion: KF Skënderbeu (second qualifying round)

CHAMPIONS LEAGUE

Cup winner: KF Laçi (first qualifying round)

FK Kukësi (first qualifying round)
FK Partizani (first qualifying round)

EUROPA LEAGUE

Top scorer	Pero Pejić (Kukës), 31 goals
Relegated clubs	KF Elbasani, KF Apolonia
Promoted clubs	KF Tërbuni, FK Bylis
Cup final	KF Laçi 2-1 FK Kukësi

Team of the season
(4-3-3)

Coach: Josa *(Skënderbeu)*

Player of the season

Pero Pejić
(FK Kukësi)

Having struck a league-best tally of 20 goals for KF Skënderbeu in their 2013/14 title-winning campaign, Pejić failed to agree new terms and left for rivals Kukës. The tall, 32-year-old Croatian striker became even more prolific at his new club, scoring 31 goals – 21 of them after Christmas – to win the Kategoria Superiore's golden boot by a landslide, his final tally more than twice as many as the next highest scorer. He also fired Kukës to the cup final with two crucial semi-final strikes against Skënderbeu.

Newcomer of the season

Arbnor Fejzullahu
(FK Partizani)

Recruited from relegated KS Besa in May 2014, Fejzullahu made such rapid progress in his debut campaign with Partizani that by the end of it he had become a senior Albanian international, making his debut as a late substitute in the June friendly win against France. A classy defender with a sure touch, the 22-year-old started 33 of Partizani's 36 league games and was a major figure in the club's title challenge, which ultimately brought a third-place finish and a return to Europe after seven years.

NATIONAL TEAM

Top five all-time caps
Lorik Cana (83); Altin Lala (78); Klodian Duro (76); Erjon Bogdani & Ervin Skela (75)

Top five all-time goals
Erjon Bogdani (18); Alban Bushi (14); Ervin Skela (13); Altin Rraklli & **Hamdi Salihi** (11)

Results 2014/15

07/09/14	Portugal (ECQ)	A	Aveiro	W	1-0	*Balaj (52)*
11/10/14	Denmark (ECQ)	H	Elbasan	D	1-1	*Lenjani (38)*
14/10/14	Serbia (ECQ)	A	Belgrade	W	3-0	*(w/o; original match abandoned after 42 mins at 0-0)*
14/11/14	France	A	Rennes	D	1-1	*Mavraj (40)*
18/11/14	Italy	A	Genoa	L	0-1	
29/03/15	Armenia (ECQ)	H	Elbasan	W	2-1	*Mavraj (77), Gashi (81)*
13/06/15	France	H	Elbasan	W	1-0	*Kaçe (43)*

Appearances 2014/15

Coach: Gianni De Biasi (ITA)	16/06/56		POR	DEN	SRB	Fra	Ita	ARM	Fra	Caps	Goals
Etrit Berisha	10/03/89	Lazio (ITA)	G	G	G	G	G	G	G	25	-
Elseid Hysaj	20/02/94	Empoli (ITA)	D	D	D	D	D74	D	D	14	-
Lorik Cana	27/07/83	Lazio (ITA)	D	D	D	D	D	D	D	83	1
Mërgim Mavraj	09/06/86	Köln (GER)	D	D	D	D	D	D		23	3
Ansi Agolli	11/10/82	Qarabağ (AZE)	D	D	D	D	D	D		54	2
Burim Kukeli	16/01/84	Zürich (SUI)	M66	M	M	M90	M67	M		10	-
Amir Abrashi	27/03/90	Grasshoppers (SUI)	M	M	M	M69	M71	M46		13	-
Taulant Xhaka	28/03/91	Basel (SUI)	M	M82	M			M		4	-
Odhise Roshi	22/05/91	FSV Frankfurt (GER)	M			s67	M69		M64	23	1
Ermir Lenjani	05/08/89	St Gallen (SUI) /Rennes (FRA)	M75	M	M	M76	M86	s46	M56	10	1
Bekim Balaj	11/01/91	Slavia Praha (CZE) /Rijeka (CRO)	A82	A69	A	s90	s86		s80	10	1
Ergys Kaçe	08/07/93	PAOK (GRE)	s66						M80	12	2
Andi Lila	12/02/86	Giannina (GRE) /Parma (ITA)	s75	M87	M	M85	M90		M18	53	-
Sokol Çikalleshi	27/07/90	Split (CRO)	s82	s69		A90	A78	A	A88	9	-
Valdet Rama	20/11/87	1860 München (GER)		s82			s90		s56	15	3
Debatik Curri	28/12/83	Tirana		s87						44	1
Ledian Memushaj	07/12/86	Pescara (ITA)				M	M	M46	s18	9	-
Arlind Ajeti	25/09/93	Basel (SUI)				s69	s74		D	3	-
Herolind Shala	01/02/92	Odd (NOR)				s76	s71			2	-
Emiljano Vila	12/03/88	Partizani				s85				27	3
Ervin Bulku	03/03/81	Tirana				s90				56	1
Hamdi Salihi	19/01/84	H. Akko (ISR) /H. Haifa (ISR)					s78	s69		50	11
Shkëlzen Gashi	15/07/88	Basel (SUI)						s46		6	1
Naser Aliji	27/12/93	Vaduz (SUI)							D	1	-
Migjen Basha	05/01/87	Torino (ITA)							M72	9	2
Armando Sadiku	27/05/91	Zürich (SUI)							s64	12	1
Sabien Lilaj	18/02/89	Skënderbeu							s72	11	-
Arbnor Fejzullahu	08/04/93	Partizani							s88	1	-

EUROPE

KF Skënderbeu

CHAMPIONS LEAGUE

Second qualifying round - FC BATE Borisov (BLR)
A 0-0
Shehi, Arapi, Progni (Jashanica 90+4), Orelesi, Shkëmbi, Osmani, Ademir (Nimaga 74), Sefa (Ribaj 90+2), Vangjeli, Radaš, Lilaj. Coach: Mirel Josa (ALB)
H 1-1 *Radaš (67)*
Shehi, Arapi, Progni, Orelesi, Shkëmbi, Osmani (Jashanica 66), Berisha (Ribaj 60), Sefa, Vangjeli, Radaš, Lilaj. Coach: Mirel Josa (ALB)

KS Flamurtari

EUROPA LEAGUE

First qualifying round - FC Sioni Bolnisi (GEO)
A 3-2 *Veliu (20), Kuqi (74), G Lika (90+3)*
I Lika, Mici, Lena, Veliu, Arbëri (Idrizaj 90+2), Muzaka (Meto 87), Telushi, Zeqiri (Shehaj 83), Kuqi, Abilaliaj, G Lika. Coach: Ernest Gjoka (ALB)
H 1-2 *Shehaj (85)*
I Lika, Mici, Lena, Veliu, Arbëri, Muzaka (Liçaj 89), Telushi, Zeqiri (Shehaj 67), Kuqi, Abilaliaj, G Lika (Meto 78). Coach: Ernest Gjoka (ALB)

Second qualifying round - FC Petrolul Ploieşti (ROU)
A 0-2
I Lika, Mici, Lena, Veliu, Arbëri, Muzaka, Telushi, Zeqiri (Gërxho 90+3), Kuqi, Abilaliaj (Shehaj 66), G Lika (Meto 75). Coach: Ernest Gjoka (ALB)
H 1-3 *Lena (37)*
I Lika, Douglas, Mici, Lena, Arbëri, Muzaka (Meto 86), Telushi (Gërxho 62), Zeqiri, Kuqi, Shehaj (Liçaj 67), G Lika. Coach: Ernest Gjoka (ALB)

FK Kukësi

EUROPA LEAGUE

First qualifying round - FC Kairat Almaty (KAZ)
A 0-1
Halili, Smajlaj, Shameti, Dushku, Lushtaku (Pericles 86), Çikalleshi, Hallaçi, Allmuça (Jefferson 18), Bicaj, Hoxha, Musolli. Coach: Agim Canaj (ALB)
H 0-0
Halili, Smajlaj, Dushku, Lushtaku (Hysa 59), Çikalleshi, Hallaçi, Allmuça (Shameti 72), Bicaj, Hoxha (Perić 80), Pejić, Musolli. Coach: Agim Canaj (ALB)

KF Laçi

EUROPA LEAGUE

First qualifying round - NK Rudar Velenje (SVN)
A 1-1 *Adeniyi (89)*
Vujadinović, Ofoyen, Çela, Sheta, Adeniyi, Sefa, Owoeye (Ndreca 39), Nimani, Teqja, Zefi, Veliaj. Coach: Stavri Nica (ALB)
H 1-1 *Adeniyi (58)* **(aet; 3-2 on pens)**
Vujadinović, Ofoyen, Çela, Sheta, Adeniyi, Sefa (Sefgjini 46), Vuçaj, Nimani (Kastrati 82), Teqja, Zefi, Veliaj (Ndreca 46). Coach: Stavri Nica (ALB)

Second qualifying round - FC Zorya Luhansk (UKR)
H 0-3
Vujadinović, Ofoyen, Çela, Sheta (Veliaj 69), Adeniyi, Vuçaj, Sefgjini (Buljan 27), Nimani, Teqja, Zefi, Morina (Sefa 40). Coach: Stavri Nica (ALB)
A 1-2 *Nimani (85)*
Vujadinović, Ofoyen, Çela (Sefgjini 69), Sheta, Adeniyi (Veliaj 81), Sefa, Vuçaj, Buljan, Nimani (Ndreca 90+1), Teqja, Zefi. Coach: Stavri Nica (ALB)

DOMESTIC LEAGUE CLUB-BY-CLUB

KF Apolonia

1925 • Loni Papuçiu (7,000) • no website
Major honours
Albanian Cup (1) 1998
Coach: Elidon Demiri;
(01/12/14) Marjol Miho;
(03/01/15) Artan Mërgjyshi

2014

24/08	a Tirana	L	0-3	
30/08	h Partizani	W	1-0	*Çamka*
10/09	a Flamurtari	L	0-3	
14/09	h Skënderbeu	D	0-0	
20/09	a Vllaznia	L	0-2	
26/09	h Kukës	L	0-1	
05/10	a Elbasan	L	0-2	
19/10	h Teuta	W	1-0	*Karakaçi*
26/10	a Laç	L	1-3	*Mitraj*
29/10	h Tirana	L	0-3	
02/11	a Partizani	L	0-1	
09/11	h Flamurtari	D	1-1	*Erkoçeviq*
23/11	a Skënderbeu	L	0-6	
29/11	h Vllaznia	L	0-1	
06/12	a Kukës	D	0-0	
13/12	h Elbasan	L	0-1	
17/12	a Teuta	L	0-1	
20/12	h Laç	L	0-2	

2015

24/01	a Tirana	L	0-2	
31/01	h Partizani	L	0-2	
08/02	a Flamurtari	L	0-1	
14/02	h Skënderbeu	L	0-1	
22/02	a Vllaznia	L	0-1	
28/02	h Kukës	D	2-2	*Fili, Uzuni*
05/03	a Elbasan	W	1-0	*Fili*
08/03	h Teuta	W	2-1	*Dimo, Fili*
16/03	a Laç	L	0-2	
22/03	h Tirana	L	0-2	
04/04	a Partizani	L	0-1	
12/04	h Flamurtari	W	2-1	*Ribaj, Fili*
18/04	a Skënderbeu	L	0-1	
25/04	h Vllaznia	W	2-0	*Dimo, Ribaj (p)*
02/05	a Kukës	L	1-2	*Ribaj*
09/05	h Elbasan	W	4-1	*Ribaj 3 (2p), Fili*
17/05	a Teuta	L	0-1	
22/05	h Laç	L	1-4	*Nako*

No	Name	Nat	DoB	Pos	Aps	(s)	Gls
42	Sulaimon Adekunle	NGA	26/10/90	M	15	(5)	
16	Dejan Andoni		23/06/95	M		(4)	
14	Kliti Arapi		16/09/91	M	1	(2)	
3	Sodiq Olodode Atanda	NGA	26/08/83	D	26		
22	Izmir Balaj		04/02/94	D	2	(8)	
13	Endri Braka		07/04/97	D	1	(1)	
5	Klajdi Broshka		18/11/93	D	19	(4)	
31	Endrit Çako		20/03/92	G	1	(1)	
33	Vilson Čaković	SRB	22/02/91	G	25		
18	Mikel Çamka		18/02/87	A	10	(5)	1
2	Amarildo Dimo		25/08/82	D	17		2
13	Djordje Djordjević	SRB	07/03/88	D	15	(5)	
22	Dejan Dosti		15/02/91	A	8	(2)	
14	Bekim Erkoçeviq		23/04/92	M	9	(3)	1
28	Realdo Fili		14/05/96	A	25	(3)	5
88	Julian Gërxho		22/01/85	M	20	(2)	
19	Taulant Hysenshahaj		26/12/91	M	19	(7)	
15	Endrit Idrizaj		14/06/89	D	5	(2)	
29	Ervis Kaja		29/07/87	D	29		
8	Abaz Karakaçi		25/08/92	M	9	(1)	1
27	Xhek Kondakçiu		02/10/95	M	1	(4)	
23	Andi Mahilaj		15/03/95	A		(3)	
1	Eduart Miço		01/12/83	G	10		
9	Aldo Mitraj		12/01/87	M	11	(4)	1
4	Renato Naçi		26/11/93	D	3	(6)	
6	Rudin Nako		20/05/87	D	30	(3)	1
17	Albi Prifti		02/10/91	M		(1)	
24	Andi Prifti		01/08/88	D	25	(4)	
99	Marko Rajković	SRB	13/11/92	A	15	(16)	
9	Andi Ribaj		21/11/89	A	13	(4)	6
77	Myrto Uzuni		31/05/95	A	17	(1)	1
3	Erjon Haki Xhafa		29/04/86	D	15	(1)	

KF Elbasani

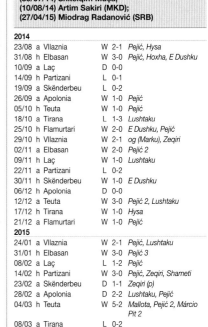

1913 • Elbasani Arena (15,000); Gjorgji Kyçyku, Pogradec (10,700); Kamza, Kamëz (4,800) • no website

Major honours
Albanian League (2) 1984, 2006; Albanian Cup (2) 1975, 1992

Coach: Ilirjan Filja; (09/09/14) Edmond Mustafaraj

2014					
22/08	h	Skënderbeu	L	0-1	
31/08	a	Kukës	L	0-3	
10/09	h	Teuta	L	1-5	*Çota*
14/09	a	Tirana	L	1-2	*Kaçuli*
20/09	h	Flamurtari	L	0-2	
27/09	a	Vllaznia	L	0-1	
05/10	h	Apolonia	W	2-0	*Çota, Musta*
18/10	h	Laç	L	0-2	
26/10	a	Partizani	L	0-1	
29/10	a	Skënderbeu	L	0-1	
02/11	h	Kukës	L	0-2	
08/11	a	Teuta	W	2-0	*Çota, Lamçja*
23/11	h	Tirana	L	2-3	*Bylykbashi 2 (1p)*
01/12	a	Flamurtari	L	0-2	
07/12	h	Vllaznia	L	1-4	*Agboyi*
13/12	a	Apolonia	W	1-0	*Lamçja*
17/12	a	Laç	L	0-1	
20/12	h	Partizani	L	0-1	
2015					
25/01	h	Skënderbeu	L	1-4	*Agboyi*
31/01	a	Kukës	L	0-3	
08/02	h	Teuta	W	1-0	*Lamçja*
14/02	a	Tirana	L	0-2	
22/02	h	Flamurtari	L	0-1	
28/02	a	Vllaznia	D	1-1	*Yontcha*
05/03	h	Apolonia	L	0-1	
08/03	h	Laç	L	0-2	
16/03	a	Partizani	L	1-4	*Malindi*
21/03	a	Skënderbeu	L	1-5	*Gava*
04/04	h	Kukës	L	0-4	
12/04	a	Teuta	L	0-1	
18/04	h	Tirana	L	1-3	*Jaupi*
25/04	a	Flamurtari	L	1-2	*Toçi (p)*
02/05	h	Vllaznia	D	1-1	*Grabova*
09/05	a	Apolonia	L	1-4	*Lamçja*
17/05	a	Laç	L	0-2	
22/05	h	Partizani	L	0-3	

No	Name	Nat	DoB	Pos	Aps	(s)	Gls
19	Ovbokha Agboyi	NGA	14/12/94	A	22	(2)	2
18	Kejvi Bardhi		07/08/96	G		(2)	
44	Elton Basriu		03/08/87	D	13	(1)	
6	Leodor Bërdufi		24/04/96	D	1		
17	Dorian Bylykbashi		08/08/80	M	10		2
44	Klaudio Cema		22/04/95	A	7		
9	Mirel Çota		14/05/88	A	13	(3)	3
7	Arbër Çyrbja		18/09/93	M	5	(2)	
10	Endri Dalipi		02/05/83	M	4		
4	Jurgen Dosti		02/11/91	D	19	(5)	
13	Endri Duka		07/10/87	D	1	(4)	
8	Orgest Gava		29/03/90	M	31		1
3	Klaus Gjorga		17/04/94	D	1	(3)	
14	John Grabova		17/12/95	M	2	(5)	1
27	Ardit Hila		06/01/93	M	26	(4)	
6	Ertigen Hoti		20/06/96	A		(2)	
6	Xhulio Jaupi		30/09/92	D	19	(1)	1
23	Ganjol Kaçuli		22/09/89	D	26		1
8	Arsen Kasa		02/05/97	D	1		
1	Elvis Kotorri		30/04/79	G	14		
12	Ted Laço		01/02/95	G		(2)	
16	Eri Lamçja		10/03/94	A	16	(8)	4
6	Jurgen Lleshi		05/04/95	M	4	(4)	
19	Shamet Luta		26/06/95	D	6	(8)	
11	Enco Malindi		15/01/88	A	21	(2)	1
18	Maurício	BRA	08/02/93	A	3	(4)	
7	Erjol Merxha		21/04/79	M	1		
19	Serxhio Mukja		15/11/96	D	2		
20	Emiljano Musta		31/01/92	M	19	(7)	1
12	Eduart Myftarago		05/02/93	G	4	(2)	
5	Arjan Pisha		18/01/77	D	20		
1	Shkëlzen Ruçi		01/07/92	G	18		
3	Elio Shazivari		14/04/85	D	8	(2)	
27	Dejan Shehi		19/03/97	M	2		
9	Kristi Shyti		05/03/95	D	2	(3)	
23	Brilant Sulaj		17/02/91	M	5	(6)	
16	Holker Suvaria		29/01/96	M	1		
9	Ornald Tafani		08/01/93	A		(1)	
14	Artnad Tahirllari		12/02/92	A	3	(7)	
15	Mateos Toçi		16/05/93	M	21	(5)	1
18	Rei Ujkashi		28/06/94	M	2	(5)	
16	Besart Veseli		24/09/92	D	2	(2)	
13	Jurgen Vogli		12/06/93	D	14	(1)	
9	Jean Paul Yontcha	CMR	15/05/83	A	7	(1)	1

KS Flamurtari

1923 • Flamurtari (9,000) • skflamurtari.com

Major honours
Albanian League (1) 1991; Albanian Cup (4) 1985, 1988, 2009, 2014

Coach: Ernest Gjoka; (30/10/14) (Luan Birçe); (03/11/14) Ernestino Ramella (ITA)

2014					
22/08	h	Teuta	W	2-1	*Abilaliaj, Gilberto*
30/08	a	Tirana	L	0-1	
10/09	h	Apolonia	W	3-0	*Telushi, Gelashvili, Muzaka (p)*
14/09	h	Vllaznia	D	0-0	
20/09	a	Elbasan	W	2-0	*Muzaka (p), Gelashvili*
27/09	h	Laç	D	1-1	*Gilberto*
04/10	a	Partizani	D	0-0	
17/10	h	Skënderbeu	D	1-1	*Abilaliaj*
25/10	a	Kukës	L	0-2	
29/10	a	Teuta	L	0-1	
02/11	h	Tirana	D	0-0	
09/11	a	Apolonia	D	1-1	*Muzaka*
22/11	a	Vllaznia	L	0-1	
01/12	h	Elbasan	W	2-0	*Douglas, Abilaliaj*
07/12	a	Laç	D	1-1	*Telushi*
13/12	h	Partizani	W	1-0	*Shehaj*
17/12	a	Skënderbeu	L	0-1	
21/12	h	Kukës	L	0-1	
2015					
24/01	h	Teuta	W	2-1	*Abilaliaj, Shehaj*
30/01	a	Tirana	L	0-1	
08/02	h	Apolonia	W	1-0	*Telushi (p)*
14/02	h	Vllaznia	W	3-0	*Abilaliaj, Buval, Maxhuni*
22/02	a	Elbasan	W	1-0	*Buval*
04/03	a	Partizani	L	1-2	*Telushi*
08/03	h	Skënderbeu	L	0-1	
12/03	h	Laç	L	0-2	
16/03	a	Kukës	L	0-4	
21/03	a	Teuta	L	0-1	
04/04	h	Tirana	L	1-2	*Bregu*
12/04	a	Apolonia	L	1-2	*Bregu*
18/04	a	Vllaznia	D	1-1	*Kruja*
25/04	h	Elbasan	W	2-1	*Bregu, Shehaj*
02/05	a	Laç	L	1-2	*Bregu*
09/05	h	Partizani	L	0-1	
16/05	a	Skënderbeu	L	0-2	
22/05	h	Kukës	L	1-2	*Bregu*

No	Name	Nat	DoB	Pos	Aps	(s)	Gls
21	Arbër Abilaliaj		06/06/86	A	18	(10)	5
32	Shahin Aliaj		21/08/96	A		(5)	
13	Polizoi Arbëri		09/09/88	D	21		
3	Halim Begaj		29/11/85	D		(1)	
13	Arbri Beqaj		29/09/98	D		(1)	
25	David Bocaj		28/03/98	M	1	(1)	
22	Dejvi Bregu		24/10/95	M	8	(6)	5
85	Bedi Buval	FRA	16/06/86	D	12	(2)	2
5	Douglas	BRA	10/04/88	D	15		1
77	Denis Duda		14/02/96	A	2	(2)	
99	Nikoloz Gelashvili	GEO	01/08/85	A	5	(5)	2
9	Gilberto	BRA	11/07/87	A	9	(3)	2
8	Julian Gjinaj		24/10/96	M	6	(1)	
9	Albin Hodza	FRA	07/02/88	A	5	(3)	
4	Hektor Idrizaj		15/04/89	D	22	(2)	
8	Gëzim Krasniqi		05/01/90	M	10	(1)	
12	Arsid Kruja		08/06/93	A	8	(6)	1
20	Taulant Kuqi		11/11/85	D	20	(6)	
10	Nijaz Lena	MKD	25/06/86	M	19	(2)	
18	Ledio Liçaj		19/01/87	M		(4)	
89	Gilman Lika		13/01/87	M	12	(1)	
89	Ilion Lika		17/05/80	G	24		
66	Aldo Llambi		06/06/96	M	4	(1)	
7	Lorik Maxhuni		02/07/92	M	9	(2)	1
6	Shkodran Metaj		05/02/88	D	7	(5)	
77	Agim Meto		02/02/86	M	1	(5)	
7	Gledian Mici		06/02/91	D	15		
14	Gjergji Muzaka		26/09/84	M	17		3
5	Baćo Nikolić	MNE	19/01/86	D	5	(2)	
15	Ardi Qejvani		28/01/93	D	1	2	
28	Artan Sakaj		08/12/80	D	1		
1	Edmir Sali		07/08/97	G		(1)	
23	Ardit Shehaj		23/09/90	A	9	(15)	3
91	Jurgen Sino		24/01/97	M	2		
17	Bruno Telushi		14/11/90	A	31		4
18	Vukašin Tomić	SRB	08/04/87	M	7	(1)	
19	Jani Urdinov	MKD	28/03/91	A	6	(2)	
11	Franc Veliu		11/11/88	M	18		
25	Erjon Vuçaj		25/12/90	M	27	(5)	
89	Klodian Xhelili		23/11/88	G	12	(1)	
3	Valto Zeqaj		24/08/95	D	7		

FK Kukësi

1930 • Zeqir Ymeri (4,500) • fk-kukesi.al

Coach: Agim Canaj; (30/07/14) Shkëlqim Muça; (10/08/14) Artim Sakiri (MKD); (27/04/15) Miodrag Radanović (SRB)

2014					
23/08	a	Vllaznia	W	2-1	*Pejić, Hysa*
31/08	h	Elbasan	W	3-0	*Pejić, Hoxha, E Dushku*
10/09	a	Laç	D	0-0	
14/09	h	Partizani	L	0-1	
19/09	a	Skënderbeu	L	0-2	
26/09	a	Apolonia	W	1-0	*Pejić*
05/10	h	Teuta	W	1-0	*Pejić*
18/10	a	Tirana	L	1-3	*Lushtaku*
25/10	h	Flamurtari	W	2-0	*E Dushku, Pejić*
29/10	h	Vllaznia	W	2-1	*og (Marku), Zeqiri*
02/11	a	Elbasan	W	2-0	*Pejić 2*
09/11	h	Laç	W	1-0	*Lushtaku*
22/11	a	Partizani	L	0-2	
30/11	h	Skënderbeu	W	1-0	*E Dushku*
06/12	h	Apolonia	D	0-0	
12/12	a	Teuta	W	3-0	*Pejić 2, Lushtaku*
17/12	h	Tirana	W	1-0	*Hysa*
21/12	a	Flamurtari	W	1-0	*Pejić*
2015					
24/01	a	Vllaznia	W	2-1	*Pejić, Lushtaku*
31/01	h	Elbasan	W	3-0	*Pejić 3*
08/02	a	Laç	L	1-2	*Pejić*
14/02	h	Partizani	W	3-0	*Pejić, Zeqiri, Shameti*
23/02	a	Skënderbeu	D	1-1	*Zeqiri (p)*
28/02	a	Apolonia	D	2-2	*Lushtaku, Pejić*
04/03	h	Teuta	W	5-2	*Mallota, Pejić 2, Márcio Pit 2*
08/03	a	Tirana	L	0-2	
16/03	h	Flamurtari	W	4-0	*E Dushku, Pejić 2, Hysa*
21/03	h	Vllaznia	W	1-0	*Pejić*
04/04	a	Elbasan	W	4-0	*Jefferson, Pejić 2 (1p), E Dushku*
13/04	h	Laç	D	0-0	
18/04	a	Partizani	D	1-1	*Pejić (p)*
26/04	h	Skënderbeu	L	0-1	
02/05	h	Apolonia	W	2-1	*Zeqiri, Hysa*
09/05	a	Teuta	W	3-2	*Pejić 3 (1p)*
17/05	h	Tirana	W	4-1	*Hysa, Pejić 3 (1p)*
22/05	a	Flamurtari	W	2-1	*Hysa, og (Gjinaj)*

No	Name	Nat	DoB	Pos	Aps	(s)	Gls
14	Igli Allmuça		25/10/80	M	2	(2)	
5	Julian Brahja		06/12/80	D		(3)	
15	Albi Dosti		13/09/91	M	1	(16)	
6	Erjon Dushku		25/02/85	D	27		5
23	Rigers Dushku		08/09/91	D	1	(3)	
25	Faramilio	BRA	30/01/88	M		(3)	
33	Ivan Gvozdenović	SRB	19/08/78	D	3	(1)	
1	Argjend Halili		16/11/82	G	31		
27	Ndriqim Halili		29/01/93	M	1	(1)	
13	Rahman Hallaçi		12/11/83	D	34		
16	Edon Hasani		09/01/92	M	15	(11)	
20	Ylli Hoxha		26/12/87	A	17	(11)	1
11	Vilfor Hysa		09/09/89	M	23	(8)	6
27	Jefferson	BRA	27/10/89	D	23	(3)	1
77	Fjoart Jonuzi		09/07/96	M		(3)	
12	Ervis Koçi		13/11/84	G	1	(1)	
10	Kushtrim Lushtaku		08/10/89	D	28	(1)	5
24	Renato Mallota		24/06/89	D	34		1
15	Márcio Pit	BRA	10/05/89	A	6	(8)	2
7	Gledi Mici		06/02/91	D	10	(1)	
2	Endri Mucmata		21/06/96	D		(1)	
23	Besar Musolli		28/02/89	M	23	(3)	
22	Pero Pejić	CRO	28/11/82	A	35		31
7	Roland Peqini		25/11/90	D	5	(2)	
88	Ivan Perić	SRB	05/05/82	A	2	(4)	
4	Ylli Shameti		07/06/84	D	13	(16)	1
2	Dritan Smajlaj		12/02/85	D	25		
98	Dmitri Stajila	MDA	02/08/91	G	4		
19	Hair Zeqiri		11/10/88	M	32	(1)	4

 # ALBANIA

KF Laçi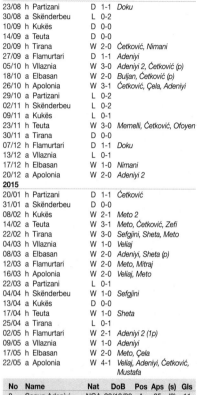

1960 • Laçi (3,500) • kflaci.com
Major honours
Albanian Cup (2) 2013, 2015
Coach: Stavri Nica;
(03/08/14) Armando Cungu

2014
23/08	h	Partizani	D	1-1	Doku
30/08	a	Skënderbeu	L	0-2	
10/09	h	Kukës	D	0-0	
14/09	a	Teuta	D	0-0	
20/09	h	Tirana	W	2-0	Ćetković, Nimani
27/09	a	Flamurtari	D	1-1	Adeniyi
05/10	h	Vllaznia	W	3-0	Adeniyi 2, Ćetković (p)
18/10	a	Elbasan	W	2-0	Buljan, Ćetković (p)
26/10	h	Apolonia	W	3-1	Ćetković, Çela, Adeniyi
29/10	a	Partizani	L	0-2	
02/11	h	Skënderbeu	L	0-2	
09/11	a	Kukës	L	0-1	
23/11	h	Teuta	W	3-0	Memelli, Ćetković, Ofoyen
30/11	a	Tirana	D	0-0	
07/12	h	Flamurtari	D	1-1	Doku
13/12	a	Vllaznia	L	0-1	
17/12	h	Elbasan	W	1-0	Nimani
20/12	a	Apolonia	W	2-0	Adeniyi 2

2015
20/01	h	Partizani	D	1-1	Ćetković
31/01	a	Skënderbeu	D	0-0	
08/02	h	Kukës	W	2-1	Meto 2
14/02	a	Teuta	W	3-1	Meto, Ćetković, Zefi
22/02	h	Tirana	W	3-0	Sefgjini, Sheta, Meto
04/03	h	Vllaznia	W	1-0	Veliaj
08/03	a	Elbasan	W	2-0	Adeniyi, Sheta (p)
12/03	a	Flamurtari	W	2-0	Meto, Mitraj
16/03	h	Apolonia	W	2-0	Veliaj, Meto
22/03	a	Partizani	L	0-1	
04/04	h	Skënderbeu	W	1-0	Sefgjini
13/04	h	Kukës	D	0-0	
17/04	h	Teuta	W	1-0	Sheta
25/04	a	Tirana	L	0-1	
02/05	h	Flamurtari	W	2-1	Adeniyi 2 (1p)
09/05	a	Vllaznia	W	1-0	Adeniyi
17/05	h	Elbasan	W	2-0	Meto, Çela
22/05	a	Apolonia	W	4-1	Veliaj, Adeniyi, Ćetković, Mustafa

No	Name	Nat	DoB	Pos	Aps	(s)	Gls
8	Segun Adeniyi	NGA	20/12/92	A	25	(2)	11
6	Mikelanxhelo Bardhi		08/01/95	M	2	(11)	
18	Mishel Bilibashi		08/03/89	M	7	(2)	
4	Stipe Buljan	CRO	21/09/83	D	35		1
3	Emiljano Çela		21/07/85	D	21	(6)	2
18	Marko Ćetković	MNE	10/07/86	M	25	(4)	8
7	Elton Doku		01/10/86	D	19	(3)	2
15	Arbër Haliti		25/01/92	A		(13)	
16	Daniel Jubani		07/12/93	D		(1)	
9	Migen Memelli		25/04/80	A	6	(5)	1
9	Agim Meto		02/02/86	A	17		7
9	Aldo Mitraj		12/01/87	M	3	(11)	1
1	Shpëtim Moçka		20/10/89	G	3		
14	Argjend Mustafa		30/08/92	D	11	(7)	1
16	Edison Ndreca		05/07/94	M	2	(5)	
19	Valdano Nimani		05/03/87	A	26	(5)	2
2	Charles Ofoyen	NGA	26/07/85	D	9	(6)	1
7	Jetmir Sefa		30/01/87	M	3	(10)	
11	Taulant Sefgjini		21/07/86	M	29	(3)	2
33	Anthimos Selala		09/02/94	A		(1)	
5	Arjan Sheta		13/02/81	D	31		3
17	Rafael Sosa	ARG	07/05/88	A	6	(4)	
21	Olsi Teqja		27/07/88	M	27	(1)	
20	Artan Thorja		09/03/93	M		(1)	
1	Eduin Ujka		10/04/95	G	1		
28	Emiljano Veliaj		09/02/85	M	30	(2)	3
31	Miroslav Vujadinović	MNE	22/04/83	G	32		
22	Alfred Zefi		20/08/91	D	26		1

FK Partizani

1946 • Qemal Stafa (16,230) • partizani.net
Major honours
Albanian League (15) 1947, 1948, 1949, 1954, 1957, 1958, 1959, 1961, 1963, 1964, 1971, 1979, 1981, 1987, 1993; Albanian Cup (15) 1948, 1949, 1957, 1958, 1961, 1964, 1966, 1968, 1970, 1973, 1980, 1991, 1993, 1997, 2004
Coach: Shpëtim Duro

2014
23/08	a	Laç	D	1-1	Račić
30/08	a	Apolonia	L	0-1	
11/09	h	Skënderbeu	W	1-0	Vila (p)
14/09	h	Kukës	W	1-0	Račić
19/09	h	Teuta	W	2-0	Račić, Fazliu
26/09	a	Tirana	D	0-0	
04/10	h	Flamurtari	D	0-0	
19/10	a	Vllaznia	W	1-0	Mazrekaj
26/10	h	Elbasan	W	1-0	Račić
29/10	h	Laç	W	2-0	Vila, Mazrekaj (p)
02/11	a	Apolonia	W	1-0	Mazrekaj
08/11	a	Skënderbeu	L	0-3	
22/11	h	Kukës	W	2-0	Ibrahimi, Nedzipi
30/11	a	Teuta	W	1-0	Osmanaj
08/12	h	Tirana	W	2-0	Nedzipi, Mazrekaj (p)
13/12	a	Flamurtari	L	0-1	
17/12	h	Vllaznia	L	0-1	
20/12	a	Elbasan	W	1-0	Račić

2015
25/01	h	Laç	D	1-1	Bylykbashi
31/01	a	Apolonia	W	2-0	Vila, Rrahmani
09/02	h	Skënderbeu	D	0-0	
14/02	a	Kukës	L	0-3	
22/02	h	Teuta	W	2-1	Fazliu, Mazrekaj
04/03	a	Flamurtari	W	2-1	Rrahmani, Račić
08/03	a	Vllaznia	L	0-1	
13/03	a	Tirana	W	2-1	Nedzipi, Račić
16/03	h	Elbasan	W	4-1	Vila, Račić 2, Rrahmani
22/03	a	Laç	W	1-0	Račić
04/04	a	Apolonia	W	1-0	Račić
13/04	h	Skënderbeu	L	2-5	Račić 2
18/04	a	Kukës	D	1-1	Račić
25/04	a	Teuta	W	1-0	Batha
04/05	h	Tirana	D	2-2	Fazliu, Mazrekaj
09/05	a	Flamurtari	W	1-0	Mazrekaj (p)
17/05	h	Vllaznia	W	1-0	Mazrekaj (p)
22/05	a	Elbasan	W	3-0	Krasniqi, Bylykbashi, Fazliu

No	Name	Nat	DoB	Pos	Aps	(s)	Gls
27	Jurgen Bardhi		06/11/97	A		(4)	
10	Idriz Batha		28/03/92	M	31		1
70	Dorian Bylykbashi		08/08/80	M	4	(5)	2
6	Ardian Cuculi	MKD	19/07/87	D	32		
21	Asjon Daja		14/03/90	M	9	(11)	
5	Ignat Dishliev	BUL	08/06/87	D	2	(1)	
9	Astrit Fazliu		28/09/87	A	17	(15)	4
4	Arbnor Fejzullahu		08/04/93	D	33		
38	Fabio Gjonikaj		25/05/95	G	1	(1)	
12	Alban Hoxha		23/11/87	G	30		
22	Labinot Ibrahimi		25/06/86	A	13	(5)	1
5	Gëzim Krasniqi		05/01/90	D	5	(3)	1
14	Mentor Mazrekaj		08/02/89	M	28	(3)	8
8	Argjend Mustafa		30/08/92	M	1	(3)	
3	Erbi Myftaraj		22/12/91	D		(1)	
11	Nderim Nedzipi	MKD	22/05/84	M	28	(3)	3
23	Liridon Osmanaj	SVN	04/01/92	M	2	(9)	1
17	Stevan Račić	SRB	17/01/84	A	31	(2)	14
18	Amir Rrahmani		24/02/94	D	33	(1)	3
20	Bunjamin Shabani	MKD	30/01/91	M	6	(13)	
19	Lorenc Trashi		19/05/92	M	28	(5)	
30	Jurgen Vatnikaj		08/08/95	D	1	(9)	
88	Emiljano Vila		12/03/88	A	33	(1)	4
44	Endrit Vrapi		23/05/82	D	23	(3)	
1	Dashamir Xhika		23/05/89	G	5		

KF Skënderbeu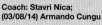

1909 • Skënderbeu (7,000) • kfskenderbeu.al
Major honours
Albanian League (6) 1933, 2011, 2012, 2013, 2014, 2015
Coach: Mirel Josa

2014
22/08	a	Elbasan	W	1-0	Sefa
30/08	h	Laç	W	2-0	Osmani, Progni
11/09	a	Partizani	L	0-1	
14/09	a	Apolonia	D	0-0	
19/09	h	Kukës	W	2-0	Sefa, Progni
27/09	a	Teuta	L	0-2	
04/10	h	Tirana	D	0-0	
17/10	a	Flamurtari	D	1-1	Vangjeli
25/10	h	Vllaznia	W	3-0	Dimo, Olayinka, Vangjeli
29/10	h	Elbasan	W	1-0	Olayinka
02/11	a	Laç	W	2-0	Olayinka, Sefa
08/11	h	Partizani	W	3-0	Dhiego Martins 2, Sefa
23/11	h	Apolonia	W	6-0	Progni 2, Shkëmbi (p), Dhiego Martins 3
30/11	a	Kukës	L	0-1	
06/12	h	Teuta	W	3-2	Shehi (p), Alikaj, Olayinka
13/12	a	Tirana	L	0-2	
17/12	h	Flamurtari	W	1-0	Olayinka
21/12	a	Vllaznia	W	1-0	Shkëmbi (p)

2015
25/01	a	Elbasan	W	4-1	Olayinka, Vangjeli, Berisha, Nimaga
31/01	h	Laç	D	0-0	
09/02	a	Partizani	D	0-0	
14/02	a	Apolonia	W	1-0	Stojkov
23/02	h	Kukës	D	1-1	Abazi
28/02	a	Teuta	W	1-0	Shkëmbi (p)
04/03	h	Tirana	W	1-0	Shkëmbi (p)
08/03	a	Flamurtari	W	1-0	Stojkov
15/03	h	Vllaznia	W	3-1	Radaš, Latifi, Lilaj
21/03	h	Elbasan	W	5-1	og (Toçi), Dhiego Martins, Nimaga 2, Latifi
04/04	a	Laç	L	0-1	
13/04	h	Partizani	W	5-2	Lilaj, Latifi, Berisha, Stojkov, Radaš
18/04	a	Apolonia	W	1-0	Sefa
26/04	a	Kukës	W	1-0	Lilaj
02/05	h	Teuta	W	4-2	Latifi, Dhiego Martins, Berisha, Sefa
09/05	a	Tirana	D	0-0	
16/05	h	Flamurtari	W	2-0	Latifi, Lilaj
22/05	a	Vllaznia	W	2-0	Berisha, Progni

No	Name	Nat	DoB	Pos	Aps	(s)	Gls
14	Leonit Abazi		05/07/93	M	14	(9)	1
9	Enkeleid Alikaj		27/12/81	M	5	(13)	1
3	Renato Arapi		28/08/86	D	33		
23	Bernard Berisha		24/10/91	M	30	(2)	4
11	Dhiego Martins	BRA	27/08/88	A	22	(7)	7
2	Amarildo Dimo		25/08/82	M	3	(5)	1
25	Bajram Jashanica		25/09/90	D	9	(13)	
27	Liridon Latifi		06/02/94	M	7	(5)	5
88	Sabien Lilaj		18/02/89	M	31	(2)	4
12	Erjon Llapanji		10/05/85	G		(1)	
4	Bruno Lulaj		02/04/95	D		(3)	
77	Marconi	BRA	22/06/88	A	1	(4)	
19	Bakary Nimaga	MLI	06/12/94	M	18	(7)	3
99	Peter Olayinka	NGA	18/11/95	A	15		6
17	Tefik Osmani		08/06/83	D	21	(1)	1
7	Gerhard Progni		06/11/86	M	30	(1)	5
33	Marko Radaš	CRO	26/10/83	D	33		2
30	Andi Ribaj		21/11/89	A	7	(4)	
29	Fatjon Sefa		23/07/84	A	9	(19)	6
1	Orges Shehi		25/09/77	G	36		1
10	Bledi Shkëmbi		13/08/78	M	31		4
99	Aco Stojkov	MKD	29/04/83	A	8	(5)	3
32	Kristi Vangjeli		05/09/85	D	33		3

KF Teuta

1920 • Niko Dovana (8,000) • kftirana.al

Major honours
Albanian League (1) 1994, Albanian Cup (0) 1005, 2000, 2005

Coach: Hasan Lika;
(24/11/14) Gentian Begeja

2014
22/08	a	Flamurtari	L	1-2	*Shabani*
31/08	h	Vllaznia	L	0-1	
10/09	a	Elbasan	W	5-1	*Pepa 2, Shabani 2, Dita*
14/09	h	Laç	D	0-0	
19/09	a	Partizani	L	0-2	
27/09	h	Skënderbeu	W	2-0	*Peposhi, Krasniqi*
05/10	a	Kukës	L	0-1	
19/10	a	Apolonia	L	0-1	
26/10	h	Tirana	L	0-1	
29/10	h	Flamurtari	W	1-0	*Rafael*
02/11	a	Vllaznia	W	2-1	*Deliallisi, Rafael*
08/11	h	Elbasan	L	0-2	
23/11	a	Laç	L	0-3	
30/11	h	Partizani	L	0-1	
06/12	a	Skënderbeu	L	2-3	*Hyseni, Dita*
12/12	h	Kukës	L	0-3	
17/12	h	Apolonia	W	1-0	*Nika (p)*
21/12	a	Tirana	L	2-4	*Hyseni, Dita*

2015
24/01	a	Flamurtari	L	1-2	*og (Tomić)*
31/01	h	Vllaznia	W	2-1	*Nika (p), Çota*
08/02	a	Elbasan	L	0-1	
14/02	h	Laç	L	1-3	*Dita*
22/02	a	Partizani	L	1-2	*Nika (p)*
28/02	h	Skënderbeu	L	0-1	
04/03	a	Kukës	L	2-5	*Kastrati, Nika*
08/03	a	Apolonia	L	1-2	*Kotobelli*
16/03	h	Tirana	D	0-0	
21/03	h	Flamurtari	W	1-0	*Nika*
04/04	a	Vllaznia	L	0-1	
12/04	h	Elbasan	W	1-0	*Hyseni*
17/04	a	Laç	L	0-1	
25/04	h	Partizani	L	0-1	
02/05	a	Skënderbeu	L	2-4	*Kotobelli, Peposhi*
09/05	h	Kukës	L	2-3	*Çota, Peposhi*
17/05	h	Apolonia	W	1-0	*Peposhi*
22/05	a	Tirana	L	0-1	

No	Name	Nat	DoB	Pos	Aps	(s)	Gls
30	Julian Ahmataj		24/05/79	M	8	(7)	
8	Florind Bardulla		19/11/92	M	3	(3)	
6	Armando Bashhysa		12/10/97	D		(1)	
16	Fabian Beqja		15/02/94	M	2	(3)	
6	Julian Brahja		06/02/80	D	15		
9	Mirel Çota		14/05/88	A	13	(4)	2
16	Alfred Deliallisi		28/03/93	M	21	(6)	1
28	Bruno Dita		18/02/93	D	22	(9)	4
10	Mokhtar Fall	SEN	24/08/90	M		(4)	
8	Nazmi Gripshi		05/07/97	M	1	(1)	
30	Bledar Hodo		21/09/85	M	24	(1)	
14	Altin Hoxha		21/10/90	M	1		
4	Erand Hoxha		25/04/85	M	32	(2)	
5	Rustem Hoxha		04/07/91	D	29		
6	Erjon Hoxhallari		15/10/95	D	25	(2)	
13	Klejdi Hyka		13/06/97	D	1	(2)	
19	Klaudio Hyseni		15/07/94	A	11	(8)	3
24	Resul Kastrati		24/01/95	A	10		1
20	Erlind Koreshi		09/02/79	D	11	(8)	
15	Blerim Kotobelli		10/08/92	D	31	(1)	2
2	Besnik Krasniqi		01/02/90	D	14	(1)	1
10	Bekim Kuli		19/09/82	A	5	(6)	
6	Endrian Magani		06/06/91	D	1	(1)	
11	Elidon Mara		27/06/97	D		(1)	
13	Vangjel Mile		01/07/86	A	2	(1)	
7	Ansi Nika		22/08/90	A	27	(2)	5
12	Alfred Osmani		20/02/83	G	2	(1)	
9	Brunild Pepa		27/11/90	A	4	(5)	2
25	Ardit Peposhi		14/09/93	M	20	(9)	4
3	Elvis Premçi		26/06/93	D	4		
16	Tedi Qehajaj		08/07/96	M		(1)	
11	Rafael	BRA	06/02/86	M	8	(2)	2
1	Marat Rexhepaj		02/07/94	G	2		
1	Bledian Rizvani		02/07/85	G	32		
24	Xhevdet Shabani		10/10/86	A	13	(1)	3
17	Shaqir Stafa		23/04/87	D	2	(2)	
21	Marvin Turtulli		17/10/94	M		(3)	

KF Tirana

1920 • Qemal Stafa (16,230) • kftirana.al

Major honours
Albanian League (24) 1930, 1931, 1932, 1934, 1936, 1937, 1965, 1966, 1968, 1970, 1982, 1985, 1988, 1989, 1995, 1996, 1997, 1999, 2000, 2003, 2004, 2005, 2007, 2009; Albanian Cup (15) 1939, 1963, 1976, 1977, 1983, 1984, 1986, 1994, 1996, 1999, 2001, 2002, 2006, 2011, 2012

Coach: Gugash Magani;
(18/05/15) Emanuel Egbo (NGA)

2014
24/08	h	Apolonia	W	3-0	*Elis Bakaj, Ndikumana, Hyshmeri*
30/08	a	Flamurtari	W	1-0	*Elis Bakaj*
11/09	a	Vllaznia	D	1-1	*Bulku*
14/09	h	Elbasan	W	2-1	*Bušić, Curri*
20/09	a	Laç	L	0-2	
26/09	h	Partizani	D	0-0	
04/10	a	Skënderbeu	D	0-0	
18/10	h	Kukës	W	3-1	*og (E Dushku), Elis Bakaj, Curri*
26/10	a	Teuta	W	1-0	*Elis Bakaj*
29/10	a	Apolonia	W	3-0	*Ndikumana, Elis Bakaj, Muça*
02/11	a	Flamurtari	D	0-0	
08/11	h	Vllaznia	W	1-0	*Taku*
23/11	a	Elbasan	W	3-2	*Muça, Elis Bakaj, Ndikumana*
30/11	h	Laç	D	0-0	
08/12	h	Partizani	L	0-2	
13/12	h	Skënderbeu	W	2-0	*Ndikumana 2*
17/12	a	Kukës	L	0-1	
21/12	h	Teuta	W	4-2	*Elis Bakaj 2, Morina, Kagere*

2015
24/01	h	Apolonia	W	2-0	*Ndikumana 2*
30/01	h	Flamurtari	W	1-0	*Ndikumana*
08/02	a	Vllaznia	W	1-0	*Elis Bakaj*
14/02	h	Elbasan	W	2-0	*Sefa, Elis Bakaj (p)*
22/02	a	Laç	L	0-3	
04/03	a	Skënderbeu	L	0-1	
08/03	h	Kukës	W	2-0	*Bušić, Muzaka*
13/03	h	Partizani	L	1-2	*Morina*
16/03	a	Teuta	D	0-0	
22/03	a	Apolonia	W	2-0	*Morina (p), Muça*
04/04	a	Flamurtari	W	2-1	*Muça, Bušić*
12/04	h	Vllaznia	W	2-1	*Muça 2*
18/04	a	Elbasan	W	3-1	*Hyshmeri, Bušić, Elis Bakaj*
25/04	h	Laç	W	1-0	*Kahata*
04/05	a	Partizani	D	2-2	*Elis Bakaj 2*
09/05	h	Skënderbeu	D	0-0	
17/05	a	Kukës	L	1-4	*Ndikumana*
22/05	h	Teuta	W	1-0	*Elis Bakaj*

No	Name	Nat	DoB	Pos	Aps	(s)	Gls
31	Edvan Bakaj		09/10/87	G	9		
19	Elis Bakaj		25/06/87	A	26	(1)	14
8	Ervin Bulku		03/03/81	M	24	(4)	1
9	Tomislav Bušić	CRO	02/02/86	A	17	(16)	4
6	Debatik Curri		28/12/83	D	26	(1)	2
1	Stivi Frashëri		29/08/90	G	27		
27	Grent Halili		24/05/98	M		(2)	
17	Renato Hyshmeri		14/03/89	M	9	(13)	2
27	Endrit Idrizaj		14/06/89	D	4	(3)	
7	Meddie Kagere	RWA	10/10/86	A	5	(11)	1
7	Francis Kahata	KEN	07/06/91	A	11	(2)	1
25	Renaldo Kalari		25/06/84	D	18	(5)	
21	Erando Karabeci		06/09/88	M	31	(1)	
18	Dorian Kërçiku		30/08/93	M	24	(1)	
23	Argjend Malaj		16/10/93	D	14	(10)	
10	Mario Morina		16/10/92	A	20	(6)	3
4	Gentian Muça		13/05/87	D	32	(1)	6
17	Gjergji Muzaka		26/09/84	A	12		1
11	Selamani Ndikumana	BDI	18/03/87	A	23	(7)	9
21	Ronald Olaki	UGA	11/06/95	M	1	(6)	
5	Entonio Pashaj		10/11/84	D	13	(6)	
25	Kire Ristevski	MKD	22/10/90	D	13		
24	Jetmir Sefa		30/01/87	M	4	(10)	1
26	Afrim Taku		04/08/89	M	33	(1)	1

KF Vllaznia

1919 • Loro Boriçi (16,000) • vllaznia.al

Major honours
Albanian League (9) 1945, 1946, 1972, 1974, 1978, 1983, 1992, 1998, 2001; Albanian Cup (6) 1965, 1972, 1979, 1981, 1987, 2008

Coach: Baldo Raineri (ITA);
(03/03/15) Luan Zmijani

2014
23/08	a	Kukës	L	1-2	*Dibra*
31/08	a	Teuta	W	1-0	*Kruja*
11/09	h	Tirana	D	1-1	*Shtupina*
14/09	a	Flamurtari	D	0-0	
20/09	h	Apolonia	W	2-0	*Shtupina 2 (1p)*
27/09	h	Elbasan	W	1-0	*Sosa*
05/10	a	Laç	L	0-3	
19/10	a	Partizani	L	0-1	
25/10	a	Skënderbeu	L	0-3	
29/10	a	Kukës	L	1-2	*Marku*
02/11	h	Teuta	L	1-2	*Sosa*
08/11	a	Tirana	L	0-1	
22/11	h	Flamurtari	W	1-0	*Hajdari*
29/11	a	Apolonia	W	1-0	*Sosa*
07/12	a	Elbasan	W	4-1	*Sosa 2, Shtupina, Kalaja*
13/12	h	Laç	W	1-0	*Beqiri*
17/12	a	Partizani	W	1-0	*Tafili*
21/12	h	Skënderbeu	L	0-1	

2015
24/01	h	Kukës	L	1-2	*Kalaja*
31/01	h	Teuta	L	1-2	*Sosa*
08/02	h	Tirana	L	0-1	
14/02	a	Flamurtari	L	0-3	
22/02	h	Apolonia	W	2-0	*Sosa, Lika*
28/02	h	Elbasan	D	1-1	*Gocaj*
04/03	a	Laç	L	0-1	
08/03	h	Partizani	W	1-0	*Çinari*
15/03	a	Skënderbeu	L	1-3	*Gocaj (p)*
21/03	a	Kukës	L	0-1	
04/04	h	Teuta	W	1-0	*og (Rizvani)*
12/04	a	Tirana	L	1-2	*Çinari*
18/04	h	Flamurtari	D	1-1	*Lika*
25/04	a	Apolonia	D	0-0	
02/05	a	Elbasan	D	1-1	*Lika*
09/05	h	Laç	L	0-1	
17/05	a	Partizani	L	0-1	
22/05	h	Skënderbeu	L	0-2	

No	Name	Nat	DoB	Pos	Aps	(s)	Gls
13	Giorginho Aguirre	URU	23/03/93	M		(1)	
16	Alis Baçi		08/02/91	D	23	(1)	
4	Florind Bardhulla		19/11/92	M	2	(3)	
18	Elvin Beqiri		27/09/80	D	27	(2)	1
27	Ergi Borshi		09/08/95	M	2	(1)	
12	Gianmarco Campironi	ITA	16/05/89	G	1		
17	Eraldo Çinari		11/10/96	A	9	(6)	2
32	Mauro Cioffi	ITA	16/05/94	A		(6)	
8	Bekim Dema		30/03/93	M	17	(6)	
44	Arenc Dibra		11/05/90	D	6	(8)	1
7	Denis Dyca		11/01/96	M	4	(4)	
22	Olsi Gocaj		30/09/89	A	31	(2)	7
3	Sidrit Guri		23/10/93	D	4	(3)	
16	Erdenis Gurishta		24/04/95	M	4	(3)	
21	Arsen Hajdari		25/02/89	A	20	(10)	1
4	Esin Hakaj		06/12/96	D	4	(1)	
19	Arlind Kalaja		27/12/95	M	3	(17)	2
14	Arsid Kruja		08/06/93	D	14	(3)	1
13	Ardit Krymi		02/05/96	D	21	(1)	
12	Gilman Lika		13/01/87	A	17		3
17	Paolo Markolaj		31/10/93	M		(3)	
3	Antonio Marku		24/03/92	M	13	(3)	1
27	Ersin Mehmedović	SRB	10/05/81	M	6	(2)	
24	Denis Pjeshka		28/05/85	D	8	(3)	
1	Erind Selimaj		22/05/89	G	28		
4	Rijat Shala		26/09/83	M	9		
30	Alen Sherri		15/12/97	G	7		
10	Ndriçim Shtupina		18/03/87	M	33	(1)	4
9	Sebastián Sosa	URU	13/03/94	A	18	(1)	7
15	Arsen Sykaj		16/04/90	D	31		
5	Alsid Tafili		20/08/87	D	34	(1)	1
23	Stivi Vecaj		29/01/94	M		(3)	

Top goalscorers

31	Pero Pejić (Kukës)
14	Stevan Račić (Partizani)
	Elis Bakaj (Tirana)
11	Segun Adeniyi (Laç)
9	Selamani Ndikumana (Tirana)
8	Marko Ćetković (Laç)
	Mentor Mazrekaj (Partizani)
7	Agim Meto (Laç)
	Dhiego Martins (Skënderbeu)
	Sebastián Sosa (Vllaznia)

Promoted clubs

KF Tërbuni

1936 • Ismail Xhemali (4,000) • no website
Coach: Elvis Plori

FK Bylis

1972 • Adush Muça (5,000) • no website
Coach: Roland Nenaj

Second level final tables 2014/15

Group A	Pld	W	D	L	F	A	Pts
1 KF Tërbuni	27	21	6	0	55	12	69
2 KF Besëlidhja	27	21	2	4	56	13	65
3 KF Mamurrasi	27	20	4	3	57	16	64
4 KF Iliria	27	9	6	12	25	25	33
5 KS Kastrioti	27	9	4	14	33	36	31
6 KS Kamza	27	9	4	14	30	47	31
7 KS Burreli	27	10	1	16	38	45	31
8 KS Ada	27	8	3	16	31	57	27
9 KS Besa	27	5	8	14	25	45	23
10 FK Veleçiku	27	3	2	22	23	77	11

Group B	Pld	W	D	L	F	A	Pts
1 FK Bylis	27	17	2	8	46	26	53
2 KS Lushnja	27	16	5	6	36	18	53
3 KS Butrinti	27	11	8	8	34	22	41
4 KF Sopoti	27	10	6	11	31	34	36
5 KS Luftëtari	27	10	4	13	24	29	34
6 FK Dinamo Tirana	27	9	9	9	27	26	33
7 KS Shkumbini	27	8	7	12	29	33	31
8 KS Pogradeci	27	8	7	12	21	29	31
9 FK Tomori	27	9	5	13	21	38	29
10 KF Naftëtari	27	4	13	10	18	32	25

NB FK Dinamo Tirana & FK Tomori – 3 pts deducted.

DOMESTIC CUP

Kupa e Shqipërisë 2014/15

FIRST ROUND

(01/10/14 & 22/10/14)
Ada 1-1, 1-2 Kastrioti *(2-3)*
Besëlidhja 0-2, 2-3 Teuta *(2-5)*
Burreli 0-1, 0-1 Lushnja *(0-2)*
Dinamo 0-4, 0-4 Apolonia *(0-8)*
Himara 1-10, 0-10 Skënderbeu *(1-20)*
Iliria 0-3, 1-2 Partizani *(1-5)*
Kamza 0-0, 0-5 Flamurtari *(0-5)*
Luftëtari 2-1, 1-3 Bylis *(3-4)*
Mamurrasi 0-2, 2-1 Vllaznia *(2-3)*
Naftëtari 0-2, 1-3 Laç *(1-5)*
Pogradec 2-0, 0-0 Butrinti *(2-0)*
Shkumbini 2-2, 1-1 Elbasan *(3-3; Elbasan on away goals)*
Sopoti 0-3, 1-1 Tirana *(1-4)*
Tomori 1-2, 1-1 Tërbuni *(2-3)*
Veleçiku 0-0, 2-2 Besa *(2-2; Veleçiku on away goals)*
Vora 1-4, 1-6 Kukës *(2-10)*

SECOND ROUND

(05/11/14 & 19/11/14)
Apolonia 2-1, 0-0 Teuta *(2-1)*
Elbasan 2-3, 0-2 Laç *(2-5)*
Kastrioti 0-4, 0-0 Vllaznia *(0-4)*
Lushnja 0-1, 1-4 Partizani *(1-5)*
Pogradec 0-2, 2-5 Kukës *(2-7)*
Veleçiku 1-6, 0-3 *(w/o)* Flamurtari *(1-9)*

(05/11/14 & 20/11/14)
Bylis 0-1, 0-6 Tirana *(0-7)*
Tërbuni 0-0, 1-6 Skënderbeu *(1-6)*

QUARTER-FINALS

(04/02/15 & 18/02/15)
Flamurtari 1-1 Skënderbeu *(Nikolić 60; Shkëmbi 77p)*
Skënderbeu 3-1 Flamurtari *(Osmani 45, Berisha 55, Shkëmbi 89; Hodza 72)*
(Skënderbeu 4-2)

Partizani 2-0 Laç *(Fazliu 9, Bylykbashi 17)*
Laç 3-0 Partizani *(Adeniyi 55p, Meto 67, Ćetković 119) (aet)*
(Laç 3-2)

Vllaznia 0-2 Kukës *(Pejić 2, Lushtaku 15p)*
Kukës 0-0 Vllaznia
(Kukës 2-0)

Tirana 2-2 Apolonia *(Morina 49, Karabeci 62; Ribaj 29, Uzuni 43)*
Apolonia 0-3 Tirana *(Pashaj 17, Taku 57, Bušić 85)*
(Tirana 5-2)

SEMI-FINALS

(08/04/15 & 22/04/15)
Kukës 1-0 Skënderbeu *(Pejić 6)*
Skënderbeu 1-1 Kukës *(Progni 15; Pejić 25)*
(Kukës 2-1)

Tirana 0-0 Laç
Laç 1-0 Tirana *(Adeniyi 62)*
(Laç 1-0)

FINAL

(29/05/15)
Qemal Stafa, Tirana
KF LAÇI 2 *(Veliaj 28, Adeniyi 61)*
FK KUKËSI 1 *(Hasani 45)*
Referee: Jemini
LAÇ: Vujadinović, Sheta, Buljan, Çela, Mustafa, Teqja, Veliaj, Sefgjini, Ćetković (Nimani 85), Meto, Adeniyi
KUKËS: A Halili, Hallaçi, Mallota, Shameti, Mici, Lushtaku (Márcio Pit 44), Jefferson, Hasani, Hysa, Zeqiri, Pejić

Laç claimed the Albanian Cup for the second time in three years

ANDORRA
Federació Andorrana de Fútbol (FAF)

Address	c/ Batlle Tomàs, 4 Baixos AD-700 Escaldes-Engordany	**President**	Victor Manuel Domingos dos Santos
Tel	+376 805 830	**General secretary**	Tomás Gea
Fax	+376 862 006	**Media officer**	Teresa Figueras
E-mail	info@faf.ad	**Year of formation**	1934
Website	faf.ad	**National stadium**	Estadi Nacional (3,306)

PRIMERA DIVISIÓ CLUBS

  1 FC Encamp

  **2** UE Engordany

  **3** Inter Club d'Escaldes

  4 FC Lusitans

5 FC Ordino

6 UE Sant Julià

7 FC Santa Coloma

8 UE Santa Coloma

PROMOTED CLUB

 9 Penya Encarnada d'Andorra

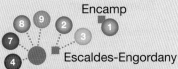

KEY:

 – UEFA Champions League

 – UEFA Europa League

 – Promoted

 – Relegated

0	10	20 km
0		10 miles

FC Santa Coloma hold their nerve

The race for the Andorran Primera Divisió title went to the wire in 2014/15, with FC Santa Coloma finishing stronger than their three rivals in the championship pool to triumph for the second season in a row and a record ninth time in all.

FC Lusitans finished runners-up, three points behind the champions, to re-qualify for continental competition after a year's absence, and the third European place was seized in the final of the Copa Constitució, where UE Sant Julià, fourth in the league, denied FC Santa Coloma the double by retaining the trophy after a penalty shoot-out.

Successful title defence for record champions

Sant Julià retain the cup in penalty shoot-out

Goals but still no points for national team

Domestic league

For the sixth season in a row the same four teams advanced through to the championship pool of the Primera Divisió. In fact, there was plenty of distance between fourth-placed UE Sant Julià and fifth-placed FC Ordino at the 14-match cut-off, whereas just four points separated the leading quartet, with FC Santa Coloma and Lusitans level on 31.

Richard Imbernón's defending champions were on a roll going into the second phase, having recovered from a disappointing start by posting six successive victories, in which they scored 27 goals, 11 of them from ace marksman Cristian Martínez. But the month's break appeared to do them no favours as they kicked off the four-team mini-league with a 1-0 defeat against UE Santa Coloma and then drew against both Lusitans and Sant Julià. Now, with three games remaining, the first-phase leaders were down in third, with both Lusitans and UE Santa Coloma two points above them.

A victory charge to the finish was imperative, and FC Santa Coloma duly delivered, Andorran international striker Gabriel Riera in particular stepping up to the plate as Imbernón's team defeated UE Santa Coloma 3-1 and Lusitans 2-1

to return to the summit and leave themselves requiring a last-day win against Sant Julià to secure the title. Goals from Riera, 35-year-old skipper Ildefons Lima and No10 Juan Carlos Toscano paved the way to a 3-1 win, which, in the event, with Lusitans simultaneously defeating UE Santa Coloma 4-2, was not actually necessary. A draw would have sufficed, and even a defeat would have given them the title on goal difference, but Imbernón and his players were more than happy to crown their achievement in style.

Domestic cup

A week after clinching the league title FC Santa Coloma met Sant Julià again, in the final of the Copa Constitució. The record champions had not won the double for 11 years, and they would be obliged to wait a little longer as Sant Julià, the holders, eked out the win they needed not only to retain the trophy but also qualify for Europe, at the expense of UE Santa Coloma, who had finished a place above them in the league. Goalless after 90 minutes, the game burst into life at the end of the first period of extra time, with in-form Riera putting the champions ahead only for Sant Julià to level soon afterwards. A penalty shoot-out ensued and it was to produce a match-winning hero in Sant Julià's Spanish keeper Jesús

Coca, who, having saved from his opposite number, Eloy Casals, then beat him with the decisive spot-kick.

Europe

Several months earlier, Casals had been a heroic headline-maker himself when he ventured up front and scored the 94th-minute goal that enabled FC Santa Coloma to eliminate Armenian club FC Banants from the UEFA Champions League first qualifying round on away goals. Thanks to their goalkeeper's dramatic intervention the club finally won a European tie at the 11th attempt.

National team

The Andorran national team's wait for a qualifying point in either the FIFA World Cup of UEFA European Championship reached unenviable milestone figures of 20 years and 50 matches as their first six games in the UEFA EURO 2016 qualifying campaign failed to stop the rot. The good news was that, unlike in their 2014 World Cup campaign, Koldo Alvarez's side actually scored a goal. In fact, they managed three – albeit two penalties and an own goal – on the artificial surface of the new Estadi Nacional, the first and third of those even giving Andorra the lead in their respective matches against Wales and Cyprus.

DOMESTIC SEASON AT A GLANCE

Primera Divisió 2014/15 final tables

FIRST PHASE

		Pld	W	D	L	F	A	Pts
1	FC Santa Coloma	14	10	1	3	53	7	31
2	FC Lusitans	14	10	1	3	45	17	31
3	UE Santa Coloma	14	9	2	3	23	8	29
4	UE Sant Julià	14	8	3	3	35	13	27
5	FC Ordino	14	6	2	6	22	22	20
6	FC Encamp	14	4	1	9	13	28	13
7	UE Engordany	14	2	1	11	11	62	7
8	Inter Club d'Escaldes	14	1	1	12	7	52	4

SECOND PHASE

Championship Pool

		Pld	W	D	L	F	A	Pts
1	**FC Santa Coloma**	**20**	**13**	**3**	**4**	**64**	**14**	**42**
2	FC Lusitans	20	12	3	5	53	26	39
3	UE Santa Coloma	20	12	2	6	33	17	38
4	UE Sant Julià	20	9	5	6	41	23	32

Relegation Pool

		Pld	W	D	L	F	A	Pts
5	FC Ordino	20	9	3	8	36	33	30
6	FC Encamp	20	8	3	9	25	34	27
7	UE Engordany	20	5	2	13	21	72	17
8	Inter Club d'Escaldes	20	1	1	18	9	63	4

European qualification 2015/16

 Champion: FC Santa Coloma (first qualifying round)

 Cup winner: UE Sant Julià (first qualifying round)
FC Lusitans (first qualifying round)

Top scorer	Cristian Martínez (FC Santa Coloma), 22 goals
Relegated club	Inter Club d'Escaldes
Promoted club	Penya Encarnada d'Andorra
Cup final	UE Sant Julià 1-1 FC Santa Coloma *(aet; 5-4 on pens)*

Team of the season
(4-3-3)

Coach: Imbernón *(FC Santa Coloma)*

Casals *(FC Santa Coloma)*
Jordi Rubio *(UE Santa Coloma)* — Muñoz *(Lusitans)* — Lima *(FC Santa Coloma)* — Wagner *(FC Santa Coloma)*
V Rodríguez *(UE Santa Coloma)* — Rebés *(FC Santa Coloma)* — Bertran *(Ordino)*
C Martínez *(FC Santa Coloma)* — Alfi *(Lusitans)* — Aguilar *(Lusitans)*

Player of the season

Cristian Martínez
(FC Santa Coloma)

With his 22 goals in 20 Primera Divisió games, Martínez scored twice as many as any other player. The 25-year-old had managed just nine the previous season for FC Lusitans, but after scoring on his league debut for FC Santa Coloma, the habit never left him. Granted, most of the Andorra international winger's goals came against the league's lesser lights during the first phase, but a double in a 3-1 win against UE Santa Coloma during the run-in proved crucial in his new team's title success.

Newcomer of the season

Marc Rebés
(FC Santa Coloma)

A prominent member of Andorra's youth selections for several years, Rebés made eight appearances in the 2015 UEFA European Under-21 Championship qualifying competition before graduating to the senior team at the end of the season, making his debut against Equatorial Guinea when he came on as a substitute for Óscar Sonejee, who was winning his 100th cap. The young midfielder had an excellent season for champions FC Santa Coloma, starting 16 of the 20 games and scoring four goals.

ANDORRA

NATIONAL TEAM

Top five all-time caps
Óscar Sonejee (101); Ildefons Lima (92); Manolo Jiménez (80); Koldo Alvarez & Josep Manel Ayala (79)

Top five all-time goals
Ildefons Lima (9); Óscar Sonejee (4); Jesús Julián Lucendo (3); Emiliano González, Marc Pujol, Justo Ruiz & Fernando Silva (2)

Results 2014/15

09/09/14	Wales (ECQ)	H	Andorra la Vella	L	1-2	Lima (6p)
10/10/14	Belgium (ECQ)	A	Brussels	L	0-6	
13/10/14	Israel (ECQ)	H	Andorra la Vella	L	1-4	Lima (15p)
16/11/14	Cyprus (ECQ)	A	Nicosia	L	0-5	
28/03/15	Bosnia & Herzegovina (ECQ)	H	Andorra la Vella	L	0-3	
06/06/15	Equatorial Guinea	H	Sant Julia	L	0-1	
12/06/15	Cyprus (ECQ)	H	Andorra la Vella	L	1-3	Dossa Júnior (2og)

Appearances 2014/15

Coach: Koldo Alvarez	04/09/70		WAL	BEL	ISR	CYP	BIH	Egg	CYP	Caps	Goals
Ferran Pol	28/02/83	FC Andorra (ESP)	G	G	G	G	G	G46	G	17	-
Jordi Rubio	01/11/87	UE Santa Coloma	D	M61	D70	D73	s85	D67	D	25	-
Ildefons Lima	10/12/79	FC Santa Coloma	D	D	D40	D49	D		s67	92	9
Emili García	11/01/89	Pennoise (FRA)	D	D	D	D				28	1
David Maneiro	16/02/89	UE Santa Coloma	D	D	D					11	-
Marc Vales	04/04/90	Zaragoza (ESP)	M	M	M	M	D	D	D	39	-
Cristian Martínez	16/10/89	FC Santa Coloma	M83	M78	M	M	s54	M	M	32	1
Edu Peppe	28/01/83	FC Andorra (ESP)	M53		M83			M46	s79	19	-
Josep Manel Ayala	08/04/80	FC Andorra (ESP) /UE Santa Coloma	M86	M	s40	s46			M60	79	-
Iván Lorenzo	15/04/86	Mollerussa (ESP)	M	s61	M	M	M85	s46		24	-
Gabriel Riera	05/06/85	FC Santa Coloma	A	A72	A	A	s59			30	1
Márcio Vieira	10/10/84	Atlético Monzón (ESP)	s53	M	M	M46	M			59	-
Óscar Sonejee	26/03/76	Lusitans	s83				M	M58	s60	101	4
Juli Sánchez	20/06/78	FC Andorra (ESP)	s86							64	1
Moisés San Nicolás	17/09/93	Ordino		D			D	s67		12	-
Marc García	21/03/88	Rubí (ESP)		s72		D	D	D	D	24	-
Sergio Moreno	25/11/87	Gzira (MLT) /Jumilla (ESP)		s78				M	M67	52	-
Marc Pujol	21/08/82	FC Santa Coloma			s70	M				65	2
Juan Carlos Toscano	14/08/84	FC Santa Coloma			s83					22	-
Victor Rodríguez	07/09/87	UE Santa Coloma				s49	M	M74	M	8	-
Adrián Rodrigues	14/08/88	Salmantino (ESP) /Marino Luanco (ESP)				s73		D	D	12	-
Ludovic Clemente	09/05/86	FC Andorra (ESP)					M54			11	-
Sebastián Gómez	01/11/83	FC Andorra (ESP)					A59	A46		25	-
José Antonio Gomes	03/12/85	UE Santa Coloma						s46		33	-
Aaron Sánchez	05/06/96	Lleida Esportiu (ESP)						s46	A	2	-
Marc Rebés	03/07/94	FC Santa Coloma						s58	M79	2	-
Leonel Alves	28/09/93	FC Andorra (ESP)						s74		2	-

EUROPE

FC Santa Coloma

First qualifying round - FC Banants (ARM)
H 1-0 *Pujol (5)*
Casals, Wagner, A Ramos, Rebés (J Martínez 58), Lima, Pujol, C Martínez, Parra (Romero 81), Juvenal, Juanfer (Mercadé 63), R Ramos. Coach: Richard Imbernón (AND)
A 2-3 *Lima (20), Casals (90+4)*
Casals, Wagner (J Martínez 82), A Ramos, Rebés, Lima (Blanco 58), Pujol, C Martínez, Parra, Juvenal, Juanfer (Juan Toscano 67), R Ramos. Coach: Richard Imbernón (AND)

Second qualifying round - Maccabi Tel-Aviv FC (ISR)
H 0-1
Casals, A Ramos, Rebés, Pujol, J Martínez (Blanco 70), Mercadé (Romero 71), C Martínez, Parra, Juan Toscano (Juanfer 58) Juvenal, R Ramos. Coach: Richard Imbernón (AND)
A 0-2
Casals, A Ramos, Rebés, Pujol, J Martínez (Blanco 49), Mercadé, C Martínez, Parra, Juan Toscano (García 82), Juvenal, Juanfer (R Ramos 52). Coach: Richard Imbernón (AND)
Red card: Mercadé 80

UE Sant Julià

First qualifying round - FK Čukarički (SRB)
A 0-4
Coca, Estepa, Fontan (Puente 76), Ruiz, Soto, Pérez, Cabezas, Rodríguez, Fábio Serra, Spano, Varela. Coach: Raúl Cañete (ESP)
H 0-0
Coca (Rivas 84), Estepa, Fontan, Ruiz, Girau (Cabezas 74), Soto, Pérez (Barra 88), Rodríguez, Fábio Serra, Spano, Varela. Coach: Raúl Cañete (ESP)

UE Santa Coloma

First qualifying round - FK Metalurg Skopje (MKD)
H 0-3
Godswill, Jesús Rubio, Maneiro, Alex Martínez (Triquell 33), Roca, Anton (Salvat 64), Vall, Bernat, Crespo (Aloy 76), Jordi Rubio, V Rodríguez. Coach: Emiliano González (AND)
A 0-2
Godswill, Maneiro, Alex Martínez, Roca, Anton (Amat 63), Salvat (Vall 73), Bernat (Pereira 53), G Lopez, Crespo, Jordi Rubio, V Rodríguez. Coach: Emiliano González (AND)

DOMESTIC LEAGUE CLUB-BY-CLUB

Stadiums

Camp d'Esports d'Aixovall, Sant Julià (520)
Centre Esportiu d'Alàs, Alàs (480)
Estadi Comunal, Andorra la Vella (1,504)

FC Encamp

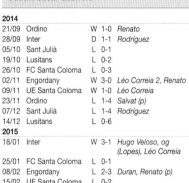

1950 • no website
Major honours
Andorran League (2) 1996, 2002
Coach: Oscar Guerrero

2014

Date	Opponent		Score	Scorers
21/09	Ordino	W	1-0	*Renato*
28/09	Inter	D	1-1	*Rodríguez*
05/10	Sant Julià	L	0-1	
19/10	Lusitans	L	0-2	
26/10	FC Santa Coloma	L	0-3	
02/11	Engordany	W	3-0	*Léo Correia 2, Renato*
09/11	UE Santa Coloma	W	1-0	*Léo Correia*
23/11	Ordino	L	1-4	*Salvat (p)*
07/12	Sant Julià	L	1-4	*Rodríguez*
14/12	Lusitans	L	0-6	

2015

Date	Opponent		Score	Scorers
18/01	Inter	W	3-1	*Hugo Veloso, og (Lopes), Léo Correia*
25/01	FC Santa Coloma	L	0-1	
08/02	Engordany	L	2-3	*Duran, Renato (p)*
15/02	UE Santa Coloma	L	0-2	
15/03	Inter	W	1-0	*Bueno*
22/03	Ordino	D	1-1	*Alves*
12/04	Engordany	W	3-0	*(w/o; original result 0-2)*
19/04	Inter	W	2-1	*Léo Correia 2*
26/04	Ordino	W	4-3	*Rodríguez, Renato 3*
03/05	Engordany	D	1-1	*og (Marques)*

No	Name	Nat	DoB	Pos	Aps	(s)	Gls
19	Helder Alves		25/01/94	D	11	(2)	1
15	Victor Bueno		23/07/94	M	14		1
16	Alex Calvo		20/02/98	A		(1)	
17	Ricardo Carvalho		02/07/91	A		(1)	
2	David De la Fuente	ESP	17/06/94	D		(2)	
17	Roberto Dos Santos		20/04/94	M	13	(2)	
9	Oscar Duran		14/05/87	A	8	(1)	1
10	Maurizio Falzone	ITA	27/01/76	M		(2)	
2	Max Ferré		05/06/92	M	1	(1)	
4	Genís Garcia		18/05/78	M	15	(2)	
19	Sergi Gómez		29/12/96	M		(2)	
11	Sandro Gutiérrez		02/01/96	M	15	(2)	
5	Hugo Veloso	POR	11/07/79	D	17	(2)	1
13	Marcos Lage		14/10/97	G	1	(2)	
20	Léo Correia	POR	10/07/83	A	15	(1)	6
12	Maicon	BRA	28/05/83	A		(2)	
3	Marcelo Monteiro	POR	27/05/94	D	5	(6)	
23	Fernando Meilan		06/08/82	D	8	(6)	
22	Paulo Bruno Monteiro		24/09/95	M	8	(1)	
14	Ferran Montobbio		10/03/94	A	3	(3)	
16	Xavier Moreno		03/12/90	D	14	(1)	
1	Israel Pérez-Serrano	ESP	08/02/75	G	19		
7	Renato	POR	19/03/80	M	17		6
13	David Ribolleda		13/02/85	D	9		
8	Xavier Rodríguez		28/04/92	M	18	(2)	3
12	Xavier Salvador	ESP	24/11/80	M		(1)	
10	Joaquim Salvat		18/12/80	A	4	(2)	1
15	Oscar San Segundo		19/11/96	A	1	(1)	
22	Alex Somoza		07/07/86	D	4	(4)	

UE Engordany

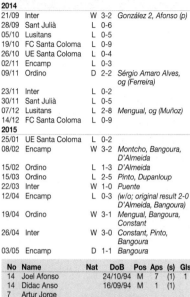

2001 • no website
Coach: Josep Mengual

2014
21/09	Inter	W 3-2	González 2, Afonso (p)
28/09	Sant Julià	L 0-6	
05/10	Lusitans	L 0-5	
19/10	FC Santa Coloma	L 0-9	
26/10	UE Santa Coloma	L 0-4	
02/11	Encamp	L 0-3	
09/11	Ordino	D 2-2	Sérgio Amaro Alves, og (Ferreira)
23/11	Inter	L 0-2	
30/11	Sant Julià	L 0-5	
07/12	Lusitans	L 2-8	Mengual, og (Muñoz)
14/12	FC Santa Coloma	L 0-9	

2015
25/01	UE Santa Coloma	L 0-2	
08/02	Encamp	W 3-2	Montcho, Bangoura, D'Almeida
15/02	Ordino	L 1-3	D'Almeida
15/03	Ordino	L 2-5	Pinto, Dupanloup
22/03	Inter	W 1-0	Puente
12/04	Encamp	L 0-3	(w/o; original result 2-0 D'Almeida, Bangoura)
19/04	Ordino	W 3-1	Mengual, Bangoura, Constant
26/04	Inter	W 3-0	Constant, Pinto, Bangoura
03/05	Encamp	D 1-1	Bangoura

No	Name	Nat	DoB	Pos	Aps	(s)	Gls
14	Joel Afonso		24/10/94	M	7	(1)	1
14	Didac Anso		16/09/94	M	1	(1)	
7	Artur Jorge Fernandes	POR	01/05/88	D	7		
20	Mamadou Bangoura	GUI	14/03/94	A	7		5
9	Jeremias Boquete	ESP	19/03/95	A	3		
15	Carlos Manuel Costa	POR	19/12/99	M	1	(1)	
9	Bruno Miguel Cerqueira		11/02/97	A	1		
7	Jean Luc Constant	FRA	06/02/96	D	2	(2)	2
11	Daniel Cortés		14/07/94	M	13	(2)	
10	Cédric D'Almeida	FRA	04/07/93	A	9		3
16	Mouhamadou Diop	SEN	15/06/94	D	2		
13	Ivan Donsion		28/02/95	G	6	(4)	
19	Laurent Dupanloup	FRA	13/06/96	D	7	(1)	1
9	Rainer Johan Ferrel	BOL	08/09/94	A	1	(2)	
8	Filipe Manuel Gonçalves	POR	21/07/98	M	1	(3)	
21	Cristian González		30/07/97	M	14	(2)	2
9	José Ricardo Guerra	PER	16/04/82	M	1		
6	Mario Herreros	ESP	14/09/85	M	4	(2)	
2	Almir David Ignacio	PER	19/11/85	D	3	(1)	
3	João Veloso	POR	04/07/75	D	1	(1)	
10	Joel Marques		17/03/95	A	7	(7)	
6	Alvaro Martins		03/11/98	M	1	(1)	
5	Carles Medina		21/12/95	D	11	(2)	
21	Brian Mengual		30/06/94	D	15		2
19	William Montcho	BEN	30/11/91	A	2	(1)	1
8	Carlos Otiniano	PER	05/12/80	D	3		
17	Luis Antonio Pajares	PER	14/10/91	M	5		
8	Víctor Pérez	MEX	12/11/90	M	7		
4	Jorge Pinto		15/05/94	M	13	(4)	2
6	Pedro Adan Puente	MEX	20/12/96	D	8	(1)	1
9	José María Ramírez	MEX	21/09/95	A	7		
18	Jorge Daniel Rivas		15/11/95	M	5	(2)	
16	Yael Servando Rivera	MEX	01/12/96	M	8		
17	Isidro Fabián Rodríguez	PER	27/02/85	M	7		
3	Sérgio Amaro Alves	POR	15/08/80	D	4	(5)	1
8	Tiago da Silva	POR	06/07/88	M		(1)	
1	Alberto Usubiaga		06/11/94	G	14		
24	Vítor Pereira	POR	23/12/82	D	12	(1)	

Inter Club d'Escaldes

1991 • no website
Coach: Carlos Sánchez (ESP)

2014
21/09	Engordany	L 2-3	Andrés, Da Silva
28/09	Encamp	D 1-1	Da Silva
05/10	Ordino	L 1-3	Lopes
19/10	UE Santa Coloma	L 0-3	
26/10	Sant Julià	L 0-3	
02/11	Lusitans	L 0-3	
09/11	FC Santa Coloma	L 0-9	
23/11	Engordany	W 2-0	Abdian, Andrés
07/12	Ordino	L 0-2	
14/12	UE Santa Coloma	L 0-3	

2015
18/01	Encamp	L 1-3	López
25/01	Sant Julià	L 0-8	
08/02	Lusitans	L 0-4	
15/02	FC Santa Coloma	L 0-7	
15/03	Encamp	L 0-1	
22/03	Engordany	L 0-1	
12/04	Ordino	L 0-2	
19/04	Encamp	L 1-2	Matos
26/04	Engordany	L 0-3	
03/05	Ordino	L 1-2	Martins

No	Name	Nat	DoB	Pos	Aps	(s)	Gls
12	Diego Abdian	ARG	02/11/82	M	8		1
2	Xavier Albarelhos		11/06/88	D	8	(3)	
6	Marc Andrés		13/03/89	M	12	(1)	2
13	Adrià Barcala		01/10/91	G	1	(1)	
16	Alexandre Barreiro		10/01/88	M	3	(1)	
18	Abdellah Bourezzaq	MAR	05/04/84	M	1	(2)	
7	Eric Buixó		07/02/89	M	5	(3)	
5	Oscar Da Cunha		18/12/78	D	12		
11	Helder Da Silva		05/08/92	M	14		2
8	Jacobo	ECU	25/03/88	A	17	(1)	
15	Iván Lage	ESP	06/08/96	M	4	(11)	
10	Joao Lopes		09/10/91	A	17	(1)	1
19	Manu López		26/11/91	A	4	(3)	1
3	André Marinho		26/03/93	D	16		
3	André Marinho		26/03/93	G	1		
9	José Antonio Martín	ESP	02/04/83	M	17		
17	Rafa Martins		07/11/91	A	20		1
12	Andreu Matos		01/12/95	A	5	(2)	1
14	Jose Carlos Medeiros		14/08/84	D	2	(3)	
20	Vicente Muñoz	ESP	02/06/81	D	16		
4	Jonathan Puente		13/12/86	M	12		
18	Pere Riba		06/05/80	A	4	(8)	
1	Josep Rivas		01/05/78	G	18		
14	Gilbert Sánchez		06/07/91	D		(1)	
7	Dinis Silva		30/03/95	A	3	(3)	

FC Lusitans

1999 • no website
Major honours
Andorran League (2) 2012, 2013
Coach: Vicenç Marqués (ESP)

2014
21/09	UE Santa Coloma	L 1-3	Luís dos Reis (p)
28/09	FC Santa Coloma	W 2-1	Aguilar 2 (1p)
05/10	Engordany	W 5-0	Pedro Reis 2, Pinto, Luís dos Reis 2
19/10	Encamp	W 2-0	Bruninho, Muñoz
26/10	Ordino	W 2-1	Muñoz, Bruninho
02/11	Inter	W 3-0	Luís dos Reis 3
09/11	Sant Julià	D 0-0	
23/11	UE Santa Coloma	L 1-2	Andorrà
30/11	FC Santa Coloma	L 1-5	Molina
07/12	Engordany	W 8-2	Bruninho 2 (1p), Pedro Reis, Aguilar 2, Pinto 2, Andorrà (p)
14/12	Encamp	W 6-0	Aguilar 2, Bruninho 2, Sonejee, Franclim Soares

2015
25/01	Ordino	W 7-1	Aguilar 2, Alfi 2, Bruninho, Rafael Brito, Franclim Soares
08/02	Inter	W 4-0	Aguilar 2 (1p), og (Muñoz), Bruninho
15/02	Sant Julià	W 3-2	Sonejee, Molina, Rafael Brito
15/03	Sant Julià	W 1-0	Bruninho
22/03	FC Santa Coloma	D 1-1	Sonejee
12/04	UE Santa Coloma	L 0-3	(w/o; original result 2-2 Alfi, Aguilar)
19/04	Sant Julià	D 1-1	Luís dos Reis
26/04	FC Santa Coloma	L 1-2	Rafael Brito
03/05	UE Santa Coloma	W 4-2	og (Anton), Alfi 2, Muñoz

No	Name	Nat	DoB	Pos	Aps	(s)	Gls
2	Carlos Acosta	ESP	15/08/89	M	14	(6)	
11	José Antonio Aguilar	ESP	11/10/89	A	16	(3)	11
7	Alfi	ESP	18/01/85	A	8		5
13	Xavier Andorrà		07/06/85	M	10	(1)	2
15	André Armada		04/03/97	A		(3)	
30	Andrés Benítez	PAR	01/01/83	G	6		
20	Bruninho	POR	11/01/86	A	20		9
7	Bruno da Silva	POR	31/12/82	M		(2)	
5	Duarte Pires	POR	07/05/89	D	2	(10)	
1	Ricard Fernández	ESP	26/05/75	G	5		
17	Joan Fonseca		08/10/97	M		(1)	
21	Franclim Soares	POR	16/05/82	D	7	(3)	2
24	Léo Maciel	POR	02/07/82	D	18	(1)	
10	Luís dos Reis	POR	22/03/81	A	10	(6)	7
23	Alberto Molina	ESP	21/04/88	M	18		2
15	Eduardo Moya	ESP	03/01/81	M	3		
3	Pedro Muñoz	ESP	09/01/88	D	20		3
30	Nuno Ribeiro	POR	30/09/84	G	9		
9	Pedro Reis	POR	08/02/85	A	10	(9)	3
8	Luis Pinto		05/03/87	M	9	(5)	3
6	Rafael Brito	POR	06/07/86	D	20		3
4	Óscar Sonejee		26/03/76	D	15	(2)	3

FC Ordino

2010 • futbolclubordino.com
**Coach: Víctor Torres Mestre (ESP);
(30/10/14) José Quereda (ESP)**

2014

21/09	Encamp	L	0-1	
28/09	UE Santa Coloma	L	0-1	
05/10	Inter	W	3-1	og (Muñoz), Jefferson, L San Nicolas
19/10	Sant Julià	W	3-0	(w/o; original result 0-2)
26/10	Lusitans	L	1-2	Da Silva
02/11	FC Santa Coloma	W	1-0	D Fatsini (p)
09/11	Engordany	D	2-2	D Fatsini (p), Jefferson
23/11	Encamp	W	4-1	Bertran 2, Marinho, Jefferson
30/11	UE Santa Coloma	D	1-1	J Fatsini
07/12	Inter	W	2-0	D Fatsini (p), Gomes
14/12	Sant Julià	L	1-2	Ribeiro

2015

25/01	Lusitans	L	1-7	Bertran
08/02	FC Santa Coloma	L	0-3	
15/02	Engordany	W	3-1	Pousa 2 (1p), Bertran
15/03	Engordany	W	5-2	Jefferson, Bertran 2, Pousa, Damià
22/03	Encamp	D	1-1	Pousa
12/04	Inter	W	2-0	Damià 2
19/04	Engordany	L	1-3	Pousa (p)
26/04	Encamp	L	3-4	Mejías, M San Nicolas, L San Nicolas
03/05	Inter	W	2-1	Jefferson, Bueno

No	Name	Nat	DoB	Pos	Aps	(s)	Gls
21	Aleix Guillem Angermair		04/03/97	M	1		
12	Guillem Aurenche		02/02/97	D		(1)	
16	Nilberthy Barbosa	ESP	14/01/91	A	2		
11	Marc Baró		31/12/96	M	1		
10	Sebastià Bertran		10/12/92	M	17	(1)	6
11	Nakor Bueno	ESP	04/03/78	A	4	(1)	1
17	Nuno Da Silva		26/01/92	A		(6)	1
18	Germán Damià	ESP	18/01/90	M	18		3
13	Hugo Do Paço		10/06/84	G	9		
23	Adel Durán	CUB	29/01/93	M	11	(6)	
11	Dani Fatsini	ESP	06/11/91	A	8	(3)	3
2	Joab Fatsini	ESP	24/07/90	D	10		1
5	Jonathan Ferreira		17/06/93	D	13	(1)	
22	Robert Flotats		11/11/97	M		(2)	
90	Joel Garcia		01/03/95	G	7	(1)	
7	Carlos Gomes		18/10/93	A	5	(6)	1
10	Rodrigo Guida		24/08/82	A	1	(3)	
22	Francisco Hernández	ESP	08/01/86	M	2	(1)	
1	Hugo Fernandes	POR	26/05/90	G	4		
19	Jefferson	BRA	06/02/95	A	10	(5)	5
8	Joel da Rocha	POR	10/06/97	M	1	(1)	
4	Diego Marinho		16/06/92	M	14	(2)	1
8	Daniel Mejías		28/06/82	M	5	(2)	1
21	Jaume Pereira		18/03/92	D	1	(1)	
6	Cristopher Pousa		29/06/92	M	11	(2)	5
3	Daniel Ribeiro		09/01/92	D	9	(3)	1
9	Luigi San Nicolas		28/06/92	A	15	(4)	2
14	Moisés San Nicolas		17/09/93	D	18		1
15	Cristian Sánchez		22/12/94	D	18		
21	Vítor Pinto	POR	07/10/82	M	5		
4	Jordi Xapell		01/06/98	D		(1)	

UE Sant Julià

1982 • no website
Major honours
Andorran League (2) 2005, 2009; Andorran Cup (5) 2008, 2010, 2011, 2014, 2015
Coach: Raúl Cañete (ESP)

2014

21/09	FC Santa Coloma	L	0-2	
28/09	Engordany	W	6-0	Varela (p), Castellano 2, Girau, Barra, Morlan
05/10	Encamp	W	1-0	Fábio Serra
19/10	Ordino	L	0-3	(w/o; original result 2-0 Morlan 2)
26/10	Inter	W	3-0	Girau, Fábio Serra, Vigo
02/11	UE Santa Coloma	W	1-0	Morlan
09/11	Lusitans	D	0-0	
23/11	FC Santa Coloma	D	2-2	Morlan, Spano
30/11	Engordany	W	5-0	Fábio Serra, Girau, Barra 2, Morlan
07/12	Encamp	W	4-1	Ruiz 2, Vigo, Girau
14/12	Ordino	W	2-1	Ruiz, Varela (p)

2015

25/01	Inter	W	8-0	Pérez, Blanco, Varela 2, Vigo, Spano, Gándara, Guida
08/02	UE Santa Coloma	D	1-1	Varela (p)
15/02	Lusitans	L	2-3	Varela (p), Gándara
15/03	Lusitans	L	0-1	
22/03	UE Santa Coloma	W	1-0	Gándara
12/04	FC Santa Coloma	D	2-2	Blanco, Ruiz
19/04	Lusitans	D	1-1	Pérez
26/04	UE Santa Coloma	L	1-3	Varela (p)
03/05	FC Santa Coloma	L	1-3	Gándara

No	Name	Nat	DoB	Pos	Aps	(s)	Gls
10	Jordi Barra		10/07/78	M	5	(5)	3
20	Luis Blanco		15/01/90	M	12	(2)	2
1	German Canal		21/10/83	G	1	(2)	
8	Alfonso Castellano	ESP	16/02/92	M	13	(1)	2
13	Jesús Coca	ESP	22/05/89	G	19		
17	Fábio Serra	POR	24/08/84	A	17		3
4	Yael Fontan	ESP	24/08/90	D	14	(1)	
9	Arturo Gándara	ESP	25/08/92	A	9		4
12	Iván Garcia		01/04/91	M	1		
7	Kiko Girau	ESP	03/06/85	M	20		4
3	Èric González		04/08/94	D	1	(2)	
21	Rodrigo Guida		24/08/82	A	1	(4)	1
18	Luís Carlos Moreira	POR	08/08/93	M		(2)	
9	Manuel Jesús Morlan	ESP	27/08/93	A	11		6
6	Christian Paredes	PER	16/04/87	D	1	(3)	
11	Carlos Pérez	ESP	14/03/89	A	9	(1)	2
14	Eric Rodríguez		02/04/93	D	18		
5	Miguel Ruiz	ESP	16/07/82	D	20		4
19	Mario Valentín Spano	ITA	07/02/86	M	11	(1)	2
23	Sebas Varela	URU	23/09/80	D	18		7
22	Iván Vigo	ESP	07/09/86	D	19		3

FC Santa Coloma

1986 • fclubsantacoloma.com
Major honours
Andorran League (9) 1995, 2001, 2003, 2004, 2008, 2010, 2011, 2014, 2015; Andorran Cup (8) 2001, 2003, 2004, 2005, 2006, 2007, 2009, 2012
Coach: Richard Imbernón

2014

21/09	Sant Julià	W	2-0	Rebés, C Martínez
28/09	Lusitans	L	1-2	C Martínez
05/10	UE Santa Coloma	L	0-1	
19/10	Engordany	W	9-0	Juanfer 3, Pujol, Mercadé 2, C Martínez 2, Riera
26/10	Encamp	W	3-0	Pujol, C Martínez 2
02/11	Ordino	L	0-1	
09/11	Inter	W	9-0	Lima, J Martínez, Pujol, Riera 2, C Martínez 2, Juanfer, Romero
23/11	Sant Julià	D	2-2	C Martínez, Pujol
30/11	Lusitans	W	5-1	Lima, J Toscano 2, Riera, C Martínez
07/12	UE Santa Coloma	W	2-0	C Martínez 2
14/12	Engordany	W	9-0	C Martínez 4 (1p), J Martínez, Riera 2, Sánchez, Silva

2015

25/01	Encamp	W	1-0	J Toscano
08/02	Ordino	W	3-0	C Martínez, J Martínez, Riera
15/02	Inter	W	7-0	Juanfer, J Martínez, A Ramos, C Martínez 3 (1p), Rebés
15/03	UE Santa Coloma	L	0-1	
22/03	Lusitans	D	1-1	Rebés
12/04	Sant Julià	D	2-2	og (Varela), Rebés
19/04	UE Santa Coloma	W	3-1	Riera, C Martínez 2
26/04	Lusitans	W	2-1	Riera 2
03/05	Sant Julià	W	3-1	Riera, Lima, J Toscano

No	Name	Nat	DoB	Pos	Aps	(s)	Gls
1	Eloy Casals	ESP	22/10/82	G	15		
18	Gabriel Fernandes		24/07/96	A		(1)	
3	Oriol Fité		02/02/89	D	8	(3)	
22	Txema Garcia		04/12/74	D	3	(4)	
23	Juanfer	ESP	05/05/83	A	17	(2)	5
14	Juvenal	EQG	03/04/79	M	16		
6	Ildefons Lima		10/12/79	D	12		3
16	Cristian Martínez		16/10/89	A	20		22
8	Joel Martínez		31/12/88	A	11	(7)	4
19	Andreu Matos		01/12/95	A		(4)	
11	Albert Mercadé	ESP	23/01/85	M	10	(5)	2
7	Marc Pujol		21/08/82	M	16		4
4	Andreu Ramos	ESP	19/01/89	D	15	(1)	1
24	Robert Ramos	ESP	11/12/92	D	16	(1)	
5	Marc Rebés		03/07/94	M	16		4
21	Gabriel Riera		05/06/85	A	12	(7)	11
20	Lucas Rodríguez	ESP	09/02/93	M	1	(3)	
9	Alejandro Romero	ARG	22/09/76	A	2	(8)	1
15	Adrià Sánchez		14/09/96	D	1	(4)	1
17	Dinis Silva		30/03/95	A		(2)	1
25	Francisco Toscano		05/02/83	G	5		
10	Juan Carlos Toscano		14/08/84	A	12	(3)	4
2	Walter Wagner	ARG	12/01/81	D	12		

 **ANDORRA**

UE Santa Coloma

1986 • uesantacoloma.com
Major honours
Andorran Cup (1) 2013
Coach: Emiliano González

2014

21/09	Lusitans	W	3-1	*Jordi Rubio, Crespo, Bernat*
28/09	Ordino	W	1-0	*Maneiro*
05/10	FC Santa Coloma	W	1-0	*V Rodríguez*
19/10	Inter	W	3-0	*Salomó, Bernat, Jesús Rubio (p)*
26/10	Engordany	W	4-0	*Vall 2, Bernat, Triquell (p)*
02/11	Sant Julià	L	0-1	
09/11	Encamp	L	0-1	
23/11	Lusitans	W	2-1	*V Rodríguez, Bernat*
30/11	Ordino	D	1-1	*V Rodríguez*
07/12	FC Santa Coloma	L	0-2	
14/12	Inter	W	3-0	*Jordi Rubio 2, V Rodríguez*

2015

25/01	Engordany	W	2-0	*Bernat, A Rodríguez*
08/02	Sant Julià	D	1-1	*Maneiro*
15/02	Encamp	W	2-0	*Crespo, V Rodríguez*
15/03	FC Santa Coloma	W	1-0	*Jordi Rubio*
22/03	Sant Julià	L	0-1	
12/04	Lusitans	W	3-0	*(w/o; original result 2-2 Jordi Rubio, V Rodríguez)*
19/04	FC Santa Coloma	L	1-3	*Jordi Rubio (p)*
26/04	Sant Julià	W	3-1	*Anton, Crespo, Salomó*
03/05	Lusitans	L	2-4	*Jordi Rubio 2 (2p)*

No	Name	Nat	DoB	Pos	Aps	(s)	Gls
4	Marc Amat		26/06/93	M	11	(8)	
9	Boris Anton		27/02/87	A	2	(1)	1
8	Josep Manel Ayala		08/04/80	M	7	(1)	
14	Víctor Bernat	ESP	17/05/87	A	17	(1)	5
15	Walid Bousenine		07/04/93	M	5	(2)	
22	Sergio Crespo		29/09/92	M	16	(3)	3
13	Friday Godswill	NGA	02/05/85	G	12		
1	Jose Antonio Gomes		03/12/85	G	7		
17	Manu López		26/11/91	A		(4)	
3	David Maneiro		16/02/89	D	17		2
5	Alex Martínez		04/03/87	D	14		
17	Alexandre Martínez		10/10/98	A		(3)	
19	Aitor Pereira		22/12/92	M	5	(5)	
1	Ivan Periánez		25/01/82	G	1		
7	Albert Ramírez		05/02/87	M		(4)	
8	Albert Ribera		10/10/89	M		(1)	
6	Alex Roca		04/07/91	D	14	(1)	
18	Albert Rodríguez		12/02/86	M	4	(6)	1
25	Victor Rodríguez		07/09/87	M	17		6
2	Jesús Rubio		09/09/94	D	16		1
23	Jordi Rubio		01/11/87	M	19	(1)	8
10	Juan Salomó		20/12/83	A	11	(9)	2
16	Enric Triquell		20/03/93	D	12	(3)	1
11	Josep Vall		21/05/91	A	13	(4)	2

Top goalscorers

22	Cristian Martínez (FC Santa Coloma)
11	José Antonio Aguilar (Lusitans)
	Gabriel Riera (FC Santa Coloma)
9	Bruninho (Lusitans)
8	Jordi Rubio (UE Santa Coloma)
7	Luís dos Reis (Lusitans)
	Sebas Varela (Sant Julià)
6	Léo Correia (Encamp)
	Renato (Encamp)
	Sebastià Bertran (Ordino)
	Manuel Jesús Morlan (Sant Julià)
	Victor Rodríguez (UE Santa Coloma)

Promoted club

Penya Encarnada d'Andorra

2009 • no website
Coach: Filipe António Busto (POR)

Second level final table 2014/15

		Pld	W	D	L	F	A	Pts
1	Penya Encarnada d'Andorra	10	8	2	0	52	16	26
2	Ranger's FC	10	8	1	1	28	11	25
3	Atlètic Club d'Escaldes	10	5	3	2	33	16	18
4	UE Santa Coloma B	10	5	2	3	42	24	17
5	FC Lusitans B	10	5	2	3	30	28	17
6	FS La Massana	10	4	3	3	33	20	15
7	FC Ordino B	10	4	1	5	25	26	13
8	UE Extremenya	10	3	3	4	15	18	12
9	FC Encamp B	10	2	3	5	17	25	9
10	UE Engordany B	10	1	0	9	11	59	3
11	CE Jenlai	10	0	0	10	5	48	0

NB After 10 rounds the top four clubs eligible for promotion enter the promotion play-offs

Promotion play-offs final table

		Pld	W	D	L	F	A	Pts
1	Penya Encarnada d'Andorra	16	13	2	1	70	23	41
2	Atlètic Club d'Escaldes	16	10	3	3	59	22	33
3	Ranger's FC	16	8	2	6	33	29	26
4	FS La Massana	16	5	4	7	41	44	19

Promotion/Relegation play-offs

(20/05/15 & 24/05/15)
Engordany 2-1 Atlètic
Atlètic 1-2 Engordany
(Engordany 4-2)

DOMESTIC CUP

Copa Constitució 2015

FIRST ROUND

(21/02/15)
UE Santa Coloma B 2-4 Ordino B

(22/02/15)
Lusitans B 0-9 FC Santa Coloma
Ranger's 0-10 Lusitans

(01/03/15)
Engordany 2-2 Encamp
Extremenya 0-5 Sant Julià
Inter 8-0 Encamp B
Ordino 11-0 Massana
Penya Encarnada 0-3 UE Santa Coloma
Replay
(05/03/15)
Engordany 0-1 Encamp

QUARTER-FINALS

(01/03/15)
FC Santa Coloma 14-0 Ordino B *(Riera 12, 27, 30p, 32, 38, 57, 64, Romero 14, Rebés 18, Flotats 25og, C Martínez 71, 89, Lima 73, 80)*

(03/03/15)
UE Santa Coloma 3-1 Inter *(V Rodríguez 37, Jordi Rubio 57, Salomó; Marinho 39)*

(04/03/15)
Lusitans 0-2 Ordino *(M San Nicolas 14, Bertran 62)*

(08/03/15)
Sant Julià 4-0 Encamp *(Girau 40, Gándara 77, 80, Guida 90)*

SEMI-FINALS

(08/03/15)
FC Santa Coloma 4-3 Ordino *(Juvenal 43, Juanfer 65, Rebés 66, Lima 78; M San Nicolas 23, Pousa 73p, Bertran 82)*

(11/03/15)
UE Santa Coloma 1-3 Sant Julià *(Bernat 38; Gándara 11, 80, Pérez 76)*

FINAL

(10/05/15)
Estadi Comunal, Andorra la Vella
UE SANT JULIÀ 1 *(Guida 104)*
FC SANTA COLOMA 1 *(Riera 100)*
(aet; 5-4 on pens)
Referee: González Salvado
SANT JULIÀ: *Coca, Ruiz, Rodríguez, Vigo, Varela, Girau, Castellano, Blanco, Gándara, Pérez, Fábio Serra (Guida 93)*
FC SANTA COLOMA: *Casals, Fité, A Ramos, Lima, Garcia (Juvenal 49), Rebés (J Toscano 83), Pujol, Mercadé, J Martínez (Juanfer 61), C Martínez, Riera*

ARMENIA
Hayastani Futboli Federacia (HFF)

Address	Khanjyan Street 27	**President**	Ruben Hayrapetyan
	AM-0010 Yerevan	**Vice-president**	Armen Minasyan
Tel	+374 10 568883	**Media officer**	Tigran Israelyan
Fax	+374 10 547173	**Year of formation**	1992
E-mail	media@ffa.am	**National stadium**	Hanrapetakan,
Website	ffa.am		Yerevan (14,400)

KEY:
● – UEFA Champions League
● – UEFA Europa League

Gyumri
Yerevan
Kapan

PREMIER LEAGUE CLUBS

 ① Alashkert FC

 ② FC Ararat

 ③ FC Banants

 ④ FC Gandzasar

 ⑤ FC Mika

 ⑥ FC Pyunik

 ⑦ FC Shirak

 ⑧ Ulisses FC

Double delight for Pyunik

Winners of the Armenian championship in the first ten years of the 21st century, FC Pyunik returned to power in 2014/15 with an exciting young team led by Armenia's record cap-holder Sargis Hovsepyan.

Ten points adrift of early front-runners Ulisses FC after ten games, Pyunik stormed back to overhaul them in the spring and eventually clinch the title ten days after winning the Armenian Cup for the third successive year. Their vanquished opponents were FC Mika, victorious in each of their previous six finals.

| Yerevan club overtake Ulisses to claim 14th title | Cup hat-trick ends Mika's flawless record in finals | Hovsepyan adds national team to Pyunik duties |

Domestic league

The new autumn-to-spring Armenian Premier League may have become a closed shop, with its eight participants free from relegation concerns, but it is nothing if not unpredictable. The 2014/15 final league table bore scant resemblance to the previous one, with only one team, FC Shirak, appearing in the top half of both. While champions FC Banants dropped down to sixth and FC Ararat from fourth to last, there was significant upward mobility for Pyunik and Ulisses, a mere sixth and seventh, respectively, in 2013/14.

Ulisses got off to an incredible start, winning 11 of their first 12 matches and drawing the other, but when they lost their next game, 3-0 at Mika, the wheels suddenly came off the wagon. Two further defeats followed, the second of them against Pyunik, who, with five successive victories, suddenly found themselves just one point behind the leaders at the winter break.

With free-scoring American striker Cesar Romero as their talisman, Pyunik's young side were a growing force, and they maintained their winning run on the resumption, finally grappling to the Premier League summit after the third fixture of the spring campaign. By now Ulisses' early form had completely deserted them, and although they beat Hovsepyan's side 2-1 at home, that was their only three-pointer over an eight-game stretch. Pyunik recovered to win their next three games – enough to elevate their points haul to a title-winning total with four matches remaining, the club's record-extending 14th championship triumph being mathematically sealed when Ulisses and Shirak both drew on 16 May.

Pyunik ended up with 61 points – 11 more than Banants had accumulated in winning the previous season's title. They also scored 58 goals, averaging over two per game. Despite losing 4-0 to Shirak on the final day, Ulisses edged their rivals into the runners-up spot, while there was a nice reward for Alashkert FC, the 2013/14 basement club, as they won their last two matches – while Mika lost theirs – to snatch the third UEFA Europa League spot.

Domestic cup

Mika would have taken that European place had they won the Armenian Cup final, but for the first time in their seven appearances they tasted defeat. Pyunik, beaten by Mika in 2006 but victorious in each of their four subsequent finals, including 2013 and 2014, duly completed the hat-trick with a 3-1 win, two goals from teenager Razmik Hakobyan and a third from Romero, all in the first half, securing a record eighth win for the Yerevan club.

Europe

Armenia suffered a whitewash in Europe, with Banants, Pyunik, Shirak and Mika all falling at the first hurdle. Banants' exit from the UEFA Champions League was the most painful as they went out to FC Santa Coloma after conceding an all-important last-gasp away goal that was scored by the Andorran champions' goalkeeper.

National team

Pyunik boss Hovsepyan, the only Armenian footballer to win a century of international caps (he ended his career in 2012 with 131), found himself committed to extra duties as the head coach of the national team when Bernard Challandes, the experienced Swiss hired to oversee the team's UEFA EURO 2016 qualifying campaign, left his post halfway through. With just one point from their first four qualifiers, Armenia's hopes of challenging for a place in France were looking increasingly forlorn.

The team put on a decent display in Hovsepyan's first game, at home to Portugal, but, as in three of the previous four matches, they took the lead – with a magnificent long-range free-kick from Marcos Pizzelli – only to end up once again defeated, albeit by the great Cristiano Ronaldo, who scored a hat-trick.

DOMESTIC SEASON AT A GLANCE

Premier League 2014/15 final table

		Pld	Home					Away					Total					Pts
			W	D	L	F	A	W	D	L	F	A	W	D	L	F	A	
1	**FC Pyunik**	**28**	**11**	**1**	**2**	**35**	**12**	**8**	**3**	**3**	**23**	**14**	**19**	**4**	**5**	**58**	**26**	**61**
2	Ulisses FC	28	8	3	3	27	15	7	2	5	16	17	15	5	8	43	32	50
3	FC Shirak	28	8	3	3	21	11	6	4	4	30	21	14	7	7	51	32	49
4	Alashkert FC	28	7	3	4	16	12	3	5	6	16	23	10	8	10	32	35	38
5	FC Mika	28	5	8	1	23	13	4	2	8	10	21	9	10	9	33	34	37
6	FC Banants	28	6	3	5	24	20	2	5	7	18	26	8	8	12	42	46	32
7	FC Gandzasar	28	5	4	5	17	19	2	4	8	14	25	7	8	13	31	44	29
8	FC Ararat	28	2	2	10	18	35	1	2	11	10	34	3	4	21	28	69	13

European qualification 2015/16

Champion/Cup winner: FC Pyunik (first qualifying round)

Ulisses FC (first qualifying round)
FC Shirak (first qualifying round)
Alashkert FC (first qualifying round)

Top scorer	Cesar Romero (Pyunik) & Jean-Jacques Bougouhi (Shirak), 21 goals
Relegated clubs	none
Promoted clubs	none
Cup final	FC Pyunik 3-1 FC Mika

Team of the season
(4-4-2)

Coach: Hovsepyan (Pyunik)

Elazyan (Shirak)

Minasyan (Alashkert) · Morozov (Ulisses) · Haroyan (Pyunik) · Hanzel (Banants)

Satumyan (Mika) · Aleksanyan (Ulisses) · Hakobyan (Shirak) · Badoyan (Pyunik)

Romero (Pyunik) · Bougouhi (Shirak)

Player of the season

Cesar Romero
(FC Pyunik)

Plucked from obscurity to lead the Pyunik attack in 2014/15, the San Diego-born former Chivas USA striker did not take long to make himself at home on the other side of the world. The goals flowed almost from day one, with 17 scored in the league before Christmas and 21 in total as he shared the golden boot with FC Shirak's Ivorian hit man Jean-Jacques Bougouhi. The 25-year-old also scored five goals in the Armenian Cup, including one in the final, as Pyunik scooped the domestic double.

Newcomer of the season

Razmik Hakobyan
(FC Pyunik)

Used sparingly in the first half of the season, Hakobyan gradually gained the trust of Pyunik boss Sargis Hovsepyan and was a first-XI regular by the time his side had begun their spring surge to the Armenian Premier League title. A confident dribbler with the strength to hold off defenders, the 19-year-old also proved his worth in front of goal, scoring five times in the league and twice more in the cup final to help Pyunik complete a successful defence of the trophy with a 3-1 win against FC Mika.

ARMENIA

NATIONAL TEAM

Top five all-time caps
Sargis Hovsepyan (131); **Roman Berezovski** (93); **Robert Arzumanyan** (71); Artur Petrosyan (69); Harutyun Vardanyan (63)

Top five all-time goals
Henrikh Mkhitaryan (16); Artur Petrosyan (11); **Gevorg Ghazaryan** & **Yura Movsisyan** (9); **Edgar Manucharyan** & **Marcos Pizzelli** (8)

Results 2014/15

03/09/14	Latvia	A	Riga	L	0-2	
07/09/14	Denmark (ECQ)	A	Copenhagen	L	1-2	*Mkhitaryan (50)*
11/10/14	Serbia (ECQ)	H	Yerevan	D	1-1	*Arzumanyan (73)*
14/10/14	France	H	Yerevan	L	0-3	
14/11/14	Portugal (ECQ)	A	Faro	L	0-1	
29/03/15	Albania (ECQ)	A	Elbasan	L	1-2	*Mavraj (4og)*
13/06/15	Portugal (ECQ)	H	Yerevan	L	2-3	*Pizzelli (14), Mkoyan (72)*

Appearances 2014/15

Coach: Bernard Challandes (SUI) /(28/04/15) Sargis Hovsepyan	26/07/51 02/11/72		Lva	DEN	SRB	Fra	POR	ALB	POR	Caps	Goals
Roman Berezovski	05/08/74	Dinamo Moskva (RUS)	G	G	G	G61	G	G	G	93	-
Kamo Hovhannisyan	05/10/92	Pyunik	D	D	D	D	D	s67	M61	22	-
Varazdat Haroyan	24/08/92	Pyunik	D	D	D	D	D			16	-
Hrayr Mkoyan	02/09/86	Esteghlal (IRN)	D	D					D	33	1
Taron Voskanyan	22/02/93	Pyunik	D68	s66	D	D	D			12	-
Levon Hayrapetyan	17/04/89	Příbram (CZE) /Pyunik	D71	D	D	D	D	D	D	29	1
Artur Yedigaryan	26/06/87	Kairat (KAZ) /Dinamo Minsk (BLR)	M76	M	M	M58	M77	M84		42	-
Rumyan Hovsepyan	13/11/91	Metalurh Donetsk (UKR)	M81	M	s52	s69			s29	8	1
Gevorg Ghazaryan	05/04/88	Olympiacos (GRE) /Kerkyra (GRE)	M84	M		M62		M	M	45	9
Henrikh Mkhitaryan	21/01/89	Dortmund (GER)	M	M71			M	M	M	52	16
Edgar Manucharyan	19/01/87	Ural (RUS)	A63	A84	A66		s62	A67		47	8
Zaven Badoyan	22/12/89	Gomel (BLR)	s63							5	-
Artur Sarkisov	19/01/87	Volga (RUS)	s68		A	M65	s77		A72	30	4
Hovhannes Hambardzumyan	04/10/90	Vardar (MKD)	s71			s65		D 70*		10	-
Karlen Mkrtchyan	25/11/88	Metalurh Donetsk (UKR) /Pyunik	s76		M52	M90		M84	M29	41	2
Marcos Pizzelli	03/10/84	Aktobe (KAZ)	s81	s71	M84	M82	s84	M	M	42	8
Norayr Aslanyan	25/03/91	Almere (NED)	s84			s90				7	-
Robert Arzumanyan	24/07/85	Aktobe (KAZ) /Amkar (RUS)		D66	D	D	D	D	D	71	5
Artak Dashyan	20/11/89	Vardar (MKD)		s84	s66	s58				7	-
Alexander Karapetyan	23/12/87	Dudelange (LUX)			s84	s82				2	-
Artem Simonyan	20/02/95	Zenit (RUS)				A69				1	-
Gevorg Kasparov	25/07/80	Mika				s61				25	-
Yura Movsisyan	02/08/87	Spartak Moskva (RUS)					A	A		31	9
Gael Andonyan	07/02/95	Marseille (FRA)						D	D	2	-
Ruslan Koryan	15/06/88	Lokomotiv Tashkent (UZB)						s84	s72	2	-
Aras Özbiliz	09/03/90	Spartak Moskva (RUS)							s61	18	4

EUROPE

DOMESTIC LEAGUE CLUB-BY-CLUB

FC Banants

CHAMPIONS LEAGUE

First qualifying round - FC Santa Coloma (AND)
A 0-1
Toroyan, Daghbashyan, Shakhnazaryan, Arakelyan, Loretsyan, Karapetyan (Muradyan 78), Azatyan (Poghosyan 59), Hovsepyan, Nranyan, Usanov (Ayvazyan 73), Fofana. Coach: Zsolt Hornyák (SVK)
H 3-2 *Hovsepyan (29, 56p), Mashumyan (47)*
Toroyan, Daghbashyan, Arakelyan, Loretsyan, Poghosyan, Azatyan (Mashumyan 46), Hovsepyan, Nranyan, Ayvazyan, Usanov (Karapetyan 25; Muradyan 90), Fofana. Coach: Zsolt Hornyák (SVK)
Red card: Nranyan 68

FC Pyunik

EUROPA LEAGUE

First qualifying round - FC Astana (KAZ)
H 1-4 *Papikyan (68)*
Harutyunyan, Haroyan (Ghukas Poghosyan 74), G Hovhannisyan, K Hovhannisyan, Gagik Poghosyan, Malakyan, Yusbashyan, Papikyan (Aslanyan 72), Minasyan, Razmik Hakobyan (Baloyan 60), T Voskanyan. Coach: Sargis Hovsepyan (ARM)
A 0-2
Ohanyan, Haroyan, G Hovhannisyan, K Hovhannisyan, Gagik Poghosyan (Aslanyan 46), Malakyan, Yusbashyan, Papikyan, Minasyan, Razmik Hakobyan (Ghukas Poghosyan 64), T Voskanyan. Coach: Sargis Hovsepyan (ARM)

FC Shirak

SHIRAK FC 1958

EUROPA LEAGUE

First qualifying round - FC Shakhter Karagandy (KAZ)
H 1-2 *Deblé (85p)*
Beglaryan, Davtyan, Deblé, Hakobyan (A Muradyan 78), Kpodo, Aleksanyan, Marikyan, K Muradyan, Ly (Diarrassouba 67), Hovhannisyan, Diop (Barikyan 46). Coach: Vardan Bichakhchyan (ARM)
A 0-4
Ermakov, Deblé, Bougouhi (Davtyan 46), Hakobyan, Kpodo, Aleksanyan, Marikyan (Darbinyan 53), K Muradyan, Ly (Barikyan 46), Hovhannisyan, Diop. Coach: Vardan Bichakhchyan (ARM)

FC Mika

EUROPA LEAGUE

First qualifying round - RNK Split (CRO)
A 0-2
Kasparov, Petrosyan, A Voskanyan, Karapetyan, Satumyan, Arakelyan (D Grigoryan 67), Barseghyan, Gevorg Poghosyan (Gor Poghosyan 22), Movsisyan, Beglaryan (H Voskanyan 83), Alex. Coach: Aram Voskanyan (ARM)
H 1-1 *Karapetyan (45+1)*
Kasparov, Petrosyan, A Voskanyan, Gor Poghosyan, Karapetyan, D Grigoryan (Ghazaryan 55), Satumyan, Barseghyan, Movsisyan (Hakobyan 77), H Voskanyan (Beglaryan 61), Alex. Coach: Aram Voskanyan (ARM)

Alashkert FC

2012 • Nairi (2,500) • fcalashkert.am
Coach: Armen Gyulbudaghyants;
(28/08/14) Abraham Khashmanyan

2014

Date		Opponent	Result	Scorers
03/08	h	Ararat	W 3-2	Arakelyan, Norayr Gyozalyan, Balabekyan
09/08	a	Mika	D 0-0	
16/08	h	Pyunik	L 0-2	
24/08	a	Gandzasar	L 0-1	
31/08	h	Ulisses	L 0-1	
13/09	h	Shirak	W 2-0	E Malakyan, Davtyan
20/09	a	Banants	L 0-1	
28/09	a	Ararat	L 1-2	Norayr Gyozalyan
05/10	h	Mika	W 2-0	Norayr Gyozalyan, Bareghamyan
18/10	a	Pyunik	D 3-3	Hovsepyan, Manasyan 2
26/10	h	Gandzasar	W 1-0	Balabekyan
01/11	a	Ulisses	L 1-5	Manasyan
09/11	a	Shirak	D 1-1	E Malakyan
22/11	h	Banants	D 0-0	
30/11	h	Ararat	D 1-1	Manasyan
2015				
01/03	a	Mika	D 1-1	Norayr Gyozalyan
07/03	h	Pyunik	L 0-1	
15/03	a	Gandzasar	W 3-2	Manasyan 2, A Hovhannisyan
22/03	h	Ulisses	W 1-0	Bareghamyan
05/04	h	Shirak	D 1-1	Bareghamyan
11/04	a	Banants	L 0-2	
19/04	a	Ararat	W 1-0	Mladenović
26/04	h	Mika	L 1-2	Manasyan
02/05	h	Pyunik	L 1-3	Norayr Gyozalyan
10/05	h	Gandzasar	W 1-0	Bareghamyan (p)
16/05	a	Ulisses	D 2-2	Vučić, Norayr Gyozalyan
24/05	a	Shirak	W 2-0	Minasyan, Manasyan
30/05	h	Banants	W 3-1	Manasyan, Balabekyan, Norayr Gyozalyan

No	Name	Nat	DoB	Pos	Aps	(s)	Gls
16	Artak Andrikyan		24/01/88	D		(1)	
6	Ararat Arakelyan		01/02/84	D	17	(2)	1
21	Arsen Balabekyan		24/11/86	A	19	(3)	3
14	Aram Bareghamyan		01/06/88	M	24	(3)	4
15	Edgar Barseghyan		19/08/97	M		(2)	
10	Narek Davtyan		24/08/88	M	12	(8)	1
25	Mamadou Sekou Fofana	MLI	26/09/89	D	11		
1	Stepan Ghazaryan		11/01/85	G	18		
18	Stanislav Gnedko	BLR	07/01/87	M	8	(3)	
20	Hovhannes Grigoryan		09/03/85	D	7		
2	Vardan Grigoryan	RUS	21/09/85	D		(1)	
8	Narek Gyozalyan		10/07/92	M	5	(5)	
22	Norayr Gyozalyan		15/03/90	A	17	(8)	7
3	Tigran Hakhnazaryan		18/04/87	D	10	(2)	
4	Aghvan Hayrapetyan		19/06/87	M	3		
16	Arman Hovhannisyan		07/07/93	D	19	(1)	1
24	Benik Hovhannisyan		01/05/93	M		(2)	
15	Aram Hovsepyan		06/06/91	M	14	(8)	1
18	Hayk Ishkhanyan		24/06/89	D	2	(2)	
55	Armen Khachatryan		25/09/84	G	10	(2)	
23	Edgar Malakyan		22/09/90	M	3	(3)	2
11	Gor Malakyan		12/06/94	M	9	(1)	
7	Mihran Manasyan		13/06/89	A	18	(3)	9
19	Vahagn Minasyan		25/04/85	D	20	(2)	1
13	Dušan Mladenović	SRB	13/10/90	M	22		1
19	Karen Muradyan		01/11/92	M	8	(1)	
9	Sargis Nasibyan		07/07/90	A		(1)	
23	Goran Obradović	SRB	25/12/86	D	4		
17	Gevorg Ohanyan		29/07/92	M		(1)	
24	Vardan Petrosyan		27/07/82	A		(1)	
5	Norayr Sahakyan		09/07/87	M	6	(4)	
6	Sergei Usenya	BLR	04/03/88	D	13		
4	Dylan Van Welkenhuysen	BEL	20/01/92	A	3	(1)	
20	Darko Vučić	MNE	23/08/91	M	4	(5)	1
3	Vachik Yeghiazaryan		08/11/92	D	2	(20)	

FC Ararat

1935 • Hrazdan (45,000) • fcararat.am

Major honours
USSR League (1) 1973; Armenian League (1) 1993;
USSR Cup (2) 1973, 1975; Armenian Cup (5) 1993,
1994, 1995, 1997, 2008

Coach: Dušan Mijić (SRB);
(27/09/14) (Samvel Darbinyan);
(01/12/14) Suren Chakhalyan;
(18/04/15) (Samvel Darbinyan);
(28/04/15) Varuzhan Sukiasyan

2014
03/08	a	Alashkert	L	2-3	Di Lauro, Rakić
09/08	h	Shirak	L	0-2	
17/08	a	Banants	L	0-3	
23/08	a	Ulisses	L	0-2	
30/08	h	Mika	W	2-0	De la Fuente, Rakić
13/09	a	Pyunik	L	0-4	
21/09	h	Gandzasar	L	1-5	De la Fuente
28/09	a	Alashkert	W	2-1	Rakić 2
04/10	a	Shirak	L	2-3	Di Lauro, Tomčić
19/10	h	Banants	L	4-6	Wallace, Rakić 2, Tomčić
25/10	h	Ulisses	L	2-3	Di Lauro 2
02/11	a	Mika	L	1-3	Rakić
08/11	h	Pyunik	L	0-3	
23/11	a	Gandzasar	L	0-1	
30/11	h	Alashkert	D	1-1	Sahakyan

2015
01/03	h	Shirak	L	2-4	Azatyan, Rakić
08/03	a	Banants	L	1-3	Rakić
14/03	a	Ulisses	D	0-0	
22/03	h	Mika	L	0-1	
04/04	a	Pyunik	L	0-4	
12/04	h	Gandzasar	L	0-2	
19/04	a	Alashkert	L	0-1	
25/04	a	Shirak	L	0-4	
03/05	h	Banants	D	2-2	Kaina, De la Fuente
09/05	h	Ulisses	L	1-3	Rakić
17/05	a	Mika	L	0-3	
23/05	h	Pyunik	D	2-2	Orozco 2
30/05	a	Gandzasar	W	3-0	Chueca 2, De la Fuente

No	Name	Nat	DoB	Pos	Aps	(s)	Gls
31	Sergey Amroyan		20/04/93	A		(1)	
10	Areg Azatyan		29/06/90	A	5	(5)	1
3	Nagui Bouras	FRA	13/12/92	M	6		
20	Zaven Bulut	FRA	05/04/92	M	14	(1)	
23	Carlo Chueca	PER	23/03/93	M	3	(7)	2
11	Bryan de la Fuente	MEX	01/07/92	M	21	(1)	4
26	Armen Derdzyan		17/11/93	M	1	(1)	
9	Robin Di Lauro	FRA	19/12/88	A	8	(3)	4
15	Armen Dorunts		01/11/90	D	9	(2)	
21	Victor Garza	USA	25/02/92	A	5	(1)	
21	David Ghandilyan		04/07/93	M	4	(4)	
3	Avetis Ghazaryan		02/08/90	D	10	(1)	
8	Davit Grigoryan		12/09/87	D	15	(7)	
24	Samvel Hakobyan		11/09/93	A		(1)	
1	Aram Hayrapetyan		22/11/86	G	9		
17	Arsen Hovhannisyan		12/05/89	D		(1)	
22	Roman Hovhannisyan		28/08/91	A	1	(1)	
22	Karen Israyelyan		26/03/93	G	4		
30	Oumarou Kaina	CMR	16/10/96	A	7	(2)	1
17	Raffi Kaya	FRA	08/06/94	M	9	(1)	
16	Gorik Khachatryan		16/06/88	M	13		
2	Karen Khachatryan		10/06/85	A	3	(5)	
52	Christian King	BRB	04/10/87	M	9	(4)	
4	Souleymane Koné	CIV	05/01/92	D	8	(1)	
17	Zdravko Kovačević	SRB	06/08/84	M	9	(1)	
1	Gor Martirosyan		04/04/93	G	8		
2	Vahe Martirosyan		19/01/88	A	5	(2)	
19	Armen Meliksetyan		21/07/95	A	4		
27	Tigran Melikyan		26/07/93	D	1		
88	Levon Minasyan		18/10/90	D	3		
14	Arayik Mkrtchyan		08/07/93	A	4	(5)	
5	Gor Mkrtumyan		24/05/92	M	2	(2)	
18	Darryl Odom	USA	23/09/87	M	2	(6)	
19	Moisés Orozco	USA	06/02/92	M	13	(3)	2
25	Ararat Poghosyan		11/09/93	M	4	(2)	
23	Nikola Prebiračević	SRB	23/01/87	D	10		
5	Nikolas Proesmans	BEL	11/05/92	M	11		
7	Aleksandar Rakić	SRB	17/01/87	A	26		10
21	Mher Sahakyan		01/01/93	M	8	(5)	1
4	Čedomir Tomčić	SRB	20/04/87	D	11	(3)	2
18	Olexandr Volchkov	UKR	18/07/85	D	11		
6	Jamel Wallace	USA	12/08/87	D	12		1

FC Banants

1992 • Banants (3,500) • fcbanants.am

Major honours
Armenian League (1) 2014; Armenian Cup (2) 1992, 2007
Coach: Zsolt Hornyák (SVK)

2014
10/08	a	Ulisses	L	0-1	
17/08	h	Ararat	W	3-0	Hovsepyan (p), Nranyan 2
23/08	a	Mika	D	1-1	Nranyan
27/08	a	Shirak	L	0-2	
14/09	a	Gandzasar	L	1-3	Karapetyan
20/09	h	Alashkert	W	1-0	Serečin
28/09	h	Shirak	D	1-1	Ayvazyan
04/10	h	Ulisses	L	0-2	
19/10	a	Ararat	W	6-4	Hanzel 2, Daghbashyan, Ayvazyan, Poghosyan, Nranyan
25/10	h	Mika	L	0-2	
02/11	a	Pyunik	L	0-1	
09/11	h	Gandzasar	D	3-3	og (A Khachatryan), Ayvazyan, Hanzel
18/11	h	Pyunik	L	2-3	Harutyunyan, Nranyan
22/11	a	Alashkert	D	0-0	
30/11	h	Shirak	D	2-2	og (Marikyan), Karapetyan

2015
01/03	a	Ulisses	L	1-2	Nranyan
08/03	h	Ararat	W	3-1	Bagi, López, og (Volchkov)
14/03	a	Mika	D	2-2	Grigoryan, Hanzel
22/03	h	Pyunik	L	1-2	Timov
05/04	a	Gandzasar	L	0-2	
11/04	h	Alashkert	W	2-0	López 2 (1p)
19/04	h	Shirak	L	3-6	Avetisyan, López, og (Hovhannisyan)
25/04	a	Ulisses	W	3-0	Minasyan, Poghosyan 2
03/05	a	Ararat	D	2-2	Shakhnazaryan, Poghosyan
09/05	h	Mika	D	0-0	
17/05	a	Pyunik	W	2-1	López, Nranyan
24/05	h	Gandzasar	W	2-0	Ayvazyan, López (p)
30/05	a	Alashkert	L	1-3	Hanzel

No	Name	Nat	DoB	Pos	Aps	(s)	Gls
5	Artashes Arakelyan		10/06/89	D	10		
11	Petros Avetisyan		07/01/96	M	6	(7)	1
18	Vahagn Ayvazyan		16/04/92	M	13	(8)	4
10	Areg Azatyan		23/06/90	A	4	(7)	
9	Tomáš Bagi	SVK	09/06/91	A	11		1
9	Sargis Baloyan		24/08/92	A	8	(3)	
3	Gagik Daghbashyan		19/10/90	D	14		1
25	Mamadou Sekou Fofana	MLI	26/09/89	D	4		
17	Norayr Grigoryan		07/01/83	M	21	(2)	1
24	Hakob Hakobyan		29/03/97	D		(1)	
19	Hovhannes Hambartsumyan		04/10/90	D	1	(5)	
14	Orbeli Hambartsumyan		26/03/96	A	1		
2	Ľuboš Hanzel	SVK	07/05/87	D	25		5
20	Karen Harutyunyan		05/08/86	M	17		1
71	Aram Hayrapetyan	RUS	22/11/86	G	8		
7	Rumyan Hovsepyan		13/11/91	M	2		1
16	Hovhannes Ilangyozyan		14/01/97	M	1	(1)	
12	Gevorg Karapetyan		10/06/90	A	9	(3)	2
15	Miguel López	ARG	09/06/88	M	11	(1)	6
7	Aram Loretsyan		07/03/93	M	20	(5)	
16	Gagik Maghakyan		07/02/96	M	1	(2)	
2	Armen Manucharyan		25/01/96	D	8	(1)	
17	Zhirayr Margaryan		13/09/97	D		(3)	
22	Garegin Mashumyan		01/09/94	A		(7)	
39	Nairi Minasyan		26/08/95	M	17	(5)	1
12	Gevorg Minasyan		09/03/86	A	21	(2)	7
14	Hovhannes Panosyan		25/03/97	A	5		
18	Narek Petrosyan		25/01/96	D	1	(3)	
22	Nika Piliev	RUS	21/03/91	M	3	(4)	
8	Valter Poghosyan		16/05/92	M	15	(6)	4
17	Hovhannes Sarafyan		03/01/94	M		(1)	
19	Filip Serečin	SVK	04/10/93	A	1	(4)	1
4	Aram Shakhnazaryan		21/04/94	D	21	(2)	1
13	Papin Tevosyan		22/03/92	G		(1)	
24	Filip Timov	MKD	22/05/92	M	9	(3)	1
1	Artur Toroyan		01/02/92	G	20		
23	Emil Yeghiazaryan		03/11/97	M		(6)	

FC Gandzasar

2002 • Lernagorts (3,500) • no website
Coach: Serhiy Puchkov (UKR);
(15/03/15) Ashot Barseghyan

2014
02/08	h	Mika	W	2-1	G Harutyunyan, H Avagyan
10/08	a	Pyunik	L	0-2	
16/08	h	Ulisses	D	0-0	
24/08	h	Alashkert	W	1-0	Melkonyan (p)
14/09	h	Banants	W	3-1	Melkonyan, Palagnyuk, H Avagyan
21/09	a	Ararat	W	5-1	Palagnyuk 2, Daudov 2, Melkonyan
27/09	a	Mika	D	1-1	Orlovskiy
05/10	h	Pyunik	L	3-4	Daudov, Palagnyuk, H Avagyan
18/10	a	Ulisses	L	1-7	Palagnyuk
26/10	a	Alashkert	L	0-1	
01/11	h	Shirak	L	0-3	
09/11	a	Banants	D	3-3	G Harutyunyan, A Grigoryan, Veranyan
18/11	a	Shirak	L	0-1	
23/11	h	Ararat	W	1-0	Palagnyuk
29/11	h	Mika	D	0-0	

2015
15/03	h	Alashkert	L	2-3	G Harutyunyan, Beglaryan
21/03	h	Shirak	L	0-2	
05/04	h	Banants	W	2-0	Beglaryan, G Harutyunyan
12/04	a	Ararat	W	2-0	G Harutyunyan 2
18/04	a	Mika	D	1-1	Alexander Petrosyan
26/04	h	Pyunik	L	0-1	
29/04	h	Ulisses	D	0-0	
02/05	a	Ulisses	D	0-0	
10/05	a	Alashkert	L	0-1	
16/05	h	Shirak	D	3-3	Beglaryan 2, A Khachatryan (p)
20/05	a	Pyunik	L	1-3	H Avagyan
24/05	a	Banants	L	0-2	
30/05	h	Ararat	L	0-3	

No	Name	Nat	DoB	Pos	Aps	(s)	Gls
61	José Alpuche	MEX	25/11/87	M	1	(3)	
5	Artur Avagyan		04/07/87	M	11	(1)	
11	Hayrapet Avagyan		08/05/89	A	3	(16)	4
3	Artur Barseghyan		16/11/86	M	6	(7)	
15	Narek Beglaryan		01/09/85	A	12		4
10	Marat Daudov	UKR	03/08/89	M	14		3
4	Armen Durunts		01/11/90	D	12	(1)	
16	Rafik Galstyan		01/01/97	M		(2)	
9	Aleksandr Golubev	RUS	27/02/86	A	2	(1)	
33	Artak Grigoryan		19/10/87	A	12	(2)	1
27	Vruyr Grigoryan		06/07/92	D	4	(7)	
29	Gustavo	BRA	30/04/93	M		(1)	
17	Alen Hambartsumyan		01/03/92	D	22		
9	Gegham Harutyunyan		23/08/90	D	26	(1)	6
19	Mher Harutyunyan		16/09/92	A		(10)	
21	Hayk Ishkhanyan		24/07/89	D	11		
2	Tigran Ivanyan		02/09/94	D	1		
16	Ara Khachatryan		21/10/81	M	27		1
26	Vardan Khachatryan		16/09/96	D		(1)	
1	Grigor Meliksetyan		18/08/86	G	9		
6	Samvel Melkonyan		15/03/84	M	25		3
22	Anton Monakhov	UKR	31/01/82	D	8		
3	Borys Orlovskiy	UKR	16/01/93	M	7	(2)	1
16	Vasyl Palagnyuk	UKR	07/03/91	A	11		6
15	Alexander Petrosyan		28/05/86	D	22		1
2	Arsen Petrosyan		18/09/92	G	11		
5	Olexiy Pinchuk	UKR	17/02/92	M	7	(2)	
89	Gevorg Prazyan		24/07/89	G	8		
18	Artem Proshenko	UKR	01/06/90	M	4	(6)	
25	Arkadi Safaryan		06/09/98	M		(1)	
27	Sergey Tumasyan	RUS	31/01/90	M		(3)	
24	Khoren Veranyan		04/09/86	M	27		1
14	Dejan Vukomanović	BIH	31/12/90	M	5	(3)	
3	Artashes Zakaryan		29/11/87	D	1	(3)	

FC Mika

1997 • Mika stadium (7,000) • no website
Major honours
Armenian Cup (6) 2000, 2001, 2003, 2005, 2006, 2011
Coach: Aram Voskanyan

2014

02/08	a	Gandzasar	L	1-2	Satumyan
09/08	h	Alashkert	D	0-0	
17/08	a	Shirak	L	0-1	
23/08	h	Banants	D	1-1	Beglaryan
30/08	a	Ararat	L	0-2	
13/09	a	Ulisses	L	1-3	H Voskanyan
21/09	h	Pyunik	D	1-1	og (T Voskanyan)
27/09	h	Gandzasar	D	1-1	og (Monakhov)
05/10	a	Alashkert	L	0-2	
19/10	h	Shirak	W	3-1	A Voskanyan, D Grigoryan, Barseghyan
25/10	a	Banants	W	2-0	A Voskanyan, Barseghyan
02/11	h	Ararat	W	3-1	Ghazaryan, Satumyan 2
08/11	h	Ulisses	W	3-0	Barseghyan, Alex, Ghazaryan
23/11	a	Pyunik	L	0-5	
29/11	a	Gandzasar	D	0-0	

2015

01/03	h	Alashkert	D	1-1	Satumyan
08/03	a	Shirak	L	0-2	
14/03	h	Banants	D	2-2	G Karapetyan 2
22/03	a	Ararat	W	1-0	Barseghyan
04/04	a	Ulisses	W	1-0	Artak Grigoryan
12/04	h	Pyunik	W	1-0	G Karapetyan
18/04	h	Gandzasar	D	1-1	Alex
26/04	a	Alashkert	W	2-1	Alex, Artak Grigoryan
03/05	h	Shirak	D	2-2	G Karapetyan, Satumyan
09/05	a	Banants	D	0-0	
17/05	h	Ararat	W	3-0	Barseghyan, G Karapetyan, Alex
23/05	h	Ulisses	L	1-2	Arakelyan
30/05	a	Pyunik	L	2-3	G Karapetyan 2

No	Name	Nat	DoB	Pos	Aps	(s)	Gls
6	Artur Adamyan	RUS	22/04/92	M	8	(3)	
22	Alex		06/01/82	D	24	(2)	4
10	Alik Arakelyan		21/05/96	M	13	(10)	1
11	Tigran Barseghyan		22/09/93	M	24		5
20	Narek Beglaryan		01/09/85	A	4	(1)	1
14	Otar Chapidze	GEO	15/10/93	M	2	(3)	
32	Armen Fishyan		02/04/86	G	3		
23	Rafayel Ghazaryan		17/05/90	M	16	(9)	2
23	Artak G Grigoryan		19/10/87	A	5	(2)	2
20	Artur Grigoryan		10/07/93	M	16	(7)	
8	Davit Grigoryan		28/12/82	M	12	(7)	1
21	Arman Hakobyan		14/03/91	M		(1)	
18	Akhmed Jindoyan		02/10/97	A		(5)	
17	Gevorg Karapetyan		10/06/90	A	9	(3)	7
7	Sargis Karapetyan		24/04/90	M	2	(7)	
1	Gevorg Kasparov		25/07/80	G	25		
15	Davit Minasyan		09/03/93	M		(4)	
16	Vardan Movsisyan		18/08/91	D	24	(1)	
2	Armen Petrosyan		26/09/85	M	21	(2)	
13	Gevorg Poghosyan		26/08/86	D	25	(1)	
5	Gor Poghosyan		11/06/88	D	16	(2)	
14	Vardan Safaryan		22/04/97	M		(3)	
9	Vardges Satumyan		07/02/90	M	26	(2)	5
3	Andranik Voskanyan		11/04/90	D	27		2
17	Hayk Voskanyan		23/06/96	M	6	(15)	1

FC Pyunik

1992 • Armenian Football Academy (1,000) • no website
Major honours
Armenian League (14) 1992 (shared), 1996, 1997, 2001, 2002, 2003, 2004, 2005, 2006, 2007, 2008, 2009, 2010, 2015; Armenian Cup (8) 1996, 2002, 2004, 2009, 2010, 2013, 2014, 2015
Coach: Sargis Hovsepyan

2014

10/08	h	Gandzasar	W	2-0	K Hovhannisyan 2
16/08	a	Alashkert	W	2-0	Romero, Baloyan
24/08	h	Shirak	W	1-0	Romero
27/08	h	Ulisses	L	0-2	
13/09	a	Ararat	W	4-0	K Hovhannisyan, Manoyan 2, Romero
21/09	a	Mika	D	1-1	Romero
27/09	a	Ulisses	L	1-2	Romero (p)
05/10	a	Gandzasar	W	4-3	og (Hambartsumyan), Romero, K Hovhannisyan, Manoyan
18/10	h	Alashkert	D	3-3	K Hovhannisyan, Romero 2
26/10	a	Shirak	D	0-0	
02/11	h	Banants	W	1-0	Ghukas Poghosyan
08/11	a	Ararat	W	3-0	Romero 3
18/11	a	Banants	W	3-2	Romero 2, K Hovhannisyan
23/11	h	Mika	W	5-0	Aslanyan 2, Romero 2, Razmik Hakobyan
29/11	h	Ulisses	W	3-0	Gagik Poghosyan, Romero 2

2015

07/03	a	Alashkert	W	1-0	Badoyan
15/03	h	Shirak	W	2-1	K Hovhannisyan, Badoyan
22/03	a	Banants	W	2-1	Badoyan, Romero
04/04	h	Ararat	W	4-0	Razmik Hakobyan 2, K Hovhannisyan, Badoyan
12/04	a	Mika	L	0-1	
19/04	a	Ulisses	L	1-2	Romero
26/04	a	Gandzasar	W	1-0	Aslanyan
02/05	h	Alashkert	W	3-1	Razmik Hakobyan, K Hovhannisyan 2
10/05	a	Shirak	W	2-0	Badoyan, Aslanyan
17/05	h	Banants	L	1-2	Badoyan
20/05	h	Gandzasar	W	3-1	Razmik Hakobyan, Badoyan, Aslanyan
23/05	a	Ararat	D	2-2	Badoyan, Romero (p)
30/05	h	Mika	W	3-2	Romero, Badoyan 2

No	Name	Nat	DoB	Pos	Aps	(s)	Gls
6	Narek Aslanyan		01/01/96	M	6	(8)	5
1	Anatoli Ayvazov	RUS	08/06/96	G	24		
7	Zaven Badoyan		22/12/89	M	12		10
20	Sargis Baloyan	RUS	24/08/92	A	4	(1)	1
17	Artavazd Boiajyan		19/12/90	M		(1)	
14	Edgar Cotto	GUA	27/01/84	M		(2)	
26	Razmik Hakobyan		09/02/96	A	13	(10)	5
16	Robert Hakobyan		22/10/96	D	6	(8)	
3	Varazdat Haroyan		24/08/92	D	24		
22	Artur Harutyunyan		02/08/85	G	4		
16	Levon Hayrapetyan		17/04/89	D	6	(1)	
21	Vahagn Hayrapetyan		14/06/97	M		(3)	
4	Grigor Hovhannisyan		08/12/93	D	22	(1)	
5	Kamo Hovhannisyan		05/10/92	D	26		10
18	Artur Kartashyan		08/01/97	D	1	(1)	
11	Davit Manoyan		05/07/90	M	8	(3)	3
25	Davit Markosyan		07/10/95	M		(1)	
17	John Lenda Matkin	USA	20/04/86	M	2	(2)	
19	Vaspurak Minasyan		29/06/94	M	22	(4)	
24	Karlen Mkrtchyan		25/11/88	M	5		
25	Erik Nazaryan		14/03/96	M		(3)	
26	Hovik Nersisyan		06/02/95	D		(5)	
22	Hovhannes Papazyan		14/07/96	M		(1)	
8	Gagik Poghosyan		04/05/93	M	25		1
10	Ghukas Poghosyan		06/02/94	M	13	(7)	1
23	Hovhannes Poghosyan		17/12/97	M		(16)	
7	Cesar Romero	USA	02/08/89	A	25		21
18	Masis Voskanyan		11/07/90	M	11	(2)	
33	Taron Voskanyan		22/02/93	D	27		
27	Karen Yesayan		10/04/96	M		(9)	
15	Artur Yusbashyan		07/09/79	M	22	(6)	

FC Shirak

1958 • Gyumri City (4,500) • fcshirak.am
Major honours
Armenian League (4) 1992 (shared), 1994, 1999, 2013; Armenian Cup (1) 2012
Coach: Vardan Bichakhchyan

2014

09/08	a	Ararat	W	2-0	Bougouhi 2
17/08	h	Mika	W	1-0	Bougouhi
24/08	a	Pyunik	L	0-1	
27/08	h	Banants	W	2-0	Bougouhi, Gyamfi
13/09	a	Alashkert	L	0-2	
20/09	h	Ulisses	L	1-2	og (Lalić)
28/09	a	Banants	D	1-1	Diarrassouba
04/10	a	Ararat	W	3-2	Marikyan, Barikyan (p), Diarrassouba
19/10	a	Mika	L	1-3	Diarrassouba
26/10	h	Pyunik	D	0-0	
01/11	a	Gandzasar	W	3-0	Bougouhi 3
09/11	h	Alashkert	D	1-1	Bougouhi (p)
18/11	a	Gandzasar	W	1-0	Hakobyan
22/11	a	Ulisses	W	2-1	Hakobyan, Diarrassouba
30/11	h	Banants	D	2-2	Bougouhi, Hakobyan

2015

01/03	a	Ararat	W	4-2	G Malakyan, Bougouhi 2 (2p), Ayvazyan
08/03	h	Mika	W	2-0	Bougouhi 2
15/03	a	Pyunik	L	1-2	Bougouhi
21/03	h	Gandzasar	W	2-0	Hakobyan 2
05/04	a	Alashkert	D	1-1	Stamenković
11/04	h	Ulisses	W	2-0	Barikyan, Hakobyan
19/04	a	Banants	W	6-3	E Malakyan, Barikyan, Bougouhi 4
25/04	a	Ararat	W	4-0	Bougouhi 2, G Malakyan, Stamenković
03/05	a	Mika	D	2-2	Diarrassouba, Marikyan
10/05	h	Pyunik	L	0-2	
16/05	a	Gandzasar	D	3-3	Bougouhi, A Muradyan, Stamenković
24/05	h	Alashkert	L	0-2	
30/05	a	Ulisses	W	4-0	Diarrassouba, Barikyan, Darbinyan, Ayvazyan

No	Name	Nat	DoB	Pos	Aps	(s)	Gls
1	Norayr Abrahamyan		30/10/85	G	2		
15	Karen Aleksanyan		17/06/80	M	17	(7)	
2	Arnold Anoma	CIV	21/01/95	D	9		
7	Viulen Ayvazyan		01/01/95	A	1	(11)	2
12	Andranik Barikyan		11/09/80	A	9	(12)	4
9	Jean-Jacques Bougouhi	CIV	12/06/92	A	24	(1)	21
23	Robert Darbinyan		04/10/95	D	15	(6)	1
25	Aghvan Davoyan		21/03/90	M	25	(1)	
5	Tigran L Davtyan		10/06/78	M	18	(7)	
36	Drissa Diarrassouba	CIV	15/11/94	A	22	(5)	6
14	Ousseynou Diop	SEN	01/01/97	M	1	(5)	
13	Gor Elazyan		01/06/91	G	26		
55	Serob Grigoryan		04/02/95	D	6	(6)	
4	Emmanuel Gyamfi	GHA	16/12/94	A	6	(4)	1
10	Davit Hakobyan		21/03/93	M	26	(1)	6
21	Gevorg Hovhannisyan		16/06/83	D	17	(1)	
22	Edgar Malakyan		22/09/90	M	13		1
8	Gor Malakyan		12/06/94	M	12		2
17	Davit Marikyan		08/05/93	D	16	(4)	2
3	Artyom Mikaelyan		12/07/91	D	5		
18	Aram Muradyan		01/01/96	A	2	(7)	1
19	Karen Muradyan		01/11/92	M	11	(1)	
11	Eduard Panosyan		11/10/92	M		(2)	
8	Miloš Stamenković	SRB	01/06/90	D	24		3
22	Arman Tadevosyan		26/09/94	M	1		
23	Aram Tosunyan		29/05/93	M		(1)	

Ulisses FC

2006 • Hanrapetakan (14,400) • fculisses.com
Major honours
Armenian League (1) 2011
Coach: Suren Chakhalyan;
(06/10/14) (Gagik Simonyan);
(18/04/15) (Suren Chakhalyan)

2014

10/08	h	Banants	W	1-0	Ovchinnikov
16/08	a	Gandzasar	D	0-0	
23/08	h	Ararat	W	2-0	Dugalić, Aleksanyan
27/08	a	Pyunik	W	2-0	Goharyan, Papikyan
31/08	a	Alashkert	W	2-0	Musonda, Goharyan
13/09	h	Mika	W	3-1	Kpodo, Goharyan, Aleksanyan (p)
20/09	a	Shirak	W	2-1	Janashia, Khubua
27/09	h	Pyunik	W	2-1	og (Haroyan), Aleksanyan
04/10	a	Banants	W	2-0	Goharyan, Aleksanyan
18/10	h	Gandzasar	W	7-1	Goharyan 3, Aleksanyan, Janashia, Dugalić, Elyazyan
25/10	a	Ararat	W	3-2	Goharyan, Aleksanyan, Musonda
01/11	h	Alashkert	W	5-1	Morozov 2, Papikyan, Khurtsidze, Elyazyan
08/11	a	Mika	L	0-3	
22/11	h	Shirak	L	1-2	Khurtsidze
29/11	a	Pyunik	L	0-3	
2015					
01/03	h	Banants	W	2-1	Aleksanyan (p), Goharyan
14/03	h	Ararat	D	0-0	
22/03	a	Alashkert	L	0-1	
04/04	h	Mika	L	0-1	
11/04	a	Shirak	L	0-2	
19/04	h	Pyunik	W	2-1	Morozov, Geperidze
25/04	a	Banants	L	0-3	
29/04	a	Gandzasar	D	0-0	
02/05	h	Gandzasar	D	0-0	
09/05	a	Ararat	W	3-1	Chezhiya, Aleksanyan, Geperidze
16/05	h	Alashkert	D	2-2	Aleksanyan, Morozov
23/05	a	Mika	W	2-1	Jarkava, Kalimulin
30/05	h	Shirak	L	0-4	

No	Name	Nat	DoB	Pos	Aps	(s)	Gls
19	Artak Aleksanyan		10/03/91	M	28		9
1	Arsen Beglaryan		18/02/93	G	27		
21	Andrei Belomitsev	RUS	29/10/94	M	11	(10)	
25	Irakli Chezhiya	RUS	22/05/92	D	12		1
26	Rade Dugalić	SRB	05/11/92	D	26		2
17	Alik Elyazyan		04/07/87	M	2	(8)	2
24	Soslan Gatagov	RUS	29/09/92	M	4	(4)	
13	Irakli Geperidze	GEO	14/02/87	A	12		2
9	Hovhannes Goharyan		18/03/88	A	17	(5)	9
11	Zamir Janashia	GEO	26/02/88	A	7	(5)	2
22	Levan Jarkava	RUS	29/03/88	D	13		1
26	Rustem Kalimulin	RUS	24/06/84	A	1	(8)	1
99	Giorgi Khubua	GEO	19/04/93	M	25	(2)	1
8	David Khurtsidze	RUS	04/07/93	M	14	(8)	2
92	Alexandre Kore	FRA	11/12/91	A		(1)	
3	Edward Kpodo	GHA	14/01/90	D	13	(1)	1
15	Slobodan Lalić	SRB	18/02/92	D	12		
23	Ivan Mamakhanov	RUS	26/02/96	M	4	(6)	
1	Grigor Meliksetyan		18/08/86	G	1		
24	Davit Minasyan		09/03/93	M		(1)	
66	Konstantin Morozov	RUS	13/05/92	D	24	(1)	4
20	Lubamba Musonda	ZAM	05/05/95	M	13		2
7	Gor Oganesyan	RUS	08/04/92	A	4	(3)	
88	Sergei Ovchinnikov	RUS	07/12/84	A	5	(9)	1
10	Aghvan Papikyan		08/02/94	M	18	(1)	2
18	Nika Piliev	RUS	21/03/91	M	8	(4)	
19	Armen Tigranyan		27/11/85	M	1	(1)	
17	Davit Zakaryan		19/04/94	M		(1)	
47	Galaktion Zoidze	GEO	13/02/89	M	6	(2)	

Top goalscorers

21	Cesar Romero (Pyunik)
	Jean-Jacques Bougouhi (Shirak)
10	Aleksandar Rakić (Ararat)
	Zaven Badoyan (Pyunik)
	Kamo Hovhannisyan (Pyunik)
9	Mihran Manasyan (Alashkert)
	Gevorg Karapetyan (Banants/Mika)
	Artak Aleksanyan (Ulisses)
	Hovhannes Goharyan (Ulisses)
7	Norayr Gyozalyan (Alashkert)
	Gevorg Nranyan (Banants)

Second level

Second level final table 2014/15

		Pld	W	D	L	F	A	Pts
1	Alashkert FC-2	28	19	6	3	83	27	63
2	FC Banants-2	28	19	3	6	73	30	60
3	FC Pyunik-2	28	16	4	8	55	39	52
4	FC Ararat-2	28	11	4	13	56	62	37
5	FC Gandzasar-2	28	7	6	15	35	77	27
6	Ulisses FC-2	28	8	2	18	49	86	26
7	FC Shirak-2	28	6	8	14	36	49	26
8	FC Mika-2	28	6	7	15	43	60	25

NB No promotion.

DOMESTIC CUP

Armenian Independence Cup 2014/15

QUARTER-FINALS

(17/09/14 & 22/10/14)
Ararat 0-2 Alashkert *(Norayr Gyozalyan 28, G Malakyan 62)*
Alashkert 4-3 Ararat *(Minasyan 17, 84, Manasyan 84, Balabekyan 90; Di Lauro 20, 70, De la Fuente 37)*
(Alashkert 6-3)

(17/09/14 & 05/11/14)
Pyunik 3-0 Shirak *(Romero 21, 57, Haroyan 90)*
Shirak 0-1 Pyunik *(Gagik Poghosyan 24)*
(Pyunik 4-0)

(01/10/14 & 22/10/14)
Mika 2-0 Gandzasar *(A Voskanyan 23, H Voskanyan 79)*
Gandzasar 0-3 Mika *(Satumyan 3, 30, Arakelyan 9)*
(Mika 5-0)

(01/10/14 & 05/11/14)
Ulisses 1-4 Banants *(Belomitsev 73; Azatyan 3, Nranyan 8, Karapetyan 38, Ayvazyan 42)*
Banants 0-2 Ulisses *(Ovchinnikov 25, Papikyan 48)*
(Banants 4-3)

SEMI-FINALS

(18/03/15 & 15/04/15)
Mika 1-2 Banants *(Alex 35p; Hanzel 28, Loretsyan 90)*
Banants 1-3 Mika *(López 1; Artak Grigoryan 22, Barseghyan 53, G Karapetyan 90)*
(Mika 4-3)

(19/03/15 & 16/04/15)
Pyunik 3-1 Alashkert *(Romero 19p, 25, Razmik Hakobyan 28; Balabekyan 32)*
Alashkert 1-0 Pyunik *(Bareghamyan 22)*
(Pyunik 3-2)

FINAL

(06/05/15)
Hanrapetakan, Yerevan
FC PYUNIK 3 *(Razmik Hakoban 4, 32, Romero 36)*
FC MIKA 1 *(Alex 11p)*
Referee: *Rocci (ITA)*
PYUNIK: *Ayvazov, K Hovhannisyan, Haroyan, T Voskanyan, G Hovhannisyan, L Hayrapetyan, Gagik Poghosyan (H Poghosyan 85), Yusbashyan, Razmik Hakobyan (M Voskanyan 58; Aslanyan 75), Badoyan (Ghukas Poghosyan 82), Romero*
MIKA: *Kasparov, Alex, Movsisyan, Gevorg Poghosyan, A Voskanyan, Arakelyan (Ghazaryan 62), Barseghyan, Petrosyan (H Voskanyan 69), Satumyan (Adamyan 79), Artak Grigoryan, G Karapetyan*
Red card: *Artak Grigoryan (72)*

Pyunik players celebrate a hat-trick of Armenian Independence Cup triumphs

AUSTRIA
Österreichischer Fussball-Bund (ÖFB)

Address	Ernst-Happel-Stadion Sektor A/F, Meiereistrasse 7 AT-1020 Wien	**President**	Leo Windtner
		General secretary	Alfred Ludwig
		Media officer	Wolfgang Gramann
Tel	+43 1 727 180	**Year of formation**	1904
Fax	+43 1 728 1632	**National stadium**	Ernst-Happel-
E-mail	office@oefb.at		Stadion, Vienna
Website	oefb.at		(50,000)

KEY:
- – UEFA Champions League
- – UEFA Europa League
- – Promoted
- – Relegated

Ried im Innkreis 6

Wien 3
(Vienna) 5

1

Mödling

Wiener Neustadt 9

Mattersburg 11

7 Salzburg

Grödig 4

Altach

2

8 Graz

Wolfsberg

10

0	100	200 km

0	100 miles

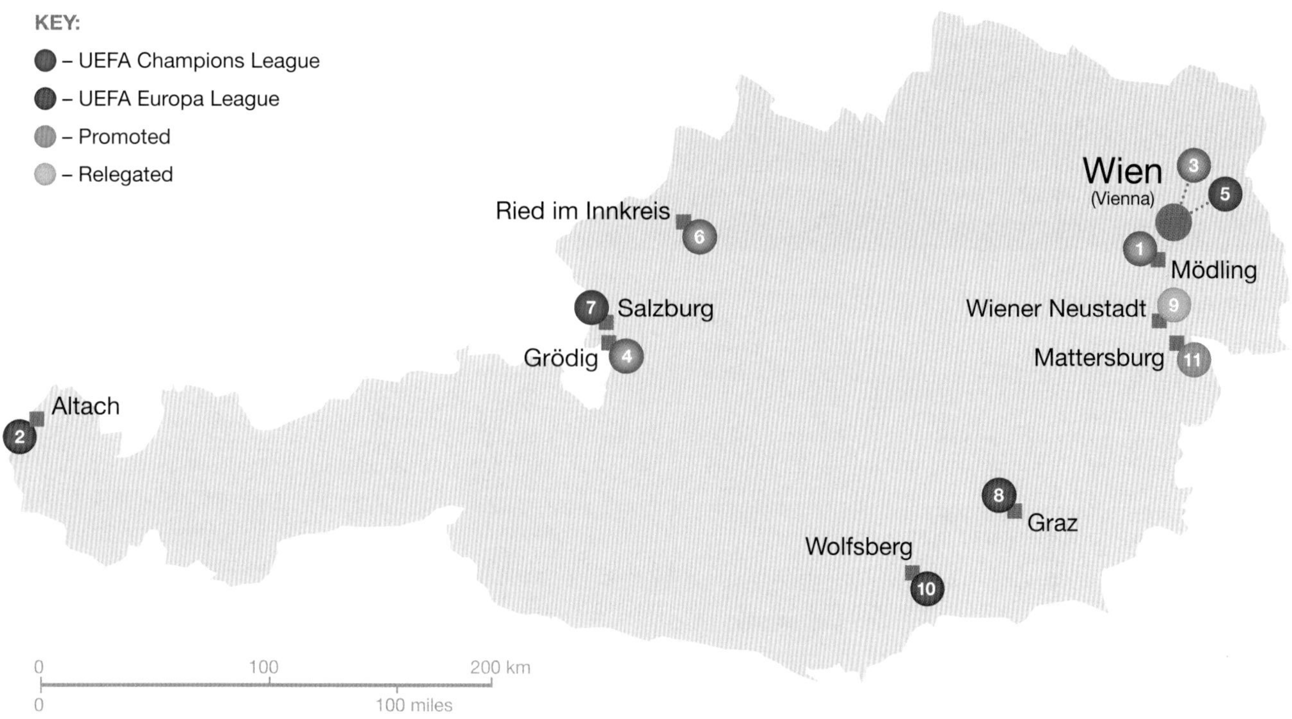

BUNDESLIGA CLUBS

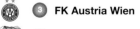 1 FC Admira Wacker Mödling

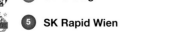 2 SCR Altach

3 FK Austria Wien

4 SV Grödig

5 SK Rapid Wien

 6 SV Ried

7 FC Salzburg

8 SK Sturm Graz

9 SC Wiener Neustadt

10 Wolfsberger AC

PROMOTED CLUB

 11 SV Mattersburg

Trophies keep coming for Salzburg

FC Salzburg's domination of Austrian football continued in 2014/15 as they won the domestic league and cup double for the third time in four seasons, new coach Adi Hütter repeating the feat of his predecessors Ricardo Moniz and Roger Schmidt.

SK Rapid Wien joined Salzburg as UEFA Champions League qualifiers by taking second place in the Bundesliga after a powerful run in the spring, while FK Austria Wien's cup final defeat left them out of Europe. It was a fabulous season, though, for Team Austria as Marcel Koller's side racked up the points in their UEFA EURO 2016 qualifying group.

New coach Hütter lands repeat domestic double	Differing fortunes for Viennese clubs Rapid and Austria	Koller's national team on course for EURO finals

Domestic league

Salzburg's sixth Bundesliga title in nine years was not quite the breeze of the previous season, but they always looked in command of proceedings – despite the sale of some important players, notably Sadio Mané in late summer and Kevin Kampl and Alan in the winter. Hütter was brought in from nearby SV Grödig, replacing Bayer 04 Leverkusen-bound Schmidt, and the former Austrian international midfielder did not disappoint.

Although Wolfsberger AC posed an unlikely threat early on, matching Salzburg's opening six wins and keeping pace with them until late October, Dietmar Kühbauer's side plummeted out of contention during a disastrous middle third of the campaign. Rapid, fuelled by the goals of Slovenian striker Robert Berič, became Salzburg's chief challengers in the spring, succumbing to defeat only once in their last 20 matches, but having been nine points adrift at the winter shutdown, they simply had too much ground to make up.

Despite scoring freely, with skipper Jonatan Soriano at the forefront with a Bundesliga-best tally of 31 for the second successive season and his precocious partner Marcel Sabitzer adding another 19, Salzburg's shaky defence often cost them points. That problem was eventually resolved,

however, as Hütter's men closed with a ten-game unbeaten run, the club's ninth title being wrapped up with a 3-0 home win over Wolfsberg in their penultimate fixture.

Austria's improved UEFA coefficient meant that the five teams in the top half of the table all qualified for Europe. Newly promoted SCR Altach caused a major surprise by finishing third, one point ahead of fourth-placed SK Sturm Graz, while Wolfsberg held on to finish fifth.

Domestic cup

Austria Wien, the 2013/14 UEFA Champions League group stage participants, would have taken Wolfsberg's UEFA Europa League berth had they defeated Salzburg in the ÖFB-Pokal final. A dismal seventh-placed finish in the league had been partially counterbalanced by a magnificent cup run, during which they won five times away without conceding. But despite having a one-man advantage for most of the game – following Salzburg keeper Péter Gulácsi's 43rd-minute expulsion – they could not exploit it, and their defence was finally breached in extra time, first by Soriano then by substitute Felipe Pires, as Salzburg ran out 2-0 winners to complete their second successive double. Surprisingly, it would be Hütter's final game in charge, a contractual disagreement provoking his departure two weeks later.

Europe

A lightweight collective effort in Europe was lifted by Salzburg's impressive form in the UEFA Europa League group stage, in which they set a new record of 21 goals scored, eight of them by Alan, the competition's joint top marksman. Of course, Salzburg would have preferred to be playing in the UEFA Champions League group stage for the first time, but they blew a big opportunity against Malmö FF, conceding a silly late goal when 2-0 up at home before crashing to a 3-0 defeat in southern Sweden.

National team

Austria had never previously enjoyed a successful UEFA European Championship qualifying campaign, but with 16 points from their first six games on the road to UEFA EURO 2016, a place in France looked highly probable for Marcel Koller's side. Having assumed Group G leadership in October, they consolidated their advantage with a precious 1-0 home win against Russia, substitute Rubin Okotie grabbing the winner – just as he had done the previous month against Montenegro. A memorable season was crowned in June by an even more impressive victory, Marc Janko's spectacular overhead kick bringing Austria another 1-0 win over Russia in Moscow, where Koller's disciplined and talented team were on top virtually from start to finish.

DOMESTIC SEASON AT A GLANCE

Bundesliga 2014/15 final table

		Pld	Home					Away					Total					Pts
			W	D	L	F	A	W	D	L	F	A	W	D	L	F	A	
1	**FC Salzburg**	36	13	1	4	59	19	9	6	3	40	23	22	7	7	99	42	73
2	SK Rapid Wien	36	10	5	3	34	13	9	5	4	34	25	19	10	7	68	38	67
3	SCR Altach	36	12	3	3	33	16	5	5	8	17	33	17	8	11	50	49	59
4	SK Sturm Graz	36	8	6	4	33	23	8	4	6	24	18	16	10	10	57	41	58
5	Wolfsberger AC	36	11	2	5	27	18	5	2	11	17	32	16	4	16	44	50	52
6	SV Ried	36	7	5	6	32	22	5	3	10	17	29	12	8	16	49	51	44
7	FK Austria Wien	36	7	6	5	26	21	3	7	8	19	30	10	13	13	45	51	43
8	SV Grödig	36	6	4	8	25	25	4	3	11	21	40	10	7	19	46	65	37
9	FC Admira Wacker Mödling	36	3	8	7	16	28	4	5	9	16	33	7	13	16	32	61	34
10	SC Wiener Neustadt	36	5	4	9	23	34	2	4	12	14	45	7	8	21	37	79	29

European qualification 2015/16

Champion/Cup winner: FC Salzburg (third qualifying round)

SK Rapid Wien (third qualifying round)

SCR Altach (third qualifying round)
SK Sturm Graz (third qualifying round)
Wolfsberger AC (second qualifying round)

Top scorer	Jonatan Soriano (Salzburg), 31 goals
Relegated club	SC Wiener Neustadt
Promoted club	SV Mattersburg
Cup final	FC Salzburg 2-0 FK Austria Wien *(aet)*

Team of the season
(4-3-3)

Coach: Canadi *(Altach)*

Stankovic *(Grödig)*

Lienhart *(Altach)* — Sonnleitner *(Rapid)* — Hinteregger *(Salzburg)* — Schrammel *(Rapid)*

Piesinger *(Sturm)* — Keïta *(Salzburg)* — Schobesberger *(Rapid)*

Berić *(Rapid)* — Jonatan Soriano *(Salzburg)* — Sabitzer *(Salzburg)*

Player of the season

Jonatan Soriano
(FC Salzburg)

Once again, Jonatan Soriano was the undisputed player of the season in Austria. The former FC Barcelona B striker has made the city of Mozart his home, and his love affair with the Salzburg fans continued as he skippered the side to a second successive domestic double, leading from the front with 31 Bundesliga goals, seven more in the Austrian Cup (including the winner in the final), and another eight in Europe. That made it a staggering 94 in all competitions over his two seasons as Salzburg captain.

Newcomer of the season

Naby Keïta
(FC Salzburg)

Salzburg's recruitment policy has repeatedly proved its worth in recent years, and the addition of Keïta to the club's roster in 2014/15 proved to be another masterstroke. The youngster was lured from French Ligue 2 side FC Istres, and although he took a few weeks to settle into his new environment, once the campaign was in full swing, so was he. Destructive and creative in equal measure, his all-purpose midfield play had many Bundesliga-watchers predicting a career at the very top for the 20-year-old.

AUSTRIA

NATIONAL TEAM

International tournament appearances

FIFA World Cup Finals (7) 1934 (4th), 1954 (3rd), 1958, 1978 (2nd phase), 1982 (2nd phase), 1990, 1998
UEFA European Championship (1) 2008

Top five all-time caps

Andreas Herzog (103); Anton Polster (95); Gerhard Hanappi (93); Karl Koller (86); Friedl Koncilia & Bruno Pezzey (84)

Top five all-time goals

Anton Polster (44); Hans Krankl (34); Johann Horvath (29); Erich Hof (28); Anton Schall (27)

Results 2014/15

08/09/14	Sweden (ECQ)	H	Vienna	D	1-1	*Alaba (7p)*
09/10/14	Moldova (ECQ)	A	Chisinau	W	2-1	*Alaba (12p), Janko (51)*
12/10/14	Montenegro (ECQ)	H	Vienna	W	1-0	*Okotie (24)*
15/11/14	Russia (ECQ)	H	Vienna	W	1-0	*Okotie (73)*
18/11/14	Brazil	H	Vienna	L	1-2	*Dragovic (75p)*
27/03/15	Liechtenstein (ECQ)	A	Vaduz	W	5-0	*Harnik (14), Janko (16), Alaba (59), Junuzovic (74), Arnautovic (90+3)*
31/03/15	Bosnia & Herzegovina	H	Vienna	D	1-1	*Janko (34)*
14/06/15	Russia (ECQ)	A	Moscow	W	1-0	*Janko (33)*

Appearances 2014/15

Coach: Marcel Koller (SUI)	11/11/60		SWE	MDA	MNE	RUS	Bra	LIE	Bih	RUS	Caps	Goals
Robert Almer	20/03/84	Hannover (GER)	G	G	G	G	G46	G		G	22	-
Florian Klein	17/11/86	Stuttgart (GER)	D	D	D	D	D	D	D	D	28	-
Aleksandar Dragovic	06/03/91	Dynamo Kyiv (UKR)	D	D	D	D86	D	D	D	D	38	1
Martin Hinteregger	07/09/92	Salzburg	D		D	D	D	D		D	9	-
Christian Fuchs	07/04/86	Schalke (GER)	D	D	D	D	D	D		D	67	1
Julian Baumgartlinger	02/01/88	Mainz (GER)	M	M	M			M	M62	M	37	1
David Alaba	24/06/92	Bayern (GER)	M	M	M			M	M46		37	9
Martin Harnik	10/06/87	Stuttgart (GER)	M86	s46	M	M	M88	M72	s62	M65	51	11
Zlatko Junuzovic	26/09/87	Bremen (GER)	M76	M86	M77	M	M71	M82	M79	M86	40	5
Marko Arnautovic	19/04/89	Stoke (ENG)	M	M79	M62	M91	M76	M	M62	M	43	8
Marc Janko	25/06/83	Sydney FC (AUS)	A68	A 82*		A59		A77	A46	A75	46	21
Rubin Okotie	06/06/87	1860 München (GER)	s68		A83	s59	A54			s75	10	2
Christoph Leitgeb	14/04/85	Salzburg	s76	s79	M						41	-
Valentino Lazaro	24/03/96	Salzburg	s86		s83						4	-
Sebastian Prödl	21/06/87	Bremen (GER)		D		s86	s88		s62	s86	50	4
Marcel Sabitzer	17/03/94	Salzburg		M46		s91	s54	s72	M90	s65	12	2
Stefan Ilsanker	18/05/89	Salzburg		s86	s77	M	M		s46	M	8	-
Lukas Hinterseer	28/03/91	Ingolstadt (GER)			s62			s82	s79		6	-
Veli Kavlak	03/11/88	Beşiktaş (TUR)				M					31	1
Ramazan Özcan	28/06/84	Ingolstadt (GER)				s46		G			4	-
Andreas Weimann	05/08/91	Aston Villa (ENG)				s71			s90		14	-
Andreas Ulmer	30/10/85	Salzburg				s76					3	-
Marco Djuricin	12/12/92	Salzburg						s77	s46		2	-
Kevin Wimmer	15/11/92	Köln (GER)							D		2	-
Markus Suttner	16/04/87	Austria Wien								D	14	-

EUROPE

FC Salzburg

CHAMPIONS LEAGUE

Third qualifying round - Qarabağ FK (AZE)
A 1-2 *Jonatan Soriano (77)*
Gulácsi, André Ramalho, Schwegler, Sabitzer (Bruno 61), Keïta (Ankersen 38), Mané, Ulmer, Leitgeb (Quaschner 90), Jonatan Soriano, Hinteregger, Kampl. Coach: Adi Hütter (AUT)
Red card: Schwegler 34
H 2-0 *Hinteregger (18, 34)*
Gulácsi, Ankersen, André Ramalho, Mané, Ilsanker (Keïta 73), Ulmer, Leitgeb, Jonatan Soriano, Alan (Sabitzer 79), Hinteregger, Kampl (Bruno 86). Coach: Adi Hütter (AUT)

Play-offs - Malmö FF (SWE)
H 2-1 *Schiemer (16), Jonatan Soriano (54)*
Gulácsi, André Ramalho, Schwegler, Sabitzer (Alan 85), Mané (Bruno 80), Ilsanker, Schiemer, Ulmer, Leitgeb (Keïta 87), Jonatan Soriano, Kampl. Coach: Adi Hütter (AUT)
A 0-3
Gulácsi, André Ramalho, Schwegler, Keïta (Ankersen 46), Ilsanker, Leitgeb (Lazaro 78), Jonatan Soriano, Alan, Hinteregger, Kampl, Bruno (Sabitzer 66). Coach: Adi Hütter (AUT)

EUROPA LEAGUE

Group D
Match 1 - Celtic FC (SCO)
H 2-2 *Alan (36), Jonatan Soriano (78)*
Gulácsi, André Ramalho, Schwegler, Sabitzer, Ilsanker, Ulmer (Ankersen 82), Leitgeb, Jonatan Soriano, Alan, Hinteregger, Kampl. Coach: Adi Hütter (AUT)
Match 2 - FC Astra Giurgiu (ROU)
A 2-1 *Kampl (36), Jonatan Soriano (42)*
Gulácsi, André Ramalho, Sabitzer, Ilsanker, Ulmer, Leitgeb, Jonatan Soriano (Quaschner 73), Alan (Bruno 83), Hinteregger, Lazaro, Kampl. Coach: Adi Hütter (AUT)
Match 3 - GNK Dinamo Zagreb (CRO)
H 4-2 *Alan (14, 45, 52), André Ramalho (49)*
Gulácsi, Ankersen, André Ramalho, Ilsanker, Ulmer (Lazaro 69), Leitgeb (Keïta 82), Jonatan Soriano, Alan (Sabitzer 70), Hinteregger, Kampl, Bruno. Coach: Adi Hütter (AUT)
Match 4 - GNK Dinamo Zagreb (CRO)
A 5-1 *Jonatan Soriano (40, 64, 85), Kampl (59), Bruno (72)*
Gulácsi, Ankersen, André Ramalho, Sabitzer (Bruno 31), Keïta (Laimer 77), Ilsanker, Ulmer, Leitgeb, Jonatan Soriano, Hinteregger (Schiemer 87), Kampl. Coach: Adi Hütter (AUT)
Match 5 - Celtic FC (SCO)
A 3-1 *Alan (8, 13), Keïta (90+2)*
Gulácsi, Schmitz, Ankersen (Schwegler 80), André Ramalho, Ilsanker, Leitgeb, Jonatan Soriano (Sabitzer 74), Alan, Hinteregger, Kampl, Bruno (Keïta 71). Coach: Adi Hütter (AUT)
Match 6 - FC Astra Giurgiu (ROU)
H 5-1 *Sabitzer (9), Kampl (34, 90+2), Alan (46, 70)*
Walke, Schmitz, Ankersen (Schwegler 78), Sabitzer, Keïta, Alan, Hinteregger (Schiemer 82), Laimer, Kampl, Ćaleta-Car, Bruno (Jonatan Soriano 74). Coach: Adi Hütter (AUT)

Round of 32 - Villarreal CF (ESP)
A 1-2 *Jonatan Soriano (48p)*
Gulácsi, André Ramalho, Schwegler, Sabitzer, Djuricin (Berisha 76), Ilsanker, Ulmer, Leitgeb (Keïta 64), Jonatan Soriano, Hinteregger, Bruno (Felipe Pires 64). Coach: Adi Hütter (AUT)
H 1-3 *Djuricin (18)*
Gulácsi, André Ramalho, Schwegler, Sabitzer, Keïta, Djuricin (Berisha 84), Ulmer, Minamino (Felipe Pires 46), Jonatan Soriano, Hinteregger, Laimer (Bruno 70). Coach: Adi Hütter (AUT)

SK Rapid Wien

EUROPA LEAGUE

Play-offs - HJK Helsinki (FIN)
A 1-2 *Schaub (58)*
Novota, Behrendt, Schrammel, Sonnleitner, Schwab (Kainz 90+1), Berič, Schaub, S Hofmann (Starkl 77), Dibon (M Hofmann 64), Pavelic, Wydra. Coach: Zoran Barisic (AUT)
H 3-3 *Schaub (10, 13), Wydra (90+4)*
Novota, Behrendt (Wydra 46), Schrammel, Sonnleitner, Schwab, Berič, Schaub, S Hofmann (Petsos 72), Kainz (Starkl 79), M Hofmann, Pavelic. Coach: Zoran Barisic (AUT)

SV Grödig

EUROPA LEAGUE

Second qualifying round - FK Čukarički (SRB)
A 4-0 *Nutz (37, 90), Schütz (80, 85)*
Stankovic, Karner, Brauer, Handle, Tomi Correa, Strobl, Reyna (Wallner 78), Huspek (Schütz 29), Nutz, Boller (Martschinko 84), Maak. Coach: Michael Baur (AUT)
H 1-2 *Karner (29)*
Stankovic, Karner, Brauer, Handle, Tomi Correa (Djuric 85), Schütz (Huspek 46), Strobl, Reyna, Nutz, Boller (Wallner 62), Maak. Coach: Michael Baur (AUT)

Third qualifying round - FC Zimbru Chisinau (MDA)
H 1-2 *Tomi Correa (89)*
Stankovic, Karner, Brauer, Handle, Tomi Correa, Strobl (Martschinko 63), Reyna, Huspek, Nutz (Djuric 74), Boller (Schütz 63), Maak. Coach: Michael Baur (AUT)
A 1-0 *Djuric (84)*
Stankovic, Karner, Brauer, Handle, Tomi Correa, Schütz (Djuric 78), Strobl, Reyna, Huspek, Nutz, Maak (Wallner 58). Coach: Michael Baur (AUT)
Red card: Tomi Correa 90+6

SKN St Pölten

EUROPA LEAGUE

Second qualifying round - PFC Botev Plovdiv (BUL)
A 1-2 *Segovia (55)*
Kostner, Huber, Wisio, Parada, Kerschbaumer, Ambichl, Hofbauer (Schibany 88), Segovia (Noel 77), Grasegger, Harti (Stec 73), Holzmann. Coach: Herbert Gager (AUT)
H 2-0 *Segovia (6, 55)*
Kostner, Huber, Wisio, Parada, Kerschbaumer, Noel (Fucik 68), Hofbauer (Ambichl 90), Segovia (Harti 86), Grasegger, Holzmann, Stec. Coach: Herbert Gager (AUT)

Third qualifying round - PSV Eindhoven (NED)
A 0-1
Kostner, Huber, Wisio, Parada, Kerschbaumer, Hofbauer, Segovia (Noel 76), Grasegger, Fucik (Harti 46), Holzmann (Ambichl 65), Stec. Coach: Herbert Gager (AUT)
H 2-3 *Segovia (56), Kerschbaumer (90)*
Riegler, Huber, Wisio, Parada (Ambichl 46), Kerschbaumer, Noel (Fucik 73), Hofbauer, Segovia, Grasegger, Holzmann, Stec (Harti 77). Coach: Herbert Gager (AUT)

DOMESTIC LEAGUE CLUB-BY-CLUB

FC Admira Wacker Mödling

1905 • BSFZ-Arena (12,000) • admirawacker.at

Major honours
Austrian League (9) 1927, 1928, 1932, 1934, 1936, 1937, 1939, 1947, 1966; Austrian Cup (6) 1928, 1932, 1934, 1947, 1964, 1966

Coach: Walter Knaller;
(06/04/15) Oliver Lederer

2014
19/07	h	Wolfsberg	L	1-4	Schicker (p)
02/08	h	Rapid	D	1-1	Schick
09/08	a	Ried	D	1-1	Auer
13/08	a	Altach	W	2-0	Zwierschitz, Schicker
16/08	h	Salzburg	L	0-3	
23/08	a	Wr Neustadt	L	4-5	Bajrami 2, Schicker, Ouédraogo
30/08	h	Austria W	W	2-1	Bajrami, Zwierschitz
13/09	a	Sturm	W	2-0	Zwierschitz, Thürauer
20/09	h	Grödig	D	0-0	
27/09	a	Wolfsberg	L	1-2	Sulimani
04/10	h	Altach	L	0-2	
18/10	a	Rapid	D	0-0	
25/10	h	Ried	D	0-0	
01/11	a	Salzburg	L	0-2	
08/11	h	Wr Neustadt	D	1-1	Thürauer
22/11	a	Austria W	L	0-4	
29/11	h	Sturm	L	0-2	
06/12	a	Grödig	L	0-5	
13/12	h	Wolfsberg	W	2-1	Windbichler (p), Thürauer

2015
14/02	a	Altach	L	0-2	
22/02	h	Rapid	D	1-1	Weber
28/02	a	Ried	D	2-2	Zwierschitz, Sulimani
04/03	h	Salzburg	L	1-4	Schicker
07/03	a	Wr Neustadt	D	0-0	
14/03	h	Austria W	D	1-1	Katzer
21/03	a	Sturm	L	1-3	Schicker
04/04	h	Grödig	L	2-3	Windbichler (p), Kerschbaumer
11/04	a	Wolfsberg	L	0-2	
18/04	h	Altach	D	2-2	Windbichler (p), Ouédraogo
25/04	a	Rapid	D	1-1	Sulimani
02/05	h	Ried	W	1-0	Sulimani
09/05	a	Salzburg	L	0-4	
16/05	h	Wr Neustadt	D	0-0	
20/05	a	Austria W	W	1-0	Schösswendter
24/05	h	Sturm	L	1-2	Windbichler (p)
31/05	a	Grödig	W	1-0	Vastic

No	Name	Nat	DoB	Pos	Aps	(s)	Gls
17	Stephan Auer		11/01/91	D	33	(1)	1
27	Eldis Bajrami	MKD	12/12/92	M	23	(8)	3
44	Markus Blutsch		01/06/95	M	1	(1)	
20	Dominik Burusic		17/03/93	A		(1)	
11	Wilfried Domoraud	FRA	18/08/88	M	2	(1)	
5	Thomas Ebner		22/02/92	D	23	(3)	
45	Marvin Egho		09/04/94	A	2	(4)	
11	Lukas Grozurek		22/12/91	M	9	(4)	
14	Markus Katzer		11/12/79	D	20	(4)	1
27	Konstantin Kerschbaumer		01/07/92	M	16		1
24	Christoph Knasmüller		30/04/92	M	6	(8)	
29	Manuel Kuttin		17/12/93	G	8		
6	Markus Lackner		05/04/91	D	21	(7)	
1	Andreas Leitner		25/03/94	G	14		
19	Nico Löffler		05/07/97	M		(1)	
22	Marcus Maier		18/12/95	M		(3)	
12	Philipp Malicsek		03/06/97	M	8	(1)	
16	Simon Manzoni	ITA	28/03/85	G	1		
9	Issiaka Ouédraogo	BFA	19/08/88	A	23	(11)	2
7	Maximilian Sax		22/11/92	M	1	(1)	
28	Thorsten Schick		19/05/90	A	5		1
18	Rene Schicker		28/09/84	A	14	(10)	5
3	Christoph Schösswendter		16/07/88	D	31	(1)	1
28	Jörg Siebenhandl		18/01/90	G	13	(1)	
23	Benjamin Sulimani		26/09/88	A	14	(12)	4
13	Lukas Thürauer		21/12/87	M	15	(1)	3
10	Daniel Toth		10/06/87	M	6	(2)	
77	Toni Vastic		17/01/93	A	2	(4)	1
31	Thomas Weber		29/04/93	D	12	(4)	1
25	Patrick Wessely		17/07/92	D	9	(2)	
2	Richard Windbichler		02/04/91	D	29	(1)	4
21	Markus Wostry		19/07/92	D	6	(1)	
26	Mustafa Yavuz		13/04/94	D		(1)	
4	Stephan Zwierschitz		17/09/90	D	29		4

SCR Altach

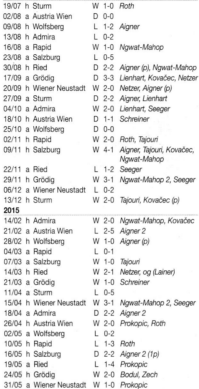

1929 • Cashpoint Arena (8,900) • scra.at

Coach: Damir Canadi

2014
19/07	h	Sturm	W	1-0	Roth
02/08	a	Austria Wien	D	0-0	
09/08	h	Wolfsberg	L	1-2	Aigner
13/08	h	Admira	L	0-2	
16/08	a	Rapid	W	1-0	Ngwat-Mahop
23/08	a	Salzburg	L	0-5	
30/08	h	Ried	D	2-2	Aigner (p), Ngwat-Mahop
17/09	a	Grödig	D	3-3	Lienhart, Kovačec, Netzer
20/09	h	Wiener Neustadt	W	2-0	Netzer, Aigner (p)
27/09	a	Sturm	D	2-2	Aigner, Lienhart
04/10	a	Admira	W	2-0	Lienhart, Seeger
18/10	h	Austria Wien	D	1-1	Schreiner
25/10	a	Wolfsberg	D	0-0	
02/11	h	Rapid	W	2-0	Roth, Tajouri
09/11	h	Salzburg	W	4-1	Aigner, Tajouri, Kovačec, Ngwat-Mahop
22/11	a	Ried	L	1-2	Seeger
29/11	h	Grödig	W	3-1	Ngwat-Mahop 2, Seeger
06/12	a	Wiener Neustadt	L	0-2	
13/12	h	Sturm	W	2-0	Tajouri, Kovačec (p)

2015
14/02	h	Admira	W	2-0	Ngwat-Mahop, Kovačec
21/02	h	Austria Wien	L	2-5	Aigner 2
28/02	h	Wolfsberg	W	1-0	Aigner (p)
04/03	a	Rapid	L	0-1	
07/03	a	Salzburg	W	1-0	Tajouri
14/03	h	Ried	W	2-1	Netzer, og (Lainer)
21/03	a	Grödig	W	1-0	Schreiner
11/04	a	Sturm	L	0-5	
15/04	h	Wiener Neustadt	W	3-1	Ngwat-Mahop 2, Seeger
18/04	a	Admira	D	2-2	Aigner 2
26/04	a	Austria Wien	W	2-0	Prokopic, Roth
02/05	a	Wolfsberg	L	0-2	
10/05	h	Rapid	L	1-3	Roth
16/05	h	Salzburg	D	2-2	Aigner 2 (1p)
23/05	a	Ried	L	1-4	Prokopic
24/05	h	Grödig	W	2-0	Bodul, Zech
31/05	a	Wiener Neustadt	W	1-0	Prokopic

No	Name	Nat	DoB	Pos	Aps	(s)	Gls
25	Hannes Aigner		16/03/81	A	28	(2)	12
9	Darko Bodul	CRO	11/01/89	A	9	(3)	1
4	Sebastian Brandner		08/02/83	G	1		
19	César Ortiz	ESP	30/01/89	D	20	(1)	
8	Ronald Gercaliu		12/02/86	D	11	(6)	
22	Lukas Jäger		12/02/94	D	8	(7)	
1	Martin Kobras		19/06/86	G	21	(1)	
20	Ivan Kovačec	CRO	27/06/88	A	16	(8)	4
7	Andreas Lienhart		28/01/86	D	36		3
12	Andreas Lukse		08/11/87	G	14		
15	Daniel Luxbacher		13/03/92	M	6	(9)	
30	Martí Riverola	ESP	26/01/91	M	2	(2)	
5	Philipp Netzer		02/10/85	M	22	(2)	1
29	Louis Ngwat-Mahop	CMR	16/09/87	A	20	(11)	8
9	Darijo Pecirep	CRO	14/08/91	A	3	(5)	
2	Alexander Pöllhuber		30/04/85	D	15	(2)	
28	Boris Prokopic		29/03/88	M	23	(4)	3
11	Felix Roth	GER	13/11/87	M	24	(6)	4
10	Patrick Salomon		10/06/88	M	17	(6)	
16	Emanuel Schreiner		02/02/89	D	24	(5)	2
26	Patrick Seeger		25/08/86	A	10	(16)	4
17	Ismael Tajouri	LBY	27/03/94	M	19	(9)	4
23	Benedikt Zech		03/11/90	D	12	(2)	1
18	Jan Zwischenbrugger		16/06/90	M	35		

FK Austria Wien

1911 • Generali-Arena (13,400) • fk-austria.at

Major honours
Austrian League (24) 1924, 1926, 1949, 1950, 1953, 1961, 1962, 1963, 1969, 1970, 1976, 1978, 1979, 1980, 1981, 1984, 1985, 1986, 1991, 1992, 1993, 2003, 2006, 2013; Austrian Cup (27) 1921, 1924, 1925, 1926, 1933, 1935, 1936, 1948, 1949, 1960, 1962, 1963, 1967, 1971, 1974, 1977, 1980, 1982, 1986, 1990, 1992, 1994, 2003, 2005, 2006, 2007, 2009

Coach: Gerald Baumgartner;
(22/03/15) Andreas Ogris

2014
20/07	h	Grödig	D	1-1	Kamara
26/07	a	Wolfsberg	L	0-4	
02/08	h	Altach	D	0-0	
09/08	a	Wr Neustadt	D	2-2	Damari, Grünwald
17/08	a	Sturm	D	1-1	Royer
24/08	h	Rapid	D	2-2	Gorgon, Damari (p)
30/08	a	Admira	L	1-2	Grünwald
13/09	h	Ried	W	3-1	Damari 2, Royer
21/09	a	Salzburg	W	3-2	Meilinger, De Paula, Damari
27/09	a	Grödig	D	0-0	
04/10	h	Wolfsberg	L	0-2	
18/10	a	Altach	D	1-1	Stryger
25/10	h	Wr Neustadt	W	2-0	Royer, Grünwald
01/11	h	Sturm	L	0-3	
09/11	a	Rapid	W	3-2	Damari 2, Royer
22/11	h	Admira	W	4-0	Damari (p), Royer, Gorgon 2
29/11	a	Ried	D	1-1	Gorgon
06/12	h	Salzburg	L	2-4	Gorgon, Grünwald
13/12	h	Grödig	W	1-0	Kvasina

2015
15/02	a	Wolfsberg	L	0-1	
21/02	h	Altach	W	5-2	Koch, Gorgon 2, Holzhauser, Stronati
28/02	a	Wr Neustadt	L	0-1	
03/03	a	Sturm	L	1-2	Grünwald
08/03	h	Rapid	W	2-1	Rotpuller, Sikov
14/03	a	Admira	D	1-1	Suttner
21/03	h	Ried	L	0-1	
04/04	a	Salzburg	L	1-3	De Paula
11/04	a	Grödig	D	1-1	Kvasina
19/04	h	Wolfsberg	D	1-1	Grünwald
26/04	a	Altach	L	0-2	
02/05	h	Wr Neustadt	W	2-1	De Paula, Grünwald
09/05	h	Sturm	D	0-0	
17/05	a	Rapid	L	1-4	De Paula
20/05	h	Admira	L	0-1	
24/05	a	Ried	W	2-0	Kvasina, Gorgon
31/05	h	Salzburg	D	1-1	Zulechner

No	Name	Nat	DoB	Pos	Aps	(s)	Gls
16	Omer Damari	ISR	24/03/89	A	13		8
23	David De Paula	ESP	03/05/84	M	16	(6)	4
41	Michael Endlicher		24/11/96	M		(1)	
37	Alexander Frank		24/03/94	D	2	(3)	
20	Alexander Gorgon		28/10/88	M	18	(3)	8
10	Alexander Grünwald		01/05/89	M	26	(5)	7
31	Osman Hadzikic		12/03/96	G	5		
9	Martin Harrer		19/05/92	A		(6)	
25	James Holland	AUS	15/05/89	M	25	(2)	
26	Raphael Holzhauser		16/02/93	M	9	(7)	1
21	Sascha Horvath		22/08/96	M	1	(1)	
11	Ola Kamara	NOR	15/10/89	A	2	(9)	1
24	Roman Kienast		29/03/84	A	2	(2)	
30	Fabian Koch		24/06/89	D	17	(1)	1
27	Marko Kvasina		20/12/96	A	9	(8)	3
6	Mario Leitgeb		30/06/88	M	19	(6)	
13	Heinz Lindner		17/07/90	G	31		
17	Florian Mader		14/09/82	M	8	(6)	
7	Marco Meilinger		03/08/91	M	25	(5)	1
14	Manuel Ortlechner		04/03/80	D	12	(1)	
15	Christian Ramsebner		26/03/89	D	9	(3)	
33	Lukas Rotpuller		31/03/91	D	26	(1)	1
28	Daniel Royer		22/05/90	M	23	(10)	5
35	Thomas Salamon		18/01/89	M	14	(5)	
36	Tarkan Serbest		02/05/94	M	5	(3)	
4	Vance Sikov	MKD	09/07/85	D	20		1
19	Patrizio Stronati	CZE	17/11/94	D	8	(1)	1
8	Jens Stryger	DEN	21/02/91	D	15	(4)	1
29	Markus Suttner		16/04/87	D	30	(1)	1
16	Philipp Zulechner		12/04/90	A	6	(4)	1

SV Grödig

1948 • DAS.GOLDBERG Stadion (4,128) •
sv-groedig.at
Coach: Michael Baur

2014

20/07	a	Austria Wien	D	1-1	*Schütz*
27/07	h	Sturm	W	2-1	*Tomi Correa, Reyna*
03/08	h	Wolfsberg	L	0-2	
10/08	a	Salzburg	L	0-8	
16/08	h	Wiener Neustadt	W	3-0	*Nutz, Reyna, Wallner*
23/08	a	Ried	D	2-2	*Reyna, Schütz*
31/08	a	Rapid	L	0-2	
17/09	h	Altach	D	3-3	*Wallner, Reyna (p), Huspek (p)*
20/09	a	Admira	D	0-0	
27/09	h	Austria Wien	D	0-0	
04/10	a	Sturm	L	0-1	
18/10	a	Wolfsberg	W	2-1	*Karner, Potzmann*
26/10	h	Salzburg	D	2-2	*Reyna, Huspek (p)*
05/11	a	Wiener Neustadt	W	4-2	*Reyna 3, Martschinko*
08/11	h	Ried	L	0-1	
22/11	h	Rapid	W	3-1	*Reyna, Huspek 2*
29/11	a	Altach	L	1-3	*Schütz*
06/12	h	Admira	W	5-0	*Reyna 2, Schütz, Nutz 2*
13/12	a	Austria Wien	L	0-1	

2015

01/03	a	Salzburg	L	1-3	*Tomi Correa*
04/03	h	Wiener Neustadt	L	1-3	*Goiginger*
07/03	a	Ried	L	1-2	*Emmanuel*
11/03	h	Sturm	L	0-2	
14/03	a	Rapid	L	0-4	
18/03	h	Wolfsberg	W	2-0	*Karner, Emmanuel*
21/03	h	Altach	L	0-1	
04/04	a	Admira	W	3-2	*Karner, Nutz (p), Hart*
11/04	h	Austria Wien	D	1-1	*Nutz*
18/04	a	Sturm	L	1-2	*Maak*
25/04	a	Wolfsberg	L	1-2	*Tomi Correa*
02/05	h	Salzburg	L	0-3	
09/05	a	Wiener Neustadt	W	4-2	*Tomi Correa, Huspek 2, Nutz*
16/05	h	Ried	W	3-2	*Völkl, og (Lainer), Tomi Correa*
24/05	a	Altach	L	0-2	
27/05	h	Rapid	L	0-2	
31/05	h	Admira	L	0-1	

No	Name	Nat	DoB	Pos	Aps	(s)	Gls
23	Sascha Boller	GER	16/02/84	M	2	(6)	
5	Timo Brauer	GER	30/05/90	M	31	(3)	
10	Sandro Djuric		15/02/94	M	8	(16)	
37	Sunday Emmanuel	NGA	20/02/90	A	5	(10)	2
27	Thomas Goiginger		15/03/93	A	3	(13)	1
21	Bernd Gschweidl		08/09/95	A	6	(4)	
7	Simon Handle		25/01/93	M	12	(3)	
14	Florian Hart		11/05/90	D	6	(6)	1
18	Philipp Huspek		05/02/91	M	31	(3)	6
13	Ione Cabrera	ESP	13/10/85	D	13	(1)	
3	Maximilian Karner		03/01/90	D	21	(2)	3
20	Roman Kerschbaum		19/01/94	M	1	(6)	
23	Lucas Henrique	BRA	14/01/95	M	8	(3)	
31	Matthias Maak		12/05/92	D	24	(1)	1
32	Christoph Martschinko		13/02/94	D	29	(5)	1
22	Stefan Nutz		15/05/92	M	31	(2)	6
19	Marvin Potzmann		07/12/93	D	25		1
17	Yordy Reyna	PER	17/09/93	A	19		11
11	Daniel Schütz		19/06/91	M	18	(7)	4
1	Cican Stankovic		04/11/92	G	35		
25	Pirmin Strasser		16/10/90	G	1	(1)	
2	Fabio Strauss		06/08/94	D	4		
12	Robert Strobl		24/10/85	D	23	(2)	
9	Tomi Correa	ESP	05/12/84	A	19	(2)	5
6	Robert Völkl		12/02/93	M	19	(2)	1
8	Roman Wallner		04/02/82	A	2	(8)	2

SK Rapid Wien

1899 • Ernst Happel-Stadion (50,000) •
skrapid.at
Major honours
*Austrian League (32) 1912, 1913, 1916, 1917, 1919,
1920, 1921, 1923, 1929, 1930, 1935, 1938, 1940, 1941,
1946, 1948, 1951, 1952, 1954, 1956, 1957, 1960, 1964,
1967, 1968, 1982, 1983, 1987, 1988, 1996, 2005, 2008;
German League (1) 1941; Austrian Cup (14) 1919, 1920,
1927, 1946, 1961, 1968, 1969, 1972, 1976, 1983, 1984,
1985, 1987, 1995; German Cup (1) 1938*
Coach: Zoran Barisic

2014

19/07	a	Salzburg	L	1-6	*S Hofmann (p)*
26/07	h	Ried	W	1-0	*Alar*
02/08	a	Admira	D	1-1	*Kainz*
09/08	h	Sturm	D	1-1	*Berič*
16/08	a	Altach	L	0-1	
24/08	a	Austria Wien	D	2-2	*Berič, Schwab*
31/08	h	Grödig	W	2-0	*Schrammel, S Hofmann*
17/09	a	Wiener Neustadt	W	5-1	*Berič 2, Schaub 2, M Hofmann*
20/09	h	Wolfsberg	W	3-0	*Berič 2, Kainz*
28/09	h	Salzburg	L	1-2	*Prosenik*
05/10	a	Ried	W	2-1	*Berič, Sonnleitner*
18/10	h	Admira	D	0-0	
25/10	a	Sturm	W	3-1	*Schwab, Berič, Dibon*
02/11	h	Altach	L	0-2	
09/11	h	Austria Wien	L	2-3	*Alar, Berič*
22/11	a	Grödig	L	1-3	*Alar*
29/11	h	Wiener Neustadt	W	3-0	*Kainz, Berič 2*
07/12	a	Wolfsberg	L	1-1	*Schwab*
14/12	a	Salzburg	W	2-1	*Berič 2*

2015

14/02	h	Ried	W	3-0	*Alar 2 (2p), Berič (p)*
22/02	a	Admira	D	1-1	*Berič*
28/02	h	Sturm	W	1-0	*Berič*
04/03	a	Altach	W	1-0	*Prosenik*
08/03	a	Austria Wien	L	1-2	*S Hofmann*
14/03	h	Grödig	W	4-0	*Pavelic, Schaub, Kainz, Schobesberger*
22/03	a	Wiener Neustadt	W	1-0	*Berič*
04/04	h	Wolfsberg	W	4-1	*Schobesberger, Schwab, Berič 2*
12/04	h	Salzburg	D	3-3	*Berič, Schobesberger, Prosenik*
18/04	a	Ried	W	1-0	*Schobesberger*
24/04	h	Admira	D	1-1	*Schobesberger*
03/05	a	Sturm	D	2-2	*Schobesberger, Petsos*
10/05	a	Altach	W	3-1	*Berič 2, Schobesberger*
17/05	h	Austria Wien	W	4-1	*Schobesberger, S Hofmann (p), Berič, Sonnleitner*
24/05	h	Wiener Neustadt	D	0-0	
27/05	a	Grödig	W	2-0	*Berič (p), Alar (p)*
31/05	a	Wolfsberg	W	5-0	*Schaub 2, Berič 3*

No	Name	Nat	DoB	Pos	Aps	(s)	Gls
33	Deni Alar		18/01/90	A	9	(16)	6
3	Brian Behrendt	GER	24/10/91	D	6	(4)	
9	Robert Berič	SVN	17/06/91	A	31	(2)	27
17	Christopher Dibon		02/11/90	D	15	(1)	1
15	Srdjan Grahovac	BIH	19/09/92	M	7	(6)	
26	Lukas Grozurek		22/12/91	M	2	(3)	
20	Maximilian Hofmann		07/08/93	D	23		1
11	Steffen Hofmann	GER	09/09/80	M	29	(7)	4
14	Florian Kainz		24/03/92	M	30	(2)	4
29	Marko Marić	CRO	03/01/96	G	7		
31	Armin Mujakic		03/07/95	M		(1)	
1	Ján Novota	SVK	29/11/83	G	29		
22	Mario Pavelic		19/09/93	D	27	(1)	1
5	Thanos Petsos	GRE	05/06/91	M	25	(2)	1
38	Philipp Prosenik		03/03/93	A	2	(15)	3
10	Louis Schaub		29/12/94	M	24	(4)	5
7	Philipp Schobesberger		10/12/93	M	14	(13)	8
4	Thomas Schrammel		05/09/87	D	33		1
8	Stefan Schwab		27/09/90	M	24	(6)	4
6	Mario Sonnleitner		08/10/86	D	33		2
23	Stefan Stangl		21/10/91	D	11	(3)	
34	Dominik Starkl		06/11/93	A	2	(13)	
39	Ferdinand Weinwurm		29/04/90	D	1		
25	Dominik Wydra		21/03/94	M	12	(6)	

SV Ried

1912 • Keine Sorgen Arena (7,680) • svried.at
Major honours
Austrian Cup (2) 1998, 2011
Coach: Oliver Glasner

2014

19/07	h	Wiener Neustadt	W	3-1	*Walch, Möschl, og (Pichlmann)*
26/07	a	Rapid	L	0-1	
02/08	h	Salzburg	L	0-2	
09/08	h	Admira	D	1-1	*Pichler*
16/08	a	Wolfsberg	L	1-4	*Kragl*
23/08	h	Grödig	D	2-2	*Fröschl, Elsneg*
30/08	a	Altach	D	2-2	*Streker, Perstaller*
13/09	a	Austria Wien	L	1-3	*Thomalla*
20/09	h	Sturm	L	0-1	
27/09	a	Wiener Neustadt	W	1-0	*Thomalla*
05/10	h	Rapid	L	1-2	*Kragl*
18/10	a	Salzburg	L	2-4	*Thomalla, Walch*
25/10	a	Admira	D	0-0	
01/11	h	Wolfsberg	W	1-0	*Murg*
08/11	a	Grödig	W	1-0	*Perstaller*
22/11	h	Altach	W	2-1	*Thomalla, Fröschl*
29/11	h	Austria Wien	D	1-1	*Vastic*
06/12	a	Sturm	L	1-3	*Kragl*
13/12	h	Wiener Neustadt	W	6-0	*Lainer, Murg, Walch, Perstaller 2, Möschl*

2015

14/02	a	Rapid	L	0-3	
22/02	h	Salzburg	D	2-2	*Thomalla 2*
28/02	h	Admira	D	2-2	*Thomalla, Filipovic*
04/03	a	Wolfsberg	W	2-1	*Möschl, Janeczek*
07/03	h	Grödig	W	2-1	*og (Ione Cabrera), Trauner*
14/03	a	Altach	L	1-2	*Reifeltshammer*
21/03	a	Austria Wien	W	1-0	*Thomalla*
05/04	a	Sturm	L	1-2	*Fröschl*
11/04	a	Wiener Neustadt	W	1-0	*Walch*
18/04	h	Rapid	L	0-1	
25/04	a	Salzburg	L	1-2	*Perstaller*
02/05	a	Admira	L	0-1	
09/05	h	Wolfsberg	W	4-0	*Walch, Filipovic, Thomalla, Fröschl*
16/05	a	Grödig	L	2-3	*Thomalla, og (Martschinko)*
19/05	h	Altach	W	4-1	*Fröschl 3, Murg*
24/05	h	Austria Wien	L	0-2	
31/05	h	Sturm	D	0-0	

No	Name	Nat	DoB	Pos	Aps	(s)	Gls
15	Julian Baumgartner		27/07/94	D		(1)	
24	Thomas Burghuber		03/05/94	D	2	(4)	
20	Dieter Elsneg		04/02/90	M	29	(7)	1
19	Petar Filipovic	GER	14/09/90	M	14		2
19	Thomas Fröschl		20/09/88	A	8	(25)	7
1	Thomas Gebauer	GER	30/06/82	G	35		
30	Lorenz Höbarth		14/09/91	G	1	(1)	
5	Bernhard Janeczek		10/03/92	D	24	(2)	1
11	Oliver Kragl	GER	12/05/90	D	30	(2)	3
29	Jakob Kreuzer		15/01/95	A		(4)	
2	Stefan Lainer		27/08/92	D	34		1
26	Luca Mayr-Fälten		06/04/96	A		(1)	
25	Patrick Möschl		06/03/93	M	17	(6)	3
10	Thomas Murg		14/11/94	M	25	(4)	3
9	Julius Perstaller		08/04/89	A	6	(18)	5
22	Harald Pichler		18/06/87	D	22	(4)	1
16	Michele Polverino	LIE	26/09/84	M	9	(1)	
28	Thomas Reifeltshammer		03/07/88	D	15	(2)	1
6	Denis Streker	GER	06/04/91	M	17	(7)	1
31	Denis Thomalla	GER	16/08/92	A	29		10
3	Gernot Trauner		25/03/92	M	27	(2)	1
17	Toni Vastic		17/01/93	A	3	(8)	1
33	Clemens Walch		10/07/87	A	23	(6)	5
4	Marcel Ziegl		20/12/92	M	26	(1)	

FC Salzburg

1933 • Bullen Arena Wals-Siezenheim (30,900)
• redbulls.com/de
Major honours
Austrian League (9) 1994, 1995, 1997, 2007, 2009, 2010,
2012, 2014, 2015; Austrian Cup (3) 2012, 2014, 2015
Coach: Adi Hütter

2014
19/07	h	Rapid	W	6-1	Ulmer, Alan, Mané, Jonatan Soriano 2, Kampl
26/07	a	Wr Neustadt	W	5-0	Sabitzer, Jonatan Soriano 2 (1p), Schwegler, Kampl
02/08	a	Ried	W	2-0	Schiemer, Bruno
10/08	h	Grödig	W	8-0	Jonatan Soriano 5, Mané, Sabitzer, Lazaro
16/08	a	Admira	W	3-0	Bruno, Schwegler, Sabitzer
23/08	h	Altach	W	5-0	Jonatan Soriano (p), Bruno, Alan 2, Lazaro
30/08	h	Sturm	L	2-3	Kampl, Jonatan Soriano
14/09	a	Wolfsberg	L	0-1	
21/09	a	Austria W	L	2-3	Alan 2
28/09	a	Rapid	W	2-1	Bruno, Alan
05/10	h	Wr Neustadt	W	4-1	Ankersen, Sabitzer, Jonatan Soriano, Kampl
18/10	h	Ried	W	4-2	Jonatan Soriano 2, Sabitzer 2
26/10	a	Grödig	D	2-2	Kampl, Sabitzer
01/11	a	Admira	W	2-0	Jonatan Soriano 2
09/11	h	Altach	L	1-4	Bruno
23/11	a	Sturm	W	2-1	Bruno, Jonatan Soriano
30/11	h	Wolfsberg	D	2-2	Jonatan Soriano 2 (2p)
06/12	a	Austria W	W	4-2	Alan 3, Sabitzer
14/12	h	Rapid	L	1-2	Sabitzer

2015
14/02	a	Wr Neustadt	W	2-0	Jonatan Soriano 2
22/02	a	Ried	D	2-2	Felipe Pires, Keïta
01/03	h	Grödig	W	3-1	Sabitzer 2, Keïta
04/03	a	Admira	W	4-1	Sabitzer, Minamino 2, Berisha
07/03	a	Altach	L	0-1	
15/03	h	Sturm	W	2-1	Djuricin, Keïta
21/03	a	Wolfsberg	L	2-3	Jonatan Soriano 2
04/04	h	Austria W	W	3-1	Sabitzer, Lazaro 2
12/04	a	Rapid	D	3-3	Berisha, Jonatan Soriano, Sabitzer
18/04	h	Wr Neustadt	W	6-0	Keïta, Berisha, Jonatan Soriano 2, Sabitzer, Hinteregger
25/04	h	Ried	W	2-1	Keïta, Jonatan Soriano
02/05	a	Grödig	W	3-0	Jonatan Soriano 2 (1p), Minamino
09/05	h	Admira	W	4-0	Jonatan Soriano, Ulmer, Sabitzer 2
16/05	a	Altach	D	2-2	Berisha, Sabitzer
20/05	a	Sturm	D	0-0	
24/05	h	Wolfsberg	W	3-0	Sabitzer, André Ramalho, Jonatan Soriano
31/05	a	Austria W	D	1-1	Djuricin

No	Name	Nat	DoB	Pos	Aps	(s)	Gls
27	Alan	BRA	10/07/89	A	13	(3)	9
5	André Ramalho	BRA	16/02/92	D	24	(7)	1
4	Peter Ankersen	DEN	22/09/90	D	15	(6)	1
14	Valon Berisha	NOR	07/02/93	M	8	(6)	4
77	Massimo Bruno	BEL	17/09/93	M	13	(11)	6
45	Duje Ćaleta-Car	CRO	17/09/96	D	7		
9	Marco Djuricin		12/12/92	A	7	(6)	2
11	Felipe Pires	BRA	18/04/95	M	2	(5)	1
47	Lukas Gugganig		14/02/95	D		(1)	
31	Péter Gulácsi	HUN	06/05/90	G	34		
36	Martin Hinteregger		07/09/92	D	31		1
13	Stefan Ilsanker		18/05/89	M	28	(3)	
26	Jonatan Soriano	ESP	24/09/85	A	29	(3)	31
44	Kevin Kampl	SVN	09/10/90	M	16	(2)	5
8	Naby Keïta	GUI	10/02/95	M	25	(5)	5
41	Konrad Laimer		27/05/97	M	5	(3)	
37	Valentino Lazaro		24/03/96	M	17	(8)	4
24	Christoph Leitgeb		14/04/85	M	17	(1)	
10	Sadio Mané	SEN	10/04/92	A	4		2
18	Takumi Minamino	JPN	16/01/95	M	9	(5)	3
46	Smail Prevljak	BIH	10/05/95	A		(1)	
42	Nils Quaschner	GER	22/04/94	A	2	(8)	
43	Ante Roguljić	CRO	11/03/96	M	1		
7	Marcel Sabitzer		17/03/94	A	26	(7)	19
15	Franz Schiemer		28/11/86	D	5	(1)	1
2	Benno Schmitz	GER	17/11/94	D	16	(5)	
6	Christian Schwegler	SUI	06/06/84	D	18	(3)	2
28	Asger Sørensen	DEN	05/06/96	D	1		
17	Andreas Ulmer		30/10/85	D	21		2
33	Alexander Walke	GER	06/06/83	G	2	(1)	

SK Sturm Graz

1909 • UPC-Arena (15,400) • sksturm.at
Major honours
Austrian League (3) 1998, 1999, 2011; Austrian
Cup (4) 1996, 1997, 1999, 2010
Coach: Darko Milanič (SVN);
(21/09/14) (Günther Neukirchner);
(30/09/14) Franco Foda (GER)

2014
19/07	a	Altach	L	0-1	
27/07	a	Grödig	L	1-2	Beichler
02/08	h	Wiener Neustadt	W	4-2	Djuricin 2 (1p), Klem, Offenbacher
09/08	a	Rapid	D	1-1	Djuricin
17/08	h	Austria Wien	D	1-1	Schloffer
23/08	h	Wolfsberg	L	1-2	Djuricin
30/08	a	Salzburg	W	3-2	Stankovic 2, Djuricin
13/09	a	Admira	L	0-2	
20/09	a	Ried	W	1-0	Spendlhofer
27/09	h	Altach	D	2-2	Offenbacher, Beichler
04/10	a	Grödig	W	1-0	Djuricin
19/10	a	Wiener Neustadt	D	0-0	
25/10	h	Rapid	L	1-3	Schick
01/11	a	Austria Wien	W	3-0	Stankovic, Djuricin 2
08/11	a	Wolfsberg	W	2-0	Schick, Offenbacher
23/11	h	Salzburg	L	1-2	Djuricin
29/11	a	Admira	W	2-0	Djuricin, Piesinger
06/12	h	Ried	W	3-1	Djuricin, og (Trauner), Piesinger
13/12	a	Altach	L	0-2	

2015
21/02	h	Wiener Neustadt	D	3-3	Kienast, Madl, Ehrenreich
28/02	a	Rapid	L	0-1	
03/03	h	Austria Wien	W	2-1	Piesinger 2
07/03	h	Wolfsberg	W	2-0	Kienast, Schick
11/03	a	Grödig	W	2-0	Kienast, Spendlhofer
15/03	a	Salzburg	L	1-2	Piesinger
21/03	a	Admira	W	3-1	Avdijaj, Piesinger, Stankovic
05/04	a	Ried	W	2-1	Kienast, Avdijaj
11/04	h	Altach	W	5-0	Schick, Avdijaj, Kienast, Gruber 2
18/04	h	Grödig	W	2-1	Piesinger, Kienast
25/04	a	Wiener Neustadt	D	4-4	Avdijaj 2, Piesinger, Kienast
03/05	h	Rapid	D	2-2	Piesinger, Beichler
09/05	a	Austria Wien	D	0-0	
16/05	a	Wolfsberg	L	0-1	
20/05	h	Salzburg	D	0-0	
24/05	a	Admira	W	2-1	Avdijaj, Hadžić
31/05	h	Ried	D	0-0	

No	Name	Nat	DoB	Pos	Aps	(s)	Gls
29	Taisuke Akiyoshi	JPN	18/04/89	M		(2)	
77	Donis Avdijaj	GER	25/08/96	A	12	(5)	6
5	Tomislav Barbarić	CRO	29/03/89	D	5	(2)	
28	Daniel Beichler		13/10/88	A	15	(6)	3
9	Marco Djuricin		12/12/92	A	18		11
34	Bright Edomwonyi	NGA	24/07/94	A	3	(3)	
17	Martin Ehrenreich		10/05/83	D	22		1
1	Christian Gratzei		19/09/81	G	31		
22	Andreas Gruber		04/07/94	A	11	(13)	2
8	Anel Hadžić	BIH	16/08/89	M	31	(1)	1
14	Florian Kainz		24/10/92	M	1		
36	Wilson Kamavuaka	COD	29/03/90	M	6	(1)	
42	Roman Kienast		29/03/84	A	9	(3)	7
37	Daniel Lácsi	CRO	19/01/95	A		(1)	
27	Christian Klem		21/04/91	D	34		1
30	Sandi Lovric		28/03/98	M	2	(6)	
15	Michael Madl		21/03/88	D	32		1
20	Daniel Offenbacher		18/02/92	M	27	(5)	3
35	Ihor Oshchypko	UKR	25/10/85	D	2	(1)	
24	Andreas Pfingstner		24/03/93	D	2		
13	Simon Piesinger		13/05/92	M	21	(11)	9
19	Benedikt Pliquett	GER	13/12/84	G	4		
21	Benjamin Rosenberger		15/06/96	D		(2)	
44	Thorsten Schick		19/05/90	M	27	(1)	4
18	David Schloffer		28/04/92	M	10	(9)	1
24	Marc Schmerböck		01/04/94	M	2	(9)	
32	Tobias Schützenauer		19/05/97	G	1	(1)	
33	Makhmadnaim Sharifi	RUS	03/06/92	D	1	(2)	
23	Lukas Spendlhofer		02/06/93	D	29	(2)	2
10	Marko Stankovic		17/02/86	M	24		4
11	Josip Tadić	CRO	22/08/87	A	3	(18)	
4	Aleksandar Todorovski	MKD	26/02/84	D	11		

SC Wiener Neustadt

2008 • Stadion Wiener Neustadt (7,500) •
scwn.at
Coach: Heimo Pfeifenberger;
(12/11/14) (Günter Kreissl & Christian Ilzer);
(24/11/14) Helgi Kolviosson (ISL)

2014
19/07	a	Ried	L	1-3	Kainz
26/07	h	Salzburg	L	0-5	
02/08	a	Sturm	L	2-4	Schöpf, Rauter
09/08	h	Austria Wien	D	2-2	Schöpf, Rauter
16/08	a	Grödig	L	0-3	
23/08	h	Admira	W	5-4	O'Brien, Dobras, Rauter, Ebenhofer, Osman Ali
30/08	a	Wolfsberg	W	1-0	Freitag
17/09	h	Rapid	L	1-5	Rauter
20/09	a	Altach	L	0-2	
27/09	h	Ried	L	0-1	
05/10	a	Salzburg	L	1-4	Rauter
19/10	h	Sturm	D	0-0	
25/10	a	Austria Wien	L	0-2	
05/11	h	Grödig	L	2-4	Dobras, Tieber
08/11	a	Admira	D	1-1	Dobras
22/11	h	Wolfsberg	L	2-4	Maierhofer, O'Brien (p)
29/11	a	Rapid	L	0-3	
06/12	h	Altach	W	2-0	Dobras, O'Brien (p)
13/12	a	Ried	L	0-6	

2015
14/02	h	Salzburg	L	0-2	
21/02	a	Sturm	D	3-3	Hellquist 2, Hofbauer
28/02	h	Austria Wien	W	1-0	O'Brien (p)
04/03	a	Grödig	W	3-1	Dobras, Hellquist, Sereinig
07/03	h	Admira	D	0-0	
14/03	a	Wolfsberg	L	0-2	
22/03	h	Rapid	L	0-1	
11/04	h	Ried	L	0-1	
15/04	a	Altach	L	1-3	Sušac
18/04	a	Salzburg	L	0-6	
25/04	h	Sturm	D	4-4	Ranftl 2, Hellquist, Kainz
02/05	a	Austria Wien	L	1-2	Hofbauer
09/05	h	Grödig	L	2-4	Ranftl 2
16/05	a	Admira	D	0-0	
20/05	h	Wolfsberg	W	2-0	Hofbauer, Ranftl
24/05	a	Rapid	D	0-0	
31/05	h	Altach	L	0-1	

No	Name	Nat	DoB	Pos	Aps	(s)	Gls
29	Lukas Denner		19/06/91	D	21	(1)	
15	Christian Deutschmann		11/02/88	D	11		
30	Kristijan Dobras		09/10/92	M	21	(4)	5
22	Mario Ebenhofer		29/07/92	M	3	(7)	1
25	Christoph Freitag		21/01/90	M	30	(1)	1
13	Philip Hellquist	SWE	12/05/91	A	11	(1)	4
28	Dominik Hofbauer		19/09/90	M	12	(1)	3
14	Tobias Kainz		31/10/92	M	23	(3)	2
8	Matthias Koch		01/04/88	M	11	(14)	
19	Daniel Maderner		12/10/95	A	8	(13)	
39	Stefan Maierhofer		16/08/82	A	4		1
24	Remo Mally		24/03/91	D	10	(1)	
6	Dennis Mimm		18/03/83	D	10	(2)	
4	Conor O'Brien	USA	20/10/88	M	28	(1)	4
7	Abd Al-Rahman Osman Ali		02/06/86	M	14	(8)	1
11	Thomas Pichlmann		24/04/81	A	3	(2)	
26	Mario Pollhammer		20/06/89	M	11	(6)	
5	Mark Prettenthaler		11/04/83	D	19	(1)	
17	Reinhold Ranftl		24/01/92	D	22	(8)	5
10	Herbert Rauter		27/01/94	A	27	(5)	5
9	Julian Salamon		01/05/91	A	3	(3)	
27	Domenik Schierl		20/07/94	G	4		
21	Daniel Schöpf		09/01/90	M	7	(9)	2
32	Matthias Sereinig		17/11/84	D	28		1
20	Adam Sušac	CRO	20/05/89	D	18		1
18	Michael Tieber		04/09/88	A	4	(13)	1
1	Thomas Vollnhofer		02/09/84	G	32		
23	Sebastian Wimmer		15/01/94	M	1	(3)	

Wolfsberger AC

1931 • Lavanttal Arena (7,300) • rzpelletswac.at
Coach: Dietmar Kühbauer

2014

19/07	a	Admira	W	4-1	Zulj, Trdina, Wernitznig 2
26/07	h	Austria Wien	W	4-0	Wernitznig, Rnić, Jacobo (p), Silvio
03/08	a	Grödig	W	2-0	Zulj, Hüttenbrenner
09/08	a	Altach	W	2-1	Trdina, Jacobo
16/08	h	Ried	W	4-1	Trdina, Wernitznig, Hüttenbrenner, Kerhe
23/08	a	Sturm	W	2-1	Kerhe, Standfest
30/08	h	Wiener Neustadt	L	0-1	
14/09	h	Salzburg	W	1-0	Trdina
20/09	a	Rapid	L	0-3	
27/09	a	Admira	W	2-1	Zulj, Standfest
04/10	a	Austria Wien	W	2-0	Zulj, Weber
18/10	h	Grödig	L	1-2	Hüttenbrenner
25/10	h	Altach	D	0-0	
01/11	a	Ried	L	0-1	
08/11	h	Sturm	L	0-2	
22/11	a	Wiener Neustadt	L	0-2	
30/11	a	Salzburg	D	2-2	Wernitznig, Putsche
07/12	h	Rapid	D	1-1	Seebacher
13/12	a	Admira	L	1-2	Trdina

2015

15/02	h	Austria Wien	W	1-0	Berger
28/02	a	Altach	L	0-1	
04/03	h	Ried	L	1-2	Putsche
07/03	a	Sturm	L	0-2	
14/03	h	Wiener Neustadt	W	2-0	Trdina, Weber
18/03	h	Grödig	L	0-2	
21/03	h	Salzburg	W	3-2	Jacobo, Silvio, Kerhe
04/04	a	Rapid	L	1-4	Jacobo (p)
11/04	h	Admira	W	2-0	Drescher, Seidl
19/04	a	Austria Wien	D	1-1	Zulj
25/04	h	Grödig	W	2-1	Silvio, Wernitznig
02/05	h	Altach	W	2-0	Silvio, Trdina
09/05	a	Ried	L	0-4	
16/05	h	Sturm	W	1-0	Kerhe
20/05	a	Wiener Neustadt	L	0-2	
24/05	a	Salzburg	L	0-3	
31/05	h	Rapid	L	0-5	

No	Name	Nat	DoB	Pos	Aps	(s)	Gls
7	Dario Baldauf		27/03/85	D	11	(6)	
18	Michael Berger		01/12/90	D	15	(1)	1
1	Christian Dobnik		10/07/86	G	6	(1)	
27	Daniel Drescher		07/10/89	D	16	(1)	1
16	Boris Hüttenbrenner		23/09/85	M	32		3
11	Jacobo	ESP	04/02/84	M	30	(3)	4
3	Manuel Kerhe		30/06/87	M	16	(15)	4
31	Alexander Kofler		06/11/86	G	30		
29	Hervé Oussalé	BFA	16/06/88	A	2	(4)	
4	Stefan Palla	PHI	15/05/89	D	24		
19	Roland Putsche		22/03/91	M	7	(4)	2
13	Maximilian Ritscher		11/01/94	D		(1)	
15	Nemanja Rnić	SRB	30/09/84	D	20	(1)	1
20	Stefan Schwendinger		27/07/94	M	2	(4)	
5	René Seebacher		24/07/88	M	10	(7)	1
22	Manuel Seidl		26/10/88	M	4	(5)	1
8	Silvio	BRA	01/02/85	A	16	(17)	4
9	Attila Simon	HUN	04/02/83	A	2	(6)	
26	Michael Sollbauer		15/05/90	D	31		
25	Joachim Standfest		30/05/80	D	32		2
17	Tadej Trdina	SVN	25/01/88	A	18	(7)	7
23	Peter Tschernegg		23/07/92	M	4	(4)	
6	Manuel Weber		28/08/85	M	25	(1)	2
24	Christopher Wernitznig		24/02/90	M	23	(10)	6
10	Peter Zulj		09/06/93	M	20	(7)	5

Top goalscorers

31	Jonatan Soriano (Salzburg)
27	Robert Berić (Rapid)
19	Marcel Sabitzer (Salzburg)
13	Marco Djuricin (Sturm/Salzburg)
12	Hannes Aigner (Altach)
11	Yordy Reyna (Grödig)
10	Denis Thomalla (Ried)
9	Alan (Salzburg)
	Simon Piesinger (Sturm)
8	Louis Ngwat-Mahop (Altach)
	Omer Damari (Austria Wien)
	Alexander Gorgon (Austria Wien)
	Philipp Schobesberger (Rapid)

Promoted club

SV Mattersburg

1922 • Pappelstadion (15,100) • svm.at
Coach: Ivica Vastic

Second level final table 2014/15

		Pld	W	D	L	F	A	Pts
1	SV Mattersburg	36	21	8	7	69	36	71
2	FC Liefering	36	20	5	11	70	55	65
3	LASK Linz	36	15	11	10	45	36	56
4	Kapfenberger SV	36	12	13	11	52	45	49
5	SKN St Pölten	36	13	10	13	39	41	49
6	FC Wacker Innsbruck	36	11	10	15	32	43	43
7	SC Austria Lustenau	36	11	9	16	49	56	42
8	Floridsdorfer AC	36	9	14	13	40	49	41
9	SV Horn	36	10	8	18	34	50	38
10	TSV Hartberg	36	10	8	18	46	65	38

DOMESTIC CUP

ÖFB-Cup 2014/15

FIRST ROUND

(11/07/14)
Amstetten 0-1 Rapid Wien *(aet)*
ATSV Wolfsberg 2-1 FC Dornbirn
Austria Klagenfurt 1-3 Vorwärts Steyr
Hard 1-2 Ritzing
Kalsdorf 2-2 Hartberg *(aet; 3-4 on pens)*
Kottingbrunn 0-7 Kapfenberg
Lendorf 0-7 Admira
Parndorf 2-3 Ried
Schwaz 1-4 Sturm Graz
Schwechat 1-4 Floridsdorfer AC
Seekirchen 1-4 LASK
Vienna 0-6 Austria Wien
Wallern 1-1 St Florian *(aet; 5-3 on pens)*
Wattens 2-4 Altach *(aet)*
Weiz 2-4 Wolfsberg

(12/07/14)
Donaufeld 1-3 Wacker Innsbruck *(aet)*
Gurten 0-6 Wiener Neustadt
Höchst 1-2 Mattersburg
Hohenems 5-1 Eugendorf
Kitzbühel 5-1 Retz
Micheldorf 2-1 Allerheiligen
Neusiedl 5-1 Neumarkt
Obergrafendorf 1-4 Lankowitz
SAK Klagenfurt 1-4 Lafnitz
Sollenau 1-10 Salzburg
St Johann 3-0 Spratzern
Wiener Sportklub 3-2 Austria Lustenau
Wimpassing 0-3 Horn

(13/07/14)
Admira Technopol 0-8 St Pölten
Gleisdorf 1-2 Kufstein
Leobendorf 1-7 Grödig

(16/07/14)
Austria Salzburg 2-0 Blau-Weiss Linz

SECOND ROUND

(22/09/14)
Lankowitz 0-3 LASK

(23/09/14)
ATSV Wolfsberg 0-3 Wacker Innsbruck
Austria Salzburg 0-5 Sturm Graz
Kufstein 1-6 Floridsdorfer AC
Lafnitz 0-2 Hartberg
Micheldorf 0-4 Mattersburg
Neusiedl 1-4 Kapfenberg
Ried 0-1 Wolfsberg
Ritzing 2-0 Horn
St Johann 1-1 St Pölten *(aet; 6-7 on pens)*
Vorwärts Steyr 0-2 Grödig

(24/09/14)
Hohenems 0-5 Altach
Kitzbühel 0-5 Austria Wien
Wallern 0-1 Rapid Wien
Wiener Neustadt 2-2 Admira *(aet; 5-3 on pens)*
Wiener Sportklub 1-12 Salzburg

THIRD ROUND

(28/10/14)
Hartberg 0-6 Austria Wien
Ritzing 1-3 Floridsdorfer AC
Wolfsberg 3-2 Wiener Neustadt

(29/10/14)
Altach 1-1 Mattersburg *(aet; 4-2 on pens)*
Kapfenberg 5-3 LASK
Rapid Wien 1-0 Sturm Graz
St Pölten 0-1 Grödig
Wacker Innsbruck 1-2 Salzburg *(aet)*

QUARTER-FINALS

(07/04/15)
Grödig 2-1 Floridsdorfer AC
(Gschweidl 15, Nutz 39; Duran 34)
Kapfenberg 0-2 Austria Wien
(De Paula 2, Kvasina 77)
Wolfsberg 2-1 Rapid Wien
(Kerhe 25, Wernitznig 28; Schobesberger 90+4)

(08/04/15)
Altach 0-4 Salzburg *(Sabitzer 4, 32, Jonatan Soriano 34, 79)*

SEMI-FINALS

(28/04/15)
Grödig 0-2 Salzburg *(Quaschner 74, Sabitzer 78)*

(29/04/15)
Wolfsberg 0-3 Austria Wien
(Rotpuller 64, Leitgeb 67, Holland 72)

FINAL

(03/06/15)
Wörthersee-Stadion, Klagenfurt
FC SALZBURG 2 *(Jonatan Soriano 96, Felipe Pires 108)*
FK AUSTRIA WIEN 0
(aet)
Referee: Drachta
SALZBURG: Gulácsi, Ankersen, Ćaleta-Car, Hinteregger, Schmitz, Minamino (Walke 43), André Ramalho, Keïta, Berisha (Quaschner 100), Jonatan Soriano, Sabitzer (Felipe Pires 81)
Red card: Gulácsi (43)
AUSTRIA WIEN: Lindner, Koch, Rotpuller, Stronati, Suttner, Ramsebner, Leitgeb (Holland 71), Gorgon (Zulechner 81), Grünwald, De Paula (Royer 46), Kvasina.
Red card: Rotpuller (120+2)

AZERBAIJAN

Azärbaycan Futbol Federasiyaları Assosiasiyası (AFFA)

Address	Nobel Prospekti 2208 AZ-1025 Bakı	**President**	Rövnaq Abdullayev
Tel	+994 12 404 27 77	**General secretary**	Elkhan Mämmädov
Fax	+994 12 404 27 72	**Media officer**	Mikayıl Narimanoğlu
E-mail	info@affa.az	**Year of formation**	1992
Website	affa.az	**National stadium**	Tofiq Bähramov adına Respublika, Baku (32,000)

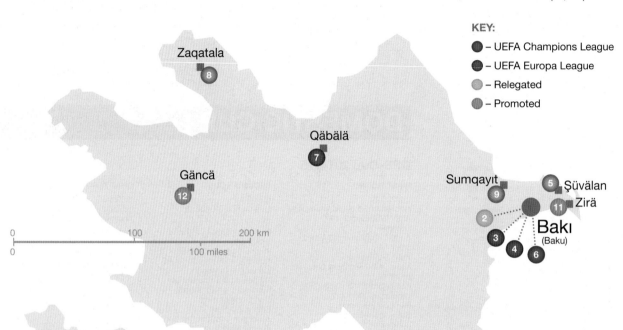

KEY:
- – UEFA Champions League
- – UEFA Europa League
- – Relegated
- – Promoted

PREMYER LİQA CLUBS

 ① Araz-Naxçıvan PFK

 ② Bakı FK

 ③ İnter Bakı PİK

 ④ Neftçi PFK

 ⑤ Olimpik-Şüvälan PFK

 ⑥ Qarabağ FK

 ⑦ Qäbälä FK

 ⑧ Simurq PFK

 ⑨ Sumqayıt FK

 ⑩ Xäzär Länkäran FK

PROMOTED CLUBS

 ⑪ Zirä FK

 ⑫ Käpäz PFK

Qarabağ prosper on all fronts

After a wait of 21 years to reclaim the Premyer Liqa title, Qarabağ FK made it two in two seasons, holding off the challenge of İnter Bakı PİK during a campaign that was reduced in mid-stream from 36 to 32 matches following the voluntary withdrawal of newly-promoted Araz-Naxçıvan PFK.

Qurban Qurbanov's men in black also won the domestic cup, defeating holders Neftçi PFK 3-1 in the final to complete the double, and they also emulated Neftçi's feat of two years previously by reaching the group stage of the UEFA Europa League.

Back-to-back titles for Qurban Qurbanov's side

Cup final victory against Neftçi completes double

Prosinečki replaces Vogts as national team coach

Domestic league

Favourites to defend their title, Qarabağ were in trouble after three matches, with just two points, but the blip was temporary and after racking up nine wins in their next ten games, albeit one of them, against Araz-Naxçıvan, subsequently annulled, they were soon in charge of the title race. At the winter break they held a five-point lead over İnter, with Neftçi three points further back in third.

Qarabağ's consistency during the spring was sufficient to keep İnter at arm's length, although Kakhabar Tskhadadze's side refused to throw in the towel. A third successive 0-0 draw against the leaders left them nine points adrift with eight games remaining, but they won their next five, and it was not until Qarabağ's penultimate fixture, against Sumqayıt FK in their temporary Bakcell Arena home, that the knockout blow was delivered, Dutch winger Leroy George scoring the only goal in a 1-0 win.

The Baku-based club originally hailing from Agdam ended up with a five-point victory margin. İnter defeated them 2-1 in their final fixture, which was only their fourth defeat, and although they registered just 51 goals in the 32 games that counted, Qarabağ had a happy habit of coming out on top in tight games, 13 of their 20 wins being achieved by one-goal margins.

With İnter taking second place, Qäbälä FK, who beat Qarabağ twice, finishing third and Neftçi a disappointingly distant fourth, the top four placings – and European qualifying spots – were identical to those of the previous season. The major surprise was that Bakı FK, fifth in 2013/14, dropped to ninth and were relegated – this despite possessing the league's leading marksman in Nurlan Novruzov, who scored 15 of their 21 goals (and of the 19 that counted).

Domestic cup

Neftçi, the country's most decorated club, were eager to make amends for a poor Premyer Liqa campaign by completing a hat-trick of domestic cup triumphs, but they had taken just one point from their four league meetings with Qarabağ and were to come a cropper once more against the champions. Brazilian striker Reynaldo, Qarabağ's leading scorer, took centre stage in the final with two goals and an assist to bring his club a 3-1 win and the trophy for the fourth time.

Europe

Qarabağ's bid to become the first Azerbaijani club to play in the UEFA Champions League group stage ended with a narrow qualifying defeat to FC Salzburg, but they did reach the UEFA Europa League equivalent, thanks to a surprise play-off success against FC Twente.

Furthermore, they almost reached the knockout phase, a disallowed winning goal in the last seconds of their final match, at home to FC Internazionale Milano, visibly shattering the Qarabağ players and the masses of supporters congregated in the Tofiq Bähramov stadium. Had that goal counted, they, not eventual finalists FC Dnipro Dnipropetrovsk, whom they defeated 1-0 in Ukraine, would have progressed to the round of 32.

National team

The six-and-a-half-year reign of Berti Vogts as Azerbaijan's head coach ended in the wake of the team's 6-0 defeat by Croatia in their third UEFA EURO 2016 qualifier. The two previous qualifying games, at home to Bulgaria and away to Italy, had both ended in gallant 2-1 defeats, but the humbling in Osijek triggered a volley of criticism towards the German that persuaded him to step down. He was eventually replaced by another foreign coach, Robert Prosinečki, and the former Yugoslavia/Croatia international made a bright start, backing up a 2-0 home win against Malta with a goalless draw in Norway.

DOMESTIC SEASON AT A GLANCE

Premyer Liqa 2014/15 final table

		Pld	Home					Away					Total					Pts
			W	D	L	F	A	W	D	L	F	A	W	D	L	F	A	
1	**Qarabağ FK**	32	11	4	1	24	10	9	4	3	27	18	20	8	4	51	28	68
2	İnter Bakı PİK	32	12	3	1	39	7	5	9	2	16	13	17	12	3	55	20	63
3	Qäbälä FK	32	6	6	4	23	17	9	3	4	23	18	15	9	8	46	35	54
4	Neftçi PFK	32	7	5	4	20	15	6	5	5	18	18	13	10	9	38	33	49
5	Simurq PFK	32	9	2	5	29	17	2	4	10	12	22	11	6	15	41	39	39
6	Olimpik-Şüvälan PFK	32	5	6	5	24	23	5	3	8	13	19	10	9	13	37	42	39
7	Xäzär Länkäran FK	32	7	5	4	25	17	1	3	12	10	29	8	8	16	35	46	32
8	Sumqayıt FK	32	5	5	6	15	13	2	5	9	17	30	7	10	15	32	43	31
9	Bakı FK	32	2	4	10	10	26	1	4	11	9	42	3	8	21	19	68	17
10	Araz-Naxçıvan PFK	0	0	0	0	0	0	0	0	0	0	0	0	0	0	0	0	0

NB Araz-Naxçıvan PFK withdrew after round 10 – all their matches were annulled.

European qualification 2015/16

Champion/Cup winner: Qarabağ FK (second qualifying round)

İnter Bakı PİK (first qualifying round)
Qäbälä FK (first qualifying round)
Neftçi PFK (first qualifying round)

Top scorer	Nurlan Novruzov (Bakı), 15 goals
Relegated clubs	Araz Naxçıvan PFK (withdrew), Bakı FK
Promoted clubs	Zirä FK, Käpäz PFK
Cup final	Qarabağ FK 3-1 Neftçi PFK

Team of the season
(4-4-2)

Coach: Qurbanov (Qarabağ)

Šehić (Qarabağ)

Medvedev (Qarabağ) Hüseynov (Qarabağ) Salukvadze (İnter) Daşdämirov (İnter)

George (Qarabağ) D Meza (İnter) Richard (Qarabağ) C Hüseynov (Qäbälä)

Reynaldo (Qarabağ) Mombongo-Dues (Olimpik-Şüvälan)

Player of the season

Cavid Hüseynov
(Qäbälä FK)

While Qarabağ FK were the best team in the 2014/15 Premyer Liqa, the leading individual was Hüseynov, Qäbälä's versatile attacking midfielder. The club's top marksman with 12 goals, he also impressed with his leadership and will to win and stood out as the inspirational figure behind Qäbälä's unbeaten closing run of ten wins and two draws that lifted them to third place. The 24-year-old also impressed in Azerbaijan's first three internationals under new coach Robert Prosinečki.

Newcomer of the season

Coşqun Diniyev
(İnter Bakı PİK)

Still only 19 at the end of a season in which he played a starring role in midfield for Premyer Liqa runners-up İnter, Diniyev left in the summer to join champions Qarabağ. A graduate of the İnter academy and son of ex-Azerbaijan national coach Şahin Diniyev, he made such rapid progress during the 2014/15 campaign, his first as a regular starter in Kakhaber Tskhadadze's side, that by the end of it he was called up to play for his country and won his first senior cap in a friendly against Serbia.

NATIONAL TEAM

Top five all-time caps
Räşad F Sadıqov (95); Aslan Kärimov (79); **Mahir Şükürov** (76); Tärlan Ähmädov (73); Mahmud Qurbanov (72)

Top five all-time goals
Qurban Qurbanov (12); **Vaqif Cavadov** (9); **Rauf Äliyev, Elvin Mämmädov** & Branimir Subašić (7)

Results 2014/15

20/08/14	Uzbekistan	H	Baku	D	0-0	
03/09/14	Russia	A	Khimki	L	0-4	
09/09/14	Bulgaria (ECQ)	H	Baku	L	1-2	*Nazarov (54)*
10/10/14	Italy (ECQ)	A	Palermo	L	1-2	*Chiellini (76og)*
13/10/14	Croatia (ECQ)	A	Osijek	L	0-6	
16/11/14	Norway (ECQ)	H	Baku	L	0-1	
28/03/15	Malta (ECQ)	H	Baku	W	2-0	*C Hüseynov (4), Nazarov (90+2)*
07/06/15	Serbia	N	St Polten (AUT)	L	1-4	*Nazarov (39)*
12/06/15	Norway (ECQ)	A	Oslo	D	0-0	

Appearances 2014/15

Coach: Berti Vogts (GER) /(18/10/14) (Mahmud Qurbanov) /(03/12/14) Robert Prosinečki (CRO)	30/12/46 10/05/73 12/01/69		Uzb	Rus	BUL	ITA	CRO	NOR	MLT	Srb	NOR	Caps	Goals
Sälahät Ağayev	04/01/91	İnter Bakı	G					G				6	-
Mahir Şükürov	12/12/82	Karşıyaka (TUR)	D60	s73	D			D				76	4
Rasim Ramaldanov	24/01/86	Xäzär Länkäran	D	D		s46	D					16	-
Ruslan Abışov	10/10/87	Qäbälä	D	M73	M74			M65		D		45	4
Ufuk Budak	26/05/90	Gaziantep BB (TUR)	D46		D90							15	-
Rahid Ämirquliyev	01/09/89	Xäzär Länkäran	M	s46		M86	M	M	M	M	M	43	1
Dimitrij Nazarov	04/04/90	Karlsruhe (GER)	M	M	M	M	M	s69	s70	M46	M93	10	3
Tuğrul Erat	17/06/92	Düsseldorf (GER)	M59									2	-
Rüfät Dadaşov	29/09/91	Zweibrücken (GER) /Saarbrücken (GER)	M	A46	A	A59						15	4
Vaqif Cavadov	25/05/89	Gaziantep BB (TUR)	M46	s46	M46			M				57	9
Rauf Äliyev	12/02/89	Xäzär Länkäran	A73		M	M	A	A				41	7
Cihan Özkara	14/07/91	Sivasspor (TUR)	s46	M57								17	1
Emin Nouri	22/07/85	Kalmar (SWE)	s46 /93									1	-
Äfran İsmayılov	08/10/88	Xäzär Länkäran /İnter Bakı	s59						M70	M61	M	21	1
İlkin Qırtımov	04/11/90	Simurq	s60	D46		D46						5	-
Cavid Hüseynov	09/03/88	Qäbälä	s73	s57		s59	s41		M	M76	M	44	2
Elnur Allahverdiyev	02/11/83	Qäbälä /Neftçi	s93			D	D66					38	-
Kamran Ağayev	09/02/86	Qäbälä /Kayserispor (TUR)	G	G	G	G			G	G	G	53	-
Räşad F Sadıqov	16/06/82	Qarabağ		D	D	D	D	D	D	D46	D	95	4
Ruslan Ämircanov	01/02/85	Qäbälä		D								5	-
Bädavi Hüseynov	11/07/91	Qarabağ		M46	D	D	D		D	s46	D	17	-
Vüqar Nadirov	15/06/87	Qarabağ		M79	s90	s86		A81		s46	s81	58	4
Qara Qarayev	12/10/92	Qarabağ		s46	M	M	M30	s65	M	s76	M	16	-
Araz Abdullayev	18/04/92	Neftçi		s79	s46	M	M	M		s61		15	-
Tärlan Quliyev	19/04/92	Qarabağ			s74		s66					2	-
Maksim Medvedev	29/09/89	Qarabağ				D	D	D			D	29	-
Ağabala Ramazanov	20/01/93	Xäzär Länkäran					s30 /41					1	-
Elvin Yunuszadä	22/08/92	Neftçi						D				3	1
Cavid İmamverdiyev	01/08/90	Elazığspor (TUR)						M69				1	-
Arif Daşdämirov	10/02/87	İnter Bakı							D	D	D	4	-
Namiq Äläsgärov	03/02/95	Qarabağ							M22			1	-
Ruslan Qurbanov	12/09/91	Hajduk Split (CRO)							s22	M61	A81	3	-
Eddy İsrafilov	02/08/92	Granada (ESP)							s81			1	-
Mähämmäd Mirzäbäyov	16/11/90	İnter Bakı								D		1	-
Mähämmäd Qurbanov	11/04/92	Sumqayıt								A46	s93	2	-
Coşqun Diniyev	13/09/95	İnter Bakı								s46		1	-
Elvin Mämmädov	18/07/88	İnter Bakı								s61		32	7

Qarabağ FK

CHAMPIONS
LEAGUE

Second qualifying round - Valletta FC (MLT)
A 1-0 *Chumbinho (18)*
Šehić, Qarayev (Yusifov 79), Reynaldo, Muarem (Danilo Dias 72), Qurbanov, Richard, Teli, Agolli, George (Nadirov 87), Hüseynov, Chumbinho. Coach: Qurban Qurbanov (AZE)
H 4-0 *Reynaldo (15), Chumbinho (48), Danilo Dias (57), George (80)*
Šehić, Qarayev, Reynaldo (Nadirov 46), Danilo Dias, Qurbanov, Richard (Yusifov 75), Teli, Agolli (Quliyev 81), George, Hüseynov, Chumbinho. Coach: Qurban Qurbanov (AZE)

Third qualifying round - FC Salzburg (AUT)
H 2-1 *Danilo Dias (2), Reynaldo (86)*
Šehić, Qarayev (Qurbanov 46), Medvedev, Reynaldo, Danilo Dias (Yusifov 70), Richard, Teli, Agolli, George (Sadıqov 57), Hüseynov, Chumbinho. Coach: Qurban Qurbanov (AZE)
Red cards: Teli 42, Reynaldo 88
A 0-2
Šehić, Qarayev, Medvedev (Quliyev 60), Danilo Dias (Chumbinho 55), Sadıqov, Nadirov, Qurbanov (Yusifov 20), Richard, Agolli, George, Hüseynov. Coach: Qurban Qurbanov (AZE)

EUROPA
LEAGUE

Play-offs - FC Twente (NED)
H 0-0
Šehić, Qarayev, Medvedev, Reynaldo, Muarem (Äläsgärov 67), Danilo Dias (Tağiyev 56), Sadıqov, Richard, Agolli, George (Nadirov 29), Hüseynov. Coach: Qurban Qurbanov (AZE)
A 1-1 *Muarem (51)*
Šehić, Qarayev, Medvedev, Reynaldo, Muarem (Danilo Dias 71), Sadıqov, Nadirov (Teli 85), Richard, Agolli, Hüseynov, Chumbinho (Yusifov 79). Coach: Qurban Qurbanov (AZE)

Group F
Match 1 - AS Saint-Étienne (FRA)
H 0-0
Šehić, Qarayev, Medvedev, Reynaldo, Muarem (Danilo Dias 80), Sadıqov, Richard, Agolli, George (Äläsgärov 70), Hüseynov, Chumbinho (Nadirov 46). Coach: Qurban Qurbanov (AZE)
Match 2 - FC Internazionale Milano (ITA)
A 0-2
Šehić, Qarayev, Yusifov (Nadirov 55), Reynaldo, Muarem, Qurbanov (Sadıqov 68), Richard, Teli, Agolli, George (Tağiyev 62), Hüseynov. Coach: Qurban Qurbanov (AZE)
Match 3 - FC Dnipro Dnipropetrovsk (UKR)
A 1-0 *Muarem (21)*
Šehić, Qarayev, Medvedev, Yusifov, Reynaldo, Muarem (Äläsgärov 90), Sadıqov, Nadirov (Tağiyev 72), Richard (Teli 82), Agolli, Hüseynov. Coach: Qurban Qurbanov (AZE)
Match 4 - FC Dnipro Dnipropetrovsk (UKR)
H 1-2 *George (36)*
Šehić, Qarayev, Medvedev, Yusifov (Tağiyev 77), Reynaldo, Muarem, Sadıqov, Richard, Agolli, George (Nadirov 65), Hüseynov. Coach: Qurban Qurbanov (AZE)

Match 5 - AS Saint-Étienne (FRA)
A 1-1 *Nadirov (15)*
Šehić, Qarayev, Medvedev, Yusifov (Teli 75), Muarem, Sadygov, Nadirov (Äläsgärov 79), Richard, Agolli, George (Qurbanov 63), Hüseynov. Coach: Qurban Qurbanov (AZE)
Match 6 - FC Internazionale Milano (ITA)
H 0-0
Šehić, Qarayev, Medvedev, Muarem, Sadıqov, Nadirov (Yusifov 43), Richard, Agolli, George, Hüseynov, Äläsgärov (Qurbanov 60). Coach: Qurban Qurbanov (AZE)

Neftçi PFK

EUROPA
LEAGUE

Second qualifying round - FC Koper (SVN)
H 1-2 *A Abdullayev (45+1)*
Stamenković, Carlos Cardoso, Yunuszadä, A Abdullayev (Mäsimov 78), Flavinho, Wobay, Ramos, Bruno Bertucci, Cauê (Seyidov 59), İsayev, Nfor (Qurbanov 73). Coach: Böyükağa Hacıyev (AZE)
A 2-0 *Seyidov (21), Carlos Cardoso (84)*
Stamenković, Carlos Cardoso, Yunuszadä, A Abdullayev (Mäsimov 72), Flavinho, Wobay, Ramos, Bruno Bertucci (Qurbanov 68), Cauê, Seyidov, Nfor (Bädälov 90+4). Coach: Böyükağa Hacıyev (AZE)

Third qualifying round - FC Chikhura Sachkhere (GEO)
H 0-0
Stamenković, Carlos Cardoso, Yunuszadä, A Abdullayev (Mäsimov 67), Flavinho, Wobay, Ramos, Bruno Bertucci, Cauê, Seyidov (İmamverdiyev 82), Nfor (Qurbanov 72). Coach: Böyükağa Hacıyev (AZE)
A 3-2 *Nfor (16, 27, 38)*
Stamenković, Carlos Cardoso, Yunuszadä, A Abdullayev (Mäsimov 72), Flavinho, Wobay (İmamverdiyev 83), Ramos, Bruno Bertucci, Cauê, Seyidov (İsayev 64), Nfor. Coach: Böyükağa Hacıyev (AZE)

Play-offs - FK Partizan (SRB)
A 2-3 *Dênis Silva (10, 17)*
Stamenković, Dênis Silva, Yunuszadä, A Abdullayev (Canales 71), Flavinho (Mäsimov 81), Wobay, Ramos, Bruno Bertucci, Cauê, Seyidov (İmamverdiyev 90+4), Nfor. Coach: Böyükağa Hacıyev (AZE)
H 1-2 *Wobay (58)*
Stamenković, Carlos Cardoso, Dênis Silva, Yunuszadä, A Abdullayev, Flavinho (Bruno Bertucci 54), Wobay (Mäsimov 83), Ramos, Cauê, Seyidov (Canales 54), Nfor. Coach: Böyükağa Hacıyev (AZE)
Red cards: Nfor 86, Ramos 90+3, Cauê 90+4

İnter Bakı PİK

EUROPA
LEAGUE

First qualifying round - FC Tiraspol (MDA)
A 3-2 *Tskhadadze (8p), E Mämmädov (10), Novicov (71og)*
Lomaia, Salukvadze, Amisulashvili, Georgievski, E Mämmädov (Mikel Álvaro 72), A Mämmädov (Hüseynpur 90+3), Bocognano, Daşdämirov, Špičić, D Meza, Tskhadadze (Madrigal 82). Coach: Kakhaber Tskhadadze (GEO)
H 3-1 *Daşdämirov (79), Tskhadadze (83p), Hüseynpur (90+1)*
Lomaia, Salukvadze, Amisulashvili, Georgievski, Mikel Álvaro, A Mämmädov (Tskhadadze 41), Bocognano, Daşdämirov, Madrigal (Hüseynpur 78), Špičić, D Meza. Coach: Zaur Svanadze (GEO)

Second qualifying round - IF Elfsborg (SWE)
A 1-0 *Georgievski (29)*
Lomaia, Salukvadze, Amisulashvili, Georgievski, Mikel Álvaro (Iván Benítez 90+3), Bocognano, Daşdämirov, Madrigal (A Mämmädov 74), Špičić, D Meza, Tskhadadze (Hüseynpur 63). Coach: Kakhaber Tskhadadze (GEO)
H 0-1 (aet; 3-4 on pens)
Lomaia, Salukvadze, Amisulashvili, Georgievski, Mikel Álvaro, Bocognano, Daşdämirov, Madrigal (A Mämmädov 70; Hüseynpur 16), Špičić, D Meza, Tskhadadze (Iván Benítez 46). Coach: Kakhaber Tskhadadze (GEO)
Red card: Salukvadze 3

Qäbälä FK

EUROPA
LEAGUE

First qualifying round - NK Široki Brijeg (BIH)
H 0-2
Ağayev, Camalov (Cristea 56), Levin, Hacıyev, Mendy, Dodô, Abışov, Tağizadä, Ropotan, Allahverdiyev, Rafael Santos. Coach: Dorinel Munteanu (ROU)
A 0-3
Ağayev, Levin (Quliyev 83), Hacıyev, Mendy, Dodô, Cristea (Camalov 65), Abışov, Tağizade (Ämircanov 46), Ropotan, Abbasov, Rafael Santos. Coach: Dorinel Munteanu (ROU)

DOMESTIC LEAGUE CLUB-BY-CLUB

Araz-Naxçıvan PFK

1967 • Naxçıvan Muxtar Respublikası adına stadion (12,800) • arazpfc.com
Coach: Äsgär Abdullayev

2014

10/08	h	Neftçi	W	3-0	Janelidze 2, Çobanov
17/08	a	Qäbälä	L	0-1	
30/08	a	Sumqayıt	L	0-1	
12/09	a	İnter	L	1-3	Zubkov
20/09	a	Xäzär Länkäran	L	0-2	
27/09	a	Bakı	L	1-2	Çobanov
18/10	h	Olimpik-Şüvälan	D	2-2	Janelidze, Soltanov
25/10	a	Simurq	L	0-4	
29/10	h	Qäbälä	L	0-1	
02/11	a	Qarabağ	L	0-4	

NB Araz-Naxçıvan withdrew from the league after 10 games; all of their matches were annulled

No	Name	Nat	DoB	Pos	Aps	(s)	Gls
23	Elnur Abdulov		18/09/92	A		(3)	
11	Vüqar Äsgärov		14/05/85	A		(2)	
12	Kamal Bayramov		15/08/85	G	10		
16	Emin Cäfärquliyev		17/06/90	D	8	(1)	
8	Elmin Çobanov		13/05/92	M	6	(2)	2
3	Älimrzä Daşzärini		23/07/92	D	3	(1)	
5	Cavid Häsänov		20/10/92	D		(4)	
2	Tural Hümbätov		24/01/94	D	4		
16	Kamil Hüseynov		04/02/92	D	3		
7	Ramal Hüseynov		16/12/84	M	9		
9	Qärib İbrahimov		11/09/88	M	2	(3)	
21	David Janelidze	GEO	12/09/89	A	7	(3)	3
18	Elgiz Kärämli		28/02/92	M	1		
2	Olexandr Krutskevich	UKR	13/11/80	D	4		
4	Azär Mämmädov		18/06/90	M	4	(2)	
13	Aqil Näbiyev		16/06/82	D	6		
11	Ruslan Näsirli		12/01/95	A		(4)	
6	Budaq Näsirov		15/07/96	M	5	(1)	
91	Kamil Nurähmädov		10/06/91	A	2	(1)	
22	Eşqin Quliyev		11/12/90	M	6	(1)	
17	Bäxtiyar Soltanov		21/06/89	A	10		1
11	Serhiy Sylyuk	UKR	05/06/85	A	3		
5	Akif Tağıyev		24/04/93	M		(1)	
19	Tärlan Xälilov		27/08/84	M	6	(1)	
44	Saşa Yunisoğlu		18/12/85	D	3		
20	Ruslan Zubkov	UKR	24/11/91	D	8		1

NB Appearances and goals for all clubs include those from the annulled matches against Araz-Naxçıvan PFK.

Bakı FK

1997 • Bakı FK training center (2,000) • fcbaku.com
Major honours
Azerbaijan League (2) 2006, 2009; Azerbaijan Cup (3) 2005, 2010, 2012
Coach: İbrahim Uzunca (TUR)

2014

16/08	a	Neftçi	L	0-1	
23/08	h	Qäbälä	L	0-2	
31/08	h	Qarabağ	D	2-2	Novruzov, Travner
14/09	h	Sumqayıt	l	1-2	Novruzov
19/09	a	İnter	L	0-7	
27/09	h	Araz-Naxçıvan	W	2-1	Qürbätov, Qurbanov (match annulled)
02/10	h	Simurq	W	1-0	Novruzov
19/10	a	Xäzär Länkäran	L	0-4	
25/10	a	Olimpik-Şüvälan	W	1-0	Novruzov
29/10	h	Neftçi	L	1-3	Novruzov
02/11	a	Qäbälä	D	1-1	Qurbanov
02/11	a	Qarabağ	L	2-4	Qurbanov, Ristović
24/11	a	Sumqayıt	D	1-1	Novruzov
29/11	h	İnter	L	0-1	
14/12	h	Xäzär Länkäran	D	0-0	
17/12	h	Olimpik-Şüvälan	L	1-3	Novruzov
22/12	a	Simurq	L	2-5	Novruzov 2 (1p)

2015

01/02	h	Qäbälä	L	0-2	
07/02	a	Qarabağ	L	1-4	Novruzov (p)
11/02	h	Sumqayıt	D	0-0	
15/02	a	İnter	L	0-4	
28/02	a	Xäzär Länkäran	L	1-2	Novruzov
08/03	a	Olimpik-Şüvälan	L	0-2	
18/03	h	Simurq	L	0-3	
01/04	a	Neftçi	L	0-2	
05/04	h	Qarabağ	D	1-1	Novruzov (p)
09/04	a	Sumqayıt	D	0-0	
17/04	h	İnter	L	1-2	Novruzov (p)
02/05	h	Xäzär Länkäran	W	2-1	Novruzov 2 (1p)
09/05	h	Olimpik-Şüvälan	L	0-2	
15/05	a	Simurq	L	0-4	
22/05	h	Neftçi	D	0-0	
28/05	a	Qäbälä	L	0-3	

No	Name	Nat	DoB	Pos	Aps	(s)	Gls
77	Ramazan Abbasov		22/09/83	M	12	(4)	
12	Elxan Ähmädov		02/07/93	G	17		
14	Elvin Äliyev		21/08/84	M	1		
56	Qeyrät Äliyev		08/11/88	M	17	(1)	
16	Rövşän Ämiraslanov		18/03/86	M		(3)	
17	Elmin Äsgärli		28/09/95	A		(7)	
26	Davud Äsgärov		30/01/95	M	1		
2	Nicat Äsgärov		01/06/95	D	13		
6	Vüqar Bäybalayev		05/08/93	M	29		
8	Lucas Horvat	ARG	13/10/85	M	13		
19	Eltun Hüseynov		27/02/93	D	29		
85	Jabá	BRA	20/05/81	A	18	(2)	
15	Azad Kärimov		31/10/94	D	5	(7)	
21	Elşad Manafov		08/03/92	D	17	(6)	
94	Qvanzan Maqomedov		08/06/94	M		(1)	
45	Mahir Mädätov		01/07/97	M	3	(14)	
30	Cämşid Mähärrämov		04/08/83	M	12	(1)	
1	Aqil Mämmädov		01/05/89	G	14		
39	Täyyar Mämmädov		02/10/96	M		(1)	
55	Aydın Mustafazadä		09/02/94	D	4	(4)	
10	Nurlan Novruzov		03/03/93	M	31		15
99	Kamil Nurähmädov		10/06/91	A	15	(1)	
5	Georgios Pelagias	CYP	02/05/87	D	21		
18	Äziz Quliyev		02/05/88	M	14	(2)	
28	Ülvi Quliyev		22/07/93	A		(3)	
7	Nuran Qurbanov		10/08/93	M	23	(6)	3
11	Tural Qürbätov		01/03/93	A	26	(6)	1
37	Mikayıl Rähimov		11/05/87	D	7		
17	Risto Ristović	SRB	05/05/88	M	12	(1)	1
16	Rüstäm Rüstämli		07/05/95	D		(1)	
1	Elçin Sadıqov		14/06/89	G	1		
20	Valeh Seyidov		04/03/96	A		(10)	
4	Ülvi Süleymanov		06/01/96	M	1	(8)	
3	Jure Travner	SVN	28/09/85	D	7		1
9	Raul Yaqubzadä		30/05/94	A		(7)	

İnter Bakı PİK

2004 • İnter Arena (6,500) • inter.az
Major honours
Azerbaijan League (2) 2008, 2010
Coach: Kakhaber Tskhadadze (GEO)

2014

10/08	h	Qäbälä	W	4-0	Amisulashvili, Mikel Álvaro 2, Mirzäbäyov
16/08	a	Qarabağ	D	0-0	
24/08	h	Sumqayıt	W	5-1	Abatsiyev, Hacıyev, Mikel Álvaro 2, A Mämmädov
29/08	a	Xäzär Länkäran	L	0-1	
12/09	h	Araz-Naxçıvan	W	3-1	Tskhadadze, Diniyev, A Mämmädov (match annulled)
19/09	h	Bakı	W	7-0	Nildo 2, Daşdämirov, Tskhadadze 2, Diniyev, Hacıyev
27/09	a	Olimpik-Şüvälan	D	1-1	Mikel Álvaro
18/10	h	Simurq	D	0-0	
26/10	a	Neftçi	D	0-0	
29/10	h	Qarabağ	D	0-0	
02/11	a	Sumqayıt	D	0-0	
20/11	h	Xäzär Länkäran	W	3-1	Nildo, Mikel Álvaro 2
29/11	a	Bakı	W	1-0	Mikel Álvaro
07/12	h	Olimpik-Şüvälan	W	1-0	Nildo
13/12	a	Simurq	D	1-1	Nildo
18/12	h	Neftçi	W	2-1	Nildo, Mirzäbäyov
21/12	a	Qäbälä	D	1-1	Mirzäbäyov

2015

30/01	h	Sumqayıt	D	0-0	
07/02	a	Xäzär Länkäran	W	2-1	Mirzäbäyov, Şpičić
15/02	h	Bakı	W	4-0	Tskhadadze 2, Ismayılov 2, Nildo
19/02	a	Olimpik-Şüvälan	D	1-1	Nildo
28/02	h	Simurq	W	2-1	Tskhadadze, E Mämmädov
08/03	a	Neftçi	W	2-0	og (İsayev), A Mämmädov
18/03	h	Qäbälä	L	1-2	Amisulashvili
02/04	a	Qarabağ	D	0-0	
05/04	h	Xäzär Länkäran	W	2-0	D Meza (p), Stanković
17/04	a	Bakı	W	2-1	C Meza 2
25/04	h	Olimpik-Şüvälan	W	2-0	Daşdämirov 2
01/05	a	Simurq	W	3-2	Daşdämirov, Mikel Álvaro, C Meza
08/05	h	Neftçi	W	4-0	Tskhadadze 2, D Meza, E Mämmädov
16/05	a	Qäbälä	D	1-1	A Mämmädov
22/05	h	Qarabağ	W	2-1	İsmayılov, Daşdämirov
28/05	a	Sumqayıt	L	1-3	Sadiqov

No	Name	Nat	DoB	Pos	Aps	(s)	Gls
7	Abdulla Abatsiyev		16/08/93	M	8	(7)	1
97	Färid Abbaslı		23/01/97	D	1		
13	Mirsahib Abbasov		19/01/93	M	1	(1)	
25	Sälahät Ağayev		04/01/91	G	28		
5	Aleksandre Amisulashvili	GEO	20/08/82	D	23		2
89	Qaraxan Äliyev		05/10/96	D	1		
24	Fuad Bayramov		30/11/94	M	2	(5)	
15	Yohan Bocognano	FRA	12/06/90	D	15	(6)	
69	Färhad Budaqov		12/10/95	M	1		
21	Arif Daşdämirov		10/02/87	D	29		5
91	Coşqun Diniyev		13/09/95	M	23	(3)	2
6	Slavco Georgievski	MKD	30/03/80	M	1		
80	Nizami Hacıyev		08/02/88	M	12	(8)	2
44	Tural Hümbätov		24/01/94	D	1		
9	Mirzağa Hüseynpur		11/03/90	M		(1)	
42	Ulvi İbazadä		26/08/96	M	1		
61	Ruzigar İbrahimzadä		06/07/97	M		(1)	
22	Äfran İsmayılov		08/10/88	M	8	(2)	3
4	Iván Benítez	ESP	31/05/88	D	2	(3)	
1	Giorgi Lomaia	GEO	08/08/79	G	4		
27	Diego Madrigal	CRC	19/03/89	A	2	(8)	
14	Mähämmäd Mirzäbäyov		26/04/96	M		(1)	
77	Vüsal Nağıyev		13/06/96	M		(1)	
18	Mansur Nähavändi		12/08/96	M	1		
11	Asif Mämmädov		05/08/86	M	9	(12)	4
10	Elvin Mämmädov		18/07/88	M	15	(10)	2
19	César Meza	PAR	05/10/91	A	4	(6)	3
88	David Meza	PAR	15/08/88	M	30		2
8	Mikel Álvaro	ESP	20/12/82	M	22	(7)	9
17	Mähämmäd Mirzäbäyov		16/11/90	D	29	(1)	4
96	Elşän Poladov		30/11/79	G	1	(1)	
45	İlkin Sadiqov		12/09/97	A	1		1
3	Lasha Salukvadze	GEO	21/12/81	D	27		
82	Ruben Schaken	NED	03/04/82	M	2	(2)	
33	Matija Şpičić	CRO	24/02/88	D	6	(1)	1
23	Vojislav Stanković	SRB	22/09/87	D	12		1
39	Elnur Süleymanov		17/09/96	M	1		
20	Särtan Taşkın		08/10/97	D	1		
28	Bachana Tskhadadze	GEO	23/10/87	A	22	(6)	7

Neftçi PFK

1937 • Bakcell Arena (11,000); İsmät Qayıbov
adına Bakıxanov qäsäbä stadionu (4,500) •
neftchipfk.com

Major honours
*Azerbaijan League (8) 1992, 1996, 1997, 2004, 2005,
2011, 2012, 2013; Azerbaijan Cup (7) 1995, 1996,
1999, 2002, 2004, 2013, 2014*

**Coach: Böyükağa Hacıyev;
(04/09/14) Arif Äsädov**

2014

10/08	a	Araz-Naxçıvan	L	0-3	*(match annulled)*
16/08	h	Bakı	W	1-0	*Wobay*
31/08	h	Simurq	W	2-1	*A Abdullayev, Wobay*
13/09	h	Xäzär Länkäran	W	1-0	*Flavinho*
21/09	a	Qäbälä	D	0-0	
27/09	h	Qarabağ	L	1-3	*Nfor*
17/10	a	Sumqayıt	W	1-0	*Nfor*
26/10	h	İnter	D	0-0	
29/10	a	Bakı	W	3-1	*Wobay, A Abdullayev,*
					Cauê
02/11	h	Olimpik-Şüvälan	W	4-0	*og (Yaqublu), Dênis Silva,*
					Canales 2
20/11	a	Simurq	L	0-1	
24/11	a	Xäzär Länkäran	D	2-2	*R Qurbanov, Seyidov*
29/11	h	Qäbälä	D	0-0	
07/12	a	Qarabağ	D	0-0	
14/12	h	Sumqayıt	W	3-2	*R Qurbanov 2,*
					A Abdullayev
18/12	a	İnter	L	1-2	*Canales*

2015

31/01	a	Olimpik-Şüvälan	L	1-2	*Canales (p)*
06/02	h	Simurq	D	0-0	
11/02	h	Xäzär Länkäran	W	2-0	*Wobay, Mäsimov*
15/02	a	Qäbälä	W	3-1	*Wobay, Dênis Silva,*
					Flavinho
19/02	h	Qarabağ	L	0-1	
24/02	a	Olimpik-Şüvälan	W	1-0	*Canales*
28/02	a	Sumqayıt	W	1-0	*Canales*
08/03	h	İnter	L	0-2	
01/04	h	Bakı	W	2-0	*Canales, Wobay*
05/04	a	Simurq	W	1-0	*Canales*
09/04	a	Xäzär Länkäran	D	2-2	*Wobay, Ramos*
17/04	h	Qäbälä	L	1-3	*Canales*
25/04	a	Qarabağ	L	2-3	*A Abdullayev, Canales*
01/05	h	Sumqayıt	D	2-2	*Canales, Mäsimov*
08/05	a	İnter	L	0-4	
22/05	h	Bakı	D	0-0	
28/05	h	Olimpik-Şüvälan	D	1-1	*E Abdullayev*

No	Name	Nat	DoB	Pos	Aps	(s)	Gls
49	Mirabdulla Abbasov		27/04/95	M		(2)	
7	Araz Abdullayev		18/04/92	M	28	(2)	4
8	Elşän Abdullayev		05/02/94	M	5	(6)	1
14	Elnur Allahverdiyev		02/11/83	D	6		
22	Rauf Äliyev		12/02/89	A	3	(8)	
1	Emil Balayev		17/04/94	G	9		
95	Elvin Bädälov		14/06/95	D	6		
16	Bruno Bertucci	BRA	20/04/90	D	2	(1)	
11	Nicolás Canales	CHI	27/06/85	A	20	(8)	11
2	Carlos Cardoso	BRA	11/09/84	D	25	(1)	
18	Cauê	BRA	24/05/89	M	21	(4)	1
3	Dênis Silva	BRA	28/12/85	D	19		2
12	Pävels Doroševs	LVA	09/10/80	G		(1)	
9	Flavinho	BRA	27/07/83	M	20	(4)	2
7	Rähman Hacıyev		25/07/93	M	3	(10)	
25	Cavid İmamverdiyev		01/08/90	M	1		
27	Mäqsäd İsayev		07/06/94	D	24		
1	Aqil Mämmädov		05/01/89	G	13		
4	Rahil Mämmädov		24/11/95	D	4	(1)	
21	Samir Mäsimov		25/08/95	M	10	(18)	2
28	Emin Mehdiyev		22/09/92	M	10	(3)	
20	Fähmin Muradbäyli		16/03/96	A		(2)	
29	Cavid Muxtarzadä		15/09/94	A		(1)	
90	Ernest Nfor	CMR	28/04/86	A	12	(5)	2
16	Äziz Quliyev		02/05/87	D	12	(2)	
17	Nicat Qurbanov		17/02/92	M	1	(2)	
23	Ruslan Qurbanov		17/02/92	A	7	(5)	3
15	Éric Ramos	PAR	12/06/87	M	24	(5)	1
19	Mirhüseyn Seyidov		10/08/92	M	20	(3)	1
30	Saša Stamenković	SRB	05/01/85	G	11	(1)	
10	Julius Wobay	SLE	19/05/84	M	26	(1)	7
5	Elvin Yunuszadä		22/08/92	D	21		

Olimpik-Şüvälan PFK

1996 • AZAL Arena (3,000) • azalpfc.az

Coach: Tärlan Ähmädov

2014

09/08	h	Xäzär Länkäran	D	1-1	*Kostadinov*
17/08	a	Simurq	L	0-2	
30/08	h	Qäbälä	W	2-1	*Abdullayev (p), Diniyev*
13/09	h	Qarabağ	L	0-3	
20/09	a	Sumqayıt	W	1-0	*Mombongo-Dues*
27/09	h	İnter	D	1-1	*Diniyev*
18/10	a	Araz-Naxçıvan	D	2-2	*Abdullayev (p), Eduardo*
					(match annulled)
25/10	h	Bakı	L	0-1	
29/10	h	Simurq	D	2-2	*Abdullayev (p), Eduardo*
02/11	a	Neftçi	L	0-4	
20/11	h	Qäbälä	D	3-3	*Eduardo, Igbekoyi,*
					Mombongo-Dues
23/11	a	Qarabağ	L	1-2	*Abdullayev (p)*
29/11	h	Sumqayıt	W	3-2	*Abdullayev, Igbekoyi,*
					Mämmädov
07/12	a	İnter	L	0-1	
17/12	a	Bakı	W	3-1	*Kostadinov 2, Kļava*
21/12	a	Xäzär Länkäran	D	1-1	*Mombongo-Dues*

2015

31/01	h	Neftçi	W	2-1	*Mombongo-Dues 2*
06/02	a	Qäbälä	W	1-0	*Abdullayev (p)*
11/02	h	Qarabağ	L	0-1	
15/02	a	Sumqayıt	D	0-0	
19/02	h	İnter	D	1-1	*Mombongo-Dues*
24/02	h	Neftçi	L	0-1	
08/03	h	Bakı	W	2-0	*Qasımov, Qurbanov*
18/03	h	Xäzär Länkäran	W	3-1	*Kutsenko,*
					Mombongo-Dues 2
01/04	a	Simurq	L	0-1	
05/04	h	Qäbälä	L	0-4	
09/04	a	Qarabağ	L	1-2	*Äsädov*
17/04	h	Sumqayıt	D	1-1	*Kutsenko*
25/04	a	İnter	L	0-2	
09/05	a	Bakı	W	2-0	*Abdullayev,*
					Mombongo-Dues
16/05	a	Xäzär Länkäran	L	0-1	
22/05	h	Simurq	W	5-0	*Mombongo-Dues 4,*
					Abdullayev
28/05	a	Neftçi	D	1-1	*Qurbanov*

No	Name	Nat	DoB	Pos	Aps	(s)	Gls
27	Räşad Abdullayev		01/10/81	M	28	(1)	8
85	Seymur Äsädov		05/05/94	M	18	(2)	1
85	Kamal Bayramov		15/08/85	G	6		
11	John Córdoba	COL	10/02/87	A	7	(2)	
5	Kärim Diniyev		05/09/93	D	20	(10)	2
6	Eduardo	BRA	12/11/86	M	13	(2)	3
17	Viktor Igbekoyi	NGA	01/09/86	M	17	(6)	2
3	Juanfran	ESP	10/01/86	D	18	(4)	
4	Lasha Kasradze	GEO	08/07/89	D	27	(6)	
15	Oskars Kļava	LVA	08/08/83	M	29		1
10	Tomi Kostadinov	BUL	15/03/91	M	9	(5)	3
25	Valeriy Kutsenko	UKR	02/11/86	A	14		2
8	Orxan Lalayev		12/10/91	M	16	(5)	
1	Ruslan Mäcidov		22/08/85	G	10		
21	Novruz Mämmädov		20/03/90	D	19	(2)	1
14	Asif Mirili		10/12/91	M	1	(1)	
33	Kamal Mirzäyev		14/09/94	M		(2)	
20	Freddy						
	Mombongo-Dues	COD	30/08/85	A	29		13
16	Stanislav Namasco	MDA	10/11/86	G	17	(1)	
23	Tural Närimanov		27/10/89	D	1		
9	Aydın Qasımov		22/09/93	D	2	(9)	1
10	Nicat Qurbanov		17/02/92	M	2	(13)	2
12	Luis Ramos	HON	11/04/85	M	9	(1)	
13	Şähriyar Rähimov		06/04/89	M	21	(1)	
23	Aleksandr Şemonayev		01/04/85	D	8	(1)	
7	Tämkin Xälilzadä		06/08/93	D	8	(15)	
22	Eltun Yaqublu		19/08/91	D	14		

Qarabağ FK

1987 • İsmät Qayıbov adına Bakıxanov
qäsäbä stadionu (4,500); İnter Arena (6,500);
Tofiq Bähramov adına Respublika stadionu (32,000);
Bakcell Arena (11,000) • qarabagh.com

Major honours
*Azerbaijan League (3) 1993, 2014, 2015; Azerbaijan
Cup (4) 1993, 2006, 2009, 2015*

Coach: Qurban Qurbanov

2014

10/08	a	Sumqayıt	L	0-3	*(w/o; original result 3-0*
					Reynaldo 2,
					og (Häsänalızadä))
16/08	h	İnter	D	0-0	
31/08	h	Bakı	D	2-2	*Chumbinho (p), Muarem*
13/09	a	Olimpik-Şüvälan	W	3-0	*Chumbinho, George,*
					Reynaldo
21/09	h	Simurq	W	1-0	*Nadirov*
27/09	a	Neftçi	W	3-1	*Richard (p), Muarem,*
					Nadirov
17/10	a	Qäbälä	W	2-0	*Nadirov, Reynaldo (p)*
26/10	h	Xäzär Länkäran	W	3-2	*Emeghara 2 (1p), Tağıyev*
29/10	a	İnter	D	0-0	
02/11	h	Araz-Naxçıvan	W	4-0	*Muarem, Emeghara,*
					Reynaldo 2 (1p)
					(match annulled)
20/11	a	Bakı	W	4-2	*Emeghara 2, Reynaldo,*
					George
23/11	h	Olimpik-Şüvälan	W	2-1	*Qurbanov, og (Yaqublu)*
30/11	a	Simurq	W	3-2	*Qurbanov, George 2*
07/12	a	Neftçi	D	0-0	
14/12	a	Qäbälä	L	1-2	*Äläsgärov*
18/12	a	Xäzär Länkäran	W	3-2	*Muarem 2, Hüseynov*
21/12	h	Sumqayıt	W	2-0	*George, og (Hüseynov)*

2015

07/02	h	Bakı	W	4-1	*Medvedev, og (Kärimov),*
					Richard 2 (1p)
11/02	a	Olimpik-Şüvälan	W	1-0	*Reynaldo*
15/02	h	Simurq	W	1-0	*Reynaldo*
19/02	a	Neftçi	W	1-0	*Reynaldo*
28/02	h	Qäbälä	L	0-1	
08/03	h	Xäzär Länkäran	W	1-0	*og (Mirzäyev)*
18/03	a	Sumqayıt	W	2-1	*Reynaldo 2*
02/04	h	İnter	D	0-0	
05/04	a	Bakı	D	1-1	*Reynaldo*
09/04	h	Olimpik-Şüvälan	W	2-1	*George, Nadirov*
17/04	a	Simurq	W	2-0	*Muarem 2*
25/04	h	Neftçi	W	3-2	*Muarem, Tağıyev, George*
02/05	a	Qäbälä	D	1-1	*Reynaldo*
08/05	a	Xäzär Länkäran	D	1-1	*George*
16/05	h	Sumqayıt	W	1-0	*George*
22/05	a	İnter	L	1-2	*George*

No	Name	Nat	DoB	Pos	Aps	(s)	Gls
25	Ansi Agolli	ALB	11/10/82	D	24	(2)	
6	Hacı Ähmädov		23/11/93	M	8	(6)	
99	Namiq Äläsgärov		03/02/95	M	9	(9)	1
33	Şähriyar Äliyev		25/12/92	D	3		
70	Chumbinho	BRA	21/09/86	M	3	(1)	2
11	Danilo Dias	BRA	06/11/85	M	2	(4)	
4	Innocent Emeghara	SUI	05/05/89	A	6	(2)	5
41	Leroy George	NED	21/04/87	M	28		10
55	Bädavi Hüseynov		11/07/91	D	28		1
5	Maksim Medvedev		29/09/89	D	23		1
10	Muarem Muarem	MKD	22/10/88	M	25	(5)	8
17	Vüqar Nadirov		15/06/87	M	15	(12)	4
2	Qara Qarayev		12/10/92	M	24	(7)	
3	Tärlan Quliyev		19/04/92	D	8		
18	İlqar Qurbanov		25/04/86	M	10	(3)	2
9	Reynaldo	BRA	24/08/89	A	22	(3)	14
20	Richard	BRA	20/03/89	M	25	(7)	3
21	Tural Rzayev		27/07/95	M		(1)	
14	Räşad F Sadıqov		16/06/82	D	21	(1)	
13	Ibrahim Šehić	BIH	02/09/88	G	29		
77	Cavid Tağıyev		22/07/92	M	21	(9)	2
24	Admir Teli	ALB	02/06/81	D	14	(4)	
1	Färhad Väliyev		01/11/80	G	4		
7	Namiq Yusifov		14/08/86	M	11	(12)	

Qäbälä FK

2005 • Qäbälä şähär stadionu (3,000) •
gabalafc.az
**Coach: Dorinel Muntoanu (ROU);
(08/12/14) (Sänan Qurbanov);
(22/12/14) Roman Hryhorchuk (UKR)**

2014

10/08	a	İnter	L 0-4	
17/08	h	Araz-Naxçıvan	W 1-0	Hüseynov (p) (match annulled)
23/08	a	Bakı	W 2-0	Mendy, Abışov
30/08	h	Olimpik-Şüvälan	L 1-2	Hüseynov (p)
13/09	a	Simurq	W 2-1	Dodô 2
21/09	h	Neftçi	D 0-0	
28/09	h	Xäzär Länkäran	D 1-1	Hüseynov
17/10	a	Qarabağ	L 0-2	
24/10	h	Sumqayıt	W 3-1	Hüseynov, Farkaš, Ehiosun
29/10	a	Araz-Naxçıvan	W 1-0	Farkaš (match annulled)
02/11	h	Bakı	D 1-1	Dodô
20/11	a	Olimpik-Şüvälan	D 3-3	og (Kasradze), Marquinhos, Hüseynov (p)
23/11	h	Simurq	L 2-3	Ehiosun, Soltanov
29/11	a	Neftçi	D 0-0	
07/12	a	Xäzär Länkäran	L 0-3	
14/12	h	Qarabağ	W 2-1	Soltanov, Dodô
18/12	a	Sumqayıt	D 1-1	Hüseynov (p)
21/12	h	İnter	D 1-1	Dodô

2015

01/02	a	Bakı	W 2-0	Hüseynov (p), og (Bäybalayev)
06/02	h	Olimpik-Şüvälan	L 0-1	
10/02	a	Simurq	L 0-2	
15/02	h	Neftçi	L 1-3	Mendy
19/02	a	Xäzär Länkäran	W 3-1	Ehiosun, Abışov, Abbasov
28/02	a	Qarabağ	W 1-0	og (Äläsgärov)
08/03	h	Sumqayıt	W 2-0	Mendy 2
18/03	a	İnter	W 2-1	Gai, Abışov
05/04	a	Olimpik-Şüvälan	W 4-0	Hüseynov 2 (1p), Mendy, Ehiosun
09/04	h	Simurq	W 1-0	Abışov
17/04	a	Neftçi	W 3-1	Gai, Hüseynov, Mendy
24/04	a	Xäzär Länkäran	W 1-0	Hüseynov
02/05	h	Qarabağ	D 1-1	Hüseynov (p)
08/05	a	Sumqayıt	W 2-0	Gai, Mendy
16/05	h	İnter	D 1-1	Gai
28/05	h	Bakı	W 3-0	Mendy, Ehiosun 2

No	Name	Nat	DoB	Pos	Aps	(s)	Gls
34	Ürfan Abbasov		14/10/92	D	26		1
15	Ruslan Abışov		10/10/87	M	28	(1)	4
1	Kamran Ağayev		09/02/86	G	17		
17	Qismät Aliyev		24/10/96	M		(1)	
7	Ruslan Ämircanov		01/02/85	D	8		
12	Alexandru Benga	ROU	15/06/89	D	8		
22	Dmytro Bezotosniy	UKR	15/11/83	G	15		
4	Elvin Camalov		04/02/95	M	23	(8)	
11	Andrei Cristea	ROU	15/05/84	A	4	(5)	
10	Dodô	BRA	16/10/87	M	19	(12)	6
90	Ekigho Ehiosun	NGA	25/06/90	A	19	(12)	6
26	Pavol Farkaš	SVK	27/03/85	D	13	(2)	2
18	Ruslan Fomin	UKR	02/03/86	A	8	(7)	
19	Olexiy Gai	UKR	06/11/82	M	16		4
14	Cavid Hüseynov		09/03/88	M	31		12
6	Volodimir Levin		23/01/84	D		(1)	
8	Marquinhos	BRA	28/05/92	M	11	(2)	1
9	Victor Mendy	SEN	22/12/81	A	20	(7)	8
13	Murad Musayev		13/06/94	D			
30	Anar Näzirov		08/09/85	G	2	(1)	
5	Sadiq Quliyev		09/03/95	D	4	(5)	
44	Rafael Santos	BRA	10/11/84	D	29		
20	Ricardinho	BRA	09/09/84	D	9	(1)	
25	Adrian Ropotan	ROU	08/05/86	M	16		
6	Räşad A Sadiqov		08/10/83	M	8	(5)	
32	Mikhail Sivakov	BLR	16/01/88	D	5	(7)	
27	Bäxtiyar Soltanov		21/06/89	M	17	(4)	2
16	Ruslan Tağızadä		09/12/93	D	11	(6)	
88	Müşfiq Teymurov		15/01/93	D	5	(1)	
21	Yazalde	POR	21/09/88	A	6	(9)	

Simurq PFK

2005 • Zaqatala şähär stadionu (3,500) •
simurqpfk.az
Coach: Giorgi Chikhradze (GEO)

2014

17/08	h	Olimpik-Şüvälan	W 2-0	Eyyubov, og (Närimanov)
24/08	h	Xäzär Länkäran	W 2-0	Ćeran, Eyyubov
31/08	a	Neftçi	L 1-2	og (Carlos Cardoso)
13/09	h	Qäbälä	L 1-2	Eyyubov (p)
21/09	a	Qarabağ	L 0-1	
28/09	h	Sumqayıt	W 3-2	Banaś, Qırtımov, Stanojević
02/10	a	Bakı	L 0-1	
18/10	a	İnter	D 0-0	
25/10	h	Araz-Naxçıvan	W 4-0	Stanojević, Eyyubov 3 (match annulled)
29/10	a	Olimpik-Şüvälan	D 2-2	Zärgärov, Gökdemir
02/11	a	Xäzär Länkäran	L 0-1	Weitzman
20/11	h	Neftçi	W 1-0	Ćeran (p)
23/11	a	Qäbälä	W 3-2	Stanojević, Ćeran 2
30/11	h	Qarabağ	L 2-3	Ćeran, Stanojević
07/12	a	Sumqayıt	L 1-2	Eyyubov
13/12	h	İnter	D 1-1	Ćeran
22/12	h	Bakı	W 5-2	Eyyubov 2, Ćeran (p), Weitzman, Zärgärov

2015

01/02	h	Xäzär Länkäran	W 2-0	E Abdullayev, Eyyubov
06/02	a	Neftçi	D 0-0	
10/02	h	Qäbälä	W 2-0	Ćeran 2 (1p)
15/02	a	Qarabağ	L 0-1	
19/02	h	Sumqayıt	D 1-1	Ćeran
28/02	h	İnter	L 1-2	Stanojević
18/03	a	Bakı	W 3-0	Zärgärov 2, Ćeran
01/04	h	Olimpik-Şüvälan	W 1-0	Ćeran (p)
05/04	h	Neftçi	L 0-1	
09/04	a	Qäbälä	L 0-1	
17/04	h	Qarabağ	L 0-2	
25/04	a	Sumqayıt	L 0-1	
01/05	h	İnter	L 2-3	Zärgärov, V Abdullayev
15/05	h	Bakı	W 4-0	Ćeran 2, Weitzman, Eyyubov
22/05	a	Olimpik-Şüvälan	L 0-5	
28/05	a	Xäzär Länkäran	D 0-0	

No	Name	Nat	DoB	Pos	Aps	(s)	Gls
7	Elnur Abdullayev		16/02/86	M	7	(6)	1
67	Särxan Abdullayev		06/08/94	A		(1)	
5	Vadim Abdullayev		17/12/94	M	16	(4)	1
35	Amil Ağacanov		24/07/83	G	6		
18	Tural Axundov		01/08/88	D	31		
42	Araz Äsädullazadä		12/01/95	D		(1)	
25	Oruc Balaşlı		23/02/94	A	1	(10)	
3	Adam Banaś	POL	25/12/82	D	11	(2)	1
11	Dragan Ćeran	SRB	06/10/87	A	25	(1)	14
10	Räşad Eyyubov		17/09/91	M	28	(1)	11
13	Ali Gökdemir		17/09/91	D	7	(13)	1
78	İlqar Hüseynov		10/01/94	M	1	(1)	
16	Mähärräm Hüseynov		05/07/92	D	1	(2)	
9	Mirzağa Hüseynpur		11/03/90	M	3	(3)	
76	Vüsal İsgändärli		03/11/95	M	1		
80	Roini İsmayılov		13/12/94	M	1		
1	Paweł Kapsa	POL	24/07/82	G	26		
70	Cavad Kazımov		08/08/94	A	1	(2)	
26	Benjamin Lambot	BEL	02/05/87	M	26		
17	Rüstäm Mämmädov		14/08/84	D	4		
4	Melli	ESP	06/06/84	D	14		
14	Vüqar Mustafayev		05/08/94	M	12	(1)	
81	Nicat Muxtarov		01/06/95	M	2	(3)	
33	Känan Müslümov		11/02/94	D	2	(3)	
8	Patrick Osiako	KEN	15/11/86	M	10	(4)	
22	Cihan Özkara		14/07/91	A	4	(8)	
25	Stjepan Poljak	CRO	17/11/83	M	15	(9)	
2	İlkin Qırtımov		04/11/90	D	30		1
32	Ülvi Quliyev		24/03/96	G	1	(1)	
21	Murad Sättarlı		09/05/92	A		(4)	
88	Marko Stanojević	SRB	22/06/88	M	24	(3)	5
83	Elmir Sulxayev		08/10/95	D		(1)	
9	Lukáš Třešňák	CZE	03/05/88	A	1	(7)	
20	Idan Weitzman	ISR	20/04/85	D	26		3
5	Samir Zärgärov		29/08/86	M	26	(3)	5

Sumqayıt FK

2010 • Kapital Bank Arena (15,000) •
sumqayitpfc.az
Coach: Aqil Mämmädov

2014

10/08	h	Qarabağ	W 3-0	(w/o; original result 0-3)
16/08	a	Xäzär Länkäran	W 1-0	Qurbanov (p)
24/08	a	İnter	L 1-5	Qurbanov
30/08	h	Araz-Naxçıvan	W 1-0	Soltanpour (match annulled)
14/09	a	Bakı	W 2-1	Qurbanov, Soltanpour
20/09	h	Olimpik-Şüvälan	L 0-1	
28/09	a	Simurq	L 2-3	Qurbanov (p), O Äliyev
17/10	h	Neftçi	L 0-1	
24/10	a	Qäbälä	L 1-3	Abbasov
29/10	h	Xäzär Länkäran	L 1-2	Qurbanov
02/11	h	İnter	D 0-0	
24/11	h	Bakı	D 1-1	Soltanpour
29/11	a	Olimpik-Şüvälan	L 2-3	O Äliyev, Mikayılov
07/12	h	Simurq	W 2-1	Mikayılov, Qurbanov
14/12	a	Neftçi	L 2-3	O Äliyev 2
18/12	a	Qäbälä	D 1-1	Qurbanov
21/12	a	Qarabağ	L 0-2	

2015

30/01	a	İnter	D 0-0	
11/02	a	Bakı	D 0-0	
15/02	h	Olimpik-Şüvälan	D 0-0	
19/02	a	Simurq	D 1-1	Qurbanov
28/02	h	Neftçi	D 0-0	
08/03	h	Qäbälä	L 0-2	
18/03	h	Qarabağ	L 1-2	Ağayev
01/04	a	Xäzär Länkäran	L 2-3	Alxasov, Chertoganov
09/04	h	Bakı	D 0-0	
17/04	a	Olimpik-Şüvälan	D 1-1	Qurbanov
25/04	h	Simurq	W 1-0	Fardjad-Azad
01/05	a	Neftçi	D 2-2	Alxasov, Qurbanov
08/05	h	Qäbälä	L 0-2	
16/05	a	Qarabağ	L 0-1	
22/05	h	Xäzär Länkäran	W 2-0	Qurbanov, Mikayılov
28/05	a	İnter	W 3-1	Fardjad-Azad, Qurbanov 2

No	Name	Nat	DoB	Pos	Aps	(s)	Gls
17	Ramazan Abbasov		22/09/83	M	8	(2)	1
45	Murad Ağayev		09/02/93	M	14	(4)	1
2	Slavik Alxasov		06/02/93	D	28	(3)	2
9	Orxan Äliyev		21/12/95	M	17	(8)	4
11	Şahin Äliyev		19/03/95	A		(3)	
10	Tärzin Cahangirov		17/01/92	M	20	(7)	
5	Ceyhun Cavadov		05/10/92	M		(1)	
18	Aleksandr Chertoganov		08/02/80	M	27	(3)	1
17	Pardis Fardjad-Azad		12/04/88	A	7	(5)	2
5	Cämil Hacıyev		24/08/94	D	19	(1)	
92	Bäxtiyar Häsänälizadä		29/12/92	D	27		
4	Vurğun Hüseynov		25/04/88	D	29	(1)	
63	Şahruddin Mähämmädäliyev		12/06/94	G	14		
15	Nodar Mämmädov		03/06/88	D	26	(2)	
77	Täväkkül Mämmädov		15/12/92	M	9	(6)	
22	Tofiq Mikayılov		11/04/86	M	25	(3)	3
97	Xäyal Näcäfov		19/12/97	M		(1)	
8	Budaq Näsirov		15/07/96	M	3	(8)	
6	Tagim Novruzov		21/11/88	M	4		
76	Uğur Pamuk		26/06/89	M	4		
7	Ruslan Poladov		30/11/79	M	27		
1	Andrey Popoviç		04/04/92	G	19		
86	Färid Quliyev		06/01/86	A		(5)	
14	Mähämmäd Qurbanov		11/04/92	A	30	(1)	13
6	Mikayıl Rähimov		11/05/87	D	2		
11	Kiyan Soltanpour	GER	23/07/89	A	3	(8)	3
23	Şähriyar Xälilov		21/08/91	D	1	(1)	

Xäzär Länkäran FK

2004 • Länkäran şähär märkäzi stadionu
(15,000); Dalğa Arena, Baku (6,700); Bayıl Arena,
Baku (3,000) • lankaranfc.com

Major honours
Azerbaijan League (1) 2007; Azerbaijan Cup (3) 2007,
2008, 2011

Coach: Oğuz Çetin (TUR);
(23/12/14) (Elbrus Mämmädov);
(08/05/15) (Yunis Hüseynov)

2014
09/08	a	Olimpik-Şüvälan	D	1-1	Äliyev
16/08	h	Sumqayıt	L	0-1	
24/08	a	Simurq	L	0-2	
29/08	h	İnter	W	1-0	Abdullayev
13/09	a	Neftçi	L	0-1	
20/09	h	Araz-Naxçıvan	W	2-0	Ivanov, Ramazanov (match annulled)
28/09	a	Qäbälä	D	1-1	Blazevski
19/10	h	Bakı	W	4-0	Sankoh (p), Ivanov, E Cäfärov, Äliyev (p)
26/10	a	Qarabağ	L	2-3	Ivanov, Äliyev
29/10	a	Sumqayıt	W	2-1	Fernando Gabriel, Sankoh
02/11	h	Simurq	W	2-1	Sadio, og (Lambot)
20/11	a	İnter	L	1-3	Fernando Gabriel
24/11	h	Neftçi	D	2-2	Ivanov, Ä İsmayılov
07/12	h	Qäbälä	W	3-0	Ivanov, og (Tağızadä), Ramazanov
14/12	a	Bakı	D	0-0	
18/12	h	Qarabağ	L	2-3	og (Qarayev), Sadio
21/12	h	Olimpik-Şüvälan	D	1-1	Fernando Gabriel

2015
01/02	a	Simurq	L	0-2	
07/02	h	İnter	L	1-2	og (Bayramov)
11/02	a	Neftçi	L	0-2	
19/02	a	Qäbälä	L	1-3	Sadio
28/02	h	Bakı	W	2-1	Ramazanov 2
08/03	a	Qarabağ	L	0-1	
18/03	a	Olimpik-Şüvälan	L	1-3	Äläkbärov
01/04	h	Sumqayıt	W	3-2	Ramaldanov, og (Poladov), Scarlatache
05/04	a	İnter	L	0-2	
09/04	h	Neftçi	D	2-2	Ämirquliyev, Scarlatache
25/04	h	Qäbälä	L	0-1	
02/05	a	Bakı	L	1-2	Sadio
08/05	h	Qarabağ	D	1-1	Ramazanov
16/05	h	Olimpik-Şüvälan	W	1-0	Ämirquliyev
22/05	a	Sumqayıt	L	0-2	
28/05	h	Simurq	D	0-0	

No	Name	Nat	DoB	Pos	Aps	(s)	Gls
10	Elnur Abdullayev		16/02/86	M	11	(4)	1
42	Kamran Abdullazadä		20/03/95	M	8	(4)	
6	İlqar Äläkbärov		06/10/93	M	1	(2)	1
11	Rauf Äliyev		12/02/89	A	12		3
14	Rahid Ämirquliyev		01/09/89	D	31		2
96	Anar Babazadä		10/04/96	D	1	(4)	
99	Dejan Blazevski	MKD	06/12/85	A	3	(2)	1
97	Elnur Cäfärov		28/03/97	A	17	(8)	1
4	Ruslan Cäfärov		26/01/93	D	1	(7)	
18	Tural Cälilov		28/11/86	D	22	(2)	
7	Mbilla Etame	CMR	22/06/88	A		(3)	
28	Fernando Gabriel	BRA	11/05/88	M	1	(11)	3
12	Cahangir Häsänzadä		04/08/79	G	6		
8	Galin Ivanov	BUL	15/04/88	M	14	(1)	5
22	Äfran İsmayılov		08/10/88	M	4	(7)	1
34	Elnur İsmayılov		24/04/94	D	2	(5)	
17	Kazım Kazımlı		05/09/93	M	10	(1)	
1	Nurxan Mänsimzadä		15/11/94	A	1		
72	Elvin Mirzäyev		11/11/93	D	14		
32	Zaman Mirzäzadä		08/02/95	D		(1)	
2	Nildo	BRA	07/12/83	A		(1)	
25	Tärlan Qasımzadä		01/01/95	D	4	(1)	
99	Mahsun Qämbärli		25/10/96	M	1	(6)	
3	Rasim Ramaldanov		24/01/86	D	22	(2)	1
10	Ağabala Ramazanov		20/01/93	M	19	(1)	5
8	Elşan Rzazadä		11/09/93	M	11	(4)	
7	Tounkara Sadio	MLI	27/04/92	M	21	(2)	4
1	Orxan Sadıqlı		19/03/93	G	8		
6	Räşad A Sadiqov		08/10/83	M	14	(1)	
63	Alfred Sankoh	SLE	22/10/88	M	25		2
12	İlyas Säfärzadä		20/01/96	M	11	(1)	
27	Adrian Scarlatache	ROU	05/12/86	D	19		2
13	Aleksandr Şemonayev		01/04/85	D	3		
9	Bähruz Teymurov		01/01/94	D		(3)	
5	Thiego	BRA	22/07/86	D	15		
19	Vjekoslav Tomić	CRO	19/07/83	D	15		
3	Vanderson	BRA	27/09/84	D	16		

Top goalscorers

15	Nurlan Novruzov (Bakı)
14	Reynaldo (Qarabağ)
	Dragan Ćeran (Simurq)
13	Freddy Mombongo-Dues (Olimpik-Şüvälan)
	Mähämmäd Qurbanov (Sumqayıt)
12	Cavid Hüseynov (Qäbälä)
11	Nicolás Canales (Neftçi)
	Räşad Eyyubov (Simurq)
10	Leroy George (Qarabağ)
9	Mikel Álvaro (İnter)

Promoted clubs

Zirä FK

2014 • Zirä qäsäbä Olimpiya İdman
Kompleksinin stadionu (1,300) • no website
Coach: Bähram Şahquliyev;
(07/04/15) Adil Şükürov

Käpäz PFK

1959 • Gäncä şähär stadionu (25,000) •
no website
Major honours
Azerbaijan League (3) 1995, 1998, 1999; Azerbaijan
Cup (4) 1994, 1997, 1998, 2000
Coach: Vidadi Rzayev;
(21/05/15) Şahin Diniyev

Second level final table 2014/15

		Pld	W	D	L	F	A	Pts
1	Neftçala FK	30	25	3	2	83	19	78
2	Ağsu FK	30	21	4	5	70	22	67
3	Rävan Bakı FK	30	21	4	5	70	22	67
4	Qaradağ Lökbatan FK	30	20	5	5	57	25	65
5	Zirä FK	30	19	6	5	61	19	63
6	Turan Tovuz İK	30	15	5	10	75	37	50
7	Şahdağ Qusar FK	30	13	8	9	40	29	47
8	Şuşa Qarabağ PFK	30	14	4	12	49	31	46
9	Käpäz PFK	30	10	8	12	37	37	38
10	Bakılı Bakı PFK	30	10	4	16	46	61	34
11	Şämkir FK	30	8	8	14	25	46	32
12	MOİK Bakı PFK	30	8	5	17	26	60	29
13	Mil-Muğan İmişli FK	30	7	5	18	30	65	26
14	Energetik Mingäçevir FK	30	5	3	22	24	82	18
15	Göyäzän Qazax FK	30	3	3	24	15	91	12
16	Lokomotiv Biläcäri FK	30	3	1	26	10	72	10

NB Lokomotiv Biläcäri FK withdrew after round 15 – their
remaining matches were awarded as 0-3 defeats;
Zirä FK & Käpäz PFK promoted as the two highest-
placed teams to obtain a Premyer Liqa licence.

DOMESTIC CUP

Azärbaycan kuboku 2014/15

1/8 FINALS

(03/12/14)
Neftçala 1-2 Olimpik-Şüvälan
Neftçi 3-0 Qaradağ Lökbatan
Qarabağ 4-2 MOİK
Qäbälä 3-0 Ağsu
Şahdağ 0-3 İnter
Simurq 6-0 Rävan
Sumqayıt 0-0 Bakı (aet; 3-4 on pens)
Xäzär Länkäran w/o Araz-Naxçıvan

QUARTER-FINALS

(04/03/15 & 13/03/15)
İnter 2-0 Xäzär Länkäran (Mikel Álvaro 41, Sankoh 69og)
Xäzär Länkäran 0-3 İnter (A Mämmädov 24, Daşdämirov 74; İsmayılov 90+1)
(İnter 5-0)

Neftçi 0-0 Olimpik-Şüvälan
Olimpik-Şüvälan 0-1 Neftçi (Wobay 19)
(Neftçi 1-0)

Qarabağ 3-0 Bakı (Reynaldo 6, 32, Nadirov 24)
Bakı 1-4 Qarabağ (Mädätov 7; Nadirov 14, 58, 69, Tağıyev 57)
(Qarabağ 7-1)

Qäbälä 0-3 Simurq (Ćeran 17, 55, Lambot 57)
Simurq 0-0 Qäbälä
(Simurq 3-0)

SEMI-FINALS

(13/04/15 & 21/04/15)
Neftçi 2-0 İnter (Canales 20, 71)
İnter 2-1 Neftçi (Daşdämirov 37, Tskhadadze 57; Canales 27)
(Neftçi 3-2)

Qarabağ 1-0 Simurq (Tağıyev 15)
Simurq 0-0 Qarabağ
(Qarabağ 1-0)

FINAL

(03/06/15)
Qäbälä şähär stadionu, Qäbälä
QARABAĞ FK 3 (Reynaldo 5, 39, Muarem 85)
NEFTÇİ PFK 1 (Nfor 77)
Referee: Häsänov
QARABAĞ: Şehić, Medvedev, Hüseynov, Sadıqov, Agolli, Qarayev, Richard, George (Nadirov 75), Tağıyev (Yusifov 82), Muarem (Qurbanov 90+2), Reynaldo
NEFTÇİ: A Mämmädov, İsayev (Mehdiyev 80), Carlos Cardoso, Dênis Silva, Bädälov, A Abdullayev (Nfor 72), E Abdullayev, Ramos, Wobay, Cauê (Mäsimov 65), Canales

BELARUS
Belorusskaja Federacija Futbola (BFF)

Address	Prospekt Pobeditelei 20/3	**President**	Sergei Roumas
	BY-220020 Minsk	**General secretary**	Sergei Safaryan
Tel	+375 17 2545 600	**Media officer**	Aleksandr Aleinik
Fax	+375 17 2544 483	**Year of formation**	1989
E-mail	info@bff.by	**National stadium**	Borisov Arena,
Website	bff.by		Borisov (13,126)

PREMIER LEAGUE CLUBS

 1 FC BATE Borisov

 2 FC Belshina Bobruisk

 3 FC Dinamo Brest

 4 FC Dinamo Minsk

 5 FC Dnepr Mogilev

 6 FC Gomel

 7 FC Minsk

 8 FC Naftan Novopolotsk

 9 FC Neman Grodno

 10 FC Shakhtyor Soligorsk

 11 SFC Slutsk

 12 FC Torpedo Zhodino

PROMOTED CLUBS

 13 FC Granit Mikashevichi

 14 FC Slavia-Mozyr

 15 FC Vitebsk

KEY:
- – UEFA Champions League
- – UEFA Europa League
- – Promoted
- – Relegated

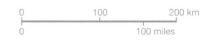

BATE strengthen their grip

The script to the 2014 Belarusian Premier League title race was a familiar one as FC BATE Borisov triumphed for the ninth successive year. In ex-player Aleksandr Yermakovich's first full season as the team's head coach, BATE lost their opening game but remained unbeaten thereafter to ward off a sustained challenge from FC Dinamo Minsk.

The country's top two clubs both extended their participation in European competition to the group stage, and there was further silverware for BATE when they ended a five-year wait by winning the 2015 Belarusian Cup.

Ninth successive league title for serial champions

Borisov club add first Belarusian Cup win in five years

Dinamo Minsk put up strong Premier League challenge

Domestic league

The 11-point victory margin posted in the final standings of the Premier League's championship pool suggested that BATE had cantered unopposed to their record-extending 11th national title. However, the truth was somewhat different. Defeated 2-0 on the opening day at FC Shakhtyor Soligorsk, BATE responded with six straight wins before drawing 0-0 at home to Dinamo Minsk, and it was the team from the capital, seeking a first national crown in a decade, that would keep the pressure on the perennial champions throughout the campaign.

Dinamo were newly led by Vladimir Zhuravel, who had won six titles as a player with the club in the 1990s and had overseen, as coach, four successive runners-up spots for Shakhtyor. His return injected fresh ambition, and Dinamo dug in hard. They ran up eight consecutive victories in June and July, and although the defending champions were proving impossible to beat after that first-day faux pas, Yermakovich's side had developed a nasty habit of drawing games they were expected to win, especially at home.

When the top two met for the fourth and final time, on 1 November in Dinamo's Traktor stadium, BATE led by a point. Although they had failed to score in the previous three encounters, Dinamo had the opportunity to overtake their rivals with a win, but they failed to seize it, two goals midway through the second half from BATE defenders Anri Khagush and Denis Polyakov setting the visitors on course for a crucial 2-1 win.

Eight days later, after a despondent Dinamo had lost again, BATE clinched the title with a 4-0 win over FC Naftan Novopolotsk in their new Borisov Arena home. They claimed a new league record 31-match unbeaten run when their campaign closed with a 1-1 draw at home to Shakhtyor, who finished third on the head-to-head rule above FC Torpedo Zhodino.

Domestic cup

Without a domestic cup victory in five years, BATE made up for lost time by winning the 2015 competition in style, defeating Dinamo Minsk in the semi-finals and then holders Shakhtyor 4-1 in a final that came alive in the second half after a goalless first period. BATE's two leading marksmen in the league triumph, Mikhail Gordeichuk and Vitali Rodionov, led the rout as the club lifted the trophy for only the third time.

Europe

Belarus's coefficient received a boost in 2014/15 as the nation's European collective chalked up 32 matches. BATE reached the UEFA Champions League group stage for the fourth time in seven seasons, Dinamo Minsk gained access to the UEFA Europa League equivalent, and Shakhtyor succumbed only in the play-offs after a remarkable 5-2 victory at SV Zulte Waregem. BATE's brightest moment was a 2-1 home win over Athletic Club, but the rest of the group stage provided only doom and gloom as they conceded a record tally of 24 goals. Dinamo also found the group stage too hot to handle before bowing out with a memorable 2-1 win at ACF Fiorentina.

National team

Joy for the Belarus national team was confined to a solitary victory in their UEFA EURO 2016 qualifying campaign, and that came after a change of coach, with Aleksandr Khatskevich, the former FC Dynamo Kyiv midfielder, overseeing a 2-1 win away to FYR Macedonia in his first game. Previous boss Georgi Kondratiev had been forced to make way after a calamitous start that brought a 1-1 draw in Luxembourg and back-to-back home defeats against Ukraine and Slovakia – the two teams with whom Belarus had hoped to contest a play-off berth. By the end of the season, however, the prospect of an improvement on their fourth place seemed forlorn.

DOMESTIC SEASON AT A GLANCE

Premier League 2014 final table

Second Phase
Championship Pool

		Pld	Home					Away					Total					
			W	D	L	F	A	W	D	L	F	A	W	D	L	F	A	Pts
1	**FC BATE Borisov**	32	8	8	0	30	6	12	3	1	38	15	20	11	1	68	21	71
2	FC Dinamo Minsk	32	10	2	4	27	14	8	5	3	17	7	18	7	7	44	21	61
3	FC Shakhtyor Soligorsk	32	8	3	5	22	13	6	5	5	13	15	14	8	10	35	28	50
4	FC Torpedo Zhodino	32	9	3	4	22	16	4	8	4	16	14	13	11	8	38	30	50
5	FC Naftan Novopolotsk	32	6	7	3	21	19	5	3	8	19	24	11	10	11	40	43	43
6	FC Gomel	32	6	3	7	18	19	4	5	7	11	22	10	8	14	29	41	38

Relegation Pool

		Pld	Home					Away					Total					
			W	D	L	F	A	W	D	L	F	A	W	D	L	F	A	Pts
7	FC Minsk	32	7	3	6	20	18	9	1	6	25	18	16	4	12	45	36	52
8	FC Neman Grodno	32	4	5	7	21	20	7	4	5	20	16	11	9	12	41	36	42
9	SFC Slutsk	32	7	5	4	15	11	4	2	10	11	23	11	7	14	26	34	40
10	FC Belshina Bobruisk	32	4	3	9	23	25	4	5	7	19	31	8	8	16	42	56	32
11	FC Dinamo Brest	32	4	3	9	15	30	3	2	11	14	38	7	5	20	29	68	26
12	FC Dnepr Mogilev	32	1	6	9	10	21	1	8	7	9	21	2	14	16	19	42	20

NB League splits into top and bottom halves after 22 games, after which the clubs play exclusively against teams in their group.

European qualification 2015/16

Champion/Cup winner: FC BATE Borisov (second qualifying round)

FC Dinamo Minsk (second qualifying round)
FC Shakhtyor Soligorsk (first qualifying round)
FC Torpedo Zhodino (first qualifying round)

Top scorer	Nikolai Yanush (Shakhtyor), 15 goals
Relegated club	FC Dnepr Mogilev
Promoted clubs	FC Granit Mikashevichi, FC Slavia-Mozyr, FC Vitebsk
Cup final	FC BATE Borisov 4-1 FC Shakhtyor Soligorsk

Team of the season
(4-1-3-2)

Coach: Yermakovich (BATE)

Kotenko (Shakhtyor)

Khagush (BATE) Filipenko (BATE) Politevich (Dinamo Minsk) Mladenović (BATE)

Nikolić (Dinamo Minsk)

Hleb (Torpedo) Krivets (BATE) Stasevich (Dinamo Minsk)

Gordeichuk (BATE) Yanush (Shakhtyor)

Player of the season

Sergei Krivets
(FC BATE Borisov)

Re-signed by BATE midway through the 2013 season, Krivets stuck around for only a year before moving abroad again, to newly promoted French Ligue 1 club FC Metz. However, during the first half of 2014 the Belarus international midfielder was in the form of his life, registering ten goals and 11 assists as BATE mounted their Premier League title assault and also firing the club into the UEFA Champions League group stage with crucial strikes against Debreceni VSC and ŠK Slovan Bratislava.

Newcomer of the season

Pavel Savitski
(FC Neman Grodno)

Savitski ended his teenage years midway through a 2014 season in which he struck a personal best tally of 11 Premier League goals for hometown club Neman and was handed his senior national team debut, scoring two goals on his second appearance in a friendly against Liechtenstein. The young striker's coming-of-age was rewarded with a loan move to title-challenging Polish Ekstraklasa outfit Jagiellonia Białystok, where, despite limited opportunities, he continued to make good progress.

BELARUS

NATIONAL TEAM

Top five all-time caps
Aleksandr Kulchy (102); Sergei Gurenko (80); Sergei Omelyanchuk (74); Sergei Shtanyuk (71); **Aleksandr Hleb** & **Timofei Kalachev** (69)

Top five all-time goals
Maksim Romashchenko (20); **Sergei Kornilenko** (16); Vitali Kutuzov (13); Vyacheslav Hleb (12); Valentin Belkevich, **Timofei Kalachev**, Vitali Rodionov & Roman Vasilyuk (10)

Results 2014/15

Date	Opponent		Venue		Score	Scorers
04/09/14	Tajikistan	H	Borisov	W	6-1	Stasevich (7), Kornilenko (55), Krivets (59), Olekhnovich (61), Kislyak (62), Aleksiyevich (75)
08/09/14	Luxembourg (ECQ)	A	Luxembourg	D	1-1	Dragun (78)
09/10/14	Ukraine (ECQ)	H	Borisov	L	0-2	
12/10/14	Slovakia (ECQ)	H	Borisov	L	1-3	Kalachev (79)
15/11/14	Spain (ECQ)	A	Huelva	L	0-3	
18/11/14	Mexico	H	Borisov	W	3-2	Kislyak (50), Signevich (56), Nekhaichik (81)
27/03/15	FYR Macedonia (ECQ)	A	Skopje	W	2-1	Kalachev (44), Kornilenko (82)
30/03/15	Gabon	N	Antalya (TUR)	D	0-0	
07/06/15	Russia	A	Khimki	L	2-4	Kislyak (51, 66)
14/06/15	Spain (ECQ)	H	Borisov	L	0-1	

Appearances 2014/15

Coach: Georgi Kondratiev 07/01/60
/(27/10/14) (Andrei Zygmantovich) 02/12/62
/(04/12/14) Aleksandr Khatskevich 19/10/73

Name	DOB	Club	Tjk	LUX	UKR	SVK	ESP	Mex	MKD	Gab	Rus	ESP	Caps	Goals
Sergei Chernik	20/07/88	BATE	G				G			s46	G46		6	-
Igor Shitov	24/10/86	Mordovia (RUS)	D	D		D76		D	D	s46	D	D	45	1
Aleksandr Martynovich	26/08/87	Krasnodar (RUS)	D	D	D87	D	D31	D			D	D	45	2
Sergei Politevich	09/04/90	Dinamo Minsk	D				D	D	D				5	-
Maksim Bordachev	18/06/86	Rostov (RUS)	D59			D	s31	s85	D			D	38	2
Yan Tigorev	10/03/84	Lokomotiv Moskva (RUS)	M18										35	1
Igor Stasevich	21/10/85	Dinamo Minsk/BATE	M46	s62	M46	s76		M79	M93	s76	s70	s81	24	2
Aleksandr Hleb	01/05/81	Konyaspor (TUR)/Gençlerbirliği (TUR)	M46						M87		M	M89	69	6
Sergei Kislyak	06/08/87	Rubin (RUS)	M	M73	s46	s80		M61	M	s46	M70	M78	53	9
Timofei Kalachev	01/05/85	Rostov (RUS)	M46	M	M	M	M	s58	M				69	10
Sergei Kornilenko	14/06/83	Krylya Sovetov (RUS)	A71	s73	s79	A67		A		s62	A71	A	68	16
Edgar Olekhnovich	17/05/87	BATE	s18	M77									14	1
Sergei Balanovich	29/08/87	Amkar (RUS)	s46	M	D	M	D						23	2
Ilya Aleksiyevich	10/02/91	BATE	s46	s77				M					9	1
Sergei Krivets	08/06/86	Metz (FRA)	s46	M	M	M	M80	s91			M46		31	4
Denis Polyakov	17/04/91	BATE	s59		D	s55				D	s67		12	-
Stanislav Dragun	04/06/88	Krylya Sovetov (RUS)	s71	A	M	M	M	s61	s87	M62	M	s78	32	4
Aleksandr Gutor	18/04/89	Dinamo Minsk		G							s46		7	-
Yegor Filipenko	10/04/88	BATE/Málaga (ESP)		D	D	D55			D	D46	D67	D	39	1
Oleg Veretilo	10/07/88	Dinamo Minsk		D62									14	-
Yuri Zhevnov	17/04/81	Torpedo Moskva (RUS)			G	G	G		G				57	-
Dmitri Verkhovtsov	10/10/86	Ufa (RUS)			D	D							44	3
Mikhail Gordeichuk	23/10/89	BATE			A79	s46		M91		M			7	1
Pavel Savitski	12/07/94	Neman			s87								3	2
Renan Bressan	03/11/88	Rio Ave (POR)				A46							18	3
Aleksei Yanushkevich	15/01/86	Shakhtyor Soligorsk					D	D					2	-
Sergei Matveichik	05/06/88	Shakhtyor Soligorsk					D	s76					2	-
Pavel Nekhaichik	15/07/88	Tom (RUS)					M	s79	s93	A76	D	M	14	1
Nikolai Signevich	20/02/92	BATE					s67	A58					2	1
Maksim Volodko	10/11/92	BATE						D76		D	s46	M81	4	-
Anton Putilo	10/06/87	Torpedo Moskva (RUS)						M85	s80	M	M	s89	49	6
Ivan Mayevski	05/05/88	Zawisza (POL)							M80	s62	M		3	-
Andrei Gorbunov	25/05/83	Atromitos (GRE)								G46	G		2	-
Aleksandr Makas	08/10/91	Minsk									A62		1	-
Nikolai Yanush	09/09/84	Shakhtyor Soligorsk									A46		1	-
Denis Laptev	01/08/91	Slavia-Mozyr									s71		1	-

EUROPE

FC BATE Borisov

CHAMPIONS LEAGUE

Second qualifying round - KF Skënderbeu (ALB)
H 0-0
Chernik, Gaiduchik, Karnitski, Aleksiyevich, Krivets (Pavlov 70), Signevich, Khagush (Gordeichuk 70), Rodionov, Filipenko, Polyakov, M Volodko. Coach: Aleksandr Yermakovich (BLR)
A 1-1 Khagush (29)
Chernik, A Volodko, Aleksiyevich (Karnitski 85), Signevich, Khagush (Gaiduchik 62), Rodionov, Filipenko, Olekhnovich, Polyakov, M Volodko, Gordeichuk (Pavlov 80). Coach: Aleksandr Yermakovich (BLR)

Third qualifying round - Debreceni VSC (HUN)
A 0-1
Chernik, A Volodko (Karnitski 81), Aleksiyevich (Pavlov 59), Signevich, Khagush, Rodionov, Filipenko, Olekhnovich, Polyakov, M Volodko, Gordeichuk (Krivets 61). Coach: Aleksandr Yermakovich (BLR)
H 3-1 A Volodko (39), Rodionov (66), Krivets (90+4)
Chernik, Likhtarovich (Olekhnovich 55), Gaiduchik (Signevich 42), A Volodko, Krivets, Khagush (Pavlov 69), Rodionov, Filipenko, Mladenović, Polyakov, Gordeichuk. Coach: Aleksandr Yermakovich (BLR)

Play-offs - ŠK Slovan Bratislava (SVK)
A 1-1 Jablonský (44og)
Chernik, Likhtarovich (Karnitski 68), A Volodko, Krivets, Khagush, Rodionov (Signevich 87), Filipenko, Mladenović, Olekhnovich, Polyakov, Gordeichuk. Coach: Aleksandr Yermakovich (BLR)
H 3-0 Gordeichuk (41), Krivets (84), Rodionov (85)
Chernik, Likhtarovich (Aleksiyevich 61), A Volodko, Krivets, Khagush, Rodionov (Signevich 87), Filipenko, Mladenović, Olekhnovich, Polyakov, Gordeichuk (Yakovlev 68). Coach: Aleksandr Yermakovich (BLR)

Group H
Match 1 - FC Porto (POR)
A 0-6
Chernik, Likhtarovich (Yakovlev 53), A Volodko, Aleksiyevich, Khagush, Rodionov (Signevich 71), Filipenko, Mladenović, Olekhnovich (Karnitski 62), Polyakov, Gordeichuk. Coach: Aleksandr Yermakovich (BLR)
Match 2 - Athletic Club (ESP)
H 2-1 Polyakov (19), Karnitski (41)
Chernik, Yablonski, Karnitski (Rodionov 86), A Volodko, Signevich, Khagush, Filipenko, Mladenović, Polyakov, M Volodko (Yakovlev 81), Gordeichuk (Olekhnovich 90+2). Coach: Aleksandr Yermakovich (BLR)
Match 3 - FC Shakhtar Donetsk (UKR)
H 0-7
Chernik, Likhtarovich (Aleksiyevich 46), Yablonski, Karnitski, Signevich (Baga 75), Khagush, Mladenović, Polyakov, M Volodko, Tubić (Gaiduchik 46), Gordeichuk. Coach: Aleksandr Yermakovich (BLR)

Match 4 - FC Shakhtar Donetsk (UKR)
A 0-5
Chernik, Gaiduchik, Yablonski (M Volodko 59), Karnitski, A Volodko, Signevich (Rodionov 70), Khagush, Mladenović, Polyakov, Gordeichuk, Yakovlev (Olekhnovich 46). Coach: Aleksandr Yermakovich (BLR)
Red card: Khagush 45+2
Match 5 - FC Porto (POR)
H 0-3
Chernik, Gaiduchik, Yablonski, Karnitski (Baga 67), A Volodko, Rodionov (Signevich 75), Mladenović (Aleksiyevich 72), Olekhnovich, M Volodko, Tubić, Gordeichuk. Coach: Aleksandr Yermakovich (BLR)
Match 6 - Athletic Club (ESP)
A 0-2
Soroko, Yablonski (Baga 77), Karnitski, A Volodko (Signevich 60), Khagush, Rodionov (Likhtarovich 83), Filipenko, Olekhnovich, M Volodko, Tubić, Gordeichuk. Coach: Aleksandr Yermakovich (BLR)

FC Shakhtyor Soligorsk

EUROPA LEAGUE

Second qualifying round - Derry City FC (IRL)
A 1-0 Yanush (28)
Kotenko, Galyuza, Matveichik, Yanushkevich, Kashevski, Yanush (Osipenko 67), Starhorodskiy, Yurevich, Balanovich (Guruli 77), Rios (Tsevan 88), Kuzmenok. Coach: Sergei Borovski (BLR)
H 5-1 Balanovich (9), Guruli (28), Osipenko (68), Yanush (81), Galyuza (90+3)
Kotenko, Matveichik, Yanushkevich, Kashevski, Guruli (Rios 73), Yanush, Starhorodskiy, Yurevich, Balanovich (Leonchik 85), Kuzmenok, Osipenko (Galyuza 79). Coach: Sergei Borovski (BLR)

Third qualifying round - SV Zulte Waregem (BEL)
A 5-2 Galyuza (4), Matveichik (12), Starhorodskiy (45+4), Yanush (78), Guruli (90+1)
Kotenko, Galyuza, Matveichik, Yanushkevich, Kashevski, Starhorodskiy, Yurevich, Balanovich, Rios (Guruli 69), Kuzmenok (Vasilevski 45+1), Osipenko (Yanush 61). Coach: Sergei Borovski (BLR)
H 2-2 Balanovich (7, 42)
Kotenko, Galyuza, Matveichik, Yanushkevich, Kashevski, Leonchik, Starhorodskiy (Vasilevski 71), Yurevich, Balanovich (Guruli 65), Rios, Osipenko (Yanush 65). Coach: Sergei Borovski (BLR)

Play-offs - PSV Eindhoven (NED)
A 0-1
Kotenko, Galyuza (Leonchik 89), Matveichik, Yanushkevich, Kashevski, Guruli (Kovalev 89), Yanush (Osipenko 85), Starhorodskiy, Yurevich, Rios, Kuzmenok. Coach: Sergei Borovski (BLR)
H 0-2
Kotenko, Galyuza (Yanush 62), Matveichik, Yanushkevich, Leonchik, Guruli (Wojciechowski 54), Starhorodskiy, Yurevich, Rios, Kuzmenok, Osipenko. Coach: Sergei Borovski (BLR)

FC Dinamo Minsk

EUROPA LEAGUE

Second qualifying round - Myllykosken Pallo -47 (FIN)
H 3-0 Udoji (25), Stasevich (61p), Nikolić (86)
Gutor, Voronkov (Bykov 66), Simović, Politevich, Nikolić, Udoji, Bangura, Zaleski, Veretilo, Stasevich (Figueredo 81), Adamović (Diomandé 73). Coach: Vladimir Zhuravel (BLR)
A 0-0
Gutor, Voronkov (Udoji 67), Simović, Politevich, Nikolić, Diomandé (Adamović 46), Karpovich, Veretilo, Figueredo (Nikitin 76), Stasevich, Kontsevoi. Coach: Vladimir Zhuravel (BLR)

Third qualifying round - CFR 1907 Cluj (ROU)
H 1-0 Adamović (54)
Gutor, Voronkov (Figueredo 62), Simović, Politevich, Nikolić, Udoji, Bangura, Zaleski (Karpovich 46), Veretilo, Stasevich, Adamović. Coach: Vladimir Zhuravel (BLR)
A 2-0 Stasevich (71), Udoji (81p)
Gutor, Voronkov (Diomandé 5), Simović, Politevich, Nikolić, Udoji, Karpovich, Bangura, Veretilo, Stasevich (Kontsevoi 90), Adamović (Figueredo 84). Coach: Vladimir Zhuravel (BLR)

Play-offs - CD Nacional (POR)
H 2-0 Stasevich (44p), Nikolić (55)
Gutor, Politevich, Nikolić, Udoji (Nikitin 89), Karpovich, Bangura, Veretilo, Figueredo (Diomandé 65), Stasevich (Molosh 90+2), Kontsevoi, Adamović. Coach: Vladimir Zhuravel (BLR)
A 3-2 Udoji (32, 63), Simović (40)
Gutor, Simović, Politevich, Nikolić, Udoji (Rassadkin 85), Karpovich, Bangura, Veretilo, Stasevich (Figueredo 77), Kontsevoi, Adamović (Voronkov 89). Coach: Vladimir Zhuravel (BLR)

Group K
Match 1 - PAOK FC (GRE)
A 1-6 Nikolić (80)
Gutor, Voronkov (Figueredo 56), Simović, Politevich, Dja Djédjé (Adamović 33), Nikolić, Udoji (Rassadkin 88), Karpovich, Bangura, Stasevich. Coach: Vladimir Zhuravel (BLR)
Red card: Simović 63
Match 2 - ACF Fiorentina (ITA)
H 0-3
Ignatovich, Voronkov, Molosh, Nikolić, Diomandé, Bangura, Veretilo, Figueredo (Dja Djédjé 62), Stasevich (Yarotski 88), Kontsevoi, Adamović (Rassadkin 86). Coach: Vladimir Zhuravel (BLR)
Match 3 - EA Guingamp (FRA)
H 0-0
Ignatovich, Voronkov (Simović 64), Politevich, Dja Djédjé (Diomandé 56), Nikolić, Karpovich, Veretilo, Figueredo (Korzun 80), Stasevich, Kontsevoi, Adamović. Coach: Vladimir Zhuravel (BLR)
Match 4 - EA Guingamp (FRA)
A 0-2
Gutor, Voronkov (Figueredo 45), Molosh, Simović, Politevich, Dja Djédjé (Stasevich 45), Nikolić, Diomandé, Udoji (Adamović 76), Veretilo, Kontsevoi. Coach: Vladimir Zhuravel (BLR)

DOMESTIC LEAGUE CLUB-BY-CLUB

Match 5 - PAOK FC (GRE)
H 0-2
Ignatovich, Simović, Politevich, Dja Djédjé (Diomandé 81), Nikolić, Udoji (Yarotski 74), Karpovich, Veretilo, Stasevich, Kontsevoi, Adamović. Coach: Vladimir Zhuravel (BLR)

Match 6 - ACF Fiorentina (ITA)
A 2-1 Kontsevoi (39), Nikolić (55)
Gutor, Voronkov (Udoji 78), Molosh, Simović, Politevich, Dja Djédjé (Karpovich 90+2), Nikolić, Veretilo, Stasevich, Kontsevoi, Adamović (Bykov 69). Coach: Vladimir Zhuravel (BLR)

Red card: Veretilo 90+2

FC Neman Grodno

Second qualifying round - FH Hafnarfjördur (ISL)
H 1-1 Savitski (66p)
Rapalis, Rakhmanov, Rovneiko (Veselinov 69), Denisevich, Rekish (Levitski 76), Zubovich (Kovalenok 76), Rybak, Vitus, Tarasovs, Legchilin, Savitski. Coach: Sergei Solodovnikov (BLR)

A 0-2
Rapalis, Denisevich, Rekish, Veselinov, Zubovich (Kovalenok 64), Rybak, Vitus, Yasinski, Tarasovs, Legchilin (Levitski 64), Savitski. Coach: Sergei Solodovnikov (BLR)

FC BATE Borisov

1996 • City Stadium (5,392);
Borisov Arena (13,126) • fcbate.by
Major honours
Belarusian League (11) 1999, 2002, 2006, 2007, 2008, 2009, 2010, 2011, 2012, 2013, 2014; Belarusian Cup (3) 2006, 2010, 2015
Coach: Aleksandr Yermakovich

2014

29/03	a	Shakhtyor	L	0-2	
05/04	h	Minsk	W	1-0	Filipenko
13/04	a	Gomel	W	3-0	Rodionov, Polyakov, Krivets (p)
19/04	h	Belshina	W	5-2	Rodionov, Gordeichuk 2, A Volodko, Krivets
27/04	a	Dinamo Brest	W	4-0	Krivets 3, Gordeichuk
04/05	a	Torpedo	W	4-1	Rodionov 2, Gordeichuk 2
10/05	h	Slutsk	W	3-0	Gordeichuk, Rodionov, Signevich
15/05	h	Dinamo Minsk	D	0-0	
26/05	h	Naftan	W	3-1	Mladenović (p), Signevich 2
01/06	a	Dnepr	W	1-0	Krivets (p)
07/06	h	Neman	D	0-0	
12/06	a	Shakhtyor	D	0-0	
16/06	a	Minsk	W	4-1	Aleksiyevich, Signevich, Krivets, Pavlov
22/06	h	Gomel	D	0-0	
29/06	a	Belshina	W	2-1	A Volodko, Signevich
05/07	h	Dinamo Brest	W	4-0	Signevich, Polyakov, Rodionov 2
10/07	h	Torpedo	D	1-1	Krivets (p)
18/07	a	Slutsk	W	3-1	M Volodko, Rodionov, Krivets
09/08	a	Naftan	D	1-1	Krivets
13/08	a	Dinamo Minsk	W	2-0	Gordeichuk, Aleksiyevich
16/08	h	Dnepr	W	3-0	Polyakov, Yakovlev, Gordeichuk
31/08	a	Neman	W	2-1	Olekhnovich, Yakovlev
13/09	h	Torpedo	D	1-1	Mladenović
22/09	h	Dinamo Minsk	D	0-0	
26/09	a	Naftan	D	2-2	Karnitski, Signevich
05/10	a	Gomel	W	2-1	Gordeichuk, Karnitski
16/10	a	Shakhtyor	W	4-1	Gordeichuk (p), Karnitski 3
27/10	a	Torpedo	D	2-2	Signevich, Yablonski
01/11	a	Dinamo Minsk	W	2-1	Khagush, Polyakov
09/11	a	Naftan	W	4-0	Gordeichuk, Rodionov 2, Karnitski
22/11	h	Gomel	W	4-0	Gordeichuk, Rodionov, Olekhnovich, Signevich
30/11	h	Shakhtyor	D	1-1	Karnitski

No	Name	Nat	DoB	Pos	Aps	(s)	Gls
9	Ilya Aleksiyevich		10/02/91	M	18	(6)	2
25	Dmitri Baga		04/01/90	M	7	(4)	
16	Sergei Chernik		20/07/88	G	29		
21	Yegor Filipenko		10/04/88	D	23		1
3	Vitali Gaiduchik		12/07/89	D	7		
62	Mikhail Gordeichuk		23/10/89	A	17	(5)	12
7	Aleksandr Karnitski		14/02/89	M	16	(11)	7
14	Anri Khagush	RUS	23/09/86	D	27	(1)	1
15	Vladislav Klimovich		12/06/96	A		(2)	
10	Sergei Krivets		08/06/86	M	19	(1)	10
2	Dmitri Likhtarovich		01/03/78	M	16		
3	Germans Māliņš	LVA	12/10/87	G	1		
22	Filip Mladenović	SRB	15/08/91	D	26		2
23	Edgar Olekhnovich		17/05/87	M	13	(9)	2
17	Aleksandr Pavlov		18/08/84	M	8	(20)	1
33	Denis Polyakov		17/04/91	D	26	(2)	4
20	Vitali Rodionov		11/12/83	A	23	(4)	11
13	Nikolai Signevich		20/02/92	A	12	(16)	9
34	Artem Soroko		01/04/92	G	2		
55	Nemanja Tubić	SRB	08/04/84	D	9		
8	Aleksandr Volodko		18/06/86	M	24	(3)	2
42	Maksim Volodko		10/11/92	M	15	(7)	1
5	Evgeni Yablonski		10/05/95	M	10	(1)	1
77	Andriy Yakovlev	UKR	20/02/89	M	4	(2)	2

FC Belshina Bobruisk

1976 • KFP, Minsk (1,500); Spartak (3,700) • fcbelshina.by
Major honours
Belarusian League (1) 2001; Belarusian Cup (3) 1997, 1999, 2001
Coach: Aleksandr Sednev

2014

30/03	a	Gomel	L	1-3	Bogunov
06/04	a	Torpedo	D	1-1	Manolo Bleda
12/04	h	Dinamo Brest	W	7-0	Bogunov, Khlebosolov (p), Ferenchak, Manolo Bleda 3, Shagoiko
19/04	a	BATE	L	2-5	Karshakevich, Khlebosolov
27/04	h	Slutsk	L	1-2	Manolo Bleda
04/05	h	Dinamo Minsk	L	1-4	Ferenchak
11/05	h	Naftan	D	1-1	Ferenchak
16/05	a	Dnepr	D	0-0	
25/05	h	Neman	L	3-4	Karshakevich, Lisitsa, Rozhkov
01/06	a	Shakhtyor	W	2-1	Lisitsa 2
06/06	h	Minsk	L	0-3	
11/06	h	Gomel	L	1-2	Alumona
15/06	h	Torpedo	L	0-1	
22/06	a	Dinamo Brest	D	2-2	og (Tatarevich), Manolo Bleda
29/06	h	BATE	L	1-2	Khlebosolov
05/07	a	Slutsk	L	0-1	
12/07	h	Dinamo Minsk	L	0-1	
19/07	a	Naftan	L	1-3	Manolo Bleda
02/08	a	Dnepr	D	0-0	
09/08	a	Neman	D	1-1	Khilkevich
15/08	h	Shakhtyor	W	2-1	Kozlov, Khlebosolov
31/08	a	Minsk	W	1-0	Khlebosolov
13/09	a	Minsk	D	1-1	Gorbachev
20/09	h	Slutsk	W	2-1	Khlebosolov, Kozlov
28/09	a	Dinamo Brest	W	1-0	Khlebosolov
05/10	a	Dnepr	W	2-1	Khlebosolov, Kozlov
19/10	h	Neman	L	1-3	Khlebosolov (p)
25/10	h	Minsk	L	1-2	og (Begunov)
01/11	a	Slutsk	L	1-3	Kozlov
08/11	h	Dinamo Brest	W	2-1	Turlin, Khlebosolov (p)
23/11	h	Dnepr	D	1-1	Rozhkov
29/11	a	Neman	L	2-5	Bukatkin, Turlin

No	Name	Nat	DoB	Pos	Aps	(s)	Gls
13	Aleksandr Alumona	RUS	18/12/83	A	5	(4)	1
93	Vadim Balbukh		04/05/93	M		(1)	
9	Olexandr Batyshchev	UKR	14/09/91	M	15		
88	Artem Bobukh	UKR	04/12/88	D	17	(4)	
93	Yaroslav Bogunov	UKR	04/09/93	A	4	(3)	2
8	Nikita Bukatkin		07/03/88	M	18	(8)	1
12	Anton Burko		16/02/95	M		(1)	
9	Serhiy Ferenchak	UKR	27/04/84	M	11		3
4	Mikhail Gorbachev		29/07/83	D	23		1
9	Roman Gribovski		17/07/95	A		(1)	
35	Dmitri Gushchenko		12/05/88	G	13		
8	Artem Kaminski		01/03/94	D		(2)	
69	Valeri Karshakevich		15/02/88	D	24	(3)	2
19	Vladimir Khilkevich		31/10/87	M	26	(5)	1
10	Dmitri Khlebosolov		07/10/90	A	25	(5)	10
81	Evgeni Kiseliov		27/02/93	M	1	(6)	
62	Mykhailo Kopolovets	UKR	29/01/84	M	3	(4)	
35	Anton Kovalevski		02/02/86	G	7		
14	Aleksei Kozlov		11/07/89	M	29		4
17	Igor Lisitsa		10/04/88	M	10	(7)	3
13	Giorgi Maghaldadze	GEO	01/01/94	M		(7)	
81	Manolo Bleda	ESP	31/07/90	A	16	(4)	7
3	Igor Rozhkov		24/06/81	M	18	(10)	2
2	Aleksandr Shagoiko		27/07/80	D	28	(1)	1
1	Andrei Shcherbakov		31/01/91	G	12	(1)	
11	Aleksei Timoshenko		09/12/86	M	29		
17	Dmitri Turlin		08/09/85	M	7	(7)	2
13	Sergei Vodyanovich		02/05/95	M		(8)	
18	Olexandr Volkov	UKR	07/02/89	M	11	(3)	

FC Dinamo Brest

1960 • GOSK Brestski (10,080) •
dynamo-brest.by
Major honours
Belarusian Cup (1) 2007
Coach: Sergei Kovalchuk

2014

29/03	a	Minsk	L	0-2	
06/04	h	Gomel	W	2-0	*Perepechko, Vergeichik*
12/04	a	Belshina	L	0-7	
18/04	a	Torpedo	L	0-2	
27/04	h	BATE	L	0-4	
04/05	a	Slutsk	L	0-1	
10/05	h	Dinamo Minsk	W	2-1	*Kurlovich, Vasilyuk*
16/05	a	Naftan	D	1-1	*Kurlovich*
25/05	h	Dnepr	L	0-2	
01/06	a	Neman	D	1-1	*Vasilyuk*
07/06	h	Shakhtyor	D	0-0	
12/06	h	Minsk	L	2-3	*Kurlovich, Shcherbo*
16/06	a	Gomel	L	3-6	*Premudrov, Matyukhevich, Solovei*
22/06	h	Belshina	D	2-2	*Perepechko, Premudrov*
28/06	h	Torpedo	W	2-1	*Semenyuk, Vergeichik*
05/07	a	BATE	L	0-4	
13/07	h	Slutsk	W	2-1	*Vergeichik, Perepechko*
20/07	a	Dinamo Minsk	L	1-3	*Vergeichik*
02/08	a	Naftan	L	0-7	
09/08	a	Dnepr	W	1-0	*Vasilyuk*
17/08	h	Neman	L	1-2	*Vasilyuk*
31/08	a	Shakhtyor	W	3-2	*Kurlovich, Perepechko, Vasilyuk*
13/09	a	Slutsk	L	0-1	
20/09	a	Dnepr	L	0-1	
28/09	h	Belshina	L	0-1	
04/10	a	Neman	W	1-0	*Vasilyuk (p)*
18/10	h	Minsk	L	1-2	*Vasilyuk*
25/10	h	Slutsk	L	0-2	
01/11	h	Dnepr	D	1-1	*Perepechko (p)*
08/11	h	Belshina	L	1-2	*Vasilyuk*
23/11	h	Neman	L	0-1	
29/11	a	Minsk	L	2-5	*Premudrov, Zhevnerov*

No	Name	Nat	DoB	Pos	Aps	(s)	Gls
19	Anton Demkov		15/10/95	M		(1)	
30	Dmitri Dudar		08/11/91	G	4		
4	Evgeni Klopotski		12/08/93	D	11	(1)	
13	Sergei Kondratiev		02/02/90	D	26		
23	Boris Konevega		06/08/95	M	5	(14)	
8	Denis Kovalevski		02/05/92	D	21	(4)	
25	Vadim Kurlovich		30/10/92	M	25	(6)	4
17	Anton Kustinski		04/04/95	D		(1)	
11	Aleksandr Matyukhevich		02/04/90	A	6	(18)	1
24	Dmitri Mulkievich		26/07/96	A		(3)	
3	Lyuben Nikolov	BUL	08/09/85	D	25	(1)	
31	Yuri Pavlyukovets		24/06/94	M	3	(6)	
7	Aleksandr Perepechko		07/04/89	M	29		5
19	Yegor Pistyk		01/02/95	A		(2)	
6	Kirill Premudrov		11/06/92	M	28	(1)	3
1	Konstantin Rudenok		15/12/90	G	28		
91	Serhiy Semenyuk	UKR	27/01/91	D	15	(4)	1
18	Vladimir Shcherbo		01/04/86	D	25	(1)	1
70	Andrei Shemruk		27/04/94	A	2	(2)	
14	Andrei Solovei		13/12/94	M	3	(6)	1
21	Artem Tatarevich		28/01/92	D	26	(2)	
2	Igor Tymonyuk		31/03/94	D	3		
10	Roman Vasilyuk		23/11/78	A	29	(1)	8
9	Kirill Vergeichik		23/08/91	A	16	(11)	4
5	Eduard Zhevnerov		01/11/87	D	22	(1)	1

FC Dinamo Minsk

1927 • KFP (1,500); Traktor (16,500) •
dinamo-minsk.by
Major honours
USSR League (1) 1982; Belarusian League (7) 1992, 1993, 1994, 1995 (spring), 1995 (autumn), 1007, 2004; Belarusian Cup (3) 1992, 1994, 2003
Coach: Vladimir Zhuravel

2014

30/03	a	Dnepr	W	1-0	*Voronkov*
06/04	h	Neman	W	1-0	*Politevich*
11/04	a	Shakhtyor	D	0-0	
19/04	h	Minsk	W	2-0	*Stasevich, Nikolić*
26/04	a	Gomel	W	2-0	*Figueredo (p), Adamović*
04/05	h	Belshina	W	4-1	*Politevich, Stasevich 2, Diomandé*
10/05	a	Dinamo Brest	L	1-2	*Bykov*
15/05	a	BATE	D	0-0	
26/05	h	Slutsk	W	3-0	*Diomandé, Stasevich, Nikitin*
31/05	a	Torpedo	L	0-1	
07/06	h	Naftan	W	2-1	*Adamović 2*
11/06	h	Dnepr	W	3-0	*Bykov (p), Udoji, Stasevich*
15/06	a	Neman	W	2-0	*Nikolić (p), Adamović*
22/06	h	Shakhtyor	W	3-0	*Udoji 2, Simović*
29/06	a	Minsk	W	2-0	*Udoji 2*
06/07	h	Gomel	W	1-0	*Figueredo*
12/07	a	Belshina	W	1-0	*Stasevich*
20/07	h	Dinamo Brest	W	3-1	*Stasevich (p), Udoji, Diomandé*
13/08	h	BATE	L	0-2	
17/08	h	Torpedo	D	0-0	
24/08	a	Slutsk	D	0-0	
31/08	a	Naftan	W	2-0	*Udoji, Stasevich*
14/09	h	Shakhtyor	L	1-4	*Adamović*
22/09	a	BATE	D	0-0	
27/09	h	Torpedo	D	1-1	*Adamović*
05/10	h	Naftan	W	2-0	*Rassadkin, Adamović*
18/10	a	Gomel	W	2-0	*Dja Djédjé, Veretilo*
27/10	a	Shakhtyor	W	2-1	*Adamović, Molosh*
01/11	h	BATE	L	1-2	*Nikolić (p)*
09/11	a	Torpedo	L	1-2	*Dja Djédjé*
22/11	a	Naftan	D	1-1	*Dja Djédjé*
30/11	h	Gomel	L	0-2	

No	Name	Nat	DoB	Pos	Aps	(s)	Gls
88	Nenad Adamović	SRB	12/01/89	M	25	(5)	8
17	Umaru Bangura	SLE	07/10/87	D	23		
7	Artem Bykov		19/10/92	M	12	(6)	2
11	Adama Diomandé	NOR	14/02/90	A	10	(13)	3
9	Franck Dja Djédjé	CIV	02/06/86	A	6	(1)	3
21	Hernán Figueredo	URU	15/05/85	M	19	(10)	2
30	Aleksandr Gutor		18/04/89	G	24		
35	Sergei Ignatovich		29/06/92	G	8		
16	Sergei Karpovich		29/03/94	D	13	(4)	
9	Vladimir Khvashchinski		10/05/90	A		(5)	
26	Sergei Kontsevoi		21/06/86	D	13	(1)	
18	Nikita Korzun		06/03/95	M	1	(3)	
3	Dmitri Molosh		10/12/81	D	8		1
5	Evgeni Nikitin		09/04/90	A	3	(7)	1
10	Nemanja Nikolić	MNE	01/01/88	M	23	(6)	3
6	Sergei Politevich		09/04/90	D	28		2
8	Hleb Rassadkin		05/04/95	A	2	(7)	1
4	Slobodan Simović	SRB	22/05/89	M	17	(6)	1
22	Igor Stasevich		21/10/85	M	30	(1)	8
15	Chigozie Udoji	NGA	16/07/86	M	26	(2)	7
20	Oleg Veretilo		10/07/88	D	27		1
2	Ihor Voronkov	UKR	24/04/81	M	18	(4)	1
23	Yaroslav Yarotski		28/03/96	M		(4)	
19	Andrei Zaleski		20/01/91	M	16	(1)	

FC Dnepr Mogilev

1960 • Spartak (7,300) • fcdnepr.by
Major honours
Belarusian League (1) 1998
Coach: Yuri Lukashov

2014

30/03	h	Dinamo Minsk	L	0-1	
05/04	a	Naftan	D	0-0	
11/04	h	Torpedo	D	2-2	*Gavryushko 2*
19/04	h	Neman	L	2-3	*Černych, Mastianica*
26/04	a	Shakhtyor	D	0-0	
04/05	h	Minsk	D	1-1	*Karamushka*
10/05	a	Gomel	D	0-0	
16/05	h	Belshina	D	0-0	
25/05	a	Dinamo Brest	W	2-0	*Černych 2*
01/06	h	BATE	D	0-0	
06/06	a	Slutsk	D	1-1	*Kugan*
11/06	a	Dinamo Minsk	L	0-3	
15/06	h	Naftan	L	0-2	
21/06	a	Torpedo	L	1-2	*Bordukov*
28/06	a	Neman	L	1-4	*Gavryushko*
04/07	h	Shakhtyor	L	0-1	
12/07	a	Minsk	L	0-1	
20/07	h	Gomel	D	1-1	*Kozlov*
02/08	a	Belshina	D	0-0	
09/08	h	Dinamo Brest	L	0-1	
16/08	a	BATE	L	0-3	
31/08	h	Slutsk	L	0-2	
14/09	a	Neman	D	1-1	*Gavryushko*
20/09	h	Dinamo Brest	W	1-0	*Gavryushko*
28/09	a	Minsk	D	1-1	*Gavryushko*
05/10	h	Belshina	L	1-2	*Shramchenko (p)*
19/10	a	Slutsk	L	0-2	
26/10	h	Neman	D	1-1	*Sazankov*
01/11	a	Dinamo Brest	D	1-1	*Shramchenko*
08/11	h	Minsk	L	0-2	
23/11	a	Belshina	D	1-1	*Markov*
29/11	h	Slutsk	D	1-1	*Tereshchenko*

No	Name	Nat	DoB	Pos	Aps	(s)	Gls
32	Vasiliy Antonenko		17/05/96	D		(1)	
16	Otar Arveladze	GEO	03/01/92	A	2	(3)	
20	Pavel Bordukov		10/04/93	M	15	(4)	1
13	Fedor Černych	LTU	21/05/91	A	10		3
78	Pavel Chelyadko		03/03/93	D	22	(4)	
9	Aleksandr Gavryushko		23/01/86	A	28	(3)	6
29	Oleh Karamushka	UKR	03/04/84	M	28		1
55	Aleksei Khodnevich		02/11/84	A	1	(3)	
7	Mikhail Kozlov		12/02/90	D	28	(1)	1
21	Aleksandr Kugan		26/05/91	M	9	(8)	1
16	Pavel Kuptsov		06/01/98	M		(1)	
15	Pavel Markov		04/12/91	D	26	(3)	1
8	Edgaras Mastianica	LTU	26/10/88	M	9	(5)	1
27	Nika Mnatobishvili	GEO	27/09/92	D	23		
4	Vladimir Moroz		04/09/85	M	2	(3)	
3	Denis Obrazov		24/06/88	D	28		
17	Vladyslav Obraztsov	UKR	02/09/94	M	10	(4)	
30	Boris Pankratov		30/12/82	G	21		
19	Sergei Rusetski		08/03/89	M	2	(4)	
23	Maksim Rybakov		23/07/93	M	5	(11)	
11	Aleksandr Sazankov		17/04/84	A	10	(2)	1
31	Anton Shepelev		08/11/89	D	4		
22	Anton Shramchenko		12/03/93	A	17	(12)	2
35	Antonio Siyaka		27/01/96	M		(2)	
10	Dmytro Tereshchenko	UKR	04/04/87	M	32		1
6	Sergei Tikhonovski		26/06/90	M	9	(6)	
1	Vladimir Zhurov		09/03/91	G	11		

FC Gomel

1995 • Central Sportkomplex (CSK) (14,307) • fcgomel.com

Major honours
Belarusian League (1) 2003; Belarusian Cup (2) 2002, 2011

Coach: Aleksei Merkulov;
(06/05/14) (Valeri Yanochkin);
(11/05/14) Vladimir Golmak

2014

30/03	h	Belshina	W	3-1	*Komarovski, Badoyan, Bliznyuk*
06/04	a	Dinamo Brest	L	0-2	
13/04	h	BATE	L	0-3	
19/04	h	Slutsk	W	1-0	*Sitko*
26/04	h	Dinamo Minsk	L	0-2	
04/05	a	Naftan	L	0-1	
10/05	h	Dnepr	D	0-0	
15/05	a	Neman	D	1-1	*Bliznyuk*
26/05	h	Shakhtyor	W	1-0	*Matveyenko*
31/05	a	Minsk	W	2-1	*Komarovski 2*
06/06	h	Torpedo	L	0-1	
11/06	a	Belshina	W	2-1	*Komarovski, Badoyan*
16/06	h	Dinamo Brest	W	6-3	*Bliznyuk, Sivakov 2, Sitko, Kirilchik, Matveyenko*
22/06	a	BATE	D	0-0	
30/06	a	Slutsk	D	0-0	
06/07	a	Dinamo Minsk	L	0-1	
13/07	h	Naftan	D	2-2	*Bliznyuk 2*
20/07	a	Dnepr	D	1-1	*Komarovski*
03/08	h	Neman	L	0-2	
10/08	a	Shakhtyor	W	1-0	*Sitko*
17/08	h	Minsk	W	1-0	*Badoyan*
31/08	a	Torpedo	D	0-0	
14/09	a	Naftan	L	1-5	*Ignatenko*
21/09	a	Torpedo	L	1-2	*Bliznyuk*
28/09	h	Shakhtyor	L	0-1	
05/10	h	BATE	L	1-2	*Bliznyuk*
18/10	a	Dinamo Minsk	L	0-2	
26/10	h	Naftan	W	3-0	*Komarovski, Sitko, Chelidze*
02/11	h	Torpedo	L	0-1	
08/11	a	Shakhtyor	L	0-3	
22/11	h	BATE	L	0-4	
30/11	a	Dinamo Minsk	W	3-0	*Komarovski, Bliznyuk*

No	Name	Nat	DoB	Pos	Aps	(s)	Gls
8	Zaven Badoyan	ARM	22/10/89	M	20	(9)	3
10	Gennadi Bliznyuk		30/07/80	A	28	(4)	8
7	Aleksandr Bychenok		30/05/85	M	22	(5)	
37	Zaza Chelidze	GEO	12/01/87	D	5	(4)	1
33	Pavel Chernyshov		12/07/95	M	1	(2)	
3	Aleksei Gavrilovich		05/01/90	D	28		
55	Dmitri Ignatenko		01/02/95	M	7	(3)	1
44	Stanislav Izhakovski		22/08/94	D		(1)	
6	Pavel Kirilchik		04/01/81	M	25	(4)	1
1	Andrei Klimovich		27/08/88	G	27		
9	Dmitri Komarovski		10/10/86	A	30		7
11	Anton Matveyenko		03/09/86	M	13	(10)	2
95	Evgeni Milevski		14/01/95	M	4	(3)	
19	Dmytro Nevmyvaka	UKR	19/03/84	D	29		
18	Azam Radzhabov		21/01/93	A	1	(1)	
30	Nikolai Romanyuk		02/06/84	G	5		
29	Maksim Sanets		04/04/97	M		(5)	
13	Evgeni Savostyanov		30/01/88	M	17	(3)	
25	Stanislav Sazonovich		06/03/92	D	12		
4	Vyacheslav Serdyuk	UKR	28/01/85	D	29		
24	Pavel Sitko		17/12/85	M	30		4
32	Mikhail Sivakov		16/01/88	M	14		2
27	Anton Tereshchenko		20/09/95	M		(1)	
17	Aleksei Teslyuk		10/01/94	A		(10)	
5	Vitali Trubilo		07/01/85	D	5		
77	Aleksandr Yanchenko		14/02/95	A		(19)	

FC Minsk

1995 • KFP (1,500); Torpedo (1,600) • fcminsk.by

Major honours
Belarusian Cup (1) 2013

Coach: Andrei Skorobogatko;
(03/06/14) Andrei Pyshnik

2014

29/03	h	Dinamo Brest	W	2-0	*Lentsevich, Mirić*
05/04	a	BATE	L	0-1	
11/04	h	Slutsk	W	1-0	*Makas*
19/04	a	Dinamo Minsk	L	0-2	
27/04	h	Naftan	L	0-1	
04/05	a	Dnepr	D	1-1	*Lentsevich*
11/05	a	Neman	W	1-0	*Makas*
15/05	a	Shakhtyor	L	1-3	*Randjelovic*
26/05	h	Torpedo	L	0-2	
31/05	h	Gomel	L	1-2	*Makas (p)*
06/06	a	Belshina	W	3-0	*Makas, Mirić, Pushnyakov*
12/06	a	Dinamo Brest	W	3-2	*Rnić, Mirić, Kutsenko (p)*
16/06	h	BATE	L	1-4	*Makas*
22/06	a	Slutsk	L	0-2	
29/06	h	Dinamo Minsk	L	0-2	
06/07	a	Naftan	W	4-0	*Mayevski, Makas 2 (1p), Randjelovic*
12/07	h	Dnepr	W	1-0	*og (Mnatobishvili)*
20/07	h	Neman	D	1-1	*Khvashchinski*
03/08	h	Shakhtyor	W	3-0	*Pushnyakov, Kovel, Shumilov*
09/08	a	Torpedo	L	0-1	
17/08	a	Gomel	L	0-1	
31/08	h	Belshina	L	0-1	
13/09	h	Belshina	D	1-1	*Vasiliyev*
21/09	a	Neman	W	4-2	*Khvashchinski 2, Makas 2*
28/09	h	Dnepr	W	2-1	*Makas 2*
04/10	a	Slutsk	D	0-0	
18/10	a	Dinamo Brest	W	2-1	*Khvashchinski, Lukić (p)*
25/10	a	Belshina	W	2-1	*Lukić, Kovel*
02/11	h	Neman	W	2-1	*Ostroukh, Mayevski*
08/11	a	Dnepr	W	2-0	*Makas, og (Markov)*
23/11	a	Slutsk	W	2-1	*Mayevski, Khvashchinski*
29/11	h	Dinamo Brest	W	5-2	*Makas 2 (1p), Begunov, Khvashchinski, Ostroukh*

No	Name	Nat	DoB	Pos	Aps	(s)	Gls
17	Ivan Bakhar		10/07/98	M		(1)	
2	Roman Begunov		22/03/93	D	28	(2)	1
1	Vladimir Bushma		24/11/83	G	31		
30	Denis Dechko		26/04/90	G	1		
19	Nikita Dudo		15/04/95	M		(2)	
37	Aleksei Ivanov		19/02/97	D		(1)	
10	Vladimir Khvashchinski		10/05/90	A	14	(2)	6
7	Vitali Kibuk		07/01/89	A	10	(14)	
77	Dmytro Korkishko	UKR	04/05/90	A	4	(3)	
22	Leonid Kovel		29/07/86	A	10	(6)	2
22	Valeriy Kutsenko	UKR	02/11/86	M	15		1
17	Dmitri Lentsevich		20/06/83	D	14		2
44	Nikola Lukić	SRB	14/05/90	M	14		2
13	Aleksandr Makas		08/10/91	A	26	(5)	14
20	Ivan Mayevski		05/05/88	M	22	(1)	3
10	Marko Mirić	SRB	26/03/87	A	14	(1)	3
21	Sergei Omelyanchuk		08/08/80	D	15		
5	Yuri Ostroukh		21/01/88	D	24	(5)	2
9	Sergei Pushnyakov		08/02/93	M	11	(14)	2
8	Predrag Randjelovic	MKD	02/03/90	M	25	(4)	2
3	Miloš Rnić	SRB	24/01/89	D	12	(4)	1
11	Aleksandr Sachivko		05/01/86	M	24	(2)	
79	Evgeni Shevchenko		06/06/96	A	4	(2)	
16	Igor Shumilov		20/10/93	M	6	(11)	1
4	Aleksandr Sverchinski		16/09/91	D	27	(4)	
6	Artem Vasiliyev		23/01/97	A		(6)	1
33	Dmitri Zinovich		29/03/95	D	1	(1)	

FC Naftan Novopolotsk

1995 • Atlant (5,300); Central, Vitebsk (8,100) • fcnaftan.com

Major honours
Belarusian Cup (2) 2009, 2012

Coach: Valeri Stripeikis

2014

29/03	h	Torpedo	W	2-0	*Kryvobok, Demidovich*
05/04	h	Dnepr	D	0-0	
11/04	a	Neman	W	2-0	*Shkabara, Demidovich*
19/04	h	Shakhtyor	D	1-1	*Hunchak*
27/04	a	Minsk	W	1-0	*Suchkov*
04/05	h	Gomel	W	1-0	*Demidovich*
11/05	a	Belshina	D	1-1	*Demidovich*
16/05	h	Dinamo Brest	D	1-1	*Suchkov*
26/05	a	BATE	L	1-3	*Hunchak*
31/05	h	Slutsk	W	1-0	*Zhukovski*
07/06	a	Dinamo Minsk	L	1-2	*Hunchak (p)*
11/06	a	Torpedo	W	1-0	*Demidovich*
15/06	a	Dnepr	W	2-0	*Zhukovski, Shkabara*
21/06	h	Neman	W	2-0	*Hunchak, Shkabara (p)*
28/06	a	Shakhtyor	L	0-2	
06/07	h	Minsk	L	0-4	
13/07	a	Gomel	D	2-2	*Hunchak (p), Demidovich*
19/07	h	Belshina	W	3-1	*Yakimov, Demidovich, Kryvobok*
02/08	a	Dinamo Brest	W	7-0	*Hunchak, Zhukovski 3, Kryvobok 3*
09/08	h	BATE	D	1-1	*Yakimov*
17/08	a	Slutsk	D	0-0	
31/08	h	Dinamo Minsk	L	0-2	
14/09	h	Gomel	W	5-1	*Demidovich, og (Chelidze), Shkabara (p), Suchkov, Zhukovski*
20/09	a	Shakhtyor	L	0-2	
26/09	h	BATE	D	2-2	*Teplov, Khotov*
05/10	a	Dinamo Minsk	L	0-2	
19/10	h	Torpedo	L	1-5	*Hunchak (p)*
26/10	a	Gomel	L	0-3	
02/11	h	Shakhtyor	D	0-0	
09/11	a	BATE	L	0-4	
22/11	h	Dinamo Minsk	D	1-1	*Demidovich*
30/11	a	Torpedo	L	1-3	*Santrapynskykh*

No	Name	Nat	DoB	Pos	Aps	(s)	Gls
31	Evgeni Berezkin		05/07/96	M		(1)	
5	Georgi Buliskeriya	RUS	07/01/89	M		(1)	
13	Vadim Demidovich		20/09/85	A	29	(2)	9
16	Igor Dovgyallo		17/07/85	G	24		
35	Ruslan Hunchak	UKR	09/08/79	M	32		7
9	Oleh Kerchu	UKR	06/07/84	D	31		
1	Yegor Khatkevich		09/07/88	G	8	(1)	
77	Mikhail Khodunov		08/12/94	M		(1)	
5	Marat Khotov	RUS	02/06/87	M	30		1
5	Vladislav Kosmynin		17/01/90	D	4	(6)	
6	Ihor Kryvobok	UKR	28/07/78	A	4	(14)	5
23	Nikita Naumov		15/11/89	D	29	(1)	
15	Simon Ogar Veron	NGA	24/04/87	M	5	(3)	
8	Mohamed Refaie	EGY	04/08/90	D		(8)	
25	Yevhen Santrapynskykh	UKR	21/10/87	M	1	(12)	1
25	Stanislav Sazanovich		06/03/92	D	2	(3)	
10	Oleg Shkabara		15/02/83	M	29		4
18	Nikita Shugunkov		17/04/92	A	1	(16)	
17	Aleksei Suchkov		10/06/81	M	26	(1)	3
37	Artem Teplov		14/01/92	D	10	(3)	1
71	Andrei Yakimov		17/11/89	M	6	(15)	2
21	Evgeni Yelezarenko		04/07/93	M	20	(5)	
11	Valeri Zhukovski		21/05/84	M	32		6
33	Igor Zyulev		05/01/84	M	29		

FC Neman Grodno

1964 • Central Sportkomplex Neman (8,404) • fcneman.by
Major honours
Belarusian Cup (1) 1993
Coach: Sergei Solodovnikov

2014

30/03	h	Slutsk	L	0-1	
06/04	a	Dinamo Minsk	L	0-1	
11/04	h	Naftan	L	0-2	
19/04	h	Dnepr	W	3-2	Karlsons, Savitski, Tarasovs
26/04	h	Torpedo	D	0-0	
07/05	h	Shakhtyor	W	3-0	Zubovich, Legchilin 2
11/05	h	Minsk	L	0-1	
15/05	h	Gomel	D	1-1	Legchilin
25/05	a	Belshina	W	4-3	Kovalenok 2, Savitski, Rekish
01/06	h	Dinamo Brest	D	1-1	Khachaturyan
07/06	a	BATE	D	0-0	
11/06	a	Slutsk	W	2-0	Zubovich, Savitski
15/06	h	Dinamo Minsk	L	0-2	
21/06	a	Naftan	L	0-2	
28/06	h	Dnepr	W	4-1	Denisevich, Savitski (p), Rekish, Zubovich
05/07	a	Torpedo	L	0-1	
11/07	a	Shakhtyor	L	0-1	
20/07	a	Minsk	D	1-1	og (Begunov)
03/08	a	Gomel	W	2-0	Savitski, Zubovich
09/08	h	Belshina	D	1-1	Savitski
17/08	a	Dinamo Brest	W	2-1	Rekish, Kovalenok
31/08	h	BATE	L	1-2	Zubovich (p)
14/09	h	Dnepr	D	1-1	Savitski
21/09	h	Minsk	L	2-4	Zubovich 2
27/09	a	Slutsk	D	0-0	
04/10	h	Dinamo Brest	L	0-1	
19/10	a	Belshina	W	3-1	Legchilin, Savitski, Zubovich
26/10	a	Dnepr	D	1-1	Savitski
02/11	h	Minsk	L	1-2	Zubovich
09/11	h	Slutsk	W	2-0	Lisitsa, Levitski
23/11	a	Dinamo Brest	W	1-0	Zubovich
29/11	h	Belshina	W	5-2	Rovneiko, Savitski 2 (1p), Zubovich 2

No	Name	Nat	DoB	Pos	Aps	(s)	Gls
14	Aleksandr Anyukevich		10/04/92	D	10	(8)	
29	Artur Bombel		14/12/92	A	1	(5)	
9	Ivan Denisevich		09/11/84	A	8	(4)	1
4	Yuri Goltsev		19/09/95	A	2	(2)	
21	Girts Karlsons	LVA	07/06/81	A	5	(4)	1
7	Andrei Khachaturyan		02/09/87	M	13		1
11	Dmitri Kovalenok		03/11/77	A	5	(19)	3
46	Aleksei Legchilin		11/04/92	M	26	(3)	4
8	Sergei Levitski		17/03/90	M	8	(4)	1
6	Igor Lisitsa		10/04/88	M	12	(1)	1
15	Anton Lukashin		21/02/95	M	1	(2)	
17	Aleksandr Poznyak		23/07/94	M	10		
4	Artem Rakhmanov		10/07/90	D	9	(3)	
1	Marius Rapalis	LTU	22/03/83	G	19	(1)	
10	Dmitri Rekish		14/09/88	M	15	(5)	3
5	Dmitri Rovneiko		13/05/80	D	22	(1)	1
18	Pavel Rybak		11/09/83	D	31		
20	Ivan Sadovnichi		11/05/87	D	10		
88	Pavel Savitski		12/07/94	A	30		11
15	Artem Solovei		01/11/90	M	2	(8)	
19	Aleksandr Sulima		01/08/79	G	13		
32	Igors Tarasovs	LVA	16/10/88	M	19	(8)	1
13	Vladimir Veselinov	SRB	25/05/84	M	19	(1)	
23	Maksim Vitus		11/02/89	D	23	(4)	
25	Igor Yasinski		04/07/90	M	13	(1)	
30	Pavel Zabelin		30/06/95	M		(4)	
9	Vasili Zhurnevich		21/02/95	A		(2)	
17	Yegor Zubovich		01/06/89	A	26	(6)	12

FC Shakhtyor Soligorsk

1961 • Stroitel (4,200) • fcshakhter.by
Major honours
Belarusian League (1) 2005; Belarusian Cup (2) 2004, 2014
Coach: Sergei Borovski

2014

29/03	h	BATE	W	2-0	og (Māliņš), Rios
05/04	a	Slutsk	W	1-0	Rios
11/04	h	Dinamo Minsk	D	0-0	
19/04	a	Naftan	D	1-1	Yanush
26/04	h	Dnepr	D	0-0	
07/05	a	Neman	L	0-3	
11/05	h	Torpedo	W	2-0	Balanovich, Osipenko
15/05	h	Minsk	W	3-1	Yanush 2 (1p), Rios
26/05	a	Gomel	L	0-1	
01/06	h	Belshina	L	1-2	Yanush
07/06	a	Dinamo Brest	D	0-0	
12/06	a	BATE	D	0-0	
16/06	h	Slutsk	W	2-0	Yanush 2
22/06	a	Dinamo Minsk	L	0-3	
28/06	h	Naftan	W	2-0	Galyuza, Yanush
04/07	a	Dnepr	W	1-0	Rios
11/07	h	Neman	W	1-0	Starhorodskiy (p)
20/07	a	Torpedo	W	1-0	Osipenko
03/08	a	Minsk	L	0-3	
10/08	h	Gomel	L	0-1	
15/08	a	Belshina	L	1-2	Osipenko
31/08	h	Dinamo Brest	L	2-3	Yanush 2
14/09	a	Dinamo Minsk	W	4-1	Yanush 3, Wojciechowski
20/09	h	Naftan	W	2-0	Wojciechowski, Galyuza
28/09	a	Gomel	W	1-0	Yanush
04/10	a	Torpedo	W	2-0	Osipenko, Yanush
16/10	h	BATE	L	1-4	Galyuza (p)
27/10	h	Dinamo Minsk	L	1-2	Galyuza
02/11	a	Naftan	D	0-0	
08/11	h	Gomel	W	3-0	Rios 2 (1p), Kuzmenok
22/11	h	Torpedo	D	0-0	
30/11	a	BATE	D	1-1	Yanush

No	Name	Nat	DoB	Pos	Aps	(s)	Gls
16	Sergei Balanovich		29/08/87	M	16	(1)	1
2	Illya Galyuza	UKR	16/11/79	M	24	(5)	4
30	Ilya Gavrilov	RUS	26/09/88	G	3		
9	Aleksandre Guruli	GEO	09/11/85	A	13	(9)	
27	Filipp Ivanov		21/07/90	A	2	(3)	
6	Nikolai Kashevski		05/10/80	D	17	(4)	
1	Artur Kotenko	EST	20/08/81	G	29		
23	Yuri Kovalev		27/01/93	M	5	(14)	
19	Igor Kuzmenok		06/07/90	D	17	(3)	1
7	Andrei Leonchik		02/01/77	M	18	(10)	
3	Sergei Matveichik		05/06/88	D	31		
13	Saulius Mikoliūnas	LTU	02/05/84	M	3	(4)	
77	Dmitri Osipenko		12/12/82	A	23	(5)	4
25	Aleksei Petrov		30/04/91	A		(2)	
17	Aleksei Rios		14/05/87	A	23	(7)	6
8	Adama Soro	CIV	20/12/81	M	3	(2)	
11	Artem Starhorodskiy	UKR	17/01/82	M	21	(1)	1
4	Andrei Tsevan		15/03/86	M	14	(5)	
21	Olexiy Tupchiy	UKR	22/08/86	M	4	(1)	
29	Aleksei Vasilevski		02/06/93	D	1	(1)	
12	Paweł Wojciechowski	POL	24/04/90	A	3	(8)	2
10	Nikolai Yanush		09/09/84	A	27	(1)	15
5	Aleksei Yanushkevich		15/01/86	D	27	(1)	
20	Vladimir Yurchenko		26/01/89	A	1	(3)	
15	Aleksandr Yurevich		08/08/79	D	27	(2)	

SFC Slutsk

1998 • Stroitel, Soligorsk (4,200); City (1,896) • sfc-slutsk.by
Coach: Yuri Krot

2014

30/03	a	Neman	W	1-0	Zenko
05/04	h	Shakhtyor	L	0-1	
11/04	a	Minsk	L	0-1	
19/04	a	Gomel	L	0-1	
27/04	a	Belshina	W	2-1	Yakovlev, Milko
04/05	h	Dinamo Brest	W	1-0	Hlebko
10/05	a	BATE	L	0-3	
16/05	a	Torpedo	L	1-4	Milko
26/05	a	Dinamo Minsk	L	0-3	
31/05	a	Naftan	L	0-1	
06/06	h	Dnepr	D	1-1	Zenko
11/06	h	Neman	L	0-2	
16/06	a	Shakhtyor	L	0-2	
22/06	h	Minsk	W	2-0	Saito, Gorbach
30/06	h	Gomel	D	0-0	
05/07	h	Belshina	W	1-0	Saito (p)
13/07	a	Dinamo Brest	L	1-2	Saito (p)
18/07	h	BATE	L	1-3	Saito
02/08	h	Torpedo	W	2-1	Yakovlev, Aliseiko
17/08	h	Naftan	D	0-0	
24/08	a	Dinamo Minsk	D	0-0	
31/08	a	Dnepr	W	2-0	Aliseiko 2
13/09	h	Dinamo Brest	W	1-0	Zenko
20/09	a	Belshina	L	1-2	Aliseiko
27/09	h	Neman	D	0-0	
04/10	a	Minsk	D	0-0	
19/10	h	Dnepr	W	2-0	Saito, Hlebko
25/10	a	Dinamo Brest	W	2-0	Zenko, Saito
01/11	h	Belshina	W	3-1	Hlebko, Saito, Aliseiko
09/11	a	Neman	L	0-2	
23/11	h	Minsk	L	1-2	Zenko
29/11	a	Dnepr	D	1-1	Milko

No	Name	Nat	DoB	Pos	Aps	(s)	Gls
16	Dmitri Aliseiko		28/08/92	D	27		5
23	Igor Bobko		09/09/85	M	23	(7)	
2	Aleksandr Bylina		26/03/81	D	27		
3	Sergei Drozd		24/06/83	D	5	(5)	
12	Vitali Ganich		29/11/93	A		(1)	
13	Stanislav Gnedko		07/01/87	M	4	(16)	
5	Ucha Gogoladze	GEO	04/09/90	A	7	(4)	
14	Andrei Gorbach		20/05/85	D	15	(4)	1
29	Vyacheslav Grigorov		08/03/83	M	27		
17	Sergei Hlebko		24/06/84	M	16	(15)	3
12	Denys Holaido	UKR	03/06/84	M	9	(1)	
8	Petro Kovalchuk	UKR	28/05/84	D	8	(1)	
27	Artur Lesko		25/05/84	G	31		
10	Evgeni Loshankov		02/01/79	M	27	(3)	
1	Sergei Mikhailov		08/06/78	G	1		
4	Vadym Milko	UKR	22/08/86	M	17	(3)	3
6	Vladyslav Mykulyak	UKR	30/08/84	M	3	(7)	
20	Anton Ryabtsev		19/02/84	D	25		
99	Yosuke Saito	JPN	07/04/88	A	16	(1)	7
18	Sergei Tsvetinski		22/02/84	D	21	(5)	
7	Andriy Yakovlev		20/02/89	M	12	(5)	2
19	Nikolai Zenko		11/03/89	A	21	(10)	5
5	Olexandr Zhdanov	UKR	27/05/84	D	10	(1)	

FC Torpedo Zhodino

1961 • Torpedo (3,020) • torpedo-belaz.by
Coach: Igor Kriushenko

2014

29/03	a	Naftan	L	0-2	
06/04	h	Belshina	D	1-1	Chelyadinski
11/04	a	Dnepr	D	2-2	Yatskevich, Vaskov
18/04	h	Dinamo Brest	W	2-0	Vaskov, Ivashko
26/04	a	Neman	D	0-0	
04/05	a	BATE	L	1-4	Vaskov
11/05	a	Shakhtyor	L	0-2	
16/05	h	Slutsk	W	4-1	Yatskevich 2, Miñano, Platonov
26/05	a	Minsk	W	2-0	Kontsevoi, Yatskevich
31/05	h	Dinamo Minsk	W	1-0	Kozeka
06/06	a	Gomel	D	0-0	
11/06	h	Naftan	L	0-1	
15/06	h	Belshina	W	1-0	Kolomyts
21/06	h	Dnepr	W	2-1	Vaskov 2
28/06	a	Dinamo Brest	L	1-2	Yatskevich
05/07	h	Neman	W	1-0	Hleb
10/07	a	BATE	D	1-1	Kontsevoi
20/07	a	Shakhtyor	L	0-1	
02/08	a	Slutsk	L	1-2	Hleb
09/08	h	Minsk	W	1-0	Melnyk
17/08	a	Dinamo Minsk	D	0-0	
31/08	h	Gomel	D	0-0	
13/09	a	BATE	D	1-1	Kozeka
21/09	h	Gomel	W	2-1	Hleb, Vaskov
27/09	a	Dinamo Minsk	D	1-1	Burko
04/10	a	Shakhtyor	L	0-2	
19/10	a	Naftan	W	5-1	Hleb 2 (1p), Platonov 2, Yatskevich
26/10	h	BATE	D	2-2	Kontsevoi, Burko
02/11	a	Gomel	W	1-0	Platonov
09/11	h	Dinamo Minsk	W	2-1	Yatskevich, Selyava
22/11	a	Shakhtyor	D	0-0	
30/11	h	Naftan	W	3-1	Shchegrikovich, Platonov 2

No	Name	Nat	DoB	Pos	Aps	(s)	Gls
5	Igor Burko		08/09/88	D	32		2
2	Artem Chelyadinski		29/12/77	M	14		1
1	Pavel Chesnovski		04/03/86	G	13		
23	Serhiy Datsenko	UKR	06/09/87	D	12		
99	Vyacheslav Hleb		12/02/83	M	16	(15)	5
9	Ruslan Ivashko	UKR	10/11/86	A	3	(12)	1
27	Vitali Kazantsev	RUS	04/07/81	D	14	(3)	
33	Vasili Khomutovski		30/08/78	G	18		
27	Yuri Kolomyts	RUS	30/04/79	D	21	(1)	1
7	Artem Kontsevoi		20/05/83	M	21	(7)	3
17	Sergei Kozeka		17/09/86	D	14	(15)	2
10	Artur Levitski		17/03/85	M	27	(1)	
4	Serhiy Melnyk	UKR	04/09/88	D	22		1
22	José Luis Miñano	ESP	22/05/87	A	10	(1)	1
25	Daniel Olcina	ESP	25/02/89	A	4		
6	Aleksei Pankovets		18/04/81	D	19	(2)	
32	Dmitri Platonov		07/02/86	A	7	(12)	6
8	Aleksandr Selyava		17/05/92	M	14	(2)	1
11	Dmitri Shchegrikovich		07/12/83	M	21	(6)	1
3	Sergei Sosnovski		14/08/81	D	1		
30	Roman Stepanov		06/08/91	G	1		
25	Denis Trapashko		17/05/90	A	2	(1)	
19	Artem Vaskov		21/10/88	D	21	(6)	6
15	Aleksandr Yatskevich		04/01/85	A	25	(7)	7

Top goalscorers

15	Nikolai Yanush (Shakhtyor)
14	Aleksandr Makas (Minsk)
12	Mikhail Gordeichuk (BATE) Yegor Zubovich (Neman)
11	Vitali Rodionov (BATE) Pavel Savitski (Neman)
10	Sergei Krivets (BATE) Dmitri Khlebosolov (Belshina)
9	Nikolai Signevich (BATE) Vadim Demidovich (Naftan)

Promoted clubs

FC Granit Mikashevichi

1978 • Polesiye, Luninets (3,090) • fcgranit.by
Coach: Valeri Bokhno

FC Slavia-Mozyr

1987 • Yunost (5,353) • no website
Major honours
Belarusian League (2) 1996, 2000; Belarusian Cup (2) 1996, 2000
Coach: Yuri Puntus

FC Vitebsk

1960 • Central (8,100) • fc.vitebsk.by
Major honours
Belarusian Cup (1) 1998
Coach: Sergei Vekhtev

Second level final table 2014

		Pld	W	D	L	F	A	Pts
1	FC Granit Mikashevichi	30	19	7	4	46	16	64
2	FC Slavia-Mozyr	30	18	6	6	55	38	60
3	FC Vitebsk	30	15	5	10	44	30	50
4	FC Smorgon	30	13	7	10	42	32	46
5	FC Rechitsa-2014	30	13	7	10	41	36	46
6	FC Gorodeya	30	11	12	7	42	26	45
7	FC Isloch	30	11	12	7	39	35	45
8	FC Khimik Svetlogorsk	30	12	7	11	34	36	43
9	FC Zvezda-BGU Minsk	30	12	4	14	50	48	40
10	FC Smolevichi-STI	30	12	4	14	37	41	40
11	FC Gomelzheldortrans Gomel	30	9	9	12	33	38	36
12	FC Bereza-2010	30	8	9	13	37	48	33
13	FC Minsk-2	30	9	6	15	41	45	33
14	FC Lida	30	10	1	19	46	64	31
15	FC Slonim	30	6	12	12	32	50	30
16	FC Volna Pinsk	30	4	8	18	26	62	20

Promotion/Relegation play-offs

(03/12/14 & 06/12/14)
Vitebsk 2-0 Dnepr
Dnepr 1-1 Vitebsk
(Vitebsk 3-1)

DOMESTIC CUP

Kubok Belarusii 2014/15

SECOND ROUND

(25/07/14)
Khimik Svetlogorsk 1-2 Gomel
Lida 0-1 Slutsk

(26/07/14)
Baranovichi 1-2 Dinamo Brest
Gomelzheldortrans Gomel 2-1 Slaviya-Mozyr
Gorodeya 0-0 Torpedo Zhodino *(aet; 3-2 on pens)*
Granit 1-0 Rechitsa-2014
Grodnensky 1-4 Belshina
Smorgon 0-2 Dnepr
Volna 2-4 Isloch
Zhdanovichi 0-4 Naftan
Zvezda-BGU Minsk 1-0 FC Minsk

(27/07/14)
Partizan Minsk 1-3 Vitebsk

Byes - BATE, Dinamo Minsk, Neman, Shakhtyor Soligorsk

THIRD ROUND

(23/08/14)
Belshina 1-0 Zvezda-BGU Minsk
Isloch 1-1 Granit *(aet; 4-5 on pens)*
Naftan 1-2 Vitebsk

(24/08/14)
Gomelzheldortrans Gomel 0-2 Dinamo Brest
Neman 5-4 Gomel *(aet)*
Shakhtyor Soligorsk 1-0 Gorodeya

(11/10/14)
BATE 2-1 Slutsk *(aet)*

(13/10/14)
Dnepr 0-1 Dinamo Minsk

QUARTER-FINALS

(21/03/15 & 04/04/15)
BATE 1-0 Neman *(Baga 41)*
Neman 1-2 BATE *(Zabelin 82; Rodionov 48, Gordeichuk 55)*
(BATE 3-1)

Belshina 0-0 Dinamo Brest
Dinamo Brest 2-1 Belshina *(Premudrov 30, Vasilyuk 42; Shagoiko 18)*
(Dinamo Brest 2-1)

(22/03/15 & 04/04/15)
Dinamo Minsk 1-2 Vitebsk *(Politevich 45; Skitov 26, Lebedev 50)*
Vitebsk 1-3 Dinamo Minsk *(Solovei 47; Bećiraj 10, 41, 92) (aet)*
(Dinamo Minsk 4-3)

Granit 0-0 Shakhtyor Soligorsk
Shakhtyor Soligorsk 3-0 *Granit (Starhorodskiy 16p, Yanush 74, 76)*
(Shakhtyor Soligorsk 3-0)

SEMI-FINALS

(15/04/15 & 29/04/15)
BATE 0-0 Dinamo Minsk
Dinamo Minsk 1-3 BATE *(Bećiraj 78; Gordeichuk 51, 69, Rodionov 58)*
(BATE 3-1)

Shakhtyor Soligorsk 0-0 Dinamo Brest
Dinamo Brest 1-2 Shakhtyor Soligorsk *(Premudrov 81; Starhorodskiy 26, Shcherbo 45og)*
(Shakhtyor Soligorsk 2-1)

FINAL

(24/05/15)
Central Sportkomplex, Gomel
FC BATE BORISOV 4 *(Gordeichuk 52, Rodionov 61, Karnitski 65, Signevich 73)*
FC SHAKHTYOR SOLIGORSK 1 *(Komarovski 72)*
Referee: *Kruk*
BATE: *Chernik, Zhavnerchik, Polyakov, Milunović, Mladenović, Karnitski, Yablonski, Stasevich (Rios 76), Baga (M Volodko 46), Gordeichuk, Rodionov (Signevich 71)*
SHAKHTYOR SOLIGORSK: *Bushma, Kobin, Matveichik, Yanushkevich, Yurevich (Martynyuk 70), Rybak, Starhorodskiy, Mikoliūnas (Shibun 73), Kovalev, Komarovski, Ćović*

BELGIUM

Union Royale Belge des Sociétés de Football Association (URBSFA) /
Koninklijke Belgische Voetbalbond (KBVB)

Address	145 Avenue Houba de Strooper BE-1020 Bruxelles
Tel	+32 2 477 1211
Fax	+32 2 478 2391
E-mail	urbsfa.kbvb@footbel.com
Website	footbel.com

President	François De Keersmaecker
General secretary (interim)	Gérard Linard
Media officer	Pierre Cornez
Year of formation	1895
National stadium	King Baudouin, Brussels (47,350)

KEY:

● – UEFA Champions League
◉ – UEFA Europa League
◐ – Promoted
○ – Relegated

PRO LEAGUE CLUBS

 ① **RSC Anderlecht**

 ② **Cercle Brugge KSV**

 ③ **R. Charleroi SC**

 ④ **Club Brugge KV**

 ⑤ **KRC Genk**

 ⑥ **KAA Gent**

 ⑦ **KV Kortrijk**

 ⑧ **K. Lierse SK**

 ⑨ **KSC Lokeren OV**

 ⑩ **KV Mechelen**

 ⑪ **R. Mouscron-Péruwelz**

 ⑫ **KV Oostende**

 ⑬ **R. Standard de Liège**

 ⑭ **Waasland-Beveren**

 ⑮ **KVC Westerlo**

⑯ **SV Zulte Waregem**

PROMOTED CLUBS

 ⑰ **K. Sint-Truidense VV**

 ⑱ **Oud-Heverlee Leuven**

Gent grab title glory

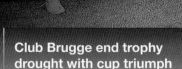

Belgium had brand new champions in 2014/15 as KAA Gent came from behind to usurp title holders RSC Anderlecht and long-time leaders Club Brugge KV and end a 115-year wait for their first league triumph.

Gent were the strongest of the six teams in the championship play-offs, which kicked off after Club Brugge had already lifted the Belgian Cup thanks to a last-gasp 2-1 win in the final against Anderlecht. The Blue-and-Blacks also reached the UEFA Europa League quarter-finals during a long and arduous campaign that took in 63 matches.

| Buffalos charge to first championship crown | Club Brugge end trophy drought with cup triumph | All-star Red Devils fail to sparkle in EURO qualifiers |

Domestic league

Just like Anderlecht the previous season, Gent timed their title-winning run in the 40-match Pro League marathon to perfection. Sitting just off the pace for most of the campaign, Hein Vanhaezebrouck's outsiders conserved their energy sufficiently to sprint clear at the finish, defeating Anderlecht 2-1 at home and Club Brugge 3-2 away before clinching that historic maiden championship triumph – and a first passport to the UEFA Champions League group stage – in the penultimate round. A convincing 2-0 victory against R. Standard de Liège sealed the deal in front of a euphoric capacity crowd in the club's new Ghelamco Arena.

The celebration party in the city of Ghent lasted several days, which was hardly surprising as no Gent fan had ever experienced anything like it. The Buffalos had won the Belgian Cup three times previously, most recently in 2010, but in all the years since the club's formation in 1900 every attempt to win the league had come to nought. The jubilation was accentuated by the fact that Gent's triumph was wholly unexpected. Even Vanhaezebrouck, newly arrived from KV Kortirjk, acknowledged that he and his players had not given serious thought to winning

the title until they defeated Anderlecht 2-1 in Brussels on the final day of the regular season.

That win – the club's fourth in a row and tenth successive match without defeat – enabled Gent to draw level with the defending champions and enter the play-off phase just two points adrift of leaders Club Brugge. A first defeat since Christmas, 2-1 at R. Charleroi SC, might have sapped the confidence of lesser sides, but Vanhaezebrouck's men displayed remarkable resilience in taking ten points from their next four games to move to the top of the table for the first time with just four fixtures remaining.

The second of those, in Bruges, proved pivotal. Gent lost the lead twice before, in the 87th minute, 20-year-old Benito Raman struck the winner to give the visitors a precious 3-2 victory, putting them five points clear of their fading hosts and four ahead of Anderlecht, held 1-1 at home by Standard. Four days later Gent and their supporters crossed the threshold to paradise as Standard were defeated 2-0, a first goal of the season from skipper Sven Kums breaking the deadlock on 18 minutes before Brazilian midfielder Renato Neto doubled Gent's advantage with a penalty early in the second half.

Even with a final-day defeat at Anderlecht, Gent boasted the best record of the six play-off teams, winning six and drawing two of their ten matches. There was no doubt that they deserved their success, although most outside observers still struggled to fathom how a team so shorn of household names could have gone the distance. With the exception of Israeli defender Rami Gershon, a former charge of Vanhaezebrouck's at Kortrijk, there were no players of international renown in the Gent squad. Several, however, advanced their careers considerably in 2014/15, notably goalkeeper Matz Sels, 13-goal striker Laurent Depoître, Swiss midfielder Danijel Milicevic and – following his mid-season arrival from FK AS Trenčín – Nigerian winger Moses Simon.

Club Brugge's failure to take first prize in a title race they bossed from halfway through the regular season was difficult to take. Without a league title since 2005, Michel Preud'homme's side simply ran out of steam in the closing weeks, three successive defeats against Standard, Anderlecht and Gent undoing all the good work that had gone before. They did, however, cling on to second place, which afforded entry to the UEFA Champions League third qualifying round.

Anderlecht's quest to win a fourth successive league title – a mission not accomplished since the 1960s – also foundered on a faltering finish. Unbeaten in their first 11 matches, Besnik Hasi's Mauves relinquished top spot to Club Brugge in November and never returned to the summit. Third place was a considerable disappointment for a team boasting the league's leading marksman in 20-goal Serbian striker Aleksandar Mitrović and two rising talents of considerable potential in 21-year-old Dennis Praet and 18-year-old Youri Tielemans.

Joining Anderlecht in the UEFA Europa League were fourth-placed Standard, who changed coach twice during a fractious campaign, and surprise package Charleroi. Felice Mazzu's side had been widely tipped for relegation at the start of term but they sneaked into the championship play-off pool thanks to a greater number of victories than KRC Genk, then finished fifth before overcoming KV Mechelen in the post-season play-offs.

Oud-Heverlee Leuven also came successfully through a play-off series to return to the Pro League after a year away, joining automatically-promoted K. Sint-Truidense VV as they sent K. Lierse SK down with Cercle Brugge KSV.

Domestic cup

The Belgian Cup was scheduled to end between the two phases of the Pro League, and it concluded with a meeting of the heavyweights at the King Baudouin stadium as Anderlecht and Club Brugge came face to face in the fixture for the first time in 21 years. The Brussels club had demolished Gent in the semi-finals, 5-0 on aggregate, but they trailed for 77 minutes of the final, to Tom De Sutter's early strike, before Mitrović snatched an equaliser. The late drama did not finish there, though, as two minutes into added time Israeli midfielder Lior Refaelov volleyed Club Brugge back in front, giving the Blue-and-Blacks their first major trophy for eight years – the club's longest sequence without silverware since the first of their 11 Belgian Cup wins back in 1968.

Europe

Belgium's five-strong European contingent amassed 46 games between them in 2014/15, with Club Brugge running up 16 alone in the UEFA Europa League as they navigated their way from the third qualifying round to the quarter-finals. They were undefeated in the first 15 of those matches – a competition record – but when that run

came to an end, it proved fatal as FC Dnipro Dnipropetrovsk beat them 1-0 in Kyiv following a first-leg 0-0 draw in Bruges. Highlights of their European tour included three wins in Denmark and a brilliant 3-1 victory over Beşiktaş JK in front of a large and hostile crowd in Istanbul.

Anderlecht also fared better than usual, avoiding last place in their UEFA Champions League group for the first time in eight attempts as they chalked up six points, one of them in a memorable fightback from 3-0 down at Arsenal FC. A third-place finish transported them into the UEFA Europa League round of 32, where they perished on entry against FC Dinamo Moskva. Standard and Lokeren both exited that competition in the group stage, the former having earlier missed out on the UEFA Champions League proper after a heavy play-off defeat by another Russian club, FC Zenit.

National team

After a quarter-final placing at the 2014 FIFA World Cup, Marc Wilmots' all-star Belgium side were expected to have little difficulty in making it two major tournament participations in a row – despite the fact that the country had not qualified for a UEFA European Championship since the last time the finals were held in neighbouring France, in 1984. However, with six of their fixtures completed, the Red Devils still had some work to do, a June defeat by Wales in Cardiff sending them home with their tails between their legs and dropping them from first place to second in the Group B standings.

Five days earlier Wilmots' men had produced their finest performance of an otherwise mediocre season in beating France 4-3 in a prestige Saint-Denis friendly, two goals from Marouane Fellaini and one apiece from Radja Nainggolan and Eden Hazard putting them 4-1 up before a late French rally. Fellaini had also struck three times in the team's two previous games to earn six qualifying points at the expense of Cyprus (5-0 in Brussels) and Israel (1-0 in Jerusalem), but the Manchester United FC midfielder was missing with injury in Cardiff, and without him and suspended skipper Vincent Kompany, Belgium succumbed to their first defeat in 16 qualifying matches.

Anderlecht striker Aleksandar Mitrović (left) is foiled by Gent goalkeeper Matz Sels

DOMESTIC SEASON AT A GLANCE

Pro League 2014/15 final tables

Championship play-offs

		Pld	Home W	D	L	F	A	Away W	D	L	F	A	Total W	D	L	F	A	Pts
1	KAA Gent	10	3	2	0	9	4	3	0	2	9	7	6	2	2	18	11	49
2	Club Brugge KV	10	4	0	1	10	6	1	1	3	6	10	5	1	4	16	16	47
3	RSC Anderlecht	10	4	1	0	12	4	1	1	3	6	9	5	2	3	18	13	46
4	R. Standard de Liège	10	4	0	1	11	4	0	1	4	3	9	4	1	5	14	13	40
5	R. Charleroi SC	10	3	0	2	10	7	0	2	3	3	8	3	2	5	13	15	36
6	KV Kortrijk	10	2	2	1	8	5	0	0	5	3	17	2	2	6	11	22	34

Pro League final table

		Pld	Home W	D	L	F	A	Away W	D	L	F	A	Total W	D	L	F	A	Pts
1	Club Brugge KV	30	10	5	0	37	11	7	5	3	32	17	17	10	3	69	28	61
2	KAA Gent	30	9	3	3	30	14	7	6	2	22	15	16	9	5	52	29	57
3	RSC Anderlecht	30	8	5	2	25	11	8	4	3	26	19	16	9	5	51	30	57
4	R. Standard de Liège	30	8	2	5	26	19	8	3	4	23	20	16	5	9	49	39	53
5	KV Kortrijk	30	8	2	5	30	17	8	1	6	24	18	16	3	11	54	35	51
6	R. Charleroi SC	30	8	3	4	23	12	6	4	5	21	19	14	7	9	44	31	49
7	KRC Genk	30	8	5	2	25	12	5	5	5	13	16	13	10	7	38	28	49
8	KSC Lokeren OV	30	7	5	3	27	18	3	7	5	11	14	10	12	8	38	32	42
9	KV Mechelen	30	7	6	2	21	11	3	5	7	16	28	10	11	9	37	39	41
10	KV Oostende	30	6	3	6	24	28	5	2	8	16	24	11	5	14	40	52	38
11	KVC Westerlo	30	5	5	5	25	21	3	4	8	17	42	8	9	13	42	63	33
12	SV Zulte Waregem	30	4	3	8	19	28	4	4	7	22	26	8	7	15	41	54	31
13	R. Mouscron-Péruwelz	30	6	2	7	23	24	1	3	11	9	27	7	5	18	32	51	26
14	Waasland-Beveren	30	5	3	7	12	18	2	2	11	18	31	7	5	18	30	49	26
15	Cercle Brugge KSV	30	4	2	9	11	22	2	4	9	10	23	6	6	18	21	45	24
16	K. Lierse SK	30	3	6	6	18	26	2	1	12	12	37	5	7	18	30	63	22

NB After 30 rounds the top six clubs enter a championship play-off, carrying forward half of their points total (half points rounded upwards); clubs placed 7-14 enter two play-off groups; clubs placed 15 &16 enter relegation play-off group.

European qualification 2015/16

Champion: KAA Gent (group stage)
Cup winner: Club Brugge KV (third qualifying round)

RSC Anderlecht (group stage)
R. Standard de Liège (third qualifying round)
R. Charleroi SC (second qualifying round)

Top scorer	Aleksandar Mitrović (Anderlecht), 20 goals
Relegated clubs	Cercle Brugge KSV, K. Lierse SK
Promoted clubs	K. Sint-Truidense VV, Oud-Heverlee Leuven
Cup final	Club Brugge KV 2-1 RSC Anderlecht

Player of the season

Víctor Vázquez
(Club Brugge KV)

There were a number of candidates for Belgium's 2015 Professional Footballer of the Year award, including other Club Brugge players such as Matthew Ryan and Lior Refaelov, but it was the team's Spanish midfield pivot, Víctor Vázquez, who scooped the prestigious end-of-season prize. A one-time team-mate of Lionel Messi at the FC Barcelona academy, he managed to put his injury troubles behind him and, in his fourth season in Bruges, play a key role in the club's long and impressive campaign on three fronts.

Newcomer of the season

Youri Tielemans
(RSC Anderlecht)

Named Belgium's young player of the year for the second successive year, Tielemans was just 17 years of age for most of the 2014/15 season, during which he played almost every game for Anderlecht, racking up 52 in total. A midfield all-rounder with abundant natural talent and an appetite for hard work, he was handed a five-year contract by the club on his 18th birthday in May. Whether he sees that out seems doubtful, however, as several of Europe's big battalions have already begun to show an interest.

Team of the season
(3-5-2)

Coach: Vanhaezebrouck *(Gent)*

Sels *(Gent)*

Deschacht *(Anderlecht)* — Mbemba *(Anderlecht)* — Jorge Teixeira *(Standard)*

Najar *(Anderlecht)* — Refaelov *(Club Brugge)* — Víctor Vázquez *(Club Brugge)* — Milicevic *(Gent)* — Obradović *(Mechelen)*

Mitrović *(Anderlecht)* — Ezekiel *(Standard)*

NATIONAL TEAM

International tournament appearances

FIFA World Cup (12) 1930, 1934, 1938, 1954, 1970, 1982 (2nd phase), 1986 (4th), 1990 (2nd round), 1994 (2nd round), 1998, 2002 (2nd round), 2014 (qtr-finals)
UEFA European Championship (4) 1972 (3rd), 1980 (runners-up), 1984, 2000

Top five all-time caps

Jan Ceulemans (96); Timmy Simons (93), Eric Gerets & Franky Van Der Elst (86); Daniel Van Buyten (85)

Top five all-time goals

Paul Van Himst & Bernard Voorhoof (30); Marc Wilmots (28); Jef Mermans (27); Raymond Braine & Robert De Veen (26)

Results 2014/15

04/09/14	Australia	H	Liège	W	2-0	Mertens (18), Witsel (77)
10/10/14	Andorra (ECQ)	H	Brussels	W	6-0	De Bruyne (31p, 34), Chadli (37), Origi (59), Mertens (65, 68)
13/10/14	Bosnia & Herzegovina (ECQ)	A	Zenica	D	1-1	Nainggolan (51)
12/11/14	Iceland	H	Brussels	W	3-1	Lombaerts (11), Origi (62), Lukaku (73)
16/11/14	Wales (ECQ)	H	Brussels	D	0-0	
28/03/15	Cyprus (ECQ)	H	Brussels	W	5-0	Fellaini (21, 66), Benteke (35), Hazard (67), Batshuayi (80)
31/03/15	Israel (ECQ)	A	Jerusalem	W	1-0	Fellaini (9)
07/06/15	France	A	Saint-Denis	W	4-3	Fellaini (17, 42), Nainggolan (50), Hazard (54p)
12/06/15	Wales (ECQ)	A	Cardiff	L	0-1	

Appearances 2014/15

Coach: Marc Wilmots	22/02/69		Aus	AND	BIH	Isl	WAL	CYP	ISR	Fra	WAL	Caps	Goals
Thibaut Courtois	11/05/92	Chelsea (ENG)	G	G	G	G	G	G	G	G	G	31	-
Toby Alderweireld	02/03/89	Southampton (ENG)	D	D	D	D	D	D	D	D	D77	48	1
Nicolas Lombaerts	20/03/85	Zenit (RUS)	D78	D	D	D	D	D	D	D	D	36	3
Vincent Kompany	10/04/86	Man. City (ENG)	D	D56	D			D	D 64*			69	4
Jan Vertonghen	24/04/87	Tottenham (ENG)	D89	D	D	D	D	D	D	D	D	71	5
Steven Defour	15/04/88	Anderlecht	M63	M	M78							48	2
Axel Witsel	12/01/89	Zenit (RUS)	M			M	M	M	M	M81	M	60	6
Kevin De Bruyne	28/06/91	Wolfsburg (GER)	M	M	M		M	M	M		M	33	8
Dries Mertens	06/05/87	Napoli (ITA)	M63	M	s57	s63	s73 /89	s69		M59	M46	38	7
Kevin Mirallas	05/10/87	Everton (ENG)	M62									50	9
Divock Origi	18/04/95	LOSC (FRA)	A81	A66	A	s46	A73		s86			14	3
Adnan Januzaj	05/02/95	Man. United (ENG)	s62			M63	s89					6	-
Nacer Chadli	02/08/89	Tottenham (ENG)	s63	M61			M62		s63	s77		30	4
Radja Nainggolan	04/05/88	Roma (ITA)	s63	M	M			M	M86	M	M	12	3
Laurent Ciman	05/08/85	Standard Liège	s78									9	-
Mousa Dembélé	16/07/87	Tottenham (ENG)	s81			M46				s81		62	5
Guillaume Gillet	09/03/84	Bastia (FRA)	s89									21	1
Sébastien Pocognoli	01/08/87	West Brom (ENG)		s56								13	-
Marouane Fellaini	22/11/87	Man. United (ENG)		s61	s78	M	M	M69	M	M77		63	14
Romelu Lukaku	13/05/93	Everton (ENG)		s66	A57	s46				s59	s46	39	11
Eden Hazard	07/01/91	Chelsea (ENG)			M	M46	M	M69	M63	M	M	58	8
Anthony Vanden Borre	24/10/87	Anderlecht				D66	D					29	1
Christian Benteke	03/12/90	Aston Villa (ENG)				A76	s62	A77	A66	A59	A	24	7
Thomas Meunier	12/09/91	Club Brugge				s66						3	-
Dennis Praet	14/05/94	Anderlecht				s76						1	-
Yannick Ferreira Carrasco	04/09/93	Monaco (FRA)						s69		s59	s77	3	-
Michy Batshuayi	02/10/93	Marseille (FRA)						s77				1	1
Jason Denayer	28/06/95	Celtic (SCO)							s66	D85	D	3	-
Leander Dendoncker	15/04/95	Anderlecht								s85		1	-

EUROPE

RSC Anderlecht

Match 1 - Galatasaray AŞ (TUR)
A 1-1 *Praet (52)*
Roef, Deschacht, Najar, Praet (Dendoncker 78), Nuytinck (Suárez 23), Defour, Acheampong, Conté, Mbemba, Tielemans, Mitrović (Kljestan 66). Coach: Besnik Hasi (ALB)
Match 2 - Borussia Dortmund (GER)
H 0-3
Proto, Deschacht, Najar, Suárez (Cyriac 82), Praet, Nuytinck, Defour, Conté (Acheampong 73), Mbemba, Tielemans, Mitrović (Kabasele 82). Coach: Besnik Hasi (ALB)
Match 3 - Arsenal FC (ENG)
H 1-2 *Najar (71)*
Proto, Deschacht, Najar, Praet (Dendoncker 88), Cyriac (Suárez 83), Defour, Acheampong, Conté, Mbemba, Tielemans, Vanden Borre. Coach: Besnik Hasi (ALB)
Match 4 - Arsenal FC (ENG)
A 3-3 *Vanden Borre (61, 73p), Mitrović (90)*
Proto, Deschacht, Najar, Praet, Cyriac (Mitrović 62), Acheampong, Kljestan, Conté (Kawaya 45), Mbemba (Dendoncker 53), Tielemans, Vanden Borre: Besnik Hasi (ALB)
Match 5 - Galatasaray AŞ (TUR)
H 2-0 *Mbemba (44, 86)*
Proto, Deschacht, Najar, Praet (Kljestan 84), Defour (Kawaya 46), Acheampong, Conté, Mbemba, Tielemans, Vanden Borre, Mitrović (Cyriac 89). Coach: Besnik Hasi (ALB)
Match 6 - Borussia Dortmund (GER)
A 1-1 *Mitrović (84)*
Proto, N'Sakala, Deschacht, Praet, Acheampong, Kljestan (Tielemans 69), Conté (Cyriac 79), Mbemba, Dendoncker, Vanden Borre, Mitrović (Heylen 89). Coach: Besnik Hasi (ALB)

Round of 32 - FC Dinamo Moskva (RUS)
H 0-0
Proto, N'Sakala, Deschacht, Najar, Rolando, Defour (Colin 67), Acheampong (Kabasele 86), Tielemans, Dendoncker, Vanden Borre (Leya Iseka 83), Mitrović. Coach: Besnik Hasi (ALB)
A 1-3 *Mitrović (29)*
Proto, N'Sakala, Deschacht, Rolando, Defour, Acheampong, Conté (Cyriac 81), Tielemans (Najar 71), Dendoncker (Leya Iseka 81), Vanden Borre, Mitrović. Coach: Besnik Hasi (ALB)

R. Standard de Liège

Third qualifying round - Panathinaikos FC (GRE)
H 0-0
Kawashima, Jorge Teixeira, Ciman (M'Poku 61), Stam (Milec 88), De Camargo, Carcela-González, Arslanagic, Van Damme, Ezekiel, Marquet, Mujangi Bia (Mbombo 82). Coach: Guy Luzon (ISR)
A 2-1 *Mbombo (36), M'Poku (42)*
Kawashima, Jorge Teixeira, Ciman, Stam, De Camargo, Mbombo (Ajdarevic 71), Carcela-González (Watt 54), Arslanagic, Van Damme, Mujangi Bia (M'Poku 20), Lumanza. Coach: Guy Luzon (ISR)

Play-offs - FC Zenit (RUS)
H 0-1
Kawashima, Faty, Jorge Teixeira, Ciman, De Camargo, Louis, Watt (Mujangi Bia 65), Arslanagic, Van Damme, M'Poku, Lumanza (Mbombo 71). Coach: Guy Luzon (ISR)
A 0-3
Kawashima, Faty, Jorge Teixeira, Ciman, De Camargo, Trebel, Louis (Ajdarevic 69), Watt (Ono 58), Van Damme, M'Poku, Mujangi Bia (Mbombo 59). Coach: Guy Luzon (ISR)
Red card: Faty 89

Group G
Match 1 - HNK Rijeka (CRO)
H 2-0 *Ciman (74), Vinícius Araújo (87)*
Kawashima, Jorge Teixeira, Ciman, De Camargo, De Sart, Trebel, Louis (Vinícius Araújo 84), Carcela-González (Jonathan Viera 56), Van Damme, Mujangi Bia (M'Poku 16), Milec. Coach: Guy Luzon (ISR)
Match 2 - Feyenoord (NED)
A 1-2 *Jonathan Viera (65)*
Kawashima, Faty, Ciman, Vinícius Araújo (Watt 70), Jonathan Viera (Ono 77), Trebel (De Camargo 89), Louis, Arslanagic, Van Damme, M'Poku, Milec. Coach: Guy Luzon (ISR)
Match 3 - Sevilla FC (ESP)
H 0-0
Thuram-Ulien, Faty, Jorge Teixeira, Ciman, De Camargo (Vinícius Araújo 90+1), Enoh (Louis 68), Trebel, Van Damme, M'Poku, Mujangi Bia (Jonathan Viera 79), Milec. Coach: Ivan Vukomanović (SRB)
Match 4 - Sevilla FC (ESP)
A 1-3 *M'Poku (32)*
Thuram-Ulien, Ciman, De Camargo, Enoh, Trebel (Lumanza 82), Louis (Watt 67), Andrade, Arslanagic, Van Damme (Mujangi Bia 63), M'Poku, Milec. Coach: Ivan Vukomanović (SRB)
Match 5 - HNK Rijeka (CRO)
A 0-2
Thuram-Ulien, Ciman, Vinícius Araújo (Watt 58), De Camargo (Lumanza 46), De Sart, Trebel, Arslanagic, Van Damme, M'Poku, Mujangi Bia (Ono 68), Milec. Coach: Ivan Vukomanović (SRB)
Red card: Arslanagic 33
Match 6 - Feyenoord (NED)
H 0-3
Kawashima, Faty (De Sart 61), Ciman, Stam, Ono (Milosevic 73), Fiore, Louis, Andrade, Watt, Mujangi Bia (De Camargo 61), Lumanza. Coach: Ivan Vukomanović (SRB)

KSC Lokeren OV

Play-offs - Hull City AFC (ENG)
H 1-0 *Vanaken (58)*
Verhulst, Scholz, Odoi, Maric, Overmeire, Persoons, Galitsios, Remacle (Ngolok 77), Júnior Dutra (Leye 83), Vanaken, De Pauw (Abdurahimi 88). Coach: Peter Maes (BEL)
A 1-2 *Remacle (49)*
Verhulst, Scholz, Odoi, Maric, Overmeire, Persoons, Galitsios, Remacle (Ngolok 88), Júnior Dutra (Leye 76), Vanaken, De Pauw (Mertens 90). Coach: Peter Maes (BEL)

Group L
Match 1 - Legia Warszawa (POL)
A 0-1
Barry, Scholz, Odoi, Maric, Overmeire, Persoons, Leye (Júnior Dutra 73), Galitsios, Remacle (Abdurahimi 65), Vanaken, De Pauw (Patosi 81). Coach: Rudi Cossey (BEL)
Match 2 - FC Metalist Kharkiv (UKR)
H 1-0 *De Pauw (74)*
Barry, Scholz, Odoi, Maric, Overmeire, Persoons, Leye (Dessers 71), Galitsios, Abdurahimi (Remacle 79), Vanaken (Ngolok 88), De Pauw. Coach: Peter Maes (BEL)
Match 3 - Trabzonspor AŞ (TUR)
A 0-2
Barry, Scholz, Odoi, Maric, Overmeire, Persoons (Remacle 76), Leye, Galitsios (Mertens 59), Abdurahimi (Júnior Dutra 63), Vanaken, De Pauw. Coach: Peter Maes (BEL)
Match 4 - Trabzonspor AŞ (TUR)
H 1-1 *Patosi (5)*
Barry, Scholz, Odoi, Maric, Overmeire (Ngolok 53), Persoons, Leye, Patosi, Galitsios, Júnior Dutra, De Pauw (Abdurahimi 79). Coach: Peter Maes (BEL)
Match 5 - Legia Warszawa (POL)
H 1-0 *Vanaken (7)*
Barry, Scholz, Odoi, Maric, Overmeire, Persoons, Patosi (Remacle 86), Galitsios, Júnior Dutra (Dessers 90), Vanaken, De Pauw (Leye 74). Coach: Peter Maes (BEL)
Match 6 - FC Metalist Kharkiv (UKR)
A 1-0 *Leye (16)*
Barry, Odoi, Mertens, Maric, Overmeire (Persoons 80), Leye, Remacle, Dessers (Ansah 78), Corryn, Ngolok (Scholz 90), De Pauw. Coach: Peter Maes (BEL)

Club Brugge KV

Third qualifying round - Brøndby IF (DEN)
H 3-0 *Duarte (14), Castillo (30), Víctor Vázquez (63)*
Ryan, Simons, Duarte, Fernando, Víctor Vázquez (Jørgensen 89), Refaelov (Storm 72), Lestienne, Meunier, De Bock, Castillo (Sobota 83), Engels. Coach: Michel Preud'homme (BEL)
A 2-0 *Castillo (38), Fernando (45+1)*
Ryan, De Fauw, Simons, Duarte (Mechele 46), Fernando, Jørgensen (Refaelov 61), Sobota, De Bock, Castillo (Lestienne 73), Engels, Storm. Coach: Michel Preud'homme (BEL)

Play-offs - Grasshopper Club Zürich (SUI)
A 2-1 *Jahić (14og), Víctor Vázquez (15)*
Ryan, Simons, Duarte, Fernando, Víctor Vázquez (Lestienne 81), Jørgensen (Odjidja-Ofoe 70), Sobota, Meunier, De Bock, Engels, Storm (Refaelov 59). Coach: Michel Preud'homme (BEL)
H 1-0 *Víctor Vázquez (62)*
Ryan, Simons, Duarte, Fernando, Víctor Vázquez (Bolingoli-Mbombo 86), Sobota (Dierckx 90), Meunier, De Bock, Castillo, Engels, Storm (Jørgensen 79). Coach: Michel Preud'homme (BEL)

Group B
Match 1 - Torino FC (ITA)
H 0-0
Ryan, Simons, Duarte, Silva, Fernando (Vormer 66), Víctor Vázquez (Storm 66), Felipe Gedoz, Meunier, Izquierdo, Mechele, Bolingoli-Mbombo (De Bock 80). Coach: Michel Preud'homme (BEL)
Match 2 - HJK Helsinki (FIN)
A 3-0 *Heikkinen (19og), De Sutter (70), De Bock (78)*
Ryan, Duarte, Silva, Fernando, Víctor Vázquez (Simons 74), Refaelov, Felipe Gedoz (Izquierdo 81), Meunier, De Bock, Mechele, Oularé (De Sutter 65). Coach: Michel Preud'homme (BEL)
Match 3 - FC København (DEN)
H 1-1 *Víctor Vázquez (90+2)*
Ryan, De Fauw, Simons, Duarte, Silva (Izquierdo 79), Víctor Vázquez, Sobota (Refaelov 56), Felipe Gedoz, De Bock, Castillo (De Sutter 69), Mechele. Coach: Michel Preud'homme (BEL)
Match 4 - FC København (DEN)
A 4-0 *Refaelov (7, 30, 36), Vormer (60)*
Ryan, De Fauw, Simons, Duarte, Víctor Vázquez (Fernando 65), Refaelov, De Sutter (Castillo 46), Felipe Gedoz (Sobota 77), Meunier, Vormer, Mechele. Coach: Michel Preud'homme (BEL)
Match 5 - Torino FC (ITA)
A 0-0
Ryan, Simons, Duarte, Silva (Vormer 63), Fernando, Víctor Vázquez (Refaelov 63), Felipe Gedoz, Meunier, De Bock, Castillo (De Sutter 88), Mechele. Coach: Michel Preud'homme (BEL)

Match 6 - HJK Helsinki (FIN)
H 2-1 *Felipe Gedoz (28p), Refaelov (88)*
Ryan, De Fauw, Simons, Duarte, Fernando (Refaelov 71), De Sutter (Oularé 79), Felipe Gedoz, Vormer, Storm, Coopman (Víctor Vázquez 71), Mechele. Coach: Michel Preud'homme (BEL)

Round of 32 - Aalborg BK (DEN)
A 3-1 *Oularé (25), Refaelov (29), Petersen (61og)*
Ryan, De Fauw, Simons, Duarte, Refaelov (De Sutter 80), Felipe Gedoz (Silva 57), Meunier, Vormer, Mechele, Oularé (Víctor Vázquez 68), Bolingoli-Mbombo. Coach: Michel Preud'homme (BEL)
H 3-0 *Víctor Vázquez (11), Oularé (64), Bolingoli-Mbombo (74)*
Ryan, De Fauw, Simons, Duarte, Víctor Vázquez (Silva 75), Refaelov, Meunier (De Bock 78), Vormer, Mechele, Oularé (Dierckx 75), Bolingoli-Mbombo. Coach: Michel Preud'homme (BEL)

Round of 16 - Beşiktaş JK (TUR)
H 2-1 *De Sutter (62), Refaelov (79p)*
Ryan, De Fauw (Oularé 61), Simons, Duarte, Refaelov, De Sutter (Dierckx 87), Meunier, Vormer, De Bock, Mechele, Bolingoli-Mbombo (Felipe Gedoz 46). Coach: Michel Preud'homme (BEL)
A 3-1 *De Sutter (61), Bolingoli-Mbombo (80, 90)*
Ryan, De Fauw (Felipe Gedoz 60), Simons, Duarte, Refaelov, De Sutter (Oularé 81), Meunier, Izquierdo (Bolingoli-Mbombo 65), Vormer, De Bock, Mechele. Coach: Michel Preud'homme (BEL)

Quarter-finals - FC Dnipro Dnipropetrovsk (UKR)
H 0-0
Ryan, De Fauw, Simons, Silva, Víctor Vázquez, Refaelov (Coopman 89), Izquierdo (Dierckx 78), Vormer, De Bock, Mechele, Oularé (De Sutter 72). Coach: Michel Preud'homme (BEL)
A 0-1
Ryan, De Fauw, Simons, Duarte, Refaelov, De Sutter (Oularé 70), Izquierdo (Dierckx 86), Vormer, De Bock, Storm (Víctor Vázquez 86), Mechele. Coach: Michel Preud'homme (BEL)

SV Zulte Waregem

Second qualifying round - Zawisza Bydgoszcz (POL)
H 2-1 *Colpaert (8), Plet (45)*
Bostyn, Cissako, Colpaert, Verboom, Plet, N'Diaye (Ekangamene 86), Skúlason, Conté (Cacérès 82), D'Haene, Aneke, Bongonda (Sylla 83). Coach: Francky Dury (BEL)
A 3-1 *Plet (1), Aneke (48), Skúlason (76)*
Bostyn, Cissako (Mendy 34), Colpaert, Verboom, Plet, N'Diaye, Skúlason, Conté (Trajkovski 73), D'Haene, Aneke, Bongonda (Sylla 64). Coach: Francky Dury (BEL)

Third qualifying round - FC Shakhtyor Soligorsk (BLR)
H 2-5 *Plet (40), Conté (75)*
Bossut, Colpaert, Plet, Sylla, N'Diaye (Sefa İşçi 25), Skúlason, Conté, Mendy (Bongonda 24), D'Haene, Aneke, Ekangamene (Trajkovski 77). Coach: Francky Dury (BEL)
Red card: Plet 44
A 2-2 *Sylla (40, 73)*
Bossut, Tiago Ferreira, Sylla, Trajkovski, N'Diaye, Conté (Hazard 69), Sefa İşçi (Skúlason 46), D'Haene, Aneke (Cacérès 69), Paye, Ekangamene. Coach: Francky Dury (BEL)

DOMESTIC LEAGUE CLUB-BY-CLUB

RSC Anderlecht

1908 • Constant Vanden Stock (28,063) • rsca.be

Major honours
UEFA Cup Winners' Cup (2) 1976, 1978; UEFA Cup (1) 1983; UEFA Super Cup (2) 1976, 1978; Belgian League (33) 1947, 1949, 1950, 1951, 1954, 1955, 1956, 1959, 1962, 1964, 1965, 1966, 1967, 1968, 1972, 1974, 1981, 1985, 1986, 1987, 1991, 1993, 1994, 1995, 2000, 2001, 2004, 2006, 2007, 2010, 2012, 2013, 2014; Belgian Cup (9) 1965, 1972, 1973, 1975, 1976, 1988, 1989, 1994, 2008

Coach: Besnik Hasi (ALB)

2014
27/07	h	Mouscron-Péruwelz	W 3-1	Acheampong, Mitrović, Suárez
01/08	a	Oostende	W 2-0	Mitrović, Suárez
10/08	h	Charleroi	W 1-0	Mitrović
17/08	a	Westerlo	D 2-2	Cyriac, Tielemans (p)
24/08	h	Waasland-Beveren	W 1-0	Kabasele
31/08	a	Club Brugge	D 2-2	Defour, Mitrović
13/09	a	Lierse	D 2-2	Acheampong, Cyriac
20/09	h	Cercle Brugge	W 3-2	Mitrović, Suárez, Najar
27/09	a	Zulte Waregem	W 2-0	Suárez, Najar
05/10	a	Genk	D 0-0	
18/10	a	Mechelen	D 1-1	Defour
26/10	h	Standard	L 0-2	
29/10	a	Kortrijk	W 3-2	Defour (p), Mitrović, Kljestan
01/11	h	Lokeren	D 1-1	Cyriac
09/11	a	Gent	W 2-0	Mitrović, Conté
22/11	a	Charleroi	L 1-3	Mitrović
30/11	h	Club Brugge	D 2-2	Praet, Deschacht
06/12	a	Mouscron-Péruwelz	L 2-4	Mbemba, Cyriac
14/12	h	Oostende	W 3-0	Praet 2, Mitrović
20/12	a	Waasland-Beveren	W 2-0	Defour (p), Praet
26/12	h	Westerlo	W 4-0	Mitrović, Conté, Praet, Colin

2015
18/01	h	Lierse	W 3-0	Tielemans (p), Dendoncker, Álvarez
25/01	a	Standard	L 0-2	
01/02	h	Zulte Waregem	D 0-0	
08/02	a	Cercle Brugge	W 2-0	Vanden Borre, Defour
15/02	h	Mechelen	D 1-1	Mitrović
22/02	a	Genk	W 1-0	Defour
01/03	a	Kortrijk	W 2-0	Mitrović, Dendoncker
07/03	a	Lokeren	W 2-1	Tielemans (p), Mitrović
15/03	h	Gent	L 1-2	Mitrović
06/04	h	Charleroi	W 1-0	Mitrović
12/04	a	Standard	L 1-3	Tielemans
19/04	a	Club Brugge	L 1-2	Mitrović
25/04	h	Kortrijk	W 5-1	Deschacht 2, Tielemans, Mitrović, Najar
30/04	a	Gent	L 1-2	Tielemans
03/05	a	Charleroi	W 1-0	Najar
10/05	h	Club Brugge	W 3-1	Najar, Mitrović, Praet
17/05	h	Standard	D 1-1	Najar
21/05	a	Kortrijk	D 2-2	Praet, Mitrović
24/05	h	Gent	W 2-1	Deschacht, Mitrović

No	Name	Nat	DoB	Pos	Aps	(s)	Gls
18	Frank Acheampong	GHA	16/10/93	A	22	(13)	2
17	Oswal Álvarez	COL	11/06/95	A	2	(3)	1
34	Samuel Bastien		26/09/96	M		(1)	
12	Maxime Colin	FRA	15/11/91	D	12	(5)	1
20	Ibrahima Conté	GUI	03/04/91	M	14	(10)	2
15	Cyriac	CIV	15/08/90	A	9	(20)	4
16	Steven Defour		15/04/88	M	29		6
32	Leander Dendoncker		15/04/95	M	17	(9)	2
3	Olivier Deschacht		16/02/81	D	40		4
24	Michaël Heylen		03/01/94	D	12	(2)	
42	Nathan Kabasele		14/01/94	A	5	(7)	1
13	Thomas Kaminski		23/10/92	G	2		
38	Andy Kawaya		23/08/96	A		(7)	
19	Sacha Kljestan	USA	09/09/85	M	5	(8)	1
35	Aaron Leya Iseka		15/11/97	A	1	(8)	
11	Marko Marin	GER	13/03/89	M	5	(1)	
22	Chancel Mbemba	COD	08/08/94	D	28		1
8	Luka Milivojević	SRB	07/04/91	M	3		
45	Aleksandar Mitrović	SRB	16/09/94	A	36	(1)	20
2	Fabrice N'Sakala	COD	21/07/90	D	23		
12	Andy Najar	HON	16/03/93	M	34	(1)	6
14	Bram Nuytinck	NED	04/05/90	D	9	(2)	
10	Dennis Praet		14/05/94	M	29	(1)	7
1	Silvio Proto		23/05/83	G	36		
33	Davy Roef		06/02/94	G	2		
13	Rolando	POR	31/08/85	D	5	(1)	
9	Matías Suárez	ARG	09/05/88	A	6	(7)	4
31	Youri Tielemans		07/05/97	M	34	(5)	6
39	Anthony Vanden Borre		24/10/87	D	20		1

Cercle Brugge KSV

1899 • Jan Breydelstadion (29,042) • cerclebrugge.be

Major honours
Belgian League (3) 1911, 1927, 1930; Belgian Cup (2) 1927, 1985

Coach: Lorenzo Staelens; (06/10/14) Arnar Vidarsson (ISL); (16/03/15) Dennis van Wijk (NED)

2014
26/07	h	Gent	D 0-0	
02/08	a	Genk	D 1-1	Bačelić-Grgić
09/08	h	Oostende	L 0-1	
15/08	a	Club Brugge	D 1-1	Kabananga
24/08	h	Lokeren	W 1-0	Kabananga
30/08	a	Mouscron-Péruwelz	L 0-4	
13/09	h	Charleroi	W 1-0	Dussenne
20/09	a	Anderlecht	L 2-3	Buyl, Kabananga
27/09	h	Westerlo	L 1-2	Van Acker
04/10	a	Waasland-Beveren	L 0-1	
18/10	h	Lierse	L 1-2	Sukuta-Pasu (p)
25/10	a	Zulte Waregem	W 2-1	Kabananga 2
29/10	h	Standard	L 0-1	
01/11	h	Kortrijk	L 0-4	
08/11	a	Mechelen	D 1-1	Kabananga
22/11	a	Gent	L 0-1	
29/11	h	Genk	L 0-1	
06/12	a	Lokeren	D 0-0	
13/12	h	Mouscron-Péruwelz	W 2-1	Kabananga, Buyl
20/12	a	Oostende	L 0-2	
27/12	h	Waasland-Beveren	W 1-0	Buyl

2015
17/01	a	Charleroi	W 2-0	Caenepeel, Buyl
25/01	h	Club Brugge	L 0-3	
31/01	a	Westerlo	L 0-1	
08/02	h	Anderlecht	L 0-2	
14/02	a	Lierse	L 1-2	D'Haene
21/02	h	Zulte Waregem	D 2-2	Kabananga, Sukuta-Pasu (p)
27/02	a	Standard	L 0-1	
07/03	a	Kortrijk	L 0-1	
15/03	h	Mechelen	L 2-3	Buyl 2
04/04	h	Lierse	L 2-3	D'Haene, Dewaele
10/04	a	Lierse	W 1-0	D'Haene
17/04	h	Lierse	L 0-2	
26/04	a	Lierse	L 1-3	Martens

No	Name	Nat	DoB	Pos	Aps	(s)	Gls
10	Stipe Bačelić-Grgić	CRO	16/02/88	M	19	(5)	1
15	Pierre Bourdin	FRA	06/01/94	D	26	(2)	
40	Stephen Buyl		02/09/92	A	17	(12)	6
4	Bart Buysse		16/10/86	D	22	(1)	
96	Jinty Caenepeel		18/07/96	A	1	(6)	1
8	Hans Cornelis		23/10/82	D	27		
30	Kristof D'Haene		06/06/90	D	25	(5)	3
24	Dennes De Kegel		07/01/94	D	8	(3)	
27	Gilles Dewaele		13/02/96	M	7	(3)	1
3	Noé Dussenne		07/04/92	D	30	(1)	1
22	Joey Godee	NED	02/03/89	A	14	(9)	
38	Faris Haroun		22/09/85	M	12	(1)	
98	Junior Kabananga	COD	04/04/89	A	29	(1)	8
33	Mathieu Maertens		27/03/95	M	9	(2)	
26	Maarten Martens		02/07/84	M	10	(1)	1
9	Albian Muzaqi		24/11/94	A		(4)	
20	Ismaïla N'Diaye	SEN	22/01/88	A	9	(2)	
7	Tim Smolders		26/08/80	M	8	(3)	
19	Richard Sukuta-Pasu	GER	24/06/90	A	16	(9)	2
11	Sam Valcke		16/12/92	A	3	(8)	
41	Thibaut Van Acker		21/11/91	D	21	(6)	1
16	Miguel Van Damme		25/09/93	G	1	(1)	
28	Karel Van Roose		01/04/90	M	11	(10)	
21	Ayron Verkindere		17/05/97	A		(3)	
1	Olivier Werner		16/04/85	G	33		
26	Stef Wils		02/08/92	D	16		

R. Charleroi SC

1904 • Pays de Charleroi (22,000) • sporting-charleroi.be
Coach: Felice Mazzu

2014

25/07	a	Standard	L	0-3
02/08	h	Westerlo	L	2-3 Fauré, Kitambala
10/08	a	Anderlecht	L	0-1
16/08	h	Waasland-Beveren	D	2-2 Saglik, Rossini
23/08	a	Lierse	W	2-0 Kitambala 2
31/08	h	Mechelen	W	2-0 Ndongala, Dewaest
13/09	a	Cercle Brugge	L	0-1
19/09	h	Zulte Waregem	W	2-1 Kitambala, Galvez-Lopez
27/09	a	Genk	D	1-1 Kebano
04/10	a	Kortrijk	L	0-2
18/10	a	Gent	D	2-2 Tainmont 2
25/10	h	Oostende	W	2-0 Houdret, Kitambala
29/10	a	Lokeren	L	2-5 Kebano 2 (1p)
02/11	h	Club Brugge	D	0-0
08/11	a	Mouscron-Péruwelz	W	2-0 Kebano 2
22/11	h	Anderlecht	W	3-1 Tainmont, Fauré 2
29/11	a	Westerlo	W	3-2 Tainmont, og (Ruyssen), Marinos
07/12	h	Standard	L	0-1
13/12	a	Waasland-Beveren	W	3-1 Dewaest, Galvez-Lopez, Coulibaly
20/12	h	Lierse	W	6-0 Fauré 2, Diandy, og (Swinkels), Coulibaly, Ndongala
26/12	a	Zulte Waregem	W	3-1 Geraerts, Fauré, Kebano

2015

17/01	a	Cercle Brugge	L	0-2
24/01	a	Kortrijk	D	0-0
31/01	h	Genk	W	1-0 Marinos
07/02	a	Mechelen	D	0-0
15/02	h	Gent	D	0-0
21/02	a	Oostende	W	3-1 Kebano 2 (1p), Dewaest
28/02	h	Lokeren	W	1-0 Tainmont
07/03	a	Club Brugge	L	0-1
15/03	h	Mouscron-Péruwelz	W	2-0 Coulibaly, Saglik
06/04	a	Anderlecht	L	0-1
11/04	h	Gent	W	2-1 Kebano 2
19/04	a	Kortrijk	D	1-1 Coulibaly
25/04	h	Standard	W	1-0 Tainmont
29/04	a	Club Brugge	L	1-3 Coulibaly
03/05	h	Anderlecht	L	0-1
08/05	a	Gent	D	1-1 Coulibaly
17/05	h	Kortrijk	W	5-2 Kebano (p), Coulibaly, Ndongala 2, Tainmont
21/05	h	Club Brugge	L	2-3 Coulibaly, Galvez-Lopez
24/05	a	Standard	L	0-2
28/05	a	Mechelen	L	1-2 Geraerts
31/05	h	Mechelen	D	2-0 Marinos, Ndongala

No	Name	Nat	DoB	Pos	Aps	(s)	Gls
19	Clinton Mata	ANG	07/11/92	A	7	(12)	
26	Kalifa Coulibaly	MLI	21/08/81	A	16	(15)	8
10	Mohamed Daf	SEN	10/03/94	M	1		
6	Sebastien Dewaest		27/05/91	D	40		3
13	Christophe Diandy	SEN	25/11/90	M	14	(7)	1
18	Cédric Fauré	FRA	14/02/79	A	21	(15)	6
22	Guillaume François		03/06/90	A	22	(4)	
20	Jessy Galvez-Lopez		17/07/95	M	8	(15)	3
23	Karel Geraerts		05/01/82	M	21	(2)	2
80	Kenneth Houdret		09/08/83	M	5	(4)	1
92	Neeskens Kebano	COD	10/03/92	M	29	(4)	11
99	Lynel Kitambala	FRA	26/10/88	A	15	(13)	5
35	Parfait Mandanda	COD	10/10/89	G	5		
25	Damien Marcq	FRA	08/12/88	D	30	(1)	
17	Stergos Marinos	GRE	17/09/87	D	32	(3)	3
8	Martos	ESP	04/01/84	D	42		
41	Francis N'Ganga	CGO	16/06/85	D	17	(2)	
88	Dieumerci Ndongala	COD	14/06/91	A	25	(7)	5
1	Nicolas Penneteau	FRA	20/02/81	G	36		
9	Giuseppe Rossini		23/08/86	A	4	(6)	1
28	Enes Saglik		08/07/91	M	22	(4)	2
7	Clément Tainmont	FRA	12/02/86	M	32	(6)	7
16	Maxime Vandermeulen		11/04/96	G	1		
8	Steeven Willems	FRA	31/08/90	D	17	(1)	

Club Brugge KV

1891 • Jan Breydelstadion (29,042) • clubbrugge.be
Major honours
Belgian League (13) 1920, 1973, 1976, 1977, 1978, 1980, 1988, 1990, 1992, 1996, 1998, 2003, 2005; Belgian Cup (11) 1968, 1970, 1977, 1986, 1991, 1995, 1996, 2002, 2004, 2007, 2015
Coach: Michel Preud'homme

2014

26/07	a	Waasland-Beveren	W	2-0 Castillo, Duarte
03/08	h	Lierse	W	1-0 Refaelov
10/08	a	Zulte Waregem	D	1-1 Castillo
15/08	h	Cercle Brugge	D	1-1 Castillo
24/08	a	Mechelen	L	1-3 Simons (p)
31/08	h	Anderlecht	D	2-2 Jørgensen, Engels
14/09	a	Genk	D	1-1 Felipe Gedoz
21/09	h	Kortrijk	W	5-0 Oularé, Víctor Vázquez, Izquierdo, Simons, Fernando
28/09	a	Oostende	D	2-2 Engels 2
05/10	h	Standard	W	3-0 Simons 2 (2p), Castillo
19/10	a	Lokeren	W	3-1 Oularé, Felipe Gedoz, Refaelov
26/10	h	Gent	D	2-2 De Sutter 2
30/10	a	Mouscron-Péruwelz	W	4-1 Felipe Gedoz, De Sutter 2, Castillo
02/11	a	Charleroi	D	0-0
09/11	h	Westerlo	W	5-0 Castillo 3, Simons (p), Duarte
22/11	a	Waasland-Beveren	W	4-2 og (Robson), Simons (p), Meunier, Vormer
30/11	a	Anderlecht	D	2-2 Víctor Vázquez 2
07/12	h	Zulte Waregem	W	2-1 Mechele, Víctor Vázquez
14/12	a	Standard	W	3-1 Refaelov, Meunier, Vormer
21/12	h	Genk	W	4-1 Duarte, Vormer, Refaelov, Izquierdo
26/12	a	Lierse	W	6-0 og 2 (Matoukou 2), Refaelov 2, Izquierdo, De Sutter

2015

16/01	h	Mechelen	D	1-1 De Sutter
25/01	a	Cercle Brugge	W	3-0 Izquierdo 2, Felipe Gedoz
30/01	h	Oostende	W	2-0 Izquierdo, Felipe Gedoz
08/02	a	Kortrijk	L	0-2
15/02	h	Lokeren	D	1-1 De Sutter
22/02	a	Gent	L	1-2 Vormer
01/03	h	Mouscron-Péruwelz	W	3-0 Izquierdo, De Sutter, Simons (p)
07/03	h	Charleroi	W	1-0 De Sutter
15/03	a	Westerlo	W	3-1 Oularé, Izquierdo 2
06/03	h	Standard	W	2-1 Refaelov 2 (2p)
11/04	a	Kortrijk	L	0-2
19/04	h	Anderlecht	W	2-1 Oularé, Vormer
26/04	a	Gent	D	2-2 Duarte, Claudemir
29/04	h	Charleroi	W	3-1 Izquierdo 2, Dierckx
02/05	a	Standard	L	0-1
10/05	a	Anderlecht	L	1-3 Refaelov
17/05	h	Gent	L	2-3 Vormer 2
21/05	a	Charleroi	W	3-2 Mechele, Refaelov, De Sutter
24/05	h	Kortrijk	W	1-0 Izquierdo

No	Name	Nat	DoB	Pos	Aps	(s)	Gls
63	Boli Bolingoli-Mbombo		01/07/95	M	6	(5)	
30	Nicolás Castillo	CHI	14/02/93	A	10	(8)	8
6	Claudemir	BRA	27/03/88	M	8	(3)	1
43	Sander Coopman		02/08/95	M	1	(5)	
28	Laurens De Bock		07/11/92	D	35	(1)	
2	Davy De Fauw		08/07/81	D	12	(6)	
9	Tom De Sutter		03/07/85	A	25	(5)	10
24	Stefano Denswil	NED	07/05/93	D	11		
55	Tuur Dierckx		09/05/95	A		(13)	1
4	Óscar Duarte	CRC	03/06/89	D	31		4
40	Björn Engels		15/09/94	D	7		3
18	Felipe Gedoz	BRA	12/07/93	M	13	(7)	5
6	Fernando	BRA	25/03/81	M	8	(2)	1
21	José Izquierdo	COL	07/07/92	A	24	(8)	13
10	Jesper Jørgensen	DEN	09/06/91	M	2	(2)	1
33	Vladan Kujović	SRB	23/08/78	G	3		
16	Maxime Lestienne		17/06/92	A	2	(2)	
44	Brandon Mechele		28/01/93	D	29	(1)	2
19	Thomas Meunier		12/09/91	D	29	(1)	2
32	Vadis Odjidja-Ofoe		21/02/89	M		(3)	
58	Obbi Oularé		08/01/96	A	5	(14)	3
8	Lior Refaelov	ISR	26/04/86	M	26	(3)	10
1	Matthew Ryan	AUS	08/04/92	G	37		
3	Francisco Silva	CHI	11/02/86	M	7	(4)	
3	Timmy Simons		11/12/76	M	39	(1)	7
17	Waldemar Sobota	POL	19/05/87	A	7	(4)	
42	Nikola Storm		30/09/94	A	10	(12)	
7	Víctor Vázquez	ESP	20/01/87	M	24	(6)	4
25	Ruud Vormer	NED	11/05/88	M	29		7

KRC Genk

1988 • Cristal Arena (25,010) • krcgenk.be
Major honours
Belgian League (3) 1999, 2002, 2011; Belgian Cup (4) 1998, 2000, 2009, 2013
Coach: Emilio Ferrera; (29/07/14) (Pierre Denier); (25/08/14) Alex McLeish (SCO)

2014

27/07	a	Mechelen	L	1-3 Hyland
02/08	h	Cercle Brugge	D	1-1 Buffel
08/08	h	Lokeren	D	0-0
16/08	a	Kortrijk	D	1-1 Mboyo
22/08	h	Gent	W	3-2 Cissé, Mboyo, Okriashvili
30/08	a	Oostende	D	1-1 Ngoncga
14/09	h	Club Brugge	D	1-1 Cissé
20/09	a	Mouscron-Péruwelz	W	2-1 Cissé, Mboyo
27/09	h	Charleroi	D	1-1 og (Marinos)
05/10	a	Anderlecht	D	0-0
19/10	h	Westerlo	W	3-1 Mboyo, Gorius, Schrijvers
25/10	a	Waasland-Beveren	W	1-0 Kagé
28/10	h	Lierse	W	3-0 Kabasele, Kagé, Buffel
31/10	a	Zulte Waregem	L	0-2
09/11	h	Standard	L	0-2
23/11	h	Mechelen	W	3-0 Cissé 2, Gerkens
29/11	a	Cercle Brugge	W	1-0 Mboyo
07/12	h	Gent	D	0-0
13/12	h	Kortrijk	W	3-0 Mboyo 2 (1p), Kabasele
21/12	a	Club Brugge	L	1-4 Mboyo

2015

18/01	a	Lokeren	D	1-1 Milinković-Savić
23/01	h	Mouscron-Péruwelz	W	2-0 Schrijvers, De Ceulaer
31/01	a	Charleroi	L	0-1
03/02	h	Oostende	D	1-1 Schrijvers
08/02	h	Waasland-Beveren	W	1-0 Milinković-Savić
13/02	a	Westerlo	W	2-1 Buffel, Kara
22/02	h	Anderlecht	L	0-1
28/02	a	Lierse	W	2-0 Schrijvers, De Ceulaer
07/03	h	Zulte Waregem	W	3-2 Milinković-Savić, Schrijvers, Kara
15/03	a	Standard	L	0-1
03/04	h	Zulte Waregem	W	1-0 De Ceulaer
11/04	a	Waasland-Beveren	W	2-0 Kagé, Buffel
18/04	a	Mechelen	L	0-4
24/04	h	Mechelen	W	1-0 Milinković-Savić
02/05	h	Waasland-Beveren	W	7-1 Buffel, Gorius, De Ceulaer, Cissé 2, Castagne, Joseph-Monrose
09/05	a	Zulte Waregem	W	3-2 Milinković-Savić, Buffel, Okriashvili

No	Name	Nat	DoB	Pos	Aps	(s)	Gls
22	Paolino Bertaccini		19/11/97	A		(2)	
1	Marco Bizot	NED	13/11/91	G	4	(1)	
19	Thomas Buffel		19/02/81	M	34		6
41	Timothy Castagne		05/12/95	D	25	(2)	1
17	Aleksandar Čavric	SRB	18/05/94	A	6	(10)	
21	Sekou Cissé	CIV	23/05/85	A	23	(6)	7
23	Benjamin De Ceulaer		19/12/83	A	11	(8)	4
39	Pieter Gerkens		17/02/95	M	15	(4)	1
10	Julien Gorius	FRA	17/08/85	M	30		2
4	Brian Hamalainen	DEN	29/05/89	D		(1)	
7	Khaleem Hyland	TRI	05/06/89	M	1	(1)	1
8	Steven Joseph-Monrose	FRA	20/07/90	A	6	(10)	1
27	Christian Kabasele		24/02/91	D	34		2
11	Hervé Kagé	COD	10/04/89	M	7	(15)	3
2	Serigne Modou Kara	SEN	11/11/89	D	30		2
26	László Köteles	HUN	01/09/84	G	32		
36	Ayub Masika	KEN	10/09/92	M	1		
99	Ilombe Mboyo		27/04/87	A	19		8
20	Sergej Milinković-Savić	SRB	27/02/95	M	18	(6)	5
25	Wilfred Ndidi	NGA	16/12/96	D	3	(3)	
16	Anele Ngcongca	RSA	20/10/87	D	30		1
49	Tornike Okriashvili	GEO	12/02/92	A	16	(7)	2
38	Siebe Schrijvers		18/07/96	A	20	(12)	5
17	Jeroen Simaeys		12/05/85	M	1		
9	Katuku Tshimanga		06/11/88	D	13	(1)	
9	Jelle Vossen		22/03/89	A	2		
36	Jarne Vrijsen		21/03/96	D		(3)	
5	Sandy Walsh	NED	14/03/95	D	9	(2)	
4	Dries Wouters		28/01/97	D		(1)	
45	Bennard Yao Kumordzi	GHA	21/03/85	M	6		

BELGIUM

KAA Gent

1898 • Ghelamco Arena (20,000) • kaagent.be
Major honours
Belgian League (1) 2015; Belgian Cup (3) 1964, 1984, 2010
Coach: Hein Vanhaezebrouck

2014

26/07	a Cercle Brugge	D	0-0	
03/08	h Mechelen	W	3-1	*Depoitre 2, Raman*
10/08	a Standard	W	1-0	*Depoitre*
17/08	a Zulte Waregem	W	3-1	*Habibou, Milicevic 2 (1p)*
22/08	a Genk	L	2-3	*Dejaegere, Milicevic*
29/08	h Kortrijk	L	0-1	
14/09	h Mouscron-Péruwelz	W	1-0	*Saief*
20/09	a Oostende	W	3-1	*Pollet, Depoitre 2*
28/09	h Lokeren	D	1-1	*Depoitre*
03/10	a Westerlo	W	1-0	
18/10	h Charleroi	D	2-2	*Foket, Raman*
26/10	a Club Brugge	D	2-2	*Milicevic, Rafinha*
29/10	h Waasland-Beveren	W	4-1	*Milicevic (p), Depoitre, Raman 2*
02/11	a Lierse	W	1-0	*Van der Bruggen*
09/11	h Anderlecht	L	0-2	
22/11	h Cercle Brugge	W	4-0	*Dejaegere, Raman, Depoitre, Pollet*
28/11	a Zulte Waregem	L	1-2	*Gershon*
07/12	h Genk	D	0-0	
12/12	a Mechelen	D	0-0	
21/12	h Standard	L	1-2	*Dejaegere*
26/12	a Kortrijk	W	3-2	*Nielsen, Raman, Depoitre*

2015

17/01	a Mouscron-Péruwelz	W	3-1	*Renato Neto, Depoitre, Dejaegere*
25/01	h Oostende	W	3-1	*Renato Neto 2, Saief*
01/02	a Lokeren	D	3-3	*Simon 3*
07/02	h Westerlo	W	4-0	*Depoitre 2, Simon, Milicevic*
15/02	a Charleroi	D	0-0	
22/02	h Club Brugge	W	2-1	*Simon, og (Simons)*
01/03	a Waasland-Beveren	W	1-0	*Simon*
07/03	h Lierse	W	2-1	*Renato Neto (p), Pedersen*
15/03	a Anderlecht	W	2-1	*Foket, Raman*
05/04	h Kortrijk	W	2-0	*Milicevic, Simon*
11/04	a Charleroi	L	1-2	*Poletanović*
17/04	a Standard	W	3-1	*Pedersen 2, Tabekou*
26/04	h Club Brugge	D	2-2	*Milicevic 2*
30/04	h Anderlecht	W	2-1	*Depoitre, Renato Neto*
03/05	a Kortrijk	W	1-0	*og (Chanot)*
08/05	h Charleroi	D	1-1	*Renato Neto*
17/05	a Club Brugge	W	3-2	*Nielsen, Dejaegere, Raman*
21/05	h Standard	W	2-0	*Kums, Renato Neto (p)*
24/05	a Anderlecht	L	1-2	*Pedersen*

No	Name	Nat	DoB	Pos	Aps	(s)	Gls
21	Nana Asare	GHA	11/07/86	D	37	(1)	
5	Karim Belhocine	FRA	02/04/78	D	5	(2)	
27	Jinty Caenepeel		18/07/96	A	1		
19	Brecht Dejaegere		29/05/91	M	31	(5)	5
9	Laurent Depoitre		07/12/88	A	32	(3)	13
32	Thomas Foket		25/09/94	M	34	(4)	2
55	Rami Gershon	ISR	12/08/88	D	38		1
7	Habib Habibou	FRA	16/04/87	A	1	(2)	1
18	Haris Hajradinović	BIH	18/02/94	M	2	(2)	
14	Sven Kums		26/02/88	M	23	(2)	1
40	Christophe Lepoint		24/10/84	M	11	(6)	
22	Sébastien Locigno		02/09/95	D		(4)	
77	Danijel Milicevic	SUI	05/01/86	M	28	(5)	9
23	Lasse Nielsen	DEN	08/01/88	D	26		2
8	Mustapha Oussalah	MAR	19/02/92	M	5	(1)	
28	Nicklas Pedersen	DEN	10/10/87	A	5	(4)	4
12	Marko Poletanović	SRB	20/07/93	M	3	(5)	1
7	David Pollet		12/08/88	A	7	(14)	2
13	Ante Puljić	CRO	05/11/87	D	4		
4	Rafinha	BRA	29/06/82	D	17	(2)	1
11	Benito Raman		07/11/94	A	20	(11)	8
10	Renato Neto	BRA	10/04/88	M	26	(8)	7
15	Kenny Saief	ISR	17/12/93	M	8	(12)	2
1	Matz Sels		26/02/92	G	39		
27	Moses Simon	NGA	12/07/95	A	13	(4)	7
24	Yaya Soumahoro	CIV	28/09/89	A	3	(8)	
22	Serge Tabekou	CMR	15/10/96	M		(2)	1
25	Brian Vandenbussche		24/09/81	G	1		
17	Hannes Van der Bruggen		01/04/93	M	15	(9)	1
2	Uroš Vitas	SRB	06/07/92	D	1	(1)	
6	Nermin Zolotić	BIH	07/07/93	M	4		

KV Kortrijk

1971 • Guldensporenstadion (9,500) • kvk.be
Coach: Yves Vanderhaeghe

2014

27/07	a Zulte Waregem	L	0-2	
02/08	h Standard	L	2-3	*Tomašević, De Mets*
09/08	a Mechelen	W	2-1	*Pavlović, Marušić*
16/08	h Genk	D	1-1	*Ulens*
23/08	h Oostende	L	0-2	
29/08	a Gent	W	1-0	*Santini*
14/09	h Lokeren	L	2-3	*Chevalier, Santini*
21/09	a Club Brugge	L	0-5	
27/09	h Mouscron-Péruwelz	W	3-0	*Santini, Chevalier 2*
04/10	a Charleroi	W	2-0	*Santini, og (Dewaest)*
18/10	h Waasland-Beveren	W	2-1	*Santini 2*
25/10	a Westerlo	L	1-2	*Chevalier*
29/10	h Anderlecht	L	2-3	*Dierckx, Pavlović*
01/11	a Cercle Brugge	W	4-0	*De Mets, Marušić 2, Matton*
08/11	h Lierse	W	1-0	*og (Wils)*
23/11	h Zulte Waregem	W	3-1	*Marušić, Chanot, Poulain*
30/11	a Standard	W	2-0	*Chevalier, Santini*
06/12	h Mechelen	W	3-0	*De Smet, Chevalier, Dierckx*
13/12	a Genk	L	0-3	
21/12	a Lokeren	W	2-1	*Tomašević, Santini*
26/12	h Gent	L	2-3	*De Smet, Matton*

2015

17/01	a Oostende	W	7-1	*Chevalier 2, Santini, De Smet, Matton 2, Dierckx*
24/01	h Charleroi	D	0-0	
31/01	a Mouscron-Péruwelz	W	3-0	*De Mets, Marušić, Tomašević*
08/02	h Club Brugge	W	2-0	*Matton, Poulain (p)*
14/02	a Waasland-Beveren	L	0-1	
21/02	h Westerlo	W	6-0	*Santini 4, Chevalier 2*
01/03	a Anderlecht	L	0-2	
07/03	h Cercle Brugge	W	1-0	*Chevalier*
15/03	a Lierse	D	0-0	
05/04	a Gent	L	0-2	
11/04	h Club Brugge	W	2-0	*De Smet (p), Capon*
19/04	h Charleroi	D	1-1	*Santini*
25/04	a Anderlecht	L	1-5	*Chevalier*
28/04	h Standard	W	3-1	*Tomašević, Van Eenoo, Capon*
03/05	h Gent	L	0-1	
10/05	a Standard	L	0-4	
17/05	a Charleroi	L	2-5	*Marušić, De Smet*
21/05	h Anderlecht	D	2-2	*Capon, Santini*
24/05	a Club Brugge	L	0-1	

No	Name	Nat	DoB	Pos	Aps	(s)	Gls
21	Brecht Capon		22/04/88	D	24	(2)	3
2	Maxime Chanot	LUX	21/11/89	D	29	(2)	1
9	Teddy Chevalier	FRA	28/06/87	A	36	(1)	12
4	Arno Claeys		05/04/94	D	1	(1)	
17	Gertjan De Mets		02/04/87	D	37		3
7	Stijn De Smet		27/03/85	A	17	(9)	5
55	Tuur Dierckx		09/05/95	A		(17)	3
27	Laurent Henkinet		14/09/92	G	18		
16	Darren Keet	RSA	05/08/89	G	22		
10	Robert Klaasen	NED	06/09/83	M	12	(9)	
19	Gregory Mahau		09/05/94	M		(7)	
11	Adam Marušić	MNE	17/10/92	M	27	(7)	6
20	Thomas Matton		24/10/85	M	24	(1)	5
14	Landry Mulemo	COD	17/09/86	D	16	(10)	
8	Nebojša Pavlović	SRB	09/04/81	M	25	(2)	2
6	Benoît Poulain	FRA	22/12/86	D	26		2
15	Dylan Ragolle		05/11/94	D	1	(4)	
14	Ivan Santini	CRO	21/05/89	A	33		15
5	Alassane També	FRA	26/01/92	D	1		
40	Tjardo Techel		24/11/95	M		(1)	
33	Žarko Tomašević	MNE	22/02/90	D	39		4
23	Baptiste Ulens		24/07/87	D	13	(13)	1
2	Victor Vandewiele		08/07/96	D		(1)	
12	Lukas Van Eenoo		06/02/91	M	17	(15)	1
31	Anthony Van Loo		05/10/88	D	10	(3)	
8	Bradley Vanneste		26/04/97	M		(1)	

K. Lierse SK

1906 • Herman Vanderpoortenstadion (14,538) • lierse.com
Major honours
Belgian League (4) 1932, 1942, 1960, 1997; Belgian Cup (2) 1969, 1999
Coach: Stanley Menzo (NED); (05/09/14) Slaviša Stojanović (SVN); (30/01/15) Olivier Guillou (FRA)

2014

26/07	h Oostende	W	2-0	*Keita 2*
03/08	a Club Brugge	L	0-1	
09/08	h Mouscron-Péruwelz	D	2-2	*Keita, Bourabia*
16/08	a Lokeren	L	0-2	
23/08	h Charleroi	L	0-2	
30/08	a Waasland-Beveren	L	0-2	
13/09	h Anderlecht	D	2-2	*Wamberto, Ngawa*
20/09	a Westerlo	L	1-6	*Hafez*
28/09	a Standard	D	2-2	*Ngawa, Vellios*
04/10	h Zulte Waregem	W	3-1	*Keita, Matoukou, Sayed (p)*
18/10	a Cercle Brugge	W	2-1	*Masika, Keita*
24/10	h Mechelen	L	0-1	
28/10	a Genk	L	0-3	
02/11	h Gent	L	0-1	
08/11	h Kortrijk	L	0-1	
22/11	h Mouscron-Péruwelz	L	1-2	*Losada*
30/11	h Lokeren	D	1-1	*Kouemaha*
06/12	a Oostende	L	1-2	*Kouemaha*
13/12	h Westerlo	D	3-3	*Bourabia, Traoré, Nwofor*
20/12	a Charleroi	L	0-6	
26/12	h Club Brugge	L	0-6	

2015

18/01	h Anderlecht	L	0-3	
24/01	h Waasland-Beveren	D	1-1	*Nwofor*
01/02	h Standard	L	2-3	*Sayed (p), Mojsov*
07/02	h Zulte Waregem	W	3-2	*Velikonja (p), Kasmi 2*
14/02	h Cercle Brugge	W	2-1	*Elgenawy, Kasmi*
22/02	a Mechelen	L	1-2	*Velikonja*
28/02	h Genk	L	0-2	
07/03	a Gent	L	1-2	*Kasmi*
15/03	h Kortrijk	D	0-0	
04/04	a Cercle Brugge	W	3-2	*Velikonja, Wamberto, Kasmi*
10/04	h Cercle Brugge	L	0-1	
17/04	h Cercle Brugge	W	2-0	*Velikonja, Hafez*
26/04	h Cercle Brugge	W	3-1	*og (Martens), Bensebaini, Diomandé*

No	Name	Nat	DoB	Pos	Aps	(s)	Gls
17	Charles Ankomah	GHA	10/04/96	A		(1)	
99	Boban Bajković	MNE	15/03/85	G	26		
15	Ramy Bensebaini	ALG	16/04/95	D	22	(1)	1
8	Manuel Benson		23/03/97	A	3	(6)	
1	Ihor Berezovskiy	UKR	24/08/90	G	8		
55	Rachid Bourabia	FRA	22/03/85	M	18		2
24	Ludovic Buyssens		20/03/80	D	3	(1)	
4	Joan Capdevila	ESP	03/02/78	D	11		
30	Souleymane Diomandé	CIV	21/02/92	M	12		1
3	Ahmed El Messaoudi	MAR	03/08/95	D	24	(2)	
16	Ahmed Elgenawy	EGY	09/12/95	M	3	(7)	1
33	Karim Hafez	EGY	12/03/96	D	16	(3)	2
21	Florent Hanin	FRA	04/02/90	D	9		
6	Mohamed Helal	EGY	08/10/95	M	1		
9	Faysel Kasmi		31/10/95	M	14	(5)	5
41	Alhassane Keita	GUI	16/04/92	M	17	(7)	5
28	Dorge Kouemaha	CMR	28/06/83	A	7	(7)	2
10	Hernán Losada	ARG	09/05/82	M	20		1
58	Manuel Curto	POR	09/07/86	M	4	(2)	
40	Ayub Masika	KEN	10/09/92	M	10	(6)	1
5	Eric Matoukou	CMR	08/07/83	D	6		1
19	Dušan Mićić	SRB	29/11/84	A	1		
19	Daniel Mojsov	MKD	25/12/87	D	13		1
55	Pierre-Yves Ngawa		09/02/92	D	14	(6)	2
39	Brice Ntambwe		29/04/93	M	1		
29	Uche Nwofor	NGA	17/09/91	A	4	(7)	2
14	Ahmed Sayed	EGY	10/01/96	M	28	(2)	2
4	Arjan Swinkels	NED	15/10/84	D	13	(1)	
20	Anas Tahiri		05/05/95	M	2	(8)	
2	Hamary Traoré	MLI	27/01/92	D	33		1
23	Etien Velikonja	SVN	26/12/88	A	9	(2)	4
7	Apostolos Vellios	GRE	08/01/92	A	2	(11)	1
27	Wamberto	BRA	07/10/94	A	16	(12)	2
18	Thomas Wils		24/04/90	M	11	(4)	

KSC Lokeren OV

1970 • Daknamstadion (9,271) • sporting.be
Major honours
Belgian Cup (2) 2012, 2014
Coach: Peter Maes

2014

26/07	a Westerlo	L	0-1	
03/08	h Zulte Waregem	W	2-1	Júnior Dutra 2
08/08	a Genk	D	0-0	
16/08	h Lierse	W	2-0	Maric (p), Abdurahimi
24/08	a Cercle Brugge	L	0-1	
31/08	h Standard	D	1-1	Leye
14/09	a Kortrijk	W	3-2	De Pauw 2, Vanaken
21/09	h Mechelen	W	3-2	Abdurahimi 2, Persoons
28/09	a Gent	D	1-1	Vanaken
05/10	h Oostende	W	3-1	De Pauw, Maric 2 (1p)
19/10	a Club Brugge	L	1-3	Vanaken
26/10	a Mouscron-Péruwelz	D	2-2	Leye, Maric (p)
29/10	h Charleroi	W	5-2	Patosi 2, Maric (p), Vanaken, Júnior Dutra
01/11	a Anderlecht	D	1-1	Júnior Dutra
09/11	h Waasland-Beveren	W	3-0	Patosi, De Pauw, Júnior Dutra
22/11	h Westerlo	D	0-0	
30/11	a Lierse	D	1-1	Leye
06/12	h Cercle Brugge	D	0-0	
14/12	a Zulte Waregem	L	0-1	
21/12	h Kortrijk	L	1-2	Overmeire
27/12	a Standard	L	0-2	

2015

18/01	h Genk	D	1-1	De Pauw
24/01	a Mechelen	W	1-0	Leye
01/02	h Gent	D	3-3	og (Gershon), Overmeire, Vanaken
07/02	a Oostende	W	1-0	Persoons
15/02	a Club Brugge	D	1-1	Maric
21/02	h Mouscron-Péruwelz	W	1-0	Maric (p)
28/02	a Charleroi	L	0-1	
07/03	h Anderlecht	L	1-2	Maric (p)
15/03	a Waasland-Beveren	D	0-0	
04/04	a Oostende	W	2-1	Leye, Vanaken
11/04	h Westerlo	D	1-1	Dessers
18/04	a Mouscron-Péruwelz	W	5-1	og (Monteyne), Maric, Ansah 2, De Pauw
25/04	h Mouscron-Péruwelz	W	2-1	Maric 2 (2p)
01/05	a Westerlo	L	3-4	Dessers, Overmeire, Abdurahimi
09/05	h Oostende	W	6-1	Vanaken 2, Dessers 2, De Pauw, Abdurahimi
16/05	h Mechelen	D	2-2	Ngolok 2
23/05	a Mechelen	L	1-2	Maric

No	Name	Nat	DoB	Pos	Aps	(s)	Gls
93	Djamel Abdoun	ALG	14/2/86	A	2	(2)	
18	Besart Abdurahimi	MKD	31/07/90	A	6	(17)	5
23	Eugene Ansah	GHA	16/12/94	A	1	(10)	2
6	Arthur Henrique	BRA	14/01/87	D	2	(3)	
1	Boubacar Barry	CIV	30/12/79	G	16		
25	Alexander Corryn		03/01/94	M		(3)	
29	Nill De Pauw		06/01/90	A	34	(1)	7
17	Cyriel Dessers		08/12/94	A	7	(16)	4
2	Georgios Galitsios	GRE	06/07/86	D	26	(1)	
9	Hamdi Harbaoui	TUN	05/01/85	A	1		
2	Sverrir Ingi Ingason	ISL	05/08/93	D	14		
19	Júnior Dutra	BRA	25/04/88	A	10	(2)	5
11	Onur Kaya		20/04/86	M	1	(7)	
9	Mbaye Leye	SEN	01/12/82	A	23	(9)	5
5	Mijat Maric	SUI	30/04/84	M	34		12
15	Dario Melnjak	CRO	31/10/92	D	7		
4	Grégory Mertens		21/02/91	D	11	(4)	
28	Evariste Ngolok		15/11/88	M	10	(7)	2
3	Denis Odoi		27/05/88	D	37		
7	Killian Overmeire		06/12/85	M	34		3
8	Ayanda Patosi	RSA	31/10/92	A	23	(5)	3
5	Koen Persoons		12/07/83	M	30	(1)	2
14	Jordan Remacle		14/02/87	M	9	(15)	
2	Alexander Scholz	DEN	24/10/92	D	21		
16	Jore Trompet		30/07/92	M		(5)	
20	Hans Vanaken		24/08/92	M	37		8
30	Davino Verhulst		25/11/87	G	22		

KV Mechelen

1904 • Veolia Stadion (13,123) • kvmechelen.be
Major honours
UEFA Cup Winners' Cup (1) 1988; UEFA Super Cup (1) 1989; Belgian League (4) 1943, 1946, 1948, 1989; Belgian Cup (1) 1987

Coach: Aleksandar Janković (SRB)

2014

27/07	h Genk	W	3-1	Hanni, Adesanya, Claes
03/08	a Gent	L	1-3	Kosanović (p)
09/08	h Kortrijk	L	1-2	Kosanović (p)
16/08	a Oostende	L	0-2	
24/08	h Club Brugge	W	3-1	Veselinović (p), Cordaro, Claes
31/08	a Charleroi	L	0-2	
13/09	h Westerlo	W	5-2	Rits 2, De Witte, Hanni, og (Godeau)
21/09	a Lokeren	L	2-3	Matthys, Bateau
27/09	h Waasland-Beveren	W	2-0	Obradović, Veselinović
04/10	a Mouscron-Péruwelz	D	1-1	Bateau
18/10	a Anderlecht	D	1-1	Cordaro
24/10	a Lierse	W	1-0	Veselinović
28/10	h Zulte Waregem	D	1-1	Veselinović
01/11	a Standard	L	0-2	
08/11	h Cercle Brugge	D	1-1	Hanni
23/11	a Genk	L	0-3	
29/11	h Oostende	D	0-0	
06/12	a Kortrijk	L	0-3	
12/12	h Gent	D	0-0	
20/12	a Westerlo	D	1-1	Veselinović
26/12	h Mouscron-Péruwelz	W	1-0	De Witte

2015

16/01	h Club Brugge	D	1-1	Naessens
24/01	h Lokeren	L	0-1	
31/01	a Waasland-Beveren	D	2-2	Veselinović, De Witte
07/02	h Charleroi	D	0-0	
15/02	a Anderlecht	D	1-1	Veselinović
22/02	h Lierse	W	2-1	De Witte, Hanni
28/02	a Zulte Waregem	W	3-2	Hanni, De Witte, Verdier
07/03	h Standard	D	1-1	Veselinović
15/03	a Cercle Brugge	W	3-2	Wolski 2, Veselinović (p)
05/04	h Waasland-Beveren	W	4-1	Hanni, Veselinović 2, Cocalić
12/04	a Zulte Waregem	W	1-0	Paulussen
18/04	h Genk	W	4-0	Hanni, Veselinović, Naessens, Obradović
24/04	a Genk	L	0-1	
02/05	h Zulte Waregem	W	3-0	Hanni 2 (1p), De Petter
09/05	a Waasland-Beveren	W	2-1	De Petter, De Witte
16/05	a Lokeren	D	2-2	Veselinović, Naessens
23/05	h Lokeren	W	2-1	Hanni, Kosanović
28/05	h Charleroi	W	2-1	Cissé, Kosanović
31/05	a Charleroi	L	0-2	

No	Name	Nat	DoB	Pos	Aps	(s)	Gls
16	Jason Adesanya		26/05/93	A	5	(11)	1
6	Sheldon Bateau	TRI	29/01/91	D	19	(1)	2
1	Wouter Biebauw		21/05/84	G	34	(1)	
9	Maxime Biset		26/03/86	M	7	(2)	
44	Ibrahima Cissé		28/02/94	D	30	(3)	1
24	Glen Claes		08/03/94	A	20	(12)	2
29	Edin Cocalić	BIH	05/12/87	D	15		1
12	Alessandro Cordaro		02/05/86	M	13	(5)	2
12	Steven De Petter		22/11/85	M	21	(1)	2
4	Seth De Witte		18/10/87	M	34	(1)	6
27	Sofiane Hanni	FRA	29/12/90	M	38	(1)	10
33	Miloš Kosanović	SRB	28/05/90	D	38		4
7	Lionel Makondi		25/02/95	A		(1)	
7	Tim Matthys		23/12/83	A	22	(6)	1
18	Jan Mertens		12/01/95	M		(1)	
49	Anthony Moris	LUX	29/04/90	G	3	(1)	
11	Jens Naessens		01/04/91	M	15	(6)	3
37	Ivan Obradović	SRB	25/07/88	D	39		2
28	Tomislav Pacovski	MKD	28/06/82	G	3		
28	Laurens Paulussen		19/07/90	D	22	(3)	1
11	Mats Rits		18/07/93	M	13	(11)	2
8	Jerry Van Dam	FRA	08/12/88	D		(4)	
3	Joachim Van Damme		23/07/91	D	13	(9)	
13	Wannes Van Tricht		13/11/93	M		(1)	
30	Jordi Vanlerberghe		27/03/96	M	1	(1)	
19	Nicolas Verdier	FRA	17/01/87	A	2	(13)	1
9	Dalibor Veselinović	SRB	21/09/87	A	31	(8)	13
10	Rafał Wolski	POL	10/11/92	M	2	(11)	2

R. Mouscron-Péruwelz

2010 • Le Canonnier (10,570) • rmp-foot.be
Coach: Rachid Chihab (FRA); (29/12/14) Fernando Da Cruz (FRA)

2014

27/07	a Anderlecht	L	1-3	Badri
02/08	h Waasland-Beveren	W	1-0	Diaby
09/08	a Lierse	D	2-2	Vandendriessche, Delacourt
15/08	h Standard	W	5-2	Diaby 2, Badri 2, Delacourt
23/08	a Zulte Waregem	D	1-1	Diaby
30/08	h Cercle Brugge	W	4-0	Diaby 2, Michel (p), Badri
14/09	a Gent	L	0-1	
20/09	h Genk	L	1-2	Diaby
27/09	a Kortrijk	L	0-3	
04/10	h Mechelen	D	1-1	Langil
18/10	a Oostende	D	0-0	
26/10	h Lokeren	D	2-2	Diaby, Dingomé
30/10	h Club Brugge	L	1-4	Perez
02/11	a Westerlo	W	3-1	Diaby, Badri 2
08/11	h Charleroi	L	0-2	
22/11	h Lierse	W	2-1	Dingomé, Diaby
29/11	a Waasland-Beveren	L	1-2	Diaby
06/12	h Anderlecht	W	4-2	Vandendriessche 2, og (Mbemba), Michel (p)
13/12	a Cercle Brugge	L	1-2	Diaby
20/12	h Zulte Waregem	L	0-1	
26/12	a Mechelen	L	0-1	

2015

17/01	h Gent	L	1-3	Verstraete
23/01	a Genk	L	0-2	
31/01	h Kortrijk	L	0-3	
06/02	a Standard	L	0-3	
14/02	h Oostende	L	0-1	
21/02	a Lokeren	L	0-1	
01/03	a Club Brugge	L	0-3	
07/03	h Westerlo	W	1-0	Rodelin
15/03	a Charleroi	L	0-2	
04/04	a Westerlo	W	3-0	Gano 3
11/04	h Oostende	W	2-0	Gano, Badri
18/04	h Lokeren	L	1-5	Boli
25/04	a Lokeren	L	1-2	Rodelin
01/05	a Oostende	W	1-0	Rodelin
09/05	h Westerlo	W	1-0	Gano

No	Name	Nat	DoB	Pos	Aps	(s)	Gls
9	Anice Badri	FRA	18/09/90	M	20	(9)	7
21	Kévin Boli	FRA	21/06/91	D	21	(1)	1
16	Yohan Brouckaert		30/10/87	D	1	(2)	
4	Alexandre Coeff	FRA	20/02/92	M	5	(4)	
18	Roy Contout	FRA	11/02/85	A	12	(3)	
1	Pierrick Cros	FRA	23/06/91	G	21	(1)	
13	Patrick De Vlamynck		01/10/77	G	9		
25	Benjamin Delacourt		10/09/85	D	29		2
23	Abdoulay Diaby	MLI	21/05/91	A	20	(1)	12
19	Tristan Dingomé	FRA	17/02/91	A	26	(6)	2
12	Jérémy Dumesnil	FRA	22/06/86	G	6		
7	Zinho Gano		13/10/93	A	7	(10)	5
22	Jérémy Houzé		28/10/96	M	1	(1)	
17	Marin Jakoliš	CRO	26/12/96	M		(2)	
15	Julian Jeanvier	FRA	30/11/91	D	11	(6)	
4	Corentin Kocur		17/10/95	D	5	(3)	
30	Steeven Langil	FRA	04/03/88	M	16	(5)	1
31	Nolan Mbemba	FRA	19/02/95	M	12	(1)	
4	Teddy Mezague	FRA	27/05/90	D	25	(1)	
10	Julian Michel	FRA	19/02/92	M	28	(1)	2
11	Dimitri Mohamed	FRA	11/06/89	A	8	(6)	
7	Pieter-Jan Monteyne		01/01/83	D	32	(1)	
27	Sébastien Pennacchio	FRA	01/02/83	M	11	(5)	
26	Nicolas Perez	FRA	26/10/90	A		(9)	1
29	Thibault Peyre	FRA	03/10/92	D	22		
23	Ronny Rodelin	FRA	18/11/89	M	12		3
24	Marvin Turcan	FRA	21/11/90	A			
26	Kévin Vandendriessche	FRA	07/08/89	D	31	(3)	3
8	Birger Verstraete		16/04/94	M	5	(6)	1

BELGIUM

KV Oostende

1981 • Albertparkstadion (8,125) • kvo.be
Coach: Frederik Vanderbiest

2014

26/07	a Lierse	L	0-2	
01/08	h Anderlecht	L	0-2	
09/08	a Cercle Brugge	W	1-0	Berrier
16/08	h Mechelen	W	2-0	De Schutter, Ruytinx
23/08	a Kortrijk	W	2-0	Coulibaly 2
30/08	h Genk	D	1-1	Ruytinx
13/09	a Standard	W	5-3	Coulibaly, Siani, og (De Sart), Fernando Canesin, De Schutter
20/09	h Gent	L	1-3	Siani (p)
28/09	h Club Brugge	D	2-2	Siani (p), Fernando Canesin
05/10	a Lokeren	L	1-3	Brillant
18/10	h Mouscron-Péruwelz	D	0-0	
25/10	a Charleroi	L	0-2	
29/10	h Westerlo	W	4-0	Coulibaly, Berrier, Siani (p), Wilmet
01/11	a Waasland-Beveren	L	0-1	
07/11	a Zulte Waregem	L	1-3	Brillant
23/11	h Standard	W	3-2	Siani 2, Coulibaly
29/11	a Mechelen	D	0-0	
06/12	h Lierse	W	2-1	Ruiz, Ruytinx
14/12	a Anderlecht	L	0-3	
20/12	h Cercle Brugge	W	2-0	Siani (p), Wilmet

2015

17/01	h Kortrijk	L	1-7	Coulibaly
25/01	a Gent	L	1-3	Siani
30/01	a Club Brugge	L	0-2	
03/02	a Genk	D	1-1	Ruiz
07/02	h Lokeren	L	0-1	
14/02	a Mouscron-Péruwelz	W	1-0	Coulibaly
21/02	h Charleroi	L	1-3	Musona
28/02	a Westerlo	L	0-3	
07/03	h Waasland-Beveren	W	4-3	Jonckheere, Musona 2, Hoefkens
15/03	a Zulte Waregem	W	4-1	Ruiz 3, Berrier
04/04	h Lokeren	L	1-2	Musona
11/04	a Mouscron-Péruwelz	L	0-1	
18/04	h Westerlo	W	2-0	Brillant, Jonckheere
25/04	a Westerlo	W	2-1	Musona, Ruiz
01/05	h Mouscron-Péruwelz	L	0-1	
09/05	a Lokeren	L	1-6	Milić

No	Name	Nat	DoB	Pos	Aps	(s)	Gls
27	Franck Berrier	FRA	02/02/84	M	29	(6)	3
21	Ante Blažević	CRO	05/05/96	A		(6)	
13	Frédéric Brillant	FRA	26/05/85	D	34		3
12	Jean Chopin	FRA	09/10/94	G	1		
16	Elimane Coulibaly	SEN	15/03/80	A	21	(7)	7
8	Niels Coussement		02/02/91	M	6	(11)	
3	Niels De Schutter		08/08/88	D	25	(3)	2
30	Jérémy Dumesnil	FRA	22/06/86	G	2	(1)	
55	Fernando Canesin	BRA	27/02/92	M	30	(5)	2
24	Jimmy Hempte		24/03/82	D	1		
4	Carl Hoefkens		06/10/78	D	18		1
15	Andile Jali	RSA	10/04/90	M	29	(1)	
20	Michiel Jonckheere		03/01/90	M	17	(9)	2
22	Sébastien Locigno		02/09/95	D	5	(2)	
2	Xavier Luissint	FRA	10/04/84	D	12		
5	Jordan Lukaku		25/07/94	D	29		
19	Antonio Milić	CRO	10/03/94	D	6	(2)	1
11	Knowledge Musona	ZIM	21/06/90	A	13	(2)	5
1	Didier Ovono	GAB	23/01/83	G	33		
29	John Jairo Ruiz	CRC	10/01/94	A	25	(5)	6
9	Bjorn Ruytinx		18/08/80	A	8	(21)	3
6	Baptiste Schmisser	FRA	26/02/86	D	16	(8)	
7	Sébastien Siani	CMR	21/12/86	A	32		8
22	Jonathan Wilmet		07/01/86	M	4	(15)	2

R. Standard de Liège

1898 • Maurice Dufrasne (27,500) • standard.be
Major honours
Belgian League (10) 1958, 1961, 1963, 1969, 1970, 1971, 1982, 1983, 2008, 2009; Belgian Cup (6) 1954, 1966, 1967, 1981, 1993, 2011
Coach: Guy Luzon (ISR);
(20/10/14) Ivan Vukomanović (SRB);
(02/02/15) José Riga

2014

25/07	h Charleroi	W	3-0	Mujangi Bia 2, Carcela-González
02/08	a Kortrijk	W	3-2	Ajdarevic, Mbombo, Mujangi Bia (p)
10/08	h Gent	L	0-1	
15/08	a Mouscron-Péruwelz	L	2-5	De Camargo, Watt
23/08	h Westerlo	D	2-2	Louis, De Camargo
31/08	a Lokeren	D	1-1	De Camargo
13/09	h Oostende	L	3-5	Louis, De Camargo, Mujangi Bia
21/09	a Waasland-Beveren	W	2-0	Jorge Teixeira, M'Poku
28/09	h Lierse	D	2-2	Van Damme 2
05/10	a Club Brugge	L	0-3	
19/10	h Zulte Waregem	L	1-2	M'Poku
26/10	a Anderlecht	W	2-0	Jorge Teixeira, M'Poku
29/10	a Cercle Brugge	W	1-0	Watt
01/11	h Mechelen	W	2-0	De Camargo, M'Poku
09/11	a Genk	W	2-0	M'Poku, Mujangi Bia
23/11	a Oostende	L	2-3	De Camargo, Mujangi Bia
30/11	h Kortrijk	L	0-2	
07/12	a Charleroi	W	1-0	De Camargo
14/12	h Club Brugge	L	1-3	Faty
21/12	a Gent	W	2-1	De Camargo, Mujangi Bia
27/12	h Lokeren	W	2-0	Arslanagic, Ono

2015

18/01	a Westerlo	D	1-1	Faty
25/01	h Anderlecht	W	2-0	Ciman, De Camargo
01/02	a Lierse	W	3-2	Louis, Mujangi Bia 2 (2p)
06/02	h Mouscron-Péruwelz	W	3-0	Carcela-González, Ezekiel, De Camargo
14/02	a Zulte Waregem	D	1-1	Arslanagic
20/02	h Waasland-Beveren	W	3-1	Ezekiel, Hamad, Carcela-González
27/02	a Cercle Brugge	W	1-0	Faty
07/03	h Mechelen	L	0-1	
15/03	h Genk	W	1-0	De Sart
06/04	h Club Brugge	L	1-2	Trebel
12/04	h Anderlecht	W	3-1	Ezekiel 2, Mujangi Bia
17/04	h Gent	L	1-3	Mujangi Bia (p)
25/04	a Charleroi	L	0-1	
28/04	a Kortrijk	L	1-3	Legear
02/05	h Club Brugge	L	1-0	Mujangi Bia
10/05	h Kortrijk	W	4-0	Mujangi Bia 2 (1p), Trebel, De Camargo
17/05	a Anderlecht	D	1-1	Ezekiel
21/05	a Gent	L	0-2	
24/05	h Charleroi	W	2-0	Ezekiel, Jorge Teixeira

No	Name	Nat	DoB	Pos	Aps	(s)	Gls
42	Astrit Ajdarevic	SWE	17/04/90	D	2	(4)	1
27	Darwin Andrade	COL	11/02/91	D	16	(3)	
36	Dino Arslanagic		24/04/93	D	26	(2)	2
33	Mehdi Carcela-González	MAR	01/07/89	M	18	(2)	3
6	Laurent Ciman		05/08/85	D	22		1
10	Igor De Camargo		12/05/83	A	35	(2)	11
15	Julien De Sart		23/12/94	M	15	(11)	1
19	Damien Dussaut	FRA	08/11/94	D	7	(1)	
21	Eyong Enoh	CMR	23/03/86	M	17		
39	Imoh Ezekiel	NGA	24/10/93	A	14		6
4	Ricardo Faty	SEN	04/08/86	M	17	(9)	3
24	Corentin Fiore		24/03/95	D		(1)	
11	Jiloan Hamad	SWE	06/11/90	M		(6)	1
11	Jonathan Viera	ESP	21/10/89	A	2	(1)	
5	Jorge Teixeira	POR	27/08/86	D	18	(1)	3
1	Eiji Kawashima	JPN	20/03/83	G	11		
30	Jonathan Legear		13/04/87	M		(3)	1
25	Jeff Louis	HAI	08/08/92	M	15	(12)	3
67	Tortol Lumanza		13/04/94	M	7	(7)	
40	Paul-José M'Poku	COD	19/04/92	M	16	(2)	5
45	François Marquet		17/04/95	M	3	(1)	
52	Yannis Mbombo		08/04/94	A	3	(1)	1
66	Martin Milec	SVN	20/09/91	D	27		
17	Deni Milosevic		09/03/95	M	1	(1)	
30	Samy Mmaee A Nwambeben		08/09/96	D	2	(2)	
63	Geoffrey Mujangi Bia		12/08/89	M	31	(3)	14
14	Yuji Ono	JPN	22/12/92	M	7	(17)	1
13	Alexander Scholz	DEN	24/10/92	D	16		
8	Ronnie Stam	NED	18/06/84	D	2		
16	Yohann Thuram-Ulien	FRA	31/10/88	G	29		
23	Adrien Trebel	FRA	03/03/91	M	30	(1)	2
37	Jelle Van Damme		10/10/83	M	24	(2)	2
9	Vinícius Araújo	BRA	22/02/93	A	3	(7)	
32	Tony Watt	SCO	29/12/93	A	3	(10)	2
56	Ali Yasar		08/03/95	D	1		

Waasland-Beveren

2010 • Freethiel (12,930) • waasland-beveren.be
Coach: Ronny Van Geneugden;
(05/01/15) Guido Brepoels

2014

26/07	h Club Brugge	L	0-2	
02/08	a Mouscron-Péruwelz	L	0-1	
09/08	h Westerlo	D	1-1	Bojović
16/08	a Charleroi	D	2-2	Destorme, Marić
24/08	a Anderlecht	L	0-1	
30/08	h Lierse	W	2-0	Robson, Emond
13/09	h Zulte Waregem	W	4-1	Robson, Baldé, Sawaneh, Vukušić
21/09	h Standard	L	0-2	
27/09	a Mechelen	L	0-2	
04/10	h Cercle Brugge	W	1-0	Vukušić
11/10	a Kortrijk	L	1-2	Emond (p)
25/10	h Genk	L	0-1	
29/10	a Gent	L	1-4	Emond
01/11	h Oostende	W	1-0	Emond
09/11	a Lokeren	L	0-3	
22/11	h Club Brugge	L	2-4	Robson, Emond
29/11	h Mouscron-Péruwelz	W	2-1	Emond, Destorme
05/12	a Westerlo	W	2-1	Destorme, Emond
13/12	h Charleroi	L	1-3	Vukušić
20/12	h Anderlecht	L	0-2	
27/12	a Cercle Brugge	L	0-1	

2015

17/01	h Zulte Waregem	L	1-3	Sawaneh
24/01	a Lierse	D	1-1	Emond
31/01	h Mechelen	D	2-2	Emond 2 (1p)
08/02	a Genk	L	0-1	
14/02	h Kortrijk	W	1-0	Marić
20/02	a Standard	L	2-3	Rowell, Emond
01/03	a Gent	L	0-1	
07/03	a Oostende	L	3-4	Emond 2, Corstjens
15/03	h Lokeren	L	0-1	
05/04	a Mechelen	L	1-4	og (Verdier)
11/04	h Genk	L	0-2	
18/04	a Zulte Waregem	D	2-2	Destorme, Emond
25/04	a Zulte Waregem	L	0-2	
02/05	a Genk	L	1-7	Corstjens
09/05	h Mechelen	L	1-2	Destorme

No	Name	Nat	DoB	Pos	Aps	(s)	Gls
7	David Addy	GHA	21/02/90	D	26	(1)	
33	Arthur Irawan	IDN	03/03/93	D		(1)	
11	Amido Baldé	POR	16/05/91	A	10	(4)	1
22	Siebe Blondelle		20/04/86	D	19	(9)	
5	Mijuško Bojović	MNE	09/08/88	D	7		1
39	Rachid Bourabia	FRA	22/03/85	M	7		
3	Hrvoje Čale	CRO	04/03/85	D	12	(7)	
26	Colin Coosemans		03/08/92	G	22		
2	Wouter Corstjens		13/02/87	D	20	(3)	2
69	Cédric D'Ulivo	FRA	29/09/89	D	16		
11	Dylan De Belder		03/04/92	A		(3)	
20	Niels De Pauw		19/01/96	D	5	(1)	
77	Daimy Deflem		04/05/94	A	1	(4)	
17	David Destorme		30/08/79	M	13	(12)	5
16	Renaud Emond		05/12/91	A	27	(7)	14
17	Nicolas Godemèche	FRA	22/06/84	M	1	(2)	
8	Robin Henkens		12/09/88	M	16	(8)	
6	David Hubert		12/02/88	M	22		
27	Hugo Sousa	POR	04/06/92	D	16	(1)	
24	Gyamfi Kyeremeh		09/03/95	M		(1)	
30	Alec Luyckx		19/05/95	M	2	(3)	
55	Zakaria M'Sila	MAR	06/04/87	M		(1)	
14	Miloš Marić	SRB	05/03/82	M	21	(5)	2
14	Aboubakar Oumarou	CMR	04/01/87	A	12	(3)	
4	Robson	BRA	10/07/83	D	30		3
15	Jonny Rowell	ENG	10/09/89	M	20	(2)	1
12	Ebrahima Ibou Sawaneh	GAM	07/09/86	A	23	(7)	2
18	Kenny Steppe		14/11/88	G	14		
25	Jerry Vandam	FRA	08/12/88	D	6		
28	Floriano Vanzo		22/04/94	A	5	(1)	
23	Jorn Vermeulen		16/04/87	D	5	(2)	
9	Ante Vukušić	CRO	04/06/91	A	9	(6)	3
32	Jonathan Wilmet		07/01/86	M	8	(3)	

KVC Westerlo

1933 • Het Kuipje (8,035) • kvcwesterlo.be
Major honours
Belgian Cup (1) 2001
Coach: Dennis van Wijk (NED);
(06/01/15) Harm van Voldhoven (NED)

2014
26/07	h	Lokeren	W 1-0	*Annys*
02/08	a	Charleroi	W 3-2	*Aoulad 2, Gounongbe*
09/08	a	Waasland-Beveren	D 1-1	*Gounongbe (p)*
17/08	h	Anderlecht	D 2-2	*og (Mbemba), Geudens*
23/08	a	Standard	D 2-2	*Gounongbe 2*
30/08	h	Zulte Waregem	D 2-2	*Gounongbe 2*
13/09	a	Mechelen	L 2-5	*Gounongbe, MacDonald*
20/09	h	Lierse	W 6-1	*Gounongbe, Aoulad 2, Koffi 2, Schouterden*
27/09	a	Cercle Brugge	W 2-1	*Lecomte, Gounongbe (p)*
03/10	h	Gent	D 0-0	
19/10	a	Genk	L 1-3	*Annys*
25/10	h	Kortrijk	W 2-1	*Schuermans, Lecomte*
29/10	a	Oostende	L 0-4	
02/11	h	Mouscron-Péruwelz	L 1-3	*Annys*
09/11	a	Club Brugge	L 0-5	
22/11	a	Lokeren	D 0-0	
29/11	h	Charleroi	L 2-3	*Schouterden, Ruyssen*
05/12	a	Waasland-Beveren	L 1-2	*Koffi*
13/12	a	Lierse	D 3-3	*Schouterden, Annys, Koffi*
20/12	h	Mechelen	D 1-1	*Molenberghs*
26/12	a	Anderlecht	L 0-4	

2015
18/01	h	Standard	D 1-1	*Koffi*
24/01	a	Zulte Waregem	W 3-1	*Diagne 2, Schouterden*
31/01	h	Cercle Brugge	W 1-0	*Apau*
07/02	a	Gent	L 0-4	
13/02	h	Genk	L 1-2	*Koffi*
21/02	a	Kortrijk	L 0-6	
28/02	h	Oostende	W 3-0	*Geudens, Schouterden (p), Aoulad*
07/03	a	Mouscron-Péruwelz	L 0-1	
15/03	h	Club Brugge	L 1-3	*Schouterden*
04/04	a	Mouscron-Péruwelz	L 0-3	
11/04	a	Lokeren	D 1-1	*Aoulad*
18/04	a	Oostende	L 0-2	
25/04	a	Oostende	L 1-2	*Diagne*
01/05	h	Lokeren	W 4-3	*Molenberghs, Apau, og (Ngolok), Koffi*
09/05	a	Mouscron-Péruwelz	D 1-1	*Geudens*

No	Name	Nat	DoB	Pos	Aps	(s)	Gls
8	Maxime Annys		24/07/86	M	29		4
14	Mohamed Aoulad		29/08/91	A	22	(3)	6
2	Mitch Apau	NED	27/04/90	D	34		2
24	Jens Cools		16/10/90	M	25	(3)	
1	Michaël Cordier		27/03/84	G	3	(2)	
10	Mbaye Diagne	SEN	28/10/91	A	7	(4)	3
20	Alassane Diallo	MLI	19/02/95	M	1	(6)	
12	Christian Cordara	GER	06/12/88	D	12	(3)	
6	Kevin Geudens		02/12/80	M	33		3
5	Bruno Godeau		10/05/92	D	17	(5)	
12	Frédéric Gounongbe	BEN	08/05/88	A	13	(4)	9
27	Faris Handžić	BIH	27/05/95	M	1	(2)	
3	Kevin Koffi	CIV	25/06/86	A	19	(13)	7
7	Raphaël Lecomte	FRA	22/05/88	M	18	(3)	2
11	Sherjill MacDonald	NED	20/11/84	A	3	(9)	1
4	Birger Maertens		28/06/80	D	26		
23	Jarno Molenberghs		11/12/89	M	25	(7)	2
14	Jordan Mustoe	ENG	28/01/91	M	13	(1)	
28	Jeffrey Rentmeister		11/07/84	D		(2)	
21	Nicolas Rommens		17/12/94	M	1	(19)	
38	Gilles Ruyssen		18/06/94	D	5	(2)	1
18	Nils Schouterden		14/12/88	M	22	(3)	6
17	Kenneth Schuermans		25/05/91	D	29		1
25	Enes Šipović	BIH	11/09/90	D	3	(1)	
10	Evander Sno	NED	09/04/87	M	2		
30	Koen Van Langendonck		09/06/89	G	33		
9	Kevin Vandenbergh		16/05/83	A		(1)	
19	Arno Verschueren		08/04/97	M		(6)	
20	Stef Vervoort		20/02/95	M		(1)	

SV Zulte Waregem

2001 • Regenboogstadion (8,500) • essevee.be
Major honours
Belgian Cup (1) 2006
Coach: Francky Dury

2014
27/07	h	Kortrijk	W 2-0	*Sylla 2*
03/08	a	Lokeren	L 1-2	*Verboom*
10/08	h	Club Brugge	D 1-1	*Plet*
17/08	a	Gent	L 1-3	*Sylla*
23/08	h	Mouscron-Péruwelz	D 1-1	*Aneke*
30/08	a	Westerlo	D 2-2	*Sylla, Messoudi*
13/09	h	Waasland-Beveren	L 1-4	*Plet*
19/09	a	Charleroi	L 1-2	*Troisi*
27/09	h	Anderlecht	L 0-2	
04/10	a	Lierse	L 1-3	*Sylla*
19/10	a	Standard	W 2-1	*Bongonda, Troisi*
25/10	h	Cercle Brugge	L 1-2	*Bongonda*
28/10	a	Mechelen	D 1-1	*D'Haene*
31/10	h	Genk	W 2-0	*Bongonda, Troisi*
07/11	a	Oostende	W 3-1	*N'Diaye, Verboom, D'Haene*
23/11	a	Kortrijk	L 1-3	*Trajkovski*
28/11	h	Gent	W 2-1	*Verboom, Cissako*
07/12	a	Club Brugge	L 1-2	*Troisi*
14/12	h	Lokeren	W 1-0	*Trajkovski*
20/12	a	Mouscron-Péruwelz	W 1-0	*Aneke*
26/12	h	Charleroi	L 1-3	*Messoudi (p)*

2015
17/01	h	Waasland-Beveren	W 3-1	*Cordaro, Gimbert, Trajkovski*
24/01	h	Westerlo	L 1-3	*Cordaro*
01/02	a	Anderlecht	D 0-0	
07/02	a	Lierse	L 2-3	*Rossi 2 (1p)*
14/02	h	Standard	D 1-1	*Troisi*
21/02	a	Cercle Brugge	D 2-2	*Jørgensen, Kaya*
28/02	h	Mechelen	L 2-3	*Gimbert, Mendy*
07/03	a	Genk	L 2-3	*Benteke, Rossi*
15/03	h	Oostende	L 1-4	*Benteke*
03/04	a	Genk	L 0-1	
12/04	h	Mechelen	L 0-1	
18/04	h	Waasland-Beveren	D 2-2	*Rossi, Gimbert*
25/04	a	Waasland-Beveren	W 2-0	*Kaya, Trajkovski*
02/05	a	Mechelen	L 0-3	
09/05	h	Genk	L 2-3	*Trajkovski, Skúlason*

No	Name	Nat	DoB	Pos	Aps	(s)	Gls
26	Chuks Aneke	ENG	03/07/93	M	20	(10)	2
15	Jonathan Benteke		01/01/95	A	1	(6)	2
27	Theo Bongonda		20/11/95	A	6	(8)	3
1	Sammy Bossut		11/08/85	G	36		
33	Sébastien Brebels		05/05/95	M	5	(2)	
19	Raphaël Cacérès	FRA	01/09/87	A		(2)	
2	Yarouba Cissako	FRA	08/01/95	D	25		1
3	Steve Colpaert		13/09/86	D	15		
17	Ibrahima Conté	GUI	03/04/91	M	5		
29	Alessandro Cordara		02/05/86	M	8		2
24	Karel D'Haene		05/09/80	D	27		2
36	Joey Dujardin		16/02/96	D	2		
43	Charni Ekangamene		16/02/94	M	12	(4)	
35	Karim Essikal	MAR	08/02/96	M	4		
14	Ghislain Gimbert	FRA	07/08/85	A	10	(1)	3
14	Kylian Hazard		05/08/96	M		(2)	
8	Jesper Jørgensen	DEN	09/05/84	M	23		1
34	Onur Kaya		20/04/86	M	13		2
4	Jérémy Labor	FRA	19/03/92	D	3	(1)	
20	Formose Mendy	FRA	08/10/93	M	21	(1)	1
21	Mohamed Messoudi		07/01/84	M	13	(7)	2
13	Mamatou N'Diaye	MLI	15/03/90	D	12	(2)	1
17	Willie Overtoom	CMR	02/09/86	M	1	(4)	
28	Djibril Paye	GUI	26/02/90	D		(2)	
9	Glynor Plet	NED	30/01/87	A	9	(9)	2
7	Tom Rosenthal		30/09/96	M	1	(3)	
19	Karim Rossi	SUI	01/05/94	A	8	(4)	4
23	Sefa İşçi	TUR	26/03/96	D	1		
16	Ólafur Ingi Skúlason	ISL	01/04/83	M	24	(2)	1
11	Idrissa Sylla	GUI	03/12/90	A	16	(4)	5
2	Tiago Ferreira	POR	10/07/93	D	2		
12	Aleksandar Trajkovski	MKD	05/09/92	A	24	(10)	5
10	James Troisi	AUS	03/07/88	M	18	(3)	5
5	Bryan Verboom		30/01/92	D	31		3

Top goalscorers

20	Aleksandar Mitrović (Anderlecht)
15	Ivan Santini (Kortrijk)
14	Geoffrey Mujangi Bia (Standard)
	Renaud Emond (Waasland-Beveren)
13	José Izquierdo (Club Brugge)
	Laurent Depoitre (Gent)
	Dalibor Veselinović (Mechelen)
12	Teddy Chevalier (Kortrijk)
	Mijat Maric (Lokeren)
	Abdoulay Diaby (Mouscron-Péruwelz)

Promoted clubs

K. Sint-Truidense VV

1924 • Stayen (14,600) • stvv.com
Coach: Yannick Ferrera

Oud-Heverlee Leuven

2002 • Den Dreef (8,700) • ohl.be
Coach: Ivan Leko (CRO);
(28/11/14) (Hans Vander Elst);
(26/12/14) Jacky Mathijssen

Second level final table 2014/15

		Pld	W	D	L	F	A	Pts
1	K. Sint-Truidense VV (*2)	34	24	7	3	62	28	79
2	Lommel United (*3)	34	21	7	6	65	27	70
3	KAS Eupen	34	20	7	7	63	30	67
4	Seraing United	34	17	10	7	69	39	61
5	Oud-Heverlee Leuven (*1)	34	17	10	7	66	39	61
6	R. Excelsior Virton	34	17	8	9	58	35	59
7	RAEC Mons	34	14	13	7	52	30	55
8	AFC Tubize	34	14	8	12	43	40	50
9	SC Eendracht Aalst	34	12	10	12	48	45	46
10	R. Antwerp FC	34	11	9	14	41	41	42
11	KSV Roeselare	34	10	12	12	44	45	42
12	R. White Star Bruxelles	34	8	16	10	43	40	40
13	AS Verbroedering Geel	34	10	9	15	42	62	39
14	KSK Heist	34	10	6	18	41	61	36
15	KFC Dessel Sport	34	7	10	17	36	58	31
16	K. Patro Eisden Maasmechelen	34	6	8	20	38	68	26
17	KRC Mechelen	34	5	4	25	23	87	19
18	KV Woluwe-Zaventem	34	3	6	25	30	81	15

NB (*) period champions.

Promotion/Relegation play-offs final table

		Pld	W	D	L	F	A	Pts
1	Oud-Heverlee Leuven	6	4	2	0	8	3	14
2	KAS Eupen	6	2	2	2	5	4	8
3	K. Lierse SK	6	2	1	3	8	10	7
4	Lommel United	6	1	1	4	6	10	4

 **BELGIUM**

Mid-table & Relegation play-offs 2014/15

Play-off 2A final table

		Pld	Home					Away					Total					Pts
			W	D	L	F	A	W	D	L	F	A	W	D	L	F	A	
1	KV Mechelen	6	3	0	0	11	1	2	0	1	3	2	5	0	1	14	3	15
2	KRC Genk	6	3	0	0	9	1	2	0	1	5	6	5	0	1	14	7	15
3	SV Zulte Waregem	6	0	1	2	4	6	1	0	2	2	4	1	1	4	6	10	4
4	Waasland-Beveren	6	0	0	3	1	6	0	1	2	4	13	0	1	5	5	19	1

Play-off 2B final table

		Pld	Home					Away					Total					Pts
			W	D	L	F	A	W	D	L	F	A	W	D	L	F	A	
1	KSC Lokeren OV	6	2	1	0	9	3	2	0	1	10	6	4	1	1	19	9	13
2	R. Mouscron-Péruwelz	6	1	1	1	4	6	2	0	1	5	2	3	1	2	9	8	10
3	KV Oostende	6	1	0	2	3	3	1	0	2	3	9	2	0	4	6	12	6
4	KVC Westerlo	6	1	0	2	5	8	0	2	1	2	4	1	2	3	7	12	5

UEFA Europa League qualification play-offs

FIRST ROUND

(16/05/15 & 23/05/15)
Lokeren 2-2 Mechelen
Mechelen 2-1 Lokeren
(Mechelen 4-3)

SECOND ROUND

(28/05/15 & 31/05/15)
Mechelen 2-1 Charleroi
Charleroi 2-0 Mechelen
(Charleroi 3-2)

Play-off 3 final table

		Pld	Home					Away					Total					Pts
			W	D	L	F	A	W	D	L	F	A	W	D	L	F	A	
1	K. Lierse SK	4	1	0	1	3	2	2	0	0	5	2	3	0	1	8	4	9
2	Cercle Brugge KSV	4	0	0	2	2	5	1	0	1	2	3	1	0	3	4	8	6

NB Cercle Brugge KSV carried 3 pts forward from the regular season; K. Lierse SK subsequently entered the promotion/relegation play-offs.

DOMESTIC CUP

Coupe de Belgique/Beker van België 2014/15

SIXTH ROUND

(24/09/14)
Antwerp 0-4 Zulte Waregem
Charleroi 2-0 Eupen
Club Brugge 6-1 Aalst
Coxyde 0-0 Mouscron-Péruwelz *(aet; 4-3 on pens)*
Dessel Sport 0-2 KV Mechelen
Genk 0-1 RC Mechelen
Heist 0-3 Standard
Leuven 1-3 Kortrijk
Lierse 4-0 Sint-Truiden
Lokeren 6-0 Sint-Eloois-Winkel
Lommel United 2-1 Waasland-Beveren
Namur 1-3 Gent
Olsa Brakel 6-1 Westerlo
Patro Maasmechelen 3-5 Anderlecht *(aet)*
Sint-Gillis-Waas 1-7 Cercle Brugge
Woluwe-Zaventem 1-3 Oostende

SEVENTH ROUND

(02/12/14)
Cercle Brugge 3-0 Coxyde *(aet)*

(03/12/14)
Anderlecht 4-1 RC Mechelen
Charleroi 2-0 Oostende
Kortrijk 0-3 Club Brugge
Lommel United 0-1 Gent
Olsa Brakel 2-3 KV Mechelen
Standard 1-4 Lokeren
Zulte Waregem 2-1 Lierse *(aet)*

QUARTER-FINALS

(17/12/14 & 20/01/15)
KV Mechelen 0-0 Club Brugge
Club Brugge 3-2 KV Mechelen *(Oularé 25, 37, Mechele 90; Bateau 18, De Witte 32p)*
(Club Brugge 3-2)

(17/12/14 & 21/01/15)
Charleroi 2-1 Cercle Brugge *(Fauré 26, 30; Smolders 40)*
Cercle Brugge 2-0 Charleroi *(Muzaqi 68, Buyl 90)*
(Cercle Brugge 3-2)

Lokeren 1-4 Gent *(Maric 42p; Depoitre 4, Milicevic 50, Saief 69, Raman 87)*
Gent 1-0 Lokeren *(Dejaegere 63)*
(Gent 5-1)

Zulte Waregem 0-3 Anderlecht *(Acheampong 72, Praet 74, Kljestan 85)*
Anderlecht 4-2 Zulte Waregem *(Kljestan 25, 44, Cyriac 40, Leya Iseka 68; Trajkovski 75p, Benteke 85)*
(Anderlecht 7-2)

SEMI-FINALS

(03/02/15 & 11/02/15)
Club Brugge 5-1 Cercle Brugge *(Felipe Gedoz 14, De Sutter 49, Víctor Vázquez 63, Izquierdo 78, Storm 88; Bačelić-Grgić 45)*
Cercle Brugge 2-3 Club Brugge *(Sukuta-Pasu 74, Buyl 89; Bolingoli-Mbombo 44, 76, De Fauw 50)*
(Club Brugge 8-3)

(04/02/15 & 12/02/15)
Gent 0-2 Anderlecht *(Najar 33, Vanden Borre 56)*
Anderlecht 3-0 Gent *(Defour 11, Mitrović 14, Tielemans 57p)*
(Anderlecht 5-0)

FINAL

(22/03/15)
King Baudouin, Brussels
CLUB BRUGGE KV 2 *(De Sutter 12, Refaelov 90+2)*
RSC ANDERLECHT 1 *(Mitrović 89)*
Referee: Gumienny
CLUB BRUGGE: *Ryan, Meunier, Duarte, Mechele, De Bock, Vormer, Simons, Refaelov, Bolingoli-Mbombo (Felipe Gedoz 60), Izquierdo (Claudemir 81), De Sutter (Oularé 73)*
ANDERLECHT: *Proto, Colin (Conté 85), Rolando, N'Sakala (Leya Iseka 76), Deschacht, Najar, Defour, Praet, Dendoncker, Marin (Acheampong 58), Mitrović*

BOSNIA&HERZEGOVINA
Nogometni / Fudbalski savez Bosne i Hercegovine (NFSBiH)

Address	Ulica Ferhadija 30	**President**	Elvedin Begić
	BA-71000 Saarajevo	**General secretary**	Jasmin Baković
Tel	+387 33 276 660	**Media officer**	Slavica Pecikoza
Fax	+387 33 444 332	**Year of formation**	1992
E-mail	nsbih@bih.net.ba	**National stadium**	Bilinjo Pole, Zenica
Website	nfsbih.ba		(12,820)

PREMIJER LIGA CLUBS

 ① **FK Borac Banja Luka**

 ② **NK Čelik Zenica**

 ③ **FK Drina Zvornik**

 ④ **FK Mladost Velika Obarska**

 ⑤ **FK Olimpic Sarajevo**

 ⑥ **FK Radnik Bijeljina**

 ⑦ **FK Sarajevo**

 ⑧ **FK Slavija Sarajevo**

 ⑨ **FK Sloboda Tuzla**

 ⑩ **NK Široki Brijeg**

 ⑪ **NK Travnik**

 ⑫ **FK Velež**

 ⑬ **NK Vitez**

 ⑭ **HŠK Zrinjski**

 ⑮ **NK Zvijezda**

 ⑯ **FK Željezničar**

KEY:

- ● – UEFA Champions League
- ● – UEFA Europa League
- ● – Promoted
- ● – Relegated

Prijedor ⑱
Gradačac ⑮ ④ ⑥
Banja Luka ① Bijeljina
Tuzla ⑨ ③ Zvornik
Travnik ⑪ ②
Vitez ⑬ Zenica
Doboj ⑰ ⑤
⑦
Sarajevo ⑧
⑯
Široki Brijeg ⑫
⑩ ⑭ Mostar

PROMOTED CLUBS

 ⑰ **FK Mladost Doboj Kakanj**

 ⑱ **FK Rudar Prijedor**

0	50	100 km
0		50 miles

Sarajevo end eight-year wait

The race for the 2014/15 Premijer Liga title was gripping from start to finish, with four clubs all fancying their chances, but in the end it was FK Sarajevo, thanks to a powerful surge at the finish, who came through to collect their first championship crown for eight years.

City rivals FK Željezničar finished second ahead of defending champions HŠK Zrinjski, while fourth-placed NK Široki Brijeg, the long-time leaders, missed out on Europe after losing the two-legged cup final on penalties to the underdogs of FK Olimpic Sarajevo.

| Strong finish settles thrilling four-horse title race | Olimpic beat Široki Brijeg on penalties in cup final | Baždarević replaces Sušić at national team helm |

Domestic league

There was never much distance between the Premijer Liga's top four teams, with Široki Brijeg generally setting the pace but unable to break clear. At the end of April, with six games remaining, just one point separated the leading quartet. The title was up for grabs, and it was Sarajevo, who had only just returned to the top of the table for the first time since August thanks to a 1-0 home win against Široki Brijeg, who came through to triumph.

While Široki Brijeg and Zrinjski both went off the boil, the two clubs from the capital responded positively to the challenge, and when Sarajevo hosted Željezničar in the Eternal Derby in round 28, they were just one point ahead of them. Billed as a title-decider, it produced no goals but left Sarajevo needing to win their last two fixtures, away to struggling NK Vitez and at home – where they were unbeaten – to mid-table FK Sloboda Tuzla. They duly delivered, winning the first game 3-0 and the second 3-1.

In common with all but one of the other 15 teams in the division, Sarajevo opted to change coach during the season. In fact, they did so twice. Although ex-FC Barcelona forward Meho Kodro was in charge for most of the campaign, the man who started and finished it was 39-year-old former midfielder Dženan Ušćuplić.

During his two spells at the helm Sarajevo did not lose a game, and they were only defeated twice all season. An excellent defence, with Bojan Puzigaća at its heart, was supplemented by the league's most potent attack, in which Macedonian striker Krste Velkoski and – in the spring – Croatian international Leon Benko were key contributors.

Željezničar, unbeaten in the spring under new boss Milomir Odović, boasted the league's top scorer in 15-goal Riad Bajić, who edged out Zrinjski's Stevo Nikolić and Široki Brijeg's Brazilian playmaker Wagner, the leading marksman from the previous campaign.

Domestic cup

Bosnia & Herzegovina is the only European country that persists with a two-legged domestic cup final, but even after 180 minutes the 2015 contest between Široki Brijeg and Olimpic could not produce a winner. A pair of 1-1 draws between two clubs that had also shared the spoils twice in the league led to a penalty shoot-out, and it was Olimpic, who had valiantly struck back with ten men in the second leg to equalise through first-leg scorer Veldin Muharemović, who prevailed to claim the club's first major honour and first qualification for Europe. It was Olimpic's second successive shoot-out success,

having also prevailed against Zrinjski in the semi-finals, and a fitting reward for the club's loyalty to Mirza Varešanović, the only Premijer Liga coach to remain in situ all season.

Europe

As ever, the country's leading clubs produced little of note in Europe, although Sarajevo did provide a memory to treasure with a 3-1 extra-time win at Atromitos FC, which carried them through to the UEFA Europa League's third qualifying round. There, rather more predictably, they were humbled by VfLBorussia Mönchengladbach, losing the second leg 7-0 in Germany.

National team

A disastrous start to Bosnia & Herzegovina's UEFA EURO 2016 qualifying campaign, which kicked off with a 2-1 home defeat to Cyprus, resulted in the departure of Safet Sušić, the man who had taken the side to the 2014 FIFA World Cup. The team's fortunes improved considerably after he left, with new boss Mehmed Baždarević overseeing successive wins against Andorra – in which all-time leading marksman Edin Džeko scored a hat-trick – and Israel, thereby reviving the team's chances of reaching the UEFA European Championship finals for the first time.

DOMESTIC SEASON AT A GLANCE

Premijer Liga 2014/15 final table

		Pld	Home					Away					Total					Pts
			W	D	L	F	A	W	D	L	F	A	W	D	L	F	A	
1	**FK Sarajevo**	30	10	5	0	31	7	9	4	2	24	10	19	9	2	55	17	66
2	FK Željezničar	30	10	3	2	27	13	8	6	1	25	9	18	9	3	52	22	63
3	HŠK Zrinjski	30	9	6	0	25	4	7	5	3	16	9	16	11	3	41	13	59
4	NK Široki Brijeg	30	11	4	0	30	8	4	7	4	16	15	15	11	4	46	23	56
5	FK Borac Banja Luka	30	11	2	2	19	9	3	5	7	7	17	14	7	9	26	26	49
6	FK Olimpic Sarajevo	30	9	1	5	26	13	4	6	5	15	21	13	7	10	41	34	46
7	NK Čelik Zenica	30	5	8	2	19	15	5	3	7	15	20	10	11	9	34	35	41
8	FK Sloboda Tuzla	30	9	3	3	23	10	2	4	9	10	18	11	7	12	33	28	40
9	FK Velež	30	10	3	2	22	9	0	5	10	10	24	10	8	12	32	33	38
10	FK Radnik Bijeljina	30	5	5	5	16	15	2	5	8	13	24	7	10	13	29	39	31
11	NK Travnik	30	8	3	4	17	14	0	4	11	5	28	8	7	15	22	42	31
12	FK Slavija Sarajevo	30	5	5	5	18	18	2	2	11	12	26	7	7	16	30	44	28
13	FK Drina Zvornik	30	4	7	4	14	10	2	2	11	12	30	6	9	15	26	40	27
14	NK Vitez	30	7	2	6	17	20	0	3	12	4	23	7	5	18	21	43	26
15	FK Mladost Velika Obarska	30	5	5	5	12	16	1	3	11	6	28	6	8	16	18	44	26
16	NK Zvijezda	30	4	6	5	18	21	1	4	10	12	32	5	10	15	30	53	25

European qualification 2015/16

Champion: FK Sarajevo (second qualifying round)

Cup winner: FK Olimpic Sarajevo (first qualifying round)
FK Željezničar (first qualifying round)
HŠK Zrinjski (first qualifying round)

Top scorer   Riad Bajić (Željezničar), 15 goals
Relegated clubs   NK Zvijezda, FK Mladost Velika Obarska
Promoted clubs   FK Mladost Doboj Kakanj, FK Rudar Prijedor
Cup final   NK Široki Brijeg 1-1; 1-1 FK Olimpic Sarajevo *(agg 2-2; 4-5 on pens)*

Team of the season
(4-3-3)

Coach: Varešanović *(Olimpic)*

Dujković *(Zrinjski)*	
Tatomirović *(Sarajevo)* **Bogdanović** *(Željezničar)* **Puzigaća** *(Sarajevo)* **Subić** *(Borac)*	
Muharemović *(Olimpic)* **Wagner** *(Široki Brijeg)* **Cimirot** *(Sarajevo)*	
Nikolić *(Zrinjski)* **Bajić** *(Željezničar)* **Velkoski** *(Sarajevo)*	

Player of the season

Riad Bajić
(FK Željezničar)

Željezničar's narrow failure to win the Premijer Liga title was certainly not the fault of Bajić, who in his first campaign as a regular starter topped the division's scoring charts with 15 goals. On target repeatedly throughout the campaign, he became only the second Željo player – after Eldin Adilović in 2011/12 – to claim the golden boot, albeit with the lowest total in the Premijer Liga's 13 seasons. His efforts were recognised with a call-up in March to the national team by new coach Mehmed Bazdarević.

Newcomer of the season

Amir Hadžiahmetović
(FK Željezničar)

Just 17 years of age at the start of the season, Hadžiahmetović ended the campaign with a growing reputation as one of the most exciting young midfield talents to have graced the Premijer Liga for many years. He announced himself in May with a first senior goal, against FK Mladost Velika Obarska, and three days later an excellent performance in the 0-0 draw against FK Sarajevo. His season ended with promotion above his age group and a place in the Bosnia & Herzegovina Under-21 squad

 **BOSNIA & HERZEGOVINA**

NATIONAL TEAM

International tournament appearances
FIFA World Cup (1) 2014

Top five all-time caps
Zvjezdan Misimović (83); **Emir Spahić** (81),
Edin Džeko (72); **Vedad Ibišević** (65);
Miralem Pjanić (59)

Top five all-time goals
Edin Džeko (42); Zvjezdan Misimović (25);
Vedad Ibišević (24); Elvir Bolić (22); Sergej
Barbarez (17)

Results 2014/15

04/09/14	Liechtenstein	H	Tuzla	W	3-0	*Ibišević (2, 14), Džeko (24)*
09/09/14	Cyprus (ECQ)	H	Zenica	L	1-2	*Ibišević (6)*
10/10/14	Wales (ECQ)	A	Cardiff	D	0-0	
13/10/14	Belgium (ECQ)	H	Zenica	D	1-1	*Džeko (28)*
16/11/14	Israel (ECQ)	A	Haifa	L	0-3	
28/03/15	Andorra (ECQ)	A	Andorra la Vella	W	3-0	*Džeko (13, 49, 62)*
31/03/15	Austria	A	Vienna	D	1-1	*Hajrović (48)*
12/06/15	Israel (ECQ)	H	Zenica	W	3-1	*Višća (42, 75), Džeko (45+2p)*

Appearances 2014/15

Coach: Safet Sušić /(13/12/14) Mehmed Baždarević	13/04/55 28/09/60		Lie	CYP	WAL	BEL	ISR	AND	Aut	ISR	Caps	Goals
Asmir Begović	20/06/87	Stoke (ENG)	G62	G	G	G	G	G	G	G	41	-
Mensur Mujdža	28/03/84	Freiburg (GER)	D46		D	D	D46	D	D	D	33	-
Toni Šunjić	15/12/88	Kuban (RUS)	D	D	D	D	D 47*		s46		15	-
Ognjen Vranješ	24/10/89	unattached /Gaziantepspor (TUR)	D					D73		D	17	-
Sejad Salihović	08/10/84	Hoffenheim (GER)	D								45	4
Sanjin Prcić	20/11/93	Rennes (FRA)	M	M62			s46		s79		4	-
Miralem Pjanić	02/04/90	Roma (ITA)	M46	M	M	M	M61	M	M46	M88	59	9
Muhamed Bešić	10/09/92	Everton (ENG)	M68	M	M	M	M46	M	s46	M	20	-
Haris Medunjanin	08/03/85	Deportivo (ESP)	M68	s62	M	M	M	s77	M55	M	45	5
Edin Džeko	17/03/86	Man. City (ENG)	A62	A	A	A		A	A	A	72	42
Vedad Ibišević	06/08/84	Stuttgart (GER)	A	A	A83	A		A67	s69	s88	65	24
Ermin Bičakčić	24/01/90	Hoffenheim (GER)	s46	D					D		11	1
Izet Hajrović	04/08/91	Bremen (GER)	s46	s62	s83		A		M82	s80	15	3
Jasmin Fejzić	15/05/86	Aalen (GER)	s62								1	-
Edin Višća	17/02/90	İstanbul Başakşehir (TUR)	s62		s71		s46	M		M80	17	2
Gojko Cimirot	19/12/92	Sarajevo	s68				s61				2	-
Goran Zakarić	07/11/92	Široki Brijeg	s68								1	-
Avdija Vršajević	06/03/86	Hajduk Split (CRO)		D					M69		16	1
Senad Lulić	18/01/86	Lazio (ITA)		D	D	D	M	M77		M85	41	1
Tino-Sven Sušić	13/02/92	Hajduk Split (CRO)		M62	M	M71			s82		8	-
Anel Hadžić	16/08/89	Sturm (AUT)			D	D	D		M79	s85	8	-
Emir Spahić	18/08/80	Leverkusen (GER) /unattached					D	D	D46	D	81	3
Zoran Kvržić	07/08/88	Rijeka (CRO)					M				3	-
Ervin Zukanović	11/02/87	Chievo (ITA)						D	D		8	-
Milan Djurić	22/05/90	Cesena (ITA)						s67			1	-
Edin Cocalić	05/12/87	Mechelen (BEL)						s73			1	-
Semir Štilić	08/10/87	Wisła Kraków (POL)							s55		7	-
Sead Kolašinac	20/06/93	Schalke (GER)								D	7	-

EUROPE

HŠK Zrinjski

CHAMPIONS
LEAGUE

Second qualifying round - NK Maribor (SVN)

H 0-0
Dujković, Graovac, Muminović, Pehar, Šćepanović, Stojkić, Zlatić, Stojanović (Durak 66), Nikolić (Kordić 82), Katanec, Djurić (Simeunović 65). Coach: Branko Karačić (CRO)
Red card: Muminović 90+1
A 0-2
Dujković, Radulović, Graovac, Pehar (Simeunović 60), Šćepanović, Blaić, Stojkić, Stojanović (Radeljić 75), Nikolić, Katanec, Djurić (Kordić 68). Coach: Branko Karačić (CRO)

FK Sarajevo

EUROPA
LEAGUE

Second qualifying round - FK Haugesund (NOR)

H 0-1
Bandović, Stojčev, Okić, Velkoski, Tatomirović (Kovačević 89), Berberović, Dupovac, Cimirot, Puzigaća, Radovac, Bilbija (Duljević 68). Coach: Dženan Uščuplić (BIH)
A 3-1 Stojčev (21), Okić (36, 82)
Bandović, Stojčev (Kovačević 82), Okić, Velkoski, Tatomirović, Duljević (Radovac 46), Berberović, Dupovac, Cimirot, Puzigaća, Bilbija (Protić 90+2). Coach: Dženan Uščuplić (BIH)
Red card: Berberović 79

Third qualifying round - Atromitos FC (GRE)

H 1-2 Puzigaća (26)
Bandović, Barić, Stojčev, Okić (Purić 82), Velkoski, Tatomirović, Dupovac, Cimirot, Puzigaća, Radovac (Kovačević 88), Bilbija (Duljević 73). Coach: Dženan Uščuplić (BIH)
A 3-1 Duljević (24), Bilbija (80, 105) **(aet)**
Bandović, Barić (Protić 99), Stojčev, Okić (Bilbija 68), Velkoski, Tatomirović, Duljević, Dupovac, Cimirot, Puzigaća, Radovac (Kovačević 68). Coach: Dženan Uščuplić (BIH)

Play-offs - VfL Borussia Mönchengladbach (GER)

H 2-3 Puzigaća (26), Duljević (59)
Bandović, Stojčev, Okić (Duljević 52), Velkoski, Tatomirović, Berberović, Dupovac, Cimirot, Puzigaća (Protić 76), Radovac (Kovačević 76), Bilbija. Coach: Dženan Uščuplić (BIH)
A 0-7
Bandović, Stojčev (Bilbija 46), Okić (Handžić 75), Velkoski, Tatomirović, Duljević, Berberović, Dupovac, Cimirot, Puzigaća (Protić 46), Radovac. Coach: Dženan Uščuplić (BIH)
Red card: Tatomirović 90

NK Široki Brijeg

EUROPA
LEAGUE

First qualifying round - Qäbälä FK (AZE)

A 2-0 Wagner (74, 89)
Bilobrk, Ćorić, Pehar, Marić, Zakarić (Kožulj 90+2), Landeka, Wagner, Peko (Ivanković 90), Brekalo, Laštro, Marković (Barišić 27). Coach: Slaven Musa (BIH)
H 3-0 Zakarić (17), Marić (29, 56)
Soldo, Barišić, Ćorić (Kožulj 78), Pehar (Ivanković 60), Marić, Zakarić, Landeka, Wagner, Peko (Čorluka 34), Brekalo, Laštro. Coach: Slaven Musa (BIH)

Second qualifying round - FK Mladá Boleslav (CZE)

A 1-2 Zakarić (51)
Soldo, Barišić (Marković 81), Ćorić, Pehar (Ivanković 56), Marić, Zakarić, Landeka, Wagner, Zadro (Kožulj 56), Brekalo, Laštro. Coach: Slaven Musa (BIH)
H 0-4
Soldo, Ćorić, Pehar (Kožulj 78), Marić, Zakarić, Landeka (Mihaljević 61), Wagner, Peko (Ljubić 61), Brekalo, Laštro, Marković. Coach: Slaven Musa (BIH)

FK Željezničar

EUROPA
LEAGUE

First qualifying round - FK Lovćen (MNE)

H 0-0
Antolović, Kvesić, Bučan, Turković (Bajić 70), Stanić, Čolić, D Sadiković (Svraka 85), Zeljković, Bogdanović, Tomić, Hasanović (Jamak 59). Coach: Admir Adžem (BIH)
A 1-0 D Sadiković (57)
Antolović, Kvesić, Bučan (Bajić 56), Turković, Stanić, Čolić (Memija 72), D Sadiković, Zeljković (Jamak 46), Bogdanović, Tomić, Hasanović. Coach: Admir Adžem (BIH)

Second qualifying round - FK Metalurg Skopje (MKD)

A 0-0
Antolović, Kvesić, Kosorić, Bučan, Turković (Bajić 72), Stanić (Nuspahić 53), Čolić, D Sadiković, Bogdanović, Tomić (Jamak 63), Hasanović. Coach: Admir Adžem (BIH)
H 2-2 Dodevski (16og), Bajić (54)
Antolović, Nuspahić (Bučan 64), Kvesić, Kosorić, Bajić (Turković 82), Stanić, Čolić, D Sadiković (Hasanović 77), Bogdanović, Jamak, Tomić. Coach: Admir Adžem (BIH)

DOMESTIC LEAGUE CLUB-BY-CLUB

FK Borac Banja Luka

1926 • Gradski (10,000) • fkborac.net
Major honours
Bosnian-Herzegovinian League (1) 2011; Yugoslav Cup (1) 1988; Bosnian-Herzegovinian Cup (1) 2010
Coach: Vinko Marinović; (25/03/15) Vlado Jagodić

2014
02/08	a	Mladost	L	0-2	
10/08	h	Sarajevo	L	1-3	Stokić
16/08	a	Travnik	W	2-1	Stokić, Kostić
23/08	h	Čelik	W	1-0	Subić
27/08	a	Olimpic	L	1-4	Stokić
30/08	h	Široki Brijeg	D	1-1	Grujić
14/09	a	Slavija	W	1-0	og (Hodžurda)
21/09	h	Zrinjski	W	1-0	Subić
27/09	a	Radnik	W	1-0	Jović
05/10	h	Željezničar	W	1-0	Stokić
18/10	a	Vitez	D	1-1	Ilić
26/10	h	Sloboda	W	1-0	Stokić
01/11	a	Zvijezda	L	0-2	
08/11	a	Drina	D	0-0	
22/11	h	Velež	W	2-1	Stokić, Grujić
2015					
28/02	h	Mladost	W	2-0	Jović, Subić
14/03	a	Sarajevo	D	0-0	
22/03	h	Travnik	W	1-0	Jović
03/04	a	Čelik	D	1-1	Stokić
08/04	h	Olimpic	L	0-1	
11/04	a	Široki Brijeg	D	0-0	
18/04	h	Slavija	W	2-0	Stokić, Subić
22/04	a	Zrinjski	L	0-2	
25/04	h	Radnik	D	1-1	Koljić
02/05	a	Željezničar	L	0-1	
09/05	h	Vitez	W	2-1	Runić, Koljić
13/05	a	Sloboda	L	0-2	
16/05	h	Zvijezda	W	1-0	Stokić (p)
23/05	h	Drina	W	2-1	Stokić, Predragović
30/05	a	Velež	L	0-1	

Name	Nat	DoB	Pos	Aps	(s)	Gls
Asmir Avdukić		13/05/81	G	27		
Srdjan Bečelić	SRB	08/06/92	D	26	(1)	
Ilija Danilović		18/06/97	M	2		
Darko Djajić		30/08/92	D	6		
Nikola Dujaković		27/06/96	M		(2)	
Siniša Dujaković		22/11/91	M	1	(11)	
Stefan Dujaković		04/08/92	M	1	(5)	
Luka Gajić	CRO	17/05/94	G	1		
Vladan Grujić		17/05/81	M	16	(8)	2
Petar Ilić	SRB	28/04/93	A	18	(4)	1
Marko Jevtić	SRB	21/05/82	D	21	(1)	
Toni Jović	CRO	02/09/92	D	18	(8)	3
Elvir Koljić	SVN	08/07/95	A	8	(7)	2
Ivan Kostić	SRB	24/06/89	M	22		1
Bojan Kremenović		17/01/97	A		(1)	
Bojan Macanović		18/03/89	M		(1)	
Aleksandar Malbašić		08/09/92	M	1	(2)	
Ognjen Petrović		08/12/97	M	1		
Borislav Pilipović		25/03/84	D	20	(4)	
Fedor Predragović		08/04/95	M	10	(10)	1
Uglješa Radinović	SRB	25/08/93	D	18	(4)	
Ajdin Redžić	SVN	05/12/89	A	14		
Nebojša Runić		18/09/92	D	11		1
Branislav Ružić		02/04/89	G	2		
Mihajlo Savanović		02/07/94	A	1	(8)	
Stefan Savić		09/01/95	M	1	(3)	
Dušan Stevandić		06/10/90	M		(1)	
Joco Stokić		07/04/87	M	26		10
Aleksandar Subić		27/09/93	D	26		4
Miloš Žeravica	SRB	22/07/88	M	19	(1)	
Mladen Žižović		27/12/80	M	13		

NK Čelik Zenica

1945 • Bilino Polje (13,000) • nkcelik.ba
Coach: Nizah Nukić;
(27/09/14) (Elvedin Beganović);
(03/10/14) Milomir Odović;
(06/01/14) (Elvedin Beganović);
(31/01/15) Boris Pavić (CRO)

2014
02/08	h	Vitez	D	0-0	
09/08	a	Sloboda	L	0-1	
16/08	h	Zvijezda	D	1-1	Kojić
23/08	a	Borac	L	0-1	
27/08	h	Velež	D	1-1	Pezer
30/08	a	Mladost	W	2-1	Kojić, Anel Dedić
13/09	h	Sarajevo	L	0-1	Kojić
20/09	a	Travnik	L	0-1	
27/09	h	Drina	L	0-1	
05/10	h	Olimpic	L	0-1	
19/10	a	Široki Brijeg	L	2-7	Djelmić, og (Marković)
25/10	h	Slavija	W	3-2	Kojić, Popović, Simić
01/11	a	Zrinjski	D	1-1	Popović
08/11	h	Radnik	W	2-1	Alen Dedić, Duvnjak
23/11	a	Željezničar	L	1-2	Kojić

2015
28/02	a	Vitez	L	0-1	
14/03	h	Sloboda	D	2-2	Selimović, Karić
22/03	a	Zvijezda	W	2-0	Bajraktarević, Popović
03/04	h	Borac	D	1-1	Selimović
08/04	a	Velež	L	0-1	
11/04	h	Mladost	W	1-0	Anel Dedić
17/04	a	Sarajevo	D	1-1	Simić
22/04	h	Travnik	W	1-0	Popović
25/04	a	Drina	W	1-0	Selimović
02/05	h	Olimpic	W	2-1	Bajraktarević, Anel Dedić
09/05	h	Široki Brijeg	W	5-3	Popović, Bajraktarević, Anel Dedić 2, Karić
13/05	a	Slavija	W	1-0	Popović
16/05	h	Zrinjski	D	0-0	
23/05	a	Radnik	D	2-2	Anel Dedić 2
30/05	h	Željezničar	D	1-1	Zec

Name	Nat	DoB	Pos	Aps	(s)	Gls
Adi Adilović		20/02/83	G	21		
Namir Alispahić		16/04/95	A	4	(4)	
Semir Bajraktarević		14/10/87	M	12	(1)	3
Petar Bašić	CRO	24/07/84	M	11		
Semir Bukvić		21/05/91	G	1		
Dženan Bureković		29/05/95	M	25	(1)	
Alen Dedić		11/05/85	M	15	(1)	1
Anel Dedić		02/05/91	M	21	(4)	7
Ognjen Djelmić		18/06/88	M	8		1
Anes Duraković		22/12/96	M		(1)	
Armin Duvnjak		15/02/97	M	1	(5)	1
Renato Gojković		10/09/95	D	21		
Vladimir Grahovac		12/01/95	M	1	(6)	
Haris Hećo		20/05/87	M	3	(9)	
Salih Hinović		09/02/90	G	8	(1)	
Emir Jusić		13/06/86	D	14		
Mahir Karić		14/12/86	M	13		2
Eldar Kavazović		13/09/91	D	2	(7)	
Zlatko Kazazić		10/02/89	D	14	(7)	
Jovo Kojić		08/08/88	D	27		5
Darko Mišić	CRO	27/07/91	D	13		
Amer Osmanagić		07/05/89	A	7	(5)	
Nebojša Pejić		05/01/88	M		(1)	
Semir Pezer		18/08/92	A	22	(3)	1
Marin Popović		18/08/94	M	17	(7)	6
Ognjen Radulović		27/01/91	A	2	(3)	
Haris Ribić		15/02/95	A	2	(5)	
Vernes Selimović		08/05/83	M	23	(1)	3
Edib Sikira		30/09/95	A		(1)	
Nikola Simić	SRB	30/07/81	M	22	(4)	2
Ante Vukušić	CRO	09/05/84	D	3		
Asim Zec		23/01/94	A	1	(8)	1

FK Drina Zvornik

1945 • Gradski (5,000) • no website
Coach: Dragan Mičić;
(22/03/15) Srdjan Bajić

2014
02/08	a	Velež	L	0-1	
09/08	h	Zrinjski	L	1-2	Ivanović
16/08	a	Mladost	W	2-0	Rustemović, Filipović
23/08	h	Radnik	W	1-0	Rustemović
30/08	h	Željezničar	L	1-2	Kostić
13/09	a	Travnik	D	2-2	Kostić, Filipović
20/09	h	Vitez	D	0-0	
24/09	a	Sarajevo	L	0-2	
27/09	a	Čelik	W	1-0	Rustemović
05/10	h	Sloboda	D	0-0	
18/10	h	Olimpic	L	2-5	Rustemović (p), Filipović
25/10	h	Zvijezda	D	1-1	Memović
02/11	a	Široki Brijeg	L	1-3	Kostić
08/11	h	Borac	D	0-0	
23/11	a	Slavija	L	1-6	Filipović

2015
28/02	h	Velež	W	3-1	Nedeljković, Ilić, Filipović
15/03	a	Zrinjski	D	1-1	Mrkaić
21/03	h	Mladost	L	0-2	
04/04	a	Radnik	L	0-1	
08/04	h	Sarajevo	D	0-0	
11/04	a	Željezničar	L	0-2	
18/04	h	Travnik	W	3-0	Ilić, Filipović 2 (1p)
22/04	a	Vitez	L	0-1	
25/04	h	Čelik	L	0-1	
02/05	a	Sloboda	L	0-2	
09/05	h	Olimpic	W	3-0	Filipović, Ilić, Nedeljković
13/05	a	Zvijezda	L	1-2	Memović
16/05	h	Široki Brijeg	D	1-1	Filipović (p)
23/05	a	Borac	L	1-2	Mrkaić
30/05	h	Slavija	D	0-0	

Name	Nat	DoB	Pos	Aps	(s)	Gls
Dejan Blagojević		18/01/90	D	11		
Darko Bošković		16/09/87	M	12		
Stefan Čolović	SRB	02/07/94	M	7	(6)	
Slavko Čulibrk	SRB	21/03/86	D	15		
Danijel Čulum		19/08/89	A		(3)	
Boban Djerić		20/10/93	D	17	(9)	
Slobodan Djurić		13/04/92	A	1	(15)	
Filip Erić	SRB	10/10/94	G	1		
Miloš Filipović	SRB	09/05/90	M	23	(1)	9
Aleksandar Ilić		08/04/94	A	21	(5)	3
Vlado Ivanović		24/01/94	D	11	(9)	1
Miloš Jokić		20/04/93	A	5	(8)	
Aleksandar Kikić	SRB	15/03/83	M	27		
Filip Kostić	SRB	08/10/93	A	15		3
Ivan Lazarević		22/01/89	M	28		
Rade Lazić		13/11/91	M	2		
Lee Ki-hyun	KOR	13/04/92	M		(1)	
Goran Maksimović		04/05/80	G	29		
Novica Marković		15/02/94	M		(2)	
Damir Memović	SRB	19/01/89	D	23		2
Nemanja Milenković	SRB	05/01/89	D	1	(2)	
David Milošević		30/12/94	D		(2)	
Vladan Milošević	SRB	05/04/90	D	11	(2)	
Momčilo Mrkaić		21/09/90	A	12		2
Nenad Nedeljković	SRB	18/10/86	A	12		2
Slaviša Radović		10/08/93	M	13		
Edin Rustemović		06/01/93	M	14	(1)	4
Dejan Uzelac	SRB	27/08/93	D	7		
Aleksandar Vasić		04/01/85	A		(1)	
Radovan Vasić		27/07/93	M	14	(15)	

FK Mladost Velika Obarska

1948 • Gradski, Bijeljina (4,000); Novi Gradski, Ugljevik (3,000) • no website
Coach: Dušan Jevrić (MNE);
(12/01/15) Slavoljub Bubanja (MNE)

2014
02/08	h	Borac	W	2-0	Dabić 2
09/08	a	Velež	D	0-0	
16/08	h	Drina	L	0-2	
24/08	h	Sarajevo	D	1-1	Komarčević
27/08	a	Travnik	L	0-1	
30/08	h	Čelik	L	1-2	Vidić
12/09	a	Olimpic	L	0-3	
20/09	h	Široki Brijeg	L	0-2	
28/09	a	Slavija	D	0-0	
05/10	h	Zrinjski	L	0-2	
18/10	a	Radnik	L	1-3	Komarčević
26/10	h	Željezničar	L	0-3	
01/11	a	Vitez	L	0-1	
08/11	h	Sloboda	W	1-0	Komarčević
22/11	a	Zvijezda	L	1-3	Mujezinović

2015
28/02	a	Borac	L	0-2	
14/03	h	Velež	D	0-0	
21/03	a	Drina	W	2-0	Perić, Komarčević
04/04	a	Sarajevo	L	0-4	
08/04	h	Travnik	W	2-1	D Marković, Mazić
11/04	a	Čelik	L	0-1	
18/04	h	Olimpic	D	0-0	
22/04	a	Široki Brijeg	L	0-2	
26/04	h	Slavija	W	2-1	D Marković, Cicmil
03/05	a	Zrinjski	D	0-0	
10/05	h	Radnik	D	1-1	Ibrić-Yüksel
13/05	a	Željezničar	L	0-4	
16/05	h	Vitez	W	1-0	D Marković
23/05	a	Sloboda	L	2-3	og (Mehmedagić), Komarčević
30/05	a	Zvijezda	D	1-1	Trifković

Name	Nat	DoB	Pos	Aps	(s)	Gls
Dragan Andjelic		03/02/80	M		(1)	
Davor Arnautović		03/09/91	D		(6)	
Mikica Blagojević		24/01/95	M	4	(12)	
Miloš Budaković	SRB	10/07/91	G	12		
Stefan Cicmil	MNE	16/08/90	D	13		1
Borislav Cicović		03/02/94	M	1		
Aleksandar Čovin	SRB	23/11/88	M	5		
Anel Ćurić		28/07/88	M	9	(3)	
Nemanja Dabić	SRB	22/09/85	D	23	(1)	2
Zoran Djurić	SRB	22/10/93	M	7	(1)	
Miloš Djurković		23/09/87	G	3		
Semir Hadžibulić		17/07/86	M	13		
Dušan Hodžić	SRB	31/10/93	D	14		
Damir Ibrić-Yüksel		30/03/84	M	6	(7)	1
Miroslav Jevtić		10/02/81	M	24	(1)	
Dragiša Komarčević		20/12/87	M	25		5
Bojan Marković		11/11/85	M	4		
Darko Marković	MNE	15/05/87	M	12		3
Nikola Mazić		23/11/86	M	17	(5)	1
Igor Mišan		05/05/90	A	11	(3)	
Saša Mišić	SRB	24/08/87	G	14		
Velibor Mitrović	CRO	15/11/91	M		(1)	
Mithad Mujezinović		02/02/93	M		(4)	1
Perica Novaković		02/01/87	G	1		
Radoslav Novaković		14/09/94	A		(1)	
Milan Perić	SRB	16/04/86	M	12		1
Anel Ramić		05/04/87	D	13		
Dragan Ristić		27/02/82	A	14	(1)	
Srđan Savić		27/09/85	M	7	(5)	
Duško Stajić		11/07/82	A	4	(2)	
Perica Trifković		17/01/79	D	16	(5)	1
Aleksandar Vasić		04/01/85	M	14	(1)	
Lazar Vidić	SRB	10/07/89	A	4	(9)	1
Filip Vujić	SRB	07/07/88	M		(10)	
Danilo Vuković	MNE	01/04/89	D	10	(2)	
Dušan Zelić	SRB	25/07/88	M	18		

FK Olimpic Sarajevo

1993 • Otoka (3,500) • olimpic.ba
Major honours
Bosnian-Herzegovinian Cup (1) 2015
Coach: Mirza Varešanović

2014

02/08	h	Željezničar	L	0-3	
09/08	a	Vitez	W	1-0	Subašić
16/08	h	Sloboda	W	1-0	Gojak
23/08	a	Drina	D	2-2	Regoje, Nukić
27/08	h	Borac	W	4-1	D Brković, Pandža, Hugo Souza, Nukić
30/08	a	Velež	D	1-1	og (Pejić)
12/09	h	Mladost	W	3-0	D Brković, Smajić, Pandža
20/09	a	Sarajevo	L	2-4	Muharemović, D Brković
27/09	h	Travnik	W	3-0	Handžić, D Brković 2
05/10	a	Čelik	W	1-0	Pandža
18/10	h	Drina	W	5-2	Smajić, Muharemović 3 (1p), Gojak
25/10	h	Široki Brijeg	D	0-0	
01/11	a	Slavija	W	3-1	Pandža 2, Muharemović
09/11	h	Zrinjski	L	0-1	
22/11	a	Radnik	D	2-2	Pandža 2

2015

01/03	a	Željezničar	L	0-3	
14/03	h	Vitez	W	2-0	Stefan, Bogičević
21/03	a	Sloboda	L	1-2	Stefan
04/04	a	Zvijezda	W	3-0	Smajić, Regoje, Stefan
08/04	a	Borac	W	1-0	Jusufović
11/04	h	Velež	W	1-0	Muharemović
18/04	a	Mladost	D	0-0	
22/04	h	Sarajevo	L	0-1	
26/04	a	Travnik	D	0-0	
02/05	h	Čelik	L	1-2	D Brković
09/05	a	Drina Zvornik	L	0-3	
13/05	h	Široki Brijeg	W	1-1	Stefan
16/05	h	Slavija	W	1-0	Pandža
23/05	a	Zrinjski	L	0-2	
30/05	h	Radnik	L	2-3	Smajić, og (Jakovljević)

Name	Nat	DoB	Pos	Aps	(s)	Gls
Jadranko Bogičević		11/03/83	D	24		1
Danijel Brković		03/06/91	A	21	(5)	6
Faruk Brković		18/07/92	M	1	(1)	
Cristiano	POR	05/10/90	M	8	(2)	
Denis Čomor		03/01/90	D	10	(12)	
Filip Gligorov	MKD	31/07/93	D	21	(1)	
Amer Gojak		13/02/97	M	6	(4)	2
Dino Hamzić		22/01/88	G	11		
Kenan Handžić		23/01/91	M	16	(4)	1
Hugo Souza	BRA	14/05/89	M	11	(4)	1
Adin Husić		14/04/96	G	1		
Aldin Husović		20/06/95	M		(1)	
Ermin Imamović		30/04/95	D	8	(4)	
Ervin Jusufović		07/05/95	M	8	(4)	1
Alem Merajić		04/02/94	M	21		
Veldin Muharemović		05/12/84	M	18	(1)	6
Aris Nukić		21/12/93	A	5	(13)	2
Amer Osmanagić		07/05/89	M	11	(1)	
Senedin Oštraković		13/04/87	G	12		
Dalibor Pandža		23/03/91	A	15	(9)	8
Muhamed Plakalo		07/07/93	D	1	(1)	
Bojan Regoje		02/12/82	D	23	(1)	2
Mirza Rizvanović		27/09/86	D	2	(1)	
Kemal Salihagić		21/02/97	A	2	(3)	
Sulejman Smajić		13/08/84	M	25		4
Stefan	BRA	16/04/88	M	11	(1)	4
Muhamed Subašić		19/03/88	D	15		1
Safet Šivšić		16/02/93	M	12	(8)	
Stefan Tomović		15/01/91	G	6	(1)	
Mak Varešanović		28/07/98	M	5	(1)	

FK Radnik Bijeljina

1945 • Gradski (4,000); Novi Gradski, Ugljevik (3,000) • no website
Coach: Srdjan Bajić;
(01/09/14) Slavko Petrović (SRB)

2014

03/08	a	Široki Brijeg	L	0-2	
10/08	h	Slavija	D	0-0	
16/08	a	Zrinjski	L	0-2	
23/08	a	Drina	L	0-1	
27/08	h	Željezničar	L	1-3	Memišević
30/08	a	Vitez	L	0-1	
13/09	h	Sloboda	W	2-0	Milović, Obradović
20/09	a	Zvijezda	D	1-1	Obradović
27/09	h	Borac	L	0-1	
05/10	a	Velež	L	0-3	
18/10	h	Mladost	W	3-1	Obradović 2, Lazić
25/10	a	Sarajevo	L	0-5	
01/11	a	Travnik	D	1-1	Vučinić
08/11	h	Čelik	L	1-2	Antić
22/11	h	Olimpic	D	2-2	Ćosović, Hasanović

2015

28/02	h	Široki Brijeg	L	1-2	Galešić
15/03	a	Slavija	W	4-0	Žižović (p), Antić, Beširević, Seratlić
22/03	h	Zrinjski	D	0-0	
04/04	h	Drina	W	1-0	Lazić
08/04	a	Željezničar	D	1-1	Vasić
12/04	h	Vitez	W	2-0	Antić, Ostojić
18/04	a	Sloboda	D	1-1	Antić
22/04	h	Zvijezda	L	0-1	
25/04	a	Borac	D	1-1	Obradović
03/05	h	Velež	W	1-0	Mašić
10/05	a	Mladost	D	1-1	Obradović
13/05	h	Sarajevo	L	0-2	
16/05	a	Travnik	L	0-1	
23/05	a	Čelik	D	2-2	Obradović, Žižović
30/05	a	Olimpic	W	3-2	Maksimović, Memišević, Mašić

Name	Nat	DoB	Pos	Aps	(s)	Gls
Sladjan Antić	SRB	11/01/92	D	15	(12)	4
Branko Bajić		04/06/98	M		(1)	
Siniša Bajić		24/02/94	M		(6)	
Milan Basrak	SRB	24/12/94	A	5	(6)	
Dino Beširević		31/01/94	M	12	(1)	1
Boriša Bodiroga		13/12/88	G	28		
Zoran Brković		02/05/84	D	3	(1)	
Aleksandar Ćosović		19/10/92	M	10	(1)	1
Marko Despotović		22/10/98	D		(1)	
Dragan Djordjić		20/04/89	G	2		
Slobodan Djurdjić		14/12/95	D	3		
Dragan Došlo		27/10/96	A	1	(2)	
Aleksandar Furtula		05/06/96	A		(1)	
Ranko Galešić		21/01/89	D	17		1
Ademin Hadžić		25/01/96	M	1	(12)	
Mirza Hasanović		05/01/88	M	14		1
Ivan Jakovljević	SRB	26/05/89	D	14		
Dalibor Jovanović		18/01/96	D		(1)	
Taulant Kadrija	SVN	18/05/93	D	2		
Željko Krsmanović		11/12/90	D	12	(8)	
Petar Kunić		15/07/93	A	2	(3)	
Milivoje Lazić		19/09/92	M	24	(1)	2
Marko Lukić		10/08/91	D	1	(2)	
Dejan Maksimović		11/10/95	D	4	(3)	1
Eldin Mašić		02/01/87	M	26		2
Samir Memišević		13/08/93	M	27		2
Nemanja Milinković		07/06/97	M		(1)	
Djoko Milović		16/09/92	D	20	(3)	1
Marko Obradović	MNE	30/06/91	A	19		7
Stanko Ostojić	SRB	18/06/91	M	26		1
Ermin Seratlić	MNE	21/09/90	M	4	(8)	1
Aleksandar Vasić		04/01/85	M	5	(4)	1
Milan Vignjević	SRB	30/03/89	M		(1)	
Jovan Vučinić	MNE	20/01/92	A	19	(6)	1
Mladen Žižović		27/12/80	M	14		2

FK Sarajevo

1946 • Olimpijski Asim Ferhatović Hase (34,600) • fcsarajevo.ba
Major honours
Yugoslav League (2) 1967, 1985; Bosnian-Herzegovinian League (2) 2007, 2015; Bosnian-Herzegovinian Cup (4) 1998, 2002, 2005, 2014
Coach: Dženan Uščuplić;
(25/09/14) (Esad Selimović);
(30/09/14) Meho Kodro;
(20/04/15) Dženan Uščuplić

2014

03/08	h	Zvijezda	W	3-0	(w/o)
10/08	a	Borac	W	3-1	Duljević, Bilbija, Todorović
16/08	h	Velež	D	1-1	Dupovac
24/08	a	Mladost	D	1-1	Stojčev
31/08	h	Travnik	D	2-2	Puzigaća, Velkoski
13/09	a	Čelik	D	1-1	Velkoski
20/09	h	Olimpic	W	4-2	Puzigaća 2, Duljević, Radovac
24/09	h	Drina	W	2-0	Puzigaća, Velkoski
28/09	a	Široki Brijeg	L	0-1	
05/10	h	Slavija	W	3-0	Okić, Dupovac, Puzigaća (p)
18/10	a	Zrinjski	D	1-1	Okić
25/10	h	Radnik	W	5-0	Okić 2, Velkoski 2, Bilbija
02/11	a	Željezničar	W	2-1	Velkoski, Duljević
08/11	h	Vitez	W	1-0	Puzigaća (p)
23/11	a	Sloboda	W	2-0	Puzigaća (p), Okić

2015

28/02	a	Zvijezda	W	3-0	Bekić, Benko 2
14/03	h	Borac	D	0-0	
21/03	a	Velež	L	0-2	
04/04	h	Mladost	W	4-0	Bilbija, Benko, Radovac, Stojčev
08/04	a	Drina	D	0-0	
11/04	a	Travnik	W	2-0	Puzigaća (p), Benko
17/04	h	Čelik	D	1-1	Benko
22/04	a	Olimpic	W	1-0	Benko
03/05	a	Slavija	W	3-2	Benko, Velkoski, Stojčev
09/05	h	Zrinjski	W	1-0	Benko
13/05	h	Radnik	W	2-0	Kallasi, Velkoski
16/05	h	Željezničar	D	0-0	
23/05	a	Vitez	W	3-0	Velkoski, Puzigaća (p), Bekić
30/05	h	Sloboda	W	3-1	Benko, Velkoski, Bilbija

Name	Nat	DoB	Pos	Aps	(s)	Gls
Mehmed Alispahić		24/11/87	A	1	(7)	
Dejan Bandović		11/06/83	G	15		
Mario Barić	CRO	15/04/85	D	13		
Amer Bekić		05/08/92	A	8	(9)	2
Leon Benko	CRO	11/11/83	A	14		9
Džemal Berberović		05/11/81	D	20	(2)	
Nemanja Bilbija		02/11/90	A	16	(4)	4
Gojko Cimirot		19/12/92	M	24	(2)	
Matej Delač	CRO	20/08/92	G	14		
Haris Duljević		16/11/93	M	15	(9)	3
Amer Dupovac		30/11/92	D	13		2
Faris Handžić		27/05/95	M		(2)	
Ahmad Kallasi	SYR	18/07/90	M	10		1
Miroljub Kostić	SRB	05/06/88	M	3	(1)	
Adnan Kovačević		09/09/93	D	4	(1)	
Marko Mihojević		21/04/96	D	4	(1)	
Šefko Okić	CRO	26/07/88	A	13	(7)	5
Radoš Protić	SRB	31/01/87	D	4	(4)	
Dario Purić		18/05/86	M	2	(3)	
Bojan Puzigaća		10/05/85	D	25	(1)	9
Samir Radovac		25/01/96	M	19	(4)	2
Edin Rustemović		06/01/93	M	8	(6)	
Miloš Stojčev	MNE	19/01/97	M	23	(5)	3
Ivan Tatomirović	SRB	11/09/89	D	27		
Ognjen Todorović		24/03/89	M	3	(6)	1
Krste Velkoski	MKD	20/02/88	A	21	(4)	11

BOSNIA & HERZEGOVINA

FK Slavija Sarajevo

1908 • SC Slavija (4,500); Gradski,
Foča (4,000) • fkslavija.com
Major honours
Bosnian-Herzegovinian Cup (1) 2009
**Coach: Dragan Radović;
(14/05/15) Milan Gutović**

2014
02/08	h	Zrinjski	D	0-0
10/08	a	Radnk	D	0-0
17/08	h	Željezničar	D	1-1	Kokot
23/08	a	Vltez	W	5 0	Kokot, Salković 2, Ivanović, Govedarica
27/08	h	Sloboda	W	2-1	Vejnović, Prodanović
30/08	a	Zvijezda	W	3-1	Govedarica, Kokot, Oglečevac
14/09	h	Borac	L	0-1	
20/09	a	Velež	L	0-2	
28/09	h	Mladost	D	0-0	
05/10	a	Sarajevo	L	0-3	
19/10	h	Travnik	W	1-0	Vejnović
25/10	a	Čelik	L	2-3	Popović, Kokot (p)
01/11	h	Olimpic	L	1-3	Lemez
08/11	a	Široki Brijeg	L	0-2	
23/11	h	Drina	W	6-1	Lemez, Salković, Popović, Lambulić 2, Kokot

2015
01/03	a	Zrinjski	L	0-2	
15/03	h	Radnik	L	0-4	
22/03	a	Željezničar	L	1-2	Kartal
04/04	h	Vitez	W	1-0	og (Kapetan)
08/04	a	Sloboda	L	0-4	
11/04	h	Zvijezda	W	2-1	Karić, Rovčanin
18/04	a	Borac	L	0-2	
22/04	h	Velež	D	1-1	Karić
26/04	a	Mladost	L	1-2	Karić
03/05	h	Sarajevo	L	2-3	Hodžurda, Radosavljević
09/05	a	Travnik	L	0-1	
13/05	h	Čelik	L	0-1	
16/05	a	Olimpic	L	0-1	
23/05	h	Široki Brijeg	D	1-1	Karić (p)
30/05	a	Drina	D	0-0	

Name	Nat	DoB	Pos	Aps	(s)	Gls
Semir Djip		23/06/92	A		(4)	
Miljan Govedarica		26/05/94	M	24		2
Emir Hodžurda		12/11/90	D	24	(2)	1
Milutin Ivanović	SRB	30/10/90	A	8	(2)	1
Mahir Karić		05/03/92	M	25	(1)	4
Nemanja Kartal	MNE	17/07/94	D	10	(1)	1
Zoran Kokot		28/06/85	A	14		5
Miloš Kubura		22/05/94	G	2	(1)	
Igor Lambulić	MNE	21/08/88	A	9	(8)	2
Mladen Lemez		25/01/90	A	9		2
Sedin Ljuca		21/03/96	A		(1)	
Mladen Lučić		06/07/85	G	28		
Petar Mitić	SRB	03/06/90	M	7	(2)	
Nedin Oglečevac		07/04/91	A	13	(12)	1
Damir Osmanković		12/09/93	D	9	(4)	
Goran Popović		28/04/89	D	27		2
Nemanja Prodanović		12/03/92	M	5	(7)	1
Aleksandar Pušara		29/11/95	M	2	(1)	
Duško Radosavljević	SRB	16/06/88	M	18		1
Nikola Radović		27/06/94	M		(10)	
Damir Rovčanin		12/03/88	A	12		1
Anel Salković		25/03/93	M	22	(2)	3
Marko Simović		13/07/96	M	2	(8)	
Armin Smječanin		21/03/95	M		(2)	
Vedad Šabanović		22/10/89	D	19		
Ranko Torbica	SRB	22/01/94	M	3	(6)	
Nemanja Vejnović		04/04/92	D	21	(2)	2
Emir Zeba		10/06/89	A	17	(6)	

FK Sloboda Tuzla

1919 • Tušanj (8,000) • fksloboda.ba
**Coach: Denis Sadiković;
(28/09/14) Alfredo Casimiro (POR);
(31/12/14) Husref Musemić**

2014
02/08	a	Travnik	W	3-0	Bajraktarević, Radovanović, J Mujkić
09/08	h	Čelik	W	1-0	Radovanović
16/08	a	Olimpic	L	0-1	
23/08	h	Široki Brijeg	L	0-1	
27/08	a	Slavija	L	1-2	J Mujkić
30/08	h	Zrlnjski	W	1 0	Radovanović
13/09	a	Radnik	L	0-2	
20/09	h	Željezničar	L	1-2	J Mujkić
27/09	a	Vitez	L	1-3	Sarić
05/10	a	Drina	D	0-0	
18/10	h	Zvijezda	D	0-0	
26/10	a	Borac	L	0-1	
01/11	h	Velež	D	1-1	Selamović
08/11	a	Mladost	L	0-1	
23/11	h	Sarajevo	L	0-2	

2015
28/02	h	Travnik	W	4-0	Bekić, Ahmetović, Mujić 2
14/03	a	Čelik	D	2-2	Moranjkić, Krpić
21/03	h	Olimpic	W	2-1	Mujić, Zeba (p)
04/04	a	Široki Brijeg	L	0-1	
08/04	h	Slavija	W	4-0	Zeba 2 (2p), Krpić, Music
11/04	a	Zrinjski	L	0-1	
18/04	h	Radnik	D	1-1	Mehidić
22/04	a	Željezničar	D	1-1	Zeba
25/04	h	Vitez	W	1-0	Mujić
02/05	a	Drina	W	2-0	Kiso, Zeba
09/05	h	Zvijezda	D	0-0	
13/05	h	Borac	W	2-0	Krpić, Mujić
16/05	a	Velež	W	1-0	Sarić (p)
23/05	h	Mladost	W	3-2	Mehidić, Ahmetović 2
30/05	a	Sarajevo	L	1-3	Zeba

Name	Nat	DoB	Pos	Aps	(s)	Gls
Mersudin Ahmetović		19/03/85	A	2	(9)	3
Semir Bajraktarević		14/10/87	M	8	(4)	1
Almir Bekić		01/06/89	M	13		1
Stefan Čolović		16/04/94	M	5	(6)	
Adin Džafić		21/05/89	A	4	(4)	
Samir Efendić		10/05/91	M	23		
Irfan Fejzić		01/07/86	G	13		
Almir Halilović		30/01/85	M	1	(2)	
Perica Ivetić		28/11/86	M	13	(1)	
Emilko Janković		27/03/84	D	8	(1)	
Nenad Kiso		30/04/89	D	20		1
Sulejman Krpić		01/01/91	A	11	(2)	3
Elmir Kuduzović		28/02/85	D	8	(2)	
Mirhad Mehanović		02/07/91	M	3		
Damir Mehidić		07/01/92	M	17	(8)	2
Haris Mehmedagić		29/03/88	D	13	(1)	
Darko Mitrović		18/07/85	D	11		
Jasmin Moranjkić		11/10/83	D	6		1
Muhamed Mujić		26/01/91	A	24	(2)	5
Adnan Mujkić		27/10/95	D		(3)	
Jasmin Mujkić		17/02/89	A	5	(10)	3
Mirza Musić		03/07/90	M	2	(9)	1
Muhamed Omić		04/04/85	D	14		
Kenan Pirić		07/07/94	G	17		
Omar Pršeš		07/05/95	M	7	(7)	
Igor Radovanović		02/08/85	A	7		3
Adnan Salihović		18/10/82	D	16	(1)	
Elvis Sarić	CRO	21/07/90	M	28		2
Mirnes Selamović		21/07/90	M	2	(8)	1
Adnan Šečerović		01/12/91	A	6	(4)	
Darko Todorović		05/05/97	M		(1)	
Zajko Zeba		22/05/83	M	14		6
Dilaver Zrnanović		17/11/84	D	9	(2)	

NK Široki Brijeg

1948 • Pecara (7,000) • nk-sirokibrijeg.com
Major honours
*Bosnian-Herzegovinian League (2) 2004, 2006;
Bosnian-Herzegovinian Cup (2) 2007, 2013*
**Coach: Slaven Musa;
(19/04/15) Blaž Slišković**

2014
03/08	h	Radnik	W	2-0	Zakarić 2
10/08	a	Željezničar	D	1-1	Wagner
17/08	h	Vitez	W	2-1	Kožulj, Zakarić
23/08	a	Sloboda	W	1-0	Wagner
27/08	h	Zvijezda	W	4-2	Kožulj, Wagner 2, Ćorić
30/08	a	Borac	D	1-1	Brekalu
14/09	h	Velež	W	2-0	Pehar, Kožulj
20/09	a	Mladost	W	2-0	Čorluka, Wagner
28/09	h	Sarajevo	W	1-0	Buhač
06/10	a	Travnik	L	1-2	Ivanković
19/10	h	Čelik	W	7-2	Čorluka 2, Kožulj, Mihaljević 2, Ćorić, Ivanković
25/10	a	Olimpic	D	0-0	
02/11	h	Drina	W	3-1	Wagner 2, Čorluka
08/11	h	Slavija	W	2-0	Buhač, Pandža
22/11	a	Zrinjski	D	0-0	

2015
28/02	a	Radnik	W	2-1	Wagner, Peko
15/03	h	Željezničar	D	0-0	
21/03	a	Vitez	W	3-1	Wagner 3
04/04	h	Sloboda	W	1-0	Pandža
08/04	a	Zvijezda	D	0-0	
11/04	h	Borac	D	0-0	
18/04	a	Velež	L	0-1	
22/04	h	Mladost	W	2-0	Ivanković (p), Kožulj
26/04	a	Sarajevo	L	0-1	
03/05	h	Travnik	W	2-0	Wagner, Plazonjić
09/05	a	Čelik	L	3-5	Kresinger, Menalo, Peko
13/05	h	Olimpic	D	1-1	Wagner
16/05	a	Drina	D	1-1	Menalo
23/05	a	Slavija	D	1-1	Menalo
30/05	h	Zrinjski	D	1-1	Zakarić

Name	Nat	DoB	Pos	Aps	(s)	Gls
Josip Barišić		12/08/83	D	10	(12)	
Slavko Brekalo		25/02/90	D	23		1
Ivan Buhač		15/12/94	A	8	(9)	2
Dino Ćorić		30/06/90	D	26	(1)	2
Josip Čorluka		03/03/95	D	19	(2)	4
Damir Džidić		15/02/87	D	3		
Ivica Džidić		08/02/84	D	5	(2)	
Jure Ivanković		15/11/85	M	5	(17)	3
Matej Karačić		04/08/94	M	6	(3)	
Danijel Kožul		01/08/88	M	2	(4)	
Zvonimir Kožulj		15/11/93	M	24	(1)	5
Dino Kresinger	CRO	20/03/82	A	8	(1)	1
Davor Landeka		18/09/84	M	16	(8)	
Neven Laštro	CRO	01/10/88	M	7		
Mario Ljubić		05/03/95	M	1	(4)	
Mirko Marić		16/05/95	M	2		
Stipo Marković		03/12/93	D	26		
Luka Menalo		22/07/96	M	2	(2)	3
Filip Mihaljević	CRO	09/05/92	A	7		2
Boris Pandža		15/12/86	D	17		2
Mate Pehar		25/02/88	M	6	(1)	1
Ivan Peko		05/01/90	A	10	(11)	2
Zoran Plazonjić	CRO	01/02/89	M	12	(7)	1
Antonio Soldo		12/01/88	G	30		
Taianan	BRA	13/03/87	M	1	(1)	
Wagner	BRA	01/01/78	M	27	(1)	13
Goran Zakarić		07/11/92	M	27	(1)	4

NK Travnik

1922 • Pirota (3,000) • no website
**Coach: Osman Bajrić;
(24/08/14) (Selver Lihovac);
(06/09/14) Husnija Arapović;
(23/04/15) Almir Memić**

2014
02/08	h	Sloboda	L	0-3
09/08	a	Zvijezda	D	0-0
16/08	h	Borac	L	1-2 *Jusufbašić*
23/08	a	Velež	L	1-2 *Adriano*
27/08	h	Mladost	W	1-0 *Nuhić*
31/08	a	Sarajevo	D	2-2 *Jusufbašić 2*
13/09	h	Drina	D	2-2 *Zajmović, Dudić (p)*
20/09	h	Čelik	W	1-0 *Music*
27/09	a	Olimpic	L	0-3
06/10	h	Široki Brijeg	W	2-1 *Dudić 2*
19/10	a	Slavija	L	0-1
25/10	h	Zrinjski	L	1-3 *Smajić*
01/11	a	Radnik	D	1-1 *Smajić*
08/11	h	Željezničar	D	0-0
23/11	a	Vitez	D	0-0

2015
28/02	a	Sloboda	L	0-4
15/03	h	Zvijezda	W	2-0 *Varupa, Hasečić*
22/03	a	Borac	L	0-1
04/04	a	Velež	W	2-1 *Music 2*
08/04	a	Mladost	L	1-2 *Dudić*
13/04	a	Sarajevo	L	0-2
18/04	a	Drina	L	0-3
22/04	a	Čelik	L	0-1
26/04	h	Olimpic	D	0-0
03/05	a	Široki Brijeg	L	0-2
09/05	h	Slavija	W	2-0 *Dudić 2 (1p)*
13/05	a	Zrinjski	L	0-5
16/05	h	Radnik	W	1-0 *Smajić*
23/05	a	Željezničar	L	0-1
30/05	h	Vitez	W	2-0 *Music, Jašarević*

Name	Nat	DoB	Pos	Aps	(s)	Gls
Adriano	BRA	15/02/92	M	3	(5)	1
Radosav Aleksić	SRB	06/03/86	D	13	(1)	
Mario Brlečić	CRO	10/01/89	M	7	(4)	
Bojan Burazor		25/12/92	A	7	(11)	
Muharem Čivić		04/01/93	D	16	(5)	
Amel Ćurić		22/02/93	M		(1)	
Anel Ćurić		28/07/88	M	13	(1)	
Fedja Dudić		01/02/83	A	28		6
Dženan Durak		04/02/91	M		(1)	
Nijaz Fazlić		08/09/93	D	1	(5)	
Adis Hasečić		11/03/87	A	9	(1)	1
Armin Helvida		20/02/86	D	13		
Irfan Jašarević		24/08/95	M	5	(11)	1
Sabahudin Jusufbašić		13/01/90	A	11	(3)	3
Sanel Kovač		31/10/96	D	21	(3)	
Armin Mahović		28/11/91	A	7	(1)	
Semir Music		20/07/95	M	27	(1)	4
Ajdin Nuhić		01/11/91	M	24	(3)	1
Adis Nurković		28/04/86	G	30		
Nihad Ribić		10/11/81	D	4	(8)	
Elvis Sadiković		29/10/83	D	27		
Irfan Smajić		08/09/90	A	10	(12)	3
Zoran Šupić	SRB	21/07/84	D	6		
Sinbad Terzić		22/02/81	D	21	(4)	
Nermin Varupa		18/04/91	M	18		1
Dženan Zajmović	BEL	11/11/94	A	9	(9)	1

FK Velež

1922 • Vrapčići (3,500) • fkvelez.ba
Major honours
Yugoslav Cup (2) 1981, 1986
**Coach: Nedim Jusufbegović;
(18/03/15) Adnan Dizdarević & Avdo Kalajdžić;
(14/05/15) Džealudin Muharemović**

2014
02/08	h	Drina	W	1-0 *Hajdarević*
09/08	h	Mladost	D	0-0
16/08	a	Sarajevo	D	1-1 *Haurdić*
23/08	a	Travnik	W	2-1 *Popović, Blagojević*
27/08	a	Čelik	D	1-1 *og (Kojić)*
30/08	h	Olimpic	D	1-1 *Janković*
14/09	a	Široki Brijeg	L	0-2
20/09	h	Slavija	W	2-0 *Zolj, Hajdarević*
27/09	a	Zrinjski	L	0-2
05/10	h	Radnik	W	3-0 *Hebibović 2, Popović (p)*
19/10	a	Željezničar	L	0-1
25/10	h	Vitez	W	4-0 *M Ćemalović, Hebibović 2, Merzić*
01/11	a	Sloboda	D	1-1 *Blagojević (p)*
08/11	h	Zvijezda	W	3-2 *Hajdarević, Popović, Pejić*
22/11	a	Borac	L	1-2 *Hajdarević*

2015
28/02	a	Drina	L	1-3 *Hebibović*
14/03	a	Mladost	D	0-0
21/03	h	Sarajevo	W	2-0 *Janković, Haurdić*
04/04	a	Travnik	L	1-2 *Hajdarević*
08/04	h	Čelik	W	1-0 *Haurdić*
11/04	a	Olimpic	L	0-1
18/04	h	Široki Brijeg	W	1-0 *Janković*
22/04	a	Slavija	D	1-1 *Janković*
26/04	h	Zrinjski	D	1-1 *Škahić*
03/05	a	Radnik	L	0-1
09/05	h	Željezničar	L	0-3
13/05	a	Vitez	L	1-3 *Demić*
16/05	h	Sloboda	L	0-1
23/05	a	Zvijezda	L	2-3 *M Ćemalović 2 (1p)*
30/05	h	Borac	W	1-0 *Maletić*

Name	Nat	DoB	Pos	Aps	(s)	Gls
Tomislav Barišić	MNE	25/12/91	D	12	(5)	
Jovan Blagojević	SRB	15/03/88	M	21	(6)	2
Adnan Bobić		04/02/87	G	13		
Dino Ćemalović		16/04/95	A	1	(6)	
Mirza Ćemalović		06/07/93	M	9	(2)	3
Riad Demić		17/11/89	M	5	(2)	1
Dušan Djokić	SRB	05/05/83	G	1		
Andrija Dragojević	MNE	25/12/91	G	16		
Nermin Hadžić		25/09/94	A	1	(3)	
Aldin-Dino Hajdarević		12/10/90	A	17	(10)	5
Anes Haurdić		01/06/90	M	17	(2)	3
Anel Hebibović		07/07/90	M	22	(3)	5
Dušan Hodžić		31/10/90	D	1	(1)	
Sinan Jakupović		27/08/94	M		(1)	
Nikola Janičijević	SRB	25/04/95	M		(3)	
Dejan Janković	SRB	06/01/86	M	20	(2)	4
Mustafa Kodro		29/08/81	M	3	(8)	
Marcel Mace		24/12/91	M		(1)	
Amer Mahinić		02/06/90	M	4		
Darko Maletić		20/10/80	M	23		1
Samir Merzić		29/06/84	D	10		1
Marko Nikolić	SRB	09/06/89	M	24		
Damir Peco		21/07/96	D		(2)	
Matijas Pejić		18/03/88	D	24	(2)	1
Mladen Popović	SRB	29/08/88	A	6	(3)	3
Miloš Reljić	SRB	12/06/89	A	9	(3)	
Ibrahim Škahić		25/10/93	D	16	(2)	1
Asim Škaljić		09/08/81	D	12	(1)	
Tin-Andre Tolić	CRO	16/10/95	M	2	(6)	
Admir Vladavić		29/06/82	M	6	(2)	
Amir Zolj		24/11/89	D	24	(2)	1
Denis Zvonić		08/02/92	D	11	(12)	

NK Vitez

1947 • Gradski (2,000); Kamberovića polje,
Zenica (5,000) • nkvitez.com
**Coach: Husnija Arapović;
(25/08/14) (Veselko Petrović);
(03/09/14) Ante Miše (CRO);
(19/04/15) Valentin Plavčić**

2014
02/08	a	Čelik	D	0-0
09/08	h	Olimpic	L	0-1
17/08	a	Široki Brijeg	L	1-2 *Pinjuh*
23/08	h	Slavija	L	0-5
27/08	a	Zrinjski	L	0-2
30/08	h	Radnik	W	1-0 *Pinjuh*
13/09	a	Željezničar	L	1-2 *M Jurčević (p)*
20/09	a	Drina	D	0-0
27/09	h	Sloboda	W	3-1 *Kapetan, Pinjuh, Smriko*
05/10	a	Zvijezda	D	1-1 *M Jurčević (p)*
18/10	h	Borac	D	1-1 *Smriko*
25/10	a	Velež	L	0-4
01/11	h	Mladost	W	2-0 *Hećo, Kapetan*
08/11	a	Sarajevo	L	0-1
23/11	h	Travnik	D	0-0

2015
28/02	h	Čelik	W	1-0 *Basara*
14/03	a	Olimpic	L	0-2
21/03	h	Široki Brijeg	L	1-3 *Smriko*
04/04	a	Slavija	L	0-1
08/04	h	Zrinjski	L	0-1
12/04	a	Radnik	L	0-2
18/04	h	Željezničar	L	1-4 *Kapetan*
22/04	h	Drina	W	1-0 *Miloš*
25/04	a	Sloboda	L	0-1
02/05	h	Zvijezda	W	3-0 *Basara, Pezo, Pinjuh*
09/05	a	Borac	L	1-2 *Jusufbašić*
13/05	h	Velež	W	3-1 *Basara, Pinjuh, Kapetan*
16/05	a	Mladost	L	0-1
23/05	h	Sarajevo	L	0-3
30/05	a	Travnik	L	0-2

Name	Nat	DoB	Pos	Aps	(s)	Gls
Sanel Alić		20/11/91	D	14	(6)	
Stjepan Badrov		01/12/87	M	1	(1)	
Hrvoje Barišić	CRO	03/02/91	M	11	(1)	
Marko Basara	SRB	29/07/84	A	9	(3)	3
Vladimir Branković	SRB	22/09/85	D	8		
Tomislav Čuljak	CRO	25/05/87	D	6	(3)	
Haris Hećo		20/05/87	M	13	(1)	1
Ante Hrkać		11/03/87	M	8	(4)	
Armin Imamović		19/08/93	D	6		
Dragan Jurčević		10/07/95	M	2	(7)	
Mladen Jurčević		04/03/83	M	15	(1)	2
Goran Jurić	CRO	22/08/83	M	26	(1)	
Sabahudin Jusufbašić		13/01/90	A	11	(2)	1
Armin Kapetan		11/03/86	A	25		4
Petar Kovač		17/07/96	G		(1)	
Ivan Livaja		01/10/87	M	27		
Toni Livančić		11/12/94	A	12	(11)	
Stipe Miloš		15/02/90	D	16		1
Andria Petrović	CRO	14/11/91	D	12	(8)	
Juraj Petrović		02/07/95	M		(5)	
Toni Pezo	CRO	14/02/87	M	19		1
Ante Pinjuh		09/10/90	A	11	(12)	5
Jasmin Smriko		20/01/91	A	19	(3)	3
Mateo Šafradin		28/03/95	D		(2)	
Josip Šantić		29/12/93	M	11	(7)	
Josip Škorić	CRO	13/02/81	G	13		
Fabijan Tomić	CRO	15/06/95	G	2		
Vedran Vidović		14/11/90	A	18	(7)	
Aleksandar Živković		18/06/87	G	15		

HŠK Zrinjski

1905 • Bijeli Brijeg (15,000) • hskzrinjski.ba
Major honours
Bosnian-Herzegovinian League (3) 2005, 2009,
2014; Bosnian-Herzegovinian Cup (1) 2008
Coach: Branko Karačić (CRO);
(27/12/14) Mišo Krstičević (CRO);
(16/03/15) (Dalibor Cvitanović & Marijo Ivanković);
(26/03/15) Vinko Marinović

2014

02/08	a	Slavija	D 0-0	
09/08	a	Drina	W 2-1	Pehar, Nikollć
16/08	h	Radnik	W 2-0	Simeunović, Crnov
23/08	a	Željezničar	W 2-0	Nikolić, Crnov
27/08	h	Vitez	W 2-0	Radulović, Djurić
30/08	a	Sloboda	L 0-1	
13/09	h	Zvijezda	W 3-0	Nikolić (p), Crnov, Stojkić
21/09	a	Borac	L 0-1	
27/09	h	Velež	W 2-0	Crnov, Nikolić
05/10	a	Mladost	W 2-0	Nikolić 2 (1p)
18/10	h	Sarajevo	D 1-1	Crnov
25/10	a	Travnik	W 3-1	Nikolić, Simeunović, Crnov
01/11	h	Čelik	D 1-1	Nikolić
09/11	a	Olimpic	W 1-0	Petrak
22/11	h	Široki Brijeg	D 0-0	
2015				
28/02	h	Slavija	W 2-0	og (Popović), Kordić (p)
15/03	h	Drina	D 1-1	Muminović
22/03	a	Radnik	D 0-0	
04/04	h	Željezničar	D 1-1	Nikolić
08/04	a	Vitez	W 1-0	Radulović
11/04	h	Sloboda	W 1-0	Šćepanović
18/04	a	Zvijezda	W 3-2	Todorović, Nikolić 2
22/04	h	Borac	W 2-0	Stojkić, Nikolić
26/04	a	Velež	D 1-1	Crnov
03/05	h	Mladost	D 0-0	
09/05	a	Sarajevo	L 0-1	
13/05	h	Travnik	W 5-0	Muminović, Nikolić, Mevlja, Vukomanović, Todorović
16/05	a	Čelik	D 0-0	
23/05	h	Olimpic	W 2-0	Nikolić, Todorović
30/05	a	Široki Brijeg	D 1-1	Crnov (p)

Name	Nat	DoB	Pos	Aps	(s)	Gls
Zvornimir Blaić	CRO	02/01/91	D	23	(2)	
Ivan Crnov	CRO	01/02/90	M	20	(4)	8
Sven Dedić	CRO	15/04/91	M		(1)	
Velibor Djurić		05/05/82	M	19	(6)	1
Ratko Dujković		16/03/83	G	30		
Dženan Durak		04/02/91	A		(1)	
Marin Galić		21/09/95	D		(1)	
Daniel Graovac		08/07/93	D	28		
Josip Jozić		10/01/95	D		(1)	
Matija Katanec	CRO	04/05/90	D	14		
Krešimir Kordić		03/09/81	A	2	(17)	1
Nejc Mevlja	SVN	12/06/90	D	9		1
Milan Muminović		02/10/83	M	18	(5)	2
Stevo Nikolić		05/12/84	A	28	(1)	14
Mile Pehar		01/02/91	D	11	(9)	1
Oliver Petrak	CRO	06/02/91	M	6	(5)	1
Nebojša Popović	CRO	04/04/92	A	2	(5)	
Anto Radeljić		31/12/90	D	10	(3)	
Aleksandar Radulović		09/02/87	M	24	(2)	2
Deni Simeunović	CRO	12/02/92	M	15	(6)	2
Danijel Stojanović	CRO	18/08/84	D	7	(10)	
Pero Stojkić		09/12/86	D	24		2
Pavle Sušić	SRB	15/04/88	M	1	(1)	
Vučina Šćepanović	SRB	17/11/82	M	20	(6)	1
Ognjen Todorović		24/03/89	D	13		3
Dejan Vukomanović		31/10/90	M		(3)	1
Ivo Zlatić		20/06/91	D	6	(1)	

NK Zvijezda

1922 • Banja Ilidža (3,500) • nkzvijezda.com
Coach: Nermin Huseinbašić;
(31/08/14) Petar Segrt (GER);
(19/04/14) Nedim Jusufbegović

2014

03/08	a	Sarajevo	L 0-3	(w/o)
09/08	h	Travnik	D 0-0	
16/08	a	Čelik	D 1-1	Stojanov
23/08	h	Olimpic	D 2-2	Diatta, Stojanov
27/08	a	Široki Brijeg	L 2-4	Stojanov, Isanović
30/08	h	Slavija	L 1-3	Stojanov
13/09	a	Zrinjski	L 0-3	
20/09	h	Radnik	D 1-1	og (Obradović)
27/09	a	Željezničar	L 3-5	Doljančić, Isanović, Stojanov
05/10	h	Vitez	D 1-1	Doljančić
18/10	a	Sloboda	D 0-0	
25/10	a	Drina	D 1-1	Diatta
01/11	h	Borac	W 2-0	Stojanov, Spasojević
08/11	a	Velež	L 2-3	Gadžo 2
22/11	h	Mladost	W 3-1	Stojanov, Diatta 2
2015				
02/03	h	Sarajevo	L 0-3	
15/03	a	Travnik	L 0-2	
22/03	h	Čelik	L 0-2	
04/04	a	Olimpic	L 0-3	
08/04	h	Široki Brijeg	D 0-0	
11/04	h	Slavija	L 1-2	Gadžo
18/04	h	Zrinjski	L 2-3	Diatta, Šerbečić
22/04	a	Radnik	W 1-0	Diatta
25/04	h	Željezničar	L 1-2	Stojanov
03/05	a	Vitez	L 0-3	
09/05	h	Sloboda	D 0-0	
13/05	h	Drina	W 2-1	Spasojević 2
16/05	a	Borac	L 0-1	
23/05	h	Velež	W 3-2	Gadžo, Diatta 2
30/05	a	Mladost	D 1-1	Stojanov

Name	Nat	DoB	Pos	Aps	(s)	Gls
Anel Alibašić		20/03/94	M	8	(2)	
André Luiz	BRA	22/12/91	M	10	(2)	
Dušan Bijelić		06/08/95	D	7	(1)	
Selmir Brkić		24/11/92	G	18		
Asif Čaušević	SRB	21/08/93	M		(1)	
Ademir Čolić		22/01/97	M		(1)	
Elvir Čolić		17/07/88	D	19		
Mehmedalija Čović		16/03/86	D	20	(1)	
Eldar Dedić-Mešanović		18/05/96	M		(2)	
Rijad Demić		17/11/89	M	6		
Secouba Diatta	SEN	22/12/92	M	22	(1)	8
Minel Doljančić		30/06/96	A	4	(3)	2
Eldin Fačić		03/09/94	M	15	(5)	
Ermin Gadžo		19/05/90	A	23		4
Kemal Hadžić		11/02/89	G	1		
Amir Hamzić		05/01/76	M		(1)	
Dženan Haračić		30/07/94	A		(6)	
Ismir Hasić		31/05/96	D	2	(2)	
Kenan Hujić		09/07/93	G	2	(1)	
Bernad Imamović		24/07/92	M		(1)	
Samir Isanović		23/07/95	M	8	(12)	2
Vernes Islamagić		27/07/94	D	21	(2)	
Go Ito	JPN	23/03/94	G	8		
Ivan Jakovljević	SRB	26/05/89	M	10		
Mahir Jašarević		14/01/92	D	1	(2)	
Stanoje Jovanović	SRB	21/08/93	D	14	(9)	
Fikret Karavdić		29/06/92	M	8	(8)	
Amer Ordagić		05/05/93	M	21	(1)	
Tomislav Puljić	CRO	05/11/92	D	22	(2)	
Mirko Radovanović	SRB	05/04/86	A	2	(1)	
Rodrigo	BRA	03/08/89	D	8		
Mirko Spasojević	MNE	10/08/90	A	7	(7)	3
Uroš Stojanov	SRB	05/01/89	A	25	(2)	9
Besim Šerbečić		01/05/98	D	3	(4)	1
Senad Zuhrić		03/03/92	M	2		
Edis Zulić		25/12/90	D	2		

FK Željezničar

1921 • Grbavica (14,000) • fkzeljeznicar.ba
Major honours
Yugoslav League (1) 1972; Bosnian-Herzegovinian
League (5) 2001, 2002, 2010, 2012, 2013;
Bosnian-Herzegovinian Cup (5) 2000, 2001, 2003,
2011, 2012
Coach: Admir Adžem;
(15/12/14) (Almir Memić);
(10/01/15) Milomir Odović

2014

02/08	a	Olimpic	W 3-0	Stanić, D Sadiković, Bajić
10/08	h	Široki Brijeg	D 1-1	Kosorić
17/08	a	Slavija	D 1-1	Memija
23/08	h	Zrinjski	L 0-2	
27/08	a	Radnik	W 3-1	Bučan, D Sadiković, Tomić
30/08	a	Drina	W 2-1	Bajić, Tomić
13/09	h	Vitez	W 2-1	Turković, Bučan
20/09	a	Sloboda	W 2-1	Varea, Turković
27/09	h	Zvijezda	W 5-3	Bučan, Varea, Bajić 3
05/10	a	Borac	L 0-1	
19/10	h	Velež	W 1-0	Tomić
26/10	a	Mladost	W 3-0	Memija, Bajić, D Sadiković
02/11	h	Sarajevo	L 1-2	Hasanović
08/11	a	Travnik	W 1-0	
23/11	h	Čelik	W 2-1	Bajić 2
2015				
01/03	h	Olimpic	W 3-0	Kokot 2, Bajić
15/03	a	Široki Brijeg	D 0-0	
22/03	h	Slavija	W 2-1	Bajić 2
04/04	a	Zrinjski	D 1-1	Djelmić
08/04	h	Radnik	D 1-1	Djelmić
11/04	h	Drina	W 2-0	Beganović, Bogdanović
18/04	a	Vitez	W 4-1	Memija, Beganović, Bajić 2
22/04	h	Sloboda	D 1-1	Kokot
25/04	a	Zvijezda	W 2-1	Djelmić, Čolić
02/05	h	Borac	W 1-0	Bogdanović
09/05	a	Velež	W 3-0	Bajić, Bogdanović, Beganović
13/05	h	Mladost	W 4-0	Djelmić, Bajić, Hadžiahmetović, Nuspahić
16/05	a	Sarajevo	D 0-0	
23/05	h	Travnik	W 1-0	Bogdanović
30/05	a	Čelik	D 1-1	Beganović

Name	Nat	DoB	Pos	Aps	(s)	Gls
Marijan Antolović	CRO	07/05/89	G	30		
Riad Bajić		06/05/94	A	27	(1)	15
Edi Baša	CRO	29/06/93	M	1	(4)	
Dženis Beganović		23/05/96	A	7	(1)	4
Jasmin Bogdanović		10/05/90	D	20	(1)	4
Sead Bučan		08/03/81	M	9	(8)	3
Benjamin Čolić		23/07/91	D	14	(6)	1
Ognjen Djelmić		18/08/88	M	14		4
Amir Hadžiahmetović		08/03/97	M	13	(8)	1
Eldar Hasanović		12/01/90	M	23	(2)	1
Nermin Jamak		25/08/86	M	4	(1)	
Zoran Kokot		28/06/85	A	13		3
Aleksandar Kosorić		30/01/87	D	27		1
Josip Kvesić		21/09/90	D	26		
Kerim Memija		06/01/96	D	21	(4)	3
Anes Nuspahić		10/01/93	M	1	(8)	1
Damir Sadiković		07/04/95	M	19	(8)	3
Enis Sadiković		07/04/95	M	1	(13)	
Srdjan Stanić		06/07/89	A	8		1
Tomislav Tomić		16/11/90	M	13		3
Nedo Turković		23/10/89	A	7	(9)	2
Dejan Uzelac	SRB	27/08/93	D	2		
Juan Manuel Varea	ARG	23/03/86	M	10	(10)	2
Mladen Zeljković	SRB	18/11/87	D	20		

Top goalscorers

15	Riad Bajić (Željezničar)
14	Stevo Nikolić (Zrinjski)
13	Wagner (Široki Brijeg)
11	Krste Velkoski (Sarajevo)
10	Joco Stokić (Borac)
9	Miloš Filipović (Drina)
	Leon Benko (Sarajevo)
	Bojan Puzigaća (Sarajevo)
	Uroš Stojanov (Zvijezda)
8	Dalibor Pandža (Olimpic)
	Ivan Crnov (Zrinjski)
	Secouba Diatta (Zvijezda)

Promoted clubs

FK Mladost Doboj Kakanj

1959 • Mladost (1,500) • mladostdk.com
Coach: Nijaz Kapo

FK Rudar Prijedor

1928 • Gradski (5,000) • rudarprijedor.com
**Coach: Darko Nestorović;
(01/01/15) Zoran Bujić**

Second level final tables 2014/15

	Prva liga FBiH	Pld	W	D	L	F	A	Pts
1	FK Mladost Doboj Kakanj	30	19	2	9	40	25	59
2	NK GOŠK Gabela	30	16	9	5	48	18	57
3	NK Bratstvo Gračanica	30	16	5	9	42	28	53
4	FK Budućnost Banovići	30	16	5	9	37	27	53
5	FK Goražde	30	14	8	8	33	19	50
6	NK Metalleghe Jajce	30	15	5	10	34	26	50
7	FK Radnički Lukavac	30	12	11	7	38	26	47
8	FK Rudar Kakanj	30	12	7	11	35	34	43
9	NK Jedinstvo Bihać	30	11	9	10	30	23	42
10	HNK Branitelj Mostar	30	8	11	11	20	25	35
11	HNK Orašje	30	9	8	13	33	42	35
12	HNK Čapljina	30	10	4	16	38	44	34
13	NK Podgrmeč Sanski Most	30	9	7	14	27	41	34
14	OFK Gradina Srebrenik	30	9	6	15	29	39	33
15	FK Turbina Jablanica	30	7	6	17	17	48	27
16	FK Igman Konjic	30	2	7	21	20	56	13

	Prva liga RS	Pld	W	D	L	F	A	Pts
1	FK Rudar Prijedor	25	15	5	5	31	13	44
2	FK Krupa	26	12	7	7	34	25	43
3	FK Leotar	25	15	3	7	29	21	42
4	FK Kozara Gradiška	26	12	5	9	44	31	41
5	FK Tekstilac Derventa	26	11	8	7	23	18	41
6	FK Sutjeska Foča	26	11	6	9	30	29	39
7	FK Sloboda Bosanski Novi	26	11	4	11	36	40	37
8	FK Vlasenica	26	10	6	10	30	32	36
9	FK Sloboda Mrkonjić Grad	26	9	3	13	28	34	33
10	FK Drina Višegrad	26	8	6	12	29	37	29
11	FK Proleter Teslić	26	9	4	12	32	35	25
12	FK Podrinje Janja	25	7	9	9	21	20	24
13	FK Mladost Gacko	26	7	3	16	28	47	24
14	FK Napredak Donji Šepak	26	5	5	16	31	44	20

NB FK Leotar, FK Podrinje Janja, FK Proleter Teslić & FK Rudar Prijedor – 6 pts deducted; FK Drina Višegrad – 1 pt deducted; Leotar v Podrinje & Proleter v Rudar in round 26 were annulled.

DOMESTIC CUP

Kup Bosne i Hercegovine 2014/15

1/16 FINALS

(16/09/14)
Bratstvo Gračanica 0-0 Olimpic Sarajevo *(3-4 on pens)*
Sloboda Mrkonjić Grad 0-2 Željezničar

(17/09/14)
Borac Banja Luka 0-0 Drina Zvornik *(3-2 on pens)*
Igman Konjic 0-3 Sarajevo
Jedinstvo Bihać 0-2 Široki Brijeg
Metalleghe Jajce 1-0 Proleter Teslić
Mladost Doboj Kakanj 1-0 Goražde
Mladost Velika Obarska 1-0 Mladost Župča
Radnik Bijeljina 1-5 Čelik
Rudar Prijedor 3-0 Podgrmeč Sanski Most
Slavija Sarajevo 1-2 Velež
Sloga Ljubuški 3-0 Drina Višegrad
Travnik 0-0 Sloboda Tuzla *(3-1 on pens)*
Vitez 1-1 Gradina Srebrenik *(5-3 on pens)*
Zrinjski 3-1 Napredak Donji Šepak
Zvijezda Gradačac 5-1 Sloboda Bosanski Novi

1/8 FINALS

(30/09/14 & 22/10/14)
Sloga Ljubuški 2-3, 1-4 Zrinjski *(3-7)*

(01/10/14 & 21/10/14)
Sarajevo 4-0, 3-2 Travnik *(7-2)*

(01/10/14 & 22/10/14)
Melalleghe Jajce 0-0, 0-1 Mladost Velika Obarska *(0-1)*
Mladost Doboj Kakanj 0-1, 0-2 Zvijezda Gradačac *(0-3)*
Olimpic Sarajevo 4-0, 0-1 Čelik *(4-1)*
Rudar Prijedor 0-1, 2-5 Borac Banja Luka *(2-6)*
Široki Brijeg 2-0, 1-1 Željezničar *(3-1)*
Velež 2-0, 3-3 Vitez *(5-3)*

QUARTER-FINALS

(11/03/15 & 18/03/15)
Mladost Velika Obarska 1-3 Široki Brijeg *(Perić 78p; Kožulj 6, Buhač 44, Jevtić 65og)*
Široki Brijeg 5-0 Mladost Velika Obarska *(Zakarić 1, Buhač 10, 45, Barišić 33, 90)*
(Široki Brijeg 8-1)
Sarajevo 1-2 Borac Banja Luka *(Okić 54; Jevtić 37, Subić 69)*
Borac Banja Luka 0-1 Sarajevo *(Velkoski 62)*
(2-2; Borac Banja Luka on away goals)
Zrinjski 2-2 Velež *(Kordić 17, Stojkić 66; Hebibović 27p, 70)*
Velež 0-2 Zrinjski *(Stojkić 45, Nikolić 90+2)*
(Zrinjski 4-2)
Zvijezda Gradačac 1-1 Olimpic Sarajevo *(Fačić 59; Bogićević 80)*
Olimpic Sarajevo 4-3 Zvijezda Gradačac *(Stefan 25, 80, Pandža 32, Hugo Souza 37; Fačić 15, Puljić 29, Isanović 64p)*
(Olimpic Sarajevo 5-4)

SEMI-FINALS

(15/04/15 & 29/04/15)
Olimpic Sarajevo 0-0 Zrinjski
Zrinjski 0-0 Olimpic Sarajevo
(0-0; Olimpic Sarajevo 5-4 on pens)

Borac Banja Luka 0-0 Široki Brijeg
Široki Brijeg 2-1 Borac Banja Luka *(Wagner 30, 84; Ilić 34)*
(Široki Brijeg 2-1)

FINAL

(20/05/15)
Pecara, Široki Brijeg
NK ŠIROKI BRIJEG 1 *(Regoje 79og)*
FK OLIMPIC SARAJEVO 1 *(Muharemović 10)*
Referee: Skakić
ŠIROKI BRIJEG: Bilobrk, Barišić, Brekalo, Marković, Zakarić (Peko 74), Landeka, Wagner, Menalo, Kožulj, Karačić, Kresinger (Buhač 66; Ivanković 83)
OLIMPIC: Hamzić, Regoje, Bogičević, Gligorov, Merajić, Muharemović, Smajić (Imamović 87), Stefan (Šivšić 80), Jusufović (Čomor 83), Brković, Pandža

(27/05/15)
Olimpijski Asim Ferhatović Hase, Sarajevo
FK OLIMPIC SARAJEVO 1 *(Muharemović 56)*
NK ŠIROKI BRIJEG 1 *(Peko 44)*
Referee: Valjić
OLIMPIC: Hamzić, Regoje, Bogičević, Gligorov, Merajić (Šivšić 81), Muharemović, Stefan, Handžić, Jusufović, Brković, Pandža (Čomor 89)
Red card: Bogičević (44)
ŠIROKI BRIJEG: Bilobrk, I Džidić, Brekalo, Marković, Ćorić, Zakarić, Landeka, Wagner, Menalo (Taianan 59), Kožulj (Kresinger 90), Peko (Ivanković 76)

(2-2; Olimpic Sarajevo 5-4 on pens)

BULGARIA
Bulgarski Futbolen Soyuz (BFS)

Address	26 Tzar Ivan Assen II Street BG-1124 Sofia	**President**	Borislav Mihaylov
Tel	+359 2 942 6202	**General secretary**	Borislav Popov
Fax	+359 2 942 6201	**Media officer**	Pavel Kolev
E-mail	bfu@bfunion.bg	**Year of formation**	1923
Website	bfunion.bg	**National stadium**	Vasil Levski, Sofia (43,230)

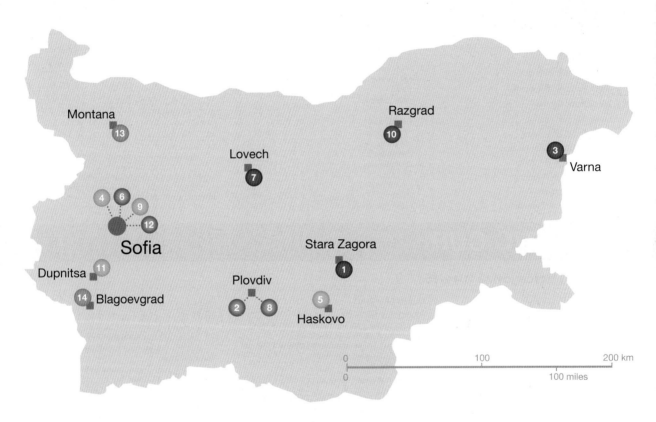

A GRUPA CLUBS

 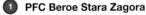 PFC Beroe Stara Zagora

  PFC Botev Plovdiv

 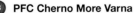 PFC Cherno More Varna

  PFC CSKA Sofia

  PFC Haskovo

 PFC Levski Sofia

 PFC Litex Lovech

  PFC Lokomotiv Plovdiv 1936

  PFC Lokomotiv Sofia

  PFC Ludogorets Razgrad

  PFC Marek Dupnitsa

 PFC Slavia Sofia

PROMOTED CLUBS

  PFC Montana 1921

  OFC Pirin Blagoevgrad

KEY:
- ⬤ – UEFA Champions League
- ◉ – UEFA Europa League
- ◯ – Promoted
- ◯ – Relegated

Four in a row for Ludogorets

The A PFG was cut to 12 teams with a reduced fixture programme of 32 matches in 2014/15, but the champions were unchanged as PFC Ludogorets Razgrad made it four league titles out of four following their promotion in 2011.

The only other club to have won four successive Bulgarian championships, PFC CSKA Sofia, looked set to halt Ludogorets' run when they led at the winter break, but a second-half-of-the-season meltdown dropped them to fifth. Worse was to follow when they and third-placed PFC Lokomotiv Sofia were demoted for financial reasons, further reducing the top division to just ten participants in 2015/16.

Razgrad club continue their domestic domination	**Collapse and relegation for record champions CSKA**	**Cherno More defeat Levski in dramatic cup final**

Domestic league

As in the previous season, Ludogorets sacked their championship-winning coach in the early weeks of the campaign, Stoycho Stoev suffering the same fate as his predecessor Ivaylo Petev when, with just one point gleaned from the first two league games and an early European exit imminent, he was dismissed by club owner Kiril Domoschiev and replaced by his assistant coach Georgi Dermendzhiev.

Once again, the move paid dividends, both in Europe and on the domestic front, where Ludogorets roared back into title contention alongside 31-times champions CSKA, who, seeking to end their longest ever wait between championship wins, were reproducing the form of old under coach Stoicho Mladenov. Defeated just once in 19 games, 1-0 at Ludogorets, they were three points clear of the defending champions at the winter break.

As title-chasing collapses go, CSKA's was pretty spectacular. With their leading scorer, Romanian striker Sergiu Buş, departed, it was as if the team's goal tap had been turned off and blocked. Incredibly, they went ten successive matches without scoring. Although they were still in contention when the league split into two, their freefall left Ludogorets unchallenged, and Dermendzhiev's men were allowed to stroll at leisure to the title, goals from Brazilian stars Marcelinho and

Juninho Quixadá (two) plus another from Dutchman Virgil Misidjan underscoring a comfortable title-clinching 4-1 home win against PFC Lokomotiv Sofia.

While Ludogorets' foreign contingent again excelled, there were some key contributions too from Bulgarians, with midfield fulcrum Svetoslav Dyakov and goalkeeper Vladislav Stoyanov particularly prominent. PFC Beroe Stara Zagora, who finished runners-up on head-to-head above Lokomotiv Sofia, also possessed a couple of fine Bulgarian defenders in Ivo Ivanov and Atanas Zahirov, but none of the top six teams could supply a single scorer with more than ten goals. Spanish striker Añete topped the charts with 14, but half of those came in the relegation pool, into which his club, PFC Levski Sofia, had surprisingly fallen after ending the first phase in seventh place.

Domestic cup

Levski, trophy-less since 2009, sought consolation by winning a record-extending 26th Bulgarian Cup. As underdogs they defeated Ludogorets in the semi-finals, but as favourites they fell in the final to PFC Cherno More Varna. It was an agonising loss for Levski but a famous win for their ten-man opponents, who equalised in added time before snatching a glorious 119th-minute winner to capture their first major trophy. Levski's defeat also meant that in 2015/16, for the

first time ever, there would be no team from Sofia participating in Europe.

Europe

Ludogorets did the country proud again as they followed up their long run in the UEFA Europa League by becoming only the second Bulgarian club (after Levski in 2006/07) to reach the UEFA Champions League group stage. Their qualification came amidst high drama as Romanian defender Cosmin Moţi replaced red-carded keeper Stoyanov in goal for a penalty shoot-out against the champions of his homeland, FC Steaua Bucureşti, and promptly saved two spot-kicks. Ludogorets then claimed Bulgaria's first group stage points by defeating FC Basel 1893 and drawing against Liverpool FC before bowing out with a visit to the Bernabéu in Madrid.

National team

Luboslav Penev's three-year reign as Bulgaria coach ended when his team could only draw 1-1 at home to Malta in a UEFA EURO 2016 qualifier. That result followed defeats against Croatia and Norway and left the team's qualifying campaign in disarray, but after ex-Ludogorets boss Petev had taken over, outside hopes of a play-off spot were rekindled by a 2-2 draw against Italy and a 1-0 win in Malta, with experienced striker Ivelin Popov scoring in both matches.

DOMESTIC SEASON AT A GLANCE

A PFG 2014/15 final table

		Pld	Home					Away					Total					Pts
			W	D	L	F	A	W	D	L	F	A	W	D	L	F	A	
1	**PFC Ludogorets Razgrad**	32	12	4	0	36	7	6	5	5	27	17	18	9	5	63	24	63
2	PFC Beroe Stara Zagora	32	8	5	3	26	16	7	5	4	20	14	15	10	7	46	30	55
3	PFC Lokomotiv Sofia	32	9	4	3	20	11	7	3	6	19	20	16	7	9	39	31	55
4	PFC Litex Lovech	32	12	2	2	30	9	4	4	8	19	27	16	6	10	49	36	54
5	PFC CSKA Sofia	32	9	5	2	26	5	5	5	6	19	22	14	10	8	45	27	52
6	PFC Botev Plovdiv	32	9	2	5	26	19	3	4	9	12	20	12	6	14	38	39	42
7	PFC Levski Sofia	32	10	3	3	43	16	7	2	7	23	17	17	5	10	66	33	56
8	PFC Chermo More Varna	32	8	3	5	19	12	7	2	7	23	24	15	5	12	42	36	50
9	PFC Slavia Sofia	32	7	2	7	24	21	5	5	6	16	17	12	7	13	40	38	43
10	PFC Lokomotiv Plovdiv 1936	32	5	3	8	17	23	4	2	10	11	29	9	5	18	28	52	32
11	PFC Marek Dupnitsa	32	3	5	8	11	26	2	0	14	3	45	5	5	22	14	71	20
12	PFC Haskovo	32	4	1	11	13	32	0	2	14	5	39	4	3	25	18	71	15

NB League splits into top and bottom halves after 22 games, after which the clubs play exclusively against teams in their group

European qualification 2015/16

 Champion: PFC Ludogorets Razgrad (second qualifying round)

 Cup winner: PFC Cherno More Varna (second qualifying round)

PFC Beroe Stara Zagora (first qualifying round)
PFC Litex Lovech (first qualifying round)

Top scorer Añete (Levski), 14 goals
Relegated clubs PFC Haskovo, PFC Marek Dupnista, PFC CSKA Sofia (excluded), PFC Lokomotiv Sofia (excluded)
Promoted clubs PFC Montana 1921, OFC Pirin Blagoevgrad
Cup final PFC Cherno More Varna 2-1 PFC Levski Sofia (aet)

Team of the season
(3-4-1-2)

Coach: Dermendzhiev (Ludogorets)

Stoyanov *(Ludogorets)*

Zehirov *(Beroe)* — Moți *(Ludogorets)* — Ivanov *(Beroe)*

Júnior Caiçara *(Ludogorets)* — Dyakov *(Ludogorets)* — Elias *(Beroe)* — Romanov *(Lokomotiv Sofia)*

Marcelinho *(Ludogorets)*

Asprilla *(Litex)* — Añete *(Levski)*

Player of the season

Marcelinho
(PFC Ludogorets Razgrad)

Voted by his fellow professionals as the A PFG player of the season, Marcelinho was a worthy recipient of the award as much for his long and loyal service to Ludogorets as his 2014/15 form. The Brazilian schemer ended the season with more top-flight games (104) and goals (32) for the club than any other player. He also had a fourth successive A PFG winner's medal to treasure as well as some happy memories from the UEFA Champions League, chief among them a brilliant goal against Real Madrid CF.

Newcomer of the season

Bozhidar Kraev
(PFC Levski Sofia)

Levski's 2014/15 season did not go as planned, but they did unearth a highly promising talent in attacking midfielder Kraev. Still only 17 when the season ended, the Vratsa-born graduate of the Hristo Stoichkov academy in Spain first hit the headlines when he scored a Bulgarian Cup hat-trick against PFC Spartak Varna. He also bagged another treble in the final game of the league campaign, against PFC Marek Dupnitsa, to double his A PFG tally before appearing as a substitute in the cup final.

International tournament appearances

FIFA World Cup (7) 1962, 1966, 1970, 1974, 1986 (2nd round), 1994 (4th), 1998
UEFA European Championship (2) 1996, 2004

Top five all-time caps

Stiliyan Petrov (106); Borislav Mihaylov (102); Hristo Bonev (96); Krasimir Balakov (92); Martin Petrov (91)

Top five all-time goals

Dimitar Berbatov (48); Hristo Bonev (47); Hristo Stoichkov (37); Emil Kostadinov (26); Lyubomir Angelov, Ivan Kolev & Petar Zhekov (25)

Results 2014/15

09/09/13	Azerbaijan (ECQ)	A	Baku	W	2-1	Micanski (14), Hristov (87)
10/10/14	Croatia (ECQ)	H	Sofia	L	0-1	
13/10/14	Norway (ECQ)	A	Oslo	L	1-2	Bodurov (43)
16/11/14	Malta (ECQ)	H	Sofia	D	1-1	Galabinov (6)
28/03/15	Italy (ECQ)	H	Sofia	D	2-2	Popov (11), Micanski (17)
08/06/15	Turkey	A	Istanbul	L	0-4	
12/06/15	Malta (ECQ)	A	Ta' Qali	W	1-0	Popov (56)

Appearances 2014/15

Coach: Luboslav Penev 31/08/66 /(07/12/14) Ivaylo Petev 09/07/75			AZE	CRO	NOR	MLT	ITA	Tur	MLT	Caps	Goals
Vladislav Stoyanov	08/06/87	Ludogorets	G	G		G				14	-
Stanislav Manolev	16/12/85	Dinamo Moskva (RUS) /Kuban (RUS)	D	M	D69	D	D	M61	M	45	4
Apostol Popov	22/12/82	CSKA Sofia	D	D	D					4	-
Nikolay Bodurov	30/05/86	Fulham (ENG)	D	D	D	D	D	D68	D	32	1
Veselin Minev	14/10/80	Levski Sofia	D		D	D				24	-
Mihail Alexandrov	11/06/89	Ludogorets	M83	s76	M	M	M	M	M75	8	-
Georgi Milanov	19/02/92	CSKA Moskva (RUS)	M	M	M	M58	M88		s75	24	2
Georgi Iliev	05/09/81	Shijiazhuang (CHN)	M74	s46	M76	M71				24	2
Svetoslav Dyakov	31/05/84	Ludogorets	M	M	M	M	M	M	M	24	-
Vladimir Gadzhev	18/07/87	Levski	M	M68			M	M60	M	28	1
Ilian Micanski	20/12/85	Karlsruhe (GER)	A58	A46			A73	A78	A90	15	4
Andrey Galabinov	27/11/88	Livorno (ITA)	s58	s46	s56	A58				6	2
Todor Nedelev	07/02/93	Mainz (GER)	s74							6	-
Ventsislav Hristov	09/11/88	Beroe	s83	A56						5	1
Petar Zanev	18/10/85	Amkar (RUS)		D46				s46		27	-
Yordan Minev	14/10/80	Ludogorets		D	s69		D	D46	D	21	-
Ivelin Popov	26/10/87	Kuban (RUS)		A	A	A	A85	A76	A81	55	12
Alexander Tonev	03/02/90	Celtic (SCO)		s68	M	s71		s61		18	3
Nikolay Mihaylov	28/06/88	Mersin (TUR)			G		G			32	-
Georgi Terziev	18/04/92	Ludogorets					D	s68		5	-
Marquinhos	30/04/82	CSKA Sofia			s58					6	-
Alexander Alexandrov	13/04/86	Ludogorets					D	D	D	5	-
Valeri Bozhinov	15/02/86	Ternana (ITA)					s73			43	6
Simeon Slavchev	25/09/93	Bolton (ENG)					s85			4	-
Ventsislav Vasilev	08/07/88	CSKA Sofia					s88			1	-
Bozhidar Mitrev	31/03/87	Lokomotiv Sofia						G	G	2	-
Ivan Bandalovski	23/11/86	Partizan (SRB)						D	D	14	-
Ivaylo Chochev	18/02/93	Palermo (ITA)						s60	s81	2	-
Kristiyan Malinov	30/03/94	Litex						s76		1	-
Radoslav Vasilev	12/10/90	Slavia Sofia						s78	s90	2	-

EUROPE

PFC Ludogorets Razgrad

Second qualifying round - F91 Dudelange (LUX)
H 4-0 *Dani Abalo (35), Bezjak (43), Anicet Abel (65), Fábio Espinho (68)*
Stoyanov, Barthe, Fábio Espinho (Wanderson 82), Bezjak, Dani Abalo, Dyakov (Zlatinski 73), Minev, Moți, Júnior Caiçara, Marcelinho (Anicet Abel 63), Misidjan. Coach: Stoycho Stoev (BUL)

A 1-1 *Bezjak (51)*
Stoyanov, Barthe (Mäntylä 73), Fábio Espinho, Bezjak, Choko, Zlatinski, Minev, Moți, Marcelinho (Wanderson 65), Misidjan (M Alexandrov 64), Lumu. Coach: Stoycho Stoev (BUL)

Third qualifying round - FK Partizan (SRB)
H 0-0
Stoyanov, M Alexandrov (Anicet Abel 75), Fábio Espinho, Bezjak, A Alexandrov, Dani Abalo (Misidjan 62), Dyakov, Moți, Vitinha (Angulo 47), Júnior Caiçara, Marcelinho. Coach: Stoycho Stoev (BUL)

A 2-2 *Marcelinho (19, 21)*
Stoyanov, M Alexandrov (Anicet Abel 78), Bezjak, A Alexandrov, Angulo, Dani Abalo (Misidjan 46), Dyakov, Zlatinski, Moți, Júnior Caiçara, Marcelinho (Fábio Espinho 85). Coach: Georgi Dermendzhiev (BUL)

Play-offs - FC Steaua București (ROU)
A 0-1
Stoyanov, M Alexandrov, Dyakov, Zlatinski (Fábio Espinho 46), Minev, Moți, Terziev, Júnior Caiçara, Marcelinho (Anicet Abel 85), Misidjan, Hamza. Coach: Georgi Dermendzhiev (BUL)

H 1-0 *Wanderson (90)* **(aet; 6-5 on pens)**
Stoyanov, M Alexandrov (Dani Abalo 82), Fábio Espinho, Bezjak (Hamza 78), Dyakov, Minev, Moți, Terziev, Júnior Caiçara, Marcelinho, Misidjan (Wanderson 85). Coach: Georgi Dermendzhiev (BUL)
Red card: Stoyanov 119

Group B
Match 1 - Liverpool FC (ENG)
A 1-2 *Dani Abalo (90+1)*
Borjan, M Alexandrov, Bezjak (Younés 86), Anicet Abel, A Alexandrov, Dyakov (Fábio Espinho 85), Minev, Moți, Júnior Caiçara, Marcelinho, Misidjan (Dani Abalo 72). Coach: Georgi Dermendzhiev (BUL)

Match 2 - Real Madrid CF (ESP)
H 1-2 *Marcelinho (6)*
Stoyanov, M Alexandrov (Misidjan 82), Fábio Espinho (Anicet Abel 82), Bezjak, A Alexandrov, Dani Abalo, Dyakov, Minev, Moți, Júnior Caiçara, Marcelinho (Wanderson 70). Coach: Georgi Dermendzhiev (BUL)

Match 3 - FC Basel 1893 (SUI)
H 1-0 *Minev (90+2)*
Stoyanov, M Alexandrov (Wanderson 81), Fábio Espinho, Bezjak (Younés 68), Dani Abalo (Misidjan 77), Dyakov, Minev, Moți, Terziev, Júnior Caiçara, Marcelinho. Coach: Georgi Dermendzhiev (BUL)

Match 4 - FC Basel 1893 (SUI)
A 0-4
Stoyanov, M Alexandrov, Fábio Espinho (Anicet Abel 64), Bezjak (Younés 46), Angulo, Dani Abalo, Dyakov, Moți (A Alexandrov 21), Terziev, Júnior Caiçara, Marcelinho. Coach: Georgi Dermendzhiev (BUL)

Match 5 - Liverpool FC (ENG)
H 2-2 *Dani Abalo (3), Terziev (88)*
Stoyanov, M Alexandrov (Wanderson 72), Fábio Espinho (Younés 81), Dani Abalo (Júnior Quixadá 69), Dyakov, Minev, Moți, Terziev, Júnior Caiçara, Marcelinho, Misidjan. Coach: Georgi Dermendzhiev (BUL)

Match 6 - Real Madrid CF (ESP)
A 0-4
Stoyanov, M Alexandrov (Wanderson 61), Fábio Espinho (Anicet Abel 63), Dani Abalo, Dyakov, Minev, Moți, Terziev, Júnior Caiçara, Marcelinho, Misidjan (Júnior Quixadá 72). Coach: Georgi Dermendzhiev (BUL)
Red card: Marcelinho 19

PFC CSKA Sofia

Second qualifying round - FC Zimbru Chisinau (MDA)
H 1-1 *Karachanakov (41)*
Diviš, Sunday (Kamburov 46), Krachunov, Toni Silva (Karachanakov 36), Joachim, Popov, Vasilev, Edenilson, Marquinhos, Supusepa, Stoyanov (Galchev 62). Coach: Stoycho Mladenov (BUL)

A 0-0
Diviš, Tunchev, Krachunov, Toni Silva, Galchev (Buş 51), Kamburov (Joachim 51), Popov, Vasilev (Supusepa 42), Edenilson, Marquinhos, I Stoyanov. Coach: Stoycho Mladenov (BUL)
Red card: Edenilson 86

PFC Litex Lovech

First qualifying round - FC Veris (MDA)
A 0-0
Pirgov, Bodurov, Mendy, Jordán (Minchev 84), Bozhikov, Vajushi (Rumenov 80), Popov, Zlatinov, Tsvetanov, Kossoko, Kolev (Tsvetkov 69). Coach: Krasimir Balakov (BUL)

H 3-0 *Mendy (27), Jordán (63, 74)*
Pirgov, Bodurov, Mendy (Nedyalkov 83), Jordán, Bozhikov, Vajushi, Popov, Zlatinov, Asprilla (Tsvetanov 79), Kossoko, Kolev (Rumenov 66). Coach: Krasimir Balakov (BUL)

Second qualifying round - Diósgyőri VTK (HUN)
H 0-2
Vinícius, Bodurov, Mendy, Jordán, Bozhikov, Vajushi, Popov, Zlatinov, Asprilla (Tsvetanov 82), Kossoko (Tsvetkov 77), Boumal (Rumenov 60). Coach: Krasimir Balakov (BUL)

A 2-1 *Asprilla (80), Jordán (85p)*
Vinícius, Nedyalkov, Bodurov, Mendy, Jordán, Vajushi, Malinov (Rumenov 77), Popov (Bozhikov 86), Tsvetkov (Angelov 66), Asprilla, Boumal. Coach: Krasimir Balakov (BUL)

PFC Botev Plovdiv

First qualifying round - AC Libertas (SMR)
H 4-0 *Ognyanov (25, 51), Tsvetkov (58), Pedro (72)*
Stachowiak, Ognyanov (Yusein 81), Curtean, Hristov, Minev, Jirsák (Vasev 69), Terziev, Tsvetkov, Kortzorg (Pedro 56), Filipov, Sarmov. Coach: Luboslav Penev (BUL)

A 2-0 *Benga (64), Filipov (87)*
Stachowiak, Benga, Ognyanov, Curtean (Vasev 46), Hristov, Pedro (Yusein 86), Jirsák, Terziev, Tsvetkov, Filipov, Sarmov (Chunchukov 71). Coach: Marin Bakalov (BUL)

Second qualifying round - SKN St Pölten (AUT)
H 2-1 *Tsvetkov (39p), Chunchukov (86)*
Stachowiak, Luchin, Benga, Ognyanov, Curtean (Gamakov 64), Hristov, Jirsák, Tsvetkov, Chunchukov, Filipov, Vasev (Marin 76; Yusein 92). Coach: Velislav Vutsov (BUL)

A 0-2
Stachowiak, Luchin, Ognyanov (Marin 77), Hristov, Jirsák, Tsvetkov, Chunchukov, Filipov, Vasev (Curtean 59), R Kolev, Gamakov (Yusein 83). Coach: Nikolai Kirov (BUL)

DOMESTIC LEAGUE CLUB-BY-CLUB

PFC Beroe Stara Zagora

1916 • Beroe (15,000) • beroe.bg

Major honours
Bulgarian League (1) 1986; Bulgarian Cup (2) 2010, 2013
Coach: Petar Hubchev

2014
20/07	h Cherno More	D	1-1	og (Stanchev)
27/07	h Botev	D	1-1	Elias
03/08	a Litex	L	1-2	Kerkar
10/08	h Levski	W	2-1	Mapuku 2
16/08	a Slavia	W	2-0	Kerkar, Hristov
24/08	h Haskovo	W	3-0	Hristov, Mapuku, Spirovski
31/08	a Ludogorets	D	1-1	Kerkar
13/09	h Marek	W	4-0	Hristov 3, Ayass
20/09	a Lokomotiv Plovdiv	W	3-0	Kostadinov, Kerkar, Hristov
28/09	h CSKA	L	1-2	Bakalov
03/10	a Lokomotiv Sofia	W	3-0	N'Diaye, Gadi 2
19/10	a Cherno More	L	0-4	
24/10	a Botev	L	1-3	Bakalov
03/11	h Litex	W	2-0	Elias 2
07/11	a Levski	W	1-0	Elias
23/11	h Slavia	D	1-1	Kerkar
29/11	a Haskovo	L	0-1	
05/12	h Ludogorets	L	0-4	
13/12	a Marek	W	3-0	Kostov, Mapuku 2

2015
28/02	h Lokomotiv Plovdiv	W	3-0	Ivanov, Kerkar, Ayass
07/03	a CSKA	W	1-0	N'Diaye
15/03	h Lokomotiv Sofia	D	0-0	
21/03	a CSKA	D	0-0	
05/04	h Lokomotiv Sofia	L	1-4	Kerkar
11/04	a Litex	D	1-1	Andonov (p)
18/04	a Botev	D	1-1	Elias
25/04	h Ludogorets	W	2-0	Ivanov, Zehirov
01/05	h CSKA	D	0-0	
11/05	a Lokomotiv Sofia	W	1-0	Kostadinov
17/05	h Levski	W	3-1	Elias 2, Zehirov
23/05	h Botev	W	2-1	Mapuku 2
31/05	a Ludogorets	D	1-1	Kostov

No	Name	Nat	DoB	Pos	Aps	(s)	Gls
10	Georgi Andonov		28/06/83	A	7	(3)	1
8	Samir Ayass		24/12/90	M	10	(3)	2
25	Dimo Bakalov		19/12/88	M	2	(11)	2
2	Valdemar Borovskij	LTU	02/05/84	D	1	(1)	
15	Georgi Dinkov		20/05/91	D	8	(2)	
27	Igor Djoman	FRA	01/05/86	M	27	(1)	
5	Tanko Dyakov		18/09/84	D	2	(6)	
21	Elias	BRA	04/09/81	M	31		7
11	Chris Gadi	FRA	09/04/92	A	7	(9)	2
10	Ventsislav Hristov		09/11/88	A	17	(1)	6
6	Ivo Ivanov		11/03/85	D	29		2
73	Ivan Karadzhov		12/07/89	G	3		
26	Salim Kerkar	FRA	04/08/87	M	30	(1)	7
70	Georgi Kostadinov		07/09/90	M	30		2
9	Stanislav Kostov		02/10/91	A	3	(17)	2
24	Mihael Kovacevic	SUI	06/03/88	D	2		
22	Blagoy Makendzhiev		11/07/88	G	22		
30	Junior Mapuku	COD	07/01/90	A	19	(7)	7
2	Iliya Munin		16/01/93	D	5	(2)	
4	Alassane N'Diaye	FRA	25/02/90	M	7	(15)	2
77	Savio Nsereko	GER	27/07/89	M	10	(1)	
7	Anton Ognyanov		30/06/88	M	1	(5)	
27	Veselin Penev		11/08/82	D	30		
23	Ilko Pirgov		23/05/86	G	7	(1)	
92	Stefan Spirovski	MKD	23/08/90	M	1	(8)	1
19	Plamen Tenev		13/06/95	D	1		
3	Vladimir Zafirov		21/03/83	D	19	(1)	
18	Atanas Zehirov		13/02/89	D	21		2

PFC Botev Plovdiv

1912 • Komatevo (3,300) • botevplovdiv.bg

Major honours
Bulgarian League (2) 1929, 1967; Bulgarian Cup (2) 1962, 1981
**Coach: Luboslav Penev;
(14/07/14) Velislav Vutsov;
(04/12/14) Petar Penchev**

2014
20/07	h Lokomotiv Sofia	W	1-0	Younés (p)
27/07	a Beroe	D	1-1	Tsvetkov
03/08	h Cherno More	W	2-1	Jirsák, Younés
09/08	h Litex	D	3-3	Tsvetkov, Baltanov, Gamakov
17/08	a Levski	L	1-2	Chunchukov
24/08	h Slavia	W	2-0	Jirsák, Baltanov
30/08	a Haskovo	W	2-1	Tsvetkov, Baltanov
12/09	h Ludogorets	L	1-2	Tsvetkov (p)
20/09	a Marek	D	1-1	Tsvetkov
27/09	h Lokomotiv Plovdiv	W	2-0	Chunchukov, Tsvetkov
03/10	a CSKA	L	0-1	
19/10	a Lokomotiv Sofia	L	1-3	Chunchukov
24/10	h Beroe	W	3-1	Gamakov, Jirsák, Tsvetkov
02/11	a Cherno More	L	1-2	Ognyanov
08/11	a Litex	W	2-1	Jirsák, A Kolev
23/11	h Levski	L	0-3	
29/11	a Slavia	L	0-3	
07/12	h Haskovo	W	2-0	Chunchukov, Baltanov
14/12	a Ludogorets	L	0-12	

2015
02/03	h Marek	W	3-0	Chunchukov, Ognyanov, Kazakov
10/03	a Lokomotiv Plovdiv	W	2-0	Baltanov, Vasev
15/03	h CSKA	W	2-0	Gamakov, Baltanov
22/03	a Ludogorets	D	0-0	
05/04	h Litex	L	0-1	
10/04	a CSKA	D	0-0	
18/04	h Beroe	D	1-1	Ognyanov
26/04	a Lokomotiv Sofia	L	0-1	
03/05	h Ludogorets	L	1-3	Jirsák
11/05	a Litex	L	0-1	
16/05	h CSKA	W	3-2	Marin, Baltanov, Tsvetkov
23/05	a Beroe	L	1-2	Marin
31/05	h Lokomotiv Sofia	L	0-2	

No	Name	Nat	DoB	Pos	Aps	(s)	Gls
2	Vladimir Aytov		12/04/96	D	1	(3)	
17	Lachezar Baltanov		11/07/88	M	24	(1)	7
23	Tsvetelin Chunchukov		10/03/93	A	23	(7)	5
95	Stanislav Dryanov		04/02/95	M	1	(8)	
28	Filip Filipov		02/08/88	D	22	(1)	
14	Goran Galešić	BIH	11/03/89	M	1	(4)	
38	Milen Gamakov		12/04/94	M	19	(9)	3
11	Yordan Hristov		12/02/84	D	31		
3	Romain Inez	FRA	30/04/88	D	9	(1)	
89	Mihail Ivanov		07/03/89	G	8		
16	Tomáš Jirsák	CZE	29/06/84	M	27		5
88	Hristiyan Kazakov		10/03/93	M		(10)	1
92	Alexander Kolev		08/12/92	M	7	(6)	1
37	Rosen Kolev		04/07/90	D	8	(3)	
4	Srdjan Luchin	ROU	04/03/86	D	2		
24	Lazar Marin		09/02/94	M	11	(5)	2
45	Nasko Milev		18/07/96	M		(4)	
22	Plamen Nikolov		12/06/85	D	23		
7	Mariyan Ognyanov		30/07/88	M	31		3
1	Adam Stachowiak	POL	18/12/86	G	24		
18	Radoslav Terziev		06/08/94	D	11	(6)	
77	Momchil Tsvetanov		03/12/90	M	9	(6)	
19	Ivan Tsvetkov		31/08/79	A	24	(5)	8
10	Vander	BRA	10/03/88	M	2		
30	Bozhidar Vasev		14/03/93	M	21	(4)	1
9	Hamza Younés	TUN	10/03/88	A	2	(2)	2
20	Serkan Yusein		31/03/96	M	1	(4)	
6	Daniel Zlatkov		06/03/89	D	10		

PFC Cherno More Varna

1945 • Ticha (8,000) • chernomorepfc.bg

Major honours
Bulgarian Cup (1) 2015
**Coach: Alexander Stankov;
(18/08/14) Nikola Spasov**

2014
20/07	a Beroe	D	1-1	Sténio
26/07	h Ludogorets	D	0-0	
03/08	a Botev	L	1-2	Sténio
09/08	h Marek	L	0-1	
15/08	a Litex	L	0-3	
23/08	h Lokomotiv Plovdiv	W	3-0	Bozhilov, Raykov 2
29/08	a Levski	L	0-1	
13/09	h CSKA	D	1-1	Petkov
19/09	a Slavia	W	3-1	Petkov, Kokonov, Raykov
28/09	h Lokomotiv Sofia	L	0-1	
03/10	a Haskovo	W	1-0	Kokonov
19/10	h Beroe	W	4-0	Manolov (p), Coureur, Kotev, Raykov
25/10	a Ludogorets	L	0-2	
02/11	h Botev	W	2-1	Coureur, Palankov
08/11	a Marek	W	3-1	Sténio, Kokonov, Manolov
22/11	h Litex	L	0-3	
29/11	a Lokomotiv Plovdiv	D	1-1	Coureur
06/12	h Levski	W	1-0	Coureur
13/12	a CSKA	L	1-3	Sténio

2015
27/02	h Slavia	W	2-0	Zlatinov (p), Hernández
09/03	a Lokomotiv Sofia	L	1-2	Kokonov
13/03	h Haskovo	W	1-0	Sténio
20/03	h Marek	W	1-0	Burkhardt
03/04	a Levski	L	2-5	Zlatinov, Raykov
10/04	h Haskovo	W	2-0	Hernández, Raykov
19/04	a Slavia	D	1-1	Burkhardt
24/04	a Lokomotiv Plovdiv	W	1-0	Kokonov
02/05	a Marek	W	2-0	Kokonov, Bizhev
09/05	h Levski	L	0-2	
18/05	a Haskovo	W	3-1	Hernández, Bizhev, Burkhardt
22/05	a Slavia	W	3-1	Bacari, Kokonov, Coureur
26/05	h Lokomotiv Plovdiv	L	1-2	Georgiev

No	Name	Nat	DoB	Pos	Aps	(s)	Gls
25	Alexander Emilov Alexandrov		30/07/86	D	16	(1)	
30	Dimo Atanasov		24/10/85	M	1	(5)	
91	Zhivko Atanasov		03/02/91	D	13	(9)	
9	Bubacar Bacari	ESP	14/03/88	A	5	(7)	1
20	Veliyan Bizhev		03/01/93	A	6	(5)	2
14	Georgi Bozhilov		12/02/87	A	16	(4)	1
18	Marcin Burkhardt	POL	25/09/83	D	15	(4)	3
40	Aleksandar Čanović	SRB	18/02/83	G	10		
23	Mamoutou Coulibaly	MLI	23/02/84	D	10		
19	Mathias Coureure	MTQ	22/03/88	A	16	(5)	5
3	Daniel Georgiev		06/11/82	M	7	(4)	1
22	Sebastián Hernández	COL	02/10/86	A	7	(4)	3
21	Emil Iliev		09/05/97	M		(1)	
33	Georgi Kitanov		06/03/95	G	12		
10	Marc Klok	NED	20/04/93	M	11	(2)	
17	Ivan Kokonov		17/08/91	A	23	(6)	7
7	Martin Kostadinov		13/05/96	M	1		
6	Kiril Kotev		04/08/82	D	25	(1)	1
22	Karen Madoyan		15/07/95	M	1		
20	Miroslav Manolov		20/05/85	A	12	(5)	2
10	Nikolay Minkov		13/08/97	M	1		
11	Iliyan Nedelchev		01/03/96	M	1		
1	Ilia Nikolov		14/07/86	G	3	(2)	
84	Todor Palankov		13/01/84	M	23		1
45	Kristian Peshkov		26/01/96	A		(1)	
11	Zhivko Petkov		03/02/93	A	8	(8)	2
26	Ilko Pirgov		23/05/86	G	7		
8	Alexander Popov		15/08/96	M	1		
7	Bekir Rasim		26/12/94	M	3	(10)	
13	Simeon Raykov		11/11/89	M	19	(4)	6
24	Slavi Stalev		28/02/94	D	5	(2)	
5	Stefan Stanchev		26/04/89	D	13	(2)	
8	Sténio	CPV	05/05/89	M	27	(1)	5
31	Toni Stoichkov		10/11/95	D	1		
4	Mihail Venkov		28/07/83	D	28		
4	Alexander Yovchev		27/10/96	D	1		
15	Petar Zlatinov		13/03/81	M	4	(1)	2

BULGARIA

PFC CSKA Sofia

1948 • Bulgarska Armia (22,000) • cska.bg

Major honours
Bulgarian League (31) 1948, 1951, 1952, 1954, 1955, 1956, 1957, 1958, 1959, 1960, 1961, 1962, 1966, 1969, 1971, 1972, 1973, 1975, 1976, 1980, 1981, 1982, 1983, 1987, 1989, 1990, 1992, 1997, 2003, 2005, 2008; Bulgarian Cup (19) 1951, 1954, 1955, 1961, 1965, 1969, 1972, 1973, 1974, 1983, 1985, 1987, 1988, 1989, 1993, 1997, 1999, 2006, 2011

**Coach: Stoycho Mladenov;
(20/03/15) (Anatoli Nankov);
(24/03/15) Galin Ivanov;
(28/04/15) Luboslav Penev**

2014
20/07	a Litex	W	1-0	Marquinhos
27/07	h Levski	W	2-0	Karachanakov, Buş
03/08	a Slavia	D	2-2	Buş, Tunchev
10/08	h Haskovo	W	4-0	Iliev, Toni Silva, Joachim, Buş
16/08	a Ludogorets	L	0-2	
22/08	h Marek	W	5-0	Buş, Karachanakov, Kukoč, Tunchev, Marquinhos
30/08	a Lokomotiv Plovdiv	W	3-0	Toni Silva, Buş, Juan Felipe
13/09	a Cherno More	D	1-1	Juan Felipe
20/09	h Lokomotiv Sofia	W	3-0	Juan Felipe, Buş, Joachim
28/09	a Beroe	W	2-1	Karachanakov, Buş
03/10	h Botev	W	1-0	Toni Silva
18/10	h Litex	W	2-0	Tunchev, Edenilson
25/10	a Levski	W	3-0	Toni Silva, Buş, Galchev
01/11	h Slavia	D	0-0	
09/11	a Haskovo	W	4-2	Karachanakov, Buş 2, Platini
22/11	h Ludogorets	D	1-1	Tunchev
30/11	a Marek	D	0-0	
06/12	h Lokomotiv Plovdiv	W	2-0	Oršulić, Joachim
13/12	h Cherno More	W	3-1	Oršulić, Joachim 2

2015
01/03	a Lokomotiv Sofia	L	0-2	
07/03	h Beroe	L	0-1	
15/03	a Botev	L	0-2	
21/03	h Beroe	D	0-0	
04/04	a Ludogorets	L	0-4	
10/04	h Botev	L	0-1	
20/04	h Lokomotiv Sofia	L	0-1	
26/04	a Litex	L	0-2	
01/05	a Beroe	D	0-0	
09/05	h Ludogorets	D	0-0	
16/05	a Botev	L	2-3	Toni Silva, Milisavljević
23/05	a Lokomotiv Sofia	D	1-1	Marquinhos
31/05	h Litex	W	3-1	Kukoč, Marković, Galchev

No	Name	Nat	DoB	Pos	Aps	(s)	Gls
5	Mario Brkljača	CRO	07/02/85	M	3	(4)	
17	Sergiu Buş	ROU	02/11/92	A	18	(1)	10
33	Jakub Diviš	CZE	27/07/86	G	24		
22	Edenilson	BRA	13/09/87	M	5	(6)	1
8	Boris Galchev		31/10/83	M	15	(9)	2
	Anatoli Gospodinov		21/04/94	G	6		
14	Valentin Iliev		11/07/80	D	11	(1)	1
13	Aurélien Joachim	LUX	10/08/86	A	6	(14)	5
70	Juan Felipe	BRA	05/12/87	A	23	(5)	3
71	Anton Karachanakov		17/01/92	M	10	(5)	4
12	Stoyan Kolev		03/02/76	G		(1)	
66	Plamen Krachunov		11/01/89	D	3	(1)	
77	Tonči Kukoč	CRO	25/09/90	D	22		2
10	Ivan Marković	SRB	20/06/94	M	2		1
28	Marquinhos		30/04/82	M	18	(6)	3
11	Nemanja Milisavljević	SRB	01/11/84	M	14	(8)	1
5	Cendrino Misidjan	NED	29/08/88	M	1		
9	Stefan Nikolić	MNE	16/04/90	A	7	(3)	
48	Marin Oršulić	CRO	25/08/87	M	14	(2)	2
20	Platini	CPV	04/04/86	M	13	(11)	1
19	Apostol Popov		22/12/82	D	17	(1)	
34	Denys Prychynenko	UKR	17/02/92	D	7	(4)	
25	Sava Savov		07/07/96	A		(1)	
73	Ivan Stoyanov		24/07/83	M	4	(2)	
4	Stephen Sunday	NGA	17/09/88	M	28		
31	Christian Supusepa	NED	29/08/88	D	6	(1)	
7	Toni Silva	POR	15/09/93	M	22	(5)	5
3	Alexander Tunchev		10/07/81	D	28		4
92	Maksims Uvarenko	LVA	17/01/87	G	2		
21	Ventsislav Vasilev		08/07/88	D	21	(1)	
16	Petar Vitanov		10/03/95	M	2		

PFC Haskovo

1957 • Dimitar Kanev (7,000) • no website

**Coach: Dimcho Nenov;
(23/09/14) (Levent Avramov);
(06/10/14) Emil Velev;
(18/03/15) Stamen Belchev**

2014
19/07	h Ludogorets	W	1-0	Atanasov
26/07	a Marek	L	1-2	Atanasov
02/08	h Lokomotiv Plovdiv	L	1-2	Lozev
10/08	a CSKA	L	0-4	
17/08	h Lokomotiv Sofia	D	0-0	
24/08	a Beroe	L	0-3	
30/08	h Botev	L	1-2	Angelov
14/09	a Litex	L	0-2	
20/09	h Levski	L	1-4	Angelov (p)
28/09	a Slavia	L	0-1	
03/10	h Cherno More	L	0-1	
17/10	a Ludogorets	L	1-3	Korudzhiev
24/10	h Marek	L	0-1	
02/11	a Lokomotiv Plovdiv	L	0-1	
09/11	h CSKA	L	2-4	Pedro Eugénio, Lozev
22/11	a Lokomotiv Sofia	L	1-2	Aleksiev
29/11	h Beroe	W	1-0	Uzunov
07/12	a Botev	L	0-2	
13/12	h Litex	L	1-4	Aleksiev

2015
27/02	a Levski	L	0-8	
13/03	a Cherno More	L	0-1	
17/03	h Slavia	L	1-5	Aleksiev
20/03	a Levski	D	1-1	Aleksiev
03/04	h Lokomotiv Plovdiv	W	2-0	Marem, Aleksiev
10/04	a Cherno More	L	0-2	
17/04	h Marek	W	1-0	Trifonov
27/04	a Slavia	D	0-0	
04/05	h Levski	L	0-5	
10/05	a Lokomotiv Plovdiv	L	0-4	
18/05	h Cherno More	L	1-3	Uzunov
21/05	a Marek	L	1-3	Uzunov
27/05	h Slavia	L	0-1	

No	Name	Nat	DoB	Pos	Aps	(s)	Gls
12	Kiril Akalski		17/10/85	G	2		
2	Orhan Aktaş	GER	21/10/94	M	10		
39	Dimitar Aleksiev		28/07/93	A	16	(5)	5
27	Dimitar Andonov		19/10/87	M	6	(5)	
9	Emil Angelov		17/07/80	A	10	(4)	2
9	Doncho Atanasov		02/04/83	M	13	(3)	2
1	Nikolay Bankov		19/11/90	G	20	(1)	
77	Beysim Beysim		04/08/93	D	8	(2)	
7	Valchan Chanev		15/07/92	M	9	(9)	
88	Atanas Chepilov		06/02/87	A	6	(10)	
27	Nikolay Dimitrov		12/06/90	M	9		
44	Galin Dimov		29/10/90	D	3	(1)	
9	Grigor Dolapchiev		23/02/94	A	5	(7)	
4	Nedyalko Hubenov		23/08/79	D	7	(4)	
2	Georgi Korudzhiev		02/03/88	M	15	(1)	1
24	Martin Kovachev		13/02/82	D	7	(1)	
17	Kircho Krumov		29/06/83	M	13	(2)	
80	Atanas Krustev		01/02/93	A	7	(3)	
6	Dzhihad Kyamil		04/08/89	M	4	(7)	
11	Deyan Lozev		26/10/93	M	20	(5)	2
89	Stanislav Malamov		21/09/89	M	8		
3	Teynur Marem		23/09/94	D	6		1
96	Eduard Mechikyan		18/02/96	G		(1)	
10	Marius Naydenov		10/07/94	M		(3)	
26	Kostadin Nichev		22/07/88	D	13	(1)	
11	Petyo Nikolov		18/06/93	D	1	(3)	
20	Pedro Eugénio	POR	26/06/90	M	13	(1)	1
21	Boyan Peykov		01/05/84	G	10		
21	Mitko Plahov		12/02/93	M	1	(6)	
19	Martin Raynov		25/04/92	M	24	(1)	
6	Yusein Sabri		16/06/98	M		(1)	
5	Oleg Shalaev	RUS	06/02/92	M	6		
14	Ivan Skerlev		28/01/86	D	30		
18	Michael Tawiah	GHA	01/12/90	M	6		
7	Tihomir Trifonov		25/11/86	D	12		1
23	Vladislav Uzunov		26/05/91	A	25	(3)	3
66	Vasil Velev		15/01/84	M	7	(1)	

PFC Levski Sofia

1914 • Georgi Asparuhov (15,000) • levski.bg

Major honours
Bulgarian League (26) 1933, 1937, 1942, 1946, 1947, 1949, 1950, 1953, 1965, 1968, 1970, 1974, 1977, 1979, 1984, 1985, 1988, 1993, 1994, 1995, 2000, 2001, 2002, 2006, 2007, 2009; Bulgarian Cup (25) 1942, 1946, 1947, 1949, 1950, 1956, 1957, 1959, 1967, 1970, 1971, 1976, 1977, 1979, 1984, 1986, 1991, 1992, 1994, 1998, 2000, 2002, 2003, 2005, 2007

**Coach: Pepe Murcia (ESP);
(04/08/14) Georgi Ivanov;
(22/12/14) Stoycho Stoev**

2014
19/07	h Lokomotiv Plovdiv	D	1-1	Domovchiyski
27/07	a CSKA	L	0 2	
02/08	h Lokomotiv Sofia	W	1-0	Procházka
10/08	a Beroe	L	1-2	Domovchiyski
17/08	h Botev	W	2-1	Gadzhev, Pedro
24/08	a Litex	L	0-3	
29/08	h Cherno More	W	1-0	Bozhinov (p)
14/09	a Slavia	W	2-0	Procházka, Añete
20/09	a Haskovo	W	4-1	Pedro, Domovchiyski, Gadzhev, Añete
27/09	h Ludogorets	W	3-2	Bedoya 2, Sarmov
04/10	a Marek	D	1-1	M Ivanov (p)
18/10	a Lokomotiv Plovdiv	D	1-1	Bedoya
25/10	h CSKA	L	0-3	
02/11	a Lokomotiv Sofia	W	1-0	Añete
07/11	h Beroe	L	0-1	
23/11	a Botev	W	3-0	Procházka, Sarmov, Bedoya
29/11	h Litex	D	2-2	Domovchiyski, Añete
06/12	a Cherno More	L	0-1	
13/12	a Slavia	L	1-3	Domovchiyski (p)

2015
27/02	h Haskovo	W	8-0	Domovchiyski 2, Añete 2, Bedoya, Kraev, Ninu, Gikiewicz
08/03	a Ludogorets	L	0-1	
14/03	h Marek	W	4-0	Añete, Gadzhev 2, Abdi
20/03	h Haskovo	D	1-1	Añete
03/04	h Cherno More	W	5-2	Abdi, Kraev, Domovchiyski, og (Coulibaly), B Tsonev
11/04	a Slavia	L	0-1	
17/04	h Lokomotiv Plovdiv	W	5-0	Domovchiyski, Procházka, Añete 3
25/04	a Marek	W	3-1	Gikiewicz, Pedro, B Tsonev (p)
04/05	a Haskovo	W	5-0	Bedoya 2, Kraev, Añete, Orachev
09/05	a Cherno More	W	2-0	Domovchiyski, Bedoya
16/05	h Slavia	L	2-3	R Tsonev 2
22/05	a Lokomotiv Plovdiv	W	1-0	Gadzhev
26/05	h Marek	W	6-0	Kraev 3, B Tsonev (p), Añete 2

No	Name	Nat	DoB	Pos	Aps	(s)	Gls
7	Liban Abdi	NOR	05/10/88	A	8	(1)	2
2	Alexander Emilov Alexandrov		30/07/86	D	5	(3)	
13	Najib Ammari	ALG	10/04/92	M	4	(2)	
20	Añete	ESP	01/10/85	A	25	(3)	14
6	Miguel Bedoya	ESP	15/04/86	M	27	(3)	8
3	Aymen Belaïd	TUN	02/01/89	D	28		
86	Valeri Bozhinov		15/02/86	A	3	(2)	1
19	Iliya Dimitrov		10/07/96	A		(2)	
20	Radoslav Dimitrov		12/08/88	D	1	(2)	
35	Plamen Dimov		29/10/90	D	5	(2)	
17	Valeri Domovchiyski		05/10/86	A	19	(10)	10
45	Vladimir Gadzhev		18/07/87	M	19	(3)	5
9	Łukasz Gikiewicz	POL	26/10/87	A	3	(3)	2
23	Plamen Iliev		30/11/91	G	17		
39	Deyan Ivanov		12/04/96	D	1		
16	Miroslav Ivanov		09/11/81	M		(4)	1
29	Bojan Jorgačević	SRB	12/02/82	G	8		
12	Bozhidar Kraev		23/06/97	M	12	(7)	6
71	Plamen Krumov		04/11/85	D	16		
32	Stefano Kunchev		20/04/91	G	3		
24	Alexander Lybenov		11/02/95	D	2		
9	Veselin Minev		14/10/80	D	24		
22	Vladislav Misyak		15/07/95	M	2	(3)	
1	Kristijan Naumovski	MKD	17/09/88	G	2	(1)	
31	Emil Ninu	ROU	28/08/86	D	7	(2)	1
7	Anton Ognyanov		30/06/88	M		(4)	
10	Miki Orachev		19/03/96	D	7	(2)	1
11	Luís Pedro	NED	27/04/90	M	20	(3)	3
15	Roman Procházka	SVK	14/03/89	M	23	(4)	4
7	Georgi Sarmov		07/09/85	M	15		2
5	Bozhidar Stoychev		26/11/86	D	28	(2)	
18	Borislav Tsonev		29/04/95	M	5	(3)	3
21	Radoslav Tsonev		29/04/95	M	4	(6)	2
77	Stefan Velev		02/05/89	D	9	(11)	

PFC Litex Lovech

1921• Gradski (7,000) • pfclitex.com
Major honours
Bulgarian League (4) 1998, 1999, 2010, 2011;
Bulgarian Cup (4) 2001, 2004, 2008, 2009
Coach: Krasimir Balakov

2014

20/07	h CSKA	L	0-1	
28/07	a Lokomotiv Sofia	L	0-2	
03/08	h Beroe	W	2-1	Angelov, Milanov
09/08	a Botev	D	3-3	Jordán, Popov, Asprilla
15/08	h Cherno More	W	3-0	Jordán 2, Galabov
24/08	h Levski	W	3-0	Asprilla, Kossoko, Zlatinov
30/08	a Slavia	W	2-0	Kossoko, og (Ristevski)
14/09	h Haskovo	W	2-0	Malinov, Jordán
21/09	a Ludogorets	L	1-4	Asprilla
29/09	h Marek	W	3-0	Jordán, Minchev 2
04/10	a Lokomotiv Plovdiv	L	0-2	
18/10	a CSKA	L	0-2	
24/10	h Lokomotiv Sofia	W	4-2	Bozhikov, Vajushi (p), Asprilla 2
03/11	a Beroe	L	0-2	
08/11	h Botev	L	1-2	Jordán
22/11	a Cherno More	W	3-0	Jordán, Asprilla, Despodov
29/11	a Levski	D	2-2	Malinov, Despodov
07/12	h Slavia	W	2-0	Asprilla, Rumenov
13/12	a Haskovo	W	4-1	Galabov, Vajushi, Jordán 2

2015

28/02	h Ludogorets	W	1-0	Asprilla
09/03	a Marek	D	0-0	
13/03	h Lokomotiv Plovdiv	W	1-0	Milanov
22/03	a Lokomotiv Sofia	D	0-0	
05/04	a Botev	W	1-0	Popov
11/04	h Beroe	D	1-1	Minchev
19/04	a Ludogorets	L	1-3	Johnsen
26/04	h CSKA	W	2-0	Asprilla 2
03/05	h Lokomotiv Sofia	D	0-0	
11/05	h Botev	W	1-0	Popov
17/05	a Beroe	L	1-3	Johnsen
23/05	h Ludogorets	W	4-2	Paulo Regula (p), Johnsen 3
31/05	a CSKA	L	1-3	Johnsen

No	Name	Nat	DoB	Pos	Aps	(s)	Gls
73	Milcho Angelov		02/01/95	A	8	(16)	1
70	Danilo Asprilla	COL	12/01/89	A	29		10
5	Nikolay Bodurov		30/05/86	D	2		
93	Petrus Boumal	CMR	20/04/93	M	24	(1)	
24	Vasil Bozhikov		02/06/88	D	25	(1)	1
99	Kiril Despodov		11/11/96	A	4	(14)	2
28	Plamen Galabov		02/11/95	D	16	(1)	2
8	Alexander Georgiev		10/10/97	M		(2)	
23	Ivan Goranov		10/06/92	D	9	(3)	
11	Bjørn Johnsen	NOR	06/11/91	A	12	(1)	6
9	Wilmar Jordán	COL	17/10/90	A	19		9
88	Nikola Kolev		06/06/95	M	15	(5)	
12	Alexander Konov		03/09/93	G	1		
78	Omar Kossoko	FRA	10/03/88	A	5	(3)	2
15	Kristiyan Malinov		30/03/94	M	28	(2)	2
6	Jackson Mendy	SEN	25/05/87	D	15		
18	Iliya Milanov		19/02/92	D	10	(4)	2
7	Georgi Minchev		20/04/95	A		(11)	3
3	Anton Nedyalkov		30/04/93	D	19	(2)	
10	Paulo Regula	POR	12/03/89	M	8	(3)	1
5	Rafael Pérez	COL	09/01/90	D	13		
11	Emil Petrov		19/06/96	M		(1)	
16	Strahil Popov		30/08/90	D	31		3
19	Rumen Rumenov		07/06/93	M	14	(13)	1
27	Momchil Tsvetanov		03/12/90	M		(1)	
21	Alexander Tsvetkov		31/08/90	M	1	(6)	
14	Armando Vajushi	ALB	03/12/91	M	13	(2)	2
31	Vinícius	BRA	19/07/85	G	31		
24	Petar Zlatinov		13/03/81	M		(3)	1

PFC Lokomotiv Plovdiv 1936

1936 • Lokomotiv (13,000) • lokomotivpd.com
Major honours
Bulgarian League (1) 2004
Coach: Nedelcho Matushev;
(01/10/14) Hristo Kolev

2014

19/07	a Levski	D	1-1	Nakov
26/07	h Slavia	D	1-1	Kiki
02/08	a Haskovo	W	2-1	Kamburov, Nakov
09/08	h Ludogorets	L	1-4	Karageren
17/08	a Marek	D	0-0	
23/08	a Cherno More	L	0-3	
30/08	h CSKA	L	0-3	
15/09	a Lokomotiv Sofia	L	0-2	
20/09	h Beroe	L	0-3	
27/09	a Botev	L	0-2	
04/10	h Litex	W	2-0	og (Bozhikov), Kamburov
18/10	a Levski	D	1-1	Kamburov
24/10	a Slavia	W	2-0	Kamburov 2
02/11	h Haskovo	W	1-0	Karageren
09/11	a Ludogorets	L	0-2	
22/11	h Marek	W	1-0	Kamburov
29/11	h Cherno More	D	1-1	Kamburov
06/12	a CSKA	L	0-2	
12/12	h Lokomotiv Sofia	L	0-4	

2015

28/02	a Beroe	L	0-3	
10/03	h Botev	L	0-2	
13/03	a Litex	L	0-1	
21/03	a Slavia	L	0-3	
03/04	a Haskovo	L	0-3	
13/04	h Marek	W	4-0	Kamburov 2 (1p), Karageren 2
17/04	a Levski	L	0-5	
24/04	h Cherno More	L	0-1	
02/05	h Slavia	L	1-2	Bourabia
10/05	h Haskovo	W	4-0	Kamburov, Kiki, Delev, Lasimant
17/05	a Marek	W	4-1	Kiki, Kamburov 3
22/05	h Levski	L	0-1	
26/05	a Cherno More	W	2-1	De Vriese, Karageren

No	Name	Nat	DoB	Pos	Aps	(s)	Gls
16	Mehdi Bourabia	FRA	07/08/91	M	9	(2)	1
17	Georgi Chukalov		25/02/98	M		(3)	
3	Emmerik De Vriese	BEL	14/02/85	M	1	(8)	1
25	Spas Delev		22/09/89	A	9		1
2	Ivaylo Dimitrov		26/06/87	M	7	(1)	
13	Radoslav Dimitrov		12/08/88	D	8	(1)	
6	Ignat Dishliev		08/07/87	D	1		
17	Bogomil Dyakov		12/04/84	D	19	(1)	
4	Venelin Filipov		20/08/90	D	22		
15	Aleksandar Goranov		27/05/88	D	3	(3)	
12	Yordan Gospodinov		15/06/78	G	19		
15	Angel Granchov		16/02/92	D	14		
3	Zdravko Iliev		19/10/84	D	11	(2)	
11	Martin Kamburov		13/10/80	A	28		13
21	Birsent Karageren		06/12/92	M	24	(6)	5
9	Dani Kiki		08/01/88	M	13	(11)	3
7	Branimir Kostadinov		04/09/89	M	1	(11)	
89	Yohann Lasimant	FRA	04/09/94	A	10	(2)	1
14	Stanislav Malamov		21/09/89	M	5	(7)	
20	Diyan Moldovanov		02/04/85	D	20		
6	Blagoy Nakov		19/03/85	M	15	(1)	2
13	Oshobe Oladele	NGA	25/11/93	M	1		
9	Shaban Osmanov		17/02/91	M		(2)	
6	Elian Parrino	ARG	03/09/88	D	8	(1)	
22	Yanko Sandanski		23/11/88	M	20	(1)	
6	Martin Sechkov		17/11/86	D	11		
12	Teodor Skorchev		04/09/86	G	7		
18	Hristo Stamov		02/01/94	M	5	(3)	
13	Georgi Stefanov		13/07/88	M	1	(2)	
1	Bozhidar Stoychev		01/05/91	G	2		
23	Vanco Trajanov	MKD	09/08/78	M	27	(2)	
5	Georgi Valchev		07/03/91	D	7	(12)	
1	Alexander Vitanov		01/05/92	G	4	(1)	
10	Alexander Yakimov		27/04/89	D	20	(4)	
16	Aykut Yanakov		08/04/95	A		(3)	

PFC Lokomotiv Sofia

1929 • Lokomotiv (15,000) •
lokomotivsofia.bg
Major honours
Bulgarian League (4) 1940, 1945, 1964, 1978; Bulgarian
Cup (4) 1948, 1953, 1982, 1995
Coach: Dimitar Vasev

2014

20/07	a Botev	L	0-1	
28/07	h Litex	W	2-0	Chehoudi, Genov
02/08	a Levski	L	0-1	
09/08	h Slavia	W	1-0	Ivanov
17/08	a Haskovo	D	0-0	
23/08	h Ludogorets	D	2-2	Helton, Tom
30/08	a Marek	W	1-0	Randjelović
15/09	h Lokomotiv Plovdiv	W	2-0	Romanov, Chehoudi
20/09	a CSKA	L	0-3	
28/09	a Cherno More	W	1-0	Branekov
03/10	h Beroe	L	0-3	
19/10	h Botev	W	3-1	Ivanov, Tom, Romanov
24/10	a Litex	L	2-4	Tom, Yordanov
02/11	h Levski	L	0-1	
08/11	h Slavia	W	2-1	Genov, Chehoudi
22/11	h Haskovo	W	2-1	Chehoudi 2
30/11	a Ludogorets	L	1-5	Romanov
06/12	h Marek	W	2-0	Chehoudi, Todorov
12/12	a Lokomotiv Plovdiv	W	4-0	Randjelović, Chehoudi 2, Genov

2015

01/03	h CSKA	W	2-0	Yordanov, Romanov
09/03	h Cherno More	W	2-1	Yordanov, Genov
15/03	a Beroe	D	0-0	
22/03	h Litex	D	0-0	
05/04	a Beroe	W	4-1	Chehoudi, Todorov, Gargorov, Romanov
13/04	h Ludogorets	D	0-0	
20/04	a CSKA	W	1-0	Romanov
26/04	h Botev	W	1-0	Gargorov
03/05	a Litex	D	0-0	
11/05	h Beroe	L	0-1	
15/05	a Ludogorets	L	1-4	Genov
23/05	a CSKA	D	1-1	Gargorov
31/05	a Botev	W	2-0	Fernando Livramento, Velkovski

No	Name	Nat	DoB	Pos	Aps	(s)	Gls
6	Alexandar Branekov		31/05/87	D	26		1
29	Lamjed Chehoudi	TUN	08/05/86	A	20	(3)	9
88	Petar Dimitrov		28/02/92	M	2	(7)	
47	Fernando Livramento	POR	03/03/82	M	30		1
21	Daniel Gadzhev		21/06/85	M	1	(7)	
23	Emil Gargorov		15/02/81	M	11	(1)	3
7	Daniel Genov		19/05/89	M	24	(2)	5
16	Kamen Hadzhiev		22/09/91	D	22	(4)	
69	Helton dos Reis	FRA	01/05/88	D	30	(2)	1
26	Ivo Ivanov		30/04/85	M	19	(5)	2
1	Alexander Manolov		03/03/91	M	2	(7)	
1	Bozhidar Mitrev		31/03/87	G	32		
5	Marko Randjelović	SRB	16/08/84	D	21	(1)	2
11	Vladislav Romanov		07/02/88	D	32		6
20	Anton Slavchev		21/06/95	M		(2)	
66	Orlin Starokin		08/01/87	D	10		
77	Yordan Todorov		27/07/81	M	7	(16)	2
33	Tom	BRA	18/03/86	M	30		3
15	Trayan Trayanov		03/08/87	D	10	(8)	
8	Rumen Trifonov		22/02/85	M	20	(7)	
14	Daniel Vasev		23/05/94	M		(7)	
19	Dimitar Velkovski		22/01/95	M		(3)	1
9	Preslav Yordanov		21/07/89	A	3	(9)	3

PFC Ludogorets Razgrad

1945 • Ludogorets Arena (5,000) •
ludogorets.com
Major honours
*Bulgarian League (4) 2012, 2013, 2014, 2015;
Bulgarian Cup (2) 2012, 2014*
**Coach: Stoycho Stoev;
(30/07/14) Georgi Dermendzhiev**

2014
19/07	a Haskovo	L	0-1		
26/07	a Cherno More	D	0-0		
02/08	h Marek	W	3-0	*og (Lahchev), Misidjan, Juninho Quixadá*	
09/08	a Lokomotiv Plovdiv	W	4-1	*Juninho Quixadá 2, Wanderson, Misidjan*	
16/08	h CSKA	W	2-0	*Misidjan, Younés*	
23/08	a Lokomotiv Sofia	D	2-2	*Anicet Abel 2*	
31/08	h Beroe	D	1-1	*Barthe*	
12/09	a Botev	W	2-1	*Dani Abalo, Bezjak*	
21/09	h Litex	W	4-1	*Marcelinho, M Alexandrov, Younés, Wanderson*	
27/09	a Levski	L	2-3	*Moţi (p), Wanderson*	
04/10	h Slavia	D	0-0		
17/10	h Haskovo	W	3-1	*Marcelinho, Moţi (p), Dani Abalo*	
25/10	h Cherno More	W	2-0	*Wanderson, Misidjan*	
31/10	a Marek	W	4-0	*Dani Abalo 2, Marcelinho, Bezjak*	
09/11	h Lokomotiv Plovdiv	W	2-0	*Dani Abalo, Younés (p)*	
22/11	a CSKA	D	1-1	*Fábio Espinho*	
30/11	h Lokomotiv Sofia	W	5-1	*Wanderson, Marcelinho 2, Younés, Dani Abalo*	
05/12	a Beroe	W	4-0	*Juninho Quixadá, Misidjan 2, Wanderson*	
14/12	h Botev	W	1-0	*Anicet Abel*	
2015					
28/02	a Litex	L	0-1		
08/03	h Levski	W	1-0	*Wanderson*	
14/03	a Slavia	W	3-0	*Fábio Espinho, Zlatinski (p), Misidjan*	
22/03	h Botev	D	0-0		
04/04	h CSKA	W	4-0	*Barthe, Marcelinho, Misidjan, Juninho Quixadá*	
13/04	a Lokomotiv Sofia	D	0-0		
19/04	h Litex	W	3-1	*Juninho Quixadá, Moţi, Dani Abalo*	
25/04	a Beroe	L	0-2		
03/05	a Botev	W	3-1	*Juninho Quixadá 2, Wanderson*	
09/05	a CSKA	D	0-0		
15/05	h Lokomotiv Sofia	W	4-1	*Marcelinho, Juninho Quixadá 2, Misidjan*	
23/05	a Litex	L	2-4	*Misidjan, Marcelinho*	
31/05	h Beroe	D	1-1	*Zlatinski (p)*	

No	Name	Nat	DoB	Pos	Aps	(s)	Gls
15	Alexander Dragomirov Alexandrov		13/04/86	D	13		
7	Mihail Alexandrov		11/06/89	M	13	(9)	1
16	Brayan Angulo	COL	02/11/89	D	17	(3)	
12	Anicet Abel	MAD	16/03/90	M	14	(8)	3
31	Georgi Argilashki		13/06/91	G	1		
5	Alexandre Barthe	FRA	05/03/86	D	12	(1)	2
9	Roman Bezjak	SVN	21/02/89	A	9	(6)	2
26	Milan Borjan	CAN	23/10/87	G	2		
20	Choko	BRA	18/01/90	D	5		
91	Ivan Čvorović		21/09/85	G	6		
17	Dani Abalo	ESP	29/09/87	M	20	(8)	7
18	Svetoslav Dyakov		31/05/84	M	24		
8	Fábio Espinho	POR	18/08/85	M	19	(4)	2
10	Sebastián Hernández	COL	10/12/86	A		(2)	
11	Juninho Quixadá	BRA	12/12/85	A	16	(9)	10
80	Júnior Caiçara	BRA	27/04/89	D	24	(2)	
13	Veselin Lyubomirov		02/02/96	M		(1)	
4	Tero Mäntylä	FIN	18/04/91	D	2		
84	Marcelinho	BRA	24/08/84	M	21	(1)	8
25	Yordan Minev		14/10/80	D	14		
93	Virgil Misidjan	NED	24/07/93	M	24	(4)	10
27	Cosmin Moţi	ROU	03/12/84	D	23		3
24	Preslav Petrov		01/05/95	D		(1)	
21	Vladislav Stoyanov		08/06/87	G	23		
55	Georgi Terziev		18/04/92	D	13		
19	Alexander Vasilev		27/04/95	D	2	(5)	
77	Vitinha	POR	11/02/86	M	2	(1)	
88	Wanderson	BRA	02/01/88	M	14	(14)	8
99	Hamza Younés	TUN	16/04/86	A	8	(9)	4
23	Hristo Zlatinski		22/01/85	M	11	(7)	2

PFC Marek Dupnitsa

1947 • Bonchuk (16,050) • no website
Major honours
Bulgarian Cup (1) 1978
**Coach: Anton Velkov;
(01/10/14) (Yanek Kyuchukov);
(06/10/14) Tencho Tenev**

2014
19/07	a Slavia	L	1-4	*Tonchev*	
26/07	h Haskovo	W	2-1	*M Vasilev, Bibishkov (p)*	
02/08	a Ludogorets	L	0-3		
09/08	a Cherno More	W	1-0	*D Petkov*	
17/08	h Lokomotiv Plovdiv	D	0-0		
22/08	a CSKA	L	0 5		
30/08	h Lokomotiv Sofia	L	0-1		
13/09	a Beroe	L	0-4		
20/09	h Botev	D	1-1	*Krastovchev (p)*	
29/09	a Litex	L	0-3		
04/10	h Levski	D	1-1	*Bonev*	
19/10	h Slavia	L	0-2		
24/10	a Haskovo	W	1-0	*Krastovchev*	
31/10	h Ludogorets	L	0-4		
08/11	h Cherno More	L	1-3	*K Petkov*	
22/11	h Lokomotiv Plovdiv	L	0-1		
30/11	h CSKA	D	0-0		
06/12	a Lokomotiv Sofia	L	0-2		
13/12	h Beroe	L	0-3		
2015					
02/03	a Botev Povdiv	L	0-3		
09/03	h Litex	D	0-0		
14/03	a Levski	L	0-2		
20/03	a Cherno More	L	0-1		
04/04	a Slavia	W	1-0	*Abushev*	
13/04	a Lokomotiv Plovdiv	L	0-4		
17/04	a Haskovo	L	0-1		
25/04	h Levski	L	1-3	*D Dimitrov*	
02/05	h Cherno More	L	0-2		
08/05	a Slavia	L	0-4		
17/05	h Lokomotiv Plovdiv	L	1-4	*Yordanov*	
21/05	h Haskovo	W	3-1	*B Nikolov, Bonev, Manolov*	
26/05	a Levski	L	0-6		

No	Name	Nat	DoB	Pos	Aps	(s)	Gls
19	Rangel Abushev		26/05/89	A	8		1
19	Dimitar Andonov		19/10/87	M	18		
20	Dimo Atanasov		24/10/85	A	10		
11	Krum Bibishkov		02/09/82	A	20		1
7	Mario Bliznakov		09/08/82	A	8	(6)	
18	Zlatko Bonev		09/06/94	M	11	(4)	2
6	Svetoslav Dikov		18/04/92	M	1	(4)	
9	Dimitar Dimitrov		06/01/90	M	8	(15)	1
8	Martin Dimitrov		17/07/87	D	25	(2)	
2	Iliyan Garov		08/01/84	M	10		
2	Daniel Georgiev		16/01/94	M	1	(1)	
20	Dimitar Iliev		27/07/86	A	18		
5	Martin Kavdanski		13/02/87	D	12		
17	Todor Kolev		22/09/89	M	4		
10	Enyo Krastovchev		07/02/84	A	14	(8)	2
4	Milen Lahchev		01/04/87	D	26	(1)	
14	Alexander Manolov		03/03/91	M	10	(2)	1
1	Emil Mihaylov		01/05/88	G	29		
12	Plamen Mladenov		04/09/87	G	2		
13	Borislav Nikolov		03/02/92	M	28		1
9	Nikolay Nikolov		26/01/81	D	9	(6)	
9	Tomislav Pavlov		10/06/91	M		(1)	
16	Dimitar Petkov		24/08/87	M	19	(1)	1
12	Kristiyan Petkov		10/08/94	A	4	(7)	1
17	Pavel Petkov		26/06/90	M	3	(4)	
4	Denis Pidev		01/11/92	M	6		
4	Angel Rusev		06/01/81	A		(3)	
6	Emil Stoyanov		11/11/96	M		(3)	
15	Petar Tonchev		08/04/89	M	11	(2)	1
2	Veselin Tsvetkovski		08/03/89	G	1		
7	Georg Vasilev		29/10/95	M		(4)	
5	Milen Vasilev		17/05/88	M	6	(2)	1
3	Emil Viyachki		18/05/90	D	23	(3)	
6	Dimitar Vladimirov		29/10/95	A		(1)	
15	Ivan Vlahov		29/04/96	M		(1)	
5	Rosen Yordanov		06/04/92	A	4	(7)	1
2	Angel Yoshev		01/01/85	D	3	(1)	

PFC Slavia Sofia

1913 • Slavia (15,000) • pfcslavia.com
Major honours
*Bulgarian League (7) 1928, 1930, 1936, 1939, 1941,
1943, 1996; Bulgarian Cup (7) 1952, 1963, 1964,
1966, 1975, 1980, 1996*
**Coach: Milen Radukanov;
(31/08/14) Ivan Kolev**

2014
19/07	h Marek	W	4-1	*Carlos Fonseca, Michel, Genchev, Bizhev*	
26/07	a Lokomotiv Plovdiv	D	1-1	*Michel*	
03/08	h CSKA	D	2-2	*Burgzorg, Michel*	
09/08	a Lokomotiv Sofia	L	0-1		
16/08	h Beroe	L	0-2		
24/08	a Botev	L	0-2		
30/08	h Litex	L	0-2		
14/09	a Levski	L	0-2		
19/09	h Cherno More	L	1-3	*Michel*	
28/09	h Haskovo	W	1-0	*R Vasilev*	
04/10	a Ludogorets	D	0-0		
19/10	a Marek	W	2-0	*R Vasilev, Michel*	
24/10	h Lokomotiv Plovdiv	L	0-2		
01/11	a CSKA	D	0-0		
08/11	h Lokomotiv Sofia	L	1-2	*Savic*	
23/11	a Beroe	D	1-1	*R Vasilev*	
29/11	h Botev	W	3-0	*Carlos Fonseca, R Vasilev 2*	
07/12	a Litex	L	0-2		
13/12	h Levski	W	3-1	*Manzorro 3*	
2015					
27/02	a Cherno More	L	0-2		
14/03	a Ludogorets	L	0-3		
17/03	h Haskovo	W	5-1	*R Vasilev 2, Atanasov, Mbarga, Manzorro*	
21/03	h Lokomotiv Plovdiv	W	3-0	*Atanasov, R Vasilev 2*	
04/04	a Marek	L	0-1		
11/04	h Levski	W	1-0	*Carlos Fonseca*	
19/04	a Cherno More	D	1-1	*Dimitrov*	
27/04	a Haskovo	D	0-0		
02/05	a Lokomotiv Plovdiv	W	2-1	*Pirgov, R Vasilev (p)*	
08/05	h Marek	W	4-0	*Carlos Fonseca 2, Manzorro 2 (1p)*	
16/05	a Levski	W	3-2	*Pirgov, Atanasov, Manzorro*	
22/05	h Cherno More	L	1-3	*Manzorro*	
27/05	a Haskovo	W	1-0	*Atanasov*	

No	Name	Nat	DoB	Pos	Aps	(s)	Gls
20	Petar Atanasov		13/10/90	A	8	(1)	4
9	Viliyan Bizhev		03/01/93	A		(10)	1
11	Mitchell Burgzorg	NED	25/07/87	M	13	(2)	1
33	Carlos Fonseca	POR	23/08/87	A	17	(1)	5
71	Diego	BRA	21/05/92	M	23	(2)	
14	Ivaylo Dimitrov		26/03/89	M	2	(2)	1
17	Kostadin Dyakov		22/08/85	M	20	(1)	
4	Fernando Silva	BRA	18/05/91	M	12	(2)	
8	Stanislav Genchev		20/03/81	M	10	(3)	1
18	Dimitar Georgiev		09/02/92	M		(4)	
88	Angel Granchov		16/10/92	D	4	(1)	
75	Yanis Karabelyov		08/03/96	M	2	(2)	
6	Fernander Kassaï	CTA	01/07/87	D	19	(1)	
13	Mario Kirev		15/08/89	G	8	(1)	
70	Plamen Krumov		04/11/85	D	7	(1)	
7	Jérémy Manzorro	FRA	11/11/91	M	25	(5)	8
5	Franck Mbarga	GER	09/01/92	M	4	(1)	1
20	Michel	BRA	08/09/83	A	15		5
25	Tsvetomir Panov		17/04/89	D	25	(1)	
1	Georgi Petkov		14/03/76	G	17		
12	Emil Petrov		22/07/83	G	7	(1)	
3	Dimitar Pirgov		23/10/89	D	15	(5)	2
4	Kire Ristevski	MKD	22/10/90	D	11	(3)	
77	Dusan Savic	MKD	01/10/85	A	8		1
22	Vladimir Semerdzhiev		27/05/95	M	10	(5)	
45	Slavcho Shokolarov		20/08/89	M	4	(4)	
77	Martin Stankev		06/04/88	M		(1)	
23	Emil Stoev		17/01/96	M		(5)	
91	Krum Stoyanov		19/11/92	M	4	(6)	
4	Dimitar Todorov		08/11/90	D		(1)	
35	Ivan Valchanov		28/09/91	M	13	(10)	
24	Kitan Vasilev		19/02/97	A		(1)	
99	Radoslav Vasilev		12/10/90	A	21	(4)	10
26	Dimitar Vezalov		13/04/87	D	25	(1)	
88	Chavdar Yankov		29/03/84	M	3	(2)	

Top goalscorers

14 Añete (Levski)

13 Martin Kamburov (Lokomotiv Plovdiv)

10 Sergiu Buş (CSKA)
Valeri Domovchiyski (Levski)
Danilo Asprilla (Litex)
Juninho Quixadá (Ludogorets)
Virgil Misidjan (Ludogorets)
Radoslav Vasilev (Slavia)

9 Wilmar Jordán (Litex)
Lamjed Chehoudi (Lokomotiv Sofia)

Promoted clubs

PFC Montana 1921

1921 • Ogosta (8,000) • no website
Coach: Ferario Spasov

OFC Pirin Blagoevgrad

1922 • Hristo Botev (7,500) • pirinfc.com
Coach: Yordan Samokovliyski;
(24/04/15) Ivo Trenchev

Second level final table 2014/15

		Pld	W	D	L	F	A	Pts
1	PFC Montana 1921	30	25	3	2	72	16	78
2	OFC Pirin Blagoevgrad	30	17	10	3	52	15	61
3	FC Lokomotiv Gorna Oryahovitsa	30	18	5	7	60	34	59
4	FC Bansko 1951	30	14	11	5	38	18	53
5	PFC Dobrudzha 1919 Dobrich	30	13	7	10	41	28	46
6	FC Sozopol	30	12	10	8	39	25	46
7	PFC Burgas	30	11	10	9	34	30	43
8	FC Botev Galabovo	30	11	9	10	35	40	42
9	FC Lokomotiv Mezdra	30	12	5	13	43	41	41
10	FC Pirin 2002 Razlog	30	10	10	10	33	38	40
11	FC Vereya Stara Zagora	30	9	10	11	25	24	37
12	FC Septemvri Simitli	30	11	3	16	30	47	36
13	OFC Botev Vratsa	30	8	5	17	26	43	29
14	PSFC Chernomorets Burgas	30	7	7	16	25	40	28
15	FC Rakovski 2011	29	6	1	22	25	71	16
16	PFC Spartak 1918 Varna	29	2	0	27	9	77	6

NB PFC Spartak 1918 Varna withdrew after round 16;
FC Rakovski 2011 withdrew after round 17 – their
remaining matches were awarded as 0-3 defeats;
FC Rakovski 2011 – 3 pts deducted.

DOMESTIC CUP

Kupa na Bulgariya 2014/15

FIRST ROUND

(23/09/14)
Lokomotiv Mezdra 0-4 Botev Plovdiv
Spartak Varna 1-7 Levski Sofia
Vereya Stara Zagora 0-2 Lokomotiv Plovdiv

(24/09/14)
Atletik Kuklen 0-6 Bansko
Botev Galabovo 1-0 Marek Dupnista
Botev Vratsa 1-5 Ludogorets Razgrad
Burgas 0-1 Beroe Stara Zagora
Chernomorets Burgas 1-3 Slavia Sofia
Dunav Ruse 4-0 Rakovski
Manastirishte 1-4 Lokomotiv Gorna Oryahovitsa
Montana 2-1 CSKA Sofia *(aet)*
Pirin Gotse Dolchev 3-0 Dobrudzha
Pirin Razlog 0-1 Lokomotiv Sofia
Septemvri Simitli 1-3 Haskovo
Sozopol 0-2 Cherno More Varna

(25/09/14)
OFC Pirin Blagoevgrad 1-2 Litex Lovech *(aet)*

SECOND ROUND

(28/10/14 & 12/11/14)
Litex Lovech 3-1, 4-0 Pirin Gotse Delchev *(7-1)*

(28/10/14 & 03/12/14)
Cherno More Varna 2-0, 2-2 Slavia Sofia *(4-2)*
Lokomotiv Plovdiv 1-1, 2-1 Botev Plovdiv *(3-2)*

(29/10/14 & 14/11/14)
Botev Galabovo 1-4, 1-5 Lokomotiv Sofia *(2-9)*

(29/10/14 & 03/12/14)
Haskovo 3-0, 0-2 Bansko *(3-2)*
Montana 2-0, 0-4 Levski Sofia *(2-4)*

(29/10/14 & 06/12/14)
Lokomotiv Gorna Oryahovitsa 1-1, 1-0 Dunav Ruse *(2-1)*

(15/02/15 & 22/02/15)
Beroe Stara Zagora 2-1, 0-1 Ludogorets Razgrad *(2-2; Ludogorets on away goal)*

QUARTER-FINALS

(21/02/15 & 03/03/15)
Levski Sofia 3-0 Haskovo *(Domovchiyski 23p, 35, Trifonov 90og)*
Haskovo 1-1 Levski Sofia *(Malamov 81; Gikiewicz 42)*
(Levski Sofia 4-1)

(21/02/15 & 05/03/15)
Cherno More Varna 1-0 Lokomotiv Gorna Oryahovitsa *(Rasim 90+2)*
Lokomotiv Gorna Oryahovitsa 0-5 Cherno More Varna *(Burkhardt 2, Kotev 23, Coulibaly 25, Bizhev 38, Sténio 44)*
(Cherno More Varna 6-0)

(22/02/15 & 04/03/15)
Lokomotiv Plovdiv 2-1 Lokomotiv Sofia *(Trajanov 9, Lasimant 60; Chehoudi 14)*
Lokomotiv Sofia 1-2 Lokomiv Plovdiv *(Trayanov 43; Lasimant 32, Delev 54)*
(Lokomotiv Plovdiv 4-2)

(04/03/15 & 18/03/15)
Litex Lovech 0-0 Ludogorets Razgrad
Ludogorets Razgrad 5-0 Litex Lovech *(Dyakov 12, Fábio Espinho 27, Barthe 62, Misidjan 84, Dani Abalo 90)*
(Ludogorets Razgrad 5-0)

SEMI-FINALS

(07/04/15 & 28/04/15)
Cherno More Varna 5-1 Lokomotiv Plovdiv *(Raykov 2, Bizhev 44, Venkov 48, Coureur 59, Bacari 76; Bourabia 69)*
Lokomotiv Plovdiv 2-3 Cherno More Varna *(Delev 39, Coulibaly 67og; Z Atanasov 4, Coureur 89, 90)*
(Cherno More Varna 8-3)

(08/04/15 & 29/04/15)
Ludogorets Razgrad 0-0 Levski Sofia
Levski Sofia 1-0 Ludogorets Razgrad *(Añete 90)*
(Levski Sofia 1-0)

FINAL

(30/05/15)
Lazur, Burgas
PFC CHERNO MORE VARNA 2 *(Bacari 90+2, Coureur 119)*
PFC LEVSKI SOFIA 1 *(Añete 72)*
(aet)
Referee: Stoyanov
CHERNO MORE: Čanović, Venkov, Z Atanasov (Bozhilov 86), Burkhardt, Palankov, Raykov (Kokonov 75), Sténio, Klok, Hernández, Coureur, Bizhev (Bacari 59)
Red card: Sténio (38)
LEVSKI: Jorgačević, Procházka, Stoychev, Belaïd (Ninu 28), Minev, Gadzhev, Bedoya, Pedro (Kraev 64), Añete (Velev 87), Abdi, Domovchiyski
Red card: Minev (120+4)

Cherno More players celebrate the club's first Bulgarian Cup win

CROATIA
Hrvatski Nogometni Savez (HNS)

Address	Vukovarska 269A	**President**	Davor Šuker
	HR-10000 Zagreb	**General secretary**	Damir Vrbanović
Tel	+385 1 2361 555	**Media officer**	Tomislav Pacak
Fax	+385 1 2441 501	**Year of formation**	1912
E-mail	info@hns-cff.hr	**National stadium**	Maksimir, Zagreb
Website	hns-cff.hr		(35,123)

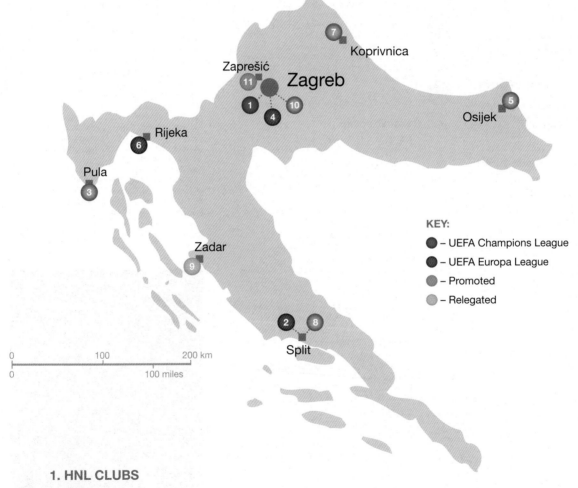

KEY:
- – UEFA Champions League
- – UEFA Europa League
- – Promoted
- – Relegated

1. HNL CLUBS

  **1** GNK Dinamo Zagreb

  **2** HNK Hajduk Split

  3 NK Istra 1961

 4 NK Lokomotiva Zagreb

 5 NK Osijek

  6 HNK Rijeka

  **7** NK Slaven Koprivnica

  8 RNK Split

  9 NK Zadar

 10 NK Zagreb

PROMOTED CLUB

  **11** NK Inter Zaprešić

Dominant Dinamo double up again

GNK Dinamo Zagreb's private possession of the Croatian league title extended to a tenth year in 2014/15, and the club marked that achievement by winning it undefeated – the first time they or any other club had completed a 1. HNL campaign without losing a game.

HNK Rijeka were by some distance the best of the rest, finishing 13 points adrift of Dinamo but a full 25 ahead of third-placed HNK Hajduk Split, whose city rivals RNK Split took Dinamo to penalties in a goalless Croatian Cup final but were unable to deny Zoran Mamić's side the double.

Tenth successive league title for Zagreb club	**First Croatian champions to end season undefeated**	**Split denied on penalties after goalless cup final**

Domestic league

Any threat to Dinamo's long reign as Croatian champions effectively ended a quarter of the way through the campaign when they consolidated a near-flawless start by winning 2-1 at in-form Rijeka. That put them four points clear, and although their sole challengers continued to impress, with ace striker Andrej Kramarić scoring for fun, Dinamo were equally relentless, and when the second summit meeting, in Zagreb, brought another Dinamo win, 3-0, that was effectively that.

Dinamo's seven-point winter-break advantage gradually increased in the spring as Rijeka, with their 21-goal hit man sold to Leicester City FC, dropped off the pace. Although Dinamo had also been weakened by mid-season transfers, with both top scorer Duje Čop and midfield schemer Marcelo Brozović departing to Italy, they had plenty in reserve to keep their unbeaten run going. In fact, they would have defeated Rijeka away again but for an extremely late equaliser. The last time the two met, on the final day, Dinamo had already been confirmed as champions for several weeks and were now concerned only with completing the season undefeated. They accomplished their mission with ease, trouncing Matjaž Kek's team 4-0 in the Maksimir.

Homegrown winger Marko Pjaca, who scored twice in the final fixture, was the revelation of Dinamo's season, but it was the club's wealth of foreign talent that set the team apart, from Portuguese internationals Eduardo and Paulo Machado to Macedonian skipper Arijan Ademi and strikers El Arbi Hillel Soudani and Ángelo Henríquez, the latter finishing one goal behind autumn goal king Kramarić in the 1. HNL scorer charts.

Elsewhere, Hajduk and NK Lokomotiva Zagreb both qualified for the UEFA Europa League, the latter on goals scored ahead of NK Zagreb, while NK Zadar's eight-year top-flight sojourn ended, with NK Inter Zaprešić replacing them. A planned promotion/relegation play-off between NK Istra 1961 and NK Sesvete was cancelled as the latter's stadium did not meet top-division licensing requirements.

Domestic cup

Without a Croatian Cup win since 2012, Dinamo avenged their 2014 final conquerors Rijeka by defeating them 2-1 in the semi-finals to set up a meeting in the Maksimir – for the competition's first one-off final in 16 years – with Split, who overcame city rivals Hajduk by the same aggregate thanks to a penalty in each leg. Spot-kicks, however, would be the underdogs' undoing as they valiantly held the champions at bay for two hours only to lose 4-2 in a shoot-out, with Marko Rog and Slavko Bogajević both missing their efforts as Dinamo's four chosen ones all scored.

Europe

As in 2013/14, Dinamo and Rijeka both competed in the UEFA Europa League group stage, but this time they made a better fist of it. Although neither club made further progress, they did both win twice at home, with three players – Dinamo's Soudani and Pjaca, and Rijeka's Kramarić – all scoring hat-tricks. The two teams from Split did not disgrace themselves either, each of them falling to narrow play-off defeats, Hajduk against eventual runners-up FC Dnipro Dnipropetrovsk.

National team

Croatia made good progress towards a fourth successive UEFA European Championship appearance as Niko Kovač's side drew twice with Italy and won their other four qualifiers – with a goal difference of 14-1 – to end the season on top of their group. It was an excellent effort from a team of many talents, including several players who shone for their clubs in 2014/15, among them Real Madrid CF's Luka Modrić, FC Barcelona's Ivan Rakitić and AS Monaco FC goalkeeper Danijel Subašić. The season also brought a 100th international cap for Ivica Olić – the fifth Croatian player to reach that milestone.

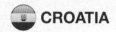

DOMESTIC SEASON AT A GLANCE

1. HNL 2014/15 final table

		Pld	Home					Away					Total					Pts
			W	D	L	F	A	W	D	L	F	A	W	D	L	F	A	
1	**GNK Dinamo Zagreb**	36	17	1	0	53	5	9	9	0	32	16	26	10	0	85	21	88
2	HNK Rijeka	36	14	3	1	56	12	8	6	4	20	17	22	9	5	76	29	75
3	HNK Hajduk Split	36	9	5	4	36	25	6	3	9	23	31	15	8	13	59	56	50
4	NK Lokomotiva Zagreb	36	7	3	8	28	31	6	1	8	31	37	13	7	16	59	68	46
5	NK Zagreb	36	8	4	6	26	24	5	3	10	19	30	13	7	16	45	54	46
6	NK Slaven Koprivnica	36	10	5	3	26	13	1	4	13	12	36	11	9	16	38	49	42
7	RNK Split	36	5	9	4	26	24	4	5	9	16	25	9	14	13	42	49	41
8	NK Osijek	36	8	4	6	25	20	2	2	14	17	39	10	6	20	42	59	36
9	NK Istra 1961	36	6	8	4	19	20	1	6	11	17	39	7	14	15	36	59	35
10	NK Zadar	36	6	4	8	24	26	2	4	12	13	49	8	8	20	37	75	32

NB HNK Hajduk Split – 3 pts deducted.

European qualification 2015/16

 Champion/Cup winner: GNK Dinamo Zagreb (second qualifying round)

 HNK Rijeka (second qualifying round)
HNK Hajduk Split (first qualifying round)
NK Lokomotiva Zagreb (first qualifying round)

Top scorer	Andrej Kramarić (Rijeka), 21 goals
Relegated club	NK Zadar
Promoted club	NK Inter Zaprešić
Cup final	GNK Dinamo Zagreb 0-0 RNK Split *(aet; 4-2 on pens)*

Team of the season
(4-1-3-2)

Coach: Mamić *(Dinamo)*

Player of the season

Ángelo Henríquez
(GNK Dinamo Zagreb)

He came up just short in the race for the 1. HNL golden boot, but 20 goals in 25 games, a tally including three hat-tricks, was an impressive return for Henríquez on his season-long loan at Dinamo from Manchester United FC. The Chilean international striker added six goals in the domestic cup and also converted Dinamo's opening penalty in the final shoot-out against RNK Split to help the club complete the double. The reward for his efforts was a place in host nation Chile's 2015 Copa América-winning squad.

Newcomer of the season

Marko Pjaca
(GNK Dinamo Zagreb)

Dinamo have a long-established reputation for producing gifted young footballers, and Pjaca, who turned 20 in the month that the club claimed their eighth Croatian league and cup double, is the latest to have turned heads with his extravagant talent. Fast, powerful and full of trickery, the young winger's first season at Dinamo, following a transfer from feeder club NK Lokomotiva Zagreb, was adorned with 11 league goals plus a memorable UEFA Europa League hat-trick at home to Celtic FC.

Kalinić *(Hajduk)*

Tomečak *(Rijeka)* | Mrčela *(Lokomotiva)* | Mitrović *(Rijeka)* | B Barišić *(Osijek)*

Ademi *(Dinamo)*

Pjaca *(Dinamo)* | Krovinović *(Zagreb)* | Sušić *(Hajduk)*

Kramarić *(Rijeka)* | Henríquez *(Dinamo)*

NATIONAL TEAM

International tournament appearances
FIFA World Cup (4) 1998 (3rd), 2002, 2006, 2014
UEFA European Championship (4) 1996 (qtr-finals), 2004, 2008 (qtr-finals), 2012

Top five all-time caps
Darijo Srna (123); Stipe Pletikosa (114); Josip Šimunić (105); **Ivica Olić** (102); Dario Šimić (100)

Top five all-time goals
Davor Šuker (45); Eduardo (29); **Darijo Srna** (21); **Ivica Olić** (20); **Mario Mandžukić** (19)

Results 2014/15

04/09/14	Cyprus	H	Pula	W	2-0	*Mandžukić (18, 58)*
09/09/14	Malta (ECQ)	H	Zagreb	W	2-0	*Modrić (46), Kramarić (81)*
10/10/14	Bulgaria (ECQ)	A	Sofia	W	1-0	*Bodurov (36og)*
13/10/14	Azerbaijan (ECQ)	H	Osijek	W	6-0	*Kramarić (11), Perišić (34, 45), Brozović (45+1), Modrić (57p), Sadıqov (61og)*
12/11/14	Argentina	N	London (ENG)	L	1-2	*Sharbini (11)*
16/11/14	Italy (ECQ)	A	Milan	D	1-1	*Perišić (15)*
28/03/15	Norway (ECQ)	H	Zagreb	W	5-1	*Brozović (30), Perišić (53), Olić (65), Schildenfeld (87), Pranjić (90+4)*
07/06/15	Gibraltar	H	Varazdin	W	4-0	*Sharbini (7), Kovačić (15), Mandžukić (53p), Kramarić (79)*
12/06/15	Italy (ECQ)	H	Split	D	1-1	*Mandžukić (11)*

Appearances 2014/15

Coach: Niko Kovač	15/10/71		Cyp	MLT	BUL	AZE	Arg	ITA	NOR	Gib	ITA	Caps	Goals
Danijel Subašić	27/10/84	Monaco (FRA)	G	G	G	G		G	G	G	G	14	-
Darijo Srna	01/05/82	Shakhtar Donetsk (UKR)	D78	D	D	D		D	D		D 90*	123	21
Dejan Lovren	05/07/89	Liverpool (ENG)	D	D								30	2
Vedran Ćorluka	05/02/86	Lokomotiv Moskva (RUS)	D69	D	D	D		D	D 74*			81	4
Ivan Strinić	17/07/87	Dnipro (UKR)	D									33	-
Marcelo Brozović	16/11/92	Dinamo Zagreb /Internazionale (ITA)	M	M	M	M		M83	M	M65	M	10	2
Luka Modrić	09/09/85	Real Madrid (ESP)	M61	M	M	M60		M28	M			84	10
Mateo Kovačić	06/05/94	Internazionale (ITA)	M78	M46	s80	M24	M46	s28		M46	M92	21	1
Alen Halilović	18/06/96	Barcelona (ESP)	M69	M67		s60	s46					7	-
Andrej Kramarić	19/06/91	Rijeka /Leicester (ENG)	A	s67		A76		s68	s70	s46		6	3
Mario Mandžukić	21/05/86	Atlético (ESP)	A61	A79	A	A		A	A87	A57	A	60	19
Duje Čop	01/02/90	Dinamo Zagreb	s61				A84					2	-
Mario Pašalić	09/02/95	Elche (ESP)	s61							s65		2	-
Ivica Olić	14/09/79	Wolfsburg (GER) /Hamburg (GER)	s69	s79	M	s76		M68	M70		M46	102	20
Domagoj Vida	29/04/89	Dynamo Kyiv (UKR)	s69		D	D		D	D		D	29	1
Tin Jedvaj	28/11/95	Leverkusen (GER)	s78				D			D		3	-
Marko Pjaca	06/05/95	Dinamo Zagreb	s78							M57		2	-
Hrvoje Milić	10/05/89	Rostov (RUS)	D				M71					6	-
Ivan Rakitić	10/03/88	Barcelona (ESP)	M	M80	M			M	M75		M	71	9
Nikica Jelavić	27/08/85	Hull (ENG)	s46									36	6
Danijel Pranjić	02/12/81	Panathinaikos (GRE)			D	D		D	D		D72	57	1
Ivan Perišić	02/02/89	Wolfsburg (GER)			M	s24		M	M	s57	M	38	9
Lovre Kalinić	03/04/90	Hajduk Split					G89					1	-
Marin Leovac	07/08/88	Rijeka					D			D	s92	3	-
Marko Lešković	27/04/91	Rijeka					D84			D		2	-
Šime Vrsaljko	10/01/92	Sassuolo (ITA)					D			D	s72	12	-
Domagoj Antolić	30/06/90	Dinamo Zagreb					M					1	-
Milan Badelj	25/02/89	Fiorentina (ITA)					M	s83	s87	M65		13	1
Anas Sharbini	21/02/87	Rijeka					M65			M46		3	2
Mato Jajalo	25/05/88	Rijeka /Palermo (ITA)					s65			s65		2	-
Ivan Tomečak	07/12/89	Rijeka					s71					1	-
Matej Mitrović	10/11/93	Rijeka					s84					1	-
Marko Rog	19/07/95	Split					s84					1	-
Ivan Vargić	15/03/87	Rijeka					s89					1	-
Gordon Schildenfeld	18/03/85	Panathinaikos (GRE)							s75		D	23	1
Ante Rebić	21/09/93	RB Leipzig (GER)								s46	s46	10	1
Nikola Kalinić	05/01/88	Dnipro (UKR)								s57		21	6

EUROPE

GNK Dinamo Zagreb

CHAMPIONS
LEAGUE

Second qualifying round - VMFD Žalgiris (LTU)
H 2-0 *Soudani (58), Antolić (70)*
Eduardo, Soudani (Pjaca 73), Ibáñez, Šimunić, Ivo Pinto, Antolić (Gonçalo Santos 85), Paulo Machado (Andrijašević 78), Ademi, Sigali, Brozović, Čop. Coach: Zoran Mamić (CRO)
A 2-0 *Soudani (46), Šimunić (49)*
Eduardo, Ibáñez, Šimunić, Šimunović, Ivo Pinto, Antolić, Paulo Machado, Radonjić (Soudani 46), Ademi (Ćorić 56), Pjaca, Brozović (Gonçalo Santos 67). Coach: Zoran Mamić (CRO)

Third qualifying round - Aalborg BK (DEN)
A 1-0 *Brozović (49)*
Eduardo, Soudani (Andrijašević 79), Šimunić, Ivo Pinto, Antolić (Gonçalo Santos 70), Paulo Machado, Ademi, Pivarić, Sigali, Brozović, Čop (Pjaca 46). Coach: Zoran Mamić (CRO)
H 0-2
Eduardo, Soudani, Šimunić, Šimunović, Ivo Pinto, Antolić (Pjaca 66), Paulo Machado (Wilson Eduardo 89), Ademi, Pivarić, Brozović, Čop. Coach: Zoran Mamić (CRO)

EUROPA
LEAGUE

Play-offs - FC Petrolul Ploiești (ROU)
A 3-1 *Čop (29p, 80), Paulo Machado (90+6)*
Eduardo, Soudani (Paulo Machado 46), Šimunić, Šimunović, Ivo Pinto, Antolić (Vukojević 72), Ademi, Pivarić, Wilson Eduardo (Pjaca 62), Brozović, Čop. Coach: Zoran Mamić (CRO)
H 2-1 *Čop (22), Antolić (90+5)*
Eduardo, Šimunić, Šimunović, Ivo Pinto, Antolić, Paulo Machado (Vukojević 64), Ademi (Ćorić 90), Pivarić, Wilson Eduardo (Soudani 71), Brozović, Čop. Coach: Zoran Mamić (CRO)

Group D
Match 1 - FC Astra Giurgiu (ROU)
H 5-1 *Soudani (17, 24, 45+1), Henríquez (70), Ćorić (90+2)*
Eduardo, Soudani, Šimunić, Ivo Pinto (Paulo Machado 72), Antolić (Ćorić 77), Ademi, Pivarić, Sigali, Wilson Eduardo, Brozović, Čop (Henríquez 67). Coach: Zoran Mamić (CRO)
Match 2 - Celtic FC (SCO)
A 0-1
Eduardo, Soudani, Šimunić, Ivo Pinto, Antolić (Ćorić 75), Ademi, Pivarić, Sigali, Wilson Eduardo (Pjaca 83), Brozović, Čop (Henríquez 60). Coach: Zoran Mamić (CRO)
Match 3 - FC Salzburg (AUT)
A 2-4 *Ademi (81), Henríquez (89)*
Eduardo, Soudani, Šimunić, Ivo Pinto (Šimunović 65), Antolić, Henríquez, Paulo Machado (Pjaca 53), Ademi, Pivarić (Vukojević 65), Sigali, Brozović. Coach: Zoran Mamić (CRO)
Match 4 - FC Salzburg (AUT)
H 1-5 *Henríquez (60)*
Eduardo, Soudani, Ibáñez, Šimunović, Ivo Pinto, Antolić (Andrijašević 69), Henríquez, Ademi, Brozović, Taravel, Čop (Fernandes 60). Coach: Zoran Mamić (CRO)

Match 5 - FC Astra Giurgiu (ROU)
A 0-1
Eduardo, Soudani, Šimunović, Ivo Pinto, Antolić, Henríquez (Čop 68), Pivarić, Wilson Eduardo (Fernandes 52), Vukojević (Paulo Machado 52), Brozović, Taravel. Coach: Zoran Mamić (CRO)
Match 6 - Celtic FC (SCO)
H 4-3 *Pjaca (14, 40, 50), Brozović (48)*
Eduardo, Soudani (Fernandes 82), Ivo Pinto, Antolić, Henríquez (Čop 65), Ademi, Pivarić, Pjaca, Sigali, Brozović, Taravel (Šimunović 11). Coach: Zoran Mamić (CRO)

HNK Rijeka

EUROPA
LEAGUE

Second qualifying round - Ferencvárosi TC (HUN)
H 1-0 *Krstanović (85p)*
Vargić, Jajala (Kramarić 57), Sharbini (Kvržić 66), Tomečak, Mitrović, Samardžič, Leovac, Brezovec, Moisés, Jugović (Jahović 82), Krstanović. Coach: Matjaž Kek (SVN)
A 2-1 *Krstanović (20p), Samardžić (37)*
Vargić, Jajalo (Kvržić 69), Sharbini (Mitrović 87), Tomečak, Lešković, Samardžič, Leovac, Brezovec, Jugović, Kramarić (Zlomislić 59), Krstanović. Coach: Matjaž Kek (SVN)
Red card: Krstanović 54

Third qualifying round - Víkingur (FRO)
A 5-1 *Lešković (14), Kvržić (45+1, 76), Jahović (52), Kramarić (81p)*
Vargić, Jajalo (Zlomislić 68), Jahović, Tomečak, Lešković, Mitrović, Kvržić, Leovac, Brezovec, Jugović (Ajayi 64), Kramarić (Čanadjija 82). Coach: Matjaž Kek (SVN)
H 4-0 *Jahović (39, 48, 64), E Jacobsen (77og)*
Prskalo, Jajalo (Čanadjija 46), Jahović, Sharbini, Boras, Mitrović, Ajayi, Samardžič, Kvržić (Kramarić 46), Zlomislić (Jugović 71), Bertoša. Coach: Matjaž Kek (SVN)

Play-offs - FC Sheriff (MDA)
H 1-0 *Leovac (85)*
Vargić, Jajalo, Jahović (Moisés 76), Tomečak, Lešković, Samardžič, Kvržić (Cvijanovič 87), Leovac, Brezovec, Jugović (Sharbini 62), Kramarić. Coach: Matjaž Kek (SVN)
A 3-0 *Ligger (29og), Kramarić (44), Moisés (61)*
Vargić, Jajalo, Sharbini (Kvržić 54), Tomečak, Lešković, Samardžič, Leovac, Brezovec, Moisés (Zlomislić 68), Jugović (Cvijanovič 81), Kramarić. Coach: Matjaž Kek (SVN)

Group G
Match 1 - R. Standard de Liège (BEL)
A 0-2
Vargić, Jajalo, Tomečak, Lešković, Cvijanovič, Samardžič, Kvržić (Vešović 66), Leovac, Jugović (Ivančić 81), Kramarić (Moisés 63), Krstanović. Coach: Matjaž Kek (SVN)
Match 2 - Sevilla FC (ESP)
H 2-2 *Kramarić (53p), Kvržić (68)*
Vargić, Jajalo, Tomečak, Lešković, Cvijanovič, Mitrović, Kvržić (Zlomislić 75), Leovac, Moisés (Vešović 88), Jugović, Kramarić (Krstanović 82). Coach: Matjaž Kek (SVN)

Match 3 - Feyenoord (NED)
H 3-1 *Kramarić (63, 71, 76p)*
Vargić, Jajalo, Sharbini, Tomečak, Lešković (Samardžič 65), Cvijanovič, Mitrović, Leovac, Moisés (Krstanović 89), Jugović (Kvržić 84), Kramarić. Coach: Matjaž Kek (SVN)
Match 4 - Feyenoord (NED)
A 0-2
Vargić, Jajalo, Sharbini (Kvržić 50), Tomečak (Vešović 79), Lešković, Cvijanovič, Samardžič, Leovac, Moisés (Krstanović 61), Jugović, Kramarić. Coach: Matjaž Kek (SVN)
Match 5 - R. Standard de Liège (BEL)
H 2-0 *Moisés (26), Kramarić (34p)*
Vargić, Jajalo (Cvijanovič 77), Sharbini (Kvržić 66), Tomečak, Lešković, Mitrović, Močinić, Vešović, Moisés (Krstanović 89), Jugović, Kramarić. Coach: Matjaž Kek (SVN)
Match 6 - Sevilla FC (ESP)
A 0-1
Vargić, Jajalo, Sharbini, Tomečak, Mitrović, Močinić (Cvijanovič 71), Samardžič, Kvržić (Jugović 67), Vešović, Moisés (Ivančić 76), Kramarić. Coach: Matjaž Kek (SVN)

HNK Hajduk Split

EUROPA
LEAGUE

Second qualifying round - Dundalk FC (IRL)
A 2-0 *Caktaš (9), Vlašić (75)*
Stipica, A Milić, Milović, Vršajević, Vlašić, Maglica (Andjelković 58), Gotal, Caktaš, Maloča, Bradarić (Maloku 82), Kouassi (Bašić 79). Coach: Igor Tudor (CRO)
H 1-2 *Kouassi (25)*
Stipica, Milović, Andjelković, Vlašić (Maloku 76), Gotal, Jozinović, Caktaš (Bradarić 46), Maloča, Nižić, Bencun, Kouassi (Maglica 62). Coach: Igor Tudor (CRO)

Third qualifying round - FC Shakhter Karagandy (KAZ)
A 2-4 *Gotal (2), Caktaš (78p)*
Stipica, Mikanović, A Milić, Andjelković, Vlašić (Maloku 88), Gotal, Jozinović, Caktaš, Maloča, Bradarić, Kouassi (Bencun 71). Coach: Igor Tudor (CRO)
H 3-0 *Sušić (14), Maglica (36), Gotal (90+5)*
Kalinić, A Milić (Nižić 66), Milović, Vršajević (Vasilj 73), Andjelković, Vlašić (Kouassi 82), Maglica, Gotal, Caktaš, Maloča, Sušić. Coach: Igor Tudor (CRO)

Play-offs - FC Dnipro Dnipropetrovsk (UKR)
A 1-2 *Sušić (47)*
Kalinić, A Milić, Milović, Vršajević, Andjelković (Mezga 71), Maglica (Milevskiy 78), Gotal (Vlašić 46), Caktaš, Maloča, Sušić, Kouassi. Coach: Igor Tudor (CRO)
H 0-0
Kalinić, A Milić, Milović, Vršajević, Andjelković (Bencun 60), Maglica, Caktaš, Maloča, Sušić (Nižić 84), Kouassi (Gotal 60), Mezga. Coach: Igor Tudor (CRO)

DOMESTIC LEAGUE CLUB-BY-CLUB

RNK Split

First qualifying round - FC Mika (ARM)
H 2-0 *Glumac (39), Vojnović (87)*
Zagorac, Glavina (Roce 63), Glumac, Vojnović, Bilić (M Galić 86), Erceg, Vidović, Rugašević, Galović, Ibriks, Belle (Bagarić 46). Coach: Ivan Matić (CRO)

A 1-1 *Bilić (88)*
Zagorac, Glavina (Rog 70), Glumac, Vojnović (Dujmović 80), Bilić, Erceg, Bagarić (Belle 59), Vidović, Rugašević, Galović, Ibriks. Coach: Ivan Matić (CRO)

Second qualifying round - Hapoel Beer Sheva FC (ISR)
H 2-1 *Dujmović (78), Bilić (86p)*
Vuković, Glavina, Glumac, Vojnović (Dujmović 46), Bilić, Erceg, Bagarić (Belle 70), Vidović, Rugašević (Rog 60), Galović, Ibriks. Coach: Ivan Matić (CRO)

A 0-0
Vuković, Glavina, Glumac, Vojnović (Kvesić 50), Bilić, Erceg, Bagarić (Belle 62), Roce (Rog 79), Vidović, Galović, Ibriks. Coach: Ivan Matić (CRO)

Third qualifying round - FC Chornomorets Odesa (UKR)
H 2-0 *Rog (25), Belle (48)*
Vuković, Glavina (Erceg 75), Glumac, Bilić (Roce 88), Radotić, Rog, Dujmović, Vidović, Rugašević, Galović, Belle (Bagarić 66). Coach: Ivan Matić (CRO)

A 0-0
Vuković, Glavina, Glumac, Bilić (Bagarić 82), Roce (Erceg 71), Radotić (Ibriks 82), Rog, Dujmović, Vidović, Galović, Belle. Coach: Ivan Matić (CRO)

Play-offs - Torino FC (ITA)
H 0-0
Vuković, Glumac, Bilić, Bagarić, Rog (Vojnović 71), Dujmović (Kvesić 87), Vidović, Rugašević, Galović, Ibriks, Belle (Roce 63). Coach: Ivan Matić (CRO)

A 0-1
Vuković, Glavina (Radotić 63), Glumac, Bilić, Bagarić, Rog, Dujmović, Vidović (Kvesić 63), Rugašević, Galović, Ibriks (Roce 84). Coach: Ivan Matić (CRO)

GNK Dinamo Zagreb

1945 • Maksimir (35,123) • gnkdinamo.hr
Major honours
Inter Cities Fairs Cup (1) 1967; Yugoslav League (4) 1948, 1954, 1958, 1982; Croatian League (17) 1993, 1996, 1997, 1998, 1999, 2000, 2003, 2006, 2007, 2008, 2009, 2010, 2011, 2012, 2013, 2014, 2015; Yugoslav Cup (7) 1951, 1960, 1963, 1965, 1969, 1980, 1983; Croatian Cup (13) 1994, 1996, 1997, 1998, 2001, 2002, 2004, 2007, 2008, 2009, 2011, 2012, 2015
Coach: Zoran Mamić

2014
18/07	h	Slaven	W 4-0	Pjaca, Brozović, Soudani, Andrijašević
25/07	a	Lokomotiva	W 4-3	og (Ćalušić), Pjaca, Soudani 2
02/08	h	Zadar	W 5-0	Čop 3, Ademi, Soudani
09/08	a	Osijek	W 2-1	Čop 2 (1p)
15/08	h	Split	W 1-0	Čop
24/08	h	Zagreb	D 1-1	Ibáñez
31/08	a	Hajduk	W 3-2	Čop 2, Henríquez
13/09	a	Istra 1961	W 2-0	Henríquez, Wilson Eduardo
21/09	a	Rijeka	W 2-1	Soudani 2
27/09	a	Slaven	D 0-0	
05/10	h	Lokomotiva	W 3-0	Henríquez 3 (1p)
18/10	a	Zadar	W 3-1	Pjaca, og (Matković), Andrijašević
26/10	h	Osijek	W 5-0	Čop, Taravel, Soudani 2, Fernandes
01/11	a	Split	D 0-0	
09/11	h	Zagreb	D 0-0	
22/11	h	Hajduk	W 3-0	(w/o)
30/11	a	Istra 1961	W 4-0	Pjaca, Soudani, Fernandes, Andrijašević
06/12	h	Rijeka	W 3-0	Ademi, Henríquez, Čop
14/12	h	Slaven	W 3-2	Pjaca, Čop 2

2015
07/02	a	Lokomotiva	W 2-1	Ademi, Henríquez
16/02	h	Zadar	W 2-0	Fernandes, Sigali
22/02	a	Osijek	D 1-1	Pavičić
28/02	h	Split	W 2-0	Henríquez (p), Fernandes
07/03	h	Zagreb	W 2-0	Henríquez 2
14/03	a	Hajduk	D 1-1	Paulo Machado
21/03	h	Istra 1961	W 4-1	Paulo Machado, Henríquez, Pjaca 2
04/04	a	Rijeka	D 2-2	Pjaca, Sigali
12/04	a	Slaven	D 0-0	
17/04	a	Lokomotiva	W 2-1	Soudani, Henríquez
24/04	a	Zadar	W 1-0	Pjaca
28/04	h	Osijek	W 3-0	Pavičić, Henríquez, Ćorić
02/05	a	Split	W 5-1	Henríquez 3 (1p), Ćorić, Hodžić
09/05	a	Zagreb	D 1-1	Henríquez
16/05	h	Hajduk	W 4-0	Ćorić, Henríquez 3
24/05	a	Istra 1961	D 1-1	Fernandes
29/05	h	Rijeka	W 4-0	Pjaca 2 (1p), Taravel, Soudani

No	Name	Nat	DoB	Pos	Aps	(s)	Gls
16	Arijan Ademi	MKD	29/05/91	M	25	(1)	3
7	Franko Andrijašević		22/06/91	M	3	(7)	3
8	Domagoj Antolić		30/06/90	M	12	(1)	
14	Ivan Boras		31/10/91	D	1		
77	Marcelo Brozović		16/11/92	M	12	(2)	1
17	Endri Çekiçi	ALB	23/11/96	M	1	(3)	
90	Duje Čop		01/02/90	A	11	(4)	12
24	Ante Ćorić		14/04/97	M	14	(10)	3
21	Dani Olmo	ESP	07/05/98	A		(5)	
34	Eduardo	POR	19/09/82	G	34		
11	Júnior Fernandes	CHI	04/10/88	A	13	(8)	5
25	Ivan Fiolić		29/04/96	M	2	(3)	
14	Amer Gojak	BIH	13/02/97	M		(1)	
23	Gonçalo	POR	15/11/86	M	13	(10)	
9	Ángelo Henríquez	CHI	13/04/94	A	17	(8)	20
15	Armin Hodžić	BIH	17/11/94	A	1	(5)	1
3	Luis Ibáñez	ARG	15/07/88	D	9		1
6	Ivo Pinto	POR	07/01/90	D	29		
1	Antonio Ježina		05/06/89	G	1		
27	Jerko Leko		09/04/80	M	1		
71	Alexandru Mățel	ROU	17/10/89	D	11	(2)	
10	Paulo Machado	POR	31/03/86	M	25	(4)	2
18	Domagoj Pavičić		09/03/94	M	3	(6)	2
19	Josip Pivarić		30/01/89	D	15	(1)	
20	Marko Pjaca		06/05/95	M	26	(6)	11
15	Dejan Radonjić		23/07/90	A	2		
22	Leonardo Sigali	ARG	29/05/87	D	26		2
4	Josip Šimunić		18/02/78	D	5		
5	Jozo Šimunović		04/08/94	D	20		
28	Borna Sosa		21/01/88	D	1		
2	El Arbi Hillel Soudani	ALG	25/11/87	A	20	(3)	11
87	Jérémy Taravel	FRA	17/04/87	D	17		2
55	Ognjen Vukojević		20/12/83	M	8	(9)	
28	Wilson Eduardo	POR	08/07/90	A	7	(3)	1

HNK Hajduk Split

1911 • Poljud (34,200) • hajduk.hr

Major honours
Yugoslav League (9) 1927, 1929, 1950, 1952, 1955,
1971, 1974, 1975, 1979; Croatian League (6) 1992,
1994, 1995, 2001, 2004, 2005; Yugoslav Cup (9) 1967,
1972, 1973, 1974, 1976, 1977, 1984, 1987, 1991;
Croatian Cup (6) 1993, 1995, 2000, 2003, 2010, 2013

Coach: Igor Tudor;
(04/02/15) (Hari Vukas);
(19/02/15) Stanko Poklepović;
(13/04/15) (Goran Vučević);
(24/04/15) (Hari Vukas)

2014
20/07	h	Istra 1961	D	1-1	Gotal
27/07	a	Rijeka	L	2-4	Kouassi, Caktaš
03/08	h	Slaven	W	2-0	Caktaš, Maglica
10/08	a	Lokomotiva	W	5-2	Kouassi 2, Gotal 2, Maloča (p)
16/08	h	Zadar	W	6-0	Caktaš (p), Maglica 2, Kouassi 2, Gotal
24/08	a	Osijek	L	0-2	
31/08	h	Dinamo	L	2-3	Sušić, A Milić
14/09	a	Zagreb	D	2-2	Vršajević, Kouassi
20/09	h	Split	D	1-1	Maglica
28/09	a	Istra 1961	W	2-0	Sušić, Bradarić
05/10	h	Rijeka	D	1-1	Caktaš (p)
19/10	a	Slaven	W	1-0	Sušić
25/10	h	Lokomotiva	D	2-2	Maloku, Milevskiy
02/11	a	Zadar	W	3-0	Vršajević, Caktaš (p), Vlašić
08/11	h	Osijek	D	2-2	Caktaš (p), Gotal
22/11	a	Dinamo	L	0-3	(w/o)
29/11	h	Zagreb	L	0-2	
07/12	h	Split	W	2-1	og (Ibriks), A Milić
13/12	h	Istra 1961	W	5-3	Caktaš 2 (2p), Gotal 2, Milevskiy

2015
15/02	h	Slaven	W	2-1	Gotal, Vlašić
18/02	a	Rijeka	L	0-3	
21/02	a	Lokomotiva	L	1-2	Maglica
01/03	h	Zadar	D	2-2	Balić, Maglica
08/03	a	Osijek	W	1-0	Balić
14/03	h	Dinamo	L	1-2	Balić
22/03	a	Zagreb	L	0-2	
04/04	h	Split	L	1-2	Milevskiy
11/04	a	Istra 1961	L	2-3	Maglica, Milović
18/04	h	Rijeka	L	1-2	Tudor
26/04	a	Slaven	L	2-3	Mezga, Tudor
29/04	h	Lokomotiva	W	2-1	Mezga 2
03/05	a	Zadar	L	0-2	
09/05	h	Osijek	W	3-2	Gotal, Balić, Caktaš
16/05	a	Dinamo	L	0-4	
23/05	h	Zagreb	W	2-1	Vlašić
30/05	a	Split	D	1-1	Maloku

No	Name	Nat	DoB	Pos	Aps	(s)	Gls
15	Temurkhuja Abdukholiqov	UZB	25/09/91	A		(1)	
7	Mislav Andjelković		22/04/88	M	7	(2)	
99	Andrija Balić		11/08/97	M	8	(6)	4
30	Josip Bašić		02/03/96	M	3	(6)	
32	Marko Bencun		09/11/92	A	2	(6)	
4	Petar Bosančić		19/04/96	D	1		
28	Filip Bradarić		11/01/92	M	10	(3)	1
18	Mijo Caktaš		08/05/92	M	29	(2)	9
11	Sandro Gotal	AUT	09/09/91	A	22	(3)	9
13	Ivo Grbić		18/01/96	G	3		
1	Ismar Hairlahović	BIH	04/03/96	M		(1)	
17	Goran Jozinović		27/08/90	D	20	(3)	
77	Josip Juranović		16/08/95	M	1	(5)	
91	Lovre Kalinić		03/04/90	G	28		
77	Jean Kouassi	CIV	25/09/94	M	15	(1)	6
9	Anton Maglica		11/11/91	A	17	(4)	7
22	Mario Maloča		04/05/89	D	28		1
19	Elvir Maloku		14/05/96	A	2	(13)	2
78	Dejan Mezga		16/07/85	M	19	(2)	3
2	Dino Mikanović		07/05/94	D	12	(1)	
10	Artem Milevskiy	UKR	12/01/85	A	11	(10)	3
4	Antonio Milić		10/03/94	D	11		2
27	Zvonimir Milić		20/02/95	D	1	(1)	
5	Goran Milović		29/01/89	D	27	(1)	1
23	Zoran Nižić		11/10/89	D	12	(4)	
24	Marko Pejić		24/02/95	D	1	(1)	
21	Ivan Prskalo		29/03/95	M	1	(1)	
7	Ruslan Qurbanov	AZE	12/09/91	M	1	(4)	
1	Marko Ranilovič	SVN	25/11/86	G	2	(1)	
25	Dante Stipica		30/05/91	G	2		
31	Tino-Sven Sušić	BIH	13/02/92	M	25	(1)	3
32	Fran Tudor		27/09/95	M	6	(1)	2
14	Ivan Anton Vasilj		05/04/91	D	4	(1)	
8	Nikola Vlašić		04/10/97	M	22	(5)	3
8	Avdija Vršajević	BIH	06/03/86	D	22		2
26	Josip Vuković		02/05/92	M	10	(10)	

NK Istra 1961

1961 • Aldo Drosina (8,923) • nkistra1961.hr
Coach: Igor Pamić

2014
20/07	a	Hajduk	D	1-1	Ivančić
28/07	a	Split	D	1-1	Blagojević
04/08	h	Rijeka	L	0-1	
09/08	a	Slaven	D	1-1	Heister
17/08	h	Lokomotiva	W	3-2	Radonjić 2, Matoš
23/08	a	Zadar	D	1-1	Radonjić
29/08	h	Osijek	D	0-0	
13/09	a	Dinamo	L	0-2	
20/09	h	Zagreb	L	1-2	Tomić
28/09	h	Hajduk	L	0-2	
04/10	a	Split	W	2-0	Radonjić 2
18/10	a	Rijeka	L	1-3	Tomić
25/10	h	Slaven	W	1-0	Horvat
03/11	a	Lokomotiva	L	2-4	Radonjić, Pamić
08/11	h	Zadar	D	1-1	Radonjić
21/11	h	Osijek	D	1-1	Radonjić
30/11	h	Dinamo	L	0-4	
05/12	a	Zagreb	L	0-1	
13/12	a	Hajduk	L	3-5	Radonjić 2 (1p), Blagojević

2015
06/02	a	Split	D	2-2	Matoš 2
15/02	h	Rijeka	D	0-0	
20/02	a	Slaven	L	1-2	Jô
27/02	a	Lokomotiva	D	1-1	Tomić
08/03	a	Zadar	L	0-2	
15/03	h	Osijek	W	1-0	Špehar
21/03	a	Dinamo	L	1-4	Špehar
03/04	a	Zagreb	W	2-1	Radonjić 2 (1p)
11/04	h	Hajduk	W	3-2	Radonjić, Pamić 2
18/04	a	Split	D	1-1	Radonjić (p)
26/04	a	Rijeka	L	0-3	
30/04	a	Slaven	D	2-2	Radonjić 2
04/05	a	Lokomotiva	W	2-1	Repić, Gregov
10/05	a	Zadar	D	0-0	
17/05	a	Osijek	L	0-1	
24/05	h	Dinamo	D	1-1	Jô
30/05	a	Zagreb	L	0-4	

No	Name	Nat	DoB	Pos	Aps	(s)	Gls
6	Luka Batur		28/11/89	D		(3)	
7	Slavko Blagojević		21/03/87	M	16		2
1	Ivan Brkić		29/06/95	G	21		
13	Chung Woon	KOR	30/06/89	D	16		
6	Dinis	POR	21/01/90	M	6	(2)	
24	Saša Dreven		27/01/90	G	12	(1)	
24	Petar Franjić		21/08/91	D	13	(6)	
25	Ivan Graf		17/06/87	D	17		
2	Šime Gregov		08/07/89	D	26	(3)	1
7	Toni Grković		29/12/90	D		(3)	
22	Adis Hadžanović	BIH	02/01/93	M	1	(1)	
26	Marcel Heister	GER	29/07/92	D	32	(2)	1
2	Ivor Horvat		18/01/90	D	5	(1)	1
21	Ermin Huseinbašić	BIH	11/07/93	A	4		
30	Kruno Ivančić		18/01/94	D	7	(5)	1
29	Božidar Janjušević	MNE	30/03/94	M		(1)	
33	Jô	BRA	19/09/88	A	17	(4)	2
11	Marko Jordan		27/10/90	A	7	(10)	
50	Sandi Križman		17/08/89	A	2		
7	Lorran	BRA	18/09/89	D		(1)	
12	Igor Lovrić		07/10/87	G	3		
15	Marin Matoš		26/01/89	M	21	(8)	3
4	Jure Obšivač		28/05/90	D	33	(1)	
20	Zvonko Pamić		04/02/91	M	17	(3)	3
16	Bojan Pavlović	SRB	01/02/85	M	25	(2)	
9	Dejan Radonjić		23/07/90	A	20	(3)	16
4	Amar Rahmanović	BIH	13/05/94	M		(6)	
24	Antonio Repić		30/03/91	M		(4)	1
21	Dennis Salanovic	LIE	26/02/96	M	2	(4)	
25	Ivan Šimurina		08/05/92	D	4		
14	Dino Špehar		08/02/94	A	24	(8)	2
17	Dario Tomić		23/06/87	D	16	(6)	3
3	Vitor Bastos	POR	01/05/90	D	7	(5)	
5	Luka Vučko		11/04/84	D	5	(1)	
5	Neven Vukman		11/04/85	M	17	(7)	
28	Marin Zulim		26/10/91	A		(1)	

NK Lokomotiva Zagreb

1914 • Maksimir (35,123) • nklokomotiva.hr
Coach: Tomislav Ivković;
(11/05/15) (Marko Pinčić)

2014
19/07	a	Osijek	W	4-1	Pavičić, Pajač, Budimir 2
25/07	h	Dinamo	L	3-4	Budimir 3
01/08	a	Zagreb	L	0-2	
10/08	h	Hajduk	L	2-5	Mišić, Mrčela
17/08	a	Istra 1961	L	2-3	Rukavina, Čabraja
24/08	h	Rijeka	W	2-1	Šovšić (p), Pavičić
30/08	a	Slaven	W	2-0	Musa, Pavičić
12/09	a	Split	D	2-2	Leko, Musa
19/09	h	Zadar	L	0-1	
28/09	h	Osijek	W	2-0	Pavičić 2
05/10	a	Dinamo	L	0-3	
19/10	h	Zagreb	W	3-0	Marić 2, Šovšić (p)
25/10	h	Hajduk	D	2-2	Marić, Pavičić
03/11	a	Istra 1961	W	4-2	Rukavina, Doležal, Šovšić (p), Kolar
09/11	a	Rijeka	L	0-6	
23/11	h	Slaven	D	0-0	
28/11	h	Split	D	1-1	Doležal
06/12	a	Zadar	W	5-2	Prenga, Pavičić 2, Doležal, Leko
13/12	a	Osijek	W	2-0	Marić, Kolar

2015
07/02	a	Dinamo	L	1-2	Doležal
14/02	a	Zagreb	W	6-0	Kolar 2, og (Kovačić), Doležal, Gržan, Marić
21/02	h	Hajduk	W	2-1	Andrijašević, Gržan
27/02	a	Istra 1961	D	1-1	Kolar
09/03	h	Rijeka	W	1-0	Leko (p)
14/03	a	Slaven	L	0-4	
21/03	a	Split	W	1-0	Andrijašević
03/04	a	Zadar	L	1-5	Kolar
10/04	h	Osijek	D	2-2	Rukavina, Andrijašević
17/04	h	Dinamo	L	1-2	Gržan
24/04	a	Zagreb	L	1-2	Kolar
29/04	a	Hajduk	L	1-2	Andrijašević
04/05	h	Istra 1961	L	1-2	Begonja
10/05	a	Rijeka	L	0-5	
15/05	h	Slaven	W	2-0	Andrijašević 2
24/05	h	Split	L	0-3	
30/05	a	Zadar	D	2-2	Marić, Leko

No	Name	Nat	DoB	Pos	Aps	(s)	Gls
6	Lee Addy	GHA	07/07/90	D	3	(1)	
18	Muhamed Alghoul		09/04/96	M	1	(1)	
16	Franko Andrijašević		22/06/91	M	14		6
16	Matko Babić		28/07/98	A		(1)	
2	Karlo Bartolec		20/04/95	D	23	(2)	
8	Luka Begonja		23/05/92	M	20	(10)	1
3	Jakov Biljan		02/08/95	M	1	(3)	
11	Karlo Bručić		17/04/92	D	26	(4)	
9	Ante Budimir		22/07/91	A	3		5
17	Dejan Čabraja		22/08/93	A		(3)	1
6	Josip Čalušić		11/10/93	D	16		
17	Denis Ceraj		02/11/95	M	1	(8)	
21	Jan Doležal		12/02/93	A	13	(10)	5
26	Toni Gorupec		04/07/93	D	1	(1)	
30	Šime Gržan		06/04/94	M	13	(9)	3
22	Marko Kolar		31/05/95	A	17	(13)	7
42	Jerko Leko		09/04/80	M	29		4
3	Petar Mamić		06/03/96	D	5	(4)	
21	Mirko Marić		16/05/95	A	9	(15)	6
8	Petar Mišić		24/07/94	A	8	(1)	1
5	Tomislav Mrčela		01/10/90	D	28	(2)	1
13	Filip Mržljak		16/04/93	M	3		
3	Mario Musa		06/07/90	D	16		2
2	Marko Pajač		11/05/93	M	4		1
10	Domagoj Pavičić		09/03/94	M	21		8
14	Dino Perić		12/07/94	D	7	(1)	
19	Herdi Prenga		31/08/94	D	28		1
55	Ante Rukavina		18/06/86	A	26	(3)	3
12	Simon Sluga		17/03/93	G	26		
7	Damir Šovšić		05/02/90	M	24		3
4	Andrej Šporčić		27/02/95	M		(1)	
24	Marko Tolić		05/07/96	M		(1)	
1	Oliver Zelenika		14/05/93	G	10		

NK Osijek

1947 • Gradski vrt (19,500) • nk-osijek.hr
Major honours
Croatian Cup (1) 1999
Coach: Tomislav Rukavina;
(10/02/15) Ivo Šušak

2014

19/07	h	Lokomotiva	L	1-4	*J Barišić*
26/07	a	Zadar	L	1-2	*J Barišić (p)*
03/08	h	Split	D	1-1	*Mišić*
09/08	h	Dinamo	L	1-2	*J Barišić (p)*
17/08	a	Zagreb	W	2-1	*Jonjić 2*
24/08	h	Hajduk	W	2-0	*Baraban, Glavaš*
29/08	a	Istra 1961	D	0-0	
13/09	h	Rijeka	L	0-1	
21/09	a	Slaven	L	0-2	
28/09	a	Lokomotiva	L	0-2	
04/10	h	Zadar	W	4-1	*Mešanović 2, Novaković, Baraban*
17/10	a	Split	L	0-3	
26/10	a	Dinamo	L	0-5	
02/11	h	Zagreb	W	1-0	*B Barišić (p)*
08/11	a	Hajduk	L	1-2	*Glavaš*
21/11	h	Istra 1961	D	1-1	*Jonjić*
01/12	a	Rijeka	L	1-2	*Jonjić*
07/12	a	Slaven	L	2-3	*Mešanović, Škorić*
13/12	h	Lokomotiva	L	0-2	

2015

08/02	a	Zadar	L	1-3	*Laštro*
14/02	h	Split	W	4-0	*Perošević, Škorić 2 (1p), Vojnović*
22/02	h	Dinamo	D	1-1	*Mešanović*
01/03	a	Zagreb	W	4-0	*Perošević, Vojnović 3*
08/03	h	Hajduk	L	0-1	
15/03	a	Istra 1961	L	0-1	
20/03	h	Rijeka	D	0-0	
02/04	a	Slaven	L	1-2	*Peev*
10/04	a	Lokomotiva	D	2-2	*Aneff, Vojnović*
19/04	a	Zadar	L	1-2	*Perošević, Laštro*
25/04	a	Split	L	2-3	*Aneff, Glavaš*
28/04	a	Dinamo	L	0-3	
02/05	h	Zagreb	W	1-0	*Škorić*
09/05	a	Hajduk	L	2-3	*Glavaš, Špoljarić*
17/05	h	Istra 1961	W	1-0	*Perošević*
23/05	a	Rijeka	L	0-3	
30/05	h	Slaven	W	3-2	*Perošević 2, Vojnović (p)*

No	Name	Nat	DoB	Pos	Aps	(s)	Gls
30	Sasha Aneff	URU	26/06/91	A	4	(4)	2
17	Lovro Anić		22/06/97	D		(1)	
14	Ivan Baraban		22/01/88	A	7	(7)	2
8	Borna Barišić		10/11/92	D	28		1
11	Josip Barišić		14/11/86	A	10	(6)	3
28	Slavko Bralić		15/12/92	D	15	(2)	
5	Tomislav Čuljak		25/05/87	D	6	(4)	
9	Marko Dugandžić		07/04/94	A	5	(1)	
18	Marin Glavaš		17/03/92	M	10	(16)	4
17	Nermin Jamak	BIH	25/08/86	M	22	(2)	
20	Matej Jonjić		29/01/91	D	18		4
4	Hrvoje Kurtović		06/10/83	M	18		
11	Neven Laštro	BIH	01/10/88	M	16		2
13	Filip Lončarić		17/09/86	G	6		
16	Andrej Lukić		02/04/94	M	5	(3)	
20	Nikola Mandić		19/03/95	A		(1)	
26	Nikola Matas		22/06/87	D	29	(2)	
3	Jasmin Mešanović	BIH	21/06/92	A	17	(12)	4
1	Zvonimir Mikulić		05/02/90	G	30		
18	Benedikt Mioc		06/10/94	M	1	(2)	
17	Josip Mišić		28/06/94	M	16		1
16	Saša Novaković		27/05/91	D	12		1
3	Antonio Pavić		07/08/94	D	6	(2)	
88	Daniel Peev	BUL	06/10/87	M	2	(2)	1
10	Antonio Perošević		06/03/92	A	19	(4)	6
2	Federico Platero	URU	07/02/91	D	1	(1)	
	Jurica Pranjić		16/02/87	D	6		
21	Mile Škorić		19/06/91	D	25	(6)	4
22	Tomislav Šorša		11/05/89	M	29	(2)	
	Davor Špehar		09/02/88	D	9	(3)	
10	Josip Špoljarić		05/01/97	M	1	(3)	1
	Steven Ugarković	AUS	19/08/94	M	2	(6)	
15	Frane Vitaić		07/06/82	M	1	(1)	
8	Aljoša Vojnović		24/10/85	M	15		6
23	Dragomir Vukobratović	SRB	12/05/88	M	5	(3)	

HNK Rijeka

1946 • Kantrida (11,000) • nk-rijeka.hr
Major honours
Yugoslav Cup (2) 1978, 1979; Croatian Cup (3) 2005, 2006, 2014
Coach: Matjaž Kek (SVN)

2014

20/07	a	Zagreb	W	3-1	*Kramarić 2 (1p), Ajayi*
27/07	h	Hajduk	W	4-2	*Kramarić 3, Sharbini*
04/08	a	Istra 1961	W	1-0	*Krstanović (p)*
10/08	a	Split	W	3-0	*Leovac, Kramarić 2*
16/08	h	Slaven	W	3-0	*Tomečak, Kramarić 2*
24/08	a	Lokomotiva	L	1-2	*Jahovic*
31/08	h	Zadar	W	6-1	*Kramarić, Tomečak, Moisés 3, Cvijanović*
13/09	a	Osijek	W	1-0	*Jugović*
21/09	h	Dinamo	L	1-2	*Kramarić*
27/09	a	Zagreb	W	4-2	*Kramarić 2, Krstanović*
05/10	a	Hajduk	D	1-1	*Kvržić*
18/10	h	Istra 1961	W	3-1	*Jajalo, Kramarić, Zec*
26/10	h	Split	W	1-0	*Kramarić*
01/11	a	Slaven	D	1-1	*Kramarić (p)*
09/11	h	Lokomotiva	W	6-0	*Kramarić 5, Ivančić*
22/11	a	Zadar	W	1-0	*Moisés*
01/12	h	Osijek	W	2-1	*Samardžić, Moisés*
06/12	a	Dinamo	L	0-3	
15/12	a	Zagreb	W	2-1	*Sharbini, og (Štiglec)*

2015

15/02	h	Istra 1961	D	0-0	
18/02	h	Hajduk	W	3-0	*Jugović 2, Balaj*
22/02	h	Split	D	1-1	*Balaj*
28/02	h	Slaven	D	1-1	*Álex*
09/03	a	Lokomotiva	L	0-1	
15/03	h	Zadar	W	4-0	*Balaj, Hristov 2, Leovac*
20/03	a	Osijek	D	0-0	
04/04	a	Dinamo	D	2-2	*Balaj, Radošević*
12/04	h	Zagreb	W	4-1	*Tomečak, Balaj, Mitrović, Tomasov*
18/04	a	Hajduk	W	2-1	*Tomečak, Vešović*
26/04	a	Istra 1961	W	3-0	*Tomasov 2, Álex*
29/04	h	Split	W	2-0	*Tomasov, og (Glavina)*
04/05	a	Slaven	D	1-1	*Balaj*
10/05	h	Lokomotiva	W	5-0	*Tomasov 2, Balaj, Bradarić, Sharbini*
17/05	a	Zadar	W	2-0	*Balaj, Samardžič*
23/05	h	Osijek	W	3-0	*Balaj, Sharbini (p), Tomasov*
29/05	a	Dinamo	L	0-4	

No	Name	Nat	DoB	Pos	Aps	(s)	Gls
17	Goodness Ajayi	NGA	06/10/94	A	2	(8)	1
8	Álex Fernández	ESP	15/10/92	M	9		2
24	Bekim Balaj	ALB	11/01/91	A	15		9
24	Mateo Bertoša		10/08/88	D	6	(3)	
18	Filip Bradarić		11/01/92	M	15		1
30	Josip Brezovec		12/03/86	M	6		
7	Dario Čanadjija		17/04/94	M		(1)	
14	Goran Cvijanović	SVN	09/09/86	M	7	(8)	1
30	Filip Dangubić		05/05/95	A		(1)	
20	Ventsislav Hristov	BUL	09/11/88	A	3	(3)	2
28	Josip Ivančić		29/03/91	A	2	(10)	1
8	Adis Jahovic	MKD	18/03/87	A	3	(1)	1
8	Mato Jajalo		25/05/88	M	15	(1)	1
89	Vedran Jugović		31/07/89	M	25	(1)	3
5	Dario Knežević		20/04/82	D	2		
91	Andrej Kramarić		19/06/91	A	18		21
99	Ivan Krstanović		05/01/83	A	8	(3)	2
10	Zoran Kvržić	BIH	07/08/88	M	9	(8)	1
22	Marin Leovac		07/08/88	D	29		2
14	Marko Lešković		27/04/91	D	26	(1)	
24	Josip Mišić		28/06/94	M	5	(6)	
15	Matej Mitrović		10/11/93	D	24	(2)	1
16	Ivan Močinić		30/04/93	M	11	(8)	
88	Moisés	BRA	17/03/88	M	9	(3)	5
32	Andrej Prskalo		01/05/87	G	8		
33	Josip Radošević		03/04/94	M	12	(4)	1
7	Rúben Lima	POR	03/10/89	D		(2)	
19	Miral Samardžič	SVN	17/02/87	D	20	(2)	2
40	Anas Sharbini		21/02/87	M	26	(3)	4
4	Jozo Špikić	BIH	31/03/94	D		(1)	
7	Marin Tomasov		31/08/87	A	10	(5)	7
11	Ivan Tomečak		07/12/89	D	32	(1)	4
25	Ivan Vargić		15/03/87	G	28		
29	Marko Vešović	MNE	28/08/91	D	8	(9)	1
9	Ermin Zec	BIH	18/02/88	A		(3)	1
21	Damir Zlomislić	BIH	20/07/91	M	3	(7)	

NK Slaven Koprivnica

1907 • Gradski (3,800) • nk-slaven-belupo.hr
Coach: Elvis Scoria;
(30/10/14) (Josip Omrčen Čeko);
(04/11/14) Ante Čačić

2014

18/07	a	Dinamo	L	0-4	
26/07	h	Zagreb	W	3-2	*Delić, Geng, Glavina*
03/08	a	Hajduk	L	0-2	
09/08	h	Istra 1961	D	1-1	*Grgić*
16/08	a	Rijeka	L	0-3	
24/08	a	Split	L	0-2	
30/08	h	Lokomotiva	L	0-2	
14/09	a	Zadar	L	0-4	
21/09	h	Osijek	W	2-0	*Ozobić, og (Jonjić)*
27/09	h	Dinamo	D	0-0	
03/10	a	Zagreb	D	1-1	*Mirić*
19/10	h	Hajduk	W	1-0	
25/10	a	Istra 1961	L	0-1	
01/11	h	Rijeka	D	1-1	*Ozobić*
07/11	h	Split	W	1-0	*Melnjak*
23/11	a	Lokomotiva	D	0-0	
29/11	h	Zadar	W	4-0	*Brlek, Mirić 2, Cesarec*
07/12	a	Osijek	W	3-2	*Mirić 2 (1p), Ozobić*
14/12	a	Dinamo	L	2-3	*Delić, Cesarec*

2015

08/02	a	Zagreb	L	0-1	
15/02	a	Hajduk	L	1-2	*Paracki*
20/02	h	Istra 1961	W	2-1	*Grgić, Mirić*
28/02	a	Rijeka	D	1-1	*Parlov*
07/03	a	Split	L	0-2	
14/03	h	Lokomotiva	W	4-0	*Mirić, Ejupi, Vugrinec 2*
22/03	a	Zadar	L	0-1	
02/04	h	Osijek	W	2-1	*Mihaljević, Crepulja*
12/04	h	Dinamo	D	0-0	
19/04	h	Zagreb	W	2-1	*Mirić 2*
26/04	h	Hajduk	L	0-2	
30/04	a	Istra 1961	D	2-2	*Ejupi 2*
04/05	h	Rijeka	D	1-1	*Mišić*
08/05	h	Split	W	1-0	*Mirić*
15/05	a	Lokomotiva	L	0-1	
22/05	h	Zadar	W	2-0	*Ejupi 2*
30/05	a	Osijek	L	2-3	*Delić, Peričić*

No	Name	Nat	DoB	Pos	Aps	(s)	Gls
13	David Arap		09/03/95	M	1	(2)	
24	Hrvoje Barišić		02/02/91	M	4	(3)	
10	Kristijan Bistrović		09/04/98	M		(1)	
10	Petar Brlek		29/01/94	M	26	(4)	1
8	Danijel Cesarec		08/01/83	A	9	(7)	2
6	Ljuban Crepulja		02/09/93	M	31	(2)	1
14	Mateas Delić		17/06/88	A	25	(5)	3
5	Edson Henrique	BRA	06/07/87	D	21	(4)	
7	Muzafer Ejupi	MKD	16/09/88	A	11	(2)	5
13	Petar Filipovic	GER	14/09/90	M		(6)	
18	Ivan Fuštar		18/08/89	D	21	(3)	
23	Stjepan Geng		02/03/93	D	10	(5)	1
9	Dominik Glavina		06/12/92	A	11	(4)	1
20	Mario Gregurina		23/03/88	M	8	(1)	
4	Mato Grgić		27/09/87	D	32	(1)	2
21	Nikola Jambor		25/09/95	M	2	(8)	
1	Ivan Kardum		18/07/87	G	24		
27	Petar Lela		17/03/94	D	1	(1)	
3	Marko Martinaga		27/05/98	D	2		
3	Dario Melnjak		31/10/92	D	19		1
9	Filip Mihaljević		09/03/92	A	3	(8)	1
19	Marko Mirić	SRB	26/03/87	A	24	(5)	10
7	Petar Mišić		18/04/94	A	10	(7)	1
22	Enes Novinić		18/07/85	A	1	(1)	
30	Filip Ozobić		08/04/91	M	24	(2)	3
11	Goran Paracki		21/01/87	M	20	(4)	1
17	Ivan Parlov		07/08/93	M	8		1
26	Špiro Peričić		08/10/93	D	2	(1)	1
12	Dominik Picak		12/02/92	G	12		
26	Hrvoje Plazanić		18/09/90	D	5	(1)	
16	Vedran Purić		16/03/86	D	29		
15	Davor Vugrinec		24/03/75	A	5	(12)	2

CROATIA

RNK Split

1912 • Park mladeži (8,000) • rnksplit.hr
Coach: Ivan Matić;
(24/12/14) Zoran Vulić

2014

21/07	a	Zadar	W	2-1	Bilić 2 (1p)
28/07	h	Istra 1961	D	1-1	Bilić (p)
03/08	a	Osijek	D	1-1	Glavina
10/08	h	Rijeka	L	0-3	
15/08	a	Dinamo	L	0-1	
24/08	h	Slaven	W	2-0	Rog, Bilić
31/08	a	Zagreb	L	1-2	Bagarić
12/09	a	Lokomotiva	D	2-2	Çikalleshi 2
20/09	h	Hajduk	D	1-1	Galović
29/09	a	Zadar	W	3-0	Galović, Rog, Çikalleshi
04/10	a	Istra 1961	L	0-2	
17/10	h	Osijek	W	3-0	Çikalleshi (p), Roce 2
26/10	a	Rijeka	D	1-1	Ibriks
01/11	h	Dinamo	D	0-0	
07/11	a	Slaven	L	0-1	
23/11	h	Zagreb	D	2-2	Çikalleshi 2 (1p)
28/11	a	Lokomotiva	D	1-1	Rog
07/12	h	Hajduk	L	1-2	Jukić
12/12	a	Zadar	D	1-1	Bagarić

2015

06/02	h	Istra 1961	D	2-2	Ibriks, Roce
14/02	a	Osijek	L	0-4	
22/02	h	Rijeka	D	1-1	Kvesić
28/02	a	Dinamo	L	0-2	
07/03	h	Slaven	W	2-0	Çikalleshi, Kvesić
13/03	a	Zagreb	W	2-1	Mršić, Bagarić
21/03	h	Lokomotiva	L	0-1	
04/04	a	Hajduk	W	2-1	Rog, Çikalleshi (p)
11/04	h	Zadar	D	1-1	Rog
18/04	a	Istra 1961	D	1-1	Çikalleshi
25/04	h	Osijek	W	3-2	Bagarić, Blagojević, Çikalleshi
29/04	a	Rijeka	L	0-2	
02/05	h	Dinamo	L	1-5	Mršić
08/05	a	Slaven	L	0-1	
16/05	h	Zagreb	L	1-2	Rog
24/05	a	Lokomotiva	W	3-0	Erceg 2, Rog
30/05	h	Hajduk	D	1-1	Vidović

No	Name	Nat	DoB	Pos	Aps	(s)	Gls
11	Dražen Bagarić		12/11/92	A	23	(8)	4
19	Tomislav Barbarić		29/03/89	D	15		
34	Henry Belle	CMR	25/01/89	A	8	(4)	
9	Mate Bilić		23/10/80	A	7	(4)	4
77	Slavko Blagojević		18/03/90	M	9	(2)	1
13	Chung Woon	KOR	30/06/89	D	9		
18	Sokol Çikalleshi	ALB	27/07/90	A	30	(2)	10
19	Tomislav Dujmović		26/02/81	M	11	(1)	
10	Ante Erceg		12/12/89	M	10	(8)	2
26	Nino Galović		07/06/92	D	32	(1)	2
3	Denis Glavina		03/03/86	M	23	(3)	1
6	Tomislav Glumac		14/05/91	D	12		
18	Luka Grubišić		09/11/97	M		(3)	
29	Ivan Ibriks		06/10/87	D	20	(2)	2
22	Ivan Jukić		21/06/96	A	1	(11)	1
15	Mario Kvesić	BIH	12/01/92	M	15	(11)	2
4	Ante Majstorović		06/11/93	D	4	(4)	
7	Tomislav Mrkonjić		22/02/94	A		(2)	
8	Antonio Mršić		05/06/87	M	11	(5)	2
10	Tomislav Radotić		13/12/81	D	15	(1)	
14	Goran Roce		12/04/86	A	11	(12)	3
17	Marko Rog		19/07/95	M	27	(3)	7
32	Marin Roglić		16/06/97	A		(2)	
26	Dario Rugašević		29/01/91	D	19	(2)	
24	Miloš Vidović	SRB	03/10/89	M	28	(3)	1
7	Aljoša Vojnović		24/10/85	M	5	(6)	
5	Branko Vrgoč		18/12/89	D	15	(3)	
30	Andrija Vuković		03/08/83	G	11		
12	Danijel Zagorac		07/02/87	G	25		

NK Zadar

1945 • Stanovi (5,860) • nkzadar.hr
Coach: Ferdo Milin;
(25/08/14) (Zvonimir Jurić);
(05/09/14) Miroslav Blažević;
(08/01/15) Igor Štimac

2014

21/07	h	Split	L	1-2	Ivančić
26/07	h	Osijek	W	2-1	Ivančić, Weitzer
02/08	a	Dinamo	L	0-5	
08/08	h	Zagreb	D	2-2	Weitzer, Ivančić
16/08	a	Hajduk	L	0-6	
23/08	h	Istra 1961	D	1-1	Šimurina
31/08	a	Rijeka	L	1-6	Terkeš
14/09	h	Slaven	W	4-0	Terkeš, Pešić, Hrgović (p), Pušić
19/09	a	Lokomotiva	W	1-0	Weitzer
29/09	a	Split	L	0-3	
04/10	a	Osijek	L	1-4	Ikić
18/10	h	Dinamo	L	1-3	Pešić
24/10	a	Zagreb	L	0-3	
02/11	h	Hajduk	L	0-3	
08/11	a	Istra 1961	D	1-1	Buljat
22/11	h	Rijeka	L	0-1	
29/11	a	Slaven	L	0-4	
06/12	h	Lokomotiva	L	2-5	Theophilus, Buljat (p)
12/12	h	Split	D	1-1	Jerbić

2015

08/02	h	Osijek	W	3-1	Pešić, L Ćirjak (p), Banović
16/02	a	Dinamo	L	0-2	
21/02	h	Zagreb	L	0-1	
01/03	h	Hajduk	D	2-2	Gabrić, L Ćirjak (p)
08/03	h	Istra 1961	W	2-0	Krstanović (p), L Ćirjak
15/03	a	Rijeka	L	0-4	
22/03	h	Slaven	W	1-0	Jerbić
03/04	a	Lokomotiva	W	5-1	Gabrić, og (Bartolec), Krstanović 3 (2p)
11/04	a	Split	D	1-1	Jerbić
19/04	a	Osijek	L	1-2	Pešić
25/04	h	Dinamo	L	0-1	
29/04	a	Zagreb	L	0-3	
03/05	h	Hajduk	W	2-0	Ikić, Krstanović
10/05	a	Istra 1961	D	0-0	
17/05	h	Rijeka	L	0-2	
22/05	a	Slaven	L	0-2	
30/05	h	Lokomotiva	D	2-2	Krstanović (p), Anić

No	Name	Nat	DoB	Pos	Aps	(s)	Gls
17	Mohammed Aliyu	NGA	05/09/95	A	2	(7)	
29	Josip Anić		09/09/96	M	1	(1)	1
22	Igor Banović		12/05/87	M	19	(1)	1
2	Josip Bilaver		14/08/84	M	13	(2)	
18	Vlatko Blažević		23/10/94	A	1	(4)	
30	Jurica Buljat		12/09/86	D	8		2
14	Frane Ćirjak		23/06/95	M		(3)	
3	Lovre Ćirjak		02/11/91	D	25	(5)	3
14	Dino Fazlić		21/11/91	D	1	(1)	
10	Drago Gabrić		27/09/86	M	12	(1)	2
12	Tomo Gluić		26/07/83	G	6		
18	Mirko Hrgović	BIH	05/02/79	D	18		1
25	Frane Ikić		19/06/94	D	20	(2)	2
9	Josip Ivančić		29/03/91	A	6		3
15	Jure Jerbić		28/06/90	M	25	(1)	3
6	Vedran Ješe		03/02/81	D	20	(3)	
5	Ivan Jovanović		22/05/91	A	1		
13	Ivan Jović		10/04/97	M	3	(1)	
27	Ivica Jurkić		22/02/94	A	6	(4)	
19	Domagoj Krajačić		14/04/87	D	8		
99	Ivan Krstanović		05/01/83	A	11	(1)	6
1	Mladen Matković		12/05/89	G	30		
9	Andrija Milinković		27/06/90	A	3	(4)	
20	Darko Mišić		27/06/91	D	12	(1)	
22	Domagoj Muić		30/09/93	M	5	(7)	
21	Tonči Mujan		19/07/95	A	1	(3)	
16	Ivan Pešić		06/04/92	A	25	(7)	4
7	Domagoj Pušić		24/10/91	M	27		1
4	Ante Sarić		17/06/92	D	12	(8)	
26	Vlatko Sutić		01/02/90	A	7	(4)	
5	Ivan Šimurina		08/05/92	D	11	(2)	1
8	Jakov Surać		12/02/75	M	4	(8)	
14	Danijel Sutić		23/09/97	M		(1)	
20	Želimir Terkeš	BIH	08/01/81	A	27	(3)	2
22	Marko Tešija		14/01/92	M		(2)	
11	Solomon Theophilus	NGA	18/01/96	A	3	(10)	1
29	Ivan Tokić		06/06/92	D	2		
30	Hrvoje Vejić		08/06/77	D	2		
23	Roberto Viduka		18/01/95	D	2	(4)	
10	Ivor Weitzer		24/05/88	M	18	(1)	3

NK Zagreb

1903 • Kranjčevićeva (8,850) • nkzagreb.hr
Major honours
Croatian League (1) 2002
Coach: Željko Kopić

2014

20/07	h	Rijeka	L	1-3	G Boban
26/07	a	Slaven	L	2-3	G Boban, Konopek
01/08	h	Lokomotiva	W	2-0	Stepčić, Šulc
08/08	a	Zadar	D	2-2	Jurendić 2 (2p)
17/08	h	Osijek	L	1-2	Jurendić
24/08	a	Dinamo	D	1-1	Stepčić
31/08	h	Split	W	2-1	G Boban 2
14/09	h	Hajduk	D	2-2	Jurendić, Medić
20/09	a	Istra 1961	W	2-1	Šulc, Bevab
27/09	a	Rijeka	L	0-3	
03/10	h	Slaven	D	1-1	Novak
19/10	a	Lokomotiva	L	0-3	
24/10	h	Zadar	W	3-0	G Boban 2, Jurendić (p)
02/11	a	Osijek	L	0-1	
09/11	h	Dinamo	D	0-0	
23/11	a	Split	D	2-2	Kolinger, G Boban
29/11	h	Hajduk	W	2-0	Krovinović, Mudražija
05/12	h	Istra 1961	W	1-0	og (Obšivač)
15/12	h	Rijeka	L	1-2	Stepčić

2015

08/02	h	Slaven	W	1-0	Medić
14/02	h	Lokomotiva	L	0-6	
21/02	a	Zadar	W	1-0	Matić
01/03	h	Osijek	L	0-4	
07/03	h	Dinamo	L	0-2	
13/03	h	Split	L	1-2	Kolinger
22/03	h	Hajduk	W	2-0	G Boban, Krovinović
03/04	a	Istra 1961	L	1-2	Stepčić
12/04	a	Rijeka	L	1-4	Jurendić (p)
19/04	a	Slaven	L	1-2	Jurendić (p)
24/04	a	Lokomotiva	W	2-1	Jurendić (p), Stepčić
29/04	h	Zadar	W	3-0	G Boban 3
02/05	a	Osijek	L	0-1	
09/05	h	Dinamo	D	1-1	Jurendić
16/05	a	Split	W	2-1	Medić, G Boban
23/05	a	Hajduk	L	0-1	
30/05	h	Istra 1961	W	4-0	G Boban, Krovinović, Štiglec, Jurilj

No	Name	Nat	DoB	Pos	Aps	(s)	Gls
14	Dino Bevab	BIH	13/01/93	D	13	(4)	1
99	Bruno Boban		12/08/92	A	4	(7)	
30	Gabrijel Boban		23/07/89	A	32	(2)	13
24	Mario Čubel		20/03/90	M		(9)	
18	Marijo Dučkić		09/02/91	M	3	(4)	
15	Jakša Herceg		15/02/89	G	1		
7	Denis Jurendić		26/04/87	D	31		9
8	Alen Jurilj	BIH	07/03/96	D	1	(4)	1
26	Vedran Jurjević		21/01/92	M		(5)	
20	Denis Kolinger		14/01/94	D	30		2
11	Miroslav Konopek		28/03/91	A	7	(14)	1
4	Dominik Kovačić		05/01/94	D	6	(1)	
10	Filip Krovinović		29/08/95	M	34	(1)	3
1	Dominik Livaković		09/01/95	G	35		
24	Ivan Ljubičić		17/01/92	M	21	(3)	
27	Bernardo Matić		27/07/94	D	13	(7)	1
9	Lovro Medić		23/10/90	A	30	(4)	3
16	Robert Mudražija		05/05/97	M	10	(7)	1
18	Domagoj Muić		05/09/93	M	6	(1)	
23	Božo Musa		15/09/88	D	32		
6	Leopold Novak		03/12/90	A	1	(3)	1
29	Edin Šehić	BIH	03/02/95	D	7	(2)	
2	Luka Šimunović		24/05/97	D			
21	Valentino Stepčić		16/01/90	M	35		5
22	Dino Štiglec		03/10/90	D	32		1
5	Roko Strika	AUS	12/02/94	A		(1)	
19	Matias Šulc		28/07/92	D	12	(5)	2

Top goalscorers

21	Andrej Kramarić (Rijeka)
20	Ángelo Henríquez (Dinamo)
16	Dejan Radonjić (Istra 1961)
13	Gabrijel Boban (Zagreb)
12	Duje Čop (Dinamo)
11	Marko Pjaca (Dinamo)
	El Arbi Hillel Soudani (Dinamo)
10	Domagoj Pavičić (Lokomotiva/Dinamo)
	Marko Mirić (Slaven)
	Sokol Çikalleshi (Split)

Promoted club

NK Inter Zaprešić

1929 • ŠRC Zaprešić (5,228) • inter.hr

Major honours
Croatian Cup (1) 1992
Coach: Samir Toplak

Second level final table 2014/15

		Pld	W	D	L	F	A	Pts
1	NK Inter Zaprešić	30	17	7	6	48	25	58
2	NK Sesvete	30	15	8	7	53	30	53
3	HNK Gorica	30	13	12	5	46	26	51
4	NK Rudeš	30	10	12	8	36	28	42
5	NK Imotski	30	9	11	10	31	38	38
6	HNK Cibalia	30	10	8	12	36	44	38
7	NK Dugopolje	30	7	13	10	27	32	34
8	HNK Segesta	30	9	7	14	31	42	34
9	NK Lučko	30	8	9	13	24	35	33
10	NK Hrvatski dragovoljac	30	8	9	13	30	42	33
11	NK Bistra	30	5	12	13	18	38	27
12	NK Pomorac Kostrena	0	0	0	0	0	0	0

NB NK Pomorac Kostrena withdrew after round 11 – all their matches were annulled.

DOMESTIC CUP

Hrvatski Nogometni Kup 2014/15

FIRST ROUND

(26/08/14)
Lekenik 2-1 Stupnik

(27/08/14)
Bijelo Brdo 4-0 Vodice
Funtana 2-0 Podravina
GOŠK 3-0 Suhopolje
Lučko 0-1 Novigrad
Mladost Antin 4-1 Mladost Pavlinovec
Opatija 3-2 Borac Imbriovec
Plitvica 1-7 Bistra
Podravac 3-2 Oriolik *(aet)*
Ponikve 4-1 Radoboj *(aet)*
Primorac Biograd 0-1 Medjimurje
Segesta 3-1 Ždralovi
Slavonija Požega 8-0 Lički Osik
Vuteks Sloga 3-0 Mladost Cernik *(aet)*
Zrinski Jurjevac 4-0 Ogulin

(03/09/14)
Split 1-0 Grabrovnica

SECOND ROUND

(23/09/14)
Bijelo Brdo 2-5 Lokomotiva

(24/09/14)
Bistra 0-2 Cibalia
Funtana 0-2 Hajduk
GOŠK 7-0 Pomorac
Medjimurje 0-2 Vinogradar
Mladost Antin 0-1 Varaždin
Novigrad 2-0 Inter Zaprešić
Opatija 3-3 Zagreb *(aet; 9-8 on pens)*
Podravac 1-3 Šibenik
Ponikve 1-2 Dinamo
Segesta 0-2 Split
Slavonija Požega 2-3 Istra 1961
Vuteks Sloga 0-3 Osijek
Zagora 1-5 Zadar
Zrinski Jurjevac 1-5 Slaven Koprivnica

(15/10/14)
Lekenik 2-4 Rijeka

THIRD ROUND

(28/10/14)
Istra 1961 2-0 Šibenik

(29/10/14)
GOŠK 0-3 Rijeka
Lokomotiva 3-2 Cibalia
Novigrad 2-3 Hajduk
Opatija 2-4 Dinamo *(aet)*

Split 2-0 Osijek
Vinogradar 3-0 Slaven Koprivnica
Zadar 5-1 Varaždin

QUARTER-FINALS

(11/02/15 & 03/03/15)
Istra 1961 0-1 Dinamo *(Fernandes 57)*
Dinamo 3-0 Istra 1961*(Fernandes 42, Hodžić 55, Ćorić 69p)*
(Dinamo 4-0)

(11/02/15 & 04/03/15)
Rijeka 4-1 Lokomotiva *(Tomečak 18, Balaj 60, Jugović 77, Lešković 88; Doležal 81)*
Lokomotiva 0-4 Rijeka *(Sharbini 36, Vešović 39, Tomasov 51, Ivančić 77)*
(Rijeka 8-1)

Vinogradar 0-3 Hajduk *(Kouassi 32, Maglica 67, 70)*
Hajduk 3-0 Vinogradar *(Jozinović 12, Balić 26, 62)*
(Hajduk 6-0)

(11/02/15 & 18/03/15)
Split 1-0 Zadar *(Mršić 49)*
Zadar 1-4 Split *(L Ćirjak 82; Mršić 4, 61, Bagarić 30, Çikalleshi 62)*
(Split 5-1)

SEMI-FINALS

(08/04/15 & 22/04/15)
Dinamo 2-1 Rijeka *(Paulo Machado 70, Henríquez 81; Lešković 6)*
Rijeka 0-0 Dinamo
(Dinamo 2-1)

Hajduk 1-1 Split *(Sušić 33; Erceg 31p)*
Split 1-0 Hajduk *(Çikalleshi 43p)*
(Split 2-1)

FINAL

(20/05/15)
Maksimir, Zagreb
GNK DINAMO ZAGREB 0
RNK SPLIT 0
(aet; 4-2 on pens)
Referee: Bebek
DINAMO: Ježina, Ivo Pinto, Šimunović, Sigali *(Taravel 52)*, Pivarić, Pjaca, Ademi, Paulo Machado, Ćorić *(Fernandes 65)*, Soudani *(Pavičić 106)*, Henríquez
SPLIT: Zagorac, Galović, Barbarić, Vrgoč, Chung Woon *(Mršić 93)*, Vidović, Blagojević, Rog, Erceg, Glavina *(Rugašević 88)*, Çikalleshi *(Majstorović 97)*
Red card: Galović *(94)*

Dinamo Zagreb players in celebratory mood after their penalty shoot-out win in the Croatian Cup final

CYPRUS

Kypriaki Omospondia Podosfairon (KOP)/ Cyprus Football Association (CFA)

Address	10 Achaion Street	**President**	Costakis
	2413 Engomi, PO Box 25071		Koutsokoumnis
	CY-1306 Nicosia	**General secretary**	Phivos Vakis
Tel	+357 22 352 341	**Media officer**	Kyriacos Giorgallis
Fax	+357 22 590 544	**Year of formation**	1934
E-mail	info@cfa.com.cy	**National stadium**	GSP, Nicosia (22,859)
Website	cfa.com.cy		

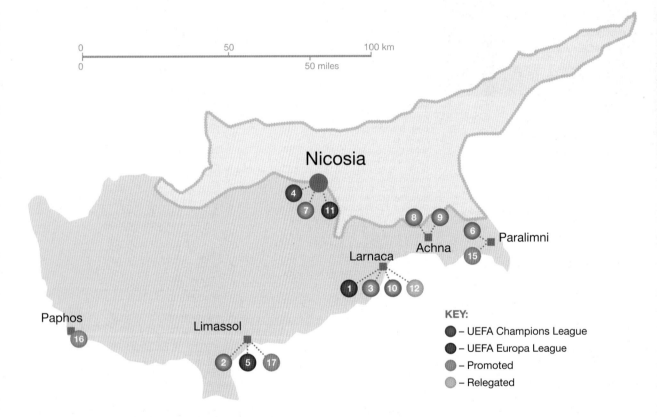

KEY:
- – UEFA Champions League
- – UEFA Europa League
- – Promoted
- – Relegated

A KATIGORIA CLUBS

 1 **AEK Larnaca FC**

 2 **AEL Limassol FC**

 3 **Anorthosis Famagusta FC**

 4 **APOEL FC**

 5 **Apollon Limassol FC**

 6 **Ayia Napa FC**

 7 **Doxa Katokopia FC**

 8 **Ermis Aradippou FC**

 9 **Ethnikos Achnas FC**

 10 **Nea Salamis Famagusta FC**

 11 **AC Omonia**

 12 **Othellos Athienou FC**

PROMOTED CLUBS

 15 **Enosis Neon Paralimni FC**

 16 **Pafos FC**

 17 **Aris Limassol FC**

All-out success for APOEL

Having captured their first domestic double for 18 years in 2013/14, APOEL FC repeated the feat 12 months later, beating AEL Limassol FC 4-2 in the cup final four days before a victory by the same score at Ermis Araddipou FC wrapped up their 24th league title.

APOEL sacked two coaches en route to their success, the first of them, Georgios Donis, having steered the club into the group stage of the UEFA Champions League. There was further reason for cheer on the international front as the Cypriot national team found some form in the UEFA EURO 2016 qualifiers.

Second straight domestic double for Nicosia club

Apollon, AEK and Omonia edged out in title race

National team rediscover winning habit at last

Domestic league

With just 12 teams taking part in the 2014/15 A Katigoria, there were four fewer matches for each club to negotiate. The two-tiered system nevertheless remained, with the top six clubs after 22 matches going forward into a championship pool. At that stage of the competition it looked like a two-horse race for the title, with Apollon Limassol FC leading the way, two points ahead of APOEL and nine in front of AC Omonia and AEK Larnaca FC.

However, as the two frontrunners stuttered in the second phase, the two pursuers began to mount a challenge. Apollon, in particular, found the pressure difficult to bear, winning only one of their first seven matches after the split, but while APOEL eventually steadied themselves, constructing a seemingly unassailable lead with three games to go, they then lost at Apollon. That led to the dismissal of coach Thorsten Fink, who had replaced Donis in January when APOEL also topped the standings. For the final week of the campaign, the job of steering the team to the double was entrusted to Gustavo Manduca, who had begun the season on the playing staff.

A 1-1 draw at home to AEK meant that, with Apollon losing and Omonia winning, APOEL held a three-point lead over all three rivals going into their final fixture. A draw against Ermis would have sufficed, but goals from Argentinian playmaker Tomás De Vincenti, captain Kostas Charalambides and top-scoring Algerian striker Rafik Djebbour (two) brought all three points and a third successive championship crown – the club's first title hat-trick since the late 1940s.

AEK, ably led by former Spain striker Thomas Christiansen, claimed the runners-up spot thanks to their superior head-to-head record over Apollon, whose last-day victory against Omonia ensured third place. All three clubs qualified for the UEFA Europa League, but AEK had the advantage of a delayed entry.

Domestic cup

Fourth place in the A Katigoria did not guarantee a European spot. Indeed, Omonia's last-day defeat at Apollon would have cost them had AEL won the Cypriot Cup earlier in the week. But the league runners-up from the previous season came second best to APOEL again, taking the lead early on before conceding four goals in the middle third of the encounter, the last of them a trademark free-kick from former Liverpool FC left-back John Arne Riise. It was APOEL's 22nd victory in the competition and second in a row.

Europe

APOEL booked into the UEFA Champions League group stage for the third time after seeing off Scandinavian opposition in HJK Helsinki and Aalborg BK, and they proved commendably obdurate early on in a tough group, but while their defence stood firm, they scored only one goal – a Manduca penalty in a 1-1 draw against AFC Ajax. Apollon made it successive qualifications for the UEFA Europa League group stage thanks to a magnificent 4-1 victory at FC Lokomotiv Moskva, but after a 3-2 home win over FC Zürich they lost their last five group games.

National team

Cyprus entered UEFA EURO 2016 qualifying in trepidation after going nine games without a goal, but coach Pambos Christodoulou's first competitive match at the helm delivered a shock 2-1 win away to Bosnia & Herzegovina, Dimitris Christofi ending the drought with a timely double. It was the team's first away win for over seven years, and although they narrowly lost their next two qualifiers against Israel and Wales, more good news followed when they beat Andorra home and away, with Georgios Efrem and Nestoras Mytidis both helping themselves to hat-tricks – a feat never previously achieved by a Cypriot international.

DOMESTIC SEASON AT A GLANCE

A Katigoria 2014/15 final table

		Pld	Home					Away					Total					Pts
			W	D	L	F	A	W	D	L	F	A	W	D	L	F	A	
1	**APOEL FC**	32	9	7	0	26	11	8	4	4	26	15	17	11	4	52	26	62
2	AEK Larnaca FC	32	11	3	2	27	11	6	5	5	29	20	17	8	7	56	31	59
3	Apollon Limassol FC	32	11	3	2	35	16	7	2	7	24	25	18	5	9	59	41	59
4	AC Omonia	32	10	3	3	32	15	7	2	7	20	19	17	5	10	52	34	56
5	Anorthosis Famagusta FC	32	11	2	3	28	14	5	2	9	22	23	16	4	12	50	37	52
6	Ermis Aradippou FC	32	7	4	5	21	26	4	3	9	17	29	11	7	14	38	55	40
7	Ethnikos Achnas FC	32	7	5	4	20	20	4	3	9	16	29	11	8	13	36	49	41
8	AEL Limassol FC	32	6	4	6	22	20	3	8	5	20	22	9	12	11	42	42	39
9	Nea Salamis Famagusta FC	32	7	4	5	22	11	2	5	9	9	26	9	9	14	31	37	36
10	Ayia Napa FC	32	4	7	5	17	25	2	5	9	15	29	6	12	14	32	54	30
11	Doxa Katokopia FC	32	3	3	10	15	33	4	4	8	14	22	7	7	18	29	55	28
12	Othellos Athienou FC	32	3	4	9	15	21	2	6	8	11	21	5	10	17	26	42	25

NB League splits into top and bottom halves after 22 games, after which the clubs play exclusively against teams in their group.

European qualification 2015/16

 Champion/Cup winner: APOEL FC (third qualifying round)

 AEK Larnaca FC (third qualifying round)
Apollon Limassol FC (first qualifying round)
AC Omonia (first qualifying round)

Top scorer	Mickaël Poté (Omonia), 17 goals
Relegated club	Othellos Athienou FC
Promoted clubs	Enosis Neon Paralimni FC, Pafos FC, Aris Limassol FC
Cup final	APOEL FC 4-2 AEL Limassol FC

Team of the season
(4-3-3)

Coach: Christiansen (AEK)

Kaminski (Anorthosis)

Demetriou (Anorthosis) — David Català (AEK) — Merkis (Apollon) — Riise (APOEL)

Efrem (APOEL) — Nuno Assis (Omonia) — Vander (AEK)

Papoulis (Apollon) — Poté (Omonia) — Makris (Anorthosis)

Player of the season

Nuno Assis
(AC Omonia)

At 37 years of age, Nuno Assis became the oldest recipient of the Cyprus FA's official player of the season award. He won no medals with his club, but the veteran Portuguese playmaker, who had three separate stints in his homeland with Vitória SC as well as four seasons with SL Benfica, combined tireless energy and exceptional creativity to lift Omonia into fourth place and help his team-mate, Benin striker Mickaël Poté, to become the A Katigoria's top marksman with 17 goals.

Newcomer of the season

Konstantinos Laifis
(Anorthosis Famagusta FC)

Anorthosis had a relatively discreet season in 2014/15, finishing fifth in the league and reaching the quarter-finals of the cup, but while some senior players disappointed, encouragement for the future was found in the performances of 22-year-old Laifis. A committed and athletic holding midfielder who can also operate in defence, he was drafted into the senior national side and won his first cap as a substitute for hat-trick hero Georgios Efrem in the UEFA EURO 2016 qualifier at home to Andorra.

NATIONAL TEAM

Top five all-time caps
Ioannis Okkas (104); Michalis Konstantinou (87); Pambos Pittas (82); **Kostas Charalambides** (77); Nicos Panayiotou (75)

Top five all-time goals
Michalis Konstantinou (32); Ioannis Okkas (26); **Kostas Charalambides** (11); Marios Agathokleous & **Efstathios Aloneftis** (10)

Results 2014/15

04/09/14	Croatia	A	Pula		L	0-2
09/09/14	Bosnia & Herzegovina (ECQ)	A	Zenica		W	2-1
10/10/14	Israel (ECQ)	H	Nicosia		L	1-2
13/10/14	Wales (ECQ)	A	Cardiff		L	1-2
16/11/14	Andorra (ECQ)	H	Nicosia		W	5-0
28/03/15	Belgium (ECQ)	A	Brussels		L	0-5
12/06/15	Andorra (ECQ)	A	Andorra la Vella		W	3-1

Results scorers:
- 09/09/14: Christofi (45, 73)
- 10/10/14: Makrides (67)
- 13/10/14: Laban (36)
- 16/11/14: Merkis (9), Efrem (31, 42, 60), Christofi (87p)
- 12/06/15: Mytidis (13, 45, 53)

Appearances 2014/15

Coach: Pambos Christodoulou	17/10/67		Cro	BIH	ISR	WAL	AND	BEL	AND	Caps	Goals
Antonis Georgallides	30/01/82	Omonia	G46	G	G			G	G	59	-
Eleftherios Mertakas	16/03/85	AEK Larnaca	D							2	-
Valentinos Sielis	01/03/90	AEL	D	s83					D	12	-
Angelis Angeli	31/05/89	Apollon	D		s29/85	D				10	-
Ilias Charalambous	25/09/80	AEK Larnaca	D							65	-
Kostakis Artymatas	15/04/93	APOEL	M46							5	-
Georgios Aresti	02/09/94	Ayia Napa	M50							2	-
Georgios Efrem	05/07/89	APOEL	M53	M71		M	M78		M	29	3
Kostas Charalambides	25/07/81	APOEL	M61	s46	M46					77	11
Nektarios Alexandrou	19/12/83	APOEL	M70	s71	s70	s68			s82	30	-
Andreas Makris	27/11/95	Anorthosis	A		M70		s46	M71		5	-
Anastasios Kissas	18/01/88	APOEL	s46			G		G		13	-
Charalambos Kyriakou	15/10/89	Omonia	s46	D	s46	D		D		8	-
Marios Nicolaou	04/10/83	AEL	s50	M	M	M68	M	M	M	47	1
Dimitris Christofi	28/09/88	Sion (SUI)	s53	A	A	A	M		M82	38	6
Konstantinos Makrides	13/01/82	Metalurh Donetsk (UKR)	s61	M83	M	M		M84	M88	72	6
Efstathios Aloneftis	29/03/83	APOEL	s70	M46			M46			60	10
Georgios Merkis	30/07/84	Apollon		D	D	D	D	D		31	1
Dossa Júnior	28/07/86	Legia (POL)		D	D29			D		15	-
Marios Antoniades	14/05/90	APOEL		D	D	D	D	D	D	8	-
Vincent Laban	09/09/84	Astra (ROU)		M	M	M	M	M57	M76	19	2
Marios Stylianou	23/09/93	Apollon		D46						2	-
Pieros Sotiriou	13/01/93	APOEL		s46	M		M		12	-
Andreas Papathanasiou	03/10/83	Ermis			s85					6	-
Jason Demetriou	18/11/87	Anorthosis					D		D	26	-
Nestoras Mytidis	01/06/81	AEK Larnaca					A63	A	A	16	3
Georgios Kolokoudias	03/05/89	Ayia Napa					s63			1	-
Konstantinos Laifis	19/05/93	Anorthosis					s78	D		2	-
Georgios Oikonomidis	10/04/90	Omonia						s57	s76	2	-
Georgios Eleftheriou	30/09/84	AEL						s71		2	-
Grigoris Kastanos	30/01/98	Juventus (ITA)						s84	s88	2	-

EUROPE

APOEL FC

Third qualifying round - HJK Helsinki (FIN)
A 2-2 *De Vincenti (71), Sheridan (74)*
Urko Pardo, João Guilherme, Carlão, Tiago Gomes, Sheridan (Adorno 79), Charalambides (Efrem 63), Antoniades (Ioannou 75), Vinícius, Nuno Morais, Mário Sérgio, De Vincenti. Coach: Georgios Donis (GRE)
H 2-0 *Sheridan (17), De Vincenti (43p)*
Urko Pardo, João Guilherme, Carlão, Tiago Gomes, Sheridan (Papazoglou 81), Charalambides (Efrem 68), Antoniades, Vinícius, Nuno Morais, Mário Sérgio, De Vincenti (Sotiriou 76). Coach: Georgios Donis (GRE)

Play-offs - Aalborg BK (DEN)
A 1-1 *Vinícius (54)*
Urko Pardo, João Guilherme, Carlão, Tiago Gomes, Sheridan (Manduca 90+3), Charalambides (Alexandrou 66), Antoniades, Vinícius, Nuno Morais, Mário Sérgio, De Vincenti (Papazoglou 82). Coach: Georgios Donis (GRE)
H 4-0 *Vinícius (29), De Vincenti (44), Aloneftis (64), Sheridan (75)*
Urko Pardo, João Guilherme, Carlão, Tiago Gomes, Sheridan (Djebbour 79), Antoniades, Vinícius, Manduca (Aloneftis 61), Nuno Morais, Mário Sérgio, De Vincenti (Efrem 82). Coach: Georgios Donis (GRE)

Group F
Match 1 - FC Barcelona (ESP)
A 0-1
Urko Pardo, João Guilherme, Carlão, Tiago Gomes (Manduca 61), Sheridan (Djebbour 75), Antoniades, Vinícius, Nuno Morais, Mário Sérgio, De Vincenti (Charalambides 79), Aloneftis. Coach: Georgios Donis (GRE)
Match 2 - AFC Ajax (NED)
H 1-1 *Manduca (31p)*
Urko Pardo, João Guilherme, Carlão, Tiago Gomes (De Vincenti 71), Sheridan (Djebbour 82), Antoniades, Vinícius, Manduca (Efrem 79), Nuno Morais, Mário Sérgio, Aloneftis. Coach: Georgios Donis (GRE)
Match 3 - Paris Saint-Germain (FRA)
H 0-1
Urko Pardo, João Guilherme, Carlão, Efrem, Tiago Gomes, Sheridan (Djebbour 67), Antoniades (Riise 41), Vinícius, Manduca, Nuno Morais (De Vincenti 80), Mário Sérgio. Coach: Georgios Donis (GRE)
Match 4 - Paris Saint-Germain (FRA)
A 0-1
Urko Pardo, João Guilherme, Carlão, Efrem, Tiago Gomes (Sheridan 46), Vinícius, Manduca (De Vincenti 59), Nuno Morais, Mário Sérgio, Ioannou, Djebbour (Aloneftis 64). Coach: Georgios Donis (GRE)
Match 5 - FC Barcelona (ESP)
H 0-4
Urko Pardo, João Guilherme, Carlão, Tiago Gomes, Sheridan, Antoniades, Vinícius (Djebbour 74), Manduca (De Vincenti 63), Nuno Morais, Mário Sérgio, Aloneftis (Efrem 46). Coach: Georgios Donis (GRE)
Red card: João Guilherme 84

Match 6 - AFC Ajax (NED)
A 0-4
Urko Pardo, Carlão, Efrem (Aloneftis 65), Tiago Gomes, Sheridan (Sotiriou 65), Alexandrou, Antoniades, Vinícius, Papazoglou, Nuno Morais (Artymatas 72), Mário Sérgio. Coach: Georgios Donis (GRE)

AEL Limassol FC

Third qualifying round - FC Zenit (RUS)
H 1-0 *Gikiewicz (64)*
Fegrouche, Sielis, Gikiewicz, Nicolaou, Danielzinho (Eleftheriou 76), Edmar, Carlitos I, Guidileye, Cadú, Adrián Sardinero (Tagbajumi 69), Zézinho (Luciano Bebê 60). Coach: Ivaylo Petev (BUL)
A 0-3
Fegrouche, Sielis, Gikiewicz (Tagbajumi 86), Nicolaou, Danielzinho, Edmar, Carlitos I, Guidileye, Cadú, Adrián Sardinero (Eleftheriou 58), Zézinho (Diego Barcelos 18). Coach: Ivaylo Petev (BUL)
Red card: Danielzinho 27

Play-offs - Tottenham Hotspur FC (ENG)
H 1-2 *Adrián Sardinero (14)*
Fegrouche, Sielis, Gikiewicz (Tagbajumi 73), Diego Barcelos (Eleftheriou 67), Nicolaou, Edmar, Luciano Bebê, Carlitos I, Guidileye, Cadú, Adrián Sardinero (Carlitos II 80). Coach: Ivaylo Petev (BUL)
A 0-3
Fegrouche (Pulpo 13), Sielis, Gikiewicz, Diego Barcelos, Nicolaou (Danielzinho 45), Edmar, Luciano Bebê, Carlitos I, Guidileye, Cadú, Adrián Sardinero (Tagbajumi 80). Coach: Ivaylo Petev (BUL)

Apollon Limassol FC

Play-offs - FC Lokomotiv Moskva (RUS)
H 1-1 *Gneki Guié (80)*
Bruno Vale, Marcos Gullón, Meriem (Rezek 69), Merkis, Gneki Guié, Robert, Papoulis, Stylianou (Mulder 70), João Paulo, Hamdani, Vasiliou (Thuram 79). Coach: Christos Christoforou (CYP)

A 4-1 *Rezek (20), Papoulis (51), Thuram (78), Hugo López (84)*
Bruno Vale, Marcos Gullón (Angeli 87), Sangoy, Rezek, Meriem (Thuram 64), Merkis, Robert, Papoulis (Hugo López 81), Stylianou, João Paulo, Hamdani. Coach: Christos Christoforou (CYP)

Group A
Match 1 - FC Zürich (SUI)
H 3-2 *Papoulis (9), Marcos Gullón (40), Koch (87og)*
Bruno Vale, Marcos Gullón, Sangoy (Hugo López 78), Rezek, Meriem, Merkis, Robert, Papoulis, Stylianou (Angeli 90+1), João Paulo, Hamdani (Thuram 67). Coach: Christos Christoforou (CYP)
Red card: Marcos Gullón 80
Match 2 - Villarreal CF (ESP)
A 0-4
Bruno Vale, Sangoy, Meriem, Merkis, Hugo López (Gneki Guié 46), Robert, Papoulis (Thuram 83), Stylianou, João Paulo, Hamdani, Vasiliou (Rezek 48). Coach: Christos Christoforou (CYP)
Match 3 - VfL Borussia Mönchengladbach (GER)
A 0-5
Bruno Vale, Mulder, Marcos Gullón (Grigore 50; João Paulo 66), Sangoy, Rezek, Merkis, Lopez, Gneki Guié (Meriem 70), Robert, Angeli, Hamdani. Coach: Ioan Andone (ROU)
Match 4 - VfL Borussia Mönchengladbach (GER)
H 0-2
Bruno Vale, Mulder (Papoulis 67), Thuram, Meriem, Merkis, Gneki Guié (Stylianou 60; Hugo López 65), Robert, Angeli, Wheeler, Hamdani, Farley. Coach: Ioan Andone (ROU)
Match 5 - FC Zürich (SUI)
A 1-3 *Farley (23)*
Bruno Vale, Thuram, Meriem (Marcos Gullón 46), Lopez, Gneki Guié (Sangoy 80), Robert, Papoulis (Olinga 55), Angeli, João Paulo, Hamdani, Farley. Coach: Ioan Andone (ROU)
Match 6 - Villarreal CF (ESP)
H 0-2
Hidi, Mulder, Marcos Gullón, Thuram, Merkis, Papoulis (Rezek 66), Angeli, Hamdani (Kyriakou 76), Farley, Olinga (Sangoy 59), Vasiliou. Coach: Ioan Andone (ROU)

Ermis Aradippou FC

Third qualifying round - BSC Young Boys (SUI)
A 0-1
Bogatinov, Žarković, Ouon (Paulinho 46), Axente (Araba 78), Taralidis, Luis Morán (Iluridze 68), China, Paulo Pina, Douglas Packer, Jonatas Belusso, Palazuelos. Coach: Nikos Panayiotou (CYP)
H 0-2
Bogatinov, Žarković (Papathanasiou 45+1), Ouon, Axente (Iluridze 77), Taralidis (Demetriou 68), China, Paulinho, Paulo Pina, Douglas Packer, Jonatas Belusso, Palazuelos. Coach: Nikos Panayiotou (CYP)
Red card: Paulinho 46

DOMESTIC LEAGUE CLUB-BY-CLUB

AC Omonia

Second qualifying round - FK Budućnost Podgorica (MNE)
A 2-0 *Roberto (36), Lobjanidze (79)*
Moreira, Lobjanidze, Rodri, Roberto (Poté 86), Grigalashvili (Álex Rubio 77), Alípio, Cristóvão, Scaramozzino (Fylaktou 82), Kyriakou, Serginho, Acquistapace. Coach: Kostas Kaiafas (CYP)
H 0-0
Moreira, Lobjanidze, Rodri, Roberto, Grigalashvili (Poté 78), Alípio (Nuno Assis 69), Cristóvão (Álex Rubio 64), Kakubava, Kyriakou, Serginho, Acquistapace. Coach: Kostas Kaiafas (CYP)

Third qualifying round - FK Metalurg Skopje (MKD)
H 3-0 *Cristóvão (9, 57), Poté (14)*
Moreira, Lobjanidze, Stepanov, Rodri, Roberto, Cristóvão, Nuno Assis (Grigalashvili 59), Fofana (Álex Rubio 64), Poté, Serginho (Fylaktou 72), Acquistapace. Coach: Kostas Kaiafas (CYP)
A 1-0 *Nuno Assis (54)*
Moreira, Lobjanidze, Stepanov, Rodri, Grigalashvili, Cristóvão, Fofana (Álex Rubio 74), Poté, Kyriakou (Nuno Assis 46), Serginho (Roushias 63), Acquistapace. Coach: Kostas Kaiafas (CYP)

Play-offs - FC Dinamo Moskva (RUS)
A 2-2 *Lobjanidze (2), Fofana (59)*
Moreira, Lobjanidze, Stepanov, Rodri, Cristóvão, Nuno Assis (Grigalashvili 77), Fofana (Kyriakou 86), Renato Margaça, Poté (Roberto 71), Serginho, Acquistapace. Coach: Kostas Kaiafas (CYP)
H 1-2 *Poté (23)*
Moreira, Lobjanidze, Stepanov, Rodri, Cristóvão, Nuno Assis (Grigalashvili 90), Fofana (Kyriakou 86), Renato Margaça, Poté (Roberto 74), Serginho, Acquistapace. Coach: Kostas Kaiafas (CYP)

AEK Larnaca FC

1994 • Neo GSZ (13,032) • aek.com.cy
Major honours
Cypriot Cup (1) 2004
Coach: Thomas Christiansen (ESP)

2014
24/08	a	Apollon	W 5-2	Boljević, Colautti 2, Joan Tomàs 2
31/08	h	APOEL	L 0-2	
15/09	a	Anorthosis	L 1-2	Colautti
21/09	a	Omonia	W 1-0	Joan Tomàs
29/09	h	Ermis	D 0-0	
05/10	a	Ayia Napa	W 2-1	Colautti, Boljević
25/10	h	AEL	D 1-1	David Català
02/11	a	Othellos	D 1-1	Mytidis
09/11	h	Nea Salamis	W 2-0	Mytidis, Joan Tomàs
24/11	a	Ethnikos	L 1-2	Pavlou
30/11	h	Doxa	W 1-0	Vander
06/12	h	Apollon	W 3-1	David Català, Jorge Larena, Englezou
15/12	a	APOEL	D 4-4	Englezou, José Kanté 2, Jorge Larena
21/12	h	Anorthosis	W 1-0	David Català

2015
03/01	h	Omonia	L 1-3	Colautti
10/01	a	Ermis	W 4-0	Monteiro 2, Vander, Jorge Larena
19/01	h	Ayia Napa	W 2-0	Colautti, Jorge Larena (p)
01/02	a	AEL	L 0-1	
07/02	h	Othellos	D 2-2	Monteiro, Jorge Larena
14/02	a	Nea Salamis	D 0-0	
22/02	h	Ethnikos	W 5-0	Joan Tomàs, Vander, Skopelitis, og (Frantzeskou), Englezou
28/02	a	Doxa	W 4-1	Vander, Mytidis 2, Colautti
08/03	h	Omonia	W 2-1	Murillo, Mytidis
14/03	a	Apollon	L 0-1	
21/03	a	Ermis	W 4-0	David Català, Mytidis, Joan Tomàs, Monteiro
04/04	h	APOEL	W 1-0	Mytidis
18/04	a	Anorthosis	L 0-3	
25/04	a	Omonia	D 1-1	José Kanté
02/05	a	Apollon	W 2-0	Mytidis, Monteiro
09/05	h	Ermis	W 2-1	Mytidis, Colautti
17/05	a	APOEL	D 1-1	Boljević (p)
24/05	h	Anorthosis	W 2-0	Englezou, Mytidis

No	Name	Nat	DoB	Pos	Aps	(s)	Gls
1	Alexandre Negri		27/03/81	G	8		
14	Vladimir Boljević	MNE	17/01/88	M	23	(7)	3
33	Ilias Charalambous		25/09/80	D	23		
9	Roberto Colautti	ISR	24/05/82	A	12	(11)	8
6	David Català	ESP	01/12/89	D	30		4
21	Nikos Englezou		11/07/93	M	14	(12)	4
17	Dimitrios Froxylias	GRE	28/06/93	M		(5)	
4	Serginho Greene	NED	24/06/82	D	4	(2)	
10	Joan Tomàs	ESP	17/05/85	M	30		6
7	Jorge Larena	ESP	29/09/81	M	27	(3)	5
29	José Kanté	ESP	27/09/90	A	9	(8)	3
8	Juanma Ortiz	ESP	01/03/82	M	29		
26	Dimitris Kyprianou		02/02/93	M	5	(10)	
2	Eleftherios Mertakas		16/03/85	D	3		
16	Miguel Massana	ESP	11/05/89	D	10	(5)	
5	Konstantinos Mintikkis		08/06/89	A	5	(1)	
7	Monteiro	POR	15/08/88	M	16	(1)	5
18	Ander Murillo	ESP	22/07/83	D	24	(1)	1
19	Nestoras Mytidis		01/06/91	A	11	(6)	10
11	Kyriakos Pavlou		04/09/86	A	5	(12)	1
3	Sipo	EQG	21/04/88	D	2		
20	Giannis Skopelitis	GRE	02/05/78	M	15	(6)	1
22	Toño	ESP	23/11/86	G	24		
12	Vander	BRA	03/10/88	M	23	(5)	4

AEL Limassol FC

1930 • Tsirion (13,331) • ael-limassol.com.cy
Major honours
Cypriot League (6) 1941, 1953, 1955, 1956, 1968, 2012;
Cypriot Cup (6) 1939, 1940, 1948, 1985, 1987, 1989
Coach: Ivaylo Petev (BUL);
(17/11/14) Christakis Christoforou

2014
24/08	a	Nea Salamis	W 2-0	Sielis, Luciano Bebê
01/09	h	Ethnikos	D 2-2	Cadú, Gikiewicz
14/09	a	Doxa	W 4-0	Danielzinho, Cadú, Gikiewicz, Diego Barcelos
22/09	h	Apollon	L 1-2	Danielzinho
27/09	a	APOEL	D 0-0	
05/10	h	Anorthosis	W 4-1	Danielzinho, Gikiewicz, Edmar, Stavrou
25/10	a	AEK	D 1-1	Diego Barcelos
02/11	h	Ermis	L 2-3	Danielzinho, Luciano Bebê
09/11	h	Ayia Napa	D 1-1	Ioniță
22/11	a	Omonia	L 0-2	
29/11	h	Othellos	W 1-0	Stavrou
06/12	h	Nea Salamis	D 1-1	Guidileye
14/12	a	Ethnikos	L 2-4	Luciano Bebê, Ioniță
21/12	h	Doxa	D 0-0	

2015
04/01	a	Apollon	D 3-3	Tagbajumi 2, Stavrou
11/01	h	APOEL	W 2-1	Tagbajumi 2 (1p)
18/01	a	Anorthosis	L 1-2	Luciano Bebê
01/02	h	AEK	W 1-0	Adrián Sardinero
09/02	a	Ermis	D 2-2	Luciano Bebê, Sambou
15/02	h	Ayia Napa	W 3-0	Luciano Bebê, Tagbajumi, og (Markovski)
21/02	h	Omonia	L 0-1	
28/02	a	Othellos	D 0-0	
08/03	a	Doxa	W 2-1	Sema, Tagbajumi
15/03	h	Ayia Napa	D 2-2	Tagbajumi 2
22/03	a	Ethnikos	D 1-1	Nicolaou
05/04	h	Othellos	L 0-1	
19/04	a	Nea Salamis	D 1-1	Stavrou
26/04	h	Doxa	L 0-4	
03/05	a	Ayia Napa	L 0-1	
10/05	h	Ethnikos	L 1-2	Adrián Sardinero
16/05	a	Othellos	L 0-3	
23/05	h	Nea Salamis	W 2-0	Ohene, Nicolaou

No	Name	Nat	DoB	Pos	Aps	(s)	Gls
77	Adrián Sardinero	ESP	13/10/90	A	24	(2)	2
49	Andreas Andreou		28/03/95	D	1		
50	Cadú	POR	21/12/81	D	12		2
23	Carlitos I	CPV	23/04/85	D	20	(2)	
11	Carlitos II	POR	09/03/93	A	8	(10)	
17	Danielzinho	BRA	21/02/88	A	8	(2)	4
10	Diego Barcelos	BRA	05/04/85	M	6	(4)	2
11	Edmar	BRA	19/04/82	M	24	(3)	1
27	Georgios Eleftheriou		30/09/84	M	10	(5)	
1	Karim Fegrouche	MAR	14/02/82	G	8		
40	Evangelos Georgiou		01/09/95	G	2		
9	Łukasz Gikiewicz	POL	26/10/87	A	9	(1)	3
33	Diallo Guidileye	MTN	30/12/89	M	19	(6)	1
32	Alexandru Ioniță	ROU	05/08/89	A	7	(6)	2
2	Jonathan Espańa	VEN	13/11/88	D	6	(2)	
45	Andreas Kyriakou		05/02/94	D	9		
14	Leandros Lillis		13/09/96	M	5	(1)	
20	Luciano Bebê	BRA	11/03/81	M	21	(2)	6
25	Bernard Mendy	FRA	20/08/81	D	12		
44	Joshua Nadeau	FRA	12/09/94	D	6	(3)	
12	Marios Nicolaou		04/10/83	M	22	(3)	2
94	Carlos Ohene	GHA	21/07/93	M	6	(5)	1
46	Paris Panayiotou		21/08/96	M	2	(1)	
53	Anthimos Panteli		11/09/97	M	2		
30	Pulpo	ESP	28/10/87	G	22		
55	Esteban Sachetti	ARG	21/11/85	M	12	(1)	
6	Massamba Sambou	SEN	17/09/86	D	11	(1)	1
16	Maic Sema	SWE	02/12/88	M	6	(5)	1
4	Valentinos Sielis		01/03/90	D	20	(3)	1
8	Andreas Stavrou		27/10/88	M	10	(13)	4
7	Marco Tagbajumi	NGA	01/08/88	A	17	(7)	8
47	Antonis Vasiliou		23/04/96	M	3	(1)	
43	Sotiris Vasiliou		29/12/95	M	1	(1)	
90	Zézinho	GNB	23/09/92	M	1	(1)	

CYPRUS

Anorthosis Famagusta FC

1911 • Antonis Papadopoulos (10,230) • anorthosisfc.com.cy

Major honours
Cypriot League (13) 1950, 1957, 1958, 1960, 1962, 1963, 1995, 1997, 1998, 1999, 2000, 2005, 2008; Cypriot Cup (10) 1949, 1959, 1962, 1964, 1971, 1975, 1998, 2002, 2003, 2007

Coach: André Paus (NED)

2014

01/09	a Omonia	L 2-3	Ede, Yakovenko
15/09	h AEK	W 2-1	Yakovenko, Toni Calvo
21/09	a Ermis	L 0-1	
24/09	a APOEL	L 0-2	
27/09	h Ayia Napa	W 4-1	og (Stathakis), Makris, Aburjania, Toni Calvo
05/10	a AEL	L 1-4	Yakovenko
26/10	h Othellos	W 1-0	Serrán
03/11	a Nea Salamis	W 3-2	Nuhu, Makris, Yakovenko
08/11	h Ethnikos	D 0-0	
22/11	a Doxa	W 4-0	Laifis, Aburjania, Makris 2
01/12	h Apollon	L 0-1	
05/12	h APOEL	L 0-1	
14/12	h Omonia	W 2-1	Laifis, Makris
21/12	a AEK	L 0-1	

2015

04/01	h Ermis	W 2-0	Toni Calvo (p), Gonzalo García
11/01	a Ayia Napa	W 5-1	Toni Calvo, Makris 2, Avraam 2
18/01	h AEL	W 2-1	Makris, Avraam
01/02	a Othellos	W 2-0	Makris, Esmaël Gonçalves
08/02	h Nea Salamis	W 1-0	Laifis
14/02	a Ethnikos	D 0-0	
22/02	h Doxa	W 1-0	Esmaël Gonçalves (p)
28/02	a Apollon	L 0-2	
07/03	a APOEL	L 0-1	
14/03	h Ermis	W 3-1	Marangos, Makris, Laifis
22/03	h Omonia	L 1-3	Esmaël Gonçalves
04/04	a Apollon	W 3-1	Ede, Toni Calvo, Esmaël Gonçalves
18/04	h AEK	W 3-0	Ede, Esmaël Gonçalves, Avraam
25/04	h APOEL	D 3-3	Esmaël Gonçalves 2, Makris
03/05	a Ermis	D 1-1	Esmaël Gonçalves
09/05	a Omonia	L 1-2	Makris
17/05	h Apollon	W 3-1	Esmaël Gonçalves, Makos, Makris
24/05	a AEK	L 0-2	

No	Name	Nat	DoB	Pos	Aps	(s)	Gls
8	Giorgi Aburjania	GEO	02/01/95	M	28	(2)	2
2	Marko Andjić	SRB	14/12/83	D	9		
36	Adamos Andreou		18/12/94	M	2	(5)	
30	Andreas Avraam		06/06/87	A	11	(10)	4
24	Jason Demetriou		18/11/87	D	25		
17	Chinedu Ede	GER	05/02/87	M	16	(6)	3
77	Esmaël Gonçalves	POR	25/06/91	A	14	(1)	9
10	Gonzalo García	ESP	13/10/83	A	8	(7)	1
15	Markus Holgersson	SWE	16/04/85	D	29		
12	Thomas Kaminski	BEL	23/10/92	G	30		
32	Gabriel Konstantinou		05/07/89	G		(1)	
28	Panagiotis Konstantinou		06/08/86	M		(5)	
38	Fytos Kyriakou		29/10/97	A	1	(5)	
34	Konstantinos Laifis		19/05/93	M	24		4
18	Irakli Maisuradze	GEO	22/02/88	M	24	(2)	
41	Grigoris Makos	GRE	18/01/87	D	25	(2)	1
33	Andreas Makris		27/11/95	M	25	(5)	13
6	Christos Marangos			M	5	(18)	1
5	Razak Nuhu	GHA	14/05/91	D	28		1
22	Dimitris Oikonomou		10/11/92	D	3	(3)	
9	Valērijs Šabala	LVA	12/10/94	A		(8)	
3	Albert Serrán	ESP	17/07/84	D	10	(2)	1
7	Toni Calvo	ESP	28/03/78	M	24		5
16	Matthieu Valverde	FRA	14/05/83	G	1		
1	Mario Vega	ARG	03/06/84	G	1		
11	Yuriy Yakovenko	UKR	03/09/93	A	9	(4)	4

APOEL FC

1926 • GSP (23,700) • apoelfc.com.cy

Major honours
Cypriot League (24) 1936, 1937, 1938, 1939, 1940, 1947, 1948, 1949, 1952, 1965, 1973, 1980, 1986, 1990, 1992, 1996, 2002, 2004, 2007, 2009, 2011, 2013, 2014, 2015; Cypriot Cup (21) 1937, 1941, 1947, 1951, 1963, 1968, 1969, 1973, 1976, 1978, 1979, 1984, 1993, 1995, 1996, 1997, 1999, 2006, 2008, 2014, 2015

**Coach: Georgios Donis (GRE);
(10/01/15) Thorsten Fink (GER);
(11/05/15) (Gustavo Manduca (BRA))**

2014

31/08	a AEK	W 2-0	Manduca 2
13/09	h Ermis	W 1-0	Sheridan
20/09	a Ayia Napa	W 3-1	Charalambides, Sotiriou, Manduca
24/09	h Anorthosis	W 2-0	Manduca, Aloneftis
27/09	h AEL	D 0-0	
06/10	a Othellos	W 2-1	Manduca, Djebbour
26/10	h Nea Salamis	W 1-0	Djebbour
01/11	a Ethnikos	W 4-0	Sheridan 2, Alexandrou, Manduca
10/11	h Doxa	D 0-0	
21/11	a Apollon	D 0-0	
30/11	h Omonia	W 1-0	Efrem
05/12	a Anorthosis	W 1-0	Djebbour
15/12	h AEK	D 4-4	Djebbour 2, Sotiriou 2
20/12	a Ermis	L 1-2	Sotiriou

2015

05/01	h Ayia Napa	D 1-1	Efrem
11/01	a AEL	L 1-2	Riise
17/01	h Othellos	D 1-1	Djebbour
31/01	a Nea Salamis	W 1-0	Djebbour
07/02	h Ethnikos	W 4-0	Lanig, Riise, Efrem, Djebbour
14/02	a Doxa	W 2-0	Riise, og (João Leonardo)
21/02	a Apollon	W 1-0	Nuno Morais
28/02	a Omonia	D 1-1	Nuno Morais
07/03	h Anorthosis	W 1-0	Riise
14/03	a Omonia	D 1-1	Djebbour
21/03	a Apollon	D 2-2	Tiago Gomes, Nafiu
04/04	a AEK	L 0-1	
19/04	h Ermis	W 3-0	Lanig, Djebbour 2
25/04	a Anorthosis	D 3-3	Charalambides, Efrem, og (Demetriou)
02/05	h Omonia	W 3-2	De Vincenti, Alexandrou, Djebbour
10/05	a Apollon	L 0-1	
16/05	h AEK	D 1-1	De Vincenti (p)
24/05	a Ermis	W 4-2	De Vincenti, Charalambides, Djebbour 2 (1p)

No	Name	Nat	DoB	Pos	Aps	(s)	Gls
11	Nektarios Alexandrou		19/12/83	M	9	(5)	2
46	Efstathios Aloneftis		29/03/83	M	4	(11)	1
15	Marios Antoniades		14/05/90	D	8	(3)	
4	Kostakis Artymatas		15/04/93	M	5	(7)	
5	Carlão	BRA	19/01/86	D	19	(1)	
10	Kostas Charalambides		25/07/81	M	14	(5)	3
22	Dionisios Chiotis	GRE	04/06/77	G	11		
25	Andreas Christofidis		14/10/92	D	1		
30	Tomás De Vincenti	ARG	09/02/89	M	21	(3)	3
7	Rafik Djebbour	ALG	08/03/84	A	23	(3)	14
7	Georgios Efrem		05/07/89	M	20	(4)	4
44	Nicholas Ioannou		10/11/95	D	2	(1)	
3	João Guilherme	BRA	21/04/86	D	23	(3)	
73	Kaká	BRA	16/05/81	D	16	(4)	
4	Alex Konstantinou		11/04/92	A		(1)	
13	Martin Lanig	GER	11/07/84	M	13		2
21	Gustavo Manduca	BRA	08/06/80	M	9	(4)	6
34	Mário Sérgio	POR	28/07/81	D	30		
34	Valmir Nafiu	MKD	03/04/94	A	3	(7)	1
26	Nuno Morais	POR	29/01/84	M	27		2
31	Vasilios Pafafotis		10/08/95	M	1	(3)	
23	Anastasios Papazoglou	GRE	24/09/88	D	7	(2)	
35	Marios Pechlivanos		23/05/95	M		(1)	
6	John Arne Riise	NOR	24/09/80	D	25		4
9	Cillian Sheridan	IRL	23/02/89	A	11	(9)	3
20	Pieros Sotiriou		13/01/93	A	5	(5)	4
8	Tiago Gomes	POR	19/08/85	M	11	(10)	1
78	Urko Pardo	ESP	28/01/83	G	21		
16	Vinícius	BRA	16/05/86	M	13	(3)	

Apollon Limassol FC

1954 • Tsirion (13,331) • apollon.com.cy

Major honours
Cypriot League (3) 1991, 1994, 2006; Cypriot Cup (7) 1966, 1967, 1986, 1992, 2001, 2010, 2013

**Coach: Christos Christoforou;
(16/10/14) Ioan Andone (ROU);
(09/04/15) Ton Caanen (NED)**

2014

24/08	h AEK	L 2-5	Robert, Papoulis
01/09	a Ermis	W 3-1	Thuram, Rezek, Meriem
13/09	h Ayia Napa	W 1-0	Sangoy
22/09	a AEL	W 2-1	Hugo López, Sangoy
27/09	h Othellos	W 4-0	Hugo López 2, Thuram, Farley
06/10	a Nea Salamıs	L 0-4	
27/10	h Ethnikos	W 3-0	Papoulis, Stojanović, Sangoy
01/11	a Doxa	W 3-1	Sangoy 2 (1p), Hugo López
10/11	h Omonia	W 3-0	Papoulis 2, Stojanović
21/11	h APOEL	D 0-0	
01/12	a Anorthosis	W 1-0	Sangoy
06/12	a AEK	L 1-3	João Paulo
15/12	h Ermis	W 3-2	Stojanović, Papoulis 2
20/12	a Ayia Napa	W 5-2	Stojanović, Gneki Guié, João Paulo, Papoulis, Marcos Gullón

2015

04/01	h AEL	D 3-3	Thuram, Gneki Guié, Merkis
12/01	a Othellos	D 2-2	Gneki Guié 2
17/01	h Nea Salamis	W 5-0	Sangoy, João Paulo, Gneki Guié, Merkis, Thuram
02/02	a Ethnikos	W 2-0	Papoulis, Gneki Guié
07/02	h Doxa	W 2-0	Papoulis (p), Gneki Guié
15/02	a Omonia	W 2-1	Gneki Guié, Papoulis
21/02	a APOEL	L 0-1	
28/02	a Anorthosis	W 2-0	Papoulis, Gneki Guié
07/03	a Ermis	L 0-1	
14/03	h AEK	W 1-0	Sangoy
21/03	a APOEL	D 2-2	Sangoy, Papoulis
04/04	h Anorthosis	L 1-3	Gneki Guié
18/04	a Omonia	L 0-1	
25/04	h Ermis	D 2-2	Nuno Lopes, Merkis
02/05	a AEK	D 0-2	
10/05	h APOEL	W 1-0	Papoulis
16/05	a Anorthosis	L 1-3	Wheeler
24/05	h Omonia	W 2-1	Papoulis, Hamdani

No	Name	Nat	DoB	Pos	Aps	(s)	Gls
27	Angelis Angeli		31/05/89	D	12	(2)	
83	Bruno Vale	POR	08/04/83	G	32		
18	Elton Figueiredo	BRA	12/02/86	M	2	(1)	
70	Farley	BRA	14/01/94	M	13	(11)	1
19	Abraham Gneki Guié	CIV	25/07/86	A	15	(7)	10
2	Nicolae Grigore	ROU	04/09/83	M		(1)	
56	Rachid Hamdani	MAR	08/04/85	M	21	(4)	1
17	Hugo López	ESP	15/05/88	M	12	(7)	4
50	João Paulo	POR	06/06/81	D	19		3
21	Georgios Kolokoudias		03/05/89	A		(7)	
48	Charalambos Kyriakou		09/02/95	M	3	(7)	
6	Marcos Gullón	ESP	20/02/89	M	13	(6)	1
4	Camel Meriem	FRA	18/10/79	M	23	(4)	1
16	Georgios Merkis		30/07/84	D	26		3
2	Dustley Mulder	CUW	27/01/85	D	9	(2)	
5	Nuno Lopes	POR	19/12/86	M	14	(1)	1
77	Fabrice Olinga	CMR	12/05/96	A		(1)	
29	Edwin Ouon	RWA	26/01/81	D	7	(3)	
41	Fotios Papoulis	GRE	22/01/85	M	26	(4)	14
41	Alastair Reynolds		02/09/96	M		(1)	
11	Jan Rezek	CZE	05/05/82	A	12	(1)	1
8	Bertrand Robert	FRA	16/11/83	M	16	(5)	1
10	Gastón Sangoy	ARG	05/10/84	A	20		9
22	Luka Stojanović	SRB	04/01/94	M	15	(3)	4
28	Marios Stylianou		23/09/93	D	2		
51	Stylianos Stylianou		06/07/95	M		(1)	
9	Thuram	BRA	01/02/91	A	15	(9)	4
88	Georgios Vasiliou		12/06/84	D	11	(3)	
42	Christos Wheeler		29/06/97	D	8	(1)	1

Ayia Napa FC

1990 • Tasos Markou, Paralimni (8,000) • aoanfc.com

Coach: Nikos Andronikou;
(23/10/14) Georgios Kosma

2014
23/08	a	Ethnikos	L 1-2	Antoniou
31/08	h	Doxa	D 2-2	Kolokoudias, Haber
13/09	a	Apollon	L 0-1	
20/09	h	APOEL	L 1-3	Panayotov
27/09	a	Anorthosis	L 1-4	Rojas
05/10	h	AEK	L 1-2	Markoski
26/10	a	Ermis	D 2-2	Kolokoudias 2
02/11	a	Omonia	W 2-1	Panayotov, Kolokoudias
09/11	h	AEL	D 1-1	Marchev
22/11	a	Othellos	L 1-2	Kolokoudias
29/11	h	Nea Salamis	D 1-1	Kolokoudias
08/12	h	Ethnikos	D 0-0	
13/12	a	Doxa	L 0-1	
20/12	a	Apollon	L 2-5	Georgiou, Marchev

2015
05/01	a	APOEL	D 1-1	Kolokoudias
11/01	h	Anorthosis	L 1-5	Panayotov
19/01	a	AEK	L 0-2	
31/01	h	Ermis	W 2-1	Curjurić 2
08/02	h	Omonia	L 1-3	Theodorou
15/02	a	AEL	L 0-3	
22/02	h	Othellos	W 1-0	Curjurić (p)
28/02	a	Nea Salamis	D 0-0	
08/03	h	Nea Salamis	D 0-0	
15/03	a	AEL	D 2-2	Felgate, Panayotov
22/03	a	Doxa	W 1-0	Antoniou
05/04	h	Ethnikos	W 1-0	Haber
19/04	a	Othellos	D 2-2	Haber, Marchev
26/04	a	Nea Salamis	L 0-3	
03/05	h	AEL	W 1-0	Panayotov
10/05	h	Doxa	D 0-0	
16/05	a	Ethnikos	L 2-3	Antolek, Mertakas (p)
23/05	h	Othellos	D 2-2	Bamba, Georgiou

No	Name	Nat	DoB	Pos	Aps	(s)	Gls
55	Ivan Antolek	CRO	27/01/93	A	7	(5)	1
24	Giannis Antoniou		21/01/90	D	22	(5)	2
88	Georgios Aresti		02/09/94	M	10	(2)	
1	Grigoris Athanasiou	GRE	09/03/84	G	17		
28	Fousseni Bamba	CIV	19/04/90	D	15	(3)	1
77	Ivan Curjurić	CRO	29/09/89	M	12	(3)	3
2	Christos Djamas		06/09/95	M	1	(3)	
3	Michael Felgate	ENG	01/04/91	D	22		1
18	Emiliano Fusco	ARG	02/03/86	D	19	(4)	
19	Elias Georgiou		24/07/97	M	3	(7)	2
10	Daniel Haber	CAN	29/05/92	A	26	(4)	3
31	Andreas Kittos		09/09/90	G	15		
21	Georgios Kolokoudias		03/05/89	A	16	(1)	7
17	Antonis Koudellis		27/06/95	D		(1)	
33	Nicolas Liotatis		17/06/90	D		(2)	
98	Antonis Machattou		08/07/98	D		(2)	
11	Veselin Marchev	BUL	07/02/90	A	24	(1)	3
7	Marko dos Santos	BRA	18/05/81	A	1	(5)	
30	Kostas Markou		27/03/88	M	4	(1)	
16	Bojan Markoski	MKD	08/08/83	D	27		1
37	Eleftherios Mertakas		16/03/85	D	15		1
27	Petros Messios		09/11/84	M	6	(15)	
43	Musawengosi Mguni	ZIM	05/04/83	A	7	(6)	
21	Vasil Panayotov	BUL	16/07/90	M	30		5
14	Fabricio Poci	ARG	10/04/86	M	4	(2)	
25	Stergios Psianos	GRE	12/09/89	M	15	(2)	
13	David Rojas	COL	13/02/92	D	7	(4)	1
12	Rômulo Santos	BRA	18/06/92	A		(3)	
29	Angelos Siathas		09/06/96	A		(1)	
4	Stavros Stathakis	GRE	30/11/87	D	7	(2)	
26	Zacharias Theodorou		07/07/93	M	18		1
20	Nektarios Tziortzis		09/11/90	M	2	(12)	

Doxa Katokopia FC

1954 • Makario, Nicosia (16,000) • doxafc.com

Coach: Demetris Ioannou;
(08/09/14) Slobodan Krčmarević (SRB);
(04/03/15) Nikos Andreou

2014
23/08	h	Ermis	L 0-2	
31/08	a	Ayia Napa	D 2-2	Ricardo Fernandes 2
14/09	h	AEL	L 0-4	
21/09	a	Othellos	L 0-2	
28/09	h	Nea Salamis	D 1-1	Paulo Jorge
04/10	a	Ethnikos	W 2-1	Diogo Ramos, Ricardo Fernandes
25/10	h	Omonia	L 0-1	
01/11	h	Apollon	L 1-3	Emmanuel
10/11	a	APOEL	D 0-0	
22/11	h	Anorthosis	L 0-4	
30/11	a	AEK	L 0-1	
07/12	a	Ermis	L 1-2	Ricardo Fernandes
13/12	h	Ayia Napa	W 1-0	Diogo Ramos
21/12	a	AEL	D 0-0	

2015
03/01	h	Othellos	D 0-0	
10/01	a	Nea Salamis	L 0-1	
18/01	h	Ethnikos	W 3-1	Ricardo Lobo, Bernardo Vasconcelos, Novoa
01/02	a	Omonia	L 2-4	Ricardo Lobo 2
07/02	a	Apollon	L 0-2	
14/02	h	APOEL	L 0-2	
22/02	a	Anorthosis	L 0-1	
28/02	h	AEK	L 1-4	Ricardo Lobo
08/03	h	AEL	L 1-2	Álvaro Ocaña
15/03	a	Othellos	W 1-0	Ricardo Lobo
22/03	h	Ayia Napa	L 0-1	
05/04	h	Nea Salamis	W 3-0	Ricardo Fernandes 2, Ricardo Lobo
19/04	a	Ethnikos	W 2-0	Diogo Ramos 2
26/04	a	AEL	W 4-0	Ricardo Lobo 3, Diogo Ramos
03/05	h	Othellos	D 3-3	Diogo Ramos 2, Ricardo Lobo
10/05	a	Ayia Napa	D 0-0	
16/05	a	Nea Salamis	D 0-6	
23/05	h	Ethnikos	L 1-5	Koukartas

No	Name	Nat	DoB	Pos	Aps	(s)	Gls
30	Livingstone Adjin	GHA	12/04/89	M	6		
15	Albert Ahulu	GHA	19/06/93	A		(1)	
21	Álvaro Ocaña	ESP	02/02/93	D	18	(6)	1
11	Gary Ambroise	HAI	17/07/85	M	5	(4)	
88	Georgios Aresti		02/09/94	M	7	(5)	
18	Bernardo Vasconcelos	POR	10/06/79	A	4	(2)	1
23	Homero Calderón	VEN	20/10/93	M	18	(3)	
13	Carlos Marques	POR	06/02/83	D	17	(4)	
99	Evagoras Chatzifragkiskou		29/10/86	G	14		
21	Konstantinos Christodoulou		22/03/96	A		(7)	
8	Dani López	ESP	31/03/92	M	8	(3)	
9	Diogo Ramos	POR	08/11/86	A	26	(3)	7
28	Richard Emmanuel	CMR	17/01/95	A	11	(13)	1
4	Ferrán Monzó	ESP	06/12/91	D	20	(3)	
20	Héctor González	VEN	04/11/77	M	8	(3)	
77	Raúl González	VEN	28/06/85	D	27	(2)	
7	José Higón	ESP	22/05/91	M	1	(3)	
33	João Leonardo	BRA	30/07/85	D	27	(1)	
39	Marios Koukartas		04/06/98	M	1	(2)	1
33	Dimos Koukou		28/01/97	D	1		
1	Luiz Fernando	BRA	20/02/88	G	3		
79	Michalis Morfis		15/01/79	G	1		
32	Savvas Nicolaou		05/08/87	M		(4)	
16	Nilson	CPV	05/08/87	D	29	(2)	
12	Christian Novoa	VEN	09/07/91	A	11	(5)	1
14	Paulo Alves	POR	19/12/93	D	6	(3)	
3	Paulo Jorge	POR	16/06/80	D	13	(1)	1
10	Ricardo Fernandes	POR	21/04/78	M	25	(2)	6
9	Ricardo Lobo	BRA	20/05/84	A	15		10
5	Elias Romero	VEN	12/07/96	M	2	(1)	
87	Giannis Siderakis	GRE	16/11/87	G	14		
6	Stefanos Siontis	GRE	04/09/87	D	12		
31	Georgios Xenofontos		01/03/96	D	1	(1)	

Ermis Aradippou FC

1958 • Dasaki, Achna (5,000); Ammochostos, Larnaca (4,000) • ermisfc.com.cy

Coach: Nikos Panayiotou;
(08/09/14) Nikodimos Papavasiliou;
(05/02/15) Mitchell van der Gaag (NED);
(28/03/15) Ioannis Okkas;
(14/05/15) (Michalis Markou)

2014
23/08	a	Doxa	W 2-0	Luis Morán, Onyilo
01/09	h	Apollon	L 1-3	Papathanasiou
13/09	a	APOEL	L 0-1	
21/09	h	Anorthosis	W 1-0	De Azevedo
29/09	a	AEK	D 0-0	
04/10	a	Omonia	L 1-2	Luis Morán
26/10	h	Ayia Napa	D 2-2	Paulo Pina, Onyilo
02/11	a	AEL	W 3-2	Ibraimi, Onyilo 2
08/11	h	Othellos	W 1-0	Onyilo
23/11	a	Nea Salamis	W 1-0	Paulo Pina
29/11	h	Ethnikos	W 2-1	China, Luis Morán
07/12	h	Doxa	W 2-1	Onyilo, De Azevedo
15/12	a	Apollon	L 2-3	Onyilo 2
20/12	h	APOEL	W 2-1	Onyilo 2

2015
04/01	a	Anorthosis	L 0-2	
10/01	h	AEK	L 0-4	
17/01	h	Omonia	D 1-1	Paulo Pina
31/01	a	Ayia Napa	L 1-2	Onyilo
09/02	h	AEL	D 2-2	Ibraimi, Paulinho
15/02	a	Othellos	W 2-0	Manú, Taralidis
21/02	h	Nea Salamis	W 3-1	Manú, Bruno Turco, China
28/02	a	Ethnikos	D 0-0	
07/03	h	Apollon	W 1-0	Onyilo
14/03	a	Anorthosis	L 1-3	Onyilo
21/03	h	AEK	L 0-4	
05/04	h	Omonia	L 0-1	
19/04	a	APOEL	L 0-3	
25/04	a	Apollon	D 2-2	Onyilo, Manú
03/05	h	Anorthosis	D 1-1	Onyilo (p)
09/05	a	AEK	L 1-2	Papathanasiou
17/05	a	Omonia	L 1-7	Katsiati
24/05	a	APOEL	L 2-4	Taralidis, Papathanasiou

No	Name	Nat	DoB	Pos	Aps	(s)	Gls
12	Aldo Adorno	PAR	08/04/82	A	1		
92	Anastasios Andreou		26/05/98	M		(1)	
75	Mathieu Bemba	FRA	04/03/88	M	9	(3)	
1	Martin Bogatinov	MKD	26/04/86	G	23		
91	Bruno Turco	BRA	30/07/91	M	11	(3)	1
20	China	POR	15/04/82	D	21	(2)	2
93	Martinos Christofi		26/07/93	D	8	(5)	
33	Athos Chrysostomou		08/07/81	G	3		
33	Marcos De Azevedo	BRA	23/11/81	M	6	(3)	2
99	Anastasis Demetriou		18/10/99	A		(3)	
8	Stelios Demetriou		04/10/90	D	2	(4)	
77	Douglas Packer	BRA	13/03/87	M	4	(4)	
95	Sergios Hadjidemetriou		18/12/98	A	1	(2)	
27	Besart Ibraimi	MKD	17/12/86	M	22	(1)	2
80	Jonatas Belusso	BRA	10/06/88	A	2	(5)	
14	Georgios Katsiati		04/02/96	A	3	(4)	1
98	Stylianos Konstantinou		26/11/99	G		(2)	
60	Lefteris Kontonicola		15/01/95	A	1		
12	Petros Kourou		03/06/96	M	4	(1)	
96	Kyriakos Kyriakou		01/03/98	M	1		
19	Luis Morán	ESP	26/07/87	M	15	(2)	3
81	Manú	POR	28/08/82	M	15		3
11	Ifeanyi Onyilo	NGA	31/10/90	A	27		15
6	Edwin Ouon	RWA	26/01/81	D	16		
22	Rubén Palazuelos	ESP	11/04/83	M	6	(1)	
29	Andreas Papathanasiou		03/10/83	A	3	(24)	3
22	Paulinho	BRA	24/08/83	D	22	(7)	1
26	Paulo Pina	CPV	04/01/81	D	26		3
62	Kyriakos Pittas		05/01/98	M		(1)	
24	Moustapha Quaynor	GHA	17/06/97	D	12	(5)	
21	Jan Rezek	CZE	05/05/82	A	9		
32	Konstantinos Samaras		18/05/84	D	18	(2)	
55	Pavlos Samboukasides		29/06/95	M	1		
84	Dimitris Stylianou		05/07/84	G	6		
17	Giannis Taralidis	GRE	17/05/81	M	26	(2)	2
97	Theofilos Theokli		13/12/98	M		(1)	
16	Georgios Tofas		17/06/89	A	1		
35	Toni	POR	23/07/79	D	12	(3)	
3	Dragan Žarković	SRB	16/04/86	D	17		

Ethnikos Achnas FC

1968 • Dasaki (5,000) • fcachna.com.cy

Coach: Apostolos Makrides;
(28/03/15) Borce Gjurev

2014
23/08	h Ayia Napa	W	2-1	Valdo, Ibson
01/09	a AEL	D	2-2	Eduardo Pincelli, Tall
15/09	h Othellos	D	0-0	
20/09	a Nea Salamis	L	1-2	Stoller
28/09	h Omonia	W	1-0	Ogungbe
04/10	h Doxa	L	1-2	Jone
27/10	a Apollon	L	0-3	
01/11	h APOEL	L	0-4	
08/11	h Anorthosis	D	0-0	
24/11	a AEK	W	2-1	Stoller, Valdo
29/11	a Ermis	L	1-2	Valdo
08/12	a Ayia Napa	D	0-0	
14/12	h AEL	W	4-2	Juninho, Ogungbe 2, Valdo
20/12	a Othellos	W	2-1	Jone, Amessan

2015
04/01	h Nea Salamis	D	1-1	Valdo
10/01	a Omonia	L	0-2	
18/01	a Doxa	L	1-3	Eduardo Pincelli
02/02	h Apollon	L	0-2	
07/02	a APOEL	L	0-4	
14/02	h Anorthosis	D	0-0	
22/02	a AEK	L	0-5	
28/02	h Ermis	D	0-0	
08/03	h Othellos	W	3-1	Valdo, Ibson, Belfort
15/03	a Nea Salamis	L	0-1	
22/03	h AEL	D	1-1	Juninho
05/04	a Ayia Napa	L	0-1	
19/04	h Doxa	L	0-2	
26/04	a Othellos	W	2-1	Eduardo Pincelli, Chatzivasilis
03/05	h Nea Salamis	W	2-1	Valdo, Belfort
09/05	a AEL	W	2-1	Valdo, Chatziaros
16/05	h Ayia Napa	W	3-2	Valdo 2, Belfort (p)
23/05	a Doxa	W	5-1	Elia 2, Valdo, Tall, Chatzivasilis

No	Name	Nat	DoB	Pos	Aps	(s)	Gls
77	Rodolph Amessan	CIV	27/09/90	A	5	(6)	1
18	Anestis Argyriou	GRE	04/01/88	D	10		
16	Kervens Belfort	HAI	16/05/92	A	14	(1)	3
7	Petros Chatziaros		10/08/82	D	7	(1)	1
19	Giannis Chatzivasilis		26/04/90	A	10	(15)	2
26	Christoforos Christofi		23/03/91	M	8	(9)	
1	Bouna Coundoul	SEN	04/03/82	G	14		
23	Andreas Dober	AUT	31/03/86	D	8		
5	Eduardo Pincelli	BRA	23/04/83	M	20	(1)	3
16	Marios Elia		19/05/96	M	1	(3)	2
44	Pavlos Engomitis		22/10/96	D	1	(1)	
4	Everton Santos	BRA	15/06/84	D	18		
4	Panagiotis Frantzeskou		12/04/91	D	8	(3)	
17	Panagiotis Giannopoulos	GRE	21/07/94	M		(1)	
8	Ibson	BRA	08/10/89	M	19	(6)	2
22	Joaquín García	ESP	12/01/86	M	9	(3)	
99	Jone	BRA	13/11/91	A	4	(6)	2
11	Juninho	BRA	29/06/89	A	16	(8)	2
45	Antonis Katsiaris		14/10/96	M		(2)	
14	Symeon Kone		15/01/98	D		(1)	
14	Paraskevas Koui		10/02/98	M		(1)	
42	Krasniqi Kreshnic	ENG	15/09/94	M		(3)	
33	Georgios Loizou		25/02/92	G	5		
25	Ganiu Ogungbe	NGA	01/12/92	D	25	(2)	3
10	Christos Poyiatzis		12/04/78	A	1	(4)	
20	Thomas Prager	AUT	13/09/85	M	27		
88	Fabian Stoller	SUI	31/03/88	M	27	(2)	2
6	Gora Tall	SEN	20/05/85	D	27		2
9	Valdo	BRA	15/06/84	A	27	(2)	11
16	Matthieu Valverde	FRA	14/05/83	G	13		
2	Mamadou Wague	FRA	19/08/90	D	16	(3)	
7	Rafael Yiangoudakis		15/08/90	M	12	(10)	

Nea Salamis Famagusta FC

1948 • Ammochostos (4,000) • neasalamina.com

Major honours
Cypriot Cup (1) 1990

Coach: Neophytos Larkou;
(16/12/14) Nikos Panayiotou;
(05/05/15) (Floros Nicolaou)

2014
24/08	h AEL	L	0-2	
30/08	a Othellos	W	1-0	Éder
14/09	h Omonia	D	1-1	Diego León
20/09	h Ethnikos	W	2-1	Henrique, Pedrito
28/09	a Doxa	D	1-1	Krstić
06/10	h Apollon	W	4-0	Krstić, Pedrito, Henrique, Gabi
26/10	a APOEL	L	0-1	
03/11	h Anorthosis	L	2-3	Chidi, Diego León
09/11	a AEK	L	0-2	
23/11	h Ermis	L	0-1	
29/11	a Ayia Napa	D	1-1	Lambropoulos
06/12	a AEL	D	1-1	Okeuhie
14/12	h Othellos	L	0-1	
20/12	a Omonia	L	0-3	

2015
04/01	a Ethnikos	D	1-1	Grigalashvili
10/01	h Doxa	W	1-0	Henrique
17/01	a Apollon	L	0-5	
31/01	h APOEL	L	0-1	
08/02	a Anorthosis	L	0-1	
14/02	h AEK	D	0-0	
21/02	a Ermis	L	1-3	Lambropoulos
28/02	h Ayia Napa	D	0-0	
08/03	a Ayia Napa	D	0-0	
15/03	h Ethnikos	W	1-0	Henrique
21/03	a Othellos	W	2-0	Gleison 2
05/04	a Doxa	L	0-3	
19/04	h AEL	D	1-1	Gleison
26/04	h Ayia Napa	W	3-0	Diego León, Gleison, Maurice
03/05	a Ethnikos	L	1-2	Pedrito
10/05	h Othellos	W	1-0	Henrique
16/05	h Doxa	W	6-0	Pedrito 2, Konstantinou 2, Kousoulos, Gleison
23/05	a AEL	L	0-2	

No	Name	Nat	DoB	Pos	Aps	(s)	Gls
15	Siaka Bamba	CIV	24/08/89	M	12	(2)	
83	Corrin Brooks-Meade	ENG	19/03/88	G	15		
15	Philip Chidi	NGA	20/02/84	A	6	(6)	1
90	Mattia Cinquini	ITA	11/05/90	D	19	(3)	
10	Diego León	ESP	16/01/84	M	25	(1)	3
5	Éder	BRA	21/09/83	D	21		1
33	Gabi	POR	20/03/81	M	8	(5)	1
38	Gleison	BRA	28/12/84	M	22	(6)	5
30	Shota Grigalashvili	GEO	21/06/86	M	1		1
50	Solomon Grimes	LBR	24/07/87	D	29	(2)	
9	Henrique	POR	31/03/80	A	16	(7)	5
63	Iasonas Ioannou		28/08/96	M	1	(1)	
32	Antonis Katsis		06/09/89	D	1	(4)	
8	Charalambos Kokkinos		14/08/97	M		(1)	
19	Stavros Konstantinou		19/03/97	M	2	(9)	2
13	Giannis Kousoulos		14/06/96	M	7	(7)	1
22	Miloš Krstić	SRB	07/03/87	M	7	(4)	2
12	Kyriakos Kyriakou		20/06/89	D	13	(4)	
21	Georgios Lambropoulos	GRE	26/10/84	M	16	(5)	2
34	Leandro	BRA	11/01/89	A	18	(2)	
16	Andreas Lemesios		24/09/97	M	2		
35	Panagiotis Loizides		28/02/95	D		(7)	
19	Chrysathos Mantzalos	ISR	04/05/96	M	1	(1)	
3	Marco Aurélio	BRA	27/03/83	D	14	(2)	
94	Jean-Eudes Maurice	HAI	21/06/86	A	3	(2)	1
77	Konstantinos Mintikkis		08/06/89	A	16	(1)	
11	Eze Vincent Okeuhie	NGA	06/06/93	M	22	(5)	1
17	Panagiotis Panayiotou		12/06/96	M		(1)	
55	Giorgi Papava	GEO	16/02/93	M	12	(2)	
7	Pedrito	ESP	28/04/89	A	26	(5)	5
29	Ellinas Sofroniou		29/01/96	G	2		
1	Ram Strauss	ISR	28/04/92	G	15		

AC Omonia

1948 • GSP (23,700) • omonoia.com.cy

Major honours
Cypriot League (20) 1961, 1966, 1972, 1974, 1975, 1976, 1977, 1978, 1979, 1981, 1982, 1983, 1984, 1985, 1987, 1989, 1993, 2001, 2003, 2010; Cypriot Cup (14) 1965, 1972, 1974, 1980, 1981, 1982, 1983, 1988, 1991, 1994, 2000, 2005, 2011, 2012

Coach: Kostas Kaiafas

2014
01/09	h Anorthosis	W	3-2	Poté 2, Roushias
14/09	a Nea Salamis	D	1-1	Poté
21/09	h AEK	L	0-1	
24/09	a Othellos	W	1-0	Poté
28/09	a Ethnikos	L	0-1	
04/10	h Ermis	W	2-1	Poté, Fofana
25/10	a Doxa	W	1-0	Kirm
02/11	h Ayia Napa	L	1-2	Poté
10/11	a Apollon	L	0-3	
22/11	h AEL	W	2-0	Poté 2 (1p)
30/11	a APOEL	L	0-1	
06/12	h Othellos	W	1-0	Poté
14/12	a Anorthosis	L	1-2	Oikonomidis
20/12	h Nea Salamis	W	3-0	Kirm, Poté, Álex Rubio

2015
03/01	h AEK	W	3-1	Poté 2, Nuno Assis
10/01	h Ethnikos	W	2-0	Nuno Assis, Schembri
17/01	a Ermis	D	1-1	Leandro
01/02	h Doxa	W	4-2	Poté 2, Cristóvão 2
08/02	h Ayia Napa	W	3-1	Poté (p), Roberto, Fofana
15/02	h Apollon	L	1-2	Runje
21/02	a AEL	W	1-0	Leandro
28/02	h APOEL	D	1-1	Fofana
08/03	a AEK	L	1-2	Leandro
14/03	h APOEL	D	1-1	Schembri
22/03	a Anorthosis	W	3-1	Roberto 2, Nuno Assis
05/04	a Ermis	W	1-0	Kirm
18/04	h Apollon	W	1-0	Schembri
25/04	h AEK	D	1-1	Lobjanidze
02/05	a APOEL	L	2-3	Nuno Assis 2
10/05	h Anorthosis	W	2-1	Fofana, Kirm
17/05	h Ermis	W	7-1	Schembri 2, Kirm 2, Goulon, Poté 2
24/05	a Apollon	L	1-2	Goulon

No	Name	Nat	DoB	Pos	Aps	(s)	Gls
89	Jonas Acquistapace	GER	18/06/89	D	13		
22	Álex Rubio	ESP	23/07/93	A	9	(8)	1
16	Cristóvão	POR	25/03/83	M	18	(3)	2
7	Marios Demetriou		25/12/92	A	9	(1)	
26	Gaoussou Fofana	CIV	17/04/84	M	16	(12)	4
20	Gerasimos Fylaktou		24/07/91	M	11	(4)	
33	Antonis Georgallides		30/01/82	G	10	(1)	
5	Hérold Goulon	FRA	12/06/88	M	11	(1)	2
10	Shota Grigalashvili	GEO	21/06/86	M	4	(5)	
30	Andraž Kirm	SVN	06/09/84	M	25	(1)	6
40	Charalambos Kyriakou		15/10/89	D	9	(1)	
44	Leandro	HUN	19/03/82	D	17		3
3	Ucha Lobjanidze	GEO	23/02/87	D	22	(2)	1
31	José Moreira	POR	20/03/82	G	15		
9	Nuno Assis	POR	25/11/77	M	24	(2)	5
23	Georgios Oikonomidis		10/04/90	M	23		1
1	Konstantinos Panagi		08/10/94	G	7		
19	Andreas Panayiotou		31/05/95	D		(2)	
39	Mickaël Poté	BEN	24/09/84	A	23	(6)	17
28	Renato Margaça	POR	17/07/85	M	25	(2)	
9	Roberto	ESP	04/02/80	A	10	(15)	3
6	Rodri	ESP	25/04/85	M	9	(3)	
8	Onisiforos Roushias		15/07/92	A		(13)	1
90	Ivan Runje	CRO	09/10/90	D	13		1
36	Jack Sammoutis	ENG	15/01/94	M		(3)	
17	Anthony Scaramozzino	FRA	30/04/85	D	10		
27	André Schembri	MLT	27/05/86	A	6	(9)	5
88	Serginho	BRA	27/04/88	M	7	(1)	
5	Milan Stepanov	SRB	02/04/83	D	6		

Othellos Athienou FC

1933 • Antonis Papadopoulos,
Larnaca (10,230) • othellosfc.com.cy
Coach: Kostas Sakkas

2014

30/08	h	Nea Salamis	L	0-1
15/09	a	Ethnikos	D	0-0
21/09	h	Doxa	W	2-0 *Thiago, Panayiotou*
24/09	h	Omonia	L	0-1
27/09	a	Apollon	L	0-4
06/10	h	APOEL	L	1-2 *Thiago*
26/10	a	Anorthosis	L	0-1
02/11	h	AEK	D	1-1 *Khmaladze*
08/11	a	Ermis	L	0-1
22/11	h	Ayia Napa	W	2-1 *Thiago 2*
29/11	a	AEL	L	0-1
06/12	a	Omonia	L	0-1
14/12	a	Nea Salamis	W	1-0 *og (Chidi)*
20/12	h	Ethnikos	L	1-2 *Grigalashvili*

2015

03/01	a	Doxa	D	0-0
12/01	h	Apollon	D	2-2 *Khmaladze, Efthymiou*
17/01	a	APOEL	D	1-1 *Grigalashvili*
01/02	h	Anorthosis	L	0-2
07/02	a	AEK	D	2-2 *Vera, Khmaladze*
15/02	h	Ermis	L	0-2
22/02	a	Ayia Napa	L	0-1
28/02	h	AEL	D	0-0
08/03	a	Ethnikos	L	1-3 *I Sassi*
15/03	h	Doxa	L	0-1
21/03	h	Nea Salamis	L	0-2
05/04	a	AEL	W	1-0 *Grigalashvili*
19/04	h	Ayia Napa	D	2-2 *Thiago, Greene*
26/04	h	Ethnikos	L	1-2 *I Sassi*
03/05	a	Doxa	D	3-3 *Thiago 2, Vera*
10/05	a	Nea Salamis	L	0-1
16/05	h	AEL	W	3-0 *I Sassi, Thiago 2*
23/05	a	Ayia Napa	D	1-2 *I Sassi, Thiago*

No	Name	Nat	DoB	Pos	Aps	(s)	Gls
23	Agapios Agapiou		18/04/96	M		(1)	
4	Alain Álvarez	ESP	13/11/89	D	22		
7	Vasilios Chatzigiannakou		10/04/91	M	26		
16	Dennis Nieblas	ESP	16/10/90	D	1	(6)	
3	Nicos Efthymiou		04/02/93	D	26	(2)	1
2	Serginho Greene	NED	24/06/82	D	11	(3)	1
30	Elguja Grigalashvili	GEO	30/12/89	M	26		3
39	Jonan García	ESP	08/01/83	M		(6)	
8	Levan Khmaladze	GEO	06/04/85	M	23		3
89	Roin Kvaskhvadze	GEO	31/05/89	G	26		
32	Evangelos Kyriakou		03/02/94	D		(12)	
5	Kyriakos Kyriakou		19/06/91	D	8	(9)	
19	Georgios Loizou		29/05/90	A	6	(12)	
24	Ulysse Ndong	GHA	24/11/92	M	26	(1)	
20	Marian Neagu	ROU	29/10/91	M	2	(2)	
77	Panagiotis Panayiotou		27/09/88	D	25	(4)	1
21	Panagiotis Papapericleous		24/10/95	M	1	(1)	
38	Marios Poutziouris		08/12/93	M	23	(8)	
9	Ismail Sassi	FRA	10/12/87	A	5	(11)	4
27	Mohamed Sassi	FRA	10/12/87	M	1	(6)	
83	Civard Sprockel	NED	10/05/83	D	6	(4)	
70	Thiago	BRA	12/07/87	A	27		10
17	Dimitris Tziakouris		28/05/94	G	6		
6	Andreas Vasiliou		02/05/88	D	28		
18	Jesús Vera	ARG	10/01/89	A	27	(1)	2

Top goalscorers

17	Mickaël Poté (Omonia)
15	Ifeanyi Onyilo (Ermis)
14	Rafik Djebbour (APOEL)
	Fotios Papoulis (Apollon)
13	Andreas Makris (Anorthosis)
11	Valdo (Ethnikos)
10	Nestoras Mytidis (AEK)
	Abraham Gneki Guié (Apollon)
	Ricardo Lobo (Doxa)
	Thiago (Othellos)

Promoted clubs

Enosis Neon Paralimni FC

1936 • Tasos Markou (8,000) • no website
**Coach: Marios Constantinou;
(01/11/14) Nikos Karageorgiou (GRE)**

Pafos FC

2014 • Pafiako (7,650) • pafosfc.com.cy
**Coach: Radmilo Ivančević (SRB);
(24/10/14) Sofoklis Sofokleous**

Aris Limassol FC

1930 • Tsirion (13,331) • no website
**Coach: Georgios Polyviou;
(14/10/14) Akis Agiomamitis**

Second level final table 2014/15

		Pld	W	D	L	F	A	Pts
1	Enosis Neon Paralimni FC	26	19	6	1	57	13	63
2	Pafos FC	26	19	5	2	55	19	62
3	Aris Limassol FC	26	16	4	6	35	25	49
4	AEZ Zakakiou	26	12	8	6	29	19	44
5	Karmiotissa Pano Polemidion	26	12	2	12	36	29	38
6	Anagennisi Derynia FC	26	10	8	8	27	26	38
7	Elpida Xylofagou	26	9	7	10	29	34	34
8	Nikos & Sokratis Erimis FC	26	8	5	13	35	48	29
9	ENAD FC	26	7	8	11	30	30	29
10	Olympiakos Nicosia FC	26	10	5	11	34	42	29
11	Omonia Aradippou FC	26	8	4	14	35	37	28
12	Enosis Neon Parekklisias FC	26	7	4	15	26	39	25
13	AS Digenis Voroklinis	26	4	6	16	16	49	18
14	APEP Kyperounda FC	26	4	2	20	18	52	8

*NB APEP Kyperounda FC & Olympiakos Nicosia FC –
6 pts deducted; Aris Limassol FC – 3 pts deducted.*

DOMESTIC CUP

Cyprus Cup 2014/15

SECOND ROUND

(29/10/14)
AEZ 2-3 Doxa
APEP 0-1 Olympiakos
Ayia Napa 3-1 EN Parekklisias
Digenis Voroklinis 0-0 Omonia Aradippou *(aet; 4-2 on pens)*
Elpida Xylofagou 1-4 Nea Salamis
ENAD 2-4 Anorthosis
Karmiotissa 2-1 Paralimni
Nikos & Sokratis 3-4 Anagennisi Derynia *(aet)*
Pafos 0-3 Othellos

(05/11/14)
Ethnikos Achnas 3-0 Aris

Byes – AEK, AEL, APOEL, Apollon, Ermis, Omonia

THIRD ROUND

(07/01/15 & 14/01/15)
AEK 1-0, 1-0 Nea Salamis *(2-0)*
Karmiotissa 2-1, 1-0 Anagennisi Derynia *(3-1)*
Doxa 1-3, 0-2 Ermis *(1-5)*

(07/01/15 & 28/01/15)
Apollon 1-1, 1-2 Othellos *(2-3)*

(14/01/15 & 28/01/15)
Olympiakos 0-1, 0-3 APOEL *(0-4)*
AEL 1-0, 2-2 Ethnikos Achnas *(3-2)*

(14/01/15 & 04/02/15)
Digenis Voroklinis 1-2, 0-2 Anorthosis *(1-4)*
Omonia 4-0, 5-0 Ayia Napa *(9-0)*

QUARTER-FINALS

(11/02/15 & 18/02/15)
Omonia 2-0 Karmiotissa *(Álex Rubio 23, Schembri 89)*
Karmiotissa 0-5 Omonia *(Schembri 51, 69, 84, Roushias 62, 73)*
(Omonia 7-0)

Othellos 1-1 AEK *(Vera 62; David Català 90)*
AEK 4-0 Othellos *(Joan Tomàs 3, 27p, Colautti 34p, Monteiro 85)*
(AEK 5-1)

(18/02/15 & 04/03/15)
AEL 1-0 Ermis *(Carlitos II 60)*
Ermis 1-1 AEL *(Mendy 83og; Tagbajumi 90)*
(AEL 2-1)

(04/03/15 & 11/03/15)
Anorthosis 0-0 APOEL
APOEL 2-0 Anorthosis *(Djebbour 67, 80)*
(APOEL 2-0)

SEMI-FINALS

(08/04/15 & 22/04/15)
APOEL 3-0 Omonia *(Lanig 35, Riise 38, De Vincenti 77)*
Omonia 0-0 APOEL
(APOEL 3-0)

AEK 2-2 AEL *(Mendy 32og, José Kanté 65; Sema 47, 89)*
AEL 1-1 AEK *(Adrián Sardinero 40; Joan Tomàs 33)*
(3-3; AEL on away goals)

FINAL

(20/05/15)
Neo GSZ, Larnaca
APOEL FC 4 *(De Vincenti 31, Efrem 45+1, 53, Riise 60)*
AEL LIMASSOL FC 2 *(Sema 11, Sielis 90)*
Referee: Královec (CZE)
APOEL: Chiotis, Mário Sérgio, Carlão, João Guilherme, Riise, Efrem (Charalambides 65), Nuno Morais, Lanig, Aloneftis (Tiago Gomes 70), De Vincenti (Alexandrou 86), Djebbour
AEL: Fegrouche, Eleftheriou, Sambou, Sielis, Carlitos I (Edmar 81) Carlitos II, Sachetti (Tagbajumi 57) Guidileye, Luciano Bebê, Sema (Ohene 81), Adrián Sardinero

CZECH REPUBLIC
Fotbalová asociace České republiky (FAČR)

Address Diskařská 2431/4
CZ-160 17 Praha
Tel +420 2 3302 9111
Fax +420 2 3335 3107
E-mail facr@fotbal.cz
Website fotbal.cz

President Miroslav Pelta
General secretary Rudolf Řepka
Media officer Ondřej Lípa
Year of formation 1901

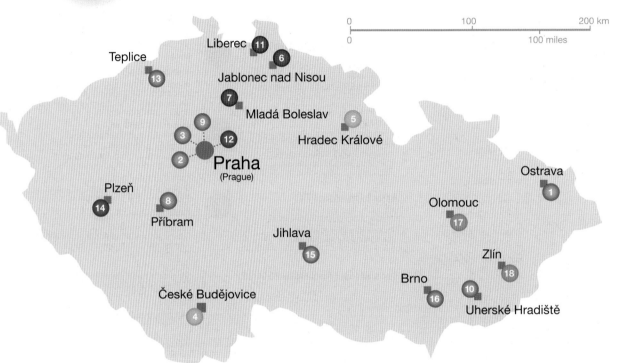

1. LIGA CLUBS

 1 FC Baník Ostrava

 2 Bohemians Praha 1905

 3 FK Dukla Praha

 4 SK Dynamo České Budějovice

 5 FC Hradec Králové

 6 FK Jablonec

 7 FK Mladá Boleslav

 8 1. FK Příbram

 9 SK Slavia Praha

 10 1. FC Slovácko

 11 FC Slovan Liberec

 12 AC Sparta Praha

 13 FK Teplice

 14 FC Viktoria Plzeň

 15 FC Vysočina Jihlava

 16 FC Zbrojovka Brno

PROMOTED CLUBS

 17 SK Sigma Olomouc

 18 FC Zlín

KEY:
 – UEFA Champions League
– UEFA Europa League
– Promoted
– Relegated

Plzeň return to the summit

Runners-up to double-winning AC Sparta Praha in both league and cup the previous season, FC Viktoria Plzeň came storming back to form under new coach Miroslav Koubek to beat the champions home and away and reclaim the Czech 1. Liga title in 2014/15.

There was a surprise in the Czech Cup as struggling FC Slovan Liberec defeated in-form local rivals FK Jablonec on penalties in the final, and another in the UEFA EURO 2016 qualifiers as the Czech national team, entering the campaign without a win under new coach Pavel Vrba, took maximum points from their first four matches.

Koubek's free-scoring side too good for Sparta	League strugglers Liberec edge Jablonec in cup final	National team off to a flier in EURO qualifiers

Domestic league

Champions in 2010/11 and 2012/13, Plzeň made it three titles in five seasons, controlling proceedings virtually from start to finish despite the close attentions of Sparta. The experienced Koubek was a surprise appointment when he replaced Dušan Uhrin Jr in August as he had overseen the club's relegation in 2000/01, but the 63-year-old soon converted the sceptics, leading the team to the league summit in his first game, then to a six-match winning streak that concluded with a 2-0 home win over Sparta.

One point ahead at the winter break, Plzeň improved their position with seven successive wins in the early spring, and although Sparta remained undefeated over the same stretch, the title was effectively decided when Koubek's side completed the double over their rivals – now under new coach Zdeněk Ščesný following the dismissal of double-winning Vítězslav Lavička – with another 2-0 win at the Letná, second-half goals from Jan Holenda and Roman Hubník putting Plzeň six points clear. With a head-to-head advantage, the leaders now needed only one more win from their last three matches to clinch the title. They did not delay, beating FC Vysočina Jihlava 2-0 at home in their next encounter with first-half headers from Hubník (again) and František Rajtoral.

Plzeň dedicated their title win to defender Marián Čišovský, who was battling a serious illness, and the final match of the season brought further emotion with the retirement of 40-year-old captain Pavel Horváth. The 5-2 win against 1. FK Příbram also hoisted the team's goal aggregate to 70, with midfielder Daniel Kolář scoring twice to become the only Plzeň player to reach double figures. Conversely, 18 of the 20 outfield players used during the campaign scored at least once. The league's top marksman, for the fourth time in five years, was Sparta's David Lafata, with 20 goals, while another fairly predictable outcome was the second relegation in three seasons of yo-yo clubs SK Dynamo České Budějovice and FC Hradec Králové.

Domestic cup

Liberec rescued an otherwise forgettable 2014/15 campaign by winning the Czech Cup, under caretaker coach David Vavruška, thanks to a late equaliser and penalty shoot-out win in the final against Jablonec. Their North Bohemian rivals, by contrast, enjoyed an excellent season in the league under Liberec's 2011/12 title-winning boss Jaroslav Šilhavý, finishing just three points behind Sparta in third – and 18 clear of fourth-placed FK Mladá Boleslav – but they could convert only one of their four spot-kicks past Liberec keeper Lukáš Hroššo.

Europe

Trophy-winning domestic campaigns for both Plzeň and Liberec were preceded by European disappointment as both crashed out against Romanian opposition in the third qualifying round of the UEFA Europa League. Sparta's UEFA Champions League challenge also ended at the same juncture, on away goals to Malmö FF, but Lavička's team did reach the UEFA Europa League group stage, where they were denied further progress only by a last-day defeat at BSC Young Boys.

National team

The Czech Republic entered the UEFA EURO 2016 qualifying campaign having failed to win in four friendlies under new boss Vrba, but an added-time tap-in from Václav Pilař brought an opening 2-1 win at home to the Netherlands, and when that was followed by further successes against Turkey, Kazakhstan and Iceland, a sixth successive participation at the UEFA European Championship finals looked imminent. However, a 1-1 home draw against Latvia – rescued by another late Pilař intervention – and a 2-1 defeat in Iceland enabled their conquerors in Rejkvaik to leapfrog them to the top of Group A, and with the Netherlands lurking dangerously behind them, a top-two final placing was far from guaranteed.

DOMESTIC SEASON AT A GLANCE

1. Liga 2014/15 final table

		Pld	Home W	D	L	F	A	Away W	D	L	F	A	Total W	D	L	F	A	Pts
1	FC Viktoria Plzeň	30	14	0	1	41	8	9	3	3	29	16	23	3	4	70	24	72
2	AC Sparta Praha	30	12	1	2	34	9	9	3	3	23	11	21	4	5	57	20	67
3	FK Jablonec	30	11	3	1	34	6	8	4	3	24	16	19	7	4	58	22	64
4	FK Mladá Boleslav	30	9	3	3	31	15	4	4	7	12	19	13	7	10	43	34	46
5	1. FK Příbram	30	9	3	3	24	16	3	4	8	16	29	12	7	11	40	45	43
6	FK Dukla Praha	30	7	5	3	23	13	4	3	8	11	27	11	8	11	34	40	41
7	FK Teplice	30	7	5	3	28	13	2	6	7	13	24	9	11	10	41	37	38
8	Bohemians Praha 1905	30	5	5	5	19	17	5	3	7	16	24	10	8	12	35	41	38
9	1. FC Slovácko	30	5	3	7	27	21	5	4	6	16	25	10	7	13	43	46	37
10	FC Vysočina Jihlava	30	6	2	7	16	12	4	4	7	17	26	10	6	14	33	38	36
11	SK Slavia Praha	30	6	4	5	26	23	3	3	9	14	22	9	7	14	40	45	34
12	FC Slovan Liberec	30	5	7	3	23	14	2	5	8	16	29	7	12	11	39	43	33
13	FC Baník Ostrava	30	5	7	3	16	16	3	2	10	7	25	8	9	13	23	41	33
14	FC Zbrojovka Brno	30	6	3	6	20	17	3	3	9	14	28	9	6	15	34	45	33
15	FC Hradec Králové	30	4	3	8	14	23	2	4	9	12	29	6	7	17	26	52	25
16	SK Dynamo České Budějovice	30	4	4	7	17	29	1	3	11	12	43	5	7	18	29	72	22

European qualification 2015/16

Champion: FC Viktoria Plzeň (third qualifying round)
AC Sparta Praha (third qualifying round)

Cup winner: FC Slovan Liberec (third qualifying round)
FK Jablonec (third qualifying round)
FK Mladá Boleslav (second qualifying round)

Top scorer	David Lafata (Sparta), 20 goals
Relegated clubs	SK Dynamo České Budějovice, FC Hradec Králové
Promoted clubs	SK Sigma Olomouc, FC Zlín
Cup final	FC Slovan Liberec 1-1 FK Jablonec (3-1 on pens)

Team of the season
(4-4-2)

Coach: Koubek (Plzeň)

Player of the season

Pavel Kadeřábek
(AC Sparta Praha)

Although Sparta failed to defend either of their domestic trophies in 2014/15, they did possess the country's outstanding individual performer in Kadeřábek. The rampaging right-back was one of Sparta's most potent attackers as well as a reliable defender, and he became a fixture of Pavel Vrba's Czech national side, scoring an important goal in the UEFA EURO 2016 qualifying win at home to Iceland. He also performed with distinction for his country on home soil at the 2015 UEFA European Under-21 Championship

Newcomer of the season

Aleš Matějů
(1. FK Příbram)

While Pavel Kadeřábek established himself as the foremost right-back in the Czech Republic in 2014/15, his summer departure for German club TSG 1899 Hoffenheim has left the door open for Matějů to assume that mantle. The 19-year-old was a revelation in the role for fifth-placed Příbram following a loan spell in the Netherlands with PSV Eindhoven's youth team, and at the end of term, with his profile duly enhanced, he left his hometown club for Czech champions FC Viktoria Plzeň.

Pavlenka (Baník)

Kadeřábek (Sparta) — Procházka (Plzeň) — Latka (Slavia) — Limberský (Plzeň)

Kopic (Jablonec) — Kolář (Plzeň) — Dočkal (Sparta) — Kovařík (Plzeň)

Škoda (Slavia) — Došek (Slovácko)

NATIONAL TEAM

International honours*
UEFA European Championship (1) 1976.

International tournament appearances*
FIFA World Cup (9) 1934 (runners-up), 1938 (qtr-finals), 1954, 1958, 1962 (runners-up), 1970, 1982, 1990 (qtr-finals), 2006
UEFA European Championship (8) 1960 (3rd), 1976 (Winners), 1980 (3rd), 1996 (runners-up), 2000, 2004 (semi-finals), 2008, 2012 (qtr-finals).

Top five all-time caps
Karel Poborský (118); **Petr Čech** (114); **Tomáš Rosický** (100); **Jaroslav Plašil** (94); Milan Baroš (93)

Top five all-time goals
Jan Koller (55); Milan Baroš (41); Antonín Puč (35); Zdeněk Nehoda (32); Oldřich Nejedlý & Pavel Kuka (29)

(* before 1996 as Czechoslovakia)

Results 2014/15

03/09/14	United States	H	Prague	L	0-1	
09/09/14	Netherlands (ECQ)	H	Prague	W	2-1	Dočkal (22), Pilař (90+1)
10/10/14	Turkey (ECQ)	A	Istanbul	W	2-1	Sivok (15), Dočkal (58)
13/10/14	Kazakhstan (ECQ)	A	Astana	W	4-2	Dočkal (13), Lafata (44), Krejčí (56), Necid (88)
16/11/14	Iceland (ECQ)	H	Plzen	W	2-1	Kadeřábek (45+1), Bödvarsson (61og)
28/03/15	Latvia (ECQ)	H	Prague	D	1-1	Pilař (90)
31/03/15	Slovakia	A	Zilina	L	0-1	
12/06/15	Iceland (ECQ)	A	Reykjavik	L	1-2	Dočkal (55)

Appearances 2014/15

Coach: Pavel Vrba	06/12/63		Usa	NED	TUR	KAZ	ISL	LVA	Svk	ISL	Caps	Goals
Petr Čech	20/05/82	Chelsea (ENG)	G	G	G	G	G	G		G	114	-
Pavel Kadeřábek	25/04/92	Sparta Praha	D46	D	D	D	D			D	8	1
Václav Procházka	08/05/84	Plzeň	D	D		s81	s92	D		D	10	-
Michal Kadlec	13/12/84	Fenerbahçe (TUR)	D	D	D	D	D	D	s61		60	8
David Limberský	06/10/83	Plzeň	D	D	D	D		D		D	32	-
Vladimír Darida	08/08/90	Freiburg (GER)	M79	M	M	M	M	M	s71	s84	25	-
Václav Pilař	13/10/88	Plzeň	M46	s66	s68	s69	s65	s46	M60	M67	22	5
Petr Jiráček	02/03/86	Hamburg (GER)	M46								28	3
Tomáš Rosický	04/10/80	Arsenal (ENG)	M	M	M		M92	M		M	100	22
Ladislav Krejčí	05/07/92	Sparta Praha	M68	M66	M68	M69	M65	M57	s60	s67	14	2
Matěj Vydra	01/05/92	Watford (ENG)	A46	s72	s84						15	4
Daniel Kolář	27/10/85	Plzeň	s46	s81		M			M71		23	2
Milan Petržela	19/06/83	Plzeň	s46								16	-
Radim Řezník	20/01/89	Plzeň	s46								1	-
Lukáš Vácha	13/05/89	Sparta Praha	s46	M81	M	M			M	M79	8	-
Daniel Pudil	27/09/85	Watford (ENG)	s68				D				27	2
Bořek Dočkal	30/09/88	Sparta Praha	s79	M	M92	M	M	M	s71	M84	17	6
David Lafata	18/09/81	Sparta Praha		A72	A84	A79	A82	A81			35	8
Tomáš Sivok	15/09/83	Beşiktaş (TUR)		D	D81	D				D	49	4
Jaroslav Plašil	05/01/82	Bordeaux (FRA)		s92			M	M46	s60	M	94	6
Tomáš Necid	13/08/89	Zwolle (NED)				s79	s82	s57	A	A	31	8
Theodor Gebre Selassie	24/12/86	Bremen (GER)						D	D61		30	1
Václav Kadlec	20/05/92	Sparta Praha							s81	M71	11	2
Tomáš Vaclík	29/03/89	Basel (SUI)							G		3	-
Mario Holek	28/10/86	Sparta Praha							D		8	-
Marek Suchý	29/03/88	Basel (SUI)							D		20	-
Adam Hloušek	20/12/88	Stuttgart (GER)							D82		7	-
Martin Pospíšil	26/06/91	Jablonec							M60		2	-
Filip Novák	26/06/90	Jablonec							s82		1	-
Milan Škoda	16/01/86	Slavia Praha								s79	1	-

AC Sparta Praha

CHAMPIONS
LEAGUE

Second qualifying round - FC Levadia Tallinn (EST)
H 7-0 *Lafata (22, 44, 45+4p, 57, 60), Tipuric (55og), Přikryl (84)*
Bičík, Švejdík, Vácha, Matějovský, Dočkal, Kadeřábek, Lafata
(Bednář 73), Hušbauer (Mareček 69), Krejčí (Přikryl 79), Holek,
Nhamoinesu. Coach: Vítězslav Lavička (CZE)
A 1-1 *Mareček (38)*
Štěch, Brabec, Vácha, Dočkal (Lafata 78), Mareček, Nešpor
(Holek 84), Kováč, Kadeřábek, Konaté, Hybš, Breznaník
(Přikryl 76). Coach: Vítězslav Lavička (CZE)

Third qualifying round - Malmö FF (SWE)
H 4-2 *Lafata (22, 51, 70), Kováč (52)*
Bičík, Vácha, Přikryl (Breznaník 71), Matějovský (Vacek 84),
Dočkal, Kováč, Kadeřábek, Lafata (Bednář 87), Hušbauer,
Holek, Nhamoinesu. Coach: Vítězslav Lavička (CZE)
A 0-2
Bičík, Švejdík, Vácha, Přikryl (Krejčí 60), Matějovský
(Bednář 74), Dočkal, Kováč, Kadeřábek, Lafata, Hušbauer,
Nhamoinesu (Breznaník 85). Coach: Vítězslav Lavička (CZE)
Red card: Vácha 90+7

EUROPA
LEAGUE

Play-offs - PEC Zwolle (NED)
A 1-1 *Krejčí (82)*
Bičík, Brabec, Matějovský, Dočkal (Vacek 76), Mareček,
Kováč, Kadeřábek, Lafata (Bednář 90+2), Hušbauer (Přikryl
66), Krejčí, Nhamoinesu. Coach: Vítězslav Lavička (CZE)
H 3-1 *Krejčí (10), Dočkal (44), Brabec (62)*
Bičík, Brabec, Matějovský, Dočkal, Mareček, Kováč,
Kadeřábek, Vacek (Konaté 83), Lafata (Nešpor 90+2), Krejčí
(Breznaník 90), Nhamoinesu. Coach: Vítězslav Lavička (CZE)

Group I
Match 1 - SSC Napoli (ITA)
A 1-3 *Hušbauer (14)*
Bičík, Brabec, Matějovský, Dočkal (Konaté 75), Mareček,
Kováč, Kadeřábek, Lafata (Schick 85), Hušbauer (Bednář 78),
Krejčí, Nhamoinesu. Coach: Vítězslav Lavička (CZE)
Match 2 - BSC Young Boys (SUI)
H 3-1 *Vácha (27), Lafata (28, 85)*
Bičík, Brabec, Vácha, Matějovský (Vacek 64), Dočkal,
Kadeřábek, Konaté (Mareček 81), Lafata, Krejčí (Kováč 90),
Holek, Nhamoinesu. Coach: Vítězslav Lavička (CZE)
Match 3 - ŠK Slovan Bratislava (SVK)
A 3-0 *Lafata (56), Konaté (61), Krejčí (81)*
Bičík, Brabec, Vácha, Matějovský (Vacek 80), Dočkal
(Mareček 90+1), Kadeřábek, Konaté, Lafata (Přikryl 86),
Krejčí, Holek, Nhamoinesu. Coach: Vítězslav Lavička (CZE)
Match 4 - ŠK Slovan Bratislava (SVK)
H 4-0 *Lafata (29, 83), Krejčí (32), Nhamoinesu (74)*
Bičík, Brabec, Vácha (Mareček 79), Matějovský, Dočkal
(Vacek 72), Kadeřábek, Konaté, Lafata (Bednář 89), Krejčí,
Holek, Nhamoinesu. Coach: Vítězslav Lavička (CZE)

Match 5 - SSC Napoli (ITA)
H 0-0
Štěch, Brabec, Matějovský (Vacek 90), Dočkal, Mareček,
Kadeřábek, Lafata, Hušbauer (Přikryl 72), Krejčí, Holek,
Nhamoinesu. Coach: Vítězslav Lavička (CZE)
Match 6 - BSC Young Boys (SUI)
A 0-2
Štěch, Brabec, Přikryl (Konaté 60), Matějovský, Dočkal,
Mareček, Kadeřábek, Hušbauer (Bednář 85), Krejčí, Holek,
Nhamoinesu (Schick 80). Coach: Vítězslav Lavička (CZE)

FC Viktoria Plzeň

EUROPA
LEAGUE

Third qualifying round - FC Petrolul Ploieşti (ROU)
A 1-1 *Kolář (90+1)*
Kozáčik, Hubník, Pilař (Kovařík 81), Hořava (Kolář 86),
Limberský, Horváth, Petržela (Hrošovský 74), Řezník, Vaněk,
Procházka, Bakoš. Coach: Dušan Uhrin Jr (CZE)
H 1-4 *Pilař (40)*
Kozáčik, Hubník, Pilař, Hořava (Vaněk 73), Limberský,
Horváth, Petržela (Tecl 66), Řezník, Procházka, Bakoš
(Chramosta 53), Kolář. Coach: Dušan Uhrin Jr (CZE)

FK Mladá Boleslav

EUROPA
LEAGUE

Second qualifying round - NK Široki Brijeg (BIH)
H 2-1 *Skalák (68), Ďuriš (76)*
Hruška, Milla (Šultes 69), Bořil (Bartl 75), Skalák, Štohanzl
(Vukadinović 59), Ďuriš, Ščuk, Rosa, Šisler, Smejkal, Hůlka.
Coach: Karel Jarolím (CZE)
A 4-0 *Skalák (19), Ďuriš (55, 85), Rosa (75)*
Hruška, Navrátil, Bořil, Skalák, Štohanzl (Vukadinović 61),
Ďuriš, Ščuk, Magera (Šultes 78), Rosa, Šisler (Milla 70),
Smejkal. Coach: Karel Jarolím (CZE)

Third qualifying round - Olympique Lyonnais (FRA)
H 1-4 *Rosa (66)*
Hruška, Navrátil, Milla, Bořil, Skalák, Štohanzl (Vukadinović
60), Ďuriš (Šisler 71), Ščuk, Magera (Šultes 46), Rosa,
Smejkal. Coach: Karel Jarolím (CZE)
A 1-2 *Milla (71p)*
Hruška, Navrátil, Milla, Bořil, Skalák (Bartl 78), Štohanzl, Ďuriš
(Šultes 68), Ščuk, Rosa, Šisler (Magera 71), Smejkal. Coach:
Karel Jarolím (CZE)

FC Slovan Liberec

EUROPA
LEAGUE

Second qualifying round - MFK Košice (SVK)
A 1-0 *Jarolím (83p)*
Hrošťo, Karišik, Coufal, Pavelka, Sackey, Jarolím (Pimpara
90), Hadaščok (Hamuľak 65), Rajnoch, Šural (Obžera 78),
Fleišman, Ďubek. Coach: Samuel Slovák (SVK)
H 3-0 *Ďubek (54), Delarge (81), Šural (90)*
Hrošťo, Karišik, Coufal, Pavelka, Sackey, Hamuľak
(Luckassen 75), Rajnoch, Šural, Fleišman, Ďubek (Hadaščok
84), Delarge (Kolár 87). Coach: Samuel Slovák (SVK)

Third qualifying round - FC Astra Giurgiu (ROU)
A 0-3
Hrošťo, Karišik (Pimpara 65), Coufal, Pavelka, Sackey,
Rajnoch, Luckassen (Hamuľak 71), Šural, Fleišman, Ďubek,
Delarge (Frýdek 78). Coach: Samuel Slovák (SVK)
H 2-3 *Šural (45), Obročník (45+3)*
Hrošťo, Frýdek (Luckassen 73), Sackey, Hamuľak (Hadaščok
53), Rajnoch, Mudra, Obročník (Delarge 65), Pimpara, Šural,
Fleišman, Ďubek. Coach: Samuel Slovák (SVK)

DOMESTIC LEAGUE CLUB-BY-CLUB

FC Baník Ostrava

1922 • Stadion Bazaly (17,372) • fcb.cz

Major honours
Czechoslovakian/Czech League (4) 1976, 1980, 1981, 2004; Czechoslovakian/Czech Cup (4) 1973, 1978, 1991, 2005

Coach: Tomáš Bernady;
(12/12/14) Petr Frňka

2014

25/07	a Dukla	D	0-0	
01/08	a Slavia	L	1-3	Baránek
08/08	h Teplice	D	1-1	Dyjan
15/08	a Sparta	W	1-0	Greguš
22/08	h Brno	W	1-0	og (Jugas)
30/08	a Liberec	L	0-6	
13/09	h Mladá Boleslav	W	1-0	Šichor
21/09	a Plzeň	L	0-2	
27/09	h Bohemians 1905	W	1-0	Stronati
04/10	a Slovácko	W	2-1	Narh, Frydrych
17/10	h Jihlava	D	0-0	
25/10	a Příbram	L	1-3	Kukec
01/11	h Hradec Králové	W	2-1	Holzer 2
08/11	a České Budějovice	L	0-1	
22/11	h Jablonec	L	1-2	Štěpán
28/11	h Slavia	D	0-0	

2015

21/02	a Teplice	L	0-1	
28/02	h Sparta	D	1-1	Baroš
06/03	a Brno	D	0-0	
14/03	h Liberec	D	3-3	Kouřil, Baroš (p), Frydrych
20/03	a Mladá Boleslav	L	0-1	
05/04	h Plzeň	L	0-2	
10/04	a Bohemians 1905	W	2-0	Narh, Frydrych
18/04	a Slovácko	L	0-2	
24/04	a Jihlava	L	0-2	
02/05	h Příbram	D	0-0	
09/05	h Hradec Králové	L	0-1	
16/05	h České Budějovice	W	4-3	Sivric, Šašinka, Frydrych, Kukec
23/05	a Jablonec	L	0-4	
30/05	h Dukla	D	1-1	Kukec

No	Name	Nat	DoB	Pos	Aps	(s)	Gls
2	Jan Baránek		26/06/93	D	12	(1)	1
33	Milan Baroš		28/10/81	A	8	(3)	2
20	Oldřich Byrtus		04/01/94	D	2	(7)	
27	Dyjan	BRA	23/06/91	M	16	(6)	1
23	Martin Foltýn		17/08/93	M	12	(1)	
19	Michal Frydrych		27/02/90	D	28	(1)	4
11	Ján Greguš	SVK	29/01/91	M	15		1
2	Matěj Helešic		12/11/96	D	5		
21	Daniel Holzer		18/08/95	M	18	(5)	2
14	Milan Jirásek		14/05/92	M	8	(2)	
5	Filip Kaša		01/01/94	D	6	(6)	
18	Martin Kouřil		24/02/91	D	14		1
10	Davor Kukec	CRO	16/03/86	A	25	(3)	3
14	Joel Lindpere	EST	05/10/81	M	15		
28	Luka Lučić	CRO	02/01/95	D	9		
6	Derrick Mensah	GHA	28/05/95	M	14	(4)	
9	Patrik Mišák	SVK	29/03/91	M	4	(8)	
15	Francis Narh	GHA	18/04/94	A	16	(7)	2
1	Jiří Pavlenka		14/04/92	G	30		
17	David Petrus		01/08/87	A	1	(3)	
20	Ondřej Pyclík		17/02/88	A		(1)	
31	Jakub Šašinka		02/10/95	A	2	(10)	1
8	Marek Šichor		17/07/90	M	10	(6)	1
17	Matej Sivrić	CRO	27/11/89	M	8	(2)	1
7	Vojtěch Štěpán		08/06/85	M	24	(3)	1
28	Patrizio Stronati		17/11/94	D	15		1
3	Ondřej Sukup		08/12/88	D	9	(7)	
25	Václav Svěrkoš		01/11/83	A	2		
12	Tomáš Vengřínek		08/06/92	D	2		
25	Victor Zapata	COL	29/09/94	A		(3)	

Bohemians Praha 1905

1905 • Ďolíček (5,000) • bohemians.cz

Major honours
Czechoslovakian League (1) 1983

Coach: Roman Pivarník

2014

25/07	h Sparta	L	1-2	Šmíd
02/08	a Slovácko	L	1-4	Mikuš
08/08	a Jihlava	W	2-1	Mikuš, Cseh
16/08	h Jablonec	L	1-2	Bratanovič
23/08	a Příbram	W	3-2	Mosquera, Moravec, Brabec
30/08	h Hradec Králové	D	1-1	Jindříšek (p)
13/09	a Dukla	W	1-0	Moravec
20/09	h Slavia	W	2-0	Jindříšek (p), Lietava
27/09	a Baník	L	0-1	
04/10	h České Budějovice	W	3-0	Mosquera, Jindříšek (p), Rada
18/10	a Teplice	L	1-4	Mikuš
25/10	h Liberec	L	2-4	Bratanovič, Jindříšek (p)
31/10	a Mladá Boleslav	L	0-1	
10/11	h Brno	D	0-0	
23/11	a Plzeň	L	1-2	Jindříšek
29/11	h Slovácko	L	1-2	Rada

2015

21/02	h Jihlava	D	0-0	
28/02	a Jablonec	L	0-3	
07/03	h Příbram	W	3-1	Škerle, Jindříšek, Mikuš
15/03	a Hradec Králové	L	0-1	
22/03	h Dukla	D	0-0	
04/04	a Slavia	D	1-1	Mikuš
10/04	h Baník	L	0-2	
18/04	a České Budějovice	W	3-2	Rada 2 (1p), Bartek
25/04	h Teplice	W	1-0	Mikuš
02/05	a Liberec	D	1-1	Rada (p)
10/05	h Mladá Boleslav	D	1-1	Mikuš
16/05	a Brno	W	1-0	Bratanovič
23/05	h Plzeň	W	3-2	Bratanovič 3
30/05	a Sparta	D	1-1	Bratanovič

No	Name	Nat	DoB	Pos	Aps	(s)	Gls
21	Roman Artemuk	UKR	12/08/95	A		(1)	
5	David Bartek		13/02/88	M	14	(11)	1
30	Erich Brabec		24/02/77	D	12		1
12	Elvis Bratanovič	SVN	21/08/92	A	18	(8)	7
23	Pavol Cicman	SVK	30/01/85	M		(2)	
27	Martin Cseh	SVK	22/08/88	D	4	(2)	1
17	Vojtěch Engelmann		04/07/89	A	6	(3)	
13	Zoran Gajić	SRB	18/05/90	D	9	(1)	
24	Milan Havel		07/08/94	M	1	(3)	
19	Jiří Havránek		09/01/87	G	1		
6	Michal Hubínek		10/11/94	M		(1)	
7	Marek Jarolím		21/05/84	M	3	(2)	
4	Josef Jindříšek		14/02/81	M	29		6
8	Václav Kalina		15/07/79	D	3	(4)	
15	Daniel Krch		20/03/92	D	5	(3)	
9	Ivan Lietava	SVK	20/07/83	A		(22)	1
10	Matúš Mikuš	SVK	08/07/91	A	29		7
16	Jan Moravec		13/07/87	M	26	(2)	2
18	Jhon Mosquera	COL	08/05/90	M	25	(2)	2
26	Petr Nerad		06/02/94	M	1	(3)	
3	Lukáš Pauschek	SVK	09/12/92	D	28		
20	Jakub Rada		05/05/87	M	30		5
13	Jan Růžička		26/08/84	D	1		
11	Radek Šírl		20/03/81	D	23	(1)	
28	Aleš Škerle		14/06/82	D	11	(1)	1
14	Michal Šmíd		20/10/86	D	21	(3)	1
26	Milan Švenger		06/07/86	G	17		
2	Radek Žaloudek		16/06/94	D	1	(3)	
30	Zdeněk Zlámal		05/11/85	G	12		

FK Dukla Praha

1958 • Škoda Transportation Arena (8,150) • fkdukla.cz

Coach: Luboš Kozel

2014

25/07	h Baník	D	0-0	
03/08	a Mladá Boleslav	W	1-0	Beauguel
09/08	h Brno	D	1-1	Marek Hanousek
15/08	a Liberec	D	0-0	
24/08	h Sparta	W	1-0	Berger
31/08	a Plzeň	L	1-2	Beauguel
13/09	h Bohemians 1905	L	0-1	
20/09	a Slovácko	L	1-5	Beauguel
27/09	h Jihlava	W	4-1	og (Krejčí), Beauguel, Krmenčík, Považanec
03/10	a Jablonec	L	0-6	
25/10	h Hradec Králové	W	4-2	Čajić, Beauguel 2, Považanec
28/10	h Příbram	D	0-0	
01/11	h České Budějovice	W	3-1	Beauguel, Néstor Albiach, Krmenčík
07/11	h Slavia	D	2-2	Marek Hanousek, Považanec
22/11	a Teplice	L	0-1	
29/11	h Mladá Boleslav	L	0-2	

2015

21/02	a Brno	W	1-0	Berger (p)
27/02	h Liberec	W	3-1	Polom, og (Brabec), Mareš
08/03	a Sparta	L	0-3	
15/03	h Plzeň	L	2-3	Marek Hanousek, og (Limberský)
22/03	a Bohemians 1905	D	0-0	
04/04	h Slovácko	D	0-0	
11/04	a Jihlava	W	2-1	Polom, Čajić
18/04	a Jablonec	W	1-0	Berger
25/04	a Příbram	L	0-3	
02/05	h Hradec Králové	W	1-0	Beauguel
09/05	a České Budějovice	L	0-1	
16/05	a Slavia	L	0-2	
23/05	h Teplice	W	5-1	Polom, Berger, Přikryl 2, Čajić
30/05	a Baník	D	1-1	Mareš

No	Name	Nat	DoB	Pos	Aps	(s)	Gls
17	Jean-David Beauguel	FRA	21/03/92	A	21	(6)	8
13	Tomáš Berger		22/08/85	M	23	(3)	4
10	Jan Blažek		20/03/88	A	4	(4)	
8	Aldin Čajić	BIH	11/09/92	M	18	(8)	3
30	Martin Chudý	SVK	23/04/89	G	10		
21	Nikolai Dergachev	RUS	24/05/94	A		(1)	
14	Patrik Gedeon		19/07/75	M	22	(1)	
5	Marek Hanousek		06/08/91	M	28	(1)	3
4	Matěj Hanousek		02/06/93	D	27		
33	Marek Hlinka	SVK	04/10/90	M	3	(8)	
2	Michal Jeřábek		10/09/93	D	13	(5)	
6	Jan Juroška		02/03/93	D	4	(4)	
39	Vyacheslav Karavaev	RUS	20/05/95	D	29		
22	Dino Kluk	CRO	13/05/91	D	1	(4)	
11	Michael Krmenčík		15/03/93	A	7	(6)	2
24	Petr Malý		01/06/84	M		(1)	
21	Budge Manzia	COD	24/09/95	A		(2)	
26	Jakub Mareš		26/01/87	M	18	(9)	2
10	Néstor Albiach	ESP	18/08/92	A	3	(7)	1
7	Roman Polom		11/01/92	D	17	(2)	3
7	Jakub Považanec	SVK	31/01/91	M	23	(3)	3
32	Tomáš Přikryl		04/07/92	A	5	(4)	2
1	Filip Rada		05/09/84	G	20		
19	Lukáš Štětina	SVK	24/07/91	D	25		
29	Daniel Tetour		17/07/94	M	1	(6)	
9	Jan Vorel		01/09/78	D	8	(2)	

 # CZECH REPUBLIC

SK Dynamo České Budějovice

1905 • Střelecký ostrov (6,681) • dynamocb.cz

Coach: Luboš Urban;
(03/03/15) František Cipro

2014

27/07	h	Liberec	D	1-1	Koreš
10/08	h	Plzeň	L	0-4	
16/08	a	Brno	D	2-2	Koreš, Hora
23/08	h	Mladá Boleslav	W	2-1	Machovec, Benát
29/08	a	Jihlava	D	0-0	
02/09	a	Teplice	L	0-4	
13/09	h	Slovácko	D	2-2	Linhart, Vošahlík
20/09	a	Jablonec	D	0-0	
27/09	h	Příbram	L	0-3	
04/10	a	Bohemians 1905	L	0-3	
18/10	a	Hradec Králové	W	3-2	Škoda 2, Hora
24/10	h	Slavia	D	1-1	Vošahlík
01/11	a	Dukla	L	1-3	Lengyel
08/11	h	Baník	W	1-0	Hora
22/11	a	Sparta	L	0-4	
28/11	h	Teplice	W	2-0	Škoda, Hora (p)

2015

21/02	a	Plzeň	L	0-6	
28/02	h	Brno	L	1-3	Kladrubský
07/03	a	Mladá Boleslav	L	1-4	Machovec
14/03	h	Jihlava	L	1-3	Kladrubský (p)
21/03	a	Slovácko	L	1-3	Benát
04/04	a	Jablonec	L	0-3	
11/04	a	Příbram	L	0-1	
18/04	h	Bohemians 1905	L	2-3	Varadi, Kladrubský (p)
25/04	h	Hradec Králové	D	2-2	Varadi, Vošahlík (p)
03/05	a	Slavia	L	0-2	
09/05	h	Dukla	W	1-0	Funda
16/05	a	Baník	L	3-4	Kalod, Janotka, Machovec
23/05	h	Sparta	L	1-3	Dvořák
30/05	a	Liberec	L	1-5	Řezáč

No	Name	Nat	DoB	Pos	Aps	(s)	Gls
7	Petr Benát		20/05/80	M	26	(3)	2
22	David Brunclík		17/04/85	M	5	(9)	
18	Martin Chrien	SVK	08/09/95	M	4	(4)	
13	Aleš Dvořák		09/03/92	M	1	(2)	1
2	Pavel Eliáš		26/11/86	M	8		
19	Tomáš Fryšták		18/08/87	G	1		
3	Jiří Funda		21/06/95	D	9	(7)	1
12	Jan Hála		03/06/96	M	6	(5)	
18	Aleš Hanzlík		06/02/87	D	8	(5)	
20	Ondřej Herzán		03/03/81	M	10	(3)	
18	Jakub Hora		23/02/91	A	15		4
20	Tomáš Janotka		04/03/82	D	13		1
27	Richard Kalod		08/05/84	A	9	(4)	1
17	Jiří Kladrubský		19/11/85	M	13		3
10	Michal Klesa		13/05/83	M	12	(1)	
21	Štěpán Koreš		14/02/89	M	7	(1)	2
30	Zdeněk Křížek		16/01/83	G	29		
6	Roman Lengyel		03/11/78	D	28		1
4	Zdeněk Linhart		05/03/94	A	12	(10)	1
23	Jaroslav Machovec	SVK	05/09/86	D	17	(2)	3
5	Pavel Novák		30/11/89	D	24	(2)	
22	Ondřej Otepka		25/07/96	M		(1)	
18	Petr Pasecký		26/08/96	A		(2)	
9	Jakub Pešek		24/06/93	M	11	(1)	
14	Matěj Podstavek	SVK	21/01/91	D	11	(2)	
7	Michal Řezáč		02/10/96	M	7	(2)	1
11	Michal Škoda		01/03/88	A	14	(9)	3
9	Filip Vaněk		15/04/96	D		(2)	
14	Adam Varadi		30/04/85	A	8	(1)	2
25	Ladislav Vološák		07/04/84	M	13	(3)	1
29	Jan Vošahlík		08/03/89	A	9	(4)	2

FC Hradec Králové

1905 • Všesportovní stadion (7,000) • fchk.cz

Major honours
Czechoslovakian League (1) 1960; Czech Cup (1) 1995

Coach: Luboš Prokopec;
(19/10/14) Róbert Barborík (SVK)

2014

26/07	h	Teplice	D	0-0	
02/08	a	Brno	L	0-3	
10/08	h	Mladá Boleslav	D	0-0	
17/08	a	Plzeň	L	0-4	
23/08	h	Slovácko	W	2-0	Dvořák, Halilović
30/08	a	Bohemians 1905	D	1-1	Dvořák (p)
13/09	h	Jihlava	L	0-3	
21/09	a	Sparta	L	1-3	Malinský
27/09	h	Jablonec	L	0-2	
04/10	a	Příbram	L	0-1	
18/10	h	České Budějovice	L	2-3	A Čermák, Dvořák
25/10	h	Dukla	L	2-4	Halilović, Dvořák
01/11	a	Baník	L	1-2	Dvořák
09/11	h	Liberec	D	0-0	
23/11	a	Slavia	D	1-1	Plašil
29/11	h	Brno	W	2-1	Štípek, Dvořák

2015

21/02	a	Mladá Boleslav	D	2-2	Dvořák, Vaněček
01/03	h	Plzeň	L	2-3	A Čermák, Halilović
07/03	a	Slovácko	W	1-0	A Čermák
15/03	h	Bohemians 1905	W	1-0	Vaněček
21/03	a	Jihlava	L	0-2	
04/04	h	Sparta	L	0-3	
10/04	a	Jablonec	L	0-4	
19/04	h	Příbram	L	2-3	Dvořák 2 (1p)
25/04	a	České Budějovice	D	2-2	Vaněček, P Čermák
02/05	a	Dukla	L	0-1	
09/05	h	Baník	W	1-0	Trubač
16/05	a	Liberec	L	0-2	
23/05	h	Slavia	L	0-1	
30/05	a	Teplice	W	3-1	Petrus, Mareš (p), Vaněček

No	Name	Nat	DoB	Pos	Aps	(s)	Gls
3	Aleš Čermák		01/10/94	M	21	(1)	3
8	Pavel Čermák		14/05/89	D	2	(3)	1
9	Pavel Černý		28/01/85	A	18	(3)	
2	Jakub Chleboun		24/03/85	D	19	(5)	
14	Pavel Dvořák		19/02/89	A	22	(4)	9
23	Jan Hable		04/01/89	M	1	(2)	
26	Emir Halilović	BIH	18/11/89	M	22	(5)	3
4	Tomáš Holeš		31/03/93	D	30		
13	Jiří Janoušek		17/11/89	M	2		
14	Matěj Kotiš		14/03/85	M	11	(2)	
1	Tomáš Koubek		26/08/92	G	26		
28	Ondřej Kraják		20/04/91	M		(1)	
22	Juraj Križko	SVK	20/09/85	M	18		
22	Martin Kuciak	SVK	15/03/82	G	4	(1)	
10	Marek Kulič		11/10/75	A	1	(4)	
6	Tomáš Malinský		25/08/91	A	14	(8)	1
19	Petr Mareš		17/01/91	M	20	(1)	1
5	Martin Nosek	SVK	26/01/87	D	4		
11	David Petrus		01/08/89	A	1	(5)	1
25	Marek Plašil		19/12/85	D	15		1
5	Hynek Prokeš		03/12/86	A	1	(7)	
16	Adrian Rolko		14/09/78	D	23	(2)	
16	Petr Schwarz		12/11/91	M	2	(1)	
18	Jan Shejbal		20/04/94	M	6	(9)	
24	David Štípek		24/05/92	M	25		1
9	Pavel Šultes		15/09/85	A		(3)	
21	Tito	ESP	02/07/88	M	1	(6)	
27	Daniel Trubač		17/07/97	M	13	(3)	1
17	David Vaněček		09/03/91	A	7	(13)	4
8	Adam Vlkanova		04/09/94	A		(1)	
7	Jan Vobejda		05/01/95	M	1		

FK Jablonec

1945 • Stadion Střelnice (6,108) • fkjablonec.cz

Major honours
Czech Cup (2) 1998, 2013

Coach: Jaroslav Šilhavý

2014

26/07	h	Brno	W	2-0	Čížek, Pospíšil
03/08	a	Plzeň	L	1-3	Doležal
09/08	h	Slovácko	D	1-1	Novák (p)
16/08	a	Bohemians 1905	W	2-1	Daniel Rossi, Kopic
23/08	h	Jihlava	W	2-0	Novák 2
31/08	a	Sparta	L	0-2	
13/09	a	Příbram	W	4-1	Romera, Jun (p), Daniel Rossi, Kopic
20/09	h	České Budějovice	D	0-0	
27/09	a	Hradec Králové	W	2-0	Pospíšil 2
03/10	h	Dukla	W	6-0	Doležal, Mingazov, og (Štětina), Novák 2, Daniel Rossi
18/10	a	Slavia	D	1-1	Novák
25/10	h	Teplice	W	4-2	Pospíšil, Kopic, Mingazov, Kubista
02/11	a	Liberec	W	1-0	Doležal
08/11	h	Mladá Boleslav	W	1-0	Mingazov
22/11	h	Baník	W	2-1	Doležal, og (Baránek)
30/11	h	Plzeň	L	1-2	Kopic

2015

20/02	a	Slovácko	W	2-1	Šabala 2
28/02	h	Bohemians 1905	W	3-0	Pospíšil, Kopic, Beneš
07/03	a	Jihlava	D	1-1	Crnkić
14/03	h	Sparta	D	0-0	
21/03	h	Příbram	W	2-0	Novák 2 (1p)
04/04	a	České Budějovice	W	3-0	og (Lengyel), Mingazov, Crnkić
10/04	h	Hradec Králové	W	4-0	Greguš 2, Masopust, Novák
18/04	a	Dukla	L	0-1	
25/04	a	Slavia	W	2-1	Novák, Pospíšil
03/05	a	Teplice	D	1-1	Greguš
10/05	h	Liberec	W	2-0	Kopic, Pospíšil
17/05	a	Mladá Boleslav	D	1-1	Mingazov
23/05	h	Baník	W	4-0	Pernica, Kopic 2, Doležal
30/05	a	Brno	W	3-2	Novák, Doležal 2

No	Name	Nat	DoB	Pos	Aps	(s)	Gls
23	Vít Beneš		12/08/88	D	15		1
22	Tomáš Čížek		27/11/78	M	2	(13)	1
9	Nermin Crnkić	BIH	31/08/92	M	11	(12)	2
8	Daniel Rossi	BRA	04/01/81	M	16	(7)	3
25	Martin Doležal		03/05/90	A	20	(8)	7
14	Antonín Fantiš		15/04/92	M		(2)	
24	Ján Greguš	SVK	29/01/91	M	13		3
30	Vlastimil Hrubý		21/02/85	G	28		
3	Tomáš Hübschman		04/09/81	M	28		
11	Tomáš Jun		17/01/83	A	5	(7)	1
10	Jan Kopic		04/06/90	M	30		8
27	Vojtěch Kubista		19/03/93	D		(6)	1
6	Marek Kysela		10/07/92	D	13		
15	Luboš Loučka		25/08/82	M	1	(1)	
28	Lukáš Masopust		12/02/93	D	4	(7)	1
17	Ondřej Mihálik		02/04/97	A		(4)	
13	Ruslan Mingazov	TKM	23/11/91	M	16	(8)	5
12	Milan Mišůn		21/02/90	D	3	(3)	
18	Pavel Moulis		07/04/91	A		(2)	
7	Filip Novák		26/06/90	D	29		11
4	Luděk Pernica		16/06/90	D	30		1
26	Martin Pospíšil		26/06/91	M	30		7
16	José Romera	ESP	08/09/87	D	28		1
11	Valērijs Šabala	LVA	12/10/94	A	6	(3)	2
1	Michal Špit		09/04/75	G	2	(1)	

FK Mladá Boleslav

1902 • Městský stadion (5,000) • fkmb.cz
Major honours
Czech Cup (1) 2011
Coach: Karel Jarolím

2014

27/07	a Jihlava	W	1-0	Šćuk (p)
03/08	h Dukla	L	0-1	
10/08	a Hradec Králové	D	0-0	
16/08	h Příbram	W	4-1	Wágner 2 (1p), Bořil, Skalák
23/08	a České Budějovice	L	1-2	Mehanović
30/08	h Slavia	W	2-1	Šćuk, Navrátil
13/09	a Baník	L	0-1	
19/09	h Teplice	W	3-0	Wágner 3 (1p)
28/09	a Liberec	D	0-0	
04/10	h Brno	W	5-1	Šćuk, Hůlka, Ďuriš 2, og (Košťál)
19/10	h Plzeň	L	0-3	
26/10	a Sparta	L	0-1	
31/10	h Bohemians 1905	W	1-0	Tavares
08/11	a Jablonec	L	0-1	
21/11	h Slovácko	W	2-0	Wágner, Ďuriš
29/11	h Dukla	W	2-0	Skalák, Wágner

2015

21/02	h Hradec Králové	D	2-2	Ďuriš, Magera
28/02	a Příbram	L	0-2	
07/03	h České Budějovice	W	4-1	Wágner, Skalák 2, Navrátil
13/03	a Slavia	W	4-3	Šćuk, Šisler, Skalák, Wágner
20/03	h Baník	W	1-0	Šćuk
04/04	a Teplice	L	0-5	
11/04	h Liberec	D	1-1	Šćuk
19/04	a Brno	L	0-1	
25/04	a Plzeň	W	2-1	Skalák, Zahuštěl
03/05	h Sparta	L	2-3	Zahuštěl, Wágner
10/05	a Bohemians 1905	D	1-1	Magera
17/05	h Jablonec	D	1-1	Magera
23/05	a Slovácko	D	1-1	Klobása
30/05	h Jihlava	W	3-0	Klobása, Šćuk, Magera

No	Name	Nat	DoB	Pos	Aps	(s)	Gls
33	Daniel Bartl		05/07/89	M	11	(4)	
8	Jan Bořil		11/01/91	D	27	(2)	1
16	Michal Ďuriš	SVK	01/06/88	A	20	(7)	4
30	Daniel Geissler		01/07/94	D	1		
13	Aleš Hruška		23/11/85	G	26		
28	Lukáš Hůlka		31/03/95	D	12	(1)	1
31	Stanislav Klobása		07/03/94	A	1	(1)	2
4	Jan Koch	GER	04/11/95	D	6		
14	Matěj Konćal		04/12/93	M	5	(2)	
34	Antonín Křapka		22/01/94	D	6		
11	Ondřej Kúdela		26/03/87	M	4	(1)	
20	Jan Kysela		17/12/85	D	17	(1)	
11	Milan Lalkovič	SVK	09/12/92	M	2	(4)	
18	Lukáš Magera		17/01/83	A	14	(14)	4
7	Mirzad Mehanović	BIH	05/01/93	M	2	(2)	1
32	Gaston Mendy	SEN	22/11/85	D	1		
6	Florian Milla	FRA	14/02/94	M	2	(2)	
3	Jakub Navrátil		01/02/84	D	22		2
9	Adam Pajer		02/05/95	D		(4)	
22	Antonín Rosa		02/05/86	D	6		
17	Jasmin Šćuk	BIH	14/07/90	M	26	(1)	7
12	Jan Šeda		17/12/85	G	4		
24	Jan Šisler		24/04/88	M	14	(3)	1
10	Jiří Skalák		12/03/92	M	23	(1)	6
25	Michal Smejkal		21/02/86	D	7	(1)	
15	Jan Štohanzl		20/03/85	M	10	(2)	
29	Igor Subbotin	EST	26/06/90	A		(1)	
29	Pavel Šultes		09/09/85	A	1	(1)	
23	Mickaël Tavares	SEN	25/10/82	M	13		1
2	Florian Thalamy	FRA	12/03/94	D		(1)	
7	Kamil Vacek		05/05/87	M	12	(1)	
26	Miljan Vukadinović	SRB	27/12/92	M	3	(11)	
19	Tomáš Wágner		06/03/90	A	18	(6)	10
21	Ondřej Zahuštěl		18/06/91	M	14	(10)	2

1. FK Příbram

1928 • Energon Arena (7,900) • fkpribram.cz
Coach: Petr Čuhel;
(15/09/14) Pavel Tobiáš

2014

26/07	h Plzeň	D	2-2	Zápotočný, Řezníček
03/08	a Liberec	D	0-0	
09/08	h Sparta	L	0-1	
16/08	a Mladá Boleslav	L	1-4	Řezníček
23/08	h Bohemians 1905	L	2-3	Fillo, Švancara
30/08	a Slovácko	L	1-4	Fillo
13/09	h Jablonec	L	1-4	Řezníček
20/09	a Jihlava	W	1-0	Řezníček
27/09	a České Budějovice	W	3-0	Hnaniček, Sus, Řezníček
04/10	h Hradec Králové	W	1-0	Nando
25/10	h Baník	W	3-1	Zeman, Řezníček 2
28/10	a Dukla	D	0-0	
01/11	a Slavia	L	2-3	Zápotočný, Řezníček
07/11	h Teplice	D	1-1	Řezníček
22/11	a Brno	L	0-1	
29/11	h Liberec	W	1-0	Hnaniček

2015

23/02	a Sparta	L	1-4	og (Kadeřábek)
28/02	h Mladá Boleslav	W	2-0	Pilík, Bednář
07/03	a Bohemians 1905	L	1-3	Bednář
14/03	h Slovácko	L	1-1	Bednář
21/03	a Jablonec	L	0-2	
04/04	a Jihlava	D	1-1	Suchan
11/04	h České Budějovice	W	1-0	Hájovský
19/04	a Hradec Králové	W	3-2	Zeman 2 (1p), Pilík
25/04	h Dukla	W	3-0	Moulis, Hnaniček, Zeman
02/05	a Baník	D	0-0	
09/05	h Slavia	W	2-1	Bednář 2
16/05	a Teplice	D	1-1	Matějů
23/05	h Brno	W	3-2	Suchan, Zeman (p), Fořt
30/05	a Plzeň	L	2-5	Bednář, Zápotočný

No	Name	Nat	DoB	Pos	Aps	(s)	Gls
19	Roman Bednář		26/03/83	A	12		6
28	Marek Boháč		31/10/88	G	20		
20	Zoran Danoski	MKD	20/10/90	A	1	(6)	
9	Simon Deli	CIV	27/10/91	D	6	(1)	
24	Josef Divíšek		24/09/90	D	5	(1)	
10/19	Martin Fillo		07/02/86	M	24		2
9	Pavel Fořt		26/06/83	A		(6)	1
4	Tomáš Hájovský	SVK	10/12/82	D	27		1
15	Levon Hayrapetyan	ARM	17/04/89	D		(1)	
29	Josef Hnaniček		28/12/86	D	30		3
15	Petr Hronek		04/07/93	D		(1)	
24	Martin Husár	SVK	10/02/85	D	1	(1)	
1	Marián Kelemen	SVK	07/12/79	G	9		
23	Martin Krameš		17/08/93	D	13	(5)	
17	Dominik Kraut		15/01/90	A		(1)	
22	Lukáš Krbeček		27/10/85	G	1	(1)	
10	Tomáš Krbeček		27/10/85	M	1	(9)	
21	Jiří Mareš		16/02/92	M	7	(9)	
3	Aleš Matějů		03/06/96	D	14	(1)	1
16	Pavel Moulis		07/04/91	A	3	(6)	1
26	Nando	CPV	09/06/78	D	16		1
7	Milan Nitrianský		13/12/90	D	12		
27	Jakub Řezníček		26/05/88	A	16		9
12	Petr Rys		15/01/96	M		(1)	
6	Jakub Šindelář		24/02/94	D		(1)	
10	Miroslav Slepička		10/11/81	A	1	(3)	
8	Lukáš Stratil		29/01/94	A		(6)	
14	Jan Suchan		18/01/96	M	8	(7)	2
16	Martin Sus		15/03/90	D	16	1	
9	Petr Švancara		05/11/77	A		(5)	1
6	Daniel Tarczal		22/03/85	M	5	(1)	
30	Marian Tregler		01/12/95	D	1	(8)	
5	Tomáš Zápotočný		13/09/80	D	28		3
11	Martin Zeman		28/03/89	M	24	(1)	5

SK Slavia Praha

1892 • Eden Arena (20,800) • slavia.cz
Major honours
Czechoslovakian/Czech League (16) 1925, 1929, 1930, 1931, 1933, 1934, 1935, 1937, 1940, 1941, 1942, 1943, 1947, 1996, 2008, 2009; Czech Cup (3) 1997, 1999, 2002
Coach: Miroslav Beránek

2014

26/07	a Slovácko	W	2-1	Škoda, Balaj
01/08	h Baník	W	3-1	Škoda, Zmrhal, Latka
10/08	h Liberec	W	4-1	Balaj, Zmrhal, Škoda 2
16/08	a Teplice	L	1-2	Škoda
23/08	h Plzeň	W	1-0	Zmrhal
30/08	a Mladá Boleslav	L	1-2	Škoda
12/09	h Brno	L	1-3	Černý
20/09	a Bohemians 1905	L	0-2	
27/09	h Sparta	L	0-2	
04/10	a Jihlava	L	0-1	
18/10	h Jablonec	D	1-1	Bílek
24/10	a České Budějovice	D	1-1	Piták (p)
01/11	h Příbram	W	3-2	Latka (p), Bílek, Balaj
07/11	a Dukla	D	2-2	Dobrotka, Škoda
23/11	a Hradec Králové	D	1-1	Škoda
28/11	a Baník	D	0-0	

2015

21/02	a Liberec	W	3-1	Škoda 3
28/02	h Teplice	D	2-2	Škoda, og (Grigar)
13/03	h Mladá Boleslav	L	3-4	Zmrhal, Kenia, Škoda
18/03	a Plzeň	L	0-1	
22/03	a Brno	L	0-3	
04/04	h Bohemians 1905	D	1-1	Vukadinović
11/04	a Sparta	L	1-2	Škoda
18/04	a Jihlava	L	1-2	Diop
25/04	a Jablonec	L	1-2	Škoda
03/05	h České Budějovice	W	2-0	Škoda 2
09/05	a Příbram	L	1-2	Škoda
16/05	h Dukla	W	2-0	Kenia, Červenka
23/05	a Hradec Králové	W	1-0	Škoda
30/05	h Slovácko	L	1-3	Bílek

No	Name	Nat	DoB	Pos	Aps	(s)	Gls
26	Aldo Baéz	ARG	05/09/88	M	19	(4)	
19	Bekim Balaj	ALB	11/01/91	A	7	(6)	3
29	Martin Berkovec		12/02/89	G	11		
20	Jiří Bílek		04/11/83	D	27		3
10	Damien Boudjemaa	FRA	17/06/85	M	4	(8)	
16	Milan Černý		16/03/88	M	15	(2)	1
27	Marek Červenka		17/12/92	A		(8)	1
9	Simon Deli	CIV	27/10/91	D	13		
17	Dame Diop	SEN	15/02/93	A		(5)	1
6	Martin Dobrotka	SVK	22/01/85	D	10	(1)	1
30	Martin Dostál		23/09/89	D	2	(4)	
27/15	Lukáš Fialka		19/09/95	D	5	(1)	
15	Marcel Gecov		01/01/88	M	4	(2)	
1	Karel Hrubeš		16/03/93	G	15		
4	Robert Hrubý		27/04/94	M	10	(9)	
9	Martin Juhar	SVK	09/03/88	D	14		
11	Levan Kenia	GEO	18/10/90	M	13	(1)	2
14	Marek Kodr		17/08/96	D	9	(6)	
28	Martin Latka		28/09/84	D	19		2
3	Jan Mikula		05/01/92	D	12	(2)	
5	Milan Nitrianský		13/12/90	D	7	(2)	
22	Jakub Petr		10/04/90	A	2	(5)	
23	Karel Piták		28/01/80	M	10	(15)	1
12	Václav Prošek		08/04/93	M	6	(1)	
34	Matej Rakovan	SVK	14/03/90	G	4		
21	Milan Škoda		16/01/86	A	28		19
2	Michal Švec		19/03/87	M	7	(1)	
6	Krisztián Tamás	HUN	18/04/95	D	11		
18	Vukadin Vukadinović	SRB	14/12/90	M	21	(1)	1
8	Jaromír Zmrhal		02/08/93	M	25	(1)	4

CZECH REPUBLIC

1. FC Slovácko

1894 • Městský fotbalový stadion
Miroslava Valenty (8,121) • fcslovacko.cz
Coach: Svatopluk Habanec

2014

26/07	h	Slavia	L	1-2	Trávník
02/08	h	Bohemians 1905	W	4-1	Došek 2, Sumulikoski, Trávník
09/08	a	Jablonec	D	1-1	Diviš
16/08	h	Jihlava	W	2-0	Došek 2
23/08	a	Hradec Králové	L	0-2	
30/08	h	Příbram	W	4-1	Došek, Kalouda 2, Diviš
13/09	a	České Budějovice	D	2-2	Kerbr, Došek
20/09	h	Dukla	W	5-1	Došek 3, Kerbr, Kalouda
26/09	a	Teplice	L	0-4	
04/10	h	Baník	L	1-2	Havlík
18/10	a	Liberec	D	2-2	Sumulikoski, Kalouda
25/10	h	Plzeň	L	0-1	
01/11	a	Brno	W	1-0	Došek
09/11	h	Sparta	L	0-2	
21/11	a	Mladá Boleslav	L	0-2	
29/11	a	Bohemians 1905	W	2-1	Došek, Břečka

2015

20/02	h	Jablonec	L	1-2	Hlúpik
27/02	a	Jihlava	W	1-0	Kalouda
07/03	h	Hradec Králové	L	0-1	
14/03	a	Příbram	L	0-1	
17/03	h	Teplice	D	2-2	Valenta, Kalouda (p)
21/03	h	České Budějovice	W	3-1	Diviš, Kalouda, Došek
04/04	a	Dukla	D	0-0	
18/04	a	Baník	W	2-0	Valenta, Kerbr
25/04	h	Liberec	L	2-3	Valenta, Došek
02/05	a	Plzeň	L	0-4	
08/05	h	Brno	D	1-1	Došek (p)
16/05	a	Sparta	L	2-5	Trávník, Diviš
23/05	h	Mladá Boleslav	D	0-0	
30/05	a	Slavia	W	3-1	Došek, Trávník, Valenta

No	Name	Nat	DoB	Pos	Aps	(s)	Gls
13	Tomáš Břečka		12/05/94	D	10	(1)	1
23	Eldar Čivić	BIH	28/05/96	M		(3)	
2	Vlastimil Daníček		15/07/91	D	1	(3)	
9	Jaroslav Diviš		09/07/86	M	26	(3)	4
23	Tomáš Dočekal		24/05/89	A	2	(4)	
7	Libor Došek		24/04/78	A	25		16
5	Petr Galuška		08/07/96	A		(3)	
15	Roman Haša		15/02/93	A		(1)	
20	Marek Havlík		08/07/95	M	9	(15)	1
29	Milan Heča		23/03/91	G	30		
8	Filip Hlúpik		30/04/91	M	9	(9)	1
10	Luboš Kalouda		20/05/87	M	19	(8)	7
21	Milan Kerbr		10/09/89	A	24	(3)	3
22	Tomáš Košút	SVK	13/01/90	D	21	(4)	
14	Marián Kovář		13/08/93	A		(1)	
17	Martin Kuncl		01/04/84	M	25		
19	Radek Mezlík		25/05/82	D	7	(2)	
3	Jakub Prajza		21/12/93	M	1	(2)	
4	Tomáš Rada		15/02/83	M	26	(1)	
6	Petr Reinberk		23/05/89	D	16	(2)	
18	Lukáš Sadílek		23/05/96	M		(3)	
12	Patrik Šimko	SVK	08/07/91	D	14	(1)	
5	Velice Sumulikoski	MKD	24/04/81	M	24	(1)	2
24	Michal Trávník		17/05/94	M	20	(4)	4
11	Jiří Valenta		14/02/88	M	21	(4)	4
23	Tomáš Zajíc		12/08/96	A		(1)	

FC Slovan Liberec

1958 • U Nisy (9,900) • fcslovanliberec.cz
Major honours
Czech League (3) 2002, 2006, 2012; Czech Cup (2) 2000, 2015

Coach: Samuel Slovák (SVK);
(17/12/14) (Jiří Kotrba);
(09/03/15) David Vavruška

2014

27/07	a	České Budějovice	D	1-1	Pavelka
03/08	h	Příbram	D	0-0	
10/08	a	Slavia	L	1-4	Šural
15/08	h	Dukla	D	0-0	
22/08	a	Teplice	D	2-2	Hadaščok, Luckassen
30/08	h	Baník	W	6-0	Šural 3, Frýdek, Ďubek, Fleišman (p)
15/09	h	Plzeň	D	1-1	Šural
20/09	a	Brno	L	0-1	
28/09	h	Mladá Boleslav	D	0-0	
05/10	a	Sparta	L	0-1	
18/10	h	Slovácko	D	2-2	Delarge, Pavelka
24/10	a	Bohemians 1905	W	4-2	Pavelka, Šural, Delarge 2
02/11	a	Jablonec	L	0-1	
09/11	h	Hradec Králové	D	0-0	
22/11	h	Jihlava	D	2-2	Šural, Hadaščok
29/11	a	Příbram	L	0-1	

2015

21/02	h	Slavia	L	1-3	Obročník
27/02	a	Dukla	L	1-3	Šural
07/03	h	Teplice	L	0-2	
14/03	a	Baník	D	3-3	Sackey, Fleišman (p), Šural
22/03	a	Plzeň	L	0-2	
05/04	h	Brno	W	1-0	Bakoš
11/04	a	Mladá Boleslav	D	1-1	Luckassen
18/04	h	Sparta	W	2-1	Delarge, Pokorný
25/04	a	Slovácko	W	3-2	og (Košút), Delarge, Frýdek
02/05	h	Bohemians 1905	D	1-1	Delarge
10/05	a	Jablonec	L	0-2	
16/05	h	Hradec Králové	W	2-0	Karišik, Šural
23/05	a	Jihlava	L	0-4	
30/05	h	České Budějovice	W	5-1	Šural 2, Breznaník, Fleišman, Hadaščok

No	Name	Nat	DoB	Pos	Aps	(s)	Gls
27	Marek Bakoš	SVK	15/04/83	A	9	(3)	1
15	Erich Brabec		24/02/77	D	6		
17	Michal Breznaník	SVK	16/12/85	M	6	(3)	1
5	Vladimír Coufal		22/08/92	D	10	(3)	
28	Dzon Delarge	CGO	23/06/90	A	17	(2)	6
24	Douglas Djika	CMR	08/03/93	M	1	(4)	
26	Tomáš Ďubek	SVK	22/01/87	M	15	(4)	1
6	Daniel Dydowicz		01/01/94	M	1	(5)	
2	Tomáš Egert		01/08/94	D		(1)	
25	Jiří Fleišman		02/10/84	D	26		3
2	Denis Frimmel		08/01/94	M	1	(1)	
11	Martin Frýdek		24/03/92	M	23	(2)	2
14	Vojtěch Hadaščok		08/01/92	A	11	(10)	3
15	Michal Hamulák	SVK	26/11/90	A	1	(6)	
30	Lukáš Hrošso	SVK	19/04/87	G	12		
13	Marek Jarolím		21/05/84	M	2	(1)	
22	Lukáš Kaiser		29/11/95	M	2	(1)	
3	Miloš Karišik	SRB	07/10/88	D	14	(2)	1
27	Ľuboš Kolár	SVK	01/09/89	M	2	(1)	
1	Ondřej Kolář		17/10/94	G	16		
19	Kevin Luckassen	NED	27/07/93	A	6	(10)	2
16	Patrik Lukáč	SVK	30/09/81	A	2		
16	Marcos Vinícius	BRA	14/06/96	M		(4)	
18	Jan Mudra		22/01/90	D	13	(5)	
9	Mouhamadou Ndiaye	SEN	24/08/94	A		(4)	
20	Michal Obročník	SVK	04/06/91	M	17	(1)	1
8	David Pavelka		18/05/91	M	19	(1)	3
21	Jiří Pimpara		04/02/87	D	17	(3)	
29	Lukáš Pokorný		05/07/93	D	18	(1)	1
17	Jan Rajnoch		30/09/81	D	3		
12	Isaac Sackey	GHA	04/04/94	M	14	(2)	1
31	Soune Soungole	CIV	26/02/95	M	10	(4)	
23	Josef Šural		30/05/90	M	25		12
4	Martin Sus		15/03/90	D	11	(2)	

AC Sparta Praha

1893 • Generali Arena (19,416) • sparta.cz
Major honours
Czechoslovakian/Czech League (33) 1926, 1927, 1932, 1936, 1938, 1939, 1944, 1946, 1948, 1952, 1954, 1965, 1967, 1984, 1985, 1987, 1988, 1989, 1990, 1991, 1993, 1994, 1995, 1997, 1998, 1999, 2000, 2001, 2003, 2005, 2007, 2010, 2014; Czechoslovakian/Czech Cup (14) 1964, 1972, 1976, 1980, 1984, 1988, 1989, 1992, 1996, 2004, 2006, 2007, 2008, 2014

Coach: Vítězslav Lavička;
(15/04/15) Zdeněk Ščasný

2014

25/07	a	Bohemians 1905	W	2-1	Nešpor, Hušbauer
02/08	h	Jihlava	W	3-0	Přikryl 2, Dočkal
09/08	a	Příbram	W	1-0	Lafata
15/08	h	Baník	L	0-1	
24/08	a	Dukla	L	0-1	
31/08	h	Jablonec	W	2-0	Lafata 2
13/09	a	Teplice	D	0-0	
21/09	h	Hradec Králové	W	3-1	Lafata 2, Hušbauer
27/09	a	Slavia	W	2-0	Lafata 2
05/10	h	Liberec	W	1-0	Dočkal (p)
18/10	a	Brno	W	3-1	Krejčí, Dočkal (p), Lafata
26/10	h	Mladá Boleslav	W	2-0	Dočkal
01/11	h	Plzeň	L	0-2	
09/11	h	Slovácko	W	2-0	Dočkal, Konaté
22/11	h	České Budějovice	W	4-0	Lafata 2, Dočkal 2
30/11	a	Jihlava	W	2-0	Hušbauer, Brabec

2015

23/02	a	Příbram	W	4-1	Lafata, Kadlec 2, og (Nitriansky)
28/02	a	Baník	D	1-1	Kadlec
08/03	h	Dukla	W	3-0	og (Štětina), Dočkal (p), Krejčí
14/03	a	Jablonec	D	0-0	
21/03	h	Teplice	W	1-0	Dočkal (p)
04/04	a	Hradec Králové	W	3-0	Kadlec, Lafata, Krejčí
11/04	h	Slavia	W	2-1	Lafata, Brabec
18/04	a	Liberec	L	1-2	Lafata
26/04	h	Brno	W	4-0	Lafata 3, Dočkal
03/05	a	Mladá Boleslav	W	3-2	Kadlec 2 (1p), Kadeřábek
09/05	h	Plzeň	L	0-2	
16/05	h	Slovácko	W	5-2	Kadeřábek, Lafata, Vácha, Kadlec 2
23/05	a	České Budějovice	W	3-1	Kadlec, Lafata, Kadeřábek
30/05	h	Bohemians 1905	D	1-1	Lafata

No	Name	Nat	DoB	Pos	Aps	(s)	Gls
29	Roman Bednář		26/03/83	A	1	(4)	
35	David Bičík		06/04/81	G	13		
5	Jakub Brabec		06/08/92	D	23		2
33	Michal Breznaník	SVK	16/12/85	M	1	(4)	
19	Juraj Chvátal	SVK	13/07/96	D		(1)	
9	Bořek Dočkal		30/09/88	M	27	(2)	10
25	Mario Holek		28/10/86	D	24		
16	Josef Hušbauer		16/03/90	M	8	(1)	3
16	Pavel Kadeřábek		25/04/92	D	25		3
3	Václav Kadlec		20/05/92	A	12	(1)	9
15	Tiémoko Konaté	CIV	03/03/90	M	7	(18)	1
15	Radoslav Kováč		27/11/79	D	10	(7)	
23	Ladislav Krejčí		05/07/92	M	27		3
21	David Lafata		18/09/81	A	29	(1)	20
11	Lukáš Mareček		17/04/90	M	12	(10)	
8	Marek Matějovský		20/12/81	M	24		
14	Martin Nešpor		05/06/90	A	1	(2)	1
26	Costa Nhamoinesu	ZIM	06/01/86	D	28		
13	Jakub Pešek		24/06/93	M		(1)	
39	Jakub Podaný		15/06/87	M	2	(2)	
7	Tomáš Přikryl		04/07/92	M	4	(6)	2
27	Jakub Řezníček		26/05/88	A	1	(7)	
49	Patrik Schick			A		(2)	
10	Herolind Shala	ALB	01/02/92	M	1	(2)	
1	Marek Štěch		28/01/90	G	17		
4	Ondřej Švejdík		03/12/82	D	4	(2)	
17	Kamil Vacek		18/05/87	M	4	(7)	
6	Lukáš Vácha		13/05/89	M	25		1

FK Teplice

1945 • Na Stínadlech (18,221) • fkteplice.cz
Major honours
Czech Cup (2) 2003, 2009
Coach: **Zdeněk Ščasný;**
(17/02/15) **Petr Rada**

2014
26/07	a	Hradec Králové	D	0-0
08/08	a	Baník	D	1-1 *Mahmutović*
16/08	h	Slavia	W	2-1 *Litsingi, og (Bílek)*
22/08	h	Liberec	D	2-2 *Vůch, Krob*
29/08	a	Brno	D	1-1 *Vůch*
02/09	h	České Budějovice	W	4-0 *Salami, Krob, Mahmutović(p), Jablonský*
13/09	h	Sparta	D	0-0
19/09	a	Mladá Boleslav	L	0-3
26/09	h	Slovácko	W	4-0 *Vůch, Litsingi, Nivaldo, Mahmutović*
05/10	a	Plzeň	L	0-1
18/10	h	Bohemians 1905	W	4-1 *Ljevaković, Mahmutović, Vůch, Salami*
25/10	a	Jablonec	L	2-4 *Nivaldo, Mahmutović*
01/11	a	Jihlava	L	2-3 *Mahmutović, Jablonský*
07/11	a	Příbram	D	1-1 *Jablonský*
22/11	h	Dukla	W	1-0 *Krob (p)*
28/11	a	České Budějovice	L	0-2

2015
21/02	h	Baník	W	1-0 *Hora*
28/02	a	Slavia	D	2-2 *Potočný 2*
07/03	a	Liberec	W	2-0 *Vachoušek, Vůch*
14/03	h	Brno	L	0-1
17/03	h	Slovácko	D	2-2 *Hora, Krob (p)*
21/03	a	Sparta	L	0-1
04/04	h	Mladá Boleslav	W	5-0 *Táborský, Litsingi 2, Potočný, Salami*
20/04	h	Plzeň	D	0-0
25/04	a	Bohemians 1905	L	0-1
03/05	h	Jablonec	D	1-1 *Hošek*
09/05	a	Jihlava	W	1-0 *Hora*
16/05	h	Příbram	D	1-1 *Potočný*
23/05	a	Dukla	L	1-5 *Kapolongo*
30/05	h	Hradec Králové	L	1-3 *Takács*

No	Name	Nat	DoB	Pos	Aps	(s)	Gls
25	Benjamin Balázs	HUN	26/04/90	M	3	(3)	
12	Chukwudi Chukwuma	NGA	17/10/87	A	1	(4)	
16	Martin Fenin		16/04/87	A		(2)	
30	Tomáš Grigar		01/02/83	G	30		
13	Jakub Hora		23/02/91	A	13		3
23	Jan Hošek		01/04/89	D	5	(2)	1
18	David Jablonský		08/10/91	D	27		3
7	Milan Jirásek		14/05/92	M	1	(4)	
14	Ulrich Kapolongo	CGO	31/07/89	A	5	(11)	1
24	Jan Krob		27/04/87	D	27		4
2	Denis Laňka		13/05/97	A		(1)	
28	Francis Litsingi	CGO	09/10/86	M	24		4
5	Admir Ljevaković	BIH	07/08/84	M	25		1
4	Michael Lüftner		14/03/94	D	22	(2)	
25	Aidin Mahmutović	BIH	24/04/86	A	9	(6)	6
20	Milan Matula		22/04/84	D	21	(5)	
15	Alen Melunović	SRB	26/01/90	A	1	(1)	
16	Václav Mozol		30/09/91	M	1		
26	Nivaldo	CPV	10/07/88	D	19		2
15	Roman Potočný		25/04/91	A	13		4
11	Eugène Salami	NGA	05/02/89	A	6	(5)	3
1	Ivo Táborský		10/05/85	A	6	(9)	1
22	Ladislav Takács		15/07/96	D	15	(6)	1
6	Otto Urma		17/08/94	D	1	(1)	
8	Štěpán Vachoušek		26/07/79	M	13	(1)	1
17	Tomáš Vondrášek		26/10/87	D	20	(5)	
27	Egon Vůch		01/02/91	M	22	(6)	5

FC Viktoria Plzeň

1911 • Doosan Arena (11,354) • fcviktoria.cz
Major honours
Czech League (3) 2011, 2013, 2015; Czech Cup (1) 2010
Coach: **Dušan Uhrin Jr;**
(12/08/14) **Miroslav Koubek**

2014
26/07	a	Příbram	D	2-2 *Bakoš, Horváth (p)*
03/08	h	Jablonec	W	3-1 *Kolář (p), og (Hrubý), Petržela*
10/08	a	České Budějovice	W	4-0 *Řezník, Chramosta 2, Kolář*
17/08	h	Hradec Králové	W	4-0 *Limberský, Chramosta, Pilař (p), Petržela*
23/08	a	Slavia	L	0-1
31/08	h	Dukla	W	2-1 *Vaněk, Procházka*
15/09	a	Liberec	D	1-1 *Pilař*
21/09	h	Baník	W	2-0 *Kolář (p), Vaněk*
27/09	a	Brno	W	3-2 *Kolář (p), Tecl, Řezník*
05/10	h	Teplice	W	1-0 *Hejda*
19/10	a	Mladá Boleslav	W	3-0 *Tecl 3*
25/10	a	Slovácko	W	1-0 *Hořava*
01/11	h	Sparta	W	2-0 *Hejda, Hořava*
09/11	a	Jihlava	L	1-2 *Limberský*
23/11	h	Bohemians 1905	W	2-1 *Hořava (p), og (Jindřišek)*
30/11	a	Jablonec	W	2-1 *Tecl, Řezník*

2015
21/02	h	České Budějovice	W	6-0 *Petržela, Kolář, Mahmutović, Rajtoral, Vaněk, Hořava*
01/03	a	Hradec Králové	W	3-2 *Kolář, Vaněk, Rajtoral*
15/03	a	Dukla	W	3-2 *Kovařík, Kolář 2 (2p)*
18/03	h	Slavia	W	1-0 *Holenda*
22/03	h	Liberec	W	2-0 *Hubník, Vaněk*
05/04	a	Baník	W	2-0 *Hořava, Rajtoral*
12/04	h	Brno	W	4-1 *Mahmutović 2, Kovařík, Hořava*
20/04	a	Teplice	D	0-0
25/04	h	Mladá Boleslav	L	1-2 *Kolář*
02/05	h	Slovácko	W	4-0 *og (Kerbr), Kovařík (p), Mahmutović*
09/05	a	Sparta	W	2-0 *Holenda, Hubník*
18/05	h	Jihlava	W	2-0 *Hubník, Rajtoral*
23/05	a	Bohemians 1905	L	2-3 *Mahmutović, Pilař*
30/05	h	Příbram	W	5-2 *Holenda 2, Pilař, Kolář 2*

No	Name	Nat	DoB	Pos	Aps	(s)	Gls
23	Marek Bakoš	SVK	15/04/83	A	2	(3)	1
22	Jan Baránek		26/06/93	D	3	(4)	
13	Petr Bolek		08/06/84	G	1		
29	Jan Chramosta		12/10/90	A	7	(3)	3
2	Lukáš Hejda		09/03/90	D	12	(1)	2
16	Jan Holenda		22/08/85	A	6	(12)	4
7	Tomáš Hořava		29/05/88	M	14	(12)	6
10	Pavel Horváth		22/04/75	M	1	(6)	1
17	Patrik Hrošovský	SVK	22/04/92	M	26	(2)	
4	Roman Hubník		06/06/84	D	18	(1)	3
26	Daniel Kolář		27/10/85	M	23	(2)	11
19	Jan Kovařík		19/06/88	M	14	(12)	3
1	Matúš Kozáčik	SVK	27/12/83	G	29		
8	David Limberský		06/10/83	D			2
25	Aidin Mahmutović	BIH	06/04/86	A	10	(4)	6
11	Milan Petržela		19/06/83	M	24	(3)	3
6	Václav Pilař		13/10/88	M	25	(3)	4
21	Václav Procházka		08/05/84	D	29	(1)	1
27	František Rajtoral		12/03/86	D	14	(2)	4
14	Radim Řezník		20/01/89	D	16		3
9	Stanislav Tecl		01/09/90	A	5	(13)	4
20	Ondřej Vaněk		05/07/90	A	25	(4)	5

FC Vysočina Jihlava

1948 • Městský stadion (4,155) • fcvysocina.cz
Coach: **Petr Rada;**
(30/09/14) (**Roman Kučera**);
(05/12/14) **Luděk Klusáček**

2014
27/07	h	Mladá Boleslav	L	0-1
02/08	a	Sparta	L	0-3
08/08	h	Bohemians 1905	L	1-2 *Kučera*
16/08	a	Slovácko	L	0-2
23/08	a	Jablonec	L	0-2
29/08	h	České Budějovice	D	0-0
13/09	h	Hradec Králové	W	3-0 *Harba 2, Kukoľ*
20/09	h	Příbram	L	0-2
27/09	a	Dukla	L	1-4 *Kovář*
04/10	h	Slavia	W	1-0 *Kukoľ*
17/10	a	Baník	D	0-0
24/10	h	Brno	W	2-0 *Mešanović, Hybš*
01/11	a	Teplice	W	3-2 *Kukoľ, Kučera, Mešanović*
09/11	h	Plzeň	W	2-1 *Mešanović, Masopust*
22/11	a	Liberec	D	2-2 *Kučera, Mešanović*
30/11	a	Sparta	L	0-2

2015
21/02	a	Bohemians 1905	D	0-0
27/02	h	Slovácko	L	0-1
07/03	h	Jablonec	D	1-1 *Šulek*
14/03	a	České Budějovice	W	3-1 *Vaculík 2 (2p), Mešanović*
21/03	h	Hradec Králové	W	2-0 *Vaculík (p), Šulek*
04/04	a	Příbram	D	1-1 *Tlustý*
11/04	h	Dukla	L	1-2 *Jánoš*
18/04	a	Slavia	W	2-1 *Šulek, Kučera*
24/04	h	Baník	W	2-0 *Harba, Kliment*
01/05	a	Brno	L	2-3 *Jungr 2*
09/05	h	Teplice	L	0-1
18/05	a	Plzeň	L	0-2
23/05	h	Liberec	W	4-0 *Kliment, Mešanović, Nerad, Harba*
30/05	a	Mladá Boleslav	L	0-3

No	Name	Nat	DoB	Pos	Aps	(s)	Gls
24	Augusto Batioja	ECU	04/05/90	A		(4)	
29	Jaromír Blažek		29/12/72	G	3		
21	Patrik Demeter		02/01/94	M	2	(2)	
7	Tomáš Duba		31/01/96	M		(1)	
22	Jakub Fulnek		26/04/94	M	14	(5)	
1	Jan Hanuš		24/04/88	G	27		
28	Haris Harba	BIH	22/07/88	A	20	(8)	4
31	Matěj Hybš		03/01/93	D	23		1
25	Christian Irobiso	NGA	28/05/93	A		(3)	
8	Adam Jánoš		20/07/92	M	19		1
9	Marek Jungr		11/04/87	M	10	(7)	2
12	Jan Kliment		01/09/93	A	7	(8)	2
21	Václav Koloušek		13/04/76	M	2	(1)	
18	Jan Kosak		03/02/92	M	1	(5)	
3	Marián Kovář		13/08/93	D	3	(4)	1
5	Jiří Krejčí		22/03/86	D	29		
15	Lukáš Kryštůfek		11/08/92	D	11	(2)	
16	Tomáš Kučera		20/07/91	M	26	(1)	4
30	Vladimír Kukoľ	SVK	08/05/86	M	21	(4)	3
27	Matúš Marcin	SVK	06/04/94	A	1	(4)	
14	Tomáš Marek		20/04/81	M	21	(3)	
26	Lukáš Masopust		12/02/93	M		(3)	1
26	Muris Mešanović	BIH	04/07/90	A	19	(8)	6
23	Mateja Mlakić	CRO	07/06/95	D		(1)	
26	Petr Nerad		06/02/94	M	3	(2)	1
6	Ondřej Šourek		26/04/83	D	5	(1)	
25	David Štěpánek		30/03/97	M		(1)	
20	Peter Šulek	SVK	21/09/88	D	17	(3)	3
17	Petr Tlustý		12/01/86	D	18	(1)	1
11	Lukáš Vaculík		06/06/83	M	23	(2)	3
24	Vlastimil Vidlička		02/07/81	D	5	(1)	

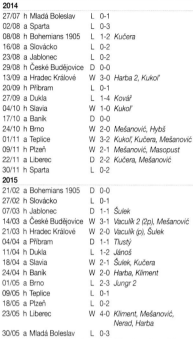

CZECH REPUBLIC

FC Zbrojovka Brno

1913 • Městský fotbalový stadion (12,550)
• fczbrno.cz
Major honours
Czechoslovakian League (1) 1978
Coach: Václav Kotal

2014
26/07	a Jablonec	L	0-2	
02/08	h Hradec Králové	W	3-0	Schuster, Jugas, Marković
09/08	a Dukla	D	1-1	Marković
16/08	h České Budějovice	D	2-2	og (Klesa), Vávra
22/08	a Baník	L	0-1	
29/08	h Teplice	D	1-1	Pašek
12/09	h Slavia	W	3-1	Vávra 2, Zavadil (p)
20/09	h Liberec	W	1-0	Sýkora
27/09	h Plzeň	L	2-3	Brigant, Lutonský
04/10	a Mladá Boleslav	L	1-5	Vávra
18/10	h Sparta	L	1-3	Košťál
24/10	a Jihlava	L	0-2	
01/11	h Slovácko	L	0-1	
11/11	h Bohemians 1905	D	0-0	
22/11	h Příbram	W	1-0	Moukanza
29/11	a Hradec Králové	L	1-2	Zavadil (p)

2015
21/02	h Dukla	L	0-1	
28/02	a České Budějovice	W	3-1	Sýkora, Jugas, Malík
06/03	h Baník	D	0-0	
14/03	a Teplice	W	1-0	Zoubele
22/03	h Slavia	W	3-0	Pašek, Čtvrtníček, Sýkora
05/04	a Liberec	L	0-1	
12/04	h Plzeň	L	1-4	Marković
19/04	h Mladá Boleslav	W	1-0	Marković (p)
26/04	a Sparta	L	0-4	
01/05	h Jihlava	W	3-2	Zavadil (p), Pašek 2
08/05	a Slovácko	D	1-1	Zavadil
16/05	h Bohemians 1905	L	0-1	
23/05	a Příbram	L	2-3	Zavadil, Hyčka
30/05	h Jablonec	L	2-3	Sýkora, Jugas

No	Name	Nat	DoB	Pos	Aps	(s)	Gls
28	Tomáš Brigant	SVK	18/10/94	A	8	(4)	1
3	Petr Buchta		11/07/92	D	11	(2)	
26	Radek Buchta		22/04/89	D	13		
6	Josef Čtvrtníček		13/02/80	A	3	(4)	1
1	Martin Doležal		18/12/80	G	1	(1)	
18	Roman Fischer		24/03/83	M	14		
17	Václav Hladký		14/11/90	G	16		
24	Alois Hyčka		22/07/90	D	10	(12)	1
4	Jakub Jugas		05/05/92	D	27	(1)	3
5	Marek Kaščák	SVK	22/05/82	M	3	(3)	
30	Miroslav Keresteš	SVK	30/07/89	D	14	(4)	
5	Václav Klán		07/09/93	A		(1)	
21	Kamil Kopúnek	SVK	18/05/84	M	4	(2)	
14	Pavel Košťál		17/09/80	D	27		1
19	Milan Lutonský		10/08/93	M	10	(4)	1
8	Jan Malík		07/04/92	D	21	(6)	1
9	Miroslav Marković	SRB	04/11/89	A	7	(5)	4
1	Dušan Melichárek		29/11/83	G	13		
10	Pavel Mezlík		25/06/83	M	1	(3)	
29	Donneil Moukanza	FRA	27/02/91	M	8	(7)	1
25	David Pašek		27/10/89	A	16	(3)	4
21	Jakub Přichystal		25/10/95	A		(1)	
22	Aleš Schuster		26/10/81	D	22	(1)	1
13	Jan Sedlák		25/10/94	M		(1)	
23	Fabián Slančík	SVK	22/09/91	A	3	(7)	
16	Šimon Šumbera		05/01/91	M	2	(8)	
15	Jan Sýkora		29/12/93	M	26		4
11	Stanislav Vávra		20/07/93	A	19	(7)	4
7	Pavel Zavadil		30/04/78	M	26		5
10	Lukáš Zoubele		20/12/85	M	5	(1)	1

Top goalscorers

20	David Lafata (Sparta)
19	Milan Škoda (Slavia)
16	Libor Došek (Slovácko)
12	Josef Šural (Liberec)
	Aidin Mahmutović (Teplice/Plzeň)
11	Filip Novák (Jablonec)
	Daniel Kolář (Plzeň)
10	Tomáš Wágner (Mladá Boleslav)
	Bořek Dočkal (Sparta)
9	Pavel Dvořák (Hradec Králové)
	Jakub Řezníček (Příbram)
	Václav Kadlec (Sparta)

Promoted clubs

SK Sigma Olomouc

1919 • Andrův stadion (12,541) •
sigmafotbal.cz
Major honours
Czech Cup (1) 2012
Coach: Leoš Kalvoda

FC Zlín

1919 • Stadion Letná (6,089) • fcfastavzlin.cz
Major honours
Czechoslovakian Cup (1) 1970
Coach: Martin Pulpit;
(25/11/14) Bohumil Pánik

Second level final table 2014/15

		Pld	W	D	L	F	A	Pts
1	SK Sigma Olomouc	30	19	6	5	64	25	63
2	FK Varnsdorf	30	17	8	5	47	27	59
3	FC Zlín	30	16	7	7	53	32	55
4	FK Viktoria Žižkov	30	16	7	7	50	23	55
5	FK Baník Sokolov	30	13	9	8	44	39	48
6	FC MAS Táborsko	30	13	8	9	55	42	47
7	MFK OKD Karviná	30	12	10	8	39	31	46
8	FK Pardubice	30	12	9	9	37	34	45
9	SFC Opava	30	11	9	10	36	35	42
10	FC Vlašim	30	11	6	13	36	50	39
11	1. SC Znojmo	30	11	5	14	37	43	38
12	FK Ústí nad Labem	30	10	4	16	34	46	34
13	FK Fotbal Třinec	30	8	6	16	33	51	30
14	MFK Frýdek-Místek	30	8	4	18	28	41	28
15	FK Baník Most	30	5	6	19	25	51	21
16	FK Kolín	30	3	6	21	26	74	15

NB FK Varnsdorf did not receive licence for 1.Liga;
FC Zlín promoted instead.

DOMESTIC CUP

Pohár České Pošty 2014/15

SECOND ROUND

(12/08/14)
Blansko 1-4 Frýdek-Místek
Hlučín 1-2 Baník Ostrava
Neratovice-Byškovice 0-2 Teplice
Písek 0-2 Příbram
Prostějov 1-4 Slovácko

(13/08/14)
Admira Praha 0-0 Baník Sokolov *(15-14 on pens)*
Bohemians Praha 2-0 Varnsdorf
Hanácká Slavia Kroměříž 1-1 Zlín *(5-6 on pens)*
Hranice 1-1 Opava *(4-5 on pens)*
Chomutov 0-5 Jablonec
Chrudim 1-3 Slavia Praha
Dobrovice 5-0 Klatovy 1898
Jíloviště 1-2 Štěchovice
Kolín 0-3 Bohemians 1905
Olympia Hradec Králové 0-6 Hradec Králové
Převýšov 0-1 Pardubice
Slovan Rosice 1-3 Znojmo
Sokol Brozany 2-6 České Budějovice
Sokol Jablonec 2-4 Vlašim
Třebíč 0-4 Zbrojovka Brno
Uničov 0-3 Fotbal Třinec
Union Nový Bydžov 0-2 Ústí nad Labem
Vysoké Mýto 0-4 Sokol Živanice
Zábřeh 0-2 Karviná

(19/08/14)
Viktoria Žižkov 2-1 Vysočina Jihlava

(20/08/14)
Jiskra Domažlice 3-1 Dukla Praha
Tachov 1-3 Táborsko

(02/09/14)
Velké Meziříčí 0-3 Sigma Olomouc

Byes - Mladá Boleslav, Slovan Liberec, Sparta
Praha, Viktoria Plzeň

THIRD ROUND

(03/09/14)
Štěchovice 0-1 Mladá Boleslav
Viktoria Žižkov 2-1 Slavia Praha

(05/09/14)
Opava 1-0 Karviná
Ústí nad Labem 0-3 Slovan Liberec
Vlašim 0-1 Příbram

(06/09/14)
Bohemians Praha 0-3 Teplice
Bohemians 1905 2-0 České Budějovice
Dobrovice 1-2 Jablonec
Sigma Olomouc 0-1 Fotbal Třinec
Zlín 0-4 Slovácko

(07/09/14)
Frýdek-Místek 1-2 Baník Ostrava
Sokol Živanice 1-3 Sparta Praha

(09/09/14)
Admira Praha 1-1 Hradec Králové *(3-4 on pens)*

(10/09/14)
Jiskra Domažlice 1-0 Pardubice

(24/09/14)
Táborsko 0-3 Viktoria Plzeň

(08/10/14)
Znojmo 1-0 Zbrojovka Brno

FOURTH ROUND

(23/09/14 & 09/10/14)
Jablonec 2-0, 2-0 Bohemians 1905 *(4-0)*

(23/09/14 & 18/10/14)
Viktoria Žižkov 1-1, 0-5 Mladá Boleslav *(1-6)*

(24/09/14 & 08/10/14)
Fotbal Třinec 2-0, 0-0 Opava *(2-0)*

(30/09/14 & 14/10/14)
Jiskra Domažlice 0-4, 2-1 Teplice *(2-5)*

(08/10/14 & 29/10/14)
Baník Ostrava 1-1, 1-1 Slovácko *(2-2; 3-4 on pens)*

(28/10/14 & 05/11/14)
Slovan Liberec 6-0, 2-1 Znojmo *(8-1)*

(04/11/14 & 19/11/14)
Hradec Králové 1-2, 0-0 Viktoria Plzeň *(1-2)*

(18/11/14 & 04/12/14)
Příbram 1-1, 1-3 Sparta Praha *(2-4)*

QUARTER-FINALS

(17/03/15 & 14/04/15)
Sparta Praha 2-1 Jablonec *(Řezníček 10, Kadlec
40; Doležal 57)*
Jablonec 2-0 Sparta Praha *(Novák 22p, Kopic 37)*
(Jablonec 3-2)

(01/04/15 & 14/04/15)
Fotbal Třinec 3-1 Slovan Liberec *(Smetana 4,
Dedič 80, Motyčka 87; Delarge 56)*
Slovan Liberec 2-0 Fotbal Třinec *(Breznaník 66,
Pavelka 89)*
(3-3; Slovan Liberec on away goal)

Slovácko 2-2 Mladá Boleslav *(Diviš 8, Košút 85;
Wágner 35, Skalák 57)*
Mladá Boleslav 5-3 Slovácko *(Wágner 21, 65p,
Skalák 54, Ďuriš 75, 90; Trávník 42, Košút 77, Diviš
90+2)*
(Mladá Boleslav 7-5)

(08/04/15 & 15/04/15)
Teplice 2-1 Viktoria Plzeň *(Potočný 80, Balázs 89;
Rajtoral 76)*
Viktoria Plzeň 2-1 Teplice *(Holenda 62, Baránek 77;
Litsingi 69)*
(3-3; Teplice 4-3 on pens)

SEMI-FINALS

(28/04/15 & 13/05/15)
Slovan Liberec 3-0 Teplice *(Djika 10, Brabec 16,
Luckassen 47)*
Teplice 3-1 Slovan Liberec *(Hošek 31, Krob 42,
Balázs 72; Frýdek 60)*
(Slovan Liberec 4-3)

(29/04/15 & 13/05/15)
Mladá Boleslav 1-2 Jablonec *(Zahuštěl 36;
Mingazov 6, Kopic 18)*
Jablonec 1-0 Mladá Boleslav *(Greguš 90)*
(Jablonec 3-1)

FINAL

(27/05/15)
Městský stadion, Mlada Boleslav
FC SLOVAN LIBEREC 1 *(Bakoš 86)*
FK JABLONEC 1 *(Doležal 38)*
(3-1 on pens)
Referee: *Proske*
LIBEREC: *Hroššo, Sus, Karišik (Pimpara 85),
Pokorný, Mudra, Soungole (Bakoš 77), Pavelka,
Šural, Delarge (Breznaník 62), Frýdek, Luckassen*
JABLONEC: *Špit, Masopust, Pernica, Beneš,
Novák, Greguš, Hübschman, Kopic, Pospíšil
(Daniel Rossi 81), Mingazov (Crnkić 60), Doležal*

Jubilant Liberec players pose with the Czech Cup

DENMARK
Dansk Boldspil-Union (DBU)

Address	House of Football	**President**	Jesper Møller
	DBU Allé 1		Christensen
	DK-2605 Brøndby	**Chief executive**	Claus Bretton-Meyer
Tel	+45 43 262 222	**Media officer**	Jacob Høyer
Fax	+45 43 262 245	**Year of formation**	1889
E-mail	dbu@dbu.dk	**National stadium**	Telia Parken (38,065)
Website	dbu.dk		

SUPERLIGA CLUBS

 ① **Aalborg BK**

 ② **Brøndby IF**

 ③ **Esbjerg fB**

 ④ **Hobro IK**

 ⑤ **FC København**

 ⑥ **FC Midtjylland**

 ⑦ **FC Nordsjælland**

 ⑧ **Odense BK**

 ⑨ **Randers FC**

 ⑩ **Silkeborg IF**

 ⑪ **SønderjyskE**

 ⑫ **FC Vestsjælland**

PROMOTED CLUBS

 ⑬ **Viborg FF**

 ⑭ **AGF Aarhus**

KEY:

● – UEFA Champions League

● – UEFA Europa League

● – Promoted

● – Relegated

Midtjylland make history

Long-time leaders in the 2013/14 Superliga title race before they eventually ended up third, FC Midtjylland managed to see the job through to its conclusion 12 months later to become champions of Denmark for the first time – just 16 years after the club's formation.

Glen Riddersholm's attack-minded side struck 24 goals more than runners-up FC København, who avoided a second successive season without a trophy by winning the Danish Cup for the sixth time, defeating relegated FC Vestsjælland 3-2 after extra time in a thrilling final.

| First Superliga title for Jutland merger club | League runners-up FC København lift the cup | National team boss Olsen announces departure |

Domestic league

If Midtjylland's near-miss of the previous season had left any scars, they were barely visible as Riddersholm's well-drilled side racked up the wins to build up a big lead during the autumn and protect it during the spring. With FCK and the rest safely out of harm's way, the club that came into being in 1999 from a merger of Ikast FS and Herning Fremad made mathematically certain of their maiden triumph with a 0-0 draw at Vestsjælland four days after they had dispelled virtually all doubts by defeating FCK 2-0 at home.

It was Midtjylland's outstanding form in the MCH Arena that propelled them into the history books. Up until the title was secure they did not drop a single point at home, and although Brøndby IF, who finished third, ended that perfect record with a party-pooping 3-2 win on the day that Ridderholm and his players celebrated the championship win with their fans, it could not detract from a magnificent campaign in which several players scaled new career heights. Among those were winger Pione Sisto, midfield dynamo Jakob Poulsen and – in the spring – fit-again defender Erik Sviatchenko and Austrian striker Martin Pusic, who, having joined in mid-season, added eight goals to the nine he had struck for Esbjerg fB to become the Superliga's top scorer.

While Midtjylland possessed the league's most potent attack, scoring 64 times, FCK's concession of just 22 goals made them the division's strongest defensive unit. Their final tally of 67 points was five more than Aalborg BK had accumulated in winning the previous season's title, but it was not enough to provide more than a cursory challenge to the champions, who had already constructed a ten-point lead over Ståle Solbakken's title favourites with just seven matches played.

Domestic cup

A second successive runners-up spot was not what the ten-time Danish champions had in mind for the Superliga, but at least they redeemed themselves by winning a sixth Danish Cup. Indeed, with the final staged in mid-May, FCK actually lifted the cup before Midtjylland got their hands on the Superliga silverware. A goal down to first-time finalists Vestsjælland before they went 2-1 up, Solbakken's troops were then pegged back to 2-2 in the 88th minute before eventually prevailing in extra time with a winning goal from 19-year-old Faroe Islands international midfielder Brandur Olsen.

Europe

Aalborg BK's disappointing defence of the two trophies they won in 2013/14 –

they finished fifth in the league and were eliminated in the quarter-finals of the cup – might have had something to do with the extra workload brought on by the club's extended European adventure, which carried them from the third qualifying round of the UEFA Champions League to the UEFA Europa League round of 32. Kent Nielsen's side were eventually removed from the latter competition by Club Brugge KV, who had previously helped to eliminate FCK in the group stage.

National team

Two victories over Serbia – the first in Belgrade (3-1), the second in Copenhagen (2-0) – appeared to have set Denmark firmly on the path to the UEFA EURO 2016 finals after an edgy start in which they came from behind to beat Armenia, dropped two points in Albania and then lost at home to a last-gasp Cristiano Ronaldo goal against Portugal.

The season was also notable for a first international hat-trick from Nicklas Bendtner – in a friendly win over the United States – and the announcement a few days earlier from Morten Olsen that he would be leaving the post of head coach he had held since 2000 once Denmark's UEFA EURO 2016 participation was over, be that at the finals in France or the end of qualification.

DOMESTIC SEASON AT A GLANCE

Superliga 2014/15 final table

		Pld	Home					Away					Total					Pts
			W	D	L	F	A	W	D	L	F	A	W	D	L	F	A	
1	**FC Midtjylland**	33	16	0	1	41	12	6	5	5	23	22	22	5	6	64	34	71
2	FC København	33	13	2	2	25	11	7	5	4	15	11	20	7	6	40	22	67
3	Brøndby IF	33	10	4	3	26	9	6	3	7	17	20	16	7	10	43	29	55
4	Randers FC	33	7	5	4	20	13	7	5	5	19	15	14	10	9	39	28	52
5	Aalborg BK	33	9	3	5	22	14	4	6	6	17	17	13	9	11	39	31	48
6	FC Nordsjælland	33	10	1	6	28	23	3	4	9	11	21	13	5	15	39	44	44
7	Hobro IK	33	6	6	4	21	18	5	4	8	19	29	11	10	12	40	47	43
8	Esbjerg fB	33	5	7	5	25	21	5	3	8	22	24	10	10	13	47	45	40
9	Odense BK	33	5	5	6	16	17	6	2	9	19	26	11	7	15	35	43	40
10	SønderjyskE	33	2	8	6	13	22	5	8	4	22	22	7	16	10	35	44	37
11	FC Vestsjælland	33	6	4	6	19	18	3	2	12	12	34	9	6	18	31	52	33
12	Silkeborg IF	33	0	5	11	13	31	2	3	12	13	28	2	8	23	26	59	14

European qualification 2015/16

 Champion: FC Midtjylland (second qualifying round)

 Cup winner: FC København (second qualifying round)
Brøndby IF (first qualifying round)
Randers FC (first qualifying round)

Top scorer	Martin Pusic (Esbjerg/Midtjylland), 17 goals
Relegated clubs	Silkeborg IF, FC Vestsjælland
Promoted clubs	Viborg FF, AGF Aarhus
Cup final	FC København 3-2 FC Vestsjælland (aet)

Team of the season
(4-4-2)

Coach: Riddersholm (Midtjylland)

Player of the season

Jakob Poulsen
(FC Midtjylland)

After an ill-fated 18-month stay in France with AS Monaco FC, Poulsen's first full season back at former club Midtjylland ended in triumph as he won the first major honour of his career in helping the Jutland side to the 2014/15 Superliga title. A key member of Glen Riddersholm's team, bringing control and experience as well as set-piece know-how, the do-it-all midfielder regained his place in the Danish national team, which he marked with a crucial goal in a UEFA EURO 2016 qualifying win against Serbia.

Newcomer of the season

Pione Sisto
(FC Midtjylland)

A brilliant run of form in the first half of the season resulted in Sisto being voted 2014 Danish players' player of the year, and although the young, Uganda-born winger missed much of the spring campaign through injury, he returned to produce a man-of-the-match display in the 2-0 win at home to FC København that all but secured Midtjylland's Superliga triumph. His season ended with a call-up by Morten Olsen and a place in Denmark's 2015 UEFA European Under-21 Championship squad.

NATIONAL TEAM

International honours
UEFA European Championship (1) 1992

International tournament appearances
FIFA World Cup (4) 1986 (2nd round), 1998 (qtr-finals), 2002 (2nd round), 2010
UEFA European Championship (8) 1964 (4th), 1984 (semi-finals), 1988, 1992 (Winners), 1996, 2000, 2004 (qtr-finals), 2012

Top five all-time caps
Peter Schmeichel (129); Dennis Rommedahl (126); Jon Dahl Tomasson (112); Thomas Helveg (109); Michael Laudrup (104)

Top five all-time goals
Poul "Tist" Nielsen & Jon Dahl Tomasson (52); Pauli Jørgensen (44); Ole Madsen (42); Preben Elkjær (38)

Results 2014/15

Date	Opponent		Venue		Score	Scorers
03/09/14	Turkey	H	Odense	L	1-2	Agger (35p)
07/09/14	Armenia (ECQ)	H	Copenhagen	W	2-1	Højbjerg (65), Kahlenberg (80)
11/10/14	Albania (ECQ)	A	Elbasan	D	1-1	Vibe (81)
14/10/14	Portugal (ECQ)	H	Copenhagen	L	0-1	
14/11/14	Serbia (ECQ)	A	Belgrade	W	3-1	Bendtner (60, 85), Kjær (62)
18/11/14	Romania	A	Bucharest	L	0-2	
25/03/15	United States	H	Aarhus	W	3-2	Bendtner (33, 83, 90)
29/03/15	France	A	Saint-Etienne	L	0-2	
08/06/15	Montenegro	H	Viborg	W	2-1	Eriksen (71), Fischer (86p)
13/06/15	Serbia (ECQ)	H	Copenhagen	W	2-0	Y Poulsen (13), J Poulsen (87)

Appearances 2014/15

Coach: Morten Olsen	14/08/49		Tur	ARM	ALB	POR	SRB	Rou	Usa	Fra	Mne	SRB	Caps	Goals
Kasper Schmeichel	05/11/86	Leicester (ENG)	G	G	G	G	G			G	G	G	12	-
Peter Ankersen	22/09/90	Salzburg (AUT)	D84	D	D71		D70						10	-
Daniel Agger	12/12/84	Brøndby	D46			D						D	67	12
Andreas Bjelland	11/07/88	Twente (NED)	D	D	D		D	D			D		21	2
Nicolai Boilesen	16/02/92	Ajax (NED)	D46	D	D	D58	D	D79	D53	D46			15	1
Pierre Højbjerg	05/08/95	Bayern (GER)/Augsburg (GER)	M	M	M79	M					M63	M	7	1
William Kvist Jørgensen	24/02/85	Wigan (ENG)	M	M74	M	M	M	M70	M46	M88	M	M77	57	2
Thomas Kahlenberg	20/03/83	Brøndby	M63	s74	s79	s84	M88						46	5
Lasse Schöne	27/05/86	Ajax (NED)	A	A56					s78	s83			22	3
Nicklas Bendtner	16/01/88	Wolfsburg (GER)	A63	A	A	A	A88	A	A	A	A46	A	68	29
Christian Eriksen	14/02/92	Tottenham (ENG)	A46	A	A	A84	A		A	A83	A81	A	53	6
Leon Andreasen	23/04/83	Hannover (GER)	s46										20	3
Jonas Knudsen	16/09/92	Esbjerg	s46										2	-
Kasper Kusk	10/11/91	Twente (NED)	s46										8	-
Andreas Cornelius	16/03/93	København	s63										8	1
Lasse Vibe	22/02/87	Göteborg (SWE)	s63	s56	s46	A46	A	A73	A74	A57		s73	9	1
Daniel Wass	31/05/89	Évian (FRA)	s84						D	M46			13	-
Simon Kjær	26/03/89	LOSC (FRA)		D57	D	D	D	D46	D	D	D63	D	50	2
Michael Krohn-Dehli	06/06/83	Celta (ESP)		M	M	M	M		M78	M	M73	M61	51	6
Jores Okore	11/08/92	Aston Villa (ENG)		s57									8	-
Yussuf Poulsen	15/06/94	RB Leipzig (GER)			A46		s88	s73			A	A73	5	1
Uffe Bech	13/01/93	Nordsjælland			s71	s46	s46						3	-
Lars Jacobsen	20/09/79	Guingamp (FRA)				D	s70	D		D	D	D	75	1
Simon Busk Poulsen	07/10/84	AZ (NED)				s58		s79	s53	s46	D73	D	31	-
Rasmus Würtz	18/09/83	AaB					s88	s27					12	-
Stephan Andersen	26/11/81	København						G	G				30	-
Anders Christiansen	08/06/90	Nordsjælland/Chievo (ITA)						M46	s46	s46			3	-
Nicolaj Thomsen	08/05/93	AaB						M					1	-
Lucas Andersen	13/09/94	Ajax (NED)							A27		s81		2	-
Jannik Vestergaard	03/08/92	Hoffenheim (GER)/Bremen (GER)						s46			s63		3	-
Kian Hansen	03/03/89	Nantes (FRA)						s70		s77			2	-
Erik Sviatchenko	04/10/91	Midtjylland							D	D77			2	-
Jakob Poulsen	07/07/83	Midtjylland							M46			s61	32	2
Thomas Delaney	03/09/91	København							s46	s88			3	-
Martin Braithwaite	05/06/91	Toulouse (FRA)							s74				8	1
Nicolai Jørgensen	15/01/91	København								s57			8	-
Morten "Duncan" Rasmussen	31/01/85	Midtjylland									s46		10	3
Andreas Christensen	10/04/96	Chelsea (ENG)									s63	s77	2	-
Viktor Fischer	09/06/94	Ajax (NED)									s73		7	1
Riza Durmisi	08/01/94	Brøndby									s73		1	-

Aalborg BK

CHAMPIONS
LEAGUE

Third qualifying round - GNK Dinamo Zagreb (CRO)
H 0-1
Larsen, Kristensen, Petersen, Enevoldsen (Helenius 72), Augustinussen, Wichmann, Jacobsen, Risgård (Thomsen 46), Thelander, Blåbjerg, Spalvis (Bruhn 73). Coach: Kent Nielsen (DEN)
A 2-0 *Jacobsen (36, 85)*
Larsen, Kristensen, Petersen, Würtz (Augustinussen 89), Wichmann (Enevoldsen 57), Jacobsen, Risgård, Thomsen, Thelander, Blåbjerg, Spalvis (Helenius 62). Coach: Kent Nielsen (DEN)

Play-offs - APOEL FC (CYP)
H 1-1 *Thomsen (16)*
Larsen, Kristensen (V Ahlmann 76), Petersen, Würtz, Helenius (Dalsgaard 76), Wichmann, Jacobsen, Risgård, Thomsen (Thrane 86), Thelander, Blåbjerg. Coach: Kent Nielsen (DEN)
A 0-4
Larsen, Kristensen (Dalsgaard 46), Petersen, Enevoldsen, Würtz, Jacobsen, Risgård, Thomsen, Børsting (Helenius 46), Thelander, Blåbjerg (Gorter 62). Coach: Kent Nielsen (DEN)

EUROPA
LEAGUE

Group J
Match 1 - FC Steaua Bucureşti (ROU)
A 0-6
Larsen, Petersen, Gorter, Frederiksen 15), Enevoldsen (Christensen 59), Würtz, Wichmann, Jacobsen (Helenius 63), Dalsgaard, Risgård, Thomsen, Thelander. Coach: Kent Nielsen (DEN)
Red card: Larsen 57
Match 2 - Rio Ave FC (POR)
H 1-0 *Helenius (46)*
Christensen, Petersen, Gorter, Würtz, Helenius (Augustinussen 78), Jacobsen (Enevoldsen 90+3), Dalsgaard, Risgård, Thomsen, Børsting (Bruhn 66), Thelander. Coach: Kent Nielsen (DEN)
Match 3 - FC Dynamo Kyiv (UKR)
H 3-0 *Enevoldsen (11), Thomsen (39, 90+1)*
Larsen, Petersen, Gorter, Enevoldsen (Frederiksen 86), Würtz (Augustinussen 83), Helenius (Jacobsen 70), Dalsgaard, Risgård, Thomsen, Thelander, Bruhn. Coach: Kent Nielsen (DEN)
Match 4 - FC Dynamo Kyiv (UKR)
A 0-2
Larsen, Petersen, Gorter, Enevoldsen (Augustinussen 66), Würtz (V Ahlmann 83), Helenius, Dalsgaard, Risgård, Thomsen, Thelander, Bruhn (Frederiksen 83). Coach: Kent Nielsen (DEN)
Match 5 - FC Steaua Bucureşti (ROU)
H 1-0 *Enevoldsen (72)*
Larsen, Petersen, Gorter, Enevoldsen (Jacobsen 74), Helenius (Augustinussen 88), Dalsgaard, Risgård, Thomsen, Thelander, Bruhn (Wichmann 77). Coach: Kent Nielsen (DEN)
Match 6 - Rio Ave FC (POR)
A 0-2
Larsen, Petersen, Gorter (Blåbjerg 11), Enevoldsen, Würtz, Helenius, Dalsgaard, Risgård (Frederiksen 74), Thomsen, Thelander, Bruhn (Jacobsen 63). Coach: Kent Nielsen (DEN)

Round of 32 - Club Brugge KV (BEL)
H 1-3 *Helenius (71p)*
Larsen, Petersen, Würtz, Helenius, Jacobsen (Enevoldsen 62), Dalsgaard, Thomsen, Børsting (Kristensen 80), Thelander, Bruhn (Augustinussen 46), Blåbjerg. Coach: Kent Nielsen (DEN)
A 0-3
Larsen, Kristensen, Petersen, Enevoldsen (Jacobsen 63), Würtz (Augustinussen 58), Helenius, Dalsgaard (Thrane 70), Risgård, Thomsen, Thelander, Bruhn. Coach: Kent Nielsen (DEN)

FC København

CHAMPIONS
LEAGUE

Third qualifying round - FC Dnipro Dnipropetrovsk (UKR)
A 0-0
Andersen, Høgli, Bengtsson, Nilsson, Delaney, Kadrii (Remmer 71), N Jørgensen (De Ridder 87), Cornelius, Amartey, M Jørgensen, Amankwaa (Toutouh 78). Coach: Ståle Solbakken (NOR)
H 2-0 *Cornelius (36), Kadrii (52)*
Andersen, Høgli, Bengtsson, Nilsson, Delaney (Antonsson 90), Kadrii (Toutouh 70), N Jørgensen, Cornelius, Amartey, M Jørgensen, Amankwaa. Coach: Ståle Solbakken (NOR)

Play-offs - Bayer 04 Leverkusen (GER)
H 2-3 *M Jørgensen (9), Amartey (13)*
Andersen, Høgli, Bengtsson, Nilsson, Claudemir (De Ridder 53), Delaney, Kadrii, Cornelius, Amartey, M Jørgensen, Amankwaa. Coach: Ståle Solbakken (NOR)
A 0-4
Andersen, Høgli, Bengtsson, Claudemir, Delaney, Kadrii, Cornelius (De Ridder 46), Antonsson, Toutouh (Gíslason 58), M Jørgensen, Amankwaa (Pourie 75). Coach: Ståle Solbakken (NOR)

EUROPA
LEAGUE

Group B
Match 1 - HJK Helsinki (FIN)
H 2-0 *N Jørgensen (68, 81)*
Andersen, Bengtsson, Nilsson (Antonsson 82), Claudemir, Kadrii (N Jørgensen 58), Cornelius, Kacaniklic, Amartey, Gíslason (Amankwaa 58), Toutouh, M Jørgensen. Coach: Ståle Solbakken (NOR)
Match 2 - Torino FC (ITA)
A 0-1
Andersen, Høgli, Bengtsson, Claudemir (Delaney 82), Kadrii (N Jørgensen 58), Cornelius, Antonsson, Amartey, Gíslason (Kacaniklic 68), Toutouh, M Jørgensen. Coach: Ståle Solbakken (NOR)
Match 3 - Club Brugge KV (BEL)
A 1-1 *Amartey (89)*
Andersen, Høgli, Bengtsson, Delaney, N Jørgensen (De Ridder 68), Cornelius, Antonsson, Kacaniklic (Gíslason 64), Amartey, M Jørgensen, Amankwaa (Claudemir 81). Coach: Ståle Solbakken (NOR)
Match 4 - Club Brugge KV (BEL)
H 0-4
Andersen, Høgli, Bengtsson (Toutouh 62), Claudemir, N Jørgensen (Amankwaa 34), Antonsson, Kacaniklic, Amartey (Delaney 46), Gíslason, De Ridder, M Jørgensen. Coach: Ståle Solbakken (NOR)

Match 5 - HJK Helsinki (FIN)
A 1-2 *Nilsson (90)*
Andersen, Høgli (Amankwaa 71), Bengtsson, Nilsson, Delaney (Toutouh 71), Cornelius, Antonsson, Kacaniklic (N Jørgensen 46), Amartey, Gíslason, De Ridder. Coach: Ståle Solbakken (NOR)
Match 6 - Torino FC (ITA)
H 1-5 *Amartey (6)*
Andersen, Høgli, Claudemir (Lindbjerg 77), Delaney, N Jørgensen (Felfel 84), Antonsson, Amartey, De Ridder (Olsen 87), Toutouh, M Jørgensen, Amankwaa. Coach: Ståle Solbakken (NOR)
Red cards: Antonsson 30, M Jørgensen 40

FC Midtjylland

EUROPA
LEAGUE

Play-offs - Panathinaikos FC (GRE)
A 1-4 *Lauridsen (13)*
Haugaard, Poulsen, Rasmussen (Onuachu 22; Janssen 85), Lauridsen, Sviatchenko, Dickoh, Banggaard, Sisto, Hassan (J Larsen 60), Uzochukwu, Igboun. Coach: Glen Riddersholm (DEN)
Red card: Sviatchenko 58
H 1-2 *Igboun (73p)*
Haugaard, Sparv (Uzochukwu 77), J Larsen, Poulsen, Andersson (Igboun 59), Lauridsen, M Larsen (Onuachu 46), Banggaard, Sisto, Rømer, Hassan. Coach: Glen Riddersholm (DEN)

Brøndby IF

EUROPA
LEAGUE

Third qualifying round - Club Brugge KV (BEL)
A 0-3
Hradecky, Almebäck, Semb Berge, Albrechtsen, Ørnskov (Nørgaard 86), Kahlenberg, Makienok, Thygesen (Rashani 76), Durmisi, Phiri, Hasani (Holst 86). Coach: Thomas Frank (DEN)
H 0-2
Hradecky, Semb Berge (Albrechtsen 46), Ørnskov, Kahlenberg (Núñez 74), Szymanowski, Makienok, Holst, Rashani (Thygesen 62), Durmisi, Phiri, Dumic. Coach: Thomas Frank (DEN)

DOMESTIC LEAGUE CLUB-BY-CLUB

Esbjerg fB

EUROPA LEAGUE

Second qualifying round - FC Kairat Almaty (KAZ)
A 1-1 *Fellah (90+2)*
Dúbravka, Jakobsen, Gomes (Askou 81), Lekven, Andersen, Van Buren (Nielsen 84), Lyng (Vestergaard 66), Laursen, Ankersen, Lucena, Fellah. Coach: Niels Frederiksen (DEN)
H 1-0 *Ankersen (38)*
Dúbravka, Jakobsen, Gomes, Bergvold (Brinch 67), Lekven, Andersen, Laursen, Nielsen (Rasmussen 72), Ankersen, Fellah, Pusic (Lyng 62). Coach: Niels Frederiksen (DEN)

Third qualifying round - Ruch Chorzów (POL)
A 0-0
Dúbravka, Jakobsen, Stenderup (Gomes 79), Andersen (Ankersen 63), Van Buren, Laursen, Nielsen, Fellah, J Andreasen (Lekven 46), Pusic, Askou. Coach: Niels Frederiksen (DEN)
H 2-2 *Nielsen (29), Pusic (85)*
Dúbravka, Jakobsen, Stenderup (Laursen 72), Gomes, Lekven, Van Buren, Nielsen (Andersen 65), Ankersen, Fellah (Rasmussen 64), Knudsen, Pusic. Coach: Niels Frederiksen (DEN)

Aalborg BK

1885 • Nordjyske Arena (13,800) • fodbold.aabsport.dk
Major honours
Danish League (4) 1995, 1999, 2008, 2014; Danish Cup (3) 1966, 1970, 2014
Coach: Kent Nielsen

2014

19/07	a	SønderjyskE	D	0-0	
26/07	h	Midtjylland	W	2-0	Jacobsen, Helenius (p)
02/08	a	OB	D	1-1	Kristensen
09/08	h	Nordsjælland	L	1-2	Helenius
16/08	h	Esbjerg	D	1-1	Petersen
31/08	a	Silkeborg	D	2-2	Jacobsen 2
13/09	h	København	W	1-0	Helenius (p)
22/09	a	Vestsjælland	L	0-1	
26/09	h	Randers	D	0-0	
05/10	a	Brøndby	L	1-2	Frederiksen
17/10	h	Hobro	D	1-1	Bruhn
27/10	a	Nordsjælland	W	1-0	og (Gregor)
03/11	a	Silkeborg	W	2-0	Jacobsen, Dalsgaard
09/11	h	Vestsjælland	W	2-0	Risgård, Wichmann
23/11	a	Midtjylland	L	0-2	
30/11	h	København	L	0-1	
06/12	h	OB	D	1-1	Enevoldsen
2015					
22/02	h	Brøndby	W	1-0	Jacobsen
02/03	a	Esbjerg	W	3-1	Jacobsen, Børsting, Enevoldsen
08/03	h	Randers	W	2-1	Petersen, Enevoldsen
16/03	a	Hobro	L	0-1	
22/03	h	SønderjyskE	L	1-4	Risgård
06/04	a	Randers	D	1-1	Risgård
12/04	h	Midtjylland	L	1-2	Enevoldsen
18/04	a	Vestsjælland	L	1-2	Helenius
26/04	a	SønderjyskE	W	3-0	Jacobsen 2, Helenius
01/05	h	Hobro	W	5-0	Helenius 3 (1p), Jacobsen, og (Justesen)
10/05	a	Brøndby	D	1-1	og (Nørgaard)
15/05	h	OB	L	0-2	
20/05	a	København	L	0-1	
26/05	h	Esbjerg	W	1-0	Bruhn
31/05	a	Silkeborg	W	2-1	Jacobsen, Jönsson
07/06	h	Nordsjælland	W	1-0	Pedersen

No	Name	Nat	DoB	Pos	Aps	(s)	Gls
3	Jakob Ahlmann		18/01/91	D	2		
28	Viktor Ahlmann		03/01/95	A	1	(6)	
9	Thomas Augustinussen		20/03/81	M	9	(13)	
14	Andreas Blomqvist	SWE	05/05/92	M		(1)	
31	Jakob Blåbjerg		11/01/95	D	17	(1)	
30	Andreas Bruhn		17/02/94	M	10	(12)	2
25	Frederik Børsting		13/02/95	M	16	(3)	1
22	Carsten Christensen		28/08/86	G	1		
20	Henrik Dalsgaard		27/07/89	D	25	(1)	1
7	Thomas Enevoldsen		27/07/87	M	20	(9)	4
19	Søren Frederiksen		08/07/89	A	3	(3)	1
6	Donny Gorter	NED	15/06/88	D	9		
11	Nicklas Helenius		08/05/91	A	20	(12)	8
18	Anders Jacobsen		27/10/89	A	26	(5)	10
10	Rasmus Jönsson	SWE	27/01/90	A	10	(5)	1
2	Patrick Kristensen		28/04/87	D	20	(1)	1
1	Nicolai Larsen		09/03/91	G	32		
32	Kasper Pedersen		13/01/93	D	16	(2)	1
5	Kenneth Emil Petersen		15/01/85	D	27		2
21	Kasper Risgård		04/01/83	M	24	(3)	3
33	Lukas Spalvis	LTU	27/07/94	A	3	(3)	
15	Gilli Sørensen	FRO	11/08/92	A	1	(8)	
26	Rasmus Thelander		09/07/91	D	16		
23	Nicolaj Thomsen		08/05/93	M	27	(2)	
16	Mathias Thrane		04/09/93	M		(3)	
14	Mathias Wichmann		06/08/91	M	5	(6)	1
8	Rasmus Würtz		18/09/83	M	23		

Brøndby IF

1964 • Brøndby Stadion (28,000) • brondby.com
Major honours
Danish League (10) 1985, 1987, 1988, 1990, 1991, 1996, 1997, 1998, 2002, 2005; Danish Cup (6) 1989, 1994, 1998, 2003, 2005, 2008
Coach: Thomas Frank

2014

20/07	a	Midtjylland	L	1-3	Makienok
28/07	h	Silkeborg	W	2-0	Núñez, Phiri
03/08	a	Hobro	L	0-2	
10/08	h	OB	D	1-1	Rashani
17/08	h	SønderjyskE	W	2-0	Makienok 2
31/08	a	Nordsjælland	W	3-0	Elmander, Semb Berge, Kahlenberg
14/09	h	Randers	L	0-2	
21/09	a	København	L	0-1	
28/09	a	Esbjerg	D	2-2	Pukki, Fridjónsson
05/10	h	AaB	W	2-1	Pukki 2
19/10	h	Vestsjælland	W	5-0	Kahlenberg, Pukki, Hjulsager, Durmisi, Rashani
26/10	a	Esbjerg	D	0-0	
02/11	h	Randers	W	1-0	Pukki
09/11	a	Hobro	L	0-3	
23/11	h	SønderjyskE	W	1-0	Hjulsager
30/11	a	Nordsjælland	L	0-2	
07/12	h	Silkeborg	W	1-0	Hasani
2015					
22/02	h	AaB	L	0-1	
01/03	h	Midtjylland	D	1-1	Hasani
08/03	a	København	L	1-3	Núñez
15/03	h	OB	W	2-0	Larsson, Pukki
22/03	h	Vestsjælland	W	1-0	Nørgaard
06/04	a	København	D	0-0	
12/04	a	SønderjyskE	W	1-0	Núñez
19/04	h	Hobro	L	0-1	
26/04	h	Vestsjælland	W	4-0	Nørgaard 2, Larsson, Laursen
03/05	a	OB	W	2-0	Durmisi, Hasani
10/05	h	AaB	D	1-1	Larsson
17/05	a	Silkeborg	W	2-0	Pukki, Hjulsager
21/05	h	Nordsjælland	W	3-1	og (Petry), Pukki, Hjulsager
25/05	a	Midtjylland	W	3-2	Pukki, Szymanowski, Agger
31/05	a	Randers	D	1-1	Durmisi
07/06	h	Esbjerg	L	0-1	

No	Name	Nat	DoB	Pos	Aps	(s)	Gls
22	Daniel Agger		12/12/84	D	19		1
5	Martin Albrechtsen		31/03/80	D	8	(7)	
23	Patrick da Silva		23/10/94	D	12	(4)	
20	Dario Dumic		30/01/92	D	25		
17	Riza Durmisi		08/01/94	D	23	(5)	3
11	Johan Elmander	SWE	27/05/81	A	13	(7)	1
25	Hólmbert Aron Fridjónsson	ISL	19/04/93	A	4	(7)	1
24	Ferhan Hasani	MKD	18/06/90	M	13	(3)	3
21	Andrew Hjulsager		15/01/95	M	17	(3)	4
12	Frederik Holst		24/09/94	D	17	(11)	
1	Lukas Hradecky	FIN	24/11/89	G	33		
7	Thomas Kahlenberg		20/03/83	M	20	(1)	2
13	Johan Larsson	SWE	05/05/90	D	16		3
29	Nikolai Laursen		19/02/98	A		(3)	1
9	Simon Makienok		21/11/90	A	5		3
10	José Ariel Núñez	PAR	12/09/88	A	10	(5)	3
19	Christian Nørgaard		10/03/94	M	17	(3)	3
18	Lebogang Phiri	RSA	09/11/94	M	20	(10)	1
9	Teemu Pukki	FIN	29/03/90	A	27		9
14	Elbasan Rashani	NOR	09/05/93	M	10	(4)	2
3	Fredrik Semb Berge	NOR	06/02/90	D	7		
8	Alexander Szymanowski	ARG	13/10/88	M	15	(9)	1
15	Mikkel Thygesen		22/10/84	M	3	(10)	
6	Martin Ørnskov		10/10/85	M	29	(1)	

 **DENMARK**

Esbjerg fB

1924 • Blue Water Arena (16,942) • efb.dk
Major honours
Danish League (5) 1961, 1962, 1963, 1965, 1979;
Danish Cup (3) 1964, 1976, 2013
Coach: Niels Frederiksen

2014
21/07	h Randers	L	0-1	
27/07	h SønderjyskE	D	1-1	*Pusic*
03/08	a Nordsjælland	L	2-3	*Pusic, Ankersen*
11/08	h Silkeborg	D	0-0	
16/08	a AaB	D	1-1	*Pusic*
31/08	a Midtjylland	L	0-2	
14/09	h Vestsjælland	W	3-0	*Söder 2, Pusic*
20/09	a Hobro	D	1-1	*Pusic*
28/09	h Brøndby	D	2-2	*Andreasen, Lekven*
05/10	a København	L	1-2	*Pusic*
20/10	h OB	W	2-0	*Ankersen (p), Söder*
26/10	h Brøndby	D	0-0	
01/11	a Vestsjælland	W	4-1	*Fellah, Pusic, Gomes, Vestergaard*
08/11	a Randers	L	2-3	*Pusic 2*
22/11	h Hobro	W	4-2	*Ankersen 3 (1p), Knudsen*
28/11	h SønderjyskE	D	0-0	
08/12	a Nordsjælland	D	0-0	

2015
21/02	a Silkeborg	W	3-1	*Rise 2, Söder*
02/03	h AaB	L	1-3	*Knudsen*
08/03	a Midtjylland	L	0-3	
15/03	h København	L	0-1	
20/03	a OB	W	2-0	*Larsson, Van Buren*
05/04	h Midtjylland	D	3-3	*Lyng, Laursen, Friberg*
10/04	a Hobro	L	1-3	*Larsson*
20/04	h Randers	D	0-0	
24/04	h OB	L	0-2	
03/05	a København	L	1-2	*og (Høgli)*
09/05	h Silkeborg	W	5-2	*Fellah, Van Buren 2, Nielsen, Mensah*
18/05	a Nordsjælland	W	3-1	*Lyng, Andreasen (p), Vestergaard*
21/05	h SønderjyskE	L	2-3	*Vestergaard 2*
26/05	a AaB	L	0-1	
31/05	h Vestsjælland	W	2-1	*Van Buren 2*
07/06	a Brøndby	W	1-0	*Fellah*

No	Name	Nat	DoB	Pos	Aps	(s)	Gls
19	Michael Almebäck	SWE	04/04/88	D	7	(2)	
8	Jeppe Andersen		06/12/92	M	18	(1)	
20	Hans Henrik Andreasen		10/01/79	M	17	(10)	2
19	Jakob Ankersen		22/09/90	M	17		5
33	Jens Berthel Askou		19/08/82	D		(2)	
5	Martin Bergvold		20/02/84	M		(1)	
25	Jeppe Brinch		30/04/95	D		(2)	
30	Martin Dúbravka	SVK	15/01/89	G	33		
22	Mohammed Fellah	NOR	24/05/89	M	17	(8)	3
18	Erik Friberg	SWE	10/02/86	M	12	(1)	1
4	Eddi Gomes		17/11/88	D	12	(1)	1
2	Michael Jakobsen		02/01/86	D	30		
23	Jonas Knudsen		16/09/92	D	27	(1)	2
32	Daniel Larsson	SWE	25/01/87	A	12	(2)	2
15	Ryan Laursen		14/04/92	D	32		1
6	Magnus Lekven	NOR	13/01/88	M	27		1
21	Jerry Lucena	PHI	11/08/80	M	1	(1)	
10	Emil Lyng		03/08/89	M	14	(4)	2
33	Kevin Mensah		15/05/91	M	5	(4)	1
17	Casper Nielsen		29/04/94	M	11	(15)	1
32	Martin Pusic	AUT	24/10/87	A	15	(2)	9
31	Jesper Rasmussen		04/01/92	M		(4)	
11	Lasse Rise		09/06/86	M	6	(9)	2
3	Daniel Stenderup		31/05/89	D	24	(1)	
27	Robin Söder	SWE	01/04/91	A	18	(3)	4
9	Mick van Buren	NED	24/08/92	A	6	(11)	5
7	Mikkel Vestergaard		22/11/92	A	2	(11)	4

Hobro IK

1913 • DS Arena (7,500) • hikfodbold.dk
Coach: Jonas Dal Andersen

2014
20/07	a OB	W	2-1	*Hvilsom 2*
27/07	a Randers	L	1-2	*Thomsen*
03/08	h Brøndby	W	2-0	*Thomsen (p), Hvilsom*
10/08	a København	W	3-0	*Antipas, Justesen, Hvilsom*
18/08	h Nordsjælland	D	0-0	
01/09	h Vestsjælland	W	3-1	*Antipas, Hvilsom, Thomsen*
15/09	a SønderjyskE	D	1-1	*Hvilsom*
20/09	h Esbjerg	D	1-1	*Thomsen*
27/09	a Silkeborg	D	2-2	*Hvilsom, Egholm*
03/10	h Midtjylland	L	1-5	*Christensen*
17/10	a AaB	D	1-1	*Antipas*
26/10	h København	L	0-2	
02/11	a OB	L	1-3	*og (Toppel)*
09/11	h Brøndby	W	3-0	*Berggreen 2, Hvilsom*
22/11	a Esbjerg	L	2-4	*Thomsen, Hvilsom*
30/11	h Randers	L	0-1	
07/12	a Vestsjælland	D	1-1	*Berggreen*

2015
22/02	h SønderjyskE	L	0-1	
28/02	h Nordsjælland	W	1-0	*Egholm*
08/03	a Silkeborg	W	1-0	*Thygesen*
16/03	h AaB	W	1-0	*Hvilsom*
21/03	a Midtjylland	L	0-3	
05/04	h Silkeborg	D	2-2	*Hvilsom 2*
10/04	h Esbjerg	W	3-1	*Antipas 2, Hvilsom*
19/04	a Brøndby	W	1-0	*Jessen*
27/04	h Midtjylland	D	0-0	
01/05	a AaB	L	0-5	
10/05	h SønderjyskE	D	2-2	*Hvilsom 2*
17/05	h Vestsjælland	L	0-1	
21/05	a Randers	W	1-0	*Hvilsom*
25/05	a Nordsjælland	L	2-4	*Mikkelsen 2*
31/05	h OB	D	2-2	*Thomsen, T Hansen*
07/06	a København	L	0-1	

No	Name	Nat	DoB	Pos	Aps	(s)	Gls
80	Quincy Antipas	ZIM	20/04/84	A	24	(2)	5
90	Mikkel Beckmann		24/10/83	A	5	(4)	
9	Emil Berggreen		10/05/93	A	17		3
20	Mathias Bersang		24/11/91	M	7	(11)	
3	Jesper Bøge		22/02/90	D	32		
5	Rasmus Lynge Christensen		12/08/91	M	8	(14)	1
12	Jonas Damborg		17/04/86	M	26		
2	Anders Egholm		15/05/83	D	29		2
7	Rasmus Hansen		12/04/86	M		(4)	
14	Thomas Hansen		18/01/83	D	9	(11)	1
17	Rune Hastrup		16/10/91	D	2	(7)	
8	Mads Hvilsom		23/08/92	A	33		16
16	Dennis Høegh		21/02/89	A	1	(6)	
7	Rasmus Ingeman		04/04/83	D	4	(2)	
1	Mads Jessen		14/10/89	M	10	(11)	1
13	Mads Justesen		31/12/82	D	32		1
26	Martin Mikkelsen		29/04/86	M	23	(6)	2
24	Ruben Nygaard		25/05/86	M		(3)	
1	Jesper Rask		18/07/88	G	33		
5	Mathias Schlie		31/01/88	M		(2)	
10	Martin Thomsen		06/08/82	M	33		6
15	Mikkel Thygesen		22/10/84	M	6	(3)	1
4	Jacob Tjørnelund		31/12/91	D	29		
23	Christoffer Østergaard		22/05/93	D		(5)	

FC København

1992 • Telia Parken (38,065) • fck.dk
Major honours
Danish League (10) 1993, 2001, 2003, 2004, 2006, 2007, 2009, 2010, 2011, 2013; Danish Cup (6) 1995, 1997, 2004, 2009, 2012, 2015
Coach: Ståle Solbakken (NOR)

2014
20/07	a Silkeborg	D	0-0	
26/07	h Nordsjælland	W	2-1	*M Jørgensen, N Jørgensen*
02/08	a Vestsjælland	D	2-2	*Cornelius 2 (1p)*
10/08	h Hobro	L	0-3	
15/08	h Midtjylland	L	1-2	*Cornelius (p)*
31/08	a OB	W	1-0	*Kadrii*
13/09	a AaB	L	0-1	
21/09	h Brøndby	W	1-0	*Kadrii*
27/09	a SønderjyskE	D	1-1	*Kacaniklic*
05/10	h Esbjerg	W	2-1	*Claudemir, Cornelius*
19/10	h Randers	W	1-0	*Kacaniklic (p)*
26/10	a Hobro	W	2-0	*N Jørgensen, Toutouh*
02/11	a SønderjyskE	D	1-1	*N Jørgensen*
09/11	a Nordsjælland	D	0-0	
22/11	h Silkeborg	W	1-0	*N Jørgensen*
30/11	a AaB	W	1-0	*Cornelius*
07/12	h Midtjylland	W	3-0	*og (J Larsen), Amankwaa, N Jørgensen*

2015
22/02	h Vestsjælland	W	2-0	*Høgli, Augustinsson*
01/03	a OB	L	0-1	
08/03	h Brøndby	W	3-1	*Amartey, N Jørgensen, Delaney*
15/03	a Esbjerg	W	1-0	*Cornelius*
22/03	h Randers	D	1-1	*N Jørgensen*
06/04	a Brøndby	D	0-0	
13/04	a Silkeborg	W	4-0	*Poulsen, Toutouh, Sigurdarson, De Ridder*
19/04	h Nordsjælland	W	2-0	*N Jørgensen 2 (1p)*
26/04	a Randers	L	0-3	
03/05	h Esbjerg	W	2-1	*Amartey, N Jørgensen*
11/05	a Vestsjælland	W	1-0	*Delaney*
17/05	a Midtjylland	L	0-2	
20/05	h AaB	W	1-0	*Gíslason*
25/05	h OB	W	1-0	*Olsen*
31/05	a SønderjyskE	W	2-1	*De Ridder, Olsen*
07/06	h Hobro	W	1-0	*Amartey*

No	Name	Nat	DoB	Pos	Aps	(s)	Gls
32	Danny Amankwaa		30/01/94	M	18	(5)	1
18	Daniel Amartey	GHA	21/12/94	M	27	(2)	3
1	Stephan Andersen		26/11/81	G	33		
15	Mikael Antonsson	SWE	31/05/81	D	23		
3	Ludwig Augustinsson	SWE	21/04/94	D	15		1
3	Pierre Bengtsson	SWE	12/04/88	D	16		
3	Claudemir	BRA	27/03/88	M	10	(4)	1
11	Andreas Cornelius		16/03/93	A	22		6
22	Steve De Ridder	BEL	25/02/87	A	15	(8)	2
8	Thomas Delaney		03/09/91	M	24	(3)	2
33	Yones Felfel		24/11/95	A	1	(5)	
16	Kevin Foley	IRL	01/11/84	D		(4)	
19	Rúrik Gíslason	ISL	25/02/88	M	19	(6)	1
2	Tom Høgli	NOR	24/02/84	D	28	(3)	1
25	Mathias "Zanka" Jørgensen		23/04/90	D	27	(2)	1
10	Nicolai Jørgensen		15/01/91	M	22	(3)	10
17	Alex Kacaniklic	SWE	13/08/91	A	7		2
9	Bashkim Kadrii		09/07/91	M	4	(4)	2
40	Marcus Mathisen		27/02/96	D		(1)	
7	Franco Mussis	ARG	19/04/92	M		(1)	
4	Per Nilsson	SWE	15/09/82	D	13	(4)	
36	Brandur H Olsen	FRO	19/12/95	M	1	(6)	2
29	Christian Poulsen		28/02/80	M	9	(7)	1
23	Marvin Pourie	GER	08/01/91	A	2	(2)	
20	Christoffer Remmer		16/01/93	D	7	(3)	
14	Björn Bergmann Sigurdarson	ISL	26/02/91	A	10	(4)	1
24	Youssef Toutouh		06/10/92	A	10	(11)	2
35	Mikkel Wohlgemuth		04/06/95	M		(1)	

FC Midtjylland

1999 • MCH Arena (11,809) • fcm.dk
Major honours
Danish League (1) 2015
Coach: Glen Riddersholm

2014

20/07	h Brøndby	W	3-1	Hassan, Rasmussen, Onuachu
26/07	a AaB	L	0-2	
04/08	h Randers	W	3-1	Sisto 2, Rasmussen
10/08	a SønderjyskE	W	3-1	Andersson, Igboun, Banggaard
15/08	a København	W	2-1	Bak, Igboun (p)
31/08	h Esbjerg	W	2-0	J Larsen, M Larsen
12/09	h OB	W	3-2	Igboun 3 (1p)
21/09	a Nordsjælland	L	1-2	Hassan
28/09	h Vestsjælland	W	1-0	Igboun
03/10	a Hobro	W	5-1	Rasmussen 3, Poulsen, Sisto
19/10	h Silkeborg	W	2-1	Rasmussen (p), Sisto
25/10	a SønderjyskE	D	1-1	Ureña
31/10	h Nordsjælland	W	2-0	Sisto 2
07/11	a Silkeborg	W	2-1	Andersson, Sisto
23/11	h AaB	W	2-0	Igboun, Ureña
01/12	h Vestsjælland	W	2-1	J Larsen, Bak
07/12	a København	L	0-3	

2015

23/02	h OB	W	3-0	Igboun, Sviatchenko, Rasmussen
01/03	a Brøndby	D	1-1	Pusic
08/03	h Esbjerg	W	3-0	Rasmussen 2, Andersson
13/03	a Randers	W	2-1	Bak, Poulsen
21/03	h Hobro	W	3-0	Pusic 2, J Larsen
05/04	a Esbjerg	D	3-3	Pusic 3
12/04	a AaB	W	2-1	Poulsen 2
17/04	a Silkeborg	W	1-0	Hassan
27/04	a Hobro	D	0-0	
04/05	h Randers	W	5-2	Andersson, Rasmussen 3, Igboun
10/05	a OB	L	1-3	Rasmussen
17/05	h København	W	2-0	Rømer, Sisto
21/05	a Vestsjælland	D	0-0	
25/05	h Brøndby	L	2-3	Pusic, Lauridsen
31/05	a Nordsjælland	L	0-1	
07/06	h SønderjyskE	W	2-1	Pusic, Ureña

No	Name	Nat	DoB	Pos	Aps	(s)	Gls
8	Petter Andersson	SWE	20/02/85	M	21	(2)	4
32	Kristian Bach Bak		20/10/82	D	19	(1)	3
26	Patrick Banggaard		04/04/94	D	25	(1)	1
16	Johan Dahlin	SWE	08/09/86	G	10		
20	Francis Dickoh	GHA	13/12/82	D	10		
22	Mikkel Duelund		29/06/97	M	2	(5)	
36	Rilwan Hassan	NGA	09/02/91	M	18	(6)	3
14	Jakob Haugaard		01/05/92	G	23		
44	Sylvester Igboun	NGA	08/09/90	A	31		9
6	Jim Larsen		06/11/85	D	14	(2)	3
19	Marco Larsen		15/05/93	M	3	(7)	1
15	Jesper Lauridsen		27/03/91	D	33		1
35	Frederik Møller		08/07/93	D		(1)	
17	Kristoffer Olsson	SWE	30/06/95	M	5	(5)	
33	Ebere Onuachu	NGA	28/05/94	A	1	(9)	1
7	Jakob Poulsen		07/07/83	M	29	(2)	4
10	Martin Pusic	AUT	24/10/87	A	12	(4)	8
9	Morten "Duncan" Rasmussen		31/01/85	A	16	(7)	13
28	André Rømer		18/07/93	M	14	(11)	1
27	Pione Sisto		04/02/95	M	16	(6)	8
3	Tim Sparv	FIN	20/02/87	M	24	(5)	
4	Erik Sviatchenko		04/10/91	D	17	(2)	1
11	Marcos Ureña	CRC	05/03/90	A	3	(18)	3
43	Izunna Uzochukwu	NGA	11/04/90	M	17	(5)	

FC Nordsjælland

2003 • Farum Park (10,300) • fcn.dk
Major honours
Danish League (1) 2012; Danish Cup (2) 2010, 2011
Coach: Ólafur Kristjánsson (ISL)

2014

18/07	h Vestsjælland	W	3-2	Aabech, Bech 2
26/07	a København	L	1-2	Aabech
03/08	h Esbjerg	W	3-2	Bech 2 (1p), John
09/08	a AaB	W	2-1	John, Lindberg
18/08	a Hobro	D	0-0	
31/08	h Brøndby	L	0-3	
14/09	a Silkeborg	W	2-1	Lorentzen, Bech
21/09	h Midtjylland	W	2-1	Bech, Lorentzen
29/09	h OB	W	2-1	Vingaard, Bech
05/10	a Randers	D	0-0	
18/10	h SønderjyskE	L	2-3	Lorentzen, Runje
27/10	h AaB	L	0-1	
31/10	a Midtjylland	L	0-2	
09/11	h København	D	0-0	
23/11	a OB	L	0-1	
30/11	h Brøndby	W	2-1	John, Lorentzen
08/12	a Esbjerg	D	0-0	

2015

20/02	h Randers	L	0-3	
28/02	a Hobro	L	0-1	
07/03	h SønderjyskE	W	4-0	John 2, Moberg Karlsson, Thychosen
15/03	h Vestsjælland	W	2-0	Baldvinsson, Moberg Karlsson
22/03	a Silkeborg	D	2-2	Moberg Karlsson, og (Nørgaard)
04/04	a SønderjyskE	W	2-1	Moberg Karlsson, og (Marxen)
12/04	h OB	L	1-2	Bech
19/04	a København	L	0-2	
25/04	h Silkeborg	W	1-0	Marcondes
03/05	a Vestsjælland	L	1-2	Bech (p)
08/05	a Randers	L	0-2	
18/05	h Esbjerg	L	1-3	Marcondes
21/05	a Brøndby	L	1-3	Marcondes
25/05	h Hobro	W	4-2	Ingvartsen 2, Marcondes, Bech
31/05	h Midtjylland	W	1-0	Marcondes
07/06	a AaB	L	0-1	

No	Name	Nat	DoB	Pos	Aps	(s)	Gls
31	Adam Örn Arnarson	ISL	27/08/95	D	7	(1)	
9	Kim Aabech		31/05/83	A	1	(1)	2
9	Gudjón Baldvinsson	ISL	15/02/86	A	7	(6)	1
7	Uffe Bech		13/01/93	A	24	(3)	10
17	Søren Christensen		29/06/86	M	15		
5	Anders Christiansen		08/06/90	M	15		
3	Pascal Gregor		18/02/94	D	32		
30	Marcus Ingvartsen		04/01/96	A	5	(9)	2
1	David Jensen		25/03/92	G	32		
12	Joshua John	NED	01/10/88	A	31		5
21	Kristian Lindberg		14/02/94	A	3	(8)	1
21	Kasper Lorentzen		19/11/85	M	12	(1)	4
18	Emiliano Marcondes		09/03/95	M	10	(14)	5
4	Andreas Maxsø		18/03/94	D	21	(6)	
15	David Moberg Karlsson	SWE	20/03/94	A	13	(12)	4
28	Nicklas Mouritsen		15/03/95	D	5	(2)	
8	Patrick Mtiliga		28/01/81	D	26		
9	Hans Mulder	NED	27/04/87	M	3	(5)	
11	Morten Nordstrand		08/06/83	A	2	(11)	
6	Lasse Petry		19/09/92	M	10	(3)	
27	Mathias Hebo Rasmussen		02/08/95	M		(3)	
16	Rúnar Alex Rúnarsson	ISL	18/02/95	G	1		
21	Ivan Runje	CRO	09/10/90	D	14	(1)	1
14	Gudmundur Thórarinsson	ISL	15/04/92	M	15		
13	Oliver Thychosen		17/01/93	A	1	(8)	1
23	Mario Tičinović	CRO	20/08/91	D	27	(1)	
10	Martin Vingaard		20/03/85	M	31		1

Odense BK

1887 • TRE-FOR Park (15,790) • ob.dk
Major honours
Danish League (3) 1977, 1982, 1989; Danish Cup (5) 1983, 1991, 1993, 2002, 2007
Coach: Troels Bech; (30/09/14) Ove Pedersen

2014

20/07	h Hobro	L	1-2	K Larsen
25/07	a Vestsjælland	L	1-3	E Larsen
02/08	a AaB	D	1-1	Falk
10/08	h Brøndby	D	1-1	Høegh
17/08	a Randers	W	2-0	E Larsen, Nielsen
31/08	h København	L	0-1	
12/09	a Midtjylland	L	2-3	K Larsen, Dvalishvili
21/09	h SønderjyskE	D	1-1	Spelman
29/09	a Nordsjælland	L	1-2	Bodul
04/10	h Silkeborg	W	2-0	Skúlason, Mikkelsen
20/10	a Esbjerg	L	0-2	
26/10	a Randers	L	0-3	
02/11	h Hobro	W	3-1	og (Justesen), Kryger, E Larsen (p)
09/11	a SønderjyskE	L	1-2	Kryger
23/11	h Nordsjælland	W	1-0	Dvalishvili
29/11	a Silkeborg	W	1-0	Spelmann
06/12	a AaB	D	1-1	Falk

2015

23/02	a Midtjylland	L	0-3	
01/03	h København	W	1-0	og (M Jørgensen)
09/03	a Vestsjælland	W	2-1	Falk, Zohore
15/03	a Brøndby	L	0-2	
20/03	h Esbjerg	L	0-2	
07/04	h Vestsjælland	L	1-2	Dalgaard
12/04	a Nordsjælland	W	2-1	Spelmann 2
19/04	a SønderjyskE	D	0-0	
24/04	a Esbjerg	W	2-0	Spelmann, Falk
03/05	a Brøndby	L	0-2	
10/05	h Midtjylland	W	3-1	og (Igboun), Falk, Høegh
15/05	a AaB	W	2-0	Skúlason (p), Nielsen
20/05	h Silkeborg	D	1-1	Høegh
25/05	a København	L	0-1	
31/05	a Hobro	D	2-2	Zohore, Greve
07/06	h Randers	L	0-2	

No	Name	Nat	DoB	Pos	Aps	(s)	Gls
10	Darko Bodul	CRO	11/01/89	A	4	(4)	1
18	Azer Busuladzic		12/11/91	M	23	(2)	
10	Thomas Dalgaard		13/04/84	A	4	(5)	1
19	Mikkel Desler		19/02/95	M	17	(10)	
6	Mohammed Diarra	FRA	20/06/92	D	3	(2)	
13	Vladimer Dvalishvili	GEO	20/04/86	A	5	(7)	2
9	Rasmus Falk		15/01/92	A	26	(1)	5
21	Mathias Greve		11/02/95	A	7	(10)	1
26	Daniel Høegh		06/01/91	D	23	(2)	3
11	Lucas Jensen		08/10/94	M	2	(12)	
4	Hallgrímur Jónasson	ISL	04/05/86	D	14	(1)	
2	Mikkel Kirkeskov		05/09/91	D	11	(3)	
5	Lasse Kryger		03/11/82	D	14	(7)	2
7	Emil Larsen		22/06/91	A	31	(1)	3
3	Kasper Larsen		25/01/93	D	12	(2)	2
22	Thomas Mikkelsen		19/01/90	A	7	(4)	1
5	Lasse Nielsen		03/03/87	D	32		2
14	Conor O'Brien	USA	20/10/88	M	1		
1	Emil Ousager		19/07/87	G	2	(1)	
24	Espen Ruud	NOR	26/02/84	D	10		
16	Jacob Schoop		23/12/88	M	2	(6)	
28	Håkon Skogseid	NOR	14/01/88	D	15		
22	Ari Freyr Skúlason	ISL	14/05/87	M	29	(1)	2
8	Martin Spelmann		21/03/87	M	31		5
14	Jens Jakob Thomasen		25/06/96	M	1	(2)	
29	Anders Thomsen		29/07/95	M		(2)	
17	Mads Toppel		30/01/82	G	31		
25	Kenneth Zohore		31/01/94	A	6	(5)	2

Randers FC

2003 • AutoC Park (10,300) • randersfc.dk
Major honours
Danish Cup (1) 2006
Coach: Colin Todd (ENG)

2014

21/07	a Esbjerg	W	1-0	Lundberg
27/07	h Hobro	W	2-1	Fall, Fisker
04/08	a Midtjylland	L	1-3	Lundberg
08/08	h Vestsjælland	W	1-0	Ishak
17/08	h OB	L	0-2	
30/08	a SønderjyskE	D	1-1	Fall
14/09	a Brøndby	W	2-0	Bjarnason, Fall
19/09	h Silkeborg	W	1-0	Lundberg
26/09	a AaB	D	0-0	
05/10	h Nordsjælland	D	0-0	
19/10	a København	L	0-1	
26/10	h OB	W	3-0	Bjarnason, Lundberg, Ishak
02/11	a Brøndby	L	0-1	
08/11	h Esbjerg	W	3-2	Ishak, Bjarnason, Lundberg
21/11	a Vestsjælland	W	1-0	Ishak
30/11	a Hobro	W	1-0	Ishak
05/12	h SønderjyskE	D	0-0	

2015

20/02	a Nordsjælland	W	3-0	Brock-Madsen, Fall 2 (1p)
01/03	h Silkeborg	L	1-2	Fall
08/03	a AaB	L	1-2	Ishak
13/03	h Midtjylland	L	1-2	Ishak
22/03	a København	D	1-1	Fall
06/04	a AaB	L	1-2	Lundberg
11/04	h Vestsjælland	D	1-1	Ishak
20/04	a Esbjerg	D	0-0	
26/04	h København	W	3-0	Ishak 2, Brock-Madsen
04/05	a Midtjylland	L	2-5	Tverskov, Brock-Madsen
08/05	h Nordsjælland	W	2-0	Brock-Madsen, Lundberg
18/05	a SønderjyskE	D	1-1	Fall
21/05	h Hobro	L	0-1	
25/05	a Silkeborg	W	2-0	Fall, Kamper
31/05	h Brøndby	D	1-1	Fischer
07/06	a OB	W	2-0	Ishak, Borring

No	Name	Nat	DoB	Pos	Aps	(s)	Gls
5	Mads Agesen		17/03/83	D	20		
20	Joel Allansson	SWE	03/11/92	M	5	(3)	
22	Jacob Degn Andersen		04/08/95	D	1		
18	Edgar Babayan		28/10/95	A		(3)	
7	Theódór Elmar Bjarnason	ISL	04/03/87	M	29		3
29	Jonas Borring		04/01/85	M	5	(6)	1
44	Nicolai Brock-Madsen		09/01/93	A	4	(13)	4
30	Baye Djiby Fall	SEN	20/04/85	A	14	(11)	9
13	Mads Fenger		10/09/90	D	32		
21	Alexander Fischer		16/09/86	D	33		1
16	Kasper Fisker		22/05/88	M	25	(3)	1
10	Mikael Ishak	SWE	31/03/93	A	23	(3)	11
1	Karl-Johan Johnsson	SWE	28/01/90	G	32		
14	Kasper Junker		05/03/94	A		(4)	
19	Mikkel Kallesøe		20/04/97	M	1	(7)	
17	Jonas Kamper		30/05/83	M	9	(9)	1
3	Christian Keller		17/08/80	M	29		
25	Ögmundur Kristinsson	ISL	19/06/89	G	1	(1)	
23	Viktor Lundberg	SWE	04/03/91	A	26	(6)	7
38	Nicolai Poulsen		15/08/93	M	25	(4)	
20	Martin Svensson		10/08/89	M		(2)	
33	Adama Tamboura	MLI	18/05/85	D	7	(9)	
4	Johnny Thomsen		26/02/82	D	29		
6	Jeppe Tverskov		12/03/93	M	13	(3)	1

Silkeborg IF

1917 • Mascot Park (10,000) • silkeborgif.com
Major honours
Danish League (1) 1994; Danish Cup (1) 2001
**Coach: Jesper Sørensen;
(08/12/14) Kim Poulsen**

2014

20/07	h København	D	0-0	
28/07	a Brøndby	L	0-2	
01/08	h SønderjyskE	L	0-2	
11/08	a Esbjerg	D	0-0	
17/08	a Vestsjælland	L	0-2	
31/08	h AaB	D	2-2	Scheel 2 (1p)
14/09	h Nordsjælland	L	1-2	Scheel
19/09	a Randers	L	0-1	
27/09	h Hobro	D	2-2	Agger, Scheel
04/10	a OB	L	0-2	
19/10	a Midtjylland	L	1-2	Skov
24/10	h Vestsjælland	L	1-2	Agger
03/11	a AaB	L	0-2	
07/11	h Midtjylland	L	1-2	Agger
22/11	a København	L	0-1	
29/11	h OB	L	0-1	
07/12	a Brøndby	L	0-1	

2015

21/02	h Esbjerg	L	1-3	Scheel
01/03	a Randers	W	2-1	Agger, Pedersen
08/03	h Hobro	L	0-1	
14/03	a SønderjyskE	W	4-1	Beck, og (Bechmann), Ritter, Runsewe
22/03	h Nordsjælland	D	2-2	Beck 2
05/04	a Hobro	D	2-2	Agger 2
13/04	h København	L	0-4	
17/04	a Midtjylland	L	0-1	
25/04	a Nordsjælland	L	0-1	
02/05	h SønderjyskE	D	2-2	Beck, og (Kanstrup)
09/05	a Esbjerg	L	2-5	Scheel, Rasmussen
17/05	h Brøndby	L	0-2	
20/05	a OB	D	1-1	Beck
25/05	h Randers	L	0-2	
31/05	h AaB	L	1-2	Agger
07/06	a Vestsjælland	L	1-3	Agger

No	Name	Nat	DoB	Pos	Aps	(s)	Gls
7	Nicolaj Agger		23/10/88	A	29		8
10	Jesper Bech		25/05/82	A	11	(5)	
9	Morten Beck		02/01/88	A	15	(12)	5
19	Gustav Dahl		21/01/96	M	1	(1)	
18	Kasper Dolberg		06/10/97	A		(3)	
14	Dennis Flinta		14/11/83	D	29	(1)	
27	Jens Martin Gammelby		05/02/95	D	26	(3)	
20	Frank Hansen		23/02/83	D	29	(2)	
23	Jeppe Illum		25/03/92	A	14	(13)	
4	Simon Jakobsen		17/11/90	D	16	(1)	
1	Kasper Jensen		07/10/82	G	10		
5	Ári Mohr Jónsson	FRO	22/07/94	D		(2)	
13	Sune Kiilerich		18/12/90	D	3		
24	Nicolaj Køhlert		21/01/93	M	2	(3)	
2	Jesper Mikkelsen		26/07/80	M	9	(1)	
16	Thomas Nørgaard		07/01/87	G	23		
6	Daniel Pedersen		27/07/92	M	23	(4)	1
17	Frans Dhia Putros		14/07/93	D	8	(4)	
26	Thorbjørn Holst Rasmussen		21/03/87	D	21	(4)	1
25	Nicolaj Ritter		08/05/92	M	31		1
11	Adeola Runsewe	NGA	01/12/89	M	15	(9)	1
28	Tobias Salquist		18/05/95	M	4	(1)	
15, 10	Emil Scheel		18/03/90	M	25	(1)	6
29	Robert Skov		20/05/96	M	16	(8)	1
3	Christian Sørensen		06/08/92	M		(9)	
8	Bjarni Thór Vidarsson	ISL	05/03/88	M	3	(1)	

SønderjyskE

2004 • Sydbank Park (10,000) • soenderjyske.dk
Coach: Lars Søndergaard

2014

19/07	h AaB	D	0-0	
27/07	a Esbjerg	D	1-1	og (Lyng)
01/08	a Silkeborg	W	2-0	Golubović, Oggesen
10/08	h Midtjylland	L	1-3	Absalonsen
17/08	a Brøndby	L	0-2	
30/08	h Randers	D	1-1	Songani
15/09	h Hobro	D	1-1	Bechmann
21/09	a OB	D	1-1	Guira
27/09	h København	D	1-1	Guira
05/10	a Vestsjælland	D	1-1	Bechmann
18/10	a Nordsjælland	W	3-2	Bechmann 2, og (Runje)
25/10	h Midtjylland	D	1-1	Pourie
02/11	a København	D	1-1	Lodberg
09/11	h OB	W	2-1	Paulsen, Pourie
23/11	a Brøndby	L	0-1	
28/11	h Esbjerg	D	0-0	
05/12	a Randers	D	0-0	

2015

22/02	h Hobro	W	1-0	Songani
27/02	a Vestsjælland	W	1-0	Paulsen
07/03	a Nordsjælland	L	0-4	
14/03	h Silkeborg	L	1-4	Pourie (p)
22/03	a AaB	W	4-1	Pourie, Songani, Paulsen, Absalonsen
04/04	h Nordsjælland	L	1-2	Songani
12/04	h Brøndby	L	0-1	
19/04	a OB	D	0-0	
26/04	h AaB	L	0-3	
02/05	a Silkeborg	D	2-2	Madsen, Songani
10/05	a Hobro	D	2-2	Mussmann, Paulsen
18/05	h Randers	D	1-1	Pourie
21/05	a Esbjerg	W	3-2	Pourie 3
24/05	h Vestsjælland	D	1-1	og (Bozga)
31/05	h København	L	1-2	Pourie
07/06	a Midtjylland	L	1-2	Bechmann

No	Name	Nat	DoB	Pos	Aps	(s)	Gls
11	Johan Absalonsen		16/09/85	A	24	(1)	2
9	Tommy Bechmann		22/12/81	A	20	(6)	5
29	Morten Beck		06/12/94	M	15	(7)	
30	Bojan Golubović	BIH	22/08/83	A	4	(5)	1
18	Adama Guira	BFA	24/04/88	M	28	(1)	2
8	Henrik Hansen		28/07/79	M	3	(16)	
2	Daniel Jensen		25/06/79	M	24	(1)	
4	Hallgrímur Jónasson	ISL	04/05/86	D	16		
26	Pierre Kanstrup		21/02/89	D	31	(1)	
5	Niels Lodberg		14/10/80	D	25	(3)	1
10	Nicolaj Madsen		16/07/88	M	17	(5)	1
7	Erik Marxen		02/12/90	D	30		
12	Søren Mussmann		29/06/93	D	11	(4)	1
24	Andreas Oggesen		18/03/94	M	6	(10)	1
20	Bjorn Paulsen		02/07/91	D	28	(4)	4
3	Marvin Pourie	GER	08/01/91	A	26		9
28	Jens Rinke		16/04/90	G	1		
22	Mees Siers	NED	06/10/87	D		(3)	
4	Baldur Sigurdsson	ISL	24/04/85	D	6	(2)	
31	Jeppe Simonsen		21/11/95	A		(6)	
1	Marin Skender	CRO	12/08/79	G	32	(1)	
23	Silas Songani	ZIM	28/06/89	A	16	(10)	5
6	Bo Storm		03/02/87	M		(3)	
21	Mikael Uhre		30/09/94	A		(2)	

FC Vestsjælland

2008 • Harboe Arena (10,000) •
fcvvikings.com
Coach: Michael Hansen

2014

18/07	a	Nordsjælland	L	2-3	*Festersen, og (Runje)*
25/07	h	OB	W	3-1	*Festersen, og (Skúlason), M Sørensen*
02/08	h	København	D	2-2	*D Sørensen, Dal Hende*
08/08	a	Randers	L	0-1	
17/08	h	Silkeborg	W	2-0	*Lund, Due*
01/09	a	Hobro	L	1-3	*Festersen*
14/09	a	Esbjerg	L	0-3	
22/09	h	AaB	W	1-0	*Festersen*
28/09	a	Midtjylland	L	0-1	
05/10	h	SønderjyskE	D	1-1	*Due*
19/10	a	Brøndby	L	0-5	
24/10	a	Silkeborg	W	2-1	*Kristiansen, Festersen (p)*
01/11	h	Esbjerg	L	1-4	*Festersen*
09/11	a	AaB	L	0-2	
21/11	h	Randers	L	0-1	
01/12	a	Midtjylland	L	1-2	*König*
07/12	h	Hobro	D	1-1	*Festersen*

2015

22/02	a	København	L	0-2	
27/02	h	SønderjyskE	L	0-1	
09/03	h	OB	L	1-2	*Festersen*
15/03	a	Nordsjælland	L	0-2	
22/03	h	Brøndby	L	0-1	
07/04	a	OB	W	2-1	*Festersen, Vellios*
11/04	a	Randers	D	1-1	*Festersen*
18/04	h	AaB	W	2-1	*Akharraz, Kure*
26/04	a	Brøndby	L	0-4	
03/05	h	Nordsjælland	W	2-1	*Kure, Akharraz*
11/05	h	København	L	0-1	
17/05	a	Hobro	W	1-0	*Bozga*
21/05	h	Midtjylland	D	0-0	
24/05	a	SønderjyskE	D	1-1	*D Sørensen*
31/05	a	Esbjerg	L	1-2	*Vellios*
07/06	h	Silkeborg	W	3-1	*Vellios (p), D Sørensen, Nymann*

No	Name	Nat	DoB	Pos	Aps	(s)	Gls
33	Osama Akharraz		26/11/90	M	4	(6)	2
26	Patrick Andersen		03/01/94	M		(1)	
24	Onur Bilgin		25/04/97	M		(1)	
13	Jean-Claude Bozga	ROU	01/06/84	D	22	(5)	1
21	Frederik Christensen		07/03/95	M	1		
3	Michael Christensen		06/02/83	D	7	(3)	
17	Marc Dal Hende		06/11/90	A	23	(3)	1
8	Anders Due		17/03/82	M	20	(3)	2
14	Rasmus Festersen		26/08/86	A	31		10
4	Eggert Gunnthór Jónsson	ISL	18/08/88	M	14		
29	Adam Kolberg		05/06/93	M		(1)	
27	Jan Kristiansen		04/08/81	M	27	(4)	1
10	Anders Kure		12/09/85	D	21	(1)	2
7	Danni König		17/12/86	M	3	(4)	1
28	Michael Lumb		09/01/88	D	8		
48	Oliver Lund		21/08/90	D	15	(8)	1
6	Henrik Madsen		25/02/83	M	20	(2)	
1	Thomas Mikkelsen		27/08/83	G	33		
4,7	Peter Nymann		22/08/82	M	30	(3)	1
23	Jukka Raitala	FIN	15/09/88	D	15		
12	Anders Randrup		16/07/88	D	1	(3)	
5	Lennard Sowah	GER	23/08/92	D	1	(2)	
11	Dennis Sørensen		24/05/81	M	12	(17)	3
20	Marc Rochester Sørensen		13/12/92	M	8	(7)	1
19	Thiago Borges	BRA	22/10/88	M	1	(4)	
22	Jean Thome	CIV	10/10/95	M	2	(3)	
15	Jonas Thomsen		05/02/91	M	5	(4)	
10	Joël Tshibamba	COD	22/09/88	A	2	(3)	
9	Apostolos Vellios	GRE	08/01/92	A	14	(2)	3
2	Anders Østli	NOR	08/01/83	D	23	(5)	

Top goalscorers

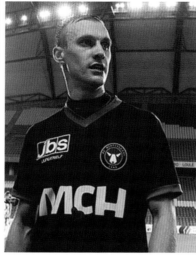

17	Martin Pusic (Esbjerg/Midtjylland)
16	Mads Hvilsom (Hobro)
13	Morten "Duncan" Rasmussen (Midtjylland)
11	Mikael Ishak (Randers)
10	Anders Jacobsen (AaB)
	Nicolai Jørgensen (København)
	Uffe Bech (Nordsjælland)
	Rasmus Festersen (Vestsjælland)
9	Teemu Pukki (Brøndby)
	Sylvester Igboun (Midtjylland)
	Baye Djiby Fall (Randers)
	Marvin Pourie (SønderjyskE)

Promoted clubs

Viborg FF

1896 • Energi Viborg Arena (10,000) • vff.dk
Major honours
Danish Cup (1) 2000
Coach: Aurelijus Skarbalius (LTU)

AGF Aarhus

1880 • NRGi Park (19,433) • agf.dk
Major honours
*Danish League (5) 1955, 1956, 1957, 1960, 1986;
Danish Cup (9) 1955, 1957, 1960, 1961, 1965, 1987,
1988, 1992, 1996*
Coach: Morten Wieghorst

Second level final table 2014/15

		Pld	W	D	L	F	A	Pts
1	Viborg FF	33	17	14	2	47	20	65
2	AGF Aarhus	33	17	10	6	59	33	61
3	Lyngby BK	33	14	9	10	49	37	51
4	Vendsyssel FF	33	13	10	10	35	29	49
5	Vejle BK	33	11	12	10	41	46	45
6	AC Horsens	33	10	12	11	43	42	42
7	HB Køge	33	10	12	11	33	35	42
8	Skive IK	33	8	17	8	40	42	41
9	FC Roskilde	33	10	8	15	40	38	38
10	FC Fredericia	33	6	16	11	28	40	34
11	Akademisk BK	33	8	8	17	35	61	32
12	Brønshøj BK	33	3	14	16	20	47	23

DOMESTIC CUP

Landspokalturneringen 2014/15

SECOND ROUND

(27/08/14)
Svebølle 1-5 Vestsjælland

(10/09/14)
Hvidovre 1-2 Roskilde *(aet)*
Ledøje-Smørum 0-1 Fremad Amager

(16/09/14)
Marstal/Rise 0-3 Jammerbugt

(23/09/14)
AGF 2-1 Hobro *(aet)*
B73 Slagelse 0-1 B1908
Brabrand 1-2 Horsens
Gilleleje 1-5 HIK
Greve 2-1 Nykøbing F
Herlev 0-2 B93
Kolding BK 1-7 Randers
Lejre 0-6 Søllerød-Vedbæk
Lindholm 0-1 Esbjerg fB
OKS 1-2 Skovbakken
Rødovre 2-1 Avedøre
Svendborg 1-0 Kjellerup *(aet)*
Sønderborg 0-7 Silkeborg

(24/09/14)
Aarhus Fremad 2-1 Fredericia
AB Tårnby 1-3 AB
Brønshøj 1-0 OB
Egedal 1-1 Nordsjælland *(aet; 4-3 on pens)*
Esbjerg IF 92 0-3 SønderjyskE
Kalundborg 0-10 Lyngby
Lyseng 1-2 Odder *(aet)*
Næsby 0-3 HB Køge
Varde 3-2 Ringkøbing

(30/09/14)
Marienlyst 1-2 Skive
Vejgaard 1-2 Vejle

Byes – AaB, Brøndby, København, Midtjylland

THIRD ROUND

(28/10/14)
Aarhus Fremad 1-5 Midtjylland
AGF 1-1 SønderjyskE *(aet; 4-5 on pens)*
Jammerbugt 0-2 Brønshøj
Rødovre 0-4 Silkeborg
Søllerød-Vedbæk 0-3 Skive

(29/10/14)
Egedal 2-3 Varde
Fremad Amager 1-3 Brøndby
Greve 1-0 B93
HB Køge 2-1 AB
HIK 1-5 Odder
Horsens 0-7 Esbjerg fB
Lyngby 0-2 Randers
Skovbakken 4-2 B1908
Svendborg 2-3 Vestsjælland

(30/10/14)
Roskilde 2-3 København
Vejle 0-1 AaB *(aet)*

FOURTH ROUND

(16/11/14)
HB Køge 0-3 Vestsjælland

(19/11/14)
Odder 2-4 AaB

(26/11/14)
Randers 1-0 Silkeborg *(aet)*

(29/11/14)
Brønshøj 1-0 Skive

(01/12/14)
Varde 0-3 SønderjyskE

(03/12/14)
Skovbakken 1-2 Brøndby *(aet)*

(04/12/14)
Esbjerg fB 3-0 Midtjylland
Greve 0-3 København

QUARTER-FINALS

(04/03/15)
Brønshøj 1-2 Vestsjælland *(Akpoveta 28; Vellios 9, Dal Hende 13)*
SønderjyskE 4-2 Brøndby *(Pourie 3, 109, Songani 65, Absalonsen 107; Elmander 24, Pukki 33) (aet)*

(05/03/15)
Esbjerg fB 4-2 AaB *(Lyng 51, Mensah 67, 72, Rise 88; Helenius 37, Enevoldsen 41)*
København 0-0 Randers *(aet; 5-4 on pens)*

SEMI-FINALS

(15/04/15 & 29/04/15)
Vestsjælland 2-0 SønderjyskE *(Jónsson 70, Vellios 85)*
SønderjyskE 1-0 Vestsjælland *(Absalonsen 5) (Vestsjælland 2-1)*

(16/04/15 & 30/04/15)
København 1-1 Esbjerg fB *(Toutouh 11; Van Buren 68)*
Esbjerg fB 0-1 København *(Augustinsson 79) (København 2-1)*

FINAL

(14/05/15)
Telia Parken, Copenhagen
FC KØBENHAVN 3 *(Nilsson 46, Sigurdarson 54, Olsen 102)*
FC VESTSJÆLLAND 2 *(Vellios 31, D Sørensen 88) (aet)*
Referee: *Tykgaard*
KØBENHAVN: *Andersen, Høgli (Remmer 46), Nilsson, M Jørgensen, Augustinsson, Delaney, Gíslason (Olsen 84), Amartey, Sigurdarson, N Jørgensen (Poulsen 70), De Ridder*
VESTSJÆLLAND: *Mikkelsen, Raitala, Østli, Kure, Lumb (Due 65), Nymann, Madsen (Kristiansen 61), Jónsson (D Sørensen 79), Dal Hende, Vellios, Festersen*

FC København enjoy the fruits of their labour after defeating Vestsjælland in an exciting Danish Cup final

The FA

ENGLAND
The Football Association (FA)

Address	Wembley Stadium PO Box 1966 GB-London SW1P 9EQ	**Chairman**	Greg Dyke
		Chief executive	Martin Glenn
		Media officer	Scott Field
Tel	+44 844 980 8200	**Year of formation**	1863
Fax	+44 844 980 8201	**National stadium**	Wembley Stadium,
E-mail	info@thefa.com		London (90,000)
Website	thefa.com		

PREMIER LEAGUE CLUBS

 1 **Arsenal FC**

 2 **Aston Villa FC**

 3 **Burnley FC**

 4 **Chelsea FC**

 5 **Crystal Palace FC**

 6 **Everton FC**

 7 **Hull City AFC**

 8 **Leicester City FC**

 9 **Liverpool FC**

 10 **Manchester City FC**

 11 **Manchester United FC**

 12 **Newcastle United FC**

 13 **Queens Park Rangers FC**

 14 **Southampton FC**

 15 **Stoke City FC**

 16 **Sunderland AFC**

 17 **Swansea City AFC**

 18 **Tottenham Hotspur FC**

 19 **West Bromwich Albion FC**

 20 **West Ham United FC**

PROMOTED CLUBS

 21 **AFC Bournemouth**

 22 **Watford FC**

 23 **Norwich City FC**

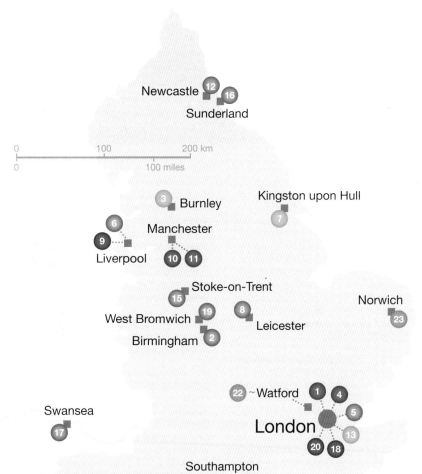

KEY:
- – UEFA Champions League
- – UEFA Europa League
- – Promoted
- – Relegated

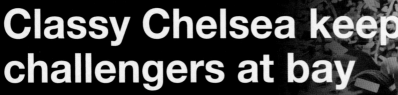

Classy Chelsea keep challengers at bay

The Premier League trophy returned to west London in 2014/15 as José Mourinho steered Chelsea FC back to the pinnacle of English football in typically artful style. The Blues led throughout, their all-round class and consistency proving too much for their rivals, none of whom mounted a sustained challenge.

While Chelsea doubled up with victory in the League Cup, Arsenal FC lifted the FA Cup for a record 12th time. It was a bad season for English clubs in Europe, with no team reaching the quarter-finals, but a very good one for Roy Hodgson's England, who won all six of their UEFA EURO 2016 qualifiers.

| Mourinho brings Premier League title back to Stamford Bridge | Arsenal retain FA Cup to post record 12th victory | Clubs flop in Europe but national team cruise towards France |

Domestic league

After the to-ing and fro-ing of the previous Premier League campaign, when the lead changed hands repeatedly before Manchester City FC triumphed, only one team ruled in 2014/15. Apart from a momentary lapse at the turn of the year, when City joined them at the top of the table with identical points and goals records, Chelsea's domination was total, their 274-day sojourn at the Premier League summit setting a new competition record.

Mourinho, whose first season back at Stamford Bridge had resulted in an untidy third-place finish, reinforced his squad with several top-grade players. Goalkeeper Thibaut Courtois returned after a three-year loan at Club Atlético de Madrid, where Chelsea did further business, bringing in left-back Filipe Luís and striker Diego Costa. With ex-Arsenal favourite Cesc Fàbregas also brought back to London from FC Barcelona, Mourinho had the team he wanted. The introduction of Costa, especially, reinvigorated the forward line, with the Spanish international scoring seven goals in his first four matches, all victories, to catapult Chelsea into first place.

By late November, Chelsea were out on their own, the only points dropped in

their opening dozen games having come at Manchester City – where Blues legend Frank Lampard, released in the summer after 13 years' service, scored the home side's equaliser – and Manchester United FC – where Robin van Persie levelled the scores in added time. However, just as talk surfaced of Mourinho's side going through the whole season undefeated, they lost 2-1 at Newcastle United FC. Their next defeat, 5-3 at Tottenham Hotspur FC on New Year's Day, was more troubling as it enabled a re-energised City to move alongside them at the Premier League summit.

No sooner had Manuel Pellegrini's defending champions risen into a challenging position, however, than they abruptly fell away again, dropping five points in their next two games while Chelsea collected two wins, the second of them a 5-0 masterclass at Swansea City AFC. A 1-1 draw between the top two at Stamford Bridge kept the gap at five points, but that would grow as winter turned to spring, with City losing four times in six outings and the other potential challengers, Arsenal and Manchester United, too far back to make their resurgent form count for anything more than a place in the top four.

Chelsea, meanwhile, carefully consolidated their position. Mourinho

was fortunate in being able to field virtually the same starting XI from one week to the next, with Costa the only one of his regulars sidelined for any length of time through injury. Following the big win at Swansea, Chelsea became more pragmatic in their play. Although they continued to pick up points, the wins were all hard-fought, with one goal invariably the difference. It was perhaps fitting, therefore, that the club's fifth league title – and third under Mourinho – should be clinched with a 1-0 victory, Eden Hazard's penalty at home to Crystal Palace FC putting the Blues out of reach with three fixtures remaining.

Hazard, the unanimous choice as the Premier League's outstanding performer, was one of three Chelsea players to start all 38 matches. The other two, captain John Terry and right-back Branislav Ivanović, even eclipsed the Belgian by never being substituted. Both defenders were immense, forming the best back line in the league alongside Gary Cahill and left-back César Azpilicueta, whose reliability kept new signing Luís in reserve. Courtois's brilliance also meant a regular place on the bench for long-serving No1 Petr Čech. Elsewhere, Fàbregas and Nemanja Matić provided a beautifully balanced central midfield, while Brazilian duo Willian and Oscar brought pace and flair to the attack,

which, when not spearheaded by the abrasive Costa, found a place for 37-year-old club icon Didier Drogba, back at the Bridge for a swansong season and – like Terry and Čech – a fourth Premier League winner's medal.

City ended strongly to finish eight points behind Chelsea in second place. Once again they boasted the Premier League's most potent attack, although this time with just 83 goals (rather than the 102 of 2013/14), 26 of them to the dynamic Sergio Agüero, who collected the golden boot. While the Argentinian striker and his Spanish midfield accomplice David Silva were as delightfully entertaining as ever, other key players, notably Yaya Touré and Vincent Kompany, did not have the impact of old, while the only new signing of incontestable merit was supersub Lampard, whose loan from MLS club New York City was extended for the full season.

Arsenal ensured an 18th successive season of UEFA Champions League football by finishing third. A strong surge in the spring, which brought eight consecutive victories, lifted them up to second but City overtook them as they faltered during the run-in. Arsène Wenger's side were never realistic title

challengers after falling 11 points behind Chelsea early on, although they did possess the Premier League's best new acquisition in Alexis Sánchez, outstanding from first kick to last as goalscorer, provider and all-round workaholic. Midfielder Santi Cazorla also excelled, but, unlike Chelsea, Arsenal were persistently troubled by injuries, with England internationals Jack Wilshere, Theo Walcott, Alex Oxlade-Chamberlain and new recruit Danny Welbeck among those sidelined for extended periods.

Manchester United also suffered with injuries, but new manager Louis van Gaal juggled his resources with sufficient dexterity to lead the club back into the UEFA Champions League (play-offs) as they ended a season of transition in a comfortable fourth place. United were far from the force of old, their fortunes fluctuating from month to month, but they were a considerable improvement on the 2013/14 side, led by the hapless David Moyes, that failed to qualify for Europe. Van Gaal's rebuilding job was assisted by a vast outlay of funds, which brought in a flood of high-profile players, among them Premier League record buy Ángel Di María and, on loan from AS Monaco FC, Radamel Falcao. Most of

the newcomers, including those two illustrious South Americans, failed to impress, however, and but for the consistent brilliance in goal of David de Gea, United would almost certainly have been returning to continental competition in the UEFA Europa League.

Tottenham Hotspur FC, Liverpool FC and Southampton FC all flirted with a top-four place, only to fade away at the finish and claim a UEFA Europa League consolation prize. Spurs, under new coach Mauricio Pochettino, were galvanised by their 21-goal striker Harry Kane but often flattered to deceive. Liverpool, who ran City so close for the 2013/14 title, were a pale imitation, the loss of strikers Luis Suárez to Barcelona and Daniel Sturridge to injury aggravated by some ineffective new signings. Long-serving skipper Steven Gerrard's farewell season did not go to plan, his final game resulting in a 6-1 mauling at Stoke City FC – the club's heaviest league defeat for 52 years. Southampton, meanwhile, performed wonders to finish seventh after having their squad ripped apart, mostly by Liverpool, in the summer. With Pochettino departed for Tottenham, new boss Ronald Koeman bought sensibly to plug the gaps and was rewarded with a brilliant start and a couple of huge wins, 8-0 against Sunderland AFC and, in the last home game, 6-1 against Aston Villa FC.

Sunderland and Villa were among several teams embroiled in a frantic fight to stave off relegation. They and, in the nick of time, Newcastle all survived, but the greatest escape of all was achieved by newly-promoted Leicester City FC. Having propped up the table for four months, they won six games out of seven before drawing 0-0 at Sunderland to preserve their status with a game to spare. Leicester's fellow newcomers Burnley FC and Queens Park Rangers FC could not emulate them, going straight back down alongside Hull City AFC, whose fate was sealed on the final day.

There was a newcomer to the Premier League ranks for 2015/16 as AFC Bournemouth continued their remarkable rise through the divisions to win the Championship (second tier) and claim automatic promotion alongside Watford FC. The third place was filled by Norwich City FC, who ensured an immediate return to the top flight with a comfortable 2-0 victory over Middlesbrough FC in the play-off final at Wembley.

Arsenal's Olivier Giroud (left) and Alexis Sánchez (right) celebrate a Premier League goal scored by Santi Cazorla (centre) against Manchester City

Domestic cups

Having lifted the FA Cup in 2014 to end a nine-year trophy famine, Arsenal made it two victories in as many years, trouncing Aston Villa 4-0 in the final to become the competition's record winners, half of their 12 victories coming during Wenger's 19-year reign. Goals from Walcott, Alexis, Per Mertesacker and Olivier Giroud ensured an easy win for the north Londoners, who had been pressed far harder in the semi-final by Championship side Reading FC. Villa were worthy semi-final winners against Liverpool, whose 2-1 defeat denied Gerrard a Wembley farewell on his 35th birthday.

The Merseysiders also lost in the League Cup semi-finals, an extra-time Ivanović strike giving Chelsea a 2-1 aggregate victory. Mourinho's side were joined at Wembley by Tottenham in a repeat of the 2008 final. Spurs had won that game 2-1, but they failed to stage an encore, a goal from Terry just before half-time giving the Blues the lead before a deflected Diego Costa strike sealed a 2-0 win to give Chelsea the trophy for the fifth time.

Europe

Chelsea's domestic achievements were scarred by an early elimination from the UEFA Champions League. They were one of three Premier League fallers in the round of 16 as England endured one of its worst ever continental campaigns, failing to take any teams through to the quarter-finals for the first time since 1992/93 – when an embryonic Premier League had provided just four European entrants.

Hull were the first of the seven 2014/15 participants to drop out, in the UEFA Europa League play-offs. The other six were still involved after Christmas, but not for long. Liverpool, who had messed up their return to the UEFA Champions League, finishing third in their group, tripped at the first hurdle of the UEFA Europa League as well, losing to Beşiktaş JK on penalties while Tottenham were bowing out at ACF Fiorentina. Everton FC lasted one round longer before they capitulated against FC Dynamo Kyiv.

In the UEFA Champions League, Manchester City did well not to share Liverpool's fate, but their reward for stirring victories against FC Bayern München and AS Roma was a second successive last-16 meeting with Barcelona. As in 2013/14, they lost both legs – despite some heroics from goalkeeper Joe Hart. Arsenal came through their group for the 15th successive season but exited in the round of 16 for the fifth year in a row, losing unexpectedly to Monaco on away goals after a shoddy 3-1 first-leg defeat in London. Chelsea also went out after sharing six goals with a French club, their inability to build on a first-leg 1-1 draw at Paris Saint-Germain and defend a lead against ten men at Stamford Bridge – both in normal time and extra time – resulting in an unexpected away-goals defeat to the team they had overcome by the same method in the 2013/14 quarter-finals.

National team

While English clubs struggled, a revived national team made the most of their good fortune in the UEFA EURO 2016 qualifying draw by winning their first six matches. In fact, Roy Hodgson's side did even better than that, avoiding defeat in four friendly internationals to complete England's first unbeaten season for 24 years. Coming in the immediate aftermath of the country's worst ever performance at a FIFA World Cup, it was quite a turnaround.

The toughest of the team's qualifying assignments came at the beginning and end of the season. First up were Switzerland in Basel, where two Welbeck goals gave Hodgson's men a very welcome 2-0 win, and in June, against Slovenia in Ljubljana, it was another Arsenal player, Wilshere, who inspired his team to victory with a brace of goals, both spectacular, before Wayne Rooney supplied a late winner to extend his scoring run in the qualifying competition to a fifth successive match and maintain his team's perfect record on the road to France.

Rooney's first season as England captain, following the retirement of Gerrard, yielded eight goals in all – a haul matched in 2014/15 only by Sweden's Zlatan Ibrahimović across all 54 European national teams – which lifted his all-time tally to 48, one shy of Bobby Charlton's 45-year-old record. Having won his 100th cap in the home fixture against Slovenia, Rooney delivered one of his best performances in an England shirt, scoring twice in a 3-1 victory at Celtic Park over Scotland. There will be two further 'Battles of Britain' in the preliminary competition for the 2018 World Cup, but first Hodgson and his players must concentrate on getting their act together across the Channel at UEFA EURO 2016.

Wayne Rooney celebrates a late winning goal against Slovenia – his 48th for England

DOMESTIC SEASON AT A GLANCE

Premier League 2014/15 final table

		Pld	Home					Away					Total					Pts
			W	D	L	F	A	W	D	L	F	A	W	D	L	F	A	
1	**Chelsea FC**	**38**	**15**	**4**	**0**	**36**	**9**	**11**	**5**	**3**	**37**	**23**	**26**	**9**	**3**	**73**	**32**	**87**
2	Manchester City FC	38	14	3	2	44	14	10	4	5	39	24	24	7	7	83	38	79
3	Arsenal FC	38	12	5	2	41	14	10	4	5	30	22	22	9	7	71	36	75
4	Manchester United FC	38	14	2	3	41	15	6	8	5	21	22	20	10	8	62	37	70
5	Tottenham Hotspur FC	38	10	3	6	31	24	9	4	6	27	29	19	7	12	58	53	64
6	Liverpool FC	38	10	5	4	30	20	8	3	8	22	28	18	8	12	52	48	62
7	Southampton FC	38	11	4	4	37	13	7	2	10	17	20	18	6	14	54	33	60
8	Swansea City AFC	38	9	5	5	27	22	7	3	9	19	27	16	8	14	46	49	56
9	Stoke City FC	38	10	3	6	32	22	5	6	8	16	23	15	9	14	48	45	54
10	Crystal Palace FC	38	6	3	10	21	27	7	6	6	26	24	13	9	16	47	51	48
11	Everton FC	38	7	7	5	27	21	5	4	10	21	29	12	11	15	48	50	47
12	West Ham United FC	38	9	4	6	25	18	3	7	9	19	29	12	11	15	44	47	47
13	West Bromwich Albion FC	38	7	4	8	24	26	4	7	8	14	25	11	11	16	38	51	44
14	Leicester City FC	38	7	5	7	28	22	4	3	12	18	33	11	8	19	46	55	41
15	Newcastle United FC	38	7	5	7	26	27	3	4	12	14	36	10	9	19	40	63	39
16	Sunderland AFC	38	4	8	7	16	27	3	9	7	15	26	7	17	14	31	53	38
17	Aston Villa FC	38	5	6	8	18	25	5	2	12	13	32	10	8	20	31	57	38
18	Hull City AFC	38	5	5	9	19	24	3	6	10	14	27	8	11	19	33	51	35
19	Burnley FC	38	4	7	8	14	21	3	5	11	14	32	7	12	19	28	53	33
20	Queens Park Rangers FC	38	6	5	8	23	24	2	1	16	19	49	8	6	24	42	73	30

European qualification 2015/16

Champion: Chelsea FC (group stage)
Manchester City FC (group stage)
Cup winner: Arsenal FC (group stage)
Manchester United FC (play-offs)

Tottenham Hotspur FC (group stage)
Liverpool FC (group stage)
Southampton FC (third qualifying round)
West Ham United FC (first qualifying round)

Top scorer	Sergio Agüero (Man. City), 26 goals
Relegated clubs	Queens Park Rangers FC, Burnley FC, Hull City AFC
Promoted clubs	AFC Bournemouth, Watford FC, Norwich City FC
FA Cup final	Arsenal FC 4-0 Aston Villa FC
League Cup final	Chelsea FC 2-0 Tottenham Hotspur FC

Team of the season
(4-1-3-2)

Coach: Mourinho (Chelsea)

Player of the season

Eden Hazard
(Chelsea FC)

An ever-present member of Chelsea's Premier League title-winning team, Hazard registered 14 goals and nine assists and was a constant crowd-pleaser with his effortless ability to glide into dangerous areas and pull defenders out of position. Twice voted player of the year in France while at LOSC Lille, his 2014/15 exploits brought him both the PFA Player of the Year and FWA Footballer of the Year awards in England. At just 24, the immensely gifted Belgian has the football world at his twinkling feet.

Newcomer of the season

Harry Kane
(Tottenham Hotspur FC)

The revelation of the 2014/15 English season by some distance, Kane had a dream campaign, scoring 21 league goals for Tottenham – a tally bettered only by Sergio Agüero – and then finding the net 79 seconds into his senior debut for England. A mere substitute for Spurs at the start of the Premier League campaign, the tall, powerful 21-year-old became a figure of worship for the White Hart Lane faithful after scoring brilliant doubles in memorable home wins against Chelsea FC and Arsenal FC.

De Gea (Man. United)
Ivanović (Chelsea) · Cahill (Chelsea) · Terry (Chelsea) · Bertrand (Southampton)
Matić (Chelsea)
Alexis Sánchez (Arsenal) · Coutinho (Liverpool) · Hazard (Chelsea)
Diego Costa (Chelsea) · Kane (Tottenham)

ENGLAND

NATIONAL TEAM

International honours
FIFA World Cup (1) 1966.

International tournament appearances
FIFA World Cup (14) 1950, 1954 (qtr-finals), 1958, 1962 (qtr-finals), 1966 (Winners), 1970 (qtr-finals), 1982 (2nd phase), 1986 (qtr-finals), 1990 (4th), 1998 (2nd round), 2002 (qtr-finals), 2006 (qtr-finals), 2010 (2nd round), 2014
UEFA European Championship (8) 1968 (3rd), 1980, 1988, 1992, 1996 (semi-finals), 2000, 2004 (qtr-finals), 2012 (qtr-finals)

Top five all-time caps
Peter Shilton (125); David Beckham (115); Steven Gerrard (114); Bobby Moore (108); Ashley Cole (107)

Top five all-time goals
Bobby Charlton (49); Gary Lineker & **Wayne Rooney** (48); Jimmy Greaves (44); Michael Owen (40)

Results 2014/15

03/09/14	Norway	H	London	W	1-0	Rooney (68p)
08/09/14	Switzerland (ECQ)	A	Basel	W	2-0	Welbeck (58, 90+4)
09/10/14	San Marino (ECQ)	H	London	W	5-0	Jagielka (25), Rooney (43p), Welbeck (49), Townsend (72), Della Valle (78og)
12/10/14	Estonia (ECQ)	A	Tallinn	W	1-0	Rooney (74)
15/11/14	Slovenia (ECQ)	H	London	W	3-1	Rooney (59p), Welbeck (66, 72)
18/11/14	Scotland	A	Glasgow	W	3-1	Oxlade-Chamberlain (32), Rooney (47, 85)
27/03/15	Lithuania (ECQ)	H	London	W	4-0	Rooney (6), Welbeck (45), Sterling (58), Kane (73)
31/03/15	Italy	A	Turin	D	1-1	Townsend (79)
07/06/15	Republic of Ireland	A	Dublin	D	0-0	
14/06/15	Slovenia (ECQ)	A	Ljubljana	W	3-2	Wilshere (57, 73), Rooney (86)

Appearances 2014/15

Coach: Roy Hodgson	09/08/47		Nor	SUI	SMR	EST	SVN	Sco	LTU	Ita	Irl	SVN	Caps	Goals
Joe Hart	19/04/87	Man. City	G	G	G	G	G		G	G	G	G	52	-
John Stones	28/05/94	Everton	D81	D									4	-
Phil Jones	21/02/92	Man. United	D	D77					D	M	D	D46	17	-
Gary Cahill	19/12/85	Chelsea	D84	D	D	D	D	D46	D		D74	D	36	3
Leighton Baines	11/12/84	Everton	D	D		D			D				30	1
Alex Oxlade-Chamberlain	15/08/93	Arsenal	M70		s46	s61	s85	M80					20	4
Jordan Henderson	17/06/90	Liverpool	M	M	M46	M64	M		M71	M74	M	M	22	-
Jack Wilshere	01/01/92	Arsenal	M70	M73	M	M	M	M87			M66	M	28	2
Raheem Sterling	08/12/94	Liverpool	M	M	M46	s64	M85	s67	A		A66	A	16	1
Wayne Rooney	24/10/85	Man. United	A70	A90	A	A	A	A	A71	M	A74	A	105	48
Daniel Sturridge	01/09/89	Liverpool	A89										16	5
James Milner	04/01/86	Man. City	s70	s73	M		s80	M			M		54	1
Fabian Delph	21/11/89	Aston Villa	s70	M		M61				M	M70		M85	6	-
Danny Welbeck	26/11/90	Arsenal	s70	A	A66	A80	A	A67	A77				33	14
Calum Chambers	20/01/95	Arsenal	s81		D	D							3	-
Phil Jagielka	17/08/82	Everton	s84	s77	D	D	D89	s46		D	s74		36	3
Rickie Lambert	16/02/82	Liverpool	s89	s90		s80		s80					11	3
Kieran Gibbs	26/09/89	Arsenal			D		D	s66		D88		D	8	-
Adam Lallana	10/05/88	Liverpool			s46	M	M80	s46			A82	s46	15	-
Andros Townsend	16/07/91	Tottenham			s66					s70	s66	A74	9	3
Nathaniel Clyne	05/04/91	Southampton				D	D	D	D	D46		s85	5	-
Chris Smalling	22/11/89	Man. United					s89	D		D44	D	D	18	-
Fraser Forster	17/03/88	Southampton						G					3	-
Luke Shaw	12/07/95	Man. United						D66					4	-
Stewart Downing	22/07/84	West Ham						M46					35	-
Ross Barkley	05/12/93	Everton						s87	s71	s55	s66		13	-
Michael Carrick	28/07/81	Man. United							M	s44			33	-
Harry Kane	28/07/93	Tottenham							s71	A			2	1
Theo Walcott	16/03/89	Arsenal							s77	A55	s82	s74	40	5
Kyle Walker	28/05/90	Tottenham								s46			11	-
Ryan Mason	13/06/91	Tottenham								s74			1	-
Ryan Bertrand	05/08/89	Southampton								s88	D		4	-
Jamie Vardy	11/01/87	Leicester									s74		1	-

EUROPE

Manchester City FC

Group E
Match 1 - FC Bayern München (GER)
A 0-1
Hart, Sagna, Kompany, Nasri (Milner 58), Džeko (Agüero 74), Jesús Navas (Kolarov 88), Silva, Clichy, Fernandinho, Demichelis, Touré. Coach: Rubén Cousillas (ESP)
Match 2 - AS Roma (ITA)
H 1-1 Agüero (4p)
Hart, Kompany, Zabaleta, Džeko (Lampard 57), Jesús Navas (Milner 46), Agüero (Jovetić 84), Silva, Clichy, Fernandinho, Demichelis, Touré. Coach: Manuel Pellegrini (CHI)
Match 3 - PFC CSKA Moskva (RUS)
A 2-2 Agüero (29), Milner (38)
Hart, Kompany, Zabaleta, Fernando (Jovetić 86), Milner, Džeko (Jesús Navas 72), Kolarov, Agüero, Mangala, Silva (Fernandinho 78), Touré. Coach: Manuel Pellegrini (CHI)
Match 4 - PFC CSKA Moskva (RUS)
H 1-2 Touré (8)
Hart, Kompany, Zabaleta, Fernando (Džeko 65), Milner, Jesús Navas (Nasri 46), Agüero, Clichy, Demichelis, Jovetić (Fernandinho 46), Touré. Coach: Manuel Pellegrini (CHI)
Red cards: Fernandinho 70, Touré 82
Match 5 - FC Bayern München (GER)
H 3-2 Agüero (22p, 85, 90+1)
Hart, Sagna (Zabaleta 68), Kompany, Fernando, Milner (Jovetić 66), Nasri, Jesús Navas, Agüero (Demichelis 90+4), Lampard, Mangala, Clichy. Coach: Manuel Pellegrini (CHI)
Match 6 - AS Roma (ITA)
A 2-0 Nasri (60), Zabaleta (86)
Hart, Zabaleta, Fernando, Milner, Nasri (Kolarov 89), Džeko (Jovetić 78), Jesús Navas (Silva 67), Mangala, Clichy, Fernandinho, Demichelis. Coach: Manuel Pellegrini (CHI)

Round of 16 - FC Barcelona (ESP)
H 1-2 Agüero (69)
Hart, Kompany, Zabaleta, Fernando, Milner, Nasri (Fernandinho 62), Džeko (Bony 68), Agüero, Silva (Sagna 78), Clichy, Demichelis. Coach: Manuel Pellegrini (CHI)
Red card: Clichy 74
A 0-1
Hart, Sagna, Kompany, Milner (Lampard 87), Nasri (Jesús Navas 46), Kolarov, Agüero, Silva, Fernandinho, Demichelis, Touré (Bony 72). Coach: Manuel Pellegrini (CHI)

Liverpool FC

Group B
Match 1 - PFC Ludogorets Razgrad (BUL)
H 2-1 Balotelli (82), Gerrard (90+3p)
Mignolet, Lovren, Gerrard, Coutinho (Lucas 68), Henderson, Sakho, Moreno, Javi Manquillo, Lallana (Borini 67), Sterling, Balotelli. Coach: Brendan Rodgers (NIR)

Match 2 - FC Basel 1893 (SUI)
A 0-1
Mignolet, José Enrique, Lovren, Gerrard, Coutinho (Lallana 70), Henderson, Javi Manquillo, Sterling, Škrtel, Balotelli, Marković (Lambert 81). Coach: Brendan Rodgers (NIR)
Match 3 - Real Madrid CF (ESP)
H 0-3
Mignolet, Johnson, Lovren, Gerrard, Coutinho (Marković 68), Henderson (Can 67), Moreno, Allen, Sterling, Škrtel, Balotelli (Lallana 46). Coach: Brendan Rodgers (NIR)
Match 4 - Real Madrid CF (ESP)
A 0-1
Mignolet, Touré, Moreno, Javi Manquillo, Lallana, Lucas (Gerrard 69), Can (Coutinho 75), Allen, Borini, Škrtel, Marković (Sterling 69). Coach: Brendan Rodgers (NIR)
Match 5 - PFC Ludogorets Razgrad (BUL)
A 2-2 Lambert (8), Henderson (37)
Mignolet, Johnson, Touré, Gerrard, Lambert, Henderson, Javi Manquillo, Lucas, Allen, Sterling (Moreno 82), Škrtel. Coach: Brendan Rodgers (NIR)
Match 6 - FC Basel 1893 (SUI)
H 1-1 Gerrard (81)
Mignolet, Johnson, José Enrique (Moreno 46), Lovren, Gerrard, Lambert (Marković 46), Henderson, Lucas (Coutinho 74), Allen, Sterling, Škrtel. Coach: Brendan Rodgers (NIR)
Red card: Marković 60

Round of 32 - Beşiktaş JK (TUR)
H 1-0 Balotelli (85p)
Mignolet, Coutinho (Balotelli 63), Henderson, Sturridge, Sakho, Moreno, Lallana (Sterling 77), Can, Allen (Lovren 63), Ibe, Škrtel. Coach: Brendan Rodgers (NIR)
A 0-1 (aet; 4-5 on pens)
Mignolet, Touré, Lovren, Sturridge (Lambert 106), Moreno, Can, Allen, Sterling, Ibe (Javi Manquillo 76), Škrtel (Lallana 82). Coach: Brendan Rodgers (NIR)

Chelsea FC

Group G
Match 1 - FC Schalke 04 (GER)
H 1-1 Fàbregas (11)
Courtois, Ivanović, Filipe Luís, Fàbregas, Ramires (Oscar 67), Hazard, Drogba (Diego Costa 74), Matić, Willian (Rémy 74), Cahill, Terry. Coach: José Mourinho (POR)
Match 2 - Sporting Clube de Portugal (POR)
A 1-0 Matić (34)
Courtois, Ivanović, Filipe Luís, Fàbregas, Oscar (Mikel 71), Hazard (Salah 84), Schürrle (Willian 58), Diego Costa, Matić, Cahill, Terry. Coach: José Mourinho (POR)
Match 3 - NK Maribor (SVN)
H 6-0 Rémy (13), Drogba (23p), Terry (31), Viler (54og), Hazard (77p, 90)
Čech, Ivanović, Filipe Luís, Fàbregas (Aké 60), Zouma, Oscar (Solanke 73), Hazard, Rémy (Drogba 16), Matić, Willian, Terry. Coach: José Mourinho (POR)
Match 4 - NK Maribor (SVN)
A 1-1 Matić (73)
Čech, Ivanović, Filipe Luís (Ramires 56), Fàbregas, Zouma, Hazard, Drogba, Schürrle (Diego Costa 46), Matić, Willian (Oscar 46), Terry. Coach: José Mourinho (POR)

Match 5 - FC Schalke 04 (GER)
A 5-0 Terry (2), Willian (29), Kirchhoff (44og), Drogba (76), Ramires (78)
Courtois, Ivanović, Fàbregas (Schürrle 79), Oscar (Ramires 75), Hazard, Diego Costa (Drogba 66), Matić, Willian, Terry, Azpilicueta. Coach: José Mourinho (POR)
Match 6 - Sporting Clube de Portugal (POR)
H 3-1 Fàbregas (8p), Schürrle (16), Mikel (56)
Čech, Filipe Luís, Fàbregas (Loftus-Cheek 83), Zouma, Mikel, Schürrle (Ramires 74), Salah (Rémy 71), Diego Costa, Matić, Cahill, Azpilicueta. Coach: José Mourinho (POR)

Round of 16 - Paris Saint-Germain (FRA)
A 1-1 Ivanović (36)
Courtois, Ivanović, Fàbregas (Oscar 84), Ramires, Hazard, Diego Costa (Rémy 81), Matić, Willian (Cuadrado 79), Cahill, Terry, Azpilicueta. Coach: José Mourinho (POR)
H 2-2 Cahill (81), Hazard (96p) (aet)
Courtois, Ivanović, Fàbregas, Ramires (Drogba 91), Oscar (Willian 46), Hazard, Diego Costa, Matić (Zouma 84), Cahill, Terry, Azpilicueta. Coach: José Mourinho (POR)

Arsenal FC

Play-offs - Beşiktaş JK (TUR)
A 0-0
Szczęsny, Debuchy, Koscielny, Arteta (Flamini 50), Wilshere, Giroud, Ramsey, Alexis Sánchez (Oxlade-Chamberlain 73), Monreal, Santi Cazorla (Rosický 90), Chambers. Coach: Arsène Wenger (FRA)
Red card: Ramsey 80
H 1-0 Alexis Sánchez (45+1)
Szczęsny, Debuchy, Mertesacker, Koscielny, Wilshere, Özil (Chambers 77), Oxlade-Chamberlain, Alexis Sánchez, Monreal, Santi Cazorla, Flamini. Coach: Arsène Wenger (FRA)
Red card: Debuchy 75

Group D
Match 1 - Borussia Dortmund (GER)
A 0-2
Szczęsny, Gibbs, Mertesacker, Koscielny, Arteta (Podolski 77), Wilshere, Özil (Oxlade-Chamberlain 62), Ramsey (Santi Cazorla 62), Alexis Sánchez, Welbeck, Bellerín. Coach: Arsène Wenger (FRA)
Match 2 - Galatasaray AŞ (TUR)
H 4-1 Welbeck (22, 30, 52), Alexis Sánchez (41)
Szczęsny, Gibbs, Mertesacker, Koscielny, Özil (Wilshere 77), Oxlade-Chamberlain (Rosický 68), Alexis Sánchez (Ospina 62), Santi Cazorla, Flamini, Chambers, Welbeck. Coach: Arsène Wenger (FRA)
Red card: Szczęsny 60
Match 3 - RSC Anderlecht (BEL)
A 2-1 Gibbs (89), Podolski (90+1)
Martínez, Gibbs, Mertesacker, Wilshere (Podolski 84), Ramsey, Alexis Sánchez, Monreal, Santi Cazorla, Flamini (Oxlade-Chamberlain 75), Chambers, Welbeck (Campbell 75). Coach: Arsène Wenger (FRA)
Match 4 - RSC Anderlecht (BEL)
H 3-3 Arteta (25p), Alexis Sánchez (29), Oxlade-Chamberlain (58)
Szczęsny, Gibbs, Mertesacker, Arteta (Flamini 62), Oxlade-Chamberlain (Rosický 83), Ramsey, Alexis Sánchez, Monreal, Santi Cazorla, Chambers, Welbeck (Podolski 83). Coach: Arsène Wenger (FRA)

Match 5 - Borussia Dortmund (GER)
H 2-0 *Sanogo (2), Alexis Sánchez (57)*
Martínez, Gibbs, Mertesacker, Arteta (Flamini 67), Oxlade-Chamberlain (Campbell 90), Ramsey, Alexis Sánchez, Monreal, Santi Cazorla, Chambers, Sanogo (Podolski 79). Coach: Arsène Wenger (FRA)
Match 6 - Galatasaray AŞ (TUR)
A 4-1 *Podolski (3, 90+2), Ramsey (11, 29)*
Szczęsny, Debuchy (O'Connor 77), Mertesacker, Podolski, Oxlade-Chamberlain, Ramsey (Maitland-Niles 46), Flamini (Zelalem 46), Chambers, Sanogo, Campbell, Bellerín. Coach: Arsène Wenger (FRA)

Round of 16 - AS Monaco FC (FRA)
H 1-3 *Oxlade-Chamberlain (90+1)*
Ospina, Gibbs, Mertesacker, Koscielny, Özil, Giroud (Walcott 60), Alexis Sánchez, Santi Cazorla (Rosický 82), Welbeck, Coquelin (Oxlade-Chamberlain 68), Bellerín. Coach: Arsène Wenger (FRA)
A 2-0 *Giroud (36), Ramsey (79)*
Ospina, Mertesacker, Koscielny, Özil, Giroud, Alexis Sánchez, Monreal (Gibbs 83), Santi Cazorla, Welbeck (Walcott 72), Coquelin (Ramsey 63), Bellerín. Coach: Arsène Wenger (FRA)

Everton FC

Group H
Match 1 - VfL Wolfsburg (GER)
H 4-1 *Rodriguez (15og), Coleman (45+1), Baines (47p), Mirallas (89)*
Howard, Baines, Jagielka, McGeady, Lukaku (Eto'o 69), Mirallas, Naismith (Gibson 82), McCarthy, Barry, Coleman (Osman 90+1), Stones. Coach: Roberto Martínez (ESP)
Match 2 - FC Krasnodar (RUS)
A 1-1 *Eto'o (82)*
Howard, Hibbert, Baines, Gibson, Eto'o, Jagielka, McGeady, Barry, Atsu (Lukaku 46), Osman, Stones. Coach: Roberto Martínez (ESP)
Match 3 - LOSC Lille (FRA)
A 0-0
Howard, Hibbert, Baines, Eto'o, Jagielka, McGeady (Atsu 82), Distin, Bešić, Barry, Barkley (McCarthy 90+2), Pienaar (Lukaku 64). Coach: Roberto Martínez (ESP)
Match 4 - LOSC Lille (FRA)
H 3-0 *Osman (27), Jagielka (42), Naismith (61)*
Howard, Hibbert, Baines, Jagielka, McGeady (Atsu 66), Lukaku, Naismith, Distin, McCarthy (Bešić 84), Barry (Gibson 67), Osman. Coach: Roberto Martínez (ESP)
Match 5 - VfL Wolfsburg (GER)
A 2-0 *Lukaku (43), Mirallas (75)*
Howard, Hibbert, Eto'o (Barkley 72), Jagielka, McGeady, Lukaku, Mirallas (Atsu 83), Distin, McCarthy (Osman 31), Bešić, Garbutt. Coach: Roberto Martínez (ESP)
Match 6 - FC Krasnodar (RUS)
H 0-1
Joel, Oviedo, Koné, Barry, Atsu (Dowell 11), Pienaar, Browning (Jones 90), Garbutt, Alcaraz, McAleny (Long 80), Ledson. Coach: Roberto Martínez (ESP)

Round of 32 - BSC Young Boys (SUI)
A 4-1 *Lukaku (24, 39, 58), Coleman (28)*
Howard, Jagielka, Oviedo (Garbutt 58), Lukaku (Atsu 85), Mirallas, Naismith, McCarthy (Alcaraz 69), Barry, Barkley, Coleman, Stones. Coach: Roberto Martínez (ESP)
Red card: Stones 63

H 3-1 *Lukaku (25p, 30), Mirallas (42)*
Howard, Gibson, Jagielka, Lukaku (Koné 49), Mirallas, Naismith (Osman 80), McCarthy (Bešić 61), Barry, Coleman, Garbutt, Alcaraz. Coach: Roberto Martínez (ESP)

Round of 16 - FC Dynamo Kyiv (UKR)
H 2-1 *Naismith (39), Lukaku (82p)*
Howard, Jagielka, Lukaku, Mirallas (Koné 64), Naismith, McCarthy, Barry, Barkley (Osman 74), Coleman, Garbutt, Alcaraz. Coach: Roberto Martínez (ESP)
A 2-5 *Lukaku (29), Jagielka (82)*
Howard, Baines, Jagielka, Lukaku, Naismith (Koné 65), McCarthy (Bešić 77), Barry, Atsu (Osman 65), Barkley, Coleman, Alcaraz. Coach: Roberto Martínez (ESP)

Tottenham Hotspur FC

Play-offs - AEL Limassol FC (CYP)
A 2-1 *Soldado (74), Kane (80)*
Lloris, Vertonghen, Paulinho (Chadli 59), Soldado, Holtby (Dembélé 66), Dier, Naughton, Townsend (Lamela 72), Kane, Davies, Bentaleb. Coach: Mauricio Pochettino (ESP)
H 3-0 *Kane (45), Paulinho (49), Townsend (66p)*
Lloris, Kaboul, Chiricheș (Veljković 86), Lennon, Paulinho, Naughton, Townsend, Kane, Dembélé, Sandro (Holtby 78), Davies. Coach: Mauricio Pochettino (ESP)

Group C
Match 1 - FK Partizan (SRB)
A 0-0
Lloris, Vertonghen, Lennon, Paulinho (Soldado 60), Naughton, Townsend (Lamela 59), Kane, Fazio, Stambouli (Capoue 72), Davies, Bentaleb. Coach: Mauricio Pochettino (ESP)
Match 2 - Beşiktaş JK (TUR)
H 1-1 *Kane (27)*
Lloris, Chiricheș, Paulinho (Lennon 60), Soldado (Adebayor 79), Dier, Townsend, Kane, Fazio, Stambouli (Dembélé 65), Davies, Bentaleb. Coach: Mauricio Pochettino (ESP)
Match 3 - Asteras Tripolis FC (GRE)
H 5-1 *Kane (13, 74, 81), Lamela (30, 66)*
Lloris, Vertonghen, Adebayor (Chadli 76), Lamela (Eriksen 76), Dier, Townsend (Lennon 83), Kane, Dembélé, Fazio, Capoue, Davies. Coach: Mauricio Pochettino (ESP)
Red card: Lloris 87
Match 4 - Asteras Tripolis FC (GRE)
A 2-1 *Townsend (36p), Kane (42)*
Vorm, Vertonghen, Lamela (Soldado 46), Dier, Townsend, Kane (Paulinho 77), Dembélé, Fazio, Eriksen (Mason 63), Stambouli, Davies. Coach: Mauricio Pochettino (ESP)
Red card: Fazio 89
Match 5 - FK Partizan (SRB)
H 1-0 *Stambouli (49)*
Lloris, Vertonghen, Chiricheș, Lennon, Paulinho (Winks 87), Soldado (Kane 66), Lamela, Naughton, Dembélé (Bentaleb 56), Stambouli, Davies. Coach: Mauricio Pochettino (ESP)
Match 6 - Beşiktaş JK (TUR)
A 0-1
Vorm, Walker (Capoue 76), Rose, Kaboul, Chiricheș, Paulinho (Lennon 69), Soldado (Lamela 69), Townsend, Dembélé, Chadli, Stambouli. Coach: Mauricio Pochettino (ESP)

Round of 32 - ACF Fiorentina (ITA)
H 1-1 *Soldado (6)*
Lloris, Walker, Vertonghen, Paulinho (Mason 84), Soldado, Townsend (Lamela 73), Fazio, Chadli (Kane 66), Eriksen, Davies, Bentaleb. Coach: Mauricio Pochettino (ESP)
A 0-2
Lloris, Vertonghen (Walker 75), Chiricheș, Soldado, Lamela, Fazio, Chadli (Townsend 63), Eriksen, Stambouli, Davies, Bentaleb (Kane 63). Coach: Mauricio Pochettino (ESP)

Hull City AFC

Third qualifying round - FK AS Trenčín (SVK)
A 0-0
McGregor, Rosenior, Bruce, Chester, Davies, Meyler (Snodgrass 65), Huddlestone, Long (Jelavić 86), Livermore, Aluko (Ince 65), Elmohamady. Coach: Steve Bruce (ENG)
H 2-1 *Elmohamady (27), Aluko (80)*
McGregor, Bruce (Ince 66), Chester, Davies, Huddlestone, Long (Aluko 74), Snodgrass, Brady (Rosenior 56), Livermore, Sagbo, Elmohamady. Coach: Steve Bruce (ENG)

Play-offs - KSC Lokeren OV (BEL)
A 0-1
McGregor, Rosenior, Figueroa, Chester, Meyler, Brady (Ince 72), Maguire, McShane, Boyd (Elmohamady 80), Sagbo (Jelavić 72), Aluko. Coach: Steve Bruce (ENG)
H 2-1 *Brady (6, 55p)*
McGregor, Rosenior (Jelavić 66), Figueroa, Chester (Huddlestone 75), Davies, Meyler (Ince 75), Brady, Livermore, Sagbo, Aluko, Elmohamady. Coach: Steve Bruce (ENG)
Red card: Sagbo 71

DOMESTIC LEAGUE CLUB-BY-CLUB

Arsenal FC

1886 • Emirates Stadium (60,272) • arsenal.com
Major honours
UEFA Cup Winners' Cup (1) 1994; Inter Cities Fairs Cup (1) 1970; English League (13) 1931, 1933, 1934, 1935, 1938, 1948, 1953, 1971, 1989, 1991, 1998, 2002, 2004; FA Cup (12) 1930, 1936, 1950, 1971, 1979, 1993, 1998, 2002, 2003, 2005, 2014, 2015; League Cup (2) 1987, 1993
Manager: Arsène Wenger (FRA)

2014
16/08	h	Crystal Palace	W	2-1	Koscielny, Ramsey
23/08	a	Everton	D	2-2	Ramsey, Giroud
31/08	a	Leicester	D	1-1	Alexis Sánchez
13/09	h	Man. City	D	2-2	Wilshere, Alexis Sánchez
20/09	a	Aston Villa	W	3-0	Özil, Welbeck, og (Cissokho)
27/09	h	Tottenham	D	1-1	Oxlade-Chamberlain
05/10	a	Chelsea	L	0-2	
18/10	h	Hull	D	2-2	Alexis Sánchez, Welbeck
25/10	a	Sunderland	W	2-0	Alexis Sánchez 2
01/11	h	Burnley	W	3-0	Alexis Sánchez 2, Chambers
09/11	a	Swansea	L	1-2	Alexis Sánchez
22/11	h	Man. United	L	1-2	Giroud
29/11	a	West Brom	W	1-0	Welbeck
03/12	h	Southampton	W	1-0	Alexis Sánchez
06/12	a	Stoke	L	2-3	Santi Cazorla (p), Ramsey
13/12	h	Newcastle	W	4-1	Giroud 2, Santi Cazorla 2 (1p)
21/12	a	Liverpool	D	2-2	Debuchy, Giroud
26/12	h	QPR	W	2-1	Alexis Sánchez, Rosický
28/12	a	West Ham	W	2-1	Santi Cazorla (p), Welbeck

2015
01/01	a	Southampton	L	0-2	
11/01	h	Stoke	W	3-0	Koscielny, Alexis Sánchez 2
18/01	a	Man. City	W	2-0	Santi Cazorla (p), Giroud
01/02	h	Aston Villa	W	5-0	Giroud, Özil, Walcott, Santi Cazorla (p), Bellerín
07/02	a	Tottenham	L	1-2	Özil
10/02	h	Leicester	W	2-1	Koscielny, Walcott
21/02	a	Crystal Palace	W	2-1	Santi Cazorla (p), Giroud
01/03	h	Everton	W	2-0	Giroud, Rosický
04/03	a	QPR	W	2-1	Giroud, Alexis Sánchez
14/03	h	West Ham	W	3-0	Giroud, Ramsey, Flamini
21/03	a	Newcastle	W	2-1	Giroud 2
04/04	h	Liverpool	W	4-1	Bellerín, Özil, Alexis Sánchez, Giroud
11/04	a	Burnley	W	1-0	Ramsey
26/04	h	Chelsea	D	0-0	
04/05	a	Hull	W	3-1	Alexis Sánchez 2, Ramsey
11/05	h	Swansea	L	0-1	
17/05	a	Man. United	D	1-1	og (Blackett)
20/05	h	Sunderland	D	0-0	
24/05	h	West Brom	W	4-1	Walcott 3, Wilshere

No	Name	Nat	DoB	Pos	Aps	(s)	Gls
38	Chuba Akpom		09/10/95	A		(3)	
17	Alexis Sánchez	CHI	19/12/88	A	34	(1)	16
8	Mikel Arteta	ESP	26/03/82	M	6	(1)	
39	Héctor Bellerín	ESP	19/03/95	D	17	(3)	2
28	Joel Campbell	CRC	26/06/92	A		(4)	
21	Calum Chambers		20/01/95	D	17	(6)	1
34	Francis Coquelin	FRA	13/05/91	M	19	(3)	
2	Mathieu Debuchy	FRA	28/07/85	D	10		1
20	Mathieu Flamini	FRA	07/03/84	M	15	(8)	1
5	Gabriel	BRA	26/11/90	D	4	(2)	
3	Kieran Gibbs		26/09/89	D	18	(4)	
12	Olivier Giroud	FRA	30/09/86	A	21	(6)	14
6	Laurent Koscielny	FRA	10/09/85	D	26	(1)	3
70	Ainsley Maitland-Niles		29/08/97	M		(1)	
26	Emiliano Martínez	ARG	02/09/92	G	3	(1)	
4	Per Mertesacker	GER	29/09/84	D	35		
18	Nacho Monreal	ESP	26/02/86	D	26	(2)	
13	David Ospina	COL	31/08/88	G	18		
15	Alex Oxlade-Chamberlain		15/08/93	M	17	(6)	1
11	Mesut Özil	GER	15/10/88	M	21	(1)	4
9	Lukas Podolski	GER	04/06/85	A		(7)	
16	Aaron Ramsey	WAL	26/12/90	M	23	(6)	6
7	Tomáš Rosický	CZE	04/10/80	M	5	(10)	2
22	Yaya Sanogo	FRA	27/01/93	A	2	(1)	
19	Santi Cazorla	ESP	13/12/84	M	33	(4)	7
1	Wojciech Szczesny	POL	18/04/90	G	17		
14	Theo Walcott		16/03/89	A	4	(10)	5
23	Danny Welbeck		26/11/90	A	18	(7)	4
10	Jack Wilshere		01/01/92	M	9	(5)	2

Aston Villa FC

1874 • Villa Park (42,682) • avfc.co.uk
Major honours
European Champion Clubs' Cup (1) 1982; UEFA Super Cup (1) 1982; English League (7) 1894, 1896, 1897, 1899, 1900, 1910, 1981; FA Cup (7) 1887, 1895, 1897, 1905, 1913, 1920, 1957; League Cup (5) 1961, 1975, 1977, 1994, 1996
Manager: Paul Lambert (SCO); (14/02/15) Tim Sherwood

2014
16/08	a	Stoke	W	1-0	Weimann
23/08	h	Newcastle	D	0-0	
31/08	h	Hull	W	2-1	Agbonlahor, Weimann
13/09	a	Liverpool	W	1-0	Agbonlahor
20/09	h	Arsenal	L	0-3	
27/09	a	Chelsea	L	0-3	
04/10	a	Man. City	L	0-2	
18/10	a	Everton	L	0-3	
27/10	a	QPR	L	0-2	
02/11	h	Tottenham	L	1-2	Weimann
08/11	a	West Ham	D	0-0	
24/11	h	Southampton	D	1-1	Agbonlahor
29/11	a	Burnley	D	1-1	Cole
02/12	h	Crystal Palace	W	1-0	Benteke
07/12	a	Leicester	W	2-1	Clark, Hutton
13/12	a	West Brom	L	0-1	
20/12	h	Man. United	D	1-1	Benteke
26/12	a	Swansea	L	0-1	
28/12	h	Sunderland	D	0-0	

2015
01/01	h	Crystal Palace	D	0-0	
10/01	a	Leicester	L	0-1	
17/01	h	Liverpool	L	0-2	
01/02	a	Arsenal	L	0-5	
07/02	h	Chelsea	L	1-2	Okore
10/02	a	Hull	L	0-2	
21/02	h	Stoke	L	1-2	Sinclair
28/02	a	Newcastle	L	0-1	
03/03	h	West Brom	W	2-1	Agbonlahor, Benteke (p)
14/03	a	Sunderland	W	4-0	Benteke 2, Agbonlahor 2
21/03	h	Swansea	L	0-1	
04/04	a	Man. United	L	1-3	Benteke
07/04	h	QPR	D	3-3	Benteke 3
11/04	a	Tottenham	W	1-0	Benteke
25/04	h	Man. City	L	2-3	Cleverley, Sánchez
02/05	h	Everton	W	3-2	Benteke 2, Cleverley
09/05	h	West Ham	W	1-0	Cleverley
16/05	a	Southampton	L	1-6	Benteke
24/05	h	Burnley	L	0-1	

No	Name	Nat	DoB	Pos	Aps	(s)	Gls
11	Gabriel Agbonlahor		13/10/86	A	30	(4)	6
7	Leandro Bacuna	NED	21/08/91	M	10	(9)	
2	Nathan Baker		23/04/91	D	8	(3)	
19	Darren Bent		06/02/84	A		(7)	
20	Christian Benteke	BEL	03/12/90	A	26	(3)	13
23	Aly Cissokho	FRA	15/09/87	D	24	(1)	
6	Ciaran Clark	IRL	26/09/89	D	22	(3)	1
8	Tom Cleverley		12/08/89	M	31		3
12	Joe Cole		08/11/81	M	3	(9)	1
16	Fabian Delph		21/11/89	M	27	(1)	
25	Carles Gil	ESP	22/11/92	M	4	(1)	
31	Shay Given	IRL	20/04/76	G	3		
40	Jack Grealish	IRL	10/09/95	M	7	(10)	
1	Brad Guzan	USA	09/09/84	G	34		
29	Rushian Hepburn-Murphy		19/09/98	A		(1)	
21	Alan Hutton	SCO	30/11/84	D	27	(3)	1
34	Matthew Lowton		09/06/89	D	8	(4)	
28	Charles N'Zogbia	FRA	28/05/86	M	19	(8)	
5	Jores Okore	DEN	11/08/92	D	22	(1)	1
18	Kieran Richardson		21/10/84	M	16	(6)	
24	Carlos Sánchez	COL	06/02/86	M	20	(8)	1
14	Philippe Senderos	SUI	14/02/85	D	7	(1)	
9	Scott Sinclair		25/03/89	A	5	(4)	1
13	Jed Steer		23/09/92	G	1		
4	Ron Vlaar	NED	16/02/85	D	19	(1)	
10	Andreas Weimann	AUT	05/08/91	A	20	(11)	3
15	Ashley Westwood		01/04/90	M	25	(2)	

Burnley FC

1882 • Turf Moor (21,401) • burnleyfootballclub.com
Major honours
English League (2) 1921, 1960; FA Cup (1) 1914
Manager: Sean Dyche

2014
18/08	h	Chelsea	L	1-3	Arfield
23/08	a	Swansea	L	0-1	
30/08	h	Man. United	D	0-0	
13/09	a	Crystal Palace	D	0-0	
20/09	h	Sunderland	D	0-0	
28/09	a	West Brom	W	4-0	
04/10	a	Leicester	D	2-2	Kightly, Wallace
18/10	h	West Ham	L	1-3	Boyd
26/10	h	Everton	L	1-3	Ings
01/11	a	Arsenal	L	0-3	
08/11	h	Hull	W	1-0	Barnes
22/11	a	Stoke	W	2-1	Ings 2
29/11	h	Aston Villa	D	1-1	Ings (p)
02/12	h	Newcastle	D	1-1	Boyd
06/12	a	QPR	L	0-2	
13/12	h	Southampton	W	1-0	Barnes
20/12	a	Tottenham	L	1-2	Barnes
26/12	h	Liverpool	L	0-1	
28/12	a	Man. City	D	2-2	Boyd, Barnes

2015
01/01	a	Newcastle	D	3-3	og (Dummett), Ings, Boyd
10/01	h	QPR	W	2-1	Arfield, Ings
17/01	h	Crystal Palace	L	2-3	Mee, Ings
31/01	a	Sunderland	L	0-2	
08/02	h	West Brom	D	2-2	Barnes, Ings
11/02	a	Man. United	L	1-3	Ings
21/02	a	Chelsea	D	1-1	Mee
28/02	h	Swansea	L	0-1	
04/03	a	Liverpool	L	0-2	
14/03	h	Man. City	W	1-0	Boyd
21/03	a	Southampton	L	0-2	
05/04	h	Tottenham	D	0-0	
11/04	h	Arsenal	L	0-1	
18/04	a	Everton	L	0-1	
25/04	a	Leicester	L	0-1	
02/05	a	West Ham	L	0-1	
09/05	a	Hull	W	1-0	Ings
16/05	h	Stoke	W	0-0	
24/05	h	Aston Villa	W	1-0	Ings

No	Name	Nat	DoB	Pos	Aps	(s)	Gls
37	Scott Arfield	SCO	01/11/88	M	36	(1)	2
30	Ashley Barnes	AUT	30/10/89	A	28	(7)	5
21	George Boyd	SCO	02/10/85	M	35		5
20	Nathaniel Chalobah		12/12/94	M		(4)	
4	Michael Duff	NIR	11/01/78	D	21		
1	Tom Heaton		15/04/86	G	38		
10	Danny Ings		23/07/92	A	35		11
14	David Jones		04/11/84	M	36		
19	Lukas Jutkiewicz		28/03/89	A	10	(15)	
25	Michael Keane		11/01/93	D	17	(4)	
11	Michael Kightly		24/01/86	M	10	(7)	1
3	Daniel Lafferty	NIR	18/05/89	D		(1)	
28	Kevin Long	IRL	18/08/90	D		(1)	
8	Dean Marney		31/01/84	M	20		
6	Ben Mee		23/09/89	D	32	(1)	2
18	Steven Reid	IRL	10/03/81	D	1	(6)	
5	Jason Shackell		27/09/83	D	38		
17	Marvin Sordell		17/02/91	A	2	(12)	
15	Matt Taylor		27/11/81	M	7	(3)	
2	Kieran Trippier		19/09/90	D	38		
20	Fredrik Ulvestad	NOR	17/06/92	M	1	(1)	
9	Sam Vokes	WAL	21/10/89	A	5	(10)	
7	Ross Wallace	SCO	23/05/85	M	1	(14)	1
23	Stephen Ward	IRL	20/08/85	D	7	(2)	

 ENGLAND

Chelsea FC

1905 • Stamford Bridge (41,798) •
chelseafc.com
Major honours
*UEFA Champions League (1) 2012; UEFA Cup
Winners' Cup (2) 1971, 1998; UEFA Europa League
(1) 2013; UEFA Super Cup (1) 1998; English League
(5) 1955, 2005, 2006, 2010, 2015; FA Cup (7) 1970,
1997, 2000, 2007, 2009, 2010, 2012; League Cup
(5) 1965, 1998, 2005, 2007, 2015*
Manager: José Mourinho (POR)

2014
18/08	a	Burnley	W	3-1	Diego Costa, Schürrle, Ivanović
23/08	h	Leicester	W	2-0	Diego Costa, Hazard
30/08	a	Everton	W	6-3	Diego Costa 2, Ivanović, og (Coleman), Matić, Ramires
13/09	h	Swansea	W	4-2	Diego Costa 3, Rémy
21/09	a	Man. City	D	1-1	Schürrle
27/09	h	Aston Villa	W	3-0	Oscar, Diego Costa, Willian
05/10	h	Arsenal	W	2-0	Hazard (p), Diego Costa
18/10	a	Crystal Palace	W	2-1	Oscar, Fàbregas
26/10	a	Man. United	D	1-1	Drogba
01/11	h	QPR	W	2-1	Oscar, Hazard (p)
08/11	a	Liverpool	W	2-1	Cahill, Diego Costa
22/11	h	West Brom	W	2-0	Diego Costa, Hazard
29/11	a	Sunderland	D	0-0	
03/12	a	Tottenham	W	3-0	Hazard, Drogba, Rémy
06/12	a	Newcastle	L	1-2	Drogba
13/12	h	Hull	W	2-0	Hazard, Diego Costa
22/12	h	Stoke	W	2-0	Terry, Fàbregas
26/12	h	West Ham	W	2-0	Terry, Diego Costa
28/12	a	Southampton	D	1-1	Hazard
2015					
01/01	a	Tottenham	L	3-5	Diego Costa, Hazard, Terry
10/01	h	Newcastle	W	2-0	Oscar, Diego Costa
17/01	a	Swansea	W	5-0	Oscar 2, Diego Costa 2, Schürrle
31/01	h	Man. City	D	1-1	Rémy
07/02	a	Aston Villa	W	2-1	Hazard, Ivanović
11/02	h	Everton	W	1-0	Willian
21/02	h	Burnley	D	1-1	Ivanović
04/03	a	West Ham	W	1-0	Hazard
15/03	a	Southampton	D	1-1	Diego Costa
22/03	a	Hull	W	3-2	Hazard, Diego Costa, Rémy
04/04	h	Stoke	W	2-1	Hazard (p), Rémy
12/04	h	QPR	W	1-0	Fàbregas
18/04	a	Man. United	L	1-0	Hazard
26/04	a	Arsenal	D	0-0	
29/04	a	Leicester	W	3-1	Drogba, Terry, Ramires
03/05	h	Crystal Palace	W	1-0	Hazard
10/05	h	Liverpool	D	1-1	Terry
18/05	a	West Brom	L	0-3	
24/05	h	Sunderland	W	3-1	Diego Costa (p), Rémy 2

No	Name	Nat	DoB	Pos	Aps	(s)	Gls
6	Nathan Aké	NED	18/02/95	D		(1)	
28	César Azpilicueta	ESP	28/08/89	D	29		
37	Isaiah Brown		07/01/97	A		(1)	
24	Gary Cahill		19/12/85	D	33	(3)	1
1	Petr Čech	CZE	20/05/82	G	6	(1)	
31	Andreas Christensen	DEN	10/04/96	D		(1)	
13	Thibaut Courtois	BEL	11/05/92	G	32		
23	Juan Cuadrado	COL	26/05/88	M	4	(8)	
19	Diego Costa	ESP	07/10/88	A	24	(2)	20
11	Didier Drogba	CIV	11/03/78	A	8	(20)	4
4	Cesc Fàbregas	ESP	04/05/87	M	33	(1)	3
3	Filipe Luís	BRA	09/08/85	D	9	(6)	
10	Eden Hazard	BEL	07/01/91	M	38		14
2	Branislav Ivanović	SRB	22/02/84	D	38		4
36	Ruben Loftus-Cheek		23/01/96	M	2	(1)	
21	Nemanja Matić	SRB	01/08/88	M	35	(1)	1
12	John Obi Mikel	NGA	22/04/87	M	6	(12)	
8	Oscar	BRA	09/09/91	M	26	(2)	6
7	Ramires	BRA	24/03/87	M	11	(12)	1
18	Loïc Rémy	FRA	02/01/87	A	6	(13)	7
17	Mohamed Salah	EGY	15/06/92	M		(3)	
14	André Schürrle	GER	06/11/90	M	5	(9)	3
26	John Terry		07/12/80	D	38		5
22	Willian	BRA	09/08/88	M	28	(8)	2
5	Kurt Zouma	FRA	27/10/94	D	7	(8)	

Crystal Palace FC

1905 • Selhurst Park (25,747) • cpfc.co.uk
**Manager: Neil Warnock;
(27/12/14) (Keith Millen);
(02/01/15) Alan Pardew**

2014
16/08	a	Arsenal	L	1-2	Hangeland
23/08	h	West Ham	L	1-3	Chamakh
30/08	a	Newcastle	D	3-3	Gayle, Puncheon, Zaha
13/09	h	Burnley	D	0-0	
21/09	a	Everton	W	3-2	Jedinak (p), Campbell, Bolasie
27/09	h	Leicester	W	2-0	Campbell, Jedinak
04/10	a	Hull	L	0-2	
18/10	a	Chelsea	L	1-2	Campbell
25/10	a	West Brom	D	2-2	Hangeland, Jedinak (p)
03/11	a	Sunderland	L	1-3	og (Brown)
08/11	a	Man. United	L	0-1	
23/11	h	Liverpool	W	3-1	Gayle, Ledley, Jedinak
29/11	a	Swansea	D	1-1	Jedinak (p)
02/12	a	Aston Villa	L	0-1	
06/12	h	Tottenham	D	0-0	
13/12	h	Stoke	D	1-1	McArthur
20/12	a	Man. City	L	0-3	
26/12	h	Southampton	L	1-3	Dann
28/12	a	QPR	D	0-0	
2015					
01/01	a	Aston Villa	D	0-0	
10/01	h	Tottenham	W	2-1	Gayle (p), Puncheon
17/01	h	Burnley	W	3-2	Gayle 2, Puncheon
31/01	h	Everton	L	0-1	
07/02	a	Leicester	W	1-0	Ledley
11/02	h	Newcastle	D	1-1	Campbell
21/02	h	Arsenal	L	1-2	Murray
28/02	a	West Ham	W	3-1	Murray 2, Dann
03/03	a	Southampton	L	0-1	
14/03	h	QPR	W	3-1	Zaha, McArthur, Ward
21/03	a	Stoke	W	2-1	Murray (p), Zaha
06/04	h	Man. City	W	2-1	Murray, Puncheon
11/04	a	Sunderland	W	4-1	Murray, Bolasie 3
18/04	h	West Brom	L	0-2	
25/04	h	Hull	L	0-2	
03/05	a	Chelsea	L	0-1	
09/05	h	Man. United	L	1-2	Puncheon
16/05	a	Liverpool	W	3-1	Puncheon, Zaha, Murray
24/05	h	Swansea	W	1-0	Chamakh

No	Name	Nat	DoB	Pos	Aps	(s)	Gls
23	Shola Ameobi	NGA	12/10/81	A		(4)	
25	Barry Bannan	SCO	01/12/89	M	2	(5)	
7	Yannick Bolasie	COD	24/05/89	M	31	(3)	4
10	Fraizer Campbell		13/09/87	A	13	(7)	4
29	Marouane Chamakh	MAR	10/01/84	A	15	(3)	2
6	Scott Dann		14/02/87	D	34		2
27	Damien Delaney	IRL	29/07/81	D	28	(1)	
9	Kevin Doyle	IRL	18/09/83	A		(3)	
19	Zeki Fryers		09/09/92	D		(1)	
8	Dwight Gayle		20/10/90	A	11	(14)	5
5	Brede Hangeland	NOR	20/06/81	D	12	(2)	2
13	Wayne Hennessey	WAL	24/01/87	G	2	(1)	
15	Mile Jedinak	AUS	03/08/84	M	24		5
34	Martin Kelly		27/04/90	D	27	(4)	
28	Joe Ledley	WAL	23/01/87	M	30	(2)	2
24	Lee Chung-yong	KOR	02/07/88	M	1	(2)	
24	Adrian Mariappa	JAM	03/10/86	D	8	(4)	
24	James McArthur	SCO	07/10/87	M	29	(5)	2
17	Glenn Murray		25/09/83	A	9	(8)	7
22	Jordon Mutch		02/12/91	M	4	(9)	
15	Stuart O'Keefe		04/03/91	M	1	(1)	
42	Jason Puncheon		26/06/86	M	31	(6)	6
9	Yaya Sanogo	FRA	27/01/93	A	3	(7)	
40	Pape Souaré	SEN	06/06/90	D	7	(2)	
1	Julián Speroni	ARG	18/05/79	G	36		
14	Jerome Thomas		23/03/83	M		(1)	
2	Joel Ward		29/10/89	D	37		1
20	Jonathan Williams	WAL	09/10/93	M		(2)	
11	Wilfried Zaha		10/11/92	M	23	(8)	4

Everton FC

1878 • Goodison Park (39,571) •
evertonfc.com
Major honours
*UEFA Cup Winners' Cup (1) 1985; English League
(9) 1891, 1915, 1928, 1932, 1939, 1963, 1970, 1985,
1987; FA Cup (5) 1906, 1933, 1966, 1984, 1995*
Manager: Roberto Martínez (ESP)

2014
16/08	a	Leicester	D	2-2	McGeady, Naismith
23/08	h	Arsenal	D	2-2	Coleman, Naismith
30/08	h	Chelsea	L	3-6	Mirallas, Naismith, Eto'o
13/09	h	West Brom	W	2-0	Lukaku, Mirallas
21/09	h	Crystal Palace	L	2-3	Lukaku, Baines (p)
27/09	a	Liverpool	D	1-1	Jagielka
05/10	a	Man. United	L	1-2	Naismith
18/10	h	Aston Villa	W	3-0	Jagielka, Lukaku, Coleman
26/10	a	Burnley	W	3-1	Eto'o 2, Lukaku
01/11	h	Swansea	D	0-0	
09/11	a	Sunderland	D	1-1	Baines (p)
22/11	h	West Ham	W	2-1	Lukaku, Osman
30/11	a	Tottenham	L	1-2	Mirallas
03/12	h	Hull	D	1-1	Lukaku
06/12	a	Man. City	L	0-1	
15/12	h	QPR	W	3-1	Barkley, Mirallas, og (Onuoha)
20/12	a	Southampton	L	0-3	
26/12	h	Stoke	L	0-1	
28/12	a	Newcastle	L	2-3	Koné, Mirallas
2015					
01/01	a	Hull	L	0-2	
10/01	h	Man. City	D	1-1	Naismith
19/01	h	West Brom`	D	0-0	
31/01	a	Crystal Palace	W	1-0	Lukaku
07/02	h	Liverpool	D	0-0	
11/02	h	Chelsea	L	0-1	
22/02	h	Leicester	D	2-2	Naismith, og (Upson)
01/03	a	Arsenal	L	0-2	
04/03	a	Stoke	L	0-2	
15/03	h	Newcastle	W	3-0	McCarthy, Lukaku (p), Barkley
22/03	h	QPR	W	2-1	Coleman, Lennon
04/04	h	Southampton	W	1-0	Jagielka
11/04	a	Swansea	D	1-1	Lennon
18/04	a	Burnley	L	0-1	Mirallas
26/04	h	Man. United	W	3-0	McCarthy, Stones, Mirallas
02/05	a	Aston Villa	L	2-3	Lukaku (p), Jagielka
09/05	h	Sunderland	L	0-2	
16/05	h	West Ham	W	2-1	Osman, Lukaku
24/05	h	Tottenham	L	0-1	

No	Name	Nat	DoB	Pos	Aps	(s)	Gls
30	Antolín Alcaraz	PAR	30/07/82	D	6	(2)	
19	Christian Atsu	GHA	10/01/92	M	1	(4)	
3	Leighton Baines		11/12/84	D	31		2
20	Ross Barkley		05/12/93	M	22	(7)	2
18	Gareth Barry		23/02/81	M	33		
17	Muhamed Bešić	BIH	10/09/92	M	15	(8)	
27	Tyias Browning		27/05/94	D		(2)	
15	Séamus Coleman	IRL	11/10/88	D	34	(1)	3
15	Sylvain Distin	FRA	16/12/77	D	12	(1)	
5	Samuel Eto'o	CMR	10/03/81	A	8	(6)	3
32	Brendan Galloway		17/03/96	D	2		
29	Luke Garbutt		21/05/93	D	3	(1)	
4	Darron Gibson	IRL	25/10/87	M	3	(6)	
2	Tony Hibbert		20/02/81	D	4		
24	Tim Howard	USA	06/03/79	G	32		
6	Phil Jagielka		17/08/82	D	37		4
1	Joel Robles	ESP	17/06/90	G	6	(1)	
9	Arouna Koné	CIV	11/11/83	A	7	(5)	1
25	Aaron Lennon		16/04/87	M	12	(2)	2
10	Romelu Lukaku	BEL	13/05/93	A	32	(4)	10
16	James McCarthy	IRL	12/11/90	M	27	(1)	2
7	Aiden McGeady	IRL	04/04/86	M	10	(6)	1
11	Kevin Mirallas	BEL	05/10/87	M	18	(11)	7
14	Steven Naismith	SCO	14/09/86	A	22	(9)	6
21	Leon Osman		17/05/81	M	13	(8)	2
8	Bryan Oviedo	CRC	18/02/90	D	2	(4)	
22	Steven Pienaar	RSA	17/03/82	M	3	(6)	
26	John Stones		28/05/94	D	23		1

Hull City AFC

1904 • KC Stadium (25,400) •
hullcitytigers.com
Manager: Steve Bruce

2014

16/08	a	QPR	W	1-0	Chester
24/08	h	Stoke	D	1-1	Jelavić
31/08	a	Aston Villa	L	1-2	Jelavić
15/09	h	West Ham	D	2-2	Hernández, Diamé
20/09	a	Newcastle	D	2-2	Jelavić, Diamé
27/09	h	Man. City	L	2-4	og (Mangala), Hernández (p)
04/10	h	Crystal Palace	W	2-0	Diamé, Jelavić
18/10	a	Arsenal	D	2-2	Diamé, Hernández
25/10	a	Liverpool	D	0-0	
01/11	h	Southampton	L	0-1	
08/11	h	Burnley	L	0-1	
23/11	h	Tottenham	L	1-2	Livermore
29/11	a	Man. United	L	0-3	
03/12	a	Everton	D	1-1	Aluko
06/12	h	West Brom	D	0-0	
13/12	a	Chelsea	L	0-2	
20/12	h	Swansea	L	0-1	
26/12	h	Sunderland	W	3-1	Ramírez, Chester, Jelavić
28/12	h	Leicester	L	0-1	

2015

01/01	h	Everton	W	2-0	Elmohamady, Jelavić
10/01	a	West Brom	L	0-1	
18/01	a	West Ham	L	0-3	
31/01	h	Newcastle	L	0-3	
07/02	a	Man. City	D	1-1	Meyler
10/02	h	Aston Villa	W	2-0	Jelavić, N'Doye
21/02	a	QPR	W	2-1	Jelavić, N'Doye
28/02	a	Stoke	L	0-1	
03/03	h	Sunderland	D	1-1	N'Doye
14/03	a	Leicester	D	0-0	
22/03	h	Chelsea	L	2-3	Elmohamady, Hernández
04/04	a	Swansea	L	1-3	McShane
11/04	a	Southampton	L	0-2	
25/04	h	Crystal Palace	W	2-0	N'Doye 2
28/04	h	Liverpool	W	1-0	Dawson
04/05	h	Arsenal	L	1-3	Quinn
09/05	h	Burnley	L	0-1	
16/05	a	Tottenham	L	0-2	
24/05	a	Man. United	D	0-0	

No	Name	Nat	DoB	Pos	Aps	(s)	Gls
24	Sone Aluko	NGA	19/02/89	A	13	(12)	1
10	Hatem Ben Arfa	FRA	07/03/87	M	5	(3)	
17	George Boyd	SCO	02/10/85	M		(1)	
11	Robbie Brady	IRL	14/01/92	M	17	(10)	
4	Alex Bruce	NIR	28/09/84	D	17	(5)	
5	James Chester	WAL	23/01/89	D	23		2
6	Curtis Davies		15/03/85	D	21		
20	Michael Dawson		18/11/83	D	28		1
17	Mohamed Diamé	SEN	14/06/87	M	10	(2)	4
27	Ahmed Elmohamady	EGY	09/09/87	M	38		2
3	Maynor Figueroa	HON	02/05/83	D	2	(1)	
22	Steve Harper		14/03/75	G	10		
9	Abel Hernández	URU	08/08/90	A	15	(10)	4
8	Tom Huddlestone		28/12/86	M	30	(1)	
23	Tom Ince		30/01/92	M	3	(4)	
16	Eldin Jakupovic	SUI	02/10/84	G	2	(1)	
18	Nikica Jelavić	CRO	27/08/85	A	21	(5)	8
14	Jake Livermore		14/11/89	M	35		1
12	Harry Maguire		05/03/93	D		(3)	
1	Allan McGregor	SCO	31/01/82	G	26		
15	Paul McShane	IRL	06/01/86	D	19	(1)	1
7	David Meyler	IRL	29/05/89	M	19	(9)	1
28	Dame N'Doye	SEN	21/02/85	A	13	(2)	5
29	Stephen Quinn	IRL	01/04/86	M	17	(11)	1
10	Gastón Ramírez	URU	02/12/90	M	11	(11)	1
26	Andrew Robertson	SCO	11/03/94	D	17	(7)	
2	Liam Rosenior		09/07/84	D	5	(8)	
20	Yannick Sagbo	CIV	12/04/88	A		(4)	
10	Robert Snodgrass	SCO	07/09/87	M	1		

Leicester City FC

1884 • King Power Stadium (32,312) •
lcfc.com
Major honours
League Cup (3) 1964, 1997, 2000
Manager: Nigel Pearson

2014

16/08	h	Everton	D	2-2	Ulloa, Wood
23/08	a	Chelsea	L	0-2	
31/08	h	Arsenal	D	1-1	Ulloa
13/09	a	Stoke	W	1-0	Ulloa
21/09	h	Man. United	W	5-3	Ulloa 2 (1p), Nugent (p), Cambiasso, Vardy
27/09	a	Crystal Palace	L	0-2	
04/10	h	Burnley	D	2-2	Schlupp, Mahrez
18/10	a	Newcastle	L	0-1	
25/10	a	Swansea	L	0-2	
01/11	h	West Brom	L	0-1	
08/11	a	Southampton	L	0-2	
22/11	h	Sunderland	D	0-0	
29/11	h	QPR	L	2-3	Cambiasso, Schlupp
02/12	h	Liverpool	L	1-3	og (Mignolet)
07/12	a	Aston Villa	L	1-2	Ulloa
13/12	h	Man. City	L	0-1	
20/12	a	West Ham	L	0-2	
26/12	h	Tottenham	L	1-2	Ulloa
28/12	a	Hull	W	1-0	Mahrez

2015

01/01	a	Liverpool	D	2-2	Nugent, Schlupp
10/01	a	Aston Villa	W	1-0	Konchesky
17/01	h	Stoke	L	0-1	
31/01	a	Man. United	L	1-3	Wasilewski
07/02	h	Crystal Palace	L	0-1	
10/02	a	Arsenal	L	1-2	Kramarić
22/02	a	Everton	D	2-2	Nugent, Cambiasso
04/03	a	Man. City	L	0-2	
14/03	h	Hull	D	0-0	
21/03	h	Tottenham	L	3-4	Vardy, Morgan, Nugent
04/04	h	West Ham	W	2-1	Cambiasso, King
11/04	a	West Brom	W	3-2	Nugent, Huth, Vardy
18/04	h	Swansea	W	2-0	Ulloa, King
25/04	h	Burnley	W	1-0	Vardy
29/04	h	Chelsea	L	1-3	Albrighton
02/05	a	Newcastle	W	3-0	Ulloa 2 (1p), Morgan
09/05	h	Southampton	W	2-0	Mahrez 2
16/05	a	Sunderland	D	0-0	
24/05	h	QPR	W	5-1	Vardy, Albrighton, Ulloa, Cambiasso, Kramarić

No	Name	Nat	DoB	Pos	Aps	(s)	Gls
11	Marc Albrighton		18/11/89	M	10	(8)	2
19	Esteban Cambiasso	ARG	18/08/80	M	27	(4)	5
2	Ritchie De Laet	BEL	28/11/88	D	20	(6)	
4	Danny Drinkwater		05/03/90	M	16	(7)	
12	Ben Hamer		20/11/87	G	8		
7	Dean Hammond		07/03/83	M	9	(3)	
14	Robert Huth	GER	18/08/84	D	14		1
8	Matty James		22/07/91	M	20	(7)	
10	Andy King	WAL	29/10/88	M	16	(8)	2
24	Anthony Knockaert	FRA	20/11/91	M	3	(6)	
3	Paul Konchesky		15/05/81	D	26		1
40	Andrej Kramarić	CRO	19/06/91	A	6	(7)	2
16	Tom Lawrence	WAL	13/01/94	M		(3)	
26	Riyad Mahrez	ALG	21/02/91	M	25	(5)	4
18	Liam Moore		31/01/93	D	10	(1)	
5	Wes Morgan	JAM	21/01/84	D	37		2
35	David Nugent		02/05/85	A	16	(13)	5
14	Nick Powell		23/03/94	M		(3)	
15	Jeff Schlupp	GHA	23/12/92	M	30	(2)	3
1	Kasper Schmeichel	DEN	05/11/86	G	24		
32	Mark Schwarzer	AUS	06/10/72	G	6		
17	Danny Simpson		04/01/87	D	13	(1)	
22	Gary Taylor-Fletcher		04/06/81	A		(1)	
23	Leonardo Ulloa	ARG	26/07/86	A	29	(8)	11
6	Matthew Upson		18/04/79	D	5		
9	Jamie Vardy		11/01/87	A	26	(8)	5
27	Marcin Wasilewski	POL	09/06/80	D	22	(3)	1
39	Chris Wood	NZL	07/12/91	A		(7)	1

Liverpool FC

1892 • Anfield (45,276) • liverpoolfc.com
Major honours
European Champion Clubs' Cup/UEFA Champions
League (5) 1977, 1978, 1981, 1984, 2005; UEFA
Cup (3) 1973, 1976, 2001; UEFA Super Cup (3)
1977, 2001, 2005; English League (18) 1901, 1906,
1922, 1923, 1947, 1964, 1966, 1973, 1976, 1977,
1979, 1980, 1982, 1983, 1984, 1986, 1988, 1990;
FA Cup (7) 1965, 1974, 1986, 1989, 1992, 2001,
2006; League Cup (8) 1981, 1982, 1983, 1984,
1995, 2001, 2003, 2012
Manager: Brendan Rodgers (NIR)

2014

17/08	h	Southampton	W	2-1	Sterling, Sturridge
25/08	a	Man. City	L	1-3	og (Zabaleta)
31/08	h	Tottenham	W	3-0	Sterling, Gerrard (p), Moreno
13/09	h	Aston Villa	L	0-1	
20/09	a	West Ham	L	1-3	Sterling
27/09	h	Everton	D	1-1	Gerrard
04/10	h	West Brom	W	2-1	Lallana, Henderson
19/10	a	QPR	W	3-2	og (Dunne), Coutinho, og (Caulker)
25/10	h	Hull	D	0-0	
01/11	a	Newcastle	L	0-1	
08/11	h	Chelsea	L	1-2	Can
23/11	a	Crystal Palace	L	1-3	Lambert
29/11	h	Stoke	W	1-0	Johnson
02/12	a	Leicester	W	3-1	Lallana, Gerrard, Henderson
06/12	h	Sunderland	D	0-0	
14/12	a	Man. United	L	0-3	
21/12	h	Arsenal	D	2-2	Coutinho, Škrtel
26/12	a	Burnley	W	1-0	Sterling
29/12	h	Swansea	W	4-1	Moreno, Lallana 2, og (Shelvey)

2015

01/01	h	Leicester	D	2-2	Gerrard 2 (2p)
10/01	a	Sunderland	W	1-0	Marković
17/01	a	Aston Villa	W	2-0	Borini, Lambert
31/01	h	West Ham	W	2-0	Sterling, Sturridge
07/02	a	Everton	D	0-0	
10/02	h	Tottenham	W	3-2	Marković, Gerrard (p), Balotelli
22/02	a	Southampton	W	2-0	Coutinho, Sterling
01/03	h	Man. City	W	2-1	Henderson, Coutinho
04/03	h	Burnley	W	2-0	Henderson, Sturridge
10/03	a	Swansea	W	1-0	Henderson
22/03	h	Man. United	L	1-2	Sturridge
04/04	a	Arsenal	L	1-4	Henderson (p)
13/04	h	Newcastle	W	2-0	Sterling, Allen
25/04	a	West Brom	D	0-0	
28/04	h	Hull	L	0-1	
02/05	h	QPR	W	2-1	Coutinho, Gerrard
10/05	a	Chelsea	D	1-1	Gerrard
16/05	h	Crystal Palace	L	1-3	Lallana
24/05	a	Stoke	L	1-6	Gerrard

No	Name	Nat	DoB	Pos	Aps	(s)	Gls
24	Joe Allen	WAL	14/03/90	M	16	(5)	1
45	Mario Balotelli	ITA	12/08/90	A	10	(6)	1
29	Fabio Borini	ITA	29/03/91	A	3	(9)	1
23	Emre Can	GER	12/01/94	M	23	(4)	
10	Philippe Coutinho	BRA	12/06/92	M	32	(3)	5
8	Steven Gerrard		30/05/80	M	25	(4)	9
14	Jordan Henderson		17/06/90	M	36	(1)	6
33	Jordon Ibe		08/12/95	M	7	(5)	
19	Javi Manquillo	ESP	05/05/94	D	10		
2	Glen Johnson		23/08/84	D	15	(4)	1
1	Brad Jones	AUS	19/03/82	G	3		
3	José Enrique	ESP	23/01/86	D	2	(2)	
20	Adam Lallana		10/05/88	M	23	(4)	5
9	Rickie Lambert		16/02/82	A	7	(18)	2
6	Dejan Lovren	CRO	05/07/89	D	22	(4)	
21	Lucas Leiva	BRA	09/01/87	M	16	(4)	
50	Lazar Marković	SRB	02/03/94	M	11	(8)	2
22	Simon Mignolet	BEL	06/08/88	G	35	(1)	
18	Alberto Moreno	ESP	05/07/92	D	26	(2)	2
17	Mamadou Sakho	FRA	13/02/90	D	15	(1)	
48	Jerome Sinclair		20/09/96	A		(2)	
37	Martin Škrtel	SVK	15/12/84	D	33		1
31	Raheem Sterling		08/12/94	A	34	(1)	7
15	Daniel Sturridge		01/09/89	A	7	(5)	4
4	Kolo Touré	CIV	19/03/81	D	7	(5)	

ENGLAND

Manchester City FC

1894 • Etihad Stadium (46,708) • mcfc.co.uk

Major honours
UEFA Cup Winners' Cup (1) 1970; English League (4) 1937, 1968, 2012, 2014; FA Cup (5) 1904, 1934, 1956, 1969, 2011; League Cup (3) 1970, 1976, 2014

Manager: Manuel Pellegrini (CHI)

2014

17/08	a	Newcastle	W	2-0	*Silva, Agüero*
25/08	h	Liverpool	W	3-1	*Jovetić 2, Agüero*
30/08	h	Stoke	L	0-1	
13/09	a	Arsenal	D	2-2	*Agüero, Demichelis*
21/09	h	Chelsea	D	1-1	*Lampard*
27/09	a	Hull	W	4-2	*Agüero, Džeko 2, Lampard*
04/10	h	Aston Villa	W	2-0	*Touré, Agüero*
18/10	h	Tottenham	W	4-1	*Agüero 4 (2p)*
25/10	a	West Ham	L	1-2	*Silva*
02/11	h	Man. United	W	1-0	*Agüero*
08/11	a	QPR	D	2-2	*Agüero 2*
22/11	h	Swansea	W	2-1	*Jovetić, Touré*
30/11	a	Southampton	W	3-0	*Touré, Lampard, Clichy*
03/12	a	Sunderland	W	4-1	*Agüero 2, Jovetić, Zabaleta*
06/12	h	Everton	W	1-0	*Touré (p)*
13/12	a	Leicester	W	1-0	*Lampard*
20/12	h	Crystal Palace	W	3-0	*Silva 2, Touré*
26/12	a	West Brom	W	3-1	*Fernando, Touré (p), Silva*
28/12	h	Burnley	D	2-2	*Silva, Fernandinho*

2015

01/01	h	Sunderland	W	3-2	*Touré, Jovetić, Lampard*
10/01	a	Everton	D	1-1	*Fernandinho*
18/01	h	Arsenal	L	0-2	
31/01	a	Chelsea	D	1-1	*Silva*
07/02	h	Hull	D	1-1	*Milner*
11/02	a	Stoke	W	4-1	*Agüero 2 (1p), Milner, Nasri*
21/02	h	Newcastle	W	5-0	*Agüero (p), Nasri, Džeko, Silva 2*
01/03	a	Liverpool	L	1-2	*Džeko*
04/03	h	Leicester	W	2-0	*Silva, Milner*
14/03	a	Burnley	L	0-1	
21/03	h	West Brom	W	3-0	*Bony, Fernando, Silva*
06/04	a	Crystal Palace	L	1-2	*Touré*
12/04	a	Man. United	L	2-4	*Agüero 2*
19/04	h	West Ham	W	2-0	*og (Collins), Agüero*
25/04	h	Aston Villa	W	3-2	*Agüero, Kolarov, Fernandinho*
03/05	a	Tottenham	W	1-0	*Agüero*
10/05	h	QPR	W	6-0	*Agüero 3 (1p), Kolarov, Milner, Silva*
17/05	a	Swansea	W	4-2	*Touré 2, Milner, Bony*
24/05	h	Southampton	W	2-0	*Lampard, Agüero*

No	Name	Nat	DoB	Pos	Aps	(s)	Gls
16	Sergio Agüero	ARG	02/06/88	A	30	(3)	26
14	Wilfried Bony	CIV	10/12/88	A	2	(8)	2
38	Dedryck Boyata	BEL	28/11/90	D	1	(1)	
13	Willy Caballero	ARG	28/09/81	G	2		
22	Gaël Clichy	FRA	26/07/85	D	23		1
26	Martín Demichelis	ARG	20/12/80	D	28	(3)	1
10	Edin Džeko	BIH	17/03/86	A	11	(11)	4
25	Fernandinho	BRA	04/05/85	M	25	(8)	3
6	Fernando	BRA	25/07/87	M	22	(3)	2
1	Joe Hart		19/04/87	G	36		
15	Jesús Navas	ESP	21/11/85	M	23	(12)	
35	Stevan Jovetić	MNE	02/11/89	A	9	(8)	5
11	Aleksandar Kolarov	SRB	10/11/85	D	16	(5)	2
4	Vincent Kompany	BEL	10/04/86	D	23	(2)	
18	Frank Lampard		20/06/78	M	10	(22)	6
20	Eliaquim Mangala	FRA	13/02/91	D	24	(1)	
7	James Milner		04/01/86	M	18	(14)	5
8	Samir Nasri	FRA	26/06/87	M	18	(6)	2
78	José Ángel Pozo	ESP	15/03/96	A	1	(2)	
3	Bacary Sagna	FRA	14/02/83	D	8	(1)	
21	David Silva	ESP	08/01/86	M	32		12
12	Scott Sinclair		25/03/89	M		(2)	
42	Yaya Touré	CIV	13/05/83	M	27	(2)	10
5	Pablo Zabaleta	ARG	16/01/85	D	29		1

Manchester United FC

1878 • Old Trafford (75,635) • manutd.com

Major honours
European Champion Clubs' Cup/UEFA Champions League (3) 1968, 1999, 2008; UEFA Cup Winners' Cup (1) 1991; UEFA Super Cup (1) 1991; European/ South American Cup (1) 1999; FIFA Club World Cup (1) 2008; English League (20) 1908, 1911, 1952, 1956, 1957, 1965, 1967, 1993, 1994, 1996, 1997, 1999, 2000, 2001, 2003, 2007, 2008, 2009, 2011, 2013; FA Cup (11) 1909, 1948, 1963, 1977, 1983, 1985, 1990, 1994, 1996, 1999, 2004; League Cup (4) 1992, 2006, 2009, 2010

Manager: Louis van Gaal (NED)

2014

16/08	h	Swansea	L	1-2	*Rooney*
24/08	a	Sunderland	D	1-1	*Mata*
30/08	a	Burnley	D	0-0	
14/09	h	QPR	W	4-0	*Di María, Ander Herrera, Rooney, Mata*
21/09	a	Leicester	L	3-5	*Van Persie, Di María, Ander Herrera*
27/09	h	West Ham	W	2-1	*Rooney, Van Persie*
05/10	h	Everton	W	2-1	*Di María, Falcao*
20/10	a	West Brom	D	2-2	*Fellaini, Blind*
26/10	h	Chelsea	D	1-1	*Van Persie*
02/11	a	Man. City	L	0-1	
08/11	h	Crystal Palace	W	1-0	*Mata*
22/11	a	Arsenal	W	2-1	*og (Gibbs), Rooney*
29/11	h	Hull	W	3-0	*Smalling, Rooney, Van Persie*
02/12	h	Stoke	W	2-1	*Fellaini, Mata*
08/12	a	Southampton	W	2-1	*Van Persie 2*
14/12	h	Liverpool	W	3-0	*Rooney, Mata, Van Persie*
20/12	a	Aston Villa	D	1-1	*Falcao*
26/12	h	Newcastle	W	3-1	*Rooney 2, Van Persie*
28/12	a	Tottenham	D	0-0	

2015

01/01	a	Stoke	D	1-1	*Falcao*
11/01	h	Southampton	L	0-1	
17/01	a	QPR	W	2-0	*Fellaini, Wilson*
31/01	h	Leicester	W	3-1	*Van Persie, Falcao, og (Morgan)*
08/02	a	West Ham	D	1-1	*Blind*
11/02	h	Burnley	W	3-1	*Smalling 2, Van Persie (p)*
21/02	a	Swansea	L	1-2	*Ander Herrera*
28/02	h	Sunderland	W	2-0	*Rooney 2 (1p)*
04/03	a	Newcastle	W	1-0	*Young*
15/03	h	Tottenham	W	3-0	*Fellaini, Carrick, Rooney*
22/03	a	Liverpool	W	2-1	*Mata 2*
04/04	h	Aston Villa	W	3-1	*Ander Herrera 2, Rooney*
12/04	h	Man. City	W	4-2	*Young, Fellaini, Mata, Smalling*
18/04	a	Chelsea	L	0-1	
26/04	a	Everton	L	0-3	
02/05	h	West Brom	L	0-1	
09/05	a	Crystal Palace	W	2-1	*Mata (p), Fellaini*
17/05	h	Arsenal	D	1-1	*Ander Herrera*
24/05	a	Hull	D	0-0	

No	Name	Nat	DoB	Pos	Aps	(s)	Gls
21	Ander Herrera	ESP	14/08/89	M	19	(7)	6
28	Anderson	BRA	13/04/88	M		(1)	
44	Andreas Pereira	BRA	01/01/96	M		(1)	
42	Tyler Blackett		02/04/94	D	6	(5)	
17	Daley Blind	NED	09/03/90	M	25		2
16	Michael Carrick		28/07/81	M	16	(2)	1
23	Tom Cleverley		12/08/89	M	1		
1	David de Gea	ESP	07/11/90	G	37		
7	Ángel Di María	ARG	14/02/88	M	20	(7)	3
6	Jonny Evans	NIR	03/01/88	D	12	(2)	
9	Radamel Falcao	COL	10/02/86	A	14	(12)	4
31	Marouane Fellaini	BEL	22/11/87	M	19	(8)	6
24	Darren Fletcher	SCO	01/02/84	M	4	(7)	
14	Javier Hernández	MEX	01/06/88	A	1		
11	Adnan Januzaj	BEL	05/02/95	M	7	(11)	
4	Phil Jones		21/02/92	D	22		
38	Michael Keane		22/01/93	D		(1)	
35	Jesse Lingard		15/12/92	M	1		
8	Juan Mata	ESP	28/04/88	M	27	(6)	9
33	Paddy McNair	NIR	27/04/95	D	12	(4)	
17	Nani	POR	17/11/86	M		(1)	
2	Rafael	BRA	09/07/90	D	6	(4)	
5	Marcos Rojo	ARG	20/03/90	D	20	(2)	
10	Wayne Rooney		24/10/85	A	33		12
3	Luke Shaw		12/07/95	D	15	(1)	
12	Chris Smalling		22/11/89	D	21	(4)	4
39	Tom Thorpe		13/01/93	D		(1)	
25	Antonio Valencia	ECU	04/08/85	M	29	(3)	
20	Robin van Persie	NED	06/08/83	A	25	(2)	10
32	Víctor Valdés	ESP	14/01/82	G	1	(1)	
19	Danny Welbeck		26/11/90	A		(2)	
49	James Wilson		01/12/95	A	2	(11)	1
18	Ashley Young		09/07/85	M	23	(3)	2

Newcastle United FC

1881 • St James' Park (52,405) • nufc.co.uk

Major honours
Inter Cities Fairs Cup (1) 1969; English League (4) 1905, 1907, 1909, 1927; FA Cup (6) 1910, 1924, 1932, 1951, 1952, 1955

Manager: Alan Pardew; (31/12/14) (John Carver)

2014

17/08	h	Man. City	L	0-2	
23/08	a	Aston Villa	D	0-0	
30/08	h	Crystal Palace	D	3-3	*Janmaat, Aarons, Williamson*
13/09	a	Southampton	L	0-4	
20/09	h	Hull	D	2-2	*Cissé 2*
29/09	a	Stoke	L	0-1	
04/10	a	Swansea	D	2-2	*Cissé 2*
18/10	h	Leicester	W	1-0	*Obertan*
26/10	a	Tottenham	W	2-1	*Ameobi, Ayoze*
01/11	h	Liverpool	W	1-0	*Ayoze*
09/11	a	West Brom	W	2-0	*Ayoze, Coloccini*
22/11	h	QPR	W	1-0	*Sissoko*
29/11	a	West Ham	L	0-1	
02/12	a	Burnley	D	1-1	*Cissé*
06/12	h	Chelsea	W	2-1	*Cissé 2*
13/12	a	Arsenal	L	1-4	*Ayoze*
21/12	h	Sunderland	L	0-1	
26/12	a	Man. United	L	1-3	*Cissé (p)*
28/12	h	Everton	W	3-2	*Cissé, Ayoze, Colback*

2015

01/01	h	Burnley	D	3-3	*S Taylor, Colback, Sissoko*
10/01	a	Chelsea	L	0-2	
17/01	h	Southampton	L	1-2	*Gouffran*
31/01	a	Hull	W	3-0	*Cabella, Ameobi, Gouffran*
08/02	h	Stoke	D	1-1	*Colback*
11/02	a	Crystal Palace	D	1-1	*Cissé*
21/02	a	Man. City	L	0-5	
28/02	h	Aston Villa	W	1-0	*Cissé*
04/03	h	Man. United	L	0-1	
15/03	a	Everton	L	0-3	
21/03	h	Arsenal	L	1-2	*Sissoko*
05/04	a	Sunderland	L	0-1	
13/04	a	Liverpool	L	0-2	
19/04	h	Tottenham	L	1-3	*Colback*
25/04	h	Swansea	L	2-3	*Ayoze, De Jong*
02/05	a	Leicester	L	0-3	
09/05	h	West Brom	D	1-1	*Ayoze*
16/05	a	QPR	L	1-2	*Rivière*
24/05	h	West Ham	W	2-0	*Sissoko, Gutiérrez*

No	Name	Nat	DoB	Pos	Aps	(s)	Gls
16	Rolando Aarons		16/11/95	M		(4)	1
30	Mehdi Abeid	ALG	06/08/92	M	7	(6)	
31	Jak Alnwick		17/06/93	G	5	(1)	
28	Sammy Ameobi		01/05/92	A	15	(10)	2
8	Vurnon Anita	NED	04/04/89	M	17	(2)	
32	Adam Armstrong		10/02/97	A	1	(10)	
17	Ayoze Pérez	ESP	23/07/93	A	25	(11)	7
20	Rémy Cabella	FRA	08/03/90	M	21	(10)	1
9	Papiss Cissé	SEN	03/06/85	A	11	(11)	11
14	Jack Colback		24/10/89	M	35		4
2	Fabricio Coloccini	ARG	22/01/82	D	32		1
10	Siem de Jong	NED	28/01/89	M	1	(3)	1
36	Paul Dummett	WAL	26/09/91	D	24	(1)	
21	Rob Elliot	IRL	30/04/86	G	3		
11	Yoan Gouffran	FRA	25/05/86	A	24	(7)	2
18	Jonas Gutiérrez	ARG	05/07/83	M	6	(4)	1
19	Massadio Haïdara	FRA	02/12/92	D	12	(3)	
22	Daryl Janmaat	NED	22/07/89	D	37		1
1	Tim Krul	NED	03/04/88	G	30		
25	Gabriel Obertan	FRA	26/02/89	A	8	(5)	1
29	Emmanuel Rivière	FRA	03/03/90	A	15	(8)	1
7	Moussa Sissoko	FRA	16/08/89	M	34		4
4	Ryan Taylor		19/08/94	M	11	(3)	
27	Steven Taylor		23/01/86	D	7	(3)	1
24	Cheick Tioté	CIV	21/06/86	M	10	(1)	
23	Haris Vukčič	SVN	21/08/92	M		(1)	
6	Mike Williamson		08/11/83	D	27	(4)	1

Queens Park Rangers FC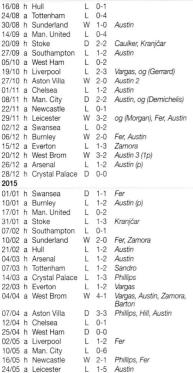

1882 • Loftus Road (18,000) • qpr.co.uk
Major honours
League Cup (1) 1967
Manager: Harry Hedknapp;
(03/02/15) (Chris Ramsey)

2014
16/08	h	Hull	L	0-1	
24/08	a	Tottenham	L	0-4	
30/08	h	Sunderland	W	1-0	*Austin*
14/09	a	Man. United	L	0-4	
20/09	h	Stoke	D	2-2	*Caulker, Kranjčar*
27/09	a	Southampton	L	1-2	*Austin*
05/10	a	West Ham	L	0-2	
19/10	h	Liverpool	L	2-3	*Vargas, og (Gerrard)*
27/10	h	Aston Villa	W	2-0	*Austin 2*
01/11	a	Chelsea	L	0-1	*Austin*
08/11	h	Man. City	D	2-2	*Austin, og (Demichelis)*
22/11	a	Newcastle	L	0-1	
29/11	h	Leicester	W	3-2	*og (Morgan), Fer, Austin*
02/12	a	Swansea	L	0-2	
06/12	h	Burnley	W	2-0	*Fer, Austin*
15/12	a	Everton	L	1-3	*Zamora*
20/12	h	West Brom	W	3-2	*Austin 3 (1p)*
26/12	a	Arsenal	L	1-2	*Austin (p)*
28/12	h	Crystal Palace	D	0-0	

2015
01/01	h	Swansea	D	1-1	*Fer*
10/01	a	Burnley	L	1-2	*Austin (p)*
17/01	h	Man. United	L	0-2	
31/01	a	Stoke	L	1-3	*Kranjčar*
07/02	h	Southampton	L	0-1	
10/02	h	Sunderland	W	2-0	*Fer, Zamora*
21/02	a	Hull	L	1-2	*Austin*
04/03	a	Arsenal	L	1-2	*Austin*
07/03	h	Tottenham	L	1-2	*Sandro*
14/03	a	Crystal Palace	L	1-3	*Phillips*
22/03	h	Everton	L	1-2	*Vargas*
04/04	a	West Brom	W	4-1	*Vargas, Austin, Zamora, Barton*
07/04	a	Aston Villa	D	3-3	*Phillips, Hill, Austin*
12/04	h	Chelsea	L	0-1	
25/04	h	West Ham	D	0-0	
02/05	a	Liverpool	L	1-2	*Fer*
10/05	a	Man. City	L	0-6	
16/05	h	Newcastle	W	2-1	*Phillips, Fer*
24/05	a	Leicester	L	1-5	*Austin*

No	Name	Nat	DoB	Pos	Aps	(s)	Gls
9	Charlie Austin		05/07/89	A	35		18
8	Joey Barton		02/09/82	M	27	(1)	1
4	Steven Caulker		29/12/91	D	34	(1)	1
41	Brandon Comley		18/11/95	M		(1)	
36	Michael Doughty		20/11/92	M		(3)	
22	Richard Dunne	IRL	21/09/79	D	22	(1)	
18	Alejandro Faurlín	ARG	09/08/86	M	1	(1)	
10	Leroy Fer	NED	05/01/90	M	27	(2)	6
5	Rio Ferdinand		07/11/78	D	11		
38	Darnell Furlong		31/10/95	D	3		
1	Robert Green		18/01/80	G	36		
39	Reece Grego-Cox	IRL	12/11/96	A	1	(3)	
20	Karl Henry		26/11/82	M	27	(6)	
6	Clint Hill		19/10/78	D	15	(4)	1
23	Junior Hoilett	CAN	05/06/90	M	9	(13)	
14	Mauricio Isla	CHI	12/06/88	M	24	(2)	
42	Cole Kpekawa		20/05/96	D		(1)	
19	Niko Kranjčar	CRO	13/08/84	M	11	(11)	2
12	Alex McCarthy		03/12/89	G	2	(1)	
18	Jordon Mutch		02/12/91	M	6	(3)	
15	Nedum Onuoha		12/11/86	D	22	(1)	
7	Matt Phillips	SCO	13/03/91	M	20	(5)	3
19	Loïc Rémy	FRA	02/01/87	A	2		
30	Sandro	BRA	15/03/89	M	17		1
2	Danny Simpson		04/01/87	D	1		
27	Adel Taarabt	MAR	24/05/89	M	3	(4)	
3	Armand Traoré	SEN	08/10/89	D	7	(9)	
24	Eduardo Vargas	CHI	20/11/89	A	16	(5)	3
11	Shaun Wright-Phillips		25/10/81	M	1	(3)	
13	Yun Suk-young	KOR	13/02/90	D	19	(4)	
25	Bobby Zamora		16/01/81	A	19	(12)	3
29	Mauro Zárate	ARG	18/03/87	A		(4)	

Southampton FC

1885 • St Mary's Stadium (32,505) •
saintsfc.co.uk
Major honours
FA Cup (1) 1976
Manager: Ronald Koeman (NED)

2014
17/08	a	Liverpool	L	1-2	*Clyne*
23/08	h	West Brom	D	0-0	
30/08	a	West Ham	W	3-1	*Schneiderlin 2, Pellè*
13/09	h	Newcastle	W	4-0	*Pellè 2, Cork, Schneiderlin*
20/09	a	Swansea	W	1-0	*Wanyama*
27/09	h	QPR	W	2-1	*Bertrand, Pellè*
05/10	a	Tottenham	L	0-1	
18/10	h	Sunderland	W	8-0	*og (Vergini), Pellè 2, Cork, og (Bridcutt), Tadić, Wanyama, og (Van Aanholt)*
25/10	h	Stoke	W	1-0	*Mané*
01/11	a	Hull	W	1-0	*Wanyama*
08/11	h	Leicester	W	2-0	*Long 2*
24/11	a	Aston Villa	W	1-0	*Clyne*
30/11	h	Man. City	L	0-3	
03/12	a	Arsenal	L	0-1	
08/12	h	Man. United	L	1-2	*Pellè*
13/12	a	Burnley	L	0-1	
20/12	h	Everton	W	3-0	*og (Lukaku), Pellè, Yoshida*
26/12	a	Crystal Palace	W	3-1	*Mané, Bertrand, Alderweireld*
28/12	h	Chelsea	D	1-1	*Mané*

2015
01/01	h	Arsenal	W	2-0	*Mané, Tadić*
11/01	a	Man. United	W	1-0	*Tadić*
17/01	h	Newcastle	W	2-1	*Elia 2*
01/02	h	Swansea	L	0-1	
07/02	a	QPR	W	1-0	*Mané*
11/02	h	West Ham	D	0-0	
22/02	h	Liverpool	L	0-2	
28/02	a	West Brom	L	0-1	
03/03	h	Crystal Palace	W	1-0	*Mané*
15/03	a	Chelsea	D	1-1	*Tadić (p)*
21/03	h	Burnley	W	2-0	*Long, og (Shackell)*
04/04	a	Everton	L	0-1	
11/04	h	Hull	W	2-0	*Ward-Prowse (p), Pellè*
18/04	a	Stoke	L	1-2	*Schneiderlin*
25/04	a	Tottenham	D	2-2	*Pellè 2*
02/05	a	Sunderland	L	1-2	*Mané*
09/05	h	Leicester	L	0-2	
16/05	h	Aston Villa	W	6-1	*Mané 3, Long 2, Pellè*
24/05	a	Man. City	L	0-2	

No	Name	Nat	DoB	Pos	Aps	(s)	Gls
17	Toby Alderweireld	BEL	02/03/89	D	26		1
21	Ryan Bertrand		05/08/89	D	34		2
2	Nathaniel Clyne		05/04/91	D	35		2
18	Jack Cork		25/06/89	M	5	(7)	2
1	Kelvin Davis		29/09/76	G	6	(1)	
8	Steven Davis	NIR	01/01/85	M	32	(3)	
15	Filip Djuričić	SRB	30/01/92	M	3	(6)	
22	Eljero Elia	NED	13/02/87	M	9	(7)	2
23	Fraser Forster		17/03/88	G	30		
46	Dominic Gape		09/09/94	M		(1)	
5	Florin Gardoş	ROU	29/10/88	D	5	(6)	
25	Paulo Gazzaniga	ARG	02/01/92	G	2		
42	Jake Hesketh		27/03/96	M	1	(1)	
27	Lloyd Isgrove	WAL	12/01/93	M		(1)	
6	José Fonte	POR	22/12/83	D	37		
7	Shane Long	IRL	22/01/87	A	16	(16)	5
10	Sadio Mané	SEN	10/04/92	A	24	(6)	10
24	Emmanuel Mayuka	ZAM	21/11/90	A		(5)	
32	Jason McCarthy		27/11/95	D		(2)	
19	Graziano Pellè	ITA	15/07/85	A	37	(1)	12
10	Gastón Ramírez	URU	02/12/90	M		(1)	
28	Harrison Reed		27/01/95	M	5	(4)	
4	Morgan Schneiderlin	FRA	08/11/89	M	24	(2)	4
45	Ryan Seager		05/02/96	A		(1)	
11	Dušan Tadić	SRB	20/11/88	M	24	(7)	4
33	Matt Targett		18/09/95	D	3	(3)	
12	Victor Wanyama	KEN	25/06/91	M	26	(6)	3
16	James Ward-Prowse		01/11/94	M	16	(9)	1
3	Maya Yoshida	JPN	24/08/88	D	18	(4)	1

Stoke City FC

1868 • Britannia Stadium (27,740) •
stokecityfc.com
Major honours
League Cup (1) 1972
Manager: Mark Hughes (WAL)

2014
16/08	h	Aston Villa	L	0-1	
24/08	a	Hull	D	1-1	*Shawcross*
30/08	a	Man. City	W	1-0	*Diouf*
13/09	h	Leicester	L	0-1	
20/09	a	QPR	D	2-2	*Diouf, Crouch*
29/09	h	Newcastle	W	1-0	*Crouch*
04/10	a	Sunderland	L	1-3	*Adam*
19/10	h	Swansea	W	2-1	*Adam (p), Walters*
25/10	a	Southampton	L	0-1	
01/11	h	West Ham	D	2-2	*Moses, Diouf*
09/11	a	Tottenham	W	2-1	*Bojan, Walters*
22/11	h	Burnley	L	1-2	*Walters*
29/11	a	Liverpool	L	0-1	
02/12	a	Man. United	L	1-2	*N'Zonzi*
06/12	h	Arsenal	W	3-2	*Crouch, Bojan, Walters*
13/12	a	Crystal Palace	D	1-1	*Crouch*
22/12	h	Chelsea	L	0-2	
26/12	a	Everton	W	1-0	*Bojan (p)*
28/12	h	West Brom	W	2-0	*Diouf 2*

2015
01/01	h	Man. United	D	1-1	*Shawcross*
11/01	a	Arsenal	L	0-3	
17/01	h	Leicester	W	1-0	*Bojan*
31/01	a	QPR	W	3-1	*Walters 3*
08/02	h	Newcastle	W	1-0	*Crouch*
11/02	h	Man. City	L	1-4	*Crouch*
21/02	a	Aston Villa	W	2-1	*Diouf, Moses (p)*
28/02	h	Hull	W	1-0	*Crouch*
04/03	h	Everton	W	2-0	*Moses, Diouf*
14/03	a	West Brom	L	0-1	
21/03	h	Crystal Palace	L	1-2	*Diouf*
04/04	a	Chelsea	L	1-2	*Adam*
11/04	h	West Ham	D	1-1	*Arnautovic*
18/04	a	Southampton	W	2-1	*Diouf, Adam*
25/04	a	Sunderland	D	1-1	*Adam*
02/05	a	Swansea	L	0-2	
09/05	h	Tottenham	W	3-0	*Adam, N'Zonzi, og (Vertonghen)*
16/05	a	Burnley	D	0-0	
24/05	a	Liverpool	W	6-1	*Diouf 2, Walters, Adam, N'Zonzi, Crouch*

No	Name	Nat	DoB	Pos	Aps	(s)	Gls
16	Charlie Adam	SCO	10/12/85	M	15	(14)	7
10	Marko Arnautovic	AUT	19/04/89	A	20	(9)	1
24	Oussama Assaidi	MAR	15/08/88	M	1	(8)	
2	Phil Bardsley	SCO	28/06/85	D	24	(1)	
1	Asmir Begović	BIH	20/06/87	G	35		
27	Bojan Krkić	ESP	28/08/90	A	14	(2)	4
22	Jack Butland		10/03/93	G	3		
20	Geoff Cameron	USA	11/07/85	D	21	(6)	
25	Peter Crouch		30/01/81	A	17	(16)	8
23	Dionatan	SVK	22/07/92	D		(1)	
18	Mame Biram Diouf	SEN	16/12/87	A	28	(6)	11
4	Robert Huth	GER	18/08/84	D		(1)	
7	Stephen Ireland	IRL	22/08/86	M	11	(7)	
13	Victor Moses	NGA	12/12/90	A	19		3
5	Marc Muniesa	ESP	27/03/92	D	14	(5)	
15	Steven N'Zonzi	FRA	15/12/88	M	38		3
9	Peter Odemwingie	NGA	15/07/81	A	1	(6)	
3	Erik Pieters	NED	07/08/88	D	29	(2)	
17	Ryan Shawcross		04/10/87	D	32		2
34	Oliver Shenton		06/11/97	M		(1)	
21	Steve Sidwell		14/12/82	M	5	(7)	
19	Jonathan Walters	IRL	20/09/83	A	28	(4)	7
6	Glenn Whelan	IRL	13/01/84	M	26	(2)	
12	Marc Wilson	IRL	17/08/87	D	25	(2)	
26	Philipp Wollscheid	GER	06/03/89	D	12		

Sunderland AFC

1879 • Stadium of Light (48,707) • safc.com

Major honours
English League (6) 1892, 1893, 1895, 1902, 1913,
1936; FA Cup (2) 1937, 1973
Manager: Gus Poyet (URU);
(17/03/15) (Dick Advocaat (NED))

2014

16/08	a	West Brom	D	2-2	*Cattermole, Larsson*
24/08	h	Man. United	D	1-1	*Rodwell*
30/08	h	QPR	L	0-1	
13/09	h	Tottenham	D	2-2	*Johnson, og (Kane)*
20/09	a	Burnley	D	0-0	
27/09	h	Swansea	D	0-0	
04/10	h	Stoke	W	3-1	*Wickham, Fletcher 2*
18/10	a	Southampton	L	0-8	
25/10	h	Arsenal	L	0-2	
03/11	a	Crystal Palace	W	3-1	*Fletcher 2, Jordi Gómez*
09/11	h	Everton	D	1-1	*Larsson*
22/11	a	Leicester	D	0-0	
29/11	h	Chelsea	D	0-0	
03/12	h	Man. City	L	1-4	*Wickham*
06/12	h	Liverpool	D	0-0	
13/12	h	West Ham	D	1-1	*Jordi Gómez (p)*
21/12	a	Newcastle	W	1-0	*Johnson*
26/12	h	Hull	L	1-3	*Johnson*
28/12	a	Aston Villa	D	0-0	

2015

01/01	a	Man. City	L	2-3	*Rodwell, Johnson (p)*
10/01	h	Liverpool	L	0-1	
17/01	a	Tottenham	L	1-2	*Larsson*
31/01	h	Burnley	W	2-0	*Wickham, Defoe*
07/02	a	Swansea	D	1-1	*Defoe*
10/02	h	QPR	L	0-2	
21/02	a	West Brom	D	0-0	
28/02	h	Man. United	L	0-2	
03/03	h	Hull	D	1-1	*Rodwell*
14/03	h	Aston Villa	L	0-4	
21/03	a	West Ham	L	0-1	
05/04	h	Newcastle	W	1-0	*Defoe*
11/04	h	Crystal Palace	L	1-4	*Wickham*
25/04	a	Stoke	D	1-1	*Wickham*
02/05	h	Southampton	W	2-1	*Jordi Gómez 2 (2p)*
09/05	a	Everton	W	2-0	*Graham, Defoe*
16/05	h	Leicester	D	0-0	
20/05	a	Arsenal	D	0-0	
24/05	a	Chelsea	L	1-3	*Fletcher*

No	Name	Nat	DoB	Pos	Aps	(s)	Gls
17	Jozy Altidore	USA	06/11/89	A	2	(9)	
26	Ricky Álvarez	ARG	12/04/88	M	5	(8)	
4	Liam Bridcutt	SCO	08/05/89	M	10	(8)	
5	Wes Brown		13/10/79	D	23	(2)	
30	Will Buckley		21/11/89	M	9	(13)	
6	Lee Cattermole		21/03/88	M	26	(2)	1
22	Sebastián Coates	URU	07/10/90	D	9	(1)	
28	Jermain Defoe		07/10/82	A	17		4
9	Steven Fletcher	SCO	26/03/87	A	20	(10)	5
23	Emanuele Giaccherini	ITA	05/05/85	M	2	(6)	
19	Danny Graham		12/08/85	A	7	(1)	1
11	Adam Johnson		14/07/87	M	23	(9)	4
28	Billy Jones		24/03/87	D	14		
14	Jordi Gómez	ESP	24/05/85	M	22	(7)	4
38	Sebastian Larsson	SWE	06/06/85	M	36		3
38	Mikael Mandron	FRA	11/10/94	A		(1)	
25	Vito Mannone	ITA	02/03/88	G	10		
16	John O'Shea	IRL	30/04/81	D	37		
1	Costel Pantilimon	ROU	01/02/87	G	28		
15	Anthony Réveillère	FRA	10/11/79	D	15	(1)	
29	Valentin Roberge	FRA	09/06/87	D	1		
8	Jack Rodwell		11/03/91	M	17	(6)	3
3	Patrick van Aanholt	NED	29/08/90	D	26	(2)	
27	Santiago Vergini	ARG	03/08/88	D	28	(3)	
10	Connor Wickham		31/03/93	A	31	(5)	5

Swansea City AFC

1912 • Liberty Stadium (20,827) • swanseacity.net

Major honours
League Cup (1) 2013; Welsh Cup (10) 1913, 1932,
1950, 1961, 1966, 1981, 1982, 1983, 1989, 1991
Manager: Garry Monk

2014

16/08	a	Man. United	W	2-1	*Ki, Sigurdsson*
23/08	h	Burnley	W	1-0	*Dyer*
30/08	h	West Brom	W	3-0	*Dyer 2, Routledge*
13/09	a	Chelsea	L	2-4	*og (Terry), Shelvey*
20/09	h	Southampton	L	0-1	
27/09	a	Sunderland	D	0-0	
04/10	h	Newcastle	D	2-2	*Bony, Routledge*
19/10	a	Stoke	L	1-2	*Bony (p)*
25/10	h	Leicester	W	2-0	*Bony 2*
01/11	a	Everton	D	0-0	
09/11	h	Arsenal	W	2-1	*Sigurdsson, Gomis*
22/11	a	Man. City	L	1-2	*Bony*
29/11	h	Crystal Palace	D	1-1	*Bony*
02/12	h	QPR	W	2-0	*Ki, Routledge*
07/12	a	West Ham	L	1-3	*Bony*
14/12	a	Tottenham	L	1-2	*Bony*
20/12	a	Hull	W	1-0	*Ki*
26/12	h	Aston Villa	W	1-0	*Sigurdsson*
29/12	a	Liverpool	L	1-4	*Sigurdsson*

2015

01/01	a	QPR	D	1-1	*Bony*
10/01	h	West Ham	D	1-1	*og (Noble)*
17/01	h	Chelsea	L	0-5	
01/02	a	Southampton	W	1-0	*Shelvey*
07/02	h	Sunderland	D	1-1	*Ki*
11/02	a	West Brom	L	0-2	
21/02	h	Man. United	W	2-1	*Ki, Gomis*
28/02	a	Burnley	W	1-0	*og (Trippier)*
04/03	h	Tottenham	L	2-3	*Ki, Sigurdsson*
16/03	a	Liverpool	L	0-1	
21/03	a	Aston Villa	W	1-0	*Gomis*
04/04	h	Hull	W	3-1	*Ki, Gomis 2*
11/04	a	Everton	D	1-1	*Shelvey (p)*
18/04	a	Leicester	L	0-2	
25/04	a	Newcastle	W	3-2	*Nélson Oliveira, Sigurdsson, Cork*
02/05	h	Stoke	W	2-0	*Montero, Ki*
11/05	a	Arsenal	W	1-0	*Gomis*
17/05	h	Man. City	L	2-4	*Sigurdsson, Gomis*
24/05	a	Crystal Palace	L	0-1	

No	Name	Nat	DoB	Pos	Aps	(s)	Gls
58	Modou Barrow	GAM	13/10/92	A	1	(10)	
27	Kyle Bartley		22/05/91	D	7		
10	Wilfried Bony	CIV	10/12/88	A	16	(4)	9
7	Leon Britton		16/09/82	M	7	(2)	
14	Tom Carroll		28/05/92	M	8	(5)	
24	Jack Cork		25/06/89	M	15		1
12	Nathan Dyer		29/11/87	M	23	(9)	3
11	Marvin Emnes	NED	27/05/88	A	3	(14)	
1	Lukasz Fabiański	POL	18/04/85	G	37		
33	Federico Fernández	ARG	21/02/89	D	27	(1)	
56	Jay Fulton	SCO	01/04/94	M	1	(1)	
18	Bafétimbi Gomis	FRA	06/08/85	A	18	(14)	7
46	Kenji Gorré	NED	29/09/94	A		(1)	
21	Matt Grimes		15/07/95	M		(3)	
2	Jordi Amat	ESP	21/03/92	D	7	(3)	
24	Ki Sung-yong	KOR	24/01/89	M	30	(3)	8
20	Jefferson Montero	ECU	01/09/89	M	15	(15)	1
26	Kyle Naughton		11/11/88	D	10		
17	Nélson Oliveira	POR	08/08/91	A	4	(6)	1
22	Ángel Rangel	ESP	28/10/82	D	22	(5)	
29	Ashley Richards	WAL	12/04/91	D	7	(3)	
15	Wayne Routledge		07/01/85	M	27	(2)	3
8	Jonjo Shelvey		27/02/92	M	28	(3)	3
23	Gylfi Thór Sigurdsson	ISL	08/09/89	M	32		7
3	Neil Taylor	WAL	07/02/89	D	34		
19	Dwight Tiendalli	NED	21/10/85	D	1	(2)	
25	Gerhard Tremmel	GER	16/11/78	G	1	(1)	
6	Ashley Williams	WAL	23/08/84	D	37		

Tottenham Hotspur FC

1882 • White Hart Lane (36,284) • tottenhamhotspur.com

Major honours
UEFA Cup Winners' Cup (1) 1963; UEFA Cup (2)
1972, 1984; English League (2) 1951, 1961; FA Cup
(8) 1901, 1921, 1961, 1962, 1967, 1981, 1982, 1991;
League Cup (4) 1971, 1973, 1999, 2008
Manager: Mauricio Pochettino (ARG)

2014

16/08	a	West Ham	W	1-0	*Dier*
24/08	h	QPR	W	4-0	*Chadli 2, Dier, Adebayor*
31/08	h	Liverpool	L	0-3	
13/09	a	Sunderland	D	2-2	*Chadli, Eriksen*
21/09	h	West Brom	L	0-1	
27/09	a	Arsenal	D	1-1	*Chadli*
05/10	h	Southampton	W	1-0	*Eriksen*
18/10	a	Man. City	L	1-4	*Eriksen*
26/10	h	Newcastle	L	1-2	*Adebayor*
02/11	a	Aston Villa	W	2-1	*Chadli, Kane*
09/11	h	Stoke	L	1-2	*Chadli*
23/11	h	Hull	W	2-1	*Kane, Eriksen*
30/11	a	Everton	W	2-1	*Eriksen, Soldado*
03/12	a	Chelsea	L	0-3	
06/12	h	Crystal Palace	D	0-0	
14/12	a	Swansea	W	2-1	*Kane, Eriksen*
20/12	h	Burnley	W	2-1	*Kane, Lamela*
26/12	a	Leicester	W	2-1	*Kane, Eriksen*
28/12	h	Man. United	D	0-0	

2015

01/01	h	Chelsea	W	5-3	*Kane 2, Rose, Townsend (p), Chadli*
10/01	a	Crystal Palace	L	1-2	*Kane*
17/01	h	Sunderland	W	2-1	*og (O'Shea), Eriksen*
31/01	a	West Brom	W	3-0	*Eriksen, Kane 2 (1p)*
07/02	a	Arsenal	W	2-1	*Kane 2*
10/02	h	Liverpool	L	2-3	*Kane, Dembélé*
22/02	h	West Ham	D	2-2	*Rose, Kane*
04/03	h	Swansea	W	3-2	*Chadli, Mason, Townsend*
07/03	a	QPR	W	2-1	*Kane 2*
15/03	a	Man. United	L	0-3	
21/03	h	Leicester	W	4-3	*Kane 3 (1p), og (Schlupp)*
05/04	a	Burnley	D	0-0	
11/04	h	Aston Villa	L	0-1	
19/04	a	Newcastle	W	3-1	*Chadli, Eriksen, Kane*
25/04	a	Southampton	D	2-2	*Lamela, Chadli*
03/05	h	Man. City	L	0-1	
09/05	a	Stoke	L	0-3	
16/05	h	Hull	W	2-0	*Chadli, Rose*
24/05	a	Everton	W	1-0	*Kane*

No	Name	Nat	DoB	Pos	Aps	(s)	Gls
10	Emmanuel Adebayor	TOG	26/02/84	A	9	(4)	2
42	Nabil Bentaleb	ALG	24/11/94	M	25	(1)	
29	Étienne Capoue	FRA	11/07/88	M	11	(1)	
22	Nacer Chadli	BEL	02/08/89	M	28	(7)	11
6	Vlad Chiricheş	ROU	14/11/89	D	8	(2)	
33	Ben Davies	WAL	24/04/93	D	9	(6)	
19	Mousa Dembélé	BEL	16/07/87	M	10	(16)	1
15	Eric Dier		15/01/94	D	25	(3)	2
23	Christian Eriksen	DEN	14/02/92	M	37	(1)	10
21	Federico Fazio	ARG	17/03/87	D	20		
14	Lewis Holtby	GER	18/09/90	M		(1)	
4	Younès Kaboul	FRA	04/01/86	D	11		
18	Harry Kane		28/07/93	A	28	(6)	21
11	Erik Lamela	ARG	04/03/92	M	25	(8)	2
7	Aaron Lennon		16/04/87	M	3	(6)	
1	Hugo Lloris	FRA	26/12/86	G	35		
38	Ryan Mason		13/06/91	M	29	(2)	1
16	Kyle Naughton		11/11/88	D	5		
8	Paulinho	BRA	25/07/88	M	3	(12)	
9	Danny Rose		02/07/90	D	27	(1)	3
9	Roberto Soldado	ESP	27/05/85	A	7	(17)	1
25	Benjamin Stambouli	FRA	13/08/90	M	4	(8)	
17	Andros Townsend		16/07/91	M	10	(7)	2
5	Jan Vertonghen	BEL	24/04/87	D	31	(1)	
13	Michel Vorm	NED	20/10/83	G	3	(1)	
2	Kyle Walker		28/05/90	D	15		
12	DeAndre Yedlin	USA	09/07/93	D		(1)	

West Bromwich Albion FC

1878 • The Hawthorns (26,445) • wba.co.uk

Major honours
English League (1) 1920; FA Cup (5) 1888, 1892, 1931, 1954, 1968; League Cup (1) 1966

Manager: Alan Irvine (SCO);
(29/12/14) (Keith Downing & Rob Kelly);
(01/01/15) Tony Pulis (WAL)

2014

16/08	h	Sunderland	D	2-2	Berahino 2 (1p)
23/08	a	Southampton	D	0-0	
30/08	a	Swansea	L	0-3	
13/09	h	Everton	L	0-2	
21/09	a	Tottenham	W	1-0	Morrison
28/09	h	Burnley	W	4-0	Dawson, Berahino 2, Dorrans
04/10	a	Liverpool	L	1-2	Berahino (p)
20/10	a	Man. United	D	2-2	Sessègnon, Berahino
25/10	h	Crystal Palace	D	2-2	Anichebe, Berahino (p)
01/11	a	Leicester	W	1-0	og (Cambiasso)
09/11	h	Newcastle	L	0-2	
22/11	a	Chelsea	L	0-2	
29/11	h	Arsenal	L	0-1	
02/12	h	West Ham	L	1-2	Dawson
06/12	a	Hull	D	0-0	
13/12	h	Aston Villa	W	1-0	Gardner
20/12	a	QPR	L	2-3	Lescott, Varela
26/12	h	Man. City	L	1-3	Ideye
28/12	a	Stoke	L	0-2	
2015					
01/01	a	West Ham	D	1-1	Berahino
10/01	h	Hull	W	1-0	Berahino
19/01	a	Everton	D	0-0	
31/01	h	Tottenham	L	0-3	
08/02	a	Burnley	D	2-2	Brunt, Ideye
11/02	h	Swansea	W	2-0	Ideye, Berahino
21/02	a	Sunderland	D	0-0	
28/02	h	Southampton	W	1-0	Berahino
03/03	a	Aston Villa	L	1-2	Berahino
14/03	h	Stoke	W	1-0	Ideye
21/03	a	Man. City	L	0-3	
04/04	h	QPR	L	1-4	Anichebe
11/04	h	Leicester	L	2-3	Fletcher, Gardner
18/04	a	Crystal Palace	W	2-0	Morrison, Gardner
25/04	h	Liverpool	D	0-0	
02/05	a	Man. United	W	1-0	Olsson
09/05	a	Newcastle	D	1-1	Anichebe
18/05	h	Chelsea	W	3-0	Berahino 2 (1p), Brunt
24/05	a	Arsenal	L	1-4	McAuley

No	Name	Nat	DoB	Pos	Aps	(s)	Gls
10	Victor Anichebe	NGA	23/04/88	A	11	(10)	3
4	Chris Baird	NIR	25/02/82	D	9	(10)	
18	Saido Berahino		04/08/93	A	32	(6)	14
28	Sebastián Blanco	ARG	15/03/88	D		(3)	
11	Chris Brunt	NIR	14/12/84	M	33	(1)	2
14	Jason Davidson	AUS	29/06/91	D	1	(1)	
25	Craig Dawson		06/05/90	D	29		2
17	Graham Dorrans	SCO	05/05/87	M	19	(2)	1
24	Darren Fletcher	SCO	01/02/84	M	15		1
1	Ben Foster		03/04/83	G	28		
16	Cristian Gamboa	CRC	24/10/89	D	1	(9)	
8	Craig Gardner		25/11/86	M	30	(5)	3
9	Brown Ideye	NGA	10/10/88	A	13	(11)	4
6	Joleon Lescott		16/08/82	D	34		1
23	Gareth McAuley	NIR	05/12/79	D	24		1
19	Callum McManaman		25/04/91	M	5	(3)	
7	James Morrison	SCO	25/05/86	M	29	(4)	2
21	Youssuf Mulumbu	COD	25/01/87	M	10	(7)	
13	Boaz Myhill	WAL	09/11/82	G	10	(1)	
3	Jonas Olsson	SWE	10/03/83	D	9	(4)	1
15	Sébastien Pocognoli	BEL	01/08/87	D	15		
30	Georgios Samaras	GRE	21/02/85	A		(5)	
29	Stéphane Sessègnon	BEN	01/06/84	M	20	(8)	1
27	Silvestre Varela	POR	02/02/85	M	3	(4)	1
2	Andre Wisdom		09/05/93	D	22	(2)	
5	Claudio Yacob	ARG	18/07/87	M	16	(4)	

West Ham United FC

1895 • Boleyn Ground (35,245) • whufc.com

Major honours
UEFA Cup Winners' Cup (1) 1965; FA Cup (3) 1964, 1975, 1980

Manager: Sam Allardyce

2014

16/08	h	Tottenham	L	0-1	
23/08	a	Crystal Palace	W	3-1	Zárate, Downing, Cole
30/08	h	Southampton	L	1-3	Noble
15/09	a	Hull	D	2-2	Valencia, Sakho
20/09	h	Liverpool	W	3-1	Reid, Sakho, Amalfitano
27/09	a	Man. United	L	1-2	Sakho
05/10	h	QPR	W	2-0	og (Onuoha), Sakho
18/10	a	Burnley	W	3-1	Sakho, Valencia, Cole
25/10	h	Man. City	W	2-1	Amalfitano, Sakho
01/11	a	Stoke	D	2-2	Valencia, Downing
08/11	h	Aston Villa	D	0-0	
22/11	a	Everton	L	1-2	Zárate
29/11	h	Newcastle	W	1-0	Cresswell
02/12	a	West Brom	W	2-1	Nolan, Tomkins
07/12	h	Swansea	W	3-1	Carroll 2, Sakho
13/12	a	Sunderland	D	1-1	Downing
20/12	h	Leicester	W	2-0	Carroll, Downing
26/12	a	Chelsea	L	0-2	
28/12	a	Arsenal	L	1-2	Kouyaté
2015					
01/01	h	West Brom	D	1-1	Sakho
10/01	a	Swansea	D	1-1	Carroll
18/01	h	Hull	W	3-0	Carroll, Amalfitano, Downing
31/01	a	Liverpool	L	0-2	
08/02	h	Man. United	D	1-1	Kouyaté
11/02	a	Southampton	D	0-0	
22/02	a	Tottenham	D	2-2	Kouyaté, Sakho
28/02	h	Crystal Palace	L	1-3	Valencia
04/03	h	Chelsea	L	0-1	
14/03	a	Arsenal	L	0-3	
21/03	h	Sunderland	W	1-0	Sakho
04/04	a	Leicester	L	1-2	Kouyaté
11/04	h	Stoke	D	1-1	Cresswell
19/04	a	Man. City	L	0-2	
25/04	a	QPR	D	0-0	
02/05	h	Burnley	W	1-0	Noble (p)
09/05	a	Aston Villa	L	0-1	
16/05	h	Everton	L	1-2	Downing
24/05	a	Newcastle	L	0-2	

No	Name	Nat	DoB	Pos	Aps	(s)	Gls
13	Adrián	ESP	03/01/87	G	38		
21	Morgan Amalfitano	FRA	20/03/85	M	14	(10)	3
32	Reece Burke		02/09/96	D	4	(1)	
9	Andy Carroll		06/01/89	A	12	(2)	5
24	Carlton Cole		12/10/83	A	8	(15)	2
19	James Collins	WAL	23/08/83	D	21	(6)	
3	Aaron Cresswell		15/12/89	D	38		2
20	Guy Demel	CIV	13/06/81	D	3	(3)	
21	Mohamed Diamé	SEN	14/06/87	M		(3)	
11	Stewart Downing		22/07/84	M	37		6
22	Jussi Jääskeläinen	FIN	19/04/75	G		(1)	
7	Matt Jarvis		22/05/86	M	4	(7)	
18	Carl Jenkinson		08/02/92	D	29	(3)	
8	Cheikhou Kouyaté	SEN	21/12/89	M	30	(1)	4
36	Elliot Lee		16/12/94	A		(1)	
15	Ravel Morrison		02/02/93	M		(1)	
12	Nenê	BRA	19/07/81	M		(8)	
16	Mark Noble		08/05/87	M	27	(1)	2
4	Kevin Nolan		24/06/82	M	19	(10)	1
17	Joey O'Brien	IRL	17/02/86	D	6	(3)	
23	Diego Poyet	URU	08/04/95	M	1	(2)	
2	Winston Reid	NZL	03/07/88	D	29	(1)	1
15	Diafra Sakho	SEN	24/12/89	A	20	(3)	10
30	Alex Song	CMR	09/09/87	M	25	(3)	
5	James Tomkins		29/03/89	D	20	(2)	1
31	Enner Valencia	ECU	04/11/89	A	25	(7)	4
12	Ricardo Vaz Té	POR	01/10/86	A	3	(1)	
10	Mauro Zárate	ARG	18/03/87	A	5	(2)	2

Top goalscorers

26	Sergio Agüero (Man. City)
21	Harry Kane (Tottenham)
20	Diego Costa (Chelsea)
18	Charlie Austin (QPR)
16	Alexis Sánchez (Arsenal)
14	Olivier Giroud (Arsenal)
	Eden Hazard (Chelsea)
	Saido Berahino (West Brom)
13	Christian Benteke (Aston Villa)
12	David Silva (Man. City)
	Wayne Rooney (Man. United)
	Graziano Pellè (Southampton)

Promoted clubs

AFC Bournemouth

1890 • Goldsands Stadium (11,700) •
afcb.co.uk
Manager: Eddie Howe

Watford FC

1881 • Vicarage Road (20,877) • watfordfc.com
**Manager: Giuseppe Sannino (ITA);
(02/09/14) Óscar García (ESP);
(29/09/14) (Billy McKinlay (SCO));
(07/10/14) Slaviša Jokanović (SRB)**

Norwich City FC

1902 • Carrow Road (27,244) • canaries.co.uk
Major honours
League Cup (2) 1986, 1996
**Manager: Neil Adams:
(09/01/15) Alex Neil (SCO)**

Second level final table 2014/15

		Pld	W	D	L	F	A	Pts
1	AFC Bournemouth	46	26	12	8	98	45	90
2	Watford FC	46	27	8	11	91	50	89
3	Norwich City FC	46	25	11	10	88	48	86
4	Middlesbrough FC	46	25	10	11	68	37	85
5	Brentford FC	46	23	9	14	78	59	78
6	Ipswich Town FC	46	22	12	12	72	54	78
7	Wolverhampton Wanderers FC	46	22	12	12	70	56	78
8	Derby County FC	46	21	14	11	85	56	77
9	Blackburn Rovers FC	46	17	16	13	66	59	67
10	Birmingham City FC	46	16	15	15	54	64	63
11	Cardiff City FC	46	16	14	16	57	61	62
12	Charlton Athletic FC	46	14	18	14	54	60	60
13	Sheffield Wednesday FC	46	14	18	14	43	49	60
14	Nottingham Forest FC	46	15	14	17	71	69	59
15	Leeds United AFC	46	15	11	20	50	61	56
16	Huddersfield Town FC	46	13	16	17	58	75	55
17	Fulham FC	46	14	10	22	62	83	52
18	Bolton Wanderers FC	46	13	12	21	54	67	51
19	Reading FC	46	13	11	22	48	69	50
20	Brighton & Hove Albion FC	46	10	17	19	44	54	47
21	Rotherham United FC	46	11	16	19	46	67	46
22	Millwall FC	46	9	14	23	42	76	41
23	Wigan Athletic FC	46	9	12	25	39	64	39
24	Blackpool FC	46	4	14	28	36	91	26

NB Rotherham United FC – 3 pts deducted.

Promotion play-offs

(08/05/15 & 15/05/15)
Brentford 1-2 Middlesbrough
Middlesbrough 3-0 Brentford
(Middlesbrough 5-1)

(09/05/15 & 16/05/15)
Ipswich 1-1 Norwich
Norwich 3-1 Ipswich
(Norwich 4-2)

(25/05/15)
Norwich 2-0 Middlesbrough

DOMESTIC CUPS

FA Cup 2014/15

THIRD ROUND

(02/01/15)
Cardiff 3-1 Colchester

(03/01/15)
Barnsley 0-2 Middlesbrough
Blyth Spartans 2-3 Birmingham
Bolton 1-0 Wigan
Brentford 0-2 Brighton
Cambridge United 2-1 Luton
Charlton 1-2 Blackburn
Derby 1-0 Southport
Doncaster 1-1 Bristol City
Fulham 0-0 Wolves
Huddersfield 0-1 Reading
Leicester 1-0 Newcastle
Millwall 3-3 Bradford
Preston 2-0 Norwich
Rochdale 1-0 Nottingham Forest
Rotherham 1-5 Bournemouth
Tranmere 2-6 Swansea
West Brom 7-0 Gateshead

(04/01/15)
Arsenal 2-0 Hull
Aston Villa 1-0 Blackpool
Chelsea 3-0 Watford
Dover 0-4 Crystal Palace
Man. City 2-1 Sheffield Wednesday
QPR 0-3 Sheffield United
Southampton 1-1 Ipswich
Stoke 3-1 Wrexham
Sunderland 1-0 Leeds
Yeovil 0-2 Man. United

(05/01/15)
Burnley 1-1 Tottenham
Wimbledon 1-2 Liverpool

(06/01/15)
Everton 1-1 West Ham
Scunthorpe 2-2 Chesterfield

Replays

(13/01/15)
Bristol City 2-0 Doncaster
Chesterfield 2-0 Scunthorpe *(aet)*
West Ham 2-2 Everton *(aet; 9-8 on pens)*
Wolves 3-3 Fulham *(aet; 3-5 on pens)*

(14/01/15)
Bradford 4-0 Millwall
Ipswich 0-1 Southampton
Tottenham 4-2 Burnley

League Cup 2014/15

QUARTER-FINALS

(16/12/14)
Derby 1-3 Chelsea *(Bryson 71; Hazard 23, Filipe Luís 56, Schürrle 82)*

Sheffield United 1-0 Southampton *(McNulty 63)*

(17/12/14)
Bournemouth 1-3 Liverpool *(Gosling 57; Sterling 20, 51, Marković 27)*

Tottenham 4-0 Newcastle *(Bentaleb 18, Chadli 46, Kane 63, Soldado 70)*

FOURTH ROUND

(23/01/15)
Cambridge United 0-0 Man. United

(24/01/15)
Birmingham 1-2 West Brom
Blackburn 3-1 Swansea
Cardiff 1-2 Reading
Chelsea 2-4 Bradford
Derby 2-0 Chesterfield
Liverpool 0-0 Bolton
Man. City 0-2 Middlesbrough
Preston 1-1 Sheffield United
Southampton 2-3 Crystal Palace
Sunderland 0-0 Fulham
Tottenham 1-2 Leicester

(25/01/15)
Aston Villa 2-1 Bournemouth
Brighton 2-3 Arsenal
Bristol City 0-1 West Ham

(26/01/15)
Rochdale 1-4 Stoke

Replays

(03/02/15)
Fulham 1-3 Sunderland
Man. United 3-0 Cambridge United
Sheffield United 1-3 Preston

(04/02/15)
Bolton 1-2 Liverpool

FIFTH ROUND

(14/02/15)
Blackburn 4-1 Stoke
Crystal Palace 1-2 Liverpool
Derby 1-2 Reading
West Brom 4-0 West Ham

(15/02/15)
Arsenal 2-0 Middlesbrough
Aston Villa 2-1 Leicester
Bradford 2-0 Sunderland

(16/02/15)
Preston 1-3 Man. United

SEMI-FINALS

(20/01/15 & 27/01/15)
Liverpool 1-1 Chelsea *(Sterling 59; Hazard 18p)*
Chelsea 1-0 Liverpool *(Ivanović 94) (aet)*
(Chelsea 2-1)

(21/01/15 & 28/01/15)
Tottenham 1-0 Sheffield United *(Townsend 74p)*
Sheffield United 2-2 Tottenham *(Adams 77, 79; Eriksen 28, 88)*
(Tottenham 3-2)

QUARTER-FINALS

(07/03/15)
Bradford 0-0 Reading
Aston Villa 2-0 West Brom
(Delph 51, Sinclair 85)

(08/03/15)
Liverpool 0-0 Blackburn

(09/03/15)
Man. United 1-2 Arsenal
(Rooney 29; Monreal 25, Welbeck 61)

Replays

(16/03/15)
Reading 3-0 Bradford *(Robson-Kanu 6, McCleary 9, Mackie 68)*
(08/04/15)
Blackburn 0-1 Liverpool
(Coutinho 70)

SEMI-FINALS

(18/04/15)
Arsenal 2-1 Reading *(Alexis Sánchez 39, 105; McCleary 54) (aet)*

(19/04/15)
Aston Villa 2-1 Liverpool *(Benteke 36, Delph 54; Coutinho 30)*

FINAL

(30/05/15)
Wembley Stadium, London
ARSENAL FC 4 *(Walcott 40, Alexis Sánchez 50, Mertesacker 62, Giroud 90+3)*
ASTON VILLA FC 0
Referee: Moss
ARSENAL: Szczęsny, Bellerín, Mertesacker, Koscielny, Monreal, Coquelin, Santi Cazorla, Ramsey, Özil (Wilshere 77), Alexis Sánchez (Oxlade-Chamberlain 90), Walcott (Giroud 77)
ASTON VILLA: Given, Hutton, Okore, Vlaar, Richardson (Bacuna 68), Cleverley, Westwood (Sánchez 71), Delph, N'Zogbia (Agbonlahor 53), Grealish, Benteke

FINAL

(01/03/15)
Wembley Stadium, London
CHELSEA FC 2 *(Terry 45, Diego Costa 56)*
TOTTENHAM HOTSPUR FC 0
Referee: Taylor
CHELSEA: Čech, Ivanović, Cahill, Terry, Azpilicueta, Ramires, Zouma, Fàbregas (Oscar 88), Willian (Cuadrado 76), Hazard, Diego Costa (Drogba 90+3)
TOTTENHAM: Lloris, Walker, Dier, Vertonghen, Rose, Bentaleb, Mason (Lamela 71), Townsend (Dembélé 62), Eriksen, Chadli (Soldado 80), Kane

ESTONIA
Eesti Jalgpalli Liit (EJL)

Address	A. Le Coq Arena, Asula 4c
	EE-11312 Tallinn
Tel	+372 627 9960
Fax	+372 627 9969
E-mail	efa@jalgpall.ee
Website	jalgpall.ee

President	Aivar Pohlak
General secretary	Anne Rei
Media officer	Mihkel Uiboleht
Year of formation	1921
National stadium	A. Le Coq Arena,
	Tallinn (9,692)

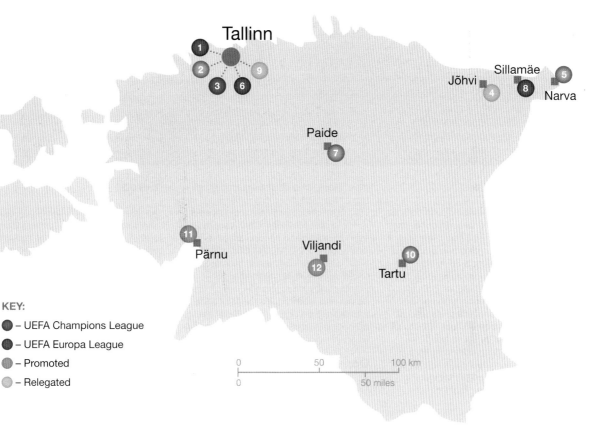

KEY:
- – UEFA Champions League
- – UEFA Europa League
- – Promoted
- – Relegated

MEISTRILIIGA CLUBS

  1 FC Flora Tallinn

  2 FC Infonet Tallinn

 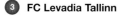 3 FC Levadia Tallinn

  4 FC Lokomotiv Jõhvi

 5 JK Narva Trans

 6 Nõmme Kalju FC

  7 Paide Linnameeskond

  8 JK Sillamäe Kalev

  9 JK Tallinna Kalev

 10 JK Tammeka Tartu

PROMOTED CLUBS

  11 Pärnu Linnameeskond

  12 JK Tulevik Viljandi

Levadia retain their title

FC Levadia Tallinn drew level with their city rivals FC Flora Tallinn in the Meistriliiga's roll of honour, claiming the championship title for a record-equalling ninth time at the end of a fascinating season in which they were challenged to the end by Flora and Nõmme Kalju FC.

Second place eventually went to another team, JK Sillamäe Kalev, thanks to a brilliant late run sparked by the league's 38-goal leading scorer, Russian striker Evgeni Kabaev, but 2012 champions Kalju, who finished fourth, returned to the trophy trail in 2015 by lifting the Estonian Cup.

Record-equalling ninth league title for Tallinn club	**Sillamäe storm to second place after three-way tussle**	**Nõmme Kalju capture Estonian Cup for first time**

Domestic league

A successful title defence did not look on the cards for Levadia's young guns when they took just one point from their first two games and won only two of the first six. But the Meistriliiga's 36-match schedule gave them ample time to recover, and with goalkeeper Roman Smishko, the club captain, going 13 matches without conceding – a total of 1,282 minutes unbeaten, just 108 shy of ex-Club Brugge KV keeper Dany Verlinden's European domestic league record – the foundation was laid for a protracted title challenge that would eventually eclipse the efforts of both Flora and Kalju.

By the start of October, with five games left, Levadia held a two-point lead over both title rivals. Their next two fixtures were at home to Kalju and away to Flora, and crucially they won them both, Estonian international Dmitri Kruglov grabbing a late double to turn potential defeat into a 3-2 victory against Kalju and top-scoring striker Igor Subbotin netting a 77th-minute winner to secure another precious comeback win in the derby.

Levadia lost next time out, 2-0 at FC Infonet, to keep things interesting, but two huge wins in their last two fixtures clinched the trophy for Marko Kristal's

men. Flora, who had spent longer at the top of the table than any other side, were still within striking distance of Levadia on the final day. However, they were unable even to hold on to second place as they went down 3-2 to fast-finishing Sillamäe, who, with their 15th win in 16 matches under new Russian coach Sergei Frantsev, therefore joined Flora on 79 points and leapfrogged them into the runners-up berth thanks to their greater number of victories. Kalju, meanwhile, finished a point further adrift in fourth.

Domestic cup

There would be no defence of the Estonian Cup for Levadia as they had to forfeit their third-round tie for fielding an ineligible player. Their early elimination opened up the field, and although both Flora's first and second teams reached the semi-finals, the two finalists were Kalju and Paide Linnameeskond, neither of whom had previously lifted the trophy. There was a double prize for the winners, with a UEFA Europa League place alongside the trophy itself, and favourites Kalju, now led by rookie coach Sergei Terehhov, claimed the booty with a comfortable 2-0 win, Artjom Dmitrijev breaking the deadlock in first-half added time before Allan Kimbaloula, who had provided the assist, made it 2-0 12 minutes from the end.

Europe

As usual, Estonian interest in Europe was short-lived. With Flora absent from continental combat for the first time in 20 years and one of the four places taken up by second-tier FC Santos Tartu, the 2013 Estonian Cup runners-up, expectations were not high. Indeed, there were predictable second qualifying round exits for Levadia, Kalju and Sillamäe, with only Kalju hinting at further progress when they defeated Poland's KKS Lech Poznań 1-0 at home in the first leg with a goal from their prolific Japanese import Hidetoshi Wakui.

National team

When Estonia opened their UEFA EURO 2016 qualifying campaign with a 1-0 win at home to Slovenia, courtesy of substitute Ats Purje's late winner, it looked as if new coach Magnus Pehrsson might be able to match the success of his predecessor Tarmo Rüütli, who took the team to the UEFA EURO 2012 qualifying play-offs. Subsequent results, however, suggested that the Swede's first competitive game in charge was a case of beginner's luck as Estonia took just one point from their next four games – and that in an embarrassing 0-0 draw against San Marino.

DOMESTIC SEASON AT A GLANCE

Meistriliiga 2014 final table

		Pld	Home W	D	L	F	A	Away W	D	L	F	A	Total W	D	L	F	A	Pts
1	FC Levadia Tallinn	36	12	3	3	57	14	14	3	1	55	5	26	6	4	112	19	84
2	JK Sillamäe Kalev	36	12	1	5	55	19	13	3	2	53	15	25	4	7	108	34	79
3	FC Flora Tallinn	36	12	3	3	43	14	12	4	2	45	22	24	7	5	88	36	79
4	Nõmme Kalju FC	36	12	3	3	43	9	12	3	3	42	10	24	6	6	85	19	78
5	FC Infonet Tallinn	36	9	4	5	48	24	10	5	3	32	20	19	9	8	80	44	66
6	Paide Linnameeskond	36	4	3	11	20	36	5	5	8	19	31	9	8	19	39	67	35
7	JK Tammeka Tartu	36	3	5	10	18	46	4	2	12	19	37	7	7	22	37	83	28
8	JK Narva Trans	36	4	6	8	21	34	2	4	12	16	45	6	10	20	37	79	28
9	FC Lokomotiv Jõhvi	36	3	3	12	17	40	1	3	14	18	75	4	6	26	35	115	18
10	JK Tallinna Kalev	36	2	2	14	11	73	1	1	16	10	73	3	3	30	21	146	12

European qualification 2015/16

Champion: FC Levadia Tallinn (first qualifying round)

Cup winner: Nõmme Kalju FC (first qualifying round)
JK Sillamäe Kalev (first qualifying round)
FC Flora Tallinn (first qualifying round)

Top scorer   Evgeni Kabaev (Sillamäe), 36 goals
Relegated clubs   JK Tallinna Kalev, FC Lokomotiv Jõhvi
Promoted clubs   Pärnu Linnameeskond, JK Tulevik Viljandi
Cup final   Nõmme Kalju FC 2-0 Paide Linnameeskond

Team of the season
(4-4-2)

Coach: Kristal (Levadia)

Smishko (Levadia)

Jürgenson (Flora)   Tipuric (Levadia)   Mets (Flora)   Kallaste (Kalju)

Alliku (Flora)   Vukobratović (Levadia)   Ratnikov (Sillamäe)   Kruglov (Levadia)

Subbotin (Levadia)   Kouakou (Infonet)

Player of the season

Igor Subbotin
(FC Levadia Tallinn)

Relocated from midfield into attack, Subbotin found the transition remarkably easy as he plundered 32 Meistriliiga goals from 33 appearances, including eight in the last two games, to help Levadia retain the title. His late flurry was not sufficient to dislodge JK Sillamäe Kalev's Evgeni Kabaev from the head of the top scorer listings, but his excellence over the season was rewarded with several call-ups to the Estonian national team and, in 2015, a move to Czech club FK Mladá Boleslav.

Newcomer of the season

Karol Mets
(FC Flora Tallinn)

With 35 starts – and 35 finishes – in Flora's 2014 Meistriliiga campaign, Mets was one of the league's most durable as well as promising participants. Still only 21 at the season's close, the tall central defender's increasing influence was recognised not only by Flora boss Norbert Hurt but also by national team coach Magnus Pehrsson, albeit in a different way as he opted to make Mets a mainstay of Estonia's midfield. As foreign interest grew, he joined Norwegian club Viking FK in December 2014.

NATIONAL TEAM

Top five all-time caps
Martin Reim (157); Marko Kristal (143); Andres Oper (134); Mart Poom (120); Kristen Viikmäe (115)

Top five all-time goals
Andres Oper (38); Indrek Zelinski (27); Eduard Ellmann-Eelma (21); Richard Kuremaa & **Konstantin Vassiljev** (19)

Results 2014/15

04/09/14	Sweden	A	Solna	L	0-2	
08/09/14	Slovenia (ECQ)	H	Tallinn	W	1-0	*Purje (86)*
09/10/14	Lithuania (ECQ)	A	Vilnius	L	0-1	
12/10/14	England (ECQ)	H	Tallinn	L	0-1	
12/11/14	Norway	A	Oslo	W	1-0	*Vassiljev (24)*
15/11/14	San Marino (ECQ)	A	Serravalle	D	0-0	
18/11/14	Jordan	H	Tallinn	W	1-0	*Henri Anier (16)*
27/12/14	Qatar	A	Doha	L	0-3	
27/03/15	Switzerland (ECQ)	A	Lucerne	L	0-3	
31/03/15	Iceland	H	Tallinn	D	1-1	*Vassiljev (59)*
09/06/15	Finland	A	Turku	W	2-0	*Purje (28, 57)*
14/06/15	San Marino (ECQ)	H	Tallinn	W	2-0	*Zenjov (35, 63)*

Appearances 2014/15

Coach:
Magnus Pehrsson (SWE) 25/05/76

			Swe	SVN	LTU	ENG	Nor	SMR	Jor	Qat	SUI	Isl	Fin	SMR	Caps	Goals
Sergei Pareiko	31/01/77	Volga (RUS) /unattached /Levadia	G	G	G	G			G		G		G		64	-
Taijo Teniste	31/01/88	Sogndal (NOR)	D46	D71			D46	D			D	D87		D	38	-
Igor Morozov	27/05/89	Debrecen (HUN)	D	D		D	D	D							29	-
Ragnar Klavan	30/10/85	Augsburg (GER)	D	D	D	D 48*					D	D	D	D	103	3
Ken Kallaste	31/08/88	Kalju	D	D	D 86*		D33				D	D	D	D	16	-
Sergei Zenjov	20/04/89	Blackpool (ENG) /unattached /Torpedo Moskva (RUS)	M65	M	M64	M80	M46	A		A66	A87	s12	M79	M89	44	9
Karol Mets	16/05/93	Flora /Viking (NOR)	M	M	M	M	M	M	s46		D	M		D	17	-
Martin Vunk	21/08/84	Kalju	M65	M	M80	M83									67	1
Joel Lindpere	05/10/81	Baník (CZE) /Kalju	M73	M85	M76	s46	s46	s46					M46	M84	100	7
Ilja Antonov	05/12/92	Levadia	M91	M67	M	M	M	M	M46	M	M	s91	M64	s79	19	-
Henri Anier	17/12/90	Erzgebirge Aue (GER) /Dundee United (SCO)	A46	A	A	A		s62	A46		A56		s64		23	6
Enar Jääger	18/11/84	unattached /Flora	s46	s71	D	D	s46		D		D	D			113	-
Henrik Ojamaa	20/05/91	Motherwell (SCO) /Sarpsborg (NOR)	s46		s64	s80	A81	A62			s56				23	-
Gert Kams	25/05/85	SJK (FIN) /Flora	s65	s67							s46		s87	s46	39	2
Ats Purje	03/08/85	KuPS (FIN) /Kalju	s65	s85	s80						s75	A64	A		50	7
Kaimar Saag	05/08/88	Assyriska (SWE)	s73												46	3
Aleksandr Dmitrijev	18/02/82	Levadia /Infonet	s91				M	M46			M63	M91	M	M	92	-
Alo Bärengrub	12/02/84	Kalju			D				D	D					48	-
Konstantin Vassiljev	16/08/84	Piast (POL)			s76	M46	M46	M			M	M	s64	M79	79	19
Artur Pikk	05/03/93	Levadia				D						D			4	-
Dmitri Kruglov	24/05/84	Levadia			s83	s33	D	D			s63	M75	s46	s84	99	3
Mihkel Aksalu	07/11/84	SJK (FIN)					G	G				G		G	16	-
Artjom Artjunin	24/01/90	Levadia					D	D74		D86					6	-
Igor Subbotin	26/06/90	Levadia /unattached					s46		M	M75					4	-
Ingemar Teever	24/02/83	Levadia					s81	s74	s64	A46				s89	29	4
Markus Jürgenson	09/09/87	Flora							D	D		D90			5	-
Sergei Mošnikov	07/01/88	Flora /unattached							M	M46					23	-
Frank Liivak	07/07/96	Napoli (ITA) /unattached							A64	s75					3	-
Rimo Hunt	05/11/85	Kaysar (KAZ)							A64						7	1
Hannes Anier	16/01/93	Erzgebirge Aue (GER)							s46	s46					4	1
Rauno Alliku	02/03/90	Flora							s64	s66	s87	M75	M46	M	8	-
Marko Meerits	26/04/92	Emmen (NED)								G					3	-
Brent Lepistu	26/03/93	Flora								M46					1	-
Andreas Raudsepp	13/12/93	Levadia								s46		s75			2	-
Vladimir Avilov	10/03/95	Infonet								s86					1	-
Raio Piiroja	11/07/79	Pärnu									A12				114	8
Artjom Dmitrijev	14/11/88	Kalju											s79		1	-
Maksim Gussev	20/07/94	Flora											s90		1	-

EUROPE

FC Levadia Tallinn

CHAMPIONS LEAGUE

First qualifying round - SP La Fiorita (SMR)
A 1-0 *Tamm (90+3)*
Smishko, Artjunin, Antonov, Subbotin, Teever, Podholjuzin, Tipuric, Pikk, Ivanov (Tamm 59), Raudsepp (Aallikko 79), Vukobratović. Coach: Marko Kristal (EST)
H 7-0 *Kulinitš (7), Subbotin (30, 72), El Hussieny (48), Artjunin (75, 90+2), Tipuric (85)*
Smishko, Artjunin, Antonov, Subbotin, Teever (Marin 71), Tamm (El Hussieny 46), Podholjuzin, Tipuric, Kulinitš, Pikk, Vukobratović (Kaljumäe 60). Coach: Marko Kristal (EST)

Second qualifying round - AC Sparta Praha (CZE)
A 0-7
Smishko, Artjunin, El Hussieny (Penić 63), Antonov (Kaljumäe 82), Subbotin, Podholjuzin, Tipuric, Kulinitš (Teever 58), Pikk, Raudsepp, Vukobratović. Coach: Marko Kristal (EST)
H 1-1 *Teever (68)*
Pikker, Penić (Marin 81), Artjunin, Antonov, Subbotin, Teever, Podholjuzin, Tipuric, Pikk, Ivanov (El Hussieny 61), Raudsepp. Coach: Marko Kristal (EST)

Nõmme Kalju FC

EUROPA LEAGUE

First qualifying round - Fram Reykjavík (ISL)
A 1-0 *Fábio Prates (61)*
Teleš, Reintam, Bärengrub, Quintieri (Mbu Alidor 85), Kimbaloula, Vunk, Kallaste, Toomet (Kirss 74), Fábio Prates, Wakui, Šišov. Coach: Igor Prins (EST)
H 2-2 *Felipe Nunes (10), Wakui (53)*
Teleš, Reintam, Bärengrub, Mbu Alidor, Quintieri (Jorge Rodrigues 89), Vunk, Kallaste, Toomet (Kirss 57), Fábio Prates, Felipe Nunes (Jevdokimov 61), Wakui. Coach: Igor Prins (EST)

Second qualifying round - KKS Lech Poznań (POL)
H 1-0 *Wakui (81)*
Teleš, Pürg (Toomet 64), Bärengrub, Jorge Rodrigues, Mbu Alidor, Mööl, Quintieri (Ainsalu 77), Vunk, Kallaste, Felipe Nunes (Kirss 62), Wakui. Coach: Igor Prins (EST)
A 0-3
Teleš, Pürg (Ainsalu 46), Bärengrub, Jorge Rodrigues, Mbu Alidor, Mööl, Quintieri, Kallaste, Kirss (Jevdokimov 68), Felipe Nunes (Ahjupera 75), Wakui. Coach: Igor Prins (EST)

JK Sillamäe Kalev

EUROPA LEAGUE

First qualifying round - FC Honka Espoo (FIN)
H 2-1 *Ratnikov (32), Kabaev (72)*
Starodubtsev, Dudarev, Sidorenkov, Cheminava (Baguzis 78), Volodin, Silich, Ratnikov, Mashichev, Tjapkin, Murikhin (Kvasov 54), Kabaev. Coach: Vadym Dobyzha (UKR)
A 2-3 *Sidorenkov (25), Kabaev (120)* **(aet)**
Starodubtsev, Dudarev, Sidorenkov, Cheminava, Volodin (Baguzis 25), Silich (Kvasov 46), Ratnikov, Mashichev (Vnukov 67), Tjapkin, Murikhin, Kabaev. Coach: Vadym Dobyzha (UKR)

Second qualifying round - FC Krasnodar (RUS)
H 0-4
Starodubtsev, Dudarev, Sidorenkov, Cheminava, Vnukov (Kvasov 81), Ratnikov, Mashichev (Silich 53), Tjapkin, Baguzis, Murikhin (Novikov 90), Kabaev. Coach: Sergei Frantsev (RUS)
A 0-5
Starodubtsev, Dudarev, Sidorenkov, Cheminava, Vnukov (Ratnikov 70), Silich (Kvasov 72), Mashichev (Novikov 83), Tjapkin, Baguzis, Murikhin, Kabaev. Coach: Sergei Frantsev (RUS)

FC Santos Tartu

EUROPA LEAGUE

First qualifying round - Tromsø IL (NOR)
H 0-7
Säesk, Teniste, Alve (Vidaja 83), Vellemaa, Sonn, K Laas, M Laas (Kartsep 75), Roops, Eessaar, Flyak (Kallandi 86), Vereshchak. Coach: Algimantas Liubinskas (LTU)
A 1-6 *Alve (39)*
Kohler, Teniste, Kallandi, Alve, Vellemaa (Laurson 34), Sonn, K Laas, M Laas (Eessaar 79), Roops, Flyak, Vereshchak (Vidaja 85). Coach: Algimantas Liubinskas (LTU)

DOMESTIC LEAGUE CLUB-BY-CLUB

FC Flora Tallinn

1990 • A. Le Coq Arena (9,692); Sportland Arena (500) • fcflora.ee
Major honours
Estonian League (9) 1994, 1995, 1998, 1998 (autumn), 2001, 2002, 2003, 2010, 2011; Estonian Cup (6) 1995, 1998, 2008, 2009, 2011, 2013
Coach: Norbert Hurt

2014

Date		Opponent	Result	Scorers
01/03	a	Lokomotiv	W 3-1	Alliku, Aloe, Jürgenson (p)
08/03	h	Paide	W 5-0	Beglarishvili, Prosa 2, Alliku, Jürgenson
14/03	h	Tammeka	W 3-0	Prosa 2, Beglarishvili
22/03	a	Kalju	D 1-1	Prosa
28/03	h	Infonet	L 2-3	Prosa, Rähn
05/04	a	Levadia	D 1-1	Alliku
12/04	h	Trans	W 1-0	Rähn
19/04	a	Tallinna Kalev	W 4-1	Alliku 3, Post
26/04	a	Sillamäe	D 1-1	
03/05	a	Sillamäe	W 2-1	Beglarishvili, Prosa
09/05	h	Tallinna Kalev	W 5-1	Alliku, og (Välja), Kase, Beglarishvili, Post
13/05	a	Trans	W 1-0	Post
20/05	h	Levadia	D 0-0	
23/05	a	Infonet	W 3-2	Beglarishvili, Prosa, Gussev
10/06	h	Kalju	W 1-0	Logua
14/06	h	Tammeka	W 1-0	Post
21/06	a	Paide	W 5-1	Prosa, Frolov, Alliku, Logua, Jürgenson
06/07	h	Lokomotiv	W 3-1	Alliku, Jürgenson, Prosa
14/07	h	Sillamäe	W 1-0	Alliku
18/07	a	Tallinna Kalev	W 2-0	Prosa, Sappinen
26/07	a	Trans	W 6-0	Rähn, Prosa, Logua, Alliku, Jürgenson, Post
04/08	a	Levadia	D 1-1	Jürgenson (p)
08/08	h	Infonet	D 2-2	Gussev, Prosa
16/08	a	Kalju	L 0-1	
19/08	a	Tammeka	D 1-1	Logua
23/08	h	Paide	W 3-0	Prosa 3
30/08	a	Lokomotiv	W 5-2	Alliku, Post 2, Prosa
13/09	h	Lokomotiv	W 6-2	Prosa, Alliku, Beglarishvili 2, Frolov, Logua
16/09	a	Paide	W 2-1	Jürgenson (p), Post
20/09	a	Tammeka	W 4-2	Prosa, Logua, Beglarishvili, Jürgenson (p)
27/09	h	Kalju	L 0-2	
03/10	a	Infonet	W 3-1	Beglarishvili, Logua 2
18/10	h	Levadia	L 1-2	Logua
25/10	a	Trans	W 5-2	Rähn, Alliku, Prosa, Logua, Jürgenson
01/11	h	Tallinna Kalev	W 2-0	Sappinen, Post
08/11	a	Sillamäe	L 2-3	Beglarishvili, Prosa

Name	Nat	DoB	Pos	Aps	(s)	Gls
Rauno Alliku		02/03/90	M	29	(5)	15
Kevin Aloe		07/05/95	D	18	(1)	1
Nikita Baranov		19/08/92	D	19		
Zakaria Beglarishvili	GEO	30/04/90	M	33	(1)	10
Andre Frolov		18/04/88	M	18	(6)	2
Maksim Gussev		20/07/94	M	12	(13)	2
Joosep Juha		05/09/96	D	2		
Erkki Junolainen		05/01/92	D	9	(3)	
Markus Jürgenson		09/09/87	D	30		9
Martin Kase		02/09/93	A	1	(13)	1
Brent Lepistu		26/03/93	M	19	(9)	
Irakli Logua	RUS	29/07/91	M	28	(7)	10
Karl-Eerik Luigend		15/01/93	M	26	(2)	
Karol Mets		16/05/93	D	35		
Sergei Mošnikov		07/01/88	M	7		
Janar Õunap		09/09/94	D		(1)	
Sander Post		10/09/84	A	6	(18)	9
Stanislav Prins		06/00/00	D	24	(1)	
Albert Prosa		01/10/90	A	30	(3)	22
Taavi Rähn		16/05/81	D	32	(1)	4
Joseph Saliste		10/04/95	M		(2)	
Rauno Sappinen		23/01/96	M	4	(8)	2
German Šlein		28/03/96	M	2	(2)	
Roman Sobtšenko		25/01/94	M		(10)	
Mait Toom		07/05/90	G	12		

FC Infonet Tallinn

2002 • Sportland Arena (500) • fcinfonet.ee
Coach: Aleksandr Puštov

2014

01/03	a	Kalju	W 0-0	(w/o; original result 0-1)
08/03	h	Tammeka	W 3-0	Lipin, Kouakou, Golovljov
15/03	a	Sillamäe	L 1-3	og (Dudarev)
21/03	h	Paide	D 1-1	Golovljov
28/03	a	Flora	W 3-2	Lipin, Kouakou, Golovljov
05/04	h	Lokomotiv	W 2-0	Elhi, Lipin
11/04	a	Levadia	L 0-3	
18/04	a	Trans	D 1-1	Melts
25/04	h	Tallinna Kalev	W 6-0	Nahk, Harin, Saarlas, Kouakou 3
02/05	a	Tallinna Kalev	W 3-1	Mones, og (A Savitski), Kouakou
09/05	h	Trans	W 4-0	Kouakou, Gurtšioglujants, Valov, Mones
12/05	h	Levadia	L 0-4	
20/05	a	Lokomotiv	D 1-1	Kalimullin
23/05	h	Flora	L 2-3	Avilov, Kouakou (p)
10/06	a	Paide	W 1-0	Harin
14/06	h	Sillamäe	D 3-3	Valov, Kouakou, Aidara
21/06	a	Tammeka	W 4-0	Aidara 2, Harin, Lipin
07/07	h	Kalju	D 0-0	
13/07	h	Tallinna Kalev	W 5-0	Kouakou 4, Malov
18/07	a	Trans	W 3-0	Golovljov, Malov, Saarlas
25/07	a	Levadia	W 3-2	Aidara, Elhi, Kouakou
01/08	h	Lokomotiv	W 10-1	Kouakou, Elhi, Valov, og (Stepanov), Semakhin 2, Nahk, Gurtšioglujants, Lipin, Melts (p)
08/08	a	Flora	D 2-2	Kouakou 2
16/08	h	Paide	D 0-0	
19/08	a	Sillamäe	L 0-3	
22/08	h	Tammeka	W 3-2	Taar, Kouakou, Malov
29/08	a	Kalju	D 1-1	Kouakou (p)
13/09	h	Kalju	L 1-3	Malov (p)
16/09	a	Tammeka	D 1-1	Kouakou (p)
19/09	h	Sillamäe	L 0-2	
27/09	a	Paide	W 1-0	Kouakou
03/10	h	Flora	L 1-3	Aidara
18/10	a	Lokomotiv	W 3-0	Kouakou 2 (1p), Aksjonov
24/10	h	Levadia	W 2-0	Kouakou 2 (1p)
01/11	h	Trans	W 5-2	Harin, Kouakou 2, Taar, Gurtšioglujants
08/11	a	Tallinna Kalev	W 4-0	Kouakou 3 (1p), Harin

Name	Nat	DoB	Pos	Aps	(s)	Gls
Kassim Aidara	FRA	12/05/87	A	23	(13)	5
Vadim Aksjonov		20/11/96	M		(2)	1
Vladimir Avilov		10/03/95	D	33		1
Artjom Dmitrijev		14/11/88	A	3	(2)	
Trevor Elhi		11/04/93	D	34	(1)	3
Eduard Golovljov		25/01/97	A		(11)	4
Jevgeni Gurtšioglujants		03/04/86	M	5	(16)	3
Evgeni Harin	RUS	11/06/95	M	20	(7)	5
Matvei Igonen		02/10/96	G	30		
Andrei Kalimullin		06/10/77	D	34		1
Ilja Kassjantšuk		06/02/86	G	5	(2)	
Fabrice Kouakou	CIV	03/10/90	A	31		30
Maksim Lipin		17/03/92	M	23	(5)	5
Vladimir Malinin	RUS	12/02/92	M	3	(6)	
Deniss Malov		08/06/80	D	22	(4)	4
Nikita Martõnov		04/09/93	M	5	(4)	
Tanel Melts		20/11/88	M	32	(2)	2
Aleks Mones		27/06/90	D	10	(5)	2
Konstantin Nahk		10/02/75	M	25		2
Vladislav Ogorodnik		18/03/95	M	4	(5)	
Marten Saarlas		29/03/95	A		(8)	2
Aleksandr Semakhin	RUS	10/01/95	D	21	(8)	2
Albert Taar		15/01/90	M	8	(2)	2
Edgar Tur		28/12/96	M		(1)	
Oleg Valov	RUS	03/01/92	M	24	(2)	3
Maksim Zelentsov		03/08/95	G	1		

FC Levadia Tallinn

1998 • Kadriorg (5,000); Sportland Arena (500) • fclevadia.ee
Major honours
Estonian League (9) 1999, 2000, 2004, 2006, 2007, 2008, 2009, 2013, 2014; Estonian Cup (8) 1999, 2000, 2004, 2005, 2007, 2010, 2012, 2014
Coach: Marko Kristal

2014

01/03	h	Paide	L 0-1	
08/03	h	Sillamäe	D 2-2	Pikk, Teever
15/03	a	Tallinna Kalev	W 8-0	Teever, Rättel 2, El Hussieny 2 (1p), Ivanov, Marin, Buinickij
22/03	h	Tammeka	W 2-0	Rättel 2
29/03	h	Kalju	D 0-0	
05/04	h	Flora	D 1-1	Subbotin
11/04	h	Infonet	W 3-0	Artjunin, Subbotin, Teever
19/04	a	Lokomotiv	W 4-0	Subbotin 2, Buinickij, Raudsepp
26/04	h	Trans	W 1-0	Jahhimovitš
03/05	h	Trans	D 0-0	
09/05	h	Lokomotiv	W 6-0	Subbotin 2, Teever, El Hussieny, Ivanov 2
12/05	a	Infonet	W 4-0	Ivanov 3 (1p), Subbotin
20/05	a	Flora	D 0-0	
23/05	h	Kalju	W 1-0	Ivanov (p)
10/06	a	Tammeka	W 7-0	Teever 2, Subbotin, Ivanov 4
15/06	h	Tallinna Kalev	W 9-0	og (Heintare), Ivanov 3, Raudsepp, Kulinitš, Subbotin 3
21/06	a	Sillamäe	W 2-0	Subbotin 2 (1p)
05/07	a	Paide	W 2-0	Teever, Kulinitš
12/07	h	Trans	W 7-0	El Hussieny, Subbotin 2, Penić, Tipuric 2, Teever
18/07	a	Lokomotiv	W 5-1	Kaljumäe, Penić, Ivanov, Tipuric, Subbotin
25/07	h	Infonet	L 2-3	Subbotin, Ivanov
04/08	h	Flora	D 1-1	Ivanov
09/08	a	Kalju	W 1-0	Teever
15/08	h	Tammeka	W 1-0	Ivanov
18/08	a	Tallinna Kalev	W 7-0	Artjunin, Ivanov, Subbotin, El Hussieny, Peetson, Penić, Kaljumäe
23/08	h	Sillamäe	L 0-3	
30/08	h	Paide	W 4-1	El Hussieny, Teever, Tipuric, Kruglov
12/09	a	Paide	W 3-0	Pikk, Subbotin, Teever
16/09	a	Sillamäe	W 1-0	Kruglov
19/09	h	Tallinna Kalev	W 5-0	Subbotin 4 (1p), Podholjuzin
26/09	a	Tammeka	W 1-0	Teever
04/10	h	Kalju	W 3-2	Teever, Kruglov 2 (1p)
18/10	a	Flora	W 2-1	Teever, Subbotin
24/10	a	Infonet	L 0-2	
02/11	h	Lokomotiv	W 9-0	Subbotin 4, Teever, Kruglov, Tipuric, Antonov, Peetson
08/11	a	Trans	W 8-1	Antonov, Subbotin 4, Vukobratović (p), Dmitrijev (p), El Hussieny

Name	Nat	DoB	Pos	Aps	(s)	Gls
Jere Aallikko	FIN	28/02/94	M	1	(6)	
Ilja Antonov		05/12/92	M	29		2
Artjom Artjunin		24/01/90	D	32	(1)	2
Arsenij Buinickij	LTU	10/10/85	A	3	(5)	2
Aleksandr Dmitrijev		18/02/82	M	11	(1)	1
Omar El Hussieny	EGY	03/11/85	M	24	(5)	7
Vladislav Ivanov	RUS	24/01/86	A	13	(8)	19
Aleksei Jahhimovitš		30/03/90	D	10		1
Marek Kaljumäe		18/02/91	M	9	(5)	2
Dmitri Kruglov		24/05/84	D	9	(1)	5
Aleksandr Kulinitš		24/05/92	M	6	(4)	2
Pavel Marin		14/06/95	M	3	(7)	1
Rasmus Peetson		03/05/95	M		(3)	2
Jan Penić	CRO	31/12/91	M	7	(7)	3
Artur Pikk		05/03/93	D	33		2
Priit Pikker		15/03/86	G	1		
Maksim Podholjuzin		13/11/92	D	31	(1)	1
Artur Rättel		08/02/93	A	11	(1)	4
Andreas Raudsepp		13/12/93	M	22	(2)	2
Henry Rohtla		22/11/91	M		(7)	
Kristen Saarts		28/10/94	A		(4)	
Roman Smishko	UKR	18/03/83	G	35		
Igor Subbotin		26/06/90	A	30	(3)	32
Heiko Tamm		18/03/87	M	6	(9)	
Ingemar Teever		24/02/83	A	32	(2)	15
Toni Tipuric	AUT	10/09/90	M	17	(1)	5
Madis Vihmann		05/10/95	D		(2)	
Olexandr Volchkov	UKR	18/06/85	D	2		
Dragomir Vukobratović	CRO	12/05/88	M	19		1

FC Lokomotiv Jõhvi

2011 • Jõhvi linnastaadion (246); Ahtme kunstmurustaadion (200) • fclokomotiv.eu
Coach: Viktors Ņesterenko (LVA);
(22/04/14) Aleksei Tikhomirov (RUS);
(01/06/14) (Andrei Škaleta);
(05/08/14) Aleksei Tikhomirov (RUS)

2014

01/03	h	Flora	L 1-3	Zahharenkov
08/03	h	Kalju	L 0-2	
15/03	a	Trans	L 0-5	
22/03	h	Tallinna Kalev	L 0-1	
29/03	h	Sillamäe	L 1-3	Jõgi
05/04	a	Infonet	L 0-2	
12/04	a	Tammeka	D 1-1	Bazyukin
19/04	h	Levadia	L 0-4	
26/04	a	Paide	L 0-3	
03/05	h	Paide	L 1-2	Mboungou
09/05	a	Levadia	L 0-6	
13/05	h	Tammeka	D 2-2	Kutuzov, Garsevanishvili
20/05	h	Infonet	D 1-1	Potapov
24/05	a	Sillamäe	L 1-6	Jõgi
09/06	a	Tallinna Kalev	L 1-2	Kutuzov
14/06	h	Trans	L 0-2	
21/06	h	Kalju	L 1-3	Bazyukin
06/07	a	Flora	L 1-3	Kulikov
11/07	h	Paide	D 0-0	
18/07	h	Levadia	L 1-5	Bazyukin
25/07	a	Tammeka	D 3-3	Jegorov, Nikulin, Alania
01/08	a	Infonet	L 1-10	Alania
08/08	h	Sillamäe	L 1-2	Nikulin
15/08	h	Tallinna Kalev	W 1-0	Nikulin (p)
19/08	a	Trans	D 2-2	Zaitsev, Smirnov
22/08	a	Kalju	L 1-5	Smirnov
30/08	h	Flora	L 2-5	Yablokov, Jõgi
13/09	a	Flora	L 2-6	Volchkov, Yablokov
16/09	a	Kalju	L 0-9	
20/09	h	Trans	W 3-2	og (Andreev), Jõgi, Naveriani
27/09	a	Tallinna Kalev	W 5-0	Nikulin 2, Jõgi, Zahharenkov, og (Stüf)
04/10	a	Sillamäe	L 0-2	
18/10	h	Infonet	L 0-3	
25/10	h	Tammeka	W 2-0	og (Lukjanov), Nikulin
02/11	a	Levadia	L 0-9	
08/11	h	Paide	L 0-1	

Name	Nat	DoB	Pos	Aps	(s)	Gls
Kostyantyn Alania	UKR	02/10/90	D	21		2
Nikita Apet		05/10/96	M		(4)	
Sergei Bazjukin		15/12/88	M	3		
Maksim Bazyukin	RUS	18/06/83	M	19	(7)	3
Dmitri Belov	RUS	13/01/98	A	2	(1)	
Malkhaz Garsevanishvili	GEO	14/02/94	A	4	(1)	1
Boriss Gritsjuk		06/07/88	D		(1)	
Viktor Gusev	RUS	23/09/96	G	1		
Aleksandr Hlobõstin		03/09/97	M		(5)	
Aleksandr Ivanjušin		07/09/95	D	9	(1)	
Rihards Ivanovs	LVA	08/04/94	A	4	(2)	
Svjatoslav Jakovlev		24/04/96	M	8	(3)	
Dmitri Jegorov		29/08/91	M	9	(6)	1
Andrei Jõgi		02/10/82	A	17	(7)	5
Martin Juhanson		25/10/97	M		(2)	
Kevin Kaivoja		06/12/95	M	20	(4)	
Deniss Kulikov		25/09/93	D	23	(2)	1
Valeri Kurlõtškin		16/09/92	D	6	(1)	
Vitali Kutuzov	RUS	29/06/90	A	15	(2)	2
Aleksei Larin		29/03/92	D	2	(3)	
Olexiy Lazebniy	UKR	06/05/93	M	4		
Aleksei Matrossov		06/04/91	G	9	(1)	
Preche Mboungou	CGO	14/10/92	M	11	(1)	1
Lasha Naveriani	GEO	22/04/90	A	24	(5)	1
Bogdans Nesterenko	LVA	16/05/84	D	6		
Aleksandr Nikulin		15/01/85	A	13		6
Sergei Paltsev		16/02/85	M	3	(3)	
Aleksandr Panfilov	RUS	17/03/90	G	2		
Egor Potapov	RUS	21/09/93	D	22	(1)	1
Jegor Rudomin		18/05/89	D	3	(3)	
Valeri Smelkov		14/09/89	A	1		
Valeri Smelkov		14/09/89	G	24		
Dmitri Smirnov		10/09/89	D	29	(2)	2
Gleb Stepanov		15/09/97	D	2	(1)	
Aleksei Tihhonov		04/05/97	M		(3)	
Anton Vasilyev	RUS	12/10/91	M	6		
Aleksandr Vladimirov		21/09/97	D	14	(5)	
Olexandr Volchkov	UKR	18/07/85	D	14		2
Nikita Volkov		21/11/95	A	4	(6)	
Stanislav Yablokov	RUS	17/01/93	M	9		2
Aleksandr Zahharenkov	RUS	09/02/87	D	21	(3)	2
Mikhail Zaitsev	RUS	08/04/93	M	9	(2)	1

JK Narva Trans

1979 • Kreenholm (1,080); Fama Kalev (1,200) • fctrans.ee
Major honours
Estonian Cup (1) 2001
Coach: Valeri Bondarenko;
(14/06/14) Aleksei Yagudin (RUS)

2014

08/03	h	Tallinna Kalev	D	1-1	Avdeev
15/03	h	Lokomotiv	W	5-0	Tenno 2, Nesterovski (p), Plotnikov 2
22/03	a	Sillamäe	D	1-1	Nesterovski (p)
29/03	a	Paide	D	0-0	
05/04	h	Kalju	L	0-4	
12/04	h	Flora	L	0-1	
18/04	h	Infonet	D	1-1	Andreev
26/04	a	Levadia	L	0-1	
03/05	h	Levadia	D	0-0	
09/05	a	Infonet	L	0-4	
13/05	h	Flora	L	0-1	
19/05	a	Kalju	L	1-2	og (Šišov)
24/05	h	Paide	W	1-0	Tenno
31/05	a	Tammeka	D	1-1	Fjodorov
07/06	h	Sillamäe	L	1-4	Tenno
14/06	a	Lokomotiv	W	2-0	Škinjov, Plotnikov
21/06	a	Tallinna Kalev	L	1-3	Plotnikov
07/07	h	Tammeka	L	1-2	Plotnikov
12/07	a	Levadia	L	0-7	
18/07	h	Infonet	L	0-3	
26/07	a	Flora	L	0-6	
02/08	h	Kalju	D	0-0	
09/08	a	Paide	D	1-1	Nesterovski (p)
16/08	a	Sillamäe	L	1-7	Nesterovski
19/08	a	Lokomotiv	D	2-2	Nesterovski, Siņicins
23/08	h	Tallinna Kalev	W	4-1	Škinjov 2, Plotnikov, Siņicins
30/08	a	Tammeka	L	1-2	Osipov
13/09	h	Tammeka	W	2-1	Jakovlev 2
16/09	a	Tallinna Kalev	W	3-0	Jakovlev, Škinjov, Plotnikov
20/09	a	Lokomotiv	L	2-3	Jakovlev, Škinjov
27/09	h	Sillamäe	L	0-1	
04/10	h	Paide	D	0-0	
18/10	a	Kalju	L	0-1	
25/10	h	Flora	L	2-5	Lvov, Plotnikov
01/11	a	Infonet	L	2-5	Plotnikov, Nesterovski (p)
08/11	h	Levadia	L	1-8	Fjodorov

Name	Nat	DoB	Pos	Aps	(s)	Gls
Vitali Andreev	RUS	22/02/86	D	29		1
Vitali Andreev	RUS	22/02/86	G	2		
Pavel Avdeev	RUS	26/09/90	D	29		1
Ilja Bordikov		03/08/94			(1)	
Aleksandr Eliseyonok	RUS	18/05/90	A	10	(1)	
Ignat Epifanov	RUS	06/04/93	M	16		
Vladislav Fjodorov		31/07/92	M	29	(4)	2
Bi Sehi Elysée Irié	CIV	13/09/89	M	14		
Svjatoslav Jakovlev		24/04/96	M	15		4
Sergei Kapustin	RUS	04/03/98	M		(2)	
Vitali Kutuzov	RUS	29/06/90	A		(6)	
Sergei Lepmets		05/04/87	G	17		
Aleksandr Lissitsõn		17/05/96	M		(9)	
German-Guri Lvov		16/01/96	A	6	(15)	1
Vadim Mihhailov		06/06/98	M	8	(11)	
Sergejs Mišlns	LVA	04/06/87	M	18		
Roman Nesterovski		09/06/89	D	34		6
Valeri Nichik	RUS	04/03/94	M		(1)	
Andrei Ornat	RUS	04/03/91	A	2	(1)	
Ilya Osipov	RUS	20/03/91	M	16		1
Viktor Plotnikov		14/07/89	M	33	(2)	9
Nikita Savenkov		28/07/98	D	2	(3)	
Dmitri Shevyakov	RUS	25/04/94	D	25	(3)	
Andrejs Siņicins	LVA	30/01/91	M	22		2
Artjom Škinjov		30/01/94	A	27	(7)	5
Tanel Tamberg		06/06/92	D	8	(1)	
Siim Tenno		04/08/90	M	17		4
Nikita Tokaitšuk		12/03/96	G	17		

Nõmme Kalju FC

1923 • Kadriorg (5,000); Hiiu (400) • jkkalju.ee
Major honours
Estonian League (1) 2012; Estonian Cup (1) 2015
Coach: Igor Prins

2014

01/03	h	Infonet	L	0-0	(w/o; original result 1-0 Neemelo)
08/03	a	Lokomotiv	W	2-0	og (Zahharenkov), Neemelo
15/03	a	Paide	W	6-0	Fábio Prates 2, Wakui, Kimbaloula 2, Kirss
22/03	h	Flora	D	1-1	Wakui
29/03	h	Levadia	D	0-0	
05/04	a	Trans	W	4-0	Neemelo 2, Reintam, Toomet
12/04	h	Tallinna Kalev	W	2-1	Mööl 2
19/04	a	Sillamäe	W	3-0	Reintam, Wakui, Kimbaloula
28/04	h	Tammeka	W	6-0	Kallaste 2, Wakui 2, Jevdokimov, Kirss
02/05	a	Tammeka	W	2-0	Neemelo, Kimbaloula
10/05	h	Sillamäe	W	1-0	Bärengrub
13/05	a	Tallinna Kalev	W	3-0	Wakui, Neemelo, Vunk
19/05	h	Trans	W	2-1	Wakui 2
23/05	a	Levadia	L	0-1	
10/06	a	Flora	L	0-1	
14/06	h	Paide	W	3-0	Toomet, Wakui 2
21/06	a	Lokomotiv	W	3-1	Quintieri, Wakui, Jevdokimov
07/07	a	Infonet	D	0-0	
14/07	a	Tammeka	W	3-0	Wakui 3
21/07	a	Sillamäe	W	3-2	Vunk, Wakui, Felipe Nunes
28/07	h	Tallinna Kalev	W	5-0	Ahjupera 3, Kallaste, Felipe Nunes
02/08	a	Trans	D	0-0	
09/08	a	Levadia	L	0-1	
16/08	h	Flora	W	1-0	Jorge Rodrigues
19/08	a	Paide	D	1-1	Puri
22/08	a	Lokomotiv	W	5-1	Wakui, Kirss 3, Neemelo
29/08	h	Infonet	D	1-1	Vunk
13/09	a	Infonet	W	3-1	Wakui (p), Neemelo, Pürg
16/09	h	Lokomotiv	W	9-0	Felipe Nunes 4, Neemelo 3, Fábio Prates 2
20/09	h	Paide	W	3-1	Felipe Nunes 2, Kallaste
27/09	a	Flora	W	2-0	Wakui (p), Neemelo
04/10	a	Levadia	L	2-3	Vunk (p), og (Pikk)
18/10	h	Trans	W	1-0	Wakui
25/10	a	Tallinna Kalev	W	7-0	Neemelo 3, Kirss 2, Felipe Nunes, Wakui
01/11	h	Sillamäe	L	0-2	
08/11	a	Tammeka	W	1-0	Wakui (p)

Name	Nat	DoB	Pos	Aps	(s)	Gls
Jarmo Ahjupera		13/04/84	A	1	(4)	3
Mihkel Ainsalu		08/03/96	M	5	(5)	
Richard Aland		15/03/94	G	1		
Alo Bärengrub		12/02/84	D	32		1
Fábio Prates	BRA	20/06/85	M	20	(6)	4
Felipe Nunes	BRA	02/03/81	A	9	(4)	9
Nicolas Galpin	FRA	27/02/93	D	2	(3)	
Andre Järva		21/11/96	A		(1)	
Juri Jevdokimov		03/06/88	A		(12)	2
Jorge Rodrigues	POR	19/03/82	D	19	(2)	1
Ken Kallaste		31/08/88	D	35		4
Allan Kimbaloula	CGO	01/01/92	M	14	(1)	4
Robert Kirss		03/09/94	A	9	(14)	7
Erik Listmann		09/02/95	M		(2)	
Martin Mägi		18/06/96	D			
Reginald Mbu Alidor	FRA	15/05/93	M	27	(5)	
Karl Mööl		04/03/92	D	25	(5)	2
Tarmo Neemelo		10/02/82	A	27	(3)	15
Hindrek Ojamaa		12/06/95	D	1		
Novo Papaz	BIH	31/12/90	M		(1)	
Henrik Pürg		03/06/96	D	8	(2)	1
Eino Puri		07/05/88	M	9	(4)	1
Damiano Quintieri	ITA	04/05/90	M	8	(6)	1
Mikk Reintam		22/05/90	D	18		2
Tihhon Šišov		11/02/83	D	19	(1)	
Vitali Teleš		17/10/83	G	35		
Janar Toomet		10/08/89	M	15	(7)	2
Martin Vunk		21/08/84	M	24	(2)	4
Hidetoshi Wakui	JPN	12/02/83	M	33		21

Paide Linnameeskond

1999 • Paide linnastaadion (450); Paide kunstmurustaadion (200) • linnameeskond.com
Coach: Meelis Rooba

2014

01/03	a	Levadia	W	1-0	Atie
08/03	a	Flora	L	0-5	
15/03	h	Kalju	L	0-6	
21/03	a	Infonet	D	1-1	Palatu
29/03	h	Trans	D	0-0	
04/04	a	Tallinna Kalev	D	1-1	Mägi (p)
12/04	h	Sillamäe	L	0-3	
18/04	a	Tammeka	W	4-2	Tomson 2, Goldberg, Köll (p)
26/04	a	Lokomotiv	W	3-0	Köll (p), Rõivassepp 2
03/05	a	Lokomotiv	W	2-1	Goldberg, Tomson
10/05	h	Tammeka	L	0-4	
13/05	a	Sillamäe	L	1-3	Rõivassepp
20/05	h	Tallinna Kalev	W	6-2	Goldberg 2, Tomson 3, Ustaal
24/05	a	Trans	L	0-1	
10/06	h	Infonet	L	0-1	
14/06	a	Kalju	L	0-3	
21/06	h	Flora	L	1-5	Paur
05/07	h	Levadia	L	0-2	
11/07	a	Lokomotiv	D	0-0	
19/07	a	Tammeka	W	4-0	Uwaegbulam, Palatu 2, Vassiljev
28/07	h	Sillamäe	L	2-3	Sinilaid, Köll (p)
02/08	a	Tallinna Kalev	W	3-0	Uwaegbulam 2, Vassiljev
09/08	h	Trans	D	1-1	Sinilaid
16/08	a	Infonet	D	0-0	
19/08	h	Kalju	D	1-1	Sinilaid
23/08	a	Flora	L	0-3	
30/08	a	Levadia	L	1-4	Vassiljev
12/09	h	Levadia	L	0-3	
16/09	h	Flora	L	1-2	Kaldoja
20/09	a	Kalju	L	1-3	Ustaal
27/09	h	Infonet	L	0-1	
04/10	a	Trans	D	0-0	
18/10	h	Tallinna Kalev	W	4-1	Sinilaid, Tomson 2, Paur
25/10	a	Sillamäe	L	0-4	
01/11	h	Tammeka	L	0-1	
08/11	h	Lokomotiv	W	1-0	Vassiljev

Name	Nat	DoB	Pos	Aps	(s)	Gls
Said Atie	SWE	13/06/92	A	7		1
Stanislav Goldberg		30/01/92	M	26	(4)	4
Markus Holst		18/01/91	D	11	(2)	
Joel Indermitte		27/12/92	D	17	(2)	
Kaspar Kaldoja		01/01/90	D	25	(5)	1
Ervin Köll		18/03/89	M	19	(2)	3
Rauno Kööp		18/08/89	A			
Dmitri Kovtunovitš		11/05/91	D	20	(3)	
Silver Kruusalu		05/08/95	D	1	(3)	
Liivo Leetma		20/01/77	D	22	(1)	
Timo Lomp		26/07/88	D	20	(1)	
Andre Mägi		14/01/88	D	6		1
Marten Mütt		25/05/92	A		(7)	
Mart-Mattis Niinepuu		23/07/92	G	13	(1)	
Karl Palatu		05/12/82	D	26	(1)	3
Siim-Sten Palm		18/08/92	G	23		
Kaspar Paur		16/02/95	M	23	(6)	2
Rene Puhke		16/08/94	M	1	(3)	
Eerik Heinsoo		12/05/88	M	19	(3)	
Karl Johann Reitalu		13/05/95	M	1	(2)	
Sander Rõivassepp		23/08/90	M	32	(3)	3
Urmas Rooba		08/07/78	D		(1)	
Sander Sinilaid		07/10/90	M	24	(1)	4
Rasmus Tomson		13/08/85	M	28	(4)	8
Carl Tubarik		31/07/81	D	1		
Rauno Tutk		10/04/88	D		(1)	
Martin Ustaal		06/02/93	M	9	(11)	2
Jasper Uwaegbulam	NGA	12/12/94	A	6	(6)	3
Elari Valmas		02/07/88	A	3	(3)	
Aleksandr Vassiljev		24/06/88	A	7	(15)	4
Andrei Veis		06/04/90	D	6	(8)	

ESTONIA

JK Sillamäe Kalev

1951 • Kalev (1,000); Sillamäe
kunstmurustaadion (490) • fcsillamae.ee
Coach: Sergei Ratnikov;
(22/04/14) (Vadym Dobyzha (UKR));
(12/07/14) Sergei Frantsev (RUS)

2014

01/03	a	Tallinna Kalev	W 6-0	Ratnikov, og (Heintare), Kabaev, Zahovaiko 2, Kvasov
08/03	a	Levadia	D 2-2	Mashichev, Ratnikov
15/03	h	Infonet	W 3-1	Kabaev 2, Ratnikov
22/03	h	Trans	D 1-1	Ratnikov
29/03	a	Lokomotiv	W 3-1	Kvasov, Ratnikov, Murikhin
05/04	h	Tammeka	W 5-0	Murikhin, Kvasov 2, Zahovaiko, Mashichev
12/04	a	Paide	W 3-0	Paponov, Zahovaiko, Kvasov
19/04	h	Kalju	L 0-3	
26/04	a	Flora	D 1-1	Kvasov
03/05	h	Flora	L 1-2	Ratnikov
10/05	a	Kalju	L 0-1	
13/05	h	Paide	W 3-1	Kabaev, Ratnikov, Mashichev
20/05	a	Tammeka	W 6-0	Kabaev 2 (1p), Murikhin 3, Kvasov
24/05	a	Lokomotiv	W 6-1	Murikhin, Kabaev 2, Volodin, Kvasov (p), Ratnikov
07/06	a	Trans	W 4-1	Kvasov, Murikhin, Volkov, Kabaev
14/06	a	Infonet	D 3-3	Aleksejev, Kabaev, Dudarev
21/06	h	Levadia	L 0-2	
07/07	h	Tallinna Kalev	W 6-1	Murikhin 2, Mashichev, Kabaev 3
14/07	a	Flora	L 0-1	
21/07	h	Kalju	L 2-3	Kabaev, Bagužis
28/07	a	Paide	W 3-2	Kabaev, Mashichev, Kvasov
01/08	h	Tammeka	W 1-0	Kabaev (p)
08/08	a	Lokomotiv	W 2-1	Kabaev 2
16/08	h	Trans	W 7-1	Kabaev 2 (1p), Bagužis, Tjapkin, Silich, Ratnikov, Dubõkin
19/08	h	Infonet	W 3-0	Kabaev, Murikhin 2
23/08	a	Levadia	W 3-0	Kabaev, Kvasov, Dubõkin
30/08	h	Tallinna Kalev	W 8-0	Kabaev 4, Murikhin 3, Volodin
13/09	a	Tallinna Kalev	W 8-1	Kabaev 3 (1p), Murikhin, Dubõkin, Silich, Dudarev, Cheminava
16/09	h	Levadia	L 0-1	
19/09	h	Infonet	W 2-0	Kabaev, Volodin
27/09	a	Trans	W 1-0	Sidorenkov
04/10	h	Lokomotiv	W 2-0	Kabaev 2
17/10	a	Tammeka	W 4-1	Murikhin, Kabaev (p), og (Ojamaa), Ratnikov
25/10	h	Paide	W 4-0	Kabaev 2, Bagužis, Kvasov
01/11	a	Kalju	W 2-0	Mashichev 2
08/11	h	Flora	W 3-2	Silich, Kabaev (p), Bagužis

Name	Nat	DoB	Pos	Aps	(s)	Gls
Pavel Aleksejev		24/02/91	D	6	(5)	1
Mindaugas Bagužis	LTU	10/04/83	D	27	(1)	4
Igor Cheminava	RUS	23/03/91	D	17	(3)	1
Aleksei Cherkasov	RUS	01/09/94	D		(1)	
Aleksandr Dubõkin		06/05/83	M	8	(8)	3
Igor Dudarev	RUS	12/08/93	D	31	(2)	2
João Paulo	BRA	19/02/92	M		(1)	
Evgeni Kabaev	RUS	28/02/88	A	35		36
Yaroslav Kvasov	UKR	05/03/92	A	15	(18)	12
Mihhail Lavrentjev		22/02/90	G	18		
Olexiy Lazebniy	UKR	06/05/93	M	3	(3)	
Artem Levizi	RUS	02/03/93	G	2		
Hiroki Maehara	JPN	12/06/94	D	10	(2)	
Nikolai Mashichev	RUS	05/12/88	M	30	(4)	7
Micha	ESP	16/08/92	M	1		
Stanislav Murikhin	RUS	21/01/92	M	24	(6)	16
Kirill Novikov		08/12/89	D	3	(8)	
Maksim Paponov		11/06/90	M	10		1
Daniil Ratnikov		10/02/88	M	30	(3)	10
Andrei Sidorenkov		12/02/84	D	25	(1)	1
Kyrylo Silich	UKR	03/08/90	M	13	(3)	3
Mihhail Starodubtsev		14/08/82	G	16		
Deniss Tjapkin		30/01/91	M	29	(3)	1
Denis Vnukov		01/11/91	M	10	(12)	
Aleksandr Volkov		11/10/94	A		(12)	1
Aleksandr Volodin		29/03/88	D	27	(3)	
Vjatšeslav Zahovaiko		29/12/81	A	6	(4)	4

JK Tallinna Kalev

1911 • Kalev (12,000); Kalevi
kunstmurustaadion (300) • jkkalev.ee
Major honours
Estonian League (2) 1923, 19302010
Coach: Tarmo Rüütli;
(06/03/14) (Daniel Meijel);
(10/03/14) Sergei Zamogilnõi

2014

01/03	h	Sillamäe	L 0-6	
08/03	a	Trans	D 1-1	Hausenberg
15/03	h	Levadia	L 0-8	
22/03	a	Lokomotiv	W 1-0	Belov
29/03	h	Tammeka	L 1-6	og (Martin Jõgi)
04/04	h	Paide	D 1-1	Omanidze
12/04	a	Kalju	L 1-2	Naariste
19/04	h	Flora	L 1-4	og (Jürgenson)
25/04	a	Infonet	L 0-6	
02/05	h	Infonet	L 1-3	Belov
09/05	a	Flora	L 1-5	Belov
13/05	h	Kalju	L 0-3	
20/05	a	Paide	L 2-6	Naariste, Armean
24/05	h	Tammeka	D 1-1	Belov (p)
09/06	h	Lokomotiv	W 2-1	Omanidze 2
15/06	a	Levadia	L 0-9	
21/06	h	Trans	W 3-1	Omanidze 2, Paal
07/07	a	Sillamäe	L 1-6	R Karpov
13/07	a	Infonet	L 0-5	
18/07	h	Flora	L 0-2	
28/07	a	Kalju	L 0-5	
02/08	h	Paide	L 0-3	
08/08	a	Tammeka	L 0-2	
15/08	a	Lokomotiv	L 0-1	
18/08	h	Levadia	L 0-7	
23/08	a	Trans	L 1-4	Omanidze
30/08	a	Sillamäe	L 0-8	
13/09	h	Sillamäe	L 1-8	R Karpov
16/09	h	Trans	L 0-3	
19/09	a	Levadia	L 0-5	
27/09	h	Lokomotiv	L 0-5	
03/10	a	Tammeka	L 1-2	Omanidze
18/10	a	Paide	L 1-4	Koger
25/10	a	Kalju	L 0-7	
01/11	a	Flora	L 0-2	
08/11	h	Infonet	L 0-4	

Name	Nat	DoB	Pos	Aps	(s)	Gls
Albert Anissimov		21/01/94	M	2	(12)	
Ionel Armean	FIN	26/10/91	D	19	(3)	1
Gregor Aru		12/03/95	M	5	(2)	
Priidu Aruste		22/07/84	M	3	(2)	
Aleksei Belov		04/03/92	A	15		4
Nikita Brõlin		17/08/95	M	8	(4)	
Edgars Butlers		27/08/94	D	24		
Juri Gavrilov		11/05/93	D	31		
Hans-Kristjan Hansberg		06/05/96	M	7		
Ando Hausenberg		10/07/87	D	6	(7)	1
Egert Heintare		13/05/92	D	35		
Oliver Heliste		07/11/94	D	8	(7)	
Marek Kahr		09/12/81	M	8	(2)	
Freddy Karpov		27/01/95	M		(2)	
Raiko Karpov		05/02/92	M	29		2
Andi Kivirand		02/04/91	D	1		
Nikita Koger		06/05/94	M	22	(6)	1
Mike Kõiv		06/09/95	A			
Ranon Kriisa		28/01/96	D		(3)	
Johannes Kukebal		19/07/93	D	27	(1)	
Aleksei Larin		29/03/92	D	8	(1)	
Artem Levizi	RUS	02/03/93	G	14		
Aleksei Naariste		30/11/89	A	6	(9)	2
Henry Niinlaub		15/10/92	M	5	(5)	
Lasha Omanidze	GEO	01/03/94	M	18	(3)	7
Innar Paal		30/06/94	M	1	(7)	1
Ivo-Henri Pikkor		15/06/93	A	2		
Ragnar Rump		12/09/91	M	5	(3)	
Aleksei Savitski		03/10/85	D	26	(3)	
Daniil Savitski		04/05/89	A		(1)	
Daniil Savitski		04/05/89	G	19		
Alen Stepanjan		23/07/91	M	1	(1)	
Edwin Stüf		30/07/89	M	9	(2)	
Sten Teino		02/04/91	M	1		
Ian-Erik Valge		12/08/91	A	6	(4)	
Lauri Välja		25/05/95	M	10	(2)	
Karl Andre Vallner		28/02/98	G	3		
Gregor Wahl		08/11/95	D	1	(6)	
Sean Whalen	USA	16/02/81	D	11	(7)	

JK Tammeka Tartu

1989 • Tamme (1,645) • jktammeka.ee
Coach: Indrek Koser

2014

08/03	a	Infonet	L 0-3	
14/03	a	Flora	L 0-3	
22/03	a	Levadia	L 0-3	
29/03	a	Tallinna Kalev	W 6-1	Tiirik 3, Ivanov, Naggel, Paju
05/04	a	Sillamäe	L 0-5	
12/04	h	Lokomotiv	D 1-1	Lorenz
18/04	h	Paide	L 2-4	Laabus, Tiirik
28/04	a	Kalju	L 0-6	
02/05	h	Kalju	L 0-2	
10/05	a	Paide	W 4-0	Tiirik 2 (1p), Valtna, Tauts
13/05	a	Lokomotiv	D 2-2	Tekko, Tiirik (p)
20/05	h	Sillamäe	L 0-6	
24/05	a	Tallinna Kalev	D 1-1	Laabus
31/05	h	Trans	D 1-1	Tiirik
10/06	h	Levadia	L 0-7	
14/06	a	Flora	L 0-1	
21/06	h	Infonet	L 0-4	
07/07	a	Trans	W 2-1	Tiirik (p), Miller
14/07	a	Kalju	L 0-3	
19/07	h	Paide	L 0-4	
25/07	h	Lokomotiv	D 3-3	Tiirik 2, Suurpere
01/08	a	Sillamäe	L 0-1	
08/08	h	Tallinna Kalev	W 2-0	Hurt, Paju
15/08	a	Levadia	L 0-1	
19/08	h	Flora	D 1-1	Hurt
22/08	a	Infonet	L 2-3	Hurt, Tiirik (p)
30/08	a	Trans	W 2-1	Paju, Rääbis
13/09	a	Trans	L 1-2	Hurt
16/09	h	Infonet	D 1-1	Kiidron
20/09	h	Flora	L 2-4	Tutk 2 (1p)
26/09	a	Levadia	L 0-1	
03/10	h	Tallinna Kalev	W 2-1	Suurpere, Tiirik
17/10	h	Sillamäe	L 1-4	Hurt
25/10	a	Lokomotiv	L 0-2	
01/11	a	Paide	W 1-0	Suurpere
08/11	h	Kalju	L 0-1	

Name	Nat	DoB	Pos	Aps	(s)	Gls
Martin Aasmäe		10/05/96	M	3	(4)	
Kevin Anderson		10/11/93	D	24	(1)	
Mihail Gutak		28/07/87	D		(3)	
Mario Hansi		21/05/87	M		(1)	
Martin Hurt		27/06/84	A	17		5
Georgi Ivanov		19/06/92	M	3	(6)	1
Markus Jõgi		30/09/96	M	5	(7)	
Martin Jõgi		05/01/95	D	6		
Tanel Joosep		08/08/90	D	2		
Siim Kask		21/03/97	D		(1)	
Kaarel Kiidron		30/04/90	D	6	(1)	1
Karli Kütt		17/02/93	G	21		
Reio Laabus		14/03/90	M	17		2
Jürgen Lorenz		11/05/93	D	23	(1)	1
Andrus Lukjanov		21/11/89	G	4		
Martin Miller		25/09/97	M	12	(4)	1
Paul Naaber		05/05/96	A		(1)	
Marek Naal		10/01/93	A	5	(10)	
Martin Naggel		22/05/90	D	29	(1)	1
Hindrek Ojamaa		12/06/95	D	11	(2)	
Andre Paju		05/01/95	M	28	(1)	3
Karl Johan Pechter		02/03/96	G	11		
Prit Peedo		18/04/95	M	2	(1)	
Kevin Rääbis		02/01/94	A	9	(9)	1
Valeri Šabanov		19/04/95	D	12	(13)	
Geir-Kristjan Suurpere		26/02/95	M	22	(5)	3
Rasmus Tauts		07/01/97	M	24	(5)	1
Tauno Tekko		14/12/94	M	32		1
Simo Tenno		05/09/92	D	9	(4)	
Kristjan Tiirik		25/08/82	M	33		13
Mario Tikerberi		01/04/98	A	2	(3)	
Rauno Tutk		10/04/88	D	12	(2)	2
Mikk Valtna		18/11/85	A	9	(16)	1
Tanel Vanaveski		28/05/91	D	3	(1)	

Top goalscorers

36	Evgeni Kabaev (Sillamäe)
32	Igor Subbotin (Levadia)
30	Fabrice Kouakou (Infonet)
22	Albert Prosa (Flora)
21	Hidetoshi Wakui (Kalju)
19	Vladislav Ivanov (Levadia)
16	Stanislav Murikhin (Sillamäe)
15	Rauno Alliku (Flora)
	Ingemar Teever (Levadia)
	Tarmo Neemelo (Kalju)

Promoted clubs

Pärnu Linnameeskond

2011 • Kalev (1,500) • no website
Coach: Gert Olesk

JK Tulevik Viljandi

1912 • Viljandi linnastaadion (1,084) • jktulevik.ee
Coach: Aivar Lillevere

Second level final table 2014

		Pld	W	D	L	F	A	Pts
1	FC Flora Tallinn II	36	24	6	6	104	40	78
2	FC Levadia Tallinn II	36	20	8	8	102	52	68
3	Pärnu Linnameeskond	36	19	3	14	109	78	60
4	Nõmme Kalju FC II	36	17	6	13	69	62	57
5	JK Tulevik Viljandi	36	14	9	13	53	51	51
6	FC Kuressaare	36	14	5	17	69	81	47
7	FC Irbis Kiviõli	36	12	11	13	72	82	47
8	JK Tarvas Rakvere	36	12	10	14	61	65	46
9	JK Vaprus Vändra	36	11	5	20	60	72	38
10	FC Puuma Tallinn	36	2	7	27	32	148	10

NB FC Flora Tallinn II, FC Levadia Tallinn II and Nõmme Kalju FC II ineligible for promotion; Pärnu Linnameeskond promoted directly; JK Tulevik Viljandi entered play-offs; FC Puuma Tallinn – 3 pts deducted.

Promotion/Relegation play-offs

(16/11/14 & 22/11/14)
Tulevik 0-0 Lokomotiv
Lokomotiv 1-1 Tulevik
(1-1; Tulevik on away goal)

DOMESTIC CUP

Eesti Karikas 2014/15

FIRST ROUND

(01/06/14)
Infonet-2 7-0 Paidelona

(04/06/14)
Emmaste 5-0 Olympic Olybet

(05/06/14)
Ararat TTÜ w/o Vinni
Depoo 3-8 Starbunker
Flora-2 4-4 Santos *(aet; 9-8 on pens)*
Kadakas Kernu 0-2 Kaitseliit Kalev
Lokomotiv Jõhvi w/o JK aameraaS
MRJK Viimsi 6-1 Järva-Jaani
Pärnu Linnameeskond 3-4 Tallinna Kalev
Rada 9-0 TÜ/Fauna
Reliikvia 0-1 Võru
Tammeka 5-2 EMÜ SK

(06/06/14)
FC Tartu 4-0 Peedu
Kalev-3 3-2 Raudne Rusikas

(07/06/14)
Dnipro w/o Vutihoolikud
Infonet 16-0 Poseidon Nirvaana
Kuressaare 7-0 Väätsa vald
Narva United 2-0 Lokomotiv Rapla

(08/06/14)
Fellin/Club Red 1-1 Raasiku valla FC *(aet; 1-4 on pens)*
Igiliikur 5-1 Virtsu
Kalev Juunior 6-1 Aseri/Askele
Lootos FCR 2-5 Tallinna Jalgpalliselts
Maardu United 8-0 Shnelli
Merkuur 10-1 Õismäe Torm
Retro 5-1 Piraaja
Taara 0-8 Vaprus Vändra
Tarvas 3-0 Castovanni Eagles
Tõrva 6-0 Aspen
Twister 1-4 Tartu Tehased

(09/06/14)
Sporting 3-1 Loo

(10/06/14)
Charma 3-2 Jalgpallihaigla

(11/06/14)
FC Lelle 1-5 FCF Tallinna Ülikool
Ganvix 11-2 Kohtla-Nõmme
Keila 12-1 Somnium
Nõmme United 10-0 Anija United
Trans 1-3 Sillamäe Kalev

(15/06/14)
Forss 6-1 Helios

(18/06/14)
Joker 1993 8-2 Viimsi Ehitus

(26/06/14)
Laagri 2-1 Eston Villa *(aet)*
Metropool 9-0 Haiba

(27/06/14)
Tääksi 1-1 Läänemaa *(aet; 5-4 on pens)*

(02/07/14)
Flora 7-0 Tulevik

SECOND ROUND

(25/06/14)
Tallinna Jalgpalliselts 0-2 Igiliikur

(28/06/14)
Kalev Juunior 0-19 Levadia

(02/07/14)
Irbis 15-0 Sporting
Navi Vutiselts 0-3 Tallinna Kalev
Paide Linnameeskond 17-0 Tartu Tehased

(05/07/14)
Noorus-96 w/o Ajax

(06/07/14)
FC Tartu 8-1 Atli
Retro 9-2 Warrior

(10/07/14)
Kaitseliit Kalev 0-3 Charma

(11/07/14)
Tammeka 4-1 Rada

(13/07/14)
Ganvix 4-1 Tõrva

(15/07/14)
Ararat TTÜ 5-0 FCF Tallinna Ülikool-2
Lokomotiv Jõhvi 2-1 Vaprus Vändra *(aet)*
Merkuur 0-4 Kuressaare
Otepää 0-2 Tarvas
Võru 5-2 Soccernet

(16/07/14)
Flora-2 3-1 Narva United
Metropool 3-1 Raasiku valla FC
Nõmme United 2-9 FCF Tallinna Ülikool
Tallinna Kalev-3 w/o IAFA

(20/07/14)
Dnipro 2-0 Maardu United
Tapa 0-4 Flora-3

(22/07/14)
Flora 5-0 Visadus
Joker 1993 0-2 Infonet
Starbunker 2-1 Emmaste

(23/07/14)
Elva 2-2 Infonet-2 *(aet; 2-3 on pens)*
Forss 1-3 Laagri
Reaal 2-4 Tääksi
Welco Elekter 0-0 Kose *(aet; 2-4 on pens)*

(05/08/14)
Sillamäe Kalev 11-0 MRJK Viimsi

(06/08/14)
Keila 2-1 Puuma

(13/08/14)
Kalju 18-0 Ambla

THIRD ROUND

(05/08/14)
Lokomotiv Jõhvi 3-1 Tallinna Kalev-3

(06/08/14)
Infonet-2 2-1 Tarvas
Metropool 3-3 Ararat TTÜ *(aet; 1-3 on pens)*
Tääksi 3-7 Irbis

(12/08/14)
Flora 13-0 Kose
Flora-2 3-1 Tammeka
Võru 0-11 Infonet

(14/08/14)
FC Tartu 2-5 Retro

(17/08/14)
Flora-3 2-3 Igiliikur

(19/08/14)
Charma 2-11 FCF Tallinna Ülikool

(26/08/14)
Noorus-96 0-1 Tallinna Kalev

(02/09/14)
Dnipro 0-13 Sillamäe Kalev
Keila 0-6 Paide Linnameeskond
Laagri w/o Levadia *(original result 0-5)*

(03/09/14)
Starbunker 5-1 Ganvix

(01/10/14)
Kalju 4-0 Kuressaare

FOURTH ROUND

(24/09/14)
FCF Tallinna Ülikool 4-3 Retro *(aet)*

(01/10/14)
Ararat TTÜ 0-3 Infonet-2

(11/10/14)
Paide Linnameeskond w/o Irbis
Starbunker 0-4 Kalju
Tallinna Kalev 0-3 Lokomotiv Jõhvi

(21/10/14)
Flora 11-0 Laagri
Sillamäe Kalev 0-0 Infonet *(aet; 4-2 on pens)*

(22/10/14)
Igiliikur 0-9 Flora-2

QUARTER-FINALS

(28/04/15)
Flora 2-1 Sillamäe Kalev
(Tukiainen 12, 85; Sidorenkov 22)

Paide Linnameeskond 3-0 Infonet-2 *(Uwaegbulam 2, 52, Varendi 53)*

(29/04/15)
FCF Tallinna Ülikool 3-5 Flora-2 *(Anniste 45, Taska 61, Klasen 74; Taska 27og, Siim 33, 90+3, Roog 41, Riiberg 45+1)*

Kalju 5-3 Lokomotiv Jõhvi *(Neemelo 3, Dmitrijev 17, 56, Järva 31, Listmann 68; Smirnov 48, 64, 74p)*

SEMI-FINALS

(12/05/15)
Flora-2 1-3 Paide Linnameeskond *(Siim 59; Varendi 8, Uwaegbulam 63, Zahovaiko 84)*

(13/05/15)
Flora 1-2 Kalju *(Jürgenson 15; Kimbaloula 75, Neemelo 83)*

FINAL

(30/05/15)
A Le Coq Arena, Tallinn
NÕMME KALJU FC 2 *(Dmitrijev 45+1, Kimbaloula 76)*
PAIDE LINNAMEESKOND 0
Referee: Frischer
KALJU: Teleš, Mööl, Jorge Rodrigues, Bärengrub, Kallaste, Listmann, Lindpere (Puri 34), Wakui, Kimbaloula (Järva 80), Purje (Neemelo 62), Dmitrijev
PAIDE: Niinepuu, Lilander, Leetma, Mägi, Lomp, Sillaste (Tomson 90+2), Ustaal, Sinilaid, Varendi (Paur 77), Zahovaiko, Uwaegbulam (Rõivassepp 90+2)

FAROE ISLANDS
Fótbóltssamband Føroya (FSF)

Address	Gundadalur, PO Box 3028	**President**	Christian Andreasen
	FO-110 Tórshavn	**General secretary**	Virgar Hvidbro
Tel	+298 351979	**Media officer**	Terji Nielsen
Fax	+298 319079	**Year of formation**	1979
E-mail	fsf@football.fo	**National stadium**	Tórsvøllur, Torshavn
Website	football.fo		(4,132)

MEISTARADEILDIN CLUBS

 ① **AB Argir**

 ② **B36 Tórshavn**

 ③ **B68 Toftir**

 ④ **EB/Streymur**

 ⑤ **HB Tórshavn**

 ⑥ **ÍF Fuglafjørdur**

 ⑦ **KÍ Klaksvík**

 ⑧ **NSÍ Runavík**

 ⑨ **Skála ÍF**

 ⑩ **Víkingur**

PROMOTED CLUBS

 ⑪ **TB Tvøroyri**

 ⑫ **FC Suduroy**

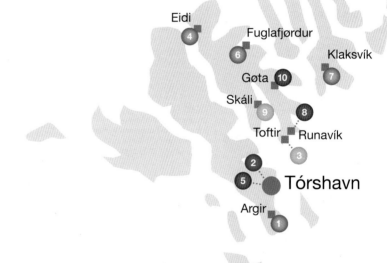

KEY:

⬤ – UEFA Champions League

⬤ – UEFA Europa League

⬤ – Promoted

⬤ – Relegated

Tenth title for B36

Unfancied at the start of the 2014 Meistardeildin, B36 Tórshavn were an unstoppable force for most of the 27-match campaign, capturing the tenth title in their history as local rivals and defending champions HB had to settle for second place.

There was another runners-up spot for HB in the domestic cup as competition specialists Víkingur, who also excelled in Europe, lifted the trophy for the third year on the trot. Eclipsing all else for the islands' football fans, though, was the national team's sensational feat of beating Greece not once but twice in the UEFA EURO 2016 qualifiers.

| Holders HB edged out by local rivals | Cup hat-trick for Víkingur | National team do double over Greece |

Domestic league

Sámal Erik Hentze had coached HB to their 2009 title win, and he was back for more with the other club from the capital in 2014. Newly recruited from AB Argir, he could hardly have got off to a better start as B36 raced to the top of the table with a 16-game unbeaten run that stretched from mid-March to early August. HB were the only club close enough to cause concern, but when B36 followed their first defeat – 1-0 at EB/Streymur – with another three wins, and thus found themselves seven points clear with seven games to go, the title appeared to be in the bag.

However, two successive home defeats, against KÍ Klaksvík and Víkingur, brought on a few jitters, and when Hentze's men then trailed 2-0 at NSÍ Runavík in their next fixture the alarm bells really started to ring. However, a stunning second-half comeback win stopped the rot, and that was followed by three further victories, the last of which, 3-1 away to B68 Toftir, secured the title with a game to spare.

HB defeated the newly-crowned champions on the final day to close the gap to a single point, but the local bragging rights were unaffected. The key men in B36's triumph were veteran skipper Jákup á Borg, 20-year-old centre-back Hørdur Askham and the team's two foreigners, Polish midfielder Łukasz Cieślewicz and 13-goal Nigerian striker Adeshina Lawal.

While HB, inspired once again by the evergreen Fródi Benjaminsen, took second place, Víkingur finished a distant third and NSÍ edged EB/Streymur for fourth spot, and a place in Europe, on goal difference, with 20-goal striker Klæmint Andrasson Olsen topping the scorer charts for the for the second year running. It was a disappointing season for ÍF Fuglafjørdur, runners-up in the previous two campaigns, as they finished seventh, while newly promoted Skála ÍF and B68 both endured immediate relegation. They were replaced by south-islanders TB Tvøroyri and FC Suduroy.

Domestic cup

For the first time since 2006 the final of the Faroe Islands Cup did not involve EB/Streymur. However, there was nothing unfamiliar about the winners as Víkingur lifted the trophy for the third year in a row. Sigfrídur Clementsen's side ended EB/Streymur's extraordinary run in the semi-finals before seeing off HB in the final with a late headed goal from Faroe Islands midfielder Hallur Hansen.

Europe

Víkingur were also the country's star performers in knockout football of an international variety as they became the first club from the islands to win two successive ties in Europe. FC Daugava Daugavpils and Tromsø IL were their victims in the first two qualifying rounds of the UEFA Europa League before they met their match in HNK Rijeka. The 2-1 win in northern Norway against Tromsø was arguably the finest result achieved by any Faroe Islands club side.

National team

There is no disputing the greatest result in the history of the Faroe Islands national team. That came on matchday four of the UEFA EURO 2016 qualifying tournament when, after defeats in their opening three matches, Lars Olsen's side beat 2004 European champions Greece 1-0 in Piraeus.

Jóan Símun Edmundsson's 61st-minute winner was no more than the team deserved, and, as if to prove the point, when Greece travelled to the North Atlantic for the re-match seven months later, the Faroe Islands beat them again, 2-1.

Hallur Hansson and 19-year-old Brandur Olsen became the latest local heroes as they found the net in another astonishing display of verve and passion from Olsen's unsung side that left the home fans eagerly anticipating the final four fixtures of the campaign.

DOMESTIC SEASON AT A GLANCE

Meistaradeildin 2014 final table

		Pld	Home					Away					Total					Pts
			W	D	L	F	A	W	D	L	F	A	W	D	L	F	A	
1	**B36 Tórshavn**	27	8	3	3	20	11	11	1	1	33	14	19	4	4	53	25	61
2	HB Tórshavn	27	10	2	2	35	11	8	4	1	24	9	18	6	3	59	20	60
3	Víkingur	27	6	5	2	29	11	7	5	2	31	19	13	10	4	60	30	49
4	NSÍ Runavík	27	7	2	5	29	18	5	2	6	24	24	12	4	11	53	42	40
5	EB/Streymur	27	7	2	5	25	16	4	5	4	16	17	11	7	9	41	33	40
6	KÍ Klaksvík	27	8	2	3	28	14	2	4	8	13	24	10	6	11	41	38	36
7	ÍF Fuglafjørdur	27	5	3	6	23	24	2	4	7	13	28	7	7	13	36	52	28
8	AB Argir	27	2	4	7	12	29	4	3	7	18	32	6	7	14	30	61	25
9	Skála ÍF	27	2	6	5	14	22	1	2	11	5	32	3	8	16	19	54	17
10	B68 Toftir	27	3	3	7	16	28	1	2	11	7	32	4	5	18	23	60	17

European qualification 2015/16

Champion: B36 Tórshavn (first qualifying round)

Cup winner: Víkingur (first qualifying round)
HB Tórshavn (first qualifying round)
NSÍ Runavík (first qualifying round)

Top scorer Klæmint Andrasson Olsen (NSÍ), 22 goals
Relegated clubs B68 Toftir, Skála ÍF
Promoted clubs TB Tvøroyri, FC Suduroy
Cup final Víkingur 1-0 HB Tórshavn

Team of the season
(4-4-2)

Coach: Hentze (B36)

Player of the season

Adeshina Lawal
(B36 Tórshavn)

With his 13 goals and 11 assists, Nigerian striker Adeshina Lawal played a huge part in B36's league triumph, not least with the double that helped his side overturn a 2-0 deficit and win a pivotal fixture at NSÍ Runavík. A skilful dribbler with plenty of pace, his second season at the club was marked by a constant desire to take on defenders and shoot on goal. It earned him not only a championship winner's medal but also the official Meistaradeildin player of the year crown.

Newcomer of the season

Hørdur Askham
(B36 Tórshavn)

Askham was a midfielder when he made his league debut for B36, aged 16, in their 2011 title triumph. By 2014, however, the youngster had developed into the linchpin of the champions' defence, his consistency of performance not only earning him a regular place in the Faroe Islands Under-21 side but also drawing words of appreciation from senior national team boss Lars Olsen. He started 23 of B36's league games and, despite his tender years, was seldom found wanting.

NATIONAL TEAM

Top five all-time caps
Fródi Benjaminsen (85); Óli Johannesen (83); Jákup Mikkelsen (73); Jens Martin Knudsen (65); Julian Johnsson (62)

Top five all-time goals
Rógvi Jacobsen (10); Todi Jónsson (9); Uni Arge (8); **Fródi Benjaminsen, Christian Lamhauge Holst** & John Petersen (6)

Results 2014/15

07/09/14	Finland (ECQ)	H	Torshavn	L	1-3	Holst (41)
11/10/14	Northern Ireland (ECQ)	A	Belfast	L	0-2	
14/10/14	Hungary (ECQ)	H	Torshavn	L	0-1	
14/11/14	Greece (ECQ)	A	Piraeus	W	1-0	Edmundsson (61)
29/03/15	Romania (ECQ)	A	Ploiesti	L	0-1	
13/06/15	Greece (ECQ)	H	Torshavn	W	2-1	Hansson (32), B Olsen (70)

Appearances 2014/15

Coach: Lars Olsen (DEN)	02/02/61		FIN	NIR	HUN	GRE	ROU	GRE	Caps	Goals
Gunnar Nielsen	07/10/86	Motherwell (SCO) /unattached /Stjarnan (ISL)	G	G	G	G	G	G	27	-
Jónas Tór Næs	27/12/86	EB/Streymur	D	D	D	D			41	-
Odmar Færø	01/11/89	B36	D		s86		M74	s74	10	-
Sonni Nattestad	05/08/94	Horsens (DEN) /Vejle (DEN)	D	D	D	D	D	D	8	-
Viljormur Davidsen	19/07/91	Vejle (DEN)	D	D	D	D	D		13	-
Fródi Benjaminsen	14/12/77	HB	M	M	M	M		M	85	6
Hallur Hansson	08/07/92	Víkingur /Vendsyssel (DEN)	M	M	M	M		M	18	4
Gilli Sørensen	11/08/92	AaB (DEN)	M76		s81		s80	D13	6	-
Róaldur Jacobsen	23/01/91	B36	M55				M80		2	-
Christian Lamhauge Holst	25/12/81	Fremad Amager (DEN)	M	M82	M69	M76	M	M74	48	6
Páll A Klettskard	17/05/90	KÍ	A46	A75					11	-
Jóan Símun Edmundsson	26/07/91	HB /Vejle (DEN)	s46	M	A76	A86	A	A92	33	3
Rógvi Baldvinsson	06/12/89	Ålgård (NOR)	s55						20	2
Ári Mohr Jónsson	22/07/94	Silkeborg (DEN)	s76						2	-
Atli Gregersen	15/06/82	Víkingur		D	D	D	D	D	28	-
Pól Jóhannus Justinussen	13/01/89	NSÍ		M91		s76			21	-
Arnbjørn T Hansen	27/02/86	EB/Streymur		s75	s76				18	3
Brandur H Olsen	19/12/95	København (DEN)		s82	M	M88	M80	M	5	1
Kaj Leo í Bartalsstovu	23/06/91	Levanger (NOR)		s91	s69				4	-
Sølvi Vatnhamar	05/05/86	Víkingur			M81	M	M	M	5	-
Klæmint A Olsen	17/07/90	NSÍ				s88			5	-
Jóhan Troest Davidsen	31/01/88	HB					D	s13	31	-
Andreas Lava Olsen	09/10/87	Víkingur					s74		8	1
René S Joensen	08/02/93	HB					s80	s92	4	-
Bardur J Hansen	13/03/92	Víkingur						D	1	-

EUROPE

HB Tórshavn

First qualifying round - Lincoln FC (GIB)
A 1-1 *Hanssen (71)*
Gestsson, Alex, Holm, Jóhan Davidsen, Vatnsdal, Benjaminsen, Edmundsson, Hanssen, K Mouritsen (Ingason 84), R Joensen, Jensen. Coach: Hedin Askham (FRO)
H 5-2 *Hanssen (11, 81), Jensen (25), Edmundsson (34), Benjaminsen (88)*
Gestsson, Alex, Holm, Jóhan Davidsen, Vatnsdal, Benjaminsen, Edmundsson, Hanssen, K Mouritsen (P Joensen 90+1), R Joensen (Jógvan Davidsen 90), Jensen (Fløtum 58). Coach: Hedin Askham (FRO)

Second qualifying round - FK Partizan (SRB)
A 0-3
Gestsson, Alex, Holm, Jóhan Davidsen, Vatnsdal, Benjaminsen, Edmundsson, Jógvan Davidsen (Fløtum 77), K Mouritsen (Ingason 66), R Joensen (Wardum 63), Jensen. Coach: Hedin Askham (FRO)
H 1-3 *Wardum (35)*
Gestsson, Holm, Jóhan Davidsen, Vatnsdal (Wardum 22), Benjaminsen, Edmundsson, Hanssen, P Joensen, Jógvan Davidsen, K Mouritsen (Fløtum 82), Jensen (Ingason 75). Coach: Hedin Askham (FRO)

Víkingur

First qualifying round - FC Daugava Daugavpils (LVA)
H 2-1 *F Justinussen (23), A Olsen (59)*
Túri, H Jacobsen, A Gregersen, Joensen (A Olsen 46; G Vatnhamar 88), Hedin Hansen (Sørensen 73), Djordjević, Hansson, B Hansen, E Jacobsen, Djurhuus, F Justinussen. Coach: Sigfrídur Clementsen (FRO)
A 1-1 *A Olsen (88)*
Túri, H Jacobsen, A Gregersen, Hedin Hansen, Djordjević (Sørensen 90+1), S Vatnhamar, Hansson, B Hansen, E Jacobsen, Djurhuus (A Olsen 73), F Justinussen. Coach: Sigfrídur Clementsen (FRO)

Second qualifying round - Tromsø IL (NOR)
H 0-0
Túri, H Jacobsen, A Gregersen, S Olsen (Sørensen 90+3), Djordjević (A Olsen 68), S Vatnhamar (Hedin Hansen 76), Hansson, B Hansen, E Jacobsen, Djurhuus, F Justinussen. Coach: Sigfrídur Clementsen (FRO)
A 2-1 *B Hansen (60), Hansson (77)*
Túri, A Olsen (Djordjević 63), H Jacobsen, A Gregersen, S Olsen (Hedin Hansen 78), S Vatnhamar (Sørensen 90+2), Hansson, B Hansen, E Jacobsen, Djurhuus, F Justinussen. Coach: Sigfrídur Clementsen (FRO)

Third qualifying round - HNK Rijeka (CRO)
H 1-5 *Hansson (35)*
Túri, A Olsen (Sørensen 77), H Jacobsen, A Gregersen, S Olsen, S Vatnhamar, Hansson (Hedin Hansen 64), B Hansen, E Jacobsen, Djurhuus (Djordjević 45+2), F Justinussen. Coach: Sigfrídur Clementsen (FRO)
A 0-4
Túri, H Jacobsen, A Gregersen, S Olsen, Djordjević (Sørensen 81), S Vatnhamar, Hansson (Hedin Hansen 80), B Hansen, E Jacobsen, Djurhuus, F Justinussen (A Olsen 71). Coach: Sigfrídur Clementsen (FRO)

ÍF Fuglafjørdur

First qualifying round - Myllykosken Pallo -47 (FIN)
A 0-1
J Mikkelsen, Á Petersen, P Mikkelsen, Lambanum, K Løkin, Lakjuni, B Petersen (Jakobsen 77), A Ellingsgaard (Joensen 90+1), Zachariassen, J Ellingsgaard, Eliasen. Coach: Albert Ellefsen (FRO)
H 0-0
J Mikkelsen, P Mikkelsen, K Løkin, B Petersen, Jakobsen (Jøkladal 88), A Ellingsgaard (Poulsen 80), Zachariassen, Joensen, Šarić, J Ellingsgaard, Eliasen. Coach: Albert Ellefsen (FRO)

B36 Tórshavn

First qualifying round - Linfield FC (NIR)
H 1-2 *Lawal (72)*
Thomsen, O Færø (Joensen 63), A Cieślewicz (Poulsen 89), H Askham, Jacobsen, Ł Cieślewicz, Eriksen, Eysturoy, Matras, Thorleifsson (Sørensen 90+3), Lawal. Coach: Sámal Erik Hentze (FRO)
A 1-1 *Lawal (48p)*
Thomsen, O Færø, H Askham, Jacobsen, Ł Cieślewicz, Poulsen, Mellemgaard, Eysturoy, Matras (Sørensen 84), Thorleifsson (A Cieślewicz 56), Lawal. Coach: Sámal Erik Hentze (FRO)

DOMESTIC LEAGUE CLUB-BY-CLUB

AB Argir

1973 • Blue Water Arena (2,000) • ab.fo
**Coach: Bill McLeod Jacobsen;
(16/04/14) Oddbjørn Joensen**

2014

15/03	a	Víkingur	W	2-0	Edmundsson, Mohr
21/03	h	B36	L	1-2	J Drangastein
30/03	a	NSÍ	L	0-3	
13/04	h	Skála	D	1-1	Anghel
17/04	a	KÍ	L	1-4	Splidt
21/04	a	B68	L	2-3	Anghel 2
04/05	h	HB	L	0-3	
11/05	a	EB/Streymur	L	0-5	
18/05	h	ÍF	W	4-1	Anghel 3, Edmundsson
25/05	h	NSÍ	L	0-7	
01/06	a	B36	D	1-1	Mohr
09/06	h	Víkingur	L	0-3	
16/06	a	KÍ	D	1-1	Joensen
22/06	a	Skála	D	0-0	
27/06	h	B68	W	3-2	Mohr, Egilsson, Splidt
27/07	h	EB/Streymur	D	2-2	Mohr, Færø
03/08	a	HB	W	2-1	J Drangastein, Hentze
10/08	a	ÍF	W	2-0	og (Isaksen), Anghel
17/08	a	Víkingur	D	2-2	Čekulajevs, Nielsen
20/08	h	B36	L	0-3	
24/08	h	EB/Streymur	D	0-0	
14/09	a	NSÍ	L	1-3	Olsen
21/09	a	ÍF	L	0-3	
01/10	h	B68	W	2-1	og (Rosenberg), Janković (p)
05/10	h	HB	L	1-3	J Drangastein
19/10	a	KÍ	L	1-5	Færø
25/10	h	Skála	L	1-2	Nolsøe

No	Name	Nat	DoB	Pos	Aps	(s)	Gls
10	Sorin Vasile Anghel		16/07/79	D	16	(2)	7
9	Aleksandrs Čekulajevs	LVA	10/09/85	A	5		1
24	Áki Dahl		04/04/93	G	1		
21	Gert Drangastein		25/08/94	M	4	(3)	
7	Jobin Drangastein		01/11/90	M	18	(4)	3
9	Jóan Símun Edmundsson		26/07/91	A	7	(2)	2
27	Magnus Egilsson		19/03/94	M	11	(10)	1
22	Beinir Ellefsen		07/04/93	M	25		
25	Sandri Færø		04/03/92	M	6	(3)	2
25	Cristian í Gardi		02/12/90	A	2	(4)	
14	Mikkjal Theodor Hentze		08/12/86	M	6	(11)	1
20	Karstin Højgaard		23/02/94	M	5	(4)	
4	Jógvan Isaksen		25/04/90	D	8	(1)	
6	Dmitrije Janković	SRB	05/11/75	D	18		1
19	Leivur Holm Joensen		08/01/88	D	6	(9)	1
3	Ari Johannesen		15/09/92	M		(1)	
1	Hans Jørgensen		13/08/90	G	6		
4	Tóki á Lofti		06/12/93	M		(1)	
3	Jørgin Martin Meinraðsson		29/12/93	D	1		
8	Martin Midjord		25/12/89	D	6	(3)	
15	Hørdur Mouritzarson Mohr		06/03/93	M	22	(3)	4
26	Kári Nielsen		03/03/81	M	22	(1)	1
23	Jógvan Andrias Nolsøe		20/05/92	A	10	(3)	1
11	Bárdur Olsen		05/12/85	M	17	(3)	1
5	Sørin Nygaard Samuelsen		29/04/92	D	6	(1)	
18	Dan í Soylu		09/07/96	M	4	(2)	
32	Dion Brynjólf Splidt		05/06/89	M	9		2
16	Hedin Stenberg		14/01/89	G	20		
13	Jónas Stenberg		07/04/87	D	26	(1)	
2	Andras Brixen Vágsheyg		01/01/92	D	10	(2)	
1	Rói Zachariasen		12/10/98	G		(1)	

B36 Tórshavn

1936 • Gundadalur (5,000) • b36.fo

Major honours
Faroe Islands League (10) 1946, 1948, 1950, 1959, 1962, 1997, 2001, 2005, 2011, 2014; Faroe Islands Cup (5) 1965, 1991, 2001, 2003, 2006
Coach: Sámal Erik Hentze

2014

15/03	h	Skála	W	2-0	Thorleifsson, Matras
21/03	a	AB	W	2-1	Jacobsen 2
28/03	h	Víkingur	D	2-2	Lawal, Borg
11/04	h	HB	D	1-1	Borg
17/04	a	B68	W	4-2	H Askham 2, Ł Cieślewicz, Borg
21/04	a	ÍF	W	5-2	Jacobsen 2, Borg, Sørensen, Lawal
04/05	h	EB/Streymur	W	3-1	og (G Hansen), Lawal, Borg
11/05	a	KÍ	W	3-1	Lawal 2, Borg
18/05	a	NSÍ	W	1-0	Lawal
25/05	a	Víkingur	W	2-1	Lawal, Ł Cieślewicz
01/06	h	AB	D	1-1	Lawal (p)
09/06	a	Skála	W	3-0	Mellemgaard, Borg, Sørensen
15/06	h	B68	W	3-0	Thorleifsson, Jacobsen, Heinesen
22/06	a	HB	D	2-2	Mellemgaard, Ł Cieślewicz
27/06	h	ÍF	W	1-0	Borg (p)
29/07	h	KÍ	W	2-1	Ł Cieślewicz, Lawal
03/08	a	EB/Streymur	L	0-1	
10/08	h	NSÍ	W	1-0	Thorleifsson
17/08	h	Skála	W	2-0	og (E Jacobsen), Ł Cieślewicz
20/08	a	AB	W	3-0	Eysturoy, Ł Cieślewicz, Lawal
24/08	h	KÍ	L	0-1	
14/09	h	Víkingur	L	0-2	
21/09	a	NSÍ	W	3-2	Jacobsen, Lawal 2
01/10	a	ÍF	W	2-1	Á Nielsen 2
05/10	h	EB/Streymur	W	1-0	Ł Cieślewicz
19/10	a	B68	W	3-1	Lawal, Mellemgaard, Matras
25/10	h	HB	L	1-2	Ł Cieślewicz

No	Name	Nat	DoB	Pos	Aps	(s)	Gls
8	Hørdur Askham		22/09/94	D	23		2
25	Trygvi Askham		28/03/88	G	1		
9	Jákup á Borg		26/10/79	A	21		8
7	Adrian Cieślewicz	POL	16/11/90	M		(3)	
11	Łukasz Cieślewicz	POL	15/11/87	M	27		8
16	Karl Martin Eivindsson Danielsen		20/04/95	D		(3)	
2	Andrias Høgnason Eriksen		22/02/94	D	19	(2)	
20	Høgni Eysturoy		14/07/90	D	27		1
5	Odmar Færø		01/11/89	D	12	(1)	
14	Sandri Færø		04/03/92	M		(3)	
18	Benjamin Heinesen		26/03/96	M		(11)	1
25	Jákup Højgaard		06/02/94	G		(1)	
10	Róaldur Jacobsen		23/01/91	M	27		6
3	Símun Joensen		12/07/83	D	5	(7)	
30	Adeshina Lawal	NGA	17/10/84	A	26		13
16	Tóki á Lofti		06/12/93	M		(3)	
22	Klæmint Matras		20/05/81	M	20	(1)	2
17	Alex Mellemgaard		27/11/91	D	27		3
7	Høgni Midjord		04/02/91	M		(3)	
18	Árni Guldborg Nielsen		22/06/93	M	1	(6)	2
6	Eli Falkvard Nielsen		23/09/92	M	1	(4)	
16	Rógvi Poulsen		31/10/89	M	4	(5)	
14	Heini í Skorini		14/05/83	M	1	(1)	
23	Rasmus Dan Sørensen		27/05/95	A	9	(8)	2
1	Tórdur Thomsen		11/06/86	G	26		
7	Hanus Thorleifsson		19/12/85	M	20	(2)	3

B68 Toftir

1962 • Svangarskard (5,000) • b68.fo

Major honours
Faroe Islands League (3) 1984, 1985, 1992
Coach: Jógvan Martin Olsen

2014

16/03	a	NSÍ	L	0-1	
22/03	h	EB/Streymur	D	1-1	og (G Hansen)
30/03	a	ÍF	L	0-3	
13/04	a	Víkingur	L	0-1	
17/04	h	B36	L	2-4	Ó Olsen 2
21/04	h	AB	W	3-2	Jóhan Højgaard, Ó Olsen, Líknargøtu
02/05	h	Skála	D	0-0	
11/05	h	HB	L	0-4	
18/05	h	KÍ	W	5-3	Líknargøtu 2, Ó Olsen 2, Edmundsson
26/05	h	ÍF	D	1-1	Ó Olsen
01/06	a	EB/Streymur	L	0-3	
09/06	h	NSÍ	L	0-2	
15/06	a	B36	L	0-3	
22/06	h	Víkingur	L	1-3	Jonleif Højgaard
27/06	a	AB	L	2-3	Brim, Petersen
28/07	a	HB	L	0-6	
02/08	a	Skála	L	0-1	
08/08	a	KÍ	D	0-0	
17/08	a	NSÍ	L	1-3	Jóhan Højgaard
20/08	h	EB/Streymur	L	0-3	
24/08	a	HB	L	0-3	
14/09	a	ÍF	W	2-1	A Olsen (p), Camara
21/09	a	KÍ	W	1-0	Camara
01/10	h	AB	L	1-2	Jóhan Højgaard
05/10	a	Skála	D	1-1	Blé
19/10	h	B36	L	1-3	Camara
25/10	a	Víkingur	L	1-3	Jonleif Højgaard

No	Name	Nat	DoB	Pos	Aps	(s)	Gls
8	Kristian Anton Andreassen		30/08/85	A	21	(3)	
7	Evrard Blé	CIV	02/01/82	M	20		1
18	Ovi Brim		12/08/86	D	21	(3)	1
29	Ibrahima Camara	SEN	30/07/91	A	7	(1)	3
15	Esmar Petur Clementsen		29/09/96	M	1	(6)	
14	Hákun Edmundsson		21/03/96	D	25	(2)	1
16	Bergur Gregersen		11/09/94	D	4	(2)	
11	Jóhan Dávur Højgaard		11/06/82	D	24	(1)	3
10	Jonleif Højgaard		26/10/88	M	17	(4)	2
5	Oddur Árnason Højgaard		12/09/89	D	4	(2)	
26	Kristian Joensen		21/12/92	D	13		
17	Ari Johannesen		07/06/96	M	1	(5)	
27	Bjarki Johannesen		31/05/92	M	6	(3)	
26	Hans Jørgensen		13/08/90	G	11		
22	Remi Langgaard		16/12/91	M		(3)	
24	Andrias Klein á Líknargøtu		09/05/90	A	13	(11)	3
25	Ragnar Lindholm		17/08/93	G	3		
32	Janus Wiberg Mortensen		21/12/90	M	8	(4)	
16	André Olsen		23/10/90	M	9		1
19	Óli Højgaard Olsen		24/11/85	A	22	(2)	6
9	Jann Ingi Petersen		07/01/84	M	22		1
3	Niklas Poulsen		30/03/89	D	17	(1)	
6	Ingvard Emil Ronaldsson		22/06/88	M	2	(7)	
20	Mads Rosenberg	DEN	30/06/86	D	26		

EB/Streymur

1993 • Vid Margáir (3,000) • eb-streymur.fo

Major honours
Faroe Islands League (2) 2008, 2012; Faroe Islands Cup (4) 2007, 2009, 2010, 2011
Coach: Rúni Nolsøe

2014

15/03	h	HB	D	1-1	Niclasen
22/03	a	B68	D	1-1	Danielsen
30/03	a	Skála	W	3-0	Justinussen, Samuelsen, B Olsen
13/04	h	KÍ	W	3-1	Samuelsen, Danielsen, Zachariasen
17/04	a	ÍF	L	0-3	
21/04	h	NSÍ	D	0-0	
04/05	a	B36	L	1-3	Bø
11/05	a	AB	W	5-0	Arnbjørn Hansen 3, Samuelsen 2
18/05	h	Víkingur	L	2-3	Justinussen, Arnbjørn Hansen
25/05	a	Skála	D	1-1	Samuelsen
01/06	h	B68	W	3-0	Samuelsen 2, Niclasen
09/06	a	HB	W	2-1	Bø, Danielsen
15/06	h	ÍF	L	1-2	Samuelsen
22/06	a	KÍ	L	1-3	Djurhuus
27/06	a	NSÍ	W	2-1	Arnbjørn Hansen, Danielsen
27/07	a	AB	D	2-2	Zachariasen, Samuelsen (p)
03/08	h	B36	W	1-0	Arnbjørn Hansen
11/08	a	Víkingur	D	1-1	Arnbjørn Hansen
17/08	h	HB	L	0-3	
20/08	a	B68	W	3-0	Zachariasen 2, Samuelsen
24/08	a	AB	D	0-0	
14/09	h	Skála	W	3-1	Samuelsen 2, Arnbjørn Hansen
21/09	h	Víkingur	L	1-3	og (A Gregersen)
01/10	h	NSÍ	L	0-2	
19/10	a	B36	L	0-1	
19/10	a	ÍF	W	2-0	Samuelsen, Arnbjørn Hansen
25/10	h	KÍ	W	2-0	Nielsen, Arnbjørn Hansen

No	Name	Nat	DoB	Pos	Aps	(s)	Gls
8	Egil á Bø		02/04/74	D	25		2
19	Arnar Dam		19/10/91	A	6	(5)	
17	Niels Pauli Bjartalid Danielsen		18/01/89	A	27		4
12	Marni Djurhuus		06/09/85	M	26		1
5	Allan Jeffrison Hansen		01/04/94	D		(1)	
22	Arnbjørn Theodor Hansen		27/02/86	A	20	(4)	10
4	Gert Åge Hansen		25/07/84	M	20		
24	Jákup Andrias Hansen		15/12/93	G	1		
20	Jóhannes Hansen		31/12/95	D	10	(3)	
7	Jan á Høgaryggi		15/06/97	A		(1)	
5	Tóki Hammershaimb Johannesen		17/03/97	M		(1)	
13	Pól Jóhannus Justinussen		13/01/89	D	13		2
6	Høgni Madsen		04/02/85	M	13	(5)	
2	Jónas Tor Næs		27/12/86	D	25	(1)	
23	Leif Niclasen		01/10/86	A	18	(8)	2
18	Rógvi Egilstoft Nielsen		07/12/92	D	19	(1)	1
18	Brian Olsen		22/08/85	M	3	(7)	1
15	Hanus Egil Olsen		15/02/90	M	1	(10)	
15	Rói Hedinsson Olsen		03/03/97	M	1	(6)	
3	Andru Poulsen		30/08/90	D		(1)	
11	Hans Pauli Samuelsen		18/10/84	M	26	(1)	13
1	René Tórgard		03/08/79	G	26		
10	Gunnar Zachariasen		22/01/92	M	17	(5)	4

FAROE ISLANDS

HB Tórshavn

1904 • Gundadalur (5,000) • hb.fo

Major honours
Faroe Islands League (22) 1955, 1960, 1963, 1964,
1965, 1971, 1973, 1974, 1975, 1978, 1981, 1982,
1988, 1990, 1998, 2002, 2003, 2004, 2006, 2009,
2010, 2013; Faroe Islands Cup (26) 1955, 1957, 1959,
1962, 1963, 1964, 1968, 1969, 1971, 1972, 1973,
1975, 1976, 1978, 1979, 1980, 1981, 1982, 1984,
1987, 1988, 1989, 1992, 1995, 1998, 2004
Coach: Hedin Askham

2014
15/03	a	EB/Streymur	D	1-1	*Benjaminsen*
22/03	h	ÍF	W	3-1	*Fløtum, C Mouritsen,*
					K Mouritsen
30/03	h	KÍ	W	2-0	*Benjaminsen, Holm*
11/04	a	B36	D	1-1	*C Mouritsen*
17/04	h	NSÍ	W	4-1	*og (K Olsen),*
					Benjaminsen, Samuelsen,
					Fløtum
21/04	h	Víkingur	D	2-2	*K Mouritsen, R Joensen*
04/05	a	AB	W	3-0	*Benjaminsen,*
					K Mouritsen, Jensen
11/05	a	B68	W	4-0	*Fløtum 2, K Mouritsen,*
					C Mouritsen
16/05	h	Skála	W	2-0	*Pál Joensen,*
					Benjaminsen
25/05	a	KÍ	W	2-1	*Benjaminsen 2*
01/06	a	ÍF	D	2-2	*C Mouritsen, R Joensen*
09/06	h	EB/Streymur	L	1-2	*Jóhan Davidsen*
15/06	a	NSÍ	W	2-1	*Ingason, Benjaminsen*
22/06	h	B36	D	2-2	*Pál Joensen, Holm*
27/06	a	Víkingur	D	0-0	
28/07	h	B68	W	6-0	*K Mouritsen,*
					Benjaminsen, R Joensen,
					Edmundsson 2,
					og (Rosenberg)
03/08	h	AB	L	1-2	*Ingason*
10/08	a	Skála	W	1-0	*Edmundsson*
17/08	a	EB/Streymur	W	3-0	*Ingason, Fløtum,*
					K Mouritsen
20/08	h	ÍF	W	2-0	*Fløtum, Vatnsdal*
24/08	h	B68	W	3-0	*Ingason, Pál Joensen,*
					Benjaminsen
14/09	a	KÍ	L	0-1	
21/09	h	Skála	W	2-0	*Edmundsson, Alex*
01/10	h	Víkingur	W	2-1	*K Mouritsen,*
					Benjaminsen (p)
05/10	a	AB	W	3-1	*Fløtum 3*
19/10	h	NSÍ	W	3-0	*Edmundsson 2, Pál*
					Joensen
25/10	a	B36	W	2-1	*Fløtum, Benjaminsen*

No	Name	Nat	DoB	Pos	Aps	(s)	Gls
2	Alex	BRA	28/03/81	D	16	(3)	1
7	Fródi Benjaminsen		14/12/77	M	26		12
19	Jógvan Rói Davidsen		09/10/91	M	21	(1)	
5	Jóhan Troest Davidsen		31/01/88	D	23		1
8	Jóan Símun Edmundsson		26/07/91	A	11		6
10	Andrew av Fløtum		13/06/79	A	20	(2)	10
1	Teitur Matras Gestsson		19/08/92	G	26		
12	Levi Hanssen		24/02/88	M	17	(7)	
22	Bárdur Johnson Heinesen		19/09/90	A		(2)	
3	Rógvi Sjúrdarson Holm		24/01/90	D	25		2
20	Poul Ingason		28/09/95	A	5	(11)	4
14	Teit Jacobsen		16/03/98	M		(4)	
22	Hilmar Leon Jakobsen		02/08/97	M		(1)	
24	Tróndur Jensen		06/02/93	M	11	(7)	1
18	Pál Mohr Joensen		20/08/92	D	17	(8)	4
8	Páll Mohr Joensen		29/06/86	A		(2)	
23	René Shaki Joensen		08/02/93	D	16	(8)	3
22	Adrian Justinussen		21/07/98	M		(1)	
16	Thomas Knudsen		24/03/93	G		(1)	
15	Heri Hjalt Mohr		13/05/97	M		(1)	
11	Christian Restorff Mouritsen		03/12/88	M	10		4
21	Kristin Restorff Mouritsen		23/04/91	M	24	(2)	7
9	Símun Samuelsen		21/05/85	M	3	(8)	1
25	Hedin Stenberg		14/01/89	G	1		
6	Heini Vatnsdal		18/10/91	M	20	(2)	1
17	Bartal Wardum		03/05/97	D	5	(4)	

ÍF Fuglafjørdur

1946 • Fløtugerdi (2,000) • if.fo

Major honours
Faroe Islands League (1) 1979
Coach: Albert Ellefsen

2014
16/03	h	KÍ	L	1-3	*K Løkin*
22/03	a	HB	L	1-3	*B Petersen (p)*
30/03	h	B68	W	3-0	*Eliasen, A Ellingsgaard 2*
13/04	h	NSÍ	W	2-1	*Clayton, Lakjuni*
17/04	h	EB/Streymur	W	3-0	*Joensen, og (Djurhuus),*
					A Ellingsgaard
21/04	h	B36	L	2-5	*Eliasen, Jakobsen*
04/05	a	Víkingur	D	1-1	*K Løkin*
11/05	a	Skála	D	2-2	*Jakobsen, Eliasen*
18/05	h	AB	L	1-4	*og (Janković)*
26/05	a	B68	D	1-1	*A Ellingsgaard*
01/06	h	HB	D	2-2	*K Løkin, Lakjuni*
09/06	a	KÍ	L	0-4	
15/06	a	EB/Streymur	W	2-1	*Lakjuni 2*
21/06	a	NSÍ	D	2-2	*og (Gaardbo), Clayton*
27/06	a	B36	L	0-1	
27/07	h	Skála	W	1-0	*Clayton*
04/08	h	Víkingur	D	2-2	*Clayton, K Løkin*
10/08	a	AB	L	0-2	
17/08	h	KÍ	D	1-1	*Isaksen*
20/08	h	HB	L	0-2	
25/08	a	Skála	W	2-0	*Eliasen, Jakobsen*
14/09	h	B68	L	1-2	*B Løkin*
21/09	h	AB	W	3-0	*Clayton 2, B Petersen*
01/10	h	B36	L	1-2	*Clayton*
05/10	a	Víkingur	L	0-5	
19/10	h	EB/Streymur	L	0-2	
25/10	a	NSÍ	L	2-4	*Clayton, Jakobsen*

No	Name	Nat	DoB	Pos	Aps	(s)	Gls
18	Clayton	BRA	24/11/78	A	24		8
76	Bartal Eliasen		23/08/76	D	25		4
10	Ari Ólavsson Ellingsgaard		03/02/93	M	19	(5)	4
37	Jan Ólavsson Ellingsgaard		26/06/90	D	6	(2)	
16	Hallgrím Gregersen Hansen		24/12/94	G	7	(2)	
23	Jógvan Isaksen		25/04/90	D	4		1
9	Kristoffur Jakobsen		07/11/88	M	22	(4)	4
20	Leivur Joensen		07/02/94	M	17	(7)	1
19	Levi Jøkladal		20/12/97	M		(1)	
12	Aleksandar Jovević	SRB	10/04/78	M		(1)	
28	Arnold Kristiansen		24/03/95	A	2	(1)	
7	Dánjal á Lakjuni		22/09/90	A	23	(4)	4
5	Fritleif í Lambanum		13/04/86	D	26		
15	Bogi Abrahamson Løkin		22/10/88	M	5	(4)	1
6	Karl Abrahamson Løkin		19/04/91	M	16		4
1	Jákup Mikkelsen		16/08/70	G	20	(1)	
3	Poul Nolsøe Mikkelsen		19/04/95	D	17	(2)	
13	Heri Hansen Nesá		07/01/90	D	4		
14	Áki Petersen		01/12/84	D	9	(3)	
8	Bogi Reinert Petersen		20/02/93	M	22	(1)	2
14	Pól Magnus Petersen		01/07/95	M		(5)	
21	Andrias Poulsen		03/08/97	M		(5)	
11	Frank Højbjerg Poulsen		03/11/88	M	6	(10)	
4	Nenad Šarić	SRB	05/07/81	M	16	(3)	
17	Høgni Justinus Zachariassen		26/08/82	D	7	(2)	

KÍ Klaksvík

1904 • Djúpumýra (3,000) • ki.fo

Major honours
Faroe Islands League (17) 1942, 1945, 1952, 1953,
1954, 1956, 1957, 1958, 1961, 1966, 1967, 1968,
1969, 1970, 1972, 1991, 1999; Faroe Islands Cup (5)
1966, 1967, 1990, 1994, 1999
Coach: Eydun Klakstein

2014
16/03	a	ÍF	W	3-1	*Danielsen, Klettskard,*
					Kalsø
23/03	h	Víkingur	W	1-0	*Klettskard*
30/03	a	HB	L	0-2	
13/04	a	EB/Streymur	L	1-3	*Gueye*
17/04	h	AB	W	4-1	*Kalsø, Elttør, Rodrigo,*
					Klettskard
21/04	h	Skála	W	1-0	*Rodrigo*
03/05	a	NSÍ	D	1-1	*H Heinesen*
11/05	h	B36	L	1-3	*Rodrigo*
18/05	a	B68	L	3-5	*Klettskard 2, Kalsø*
25/05	h	HB	L	1-2	*Rodrigo*
31/05	h	Víkingur	L	2-4	*Klettskard, Gueye*
09/06	h	ÍF	W	4-0	*Gueye, Jacobsen,*
					Í Simonsen, Klettskard
16/06	a	AB	D	1-1	*Gueye*
22/06	h	EB/Streymur	W	3-1	*Elttør, Gueye,*
					Danielsen (p)
27/06	a	Skála	L	0-2	
29/07	a	B36	L	1-2	*Elttør*
03/08	a	NSÍ	D	2-2	*Klettskard (p), Klakstein*
08/08	h	B68	D	0-0	
17/08	a	ÍF	D	1-1	*Gueye*
20/08	a	Víkingur	D	1-1	*Klettskard*
24/08	a	B36	W	1-0	*B Heinesen*
14/09	h	HB	W	1-0	*Elttør*
21/09	a	B68	L	0-1	
01/10	h	Skála	W	3-0	*Klettskard 3*
05/10	a	NSÍ	L	0-2	
19/10	h	AB	W	5-1	*Lakjuni 2, H Heinesen,*
					Jacobsen, Elttør
25/10	a	EB/Streymur	L	0-2	

No	Name	Nat	DoB	Pos	Aps	(s)	Gls
25	Jákup Biskopstø Andreasen		31/05/98	M		(1)	
17	Álvur Fuglø Christiansen		29/05/89	M	13	(7)	
2	Gunnar Christiansen		08/08/92	D	8	(6)	
11	Atli Danielsen		15/08/83	M	13		2
5	Rudolf Eliasen		23/02/87	D		(1)	
11	Hjalgrím Elttør		03/03/83	M	24	(1)	5
15	Ndende Adama Gueye	SEN	05/01/83	M	27		6
11	Bárdur Johnson Heinesen		19/09/90	A		(9)	1
12	Henry Heinesen		01/06/88	M	12	(6)	2
19	Johan Jacobsen		02/07/92	A	21	(2)	2
7	Ivan Joensen		20/02/92	M	16	(6)	
16	Meinhard Joensen		27/11/79	G	27		
14	Tórur Justesen		04/01/95	D	13	(5)	
6	Sørmundur Árni Kalsø		20/01/92	D	23	(1)	3
21	Hedin Klakstein		30/04/92	M	18	(7)	1
9	Páll Andrasson Klettskard		17/05/90	A	26		12
18	Hedin á Lakjuni		19/02/78	D	19	(3)	2
4	Jonas Flindt Rasmussen	DEN	07/11/88	D	20		
20	Rodrigo	BRA	16/11/82	A	11	(6)	4
12	Eli Simonsen		03/09/90	M		(1)	
3	Ísak Simonsen		12/10/93	D	6	(8)	1

NSÍ Runavík

1957 • Vid Løkin (2,000) • nsi.fo

Major honours
Faroe Islands League (1) 2007; Faroe Islands Cup (2) 1986, 2002

Coach: Trygvi Mortensen

2014

16/03	h	B68	W	1-0	K Olsen (p)
23/03	a	Skála	W	5-1	K Olsen 3, Magnus Olsen, Á Frederiksberg
30/03	h	AB	W	3-0	Mortensen, K Olsen 2
13/04	a	ÍF	L	1-2	Á Frederiksberg
17/04	a	HB	L	1-4	Magnus Olsen
21/04	a	EB/Streymur	D	0-0	
03/05	h	KÍ	D	1-1	Danielsen
09/05	a	Víkingur	L	0-3	
18/05	h	B36	L	0-1	
25/05	a	AB	W	7-0	K Olsen 4, og (Isaksen), A Olsen, Á Frederiksberg
01/06	h	Skála	W	6-1	Á Frederiksberg 3, K Olsen, og (P Mikkelsen), Magnus Olsen
09/06	a	B68	W	2-0	A Olsen, Á Frederiksberg
15/06	h	HB	L	1-2	K Olsen
21/06	h	ÍF	D	2-2	K Olsen 2
27/06	h	EB/Streymur	L	1-2	K Olsen
03/08	a	KÍ	D	2-2	Á Frederiksberg, C Jacobsen
10/08	a	B36	L	0-1	
17/08	h	B68	W	3-1	C Jacobsen 2, Magnus Olsen
20/08	a	Skála	W	3-2	A Olsen, K Olsen, Magnus Olsen
24/08	a	Víkingur	L	1-6	Á Frederiksberg
14/09	h	AB	W	3-1	K Olsen 3 (1p)
17/09	h	Víkingur	L	0-2	
21/09	h	B36	L	2-3	K Olsen, Justinussen
01/10	a	EB/Streymur	W	2-0	E Hansen, Á Frederiksberg
05/10	h	KÍ	W	2-0	og (Klettskard), K Olsen
19/10	a	HB	L	0-3	
25/10	h	ÍF	W	4-2	Joensen, C Jacobsen, K Olsen, A Olsen

No	Name	Nat	DoB	Pos	Aps	(s)	Gls
9	Debes Danielsen		12/08/86	M		(6)	1
11	Árni Frederiksberg		13/06/92	M	26		10
17	Jónhard Frederiksberg		27/08/80	D	27		
5	Jákup Andrias Gaardbo		22/09/95	D	3	(2)	
1	András Gángó	HUN	02/03/84	G	27		
12	Einar Tróndargjógv Hansen		02/04/88	D	25		1
6	Justinus Ragnhardson Hansen		14/05/85	M	5	(6)	
19	Haraldur Reinert Højgaard		21/03/95	M	8	(17)	
22	Leivur Højgaard		03/01/96	D		(2)	
23	Christian Høgni Jacobsen		12/05/80	A	3	(2)	4
3	Monrad Holm Jacobsen		23/04/91	D	15		
21	Sjúrdur Jacobsen		29/08/76	D	16	(6)	
4	Jens Joensen		17/05/89	D	22		1
13	Pól Jóhannus Justinussen		13/01/89	D	11		1
22	Petur Knudsen		24/04/98	M		(1)	
2	Per Langgaard		30/05/91	D	11	(2)	
7	Jann Martin Mortensen		18/07/89	M	23	(2)	1
27	Andy Ólavur Olsen		03/12/84	M	24	(3)	4
10	Klæmint Andrasson Olsen		17/07/90	A	27		22
18	Magnus Hendriksson Olsen		26/10/86	M	24	(1)	5
14	Meinhard Egilsson Olsen		10/04/97	M		(22)	
15	Michal Przybylski		29/12/97	M		(3)	

Skála ÍF

1965 • Undir Mýruhjalla (2,000) • skalaif.fo

Coach: Eliesar Jónsson Olsen;
(17/06/14) Pauli Poulsen

2014

15/03	a	B36	L	0-2	
23/03	h	NSÍ	L	1-5	B Jacobsen
30/03	a	EB/Streymur	L	0-3	
13/04	a	AB	D	1-1	Jákup Johansen
17/04	h	Víkingur	D	1-1	B Jacobsen
21/04	a	KÍ	L	0-1	
02/05	a	B68	D	0-0	
11/05	h	ÍF	D	2-2	Ó Mikkelsen, Jákup Johansen
16/05	a	HB	L	0-2	
25/05	a	EB/Streymur	D	1-1	Ó Mikkelsen
01/06	a	NSÍ	L	1-6	B Jacobsen
09/06	h	B36	L	0-3	
15/06	a	Víkingur	L	0-5	
22/06	a	AB	D	0-0	
27/06	h	KÍ	W	2-0	Durhuus, Ó Mikkelsen
27/07	a	ÍF	L	0-1	
02/08	h	B68	W	1-0	P Jacobsen
10/08	h	HB	L	0-1	
17/08	a	B36	L	0-2	
20/08	h	NSÍ	L	2-3	B Jacobsen 2
25/08	h	ÍF	L	0-2	
14/09	a	EB/Streymur	L	1-3	Keita
21/09	a	HB	L	0-2	
01/10	a	KÍ	L	0-3	
05/10	h	B68	D	1-1	Jákup Johansen
19/10	h	Víkingur	D	3-3	E Jacobsen, Jákup Johansen, Durhuus
25/10	a	AB	W	2-1	P Mikkelsen, Jóhan Johansen

No	Name	Nat	DoB	Pos	Aps	(s)	Gls
11	Holgar Durhuus		29/10/92	A	25	(2)	2
12	Suni Ernstsson		16/03/91	G	9	(1)	
21	Rói av Fløtum		30/12/94	D	2	(2)	
8	Andras Frederiksberg		02/12/92	M	26		
14	Hendrik á Fridriksmørk		29/10/94	A		(6)	
14	Jan Ingason Hansen		08/10/97	M		(2)	
16	Pauli Gregersen Hansen		09/04/80	M	13		
9	Brian Jacobsen		04/11/91	A	22	(2)	5
20	Edvin Jacobsen		12/04/91	M	25		1
4	Jákup Jacobsen		22/11/92	D	17		
24	Pætur Dam Jacobsen		05/12/82	D	20	(2)	1
17	Uni Jacobsen		18/11/92	A	5	(8)	
5	Teitur Reinert Joensen		10/11/86	D	18		
21	Alexandur Johansen		07/06/79	A		(5)	
10	Jákup Johansen		27/04/93	M	25		4
9	Jóhan Bergsson Johansen		11/06/93	A	3	(2)	1
15	Karstin Justesen		28/11/86	M	3	(13)	
23	Ahmed Keita	SEN	12/05/87	A	5	(2)	1
16	Predrag Marković	SRB	01/02/77	D	1		
14	Høgni Midjord		04/02/91	A	1	(2)	
7	Ólavur Mikkelsen		11/01/92	M	24	(3)	3
3	Petur Pauli Mikkelsen		20/06/90	D	26	(1)	1
4	Ari Olsen		09/09/98	D	4		
22	Marnar Poulsen		09/02/95	M		(3)	
23	Poul Narvi Poulsen		22/09/86	M	5	(2)	
6	Símun Petur Poulsen		16/11/94	M	1	(4)	
1	Mark Ryutin	RUS	26/03/88	G	17		

Víkingur

2008 • Sarpugerdi (2,000) • vikingur.fo

Major honours
Faroe Islands League (6) 1983, 1986, 1993, 1994, 1995, 1996 (as GÍ Gøta); Faroe Islands Cup (10) 1983, 1985, 1996, 1997, 2000, 2005 (as GÍ Gøta), 2009, 2012, 2013, 2014

Coach: Sigfrídur Clementsen

2014

15/03	h	AB	L	0-2	
23/03	a	KÍ	L	0-1	
28/03	a	B36	D	2-2	og (Joensen), S Olsen
13/04	h	B68	W	1-0	Hedin Hansen
17/04	a	Skála	D	1-1	S Olsen (p)
21/04	a	HB	D	2-2	F Justinussen 2
04/05	h	ÍF	D	1-1	B Hansen
09/05	h	NSÍ	W	3-0	og (E Hansen), F Justinussen 2
18/05	h	EB/Streymur	W	3-2	Hedin Hansen, F Justinussen, Djurhuus
25/05	h	B36	L	1-2	F Justinussen
31/05	a	KÍ	W	4-2	F Justinussen 2, Hedin Hansen, S Olsen
09/06	a	AB	W	3-0	S Olsen 2, F Justinussen
15/06	h	Skála	W	5-0	Hedin Hansen, H Jacobsen, S Olsen 2, Jarnskor
22/06	a	B68	W	3-1	B Hansen, Hansson, H Jacobsen (p)
27/06	h	HB	D	0-0	
04/08	a	ÍF	D	2-2	B Hansen, F Justinussen
11/08	h	EB/Streymur	D	1-1	F Justinussen
17/08	h	AB	D	2-2	Djordjević, Hedin Hansen
20/08	a	KÍ	D	1-1	og (H Heinesen)
24/08	a	NSÍ	W	6-1	F Justinussen 2, S Olsen, Hansson, S Vatnhamar 2
14/09	a	B36	W	2-0	F Justinussen 2
17/09	a	NSÍ	W	2-0	Hansson, S Vatnhamar
21/09	a	EB/Streymur	W	3-1	H Jacobsen 2, S Olsen (p)
01/10	a	HB	L	1-2	F Justinussen
05/10	h	ÍF	W	5-0	Hansson 3, S Olsen, S Vatnhamar
19/10	a	Skála	D	3-3	A Olsen, F Justinussen, S Vatnhamar
25/10	h	B68	W	3-1	H Jacobsen, F Justinussen 2

No	Name	Nat	DoB	Pos	Aps	(s)	Gls
9	Filip Djordjević	SRB	07/03/94	M	22	(4)	1
16	Hans Jørgin Djurhuus		29/11/78	M	15	(3)	1
4	Atli Gregersen		15/06/82	D	22	(1)	
2	Bergur Gregersen		11/09/94	D		(1)	
12	Bárdur Jógvansson Hansen		13/03/92	D	25		3
8	Hedin Hansen		30/07/91	M	19	(7)	5
25	Hjartvard Hansen		17/09/88	M	2		
11	Hallur Hansson		08/07/92	M	24	(1)	6
13	Erling Dávidsson Jacobsen		13/02/90	D	27		
3	Hanus Jacobsen		25/05/85	D	26	(1)	5
14	Magnus Jarnskor		14/12/95	M		(15)	1
6	Sámal Jákup Joensen		07/04/93	M	5	(8)	
17	Finnur Justinussen		30/03/89	A	27		19
14	Svein Justinussen		05/09/95	A		(2)	
5	Dánjal Pauli Lervig		26/04/91	D	2		
2	Andreas Lava Olsen		09/10/87	A	5	(3)	1
19	Martin Olsen		22/12/89	A		(2)	
7	Súni Olsen		07/03/81	M	24	(1)	10
7	Elias Rasmussen		13/05/96	G	1		
22	Ingi Sørensen		24/11/90	M	3	(5)	
20	Hjalti Strømsten		21/01/97	M	1	(1)	
1	Géza Tamás Túri	HUN	11/03/74	G	26		
24	Gunnar Vatnhamar		29/03/95	D	2	(11)	
10	Sølvi Vatnhamar		05/05/86	M	19	(2)	5

Top goalscorers

22	Klæmint Andrasson Olsen (NSÍ)
19	Finnur Justinussen (Víkingur)
13	Adeshina Lawal (B36)
	Hans Pauli Samuelsen (EB/Streymur)
12	Fródi Benjaminsen (HB)
	Páll Andrasson Klettskard (KÍ)
10	Arnbjørn Theodor Hansen (EB/Streymur)
	Andrew av Fløtum (HB)
	Árni Frederiksberg (NSÍ)
	Súni Olsen (Víkingur)

Promoted clubs

TB Tvøroyri

1892 • Vid Stórá (3,000) • tb.fo
Major honours
*Faroe Islands League (7) 1943, 1949, 1951, 1976,
1977, 1980, 1987; Faroe Islands Cup (5) 1956, 1958,
1960, 1961, 1977*
Coach: Páll Gudlaugsson (ISL)

FC Suduroy

2010 • Vesturi á Eidinum (3,000) •
fcsuduroy.com
Major honours
*Faroe Islands League (1) 2000 (as VB Vágur);
Faroe Islands Cup (1) 1974 (as VB Vágur)*
**Coach: Jón Johannesen;
(01/08/14) Jón Pauli Olsen**

Second level final table 2014

		Pld	W	D	L	F	A	Pts
1	TB Tvøroyri	27	21	4	2	73	21	67
2	FC Suduroy	27	14	6	7	54	34	48
3	07 Vestur	27	14	5	8	54	41	47
4	B36 Tórshavn II	27	10	6	11	53	52	36
5	AB Argir II	27	9	8	10	49	46	35
6	NSÍ Runavík II	27	10	4	13	54	52	34
7	Víkingur II	27	9	7	11	41	51	34
8	KÍ Klaksvík II	27	7	8	12	44	62	29
9	HB Tórshavn II	27	8	5	14	41	65	29
10	EB/Streymur II	27	4	5	18	32	71	17

DOMESTIC CUP

Løgmanssteypid 2014

SECOND ROUND

(05/04/14)
AB 1-1 TB *(aet; 3-1 on pens)*
B68 8-0 Royn
Giza/Hoyvík 1-6 EB/Streymur
ÍF 14-1 Undrid
KÍ 5-0 07 Vestur
Suduroy 0-4 NSÍ
Víkingur 2-0 Skála

(06/04/14)
HB 3-2 B36

QUARTER-FINALS

(27/04/14)
AB 0-2 HB *(Vatnsdal 17, Fløtum 81)*
EB/Streymur 4-3 NSÍ *(Danielsen 79,
Arnbjørn Hansen 81, 89, 95; Á Frederiksberg 22,
K Olsen 45, 66) (aet)*
Víkingur 3-0 KÍ *(F Justinussen 8, 90+2,
H Jacobsen 49)*

(14/05/14)
B68 4-3 ÍF *(Eliasen 18og, Edmundsson 20,
Rosenberg 26, P Mikkelsen 75og; Clayton 24, 86,
F Poulsen 56)*

SEMI-FINALS

(21/05/14 & 18/06/14)
Víkingur 4-1 EB/Streymur *(S Olsen 34, 62,
Hansson 56, Djordjević 90; Danielsen 68)*
EB/Streymur 2-0 Víkingur *(Túri 5og, Samuelsen 65)*
(Víkingur 4-3)

(05/06/14 & 18/06/14)
B68 0-1 HB *(Hanssen 57)*
HB 1-0 B68 *(R Joensen 51)*
(HB 2-0)

FINAL

(30/08/14)
Tórsvøllur, Torshavn
VÍKINGUR 1 *(Hansson 89)*
HB TÓRSHAVN 0
Referee: *Müller*
VÍKINGUR: *Túri, B Hansen, A Gregersen,
E Jacobsen, H Jacobsen, S Olsen, Djurhuus
(A Olsen 60), S Vatnhamar, Hansson (Djordjević 64),
Hedin Hansen, F Justinussen*
HB: *Gestsson, Alex, Jóhan Davidsen, Holm,
R Joensen, Vatnsdal, Hanssen, Benjaminsen,
Jógvan Davidsen, Fløtum, Ingason (Pál Joensen 69)*
Red card: *Alex (90+5)*

Víkingur claimed a hat-trick of domestic cup triumphs with their 1-0 win over HB at the Tórsvøllur

FINLAND

Suomen Palloliitto – Finlands Bollförbund (SPL-FBF)

Address	Urheilukatu 5, PO Box 191 FI-00251 Helsinki	**President**	Pertti Alaja
Tel	+358 9 742 151	**General secretary**	Marco Casagrande
Fax	+358 9 454 3352	**Media officer**	Sami Terävä
E-mail	sami.terava@palloliitto.fi	**Year of formation**	1907
Website	palloliitto.fi	**National stadium**	Olympic Stadium, Helsinki (40,682)

VEIKKAUSLIIGA CLUBS

 1 **HJK Helsinki**

 2 **FC Honka Espoo**

3 **FC Inter Turku**

 4 **FF Jaro**

 5 **KuPS Kuopio**

 6 **FC Lahti**

 7 **IFK Mariehamn**

 8 **Myllykosken Pallo -47**

 9 **RoPS Rovaniemi**

 10 **SJK Seinäjoki**

 11 **TPS Turku**

 12 **VPS Vaasa**

PROMOTED CLUBS

 13 **HIFK Helsinki**

 14 **FC KTP Kotka**

15 **FC Ilves**

KEY:

 – UEFA Champions League

 – UEFA Europa League

 – Promoted

– Relegated

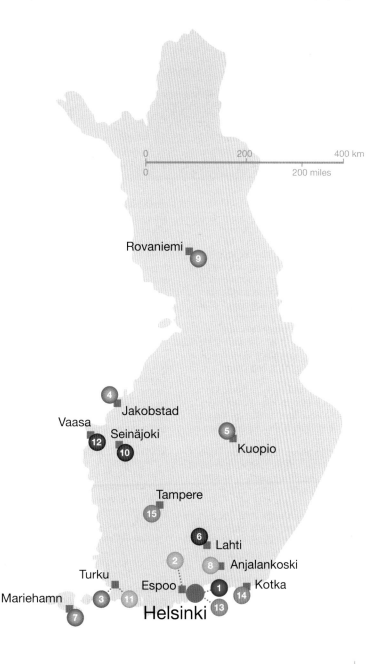

Lehkosuo lifts HJK to new level

The 2014 Finnish football season belonged to HJK Helsinki, with the club from the capital prospering both at home and abroad under their new coach Mika Lehkosuo.

The former HJK captain replaced Sixten Boström early in the campaign and steered the men in the blue and white stripes to a domestic double as well a place in the group stage of the UEFA Europa League. Newly promoted SJK Senäjoki were surprise runners-up in the Veikkausliiga, finishing a point ahead of FC Lahti.

| Helsinki club add cup win to sixth successive league title | New coach also oversees extended European run | Paatelainen out as EURO qualifying hopes fade |

Domestic league

HJK's quest for a sixth successive Veikkausliiga title – and 27th in all – appeared to be under little threat when they won their opening two matches, but as the first month of the season ended, they had acquired just one additional point. That prompted a change of coach, with legendary former midfielder Lehkosuo, who had spent several seasons in charge of local rivals FC Honka Espoo, called in to replace Boström after just five matches of the campaign.

Lehkosuo's arrival transformed HJK's fortunes at a stroke. His impact was immediate and devastating as the team went nine games without conceding a goal, winning eight of them, and continued to avoid defeat under their new boss until late August – a run of 18 matches – when they lost 2-0 at SJK. With Simo Valakari's side performing wonders in the club's first ever Veikkausliiga campaign, that result reduced HJK's lead to five points, but the defending champions responded with renewed vigour, winning four of their next five games, the last of them at TPS Turku, where the title was duly retained with a handsome 4-1 victory.

Four games later the season was over and HJK had a 13-point victory margin over SJK. It was not quite the gung-ho goalfest of the previous campaign under Boström, but with 65 goals scored (as opposed to 78 in 2013) and 22 conceded Lehkosuo's side headed both categories. They also boasted some of the league's top performers, from veteran Finnish internationals Markus Heikkinen, Mika Väyrynen, Teemu Tainio and Mikael Forssell to African imports Demba Savage and Macoumba Kandji and dazzling young midfielder Robin Lod.

Lehkosuo's former team Honka, whom he led to second place in 2013, endured a disastrous season, finishing 11th, and it got worse when they were refused a licence to compete in the 2015 Veikkausliiga. The same fate befell top-flight mainstays Myllykosken Pallo -47.

Domestic cup

The last team other than HJK to win the Veikkausliiga were FC Inter Turku, in 2008, and they were tasked with preventing the champions from completing only the fourth domestic double in their history when they met in the Finnish Cup final. Despite being rank outsiders in the Sonera Stadium, HJK's home, the team that finished ninth in the league came extremely close to an upset, succumbing only in a penalty shoot-out after 120 goalless minutes. While HJK converted all five of their spot-kicks, Inter midfielder Ari Nyman had his effort saved, giving Klubi the trophy for the 12th time.

Europe

The domestic cup final was just one fixture on HJK's post-Veikkausliiga schedule. They were also still involved in Europe, having defied the odds by becoming the first Finnish participant in the UEFA Europa League group stage. Although initially enrolled in the UEFA Champions League, Lehkosuo's men made a successful crossover, defeating SK Rapid Wien in the play-offs after a thrilling 3-3 draw in Vienna. Although they lost their first three group games without scoring, two home wins over Torino FC and FC København meant the round of 32 was still reachable going into their final match. However, their 12-game European run was brought to a halt by a 2-1 defeat at Club Brugge KV.

National team

HJK's European success was not matched by the national team as they played themselves out of contention for a place at UEFA EURO 2016 with a series of disappointing displays that left them with just one win in six matches. A 1-0 home defeat to Hungary in June – Finland's fourth loss in as many qualifiers – led to the termination of head coach Mixu Paatelainen's contract and the end of his four-year reign.

DOMESTIC SEASON AT A GLANCE

Veikkausliiga 2014 final table

		Pld	Home					Away					Total					Pts
			W	D	L	F	A	W	D	L	F	A	W	D	L	F	A	
1	**HJK Helsinki**	**33**	**12**	**4**	**1**	**37**	**8**	**9**	**5**	**2**	**28**	**14**	**21**	**9**	**3**	**65**	**22**	**72**
2	SJK Seinäjoki	33	10	4	2	23	10	6	7	4	17	16	16	11	6	40	26	59
3	FC Lahti	33	8	6	3	25	13	7	7	2	20	10	15	13	5	45	23	58
4	VPS Vaasa	33	7	4	6	23	18	6	5	5	16	16	13	9	11	39	34	48
5	IFK Mariehamn	33	9	3	5	32	25	5	3	8	17	30	14	6	13	49	55	48
6	FF Jaro	33	6	4	6	19	24	6	4	7	28	23	12	8	13	47	47	44
7	KuPS Kuopio	33	8	4	4	22	16	3	7	7	22	28	11	11	11	44	44	44
8	Myllykosken Pallo -47	33	8	7	2	34	23	2	2	12	7	31	10	9	14	41	54	39
9	FC Inter Turku	33	6	6	4	22	18	2	6	9	20	29	8	12	13	42	47	36
10	RoPS Rovaniemi	33	6	3	7	17	15	4	2	11	17	29	10	5	18	34	44	35
11	FC Honka Espoo	33	5	8	4	21	23	1	5	10	17	34	6	13	14	38	57	31
12	TPS Turku	33	5	3	8	19	26	1	3	13	10	34	6	6	21	29	60	24

European qualification 2015/16

Champion/ Cup winner: HJK Helsinki (second qualifying round)

SJK Senäjoki (second qualifying round)
FC Lahti (second qualifying round)
VPS Vaasa (second qualifying round)

Top scorers   Jonas Emet (Jaro) & Luis Solignac (Mariehamn), 14 goals
Relegated clubs   TPS Turku, FC Honka Espoo (excluded), Myllykosken Pallo -47 (excluded)
Promoted clubs   HIFK Helsinki, FC KTP Kotka, Ilves Tampere
Cup final   HJK Helsinki 0-0 FC Inter Turku (aet; 5-3 on pens)

Team of the season
(4-2-3-1)

Coach: Valakari (SJK)

Moisander (Lahti)

Sorsa (HJK)   Heikkinen (HJK)   Gogoua (SJK)   Rannankari (KuPS)

Tainio (HJK)   Laaksonen (SJK)

Emet (Jaro)   Lod (HJK)   Savage (HJK)

Rafael (Lahti)

Player of the season

Robin Lod
(HJK Helsinki)

The leading light for Finland's Under-21 team in the qualifying campaign for the 2015 European finals, Lod made an even greater impression with his outstanding form for HJK in 2014, providing six goals and six assists to the club's Veikkausliiga title triumph and a series of outstanding performances in the club's lengthy European run. A first senior cap for Finland was an inevitable consequence, and in May 2015 the 22-year-old schemer signed a three-year contract with Panathinaikos FC.

Newcomer of the season

Johannes Laaksonen
(SJK Seinäjoki)

A prominent member of SJK's promotion-winning side of 2013, Laaksonen cut quite a dash in his debut Veikkausliiga campaign to help the team exceed all expectations with a second-place finish. The young all-purpose midfielder was a figure of authority in the SJK midfield, his height and power matched by composure on the ball, an indefatigable energy and a powerful right-foot shot. He was rewarded with a first cap for Finland in a winter friendly against Sweden in the Middle East.

NATIONAL TEAM

Top five all-time caps
Jari Litmanen (137); Sami Hyypiä & Jonatan Johansson (105); Ari Hjelm (100); Joonas Kolkka (98)

Top five all-time goals
Jari Litmanen (32); Mikael Forssell (29); Jonatan Johansson (22); Ari Hjelm (20); Mixu Paatelainen (18)

Results 2014/15

07/09/14	Faroe Islands (ECQ)	A	Torshavn	W	3-1	Riku Riski (53, 78), Eremenko (82)
11/10/14	Greece (ECQ)	H	Helsinki	D	1-1	Hurme (55)
14/10/14	Romania (ECQ)	H	Helsinki	L	0-2	
14/11/14	Hungary (ECQ)	A	Budapest	L	0-1	
18/11/14	Slovakia	A	Zilina	L	1-2	Hubočan (45+1og)
19/01/15	Sweden	N	Abu Dhabi (UAE)	W	1-0	Roope Riski (63)
22/01/15	Yemen	N	Dubai (UAE)	D	0-0	
29/03/15	Northern Ireland (ECQ)	A	Belfast	L	1-2	Sadik (90+1)
09/06/15	Estonia	H	Turku	L	0-2	
13/06/15	Hungary (ECQ)	H	Helsinki	L	0-1	

Appearances 2014/15

Coach: Mixu Paatelainen	03/02/67		FRO	GRE	ROU	HUN	Svk	Swe	Yem	NIR	Est	HUN	Caps	Goals
Niki Mäenpää	23/01/85	VVV (NED)	G	G	G						G		25	-
Kari Arkivuo	23/06/83	Häcken (SWE)	D	D	D		D86	D	s61			D	38	1
Joona Toivio	10/03/88	Molde (NOR)	D	D	D	D				D46	D		32	2
Niklas Moisander	29/09/85	Ajax (NED)	D	D	D	D	D			D	D61	D	50	2
Jere Uronen	13/07/94	Helsingborg (SWE)	D75			D	D	D	s46	D			12	-
Alexander Ring	09/04/91	Kaiserslautern (GER)	M	M	M 56*						M		30	1
Tim Sparv	20/02/87	Midtjylland (DEN)	M	M	M	M	M	M	M	M		M	47	1
Perparim Hetemaj	12/12/86	Chievo (ITA)	M	M46	M64	M	M73				M84	M	36	4
Roman Eremenko	19/03/87	CSKA Moskva (RUS)	M	M	M	M				M	M	M	68	5
Riku Riski	16/08/89	Rosenborg (NOR)	M	M88	s46	s82	M				M72	s46	25	4
Teemu Pukki	29/03/90	Brøndby (DEN)	A88	A70	A46	A65	s46	A60		A70	s46	A46	41	8
Eero Markkanen	03/07/91	Real Madrid (ESP)	s75		s74	s85					s72		5	-
Joel Pohjanpalo	13/09/94	Düsseldorf (GER)	s88	s70	s64	s65	A46			s43	A46	s85	14	1
Jarkko Hurme	04/06/86	Odd (NOR)		D	D	D							11	1
Kasper Hämäläinen	08/08/86	Lech (POL)		s46	M74	M82	s73			M43		M	45	7
Teemu Tainio	27/11/79	HJK		s88									64	6
Lukas Hradecky	24/11/89	Brøndby (DEN)				G	G	G		G		G	22	-
Markus Halsti	19/03/84	Malmö (SWE) /DC United (USA)					M85	D			s61	D	23	-
Joni Kauko	12/07/90	FSV Frankfurt (GER)					M73				M46		6	-
Sakari Mattila	14/07/89	Aalesund (NOR)					s73	M	M			M85	6	-
Veli Lampi	18/07/84	HJK					s86	D46					33	-
Valtteri Moren	15/06/91	HJK						D	D				3	1
Hannu Patronen	23/05/84	Sogndal (NOR)						D	D				4	-
Toni Kolehmainen	20/07/88	Hønefoss (NOR)						M75					10	3
Rasmus Schüller	18/06/91	HJK						M90	s70				11	-
Petteri Forsell	16/10/90	Mariehamn						M75	M				4	1
Erfan Zeneli	28/12/86	HJK						M60	s85				6	-
Mika Väyrynen	28/12/81	HJK						s60	M46				63	5
Roope Riski	16/08/91	Hønefoss (NOR)						s60	A85				2	1
Johannes Laaksonen	13/12/90	SJK						s75					1	-
Tim Väyrynen	30/03/93	Dortmund (GER) /Viktoria Köln (GER)						s75	s46		s46		4	-
Robin Lod	17/04/93	HJK						s90	M70		s84		3	-
Henrik Moisander	29/09/85	Lahti							G				1	-
Ville Jalasto	19/04/86	Stabæk (NOR)							D61				4	-
Sebastian Sorsa	25/01/84	HJK								D			6	-
Paulus Arajuuri	15/06/88	Lech (POL)								s46			7	-
Berat Sadik	14/09/86	Thun (SUI)								s70			9	1
Boris Rotenberg	19/05/86	Dinamo Moskva (RUS)									D46		1	-
Jukka Raitala	15/09/88	Vestsjælland (DEN)									D	D	26	-
Thomas Lam	18/12/93	Zwolle (NED)									M		1	-
Mikko Sumusalo	12/03/90	Rostock (GER)									s46		4	1

EUROPE

HJK Helsinki

CHAMPIONS
LEAGUE

Second qualifying round - FK Rabotnicki (MKD)
A 0-0
Tørnes, Väyrynen, Heikkinen, Savage, Tainio, Lampi, Moren, Alho (Schüller 71), Sorsa, Lod, Kandji. Coach: Mika Lehkosuo (FIN)
H 2-1 Lod (22), Moren (26)
Tørnes, Heikkinen, Savage (Baah 90+3), Tainio, Lampi, Moren, Alho, Sorsa, Schüller, Lod, Kandji (Väyrynen 88). Coach: Mika Lehkosuo (FIN)

Third qualifying round - APOEL FC (CYP)
H 2-2 Savage (11, 45+1p)
Tørnes, Heikkinen, Savage, Tainio, Lampi, Moren, Alho (Baah 77), Sorsa, Schüller (Väyrynen 76), Lod (Mannström 87), Kandji. Coach: Mika Lehkosuo (FIN)
Red card: Kandji 48
A 0-2
Tørnes, Väyrynen (Baah 46), Heikkinen, Savage, Tainio (Forssell 74), Lampi, Moren, Alho, Sorsa (Mannström 78), Schüller, Lod. Coach: Mika Lehkosuo (FIN)

EUROPA
LEAGUE

Play-offs - SK Rapid Wien (AUT)
H 2-1 Lod (63), Väyrynen (74)
Doblas, Väyrynen (Heikkilä 90+2), Heikkinen, Savage, Lampi, Moren, Alho (Zeneli 71), Perovuo, Sorsa (Baah 75), Lod, Kandji. Coach: Mika Lehkosuo (FIN)
A 3-3 Kandji (15), Alho (77), Savage (88p)
Doblas, Heikkinen, Savage, Tainio, Lampi, Moren, Alho (Heikkilä 90+4), Sorsa, Schüller (Zeneli 68), Lod, Kandji (Perovuo 88). Coach: Mika Lehkosuo (FIN)

Group B
Match 1 - FC København (DEN)
A 0-2
Doblas, Heikkinen, Savage (Zeneli 77), Tainio, Lampi, Moren, Sorsa, Bancé, Lod, Annan, Porokara (Kandji 71). Coach: Mika Lehkosuo (FIN)
Match 2 - Club Brugge KV (BEL)
H 0-3
Doblas, Baah, Väyrynen (Zeneli 46), Heikkinen, Savage, Tainio, Lampi, Sorsa, Bancé (Porokara 67), Lod (Kandji 43), Annan. Coach: Mika Lehkosuo (FIN)
Match 3 - Torino FC (ITA)
A 0-2
Doblas (Eriksson 46), Baah, Heikkinen, Savage, Tainio (Väyrynen 76), Lampi, Sorsa, Lod, Annan, Zeneli, Alho (Kandji 67). Coach: Mika Lehkosuo (FIN)
Match 4 - Torino FC (ITA)
H 2-1 Baah (60), Moren (81)
Doblas, Baah, Väyrynen (Perovuo 75), Savage, Lampi, Moren, Sorsa, Lod, Annan, Zeneli (Alho 86), Kandji (Heikkilä 90). Coach: Mika Lehkosuo (FIN)

Match 5 - FC København (DEN)
H 2-1 Baah (29), Kandji (90+3)
Doblas, Baah, Väyrynen (Heikkilä 70), Heikkinen, Tainio (Schüller 54), Moren, Alho, Sorsa, Lod, Zeneli (Perovuo 80), Kandji. Coach: Mika Lehkosuo (FIN)
Match 6 - Club Brugge KV (BEL)
A 1-2 Kandji (51)
Doblas, Baah, Väyrynen (Perovuo 83), Heikkinen, Moren, Sorsa, Schüller, Lod, Annan, Zeneli (Porokara 63), Kandji. Coach: Mika Lehkosuo (FIN)

RoPS Rovaniemi

EUROPA
LEAGUE

Second qualifying round - Asteras Tripolis FC (GRE)
H 1-1 Lahdenmäki (2)
Sahlgren, Lahdenmäki, Okkonen, Mäkitalo, Otaru (Virtanen 88), Kokko (Lahtinen 23), Gay, Saxman, Majava, Nyassi (Emenike 90+3), Obilor. Coach: Juha Malinen (FIN)
A 2-4 Mäkitalo (53), Lahdenmäki (62)
Sahlgren, Lahdenmäki, Okkonen, Mäkitalo, Otaru (Forsman 45+5), Kokko (Emenike 71), Gay, Saxman, Majava, Nyassi (Lahtinen 84), Obilor. Coach: Juha Malinen (FIN)
Red card: Sahlgren 45+2

FC Honka Espoo

EUROPA
LEAGUE

First qualifying round - JK Sillamäe Kalev (EST)
A 1-2 Kabashi (82)
Viitala, Aalto, Anyamele (Mombilo 68), Mäkijärvi, Äijälä, Väisänen, Hatakka, Levänen (Jokinen 46), Porokara, Hetemaj, Kabashi. Coach: Shefki Kuqi (FIN)
H 3-2 Äijälä (45), Mombilo (90), Porokara (105) **(aet)**
Kollar, Aalto, Anyamele (Mombilo 46), Mäkijärvi, Äijälä, Väisänen, Tuomela (Saarinen 52), Hatakka, Porokara, Hetemaj, Kabashi (Levänen 81). Coach: Shefki Kuqi (FIN)

VPS Vaasa

EUROPA
LEAGUE

First qualifying round - IF Brommapojkarna (SWE)
H 2-1 Strandvall (53), Parikka (54)
Henriksson, Koskimaa, Engström, Nganbe Nganbe, Strandvall, Parikka (Linjala 82), Björk, Honkaniemi, Dafaa, Brown, Stewart (Seabrook 69). Coach: Olli Huttunen (FIN)
A 0-2
Henriksson, Koskimaa, Engström, Nganbe Nganbe, Strandvall, Parikka (Seabrook 46), Björk, Honkaniemi, Dafaa, Brown (Simpson 10), Stewart (Linjala 81). Coach: Olli Huttunen (FIN)

Myllykosken Pallo -47

EUROPA
LEAGUE

First qualifying round - ÍF Fuglafjørdur (FRO)
H 1-0 Abdulahi (76)
Iiskola, Vesala (Salmikivi 90+1), Dema (Minkenen 72), Abdulahi, Pirinen, Sihvola, Bah, Soiri (Ristola 63), Koskinen, Aho, A Lody. Coach: Antti Muurinen (FIN)
A 0-0
Iiskola, Vesala (Hoivala 90), Dema, Abdulahi, Salmikivi (Leandro Motta 72), Pirinen, Soiri (Ristola 77), Koskinen, Aho, A Lody, Minkenen. Coach: Antti Muurinen (FIN)

Second qualifying round - FC Dinamo Minsk (BLR)
A 0-3
Iiskola, Vesala (Ristola 70), Dema, Abdulahi, Pirinen, Bah, Soiri (Salmikivi 84), Koskinen, Aho, A Lody, Minkenen (Leandro Motta 62). Coach: Antti Muurinen (FIN)
H 0-0
Iiskola, Hoivala, Abdulahi (Minkenen 62), Salmikivi, Sihvola, Bah, Soiri (Ristola 72), Koskinen, Leandro Motta (Dema 58), Aho, A Lody. Coach: Antti Muurinen (FIN)

DOMESTIC LEAGUE CLUB-BY-CLUB

HJK Helsinki

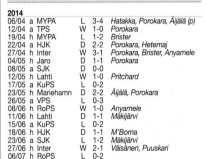

1907 • Sonera Stadium (10,800) • hjk.fi

Major honours
Finnish League (27) 1911, 1912, 1917, 1918, 1919, 1923, 1925, 1936, 1938, 1964, 1973, 1978, 1981, 1985, 1987, 1988, 1990, 1992, 1997, 2002, 2003, 2009, 2010, 2011, 2012, 2013, 2014; Finnish Cup (12) 1966, 1981, 1984, 1993, 1996, 1998, 2000, 2003, 2006, 2008, 2011, 2014

Coach: Sixten Boström;
(29/04/14) Mika Lehkosuo

2014

06/04	h Jaro	W	1-0	Tainio
12/04	h KuPS	W	3-1	Kandji, Lod, Forssell (p)
19/04	a Lahti	L	1-3	Baah
22/04	h Honka	D	2-2	Forssell, Alho
26/04	h TPS	L	0-1	
04/05	a VPS	W	2-0	Mannström 2
08/05	h Mariehamn	W	1-0	Savage
12/05	a RoPS	W	1-0	og (Alison)
16/05	h MYPA	W	4-0	Kandji, Lampi, Alho, Schüller
26/05	h SJK	W	1-0	Kandji
04/06	a Inter	W	2-0	Forssell, Kandji
08/06	a Jaro	W	2-0	Kandji, Savage
11/06	a RoPS	D	0-0	
14/06	h VPS	W	3-0	Alho, Savage, Lod
18/06	a Honka	D	1-1	Kandji
23/06	h TPS	W	5-0	Heikkilä, Forssell, Savage 2, Lod
27/06	a Mariehamn	W	2-0	Alho, Konan
02/07	h Lahti	D	0-0	
06/07	a KuPS	D	2-2	Alho, Savage
19/07	h SJK	W	2-0	Forssell (p), Konan
26/07	a Inter	D	3-3	Forssell, Sorsa, Savage (p)
02/08	a MYPA	W	1-0	Lod
13/08	h Inter	W	2-0	Alho, Forssell
24/08	a SJK	L	0-2	
31/08	a Jaro	W	4-1	Mannström, Baah, Konan 2
12/09	h KuPS	D	2-2	Heikkilä 2
21/09	h Mariehamn	W	5-1	Savage 3, Bancé, Väyrynen
25/09	a Lahti	W	2-0	Lod, Porokara
28/09	h TPS	W	4-1	Väyrynen, Zeneli 2 (2p), Lod
05/10	h Honka	D	1-1	Savage
16/10	h MYPA	W	2-0	Zeneli, Alho
19/10	a VPS	D	1-1	Mannström
26/10	h RoPS	W	3-0	(w/o; original result 0-3)

No	Name	Nat	DoB	Pos	Aps	(s)	Gls
17	Nikolai Alho		12/03/93	A	15	(7)	7
20	Anthony Annan	GHA	21/07/86	M	4	(3)	
3	Gideon Baah	GHA	01/10/91	D	23	(2)	2
30	Aristide Bancé	BFA	19/09/84	A	2	(2)	1
12	Toni Doblas	ESP	05/08/80	G	5		
13	Carljohan Eriksson		25/04/95	G	6		
9	Mikael Forssell		15/03/81	A	14	(3)	7
18	Emerik Grönroos		06/07/94	M		(2)	
5	Tapio Heikkilä		08/04/90	D	26	(2)	3
6	Markus Heikkinen		13/10/78	D	20	(3)	
14	Joevin Jones	TRI	03/08/91	M	5	(1)	
99	Macoumba Kandji	SEN	02/08/85	M	19	(5)	6
15	Oussou Konan	CIV	23/01/89	A	8	(10)	4
11	Veli Lampi		18/07/84	D	21	(2)	1
22	Fredrik Lassas		01/10/96	M	9	(5)	
2	Alex Lehtinen		09/04/96	D	4	(3)	
31	Robin Lod		17/04/93	M	24	(4)	6
26	Obed Malolo		18/04/97	M		(4)	
7	Sebastian Mannström		29/10/88	M	16	(9)	4
16	Valtteri Moren		15/06/91	D	25		
42	Joel Perovuo		11/08/85	M	8	(2)	
33	Roni Porokara		12/12/83	A	2	(2)	1
8	Demba Savage	GAM	17/06/88	A	19	(5)	11
28	Rasmus Schüller		18/06/91	M	10	(1)	1
27	Sebastian Sorsa		25/01/84	D	10	(9)	1
10	Teemu Tainio		27/11/79	M	14	(2)	1
21	Michael Tørnes	DEN	08/01/86	G	22		
25	Mikko Viitikko		18/04/95	D	3		
4	Mika Väyrynen		28/12/81	M	21	(4)	2
80	Erfan Zeneli		28/12/86	M	8	(1)	3

FC Honka Espoo

1957 • Tapiolan urheilupuisto (5,000) • fchonkaespoo.com

Major honours
Finnish Cup (1) 2012

Coach: Shefki Kuqi

2014

06/04	a MYPA	L	3-4	Hatakka, Porokara, Äijälä (p)
12/04	a TPS	W	1-0	Porokara
19/04	h MYPA	L	1-2	Brister
22/04	a HJK	D	2-2	Porokara, Hetemaj
27/04	h Inter	W	3-1	Porokara, Brister, Anyamele
04/05	a Jaro	D	1-1	Porokara
08/05	a SJK	D	0-0	
12/05	h Lahti	W	1-0	Pritchard
17/05	a KuPS	L	0-2	
23/05	h Mariehamn	D	2-2	Äijälä, Porokara
26/05	a VPS	L	0-3	
08/06	h RoPS	W	1-0	Anyamele
11/06	h Lahti	D	1-1	Mäkijärvi
15/06	a KuPS	L	0-2	
18/06	h HJK	D	1-1	M'Boma
23/06	a SJK	L	1-2	Mäkijärvi
27/06	h Inter	W	2-1	Väisänen, Puuskari
06/07	h RoPS	L	0-2	
12/07	a VPS	L	1-3	Mombilo
20/07	h Jaro	L	0-5	
27/07	h TPS	D	1-1	Anyamele
03/08	h Mariehamn	D	1-1	Björs
10/08	a Mariehamn	L	1-4	Caloi
13/08	a TPS	L	1-2	Porokara
24/08	a Jaro	D	3-3	P Couñago (p), Y Couñago, Porokara
31/08	h VPS	L	1-2	Y Couñago
14/09	a RoPS	L	1-2	P Couñago (p)
17/09	h MYPA	W	2-0	Y Couñago, P Couñago
22/09	a Inter	D	2-2	P Couñago, Vasara
28/09	h SJK	D	1-1	Mäkijärvi
05/10	a HJK	D	1-1	Mäkijärvi
18/10	h KuPS	D	2-2	P Couñago, Vasara
25/10	a Lahti	L	0-2	

No	Name	Nat	DoB	Pos	Aps	(s)	Gls
5	Henri Aalto		20/04/89	D	32		
7	Nnaemeka Anyamele		16/05/94	M	17	(14)	3
11	Ilari Äijälä		30/09/86	D	29		2
37	Albinot Bekaj		27/02/93	A		(3)	
37	Markus Björs		17/09/95	D	1	(2)	1
21	Alex Brister	ENG	19/12/93	D	10		2
8	Carlos Caloi	ESP	11/02/87	M	9	(1)	1
38	Pablo Couñago	ESP	09/08/79	A	8		5
21	Yerai Couñago	ESP	11/10/91	M	10		3
2	Martín Fernández	ESP	11/06/89	D	2		
34	Lucas García	ARG	13/01/88	M	3		
3	Abel Gebor	LBR	27/08/90	M	1	(1)	
25	Gladson	BRA	18/09/90	M	5	(2)	
36	Eero Haapala		24/04/96	D		(2)	
3	Aapo Halme		22/05/98	A		(1)	
26	Dani Hatakka		12/03/94	D	22	(2)	1
31	Reza Heidari		18/04/96	M		(1)	
6	Marcus Heimonen		11/10/93	M	6	(2)	
58	Mehmet Hetemaj		08/12/87	M	15	(1)	1
34	Jani Jokinen		23/04/93	M	3	(2)	
68	Armend Kabashi		09/12/95	M	21	(5)	
12	Daniel Kollar		29/03/94	G	18		
99	Albert Kuqi		14/02/92	A	1	(4)	
36	Jatuli Laevuo		19/05/95	D	1	(1)	
27	Jonas Levänen		12/01/94	M	2	(3)	
37	Aristote M'Boma		30/06/94	A	2	(1)	1
31	Jeremie Malolo		21/11/91	M		(3)	
23	Kosta Manev		07/04/93	D	10	(1)	
22	Miloš Milović	MNE	22/12/95	D	7		
22	Kevin Mombilo		06/05/93	A	3	(5)	1
10	Antti Mäkijärvi		08/12/93	M	14	(9)	4
17	Janne Paukkonen		16/01/95	A	2	(4)	
36	Julius Perovuo		22/12/94	D	1	(1)	
33	Roni Porokara		12/12/83	A	25		8
23	Joshua Pritchard	WAL	23/09/92	M	5	(1)	1
36	Miko Puuskari		13/05/95	M	3	(4)	1
19	Youness Rahimi		13/02/95	A	1	(6)	
22	Sakir Redzepi	MKD	21/10/87	D	4		
4	Lum Rexhepi		03/08/92	D	20	(2)	
31	Valtteri Rönnberg		19/06/96	M	2	(2)	
22	Tommi Saarinen		31/01/95	M	1		
69	Toni Sjöstedt		24/02/97	D		(1)	
8	Ghassimu Sow	LBR	10/04/95	M	4	(3)	
8	Ville Tuomela		03/11/96	M	1	(2)	
9	Jussi Vasara		14/05/87	M	13	(2)	2
1	Walter Viitala		09/01/92	G	14		
15	Sauli Väisänen		05/06/94	D	14	(1)	1

FC Inter Turku

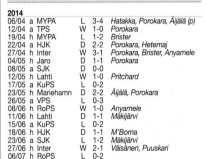

1990 • Veritas Stadion (9,300) • fcinter.com

Major honours
Finnish League (1) 2008; Finnish Cup (1) 2009

Coach: Job Dragtsma (NED)

2014

13/04	a Jaro	W	2-0	Gruborovics, Ojala (p)
19/04	h SJK	W	2-1	Sirbiladze, Gruborovics (p)
23/04	a RoPS	L	0-1	
27/04	a Honka	L	1-3	Lehtonen
04/05	a KuPS	D	1-1	Sirbiladze
08/05	a Lahti	D	0-0	
12/05	a Mariehamn	D	2-2	Ojala, Kauppi
17/05	h VPS	D	0-0	
26/05	h MYPA	D	1-1	Duah
04/06	h HJK	L	0-2	
08/06	h TPS	W	2-1	Suárez, Sirbiladze
11/06	a Jaro	L	0-1	
15/06	h MYPA	W	1-0	Lehtonen
18/06	a RoPS	L	0-3	
23/06	h VPS	W	3-0	Lindström, Lehtonen, Duah
27/06	a Honka	L	1-2	Duah
02/07	h TPS	W	3-2	Lehtonen, Onovo, Sirbiladze
06/07	a Mariehamn	L	1-3	Suárez
14/07	h Lahti	L	0-1	
20/07	a KuPS	L	2-4	Sirbiladze 2
26/07	h HJK	D	3-3	Onovo, Lindström, Miftari
03/08	a SJK	D	2-2	Paajanen, Hämäläinen
09/08	h SJK	D	1-1	Salminen
13/08	a HJK	L	0-2	
25/08	h KuPS	D	0-0	
31/08	a Lahti	L	0-2	
13/09	h Mariehamn	L	0-2	
17/09	a TPS	W	6-1	Sirbiladze 3, Lindström, Ojala (p), Lehtonen
22/09	h Honka	D	2-2	Onovo, Ojala (p)
28/09	a VPS	L	0-1	
05/10	h RoPS	W	4-1	Duah 2, Diogo, Ojala
19/10	a MYPA	D	2-2	Lehtonen, Ojala (p)
25/10	a Jaro	L	0-1	

No	Name	Nat	DoB	Pos	Aps	(s)	Gls
14	Joni Aho		12/04/86	D	16	(2)	
1	Magnus Bahne		15/03/79	G	27		
26	Demba Camara	GUI	11/08/95	A	3	(6)	
19	Diogo	BRA	14/01/88	M	3	(2)	1
21	Solomon Duah		07/01/93	A	13	(11)	5
6	Tamás Gruborovics	HUN	03/07/84	M	23	(5)	2
3	Juuso Hämäläinen		08/12/93	D	27	(4)	1
22	Kaan Kairinen		22/12/98	M		(1)	
16	Kalle Kauppi		06/05/92	M	14	(12)	1
12	Jere Koponen		23/05/92	G	6	(1)	
12	Joonas Lahti		15/04/95	M		(1)	
27	Aleksi Laiho		17/06/93	M	1	(2)	
1	Henri Lehtonen		28/07/80	M	25	(1)	6
5	Mathias Lindström		14/01/81	D	24	(2)	3
20	Stefan Marinkovic	SUI	20/02/94	D	16	(4)	
11	Blend Miftari		03/12/95	A	2	(6)	1
23	Ville Nikkari		05/11/88	D	11	(2)	
7	Ari Nyman		07/02/84	M	28	(1)	
17	Mika Ojala		21/06/88	M	18	(1)	6
24	Vincent Onovo	NGA	10/12/95	M	24	(2)	3
24	Daniel Osinachi	NGA	25/08/89	A		(2)	
15	Severi Paajanen		23/10/86	M	32	(1)	1
28	Oskari Qvick		15/12/97	M		(2)	
25	Renan	BRA	17/11/90	D	4	(2)	
4	Juho Salminen		08/08/95	D	4	(11)	1
10	Irakli Sirbiladze	GEO	27/09/82	A	30		9
18	Francis Suárez	ESP	06/01/87	M	12	(8)	2

FF Jaro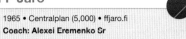

1965 • Centralplan (5,000) • ffjaro.fi
Coach: Alexei Eremenko Sr

2014

06/04	a	HJK	L	0-1	
13/04	h	Inter	L	0-2	
19/04	a	KuPS	W	4-1	Helmke, Winchester, David, Carlsson
23/04	h	Lahti	W	2-1	Helmke, Emet (p)
27/04	a	Mariehamn	W	3-1	Vaganov, Emet, Helmke (p)
04/05	a	Honka	D	1-1	Helmke
08/05	h	VPS	W	1-0	Emet
12/05	a	MYPA	L	2-3	Vaganov, Brunell
17/05	h	TPS	W	2-0	Winchester, Fondacaro
23/05	a	SJK	W	1-0	Winchester
26/05	a	RoPS	L	1-2	Winchester
08/06	h	HJK	L	0-2	
11/06	h	Inter	W	2-0	Brunell, Emet (p)
15/06	a	Mariehamn	L	2-4	Winchester, Emet
18/06	a	MYPA	D	1-1	Winchester
24/06	a	Lahti	L	0-1	
27/06	h	RoPS	D	1-1	Fondacaro
02/07	a	KuPS	D	1-1	Helmke
06/07	h	VPS	L	1-2	Fondacaro
20/07	a	Honka	W	5-0	Emet 2, David, Winchester, Larsson
26/07	h	SJK	L	0-1	
03/08	a	TPS	D	2-2	Vaganov, Helmke
10/08	h	TPS	D	1-1	Emet
13/08	a	SJK	L	0-1	
24/08	a	Honka	D	3-3	Emet 2 (1p), Helmke
31/08	a	HJK	L	1-4	Helmke
14/09	a	VPS	D	3-3	Emet 2, David
19/09	a	KuPS	W	3-2	Emet (p), Winchester, Denis
22/09	a	RoPS	W	1-0	Denis
28/09	h	Lahti	L	0-4	
05/10	a	MYPA	L	1-2	Denis
18/10	h	Mariehamn	W	1-0	Winchester
26/10	a	Inter	W	1-0	Emet

No	Name	Nat	DoB	Pos	Aps	(s)	Gls
30	Edgar Bernhardt	GER	30/03/86	A	4	(3)	
6	Johan Brunell		29/05/91	D	16	(2)	2
21	Patrick Byskata		13/08/90	M	6	(1)	
9	David Carlsson	SWE	07/03/83	A	3	(22)	1
2	Aubrey David	TRI	11/10/90	D	31		3
33	Denis	BRA	29/12/89	A	5	(2)	3
19	Iidle Elmi		01/01/95	A		(9)	
10	Jonas Emet		13/02/88	M	32		14
13	Sergei Eremenko		06/01/99	M		(1)	
32	Carlos Fondacaro	ARG	21/05/87	D	28		3
11	Hendrik Helmke	GER	13/07/87	A	31		8
15	Markus Kronholm		02/04/91	M	11	(12)	
4	Mathias Kullström		02/01/87	D	21	(3)	
23	Kevin Larsson		31/01/96	A	1	(9)	1
18	Peter Opiyo	KEN	01/08/92	M	27	(1)	
16	Antti Palohuhta		01/05/94	A		(1)	
17	Kevin Peth		26/04/93	D	13	(6)	
8	Jari Sara		25/04/89	D	10	(5)	
7	Fredrik Svanbäck		12/05/79	M	29		
13	Aleksandr Tumasyan	ARM	15/10/92	M	1		
27	Ilya Vaganov	RUS	15/01/89	D	31		3
22	Shahdon Winchester	TRI	08/01/92	A	30	(1)	9
25	Emil Öhberg		20/06/93	G	9		
1	Jesse Öst		20/10/90	G	24		

KuPS Kuopio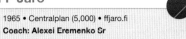

1923 • Savon Sanomat Areena (3,700) • kups.fi
Major honours
Finnish League (5) 1956, 1958, 1966, 1974, 1976;
Finnish Cup (2) 1968, 1989
Coach: Esa Pekonen;
(24/04/14) (Tero Taipale);
(02/05/14) Marko Rajamäki

2014

12/04	a	HJK	L	1-3	Ilo
19/04	h	Jaro	L	1-4	Ilo
23/04	a	SJK	L	0-2	
27/04	h	Lahti	L	0-2	
04/05	a	Inter	D	1-1	Purje
08/05	h	RoPS	W	1-0	Colley
12/05	a	VPS	D	1-1	Catovic
17/05	h	Honka	W	2-0	Catovic, Paananen
23/05	a	MYPA	L	0-2	
26/05	a	TPS	W	3-0	Colley, Purje, Chibuike
08/06	h	Mariehamn	W	4-0	Chibuike 2, Colley, Catovic
11/06	a	VPS	W	3-0	Markić, Cox, Trafford
15/06	a	Honka	W	2-0	og (Hatakka), Catovic
18/06	a	TPS	D	1-1	Cox
23/06	h	Mariehamn	L	1-3	Markić
27/06	a	Lahti	W	1-0	Ilo
02/07	a	Jaro	D	1-1	Purje
06/07	h	HJK	D	2-2	Purje 2 (1p)
12/07	a	SJK	D	0-0	
20/07	a	Inter	W	4-2	Purje, Ilo, Catovic 2
27/07	a	MYPA	L	3-5	Purje 2 (2p), Paananen
03/08	a	RoPS	L	1-3	Purje
10/08	h	RoPS	W	1-0	Niskanen
13/08	h	MYPA	W	1-0	Trafford
25/08	a	Inter	D	0-0	
31/08	h	SJK	D	0-0	
12/09	h	HJK	D	2-2	Hakola, Ilo
19/09	a	Jaro	L	2-3	Ilo, Trafford
22/09	h	Lahti	D	1-1	Colley
28/09	a	Mariehamn	L	1-3	Chibuike
05/10	h	TPS	W	1-0	Chibuike
18/10	a	Honka	D	2-2	Markić, Ilo
25/10	h	VPS	L	0-1	

No	Name	Nat	DoB	Pos	Aps	(s)	Gls
7	Ali Al-Musawi		12/09/96	A		(1)	
17	Admir Catovic	SWE	05/09/87	A	26	(5)	6
30	Francis Chibuike	NGA	07/06/93	A	17	(4)	5
15	Omar Colley	GAM	24/10/92	D	32		4
9	Michael Cox	CAN	02/08/92	A	3	(8)	2
25	Juha Hakola		27/10/87	A	4	(4)	1
20	Miikka Ilo		09/05/82	A	26	(4)	7
25	Joona Kemppainen		05/06/88	M		(2)	
18	Jussi Kujala		04/04/83	M	2	(4)	
1	Tomi Maanoja		12/09/86	G	33		
26	Jani Mahanen		12/01/90	M	1	(5)	
14	Toni Markić	BIH	25/10/90	D	29		3
11	Ilmari Niskanen		27/10/97	A	1	(3)	1
25	Joonas Nissinen		24/04/97	M		(1)	
29	Joonas Ojantie		11/10/91	D	3	(6)	
13	Aleksi Paananen		25/01/93	M	28	(5)	2
9	Mikko Pitkänen		07/02/97	D		(2)	
10	Ats Purje	EST	03/08/85	A	28	(1)	9
21	Peetu Pöyhönen		09/11/96	M		(3)	
32	Tuomas Rannankari		21/05/91	D	32	(1)	
28	Lamin Samateh	GAM	26/06/92	D	2		
6	Saku Savolainen		13/08/96	A	3	(14)	
23	Ebrima Sohna	GAM	14/12/88	M	31		
4	Tero Taipale		14/12/72	M	6	(4)	
19	Charlie Trafford	CAN	24/05/92	M	21		3
22	Joel Vartiainen		14/03/94	M	14	(6)	
8	Jerry Voutilainen		29/03/95	M	21	(7)	

FC Lahti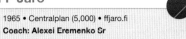

1996 • Lahden stadion (7,400);
Kisapuisto (3,000) • fclahti.fi
Coach: Toni Korkeakunnas

2014

13/04	a	MYPA	D	1-1	Drilon Shala
19/04	h	HJK	W	3-1	Drilon Shala 2, Hauhia
23/04	a	Jaro	L	1-2	Ngueukam
27/04	a	KuPS	W	2-0	Klinga, Rafael
04/05	h	SJK	D	1-1	Salimäki
08/05	h	Inter	D	0-0	
12/05	a	Honka	L	0-1	
17/05	h	RoPS	W	1-0	Ngueukam
23/05	h	TPS	W	2-0	Hertsi, Rafael
26/05	a	Mariehamn	D	0-0	
04/06	h	TPS	W	2-0	Rafael (p), Klinga
08/06	h	VPS	D	1-1	Hovi
11/06	a	Honka	D	1-1	Tanska
18/06	a	Mariehamn	W	1-0	Rafael
24/06	a	Jaro	W	1-0	Rafael
27/06	h	KuPS	L	0-1	
02/07	a	HJK	D	0-0	
07/07	h	SJK	D	1-1	Rafael (p)
14/07	a	Inter	W	1-0	Rafael
20/07	h	MYPA	W	3-0	Tanska, Hertsi, Rafael
27/07	a	RoPS	W	1-0	Tanska
03/08	a	VPS	W	3-1	Joenmäki, Ngueukam 2
10/08	h	VPS	W	4-1	Joenmäki, Ngueukam, Klinga, Sesay
13/08	h	RoPS	L	3-4	Hertsi, Rafael 2
24/08	a	MYPA	D	2-2	Korte, Sesay
31/08	h	Inter	D	0-0	
13/09	a	SJK	D	1-1	Gela
22/09	a	KuPS	D	1-1	Rafael
25/09	h	HJK	L	0-2	
28/09	a	Jaro	W	4-0	Rafael 2, Hertsi, Ngueukam
05/10	h	Mariehamn	D	1-1	Sesay
18/10	a	TPS	W	1-0	Pasanen
25/10	h	Honka	W	2-0	Drilon Shala, Ngueukam

No	Name	Nat	DoB	Pos	Aps	(s)	Gls
4	Xhevdet Gela		14/11/89	M	7	(2)	1
3	Mikko Hauhia		03/09/84	D	33		1
22	Loorens Hertsi		13/11/92	M	25	(6)	4
21	Jaakko Hietikko		13/01/94	A	3	(2)	
19	Kimmo Hovi		31/05/94	A	4	(7)	1
13	Markus Joenmäki		11/02/88	D	25	(2)	2
10	Matti Klinga		10/12/94	M	20	(3)	3
17	Eero Korte		20/09/87	M	13	(9)	1
6	Pyry Kärkkäinen		10/11/86	D	28		
8	Onuray Köse		11/02/96	M		(2)	
12	Joonas Meronen		11/06/93	G	4		
1	Henrik Moisander		29/09/85	G	29		
11	Ariel Ngueukam	CMR	15/11/88	M	25	(4)	7
24	Petri Pasanen		24/09/80	D	10	(1)	1
9	Rafael	BRA	01/08/78	A	24	(4)	13
15	Tomi Saarelma		30/11/88	A		(2)	
34	Hafid Salhi	NED	04/01/93	M	15	(8)	
5	Mikael Salimäki		27/08/92	D		(12)	1
20	Hassan Sesay	SLE	22/10/87	A	20	(3)	4
7	Drilon Shala		20/03/87	A	15	(7)	4
28	Driton Shala		26/05/97	A		(1)	
2	Jani Tanska		29/07/88	D	31		3
16	Henri Toivomäki		21/02/91	D	32		

IFK Mariehamn

1919 • Wiklöf Holding Arena (4,000) • ifkmariehamn.com
Coach: Pekka Lyyski

2014

13/04	h VPS	L	0-3	(w/o; original result 1-0 Hradecky)
19/04	h RoPS	W	2-0	Solignac, Forsell
23/04	a TPS	W	1-0	Lyyski
27/04	h Jaro	L	1-3	Forsell (p)
04/05	h MYPA	W	2-1	Forsell, Solignac
08/05	a HJK	L	0-1	
12/05	h Inter	D	2-2	Ekhalie, Solignac
17/05	a SJK	L	0-3	
23/05	a Honka	D	2-2	Diego Assis, Solignac
26/05	h Lahti	D	0-0	
08/06	h KuPS	L	0-4	
11/06	a TPS	L	1-3	Diego Assis
15/06	h Jaro	W	4-2	Forsell 2, Orgill, Ekhalie
18/06	h Lahti	L	0-1	
23/06	a KuPS	W	3-1	Forsell, Solignac 2
27/06	h HJK	L	0-2	
02/07	a SJK	L	0-3	
06/07	h Inter	W	3-1	Solignac 2, Diego Assis
13/07	a MYPA	L	0-3	
20/07	h RoPS	L	2-4	Solignac, Forsell
27/07	a VPS	W	2-1	Diego Assis, Lyyski
03/08	a Honka	D	1-1	Forsell
10/08	h Honka	W	4-1	Diego Assis 3, Solignac
13/08	h VPS	W	1-0	Ibrahim
24/08	a RoPS	W	3-1	Ekhalie, Forsell, Diego Assis
31/08	h MYPA	W	3-1	Tammilehto, Forsell, Solignac
13/09	a Inter	W	2-0	Solignac, Ramandingaye
17/09	h SJK	D	2-2	Kojola, Lyyski
21/09	a HJK	L	1-5	Forsell (p)
28/09	h KuPS	W	3-1	Diego Assis, Ekhalie, Ramandingaye
05/10	a Lahti	D	1-1	Solignac
18/10	a Jaro	L	0-1	
25/10	h TPS	W	3-1	Diego Assis 2, Solignac

No	Name	Nat	DoB	Pos	Aps	(s)	Gls
3	Rezgar Amani		01/06/92	M		(1)	
27	Bernardo	BRA	09/10/89	M	13	(6)	
90	Patrick Byskata		13/08/90	M	12	(2)	
25	Diego Assis	BRA	14/09/87	M	22	(3)	11
15	Amos Ekhalie	KEN	08/07/88	M	18	(9)	4
10	Petteri Forsell		16/10/90	M	31		11
24	Oscar Forsström		15/10/82	G	2		
55	Bobbie Friberg da Cruz	SWE	16/02/82	D	32		
2	Albin Granlund		01/09/89	D	30		
20	Tomas Hradecky		13/10/92	D	18	(8)	1
7	Josef Ibrahim	SWE	13/03/91	M	6	(6)	1
3	Kristian Kojola		12/09/86	D	11		1
26	Erik Lundberg		20/03/94	D	3	(2)	
8	Jani Lyyski		16/03/83	D	25		3
35	Juho Mäkelä		23/06/83	A		(6)	
18	Thomas Mäkinen		30/01/97	M		(1)	
30	Marc Nordqvist		01/11/97	G		(1)	
21	Simon Nurme	SWE	24/11/82	G	14		
5	Dever Orgill	JAM	08/03/90	A	5	(7)	1
14	David Ramandingaye		14/09/89	A	22	(4)	2
19	Robin Sid		21/09/94	M		(5)	
9	Luis Solignac	ARG	16/02/91	A	32		14
6	Duarte Tammilehto		15/02/90	M	19	(5)	1
4	Roger Thompson	CAN	19/12/91	D	11	(9)	
1	Otso Virtanen		03/04/94	G	17		
11	Tommy Wirtanen		19/01/83	M	17	(1)	
16	Robin Östlind	SWE	14/03/90	M	3	(5)	

Myllykosken Pallo -47

1947 • Saviniemen jalkapallostadion (4,100) • mypa.fi
Major honours
Finnish League (1) 2005; Finnish Cup (3) 1992, 1995, 2004
Coach: Antti Muurinen

2014

06/04	h Honka	W	4-3	Vesala 2, Sihvola, Lindberg
13/04	h Lahti	D	1-1	Minkenen
19/04	a Honka	W	2-1	Abdulahi, Sihvola
23/04	h VPS	D	1-1	Abdulahi
27/04	a RoPS	W	1-0	Bah
04/05	a Mariehamn	L	1-2	Ristola
08/05	h TPS	W	4-1	Abdulahi, Sihvola, Stéfano 2
12/05	h Jaro	W	3-2	Bah 2, Stéfano
16/05	a HJK	L	0-4	
23/05	h KuPS	W	2-0	Stéfano, Ristola
26/05	h Inter	D	1-1	Sihvola
04/06	a SJK	L	0-1	
11/06	h SJK	L	1-3	Abdulahi
15/06	a Inter	L	0-1	
18/06	a Jaro	D	1-1	Aho
23/06	h RoPS	D	1-1	Sihvola
27/06	a VPS	L	0-4	
07/07	a TPS	L	0-1	
13/07	h Mariehamn	W	3-0	Bah, Sihvola, Ristola
20/07	a Lahti	L	0-3	
27/07	h KuPS	W	5-3	Ristola 2, Sihvola, Minkenen (p), Salmikivi
02/08	h HJK	L	0-1	
13/08	a KuPS	L	0-1	
24/08	h Lahti	D	2-2	Salmikivi, Abdulahi
31/08	a Mariehamn	L	1-3	Abdulahi
14/09	h TPS	W	2-1	Soiri, Stéfano
17/09	a Honka	L	0-2	
21/09	h VPS	D	0-0	
28/09	a RoPS	D	0-0	
05/10	h Jaro	W	2-1	Stéfano 2
16/10	a HJK	L	0-2	
19/10	h Inter	D	2-2	Ristola, Dema (p)
25/10	a SJK	L	1-3	Salmikivi

No	Name	Nat	DoB	Pos	Aps	(s)	Gls
19	Nosh A Lody		17/07/89	D	23	(1)	
6	Denis Abdulahi		22/05/90	M	31		6
30	Tuomas Aho		27/05/81	D	24		1
30	Sasha Anttilainen		19/12/86	A	3	(1)	
10	Dawda Bah	GAM	18/11/83	A	24	(3)	4
4	Dema	BRA	28/04/83	M	27	(1)	1
26	Jari Hassel		26/05/97	M		(1)	
2	Atte Hoivala		10/02/92	D	13	(8)	
1	Ville Iiskola		26/04/85	G	20	(1)	
14	Kassiano Soares	BRA	24/04/95	M	1	(5)	
7	Antti Koskinen		19/07/88	D	29	(2)	
17	Leandro Motta	BRA	14/01/92	M	10	(16)	
5	Toni Lindberg		23/09/85	D	13	(2)	1
25	Simo Majander		02/08/96	A	4	(6)	
20	Valeri Minkenen		09/04/89	M	14	(2)	2
23	Alex Oikkonen	PUR	15/10/94	M		(3)	
23	Esko-Petteri Pesari		02/11/96	M		(2)	
8	Juha Pirinen		22/10/91	M	22	(2)	
12	Jere Pyhäranta		06/07/92	G	13		
15	Aleksi Ristola		06/11/89	A	19	(8)	6
7	Ville Salmikivi		20/05/92	A	7	(8)	3
9	Pekka Sihvola		22/04/84	A	19		7
11	Pyry Soiri		22/09/94	A	15	(10)	1
22	Stéfano	BRA	12/01/91	A	18	(2)	7
3	Tommi Vesala		12/01/86	D	14	(4)	2

RoPS Rovaniemi

1950 • Keskuskenttä (3,400) • rops.fi
Major honours
Finnish Cup (2) 1986, 2013
Coach: Juha Malinen

2014

06/04	h VPS	L	0-2	
12/04	h SJK	D	1-1	Kokko
19/04	a Mariehamn	L	0-2	
23/04	h Inter	W	1-0	Pennanen
27/04	h MYPA	L	0-1	
03/05	a TPS	W	2-0	Pennanen, Mäkitalo
08/05	a KuPS	L	0-1	
12/05	h HJK	L	0-1	
17/05	a Lahti	L	0-1	
23/05	a VPS	L	0-2	
26/05	h Jaro	W	2-1	Roiha 2
08/06	a Honka	L	0-1	
11/06	h HJK	D	0-0	
15/06	a SJK	L	0-1	
18/06	h Inter	W	3-0	Gay, Kokko, Lahdenmäki
23/06	a MYPA	D	1-1	Majava
27/06	a Jaro	D	1-1	Nyassi
06/07	h Honka	W	2-0	Kokko 2 (1p)
12/07	h TPS	W	3-0	Kokko 2, Mäkitalo
20/07	a Mariehamn	W	4-2	Emenike 2, Mäkitalo, Lahtinen
27/07	h Lahti	L	0-1	
03/08	h KuPS	W	3-1	Kokko 2 (1p), Roiha
10/08	a KuPS	L	0-1	
13/08	a Lahti	W	4-3	Alison, Saxman, Nyassi, Gay
24/08	h Mariehamn	L	1-3	Roiha
31/08	a TPS	L	2-4	Kokko, og (Rähmönen)
14/09	h Honka	W	2-1	Nyassi, Obilor
17/09	a VPS	L	0-2	
22/09	a Jaro	L	0-1	
28/09	h MYPA	D	0-0	
05/10	a Inter	L	1-4	Alison
18/10	h SJK	L	1-2	Roiha
26/10	a HJK	L	0-3	(w/o; original result 3-0 Roiha, Okkonen, Nyassi)

No	Name	Nat	DoB	Pos	Aps	(s)	Gls
13	Jesse Ahonen		22/06/92	M	2	(5)	
6	Ndukaku Alison	NGA	12/08/91	D	17	(2)	2
31	Patrick Bantamoi	SLE	24/05/86	G	2	(1)	
21	Mbachu Emenike	NGA	21/05/89	A	2	(10)	2
12	Oskari Forsman		28/01/88	G	2		
14	Jamal Gay	TRI	09/02/89	A	25	(5)	2
11	Aleksandr Kokko		04/06/87	A	16	(4)	9
19	Santeri Kumpula		22/11/96	M		(2)	
3	Jarkko Lahdenmäki		16/04/91	D	18	(1)	1
9	Mika Lahtinen		30/04/85	A	4	(7)	1
18	Juuso Majava		07/04/89	M	15	(4)	1
7	Mika Mäkitalo		12/06/85	M	30		3
2	Lassi Nurmos		24/07/94	D	12	(4)	
24	Sainey Nyassi	GAM	31/01/89	A	17	(2)	4
80	Faith Obilor	NGA	05/03/91	D	31		1
4	Antti Okkonen		06/06/82	M	32		1
10	Nicholas Otaru		15/07/86	A	28		
45	Petteri Pennanen		19/09/90	M	7		2
23	Antti Peura		27/12/84	D	10	(3)	
17	Olli Pöyliö		11/08/95	M	5	(9)	
20	Simo Roiha		27/12/91	A	11	(14)	6
1	Saku-Pekka Sahlgren		08/04/92	G	29	(1)	
5	Janne Saksela		14/03/93	D	10	(2)	
16	Ville Saxman		15/11/89	M	27	(6)	1
8	Jani Virtanen		06/05/88	M	11	(9)	

SJK Seinäjoki

2007 • Seinäjoen keskuskenttä (3,500) •
sjk2007.fi
Coach: Simo Valakari

2014

12/04	a	RoPS	D	1-1	Milosavljević
19/04	a	Inter	L	1-2	Pelvas
23/04	h	KuPS	W	2-0	Carlos López 2 (1p)
04/05	a	Lahti	D	1-1	Lähde
08/05	h	Honka	D	0-0	
12/05	a	TPS	L	0-2	
17/05	h	Mariehamn	W	3-0	Moose, Laaksonen, Lehtinen
23/05	h	Jaro	L	0-1	
26/05	a	HJK	L	0-1	
04/06	a	MYPA	W	1-0	Lehtinen (p)
11/06	a	MYPA	W	3-1	og (Abdulahi), Pelvas, Moose
15/06	h	RoPS	W	1-0	Dorman
18/06	a	VPS	W	1-0	Laaksonen
23/06	h	Honka	W	2-1	Lehtinen (p), Moose
27/06	a	TPS	W	1-0	Lehtinen
02/07	h	Mariehamn	W	3-0	Lehtinen 2, Tahvanainen
07/07	a	Lahti	D	1-1	Laaksonen
12/07	h	KuPS	D	0-0	
19/07	a	HJK	L	0-2	
26/07	a	Jaro	W	1-0	Pelvas
03/08	h	Inter	D	2-2	Pelvas, Lehtinen
09/08	a	Inter	D	1-1	Laaksonen
13/08	h	Jaro	W	1-0	Lehtinen (p)
17/08	a	VPS	W	1-0	Savić
24/08	h	HJK	W	2-0	Pelvas 2 (1p)
31/08	a	KuPS	D	0-0	
13/09	h	Lahti	D	1-1	Pelvas
17/09	a	Mariehamn	D	2-2	Pelvas, Kams
21/09	h	TPS	W	2-1	Lähde, Pelvas
28/09	a	Honka	D	1-1	Laaksonen
05/10	h	VPS	L	0-3	
18/10	a	RoPS	W	2-1	Pelvas 2 (1p)
25/10	h	MYPA	W	3-1	Kams 2, Gogoua

No	Name	Nat	DoB	Pos	Aps	(s)	Gls
33	Mihkel Aksalu	EST	07/11/84	G	30		
28	Felipe Aspegren		12/02/94	D	2		
10	Wayne Brown	ENG	06/08/88	M	11		
9	Carlos López	ESP	01/01/87	A	5	(5)	2
2	Richard Dorman	WAL	14/06/88	D	27	(2)	1
27	Cédric Gogoua	CIV	10/07/94	D	23		1
6	Héctor García	ESP	25/09/92	M	1	(2)	
25	Josué	ESP	27/02/93	M	3	(3)	
19	Gert Kams	EST	25/05/85	D	23	(7)	3
8	Johannes Laaksonen		13/12/90	M	29	(2)	5
14	Toni Lehtinen		05/05/84	A	24	(6)	8
1	Luis Fernando	BRA	06/06/79	G	3		
11	Juho Lähde		11/02/91	M	17	(9)	2
22	Matti Lähitie		13/12/85	D	6	(4)	
20	Marco Matrone		02/07/87	M	29	(3)	
5	Pavle Milosavljević	SRB	21/06/87	D	20		1
18	Justin Moose	USA	23/11/83	M	30	(2)	3
9	Juho Mäkelä		23/06/83	A	1	(5)	
16	Akseli Pelvas		08/02/89	A	22	(7)	11
17	Teemu Penninkangas		24/07/92	A	6	(5)	
26	Jesse Sarajärvi		20/05/95	M	1	(2)	
15	Željko Savić	SRB	18/03/88	D	33		1
7	Timo Tahvanainen		26/06/86	M	17	(9)	1

TPS Turku

1922 • Veritas Stadion (9,300) • fctps.fi
Major honours
*Finnish League (0) 1928, 1939, 1941, 1949, 1968,
1971, 1972, 1975; Finnish Cup (3) 1991, 1994, 2010*
Coach: Mika Laurikainen

2014

12/04	h	Honka	L	0-1	
19/04	a	VPS	L	0-1	
23/04	h	Mariehamn	L	0-1	
26/04	a	HJK	W	1-0	Brown
03/05	h	RoPS	L	0-2	
08/05	a	MYPA	L	1-4	Brown
12/05	h	SJK	W	2-0	Jovanovic, Brown
17/05	a	Jaro	L	0-2	
23/05	a	Lahti	L	0-2	
26/05	h	KuPS	L	0-3	
04/06	a	Lahti	L	0-2	
08/06	a	Inter	L	1-2	Tamminen
11/06	h	Mariehamn	W	3-1	Tamminen 2, Lehtonen
18/06	h	KuPS	D	1-1	Brechtel (p)
23/06	a	HJK	L	0-5	
27/06	h	SJK	L	0-1	
02/07	a	Inter	L	2-3	S Peltola, De John
07/07	h	MYPA	W	3-0	Hyyrynen, Lehtonen, Tamminen
12/07	a	RoPS	L	0-3	
20/07	h	VPS	D	0-0	
27/07	a	Honka	D	1-1	Hyyrynen
03/08	a	Jaro	D	2-2	Rähmönen 2
10/08	a	Jaro	D	1-1	Osvold
13/08	h	Honka	W	2-1	Hyyrynen 2
25/08	a	VPS	D	0-0	
31/08	h	RoPS	W	4-2	Tamminen, Osvold 2 (1p), Tenho
14/09	a	MYPA	L	1-2	Ääritalo
17/09	h	Inter	L	1-6	Ääritalo
21/09	a	SJK	L	1-2	Rähmönen
28/09	h	HJK	L	1-4	Lomski
05/10	a	KuPS	L	0-1	
18/10	h	Lahti	L	0-1	
25/10	a	Mariehamn	L	1-3	Lehtonen

No	Name	Nat	DoB	Pos	Aps	(s)	Gls
8	Hushyar Aftab		01/07/93	M		(1)	
21	Thomas Agyiri	GHA	28/04/94	M	9	(5)	
28	Felipe Aspegren		12/02/94	D	7	(3)	
11	Mika Ääritalo		25/07/83	A	6		2
22	Niklas Blomqvist		08/02/96	M	6	(3)	
4	Jesper Brechtel		21/01/94	M	19	(3)	1
10	Wayne Brown	ENG	06/08/88	M	11		3
5	Alex De John	USA	10/05/91	D	28		1
21	Niklas Friberg		14/03/96	D	7	(4)	
6	Matej Hradecky		17/04/95	M	24	(3)	
18	Mikko Hyyrynen		01/11/77	A	27	(2)	4
23	Igor Jovanovic	GER	02/12/88	D	13		1
33	Kevin Kauber	EST	23/03/95	A		(2)	
31	Juri Kinnunen		09/03/90	D	11		
9	Juho Lehtonen		03/08/92	A	15	(14)	3
12	Jukka Lehtovaara		15/03/88	G	27		
27	Patrik Lomski		03/02/89	M	16	(6)	1
17	Matias Louanto		22/12/95	M		(1)	
8	Leroy Maluka	RSA	22/12/85	M	4	(4)	
25	Santeri Mäkinen		09/04/92	M		(5)	
2	Aleksi Ojanperä		16/02/96	D		(1)	
24	Dennis Okaru	NGA	02/03/91	A		(7)	
29	Joachim Osvold	NOR	23/09/94	A	11		3
16	Santeri Peltola		02/10/93	M	21	(9)	1
36	Waltteri Peltola		11/04/96	D		(1)	
14	Ville Rannikko		24/01/94	D	4	(4)	
7	Sami Rähmönen		19/04/87	M	25	(1)	3
20	Riku Sjöroos		10/03/95	M		(1)	
3	Ville-Valtteri Starck		03/02/95	D	14	(4)	
19	Eero Tamminen		19/05/95	M	20	(5)	5
15	Miro Tenho		02/04/95	D	30		1
8	Charlie Trafford	CAN	24/05/92	M	2	(3)	
1	Jani Tuomala		03/02/77	G		(1)	
30	Arnold Uschanoff		12/05/95	G	6		

VPS Vaasa

1924 • Hietalahden jalkapallostadion (4,600)
• vepsu.fi
Major honours
Finnish League (2) 1945, 1948
Coach: Olli Huttunen

2014

06/04	a	RoPS	W	2-0	Koskimaa, Strandvall
13/04	a	Mariehamn	W	3-0	(w/o; original result 0-1)
19/04	h	TPS	W	1-0	Linjala
23/04	a	MYPA	D	1-1	Simpson
04/05	a	HJK	L	0-2	
08/05	a	Jaro	L	0-1	
12/05	h	KuPS	D	1-1	Seabrook
17/05	a	Inter	D	0-0	
23/05	h	RoPS	W	2-0	Simpson, Lahti
26/05	h	Honka	W	3-0	Parikka, Koskimaa, Strandvall
08/06	a	Lahti	D	1-1	Simpson
11/06	h	KuPS	L	0-3	
14/06	a	HJK	L	0-3	
18/06	h	SJK	L	0-1	
23/06	a	Inter	L	0-3	
27/06	h	MYPA	W	4-0	og 2 (Aho 2), Honkaniemi, Stewart
06/07	a	Jaro	W	2-1	Kula, Seabrook
13/07	h	Honka	W	3-1	Nganbe Nganbe, Seabrook, Björk
20/07	a	TPS	D	0-0	
27/07	h	Mariehamn	L	1-2	Strandvall
03/08	a	Lahti	L	1-3	Seabrook
10/08	a	Lahti	L	1-4	Nganbe Nganbe
13/08	a	Mariehamn	L	0-1	
17/08	h	SJK	L	0-1	
25/08	h	TPS	D	0-0	
31/08	a	Honka	W	2-1	Morrissey, Stewart
14/09	a	Jaro	D	3-3	Stewart, Strandvall, Seabrook
17/09	h	RoPS	D	2-0	Morrissey, Kula
21/09	a	MYPA	D	0-0	
28/09	h	Inter	W	1-0	Stewart
05/10	a	SJK	W	3-0	Stewart, Morrissey, Seabrook
19/10	h	HJK	D	1-1	Strandvall
25/10	a	KuPS	W	1-0	Strandvall

No	Name	Nat	DoB	Pos	Aps	(s)	Gls
21	Andrew Barsalona	CAN	03/08/90	M	2		
10	Tony Björk		25/10/83	M	19	(12)	1
25	Jordaan Brown	ENG	13/03/92	D	5	(1)	
18	Anthony Dafaa	KEN	26/06/88	M	26	(2)	
4	Jesper Engström		24/04/92	M	31		
12	Karl-Filip Eriksson		16/02/94	G	2	(1)	
6	Cheyne Fowler	RSA	08/03/82	M	8	(6)	
1	Janne Henriksson		05/08/81	G	14	(1)	
16	Teemu Honkaniemi		20/01/91	D	28		1
3	Ville Koskimaa		21/05/83	D	32		2
15	Thomas Kula		24/05/91	M	28	(1)	2
2	Timi Lahti		28/06/90	D	17	(1)	1
20	Lasse Linjala		15/08/87	A	10	(7)	1
26	Steven Morrissey	JAM	25/07/86	A	11	(5)	3
7	Jean Fridolin Nganbe Nganbe	CMR	11/05/88	A	16	(10)	2
23	Miika Niemi		04/03/94	D	1	(8)	
9	Jarno Parikka		21/07/86	A	8	(3)	1
19	Jordan Seabrook	USA	27/06/87	A	24	(8)	6
32	Henri Sillanpää		04/06/79	G	17		
14	Keithy Simpson	JAM	19/04/90	D	21	(2)	3
39	Cornelius Stewart	VIN	07/10/89	A	13	(15)	5
8	Sebastian Strandvall		16/09/86	M	30	(1)	6

 **FINLAND**

Top goalscorers

14	Jonas Emet (Jaro)
	Luis Solignac (Mariehamn)
13	Rafael (Lahti)
11	Demba Savage (HJK)
	Diego Assis (Mariehamn)
	Petteri Forsell (Mariehamn)
	Akseli Pelvas (SJK)
9	Roni Porokara (Honka/HJK)
	Irakli Sirbiladze (Inter)
	Shahdon Winchester (Jaro)
	Ats Purje (KuPS)
	Aleksandr Kokko (RoPS)

Promoted clubs

HIFK Helsinki

1897 • Töölön Pallokenttä (3,000) •
hifkfotboll.fi
Major honours
*Finnish League (7) 1930, 1931, 1933, 1937, 1947,
1959, 1961*
Coach: Jani Honkavaara

FC KTP Kotka

1927 • Arto Tolsa Areena (4,230) • fcktp.fi
Major honours
*Finnish League (2) 1951, 1952; Finnish Cup (4)
1958, 1961, 1967, 1980*
Coach: Sami Ristilä

FC Ilves Tampere

1931 • Tammelan stadion (5,000) •
ilvesedustus.com
Major honours
Finnish League (1) 1983; Finnish Cup (2) 1979, 1990
Coach: Mika Malinen

Second level final table 2014

		Pld	W	D	L	F	A	Pts
1	HIFK Helsinki	27	15	5	7	63	30	50
2	FC KTP Kotka	27	15	5	7	57	33	50
3	Ilves Tampere	27	14	5	8	45	29	47
4	AC Oulu	27	13	8	6	46	32	47
5	Valkeakosken Haka	27	13	7	7	55	32	46
6	PK-35 Vantaa	27	12	10	5	40	28	46
7	JJK Jyväskylä	27	11	5	11	40	46	38
8	FC Jazz Pori	27	6	7	14	31	48	25
9	JIPPO Joensuu	27	5	5	17	19	56	20
10	FC Viikingit	27	1	3	23	19	81	6

*NB FC KTP Kotka and Ilves Tampere were
subsequently invited to Veikkausliiga 2015.*

DOMESTIC CUP

Suomen Cup 2014

FOURTH ROUND

(08/03/14)
Peltirumpu 1-2 Atlantis

(12/03/14)
KäPa 1-2 Lahti *(aet)*
Nekalan Pallo 0-3 RoPS

(15/03/14)
ÅIFK 1-4 Ilves
Hämeenlinna 2-1 Jaro
HJK Töölö 3-0 Gnistan Ogeli
JäPS 1-0 KTP
PS Kemi 3-1 AC Kajaani
Kontu 0-8 HIFK
Sudet 1-2 SiPS
TPV 3-1 P-Iirot
VIFK 3-2 FC Jazz *(aet)*

(16/03/14)
LeKi 0-2 JBK
NJS 1-0 FC Viikkarit

(19/03/14)
BK-46 3-3 Viikingit *(aet; 7-6 on pens)*
EsPa 0-4 JJK
Kiffen 1-2 GrIFK *(aet)*
Klubi 04 3-4 Haka *(aet)*
AC Oulu 0-4 TPS

(22/03/14)
Futura 0-0 EIF *(aet; 4-2 on pens)*

FIFTH ROUND

(22/03/14)
Ilves 0-3 RoPS

(23/03/14)
VIFK 0-2 Inter

(27/03/14)
NJS 0-6 Lahti

(28/03/14)
HIFK 7-1 Futura

(29/03/14)
Hämeenlinna 3-2 TPV *(aet)*
JBK 1-3 Honka

(30/03/14)
GrIFK 0-2 MYPA

(01/04/14)
JäPS 1-3 JJK

(02/04/14)
PS Kemi 1-1 TPS *(aet; 3-4 on pens)*

(03/04/14)
Atlantis 2-0 BK-46

(04/04/14)
HJK Töölö 0-8 KuPS

(05/04/14)
SiPS 0-5 Haka

SIXTH ROUND

(15/04/14)
HIFK 0-1 SJK *(aet)*

(16/04/14)
Hämeenlinna 2-4 Mariehamn
HJK 2-0 RoPS
Honka 0-3 KuPS
Inter 3-0 MYPA
JJK 1-0 TPS
VPS 0-1 Lahti *(aet)*

(17/04/14)
Atlantis 1-4 Haka

QUARTER-FINALS

(30/04/14)
Haka 0-3 HJK *(Konan 58, Lod 75, Alho 88)*
KuPS 1-2 Inter *(Markić 72; Hämäläinen 10,
Sirbiladze 50)*
Mariehamn 2-0 JJK *(Sid 30, Bernardo 68)*
SJK 0-1 Lahti *(Ngueukam 44p))*

SEMI-FINALS

(16/08/14)
Lahti 1-2 Inter *(Ngueukam 78; Hämäläinen 45+1,
Sirbiladze 97) (aet)*
Mariehamn 1-2 HJK *(Solignac 70; Baah 29,
Kandji 51)*

FINAL

(01/11/14)
Sonera Stadium, Helsinki
HJK HELSINKI 0
FC INTER TURKU 0
(aet; 5-3 on pens)
Referee: *Nevalainen*
HJK: *Doblas, Sorsa, Heikkinen, Baah, Lampi,
Tainio (Alho 95), Annan, Lod (Perovuo 106), Zeneli
(Väyrynen 91), Kandji, Savage*
INTER: *Bahne, Aho, Hämäläinen, Lindström,
Salminen (Duah 70), Nyman, Lehtonen, Ojala,
Gruborovics, Onovo (Paajanen 104), Sirbiladze*

HJK's penalty shoot-out win over Inter in the Finnish Cup final completed the club's fourth domestic double

FRANCE
Fédération Française de Football (FFF)

Address	87 boulevard de Grenelle FR-75738 Paris, Cedex 15	**President**	Noël Le Graët
		Chief executive	Florence Hardouin
Tel	+33 1 4431 7300	**Media officer**	Yann Perrin
Fax	+33 1 4431 7373	**Year of formation**	1919
E-mail	competitions. internationales@fff.fr	**National stadium**	Stade de France, Saint-Denis (81,338)
Website	fff.fr		

LIGUE 1 CLUBS

1. SC Bastia
2. FC Girondins de Bordeaux
3. SM Caen
4. Évian Thonon Gaillard FC
5. EA Guingamp
6. RC Lens
7. LOSC Lille
8. FC Lorient
9. Olympique Lyonnais
10. Olympique de Marseille
11. FC Metz
12. AS Monaco FC
13. Montpellier Hérault SC
14. FC Nantes
15. OGC Nice
16. Paris Saint-Germain
17. Stade de Reims
18. Stade Rennais FC
19. AS Saint-Étienne
20. Toulouse FC

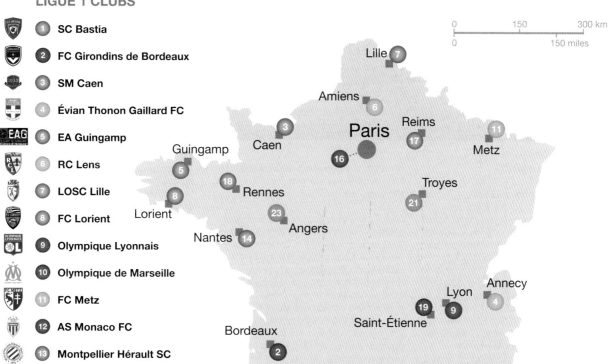

PROMOTED CLUBS

 21. ES Troyes AC

 22. GFC Ajaccio

 23. Angers SCO

KEY:

- – UEFA Champions League
- – UEFA Europa League
- – Promoted
- – Relegated

All-conquering Paris make history

Kings of France for the third season running, Paris Saint-Germain did not limit themselves to retaining the Ligue 1 title. They also won every other domestic competition they entered – the pre-season Champions Trophy, the League Cup and, with a 1-0 win in the final against Ligue 2 opponents AJ Auxerre, the Coupe de France.

There would be no big breakthrough in Europe, however, for Laurent Blanc's side as they bowed to the might of FC Barcelona in the UEFA Champions League quarter-finals. AS Monaco FC also reached that stage of the competition while taking third place in Ligue 1 behind surprise runners-up Olympique Lyonnais.

| Clean sweep of domestic trophies for Blanc's men | Quarter-final curse strikes again in Europe | Mixed results for Les Bleus in EURO countdown |

Domestic league

Comfortable winners of Ligue 1 in Blanc's first season at the Parc des Princes, Paris were pressed much harder for the title in his second. They spent the majority of the campaign as the hunters rather than the hunted, with their arch-rivals from the south, Olympique de Marseille, leading the championship race for most of the autumn before Lyon took command after Christmas. It was not until the end of March that Paris went top of the table for the first time. Unlike their two predecessors in pole position, however, they had the strength in depth and durability to stay there. Victories in each of their last nine matches catapulted the defending champions out of reach, enabling them to become the fourth club – after AS Saint-Étienne, Marseille and Lyon – to complete a hat-trick of French league titles.

The final table of a 38-match season never lies, but Paris's eight-point victory margin was a touch flattering. It certainly failed to tell the full story of a campaign that for the most part was one of frustration for the PSG fans, with the talismanic Zlatan Ibrahimović missing large chunks of it, either through injury or suspension. Although Blanc's team did not lose until mid-December, when they went down 1-0 at EA Guingamp, six

draws in their opening nine matches, including two at home against Lyon and Monaco, left them off the pace.

Given the club's superior resources, it seemed only a matter of time before PSG would work their way to the top of the Ligue 1 standings, but despite a good run in October and November, they could not dislodge Marseille. Then, after a mid-season mini-crisis in which they picked up just one point from three games and Blanc's position was called into question, they were forced to regroup and go again as Lyon suddenly came to the fore. Again, they kept knocking, but the door to the summit would not open.

Finally, however, in the closing weeks of the campaign, they made it through. The catalyst to their powerful title-winning burst was a dramatic 3-2 win in the Stade Vélodrome, where they twice came from behind to take all three points and effectively eliminate hosts Marseille from the running. Ibrahimović missed the next three games with a ban imposed for some ill-advised and over-the-top comments he made after a 3-2 defeat at FC Girondins de Bordeaux, but as he sat idly in the stands, his strike partner Edinson Cavani found the best form of his two seasons in Paris. The expensively-recruited Uruguayan went on to score ten goals in

the last seven matches, ending the campaign with 18 – just one fewer than his Swedish team-mate. The only fixture during that sequence in which Cavani did not score was the 2-1 win at Montpellier Hérault SC that clinched the title with a game to spare.

Blanc's championship-winning squad was not far removed from that of the previous season, with Brazilian defender David Luiz the only significant newcomer. He and his compatriot Thiago Silva formed a solid central defensive alliance, with another Brazilian, Maxwell, also enjoying a fine season at left-back. The main men in midfield were Marco Verratti, for his terrier-like application and ball-winning, and Javier Pastore, for his skill and creativity, while Ibrahimović and Cavani, though seldom in harmony as a pair, banged in the goals when they were needed.

If Blanc's trophy haul made him the obvious winner of France's coach of the season award, he had strong competition from Lyon's Hubert Fournier. Brought in from Stade de Reims to replace Rémi Garde, the ex-Dogues defender got off a to a poor start, but in his own quiet way he transformed a young team full of academy graduates into a side that not only challenged Paris for the title but pushed them virtually all the way to the

finish. Lyon lost only once in 22 league matches from early September to late February, stringing together seven successive victories around the turn of the year to move into first place. The player who did most to take them there was forward Alexandre Lacazette, who struck 27 goals in his 33 starts to win the Ligue 1 golden boot. Many of those were set up by his young accomplice, Nabil Fekir, who also scored 13 times himself.

Lyon's second place returned them to the UEFA Champions League after a four-year absence, but there would be no place at Europe's top table for Marseille, who followed a fabulous autumn, in which they posted eight successive victories, with a lousy spring. High-profile new coach Marcelo Bielsa was praised and pilloried in equal measure for his maverick ways by the French media as the season unfolded, but ultimately fourth place was a grave disappointment for a team that had promised so much more. There were further post-season blues for the OM fans when the team's two most productive players, André-Pierre Gignac and Dimitri Payet, both left for pastures new.

Marseille won their last four matches, including the Cote d'Azur derby against Monaco, but it was not enough to prevent their south coast rivals from pipping them to the UEFA Champions League qualifying slot. The previous season's runners-up had lost Colombian stars James Rodríguez and Radamel Falcao as previously free-spending Russian owner Dmitry Rybolovlev moved towards a policy of austerity, but under new coach Leonardo Jardim – the replacement for Claudio Ranieri – the remodelled Monaco defied the sceptics, lifting themselves all the way from the relegation zone – where they spent the early weeks of the campaign – to third place. The key to their success was a formidable defensive unit, underpinned by Croatian goalkeeper Danijel Subašić, which kept 20 clean sheets, but they were full of enterprise going forward too, with young guns Bernardo Silva, Anthony Martial and Yannick Ferreira Carrasco all lighting up the league, especially in the final third of the season.

Marseille were accompanied into the UEFA Europa League by St-Étienne and Bordeaux, who finished fifth and sixth respectively. Les Verts continued to progress under coach Christophe Galtier, finishing in the top five and qualifying for Europe for the third season running. Their star performer was Ivory Coast midfielder Max-Alain Gradel, who scored 17 goals – a third of their total – while Bordeaux, with ex-France right-back Willy Sagnol at the controls, owed their European return to a happy habit of winning matches by the odd goal, 15 of their 17 victories coming by that narrowest of margins.

At the bottom there were immediate returns to Ligue 2 for RC Lens and FC Metz. The other newly-promoted club, SM Caen, looked like joining them before they suddenly sprang to life in January, winning six matches out of seven – and drawing the other in Paris – to leap clear. The Normandy club closed their campaign with a 3-2 win over Évian Thonon Gaillard FC, the third team to go down, while Ligue 2 was dominated by ES Troyes AC, who went up in the company of Angers SCO and GFC Ajaccio, the low-budget Corsican club that had never previously rubbed shoulders with French football's elite.

Domestic cups

Paris's one-two in the domestic knockout competitions began with the retention of the Coupe de la Ligue. They reached the final with hard-fought 1-0 victories at St-Étienne and LOSC Lille, but they were never fully tested in the final by an SC Bastia side that had caused a big shock in the semis by knocking out Monaco in a penalty shoot-out but were reduced to ten men early on at the Stade de France by Sébastien Squillaci's 20th-minute red card. Ibrahimović scored twice in the first half and Cavani twice in the second as the holders cruised to victory, claiming the trophy for a record sixth time.

PSG's ninth Coupe de France victory – one shy of Marseille's record – was achieved in less convincing fashion, a powerful Cavani header off the underside of the bar from Gregory van der Wiel's cross proving sufficient to defeat mid-table Ligue 2 side Auxerre at the Stade de France. It was only the second goal conceded in the competition by the Burgundy club during a run of eight matches that featured two penalty shoot-out successes and a semi-final victory against holders Guingamp. PSG's path to the final was more demanding as they

Javier Pastore (second from left) scores for Paris Saint-Germain in a 3-1 victory at Nice

Raphaël Varane leaps high to score for France against Brazil

were drawn against Ligue 1 opposition in every round, eliminating Montpellier, Bordeaux, FC Nantes, Monaco and – thanks to a semi-final hat-trick from Ibrahimović – St-Étienne.

Europe

PSG's Qatari owners are eager for the club to rule Europe as well as France, but there was no progress on that front in 2014/15 as they fell at the quarter-final stage of the UEFA Champions League for the third successive season. As in 2012/13, it was Barcelona who barred their route, the eventual champions ending Paris's 33-game unbeaten home record in Europe on the way to a 5-1 aggregate victory. Blanc's men had already beaten Barça 3-2 at home, minus the injured Ibrahimović, in the group stage, but when the Swede was missing again, through suspension, in

the spring, Luis Enrique's side were simply too good for the French champions.

The previous round had provided a double boost to Ligue 1's international profile as Paris exacted revenge on their 2013/14 quarter-final conquerors, Chelsea FC, with a brilliant ten-man display at Stamford Bridge – after Ibrahimović's early sending-off – to go through after extra time on away goals, while Monaco also profited from that rule to knock out another London club, Arsenal FC. A shock 3-1 away win paved the way to the quarter-finals for Jardim's side, who would only go out to Juventus 1-0 on aggregate after conceding a penalty in Turin. A last-eight placing was an impressive achievement for a club making their first appearance in European competition for nine years.

Not for the first time, however, the UEFA Europa League provided little cheer for French clubs. Lyon, the only Ligue 1 side to have reached the quarter-finals of the competition, in 2013/14, fell unexpectedly in the play-offs to FC Astra Giurgiu, while St-Étienne and LOSC both crashed out at the group stage without a win between them. Guingamp were the only knockout phase survivors, thanks chiefly to the goalscoring exploits of Claudio Beauvue, but Jocelyn Gourvennec's side advanced no further after failing to protect a 2-1 first-leg lead against FC Dynamo Kyiv.

National team

As the hosts of UEFA EURO 2016, France had no competitive action during the 2014/15 season, but Didier Deschamps' side did play ten games, including six centralised friendlies against the teams in European Qualifiers Group I. Preparations for the main event looked to be going well until June, when Les Bleus lost twice in a week, 4-3 at home to Belgium and 1-0 away to Albania. Their only other defeat of the season had come in March when they were beaten 3-1 at the Stade de France by Brazil.

On the positive side, the season of planning and experimentation brought home wins against Spain, Portugal and Sweden plus further opportunities for the team's younger element to gain valuable international experience. Real Madrid CF defender Raphaël Varane certainly got plenty, starting and finishing all ten matches, while newcomers such as Lacazette, Fekir and Monaco pair Layvin Kurzawa and Geoffrey Kondogbia were all given the chance to show what they were made of at the highest level.

As the team counted down to UEFA EURO 2016, so did the country, with all of the tournament's ten stadiums being made ready, either through refurbishment or – in the case of Bordeaux, Lille, Lyon and Nice – from scratch. France's three group games will be played in Saint-Denis, Marseille and Lille, with a trip to Lyon next up should they win Group A. Having triumphed at major tournaments on home soil in 1984 and 1998, Les Bleus will undoubtedly be the team to beat as 23 nations arrive in France for the biggest-ever UEFA European Championship finals next summer.

DOMESTIC SEASON AT A GLANCE

Ligue 1 2014/15 final table

		Pld	Home					Away					Total					Pts
			W	D	L	F	A	W	D	L	F	A	W	D	L	F	A	
1	**Paris Saint-Germain**	**38**	**15**	**4**	**0**	**52**	**14**	**9**	**7**	**3**	**31**	**22**	**24**	**11**	**3**	**83**	**36**	**83**
2	Olympique Lyonnais	38	14	3	2	40	11	8	6	5	32	22	22	9	7	72	33	75
3	AS Monaco FC	38	8	9	2	23	10	12	2	5	28	16	20	11	7	51	26	71
4	Olympique de Marseille	38	13	2	4	40	22	8	4	7	36	20	21	6	11	76	42	69
5	AS Saint-Étienne	38	12	5	2	32	11	7	7	5	19	19	19	12	7	51	30	69
6	FC Girondins de Bordeaux	38	12	5	2	31	23	5	7	7	16	21	17	12	9	47	44	63
7	Montpellier Hérault SC	38	11	2	6	30	21	5	6	8	16	18	16	8	14	46	39	56
8	LOSC Lille	38	11	5	3	26	12	5	3	11	17	30	16	8	14	43	42	56
9	Stade Rennais FC	38	8	5	6	22	22	5	6	8	13	20	13	11	14	35	42	50
10	EA Guingamp	38	9	1	9	23	25	6	3	10	18	30	15	4	19	41	55	49
11	OGC Nice	38	6	6	7	21	24	7	3	9	23	29	13	9	16	44	53	48
12	SC Bastia	38	8	7	4	24	18	4	4	11	13	28	12	11	15	37	46	47
13	SM Caen	38	7	3	9	26	25	5	7	7	28	30	12	10	16	54	55	46
14	FC Nantes	38	7	7	5	17	17	4	5	10	12	23	11	12	15	29	40	45
15	Stade de Reims	38	8	3	8	24	29	4	5	10	23	37	12	8	18	47	66	44
16	FC Lorient	38	6	5	8	17	17	6	2	11	27	33	12	7	19	44	50	43
17	Toulouse FC	38	8	6	5	28	29	4	0	15	15	35	12	6	20	43	64	42
18	Évian Thonon Gaillard FC	38	7	2	10	20	25	4	2	13	21	37	11	4	23	41	62	37
19	FC Metz	38	6	4	9	26	32	1	5	13	5	29	7	9	22	31	61	30
20	RC Lens	38	5	4	10	14	24	2	4	13	18	37	7	8	23	32	61	29

European qualification 2015/16

Champion/Cup winner: Paris Saint-Germain (group stage)
Olympique Lyonnais (group stage)
AS Monaco FC (play-offs)

Olympique de Marseille (group stage)
AS Saint-Étienne (third qualifying round)
FC Girondins de Bordeaux (third qualifying round)

Top scorer	Alexandre Lacazette (Lyon), 27 goals
Relegated clubs	RC Lens, FC Metz, Évian Thonon Gaillard FC
Promoted clubs	ES Troyes AC, GFC Ajaccio, Angers SCO
French Cup final	Paris Saint-Germain 1-0 AJ Auxerre
League Cup final	Paris Saint-Germain 4-0 SC Bastia

Team of the season
(4-3-3)

Coach: Blanc (Paris)

Player of the season

Alexandre Lacazette
(Olympique Lyonnais)

Zlatan Ibrahimović was denied a third successive Ligue 1 golden boot as Lacazette struck 27 goals to finish eight clear of the Swede – and six ahead of runner-up André-Pierre Gignac – at the top of the standings. It was a magnificent effort from the 24-year-old striker – the highest tally ever registered by a Lyon player in a top-flight campaign – and almost helped his club to a first league title in seven years. His season was further embellished by a first goal for France and the official Ligue 1 player of the year award.

Newcomer of the season

Nabil Fekir
(Olympique Lyonnais)

Didier Deschamps was delighted when Fekir opted to pursue his international career with France rather than Algeria, for the 22-year-old was one of Ligue 1's leading attractions in 2014/15. Barely used by previous Lyon boss Rémi Garde, the young winger flourished under Hubert Fournier, contributing to the club's title challenge with 13 goals and nine assists. A dazzling dribbler in the mould of – though clearly not in the class of – Lionel Messi, he was a worthy recipient of the Ligue 1 young player of the year prize.

FRANCE

NATIONAL TEAM

International honours
FIFA World Cup (1) 1998
UEFA European Championship (2) 1984, 2000
FIFA Confederations Cup (2) 2001, 2003

International tournament appearances
FIFA World Cup (13) 1930, 1938 (2nd round), 1954, 1958 (3rd), 1966, 1978, 1982 (4th), 1986 (3rd), 1998 (Winners), 2002, 2006 (runners-up), 2010, 2014 (qtr-finals)
UEFA European Championship (8) 1960 (4th), 1984 (Winners), 1992, 1996 (semi-finals), 2000 (Winners), 2004 (qtr-finals), 2008, 2012 (qtr-finals)

Top five all-time caps
Lilian Thuram (142); Thierry Henry (123); Marcel Desailly (116); Zinédine Zidane (108); Patrick Vieira (107)

Top five all-time goals
Thierry Henry (51); Michel Platini (41); David Trezeguet (34); Zinédine Zidane (31); Just Fontaine & Jean-Pierre Papin (30)

Results 2014/15

04/09/14	Spain	H	Saint-Denis	W	1-0	*Rémy (74)*
07/09/14	Serbia	A	Belgrade	D	1-1	*Pogba (13)*
11/10/14	Portugal	H	Saint-Denis	W	2-1	*Benzema (3), Pogba (69)*
14/10/14	Armenia	A	Yerevan	W	3-0	*Rémy (7), Gignac (55p), Griezmann (83)*
14/11/14	Albania	H	Rennes	D	1-1	*Griezmann (73)*
18/11/14	Sweden	H	Marseille	W	1-0	*Varane (83)*
26/03/15	Brazil	H	Saint-Denis	L	1-3	*Varane (21)*
29/03/15	Denmark	H	Saint-Etienne	W	2-0	*Lacazette (14), Giroud (38)*
07/06/15	Belgium	H	Saint-Denis	L	3-4	*Valbuena (53p), Fekir (89), Payet (90+1)*
13/06/15	Albania	A	Elbasan	L	0-1	

Appearances 2014/15

Coach: Didier Deschamps	15/10/68		Esp	Srb	Por	Arm	Alb	Swe	Bra	Den	Bel	Alb	Caps	Goals
Hugo Lloris	26/12/86	Tottenham (ENG)	G	G			G				G	G	67	-
Mathieu Debuchy	28/07/85	Arsenal (ENG)	D										26	2
Raphaël Varane	25/04/93	Real Madrid (ESP)	D	D	D	D	D	D	D	D	D	D	21	2
Mamadou Sakho	13/02/90	Liverpool (ENG)	D						D			D	26	2
Patrice Evra	15/05/81	Juventus (ITA)	D68		D				D			D	66	-
Blaise Matuidi	09/04/87	Paris	M68	s74	M	M46		M	M84	s71	M		35	4
Paul Pogba	15/03/93	Juventus (ITA)	M	M74	M	s46	M	M	M74		M	s46	23	5
Moussa Sissoko	16/08/89	Newcastle (ENG)	M78	M82	s71	M60	M70	s61					29	1
Mathieu Valbuena	28/09/84	Dinamo Moskva (RUS)	M75	s82	A58	s73	M85	M68	A82	s83	A73	s59	48	7
Antoine Griezmann	21/03/91	Atlético (ESP)	M59		A84	s60	s59	M	A74	A60	A46	A59	18	5
Karim Benzema	19/12/87	Real Madrid (ESP)	A	s60	A90	s87	A	s68	A				78	25
Loïc Rémy	02/01/87	Chelsea (ENG)	s59	A60		M73							30	7
Yohan Cabaye	14/01/86	Paris	s68	M	M71		M59				M46		39	3
Lucas Digne	20/07/93	Paris	s68	D		D	D70	s78					8	-
Rémy Cabella	08/03/90	Newcastle (ENG)	s75	M60		s60							4	-
Morgan Schneiderlin	08/11/89	Southampton (ENG)	s78	M	s84	M	s80		M	M82			9	-
Bacary Sagna	14/02/83	Man. City (ENG)		D	D			D	D	s90	D	s71	49	-
Jérémy Mathieu	29/10/83	Barcelona (ESP)		D	D								4	-
Alexandre Lacazette	28/05/91	Lyon		s60			A69	s68		A71	s46	A	8	1
Steve Mandanda	28/03/88	Marseille			G	G		G	G				20	-
Eliaquim Mangala	13/02/91	Man. City (ENG)			D				D				5	-
Dimitri Payet	29/03/87	Marseille			s58	M60	s85	M61	s82	M83	s46	M46	15	1
André-Pierre Gignac	05/12/85	Marseille			s90	A87	s69	A68					21	5
Christophe Jallet	31/10/83	Lyon				D	D			D90		D71	9	1
Mapou Yanga-Mbiwa	15/05/89	Roma (ITA)					D						4	-
Layvin Kurzawa	04/09/92	Monaco					s70	D78					2	-
Josuha Guilavogui	19/09/90	Wolfsburg (GER)						M86		s60			7	-
Maxime Gonalons	10/03/89	Lyon						s86			M59		8	-
Geoffrey Kondogbia	15/02/93	Monaco							s74	M60		M	4	-
Nabil Fekir	18/07/93	Lyon							s74	s60	s73	s46	4	1
Olivier Giroud	30/09/86	Arsenal (ENG)							s84	A	A80	A46	39	10
Stéphane Ruffier	27/09/86	St-Étienne								G			3	-
Laurent Koscielny	10/09/85	Arsenal (ENG)								D	D		23	-
Benoît Trémoulinas	28/12/85	Sevilla (ESP)								D	D		4	-
Kurt Zouma	27/10/94	Chelsea (ENG)							s82				1	-
Paul-Georges Ntep	29/07/92	Rennes									s80	s59	2	-

Paris Saint-Germain

Group F
Match 1 - AFC Ajax (NED)
A 1-1 *Cavani (14)*
Sirigu, Marquinhos, Lucas (Lavezzi 81), Thiago Motta, Cavani, Ibrahimović, Matuidi, Maxwell, Van der Wiel, Verratti (Pastore 81), David Luiz. Coach: Laurent Blanc (FRA)

Match 2 - FC Barcelona (ESP)
H 3-2 *David Luiz (10), Verratti (26), Matuidi (54)*
Sirigu, Marquinhos, Lucas (Bahebeck 90+1), Thiago Motta, Cavani, Matuidi, Maxwell, Van der Wiel, Verratti (Cabaye 71), Pastore (Chantôme 86), David Luiz. Coach: Laurent Blanc (FRA)

Match 3 - APOEL FC (CYP)
A 1-0 *Cavani (87)*
Sirigu, Thiago Silva, Lucas (Chantôme 89), Thiago Motta, Cavani, Matuidi, Maxwell, Van der Wiel, Verratti (Bahebeck 70), Pastore (Cabaye 70), David Luiz. Coach: Laurent Blanc (FRA)

Match 4 - APOEL FC (CYP)
H 1-0 *Cavani (1)*
Sirigu, Thiago Silva, Lucas (Cabaye 86), Thiago Motta, Cavani, Matuidi, Maxwell, Lavezzi (Bahebeck 78), Van der Wiel, Pastore, David Luiz. Coach: Laurent Blanc (FRA)

Match 5 - AFC Ajax (NED)
H 3-1 *Cavani (33, 83), Ibrahimović (78)*
Sirigu, Marquinhos, Cavani, Ibrahimović (Digne 86), Matuidi, Maxwell, Lavezzi (Lucas 68), Van der Wiel, Rabiot (Chantôme 75), Pastore, David Luiz. Coach: Laurent Blanc (FRA)

Match 6 - FC Barcelona (ESP)
A 1-3 *Ibrahimović (15)*
Sirigu, Thiago Silva, Lucas, Thiago Motta, Cavani, Ibrahimović, Matuidi (Lavezzi 75), Maxwell, Van der Wiel, Verratti (Pastore 62), David Luiz. Coach: Laurent Blanc (FRA)

Round of 16 - Chelsea FC (ENG)
H 1-1 *Cavani (54)*
Sirigu, Thiago Silva, Marquinhos, Cavani, Ibrahimović, Matuidi, Maxwell, Lavezzi (Pastore 81), Van der Wiel, Verratti, David Luiz. Coach: Laurent Blanc (FRA)

A 2-2 *David Luiz (86), Thiago Silva (114)* (aet)
Sirigu, Thiago Silva, Marquinhos, Thiago Motta, Cavani, Ibrahimović, Matuidi (Rabiot 81), Maxwell, Verratti (Lavezzi 81), Pastore (Van der Wiel 118), David Luiz. Coach: Laurent Blanc (FRA)
Red card: Ibrahimović 31

Quarter-finals - FC Barcelona (ESP)
H 1-3 *Mathieu (82og)*
Sirigu, Thiago Silva (David Luiz 21), Cabaye, Marquinhos, Cavani, Matuidi, Maxwell, Lavezzi, Van der Wiel, Rabiot (Lucas 65), Pastore. Coach: Laurent Blanc (FRA)

A 0-2
Sirigu, Cabaye (Lucas 66), Marquinhos, Cavani (Lavezzi 80), Ibrahimović, Matuidi (Rabiot 80), Maxwell, Van der Wiel, Verratti, Pastore, David Luiz. Coach: Laurent Blanc (FRA)

AS Monaco FC

Group C
Match 1 - Bayer 04 Leverkusen (GER)
H 1-0 *João Moutinho (61)*
Subašić, Fabinho, Kurzawa, Ricardo Carvalho (Wallace 90+4), João Moutinho, Berbatov, Ocampos (Bernardo Silva 57), Ferreira Carrasco (Dirar 86), Kondogbia, Raggi, Toulalan. Coach: Leonardo Jardim (POR)

Match 2 - FC Zenit (RUS)
A 0-0
Subašić, Fabinho, Kurzawa, Ricardo Carvalho, Dirar, João Moutinho (Bakayoko 90+2), Berbatov (Ferreira Carrasco 52), Ocampos (Germain 80), Kondogbia, Raggi, Toulalan. Coach: Leonardo Jardim (POR)

Match 3 - SL Benfica (POR)
H 0-0
Subašić, Fabinho, Kurzawa, Ricardo Carvalho, Dirar, João Moutinho (Bernardo Silva 82), Berbatov (Martial 34), Ocampos (Ferreira Carrasco 62), Kondogbia, Raggi, Toulalan. Coach: Leonardo Jardim (POR)

Match 4 - SL Benfica (POR)
A 0-1
Subašić, Fabinho, Kurzawa, Ricardo Carvalho, João Moutinho, Ocampos (Dirar 63), Ferreira Carrasco (Martial 72), Kondogbia (Germain 86), Raggi, Toulalan. Coach: Leonardo Jardim (POR)

Match 5 - Bayer 04 Leverkusen (GER)
A 1-0 *Ocampos (72)*
Subašić, Abdennour, Ricardo Carvalho, Dirar (Fabinho 83), João Moutinho, Berbatov (L Traoré 90), Bakayoko, Ferreira Carrasco (Ocampos 70), Echijile, Raggi, Toulalan. Coach: Leonardo Jardim (POR)

Match 6 - FC Zenit (RUS)
H 2-0 *Abdennour (63), Fabinho (89)*
Subašić, Fabinho, Abdennour, Dirar (Bernardo Silva 90), João Moutinho, Berbatov (Martial 56), Wallace, Bakayoko, Ferreira Carrasco (Ocampos 90+2), Raggi, Toulalan. Coach: Leonardo Jardim (POR)

Round of 16 - Arsenal FC (ENG)
A 3-1 *Kondogbia (38), Berbatov (53), Ferreira Carrasco (90+4)*
Subašić, Fabinho, Abdennour, Dirar (Kurzawa 82), João Moutinho, Berbatov (Ferreira Carrasco 76), Wallace, Echijile, Kondogbia, Martial (Bernardo Silva 84), Touré. Coach: Leonardo Jardim (POR)

H 0-2
Subašić, Fabinho, Kurzawa, Abdennour, Dirar (Echijile 86), João Moutinho, Berbatov (Bernardo Silva 70), Wallace, Kondogbia, Martial (Ferreira Carrasco 60), Toulalan. Coach: Leonardo Jardim (POR)

Quarter-finals - Juventus (ITA)
A 0-1
Subašić, Fabinho, Kurzawa, Abdennour, Ricardo Carvalho, Dirar (Bernardo Silva 51), João Moutinho, Ferreira Carrasco, Kondogbia, Martial (Matheus Carvalho 87), Raggi (Berbatov 71). Coach: Leonardo Jardim (POR)

H 0-0
Subašić, Fabinho, Kurzawa, Abdennour, João Moutinho, Bernardo Silva, Ferreira Carrasco (Matheus Carvalho 87), Kondogbia, Martial (Germain 76), Raggi, Toulalan (Berbatov 46). Coach: Leonardo Jardim (POR)

LOSC Lille

Third qualifying round - Grasshopper Club Zürich (SUI)
A 2-0 *Corchia (29), Ryan Mendes (49)*
Elana, Corchia, Balmont, Gueye, Delaplace (Meïté 80), Rodelin (Sidibé 90+4), Kjær, Béria, Ryan Mendes (Roux 71), Souaré, Baša. Coach: René Girard (FRA)

H 1-1 *Balmont (19)*
Enyeama, Corchia, Balmont, Gueye, Rodelin, Meïté (Delaplace 56), Kjær, Béria, Origi (84), Ryan Mendes (Kalou 76), Souaré, Baša. Coach: René Girard (FRA)

Play-offs - FC Porto (POR)
H 0-1
Enyeama, Corchia, Balmont (Marcos Lopes 62), Gueye, Kalou (Roux 76), Kjær, Béria, Souaré, Mavuba, Baša, Origi (Ryan Mendes 71). Coach: René Girard (FRA)

A 0-2
Enyeama, Corchia (Marcos Lopes 71), Balmont, Gueye (Delaplace 77), Kjær, Béria, Rozehnal, Souaré, Mavuba, Roux (Ryan Mendes 67), Origi. Coach: René Girard (FRA)

Group H
Match 1 - FC Krasnodar (RUS)
H 1-1 *Kjær (63)*
Enyeama, Corchia, Balmont (Ryan Mendes 77), Gueye, Kjær, Marcos Lopes, Souaré, Mavuba (Delaplace 46), Baša, Roux (Frey 46), Origi. Coach: René Girard (FRA)

Match 2 - VfL Wolfsburg (GER)
A 1-1 *Origi (77p)*
Enyeama, Corchia, Balmont, Gueye, Kjær, Béria, Ryan Mendes (Roux 46), Rozehnal, Souaré (Sidibé 43), Baša, Origi (Rodelin 85). Coach: René Girard (FRA)

Match 3 - Everton FC (ENG)
H 0-0
Enyeama, Corchia, Balmont, Gueye, Rodelin (Ryan Mendes 73), Kjær, Béria, Souaré, Mavuba (Martin 86), Baša, Origi. Coach: René Girard (FRA)

Match 4 - Everton FC (ENG)
A 0 3
Enyeama, Corchia (Rodelin 75), Balmont, Gueye, Frey (Roux 63), Kjær, Ryan Mendes (Béria 64), Souaré, Mavuba, Baša, Origi. Coach: René Girard (FRA)

Match 5 - FC Krasnodar (RUS)
A 1-1 *Roux (79)*
Enyeama, Corchia, Balmont, Gueye, Delaplace (Mavuba 62), Martin (Rodelin 67), Frey (Ryan Mendes 80), Béria, Rozehnal, Baša, Roux. Coach: René Girard (FRA)

Match 6 - VfL Wolfsburg (GER)
H 0-3
Enyeama, Corchia (Rodelin 67), Balmont, Gueye (Meïté 83), Kjær, Sidibé, Ryan Mendes (Roux 67), Souaré, Mavuba, Baša, Origi. Coach: René Girard (FRA)

EA Guingamp

Group K
Match 1 - ACF Fiorentina (ITA)
A 0-3
Samassa, Angoua, Sankoh, Diallo, Lévêque, Beauvue, Mandanne (Douniama 71), Mathis, Marveaux (Yatabaré 52), Pied (Giresse 62), Kerbrat. Coach: Jocelyn Gourvennec (FRA)
Red card: Diallo 38
Match 2 - PAOK FC (GRE)
H 2-0 *Marveaux (47, 50)*
Lössl, Jacobsen, Lévêque, Schwartz (Mandanne 73), Sankharé, Beauvue, Sorbon, Mathis, Marveaux (Giresse 78), Pied (Yatabaré 54), Kerbrat. Coach: Jocelyn Gourvennec (FRA)
Match 3 - FC Dinamo Minsk (BLR)
A 0-0
Lössl, Jacobsen, Angoua, Sankharé (Diallo 80), Beauvue, Sorbon, Alioui, Mathis, Dos Santos, Marveaux (Mandanne 71), Yatabaré. Coach: Jocelyn Gourvennec (FRA)
Match 4 - FC Dinamo Minsk (BLR)
H 2-0 *Beauvue (44), Mandanne (86)*
Lössl, Angoua, Sankoh, Diallo (Pied 74), Beauvue, Mandanne, Mathis, Dos Santos (Baca 83), Marveaux (Sankharé 64), Yatabaré, Kerbrat. Coach: Jocelyn Gourvennec (FRA)
Match 5 - ACF Fiorentina (ITA)
H 1-2 *Beauvue (45p)*
Lössl, Jacobsen, Sankoh, Diallo, Beauvue, Sorbon, Mathis, Marveaux (Giresse 90+1), Pied (Schwartz 78), Yatabaré, Kerbrat. Coach: Jocelyn Gourvennec (FRA)
Match 6 - PAOK FC (GRE)
A 2-1 *Beauvue (7, 83)*
Lössl, Jacobsen, Angoua, Lévêque, Sankharé, Beauvue, Mandanne (Kerbrat 75), Sorbon, Mathis, Yatabaré (Pied 46), Giresse (Dos Santos 86). Coach: Jocelyn Gourvennec (FRA)

Round of 32 - FC Dynamo Kyiv (UKR)
H 2-1 *Beauvue (72), Diallo (75)*
Lössl, Jacobsen, Lévêque, Sankharé, Beauvue, Mandanne (Marveaux 46), Sorbon, Mathis (Diallo 73), Pied, Yatabaré (Giresse 68), Kerbrat. Coach: Jocelyn Gourvennec (FRA)
A 1-3 *Mandanne (66)*
Lössl, Jacobsen, Angoua, Lévêque, Sankharé, Beauvue, Mandanne, Sorbon, Mathis (Diallo 61), Pied, Giresse (Yatabaré 77). Coach: Jocelyn Gourvennec (FRA)

AS Saint-Étienne

Play-offs - Kardemir Karabükspor (TUR)
A 0-1
Ruffier, Clément, Gradel, Mevlüt Erdinç, Cohade, Lemoine (Corgnet 80), Brison, Hamouma (Monnet-Paquet 57), Perrin, Bayal Sall, Tabanou. Coach: Christophe Galtier (FRA)
H 1-0 *Monnet-Paquet (13)*
Ruffier, Théophile-Catherine, Clément, Gradel, Mevlüt Erdinç (Van Wolfswinkel 66), Lemoine, Hamouma (Cohade 77), Monnet-Paquet, Perrin (Pogba 46), Bayal Sall, Tabanou. Coach: Christophe Galtier (FRA)

Group F
Match 1 - Qarabağ FK (AZE)
A 0-0
Ruffier, Clément, Gradel, Corgnet (Saint-Maximin 50), Mevlüt Erdinç (Lemoine 75), Cohade (Diomandé 87), Pogba, Brison, Monnet-Paquet, Baysse, Bayal Sall. Coach: Christophe Galtier (FRA)
Match 2 - FC Dnipro Dnipropetrovsk (UKR)
H 0-0
Ruffier, Clément, Gradel, Cohade (Corgnet 75), Van Wolfswinkel, Lemoine, Monnet-Paquet, Perrin, Bayal Sall, Tabanou, Clerc. Coach: Christophe Galtier (FRA)
Match 3 - FC Internazionale Milano (ITA)
A 0-0
Ruffier, Théophile-Catherine, Clément, Van Wolfswinkel (Monnet-Paquet 65), Lemoine, Pogba (Baysse 78), Hamouma, Perrin, Bayal Sall, Tabanou, Diomandé (Cohade 85). Coach: Christophe Galtier (FRA)
Match 4 - FC Internazionale Milano (ITA)
H 1-1 *Bayal Sall (50)*
Ruffier, Théophile-Catherine, Clément, Gradel, Mevlüt Erdinç (Diomandé 56), Lemoine, Pogba, Hamouma (Van Wolfswinkel 68), Perrin, Bayal Sall, Tabanou. Coach: Christophe Galtier (FRA)
Match 5 - Qarabağ FK (AZE)
H 1-1 *Van Wolfswinkel (21)*
Ruffier, Théophile-Catherine, Clément, Gradel, Cohade (Mollo 68), Van Wolfswinkel (Pogba 90+1), Lemoine, Brison, Hamouma (Monnet-Paquet 63), Perrin, Bayal Sall. Coach: Christophe Galtier (FRA)
Match 6 - FC Dnipro Dnipropetrovsk (UKR)
A 0-1
Ruffier, Théophile-Catherine, Gradel, Mollo (Hamouma 60), Van Wolfswinkel, Lemoine, Pogba, Brison (Tabanou 83), Monnet-Paquet (Cohade 80), Perrin, Diomandé. Coach: Christophe Galtier (FRA)

Olympique Lyonnais

Third qualifying round - FK Mladá Boleslav (CZE)
A 4-1 *Yattara (9, 47), Gonalons (36), Umtiti (67)*
Lopes, B Koné (Bedimo 71), Biševac, Lacazette, Ferri, Jallet, Malbranque (Fekir 64), Yattara (Benzia 70), Gonalons, Umtiti, Mvuemba. Coach: Hubert Fournier (FRA)
H 2-1 *Lacazette (58), Njie (89)*
Lopes, Bedimo (B Koné 36), Lacazette (Njie 73), Jallet, Malbranque, Fekir, Gonalons, Rose (Ferri 53), Umtiti, Benzia. Coach: Hubert Fournier (FRA)

Play-offs - FC Astra Giurgiu (ROU)
H 1-2 *Malbranque (25)*
Lopes, B Koné, Lacazette, Ferri, Jallet, Malbranque (Grenier 76), Yattara (Ghezzal 81), Gonalons, Rose, Tolisso, Bahlouli (Mvuemba 68). Coach: Hubert Fournier (FRA)
Red card: Rose 78
A 1-0 *Ferri (23)*
Lopes, Zeffane (Bahlouli 73), B Koné, Lacazette, Ghezzal (Danic 65), Ferri, Jallet, Malbranque (Mvuemba 80), Njie, Gonalons, Tolisso. Coach: Hubert Fournier (FRA)

DOMESTIC LEAGUE CLUB-BY-CLUB

SC Bastia

1905 • Armand-Cesari (17,600) • sc-bastia.net

Major honours
French Cup (1) 1981
Coach: Claude Makélélé;
(03/11/14) (Ghislain Printant & Herve Sakli);
(27/11/14) Ghislain Printant

2014
09/08	h	Marseille	D	3-3	Maboulou 2, Tallo (p)
16/08	a	Paris	L	0-2	
23/08	h	Toulouse	W	1-0	Boudebouz (p)
31/08	a	Bordeaux	D	1-1	Tallo
13/09	h	Lens	D	1-1	Gillet
20/09	a	Metz	L	1-3	Ayité
24/09	h	Nantes	D	0-0	
27/09	a	LOSC	L	0-1	
04/10	h	Lorient	L	0-2	
18/10	a	Nice	W	1-0	Ayité
25/10	h	Monaco	L	1-3	Maboulou
01/11	a	Guingamp	L	0-1	
08/11	h	Montpellier	W	2-0	Tallo 2
22/11	h	Lyon	D	0-0	
29/11	a	Reims	L	1-2	Modesto
03/12	h	Évian	L	1-2	og (Abdallah)
06/12	a	St-Étienne	L	0-1	
13/12	a	Rennes	W	2-0	Boudebouz, Cahuzac
20/12	a	Caen	D	1-1	Kamano

2015
10/01	h	Paris	W	4-2	Boudebouz (p), Modesto, Palmieri 2
17/01	a	Toulouse	D	1-1	og (Ahamada)
24/01	h	Bordeaux	D	0-0	
31/01	a	Lens	D	1-1	Boudebouz (p)
07/02	h	Metz	W	2-0	Kamano, Boudebouz (p)
14/02	a	Nantes	W	2-0	Sio, Ayité
21/02	h	LOSC	W	2-1	Sio, Ayité
28/02	a	Lorient	L	0-2	
07/03	h	Nice	W	2-1	Gillet, Sio
13/03	a	Monaco	L	0-3	
21/03	h	Guingamp	D	0-0	
04/04	a	Montpellier	L	1-3	Sio
15/04	a	Lyon	L	0-2	
18/04	h	Reims	L	1-2	Sio
25/04	a	Évian	W	2-1	Kamano 2
02/05	h	St-Étienne	W	1-0	Ayité
09/05	a	Rennes	W	1-0	Danic
16/05	h	Caen	D	1-1	Ayité
23/05	a	Marseille	L	0-3	

No	Name	Nat	DoB	Pos	Aps	(s)	Gls
1	Alphonse Areola		27/02/93	G	35		
7	Floyd Ayité	TOG	15/12/88	M	26	(4)	6
8	El Hadji Ba		05/03/93	M	7		
10	Ryad Boudebouz	ALG	19/02/90	M	32	(2)	5
26	Brandão	BRA	16/06/80	A	7	(2)	
18	Yannick Cahuzac		18/01/85	M	21		1
29	Gilles Cioni		14/06/84	D	10	(4)	
9	Djibril Cissé		12/08/81	A		(8)	
28	Gaël Danic		19/11/81	M	14	(1)	1
23	Drissa Diakité	MLI	18/02/85	M	22		
33	Alexander Djiku		09/08/94	D	2		
27	Guillaume Gillet	BEL	09/03/84	D	37	(1)	2
24	Lyes Houri		19/01/96	M		(1)	
25	François Kamano	GUI	01/05/96	A	19	(5)	4
13	Abdoulaye Keita	MLI	05/01/94	M	2	(3)	
14	Famoussa Koné	MLI	05/03/94	A	2	(2)	
16	Jean-Louis Leca		21/09/85	G	3		
22	Christophe Maboulou		19/03/90	M	14	(6)	3
4	Florian Marange		03/03/86	D	15	(3)	
20	François Modesto		19/08/78	D	25	(4)	2
19	Benjamin Mokulu	BEL	11/10/89	A		(4)	
3	Hervin Ongenda		24/06/95	A	6	(10)	
15	Julian Palmieri		17/12/86	D	34	(1)	2
17	Mathieu Peybernes		21/10/90	D	24	(6)	
12	Juan Pablo Piño	COL	30/03/87	M	2	(2)	
12	Joao Rodríguez	COL	19/05/96	A		(5)	
34	Julien Romain		23/02/96	M		(1)	
6	Romaric	CIV	04/06/83	M	15	(11)	
19	Giovanni Sio	CIV	31/03/89	A	9	(4)	5
5	Sébastien Squillaci		11/08/80	D	25		
11	Junior Tallo	CIV	21/12/92	A	10		4

FC Girondins de Bordeaux ◀

1881 • Chaban-Delmas (34,614); Nouveau Stade Bordeaux (42,115) • girondins.com

Major honours
French League (6) 1950, 1984, 1985, 1987, 1999, 2009; French Cup (4) 1941, 1986, 1987, 2013; League Cup (3) 2002, 2007, 2009
Coach: Willy Sagnol

2014
09/08	a	Montpellier	W	1-0	Diabaté
17/08	h	Monaco	W	4-1	Rolán 2, Sala (p), Khazri (p)
23/08	a	Nice	W	3-1	Diabaté (p), Maurice-Belay, Sertic
31/08	h	Bastia	D	1-1	Rolán
14/09	a	Guingamp	L	1-2	Diabaté
19/09	h	Évian	W	2-1	Rolán, Khazri
25/09	a	St-Étienne	D	1-1	Thiago Ilori
28/09	h	Rennes	W	2-1	Khazri, Touré
03/10	a	Reims	L	0-1	
19/10	a	Caen	D	1-1	Diabaté (p)
25/10	a	Paris	L	0-3	
02/11	h	Toulouse	W	2-1	Planus, Rolán
08/11	a	Lens	W	2-1	Khazri, Diabaté
23/11	a	Marseille	L	1-3	Touré
30/11	h	LOSC	W	1-0	Diabaté
03/12	a	Metz	D	0-0	
06/12	h	Lorient	W	3-2	Khazri, Diabaté 2
13/12	a	Nantes	L	1-2	og (Hansen)
21/12	h	Lyon	L	0-5	

2015
11/01	a	Monaco	D	0-0	
16/01	h	Nice	L	1-2	Rolán (p)
24/01	a	Bastia	D	0-0	
01/02	h	Guingamp	D	1-1	Poundjé
07/02	a	Évian	W	1-0	Khazri
15/02	h	St-Étienne	D	1-1	Rolán
21/02	a	Rennes	D	1-1	Khazri (p)
28/02	h	Reims	D	1-1	Kiese Thelin
07/03	a	Caen	W	2-1	Rolán 2 (1p)
15/03	h	Paris	W	3-2	Sané, Khazri, Rolán
21/03	a	Toulouse	L	1-2	Rolán
05/04	a	Lens	W	2-1	Mariano, Maurice-Belay
12/04	h	Marseille	W	1-0	Yambere
19/04	a	LOSC	L	0-2	
25/04	h	Metz	W	1-0	Khazri
02/05	a	Lorient	D	0-0	
09/05	h	Nantes	W	2-1	Rolán 2 (1p)
15/05	a	Lyon	D	0-0	Crivelli
23/05	h	Montpellier	W	2-1	Rolán 2

No	Name	Nat	DoB	Pos	Aps	(s)	Gls
17	André Biyogo Poko	GAB	01/01/93	M	11	(5)	
16	Cédric Carrasso		30/12/81	G	37		
11	Clément Chantôme		11/09/87	M	13		
3	Diego Contento	GER	01/05/90	D	23	(2)	
34	Enzo Crivelli		06/02/95	A	1	(10)	1
33	Sessi D'Almeida		20/11/95	M		(2)	
14	Cheick Diabaté	MLI	25/04/88	A	13	(2)	8
28	David Djigla	BEN	23/08/95	A		(1)	
22	Julien Faubert		01/08/83	D	11	(2)	
33	Frédéric Guilbert		24/12/94	D	1	(2)	
1	Ažbe Jug	SVN	03/03/92	G	1	(1)	
24	Younès Kaabouni		23/05/95	M	2	(10)	
24	Wahdi Khazri	TUN	08/02/91	M	29	(2)	9
12	Isaac Kiese Thelin	SWE	24/06/92	A	12	(3)	1
2	Mariano	BRA	23/06/86	D	31		1
19	Nicolas Maurice-Belay		19/04/85	M	15	(17)	2
5	Nicolas Pallois		19/09/87	D	33	(1)	
27	Marc Planus		07/03/82	D	6	(2)	1
18	Jaroslav Plašil	CZE	05/01/82	M	31	(3)	
29	Maxime Poundjé		16/08/92	D	12		1
9	Diego Rolán	URU	24/03/93	A	28	(8)	15
12	Hadi Sacko		24/03/94	A		(2)	
10	Henri Saivet	SEN	26/10/90	A	7	(7)	
5	Emiliano Sala	ARG	31/10/90	A	4	(7)	1
6	Lamine Sané	SEN	22/03/87	D	22	(1)	1
8	Grégory Sertic		05/08/89	M	24	(3)	1
13	Thiago Ilori	POR	26/02/93	D	12		1
7	Abdou Traoré	MLI	17/01/88	M	8	(9)	
33	Cédric Yambere		06/11/90	D	15	(1)	1

SM Caen

1913 • Michel d'Ornano (21,250) • smcaen.fr

Coach: Patrice Garand

2014
09/08	a	Évian	W	3-0	Kanté, Duhamel 2
15/08	h	LOSC	L	0-1	
23/08	a	Reims	W	2-0	Kanté, Bazile
30/08	h	Rennes	L	0-1	
13/09	a	St-Étienne	L	0-1	
20/09	a	Toulouse	D	3-3	Raspentino, Nangis, Calvé
24/09	h	Paris	L	0-2	
28/09	a	Lens	D	0-0	
04/10	h	Marseille	L	1-2	Musavu-King
19/10	a	Bordeaux	D	1-1	Bazile
25/10	h	Lorient	W	2-1	Nangis, Duhamel (p)
01/11	a	Metz	L	2-3	Calvé, Koita
08/11	h	Nantes	L	1-2	Duhamel
22/11	a	Monaco	D	2-2	Koita, og (Kondogbia)
29/11	h	Montpellier	D	1-1	Duhamel
03/12	a	Guingamp	L	1-5	Yahia
06/12	h	Nice	L	2-3	Duhamel (p), Nangis
12/12	a	Lyon	L	0-3	
20/12	h	Bastia	D	1-1	Féret

2015
10/01	a	LOSC	L	0-1	
17/01	h	Reims	W	4-1	og (Roberge), Privat, Yahia, Koita (p)
25/01	a	Rennes	W	4-1	Privat, Nangis, Féret, Da Silva
01/02	h	St-Étienne	W	1-0	Féret
07/02	h	Toulouse	W	2-0	Privat, Féret (p)
14/02	a	Paris	D	2-2	Sala, Bazile
21/02	h	Lens	W	4-1	Féret (p), Sala 2, Bazile
27/02	a	Marseille	W	3-2	Seube, Sala, Benezet
07/03	h	Bordeaux	L	1-2	Privat
14/03	a	Lorient	L	1-2	Bazile
21/03	h	Metz	D	0-0	
05/04	a	Nantes	W	2-1	Sala (p), Lemar
10/04	h	Monaco	L	0-3	
19/04	a	Montpellier	L	0-1	
25/04	h	Guingamp	L	0-2	
02/05	a	Nice	D	1-1	Benezet
09/05	h	Lyon	W	3-0	Benezet 2, Privat
16/05	a	Bastia	D	1-1	Privat
23/05	h	Évian	W	3-2	Bazile 2, og (Modou Sougou)

No	Name	Nat	DoB	Pos	Aps	(s)	Gls
18	Jordan Adéoti	BEN	12/03/89	M	18	(10)	
12	Dennis Appiah		09/06/92	D	29	(1)	
20	Hervé Bazile	HAI	18/03/90	A	19	(11)	7
7	Nicolas Benezet		24/02/91	M	5	(7)	4
23	Jean Calvé		30/04/84	D	14	(2)	2
28	Damien Da Silva		17/05/88	D	35		1
4	Mathieu Duhamel		12/07/84	A	15	(4)	6
19	Felipe Saad	BRA	11/09/83	D	7	(3)	
25	Julien Féret		05/07/82	M	33	(4)	5
15	Emmanuel Imorou	BEN	16/09/88	D	30		
17	N'Golo Kanté		29/03/91	M	36	(1)	2
11	Bangaly-Fodé Koita		21/10/90	A	22	(7)	3
27	Thomas Lemar		12/11/95	M	6	(19)	1
29	Yrondu Musavu-King	GAB	08/01/92	D	6		1
10	Lenny Nangis		24/03/94	A	28	(6)	4
13	Jean-Jacques Pierre	HAI	23/01/81	D	11	(1)	
9	Sloan Privat		24/07/89	A	13	(7)	6
24	Florian Raspentino		06/06/89	A	9	(8)	1
21	José Saez		07/05/82	M	1	(1)	
14	Emiliano Sala	ARG	30/10/90	A	7	(6)	5
2	Nicolas Seube		11/08/79	M	22	(2)	1
1	Rémy Vercoutre		26/06/80	G	38		
5	Alaeddine Yahia	TUN	26/09/81	D	14	(4)	2

FRANCE

Évian Thonon Gaillard FC

2007 • Parc des Sports d'Annecy (15,714) •
etgfc.com

Coach: Pascal Dupraz

2014

09/08	h	Caen	L 0-3
16/08	a	Rennes	L 2-6 Wass 2
22/08	h	Paris	D 0-0
30/08	a	Toulouse	L 0-1
14/09	h	Marseille	L 1-3 N'Sikulu
19/09	a	Bordeaux	L 1-2 Tejeda
24/09	h	Lens	W 2-1 Wass, Mensah
27/09	a	Lorient	W 2-0 Koné, Barbosa
04/10	h	Metz	W 3-0 og (Doukouré), Wass (p), Bruno
18/10	a	Monaco	L 0-1
25/10	h	Nantes	L 0-2
01/11	a	Montpellier	L 0-2
08/11	h	Nice	W 1-0 Wass
30/11	h	Guingamp	W 2-0 Wass, Nielsen
03/12	a	Bastia	W 2-1 Wass, N'Sikulu
07/12	h	Lyon	L 2-3 Barbosa 2
13/12	a	Reims	W 2-1 Wass, Cambon
21/12	a	St-Étienne	L 0-3

2015

07/01	h	LOSC	L 0-1
10/01	h	Rennes	D 1-1 Thomasson
18/01	a	Paris	L 2-4 Barbosa, og (Van der Wiel)
25/01	h	Toulouse	W 1-0 Thomasson
31/01	a	Marseille	L 0-1
07/02	a	Bordeaux	L 0-1
14/02	h	Lens	W 2-0 Duhamel 2
28/02	a	Metz	W 2-1 og (Carrasso), Sunu
04/03	h	Lorient	W 1-0 N'Sikulu
07/03	a	Monaco	L 1-3 Modou Sougou
14/03	a	Nantes	L 1-2 N'Sikulu
21/03	h	Montpellier	L 1-2 N'Sikulu
04/04	a	Nice	D 2-2 Nounkeu, og (Gomis)
12/04	h	LOSC	L 0-1
18/04	a	Guingamp	D 1-1 Blandi
25/04	h	Bastia	L 1-2 Sunu
02/05	a	Lyon	L 0-2
09/05	h	Reims	L 2-3 Sunu, Duhamel
16/05	h	St-Étienne	L 1-2 Duhamel
23/05	a	Caen	L 2-3 Sorlin, Modou Sougou

No	Name	Nat	DoB	Pos	Aps	(s)	Gls
2	Kassim Abdallah	COM	09/04/87	D	29	(1)	
17	Aldo Angoula		04/05/81	D	7	(1)	
14	Cédric Barbosa		06/03/76	M	19	(10)	4
9	Nicolas Benezet		24/02/91	M	7	(4)	
9	Nicolás Blandi	ARG	31/01/90	A	1	(5)	1
33	Jordan Boy		20/03/94	D		(1)	
9	Gianni Bruno	BEL	19/08/91	A	10	(7)	1
22	Cédric Cambon		20/09/86	D	24	(2)	1
11	Fabien Camus	TUN	28/02/85	M	8	(11)	
10	Mathieu Duhamel		12/07/84	A	11		4
33	Alioune Fall		20/12/90	D	3	(5)	
12	Gaël Givet		09/10/81	D	1		
30	Jesper Hansen	DEN	31/03/85	G	15		
26	Jesper Juelsgård	DEN	26/01/89	D	10	(1)	
6	Djakaridja Koné	BFA	22/07/86	M	22	(4)	1
40	Benjamin Leroy		23/07/90	G	23		
25	Jonathan Mensah	GHA	13/07/90	D	10	(1)	1
20	Modou Sougou	SEN	18/12/84	A	9	(15)	2
21	Cédric Mongongu	COD	22/06/89	D	19	(5)	
27	Clarck N'Sikulu	COD	10/07/92	A	20	(8)	5
23	Nicki Bille Nielsen	DEN	07/02/88	A	7	(12)	1
5	Miloš Ninković	SRB	25/12/84	M	10	(5)	
13	Dany Nounkeu	CMR	11/04/86	D	14		1
12	David Ramírez	CRC	28/05/93	A	2	(4)	
19	Youssouf Sabaly		05/03/93	D	29		
24	Olivier Sorlin		09/04/79	M	26	(4)	1
15	Gilles Sunu		30/03/91	M	9	(1)	3
8	Yeltsin Tejeda	CRC	17/03/92	M	25	(2)	1
7	Adrien Thomasson		10/12/93	A	20	(1)	2
18	Daniel Wass	DEN	31/05/89	M	28	(4)	8

EA Guingamp

1912 • Roudourou (18,256) • eaguingamp.com

Major honours
French Cup (2) 2009, 2014

Coach: Jocelyn Gourvennec

2014

09/08	h	St-Étienne	L 0-2
16/08	a	Lens	W 1-0 Douniama
23/08	h	Marseille	L 0-1
30/08	a	Lorient	L 0-4
14/09	h	Bordeaux	W 2-1 Diallo, Mandanne (p)
21/09	a	Monaco	L 0-1
24/09	h	Metz	L 0-1
27/09	a	Montpellier	L 1-2 Beauvue
05/10	h	Nantes	L 0-1
18/10	a	LOSC	W 2-1 Beauvue, Schwartz
26/10	h	Nice	L 2-7 Beauvue, Schwartz
01/11	h	Bastia	W 1-0 S Yatabaré
09/11	a	Lyon	L 1-3 og (Anthony Lopes)
22/11	h	Rennes	L 0-1
30/11	a	Évian	L 0-2
03/12	h	Caen	W 5-1 Mandanne 2, Giresse, Beauvue 2 (1p)
07/12	a	Reims	W 3-2 Jacobsen, Mandanne, Beauvue
14/12	h	Paris	W 1-0 Pied
20/12	a	Toulouse	D 1-1 Giresse

2015

10/01	h	Lens	W 2-0 Mandanne, Beauvue (p)
18/01	a	Marseille	L 1-2 Beauvue (p)
24/01	h	Lorient	W 3-2 Beauvue 2 (1p), Mandanne
01/02	a	Bordeaux	D 1-1 Beauvue
08/02	h	Monaco	L 0-1 Lévêque
15/02	a	Metz	W 2-0 Mandanne, Pied
22/02	h	Montpellier	L 0-2
01/03	a	Nantes	L 0-1
08/03	h	LOSC	L 0-1
13/03	a	Nice	W 2-1 Mandanne 2
21/03	a	Bastia	D 0-0
04/04	h	Lyon	L 1-3 Beauvue
12/04	a	Rennes	L 0-1
18/04	h	Évian	D 1-1 Beauvue
25/04	a	Caen	W 2-0 Beauvue, Marveaux
02/05	h	Reims	W 2-0 Beauvue (p), Mandanne
08/05	a	Paris	L 0-6
15/05	h	Toulouse	W 2-1 Mandanne, Beauvue
23/05	a	St-Étienne	L 1-2 Beauvue (p)

No	Name	Nat	DoB	Pos	Aps	(s)	Gls
32	Karim Achahbar	MAR	03/01/96	A		(1)	
17	Rachid Alioui	MAR	18/06/92	A	2	(5)	
3	Benjamin Angoua	CIV	28/11/86	D	16	(5)	
6	Maxime Baca		02/06/83	D	12	(2)	
12	Claudio Beauvue		16/04/88	M	34	(2)	17
22	Julien Cardy		29/09/81	M		(2)	
5	Marcus Coco		24/06/96	M	2	(1)	
5	Moustapha Diallo	SEN	14/05/86	M	20	(12)	1
20	Laurent Dos Santos		21/03/93	M	5	(5)	
14	Ladislas Douniama	CGO	24/05/86	A		(9)	1
26	Thibault Giresse		25/05/81	M	26	(6)	2
2	Lars Jacobsen	DEN	20/09/79	D	24	(1)	1
29	Christophe Kerbrat		02/08/86	D	27	(5)	
25	Reynald Lemaître		28/06/83	D	12	(3)	
7	Dorian Lévêque		22/11/89	D	17	(1)	1
1	Jonas Lössl	DEN	01/02/89	G	30		
13	Christophe Mandanne		07/02/85	A	25	(6)	11
21	Sylvain Marveaux		15/04/86	M	19	(5)	1
18	Lionel Mathis		04/10/81	M	27	(4)	
23	Jérémy Pied		23/02/89	M	23	(5)	2
23	Yannis Salibur		21/01/91	M	5	(5)	
30	Mamadou Samassa	MLI	16/02/90	G	8	(1)	
10	Younousse Sankharé		10/09/89	M	25	(4)	
4	Baïssama Sankoh	GUI	20/03/92	D	8	(1)	
8	Ronnie Schwartz	DEN	29/09/89	A	8	(6)	2
15	Jérémy Sorbon		05/08/83	D	35		
9	Mustapha Yatabaré	MLI	26/01/86	A	2	(2)	
24	Sambou Yatabaré	MLI	02/03/89	M	11	(8)	1

RC Lens

1906 • Stade de la Licorne, Amiens (12,097);
Stade de France, Saint-Denis (81,338) • rclens.fr

Major honours
French League (1) 1998; League Cup (1) 1999

Coach: Antoine Kombouaré

2014

09/08	a	Nantes	L 0-1
16/08	h	Guingamp	L 0-1
24/08	a	Lyon	W 1-0 Nomenjanahary
30/08	h	Reims	W 4-2 Cyprien, Chavarría, Touzghar (p), Coulibaly (p)
13/09	a	Bastia	D 1-1 Chavarría
21/09	h	St-Étienne	L 0-1
24/09	a	Évian	L 1-2 Touzghar
28/09	h	Caen	D 0-0
04/10	a	Rennes	L 0-2
17/10	h	Paris	L 1-3 Coulibaly
24/10	a	Toulouse	W 2-0 El Jadeyaoui, Bourigeaud
02/11	a	Marseille	L 1-2 Guillaume
08/11	h	Bordeaux	L 1-2 Touzghar (p)
22/11	a	Lorient	L 0-1
29/11	h	Metz	W 2-0 El Jadeyaoui, Bourigeaud
02/12	a	Monaco	L 0-2
07/12	h	LOSC	D 1-1 Coulibaly
13/12	a	Montpellier	D 3-3 Valdivia, Guillaume, Touzghar
19/12	h	Nice	W 2-0 Cyprien, Coulibaly

2015

10/01	a	Guingamp	L 0-2
17/01	h	Lyon	L 0-2
25/01	a	Reims	D 0-0
31/01	h	Bastia	D 1-1 Kantari (p)
06/02	a	St-Étienne	D 3-3 Touzghar 2 (1p), Chavarría
14/02	h	Évian	L 0-2
21/02	a	Caen	L 1-4 El Jadeyaoui
28/02	h	Rennes	L 0-1
07/03	a	Paris	L 1-4 Touzghar
14/03	h	Toulouse	W 1-0 Chavarría
22/03	h	Marseille	L 0-4
05/04	a	Bordeaux	L 1-2 Chavarría
12/04	h	Lorient	D 0-0
18/04	a	Metz	L 1-3 Madiani
26/04	h	Monaco	L 0-3
03/05	a	LOSC	L 1-2 Chavarría
10/05	h	Montpellier	L 0-1
16/05	h	Nice	L 1-2 Touzghar
23/05	h	Nantes	W 1-0 Chavarría

No	Name	Nat	DoB	Pos	Aps	(s)	Gls
16	Samuel Atrous		15/02/90	G	1		
33	Abdoul Ba	MTN	08/02/94	D	4	(5)	
24	Ludovic Baal		24/05/86	D	27		
40	Valentin Belon		05/07/95	G	5	(1)	
27	Benjamin Boulenger		01/03/90	D	9	(4)	
29	Benjamin Bourigeaud		14/01/94	M	12	(8)	2
33	Dimitri Cavare		05/02/95	D	16	(4)	
11	Pablo Chavarría	ARG	02/01/88	A	27	(4)	7
9	Adamo Coulibaly		14/08/81	A	28	(5)	4
23	Wylan Cyprien		28/01/95	M	27	(6)	2
21	Alharbi El Jadeyaoui	MAR	08/08/86	M	13	(13)	3
15	Patrick Fradj		11/03/92	D		(1)	
25	Jean-Philippe Gbamin		25/09/95	D	29	(4)	
19	Baptiste Guillaume	BEL	16/06/95	A	15	(12)	2
4	Ahmed Kantari	MAR	28/06/85	D	31		1
22	Loïck Landre		05/05/92	D	26		
6	Jérôme Le Moigne		15/02/83	M	31		
34	Quentin Lecoeuche		04/02/94	D	1	(1)	
34	Aristote Madiani		22/08/95	A	1	(15)	1
35	Taylor Moore	ENG	12/05/97	D	4		
14	Dème N'Diaye	SEN	06/02/85	A	3	(4)	
20	Lalaina Nomenjanahary	MAD	16/01/89	M	17	(9)	1
1	Rudy Riou		22/01/80	G	32		
34	El Hadji Malick Seck	SEN	09/02/90	A		(1)	
34	Boubacar Sylla	MLI	17/04/91	D	5	(2)	
7	Yohann Touzghar	TUN	29/11/86	A	22	(7)	8
18	Pierrick Valdivia		18/04/88	M	32	(3)	1

LOSC Lille

1944 • Pierre-Mauroy (50,157) • losc.fr
Major honours
French League (3) 1946, 1954, 2011; French Cup (6) 1946, 1947, 1948, 1953, 1955, 2011
Coach: René Girard

2014
09/08	h	Metz	D	0-0	
15/08	a	Caen	W	1-0	*Origi (p)*
23/08	h	Lorient	W	2-0	*Delaplace, Kjær*
30/08	a	Monaco	D	1-1	*Roux*
14/09	h	Nantes	W	2-0	*Origi, Marcos Lopes*
21/09	h	Montpellier	D	0-0	
24/09	a	Nice	L	0-1	
27/09	h	Bastia	W	1-0	*Origi*
05/10	a	Lyon	L	0-3	
18/10	h	Guingamp	L	1-2	*Mavuba*
26/10	a	Rennes	L	0-2	
01/11	h	St-Étienne	D	1-1	*Frey*
09/11	a	Reims	L	0-2	
30/11	a	Bordeaux	L	0-1	
03/12	h	Paris	D	1-1	*og (Sirigu)*
07/12	h	Lens	L	0-1	*Gueye*
14/12	a	Toulouse	W	3-0	*Sidibé, Ryan Mendes, Roux*
21/12	a	Marseille	L	1-2	*Gueye*

2015
07/01	h	Évian	W	1-0	*Traoré*
10/01	h	Caen	W	1-0	*Frey*
17/01	a	Lorient	L	0-1	
24/01	h	Monaco	L	0-1	
31/01	a	Nantes	D	1-1	*Delaplace*
07/02	h	Montpellier	W	2-1	*Roux, Marcos Lopes*
14/02	h	Nice	D	0-0	
21/02	a	Bastia	L	1-2	*Ryan Mendes*
28/02	h	Lyon	W	2-1	*Gueye, Marcos Lopes*
08/03	a	Guingamp	W	1-0	*Roux*
15/03	h	Rennes	W	3-0	*Origi 3 (1p)*
22/03	a	St-Étienne	L	0-2	
04/04	h	Reims	W	3-1	*Corchia, Origi, Roux*
12/04	a	Évian	W	1-0	*Boufal (p)*
19/04	h	Bordeaux	W	2-0	*Roux, Traoré*
25/04	a	Paris	L	1-6	*Baša*
03/05	h	Lens	W	3-1	*Boufal (p), Sidibé, Origi*
09/05	a	Toulouse	L	2-3	*Roux, Boufal*
16/05	h	Marseille	L	0-4	
23/05	a	Metz	W	4-1	*Balmont, Gueye, Roux 2 (1p)*

No	Name	Nat	DoB	Pos	Aps	(s)	Gls
4	Florent Balmont		02/02/80	M	25	(5)	1
25	Marko Baša	MNE	29/12/82	D	30		1
18	Franck Béria		23/05/83	D	16	(1)	
7	Sofiane Boufal	MAR	17/09/93	M	11	(3)	3
2	Sébastien Corchia		01/11/90	D	29	(2)	1
6	Jonathan Delaplace		01/03/86	M	12	(9)	2
21	Abdoulay Diaby	MLI	21/05/91	A		(3)	
1	Vincent Enyeama	NGA	29/08/82	G	38		
11	Michael Frey	SUI	19/07/94	M	7	(8)	2
5	Idrissa Gueye	SEN	26/09/89	M	30	(2)	4
8	Salomon Kalou	CIV	05/08/85	A	1		
14	Simon Kjær	DEN	26/03/89	D	31		1
35	Kévin Koubemba	CGO	23/03/93	A	5	(3)	
17	Marcos Lopes	POR	28/12/95	M	18	(5)	3
10	Marvin Martin		10/01/88	M	5	(1)	
24	Rio Mavuba		08/03/84	M	30		1
12	Soualiho Meïté		17/03/94	M	1	(7)	
27	Divock Origi	BEL	18/04/95	A	22	(11)	8
34	Benjamin Pavard		28/03/96	D	5	(3)	
9	Ronny Rodelin		18/11/89	A	5	(10)	
26	Nolan Roux		01/03/88	A	29	(4)	9
22	David Rozehnal	CZE	05/07/80	D	14	(4)	
20	Ryan Mendes	CPV	08/01/90	A	11	(8)	2
15	Djibril Sidibé		29/07/92	D	23	(2)	2
23	Pape Souaré	SEN	06/06/90	D	9	(3)	
13	Adama Soumaoro		18/06/92	D	1		
8	Adama Traoré	MLI	28/06/95	M	10	(10)	2

FC Lorient

1926 • Le Moustoir-Yves-Allainmat (18,110) • fclweb.fr
Major honours
French Cup (1) 2002
Coach: Sylvain Ripoll

2014
10/08	a	Monaco	W	2-1	*Aboubakar (p), Lavigne*
16/08	h	Nice	D	0-0	
23/08	a	LOSC	L	0-2	
30/08	h	Guingamp	W	4-0	*Jeannot, Lavigne 2, Ayew*
13/09	a	Montpellier	L	0-1	
20/09	h	Reims	L	0-1	
24/09	a	Lyon	L	0-4	
27/09	h	Évian	L	0-1	
04/10	a	Bastia	W	2-0	*og (Peybernes), Sunu*
18/10	h	St-Étienne	L	0-1	
25/10	a	Caen	L	1-2	*Ayew (p)*
01/11	h	Paris	L	1-2	*Raphael Guerreiro*
07/11	a	Rennes	L	0-1	
22/11	h	Lens	W	1-0	*Raphael Guerreiro*
29/11	a	Toulouse	W	3-2	*Raphael Guerreiro, Jeannot, Ayew (p)*
02/12	h	Marseille	D	1-1	*Ayew (p)*
06/12	a	Bordeaux	L	2-3	*Jeannot, Le Goff*
13/12	h	Metz	W	3-1	*Ayew, Raphael Guerreiro, Jeannot*
20/12	h	Nantes	L	1-2	*Ayew*

2015
10/01	a	Nice	L	1-3	*Jeannot*
17/01	h	LOSC	W	1-0	*Raphael Guerreiro*
24/01	a	Guingamp	L	2-3	*Jeannot (p), og (Lévêque)*
31/01	h	Montpellier	D	0-0	
07/02	a	Reims	W	3-1	*Gassama, Raphael Guerreiro, Jeannot*
15/02	h	Lyon	D	1-1	*Ayew*
28/02	h	Bastia	W	2-0	*Bellugou, Bruno*
04/03	a	Évian	L	0-2	
08/03	a	St-Étienne	L	0-2	
14/03	h	Caen	W	2-1	*Raphael Guerreiro, Ayew*
20/03	h	Paris	L	1-3	*Ayew*
04/04	h	Rennes	L	0-3	
12/04	a	Lens	D	0-0	
18/04	a	Toulouse	L	0-1	
24/04	a	Marseille	W	5-3	*Ayew 2, Bellugou, Philippoteaux, Autret*
02/05	h	Bordeaux	D	0-0	
09/05	a	Metz	W	4-0	*Mostefa, Philippoteaux, Koné, Ayew*
16/05	h	Nantes	D	1-1	*og (Djilobodji)*
23/05	h	Monaco	L	0-1	

No	Name	Nat	DoB	Pos	Aps	(s)	Gls
13	Raffidine Abdullah		15/01/94	M	18	(5)	
9	Vincent Aboubakar	CMR	22/01/92	A	2		1
16	Fabien Audard		28/03/78	G		(1)	
23	Mathias Autret		01/03/91	M	3	(4)	1
9	Jordan Ayew	GHA	11/09/91	A	29	(2)	12
28	Maxime Barthelmé		08/09/88	M	9	(11)	
6	François Bellugou		25/04/87	D	19	(1)	2
32	Didier Bouanga		12/12/94	M		(1)	
39	Gianni Bruno	BEL	19/08/91	A	3	(9)	1
10	Mathieu Coutadeur		20/06/86	M	8	(3)	
7	Sadio Diallo	GUI	28/12/90	M	4	(6)	
5	Bruno Ecuélé Manga	GAB	16/07/88	D	3		
34	Marvin Gakpa		01/11/93	M		(2)	
25	Lamine Gassama	SEN	20/10/89	D	31		1
22	Benjamin Jeannot		22/01/92	A	25	(6)	7
8	Yann Jouffre		23/07/84	M	12	(6)	
2	Lamine Koné		01/02/89	D	30		1
24	Wesley Lautoa		25/08/87	D	26		
33	Valentin Lavigne		04/06/94	A	4	(11)	3
4	Vincent Le Goff		15/09/89	D	25	(3)	1
1	Benjamin Lecomte		26/04/91	G	38		
17	Walid Mesloub	ALG	04/09/85	M	29	(3)	
32	Mehdi Mostefa	ALG	30/08/83	M	19	(4)	1
11	Didier N'Dong	GAB	17/06/94	M	9	(3)	
3	Pedrinho	POR	06/03/85	D	7	(2)	
19	Bryan Pelé		25/03/92	M	5	(5)	
19	Romain Philippoteaux		02/03/88	M	13	(2)	2
14	Raphael Guerreiro	POR	22/12/93	D	33	(1)	7
15	Fabien Robert		06/01/89	A		(3)	
18	Gilles Sunu		30/03/91	A	9	(8)	1
21	Alain Traoré	BFA	31/12/88	M		(3)	
26	Yoanni Wachter		07/04/92	D	5	(3)	

Olympique Lyonnais

1950 • Gerland (42,591) • olweb.fr
Major honours
French League (7) 2002, 2003, 2004, 2005, 2006, 2007, 2008; French Cup (5) 1964, 1967, 1973, 2008, 2012; League Cup (1) 2001
Coach: Hubert Fournier

2014
10/08	h	Rennes	W	2-0	*Malbranque, Lacazette (p)*
16/08	a	Toulouse	L	1-2	*Lacazette*
24/08	a	Lens	L	0-1	
31/08	h	Metz	L	1-2	*Lacazette*
12/09	h	Monaco	W	2-1	*Fekir, Tolisso*
21/09	a	Paris	D	1-1	*Umtiti*
24/09	a	Lorient	W	4-0	*Lacazette, Fekir 2, Njie*
28/09	a	Nantes	D	1-1	*Koné*
05/10	h	LOSC	W	3-0	*Lacazette 3*
19/10	h	Montpellier	W	5-1	*Gourcuff 2, Fekir, Lacazette, Malbranque*
26/10	h	Marseille	W	1-0	*Gourcuff*
01/11	a	Nice	W	3-1	*Malbranque, Lacazette 2*
09/11	h	Guingamp	W	3-1	*Lacazette, Fekir 2*
22/11	a	Bastia	D	0-0	
30/11	a	St-Étienne	L	0-3	
04/12	h	Reims	W	2-1	*Tolisso, og (Placide)*
07/12	a	Évian	W	3-2	*Benzia, Lacazette 2 (1p)*
12/12	h	Caen	W	3-0	*Lacazette 2 (1p), Benzia*
21/12	a	Bordeaux	W	5-0	*Lacazette 2, Tolisso, Fekir, Ferri*

2015
11/01	h	Toulouse	W	3-0	*Lacazette 2, Fekir*
17/01	a	Lens	W	2-0	*og (Gbamin), Lacazette (p)*
25/01	h	Metz	W	2-0	*Lacazette (p), Tolisso*
01/02	a	Monaco	D	0-0	
08/02	h	Paris	D	1-1	*Njie*
15/02	a	Lorient	D	1-1	*Njie*
22/02	h	Nantes	W	1-0	*Fekir*
28/02	a	LOSC	L	1-2	*Tolisso*
08/03	a	Montpellier	W	5-1	*Lacazette 2 (1p), Fekir 2, Tolisso*
15/03	a	Marseille	D	0-0	
21/03	h	Nice	L	1-2	*Gonalons (p)*
04/04	a	Guingamp	W	3-1	*Fekir, Lacazette (p), Njie*
15/04	h	Bastia	W	2-0	*Yattara, Lacazette*
19/04	h	St-Étienne	D	2-2	*Njie, Jallet*
26/04	h	Reims	W	4-2	*Tolisso, Lacazette, Njie, og (Tacalfred)*
02/05	a	Évian	W	2-0	*Grenier, Lacazette (p)*
09/05	a	Caen	L	0-3	
16/05	h	Bordeaux	D	1-1	*Fekir*
23/05	a	Rennes	W	1-0	*Njie*

No	Name	Nat	DoB	Pos	Aps	(s)	Gls
1	Anthony Lopes	POR	01/10/90	G	38		
29	Farès Bahlouli		08/04/95	M		(4)	
3	Henri Bedimo	CMR	04/06/84	D	25	(2)	
25	Yassine Benzia		08/09/94	A	3	(7)	2
5	Milan Biševac	SRB	31/08/83	D	13		
27	Maxwell Cornet		27/09/96	A	1	(3)	
14	Mouhamadou Dabo		28/11/86	D	13		
26	Gaël Danic		19/11/81	M	1		
18	Nabil Fekir		18/07/93	M	34		13
12	Jordan Ferri		12/03/92	M	30	(5)	1
6	Gueïda Fofana		16/05/91	M		(2)	
11	Rachid Ghezzal	ALG	09/05/92	M	6	(13)	
21	Maxime Gonalons		10/03/89	M	35		1
8	Yoann Gourcuff		11/07/86	M	8	(9)	3
13	Christophe Jallet		31/10/83	D	32		1
4	Bakary Koné	BFA	27/04/88	D	14	(3)	1
10	Alexandre Lacazette		28/05/91	A	33		27
28	Steed Malbranque		06/01/80	M	13	(15)	3
28	Arnold Mvuemba		28/01/85	M	10	(10)	
20	Clinton Njie	CMR	15/08/93	A	15	(15)	7
22	Lindsay Rose		08/02/92	D	13	(2)	
24	Corentin Tolisso		03/08/94	M	37	(1)	7
23	Samuel Umtiti		14/11/93	D	35		1
19	Mohamed Yattara	GUI	28/07/93	A	4	(17)	1
2	Mehdi Zeffane	ALG	19/05/92	D	1	(3)	

FRANCE

Olympique de Marseille

1899 • Vélodrome (67,054) • om.net

Major honours
UEFA Champions League (1) 1993; French League (9) 1937, 1948, 1971, 1972, 1989, 1990, 1991, 1992, 2010; French Cup (10) 1924, 1926, 1927, 1935, 1938, 1943, 1969, 1972, 1976, 1989; League Cup (3) 2010, 2011, 2012

Coach: Marcelo Bielsa (ARG)

2014
09/08	a	Bastia	D	3-3	Gignac 2 (1p), og (Romaric)
17/08	h	Montpellier	L	0-2	
23/08	a	Guingamp	W	1-0	Gignac
29/08	h	Nice	W	4-0	Payet 2, Thauvin, Barrada
14/09	a	Évian	W	3-1	Gignac, og (Mensah), Thauvin
20/09	h	Rennes	W	3-0	Gignac 2, Alessandrini
23/09	a	Reims	W	5-0	Gignac 2, Ayew 2, Imbula
28/09	h	St-Étienne	W	2-1	Imbula, Payet
04/10	a	Caen	W	2-1	Romao, Gignac
19/10	h	Toulouse	W	2-1	N'Koulou, Gignac
26/10	a	Lyon	L	0-1	
02/11	h	Lens	W	2-1	N'Koulou, Thauvin
09/11	a	Paris	L	0-2	
23/11	h	Bordeaux	W	3-1	Lemina, Gignac, Batshuayi
28/11	h	Nantes	W	2-0	Thauvin, Fanni
02/12	a	Lorient	D	1-1	Payet
07/12	h	Metz	W	3-1	Gignac, Ayew, Payet
14/12	a	Monaco	L	0-1	
21/12	h	LOSC	W	2-1	og (Roux), Batshuayi

2015
09/01	a	Montpellier	L	1-2	Omrani
18/01	h	Guingamp	W	2-1	Lemina, Gignac
23/01	a	Nice	L	1-2	Thauvin
31/01	h	Évian	W	1-0	Gignac (p)
07/02	a	Rennes	D	1-1	Ocampos
13/02	h	Reims	D	2-2	Payet, Ayew
22/02	a	St-Étienne	D	2-2	Batshuayi 2
27/02	h	Caen	L	2-3	Ayew, Gignac
06/03	a	Toulouse	W	6-1	Batshuayi 2, Aloé, og (Moubandje), Ayew, Gignac
15/03	h	Lyon	D	0-0	
22/03	h	Lens	W	4-0	Batshuayi 2, Romao, Ayew
05/04	h	Paris	L	2-3	Gignac 2
12/04	a	Bordeaux	L	0-1	
17/04	a	Nantes	L	0-1	
24/04	h	Lorient	L	3-5	Ayew, Morel, Batshuayi
01/05	a	Metz	W	2-0	Gignac 2
10/05	h	Monaco	W	2-1	Ayew, Alessandrini
16/05	a	LOSC	W	4-0	Gignac, Fanni, Alessandrini, Ayew
23/05	h	Bastia	W	3-0	Payet, og (Djiku), Ocampos

No	Name	Nat	DoB	Pos	Aps	(s)	Gls
11	Romain Alessandrini		03/04/89	M	13	(13)	3
2	Baptiste Aloé		29/06/94	D	4	(10)	1
12	Gael Andonyan	ARM	07/02/95	D		(1)	
10	André Ayew	GHA	17/12/89	A	27	(1)	10
27	Abdelaziz Barrada	MAR	19/06/89	M	3	(6)	1
22	Michy Batshuayi	BEL	02/10/93	A	6	(20)	9
33	Bilel Boutobba		29/08/98	A		(3)	
26	Brice Dja Djédjé	CIV	23/12/90	D	33		
24	Rod Fanni		06/12/81	D	24	(3)	2
9	André-Pierre Gignac		05/12/85	A	36	(2)	21
25	Giannelli Imbula		12/09/92	M	37		2
8	Mario Lemina		01/09/93	M	13	(10)	2
4	Lucas Mendes	BRA	03/07/90	D		(1)	
30	Steve Mandanda		28/03/85	G	38		
23	Benjamin Mendy		17/07/94	D	33		
15	Jérémy Morel		02/04/84	D	30	(1)	1
3	Nicolas N'Koulou	CMR	27/03/90	D	23	(1)	2
7	Lucas Ocampos	ARG	11/07/94	M	3	(11)	2
19	Billel Omrani		21/06/93	A		(4)	1
17	Dimitri Payet		29/03/87	M	35	(1)	7
29	Jérémie Porsan-Clemente		16/12/97	A		(1)	
20	Alaixys Romao	TOG	18/01/84	M	27	(5)	2
5	Stéphane Sparagna		17/02/95	M	1	(3)	
14	Florian Thauvin		26/01/93	M	32	(4)	5
18	Bill Tuiloma	NZL	27/03/95	M		(2)	

FC Metz

1932 • Municipal Saint-Syphorien (26,671) • fcmetz.com

Major honours
French Cup (2) 1984, 1988; League Cup (1) 1996

Coach: Albert Cartier

2014
09/08	a	LOSC	D	0-0	
16/08	h	Nantes	D	1-1	N'Gbakoto (p)
23/08	a	Montpellier	D	0-0	
31/08	h	Lyon	W	2-1	N'Gbakoto (p), Falcón
13/09	a	Nice	L	0-1	
20/09	h	Bastia	W	3-1	Krivets, Milán, Falcón
24/09	a	Guingamp	W	1-0	Bussmann
27/09	h	Reims	W	3-0	Falcón 2, Kashi
04/10	a	Évian	L	0-3	
18/10	h	Rennes	D	0-0	
26/10	a	St-Étienne	L	0-1	
01/11	h	Caen	W	3-2	Maïga 2, Malouda (p)
08/11	a	Toulouse	L	0-2	
21/11	h	Paris	L	2-3	Maïga 2 (2p)
29/11	a	Lens	L	0-2	
03/12	a	Bordeaux	D	0-0	
07/12	h	Marseille	L	1-3	Malouda
13/12	a	Lorient	L	1-3	N'Gbakoto
20/12	h	Monaco	L	0-1	

2015
11/01	a	Nantes	D	0-0	
17/01	h	Montpellier	L	2-3	N'Gbakoto (p), Bussmann
25/01	a	Lyon	L	0-2	
31/01	h	Nice	D	0-0	
07/02	a	Bastia	L	0-2	
15/02	h	Guingamp	L	0-2	
22/02	a	Reims	D	0-0	
28/02	h	Évian	L	1-2	Sarr
07/03	a	Rennes	L	0-1	
14/03	h	St-Étienne	L	2-3	Lejeune, N'Gbakoto (p)
21/03	a	Caen	D	0-0	
04/04	h	Toulouse	W	3-2	Maïga 3
18/04	h	Lens	W	3-1	Malouda, Sarr (p), Maïga
25/04	a	Bordeaux	D	1-1	Sassi
28/04	a	Paris	L	1-3	Maïga
01/05	h	Marseille	L	0-2	
09/05	h	Lorient	L	0-4	
16/05	a	Monaco	L	0-2	
23/05	h	LOSC	L	1-4	Palomino

No	Name	Nat	DoB	Pos	Aps	(s)	Gls
11	Federico Andrada	ARG	03/03/94	A	2	(10)	
17	Fakhreddine Ben Youssef	TUN	21/06/91	A	2	(4)	
24	Gaëtan Bussmann		02/02/91	D	31		2
1	Johann Carrasso		07/05/88	G	21		
18	Jérémy Choplin		09/02/85	D	20	(1)	
8	Cheick Doukouré	CIV	11/09/92	M	12	(8)	
9	Juan Falcón	VEN	24/02/89	A	14	(7)	4
4	Moussa Gueye	SEN	20/02/89	A		(3)	
28	Jānis Ikaunieks	LVA	16/02/95	M	2	(2)	
21	Ahmed Kashi	ALG	18/11/88	M	15	(4)	1
29	Sergei Krivets	BLR	08/06/86	M	15	(7)	1
2	Kevin Lejeune		22/01/95	M	27	(5)	1
20	Modibo Maïga	MLI	03/09/87	A	19		9
13	Florent Malouda		13/06/80	M	28		3
4	Sylvain Marchal		10/02/80	D	15	(2)	
15	Roman Métanire		28/03/90	D	33	(1)	
16	Anthony Mfa Mezui	GAB	07/03/91	G	16		
5	Guido Milán	ARG	03/07/87	D	22	(2)	1
25	Guirane N'Daw	SEN	24/04/84	M	25	(2)	
28	Mayoro N'Doye-Baye	SEN	18/12/91	M		(1)	
23	Yeni N'Gbakoto		23/01/92	M	19	(11)	5
12	Kwame N'Sor	GHA	01/08/92	A	2	(5)	
30	David Oberhauser		29/11/91	G	1	(2)	
27	José Luis Palomino	ARG	05/04/90	D	21	(3)	1
26	Chris Philipps	LUX	08/03/94	D	9		
3	Jonathan Rivierez		15/05/89	D	7	(1)	
7	Romain Rocchi		02/10/81	M	3		
10	Bouna Sarr	GUI	31/01/92	M	23	(7)	2
6	Ferjani Sassi	TUN	18/03/92	M	12	(1)	1
14	Fadil Sido	BFA	13/04/93	M	1	(4)	
19	Thibaut Vion		13/12/93	A	1	(4)	

AS Monaco FC

1919 • Louis-II (18,523) • asm-fc.com

Major honours
French League (7) 1961, 1963, 1978, 1982, 1988, 1997, 2000; French Cup (5) 1960, 1963, 1980, 1985, 1991; League Cup (1) 2003

Coach: Leonardo Jardim (POR)

2014
10/08	h	Lorient	L	1-2	Falcao (p)
17/08	a	Bordeaux	L	1-4	Berbatov
24/08	a	Nantes	W	1-0	Falcao
30/08	h	LOSC	D	1-1	Berbatov
12/09	a	Lyon	L	1-2	Ocampos
21/09	h	Guingamp	W	1-0	Dirar
24/09	a	Montpellier	W	1-0	Germain
27/09	h	Nice	L	0-1	
05/10	a	Paris	D	1-1	Martial
18/10	h	Évian	W	2-0	João Moutinho (p), Ferreira Carrasco
25/10	a	Bastia	W	3-1	Germain, Kondogbia, Ferreira Carrasco
31/10	h	Reims	D	1-1	Echijile
09/11	a	St-Étienne	D	1-1	L Traoré
22/11	h	Caen	D	2-2	og (Imorou), João Moutinho
29/11	a	Rennes	L	0-2	
02/12	h	Lens	W	2-0	Berbatov (p), Ferreira Carrasco
05/12	a	Toulouse	W	2-0	Berbatov 2 (1p)
14/12	h	Marseille	W	1-0	Bernardo Silva
20/12	a	Metz	W	1-0	Ferreira Carrasco

2015
11/01	h	Bordeaux	D	0-0	
17/01	h	Nantes	W	1-0	Bernardo Silva
24/01	a	LOSC	W	1-0	Berbatov
01/02	h	Lyon	D	0-0	
08/02	a	Guingamp	L	0-1	
20/02	a	Nice	W	1-0	Bernardo Silva
01/03	h	Paris	D	0-0	
07/03	a	Évian	W	3-1	Martial, og (Abdallah), Touré
13/03	h	Bastia	W	3-0	Martial 2, Matheus Carvalho
22/03	a	Reims	W	3-1	Fabinho, Martial, Dirar
03/04	h	St-Étienne	D	1-1	Martial
07/04	h	Montpellier	D	0-0	
10/04	h	Caen	W	3-0	Martial, Bernardo Silva 2
18/04	a	Rennes	W	1-0	Bernardo Silva
26/04	a	Lens	W	3-0	Ferreira Carrasco, Martial, Bernardo Silva
03/05	h	Toulouse	W	4-1	Bernardo Silva, Martial (p), João Moutinho, Germain
10/05	a	Marseille	L	1-2	João Moutinho
16/05	h	Metz	W	2-0	Bernardo Silva, Germain
23/05	a	Lorient	W	1-0	Ferreira Carrasco

No	Name	Nat	DoB	Pos	Aps	(s)	Gls
5	Aymen Abdennour	TUN	06/08/89	D	17	(1)	
14	Tiémoué Bakayoko		17/08/94	M	10	(2)	
10	Dimitar Berbatov	BUL	30/01/81	A	18	(8)	6
15	Bernardo Silva	POR	10/08/94	M	25	(7)	9
34	Abdou Diallo		04/05/96	D	1	(4)	
7	Nabil Dirar	MAR	25/02/86	M	13	(14)	2
21	Elderson Echijile	NGA	20/01/88	D	10	(2)	1
2	Fabinho	BRA	23/10/93	D	35	(1)	1
9	Radamel Falcao	COL	10/02/86	A	1	(2)	2
17	Yannick Ferreira Carrasco	BEL	04/09/93	M	33	(3)	6
18	Valère Germain		17/04/90	A	9	(20)	4
8	João Moutinho	POR	08/09/86	M	35	(2)	4
33	Aboubakar Kamara		07/03/95	A		(2)	
22	Geoffrey Kondogbia		15/02/93	M	22	(1)	1
3	Layvin Kurzawa		04/09/92	D	25	(2)	
23	Anthony Martial		05/12/95	A	19	(16)	9
12	Matheus Carvalho	BRA	11/03/92	A	4	(4)	1
10	Lucas Ocampos	ARG	11/07/94	M	7	(10)	1
24	Andrea Raggi	ITA	24/06/84	D	27		
6	Ricardo Carvalho	POR	18/05/78	D	23	(2)	
16	Maarten Stekelenburg	NED	22/09/82	G	1		
1	Danijel Subašić	CRO	27/10/84	G	37		
28	Jérémy Toulalan		10/09/83	M	28		
38	Almamy Touré	MLI	28/04/96	D	4	(1)	1
25	Alain Traoré	BFA	01/01/88	M		(1)	
19	Lacina Traoré	CIV	20/08/90	A	3	(3)	1
13	Wallace	BRA	14/10/94	D	11	(3)	

Montpellier Hérault SC

1974 • La Mosson (32,950) • mhscfoot.com
Major honours
French League (1) 2012; French Cup (1) 1990
Coach: Rolland Courbis

2014

09/08	h	Bordeaux	L	0-1	
17/08	a	Marseille	W	2-0	Mounier, Sanson
23/08	h	Metz	W	2-0	Tiéné, Camara
30/08	a	Nantes	L	0-1	
13/09	h	Lorient	W	1-0	og (Koné)
21/09	a	LOSC	D	0-0	
24/09	h	Monaco	L	0-1	
27/09	h	Guingamp	W	2-1	Camara, Montaño
04/10	h	Nice	D	1-1	Hilton
19/10	a	Lyon	L	1-5	Tiéné
25/10	a	Reims	L	0-1	
01/11	h	Évian	W	2-0	Bérigaud, Mounier
08/11	a	Bastia	L	0-2	
23/11	h	Toulouse	W	2-0	Mounier, Camara
29/11	h	Caen	D	1-1	Hilton
03/12	h	St-Étienne	L	0-2	
06/12	a	Rennes	W	4-0	Martin, Sanson, Barrios, Mounier
13/12	h	Lens	D	3-3	Sanson, Barrios, Mounier
20/12	a	Paris	D	0-0	

2015

09/01	h	Marseille	W	2-1	Bérigaud, Lasne
17/01	a	Metz	W	3-2	Barrios 3 (1p)
24/01	h	Nantes	W	4-0	Lasne, Bérigaud, Mounier, Barrios
31/01	a	Lorient	D	0-0	
07/02	h	LOSC	L	1-2	Dabo
22/02	a	Guingamp	W	2-0	Sanson, Bérigaud
01/03	h	Nice	W	2-1	Dabo, Barrios
08/03	h	Lyon	L	1-5	Barrios
14/03	h	Reims	W	3-1	Barrios 2, Sanson
21/03	a	Évian	L	0-1	
04/04	h	Bastia	W	3-1	Barrios (p), Mounier (p), Sanson
07/04	a	Monaco	D	0-0	
12/04	a	Toulouse	L	0-1	
19/04	h	Caen	W	1-0	Hilton
26/04	a	St-Étienne	L	0-1	
02/05	h	Rennes	D	0-0	
10/05	a	Lens	W	1-0	Mounier
16/05	h	Paris	L	1-2	Mounier
23/05	a	Bordeaux	L	1-2	Bakar

No	Name	Nat	DoB	Pos	Aps	(s)	Gls
28	Djamel Bakar		06/04/89	A	1	(13)	1
10	Lucas Barrios	ARG	13/11/84	A	30	(1)	11
9	Kévin Bérigaud		09/05/88	A	23	(10)	4
19	Souleymane Camara	SEN	22/12/82	A	7	(30)	3
3	Daniel Congré		05/04/85	D	26	(4)	
14	Bryan Dabo		18/02/92	M	20	(1)	2
25	Mathieu Deplagne		01/10/91	D	23	(8)	
24	Jean Deza	PER	09/06/93	A		(2)	
21	Abdelhamid El Kaoutari	MAR	17/03/90	D	37	(1)	
13	Dylan Gissi	SUI	27/04/91	D	1		
4	Hilton	BRA	13/09/77	D	37		3
16	Geoffrey Jourdren		04/02/86	G	29		
17	Paul Lasne		16/01/89	M	21	(10)	2
30	Jonathan Ligali		28/05/91	G	6		
8	Jonas Martin		09/04/90	M	27	(4)	1
6	Joris Marveaux		15/08/82	D	20	(9)	
11	Victor Montaño	COL	01/05/84	A	2	(7)	1
7	Anthony Mounier		27/09/87	A	36		9
34	Mamadou N'Diaye	SEN	28/05/95	D		(1)	
1	Laurent Pionnier		24/05/82	G	3		
33	Anthony Ribelin		08/04/96	M		(7)	
23	Jamel Saïhi	TUN	27/01/87	M	20	(1)	
20	Morgan Sanson		18/08/94	M	30	(2)	6
33	Ellyes Skhiri		10/05/95	M	1	(1)	
22	Benjamin Stambouli			D	2		
5	Siaka Tiéné	CIV	22/02/82	D	15	(2)	2
22	Sébastien Wüthrich	SUI	29/05/90	M	1		

FC Nantes

1943 • La Beaujoire (38,004) • fcnantes.com
Major honours
French League (8) 1965, 1966, 1973, 1977, 1980, 1983, 1995, 2001; French Cup (3) 1979, 1999, 2000
Coach: Michel Der Zakarian (ARM)

2014

09/08	h	Lens	W	1-0	Bammou
16/08	a	Metz	D	1-1	Veretout
24/08	h	Monaco	D	0-0	
30/08	h	Montpellier	W	1-0	Gakpé
14/09	a	LOSC	L	0-2	
20/09	h	Nice	W	2-1	og (Amavi), Shechter
24/09	a	Bastia	D	0-0	
28/09	h	Lyon	D	1-1	Veretout (p)
05/10	a	Guingamp	W	1-0	N'Koudou
18/10	h	Reims	D	1-1	Audel
25/10	a	Évian	W	2-0	Veretout (p), Bammou
02/11	h	Rennes	D	1-1	og (Armand)
08/11	a	Caen	W	2-1	Vizcarrondo, Veretout
23/11	a	St-Étienne	D	0-0	
28/11	h	Marseille	L	0-2	
02/12	h	Toulouse	L	1-2	Veretout (p)
06/12	a	Paris	L	1-2	Bedoya
13/12	h	Bordeaux	W	2-1	Veretout, og (Jug)
20/12	a	Lorient	W	2-1	Bammou, Audel

2015

11/01	h	Metz	D	0-0	
17/01	a	Monaco	L	0-1	
24/01	a	Montpellier	L	0-4	
31/01	h	LOSC	D	1-1	Vizcarrondo
08/02	h	Nice	D	0-0	
14/02	h	Bastia	L	0-2	
22/02	a	Lyon	L	0-1	
01/03	h	Guingamp	W	1-0	Bammou
07/03	a	Reims	L	1-3	Bangoura
14/03	h	Évian	W	2-1	N'Koudou, Gakpé
21/03	a	Rennes	D	0-0	
05/04	h	Caen	L	1-2	Bedoya
12/04	a	St-Étienne	L	0-1	
17/04	h	Marseille	W	1-0	Gakpé
25/04	a	Toulouse	D	1-1	Bedoya
03/05	h	Paris	L	0-2	
09/05	a	Bordeaux	L	1-2	Veretout (p)
16/05	h	Lorient	D	1-1	Audel
23/05	a	Lens	L	0-1	

No	Name	Nat	DoB	Pos	Aps	(s)	Gls
24	Chaker Alhadhur	COM	04/12/91	D	12	(3)	
10	Fernando Aristeguieta	VEN	09/04/92	A	2	(4)	
21	Johan Audel		12/12/83	A	14	(10)	3
23	Yacine Bammou	MAR	21/11/91	A	25	(12)	4
11	Ismaël Bangoura	GUI	02/01/85	A	9		1
7	Alejandro Bedoya	USA	29/04/87	M	20	(8)	3
8	Vincent Bessat		08/11/85	M	19	(8)	
22	Issa Cissokho	SEN	23/02/85	D	32	(1)	
18	Lucas Déaux		26/12/88	M	23	(11)	
26	Koffi Djidji		30/11/92	D	4	(1)	
3	Papy Mison Djilobodji	SEN	01/12/88	D	30	(1)	
15	Léo Dubois		14/09/94	D	1	(1)	
30	Maxime Dupé		04/03/93	G	6		
13	Serge Gakpé	TOG	07/05/87	A	25	(9)	3
6	Rémi Gomis	SEN	14/02/84	M	15	(5)	
2	Kian Hansen	DEN	03/03/89	D	28	(1)	
33	Jules Iloki		14/01/92	M		(2)	
38	Aristode N'Dongala	COD	19/01/94	A		(1)	
14	Georges-Kévin N'Koudou		13/02/95	M	16	(12)	2
27	Adama Niane	MLI	16/06/93	A		(3)	
1	Rémy Riou		06/08/87	G	32		
28	Valentina Rongier		07/12/94	M	3	(3)	
9	Itay Shechter	ISR	22/02/87	A	6	(7)	1
3	Birama Touré	MLI	06/06/92	M		(1)	
5	Olivier Veigneau		16/07/85	D	24		
25	Jordan Veretout		01/03/93	M	36		7
4	Oswaldo Vizcarrondo	VEN	31/05/84	D	36		2

OGC Nice

1904 • Allianz Riviera (35,624) • ogcnice.com
Major honours
French League (4) 1951, 1952, 1956, 1959; French Cup (3) 1952, 1954, 1997
Coach: Claude Puel

2014

09/08	h	Toulouse	W	3-2	Cvitanich 2, Bosetti
16/08	a	Lorient	D	0-0	
23/08	h	Bordeaux	L	1-3	Bosetti
29/08	h	Marseille	L	0-4	
13/09	h	Metz	W	1-0	Bosetti
20/09	h	Nantes	L	1-2	Amavi
24/09	h	LOSC	L	0-1	Bodmer
27/09	a	Monaco	W	1-0	Carlos Eduardo
04/10	h	Montpellier	D	1-1	Palun
18/10	h	Bastia	L	0-1	
26/10	h	Guingamp	W	7-2	Carlos Eduardo 5, Pléa, Bauthéac
01/11	h	Lyon	L	1-3	G Puel
08/11	a	Évian	L	0-1	
22/11	h	Reims	D	0-0	
29/11	h	Paris	L	0-1	
03/12	h	Rennes	L	1-2	Cvitanich
06/12	a	Caen	W	3-2	Amavi, Bauthéac (p), Pléa
14/12	a	St-Étienne	D	0-0	
19/12	h	Lens	L	0-2	

2015

10/01	h	Lorient	W	3-1	Bauthéac (p), Bosetti, Carlos Eduardo
16/01	a	Bordeaux	W	2-1	Amavi, Pléa
23/01	h	Marseille	W	2-1	Genevois, Hult
31/01	a	Metz	D	0-0	
08/02	h	Nantes	D	0-0	
14/02	a	LOSC	D	0-0	
20/02	a	Monaco	L	0-1	
01/03	a	Montpellier	L	1-2	Bauthéac (p)
07/03	a	Bastia	L	1-2	Carlos Eduardo
13/03	h	Guingamp	L	1-2	Bauthéac
21/03	a	Lyon	W	2-1	Carlos Eduardo, Eysseric (p)
04/04	h	Évian	D	2-2	Bosetti, Eysseric
12/04	a	Reims	W	1-0	Benrahma
18/04	h	Paris	L	1-3	Bodmer
24/04	a	Rennes	L	1-2	Bauthéac
02/05	h	Caen	D	1-1	Carlos Eduardo
10/05	a	St-Étienne	L	0-5	
16/05	h	Lens	W	2-1	Amavi, Digard
23/05	a	Toulouse	W	3-2	Maupay, Bauthéac 2

No	Name	Nat	DoB	Pos	Aps	(s)	Gls
19	Jordan Amavi		09/03/94	D	36		4
11	Éric Bauthéac		24/08/87	M	29	(6)	8
35	Saïd Benrahma	ALG	10/08/95	A	3		1
24	Mathieu Bodmer		22/11/82	D	21	(1)	2
34	Olivier Boscagli		18/11/97	D	2		
23	Alexy Bosetti		23/04/93	A	13	(14)	5
3	Carlos Eduardo	BRA	18/07/87	M	29	(1)	10
34	Bryan Constant		27/03/94	A		(2)	
12	Dario Cvitanich	ARG	16/05/84	A	5	(4)	3
16	Joris Delle		29/03/90	G		(1)	
20	Souleymane Diawarra	SEN	24/12/78	D	12	(2)	
6	Didier Digard		12/07/86	M	9	(5)	1
10	Valentin Eysseric		25/03/92	M	24	(12)	2
25	Romain Genevois	HAI	28/10/87	D	34		1
5	Kévin Gomis		20/01/89	D	11	(5)	
40	Mouez Hassen		05/03/95	G	30		
34	Franck Honorat		11/08/96	A	1	(4)	
13	Niklas Hult	SWE	13/02/90	M	20	(10)	1
34	Vincent Koziello		28/10/95	M	3	(4)	
18	Neal Maupay		14/08/96	A	3	(10)	1
22	Nampalys Mendy		23/06/92	M	36		
21	Lloyd Palun	GAB	28/11/88	M	19	(2)	1
14	Jérémy Pied		23/02/89	A	2		
10	Alassane Pléa		10/03/93	A	27	(6)	3
16	Simon Pouplin		28/05/85	G	8		
15	Grégoire Puel		20/02/92	A	26	(1)	1
35	Paulin Puel		09/05/91	A		(1)	
33	Albert Rafetraniaina	MAD	09/09/96	D	12	(9)	
34	Sada Thioub		01/06/95	A		(2)	
7	Julien Vercauteren	BEL	12/01/93	M	3	(6)	

Paris Saint-Germain

1970 • Parc des Princes (48,527) • psg.fr

Major honours
UEFA Cup Winners' Cup (1) 1996; French League
(5) 1986, 1994, 2013, 2014, 2015; French Cup (9)
1982, 1983, 1993, 1995, 1998, 2004, 2006, 2010,
2015; League Cup (5) 1995, 1998, 2008, 2014, 2015
Coach: Laurent Blanc

2014

08/08	a	Reims	D	2-2	Ibrahimović 2
16/08	h	Bastia	W	2-0	Lucas, Cavani
22/08	a	Évian	D	0-0	
31/08	a	St-Étienne	W	5-0	og (Ruffier), Ibrahimović 3, Cavani
13/09	a	Rennes	D	1-1	Camara
21/09	h	Lyon	W	1-0	Cavani
24/09	a	Caen	W	2-0	Lucas, Marquinhos
27/09	a	Toulouse	D	1-1	Bahebeck
05/10	h	Monaco	D	1-1	Lucas
17/10	a	Lens	W	3-1	Cabaye, Maxwell, Cavani (p)
25/10	h	Bordeaux	W	3-0	Lucas 2 (2p), Lavezzi
01/11	a	Lorient	W	2-1	Cavani, Bahebeck
09/11	h	Marseille	W	2-0	Lucas, Cavani
21/11	a	Metz	W	3-2	Pastore, og (Bussmann), Lavezzi
29/11	h	Nice	W	1-0	Ibrahimović (p)
03/12	a	LOSC	D	1-1	Cavani
06/12	h	Nantes	W	2-1	Ibrahimović 2
14/12	a	Guingamp	L	0-1	
20/12	h	Montpellier	D	0-0	

2015

10/01	a	Bastia	L	2-4	Lucas, Rabiot
18/01	h	Évian	W	4-2	David Luiz, Verratti, Pastore, Cavani
25/01	a	St-Étienne	W	1-0	Ibrahimović (p)
30/01	h	Rennes	W	1-0	Lavezzi
08/02	a	Lyon	D	1-1	Ibrahimović (p)
14/02	h	Caen	D	2-2	Ibrahimović, Lavezzi
21/02	a	Toulouse	W	3-1	Rabiot 2, Thiago Silva
01/03	a	Monaco	D	0-0	
07/03	h	Lens	W	4-1	David Luiz, Ibrahimović (p), Matuidi, Pastore
15/03	a	Bordeaux	L	2-3	Ibrahimović 2 (1p)
20/03	a	Lorient	W	3-1	Ibrahimović 3 (2p)
05/04	a	Marseille	W	3-2	Matuidi, Marquinhos, og (Morel)
18/04	a	Nice	W	3-1	Pastore 2, Cavani (p)
25/04	h	LOSC	W	6-1	Maxwell, Cavani 2 (1p), Lavezzi 3
28/04	h	Metz	W	3-1	Verratti, Cavani, Van der Wiel
03/05	a	Nantes	W	2-0	Cavani, Matuidi
08/05	h	Guingamp	W	6-0	Cavani 3, Ibrahimović 2 (1p), Maxwell
16/05	a	Montpellier	W	2-1	Matuidi, Lavezzi
23/05	h	Reims	W	3-2	Cavani 2, Rabiot

No	Name	Nat	DoB	Pos	Aps	(s)	Gls
19	Serge Aurier	CIV	24/12/92	D	12	(2)	
15	Jean-Christophe Bahebeck		01/05/93	A	3	(12)	2
4	Yohan Cabaye		14/01/86	M	13	(11)	1
6	Zoumana Camara		03/04/79	D	6	(2)	1
9	Edinson Cavani	URU	14/02/87	A	30	(5)	18
20	Clément Chantôme		11/09/87	M		(6)	
32	David Luiz	BRA	22/04/87	D	26	(2)	2
21	Lucas Digne		20/07/93	D	14	(1)	
1	Nicolas Douchez		22/04/80	G	4	(1)	
10	Zlatan Ibrahimović	SWE	03/10/81	A	23	(1)	19
34	Presnel Kimpembe		13/08/95	D		(1)	
22	Ezequiel Lavezzi	ARG	03/05/85	A	19	(12)	8
7	Lucas	BRA	13/08/92	M	22	(7)	7
5	Marquinhos	BRA	14/05/94	D	21	(4)	2
14	Blaise Matuidi		09/04/87	M	25	(9)	4
17	Maxwell	BRA	27/08/81	D	24	(2)	3
27	Javier Pastore	ARG	20/06/89	M	31	(3)	5
25	Adrien Rabiot		03/04/95	M	10	(11)	4
30	Salvatore Sirigu	ITA	12/01/87	G	34		
8	Thiago Motta		28/08/82	M	25	(2)	
2	Thiago Silva	BRA	22/09/84	D	26		1
23	Gregory van der Wiel	NED	03/02/88	D	22	(3)	1
24	Marco Verratti	ITA	05/11/92	M	28	(4)	2

Stade de Reims

1911 • Auguste-Delaune (21,628) •
stade-de-reims.com

Major honours
French League (6) 1949, 1953, 1955, 1958, 1960,
1962; French Cup (2) 1950, 1958
**Coach: Jean-Luc Vasseur;
(08/04/15) Olivier Guégan**

2014

08/08	h	Paris	D	2-2	Oniangué, Devaux
17/08	a	St-Étienne	L	1-3	og (Perrin)
23/08	h	Caen	L	0-2	
30/08	a	Lens	L	2-4	Mandi, Courtet
13/09	h	Toulouse	W	2-0	N'Gog, Courtet
20/09	a	Lorient	W	1-0	Moukandjo
23/09	h	Marseille	L	0-5	
27/09	a	Metz	L	0-3	
03/10	h	Bordeaux	W	1-0	Odair Fortes
18/10	a	Nantes	D	1-1	Diego
25/10	h	Montpellier	L	0-1	Moukandjo
31/10	a	Monaco	D	1-1	Moukandjo
09/11	h	LOSC	W	2-0	Moukandjo (p), Mandi
22/11	a	Nice	D	0-0	
29/11	h	Bastia	W	2-1	N'Gog, Moukandjo
04/12	a	Lyon	L	1-2	Moukandjo
07/12	h	Guingamp	L	2-3	Charbonnier, Oniangué
13/12	h	Évian	W	3-2	Diego 2, Mandi
20/12	a	Rennes	W	3-1	Charbonnier, Odair Fortes, De Préville

2015

10/01	h	St-Étienne	L	1-2	Diego
17/01	a	Caen	L	1-4	Charbonnier (p)
25/01	h	Lens	D	0-0	
31/01	a	Toulouse	L	0-1	
07/02	h	Lorient	L	1-3	Moukandjo
13/02	a	Marseille	D	2-2	De Préville, N'Gog
22/02	h	Metz	D	0-0	
28/02	a	Bordeaux	D	1-1	Charbonnier
07/03	h	Nantes	W	3-1	Bourillon, Mandi, N'Gog
14/03	a	Montpellier	L	1-3	Oniangué
22/03	h	Monaco	L	1-3	Diego
04/04	a	LOSC	L	1-3	De Préville
12/04	h	Nice	L	0-1	
18/04	a	Bastia	W	2-1	N'Gog, Mandi
26/04	h	Lyon	L	2-4	Peuget, Charbonnier
02/05	a	Guingamp	L	0-2	
09/05	a	Évian	W	3-2	N'Gog 2, Moukandjo
16/05	h	Nantes	W	1-0	Charbonnier (p)
23/05	a	Paris	L	2-3	Mandi, Kyei

No	Name	Nat	DoB	Pos	Aps	(s)	Gls
16	Kossi Agassa	TOG	07/07/78	G	16	(1)	
17	Mads Albæk	DEN	14/01/90	M	8	(4)	
9	Eliran Atar	ISR	17/02/87	A		(1)	
40	Sacha Bastien		22/01/95	G	1		
5	Grégory Bourillon		01/07/84	M	18	(3)	1
21	Bocundji Ca	GNB	28/12/86	M		(5)	
10	Gaëtan Charbonnier		27/12/88	A	29	(4)	6
28	Antoine Conte		29/01/94	D	29		
18	Gaëtan Courtet		22/02/89	A	3	(14)	2
12	Nicolas De Préville		08/01/91	A	13	(12)	3
6	Antoine Devaux		23/02/85	M	27	(1)	1
11	Diego	BRA	09/03/88	M	28	(3)	5
2	Mohamed Fofana	MLI	07/03/85	D	10	(2)	
50	Cyriack Garel		13/07/96	G		(1)	
27	Christopher Glombard		05/06/89	D	3	(8)	
29	Grejohn Kyei		12/08/95	A		(3)	1
26	Omenuke M'Fulu	COD	20/03/94	D	1	(6)	
23	Aïssa Mandi	ALG	22/10/91	D	32		6
15	Chris Mavinga	COD	26/05/91	D	7	(2)	
14	Benjamin Moukandjo	CMR	12/11/88	M	19	(12)	8
24	David N'Gog		01/04/89	A	22	(6)	7
8	Odair Fortes	CPV	31/03/87	A	24	(9)	2
8	Prince Oniangué	CGO	04/11/88	M	30	(2)	3
30	Alexi Peuget		18/12/90	M	5	(4)	1
19	Johnny Placide	HAI	29/01/88	G	21	(1)	
4	Valentin Roberge		09/06/87	D	11		
33	Theoson Jordan Siebatcheu		26/04/96	A		(1)	
3	Franck Signorino		19/09/81	D	26		
22	Mickaël Tacalfred		23/04/81	D	27	(2)	
25	Anthony Weber		11/06/87	D	8	(5)	

Stade Rennais FC

1901 • Route de Lorient (29,778) •
staderennais.com

Major honours
French Cup (2) 1965, 1971
Coach: Philippe Montanier

2014

10/08	a	Lyon	L	0-2	
16/08	h	Évian	W	6-2	Toivonen 2, Mexer 2, Ntep 2
24/08	a	St-Étienne	D	0-0	
30/08	a	Caen	W	1-0	Toivonen (p)
13/09	h	Paris	D	1-1	og (Maxwell)
20/09	a	Marseille	L	0-3	
23/09	h	Toulouse	L	0-3	
28/09	a	Bordeaux	L	1-2	Habibou
04/10	h	Lens	W	2-0	Ntep 2
18/10	a	Metz	D	0-0	
26/10	h	LOSC	W	2-0	Habibou, Doucouré
02/11	a	Nantes	D	1-1	Pedro Henrique
07/11	h	Lorient	W	1-0	Pedro Henrique
22/11	a	Guingamp	W	1-0	Ntep
29/11	h	Monaco	W	2-0	og (Abdennour), Toivonen
03/12	a	Nice	W	2-1	Ntep, Konradsen
06/12	h	Montpellier	L	0-4	
13/12	a	Bastia	L	0-2	
20/12	h	Reims	L	1-3	Mexer

2015

10/01	a	Évian	D	1-1	Ntep
18/01	h	St-Étienne	D	0-0	
25/01	h	Caen	L	1-4	André
30/01	a	Paris	L	0-1	
07/02	h	Marseille	D	1-1	Toivonen
14/02	a	Toulouse	L	1-2	Toivonen
21/02	h	Bordeaux	D	1-1	Ntep
28/02	a	Lens	W	1-0	Doucouré
07/03	h	Metz	W	1-0	Ntep
15/03	a	LOSC	L	0-3	
21/03	h	Nantes	D	0-0	
04/04	a	Lorient	W	3-0	Mexer, Armand, Doucouré
12/04	h	Guingamp	W	1-0	Toivonen
18/04	a	Monaco	D	1-1	Habibou
25/04	h	Nice	W	2-1	Prcić, Konradsen
02/05	a	Montpellier	D	0-0	
09/05	h	Bastia	L	0-1	
16/05	a	Reims	L	0-1	
23/05	h	Lyon	L	0-1	

No	Name	Nat	DoB	Pos	Aps	(s)	Gls
21	Benjamin André		03/08/90	M	16	(6)	1
22	Sylvain Armand		01/08/80	D	36		1
13	Christian Brüls	BEL	30/09/88	D	6	(3)	
1	Benoît Costil		03/07/87	G	38		
29	Romain Danzé		03/07/86	D	29	(2)	
14	Fallou Diagné	SEN	14/08/89	D	13	(2)	
8	Abdoulaye Doucouré		01/01/93	M	31	(4)	3
6	Gelson Fernandes	SUI	02/09/86	M	32	(1)	
10	Kamil Grosicki	POL	08/06/88	M	9	(10)	
11	Habib Habibou	CTA	16/04/87	A	8	(18)	3
11	Philipp Hosiner	AUT	15/05/89	A	3	(9)	
23	Anders Konradsen	NOR	18/07/90	M	10	(9)	2
19	Ermir Lenjani	ALB	05/08/89	D	1	(2)	
3	Cheikh M'Bengue	SEN	23/07/88	D	32		
15	Jean II Makoun	CMR	29/05/83	M	1		
4	Mexer	MOZ	08/12/88	D	35		4
12	Steven Moreira		13/08/94	D	13	(10)	
7	Paul-Georges Ntep		29/07/92	A	29	(6)	9
17	Vincent Pajot		18/09/90	M	20	(3)	
18	Pedro Henrique	BRA	14/05/88	M	21	(13)	2
24	Sanjin Prcić	BIH	20/11/93	M	7	(10)	1
9	Ola Toivonen	SWE	03/07/86	A	28	(2)	7

AS Saint-Étienne

1933 • Geoffroy-Guichard (38,458) • asse.fr
Major honours
French League (10) 1957, 1964, 1967, 1968, 1969, 1970, 1974, 1975, 1976, 1981; French Cup (6) 1962, 1968, 1970, 1974, 1975, 1977; League Cup (1) 2013
Coach: Christophe Galtier

2014
09/08	a	Guingamp	W 2-0	Mevlüt 2 (1p)
17/08	h	Reims	W 3-1	Gradel, Monnet-Paquet, Mevlüt
24/08	h	Rennes	D 0-0	
31/08	a	Paris	L 0-5	
13/09	h	Caen	W 1-0	og (Pierre)
21/09	a	Lens	W 1-0	Lemoine
25/09	h	Bordeaux	D 1-1	Van Wolfswinkel
28/09	a	Marseille	L 1-2	Brison
05/10	h	Toulouse	L 0-1	
18/10	a	Lorient	W 1-0	Lemoine
26/10	h	Metz	W 1-0	Gradel
01/11	a	LOSC	D 1-1	Gradel
09/11	h	Monaco	D 1-1	Van Wolfswinkel
23/11	a	Nantes	D 0-0	
30/11	a	Lyon	W 3-0	Bayal Sall, Van Wolfswinkel, Cohade
03/12	a	Montpellier	W 2-0	Pogba, Baysse
06/12	h	Bastia	W 1-0	Van Wolfswinkel
14/12	a	Nice	D 0-0	
21/12	h	Évian	W 3-0	Gradel, Van Wolfswinkel, Hamouma

2015
10/01	a	Reims	W 2-1	Mollo, Hamouma
18/01	a	Rennes	D 0-0	
25/01	h	Paris	L 0-1	
01/02	a	Caen	W 1-0	
06/02	h	Lens	D 3-3	N'Guémo, Mollo, Mevlüt
15/02	a	Bordeaux	L 0-1	
22/02	h	Marseille	D 2-2	Gradel (p), Mevlüt
28/02	a	Toulouse	D 1-1	Gradel (p)
08/03	h	Lorient	W 2-0	Mollo, Gradel
14/03	a	Metz	W 3-2	Gradel, Mevlüt, Mollo
22/03	h	LOSC	W 2-0	Gradel 2
03/04	a	Monaco	D 1-1	Mevlüt
12/04	h	Nantes	W 1-0	Tabanou
19/04	a	Lyon	D 2-2	Gradel (p), Hamouma
26/04	h	Montpellier	W 1-0	Gradel
02/05	a	Bastia	L 0-1	
10/05	h	Nice	W 5-0	Perrin, Clément, Mevlüt, Gradel, Monnet-Paquet
16/05	a	Évian	W 2-1	Gradel 2 (1p)
23/05	h	Guingamp	W 2-1	Gradel 2

No	Name	Nat	DoB	Pos	Aps	(s)	Gls
33	Jonathan Bamba		26/03/96	M		(3)	
26	Moustapha Bayal Sall	SEN	30/11/85	D	23		1
23	Paul Baysse		18/05/88	D	8	(1)	1
20	Jonathan Brison		07/02/83	D	9	(9)	1
6	Jérémy Clément		26/08/84	M	28	(1)	1
29	François Clerc		18/04/83	D	15		
10	Renaud Cohade		29/09/84	M	11	(6)	1
8	Benjamin Corgnet		04/04/87	M	15	(10)	
28	Ismaël Diomandé	CIV	28/08/92	M	12	(8)	
7	Max-Alain Gradel	CIV	30/11/87	M	23	(8)	17
21	Romain Hamouma		29/03/87	M	23	(3)	3
31	Ben-Kantie Karamoko		17/05/95	D	1	(1)	
18	Fabien Lemoine		16/03/87	M	31	(4)	2
9	Mevlüt Erdinç	TUR	25/02/87	A	20	(6)	8
11	Yohan Mollo		18/07/89	A	12	(11)	4
22	Kévin Monnet-Paquet		19/08/88	A	18	(12)	2
9	Landry N'Guémo	CMR	28/11/85	M	11	(3)	
24	Loïc Perrin		07/08/85	D	27	(1)	1
19	Florentin Pogba	GUI	19/08/90	D	12	(4)	1
16	Stéphane Ruffier		27/09/86	G	38		
12	Allan Saint-Maximin		12/03/97	A	3		
27	Franck Tabanou		30/01/89	M	30	(1)	1
2	Kévin Théophile-Catherine		28/10/89	D	30	(1)	
13	Ricky van Wolfswinkel	NED	27/01/89	A	18	(10)	5

Toulouse FC

1937 • Stadium Municipal (22,814) • tfc.info
Major honours
French Cup (1) 1957
Coach: Alain Casanova; (16/03/15) Dominique Arribagé

2014
09/08	a	Nice	L 2-3	Braithwaite, Ben Yedder
16/08	h	Lyon	W 2-1	Akpa-Akpro, Ben Yedder
23/08	a	Bastia	L 0-1	
30/08	h	Évian	W 1-0	Regattin
13/09	a	Reims	L 0-2	
20/09	h	Caen	D 3-3	Ben Yedder (p), Regattin (p), Ninkov
23/09	a	Rennes	W 3-0	Pešić, og (Diagné), Ben Yedder
27/09	h	Paris	D 1-1	Ben Yedder
05/10	a	St-Étienne	W 1-0	Ben Yedder
19/10	a	Marseille	L 0-2	
24/10	h	Lens	L 0-2	
02/11	a	Bordeaux	L 1-2	Pešić
08/11	h	Metz	W 3-0	Sirieix, Ben Yedder, Pešić
23/11	a	Montpellier	L 0-2	
29/11	h	Lorient	L 2-3	Doumbia, Pešić
02/12	h	Nantes	W 2-1	Sylla, Braithwaite
05/12	h	Monaco	L 0-1	
14/12	a	LOSC	L 0-3	
20/12	h	Guingamp	D 1-1	Doumbia

2015
11/01	a	Lyon	L 0-3	
17/01	h	Bastia	D 1-1	Braithwaite
25/01	a	Évian	L 0-1	
31/01	h	Reims	W 1-0	Pešić
07/02	a	Caen	L 0-2	
14/02	h	Rennes	W 2-1	Trejo, Pešić
21/02	a	Paris	L 1-3	Ben Yedder
28/02	h	St-Étienne	D 1-1	Akpa-Akpro
06/03	h	Marseille	L 1-6	Ben Yedder
14/03	a	Lens	L 0-1	
21/03	h	Bordeaux	W 2-1	Ben Yedder, Kana-Biyik
04/04	a	Metz	L 2-3	Ben Yedder, Doumbia
12/04	h	Montpellier	W 1-0	Trejo
18/04	a	Lorient	W 1-0	Braithwaite
25/04	h	Nantes	D 1-1	Regattin
03/05	a	Monaco	L 1-4	Braithwaite
09/05	h	LOSC	W 3-2	Ben Yedder, Trejo, Braithwaite
16/05	a	Guingamp	L 1-2	Ben Yedder (p)
23/05	h	Lyon	L 2-3	Ben Yedder, Trejo

No	Name	Nat	DoB	Pos	Aps	(s)	Gls
21	Abel Aguilar	COL	06/01/85	M	18	(3)	
30	Ali Ahamada		14/07/90	G	23	(9)	
4	Jean-Daniel Akpa-Akpro	CIV	11/10/92	M	25	(7)	2
10	Wissam Ben Yedder		12/08/90	A	34	(2)	14
33	Youssef Benali		04/02/95	A		(3)	
4	Alexis Blin		16/09/96	M	3	(3)	
34	Yann Bodiger		09/02/95	M	10		
1	Zacharie Boucher		07/03/92	G	15		
7	Martin Braithwaite	DEN	05/06/91	A	22	(12)	6
4	Étienne Didot		24/07/83	M	16	(4)	
4	Tongo Doumbia	MLI	06/08/89	M	22	(2)	3
25	Dragoş Grigore	ROU	07/09/86	D	25	(2)	
3	Jean-Armel Kana-Biyik	CMR	03/07/89	D	13		1
35	Sami Larabi		13/04/96	D		(1)	
33	Zinédine Machach		05/01/96	A		(1)	
29	François Moubandje	SUI	21/06/90	D	30	(1)	
24	Pavle Ninkov	SRB	20/04/85	D	15	(6)	1
11	Aleksandar Pešić	SRB	21/04/92	A	22	(12)	6
17	Adrien Regattin	MAR	22/08/91	M	17	(17)	3
14	François Sirieix		07/10/80	M	7	(7)	1
15	Uroš Spajić	SRB	13/02/93	D	17		
2	Maxime Spano		31/10/94	D	2	(1)	
5	Issiaga Sylla	GUI	01/01/93	D	9	(3)	1
18	Óscar Trejo	ARG	26/04/88	M	25	(6)	4
22	Dušan Veškovac	SRB	16/03/86	D	13		
6	William Matheus	BRA	02/04/90	D	6	(4)	
20	Steeve Yago	BFA	16/12/92	D	12	(2)	

Top goalscorers

27	Alexandre Lacazette (Lyon)
21	André-Pierre Gignac (Marseille)
19	Zlatan Ibrahimović (Paris)
18	Edinson Cavani (Paris)
17	Claudio Beauvue (Guingamp)
	Max-Alain Gradel (St-Étienne)
15	Diego Rolán (Bordeaux)
14	Wissam Ben Yedder (Toulouse)
13	Nabil Fekir (Lyon)
12	Jordan Ayew (Lorient)

Promoted clubs

ES Troyes AC

1986 • L'Aube (20,842) • estac.fr
Coach: Jean-Marc Furlan

GFC Ajaccio

1910 • Ange Casanova (2,885) • gfca-foot.com
Coach: Thierry Laurey

Angers SCO

1919 • Jean Bouin (17,835) • angers-sco.fr
Coach: Stéphane Moulin

Second level final table 2014/15

		Pld	W	D	L	F	A	Pts
1	ES Troyes AC	38	24	6	8	61	24	78
2	GFC Ajaccio	38	18	11	9	49	37	65
3	Angers SCO	38	18	10	10	47	30	64
4	Dijon FCO	38	17	10	11	44	34	61
5	AS Nancy-Lorraine	38	15	13	10	53	39	58
6	Stade Brestois 29	38	14	15	9	41	27	57
7	Le Havre AC	38	13	13	11	47	37	55
8	Stade Lavallois MFC	38	11	21	6	41	34	54
9	AJ Auxerre	38	12	16	10	48	42	52
10	FC Sochaux-Montbéliard	38	13	13	12	39	37	52
11	Chamois Niortais FC	38	11	17	10	41	42	50
12	Clermont Foot Auvergne	38	12	13	13	43	47	49
13	Nîmes Olympique	38	12	10	16	44	57	46
14	US Créteil	38	10	15	13	44	52	45
15	Tours FC	38	12	8	18	49	54	44
16	Valenciennes FC	38	10	12	16	34	51	42
17	AC Ajaccio	38	9	14	15	32	42	41
18	US Orléans	38	9	13	16	36	47	40
19	LB Châteauroux	38	7	11	20	31	63	32
20	AC Arles-Avignon	38	7	9	22	31	59	30

DOMESTIC CUPS

Coupe de France 2014/15

1/32 FINALS

(03/01/15)
Andrézieux 2-0 St-Priest
Avranches 1-0 Lorient
SC Bastia 2-0 LOSC
Bobigny 0-3 Évian
Boulogne 5-4 Sarre Union
Bressuire 2-1 Amiens
Brest 1-0 Laval
Concarneau 1-0 Niort
Jura Sud 3-0 St-Louis Neuweg
Le Mans 1-3 Tours
Le Poiré-sur-Vie 3-1 Plabennec
Luçon 0-1 Châteauroux
Lusitanos 1-3 Reims
Nantes 4-0 Franciscain
Quevilly 3-3 Orleans *(aet; 5-3 on pens)*
Red Star 2-1 Arles-Avignon
St-Omer 0-5 IC Croix
Valenciennes 2-0 Nice

(04/01/15)
Auxerre 1-0 Strasbourg
Beauvais 0-0 Cholet *(aet; 5-6 on pens)*
Bordeaux 2-1 Toulouse
Caen 2-3 Dijon *(aet)*
Consolat Marseille 3-0 AC Ajaccio
Dinan-Léhon 0-3 Guingamp
Dunkerque 1-2 Rennes
Épinal 1-2 Metz
Grenoble 3-3 Marseille *(aet; 5-4 on pens)*
Lens 2-3 Lyon
Nîmes 0-2 Monaco
Pagny Sur Moselle 1-3 Yzeure
St-Étienne 1-0 Nancy *(aet)*

(05/01/15)
Montpellier 0-3 Paris

1/16 FINALS

(20/01/15)
Andrézieux 1-2 IC Croix
Avranches 0-3 Metz *(aet)*
Concarneau 1-0 Dijon *(aet)*
Jura Sud 0-1 Auxerre
Nantes 3-2 Lyon
Quevilly 1-1 SC Bastia *(aet; 3-1 on pens)*
Yzeure 2-0 Valenciennes

(21/01/15)
Boulogne 1-0 Grenoble
Bressuire 0-1 Le Poiré-sur-Vie *(aet)*
Cholet 1-3 Brest *(aet)*
Guingamp 2-0 Châteauroux
Monaco 2-0 Évian
Paris 2-1 Bordeaux
Tours 3-5 St-Étienne *(aet)*

(22/01/15)
Rennes 1-1 Reims *(aet; 5-4 on pens)*

(23/01/15)
Red Star 2-0 Consolat Marseille

1/8 FINALS

(10/02/15)
Boulogne 2-0 Quevilly
IC Croix 0-0 Concarneau *(aet; 1-4 on pens)*
Le Poiré-sur-Vie 1-1 Auxerre *(aet; 5-6 on pens)*
Red Star 1-2 St-Étienne

(11/02/15)
Monaco 3-1 Rennes
Paris 2-0 Nantes
Yzeure 1-3 Guingamp *(aet)*

(12/02/15)
Metz 0-0 Brest *(aet; 3-4 on pens)*

QUARTER-FINALS

(03/03/15)
Boulogne 1-1 St-Étienne *(Soubervie 80p; Corgnet 85)*
(aet; 3-4 on pens)

(04/03/15)
Paris 2-0 Monaco *(David Luiz 3, Cavani 52)*

(05/03/15)
Brest 0-0 Auxerre *(aet; 2-4 on pens)*
Concarneau 1-2 Guingamp *(Gourmelon 22; Mandanne 3, Beauvue 90+2)*

SEMI-FINALS

(07/04/15)
Auxerre 1-0 Guingamp *(Sammaritano 15)*

(08/04/15)
Paris 4-1 St-Étienne *(Ibrahimović 21p, 81, 90+2, Lavezzi 60; Hamouma 25)*

FINAL

(30/05/15)
Stade de France, Saint-Denis
PARIS SAINT-GERMAIN 1 *(Cavani 64)*
AJ AUXERRE 0
Referee: *Gautier*
PARIS: *Douchez, Van der Wiel, Thiago Silva, David Luiz, Maxwell, Matuidi, Thiago Motta, Verratti, Lucas (Lavezzi 73), Cavani, Ibrahimović*
AUXERRE: *Léon, Aguilar, Puygrenier, Fontaine, Djellabi, Aït-Ben-Idir, Mulumba (Vincent 86), Berthier (Nabab 80), Sammaritano, Baby (Viale 82), Diarra*

Coupe de la Ligue 2014/15

QUARTER-FINALS

(13/01/15)
SC Bastia 3-1 Rennes *(Squillaci 47, Danzé 71og, Cissé 90; Armand 12)*
St-Étienne 0-1 Paris *(Ibrahimović 72)*

(14/01/15)
Monaco 2-0 Guingamp *(Berbatov 8, Martial 90+4)*
LOSC 2-0 Nantes *(Corchia 9, Kjær 69)*

SEMI-FINALS

(03/02/15)
LOSC 0-1 Paris *(Maxwell 27)*

(04/02/15)
Monaco 0-0 SC Bastia *(aet; 6-7 on pens)*

FINAL

(11/04/15)
Stade de France, Saint-Denis
PARIS SAINT-GERMAIN 4 *(Ibrahimović 21p, 41, Cavani 80, 90+2)*
SC BASTIA 0
Referee: *Bastien*
PARIS: *Douchez, Aurier, Thiago Silva, Marquinhos, Maxwell, Matuidi, Verratti, Rabiot (Cabaye 77), Pastore (Lucas 72), Ibrahimović, Lavezzi (Cavani 63)*
BASTIA: *Areola, Cioni, Squillaci, Modesto, Marange, Cahuzac, Gillet, Boudebouz, Palmieri (Ayité 68), Danic (Peybernes 22), Sio (Brandão 81)*
Red card: Squillaci (20)

Paris completed a clean sweep of domestic silverware with victory in the Coupe de France final

GEORGIA
Georgian Football Federation (GFF)

Address	76a Chavchavadze Ave. GE-0179 Tbilisi	**President**	Domenti Sichinava
Tel	+995 32 291 2670	**General secretary**	Revaz Arveladze
Fax	+995 32 291 5995	**Media officer**	Otar Giorgadze
E-mail	gff@gff.ge	**Year of formation**	1990
Website	gff.ge	**National stadium**	Boris Paichadze Dinamo Arena (53,233)

KEY:
- – UEFA Champions League
- – UEFA Europa League
- – Promoted
- – Relegated

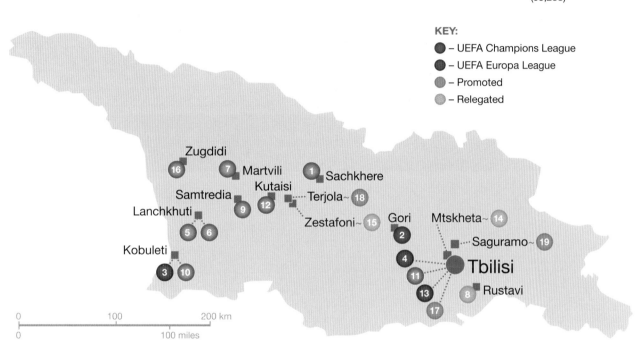

UMAGLESI LIGA CLUBS

  1 FC Chikhura Sachkhere

  2 FC Dila Gori

  3 FC Dinamo Batumi

  4 FC Dinamo Tbilisi

  5 FC Guria Lanchkhuti

  6 FC Kolkheti Poti

  7 FC Merani Martvili

  8 FC Metalurgi Rustavi

  9 FC Samtredia

  10 FC Shukura Kobuleti

  11 FC Sioni Bolnisi

  12 FC Torpedo Kutaisi

  13 FC Tskhinvali

  14 FC WIT Georgia

  15 FC Zestafoni

  16 FC Zugdidi

PROMOTED CLUBS

  17 FC Saburtalo Tbilisi

  18 FC Sapovnela Terjola

  19 FC Lokomotivi Tbilisi

Faith in youth rewards Dila

FC Dila Gori sprang a major surprise in 2014/15 to become champions of Georgia for the first time. Led by the remarkable Ucha Sosiashvili, who only turned 25 on the eve of the season, the club from the mountainous region to the north-west of Tbilisi took the title despite failing to win any of their four games against closest pursuers FC Dinamo Batumi and FC Dinamo Tbilisi.

Compensaton for the latter's failure to defend the Umaglesi Liga title came in the Georgian Cup, which they won for the third year running, and the 12th time in all, thanks to a 5-0 rout of FC Samtredia in the final.

| Gori club led to first title by 25-year-old coach | Dinamo Tbilisi complete domestic cup hat-trick | Zestafoni excluded and two former champions relegated |

Domestic league

A Georgian Cup win in 2011/12 and a runners-up placing in the 2012/13 Umaglesi Liga had led to two successive runs to the UEFA Europa League play-offs, but Dila, who finished ninth out of 12 teams in 2013/14, were certainly not among the favourites for the 2014/15 title, especially when they presented the fresh-faced, inexperienced Sosiashvili as their new coach.

With the top division back to 16 teams – among them newly promoted Dinamo Batumi and Samtredia, whose licences to compete had initially been revoked – and every club playing the other twice on a conventional home-and-away basis, there appeared to be a restoration of traditional order to elite football in Georgia, but the 26th season of the Umaglesi Liga was to deliver some unusual and unexpected outcomes.

While Dila claimed an against-the-odds first title, FC Spartaki Tskhinvali changed their name in mid-season and finished fourth, while FC Zestafoni, the champions of 2010/11 and 2011/12 and runners-up in 2013/14, were punished for failing to fulfil their home fixture against Dila in April with ejection from the league. Furthermore, the two teams that would later accompany them out of the division were also double Georgian champions, FC WIT Georgia being relegated

automatically and FC Metalurgi Rustavi following them down after a play-off.

Although Dila gave notice of their championship ambitions during the autumn, it was at the business end of the campaign that they produced their very best form, a six-match victory charge ending with a 1-0 win at Samtredia that clinched the title with two games to spare. Their six-point advantage over Dinamo Tbilisi proved sufficient as they held a head-to-head advantage on away goals after drawing 0-0 at home and 2-2 away against the defending champions. Dila's two stand-out performers were striker Irakli Modebadze, who topped the league's scoring charts with 16 goals, and midfield orchestrator Nika Kvekveskiri, who also bagged seven goals himself.

Domestic cup

Dinamo Tbilisi's failure to win the league resulted in the sacking of coach Kakhi Gogichaishvili. He was replaced for the cup final against Samtredia by the returning Gia Geguchadze, who had led the club a decade earlier before making his name with Zestafoni. The new man appeared to have the magic touch, steering his new charges to a one-sided 5-0 win, in which the team's 19-year-old starlet Giorgi Papunashvili and new Spanish striker Manuel Onwu – a mid-season replacement for prolific compatriot Xisco – both scored twice.

Europe

Dinamo Tbilisi's 4-0 aggregate defeat to FC Aktobe in the UEFA Champions League second qualifying round brought about the dismissal of their new coach, ex-Czech Republic national team boss Michal Bílek, before he had even taken charge of a domestic fixture. In the UEFA Europa League, meanwhile, only FC Chikhura Sachkhere won a tie – two, in fact, as they reached the third qualifying round after a couple of goalless draws and a penalty shot-out against Turkish club Bursaspor.

National team

While the lack of international success for Georgia's clubs was not entirely unexpected, there was widespread local dismay at the repeated failures of the national team in their first six UEFA EURO 2016 qualifiers. Five of them resulted in defeat, the only exception being a 3-0 away win against the easy meat of Gibraltar. Coach Temur Ketsbaia stepped down after a 4-0 home loss to Poland, and his successor, Kakhaber Tskhadadze, suffered an identical result against the group leaders when, in the final qualifier of the season, three late goals were conceded in Warsaw, all to star striker Robert Lewandowski, shortly after Georgia had come desperately close to scoring a deserved equaliser.

DOMESTIC SEASON AT A GLANCE

Umaglesi Liga 2014/15 final table

		Pld	W	D	Home L	F	A	W	D	Away L	F	A	W	D	Total L	F	A	Pts
1	**FC Dila Gori**	30	12	2	1	29	9	7	5	3	21	12	19	7	4	50	21	64
2	FC Dinamo Batumi	30	10	3	2	21	8	8	1	6	19	16	18	4	8	40	24	58
3	FC Dinamo Tbilisi	30	11	2	2	41	11	6	5	4	15	17	17	7	6	56	28	58
4	FC Tskhinvali	30	11	1	3	29	11	5	4	6	18	26	16	5	9	47	37	53
5	FC Chikhura Sachkhere	30	11	1	3	26	14	2	6	7	13	22	13	7	10	39	36	46
6	FC Samtredia	30	10	1	4	29	13	3	5	7	11	18	13	6	11	40	31	45
7	FC Shukura Kobuleti	30	6	4	5	19	15	5	4	6	17	23	11	8	11	36	38	41
8	FC Torpedo Kutaisi	30	4	7	4	17	16	6	4	5	22	17	10	11	9	39	33	41
9	FC Guria Lanchkhuti	30	8	6	1	25	12	2	3	10	13	31	10	9	11	38	43	39
10	FC Kolkheti Poti	30	6	5	4	18	12	3	5	7	13	19	9	10	11	31	31	37
11	FC Merani Martvili	30	7	5	3	18	9	2	4	9	11	24	9	9	12	29	33	36
12	FC Zugdidi	30	5	5	5	16	19	3	4	8	8	26	8	9	13	24	45	33
13	FC Sioni Bolnisi	30	7	3	5	21	22	2	2	11	11	24	9	5	16	32	46	32
14	FC Metalurgi Rustavi	30	3	7	5	14	16	3	1	11	11	30	6	8	16	25	46	26
15	FC WIT Georgia	30	4	3	8	16	18	3	2	10	11	22	7	5	18	27	40	26
16	FC Zestafoni	30	4	4	7	23	26	2	4	9	17	35	6	8	16	40	61	26

NB FC Spartaki Tskhinvali changed their name to FC Tskhinvali in mid-season; FC Zestafoni were excluded after round 23 – their remaining matches were awarded as 0-3 defeats.

European qualification 2015/16

Champion: FC Dila Gori (second qualifying round)

Cup winner: FC Dinamo Tbilisi (first qualifying round)

FC Dinamo Batumi (first qualifying round)
FC Tskhinvali (first qualifying round)

Top scorer	Irakli Modebadze (Dila), 16 goals
Relegated clubs	FC Zestafoni (excluded), FC WIT Georgia, FC Metalurgi Rustavi
Promoted clubs	FC Saburtalo Tbilisi, FC Sapovnela Terjola, FC Lokomotivi Tbilisi
Cup final	FC Dinamo Tbilisi 5-0 FC Samtredia

Team of the season
(4-4-2)

Coach: Sosiashvili (Dila)

Alavidze
(Dinamo Batumi)

Khurtsilava (Dila) — Rene (Zestafoni/ Dinamo Tbilisi) — Makharadze (Dinamo Batumi) — Totadze (Dinamo Tbilisi)

Papunashvili (Dinamo Tbilisi) — Tsintsadze (Dinamo Tbilisi) — Kvekveskiri (Dila) — Shalamberidze (Guria)

Modebadze (Dila) — Kacharava (Tskhinvali)

Player of the season

Giorgi Papunashvili
(FC Dinamo Tbilisi)

While FC Dila Gori were led to the league title by a 25-year-old coach, Dinamo Tbilisi also drew on youth to win the Georgian Cup, 19-year-old Papunashvili crowning a brilliant first full season at the club with two goals in the final against FC Samtredia. Following the mid-season departure of Xisco, the Umaglesi Liga's top scorer in each of the previous two seasons, the young Georgian international midfielder became Dinamo's primary source of goals, striking 14 in just 21 league games.

Newcomer of the season

Nika Kacharava
(FC Tskhinvali)

Having started the season as FC Spartaki Tskhinvali, the newly-named club finished it strongly to take fourth place – six positions higher than in 2013/14 – and claim European qualification for the first time. It was a father-and-son pairing that did most to take them there, coach Kahi Kacharava bringing son Nika back from Russia and watching on proudly as he led the attack with pace and purpose, scoring 12 goals – just four behind the Umaglesi Liga's top marksman, FC Dila Gori's Irakli Modebadze.

NATIONAL TEAM

Top five all-time caps
Levan Kobiashvili (100); Zurab Khizanishvili (91); Kakha Kaladze (83); Giorgi Nemsadze (69); Aleksandre Iashvili (67)

Top five all-time goals
Shota Arveladze (26); Temur Ketsbaia (17); Aleksandre Iashvili (15); Giorgi Demetradze & Levan Kobiashvili (12)

Results 2014/15

07/09/14	Republic of Ireland (ECQ)	H	Tbilisi	L	1-2	*Okriashvili (38)*
11/10/14	Scotland (ECQ)	A	Glasgow	L	0-1	
14/10/14	Gibraltar (ECQ)	A	Faro (POR)	W	3-0	*Gelashvili (9), Okriashvili (19), Kankava (69)*
14/11/14	Poland (ECQ)	H	Tbilisi	L	0-4	
25/03/15	Malta	H	Tbilisi	W	2-0	*Kankava (85), Kazaishvili (90)*
29/03/15	Germany (ECQ)	H	Tbilisi	L	0-2	
09/06/15	Ukraine	N	Linz (AUT)	L	1-2	*Vatsadze (81)*
13/06/15	Poland (ECQ)	A	Warsaw	L	0-4	

Appearances 2014/15

Coach: Temur Ketsbaia /(25/12/14) Kakhaber Tskhadadze	18/03/68 07/09/68		IRL	SCO	GIB	POL	Mlt	GER	Ukr	POL	Caps	Goals
Giorgi Loria	27/01/86	OFI (GRE)	G46	G	G	G	G46	G	G	G	33	-
Ucha Lobjanidze	23/02/87	Omonia (CYP)	D	D	D	D		D	D70	D	42	1
Solomon Kverkvelia	06/02/92	Rubin (RUS)	D	D	D	D	D46	D			9	-
Akaki Khubutia	17/03/86	H. Petach-Tikva (ISR) /unattached	D	D	D	D					20	
David Kvirkvelia	27/06/80	Samtredia	D	M46							59	-
Jaba Kankava	18/03/86	Dnipro (UKR)	M	M	M	M	M	M			55	6
Guram Kashia	04/07/87	Vitesse (NED)	M			M	D	D	D46	D	37	1
Murtaz Daushvili	01/05/89	Karpaty (UKR)	M	M		M				s46	25	
Jano Ananidze	10/10/92	Spartak Moskva (RUS)	M63		M80	M59			M	M	29	3
Tornike Okriashvili	12/02/92	Genk (BEL)	M88	s46	M	s59	A70	M46	M46	M46	22	4
Nikoloz Gelashvili	05/08/85	Flamurtari (ALB)	A	A	A67						23	1
Roin Kvaskhvadze	31/05/89	Othellos (CYP)	s46								3	-
David Targamadze	22/08/89	Illychivets (UKR)	s63								20	2
Levan Mchedlidze	24/03/90	Empoli (ITA)	s88			A68	A70	A			25	2
Gia Grigalava	05/08/89	Anji (RUS)		D	D	D					20	-
Giorgi Papava	16/02/93	Dinamo Tbilisi		M70							3	
Valeri Kazaishvili	29/01/93	Vitesse (NED)		M80			s63		M70	M	7	1
Irakli Dzaria	01/12/87	Dinamo Tbilisi		s70	M						10	1
Giorgi Chanturia	11/04/93	CFR Cluj (ROU)		s80	M76	s68	A63	s46	s46	s63	8	1
Giorgi Papunashvili	02/09/95	Dinamo Tbilisi		s67							2	-
Vladimer Dvalishvili	20/04/86	OB (DEN)		s76							32	5
Avtandil Ebralidze	03/10/91	Gil Vicente (POR)		s80							3	-
Aleksandre Kobakhidze	11/02/87	Volyn (UKR)				M88	M85	M	M	M76	27	3
Nika Dzalamidze	06/01/92	Jagiellonia (POL)				s88	s85				6	-
Aleksandre Amisulashvili	20/08/82	İnter Bakı (AZE)					D	D4	D	D	39	3
Kakha Makharadze	20/10/87	Pakhtakor (UZB)					M	M63			3	-
Giorgi Navalovski	28/06/86	Tosno (RUS)					M	D	D	D	6	-
Nukri Revishvili	02/03/87	Tosno (RUS)					s46				24	-
Levan Kenia	18/10/90	Slavia Praha (CZE)					s46	s63	s46		26	3
Mate Vatsadze	17/12/88	AGF (DEN)					s70		s70	A63	10	2
Bachana Tskhadadze	23/10/87	İnter Bakı (AZE)					s70		A46	s76	5	-
Lasha Dvali	14/05/95	Kasımpaşa (TUR)						s4	D	D	3	-
Lasha Salukvadze	21/12/81	İnter Bakı (AZE)							s46		38	1
Kakhaber Aladashvili	11/08/83	SKA-Energia (RUS)							s70		8	-

EUROPE

FC Dinamo Tbilisi

DINAMO TBILISI
1925

Second qualifying round - FC Aktobe (KAZ)
H 0-1
Loria, Totadze, Janelidze (Xisco 46), Merebashvili (Martsvaladze 66), Grigalashvili, Papava, Dosoudil, Gvelesiani, Shergelashvili, Dzaria, Vouho (Jordá 79). Coach: Michal Bílek (CZE)
A 0-3
Loria, Khurtsilava, Totadze, Merebashvili (Martsvaladze 63), Jordá, Grigalashvili, Papava (Vouho 77), Xisco, Dosoudil, Gvelesiani, Dzaria. Coach: Michal Bílek (CZE)

FC Zestafoni

Second qualifying round - FC Spartak Trnava (SVK)
H 0-0
Pavlović, Gongadze, Gelashvili (Tatanashvili 65), Kukhianidze (Chanturishvili 84), Dvali (Pantsulaia 78), Sharikadze, Guruli, Dolidze, Rene, Chelidze, Getsadze. Coach: Gia Geguchadze (GEO)
A 0-3
Pavlović, Gongadze (Grigalashvili 72), Gelashvili, Kukhianidze, Dvali (Gvalia 46), Sharikadze, Guruli, Dolidze, Rene, Chelidze, Getsadze (Pantsulaia 53). Coach: Gia Geguchadze (GEO)

FC Sioni Bolnisi

First qualifying round - KS Flamurtari (ALB)
H 2-3 Isiani (27, 30)
Merlani, Tskhadaia, Kandelaki, Svanidze, Kakhelishvili, Isiani, Lobjanidze (Ugulava 54), Imedashvili, Aptsiauri (Samkharadze 74), D Popkhadze, Gureshidze (Adamia 85). Coach: Armaz Jeladze (GEO)
A 2-1 Ugulava (56), Kuqi (83og)
Merlani, Kandelaki, Svanidze, Gogoberishvili, Ganugrava (Samkharadze 65), Isiani, Lobjanidze, Imedashvili, Aptsiauri, D Popkhadze (Adamia 81), Gureshidze (Ugulava 54). Coach: Armaz Jeladze (GEO)

FC Chikhura Sachkhere

First qualifying round - FK Turnovo (MKD)
A 1-0 Kuchukhidze (31)
Somkhishvili, Chelidze, Gabedava, Kuchukhidze (Mumladze 86), Chikvaidze, Datunaishvili, Bechvaia, Kashia, Odikadze, Dekanoidze (Koripadze 79), Rekhviashvili. Coach: Soso Pruidze (GEO)
Red card: Chikvaidze 42
H 3-1 Gabedava (6, 67), Rekhviashvili (75)
Somkhishvili, Chelidze, Kimadze, Gabedava (Koripadze 80), Kuchukhidze (Mumladze 79), Datunaishvili, Bechvaia, Kashia, Odikadze, Dekanoidze, Rekhviashvili. Coach: Soso Pruidze (GEO)

Second qualifying round - Bursaspor (TUR)
A 0-0
Kvilitaia, Jigauri, Kimadze, Gabedava, Kuchukhidze, Datunaishvili, Bechvaia, Kashia, Odikadze, Dekanoidze (Koripadze 90+1), Rekhviashvili. Coach: Soso Pruidze (GEO)
H 0-0 (aet; 4-1 on pens)
Kvilitaia, Jigauri, Kimadze (Chikvaidze 117), Gabedava, Kuchukhidze (Mumladze 119), Datunaishvili, Bechvaia, Kashia, Odikadze, Dekanoidze (Koripadze 90), Rekhviashvili. Coach: Soso Pruidze (GEO)

Third qualifying round - Neftçi PFK (AZE)
A 0-0
Kvilitaia, Jigauri, Kimadze, Gabedava, Kuchukhidze, Koripadze (Chelidze 81), Datunaishvili, Kashia, Odikadze, Dekanoidze (Chikvaidze 89), Rekhviashvili. Coach: Soso Pruidze (GEO)
H 2-3 Gabedava (30, 50)
Kvilitaia, Jigauri, Kimadze, Gabedava, Kuchukhidze, Koripadze (Mumladze 79), Datunaishvili, Kashia, Odikadze, Dekanoidze, Rekhviashvili. Coach: Soso Pruidze (GEO)

FC Chikhura Sachkhere

1938 • Central (750) • no website
Coach: Soso Pruidze

2014

11/08	a	Sioni	L	0-1	
16/08	h	Zestafoni	W	2-1	Jigauri, Mumladze
24/08	a	Shukura	D	1-1	Kuchukhidze
11/09	a	Kolkheti	L	0-1	
17/09	h	Metalurgi	W	2-1	Gongadze (p), og (Khizaneishvili)
21/09	h	Dila	W	2-1	Jigauri, og (Adamadze)
27/09	a	Merani	L	0-2	
05/10	h	WIT Georgia	W	2-0	Gongadze (p), Mumladze
19/10	a	Spartaki	L	1-2	Koripadze
26/10	h	Torpedo	D	2-2	Mumladze, Kashia
02/11	a	Dinamo Batumi	D	0-0	
06/11	h	Zugdidi	W	1-0	Mumladze
22/11	a	Guria	D	2-2	Koripadze, Chelidze
30/11	a	Samtredia	L	1-3	Sikharulia
07/12	h	Dinamo Tbilisi	W	1-0	Mumladze

2015

22/02	h	Sioni	W	2-0	Mandzhgaladze, Koripadze
01/03	a	Zestafoni	D	2-2	Mumladze, Chikvaidze
05/03	h	Shukura	L	0-2	
14/03	a	Metalurgi	D	0-0	
18/03	h	Kolkheti	W	5-1	Kuchukhidze 2, Mumladze, og (Chaduneli), Sardalishvili
22/03	a	Dila	L	1-2	Dekanoidze
03/04	h	Merani	W	2-0	Ivanishvili, Dekanoidze
11/04	a	WIT Georgia	W	2-1	Ganugrava, Troyanovskiy
19/04	h	Tskhinvali	L	1-3	Troyanovskiy
24/04	a	Torpedo	W	2-1	Odikadze, Sardalishvili
02/05	h	Dinamo Batumi	L	0-1	
09/05	a	Zugdidi	D	1-1	Chikvaidze
13/05	h	Guria	W	2-1	Kuchukhidze, Odikadze (p)
17/05	h	Samtredia	W	2-1	Koripadze, Kuchukhidze
22/05	a	Dinamo Tbilisi	L	0-3	

Name	Nat	DoB	Pos	Aps	(s)	Gls
Archil Bajelidze		07/04/86	D	9	(4)	
Lasha Chelidze		13/03/85	D	24		1
Lasha Chikvaidze		04/10/89	D	24	(4)	2
Besik Dekanoidze		01/03/92	M	23	(4)	2
Denis Dobrovolski		10/10/85	M	26		
Giorgi Ganugrava		21/02/88	M	12	(1)	1
Teimuraz Gongadze		08/09/85	D	16		2
Aleksandre Ivanishvili		01/01/91	M	3	(6)	1
Jaba Jigauri		08/07/92	M	10		2
Kakhaber Kakashvili		26/06/93	M	2	(5)	
Shota Kashia		22/10/84	D	25		1
Giorgi Kimadze		11/02/92	D	14		
Giorgi Koripadze		13/10/89	M	30		4
Lasha Kuchukhidze		14/03/92	A	15	(7)	5
Maksime Kvilitaia		17/09/85	G	27		
Serhiy Lyubchak	UKR	15/04/86	D	11	(1)	
Giuly Mandzhgaladze	UKR	09/09/92	M	6	(2)	1
Tornike Mumladze		23/07/92	A	14	(12)	7
Temur Nadiradze		19/03/92	A		(2)	
Zaza Nadiradze		21/01/93	M		(1)	
David Odikadze		14/04/84	D	16	(2)	2
Mikheil Sardalishvili		17/02/92	A	9	(6)	2
Zviad Sikharulia		01/08/92	M	5	(4)	1
Yevhen Troyanovskiy	UKR	02/07/93	A	6	(4)	2
Tornike Zarkua		01/09/90	G	3		

FC Dila Gori

1936 • Tengiz Burjanadze (4,483) • fcdila.ge
Major honours
Georgian League (1) 2015; Georgian Cup (1) 2012
Coach: Ucha Sosiashvili

2014

10/08	h	Spartaki	W	2-0	Modebadze, Kvekveskiri
15/08	a	Torpedo	D	0-0	
23/08	h	Dinamo Batumi	L	0-1	
11/09	h	Guria	W	2-0	Kvekveskiri, Modebadze (p)
17/09	a	Zugdidi	W	3-0	Modebadze, Razmadze (p), Eristavi
21/09	a	Chikhura	L	1-2	Karkuzashvili
26/09	h	Dinamo Tbilisi	D	0-0	
04/10	a	Sioni	W	4-1	Modebadze 2, Arabuli, Akhalkatsi
19/10	h	Zestafoni	D	2-2	og (Khidesheli), Modebadze
25/10	a	Shukura	L	0-3	(w/o; original match abandoned after 50 mins at 0-0)
01/11	h	Metalurgi	W	3-2	Karkuzashvili, Modebadze, Kvekveskiri
07/11	a	Kolkheti	W	1-0	Seturidze
21/11	h	Samtredia	W	1-0	Adamadze
30/11	h	Merani	W	1-0	Akhalkatsi
07/12	a	WIT Georgia	D	2-2	Modebadze, Adamadze

2015

22/02	a	Tskhinvali	W	1-0	Gorelishvili
01/03	h	Torpedo	W	2-1	Kvekveskiri, og (Chikviladze)
05/03	a	Dinamo Batumi	L	0-1	
14/03	h	Zugdidi	W	4-0	Kvekveskiri 3, Gorelishvili
18/04	a	Guria	D	0-0	
22/03	h	Chikhura	W	2-1	Modebadze 2
03/04	a	Dinamo Tbilisi	D	2-2	og (Gvelesiani), Eristavi
11/04	h	Sioni	W	1-0	Eristavi
19/04	a	Zestafoni	W	3-0	(w/o)
24/04	h	Shukura	W	5-2	Gorelishvili 2, Eristavi, Modebadze 2
02/05	a	Metalurgi	W	2-0	Gorelishvili, Modebadze
09/05	h	Kolkheti	W	1-0	Modebadze
13/05	a	Samtredia	W	1-0	Kvakhadze
17/05	a	Merani	D	1-1	Akhalkatsi
22/05	h	WIT Georgia	W	3-0	Modebadze 2, Eristavi

Name	Nat	DoB	Pos	Aps	(s)	Gls
Guram Adamadze		31/08/88	D	13	(1)	2
Roman Akhalkatsi		20/02/81	M	15	(6)	3
Bachana Arabuli		05/01/94	A	2	(7)	1
Alan Bagaev	RUS	07/04/91	D	13		
Giorgi Beridze		12/05/97	A	2	(3)	
Ilia Buzaladze		29/02/92	A		(1)	
Chiaber Chechelashvili		10/10/95	M	3	(4)	
Irakli Dzaria		01/12/87	M		(3)	
Giorgi Eristavi		04/02/94	M	11	(13)	5
Mikheil Gorelishvili	RUS	29/05/93	A	10	(2)	5
Lasha Gvalia		06/10/91	M	10	(1)	
Lasha Japaridze		16/04/85	D	21	(2)	
Givi Karkuzashvili		20/09/86	D	22	(1)	2
Giorgi Khidesheli		23/01/88	D	1		
David Khurtsilava		09/03/88	D	23		
Aleksandre Kvakhadze		17/08/84	D	12		1
Nika Kvekveskiri		29/05/92	M	23	(4)	7
Ilia Lomidze		04/11/89	D	2	(1)	
Slavko Marić	SRB	07/03/84	D	7	(2)	
Omar Migineishvili		02/06/84	G	10		
Irakli Modebadze		04/10/84	A	22	(1)	16
Guga Palavandishvili		14/08/93	M	22	(2)	
Luka Razmadze		30/12/83	M	17	(3)	1
Nikoloz Sadagashvili		10/10/88	A		(6)	
Giga Samkharadze		28/04/95	M	1		
Giorgi Seturidze		01/10/85	M	19	(8)	1
Beka Shekriladze		28/11/83	G	7		
Giorgi Somkhishvili		27/11/80	G	12		
Giorgi Tekturmanidze		17/09/90	M	4	(4)	
Tengiz Tsikaridze		21/12/95	M	15	(4)	

FC Dinamo Batumi

1923 • Chele Arena, Kobuleti (3,800) • no website
Major honours
Georgian Cup (1) 1998
Coach: Levan Khomeriki

2014

09/08	a	Metalurgi	L	1-2	Shonia
15/08	h	Kolkheti	W	1-0	Tetunashvili
23/08	a	Dila	W	1-0	Chirikashvili
12/09	a	WIT Georgia	L	0-2	
16/09	h	Merani	W	3-1	Tetunashvili 2, Mujiri
20/09	h	Spartaki	L	0-1	
27/09	a	Torpedo	D	2-2	Beriashvili, Diasamidze
05/10	a	Samtredia	L	0-2	
19/10	h	Zugdidi	W	2-0	Tatanashvili, Tevdoradze (p)
25/10	a	Guria	L	0-1	
02/11	h	Chikhura	D	0-0	
06/11	a	Dinamo Tbilisi	W	1-0	Gogitidze
21/11	h	Sioni	W	2-1	Mujiri, Shonia
30/11	a	Zestafoni	W	4-2	Shonia, Tatanashvili, Gogitidze, Beriashvili
06/12	h	Shukura	D	0-0	

2015

22/02	h	Metalurgi	W	2-0	Beriashvili, Tatanashvili
28/02	a	Kolkheti	W	2-0	Tatanashvili (p), Beriashvili (p)
05/03	h	Dila	W	1-0	Shonia
13/03	a	Merani	W	2-1	Beriashvili, Kavtaradze
18/03	h	WIT Georgia	W	2-1	Kavtaradze, Beriashvili
22/03	a	Tskhinvali	W	1-0	Koridze
03/04	h	Torpedo	L	2-3	Tatanashvili, Shonia
11/04	h	Samtredia	W	1-0	og (Kakubava)
18/04	a	Zugdidi	L	1-2	Kavtaradze
25/04	h	Guria	W	2-1	Beriashvili 2
02/05	a	Chikhura	W	1-0	Mgeladze
09/05	h	Dinamo Tbilisi	D	0-0	
13/05	a	Sioni	W	1-0	
17/05	h	Zestafoni	W	3-0	(w/o)
22/05	a	Shukura	W	3-1	Shonia, Beriashvili, Makharadze (p)

Name	Nat	DoB	Pos	Aps	(s)	Gls
Amiran Abuselidze		16/03/93	M	1	(13)	
Mikheil Alavidze		05/11/87	G	20		
Giorgi Beriashvili		10/10/86	A	26		9
Irakli Chirikashvili		10/01/87	M	16	(1)	1
Beka Chkuaseli		12/10/96	M	11	(7)	
Nika Diasamidze		02/09/94	M	9	(8)	1
Giorgi Gavashelishvili		31/10/99	D	6		
Gela Gogitidze		25/11/90	M	9	(3)	2
Mikheil Kakaladze		06/06/82	A	5	(2)	
Giorgi Kavtaradze		01/01/89	M	14		3
Vaja Koridze		05/01/87	D	9	(3)	1
Karen Makariani		03/03/88	D	6	(8)	
Boris Makharadze		08/11/90	D	26		1
Shota Maminashvili		30/08/86	G	9		
Nika Mgeladze		20/12/85	D	24		1
Amiran Mujiri		20/02/74	M	9	(7)	2
Dimitri Pachkoria		07/12/91	M		(1)	
Mirza Partenadze		16/05/90	M		(2)	
Teimuraz Shonia		28/05/90	M	28		6
Anzor Sukhiashvili		27/10/88	D	28		
Dimitri Tatanashvili		19/10/83	A	19	(3)	5
Arnaud Tchuensu	CMR	28/10/91	D	1		
Badri Tetunashvili		09/02/90	D	26	(2)	3
Valerian Tevdoradze		11/10/93	M	7	(12)	1
Beka Varshanidze		12/05/93	M	10	(13)	

FC Dinamo Tbilisi

1925 • Boris Paichadze Dinamo Arena (53,233) • fcdinamo.ge
Major honours
UEFA Cup Winners Cup (1) 1981; USSR League (2) 1964, 1978; Georgian League (15) 1990, 1991, 1992, 1993, 1994, 1995, 1996, 1997, 1998, 1999, 2003, 2005, 2008, 2013, 2014; USSR Cup (2) 1976, 1979; Georgian Cup (12) 1992, 1993, 1994, 1995, 1996, 1997, 2003, 2004, 2009, 2013, 2014, 2015
**Coach: Michal Bílek (CZE);
(01/08/14) Kakhi Gogichaishvili;
(20/05/15) Gia Geguchadze**

2014

10/08	h	Samtredia	W	2-0	Xisco, Papunashvili
17/08	h	Sioni	W	1-0	Xisco
23/08	a	Zestafoni	W	3-2	Papunashvili, Dzaria 2
11/09	a	Metalurgi	L	0-3	
16/09	h	Shukura	W	6-0	Sabanadze 2, Lobjanidze, Shergelashvili, Papunashvili, Chirgadze
21/09	h	Kolkheti	W	2-1	Sabanadze, Chirgadze
26/09	a	Dila	D	0-0	
05/10	h	Merani	D	0-0	
18/10	a	WIT Georgia	W	1-0	Xisco
24/10	h	Spartaki	W	6-1	Papunashvili 3, Parunashvili, Dzaria, Tsintsadze
02/11	a	Torpedo	W	2-1	Sabanadze
06/11	h	Dinamo Batumi	L	0-1	
22/11	a	Zugdidi	W	2-1	Papunashvili, Xisco
30/11	h	Guria	L	1-2	Shergelashvili
07/12	a	Chikhura	L	0-1	

2015

22/02	a	Samtredia	W	1-0	Onwu
01/03	a	Sioni	L	1-2	Tsintsadze
05/03	h	Zestafoni	W	3-2	Onwu 2, Totadze
14/03	a	Shukura	W	1-0	Parunashvili
18/03	h	Metalurgi	W	2-0	Chirgadze 2
22/03	a	Kolkheti	D	0-0	
03/04	h	Dila	D	2-2	Chanturishvili 2
11/04	a	Merani	D	1-1	Papunashvili
19/04	h	WIT Georgia	W	3-0	Papunashvili 2, Tsintsadze
24/04	a	Tskhinvali	L	1-4	Tsintsadze
02/05	h	Torpedo	W	3-2	Totadze, Papunashvili, Jigauri
09/05	a	Dinamo Batumi	D	0-0	
13/05	h	Zugdidi	W	7-0	Chanturishvili 2, Papunashvili, Chirgadze 3, Jigauri
17/05	a	Guria	D	2-2	Chanturishvili, Papunashvili (p)
22/05	h	Chikhura	W	3-0	Papunashvili, Totadze, Chanturishvili

Name	Nat	DoB	Pos	Aps	(s)	Gls
Stefan Bukorac	SRB	15/02/91	M	4	(3)	
Nika Chanturia		19/01/95	D	12		
Vakhtang Chanturishvili		05/08/93	M	12	(1)	6
Giorgi Chirgadze		23/11/90	A	15	(13)	7
Nika Daushvili		16/10/89	G	6	(1)	
Irakli Dzaria		01/12/87	M	12	(1)	3
Giorgi Gvelesiani		05/05/91	D	13	(2)	
Libor Hrdlička	SVK	02/01/86	G	10		
Giorgi Janelidze		25/09/89	M	9	(6)	
Jambul Jigauri		08/07/92	M	4	(8)	2
David Jikia		10/01/95	A		(2)	
Otar Kakabadze		27/06/96	D	19	(4)	
Zurab Khizanishvili		06/10/81	D	3	(1)	
Otar Kiteishvili		26/03/96	M	10	(4)	
Saba Lobjanidze		18/12/94	M	11	(13)	1
Giorgi Mchedlishvili		18/01/92	D	2	(4)	
Omar Migineishvili		02/06/84	G	14		
Manuel Onwu	ESP	11/01/88	A	8	(2)	3
Giorgi Papava		16/02/93	M	13	(1)	
Giorgi Papunashvili		02/09/95	M	20	(1)	14
Lasha Parunashvili		14/02/93	M	21	(4)	2
Rene	BRA	21/04/92	M	14		
Nika Sabanadze		02/05/91	A	9	(3)	5
David Sajaia		23/08/93	D	2	(1)	
Lasha Shergelashvili		17/01/92	D	20	(7)	2
Vaja Tabatadze		01/02/91	D	4	(2)	
Lasha Totadze		24/08/88	D	26		3
Mate Tsintsadze		07/01/95	M	28	(1)	4
David Volkovi		03/06/95	A		(1)	
Xisco	ESP	05/09/80	A	9	(3)	4
Budu Zivzivadze		10/03/94	A		(1)	

FC Guria Lanchkhuti

1924 • Evgrapi Shevardnadze (4,500) •
no website
Major honours
Georgian Cup (1) 1990
Coach: Teimuraz Loria;
(20/04/15) Gigla Imnadze

2014

09/08	a	Zestafoni	L	0-6
15/08	h	Shukura	D	0-0
24/08	a	Metalurgi	D	0-0
11/09	a	Dila	L	0-2
17/09	h	Kolkheti	W	3-2 Kiladze, Lomia 2
21/09	h	Merani	W	1-0 Jvania (p)
26/09	a	WIT Georgia	D	2-2 Shalamberidze, Jvania
04/10	a	Spartaki	D	1-1 Shalamberidze (p)
19/10	a	Torpedo	D	2-2 og (Bondarenko), Shalamberidze (p)
25/10	h	Dinamo Batumi	W	1-0 Shalamberidze
01/11	a	Zugdidi	L	1-2 Koshkadze
07/11	a	Samtredia	L	1-3 Lomia
22/11	h	Chikhura	D	2-2 Megrelishvili, Gabrichidze
30/11	a	Dinamo Tbilisi	W	2-1 Koshkadze, Shalamberidze
07/12	h	Sioni	D	0-0

2015

21/02	h	Zestafoni	W	1-0 Mosiashvili
28/02	a	Shukura	L	0-2
05/03	a	Metalurgi	W	1-0 Mosiashvili
14/03	h	Kolkheti	W	1-0 Koshkadze
18/03	h	Dila	D	0-0
22/03	a	Merani	L	0-1
03/04	h	WIT Georgia	W	4-1 Tsilosani, Mosiashvili 2, Shalamberidze
11/04	a	Tskhinvali	L	0-3
19/04	h	Torpedo	L	1-3 Isiani
25/04	a	Dinamo Batumi	L	1-2 Gogiashvili
01/05	h	Zugdidi	W	5-0 Shalamberidze, Benashvili, Isiani 2, Kiladze
09/05	h	Samtredia	W	3-1 Isiani, Zozulia, Shevel
13/05	a	Chikhura	L	1-2 Zozulia
17/05	h	Dinamo Tbilisi	D	2-2 Mchedlishvili, Koshkadze
22/05	a	Sioni	L	2-3 Mosiashvili 2

Name	Nat	DoB	Pos	Aps	(s)	Gls
Aleksi Benashvili		20/03/89	M	11	(3)	1
Giga Cheishvili		17/09/93	D	25		
Shota Gabrichidze		31/03/90	M	12	(5)	1
Konstantine Gaganidze		03/02/93	M	4	(6)	
Jemal Gogiashvili		06/05/88	D	17	(1)	1
Mikheil Goguadze		29/06/89	G	8		
Robert Imerlishvili		24/07/93	D	3	(1)	
Levan Ingorokva		08/07/94	D	9	(11)	
Vili Isiani		22/03/91	A	9	(2)	4
Nikoloz Jishkariani		04/06/90	D	6	(3)	
Vladimer Jojua		05/12/80	M	15		
Giga Jvania		16/01/82	D	12	(1)	2
Nikoloz Kharabadze		03/10/90	M	3		
Erekle Kiladze		11/01/90	M	21	(6)	2
Nikita Konovalov	UKR	10/06/94	M	1	(4)	
Aleksandre Koshkadze		04/12/81	M	26		4
Tariel Kukuladze		20/11/82	M	2	(3)	
Shalva Kvantaliani		26/03/91	A		(3)	
Giga Kverenchkhiladze		21/02/85	A	6	(4)	
Saba Lomia		07/07/90	A	10	(2)	3
Vaja Matiashvili		22/03/94	A	4	(8)	
Giorgi Mchedlishvili		18/01/92	D	14		1
David Megrelishvili		25/09/91	D	13		1
Giorgi Mikaberidze		17/02/88	M	12	(2)	
Tornike Mosiashvili		09/10/91	M	14	(1)	6
Aleksandre Rekhviashvili		23/03/93	A	1	(1)	
Koba Shalamberidze		15/10/84	M	27		7
Yuriy Shevel	UKR	29/01/88	M	1	(4)	1
Gabriel Tebidze		20/01/94	G	7		
Vano Tsilosani		14/02/94	M	5	(11)	1
Bidzina Tsintsadze		04/06/89	D	9		
Konstantine Zarnadze		13/01/93	M	1		
Dmytro Zozulia		09/06/88	M	10	(2)	2
Vladimer Zukhbaia		31/01/86	G	12		

FC Kolkheti Poti

1913 • Evgrapi Shevardnadze, Lanchkhuti
(4,500); Chele Arena, Kobuleti (3,800) • no website
Coach: Zaza Inashvili

2014

09/08	h	Torpedo	L	0-3
15/08	a	Dinamo Batumi	L	0-1
24/08	h	Zugdidi	D	1-1 Ambroladze
11/09	h	Chikhura	W	1-0 Jikia
17/09	a	Guria	L	2-3 Ambroladze, Jishkariani
21/09	a	Dinamo Tbilisi	L	1-2 Guguchia
26/09	h	Sioni	W	1-0 D Sichinava
04/10	a	Zestafoni	D	1-1 D Sichinava
19/10	a	Shukura	D	2-2 D Sichinava, N Sichinava
25/10	a	Metalurgi	L	0-1
01/11	h	Samtredia	D	0-0
07/11	h	Dila	L	0-1
21/11	a	Merani	D	0-0
30/11	h	WIT Georgia	W	2-1 D Sichinava, Jikia
06/12	a	Spartaki	W	2-1 D Sichinava 2

2015

22/02	a	Torpedo	D	0-0
28/02	h	Dinamo Batumi	L	0-2
06/03	a	Zugdidi	W	2-0 Gogonaia, Shengelia
14/03	a	Guria	L	0-1
18/03	a	Chikhura	L	1-5 Jikia
22/03	h	Dinamo Tbilisi	D	0-0
03/04	a	Sioni	W	2-1 Shengelia, Tevzadze
11/04	h	Zestafoni	W	4-0 Shengelia 2, Jishkariani, Ambroladze
18/04	h	Shukura	D	1-1 Jishkariani
24/04	h	Metalurgi	W	3-0 Gureshidze, Gogonaia, Gigauri
02/05	a	Samtredia	D	1-1 N Sichinava
09/05	a	Dila	L	0-1
13/05	h	Merani	W	3-0 Jikia, T Kakulia, Gigauri
17/05	a	WIT Georgia	L	0-1
22/05	h	Tskhinvali	D	1-1 N Sichinava

Name	Nat	DoB	Pos	Aps	(s)	Gls
Ibrahim Adamu	GHA	13/12/93	M	1		
Giga Ambroladze		28/12/90	A	13	(9)	3
Konstantine Baramidze		12/01/91	M	7	(8)	
Temur Bechekhia		16/04/94	M		(1)	
Gia Chaduneli		15/05/94	D	18		
Aliko Chakvetadze		26/03/95	M	13		
Lasha Dzagania		14/01/88	G	5		
Merab Gigauri		05/06/93	M	13	(1)	2
Omar Gogonaia		24/01/89	M	25		2
Luka Guguchia		10/12/91	M	10	(1)	1
Amiran Gugushvili		02/06/95	M	1	(8)	
Levan Gulua		06/05/91	M		(2)	
Guram Gureshidze		08/10/89	M	14		1
Shota Jikia		30/12/84	A	18	(4)	4
Tamaz Jishkariani		13/03/93	A	14	(7)	1
Levan Kakulia		28/07/92	M	11	(4)	
Tedo Kakulia		26/09/92	D	12	(4)	1
Giorgi Kilasonia		21/05/86	D	27		
Aleksandre Korchilava		11/09/91	M	5	(17)	
Giorgi Lemonjava		20/11/90	D	23	(1)	
Charles Nwuocho	NGA	14/03/85	A	7	(2)	
Teimuraz Parulava		20/07/83	D	8		
Apalon Sarsania		10/10/91	M	3		
Konstantine Sepiashvili		19/03/86	G	25		
Teimuraz Sharashenidze		21/01/92	A	3		
Levan Shengelia		27/10/95	M	9	(2)	4
Data Sichinava		21/03/89	M	13	(2)	6
Nika Sichinava		17/07/94	M	12	(12)	3
Zurab Tevzadze		28/08/94	D	22	(1)	1
Paata Tskhvitaria		17/09/89	A	1		

FC Merani Martvili

1936 • Erosi Manjgaladze, Samtredia (3,000);
David Abashidze, Zestafoni (5,000); Murtaz
Khurtsilava (3,000) • fcmerani.ge
Coach: Shalva Gongadze

2014

10/08	h	WIT Georgia	L	0-2
15/08	a	Spartaki	L	0-1
24/08	h	Torpedo	W	3-1 Chimakadze 2, Poniava
12/09	h	Zugdidi	D	0-0
16/09	a	Dinamo Batumi	L	1-3 Tskarozia
21/09	a	Guria	L	0-1
27/09	h	Chikhura	W	2-0 D Tsitskhvaia 2
05/10	a	Dinamo Batumi	D	0-0
18/10	h	Sioni	W	2-0 Poniava, D Tsitskhvaia
26/10	a	Zestafoni	W	1-0
02/11	h	Shukura	W	1-0 Jgamaia
08/11	a	Metalurgi	W	2-1 Bolkvadze (p), Chimakadze
21/11	h	Kolkheti	D	0-0
30/11	a	Dila	L	0-1
07/12	h	Samtredia	D	0-0

2015

22/02	a	WIT Georgia	D	2-2 Tsurtsumia, Tskarozia
01/03	h	Tskhinvali	L	0-2
05/03	a	Torpedo	D	1-1 Lomia
13/03	h	Dinamo Batumi	L	1-2 Gegechkori
18/03	a	Zugdidi	L	0-3
22/03	h	Guria	W	1-0 Gegechkori
03/04	a	Chikhura	L	0-2
11/04	h	Dinamo Tbilisi	D	1-1 D Tsitskhvaia
18/04	a	Sioni	L	0-1
25/04	h	Zestafoni	W	3-0 (w/o)
01/05	a	Shukura	W	3-1 Pipia, Jgamaia, Kikava
08/05	h	Metalurgi	W	3-0 Shulaia, D Tsitskhvaia, Kiknavelidze
13/05	a	Kolkheti	L	0-3
17/05	h	Dila	D	1-1 D Tsitskhvaia
22/05	a	Samtredia	L	2-4 Pipia, Tskarozia

Name	Nat	DoB	Pos	Aps	(s)	Gls
Giorgi Begashvili		12/02/91	G	4		
David Bolkvadze		05/06/80	M	12	(1)	1
Besik Chimakadze		24/06/88	A	12	(2)	3
Levan Gegechkori		05/06/94	D	21	(1)	2
Giorgi Gegia		25/08/95	M	5		
Beka Gotsiridze		17/08/88	A		(1)	
Lasha Jgamaia		03/10/95	D	16	(11)	2
Mikheil Kajaia		02/03/95	M		(3)	
Teimuraz Kharchiladze		05/12/83	A		(2)	
Vaja Kikava		28/12/95	M	9	(3)	1
Nodar Kiknavelidze		25/04/93	M	22	(3)	1
Aleksandre Kokhadze		04/12/81	M	1		
Yevhen Kushnir	UKR	11/03/96	M	1	(1)	
Vaja Lomashvili		04/09/85	D	27		
Saba Lomia		07/07/90	A	9	(3)	1
Zurab Mamaladze		10/02/82	G	25		
Dimitri Margvelashvili		05/02/96	M		(4)	
Kichi Meliava		14/04/92	D	28		
Sergi Orbeladze		01/05/82	M	27	(1)	
David Petava		27/10/95	M		(1)	
Gogi Pipia		04/02/85	A	8	(3)	2
Papuna Poniava		10/03/94	M	24	(1)	2
Mikheil Rukhaia		23/08/96	M		(1)	
Akaki Shulaia		06/09/96	M	16	(10)	1
Beka Tsikolia		28/02/94	M		(2)	
David Tsitskhvaia		30/11/83	A	20	(8)	6
Irakli Tsitskhvaia		28/01/95	D	5		
Akaki Tskarozia		02/08/88	M	20	(2)	3
Data Tsulaia		31/07/94	M	2	(4)	
Giga Tsurtsumia		14/04/97	M	5	(13)	1

GEORGIA

FC Metalurgi Rustavi

1948 • Poladi (4,656) • no website
Major honours
Georgian League (2) 2007, 2010
Coach: Varlam Kilasonia

2014

09/08	h	Dinamo Batumi	W 2-1	Sikharulidze, Tsnobiladze
16/08	a	Zugdidi	D 0-0	
24/08	a	Guria	D 0-0	
11/09	h	Dinamo Tbilisi	W 3-0	Kavtaradze, Jokhadze, Sikharulidze
17/09	a	Chikhura	L 1-2	Tsnobiladze
21/09	a	Sioni	L 1-3	D Gelashvili
26/09	h	Zestafoni	D 2-2	V Kilasonia 2 (1p)
05/10	a	Shukura	W 1-0	V Kilasonia (p)
18/10	h	Samtredia	D 1-1	Sikharulidze
25/10	h	Kolkheti	W 1-0	Tsnobiladze
01/11	a	Dila	L 2-3	Tsnobiladze, Alaverdashvili
08/11	h	Merani	L 1-2	Kavtaradze
21/11	a	WIT Georgia	W 2-0	D Gelashvili 2
30/11	h	Spartaki	D 1-1	Tsnobiladze
07/12	a	Torpedo	W 1-0	Kavtaradze

2015

22/02	a	Dinamo Batumi	L 0-2	
01/03	h	Zugdidi	L 0-1	
05/03	a	Guria	L 0-1	
14/03	h	Chikhura	D 0-0	
18/03	a	Dinamo Tbilisi	L 1-2	
22/03	h	Sioni	L 1-2	Nozadze
03/04	a	Zestafoni	L 0-2	
11/04	h	Shukura	L 1-3	Barabadze
19/04	a	Samtredia	L 1-2	Mikautadze
24/04	h	Kolkheti	L 0-3	
02/05	h	Dila	L 0-2	
08/05	a	Merani	L 0-3	
13/05	h	WIT Georgia	D 0-0	
17/05	a	Tskhinvali	L 2-7	Beruashvili, Zviadadze
22/05	h	Torpedo	D 1-1	Barabadze

Name	Nat	DoB	Pos	Aps	(s)	Gls
Giorgi Alaverdashvili		21/11/87	A	5	(3)	1
Revaz Barabadze		04/10/88	A	12	(1)	2
Revaz Baramidze		19/07/96	M	9		
Grigol Bediashvili		07/02/80	G	22		
Levan Beruashvili		09/12/91	A	11		1
Shota Bitskinashvili		25/01/94	M	2	(3)	
Konstantine Broladze		22/01/89	M	4		
Giorgi Chikvaidze		11/09/89	M	5	(2)	
Shalva Ekvtimishvil		05/01/94	A	10	(2)	
Konstantine Gabashvili		06/02/92	A	5	(6)	
David Gelashvili		08/04/93	A	3	(6)	3
Zurab Gelashvili		09/09/96	M	2	(2)	
Giorgi Gotsadze		26/10/96	D	1	(3)	
Avtandil Gujabidze		06/07/97	D	4		
Soso Gulua		15/03/96	M		(1)	
Giorgi Jokhadze		24/03/90	M	14	(3)	1
Kakhaber Kakashvili		26/03/93	M	13	(1)	
Soso Kardava		08/12/97	G	1		
Giorgi Kavtaradze		01/01/89	M	14		3
Ivane Khabelashvili		05/09/93	M	3	(1)	
Konstantine Khizaneishvili		30/04/93	D	22		
Irakli Khuchua		29/04/92	M	4		
Giorgi Kilasonia		04/05/96	M	11	(5)	
Varlav Kilasonia		09/01/93	D	12	(1)	3
Otar Kiteishvili		26/03/96	M	4	(10)	
Lasha Maisuradze		14/02/96	M		(1)	
Lasha Mchedlishvil		07/02/93	D	6	(1)	
Rostom Mikautadze		28/11/93	M	15	(1)	1
Bachana Mikeladze		31/05/96	M		(1)	
Guram Mindorashvili		16/02/90	D	5	(1)	
Giorgi Nadiradze		04/03/96	G	7		
Giorgi Narimanidze		25/11/93	M	23		
Luka Nozadze		25/12/96	M	11		1
Beka Okropiridze		29/08/94	M	2	(6)	
Lasha Paksashvili		12/04/96	M		(4)	
Aleksandre Sarishvili		08/04/95	M	11	(2)	
Aleksandre Shengelia		27/06/89	M	1		
Giorgi Shushiashvili		20/06/90	M	4		
Irakli Sikharulidze		18/07/90	A	11	(2)	3
Tornike Stepniashvili		10/11/92	M	2	(2)	
Mamuka Toronjadze		13/05/86	A	4	(6)	
Zaza Tsitskishvili		04/07/95	M	4	(8)	
Dachi Tsnobiladze		28/01/94	D	15		5
Giorgi Vasadze		14/06/89	M	11	(3)	
Giorgi Zviadadze		15/09/91	D	6		1

FC Samtredia

1936 • Erosi Manjgaladze (3,000) • no website
Coach: Gela Sanaia;
(27/10/14) Zaza Zamtaradze

2014

10/08	a	Dinamo Tbilisi	L 0-2	
16/08	h	WIT Georgia	W 1-0	og (Getiashvili)
24/08	a	Sioni	D 2-2	Bakuradze, Dolidze
12/09	h	Zestafoni	W 1-0	Datunaishvili
16/09	h	Spartaki	W 3-1	Bechvaia, Kvirkvelia, Gabedava
21/09	h	Torpedo	L 0-1	
27/09	a	Shukura	W 1-0	Gorgiashvili
05/10	h	Dinamo Batumi	W 2-0	Pachkoria, Melkadze
18/10	a	Metalurgi	D 1-1	Gorgiashvili
25/10	h	Zugdidi	L 0-1	
01/11	a	Kolkheti	D 0-0	
07/11	a	Guria	W 3-1	Kakubava, Dolidze, Kvirkvelia
21/11	a	Dila	L 0-1	
30/11	h	Chikhura	W 3-1	Gorgiashvili, I Kerdzevadze 2
07/12	a	Merani	D 0-0	

2015

22/02	h	Dinamo Tbilisi	L 0-1	
01/03	a	WIT Georgia	W 1-0	I Kerdzevadze
05/03	h	Sioni	W 3-1	Khizanishvili, Getsadze, Kapanadze
13/03	a	Tskhinvali	L 1-2	Kakubava
18/03	h	Zestafoni	W 3-0	Kapanadze 2, Kvirkvelia
22/03	h	Torpedo	L 1-3	og (Kimadze)
03/04	h	Shukura	W 4-1	Gorgiashvili, Iashvili, Dolidze, Kapanadze
11/04	a	Dinamo Batumi	L 0-1	
19/04	h	Metalurgi	W 2-1	Getsadze, Dolidze
24/04	a	Zugdidi	D 1-1	Kakubava
02/05	h	Kolkheti	D 1-1	Tedore Grigalashvili
09/05	a	Guria	L 1-3	og (Zozulia)
13/05	h	Dila	L 0-1	
17/05	a	Chikhura	L 1-2	Sharikadze
22/05	h	Merani	W 4-2	Guruli, Gabedava, Iashvili (p), Leonardo

Name	Nat	DoB	Pos	Aps	(s)	Gls
Levan Bakuradze		18/01/86	M	12		1
Giga Bechvaia		29/08/86	M	24	(1)	1
Giorgi Begashvili		12/02/91	G	11	(1)	
David Bolkvadze		05/06/80	M	7	(4)	
Giorgi Datunaishvili		09/02/85	M	23	(2)	1
Grigol Dolidze		25/10/82	M	22	(2)	4
Akaki Dvalishvili		30/06/91	D		(3)	
Giorgi Gabedava		10/03/89	A	13	(7)	2
Bichiko Gedenidze		11/11/91	M	2	(5)	
Revaz Getsadze		11/01/85	M	24	(2)	2
Tornike Gorgiashvili		27/08/88	M	22	(3)	4
Tedore Grigalashvili		12/05/93	M	4	(1)	1
Tornike Grigalashvili		28/01/93	D	4	(2)	
Aleksandre Guruli		09/11/85	A	5	(3)	1
Aleksandre Iashvili		23/10/77	A	6	(4)	2
Levan Kakubava		15/10/90	D	21	(1)	3
Tornike Kakushadze		02/01/91	M	3		
Zviad Kantaria		03/06/90	A	4	(5)	
Tornike Kapanadze		04/06/92	A	6	(7)	4
Lasha Kebadze		27/08/83	M	2	(2)	
Ilia Kerdzevadze		19/01/96	A	8	(7)	3
Shota Kerdzevadze		20/03/93	M	3	(5)	
Zurab Khizanishvili		06/10/81	D	14		1
Tamaz Kikabidze		17/03/92	M	2	(2)	
David Kvirkvelia		27/06/80	D	24	(1)	3
Leonardo	BRA	24/11/84	A	9	(4)	1
Giorgi Melkadze		30/04/84	G	7		
Mikheil Mujrishvili		29/05/89	D	7		1
Giorgi Pachkoria		02/08/89	A	1	(6)	
Ilia Pavlishvili		12/08/89	A	1		
Tornike Shalikashvili		24/10/90	D	10		
Levan Sharikadze		16/07/89	M	6	(2)	1
Revaz Tevdoradze		14/02/88	G	12	(1)	
Giorgi Tevzadze		25/08/96	D	4	(2)	
Gulverd Tomashvili		13/10/88	D	4		

FC Shukura Kobuleti

1936 • Chele Arena (3,800) • no website
Coach: Besik Sherozia;
(28/08/14) Amiran Gogitidze;
(09/02/15) Gela Sanaia

2014

09/08	h	Zugdidi	W 2-1	Metreveli, Chelebadze (p)
15/08	a	Guria	D 0-0	
24/08	h	Chikhura	D 1-1	Chelebadze (p)
12/09	h	Sioni	D 1-1	Tugushi
16/09	a	Dinamo Tbilisi	L 0-6	
20/09	a	Zestafoni	D 1-1	Chaladze
27/09	h	Samtredia	L 0-1	
05/10	h	Metalurgi	L 0-1	
19/10	a	Kolkheti	D 2-2	Chelebadze, Metreveli
25/10	h	Dila	W 3-0	(w/o; original match abandoned after 50 mins at 0-0)
02/11	a	Merani	L 0-1	
08/11	h	WIT Georgia	W 2-0	Tugushi, Metreveli
22/11	a	Spartaki	L 0-1	
30/11	h	Torpedo	W 2-1	Khocholava, Tugushi
06/12	a	Dinamo Batumi	D 0-0	

2015

21/02	a	Zugdidi	L 0-1	
28/02	h	Guria	W 2-0	Chapidze, Pukanych
05/03	a	Chikhura	W 2-0	Metreveli, Kukhianidze (p)
14/03	h	Dinamo Tbilisi	L 0-1	
18/03	a	Sioni	W 3-1	Luizinho, Paulo Victor, Pukanych
22/03	h	Zestafoni	W 3-1	Tukhareli, Chelebadze, Pukanych
03/04	a	Samtredia	L 1-4	Paulo Victor
11/04	a	Metalurgi	W 3-1	Guruli, Chelebadze, Malania
18/04	h	Kolkheti	D 1-1	Guruli
24/04	a	Dila	L 2-5	Chelebadze, Tukhareli
01/05	h	Merani	L 1-3	Tukhareli
08/05	a	WIT Georgia	W 1-0	Metreveli
13/05	h	Tskhinvali	D 0-0	
17/05	a	Torpedo	W 2-0	Kukhianidze, Guruli
22/05	h	Dinamo Batumi	L 1-3	Chelebadze

Name	Nat	DoB	Pos	Aps	(s)	Gls
Levan Ananidze		03/08/96	M		(2)	
Levan Beruashvili		09/02/91	A	4	(5)	
Lasha Chaladze		06/11/87	D	26	(1)	1
Lasha Chapidze		08/07/92	A	13	(6)	1
Giorgi Chelebadze		01/01/92	M	27	(1)	7
Anri Chkhaidze		28/06/96	M		(1)	
Azamat Dzhioev	RUS	23/11/91	G	17		
Felipe Bezerra	BRA	03/04/94	M	2	(3)	
Giorgi Germozashvili		24/06/95	M		(1)	
Maksim Golikhin	RUS	08/09/94	M		(1)	
Giorgi Guruli		31/07/88	D	26		3
Teimuraz Kakaladze		06/05/88	G	13		
Lasha Kalandadze		17/06/91	D	9	(1)	
David Khocholava		08/02/93	D	24	(1)	1
Irakli Khuchua		29/04/92	M	3	(4)	
Irakli Komakhidze		26/03/97	M	6	(4)	
Merab Kopaliani		31/03/92	A	3	(8)	
Giorgi Kukhianidze		01/07/92	M	27	(1)	2
Levan Kutalia		19/07/89	M	11		
Ramaz Kveseishvili		20/02/96	M		(1)	
Bakar Lagadze		23/08/95	M	1		
Robert Lobe	CMR	10/10/88	M	6	(3)	
Lucas	BRA	11/10/89	M	1	(2)	
Luizinho	BRA	04/05/92	M	6		1
Zurab Malania		17/10/96	D	11		1
Tsotne Meskhi		31/05/96	M	3	(8)	
Zviad Metreveli		28/11/85	A	14	(11)	5
Kakhaber Mjavanadze		02/10/78	D	4	(2)	
Paulo Victor	BRA	11/05/94	A	10	(1)	2
Adrian Pukanych	UKR	22/06/83	M	15		3
Irakli Takidze		02/01/92	D	5	(5)	
Zaza Tugushi		08/07/92	M	9	(6)	3
Tornike Tukhareli		11/09/91	M	14	(5)	3
Archil Tvildiani		31/01/93	D	20		

FC Sioni Bolnisi

1936 • Mikheil Meskhi, Tbilisi (24,939);
Tengiz Burjanadze, Gori (4,843) • no website
Major honours
Georgian League (1) 2006
Coach: Armaz Jeladze

2014

11/08	h	Chikhura	W	1-0	Siradze
17/08	a	Dinamo Tbilisi	L	0-1	
24/08	h	Samtredia	D	2-2	Siradze 2
12/09	a	Shukura	D	1-1	Ugulava
16/09	h	Zestafoni	L	1-3	Kvaratskhelia
21/09	h	Metalurgi	W	3-1	Kvaratskhelia, Ugulava (p), Lobjanidze
26/09	a	Kolkheti	L	0-1	
04/10	h	Dila	L	1-4	G Popkhadze
18/10	a	Merani	L	0-2	
24/10	h	WIT Georgia	D	0-0	
02/11	a	Spartaki	L	1-2	Gogoberishvili
06/11	h	Torpedo	W	1-0	Kvaratskhelia
21/11	a	Dinamo Batumi	L	1-2	Lobjanidze
30/11	h	Zugdidi	D	0-0	
07/12	a	Guria	D	0-0	

2015

22/02	a	Chikhura	L	0-2	
01/03	h	Dinamo Tbilisi	W	2-1	Luís Alberto, Tsnobiladze
05/03	a	Samtredia	L	1-3	Keburia
13/03	a	Zestafoni	L	2-4	Sichinava, Mikaberidze
18/03	h	Shukura	L	1-3	Sajaia
22/03	a	Metalurgi	W	2-1	Sichinava, Ugulava
03/04	h	Kolkheti	L	1-2	Luís Alberto
11/04	a	Dila	L	0-1	
18/04	h	Merani	W	1-0	Luís Alberto
24/04	a	WIT Georgia	L	0-2	
02/05	h	Tskhinvali	L	3-4	Ugulava 2 (2p), Sichinava
09/05	a	Torpedo	L	0-1	
13/05	h	Dinamo Batumi	L	0-1	Luís Alberto
17/05	a	Zugdidi	W	3-1	Ugulava, Luís Alberto, Chankotadze
22/05	h	Guria	W	3-2	Chikoia 2, Chankotadze

Name	Nat	DoB	Pos	Aps	(s)	Gls
Giorgi Adamia		10/03/81	A	1		
Tornike Aptsiauri		28/11/79	M	3	(3)	
Zurab Batiashvili		06/02/80	G	15	(1)	
Giorgi Chankotadze		06/05/91	A	10	(4)	2
Soso Chikaidze		22/07/87	A	7	(10)	
Felipe Lima	BRA	02/02/89	M	4		
Giorgi Ganugrava		21/02/88	M	7	(4)	
Giorgi Gaprindashvili		06/05/95	M	17	(3)	
Guram Giorbelidze		25/02/96	D	2		
Aleksandre Gogoberishvili		22/07/77	M	21	(5)	1
Aleksandre Gureshidze		23/04/95	D	10		
Guram Gureshidze		08/10/89	M	3	(5)	
Héndrio Araújo	BRA	16/05/94	M	3	(6)	
David Imedashvili		15/12/84	D	5		
Aleksandre Intskirveli		24/08/81	D	4	(1)	
Vili Isiani		22/03/91	A	9	(2)	
Gela Jincharashvili		21/01/94	M	2		
Ilia Kandelaki		26/12/81	D	11		
Tsotne Keburia		24/02/95	M	3	(3)	1
Otar Khizaneishvili		26/08/81	D	4		
Givi Kvaratskheli		05/11/79	D	13		3
Zviad Lobjanidze		19/04/90	M	19	(6)	2
Luís Alberto	POR	12/10/91	A	12		5
Mirza Merlani		25/10/80	G	15		
Giorgi Mikaberidze		17/02/88	M	5	(2)	1
Papuna Mosemgvdlishvili		27/04/94	M	9	(2)	
Giorgi Otarishvili		12/12/90	M		(2)	
Dachi Popkhadze		27/01/84	D	20	(1)	
Giorgi Popkhadze		25/09/86	D	5	(1)	1
David Sajaia		23/08/93	D	10	(2)	1
Irakli Samkharadze		12/02/83	M		(5)	
Data Sichinava		21/03/89	M	13	(1)	5
David Siradze		21/10/81	A	8	(4)	3
David Svanidze		14/10/79	D	14		
Giorgi Tskhadaia		23/04/88	M	23	(3)	
Dachi Tsnobiladze		18/01/94	D	10		1
Vladimer Ugrekhalidze		24/11/85	M		(3)	
Jaba Ugulava		08/04/92	M	13	(10)	6

FC Torpedo Kutaisi

1946 • Central (11,880) • fctorpedo.ge
Major honours
Georgian League (3) 2000, 2001, 2002; Georgian
Cup (2) 1999, 2001
**Coach: Revaz Dzodzuashvili;
(15/12/14) Giorgi Daraselia**

2014

09/08	a	Kolkheti	W	3-0	Kvaskhvadze, Kvernadze, Chikviladze
15/08	h	Dila	D	0-0	
24/08	a	Merani	L	1-3	Kvernadze
12/09	a	Spartaki	D	0-0	
16/09	h	WIT Georgia	W	1-0	Bondarenko
21/09	a	Samtredia	W	1-0	Kvernadze
27/09	h	Dinamo Batumi	D	2-2	Kvernadze, Abramidze
05/10	a	Zugdidi	D	0-0	
19/10	h	Guria	D	2-2	Kvernadze 2
26/10	a	Chikhura	D	2-2	Chikviladze, Tugushi
02/11	h	Dinamo Tbilisi	L	1-2	Chikviladze
06/11	a	Sioni	L	0-1	
22/11	h	Zestafoni	D	3-3	Mamasakhlisi 2, Kvernadze
30/11	a	Shukura	L	1-2	Pipia
07/12	h	Metalurgi	L	0-1	

2015

22/02	h	Kolkheti	D	0-0	
01/03	a	Dila	L	1-2	Sabanadze
05/03	h	Merani	D	1-1	Sabanadze
14/03	a	WIT Georgia	W	1-0	Babunashvili
18/03	h	Tskhinvali	W	2-0	Klimiashvili, Tugushi (p)
22/03	a	Samtredia	W	3-1	Kvernadze, Klimiashvili, Tugushi
03/04	a	Dinamo Batumi	W	3-2	Adamadze, Kirkitadze, Kvernadze
11/04	h	Zugdidi	D	0-0	
19/04	a	Guria	W	3-1	Kirkitadze, Kimadze, Kvaratskhelia
24/04	h	Chikhura	L	1-2	Adamadze
02/05	a	Dinamo Tbilisi	L	2-3	Adamadze, Kvaratskhelia
09/05	h	Sioni	W	1-0	Kvaratskhelia
13/05	a	Zestafoni	W	3-0	(w/o)
17/05	h	Shukura	L	0-2	
22/05	a	Metalurgi	D	1-1	Kvernadze

Name	Nat	DoB	Pos	Aps	(s)	Gls
Valeri Abramidze		17/01/80	D	12		1
Guram Adamadze		31/08/88	D	12	(1)	3
Shota Babunashvili		17/11/80	M	11	(15)	1
Ushangi Bandzeladze		09/02/93	D	2		
Aleksi Benashvili		20/03/89	M		(1)	
Mindia Bobgiashvili		02/06/83	D	1		
Valeriy Bondarenko	UKR	03/02/94	D	12		1
Tornike Chaduneli		04/04/91	D	4	(3)	
Aliko Chakvetadze		26/03/95	M	15		
Zaza Chelidze		12/01/87	D	13		
Tengiz Chikviladze		12/08/83	M	14	(3)	3
Ilya Dreval	UKR	24/10/95	M	4		
Zaal Eliava		02/01/85	D	2		
Zurab Gelashvili		04/09/96	D	4	(5)	
Giorgi Giorgadze		23/10/94	M		(1)	
Gogi Gogichaishvili		26/03/94	M	1	(2)	
Zaur Goguadze		12/08/96	M	1	(5)	
Givi Ioseliani		25/10/90	D	8		
Romeo Kankia		27/05/92	M	3		
Lasha Kebadze		27/08/83	M	3	(1)	
Tsotne Keburia		24/02/95	M	4	(6)	
Giorgi Kimadze		11/02/92	D	13	1	1
David Kirkitadze		03/09/92	A	13	(1)	2
Irakli Klimiashvili		30/05/88	M	12		2
Vakhtang Kvaratskhella		30/03/88	A	4	(5)	3
Hika Kvaskhvadze		15/04/88	M	2	(3)	1
Otar Kvernadze		10/09/93	A	18	(6)	10
Mikheil Makhviladze		22/07/78	D	11		
Oleg Mamasakhlisi		25/11/95	D	12	(2)	2
Teimuraz Markozashvili		09/08/94	M	4	(5)	
Bakar Mirtskhulava		24/05/92	D	14		
Gogi Pipia		04/02/85	A	13	(2)	1
Inal Pukhaev	RUS	28/01/92	M	3	(2)	
Nika Sabanadze		02/05/91	A	5	(2)	2
Beka Shekriladze		28/02/83	G	10		
Levan Shengelia		27/10/95	M		(1)	
Olexiy Shevchenko	UKR	24/02/92	G	4		
Vaja Tabatadze		01/02/91	D	12		
Gabriel Tebidze		20/01/94	G	10		
Sevasti Todua		13/05/76	D	11	(1)	
Saba Tsabutashvili		25/05/94	G	2		
Beka Tugushi		24/01/89	A	16	(5)	3
Budu Zivzivadze		10/03/94	A	2	(6)	

FC Tskhinvali

2007 • Mikheil Meskhi reserve pitch,
Tbilisi (2,000) • fcspartak.ge
Coach: Kakhi Kacharava

2014

10/08	a	Dila	L	0-2	
15/08	h	Merani	W	1-0	Burdzenadze (p)
24/08	a	WIT Georgia	W	1-0	Ivanishvili
12/09	h	Torpedo	D	0-0	
16/09	a	Samtredia	L	1-3	Kachkachishvili
20/09	a	Dinamo Batumi	W	1-0	Chapodze
25/09	h	Zugdidi	W	2-1	Shindagoridze, Ivanishvili
04/10	a	Guria	D	1-1	Kacharava
19/10	h	Chikhura	W	2-1	Lekvtadze 2
24/10	a	Dinamo Tbilisi	L	1-6	Gigauri
02/11	h	Sioni	W	2-1	Tsertsvadze, Kemoklidze
06/11	a	Zestafoni	L	0-3	
22/11	h	Shukura	W	1-0	Shindagoridze
30/11	a	Metalurgi	D	1-1	Kacharava (p)
06/12	h	Kolkheti	L	1-2	Gigauri

2015

22/02	h	Dila	L	0-1	
01/03	a	Merani	W	2-0	Markozashvili, Shindagoridze
05/03	h	WIT Georgia	W	1-0	Shindagoridze
13/03	a	Samtredia	W	2-0	Shindagoridze, Tsatskrialashvili
18/03	a	Torpedo	L	0-2	
22/03	h	Dinamo Batumi	L	0-1	
03/04	a	Zugdidi	L	2-3	Makharoblidze 2
11/04	h	Guria	W	3-0	Kacharava 2, Shindagoridze
19/04	a	Chikhura	W	3-1	Maisashvili, Kacharava 2
24/04	h	Dinamo Tbilisi	W	4-1	Ivanishvili, Kacharava, Makharoblidze, Tsatskrialashvili
02/05	a	Sioni	W	4-3	Makharoblidze, Kacharava, Ivanishvili, Shindagoridze (p)
09/05	h	Zestafoni	W	3-0	(w/o)
13/05	a	Shukura	D	0-0	
17/05	h	Metalurgi	W	7-2	Ivanishvili, Kacharava 3, Shindagoridze, Tsertsvadze, Kochladze
22/05	a	Kolkheti	D	1-1	Kacharava (p)

Name	Nat	DoB	Pos	Aps	(s)	Gls
Bachana Arabuli		05/01/94	A		(4)	
Vasiko Bachiashvili		04/11/92	D	8		
Ucha Burdzenadze		23/04/93	D	5	(5)	1
Levan Chapodze		21/10/88	D	7		1
Chiaber Chechelashvili		10/10/95	M	2	(1)	
Merab Gigauri		05/06/93	M	14		2
David Imedashvili		15/12/84	D	6	(2)	
Givi Ioseliani		25/10/90	D	15		
Giorgi Ivanishvili		18/10/89	A	22	(2)	5
Nikoloz Jishkariani		04/06/90	D	6	(1)	
Nika Kacharava		13/01/94	A	23	(2)	12
Giorgi Kachkachishvili		08/08/90	D	24	(1)	1
Bakar Kardava		04/11/94	M	10	(2)	
Revaz Kemoklidze		13/03/79	D	4	(3)	1
Lasha Kemukhtashvili		09/04/94	A		(1)	
Varlam Kilasonia		09/01/93	D	10		
Lasha Kochladze		22/08/95	M		(4)	1
Irakli Lekvtadze		30/08/91	M	9	(15)	2
David Maisashvili		18/02/89	D	17	(5)	1
Tamaz Makatsaria		03/10/95	M	1	(9)	
Bidzina Makharoblidze		10/10/92	M	26		4
Teimuraz Markozashvili		09/08/94	M	2	(4)	1
Beka Mumladze		17/12/92	A		(4)	
Giorgi Nadiradze		14/03/92	G	28		
Soslan Naniev	RUS	08/12/89	G	1		
Giorgi Pantsulaia		06/01/94	A		(1)	
Buba Rukhadze		22/01/93	M		(1)	
Lasha Shindagoridze		30/01/93	M	23	(5)	8
Tornike Tarkhnishvili		30/06/90	M	9	(2)	
Giorgi Tekturmanidze		17/09/90	M	15		
Rati Tsatskrialashvili		11/10/93	M	8	(4)	2
Giorgi Tsertsvadze		15/11/94	M	24	(2)	2

GEORGIA

FC WIT Georgia

1968 • Mtskheta Park, Mtskheta (2,000) •
witgeorgia.ge
Major honours
Georgian League (2) 2004, 2009; Georgian Cup (1)
2010
Coach: Zurab Beridze;
(06/03/15) Tengiz Kobiashvili

2014
10/08	a	Merani	W 2-0	Kvirkvia 2
16/08	a	Samtredia	L 0-1	
24/08	h	Spartaki	L 0-1	
12/09	h	Dinamo Batumi	W 2-0	Kakhabrishvili, Kalandia
16/09	a	Torpedo	L 0-1	
21/09	h	Zugdidi	W 3-1	Kvirkvia, Murusidze, Dadiani
26/09	h	Guria	D 2-2	Kurdgelashvili, Lobjanidze
05/10	a	Chikhura	L 0-2	
18/10	h	Dinamo Tbilisi	L 0-1	
24/10	a	Sioni	D 0-0	
02/11	h	Zestafoni	L 2-3	Sabadze 2
08/11	h	Shukura	L 0-2	
21/11	h	Metalurgi	L 0-2	
30/11	h	Kolkheti	L 1-2	Kukhaleishvili
07/12	h	Dila	D 2-2	Davlashelidze, Sabadze

2015
22/02	h	Merani	D 2-2	Kurdgelashvili 2
01/03	h	Samtredia	L 0-1	
05/03	a	Tskhinvali	L 0-1	
14/03	h	Torpedo	L 0-1	
18/03	a	Dinamo Batumi	L 1-2	Lobjanidze
22/03	h	Zugdidi	W 2-0	Lobjanidze, Kurdgelashvili
03/04	a	Guria	L 1-4	Kurdgelashvili
11/04	h	Chikhura	L 1-2	Chitishvili
19/04	a	Dinamo Tbilisi	L 0-3	
24/04	h	Sioni	W 2-0	Lobjanidze, Kakhabrishvili
02/05	a	Zestafoni	W 3-0	(w/o)
08/05	h	Shukura	L 0-1	
13/05	a	Metalurgi	D 0-0	
17/05	h	Kolkheti	W 1-0	Kakhabrishvili
22/05	a	Dila	L 0-3	

Name	Nat	DoB	Pos	Aps	(s)	Gls
Giorgi Bunturi		31/03/96	M		(2)	
Revaz Chitishvili		19/05/94	M	7		1
Nikoloz Dadiani		08/07/95	M	5	(7)	1
Goga Danelia		14/09/95	D	10	(2)	
Shota Davlashelidze		25/03/93	M	24	(2)	1
Badri Demetrashvili		01/03/91	D	10	(3)	
Valiko Gakharia		23/01/94	M	24	(2)	
Giorgi Getiashvili		07/03/90	D	29		
Irakli Gibradze		26/10/91	M	6	(10)	
Giorgi Giorgadze		29/11/93	M		(1)	
Levan Isergishvili		08/03/94	G		(1)	
Kakha Kakhabrishvili		08/07/93	M	15	(8)	3
Iona Kalajishvili		22/08/96	M		(1)	
Giorgi Kalandia		18/01/93	M	24		1
Erekle Khvistani		09/01/94	M	1	(16)	
Levan Kukhaleishvili		24/02/92	A	3	(10)	1
Vano Kurdgelashvili		17/10/95	M	23	(2)	5
Mate Kvirkvia		14/06/96	M	10		3
Erekle Lebanidze		25/03/97	M	2	(2)	
Elguja Lobjanidze		17/09/92	A	26	(2)	4
Nikoloz Maisuradze		29/03/89	M	23	(4)	
Vaja Merabishvili		17/05/96	M		(1)	
Besik Murusidze		25/03/95	D	9		1
Levan Sabadze		17/03/92	D	27		3
Joni Sherozia		09/09/90	G	29		
Luka Tatkhashvili		18/02/93	D	12	(8)	

FC Zestafoni

2004 • David Abashidze (5,000) •
fczestafoni.ge
Major honours
Georgian League (2) 2011, 2012; Georgian Cup (1)
2008
Coach: Gia Geguchadze;
(27/01/15) Giorgi Mikadze

2014
09/08	h	Guria	W 6-0	Dvali 2, Gongadze, Pantsulaia, Tedore Grigalashvili, Gvalia
16/08	a	Chikhura	L 1-2	Chankotadze
23/08	h	Dinamo Tbilisi	L 2-3	Sardalishvili, Dvali
12/09	h	Samtredia	L 0-1	
16/09	a	Sioni	W 3-1	Chanturishvili, Iluridze, Kapanadze
20/09	h	Shukura	D 1-1	Iluridze
26/09	a	Metalurgi	D 2-2	Pantsulaia, Sharikadze (p)
04/10	h	Kolkheti	D 1-1	Dvali
19/10	a	Dila	D 2-2	Dvali 2 (1p)
26/10	h	Merani	D 0-0	
02/11	a	WIT Georgia	W 3-2	Dvali 2 (1p), Kapanadze
06/11	h	Spartaki	W 3-0	Kapanadze, Dvali, Sharikadze
22/11	a	Torpedo	D 3-3	Sardalishvili, Iluridze, Dvali
30/11	h	Dinamo Batumi	L 2-4	Iluridze, Khidesheli
07/12	a	Zugdidi	D 0-0	

2015
21/02	a	Guria	L 0-1	
01/03	h	Chikhura	D 2-2	Sikharulidze, Iluridze
05/03	a	Dinamo Tbilisi	L 2-3	Sikharulia, Samushia
13/03	h	Sioni	W 4-2	Sikharulidze 2, Khizaneishvili, Iluridze
18/03	a	Samtredia	L 0-3	
22/03	h	Shukura	L 1-3	Gagoshidze
03/04	h	Metalurgi	W 2-0	Jeremiah 2
11/04	a	Kolkheti	L 0-4	
19/04	h	Dila	L 0-3	(w/o)
25/04	a	Merani	L 0-3	(w/o)
02/05	h	WIT Georgia	L 0-3	(w/o)
09/05	a	Tskhinvali	L 0-3	(w/o)
13/05	h	Torpedo	L 0-3	(w/o)
17/05	a	Dinamo Batumi	L 0-3	(w/o)
22/05	h	Zugdidi	L 0-3	(w/o)

Name	Nat	DoB	Pos	Aps	(s)	Gls
Giorgi Beridze		12/05/97	M	3	(5)	
Giorgi Chankotadze		06/05/91	A	8	(5)	1
Vakhtang Chanturishvili		05/08/93	M	14		1
Giorgi Chikhradze		04/08/87	M		(1)	
Jaba Dvali		08/02/85	A	12		10
Avto Endeladze		17/09/94	M	4	(6)	
Nodar Gachechiladze		05/01/93	M	1	(4)	
Malkhaz Gagoshidze		20/02/93	D	19	(2)	1
Teimuraz Gongadze		08/09/85	D	2		1
Tedore Grigalashvili		12/05/93	M	13	(1)	1
Tornike Grigalashvili		28/01/93	D	7	(1)	
Lasha Gvalia		06/10/91	M	10		1
Giorgi Iluridze		04/06/92	A	16	(2)	6
John Jeremiah	NGA	02/09/93	A	4	(2)	2
Tornike Kapanadze		04/06/92	A	4	(11)	3
Ivane Khabelashvili		05/09/93	M	1	(1)	
Giorgi Khidesheli		23/01/88	D	10		1
Otar Khizaneishvili		26/06/81	D	6	(1)	1
David Kupatadze		06/06/91	G	8		
Mate Kvirkvia		14/06/96	A	1	(4)	
David Lomaia		18/05/85	D	1	(1)	
Piruz Marakvelidze		21/01/95	M	2		
Lasha Mchedlishvili		07/02/93	D	4		
Beka Mikeltadze		26/11/97	M		(6)	
David Mtivlishvili		26/10/94	D	8		
Vaja Nemsadze		07/12/90	M	1		
Giorgi Pantsulaia		06/01/94	A	5	(9)	2
Bojan Pavlović	SRB	08/11/86	G	15		
David Rajamashvili		28/10/88	M	7		
Rene	BRA	21/04/92	D	14		
Mirian Robakidze		14/03/95	M	6	(1)	
Guram Samushia		05/09/94	M	3	(3)	1
Mikheil Sardalishvili		19/09/92	A	14		2
Levan Sharikadze		16/07/89	M	13		2
Zviad Sikharulia		01/08/92	M	5	(2)	1
Irakli Sikharulidze		18/07/90	A	4	(1)	3
Giorgi Vasadze		14/06/89	M	8		

FC Zugdidi

2005 • Baia (1,000); Central, Kutaisi (11,880) •
fczugdidi.ge
Coach: Nestor Mumladze;
(20/10/14) Besik Sherozia

2014
09/08	a	Shukura	L 1-2	Lomia
16/08	h	Metalurgi	D 0-0	
24/08	a	Kolkheti	D 1-1	Lomia
12/09	a	Merani	D 0-0	
17/09	h	Dila	L 0-3	
21/09	h	WIT Georgia	L 1-3	Lomia
25/09	a	Spartaki	L 1-2	Lomia
05/10	h	Torpedo	D 0-0	
19/10	a	Dinamo Batumi	L 0-2	
25/10	a	Samtredia	W 1-0	Tsurtsumia
01/11	h	Guria	W 2-1	Lomia (p), Ekhvaia
06/11	a	Chikhura	L 0-1	
22/11	h	Dinamo Tbilisi	L 1-2	Ekhvaia
30/11	a	Sioni	D 0-0	
07/12	h	Zestafoni	D 0-0	

2015
21/02	h	Shukura	W 1-0	Kobalia
01/03	a	Metalurgi	W 1-0	Guguchia
06/03	h	Kolkheti	L 0-2	
14/03	a	Dila	L 0-4	
18/03	h	Merani	W 3-0	Gongadze, Lomia, Tsurtsumia
22/03	a	WIT Georgia	L 0-2	
03/04	h	Tskhinvali	W 3-2	Lomia 2, Rigvava
11/04	a	Torpedo	D 0-0	
18/04	h	Dinamo Batumi	W 2-1	Lomia (p), Kukava
24/04	h	Samtredia	D 1-1	Gongadze
01/05	a	Guria	L 0-5	
09/05	h	Chikhura	D 1-1	Megrelishvili
13/05	a	Dinamo Tbilisi	L 0-7	
17/05	h	Sioni	L 1-3	Kukava
22/05	a	Zestafoni	W 3-0	(w/o)

Name	Nat	DoB	Pos	Aps	(s)	Gls
Levan Akobia		11/02/80	D	16	(1)	
Mindia Bobgiashvili		02/08/83	G	12		
Giorgi Bulia		06/05/94	M		(2)	
Giorgi Chaava		27/11/91	D		(2)	
Irakli Devadze		26/03/89	G	1		
Irakli Ekhvaia		09/01/89	A	16	(5)	2
Avto Endeladze		17/09/94	M	8	(5)	
Lasha Gongadze		01/03/90	D	17	(2)	2
Luka Guguchia		10/12/91	M	13		1
Levan Gulordava		16/05/88	M	2	(6)	
Shota Gvazava		26/10/92	M	4	(1)	
Manuchar Ivardava		23/07/82	G	2		
Otar Javashvili		17/08/93	D	12		
Data Kiria		17/06/95	M	15	(6)	
Nika Kiria		04/01/94	M	2	(1)	
Irakli Kobalia		13/03/92	A	2		1
Luka Koberidze		09/09/94	M	16	(6)	
Koka Kometiani		10/03/94	M	1	(1)	
Lasha Kukava		12/01/92	M	7	(16)	2
Levan Kurdadze		03/09/90	D	7	(2)	
Levan Kutalia		19/07/89	M	12		
Vakhtang Kvaratskhelia		30/03/88	A	8	(3)	
David Lomaia		18/05/85	D	6	(2)	
Shota Lomia		13/02/84	M	27		9
Goderdzi Machaidze		17/07/92	D	12		
David Megrelishvili		25/09/91	D	5	(2)	1
Bakar Mirtskhulava		24/05/92	D	10		
Giorgi Pachkoria		29/05/89	D	9		
Akaki Parjikia		25/09/93	M	6	(13)	
Data Rigvava		22/10/91	D	20	(1)	1
Tsotne Samushia		24/10/94	M		(4)	
Aleksandre Shengelia		27/06/89	M	1	(2)	
Revaz Tevdoradze		14/02/88	G	14		
Valiko Tkemaladze		14/11/87	M	13		
Levan Tsurtsumia		28/01/89	M	23	(2)	2
Dimitri Tutberidze		22/03/97	M		(1)	

Top goalscorers

16	Irakli Modebadze (Dila)
14	Giorgi Papunashvili (Dinamo Tbilisi)
12	Nika Kacharava (Tskhinvali)
11	Data Sichinava (Kolkheti/Sioni)
10	Otar Kvernadze (Torpedo) Jaba Dvali (Zestafoni)
9	Giorgi Beriashvili (Dinamo Batumi) Shota Lomia (Zugdidi)
8	Lasha Shindagoridze (Tskhinvali)
7	Tornike Mumladze (Chikhura) Nika Kvekveskiri (Dila) Koba Shalamberidze (Guria) Giorgi Chirgadze (Dinamo Tbilisi) Nika Sabanadze (Dinamo Tbilisi/Torpedo) Giorgi Chelebadze (Shukura) Vakhtang Chanturishvili (Zestafoni/ Dinamo Tbilisi) Tornike Kapanadze (Zestafoni/Samtredia)

Promoted clubs

FC Saburtalo Tbilisi

1999 • Bendela (1,100) • fcsaburtalo.ge
Coach: Giorgi Chiabrishvili

FC Sapovnela Terjola

1936 • Central (2,500) • no website
Coach: Mirian Getsadze

FC Lokomotivi Tbilisi

1936 • Saguramo (700) • fcloco.ge
Coach: Vasil Maisuradze

Second level final tables 2014/15

Group A		Pld	W	D	L	F	A	Pts
1	FC Saburtalo Tbilisi	36	28	3	5	92	25	87
2	FC Lokomotivi Tbilisi	36	21	5	10	87	42	68
3	FC Lazika Zugdidi	36	20	6	10	69	41	66
4	FC Samgurali Tskhaltubo	36	19	3	14	76	50	60
5	FC Chiatura	36	17	3	16	53	52	54
6	FC Machakhela Khelvachauri	36	14	3	19	48	66	45
7	FC Sasko-Tiflisi Tbilisi	36	11	9	16	61	67	42
8	FC Chkherimela Kharagauli	36	12	4	20	35	71	40
9	FC STU-N. Dinamo Tbilisi	36	11	2	23	47	97	35
10	FC Adeli Batumi	36	6	4	26	37	94	22

Group B		Pld	W	D	L	F	A	Pts
1	FC Sapovnela Terjola	36	23	8	5	64	28	77
2	FC Borjomi	36	16	6	14	40	43	54
3	FC Gagra	36	15	5	16	59	47	50
4	FC Betlemi Keda	36	14	7	15	51	50	49
5	FC Mertskhali Ozurgeti	36	13	9	14	45	68	48
6	FC Algeti Marneuli	36	12	11	13	47	39	47
7	FC Meshakhte Tkibuli	36	14	5	17	57	55	47
8	FC Kolkheti Khobi	36	12	10	14	46	51	46
9	FC Skuri Tsalenjikha	36	11	13	12	47	55	46
10	FC Dinamo-2 Tbilisi	36	9	6	21	42	68	33

Promotion/Relegation play-offs

(23/05/15)
Lokomotivi Tbilisi 3-3 Borjomi *(aet; 4-2 on pens)*

(27/05/15)
Metalurgi Rustavi 0-5 Lokomotivi Tbilisi

DOMESTIC CUP

Sakartvelos Tasi 2014/15

FIRST ROUND

(19/08/14 & 30/09/14)
Lokomotivi Tbilisi 1-3, 0-1 Dila *(1-4)*

(19/08/14 & 01/10/14)
Dinamo Batumi 5-0, 0-2 Chiatura *(5-2)*
Samgurali 1-1, 1-1 Shukura *(aet; 2-2, 3-4 on pens)*

(20/08/14 & 30/09/14)
Metalurgi 1-1, 2-2 Sasko Tbilisi *(3-3; Metalurgi on away goals)*
Samtredia 3-0, 4-1 Betlemi *(7-1)*
Sapovnela 2-1, 1-2 Guria *(aet; 3-3, 3-0 on pens)*
Skuri 0-1, 0-6 Kolkheti Poti *(0-7)*
Spartaki Tskhinvali 1-2, 3-0 Saburtalo *(4-2)*
Zugdidi 2-0, 2-3 Machakhela *(4-3)*

(20/08/14 & 01/10/14)
Chkherimela 0-1, 2-5 Torpedo *(2-6)*
Gagra 2-4, 1-2 WIT Georgia *(3-6)*
Mertskhali 1-4, 2-3 Merani Martvili *(3-7)*

Byes – Chikhura, Dinamo Tbilisi, Sioni, Zestafoni

SECOND ROUND

(17/11/14 & 25/11/14)
Dinamo Batumi 4-1, 0-3 Samtredia *(4-4; Samtredia on away goal)*
WIT Georgia 1-0, 3-3 Sioni *(4-3)*

(17/11/14 & 26/11/14)
Dila 0-0, 1-1 Kolkheti Poti *(1-1; Dila on away goal)*
Spartaki Tskhinvali 3-0, 0-0 Sapovnela *(3-0)*

Merani Martvili 0-3, 4-3 Torpedo *(4-6)*
Zugdidi 0-2, 0-5 Metalurgi *(0-7)*
Chikhura 0-0, 1-0 Zestafoni *(1-0)*

(18/11/14 & 26/11/14)
Shukura 1-1, 1-3 Dinamo Tbilisi *(2-4)*

QUARTER-FINALS

(18/02/15 & 09/03/15)
Dila 0-0 Dinamo Tbilisi
Dinamo Tbilisi 1-0 Dila *(Kakabadze 21)*
(Dinamo Tbilisi 1-0)

Samtredia 2-1 Torpedo *(Kapanadze 65, 67; Tugushi 42)*
Torpedo 0-0 Samtredia
(Samtredia 2-1)

Tskhinvali 4-5 WIT Georgia *(Kacharava 5, 63, Ivanishvili 12, Kachkachishvili 48; Sabadze 10, Davlashelidze 17, Tatkhashvili 22, 55, Kurdgelashvili 86)*
WIT Georgia 1-4 Tskhinvali *(Gibradze 81p; Tsatskrialashvili 22, 55, Makharoblidze 51, Lekvtadze 70)*
(Tskhinvali 8-6)

Metalurgi 0-0 Chikhura
Chikhura 3-0 Metalurgi *(Mumladze 6, Troyanovskiy 44, Dobrovolski 59)*
(Chikhura 3-0)

NB Spartaki Tskhinvali changed name to Tskhinvali before quarter-finals.

SEMI-FINALS

(07/04/15 & 28/04/15)
Chikhura 0-1 Samtredia *(Tevzadze 48)*
Samtredia 3-0 Chikhura *(Iashvili 28, Gorgiashvili 62, Kapanadze 71)*
(Samtredia 4-0)

Dinamo Tbilisi 2-0 Tskhinvali *(Tsintsadze 22p, Volkovi 79)*
Tskhinvali 1-0 Dinamo Tbilisi *(Ivanishvili 38)*
(Dinamo Tbilisi 2-1)

FINAL

(26/05/15)
Mikheil Meskhi stadium, Tbilisi
FC DINAMO TBILISI 5 *(Papunashvili 14, 53, Onwu 50, 68, Volkovi 87)*
FC SAMTREDIA 0
Referee: *Fritz (GER)*
DINAMO TBILISI: Hrdlička, Kakabadze, Rene, Gvelesiani, Totadze, Tsintsadze, Janelidze, Kiteishvili *(Parunashvili 75)*, Papunashvili, Chanturishvili *(Volkovi 85)*, Onwu *(Lobjanidze 69)*
SAMTREDIA: Tevdoradze, Kakubava, Kvirkvelia, Khizanishvili, Datunaishvili *(Gorgiashvili 58)*, Tedore Grigalashvili *(Bechvaia 46)*, Dolidze, Sharikadze, Getsadze *(Kapanadze 66)*, Iashvili, Gabedava

GERMANY
Deutscher Fussball-Bund (DFB)

Address	Otto-Fleck-Schneise 6
	Postfach 710265
	DE-60492 Frankfurt
	am Main
Tel	+49 69 67 880
Fax	+49 69 67 88266
E-mail	info@dfb.de
Website	dfb.de

President	Wolfgang Niersbach
General secretary	Helmut Sandrock
Media officer	Ralf Köttker
Year of formation	1900

BUNDESLIGA CLUBS

 1 FC Augsburg

 2 Bayer 04 Leverkusen

 3 FC Bayern München

 4 Borussia Dortmund

 5 VfL Borussia Mönchengladbach

 6 Eintracht Frankfurt

 7 SC Freiburg

 8 Hamburger SV

 9 Hannover 96

 10 Hertha BSC Berlin

 11 TSG 1899 Hoffenheim

 12 1. FC Köln

 13 1. FSV Mainz 05

 14 SC Paderborn 07

 15 FC Schalke 04

 16 VfB Stuttgart

 17 SV Werder Bremen

 18 VfL Wolfsburg

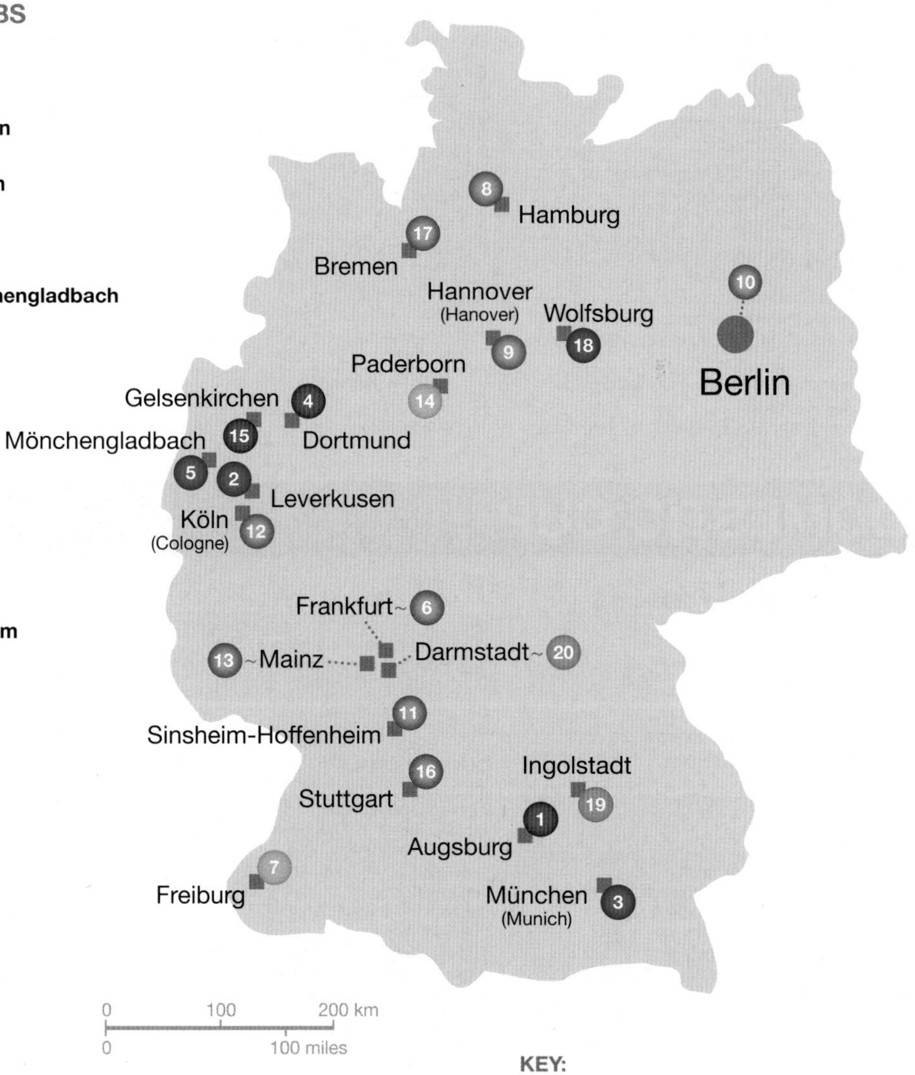

PROMOTED CLUBS

 19 FC Ingolstadt 04

 20 SV Darmstadt 98

8 Hamburg

17 Bremen

Hannover
(Hanover) 9 Wolfsburg 18

10 Berlin

Paderborn 14

Gelsenkirchen 4

Mönchengladbach 15 Dortmund

5 2 Leverkusen

Köln 12
(Cologne)

Frankfurt ~ 6

13 ~ Mainz · · · · · Darmstadt ~ 20

11 Sinsheim-Hoffenheim

16 Ingolstadt

Stuttgart

1 19

Augsburg

7 München 3
Freiburg (Munich)

0	100	200 km
0		100 miles

KEY:
● – UEFA Champions League

● – UEFA Europa League

● – Promoted

● – Relegated

Another title romp for Bayern

For the third season in a row the Bundesliga title was claimed with crushing conviction by FC Bayern München, Josep 'Pep' Guardiola's power-packed team shrugging off a spate of injuries to retain their crown with consummate ease.

For the first time since 2001, however, Bayern did not supplement their league triumph with success in the German Cup. That prize went to Bundesliga runners-up VfL Wolfsburg, 3-1 conquerors in the Berlin final of a Borussia Dortmund side bidding farewell to their charismatic coach Jürgen Klopp after seven highly eventful years.

Bundesliga triumph a formality for Guardiola's side

League runners-up Wolfsburg lift the cup

Klopp ends seven-year reign at Dortmund

Domestic league

Omnipotent in the previous two seasons, Bayern's title hat-trick – and record-extending 25th German championship win – was never in doubt once they had climbed to the top of the table after five matches. The strength in depth of the squad at Guardiola's disposal was so superior to those elsewhere that he could have fielded two teams capable of winning the Bundesliga. As it turned out, the ex-FC Barcelona boss was obliged to draw on his full roster, with a number of key players sidelined at various stages of the campaign. Those forced out of action for extended periods included Javi Martínez, Thiago Alcántara, Franck Ribéry, Bastian Schweinsteiger, David Alaba, Arjen Robben and even the normally unbreakable club captain Philipp Lahm.

Despite the potential for post-FIFA World Cup withdrawal and fatigue, Bayern – who had six German world champions in their squad (a seventh, Toni Kroos, had departed for Real Madrid CF) – remained invincible throughout the first half of the Bundesliga campaign. Indeed, they dropped only six points – in away draws at FC Schalke 04, Hamburger SV and VfL Borussia Mönchengladbach – and, even more impressively, conceded just four goals. They powered into the winter break with eight wins on the spin, the last of them courtesy of an added-time Robben strike at 1. FSV Mainz 05, to go 11 points clear at the top – a new record margin for a Bundesliga halfway lead.

Second-in-the-table Wolfsburg reduced that advantage when they thrashed Bayern 4-1 in the first fixture of the spring campaign, and when the leaders followed that first defeat by dropping their first points at home, in a 1-1 draw with Schalke, it looked as if there might be a chink in the armour of Guardiola's all-conquering juggernaut. But that hypothesis was swiftly deconstructed as Bayern stormed to six successive victories, during which they smashed in 27 goals, eight of them in an Allianz-Arena rout of their traditional northern rivals Hamburg.

A first home defeat in 11 months, by Mönchengladbach, brought that sequence to a brusque halt, but by then it was just a question of when Bayern's title triumph would be confirmed. That came four wins later, although it was actually a day after the last of those victories – 1-0 against Hertha BSC Berlin in Munich – that mathematical certainty was provided by Wolfsburg's 1-0 defeat at Mönchengladbach. With the Bundesliga booty in their possession, Bayern then took their foot off the accelerator and, alarmingly if insignificantly, lost three matches in a row. That brought a reduced final points tally of 79 (compared to 90 in 2013/14) and a final victory margin of just ten (as opposed to the 19 of Guardiola's first season).

Despite the excellent debut campaign of their new recruit from Dortmund, Robert Lewandowski, who had replaced Club Atlético de Madrid-bound Mario Mandžukić as the team's main striker, Bayern's final goal count was also down (from 94 to 80), but the defensive figures were an improvement (from 23 to 18), with Manuel Neuer continuing to reinforce his standing as the world's best goalkeeper and Jérôme Boateng establishing himself as the dominant figure in central defence. Elsewhere the versatile Thomas Müller was as reliable as ever, and new signing Xabi Alonso stood in superbly for injured compatriot Martínez in midfield. Robben, the dazzling Dutchman, was the brightest spark of all, scoring 17 goals – the same number as Lewandowski – and driving Bundesliga defences to weekly distraction with his skills until he missed the final two months of the campaign through injury.

While Bayern continued to reign supreme, there was a shift in power among the teams vying to join them in

the UEFA Champions League. The big story for much of the campaign was the dramatic decline of Dortmund. Champions in 2010/11 and 2011/12, and runners-up in 2012/13 and 2013/14, Klopp's Yellow-and-Black army fell so deep into retreat that by early February they were propping up the Bundesliga table. A hideous first half of the season that started with the concession of a goal against Bayer 04 Leverkusen after just nine seconds – the fastest in Bundesliga history – yielded ten defeats. Mercifully for their legions of fans, Dortmund recovered in the spring and climbed all the way up to seventh to re-qualify for Europe, but there was bad news among the good as Klopp announced in mid-April that he would be leaving the club in the summer, passing on the baton to much-lauded ex-Mainz boss Thomas Tuchel.

Dortmund's local rivals Schalke also parted company with a high-profile coach at the season's end, although, unlike Klopp, Roberto Di Matteo left few happy memories behind him. His sojourn in Gelsenkirchen lasted only seven months, and it ended with Schalke dropping to sixth place, just two points ahead of Dortmund. Above both of the big Ruhr rivals were the remarkable, low-budget Bavarians of FC Augsburg, whose fifth-place finish was the highest in the club's history and earned them a first crack at European

competition. Coach Markus Weinzierl's stock continued to rise as he drew the maximum from a largely unheralded group of players. Augsburg may have lost as many games as they won, but among the opponents they defeated were Bayern, Wolfsburg and Mönchengladbach – the top three teams in the division.

Wolfsburg enjoyed a fabulous season on all fronts under Dieter Hecking, and although Bayern's irrepressible front-running gave them no chance of reprising their 2008/09 Bundesliga triumph, the Green-and-Whites were more than worthy runners-up. Undefeated at home, they also entertained on their travels, notably at the start of the spring when, with Dutch striker Bas Dost in scintillating form following his brace in the momentous 4-1 win against Bayern, they posted back-to-back five-goal victories at Leverkusen and SV Werder Bremen. The standout individual in Wolfsburg's success was brilliant playmaker Kevin De Bruyne, with full-backs Vieirinha and Ricardo Rodriguez, and Brazilian duo Naldo and Luiz Gustavo, also catching the eye.

Mönchengladbach's season was as memorable as Wolfsburg's, with Swiss coach Lucien Favre leading the club to third place and a guaranteed first participation in the UEFA Champions

League group stage. A positive, unbeaten start was followed by a late-autumn dip, but post-Christmas, with Favre's Swiss compatriots Yann Sommer (in goal) and Granit Xhaka (in midfield) to the fore, Gladbach rose again, going 13 matches without defeat. Among the goals during that spell were Brazilian striker Raffael and German internationals Max Kruse and Patrick Herrmann, all of whom reached double figures for the season.

Leverkusen finished fourth for the second year in a row, new boss Roger Schmidt acquitting himself well in his debut season as a Bundesliga coach. A seven-match winning stretch in the spring ensured that the Rhinelanders would gain ample reward for a solid campaign in which attacking midfielders Karim Bellarabi and Hakan Çalhanoğlu were especially impressive. The 2014/15 season was a positive one also for TSG 1899 Hoffenheim, inspired by Brazilian schemer Roberto Firmino, and Eintracht Frankfurt, who boasted the Bundesliga's leading marksman in 19-goal Alexander Meier, but Dortmund were not the only traditional heavyweight club to endure a fraught campaign.

Bremen, bottom in December, lifted themselves clear of the relegation battle in good time, but VfB Stuttgart and Hamburg were still in the thick of it at the finish. However, in a repeat scenario of the previous season, both clubs extracted themselves from disaster by the skin of their teeth. Stuttgart were rescued again by Dutch coach Huub Stevens as they won their final three fixtures, the last of them at Bundesliga debutants SC Paderborn 07, who therefore went down instead – along with fellow last-day losers SC Freiburg, defeated 2-1 by another endangered team, Hannover 96.

Hamburg, just like 12 months before, had to undergo the ordeal of the play-offs, but once again they survived, preserving their unique status as the only ever-present Bundesliga club thanks to a last-gasp equaliser and extra-time winner in the second leg against Karlsruher SC. There was intrigue in the identity of the two promoted clubs as FC Ingolstadt 04 qualified for the Bundesliga for the first time and SV Darmstadt 98 ended a 33-year absence from Germany's elite.

Wolfsburg's Bas Dost scores the first of his two goals in a 4-1 Bundesliga win at home to Bayern

Domestic cup

Bayern's grip on the DFB-Pokal was released in extraordinary circumstances as they lost their home semi-final against Dortmund on penalties after missing all four spot kicks, with Lahm, Xabi Alonso, Mario Götze and goalkeeper Neuer the guilty parties. That enabled Dortmund to give Klopp the perfect send-off in the season's curtain-closer in Berlin, but Wolfsburg, who cruised past giant-killing DSC Arminia Bielefeld in the other semi, had other ideas.

The Lower Saxony club had never lifted the trophy but, having displaced Dortmund as the Bundesliga's second-best side, were eager to cement the changing of the order in the cup final. First blood in the Olympiastadion went to Dortmund when their player of the season, Pierre-Emerick Aubameyang, struck after five minutes, but Wolfsburg responded brilliantly with three goals in a riveting 16-minute spell, Luiz Gustavo equalising before De Bruyne and Dost gave their team a two-goal advantage that they would preserve through to the final whistle, bringing coach Hecking his first major trophy.

Europe

For the second straight season Germany's four-strong UEFA Champions League collective of Bayern, Dortmund, Schalke and Leverkusen progressed en bloc to the knockout phase. Three of the teams would fall at the same hurdle as 12 months previously, the odd one out being 2013/14 quarter-finalists Dortmund, who crashed out alongside Schalke and Leverkusen in the round of 16. Juventus proved far too strong for Klopp's side, winning 5-1 on aggregate, while the city of Madrid proved to be the final outpost for both Schalke and Leverkusen as they came frustratingly close to eliminating the previous season's finalists, Di Matteo's side posting a famous 4-3 win over Real Madrid in the Santiago Bernabéu but losing 5-4 on aggregate and Schmidt's team losing on penalties to Atlético in the Vicente Calderón.

Bayern produced an astonishing display to crush AS Roma 7-1 at the Stadio Olimpico in the group stage, but they failed to win any of their four subsequent away fixtures. Imperious home form took them past FC Shakhtar Donetsk and FC Porto, but a 3-0 semi-final first-leg defeat

Arjen Robben opens the scoring in Bayern's brilliant 7-1 victory at Roma in the UEFA Champions League

at Guardiola's former fiefdom, the Camp Nou, was a setback from which they could not recover, resulting in a second successive last-four elimination by Spanish opposition.

Wolfsburg were Germany's most effective UEFA Europa League performers, reaching the quarter-finals at the expense of FC Internazionale Milano but then going out to another Serie A club, SSC Napoli, following a devastating 4-1 first-leg defeat at the Volkswagen-Arena. Whereas Mainz exited early, Mönchengladbach came through the play-offs and group stage undefeated before losing both round of 32 legs to eventual winners Sevilla FC.

National team

Having claimed sport's most coveted team prize in Brazil, Joachim Löw's FIFA World Cup winners were probably entitled to a bit of down-time in the season that followed. The UEFA EURO 2016 qualifying campaign did not afford them that luxury, however, and with a number of senior figures having ended their international careers, including captain Lahm and record goalscorer Miroslav Klose, it was perhaps unsurprising that Germany struggled to impose their usual authority at the start of their journey to France.

A fortunate 2-1 win at home to Scotland, thanks to a Müller double, was followed by a shock 2-0 defeat in Poland – Germany's first loss in a qualifying fixture for seven years – and more dropped points in a 1-1 draw at home to the Republic of Ireland.

Even a home fixture against Gibraltar did not deliver the expected flood of goals, but a 4-0 win in Nuremberg stopped the rot and was followed by a 2-0 success in Georgia and, in June, another victory over Gibraltar (7-0), enabling German fans to sleep a bit more easily in advance of the team's final four fixtures.

Other than that scrappy win against Scotland in Dortmund, however, Löw's side gave their home supporters little to celebrate. A re-run of the World Cup final in Dusseldorf – less than two months after the main event – ended in a 4-2 defeat by Argentina, and further friendlies brought a 2-2 draw with Australia in Kaiserslautern and a 2-1 defeat by Jürgen Klinsmann's USA in Cologne. Germany's only friendly win was nevertheless a prestigious one as they overcame Spain 1-0 in Vigo thanks to a late winner from new Real Madrid recruit Kroos, who in January was voted as the world champions' 2014 player of the year.

DOMESTIC SEASON AT A GLANCE

Bundesliga 2014/15 final table

		Pld	Home					Away					Total					Pts
			W	D	L	F	A	W	D	L	F	A	W	D	L	F	A	
1	**FC Bayern München**	**34**	**14**	**1**	**2**	**46**	**7**	**11**	**3**	**3**	**34**	**11**	**25**	**4**	**5**	**80**	**18**	**79**
2	VfL Wolfsburg	34	13	4	0	38	13	7	5	5	34	25	20	9	5	72	38	69
3	VfL Borussia Mönchengladbach	34	12	3	2	32	14	7	6	4	21	12	19	9	6	53	26	66
4	Bayer 04 Leverkusen	34	10	6	1	39	15	7	4	6	23	22	17	10	7	62	37	61
5	FC Augsburg	34	9	4	4	28	21	6	0	11	15	22	15	4	15	43	43	49
6	FC Schalke 04	34	10	5	2	26	14	3	4	10	16	26	13	9	12	42	40	48
7	Borussia Dortmund	34	9	3	5	26	15	4	4	9	21	27	13	7	14	47	42	46
8	TSG 1899 Hoffenheim	34	9	3	5	31	26	3	5	9	18	29	12	8	14	49	55	44
9	Eintracht Frankfurt	34	9	5	3	36	26	2	5	10	20	36	11	10	13	56	62	43
10	SV Werder Bremen	34	8	4	5	25	24	3	6	8	25	41	11	10	13	50	65	43
11	1. FSV Mainz 05	34	6	6	5	27	19	3	7	7	18	28	9	13	12	45	47	40
12	1. FC Köln	34	4	9	4	18	17	5	4	8	16	23	9	13	12	34	40	40
13	Hannover 96	34	6	4	7	21	25	3	6	8	19	31	9	10	15	40	56	37
14	VfB Stuttgart	34	5	4	8	18	28	4	5	8	24	32	9	9	16	42	60	36
15	Hertha BSC Berlin	34	6	4	7	17	22	3	4	10	19	30	9	8	17	36	52	35
16	Hamburger SV	34	6	5	6	16	18	3	3	11	9	32	9	8	17	25	50	35
17	SC Freiburg	34	5	6	6	21	22	2	7	8	15	25	7	13	14	36	47	34
18	SC Paderborn 07	34	4	6	7	21	31	3	4	10	10	34	7	10	17	31	65	31

European qualification 2015/16

Champion: FC Bayern München (group stage)

Cup winner: VfL Wolfsburg (group stage)
VfL Borussia Mönchengladbach (group stage)
Bayer 04 Leverkusen (play-offs)

FC Augsburg (group stage)
FC Schalke 04 (group stage)
Borussia Dortmund (third qualifying round)

Top scorer	Alexander Meier (Frankfurt), 19 goals
Relegated clubs	SC Paderborn 07, SC Freiburg
Promoted clubs	FC Ingolstadt 04, SV Darmstadt 98
Cup final	VfL Wolfsburg 3-1 Borussia Dortmund

Team of the season
(4-1-4-1)

Coach: Hecking (Wolfsburg)

Neuer
(Bayern)

Vieirinha (Wolfsburg) — Naldo (Wolfsburg) — Boateng (Bayern) — Rodriguez (Wolfsburg)

Xhaka (M'gladbach)

Robben (Bayern) — Herrmann (M'gladbach) — De Bruyne (Wolfsburg) — Reus (Dortmund)

Lewandowski (Bayern)

Player of the season

Kevin De Bruyne
(VfL Wolfsburg)

With 16 goals and 28 assists in all competition during the 2014/15 season, it was hardly surprising that De Bruyne collected over half the votes in the Bundesliga Player of the Year poll. The young Belgian international's first full season at Wolfsburg exceeded all expectations as he put a difficult spell at Chelsea FC firmly behind him, producing one masterful performance after another to help his team to second place in the Bundesliga, the quarter-finals of the UEFA Europa League and victory in the German Cup.

Newcomer of the season

Jonas Hector
(1. FC Köln)

New to the Bundesliga in 2014/15 following his promotion to the top flight with Köln, Hector went on to be one of the revelations of the season, starting all but one of the Rhinelanders' 34 matches and scoring two goals. While Peter Stöger's side achieved their objective of staying in the division, eventually finishing 12th, their consistently impressive rookie left-back advanced his career to such an extent that by the end of term he had become the first choice in that position for the German national team.

NATIONAL TEAM

International honours*
FIFA World Cup (4) 1954, 1974, 1990, 2014
UEFA European Championship (3) 1972, 1980, 1996

International tournament appearances*
FIFA World Cup (18) 1934 (3rd), 1938, 1954 (Winners), 1958 (4th), 1962 (qtr-finals), 1966 (runners-up), 1970 (3rd), 1974 (Winners), 1978 (2nd phase), 1982 (runners-up), 1986 (runners-up), 1990 (Winners), 1994 (qtr-finals), 1998 (qtr-finals), 2002 (runners-up), 2006 (3rd), 2010 (3rd), 2014 (Winners)
UEFA European Championship (11) 1972 (Winners), 1976 (runners-up), 1980 (Winners), 1984, 1988 (semi-finals), 1992 (runners-up), 1996 (Winners), 2000, 2004, 2008 (runners-up), 2012 (semi-finals)

Top five all-time caps
Lothar Matthäus (150); Miroslav Klose (137); **Lukas Podolski** (125); Philipp Lahm (113); **Bastian Schweinsteiger** (111)

Top five all-time goals
Miroslav Klose (71); Gerd Müller (68); **Lukas Podolski** (48); Jürgen Klinsmann & Rudi Völler (47)

(* before 1992 as West Germany)

Results 2014/15

03/09/14	Argentina	H	Dusseldorf	L	2-4	Schürrle (52), Götze (78)
07/09/14	Scotland (ECQ)	H	Dortmund	W	2-1	Müller (18, 70)
11/10/14	Poland (ECQ)	A	Warsaw	L	0-2	
14/10/14	Republic of Ireland (ECQ)	H	Gelsenkirchen	D	1-1	Kroos (71)
14/11/14	Gibraltar (ECQ)	H	Nuremberg	W	4-0	Müller (12, 29), Götze (38), Santos (67og)
18/11/14	Spain	A	Vigo	W	1-0	Kroos (89)
25/03/15	Australia	H	Kaiserslautern	D	2-2	Reus (17), Podolski (81)
29/03/15	Georgia (ECQ)	A	Tbilisi	W	2-0	Reus (39), Müller (44)
10/06/15	United States	H	Cologne	L	1-2	Götze (12)
13/06/15	Gibraltar (ECQ)	A	Faro (POR)	W	7-0	Schürrle (28, 65, 71), Kruse (47, 81), Gündoğan (51), Bellarabi (57)

Appearances 2014/15

Coach: Joachim Löw	03/02/60		Arg	SCO	POL	IRL	GIB	Esp	Aus	GEO	Usa	GIB	Caps	Goals
Manuel Neuer	27/03/86	Bayern	G46	G	G	G	G			G			58	-
Kevin Grosskreutz	19/07/88	Dortmund	D										6	-
Benedikt Höwedes	29/02/88	Schalke	D77	D			D	D					32	2
Matthias Ginter	19/01/94	Dortmund	D	s92		M46							5	-
Erik Durm	12/05/92	Dortmund	D	D	D	D	D72	D					7	-
Christoph Kramer	19/02/91	Mönchengladbach	M	M	M71				s63		s60		10	-
Toni Kroos	04/01/90	Real Madrid (ESP)	M71	M	M	M	M79	M		M			58	9
André Schürrle	06/11/90	Chelsea (ENG)/Wolfsburg	M57	M84	M77				s63	s86	M46	A	46	20
Marco Reus	31/05/89	Dortmund	M	M92					A73	M			25	9
Julian Draxler	20/09/93	Schalke	M34		s71	M70							15	1
Mario Gomez	10/07/85	Fiorentina (ITA)	A58										60	25
Lukas Podolski	04/06/85	Arsenal (ENG)/Internazionale (ITA)	s34	s84	s77	s46	M		s73	s87	s46	s56	125	48
Roman Weidenfeller	06/08/80	Dortmund	s46									G	5	-
Thomas Müller	13/09/89	Bayern	s57	M	A	A	A	M22		M86			63	27
Mario Götze	03/06/92	Bayern	s58	A	M	M	M	A84	A73	A87	A73	A36	45	14
Sebastian Rudy	28/02/90	Hoffenheim	s71	D		s86		D	s46	D	D	D	9	-
Antonio Rüdiger	03/03/93	Stuttgart	s77		D83	D		D			D		6	-
Jérôme Boateng	03/09/88	Bayern		D	D	D	D			D		D	52	-
Mats Hummels	16/12/88	Dortmund			D	D				D			39	4
Karim Bellarabi	08/04/90	Leverkusen			M	M86	M	s22	M63		s73	M	7	1
Max Kruse	19/03/88	Mönchengladbach			s83	s70	A	s84	s73		s73	s36	13	3
Shkodran Mustafi	17/04/92	Valencia (ESP)					D	D	D		D		8	-
Sami Khedira	04/04/87	Real Madrid (ESP)					M60	M92	M63		s46	s67	56	5
Kevin Volland	30/07/92	Hoffenheim					s60	M					3	-
Jonas Hector	27/05/90	Köln					s72		M	D	D	D	5	-
Lars Bender	27/04/89	Leverkusen					s79	s92					19	4
Ron-Robert Zieler	12/02/89	Hannover					G	G		G			6	-
Holger Badstuber	13/03/89	Bayern							D46				31	1
Mesut Özil	15/10/88	Arsenal (ENG)							M	M	M	M	66	18
İlkay Gündoğan	24/10/90	Dortmund							M		M60	M67	11	3
Bastian Schweinsteiger	01/08/84	Bayern							M	M46	M		111	23
Patrick Herrmann	12/02/91	Mönchengladbach									M73	M56	2	-

FC Bayern München

Group E

Match 1 - Manchester City FC (ENG)
H 1-0 *Boateng (90)*
Neuer, Xabi Alonso, Benatia (Dante 85), Lewandowski, Rafinha (Pizarro 84), Boateng, Bernat, Götze, Lahm, Müller (Robben 76), Alaba. Coach: Josep Guardiola (ESP)

Match 2 - PFC CSKA Moskva (RUS)
A 1-0 *Müller (22p)*
Neuer, Xabi Alonso, Dante, Benatia, Lewandowski (Pizarro 90), Robben (Rafinha 81), Bernat, Götze (Shaqiri 77), Lahm, Müller, Alaba. Coach: Josep Guardiola (ESP)

Match 3 - AS Roma (ITA)
A 7-1 *Robben (9, 30), Götze (23), Lewandowski (25), Müller (36p), Ribéry (78), Shaqiri (80)*
Neuer, Xabi Alonso, Benatia, Lewandowski (Ribéry 68), Robben, Boateng, Bernat, Götze (Shaqiri 79), Lahm, Müller (Rafinha 60), Alaba. Coach: Josep Guardiola (ESP)

Match 4 - AS Roma (ITA)
H 2-0 *Ribéry (38), Götze (64)*
Neuer, Xabi Alonso (Shaqiri 72), Benatia, Ribéry, Lewandowski, Rafinha, Boateng, Bernat, Götze, Lahm (Højbjerg 88), Alaba (Rode 81). Coach: Josep Guardiola (ESP)

Match 5 - Manchester City FC (ENG)
A 2-3 *Xabi Alonso (40), Lewandowski (45)*
Neuer, Xabi Alonso, Benatia, Ribéry (Schweinsteiger 81), Lewandowski (Shaqiri 84), Robben, Rafinha, Boateng, Bernat, Rode (Dante 25), Højbjerg. Coach: Josep Guardiola (ESP)
Red card: Benatia 20

Match 6 - PFC CSKA Moskva (RUS)
H 3-0 *Müller (18p), Rode (84), Götze (90)*
Neuer, Dante, Ribéry (Lewandowski 46), Gaudino (Weiser 73), Boateng, Bernat, Götze, Rode, Müller (Robben 46), Schweinsteiger, Højbjerg. Coach: Josep Guardiola (ESP)

Round of 16 - FC Shakhtar Donetsk (UKR)
A 0-0
Neuer, Xabi Alonso, Ribéry, Robben, Rafinha, Boateng, Bernat, Götze (Lewandowski 75), Müller (Badstuber 70), Alaba, Schweinsteiger. Coach: Josep Guardiola (ESP)
Red card: Xabi Alonso 65
H 7-0 *Müller (4p, 52), Boateng (34), Ribéry (49), Badstuber (63), Lewandowski (75), Götze (87)*
Neuer, Ribéry (Bernat 59), Lewandowski, Robben (Rode 19), Rafinha, Boateng, Götze, Müller, Alaba, Badstuber (Dante 67), Schweinsteiger. Coach: Josep Guardiola (ESP)

Quarter-finals - FC Porto (POR)
A 1-3 *Thiago (28)*
Neuer, Xabi Alonso (Badstuber 74), Dante, Thiago, Lewandowski, Rafinha, Boateng, Bernat, Götze (Rode 56), Lahm, Müller. Coach: Josep Guardiola (ESP)
H 6-1 *Thiago (14), Boateng (22), Lewandowski (27,40), Müller (36), Xabi Alonso (88)*
Neuer, Xabi Alonso, Thiago (Dante 90), Lewandowski, Rafinha (Rode 72), Boateng, Bernat, Götze (Weiser 86), Lahm, Müller, Badstuber. Coach: Josep Guardiola (ESP)

Semi-finals - FC Barcelona (ESP)
A 0-3
Neuer, Xabi Alonso, Benatia, Thiago, Lewandowski, Rafinha, Boateng, Bernat, Lahm, Müller (Götze 79), Schweinsteiger. Coach: Josep Guardiola (ESP)
H 3-2 *Benatia (7), Lewandowski (59), Müller (74)*
Neuer, Xabi Alonso, Benatia, Thiago, Lewandowski, Rafinha, Boateng, Bernat, Lahm (Rode 68), Müller (Götze 87), Schweinsteiger (Javi Martínez 87). Coach: Josep Guardiola (ESP)

Borussia Dortmund

Group D

Match 1 - Arsenal FC (ENG)
H 2-0 *Immobile (45), Aubameyang (48)*
Weidenfeller, Subotić, Kehl (Ginter 46), Bender, Immobile (Ramos 86), Mkhitaryan, Aubameyang, Grosskreutz, Papastathopoulos, Schmelzer (Jojić 79), Durm. Coach: Jürgen Klopp (GER)

Match 2 - RSC Anderlecht (BEL)
A 3-0 *Immobile (3), Ramos (69, 79)*
Weidenfeller, Subotić, Kehl, Bender (Hummels 82), Kagawa, Immobile (Durm 72), Aubameyang, Grosskreutz (Ramos 65), Papastathopoulos, Piszczek, Schmelzer. Coach: Jürgen Klopp (GER)

Match 3 - Galatasaray AŞ (TUR)
A 4-0 *Aubameyang (6, 18), Reus (41), Ramos (83)*
Weidenfeller, Subotić, Kehl, Bender (Ginter 55), Kagawa (Ramos 82), Mkhitaryan, Reus, Hummels (Gündogan 69), Aubameyang, Papastathopoulos, Piszczek. Coach: Jürgen Klopp (GER)

Match 4 - Galatasaray AŞ (TUR)
H 4-1 *Reus (39), Papastathopoulos (56), Immobile (74), Semih Kaya (85og)*
Weidenfeller, Subotić, Kehl, Bender (Ramos 85), Kagawa (Gündogan 63), Mkhitaryan, Reus (Immobile 71), Aubameyang, Papastathopoulos, Piszczek, Durm. Coach: Jürgen Klopp (GER)

Match 5 - Arsenal FC (ENG)
A 0-2
Weidenfeller, Subotić, Bender, Gündogan, Immobile (Kagawa 61), Mkhitaryan, Aubameyang (Ramos 61), Grosskreutz (Jojić 78), Piszczek, Ginter, Schmelzer. Coach: Jürgen Klopp (GER)

Match 6 - RSC Anderlecht (BEL)
H 1-1 *Immobile (58)*
Langerak, Subotić, Kagawa (Błaszczykowski 84), Gündogan (Kirch 66), Immobile, Mkhitaryan, Nuri Sahin, Grosskreutz, Ginter, Schmelzer (Aubameyang 75), Durm. Coach: Jürgen Klopp (GER)

Round of 16 - Juventus (ITA)
A 1-2 *Reus (18)*
Weidenfeller, Gündoğan, Immobile (Błaszczykowski 76), Mkhitaryan, Reus, Hummels, Aubameyang, Nuri Şahin, Papastathopoulos (Kirch 46), Piszczek (Ginter 32), Schmelzer. Coach: Jürgen Klopp (GER)
H 0-3
Weidenfeller, Subotić, Bender (Ramos 63), Gündoğan, Mkhitaryan (Błaszczykowski 63), Reus, Hummels, Aubameyang, Kampl, Papastathopoulos, Schmelzer (Kirch 46). Coach: Jürgen Klopp (GER)

FC Schalke 04

Group G

Match 1 - Chelsea FC (ENG)
A 1-1 *Huntelaar (62)*
Fährmann, Meyer (Choupo-Moting 74), Boateng, Draxler (Obasi 86), Höger, Aogo, Sam (Barnetta 78), Fuchs, Kaan Ayhan, Huntelaar, Neustädter. Coach: Jens Keller (GER)

Match 2 - NK Maribor (SVN)
H 1-1 *Huntelaar (56)*
Fährmann, Boateng (Meyer 79), Draxler, Choupo-Moting (Obasi 66), Aogo, Fuchs, Kaan Ayhan (Uchida 46), Huntelaar, Barnetta, Matip, Neustädter. Coach: Jens Keller (GER)

Match 3 - Sporting Clube de Portugal (POR)
H 4-3 *Obasi (34), Huntelaar (51), Höwedes (60), Choupo-Moting (90+3p)*
Fährmann, Höwedes, Boateng (Choupo-Moting 46), Draxler (Sam 82), Höger, Aogo, Obasi (Meyer 65), Uchida, Kaan Ayhan, Huntelaar, Neustädter. Coach: Roberto Di Matteo (ITA)

Match 4 - Sporting Clube de Portugal (POR)
A 2-4 *Slimani (17og), Aogo (88)*
Fährmann, Höwedes, Meyer (Boateng 65), Höger, Choupo-Moting, Aogo, Obasi (Sam 69), Uchida, Fuchs (Kirchhoff 78), Huntelaar, Neustädter. Coach: Roberto Di Matteo (ITA)

Match 5 - Chelsea FC (ENG)
H 0-5
Fährmann, Kirchhoff (Clemens 46), Höwedes, Felipe Santana, Boateng (Meyer 63), Höger, Choupo-Moting, Aogo, Uchida, Huntelaar, Neustädter. Coach: Roberto Di Matteo (ITA)

Match 6 - NK Maribor (SVN)
A 1-0 *Meyer (62)*
Fährmann, Kirchhoff, Höwedes, Höger (Kaan Ayhan 88), Choupo-Moting, Aogo, Uchida, Fuchs, Huntelaar (Friedrich 90+2), Barnetta (Meyer 56), Neustädter. Coach: Roberto Di Matteo (ITA)

Round of 16 - Real Madrid CF (ESP)
H 0-2
Wellenreuther, Höwedes, Boateng, Höger (Meyer 80), Choupo-Moting, Aogo, Uchida, Huntelaar (Platte 33), Nastasić, Matip, Neustädter (Kirchhoff 57). Coach: Roberto Di Matteo (ITA)
A 4-3 *Fuchs (20), Huntelaar (40, 84), Sané (57)*
Wellenreuther, Höwedes, Meyer, Höger (Goretzka 57), Choupo-Moting (Sané 29), Fuchs, Huntelaar, Barnetta (Uchida 81), Nastasić, Matip, Neustädter. Coach: Roberto Di Matteo (ITA)

Bayer 04 Leverkusen

Play-offs - FC København (DEN)
A 3-2 *Kiessling (5), Bellarabi (31), Son (42)*
Leno, Spahić, Rolfes, Son, Hakan Çalhanoglu (Drmic 88), Kiessling, Boenisch, Ömer Toprak, Donati (Jedvaj 46), Castro, Bellarabi (Brandt 83). Coach: Roger Schmidt (GER)

H 4-0 *Son (2), Hakan Çalhanoğlu (7), Kiessling (31p, 65)*
Leno, Spahić, Rolfes (Reinartz 65), Son, Hakan Çalhanoglu, Kiessling (Drmic 73), Jedvaj, Boenisch, Ömer Toprak (Papadopoulos 54), Castro, Bellarabi. Coach: Roger Schmidt (GER)

Group C
Match 1 - AS Monaco FC (FRA)
A 0-1
Leno, Spahić, Son, Bender (Drmic 75), Hakan Çalhanoglu, Kiessling, Jedvaj (Donati 65), Boenisch, Ömer Toprak (Reinartz 71), Castro, Bellarabi. Coach: Roger Schmidt (GER)
Match 2 - SL Benfica (POR)
H 3-1 *Kiessling (25), Son (34), Hakan Çalhanoglu (64p)*
Leno, Reinartz, Spahić, Son, Bender (Donati 82), Hakan Çalhanoglu, Kiessling (Drmic 76), Hilbert, Wendell, Ömer Toprak, Bellarabi (Öztunali 70). Coach: Roger Schmidt (GER)
Match 3 - FC Zenit (RUS)
H 2-0 *Donati (58), Papadopoulos (63)*
Leno, Reinartz, Spahić (Papadopoulos 60), Son, Bender, Hakan Çalhanoglu (Jedvaj 82), Kiessling, Wendell, Ömer Toprak, Donati, Bellarabi (Brandt 85). Coach: Roger Schmidt (GER)
Red card: Wendell 79
Match 4 - FC Zenit (RUS)
A 2-1 *Son (68, 73)*
Leno, Spahić, Son, Bender, Hakan Çalhanoglu, Kiessling (Kruse 90+1), Jedvaj (Boenisch 65), Brandt (Drmic 53), Ömer Toprak, Donati, Bellarabi. Coach: Roger Schmidt (GER)
Match 5 - AS Monaco FC (FRA)
H 0-0
Leno, Spahić, Son (Drmic 59), Bender (Rolfes 76), Hakan Çalhanoglu, Kiessling, Wendell, Ömer Toprak, Donati, Castro, Bellarabi (Brandt 77). Coach: Roger Schmidt (GER)
Match 6 - SL Benfica (POR)
A 0-0
Leno, Spahić, Rolfes (Kiessling 83), Drmic (Son 71), Hakan Çalhanoglu, Hilbert, Boenisch, Ömer Toprak, Kruse (Brandt 46), Castro, Bellarabi. Coach: Roger Schmidt (GER)
Red card: Ömer Toprak 90+1

Round of 16 - Club Atlético de Madrid (ESP)
H 1-0 *Hakan Çalhanoğlu (57)*
Leno, Spahić, Son, Bender (Rolfes 68), Drmic (Kiessling 80), Hakan Çalhanoglu (Brandt 87), Hilbert, Papadopoulos, Wendell, Castro, Bellarabi. Coach: Roger Schmidt (GER)
A 0-1 *(aet; 2-3 on pens)*
Leno, Spahić, Son (Rolfes 77), Bender (Papadopoulos 104), Drmic (Kiessling 69), Hakan Çalhanoğlu, Hilbert, Wendell, Ömer Toprak, Castro, Bellarabi. Coach: Roger Schmidt (GER)

VfL Wolfsburg

Group H
Match 1 - Everton FC (ENG)
A 1-4 *Rodriguez (90+4)*
Benaglio, Caligiuri (Bendtner 61), Olić, De Bruyne, Malanda (Hunt 46), Luiz Gustavo (Guilavogui 77), Jung, Naldo, Arnold, Knoche, Rodriguez. Coach: Dieter Hecking (GER)
Match 2 - LOSC Lille (FRA)
H 1-1 *De Bruyne (82)*
Benaglio, Perišić, Hunt, Olić (Bendtner 62), De Bruyne, Luiz Gustavo, Guilavogui, Jung (Vieirinha 62), Naldo, Knoche (Caligiuri 79), Rodriguez. Coach: Dieter Hecking (GER)

Match 3 - FC Krasnodar (RUS)
A 4-2 *Granqvist (37og), De Bruyne (46, 80), Luiz Gustavo (64)*
Benaglio, Schäfer, Caligiuri, Perišić (Vieirinha 61), Olić (Dost 78), De Bruyne (Arnold 86), Luiz Gustavo, Guilavogui, Jung, Naldo, Knoche. Coach: Dieter Hecking (GER)
Match 4 - FC Krasnodar (RUS)
H 5-1 *Hunt (47, 57), Guilavogui (73), Bendtner (89p, 90+1)*
Benaglio, Schäfer (Klose 39), Vieirinha, Perišić (Hunt 46), Dost (Bendtner 75), De Bruyne, Träsch, Luiz Gustavo, Guilavogui, Naldo, Knoche. Coach: Dieter Hecking (GER)
Match 5 - Everton FC (ENG)
H 0-2
Benaglio, Bendtner (Olić 75), Schäfer, Vieirinha, Perišić, Hunt (Arnold 75), De Bruyne, Malanda (Caligiuri 63), Luiz Gustavo, Naldo, Knoche. Coach: Dieter Hecking (GER)
Match 6 - LOSC Lille (FRA)
A 3-0 *Vieirinha (45+1), Rodriguez (65, 89p)*
Benaglio, Vieirinha (Malanda 58), Perišić, Olić (Dost 46), De Bruyne (Caligiuri 85), Luiz Gustavo, Guilavogui, Jung, Naldo, Knoche, Rodriguez. Coach: Dieter Hecking (GER)
Red card: Guilavogui 55

Round of 32 - Sporting Clube de Portugal (POR)
H 2-0 *Dost (46, 63)*
Benaglio, Vieirinha (Schäfer 89), Hunt (Arnold 41), Dost, De Bruyne, Träsch, Schürrle (Caligiuri 79), Jung, Naldo, Knoche, Rodriguez. Coach: Dieter Hecking (GER)
A 0-0
Benaglio, Vieirinha (Schäfer 76), Dost, De Bruyne (Arnold 90+1), Träsch, Schürrle (Caligiuri 61), Luiz Gustavo, Guilavogui, Naldo, Knoche, Rodriguez. Coach: Dieter Hecking (GER)

Round of 16 - FC Internazionale Milano (ITA)
H 3-1 *Naldo (28), De Bruyne (63, 76)*
Benaglio, Caligiuri, Vieirinha (Perišić 87), Dost (Bendtner 70), De Bruyne, Schürrle (Träsch 46), Luiz Gustavo, Guilavogui, Naldo, Knoche, Rodriguez. Coach: Dieter Hecking (GER)
A 2-1 *Caligiuri (24), Bendtner (89)*
Benaglio, Klose, Caligiuri (Perišić 73), Vieirinha (Arnold 85), Dost (Bendtner 64), De Bruyne, Träsch, Luiz Gustavo, Guilavogui, Knoche, Rodriguez. Coach: Dieter Hecking (GER)

Quarter-finals - SSC Napoli (ITA)
H 1-4 *Bendtner (80)*
Benaglio, Caligiuri, Vieirinha, Dost (Bendtner 57), De Bruyne, Schürrle (Perišić 64), Luiz Gustavo, Guilavogui (Arnold 70), Naldo, Knoche, Rodriguez. Coach: Dieter Hecking (GER)
A 2-2 *Klose (71), Dost (73)*
Benaglio, Bendtner, Klose, Caligiuri, Perišić, Träsch (Dost 79), Luiz Gustavo, Guilavogui (Jung 75), Naldo, Arnold, Rodriguez (Schäfer 66). Coach: Dieter Hecking (GER)

VfL Borussia Mönchengladbach

Play-offs - FK Sarajevo (BIH)
A 3-2 *Hahn (11), Hrgota (41, 73)*
Sommer, Traoré (Herrmann 46), Raffael (Hazard 82), Álvaro Domínguez, Nordtveit, Johnson, Jantschke, Hahn (Korb 65), Hrgota, Xhaka, Stranzl. Coach: Lucien Favre (SUI)
H 7-0 *Hahn (20), Xhaka (24), Hrgota (34, 67, 82), Hazard (74p, 90+2)*
Sommer, Raffael (Hazard 70), Álvaro Domínguez, Johnson, Kramer (Dahoud 55), Jantschke, Korb, Hahn (Herrmann 64), Hrgota, Xhaka, Stranzl. Coach: Lucien Favre (SUI)

Group A
Match 1 - Villarreal CF (ESP)
H 1-1 *Herrmann (21)*
Sommer, Herrmann (Traoré 74), Kruse, Álvaro Domínguez, Wendt, Johnson (Hahn 62), Kramer, Jantschke, Hrgota (Raffael 77), Xhaka, Stranzl. Coach: Lucien Favre (SUI)
Match 2 - FC Zürich (SUI)
A 1-1 *Nordtveit (25)*
Sommer, Kruse, Álvaro Domínguez (Wendt 84), Nordtveit, Jantschke, Hazard (Traoré 67), Korb, Hahn (Herrmann 73), Hrgota, Xhaka, Stranzl. Coach: Lucien Favre (SUI)
Match 3 - Apollon Limassol FC (CYP)
H 5-0 *Traoré (11, 67), Hrgota (56), Herrmann (83), Angeli (90+1og)*
Sommer, Traoré, Kruse (Raffael 46), Nordtveit, Wendt, Jantschke, Hazard, Korb, Hrgota (Herrmann 79), Xhaka (Dahoud 70), Stranzl. Coach: Lucien Favre (SUI)
Match 4 - Apollon Limassol FC (CYP)
A 2-0 *Raffael (56), Herrmann (90+5)*
Sommer, Traoré (Hahn 79), Raffael, Nordtveit, Wendt, Johnson, Kramer, Jantschke, Hazard (Brouwers 90+1), Hrgota (Herrmann 72), Stranzl. Coach: Lucien Favre (SUI)
Match 5 - Villarreal CF (ESP)
A 2-2 *Raffael (55), Xhaka (67)*
Sommer, Brouwers, Traoré (Herrmann 71), Raffael, Álvaro Domínguez, Nordtveit, Jantschke, Hazard, Korb, Hrgota (Kruse 71), Xhaka. Coach: Lucien Favre (SUI)
Match 6 - FC Zürich (SUI)
H 3-0 *Herrmann (31), Hrgota (59, 64)*
Sommer, Brouwers, Herrmann (Hazard 67), Traoré (Johnson 78), Raffael (Kruse 67), Álvaro Domínguez, Wendt, Kramer, Jantschke, Hrgota, Xhaka. Coach: Lucien Favre (SUI)

Round of 32 - Sevilla FC (ESP)
A 0-1
Sommer, Raffael (Kruse 79), Álvaro Domínguez, Wendt, Johnson, Kramer, Jantschke, Hazard, Hrgota (Herrmann 69), Xhaka, Stranzl. Coach: Lucien Favre (SUI)
H 2-3 *Xhaka (19), Hazard (29)*
Sommer, Herrmann (Traoré 72), Kruse, Raffael, Álvaro Domínguez (Hrgota 77), Wendt, Kramer, Jantschke (Johnson 78), Hazard, Xhaka, Stranzl. Coach: Lucien Favre (SUI)
Red card: Xhaka 69

1. FSV Mainz 05

Third qualifying round - Asteras Tripolis FC (GRE)
H 1-0 *Okazaki (45)*
Karius, Jara, Noveski, Geis, Moritz, Malli, Koo (Zimling 78), Baumgartlinger (Brosinski 61), Bell, Okazaki, Park (Júnior Díaz 70). Coach: Kasper Hjulmand (DEN)
A 1-3 *Koo (39)*
Karius, Noveski, Geis, Moritz, Malli (Soto 85), Koo (Jara 69), Baumgartlinger, Bell, Brosinski, Okazaki, Park (Júnior Díaz 74). Coach: Kasper Hjulmand (DEN)

GERMANY

DOMESTIC LEAGUE CLUB-BY-CLUB

FC Augsburg

1907 • SGL-Arena (30,660) • fcaugsburg.de
Coach: Markus Weinzierl

2014

22/08	a Hoffenheim	L	0-2	
29/08	h Dortmund	L	2-3	Bobadilla, Matavž
14/09	a Frankfurt	W	1-0	Bobadilla
20/09	h Bremen	W	4-2	Baier, Verhaegh (p), Werner, Matavž
24/09	a Leverkusen	L	0-1	
28/09	h Hertha	W	1-0	Verhaegh (p)
05/10	a Wolfsburg	L	0-1	
18/10	a Mainz	L	1-2	Werner
25/10	h Freiburg	W	2-0	Verhaegh (p), Halil
31/10	a Schalke	L	0-1	
08/11	h Paderborn	W	3-0	Werner 2, Callsen-Bracker
23/11	a Stuttgart	W	1-0	Verhaegh (p)
29/11	h Hamburg	W	3-1	Halil, Bobadilla, Verhaegh (p)
06/12	a Köln	W	2-1	Djurdjić, Esswein
13/12	h Bayern	L	0-4	
16/12	h Hannover	L	0-2	
20/12	a Mönchengladbach	W	2-1	Feulner, Bobadilla

2015

01/02	h Hoffenheim	W	3-1	Halil, Werner, Bobadilla
04/02	a Dortmund	W	1-0	Bobadilla
08/02	h Frankfurt	D	2-2	Klavan, Bobadilla
14/02	a Bremen	L	2-3	Klavan, Werner
21/02	h Leverkusen	D	2-2	Caiuby, Hitz
28/02	a Hertha	L	0-1	
07/03	h Wolfsburg	W	1-0	Kohr
14/03	h Mainz	L	0-2	
21/03	a Freiburg	L	0-2	
05/04	h Schalke	D	0-0	
11/04	a Paderborn	L	1-2	Højbjerg
18/04	h Stuttgart	W	2-1	Werner, Bobadilla
25/04	a Hamburg	L	2-3	Bobadilla, Werner
02/05	h Köln	D	0-0	
09/05	a Bayern	W	1-0	Bobadilla
16/05	h Hannover	L	1-2	Verhaegh (p)
23/05	a Mönchengladbach	W	3-1	Højbjerg, Matavž, Mölders

No	Name	Nat	DoB	Pos	Aps	(s)	Gls
12	Abdul Rahman Baba	GHA	02/07/94	D	29	(2)	
10	Daniel Baier		18/05/84	M	34		1
25	Raúl Bobadilla	PAR	18/06/87	A	31	(1)	10
30	Caiuby	BRA	14/07/88	M	6	(16)	1
18	Jan-Ingwer Callsen-Bracker		23/09/84	D	22	(1)	1
17	Marcel de Jong	CAN	15/10/86	D	1		
34	Nikola Djurdjić	SRB	01/04/86	A	7	(9)	1
11	Alexander Esswein		25/03/90	M	10	(9)	1
7	Markus Feulner		12/02/82	M	23	(1)	1
7	Halil Altintop	TUR	08/12/82	M	30	(1)	3
35	Marwin Hitz	SUI	18/09/87	G	25		1
19	Pierre Højbjerg	DEN	05/08/95	M	10	(6)	2
20	Hong Jeong-ho	KOR	12/08/89	D	10	(7)	
16	Christoph Janker		14/02/85	D	1	(1)	
24	Ji Dong-won	KOR	28/05/91	A	7	(5)	
5	Ragnar Klavan	EST	30/10/85	D	34		2
21	Dominik Kohr		31/01/94	M	19	(7)	1
1	Alex Manninger	AUT	04/06/77	G	9		
23	Tim Matavž	SVN	13/01/89	A	4	(12)	3
33	Sascha Mölders		22/03/85	A	4	(8)	1
9	Shawn Parker		07/03/93	M	1	(1)	
3	Ronny Philp		28/01/89	D		(2)	
39	Erik Thommy		20/08/94	M		(3)	
2	Paul Verhaegh	NED	01/09/83	D	27		6
13	Tobias Werner		19/07/85	M	30	(1)	8

Bayer 04 Leverkusen

1904 • BayArena (30,210) • bayer04.de
Major honours
German Cup (1) 1993; UEFA Cup (1) 1988
Coach: Roger Schmidt

2014

23/08	a Dortmund	W	2-0	Bellarabi, Kiessling
30/08	h Hertha	W	4-2	Jedvaj, Spahić, Brandt, Bellarabi
12/09	h Bremen	D	3-3	Jedvaj, Hakan, Son
21/09	a Wolfsburg	L	1-4	Drmic
24/09	a Augsburg	W	1-0	Son
27/09	h Freiburg	D	0-0	
04/10	h Paderborn	D	2-2	Bender, Bellarabi
18/10	a Stuttgart	D	3-3	Son 2, Bellarabi
25/10	h Schalke	W	1-0	Hakan
01/11	a Hamburg	L	0-1	
08/11	h Mainz	D	0-0	
22/11	a Hannover	W	3-1	Kiessling, Son, Bellarabi
29/11	h Köln	W	5-1	Bellarabi 2, Hakan, Drmic 2
06/12	a Bayern	L	0-1	
14/12	h Mönchengladbach	D	1-1	Hakan
17/12	h Hoffenheim	W	1-0	Kiessling
20/12	h Frankfurt	D	1-1	Bellarabi

2015

31/01	h Dortmund	D	0-0	
04/02	h Hertha	W	1-0	Kiessling
08/02	h Bremen	L	1-2	Hakan
14/02	h Wolfsburg	L	4-5	Son 3, Bellarabi
21/02	a Augsburg	D	2-2	Drmic, Reinartz
28/02	h Freiburg	W	1-0	Rolfes
08/03	a Paderborn	W	3-0	Papadopoulos, Son 2
13/03	h Stuttgart	W	4-0	Wendell, Drmic 2, Bellarabi
21/03	a Schalke	W	1-0	Bellarabi
04/04	h Hamburg	W	4-0	Castro 2, Kiessling 2
11/04	a Mainz	W	3-2	Son, Kiessling, Hakan
18/04	a Hannover	W	4-0	Ömer, Brandt, Papadopoulos, Kiessling
25/04	a Köln	D	1-1	Brandt
02/05	h Bayern	W	2-0	Hakan, Brandt
09/05	a Mönchengladbach	L	0-3	
16/05	h Hoffenheim	W	2-0	Hakan, Kiessling
23/05	a Frankfurt	L	1-2	Bellarabi

No	Name	Nat	DoB	Pos	Aps	(s)	Gls
38	Karim Bellarabi		08/04/90	M	32	(1)	12
8	Lars Bender		27/04/89	M	25	(1)	1
17	Sebastian Boenisch	POL	01/02/87	D	9	(3)	
19	Julian Brandt		02/05/96	A	10	(15)	4
27	Gonzalo Castro		11/06/87	D	19	(3)	2
26	Giulio Donati	ITA	05/02/90	D	4	(4)	
9	Josip Drmic	SUI	08/08/92	A	5	(20)	6
10	Hakan Çalhanoğlu	TUR	08/02/94	M	31	(2)	8
14	Roberto Hilbert		16/10/84	D	21	(2)	
16	Tin Jedvaj	CRO	28/11/95	D	18	(4)	2
11	Stefan Kiessling		25/01/84	A	31	(3)	9
23	Robbie Kruse	AUS	05/10/88	M		(4)	
	Bernd Leno		04/03/92	G	34		
21	Ömer Toprak	TUR	21/07/89	D	27	(2)	1
15	Levin Öztunali		15/03/96	M	2	(4)	
14	Kyriakos Papadopoulos	GRE	23/02/92	D	9	(5)	2
3	Stefan Reinartz		01/01/89	M	9	(8)	1
6	Simon Rolfes		21/01/82	M	13	(11)	1
24	Son Heung-min	KOR	08/07/92	A	28	(2)	11
5	Emir Spahić	BIH	18/08/80	D	22		1
18	Wendell	BRA	20/07/93	D	25	(1)	1
35	Vladlen Yurchenko	UKR	22/01/94	M		(3)	

FC Bayern München

1900 • Allianz-Arena (75,024) • fcbayern.de
Major honours
European Champion Clubs' Cup/UEFA Champions League (5) 1974, 1975, 1976, 2001, 2013; UEFA Cup Winners' Cup (1) 1967; UEFA Cup (1) 1996; UEFA Super Cup (1) 2013; European/South American Cup (2) 1976, 2001; FIFA Club World Cup (1) 2013; German League (25) 1932, 1969, 1972, 1973, 1974, 1980, 1981, 1985, 1986, 1987, 1989, 1990, 1994, 1997, 1999, 2000, 2001, 2003, 2005, 2006, 2008, 2010, 2013, 2014, 2015; German Cup (17) 1957, 1966, 1967, 1969, 1971, 1982, 1984, 1986, 1998, 2000, 2003, 2005, 2006, 2008, 2010, 2013, 2014
Coach: Josep Guardiola (ESP)

2014

22/08	h Wolfsburg	W	2-1	Müller, Robben
30/08	a Schalke	D	1-1	Lewandowski
13/09	h Stuttgart	W	2-0	Götze, Ribéry
20/09	a Hamburg	D	0-0	
23/09	h Paderborn	W	4-0	Götze 2, Lewandowski, Müller
27/09	a Köln	W	2-0	Götze, og (Halfar)
04/10	h Hannover	W	4-0	Lewandowski 2, Robben 2
18/10	h Bremen	W	6-0	Lahm 2, Xabi Alonso, Müller (p), Götze 2
26/10	a M'gladbach	D	0-0	
01/11	h Dortmund	W	2-1	Lewandowski, Robben (p)
08/11	h Frankfurt	W	4-0	Müller 3, Shaqiri
22/11	a Hoffenheim	W	4-0	Götze, Lewandowski, Robben, Rode
29/11	a Hertha	W	1-0	Robben
06/12	h Leverkusen	W	1-0	Ribéry
13/12	a Augsburg	W	4-0	Benatia, Robben 2, Lewandowski
16/12	h Freiburg	W	2-0	Robben, Müller
19/12	a Mainz	W	2-1	Schweinsteiger, Robben

2015

30/01	a Wolfsburg	L	1-4	Bernat
03/02	h Schalke	D	1-1	Robben
07/02	a Stuttgart	W	2-0	Robben, Alaba
14/02	h Hamburg	W	8-0	Müller 2 (1p), Götze 2, Robben 2, Lewandowski, Ribéry
21/02	a Paderborn	W	6-0	Lewandowski 2, Robben 2 (1p), Ribéry, Weiser
27/02	h Köln	W	4-1	Schweinsteiger, Ribéry, Robben, Lewandowski
07/03	a Hannover	W	3-1	Xabi Alonso, Müller 2 (1p)
14/03	a Bremen	W	4-0	Müller, Alaba, Lewandowski 2
22/03	h M'gladbach	L	0-2	
04/04	a Dortmund	W	1-0	Lewandowski
11/04	h Frankfurt	W	3-0	Lewandowski 2, Müller
18/04	a Hoffenheim	W	2-0	Rode, og (Beck)
25/04	h Hertha	W	1-0	Schweinsteiger
02/05	a Leverkusen	L	0-2	
09/05	h Augsburg	L	0-1	
16/05	a Freiburg	L	1-2	Schweinsteiger
23/05	h Mainz	W	2-0	Lewandowski (p), Schweinsteiger

No	Name	Nat	DoB	Pos	Aps	(s)	Gls
27	David Alaba	AUT	24/06/92	D	19		2
28	Holger Badstuber		13/03/89	D	9	(1)	
5	Medhi Benatia	MAR	17/04/87	D	13	(2)	1
18	Juan Bernat	ESP	01/03/93	D	28	(3)	1
17	Jérôme Boateng		03/09/88	D	25	(2)	
4	Dante	BRA	18/10/83	D	21	(6)	
16	Gianluca Gaudino		11/11/96	M	4	(4)	
40	Lukas Görtler		15/06/94	A		(1)	
19	Mario Götze		03/06/92	M	28	(4)	9
34	Pierre Højbjerg	DEN	05/08/95	M	3	(5)	
8	Javi Martínez	ESP	02/09/88	M	1		
24	Sinan Kurt		23/07/96	A		(1)	
21	Philipp Lahm		11/11/83	D	17	(3)	2
9	Robert Lewandowski	POL	21/08/88	A	28	(3)	17
25	Thomas Müller		13/09/89	A	28	(4)	13
1	Manuel Neuer		27/03/86	G	31	(1)	
14	Claudio Pizarro	PER	03/10/78	A	2	(11)	
13	Rafinha	BRA	07/09/85	D	24	(2)	
23	Pepe Reina	ESP	31/08/82	G	3		
7	Franck Ribéry	FRA	07/04/83	M	9	(6)	5
10	Arjen Robben	NED	23/01/84	A	21	(1)	17
20	Sebastian Rode		11/10/90	M	8	(15)	2
31	Bastian Schweinsteiger		01/08/84	M	15	(5)	5
11	Xherdan Shaqiri	SUI	10/10/91	M	3	(6)	1
39	Rico Strieder		06/07/92	M	1		
6	Thiago Alcántara	ESP	11/04/91	M	2	(5)	
23	Mitchell Weiser		21/04/94	M	8	(5)	1
3	Xabi Alonso	ESP	25/11/81	M	24	(2)	2

Borussia Dortmund

1909 • Signal-Iduna-Park (80,667) • bvb.de

Major honours
UEFA Champions League (1) 1997; UEFA Cup Winners' Cup (1) 1966; European/South American Cup (1) 1997; German League (8) 1956, 1957, 1963, 1995, 1996, 2002, 2011, 2012; German Cup (3) 1965, 1989, 2012
Coach: Jürgen Klopp

2014

23/08	h	Leverkusen	L	0-2
29/08	a	Augsburg	W	3-2 Reus, Papastathopoulos, Ramos
13/09	h	Freiburg	W	3-1 Ramos, Kagawa, Aubameyang
20/09	a	Mainz	L	0-2
24/09	h	Stuttgart	D	2-2 Aubameyang, Immobile
27/09	a	Schalke	L	1-2 Aubameyang
04/10	h	Hamburg	L	0-1
18/10	h	Köln	L	1-2 Immobile
25/10	h	Hannover	L	0-1
01/11	a	Bayern	L	1-2 Reus
09/11	h	Mönchengladbach	W	1-0 og (Kramer)
22/11	a	Paderborn	D	2-2 Aubameyang, Reus
30/11	h	Frankfurt	L	0-2
05/12	h	Hoffenheim	W	1-0 Gündoğan
13/12	h	Hertha	L	0-1
17/12	h	Wolfsburg	D	2-2 Aubameyang, Immobile
20/12	a	Bremen	L	1-2 Hummels

2015

31/01	a	Leverkusen	D	0-0
04/02	h	Augsburg	L	0-1
07/02	a	Freiburg	W	3-0 Reus, Aubameyang 2
13/02	h	Mainz	W	4-2 Subotić, Reus, Aubameyang, Nuri
20/02	a	Stuttgart	W	3-2 Aubameyang, Gündoğan, Reus
28/02	h	Schalke	W	3-0 Aubameyang, Mkhitaryan, Reus
07/03	a	Hamburg	D	0-0
14/03	h	Köln	D	0-0
21/03	a	Hannover	W	3-2 Aubameyang 2, Kagawa
04/04	h	Bayern	L	0-1
11/04	a	Mönchengladbach	L	1-3 Gündoğan
18/04	h	Paderborn	W	3-0 Mkhitaryan, Aubameyang, Kagawa
25/04	h	Frankfurt	W	2-0 Aubameyang (p), Kagawa
02/05	a	Hoffenheim	D	1-1 Hummels
09/05	h	Hertha	W	2-0 Subotić, Durm
16/05	a	Wolfsburg	L	1-2 Aubameyang (p)
23/05	h	Bremen	W	3-2 Kagawa, Aubameyang, Mkhitaryan

No	Name	Nat	DoB	Pos	Aps	(s)	Gls
17	Pierre-Emerick Aubameyang	GAB	18/06/89	A	31	(2)	16
6	Sven Bender		27/04/89	M	14	(6)	
16	Jakub Błaszczykowski	POL	14/12/85	M	6	(7)	
40	Jeremy Dudziak		28/08/95	D		(3)	
37	Erik Durm		12/05/92	D	18		1
28	Matthias Ginter		19/01/94	D	9	(5)	
19	Kevin Grosskreutz		19/07/88	M	12	(5)	
8	İlkay Gündoğan		24/10/90	M	22	(1)	3
38	Jospeh-Claude Gyau	USA	16/09/92	M		(1)	
7	Jonas Hofmann		14/07/92	M		(2)	
15	Mats Hummels		16/12/88	D	23	(1)	2
9	Ciro Immobile	ITA	20/02/90	A	9	(15)	3
14	Miloš Jojić	SRB	19/03/92	M	5	(5)	
7	Shinji Kagawa	JPN	17/03/89	M	23	(5)	5
23	Kevin Kampl	SVN	09/10/90	M	8	(5)	
5	Sebastian Kehl		13/02/80	M	20	(1)	
21	Oliver Kirch		21/08/82	D	5	(1)	
20	Mitchell Langerak	AUS	22/01/88	G	9		
31	Mitsuru Maruoka	JPN	06/01/96	M		(1)	
10	Henrikh Mkhitaryan	ARM	21/01/89	M	21	(7)	3
18	Nuri Şahin	TUR	05/09/88	M	6	(1)	1
25	Sokratis Papastathopoulos	GRE	09/06/88	D	19	(2)	1
26	Łukasz Piszczek	POL	03/06/85	D	19	(3)	
20	Adrián Ramos	COL	22/01/86	A	6	(12)	2
11	Marco Reus		31/05/89	M	18	(2)	7
29	Marcel Schmelzer		13/02/88	D	22		
4	Neven Subotić	SRB	10/12/88	D	24	(4)	2
1	Roman Weidenfeller		06/08/80	G	25		

VfL Borussia Mönchengladbach

1900 • Borussia-Park (54,010) • borussia.de

Major honours
UEFA Cup (2) 1975, 1979; German League (5) 1970, 1971, 1975, 1976, 1977; German Cup (3) 1960, 1973, 1995
Coach: Lucien Favre (SUI)

2014

24/08	h	Stuttgart	D	1-1 Kramer
31/08	a	Freiburg	D	0-0
13/09	h	Schalke	W	4-1 Hahn 2, Kruse, Raffael
21/09	a	Köln	D	0-0
24/09	h	Hamburg	W	1-0 Kruse
27/09	a	Paderborn	W	2-1 Herrmann, Raffael
05/10	h	Mainz	D	1-1 Kruse
18/10	h	Hannover	W	3-0 Kruse 2, Xhaka
26/10	h	Bayern	D	0-0
02/11	h	Hoffenheim	W	3-1 Hahn, Herrmann 2
09/11	a	Dortmund	L	0-1
22/11	h	Frankfurt	L	1-3 Nordtveit
30/11	a	Wolfsburg	L	0-1
06/12	h	Hertha	W	3-2 Jantschke, Raffael, Hazard
14/12	a	Leverkusen	D	1-1 Brouwers
17/12	h	Bremen	W	4-1 Kruse (p), Wendt, Kramer, Hrgota
20/12	a	Augsburg	L	1-2 Kruse (p)

2015

31/01	a	Stuttgart	W	1-0 Herrmann
03/02	h	Freiburg	W	1-0 Herrmann
06/02	a	Schalke	L	0-1
14/02	h	Köln	W	1-0 Xhaka
22/02	a	Hamburg	D	1-1 Hrgota
01/03	h	Paderborn	W	2-0 Johnson, Herrmann
07/03	a	Mainz	D	2-2 Raffael 2
15/03	h	Hannover	W	2-0 Herrmann 2
22/03	a	Bayern	W	2-0 Raffael 2
04/04	a	Hoffenheim	W	4-1 Kruse (p), Herrmann 2, Raffael
11/04	h	Dortmund	W	3-1 Wendt, Raffael, Nordtveit
17/04	a	Frankfurt	D	0-0
26/04	h	Wolfsburg	W	1-0 Kruse
03/05	a	Hertha	W	2-1 Kruse, Traoré
09/05	h	Leverkusen	W	3-0 Kruse, Herrmann, Traoré
16/05	a	Bremen	W	2-0 Raffael 2
23/05	h	Augsburg	L	1-3 Raffael

No	Name	Nat	DoB	Pos	Aps	(s)	Gls
15	Álvaro Domínguez	ESP	16/05/89	D	23	(1)	
4	Roel Brouwers	NED	28/11/81	D	15	(5)	1
6	Mahmoud Dahoud		01/01/96	M		(1)	
28	André Hahn		13/08/90	M	15	(8)	3
26	Thorgan Hazard	BEL	29/03/93	M	7	(21)	1
7	Patrick Herrmann		12/02/91	M	26	(6)	11
31	Branimir Hrgota	SWE	12/01/93	A	8	(9)	2
24	Tony Jantschke		07/04/90	D	31		1
19	Fabian Johnson	USA	11/12/87	D	15	(9)	1
27	Julian Korb		21/03/92	M	23	(1)	
23	Christoph Kramer		19/02/91	M	28	(2)	2
10	Max Kruse		19/03/88	A	29	(3)	11
16	Håvard Nordtveit	NOR	21/06/90	M	11	(11)	2
11	Raffael	BRA	28/03/85	A	28	(3)	12
1	Yann Sommer	SUI	17/12/88	G	34		
39	Martin Stranzl	AUT	16/06/80	D	18	(1)	
8	Ibrahima Traoré	GUI	21/04/88	M	8	(16)	2
17	Oscar Wendt	SWE	24/10/85	D	25	(1)	2
34	Granit Xhaka	SUI	27/09/92	M	30		2

Eintracht Frankfurt

1899 • Commerzbank-Arena (51,500) • eintracht.de

Major honours
UEFA Cup (1) 1980; German League (1) 1959; German Cup (4) 1974, 1975, 1981, 1988
Coach: Thomas Schaaf

2014

23/08	h	Freiburg	W	1-0 Seferovic
30/08	a	Wolfsburg	D	2-2 og (Jung), Kadlec
14/09	h	Augsburg	L	0-1
20/09	a	Schalke	D	2-2 Meier, Russ
23/09	h	Mainz	D	2-2 Meier, Seferovic
28/09	a	Hamburg	W	2-1 Seferovic, Lucas Piazón
04/10	h	Köln	W	3-2 Meier 2, og (Wimmer)
19/10	a	Paderborn	L	1-3 Meier
25/10	h	Stuttgart	L	4-5 Madlung 2, Meier, Aigner
01/11	a	Hannover	L	0-1
08/11	h	Bayern	L	0-4
22/11	a	Mönchengladbach	W	3-1 Stendera, Meier, Inui
30/11	h	Dortmund	W	2-0 Meier, Seferovic
07/12	h	Bremen	W	5-2 Meier 2, Seferovic, Aigner, Stendera
12/12	a	Hoffenheim	L	2-3 Aigner, Seferovic
17/12	h	Hertha	D	4-4 Aigner, Seferovic, Meier 2
20/12	a	Leverkusen	D	1-1 Meier (p)

2015

31/01	a	Freiburg	L	1-4 Russ
03/02	h	Wolfsburg	D	1-1 Aigner
08/02	h	Augsburg	D	2-2 Aigner, Meier
14/02	h	Schalke	W	1-0 Lucas Piazón
21/02	a	Mainz	L	1-3 Aigner
28/02	h	Hamburg	W	2-1 Meier 2 (1p)
08/03	a	Köln	L	2-4 Meier 2 (1p)
14/03	h	Paderborn	W	4-0 Meier, Stendera, Aigner, Valdez
21/03	a	Stuttgart	L	1-3 Seferovic
04/04	h	Hannover	D	2-2 Madlung, Aigner
11/04	a	Bayern	L	0-3
17/04	h	Mönchengladbach	D	0-0
25/04	a	Dortmund	L	0-2
02/05	a	Bremen	L	0-1
09/05	h	Hoffenheim	W	3-1 Oczipka, Seferovic, Chandler
16/05	a	Hertha	D	0-0
23/05	h	Leverkusen	W	2-1 Seferovic, Madlung

No	Name	Nat	DoB	Pos	Aps	(s)	Gls
16	Stefan Aigner		20/08/87	M	23	(5)	9
23	Anderson Bamba	BRA	10/01/88	D	19	(3)	
22	Timothy Chandler	USA	29/03/90	D	25	(4)	1
15	Constant Djakpa	CIV	17/10/86	D	5	(1)	
18	Johannes Flum		14/12/87	M		(7)	
20	Makoto Hasebe	JPN	18/01/84	M	33		
26	Timo Hildebrand		05/04/79	G	3		
27	Aleksandar Ignjovski	SRB	27/01/91	D	14	(3)	
8	Takashi Inui	JPN	02/06/88	M	21	(6)	1
10	Václav Kadlec	CZE	20/05/92	A	1	(3)	1
31	David Kinsombi		12/12/95	D	2		
28	Sony Kittel		06/01/93	M	7	(11)	
13	Martin Lanig		11/07/84	M	1	(2)	
19	Lucas Piazón	BRA	20/01/94	M	11	(11)	2
39	Alexander Madlung		11/07/82	D	14	(8)	4
25	Slobodan Medojević	SRB	20/11/90	M	10	(4)	
14	Alexander Meier		17/01/83	M	24	(2)	19
6	Bastian Oczipka		12/01/89	D	28	(2)	1
4	Marco Russ		04/08/85	D	26		2
9	Haris Seferovic	SUI	22/02/92	A	32		10
21	Marc Stendera		10/11/95	M	21	(5)	3
1	Kevin Trapp		08/07/90	G	22		
11	Nelson Valdez	PAR	28/11/83	A	6	(4)	1
24	Luca Waldschmidt		19/05/96	A	1	(2)	
30	Felix Wiedwald		15/03/90	G	9	(1)	
5	Carlos Zambrano	PER	10/07/89	D	16	(1)	

SC Freiburg

1904 • Schwarzwald-Stadion (24,000) • scfreiburg.com
Coach: Christian Streich

2014

23/08	a	Frankfurt	L	0-1
31/08	h	Mönchengladbach	D	0-0
13/09	a	Dortmund	L	1-3	Sorg
19/09	h	Hertha	D	2-2	Kempf, Klaus
23/09	a	Hoffenheim	D	3-3	Frantz 2, Darida (p)
27/09	h	Leverkusen	D	0-0
04/10	a	Bremen	D	1-1	Darida (p)
18/10	h	Wolfsburg	L	1-2	Kerk
25/10	a	Augsburg	L	0-2
02/11	a	Köln	W	1-0	Darida (p)
08/11	h	Schalke	W	2-0	Günter, Schmid
22/11	a	Mainz	D	2-2	Schmid, Mehmedi
28/11	h	Stuttgart	L	1-4	Darida
06/12	a	Paderborn	D	1-1	Darida (p)
13/12	h	Hamburg	D	0-0
16/12	a	Bayern	L	0-2
21/12	h	Hannover	D	2-2	Frantz, Kempf

2015

31/01	h	Frankfurt	W	4-1	Darida (p), Petersen 3
03/02	a	Mönchengladbach	L	0-1
07/02	h	Dortmund	L	0-3
15/02	a	Hertha	W	2-0	Klaus, Philipp
21/02	h	Hoffenheim	D	1-1	Höhn
28/02	a	Leverkusen	L	0-1
07/03	h	Bremen	L	0-1
15/03	a	Wolfsburg	L	0-3
21/03	h	Augsburg	W	2-0	Schmid, Petersen
04/04	a	Köln	W	1-0	Frantz
11/04	h	Schalke	D	0-0
18/04	h	Mainz	L	2-3	Mehmedi, Schmid
25/04	a	Stuttgart	D	2-2	Petersen 2 (1p)
02/05	h	Paderborn	L	1-2	Petersen
08/05	a	Hamburg	D	1-1	Mehmedi
16/05	h	Bayern	W	2-1	Mehmedi, Petersen
23/05	a	Hannover	L	1-2	Petersen

No	Name	Nat	DoB	Pos	Aps	(s)	Gls
1	Roman Bürki	SUI	14/11/90	G	34		
16	Mats Møller Dæhli	NOR	02/03/95	M	2		
7	Vladimír Darida	CZE	08/08/90	M	27	(4)	6
8	Mike Frantz		14/10/86	M	14	(11)	4
35	Sebastian Freis		23/04/85	A	4	(3)	
31	Karim Guédé	SVK	07/01/85	A	12	(6)	
30	Christian Günter		28/02/93	D	32	(2)	1
27	Nicolas Höfler		09/03/90	M	15	(5)	
41	Immanuel Höhn		23/12/91	D	6	(1)	1
5	Christopher Jullien	FRA	22/03/93	D		(1)	
51	Florian Kath		21/10/94	M		(1)	
20	Marc-Oliver Kempf		28/01/95	D	10	(3)	2
37	Sebastian Kerk		17/04/94	M	2	(7)	1
36	Felix Klaus		13/09/92	M	27	(4)	2
2	Pavel Krmaš	CZE	03/03/80	D	22		
14	Admir Mehmedi	SUI	16/03/91	A	26	(2)	4
15	Stefan Mitrović	SRB	22/05/90	D	13	(1)	
24	Mensur Mujdža	BIH	28/03/84	D	5	(5)	
9	Nils Petersen		06/12/88	A	5	(7)	9
42	Maximilian Philipp		01/03/94	A	10	(14)	1
22	Sascha Riether		23/03/83	D	16	(3)	
11	Dani Schahin		09/07/89	A	1	(11)	
17	Jonathan Schmid	FRA	26/06/90	M	32	(1)	4
23	Julian Schuster		15/04/85	M	18	(3)	
25	Oliver Sorg		29/05/90	D	24	(1)	1
3	Marc Torrejon	ESP	18/02/86	D	17	(2)	
15	Philipp Zulechner	AUT	12/04/90	A		(2)	

Hamburger SV

1887 • Imtech-Arena (57,000) • hsv.de
Major honours
European Champion Clubs' Cup (1) 1983; UEFA Cup Winners' Cup (1) 1977; German League (6) 1923, 1928, 1960, 1979, 1982, 1983; German Cup (3) 1963, 1976, 1987
Coach: Mirko Slomka; (16/09/14) Josef Zinnbauer; (22/03/15) Peter Knäbel; (15/04/15) Bruno Labbadia

2014

23/08	a	Köln	D	0-0
30/08	h	Paderborn	L	0-3
14/09	a	Hannover	L	0-2
20/09	h	Bayern	D	0-0
24/09	a	Mönchengladbach	L	0-1
28/09	h	Frankfurt	L	1-2	Müller
04/10	a	Dortmund	W	1-0	Lasogga
19/10	h	Hoffenheim	D	1-1	Lasogga
25/10	a	Hertha	L	0-3
01/11	h	Leverkusen	W	1-0	Van der Vaart (p)
09/11	a	Wolfsburg	L	0-2
23/11	h	Bremen	W	2-0	Rudņevs, og (Wolf)
29/11	a	Augsburg	L	1-3	Van der Vaart
07/12	h	Mainz	W	2-1	Cléber, Van der Vaart (p)
13/12	a	Freiburg	D	0-0
16/12	h	Stuttgart	D	0-1
20/12	a	Schalke	D	0-0

2015

31/01	h	Köln	L	0-2
04/02	a	Paderborn	W	3-0	Van der Vaart (p), Jansen, Stieber
07/02	h	Hannover	W	2-1	og (Marcelo), Jansen
14/02	a	Bayern	L	0-8
22/02	h	Mönchengladbach	D	1-1	Stieber
28/02	a	Frankfurt	L	1-2	Stieber
07/03	h	Dortmund	D	0-0
14/03	a	Hoffenheim	L	0-3
20/03	h	Hertha	L	0-1
04/04	a	Leverkusen	L	0-4
11/04	h	Wolfsburg	L	0-2
19/04	a	Bremen	L	0-1
25/04	h	Augsburg	W	3-2	Olić, Lasogga 2
03/05	a	Mainz	W	2-1	og (Baumgartlinger), Kačar
08/05	h	Freiburg	D	1-1	Kačar
16/05	a	Stuttgart	L	1-2	Kačar
23/05	h	Schalke	W	2-0	Olić, Rajković

No	Name	Nat	DoB	Pos	Aps	(s)	Gls
15	René Adler		15/01/85	G	11	(1)	
14	Tolgay Arslan		16/08/90	M	8	(5)	
14	Milan Badelj	CRO	25/02/89	M	2		
21	Valon Behrami	SUI	19/04/85	M	22		
21	Maximilian Beister		06/09/90	M		(5)	
3	Cléber	BRA	05/12/90	D	11	(1)	1
20	Marcelo Díaz	CHI	30/12/86	M	4	(2)	
5	Dennis Diekmeier		20/10/89	D	19	(2)	
5	Johan Djourou	SUI	18/01/87	D	32		
1	Jaroslav Drobný	CZE	18/10/79	G	23		
39	Ashton-Phillip Götz		16/07/93	M	5	(5)	
25	Mohamed Gouaida	TUN	15/05/93	M	8	(3)	
37	Julian Green	USA	06/06/95	M	1	(4)	
18	Lewis Holtby		18/09/90	M	17	(5)	
11	Ivo Iličević	CRO	14/11/86	M	9		
18	Marcell Jansen		04/11/85	M	11	(4)	2
19	Petr Jiráček	CZE	02/03/86	M	9	(10)	
40	Gojko Kačar	SRB	26/01/87	M	7	(6)	3
20	Pierre-Michel Lasogga		15/12/91	A	22	(4)	4
31	Ronny Marcos		01/10/93	D	7	(2)	
27	Nicolai Müller		25/09/87	M	24	(3)	1
34	Valmir Nafiu	MKD	23/04/94	M		(2)	
9	Ivica Olić	CRO	14/09/79	A	16		2
22	Matthias Ostrzolek		05/06/90	D	23	(2)	
24	Slobodan Rajković	SRB	03/02/89	D	11		1
10	Artjoms Rudņevs	LVA	13/01/88	A	7	(15)	1
24	Ville Matti Steinmann		08/01/95	M		(1)	
17	Zoltán Stieber	HUN	16/10/88	M	16	(9)	3
35	Tolcay Ciğerci	TUR	24/01/95	M		(1)	
23	Rafael van der Vaart	NED	11/12/83	M	22	(2)	4
4	Heiko Westermann		14/08/83	D	27	(1)	

Hannover 96

1896 • HDI-Arena (49,000) • hannover96.de
Major honours
German League (2) 1938, 1954; German Cup (1) 1992
Coach: Tayfun Korkut (TUR); (20/04/15) Michael Frontzeck

2014

23/08	h	Schalke	W	2-1	Prib, Joselu
31/08	a	Mainz	D	0-0
14/09	h	Hamburg	W	2-0	Andreasen, Sobiech
20/09	a	Paderborn	L	0-2
24/09	h	Köln	W	1-0	Joselu
27/09	a	Stuttgart	L	0-1
04/10	a	Bayern	L	0-4
18/10	h	Mönchengladbach	L	0-3
25/10	a	Dortmund	W	1-0	Kiyotake
01/11	a	Frankfurt	W	1-0	og (Madlung)
07/11	h	Hertha	W	2-0	Briand, Kiyotake
22/11	a	Leverkusen	L	1-3	Ceyhun
29/11	a	Hoffenheim	L	3-4	Stindl 2, Joselu
06/12	h	Wolfsburg	L	1-3	Joselu
13/12	a	Bremen	D	3-3	Stindl, Joselu, Kiyotake
16/12	a	Augsburg	W	2-0	Sané, Joselu (p)
21/12	a	Freiburg	D	2-2	Bittencourt, Joselu

2015

31/01	a	Schalke	L	0-1
03/02	h	Mainz	D	1-1	Briand
07/02	a	Hamburg	L	1-2	Sobiech
15/02	h	Paderborn	L	1-2	Marcelo
21/02	a	Köln	D	1-1	Joselu
28/02	h	Stuttgart	D	1-1	Stindl
07/03	h	Bayern	L	1-3	Kiyotake
15/03	a	Mönchengladbach	L	0-2
21/03	h	Dortmund	L	2-3	Stindl 2
04/04	a	Frankfurt	D	2-2	Marcelo, Ya Konan
10/04	h	Hertha	D	1-1	Schulz
18/04	a	Leverkusen	L	0-4
25/04	h	Hoffenheim	L	1-2	Stindl (p)
02/05	h	Wolfsburg	D	2-2	Briand, Sané
09/05	h	Bremen	D	1-1	Stindl
16/05	a	Augsburg	W	2-1	Stindl 2
23/05	h	Freiburg	W	2-1	Kiyotake, og (Krmaš)

No	Name	Nat	DoB	Pos	Aps	(s)	Gls
3	Miiko Albornoz	CHI	30/11/90	D	25	(3)	
2	Leon Andreasen	DEN	23/04/83	M	11	(6)	1
32	Leonardo Bittencourt		19/12/93	M	15	(11)	1
21	Jimmy Briand	FRA	02/08/85	A	25	(4)	3
6	Ceyhun Gülselam	TUR	25/12/87	M	14	(4)	1
20	Felipe	BRA	15/05/87	D	6	(5)	
35	Maurice Hirsch		30/05/93	M	5	(2)	
7	João Pereira	POR	25/02/84	D	4	(1)	
11	Joselu	ESP	27/03/90	A	28	(2)	8
26	Kenan Karaman	TUR	05/03/94	A		(11)	
25	Hiroshi Kiyotake	JPN	12/11/89	M	29	(3)	5
25	Marcelo	BRA	20/05/87	D	34		2
24	Christian Pander		28/08/83	D	4	(4)	
7	Edgar Prib		15/12/89	M	11	(9)	1
4	Hiroki Sakai	JPN	12/04/90	D	27		
5	Salif Sané	SEN	25/08/90	D	16	(2)	2
13	Jan Schlaudraff		18/07/83	A		(5)	
8	Manuel Schmiedebach		05/12/88	M	26	(1)	
19	Christian Schulz		01/04/83	D	31		1
9	Artur Sobiech	POL	12/06/90	A	4	(15)	2
18	Marius Stankevičius	LTU	15/07/81	D	1	(1)	
28	Lars Stindl		26/08/88	M	20	(1)	10
17	Stefan Thesker		11/04/91	D	1	(1)	
14	Didier Ya Konan	CIV	22/05/84	A	3	(4)	1
1	Ron-Robert Zieler		12/02/89	G	34		

Hertha BSC Berlin

1892 • Olympiastadion (74,649) •
herthabsc.de
Major honours
German League (2) 1930, 1931
Coach: Jos Luhukay (NED);
(05/02/15) Pál Dárdai (HUN)

2014

23/08	h Bremen	D	2-2	Schieber 2
30/08	a Leverkusen	L	2-4	og (Jedvaj), Schieber
13/09	h Mainz	L	1-3	Ronny (p)
19/09	a Freiburg	D	2-2	Ronny 2
24/09	h Wolfsburg	W	1-0	Kalou
28/09	a Augsburg	L	0-1	
03/10	h Stuttgart	W	3-2	Kalou 2 (1p), Beerens
18/10	a Schalke	L	0-2	
25/10	h Hamburg	W	3-0	Ben-Hatira 2, Heitinga
02/11	a Paderborn	L	1-3	Kalou
07/11	h Hannover	L	0-2	
22/11	a Köln	W	2-1	Beerens, Ndjeng
29/11	h Bayern	L	0-1	
06/12	a Mönchengladbach	L	2-3	Schieber, Kalou (p)
13/12	h Dortmund	W	1-0	Schieber
17/12	a Frankfurt	D	4-4	Brooks, Ben-Hatira, Schieber, Niemeyer
21/12	h Hoffenheim	L	0-5	

2015

01/02	a Bremen	L	0-2	
04/02	h Leverkusen	L	0-1	
07/02	a Mainz	W	2-0	Hegeler (p), Beerens
15/02	h Freiburg	L	0-2	
22/02	a Wolfsburg	L	1-2	Schieber
28/02	h Augsburg	W	1-0	Kalou
06/03	a Stuttgart	D	0-0	
14/03	h Schalke	D	2-2	Ben-Hatira, Haraguchi
20/03	a Hamburg	W	1-0	Langkamp
05/04	h Paderborn	W	2-0	Stocker, Schulz
10/04	a Hannover	D	1-1	Stocker
18/04	h Köln	D	0-0	
25/04	a Bayern	L	0-1	
03/05	h Mönchengladbach	L	1-2	Stocker
09/05	a Dortmund	L	0-2	
16/05	h Frankfurt	D	0-0	
23/05	a Hoffenheim	L	1-2	Beerens

No	Name	Nat	DoB	Pos	Aps	(s)	Gls
11	Sami Allagui	TUN	28/05/86	A		(1)	
27	Roy Beerens	NED	22/12/87	M	24	(3)	4
10	Änis Ben-Hatira	TUN	18/07/88	M	11	(4)	4
25	John Brooks	USA	28/01/93	D	24	(3)	1
30	Sascha Burchert		30/10/89	G		(1)	
24	Genki Haraguchi	JPN	09/05/91	M	14	(7)	1
13	Jens Hegeler		22/01/88	M	14	(10)	1
5	John Heitinga	NED	15/11/83	D	11	(2)	1
7	Hajime Hosogai	JPN	10/06/86	M	16	(4)	
22	Rune Almenning Jarstein	NOR	29/09/84	G	1		
11	Salomon Kalou	CIV	05/08/85	A	21	(6)	6
1	Thomas Kraft		22/07/88	G	32		
15	Sebastian Langkamp		15/01/88	D	15	(1)	1
28	Fabian Lustenberger	SUI	02/05/88	M	26	(1)	
8	Marcel Ndjeng	CMR	06/05/82	M	11	(5)	1
18	Peter Niemeyer		22/11/83	M	9	(8)	1
2	Peter Pekarík	SVK	30/10/86	D	30		
21	Marvin Plattenhardt		26/01/92	D	14	(1)	
12	Ronny	BRA	11/05/86	M	9	(10)	3
16	Julian Schieber		13/02/89	A	15	(1)	7
26	Nico Schulz		01/04/93	D	24	(4)	1
13	Per Ciljan Skjelbred	NOR	16/06/87	M	26		
14	Valentin Stocker	SUI	12/04/89	M	22	(4)	3
17	Tolga Ciğerci	TUR	23/03/92	M		(2)	
23	Johannes van den Bergh		21/11/86	D	4	(2)	
33	Sandro Wagner		29/11/87	A		(15)	

TSG 1899 Hoffenheim

1899 • Rhein-Neckar-Arena (30,150) •
achtzehn99.de
Coach: Markus Gisdol

2014

23/08	h Augsburg	W	2-0	Szalai, Elyounoussi
30/08	a Bremen	D	1-1	Roberto Firmino
13/09	h Wolfsburg	D	1-1	Modeste
20/09	a Stuttgart	W	2-0	Modeste, Elyounoussi
23/09	h Freiburg	D	3-3	Elyounoussi, Rudy, Vestergaard
26/09	a Mainz	D	0-0	
04/10	h Schalke	W	2-1	Elyounoussi, Szalai
19/10	a Hamburg	D	1-1	Modeste
25/10	h Paderborn	W	1-0	Volland
02/11	a Mönchengladbach	L	1-3	Modeste
08/11	h Köln	L	3-4	Roberto Firmino 2
22/11	a Bayern	L	0-4	
29/11	h Hannover	W	4-3	Schwegler, Volland, Polanski, Süle
05/12	a Dortmund	L	0-1	
12/12	h Frankfurt	W	3-2	Volland, Szalai, Roberto Firmino
17/12	h Leverkusen	L	0-1	
21/12	a Hertha	W	5-0	og (Brooks), Salihović 2 (2p), Schipplock, Rudy

2015

01/02	a Augsburg	L	1-3	Roberto Firmino
04/02	h Bremen	L	1-2	Bičakčić
07/02	a Wolfsburg	L	0-3	
14/02	h Stuttgart	W	2-1	Roberto Firmino, Rudy
21/02	a Freiburg	D	1-1	Volland
28/02	h Mainz	W	2-0	Volland, Polanski
07/03	a Schalke	L	1-3	Volland
14/03	h Hamburg	W	3-0	Polanski 2 (1p), Rudy
21/03	a Paderborn	D	0-0	
04/04	h Mönchengladbach	L	1-4	Schipplock
12/04	a Köln	L	2-3	Polanski (p), Modeste
18/04	h Bayern	L	0-2	
25/04	a Hannover	W	2-1	Modeste, Schipplock
02/05	h Dortmund	D	1-1	Volland
09/05	a Frankfurt	L	1-3	Volland
16/05	a Leverkusen	L	0-2	
23/05	h Hertha	W	2-1	Modeste, Roberto Firmino

No	Name	Nat	DoB	Pos	Aps	(s)	Gls
12	David Abraham	ARG	15/07/86	D	9	(5)	
34	Nadiem Amiri		27/10/96	M	4	(8)	
1	Oliver Baumann		02/06/90	G	34		
2	Andreas Beck		13/03/87	D	33		
4	Ermin Bičakčić	BIH	24/01/90	D	24		1
14	Tarik Elyounoussi	NOR	23/02/88	A	17	(8)	4
11	Jiloan Hamad	SWE	06/11/90	M		(1)	
38	Kai Herdling		27/06/84	M		(1)	
20	Kim Jin-su	KOR	13/06/92	D	17	(2)	
27	Nadiem Modeste	FRA	14/04/88	A	16	(10)	7
8	Eugen Polanski	POL	17/03/86	M	29	(1)	5
10	Roberto Firmino	BRA	02/10/91	A	33		7
6	Sebastian Rudy		28/02/90	M	25	(4)	4
23	Sejad Salihović	BIH	08/10/84	M	5	(8)	2
9	Sven Schipplock		08/11/88	A	8	(17)	3
16	Pirmin Schwegler	SUI	09/03/87	M	26	(2)	1
12	Tobias Strobl		12/05/90	D	26	(4)	
25	Niklas Süle		03/09/95	D	15		1
28	Ádám Szalai	HUN	09/12/87	A	13	(13)	4
36	Jeremy Toljan		08/08/94	D	4	(2)	
29	Jannik Vestergaard	DEN	03/08/92	D	1	(5)	1
31	Kevin Volland		30/07/92	A	30	(2)	8
17	Steven Zuber	SUI	17/08/91	M	5	(12)	

1. FC Köln

1948 • Rhein-Energie-Stadion (49,968) •
fc-koeln.de
Major honours
German League (3) 1962, 1964, 1978; German Cup (4)
1968, 1977, 1978, 1983
Coach: Peter Stöger (AUT)

2014

23/08	h Hamburg	D	0-0	
30/08	a Stuttgart	W	2-0	Osako, Ujah
13/09	h Paderborn	D	0-0	
21/09	h Mönchengladbach	D	0-0	
24/09	a Hannover	L	0-1	
27/09	h Bayern	L	0-1	
04/10	a Frankfurt	L	2-3	Risse, Hector
18/10	h Dortmund	W	2-1	Vogt, Zoller
24/10	a Bremen	W	1-0	Ujah
02/11	h Freiburg	L	0-1	
08/11	a Hoffenheim	W	4-3	Olkowski 2, Lehmann, Ujah
22/11	h Hertha	L	1-2	Ujah
29/11	h Leverkusen	L	1-5	Lehmann (p)
06/12	h Augsburg	L	1-2	Ujah
13/12	a Schalke	W	2-1	Ujah, Lehmann (p)
16/12	h Mainz	D	0-0	
20/12	a Wolfsburg	L	1-2	Maroh

2015

31/01	a Hamburg	W	2-0	Risse 2
04/02	h Stuttgart	D	0-0	
07/02	a Paderborn	D	0-0	
14/02	a Mönchengladbach	L	0-1	
21/02	h Hannover	D	1-1	Ujah
27/02	a Bayern	L	1-4	Ujah
08/03	a Frankfurt	W	4-2	Deyverson, Risse, Osako, Ujah
14/03	a Dortmund	D	0-0	
21/03	a Bremen	D	1-1	Lehmann (p)
04/04	a Freiburg	L	0-1	
12/04	h Hoffenheim	W	3-2	Lehmann (p), Ujah, Hector
18/04	a Hertha	D	0-0	
25/04	h Leverkusen	D	1-1	Finne
02/05	a Augsburg	D	0-0	
10/05	h Schalke	W	2-0	Risse, Gerhardt
16/05	a Mainz	L	0-2	
23/05	h Wolfsburg	D	2-2	Osako, og (Knoche)

No	Name	Nat	DoB	Pos	Aps	(s)	Gls
2	Mišo Brečko	SVN	01/05/84	D	17	(2)	
11	Thomas Bröcker		22/01/85	A		(4)	
20	Deyverson	BRA	08/05/91	A	4	(4)	1
26	Bård Finne	NOR	13/02/95	A	2	(8)	1
31	Yannick Gerhardt		13/03/94	M	9	(7)	1
22	Daniel Halfar		07/01/86	M	14	(8)	
14	Jonas Hector		27/05/90	D	33		2
1	Timo Horn		12/05/93	G	33		
18	Thomas Kessler		20/01/86	G	1		
33	Matthias Lehmann		28/05/83	M	32		5
5	Dominic Maroh	SVN	04/03/87	D	26	(3)	1
8	Adam Matuszczyk	POL	14/02/89	M	4	(6)	
19	Mërgim Mavraj	ALB	09/06/86	D	11	(4)	
25	Kazuki Nagasawa	JPN	16/12/91	M	5	(5)	
9	Paweł Olkowski	POL	13/02/90	D	24	(3)	2
13	Yuya Osako	JPN	18/05/90	A	16	(12)	3
17	Sławomir Peszko	POL	19/02/85	M	10	(8)	
29	Marcel Risse		17/12/89	M	26	(3)	5
29	Dušan Švento	SVK	01/08/85	M	12	(7)	
9	Anthony Ujah	NGA	14/10/90	A	28	(4)	10
6	Kevin Vogt		23/09/91	M	30	(2)	1
28	Kevin Wimmer	AUT	15/11/92	D	32		
23	Simon Zoller		26/06/91	A	5	(4)	1

1. FSV Mainz 05

1905 • Coface-Arena (34,034) • mainz05.de
Coach: Kasper Hjulmand (DEN);
(17/02/15) Martin Schmidt (SUI)

2014

24/08	a	Paderborn	D 2-2	Okazaki, Koo (p)
31/08	h	Hannover	D 0-0	
13/09	a	Hertha	W 3-1	Okazaki 2, Allagui
20/09	h	Dortmund	W 2-0	Okazaki, og (Ginter)
23/09	a	Frankfurt	D 2-2	Hofmann, Okazaki
26/09	h	Hoffenheim	D 0-0	
05/10	a	Mönchengladbach	D 1-1	Hofmann (p)
18/10	h	Augsburg	W 2-1	Hofmann, Jairo Samperio
26/10	a	Wolfsburg	L 0-3	
01/11	h	Bremen	L 1-2	Okazaki
08/11	a	Leverkusen	D 0-0	
22/11	h	Freiburg	D 2-2	Júnior Díaz, Bell
29/11	a	Schalke	L 1-4	Okazaki
07/12	a	Hamburg	L 1-2	Okazaki
13/12	h	Stuttgart	D 1-1	Geis
16/12	a	Köln	D 0-0	
19/12	h	Bayern	L 1-2	Soto

2015

31/01	h	Paderborn	W 5-0	Malli 2, De Blasis, Allagui, Geis (p)
03/02	a	Hannover	D 1-1	Soto
07/02	h	Hertha	L 0-2	
13/02	a	Dortmund	L 2-4	Soto, Malli
21/02	h	Frankfurt	W 3-1	Clemens, Geis, Malli
28/02	a	Hoffenheim	L 0-2	
07/03	h	Mönchengladbach	D 2-2	Geis, Okazaki
14/03	a	Augsburg	W 2-0	Okazaki, Koo
22/03	h	Wolfsburg	D 1-1	Bungert
04/04	a	Bremen	D 0-0	
11/04	h	Leverkusen	L 2-3	Koo 2 (2p)
18/04	a	Freiburg	W 3-2	Okazaki 2, Malli
24/04	h	Schalke	W 2-0	Bell 2
03/05	h	Hamburg	L 1-2	Malli
09/05	a	Stuttgart	L 0-2	
16/05	h	Köln	W 2-0	Koo, Jairo Samperio
23/05	a	Bayern	L 0-2	

No	Name	Nat	DoB	Pos	Aps	(s)	Gls
9	Sami Allagui	TUN	28/05/86	A	9	(10)	2
14	Julian Baumgartlinger	AUT	02/01/88	M	26		
16	Stefan Bell		24/08/91	D	31		3
7	Pierre Bengtsson	SWE	12/04/88	D	10	(3)	
18	Daniel Brosinski		17/07/88	D	32		
26	Niko Bungert		24/10/86	D	23	(3)	1
22	Nicolás Castillo	CHI	14/02/93	A		(1)	
27	Christian Clemens		04/08/91	M	6	(3)	1
15	Pablo De Blasis	ARG	04/02/88	M	13	(7)	1
10	Filip Djuričić	SRB	30/01/92	M	6	(5)	
6	Johannes Geis		17/08/93	M	33	(1)	4
31	Jonas Hofmann		14/07/92	M	8	(2)	3
17	Jairo Samperio	ESP	11/07/93	M	11	(11)	2
2	Gonzalo Jara	CHI	29/08/85	D	9	(8)	
20	Júnior Díaz	CRC	12/09/83	D	17	(2)	1
1	Stefanos Kapino	GRE	18/03/94	G	1	(1)	
21	Loris Karius		22/06/93	G	33		
22	Julian Koch		11/11/90	D		(1)	
13	Koo Ja-cheol	KOR	27/02/89	M	16	(7)	5
11	Yunus Malli		24/02/92	M	24	(7)	6
8	Christoph Moritz		27/01/90	M	6	(3)	
4	Nikolce Noveski	MKD	04/04/79	D	7	(2)	
23	Shinji Okazaki	JPN	16/04/86	A	31	(1)	12
24	Park Joo-ho	KOR	16/01/87	D	16		
29	Devante Parker		16/03/96	A		(1)	
30	Patrick Pflücke		30/11/96	M		(1)	
35	Petar Slišković	CRO	21/02/91	A		(2)	
19	Elkin Soto	COL	04/08/80	M	4	(12)	3
3	Philipp Wollscheid		06/03/89	D	2	(3)	

SC Paderborn 07

1985 • Benteler-Arena (15,000) •
scpaderborn07.de
Coach: André Breitenreiter

2014

24/08	h	Mainz	D 2-2	Kachunga, Hünemeier
30/08	a	Hamburg	W 3-0	Kachunga, Vrančić, Stoppelkamp
13/09	h	Köln	D 0-0	
20/09	h	Hannover	W 2-0	Kachunga, Stoppelkamp
23/09	a	Bayern	L 0-4	
27/09	h	Mönchengladbach	L 1-2	Wemmer
04/10	a	Leverkusen	D 2-2	Koç, Stoppelkamp
19/10	h	Frankfurt	W 3-1	Ducksch, Hünemeier, Kutschke
25/10	a	Hoffenheim	L 0-1	
02/11	h	Hertha	W 3-1	Bakalorz, Kachunga, Meha
08/11	a	Augsburg	L 0-3	
22/11	h	Dortmund	D 2-2	Rupp, Mahir
29/11	a	Bremen	L 0-4	
06/12	h	Freiburg	D 1-1	Kachunga
14/12	a	Wolfsburg	D 1-1	Meha (p)
17/12	h	Schalke	L 1-2	og (Kaan)
20/12	h	Stuttgart	D 0-0	

2015

31/01	a	Mainz	L 0-5	
04/02	h	Hannover	L 0-3	
07/02	a	Köln	D 0-0	
15/02	a	Hannover	W 2-1	Lakić, Meha
21/02	h	Bayern	L 0-6	
01/03	a	Mönchengladbach	L 0-2	
08/03	h	Leverkusen	L 0-3	
14/03	a	Frankfurt	L 0-4	
21/03	h	Hoffenheim	D 0-0	
05/04	a	Hertha	L 0-2	
11/04	h	Augsburg	W 2-1	Kachunga, Lakić
18/04	a	Dortmund	L 0-3	
26/04	h	Bremen	D 2-2	Vrančić, Stoppelkamp
02/05	a	Freiburg	W 2-1	Rupp 2
10/05	h	Wolfsburg	L 1-3	Rupp
16/05	a	Schalke	L 0-1	
23/05	h	Stuttgart	L 1-2	Vucinovic

No	Name	Nat	DoB	Pos	Aps	(s)	Gls
6	Marvin Bakalorz		13/09/89	M	26	(3)	1
14	Thomas Bertels		05/11/86	D		(1)	
21	Daniel Brückner		14/02/81	D	23		
34	Marvin Ducksch		07/03/94	A	1	(8)	1
26	Florian Hartherz		29/05/93	D	9	(1)	
22	Michael Heinloth		09/02/92	D	19	(2)	
2	Uwe Hünemeier		09/01/86	D	32		2
15	Elias Kachunga		22/04/92	A	24	(8)	6
30	Süleyman Koç		09/06/89	M	23	(6)	1
1	Lukas Kruse		09/07/83	G	34		
29	Stefan Kutschke		03/11/88	A	7	(12)	1
29	Srdjan Lakić	CRO	02/10/83	A	10	(7)	2
10	Mahir Sağlık	TUR	02/10/83	A	3	(8)	1
17	Alban Meha	ALB	26/04/86	M	13	(5)	3
27	Idir Ouali	ALG	21/05/88	M	4	(2)	
23	Mirnes Pepić	MNE	19/12/95	M		(2)	
3	Rafa López	ESP	09/04/85	D	16		
4	Lukas Rupp		08/01/91	M	21	(10)	4
11	Moritz Stoppelkamp		11/12/86	M	25	(2)	4
13	Christian Strohdiek		22/01/88	D	18	(4)	
8	Mario Vrančić	BIH	23/05/89	M	23	(7)	2
20	Marc Vucinovic		19/09/88	M	3	(5)	1
7	Jens Wemmer		31/10/85	D	17	(4)	1
5	Patrick Ziegler		09/02/90	D	23	(4)	

FC Schalke 04

1904 • Veltins-Arena (61,973) • schalke04.de
Major honours
UEFA Cup (1) 1997; German League (7) 1934, 1935, 1937, 1939, 1940, 1942, 1958; German Cup (5) 1937, 1972, 2001, 2002, 2011
Coach: Jens Keller;
(07/10/14) Roberto Di Matteo (ITA)

2014

23/08	a	Hannover	L 1-2	Huntelaar
30/08	h	Bayern	D 1-1	Höwedes
13/09	h	Mönchengladbach	L 1-4	Choupo-Moting (p)
20/09	h	Frankfurt	D 2-2	Choupo-Moting (p), Draxler
23/09	a	Bremen	W 3-0	Meyer, Neustädter, Barnetta
27/09	h	Dortmund	W 2-1	Matip, Choupo-Moting
04/10	a	Hoffenheim	L 1-2	Huntelaar
18/10	h	Hertha	W 2-0	Huntelaar, Draxler
25/10	a	Leverkusen	L 0-1	
31/10	a	Augsburg	W 1-0	Huntelaar
08/11	a	Freiburg	L 0-2	
22/11	h	Wolfsburg	W 3-2	Choupo-Moting 2, Fuchs
29/11	h	Mainz	W 4-1	Huntelaar 3, Barnetta
06/12	a	Stuttgart	W 4-0	Choupo-Moting 3, Meyer
13/12	h	Köln	L 1-2	Sané
17/12	a	Paderborn	W 2-1	Choupo-Moting, Neustädter
20/12	h	Hamburg	D 0-0	

2015

31/01	h	Hannover	W 1-0	Höger
03/02	a	Bayern	D 1-1	Höwedes
06/02	h	Mönchengladbach	W 1-0	Barnetta
14/02	a	Frankfurt	L 0-1	
21/02	h	Bremen	D 1-1	Meyer
28/02	a	Dortmund	L 0-3	
07/03	h	Hoffenheim	W 3-1	Fuchs, Meyer 2
14/03	a	Hertha	D 2-2	Sané, Matip
21/03	h	Leverkusen	L 0-1	
05/04	a	Augsburg	D 0-0	
11/04	h	Freiburg	D 0-0	
19/04	a	Wolfsburg	D 1-1	Sané
24/04	a	Mainz	L 0-2	
02/05	h	Stuttgart	W 3-2	Huntelaar 2, og (Klein)
10/05	a	Köln	L 0-2	
16/05	h	Paderborn	W 1-0	og (Hünemeier)
23/05	a	Hamburg	L 0-2	

No	Name	Nat	DoB	Pos	Aps	(s)	Gls
15	Dennis Aogo		14/01/87	D	20	(5)	
27	Tranquillo Barnetta	SUI	22/05/85	M	10	(12)	3
9	Kevin-Prince Boateng	GHA	06/03/87	M	11	(7)	
13	Eric Maxim Choupo-Moting	CMR	23/03/89	A	30	(1)	9
11	Christian Clemens		04/08/91	M	1	(7)	
20	Julian Draxler		20/09/93	M	8	(7)	2
1	Ralf Fährmann		27/09/88	G	25		
17	Jefferson Farfán	PER	26/10/84	A	6	(3)	
5	Felipe Santana	BRA	17/03/86	D	3	(1)	
2	Marvin Friedrich		13/12/95	D	2	(3)	
23	Christian Fuchs	AUT	07/04/86	D	20	(5)	2
34	Fabian Giefer		17/05/90	G	2		
8	Leon Goretzka		06/02/95	M	3	(7)	
12	Marco Höger		16/09/89	M	26		1
6	Benedikt Höwedes		29/02/88	D	28		2
25	Klaas-Jan Huntelaar	NED	12/08/83	A	27	(1)	9
24	Kaan Ayhan	TUR	10/11/94	D	10	(5)	
3	Jan Kirchhoff		01/10/90	D	12	(2)	
4	Sead Kolašinac	BIH	20/06/93	D	6		
32	Joël Matip	CMR	08/08/91	D	17	(4)	2
7	Max Meyer		18/09/95	M	22	(6)	5
31	Matija Nastasić	SRB	28/03/93	D	16		
33	Roman Neustädter		18/02/88	M	28	(1)	2
19	Chinedu Obasi	NGA	01/06/86	A	1	(5)	
36	Felix Platte		11/02/96	A	1	(1)	
18	Sidney Sam		31/01/88	A	7	(4)	
13	Leroy Sané		11/01/96	M	7	(6)	3
22	Atsuto Uchida	JPN	27/03/88	D	18	(1)	
40	Timon Wellenreuther		03/12/95	G	7	(1)	

VfB Stuttgart

1893 • Mercedes-Benz-Arena (60,441) • vfb.de

Major honours
German League (5) 1950, 1952, 1984, 1992, 2007; German Cup (3) 1954, 1958, 1997

Coach: Armin Veh; (25/11/14) Huub Stevens (NED)

2014

24/08	a	Mönchengladbach	D	1-1	*Maxim*
30/08	h	Köln	L	0-2	
13/09	a	Bayern	L	0-2	
20/09	h	Hoffenheim	L	0-2	
24/09	a	Dortmund	D	2-2	*Didavi 2*
27/09	h	Hannover	W	1-0	*Schwaab*
03/10	a	Hertha	L	2-3	*Leitner, og (Wagner)*
18/10	h	Leverkusen	D	3-3	*Werner, Klein, Harnik*
25/10	a	Frankfurt	W	5-4	*Harnik 2, Gentner 2, Werner*
01/11	h	Wolfsburg	L	0-4	
08/11	a	Bremen	L	0-2	
23/11	h	Augsburg	L	0-1	
28/11	a	Freiburg	W	4-1	*Harnik 2, Gruezo, Werner*
06/12	h	Schalke	L	0-4	
13/12	a	Mainz	D	1-1	*Kostić*
16/12	a	Hamburg	W	1-0	*Klein*
20/12	h	Paderborn	D	0-0	

2015

31/01	h	Mönchengladbach	L	0-1	
04/02	a	Köln	D	0-0	
07/02	h	Bayern	L	0-2	
14/02	h	Hoffenheim	L	1-2	*Sakai*
20/02	h	Dortmund	L	2-3	*Klein (p), Niedermeier*
28/02	a	Hannover	D	1-1	*Gentner*
06/03	h	Hertha	D	0-0	
13/03	a	Leverkusen	L	0-4	
21/03	h	Frankfurt	W	3-1	*Ginczek 2, Maxim*
04/04	a	Wolfsburg	L	1-3	*Harnik*
12/04	h	Bremen	W	3-2	*Gentner, Ginczek 2*
18/04	a	Augsburg	L	1-2	*Ginczek*
25/04	h	Freiburg	D	2-2	*Ginczek, Harnik*
02/05	a	Schalke	L	2-3	*Harnik, Kostić*
09/05	h	Mainz	W	2-0	*Didavi, Kostić*
16/05	h	Hamburg	W	2-1	*Gentner, Harnik*
23/05	a	Paderborn	W	2-1	*Didavi, Ginczek*

No	Name	Nat	DoB	Pos	Aps	(s)	Gls
32	Timo Baumgartl		04/03/96	D	18	(2)	
10	Daniel Didavi		21/02/90	D	9	(2)	4
20	Christian Gentner		14/08/85	M	33		5
33	Daniel Ginczek		13/04/91	A	14	(4)	7
11	Carlos Gruezo	ECU	19/04/95	M	6	(2)	1
7	Martin Harnik	AUT	10/06/87	A	26	(2)	9
21	Adam Hloušek	CZE	20/12/88	M	17	(5)	
9	Vedad Ibišević	BIH	06/08/84	A	6	(8)	
20	Jerome Kiesewetter	USA	09/02/93	M		(2)	
22	Thorsten Kirschbaum		20/04/87	G	6		
16	Florian Klein	AUT	17/11/86	D	33	(1)	3
18	Filip Kostić	SRB	01/11/92	M	15	(14)	3
8	Moritz Leitner		08/12/92	M	13	(6)	1
44	Alexandru Maxim	ROU	08/07/90	M	15	(11)	2
6	Georg Niedermeier		26/02/86	D	19	(3)	1
13	Oriol Romeu	ESP	24/09/91	M	20	(7)	
34	Konstantin Rausch		15/03/90	D		(4)	
24	Antonio Rüdiger		03/03/93	D	18	(1)	
2	Gotoku Sakai	JPN	14/03/91	D	17	(1)	1
3	Daniel Schwaab		23/08/88	D	27	(4)	1
23	Sercan Sararer	TUR	27/11/89	M	6	(1)	
26	Serey Dié	CIV	07/11/84	M	12	(1)	
1	Sven Ulreich		03/08/88	G	28		
19	Timo Werner		06/03/96	A	16	(16)	3

SV Werder Bremen

1899 • Weserstadion (42,500) • werder.de

Major honours
UEFA Cup Winners' Cup (1) 1992; German League (4) 1965, 1988, 1993, 2004; German Cup (6) 1961, 1991, 1994, 1999, 2004, 2009

Coach: Robin Dutt; (25/10/14) Viktor Skrypnyk (UKR)

2014

23/08	a	Hertha	D	2-2	*Lukimya, Di Santo*
30/08	h	Hoffenheim	D	1-1	*Gálvez*
12/09	a	Leverkusen	D	3-3	*Bartels, Di Santo, Prödl*
20/09	a	Augsburg	L	2-4	*Selke, Di Santo (p)*
23/09	h	Schalke	L	0-3	
27/09	a	Wolfsburg	L	1-2	*Busch*
04/10	h	Freiburg	D	1-1	*Di Santo*
18/10	a	Bayern	L	0-6	
24/10	h	Köln	L	0-1	
01/11	a	Mainz	W	2-1	*Di Santo 2*
08/11	h	Stuttgart	W	2-0	*Prödl, Bartels*
23/11	a	Hamburg	L	0-2	
29/11	h	Paderborn	W	4-0	*Junuzovic, Selke, Bartels, Ayçiçek*
07/12	a	Frankfurt	L	2-5	*Gebre Selassie, Caldirola*
13/12	h	Hannover	D	3-3	*Junuzovic, Lorenzen, Selke*
17/12	a	Mönchengladbach	L	1-4	*Junuzovic*
20/12	h	Dortmund	W	2-1	*Selke, Bartels*

2015

01/02	h	Hertha	W	2-0	*Di Santo 2*
04/02	a	Hoffenheim	W	2-1	*Di Santo, Bargfrede*
08/02	h	Leverkusen	W	2-1	*Selke, Junuzovic*
14/02	a	Augsburg	W	3-2	*Lukimya, Di Santo (p), Gebre Selassie*
21/02	a	Schalke	D	1-1	*Prödl*
01/03	a	Wolfsburg	L	3-5	*Junuzovic, Di Santo, og (Vieirinha)*
07/03	a	Freiburg	W	1-0	*Di Santo*
14/03	h	Bayern	L	0-4	
21/03	a	Köln	D	1-1	*Selke*
04/04	h	Mainz	D	0-0	
12/04	a	Stuttgart	L	2-3	*Selke, Vestergaard*
19/04	h	Hamburg	W	1-0	*Di Santo (p)*
26/04	a	Paderborn	D	2-2	*Selke, Hajrovic*
02/05	h	Frankfurt	W	1-0	*Selke*
09/05	a	Hannover	W	1-0	*Junuzovic*
16/05	h	Mönchengladbach	L	0-2	
23/05	a	Dortmund	L	2-3	*Öztunali, Gebre Selassie*

No	Name	Nat	DoB	Pos	Aps	(s)	Gls
28	Levent Ayçiçek		12/02/94	M	5	(6)	1
44	Philipp Bargfrede		03/03/89	M	15	(1)	1
22	Fin Bartels		07/02/87	M	27	(2)	4
38	Marnon Busch		08/12/94	D	4	(5)	1
3	Luca Caldirola	ITA	01/02/91	D	5	(2)	1
20	Koen Casteels	BEL	25/06/92	G	14		
9	Franco Di Santo	ARG	07/04/89	A	26		13
35	Maximilian Eggestein		08/12/96	M		(2)	
11	Eljero Elia	NED	13/02/87	A	8	(1)	
8	Clemens Fritz		07/12/80	D	26	(1)	
39	Lukas Fröde		23/01/95	M		(1)	
4	Alejandro Gálvez	ESP	06/06/89	D	18	(2)	1
2	Santiago García	ARG	08/07/88	D	20	(4)	
2	Theodor Gebre Selassie	CZE	24/12/86	D	25	(1)	3
14	Izet Hajrović	BIH	04/08/91	M	8	(11)	1
25	Oliver Hüsing		17/02/93	D		(2)	
16	Zlatko Junuzovic	AUT	26/09/87	M	32	(1)	6
18	Felix Kroos		12/03/91	M	14	(12)	
22	Melvyn Lorenzen		26/11/94	A	2	(1)	1
5	Assani Lukimya	COD	25/01/86	D	18	(4)	2
6	Cédric Makiadi	COD	23/02/84	M	6	(12)	
7	Ludovic Obraniak	POL	10/11/84	M	1	(1)	
11	Levin Öztunali		15/03/96	M	8	(8)	1
24	Nils Petersen		06/12/88	A	2	(5)	
15	Sebastian Prödl	AUT	21/06/87	D	20	(2)	3
26	Davie Selke		20/01/95	A	22	(8)	9
37	Janek Sternberg		19/10/92	D	12	(2)	
30	Richard Strebinger	AUT	14/02/93	G	1	(1)	
7	Jannik Vestergaard	DEN	03/08/92	D	15		1
20	Raphael Wolf		06/06/88	G	27		
17	Özkan Yıldırım		10/04/93	M	1		

VfL Wolfsburg

1945 • Volkswagen-Arena (30,000) • vfl-wolfsburg.de

Major honours
German League (1) 2009; German Cup (1) 2015

Coach: Dieter Hecking

2014

22/08	a	Bayern	L	1-2	*Olić*
30/08	h	Frankfurt	D	2-2	*Naldo, Arnold*
13/09	a	Hoffenheim	D	1-1	*Olić*
21/09	h	Leverkusen	W	4-1	*Rodriguez 2 (1p), Vieirinha, Hunt*
24/09	a	Hertha	L	0-1	
27/09	h	Bremen	W	2-1	*Rodriguez, Olić*
05/10	h	Augsburg	W	1-0	*Naldo*
18/10	a	Freiburg	W	2-1	*Caligiuri 2*
26/10	h	Mainz	W	3-0	*Naldo, Perišić, Caligiuri*
01/11	a	Stuttgart	W	4-0	*Perišić, Knoche, De Bruyne*
09/11	h	Hamburg	W	2-0	*Olić, Hunt*
22/11	a	Schalke	L	2-3	*Olić, Bendtner*
30/11	a	Mönchengladbach	W	1-0	*Knoche*
06/12	h	Hannover	W	3-1	*De Bruyne, Dost, Arnold*
14/12	a	Paderborn	D	1-1	*og (Rafa López)*
17/12	a	Dortmund	D	2-2	*De Bruyne, Naldo*
20/12	h	Köln	W	2-1	*Dost, Naldo*

2015

30/01	h	Bayern	W	4-1	*Dost 2, De Bruyne 2*
03/02	a	Frankfurt	D	1-1	*De Bruyne*
07/02	h	Hoffenheim	W	3-0	*Dost, De Bruyne 2*
14/02	a	Leverkusen	W	5-4	*Dost 4, Naldo*
22/02	h	Hertha	W	2-1	*Dost 2*
01/03	a	Bremen	W	5-3	*Caligiuri 2, Arnold, Dost 2*
07/03	a	Augsburg	L	0-1	
15/03	h	Freiburg	W	3-0	*De Bruyne, Rodriguez (p), Arnold*
22/03	a	Mainz	D	1-1	*Luiz Gustavo*
04/04	a	Stuttgart	W	3-1	*Rodriguez 2 (1p), Schürrle*
11/04	a	Hamburg	W	2-0	*Guilavogui, Caligiuri*
19/04	a	Schalke	D	1-1	*De Bruyne*
26/04	a	Mönchengladbach	L	0-1	
02/05	h	Hannover	D	2-2	*Dost, Perišić*
10/05	a	Paderborn	W	3-1	*Klose, Dost 2*
16/05	h	Dortmund	W	2-1	*Caligiuri, Naldo*
23/05	a	Köln	D	2-2	*Luiz Gustavo, Perišić*

No	Name	Nat	DoB	Pos	Aps	(s)	Gls
27	Maximilian Arnold		27/05/94	M	17	(10)	4
1	Diego Benaglio	SUI	08/09/83	G	31		
3	Nicklas Bendtner	DEN	16/01/88	A	5	(13)	1
7	Daniel Caligiuri	ITA	15/01/88	M	18	(10)	7
14	Kevin De Bruyne	BEL	28/06/91	M	34		10
12	Bas Dost	NED	31/05/89	A	17	(4)	16
20	Max Grün		05/04/87	G	3		
23	Josuha Guilavogui	FRA	19/09/90	M	21	(6)	1
10	Aaron Hunt		04/09/86	M	3	(12)	2
24	Sebastian Jung		22/06/90	D	17	(5)	
5	Timm Klose	SUI	09/05/88	D	11	(1)	1
31	Robin Knoche		22/05/92	D	25	(2)	2
22	Luiz Gustavo	BRA	23/07/87	M	30	(1)	2
19	Junior Malanda	BEL	28/08/94	M	4	(6)	
25	Naldo	BRA	10/09/82	D	32		7
11	Ivica Olić	CRO	14/09/79	A	12	(2)	5
9	Ivan Perišić	CRO	02/02/89	M	21	(3)	5
34	Ricardo Rodriguez	SUI	25/08/92	D	26		6
4	Marcel Schäfer		07/06/84	D	7	(1)	
17	André Schürrle		06/11/90	M	7	(7)	1
15	Christian Träsch		01/09/87	D	8	(4)	
8	Vieirinha	POR	24/01/86	D	25	(6)	1

GERMANY

Top goalscorers

19	Alexander Meier (Frankfurt)
17	Robert Lewandowski (Bayern)
	Arjen Robben (Bayern)
16	Pierre-Emerick Aubameyang (Dortmund)
	Bas Dost (Wolfsburg)
13	Thomas Müller (Bayern)
	Franco Di Santo (Bremen)
12	Karim Bellarabi (Leverkusen)
	Shinji Okazaki (Mainz)
	Raffael (Mönchengladbach)

Promoted clubs

FC Ingolstadt 04

2004 • Audi Sportpark (15,690) •
fcingolstadt.de
Coach: Ralph Hasenhüttl (AUT)

SV Darmstadt 98

1898 • Böllenfalltor (16,500) • sv98.de
Coach: Dirk Schuster

Second level final table 2014/15

		Pld	W	D	L	F	A	Pts
1	FC Ingolstadt 04	34	17	13	4	53	32	64
2	SV Darmstadt 98	34	15	14	5	44	26	59
3	Karlsruher SC	34	15	13	6	46	26	58
4	1. FC Kaiserslautern	34	14	14	6	45	31	56
5	RB Leipzig	34	13	11	10	39	31	50
6	TSV Eintracht Braunschweig	34	15	5	14	44	41	50
7	1. FC Union Berlin	34	12	11	11	46	51	47
8	1. FC Heidenheim	34	12	10	12	49	44	46
9	1. FC Nürnberg	34	13	6	15	42	47	45
10	Fortuna Düsseldorf	34	11	11	12	48	52	44
11	VfL Bochum	34	9	15	10	53	55	42
12	SV Sandhausen	34	10	12	12	32	37	39
13	FSV Frankfurt	34	10	9	15	41	53	39
14	SpVgg Greuther Fürth	34	8	13	13	34	42	37
15	FC St Pauli	34	10	7	17	40	51	37
16	TSV 1860 München	34	9	9	16	41	51	36
17	FC Erzgebirge Aue	34	9	9	16	32	47	36
18	VfR Aalen	34	7	12	15	34	46	31

NB SV Sandhausen – 3 pts deducted; VfR Aalen – 2 pts deducted

Promotion/Relegation play-offs

(28/05/15 & 01/06/15)
Hamburg 1-1 Karlsruhe
Karlsruhe 1-2 Hamburg *(aet)*
(Hamburg 3-2)

DOMESTIC CUP

DFB-Pokal 2014/15

FIRST ROUND

(15/08/14)
Chemnitz 5-5 Mainz *(aet; 5-4 on pens)*
Duisburg 1-0 Nürnberg
Waldalgesheim 0-6 Leverkusen

(16/08/14)
Bochum 2-0 Stuttgart
Bremer SV 0-1 Eintracht Braunschweig
FT Braunschweig 0-4 1. FC Köln
Homburg 1-3 Mönchengladbach
Rathenow 1-3 St Pauli
Siegen 3-3 FSV Frankfurt *(aet; 4-5 on pens)*
Stuttgarter Kickers 1-4 Dortmund
Viktoria Berlin 0-2 Eintracht Frankfurt
Viktoria Köln 2-4 Hertha BSC
Waldkirch 0-3 Greuther Fürth
Walldorf 1-3 Hannover
Wehen 0-0 Kaiserslautern *(aet; 3-5 on pens)*

(17/08/14)
Bielefeld 4-1 Sandhausen
Carl Zeiss Jena 0-1 Aue
Darmstadt 0-0 Wolfsburg *(aet; 4-5 on pens)*
Illertissen 2-3 Werder Bremen *(aet)*
Kiel 1-2 1860 München
Magdeburg 1-0 Augsburg
Münster 1-4 Bayern
Neubrandenburg 1-3 Karlsruhe
Paloma Hamburg 0-9 Hoffenheim
RB Leipzig 2-1 Paderborn *(aet)*
Rehden 1-1 Aalen *(aet; 3-4 on pens)*
Trier 0-2 Freiburg
Würzburg 3-2 Düsseldorf *(aet)*

(18/08/14)
Cottbus 2-2 Hamburger SV *(aet; 1-4 on pens)*
Dresden 2-1 Schalke
Heidenheim 2-1 Union Berlin
Offenbach 0-0 Ingolstadt *(aet; 4-2 on pens)*

SECOND ROUND

(28/10/14)
Aalen 2-0 Hannover
Bielefeld 0-0 Hertha BSC *(aet; 4-2 on pens)*
Chemnitz 0-2 Werder Bremen
Dresden 2-1 Bochum *(aet)*
Duisburg 0-0 1. FC Köln *(aet; 1-4 on pens)*
Kaiserslautern 2-0 Greuther Fürth
Offenbach 1-0 Karlsruhe
St Pauli 0-3 Dortmund

(29/10/14)
1860 München 2-5 Freiburg
Eintracht Frankfurt 1-2 Mönchengladbach
Hamburger SV 1-3 Bayern
Hoffenheim 5-1 FSV Frankfurt
Magdeburg 2-2 Leverkusen *(aet; 4-5 on pens)*
RB Leipzig 3-1 Aue *(aet)*
Wolfsburg 4-1 Heidenheim
Würzburg 0-1 Eintracht Braunschweig

THIRD ROUND

(03/03/15)
Aalen 0-2 Hoffenheim
Dresden 0-2 Dortmund
Freiburg 2-1 1. FC Köln
Leverkusen 2-0 Kaiserslautern *(aet)*

(04/03/15)
Bayern 2-0 Eintracht Braunschweig
Bielefeld 3-1 Werder Bremen
RB Leipzig 0-2 Wolfsburg
Offenbach 0-2 Mönchengladbach

QUARTER-FINALS

(07/04/15)
Dortmund 3-2 Hoffenheim *(Subotić 19, Aubameyang 57, Kehl 107; Volland 21, Roberto Firmino 28) (aet)*

Wolfsburg 1-0 Freiburg *(Rodriguez 72p)*

(08/04/15)
Bielefeld 1-1 Mönchengladbach *(Junglas 26; Kruse 32p) (aet; 5-4 on pens)*

Leverkusen 0-0 Bayern *(aet; 3-5 on pens)*

SEMI-FINALS

(28/04/15)
Bayern 1-1 Dortmund *(Lewandowski 29; Aubameyang 75) (aet; 0-2 on pens)*

(29/04/15)
Bielefeld 0-4 Wolfsburg *(Arnold 8, 55, Luiz Gustavo 31, Perišić 51)*

FINAL

(30/05/15)
Olympiastadion, Berlin
VFL WOLFSBURG 3 *(Luiz Gustavo 22, De Bruyne 33, Dost 38)*
BORUSSIA DORTMUND 1 *(Aubameyang 5)*
Referee: *Brych*
WOLFSBURG: Benaglio, Vieirinha, Naldo, Klose, Rodriguez, Arnold (Schürrle 81), Luiz Gustavo, Perišić (Guilavogui 74), De Bruyne, Caligiuri (Träsch 85), Dost
DORTMUND: Langerak, Durm (Błaszczykowski 68), Subotić, Hummels, Schmelzer, Gündoğan, Kehl (Piszczek 68), Mkhitaryan, Kagawa, Reus (Immobile 79), Aubameyang

Wolfsburg captain Diego Benaglio raises the DFB-Pokal

GIBRALTAR
Gibraltar Football Association (GFA)

Address	PO Box 513	**President**	Michael Llamas
	32 A Rosia Road	**General secretary**	Richard Manning
	GX11 1AA Gibraltar	**Media officer**	Steven Gonzalez
Tel	+350 200 42 941	**Year of formation**	1895
Fax	+350 200 42 211	**National stadium**	Victoria Stadium
E-mail	info@gibraltarfa.com		(5,000)
Website	gibraltarfa.com		

PREMIER DIVISION CLUBS

 ① **FC Britannia XI**

 ② **College Europa FC**

NB Renamed Europa FC for 2015/16 season

 ③ **Glacis United FC**

 ④ **Lincoln FC**

 ⑤ **Lions Gibraltar FC**

 ⑥ **Lynx FC**

 ⑦ **Manchester 62 FC**

 ⑧ **St Joseph's FC**

PROMOTED CLUBS

 ⑨ **Gibraltar United FC**

 ⑩ **Angels FC**

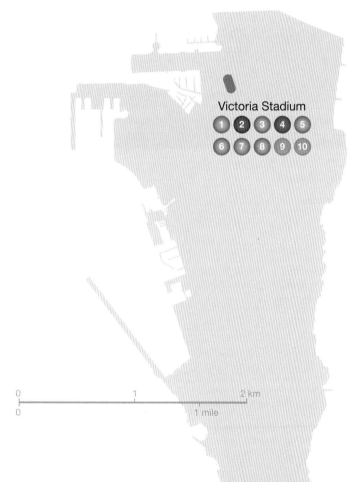

Victoria Stadium

KEY:

⬤ – UEFA Champions League

⬤ – UEFA Europa League

⬤ – Promoted

Lincoln in a different league

Football in Gibraltar entered a new era in 2014/15 with the admission of the country's leading clubs and national team into top-level UEFA competition. An extended domestic championship was also introduced, with the eight Premier Division teams playing 21 matches rather than 14.

However, there was no novel outcome to either the league title race or the Rock Cup as Lincoln FC captured their 14th domestic double, making it 13 successive Premier Division championship triumphs in the process.

Red Imps cruise to 13th successive league title	Back-to-back doubles secured with Rock Cup win	Clubs and national team enter competitive arena

Domestic league

Although Lincoln again made light work of winning the league, recording 19 victories, amassing 80 goals – almost twice as many as other team – and finishing 16 points clear of runners-up College Europa FC, the difference in 2014/15 was that they did so under a new coach. Mick McElwee, the Englishman who had taken the Red Imps to the title in each of the previous 11 seasons, stood down in July 2014 and handed over the reins to Spaniard Raúl Procopio.

There was some concern when the new man oversaw a shock 1-0 defeat on the opening day to Lynx FC, but that would be the only game Lincoln lost all season, a relentless winning streak thereafter being interrupted only by a 2-2 draw against College Europa in mid-January. It was against the same opponents, with a 5-0 win in early May, that the club's record 21st league title was confirmed. Three weeks later the Red Imps closed the campaign with their biggest win, thrashing Lions Gibraltar FC 9-0.

Striker Lee Casciaro scored twice in that final fixture to cement his position as the Premier Division's top marksman, with 18 goals. He was one of four Lincoln players on double figures, alongside Joseph Chipolina (13), Liam Walker (12) and 2013/14 golden boot winner John Paul Duarte (10).

While Lincoln cruised unopposed to the title, the more interesting battle was for second place. Three teams – College Europa, Lynx and St Joseph's FC – were all in the running, but it was the former who clinched it in advance of their final fixture against Lynx, which therefore became a dead rubber.

Also of little consequence was the battle to avoid finishing bottom – one lost by Lions Gibraltar – as the increase of the Premier Division in 2015/16 to ten teams meant a season without relegation. There was an almighty three-way scrap, however, for the two promotion places, with Europa Point FC just missing out – despite scoring 123 goals – to Angels FC and Gibraltar United FC, the last team other than Lincoln to have been crowned league champions, in 2002.

Domestic cup

With only one UEFA Europa League place available to Gibraltar, Lynx had the opportunity to snatch it from College Europa if they could win the Rock Cup – and thereby claim their first major trophy. Unfortunately, their opponents in the final were Lincoln, and although the underdogs grabbed an early lead, two goals apiece from Duarte and Walker eventually saw the champions through to a comfortable 4-1 victory.

Europe

McElwee's last stand with Lincoln brought a 6-2 aggregate defeat by HB Tórshavn in the first qualifying round of the UEFA Champions League. The tie started well, with Joseph Chipolina putting Gibraltar's finest in front with the country's historic first goal in UEFA club competition, but that was as good as it got. In the UEFA Europa League, College Europa fell at the first hurdle to FC Vaduz, losing 4-0 on aggregate.

National team

As expected, Gibraltar's introduction to competitive international football proved to be something of an ordeal. They played six UEFA EURO 2016 qualifiers and lost them all, conceding 34 goals, with four opposition players helping themselves to hat-tricks.

On the plus side, they did score once themselves, Lee Casciaro entering the history books with his equaliser in the 6-1 defeat by Scotland at Hampden Park – a match for which Gibraltar had a Scot in charge, David Wilson having moved up from assistant to caretaker coach following the resignation of Allen Bula. By July a new permanent coach had been found, with Lions Gibraltar's Jeff Wood, an Englishman, stepping into the breach.

DOMESTIC SEASON AT A GLANCE

Premier Division 2014/15 final table

		Pld	W	D	L	F	A	Pts
1	**Lincoln FC**	**21**	**19**	**1**	**1**	**80**	**12**	**58**
2	College Europa FC	21	12	6	3	42	14	42
3	Lynx FC	21	10	8	3	36	18	38
4	St Joseph's FC	21	12	2	7	36	18	38
5	Manchester 62 FC	21	7	6	8	22	25	27
6	Glacis United FC	21	4	3	14	14	50	15
7	FC Britannia XI	21	2	3	16	13	67	9
8	Lions Gibraltar FC	21	1	5	15	9	48	8

European qualification 2015/16

Champion/Cup winner: Lincoln FC (first qualifying round)

College Europa FC (first qualifying round)

Top scorer Lee Casciaro (Lincoln), 18 goals
Relegated clubs None
Promoted clubs Gibraltar United FC, Angels FC
Cup final Lincoln FC 4-1 Lynx FC

Team of the season
(4-3-3)

Coach: Procopio (Lincoln)

Navas (Lincoln)

Garcia (Lincoln) R Chipolina (Lincoln) E Montes (St Joseph's) J Chipolina (Lincoln)

Rodriguez (Glacis) Márquez (St Joseph's) Walker (Lincoln)

JP Duarte (Lincoln) L Casciaro (Lincoln) K Casciaro (Lincoln)

Player of the season

Liam Walker
(Lincoln FC)

After several years playing abroad in Spain, England and Israel, Gibraltar international Walker returned home in 2014 to add further strength to perennial champions Lincoln's squad. The former Portsmouth FC midfielder found easy pickings in the Premier Division and scored 12 goals. He also proved a key player in the team's Rock Cup triumph, scoring the winner in the quarter-final and a double in the final, and he did not miss a minute of Gibraltar's first six UEFA EURO 2016 qualifiers.

Newcomer of the season

Anthony Bardon
(Lincoln FC)

A fringe member of the Manchester 62 FC side that finished runners-up in the 2013/14 Premier Division, Bardon left for Lincoln and forced his way into the champions' first XI with some excellent midfield displays. The 22-year-old made his competitive international debut for Gibraltar in March 2015 against Scotland and a few weeks later struck his first league goal for Lincoln in the 5-0 win against College Europa FC that sealed the title. He also played the full 90 minutes of the Rock Cup final.

GIBRALTAR

NATIONAL TEAM

Top five all-time caps
Ryan Casciaro & Joseph Chipolina (12);
Roy Chipolina, Adam Priestley & Liam Walker (11)

Top five all-time goals
Kyle Casciaro, Lee Casciaro, Roy Chipolina & Jake Gosling (1)

Results 2014/15

07/09/14	Poland (ECQ)	H	Faro (POR)	L	0-7	
11/10/14	Republic of Ireland (ECQ)	A	Dublin	L	0-7	
14/10/14	Georgia (ECQ)	H	Faro (POR)	L	0-3	
14/11/14	Germany (ECQ)	A	Nuremberg	L	0-4	
29/03/15	Scotland (ECQ)	A	Glasgow	L	1-6	L Casciaro (19)
07/06/15	Croatia	A	Varazdin	L	0-4	
13/06/15	Germany (ECQ)	H	Faro (POR)	L	0-7	

Appearances 2014/15

Coach: Allen Bula 04/01/65 /(06/03/15) David Wilson (SCO) 22/02/74			POL	IRL	GEO	GER	SCO	Cro	GER	Caps	Goals
Jordan Perez	13/11/86	Lincoln /Lions Gibraltar	G	G60				G46	G	9	-
Scott Wiseman	09/10/85	Preston (ENG)	D	D	D	D	D			7	-
Joseph Chipolina	14/12/87	Lincoln	D	D	D	D	D	s46	D	12	-
David Artell	22/11/80	Bala (WAL)	D88			D	D53			7	-
Ryan Casciaro	11/05/84	Lincoln	D	D	D	D	D	D	D	12	-
Roy Chipolina	20/01/83	Lincoln	D	D57	s76	M	M74		D	11	1
Lee Casciaro	29/09/81	Lincoln	M	A	M	A71	M		M	6	1
Rafael Bado	30/12/84	Lynx	M46	M46						2	-
Liam Walker	13/04/88	Lincoln	M	M	M	M	M	M	M	11	-
Brian Perez	16/09/86	Lincoln	M	M	M	M91				4	-
Kyle Casciaro	02/12/87	Lincoln	A63		A46	s71		s75	M78	10	1
Jake Gosling	11/08/93	Bristol Rovers (ENG)	s46	M	s75		s74	M75	M	8	1
Adam Priestley	01/01/90	Farsley (ENG)	s63		s46	s91	A	M	A61	11	-
Aaron Payas	24/05/85	Manchester 62	s88	M			M		M82	6	-
Robert Guiling	14/10/80	Lynx		s46	M75			M46		6	-
Yogen Santos	15/01/85	Manchester 62		s57	D76	s58				5	-
Jamie Robba	26/10/91	College Europa		s60	G	G	G	s46		6	-
Jean-Carlos Garcia	05/07/92	Lincoln			D	D	s53	D75	D	7	-
Jack Sergeant	27/02/95	Manchester 62				M58		s46	s82	8	-
Anthony Bardon	19/01/93	Lincoln					M82	M46		4	-
Daniel Duarte	25/10/79	Lincoln					s82			4	-
Jamie Bosio	24/09/91	College Europa						D	s78	2	-
Justin Rovegno	17/07/89	Manchester 62						D46		1	-
John Paul Duarte	13/12/86	Lincoln						A		5	-
Jamie Coombes	27/05/96	Manchester 62						s46	s61	2	-
Jeremy Lopez	09/07/89	Manchester 62						s75		4	-

EUROPE

DOMESTIC LEAGUE CLUB-BY-CLUB

Lincoln FC

CHAMPIONS LEAGUE

First qualifying round - HB Tórshavn (FRO)
H 1-1 *J Chipolina (18p)*
J Perez, K Casciaro, R Casciaro, L Casciaro, Guiling (Cabrera 68), D Duarte (Payas 77), R Chipolina, JP Duarte (B Perez 83), Clarke, J Chipolina, Garcia. Coach: Mick McElwee (ENG)
A 2-5 *Cabrera (50), J.P Duarte (77)*
J Perez, K Casciaro (L Casciaro 46), R Casciaro, B Perez, R Chipolina, Payas (Guiling 86), Clarke, Cabrera, Pons (JP Duarte 68), J Chipolina, Garcia. Coach: Mick McElwee (ENG)

College Europa FC

EUROPA LEAGUE

First qualifying round - FC Vaduz (LIE)
A 0-3
Cafer, Soto, L Coombes, Pereyra, Tamayo (Molina 59), Toncheff (Montovio 81), Mouelhi, Saavedra (J Coombes 67), Pegalajar, Delgado, Bosio. Coach: José Requena (ESP)
H 0-1
Robba, L Coombes, Jolley, Molina (Marquez 79), Pereyra, Toncheff, J Coombes (Saavedra 52), Mouelhi, Bakkari, Pegalajar, Bosio (Briones 63). Coach: José Requena (ESP)
Red card: L Coombes 70

Stadium

Victoria Stadium (5,000)

FC Britannia XI

1907• fcbritanniaxi.co.uk
Major honours
Gibraltar League (14) 1908, 1912, 1913, 1918, 1920, 1937, 1940, 1955, 1956, 1957, 1958, 1959, 1961, 1963; Gibraltar Cup (3) 1937, 1940, 1948
Coach: Juan Luis Pérez Herrera (ESP); (20/02/15) Alexander Oprey (ENG)

2014
20/09	St Joseph's	L	1-2	*Cuesta*
30/09	Lions Gibraltar	D	1-1	*Roche (p)*
05/10	Lincoln	L	0-2	
20/10	Manchester 62	L	2-5	*Cuesta 2*
25/10	Lynx	L	0-3	
01/11	College Europa	L	0-9	
06/11	Glacis	D	1-1	*Pacheco Exposito*
22/11	St Joseph's	L	0-4	
28/11	Lions Gibraltar	L	1-3	*Guei*

2015
09/01	Lincoln	L	0-7	
16/01	Manchester 62	L	0-1	
06/02	Lynx	L	1-2	*Roche*
21/02	College Europa	D	0-0	
06/03	Glacis	L	1-2	*og (Rodriguez)*
21/03	St Joseph's	L	1-2	*André Santos*
13/04	Lions Gibraltar	W	2-1	*Vázquez Evuy 2*
18/04	Lincoln	L	0-7	
02/05	Manchester 62	L	1-2	*Renan Bernardes*
09/05	Lynx	L	0-8	
15/05	College Europa	L	0-5	
26/05	Glacis	W	1-0	*Vázquez Evuy*

No	Name	Nat	DoB	Pos	Aps	(s)	Gls
81	Alan Arruda	BRA	12/09/81	D	9	(1)	
2	André Santos	BRA	19/02/92	D	10		1
13	Jason Baker	ENG	13/10/83	M	3	(4)	
30	Louie Barnfather Marfe		07/10/92	G	5	(1)	
21	Kevin Boateng	ENG	08/09/92	M	1	(1)	
18	Christian Caetano		30/04/86	M	4	(4)	
25	Daniel Cameron	ESP	12/06/95	M	6		
22	Sebastián Campillo	ARG	02/06/84	A	1		
20	Fernando Cuesta	ESP	20/07/91	A	6	(2)	3
10	Kristian D'Rosario	ENG	11/06/89	A	9	(5)	
22	Moussa Dia	SEN	01/06/94	D	5	(2)	
5	Imanol Fernández Pérez	ESP	29/03/95	D	4		
32	José Miguel González Rodríguez	ESP	08/04/93	G	4		
20	Marius Guei	CIV	25/08/86	M	2	(2)	1
16	José Manuel Guerra	ESP	03/11/93	M	6		
26	Juan Carlos Gutiérrez	ESP	12/12/80	D	2		
11	Stefan Jarv	EST	07/07/91	D	3		
24	Risto Kägo	EST	04/08/89	M	16		
25	Martin Lobb	ENG	15/01/87	A	2	(1)	
17	Christopher Mousdell	ENG	23/04/86	D	7	(1)	
13	Luke Nixon	IRL	14/09/86	D	7		
15	Diego Pacheco Exposito	ESP	06/09/96	D	16	(1)	1
6	Karl Parody		21/09/93	D	6	(3)	
3	Nicholas Pecino		08/07/85	D	5		
30	Anthony Perez		02/12/85	G	2		
4	Renan Bernardes	BRA	21/03/92	M	9		1
1	Philip Reyes		28/09/92	G	10		
8	Liam Roche		11/12/85	M	14	(3)	2
2	Sebastian Rodriguez		14/03/84	M	5		
4	Julian Sacarello		15/05/86	D	1	(2)	
21	Leone Seatory		21/06/97	A	2	(2)	
7	Alen Stepanjan	EST	23/07/91	D	3	(4)	
9	Matthew Thompson	ENG	17/07/87	D	1		
17	Jesús Vázquez Evuy	ESP	20/04/93	A	11	(1)	3
11	Liam Victor		22/07/85	M	6	(5)	
23	Peter Warren	ENG	11/06/89	A	11	(3)	
14	James Watson		30/04/83	D	8	(3)	
16	Tim Whittle	ENG	28/07/86	D	2	(1)	
21	Pierre Yamfam	ENG	03/10/95	M	1	(2)	
12	Alexis Zamboglou	IRL	29/10/82	D	6	(2)	

College Europa FC

1925 • no website
Coach: José Requena (ESP); (06/11/14) Bruno Akrapović (BIH)

2014
22/09	Glacis	W	6-0	*Pegalajar 2, Toncheff 2, Saavedra, Tamayo*
26/09	St Joseph's	W	1-0	*Toncheff*
05/10	Lions Gibraltar	W	3-0	*Molina 2, Tamayo*
18/10	Lincoln	L	0-3	
25/10	Manchester 62	D	0-0	
01/11	Britannia XI	W	9-0	*Toncheff 4, Pegalajar 2, Delgado, Dechraoui, og (Parody)*
08/11	Lynx	W	1-0	*Mouelhi*
21/11	Glacis	W	1-0	*Pegalajar*
29/11	St Joseph's	W	2-0	*Pegalajar, Pereyra*

2015
12/01	Lions Gibraltar	W	2-0	*Pegalajar (p), Toncheff*
19/01	Lincoln	D	2-2	*Toncheff, Tamayo*
07/02	Manchester 62	D	1-1	*Delgado*
21/02	Britannia XI	D	0-0	
04/03	Lynx	D	1-1	*Toncheff*
20/03	Glacis	W	2-1	*Tamayo, Dechraoui*
10/04	St Joseph's	L	0-1	
18/04	Lions Gibraltar	W	3-0	*Briones, Toncheff, Sokol*
02/05	Lincoln	L	0-5	
08/05	Manchester 62	W	3-0	*Toncheff (p), Plazanić, Akrapovic*
15/05	Britannia XI	W	5-0	*Duvnjak 2, Toncheff 2 (1p), Saavedra*
23/05	Lynx	D	0-0	

No	Name	Nat	DoB	Pos	Aps	(s)	Gls
20	Aaron Akrapovic	ITA	02/03/94	M	12		1
19	Abderkahman Bakkari		22/02/88	M		(1)	
24	Jamie Bosio		24/09/91	M	16	(1)	
6	Carlos Martin Briones	EQG	18/02/90	D	8	(5)	1
1	Matthew Cafer	ENG	27/09/94	G	6		
11	Jamie Coombes		27/05/96	A		(3)	
3	Lee Coombes		30/06/96	D	4		
22	Karim Dechraoui		30/04/92	D	12	(4)	2
23	Juan Carlos Delgado	ESP	09/10/95	D	14	(1)	2
17	Armin Duvnjak	BIH	15/02/90	M	5	(1)	2
5	Walter Fiumano	ITA	01/01/85	M	10	(3)	
21	Kresmir Frigen	CRO	27/02/97	M		(4)	
8	Paul Gomez		13/01/98	M		(1)	
3	Jonathan Hernández	MEX	27/10/86	M	2	(1)	
4	Ethan Jolley		02/04/97	D	3	(3)	
12	Boris Jukić	CRO	19/06/88	M	9	(2)	
5	Juan Diego Molina	ESP	05/11/93	M	3	(3)	2
7	Robert Montovio		03/08/84	A		(4)	
7	Kelvin Morgan		14/11/97	D		(1)	
15	Aymen Mouelhi	TUN	14/09/86	D	15		1
21	Juan Sebastián Pegalajar	ESP	19/04/89	M	14	(1)	7
8	Leandro Pereyra	ARG	27/02/85	M	10	(5)	1
18	Hrvoje Plazanić	CRO	18/09/90	D	11		1
13	Jamie Robba		26/10/91	G	15		
16	Ramon Saavedra	ESP	17/01/96	M	10	(4)	2
11	Ante Sokol	CRO	08/11/93	D	11		1
2	Pedro Soto	ESP	24/04/92	D	11	(1)	
9	Francisco Javier Tamayo	ESP	26/02/91	A	11	(4)	4
10	Cristian Toncheff	ARG	25/03/82	A	19		14

Glacis United FC

1965 • no website
Major honours
Gibraltar League (17) 1966, 1967, 1968, 1969, 1970,
1971, 1972, 1973, 1974, 1976, 1981, 1982, 1983,
1985, 1989, 1997, 2000; Gibraltar Cup (4) 1975,
1981, 1982, 1996
Coach: Javier Sánchez Alfaro (ESP)

2014
22/09	College Europa	L 0-6	
28/09	Lynx	L 0-4	
06/10	St Joseph's	L 1-5	*Martinez*
18/10	Lions Gibraltar	W 2-1	*Martinez 2 (1p)*
24/10	Lincoln	L 0-1	
31/10	Manchester 62	W 2-1	*Moreno, Anderson Pinto (p)*
06/11	Britannia XI	D 1-1	*Martinez*
21/11	College Europa	L 0-1	
29/11	Lynx	L 1-3	*Currer*

2015
10/01	St Joseph's	L 0-4	
17/01	Lions Gibraltar	D 0-0	
07/02	Lincoln	L 1-6	*Bado (p)*
23/02	Manchester 62	L 0-1	
06/03	Britannia XI	W 2-1	*Campoy, Rodriguez*
20/03	College Europa	L 1-2	*Del Rio*
11/04	Lynx	L 0-5	
20/04	St Joseph's	L 0-2	
30/04	Lions Gibraltar	W 2-0	*Panzavechia, Currer*
11/05	Lincoln	L 0-4	
16/05	Manchester 62	D 1-1	*Rodriguez*
26/05	Britannia XI	L 0-1	

Name	Nat	DoB	Pos	Aps	(s)	Gls
Moussa Aitlachen	MAR	31/07/85	A		(2)	
Anderson Pinto	POR	11/02/94	A	4	(1)	1
Julio Bado		03/06/83	M	6	(2)	1
Tomas Barletta	ARG	10/01/92	A	9		
Kyle Bear		20/08/85	D	3	(2)	
Kevin Boateng	ENG	08/09/92	M	3		
Jeremias Campos	ESP	31/07/95	M	5	(2)	
José Antonio Campoy	ESP	09/02/95	A	4	(3)	1
Steffan Cardona		03/03/92	D	15	(1)	
Andres Castro	ESP	06/06/91	M		(1)	
James Currer		29/06/92	A	8	(1)	2
Alberto Del Rio	ESP	13/09/90	M	18	(1)	1
Borja González	ESP	14/02/92	M		(1)	
Paul Grech		08/12/86	D	4	(1)	
Al Greene		05/05/78	A	3	(1)	
Marius Guei	CIV	25/08/86	M	2	(2)	
Amael Jiménez	ESP	08/08/87	M	1	(1)	
Julian Lavagna		30/10/91	A		(3)	
Marius Loghin	ROU	16/12/87	M		(2)	
Dylan Martinez		29/12/84	A	11	(2)	4
Sean Mascarenhas		26/11/84	D	5		
Sergio Mata	ESP	11/10/85	M	4	(4)	
Jamie McCarthy		21/07/92	M		(1)	
David Mena	ESP	15/04/83	D	4	(1)	
Carlos Méndez	ESP	23/06/87	D	14		
Sergio Méndez	ESP	14/12/85	M	2	(3)	
Kyle Moreno		27/08/92	D	10	(4)	1
Liam Neale		01/12/96	G	20		
Dexter Panzavechia		30/12/90	M	9	(2)	1
Ashley Rodriguez		13/11/89	M	19		2
Emerson Rovegno		10/06/81	D	8	(4)	
Álex Ruesca	ESP	01/11/85	M	13	(3)	
Juan José Ruesca	ESP	24/11/90	D	21		
Manuel Ruiz Vecino	ESP	25/08/84	D	2	(4)	
Youseff Sabbari	MAR	03/04/93	G	1		
Francisco Santiago	ESP	25/08/91	M		(1)	
Andy Storey		22/07/87	M	3	(3)	

Lincoln FC

1975 • no website
Major honours
Gibraltar League (21) 1985 (shared), 1986, 1990,
1991, 1992, 1993, 1994, 2001, 2003, 2004, 2005,
2006, 2007, 2008, 2009, 2010, 2011, 2012, 2013,
2014, 2015; Gibraltar Cup (16) 1986, 1989, 1990,
1993, 1994, 2002, 2004, 2005, 2006, 2007, 2008,
2009, 2010, 2011, 2014, 2015
Coach: Mick McElwee (ENG);
(21/07/14) Raúl Procopio (ESP)

2014
19/09	Lynx	L 0-1	
29/09	Manchester 62	W 2-1	*L Casciaro 2*
05/10	Britannia XI	W 2-0	*Walker, L Casciaro*
18/10	College Europa	W 3-0	*J Chipolina, R Chipolina, og (Cafer)*
24/10	Glacis	W 1-0	*Walker*
01/11	St Joseph's	W 2-0	*Walker 2*
08/11	Lions Gibraltar	W 3-0	*JP Duarte, R Casciaro, J Chipolina*
24/11	Lynx	W 6-1	*J Chipolina (p), L Casciaro, Mejías, K Casciaro, JP Duarte, Walker*
01/12	Manchester 62	W 3-1	*L Casciaro 2, J Chipolina*

2015
09/01	Britannia XI	W 7-0	*K Casciaro 2, L Casciaro, JP Duarte, J Chipolina, Walker, Cristori*
19/01	College Europa	D 2-2	*L Casciaro, Walker*
07/02	Glacis	W 6-1	*L Casciaro 2, Walker, Mejías, J Chipolina, Parker*
21/02	St Joseph's	W 4-2	*K Casciaro 2, JP Duarte, J Chipolina*
08/03	Lions Gibraltar	W 4-0	*K Casciaro 2, L Casciaro, JP Duarte*
19/03	Lynx	W 4-1	*J Chipolina 3, L Casciaro*
11/04	Manchester 62	W 4-1	*J Chipolina, K Casciaro, Walker 2*
18/04	Britannia XI	W 7-0	*L Casciaro 4, JP Duarte, Cristori 2*
02/05	College Europa	W 5-0	*JP Duarte, Bardon, Walker, Cristori 2*
11/05	Glacis	W 4-0	*Cristori, og (C Méndez), J Chipolina, Garcia*
16/05	St Joseph's	W 2-1	*Bardon, Walker*
23/05	Lions Gibraltar	W 9-0	*K Chipolina, JP Duarte 3, Parker, R Casciaro, J Chipolina, L Casciaro 2*

No	Name	Nat	DoB	Pos	Aps	(s)	Gls
23	Graham Alvez		05/11/76	A		(2)	
55	Adolfo Pitu Anes		28/12/84	M		(1)	
21	Anthony Bardon		19/01/93	M	17	(1)	2
2	Francisco Belmonte	ESP	25/05/89	D	3		
11	George Cabrera		14/12/88	A		(1)	
8	Kyle Casciaro		02/12/87	M	15		8
7	Lee Casciaro		29/09/81	A	19	(1)	18
5	Ryan Casciaro		11/05/84	D	19	(1)	2
3	Joseph Chipolina		14/12/87	D	18	(2)	13
81	Kenneth Chipolina		08/04/94	D	1		1
14	Roy Chipolina		20/01/83	D	13	(2)	1
29	Tarik Chrayeh		05/11/86	D	2	(2)	
6	Liam Clarke		04/12/87	M	1	(2)	
17	Leon Clinton		19/07/98	A	1	(3)	
13	Dayle Coleing		23/10/96	G	2	(1)	
26	Emmanuel Cristori	ARG	23/01/86	A	1	(8)	6
25	Daniel Duarte		25/10/79	M	3	(3)	
16	John Paul Duarte		13/12/86	A	15	(3)	10
37	Jean-Carlos Garcia		05/07/92	D	17	(1)	1
19	Sergio Iglecias		31/12/79	M	5	(8)	
4	Ethan Jolley		29/03/97	D	2	(5)	
9	Francisco Mejías	ESP	05/05/87	M	15	(1)	2
30	Raúl Navas	ESP	03/05/78	G	19		
80	Alan Parker		15/05/96	D	2	(3)	2
10	Brian Perez		16/09/86	M	7	(2)	
17	Ian Rodriguez		20/07/88	M		(2)	
27	António Sambruno	ESP	15/07/78	D	16		
88	Liam Walker		13/04/88	M	18	(1)	12
26	Adrian Wojcik	ESP	25/05/94	A		(1)	

Lions Gibraltar FC

1966 • lionsgibraltarfc.com
Coach: Jeff Wood (ENG)

2014
20/09	Manchester 62	L 0-4	
30/09	Britannia XI	D 1-1	*Marquez*
05/10	College Europa	L 0-3	
18/10	Glacis	L 1-2	*Soussi*
27/10	St Joseph's	L 0-4	
03/11	Lynx	D 0-0	
08/11	Lincoln	L 0-3	
22/11	Manchester 62	L 0-1	
28/11	Britannia XI	W 3-1	*Soussi, Gonzalez, García Viñas*

2015
12/01	College Europa	L 0-2	
17/01	Glacis	D 0-0	
09/02	St Joseph's	L 0-2	
20/02	Lynx	D 1-1	*og (Vela)*
08/03	Lincoln	L 0-4	
21/03	Manchester 62	L 0-1	
13/04	Britannia XI	L 1-2	*Garro*
18/04	College Europa	L 0-3	
30/04	Glacis	L 0-2	
09/05	St Joseph's	L 1-2	*E Moreno*
18/05	Lynx	D 1-1	*López Luque*
23/05	Lincoln	L 0-9	

Name	Nat	DoB	Pos	Aps	(s)	Gls
Salvador Arguez	ESP	16/02/86	A	3		
Jesse Ballester		30/06/93	D	1		
Bradley Banda		20/01/98	G	1		
Erin Barnett		02/09/96	D	17		
Jamie Carlin		27/08/92	G	5		
Israel Castillo	ESP	31/07/93	A	4	(4)	
Jaydan Catania		06/03/93	D	17		
Luis Consigliero		16/08/89	A	1	(2)	
Jansen Dalli		25/09/85	M	6		
Shaun De Los Santos		26/01/98	D	5	(2)	
Byron Espinosa		15/03/99	A	6	(2)	
Ismael Fernández	ESP	13/10/86	D	7	(1)	
Aidon Garcia		16/08/94	G		(1)	
Angel García Viñas	ESP	27/06/89	A	2	(3)	1
Sykes Garro		26/02/93	M	19		1
Aidan Ghio		22/09/98	A	5	(1)	
Alex Gonzalez		02/01/96	A	9	(3)	1
Cian Green		23/08/96	M	1		
Evan Green		13/03/93	M	14	(1)	
Jonay López Luque	ESP	17/01/91	M	8	(1)	1
Jorge Manrique	ESP	25/12/85	D	3		
Lython Marquez		06/02/95	A	12	(4)	1
Enrique Moreno	ESP	09/01/92	M	7	(1)	1
Stefan Moreno		23/09/94	D	1		
Jayce Olivero		02/07/98	D	9		
Jules Origo		03/06/97	M	19		
Richie Parral		23/03/99	M	1	(2)	
Jordan Perez		13/11/86	G	15		
Adrián Pino	ESP	17/08/92	M	1		
Stefan Ramirez		18/11/98	D	3	(1)	
Nicholas Reyes		11/07/92	D	2		
Iván Rodríguez	ESP	24/12/90	D	4	(3)	
Emilio Sansolini	ITA	04/08/84	M	12	(5)	
Jon Shiels	ENG	13/03/92	A	1	(4)	
Steven Soussi		30/07/92	A	8	(5)	2
Nicholas Thompson	ENG	17/03/87	M	2	(1)	

Lynx FC

2007 • no website
Coach: Albert Parody

2014
19/09	Lincoln	W	1-0	*Guiling*
28/09	Glacis	W	4-0	*Gonzalez, Funes, Trofimenko, Ruiz*
03/10	Manchester 62	W	1-0	*Gonzalez*
25/10	Britannia XI	W	3-0	*Bado (p), Ponce, Funes*
03/11	Lions Gibraltar	D	0-0	
08/11	College Europa	L	0-1	
19/11	St Joseph's	D	0-0	
24/11	Lincoln	L	1-6	*Vela*
29/11	Glacis	W	3-1	*Avalos, Jaydan Parody, Gonzalez*

2015
10/01	Manchester 62	D	1-1	*Bado (p)*
17/01	St Joseph's	W	2-1	*Helvida, Caballero*
06/02	Britannia XI	W	2-1	*King, Sánchez*
20/02	Lions Gibraltar	D	1-1	*King*
04/03	College Europa	D	1-1	*King*
19/03	Lincoln	L	1-4	*King*
11/04	Glacis	W	5-0	*King 2, Helvida, Hassan, Trofimenko*
17/04	Manchester 62	D	0-0	
04/05	St Joseph's	W	1-0	*El-Hussiny*
09/05	Britannia XI	W	8-0	*Caballero, Bado 2 (2p), King 4, Cuby*
18/05	Lions Gibraltar	D	1-1	*Sánchez*
23/05	College Europa	D	0-0	

No	Name	Nat	DoB	Pos	Aps	(s)	Gls
14	Mariano Abeleira	ARG	31/12/92	D		(1)	
26	Daniel Avalos	ESP	28/01/85	A	4	(5)	1
11	Rafael Bado		30/12/84	M	18	(2)	4
5	Mohamed Bilaa	ESP	08/03/83	M	1	(1)	
20	Ichor Borg		13/06/78	A	3	(1)	
15	Álvaro Caballero	ESP	06/01/87	D	12	(1)	2
13	Adrian Castro	ESP	17/12/90	M	5	(4)	
14	Alberto Castro	ESP	23/03/90	M	11		
25	Joshua Cuby		25/05/92	M	1	(15)	1
66	Vedad Džafić	BIH	19/02/89	D	6		
4	Mahmoud El-Hussiny	EGY	23/04/89	M	7		1
1	Christian Fraiz	ESP	22/02/88	G	20		
10	Sacha Funes	ITA	15/08/84	M	11	(8)	2
14	Geno Gaivizo		18/07/85	D	1		
18	Alonso García	ESP	18/06/88	G	1		
7	Gabriel Gonzalez		16/07/91	A	13	(5)	3
9	Robert Guiling		14/10/80	M	17		1
5	Victor Guirado	ESP	17/01/81	D	1	(2)	
88	Mohamed Hassan	EGY	25/11/89	M	1	(4)	1
6	Armin Helvida	BIH	20/02/86	D	11		2
20	Raducio King	NED	11/08/90	A	8	(1)	10
6	Daniel Mejías	ESP	31/07/88	D	4		
88	Javan Parody		06/04/88	D	1		
30	Jaydan Parody		08/05/98	M	1	(1)	1
3	Kailan Perez		22/08/88	D	19	(1)	
22	Fernando Ponce	ARG	23/07/92	D	7		1
88	Tyson Ruiz		10/03/88	M	8		1
2	Nicholas Rumbo		10/07/86	M		(2)	
8	Carlos Sánchez	ESP	28/12/87	M	18	(1)	2
22	Ethan Santos		22/12/98	D		(1)	
23	Kirill Trofimenko	RUS	19/12/96	M	2	(3)	2
19	Leonardo Vela	ITA	05/02/82	D	19		1

Manchester 62 FC

1962 • man62fc.com
Major honours
Gibraltar League (7) 1975, 1977, 1979, 1980, 1984, 1995, 1999; Gibraltar Cup (3) 1977, 1980, 2003
**Coach: Aaron Asquez;
(27/02/15) Juan Luis Pérez Herrera (ESP)**

2014
20/09	Lions Gibraltar	W	4-0	*J Lopez, Victory, Gines, Payas*
29/09	Lincoln	L	1-2	*og (J Chipolina)*
03/10	Lynx	L	0-1	
20/10	Britannia XI	W	5-2	*Morente, Gines 2, Isola, El Andaloussi*
25/10	College Europa	D	0-0	
31/10	Glacis	L	1-2	*og (Rodriguez)*
07/11	St Joseph's	L	0-2	
22/11	Lions Gibraltar	W	1-0	*J Lopez*
01/12	Lincoln	L	1-3	*Navarro*

2015
10/01	Lynx	D	1-1	*Anthony Hernandez (p)*
16/01	Britannia XI	W	1-0	*Gareth Lopez*
07/02	College Europa	D	1-1	*Gareth Lopez*
23/02	Glacis	W	1-0	*J Coombes*
05/03	St Joseph's	D	0-0	
21/03	Lions Gibraltar	W	1-0	*J Coombes*
11/04	Lincoln	L	1-4	*Anthony Hernandez*
17/04	Lynx	D	0-0	
02/05	Britannia XI	W	2-1	*Morente, J Coombes*
08/05	College Europa	L	0-3	
16/05	Glacis	D	1-1	*J Coombes*
22/05	St Joseph's	L	0-2	

No	Name	Nat	DoB	Pos	Aps	(s)	Gls
17	Leigh Adnett		10/11/86	M	1		
28	Julio Bado		03/06/83	M	1		
11	Scott Ballantine		12/04/96	M	8	(6)	
88	Bradley Banda		20/01/98	G	1		
41	Louie Barnfather Marfe		07/10/92	G	4	(1)	
20	Francisco Belmonte		15/07/85	D	8		
26	Shea Breakspear		22/11/91	D	13		
15	Miguel Coll	ESP	12/06/95	M	3		
23	Jamie Coombes		27/05/96	A	9		4
2	Lee Coombes		20/06/96	D	3	(1)	
4	Max Cottrell		15/09/99	M		(1)	
17	Liam Crisp		23/09/99	M		(1)	
1	Kevin De Los Santos		18/01/78	G	16		
69	Ernest De Torres		27/11/97	M		(1)	
10	Naoufal El Andaloussi		07/03/91	M	6	(5)	1
3	Philip Gillingwater Pedersen		16/01/99	D	1		
34	Sergio Gines	ESP	27/12/78	A	5	(1)	3
18	Francisco González	ESP	04/05/86	D		(1)	
5	Dion Hammond		18/08/94	D		(2)	
44	Andrew Hernandez		10/01/99	M	4	(7)	
32	Anthony Hernandez		03/02/95	M	2	(1)	2
14	Thomas Isola		1/01/96	M	10	(1)	1
35	Angelo Lavagna		23/02/95	M		(1)	
16	Gareth Lopez		18/02/86	M	5	(4)	2
31	Giles Lopez		29/06/92	A		(1)	
7	Jeremy Lopez		09/07/89	M	10	(6)	2
24	Kevin Martínez	ESP	21/10/93	D	4		
8	Estiven Morente		16/02/91	M	15		2
9	Álvaro Navarro	ESP	14/04/91	A	11	(4)	1
12	Aaron Payas		04/05/85	M	17	(1)	1
3	Ashley Perez		22/02/89	D	9	(2)	
80	Theo Pizarro		10/07/98	A	3	(4)	
29	Karl Poggio		08/06/98	M		(1)	
55	Jason Pusey		18/02/89	D	5	(1)	
4	Matthew Reoch		25/02/83	D	4	(1)	
30	Justin Rovegno		17/07/89	D	13	(1)	
33	Yogen Santos		15/01/85	D	8	(2)	
40	Leone Seatory		21/06/97	A	1		
6	Jack Sergeant		27/02/95	D	16		
13	Garry Turner-Bone	ENG	11/07/83	D		(1)	
66	Jesse Victory		02/04/96	M	15		1

St Joseph's FC

1912 • no website
Major honours
Gibraltar League (1) 1996; Gibraltar Cup (9) 1979, 1983, 1984, 1985, 1987, 1991, 1995, 2012, 2013
**Coach: Jerry Aguilera;
(11/03/15) Alfonso Cortijo Cabrera (ESP)**

2014
20/09	Britannia XI	W	2-1	*og (Zamboglou), Bezares (p)*
26/09	College Europa	L	0-1	
06/10	Glacis	W	5-1	*Romero 3, Bezares, Nieto*
27/10	Lions Gibraltar	W	4-0	*Bezares, Gutiérrez, Gómez (p), K Ruiz*
01/11	Lincoln	L	0-2	
07/11	Manchester 62	W	2-0	*Romero, Paz*
19/11	Lynx	D	0-0	
22/11	Britannia XI	W	4-0	*K Ruiz, Sanz, Romero, Santos*
29/11	College Europa	L	0-2	

2015
10/01	Glacis	W	4-0	*Romero, Segura, E Montes, Santos*
17/01	Lynx	L	1-2	*Sanz*
09/02	Lions Gibraltar	W	2-0	*Sanz, Acedo*
21/02	Lincoln	L	2-4	*Romero, Gómez*
05/03	Manchester 62	D	0-0	
21/03	Britannia XI	W	2-1	*Sanz, Romero*
10/04	College Europa	W	1-0	*E Montes*
20/04	Glacis	W	2-0	*og (Del Rio), Acedo*
04/05	Lynx	L	0-1	
09/05	Lions Gibraltar	W	2-1	*Acedo (p), V Ruiz*
16/05	Lincoln	L	1-2	*Romero*
22/05	Manchester 62	W	2-0	*Romero 2*

Name	Nat	DoB	Pos	Aps	(s)	Gls
Francisco Acedo	ESP	14/02/91	A	6	(3)	3
Juan Miguel Arguez	ESP	19/06/92	M	3	(3)	
Hugo Becerra	ESP	13/06/92	A		(2)	
Nicolas Bezares	ESP	02/08/87	A	6		3
Josue Castro	ESP	29/03/94	D	3	(1)	
James Currer		29/06/92	A		(3)	
Haitam Fakir Sellam	MAR	09/04/94	A		(1)	
Carlos Fernández	ESP	20/11/94	G	5	(1)	
Liam Franco		31/03/92	D	18		
Borja Gómez	ESP	13/08/92	A	9	(6)	2
Unai Gutiérrez	ESP	15/02/91	M	10	(5)	1
Iván Lobato	ESP	28/05/91	D	20		
Kaaron Macedo		27/03/84	G	9		
Francisco Márquez	ESP	09/04/84	M	20	(1)	
Carlos Méndez	ESP	23/06/87	D	1		
Esteban Montes	ESP	03/04/88	D	20		2
José Luis Montes	ESP	24/02/85	M	13	(3)	
Juan Morales	ESP	11/07/89	M		(5)	
Francisco Nieto	ESP	13/03/91	A		(2)	1
Jovan Ocaña		15/01/91	D	3	(1)	
Damián Paz	ESP	15/03/92	D	5		1
Giles Ramirez		16/02/90	D		(2)	
José Antonio Rico	ESP	21/10/86	G	7		
José Luis Romero	ESP	19/07/92	A	18	(1)	11
Kevin Ruiz	ESP	06/06/94	A	4	(3)	2
Víctor Ruiz	ESP	19/06/92	M	11		1
Nathan Santos		11/10/88	A	6	(8)	2
Juan Miguel Sanz	ESP	24/06/93	A	13	(3)	4
Raúl Segura	ESP	11/04/91	M	7	(3)	1
Federico Tobler	ITA	15/05/92	D	14	(1)	

 **GIBRALTAR**

Top goalscorers

18	Lee Casciaro (Lincoln)
14	Cristian Toncheff (College Europa)
13	Joseph Chipolina (Lincoln)
12	Liam Walker (Lincoln)
11	José Luis Romero (St Joseph's)
10	John Paul Duarte (Lincoln)
	Raducio King (Lynx)
8	Kyle Casciaro (Lincoln)
7	Juan Sebastián Pegalajar (College Europa)
6	Emmanuel Cristori (Lincoln)

Promoted clubs

Gibraltar United FC

1943 • gibraltarunitedfc.wordpress.com
Major honours
Gibraltar League (11) 1947, 1948, 1949, 1950, 1951, 1954, 1960, 1962, 1964, 1965, 2002; Gibraltar Cup (3) 1947, 2000, 2001
Coach: Randall Aldorino;
(24/02/15) Ian Mañasco

Angels FC

2014 • no website
Coach: Juan Fernández Molina (ESP)

Second level final table 2014/15

		Pld	W	D	L	F	A	Pts
1	Gibraltar United FC	26	21	3	2	99	15	66
2	Angels FC	26	21	2	3	76	20	65
3	Europa Point FC	26	20	3	3	123	20	63
4	Gibraltar Phoenix FC	26	16	3	7	66	43	51
5	Gibraltar Scorpions FC	26	16	2	8	95	33	50
6	Red Imps FC	26	12	4	10	56	57	40
7	FC Olympique 13	26	11	4	11	44	52	37
8	Mons Calpe SC	26	10	3	13	62	63	33
9	Bruno's Magpies FC	26	9	3	14	38	79	30
10	Boca Juniors Gibraltar FC	26	5	8	13	35	60	23
11	FC Hound Dogs	26	7	0	19	35	65	21
12	College Pegasus FC	26	6	2	18	29	84	20
13	Leo FC	26	4	5	17	35	92	17
14	Cannons FC	26	3	0	23	21	131	9

DOMESTIC CUP

Rock Cup 2014/15

SECOND ROUND

(30/01/15)
Lynx 5-0 Boca Juniors Gibraltar

(31/01/15)
College Europa 2-1 Manchester 62
Lions Gibraltar 2-0 Glacis

(02/02/15)
Gibraltar Utd 1-6 Lincoln

(27/02/15)
Red Imps 0-3 Gibraltar Scorpions *(w/o)*

(28/02/15)
Angels 0-2 Britannia XI
St Joseph's 3-0 Bruno's Magpies *(w/o)*

(02/03/15)
Europa Point 5-0 Gibraltar Phoenix

QUARTER-FINALS

(13/03/15)
St Joseph's 2-1 Lions Gibraltar *(Santos 31, Sanz 63; Sansolini 51)*

(14/03/15)
Britannia XI 2-0 Gibraltar Scorpions *(Guerra 50, Nixon 78)*

Europa Point 1-2 Lynx *(Villegas 63; Sánchez 25, Bado 86)*

(15/03/15)
College Europa 0-1 Lincoln *(Walker 89)*

SEMI-FINALS

(25/04/15)
Britannia XI 1-2 Lynx *(Renan Bernardes 88; Bado 31p, 60p)*

Lincoln 2-0 St Joseph's *(Cristori 112, 120) (aet)*

FINAL

(30/05/15)
Victoria Stadium, Gibraltar
LINCOLN FC 4 *(JP Duarte 9, 18, Walker 78, 89)*
LYNX FC 1 *(Vela 4)*
Referee: *Borg*
LINCOLN: *Navas, Sambruno, R Chipolina, R Casciaro, J Chipolina, Mejías, Bardon, Walker, K Casciaro (Cristori 58), JP Duarte (Garcia 75), L Casciaro (Iglecias 82)*
LYNX: *Fraiz, Perez (Trofimenko 75), El-Hussiny, Caballero, Vela, Helvida, Sánchez, Guiling (King 63), Bado, Alberto Castro, Gonzalez (Cuby 57)*

Lincoln players in familiar pose with the Rock Cup

GREECE
Ellinikos Podosfairikos Omospondia (EPO)

Address   Goudi Park
          PO Box 14161
          GR-11510 Athens
Tel   +30 210 930 6000
Fax   +30 210 935 9666
E-mail   epo@epo.gr
Website   epo.gr

President   Georgios Girtzikis
General secretary Pafsanias
                  Papanikolaou
Media officer   Michalis Tsapidis
Year of formation 1926
National stadium Georgios Karaiskakis,
                  Piraeus (32,130)

SUPERLEAGUE CLUBS

  **1** Asteras Tripolis FC

  2 Atromitos FC

  3 Ergotelis FC

 4 Kalloni FC

 5 Kerkyra FC

 6 Levadiakos FC

 7 Niki Volou FC

 8 OFI Crete FC

 9 Olympiacos FC

 10 Panathinaikos FC

 11 Panetolikos GFS

 12 Panionios GSS

 13 Panthrakikos FC

 14 PAOK FC

 15 PAS Giannina FC

 16 Platanias FC

 17 Veria FC

 18 Xanthi FC

PROMOTED CLUBS

  **19** AEK Athens FC

20 Iraklis FC

KEY:

● – UEFA Champions League
● – UEFA Europa League
● – Promoted
● – Relegated

Olympiacos out of reach

There was yet more silverware to add to Olympiacos FC's copious trophy collection in 2014/15 as the perennial champions from Piraeus not only retained the Superleague title – their 42nd triumph – but also reclaimed the Greek Cup, which they lifted for the 27th time to complete a 17th domestic double.

PAOK FC led the league in the autumn before falling apart in the spring, which left Panathinaikos FC to take second place after the end-of-season play-offs. The Greek national team suffered complete meltdown in the UEFA EURO 2016 qualifiers, with a place in France practically out of reach after just six matches.

| **Spring surge carries Piraeus club to 42nd title** | **Cup final win against Xanthi completes 17th double** | **Horror show for national team in EURO qualifiers** |

Domestic league

When PAOK, 30 years without a championship title, defeated Olympiacos 2-1 in Piraeus in early December to move five points clear at the top of the Superleague table, the prospects of a thrilling title race, perhaps even of a major upset, were genuine. But the pressure of providing a concerted challenge to Olympiacos's omnipotence was to prove too much for Angelos Anastasiadis's side. Victory in the Georgios Karaiskakis stadium was followed by a complete loss of away form, and by the time the title holders visited the Toumbas stadium two months later – with a new coach, Vítor Pereira having replaced Míchel – PAOK had not just lost the lead but fallen eight points behind.

A goalless draw left the status quo unchanged, and PAOK's subsequent 4-0 defeat at Atromitos FC extinguished their title hopes altogether. Olympiacos were not quite in the clear yet, however, as while they had been compiling a lengthy unbeaten run, so too had Panathinaikos. Going into the big derby, in Pana's Apostolos Nikolaidis stadium, Olympiacos held a six-point lead, and although they were to lose the game 2-1, major incidents on and off the pitch led to a three-point punishment for the home side. The disturbances at the game were so grave, in fact, that the Superleague was suspended for a week, and when Panathinaikos beat

PAOK 4-3 in their next home game, they did so in an empty stadium.

Olympiacos were experienced and confident frontrunners, and when Panathinaikos succumbed to a third away defeat on the trot, at Panthrakikos FC, on the afternoon of 19 April, the title race was over. Later the same day Olympiacos treated their celebrating fans to a 4-0 win over Levadiakos FC, inspirational playmaker Alejandro Domínguez leading the way with a double.

Panathinaikos edged PAOK to finish second in a Superleague distorted by the premature exclusions of Niki Volou FC – after 14 games – and OFI Crete FC – after 28. Ioannis Anastasiou's side also topped the UEFA Champions League qualification standings, leaving UEFA Europa League places for the other three participants – Asteras Tripolis FC, who supplied the Superleague's leading marksman in 17-goal Jerónimo Barrales, Atromitos, unbeaten at home all season, and PAOK. The other post-season play-offs, to determine promotion, brought a welcome return to the elite for AEK Athens FC and Iraklis FC.

Domestic cup

Five weeks after clinching the Superleague title, Olympiacos completed the double with a 3-1 win against first-time cup finalists Xanthi FC. Again

Domínguez was the star of the show, capping a vintage display with a brilliant solo goal.

Europe

Olympiacos's UEFA Champions League campaign had a familiar storyline as they won all three home games but picked up no points on their travels, ultimately dropping into the UEFA Europa League, where they fell at the first hurdle. PAOK, Panathinaikos, Asteras Tripolis and Atromitos all departed the UEFA Europa League before Olympiacos arrived, with the first three reaching the group stage.

National team

A penalty shoot-out away from the quarter-finals of the 2014 FIFA World Cup, the Greek national team suffered a sharp and severe decline to end the season with virtually no hope of stretching their sequence of successive major tournament qualifications to five.

A pitiful return of just two points and two goals from six games left the 2004 European champions not just bottom of their group but also having to deal with the embarrassment of being defeated home and away by the Faroe Islands – 1-0 in Piraeus under new coach Claudio Ranieri, which cost the Italian his job, then 2-1 in Torshavn under his replacement, Sergio Markarián.

DOMESTIC SEASON AT A GLANCE

Superleague 2014/15 final table

		Pld	Home					Away					Total					Pts
			W	D	L	F	A	W	D	L	F	A	W	D	L	F	A	
1	**Olympiacos FC**	34	15	1	1	45	8	9	5	3	34	15	24	6	4	79	23	78
2	Panathinaikos FC	34	15	1	1	38	11	6	5	6	21	20	21	6	7	59	31	66
3	PAOK FC	34	11	4	2	30	14	9	1	7	27	28	20	5	9	57	42	65
4	Asteras Tripolis FC	34	13	4	0	33	9	4	4	9	19	28	17	8	9	52	37	59
5	Atromitos FC	34	12	5	0	30	7	2	7	8	13	20	14	12	8	43	27	54
6	PAS Giannina FC	34	9	6	2	29	15	4	8	5	18	18	13	14	7	47	33	53
7	Panetolikos GFS	34	10	3	4	29	11	4	7	6	12	17	14	10	10	41	28	52
8	Xanthi FC	34	8	7	2	25	14	4	4	9	19	27	12	11	11	44	41	47
9	Platanias FC	34	8	4	5	20	16	4	4	9	12	14	12	8	14	32	30	44
10	Kerkyra FC	34	9	4	4	26	14	3	4	10	13	24	12	8	14	39	38	44
11	Kalloni FC	34	10	5	2	23	11	1	6	10	11	28	11	11	12	34	39	44
12	Panthrakikos FC	34	9	7	1	22	11	2	3	12	13	33	11	10	13	35	44	43
13	Panionios GSS	34	8	7	2	24	15	3	3	11	19	27	11	10	13	43	42	43
14	Veria FC	34	9	3	5	28	19	3	4	10	17	35	12	7	15	45	54	43
15	Levadiakos FC	34	6	5	6	24	18	6	2	9	17	16	12	7	15	41	34	43
16	Ergotelis FC	34	4	4	9	22	33	4	4	9	13	27	8	8	18	35	60	32
17	OFI Crete FC	34	6	1	10	17	27	1	1	15	9	45	7	2	25	26	72	-6
18	Niki Volou FC	34	2	1	14	4	37	0	0	17	3	47	2	1	31	7	84	-6

NB OFI Crete FC – 29 pts deducted; Niki Volou FC – 13pts deducted; Panathinaikos FC – 3 pts deducted; Niki Volou FC withdrew after 14 matches; OFI Crete FC withdrew after 28 matches – their remaining matches were awarded as 0-3 defeats.
UEFA Champions League qualification play-offs are on page 396.

European qualification 2015/16

 Champion/Cup winner: Olympiacos FC (group stage)
Panathinaikos FC (third qualifying round)

 Asteras Tripolis FC (group stage)
Atromitos FC (third qualifying round)
PAOK FC (second qualifying round)

Top scorer	Jerónimo Barrales (Asteras), 17 goals
Relegated clubs	Niki Volou FC, OFI Crete FC, Ergotelis FC, Levadiakos FC
Promoted clubs	AEK Athens FC, Iraklis FC
Cup final	Olympiacos FC 3-1 Xanthi FC

Team of the season
(4-1-3-2)

Coach: Vergetis (Asteras)

Roberto (Olympiacos)
Elabdellaoui (Olympiacos) Schildenfeld (Panathinaikos) M'Bow (Panthrakikos) Masuaku (Olympiacos)
Tzandaris (PAOK)
Martínez (Panetolikos) Domínguez (Olympiacos) Kolovos (Panionios)
Mitroglou (Olympiacos) Barrales (Asteras)

Player of the season

Alejandro Domínguez
(Olympiacos FC)

Once a leading performer in Russia, at FC Zenit and FC Rubin Kazan, Domínguez illuminated the Greek Superleague with his array of skills in 2014/15. His second season at Olympiacos was an absolute triumph as he produced, at 33, arguably the most consistent football of his career. 'Chori' chalked up 15 goals and 11 assists in the league to help his team claim a 17th title in 19 years, and he was voted man of the match in the Greek Cup final, in which Olympiacos beat Xanthi FC 3-1 to complete the double.

Newcomer of the season

Nikolaos Karelis
(Panathinaikos FC)

A goalscorer for Panathinaikos in the 2014 Greek Cup final, in which his strike partner Marcus Berg hit a hat-trick, Karelis matched the Swede as the star of the Greens' attack in 2014/15. Both players struck 13 league goals and another three in the UEFA Champions League qualification series, with the Greek international also finding the net for his country on his senior debut – in a UEFA EURO 2016 qualifier against Finland. Quick and powerful, the 23-year-old looks set for a bright future.

NATIONAL TEAM

International honours
UEFA European Championship (1) 2004

International tournament appearances
FIFA World Cup (3) 1994, 2010, 2014 (2nd round)

UEFA European Championship (4) 1980, 2004 (Winners), 2008, 2012 (qtr-finals)

Top five all-time caps
Georgios Karagounis (139); Theodoros Zagorakis (120); **Kostas Katsouranis** (116); Angelos Basinas (100); Efstratios Apostolakis (96)

Top five all-time goals
Nikolaos Anastopoulos (29); Angelos Charisteas (25); **Theofanis Gekas** (24); Dimitrios Saravakos (22); Dimitrios "Mimis" Papaioannou (20)

Results 2014/15

07/09/14	Romania (ECQ)	H	Piraeus	L	0-1	
11/10/14	Finland (ECQ)	A	Helsinki	D	1-1	*Karelis (24)*
14/10/14	Northern Ireland (ECQ)	H	Piraeus	L	0-2	
14/11/14	Faroe Islands (ECQ)	H	Piraeus	L	0-1	
18/11/14	Serbia	H	Chania	L	0-2	
29/03/15	Hungary (ECQ)	A	Budapest	D	0-0	
13/06/15	Faroe Islands (ECQ)	A	Torshavn	L	1-2	*Papastathopoulos (84)*
16/06/15	Poland	A	Gdansk	D	0-0	

Appearances 2014/15

Coach: Claudio Ranieri (ITA) 20/10/51 /(15/11/14) (Kostas Tsanas) 22/08/67 /(12/02/15) Sergio Markarián (URU) 01/11/44			ROU	FIN	NIR	FRO	Srb	HUN	FRO	Pol	Caps	Goals
Orestis Karnezis	11/07/85	Udinese (ITA)	G	G	G	G		G	G		29	-
Vasilios Torosidis	10/06/85	Roma (ITA)	D	D	D	D	D61	D	D		77	7
Kostas Manolas	14/06/91	Roma (ITA)	D	D	D	D	D73	D	D		20	-
Sokratis Papastathopoulos	09/06/88	Dortmund (GER)	D	D	D			D	D	D46	57	2
José Holebas	27/06/84	Roma (ITA)	D								27	1
Andreas Samaris	13/06/89	Benfica (POR)	M65	M	s46	M	M79	M	M	s90	14	1
Panagiotis Tachtsidis	15/02/91	Verona (ITA)	M	M	M					M	10	-
Petros Mantalos	31/08/91	AEK	M65			s78	s79				3	-
Georgios Samaras	21/02/85	West Brom (ENG)	A46	s81	M67						81	9
Kostas Mitroglou	12/03/88	Olympiacos	A	s84	A				A	s60	40	8
Dimitrios Salpingidis	18/08/81	PAOK	A		s67						82	13
Dimitrios Diamantakos	05/03/93	Olympiacos	s46								1	-
Panagiotis Kone	26/07/87	Udinese (ITA)	s65			M	M64	M77	M81		24	1
Lazaros Christodoulopoulos	19/12/86	Verona (ITA)	s65			A	A	A69	M46		26	1
Loukas Vyntra	05/02/81	Levante (ESP)		D	D16		D			D	54	-
Ioannis Maniatis	12/10/86	Olympiacos		M	M	M	M				38	-
Charalambos Mavrias	21/02/94	Sunderland (ENG)		M70		s62	M71				5	-
Nikolaos Karelis	24/02/92	Panathinaikos		A81	A	A62			A	A60	5	1
Stefanos Athanasiadis	24/12/88	PAOK		A84	A46	s46	A64	A			11	-
Vangelis Moras	26/08/81	Verona (ITA)		s70		D	s73			D	23	-
Kostas Stafylidis	02/12/93	Fulham (ENG)			s16			D	D	D	5	-
Nikolaos Karabelas	20/12/84	Levante (ESP)				D78					1	-
Theofanis Gekas	23/05/80	Akhisar (TUR)				A46	s64				78	24
Panagiotis Glykos	10/10/86	PAOK					G				4	-
Avraam Papadopoulos	03/12/84	Trabzonspor (TUR)					D				37	-
Mihail Bakakis	18/03/91	AEK					s61				1	-
Alexandros Tziolis	13/02/85	PAOK					s64			M	51	1
Dimitrios Kolovos	27/04/93	Panionios					s71		s71	s77	3	-
Kyriakos Papadopoulos	23/02/92	Leverkusen (GER)						M			17	4
Ioannis Fetfatzidis	21/12/90	Chievo (ITA)						A77	A71	s71	24	3
Kostas Fortounis	16/10/92	Olympiacos						s69			13	-
Kostas Katsouranis	21/06/79	Atromitos						s77		M90	116	10
Ioannis Gianniotas	29/04/93	Asteras						s77			1	-
Sotirios Ninis	03/04/90	Panathinaikos							s46	M71	33	3
Taxiarhis Fountas	04/09/95	Panionios							s81	M77	2	-
Stefanos Kapino	18/03/94	Mainz (GER)								G92	3	-
Efstathios Tavlaridis	25/01/80	Panathinaikos								s46	3	-
Markos Vellidis	04/04/87	Giannina								s92	1	-

EUROPE

Olympiacos FC

Group A
Match 1 - Club Atlético de Madrid (ESP)
H 3-2 *Masuaku (13), Afellay (31), Mitroglou (73)*
Roberto, Maniatis, Botía, Milivojević, Afellay (N'Dinga 69), Mitroglou, Domínguez (David Fuster 57), Kasami (Giannoulis 84), Elabdellaoui, Abidal, Masuaku. Coach: Míchel (ESP)
Match 2 - Malmö FF (SWE)
A 0-2
Roberto, Maniatis, Botía, Milivojević, Afellay (Diamantakos 79), Mitroglou, N'Dinga (Domínguez 57), Kasami (Durmaz 69), Elabdellaoui, Abidal, Masuaku. Coach: Míchel (ESP)
Match 3 - Juventus (ITA)
H 1-0 *Kasami (36)*
Roberto, Maniatis, Botía, Milivojević, Mitroglou (Afellay 69), N'Dinga, Domínguez (David Fuster 85), Kasami (Giannoulis 90+1), Elabdellaoui, Abidal, Masuaku. Coach: Míchel (ESP)
Match 4 - Juventus (ITA)
A 2-3 *Botía (24), N'Dinga (61)*
Roberto, Maniatis (Diamantakos 83), Botía, Milivojević, Afellay, Mitroglou, N'Dinga (Kasami 77), Domínguez (David Fuster 72), Elabdellaoui, Abidal, Masuaku. Coach: Míchel (ESP)
Match 5 - Club Atlético de Madrid (ESP)
A 0-4
Roberto, Maniatis (David Fuster 46), Botía, Milivojević, Afellay (Kasami 46), Mitroglou, N'Dinga, Domínguez (Bouhalakis 72), Elabdellaoui, Abidal, Masuaku. Coach: Míchel (ESP)
Match 6 - Malmö FF (SWE)
H 4-2 *David Fuster (22), Domínguez (63), Mitroglou (87), Afellay (90)*
Roberto, Maniatis, Botía, Mitroglou (Benítez 88), N'Dinga, Domínguez (Siovas 90), Kasami, Elabdellaoui, David Fuster (Afellay 77), Abidal, Masuaku. Coach: Míchel (ESP)

Round of 32 - FC Dnipro Dnipropetrovsk (UKR)
A 0-2
Roberto, Maniatis, Afellay, Mitroglou, Domínguez (Fortounis 57), Kasami, Elabdellaoui, Siovas, Masuaku, Felipe Santana (Milivojević 57), Dossevi (Durmaz 71). Coach: Vítor Pereira (POR)
H 2-2 *Mitroglou (14), Domínguez (90p)*
Roberto, Milivojević, Afellay (Fortounis 65), Mitroglou, Durmaz (Dossevi 65), Domínguez, Kasami, Elabdellaoui, Siovas, Masuaku, Felipe Santana. Coach: Vítor Pereira (POR)
Red card: Milivojević 51

Panathinaikos FC

Third qualifying round - R Standard de Liège (BEL)
A 0-0
Kotsolis, Koutroumbis, Triantafyllopoulos, Mendes da Silva (Karelis 71), Lagos, Berg, Zeca, Ajagun (Klonaridis 85), Nano, Schildenfeld, Petrić (Pranjić 64). Coach: Ioannis Anastasiou (GRE)
H 1-2 *Arslanagic (17og)*
Kotsolis, Koutroumbis, Triantafyllopoulos, Mendes da Silva (Karelis 56), Berg, Zeca, Ajagun, Nano, Schildenfeld, Pranjić, Petrić (Klonaridis 56; Dinas 65). Coach: Ioannis Anastasiou (GRE)

Play-offs - FC Midtjylland (DEN)
H 4-1 *Berg (21p, 24, 45, 89)*
Kotsolis, Triantafyllopoulos, Mendes da Silva, Lagos (Bouy 78), Berg, Zeca, Karelis (Petrić 78), Nano, Schildenfeld, Dinas (Ajagun 67), Pranjić. Coach: Ioannis Anastasiou (GRE)
Red card: Triantafyllopoulos 81
A 2-1 *Nano (55), Klonaridis (74)*
Kotsolis, Mendes da Silva (Donis 79), Lagos (Bouy 60), Zeca, Ajagun, Karelis (Klonaridis 66), Nano, Schildenfeld, Risvanis, Bourbos, Pranjić. Coach: Ioannis Anastasiou (GRE)

Group E
Match 1 - FC Dinamo Moskva (RUS)
H 1-2 *Dinas (63)*
Kotsolis, Triantafyllopoulos, Mendes da Silva, Klonaridis (Donis 58), Lagos (Petrić 75), Zeca, Karelis, Nano, Schildenfeld, Dinas, Pranjić (Koutroumbis 80). Coach: Ioannis Anastasiou (GRE)
Match 2 - Estoril Praia (POR)
A 0-2
Kotsolis, Triantafyllopoulos, Zeca, Bajrami (Karelis 46), Ajagun, Nano, Schildenfeld, Dinas (Donis 56), Bourbos, Pranjić (Lagos 75), Petrić. Coach: Ioannis Anastasiou (GRE)
Match 3 - PSV Eindhoven (NED)
A 1-1 *Karelis (87)*
Steele, Koutroumbis, Triantafyllopoulos, Klonaridis (Petrić 75), Zeca, Donis, Nano, Bouy, Schildenfeld, Dinas (Ajagun 24), Pranjić (Karelis 60). Coach: Ioannis Anastasiou (GRE)
Match 4 - PSV Eindhoven (NED)
H 2-3 *Ajagun (11), Petric (43)*
Steele, Triantafyllopoulos, Mendes da Silva, Lagos (Donis 44), Zeca, Karelis (Bouy 72), Karelis, Nano, Schildenfeld, Pranjić, Petrić (Berg 63). Coach: Ioannis Anastasiou (GRE)
Match 5 - FC Dinamo Moskva (RUS)
A 1-2 *Berg (14)*
Kotsolis, Triantafyllopoulos, Mendes da Silva (Pranjić 86), Lagos, Berg (Klonaridis 78), Bajrami, Donis, Nano, Schildenfeld, Bourbos (Koutroumbis 56), Petrić. Coach: Ioannis Anastasiou (GRE)
Match 6 - Estoril Praia (POR)
H 1-1 *Karelis (55)*
Steele, Chouchoumis, Koutroumbis, Lagos, Ajagun (Pranjić 60), Donis, Karelis, Bouy, Risvanis, Dinas (Berg 68), Bourbos (Triantafyllopoulos 28). Coach: Ioannis Anastasiou (GRE)

PAOK FC

Play-offs - FC Zimbru Chisinau (MDA)
A 0-1
Glykos, Skondras, Katsikas, Raţ, Tziolis (Pereyra 67), Maduro, Mak (Martens 67), Salpingidis, Kaçe, Athanasiadis, Kitsiou (Spyropoulos 79). Coach: Angelos Anastasiadis (GRE)
H 4-0 *Pereyra (11), Athanasiadis (45), Mak (79), Martens (84)*
Glykos, Skondras, Tzavellas, Raţ, Tziolis, Maduro (Kaçe 52), Pereyra, Mak (Pozoglou 83), Salpingidis (Martens 62), Athanasiadis, Kitsiou. Coach: Angelos Anastasiadis (GRE)

Group K
Match 1 - FC Dinamo Minsk (BLR)
H 6-1 *Nikolić (3og), Athanasiadis (11, 16, 28), Papadopoulos (50), Tzandaris (90)*
Glykos, Skondras, Katsikas, Raţ (Spyropoulos 72), Tziolis, Mak (Papadopoulos 46), Salpingidis, Miguel Vítor, Kaçe, Tzandaris, Athanasiadis (Golasa 67). Coach: Angelos Anastasiadis (GRE)
Match 2 - EA Guingamp (FRA)
A 0-2
Glykos, Skondras (Golasa 75), Katsikas, Raţ, Tziolis (Martens 55), Mak (Papadopoulos 63), Salpingidis, Miguel Vítor, Kaçe, Tzandaris, Athanasiadis. Coach: Angelos Anastasiadis (GRE)
Match 3 - ACF Fiorentina (ITA)
H 0-1
Glykos, Skondras (Kitsiou 11), Katsikas, Raţ, Tziolis, Pereyra (Golasa 54), Salpingidis (Papadopoulos 80), Miguel Vítor, Kaçe, Tzandaris, Athanasiadis. Coach: Angelos Anastasiadis (GRE)
Match 4 - ACF Fiorentina (ITA)
A 1-1 *Martens (81)*
Glykos, Katsikas, Tziolis, Golasa, Pereyra (Maduro 46), Salpingidis (Martens 71), Miguel Vitor, Spyropoulos (Tzavellas 90), Tzandaris, Athanasiadis, Kitsiou. Coach: Angelos Anastasiadis (GRE)
Match 5 - FC Dinamo Minsk (BLR)
A 2-0 *Athanasiadis (82, 88)*
Glykos, Skondras, Katsikas (Tzavellas 28), Raţ, Tziolis, Pereyra, Salpingidis (Golasa 46), Miguel Vítor, Kaçe, Tzandaris, Athanasiadis (Papadopoulos 89). Coach: Angelos Anastasiadis (GRE)
Match 6 - EA Guingamp (FRA)
H 1-2 *Athanasiadis (22p)*
Glykos, Skondras, Tzavellas, Raţ, Golasa (Martens 53), Pereyra (Papadopoulos 61), Salpingidis, Miguel Vitor, Kaçe (Maduro 77), Tzandaris, Athanasiadis. Coach: Angelos Anastasiadis (GRE)

Atromitos FC

Third qualifying round - FK Sarajevo (BIH)
A 2-1 *Fitanidis (11), Nastos (75)*
Cennamo, Tavlaridis, Fytanidis, Eduardo Brito (Fábio 68), Napoleoni (Tatos 61), Nastos, Giannoulis, Karamanos, Dimoutsos (Ballas 90+2), Lazaridis, Pitu. Coach: Georgios Parashos (GRE)
H 1-3 *Tavlaridis (86)*
Cennamo, Tavlaridis, Fytanidis, Eduardo Brito (Ballas 75), Nastos (Napoleoni 65), Fábio (Tatos 46), Giannoulis, Karamanos, Dimoutsos, Lazaridis, Pitu. Coach: Georgios Parashos (GRE)

DOMESTIC LEAGUE CLUB-BY-CLUB

Asteras Tripolis FC

Second qualifying round - RoPS Rovaniemi (FIN)
A 1-1 *Sankaré (10)*
Bantis, Panteliadis, Usero, Barrales, Rolle (Munafo 73), Bakasetas (Badibanga 65), Sankaré, Kourbelis, Lluy, Goian, De Blasis (Zisopoulos 90+3). Coach: Staikos Vergetis (GRE)
H 4-2 *Kourbelis (12), De Blasis (45+6p, 73), Bakasetas (81)*
Bantis, Panteliadis, Mazza (Munafo 75), Usero, Barrales (Badibanga 69), Rolle, Sankaré, Kourbelis (Bakasetas 72), Lluy, Goian, De Blasis. Coach: Staikos Vergetis (GRE)

Third qualifying round – 1. FSV Mainz 05 (GER)
A 0-1
Theodoropoulos, Panteliadis, Munafo (Tsokanis 72), Mazza, Rolle (Sankaré 64), Zisopoulos, Kourbelis, Lluy, De Blasis, Badibanga (Kitoko 81). Coach: Staikos Vergetis (GRE)
H 3-1 *De Blasis (30), Mazza (68, 86)*
Theodoropoulos, Panteliadis (Sankaré 83), Munafo (Bakasetas 59), Mazza, Rolle, Zisopoulos, Kourbelis, Lluy, Goian, De Blasis, Badibanga (Usero 29). Coach: Staikos Vergetis (GRE)

Play-offs - Maccabi Tel-Aviv FC (ISR)
H 2-0 *Mazza (29), Zisopoulos (47)*
Theodoropoulos, Panteliadis, Munafo, Mazza, Barrales 79), Usero, Rolle, Sankaré (Tié Bi 88), Goian, De Blasis. Coach: Staikos Vergetis (GRE)
A 1-3 *Goian (23)*
Theodoropoulos, Panteliadis, Munafo, Mazza, Tié Bi 59), Usero, Rolle, Sankaré (Sankaré 77), Zisopoulos, Kourbelis, Lluy, Goian, De Blasis (Parra 86). Coach: Staikos Vergetis (GRE)

Group C
Match 1 - Beşiktaş JK (TUR)
A 1-1 *Parra (88)*
Košický, Panteliadis (Munafo 76), Mazza, Usero, Barrales (Gianniotas 85), Rolle, Zisopoulos, Sankaré, Lluy, Goian, Badibanga (Parra 69). Coach: Staikos Vergetis (GRE)
Match 2 - FK Partizan (SRB)
H 2-0 *Usero (22), Parra (52)*
Košický, Panteliadis, Mazza, Usero, Rolle (Munafo 90), Zisopoulos, Sankaré, Parra (Barrales 59), Lluy, Goian, Gianniotas (Kitoko 73). Coach: Staikos Vergetis (GRE)
Match 3 - Tottenham Hotspur FC (ENG)
A 1-5 *Barrales (89)*
Košický, Panteliadis, Munafo, Mazza (Bakasetas 82), Usero, Rolle (Barrales 73), Zisopoulos, Sankaré, Tsokanis, Parra (Fernández 80), Lluy. Coach: Staikos Vergetis (GRE)
Match 4 - Tottenham Hotspur FC (ENG)
H 1-2 *Barrales (90p)*
Košický, Panteliadis, Munafo (Gianniotas 81), Mazza, Usero, Rolle, Zisopoulos, Sankaré, Tsokanis (Badibanga 60), Parra (Barrales 84), Lluy. Coach: Staikos Vergetis (GRE)
Match 5 - Beşiktaş JK (TUR)
H 2-2 *Barrales (72), Parra (83)*
Košický, Panteliadis, Mazza, Fernández (Bakasetas 77), Zisopoulos, Sankaré, Parra, Kourbelis (Usero 62), Lluy, Goian, Gianniotas (Barrales 46). Coach: Staikos Vergetis (GRE)
Match 6 - FK Partizan (SRB)
A 0-0
Theodoropoulos, Panteliadis, Tié Bi (Mazza 75), Munafo, Barrales, Zisopoulos, Bakasetas (Badibanga 72), Sankaré, Tsokanis, Lluy, Gianniotas (Fernández 63). Coach: Staikos Vergetis (GRE)

Asteras Tripolis FC

1931 • Theodoros Kolokotronis (7,493) • asterastripolis.gr
Coach: Staikos Vergetis

2014
24/08	a	Giannina	L	1-3	*Barrales*
31/08	h	Levadiakos	W	2-1	*Rolle 2*
14/09	a	Panionios	L	1-2	*Parra*
21/09	h	Kalloni	W	1-0	*Mazza*
27/09	a	Platanias	W	1-0	*Barrales*
18/10	h	Panetolikos	D	1-1	*Barrales*
26/10	a	OFI	W	3-2	*Usero (p), Mazza, Tsokanis*
01/11	h	Olympiacos	D	0-0	
10/11	a	Atromitos	L	3-4	*Parra (p), Barrales, Fernández*
30/11	h	Ergotelis	W	4-1	*Barrales (p), Fernández, Gianniotas, Parra*
04/12	a	Niki Volou	W	2-0	*Bakasetas, Mazza*
07/12	h	Panathinaikos	D	1-1	*Sankaré*
14/12	a	Veria	W	2-0	*Mazza, Barrales*
17/12	a	Panthrakikos	D	1-1	*Goian*
21/12	h	Xanthi	W	2-1	*Gianniotas, Mazza*

2015
03/01	a	Kerkyra	L	0-1	
10/01	h	PAOK	W	3-0	*Gianniotas 2, Sankaré*
14/01	a	Giannina	D	2-2	*Rolle, Barrales*
18/01	a	Levadiakos	L	1-3	*Barrales*
24/01	h	Panionios	W	2-0	*Sankaré, Barrales*
31/01	a	Kalloni	L	0-1	
04/02	h	Platanias	W	1-0	*Iglesias*
08/02	h	Niki Volou	W	3-0	*(w/o)*
14/02	a	Panetolikos	L	0-2	
22/02	h	OFI	W	6-1	*Barrales 3, Mazza 2, Parra*
07/03	a	Atromitos	W	1-0	*Barrales*
14/03	a	PAOK	D	0-0	
19/03	a	Olympiacos	L	0-2	
22/03	h	Ergotelis	W	2-1	*Kourbelis, Barrales (p)*
04/04	a	Panathinaikos	D	2-2	*Barrales 2 (1p)*
20/04	a	Veria	L	0-4	
26/04	h	Panthrakikos	W	2-1	*Barrales, Rolle*
03/05	a	Xanthi	D	0-0	
10/05	h	Kerkyra	W	2-0	*Parra, Fernández*

No	Name	Nat	DoB	Pos	Aps	(s)	Gls
6	Fernando Alloco	ARG	30/04/86	D	3	(3)	
39	Ziguy Badibanga	BEL	26/11/91	A	3	(7)	
14	Anastasios Bakasetas		28/06/93	A	3	(5)	1
9	Jerónimo Barrales	ARG	28/01/87	A	22	(5)	17
86	Ederson	BRA	14/01/86	M		(2)	
11	Nicolás Fernández	ARG	17/11/86	M	9	(11)	3
70	Ioannis Gianniotas		29/04/93	A	21	(6)	4
30	Dorin Goian	ROU	12/12/80	D	22		1
62	Walter Iglesias	ARG	18/04/85	M	11	(1)	1
77	Georgios Kiriakopoulos		05/02/96	D		(1)	
17	Ritchie Kitoko	BEL	11/06/88	M	2		
1	Tomáš Košický	SVK	11/03/86	G	20		
25	Dimitrios Kourbelis		02/11/93	D	16	(6)	1
27	Braian Lluy	ARG	25/04/89	D	31		
20	Cristian Lobato	ESP	07/03/89	M	2	(1)	
7	Pablo Mazza	ARG	21/12/87	A	30		7
94	Hervaine Moukam	FRA	24/05/94	M		(5)	
17	Juan Munafo	ARG	20/03/83	M	23	(8)	
8	Athanasios Panteliadis		06/09/87	D	18	(3)	
93	Anastasios Papachristos		05/03/93	D	1	(1)	
23	Facundo Parra	ARG	15/06/85	A	13	(11)	5
10	Martín Rolle	ARG	02/02/85	M	23	(2)	4
15	Khalifa Sankaré	SEN	15/08/84	D	23		3
12	Vasil Shkurtaj	ALB	27/02/92	A	2	(1)	
21	Konstantinos Theodoropoulos		27/03/90	G	13		
4	Éric Tié Bi	CIV	20/07/90	M	8	(4)	
24	Anastasios Tsokanis		02/05/91	M	15	(7)	1
8	Fernando Usero	ESP	27/03/84	M	8	(1)	1
13	Georgios Zisopoulos		23/05/84	M	21	(1)	

Atromitos FC

1923 • Dimotiko Peristeriou (9,000) • atromitosfc.gr
Coach: Georgios Parashos; (24/09/14) Ricardo Sá Pinto (POR); (05/02/15) Georgios Korakakis); (09/02/15) Nikos Nioplias

2014
24/08	h	Platanias	W	1-0	*Papazoglou*
31/08	a	Niki Volou	W	1-0	*Fitanidis*
14/09	h	Panetolikos	D	0-0	
20/09	a	OFI	L	0-1	
27/09	h	Olympiacos	W	1-0	*Karamanos*
19/10	a	PAOK	L	1-2	*Umbides*
25/10	h	Ergotelis	D	1-1	*Lazaridis*
02/11	a	Panathinaikos	L	0-2	
10/11	h	Asteras	W	4-3	*Karamanos, Napoleoni 3*
29/11	h	Xanthi	W	2-0	*Umbides 2*
03/12	a	Veria	D	0-0	
06/12	a	Kerkyra	D	1-1	*Lazaridis*
14/12	a	Giannina	L	0-1	
17/12	h	Levadiakos	W	1-0	*Papazoglou*
21/12	a	Panionios	D	2-2	*Napoleoni 2*

2015
04/01	h	Kalloni	D	0-0	
11/01	h	Panthrakikos	D	1-1	*Papazoglou*
15/01	a	Platanias	D	0-0	
18/01	h	Niki Volou	W	3-0	*(w/o)*
26/01	a	Panetolikos	D	1-1	*Umbides*
04/02	a	Olympiacos	L	1-2	*Marcelinho*
07/02	a	Veria	D	1-1	*Eduardo Brito*
15/02	h	PAOK	W	4-0	*Dimoutsos, Umbides, Katsouranis, Marcelinho*
23/02	a	Ergotelis	W	2-1	*Napoleoni, Marcelinho*
07/03	a	Asteras	L	0-1	
14/03	h	Panthrakikos	W	2-0	*Marcelinho, Umbides*
18/03	h	Panathinaikos	W	2-0	*Marcelinho, Umbides (p)*
22/03	a	Xanthi	L	0-1	
15/04	h	OFI	W	3-0	*(w/o)*
06/04	a	Kerkyra	W	2-1	*Napoleoni 2*
19/04	a	Giannina	D	1-1	*Pitu*
25/04	a	Levadiakos	L	1-2	*Napoleoni*
03/05	h	Panionios	W	3-1	*Napoleoni 3*
10/05	a	Kalloni	D	1-1	*Papazoglou*

No	Name	Nat	DoB	Pos	Aps	(s)	Gls
5	Laurent Agouazi	ALG	16/03/84	M	16	(5)	
16	Panagiotis Ballas		06/09/93	M	3	(8)	
32	Mauricio Carrasco	ARG	24/09/87	A	3	(7)	
1	Luigi Cennamo	ITA	07/02/80	G	9		
21	Elini Dimoutsos		18/06/88	M	21	(7)	1
7	Eduardo Brito	BRA	21/09/82	M	11	(11)	1
23	Fábio	POR	26/03/88	A		(6)	
6	Sokratis Fitanidis		25/05/84	D	30		1
8	Fotios Georgiou		19/07/85	M	4	(7)	
18	Konstantinos Giannoulis		09/12/87	D	2		
30	Andrei Gorbunov	BLR	25/05/83	G	23		
20	Anastasios Karamanos		21/09/90	A	14	(6)	2
2	Kostas Katsouranis		21/06/79	M	14	(2)	1
33	Ioannis Kontoes		24/05/86	D	17	(1)	
3	Alexandros Kouros		21/08/93	D	13	(4)	
19	Kyriakos Kyvrakidis		21/07/92	D	16	(3)	
24	Nikolaos Lazaridis		12/07/79	D	19	(5)	2
29	Dimitrios Limnios		27/05/98	A		(1)	
18	Marcelinho	BRA	22/06/87	M	7	(4)	4
9	Stefano Napoleoni	ITA	26/06/86	A	27	(3)	13
13	Evangelos Nastos		13/09/80	M	16		
11	Athanasios Papazoglou		30/03/88	A	18	(7)	4
26	Pitu	ARG	27/01/84	M	26	(1)	1
10	Andreas Tatos		11/05/89	M	3	(6)	
4	Efstathios Tavlaridis		25/01/80	D	10		
33	Javier Umbides	ARG	09/02/82	M	30		7

Ergotelis FC

1929 • Pagrition (27,574) • ergotelis.gr

Coach: Juan Ferrando (ESP);
(05/09/14) Pavlos Dermitzakis;
(16/12/14) (Ioannis Taousianis);
(12/02/15) (Stavros Lambrakis);
(15/02/15) Ioannis Matzourakis;
(28/02/15) (Ioannis Taousianis)

2014
25/08	a	Panionios	L	1-2	Melli
30/08	a	Kalloni	L	0-2	
15/09	h	Platanias	L	0-3	
22/09	a	Niki Volou	W	4-1	Bogdanov, Nosković, Halkiadakis, Youssouf
28/09	h	Panetolikos	D	1-1	Likogiannis
18/10	h	Olympiacos	L	2-3	Youssouf, Abdelchadi
25/10	a	Atromitos	D	1-1	Halkiadakis
02/11	h	PAOK	L	0-2	
08/11	h	Veria	D	2-2	Halkiadakis, Youssouf
30/11	h	Asteras	L	1-4	Jovanović
04/12	a	OFI	L	0-1	
08/12	a	Panthrakikos	D	0-0	
14/12	h	Xanthi	L	0-2	
17/12	a	Kerkyra	L	1-3	Fideleff
21/12	h	Giannina	W	1-0	Youssouf
2015
04/01	a	Levadiakos	D	1-1	Youssouf
11/01	a	Panathinaikos	L	0-5	
19/01	h	Kalloni	D	3-3	Abdelchadi 2, Kozoronis
26/01	a	Platanias	W	2-1	Élton Calé, Youssouf
01/02	h	Niki Volou	W	3-0	(w/o)
04/02	a	Panetolikos	L	0-4	
07/02	a	OFI	W	3-2	Boé-Kane, Djilas, Gorkšs
14/02	a	Olympiacos	L	0-3	
18/02	h	Panionios	D	2-2	Houla (p), Olaitan
23/02	a	Atromitos	L	1-2	Solari (p)
07/03	a	Veria	W	1-0	Gorkšs
14/03	h	Panathinaikos	L	0-2	
18/03	h	PAOK	L	0-1	
22/03	a	Asteras	L	0-1	
05/04	h	Panthrakikos	W	2-1	Halkiadakis, Djilas
18/04	a	Xanthi	W	1-0	Djilas (p)
27/04	h	Kerkyra	L	1-2	Halkiadakis
03/05	a	Giannina	D	0-0	
10/05	h	Levadiakos	L	0-2	

No	Name	Nat	DoB	Pos	Aps	(s)	Gls
10	Angelos Abdelchadi		07/09/89	A	19	(3)	3
42	Alan	BRA	09/12/87	A	1	(4)	
47	Marcos Bambam	BRA	19/03/91	A	1	(4)	
15	Yann Boé-Kane	FRA	05/04/91	M	11	(2)	1
90	Andriy Bogdanov	UKR	21/01/90	M	9	(4)	1
8	Antonios Bourselis		06/07/94	M	1	(3)	
1	Tomáš Černý	CZE	10/04/85	G	11		
91	Vladimir Djilas	SRB	03/03/83	M	6	(7)	3
19	Élton Calé	BRA	12/07/88	M	7	(5)	1
39	Ignacio Fideleff	ARG	04/07/89	D	7		1
33	Savvas Gentsoglou		19/09/90	D	20	(6)	
25	Kaspars Gorkšs	LVA	06/11/81	D	13		2
21	Bruno Halkiadakis		07/04/93	M	22	(5)	5
88	Greg Houla	FRA	19/07/88	M	9	(4)	1
5	Borislav Jovanović	SRB	16/08/86	D	11	(1)	1
31	Zaharias Kavousakis		11/01/89	G	9	(2)	
16	Konstantinos Kaznaferis		22/06/87	M	18	(4)	
23	Leonardo Koutris		23/07/95	M	3	(8)	
22	Chrisovalantis Kozoronis		03/08/92	M	21	(1)	1
27	Robert Kurež	SVN	20/07/91	M		(2)	
3	Charalambos Likogiannis		22/10/93	D	20	(2)	1
26	Cyriaque Louvion	FRA	24/07/87	D	15		
6	Melli	ESP	06/06/84	D	10		1
55	Aleksandar Nosković	SRB	12/12/88	A	4	(5)	1
93	Michael Olaitan	NGA	01/01/93	A	6	(6)	1
12	Georgios Pamlidis		13/11/93	M	7	(7)	
32	Epaminondas Pantelakis		10/02/95	D	1		
24	Minas Pitsos		08/10/80	D	15	(2)	
11	Vasilios Rentzas		19/11/93	M	12		
4	Joris Sainati	FRA	25/09/88	D	2	(2)	
50	Bojan Šaranov	SRB	22/09/87	G	13		
29	Esteban Solari	ARG	02/06/80	A	5	(4)	1
99	Nikola Stojanović	SRB	17/02/95	M	1	(2)	
40	Rok Štraus	SVN	03/03/87	M	1		
17	Emmanouil Tzanakakis		30/04/92	M	23		
9	Panagiotis Vlahodimos		11/10/91	A	3	(1)	
77	Mohamed Youssouf	COM	26/03/88	M	26	(1)	6

Kalloni FC

1994 • Dimotiko Stadio Mytilinis "Tarlas" (3,000)
• kallonifc.gr

Coach: Ioannis Matzourakis;
(16/01/15) Vangelis Vlachos

2014
24/08	a	PAOK	D	1-1	Camara
30/08	h	Ergotelis	W	2-0	Kaltsas, Raúl Llorente
14/09	h	Panathinaikos	W	1-0	Leozinho
21/09	a	Asteras	L	0-1	
29/09	h	Panthrakikos	W	2-0	Anastasiadis, Manousos
19/10	h	Kerkyra	W	1-0	Adejo
25/10	a	Giannina	D	0-0	
03/11	a	Levadiakos	D	0-0	
09/11	a	Panionios	W	2-0	Keita, Juanma
29/11	h	Platanias	D	0-0	
03/12	a	Xanthi	L	1-2	Valios
07/12	a	Niki Volou	L	0-2	
13/12	h	Panetolikos	L	0-2	
17/12	a	OFI	D	1-1	Juanma (p)
20/12	h	Olympiacos	L	0-5	
2015
04/01	a	Atromitos	D	0-0	
10/01	a	Veria	D	1-1	Juanma
14/01	h	PAOK	L	1-2	Kaltsas
19/01	a	Ergotelis	D	3-3	Leozinho (p), Juanma, Mingas
24/01	a	Panathinaikos	L	0-1	
31/01	h	Asteras	W	1-0	Tsabouris
05/02	a	Panthrakikos	L	1-2	Manousos 2 (1p)
09/02	h	Xanthi	D	2-2	Juanma 2
15/02	a	Kerkyra	L	0-2	
21/02	h	Giannina	W	1-0	Petropoulos
08/03	h	Panionios	W	1-0	Petropoulos
15/03	h	Veria	W	4-1	Juanma, Leozinho 2, Adejo
18/03	a	Levadiakos	L	0-3	
23/03	a	Platanias	L	0-1	
04/04	h	Niki Volou	W	3-0	(w/o)
18/04	a	Panetolikos	L	0-2	
25/04	h	OFI	W	3-0	(w/o)
03/05	a	Olympiacos	L	0-5	
10/05	h	Atromitos	D	1-1	Mingas

No	Name	Nat	DoB	Pos	Aps	(s)	Gls
4	Daniel Adejo	NGA	07/08/89	D	31		2
13	Anestis Agritis		16/04/81	A		(4)	
77	Branimir Aleksić	SRB	24/12/90	G	3		
14	Anestis Anastasiadis		21/01/83	D	29		1
7	Salim Arrache	ALG	14/07/82	M		(5)	
2	Marcos Barrera	ARG	02/03/84	D	3	(7)	
22	Henri Camara	SEN	10/05/77	A	6	(7)	1
22	Ioannis Giorgou		05/08/96	M		(2)	
1	Andrew Hogg	MLT	02/03/85	G	29		
12	Georgios Horianopoulos		15/01/79	D	4	(4)	
32	Abdul Razak Isa	GHA	20/09/90	M		(1)	
20	Jordi Vidal	ESP	07/02/91	M	1		
19	Juanma	ESP	17/11/90	A	24	(2)	7
27	Nikolaos V Kaltsas		28/06/89	M	26	(2)	2
24	Paul Keita	SEN	26/06/92	M	26	(2)	1
6	Mihail Kripidiris		08/03/81	M	4	(1)	
28	Theodosis Kyprou	CYP	24/02/92	A		(7)	
10	Leozinho	BRA	12/12/85	M	25	(4)	4
9	Georgios Manousos		03/12/87	A	27	(1)	3
18	Marcelo Goianira	BRA	06/08/80	M	5	(5)	
33	Christos Mingas		15/04/84	M	11	(9)	2
99	Antonios Petropoulos		28/01/86	A	8	(3)	2
3	Christos Pipinis		01/11/84	D	14	(7)	
21	Raúl Llorente	ESP	02/04/86	D	23	(3)	1
16	Ljubomir Stevanović	SRB	08/08/86	M	6	(7)	
31	Savvas Tsabouris		16/07/86	M	18	(1)	1
55	Efstratios Valios		09/01/89	D	16		1
25	Ximo Navarro	ESP	12/09/88	D	13	(10)	
28	Georgios Xydas		14/04/97	A		(2)	

Kerkyra FC

1968 • Ethniko Athlitiko Kentro (EAK)
Kerkyras (2,685) • kerkyrafc.gr

Coach: Mihail-Rizos Grigoriou

2014
23/08	h	Panthrakikos	W	2-1	Nayar, Kajkut
31/08	a	Xanthi	D	0-0	
13/09	a	Veria	L	1-2	Javito
21/09	h	Giannina	W	2-0	og (Mihail), Zorbas
28/09	a	Levadiakos	W	3-2	Javito 2, Markovski
19/10	a	Kalloni	L	0-1	
26/10	h	Platanias	L	1-2	Markovski
02/11	a	Niki Volou	D	0-0	
08/11	h	Panetolikos	L	1-2	Gomes
30/11	h	Olympiacos	L	0-4	
03/12	h	Panionios	W	1-0	Kontos
06/12	h	Atromitos	D	1-1	Kontos
14/12	a	PAOK	L	1-2	Nayar
17/12	h	Ergotelis	W	3-1	Kajkut 2, Markovski
22/12	a	Panathinaikos	L	0-2	
2015
03/01	h	Asteras	W	1-0	Nayar
11/01	a	OFI	L	2-3	Kajkut, Markovski
14/01	a	Panthrakikos	L	0-1	
17/01	h	Xanthi	D	0-0	
24/01	h	Veria	W	4-0	Markovski 2, og (Vergonis), Kontos
01/02	a	Giannina	L	1-2	Javito
04/02	h	Levadiakos	D	0-0	
08/02	a	Panionios	D	0-0	
15/02	h	Kalloni	W	2-0	Kajkut (p), Jordão Diogo
22/02	a	Platanias	D	1-1	Fábio
08/03	a	Panetolikos	W	1-0	Ghazaryan
14/03	h	OFI	W	4-1	Kontos 2 (1p), Andreopoulos, Gomes
18/03	h	Niki Volou	W	3-0	(w/o)
22/03	a	Olympiacos	L	0-3	
06/04	a	Atromitos	L	1-2	Kontos
18/04	h	PAOK	L	0-1	
27/04	a	Ergotelis	W	2-1	Dimitrovski, Kontos
03/05	h	Panathinaikos	D	1-1	Kontos (p)
10/05	a	Asteras	L	0-1	

No	Name	Nat	DoB	Pos	Aps	(s)	Gls
29	Kyriakos Andreopoulos		18/01/94	M	18	(8)	1
12	Asael Ben Shabat	ISR	09/05/88	D	4		
21	Borja Sánchez	ESP	14/02/87	M	2	(2)	
14	Horacio Cardozo	ARG	29/11/79	M	19	(2)	
23	Vladimir Dimitrovski	MKD	30/11/88	D	23	(4)	1
88	Fábio	POR	26/03/88	A	4	(7)	1
77	Konstantinos Georgakopoulos		03/01/94	A	1	(5)	
10	Gevorg Ghazaryan	ARM	05/04/88	M	8		1
11	Mathieu Gomes	FRA	06/03/85	M	25	(1)	2
20	Javito	ESP	04/11/83	A	27	(3)	4
30	Jordão Diogo	POR	12/11/85	D	20	(2)	1
9	Saša Kajkut	BIH	07/07/84	A	17	(10)	5
6	Petros Kanakoudis		16/04/84	M	5		
35	Akaki Khubutia	GEO	17/03/90	D	3	(1)	
19	Alexandros Kontos		12/09/86	M	21	(9)	8
13	Fotios Koutzavasilis		11/03/89	G	12		
16	Nikolaos Kritikos		01/11/94	M	5	(10)	
99	Sergio Leal	URU	25/09/82	A	4	(5)	
3	Kostas S Manolas		26/03/93	D	3	(1)	
3	Stilianos Marangos		04/05/89	M	11	(1)	
15	Marko Markovski	SRB	26/05/86	A	23	(6)	6
25	Nikolaos Mentis		14/10/95	D		(2)	
8	Sebastián Nayar	ARG	10/05/88	M	15	(2)	3
22	Nemanja Obradović	SRB	29/05/89	A	3	(2)	
6	Georgios Paraskevaidis		09/10/82	D	3	(2)	
10	Ángel Rojas	CHI	10/04/85	M	7	(4)	
1	Ernestas Šetkus	LTU	25/05/85	G	21		
22	Stefanos Siondis		04/09/87	D	14	(2)	
5	Anastasios Venetis		24/03/80	D	29		
7	Panagiotis Zorbas		21/04/87	M	14	(8)	1
31	Angelos Zoumboulakis		23/05/89	M	2		

GREECE

Levadiakos FC

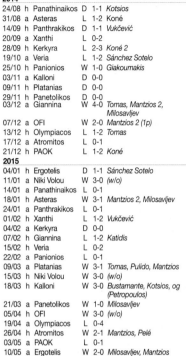

1961 • Dimotiko Livadias (6,200) • levadiakosfc.gr

Coach: Savvas Pantelidis;
(09/02/15) Apostolos Mantzios

2014
24/08	h	Panathinaikos	D	1-1	Kotsios
31/08	a	Asteras	L	1-2	Koné
14/09	h	Panthrakikos	D	1-1	Vukčević
20/09	a	Xanthi	L	0-2	
28/09	h	Kerkyra	L	2-3	Koné 2
19/10	a	Veria	L	1-2	Sánchez Sotelo
25/10	h	Panionios	W	1-0	Giakoumakis
03/11	a	Kalloni	D	0-0	
09/11	h	Platanias	D	0-0	
29/11	h	Panetolikos	D	0-0	
03/12	a	Giannina	W	4-0	Tomas, Mantzios 2, Milosavljev
07/12	a	OFI	W	2-0	Mantzios 2 (1p)
13/12	a	Olympiacos	L	1-2	Tomas
17/12	a	Atromitos	L	0-1	
21/12	h	PAOK	L	1-2	Koné

2015
04/01	h	Ergotelis	D	1-1	Sánchez Sotelo
11/01	h	Niki Volou	W	3-0	(w/o)
14/01	a	Panathinaikos	L	0-1	
18/01	a	Asteras	W	3-1	Mantzios 2, Milosavljev
24/01	a	Panthrakikos	L	0-1	
01/02	h	Xanthi	L	1-2	Vukčević
04/02	a	Kerkyra	D	0-0	
07/02	h	Giannina	L	1-2	Katidis
15/02	h	Veria	L	0-2	
22/02	h	Panionios	L	0-1	
09/03	a	Platanias	W	3-1	Tomas, Pulido, Mantzios
15/03	h	Niki Volou	W	3-0	(w/o)
18/03	h	Kalloni	W	3-0	Bustamante, Kotsios, og (Petropoulos)
21/03	a	Panetolikos	W	1-0	Milosavljev
05/04	h	OFI	W	3-0	(w/o)
19/04	a	Olympiacos	L	0-4	
26/04	h	Atromitos	W	2-1	Mantzios, Pelé
03/05	a	PAOK	L	0-1	
10/05	a	Ergotelis	W	2-0	Milosavljev, Mantzios

No	Name	Nat	DoB	Pos	Aps	(s)	Gls
20	Armiche	ESP	12/06/88	M	17	(2)	
22	Fabián Bordagaray	ARG	15/02/87	A	4	(4)	
28	Luis Bustamante	ARG	11/12/85	M	9	(2)	1
55	Carlos Milhazes	POR	17/03/81	D	13		
55	Nikolaos Georgiadis		23/03/83	D	12	(1)	
20	Petros Giakoumakis		03/07/92	M	7	(9)	1
8	Rubén Gómez	ARG	26/01/84	M	14	(8)	
18	Georgios Katidis		12/02/93	M	2	(7)	1
21	Emmanuel Koné	CIV	31/12/86	A	14		4
14	Elias Kotsios		25/04/77	D	25		2
16	Antonios Magas		28/02/94	M	1	(8)	
6	Dimitrios Maheras		16/08/90	M	13	(2)	
9	Evangelos Mantzios		22/04/83	A	22	(4)	9
27	Vladan Milosavljev	SRB	01/02/87	M	14	(10)	4
99	Miljan Mrdaković	SRB	09/05/82	A		(3)	
13	Emmanouil Nikolakakis		19/02/91	D	4	(5)	
33	Konstantinos Pappas		30/11/91	A		(2)	
15	Pelé	POR	14/09/87	M	8	(2)	1
5	Ádám Pintér	HUN	12/06/88	D	13	(1)	
15	Josip Projić	SRB	23/08/87	D	5	(2)	
81	Sebastian Przyrowski	POL	30/11/81	G	1		
71	Alan Pulido	MEX	08/03/91	A	6		1
32	Matías Sánchez	ARG	18/08/87	M	7	(1)	
26	Juan Sánchez Sotelo	ARG	02/10/87	A	6	(7)	2
30	Mihail Sifakis		09/09/84	G	25		
12	Nikolaos Skebis		02/11/92	D	5	(2)	
87	Ioannis Stathis		20/05/87	D	11		
29	Kiriakos Stratilatis		05/01/88	G	4	(1)	
4	Xavier Tomas	FRA	04/01/86	D	28	(1)	3
2	Theodoros Tripotseris		04/03/86	D	5	(3)	
1	Panagiotis Tsintonas		04/07/93	G	1		
3	Simon Vukčević	MNE	29/01/86	M	22	(3)	2
11	Eric Warden	GHA	13/12/92	A	1		
23	Mekeme Tamla Zito	CIV	19/09/85	M	22	(2)	

Niki Volou FC

1924 • Panthessaliko (22,307) • nikivoloufc.gr

Coach: Wiljan Vloet (NED);
(15/09/14) Sven Vandenbroeck (BEL);
(01/10/14) Panagiotis Tzanavaras

2014
23/08	a	Olympiacos	L	1-3	Shkurtaj
31/08	h	Atromitos	L	0-1	
13/09	a	PAOK	L	0-3	
21/09	h	Ergotelis	L	1-4	Ivens
28/09	a	Panathinaikos	L	0-1	
18/10	h	Panthrakikos	W	1-0	Rogério Martins
27/10	a	Xanthi	L	0-2	
02/11	h	Kerkyra	D	0-0	
09/11	a	Giannina	L	0-4	
30/11	a	Panionios	L	1-2	Anastasopoulos
04/12	a	Asteras	L	0-2	
07/12	h	Kalloni	W	2-0	Shkurtaj 2
13/12	a	Platanias	L	1-3	Shkurtaj
17/12	a	Veria	L	0-2	
21/12	h	Panetolikos	L	0-3	(w/o)

2015
03/01	a	OFI	L	0-3	(w/o)
11/01	h	Levadiakos	L	0-3	(w/o)
15/01	h	Olympiacos	L	0-3	(w/o)
18/01	a	Atromitos	L	0-3	(w/o)
25/01	h	PAOK	L	0-3	(w/o)
01/02	a	Ergotelis	L	0-3	(w/o)
04/02	h	Panathinaikos	L	0-3	(w/o)
08/02	a	Asteras	L	0-3	(w/o)
15/02	a	Panthrakikos	L	0-3	(w/o)
21/02	h	Xanthi	L	0-3	(w/o)
08/03	h	Giannina	L	0-3	(w/o)
15/03	a	Levadiakos	L	0-3	(w/o)
18/03	a	Kerkyra	L	0-3	(w/o)
21/03	h	Panionios	L	0-3	(w/o)
05/04	a	Kalloni	L	0-3	(w/o)
19/04	h	Platanias	L	0-3	(w/o)
26/04	h	Veria	L	0-3	(w/o)
03/05	a	Panetolikos	L	0-3	(w/o)
10/05	h	OFI	L	0-3	(w/o)

No	Name	Nat	DoB	Pos	Aps	(s)	Gls
15	Evangelos Anastasopoulos		07/03/94	M	3	(1)	1
24	Nikolaos Argyriou		04/04/94	D	1	(1)	
18	Angelos Argyris		06/05/94	M	6	(2)	
25	Georgios Dimizas		24/07/94	G	1		
10	Nikolaos Giannitsanis		16/02/94	A	4	(2)	
4	Jonas Ivens	BEL	14/10/84	D	14		1
17	Aristotelis Karasalidis		03/05/91	D	10		
8	Grigorios Kiziridis		24/10/90	M	5	(2)	
7	Ioannis Koretas		20/10/92	A		(4)	
22	Konstantinos Kotsaridis		12/06/92	M	10	(2)	
6	Kees Luijckx	NED	11/02/86	M	10		
3	Georgios Mahlelis		10/05/91	D	8	(2)	
26	Nikolaos Marinakis		12/09/93	D	13		
20	Neshat Meçe	ALB	11/08/95	M	3	(3)	
11	Alexandros Mouzakitis		04/08/94	M	9	(1)	
23	Georgios Niklitsiotis		23/03/91	M	8	(2)	
2	Theodoros Papoutsogiannopoulos		06/07/94	D	1		
14	Rogério Martins	BRA	19/11/84	M	7	(3)	1
9	Vasil Shkurtaj	ALB	27/02/92	A	8	(2)	4
16	Ioannis Sotirakos		19/01/95	D	3	(1)	
19	Robert Stambolziev	AUS	26/10/90	A	2	(6)	
1	Dimitrios Tairis		03/12/92	G	9		
12	Alexis Tambakis		08/12/92	G	14		
5	Stilianos Tsoukanis		27/02/90	M	8	(1)	
66	Christos Tzioras		05/10/88	A	7	(4)	

OFI Crete FC

1925 • Thodoros Vardinoyannis (8,150) • ofifc.gr

Major honours
Greek Cup (1) 1987

Coach: Gennaro Gattuso (ITA);
(06/01/15) Nikolaos Anastopoulos

2014
23/08	h	Panetolikos	W	1-0	Petropoulos
01/09	h	Veria	L	0-1	
13/09	a	Olympiacos	L	0-3	
20/09	h	Atromitos	W	1-0	Perogamvrakis
28/09	a	PAOK	L	0-4	
19/10	a	Panathinaikos	W	2-1	Merebashvili, Makris
26/10	h	Asteras	L	2-3	Carlos Milhazes, Merebashvili
02/11	a	Panthrakikos	D	0-0	
08/11	h	Xanthi	L	1-2	Petropoulos
30/11	a	Giannina	L	0-3	
04/12	h	Ergotelis	W	1-0	Carlos Milhazes (p)
07/12	h	Levadiakos	L	0-2	
14/12	a	Panionios	L	0-2	
17/12	h	Kalloni	D	1-1	Makris
20/12	a	Platanias	L	0-1	

2015
03/01	h	Niki Volou	W	3-0	(w/o)
11/01	h	Kerkyra	W	3-2	Carlos Milhazes 3 (2p)
14/01	h	Panetolikos	L	1-3	og (Koutromanos)
17/01	a	Veria	L	1-4	Makris
24/01	h	Olympiacos	L	0-3	
04/02	h	PAOK	W	3-1	George, Lambropoulos (p), Koutsianikoulis
07/02	a	Ergotelis	L	2-3	Makris, Merebashvili
15/02	h	Panathinaikos	L	2-3	Moniakis, Merebashvili (p)
22/02	a	Asteras	L	1-6	Lambropoulos (p)
08/03	h	Xanthi	L	0-1	
15/03	a	Kerkyra	L	1-4	George (p)
18/03	h	Panthrakikos	L	0-1	
21/03	h	Giannina	L	0-3	(w/o)
05/04	a	Levadiakos	L	0-3	(w/o)
15/04	a	Atromitos	L	0-3	(w/o)
19/04	h	Panionios	L	0-3	(w/o)
26/04	a	Kalloni	L	0-3	(w/o)
03/05	h	Platanias	L	0-3	(w/o)
10/05	a	Niki Volou	L	0-0	(w/o)

No	Name	Nat	DoB	Pos	Aps	(s)	Gls
3	Ayodele Adeleye	NGA	25/12/88	D	14		
92	Mihail Agrimakis		28/07/92	G	1		
32	Apoño	ESP	13/02/84	M	1	(2)	
4	Konstantinos Banousis		23/01/88	M	9	(2)	
30	Emmanouil Bolakis		20/10/94	D	8		
55	Carlos Milhazes	POR	17/03/81	D	12		5
5	Charalambos Damianakis		14/06/95	D	7		
17	Dani Fernández	ESP	20/01/83	D	11	(1)	
33	Emmanouil Fazos		12/08/95	D	8	(2)	
12	Islam Feruz	SCO	10/09/95	A		(1)	
11	Mayron George	CRC	23/10/94	A	10	(10)	2
44	Željko Kalajdžić	SRB	11/05/78	M	10	(3)	
8	Vasilios Koutsianikoulis		09/08/88	M	14	(6)	1
18	Andreas Lambropoulos		30/07/88	A	19	(3)	2
77	Giorgi Loria	GEO	27/01/86	G	25		
54	Georgios Makris		15/11/84	M	25	(1)	4
24	Panagiotis Manidakis		22/06/95	A	2	(5)	
31	Zacharias Marathianos		28/03/94	A	3	(6)	
19	Abdoulaye Méïté	CIV	06/10/80	D	8	(1)	
20	Giorgi Merebashvili	GEO	15/08/86	M	16	(1)	4
6	Emmanouil Moniakis		09/11/88	D	15	(1)	1
21	Alexandros Perogamvrakis		20/01/88	A	9	(2)	1
9	Antonios Petropoulos		28/01/86	A	11	(3)	2
15	Abdul Razak	CIV	11/11/92	M	8	(1)	
14	Emmanouil Rovithis		16/09/92	D	8	(9)	
7	Mirnes Šišič	SVN	08/08/81	M		(4)	
25	Ioannis Stathis		20/05/87	D	16		
2	Theodoros Tripotseris		04/03/86	D	16		

Olympiacos FC

1925 • Georgios Karaiskakis (32,130) •
olympiacos.org
Major honours
*Greek League (42) 1931, 1933, 1934, 1936, 1937, 1938,
1947, 1948, 1951, 1954, 1955, 1956, 1957, 1958, 1959,
1966, 1967, 1973, 1974, 1975, 1980, 1981, 1982, 1983,
1987, 1997, 1998, 1999, 2000, 2001, 2002, 2003, 2005,
2006, 2007, 2008, 2009, 2011, 2012, 2013, 2014, 2015;
Greek Cup (27) 1947, 1951, 1952, 1953, 1954, 1957,
1958, 1959, 1960, 1961, 1963, 1965, 1968, 1971, 1973,
1975, 1981, 1990, 1992, 1999, 2005, 2006, 2008, 2009,
2012, 2013, 2015*
**Coach: Míchel (ESP);
(06/01/15) (Antonios Nikopolidis);
(08/01/15) Vítor Pereira (POR)**

2014
23/08	h	Niki Volou	W	3-1	*Kasami, Diamantakos, Afellay*
30/08	a	Panetolikos	D	1-1	*Kasami*
13/09	h	OFI	W	3-0	*og (Adeleye), Durmaz, Domínguez*
20/09	h	Veria	W	3-2	*Mitroglou (p), Benítez, Kasami*
27/09	a	Atromitos	L	0-1	
18/10	a	Ergotelis	W	3-2	*Mitroglou 2, Domínguez (p)*
26/10	h	Panathinaikos	W	1-0	*Avlonitis*
01/11	a	Asteras	D	0-0	
09/11	h	Panthrakikos	W	5-1	*Domínguez (p), Bouhalakis, Avlonitis, Diamantakos, Mitroglou*
30/11	a	Kerkyra	W	4-0	*David Fuster, Domínguez 2 (1p), Elabdellaoui*
03/12	h	PAOK	L	1-2	*David Fuster*
06/12	h	Giannina	D	2-2	*Fortounis (p), Kasami*
13/12	a	Levadiakos	W	1-0	*Afellay, Mitroglou*
17/12	h	Panionios	W	2-0	*Mitroglou 2*
20/12	a	Kalloni	W	5-0	*Maniatis, Domínguez (p), Benítez 2, Bouhalakis*

2015
04/01	h	Platanias	W	2-1	*N'Dinga, Mitroglou*
11/01	a	Xanthi	W	3-1	*Mitroglou 2, Dossevi*
15/01	a	Niki Volou	W	3-0	*(w/o)*
18/01	h	Panetolikos	W	2-0	*Dossevi, Maniatis*
24/01	a	OFI	W	3-0	*Domínguez (p), Fortounis, Mitroglou*
01/02	a	Veria	W	2-0	*Mitroglou, Dossevi*
04/02	h	Atromitos	W	2-1	*Afellay, Mitroglou*
08/02	a	PAOK	D	0-0	
14/02	h	Ergotelis	W	3-0	*Durmaz, Fortounis 2*
22/02	a	Panathinaikos	L	1-2	*Domínguez*
15/03	h	Xanthi	W	2-0	*Domínguez, Afellay*
19/03	a	Asteras	W	2-0	*Domínguez, Fortounis*
22/03	h	Kerkyra	W	3-0	*Domínguez, Botía, Jara*
05/04	a	Giannina	L	1-3	*Milivojević*
15/04	a	Panthrakikos	W	3-1	*Benítez, Jara, Milivojević*
19/04	a	Levadiakos	W	4-0	*Domínguez 2, Benítez, Fortounis*
26/04	a	Panionios	D	2-2	*Mitroglou, Domínguez*
03/05	h	Kalloni	W	5-0	*Benítez, Fortounis, Domínguez, Mitroglou 2 (1p)*
10/05	a	Platanias	D	1-1	*Jara*

No	Name	Nat	DoB	Pos	Aps	(s)	Gls
22	Éric Abidal	FRA	11/09/79	D	9		
6	Ibrahim Afellay	NED	02/04/86	M	16	(3)	4
24	Anastasios Avlonitis		01/01/90	D	17	(1)	2
27	Jorge Benítez	PAR	02/09/92	A	8	(13)	6
3	Alberto Botía	ESP	27/01/89	D	17		1
18	Andreas Bouhalakis		05/04/93	M	3	(6)	2
19	David Fuster	ESP	03/02/82	M	6	(7)	2
17	Dimitrios Diamantakos		05/03/93	A	4	(4)	2
10	Alejandro Domínguez	ARG	10/06/81	M	26	(4)	15
77	Mathieu Dossevi	TOG	12/02/88	M	20	(6)	3
9	Jimmy Durmaz	SWE	22/03/89	M	7	(12)	2
14	Omar Elabdellaoui	NOR	05/12/91	D	23	(1)	1
45	Felipe Santana	BRA	17/03/86	D	5		
25	Kostas Fortounis		16/10/92	A	10	(15)	7
10	Gevorg Ghazaryan	ARM	05/04/88	M		(3)	
20	Konstantinos Giannoulis		09/12/87	D	7		
12	Franco Jara	ARG	15/07/88	A	7	(3)	3
11	Pajtim Kasami	SUI	02/06/92	M	20	(4)	4
30	Leandro Salino	BRA	22/04/85	D	11		
2	Ioannis Maniatis		12/10/86	M	17		2
26	Arthur Masuaku	FRA	07/11/93	D	26	(1)	
42	Balázs Megyeri	HUN	31/03/90	G	4		
5	Luka Milivojević	SRB	07/04/91	M	21	(2)	2
7	Kostas Mitroglou		12/03/88	A	20	(4)	16
8	Delvin N'Dinga	CGO	14/03/88	M	12	(5)	1
21	Avraam Papadopoulos		03/12/84	D		(1)	
16	Roberto	ESP	10/02/86	G	29		
7	Javier Saviola	ARG	11/12/81	A		(1)	
23	Dimitrios Siovas		16/09/88	D	18	(2)	
29	Praxitelis Vouros		05/05/95	D		(1)	

Panathinaikos FC

1908 • Apostolos Nikolaidis (16,003) • pao.gr
Major honours
*Greek League (20) 1930, 1949, 1953, 1960, 1961,
1962, 1964, 1965, 1969, 1970, 1972, 1977, 1984,
1986, 1990, 1991, 1995, 1996, 2004, 2010;
Greek Cup (18) 1940, 1948, 1955, 1967, 1969,
1977, 1982, 1984, 1986, 1988, 1989, 1991, 1993,
1994, 1995, 2004, 2010, 2014*
Coach: Ioannis Anastasiou

2014
24/08	a	Levadiakos	D	1-1	*Pranjić (p)*
31/08	h	Panionios	W	2-1	*Ajagun, Petrić*
14/09	a	Kalloni	L	0-1	
21/09	a	Platanias	W	3-2	*Karelis, Dinas, Zeca*
28/09	h	Niki Volou	W	1-0	*Ajagun*
19/10	h	OFI	L	1-2	*Koutroumbis*
26/10	a	Olympiacos	L	0-1	
02/11	h	Atromitos	W	2-0	*og (Lazaridis), Karelis*
09/11	a	PAOK	W	2-1	*Ajagun, Karelis*
30/11	h	Veria	W	2-1	*Pranjić (p), Berg*
04/12	a	Panetolikos	W	1-0	*Petrić*
07/12	a	Asteras	D	1-1	*Lagos*
14/12	h	Panthrakikos	W	4-0	*Karelis, Petrić, Zeca, Berg*
18/12	a	Xanthi	L	2-4	*Karelis 2*
22/12	h	Kerkyra	W	2-0	*Karelis, Chouchoumis*

2015
05/01	a	Giannina	D	0-0	
11/01	h	Ergotelis	W	5-0	*Klonaridis 2, Berg 3*
14/01	h	Levadiakos	W	1-0	*Petrić*
17/01	a	Panionios	D	1-1	*Berg*
24/01	h	Kalloni	W	1-0	*Berg*
01/02	a	Platanias	W	3-0	*Petrić, Triantafyllopoulos, Klonaridis*
04/02	a	Niki Volou	W	3-0	*(w/o)*
08/02	h	Panetolikos	W	1-0	*Petrić*
15/02	a	PAOK	W	3-2	*Karelis 2, Pranjić*
22/02	h	Olympiacos	W	2-1	*og (Masuaku), Petrić*
08/03	h	PAOK	W	4-3	*Berg 3, Karelis*
14/03	a	Ergotelis	W	2-0	*Berg, Ajagun*
18/03	a	Atromitos	L	0-1	
22/03	a	Veria	L	0-1	
04/04	h	Asteras	D	2-2	*Berg 2*
19/04	a	Panthrakikos	L	1-2	*Schildenfeld*
25/04	h	Xanthi	W	2-0	*Karelis, Pranjić (p)*
03/05	a	Kerkyra	D	1-1	*Karelis*
10/05	h	Giannina	W	3-1	*Klonaridis, Karelis, Lagos*

No	Name	Nat	DoB	Pos	Aps	(s)	Gls
14	Abdul Ajagun	NGA	10/02/93	M	16	(9)	4
16	Vasilios Angelopoulos		12/02/97	M		(1)	
11	Emir Bajrami	SWE	07/03/88	M	2	(2)	
9	Marcus Berg	SWE	17/08/86	A	17	(2)	13
17	Valmir Berisha	SWE	06/06/96	A		(1)	
31	Christos Bourbos		01/06/93	D	19	(1)	
22	Ouasim Bouy	NED	11/06/93	M	9	(4)	
3	Adamantios Chouchoumis		17/07/94	D	13	(1)	1
26	Athanasios Dinas		12/11/89	A	6	(1)	1
18	Christos Donis		09/10/94	M	7	(11)	
19	Nikolaos Karelis		24/02/92	A	20	(10)	13
7	Viktor Klonaridis	BEL	28/07/92	A	18	(9)	4
1	Stefanos Kotsolis		05/06/79	G	4		
6	Georgios Koutroumbis		10/02/91	D	13	(5)	1
8	Anastasios Lagos		12/04/92	M	22	(7)	2
27	Charalambos Mavrias		21/02/94	A	2	(1)	
6	David Mendes da Silva	NED	04/08/82	M	9	(6)	
21	Nano	ESP	27/10/84	D	20	(3)	
29	Sotirios Ninis		03/04/90	M	3	(7)	
33	Mladen Petrić	CRO	01/01/81	A	23	(6)	7
32	Danijel Pranjić	CRO	02/12/81	M	24	(2)	4
24	Spiridon Risvanis		03/01/94	D	11	(2)	
23	Gordon Schildenfeld	CRO	18/03/85	D	25		1
15	Luke Steele	ENG	24/09/84	G	29		
20	Efstathios Tavlaridis		25/01/80	D	14	(1)	
5	Konstantinos Triantafyllopoulos		03/04/93	D	19	(1)	1
10	Zeca	POR	31/08/88	M	28	(1)	2

Panetolikos GFS

1926 • Panetolikou (6,000) • panetolikos.gr
Coach: Ioakim Havos

2014
23/08	a	OFI	L	0-1	
30/08	h	Olympiacos	D	1-1	*Kousas*
14/09	a	Atromitos	D	0-0	
22/09	h	PAOK	L	0-1	
28/09	a	Ergotelis	D	1-1	*Moreno*
18/10	a	Asteras	D	1-1	
26/10	h	Panthrakikos	W	3-1	*Moreno 3 (1p)*
02/11	h	Xanthi	W	5-2	*Villafáñez 2, Edjenguélé, Martínez, Kappel*
08/11	a	Kerkyra	W	2-1	*Villafáñez, Kappel*
29/11	a	Levadiakos	D	0-0	
04/12	h	Panathinaikos	L	0-1	
07/12	h	Panionios	W	2-1	*Kappel, Malezas*
13/12	a	Kalloni	D	0-0	
17/12	h	Platanias	W	1-0	*Bejarano*
21/12	a	Niki Volou	W	3-0	*(w/o)*

2015
03/01	a	Veria	W	3-1	*Kappel, Villafáñez 2*
11/01	h	Giannina	D	0-0	
14/01	h	OFI	W	3-1	*Kevin 2, Kousas*
18/01	a	Olympiacos	L	0-2	
26/01	a	Atromitos	D	1-1	*Bejarano*
31/01	a	PAOK	W	2-1	*André Alves 2 (1p)*
04/02	h	Ergotelis	W	4-0	*Fotakis, André Alves 2, Kappel*
08/02	a	Panathinaikos	L	0-1	
14/02	h	Asteras	W	2-0	*Villafáñez, André Alves (p)*
21/02	a	Panthrakikos	D	0-0	
08/03	h	Kerkyra	L	0-1	
15/03	a	Giannina	D	0-0	
18/03	a	Xanthi	L	0-3	
21/03	h	Levadiakos	L	0-3	
05/04	a	Panionios	L	0-3	
18/04	h	Kalloni	W	2-0	*Martínez, og (Tsabouris)*
26/04	a	Platanias	L	0-2	
03/05	h	Niki Volou	W	3-0	*(w/o)*
10/05	a	Veria	W	2-0	*Martínez, Moreno*

No	Name	Nat	DoB	Pos	Aps	(s)	Gls
9	André Alves	BRA	15/10/83	A	22	(5)	5
8	Diego Bejarano	BOL	24/08/91	D	22	(2)	2
23	William Edjenguélé	FRA	07/05/87	D	21	(1)	1
32	Georgios Fotakis		29/10/81	M	26		1
15	Fernando Godoy	ARG	01/05/90	M	28		
20	Alexandros Kalogeris		14/05/86	M	1	(8)	
11	Leandro Kappel	NED	14/11/89	A	26	(5)	5
3	Kevin	ESP	08/09/89	D	25	(1)	2
7	Panagiotis Korbos		11/09/86	M	4	(7)	
5	Georgios Kousas		12/08/82	D	21		2
2	Dimitrios Koutromanos		25/02/87	D	12	(7)	
25	Costin Lazăr	ROU	24/04/81	M	4	(6)	
13	Stilianos Malezas		11/03/85	D	22	(3)	1
20	Nicolás Martínez	ARG	25/09/87	M	32		3
22	Georgios Migas		07/04/94	M	9	(10)	
19	Nikolaos Milios		01/08/95	A		(2)	
16	Erik Moreno	COL	24/11/91	A	16	(5)	6
28	Stefanos Papoutsogiannopoulos		10/08/94	M	2	(4)	
1	Rafael	BRA	05/05/81	G	25		
31	Simos Rouboulakou		30/12/91	D		(1)	
7	Sebastián Rusculleda	ARG	28/04/85	M	4	(6)	
17	Anthony Scaramozzino	FRA	30/04/85	D	6	(2)	
21	Emmanouil Stefanakos		17/08/89	G	7		
10	Georgios S Theodoridis		03/07/80	M	4	(9)	
29	Stilianos Vasiliou		29/04/91	A	1	(10)	
18	Lucas Villafáñez	ARG	04/10/91	M	18	(1)	6

Panionios GSS

1890 • Panionios GSS (16,800) • panionios.gr
Major honours
Greek Cup (2) 1979, 1998
**Coach: Dimitrios Terezopoulos;
(09/12/14) Marinos Ouzounidis**

2014
25/08	h	Ergotelis	W	2-1	*Giannou 2*
31/08	a	Panathinaikos	L	1-2	*Boumale*
14/09	a	Asteras	W	2-1	*Mitropoulos, Boumale*
21/09	a	Panthrakikos	L	0-1	
27/09	h	Xanthi	D	1-1	*Kolovos (p)*
20/10	h	Giannina	L	0-1	
25/10	a	Levadiakos	L	0-1	
01/11	a	Veria	D	2-2	*Giannou 2*
09/11	h	Kalloni	L	0-2	
30/11	h	Niki Volou	W	2-1	*Fountas, Kolovos (p)*
03/12	a	Kerkyra	L	0-1	
07/12	a	Panetolikos	L	1-2	*Giannou*
14/12	h	OFI	W	2-0	*Kolovos, Giannou*
17/12	a	Olympiacos	L	0-2	
21/12	a	Atromitos	D	2-2	*Kolovos 2 (1p)*
2015					
03/01	a	PAOK	L	2-3	*Giannou, Kolovos (p)*
10/01	a	Platanias	L	0-3	
17/01	h	Panathinaikos	D	1-1	*Boumale*
24/01	a	Asteras	L	0-2	
31/01	a	Panthrakikos	W	2-1	*Mitropoulos, Giannou*
04/02	a	Xanthi	D	1-1	*Bakasetas*
08/02	h	Kerkyra	D	0-0	
14/02	a	Giannina	W	3-1	*Boumale, Ikonomou, Hatziisaias*
18/02	a	Ergotelis	D	2-2	*og (Tzanakakis), Fountas*
22/02	h	Levadiakos	W	1-0	*Ikonomou*
08/03	a	Kalloni	L	0-1	
15/03	h	Platanias	D	0-0	
18/03	h	Veria	W	4-2	*Kolovos, Fountas 2, Giannou*
21/03	a	Niki Volou	W	3-0	*(w/o)*
05/04	h	Panetolikos	W	3-0	*Kolovos 2, Giannou*
19/04	a	OFI	W	3-0	*(w/o)*
26/04	h	Olympiacos	D	2-2	*Kolovos, Boumale*
03/05	a	Atromitos	L	1-3	*Kolovos*
10/05	h	PAOK	D	0-0	

No	Name	Nat	DoB	Pos	Aps	(s)	Gls
20	Leonidas Argiropoulos		29/05/90	D	24		
14	Anastasios Bakasetas		28/06/93	A	9	(4)	1
10	Olivier Boumale	CMR	17/09/89	M	29	(2)	5
8	Vasilios Bouzas		30/06/93	M	6	(7)	
96	Fiorin Durmishaj	ALB	14/11/96	A		(2)	
21	Taxiarhis Fountas		04/09/95	M	19	(7)	4
22	Kosmas Gezos		15/08/92	D	3	(6)	
31	Nikolaos Giannakopoulos		19/02/93	G	8		
99	Apostolos Giannou		25/01/90	A	28	(4)	10
33	Damian Gjini	ALB	06/04/95	M	1	(5)	
4	Dimitrios Hatziisaias		23/09/92	D	15		1
7	Ariel Ibagaza	ARG	27/10/76	M	12	(11)	
6	Evangelos Ikonomou		18/07/87	D	21	(2)	2
17	Nikolaos Katharios		07/10/94	M		(5)	
11	Dimitrios Kolovos		27/04/93	M	23	(6)	11
30	Panagiotis Korbos		11/09/86	M	14	(1)	
19	Georgios Masouras		01/01/94	M	2	(12)	
82	Pavlos Mitropoulos		04/04/90	M	30		2
25	Xenophon Panos		25/08/89	D	10	(7)	
5	Nikolaos Pantidos		19/04/91	D	19		
1	Nikolaos G Papadopoulos		11/04/90	G	24		
49	Spiridon Risvanis		03/01/94	D	9	(2)	
21	Emmanouil Siopis		14/05/94	M	17	(4)	
15	Alexandros Smirlis		07/02/93	A		(4)	
3	Christos Tasoulis		03/05/91	D	29		
37	Valentinos Vlahos		14/01/92	M		(1)	

Panthrakikos FC

1963 • Dimotiko Komotinis (3,000) • panthrakikos.com
**Coach: Apostolos Mantzios;
(05/11/14) (Nikolaos Bacharidis);
(10/11/14) José Manuel Roca Cases (ESP)**

2014
23/08	h	Kerkyra	L	1-2	*Igor*
30/08	h	Giannina	D	1-1	*Tzanis*
14/09	a	Levadiakos	D	1-1	*Igor*
21/09	h	Panionios	W	1-0	*Igor (p)*
29/09	a	Kalloni	L	0-2	
18/10	a	Niki Volou	L	0-1	
26/10	h	Panetolikos	L	1-3	*Cases*
02/11	h	OFI	D	0-0	
09/11	a	Olympiacos	L	1-5	*Cases (p)*
30/11	a	PAOK	L	2-3	*Diguiny, Tsoumanis*
03/12	h	Platanias	W	1-0	*Diguiny*
08/12	h	Ergotelis	D	0-0	
14/12	a	Panathinaikos	L	0-4	
17/12	h	Asteras	D	1-1	*Tzanis*
20/12	h	Veria	D	1-1	*Tzanis*
2015					
05/01	h	Xanthi	D	0-0	
11/01	h	Atromitos	D	1-1	*Igor (p)*
14/01	h	Kerkyra	W	1-0	*Igor (p)*
18/01	a	Giannina	D	2-2	*Hasomeris, Cases*
24/01	h	Levadiakos	W	1-0	*Diguiny*
31/01	a	Panionios	L	1-2	*Tzanis*
05/02	h	Kalloni	W	3-2	*M'Bow, Igor (p), og (Tsabouris)*
08/02	a	Platanias	L	0-2	
15/02	h	Niki Volou	W	3-0	*(w/o)*
21/02	h	Panetolikos	D	0-0	
14/03	a	Atromitos	L	0-2	
18/03	a	OFI	W	1-0	*Igor*
21/03	h	PAOK	W	3-1	*Diguiny, Tzanis, Igor (p)*
05/04	a	Ergotelis	L	1-2	*Mejía*
15/04	h	Olympiacos	L	1-3	*Baykara*
19/04	h	Panathinaikos	W	2-1	*Igor, Tzanis*
26/04	a	Asteras	L	1-2	*Tzanis*
03/05	a	Veria	W	1-0	*Igor (p)*
10/05	h	Xanthi	W	2-0	*Cases, Igor*

No	Name	Nat	DoB	Pos	Aps	(s)	Gls
32	Hakeem Araba	ENG	12/02/91	A	1	(6)	
30	Georgios Athanasiadis		07/04/93	G	25		
10	José María Cases	ESP	23/11/86	M	20	(8)	4
13	Sofyane Cherfa	ALG	13/08/84	D	13	(1)	
21	Ioannis Christou		05/03/81	D	8	(3)	
1	Daniel Fernandes	POR	25/09/83	G	4		
20	Deniz Baykara	TUR	13/03/84	M	27	(1)	1
9	Nicolas Diguiny	FRA	31/05/88	M	25	(5)	4
5	Guille	ESP	11/01/87	M	5	(5)	
11	Dimitrios Hasomeris		23/06/89	A	8	(13)	1
99	Igor	BRA	19/02/80	A	22	(5)	11
22	Stilianos Iliadis		03/06/86	M	4	(4)	
22	Nikolaos Katharios		07/10/94	M	1	(1)	
84	Antonios Ladakis		25/01/82	M	16	(1)	
70	Georgios Litskas		16/06/95	A		(2)	
15	Pape M'Bow	SEN	22/05/88	D	30		1
17	Manu Balda	ECU	21/02/92	A		(8)	
6	Alfredo Mejía	HON	03/04/90	M	26	(2)	1
4	Christos Melissis		01/12/82	D	16		
25	Princewill Okachi	NGA	20/06/91	M		(3)	
2	Athanasios Papageorgiou		09/05/87	D	13	(3)	
24	Alexandros Pashalakis		28/07/89	G	4		
92	Ioannis Potouridis		27/02/92	D	28	(2)	
8	Rogério Martins	BRA	19/11/84	M	2	(7)	
23	Romeu	BRA	13/02/85	M	16	(2)	
27	Sebastián Setti	ARG	09/02/84	D		(2)	
8	Vasilios Triantafillakos		16/07/91	A	1		
18	Nicolaos Tsoumanis		08/06/90	M	20	(2)	1
7	Christos Tzanis		22/04/85	A	24	(7)	7
28	Santiago Villafañe	ARG	19/05/88	D	3	(1)	
19	Konstantinos Zdravos-Rizos		16/08/93	M	1	(3)	

PAOK FC

1926 • Toumbas (31,060) • paokfc.gr
Major honours
Greek League (2) 1976, 1985; Greek Cup (4) 1972, 1974, 2001, 2003
**Coach: Angelos Anastasiadis;
(16/03/15) (Georgios H Georgiadis)**

2014
24/08	h	Kalloni	D	1-1	*Pereyra*
31/08	a	Platanias	W	4-0	*Athanasiadis, Salpingidis, Mak, Skondras*
13/09	h	Niki Volou	W	3-0	*Athanasiadis, Pereyra, Mak (p)*
22/09	a	Panetolikos	W	1-0	*Mak (p)*
28/09	h	OFI	W	4-0	*Raţ 2, Mak, Athanasiadis*
19/10	h	Atromitos	W	2-1	*Kaçe, Raţ*
26/10	h	Veria	W	4-1	*Mak, Salpingidis, Kaçe, Athanasiadis*
02/11	a	Ergotelis	W	2-0	*Athanasiadis 2*
09/11	h	Panathinaikos	L	1-2	*Pereyra*
30/11	h	Panthrakikos	W	3-2	*Salpingidis, Papadopoulos, Pereyra*
03/12	a	Olympiacos	W	2-1	*Athanasiadis, Pereyra*
07/12	a	Xanthi	L	2-4	*Athanasiadis, Mak*
14/12	h	Kerkyra	W	2-1	*Pereyra, Kaçe*
18/12	a	Giannina	L	0-3	
21/12	a	Levadiakos	W	2-1	*Tzavellas, Pereyra*
2015					
03/01	h	Panionios	W	3-2	*Miguel Vítor, Maduro, Athanasiadis (p)*
10/01	a	Asteras	L	0-3	
14/01	a	Kalloni	W	2-1	*Pereyra 2*
18/01	h	Platanias	W	1-0	*Athanasiadis*
25/01	a	Niki Volou	W	3-0	*(w/o)*
31/01	h	Panetolikos	L	1-2	*Mak*
04/02	a	OFI	L	1-2	*Papadopoulos*
08/02	h	Olympiacos	D	0-0	
15/02	a	Atromitos	L	0-4	
21/02	a	Veria	W	3-1	*Pereyra, Miguel Vítor, Noboa*
08/03	h	Panathinaikos	L	3-4	*Athanasiadis, Skondras, Noboa*
14/03	a	Asteras	D	0-0	
18/03	h	Ergotelis	W	1-0	*Papadopoulos*
21/03	a	Panthrakikos	L	1-3	*Papadopoulos*
05/04	h	Xanthi	W	2-1	*Papadopoulos 2*
18/04	a	Kerkyra	W	1-0	*Kaçe*
26/04	a	Giannina	D	1-1	*Pereyra*
03/05	h	Levadiakos	W	1-0	*Papadopoulos (p)*
10/05	a	Panionios	D	0-0	

No	Name	Nat	DoB	Pos	Aps	(s)	Gls
33	Stefanos Athanasiadis		24/12/88	A	24	(2)	11
23	Panagiotis Deligiannidis		29/08/96	A		(1)	
71	Panagiotis Glykos		10/10/86	G	15		
7	Eyal Golasa	ISR	07/10/91	M	14	(10)	
1	Charles Itandje	CMR	02/11/82	G	18	(1)	
26	Ergys Kaçe	ALB	08/07/93	M	25		4
4	Georgios Katsikas		14/06/90	D	10	(2)	
70	Stilianos Kitsiou		28/09/93	D	9	(9)	
22	Dimitrios Konstantinidis		02/06/94	D	9	(3)	
18	Efthimios Koulouris		06/03/96	A	3	(7)	
8	Hedwiges Maduro	NED	13/02/85	M	8	(2)	1
3	Róbert Mak	SVK	08/03/91	A	22	(3)	7
40	Maarten Martens	BEL	02/07/84	M	2	(6)	
15	Miguel Vítor	POR	30/06/89	D	29		2
16	Christian Noboa	ECU	09/04/85	M	12	(2)	2
9	Dimitrios Papadopoulos		20/10/81	A	9	(11)	7
13	Sotirios Papagiannopoulos		05/09/90	D	3	(4)	
10	Facundo Pereyra	ARG	03/09/87	M	26	(4)	11
44	Achilleas Pougouras		13/12/95	D		(1)	
24	Stilianos Pozatzidis		24/06/94	D	1	(4)	
96	Stilianos Pozoglou		22/01/96	M	1	(4)	
5	Răzvan Raţ	ROU	26/05/81	D	23	(2)	3
20	Ricardo Costa	POR	16/05/81	D	9	(1)	
14	Dimitrios Salpingidis		18/08/81	A	19	(3)	3
88	Kyriakos Savvidis		20/06/95	M		(4)	
2	Ioannis Skondras		21/02/90	D	23	(3)	2
21	Nikolaos Spyropoulos		10/10/83	D	5	(1)	
32	Theofanis Tzandaris		13/06/93	M	16	(4)	
3	Georgios Tzavellas		26/11/87	D	12	(1)	1
6	Alexandros Tziolis		13/02/85	M	16	(4)	

PAS Giannina FC

1966 • Oi Zosimades (7,652) • pasgiannina.gr
Coach: Ioannis Petrakis

2014
24/08	h	Asteras	W	3-1	*Chávez, Ilić, Tzimopoulos*
30/08	a	Panthrakikos	D	1-1	*Noé Acosta*
14/09	h	Xanthi	D	2-2	*Ilić, Chávez*
21/09	a	Kerkyra	L	0-2	
28/09	a	Veria	L	0-2	
20/10	a	Panionios	W	1-0	*Noé Acosta*
25/10	h	Kalloni	D	0-0	
01/11	a	Platanias	D	0-0	
09/11	h	Niki Volou	W	4-3	*Mihail, Manias, Ilić, Tsoukalas*
30/11	a	OFI	W	3-0	*Chávez 2 (1p), Ilić (p)*
03/12	h	Levadiakos	L	0-4	
06/12	a	Olympiacos	D	2-2	*Mihail, Giakos*
14/12	h	Atromitos	W	1-0	*Chávez*
18/12	h	PAOK	W	3-0	*Lila, Korovesis, Manias*
21/12	a	Ergotelis	L	0-1	

2015
05/01	h	Panathinaikos	D	0-0	
11/01	a	Panetolikos	D	0-0	
14/01	a	Asteras	D	2-2	*Korovesis 2*
18/01	h	Panthrakikos	D	2-2	*Manias 2*
24/01	a	Xanthi	D	1-1	*Chávez*
01/02	h	Kerkyra	W	2-1	*Ilić, Manias*
04/02	h	Veria	W	4-1	*Tsoukalas, Manias, Tzimopoulos 2*
07/02	a	Levadiakos	W	2-1	*Tzimopoulos, Manias*
14/02	h	Panionios	L	1-3	*Tsoukalas*
21/02	a	Kalloni	L	0-1	
08/03	h	Niki Volou	W	3-0	*(w/o)*
15/03	h	Panetolikos	D	0-0	
18/03	h	Platanias	W	1-0	*Noé Acosta*
21/03	a	OFI	W	3-0	*(w/o)*
05/04	h	Olympiacos	W	3-1	*Ilić, Manias, Noé Acosta*
19/04	a	Atromitos	D	1-1	*Chávez*
26/04	a	PAOK	D	1-1	*Chávez*
03/05	h	Ergotelis	D	0-0	
10/05	a	Panathinaikos	L	1-3	*Ilić*

No	Name	Nat	DoB	Pos	Aps	(s)	Gls
18	Mihail Avgenikou		25/01/93	M	2	(2)	
4	Theodoros Berios		21/03/89	D	16	(6)	
15	Charilaos Charisis		12/01/95	M	14	(8)	
10	Cristian Chávez	ARG	04/06/87	M	28		8
2	Georgios Dasios		12/05/83	D	13	(6)	
17	Fonsi	ESP	22/01/86	D	13	(6)	
93	Iraklis Garoufalias		01/05/93	D	1		
7	Evripidis Giakos		09/04/91	A	9	(14)	1
19	Antonios Iliadis		27/07/93	A		(2)	
9	Brana Ilić	SRB	16/02/85	A	29	(2)	7
33	Nikolaos Korovesis		10/06/91	D	18	(6)	3
25	Anastasios G Kritikos		25/01/95	M	1	(2)	
3	Andi Lila	ALB	12/02/86	D	13	(1)	1
33	Mihail Manias		20/02/90	A	19	(9)	8
6	Alexios Mihail		18/08/86	D	31		2
11	Noé Acosta	ESP	10/12/83	M	22	(6)	4
90	Stamatis Sapalidis		05/07/90	A	1	(12)	
44	Apostolos Skondras		29/12/88	D	2	(7)	
77	Dimitrios Sotiriou		13/09/87	G		(1)	
23	Andraž Struna	SVN	23/04/89	D	30		
28	Stavros Tsoukalas		23/05/88	M	30	(1)	3
8	Themistoklis Tzimopoulos		20/11/85	M	28		4
1	Markos Vellidis		04/04/87	G	32		

Platanias FC

1931 • Dimotiko Perivolion (3,700) • fcplatanias.gr
Coach: Ioannis Christopoulos; (12/03/15) (Ioannis Thomaidis); (17/03/15) Georgios Parashos

2014
24/08	a	Atromitos	L	0-1	
31/08	h	PAOK	L	0-4	
15/09	a	Ergotelis	W	3-0	*Tsourakis, Gilvan Gomes, David Torres*
21/09	h	Panathinaikos	L	2-3	*Coulibaly, David Torres*
27/09	h	Asteras	W	1-0	*Nazlidis (p)*
19/10	a	Xanthi	W	1-0	*Nazlidis (p)*
26/10	a	Kerkyra	W	2-1	*Nazlidis (p), Juan Aguilera*
01/11	h	Giannina	D	0-0	
09/11	a	Levadiakos	D	0-0	
29/11	a	Kalloni	D	0-0	
03/12	a	Panthrakikos	L	0-1	
06/12	h	Veria	L	0-2	
13/12	h	Niki Volou	W	3-1	*Nazlidis, Gilvan Gomes 2*
17/12	a	Panetolikos	L	0-1	
20/12	h	OFI	W	1-0	*Tetteh*

2015
04/01	a	Olympiacos	L	1-2	*Juan Aguilera*
10/01	h	Panionios	W	3-0	*Milunović 2, David Torres*
15/01	a	Atromitos	D	0-0	
18/01	a	PAOK	L	0-1	
26/01	h	Ergotelis	L	1-2	*Goundoulakis*
01/02	a	Panathinaikos	L	0-3	
04/02	a	Asteras	L	0-1	
08/02	h	Panthrakikos	W	2-0	*Coulibaly, Milunović*
16/02	a	Xanthi	D	0-0	
22/02	h	Kerkyra	D	1-1	*Tetteh*
09/03	h	Levadiakos	L	1-3	*Tetteh*
15/03	a	Panionios	D	0-0	
18/03	a	Giannina	L	0-1	
23/03	h	Kalloni	W	1-0	*David Torres*
04/04	h	Veria	W	1-0	*David Torres*
19/04	a	Niki Volou	W	3-0	*(w/o)*
26/04	h	Panetolikos	W	2-0	*David Torres, Giakoumakis*
03/05	a	OFI	W	3-0	*(w/o)*
10/05	h	Olympiacos	D	1-1	*og (Avlonitis)*

No	Name	Nat	DoB	Pos	Aps	(s)	Gls
77	Alexandros Apostolopoulos		07/11/91	D	15	(5)	
3	Yaya Banana	CMR	29/07/91	D	25	(1)	
45	Herron Berrian	LBR	31/07/94	A	4	(2)	
16	Cássio	BRA	20/08/90	A	7	(2)	
23	Ousmane Coulibaly	MLI	09/07/89	D	22	(2)	2
9	David Torres	ESP	16/06/86	A	21	(7)	6
5	Alkiviadis Dimitris		23/07/80	D	17	(5)	
18	Walter Figueira	ENG	17/03/95	M	1	(7)	
10	Jaime Gavilán	ESP	12/05/85	M	4	(4)	
94	Georgios Giakoumakis		09/12/94	A	4	(5)	1
84	Gilvan Gomes	BRA	09/04/84	A	12	(3)	3
20	Fanourios Goundoulakis		07/03/87	M	7	(7)	1
14	Juan Aguilera	ESP	13/09/85	M	26		2
8	Azrack-Yassine Mahamat	CHA	24/03/88	M	25	(7)	
33	Georgios Mahelis		10/05/91	D	2		
7	Konstantinos Mendrinos		28/05/85	M	15	(6)	
11	Luka Milunović	SRB	21/12/92	A	14	(9)	3
10	Thomas Nazlidis		23/10/87	A	8	(5)	3
17	Yevhen Neplyakh	UKR	11/05/92	D	7	(1)	
1	Kévin Olimpa	FRA	10/03/88	G	30		
22	Bernard Onanga Itoua	FRA	07/09/88	D	26	(2)	
91	Konstantinos Peristeridis		24/01/91	G	2		
55	Abdul Aziz Tetteh	GHA	25/05/90	M	23	(4)	3
19	Nikiforos Tsontakis		12/04/94	M		(2)	
21	Athanasios Tsourakis		12/05/90	A	19	(4)	1
31	Ioannis Zaradoukas		12/12/85	D	16	(5)	
33	Angelos Zoumboulakis		23/05/89	M		(1)	

Veria FC

1960 • Dimotikon Verias (7,000) • veriafc.gr
Coach: José Carlos Granero (ESP); (20/03/15) (Stefanos Gaitanos); (03/04/15) (Giorgos Lanaris); (06/04/15) (Stefanos Gaitanos)

2014
24/08	h	Xanthi	W	3-2	*Vergonis, Ben Nabouhane, Dumitru*
01/09	a	OFI	W	1-0	*Kaltsas*
13/09	h	Kerkyra	W	2-1	*Cámpora, Dumitru*
20/09	a	Olympiacos	L	0-3	
28/09	h	Giannina	W	2-0	*Cámpora, Kaltsas*
19/10	h	Levadiakos	W	2-1	*Battión, Dumitru*
26/10	a	PAOK	L	1-4	*Ben Nabouhane*
01/11	h	Panionios	D	2-2	*Cámpora, Raúl Bravo*
08/11	a	Ergotelis	D	2-2	*Kaltsas, Ben Nabouhane (p)*
30/11	a	Panathinaikos	L	1-2	*Kaltsas*
03/12	a	Atromitos	D	0-0	
06/12	h	Platanias	W	2-0	*Balafas, Cámpora*
14/12	a	Asteras	L	0-2	
17/12	h	Niki Volou	W	2-0	*Cámpora, Kaltsas*
20/12	a	Panthrakikos	D	1-1	*Kaltsas*

2015
03/01	h	Panetolikos	L	1-3	*Kaltsas*
10/01	h	Kalloni	D	1-1	*Kaltsas*
14/01	a	Xanthi	D	2-2	*Ben Nabouhane, Kaltsas*
17/01	h	OFI	W	4-1	*Ben Nabouhane 2 (1p), Pavlidis, Kaltsas*
24/01	a	Kerkyra	L	0-4	
01/02	h	Olympiacos	L	0-2	
04/02	a	Giannina	L	1-4	*Vergonis*
07/02	h	Atromitos	D	1-1	*Dumitru*
15/02	a	Levadiakos	W	2-0	*Marangos, Kaltsas*
21/02	h	PAOK	L	1-3	*Dumitru*
07/03	h	Ergotelis	L	0-1	
15/03	a	Kalloni	L	1-4	*Kaltsas*
18/03	h	Panionios	L	2-4	*Bargan, Ben Nabouhane*
22/03	h	Panathinaikos	W	1-0	*Ben Nabouhane*
04/04	a	Platanias	L	0-1	
20/04	h	Asteras	W	4-0	*Dumitru, Ben Nabouhane 2 (1p), Caballero*
26/04	h	Niki Volou	W	3-0	*(w/o)*
03/05	a	Panthrakikos	L	0-1	
10/05	a	Panetolikos	L	0-2	

No	Name	Nat	DoB	Pos	Aps	(s)	Gls
23	Dimitrios Amarantidis		27/07/86	D	20		
15	Pedro Arce	MEX	25/11/91	M		(4)	
25	Sotirios Balafas		19/08/86	M	15	(1)	1
11	Kenan Bargan		25/10/88	A	11	(12)	1
6	Roberto Battión	ARG	02/03/82	M	20	(2)	1
31	El Fardou Ben Nabouhane	COM	10/06/89	A	22	(6)	10
30	Carlos Caballero	ESP	05/10/84	M	3	(4)	1
9	Javier Cámpora	ARG	07/01/80	A	18	(10)	5
14	David Vázquez	ESP	21/03/86	M	12	(5)	
12	Nicolao Dumitru	ITA	12/10/91	A	21	(6)	6
77	Georgios K Georgiadis		14/11/87	A	11	(8)	
10	Nigel Hasselbaink	NED	21/11/90	A		(1)	
18	Iván Malón	ESP	26/08/86	D	20		
24	Jokin Esparza	ESP	15/06/88	A	1	(3)	
4	José Catalá	ESP	01/01/85	D	1	(3)	
3	Cyril Kali	FRA	21/04/84	D	14	(2)	
7	Nikolaos A Kaltsas		03/05/90	M	29	(1)	12
1	Georgios Kantimiris		19/09/82	G	28		
16	Georgios Katidis		12/02/93	M		(4)	
19	Cédric Mandjeck	CMR	08/04/93	M	1	(1)	
55	Stilianos Marangos		04/05/89	M	10		1
13	Thomas Nazlidis		23/10/87	A	2	(5)	
16	Neto	BRA	07/02/81	D	7	(1)	
8	Branko Ostojić	SRB	03/01/84	M	14	(4)	
32	Charalambos Pavlidis		06/05/91	M	6	(1)	1
2	Raúl Bravo	ESP	14/04/81	D	23		1
29	Andreas Tatos		11/05/89	M	6	(4)	
55	Evangelos Tsiamis		14/07/91	M	1		
21	Alexandros Vergonis		01/12/85	M	19	(6)	2
5	Angelos Vertzos		27/05/83	D	23		
99	Zvonimir Vukić	SRB	19/07/79	M		(3)	
22	Xavi Ginard	ESP	11/10/86	G	5		

Xanthi FC

1967 • Škoda Xanthi Arena (7,500) •
skodaxanthifc.gr

Coach: Sakis Tsiolis;
(16/09/14) (Nikolaos Nentidis);
(24/09/14) Răzvan Lucescu (ROU)

2014

24/08	a	Veria	L	2-3	Obodo, Lucero
31/08	h	Kerkyra	D	0-0	
14/09	a	Giannina	D	2-2	Soltani 2
20/09	h	Levadiakos	W	2-0	Kapetanos, Cleyton
27/09	a	Panionios	D	1-1	Kapetanos
19/10	a	Platanias	L	0-1	
27/10	h	Niki Volou	W	2-0	Cleyton, Soltani
02/11	a	Panetolikos	L	2-5	Lisgaras, Lucero
08/11	h	OFI	W	2-1	Lisgaras, Cleyton
29/11	a	Atromitos	L	0-2	
03/12	h	Kalloni	W	2-1	Soltani, Cleyton (p)
07/12	h	PAOK	W	4-2	Kapetanos 2, Lucero, Cleyton
14/12	a	Ergotelis	W	2-0	Lisgaras, Obodo
18/12	h	Panathinaikos	W	4-2	Goutas, Vasilakakis, Soltani, Kapetanos
21/12	a	Asteras	L	1-2	Cleyton (p)

2015

05/01	h	Panthrakikos	D	0-0	
11/01	h	Olympiacos	L	1-3	Lucero
14/01	h	Veria	D	2-2	Kapetanos, Goutas
17/01	h	Kerkyra	D	0-0	
24/01	h	Giannina	D	1-1	Cleyton
01/02	a	Levadiakos	W	2-1	Ghomsi, Kapetanos
04/02	h	Panionios	D	1-1	Kapetanos
09/02	a	Kalloni	D	2-2	Soltani, Lucero
16/02	h	Platanias	D	0-0	
21/02	a	Niki Volou	W	3-0	(w/o)
08/03	h	OFI	W	1-0	Kapetanos
15/03	a	Olympiacos	L	0-2	
18/03	h	Panetolikos	W	3-0	Papazoglou, Cleyton, Kapetanos
22/03	h	Atromitos	W	1-0	Cleyton
05/04	a	PAOK	L	1-2	Cleyton
18/04	h	Ergotelis	L	0-1	
25/04	a	Panathinaikos	L	0-2	
03/05	h	Asteras	D	0-0	
10/05	a	Panthrakikos	L	0-2	

No	Name	Nat	DoB	Pos	Aps	(s)	Gls
5	Dimosthenis Baxevanidis		14/04/88	M	20	(5)	
88	Nikola Beljić	SRB	14/05/83	M	6	(2)	
4	Emmanouil Bertos		13/05/89	D	18	(2)	
20	Cleyton	BRA	08/03/83	M	22	(3)	10
21	Konstantinos Fliskas		22/12/80	D	17	(6)	
1	Athanasios Garavelis		06/08/92	G	1		
3	Antonio Ghomsi	CMR	22/04/86	D	9		1
28	Dimitrios Goutas		04/04/94	D	21	(2)	2
30	Pantelis Kapetanos		08/06/83	A	27	(4)	10
55	Christos Karipidis		02/12/82	D	18	(1)	
23	Dimitrios Komesidis		02/02/88	D	5	(1)	
82	Dimitrios Kyriakidis		24/06/86	G	27		
31	Christos Lisgaras		12/02/86	D	17		3
11	Adrián Lucero	ARG	16/08/84	M	28	(4)	5
15	Christian Obodo	NGA	11/05/84	M	17	(11)	2
24	Petros Orfanidis		23/03/96	M		(1)	
17	Emmanouil Papasterianos		15/08/87	M	16	(10)	
12	Anastasios Papazoglou		24/09/88	D	9		1
99	Antonios Ranos		15/06/93	A	4	(12)	
77	Rennan	BRA	01/08/91	M	3	(4)	
14	Rudy	POR	05/01/89	A	2	(5)	
9	Karim Soltani	ALG	29/08/84	A	26	(2)	6
7	Panagiotis Triadis		09/09/92	A	2	(1)	
16	Theodoros Vasilakakis		20/07/88	M	21	(9)	1
8	Wallace	BRA	29/10/86	D	16	(5)	
14	Walter Fernández	ESP	14/08/89	M	6	(8)	
91	Mihail Zaropoulos		12/07/91	G	5		

Top goalscorers

17	Jerónimo Barrales (Asteras)
16	Kostas Mitroglou (Olympiacos)
15	Alejandro Domínguez (Olympiacos)
13	Stefano Napoleoni (Atromitos)
	Marcus Berg (Panathinaikos)
	Nikolaos Karelis (Panathinaikos)
12	Nikolaos A Kaltsas (Veria)
11	Dimitrios Kolovos (Panionios)
	Igor (Panthrakikos)
	Stefanos Athanasiadis (PAOK)
	Facundo Pereyra (PAOK)

Promoted clubs

AEK Athens FC

1924 • OACA Spyro Louis (74,767) • aekfc.gr

Major honours
Greek League (11) 1939, 1940, 1963, 1968, 1971,
1978, 1979, 1989, 1992, 1993, 1994; Greek Cup
(14) 1932, 1939, 1949, 1950, 1956, 1964, 1966,
1978, 1983, 1996, 1997, 2000, 2002, 2011

Coach: Traianos Dellas

Iraklis FC

1908 • Kaftanzoglio (29,080) • fciraklis.gr

Major honours
Greek Cup (1) 1976

Coach: Nikos Papadopoulos

Second level final tables 2014/15

North		Pld	W	D	L	F	A	Pts
1	Iraklis FC	24	17	6	1	34	8	57
2	Olympiacos Volou FC	24	14	3	7	33	21	45
3	Larissa FC	24	14	3	7	27	11	45
4	PAS Lamia 1964	24	12	7	5	24	17	43
5	Zakynthos FC	24	11	6	7	26	27	39
6	Anagennisis Karditsas FC	24	10	2	12	26	27	32
7	Aiginiakos Aiginiou FC	24	8	6	10	23	19	30
8	Pierikos FC	24	7	9	8	19	29	30
9	Agrotikos Asteras FC	24	8	5	11	23	27	29
10	Tyrnavos FC	24	7	8	9	16	24	29
11	Apollon Kalamarias FC	24	7	5	12	19	23	26
12	Ethnikos Gazoros FC	24	3	6	15	11	30	15
13	Fokikos FC	24	2	6	16	12	30	12

South		Pld	W	D	L	F	A	Pts
1	AEK Athens FC	24	22	2	0	67	10	65
2	Panachaiki FC	24	14	4	6	41	22	46
3	Apollon Smyrnis FC	24	13	6	5	32	17	45
4	AO Chania FC	24	12	6	6	28	20	42
5	AE Ermionidas FC	24	12	5	7	30	28	41
6	Panegialios FC	24	11	7	6	24	12	40
7	Acharnaikos FC	24	9	8	7	28	22	35
8	Kallithea FC	24	9	6	9	25	25	33
9	Episkopi FC	24	7	5	12	25	34	26
10	Iraklis Psachna FC	24	6	5	13	23	37	23
11	AOT Alimos	24	5	6	13	15	25	21
12	Fostiras FC	24	4	3	17	20	43	15
13	Paniliakos FC	24	0	1	23	7	70	-1

*NB AEK Athens FC – 3 pts deducted; Paniliakos FC –
2 pts deducted; Paniliakos FC withdrew after round 8 –
their remaining matches were awarded as 0-3 defeats.*

Promotion play-offs final table

		Pld	W	D	L	F	A	Pts
1	AEK Athens FC	10	5	3	2	14	9	28
2	Iraklis FC	10	6	1	3	10	5	26
3	Apollon Smyrnis FC	10	6	2	2	16	10	20
4	Larissa FC	10	4	1	5	10	11	13
5	Olympiacos Volou FC	10	3	1	6	8	12	10
6	Panachaiki FC	10	1	2	7	12	23	5

*NB Points carried forward from first stage – AEK Athens
FC 10 pts, Iraklis FC 7 pts, Apollon Smyrnis FC, Larissa
FC, Olympiacos Volou FC & Panachaiki FC 0 pts.*

UEFA Champions League qualification play-offs 2014/15

(20/05/15)
Asteras 0-4 Panathinaikos
(Schildenfeld 23, Karelis 45, 55,
Berg 82)
Atromitos 1-1 PAOK (Agouazi 7;
Pereyra 32)

(24/05/15)
Panathinaikos 2-0 Atromitos
(Berg 61, 67)
PAOK 0-0 Asteras

(27/05/15)
Atromitos 0-0 Asteras
PAOK 0-1 Panathinaikos
(Tavlaridis 43)

(31/05/15)
Asteras 1-0 Atromitos
(Kourbelis 66)
Panathinaikos 2-0 PAOK (Mavrias
10, Karelis 28)

(03/06/15)
Panathinaikos 0-0 Asteras
PAOK 0-1 Atromitos
(Karamanos 45)

(07/06/15)
Asteras 1-0 PAOK (Iglesias 77)
Atromitos 2-0 Panathinaikos
(Katsouranis 41, 61)

			Home				Away					Total					
		Pld	W	D	L	F	A	W	D	L	F	A	W	D	L	F	A	Pts
2	Panathinaikos FC	6	2	1	0	4	0	2	0	1	5	2	4	1	1	9	2	15
3	Asteras Tripolis FC	6	2	0	1	2	4	0	3	0	0	0	2	3	1	2	4	10
4	Atromitos FC	6	1	2	0	3	1	1	0	2	1	3	2	2	2	4	4	8
5	PAOK FC	6	0	1	2	0	2	0	1	2	1	4	0	2	4	1	6	4

NB Points carried forward from Superleague – Panathinaikos & PAOK 2 pts, Asteras 1 pt, Atromitos 0 pts

DOMESTIC CUP

Kypello Ellados 2014/15

SECOND ROUND

Group 1

(23/09/14)
Panachaiki 0-1 Olympiacos
(24/09/14)
Panionios 0-0 Fostiras
(28/10/14)
Fostiras 0-2 Panachaiki
(29/10/14)
Olympiacos 1-1 Panionios
(07/01/15)
Fostiras 0-2 Olympiacos
Panionios 4-0 Panachaiki

Final standings
1 Olympiacos 7 pts; 2 Panionios 5 pts *(qualified)*;
3 Panachaiki 3 pts; 4 Fostiras 1 pt *(eliminated)*

Group 2

(25/09/14)
Apollon Kalamarias 1-0 PAOK
Giannina 1-0 Kerkyra
(29/10/14)
PAOK 1-1 Giannina
(30/10/14)
Kerkyra 3-0 Apollon Kalamarias
(07/01/15)
Giannina 2-1 Apollon Kalamarias
Kerkyra 0-0 PAOK

Final standings
1 Giannina 7 pts; 2 Kerkyra 4 pts *(qualified)*;
3 Apollon Kalamarias 3 pts; 4 PAOK 2 pts
(eliminated)

Group 3

(24/09/14)
Xanthi 1-0 Niki Volou
Zakynthos 1-1 OFI
(30/10/14)
Niki Volou 0-3 Zakynthos *(w/o)*
OFI 1-0 Xanthi
(08/01/15)
Niki Volou 0-3 OFI *(w/o)*
Xanthi 3-1 Zakynthos

Final standings
1 OFI 7 pts; 2 Xanthi 6 pts *(qualified)*;
3 Zakynthos 4 pts; 4 Niki Volou 0 pts *(eliminated)*

Group 4

(23/09/14)
Iraklis 1-1 Levadiakos
(24/09/14)
Platanias 3-1 Ethnikos Gazoros
(28/10/14)
Ethnikos Gazoros 1-2 Iraklis
(29/10/14)
Levadiakos 2-0 Platanias
(07/01/15)
Ethnikos Gazoros 0-2 Levadiakos
Platanias 0-0 Iraklis

Final standings
1 Levadiakos 7 pts; 2 Iraklis 5 pts *(qualified)*;
3 Platanias 4 pts; 4 Ethnikos Gazoros 0 pts
(eliminated)

Group 5

(23/09/14)
Iraklis Psachna 0-1 Atromitos
(24/09/14)
Panthrakikos 0-0 AEK
(28/10/14)
AEK 3-0 Iraklis Psachna
(29/10/14)
Atromitos 1-1 Panthrakikos
(08/01/15)
AEK 3-0 Atromitos
Panthrakikos 2-1 Iraklis Psachna

Final standings
1 AEK 7 pts; 2 Panthrakikos 5 pts *(qualified)*;
3 Atromitos 4 pts; 4 Iraklis Psachna 0 pts
(eliminated)

Group 6

(24/09/14)
Apollon Smirnis 2-2 Ergotelis
Veria 4-1 AE Ermionidas
(29/10/14)
Ergotelis 0-2 Veria
(30/10/14)
AE Ermionidas 0-1 Apollon Smirnis
(07/01/15)
AE Ermionidas 2-0 Ergotelis
Veria 1-1 Apollon Smirnis

Final standings
1 Veria 7 pts; 2 Apollon Smirnis 5 pts *(qualified)*;
3 AE Ermionidas 3 pts; 4 Ergotelis 1 pt *(eliminated)*

Group 7

(24/09/14)
Aiginiakos Aiginiou 1-4 Asteras Tripolis
Kalloni 1-1 Tyrnavos
(28/10/14)
Tyrnavos 2-1 Aiginiakos Aiginiou
(29/10/14)
Asteras Tripolis 2-1 Kalloni
(07/01/15)
Kalloni 5-0 Aiginiakos Aiginiou
Tyrnavos 1-1 Asteras Tripolis

Final standings
1 Asteras Tripolis 7 pts; 2 Tyrnavos 5 pts *(qualified)*;
3 Kalloni 4 pts; 4 Aiginiakos Aiginiou 0 pts *(eliminated)*

Group 8

(24/09/14)
Olympiacos Volou 0-1 Panathinaikos
(25/09/14)
Panetolikos 0-1 AO Chania
(28/10/14)
AO Chania 0-0 Olympiacos Volou
(30/10/14)
Panathinaikos 3-1 Panetolikos
(08/01/15)
AO Chania 2-2 Panathinaikos
Panetolikos 0-2 Olympiacos Volou

Final standings
1 Panathinaikos 7 pts; 2 AO Chania 5 pts
(qualified);
3 Olympiacos Volou 4 pts; 4 Panetolikos 0 pts
(eliminated)

THIRD ROUND

(20/01/15 & 28/01/15)
Panionios 2-1, 1-1 Veria *(3-2)*

(21/01/15 & 27/01/15)
Apollon Smirnis 1-1, 4-1 Levadiakos *(5-2)*
Iraklis 1-1, 1-0 Asteras Tripolis *(2-1)*

(21/01/15 & 28/01/15)
AO Chania 1-2, 2-1 Giannina *(aet; 3-3; 5-3 on pens)*
Tyrnavos 0-3, 0-8 Olympiacos *(0-11)*

(21/01/15 & 29/01/15)
Kerkyra 1-1, 0-2 AEK *(1-3)*
Xanthi 1-1, 1-0 Panathinaikos *(2-1)*

(22/01/15 & 27/01/15)
Panthrakikos 0-4, 0-1 OFI *(0-5)*

QUARTER-FINALS

(11/02/15 & 04/03/15)
Iraklis 2-0 Panionios *(Korbos 15og, Romano 74)*
Panionios 2-0 Iraklis *(Kolovos 19p, Boumale 45) (aet)*
(2-2; Iraklis 4-3 on pens)

(11/02/15 & 11/03/15)
Olympiacos 1-1 AEK *(Milivojević 48; Aravidis 14)*
AEK 0-3 Olympiacos *(w/o; original match
abandoned after 90 mins at 0-1 Jara 89)*
(Olympiacos 4-1)

(12/02/15 & 05/03/15)
AO Chania 1-1 Apollon Smirnis *(Kritikos 81;
Souanis 76p)*
Apollon Smirnis 3-1 AO Chania *(Angulo 39,
Farinola 59, Souanis 66; Kritikos 43)*
(Apollon Smirnis 4-2)

OFI 1-1 Xanthi *(Koutsianikoulis 48; Soltani 52)*
Xanthi 3-0 OFI *(Soltani 18, 85, Cleyton 26p)*
(Xanthi 4-1)

SEMI-FINALS

(08/04/15 & 29/04/15)
Apollon Smirnis 0-3 Olympiacos *(Botía 20, Jara 26,
Dossevi 57)*
Olympiacos 1-1 Apollon Smirnis *(Benítez 84;
Angulo 43)*
(Olympiacos 4-1))

(09/04/15 & 29/04/15)
Iraklis 0-1 Xanthi *(Cleyton 7)*
Xanthi 0-0 Iraklis
(Xanthi 1-0)

FINAL

(23/05/15)
OACA Spyro Louis, Athens
OLYMPIACOS FC 3 *(Jara 45+1, Dominguez 63,
Fortounis 80)*
XANTHI FC 1 *(Kapetanos 87)*
Referee: *Koukoulakis*
OLYMPIACOS: *Roberto, Botía, Siovas (Kasami 84),
Masuaku, Leandro Salino, Milivojević, N'Dinga,
Domínguez (Mitroglou 79), David Fuster (Fortounis
65), Dossevi, Jara*
Red card: *Botía (90+1)*
XANTHI: *Kyriakidis, Bertos (Baxevanidis 78),
Wallace, Goutas, Karipidis, Obodo (Walter
Fernández 79), Papasterianos (Kapetanos 66),
Vasilakakis, Cleyton, Lucero, Soltani*

HUNGARY
Magyar Labdarúgó Szövetség (MLSZ)

Address	Kánai út 2.D	**President**	Sándor Csányi
	HU-1112 Budapest	**General secretary**	Márton Vági
Tel	+36 1 577 9500	**Media officer**	Márton Dinnyés
Fax	+36 1 577 9503	**Year of formation**	1901
E-mail	mlsz@mlsz.hu		
Website	mlsz.hu		

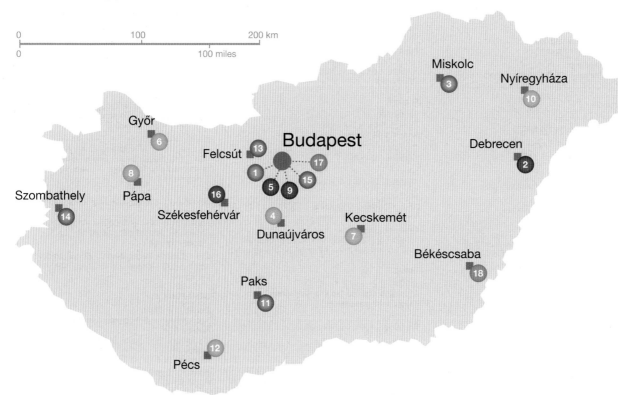

NB 1 CLUBS

 1 Budapest Honvéd FC

 2 Debreceni VSC

 3 Diósgyőri VTK

 4 Dunaújváros PASE

 5 Ferencvárosi TC

 6 Győri ETO FC

 7 Kecskeméti TE

 8 Lombard Pápa TFC

 9 MTK Budapest

 10 Nyíregyháza Spartacus FC

 11 Paksi FC

 12 Pécsi MFC

 13 Puskás Akadémia FC

 14 Szombathelyi Haladás

 15 Újpest FC

 16 Videoton FC

PROMOTED CLUBS

 17 Vasas SC

 18 Békéscsaba 1912 Előre SE

KEY:

● – UEFA Champions League

● – UEFA Europa League

● – Promoted

● – Relegated

Videoton fast-forward to victory

The 2014/15 Hungarian NB I title was won in commanding style by Videoton FC, who sped out of the blocks under their new head coach Joan Carrillo, posting ten successive wins, and were never seriously challenged thereafter.

While Videoton added a second league title to the one they had won in 2010/11, Ferencváros ended an 11-year wait for silverware by thrashing the champions 4-0 in the Hungarian Cup final. The match was staged in their new Groupama Aréna home, where they remained unbeaten all season.

Szekesfehervar club storm to second NB I title	Revitalised Ferencváros enjoy comforts of new home	Dárdai steps in to raise EURO qualifying hopes

Domestic league

Although Videoton were also fast starters in 2013/14, they eventually dropped down to fourth place and out of Europe, which resulted in Portuguese coach José Gomes being relieved of his duties. Impressed by Carillo's three-year service as an assistant, the powers-that-be at the Szekesfehervar club decided to hand the Spaniard the top job. It proved to be a masterstroke.

The Videoton squad was not significantly different from that of the previous season, but Carrillo somehow managed to raise the game of virtually every key player, from his compatriot Juan Cataluyd in goal through long-serving Hungarian international Roland Juhász in defence, playmakers Filipe Oliveira and Ádám Gyurcsó in midfield to top-scoring Nemanja Nikolić in attack.

The team's flawless opening surge, embellished by 27 goals, was eventually halted when they lost 2-1 at home to defending champions Debreceni VSC, but that proved to be a mere blip. It was followed by a 15-game unbeaten run – incorporating matches against every other team in the division – that concluded with a revenge 2-1 win at Debrecen, a result that wrapped up the title with four matches still to play.

Videoton won only one of those, enabling in-form Ferencváros, unbeaten in 20 games, to close the gap to a somewhat flattering seven points. The same margin separated Fradi from third-placed MTK Budapest, while Debrecen's disappointing title defence left them a further three points back in fourth. There was grimmer news for 2012/13 champions Győri ETO FC, whose financial problems escalated to such a degree that they were one of four clubs – alongside Kecskeméti TE, Pécsi MFC and Nyíregyháza Spartacus FC – denied a licence to compete in the 2015/16 NB I, which was consequently reduced from 16 to 12 teams.

Domestic cup

Fallen giants Ferencváros enjoyed a fabulous first season in their new stadium. It was also the first full campaign under their German coach Thomas Doll, who had arrived midway through the previous one, and with club icon Zoltán Gera back in green and white stripes after a decade in England, the club looked in its best shape for years. Although their league charge came too late to trouble Videoton, they were far too strong for the champions in the cup final, a four-goal second-half blitz inspired by mid-season signing Roland Varga bringing Fradi a first major trophy since their 2003/04 double.

Europe

Highlights for Hungarian clubs in Europe during the summer of 2014 were few and far between as all four clubs made early exits. The most satisfying result was probably Diósgyőri VTK's 2-0 win in Bulgaria against PFC Litex Lovech, but that took them into the third qualifying round of the UEFA Europa League, where they were left battered and bruised by an 8-1 aggregate defeat to FC Krasnodar.

National team

Attila Pintér became the first coaching casualty of the UEFA EURO 2016 qualifying campaign when he was dismissed following Hungary's opening 2-1 home defeat by Northern Ireland – a game in which they went 1-0 up with just 15 minutes left. The team's fortunes were lifted, however, by his replacement, Pál Dárdai, who kicked off with a remedial 1-1 draw in Romania before steering the side to successive 1-0 wins over the Faroe Islands and Finland. The disappointment of a goalless draw at home to Greece was then outweighed by another 1-0 win against Finland in Helsinki – a result that enabled Hungary to strengthen their grip on third place in Group F and look forward with optimism to the autumn and the prospect of qualifying for a major tournament for the first time in 30 years.

DOMESTIC SEASON AT A GLANCE

NB I 2014/15 final table

		Pld	Home					Away					Total					Pts
			W	D	L	F	A	W	D	L	F	A	W	D	L	F	A	
1	**Videoton FC**	**30**	**13**	**1**	**1**	**40**	**5**	**9**	**4**	**2**	**24**	**9**	**22**	**5**	**3**	**64**	**14**	**71**
2	Ferencvárosi TC	30	12	3	0	28	4	7	4	4	21	15	19	7	4	49	19	64
3	MTK Budapest	30	11	1	3	23	9	7	2	6	16	16	18	3	9	39	25	57
4	Debreceni VSC	30	10	3	2	31	7	5	6	4	13	12	15	9	6	44	19	54
5	Paksi FC	30	9	3	3	24	11	5	6	4	20	16	14	9	7	44	27	51
6	Újpest FC	30	9	3	3	22	10	5	6	4	18	18	14	9	7	40	28	51
7	Diósgyőri VTK	30	10	3	2	30	18	3	6	6	13	18	13	9	8	43	36	48
8	Győri ETO FC	30	5	6	4	23	19	5	2	8	18	25	10	8	12	41	44	38
9	Kecskeméti TE	30	7	4	4	16	13	3	4	8	14	26	10	8	12	30	39	38
10	Puskás Akadémia FC	30	6	4	5	24	18	4	1	10	11	22	10	5	15	35	40	35
11	Pécsi MFC	30	4	4	7	15	23	4	3	8	17	28	8	7	15	32	51	31
12	Nyíregyháza Spartacus FC	30	4	5	6	19	18	4	1	10	14	31	8	6	16	33	49	30
13	Budapest Honvéd FC	30	5	5	5	18	15	1	5	9	8	21	6	10	14	26	36	28
14	Szombathelyi Haladás	30	5	2	8	18	25	2	2	11	8	28	7	4	19	26	53	25
15	Dunaújváros PASE	30	4	5	6	13	18	1	3	11	13	31	5	8	17	26	49	22
16	Lombard Pápa TFC	30	3	5	7	8	21	1	2	12	6	36	4	7	19	14	57	19

NB Dunaújváros PASE – 1 pt deducted.

European qualification 2015/16

Champion: Videoton FC (second qualifying round)

Cup winner: Ferencvárosi TC (first qualifying round)
MTK Budapest (first qualifying round)
Debreceni VSC (first qualifying round)

Top scorer	Nemanja Nikolić (Videoton), 21 goals
Relegated clubs	Lombard Pápa TFC, Dunaújváros PASE, Nyíregyháza Spartacus FC (excluded), Pécsi MFC (excluded), Kecskeméti TE (excluded), Győri ETO FC (excluded)
Promoted clubs	Vasas SC, Békéscsaba 1912 Előre SE
Cup final	Ferencvárosi TC 4-0 Videoton FC

Team of the season
(4-2-3-1)

Coach: Joan Carrillo *(Videoton)*

Player of the season

Nemanja Nikolić
(Videoton FC)

Videoton's feat in winning their opening ten league fixtures of the 2014/15 NB I was impressive enough, yet it was eclipsed by the fact that Nikolić scored in every one of them. Inevitably his output slowed up as the season progressed, but the Serbia-born Hungarian international, who played in all of his country's first six UEFA EURO 2016 qualifiers, still managed to end up as the division's top marksman by some distance, his 21 goals enabling him to retain the golden boot he had shared in 2013/14.

Newcomer of the season

Roland Sallai
(Puskás Akadémia FC)

Just 17 years old for most of the 2014/15 season, Sallai looked like being the star graduate of the Ferenc Puskás Academy when he scored two goals in consecutive NB I games in September. Although no further goals followed in the young attacking midfielder's first top-flight campaign, it was plain to see that he possessed the same footballing gifts displayed by his father Tibor and especially his uncle Sándor, who won 55 caps for Hungary and appeared at the FIFA World Cup finals of 1982 and 1986.

Tujvel
(Kecskemét)

Lázár *(Debrecen)* Juhász *(Videoton)* Kádár *(Diósgyőr)* Korhut *(Debrecen)*

Varga *(Debrecen)* Elek *(Diósgyőr)*

Bódi *(Debrecen)* Gera *(Ferencváros)* Filipe Oliveira *(Videoton)*

Nikolić *(Videoton)*

NATIONAL TEAM

International tournament appearances

FIFA World Cup (9) 1934 (2nd round), 1938 (runners-up), 1954 (runners-up), 1958, 1962 (qtr-finals), 1966 (qtr finals), 1978, 1982, 1986
UEFA European Championship (2) 1964 (3rd), 1972 (4th)

Top five all-time caps
József Bozsik (101); **Gábor Király** (95); László Fazekas (92); **Roland Juhász** (87); Gyula Grosics (86)

Top five all-time goals
Ferenc Puskás (84); Sándor Kocsis (75); Imre Schlosser (59); Lajos Tichy (51); György Sárosi (42)

Results 2014/15

07/09/14	Northern Ireland (ECQ)	H	Budapest	L	1-2	*Priskin (75)*
11/10/14	Romania (ECQ)	A	Bucharest	D	1-1	*Dzsudzsák (82)*
14/10/14	Faroe Islands (ECQ)	A	Torshavn	W	1-0	*Szalai (21)*
14/11/14	Finland (ECQ)	H	Budapest	W	1-0	*Gera (84)*
18/11/14	Russia	H	Budapest	L	1-2	*Nikolić (86)*
29/03/15	Greece (ECQ)	H	Budapest	D	0-0	
05/06/15	Lithuania	H	Debrecen	W	4-0	*Stieber (15), Dzsudzsák (20), Nikolić (29), Priskin (31)*
13/06/15	Finland (ECQ)	A	Helsinki	W	1-0	*Stieber (82)*

Appearances 2014/15

Coach: Attila Pintér /(18/09/14) Pál Dárdai	07/05/66 16/03/76		NIR	ROU	FRO	FIN	Rus	GRE	Ltu	FIN	Caps	Goals
Péter Gulácsi	06/05/90	Salzburg (AUT)	G								2	-
Vilmos Vanczák	20/06/83	Sion (SUI)	D								78	4
Roland Juhász	01/07/83	Videoton	D	D	D	D57	D	D		D	87	6
Zoltán Lipták	10/12/84	Győr	D								18	1
Ádám Gyurcsó	06/03/91	Videoton	M58				s65				12	1
József Varga	06/06/88	Debrecen	M	D	M						31	-
Dániel Tőzsér	12/05/85	Watford (ENG)	M	s77	M73	M	M	M	M	M	29	1
Balázs Balogh	11/06/90	Újpest	M									
Balázs Dzsudzsák	23/12/86	Dinamo Moskva (RUS)	M	M	M	M	M65	M	M	M88	69	17
Nemanja Nikolić	31/12/87	Videoton	A46	s46	A46	s63	s46	s68	A46	s77	13	3
Gergely Rudolf	09/03/85	Győr	A70								28	10
Tamás Priskin	27/09/86	Győr	s46		s84		s46		A46	A46	49	16
Gergő Lovrencsics	01/09/88	Lech (POL)	s58	M63		s77	M46				8	-
István Kovács	27/03/92	Videoton	s70				M46				5	-
Gábor Király	01/04/76	Fulham (ENG)		G		G		G	s46	G	95	-
Zsolt Korcsmár	09/01/89	Greuther Fürth (GER)		D							24	-
Tamás Kádár	14/03/90	Diósgyőr /Lech (POL)		D	D	D	D		D	D	22	-
Zoltán Gera	22/04/79	Ferencváros		M77	M	M		M		M	82	24
Zoltán Stieber	16/10/88	Hamburg (GER)		M46			s46	M	M46	M	9	2
Ákos Elek	21/07/88	Diósgyőr /Changchun Yatai (CHN)		M		M			M70		32	1
Ádám Szalai	09/12/87	Hoffenheim (GER)		A	A84	A63	A46	A68	s46	A77	26	8
Krisztián Simon	10/06/91	Újpest		s63	D	M77					4	-
Dénes Dibusz	16/11/90	Ferencváros			G		G		G46		3	-
Mihály Korhut	01/12/88	Debrecen			D						4	-
Attila Fiola	17/02/90	Paks /Puskás Akadémia		s46	D	D57		D	D46	D	6	-
Zsolt Kalmár	09/06/95	RB Leipzig (GER)			s73		M46				5	-
Ádám Lang	17/01/93	Győr				D			D	D	6	-
Gyula Forró	06/06/88	Újpest				s57	D		D46		3	-
Ádám Simon	30/03/90	Videoton					s46		M	s88	3	-
Patrik Poór	15/11/93	MTK					s57				1	-
Leandro	19/03/82	Omonia (CYP)						D	s46		13	-
Ádám Pintér	12/06/88	Levadiakos (GRE)						s70			18	-
Roland Szolnoki	21/01/92	Videoton							D		1	-
Krisztián Németh	05/01/89	Kansas City (USA)							s46	s46	17	1
Zoltán Szélesi	22/11/81	Puskás Akadémia							s46		28	-
Roland Varga	23/01/90	Ferencváros							s46		4	2

EUROPE

Debreceni VSC

Second qualifying round - Cliftonville FC (NIR)
A 0-0
Novaković, Bouadla, Lázár, Mészáros, Máté, Sidibé, Bódi (Mihelič 79), Varga, Tisza (Seydi 45+1), Korhut, Jovanović (Zsidai 86). Coach: Elemér Kondás (HUN)
H 2-0 Mihelič (55), Sidibé (79)
Novaković, Mihelič, Mészáros, Máté, Volaš, Sidibé (Tisza 83), Bódi (Zsidai 80), Varga, Szakály (Vadnai 72), Korhut, Jovanović. Coach: Elemér Kondás (HUN)

Third qualifying round - FC BATE Borisov (BLR)
H 1-0 Sidibé (56p)
Novaković, Zsidai, Mihelič (Bódi 32), Mészáros, Máté, Volaš (Seydi 62), Sidibé, Varga, Szakály (Bouadla 80), Korhut, Jovanović. Coach: Elemér Kondás (HUN)
A 1-3 Sidibé (20p)
Novaković, Zsidai (Ludánszki 65), Bouadla, Mészáros (Brković 84), Máté, Sidibé, Varga, Szakály (Bódi 71), Korhut, Jovanović, Seydi. Coach: Elemér Kondás (HUN)
Red card: Bouadla 38

Play-offs - BSC Young Boys (SUI)
A 1-3 Sidibé (39)
Poleksić, Zsidai, Mészáros, Máté, Sidibé, Bódi, Varga, Szakály, Korhut, Jovanović, Seydi (Kulcsár 74). Coach: Elemér Kondás (HUN)
H 0-0
Novaković, Zsidai, Vadnai (Ferenczi 79), Mészáros (Morozov 46), Máté, Sidibé, Bódi, Varga, Korhut, Kulcsár (Seydi 65), Jovanović. Coach: Elemér Kondás (HUN)
Red card: Seydi 90

Győri ETO FC

Second qualifying round - IFK Göteborg (SWE)
H 0-3
Kamenár, Dinjar, Had, Dudás, Kronaveter (Koltai 57), Rudolf, Pátkai, Andrić, Švec (Varga 46), Windecker (Trajković 59), Kamber. Coach: Ferenc Horváth (HUN)
A 1-0 Andrić (68)
Kočić, Kronaveter (Koltai 71), Varga (Illés 83), Rudolf, Völgyi, Pátkai (Windecker 75), Lang, Andrić, Švec, Kamber, Wolfe. Coach: Ferenc Horváth (HUN)
Red card: Rudolf 66

Ferencvárosi TC

First qualifying round - Sliema Wanderers FC (MLT)
A 1-1 Nalepa (77)
Dibusz, Bönig, Lauth, Böde, Kukuruzović (Holman 82), Gyömbér, Busai (Somália 46), Dániel Nagy (Čukić 46), Nalepa, Bošnjak, Mateos. Coach: Thomas Doll (GER)
H 2-1 Ugrai (14p), Busai (56)
Dibusz, Lauth (Dániel Nagy 73), Kukuruzović (Čukić 88), Gyömbér, Busai (Böde 70), Nalepa, Bošnjak, Mateos, Dilaver, Ugrai, Somália. Coach: Thomas Doll (GER)

Second qualifying round - HNK Rijeka (CRO)
A 0-1
Dibusz, Havojić, Kukuruzović, Gyömbér, Nalepa (Busai 90), Bošnjak, Pavlović, Mateos, Dilaver, Ugrai (Lauth 79), Somália. Coach: Thomas Doll (GER)
H 1-2 Ugrai (65p)
Dibusz, Lauth, Gyömbér, Gera (Böde 61), Nalepa (Kukuruzović 66), Bošnjak, Pavlović, Mateos, Dilaver, Ugrai (Busai 79), Somália. Coach: Thomas Doll (GER)

Diósgyőri VTK

First qualifying round - Birkirkara FC (MLT)
H 2-1 Barczi (33), Bacsa (90+3)
Radoš, Husić (Marjanović 67), Kádár, William Alves, Okuka, Bacsa, Gosztonyi (Bori 55), Grumić, Nikházi, Elek, Barczi. Coach: Tomislav Sivić (SRB)
A 4-1 Elek (30), Husić (62), Barczi (66), Marjanović (90+1)
Antal, Husić, Kádár, William Alves, Okuka, Bacsa (Barczi 61), Debreceni (Marjanović 71), Gosztonyi, Grumić, Bori (Nikházi 71), Elek. Coach: Tomislav Sivić (SRB)

Second qualifying round - PFC Litex Lovech (BUL)
A 2-0 Németh (83), Grumić (90)
Antal, Husić, Kádár, Okuka, Bacsa (Marjanović 78), Debreceni, Egerszegi, Gosztonyi (Grumić 59), Elek, Németh, Barczi (Bognár 50). Coach: Tomislav Sivić (SRB)
H 1-2 Gosztonyi (38p)
Antal, Husić, Kádár, Okuka, Bacsa (Bognár 63), Debreceni, Egerszegi, Gosztonyi (Bori 73), Grumić (Németh 82), Elek. Coach: Tomislav Sivić (SRB)

Third qualifying round - FC Krasnodar (RUS)
H 1-5 Bacsa (49)
Antal (Radoš 80), Husić, Kádár, William Alves, Bacsa, Debreceni (Grumić 46), Egerszegi, Gosztonyi, Elek, Németh, Eperjesi (Bognár 46). Coach: Tomislav Sivić (SRB)
A 0-3
Radoš, Kádár, Okuka, Takács, Debreceni, Egerszegi (Bognár 39), Gosztonyi (Csirszki 70), Nikházi, Bori, Németh, Marjanović (Bacsa 70). Coach: Tomislav Sivić (SRB)

DOMESTIC LEAGUE CLUB-BY-CLUB

Budapest Honvéd FC

1909 • Bozsik József (13,500) • honvedfc.hu
Major honours
Hungarian League (13) 1950, 1950 (autumn), 1952, 1954, 1955, 1980, 1984, 1985, 1986, 1988, 1989, 1991, 1993; Hungarian Cup (7) 1926, 1964, 1985, 1989, 1996, 2007, 2009
Coach: Pietro Vierchowod (ITA); (06/10/14) (Jasper de Muijnck (NED)); (26/10/14) József Csábi; (07/02/15) Marco Rossi (ITA)

2014

26/07	h	Dunaújváros	W 3-0	Holender, Youla, Traoré
03/08	a	Győr	L 1-3	Youla
09/08	h	Nyíregyháza	L 0-1	
16/08	a	MTK	L 0-2	
22/08	h	Puskás Akadémia	W 1-0	Alcibiade
30/08	a	Újpest	D 0-0	
13/09	h	Haladás	W 2-0	Portilla, Hidi
20/09	a	Diósgyőr	L 1-2	Hidi
26/09	h	Pécs	L 1-2	Youla (p)
04/10	a	Debrecen	L 0-4	
18/10	h	Paks	D 0-0	
25/10	a	Kecskemét	L 0-1	
02/11	a	Videoton	L 0-1	
07/11	h	Ferencváros	L 2-3	Youla 2 (2p)
22/11	a	Pápa	D 1-1	Baráth
28/11	a	Dunaújváros	D 0-0	
06/12	h	Győr	L 0-2	

2015

28/02	h	Nyíregyháza	L 0-2	
08/03	h	MTK	L 0-2	
14/03	a	Puskás Akadémia	D 1-1	Punošević
21/03	h	Újpest	D 2-2	Hidi, Prosser
05/04	a	Haladás	W 3-1	Ignjatović, Prosser, Punošević
11/04	h	Diósgyőr	D 1-1	Hidi
18/04	a	Pécs	L 1-2	Holender
26/04	h	Debrecen	D 1-1	Youla
01/05	a	Paks	D 0-0	
09/05	h	Kecskemét	W 2-0	Youla, Holender
16/05	h	Videoton	D 1-1	Youla
24/05	a	Ferencváros	L 0-1	
30/05	h	Pápa	W 2-0	Ignjatović, Youla

No	Name	Nat	DoB	Pos	Aps	(s)	Gls
13	Raffaele Alcibiade	ITA	23/05/90	D	13		1
36	Botond Baráth		21/04/92	D	16	(3)	1
9	Gergely Bobál		31/08/95	A	2	(4)	
21	Endre Botka		25/04/94	D	7	(3)	
16	Mihály Csábi		25/05/95	M		(1)	
28	Richárd Czár		13/08/92	M	2	(5)	
19	Josip Elez	CRO	25/04/94	D	12	(1)	
21	János Fejes		09/05/93	M	2	(2)	
25	Dániel Gazdag		02/03/96	M	3	(9)	
22	Dániel Göblyös		09/04/96	M		(1)	
20	Aníbal Godoy	PAN	10/02/90	M	17	(1)	
26	Patrik Hidi		27/11/90	A	24	(5)	4
57	Filip Holender	SRB	27/07/94	A	14	(6)	3
18	András Horváth		03/02/98	G		(1)	
5	Aleksandar Ignjatović	SRB	11/04/88	D	22	(1)	2
94	Sebestyén Ihrig Farkas		28/04/94	A		(4)	
8	George Ikenne	NGA	29/10/92	M	24	(2)	
11	David Izazola	MEX	23/10/91	A	1	(1)	
41	Thomas Job	CMR	20/08/84	M	9	(2)	
22	Valér Kapacina		14/07/93	M		(1)	
71	Szabolcs Kemenes		18/05/86	G	30		
39	Francis Koné	TOG	22/11/90	A		(1)	
66	Jevrem Kosnić	SRB	28/04/93	D	11		
38	Márk Koszta		26/09/96	A		(1)	
29	Attila Lőrinczy		08/04/94	M	1		
4	Andrea Mancini	ITA	13/09/92	A		(2)	
3	Kristi Marku	ALB	13/04/95	D	8		
92	Aníbal Mello	PAN	14/01/91	D	1		
44	Jesús Meza	VEN	01/01/86	M	3	(1)	
34	Jean-Pierre Morgan	FRA	30/10/92	D	4		
77	Gergő Nagy		07/01/93	M	19	(2)	
7	Lucas Ontivero	ARG	09/09/94	A		(1)	
6	Cristian Portilla	ESP	28/08/88	D	9		1
15	Josip Projić	SRB	23/08/87	D	9		
17	Dániel Prosser		15/06/94	M	12	(10)	2
13	Bratislav Punošević	SRB	09/07/87	A	7	(4)	2
67	Anatolis Saundas	ROU	22/01/94	D	1		
15	Kandia Traoré	CIV	05/07/80	A	6	(5)	1
30	Bálint Vécsei		13/07/93	A	18	(3)	
88	Marko Vidović	MNE	03/06/88	D	6	(3)	
99	Souleymane Youla	GUI	29/11/81	A	25	(1)	9

Debreceni VSC

1902 • Nagyerdei (20,000) • dvsc.hu

Major honours
Hungarian League (7) 2005, 2006, 2007, 2009, 2010, 2012, 2014; Hungarian Cup (6) 1999, 2001, 2008, 2010, 2012, 2013
Coach: Elemér Kondás

2014

25/07	a	Nyíregyháza	D	1-1	*Seydi*
01/08	a	MTK	L	0-1	
09/08	h	Puskás Akadémia	W	2-0	*Zsidai 2*
16/08	a	Újpest	L	0-1	
24/08	h	Haladás	W	1-0	*Kulcsár*
31/08	a	Diósgyőr	D	1-1	*Seydi*
13/09	h	Pécs	L	0-2	
21/09	h	Kecskemét	D	0-0	
27/09	a	Paks	L	1-2	*Kulcsár*
04/10	a	Honvéd	W	4-0	*Tisza, Sidibé, Vadnai, Varga*
19/10	a	Videoton	W	2-1	*Kulcsár 2*
26/10	h	Ferencváros	D	2-2	*Varga, Szakály*
01/11	h	Pápa	W	2-1	*Brković, Lázár*
08/11	h	Dunaújváros	W	2-0	*Máté, Brković*
23/11	a	Győr	W	1-0	*Tisza*
30/11	h	Nyíregyháza	W	5-0	*Sidibé 2, Tisza 2 (1p), Szakály (p)*
07/12	h	MTK	W	2-1	*Varga, Tisza (p)*

2015

28/02	a	Puskás Akadémia	W	1-0	*Tisza*
08/03	h	Újpest	D	0-0	
14/03	a	Haladás	L	0-2	
22/03	h	Diósgyőr	W	1-0	*Tisza*
04/04	a	Pécs	D	0-0	
10/04	a	Kecskemét	W	2-1	*Bódi, Jovanović*
18/04	h	Paks	W	2-0	*og (Rodenbücher), Sidibé*
26/04	a	Honvéd	D	1-1	*Bouadla*
02/05	a	Videoton	L	1-2	*Bódi*
10/05	a	Ferencváros	D	1-1	*Bódi*
17/05	h	Pápa	W	4-0	*Szakály, Mihelič (p), Balogh 2*
22/05	a	Dunaújváros	D	0-0	
31/05	h	Győr	W	5-0	*Ferenczi, Bódi 3, Sós*

No	Name	Nat	DoB	Pos	Aps	(s)	Gls
16	Norbert Balogh		21/02/96	A	6	(9)	2
53	Péter Berdó		14/01/93	M		(1)	
23	Dániel Bereczki		02/06/95	A		(1)	
27	Ádám Bódi		18/10/90	M	20	(6)	6
8	Selim Bouadla	FRA	26/08/88	M	17	(2)	1
25	Dušan Brković	SRB	20/01/89	D	21		2
4	Joël Damahou	CIV	28/01/87	M		(1)	
11	János Ferenczi		03/04/91	M	4	(3)	1
77	Aleksandar Jovanović	BIH	26/10/84	M	26		1
69	Mihály Korhut		01/12/88	D	29		
70	Tamás Kulcsár		13/10/82	A	15	(4)	4
13	Pál Lázár		11/03/88	D	16		1
21	Bence Ludánszki		25/10/90	M	3	(2)	
18	Péter Máté		02/12/84	D	19	(1)	1
17	Norbert Mészáros		19/08/80	D	13	(1)	
10	René Mihelič	SVN	05/07/88	M	7	(8)	1
24	Igor Morozov	EST	27/05/89	D	8	(3)	
28	Zoltán Nagy		25/10/85	D	5	(1)	
45	Nenad Novaković	SRB	17/07/82	G	17		
1	Vukašin Poleksić	MNE	30/08/82	G	4		
88	L'Imam Seydi	SEN	31/08/85	A	2	(6)	2
26	Ibrahima Sidibé	SEN	10/08/80	A	12	(6)	4
15	Bence Sós		10/05/94	M		(1)	1
55	Péter Szakály		17/08/86	M	18	(6)	3
3	Csaba Szatmári		14/06/94	D	1		
66	Márk Szécsi		22/05/94	A		(3)	
44	Tibor Tisza		10/11/84	A	16	(8)	7
14	Dániel Vadnai		19/02/88	M	5	(6)	1
33	József Varga		06/06/88	M	26		3
87	István Verpecz		04/02/87	G	9	(1)	
19	Dalibor Volaš	SVN	27/02/87	A	4	(1)	
20	Dávid Wittrédi		17/06/87	A		(1)	
6	László Zsidai		16/07/86	M	8	(4)	2

Diósgyőri VTK

1910 • Borsodi (12,000) • dvtk.eu

Major honours
Hungarian Cup (2) 1977, 1980
**Coach: Tomislav Sivić (SRB);
(28/04/15) Zoltán Vitelki**

2014

27/07	h	Puskás Akadémia	W	2-1	*Husić, Bacsa*
03/08	a	Újpest	D	1-1	*Grumić*
10/08	h	Haladás	W	3-0	*og (Jagodics), Németh, og (Fehér)*
17/08	h	Kecskemét	W	2-1	*Grumić, Takács*
24/08	a	Pécs	W	2-1	*Gosztonyi 2*
31/08	h	Debrecen	D	1-1	*Griffiths*
20/09	h	Honvéd	W	2-1	*Bognár (p), Takács*
28/09	a	Videoton	L	1-2	*Grumić*
04/10	h	Ferencváros	W	2-1	*Grumić, Takács*
18/10	a	Pápa	D	0-0	
22/10	h	Paks	L	1-3	*Bacsa*
25/10	h	Dunaújváros	D	3-3	*Bacsa, Grumić, Marjanović*
01/11	a	Győr	D	1-1	*Marjanović*
09/11	h	Nyíregyháza	W	2-1	*Griffiths, Marjanović*
22/11	h	MTK	W	2-0	*Griffiths 2*
29/11	a	Puskás Akadémia	L	0-1	
07/12	h	Újpest	W	2-1	*Elek, Griffiths*

2015

28/02	a	Haladás	D	1-1	*Krstić*
07/03	a	Kecskemét	L	1-2	*Takács*
13/03	h	Pécs	D	2-2	*Bacsa, Marjanović*
22/03	a	Debrecen	L	0-1	
04/04	h	Paks	L	1-2	*Griffiths*
11/04	a	Honvéd	D	1-1	*Marjanović*
19/04	h	Videoton	L	1-2	*Griffiths*
25/04	a	Ferencváros	L	0-3	
02/05	h	Pápa	W	2-1	*Bacsa, Egerszegi*
09/05	a	Dunaújváros	D	0-0	
17/05	h	Győr	W	4-1	*Bognár, Okuka, og (Tóth), Takács*
23/05	a	Nyíregyháza	W	2-1	*Grumić, Boros*
31/05	h	MTK	W	1-0	*Bacsa*

No	Name	Nat	DoB	Pos	Aps	(s)	Gls
99	Botond Antal		22/08/91	G	25		
9	Patrik Bacsa		03/06/92	A	17	(11)	6
31	Dávid Barczi		01/02/89	M	11	(7)	
10	István Bognár		06/05/91	M	17	(5)	2
21	Gábor Bori		16/01/84	M	6	(1)	
91	Gábor Boros		26/09/97	M		(2)	1
4	Milán Csicsvári		02/06/96	D		(1)	
17	Tamás Egerszegi		02/08/91	M	18	(4)	1
25	Ákos Elek		21/07/88	M	14	(1)	1
94	Gábor Eperjesi		12/01/94	D	7		
18	András Gosztonyi		07/11/90	A	16	(9)	2
7	Miroslav Grumić	SRB	29/06/84	A	19	(6)	6
3	Senad Husić	BIH	12/04/90	D	20		1
27	Julian Jenner	NED	28/02/84	A	1	(5)	
4	Tamás Kádár		14/03/90	D	16		
8	Kim Ho-young	KOR	03/10/90	M	4		
78	Vladimir Koman		16/03/89	M	7	(3)	
14	Miloš Krstić	SRB	07/03/87	M	6	(2)	1
89	Lazar Marjanović	SRB	08/09/89	M	12	(8)	5
92	Milán Imre Nemes		27/09/96	D	3		
29	Milán Németh		29/05/88	D	14	(2)	1
20	Márk Nikházi		02/02/89	M	3	(1)	
7	Dražen Okuka	SRB	05/03/86	D	28		1
22	Ivan Radoš	CRO	21/02/84	G	5	(1)	
27	Vilmos Szalai		11/08/91	D	12	(1)	
11	Tamás Takács		20/02/91	A	12	(14)	5
5	William Alves	BRA	07/05/86	D	20		

Dunaújváros PASE

1998 • Dunaferr Aréna (10,046) • dpase.hu

**Coach: Barna Dobos;
(01/04/15) Tamás Artner**

2014

26/07	a	Honvéd	L	0-3	
02/08	a	Videoton	L	0-3	
16/08	h	Pápa	D	1-1	*Orosz*
23/08	a	Kecskemét	D	0-0	
27/08	a	Ferencváros	L	0-2	
31/08	a	Győr	L	3-4	*Perić, Böőr 2 (2p)*
13/09	a	Nyíregyháza	D	0-0	
20/09	h	MTK	L	0-2	
27/09	a	Puskás Akadémia	L	2-3	*Orosz, Perić*
04/10	a	Újpest	L	0-3	
17/10	h	Haladás	W	1-0	*Nikházi*
25/10	a	Diósgyőr	D	3-3	*Böőr 2 (1p), Nikházi*
01/11	h	Pécs	W	3-2	*Petneházi, Böőr, Godslove*
08/11	a	Debrecen	L	0-2	
22/11	h	Paks	W	1-0	*Nikházi*
28/11	h	Honvéd	W	1-0	
06/12	h	Videoton	L	1-4	*Böőr (p)*

2015

01/03	h	Ferencváros	L	0-1	
07/03	a	Pápa	L	0-1	
14/03	h	Kecskemét	L	0-2	
21/03	h	Győr	L	0-2	
04/04	a	Nyíregyháza	W	3-0	*Nikházi 2 (1p), Eppel*
11/04	h	MTK	D	0-0	
18/04	h	Puskás Akadémia	L	2-3	*Csehi, Böőr (p)*
24/04	h	Újpest	L	1-3	*Nikházi*
02/05	a	Haladás	W	4-1	*Eppel 2, og (Devecseri), Jakab*
09/05	h	Diósgyőr	D	0-0	
16/05	a	Pécs	L	0-2	
22/05	h	Debrecen	D	0-0	
30/05	a	Paks	L	1-2	*Hidvégi*

No	Name	Nat	DoB	Pos	Aps	(s)	Gls
10	Zoltán Böőr		14/08/78	M	25	(3)	7
19	Bruno Pascua	ESP	21/02/90	A	2	(4)	
9	Tamás Csehi		06/02/84	D	28		1
23	Timotej Dodlek	SVN	23/11/89	M	4	(2)	
14	Márton Eppel		26/10/91	M	11		3
6	Viktor Farkas		05/10/78	D	18	(4)	
4	Dino Gavrić	CRO	11/04/89	D	9		
17	Egejuru Godslove	NGA	04/12/86	A	3	(9)	1
44	Nikola Grubješić	SRB	29/06/84	A	2	(4)	
28	Szilveszter Hangya		02/01/94	M		(1)	
4	Sándor Hidvégi		09/04/83	D	12		1
1	Safet Jahić	SVN	25/01/87	G	1		
25	Dávid Jakab		21/05/93	M	11	(8)	1
8	György Józsi		31/01/83	M	6	(3)	
14	Gábor Kocsis		30/11/85	M		(2)	
7	Zsolt Lázár		07/11/85	M	13	(5)	
1	Árpád Milinte		04/05/76	G	9		
24	Rowen Muscat	MLT	05/06/91	M	4	(3)	
33	Gergely Nagy		27/05/94	G	20		
30	Márk Nikházi		02/02/89	M	23		6
8	Márk Orosz		24/10/89	M	20	(5)	2
8	Máté Papp		12/03/93	M	2	(1)	
3	Milan Perić	SRB	16/04/86	A	5	(2)	2
15	Márk Petneházi		24/04/96	M	24	(2)	1
12	Norbert Sárközi		05/03/93	D	8		
21	Tibor Sóron		18/01/93	A		(6)	
11	Tamás Szalai		10/01/80	M	1	(2)	
32	Adrián Szekeres		21/04/89	D	18		
16	Thiago	BRA	23/01/85	M	3	(17)	
13	Péter Urbin		17/09/84	A	3		
23	Tamás Vaskó		20/02/84	D	9		
2	Balázs Villám		02/06/89	D	24	(1)	
20	Donát Zsótér		06/01/96	A	12	(2)	

Ferencvárosi TC

1899 • Groupama Aréna (22,000) • fradi.hu

Major honours
*Inter Cities Fairs Cup (1) 1965; Hungarian League
(28) 1903, 1905, 1907, 1909, 1910, 1911, 1912,
1913, 1926, 1927, 1928, 1932, 1934, 1938, 1940,
1941, 1949, 1963, 1964, 1967, 1968, 1976, 1981,
1992, 1995, 1996, 2001, 2004; Hungarian Cup (21)
1913, 1922, 1927, 1928, 1933, 1935, 1942, 1943,
1944, 1958, 1972, 1974, 1976, 1978, 1991, 1993,
1994, 1995, 2003, 2004, 2015*

Coach: Thomas Doll (GER)

2014
27/07	a Kecskemét	W 3-1	Böde 3	
03/08	a Pápa	L 0-1		
17/08	a Győr	W 1-0	Busai	
24/08	h Nyíregyháza	W 3-1	Busai, Gera, Mateos (p)	
27/08	h Dunaújváros	W 2-0	Ugrai, Böde	
31/08	a MTK	L 1-2	Lauth	
14/09	h Puskás Akadémia	W 2-1	Lauth, Böde	
21/09	a Újpest	L 1-2	Mateos (p)	
28/09	h Haladás	D 0-0		
04/10	a Diósgyőr	L 1-2	Gera	
18/10	h Pécs	W 2-0	Dominik Nagy, Busai	
26/10	a Debrecen	D 2-2	Ugrai, Lauth	
01/11	h Paks	D 0-0		
07/11	a Honvéd	W 3-2	Böde, Lauth, Lamah (p)	
23/11	a Videoton	D 0-0		
29/11	h Kecskemét	W 3-1	Lauth 2, Lamah	
05/12	h Pápa	W 2-0	Kukuruzović, Gera (p)	

2015
01/03	a Dunaújváros	W 1-0	Lamah	
07/03	h Győr	W 3-0	Lamah, Hajnal, Varga	
14/03	a Nyíregyháza	D 0-0		
22/03	h MTK	W 2-0	Mateos (p), Busai	
03/04	a Puskás Akadémia	W 2-1	Böde 2	
12/04	h Újpest	W 2-0	Hajnal, Varga	
18/04	a Haladás	W 3-0	Böde 2, Varga	
25/04	h Diósgyőr	W 3-0	Mateos (p), Böde, Lamah	
03/05	a Pécs	D 2-2	Böde, Mateos (p)	
10/05	h Debrecen	D 1-1	Pavlović	
16/05	a Paks	W 1-0	Gyömbér	
24/05	h Honvéd	W 1-0	Somália	
30/05	h Videoton	W 2-0	Böde, Čukić	

No	Name	Nat	DoB	Pos	Aps	(s)	Gls
22	Bence Batik		08/11/93	M	4	(3)	
13	Dániel Böde		24/10/86	A	28	(1)	13
5	Philipp Bönig	GER	20/03/80	D	14	(5)	
35	Predrag Bošnjak		13/11/85	D	1		
22	Attila Busai		21/01/89	M	11	(11)	4
34	Ádám Csillus		18/11/96	M		(1)	
30	Vladan Čukić	SRB	27/06/80	M	9	(6)	1
90	Dénes Dibusz		16/11/90	G	30		
66	Emir Dilaver	AUT	07/05/91	D	29		
20	Zoltán Gera		22/04/79	M	25	(1)	3
19	Gábor Gyömbér		27/02/88	M	15	(8)	1
15	Tamás Hajnal		15/03/81	M	6		2
95	Attila Haris		23/01/97	M		(1)	
8	Tomislav Havojić	CRO	10/03/89	M		(3)	
17	Stjepan Kukuruzović	CRO	07/06/89	M	6	(5)	1
24	Roland Lamah	BEL	31/12/87	A	19	(2)	5
11	Benjamin Lauth	GER	04/08/81	A	12	(11)	6
44	David Mateos	ESP	22/04/87	D	19		5
99	Ádám Nagy		17/06/95	M		(1)	
23	Dániel Nagy		15/03/91	M	4	(7)	
14	Dominik Nagy		08/05/95	M	5	(5)	1
27	Michał Nalepa	POL	22/01/93	D	19	(4)	
39	Mateo Pavlović	CRO	09/06/90	D	18		1
94	Patrik Popov		12/10/97	A		(1)	
77	Cristian Ramírez	ECU	08/12/94	D	13		
88	Somália	BRA	28/09/88	M	24		1
70	Roland Ugrai		13/11/92	A	6	(8)	2
97	Roland Varga		23/01/90	A	13		3

Győri ETO FC

1904 • ETO Park (16,000) • eto.hu

Major honours
*Hungarian League (4) 1963 (autumn), 1982, 1983,
2013; Hungarian Cup (4) 1965, 1966, 1967, 1979*

**Coach: Ferenc Horváth;
(31/10/14) Tibor Tokody;
(27/11/14) Vasile Miriuţă**

2014
27/07	a Paks	L 0-2		
03/08	h Honvéd	W 3-1	Priskin, Rudolf (p), Pátkai	
09/08	a Videoton	L 2-3	Pátkai, Rudolf	
17/08	h Ferencváros	L 0-1		
23/08	a Pápa	D 0-0		
31/08	h Dunaújváros	W 4-3	Rudolf (p), Pátkai 3	
20/08	a Nyíregyháza	W 3-2	Rudolf 2, Priskin	
27/09	h MTK	L 1-2	Střeštík	
03/10	a Puskás Akadémia	L 1-2	Rudolf (p)	
19/10	h Újpest	D 0-0		
22/10	a Kecskemét	D 1-1	Lipták	
26/10	a Haladás	W 2-0	Völgyi, Varga	
01/11	h Diósgyőr	D 1-1	Priskin	
08/11	a Pécs	W 3-0	Martínez 2, Priskin	
23/11	h Debrecen	L 0-1		
30/11	h Paks	D 2-2	Kvilitaia, Lipták	
06/12	h Honvéd	W 2-0	Koltai 2	

2015
01/03	h Videoton	D 2-2	Koltai (p), Priskin	
07/03	a Ferencváros	L 0-3		
16/03	h Pápa	D 0-0		
21/03	a Dunaújváros	W 2-0	Windecker, Pátkai	
04/04	h Kecskemét	D 1-1	Priskin	
11/04	h Nyíregyháza	L 2-3	Lipták, Mayer	
18/04	a MTK	L 1-2	Priskin	
26/04	h Puskás Akadémia	W 1-0	Priskin	
03/05	a Újpest	L 0-1		
09/05	h Haladás	W 3-2	Rudolf, Koltai, Lipták	
17/05	a Diósgyőr	L 1-4	Priskin	
23/05	h Pécs	W 3-0	Priskin 2 (1p), Pátkai	
31/05	a Debrecen	L 0-5		

No	Name	Nat	DoB	Pos	Aps	(s)	Gls
19	Nemanja Andrić	SRB	13/06/87	M	3	(9)	
27	László Bénes	SVK	09/09/97	M		(1)	
7	Vladica Brdarovski	MKD	07/02/90	D	11		
5	Dan Bucşă	ROU	23/06/88	M	8	(2)	
30	Jaroslav Cellár	SVK	19/11/95	G	2		
3	Marko Dinjar	CRO	21/05/86	M	10		
8	Ádám Dudás		12/02/89	M	1	(3)	
43	Dániel Horváth		05/03/96	G	1		
22	Luis Ibáñez	ARG	15/07/88	D	10	(1)	
28	Dávid Illés		18/02/94	A		(1)	
24	Djordje Kamber	SRB	20/11/83	M	18	(5)	
26	Ľuboš Kamenár	SVK	17/06/87	G	7		
16	Márk Kelemen		17/01/94	D	1		
37	Dávid Kerékgyártó		29/09/95	M	2	(1)	
30	Miloš Kočić	SRB	04/06/85	G	10		
29	Tamás Koltai		30/04/87	M	21	(4)	4
9	Rok Kronaveter	SVN	07/12/86	M	2	(2)	
13	Giorgi Kvilitaia	GEO	01/10/93	A	4	(7)	1
18	Ádám Lang		17/01/93	D	28		
41	András Lénárt	SVK	14/04/98	D		(1)	
21	Zoltán Lipták		10/12/84	D	27	(1)	4
10	Leandro Martínez	ITA	15/10/89	A	6	(2)	2
35	Milán Mayer		24/05/96	A	1	(5)	1
9	Sinan Medgyes	SVK	30/06/93	A	1		
41	Bence Mervó		05/03/95	M	1	(4)	
6	Ádám Nagy		20/01/96	D	3	(4)	
2	Bálint Nagy		20/01/96	D	1		
31	Márk Németh		30/09/96	D	1		
20	Tamás Priskin		27/09/86	A	23	(4)	11
11	Njongo Priso	CMR	24/12/88	A	3	(3)	
14	Gergely Rudolf		09/03/85	A	25		7
10	Miroslav Stevanović	BIH	29/07/90	A	1	(2)	
7	András Stieber		08/10/91	M	1	(1)	
6	Marek Střeštík	CZE	01/02/87	M	7	(3)	1
6	Dániel Sváb		02/09/90	D	1	(1)	
22	Michal Švec	CZE	19/03/87	M	11		
7	Bence Szabó		25/04/95	A	1		
32	László Szabó		14/02/95	M	1		
21	Tibor Szabó		26/07/96	M		(1)	
33	Ádám Gábor Szalai		23/07/97	M		(1)	
36	Dávid Tóth		09/07/98	D	1	(1)	
12	Nikola Trajković	SRB	05/01/81	M		(8)	
11	Roland Varga		23/01/90	A	7	(4)	1
15	Dániel Völgyi		07/06/87	M	8		1
23	József Windecker		02/12/92	M	19	(1)	1
25	Rafe Wolfe	JAM	19/12/85	D	7	(2)	

Kecskeméti TE

1911 • Széktói (6,500) • kecskemetite.hu

Major honours
Hungarian Cup (1) 2011

Coach: Balázs Bekő

2014
27/07	h Ferencváros	L 1-3	Kitl	
02/08	h Haladás	L 0-1		
09/08	a Pápa	L 2-3	Novák, Pavićević	
17/08	a Diósgyőr	L 1-2	Vukasović	
23/08	h Dunaújváros	D 0-0		
30/08	a Pécs	W 2-1	Bebeto, Balázs	
21/09	a Debrecen	D 0-0		
27/09	h Nyíregyháza	W 1-0	Bebeto	
04/10	a Paks	W 3-2	Bebeto, Botka, Balázs	
18/10	h MTK	L 0-1		
22/10	h Győr	D 1-1	Bebeto (p)	
25/10	h Honvéd	W 1-0	Balázs	
31/10	h Puskás Akadémia	W 2-1	Varga, Bebeto	
08/11	h Videoton	D 0-0		
21/11	h Újpest	W 2-0	og (Ojo), og (Balogh)	
29/11	a Ferencváros	L 1-3	Vukasović (p)	
06/12	a Haladás	L 1-3	Novák	

2015
28/02	h Pápa	W 3-2	Kitl, Bebeto 2	
07/03	h Diósgyőr	W 2-1	Novák, Karan	
14/03	a Dunaújváros	W 2-0	Savić, Novák	
21/03	h Pécs	W 1-0	Bebeto	
04/04	a Győr	D 1-1	Bebeto	
10/04	h Debrecen	L 1-2	Kitl	
17/04	a Nyíregyháza	D 1-1	Novák	
25/04	h Paks	D 1-1	Kitl	
02/05	a MTK	D 0-0		
09/05	h Honvéd	L 0-2		
16/05	a Puskás Akadémia	L 0-4		
24/05	a Videoton	L 0-1		
30/05	a Újpest	L 0-3		

No	Name	Nat	DoB	Pos	Aps	(s)	Gls
7	Zsolt Balázs		11/08/88	A	15	(1)	3
91	Bebeto	SEN	31/12/91	A	25	(3)	9
26	Endre Botka		25/04/94	D	15		1
26	Dárius Csillag		29/01/95	A		(2)	
77	Dániel Dudás		12/04/96	M	1	(1)	
30	Henri Eninful	TOG	21/07/92	M	12	(8)	
92	András Farkas		12/03/92	D	4	(1)	
3	Dominik Fótyik	SVK	16/09/90	M	8	(6)	
19	Gábor Gréczi		03/05/93	A	2	(13)	
15	Attila Gyagya		30/03/82	D	15	(3)	
3	Dejan Karan	SRB	25/08/88	D	28		1
17	Miklós Kitl		01/06/97	M	25	(1)	4
86	Zsolt Laczkó		18/12/86	M	14	(1)	
72	Norbert Lévai		24/05/96	M	1	(2)	
16	Ivan Lovrić	CRO	11/07/85	D	26		
9	Csanád Novák		24/09/94	A	16	(10)	5
8	Zsolt Patvaros		18/02/93	D	3	(13)	
7	Darko Pavićević	MNE	24/06/85	A	2	(1)	1
29	Stojan Pilipović	SRB	02/02/87	M	2	(3)	
23	Kristóf Polyák		28/09/95	D	3		
7	Stefan Radoja	SRB	16/01/90	M	4	(3)	
7	Vladan Savić	MNE	26/07/79	M	25	(2)	1
40	Zsolt Selyem		07/03/98	A		(1)	
4	Nebojša Skopljak	SRB	12/05/87	D	13		
16	Dániel Szalai		05/09/96	A	3	(4)	
6	Donát Szivacski		18/01/97	M	2	(5)	
88	Viktor Tölgyesi		18/01/92	M		(1)	
1	Tomáš Tujvel	SVK	19/09/83	G	30		
4	Róbert Varga		25/11/86	D	13	(2)	1
14	Marko Vukasović	MNE	10/09/90	M	23	(1)	2

Lombard Pápa TFC

1995 • Perutz (8,000) • lombardfcpapa.hu

Coach: János Mátyus;
(04/09/14) László Kovács;
(10/11/14) Ferenc Lengyel;
(21/04/15) László Kovács

2014

26/07	a	Videoton	L 0-3	
03/08	h	Ferencváros	W 1-0	Popin
09/08	h	Kecskemét	W 3-2	Sluka, Csizmadia, Popin
16/08	a	Dunaújváros	D 1-1	Nagy
23/08	h	Győr	D 0-0	
30/08	a	Nyíregyháza	L 0-3	
12/09	h	MTK	L 0-1	
20/09	a	Puskás Akadémia	L 0-3	
27/09	h	Újpest	D 0-0	
05/10	a	Haladás	L 0-2	
18/10	h	Diósgyőr	D 0-0	
25/10	a	Pécs	W 2-1	Žuļevs, Coroian
01/11	h	Debrecen	L 0-2	
08/11	a	Paks	L 0-3	
22/11	h	Honvéd	D 1-1	Csizmadia (p)
29/11	h	Videoton	L 0-5	
05/12	a	Ferencváros	L 0-2	

2015

28/02	a	Kecskemét	L 2-3	Seye, Waltner
07/03	h	Dunaújváros	W 1-0	Seye
16/03	a	Győr	D 0-0	
21/03	h	Nyíregyháza	L 0-1	
04/04	a	MTK	L 0-3	
11/04	h	Puskás Akadémia	L 0-1	
19/04	a	Újpest	L 0-4	
25/04	h	Haladás	D 2-2	Popin, Seye
02/05	a	Diósgyőr	L 1-2	Seye
09/05	h	Pécs	L 0-2	
17/05	a	Debrecen	L 0-4	
23/05	h	Paks	L 0-4	
30/05	a	Honvéd	L 0-2	

No	Name	Nat	DoB	Pos	Aps	(s)	Gls
83	Euloge Ahodikpé	TOG	01/05/83	A	2	(1)	
28	Krisztián Benkő		03/06/94	M	1	(10)	
10	Bernardo Frizoni	BRA	12/03/90	A	25	(2)	
55	Milan Bogunović	SRB	31/05/83	D	26	(1)	
97	Bálint Böröczky		18/03/94	D		(3)	
24	Andrei Coroian	ROU	28/01/91	M	4	(3)	1
13	Tamás Csilus		08/05/95	M	17	(4)	
85	Csaba Csizmadia		30/05/85	D	30		2
7	Milán Faggyas		01/06/89	A	4	(4)	
17	Andrei Florean	ROU	03/04/92	M	6	(1)	
25	Szabolcs Gál		31/03/92	D	1	(5)	
23	Gábor Horváth		24/08/90	G	1		
63	Martin Iványi		16/08/95	M		(1)	
5	Bence Jagodics		31/03/94	D	18	(1)	
33	Dániel Juhász		17/05/92	D	4	(2)	
19	Krisztián Kenesei		07/01/77	A	11	(3)	
31	Botond Király		26/10/94	M	6	(7)	
65	Yannick Mbengono	CMR	11/06/87	A	1	(2)	
8	Tamás Nagy		18/01/88	D	18	(4)	1
66	Viktor Pongrácz		18/05/94	M	8	(1)	
89	Saša Popin	SRB	28/10/89	A	24	(2)	3
99	Aleksandar Randjelović	SRB	09/12/87	M	6	(3)	
61	Máté Schmid		08/07/96	M		(4)	
6	Mouhamadou Seye	SEN	10/10/88	A	11		4
19	Marián Sluka	SVK	22/07/79	M	18	(3)	1
20	András Stieber		08/10/91	M	8		
27	Lajos Szűcs		08/08/73	G	29		
4	Gábor Tóth		26/03/87	D	16		
7	Imre Vankó		17/04/94	A	4	(4)	
15	Dániel Völgyi		07/06/87	M	9		
9	Róbert Waltner		20/09/77	A	3	(14)	1
11	Vadims Žuļevs	LVA	01/03/88	M	19	(1)	1

MTK Budapest

1888 • Bozsik József (13,500) • mtk.hu

Major honours
Hungarian League (23) 1904, 1908, 1914, 1917, 1918, 1919, 1920, 1921, 1922, 1923, 1924, 1925, 1929, 1936, 1937, 1951, 1953, 1958, 1987, 1997, 1999, 2003, 2008; Hungarian Cup (12) 1910, 1911, 1912, 1914, 1923, 1925, 1932, 1952, 1968, 1997, 1998, 2000

Coach: József Garami

2014

26/07	a	Pécs	W 4-0	Horváth, Kanta 2, Frank
01/08	h	Debrecen	W 1-0	Horváth
08/08	h	Paks	L 0-3	
16/08	h	Honvéd	W 2-0	Kanta 2 (1p)
23/08	a	Videoton	L 0-5	
31/08	h	Ferencváros	W 2-1	Poór, Horváth
12/09	a	Pápa	W 1-0	P Vass
20/09	h	Dunaújváros	W 2-0	Pölöskei, Kanta (p)
27/09	a	Győr	W 2-1	og (Střeštík), Hrepka
05/10	h	Nyíregyháza	W 2-0	Torghelle, Hidvégi
18/10	a	Kecskemét	W 1-0	Kanta (p)
25/10	a	Puskás Akadémia	W 1-0	Pölöskei
02/11	h	Újpest	L 0-1	
09/11	a	Haladás	W 3-0	Hrepka, Torghelle, Bese
22/11	h	Diósgyőr	L 0-2	
29/11	h	Pécs	W 3-2	Torghelle, Csiki 2
07/12	a	Debrecen	L 1-2	Pölöskei

2015

27/02	h	Paks	W 3-1	Bese, Pölöskei, Horváth
08/03	h	Honvéd	W 2-0	Kanta, Csiki
14/03	h	Videoton	L 0-1	
22/03	a	Ferencváros	L 0-2	
04/04	h	Pápa	W 3-0	Kanta (p), Torghelle, Csiki
11/04	a	Dunaújváros	D 0-0	
18/04	h	Győr	W 2-1	Pölöskei, Csiki
25/04	a	Nyíregyháza	D 1-1	Thiam
02/05	h	Kecskemét	D 0-0	
06/05	h	Puskás Akadémia	W 1-0	Csiki
16/05	a	Újpest	L 0-1	
23/05	h	Haladás	W 2-0	Torghelle 2
31/05	a	Diósgyőr	L 0-1	

No	Name	Nat	DoB	Pos	Aps	(s)	Gls
4	Ákos Baki		24/08/94	D	10		
18	Barnabás Bese		06/05/94	A	15	(12)	2
22	Benjámin Cseke		22/07/94	M	1	(3)	
8	Norbert Csiki		21/05/91	A	11	(6)	6
32	Richárd Frank		28/09/90	A		(6)	1
33	Dániel Gera		29/08/95	A	1	(1)	
28	Federico Groppioni	ITA	17/06/84	G	1		
27	Ramon Halmai		18/04/94	M		(1)	
6	Ádám Hajdú		16/01/93	M	6	(4)	
1	Lajos Hegedűs		19/12/87	G	29		
4	Sándor Hidvégi		09/04/83	D	13		1
7	Zsolt Horváth		19/05/88	A	24	(4)	4
13	Ádám Hrepka		15/04/87	A	10	(5)	2
12	Dávid Kálnoki Kis		06/08/91	D	9		
19	József Kanta		24/03/84	M	29		8
5	Dávid Kelemen		24/05/92	D	9	(1)	
2	Tibor Nagy		14/08/91	D	17	(1)	
16	Zsolt Pölöskei		19/02/91	A	28		5
24	Patrik Poór		15/11/93	D	18	(3)	1
39	Ádám Schrammel		19/07/96	M		(1)	
9	Sergio Tamayo	ESP	28/03/91	A	5	(1)	
26	István Szatmári		27/05/97	A		(1)	
15	Khaly Thiam	SEN	07/01/94	M	10	(6)	1
30	Sándor Torghelle		05/05/82	A	18	(4)	6
11	Dániel Vadnai		19/02/88	M	7	(2)	
38	Ádám Vass		09/08/88	M	24	(3)	
17	Patrik Vass		17/01/93	A	7	(4)	1
43	Bálint Vogyicska		27/02/98	M	1	(1)	
21	Dragan Vukmir	SRB	02/08/78	D	27		

Nyíregyháza Spartacus FC

1959 • Városi Stadion (11,500) • nyiregyhazaspartacus.hu

Coach: József Csábi;
(21/10/14) János Mátyus

2014

25/07	h	Debrecen	D 1-1	Pekár (p)
02/08	h	Paks	L 0-3	
09/08	a	Honvéd	W 1-0	Bajzát
16/08	h	Videoton	L 0-2	
24/08	a	Ferencváros	L 1-3	Bajzát
30/08	h	Pápa	W 3-0	Abdouraman, Bajzát, Pekár
13/09	a	Dunaújváros	D 0-0	
20/09	h	Győr	L 2-3	Pákolicz, Bajzát
27/09	a	Kecskemét	L 0-1	
05/10	a	MTK	L 0-2	
18/10	h	Puskás Akadémia	L 0-1	
24/10	a	Újpest	L 2-3	Pekár, Molnár
01/11	h	Haladás	W 2-0	Koller, Törtei
09/11	a	Diósgyőr	L 1-2	Pákolicz
22/11	h	Pécs	W 4-0	Szokol, Pekár (p), Koller, Pákolicz
30/11	a	Debrecen	L 0-5	

2015

21/02	a	Paks	D 1-1	Törtei
28/02	h	Honvéd	W 2-0	Abdouraman, Seydi
07/03	a	Videoton	L 0-3	
14/03	h	Ferencváros	D 0-0	
21/03	a	Pápa	W 1-0	Pekár (p)
04/04	a	Dunaújváros	L 0-3	
11/04	a	Győr	W 3-2	og (Lang), Fodor, Pekár
17/04	h	Kecskemét	W 1-0	Pekár
25/04	a	MTK	D 1-1	Rezes
02/05	a	Puskás Akadémia	W 2-1	Pekár, og (Tar)
09/05	h	Újpest	L 2-4	Seydi, Pekár
15/05	a	Haladás	L 1-3	Halenár
23/05	h	Diósgyőr	L 1-2	Fodor
29/05	a	Pécs	L 1-2	Karacs

No	Name	Nat	DoB	Pos	Aps	(s)	Gls
10	Mohamadou Abdouraman	CMR	24/01/85	M	13	(7)	2
55	Zurab Arziani	GEO	19/10/87	M	6	(3)	
54	István Bagi		04/07/96	M		(1)	
18	Péter Bajzát		22/06/81	A	10	(2)	4
47	János Balogh		29/11/82	G	25		
35	Predrag Bošnjak		13/11/85	D	8		
11	Dato Dartsimelia	GEO	28/01/95	A	2	(6)	
5	Ferenc Fodor		22/03/91	D	22	(1)	2
26	Gergő Gengelíczki		08/06/93	D	8	(2)	
91	Juraj Halenár	SVK	28/06/83	A	13		1
1	Alex Hrabina		05/04/95	A		(1)	
4	Tamás Huszák		02/10/88	M	1	(1)	
26	Deniss Ivanovs	LVA	11/01/84	D	8	(1)	
28	Gábor Jánvári		25/04/90	D	8		
8	Péter Karacs		01/10/94	A		(1)	1
11	Krisztián Koller		08/05/83	A	14	(7)	2
11	Zoran Kostić	SRB	14/11/82	M	25	(2)	
22	Mihael Kovacevic	SUI	30/03/88	D	13		
22	Bence Lázár		21/03/91	A	1	(4)	
53	Dávid Markovics		27/02/90	M		(1)	
42	Marcell Molnár		26/08/90	A	1	(4)	1
28	Zoltán Nagy		25/10/85	D	8		
78	Volodymyr Ovsiyenko	UKR	30/10/78	G	5	(2)	
78	Volodymyr Ovsiyenko	UKR	30/10/78	A	1		
19	Dávid Pákolicz		13/09/84	A	14	(5)	3
11	János Pátyly		29/11/88	D	1		
77	László Pekár		20/01/93	M	27	(1)	9
31	Krisztián Póti		28/05/89	D	2	(1)	
99	László Rezes		12/08/87	M	9	(4)	1
13	Tamás Rubus		13/07/89	D	13	(3)	
29	István Sándor		04/04/94	M	4	(5)	
16	L'Imam Seydi	SEN	31/08/85	A	7	(5)	2
23	István Spitzmüller		14/05/86	M	6	(2)	
17	Márk Szécsi		22/05/94	A	4	(1)	
21	Zsolt Szokol		16/03/90	D	19	(3)	1
85	Tamás Törtei		02/10/85	D	18	(2)	2
56	Márk Vámos		24/09/96	M	1	(1)	
33	Boris Živanović	SRB	18/07/89	D	1	(2)	
7	Igor Žofčák	SVK	10/04/83	M	12		

Paksi FC

1952 • Városi (5,000) • paksifc.hu
Coach: Aurél Csertői

2014

27/07	h	Győr	W 2-0 Kecskés, Heffler
02/08	a	Nyíregyháza	W 3-0 Eppel, Heffler, Könyves
08/08	h	MTK	W 3-0 Bartha, Eppel, Könyves
15/08	a	Puskás Akadémia	D 1-1 Könyves
23/08	h	Újpest	D 0-0
29/08	a	Haladás	W 3-1 Fiola, Könyves 2
19/09	a	Pécs	D 1-1 Bartha
27/09	h	Debrecen	W 2-1 Bartha, Báló
04/10	a	Kecskemét	L 2-3 Kovács, Haraszti
18/10	a	Honvéd	D 0-0
22/10	h	Diósgyőr	W 3-1 Gévay, Bartha 2
25/10	a	Videoton	L 0-2
01/11	a	Ferencváros	D 0-0
08/11	h	Pápa	W 3-0 Báló (p), Haraszti, Bor
22/11	a	Dunaújváros	L 0-1
30/11	a	Győr	D 2-2 Simon, Bartha

2015

21/02	h	Nyíregyháza	D 1-1 Vági
27/02	a	MTK	L 1-3 Báló (p)
06/03	h	Puskás Akadémia	W 2-1 Bartha 2
14/03	a	Újpest	W 2-1 Haraszti, Bertus
20/03	h	Haladás	L 1-2 Balázs
04/04	a	Diósgyőr	W 2-1 Könyves 2
11/04	h	Pécs	W 2-0 Báló (p), Könyves
18/04	a	Debrecen	L 0-2
25/04	a	Kecskemét	D 1-1 Balázs
01/05	h	Honvéd	D 0-0
10/05	h	Videoton	W 1-0 Könyves
16/05	h	Ferencváros	L 0-1
23/05	a	Pápa	W 4-0 Kecskés, Haraszti, Vági, Hahn
30/05	h	Dunaújváros	W 2-1 Könyves, Bertus

No	Name	Nat	DoB	Pos	Aps	(s)	Gls
92	Zsolt Balázs		11/08/88	A	7	(6)	2
7	Tamás Báló		12/01/84	M	26		4
39	László Bartha		09/02/87	A	29		8
26	Lajos Bertus		26/09/90	M	30		2
95	Dávid Bor		10/12/94	A		(1)	1
24	Norbert Csernyánszki		01/02/76	G	1		
25	Márton Eppel		26/10/91	M	5		2
18	Attila Fiola		17/02/90	D	8	(5)	1
5	Zsolt Gévay		19/11/87	D	28		1
9	János Hahn		15/05/95	A	3	(19)	1
88	Zsolt Haraszti		04/11/91	A	22	(2)	4
16	Tibor Heffler		17/05/87	M	5		2
8	Tamás Kecskés		15/01/86	M	25	(2)	2
19	Barna Kesztyűs		04/09/93	M	11	(3)	
10	Tamás Kiss		27/09/79	A	1	(10)	
42	Norbert Könyves	SRB	10/06/89	A	19	(3)	10
6	Gábor Kovács		04/09/87	D	16		1
77	Dávid Kulcsár		25/02/88	M	16	(8)	
96	Bence Lenzsér		09/06/96	D	4	(1)	
1	Péter Molnár	SVK	14/12/83	G	29		
12	Richárd Nagy		15/08/95	M		(3)	
20	István Rodenbücher		22/02/84	D	9		
46	András Simon		30/03/90	A	4	(10)	1
30	János Szabó		11/07/89	D	6	(1)	
21	Zsolt Tamási		25/06/90	M	21	(1)	
22	András Vági		25/12/88	D	5	(7)	2

Pécsi MFC

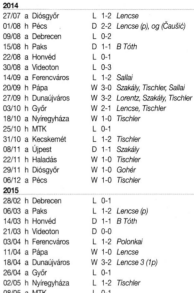

1973 • PMFC (10,000) • pmfc.hu
Major honours
Hungarian Cup (1) 1990
Coach: György Véber;
(26/10/14) Árpád Kulcsár;
(24/11/14) Robert Jarni (CRO)

2014

26/07	h	MTK	L 0-4
01/08	a	Puskás Akadémia	D 2-2 Márkvárt, Kővári
09/08	a	Újpest	D 1-1 Mohl (p)
17/08	a	Haladás	D 1-1 Heffler
24/08	h	Diósgyőr	L 1-2 Wittrédi (p)
30/08	h	Kecskemét	L 1-2 Pölöskey
13/09	a	Debrecen	W 2-0 Mohl (p), Pölöskey
19/09	h	Paks	D 1-1 og (Kovács)
26/09	a	Honvéd	W 2-1 Kővári, Szatmári
04/10	a	Videoton	L 0-2
18/10	a	Ferencváros	L 0-2
25/10	h	Pápa	L 1-2 Márkvárt
01/11	a	Dunaújváros	L 2-3 Balogh, Márkvárt
08/11	h	Győr	L 0-3
22/11	a	Nyíregyháza	L 0-4
29/11	h	MTK	L 2-3 Frank, Nagy
06/12	h	Puskás Akadémia	L 0-1

2015

28/02	a	Újpest	W 2-0 Manjrekar, Rácz
07/03	h	Haladás	W 2-1 Pauljević, Uzoma
13/03	a	Diósgyőr	D 2-2 Makriev, Rácz
21/03	a	Kecskemét	L 0-1
04/04	h	Debrecen	D 0-0
11/04	a	Paks	L 0-2
18/04	h	Honvéd	W 2-1 Ojdanić, Makriev
25/04	a	Videoton	L 0-4
03/05	h	Ferencváros	D 2-2 Szatmári 2
09/05	a	Pápa	W 2-0 Pauljević, Fröhlich
16/05	h	Dunaújváros	W 2-0 Fröhlich, Frank
23/05	a	Győr	L 0-3
29/05	h	Nyíregyháza	W 2-1 Heffler, Pauljević

No	Name	Nat	DoB	Pos	Aps	(s)	Gls
6	Béla Balogh		30/12/84	D	26		1
14	Andrej Čaušić	CRO	19/02/90	D	12	(4)	
29	Richárd Frank		28/09/90	A	4	(6)	2
10	Roland Fröhlich		08/08/88	A	14	(14)	2
1	Gergő Gőcze		30/04/90	G	8	(2)	
11	Patrik Gránicz		09/01/95	A		(2)	
9	Norbert Heffler		24/05/90	M	9	(8)	2
4	Donát Helesfay		19/07/90	G	4		
17	Adrián Horváth		20/11/87	M	25	(2)	
27	Róbert Kővári		23/11/95	A	13	(8)	2
18	Levente Lantos		26/07/80	M		(2)	
1	Dimitar Makriev	BUL	07/01/84	A	10		2
5	James Manjrekar	CAN	05/08/93	M	13	(3)	1
8	Dávid Márkvárt		20/09/94	A	29		3
22	Dávid Mohl		28/04/85	D	14		2
4	József Nagy		01/01/88	D	25	(1)	1
15	Branko Ojdanić	BIH	21/06/90	D	7	(2)	1
49	Branko Pauljević	SRB	12/06/89	M	12	(1)	3
93	Bence Pávkovics		27/03/97	M		(1)	
44	Vukašin Poleksić	MNE	30/08/82	G	18		
60	Péter Pölöskey		11/08/88	A	6	(8)	2
25	Ferenc Rácz		28/03/91	A	4	(13)	2
21	Danijel Romić	CRO	19/03/93	D	14		
32	Lóránd Szatmári		03/10/88	M	29	(1)	3
28	Mario Tadejević	CRO	28/08/89	D	2	(2)	
33	Eke Uzoma	NGA	11/08/89	M	19	(2)	1
7	Ivor Weitzer	CRO	24/05/88	M	10	(2)	
7	Dávid Wittrédi		17/06/87	A	3	(5)	1

Puskás Akadémia FC

2012 • Pancho (3,500) • puskasakademia.hu
Coach: Miklós Benczés

2014

27/07	a	Diósgyőr	L 1-2 Lencse
01/08	h	Pécs	D 2-2 Lencse (p), og (Čaušić)
09/08	a	Debrecen	L 0-2
15/08	h	Paks	D 1-1 B Tóth
22/08	a	Honvéd	L 0-1
30/08	a	Videoton	L 0-3
14/09	a	Ferencváros	L 1-2 Sallai
20/09	h	Pápa	W 3-0 Szakály, Tischler, Sallai
27/09	h	Dunaújváros	W 3-2 Lorentz, Szakály, Tischler
03/10	h	Győr	W 2-1 Lencse, Tischler
18/10	a	Nyíregyháza	W 1-0 Tischler
25/10	h	MTK	L 0-1
31/10	a	Kecskemét	L 1-2 Tischler
08/11	a	Újpest	D 1-1 Szakály
22/11	h	Haladás	W 1-0 Tischler
29/11	h	Diósgyőr	W 1-0 Gohér
06/12	a	Pécs	W 1-0 Tischler

2015

28/02	h	Debrecen	L 0-1
06/03	a	Paks	L 1-2 Lencse (p)
14/03	h	Honvéd	D 1-1 B Tóth
21/03	h	Videoton	D 0-0
03/04	h	Ferencváros	L 1-2 Polonkai
11/04	a	Pápa	W 1-0 Lencse
18/04	a	Dunaújváros	W 3-2 Lencse 3 (1p)
26/04	a	Győr	L 0-1
02/05	h	Nyíregyháza	L 1-2 Tischler
08/05	a	MTK	L 0-1
16/05	h	Kecskemét	W 4-0 Tischler 3, Lencse
23/05	h	Újpest	L 4-5 Tischler 4
30/05	a	Haladás	L 0-3

No	Name	Nat	DoB	Pos	Aps	(s)	Gls
77	Péter Czvitkovics		10/02/83	M	8	(3)	
44	Branislav Danilović	SRB	24/06/88	G	27		
14	Stefan Denković	MNE	16/06/91	M	5	(4)	
2	Fábio Guarú	BRA	03/09/87	D	7	(2)	
24	Attila Fiola		17/02/90	D	13		
6	Gergő Gohér		16/06/87	D	9	(2)	1
21	Ľuboš Hajdúch	SVK	06/03/80	G	3	(1)	
9	Zoltán Harsányi	SVK	01/06/87	A	9	(9)	
7	Martin Hudák	SVK	22/02/94	M	2	(2)	
3	Renato Kelić	CRO	31/03/91	D	25	(1)	
8	László Kleinheisler		08/04/94	M	11	(1)	
29	László Lencse		02/07/88	A	28	(1)	9
42	Márton Lorentz		01/02/95	M	3	(7)	1
99	Gábor Makrai		26/06/96	A	3	(6)	
17	Andor Margitics		03/01/91	M	6	(2)	
52	Dávid Mészáros		31/07/96	M		(2)	
25	Zsolt Nagy		25/05/93	D		(1)	
8	Máté Papp		12/03/93	M	1	(4)	
53	Bence Pintér		02/04/96	M		(1)	
18	Attila Polonkai		12/06/78	M	22	(2)	1
11	Roland Sallai		22/05/97	M	5	(11)	2
23	Csaba Spandler		07/03/96	D	13	(1)	
88	Dénes Szakály		15/03/88	M	14	(7)	3
5	Zoltán Szélesi		22/11/81	D	27	(1)	
4	Márk Tamás		28/10/93	D	14	(2)	
22	Zsolt Tar		13/02/93	D	15	(1)	
9	Patrik Tischler		30/07/91	A	24	(6)	15
20	Balázs Tóth		24/09/81	M	17	(1)	2
70	László Tóth		09/07/95	M	1		
91	Gergő Vaszicsku		30/06/91	D	13	(2)	
27	Donát Zsótér		06/01/96	A	5	(5)	

Szombathelyi Haladás

1919 • Rohonci úti (12,500) •
haladasfc.nyugat.hu
Coach: Tamás Artner;
(21/10/14) Lázár Szentes;
(20/04/15) Attila Kuttor;
(05/05/15) Géza Mészöly

2014

26/07	h	Újpest	L	0-1
02/08	a	Kecskemét	W	1-0	O Nagy
10/08	a	Diósgyőr	L	0-3
17/08	h	Pécs	D	1-1	Halmosi
24/08	a	Debrecen	L	0-1
29/08	h	Paks	L	1-3	Gaál
13/09	a	Honvéd	L	0-2
20/09	h	Videoton	L	0-2
28/09	a	Ferencváros	D	0-0
05/10	h	Pápa	W	2-0	Rocchi, Gyurján
17/10	a	Dunaújváros	L	0-1
26/10	h	Győr	L	0-2
01/11	a	Nyíregyháza	L	0-2
09/11	h	MTK	L	0-3
22/11	a	Puskás Akadémia	L	0-1
29/11	a	Újpest	L	0-1
06/12	h	Kecskemét	W	3-1	Iszlai (p), og (Varga), Devecseri

2015

28/02	h	Diósgyőr	D	1-1	Németh
07/03	a	Pécs	L	1-2	Martínez
14/03	h	Debrecen	W	2-0	Martínez 2
20/03	a	Paks	W	2-1	Halmosi, Martínez (p)
05/04	a	Honvéd	L	1-3	Radó
12/04	a	Videoton	L	0-7
18/04	h	Ferencváros	L	0-3
25/04	a	Pápa	D	2-2	Jagodics, Radó
02/05	h	Dunaújváros	L	1-4	Rocchi
09/05	a	Győr	L	2-3	Martínez, Radó
15/05	h	Nyíregyháza	W	3-1	Radó 2, Halmosi
23/05	a	MTK	L	0-2
30/05	h	Puskás Akadémia	W	3-0	Martínez (p), Rocchi, Radó

No	Name	Nat	DoB	Pos	Aps	(s)	Gls
13	Raffaele Alcibiade	ITA	23/05/90	D	10	(1)	
24	Zsolt Angyal		24/03/94	D	10	(1)	
1	Laurențiu Brănescu	ROU	30/03/94	G	2		
85	Arnaud Bühler	SUI	17/01/85	D	3	(4)	
19	Máté Czingraber		13/06/97	D		(2)	
12	Szilárd Devecseri		13/02/90	D	22		1
14	Gábor Dvorschák		14/09/89	D	12	(1)	
8	Andriy Efremov	UKR	14/03/93	M	1	(2)	
33	Márk Farkas		13/01/92	D	1	(1)	
3	Zoltán Fehér		12/06/81	D	17		
32	Bálint Gaál		14/07/91	A	22	(5)	1
30	Bence Grabant		06/05/96	A		(2)	
13	Bence Gyurján		21/02/92	M	2	(7)	1
75	László Gyűrű		02/05/92	G	2		
79	Péter Halmosi		25/09/79	M	23	(1)	3
35	János Hegedűs		04/10/96	D	2		
90	Bence Iszlai		29/05/90	D	24	(1)	1
26	Márk Jagodics		12/04/92	D	14	(3)	1
12	András Jancsó		22/04/96	M	3	(7)	
4	Gábor Jánvári		25/04/90	D	10	(1)	
90	Máté Katona		16/02/90	D	11	(1)	
41	Kamil Kopúnek	SVK	18/05/84	M	6	(1)	
10	Andrea Mancini	ITA	13/09/92	A		(2)	
9	Leandro Martínez	ITA	15/10/89	A	10		6
77	Zoltán Medgyes		23/07/95	A	3		
91	Roland Mursits		14/03/91	G	1		
23	Olivér Nagy		30/01/89	M	12	(1)	1
17	Patrik Nagy		16/02/91	M	9	(3)	
45	Márió Németh		01/05/95	A	8	(7)	1
16	Barnabás Rácz		26/04/96	M		(4)	
7	András Radó		09/09/93	A	23		6
18	Tommaso Rocchi	ITA	19/09/77	A	10	(1)	3
66	Dániel Rózsa		24/11/84	G	25		
23	Szabolcs Schimmer		24/02/84	M	17	(4)	
6	Attila Szakály		30/06/92	M	8	(3)	
21	Olivér Tihanyi		17/12/97	A		(2)	
11	Gábor Varga		20/08/85	D		(3)	
20	Viktor Városi		21/10/93	A	2	(5)	
92	Balázs Zamostny		31/01/92	A	3	(4)	
5	Martin Zsirai		19/03/94	D	2		

Újpest FC

1885 • Szusza Ferenc (13,500) • ujpestfc.hu
Major honours
Hungarian League (20) 1930, 1931, 1933, 1935,
1939, 1945, 1946, 1947, 1960, 1969, 1970, 1971,
1972, 1973, 1974, 1975, 1978, 1979, 1990, 1998;
Hungarian Cup (9) 1969, 1970, 1975, 1982, 1983,
1987, 1992, 2002, 2014
Coach: Nebojša Vignjević (SRB)

2014

26/07	a	Haladás	W	1-0	Suljić
03/08	h	Diósgyőr	D	1-1	Suljić
09/08	a	Pécs	D	1-1	Simon
16/08	h	Debrecen	W	1-0	Simon
23/08	a	Paks	D	0-0
30/08	h	Honvéd	D	0-0
14/09	a	Videoton	L	0-2
21/09	h	Ferencváros	W	2-1	Vasiljević (p), Simon
27/09	a	Pápa	D	0-0
04/10	h	Dunaújváros	W	3-0	Vasiljević (p), Simon, Stanisavljević
19/10	a	Győr	D	0-0
24/10	h	Nyíregyháza	W	3-2	Simon, Bardi, Stanisavljević
02/11	a	MTK	W	1-0	Balogh
08/11	h	Puskás Akadémia	D	1-1	Simon
21/11	a	Kecskemét	L	0-2
29/11	h	Haladás	W	1-0	Stanisavljević
07/12	a	Diósgyőr	L	1-2	Suljić

2015

28/02	h	Pécs	L	0-2
08/03	a	Debrecen	D	0-0
14/03	h	Paks	L	1-2	Bardi
21/03	a	Honvéd	D	2-2	Vasiljević (p), Andrić
05/04	h	Videoton	L	0-1
12/04	a	Ferencváros	L	0-2
19/04	h	Pápa	W	4-0	Litauszki, Balogh, Ojo (p), Nego
24/04	a	Dunaújváros	W	3-1	Perović, Heris 2
03/05	h	Győr	W	1-0	Perović
09/05	a	Nyíregyháza	W	4-2	Stanisavljević, Ojo 2, Andrić
16/05	h	MTK	W	1-0	Litauszki
23/05	a	Puskás Akadémia	W	5-4	Andrić 2, Heris, og (Kelić), Nego
30/05	h	Kecskemét	W	3-0	Ojo, Andrić, Perović

No	Name	Nat	DoB	Pos	Aps	(s)	Gls
19	Berat Ahmeti	ALB	26/01/95	A		(4)	
2	Darwin Andrade	COL	11/02/91	D	1		
19	Nemanja Andrić	SRB	13/06/87	M	10		5
1	Szabolcs Balajcza		14/07/79	G	30		
8	Balázs Balogh		11/06/90	M	29		2
23	Dávid Banai		09/05/94	G		(1)	
29	Enis Bardi	MKD	02/07/95	M	16	(5)	2
20	Aaron Dankwah	GHA	06/01/93	M	2	(5)	
17	Gyula Forró		06/06/88	D	27	(2)	
3	Jonathan Heris	BEL	03/09/90	D	27		3
26	David Hudák	SVK	21/03/93	D	8	(1)	
22	Péter Kabát		25/09/77	A		(2)	
10	Nebojša Kosović	MNE	24/02/95	M	2	(11)	
29	Róbert Litauszki		15/03/90	D	29		2
15	Aristote Mboma	FIN	30/06/94	A	3	(4)	
14	Gábor Nagy		16/10/85	M	25	(1)	
28	János Nagy		01/07/91	D	1	(1)	
2	Loïc Nego	FRA	15/01/91	D	19	(4)	2
9	Kim Ojo	NGA	02/12/88	M	11	(4)	4
11	Mihailo Perović	MNE	23/01/97	A	4	(5)	3
1	Daniel Ponce	ESP	16/05/91	A		(2)	
16	Rodrigo Rojo	URU	21/07/89	D		(6)	
18	Bojan Sanković	MNE	21/11/93	M		(4)	
7	Krisztián Simon		10/06/91	M	17		6
4	Filip Stanisavljević	SRB	20/05/87	M	17	(9)	4
99	Asmir Suljić	BIH	11/09/91	A	24	(2)	3
55	Sandro Tsveiba	RUS	05/09/93	D		(2)	
25	Viktor Vadász		15/08/86	D	11	(3)	
6	Dušan Vasiljević	SRB	07/05/82	M	17	(2)	3

Videoton FC

1941 • Sóstói (15,000) • vidi.hu
Major honours
Hungarian League (2) 2011, 2015; Hungarian Cup
(1) 2006
Coach: Joan Carrillo (ESP)

2014

26/07	h	Pápa	W	3-0	Juhász 2, Nikolić
02/08	h	Dunaújváros	W	3-0	Filipe Oliveira, Sándor, Nikolić
09/08	h	Győr	W	3-2	og (Wolfe), Juhász, Nikolić
16/08	a	Nyíregyháza	W	2-0	Kovács, Nikolić
23/08	h	MTK	W	5-0	Kovács 2, Gyurcsó, Nikolić, Feczesin
30/08	h	Puskás Akadémia	W	3-0	Gyurcsó, Nikolić 2
14/09	h	Újpest	W	2-0	Juhász, Nikolić
20/09	a	Haladás	W	2-0	Nikolić 2
28/09	h	Diósgyőr	W	2-1	Nikolić, og (William Alves)
04/10	a	Pécs	W	2-0	Nikolić, og (Čaušić)
19/10	h	Debrecen	L	1-2	Kovács
25/10	h	Paks	W	2-0	Filipe Oliveira, Nikolić
02/11	h	Honvéd	W	1-0	Kovács
08/11	a	Kecskemét	D	0-0
23/11	a	Ferencváros	D	0-0
29/11	a	Pápa	W	5-0	Nikolić 2, Gyurcsó, Stopira, Feczesin
06/12	a	Dunaújváros	W	4-1	Nikolić, Gyurcsó, Álvarez, Paulo Vinícius

2015

01/03	a	Győr	D	2-2	Nikolić, Juhász
07/03	h	Nyíregyháza	W	3-0	Paulo Vinícius, Álvarez, Nikolić (p)
14/03	a	MTK	W	1-0	Feczesin
21/03	a	Puskás Akadémia	D	0-0
05/04	a	Újpest	W	1-0	Filipe Oliveira
12/04	h	Haladás	W	7-0	Nikolić, Feczesin 2, Trebotić 2, Filipe Oliveira, og (Fehér)
19/04	a	Diósgyőr	W	2-1	Filipe Oliveira, Feczesin
25/04	a	Pécs	W	4-0	Gyurcsó, Filipe Oliveira, Nikolić 2
02/05	a	Debrecen	W	2-1	Gyurcsó, Feczesin
10/05	a	Paks	L	0-1
16/05	a	Honvéd	D	1-1	Ivanovski
24/05	h	Kecskemét	W	1-0	Trebotić
30/05	a	Ferencváros	L	0-2

No	Name	Nat	DoB	Pos	Aps	(s)	Gls
23	Arturo Álvarez	SLV	28/06/85	A	10	(13)	2
2	Álvaro Brachi	ESP	06/01/86	D	5	(2)	
1	Juan Calatayud	ESP	21/12/79	G	29		
14	Sofian Chakla	MAR	02/09/93	D	5	(1)	
9	Róbert Feczesin		22/02/86	A	9	(11)	7
6	András Fejes		26/08/88	D	6	(2)	
16	Filipe Oliveira	POR	27/05/84	M	23	(3)	6
77	Ádám Gyurcsó		06/03/91	M	25	(1)	6
5	Tibor Heffler		17/05/87	D	1	(11)	
19	Mirko Ivanovski	MKD	31/10/89	A	3	(5)	1
23	Roland Juhász		01/07/83	D	25		5
8	László Kleinheisler		08/04/94	M	3	(8)	
64	Gergő Kocsis		07/03/94	D	1		
10	István Kovács		27/03/92	M	23	(3)	5
4	Kees Luijckx	NED	11/02/86	D	2		
4	Marco Caneira		09/02/79	D	1	(2)	
24	Rémi Maréval	FRA	24/02/83	D	2	(1)	
17	Nemanja Nikolić		31/12/87	A	24	(1)	21
41	Filip Pajović	SRB	30/03/93	G	1		
3	Paulo Vinícius	BRA	21/02/90	D	25		2
11	György Sándor		20/03/84	M	24	(2)	1
46	Ádám Simon		30/03/90	M	21	(7)	
22	Stopira	CPV	20/05/88	D	25		1
30	Roland Szolnoki		21/01/92	D	25		
33	Dinko Trebotić	CRO	30/07/90	M	13	(15)	3

HUNGARY

Top goalscorers

21	Nemanja Nikolić (Videoton)
15	Patrik Tischler (Puskás Akadémia)
13	Dániel Böde (Ferencváros)
11	Tamás Priskin (Győr)
10	Norbert Könyves (Paks)
9	Souleymane Youla (Honvéd)
	Bebeto (Kecskemét)
	László Pekár (Nyíregyháza)
	László Lencse (Puskás Akadémia)
8	József Kanta (MTK)
	László Bartha (Paks)

Promoted clubs

Vasas SC

1911 • Illovszky Rudolf (18,000) •
vasasfutballclub.hu
Coach: Károly Szanyó

Békéscsaba 1912 Előre SE

1912 • Kórház utcai (13,000) • 1912elore.hu
Coach: Zoran Spisljak (SRB)

Second level final table 2014/15

		Pld	W	D	L	F	A	Pts
1	Vasas SC	30	21	3	6	68	31	66
2	Békéscsaba 1912 Előre SE	30	18	7	5	42	23	61
3	Gyirmót SE	30	16	11	3	54	32	59
4	Mezőkövesd-Zsóry SE	30	13	9	8	53	37	48
5	Soproni VSE	30	12	12	6	46	38	48
6	Szolnoki MÁV FC	30	13	7	10	50	47	46
7	Szeged 2011	30	13	6	11	36	32	45
8	Zalaegerszegi TE	30	10	8	12	42	47	38
9	Soroksár SC	30	9	6	15	32	41	33
10	Szigetszentmiklósi TK	30	7	12	11	24	35	33
11	FC Ajka	30	8	8	14	43	46	32
12	Csákvári TK	30	8	8	14	44	56	32
13	Balmazújvárosi FC	30	8	8	14	35	52	32
14	BFC Siófok	30	7	10	13	40	52	31
15	Ceglédi VSE	30	6	9	15	33	56	27
16	Kaposvári Rákóczi FC	30	5	8	17	30	47	23

DOMESTIC CUP

Magyar Kupa 2014/15

FIRST ROUND

(07/08/14)
Újbuda 1-2 Zalaegerszeg *(aet)*
(09/08/14)
Alsózsolca 2-3 Velence *(aet)*
Balatoni Vasas 0-0
Fertőszentmiklós *(aet; 4-5 on pens)*
Celldömölk 3-0 Sárvár
Cigánd 2-3 Szigetszentmiklós
Csepel 12-0 Létavértes
Dunaharaszti 1-2 Békéscsaba
Gyulaháza 0-3 Ajka
Hatvan 2-3 Csákvár
Ikarus BSE 1-0 Kondoros
Iváncsa 1-0 Hajduböszörmény
Jászfényszaru 0-1 Baja *(aet)*
Kisújszállás 1-3 Tiszaújváros
Kozármisleny 5-1 Diósdi TC
Körmend 0-5 Gyirmót
Kunszállás 3-0 Rákosmenti KSK
Majos 0-8 Cegléd
Mezőkovácsház 0-7
Mezőkövesd-Zsóry
Monor 2-4 Balmazújváros *(aet)*
Mórahalom 3-2 Maglód
Nőtincs 5-1 Rákóczi FSE
Nyírbátor 1-5 Vác
Ónod 0-6 Siófok
Orosháza 1-0 Dunaújváros
Pétervására 1-2 BKV Előre
Püspökladány 1-2
Győrsövényház *(aet)*
Sajóbábony 5-2 Nagybajom
Sárisáp 1-2 Jászapáti
Sárosd 3-2 Mosonmagyaróvár
Semjénháza 2-4 SZEOL
Soltvadkert 2-0 Ebes
Tatabánya 2-3 Szeged *(aet)*
Várda 4-1 Tököl
Veresegyháza 0-7 Bölcske

(10/08/14)
Babócsa 0-2 Kazincbarcika *(aet)*
Dabas 1-3 ESMTK
Füzfő 0-6 Vecsés
Gyöngyös 2-3 Putnok *(aet)*
Győrszemere 1-2 Kaposvári Rákóczi
Hímesháza 2-1 Csácsbozsok-Nemesapáti
Kótaj 0-1 REAC
Nagykáta 0-4 Balatonfüred
Répcelak 0-1 Nagyatád
Szerencs 3-1 Komló
Taksony 1-3 Szolnoki MÁV
Taliándörögd 0-2 Veszprém
Tata 3-9 Salgótarján
Tevel 7-2 Csetény
Voyage 1-2 Gyula *(aet)*

(12/08/14)
Andráshida 1-3 Puskás Akadémia
Felsőtárkány 2-1 Paks
Szentlőrinc 0-2 MTK

(13/08/14)
Budaörs 1-3 Újpest
Csorna 0-2 Honvéd
Dorog 1-4 Haladás
Hévíz 0-8 Ferencváros
Kalocsa 0-8 Nyíregyháza
Nyíradony 0-8 Kecskemét
Soroksár 2-0 Pápa

Szászvár 0-3 Pécs
Szekszárd 0-3 Debrecen
Testvériség 0-7 Videoton
Vasas 0-4 Diósgyőr

(27/08/14)
Soproni VSE 0-1 Győri ETO

SECOND ROUND

(02/09/14)
Nagyatád 2-0 Veszprém

(09/09/14)
Békéscsaba 3-1 Siófok
Felsőtárkány 0-1 Honvéd
Hímesháza 0-13 Újpest
Orosháza 1-5 Puskás Akadémia
Szeged 0-1 Szigetszentmiklós
Tevel 2-7 MTK
Tiszaújváros 0-3 Mezőkövesd-Zsóry
Velence 1-2 Kaposvári Rákóczi

(10/09/14)
Baja 1-4 Soroksár
Balatonfüred 1-2 Vác
Bölcske 0-5 Gyirmót
Celldömölk 0-4 Ajka
Csepel 3-4 Szolnoki MÁV
Fertőszentmiklós 0-7 Haladás
Győrsövényház 0-8 Nyíregyháza
Ikarus BSE 1-5 Csákvár
Iváncsa 0-4 Diósgyőr
Jászapáti 3-1 Gyula
Kazincbarcika 4-1 REAC
Kozármisleny 2-1 Balmazújváros
Kunszállás 0-8 Videoton
Mórahalom 0-6 Debrecen
Putnok 1-3 Győri ETO
Sajóbábony 2-1 Nőtincs
Sárosd 1-2 Salgótarján
Soltvadkert 1-6 BKV Előre
SZEOL 1-4 Pécs
Szerencs 0-10 ESMTK
Várda 2-0 Cegléd
Vecsés 1-6 Ferencváros
Zalaegerszeg 2-3 Kecskemét

THIRD ROUND

(23/09/14)
BKV Előre 1-3 Honvéd
Kazincbarcika 1-2 Csákvár
Kozármisleny 0-5 Pécs
Nagyatád 0-2 Szolnoki MÁV
Szigetszentmiklós 1-2 Videoton

(24/09/14)
Ajka 2-1 Soroksár
ESMTK 0-3 Ferencváros
Gyirmót 1-0 Kaposvári Rákóczi
Jászapáti 0-9 MTK
Mezőkövesd-Zsóry 1-2 Győri ETO
Puskás Akadémia 0-2 Debrecen
Sajóbábony 1-4 Diósgyőr
Salgótarján 1-8 Békéscsaba
Újpest 2-0 Haladás
Vác 5-2 Kecskemét *(aet)*
Várda 3-2 Nyíregyháza

FOURTH ROUND

(28/10/14)
Videoton 2-1 Diósgyőr

(29/10/14)
Ajka 1-1 Újpest *(aet; 3-5 on pens)*
Csákvár 2-1 Békéscsaba
Gyirmót 2-0 Győri ETO
Honvéd 0-0 Ferencváros *(aet; 1-3 on pens)*
Pécs 1-0 Debrecen
Szolnoki MÁV 2-1 MTK
Várda 4-0 Vác

QUARTER-FINALS

(04/03/15 & 31/03/15)
Ferencváros 5-0 Csákvár *(Busai 7, 62, 70, Lamah 37, Ramírez 64)*
Csákvár 0-5 Ferencváros *(Kukuruzović 27, Čukić 33, Dominik Nagy 41, 76, Ugrai 54)*
(Ferencváros 10-0)

Várda 1-3 Szolnoki MÁV *(Szűcs 81; Nagy 5, Fritz 41, Vári 62p)*
Szolnoki MÁV 1-1 Várda *(Vári 7p; Myke Ramos 73)*
(Szolnoki MÁV 4-2)

(04/03/15 & 01/04/15)
Gyirmót 0-0 Újpest
Újpest 4-0 Gyirmót *(Balogh 8, Suljić 18, Litauszki 20, Ojo 82)*
(Újpest 4-0)

Videoton 2-1 Pécs *(Feczesin 66, Álvarez 90+4p; Fröhlich 44)*
Pécs 0-3 Videoton *(Feczesin 13p, Ivanovski 60, Trebotić 85)*
(Videoton 5-1)

SEMI-FINALS

(07/04/15 & 29/04/15)
Szolnoki MÁV 0-2 Ferencváros *(Lengyel 3og, Varga 30)*
Ferencváros 1-1 Szolnoki MÁV *(Lamah 20; Papucsek 75)*
(Ferencváros 3-1)

(08/04/15 & 28/04/15)
Videoton 1-0 Újpest *(Gyurcsó 43)*
Újpest 1-4 Videoton *(Litauszki 39; Nikolić 22, 71, Feczesin 88, Filipe Oliveira 90+3)*
(Videoton 5-1)

FINAL

(20/05/15)
Groupama Aréna, Budapest
FERENCVÁROSI TC 4 *(Varga 53, Batik 60, Lamah 69, Szolnoki 86og)*
VIDEOTON FC 0
Referee: *Iványi*
FERENCVÁROS: *Dibusz, Dilaver, Pavlović, Batik, Ramírez (Bönig 89), Gera (Čukić 87), Somália, Á Nagy (Gyömbér 70), Varga, Böde, Lamah*
VIDEOTON: *Calatayud, Szolnoki, Juhász, Paulo Vinícius, Stopira, Sándor, Simon (Trebotić 63), Gyurcsó, Kovács (Feczesin 71), Filipe Oliveira (Álvarez 63), Nikolić*

ICELAND
Knattspyrnusamband Íslands (KSÍ)

Address	Laugardal	**President**	Geir Thorsteinsson
	IS-104 Reykjavík	**Media officer**	Ómar Smarsson
Tel	+354 510 2900	**Year of formation**	1947
Fax	+354 568 9793	**National stadium**	Laugardalsvöllur,
E-mail	ksi@ksi.is		Reykjavik (15,182)
Website	ksi.is		

Akureyri

⑩

① ~Kópavogur
⑭ Akranes
② ~Hafnarfjördur
Reykjavík~ ③ ④ ⑤ ⑧ ⑪ ⑫ ⑬
Keflavík
⑦ Gardabær~ ⑨

 Vestmannaeyjar
⑥

KEY:

● – UEFA Champions League
● – UEFA Europa League
○ – Promoted
○ – Relegated

ÚRVALSDEILDIN CLUBS

  ① Breidablik

  **② FH Hafnarfjördur**

  ③ Fjölnir

  **④ Fram Reykjavík**

  ⑤ Fylkir

  **⑥ ÍBV Vestmannaeyjar**

  ⑦ Keflavík

  ⑧ KR Reykjavík

  ⑨ Stjarnan

  ⑩ Thór Akureyri

  **⑪ Valur Reykjavík**

 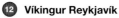 **⑫ Víkingur Reykjavík**

PROMOTED CLUBS

  **⑬ Leiknir Reykjavík**

  ⑭ ÍA Akranes

Stjarnan in dreamland

In one of the most extraordinary climaxes to any European league campaign, Stjarnan became the champions of Iceland for the first time, leapfrogging FH Hafnarfjördur into first place when they beat them with a last-gasp penalty on the final day of the season.

There was late drama too in the domestic cup final as KR Reykjavík struck a 92nd-minute winner to defeat Keflavík, while the repeated heroics of Lars Lagerbäck's national side were the talk of the nation as Iceland, with five wins in six UEFA EURO 2016 qualifiers, closed in on a first ever major tournament appearance.

| **Dramatic denouement to first title win** | **FH foiled by late penalty on final day** | **National team top EURO qualifying group** |

Domestic league

The Úrvalsdeild had produced a number of last-day thrillers in the past, but nothing that had gone before could rival the drama offered up in the 2014 title showdown between Stjarnan and FH. Having tracked each other throughout the campaign, the two clubs went into the season's finale, at FH's Kaplakriki stadium, with unbeaten records. The home side, champions six times in the previous decade, had the double advantage of playing in front of their own fans and holding a one-point lead. The visitors, who had never won a major trophy, appeared to have it all to do.

With a sell-out crowd of 6,450 watching on, it was Stjarnan who drew first blood, leading scorer Ólafur Karl Finsen finding the net just before half-time. But the pendulum swung in FH's favour when in the space of five second-half minutes Stjarnan lost their captain, Veigar Páll Gunnarsson, to a red card and Scotsman Steve Lennon drew the home side level. Despite their reduced numbers Stjarnan threw everything at FH in search of the winning goal, and two minutes into stoppage time, to gasps of horror from the locals, they were awarded a penalty. It was a do-or-die moment for Finsen, and the Stjarnan striker duly delivered, coolly sending FH keeper Robert Örn

Óskarsson the wrong way. A couple of minutes later the game was over and Stjarnan's wild celebrations began.

If Finsen was Stjarnan's championship-clinching hero, coach Rúnar Páll Sigmundsson merited equal adulation. In his first season he had not only taken the team to the title but done so without losing a game. After two successive Icelandic Cup final defeats, it was third time lucky for the Gardabaer club, but, equally, Heimir Gudjónsson's FH were entitled to bemoan their ill fortune, having scored more and conceded fewer goals than the champions and found the net in every game.

Domestic cup

As 2013 Icelandic Cup winners Fram Reykjavík suffered relegation, they returned the trophy to the team that had won it in the two seasons before them, KR. A closely-contested final against Keflavík was decided in favour of Rúnar Kristinsson's team – who had finished a distant third in the league – by striker Kjartan Henry Finnbogason's 92nd-minute winner. It was KR's 14th cup win, extending their competition record.

Europe

Stjarnan's title triumph was supplemented by a magnificent debut

campaign in Europe that lasted from the first qualifying round of the UEFA Europa League to the play-offs. Bangor City FC, Motherwell FC (with the help of three Finsen penalties) and KKS Lech Poznań were all eliminated before Italian giants FC Internazionale Milano brought Sigmundsson and his players back to earth with a bump. FH almost matched Stjarnan's efforts but lost out in the third qualifying round to IF Elfsborg.

National team

Iceland responded to the disappointment of 2014 FIFA World Cup qualifying play-off defeat by storming to three successive victories at the start of the UEFA EURO 2016 qualifying campaign. Turkey (home), Latvia (away) and, most thrillingly, the Netherlands (home) were all comprehensively defeated without the concession of a goal before the Czech Republic dislodged them from the Group A summit with a 2-1 win in Plzen. By the end of the season, however, Lagerbäck's effervescent side were back in command, a reversal of that result against the Czechs in Reykjavik following another thumping win in Kazakhstan. There were still four matches to play, but the consistent quality of Iceland's performances, with Gylfi Sigurdsson and Kolbeinn Sigthórsson to the fore, suggested that the team were more than capable of seeing the job through to the finish.

DOMESTIC SEASON AT A GLANCE

Úrvalsdeildin 2014 final table

		Pld			Home					Away					Total			Pts
			W	D	L	F	A	W	D	L	F	A	W	D	L	F	A	
1	Stjarnan	22	7	4	0	20	8	8	3	0	22	13	15	7	0	42	21	52
2	FH Hafnarfjördur	22	7	3	1	21	8	8	3	0	25	9	15	6	1	46	17	51
3	KR Reykjavík	22	6	2	3	20	13	7	2	2	20	11	13	4	5	40	24	43
4	Víkingur Reykjavík	22	5	1	5	15	14	4	2	5	10	15	9	3	10	25	29	30
5	Valur Reykjavík	22	5	0	6	20	21	3	4	4	11	15	8	4	10	31	36	28
6	Fylkir	22	5	2	4	18	18	3	2	6	16	22	8	4	10	34	40	28
7	Breidablik	22	4	5	2	26	19	1	7	3	10	14	5	12	5	36	33	27
8	Keflavík	22	3	3	5	15	15	3	4	4	14	17	6	7	9	29	32	25
9	Fjölnir	22	3	6	2	18	13	2	2	7	15	23	5	8	9	33	36	23
10	ÍBV Vestmannaeyjar	22	3	3	5	17	18	2	4	5	11	20	5	7	10	28	38	22
11	Fram Reykjavík	22	3	3	5	12	20	3	0	8	18	28	6	3	13	30	48	21
12	Thór Akureyri	22	3	2	6	14	15	0	1	10	10	29	3	3	16	24	44	12

European qualification 2015/16

Champion: Stjarnan (second qualifying round)

Cup winner: KR Reykjavík (first qualifying round)
FH Hafnarfjördur (first qualifying round)
Víkingur Reykjavík (first qualifying round)

Top scorer Gary Martin (KR), 13 goals
Relegated clubs Thór Akureyri, Fram Reykjavík
Promoted clubs Leiknir Reykjavík, ÍA Akranes
Cup final KR Reykjavík 2-1 Keflavík

Team of the season
(4-3-3)

Coach: Sigmundsson (Stjarnan)

Player of the season

Ingvar Jónsson
(Stjarnan)

Jónsson's fourth season at Stjarnan turned out to be his last as he left for Norwegian club IK Start, but it was also far and away his best. The 25-year-old goalkeeper missed only one game in the club's Úrvalsdeild title triumph and was an ever-present in the UEFA Europa League run. Agile and dependable, he proved his worth on numerous occasions with timely saves and impressed sufficiently to gain a call-up to the Icelandic national side, making his debut in a November friendly against Belgium.

Newcomer of the season

Elías Már Ómarsson
(Keflavík)

Ómarsson spent his final year as a teenager making a name for himself in the Keflavík attack, scoring six goals in 20 league appearances and also helping his team into the Icelandic Cup final. His talent on the ball was plain for all to see, and he graduated from his country's Under-19 side via the Under-21s to the seniors, making his first two appearances for Lars Lagerbäck's team in two winter friendlies against Canada in Florida. A few weeks later he joined Norwegian club Vålerenga Fotball.

ICELAND

NATIONAL TEAM

Top five all-time caps
Rúnar Kristinsson (104); Hermann Hreidarsson (89); Gudni Bergsson (80); **Eidur Smári Gudjohnsen** (79); Brynjar Björn Gunnarsson & Birkir Kristinsson (74)

Top five all-time goals
Eidur Smári Gudjohnsen (25); Ríkhardur Jónsson & **Kolbeinn Sigthórsson** (17); Ríkhardur Dadason & Arnór Gudjohnsen (14)

Results 2014/15

09/09/14	Turkey (ECQ)	H	Reykjavik	W	3-0	Bödvarsson (18), G Sigurdsson (76), Sigthórsson (77)
10/10/14	Latvia (ECQ)	A	Riga	W	3-0	G Sigurdsson (66), Gunnarsson (77), Gíslason (90)
13/10/14	Netherlands (ECQ)	H	Reykjavik	W	2-0	G Sigurdsson (10p, 42)
12/11/14	Belgium	A	Brussels	L	1-3	Finnbogason (13)
16/11/14	Czech Republic (ECQ)	A	Plzen	L	1-2	R Sigurdsson (9)
16/01/15	Canada	N	Orlando (USA)	W	2-1	Steindórsson (6), Vilhjálmsson (42)
19/01/15	Canada	N	Orlando (USA)	D	1-1	Fridjónsson (65p)
28/03/15	Kazakhstan (ECQ)	A	Astana	W	3-0	Gudjohnsen (20), B Bjarnason (32, 90+1)
31/03/15	Estonia	A	Tallinn	D	1-1	Gíslason (9)
12/06/15	Czech Republic (ECQ)	H	Reykjavik	W	2-1	Gunnarsson (60), Sigthórsson (76)

Appearances 2014/15

Coach: Lars Lagerbäck (SWE) 16/07/48 & Heimir Hallgrímsson 10/06/67			TUR	LVA	NED	Bel	CZE	Can	Can	KAZ	Est	CZE	Caps	Goals
Hannes Thór Halldórsson	27/04/84	Sandnes Ulf (NOR)	G	G	G		G	G65		G		G	28	-
Theódór Elmar Bjarnason	04/03/87	Randers (DEN)	D	D	D		D62	D					19	-
Kári Árnason	13/10/82	Rotherham (ENG)	D	D	D		D			D		D	40	2
Ragnar Sigurdsson	19/06/86	Krasnodar (RUS)	D	D	D	D84	D			D	s46	D	45	1
Ari Freyr Skúlason	14/05/87	OB (DEN)	D	D	D46		D			D	s46	D	29	-
Birkir Bjarnason	27/05/88	Pescara (ITA)	M70	M	M	s46	M77			M		M	38	6
Aron Einar Gunnarsson	22/04/89	Cardiff (ENG)	M	M	M	M46	M			M72		M	51	2
Gylfi Thór Sigurdsson	08/09/89	Swansea (ENG)	M89	M80	M		M			M		M	30	9
Emil Hallfredsson	29/06/84	Verona (ITA)	M	M87	M		M62			s72	M59	M63	49	1
Jón Dadi Bödvarsson	25/05/92	Viking (NOR)	A92	A77	A89	s74	A	A72	A46	s70	M46	s63	13	1
Kolbeinn Sigthórsson	14/03/90	Ajax (NED)	A	A	A		A			A70		A93	29	17
Rúrik Gíslason	25/02/88	København (DEN)	s70	s87	s89	M	s62	M87	M46		M85	s93	37	3
Ólafur Ingi Skúlason	01/04/83	Zulte Waregem (BEL)	s89	s80		s72					s46		25	1
Vidar Örn Kjartansson	11/03/90	Vålerenga (NOR) /Jiangsu Sainty (CHN)	s92		A74					A			4	-
Alfred Finnbogason	01/02/89	Real Sociedad (ESP)		s77	A					s83	A		25	5
Birkir Már Sævarsson	11/11/84	Brann (NOR) /Hammarby (SWE)		s46	D	s62				D	s85	D	48	-
Ögmundur Kristinsson	19/06/89	Randers (DEN)			G46			G		G			4	-
Hallgrímur Jónasson	04/05/86	SønderjyskE (DEN) /OB (DEN)			D				D		D		14	3
Hördur Björgvin Magnússon	11/02/93	Cesena (ITA)			D					D46			2	-
Helgi Valur Daníelsson	13/07/81	AGF (DEN)			M72								33	-
Jóhann Berg Gudmundsson	27/10/90	Charlton (ENG)			M	s77				M	s46	A	37	5
Ingvar Jónsson	18/10/89	Stjarnan /Start (NOR)			s46		s65						2	-
Hólmar Örn Eyjólfsson	06/08/90	Rosenborg (NOR)			s84								2	-
Sölvi Geir Ottesen	18/02/84	Ural (RUS)				D							26	-
Sverrir Ingi Ingason	05/08/93	Viking (NOR)				D							2	-
Hjörtur Logi Valgardsson	27/09/88	Sogndal (NOR)				D							9	-
Rúnar Már Sigurjónsson	18/06/90	Sundsvall (SWE)				M	M46		s59				4	1
Gudlaugur Victor Pálsson	30/04/91	Helsingborg (SWE)				M46	s46		M46				4	-
Kristinn Steindórsson	29/04/90	Columbus Crew (USA)				M46							1	1
Matthías Vilhjálmsson	30/01/87	Start (NOR)				A46	s46		s72				13	2
Björn Daníel Sverrisson	29/05/90	Viking (NOR)				s46	s72						4	-
Hólmbert Aron Fridjónsson	19/04/93	Brøndby (DEN)				s46	A						2	1
Thórarinn Ingi Valdimarsson	23/04/90	FH				s46	M61						3	-
Ólafur Karl Finsen	30/03/92	Stjarnan				s72	s61						2	-
Elías Már Ómarsson	18/01/95	Keflavík				s87	s46						2	-
Haukur Heidar Hauksson	01/09/91	AIK (SWE)					D		D				2	-
Jón Gudni Fjóluson	10/04/89	Sundsvall (SWE)					D		D46				7	-
Hördur Árnason	19/05/89	Stjarnan					D						1	-
Gudmundur Thórarinsson	15/04/92	Sarpsborg (NOR)					M72							-
Eidur Smári Gudjohnsen	15/09/78	Bolton (ENG)					A83						79	25

EUROPE

KR Reykjavík

Second qualifying round - Celtic FC (SCO)
H 0-1
Magnússon, Sigurdarson, H Hauksson, Balbi (Zato-Arouna 58), Martin (Ragnarsson 81), Sigurdsson, Finnbogason, Atlason (Ormarsson 88), Sævarsson, Jósepsson, Gudmundur Gunnarsson. Coach: Rúnar Kristinsson (ISL)
A 0-4
Magnússon, Sigurdarson, H Hauksson, Balbi (Jónsson 73), Gunnar Gunnarsson, Martin, Sigurdsson, Finnbogason, Atlason (Ormarsson 46), Sævarsson (Zato-Arouna 57), Jósepsson. Coach: Rúnar Kristinsson (ISL)

Fram Reykjavík

First qualifying round - Nõmme Kalju FC (EST)
H 0-1
Kristinsson, T Bjarnason, Briem, Atlason, Gudmundsson, Gudjónsson, Marteinsson (Albertsson 63), V Arnarsson, H Arnarsson, Gunnarsson, Takefusa (Thorláksson 72). Coach: Bjarni Gudjónsson (ISL)
A 2-2 *Ómarsson (25), T Bjarnason (64)*
Kristinsson, Traustason (Thorláksson 61), T Bjarnason, Atlason, Ómarsson, Baldvinsson, Gudjónsson, Marteinsson (Albertsson 57), V Arnarsson, Gunnarsson (H Arnarsson 81), Takefusa. Coach: Bjarni Gudjónsson (ISL)

FH Hafnarfjördur

First qualifying round - Glenavon FC (NIR)
H 3-0 *I Óskarsson (82), Gudnason (90, 90+3)*
R Óskarsson, P Vidarsson, Hewson (Rúnarsson 78), D Vidarsson, Gudnason, Emilsson (I Óskarsson 70), Jónsson (Pálsson 70), Björnsson, Doumbia, Bödvarsson, Snorrason. Coach: Heimir Gudjónsson (ISL)
A 3-2 *I Óskarsson (3), Emilsson (37, 69p)*
R Óskarsson, Reynolds, Hewson (Ingason 75), I Óskarsson, Pálsson, Emilsson, Jónsson, Doumbia, Bödvarsson (Gudmundsson 70), Snorrason (Gudnason 46), Rúnarsson. Coach: Heimir Gudjónsson (ISL)

Second qualifying round - FC Neman Grodno (BLR)
A 1-1 *Emilsson (55)*
R Óskarsson, Vidarsson, Hewson (Reynolds 70), D Vidarsson, Gudnason (I Óskarsson 82), Emilsson, Jónsson, Doumbia, Snorrason, Rúnarsson (Pálsson 84), Hendrickx. Coach: Heimir Gudjónsson (ISL)
Red card: Hendrickx 65
H 2-0 *Gudnason (42), Björnsson (80)*
R Óskarsson, Vidarsson, Hewson (Björnsson 57), Pálsson, D Vidarsson, Gudnason, Jónsson, Doumbia, Bödvarsson, Snorrason (I Óskarsson 76), Rúnarsson. Coach: Heimir Gudjónsson (ISL)

Third qualifying round - IF Elfsborg (SWE)
A 1-4 *Lennon (61)*
R Óskarsson, Vidarsson, Pálsson, D Vidarsson, Gudnason (I Óskarsson 79), Jónsson, Lennon, Doumbia, Snorrason, Rúnarsson (Hewson 79), Hendrickx. Coach: Heimir Gudjónsson (ISL)
H 2-1 *Gudnason (17), Doumbia (76)*
R Óskarsson, Vidarsson, Pálsson (Björnsson 68), D Vidarsson, Gudnason, Jónsson, Lennon, Doumbia, Snorrason (I Óskarsson 74), Rúnarsson (Hewson 85), Hendrickx. Coach: Heimir Gudjónsson (ISL)

Stjarnan

First qualifying round - Bangor City FC (WAL)
H 4-0 *Finsen (13p, 54), Gunnarsson (16), Björgvinsson (70)*
Jónsson, Vemmelund, Præst, A Jóhannsson, Punyed, D Laxdal, Gunnarsson (G Jóhannsson 62), Björgvinsson (Ottesen 75), Árnason, Finsen (Ægisson 88), Rauschenberg. Coach: Rúnar Páll Sigmundsson (ISL)
A 4-0 *Rauschenberg (53), Björgvinsson (68, 81), A Jóhannsson (85)*
Jónsson, Præst, A Jóhannsson, Punyed, D Laxdal, Árnason, Finsen (Gunnarsson 45+2), Ottesen (Björgvinsson 55), Sturluson, G Jóhannsson (Blöndal 71), Rauschenberg. Coach: Rúnar Páll Sigmundsson (ISL)

Second qualifying round - Motherwell FC (SCO)
A 2-2 *Finsen (35p, 90+2p)*
Jónsson, Vemmelund, Præst, A Jóhannsson, Punyed, D Laxdal, Gunnarsson (Toft 88), Björgvinsson, Árnason, Finsen, Rauschenberg. Coach: Rúnar Páll Sigmundsson (ISL)
H 3-2 *Finsen (38p), Toft (85), A Jóhannsson (114)* **(aet)**
Jónsson, Vemmelund, Præst, A Jóhannsson, Punyed, D Laxdal, Gunnarsson (Toft 26), Ægisson (17), Björgvinsson (Ottesen 105), Árnason, Finsen, Rauschenberg. Coach: Rúnar Páll Sigmundsson (ISL)

Third qualifying round - KKS Lech Poznań (POL)
H 1-0 *Toft (48)*
Jónsson, Vemmelund, Præst, A Jóhannsson, Punyed (Ægisson 90+3), D Laxdal, Björgvinsson (J Laxdal 84), Árnason, Finsen, Toft, Rauschenberg. Coach: Rúnar Páll Sigmundsson (ISL)
A 0-0
Jónsson, Vemmelund, Præst (Rúnarsson 74), A Jóhannsson, Punyed, D Laxdal, Björgvinsson (J Laxdal 79), Árnason, Finsen, Toft (Ægisson 22), Rauschenberg. Coach: Rúnar Páll Sigmundsson (ISL)

Play-offs - FC Internazionale Milano (ITA)
H 0-3
Jónsson, Vemmelund, A Jóhannsson, Punyed, D Laxdal, Gunnarsson (G Jóhannsson 70), Björgvinsson, Árnason, Rúnarsson (Toft 70), Finsen, Rauschenberg. Coach: Rúnar Páll Sigmundsson (ISL)
A 0-6
Jónsson, Vemmelund, A Jóhannsson (Rúnarsson 64), Punyed, D Laxdal, Gunnarsson (G Jóhannsson 59), Björgvinsson, Árnason, Finsen (Ægisson 64), Toft, Rauschenberg. Coach: Rúnar Páll Sigmundsson (ISL)

DOMESTIC LEAGUE CLUB-BY-CLUB

Breidablik

1950 • Kópavogsvöllur (3,009);
Stjörnuvöllur (1,400) • breidablik.is
Major honours
Icelandic League (1) 2010; Icelandic Cup (1) 2009
Coach: Ólafur Helgi Kristjánsson;
(03/06/14) Gudmundur Benediktsson

2014

05/05	a	FH	D	1-1	*Gardarsson*
08/05	h	KR	L	1-2	*E Adalsteinsson*
12/05	a	Keflavík	L	0-2	
18/05	h	Fjölnir	D	2-2	*Vilhjálmsson, Ólafsson*
22/05	a	Fram	D	1-1	*Lýdsson (p)*
02/06	h	Stjarnan	D	1-1	*Sigurdsson*
11/06	a	Fylkir	D	1-1	*Lýdsson*
15/06	h	ÍBV	D	1-1	*Vilhjálmsson*
22/06	a	Víkingur	L	0-1	
02/07	h	Thór	W	3-2	*E Adalsteinsson, E Helgason, Vilhjálmsson*
14/07	a	Valur	W	2-1	*E Adalsteinsson 2*
21/07	h	FH	L	2-4	*Vilhjálmsson, A Adalsteinsson*
27/07	a	KR	D	1-1	*Vilhjálmsson*
06/08	h	Keflavík	D	4-4	*Lýdsson, Gunnlaugsson, Gíslason, Sturluson*
11/08	a	Fjölnir	D	1-1	*Vilhjálmsson*
16/08	h	Fram	W	3-0	*Vilhjálmsson, Lýdsson, E Adalsteinsson*
24/08	a	Stjarnan	D	2-2	*Lýdsson, Muminovic*
31/08	h	Fylkir	D	2-2	*Sigurdsson, Hreinsson*
14/09	a	ÍBV	D	1-1	*Muminovic*
21/09	h	Víkingur	W	4-1	*Vilhjálmsson 3, Hreinsson*
28/09	a	Thór	L	0-2	
04/10	h	Valur	W	3-0	*Lýdsson 2 (1p), Hreinsson*

No	Name	Nat	DoB	Pos	Aps	(s)	Gls
29	Arnór Sveinn Adalsteinsson		26/01/86	D	16	(1)	1
9	Elfar Árni Adalsteinsson		12/08/90	A	12	(7)	5
19	Gunnlaugur Birgisson		04/06/95	M		(1)	
16	Ernir Bjarnason		22/08/97	M		(1)	
21	Gudmundur Fridriksson		06/02/94	D	3		
27	Tómas Óli Gardarsson		25/10/93	M	7	(2)	1
7	Stefán Gíslason		15/03/80	M	10	(3)	1
14	Höskuldur Gunnlaugsson		26/09/94	M	14	(1)	1
1	Gunnleifur Gunnleifsson		14/07/75	G	22		
6	Jordan Halsman	SCO	13/06/91	D	4	(3)	
5	Elfar Freyr Helgason		27/07/89	D	21	(1)	1
2	Gísli Páll Helgason		08/04/91	D	9		
22	Ellert Hreinsson		12/10/86	A	7	(8)	3
10	Gudjón Pétur Lýdsson		28/12/87	M	18	(1)	7
8	Finnur Orri Margeirsson		08/03/91	M	21		
4	Damir Muminovic		13/05/90	D	15		2
28	Davíd Kristján Ólafsson		15/05/95	D	4	(5)	1
17	Elvar Páll Sigurdsson		30/07/91	A	10	(5)	2
11	Olgeir Sigurgeirsson		22/10/82	M	2	(9)	
3	Oliver Sigurjónsson		03/03/95	M	1	(4)	
21	Baldvin Sturluson		09/04/89	M	3	(3)	1
26	Páll Olgeir Thorsteinsson		30/10/95	M	4	(2)	
23	Árni Vilhjálmsson		09/05/94	A	19	(1)	10
30	Andri Rafn Yeoman		18/04/92	M	18	(2)	

FH Hafnarfjördur

1929 • Kaplakriki (6,450) • fh.is
Major honours
Icelandic League (6) 2004, 2005, 2006, 2008, 2009, 2012; Icelandic Cup (2) 2007, 2010
Coach: Heimir Gudjónsson

2014

05/05	h	Breidablik	D	1-1	*Rúnarsson*
08/05	h	Fylkir	W	3-0	*Gudnason, Emilsson, Doumbia*
12/05	a	KR	W	1-0	*Emilsson*
18/05	h	ÍBV	W	1-0	*Björnsson*
22/05	a	Keflavík	D	1-1	*Björnsson*
01/06	h	Víkingur	W	1-0	*Björnsson*
11/06	a	Fjölnir	W	1-0	*Gudnason*
15/06	h	Thór	W	1-0	*Emilsson*
23/06	a	Fram	W	4-0	*Emilsson 2, Björnsson, og (T Bjarnason)*
27/06	h	Valur	W	2-1	*Gudnason 2 (1p)*
13/07	a	Stjarnan	D	2-2	*Björnsson, og (Rauschenberg)*
21/07	a	Breidablik	W	4-2	*I Óskarsson, Björnsson, Doumbia, Jónsson*
27/07	a	Fylkir	W	2-0	*I Óskarsson, Pálsson*
10/08	a	ÍBV	D	1-1	*Lennon*
20/08	h	Keflavík	W	2-0	*og (Matthíasson), Lennon*
25/08	a	Víkingur	W	3-2	*I Óskarsson, Björnsson, og (Tasković)*
31/08	h	Fjölnir	W	4-0	*I Óskarsson, Gudnason, Lennon 2*
14/09	a	Thór	W	2-0	*Doumbia 2*
18/09	h	KR	D	1-1	*Gudnason*
21/09	h	Fram	W	4-2	*Gudnason, Pálsson, Hewson, Björnsson*
28/09	a	Valur	W	4-1	*Gudnason 3, Lennon*
04/10	h	Stjarnan	L	1-2	*Lennon*

No	Name	Nat	DoB	Pos	Aps	(s)	Gls
3	Gudjón Árni Antoníusson		03/09/83	D	3	(3)	
17	Atli Vidar Björnsson		04/01/80	A	8	(10)	8
21	Bödvar Bödvarsson		09/04/95	D	10	(1)	
20	Kassim Doumbia	MLI	18/06/90	D	18		4
13	Kristján Gauti Emilsson		26/04/93	A	7	(2)	5
23	Brynjar Ásgeir Gudmundsson		22/06/92	A	2	(2)	
11	Atli Gudnason		28/09/84	M	18	(4)	10
26	Jonathan Hendrickx	BEL	25/12/93	D	11		
6	Sam Hewson	ENG	28/11/88	M	12	(8)	1
14	Albert Brynjar Ingason		16/01/86	A	2	(3)	
16	Jón Ragnar Jónsson		30/10/85	D	18	(2)	1
19	Steven Lennon	SCO	20/01/88	M	9	(1)	6
7	Ingimundur Níels Óskarsson		04/02/86	A	14	(6)	4
1	Róbert Örn Óskarsson		27/03/87	G	22		
2	Emil Pálsson		10/06/93	M	12	(9)	2
2	Sean Reynolds	USA	11/04/90	D	7	(2)	
25	Hólmar Örn Rúnarsson		10/12/81	M	14	(6)	1
22	Ólafur Páll Snorrason		22/04/82	A	17	(3)	
10	Davíd Thór Vidarsson		24/04/84	M	18	(2)	
5	Pétur Vidarsson		25/11/87	D	20		

Fjölnir

1988 • Fjölnisvöllur (1,190) • fjolnir.is
Coach: Ágúst Thór Gylfason

2014

04/05	h	Víkingur	W	3-0	*Leósson, Gunnar Gudmundsson, Óskarsson*
08/05	a	Thór	W	2-1	*Gunnar Gudmundsson, T Gudjónsson*
11/05	h	Valur	D	1-1	*Ingvarsson*
18/05	a	Breidablik	D	2-2	*Gudmundur Gudmundsson, T Gudjónsson*
22/05	h	KR	D	1-1	*Lárusson*
01/06	a	Keflavík	D	1-1	*Tsonis*
11/06	h	FH	L	0-1	
15/06	h	Fram	L	1-4	*Sigurdarson*
22/06	a	Stjarnan	L	1-2	*B Ólafsson*
02/07	h	Fylkir	D	3-3	*Tsonis, Gunnar Gudmundsson, I Gunnarsson*
13/07	a	ÍBV	L	2-4	*Tsonis 2*
21/07	a	Víkingur	L	0-1	
27/07	h	Thór	W	4-1	*B Ólafsson, Gudmundur Gudmundsson, Gunnar Gudmundsson, Arnarson*
06/08	a	Valur	L	3-4	*T Gudjónsson, Sigurdarson 2*
11/08	h	Breidablik	D	1-1	*Magee*
20/08	a	KR	L	0-1	
25/08	h	Keflavík	L	0-1	*T Gudjónsson*
31/08	a	FH	L	0-4	
15/09	a	Fram	W	3-1	*Gunnar Gudmundsson, T Gudjónsson, Leósson*
23/09	h	Stjarnan	D	0-0	
28/09	a	Fylkir	L	1-2	*B Ólafsson*
04/10	h	ÍBV	W	3-0	*T Gudjónsson, B Ólafsson, Leósson*

No	Name	Nat	DoB	Pos	Aps	(s)	Gls
14	Ágúst Örn Arnarson		15/08/91	A		(1)	1
17	Magnús Pétur Bjarnason		26/01/96	A		(1)	
16	Gudmundur Gudjónsson		03/08/89	M	13	(7)	
9	Thórir Gudjónsson		07/04/91	A	16	(1)	6
29	Gudmundur Karl Gudmundsson		30/03/91	M	21		2
4	Gunnar Már Gudmundsson		15/12/83	M	20		5
3	Árni Kristinn Gunnarsson		10/04/80	D	12		
2	Gunnar Valur Gunnarsson		16/02/82	D	14	(2)	
20	Illugi Thór Gunnarsson		22/06/88	M	13	(1)	1
21	Magnús Páll Gunnarsson		26/05/80	A		(4)	
12	Thórdur Ingason		30/03/88	G	22		
25	Einar Karl Ingvarsson		08/10/93	M	2	(6)	1
19	Marinó Thór Jakobsson		06/02/90	D		(1)	
11	Vidar Ari Jónsson		10/03/94	M	1	(9)	
23	Gudmundur Thór Júlíusson		29/12/92	D	3	(1)	
15	Haukur Lárusson		01/07/87	D	12	(3)	1
8	Ragnar Leósson		20/03/91	A	20	(2)	3
7	Mark Magee	ENG	03/10/89	A	6	(2)	1
31	Arnar Freyr Ólafsson		06/03/93	G		(1)	
5	Bergsveinn Ólafsson		09/09/92	D	21		4
7	Júlíus Orri Óskarsson		14/08/93	A	1		1
22	Matthew Ratajczak	USA	22/05/91	D	15	(1)	
10	Aron Sigurdarson		08/10/93	A	13	(5)	3
6	Atli Már Thorbergsson		13/03/92	D	10	(2)	
28	Christopher Tsonis	USA	02/04/91	A	7	(12)	4

Fram Reykjavík

1908 • Laugardalsvöllur (15,182);
Þróttarvöllur (2,000) • fram.is

Major honours
*Icelandic League (18) 1913, 1914, 1915, 1916,
1917, 1918, 1921, 1922, 1923, 1925, 1939, 1946,
1947, 1962, 1972, 1988, 1990; Icelandic Cup
(8) 1970, 1973, 1979, 1980, 1985, 1987, 1989, 2013*

Coach: Bjarni Gudjónsson

2014

04/05	h	ÍBV	D 1-1	Atlason
08/05	a	Víkingur	L 1-2	Thorláksson
12/05	h	Þór	W 1-0	Gudjónsson (p)
19/05	a	Valur	L 3-5	Traustason, Briem 2
22/05	h	Breidablik	D 1-1	Briem
02/06	a	KR	L 2-3	Marteinsson, V Arnarsson
10/06	h	Keflavík	D 1-1	Jónsson
15/06	a	Fjölnir	W 4-1	T Bjarnason, Marteinsson, Atlason, Albertsson
23/06	h	FH	L 0-4	
27/06	h	Stjarnan	L 1-2	Marteinsson
14/07	a	Fylkir	L 0-2	
20/07	a	ÍBV	L 0-2	
27/07	h	Víkingur	L 0-3	
06/08	a	Þór	W 2-0	Hafsteinsson 2
11/08	h	Valur	W 1-0	Jónsson
18/08	a	Breidablik	L 0-3	
25/08	h	KR	L 1-2	Baldvinsson
31/08	a	Keflavík	W 4-2	Briem, A Bjarnason, Gudjónsson, Hafsteinsson
15/09	h	Fjölnir	L 1-3	A Bjarnason
21/09	a	FH	L 2-4	Gunnarsson, A Bjarnason
28/09	a	Stjarnan	L 0-4	
04/10	h	Fylkir	W 4-3	A Bjarnason, Atlason, Hafsteinsson 2

No	Name	Nat	DoB	Pos	Aps	(s)	Gls
27	Hafthór Mar Adalgeirsson		13/08/94	A	1	(2)	
17	Aron Thórdur Albertsson		27/06/96	M	6	(6)	1
14	Halldór Arnarsson		25/12/89	D	8	(4)	
13	Viktor Bjarki Arnarsson		22/01/83	M	16	(4)	1
6	Arnthór Ari Atlason		12/10/93	A	16	(4)	3
9	Haukur Baldvinsson		05/05/90	A	16	(6)	1
16	Aron Bjarnason		14/10/95	M	10	(7)	4
23	Benedikt Októ Bjarnason		03/04/95	D		(1)	
3	Tryggvi Sveinn Bjarnason		16/01/83	D	18		1
26	Hördur Fannar Björgvinsson		26/06/97	G	4	(1)	
4	Hafsteinn Briem		28/02/91	M	16	(2)	4
1	Denis Cardaklija		11/10/88	G	8		
10	Jóhannes Karl Gudjónsson		25/05/80	M	18		2
7	Dadi Gudmundsson		11/02/81	D	4		
19	Orri Gunnarsson		05/04/92	M	17		1
22	Gudmundur Steinn Hafsteinsson		14/06/89	A	11	(1)	5
15	Ingiberg Ólafur Jónsson		03/03/95	D	15	(1)	2
1	Ögmundur Kristinsson		19/06/89	G	10		
21	Gudmundur Magnússon		10/06/91	A	1	(2)	
11	Ásgeir Marteinsson		07/07/94	M	8	(5)	3
8	Einar Bjarni Ómarsson		21/11/90	D	16	(2)	
30	Björgólfur Takefusa		11/05/80	A	7	(1)	
18	Alexander Már Thorláksson		02/08/95	A	2	(11)	1
20	Einar Már Thórisson		12/08/91	M		(2)	
2	Ósvald Jarl Traustason		22/10/95	D	14	(1)	1

Fylkir

1967 • Fylkisvöllur (1,900) • fylkir.com

Major honours
Icelandic Cup (2) 2001, 2002

Coach: Ásmundur Arnarsson

2014

04/05	a	Stjarnan	L 0-1	
08/05	a	FH	L 0-3	
12/05	a	ÍBV	W 3-1	Sousa, G Jónsson, Jóhannesson
19/05	a	Víkingur	W 2-1	Arnthórsson, Zekovic
22/05	a	Þór	L 2-5	Maduro (p), H Jónsson
02/06	a	Valur	L 0-1	
11/06	h	Breidablik	D 1-1	Björnsson
15/06	a	KR	L 0-1	
22/06	h	Keflavík	L 2-4	O Gudmundsson, Björnsson (p)
02/07	a	Fjölnir	D 3-3	Gudlaugsson, Valdimarsson, Sousa
14/07	h	Fram	W 2-0	Björnsson (p), og (T Bjarnason)
20/07	h	Stjarnan	L 1-3	Arnthórsson
27/07	h	FH	L 0-2	
06/08	a	ÍBV	W 3-1	Magnússon, Ingason, og (Sigurbjörnsson)
10/08	h	Víkingur	D 1-1	Ingason
18/08	h	Þór	W 4-1	Ingason 2, Gudlaugsson, O Gudmundsson
25/08	h	Valur	W 2-0	Eythórsson, O Gudmundsson (p)
31/08	a	Breidablik	D 2-2	G Jónsson, Breiddal
14/09	h	KR	L 0-4	
21/09	a	Keflavík	W 1-0	Sousa
28/09	h	Fjölnir	W 2-1	Ingason, Sousa
04/10	a	Fram	L 3-4	Ingason, Sousa, Arnthórsson

No	Name	Nat	DoB	Pos	Aps	(s)	Gls
17	Ásgeir Örn Arnthórsson		02/05/90	M	18	(2)	3
5	Davíd Þór Ásbjörnsson		24/02/92	D	3	(2)	
13	Magnús Otti Benediktsson		12/04/94	A		(1)	
24	Elis Rafn Björnsson		13/10/92	M	14		3
11	Kjartan Ágúst Breiddal		20/03/86	M	3	(10)	1
29	Ásgeir Eythórsson		29/04/93	D	21		1
20	Stefán Ragnar Gudlaugsson		19/03/91	D	20		2
19	Oddur Ingi Gudmundsson		28/01/89	M	16	(1)	3
8	Viktor Örn Gudmundsson		09/11/89	M	5	(3)	
1	Bjarni Halldórsson		26/07/83	G	20		
8	Kristján Hauksson		03/02/86	D		(2)	
22	Albert Brynjar Ingason		16/01/86	A	9	(1)	6
10	Andrés Már Jóhannesson		21/12/88	M	9	(9)	1
7	Gunnar Örn Jónsson		30/04/85	A	18	(3)	2
15	Hákon Ingi Jónsson		10/11/95	A	2	(4)	1
22	Ryan Maduro	USA	06/04/86	M	5	(1)	1
25	Agnar Bragi Magnússon		03/02/87	D	9	(3)	1
21	Dadi Ólafsson		05/01/94	M	4	(8)	
4	Finnur Ólafsson		30/01/84	M	8		
6	Andrew Sousa	USA	26/09/89	M	10	(5)	5
32	Björn Hákon Sveinsson		05/06/84	G	2		
9	Ragnar Bragi Sveinsson		18/12/94	M	13	(4)	
16	Tómas Thorsteinsson		08/12/88	D	20		
2	Kristján Valdimarsson		12/05/84	D	8	(1)	1
26	Sadmir Zekovic	SWE	29/04/94	A	5	(4)	1

ÍBV Vestmannaeyjar

1945 • Hásteinsvöllur (3,000) • ibv.is

Major honours
*Icelandic League (3) 1979, 1997, 1998; Icelandic
Cup (4) 1968, 1972, 1981, 1998*

Coach: Sigurdur Ragnar Eyjólfsson

2014

04/05	a	Fram	D 1-1	Gunnarsson
08/05	h	Stjarnan	L 1-2	Bergsson (p)
12/05	h	Fylkir	L 1-3	Glenn
18/05	a	FH	L 0-1	
22/05	h	Víkingur	L 1-2	Thorvardarson (p)
01/06	a	Þór	D 1-1	Gudjónsson
09/06	h	Valur	D 2-2	Garner, Glenn
15/06	a	Breidablik	D 1-1	Glenn
22/06	h	KR	L 2-3	Glenn, Thorvardarson
02/07	a	Keflavík	W 2-1	Thorvardarson (p), Jónsson
13/07	a	Fjölnir	W 4-2	Glenn 2, Jónsson, Thorvardarson
20/07	h	Fram	W 2-0	Thorvardarson, Glenn
27/07	a	Stjarnan	L 0-2	
06/08	a	Fylkir	L 1-3	Ólafsson
10/08	h	FH	D 1-1	Glenn
18/08	a	Víkingur	W 2-1	Jeffs, Bergsson
24/08	h	Þór	W 2-0	Glenn 2 (1p)
31/08	a	Valur	L 0-3	
14/09	h	Breidablik	D 1-1	Gudjónsson
21/09	a	KR	D 3-3	Glenn 2 (1p), Thorsteinsson
28/09	h	Keflavík	L 0-2	
04/10	h	Fjölnir	L 0-3	

No	Name	Nat	DoB	Pos	Aps	(s)	Gls
21	Dominic Adams	TRI	10/02/88	M	1	(6)	
9	Arnar Bragi Bergsson		30/04/93	M	13	(5)	2
1	Abel Dhaira	UGA	09/09/87	G	18		
7	Jökull Elísabetarson		26/04/84	D	18	(1)	
3	Matt Garner	ENG	09/04/84	D	19		1
17	Jonathan Glenn	TRI	27/08/87	A	20	(1)	12
2	Brynjar Gauti Gudjónsson		27/02/92	A	20		2
10	Bjarni Gunnarsson		29/01/93	M	8	(8)	1
16	Jón Ingason		21/09/95	D	15	(5)	
30	Ian Jeffs	ENG	12/10/82	M	17	(3)	1
14	Atli Fannar Jónsson		31/08/95	A	6	(13)	2
4	Dean Martin	ENG	31/08/72	M	14	(2)	
13	Isak Nylén	SWE	18/02/95	A		(3)	
32	Andri Ólafsson		26/06/85	M	6	(2)	1
24	Óskar Elías Óskarsson		04/11/95	D	4	(2)	
23	Eidur Aron Sigurbjörnsson		26/02/90	D	13		
25	Gudjón Orri Sigurjónsson		01/12/92	G	4		
6	Gunnar Thorsteinsson		01/02/94	M	17		1
11	Vídir Thorvardarson		07/07/92	A	21		5
20	Hafsteinn Valdimarsson		11/10/96	M		(1)	
5	Thórarinn Ingi Valdimarsson		23/04/90	M	8		

Keflavík

1929 • Nettóvöllurinn (2,658) • keflavik.is
Major honours
Icelandic League (4) 1964, 1969, 1971, 1973;
Icelandic Cup (4) 1975, 1997, 2004, 2006
Coach: Kristján Gudmundsson

2014

Date		Opp	Res		Scorers
04/05	h	Thór	W	3-1	J Gudmundsson, Sveinsson 2 (1p)
08/05	a	Valur	W	1-0	Matthíasson
12/05	h	Breidablik	W	2-0	Ómarsson 2
18/05	h	KR	L	0-1	
22/05	h	FH	D	1-1	Ómarsson
01/06	h	Fjölnir	D	1-1	Sveinsson
10/06	a	Fram	D	1-1	J Gudmundsson
15/06	h	Stjarnan	D	2-2	Magnússon 2
22/06	a	Fylkir	W	4-2	Thorsteinsson 2, Sveinsson 2
02/07	h	ÍBV	L	1-2	Thorsteinsson
14/07	a	Víkingur	L	1-3	Sveinsson
20/07	a	Thór	D	0-0	
27/07	h	Valur	L	1-2	Einarsson
06/08	a	Breidablik	D	4-4	Heiddal, Ómarsson, Sveinsson, Elvarsson
11/08	a	KR	L	0-2	
20/08	a	FH	L	0-2	
25/08	a	Fjölnir	D	1-1	J Gudmundsson
31/08	h	Fram	L	2-4	Sveinsson 2
14/09	a	Stjarnan	L	0-2	
21/09	h	Fylkir	L	0-1	
28/09	a	ÍBV	W	2-0	Ómarsson, Elvarsson
04/10	h	Víkingur	W	2-0	Ómarsson, Sveinsson

No	Name	Nat	DoB	Pos	Aps	(s)	Gls
12	Árni Freyr Ásgeirsson		10/03/92	G	2		
16	Endre Ove Brenne	NOR	14/04/88	D	11		
6	Einar Orri Einarsson		28/10/89	M	14		1
9	Sigurbergur Elísson		10/06/92	M	9	(6)	
25	Frans Elvarsson		14/08/90	M	12	(3)	2
5	Andri Fannar Freysson		27/08/92	M		(3)	
26	Ari Steinn Gudmundsson		31/12/96	D		(1)	
4	Haraldur Freyr Gudmundsson		14/12/81	D	19		
7	Jóhann Birnir Gudmundsson		05/12/77	M	11	(3)	3
17	Daníel Gylfason		30/07/93	A	3	(2)	
14	Halldór Kristinn Halldórsson		13/04/88	D	13		
18	Theodór Gudni Halldórsson		24/05/93	A	3	(7)	
20	Aron Heiddal		30/01/95	D	5	(2)	1
5	Hilmar Thór Hilmarsson		20/09/90	D	2	(2)	
17	Aron Grétar Jafetsson		06/10/94	D	5	(2)	
27	Ray Anthony Jónsson	PHI	03/02/79	D		(7)	
8	Bojan Stefán Ljubicic		22/06/92	M	13	(5)	
23	Sindri Snær Magnússon		18/02/92	M	22		2
3	Magnús Thórir Matthíasson		22/01/90	D	20		1
17	Hilmar Andrew McShane		09/08/99	A		(1)	
15	Paul McShane	SCO	13/04/78	M	2	(2)	
21	Sindri Kristinn Ólafsson		19/01/97	G	1	(1)	
28	Elías Már Ómarsson		18/01/95	A	20		6
1	Jonas Sandqvist	SWE	06/05/81	G	19		
19	Leonard Sigurdsson		30/04/96	M		(1)	
10	Hördur Sveinsson		24/03/83	A	19	(1)	10
29	Fannar Orri Sævarsson		28/10/97	M		(4)	
11	Magnús Sverrir Thorsteinsson		22/09/82	A	7	(6)	3
13	Unnar Már Unnarsson		25/09/94	D	10		

KR Reykjavík

1899 • KR-völlur (2,801); Thróttarvöllur (2,000) • kr.is
Major honours
Icelandic League (26) 1912, 1919, 1926, 1927,
1928, 1929, 1931, 1932, 1934, 1941, 1948, 1949,
1950, 1952, 1955, 1959, 1961, 1963, 1965, 1968,
1999, 2000, 2002, 2003, 2011, 2013; Icelandic Cup
(14) 1960, 1961, 1962, 1963, 1964, 1966, 1967,
1994, 1995, 1999, 2008, 2011, 2012, 2014
Coach: Rúnar Kristinsson

2014

Date		Opp	Res		Scorers
04/05	h	Valur	L	1-2	Martin
08/05	a	Breidablik	W	2-1	H Hauksson, Ó Hauksson
12/05	h	FH	L	0-1	
18/05	a	Keflavík	W	1-0	Ó Hauksson
22/05	a	Fjölnir	D	1-1	Martin
02/06	h	Fram	W	3-2	Sigurdsson, Ragnarsson, Finnbogason
11/06	a	Stjarnan	L	1-2	Sigurdarson
15/06	h	Fylkir	W	1-0	Sigurdarson
22/06	a	ÍBV	W	3-2	Martin 2, Finnbogason
02/07	a	Víkingur	W	2-0	Ó Hauksson, Sigurjónsson
10/07	a	Thór	L	0-2	
19/07	a	Valur	W	4-1	Jósepsson, Finnbogason, Ormarsson, Martin
27/07	h	Breidablik	D	1-1	Finnbogason
11/08	h	Keflavík	W	2-0	Ormarsson 2
20/08	h	Fjölnir	W	1-0	Martin
25/08	a	Fram	W	2-1	Sigurdsson, Finnbogason
31/08	h	Stjarnan	L	2-3	Jósepsson, Ó Hauksson
14/09	a	Fylkir	W	4-0	Sigurjónsson, Jósepsson (p), Atlason, Martin (p)
18/09	a	FH	D	1-1	Martin
21/09	h	ÍBV	D	3-3	Martin 2, Atlason
28/09	a	Víkingur	W	1-0	Sigurdarson
04/10	h	Thór	W	4-1	Martin 3 (2p), Ormarsson

No	Name	Nat	DoB	Pos	Aps	(s)	Gls
15	Emil Atlason		22/07/93	A	9	(5)	2
4	Gonzalo Balbi	URU	05/06/92	M	9	(5)	
10	Kjartan Henry Finnbogason		09/07/86	A	9	(6)	5
28	Ivar Furu	NOR	07/05/94	D	6	(1)	
21	Gudmundur Reynir Gunnarsson		21/01/89	D	12	(1)	
6	Gunnar Thór Gunnarsson		04/10/85	D	10	(1)	
3	Haukur Heidar Hauksson		01/09/91	D	21		1
11	Óskar Örn Hauksson		22/08/84	A	19	(1)	4
12	Sindri Snær Jensson		12/08/86	G	1	(2)	
5	Egill Jónsson		15/02/91	M	7	(5)	
18	Aron Bjarki Jósepsson		21/11/89	D	19		3
1	Stefán Logi Magnússon		05/09/80	G	21		
7	Gary Martin	ENG	10/10/90	A	19	(2)	13
14	Almarr Ormarsson		25/02/88	A	10	(7)	4
9	Thorsteinn Már Ragnarsson		19/04/90	A	2	(7)	1
2	Grétar Sigurdarson		09/10/82	D	19		3
8	Baldur Sigurdsson		24/04/85	M	20		2
23	Atli Sigurjónsson		01/07/91	M	11		2
16	Jónas Gudni Sævarsson		28/11/83	M	8	(4)	
26	Björn Thorláksson		21/06/95	A		(2)	
24	Farid Zato-Arouna	TOG	23/04/92	M	10	(6)	

Stjarnan

1960 • Stjörnuvöllur (1,400) • stjarnan.is
Major honours
Icelandic League (1) 2014
Coach: Rúnar Páll Sigmundsson

2014

Date		Opp	Res		Scorers
04/05	h	Fylkir	W	1-0	Finsen (p)
08/05	a	ÍBV	W	2-1	Finsen, og (Garner)
12/05	h	Víkingur	D	0-0	
18/05	a	Thór	W	4-3	Björgvinsson, Finsen, Hansen, Gunnarsson
22/05	h	Valur	D	1-1	Björgvinsson
02/06	a	Breidablik	D	1-1	Vemmelund
11/06	h	KR	W	2-1	Finsen, Hansen
15/06	a	Keflavík	D	2-2	Hansen, Finsen (p)
22/06	h	Fjölnir	W	2-1	Hansen, G Jóhannsson
27/06	a	Fram	W	2-1	Hansen 2
13/07	h	FH	D	2-2	Björgvinsson, Gunnarsson
20/07	a	Fylkir	W	3-1	Björgvinsson, Toft, Vemmelund
27/07	h	ÍBV	W	2-0	Finsen, G Jóhannsson
11/08	h	Thór	W	2-1	Björgvinsson, Punyed
15/08	a	Valur	W	2-1	Björgvinsson, Toft
24/08	h	Breidablik	D	2-2	Finsen (p), Gunnarsson
31/08	a	KR	W	3-2	Gunnarsson, Finsen 2
14/09	h	Keflavík	W	2-0	Punyed, Gunnarsson
18/09	a	Víkingur	W	1-0	Toft
23/09	h	Fjölnir	D	0-0	
28/09	h	Fram	W	4-0	Toft 3, Gunnarsson
04/10	a	FH	W	2-1	Finsen 2 (1p)

No	Name	Nat	DoB	Pos	Aps	(s)	Gls
14	Hördur Árnason		19/05/89	D	19		
18	Jón Arnar Barddal		07/10/95	A		(4)	
11	Arnar Már Björgvinsson		10/02/90	A	21		6
23	Snorri Páll Blöndal		23/03/94	D		(4)	
17	Ólafur Karl Finsen		30/03/92	A	20	(1)	11
10	Veigar Páll Gunnarsson		21/03/80	A	14	(3)	6
19	Jeppe Hansen	DEN	10/02/89	A	9		6
25	Sveinn Jóhannesson		22/01/95	G	1	(1)	
7	Atli Jóhannsson		05/10/82	M	17	(4)	
27	Gardar Jóhannsson		01/04/80	A		(9)	2
1	Ingvar Jónsson		18/10/89	G	21		
22	Thórhallur Kári Knútsson		16/05/95	A		(1)	
9	Daníel Laxdal		22/09/86	D	22		
33	Jóhann Laxdal		27/01/90	D	3	(2)	
20	Atli Freyr Ottesen		24/04/95	M	2	(6)	
5	Michael Præst	DEN	25/07/86	M	12		
8	Pablo Punyed	SLV	18/04/90	M	15	(5)	2
29	Martin Rauschenberg	DEN	15/01/92	D	21		
16	Thorri Geir Rúnarsson		24/04/95	M	12	(4)	
21	Baldvin Sturluson		09/04/89	M		(1)	
24	Rolf Toft	DEN	04/08/92	A	10	(1)	6
4	Niclas Vemmelund	DEN	02/10/92	D	17	(1)	2
12	Heidar Ægisson		10/08/95	M	6	(7)	

Thór Akureyri

1915 • Thórsvöllur (2,984) • thorsport.is
Coach: Páll Vidar Gíslason

2014

04/05	a	Keflavík	L	1-3	Ævarsson
08/05	h	Fjölnir	L	1-2	Ævarsson (p)
12/05	a	Fram	L	0-1	
18/05	h	Stjarnan	L	3-4	Nicklaw, Kristjánsson, Hannesson (p)
22/05	h	Fylkir	W	5-2	Hannesson, Hjaltalín, og (Valdimarsson), Björnsson, Jónsson
01/06	h	ÍBV	D	1-1	Björnsson
09/06	a	Víkingur	L	2-3	Hannesson 2
15/06	a	FH	D	1-1	Hannesson
22/06	h	Valur	L	0-1	
02/07	a	Breidablik	L	2-3	Jónsson, Birgisson
10/07	h	KR	W	2-0	Ævarsson, Nicklaw
20/07	a	Keflavík	D	0-0	
27/07	a	Fjölnir	L	1-4	Birgisson
06/08	h	Fram	L	0-2	
11/08	a	Stjarnan	L	1-2	Nicklaw
18/08	a	Fylkir	L	1-4	Magnússon
24/08	a	ÍBV	L	0-2	
31/08	h	Víkingur	L	0-1	
14/09	h	FH	L	0-2	
21/09	a	Valur	L	0-2	
28/09	h	Breidablik	W	2-0	Hannesson, Rósbergsson
04/10	a	KR	L	1-4	Hannesson

No	Name	Nat	DoB	Pos	Aps	(s)	Gls
5	Atli Jens Albertsson		20/04/86	D	16	(3)	
12	Thórdur Birgisson		04/02/83	A	7	(10)	2
3	Alexander Ívan Bjarnason		31/07/98	A		(1)	
8	Kristinn Thór Björnsson		11/11/89	M	8	(10)	2
23	Chukwudi Chijindu	USA	20/02/86	A	10	(1)	
9	Jóhann Helgi Hannesson		21/04/90	A	21		7
1	Hjörtur Geir Heimisson		01/05/91	G	2	(1)	
13	Ingi Freyr Hilmarsson		10/09/87	D	15		
11	Orri Freyr Hjaltalín		01/07/80	D	22		1
17	Halldór Orri Hjaltason		08/10/92	M	3	(5)	
21	Bergvin Jóhannsson		22/01/95	M		(3)	
10	Sveinn Elías Jónsson		11/10/86	M	20		2
19	Sigurdur Marinó Kristjánsson		05/10/91	M	15	(6)	1
14	Hlynur Atli Magnússon		11/09/90	D	16	(1)	1
28	Sándor Matus	HUN	31/10/76	G	20		
4	Shawn Nicklaw	GUM	15/04/89	D	15	(1)	3
16	Kristinn Thór Rósbergsson		01/07/92	A	2	(2)	1
18	Jónas Björgvin Sigurbergsson		25/08/94	M	16	(3)	
7	Orri Sigurjónsson		11/12/94	M	9	(2)	
20	Jóhann Thórhallsson		07/01/80	A	4	(5)	
	Janez Vrenko	SVN	17/08/82	D	1	(1)	
6	Ármann Pétur Ævarsson		28/10/84	M	20		3

Valur Reykjavík

1911 • Vodafonevöllurinn (2,465); Thróttarvöllur (2,000) • valur.is

Major honours
Icelandic League (20) 1930, 1933, 1935, 1936, 1937, 1938, 1940, 1942, 1943, 1944, 1945, 1956, 1966, 1967, 1976, 1978, 1980, 1985, 1987, 2007; Icelandic Cup (9) 1965, 1974, 1976, 1977, 1988, 1990, 1991, 1992, 2005

Coach: Magnús Gylfason

2014

04/05	a	KR	W	2-1	Williamson, Halldórsson
08/05	h	Keflavík	L	0-1	
11/05	a	Fjölnir	D	1-1	Kárason
19/05	h	Fram	W	5-3	Pedersen 2, Eiríksson, Halldórsson, Thorláksson
22/05	a	Stjarnan	D	1-1	Kárason
02/06	h	Fylkir	W	1-0	Nielsen
09/06	a	ÍBV	D	2-2	Lúdvíksson, G Gunnarsson
15/06	h	Víkingur	L	1-2	Williamson
22/06	a	Thór	W	1-0	H Sigurdsson
27/06	a	FH	L	1-2	og (Doumbia)
14/07	h	Breidablik	L	1-2	Kárason
19/07	h	KR	L	1-4	Mawejje
27/07	a	Keflavík	W	2-1	Pedersen, Bergsson
06/08	h	Fjölnir	W	4-3	Lárusson, Bergsson 2, Halldórsson
11/08	a	Fram	L	0-1	
15/08	h	Stjarnan	L	1-2	Pedersen
24/08	a	Fylkir	L	0-2	
31/08	h	ÍBV	W	3-0	H Sigurdsson, Hreidarsson, Pedersen
14/09	a	Víkingur	D	1-1	Hreidarsson
21/09	h	Thór	W	2-0	Lúdvíksson, Pedersen
28/09	h	FH	L	1-4	Lúdvíksson
04/10	a	Breidablik	L	0-3	

No	Name	Nat	DoB	Pos	Aps	(s)	Gls
6	Dadí Bergsson		11/03/95	A	3	(1)	3
2	Billy Berntsson	SWE	06/01/84	D	11		
12	Anton Ari Einarsson		25/08/94	G	6		
21	Bjarni Ólafur Eiríksson		28/03/82	D	22		1
11	Arnar Sveinn Geirsson		30/08/91	A	5	(2)	
14	Gunnar Gunnarsson		22/09/93	D	5	(5)	1
29	Ragnar Thór Gunnarsson		07/06/94	A		(3)	
8	Kristinn Ingi Halldórsson		08/04/89	M	13	(6)	3
18	Haukur Ásberg Hilmarsson		18/05/95	M		(5)	
15	Thórdur Steinar Hreidarsson		13/12/86	D	7		2
2	James Hurst	ENG	31/01/92	D	7		
13	Matarr Jobe	GAM	22/03/92	D	1	(1)	
16	Halldór Hermann Jónsson		01/10/84	M	8	(9)	
9	Kolbeinn Kárason		02/04/91	A	5	(14)	3
4	Sigurdur Egill Lárusson		22/01/92	M	18	(3)	1
5	Magnús Már Lúdvíksson		30/05/81	D	22		3
20	Tonny Mawejje	UGA	15/12/86	M	10	(1)	1
26	Mads Nielsen	DEN	26/03/94	D	14		1
6	Lucas Ohlander	SWE	19/02/93	M	3	(3)	
19	Patrick Pedersen	DEN	25/11/91	A	12	(1)	6
7	Haukur Páll Sigurdsson		05/08/87	M	14	(2)	2
10	Kristinn Freyr Sigurdsson		25/12/91	M	18	(3)	
23	Andri Fannar Stefánsson		22/04/91	M		(2)	
1	Fjalar Thorgeirsson		18/01/77	G	16		
20	Indridi Áki Thorláksson		02/08/95	A	5	(3)	1
3	Iain Williamson	SCO	12/01/88	M	17	(1)	2

Víkingur Reykjavík

1908 • Víkingsvöllur (1,449); Thróttarvöllur (2,000) • vikingur.is

Major honours
Icelandic League (5) 1920, 1924, 1981, 1982, 1991; Icelandic Cup (1) 1971

**Coach: Ólafur Thórdarson;
(15/09/14) Ólafur Thórdarson & Milos Milojevic**

2014

04/05	a	Fjölnir	L	0-3	
08/05	h	Fram	W	2-1	Jónasson, Faye
12/05	a	Stjarnan	D	0-0	
19/05	h	Fylkir	L	1-2	Faye
22/05	a	ÍBV	W	2-1	Kristinsson, Thrándarson
01/06	a	FH	L	0-1	
09/06	h	Thór	W	3-2	Faye 2, Thrándarson
15/06	a	Valur	W	2-1	Thrándarson, Monaghan
22/06	h	Breidablik	W	1-0	Faye
02/07	a	KR	L	0-2	
14/07	h	Keflavík	W	3-1	Thrándarson 2, Sverrisson
21/07	h	Fjölnir	W	1-0	Tasković
27/07	a	Fram	W	3-0	Tasković 2, Gudmundsson
10/08	a	Fylkir	D	1-1	Faye
18/08	h	ÍBV	L	1-2	Faye
25/08	h	FH	L	2-3	Abnett, Hjaltested
31/08	a	Thór	W	1-0	Abnett
14/09	h	Valur	D	1-1	Faye
18/09	h	Stjarnan	L	0-1	
21/09	a	Breidablik	L	1-4	Í Jónsson (p)
28/09	h	KR	L	0-1	
04/10	a	Keflavík	L	0-2	

No	Name	Nat	DoB	Pos	Aps	(s)	Gls
7	Michael Abnett	ENG	27/12/90	M	9	(2)	2
26	Ásgeir Frank Ásgeirsson		02/08/96	M		(1)	
18	Kjartan Dige Baldursson		22/11/89	D	18		
12	Sigurdur Hrannar Björnsson		26/12/93	G		(1)	
20	Pape Mamadou Faye		06/03/91	A	17	(3)	8
2	Ómar Fridriksson		05/03/93	D	4		
14	Iliyan Garov	BUL	08/01/84	D	3		
5	Tómas Gudmundsson		10/02/92	D	2	(1)	1
16	Stefán Bjarni Hjaltested		14/06/97	M		(5)	1
23	Todor Hristov	BUL	25/09/87	M	8		
31	Ventsislav Ivanov	BUL	20/05/82	A	4	(3)	
9	Sveinbjörn Jónasson		17/07/86	A	3	(1)	1
3	Ívar Örn Jónsson		02/02/94	M	12	(5)	1
24	Viktor Jónsson		23/06/94	A	3	(6)	
1	Ingvar Thór Kale		08/12/83	G	22		
25	Darri Steinn Konrádsson		15/01/93	M		(4)	
13	Arnthór Ingi Kristinsson		15/03/90	M	6	(3)	1
22	Alan Lowing	SCO	07/01/88	D	19		
8	Kristinn Magnússon		29/04/84	M	22		
15	Óttar Steinn Magnússon		08/02/89	D	11	(2)	
19	Harry Monaghan	SCO	24/03/93	M	7	(9)	1
21	Bjarni Páll Runólfsson		10/09/96	A		(1)	
6	Halldór Smári Sigurdsson		04/10/88	D	13		
11	Dofri Snorrason		21/07/90	A	18	(1)	
28	Eiríkur Stefánsson		01/12/96	A	1	(4)	
29	Agnar Darri Sverrisson		24/11/94	A	5	(6)	1
4	Igor Tasković	SRB	04/01/82	M	21		3
23	Páll Olgeir Thorsteinsson		30/10/95	M	3	(3)	
10	Aron Elís Thrándarson		10/11/94	M	11	(5)	5

Top goalscorers

13	Gary Martin (KR)
12	Jonathan Glenn (ÍBV)
11	Ólafur Karl Finsen (Stjarnan)
10	Árni Vilhjálmsson (Breidablik)
	Atli Gudnason (FH)
	Hördur Sveinsson (Keflavík)
8	Atli Vidar Björnsson (FH)
	Pape Mamadou Faye (Víkingur)
7	Gudjón Pétur Lýdsson (Breidablik)
	Jóhann Helgi Hannesson (Thór)

Promoted clubs

Leiknir Reykjavík

1973 • Leiknisvöllur (1,025) • leiknir.com

Coach: Freyr Alexandersson & David Snorri Jónasson

ÍA Akranes

1946 • Nordurálsvöllur (5,550) • kfia.is

Major honours
Icelandic League (18) 1951, 1953, 1954, 1957, 1958, 1960, 1970, 1974, 1975, 1977, 1983, 1984, 1992, 1993, 1994, 1995, 1996, 2001; Icelandic Cup (9) 1978, 1982, 1983, 1984, 1986, 1993, 1996, 2000, 2003

Coach: Gunnlaugur Jónsson

Second level final table 2014

		Pld	W	D	L	F	A	Pts
1	Leiknir Reykjavík	22	14	6	2	43	19	48
2	ÍA Akranes	22	14	1	7	46	24	43
3	Thróttur Reykjavík	22	11	4	7	35	27	37
4	Víkingur Ólafsvík	22	11	3	8	38	32	36
5	Grindavík	22	10	5	7	39	24	35
6	HK Kópavogur	22	9	7	6	34	28	34
7	Haukar	22	9	5	8	37	32	32
8	KA Akureyri	22	8	7	7	42	33	31
9	Selfoss	22	7	5	10	24	33	26
10	BÍ/Bolungarvík	22	7	4	11	34	45	25
11	KV Reykjavík	22	5	3	14	34	53	18
12	Tindastóll	22	0	4	18	15	71	4

DOMESTIC CUP

Bikarkeppnin 2014

THIRD ROUND

(26/05/14)
HK 1-2 Breidablik

(27/05/14)
Fram 1-0 KA
Fylkir 3-1 Njardvík
Hamar 3-2 KF
ÍBV 3-0 Haukar
ÍH 1-5 Thór
Sindri 0-2 KV
Vídir 0-1 Valur

(28/05/14)
Afturelding 1-1 ÍR *(aet; 5-6 on pens)*
Augnablik 0-5 Keflavík
BÍ/Bolungarvík 4-2 Fjardabyggd
Fjölnir 1-0 Dalvík/Reynir
KFG 0-4 Thróttur R.
KR 1-0 FH
Stjarnan 6-0 Selfoss
Víkingur R. 4-1 Grindavík *(aet)*

FOURTH ROUND

(17/06/14)
BÍ/Bolungarvík 5-2 ÍR *(aet)*

(18/06/14)
ÍBV 3-0 Valur
KV 3-5 Fram
Stjarnan 0-1 Thróttur R. *(aet)*
Víkingur R. 5-1 Fylkir

(19/06/14)
Breidablik 3-1 Thór *(aet)*
Keflavík 6-1 Hamar
KR 4-2 Fjölnir

QUARTER-FINALS

(06/07/14)
Breidablik 0-2 KR *(Ó Hauksson 14, Sigurdsson 34)*
Fram 1-3 Keflavík *(Takefusa 90; Sveinsson 23, Magnússon 58, Matthíasson 75)*

(07/07/14)
BÍ/Bolungarvík 0-3 Víkingur R. *(Snorrason 54, Í Jónsson 68, 90)*
Thróttur R. 0-1 ÍBV *(Thorsteinsson 113) (aet)*

SEMI-FINALS

(30/07/14)
Keflavík 0-0 Víkingur R. *(aet; 4-2 on pens)*

(31/07/14)
ÍBV 2-5 KR *(Glenn 47, Ólafsson 86; Finnbogason 31, 64, Sigurdsson 45, Balbi 76, Ó Hauksson 83)*

FINAL

(16/08/14)
Laugardalsvöllur, Reykjavik
KR REYKJAVÍK 2 *(Sigurdarson 17, Finnbogason 90+2)*
KEFLAVÍK 1 *(Sveinsson 14)*
Referee: Hinriksson
KR: *Magnússon, H Hauksson, Sigurdarson, Jósepsson, Gudmundur Gunnarsson, Sævarsson (Zato-Arouna 76), Sigurdsson, Ormarsson, Finnbogason, Martin, Ó Hauksson.*
KEFLAVÍK: *Sandqvist, Heiddal, H Halldórsson (Ljubicic 90), H Gudmundsson, Matthíasson, Einarsson, Magnússon (Elísson 78), Elvarsson, J Gudmundsson (Thorsteinsson 68), Ómarsson, Sveinsson*

KR celebrate their third Icelandic Cup win in four years

ISRAEL
Israel Football Association (IFA)

Address	Ramat Gan Stadium
	299 Aba Hillel Street
	PO Box 3591
	Il-52134 Ramat Gan
Tel	+972 3 617 1500
Fax	+972 3 570 2044
E-Mail	info@football.org.il
Website	football.org.il

President	Ofer Eini
Chief executive	Rotem Kamer
Media officer	Shlomi Barzel
Year of formation	1928
National stadium	Ramat Gan (41,583)

LIGAT HA'AL CLUBS

 1 **FC Ashdod**

 2 **Beitar Jerusalem FC**

 3 **Bnei Sakhnin FC**

 4 **Hapoel Akko FC**

 5 **Hapoel Beer Sheva FC**

 6 **Hapoel Haifa FC**

 7 **Hapoel Kiryat Shmona FC**

 8 **Hapoel Petach-Tikva FC**

 9 **Hapoel Ra'anana FC**

 10 **Hapoel Tel-Aviv FC**

 11 **Maccabi Haifa FC**

 12 **Maccabi Netanya FC**

 13 **Maccabi Petach-Tikva FC**

 14 **Maccabi Tel-Aviv FC**

PROMOTED CLUBS

 15 **Bnei Yehuda Tel-Aviv FC**

 16 **Hapoel Kfar Saba FC**

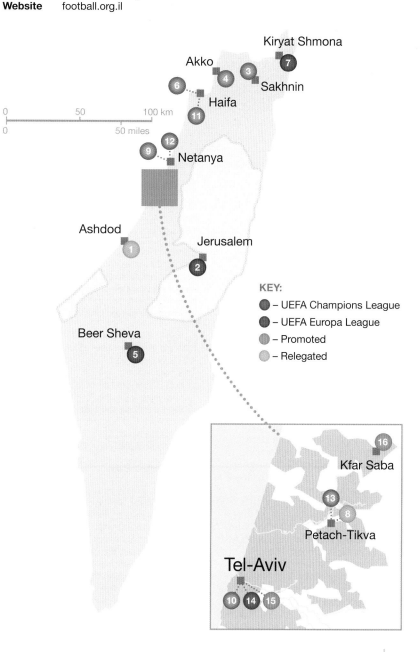

KEY:
- – UEFA Champions League
- – UEFA Europa League
- – Promoted
- – Relegated

Maccabi Tel-Aviv show their might

Record champions Maccabi Tel-Aviv FC completed a hat-trick of Israeli league titles for the first time in their history. It was a triumph that, despite a strong initial challenge from Hapoel Kiryat Shmona FC, turned out to be every bit as convincing as the previous two.

The club's new coach, Spaniard Pako Ayestarán, not only emulated the achievement of his title-winning predecessors Óscar García and Paulo Sousa but also added victory in the State Cup, with a 6-2 trouncing of third-placed Hapoel Beer Sheva FC, to complete the club's first double since 1996.

| Yellows capture league and cup double | History made with hat-trick of league titles | Disastrous European campaign for Israeli clubs |

Domestic league

Pako, a former assistant to Rafael Benítez at Liverpool FC, was brought in by the defending champions at the end of August – midway through a UEFA Europa League play-off tie – following the sudden departure of Óscar García. The club's 2012/13 title-winning boss had been re-recruited by Maccabi Tel-Aviv after Paulo Sousa's move to FC Basel 1893, but his second spell proved to be extremely brief. The club failed to survive in Europe, but on the domestic front Pako more than proved his worth as a replacement, leading Maccabi to one of the most memorable seasons in their 109-year existence.

Kiryat Shmona, the 2011/12 champions, provided Pako's men with a stern challenge to start with, remaining unbeaten in their first 16 matches and defeating the defending champions 2-1 at home in November. Maccabi, however, were also going well thanks to the phenomenal goalscoring of their Israeli international Eran Zahavi, who scored at least once in each of his first 13 league appearances. The only Maccabi scoresheet in the first three months of competition that did not feature his name was a 3-1 home win against Maccabi Netanya FC, for which he was suspended following a red card received a week earlier in an overheated

derby with Hapoel Tel-Aviv FC – a match abandoned because of crowd trouble and for which both clubs were docked two points.

Zahavi continued to find the net with regularity in the second half of the season, and his goals came a sufficient number of points to carry Maccabi Tel-Aviv clear at the top of the table as Kiryat Shmona crumbled.

Fittingly, it was against Kiryat Shmona that the Yellows secured the title, with a 2-1 win at Bloomfield in mid-May. Their opponents, who had sacked coach Barak Bakhar before that game, did however rally the following week to beat third-placed Hapoel Beer Sheva FC – where Bakhar was to end up, replacing Elisha Levi – and clinch the runners-up spot.

Domestic cup

Three days after wrapping up the league title, Maccabi Tel-Aviv completed the double by putting Beer Sheva to the sword in the State Cup final at the newly constructed Sammy Ofer stadium in Haifa. The Reds had no answer to the might of the Yellows as Maccabi ran in six goals, including three from Swedish international Rade Prica, to claim the trophy for the first time in a decade, making it a record 23 wins overall. Maccabi's double was in fact a treble as

back in December they had also win the Toto Cup, a knockout competition reserved for top-flight clubs, defeating Maccabi Haifa FC 2-1 in the final.

Europe

The 2014/15 season was a calamitous one for Israeli clubs. Between them the four Ligat Ha'al representatives played a mere 12 matches, and the only tie any of them won was against opposition from Andorra. It was the first time since 2008/09 that Israel had no group stage involvement in either of the two competitions.

National team

After their opening UEFA EURO 2016 qualifying tie at home to Belgium had been postponed for security reasons, Israel made an excellent start to their campaign, taking nine points from their first three matches, with striker Omer Damari scoring six goals in the process.

However, those three wins were followed by three straight defeats as Eli Gutman's side lost twice at home in quick succession to Wales and Belgium and then surrendered a lead to go down 3-1 in Zenica to Bosnia & Herzegovina – the team that were shaping up to be their chief rivals for a play-off spot over the final four fixtures.

DOMESTIC SEASON AT A GLANCE

Ligat Ha'al 2014/15 final table

		Pld		Home						Away						Total					Pts
			W	D	L	F	A	W	D	L	F	A	W	D	L	F	A	
1	**Maccabi Tel-Aviv FC**	36	14	3	1	41	12	7	6	5	26	20	21	9	6	67	32	70
2	Hapoel Kiryat Shmona FC	36	10	6	2	29	14	8	4	6	24	24	18	10	8	53	38	64
3	Hapoel Beer Sheva FC	36	13	4	1	38	11	4	7	7	25	29	17	11	8	63	40	62
4	Beitar Jerusalem FC	36	6	7	5	23	17	7	6	5	25	26	13	13	10	48	43	51
5	Maccabi Haifa FC	36	11	2	5	33	17	3	6	9	18	20	14	8	14	51	37	50
6	Maccabi Petach-Tikva FC	36	6	5	7	18	21	6	7	5	16	20	12	12	12	34	41	48
7	Bnei Sakhnin FC	33	6	7	4	20	18	5	4	7	23	26	11	11	11	43	44	44
8	Hapoel Tel-Aviv FC	33	8	4	5	23	18	4	4	8	13	22	12	8	13	36	40	42
9	Maccabi Netanya FC	33	6	5	6	27	28	5	3	8	19	26	11	8	14	46	54	41
10	Hapoel Ra'anana FC	33	6	5	6	21	16	4	4	8	14	20	10	9	14	35	36	39
11	Hapoel Akko FC	33	5	5	6	14	18	4	6	7	14	24	9	11	13	28	42	38
12	Hapoel Haifa FC	33	5	4	7	17	24	4	3	10	8	23	9	7	17	25	47	34
13	Hapoel Petach-Tikva FC	33	4	4	8	21	26	4	4	9	22	33	8	8	17	43	59	32
14	FC Ashdod	33	2	8	6	17	22	4	5	8	15	29	6	13	14	32	51	31

NB League splits into top 6 and bottom 8 after 26 games, after which the clubs play exclusively against teams in their group; Hapoel Tel-Aviv FC & Maccabi Tel-Aviv – 2 pts deducted; FC Beitar Jerusalem FC – 1 pt deducted.

European qualification 2015/16

Champion/Cup winner: Maccabi Tel-Aviv FC (second qualifying round)

Hapoel Kiryat Shmona FC (third qualifying round)
Hapoel Beer Sheva FC (second qualifying round)
Beitar Jerusalem FC (first qualifying round)

Top scorer	Eran Zahavi (M. Tel-Aviv), 28 goals
Relegated clubs	FC Ashdod, Hapoel Petach-Tikva FC
Promoted clubs	Bnei Yehuda Tel-Aviv FC, Hapoel Kfar Saba FC
Cup final	Maccabi Tel-Aviv FC 6-2 Hapoel Beer Sheva FC

Team of the season
(4-4-1-1)

Coach: Pako Ayestarán (M. Tel-Aviv)

Haimov
(H. Kiryat Shmona)

Dasa (Beitar) — Tzedek (H. Kiryat Shmona) — Tibi (M. Tel-Aviv) — Ben Harush (M. Tel-Aviv)

Kehat (H. Kiryat Shmona) — Alberman (M. Tel-Aviv) — Micha (M. Tel-Aviv) — Buzaglo (H. Beer Sheva)

Zahavi (M. Tel-Aviv)

Ghadir (Bnei Sakhnin)

Player of the season

Eran Zahavi
(Maccabi Tel-Aviv FC)

Having scored in each of Maccabi Tel-Aviv's last five league games in 2013/14 en route to capturing the Ligat Ha'al's golden boot, Israeli international Zahavi also struck in every one of the club's first 13 matches of the 2014/15 season (including the abandoned derby against Hapoel Tel-Aviv FC). The astonishingly prolific attacking midfielder would go on to top the charts again with 28 goals – one fewer than the previous season but 12 more than any other player – as Maccabi completed a historic title hat-trick.

Newcomer of the season

Olarenwaju Kayode
(Maccabi Netanya FC)

Following a successful loan spell at Maccabi Netanya in their 2013/14 promotion-winning season, Kayode made his mark in the Israeli top flight, scoring 13 goals – the joint third highest figure in the division. The 22-year-old Nigerian youth international's efforts – which also included six assists – were crucial in helping to steer his club clear of relegation, and at the end of the season he was snapped up by FK Austria Wien, joining the Viennese club for €800,000 on a four-year contract.

ISRAEL

NATIONAL TEAM

International tournament appearances
FIFA World Cup (1) 1970

Top five all-time caps
Yossi Benayoun (96); Arik Benado (94); Alon Harazi (88); **Tal Ben Haim I** (87), Amir Shelache (85)

Top five all-time goals
Mordechay Shpiegler (33); Yossi Benayoun & Yehushua Feigenboim (24); Ronen Harazi (23); Nahum Stelmach (22)

Results 2014/15

Date	Opponent				Result	Scorers
10/10/14	Cyprus (ECQ)	A	Nicosia	W	2-1	*Damari (38), Ben Haim II (45)*
13/10/14	Andorra (ECQ)	A	Andorra la Vella	W	4-1	*Damari (3, 41, 82), Hemed (90+6p)*
16/11/14	Bosnia & Herzegovina (ECQ)	H	Haifa	W	3-0	*Vermouth (36), Damari (45), Zahavi (70)*
28/03/15	Wales (ECQ)	H	Haifa	L	0-3	
31/03/15	Belgium (ECQ)	H	Jerusalem	L	0-1	
12/06/15	Bosnia & Herzegovina (ECQ)	A	Zenica	L	1-3	*Ben Haim II (41)*

Appearances 2014/15

Coach: Eli Gutman	24/02/58		CYP	AND	BIH	WAL	BEL	BIH	Caps	Goals
Ofir Marciano	07/10/89	Ashdod	G	G	G	G	G	G	6	-
Eyal Meshumar	10/08/83	M. Haifa	D	D	D				10	-
Tal Ben Haim I	31/03/82	Charlton (ENG)	D	D	D	D	D	D	87	1
Eitan Tibi	16/11/87	M. Tel-Aviv	D	D	D	D 51*			20	-
Omri Ben Harush	07/03/90	M. Tel-Aviv	D		D78	D	D84	D	11	-
Sheran Yeini	08/12/86	M. Tel-Aviv	M		M	M	M66	M46	15	-
Gil Vermouth	05/08/85	H. Tel-Aviv	M82	M65	M70				26	2
Bebras Natcho	18/02/88	CSKA Moskva (RUS)	M	M	M74	M	M	M	39	1
Eran Zahavi	25/07/87	M. Tel-Aviv	M	M70	M	M70	M	A	26	3
Tal Ben Haim II	05/08/89	M. Tel-Aviv	M73	M	M	M60	s46	A	13	3
Omer Damari	24/03/89	Austria Wien (AUT) /RB Leipzig (GER)	A70	A84	A	A43		s46	19	9
Itay Shechter	22/02/87	Nantes (FRA)	s70	s65					24	4
Lior Refaelov	26/04/86	Club Brugge (BEL)	s73	s70	s70	M	s66		35	5
Nir Biton	30/10/91	Celtic (SCO)	s82	M	s74	s60	M	M80	13	-
Taleb Tawatha	21/06/92	M. Haifa		D					4	-
Tomer Hemed	02/05/87	Almería (ESP)		s84		s43	A46		17	10
Ofir Davidzada	05/05/91	H. Beer Sheva			s78				4	-
Orel Dgani	08/01/89	M. Haifa				D	D	D	5	-
Ben Sahar	10/08/89	Willem II (NED)				s70	M	M62	36	6
Rami Gershon	12/08/88	Gent (BEL)					D	D	21	2
Elyaniv Barda	15/12/81	H. Beer Sheva					s84		37	12
Maor Buzaglo	14/01/88	H. Beer Sheva						s62	17	1
Roi Kehat	12/05/92	H. Kiryat Shmona						s80	1	-

EUROPE

Maccabi Tel-Aviv FC

Second qualifying round - FC Santa Coloma (AND)
A 1-0 *Prica (64)*
Juan Pablo, Alberman, Zahavi, Radi (Einbinder 64), Ben Haim (Margoulis 85), Micha, Tibi, Ben Harush, Yeini, Prica (Badash 85), Carlos García. Coach: Óscar García (ESP)
H 2-0 *Zahavi (62p), Ben Haim (90)*
Juan Pablo, Alberman, Zahavi, Ben Haim, Micha (Lugasi 80), Einbinder (Radi 68), Tibi, Ben Harush, Yeini, Prica (Badash 65), Carlos García. Coach: Óscar García (ESP)
Red card: Badash 78

Third qualifying round - NK Maribor (SVN)
A 0-1
Juan Pablo, Shpungin, Ben Basat, Alberman (Ben Harush 46), Zahavi, Radi, Ben Haim (Margoulis 89), Tibi, Yeini, Carlos García, Igiebor (Einbinder 58). Coach: Óscar García (ESP)
H 2-2 *Ben Haim (42), Ben Basat (54)*
Juan Pablo, Shpungin, Ben Basat, Zahavi, Radi, Ben Haim (Einbinder 71), Micha, Tibi, Ben Harush (Igiebor 63), Yeini, Carlos García (Prica 46). Coach: Óscar García (ESP)

Play-offs - Asteras Tripolis FC (GRE)
A 0-2
Juan Pablo, Shpungin, Ben Basat (Prica 66), Alberman, Zahavi, Radi (Lugasi 86), Micha (Ben Haim 76), Tibi, Yeini, Carlos García, Igiebor. Coach: Óscar García (ESP)
H 3-1 *Badash (27), Zahavi (54p), Prica (75)*
Juan Pablo, Ben Basat (Prica 72), Alberman, Zahavi, Micha, Tibi, Ben Harush, Yeini, Badash (Radi 85), Carlos García, Igiebor (Ben Haim 62). Coach: Pako Ayestarán (ESP)

Hapoel Kiryat Shmona FC

Third qualifying round - FC Dinamo Moskva (RUS)
A 1-1 *Kola (63)*
Haimov, Kassio, Tzedek, Dilmoni, Abed (Mizrahi 84), Kola (Mayo 90+2), Manga (Rochet 71), Elkayam, Broun, Panka, Kehat. Coach: Barak Bakhar (ISR)
H 1-2 *Kehat (11)*
Haimov, Kassio, Tzedek, Dilmoni (Pinas 72), Abed (Rochet 84), Kola, Manga, Elkayam, Broun, Panka (Mizrahi 75), Kehat. Coach: Barak Bakhar (ISR)

Hapoel Beer Sheva FC

Second qualifying round - RNK Split (CRO)
A 1-2 *Buzaglo (31)*
Ejide, Biton, Arel, Barda, Buzaglo (Naser 80), Davidzada, Gabay (Melikson 63), Pajović, William, Arbeitman (Malul 74), Gordana. Coach: Elisha Levi (ISR)
H 0-0
Ejide, Biton (Malul 85), Arel (Gabay 67), Barda, Buzaglo (Naser 80), Davidzada, Pajović, Melikson, William, Arbeitman, Gordana. Coach: Elisha Levi (ISR)

Hapoel Tel-Aviv FC

Second qualifying round - FC Astana (KAZ)
A 0-3
Amos, Cohen (Chekul 70), Colin, Zaguri, Shrem (Fadida 66), Lucas Sasha, Dgani, Vermouth, Malka (Levi 20), Abutbul, Gerzicich. Coach: Asi Domb (ISR)
Red card: Dgani 14
H 1-0 *Lucas Sasha (57p)*
Almadon, Cohen, Colin, Zaguri, Lucas Sasha (Fadida 89), Vermouth, Malka, Abutbul, Gozlan (Lazmi 69), Chekul (Dado 77), Levi. Coach: Asi Domb (ISR)

FC Ashdod

1999 • Yud Alef (7,354)• no website
Coach: Nir Klinger

2014
Date		Opponent	Res	Score	Scorers
13/09	h	H. Kiryat Shmona	D	0-0	
20/09	a	H. Haifa	W	2-0	Abu Anzeh, Inbrom
27/09	h	Bnei Sakhnin	D	2-2	Zrihan, Abu Anzeh
19/10	a	Beitar	D	1-1	Solari
25/10	h	H. Petach-Tikva	L	1-3	Solari (p)
29/10	h	M. Tel-Aviv	L	2-5	Rosh, Bello (p)
01/11	h	H. Ra'anana	L	1-2	Davidov
08/11	a	H. Beer Sheva	L	1-2	Zrihan
22/11	h	M. Haifa	W	1-0	og (Michel)
29/11	a	H. Akko	W	1-0	Abu Anzeh
04/12	a	M. Petach-Tikva	D	1-1	Solari
07/12	h	H. Tel-Aviv	W	3-1	Solari, Bello 2
13/12	a	M. Netanya	D	0-0	
20/12	a	H. Kiryat Shmona	L	0-1	
27/12	h	H. Haifa	L	0-1	

2015
Date		Opponent	Res	Score	Scorers
03/01	h	Bnei Sakhnin	W	3-2	Inbrom 2, Mund
10/01	h	Beitar	D	3-3	Davidov, Solari, Ohana
17/01	h	H. Petach-Tikva	W	2-1	Lenkebe, Ohana
24/01	h	M. Tel-Aviv	L	0-1	
02/02	a	H. Ra'anana	L	0-2	
07/02	h	H. Beer Sheva	D	2-2	Davidov, Bello (p)
14/02	a	M. Haifa	L	0-5	
21/02	h	H. Akko	D	0-0	
28/02	h	M. Petach-Tikva	D	0-0	
07/03	h	H. Tel-Aviv	L	1-3	Mund
14/03	h	M. Netanya	L	2-3	Mund, Kinda
21/03	h	H. Ra'anana	L	0-4	
11/04	h	H. Akko	D	0-0	
18/04	a	M. Netanya	D	0-0	
25/04	h	M. Haifa	D	0-0	
02/05	a	Bnei Sakhnin	D	1-1	Davidov
09/05	h	H. Petach-Tikva	L	2-4	Zrihan 2
16/05	a	H. Tel-Aviv	L	0-1	

No	Name	Nat	DoB	Pos	Aps	(s)	Gls
7	Murad Abu Anzeh		08/11/86	A	14	(11)	3
4	Elio Odu Abubaker	NGA	15/09/96	D	1		
17	Timor Avitan		27/11/91	A	1		
17	Gal Barel		15/06/90	M	3	(3)	
11	Roee Bekel		07/10/87	M	5		
9	Yero Bello	NGA	11/12/87	M	19	(9)	4
15	Tom Ben Zaken		29/10/94	D	4	(1)	
8	Rahamim Checkul		08/05/88	D	21	(2)	
10	Aleksandar Davidov	SRB	07/10/83	A	31		4
32	Nicolás Falczuk	ARG	16/11/86	A	5	(4)	
14	Shay Hadad		02/07/87	D	2	(5)	
25	Abed Hatem Elhamid		18/03/91	M	7	(5)	
12	Or Inbrom		12/01/96	M	15	(10)	3
14	Gadi Kinda		23/03/94	M	29	(1)	1
6	Paty Yeye Lenkebe	COD	02/02/82	D	31		1
1	Ofir Marciano		07/10/89	G	33		
16	Benzion Moshal		13/07/93	M	1	(5)	
17	Tom Mund		06/07/91	M	17	(2)	3
16	Michael Ohana		04/10/95	M	23	(8)	2
18	Juwon Oshaniwa	NGA	14/09/90	D	13		
5	Israel Rosh		05/03/88	D	13	(5)	1
19	Michael Ross		16/06/91	A		(4)	
20	Micky Sirushtan		25/04/89	M	26		
32	David Solari	ARG	21/03/86	M	10	(8)	5
3	Yom Tov Werta		23/05/90	D	23	(1)	
19	Niv Zrihan		24/05/94	A	16	(9)	4

Beitar Jerusalem FC

1939 • Teddy (34,000) • beitarfc.co.il

Major honours
Israeli League (6) 1987, 1993, 1997, 1998, 2007, 2008;
Israeli Cup (7) 1976, 1979, 1985, 1986, 1989, 2008,
2009

Coach: Meni Koretzki;
(28/01/15) Guy Levi

2014
13/09 a	H. Beer Sheva	D	1-1	Korać (p)
22/09 h	M. Haifa	W	1-0	Azulay
27/09 a	H. Akko	D	1-1	Dasa
19/10 h	Ashdod	D	1-1	Maman
27/10 a	H. Tel-Aviv	W	2-0	Korać, Maman
30/10 h	M. Netanya	D	1-1	Korać
03/11 a	H. Kiryat Shmona	D	1-1	Maman
08/11 h	H. Haifa	L	0-1	
23/11 a	Bnei Sakhnin	L	0-1	
01/12 h	M. Petach-Tikva	L	2-3	I Cohen, Korać (p)
04/12 h	H. Petach-Tikva	W	3-1	Claudemir, Azulay, Korać
08/12 a	M. Tel-Aviv	D	1-1	Atzili
15/12 h	H. Ra'anana	D	0-0	
22/12 h	H. Beer Sheva	L	0-3	
27/12 a	M. Haifa	W	3-1	I Cohen 2, Swissa

2015
03/01 h	H. Akko	W	4-0	Swissa, I Cohen, Atzili, Azulay
10/01 a	Ashdod	D	3-3	Atzili, Azulay, I Cohen
19/01 h	H. Tel-Aviv	D	1-1	Khila
26/01 a	M. Netanya	L	0-2	
01/02 h	H. Kiryat Shmona	W	3-1	og 2 (Tzedek 2), Kriaf
09/02 a	H. Haifa	W	4-3	I Cohen, Antal (p), L Cohen 2
15/02 h	Bnei Sakhnin	L	1-2	Maman
22/02 a	M. Petach-Tikva	D	1-1	Dasa
28/02 a	H. Petach-Tikva	W	1-0	Atzili
09/03 h	M. Tel-Aviv	W	1-0	Atzili
14/03 a	H. Ra'anana	W	2-0	Claudemir, L Cohen
22/03 a	H. Kiryat Shmona	W	2-1	Antal 2
06/04 a	M. Haifa	L	0-1	
12/04 h	M. Petach-Tikva	D	0-0	
19/04 a	M. Tel-Aviv	L	1-4	I Cohen
26/04 h	H. Beer Sheva	D	1-1	Kriaf
02/05 h	H. Kiryat Shmona	L	0-1	
10/05 h	M. Haifa	D	1-1	L Cohen
18/05 a	M. Petach-Tikva	W	2-1	L Cohen, Atzili
25/05 h	H. Tel-Aviv	W	3-0	L Cohen, Maman, I Cohen
30/05 a	H. Beer Sheva	L	0-4	

No	Name	Nat	DoB	Pos	Aps	(s)	Gls
28	Liviu Antal	ROU	02/06/89	M	14		3
7	Omer Atzili		27/07/93	M	19	(11)	6
8	Shlomi Azulay		18/10/89	A	31	(3)	4
5	César Arzo	ESP	21/06/86	D	26	(1)	
14	Claudemir	BRA	17/08/84	M	34		2
12	Avishay Cohen		19/06/95	A		(3)	
9	Itzhak Cohen		01/01/90	A	17	(9)	8
11	Lidor Cohen		16/12/92	A	24	(10)	6
2	Eli Dasa		03/12/92	D	32		2
21	Sani Emmanuel	NGA	23/12/92	A		(1)	
4	Zeev Haimovich		07/04/83	D	23	(1)	
6	Tal Khila		26/06/92	D	15	(4)	1
1	Boris Kleiman		26/10/90	G	35		
25	Žarko Korać	MNE	11/06/87	A	11	(3)	5
24	Ofir Kriaf		17/03/91	M	16	(7)	2
28	Ben Malka		06/12/89	M		(3)	
15	Shmuel Malul		03/04/93	D	5	(5)	
10	Hanan Maman		28/08/89	M	27	(8)	5
81	Dušan Matović	SRB	08/07/83	D	35		
20	Omer Nachmani		29/01/93	M	10	(5)	
18	Dani Prada		01/04/87	M	10	(11)	
77	Ben Rahav		29/04/89	G	1		
26	Mor Shaked		23/12/86	A		(2)	
19	Tomer Swissa		21/12/80	A	5	(12)	2
21	Or Vaaknin		21/09/95	M	1		
23	Tomer Yerouham		16/04/93	D	5	(5)	

Bnei Sakhnin FC

1993 • Doha (8,500) • skhnin.com

Major honours
Israeli Cup (1) 2004

Coach: Guy Levi;
(06/12/14) Eli Cohen

2014
15/09 a	M. Haifa	L	2-4	Papadopoulos, Nahya
20/09 h	H. Akko	D	1-1	Ghadir
27/09 a	Ashdod	D	2-2	Papadopoulos, Ghadir
18/10 h	H. Tel-Aviv	D	1-1	Abraham Paz
25/10 h	M. Netanya	L	1-2	og (S Harush)
28/10 h	H. Kiryat Shmona	L	1-4	Mugrabi
01/11 a	H. Haifa	W	3-0	Ghadir 2, Osman
11/11 h	M. Petach-Tikva	D	1-1	Ghadir
23/11 h	Beitar	W	1-0	Rian
29/11 a	H. Petach-Tikva	L	1-2	Osman
03/12 h	M. Tel-Aviv	L	1-3	Ghadir
06/12 a	H. Ra'anana	D	1-1	Mugrabi (p)
13/12 h	H. Beer Sheva	W	2-0	Mugrabi (p), Ghadir
20/12 h	M. Haifa	D	1-1	Bojović
27/12 a	H. Akko	W	3-1	Ghadir, Mugrabi, Rian

2015
03/01 a	Ashdod	L	2-3	Ghadir, Mugrabi
10/01 a	H. Tel-Aviv	D	1-1	Rian
19/01 h	M. Netanya	L	0-2	
25/01 a	H. Kiryat Shmona	D	1-1	Cohen
31/01 h	H. Haifa	W	2-0	Ghadir, Rian
07/02 a	M. Petach-Tikva	L	0-2	
15/02 a	Beitar	W	2-1	Ghadir 2
21/02 h	H. Petach-Tikva	D	0-0	
28/02 a	M. Tel-Aviv	L	0-2	
07/03 h	H. Ra'anana	W	2-0	Ghadir, Mugrabi
15/03 a	H. Beer Sheva	L	0-2	
21/03 h	H. Haifa	W	1-0	Cohen
11/04 h	H. Petach-Tikva	W	3-2	og (Musa), Diogo Kachuba, Mugrabi
18/04 h	H. Ra'anana	D	1-1	Mugrabi
25/04 a	M. Netanya	W	3-2	Ghadir (p), Jaber, Diogo Kachuba
02/05 a	Ashdod	D	1-1	Ghadir
09/05 h	H. Tel-Aviv	W	2-0	Mugrabi, Ghadir
16/05 a	H. Akko	L	0-1	

No	Name	Nat	DoB	Pos	Aps	(s)	Gls
23	Marae Abo Raya		16/04/93	M	1	(1)	
19	Yosef Abolabn		26/05/92	A	3	(5)	
5	Abraham Paz	ESP	29/07/88	D	20		1
8	Allah Abu Salah		25/06/87	D	17	(2)	
20	Muamen Agbaria		24/08/93	D	1	(6)	
10	Mohamad Badrana		15/11/95	M		(2)	
88	Milan Bojović	SRB	13/04/87	A	3	(7)	1
3	Itzhak Cohen		22/04/83	D	9	(1)	2
88	Diogo Kachuba	BRA	16/02/90	M	11	(1)	2
17	Hamed Ganaym		08/07/87	M	16	(7)	
10	Muhammad Ghadir		21/01/91	A	29		16
9	Ayed Habashi		10/05/95	D	13		
11	Amir Halaula		21/03/97	A		(1)	
15	Haled Halaula		16/12/82	A	23	(4)	
33	Mohamad Hamza		23/09/93	G		(1)	
23	Ataa Jaber		03/10/94	M	10		1
68	Igor Jovanovic	GER	03/05/89	D	21	(3)	
1	Ran Kadosh		04/10/85	G	20	(1)	
10	Mohamed Kalebat		15/06/90	A	8	(1)	
22	Mahmoud Kandil		11/08/88	G	13		
18	Ahmed Kasum		25/01/85	M	6	(6)	
6	Miha Mevlja	SVN	12/06/90	D	19	(3)	
26	Firas Mugrabi		24/07/91	M	29	(2)	9
20	Ahmad Nahya		07/07/91	A	5	(10)	1
18	Ali Osman		08/02/87	D	25		2
16	Ioannis Papadopoulos	GRE	09/03/89	M	11	(7)	2
77	Ismail Rian		24/04/94	A	22	(7)	4
2	Tambi Sagas		21/10/94	D	7	(7)	
14	Ahmed Sayed		22/02/94	A	2	(1)	
4	Ehab Shami		18/09/93	D	8	(4)	
7	Mohamed Zbedat		15/11/91	D	11	(5)	

Hapoel Akko FC

1946 • Akko Municipal (5,000) • no website

Coach: Alon Harazi;
(08/01/15) Shlomi Dora

2014
13/09 h	H. Haifa	D	1-1	Tzemach
20/09 a	Bnei Sakhnin	D	1-1	Hadžić
27/09 h	Beitar	D	1-1	Salihi
18/10 a	H. Petach-Tikva	L	1-4	Taga
26/10 h	M. Tel-Aviv	L	0-1	
29/10 a	H. Ra'anana	W	2-0	Salihi 2
01/11 h	H. Beer Sheva	D	1-1	Abu-El-Nir
08/11 a	M. Haifa	L	0-1	
22/11 a	H. Petach-Tikva	D	0-0	
29/11 h	Ashdod	D	0-1	
03/12 a	H. Tel-Aviv	W	3-1	Abu-El-Nir, Salihi, Jovanović
06/12 h	M. Netanya	L	1-2	Salihi
13/12 a	H. Kiryat Shmona	D	2-2	Salihi, Stain
20/12 a	M. Haifa	L	0-1	
27/12 h	Bnei Sakhnin	L	1-3	Abu-El-Nir

2015
03/01 a	Beitar	L	0-4	
10/01 h	H. Petach-Tikva	D	1-1	Gotlib
17/01 a	M. Tel-Aviv	L	0-3	
24/01 h	H. Ra'anana	L	0-2	
31/01 h	H. Beer Sheva	L	0-3	
07/02 h	M. Haifa	D	0-0	
14/02 h	M. Petach-Tikva	L	0-2	
21/02 a	Ashdod	D	0-0	
28/02 h	H. Tel-Aviv	W	1-0	Avidor
07/03 a	M. Haifa	D	1-1	Gotlib
14/03 h	H. Kiryat Shmona	W	2-0	Papadopoulos, Kasum
21/03 a	H. Tel-Aviv	L	0-1	
11/04 a	Ashdod	D	0-0	
18/04 h	H. Haifa	W	1-0	Saider
25/04 a	H. Petach-Tikva	W	2-0	Jovanović, Gotlib
02/05 h	H. Ra'anana	W	2-0	Abu-El-Nir, Tzemach
11/05 a	M. Netanya	W	2-1	Jovanović, Papadopoulos
16/05 h	Bnei Sakhnin	W	1-0	Saider

No	Name	Nat	DoB	Pos	Aps	(s)	Gls
25	Amir Abu-El-Nir		27/02/89	A	24	(5)	4
7	Namor Aga		13/01/95	M		(1)	
15	Amit Amzaleg		07/04/94	M		(8)	
11	Yuval Avidor		19/10/86	A	19	(12)	1
4	Daniel Borhel		14/06/91	D	13		
4	Uri Cohen		26/05/92	D	3		
26	Yossi Dora		25/08/81	M	31		
1	Dudu Goresh		01/02/80	G	32		
6	Edi Gotlib		16/08/92	D	31		3
99	Emir Hadžić	BIH	19/07/84	A	11	(12)	1
21	Branislav Jovanović	SRB	21/09/85	M	29		3
80	Juliano Spadacio	BRA	16/11/80	M	15	(1)	
18	Ahmed Kasum		25/01/85	M	13		1
9	Ezat Khlaily		27/03/94	A		(2)	
77	Adi Konstantinos		09/11/94	M	10	(15)	
33	Yarden Krishtul		19/10/94	G	1		
5	Moshe Mishaelov		14/09/83	D	20	(6)	
24	Snir Mishan		13/11/88	D	24		
19	Ioannis Papadopoulos	GRE	09/03/89	M	12		2
16	Elior Saider		17/11/91	A	11	(9)	2
14	Hamdi Salihi	ALB	19/01/84	A	20		7
10	Shadi Shaben		04/03/92	M	1	(6)	
7	Raz Stain		23/02/94	A	7	(3)	1
14	Amaya Taga		04/02/85	M	19	(7)	1
3	Ben Turjeman		09/01/89	D	16		
80	Zion Tzemach		19/01/90	M	1	(10)	2
17	Eli Zizov		30/01/91	M		(1)	

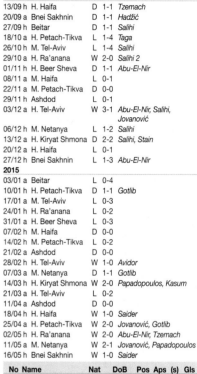

Hapoel Beer Sheva FC

1949 • Artur Vasermil (13,000) • hapoelb7.co.il
Major honours
Israeli League (2) 1975, 1976; Israeli Cup (1) 1997
Coach: Elisha Lovi

2014

13/09 h	Beitar	D	1-1	William
20/09 a	H. Petach-Tikva	W	3-1	Gordana, Gabay 2
29/09 h	M. Tel-Aviv	W	3-2	Barda 3
18/10 a	H. Ra'anana	D	1-1	Melikson (p)
25/10 a	M. Petach-Tikva	W	4-0	Gabay, Gordana, Buzaglo, Arbeitman (p)
28/10 h	M. Haifa	W	2-0	Arbeitman, Gordana
01/11 h	H. Akko	D	1-1	Buzaglo (p)
08/11 h	Ashdod	W	2-1	Arbeitman, Buzaglo
22/11 a	H. Tel-Aviv	L	2-3	Buzaglo 2
29/11 h	M. Netanya	W	4-0	Arbeitman, William, Ogu, Buzaglo (p)
02/12 a	H. Kiryat Shmona	D	1-1	Biton
06/12 h	H. Haifa	W	4-0	Buzaglo, Gordana, Arbeitman 2
13/12 a	Bnei Sakhnin	L	0-2	
22/12 a	Beitar	W	3-0	Buzaglo 2, William
27/12 h	H. Petach-Tikva	W	2-1	Ogu, Naser

2015

05/01 a	M. Tel-Aviv	D	0-0	
10/01 h	H. Ra'anana	L	0-1	
17/01 h	M. Petach-Tikva	W	1-0	Ogu
24/01 a	M. Haifa	L	0-1	
31/01 h	H. Akko	W	3-0	Arbeitman 2, Gordana
07/02 a	Ashdod	D	2-2	Arbeitman 2
14/02 h	H. Tel-Aviv	W	1-0	Arbeitman
21/02 a	M. Netanya	L	2-4	Gabay, Ogu
01/03 h	H. Kiryat Shmona	W	2-1	Barda 2
07/03 a	H. Haifa	D	1-1	Gabay
15/03 h	Bnei Sakhnin	W	2-0	Barda 2
21/03 h	M. Petach-Tikva	W	3-0	Gabay (p), Buzaglo 2
06/04 a	M. Tel-Aviv	L	1-3	Buzaglo
12/04 h	M. Haifa	D	1-1	Buzaglo
19/04 h	H. Kiryat Shmona	D	2-2	Gordana, Naser
26/04 a	Beitar	D	1-1	Barda
03/05 a	M. Petach-Tikva	W	2-1	Gabay 2 (1p)
11/05 h	M. Tel-Aviv	D	1-1	Hoban
16/05 a	M. Haifa	L	0-4	
24/05 a	H. Kiryat Shmona	L	1-3	Gabay (p)
30/05 h	Beitar	W	4-0	William, Gabay, Melikson, Gordana

No	Name	Nat	DoB	Pos	Aps	(s)	Gls
19	Yosef Abolabn		26/05/92	A		(11)	
18	Shlomi Arbeitman		14/05/85	A	25	(7)	11
8	Gal Arel		09/07/89	D	4	(8)	
3	Joakim Askling		04/01/90	D	1		
8	Hadar Barad		20/11/95	M		(1)	
10	Elyaniv Barda		15/12/82	A	27	(6)	8
2	Ben Biton		03/01/91	D	29	(1)	1
11	Maor Buzaglo		14/01/88	M	34	(1)	13
13	Ofir Davidzada		05/05/91	D	32		
1	Austin Ejlde	NGA	08/04/84	G	34		
16	Dovev Gabay		01/04/87	A	12	(11)	10
5	Roei Gordana		06/07/90	M	20	(11)	7
28	Or Havivyan		27/12/94	M		(1)	
12	Ovidiu Hoban	ROU	27/12/82	M	33		1
14	Avyatar Ilouz		04/11/83	D	3	(3)	
22	Robi Levkovic		31/08/88	G	2		
4	Dor Malul		30/04/89	D	4	(17)	
24	Maor Melikson		30/10/84	M	24	(6)	2
7	Siraj Naser		02/09/90	M	6	(19)	2
30	John Ogu	NGA	20/04/88	M	34		4
23	Tomislav Pajović	SRB	15/03/86	D	26	(1)	
16	Bar Shalom		31/01/96	A		(1)	
20	Loai Taha		26/11/89	D	8		
5	Dudi Twito		06/02/94	D	4		
21	Or Vaaknin		21/09/95	M		(1)	
25	William	BRA	07/02/85	D	34		4

Hapoel Haifa FC

1924 • Sammy Ofer (30,974) • hapoel-haifa.org.il
Major honours
Israeli League (1) 1999; Israeli Cup (3) 1963, 1966, 1974
Coach: Reuven Atar;
(16/02/15) Tal Banin

2014

13/09 h	H. Akko	D	1-1	Kalonas (p)
20/09 h	Ashdod	L	0-2	
27/09 a	H. Tel-Aviv	L	0-3	
18/10 h	M. Netanya	W	3-2	Kijanskas, G Cohen, Shukrani
25/10 a	H. Kiryat Shmona	L	0-1	
28/10 h	M. Petach-Tikva	L	0-1	
01/11 h	Bnei Sakhnin	L	0-3	
08/11 a	Beitar	W	1-0	Al Lala
22/11 h	H. Petach-Tikva	W	1-0	Al Lala
29/11 a	M. Tel-Aviv	L	0-3	
02/12 h	H. Ra'anana	W	1-0	Kiwan
06/12 a	H. Beer Sheva	L	0-4	
14/12 h	M. Haifa	L	0-4	
20/12 h	H. Akko	W	1-0	G Cohen
27/12 a	Ashdod	W	1-0	Al Lala

2015

03/01 h	H. Tel-Aviv	D	1-1	Al Lala
10/01 a	M. Netanya	W	2-0	og (Hassan), Ostaynd
17/01 h	H. Kiryat Shmona	L	1-2	Al Lala
24/01 a	M. Petach-Tikva	D	0-0	
31/01 a	Bnei Sakhnin	L	0-2	
09/02 h	Beitar	L	3-4	Al Lala 2, Ricketts
14/02 a	H. Petach-Tikva	L	1-2	Al Lala
21/02 h	M. Tel-Aviv	W	2-0	Al Lala, Kijanskas
28/02 a	H. Ra'anana	L	0-2	
07/03 h	H. Beer Sheva	D	1-1	Al Lala
14/03 a	M. Haifa	L	0-2	
21/03 a	Bnei Sakhnin	L	0-1	
11/04 h	H. Tel-Aviv	L	0-1	
18/04 a	H. Akko	L	0-1	
25/04 a	Ashdod	D	0-0	
02/05 h	H. Petach-Tikva	W	3-2	Salihi 2, Roash
09/05 a	H. Ra'anana	W	2-1	Salihi 2
16/05 h	M. Netanya	D	0-0	

No	Name	Nat	DoB	Pos	Aps	(s)	Gls
27	Maharan Abou Raya		22/01/83	D		(1)	
17	Maaran Al Lala		07/03/82	A	24	(7)	10
27	Oren Biton		17/01/94	D	5	(4)	
6	Gal Cohen		14/08/82	D	20		2
26	Stephen Cohen	FRA	27/02/86	M	18	(5)	
17	Kobi Dajani		05/11/84	M	18	(5)	
3	Ofek Fishler		24/08/96	D	3		
20	Tariko Getahon		01/01/95	M	1		
10	Idan Golan		29/02/96	A		(4)	
10	Mindaugas Kalonas	LTU	28/02/84	A	4	(5)	1
2	Tadas Kijanskas	LTU	06/09/85	D	30		2
8	Hiasham Kiwan		17/05/87	M	13	(10)	1
25	Žarko Korać	MNE	11/06/87	A	4	(11)	
16	Přemysl Kovář	CZE	14/10/85	G	33		
9	Osei Mawuli	GHA	02/10/89	A	6	(4)	
15	Haim Megrelashvili		04/07/82	D	24		
14	Almog Ohayon		05/08/94	M		(1)	
4	Or Ostaynd		18/12/87	M	26	(6)	1
7	Maxim Plakushchenko		04/01/96	M		(1)	
9	Tosaint Ricketts	CAN	06/08/87	A	23	(7)	1
21	Oshri Roash		25/07/88	D	19	(6)	1
14	Hamdi Salihi	ALB	19/01/84	A	9	(1)	4
24	Liran Sardal		02/07/94	D	23	(3)	
18	Yuval Shabtay		18/12/86	D	22	(8)	
28	Aner Shechter		29/04/87	A	1	(2)	
5	Roee Shukrani		26/07/90	M	29	(3)	1
9	Omer Vered		25/01/90	M	8	(4)	

Hapoel Kiryat Shmona FC

2000 • Kiryat Shmona Municipal (5,300) • iturank8.co.il
Major honours
Israeli League (1) 2012; Israeli Cup (1) 2014
Coach: Barak Bakhar;
(14/05/15) Beni Ben Zaken

2014

13/09 a	Ashdod	D	0-0	
20/09 h	H. Tel-Aviv	W	3-0	Panka, Kehat, Kola
27/09 a	M. Netanya	W	2-1	Mizrahi, Kassio
18/10 h	M. Petach-Tikva	W	3-0	Tzedek, Kola, Azam
25/10 h	H. Haifa	W	1-0	Mizrahi
28/10 a	Bnei Sakhnin	W	4-1	Kehat 2, Manga, Mizrahi
03/11 h	Beitar	D	1-1	Abed
08/11 a	H. Petach-Tikva	W	3-1	Kassio, Kola, og (Abu Zeid)
24/11 h	M. Tel-Aviv	W	2-1	Kola, Kehat
29/12 a	H. Ra'anana	D	0-0	
02/12 h	H. Beer Sheva	D	1-1	Kola (p)
06/12 a	M. Haifa	W	3-1	Kola 2, Mizrahi
13/12 h	H. Akko	D	2-2	Mizrahi, Manga
20/12 a	Ashdod	W	1-0	Abed
29/12 a	H. Tel-Aviv	W	1-0	Manga

2015

03/01 h	M. Netanya	W	3-1	Kehat 2 (1p), Manga
10/01 a	M. Petach-Tikva	L	0-3	
17/01 a	H. Haifa	W	2-1	Rochet, Kola
25/01 h	Bnei Sakhnin	D	1-1	Manga
01/02 a	Beitar	L	1-3	Rochet
07/02 a	H. Petach-Tikva	W	3-2	Abuhazira 2, Manga
16/02 a	M. Tel-Aviv	D	1-1	Broun
21/02 h	H. Ra'anana	D	1-1	Manga
01/03 a	H. Beer Sheva	L	1-2	Kehat
08/03 h	M. Haifa	L	0-1	
14/03 a	H. Akko	L	0-2	
22/03 h	Beitar	L	1-2	Kehat
06/04 a	M. Petach-Tikva	W	1-0	Panka
13/04 h	M. Tel-Aviv	D	0-0	
19/04 a	H. Beer Sheva	D	2-2	Kola, Mizrahi
27/04 h	M. Haifa	W	1-0	Kola
02/05 a	Beitar	W	1-0	Abed
09/05 h	M. Petach-Tikva	W	2-0	Kola, Rochet
17/05 a	M. Netanya	L	1-2	Kehat
24/05 h	H. Beer Sheva	W	3-1	Kehat 3
30/05 a	M. Haifa	L	1-4	Rochet

No	Name	Nat	DoB	Pos	Aps	(s)	Gls
7	Ahmed Abed		30/03/90	M	25	(10)	3
19	Shimon Abuhazira		10/10/86	A	13	(1)	2
27	Moshe Abutbul		11/08/84	D		(1)	
5	Shekh Tamer Ahmad		08/01/95	M	1		
77	Ahad Azam		14/01/92	D	18	(10)	1
7	Eran Azrad		01/07/94	D	1	(2)	
15	Vladimir Broun		06/05/89	M	24	(3)	1
9	Yoel Chejanavich		26/07/93	A		(14)	
2	Hen Dilmoni		07/05/89	D	16		
14	Odod Elkayam		09/02/88	D	32	(2)	
55	Guy Haimov		09/03/86	G	33		
24	Dor Jan		16/12/94	A	1	(10)	
2	Kassio	BRA	11/02/87	D	30		2
9	Roi Kehat		12/05/92	M	35		12
10	Rodgers Kola	ZAM	04/07/89	A	23	(8)	11
26	Dean Maimoni		04/05/90	D	8	(4)	
11	David Manga	CTA	03/02/89	A	25	(1)	7
8	Ofir Mizrahi		04/12/93	M	21	(12)	6
3	Amir Nasar		24/11/96	D		(1)	
18	Mindaugas Panka	LTU	01/05/84	M	21	(7)	2
4	Touvarno Pinas	SUR	25/11/85	D	17	(1)	
23	Adrian Rochet		26/07/87	M	15	(15)	4
28	Eden Shamir		25/06/95	M	1	(5)	
5	Shir Tzedek		22/08/89	D	33		1
45	Mahdi Zoabi		15/07/95	G	3		

ISREAL

Hapoel Petach-Tikva FC

1935 • HaMoshava (11,500) • no website
Major honours
Israeli League (6) 1955, 1959, 1960, 1961, 1962, 1963; Israeli Cup (2) 1957, 1992
Coach: Idan Bar-On;
(09/02/15) Meni Koretzki

2014
13/09 a	H. Ra'anana	L	0-4	
20/09 h	H. Beer Sheva	L	1-3	*Asulin*
28/09 a	M. Haifa	L	1-3	*Abu Zeid*
18/10 h	H. Akko	W	4-1	*Hirsh 2, Dayan, Hugy*
25/10 a	Ashdod	W	3-1	*og (Davidov), S Cohen, Abu Zeid*
30/10 h	H. Tel-Aviv	L	0-1	
02/11 a	M. Netanya	L	1-3	*Hirsh*
08/11 h	H. Kiryat Shmona	L	1-3	*Hirsh*
22/11 a	H. Haifa	L	1-3	*Zhairi*
29/11 h	Bnei Sakhnin	W	2-1	*og (Kandil), Hirsh*
04/12 a	Beitar	L	1-3	*Oremuš*
08/12 a	M. Petach-Tikva	W	2-1	*Zhairi, Altman*
13/12 h	M. Tel-Aviv	L	1-3	*Hirsh*
20/12 h	H. Ra'anana	D	0-0	
27/12 a	H. Beer Sheva	L	1-2	*Kochav*

2015
04/01 h	M. Haifa	D	2-2	*Altman, Dayan (p)*
10/01 a	H. Akko	D	1-1	*Altman*
17/01 h	Ashdod	L	1-2	*Hugy*
24/01 a	H. Tel-Aviv	D	0-0	
31/01 h	M. Netanya	D	1-1	*Dayan*
07/02 a	H. Kiryat Shmona	L	2-3	*Hirsh, Peso*
14/02 h	H. Haifa	W	2-1	*Ben Yair, Hirsh (p)*
21/02 a	Bnei Sakhnin	D	0-0	
28/02 h	Beitar	L	0-1	
07/03 h	M. Petach-Tikva	D	0-0	
16/03 a	M. Tel-Aviv	L	0-2	
21/03 a	M. Netanya	L	1-3	*Altman (p)*
11/04 h	Bnei Sakhnin	L	2-3	*Arel, Hirsh*
18/04 a	H. Tel-Aviv	W	2-1	*Abu Zeid, Oremuš*
25/04 h	H. Akko	L	0-2	
02/05 a	H. Haifa	L	2-3	*Hugy 2*
09/05 a	Ashdod	W	4-2	*Hugy 2 (1p), Tukura, Zhairi*
16/05 h	H. Ra'anana	W	4-2	*Hugy, Zhairi, Jan, Kochav*

No	Name	Nat	DoB	Pos	Aps	(s)	Gls
6	Hassan Abu Zeid		04/02/91	M	23	(2)	3
28	Omri Altman		23/03/94	M	25	(4)	4
23	Gal Arel		09/07/89	D	10	(1)	1
10	Lior Asulin		06/10/80	A	6	(2)	1
14	Matan Baltaxa		20/09/95	A		(1)	
7	Ben Ben Yair		23/12/92	A	2	(6)	1
22	Orel Cohen		22/04/91	G	5		
17	Sagiv Cohen		20/09/87	D	8	(14)	1
25	Sekou Conde	GUI	09/06/93	D	1	(2)	
8	Guy Dayan		20/08/86	A	16	(6)	3
26	Itai Elkaslasi	ESP	15/06/88	M		(1)	
13	Gaël Etock	CMR	05/07/93	A	2	(1)	
26	Oded Gavish		23/06/89	D	7	(2)	
19	Shahar Hirsh		13/02/93	A	27	(1)	9
11	Dor Hugy		10/07/95	A	9	(15)	7
14	Dor Jan		16/12/94	A	1	(2)	1
1	Tvrtko Kale	CRO	05/06/74	G	28		
15	Dor Kochav		06/05/93	A	12	(12)	2
2	Chimezie Mbah		10/11/92	M	19	(10)	
4	Kobi Musa		18/04/82	D	31		
7	Mirko Oremuš	CRO	06/09/88	M	29		2
14	Reef Peretz		25/02/91	M	2	(9)	
5	Ori Peso		08/01/87	D	29	(2)	1
13	Michael Semama		13/04/94	M		(1)	
24	Omer Sharabi		16/03/94	D	2		
3	Amiran Shkalim		23/03/88	D	11	(4)	
21	Michael Tukura	NGA	19/10/88	M	29		1
27	Ben Turjeman		09/01/89	D	9		
10	Liroy Zhairi		02/03/89	M	20	(3)	4

Hapoel Ra'anana FC

1972 • Municipal, Netanya (13,800) • hapoel-raanana.co.il
Coach: Haim Silvas

2014
13/09 h	H. Petach-Tikva	W	4-0	*Shoker, Mbola, Babayev, Thiam*
21/09 a	M. Tel-Aviv	L	0-2	
27/09 a	M. Petach-Tikva	L	2-3	*Nwakaeme, Thiam (p)*
18/10 h	H. Beer Sheva	D	1-1	*Nwakaeme*
25/10 a	M. Haifa	W	2-0	*Kangwa, Nwakaeme*
29/10 h	H. Akko	L	0-2	
01/11 h	Ashdod	W	2-1	*Kangwa 2*
09/11 h	H. Haifa	L	0-1	
22/11 a	M. Netanya	L	0-1	
29/11 h	H. Kiryat Shmona	D	0-0	
02/12 a	H. Haifa	L	0-1	
06/12 h	Bnei Sakhnin	D	1-1	*Thiam*
15/12 a	Beitar	D	0-0	
20/12 a	H. Petach-Tikva	D	0-0	
28/12 h	M. Tel-Aviv	L	0-2	

2015
03/01 h	M. Petach-Tikva	D	0-0	
10/01 a	H. Beer Sheva	W	1-0	*Thiam*
18/01 h	M. Haifa	W	1-0	*Thiam*
24/01 h	H. Akko	W	2-0	*Nwakaeme, Lipka*
02/02 h	Ashdod	W	2-0	*Thiam, Vahaba*
07/02 a	H. Tel-Aviv	L	1-2	*Gozlan*
14/02 h	M. Netanya	W	2-1	*Shoker, Nwakaeme*
21/02 a	H. Kiryat Shmona	D	1-1	*Gozlan*
28/02 h	H. Haifa	W	2-0	*Abutbul, Gozlan*
07/03 a	Bnei Sakhnin	L	0-2	
14/03 h	Beitar	L	0-2	
21/03 h	Ashdod	W	4-0	*Nwakaeme 2, Kangwa, Gozlan*
11/04 h	M. Netanya	L	1-2	*Thiam*
18/04 a	Bnei Sakhnin	D	1-1	*Vahaba*
25/04 h	H. Tel-Aviv	D	2-2	*Gozlan, Babayev*
02/05 h	H. Akko	L	0-2	
09/05 h	H. Haifa	L	1-2	*Babayev*
16/05 h	H. Petach-Tikva	L	2-4	*Gozlan 2*

No	Name	Nat	DoB	Pos	Aps	(s)	Gls
28	Moshe Abutbul		11/08/84	D	4	(4)	1
7	Eli Babayev		01/11/90	A	19	(7)	3
9	Sahar Benbenisti		26/11/91	M	18	(8)	
19	Ben Binyamin		17/12/85	M	31		
21	Gil Blumstein		21/05/90	M		(2)	
28	Raz Cohen		10/03/90	A		(4)	
14	Sagi Dror		07/08/95	A		(7)	
27	Ori Or Eiloz		12/01/96	M		(2)	
77	Yoav Gerafi		29/08/93	G	1	(1)	
33	Omri Glazer		11/03/96	G	1		
15	Shoval Gozlan		25/04/94	A	14	(1)	7
11	Evans Kangwa	ZAM	09/10/92	A	12	(11)	4
26	Yaniv Lavie		09/09/77	D	30		
25	Yogev Lerman		20/10/91	D	20	(3)	
1	Daniel Lifshitz		24/04/88	G	26		
24	Guy Lipka		03/04/91	D	24	(3)	1
23	Emmanuel Mbola	ZAM	10/05/93	D	26		1
27	Adi Nimni		27/08/91	D	15	(1)	
10	Anthony Nwakaeme	NGA	21/03/89	A	25		7
26	Eden Oleery		18/03/96	D		(1)	
55	Pedro Sass	BRA	15/09/90	A	13	(1)	
17	Eran Rozenbaum		26/08/92	M	2	(9)	
4	Yakir Shina		25/09/85	D	11		
8	Snir Shoker		08/05/89	A	18	(12)	2
20	Loai Taha		26/11/89	D	9		
18	Mamadou Thiam	SEN	22/10/92	A	26	(5)	7
16	Ben Vahaba		27/03/92	D	12	(4)	2
12	Bamidele Yampolski		27/08/88	A	1	(10)	
22	Arik Yanko		21/12/91	G	5		

Hapoel Tel-Aviv FC

1927 • Bloomfield (14,413) • hapoelta-fc.co.il
Major honours
Israeli League (13) 1934, 1935, 1938, 1940, 1944, 1957, 1966, 1969, 1981, 1986, 1988, 2000, 2010; Israeli Cup (15) 1928 (shared), 1934, 1937, 1938, 1939, 1961, 1972, 1983, 1999, 2000, 2006, 2007, 2010, 2011, 2012
Coach: Asi Domb;
(30/01/15) Eli Cohen

2014
13/09 h	M. Netanya	W	1-0	*og (Giurgiu)*
20/09 h	H. Kiryat Shmona	L	0-3	
27/09 h	H. Haifa	W	3-0	*Vermouth, Gozlan, Lucas Sasha*
18/10 a	Bnei Sakhnin	D	1-1	*og (Abu Salah)*
27/10 h	Beitar	D	0-0	
30/10 a	H. Petach-Tikva	W	1-0	*Yehezkel*
03/11 h	M. Tel-Aviv	D	0-0	*(w/o; original match abandoned after 44 mins at 1-1 Moshe Ohayon)*
09/11 a	H. Ra'anana	W	1-0	*Gozlan*
22/11 h	H. Beer Sheva	W	3-2	*Ikande, Abutbul, Vermouth (p)*
30/11 a	M. Haifa	L	1-3	*Vermouth (p)*
03/12 h	H. Akko	L	1-3	*Moshe Ohayon*
07/12 a	Ashdod	L	1-3	*Gozlan*
13/12 h	M. Petach-Tikva	L	1-2	*Lucas Sasha*
20/12 a	M. Netanya	W	2-0	*Zaguri, Azulay*
29/12 h	H. Kiryat Shmona	L	0-1	

2015
03/01 a	H. Haifa	D	1-1	*Azulay*
10/01 h	Bnei Sakhnin	D	1-1	*Safuri*
19/01 a	Beitar	D	1-1	*Safuri*
24/01 h	H. Petach-Tikva	D	0-0	
02/02 a	M. Tel-Aviv	L	0-2	
07/02 h	H. Ra'anana	W	2-1	*og (Vahaba), Matan Ohayon*
14/02 a	H. Beer Sheva	L	0-1	
23/02 h	M. Haifa	D	2-2	*Azulay, Reichert*
28/02 a	H. Akko	L	0-1	
07/03 h	Ashdod	W	3-1	*og (Lenkebe), Yehezkel, Biton*
14/03 a	M. Petach-Tikva	L	1-2	*Lucas Sasha (p)*
21/03 h	H. Akko	W	2-0	*Biton, Azulay*
04/11 a	H. Haifa	W	1-0	*Lazmi*
18/04 h	H. Petach-Tikva	L	1-2	*Reichert*
25/04 a	H. Ra'anana	D	2-2	*Abutbul, Izogbu*
02/05 h	M. Netanya	W	2-1	*Azulay, Falach*
09/05 a	Bnei Sakhnin	L	0-2	
16/05 h	Ashdod	W	1-0	*Abutbul (p)*

No	Name	Nat	DoB	Pos	Aps	(s)	Gls
23	Mohammed Abu El Hija		11/01/95	D	16	(1)	
15	Philipe Abu-Mana		16/05/91	M	2	(3)	
18	Shay Abutbul		16/01/83	M	26	(1)	3
22	Tom Almadon		30/11/84	G	12	(2)	
13	Dani Amos		02/02/87	G	13		
13	Shlomi Azulay		18/10/89	A	15	(12)	5
28	Amido Baldé	POR	16/05/91	A	5	(4)	
3	Francis Benjamin	NGA	02/01/93	D	2	(1)	
25	Dudu Biton		01/03/88	A	12		2
25	Avrahm Chekul		20/01/92	D	10	(3)	
4	Jürgen Colin	NED	20/01/81	D	21	(1)	
30	Apoula Edima Édel	ARM	17/06/86	G	8		
5	Sari Falach		22/11/91	D	26		1
3	Sean Goldberg		13/06/95	D	7	(2)	
24	Shoval Gozlan		25/04/94	A	16		3
19	Gay Hadida		23/07/95	M		(2)	
19	Harmony Ikande	NGA	17/09/90	M	12		1
23	Abonima Izogbu	NGA	27/11/94	D	6		1
77	Obeida Khattab		19/07/92	A		(1)	
17	Matan Lazmi		17/04/94	A	1	(10)	1
30	Lior Levi		26/10/87	D	22		
10	Lucas Sasha	BRA	01/03/90	M	25		3
7	Shon Malka		27/09/93	M	3	(7)	
24	Matan Ohayon		25/02/86	D	14		1
26	Moshe Ohayon		24/05/83	A	11	(11)	2
9	Ben Reichert		04/03/94	M	10		2
21	Ramzi Safuri		21/10/93	A	14	(14)	2
9	Eden Shrem		09/03/93	A		(6)	
14	Gil Vermouth		05/08/85	M	18		3
6	Sagiv Yehezkel		21/03/95	A	10	(6)	2
8	Israel Zaguri		29/01/90	M	26	(5)	1

Maccabi Haifa FC

1913 • Sammy Ofer (30,974) •
maccabi-haifafc.walla.co.il

Major honours
*Israeli League (12) 1984, 1985, 1989, 1991, 1994,
2001, 2002, 2004, 2005, 2006, 2009, 2011; Israeli
Cup (5) 1962, 1991, 1993, 1995, 1998*

**Coach: Aleksandar Stanojević (SRB);
(28/12/14) Marko Balbul**

2014

15/09 h	Bnei Sakhnin	W	4-2	Ezra, Rayo 2, Abuhazira
22/09 a	Beitar	L	0-1	
28/09 h	H. Petach-Tikva	W	3-1	Ezra, Turgeman, Amasha
20/10 a	M. Tel-Aviv	L	1-3	Rayo (p)
25/10 h	H. Ra'anana	L	0-2	
28/10 a	H. Beer Sheva	L	0-2	
01/11 a	M. Petach-Tikva	L	0-1	
08/11 h	H. Akko	W	1-0	Abuhazira
22/11 a	Ashdod	L	0-1	
30/11 h	H. Tel-Aviv	W	3-1	Ezra, Amasha, Vered
03/12 a	M. Netanya	W	4-0	Amasha 3, Vered
06/12 h	H. Kiryat Shmona	L	1-3	Vered
14/12 a	H. Haifa	W	4-0	Benayoun, Vered, Míchel, Abuhazira
20/12 a	Bnei Sakhnin	D	1-1	Cocalić
27/12 h	Beitar	L	1-3	Turgeman

2015

04/01 h	H. Petach-Tikva	D	2-2	Vered, Ezra
11/01 h	M. Tel-Aviv	L	0-1	
18/01 a	H. Ra'anana	L	0-1	
24/01 h	H. Beer Sheva	W	1-0	Rayo (p)
31/01 h	M. Petach-Tikva	L	0-1	
07/02 a	H. Akko	D	0-0	
14/02 h	Ashdod	W	5-0	Shechter, Ezra 2, Kamara, Atar
23/02 a	H. Tel-Aviv	D	2-2	Atar 2
02/03 h	M. Netanya	W	2-1	Atar, Benayoun
08/03 a	H. Kiryat Shmona	W	1-0	Benayoun
14/03 h	H. Haifa	W	2-0	Tawatha, Vered
22/03 a	M. Tel-Aviv	L	1-2	Atar
06/04 h	Beitar	W	1-0	Benayoun
12/04 a	H. Beer Sheva	D	1-1	Amasha
20/04 h	M. Petach-Tikva	D	0-0	
27/04 a	H. Kiryat Shmona	L	0-1	
04/05 h	M. Tel-Aviv	D	1-1	Rayo
10/05 a	Beitar	D	1-1	Amasha
16/05 h	H. Beer Sheva	W	4-0	Ezra 2, Benayoun, Turgeman
25/05 a	M. Petach-Tikva	L	0-1	
30/05 h	H. Kiryat Shmona	W	4-1	Keinan, Atar, Rayo (p), Shechter (p)

No	Name	Nat	DoB	Pos	Aps	(s)	Gls
5	Abraham Paz	ESP	29/07/88	M	13		
19	Shimon Abuhazira		10/10/86	A	7	(8)	3
14	Viam Amasha		08/08/85	A	16	(10)	7
16	Eliran Atar		17/02/87	A	12	(3)	6
15	Yossi Benayoun		05/05/80	A	24	(2)	5
25	Edin Cocalić	BIH	05/12/87	D	14		1
12	Orel Dgani		08/01/89	D	33		
8	Hen Ezra		19/01/89	M	32	(4)	8
30	Elad Gabai		15/11/85	D	12	(1)	
7	Gustavo Boccoli	BRA	16/02/78	M	10	(2)	
9	Mohammadou Idrissou	CMR	08/03/80	A	5		
23	Ataa Jaber		03/10/94	M	10	(3)	
26	Mohamed Kalebat		15/06/90	A	3	(4)	
4	Mohammed Kamara	SLE	16/11/87	M	16		1
21	Dekel Keinan		15/09/84	D	14		1
44	Ohad Levite		17/02/86	G	1		
27	Eyal Meshumar		10/08/83	D	18	(1)	
24	Míchel	ESP	08/11/85	M	16	(9)	1
32	Kobi Moyal		12/06/87	M	5	(3)	
4	Mattan Ohayon		25/02/86	D	4	(5)	
10	Rayo	ESP	21/06/86	M	17	(10)	6
18	Samuel Scheimann		03/11/87	D	6	(3)	
9	Itay Shechter		22/02/87	A	10	(4)	2
38	Vladimir Stojković	SRB	28/07/83	G	35		
13	Taleb Tawatha		21/06/92	D	30		1
17	Alon Turgeman		09/06/91	A	11	(12)	3
11	Idan Vered		25/05/89	M	8	(20)	6
28	Shon Weissman		14/02/96	A		(2)	
26	Avihai Yadin		26/10/86	M	14	(1)	

Maccabi Netanya FC

1934 • Municipal (13,800) • fcmn.co.il

Major honours
*Israeli League (5) 1971, 1974, 1978, 1980, 1983;
Israeli Cup (1) 1978*

**Coach: Yossi Mizrahi;
(14/01/15) Ronny Levi**

2014

13/09 a	H. Tel-Aviv	L	0-1	
20/09 h	M. Petach-Tikva	D	4-4	og (Dimov), E Levi (p), Ben Shoshan, Kayode
27/09 h	H. Kiryat Shmona	L	1-2	Tchalisher
18/10 a	H. Haifa	L	2-3	og (Kijanskas), S Harush
25/10 h	Bnei Sakhnin	W	2-1	Sîrghi, Shriki
30/10 a	Beitar	D	1-1	Kayode
02/11 h	H. Petach-Tikva	W	3-1	E Levi (p), Kayode 2
09/11 a	M. Tel-Aviv	L	1-3	Kayode
22/11 h	H. Ra'anana	W	1-0	S Harush
29/11 a	H. Beer Sheva	L	0-4	
03/12 a	M. Haifa	L	0-4	
06/12 a	H. Akko	W	2-1	Sîrghi, E Levi
13/12 h	Ashdod	D	0-0	
20/12 h	H. Tel-Aviv	L	0-2	
27/12 a	M. Petach-Tikva	W	1-0	Saba

2015

03/01 h	H. Kiryat Shmona	L	1-3	Hassan
10/01 h	H. Haifa	L	0-2	
19/01 h	Bnei Sakhnin	W	2-0	E Levi, Kayode
26/01 h	Beitar	W	2-0	Roll, E Levi
31/01 A	H. Petach-Tikva	D	1-1	Barouch
08/02 h	M. Tel-Aviv	D	3-3	Kayode 2, Saba
14/02 a	H. Ra'anana	L	1-2	E Levi (p)
21/02 h	H. Beer Sheva	W	4-2	Kayode 2, E Levi (p), Romário
02/03 a	M. Haifa	L	1-2	E Levi
07/03 h	H. Akko	D	1-1	E Levi (p)
14/03 a	Ashdod	W	3-2	Saba, Shitrit, Abu Abaid
21/03 h	H. Petach-Tikva	W	3-1	Barouch, Saba, Giurgiu
11/04 a	H. Ra'anana	W	2-1	Peretz, Kayode
18/04 h	Ashdod	D	0-0	
25/04 h	Bnei Sakhnin	L	2-3	E Levi (p), Kayode
02/05 a	H. Tel-Aviv	L	1-2	Kayode
11/05 h	H. Haifa	L	1-2	E Levi (p)
16/05 a	H. Haifa	D	0-0	

No	Name	Nat	DoB	Pos	Aps	(s)	Gls
11	Nir Abergil		12/09/90	A		(6)	
18	Eyad Abu Abaid		31/12/94	D	28		1
15	Or Barouch		29/11/91	A	9	(16)	2
7	Amit Ben Shoshan		23/05/85	A	13	(7)	1
11	Anes Dabour		29/04/91	D	3	(2)	
13	Snir Dori		04/12/87	G	2		
5	Oded Gavish		23/06/89	D	2	(3)	
14	Josef Genda		10/03/97	M		(1)	
29	Gabriel Giurgiu	ROU	03/09/82	M	24	(2)	1
24	Raul Gorshumov		13/08/94	M	1	(1)	
1	Ariel Harush		20/02/87	G	31		
16	Shimon Harush		20/02/87	D	20		2
12	Yarin Hassan		22/03/94	D	18		1
21	Viki Kahlon		15/01/93	D	4	(3)	
8	Olarenwaju Kayode	NGA	08/05/93	A	30	(1)	13
23	Omri Kende		06/07/86	D	1	(2)	
99	Eran Levi		04/08/85	M	31		11
1	Ido Levi		31/07/90	D	23		
7	Amer Masarwa		26/03/95	D	1		
14	Nevo Mizrahi		26/07/87	A		(9)	
25	Omer Peretz		26/01/86	A	13	(4)	1
9	Ran Roll		17/11/87	A	21	(3)	1
52	Romário	BRA	16/01/89	M	27		1
10	Dia Saba		18/11/92	M	13	(16)	4
26	Uri Shitrit		21/01/86	D	12	(2)	1
14	Idan Shriki		30/11/81	A	3	(7)	1
3	Cristian Sîrghi	ROU	23/11/86	D	19		2
19	Omer Tchalisher		22/01/93	M	14	(6)	1

Maccabi Petach-Tikva FC

1912 • HaMoshava (11,500) • m-pt.co.il

Major honours
Israeli Cup (2) 1935, 1952

Coach: Ran Ben Shimon

2014

14/09 h	M. Tel-Aviv	L	0-3	
20/09 a	M. Netanya	D	4-4	Jakobovich, Ben Dayan, Melamed, Peretz
27/09 h	H. Ra'anana	W	3-2	Melamed, Lugasi, Hazurov
18/10 a	H. Kiryat Shmona	L	0-3	
25/10 h	H. Beer Sheva	L	0-4	
28/10 a	H. Haifa	W	1-0	Gerzicich
01/11 h	M. Haifa	W	1-0	Mununga
11/11 a	Bnei Sakhnin	D	1-1	Goldenberg
22/11 h	H. Akko	D	0-0	
01/12 a	Beitar	W	3-2	Mununga 2, Peretz
04/12 h	Ashdod	D	1-1	Dimov
08/12 h	H. Petach-Tikva	L	1-2	Ben Dayan
13/12 a	H. Tel-Aviv	W	2-1	Kanuk, Peretz
21/12 a	M. Tel-Aviv	L	0-3	
27/12 h	M. Netanya	L	0-1	

2015

03/01 a	H. Ra'anana	D	0-0	
10/01 h	H. Kiryat Shmona	W	3-0	Shemesh, Paser, Kabaha
17/01 a	H. Beer Sheva	L	0-1	
24/01 h	H. Haifa	D	0-0	
31/01 a	M. Haifa	W	1-0	Dimov
07/02 h	Bnei Sakhnin	W	2-0	Shemesh, Goldenberg
14/02 a	H. Akko	W	2-0	Shemesh, Peretz
22/02 h	Beitar	D	1-1	Mununga
28/02 a	Ashdod	D	0-0	
07/03 h	H. Petach-Tikva	D	0-0	
14/03 h	H. Tel-Aviv	W	2-1	Melamed, Kanuk
21/03 a	H. Beer Sheva	L	0-3	
06/04 h	H. Kiryat Shmona	L	0-1	
12/04 a	Beitar	D	0-0	
20/04 h	M. Haifa	D	0-0	
25/04 h	M. Tel-Aviv	D	1-1	Dayan (p)
03/05 h	H. Beer Sheva	L	1-2	Melamed
09/05 a	H. Kiryat Shmona	L	0-2	
18/05 h	Beitar	L	1-2	Kabaha
25/05 h	M. Haifa	W	1-0	Danino
01/06 a	M. Tel-Aviv	W	2-0	Kanuk, Rotman

No	Name	Nat	DoB	Pos	Aps	(s)	Gls
23	Hassan Abu Zeid		04/02/91	M	1		
21	Lior Bartkovski		27/01/91	A	1		
19	Dedi Ben Dayan		27/11/78	D	17	(2)	2
99	Ben Ben Yair		23/12/92	A	3	(3)	
3	Omer Danino		17/02/95	D	27	(1)	1
9	Roei Dayan		19/09/84	A	10	(8)	1
28	Daniel Dimov	BUL	21/01/89	M	28		2
5	Tomer Elbaz		03/07/89	D	4	(2)	
18	Dor Elo		26/09/93	D	22	(5)	
7	Nicolás Falczuk	ARG	16/11/86	A	2	(2)	
31	Bryan Gerzicich	USA	30/04/81	M	30		1
22	Itzhak Gigi		01/12/88	G	14		
7	Hagai Goldenberg		15/09/90	D	28	(3)	2
24	Kostadin Hazurov	BUL	05/08/85	A	9	(4)	1
29	Ivan Herceg	CRO	10/02/90	D	26	(1)	
23	Mor Hozez		06/02/95	M		(1)	
16	Yuval Jakobovich		09/11/92	M	23	(3)	1
8	Marwan Kabaha		23/02/91	M	24	(7)	2
10	Gidi Kanuk		11/02/93	M	6	(15)	3
23	Moshe Lugasi		04/02/91	M	6	(10)	1
20	Guy Melamed		21/12/92	A	23	(4)	4
39	Joachim Mununga	BEL	30/06/88	M	24	(3)	4
1	Itamar Nitzan		23/06/87	G	22		
99	Almog Ohayon		05/08/94	M		(1)	
11	Naor Paser		18/10/85	D	20	(3)	1
14	Oz Peretz		19/04/94	A	7	(21)	4
77	Liran Rotman		07/06/96	M		(1)	1
70	Idan Shemesh		06/08/90	A	17	(4)	3
24	David Solari	ARG	21/03/86	M	2	(4)	

Maccabi Tel-Aviv FC

1906 • Bloomfield (14,413) • maccabi-tlv.co.il

Major honours
Israeli League (21) 1936, 1937, 1942, 1947, 1950, 1952, 1954, 1956, 1958, 1968, 1970, 1972, 1977, 1979, 1992, 1995, 1996, 2003, 2013, 2014, 2015; Israeli Cup (23) 1929, 1930, 1933, 1941, 1946, 1947, 1954, 1955, 1958, 1959, 1964, 1965, 1967, 1970, 1977, 1987, 1988, 1994, 1996, 2001, 2002, 2005, 2015

**Coach: Óscar García (ESP);
(26/08/14) Pako Ayestarán (ESP)**

2014

14/09	a	M. Petach-Tikva	W	3-0	Radi, Zahavi, Prica
21/09	h	H. Ra'anana	W	2-0	Ben Haim, Zahavi
29/09	a	H. Beer Sheva	L	2-3	Zahavi (p), Ben Haim
20/10	h	M. Haifa	W	3-1	og (Tawatha), Zahavi, Ben Basat
26/10	a	H. Akko	W	4-1	Zahavi 2 (1p), Ben Harush, Badash
29/10	h	Ashdod	W	5-2	Zahavi 2, Ben Harush, Igiebor, Ben Haim
03/11	a	H. Tel-Aviv	D	0-0	(w/o; original match abandoned after 44 mins at 1-1 Zahavi (p))
09/11	h	M. Netanya	W	3-1	Prica 2, Tibi
24/11	a	H. Kiryat Shmona	L	1-2	Zahavi (p)
29/11	h	H. Haifa	W	3-0	Zahavi 2, Ben Basat
03/12	a	Bnei Sakhnin	W	3-1	Zahavi, Ben Basat, Badash
08/12	h	Beitar	D	1-1	Zahavi
13/12	a	H. Petach-Tikva	W	3-1	Radi, Zahavi 2 (1p)
21/12	h	M. Petach-Tikva	W	3-0	Zahavi, Ben Haim 2
28/12	h	H. Ra'anana	W	2-0	Ben Basat, Carlos García

2015

05/01	h	H. Beer Sheva	D	0-0	
11/01	h	M. Haifa	W	1-0	Zahavi (p)
17/01	h	H. Akko	W	3-0	Zahavi, Ben Haim, Ben Basat (p)
24/01	a	Ashdod	W	1-0	Mitrović
02/02	h	H. Tel-Aviv	W	2-0	Radi, Mitrović
08/02	a	M. Netanya	D	3-3	Micha, Ben Basat, Zahavi
16/02	h	H. Kiryat Shmona	D	1-1	Badash
21/02	a	H. Haifa	L	0-2	
28/02	h	Bnei Sakhnin	W	2-0	Zahavi, Micha
09/03	a	Beitar	L	0-1	
16/03	h	H. Petach-Tikva	W	2-0	Zahavi, Micha
22/03	h	M. Haifa	W	2-1	Igiebor, Zahavi
06/04	h	H. Beer Sheva	W	3-1	Zahavi 2, Ben Haim
13/04	a	H. Kiryat Shmona	D	0-0	
19/04	h	Beitar	W	4-1	Micha 2, Prica, Zahavi
25/04	a	M. Petach-Tikva	D	1-1	Zahavi (p)
04/05	a	M. Haifa	D	1-1	Zahavi
11/05	a	H. Beer Sheva	D	1-1	Igiebor
17/05	h	H. Kiryat Shmona	W	2-1	Prica, Radi
25/05	a	Beitar	L	0-3	
01/06	h	M. Petach-Tikva	L	0-2	

No	Name	Nat	DoB	Pos	Aps	(s)	Gls
6	Gal Alberman		17/04/83	M	30	(2)	
23	Barak Badash		30/08/82	A	5	(11)	3
99	Eden Ben Basat		08/09/86	A	14	(10)	6
11	Tal Ben Haim		05/08/89	A	22	(8)	7
20	Omri Ben Harush		07/03/90	D	28		2
31	Carlos García	ESP	29/04/84	D	24	(1)	1
17	Dan Einbinder		16/02/89	M	6	(5)	
28	Sean Goldberg		13/06/95	D		(1)	
40	Emmanuel Nosa Igiebor	NGA	09/11/90	M	26	(3)	3
10	Barak Itzhaki		25/09/84	A	1	(6)	
25	Juan Pablo	ESP	02/09/78	G	28		
1	Barak Levi		07/01/93	G	8	(1)	
91	Moshe Lugasi		04/02/91	M	1		
30	Gael Margoulis		03/04/94	A	3	(1)	
15	Dor Micha		02/03/92	M	26	(7)	5
24	Nikola Mitrović	SRB	02/01/87	M	30	(4)	2
42	Dor Peretz		17/05/95	M	14	(5)	
22	Rade Prica	SWE	30/06/80	A	6	(11)	5
9	Maharan Radi		01/07/82	M	13	(11)	4
16	Ben Reichert		04/03/94	M		(5)	
3	Yuval Shpungin		30/04/87	D	2	(1)	
18	Eitan Tibi		16/11/87	D	32		1
28	Gil Vermouth		05/08/85	M	1	(2)	
21	Sheran Yeini		08/12/86	D	32	(1)	
7	Eran Zahavi		25/07/87	M	33	(1)	28
14	Yoav Ziv		16/03/81	D	12	(3)	

Top goalscorers

28	Eran Zahavi (M. Tel-Aviv)
16	Muhammad Ghadir (Bnei Sakhnin)
13	Maor Buzaglo (H. Beer Sheva)
	Olarenwaju Kayode (M. Netanya)
12	Roi Kehat (H. Kiryat Shmona)
11	Hamdi Salihi (H. Akko/H. Haifa)
	Shlomi Arbeitman (H. Beer Sheva)
	Rodgers Kola (H. Kiryat Shmona)
	Eran Levi (M. Netanya)
10	Dovev Gabay (H. Beer Sheva)
	Maaran Al Lala (H. Haifa)
	Shoval Gozlan (H. Tel-Aviv/H. Ra'anana)

Promoted clubs

Bnei Yehuda Tel-Aviv FC

1936 • Bloomfield (14,413) • bneiyehuda.com

Major honours
Israeli League (1) 1990; Israeli Cup (2) 1968, 1981

Coach: Yossi Abuksis

Hapoel Kfar Saba FC

1928 • Levita (5,800) • hapoel-kfs.org.il

Major honours
Israeli League (1) 1982; Israeli Cup (3) 1975, 1980, 1990

Coach: Felix Naim

Second level final table 2014/15

	Pld	W	D	L	F	A	Pts
1 Bnei Yehuda Tel-Aviv FC	37	21	13	3	69	26	76
2 Hapoel Kfar Saba FC	37	21	10	6	61	28	73
3 Hapoel Bnei Lod FC	37	20	11	6	56	32	71
4 Hapoel Afula FC	37	15	12	10	56	42	57
5 Maccabi Kiryat Gat FC	37	13	10	14	36	36	49
6 Hapoel Ramat Gan FC	37	11	14	12	39	47	47
7 Maccabi Ahi Nazareth FC	37	11	12	14	54	67	45
8 Maccabi Yavne FC	37	11	12	14	47	62	45
9 Hapoel Jerusalem FC	37	12	14	11	47	47	50
10 Hapoel Ironi Rishon-LeZion FC	37	13	9	15	51	50	48
11 Hapoel Ironi Nir Ramat HaSharon FC	37	12	12	13	39	40	48
12 Beitar Tel-Aviv Ramla FC	37	12	11	14	44	53	47
13 Maccabi Herzliya FC	37	11	11	15	42	44	44
14 Hapoel Nazareth Illit FC	37	9	12	16	41	54	39
15 Ironi Tiberias FC	37	9	10	18	38	50	37
16 Hakoah Maccabi Amidar Ramat Gan FC	37	5	7	25	19	59	22

NB League splits into top and bottom halves after 30 games, after which the clubs play exclusively against teams in their group.

DOMESTIC CUP

G'Viaa Hamedina (State Cup) 2014/15

THIRD ROUND

(13/01/15)
Bnei Eilat 1-2 H. Kfar-Saba
H. Akko 0-2 H. Kiryat Shmona
H. Giv'at Olga 1-2 M. Petach-Tikva
H. Haifa 0-0 Ashdod (aet; 2-4 on pens)
H. Marmorek 0-3 H. Afula
H. Petach-Tikva 2-1 H. Bnei Lod
H. Ra'anana 2-1 Bnei Yehuda
M. Ahi Nazareth 3-1 M. Netanya
M. Herzliya 0-1 H. Beer Sheva
M. Shichon H'amizrah 1-0 H. Migdal H'aemek
Moadon Caduregel Holon Yaniv 1-4 M. Ma'alot Tarshiha

(14/01/15)
Beitar Tel-Aviv Ramla 1-4 M. Tel-Aviv
H. Ramat HaSharon 1-3 M. Haifa (aet)

(15/01/15)
H. Ashkelon 3-3 Beitar Jerusalem (aet; 3-1 on pens)
H. Rishon LeZion 1-2 H. Tel-Aviv
M. Yavne 1-0 Bnei Sakhnin

FOURTH ROUND

(27/01/15)
M. Petach-Tikva 1-0 H. Petach-Tikva
M. Tel-Aviv 1-0 H. Ashkelon

(28/01/15)
H. Ra'anana 0-1 H. Beer Sheva (aet)
H. Tel-Aviv 0-2 H. Kfar-Saba
M. Haifa 1-1 H. Kiryat Shmona (aet; 1-3 on pens)

(29/01/15)
H. Afula 3-0 M. Ma'alot Tarshiha
M. Ahi Nazareth 2-1 Ashdod
M. Yavne 5-1 M. Shichon H'amizrah

QUARTER-FINALS

(10/02/15 & 04/03/15)
H. Afula 0-0 M. Petach-Tikva
M. Petach-Tikva 2-2 H. Afula (Goldenberg 11, Peretz 54; Kehinde 63, Hanuka 66)
(2-2; H. Afula on away goals)

H. Kfar-Saba 1-1 M. Ahi Nazareth (Saimon 45; David Gomes 11)
M. Ahi Nazareth 1-0 H. Kfar-Saba (Exbard 15)
(M. Ahi Nazareth 2-1)

H. Beer Sheva 1-1 M. Yavne (Gabay 64; Gertz 90)
(H. Beer Sheva 4-1)

(25/02/15 & 04/03/15)
H. Kiryat Shmona 1-1 M. Tel-Aviv (Abuhazira 90; Zahavi 44)
M. Tel-Aviv 3-0 H. Kiryat Shmona (Badash 26, Zahavi 29, 68p)
(M. Tel-Aviv 4-1)

SEMI-FINALS

(29/04/15)
H. Afula 0-7 H. Beer Sheva (Gabay 3, 68, 80, Arbeitman 7, 31, Melikson 44, Ilouz 71)
M. Tel-Aviv 3-0 M. Ahi Nazareth (Zahavi 2, Prica 82, Mitrović 89)

FINAL

(20/05/15)
Sammy Offer, Haifa
MACCABI TEL-AVIV FC 6 (Prica 20, 47, 52, Ziv 28, Zahavi 58, Radi 62)
HAPOEL BEER SHEVA FC 2 (Hoban 34, Buzaglo 57)
Referee: Adler
M. TEL-AVIV: Juan Pablo, Shpungin, Ben Harush, Ziv, Alberman, Mitrović, Einbinder, Radi, Zahavi (Itzhaki 87), Micha (Ben Haim 81), Prica (Badash 73)
H. BEER SHEVA: Ejide, Biton, William, Pajović (Gordana 35), Davidzada, Hoban, Ogu, Buzaglo, Gabay, Barda (Melikson 53), Arbeitman (Naser 66)
Red card: Buzaglo (90)

ITALY

Federazione Italiana Giuoco Calcio (FIGC)

Address Via Gregorio Allegri 14
CP 2450
IT-00198 Roma
Tel +39 0684 912 553
Fax +39 0625 496 455
E-mail international@figc.it
Website figc.it

President Carlo Tavecchio
General secretary Michele Uva
Media officer Antonello Valentini
Year of formation 1898

SERIE A CLUBS

  1 Atalanta BC

  2 Cagliari Calcio

  3 AC Cesena

 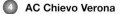 **4** AC Chievo Verona

  5 Empoli FC

 6 ACF Fiorentina

 7 Genoa CFC

 8 FC Internazionale Milano

 9 Juventus

 10 SS Lazio

 11 AC Milan

 12 SSC Napoli

  13 US Città di Palermo

 14 Parma FC

 15 AS Roma

 16 UC Sampdoria

 17 US Sassuolo Calcio

 18 Torino FC

 19 Udinese Calcio

20 Hellas Verona FC

PROMOTED CLUBS

 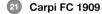 **21** Carpi FC 1909

 22 Frosinone Calcio

 23 Bologna FC

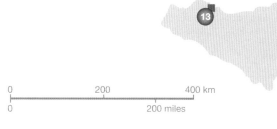

KEY:
● – UEFA Champions League
● – UEFA Europa League
● – Promoted
● – Relegated

Dominant Juventus a class apart

After three league titles in three seasons under Antonio Conte, Juventus maintained their Serie A stranglehold under new coach Massimiliano Allegri, claiming the scudetto for the 31st time with another comprehensive triumph.

The Bianconeri also won the Coppa Italia for the first time in 20 years to complete their third domestic double. Dreams of a first treble, however, turned to dust with defeat by FC Barcelona in the UEFA Champions League final. Capital city clubs AS Roma and SS Lazio finished second and third, respectively, in Serie A, but it was a woeful season for the two fallen giants from Milan.

| New boss Allegri leads Bianconeri to domestic double | Turin giants also reach UEFA Champions League final | Milan and Inter fail to qualify for Europe |

Domestic league

Conte's resignation in July 2014 came as quite a shock, but within 24 hours Juventus had replaced him with Allegri. As a former coach of traditional rivals AC Milan, his appointment drew dissent from some Juve diehards, but the 47-year-old, who had won the scudetto in his first season with the Rossoneri (2010/11), was to win over the sceptics by doing even better with the Bianconeri, leading Juventus to the brink of their greatest season of all time.

Allegri inherited a powerful squad, to which only a couple of significant newcomers, left-back Patrice Evra and striker Álvaro Morata, were added. The transition from one coaching regime to another was barely detectable as Juve won their first five league games without conceding – an unprecedented Serie A feat – then prevailed 3-2 in a stormy top-of-the-table clash with Roma, who had also opened with 15 points, thanks to two hotly-disputed Carlos Tévez penalties and a late winner from defender Leonardo Bonucci.

Roma recovered to keep the defending champions within touching distance during the autumn, but despite a 1-0 defeat at Genoa CFC and a 1-1 draw against UC Sampdoria in the Juventus

Stadium – the first points they had surrendered at home in 25 Serie A fixtures – Juve went into the festive break with a three-point lead. That had increased by the halfway point, and as Roma, hampered by the lack of a regular goalscorer and the extended absence of winger Gervinho at the Africa Cup of Nations, consistently failed to convert draws into victories, the gap at the top began to increase almost with every passing week.

Juve were far from perfect, but they were remarkably consistent. They won at SSC Napoli for the first time in 15 years, avenging their 2013/14 defeat at the Stadio San Paolo with a resounding 3-1 victory, and also completed the double over Milan with another 3-1 win in Turin. Any last doubts about the destination of the scudetto were extinguished when Juve held Roma 1-1 at the Stadio Olimpico – the Giallorossi's sixth successive home draw – to remain nine points clear. Two weeks later, after Rudi Garcia's team had ended that run of one-pointers with a 2-0 home defeat by Sampdoria, the champions were home and dry.

Juve were so far out in front that they could even afford a couple of humiliating defeats – 1-0 away at financially-crippled bottom club Parma FC and 2-1

to Torino FC, their first derby loss in 20 years – and still wrap up proceedings with four games to go. It was away to Sampdoria, on the first weekend of May, that Juventus confirmed the inevitable in a 1-0 win provided by a 32nd-minute strike from Arturo Vidal. A more fitting scorer would probably have been Tévez, who, as in 2013/14, played majestically throughout the campaign, finding the net on 20 occasions. Juve's other area of strength, as ever, was their defence, with 37-year-old goalkeeper Gianluigi Buffon showing no evident signs of wear and tear and fellow Italian internationals Bonucci and Giorgio Chiellini continuing to perform with metronomic consistency in front of him.

As the thoughts of Juventus players and fans turned to other things in the final few weeks, an exciting battle raged for the two remaining UEFA Champions League berths, with group entry going to the Serie A runners-up and a play-off spot to the team finishing third. Roma's spring decline had enabled city rivals Lazio, thanks to a burst of eight successive victories and some fabulous performances from their two midfield stars, Felipe Anderson and Antonio Candreva, to catch and overtake them into second place. But Stefano Pioli's side could not maintain that form, and when Roma beat them 2-1 in round 37

– having come from 2-0 down to draw the first derby, in January, with a double from evergreen skipper Francesco Totti – the Giallorossi's second successive runners-up spot was secure.

Lazio's defeat left them in danger of missing out on UEFA Champions League qualification entirely. Their last fixture was away to Napoli, who, although three points behind, had already beaten Lazio in Rome and would therefore claim the head-to-head advantage with another victory in Naples. It was the classic scenario of the home team needing a win and the away team a draw, and it produced arguably the most exciting match of the Serie A season, with Lazio going 2-0 up, Napoli pulling two goals back through leading marksman Gonzalo Higuaín, but the Argentinian striker missing a penalty to give his team the lead before the visitors struck on the counterattack with two late goals to win 4-2.

While Lazio's victory clinched third place, Napoli's defeat – a disappointing finale to coach Rafael Benítez's two-year tenure – dropped them to fifth, with Vincenzo Montella's ACF Fiorentina finishing fourth for the third season running thanks to a powerful surge which brought them 15 points – and 15 goals – from their last five

matches. Despite that, Montella was sacked and replaced for the 2015/16 campaign by Portuguese coach Paulo Sousa. Taking over from Real Madrid CF-bound Benítez in the Napoli hot seat, meanwhile, was Maurizio Sarri, rewarded for an excellent season with newly-promoted Empoli FC, who defied most pre-season predictions by staying up.

US Città di Palermo, the 2013/14 Serie B champions, were the best of the three new arrivals, the Sicilian club finishing 11th thanks to the potent partnership formed up front by Paulo Dybala and Franco Vázquez. AC Cesena, on the other hand, went straight back down. They would have finished last but for the seven-point penalty imposed on Parma, whose spiralling debts resulted in postponed fixtures, bankruptcy and, at the end of the season, a cessation of their 102-year existence as a professional club.

Cagliari Calcio were also relegated, their decision to appoint as coach a great former player, Gianfranco Zola, proving as ill-fated as that of Milan, who, having replaced one club icon, Clarence Seedorf, with another, Filippo Inzaghi, huffed and puffed their way to a mediocre 10th-place finish. The goals and trickery of free-transfer signing

Jérémy Ménez were virtually the only bright spot of a laboured campaign that would have brought more defeats than victories but for a mini-revival in the final month. That parting salvo could not keep Inzaghi in his job, however, and he was replaced by Siniša Mihajlović, who had just led Sampdoria into seventh place and – because sixth-placed city rivals Genoa failed to receive a European licence – into the UEFA Europa League.

The only European football scheduled for the San Siro in 2015/16 would be the UEFA Champions League final as, like Milan, FC Internazionale Milano failed to qualify, finishing eighth. The decision in November to sack Walter Mazzarri and reappoint Roberto Mancini, a three-time scudetto winner during his first spell, from 2004-08, did not yield the expected dividends. But for the goals of forward Mauro Icardi, who scored as many as his age (22), Inter would almost certainly have finished even lower than Milan. The young Argentinian striker shared the league's top scorer crown with a player 16 years his senior as the remarkable Luca Toni made it 42 goals in two seasons with Hellas Verona FC, becoming Serie A's oldest ever capocannoniere.

History of another kind was made in Serie B as both automatically promoted clubs, Carpi FC 1909 and Frosinone Calcio, reached Italy's top division for the first time. The name that emerged from the post-season play-offs with the third promotion place was more familiar as seven-time champions Bologna FC made it back to Serie A after just one season away. They needed considerable help from a favourable local rule, however, coming through both of their drawn two-legged ties against AS Avellino and Pescara Calcio on the basis of having finished higher than their opponents in the regular season.

Domestic cup

The Coppa Italia has not always enjoyed the same status as other European domestic cup competitions, which may explain why Juventus had gone 20 years without winning it before they overcame Lazio 2-1 in the 2015 final. The victory at the Stadio Olimpico sealed the Bianconeri's first league and cup double since that 1994/95 season, but they were made to work overtime for their victory – literally – by the 2013 winners,

Palermo's Franco Vázquez (bottom) and Paulo Dybala played a major role in keeping the newly-promoted Sicilian club in Serie A

who, after an exchange of goals in the early stages, came close to winning it in the second half when Filip Djordjević's shot struck the inside of both posts before rebounding clear. Juventus took advantage of their good fortune as forgotten man Alessandro Matri, who had returned to Turin on loan from Milan in January, scored the extra-time winner.

Matri had also been on the scoresheet in the second leg of the semi-final, when Juventus beat Fiorentina 3-0 in Florence to turn the tie around after a double from the Viola's in-form on-loan midfielder Mohamed Salah had ended Juventus's 47-match unbeaten home run in all competitions in the first leg. Lazio also relied on excellent away form, winning at Torino, Milan and, in the second leg of the semi-final, Napoli.

Europe

Juventus reached the final of the UEFA Champions League for the first time since 2003, going unbeaten through the knockout phase as they saw off Borussia Dortmund, AS Monaco FC and, in the semi-finals, holders Real Madrid. In Berlin, however, they came up short against Barcelona, going down 3-1 and therefore becoming the first club to lose six European Cup finals. An unhappy ending, however, could not detract from Juve's accomplishment in getting to the final, which, after two defeats in their first three group games,

looked a remote possibility. The goals of Tévez and, in the latter stages, Morata, who scored in both legs against former club Madrid, were crucial – as was the team's superbly drilled defence, cruelly denied the services of the injured Chiellini for the final.

Juventus were Italy's only surviving UEFA Champions League participant after Christmas, with Napoli removed in the play-offs and Roma knocked out at the group stage. Both clubs resurfaced in the UEFA Europa League, where Serie A had a record representation of five teams in the knockout phase. That even extended into the round of 16, with Napoli, Roma, Fiorentina, Inter and Torino all coming through testing ties in the round of 32.

Hopes were understandably high that Italy would provide a first UEFA Europa League finalist, but it did not come to pass. Fiorentina and Napoli emulated Juventus's achievement of the previous season in reaching the semi-finals, but neither could go all the way, the Viola enduring a 5-0 aggregate drubbing from Sevilla FC while Napoli, unexpectedly and perhaps unluckily, lost 2-1 over the two legs against Ukrainian upstarts FC Dnipro Dnipropetrovsk.

National team

Having left Juventus, Conte found new employment as the head coach of Italy, replacing Cesare Prandelli, who had quit

after the Azzurri's FIFA World Cup flop in Brazil. The UEFA EURO 2016 qualifying campaign began well enough, with three wins out of three, but three successive draws followed – two against Croatia and one away to Bulgaria – which left the 2012 runners-up second in the Group H table. Following the 1-1 draw against Croatia in June, played behind closed doors in Split, Italy remained two points behind their opponents, but that deficit was halved when Croatia were subseqently docked a point.

With their most difficult fixtures out of the way, Italy were well positioned to claim an automatic qualifying place. While the team's defence remained as resolute as ever, the lack of a reliable goalscorer, which hurt the Azzurri in Brazil, remained a burning issue.

Conte sought to address it by trying out a number of different options up front, and no fewer than three debutants – Simone Zaza, Graziano Pellè and naturalised Brazilian Éder – all rose to the challenge, each marking his first qualifying appearance with a crucial goal. Winger Candreva also opened his international goalscoring account by finding the net in both games against Croatia, but as the new coach's first season closed with a first defeat, 1-0 in a Geneva friendly against Portugal, the need to strengthen the Azzurri attack in time for the finals in France remained his number one priority.

Graziano Pellè (No17) scores the winning goal on his debut for Italy in a UEFA EURO 2016 qualifier away to Malta

DOMESTIC SEASON AT A GLANCE

Serie A 2014/15 final table

		Pld	Home					Away					Total					Pts
			W	D	L	F	A	W	D	L	F	A	W	D	L	F	A	
1	Juventus	38	16	3	0	45	11	10	6	3	27	13	26	9	3	72	24	87
2	AS Roma	38	10	7	2	31	14	9	6	4	23	17	19	13	6	54	31	70
3	SS Lazio	38	12	1	6	40	18	9	5	5	31	20	21	6	11	71	38	69
4	ACF Fiorentina	38	9	6	4	30	17	9	4	6	31	29	18	10	10	61	46	64
5	SSC Napoli	38	11	5	3	46	28	7	4	8	24	26	18	9	11	70	54	63
6	Genoa CFC	38	9	6	4	33	21	7	5	7	29	26	16	11	11	62	47	59
7	UC Sampdoria	38	7	10	2	23	15	6	7	6	25	27	13	17	8	48	42	56
8	FC Internazionale Milano	38	7	7	5	33	23	7	6	6	26	25	14	13	11	59	48	55
9	Torino FC	38	8	7	4	25	14	6	5	8	23	31	14	12	12	48	45	54
10	AC Milan	38	9	5	5	30	19	4	8	7	26	31	13	13	12	56	50	52
11	US Città di Palermo	38	8	6	5	30	25	4	7	8	23	30	12	13	13	53	55	49
12	US Sassuolo Calcio	38	7	8	4	25	22	5	5	9	24	35	12	13	13	49	57	49
13	Hellas Verona FC	38	7	5	7	27	30	4	8	7	22	35	11	13	14	49	65	46
14	AC Chievo Verona	38	4	9	6	16	19	6	4	9	12	22	10	13	15	28	41	43
15	Empoli FC	38	6	8	5	26	22	2	10	7	20	30	8	18	12	46	52	42
16	Udinese Calcio	38	6	5	8	26	29	4	6	9	17	27	10	11	17	43	56	41
17	Atalanta BC	38	4	7	8	22	33	3	9	7	16	24	7	16	15	38	57	37
18	Cagliari Calcio	38	4	4	11	24	36	4	6	9	24	32	8	10	20	48	68	34
19	AC Cesena	38	3	7	9	19	31	1	5	13	17	42	4	12	22	36	73	24
20	Parma FC	38	5	4	10	19	27	1	4	14	14	48	6	8	24	33	75	19

NB Parma FC – 7 pts deducted.

European qualification 2015/16

Champion/Cup winner: Juventus (group stage)
AS Roma (group stage)
SS Lazio (play-offs)

ACF Fiorentina (group stage)
SSC Napoli (group stage)
UC Sampdoria (third qualifying round)

Top scorer	Mauro Icardi (Internazionale) & Luca Toni (Verona), 22 goals
Relegated clubs	Parma FC, AC Cesena, Cagliari Calcio
Promoted clubs	Carpi FC 1909, Frosinone Calcio, Bologna FC
Cup final	Juventus 2-1 SS Lazio (aet)

Team of the season
(3-4-3)

Coach: Coach: Allegri *(Juventus)*

Buffon *(Juventus)*

De Vrij *(Lazio)* — Glik *(Torino)* — Bonucci *(Juventus)*

Nainggolan *(Roma)* — Pogba *(Juventus)*

Candreva *(Lazio)* — Felipe Anderson *(Lazio)*

Icardi *(Internazionale)* — Toni *(Verona)* — Tévez *(Juventus)*

Player of the season

Carlos Tévez
(Juventus)

Tévez's first season at Juventus, in 2013/14, was pretty special, yet his second was even better. The striker's alertness and accuracy in the penalty area brought him a glut of goals – 29 in all competitions – while his ceaseless endeavour all over the pitch served as an inspiration to those around him and also cemented his standing as a cult hero with the Juve fans. His second season in Turin, however, would also be his last as the appeal of a return to first club CA Boca Juniors lured the 31-year-old back to Argentina.

Newcomer of the season

Daniele Rugani
(Empoli FC)

A prominent member of Empoli's 2013/14 promotion-winning side, Rugani, who was co-owned by Juventus, remained with the Tuscan outfit for the 2014/15 campaign and played with such authority that an end-of-term return to Turin was inevitable. Strong and commanding, the Italian Under-21 international was the only player in the entire league to start and finish all 38 matches. Furthermore, despite being up against some of the world's trickiest attackers, he did not receive a single card – red or yellow.

ITALY

NATIONAL TEAM

International honours
FIFA World Cup (4) 1934, 1938, 1982, 2006
UEFA European Championship (1) 1968

International tournament appearances
FIFA World Cup (18) 1934 (Winners), 1938 (Winners), 1950, 1958, 1962, 1966, 1970 (runners-up), 1974, 1978 (4th), 1982 (Winners), 1986 (2nd round), 1990 (3rd), 1994 (runners-up), 1998 (qtr-finals), 2002 (2nd round), 2006 (Winners), 2010, 2014
UEFA European Championship (8) 1968 (Winners), 1980 (4th), 1988 (semi-finals), 1996, 2000 (runners-up), 2004, 2008 (qtr-finals), 2012 (runners-up)

Top five all-time caps
Gianluigi Buffon (148); Fabio Cannavaro (136); Paolo Maldini (126); **Andrea Pirlo** (115); Dino Zoff (112)

Top five all-time goals
Luigi Riva (35); Giuseppe Meazza (33); Silvio Piola (30); Roberto Baggio & Alessandro Del Piero (27)

Results 2014/15

Date	Opponent		Venue	Result	Scorers
04/09/14	Netherlands	H	Bari	W 2-0	Immobile (3), De Rossi (10p)
09/09/14	Norway (ECQ)	A	Oslo	W 2-0	Zaza (16), Bonucci (62)
10/10/14	Azerbaijan (ECQ)	H	Palermo	W 2-1	Chiellini (44, 82)
13/10/14	Malta (ECQ)	A	Ta' Qali	W 1-0	Pellè (24)
16/11/14	Croatia (ECQ)	H	Milan	D 1-1	Candreva (11)
18/11/14	Albania	H	Genoa	W 1-0	Okaka (82)
28/03/15	Bulgaria (ECQ)	A	Sofia	D 2-2	Y Minev (4og), Éder (84)
31/03/15	England	H	Turin	D 1-1	Pellè (29)
12/06/15	Croatia (ECQ)	A	Split	D 1-1	Candreva (36p)
16/06/15	Portugal	N	Geneva (SUI)	L 0-1	

Appearances 2014/15

Coach: Antonio Conte 31/07/69		Ned	NOR	AZE	MLT	CRO	Alb	BUL	Eng	CRO	Por	Caps	Goals
Salvatore Sirigu	12/01/87 Paris (FRA)	G					G73	G		s46	G	14	-
Andrea Ranocchia	16/02/88 Internazionale	D	D	D		D			D	s80	D	20	-
Leonardo Bonucci	01/05/87 Juventus	D	D	D	D 73*		D82	D	D	D	D	47	3
Davide Astori	07/01/87 Roma	D	D							D		10	1
Matteo Darmian	02/12/89 Torino	M72	M61	M81	D	D		M	M73	D	D	13	-
Claudio Marchisio	19/01/86 Juventus	M63		M	M	M				M		52	4
Daniele De Rossi	24/07/83 Roma	M67	M			M						100	16
Emanuele Giaccherini	05/05/85 Sunderland (ENG)	M	M									21	3
Mattia De Sciglio	20/10/92 Milan	M67	M	M		M				s27	D73	18	-
Ciro Immobile	20/02/90 Dortmund (GER)	A77	A	A	A65	A52	A	s60			A73	12	1
Simone Zaza	25/06/91 Sassuolo	A72	A83	A		A63		A58				5	1
Marco Verratti	05/11/92 Paris (FRA)	s63					M	M	s67			12	1
Marco Parolo	25/01/85 Lazio	s67						M	M	M	s76	11	-
Manuel Pasqual	13/03/82 Fiorentina	s67	s61		M	M28					s73	10	-
Antonio Candreva	28/02/87 Lazio	s72		s81	M	M		M		A	A64	29	2
Mattia Destro	20/03/91 Roma	s72	s83				A65					8	1
Sebastian Giovinco	26/01/87 Juventus	s77		s77	s65		A65					21	-
Gianluigi Buffon	28/01/78 Juventus		G	G	G	G			G	G46		148	-
Alessandro Florenzi	11/03/91 Roma		M87	M77	M59				M60			8	1
Andrea Poli	29/09/89 Milan		s87									5	1
Giorgio Chiellini	14/08/84 Juventus			D	D	D		D	D72			76	6
Andrea Pirlo	19/05/79 Juventus		M73						M	M		115	13
Alberto Aquilani	07/07/84 Fiorentina			s73	s59		M					38	5
Graziano Pellè	15/07/85 Southampton (ENG)				A75	s63			A60	A		4	2
Angelo Ogbonna	23/05/88 Juventus				s75							10	-
Roberto Soriano	08/02/91 Sampdoria					s28		s72	M		M58	4	-
Stephan El Shaarawy	27/10/92 Milan					s52			A80	A68		13	1
Lorenzo De Silvestri	23/05/88 Sampdoria						D		D27			4	-
Emiliano Moretti	11/06/81 Torino						D	s72				2	-
Andrea Bertolacci	11/01/91 Genoa					M70	M72				M76	3	-
Luca Antonelli	11/02/87 Genoa/Milan					M		M77	s73			9	-
Alessio Cerci	23/07/87 Atlético (ESP)					M77						14	-
Alessandro Matri	19/08/84 Genoa/Juventus						s65				s73	7	1
Stefano Okaka	09/08/89 Sampdoria						s65					1	1
Giacomo Bonaventura	22/08/89 Milan						s70					2	-
Mattia Perin	10/11/92 Genoa						s73					1	-
Manolo Gabbiadini	26/11/91 Sampdoria/Napoli						s77	s77			s64	4	-
Francesco Acerbi	10/02/88 Sassuolo						s82					1	-
Andrea Barzagli	08/05/81 Juventus							D				51	-
Éder	15/11/86 Sampdoria							s58	A60			2	1
Mirko Valdifiori	21/04/86 Empoli								M67			1	-
Ignazio Abate	12/11/86 Milan								s60			22	1
Franco Vázquez	22/02/89 Palermo								s60		s58	2	-
Nicola Sansone	10/09/91 Sassuolo										s68	1	-

EUROPE

Juventus

CHAMPIONS LEAGUE

Group A
Match 1 - Malmö FF (SWE)
H 2-0 *Tévez (59, 90)*
Buffon, Chiellini, Cáceres, Pogba, Marchisio, Tévez (Giovinco 90+1), Llorente (Morata 86), Bonucci, Asamoah, Lichtsteiner (Rômulo 90+1), Evra. Coach: Massimiliano Allegri (ITA)
Match 2 - Club Atlético de Madrid (ESP)
A 0-1
Buffon, Chiellini, Cáceres (Pereyra 78), Pogba, Marchisio, Tévez, Llorente, Bonucci, Vidal (Morata 83), Lichtsteiner (Giovinco 90), Evra. Coach: Massimiliano Allegri (ITA)
Match 3 - Olympiacos FC (GRE)
A 0-1
Buffon, Chiellini, Ogbonna (Pereyra 77), Pogba (Giovinco 87), Morata, Tévez, Bonucci, Pirlo (Marchisio 57), Asamoah, Vidal, Lichtsteiner. Coach: Massimiliano Allegri (ITA)
Match 4 - Olympiacos FC (GRE)
H 3-2 *Pirlo (21), Roberto (65og), Pogba (66)*
Buffon, Chiellini, Pogba, Marchisio (Padoin 71), Morata (Llorente 58), Tévez, Bonucci, Pirlo, Asamoah (Pereyra 83), Vidal, Lichtsteiner. Coach: Massimiliano Allegri (ITA)
Match 5 - Malmö FF (SWE)
A 2-0 *Llorente (49), Tévez (88)*
Buffon, Chiellini, Pogba, Marchisio (Pereyra 83), Tévez, Llorente (Morata 72), Bonucci, Padoin, Pirlo, Vidal, Lichtsteiner. Coach: Massimiliano Allegri (ITA)
Match 6 - Club Atlético de Madrid (ESP)
H 0-0
Buffon, Chiellini, Pogba, Tévez, Llorente, Bonucci, Pirlo, Vidal, Lichtsteiner, Evra, Pereyra. Coach: Massimiliano Allegri (ITA)

Round of 16 - Borussia Dortmund (GER)
H 2-1 *Tévez (13), Morata (43)*
Buffon, Chiellini, Pogba, Marchisio, Morata, Tévez (Coman 89), Bonucci, Pirlo (Pereyra 37), Vidal (Padoin 86), Lichtsteiner, Evra. Coach: Massimiliano Allegri (ITA)
A 3-0 *Tévez (3, 79), Morata (5)*
Buffon, Chiellini, Pogba (Barzagli 27), Marchisio, Morata (Matri 78), Tévez (Pepe 81), Bonucci, Vidal, Lichtsteiner, Evra, Pereyra. Coach: Massimiliano Allegri (ITA)

Quarter-finals - AS Monaco FC (FRA)
H 1-0 *Vidal (57p)*
Buffon, Chiellini, Marchisio, Morata (Matri 83), Tévez, Bonucci, Pirlo (Barzagli 74), Vidal, Lichtsteiner, Evra, Pereyra (Sturaro 87). Coach: Massimiliano Allegri (ITA)
A 0-0
Buffon, Chiellini, Marchisio, Morata (Llorente 69), Tévez, Barzagli, Bonucci, Pirlo, Vidal (Pereyra 77), Lichtsteiner, Evra (Padoin 89). Coach: Massimiliano Allegri (ITA)

Semi-finals - Real Madrid CF (ESP)
H 2-1 *Morata (8), Tévez (58p)*
Buffon, Chiellini, Marchisio, Morata (Llorente 78), Tévez (Pereyra 86), Bonucci, Pirlo, Vidal, Lichtsteiner, Sturaro (Barzagli 64), Evra. Coach: Massimiliano Allegri (ITA)
A 1-1 *Morata (57)*
Buffon, Chiellini, Pogba (Pereyra 89), Marchisio, Morata (Llorente 84), Tévez, Bonucci, Pirlo (Barzagli 79), Vidal, Lichtsteiner, Evra. Coach: Massimiliano Allegri (ITA)

Final - FC Barcelona (ESP)
N 1-3 *Morata (55)*
Buffon, Pogba, Marchisio, Morata (Llorente 85), Tévez, Barzagli, Bonucci, Pirlo, Vidal (Pereyra 79), Lichtsteiner, Evra (Coman 89). Coach: Massimiliano Allegri (ITA)

AS Roma

CHAMPIONS LEAGUE

Group E
Match 1 - PFC CSKA Moskva (RUS)
H 5-1 *Iturbe (6), Gervinho (10, 31), Maicon (20), Ignashevich (50og)*
De Sanctis, Nainggolan, Iturbe (Florenzi 26), Totti, Maicon, Pjanić, Keita, Astori, Gervinho (Ljajić 71), Torosidis, Manolas (Yanga-Mbiwa 76). Coach: Rudi Garcia (FRA)
Match 2 - Manchester City FC (ENG)
A 1-1 *Totti (23)*
Skorupski, Yanga-Mbiwa, Cole, Nainggolan, Totti (Iturbe 72), Maicon (Torosidis 89), Pjanić, Keita, Florenzi (Holebas 83), Gervinho, Manolas. Coach: Rudi Garcia (FRA)
Match 3 - FC Bayern München (GER)
H 1-7 *Gervinho (66)*
De Sanctis, Yanga-Mbiwa, Cole (Holebas 46), Nainggolan, Iturbe, Totti (Florenzi 46), Pjanić (Ljajić 79), De Rossi, Gervinho, Torosidis, Manolas. Coach: Rudi Garcia (FRA)
Match 4 - FC Bayern München (GER)
A 0-2
Skorupski, Yanga-Mbiwa, Nainggolan, Iturbe (Gervinho 74), De Rossi, Keita, Destro, Florenzi (Pjanić 58), Holebas (Cole 46), Torosidis, Manolas. Coach: Rudi Garcia (FRA)
Match 5 - PFC CSKA Moskva (RUS)
A 1-1 *Totti (43)*
De Sanctis, Nainggolan (Strootman 83), Ljajić (Pjanić 87), Totti, De Rossi, Keita, Astori, Florenzi, Holebas, Gervinho (Iturbe 77), Manolas. Coach: Rudi Garcia (FRA)
Match 6 - Manchester City FC (ENG)
H 0-2
De Sanctis, Yanga-Mbiwa, Nainggolan, Ljajić (Iturbe 67), Totti (Destro 70), Maicon (Florenzi 78), Pjanić, Keita, Holebas, Gervinho, Manolas. Coach: Rudi Garcia (FRA)

EUROPA LEAGUE

Round of 32 - Feyenoord (NED)
H 1-1 *Gervinho (22)*
Skorupski, Yanga-Mbiwa, Nainggolan, Totti (Doumbia 65), Pjanić, De Rossi (Keita 65), Holebas, Gervinho, Torosidis, Manolas, Verde (Florenzi 75). Coach: Rudi Garcia (FRA)
A 2-1 *Ljajić (45+2), Gervinho (60)*
Skorupski, Yanga-Mbiwa, Ljajić (Iturbe 74), Totti (Paredes 80), Pjanić (Nainggolan 74), De Rossi, Keita, Holebas, Gervinho, Torosidis, Manolas. Coach: Rudi Garcia (FRA)

Round of 16 - ACF Fiorentina (ITA)
A 1-1 *Keita (77)*
Skorupski, Yanga-Mbiwa, Nainggolan, Iturbe, Ljajić (Gervinho 75), De Rossi (Pjanić 22), Keita, Florenzi, Holebas, Torosidis, Manolas (Astori 26). Coach: Rudi Garcia (FRA)
H 0-3
Skorupski, Yanga-Mbiwa (Astori 58), Ljajić, Pjanić, De Rossi, Keita (Verde 44), Florenzi, Holebas, Gervinho, Torosidis (Iturbe 27), Manolas. Coach: Rudi Garcia (FRA)
Red card: Ljajić 88

SSC Napoli

CHAMPIONS LEAGUE

Play-offs - Athletic Club (ESP)
H 1-1 *Higuaín (68)*
Rafael Cabral, Britos, Callejón, Jorginho, Higuaín, Maggio, Hamšík (Michu 78), Insigne (Mertens 60), Koulibaly, Albiol, Gargano. Coach: Rafael Benítez (ESP)
A 1-3 *Hamšík (47)*
Rafael Cabral, Callejón, Jorginho, Higuaín, Maggio, Mertens (Zapata 77), Hamšík (Insigne 70), Koulibaly, Ghoulam (Britos 56), Albiol, Gargano. Coach: Rafael Benítez (ESP)

EUROPA LEAGUE

Group I
Match 1 - AC Sparta Praha (CZE)
H 3-1 *Higuaín (23p), Mertens (51, 81)*
Rafael Cabral, Henrique, Britos, Callejón (David López 84), Higuaín (Michu 70), Mertens, Hamšík (Zúñiga 82), Koulibaly, Albiol, Gargano, Inler. Coach: Rafael Benítez (ESP)
Match 2 - ŠK Slovan Bratislava (SVK)
A 2-0 *Hamšík (35), Higuaín (74)*
Rafael Cabral, Britos, De Guzmán (Callejón 63), Maggio, Mertens, Hamšík (Mesto 79), David López, Koulibaly, Ghoulam, Inler, Zapata (Higuaín 73). Coach: Rafael Benítez (ESP)
Match 3 - BSC Young Boys (SUI)
A 0-2
Rafael Cabral, Henrique, De Guzmán (Higuaín 84), Jorginho (Callejón 75), Maggio, Mertens, Michu (Hamšík 62), Ghoulam, Albiol, Inler, Zapata. Coach: Rafael Benítez (ESP)
Match 4 - BSC Young Boys (SUI)
H 3-0 *De Guzmán (45+2, 65, 83)*
Rafael Cabral, Henrique, Britos (Ghoulam 38), De Guzmán, Mertens, Insigne (Callejón 73), Koulibaly, Gargano, Inler, Zapata (Higuaín 79). Coach: Rafael Benítez (ESP)
Match 5 - AC Sparta Praha (CZE)
A 0-0
Rafael Cabral, Britos, Callejón, Jorginho (Ghoulam 77), Higuaín (Zapata 69), Mesto, Hamšík, David López, Koulibaly, Albiol, Gargano. Coach: Rafael Benítez (ESP)
Match 6 - ŠK Slovan Bratislava (SVK)
H 3-0 *Mertens (6), Hamšík (16), Zapata (75)*
Andújar, Britos, Callejón (Mesto 74), Maggio, Mertens (De Guzmán 63), Hamšík, Koulibaly, Ghoulam, Gargano, Inler, Zapata (Higuaín 78). Coach: Rafael Benítez (ESP)

Round of 32 - Trabzonspor AŞ (TUR)
A 4-0 *Henrique (6), Higuaín (20), Gabbiadini (27), Zapata (90+2)*
Andújar, Henrique, De Guzmán (Callejón 70), Higuaín (Zapata 80), Mertens, Gabbiadini, Koulibaly, Ghoulam, Albiol, Gargano (David López 46), Inler. Coach: Rafael Benítez (ESP)
H 1-0 *De Guzmán (19)*
Rafael Cabral, Henrique, Britos, De Guzmán (Gabbiadini 69), Callejón (Hamšík 77), Jorginho, Higuaín (Zapata 63), Mertens, Mesto, Ghoulam, Inler. Coach: Rafael Benítez (ESP)

Round of 16 - FC Dinamo Moskva (RUS)
H 3-1 *Higuaín (25, 31p, 55)*
Andújar, Henrique, Britos, De Guzmán (Hamšík 70), Callejón (Zúñiga 82), Jorginho, Higuaín, Mertens, Koulibaly (Albiol 8), Ghoulam, Inler. Coach: Rafael Benítez (ESP)
A 0-0
Andújar, Britos, Callejón, Jorginho, Higuaín (Zúñiga 81), Maggio, Mertens (De Guzmán 63), David López, Gabbiadini (Hamšík 71), Ghoulam, Albiol. Coach: Rafael Benítez (ESP)

Quarter-finals - VfL Wolfsburg (GER)
A 4-1 *Higuaín (15), Hamšík (23, 64), Gabbiadini (77)*
Andújar, Britos, Callejón, Higuaín (Henrique 86), Maggio, Mertens (Insigne 60), Hamšík (Gabbiadini 75), David López, Ghoulam, Albiol, Inler. Coach: Rafael Benítez (ESP)
H 2-2 *Callejón (50), Mertens (65)*
Andújar, Britos, Callejón, Higuaín (Zapata 68), Mertens (Henrique 83), Mesto, Hamšík (Insigne 60), David López, Ghoulam, Albiol, Inler. Coach: Rafael Benítez (ESP)

Semi-finals - FC Dnipro Dnipropetrovsk (UKR)
H 1-1 *David López (50)*
Andújar, Britos, Callejón (Gabbiadini 77), Jorginho, Higuaín, Maggio, Hamšík, David López (Gargano 71), Insigne (Mertens 82), Ghoulam, Albiol. Coach: Rafael Benítez (ESP)
A 0-1
Andújar, Britos, Callejón, Higuaín, Maggio, David López (Henrique 79), Gabbiadini (Hamšík 55), Insigne (Mertens 61), Ghoulam, Albiol, Inler. Coach: Rafael Benítez (ESP)

ACF Fiorentina

Group K
Match 1 - EA Guingamp (FRA)
H 3-0 *Vargas (34), Cuadrado (67), Bernardeschi (88)*
Tătărușanu, Vargas, Pizarro, Cuadrado (Bernardeschi 72), Savić (Richards 57), Kurtić, Basanta, Borja Valero (Badelj 46), Pasqual, Gomez, Tomović. Coach: Vincenzo Montella (ITA)
Match 2 - FC Dinamo Minsk (BLR)
A 3-0 *Aquilani (33), Iličič (62), Bernardeschi (67)*
Tătărușanu, Richards (Alonso 41), Badelj, Vargas, Aquilani (Pizarro 46), Basanta, Borja Valero (Badelj 60), Pasqual, Bernardeschi, Tomović, Iličič. Coach: Vincenzo Montella (ITA)
Match 3 - PAOK FC (GRE)
A 1-0 *Vargas (38)*
Tătărușanu, Richards, Badelj, Vargas, Kurtić, Basanta, Borja Valero (Lazzari 65), Pasqual, Bernardeschi (Cuadrado 55), Tomović, Iličič (Marin 77). Coach: Vincenzo Montella (ITA)
Match 4 - PAOK FC (GRE)
H 1-1 *Pasqual (88)*
Tătărușanu, Gonzalo Rodríguez, Vargas (Borja Valero 70), Pizarro, Cuadrado, Kurtić, Basanta, Pasqual, Lazzari (Marin 57), Gomez, Tomović (Babacar 86). Coach: Vincenzo Montella (ITA)
Match 5 - EA Guingamp (FRA)
A 2-1 *Marin (6), Babacar (13)*
Tătărușanu, Richards, Badelj (Alonso 70), Vargas, Marin (Savić 52), Aquilani, Kurtić, Basanta, Babacar, Lazzari (Cuadrado 53), Tomović. Coach: Vincenzo Montella (ITA)
Red card: Basanta 44
Match 6 - FC Dinamo Minsk (BLR)
H 1-2 *Marin (88)*
Tătărușanu, Gonzalo Rodríguez (Pizarro 59), Richards, Badelj, Vargas, Marin, Cuadrado (Minelli 24), Kurtić, Lazzari, Gomez (Iličič 46), Tomović. Coach: Vincenzo Montella (ITA)

Round of 32 - Tottenham Hotspur FC (ENG)
A 1-1 *Basanta (36)*
Tătărușanu, Gonzalo Rodríguez, Pizarro, Fernández, Savić, Joaquín, Basanta, Borja Valero (Badelj 78), Pasqual (Alonso 66), Gomez (Iličič 85), Salah. Coach: Vincenzo Montella (ITA)
H 2-0 *Gomez (54), Salah (71)*
Neto, Richards, Badelj, Pizarro, Fernández (Aquilani 25), Savić, Joaquín (Pasqual 84), Basanta (Gonzalo Rodríguez 57), Alonso, Gomez, Salah. Coach: Vincenzo Montella (ITA)

Round of 16 - AS Roma (ITA)
H 1-1 *Iličič (17)*
Neto, Gonzalo Rodríguez, Badelj, Pizarro (Fernández 45+1), Joaquín, Basanta, Borja Valero (Aquilani 72), Alonso, Tomović, Iličič (Babacar 81), Salah. Coach: Vincenzo Montella (ITA)
A 3-0 *Gonzalo Rodríguez (10p), Alonso (18), Basanta (22)*
Neto, Gonzalo Rodríguez, Badelj, Fernández, Savić (Tomović 41), Joaquín, Basanta, Borja Valero (Aquilani 79), Alonso, Babacar (Vargas 63), Salah. Coach: Vincenzo Montella (ITA)

Quarter-finals - FC Dynamo Kyiv (UKR)
A 1-1 *Babacar (90+2)*
Neto, Gonzalo Rodríguez, Badelj, Fernández, Savić, Joaquín (Vargas 66), Borja Valero (Aquilani 83), Alonso, Gomez (Babacar 77), Tomović, Salah. Coach: Vincenzo Montella (ITA)
H 2-0 *Gomez (43), Vargas (90+4)*
Neto, Gonzalo Rodríguez (Aquilani 84), Fernández, Savić, Joaquín, Borja Valero (Badelj 79), Alonso, Gomez, Tomović, Salah (Vargas 88). Coach: Vincenzo Montella (ITA)

Semi-finals - Sevilla FC (ESP)
A 0-3
Neto, Gonzalo Rodríguez, Badelj (Pizarro 68), Fernández, Savić, Joaquín, Borja Valero, Alonso, Gomez (Iličič 80), Tomović (Richards 46), Salah. Coach: Vincenzo Montella (ITA)
H 0-2
Neto, Gonzalo Rodríguez, Pizarro, Fernández (Badelj 67), Savić, Joaquín, Basanta (Pasqual 46), Borja Valero (Lazzari 85), Alonso, Iličič, Salah. Coach: Vincenzo Montella (ITA)

FC Internazionale Milano

Play-offs - Stjarnan (ISL)
A 3-0 *Icardi (41), Dodô (48), D'Ambrosio (89)*
Handanovič, Jonathan (D'Ambrosio 75), Juan, Icardi, Kovačić, Vidić, Botta (Osvaldo 61), Dodô, Ranocchia, Hernanes (Kuzmanović 88), M'Vila. Coach: Walter Mazzarri (ITA)
H 6-0 *Kovačić (28, 33, 51), Osvaldo (47), Icardi (69, 80)*
Carrizo, Juan, Andreolli, Osvaldo, Kovačić (Icardi 53), Obi (Kuzmanović 59), Ranocchia, D'Ambrosio, Nagatomo, Hernanes (Jonathan 67), M'Vila. Coach: Walter Mazzarri (ITA)

Group F
Match 1 - FC Dnipro Dnipropetrovsk (UKR)
A 1-0 *D'Ambrosio (71)*
Handanovič, Juan, Icardi, Guarín, Campagnaro, Vidić, Kuzmanović (Osvaldo 62), Dodô, D'Ambrosio, Hernanes (Jonathan 76), M'Vila. Coach: Walter Mazzarri (ITA)
Match 2 - Qarabağ FK (AZE)
H 2-0 *D'Ambrosio (18), Icardi (85)*
Carrizo, Juan, Andreolli, Icardi, Guarín (Osvaldo 63), Kuzmanović (Medel 59), Ranocchia, D'Ambrosio, Nagatomo, Hernanes (Obi 72), M'Vila. Coach: Walter Mazzarri (ITA)
Match 3 - AS Saint-Étienne (FRA)
H 0-0
Carrizo, Juan, Andreolli, Icardi, Kovačić, Guarín (Palacio 70), Vidić, Kuzmanović (Krhin 85), Dodô, Mbaye, M'Vila (Hernanes 53). Coach: Walter Mazzarri (ITA)
Match 4 - AS Saint-Étienne (FRA)
A 1-1 *Dodô (33)*
Carrizo, Juan, Andreolli, Palacio, Kovačić (Osvaldo 74), Vidić, Kuzmanović (Palazzi 83), Medel, Dodô, Mbaye, Bonazzoli (Obi 86). Coach: Walter Mazzarri (ITA)
Match 5 - FC Dnipro Dnipropetrovsk (UKR)
H 2-1 *Kuzmanović (30), Osvaldo (50)*
Handanovič, Juan, Osvaldo, Icardi (Andreolli 55), Guarín, Kuzmanović, Medel, Dodô, Ranocchia, Nagatomo (Campagnaro 37), Hernanes (Obi 60). Coach: Giulio Nuciari (ITA)
Red card: Ranocchia 46

Match 6 - Qarabağ FK (AZE)
A 0-0
Carrizo, Juan, Andreolli, Osvaldo, Campagnaro, Obi (Baldini 90+1), Mbaye, D'Ambrosio (Dimarco 84), Krhin, Donkor, M'Vila, Bonazzoli. Coach: Roberto Mancini (ITA)

Round of 32 - Celtic FC (SCO)
A 3-3 *Shaqiri (4), Palacio (13, 45)*
Carrizo, Juan, Palacio, Icardi (Kovačić 75), Guarín, Campagnaro, Kuzmanović (Dodô 79), Medel, Santon, Ranocchia, Shaqiri. Coach: Roberto Mancini (ITA)
H 1-0 *Guarín (88)*
Carrizo, Juan, Palacio (Puşcaş 89), Icardi, Guarín, Medel, Santon, Ranocchia, D'Ambrosio (Campagnaro 81), Hernanes (Kovačić 80), Shaqiri. Coach: Roberto Mancini (ITA)

Round of 16 - VfL Wolfsburg (GER)
A 1-3 *Palacio (6)*
Carrizo, Juan, Palacio, Icardi, Guarín, Medel, Santon (Kuzmanović 82), Ranocchia, D'Ambrosio, Hernanes (Vidić 58), Shaqiri (Kovačić 82). Coach: Roberto Mancini (ITA)
H 1-2 *Palacio (71)*
Carrizo, Juan, Palacio, Icardi, Kovačić (Kuzmanović 55), Guarín, Campagnaro (D'Ambrosio 68), Medel, Santon, Ranocchia, Hernanes. Coach: Roberto Mancini (ITA)

Torino FC

Third qualifying round - IF Brommapojkarna (SWE)
A 3-0 *Larrondo (45p, 53), Barreto (58)*
Padelli, Molinaro, Bovo, El Kaddouri (Rubén Pérez 84), Larrondo, Barreto (Martínez 70), Vives, Nocerino, Moretti, Glik, Vešović (Benassi 74). Coach: Giampiero Ventura (ITA)
Red card: Vives 61
H 4-0 *Jónsson (4og), Darmian (37), Quagliarella (80p), Martínez (90)*
Padelli, Molinaro, Bovo, Rubén Pérez, Larrondo (Quagliarella 55), Barreto (Martínez 63), Nocerino, Moretti, Glik (Jansson 81), Darmian, Benassi. Coach: Giampiero Ventura (ITA)

Play-offs - RNK Split (CRO)
A 0-0
Padelli, Molinaro, Bovo, El Kaddouri, Larrondo, Barreto (Quagliarella 68), Vives, Nocerino (Benassi 62), Moretti, Glik, Darmian. Coach: Giampiero Ventura (ITA)
H 1-0 *El Kaddouri (22p)*
Padelli, Molinaro, El Kaddouri (Gazzi 90+1), Barreto (Martínez 64), Maksimović, Vives, Moretti, Glik, Quagliarella, Darmian, Benassi (Nocerino 58). Coach: Giampiero Ventura (ITA)

Group B
Match 1 - Club Brugge KV (BEL)
A 0-0
Gillet, Molinaro, Gazzi, Jansson, Maksimović, Silva, Amauri, Quagliarella (Martínez 70), Sánchez Miño (Nocerino 84), Darmian, Benassi (El Kaddouri 65). Coach: Giampiero Ventura (ITA)
Match 2 - FC København (DEN)
H 1-0 *Quagliarella (90+4p)*
Gillet, Molinaro, Gazzi, Martínez (Quagliarella 72), Maksimović, Amauri (Larrondo 78), Moretti, Glik, Sánchez Miño (El Kaddouri 69), Darmian, Benassi. Coach: Giampiero Ventura (ITA)
Match 3 - HJK Helsinki (FIN)
H 2-0 *Molinaro (35), Amauri (58)*
Padelli, Molinaro, El Kaddouri, Martínez (Barreto 76), Jansson, Maksimović, Vives, Silva, Amauri (Quagliarella 67), Darmian, Benassi (Nocerino 71). Coach: Giampiero Ventura (ITA)

Match 4 - HJK Helsinki (FIN)
A 1-2 *Quagliarella (90)*
Padelli, Gazzi, Martínez (Larrondo 55), Jansson, Silva, Glik, Quagliarella, Sánchez Miño, Masiello (Molinaro 71), Darmian, Benassi (El Kaddouri 64). Coach: Giampiero Ventura (ITA)
Match 5 - Club Brugge KV (BEL)
H 0-0
Padelli, Molinaro, Bovo, El Kaddouri, Gazzi, Martínez (Larrondo 88), Jansson, Amauri, Moretti, Darmian, Benassi (Vives 78). Coach: Giampiero Ventura (ITA)
Match 6 - FC København (DEN)
A 5-1 *Martínez (15, 47), Amauri (42p), Darmian (49), Silva (53)*
Padelli, Bovo, El Kaddouri (Graziano 66), Gazzi, Martínez (Quagliarella 58), Maksimović (Jansson 60), Silva, Amauri, Moretti, Glik, Darmian. Coach: Giampiero Ventura (ITA)

Round of 32 - Athletic Club (ESP)
H 2-2 *Maxi López (18,42)*
Padelli, Molinaro, El Kaddouri (Farnerud 76), Maxi López (Amauri 72), Gazzi, Martínez (Quagliarella 58), Maksimović, Moretti, Glik, Darmian, Benassi. Coach: Giampiero Ventura (ITA)
A 3-2 *Quagliarella (16p), Maxi López (45+2), Darmian (68)*
Padelli, Molinaro, El Kaddouri (Farnerud 83), Maxi López (Martínez 73), Gazzi, Maksimović, Vives, Moretti, Glik, Quagliarella, Darmian. Coach: Giampiero Ventura (ITA)

Round of 16 - FC Zenit (RUS)
A 0-2
Padelli, Molinaro, El Kaddouri, Gazzi, Martínez (Vives 34; Farnerud 51), Maksimović, Moretti, Glik, Quagliarella (Maxi López 74), Darmian, Benassi. Coach: Giampiero Ventura (ITA)
Red card: Benassi 28
H 1-0 *Glik (90)*
Padelli, Molinaro (Amauri 82), El Kaddouri (Martínez 76), Farnerud (Bovo 64), Maxi López, Gazzi, Maksimović, Moretti, Glik, Quagliarella, Darmian. Coach: Giampiero Ventura (ITA)

NB A technical error resulted in the incorrect league results for Genoa CFC being published in the 2014/15 edition. Below is the correct data:

2013					
25/08	a	Internazionale	L	0-2	
01/09	h	Fiorentina	L	2-5	*Gilardino, Lodi (p)*
15/09	a	Sampdoria	W	3-0	*Antonini, Calaiò, Lodi*
21/09	h	Livorno	D	0-0	
24/09	a	Udinese	L	0-1	
28/09	h	Napoli	L	0-2	
06/10	a	Catania	D	1-1	*og (Legrottaglie)*
20/10	h	Chievo	W	2-1	*Gilardino 2*
27/10	a	Juventus	L	0-2	
30/10	h	Parma	W	1-0	*Gilardino*
03/11	a	Lazio	W	2-0	*Kucka, Gilardino (p)*
10/11	h	Verona	W	2-0	*Portanova, Kucka*
23/11	a	Milan	D	1-1	*Gilardino (p)*
30/11	h	Torino	D	1-1	*Biondini*
08/12	a	Cagliari	L	1-2	*Gilardino*
15/12	h	Atalanta	D	1-1	*Bertolacci*
22/12	a	Bologna	L	0-1	
2014					
06/01	h	Sassuolo	W	2-0	*Gilardino (p), Bertolacci*
12/01	a	Roma	L	0-4	
19/01	h	Internazionale	W	1-0	*Antonelli*
26/01	a	Fiorentina	D	3-3	*Gilardino (p), Antonini, De Maio*
03/02	h	Sampdoria	L	0-1	
09/02	a	Livorno	W	1-0	*Antonelli*
16/02	h	Udinese	D	3-3	*Konaté, Gilardino 2*
24/02	a	Napoli	D	1-1	*Calaiò*
02/03	h	Catania	W	2-0	*Antonelli, Sturaro*
09/03	a	Chievo	L	1-2	*Gilardino*
16/03	h	Juventus	L	0-1	
23/03	a	Parma	D	1-1	*Cofie*
26/03	h	Lazio	W	2-0	*Gilardino, Fetfatzidis*
30/03	a	Verona	L	0-3	
07/04	h	Milan	L	1-2	*og (Abbiati)*
13/04	a	Torino	L	1-2	*Gilardino*
19/04	h	Cagliari	L	1-2	*De Maio*
27/04	a	Atalanta	D	1-1	*De Ceglie*
04/05	h	Bologna	D	0-0	
11/05	a	Sassuolo	L	2-4	*Calaiò, Gilardino*
18/05	h	Roma	W	1-0	*Fetfatzidis*

DOMESTIC LEAGUE CLUB-BY-CLUB

Atalanta BC

1907 • Atleti Azzurri d'Italia (26,542) • atalanta.it
Major honours
Italian Cup (1) 1963
Coach: Stefano Colantuono; (04/03/15) Edoardo Reja

2014					
31/08	h	Verona	D	0-0	
14/09	a	Cagliari	W	2-1	*Estigarribia, Boakye*
21/09	h	Fiorentina	L	0-1	
24/09	a	Internazionale	L	0-2	
27/09	h	Juventus	L	0-3	
05/10	a	Sampdoria	L	0-1	
19/10	h	Parma	W	1-0	*Boakye*
26/10	a	Udinese	L	0-2	
29/10	h	Napoli	D	1-1	*Denis*
02/11	a	Torino	D	0-0	
08/11	a	Sassuolo	D	0-0	
22/11	h	Roma	L	1-2	*Moralez*
30/11	a	Empoli	D	0-0	
07/12	h	Cesena	W	3-2	*Benalouane, Stendardo, Moralez*
13/12	a	Lazio	L	0-3	
21/12	h	Palermo	D	3-3	*Denis 2 (1p), Moralez*
2015					
06/01	a	Genoa	D	2-2	*Zappacosta, Moralez*
11/01	h	Chievo	D	1-1	*Zappacosta*
18/01	a	Milan	W	1-0	*Denis*
25/01	a	Verona	L	0-1	
01/02	h	Cagliari	W	2-1	*Biava, Pinilla*
08/02	a	Fiorentina	L	2-3	*Zappacosta, Boakye*
15/02	h	Internazionale	L	1-4	*Moralez*
20/02	a	Juventus	L	1-2	*Migliaccio*
01/03	h	Sampdoria	L	1-2	*Stendardo*
08/03	a	Parma	D	0-0	
15/03	h	Udinese	D	0-0	
22/03	a	Napoli	D	1-1	*Pinilla*
04/04	h	Torino	L	1-2	*Pinilla*
12/04	h	Sassuolo	W	2-1	*Denis 2 (1p)*
19/04	a	Roma	D	1-1	*Denis (p)*
26/04	h	Empoli	D	2-2	*Gómez, Denis*
29/04	a	Cesena	D	2-2	*Pinilla 2*
03/05	h	Lazio	D	1-1	*Biava*
10/05	a	Palermo	W	3-2	*Baselli, og (Andjelkovič), Gómez*
17/05	h	Genoa	L	1-4	*Pinilla (p)*
24/05	a	Chievo	D	1-1	*Gómez*
30/05	h	Milan	L	1-3	*Baselli*

No	Name	Nat	DoB	Pos	Aps	(s)	Gls
1	Vlada Avramov	SRB	04/05/79	G	1		
16	Daniele Baselli		12/03/92	M	15	(7)	2
6	Gianpaolo Bellini		27/03/80	D	15		
29	Yohan Benalouane	FRA	28/03/87	D	25	(2)	1
9	Rolando Bianchi		15/02/83	A	3	(18)	
20	Giuseppe Biava		08/05/77	D	18		2
99	Richmond Boakye	GHA	28/01/93	A	8	(11)	3
10	Giacomo Bonaventura		22/08/89	M	1		
17	Carlos Carmona	CHI	21/02/87	M	32	(1)	
33	Nicolò Cherubin		02/12/86	D	10	(3)	
21	Luca Cigarini		20/06/86	M	30	(3)	
7	Marco D'Alessandro		17/02/91	M	9	(16)	
3	Cristiano Del Grosso		24/03/83	D	9	(4)	
19	Germán Denis	ARG	10/09/81	A	27	(5)	8
93	Boukary Dramé	SEN	22/07/85	D	27	(2)	
28	Urby Emanuelson	NED	16/06/86	D	4	(5)	
18	Marcelo Estigarribia	PAR	21/09/87	M	8	(1)	1
78	Giorgio Frezzolini		21/01/76	G		(1)	
10	Alejandro Gómez	ARG	15/02/88	M	18	(6)	3
95	Alberto Grassi		07/03/95	M	2	(1)	
13	Andrea Masiello		05/02/86	D	12	(2)	
8	Giulio Migliaccio		23/06/81	M	12	(8)	1
31	Salvatore Molina		01/01/92	M	2	(2)	
11	Maximiliano Moralez	ARG	27/02/87	M	26	(4)	5
51	Mauricio Pinilla	CHI	04/02/84	A	12	(2)	6
77	Cristian Raimondi		30/04/81	M	4	(2)	
27	Lorenzo Rosseti		05/08/94	A		(1)	
5	Lionel Scaloni	ARG	16/05/78	D	1	(2)	
25	Leonardo Spinazzola		25/03/93	M		(2)	
57	Marco Sportiello		10/05/92	G	37		
2	Guglielmo Stendardo		06/05/81	D	23	(1)	2
22	Davide Zappacosta		11/06/92	D	27	(2)	3

Cagliari Calcio

1920 • Sant'Elia (16,000) • cagliaricalcio.net
Major honours
Italian League (1) 1970
Coach: Zdeněk Zeman (CZE); (24/12/14) Gianfranco Zola; (09/03/15) Zdeněk Zeman (CZE); (22/04/15) Gianluca Festa

2014					
31/08	a	Sassuolo	D	1-1	*Sau*
14/09	h	Atalanta	L	1-2	*Cossu (p)*
21/09	a	Roma	L	0-2	
24/09	h	Torino	L	1-2	*Cossu*
28/09	a	Internazionale	W	4-1	*Sau, Ekdal 3*
04/10	a	Verona	L	0-1	
19/10	h	Sampdoria	D	2-2	*Danilo Avelar (p), Sau*
25/10	a	Empoli	W	4-0	*Sau, Danilo Avelar 2 (1p), Ekdal*
29/10	h	Milan	D	1-1	*Ibarbo*
03/11	a	Lazio	L	2-4	*og (Braafheid), João Pedro*
09/11	h	Genoa	D	1-1	*Diego Farias*
23/11	a	Napoli	D	3-3	*Ibarbo, Diego Farias 2*
30/11	h	Fiorentina	L	0-4	
08/12	h	Chievo	L	0-2	
14/12	a	Parma	D	0-0	
18/12	h	Juventus	L	1-3	*Rossettini*
2015					
06/01	a	Palermo	L	0-5	
11/01	h	Cesena	W	2-1	*João Pedro, Donsah*
18/01	a	Udinese	D	2-2	*João Pedro, Danilo Avelar (p)*
24/01	h	Sassuolo	W	2-1	*Rossettini, Čop*
01/02	a	Atalanta	L	1-2	*Dessena*
08/02	h	Roma	L	1-2	*M'Poku*
15/02	a	Torino	D	1-1	*Donsah*
23/02	h	Internazionale	L	1-2	*og (Carrizo)*
01/03	h	Verona	L	1-2	*Conti*
07/03	a	Sampdoria	L	0-2	
14/03	h	Empoli	D	1-1	*João Pedro*
21/03	a	Milan	L	1-3	*Diego Farias*
04/04	h	Lazio	L	1-3	*Sau*
11/04	a	Genoa	L	0-2	
19/04	h	Napoli	L	0-3	
26/04	a	Fiorentina	W	3-1	*Čop 2, Diego Farias*
29/04	a	Chievo	L	0-1	
04/05	h	Parma	W	4-0	*Ekdal, Diego Farias, M'Poku, Čop*
09/05	a	Juventus	D	1-1	*Rossettini*
17/05	h	Palermo	L	0-1	
24/05	a	Cesena	W	1-0	*Sau*
31/05	h	Udinese	W	4-3	*Sau, João Pedro, M'Poku, og (Bruno Fernandes)*

No	Name	Nat	DoB	Pos	Aps	(s)	Gls
21	Antonio Balzano		13/06/86	D	21	(4)	
18	Nicolò Barella		07/02/97	M	1	(2)	
24	Simone Benedetti		03/04/92	D	4	(1)	
44	Željko Brkić	SRB	09/07/86	G	21		
13	Caio Rangel	BRA	16/01/96	A		(6)	
33	Marco Capuano		14/10/91	D	12	(3)	
32	Luca Ceppitelli		08/11/89	D	22	(3)	
1	Simone Colombi		01/07/91	G	3		
5	Daniele Conti		09/01/79	M	17	(1)	1
90	Duje Čop	CRO	01/02/90	A	9	(7)	4
7	Andrea Cossu		03/05/80	M	19	(3)	2
27	Alessio Cragno		28/06/94	G	14		
4	Lorenzo Crisetig		20/01/93	M	26	(2)	
8	Danilo Avelar	BRA	09/06/89	D	29	(2)	4
16	Daniele Dessena		10/05/87	M	21	(7)	1
37	Modibo Diakité	FRA	02/03/87	D	8	(1)	
17	Diego Farias	BRA	10/05/90	A	20	(9)	6
30	Godfred Donsah	GHA	07/06/96	D	13	(8)	2
20	Albin Ekdal	SWE	28/07/89	M	32	(1)	5
2	Alejandro González	URU	23/03/88	D	6	(1)	
22	Josef Hušbauer	CZE	16/03/90	M		(2)	
23	Víctor Ibarbo	COL	19/05/90	A	12	(1)	2
10	João Pedro	BRA	09/03/92	M	15	(14)	5
9	Samuele Longo		12/01/92	A	9	(18)	
40	Paul-José M'Poku	COD	19/04/92	M	14	(2)	3
3	Nicola Murru		16/12/94	D	6	(2)	
14	Francesco Pisano		29/04/86	D	12	(1)	
15	Luca Rossettini		09/05/85	D	32		3
25	Marco Sau		03/11/87	A	20	(8)	7

ITALY

AC Cesena

1940 • Dino Manuzzi (23,860) • cesenacalcio.it

**Coach: Pierpaolo Bisoli;
(08/12/14) Domenico Di Carlo**

2014
31/08	h	Parma	W	1-0	Rodríguez
14/09	a	Lazio	L	0-3	
20/09	h	Empoli	D	2-2	Marilungo, Defrel
24/09	a	Juventus	L	0-3	
28/09	h	Milan	D	1-1	Succi
05/10	a	Udinese	D	1-1	Cascione (p)
19/10	a	Palermo	L	1-2	Rodríguez (p)
26/10	h	Internazionale	L	0-1	
29/10	a	Roma	L	0-2	
03/11	h	Verona	D	1-1	Defrel
09/11	a	Chievo	L	1-2	Djurić
23/11	h	Sampdoria	D	1-1	Lucchini
30/11	h	Genoa	L	0-3	
07/12	a	Atalanta	L	2-3	Defrel 2
14/12	a	Fiorentina	L	1-4	og (Savić)
20/12	a	Sassuolo	D	1-1	Zé Eduardo

2015
06/01	h	Napoli	L	1-4	Brienza
11/01	a	Cagliari	L	1-2	Brienza
18/01	h	Torino	L	2-3	Brienza 2 (2p)
25/01	a	Parma	W	2-1	Pulzetti, Rodríguez
01/02	a	Lazio	W	2-1	Defrel, og (Cataldi)
08/02	a	Empoli	L	0-2	
15/02	h	Juventus	D	2-2	Djurić, Brienza
22/02	a	Milan	L	0-2	
01/03	h	Udinese	W	1-0	Rodríguez
08/03	h	Palermo	L	0-0	
15/03	a	Internazionale	D	1-1	Defrel
22/03	h	Roma	L	0-1	
04/04	a	Verona	D	3-3	Carbonero, Brienza, Succi
12/04	h	Chievo	D	0-0	
18/04	a	Sampdoria	D	0-0	
26/04	a	Genoa	L	1-3	Carbonero
29/04	h	Atalanta	D	2-2	Brienza (p), Carbonero
03/05	a	Fiorentina	L	1-3	Rodríguez
10/05	h	Sassuolo	L	2-3	Defrel, Brienza
18/05	a	Napoli	L	2-3	Defrel 2
24/05	h	Cagliari	L	0-1	
31/05	a	Torino	L	0-5	

No	Name	Nat	DoB	Pos	Aps	(s)	Gls
30	Federico Agliardi		11/02/83	G	9	(1)	
81	Walter Bressan		26/01/81	G	1		
11	Franco Brienza		19/03/79	A	29	(1)	8
25	Daniele Capelli		20/06/86	D	29	(1)	
7	Carlos Carbonero	COL	25/07/90	M	15	(7)	3
34	Emmanuel Cascione		22/09/83	M	24	(5)	1
44	Riccardo Cazzola		08/10/85	M		(5)	
10	Manuel Coppola		11/05/82	M	10	(1)	
27	Nicola Dal Monte		13/09/97	A	1	(3)	
8	Giuseppe De Feudis		10/07/83	M	23	(2)	
92	Grégoire Defrel	FRA	17/06/91	A	31	(3)	9
18	Milan Djurić	BIH	22/05/90	A	17	(11)	2
61	Luca Garritano		11/02/94	A	1	(5)	
5	Luigi Giorgi		19/04/87	M	24	(3)	
27	Hugo Almeida	POR	23/05/84	A	7	(3)	
15	Luka Krajnc	SVN	19/09/94	D	20	(2)	
1	Nicola Leali		17/02/93	G	28		
6	Stefano Lucchini		02/10/80	D	26	(2)	1
17	Hördur Björgvin Magnússon	ISL	11/02/93	D	12		
89	Guido Marilungo		09/08/89	A	8		1
3	Antonio Mazzotta		02/08/89	D	7	(3)	
32	Gabriele Moncini		26/04/96	A		(2)	
26	Gaby Mudingayi	BEL	01/10/81	M	8	(1)	
2	Constantin Nica	ROU	18/03/93	D	4	(4)	
24	Gabriele Perico		11/03/84	D	18	(3)	
56	Nico Pulzetti		13/02/84	M	4	(5)	1
33	Francesco Renzetti		22/01/88	D	21	(2)	
9	Alejandro Rodríguez	ESP	30/07/91	A	6	(19)	5
19	Davide Succi		11/10/81	A	4	(5)	2
23	Andrea Tabanelli		02/02/90	M	3	(4)	
4	Luca Valzania		05/03/96	M	2		
14	Massimo Volta		14/05/87	D	19	(5)	
77	Zé Eduardo	BRA	16/08/91	M	7	(6)	1

AC Chievo Verona

1929 • Marc'Antonio Bentegodi (38,402) • chievoverona.it

**Coach: Eugenio Corini;
(19/10/14) Rolando Maran**

2014
30/08	h	Juventus	L	0-1	
14/09	a	Napoli	W	1-0	Maxi López
21/09	h	Parma	L	2-3	Izco, Paloschi
24/09	a	Sampdoria	L	1-2	Paloschi
28/09	h	Empoli	L	1-1	Meggiorini
04/10	a	Milan	L	0-2	
18/10	a	Roma	L	0-3	
26/10	h	Genoa	L	1-2	Zukanović
29/10	a	Palermo	L	0-1	
02/11	h	Sassuolo	D	0-0	
09/11	h	Cesena	W	2-1	Pellissier 2
23/11	a	Udinese	D	1-1	Radovanović
29/11	h	Lazio	D	0-0	
08/12	a	Cagliari	W	2-0	Meggiorini, Paloschi
15/12	a	Internazionale	L	0-2	
21/12	a	Verona	W	1-0	Paloschi

2015
06/01	h	Torino	D	0-0	
11/01	a	Atalanta	D	1-1	Lazarevič
18/01	h	Fiorentina	L	1-2	Pellissier
25/01	a	Juventus	L	0-2	
01/02	h	Napoli	L	1-2	og (Britos)
11/02	a	Parma	W	1-0	Zukanović
15/02	h	Sampdoria	W	2-1	Izco, Meggiorini
22/02	a	Empoli	L	0-3	
28/02	h	Milan	D	0-0	
08/03	h	Roma	D	0-0	
15/03	a	Genoa	W	2-0	Paloschi 2
21/03	h	Palermo	W	1-0	Paloschi
04/04	a	Sassuolo	L	0-1	
12/04	a	Cesena	D	0-0	
19/04	a	Udinese	D	1-1	Pellissier
26/04	a	Lazio	D	1-1	Paloschi
29/04	h	Cagliari	W	1-0	Meggiorini
03/05	a	Internazionale	D	0-0	
10/05	h	Verona	D	2-2	Paloschi, Pellissier (p)
17/05	a	Torino	L	0-2	
24/05	h	Atalanta	D	1-1	Pellissier
31/05	a	Fiorentina	L	0-3	

No	Name	Nat	DoB	Pos	Aps	(s)	Gls
25	Francesco Bardi		18/01/92	G	10		
63	Nicola Bellomo		18/02/91	M		(5)	
34	Cristiano Biraghi		01/09/92	D	13	(5)	
23	Valter Birsa	SVN	07/08/86	M	30	(5)	
1	Albano Bizzarri	ARG	09/11/77	G	28		
19	Rubén Botta	ARG	31/01/90	M	5	(16)	
10	Anders Christiansen	DEN	08/06/90	M	2	(2)	
14	Isaac Cofie	GHA	20/09/91	M	8	(10)	
3	Dario Dainelli		09/06/79	D	28	(2)	
26	Edimar	BRA	21/05/86	D		(1)	
18	Ioannis Fetfatzidis	GRE	21/12/90	M		(4)	
21	Nicolas Frey	FRA	06/03/84	D	31		
5	Alessandro Gamberini		27/08/81	D	15	(5)	
56	Perparim Hetemaj	FIN	12/12/86	M	31	(1)	
7	Mariano Izco	ARG	13/03/83	M	28		2
7	Dejan Lazarević	SVN	15/02/90	M	2	(6)	1
84	Thomas Mangani	FRA	29/04/87	M	1		
7	Federico Mattiello		14/07/95	M	2	(1)	
7	Maxi López	ARG	03/04/84	A	7	(6)	1
69	Riccardo Meggiorini		04/09/85	A	22	(8)	4
43	Alberto Paloschi		04/01/90	A	30	(7)	9
31	Sergio Pellissier		12/04/79	A	10	(17)	7
20	Ivan Radovanović	SRB	29/08/88	M	29	(2)	1
20	Gennaro Sardo		08/05/79	D	5	(2)	
24	Ezequiel Schelotto		23/05/89	M	26	(3)	
87	Ervin Zukanović	BIH	11/02/87	D	28	(1)	2

Empoli FC

1920 • Carlo Castellani (21,113) • empolicalcio.it

Coach: Maurizio Sarri

2014
31/08	a	Udinese	L	0-2	
13/09	h	Roma	L	0-1	
20/09	a	Cesena	D	2-2	Tavano (p), Rugani
23/09	h	Milan	D	2-2	Tonelli, Pucciarelli
28/09	a	Chievo	D	1-1	Pucciarelli
05/10	h	Palermo	W	3-0	Maccarone, Tonelli, Pucciarelli
20/10	a	Genoa	D	1-1	Tonelli
25/10	a	Cagliari	L	0-4	
28/10	a	Sassuolo	L	1-3	Croce
01/11	h	Juventus	L	0-2	
09/11	h	Lazio	W	2-1	Barba, Maccarone
23/11	a	Parma	W	2-0	Vecino, Tavano
30/11	h	Atalanta	D	0-0	
07/12	a	Napoli	D	2-2	Verdi, Rugani
15/12	h	Torino	D	0-0	
21/12	a	Fiorentina	D	1-1	Tonelli

2015
06/01	h	Verona	D	0-0	
11/01	h	Sampdoria	L	0-1	
17/01	a	Internazionale	D	0-0	
26/01	h	Udinese	L	1-2	Saponara (p)
31/01	a	Roma	D	1-1	Maccarone (p)
08/02	h	Cesena	W	2-0	Maccarone, Signorelli
15/02	a	Milan	D	1-1	Maccarone
22/02	h	Chievo	W	3-0	Rugani, Maccarone 2
01/03	a	Palermo	D	0-0	
08/03	h	Genoa	D	1-1	Barba
14/03	a	Cagliari	D	1-1	Vecino
22/03	h	Sassuolo	W	3-1	Saponara 2, Mchedlidze
04/04	a	Juventus	L	0-2	
12/04	a	Lazio	L	0-4	
19/04	a	Parma	D	2-2	Maccarone, Tonelli
26/04	a	Atalanta	D	2-2	Saponara, Maccarone
30/04	h	Napoli	W	4-2	Maccarone, og (Britos), Saponara, og (Albiol)
06/05	a	Torino	W	1-0	og (Padelli)
10/05	h	Fiorentina	L	2-3	Saponara, Mchedlidze
17/05	a	Verona	L	1-2	Saponara
24/05	h	Sampdoria	D	1-1	Pucciarelli
31/05	a	Internazionale	L	3-4	Mchedlidze 2, Pucciarelli

No	Name	Nat	DoB	Pos	Aps	(s)	Gls
99	Rodrigo Aguirre	URU	01/10/94	A		(1)	
19	Federico Barba		01/09/93	D	12	(6)	2
28	Davide Bassi		12/04/85	G	7		
22	Matteo Bianchetti		17/03/93	D		(1)	
25	Joshua Brillante	AUS	25/03/93	M		(1)	
11	Daniele Croce		09/09/82	M	35	(2)	1
17	Tiberio Guarente		01/11/85	M		(1)	
23	Elseid Hysaj	ALB	20/02/94	D	33	(3)	
13	Vincent Laurini	FRA	10/06/89	D	14	(1)	
13	Diego Laxalt	URU	07/02/93	M		(4)	
7	Massimo Maccarone		06/09/79	A	30	(4)	10
21	Mário Rui	POR	27/05/91	D	28	(6)	
4	Levan Mchedlidze	GEO	24/03/90	A	6	(19)	4
5	Davide Moro		02/01/82	M		(1)	
20	Manuel Pucciarelli		17/06/91	A	25	(9)	5
24	Daniele Rugani		29/07/94	D	38		3
5	Riccardo Saponara		21/12/91	A	17		7
33	Luigi Sepe		08/05/91	G	31		
8	Franco Signorelli	VEN	01/01/91	M	4	(9)	1
10	Michele Somma		16/03/95	D		(1)	
10	Francesco Tavano		02/03/79	A	15	(11)	2
26	Lorenzo Tonelli		17/01/90	D	27	(1)	5
6	Mirko Valdifiori		21/04/86	M	36		
88	Matías Vecino	URU	24/08/91	M	36		2
18	Simone Verdi		12/07/92	A	17	(9)	1
27	Piotr Zieliński	POL	20/05/94	M	7	(21)	

ACF Fiorentina

1926 • Artemio Franchi (43,147) • violachannel.tv

Major honours

UEFA Cup Winners' Cup (1) 1961; Italian League (2) 1956, 1969; Italian Cup (6) 1940, 1961, 1966, 1975, 1996, 2001

Coach: Vincenzo Montella

2014

30/08	a	Roma	L	0-2	
14/09	h	Genoa	D	0-0	
21/09	a	Atalanta	W	1-0	*Kurtič*
24/09	h	Sassuolo	D	0-0	
28/09	a	Torino	D	1-1	*Babacar*
05/10	h	Internazionale	W	3-0	*Babacar, Cuadrado, Tomović*
19/10	h	Lazio	L	0-2	
26/10	a	Milan	D	1-1	*Iličič*
29/10	h	Udinese	W	3-0	*Babacar 2, Borja Valero*
02/11	a	Sampdoria	L	1-3	*Savić*
09/11	h	Napoli	L	0-1	
23/11	a	Verona	W	2-1	*Gonzalo Rodríguez, Cuadrado*
30/11	a	Cagliari	W	4-0	*Fernández 2, Gomez, Cuadrado*
05/12	h	Juventus	D	0-0	
14/12	a	Cesena	W	4-1	*Borja Valero, Savić, Gonzalo Rodríguez, El Hamdaoui*
21/12	h	Empoli	D	1-1	*Vargas*

2015

06/01	a	Parma	L	0-1	
11/01	h	Palermo	W	4-3	*Pasqual, Basanta, Cuadrado, Joaquín*
18/01	a	Chievo	W	2-1	*Gonzalo Rodríguez, Babacar*
25/01	h	Roma	D	1-1	*Gomez*
31/01	a	Genoa	D	1-1	*Gonzalo Rodríguez*
08/02	h	Atalanta	W	3-2	*Basanta, Diamanti, Pasqual*
14/02	a	Sassuolo	W	3-1	*Salah, Babacar 2*
22/02	h	Torino	D	1-1	*Salah*
01/03	a	Internazionale	W	1-0	*Salah*
09/03	a	Lazio	L	0-4	
16/03	h	Milan	W	2-1	*Gonzalo Rodríguez, Joaquín*
22/03	a	Udinese	D	2-2	*Gomez 2*
04/04	h	Sampdoria	W	2-0	*Diamanti, Salah*
12/04	a	Napoli	L	0-3	
20/04	a	Verona	L	0-1	
26/04	h	Cagliari	L	1-3	*Gilardino*
29/04	a	Juventus	L	2-3	*Gonzalo Rodríguez (p), Iličič*
03/05	h	Cesena	W	3-1	*Iličič 2 (1p), Gilardino*
10/05	a	Empoli	W	3-2	*Iličič 2, Salah*
18/05	h	Parma	W	3-0	*Gonzalo Rodríguez, Gilardino, Salah*
24/05	a	Palermo	W	3-2	*Iličič, Gilardino, Alonso*
31/05	h	Chievo	W	3-0	*Iličič, Bernardeschi, Badelj*

No	Name	Nat	DoB	Pos	Aps	(s)	Gls
28	Marcos Alonso	ESP	28/12/90	D	19	(3)	1
10	Alberto Aquilani		07/07/84	M	17	(8)	
30	Khouma Babacar	SEN	17/03/93	A	14	(6)	7
5	Milan Badelj	CRO	25/02/89	M	18	(3)	1
35	Ricardo Bagadur	CRO	16/09/95	D		(1)	
19	José María Basanta	ARG	03/04/84	D	23	(1)	2
29	Federico Bernardeschi		16/02/94	A	1	(6)	1
20	Borja Valero	ESP	12/01/85	M	25	(3)	2
25	Joshua Brillante	AUS	25/03/93	M	1	(1)	
11	Juan Cuadrado	COL	26/05/88	M	17		4
18	Alessandro Diamanti		02/05/83	A	9	(2)	2
77	Mounir El Hamdaoui	MAR	14/07/84	A		(3)	1
14	Matías Fernández	CHI	15/05/86	M	23	(6)	2
9	Alberto Gilardino		05/07/82	A	8	(6)	4
33	Mario Gomez	GER	10/07/85	A	16	(4)	4
2	Gonzalo Rodríguez	ARG	10/04/84	D	30		7
72	Josip Iličič	SVN	29/01/88	M	17	(8)	8
17	Joaquín	ESP	21/07/81	M	14	(9)	2
16	Jasmin Kurtič	SVN	10/01/89	M	15	(6)	1
32	Andrea Lazzari		03/12/84	M	1	(2)	
1	Neto	BRA	19/07/89	G	29		
23	Manuel Pasqual		13/03/82	D	16	(4)	2
7	David Pizarro	CHI	11/09/79	M	18	(8)	
4	Micah Richards	ENG	24/06/88	D	7	(3)	
38	Aleandro Rosi		17/05/87	D	3	(1)	
74	Mohamed Salah	EGY	15/06/92	M	10	(6)	6
15	Stefan Savić	MNE	08/01/91	D	28	(1)	2
12	Ciprian Tătăruşanu	ROU	09/02/86	G	9		
40	Nenad Tomović	SRB	30/08/87	D	22	(2)	1
6	Juan Manuel Vargas	PER	05/10/83	M	8	(11)	1

Genoa CFC

1893 • Luigi Ferraris (36,599) • genoacfc.it

Major honours

Italian League (9) 1898, 1899, 1900, 1902, 1903, 1904, 1915, 1923, 1924; Italian Cup (1) 1937

Coach: Gian Piero Gasperini

2014

31/08	h	Napoli	L	1-2	*Pinilla*
14/09	a	Fiorentina	D	0-0	
21/09	h	Lazio	W	1-0	*Pinilla*
24/09	a	Verona	D	2-2	*Matri 2*
28/09	h	Sampdoria	L	0-1	
05/10	a	Parma	W	2-1	*Perotti, Matri*
20/10	h	Empoli	D	1-1	*Bertolacci*
26/10	a	Chievo	W	2-1	*Matri, Pinilla*
29/10	h	Juventus	W	1-0	*Antonini*
02/11	a	Udinese	W	4-2	*Marchese, Iago Falqué, Matri, Kucka*
09/11	a	Cagliari	D	1-1	*og (Rossettini)*
24/11	h	Palermo	D	1-1	*Antonelli*
30/11	a	Cesena	W	3-0	*Matri, Antonelli, og (Volta)*
07/12	h	Milan	W	1-0	*Antonelli*
14/12	h	Roma	L	0-1	
21/12	a	Torino	L	1-2	*Iago Falqué*

2015

06/01	h	Atalanta	D	2-2	*Iago Falqué (p), Matri*
11/01	a	Internazionale	L	1-3	*Izzo*
18/01	h	Sassuolo	D	3-3	*Iago Falqué, Fetfatzidis 2 (1p)*
26/01	a	Napoli	L	1-2	*Iago Falqué*
31/01	h	Fiorentina	D	1-1	*og (Tătăruşanu)*
09/02	a	Lazio	W	1-0	*Perotti (p)*
15/02	h	Verona	W	5-2	*og (Agostini), Niang 2, Bertolacci, Perotti*
24/02	a	Sampdoria	D	1-1	*Iago Falqué*
08/03	a	Empoli	D	1-1	*Niang*
15/03	h	Chievo	L	0-2	
22/03	a	Juventus	L	0-1	
04/04	h	Udinese	D	1-1	*De Maio*
11/04	h	Cagliari	W	2-0	*Niang, Iago Falqué*
15/04	h	Parma	W	2-0	*Iago Falqué, Pavoletti*
19/04	a	Palermo	L	1-2	*Iago Falqué*
26/04	h	Cesena	W	3-1	*Bertolacci, Perotti (p), Pavoletti*
29/04	a	Milan	W	3-1	*Bertolacci, Niang, Iago Falqué (p)*
03/05	a	Roma	L	0-2	
11/05	h	Torino	W	5-1	*Iago Falqué, Tino Costa 2, Bertolacci, Pavoletti*
17/05	a	Atalanta	W	4-1	*Pavoletti, Bertolacci, Iago Falqué 2*
23/05	h	Internazionale	W	3-2	*Pavoletti, Lestienne, Kucka*
31/05	a	Sassuolo	L	1-3	*Pavoletti*

No	Name	Nat	DoB	Pos	Aps	(s)	Gls
13	Luca Antonelli		11/02/87	D	18	(1)	3
3	Luca Antonini		04/08/82	D	3	(4)	1
18	Zakarya Bergdich	MAR	07/01/89	D	9	(2)	
91	Andrea Bertolacci		11/01/91	M	31	(3)	6
22	Marco Borriello		18/06/82	A	3	(5)	
8	Nicolás Burdisso	ARG	12/04/81	D	30		
4	Sebastian De Maio	FRA	05/03/87	D	31	(2)	1
21	Edenílson	BRA	18/12/89	M	28	(2)	
18	Ioannis Fetfatzidis	GRE	21/12/90	M	2	(3)	2
19	Leandro Greco		19/07/86	M	3	(4)	
24	Iago Falqué	ESP	04/01/90	M	28	(4)	13
5	Armando Izzo		02/03/92	D	11	(9)	1
33	Juraj Kucka	SVK	26/02/87	M	19	(15)	2
23	Eugenio Lamanna		07/08/89	G	6	(2)	
93	Diego Laxalt	URU	07/02/93	M	1	(7)	
16	Maxime Lestienne	BEL	17/06/92	A	10	(13)	1
38	Rolando Mandragora		29/09/97	M	2	(3)	
15	Giovanni Marchese		17/10/84	D	10	(1)	1
32	Alessandro Matri		19/08/84	A	12	(4)	7
92	Franco Mussis	ARG	19/04/92	M		(1)	
11	M'Baye Niang	FRA	19/12/94	A	12	(2)	5
37	Giuseppe Panico		10/05/97	A		(1)	
19	Leonardo Pavoletti		26/11/88	A	4	(6)	6
1	Mattia Perin		10/11/92	G	32		
10	Diego Perotti	ARG	26/07/88	M	27		4
9	Mauricio Pinilla	CHI	04/02/84	A	6	(6)	3
27	Antonino Ragusa		27/03/90	A		(1)	
88	Tomás Rincón	COL	13/01/88	M	27	(2)	
14	Facundo Roncaglia	ARG	10/02/87	D	32		
87	Aleandro Rosi		17/05/87	D	4	(3)	
69	Stefano Sturaro		09/03/93	M	13		
2	Alassane També	FRA	26/01/92	D	2	(4)	
20	Tino Costa	ARG	09/01/85	M	2	(4)	2

FC Internazionale Milano

1908 • Giuseppe Meazza (80,018) • inter.it

Major honours

European Champion Clubs' Cup/UEFA Champions League (3) 1964, 1965, 2010; UEFA Cup (3) 1991, 1994, 1998; European/South American Cup (2) 1964, 1965; FIFA Club World Cup (1) 2010; Italian League (18) 1910, 1920, 1930, 1938, 1940, 1953, 1954, 1963, 1965, 1966, 1971, 1980, 1989, 2006, 2007, 2008, 2009, 2010; Italian Cup (7) 1939, 1978, 1982, 2005, 2006, 2010, 2011

Coach: Walter Mazzarri; (14/11/14) Roberto Mancini

2014

31/08	a	Torino	D	0-0	
14/09	h	Sassuolo	W	7-0	*Icardi 3, Kovačić, Osvaldo 2, Guarín*
21/09	a	Palermo	D	1-1	*Kovačić*
24/09	h	Atalanta	W	2-0	*Osvaldo, Hernanes*
28/09	h	Cagliari	L	1-4	*Osvaldo*
05/10	a	Fiorentina	L	0-3	
19/10	h	Napoli	D	2-2	*Guarín, Hernanes*
26/10	a	Cesena	W	1-0	*Icardi (p)*
29/10	h	Sampdoria	W	1-0	*Icardi (p)*
01/11	a	Parma	L	0-2	
09/11	h	Verona	D	2-2	*Icardi 2*
23/11	a	Milan	D	1-1	*Obi*
30/11	a	Roma	L	2-4	*Ranocchia, Osvaldo*
07/12	h	Udinese	L	1-2	*Icardi*
15/12	a	Chievo	W	2-0	*Kovačić, Ranocchia*
21/12	h	Lazio	D	2-2	*Kovačić, Palacio*

2015

06/01	a	Juventus	D	1-1	*Icardi*
11/01	h	Genoa	W	3-1	*Palacio, Icardi, Vidić*
17/01	a	Empoli	D	0-0	
25/01	h	Torino	L	0-1	
01/02	a	Sassuolo	L	1-3	*Icardi*
08/02	h	Palermo	W	3-0	*Guarín, Icardi 2*
15/02	a	Atalanta	W	4-1	*Shaqiri (p), Guarín 2, Palacio*
23/02	a	Cagliari	W	2-1	*Kovačić, Icardi*
01/03	h	Fiorentina	L	0-1	
08/03	a	Napoli	D	2-2	*Palacio, Icardi (p)*
15/03	h	Cesena	D	1-1	*Palacio*
22/03	a	Sampdoria	L	0-1	
04/04	h	Parma	D	1-1	*Guarín*
11/04	a	Verona	W	3-0	*Icardi, Palacio, og (Moras)*
19/04	h	Milan	D	0-0	
25/04	h	Roma	W	2-1	*Hernanes, Icardi*
28/04	a	Udinese	W	2-1	*Icardi (p), Podolski*
03/05	h	Chievo	D	0-0	
10/05	a	Lazio	W	2-1	*Hernanes 2*
16/05	h	Juventus	L	1-2	*Icardi*
23/05	a	Genoa	L	2-3	*Icardi, Palacio*
31/05	h	Empoli	W	4-3	*Palacio, Icardi 2, Brozović*

No	Name	Nat	DoB	Pos	Aps	(s)	Gls
6	Marco Andreolli		10/06/86	D	5	(1)	
97	Federico Bonazzoli		21/05/97	A		(4)	
77	Marcelo Brozović	CRO	16/11/92	M	13	(2)	1
29	Gaston Camara	GUI	31/03/96	M		(2)	
14	Hugo Campagnaro	ARG	27/06/80	D	8	(2)	
30	Juan Pablo Carrizo	ARG	06/05/84	G	1		
33	Danilo D'Ambrosio		09/09/88	D	19	(4)	
93	Federico Dimarco		10/11/97	D		(1)	
22	Dodô	BRA	06/02/92	D	16	(4)	
54	Isaac Donkor	GHA	15/08/95	D	1	(1)	
26	Felipe	BRA	31/07/84	D	3	(1)	
27	Assane Gnoukouri	CIV	28/09/96	M	2	(3)	
13	Fredy Guarín	COL	30/06/86	M	25	(3)	6
1	Samir Handanovič	SVN	14/07/84	G	37		
88	Hernanes	BRA	29/05/85	M	17	(9)	5
9	Mauro Icardi	ARG	19/02/93	A	33	(3)	22
2	Jonathan	BRA	27/02/86	D	2		
5	Juan	BRA	10/06/91	D	32		
10	Mateo Kovačić	CRO	06/05/94	M	26	(9)	5
44	René Krhin	SVN	21/05/90	M		(3)	
17	Zdravko Kuzmanović	SRB	22/09/87	M	10	(4)	
90	Yann M'Vila	FRA	29/06/90	M	3	(5)	
25	Ibrahima Mbaye	SEN	19/11/94	D		(4)	
18	Gary Medel	CHI	03/08/87	M	34	(1)	
55	Yuto Nagatomo	JPN	12/09/86	D	11	(3)	
20	Joel Obi	NGA	22/05/91	M	6	(5)	1
7	Pablo Osvaldo		12/01/86	A	5	(7)	5
8	Rodrigo Palacio	ARG	05/02/82	A	30	(5)	8
11	Lukas Podolski	GER	04/06/85	A	8	(9)	1
28	George Puşcaş	ROU	08/04/96	A	1	(3)	
23	Andrea Ranocchia		16/02/88	D	32	(1)	2
21	Davide Santon		02/01/91	D	7	(2)	
91	Xherdan Shaqiri	SUI	10/10/91	M	8	(7)	1
15	Nemanja Vidić	SRB	21/10/81	D	23		1

ITALY

Juventus

1897 • Juventus Stadium (41,254) • juventus.com

Major honours
European Champion Clubs' Cup/UEFA Champions League (2) 1985, 1996; UEFA Cup Winners' Cup (1) 1984; UEFA Cup (3) 1977, 1990, 1993; UEFA Super Cup (2) 1984, 1997; European/South American Cup (2) 1985, 1996; Italian League (31) 1905, 1926, 1931, 1932, 1933, 1934, 1935, 1950, 1952, 1958, 1960, 1961, 1967, 1972, 1973, 1975, 1977, 1978, 1981, 1982, 1984, 1986, 1995, 1997, 1998, 2002, 2003, 2012, 2013, 2014, 2015; Italian Cup (10) 1938, 1942, 1959, 1960, 1965, 1979, 1983, 1990, 1995, 2015

Coach: Massimiliano Allegri

2014					
30/08	a	Chievo	W	1-0	*og (Biraghi)*
13/09	h	Udinese	W	2-0	*Tévez, Marchisio*
20/09	a	Milan	W	1-0	*Tévez*
24/09	h	Cesena	W	3-0	*Vidal 2 (1p), Lichtsteiner*
27/09	a	Atalanta	W	3-0	*Tévez 2, Morata*
05/10	h	Roma	W	3-2	*Tévez 2 (2p), Bonucci*
18/10	a	Sassuolo	D	1-1	*Pogba*
26/10	h	Palermo	W	2-0	*Vidal, Llorente*
29/10	a	Genoa	L	0-1	
01/11	a	Empoli	W	2-0	*Pirlo, Morata*
09/11	h	Parma	W	7-0	*Llorente 2, Lichtsteiner, Tévez 2, Morata 2*
22/11	a	Lazio	W	3-0	*Pogba 2, Tévez*
30/11	h	Torino	W	2-1	*Vidal (p), Pirlo*
05/12	a	Fiorentina	D	0-0	
14/12	h	Sampdoria	D	1-1	*Evra*
18/12	a	Cagliari	W	3-1	*Tévez, Vidal, Llorente*
2015					
06/01	h	Internazionale	D	1-1	*Tévez*
11/01	a	Napoli	W	3-1	*Pogba, Cáceres, Vidal*
18/01	h	Verona	W	4-0	*Pogba, Tévez 2, Pereyra*
25/01	h	Chievo	W	2-0	*Pogba, Lichtsteiner*
01/02	a	Udinese	D	0-0	
07/02	h	Milan	W	3-1	*Tévez, Bonucci, Morata*
15/02	a	Cesena	D	2-2	*Morata, Marchisio*
20/02	h	Atalanta	W	2-1	*Llorente, Pirlo*
02/03	a	Roma	D	1-1	*Tévez*
09/03	h	Sassuolo	W	1-0	*Pogba*
14/03	a	Palermo	W	1-0	*Morata*
22/03	h	Genoa	W	1-0	*Tévez*
04/04	h	Empoli	W	2-0	*Tévez, Pereyra*
11/04	a	Parma	L	0-1	
18/04	h	Lazio	W	2-0	*Tévez, Bonucci*
26/04	a	Torino	L	1-2	*Pirlo*
29/04	h	Fiorentina	W	3-2	*Llorente, Tévez 2*
02/05	a	Sampdoria	W	1-0	*Vidal*
09/05	h	Cagliari	D	1-1	*Pogba*
16/05	a	Internazionale	W	2-1	*Marchisio (p), Morata*
23/05	h	Napoli	W	3-1	*Pereyra, Sturaro, Pepe (p)*
30/05	a	Verona	D	2-2	*Pereyra, Llorente*

No	Name	Nat	DoB	Pos	Aps	(s)	Gls
22	Kwadwo Asamoah	GHA	09/12/88	M	7		
15	Andrea Barzagli		08/05/81	D	9	(1)	
19	Leonardo Bonucci		01/05/87	D	33	(1)	3
1	Gianluigi Buffon		28/01/78	G	33		
4	Martín Cáceres	URU	07/04/87	D	10		1
3	Giorgio Chiellini		14/08/84	D	27	(1)	
11	Kingsley Coman	FRA	13/06/96	A	5	(9)	
17	Paolo De Ceglie		17/09/86	D	1	(1)	
33	Patrice Evra	FRA	15/05/81	D	21		1
12	Sebastian Giovinco		26/01/87	A	2	(5)	
26	Stephan Lichtsteiner	SUI	16/01/84	D	26	(6)	3
14	Fernando Llorente	ESP	26/02/85	A	25	(6)	7
8	Claudio Marchisio		19/01/86	M	33	(2)	3
32	Alessandro Matri		19/08/84	A	4	(1)	
38	Federico Mattiello		14/07/95	M		(2)	
9	Álvaro Morata	ESP	23/10/92	A	11	(18)	8
5	Angelo Ogbonna		23/05/88	D	18	(7)	
20	Simone Padoin		18/03/84	M	14	(11)	
7	Simone Pepe		30/08/83	M	1	(11)	1
37	Roberto Pereyra	ARG	07/01/91	M	27	(8)	4
21	Andrea Pirlo		19/05/79	M	19	(1)	4
6	Paul Pogba	FRA	15/03/93	M	24	(2)	8
2	Rômulo		22/05/87	M	3	(1)	
30	Marco Storari		07/01/77	G	5		
27	Stefano Sturaro		09/03/93	M	8	(4)	1
10	Carlos Tévez	ARG	05/02/84	A	29	(3)	20
23	Arturo Vidal	CHI	22/05/87	M	23	(5)	7
24	Mattia Vitale		01/10/97	M		(2)	

SS Lazio

1900 • Olimpico (70,634) • sslazio.it

Major honours
UEFA Cup Winners' Cup (1) 1999; UEFA Super Cup (1) 1999; Italian League (2) 1974, 2000; Italian Cup (6) 1958, 1998, 2000, 2004, 2009, 2013

Coach: Stefano Pioli

2014					
31/08	a	Milan	L	1-3	*og (Alex)*
14/09	h	Cesena	W	3-0	*Candreva, Parolo, Mauri*
21/09	a	Genoa	L	0-1	
25/09	h	Udinese	L	0-1	
29/09	a	Palermo	W	4-0	*Djordjević 3, Parolo*
05/10	h	Sassuolo	W	3-2	*Mauri, Djordjević, Candreva*
19/10	a	Fiorentina	W	2-0	*Djordjević, Lulić*
26/10	h	Torino	W	2-1	*Biglia, Klose*
30/10	a	Verona	D	1-1	*Lulić*
03/11	h	Cagliari	W	4-2	*Mauri, Klose 2, Ederson*
09/11	a	Empoli	L	1-2	*Djordjević*
22/11	h	Juventus	L	0-3	
29/11	a	Chievo	D	0-0	
07/12	a	Parma	W	2-1	*Mauri, Felipe Anderson*
13/12	h	Atalanta	W	3-0	*Mauri 2, Lulić*
21/12	a	Internazionale	D	2-2	*Felipe Anderson 2*
2015					
05/01	h	Sampdoria	W	3-0	*Parolo, Felipe Anderson, Djordjević*
11/01	a	Roma	D	2-2	*Mauri, Felipe Anderson*
18/01	h	Napoli	L	0-1	
24/01	h	Milan	W	3-1	*Parolo 2, Klose*
01/02	a	Cesena	L	1-2	*Klose*
09/02	h	Genoa	L	0-1	
15/02	a	Udinese	W	1-0	*Candreva (p)*
22/02	h	Palermo	W	2-1	*Mauri, Candreva*
01/03	a	Sassuolo	W	3-0	*Felipe Anderson, Klose, Parolo*
09/03	h	Fiorentina	W	4-0	*Biglia, Candreva (p), Klose 2*
16/03	a	Torino	W	2-0	*Felipe Anderson 2*
22/03	h	Verona	W	2-0	*Felipe Anderson, Candreva*
04/04	a	Cagliari	W	3-1	*Klose, Biglia (p), Parolo*
12/04	h	Empoli	W	4-0	*Mauri, Klose, Candreva, Felipe Anderson*
18/04	a	Juventus	L	0-2	
26/04	h	Chievo	D	1-1	*Klose*
29/04	h	Parma	W	4-0	*Parolo, Klose, Candreva, Baldé*
03/05	a	Atalanta	D	1-1	*Parolo*
10/05	h	Internazionale	L	1-2	*Candreva*
16/05	a	Sampdoria	W	1-0	*Gentiletti*
25/05	h	Roma	L	1-2	*Djordjević*
31/05	a	Napoli	W	4-2	*Parolo, Candreva, Onazi, Klose*

No	Name	Nat	DoB	Pos	Aps	(s)	Gls
14	Keita Baldé	SEN	08/03/95	A	6	(17)	1
8	Dušan Basta	SRB	18/08/84	D	27		
1	Etrit Berisha	ALB	10/03/89	G	8	(2)	
20	Lucas Biglia	ARG	30/01/86	M	27		3
17	Bruno Pereirinha	POR	02/03/88	M	2	(1)	
5	Edson Braafheid	NED	08/04/83	D	12	(4)	
27	Lorik Cana	ALB	27/07/83	D	15	(2)	
87	Antonio Candreva		28/02/87	M	31	(3)	10
32	Danilo Cataldi		06/08/94	M	11	(5)	
39	Luis Cavanda	COD	02/01/91	D	10	(6)	
2	Michaël Ciani	FRA	06/04/84	D	9	(3)	
3	Stefan de Vrij	NED	05/02/92	D	29	(1)	
9	Filip Djordjević	SRB	28/09/87	A	15	(9)	8
10	Ederson	BRA	13/01/86	M		(4)	1
7	Felipe Anderson	BRA	15/04/93	M	23	(9)	10
18	Santiago Gentiletti	ARG	09/01/85	D	5		1
15	Álvaro González	URU	29/10/84	M	2	(2)	
11	Miroslav Klose	GER	09/06/78	A	21	(13)	13
13	Abdoulay Konko	FRA	09/03/84	D	1	(1)	
24	Cristian Ledesma		24/09/82	M	7	(6)	
19	Senad Lulić	BIH	18/01/86	M	22	(3)	3
22	Federico Marchetti		07/02/83	G	30		
6	Stefano Mauri		08/01/80	M	25	(4)	9
33	Maurício	BRA	20/09/88	D	14	(1)	
85	Diego Novaretti	ARG	09/05/85	D	2	(3)	
23	Ogenyi Onazi	NGA	25/12/92	M	6	(10)	1
16	Marco Parolo		25/01/85	M	34		10
34	Brayan Perea	COL	25/02/93	A		(5)	
26	Ştefan Radu	ROU	22/10/86	D	24		

AC Milan

1899 • Giuseppe Meazza (80,018) • acmilan.com

Major honours
European Champion Clubs' Cup/UEFA Champions League (7) 1963, 1969, 1989, 1990, 1994, 2003, 2007; UEFA Cup Winners' Cup (2) 1968, 1973; UEFA Super Cup (5) 1989, 1990, 1995, 2003, 2007; European/ South American Cup (3) 1969, 1989, 1990; FIFA Club World Cup (1) 2007; Italian League (18) 1901, 1906, 1907, 1951, 1955, 1957, 1959, 1962, 1968, 1979, 1988, 1992, 1993, 1994, 1996, 1999, 2004, 2011; Italian Cup (5) 1967, 1972, 1973, 1977, 2003

Coach: Filippo Inzaghi

2014					
31/08	h	Lazio	W	3-1	*Honda, Muntari, Ménez (p)*
14/09	a	Parma	W	5-4	*Bonaventura, Honda, Ménez 2 (1p), De Jong*
20/09	h	Juventus	L	0-1	
23/09	a	Empoli	D	2-2	*Fernando Torres, Honda*
28/09	a	Cesena	D	1-1	*Rami*
04/10	h	Chievo	W	2-0	*Muntari, Honda*
19/10	a	Verona	W	3-1	*og (Rafael Marques), Honda 2*
26/10	h	Fiorentina	D	1-1	*De Jong*
29/10	a	Cagliari	D	1-1	*Bonaventura*
02/11	h	Palermo	L	0-2	
08/11	a	Sampdoria	D	2-2	*El Shaarawy, Ménez (p)*
23/11	h	Internazionale	D	1-1	*Ménez*
30/11	h	Udinese	W	2-0	*Ménez 2 (1p)*
07/12	a	Genoa	L	0-1	
14/12	h	Napoli	W	2-0	*Ménez, Bonaventura*
20/12	a	Roma	D	0-0	
2015					
06/01	h	Sassuolo	L	1-2	*Poli*
10/01	a	Torino	D	1-1	*Ménez (p)*
18/01	h	Atalanta	L	0-1	
24/01	a	Lazio	L	1-3	*Ménez*
01/02	h	Parma	W	3-1	*Ménez 2 (1p), Zaccardo*
07/02	a	Juventus	L	1-3	*Antonelli*
15/02	h	Empoli	D	1-1	*Destro*
22/02	h	Cesena	W	2-0	*Bonaventura, Pazzini (p)*
28/02	a	Chievo	D	0-0	
07/03	h	Verona	D	2-2	*Ménez (p), og (Tachtsidis)*
16/03	a	Fiorentina	L	1-2	*Destro*
21/03	h	Cagliari	W	3-1	*Ménez 2 (1p), Mexès*
04/04	a	Palermo	W	2-1	*Cerci, Ménez*
12/04	h	Sampdoria	D	1-1	*De Jong*
19/04	a	Internazionale	D	0-0	
25/04	a	Udinese	L	1-2	*Pazzini*
29/04	h	Genoa	L	1-3	*Mexès*
03/05	a	Napoli	L	0-3	
09/05	h	Roma	W	2-1	*Van Ginkel, Destro*
17/05	a	Sassuolo	L	2-3	*Bonaventura, Alex*
24/05	h	Torino	W	3-0	*El Shaarawy 2, Pazzini (p)*
30/05	a	Atalanta	W	3-1	*Pazzini (p), Bonaventura 2*

No	Name	Nat	DoB	Pos	Aps	(s)	Gls
20	Ignazio Abate		12/11/86	D	21	(2)	
32	Christian Abbiati		08/07/77	G	10	(1)	
33	Alex	BRA	17/06/82	D	18	(3)	1
31	Luca Antonelli		11/02/87	D	12		1
27	Pablo Armero	COL	02/11/86	D	6	(2)	
19	Salvatore Bocchetti		30/11/86	D	6	(3)	
28	Giacomo Bonaventura		22/08/89	M	28	(5)	7
25	Daniele Bonera		31/05/81	D	13	(3)	
96	Davide Calabria		06/12/96	D		(1)	
22	Alessio Cerci		23/07/87	M	7	(9)	1
34	Nigel de Jong	NED	30/11/84	M	29		3
2	Mattia De Sciglio		20/10/92	D	16	(1)	
9	Mattia Destro		20/03/91	A	11	(4)	3
23	Diego López	ESP	03/11/81	G	28		
35	Davide Di Molfetta		23/06/96	A		(1)	
92	Stephan El Shaarawy		27/10/92	A	14	(4)	3
15	Michael Essien	GHA	03/12/82	M	7	(6)	
37	Gian Filippo Felicioli		30/09/97	M		(1)	
9	Fernando Torres	ESP	20/03/84	A	7	(3)	1
10	Keisuke Honda	JPN	13/06/86	M	26	(3)	6
36	Alessandro Mastalli		07/02/96	M		(1)	
7	Jérémy Ménez	FRA	07/05/87	A	31	(2)	16
5	Philippe Mexès	FRA	30/03/82	D	18	(2)	2
18	Riccardo Montolivo		18/01/85	M	9	(1)	
4	Sulley Ali Muntari	GHA	27/08/84	M	12	(4)	2
19	M'Baye Niang	FRA	19/12/94	A	1	(4)	
29	Gabriel Paletta		15/02/86	D	13	(1)	
11	Giampaolo Pazzini		02/08/84	A	4	(22)	4
16	Andrea Poli		29/09/89	M	23	(10)	1
13	Adil Rami	FRA	27/12/85	D	18	(3)	1
8	Riccardo Saponara		21/12/91	M	1		
8	Suso	ESP	19/11/93	M	2	(3)	
21	Marco van Ginkel	NED	01/12/92	M	16	(1)	1
81	Cristian Zaccardo		21/12/81	D	3		1
17	Cristián Zapata	COL	30/09/86	D	8	(4)	

SSC Napoli

1926 • San Paolo (60,240) • sscnapoli.it

Major honours
UEFA Cup (1) 1989; Italian League (2) 1987, 1990;
Italian Cup (5) 1962, 1976, 1987, 2012, 2014

Coach: Rafael Benítez (ESP)

2014

31/08	a	Genoa	W	2-1	Callejón, De Guzmán
14/09	h	Chievo	L	0-1	
21/09	a	Udinese	L	0-1	
24/09	h	Palermo	D	3-3	Koulibaly, Zapata, Callejón
28/09	a	Sassuolo	W	1-0	Callejón
05/10	h	Torino	L	0-1	
19/10	a	Internazionale	D	2-2	Callejón 2
26/10	h	Verona	W	6-2	Hamšík 2, Higuaín 3 (1p), Callejón
29/10	a	Atalanta	D	1-1	Higuaín
01/11	h	Roma	W	2-0	Higuaín, Callejón
09/11	a	Fiorentina	W	1-0	Higuaín
23/11	h	Cagliari	D	3-3	Higuaín, Inler, De Guzmán
01/12	a	Sampdoria	D	1-1	Zapata
07/12	h	Empoli	D	2-2	Zapata, De Guzmán
14/12	a	Milan	L	0-2	
18/12	h	Parma	W	2-0	Zapata, Mertens (p)

2015

06/01	a	Cesena	W	4-1	Callejón, Higuaín 2, og (Capelli)
11/01	h	Juventus	L	1-3	Britos
18/01	a	Lazio	W	1-0	Higuaín
26/01	h	Genoa	W	2-1	Higuaín 2 (1p)
01/02	a	Chievo	W	2-1	og (Cesar), Gabbiadini
08/02	h	Udinese	W	3-1	Mertens, Gabbiadini, og (Théréau)
14/02	a	Palermo	L	1-3	Gabbiadini
23/02	h	Sassuolo	W	2-0	Zapata, Hamšík
01/03	a	Torino	L	0-1	
08/03	h	Internazionale	D	2-2	Hamšík, Higuaín
15/03	a	Verona	L	0-2	
22/03	h	Atalanta	D	1-1	Zapata
04/04	a	Roma	L	0-1	
12/04	h	Fiorentina	W	3-0	Mertens, Hamšík, Callejón
19/04	a	Cagliari	W	3-0	Callejón, og (Balzano), Gabbiadini
26/04	h	Sampdoria	W	4-2	Gabbiadini, Higuaín 2 (1p), Insigne
30/04	a	Empoli	L	2-4	og (Laurini), Hamšík
03/05	h	Milan	W	3-0	Hamšík, Higuaín, Gabbiadini
10/05	a	Parma	D	2-2	Gabbiadini, Mertens
18/05	h	Cesena	W	3-2	Mertens 2, Gabbiadini
23/05	a	Juventus	L	1-3	David López
31/05	h	Lazio	L	2-4	Higuaín 2

No	Name	Nat	DoB	Pos	Aps	(s)	Gls
33	Raúl Albiol	ESP	04/09/85	D	34	(1)	
45	Mariano Andújar	ARG	30/07/83	G	15		
5	Miguel Britos	URU	17/07/85	D	17	(2)	1
7	José Callejón	ESP	11/02/87	M	33	(5)	11
19	David López	ESP	09/10/89	M	29	(3)	1
6	Jonathan de Guzmán	NED	13/09/07	M	12	(11)	0
23	Manolo Gabbiadini		26/11/91	A	8	(12)	8
77	Walter Gargano	URU	23/07/84	M	17	(7)	
31	Faouzi Ghoulam	ALG	01/02/91	D	20	(1)	
17	Marek Hamšík	SVK	27/07/87	M	28	(7)	7
4	Henrique	BRA	14/10/86	D	9	(2)	
9	Gonzalo Higuaín	ARG	10/12/87	A	31	(6)	18
88	Gökhan Inler	SUI	27/06/84	M	16	(3)	1
24	Lorenzo Insigne		04/06/91	A	13	(7)	2
8	Jorginho		20/12/91	M	14	(9)	
26	Kalidou Koulibaly	FRA	20/06/91	D	27	(1)	1
96	Sebastiano Luperto		06/09/96	D		(1)	
11	Christian Maggio		11/02/82	M	29		
14	Dries Mertens	BEL	06/05/87	M	17	(14)	6
16	Giandomenico Mesto		25/05/82	M	3	(4)	
21	Michu	ESP	21/03/86	A	2	(1)	
22	Josip Radošević	CRO	03/04/94	M		(1)	
1	Rafael Cabral	BRA	20/05/90	G	23		
3	Ivan Strinić	CRO	17/07/87	D	9		
91	Duván Zapata	COL	01/04/91	A	6	(15)	6
18	Juan Camilo Zúñiga	COL	14/12/85	D	6	(1)	

US Città di Palermo

1900 • Renzo Barbera (36,349) •
palermocalcio.it

Coach: Giuseppe Iachini

2014

31/08	h	Sampdoria	D	1-1	Dybala
15/09	a	Verona	L	1-2	Vázquez
21/09	h	Internazionale	D	1-1	Vázquez
24/09	a	Napoli	D	3-3	Belotti 2, Vázquez
29/09	h	Lazio	L	0-4	
05/10	a	Empoli	L	0-3	
19/10	h	Cesena	W	2-1	Dybala, González
26/10	a	Juventus	L	0-2	
29/10	h	Chievo	W	1-0	Rigoni
02/11	a	Milan	W	2-0	og (Zapata), Dybala
09/11	h	Udinese	D	1-1	Dybala (p)
24/11	a	Genoa	D	1-1	Dybala
30/11	h	Parma	W	2-1	Dybala, Barreto
06/12	a	Torino	D	2-2	Rigoni, Dybala
13/12	h	Sassuolo	W	2-1	Rigoni, Belotti
21/12	a	Atalanta	D	3-3	Rigoni, Vázquez 2

2015

06/01	h	Cagliari	W	5-0	Morganella, Muñoz, Dybala 2 (1p), Barreto
11/01	a	Fiorentina	L	3-4	Quaison 2, Belotti (p)
17/01	h	Roma	D	1-1	Vázquez
25/01	a	Sampdoria	D	1-1	Vázquez
01/02	h	Verona	W	2-1	Dybala, Belotti
08/02	a	Internazionale	L	0-3	
14/02	h	Napoli	W	3-1	Lazaar, Vázquez, Rigoni
22/02	a	Lazio	L	1-2	Dybala
01/03	h	Empoli	D	0-0	
08/03	a	Cesena	D	0-0	
14/03	h	Juventus	L	0-1	
21/03	a	Chievo	L	0-1	
04/04	h	Milan	L	1-2	Dybala (p)
12/04	a	Udinese	W	3-1	Lazaar, Rigoni, Chochev
19/04	h	Genoa	W	2-1	Chochev 2
26/04	a	Parma	L	0-1	
29/04	h	Torino	D	2-2	Vitiello, Rigoni
02/05	a	Sassuolo	D	0-0	
10/05	h	Atalanta	L	2-3	Vázquez, Rigoni
17/05	a	Cagliari	W	1-0	Vázquez
24/05	h	Fiorentina	L	2-3	Jajalo, Rigoni
31/05	a	Roma	W	2-1	Vázquez (p), Belotti

No	Name	Nat	DoB	Pos	Aps	(s)	Gls
4	Siniša Andjelković	SVN	13/02/86	D	32		
22	Sol Bamba	CIV	13/01/85	D	1		
8	Édgar Barreto	PAR	15/07/84	M	24		2
99	Andrea Belotti		20/12/93	A	9	(29)	6
96	Accursio Bentivegna		21/06/96	A		(3)	
15	Francesco Bolzoni		07/05/89	M	12	(11)	
18	Ivaylo Chochev	BUL	18/02/93	M	13	(5)	3
33	Fabio Daprelà	SUI	19/02/91	D	11	(11)	
14	Francesco Della Rocca		14/09/87	M	1	(4)	
9	Paulo Dybala	ARG	15/11/93	A	34		13
5	Emerson		03/08/94	D		(9)	
23	Zouhair Feddal	MAR	01/01/90	D	7		
12	Giancarlo González	CRC	08/02/88	D	28		1
28	Mato Jajalo	CRO	25/05/88	M	14	(2)	1
10	João Silva	POR	21/05/90	A		(1)	
54	Antonino La Gumina		06/03/96	A		(1)	
7	Achraf Lazaar	MAR	22/01/92	D	27	(2)	2
11	Simon Makienok	DEN	21/11/90	A		(4)	
25	Enzo Maresca		10/02/80	M	14	(5)	
89	Michel Morganella	SUI	17/05/89	D	20		1
6	Ezequiel Muñoz	ARG	08/10/90	D	13		1
17	Granddi Ngoyi	FRA	17/05/88	M		(5)	
3	Eros Pisano		31/03/87	D	4		
21	Robin Quaison	SWE	09/10/93	M	8	(11)	2
27	Luca Rigoni		07/12/84	M	31		9
3	Andrea Rispoli		29/09/88	D	9	(6)	
70	Stefano Sorrentino		28/03/79	G	35		
19	Claudio Terzi		19/06/84	D	14	(1)	
1	Samir Ujkani	ALB	05/07/88	G	3		
20	Franco Vázquez		22/02/89	M	37		10
2	Roberto Vitiello		08/05/83	D	17	(2)	1

Parma FC

1913 • Ennio Tardini (21,473) • fcparma.com

Major honours
UEFA Cup Winners' Cup (1) 1993; UEFA Cup (2)
1995, 1999; UEFA Super Cup (1) 1994; Italian Cup
(3) 1992, 1999, 2002

Coach: Roberto Donadoni

2014

31/08	a	Cesena	L	0-1	
14/09	h	Milan	L	4-5	Cassano, Felipe, Lucarelli, og (De Sciglio)
21/09	a	Chievo	W	3-2	Cassano 2, Coda
24/09	h	Roma	L	1-2	De Ceglie
29/09	a	Udinese	L	2-4	Mauri, Cassano (p)
05/10	h	Genoa	L	1-2	Coda
19/10	a	Atalanta	L	0-1	
25/10	h	Sassuolo	L	1-3	Cassano
29/10	a	Torino	L	0-1	
01/11	h	Internazionale	W	2-0	De Ceglie 2
09/11	a	Juventus	L	0-7	
23/11	h	Empoli	L	0-2	
30/11	a	Palermo	L	1-2	Palladino
07/12	h	Lazio	L	1-2	Palladino
14/12	a	Cagliari	D	0-0	
18/12	h	Napoli	L	0-2	

2015

06/01	h	Fiorentina	W	1-0	Costa
11/01	a	Verona	L	1-3	Lodi
18/01	h	Sampdoria	L	0-1	
25/01	h	Cesena	L	1-2	og (Cascione)
01/02	a	Milan	L	1-3	Nocerino
11/02	h	Chievo	L	0-1	
15/02	a	Roma	L	0-0	
08/03	h	Atalanta	D	0-0	
15/03	a	Sassuolo	L	1-4	Lila
22/03	h	Torino	L	0-2	
04/04	a	Internazionale	D	1-1	Lila
08/04	h	Udinese	W	1-0	Varela
11/04	h	Juventus	W	1-0	Mauri
15/04	a	Genoa	L	0-2	
19/04	a	Empoli	D	2-2	Lodi, Belfodil
26/04	h	Palermo	W	1-0	Nocerino (p)
29/04	a	Lazio	L	0-4	
03/05	a	Cagliari	L	0-4	
10/05	h	Napoli	D	2-2	Palladino, Jorquera
18/05	a	Fiorentina	L	0-3	
24/05	h	Verona	D	2-2	Nocerino, Varela
31/05	a	Sampdoria	D	2-2	Palladino, Varela

No	Name	Nat	DoB	Pos	Aps	(s)	Gls
30	Afriyie Acquah	GHA	05/01/92	M	12	(2)	
11	Amauri		03/06/80	A		(1)	
10	Ishak Belfodil	ALG	12/01/92	A	13	(10)	1
7	Jonathan Biabiany	FRA	28/04/88	A	1		
20	Soufiane Bidaoui	MAR	20/04/90	A	1	(3)	
37	Jeremy Broh	FRA	21/03/97	M		(1)	
2	Mattia Cassani		26/08/83	D	13	(5)	
99	Antonio Cassano		12/07/82	A	18	(1)	5
88	Massimo Coda		10/11/88	A	9	(9)	2
15	Andrea Costa		01/02/86	D	20	(2)	1
11	Paolo De Ceglie		17/09/86	D	11		3
58	Mirko Esposito		08/04/96	D			
28	Zouhair Feddal	MAR	01/01/89	D	12	(1)	
19	Felipe	BRA	31/07/84	D	11		1
14	Daniele Galloppa		15/05/85	M	8	(9)	
5	Abdelkader Ghezzal	ALG	05/12/84	A	10	(9)	
18	Massimo Gobbi		31/10/80	D	30	(3)	
34	Lukáš Haraslín	SVK	26/05/96	M		(2)	
22	Alessandro Iacobucci		03/06/91	G	5	(2)	
80	Cristóbal Jorquera	CHI	04/08/88	M	14	(3)	1
3	Andi Lila	ALB	12/02/86	D	9	(4)	2
21	Francesco Lodi		23/03/84	M	20	(3)	2
6	Alessandro Lucarelli		22/07/77	D	28		1
70	Lucas	BRA	09/01/98	D			
31	McDonald Mariga	KEN	04/04/87	M	4	(5)	
8	José Mauri		16/05/96	M	29	(4)	2
83	Antonio Mirante		08/07/83	G	33		
23	Antonio Nocerino		09/04/85	M	19	(1)	3
29	Gabriele Paletta		15/02/86	D	6	(1)	
17	Raffaele Palladino		17/04/84	M	16	(6)	4
4	Pedro Mendes	POR	01/10/90	D	17	(4)	
9	Nicola Pozzi		30/06/86	A		(3)	
13	Giuseppe Prestia		13/11/93	D		(1)	
33	Andrea Rispoli		13/09/88	D	7	(7)	
13	Stefan Ristovski	MKD	12/02/92	D	4	(2)	
24	Cristian Rodríguez	URU	30/09/85	M	5		
27	Fabiano Santacroce		24/08/86	D	12	(3)	
26	Silvestre Varela	POR	02/02/85	A	19		3

AS Roma

1927 • Olimpico (70,634) • asroma.it
Major honours
Inter Cities Fairs Cup (1) 1961; Italian League (3)
1942, 1983, 2001; Italian Cup (9) 1964, 1969, 1980,
1981, 1984, 1986, 1991, 2007, 2008
Coach: Rudi Garcia (FRA)

2014

30/08	h	Fiorentina	W	2-0	Nainggolan, Gervinho
13/09	a	Empoli	W	1-0	og (Sepe)
21/09	h	Cagliari	W	2-0	Destro, Florenzi
24/09	a	Parma	W	2-1	Ljajić, Pjanić
27/09	h	Verona	W	2-1	Florenzi, Destro
05/10	a	Juventus	L	2-3	Totti (p), Iturbe
18/10	h	Chievo	W	3-0	Destro, Ljajić, Totti (p)
25/10	a	Sampdoria	D	0-0	
29/10	h	Cesena	W	2-0	Destro, De Rossi
01/11	a	Napoli	L	0-2	
09/11	h	Torino	W	3-0	Torosidis, Keita, Ljajić
22/11	a	Atalanta	W	2-1	Ljajić, Nainggolan
30/11	h	Internazionale	W	4-2	Gervinho, Holebas, Pjanić 2
06/12	h	Sassuolo	D	2-2	Ljajić 2 (1p)
14/12	a	Genoa	W	1-0	Nainggolan
20/12	h	Milan	D	0-0	

2015

06/01	a	Udinese	W	1-0	Astori
11/01	h	Lazio	D	2-2	Totti 2
17/01	a	Palermo	D	1-1	Destro
25/01	a	Fiorentina	D	1-1	Ljajić
31/01	h	Empoli	D	1-1	Maicon
08/02	a	Cagliari	W	2-1	Ljajić, Paredes
15/02	h	Parma	D	0-0	
22/02	a	Verona	D	1-1	Totti
02/03	h	Juventus	D	1-1	Keita
08/03	h	Chievo	D	0-0	
16/03	h	Sampdoria	L	0-2	
22/03	a	Cesena	W	1-0	De Rossi
04/04	h	Napoli	W	1-0	Pjanić
12/04	a	Torino	D	1-1	Florenzi (p)
19/04	h	Atalanta	D	1-1	Totti (p)
25/04	a	Internazionale	L	1-2	Nainggolan
29/04	h	Sassuolo	W	3-0	Doumbia, Florenzi, Pjanić
03/05	h	Genoa	W	2-0	Doumbia, Florenzi
09/05	a	Milan	L	1-2	Totti (p)
17/05	h	Udinese	W	2-1	Nainggolan, Torosidis
25/05	a	Lazio	W	2-1	Iturbe, Yanga-Mbiwa
31/05	h	Palermo	L	1-2	Totti

No	Name	Nat	DoB	Pos	Aps	(s)	Gls
23	Davide Astori		07/01/87	D	22	(2)	1
42	Federico Balzaretti		06/12/81	D	1		
3	Ashley Cole	ENG	20/12/80	D	11		
16	Daniele De Rossi		24/07/83	M	25	(1)	2
26	Morgan De Sanctis		26/03/77	G	35		
22	Mattia Destro		20/03/91	A	8	(8)	5
88	Seydou Doumbia	CIV	31/12/87	A	6	(7)	2
82	Urby Emanuelson	NED	16/06/86	D		(2)	
24	Alessandro Florenzi		11/03/91	M	24	(11)	5
27	Gervinho	CIV	27/05/87	A	21	(3)	2
25	José Holebas	GRE	27/06/84	D	23	(1)	1
19	Víctor Ibarbo	COL	19/05/90	A	6	(4)	
7	Juan Manuel Iturbe	ARG	04/06/93	A	17	(10)	2
20	Seydou Keita	MLI	16/01/80	M	18	(8)	2
5	Leandro Castán	BRA	05/11/86	D	1		
4	Adem Ljajić	SRB	29/09/91	M	23	(9)	6
13	Maicon	BRA	26/07/81	D	11	(3)	1
44	Kostas Manolas	GRE	14/06/91	D	30		
4	Radja Nainggolan	BEL	04/05/88	M	30	(5)	5
32	Leandro Paredes	ARG	29/06/94	M	4	(6)	1
52	Lorenzo Pellegrini		19/06/96	M		(1)	
15	Miralem Pjanić	BIH	02/04/90	M	28	(6)	5
48	Salih Uçan	TUR	06/01/94	M	2	(2)	
96	Antonio Sanabria	PAR	04/03/96	A		(2)	
28	Łukasz Skorupski	POL	05/05/91	G	3		
50	Michele Somma		16/03/95	D		(1)	
33	Nicolás Spolli	ARG	20/02/83	D	1		
6	Kevin Strootman	NED	13/02/90	M	4	(2)	
35	Vasilios Torosidis	GRE	10/06/85	D	17	(3)	2
10	Francesco Totti		27/09/76	A	24	(3)	8
53	Daniele Verde		20/06/96	A	1	(6)	
2	Mapou Yanga-Mbiwa	FRA	15/05/89	D	22	(6)	1

UC Sampdoria

1946 • Luigi Ferraris (36,599) • sampdoria.it
Major honours
UEFA Cup Winners' Cup (1) 1990; Italian League (1)
1991; Italian Cup (4) 1985, 1988, 1989, 1994
Coach: Siniša Mihajlović (SRB)

2014

31/08	a	Palermo	D	1-1	Gastaldello
14/09	h	Torino	W	2-0	Gabbiadini, Okaka
21/09	a	Sassuolo	D	0-0	
24/09	h	Chievo	W	2-1	Gastaldello, Romagnoli
28/09	a	Genoa	W	1-0	Gabbiadini
05/10	h	Atalanta	W	1-0	Gabbiadini
19/10	a	Cagliari	D	2-2	Gabbiadini, Pedro Obiang
25/10	h	Roma	D	0-0	
29/10	a	Internazionale	L	0-1	
02/11	h	Fiorentina	W	3-1	Palombo (p), Rizzo, Éder
08/11	h	Milan	D	2-2	Okaka, Éder
23/11	a	Cesena	D	1-1	og (Nica)
01/12	h	Napoli	D	1-1	Éder
08/12	a	Verona	W	3-1	Éder (p), Okaka, Gabbiadini
14/12	a	Juventus	D	1-1	Gabbiadini
21/12	h	Udinese	D	2-2	Pedro Obiang, Gabbiadini

2015

05/01	a	Lazio	L	0-3	
11/01	h	Empoli	W	1-0	Éder
18/01	a	Parma	W	2-0	Bergessio, Soriano
25/01	h	Palermo	D	1-1	Éder
01/02	a	Torino	L	1-5	Pedro Obiang
08/02	h	Sassuolo	D	1-1	Éder
15/02	a	Chievo	L	1-2	Muriel
24/02	h	Genoa	D	1-1	Éder
01/03	a	Atalanta	W	2-1	Muriel, Okaka
07/03	a	Cagliari	W	2-0	De Silvestri, Eto'o
16/03	a	Roma	W	2-0	De Silvestri, Muriel
22/03	h	Internazionale	W	1-0	Éder
04/04	a	Fiorentina	L	0-2	
12/04	a	Milan	D	1-1	Soriano
18/04	h	Cesena	D	0-0	
26/04	a	Napoli	L	2-4	og (Albiol), Muriel
29/04	h	Verona	D	1-1	De Silvestri
02/05	h	Juventus	L	0-1	
10/05	a	Udinese	W	4-1	Soriano 2, Acquah, Duncan
16/05	h	Lazio	L	0-1	
24/05	a	Empoli	D	1-1	Eto'o
31/05	h	Parma	D	2-2	Romagnoli, De Silvestri

No	Name	Nat	DoB	Pos	Aps	(s)	Gls
30	Afriyie Acquah	GHA	05/01/92	M	10		1
18	Gonzalo Bergessio	ARG	20/07/84	A	7	(16)	1
86	Fabrizio Cacciatore		08/10/86	D	8	(3)	
25	Andrea Coda		25/04/85	D		(2)	
8	Joaquín Correa	ARG	13/08/94	M	2	(4)	
17	Lorenzo De Silvestri		23/05/88	D	33		4
27	Luka Djordjević	MNE	09/07/94	A	1	(2)	
6	Alfred Duncan	GHA	10/03/93	M	13	(13)	1
23	Éder		15/11/86	A	28	(2)	9
99	Samuel Eto'o	CMR	10/03/81	A	13	(5)	2
7	Francesco Fedato		15/10/92	A		(1)	
21	Manolo Gabbiadini		26/11/91	A	11	(2)	7
28	Daniele Gastaldello		25/06/83	D	13	(1)	2
10	Nenad Krstičić	SRB	03/07/90	M	2	(10)	
32	Marco Marchionni		22/07/80	M	1		
33	Djamel Mesbah	ALG	09/10/84	D	12	(4)	
20	Ezequiel Muñoz	ARG	08/10/90	D	3	(1)	
24	Luis Muriel	COL	16/04/91	A	11	(5)	4
9	Stefano Okaka		09/08/89	A	26	(6)	4
17	Angelo Palombo		25/09/81	M	34	(2)	1
14	Pedro Obiang	ESP	27/03/92	M	32	(2)	3
23	Vasco Regini		09/09/90	D	25	(3)	
22	Luca Rizzo		24/04/92	M	7	(8)	1
5	Alessio Romagnoli		12/01/95	D	28	(2)	2
33	Sergio Romero	ARG	22/02/87	G	9	(1)	
12	Gianluca Sansone		12/05/87	M	1	(3)	
26	Matías Silvestre	ARG	25/09/84	D	28	(1)	
21	Roberto Soriano		08/02/91	M	29	(4)	4
2	Emiliano Viviano		01/12/85	G	29		
77	Paweł Wszołek	POL	30/04/92	M	2	(4)	

US Sassuolo Calcio

1922 • Città del Tricolore, Reggio
Emilia (21,584) • sassuolocalcio.it
Coach: Eusebio Di Francesco

2014

31/08	h	Cagliari	D	1-1	Zaza
14/09	a	Internazionale	L	0-7	
21/09	h	Sampdoria	D	0-0	
24/09	a	Fiorentina	D	0-0	
28/09	h	Napoli	L	0-1	
05/10	a	Lazio	L	2-3	Berardi 2 (1p)
18/10	h	Juventus	D	1-1	Zaza
25/10	a	Parma	W	3-1	Floccari, Acerbi, Taïder
28/10	h	Empoli	D	3-1	Missiroli, Floccari, Berardi
02/11	a	Chievo	D	0-0	
08/11	h	Atalanta	D	0-0	
23/11	a	Torino	W	1-0	Floro Flores
29/11	h	Verona	W	2-1	Sansone, Taïder
06/12	a	Roma	D	2-2	Zaza 2
13/12	a	Palermo	L	1-2	Pavoletti
20/12	h	Cesena	D	1-1	Zaza (p)

2015

06/01	a	Milan	W	2-1	Sansone, Zaza
10/01	h	Udinese	D	1-1	Zaza
18/01	a	Genoa	D	3-3	Berardi 2 (1p), Missiroli
24/01	a	Cagliari	L	1-2	Acerbi
01/02	h	Internazionale	W	3-1	Zaza, Sansone, Berardi (p)
08/02	a	Sampdoria	D	1-1	Acerbi
14/02	h	Fiorentina	L	1-3	Berardi
23/02	a	Napoli	L	0-2	
01/03	h	Lazio	L	0-3	
09/03	a	Juventus	L	0-1	
15/03	h	Parma	W	4-1	Sansone 2, Berardi (p), Missiroli
22/03	a	Empoli	L	1-3	og (Rugani)
04/04	a	Chievo	W	1-0	Berardi (p)
12/04	a	Atalanta	L	1-2	Berardi
19/04	h	Torino	D	1-1	Berardi (p)
26/04	a	Verona	L	2-3	og (Moras), Floro Flores
29/04	h	Roma	L	0-3	
02/05	h	Palermo	D	0-0	
10/05	a	Cesena	W	3-2	Zaza, Taïder, Missiroli
17/05	h	Milan	W	3-2	Berardi 3
24/05	a	Udinese	W	1-0	Magnanelli
31/05	h	Genoa	W	3-1	Berardi, Zaza 2

No	Name	Nat	DoB	Pos	Aps	(s)	Gls
15	Francesco Acerbi		10/02/88	D	32		3
5	Luca Antei		19/04/92	D	5	(3)	
25	Lorenzo Ariaudo		11/06/89	D	2		
25	Domenico Berardi		01/08/94	A	32		15
20	Paolo Bianco		20/08/77	D	1	(2)	
8	Davide Biondini		24/01/83	M	17	(11)	
33	Matteo Brighi		14/02/81	M	14	(9)	
28	Paolo Cannavaro		26/06/81	D	25		
47	Raman Chibsah	GHA	10/03/93	M	3	(5)	
47	Andrea Consigli		27/01/87	G	35		
99	Sergio Floccari		12/11/81	A	10	(17)	2
83	Antonio Floro Flores		18/06/83	A	11	(18)	2
21	Leonardo Fontanesi		20/02/96	D	3		
23	Marcello Gazzola		03/04/85	D	14	(4)	
30	Dejan Lazarević	SVN	15/02/90	M	4	(6)	
3	Alessandro Longhi		25/06/89	D	17	(2)	
4	Francesco Magnanelli		12/11/84	M	28	(1)	1
7	Simone Missiroli		23/05/86	M	30	(3)	4
32	Cesare Natali		05/04/79	D		(3)	
10	Leonardo Pavoletti		26/11/88	A		(9)	1
31	Federico Peluso		20/01/84	D	26	(2)	
1	Alberto Pomini		17/03/81	G	3	(1)	
17	Nicola Sansone		10/09/91	A	30	(5)	5
19	Saphir Taïder	ALG	29/02/92	M	19	(8)	3
26	Emanuele Terranova		14/04/87	D	9		
11	Šime Vrsaljko	CRO	10/01/92	D	19	(2)	
10	Simone Zaza		25/06/91	A	29	(2)	11

Torino FC

1906 • Olimpico (27,958) • torinofc.it

Major honours
Italian League (7) 1928, 1943, 1946, 1947, 1948, 1949, 1976; Italian Cup (5) 1936, 1943, 1968, 1971, 1993

Coach: Giampiero Ventura

2014
31/08	h	Internazionale	D	0-0
14/09	a	Sampdoria	L	0-2
21/09	a	Verona	L	0-1
24/09	a	Cagliari	W	2-1	Glik, Quagliarella
28/09	h	Fiorentina	D	1-1	Quagliarella
05/10	a	Napoli	L	0-1	Quagliarella
19/10	h	Udinese	W	1-0	Quagliarella
26/10	a	Lazio	L	1-2	Farnerud
29/10	h	Parma	W	1-0	Darmian
02/11	h	Atalanta	D	0-0	
09/11	a	Roma	L	0-3	
23/11	h	Sassuolo	L	0-1	
30/11	a	Juventus	L	1-2	Bruno Peres
06/12	h	Palermo	D	2-2	Martínez, Glik
15/12	a	Empoli	D	0-0	
21/12	h	Genoa	W	2-1	Glik 2

2015
06/01	a	Chievo	D	0-0	
10/01	h	Milan	D	1-1	Glik
18/01	a	Cesena	W	3-2	Benassi, Quagliarella, Maxi López
25/01	a	Internazionale	W	1-0	Moretti
01/02	h	Sampdoria	W	5-1	Quagliarella 3 (1p), Amauri, Bruno Peres
07/02	a	Verona	W	3-1	Martínez, Quagliarella (p), El Kaddouri
15/02	h	Cagliari	D	1-1	El Kaddouri
22/02	a	Fiorentina	D	1-1	Vives
01/03	h	Napoli	W	1-0	Glik
08/03	a	Udinese	L	2-3	Quagliarella, Benassi
16/03	h	Lazio	L	0-2	
22/03	a	Parma	W	2-0	Maxi López, Basha
04/04	a	Atalanta	W	2-1	Quagliarella, Glik
12/04	h	Roma	D	1-1	Maxi López
19/04	a	Sassuolo	D	1-1	Quagliarella (p)
26/04	h	Juventus	W	2-1	Darmian, Quagliarella
29/04	a	Palermo	D	2-2	Bruno Peres, Maxi López
06/05	h	Empoli	L	0-1	
11/05	a	Genoa	L	1-5	El Kaddouri
17/05	h	Chievo	W	2-0	Maxi López 2
24/05	a	Milan	L	0-3	
31/05	h	Cesena	W	5-0	Martínez, Maxi López 2, Benassi, Moretti

No	Name	Nat	DoB	Pos	Aps	(s)	Gls
22	Amauri		03/06/80	A	7	(13)	1
10	Barreto	BRA	12/07/85	A		(1)	
4	Migjen Basha	ALB	05/01/87	M	1	(5)	1
94	Marco Benassi		08/09/94	M	17	(8)	3
5	Cesare Bovo		14/01/83	D	14	(1)	
33	Bruno Peres	BRA	01/03/90	D	28	(6)	3
36	Matteo Darmian		02/12/89	D	28	(5)	2
7	Omar El Kaddouri	MAR	21/08/90	M	25	(7)	3
8	Alexander Farnerud	SWE	01/05/84	M	15	(7)	1
14	Alessandro Gazzi		28/01/83	M	27	(3)	
1	Jean-François Gillet	BEL	31/05/79	G	12		
25	Kamil Glik	POL	03/02/88	D	31	(1)	7
15	Álvaro González	URU	29/10/84	M	1	(3)	
1	Salvador Ichazo	URU	26/01/92	G	1		
18	Pontus Jansson	SWE	13/02/91	D	7	(2)	
9	Marcelo Larrondo	ARG	16/08/88	A	3	(2)	
45	Facundo Lescano	URU	18/08/96	A		(1)	
19	Nikola Maksimović	SRB	25/11/91	D	27		
17	Josef Martínez	VEN	19/05/93	A	20	(6)	3
32	Salvatore Masiello		31/01/82	D		(1)	
11	Maxi López	ARG	03/04/84	A	8	(10)	8
3	Cristian Molinaro		30/07/83	D	17	(7)	
24	Emiliano Moretti		11/06/81	D	35		2
23	Antonio Nocerino		09/04/85	M	2	(3)	
30	Daniele Padelli		25/10/85	G	25		
27	Fabio Quagliarella		31/01/83	A	33	(1)	13
90	Simone Rosso		10/11/95	M		(2)	
6	Rubén Pérez	ESP	26/04/89	M		(6)	
28	Juan Sánchez Miño	ARG	01/01/90	M	4	(7)	
21	Gastón Silva	URU	05/03/94	D	4	(2)	
20	Giuseppe Vives		14/07/80	M	26	(2)	1

Udinese Calcio

1896 • Friuli (12,432) • udinese.it

Coach: Andrea Stramaccioni

2014
31/08	h	Empoli	W	2-0	Di Natale 2
13/09	a	Juventus	L	0-2	
21/09	h	Napoli	W	1-0	Danilo
25/09	a	Lazio	W	1-0	Théréau
29/09	h	Parma	W	4-2	Di Natale 2, Heurtaux, Théréau
05/10	h	Cesena	D	1-1	Bruno Fernandes
19/10	a	Torino	L	0-1	
26/10	h	Atalanta	W	2-0	Di Natale, Théréau
29/10	a	Fiorentina	L	0-3	
02/11	h	Genoa	L	2-4	Di Natale, Widmer
09/11	a	Palermo	D	1-1	Théréau
23/11	h	Chievo	D	1-1	Di Natale
30/11	a	Milan	L	1-2	
07/12	a	Internazionale	W	2-1	Bruno Fernandes, Théréau
14/12	h	Verona	L	1-2	Di Natale
21/12	a	Sampdoria	D	2-2	Geijo, Danilo

2015
06/01	h	Roma	L	0-1	
10/01	a	Sassuolo	D	1-1	Théréau
18/01	a	Cagliari	D	2-2	Allan, Théréau
26/01	a	Empoli	W	2-1	Di Natale, Widmer
01/02	h	Juventus	D	0-0	
08/02	a	Napoli	L	1-3	Théréau
15/02	h	Lazio	L	0-1	
01/03	a	Cesena	L	0-1	
08/03	h	Torino	W	3-2	Di Natale, og (Molinaro), Wagué
15/03	a	Atalanta	D	0-0	
22/03	h	Fiorentina	D	2-2	Wagué, Kone
04/04	a	Genoa	D	1-1	Théréau
08/04	a	Parma	L	0-1	
12/04	h	Palermo	L	1-3	Di Natale
19/04	a	Chievo	D	1-1	og (Cesar)
25/04	h	Milan	W	2-1	Pinzi, Agyemang-Badu
28/04	h	Internazionale	L	1-2	Di Natale
03/05	a	Verona	W	1-0	Di Natale
10/05	h	Sampdoria	L	1-4	Di Natale (p)
17/05	a	Roma	L	1-2	Perica
24/05	h	Sassuolo	L	0-1	
31/05	a	Cagliari	L	3-4	Aguirre, Bruno Fernandes, Théréau

No	Name	Nat	DoB	Pos	Aps	(s)	Gls
94	Rodrigo Aguirre	URU	01/10/94	A	1	(6)	1
7	Emmanuel Agyemang-Badu	GHA	02/12/90	M	20	(7)	1
6	Allan	BRA	08/01/91	M	33	(2)	1
14	Nicola Belmonte		15/04/87	D		(2)	
8	Bruno Fernandes	POR	08/09/94	M	16	(15)	3
18	Igor Bubnjić	CRO	17/07/92	D	5	(1)	
5	Danilo	BRA	10/05/84	D	37		2
10	Antonio Di Natale		13/10/77	A	27	(6)	14
11	Maurizio Domizzi		28/06/80	D	10	(1)	
34	Gabriel Silva	BRA	13/05/91	D	8	(3)	
82	Alexandre Geijo	ESP	11/03/82	A	5	(8)	1
19	Guilherme	BRA	05/04/91	M	32	(2)	
21	Melker Hallberg	SWE	20/10/95	M	2	(2)	
75	Thomas Heurtaux	FRA	03/07/88	D	24	(2)	1
31	Orestis Karnezis	GRE	11/07/85	G	37		
33	Panagiotis Kone	GRE	26/07/87	M	20	(8)	1
95	Lucas Evangelista	BRA	06/05/95	M	1	(3)	
24	Luis Muriel	COL	16/04/91	A	5	(6)	
29	Giovanni Pasquale		05/01/82	D	14	(7)	
9	Stipe Perica	CRO	07/07/95	A	5	(4)	1
66	Giampiero Pinzi		11/03/81	M	14	(5)	1
89	Iván Piris	PAR	10/03/89	D	31		
49	Simone Pontisso		20/03/97	M		(1)	
22	Simone Scuffet		31/05/96	G	1	(1)	
77	Cyril Théréau	FRA	24/04/83	A	25	(12)	10
2	Molla Wagué	MLI	21/02/91	D	10		2
27	Silvan Widmer	SUI	05/03/93	D	35	(1)	2
13	Alexis Zapata	COL	10/05/95	M		(1)	

Hellas Verona FC

1903 • Marc'Antonio Bentegodi (38,402) • hellasverona.it

Major honours
Italian League (1) 1985

Coach: Andrea Mandorlini

2014
31/08	a	Atalanta	D	0-0	
15/09	h	Palermo	W	2-1	Toni (p), og (Pisano)
21/09	a	Torino	W	1-0	Ionita
24/09	a	Genoa	D	2-2	Tachtsidis, Ionita
27/09	a	Roma	L	0-2	
04/10	h	Cagliari	W	1-0	Tachtsidis
19/10	a	Milan	L	1-3	López
26/10	h	Napoli	L	2-6	Hallfredsson, López
30/10	h	Lazio	D	1-1	Toni (p)
03/11	a	Cesena	D	1-1	Gómez Taleb
09/11	a	Internazionale	D	2-2	Toni, López
23/11	h	Fiorentina	L	1-2	López
29/11	a	Sassuolo	L	1-2	Moras
08/12	h	Sampdoria	L	1-3	Toni
14/12	a	Udinese	W	2-1	Toni, Christodoulopoulos
21/12	h	Chievo	L	0-1	

2015
06/01	a	Empoli	D	0-0	
11/01	h	Parma	W	3-1	Sala, Toni, Valoti
18/01	a	Juventus	L	0-4	
25/01	a	Atalanta	W	1-0	Saviola
01/02	a	Palermo	L	1-2	Tachtsidis
07/02	h	Torino	L	1-3	Toni
15/02	a	Genoa	L	2-5	Toni 2
22/02	h	Roma	D	1-1	Janković
01/03	a	Cagliari	W	2-1	Toni, Gómez Taleb
07/03	a	Milan	D	2-2	Toni (p), López
15/03	h	Napoli	W	2-0	Toni 2
22/03	a	Lazio	L	0-2	
04/04	h	Cesena	D	3-3	Toni 2, Gómez Taleb
11/04	h	Internazionale	L	0-3	
20/04	a	Fiorentina	W	1-0	Obbadi
26/04	h	Sassuolo	W	3-2	Gómez Taleb, Toni 2
29/04	a	Sampdoria	D	1-1	Toni
03/05	h	Udinese	L	0-1	
10/05	a	Chievo	D	2-2	Gómez Taleb, Toni
17/05	h	Empoli	W	2-1	Moras, Sala
24/05	a	Parma	D	2-2	Toni 2 (1p)
30/05	h	Juventus	D	2-2	Toni, Gómez Taleb

No	Name	Nat	DoB	Pos	Aps	(s)	Gls
33	Alessandro Agostini		23/07/79	D	21	(1)	
22	Francesco Benussi		15/10/81	G	15	(1)	
28	Davide Brivio		17/03/88	D	12	(1)	
20	Lazaros Christodoulopoulos	GRE	19/12/86	M	12	(10)	1
93	Mohamed Fares	FRA	15/02/96	A		(1)	
70	Fernandinho	BRA	25/11/85	A	1	(5)	
95	Pierluigi Gollini		18/03/95	G	3		
21	Juanito Gómez Taleb	ARG	20/05/85	A	20	(6)	6
40	Alejandro González	URU	23/03/88	D	3	(2)	
19	Leandro Greco		19/07/86	M	13	(5)	
30	Gustavo Campanharo	BRA	04/04/92	M	4	(11)	
10	Emil Hallfredsson	ISL	29/06/84	M	26	(2)	1
23	Artur Ionita	MDA	17/08/90	M	13	(5)	2
11	Boško Janković	SRB	01/03/84	M	11	(1)	1
17	Nicolás López	URU	01/10/93	A	10	(14)	6
4	Rafael Márquez	MEX	13/02/79	D	26		
71	Ivan Martić	CRO	02/10/90	D	13	(3)	
18	Vangelis Moras	GRE	26/08/81	D	35		2
99	Nenê	BRA	28/07/83	A	3	(5)	
8	Mounir Obbadi	MAR	04/04/83	M	14	(8)	1
3	Eros Pisano		31/03/87	D	15		
1	Rafael	BRA	03/03/82	G	20		
25	Rafael Marques	BRA	21/09/83	D	14	(4)	
2	Guillermo Rodríguez	URU	23/03/84	D	11	(2)	
26	Jacopo Sala		05/12/91	M	16		2
7	Javier Saviola	ARG	11/12/81	A	4	(11)	1
5	Frederik Sørensen	DEN	14/04/92	D	6	(4)	
77	Panagiotis Tachtsidis	GRE	15/02/91	M	34		3
9	Luca Toni		26/05/77	A	36	(2)	22
27	Mattia Valoti		06/09/93	M	1	(9)	1

Top goalscorers

22	Mauro Icardi (Internazionale)
	Luca Toni (Verona)
20	Carlos Tévez (Juventus)
18	Gonzalo Higuaín (Napoli)
16	Jérémy Ménez (Milan)
15	Manolo Gabbiadini (Sampdoria/Napoli)
	Domenico Berardi (Sassuolo)
14	Antonio Di Natale (Udinese)
13	Iago Falqué (Genoa)
	Miroslav Klose (Lazio)
	Paulo Dybala (Palermo)
	Fabio Quagliarella (Torino)

Promoted clubs

Carpi FC 1909

1909 • Sandro Cabassi (4,144) • carpifc1909.it
Coach: Fabrizio Castori

Frosinone Calcio

1928 • Matusa (9,680) • frosinonecalcio.com
Coach: Roberto Stellone

Bologna FC

1909 • Renato Dall'Ara (39,444) • bolognafc.it
Major honours
*Italian League (7) 1925, 1929, 1936, 1937, 1939,
1941, 1964; Italian Cup (2) 1970, 1974*
**Coach: Diego López (URU);
(04/05/15) Delio Rossi**

Second level final table 2014/15

		Pld	W	D	L	F	A	Pts
1	Carpi FC 1909	42	22	14	6	59	28	80
2	Frosinone Calcio	42	20	11	11	62	49	71
3	Vicenza Calcio	42	18	14	10	44	37	68
4	Bologna FC	42	17	17	8	49	35	68
5	Spezia Calcio	42	18	13	11	59	40	67
6	AC Perugia	42	16	18	8	49	40	66
7	Pescara Calcio	42	16	13	13	69	55	61
8	AS Avellino	42	15	14	13	42	42	59
9	AS Livorno Calcio	42	15	14	13	57	50	59
10	FC Bari 1908	42	14	12	16	43	49	54
11	Trapani Calcio	42	13	14	15	56	67	53
12	Ternana Calcio	42	13	12	17	36	47	51
13	Latina Calcio	42	11	17	14	38	41	50
14	Virtus Lanciano	42	10	20	12	49	48	50
15	Calcio Catania	42	12	13	17	59	60	49
16	FC Pro Vercelli 1892	42	12	13	17	46	57	49
17	FC Crotone	42	12	12	18	42	52	48
18	Modena FC	42	10	17	15	37	39	47
19	Virtus Entella	42	10	17	15	37	52	47
20	AS Cittadella	42	9	17	16	47	56	44
21	Brescia Calcio	42	12	12	18	54	63	42
22	AS Varese	42	9	12	21	40	67	35

*NB Brescia Calcio – 6 pts deducted; AS Varese – 4 pts
deducted*

Promotion play-offs

(26/05/15)
Perugia 1-2 Pescara
Spezia 1-2 Avellino *(aet)*

(29/05/15 & 02/06/15)
Avellino 0-1, 3-2 Bologna *(3-3; Bologna on higher
position in regular season)*
Pescara 1-0, 2-2 Vicenza *(Pescara 3-2)*

(05/06/15 & 09/06/15)
Pescara 0-0, 1-1 Bologna *(1-1; Bologna on higher
position in regular season)*

DOMESTIC CUP

Coppa Italia 2014/15

THIRD ROUND

(21/08/14)
Sassuolo 4-1 Cittadella
(22/08/14)
Pescara 1-0 Chievo
(23/08/14)
Atalanta 2-0 Pisa
Bari 1-2 Avellino
Cagliari 2-0 Catania
Palermo 0-3 Modena
Perugia 2-1 Spezia *(aet)*
Varese 1-0 Virtus Entella
(24/08/14)
Brescia 1-0 Latina
Cesena 1-0 Casertana
Empoli 3-0 L'Aquila
Lazio 7-0 Bassano Virtus
Sampdoria 4-1 Como
Udinese 5-1 Ternana
Verona 3-0 Cremonese
Virtus Lanciano 0-1 Genoa

FOURTH ROUND

02/12/14)
Lazio 3-0 Varese
Sassuolo 1-0 Pescara
Verona 1-0 Perugia
(03/12/14)
Atalanta 2-0 Avellino
Empoli 2-0 Genoa
Udinese 4-2 Cesena *(aet)*
(04/12/14)
Cagliari 4-4 Modena *(aet; 5-4 on pens)*
Sampdoria 2-0 Brescia

FIFTH ROUND

(13/01/15)
Milan 2-1 Sassuolo
(14/01/15)
Parma 2-1 Cagliari
Torino 1-3 Lazio
(15/01/15)
Juventus 6-1 Verona
(20/01/15)
Roma 2-1 Empoli *(aet)*
(21/01/15)
Fiorentina 3-1 Atalanta
Internazionale 2-0 Sampdoria
(22/01/15)
Napoli 2-2 Udinese *(aet; 5-4 on pens)*

QUARTER-FINALS

(27/01/15)
Milan 0-1 Lazio *(Biglia 38p)*
(28/01/15)
Parma 0-1 Juventus *(Morata 89)*
(03/02/15)
Roma 0-2 Fiorentina *(Gomez 65, 89)*
(04/02/15)
Napoli 1-0 Internazionale *(Higuaín 90+3)*

SEMI-FINALS

(04/03/15 & 08/04/15)
Lazio 1-1 Napoli *(Klose 33; Gabbiadini 57)*
Napoli 0-1 Lazio *(Lulić 79)*
(Lazio 2-1)

(05/03/15 & 07/04/15)
Juventus 1-2 Fiorentina *(Llorente 24; Salah 11, 56)*
Fiorentina 0-3 Juventus *(Matri 21, Pereyra 44,
Bonucci 59)*
(Juventus 4-2)

FINAL

(20/05/15)
Stadio Olimpico, Rome
JUVENTUS 2 *(Chiellini 11, Matri 97)*
SS LAZIO 1 *(Radu 4)*
(aet)
Referee: Orsato
JUVENTUS: Storari, Barzagli, Bonucci, Chiellini,
Lichtsteiner *(Padoin 115)*, Vidal, Pirlo, Pogba
(Pereyra 78), Evra, Llorente *(Matri 84)*, Tévez
LAZIO: Berisha, Basta, De Vrij *(Baldé 106)*, Gentiletti,
Radu *(Maurício 71)*, Parolo, Cataldi, Lulić, Candreva,
Felipe Anderson, Klose *(Djordjević 82)*

Giorgio Chiellini lifts the Coppa Italia for Juventus

KAZAKHSTAN

Kazakhstanning Futbol Federatsiyasi (KFF)

Address   29 Syganak Street
9th floor
KZ-010000 Astana
Tel   +7 7172 790780
Fax   +7 7172 790788
E-mail   info@kff.kz
Website   kff.kz

President   Yerlan Kozhagapanov
General secretary   Allen Chaizhunussov
Media officer   Izmail Bzarov
Year of formation   1992
National stadium   Astana Arena, Astana (30,200)

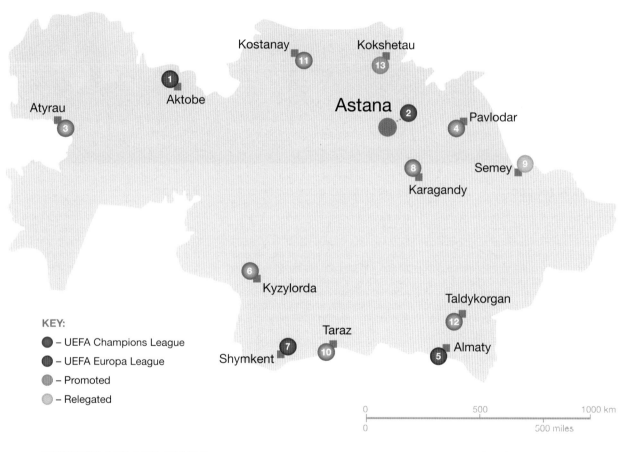

KEY:

● – UEFA Champions League
● – UEFA Europa League
● – Promoted
● – Relegated

PREMIER LEAGUE CLUBS

  FC Aktobe

  FC Astana

  FC Atyrau

 FC Irtysh Pavlodar

 **FC Kairat Almaty**

  **FC Kaysar Kyzylorda**

 FC Ordabasy Shymkent

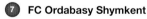 **FC Shakhter Karagandy**

 **FC Spartak Semey**

 **FC Taraz**

  FC Tobol Kostanay

 **FC Zhetysu Taldykorgan**

PROMOTED CLUB

   **FC Okzhetpes Kokshetau**

Astana power to first title

After narrowly missing out on a first Kazakh Premier League title in 2013, FC Astana made amends 12 months later, an irrepressible surge of form in the second phase of the competition under new Bulgarian coach Stanimir Stoilov seeing off the dual threat of FC Kairat Almaty and defending champions FC Aktobe.

Those two teams met in the domestic cup final, and it was to be Kairat's day in the Astana Arena as Vladimír Weiss's side romped to a 4-1 win, claiming the trophy for a record-extending sixth time.

Autumn charge leaves rivals in their wake	First phase leaders Aktobe finish runners-up	Record sixth cup triumph for Kairat

Domestic league

That Astana wrapped up the league title with two games to spare was a prospect few would have foreseen at the 22-match split. At that stage the champions-to-be were in third place, with both Aktobe and Kairat above them – albeit by just two points and one point respectively after the first-phase totals had been halved. The good news for Astana fans was that the team's form had picked up markedly following the mid-season arrival of Stoilov. The former Bulgaria boss, who had twice led PFC Levski Sofia to league titles in his homeland, replaced Grigori Babayan in late June and was yet to oversee a defeat.

After a six-week break from league action, Astana had no trouble picking up where they had left off. Indeed, they raised their game to a new level in the second phase, not only maintaining their unbeaten run under Stoilov but thrashing both Aktobe (6-1) and Kairat (5-1) in back-to-back home fixtures. Such was the impact of those two results that when they won their next home game – 3-0 against the season's surprise package, newly-promoted FC Kaysar Kyzylorda – it was enough to clinch first place.

With the job completed, there may have been a touch of post-title-winning

fatigue in the 3-0 defeat at Aktobe four days later, but Stoilov's men rounded off the season nicely with a 3-2 win at Kairat, in which dazzling winger Foxi Kéthévoama scored his 16th goal of the campaign – and eighth of the second phase – to cement his position at the head of the league's scoring charts. Another African import, Ghanaian Patrick Twumasi, who returned in August from a loan spell in Russia, also proved hugely influential in the title run-in, scoring ten goals including a hat-trick against Aktobe.

Domestic cup

Aktobe and Kairat were ultimately left standing in the league, with the latter winning only one of their last six matches, but both teams made it through to the Kazakh Cup final, Aktobe at the expense of Astana in a semi-final penalty shoot-out. A closely-contested affair was anticipated in the Astana Arena, but once Kairat's prolific Ivorian striker Gerard Gohou had put his team 2-1 up just after the half-hour mark, there was only one team in it. Gohou added a second midway through the second half before midfielder Aslan Darabayev made it 4-1 late on, enabling Baurzhan Islamkhan to become the first Kairat captain to lift the trophy since 2003.

Europe

FC Shakhter Karagandy had become the first Kazakh club to reach the UEFA Europa League group stage in 2013/14, but despite valiant efforts from the country's 2014/15 collective, the feat was not repeated. While Shakhter themselves bowed out in the third qualifying round, and Kairat a round earlier, Aktobe and Astana both reached the play-offs, the latter thanks to an impressive 3-0 win at AIK Solna. However, Legia Warszawa and Villarreal CF, respectively, proved too strong for Kazakhstan's finest as Aktobe and Astana lost both legs without scoring.

National team

A challenging UEFA EURO 2016 qualifying group was made to look especially difficult as Kazakhstan, under Russian coach Yuri Krasnozhan, struggled from one matchday to the next. They opened the campaign with a disappointing goalless draw at home to Latvia, and that turned out to be the only point the team collected from their first six games, four of which were at home. The only highlight came in their second encounter, against the Netherlands in Amsterdam, when defender Renat Abdulin headed Kazakhstan into an early lead, which they protected for an hour until the Oranje fought back to win 3-1.

DOMESTIC SEASON AT A GLANCE

Premier League 2014 final table

		Pld	Home					Away					Total					Pts
			W	D	L	F	A	W	D	L	F	A	W	D	L	F	A	
1	**FC Astana**	32	12	3	1	45	10	6	7	3	18	16	18	10	4	63	26	45
2	FC Aktobe	32	12	4	0	33	5	5	6	5	19	26	17	10	5	52	31	40
3	FC Kairat Almaty	32	11	2	3	37	13	7	3	6	21	18	18	5	9	58	31	38
4	FC Ordabasy Shymkent	32	9	2	5	21	16	4	3	9	13	28	13	5	14	34	44	27
5	FC Kaysar Kyzylorda	32	6	7	3	17	14	4	6	6	13	20	10	13	9	30	34	27
6	FC Shakhter Karagandy	32	8	6	2	25	12	3	0	13	16	37	11	6	15	41	49	21
7	FC Tobol Kostanay	32	7	6	3	19	13	3	6	7	16	22	10	12	10	35	35	26
8	FC Zhetysu Taldykorgan	32	8	3	5	12	11	2	5	9	9	20	10	8	14	21	31	25
9	FC Atyrau	32	7	4	5	19	20	3	3	10	11	23	10	7	15	30	43	25
10	FC Irtysh Pavlodar	32	7	5	4	23	15	2	5	9	16	29	9	10	13	39	44	25
11	FC Taraz	32	7	3	6	24	24	2	4	10	8	21	9	7	16	32	45	25
12	FC Spartak Semey	32	7	5	4	21	16	0	2	14	9	36	7	7	18	30	52	21

NB League splits into top and bottom halves after 22 games, after which the clubs play exclusively against teams in their group.
Points obtained during the regular season are halved (and rounded upwards). FC Tobol Kostanay – 3 pts deducted.

European qualification 2015/16

CHAMPIONS LEAGUE

Champion: FC Astana (second qualifying round)

EUROPA LEAGUE

Cup winner: FC Kairat Almaty (first qualifying round)
FC Aktobe (first qualifying round)
FC Ordabasy Shymkent (first qualifying round)

Top scorer	Foxi Kéthévoama (Astana), 16 goals
Relegated club	Spartak Semey
Promoted club	FC Okzhetpes Kokshetau
Cup final	FC Kairat Almaty 4-1 FC Aktobe

Team of the season
(4-4-2)

Coach: Weiss (Kairat)

Sidelnikov (Aktobe)

Miroshnichenko (Aktobe) Dmitrenko (Astana) Smakov (Kairat) Shomko (Astana)

Khairullin (Aktobe) Darabayev (Kairat) Islamkhan (Kairat) Kéthévoama (Astana)

Shchetkin (Taraz) Gohou (Kairat)

Player of the season

Baurzhan Islamkhan
(FC Kairat Almaty)

After an ill-fated move to FC Kuban Krasnodar and a disappointing loan spell in 2013 at FC Astana, Islamkhan returned to form with a bang in 2014, skippering Kairat to victory in the Kazakh Cup and inspiring the side with his clever midfield promptings throughout the league campaign. A favourite of Kairat coach Vladimír Weiss, he was also regularly selected by Kazakhstan boss Yuri Krasnozhan and scored his first two international goals in friendly wins against Tajikistan and Kyrgyzstan.

Newcomer of the season

Dmitri Miroshnichenko
(FC Aktobe)

Although Aktobe were unable to defend their league title in 2014 and also finished runners-up in the Kazakh Cup, the season was a resounding success for the club's 22-year-old right-back. Miroshnichenko was Aktobe's most prominent performer in a number of games, including several in Europe, and after winning his first senior cap for Kazakhstan in August, he was selected to start each of his country's first three UEFA EURO 2016 qualifiers against Latvia, the Netherlands and the Czech Republic.

KAZAKHSTAN

NATIONAL TEAM

Top five all-time caps
Ruslan Baltiyev (73); **Samat Smakov** (67); Nurbol Zhumaskaliyev (58); **Andrei Karpovich** (55); Sergei Ostapenko (42)

Top five all-time goals
Ruslan Baltiyev (13); Viktor Zubarev (12); Dmitri Byakov (8); Nurbol Zhumaskaliyev (7); Igor Avdeev, **Sergei Khizhnichenko**, Oleg Litvinenko & Sergei Ostapenko (6)

Results 2014/15

Date	Opponent		Venue	Res	Score	Scorers
12/08/14	Tajikistan	H	Almaty	W	2-1	*Islamkhan (36), Konysbayev (63)*
05/09/14	Kyrgyzstan	H	Astana	W	7-1	*Khizhnichenko (27, 42), Nuserbayev (36), Islamkhan (54), Dzholchiev (69), Konysbayev (80), Nurgaliyev (86)*
09/09/14	Latvia (ECQ)	H	Astana	D	0-0	
10/10/14	Netherlands (ECQ)	A	Amsterdam	L	1-3	*Abdulin (17)*
13/10/14	Czech Republic (ECQ)	H	Astana	L	2-4	*Logvinenko (84, 90+1)*
16/11/14	Turkey (ECQ)	A	Istanbul	L	1-3	*Smakov (87p)*
18/02/15	Moldova	N	Antalya (TUR)	D	1-1	*Shchetkin (48)*
28/03/15	Iceland (ECQ)	H	Astana	L	0-3	
31/03/15	Russia	A	Khimki	D	0-0	
12/05/15	Burkina Faso	H	Almaty	D	0-0	
12/06/15	Turkey (ECQ)	H	Almaty	L	0-1	

Appearances 2014/15

Coach: Yuri Krasnozhan (RUS) 07/06/63		Club	Tjk	Kgz	LVA	NED	CZE	TUR	Mda	ISL	Rus	Bfa	TUR	Caps	Goals
Aleksandr Mokin	19/06/81	Shakhter	G	s46		G		G						21	-
Dmitri Miroshnichenko	26/02/92	Aktobe	D	D	D	D	D83							5	-
Sergei Maliy	05/06/90	Shakhter /Ordabasy	D					s76	s46		D	D	D	8	-
Renat Abdulin	14/04/82	Atyrau /Ordabasy	D46	D	D	D	D	D76	D46	D80		D	D	29	2
Viktor Dmitrenko	04/04/91	Astana	D			D72								14	1
Gafurzhan Suyumbayev	19/08/90	Ordabasy	D46			D			D46	D				5	-
Yuri Logvinenko	22/07/88	Aktobe	M	D	D		D	D	D	D			D	30	3
Baurzhan Islamkhan	23/02/93	Kairat	M64	M64	M82		M	M	s46	M	M	s60	M85	16	2
Anatoli Bogdanov	07/08/81	Tobol	M	M	M	M			s53					14	-
Baurzhan Dzholchiev	08/05/90	Astana	M46	s58	s73	M 64*					A43			12	3
Tanat Nuserbayev	01/01/87	Astana	A57	M46	M73		M					A78		21	2
Aslan Darabayev	21/01/89	Kairat	s46 /90	s78					M					3	-
Ulan Konysbayev	28/05/89	Shakhter /Astana	s46	s46			s58	M	M46	s56	M78	M74	M	25	3
Dmitri Shomko	19/03/90	Astana	s46	D	D	M	D	D	s46		D	D	D	19	2
Aleksei Shchetkin	21/05/91	Taraz /Astana	s57					s73	A	s80	s82	s70		13	1
Azat Nurgaliyev	30/06/86	Ordabasy	s64	s64	s82	s90	s70	s82	M74	M56		M60		25	1
Baurzhan Baytana	06/06/92	Kairat	s90											1	-
Andrei Sidelnikov	08/03/80	Aktobe /Ordabasy		G46	G		G				G			29	-
Ilya Vorotnikov	01/02/86	Taraz		D	D	D	D		D	D				6	-
Samat Smakov	08/12/78	Kairat /Irtysh		M78	M			M	M53	M	M	M	M67	67	2
Sergei Khizhnichenko	17/07/91	Korona (POL) /Aktobe		A58	A	A90	A70	A82				s78	A	31	6
Andrei Karpovich	18/01/81	Atyrau				M79	M58							55	3
Mark Gurman	09/02/89	Kairat				s72		D		D67	D	D	D78	22	-
Valeri Korobkin	02/07/84	Aktobe				s79								13	-
Askhat Tagybergen	09/08/90	Aktobe					M	M		M			s78	5	-
Abzal Beysebekov	30/11/92	Astana					s83				s86	D81	s67	4	-
Stanislav Lunin	02/05/93	Kairat						M73						2	-
Nenad Erić	26/05/82	Astana							G					1	-
Pirali Aliyev	13/01/84	Irtysh							D					5	-
Zhakyp Kozhamberdy	26/02/92	Taraz						s74		s78				2	-
Daurenbek Tazhimbetov	02/07/85	Ordabasy								A				5	3
Yermek Kuantayev	13/10/90	Kairat								s67				1	-
Stas Pokatilov	08/12/92	Aktobe									G	G	G	3	-
Konstantin Engel	27/07/88	Ingolstadt (GER)									D			9	-
Georgi Zhukov	19/11/94	Astana									M86	M70		2	-
Tokhtar Zhangylyshbay	25/05/93	Astana									s43 /82			1	-
Timur Dosmagambetov	01/05/89	Taraz										s74		1	-
Sanat Zhumakhanov	30/01/88	Taraz										s81		1	-
Geynrikh Schmidtgal	20/11/85	Düsseldorf (GER)											M	14	1
Zhambyl Kukeyev	20/09/88	Kairat											s85	28	2

EUROPE

FC Aktobe

Second qualifying round - FC Dinamo Tbilisi (GEO)
A 1-0 *Danilo Neco (51)*
Sidelnikov, Tsarikayev, Miroshnichenko, Pizzelli (Zenkovich 61), Khairullin, Danilo Neco (Shabalin 81), Arzumanyan, Korobkin, Logvinenko, Anderson Mineiro, Antonov (Kapadze 72). Coach: Vladimir Gazzaev (RUS)
H 3-0 *Antonov (75), Zenkovich (82), Aimbetov (90+4)*
Sidelnikov, Muldarov, Tsarikayev, Miroshnichenko, Pizzelli (Tagybergen 84), Khairullin, Danilo Neco (Aimbetov 86), Arzumanyan, Korobkin, Anderson Mineiro, Antonov (Zenkovich 81). Coach: Vladimir Gazzaev (RUS)

Third qualifying round - FC Steaua Bucureşti (ROU)
H 2-2 *Korobkin (58), Arzumanyan (87)*
Sidelnikov, Muldarov, Tsarikayev, Miroshnichenko, Pizzelli, Khairullin (Kapadze 55), Danilo Neco, Arzumanyan, Korobkin, Anderson Mineiro, Antonov (Zenkovich 75). Coach: Vladimir Gazzaev (RUS)
A 1-2 *Kapadze (85)*
Sidelnikov, Tsarikayev, Miroshnichenko, Pizzelli (Shabalin 80), Khairullin (Kapadze 61), Danilo Neco, Arzumanyan, Korobkin, Logvinenko, Anderson Mineiro, Antonov (Aimbetov 68). Coach: Vladimir Gazzaev (RUS)
Red card: Logvinenko 57

Play-offs - Legia Warszawa (POL)
H 0-1
Sidelnikov, Muldarov, Miroshnichenko (Tsarikayev 33), Pizzelli, Khairullin (Aimbetov 66), Danilo Neco, Arzumanyan, Tagybergen, Korobkin, Anderson Mineiro, Antonov (Zenkovich 56). Coach: Vladimir Gazzaev (RUS)
A 0-2
Sidelnikov, Muldarov, Tsarikayev (Aimbetov 71), Miroshnichenko, Khairullin, Danilo Neco, Tagybergen, Korobkin (Kapadze 42), Logvinenko, Anderson Mineiro, Antonov (Zenkovich 57). Coach: Vladimir Gazzaev (RUS)

FC Shakhter Karagandy

First qualifying round - FC Shirak (ARM)
A 2-1 *Topčagić (71), Maliy (83)*
Mokin, Vičius, Topčagić (Murzoev 89), Konysbayev (Salomov 79), Finonchenko, Pokrivač (Bayzhanov 90+2), Džidić, Maliy, Maslo, Kirov, Simčević. Coach: Viktor Kumykov (RUS)

H 4-0 *Kpodo (12og), Konysbayev (29), Pokrivač (45+1), Finonchenko (49)*
Mokin, Vičius, Topčagić (Murtazayev 71), Konysbayev (Murzoev 78), Finonchenko, Pokrivač, Džidić (Bayzhanov 62), Maliy, Maslo, Kirov, Simčević. Coach: Viktor Kumykov (RUS)

Second qualifying round - FK Atlantas (LTU)
A 0-0
Mokin, Vičius, Topčagić (Murzoev 84), Konysbayev (Salomov 89), Finonchenko (Murtazayev 90+1), Pokrivač, Džidić, Maliy, Maslo, Kirov, Simčević. Coach: Viktor Kumykov (RUS)
H 3-0 *Topčagić (46), Konysbayev (61), Murtazayev (90+3)*
Mokin, Vičius, Topčagić (Murzoev 84), Konysbayev, Finonchenko (Murtazayev 89), Pokrivač (Bayzhanov 68), Džidić, Maliy, Maslo, Kirov, Simčević. Coach: Viktor Kumykov (RUS)

Third qualifying round - HNK Hajduk Split (CRO)
H 4-2 *Topčagić (11), Finonchenko (21), Džidić (71), Zhangylyshbay (90+4)*
Mokin, Vičius, Topčagić (Zhangylyshbay 83), Konysbayev, Finonchenko (Murzoev 86), Poryvaev, Pokrivač (Bayzhanov 60), Džidić, Maliy, Maslo, Kirov. Coach: Viktor Kumykov (RUS)
A 0-3
Mokin, Vičius, Topčagić, Konysbayev, Poryvaev (Murtazayev 53), Pokrivač, Džidić, Maliy, Maslo (Zhangylyshbay 60), Kirov, Simčević. Coach: Viktor Kumykov (RUS)

FC Astana

First qualifying round - FC Pyunik (ARM)
A 4-1 *Nuserbayev (40), Dzholchiev (67), Kéthévoama (71), Kurdov (84)*
Erić, Dmitrenko, Aničić, Nurdauletov (Kurdov 46), Kéthévoama, Pikalkin, Nuserbayev (Shakhmetov 59), Zhukov, Dzholchiev (Beysebekov 80), Shomko, Cañas. Coach: Stanimir Stoilov (BUL)
H 2-0 *Dzholchiev (13), Shomko (78)*
Erić, Aničić, Kojašević (Kéthévoama 46), Pikalkin, Beysebekov, Nuserbayev, Dzholchiev, Postnikov, Kurdov (Zhukov 57), Shomko, Cañas (Muzhikov 82). Coach: Stanimir Stoilov (BUL)

Second qualifying round - Hapoel Tel-Aviv FC (ISR)
H 3-0 *Cañas (16p), Nuserbayev (58), Beysebekov (69)*
Erić, Akhmetov, Dmitrenko, Kéthévoama (Muzhikov 85), Beysebekov, Nuserbayev (Kurdov 80), Zhukov, Dzholchiev (Kojašević 90+3), Essame, Postnikov, Cañas. Coach: Stanimir Stoilov (BUL)
A 0-1
Erić, Akhmetov, Dmitrenko, Kéthévoama (Twumasi 89), Pikalkin, Beysebekov, Nuserbayev (Shomko 88), Zhukov, Essame (Muzhikov 90+1), Postnikov, Cañas. Coach: Stanimir Stoilov (BUL)

Third qualifying round - AIK Solna (SWE)
H 1-1 *Nuserbayev (42)*
Erić, Akhmetov, Dmitrenko, Kéthévoama, Beysebekov, Nuserbayev, Zhukov (Twumasi 46), Dzholchiev (Muzhikov 82), Essame, Postnikov, Cañas. Coach: Stanimir Stoilov (BUL)

A 3-0 *Kéthévoama (36), Shomko (54), Dzholchiev (71)*
Erić, Dmitrenko, Aničić, Kéthévoama (Muzhikov 87), Beysebekov, Nuserbayev (Twumasi 63), Zhukov, Dzholchiev (Kurdov 85), Essame, Postnikov, Shomko. Coach: Stanimir Stoilov (BUL)

Play-offs - Villarreal CF (ESP)
H 0-3
Erić, Aničić, Kéthévoama, Beysebekov, Nuserbayev (Muzhikov 80), Zhukov, Dzholchiev (Akhmetov 62), Essame (Twumasi 57), Postnikov, Shomko, Cañas. Coach: Stanimir Stoilov (BUL)
Red card: Aničić 60
A 0-4
Loginovski, Dmitrenko, Kéthévoama (Kojašević 77), Beysebekov, Nuserbayev (Essame 62), Twumasi (Kurdov 71), Zhukov, Dzholchiev, Postnikov, Shomko, Cañas. Coach: Stanimir Stoilov (BUL)

FC Kairat Almaty

First qualifying round - FK Kukësi (ALB)
H 1-0 *Darabayev (89)*
Khomich, Pliev, Gurman, Kislitsyn, Smakov, Islamkhan, Bakaev, Michalík (Baytana 82), Yedigaryan (Darabayev 66), Gohou, Isael (Knežević 66). Coach: Vladimír Weiss (SVK)
A 0-0
Khomich, Pliev, Gurman, Kislitsyn, Smakov, Islamkhan (Li 90+1), Knežević (Lunin 46), Bakaev, Michalík, Yedigaryan (Isael 63), Gohou. Coach: Vladimír Weiss (SVK)

Second qualifying round - Esbjerg fB (DEN)
H 1-1 *Knežević (50p)*
Khomich, Pliev, Kislitsyn, Smakov, Islamkhan (Gurman 90+1), Knežević (Isael 86), Kuantayev, Bakaev, Michalík, Yedigaryan (Lunin 62), Gohou. Coach: Vladimír Weiss (SVK)
A 0-1
Khomich, Pliev, Kislitsyn, Smakov, Islamkhan, Kuantayev (Sito Riera 78), Baytana (Knežević 32), Bakaev, Michalík, Gohou, Isael (Lunin 86). Coach: Vladimír Weiss (SVK)

DOMESTIC LEAGUE CLUB-BY-CLUB

FC Aktobe

1967 • Koblandy Batyr (12,729) •
fc-aktobe.kz
Major honours
Kazakhstan League (5) 2005, 2007, 2008, 2009,
2013; Kazakhstan Cup (1) 2008
Coach: Vladimir Nikitenko;
(10/07/14) Vladimir Gazzaev (RUS)

2014
15/03	a	Taraz	W	2-0	*Khairullin (p), og (Bandjar)*
22/03	a	Shakhter	D	1-1	*Logvinenko*
29/03	h	Spartak	W	3-0	*Zenkovich 2, Shabalin*
05/04	a	Atyrau	D	0-0	
09/04	h	Zhetysu	W	1-0	*Pizzelli*
13/04	a	Ordabasy	L	0-1	
19/04	h	Kaysar	W	3-0	*Geynrikh, Danilo Neco,* *Miroshnichenko*
27/04	a	Astana	W	2-1	*Zenkovich, Khairullin*
01/05	h	Kairat	W	1-0	*Khairullin*
06/05	a	Tobol	W	2-0	*Danilo Neco, Kapadze*
10/05	a	Irtysh	W	3-0	*Khairullin, Pizzelli,* *Geynrikh (p)*
18/05	h	Shakhter	W	4-0	*Danilo Neco,* *Miroshnichenko, Geynrikh,* *Pizzelli*
24/05	a	Spartak	W	1-0	*Pizzelli*
28/05	h	Atyrau	D	0-0	
01/06	a	Zhetysu	L	0-1	
14/06	h	Ordabasy	D	1-1	*Zenkovich (p)*
22/06	a	Kaysar	D	2-2	*Zenkovich (p), Pizzelli*
27/06	h	Astana	D	1-1	*Korobkin*
06/07	a	Kairat	L	1-7	*Antonov*
11/07	h	Tobol	W	3-1	*Logvinenko, Antonov,* *Zenkovich*
26/07	a	Irtysh	D	1-1	*Anderson Mineiro*
02/08	h	Taraz	W	2-0	*Arzumanyan, Khairullin*
14/09	a	Shakhter	D	1-1	*Khairullin*
20/09	h	Kaysar	D	0-0	
28/09	a	Kairat	L	0-2	
04/10	h	Astana	L	1-6	*Antonov*
18/10	h	Shakhter	W	3-1	*Antonov 2, Pizzelli*
22/10	h	Ordabasy	W	4-1	*Danilo Neco 2, Pizzelli,* *Khairullin*
26/10	a	Kaysar	D	2-2	*Antonov 2*
01/11	h	Kairat	W	1-0	*Zhalmukan*
05/11	h	Astana	W	3-0	*Antonov, Tagybergen,* *Khairullin*
09/11	a	Ordabasy	W	3-1	*Pizzelli, Khairullin, Korobkin*

No	Name	Nat	DoB	Pos	Aps	(s)	Gls
95	Abat Aimbetov		07/08/95	A	2	(11)	
70	Anderson Mineiro	BRA	24/04/86	D	15		1
86	Olexiy Antonov	UKR	08/05/86	A	13	(3)	8
16	Robert Arzumanyan	ARM	24/07/85	D	26		1
5	Petr Badlo		24/05/76	D	11		
40	Almat Bekbaev		14/07/84	G	1		
11	Danilo Neco	BRA	27/01/86	A	21	(4)	5
50	Aleksandr Geynrikh	UZB	06/10/84	A	9	(4)	3
80	Timur Kapadze	UZB	05/09/81	M	21	(6)	1
10	Marat Khairullin		26/04/84	M	25	(3)	9
21	Valeri Korobkin		02/07/84	M	30		2
20	Evgeni Levin		12/07/92	M	3	(2)	
23	Yuri Logvinenko		22/07/88	D	21	(1)	2
7	Dmitri Miroshnichenko		26/02/92	M	26		2
3	Aleksei Muldarov		24/04/84	D	23		
35	Stanislav Pavlov		30/05/94	G	1		
9	Marcos Pizzelli	ARM	03/10/84	M	17	(11)	8
12	Robert Primus	TRI	10/11/90	D	1		
18	Pavel Shabalin		23/10/88	M	8	(14)	1
55	Andrei Sidelnikov		08/03/80	G	30		
17	Askhat Tagybergen		09/08/90	M	14	(12)	1
6	Taras Tsarikayev		17/06/89	M	18	(5)	
78	Igor Zenkovich	BLR	17/09/87	A	16	(11)	6
73	Didar Zhalmukan		22/05/96	M		(3)	1

FC Astana

2009 • Astana Arena (30,200) • fca.kz
Major honours
Kazakhstan League (1) 2014; Kazakhstan Cup (2)
2010, 2012
Coach: Grigori Babayan;
(21/06/14) Stanimir Stoilov (BUL)

2014
15/03	h	Zhetysu	D	0-0	
22/03	a	Ordabasy	W	1-0	*Cicero*
29/03	h	Kaysar	W	1-0	*Kojašević (p)*
05/04	h	Taraz	W	1-0	*Dzholchiev*
09/04	a	Kairat	D	0-0	
13/04	h	Tobol	W	1-0	*Kojašević (p)*
19/04	h	Irtysh	W	4-3	*Nuserbayev, Kurdov 3*
27/04	h	Aktobe	L	1-2	*Kéthévoama*
01/05	a	Shakhter	D	0-0	
06/05	h	Spartak	W	5-0	*Nuserbayev 2, Dmitrenko,* *Kéthévoama, Cicero*
10/05	a	Atyrau	L	0-1	
18/05	h	Ordabasy	L	0-1	*Dzholchiev*
24/05	a	Kaysar	L	0-1	
28/05	a	Taraz	W	2-1	*Dzholchiev, Kurdov*
01/06	h	Kairat	D	2-2	*Renan Bressan, Dzholchiev*
14/06	a	Tobol	D	1-1	*Kéthévoama*
22/06	h	Irtysh	W	5-3	*Kéthévoama, Cicero 2,* *Kojašević, Dzholchiev*
27/06	a	Aktobe	D	1-1	*Cicero*
06/07	h	Shakhter	W	4-0	*Beysebekov, Kéthévoama,* *Dzholchiev, Nuserbayev*
13/07	a	Spartak	D	1-1	*og (Obradović)*
27/07	h	Atyrau	W	3-0	*Kéthévoama 3*
03/08	a	Zhetysu	D	0-0	
14/09	h	Ordabasy	W	5-0	*Twumasi 2, Kéthévoama 2,* *Nuserbayev*
20/09	h	Shakhter	W	2-0	*Shomko, Twumasi*
28/09	a	Kaysar	D	1-1	*Cañas*
04/10	a	Aktobe	W	6-1	*Twumasi 3, Kéthévoama 2,* *Kojašević (p)*
18/10	a	Ordabasy	W	2-1	*Kéthévoama, Twumasi*
22/10	h	Kairat	W	5-1	*Cañas 2, Nuserbayev,* *Kéthévoama, Twumasi*
26/10	a	Shakhter	W	2-0	*Kurdov 2 (1p)*
01/11	h	Kaysar	W	3-0	*Twumasi, Shomko,* *Kéthévoama*
05/11	a	Aktobe	L	0-3	
09/11	a	Kairat	W	3-2	*Twumasi, Muzhikov,* *Kéthévoama*

No	Name	Nat	DoB	Pos	Aps	(s)	Gls
2	Eldos Akhmetov		01/06/90	D	9	(4)	
5	Marin Aničić	BIH	17/08/89	D	27		
80	Adyl Balgabayev		13/07/95	A		(1)	
15	Abzal Beysebekov		30/11/92	D	13	(2)	1
88	Roger Cañas	COL	27/03/90	M	29	(1)	3
11	Cicero	GNB	08/05/86	A	11	(1)	5
4	Viktor Dmitrenko		04/04/91	D	23	(3)	1
22	Baurzhan Dzholchiev		08/05/90	A	18	(6)	6
2	Nenad Erić		26/05/82	G	14		
25	Guy Stéphane Essame	CMR	25/11/84	M	10	(1)	
16	Evgeni Goriachiy		02/02/91	D	1		
10	Foxi Kéthévoama	CTA	30/05/86	M	25		16
32	Rinat Khairullin		19/02/94	M	1		
55	Pavel Khalezov		10/08/94	D		(1)	
7	Damir Kojašević	MNE	03/06/87	M	5	(16)	4
23	Islambek Kuat		12/01/93	M		(1)	
37	Islambek Kulekenov		15/09/94	M		(1)	
76	Atanas Kurdov	BUL	28/09/88	A	16	(9)	6
33	Vitali Li		13/03/94	A	3	(2)	
85	Vladimir Loginovski		08/10/85	G	18		
96	Vladislav Mendybayev		01/05/96	M	1		
13	Serikzhan Muzhikov		17/06/89	M	10	(7)	1
16	Kairat Nurdauletov		06/11/82	D	13	(7)	
17	Tanat Nuserbayev		01/01/87	A	19	(7)	6
9	Sergei Ostapenko		23/02/86	A	2	(5)	
19	Igor Pikalkin		19/03/92	D	18	(2)	
44	Evgeni Postnikov		16/04/86	D	12	(2)	
20	Renan Bressan	BLR	03/11/88	M	3	(3)	1
8	Marat Shakhmetov		06/02/89	A	9	(3)	
77	Dmitri Shomko		19/03/90	D	27		2
18	Patrick Twumasi	GHA	09/05/94	A	10	(1)	10
19	Georgi Zhukov		19/11/94	M	5	(7)	

FC Atyrau

1980 • Munayshi (8,700) • rfcatyrau.kz
Major honours
Kazakhstan Cup (1) 2009
Coach: Anatoli Yurevich (BLR) &
Vladimir Belyavski (BLR);
(22/07/14) Vladimir Nikitenko

2014
15/03	a	Kairat	W	1-0	*Nsereko*
22/03	h	Tobol	D	0-0	
29/03	a	Irtysh	W	1-0	*Trifunović*
05/04	a	Aktobe	D	0-0	
09/04	a	Shakhter	L	0-2	
13/04	h	Spartak	W	2-1	*Rudik (p), Gridin*
19/04	a	Taraz	D	3-3	*Essame 2, Trifunović*
27/04	a	Zhetysu	L	0-1	
01/05	h	Ordabasy	D	1-1	*Trifunović*
06/05	a	Kaysar	L	1-2	*Parkhachev*
10/05	h	Astana	W	1-0	*Trifunović (p)*
18/05	a	Tobol	D	0-0	
24/05	h	Irtysh	L	0-1	
28/05	a	Aktobe	D	0-0	
01/06	h	Shakhter	W	3-2	*Karpovich, Blažić,* *Trifunović (p)*
14/06	a	Spartak	L	1-2	*Trifunović (p)*
22/06	h	Taraz	W	3-0	*Trifunović 2 (1p), Odibe*
28/06	h	Zhetysu	L	1-2	*og (Rodionov)*
05/07	a	Ordabasy	L	0-1	
13/07	h	Kaysar	L	1-3	*Trifunović*
27/07	a	Astana	L	0-3	
03/08	a	Kairat	L	0-3	
23/08	a	Tobol	W	2-1	*Nuribekov, Abdulin*
29/08	h	Irtysh	W	2-1	*Adiyiah, Trifunović (p)*
14/09	a	Zhetysu	L	0-1	
20/09	a	Taraz	L	1-2	*Trifunović*
28/09	h	Spartak	D	1-1	*Trifunović*
04/10	a	Irtysh	L	0-2	
19/10	h	Zhetysu	W	1-0	*Odibe*
25/10	h	Taraz	W	3-2	*Trifunović (p), Shakin,* *Karpovich*
01/11	a	Spartak	L	1-3	*og (Genev)*
09/11	h	Tobol	L	0-3	

No	Name	Nat	DoB	Pos	Aps	(s)	Gls
23	Renat Abdulin		14/04/82	D	31		1
40	Dominic Adiyiah	GHA	29/11/89	A	10	(4)	1
18	Mikhail Afanasiyev	BLR	04/11/86	M	22	(6)	
46	Marko Blažić	SRB	02/08/85	M	28	(2)	1
33	Marat Butuev		08/05/92	D	29	(2)	
8	Valentin Chureev		29/08/86	D	10	(4)	
7	Guy Stéphane Essame	CMR	25/11/84	M	17	(1)	2
17	Sergei Gridin		20/05/87	A		(6)	1
21	Andrei Karpovich		18/01/81	M	25		2
24	Zhaksylyk Khalelov		14/01/95	D		(1)	
27	Evgeni Kostrub		27/08/82	M	22	(4)	
86	Aleksei Kuchuk	BLR	09/09/86	A		(5)	
77	Savio Nsereko	GER	27/07/89	M	10		1
13	Aybar Nuribekov		29/12/92	A	5	(10)	1
28	Mike Odibe	NGA	23/07/88	D	27		2
28	Dmitri Parkhachev	BLR	02/01/85	M	13	(10)	1
5	Kirill Pasichnik		24/05/93	D	1		
10	Giorgi Peikrishvili	GEO	28/02/83	M	3	(6)	
3	Pavel Plaskonny	BLR	29/01/85	D	19	(3)	
22	Filipp Rudik	BLR	22/03/87	M	8	(4)	1
1	Andrei Shabanov		17/11/86	G	29		
	Marat Shakhmetov		06/02/89	M	5	(5)	
6	Aleksei Shakin		06/08/84	M	4	(10)	1
9	Aleksei Shchetkin		21/05/91	A		(2)	
14	Miloš Trifunović	SRB	15/10/84	A	31	(1)	13
30	Anton Tsirin		20/05/87	D	3		

FC Irtysh Pavlodar

1965 • Tsentralny (11,828) • fcirtysh.kz
Major honours
Kazakhstan League (5) 1993, 1997, 1999, 2002, 2003; Kazakhstan Cup (1) 1998

Coach: Tarmo Rüütli (EST);
(02/05/14) Oyrat Saduov;
(27/10/14) Dmitri Cheryshev (RUS)

2014

15/03	h	Shakhter	W	1-0	Averchenko
22/03	a	Spartak	D	0-0	
29/03	h	Atyrau	L	0-1	
05/04	a	Zhetysu	D	0-0	
09/04	h	Ordabasy	W	2-0	Burzanović 2
13/04	a	Kaysar	L	2-4	Yurin, Begalyn
19/04	h	Astana	L	3-4	Džudović, Bakayev 2 (1p)
27/04	a	Kairat	L	1-2	Govedarica
01/05	h	Tobol	L	0-3	
06/05	h	Taraz	W	2-0	Dudchenko, Bakayev
10/05	a	Aktobe	L	0-3	
18/05	h	Spartak	W	5-0	Yurin, Dudchenko, Chichulin (p), Ayaganov, Korobov
24/05	a	Atyrau	W	1-0	Dudchenko
28/05	h	Zhetysu	W	1-0	Dudchenko
01/06	a	Ordabasy	L	1-2	Ayaganov
14/06	h	Kaysar	D	1-1	Dudchenko, Totay
22/06	a	Astana	L	3-5	Bakayev, Dudchenko, Totay
27/06	h	Kairat	L	0-1	
06/07	a	Tobol	D	1-1	Dudchenko
12/07	a	Taraz	L	1-5	Mukhutdinov
26/07	h	Aktobe	D	1-1	Dudchenko
03/08	a	Shakhter	D	2-2	Dudchenko 2
23/08	h	Zhetysu	D	1-1	Burzanović
29/08	a	Atyrau	L	1-2	Burzanović
14/09	h	Spartak	W	3-2	Totay, Amanow, Dudchenko (p)
20/09	a	Tobol	D	0-0	
28/09	h	Taraz	D	0-0	
04/10	h	Atyrau	W	2-0	Chernyshov, Yurin
19/10	a	Spartak	L	0-2	
25/10	h	Tobol	D	1-1	Begalyn
01/11	a	Taraz	W	3-0	Valeyev, Begalyn, Ivanov
09/11	a	Zhetysu	L	0-1	

No	Name	Nat	DoB	Pos	Aps	(s)	Gls
7	Arslanmyrat Amanow	TKM	28/03/90	M	15	(9)	1
8	Evgeni Averchenko		06/04/82	M	21	(8)	1
13	Alibek Ayaganov		13/01/92	M	8	(7)	2
10	Ulugbek Bakayev	UZB	28/11/78	A	14	(2)	4
90	Timur Bayzhanov		30/03/90	A		(1)	
9	Kuanysh Begalyn		05/09/92	A	5	(12)	3
50	Semion Bulgaru	MDA	26/05/85	D	9	(3)	
98	Igor Burzanović	MNE	25/08/85	M	16	(10)	4
3	Vladislav Chernyshov		16/03/81	D	20	(4)	1
6	Anton Chichulin		27/10/84	D	14		1
25	Ihor Chuchman	UKR	15/02/85	M	12	(1)	
	Altynbek Dauletkhanov		18/05/93	A		(1)	
30	Kostyantyn Dudchonko	UKR	08/07/86	A	18	(3)	11
1	Nemanja Džodžo	SRB	12/12/86	G	3		
4	Miodrag Džudović	MNE	06/09/79	D	26		1
5	Predrag Govedarica	SRB	21/10/84	M	15		1
11	Sergei Ivanov		30/05/80	M	6	(7)	1
21	Nikita Kalmykov		24/08/89	G	3		
15	Yakub Khleboun	CZE	24/03/85	D	9		
23	Zakhar Korobov		18/05/88	D	16	(3)	1
33	Vyacheslav Kotlyar		03/03/82	G	26		
2	Bakdaulet Kozhabayev		19/06/92	D	3	(2)	
77	Almir Mukhutdinov		09/06/85	M	27	(1)	1
19	Grigory Sartakov		19/08/94	D	13		
60	Orlin Starokin	BUL	03/01/87	D	5	(5)	
20	Abylaykhan Totay		16/02/92	M	11	(1)	2
	Bagdat Urazaliyev		11/01/96	M		(1)	
24	Rinar Valeyev	UKR	22/08/87	M	12	(1)	1
	Vladimir Vomenko		22/05/95	M		(1)	
14	Igor Yurin		03/07/82	M	25	(5)	3

FC Kairat Almaty

1954 • Tsentralny (26,242) • fckairat.kz
Major honours
Kazakhstan League (2) 1992, 2004; Kazakhstan Cup (6) 1992, 1996, 2000, 2001 (autumn), 2003, 2014

Coach: Vladimír Weiss (SVK)

2014

15/03	h	Atyrau	L	0-1	
22/03	a	Zhetysu	L	0-1	
29/03	h	Ordabasy	L	0-1	
05/04	a	Kaysar	W	1-0	Darabayev
09/04	h	Astana	D	0-0	
13/04	a	Taraz	W	3-1	Marković, Knežević, Kislitsyn
19/04	a	Tobol	D	2-2	Ceesay, Knežević
27/04	h	Irtysh	W	2-1	Kuantayev, Darabayev
01/05	a	Aktobe	L	0-1	
06/05	h	Shakhter	W	2-0	Knežević, Ceesay
10/05	a	Spartak	W	5-2	Ceesay 2 (1p), Marković, Knežević, Darabayev
18/05	h	Zhetysu	W	2-1	Ceesay, Lačný
24/05	a	Ordabasy	L	0-1	
28/05	h	Kaysar	W	1-0	Darabayev
01/06	a	Astana	D	2-2	Pliev, Darabayev
14/06	a	Taraz	W	3-2	Islamkhan 2, Marković
22/06	h	Tobol	W	3-1	Pliev, Kuantayev, Islamkhan
27/06	a	Irtysh	W	1-0	Baytana
06/07	h	Aktobe	W	7-1	Gohou 3, Knežević 2 (1p), Pliev, Islamkhan
13/07	a	Shakhter	L	0-1	
27/07	h	Spartak	W	4-1	og (Kutsov), Gohou 2, Kislitsyn
03/08	a	Atyrau	W	3-0	Gohou, og (Abdulin), Darabayev
29/08	h	Shakhter	W	6-1	Kislitsyn, Isael 2, Gohou 2, Darabayev
14/09	a	Kaysar	W	2-0	Gohou 2
20/09	a	Ordabasy	W	1-0	Isael
28/09	h	Aktobe	W	2-0	Isael, Islamkhan
04/10	a	Shakhter	D	0-0	
18/10	h	Kaysar	D	1-1	og (Coulibaly)
22/10	a	Astana	L	1-5	Isael
26/10	h	Ordabasy	W	2-0	Darabayev, Sito Riera
01/11	a	Aktobe	L	0-1	
09/11	h	Astana	L	2-3	Gohou 2

No	Name	Nat	DoB	Pos	Aps	(s)	Gls
19	Mikhail Bakaev		05/08/87	M	27	(1)	
11	Sherkhan Bauyrzhan		28/08/92	M	1	(9)	
14	Baurzhan Baytana		06/06/92	M	5	(3)	1
21	Momodou Ceesay	GAM	24/12/88	A	13		5
17	Aslan Darabayev		21/01/89	M	16	(9)	8
30	Gerard Gohou	CIV	29/12/88	A	9	(4)	12
3	Mark Gurman		09/02/89	D	18	(5)	
31	Isael	BRA	13/05/88	M	13	(1)	5
9	Baurzhan Islamkhan		23/02/93	M	28	(3)	5
16	Dmitri Khomich		04/10/84	G	26		
5	Aleksandr Kislitsyn		08/03/86	D	26	(2)	3
10	Josip Knežević	CRO	03/10/88	M	14	(3)	6
13	Yermek Kuantayev		13/10/90	M	23	(2)	2
32	Islambek Kuat		12/01/93	M	3	(3)	
77	Zhambyl Kukeyev		20/09/88	M		(1)	
23	Miloš Lačný	SVK	08/03/88	A	8	(3)	1
29	Vitali Li		13/03/94	A		(5)	
1	David Loria		31/10/81	G	3		
28	Stanislav Lunin		02/05/93	A	5	(10)	
6	Žarko Marković	SRB	28/01/87	D	17	(1)	3
20	Ľubomír Michalík	SVK	13/08/83	D	14	(3)	
25	Vladislav Nekhty		19/12/91	A		(5)	
	Rifat Nurmugamet		22/05/96	M		(1)	
22	Aslan Orazayev		07/05/92	M		(1)	
2	Zaurbek Pliev		27/09/91	D	24		3
	Timur Rudoselskiy		21/12/94	D	3	(2)	
15	Vladimir Sedelnikov		15/10/91	D		(9)	
26	Sito Riera	ESP	05/01/87	A	9	(3)	1
8	Samat Smakov		08/12/75	D	24	(1)	
24	Sergei Tkachuk		15/02/92	G	3		
27	Artur Yedigaryan	ARM	26/06/87	M	20	(5)	

FC Kaysar Kyzylorda

1968 • Ghani Muratbayev (7,000) • fckaysar.kz
Major honours
Kazakhstan Cup (1) 1999

Coach: Dmitri Ogay

2014

15/03	h	Ordabasy	W	1-0	Savic (p)
22/03	h	Taraz	D	0-0	
29/03	a	Astana	L	0-1	
05/04	h	Kairat	L	0-1	
09/04	a	Tobol	D	1-1	Strukov
13/04	h	Irtysh	W	4-2	Savic 2 (1p), Strukov, Zemlyanukhin
19/04	a	Aktobe	L	0-3	
27/04	h	Shakhter	W	1-0	Kalinin
01/05	a	Spartak	D	1-1	Strukov
06/05	h	Atyrau	W	2-1	Hunt 2
10/05	a	Zhetysu	D	1-1	Hunt, Strukov
18/05	h	Taraz	W	1-0	Hunt
24/05	h	Astana	W	1-0	og (Dmitrenko)
28/05	a	Kairat	L	0-1	
01/06	h	Tobol	D	0-0	
14/06	a	Irtysh	D	1-1	Rozybakiev
22/06	h	Aktobe	D	2-2	Zemlyanukhin, Hunt
29/06	a	Shakhter	L	1-4	Hunt
05/07	h	Spartak	D	1-1	Strukov
13/07	a	Atyrau	W	3-1	Hunt 2, Coulibaly
26/07	h	Zhetysu	D	0-0	
03/08	a	Ordabasy	L	1-2	Altynbekov
24/08	a	Shakhter	D	0-0	
29/08	a	Ordabasy	W	1-0	Furdui
14/09	h	Kairat	L	0-2	
20/09	a	Aktobe	D	0-0	
28/09	h	Astana	D	1-1	Zemlyanukhin
04/10	h	Ordabasy	L	0-1	
18/10	a	Kairat	D	1-1	Nekhty
26/10	h	Aktobe	D	2-2	Zemlyanukhin (p), Furdui
01/11	a	Astana	L	0-3	
09/11	h	Shakhter	W	2-1	Moldakaraev 2 (2p)

No	Name	Nat	DoB	Pos	Aps	(s)	Gls
2	Olzhas Altaev		15/07/89	D	4		
11	Elzhas Altynbekov		22/11/93	A	1	(5)	1
3	Aldan Baltaev		15/01/89	D	13	(2)	
4	Mamoutou Coulibaly	MLI	23/02/84	D	29	(1)	1
5	Damir Dautov		03/03/90	D	26		
27	Valentin Furdui	MDA	01/09/87	M	11	(1)	2
29	Kazbek Geteriev		30/06/85	M		(2)	
28	Rimo Hunt	EST	05/11/85	A	19	(8)	8
15	Miljan Jablan	SRB	30/01/85	D	14	(4)	
77	Ilya Kalinin	CZE	03/02/92	M	18	(5)	1
44	Martin Klein	CZE	02/07/84	D	24		
32	Nurzharyk Kunov		22/10/93	D	5	(11)	
19	Syjundik Kushekov		07/05/90	D		(1)	
90	Matic Maruško	SVN	30/11/90	M	24	(2)	
7	Zhasulan Moldakaraev		07/05/87	A	6	(13)	2
7	Sergei Mošnikov	EST	07/01/88	M	8	(10)	
8	Duman Narzildgam		06/09/93	A	9	(6)	
20	Vladislav Nekhty		19/12/91	M	5		1
23	Sergei Ostapenko		23/02/86	A	4	(7)	
13	Kirill Pryadkin	KGZ	06/07/77	G	32		
6	Rakhimzhan Rozybakiev		02/01/91	M	25	(3)	1
25	Dusan Savic	MKD	01/10/85	A	12	(6)	3
22	Kirill Shestakov		14/11/85	M	18	(3)	
14	Sergei Shevtsov		29/10/90	A	2	(1)	
9	Sergei Strukov	RUS	17/09/82	A	25	(1)	5
10	Anton Zemlyanukhin	KGZ	11/12/88	M	18	(3)	4

FC Ordabasy Shymkent

1998 • Kazhimukan (20,000) • fcordabasy.kz

Major honours
Kazakhstan Cup (1) 2011

Coach: Kuanysh Karakulov;
(03/04/14) Saulius Širmelis (LTU)

2014

15/03	a	Kaysar	L	0-1	
22/03	h	Astana	L	0-1	
29/03	a	Kairat	W	1-0	Junuzović
05/04	h	Tobol	W	3-0	Diakhate, Junuzović 2
09/04	a	Irtysh	L	0-2	
13/04	h	Aktobe	W	1-0	Junuzović
19/04	a	Shakhter	L	1-3	Tolebek
27/04	h	Spartak	W	2-1	Mwesigwa 2
01/05	a	Atyrau	D	1-1	Kasyanov
06/05	h	Zhetysu	D	1-1	Nurgaliyev (p)
10/05	a	Taraz	L	1-2	Nurgaliyev
18/05	h	Astana	D	1-1	Diakhate
24/05	h	Kairat	W	1-0	og (Bakaev)
28/05	a	Tobol	L	1-2	Junuzović
01/06	h	Irtysh	W	2-1	Ashirbekov, Freire
14/06	a	Aktobe	D	1-1	Ashirbekov
22/06	h	Shakhter	W	2-1	Kasyanov, Nurgaliyev
28/06	a	Spartak	L	0-2	
05/07	a	Atyrau	W	1-0	Kasyanov
12/07	a	Zhetysu	W	1-0	Kasyanov
26/07	h	Taraz	D	1-1	Kasyanov
03/08	h	Kaysar	W	2-1	og (Klein), Tazhimbetov
29/08	a	Kaysar	L	0-1	
14/09	a	Astana	L	0-5	
20/09	h	Kairat	L	0-1	
28/09	a	Shakhter	W	3-2	Nurgaliyev, Tunggyshbayev, Beysenov
04/10	a	Kaysar	W	1-0	Kasyanov
18/10	h	Astana	L	1-2	Tazhimbetov
22/10	a	Aktobe	L	1-4	Ashirbekov
26/10	a	Kairat	L	0-2	
01/11	h	Shakhter	W	3-2	Nurgaliyev, Kasyanov, Tazhimbetov
09/11	h	Aktobe	L	1-3	Ashirbekov

No	Name	Nat	DoB	Pos	Aps	(s)	Gls
77	Talgat Adyrbekov		26/01/89	D	2	(2)	
6	Pirali Aliyev		13/01/84	D	9	(1)	
10	Kairat Ashirbekov		21/10/82	M	26	(3)	4
8	Bekzat Beysenov		18/02/87	M	14	(7)	1
89	Pavel Černý	CZE	28/01/85	A	2	(6)	
25	Abdoulaye Diakhate	SEN	16/01/88	M	31		2
39	Maksim Filchakov		28/12/93			(2)	
2	Freire	BRA	21/08/89	D	28		1
33	Kazbek Geteriev		30/06/85	M	7	(3)	
	Sergei Gridin		20/05/87	A	2	(5)	
1	Aleksandr Grigorenko		06/02/85	G	26	(1)	
55	Farhadbek Irismetov		10/08/81	D	1	(1)	
28	Edin Junuzović	CRO	28/04/86	A	17		5
12	Artem Kasyanov	UKR	20/04/83	M	26	(3)	7
23	Bakdaulet Kozhabayev		19/06/92	D	5	(4)	
11	Ondřej Kúdela	CZE	26/03/87	D	14		
20	Evgeni Levin		12/07/92	M	12	(1)	
33	Argen Manekeyev		24/05/96	D		(1)	
4	Mukhtar Mukhtarov		01/01/86	D	21		
14	Andrew Mwesigwa	UGA	24/04/84	D	19	(3)	2
7	Azat Nurgaliyev		30/06/86	M	22	(5)	5
32	Samat Otarbayev		18/02/90	G	3	(1)	
5	Gafurzhan Suyumbayev		19/08/90	D	31		
18	Daurenbek Tazhimbetov		02/07/85	A	11	(14)	3
17	Mardan Tolebek		18/12/90	M	5	(19)	1
27	Andrei Tsvetkov		20/03/80	G	3		
21	Yerkebulan Tunggyshbayev		14/01/95	A	15	(4)	1

FC Shakhter Karagandy

1958 • Shakhter (19,500) • shahter.kz

Major honours
Kazakhstan League (2) 2011, 2012; Kazakhstan Cup (1) 2013

Coach: Viktor Kumykov (RUS)

2014

15/03	a	Irtysh	L	0-1	
22/03	h	Aktobe	D	1-1	Zhangylyshbay
29/03	a	Taraz	W	5-1	Vičius, Konysbayev, Salomov 2, Finonchenko
05/04	a	Spartak	W	1-0	Vasiljević
09/04	h	Atyrau	W	2-0	Poryvaev, og (Odibe)
13/04	a	Zhetysu	W	2-1	Bayzhanov, Zhangylyshbay
19/04	h	Ordabasy	W	3-1	Bayzhanov, Salomov, Vičius
27/04	a	Kaysar	L	0-1	
01/05	h	Astana	D	0-0	
06/05	a	Kairat	L	0-2	
10/05	h	Tobol	W	4-1	Konysbayev 2, Topčagić, Finonchenko
18/05	a	Aktobe	L	0-4	
24/05	h	Taraz	W	1-0	Topčagić
28/05	h	Spartak	W	1-0	Vičius
01/06	a	Atyrau	L	2-3	Yago Fernandes, Zhangylyshbay
14/06	h	Zhetysu	W	3-0	Vasiljević, Topčagić 2
22/06	a	Ordabasy	L	1-2	Poryvaev
27/06	h	Kaysar	W	4-1	Konysbayev, Topčagić 2, Murtazayev
06/07	a	Astana	L	0-4	
13/07	h	Kairat	W	1-0	Topčagić
27/07	a	Tobol	L	0-2	
03/08	h	Irtysh	D	2-2	Topčagić, Vičius
24/08	h	Kaysar	D	0-0	
29/08	a	Kairat	L	1-6	Vičius
14/09	h	Aktobe	D	1-1	Finonchenko
20/09	a	Astana	L	0-1	
28/09	h	Ordabasy	L	2-3	Topčagić 2 (1p)
04/10	h	Kairat	D	0-0	
18/10	a	Aktobe	L	1-3	Finonchenko
26/10	h	Astana	L	0-2	
01/11	a	Ordabasy	L	2-3	Murtazayev, Gabyshev
09/11	h	Kaysar	L	1-2	Maslo

No	Name	Nat	DoB	Pos	Aps	(s)	Gls
15	Sherkhan Bauyrzhan		28/08/92	M	2	(7)	
7	Maksat Bayzhanov		06/08/84	M	19	(5)	2
5	Askhat Borantayev		22/08/78	M	1	(1)	
20	Aldin Džidić	BIH	30/08/83	D	6		
14	Andrei Finonchenko		21/06/82	A	22	(4)	4
22	Mikhail Gabyshev		02/01/90	D	9	(6)	1
21	Aleksandr Kirov		04/06/84	D	13	(1)	
10	Ulan Konysbayev		28/05/89	M	25	(4)	4
77	Stanislav Lunin		02/05/93	M	7	(5)	
25	Sergei Maliy		05/06/90	D	28		
52	Ján Maslo	SVK	05/02/86	D	10		1
35	Aleksandr Mokin		19/06/81	G	26		
45	Roman Murtazayev		10/09/93	A	14	(8)	2
27	Kamoliddin Murzoev	UZB	17/02/87	M	12	(10)	
1	Stas Pokatilov		08/12/92	G	6		
18	Nikola Pokrivač	CRO	26/11/85	M	8	(1)	
17	Andrei Poryvaev	BLR	03/01/82	D	23	(2)	2
29	Shavkat Salomov	UZB	13/11/85	M	22	(6)	3
87	Aleksandar Simčević	SRB	15/02/87	D	24	(1)	
19	Evgeni Tarasov		16/04/85	D	9	(2)	
9	Mihret Topčagić	BIH	21/06/88	A	13	(12)	10
4	Nikola Vasiljević	BIH	19/12/83	D	11		2
3	Gediminas Vičius	LTU	05/07/85	M	27	(2)	5
1	Yago Fernandes	POR	05/01/88	D	6	(3)	1
44	Kuanysh Yermekov		14/04/94	M		(3)	
21	Tokhtar Zhangylyshbay		25/05/93	A	9	(8)	3

FC Spartak Semey

1964 • Spartak (10,000) • spartak-kz.ru

Major honours
Kazakhstan League (3) 1994, 1995, 1998; Kazakhstan Cup (1) 1995

Coach: Almas Kulshinbayev;
(29/04/14) (Konstantin Fridental);
(19/05/14) Aleksei Petrushin (RUS)

2014

15/03	a	Tobol	L	1-2	Azovskiy
22/03	h	Irtysh	D	0-0	
29/03	a	Aktobe	L	0-3	
05/04	h	Shakhter	L	0-1	
09/04	h	Taraz	L	0-2	
13/04	a	Atyrau	L	1-2	Čović
19/04	h	Zhetysu	D	1-1	Kovačević
27/04	a	Ordabasy	L	1-2	
01/05	h	Kaysar	D	1-1	Jovanović
06/05	a	Astana	L	0-5	
10/05	h	Kairat	L	2-5	Čović, Jovanović
18/05	a	Irtysh	L	0-5	
24/05	h	Aktobe	L	0-1	
28/05	a	Shakhter	L	0-1	
01/06	h	Taraz	L	0-1	
14/06	a	Atyrau	W	2-1	Ersalimov, Azovskiy
22/06	a	Zhetysu	L	0-1	
28/06	h	Ordabasy	W	2-0	Rudik, Akhmeev
05/07	a	Kaysar	D	1-1	Peev
13/07	h	Astana	D	1-1	Peev
27/07	a	Kairat	L	1-4	Jovanović
03/08	h	Tobol	W	2-1	Jovanović (p), Genev
23/08	a	Taraz	D	0-0	
29/08	h	Tobol	W	2-1	Azovskiy, Peev (p)
14/09	a	Irtysh	L	2-3	Nurgaliyev 2
20/09	h	Zhetysu	W	3-1	Azovskiy, Peev, Jovanović (p)
28/09	a	Atyrau	D	1-1	Jovanović
04/10	a	Tobol	L	0-1	
19/10	h	Irtysh	W	2-0	Jovanović, Nurgaliyev
26/10	a	Zhetysu	L	1-2	Kutsov
01/11	h	Atyrau	W	3-1	Nurlybaev, Dyulgerov, Sakenov
09/11	a	Taraz	L	0-1	

No	Name	Nat	DoB	Pos	Aps	(s)	Gls
92	Vladislav Akhmeev		19/12/92	M	3	(7)	1
11	Stanislav Akhmetov		09/10/96	M	7	(2)	
26	Nurlan Akinzhanov		14/01/93	D		(2)	
13	Ilias Amirseitov		22/10/89	D	8	(1)	
32	Artur Avagyan	ARM	04/07/87	M	10	(1)	
18	Maksim Azovskiy		04/06/86	M	17	(5)	4
29	Sergei Boychenko		27/09/77	G	12	(1)	
91	Nemanja Čović	SRB	18/06/91	M	8	(1)	3
88	Ognjen Djelmić	BIH	18/08/88	A	1	(1)	
71	Nikolay Dyulgerov	BUL	10/03/88	M	14	(8)	1
19	Azat Ersalimov		19/07/88	M	26	(3)	1
52	Viktor Genev	BUL	27/10/88	D	29		1
84	Nemanja Jovanović	SRB	03/03/84	A	30		7
23	Savo Kovačević	SRB	15/08/88	A	2	(6)	1
20	Sergei Kutsov	KGZ	23/04/77	D	16	(7)	1
15	Timur Muldinov		19/09/93	A		(4)	
22	Vildam Nasibullin		28/01/94	D		(1)	
8	Yerkebulan Nurgaliyev		12/09/93	M	18	(8)	3
27	Bagdat Nurlybaev		03/07/93	M	4	(3)	1
31	Goran Obradović	SRB	25/12/86	D	9	(1)	
17	Evgeni Ovshinov		17/10/80	D	23	(1)	
77	Daniel Peev	BUL	06/10/84	M	28	(2)	4
30	Daniil Rikhard		27/02/74	D	20		
2	Filipp Rudik	BLR	22/03/87	M	12		1
40	Serik Sagyndykov		09/01/84	D	20	(4)	
14	Alibek Sakenov		30/07/91	D	14	(3)	1
7	Ruslan Sakhalbaev		27/06/84	M	7	(2)	
5	Maksim Samchenko		05/05/79	D	7		
9	Baurzhan Turysbek		15/10/91	A	7	(6)	
93	Zhalyn Zhaksylykov		16/01/93	D		(2)	

FC Taraz

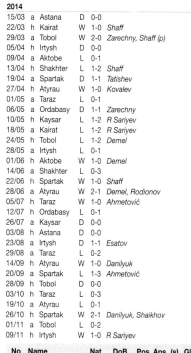

1960 • Tsentralny (12,527) • fctaraz.kz
Major honours
Kazakhstan League (1) 1996; Kazakhstan Cup (1) 2004
**Coach: Arno Pijpers (NED);
(17/04/14) (Nurmat Mirzabayev);
(09/06/14) Evgeni Yarovenko**

2014

15/03	h	Aktobe	L	0-2	
22/03	a	Kaysar	D	0-0	
29/03	h	Shakhter	L	1-5	Roj
05/04	a	Astana	L	0-1	
09/04	h	Spartak	W	2-0	Skorykh, Shchetkin
13/04	a	Kairat	L	1-3	Shchetkin
19/04	h	Atyrau	D	3-3	Dosmagambetov, Tleshev, Golić
27/04	a	Tobol	L	0-1	
01/05	h	Zhetysu	W	1-0	Shchetkin
06/05	a	Irtysh	L	0-2	
10/05	h	Ordabasy	W	2-1	Shchetkin, Vorotnikov
18/05	h	Kaysar	L	0-1	
24/05	a	Shakhter	L	0-1	
28/05	h	Astana	L	1-2	Tleshev
01/06	a	Spartak	W	1-0	Tleshev
14/06	h	Kairat	L	2-3	Tleshev, Skorykh
22/06	a	Atyrau	L	0-3	
28/06	h	Tobol	D	1-1	Tleshev
05/07	a	Zhetysu	L	0-1	
12/07	h	Irtysh	W	5-1	Tleshev 2, Kozhamberdy, Ubbink, Yarovenko
26/07	a	Ordabasy	D	1-1	Yarovenko
02/08	a	Aktobe	L	0-2	
23/08	a	Spartak	D	0-0	
29/08	h	Zhetysu	W	2-0	Kozhamberdy, Nedashkovsky
14/09	a	Tobol	L	0-3	
20/09	h	Atyrau	W	2-1	Yarovenko, Dosmagambetov
28/09	a	Irtysh	D	0-0	
03/10	a	Zhetysu	W	3-0	Shchetkin, Kozhamberdy, Yarovenko
19/10	h	Tobol	D	1-1	Shchetkin
25/10	a	Atyrau	L	2-3	Dosmagambetov 2
01/11	h	Irtysh	L	0-3	
09/11	a	Spartak	W	1-0	Shchetkin (p)

No	Name	Nat	DoB	Pos	Aps	(s)	Gls
22	Maksat Amirkhanov		10/02/92	M	10	(7)	
14	Berik Aytbaev		26/06/91	D	10	(2)	
24	Dzhurakhon Babakhanov		31/10/91	G	12		
2	Sigourney Bandjar	NED	18/08/84	D	9	(2)	
19	Richard Barroilhet	FRA	29/08/92	A	5	(4)	
28	Dmytro Bashlay	UKR	25/04/90	D	15		
21	Daniyar Bayaliev		30/01/93	D	6	(6)	
10	Baurzhan Baytana		06/06/92	M	12	(2)	
11	Timur Dosmagambetov		01/05/89	M	12	(12)	4
18	Jovan Golić	SRB	18/09/86	M	25	(1)	1
23	Zhakyp Kozhamberdy		26/02/92	M	14	(10)	3
3	Aleksandr Kuchma		09/12/80	D	12		
77	Zhasur Narzikulov		13/04/84	D	13		
17	Oleg Nedashkovsky		09/09/87	M	12	(1)	1
1	Ramil Nurmukhametov		21/12/87	G	7		
15	Rok Roj	SVN	10/10/86	D	24		1
7	Eduard Sergienko		18/02/83	M	24	(3)	
9	Aleksei Shchetkin		21/05/91	A	17	(7)	7
5	Sergei Skorykh		25/05/84	D	23	(4)	2
9	Murat Tleshev		12/10/80	A	6	(18)	7
20	Desley Ubbink	NED	15/06/93	M	17	(3)	1
26	Denys Vasilyev	UKR	08/05/87	D	15		
4	Ilya Vorotnikov		01/02/86	D	23		1
27	Olexandr Yarovenko	UKR	19/12/87	A	7	(7)	4
6	Dmitri Yevstigneev		27/11/86	M	18	(4)	
8	Vitali Yevstigneev		08/05/85	M	4	(1)	

FC Tobol Kostanay

1967 • Tsentralny (8,050) • fc-tobol.kz
Major honours
Kazakhstan League (1) 2010; Kazakhstan Cup (1) 2007
**Coach: Sergei Maslenov;
(23/04/14) Vardan Minasyan (ARM)**

2014

15/03	h	Spartak	W	2-1	Bogdanov, Krasić
22/03	a	Atyrau	D	0-0	
29/03	h	Zhetysu	D	0-0	
05/04	a	Ordabasy	L	0-3	
09/04	h	Kaysar	D	1-1	Simkovic
13/04	a	Astana	L	0-1	
19/04	h	Kairat	D	2-2	Bogdanov, Krasić
27/04	h	Taraz	W	1-0	Bogdanov
01/05	a	Irtysh	W	3-0	Zhumaskaliyev, Jeslínek 2
06/05	h	Aktobe	L	0-2	
10/05	a	Shakhter	L	1-4	Dzhalilov
18/05	h	Atyrau	D	0-0	
24/05	a	Zhetysu	W	2-1	Simkovic, Bugaiov
28/05	h	Ordabasy	W	2-1	Bugaiov 2
01/06	a	Kaysar	D	0-0	
14/06	a	Astana	D	1-1	Simkovic
22/06	a	Kairat	L	1-3	Volkov
28/06	a	Taraz	D	1-1	Bugaiov
06/07	h	Irtysh	D	1-1	Kušnír
11/07	a	Aktobe	L	1-3	Simkovic
27/07	h	Shakhter	W	2-0	Simkovic, Jeslínek
03/08	a	Spartak	L	1-2	Jeslínek
23/08	a	Atyrau	L	1-2	Zhumaskaliyev
29/08	a	Spartak	L	1-2	Bogdanov
14/09	h	Taraz	W	3-0	Zhumaskaliyev, Jeslínek, Kušnír
20/09	h	Irtysh	D	0-0	
28/09	a	Zhetysu	D	0-0	
04/10	h	Spartak	W	1-0	Sadovnichi
19/10	a	Taraz	D	1-1	Krasić
25/10	a	Irtysh	D	1-1	Dzhalilov
01/11	h	Zhetysu	W	2-0	Suley, Zhumaskaliyev
09/11	a	Atyrau	W	3-0	Zhumaskaliyev, Krasić, Dzhalilov

No	Name	Nat	DoB	Pos	Aps	(s)	Gls
22	Beybit Abishev		09/02/92	M		(5)	
37	Rafkat Aslan		02/02/94	D	15	(2)	
5	Anatoli Bogdanov		07/08/81	M	26		4
10	Igor Bugaiov	MDA	26/06/84	A	13	(9)	4
23	Raul Dzhalilov		20/07/94	M	18	(8)	3
87	Łukasz Gikiewicz	POL	26/10/87	A	7	(5)	
14	Farhadbek Irismetov		10/08/81	D	7	(6)	
99	Jiří Jeslínek	CZE	30/09/87	M	16	(11)	5
24	Ognjen Krasić	SRB	04/08/88	M	23	(7)	4
25	Štěpán Kučera	CZE	11/06/84	D	30		
17	Nurtas Kurgulin		20/09/86	D	24	(1)	
13	Ondřej Kušnír	CZE	05/04/84	D	12	(4)	2
21	Aleksei Malyshev		24/06/89	M	2	(2)	
12	Yermek Nurgaliyev		08/08/86	M		(1)	
35	Aleksandr Petukhov		11/01/85	G	28		
20	Ivan Sadovnichi	BLR	11/05/87	D	11	(2)	1
77	Arslan Satybaldin		14/08/84	G	4	(2)	
81	Tomas Simkovic	AUT	16/04/87	M	24	(2)	5
8	Nenad Šljivić	SRB	16/04/87	M	18	(3)	
6	Alisher Suley		01/11/95	A	4	(15)	1
33	Nikola Tonev	MKD	12/11/85	D	18		
11	Vitali Volkov	RUS	22/03/81	M	27	(2)	1
9	Nurbol Zhumaskaliyev		11/05/81	M	25	(3)	5

FC Zhetysu Taldykorgan

1981 • Zhetysu (5,550) • fc-zhetisu.kz
**Coach: Omari Tetradze (RUS);
(25/09/14) Askar Kozhabergenov**

2014

15/03	a	Astana	D	0-0	
22/03	h	Kairat	W	1-0	Shaff
29/03	a	Tobol	W	2-0	Zarechny, Shaff (p)
05/04	h	Irtysh	D	0-0	
09/04	a	Aktobe	L	0-1	
13/04	h	Shakhter	L	1-2	Shaff
19/04	a	Spartak	D	1-1	Tatishev
27/04	h	Atyrau	W	1-0	Kovalev
01/05	a	Taraz	L	0-1	
06/05	a	Ordabasy	D	1-1	Zarechny
10/05	h	Kaysar	L	1-2	R Sariyev
18/05	a	Kairat	L	1-2	R Sariyev
24/05	h	Tobol	L	1-2	Demel
28/05	a	Irtysh	L	0-1	
01/06	h	Aktobe	W	1-0	Demel
14/06	a	Shakhter	L	0-3	
22/06	h	Spartak	W	1-0	Shaff
28/06	a	Atyrau	W	2-1	Demel, Rodionov
05/07	h	Taraz	W	1-0	Ahmetović
12/07	h	Ordabasy	L	0-1	
26/07	a	Kaysar	D	0-0	
03/08	h	Astana	D	0-0	
23/08	a	Irtysh	D	1-1	Esatov
29/08	a	Taraz	L	0-2	
14/09	h	Atyrau	W	1-0	Danilyuk
20/09	a	Spartak	L	1-3	Ahmetović
28/09	h	Tobol	D	0-0	
03/10	h	Taraz	L	0-3	
19/10	a	Atyrau	L	0-1	
26/10	h	Spartak	W	2-1	Danilyuk, Shaikhov
01/11	a	Tobol	L	0-2	
09/11	h	Irtysh	W	1-0	R Sariyev

No	Name	Nat	DoB	Pos	Aps	(s)	Gls
2	Timerlan Adilkhanov		28/03/94	D	8	(5)	
21	Mersudin Ahmetović	BIH	19/02/85	A	6	(10)	2
19	Taras Danilyuk		29/01/84	M	20	(1)	2
79	Boti Demel	CIV	03/03/89	A	12	(10)	3
86	Marko Djalović	SRB	19/06/86	M	14		
8	Davron Erghashev	TJK	19/03/88	D	11	(1)	
12	Ruslan Esatov		31/10/84	D	9	(6)	1
4	Didier Kadio	CIV	05/04/90	D	24		
29	Arūnas Klimavičius	LTU	05/10/82	D	25		
24	Viktor Kovalev		25/08/80	D	17	(5)	1
28	Vladislav Kuzmin		03/07/87	D	20	(1)	
20	Andrei Pasechenko		09/08/87	G	17		
33	Vladimir Plotnikov		03/04/86	G	15		
77	Marko Putinčanin	SRB	16/12/87	M	30		
6	Denis Rodionov		26/07/85	M	13	(2)	1
8	Rauan Sariyev		22/01/94	A	21	(4)	3
22	Sauyat Sariyev		15/10/92	M	4	(11)	
7	Sergei Shaff		15/04/88	A	24	(8)	4
23	Berik Shaikhov		20/02/94	M	19	(5)	1
9	Beybit Tatishev		24/07/84	A	7	(15)	1
17	Abylaykhan Totay		16/02/92	M	9	(3)	
47	Alisher Yesimkhanov		14/09/93	A		(1)	
10	Konstantin Zarechny		14/02/84	M	13	(3)	2
11	Konstantin Zotov		14/01/86	M	14		

Top goalscorers

16	Foxi Kéthévoama (Astana)
13	Miloš Trifunović (Atyrau)
12	Gerard Gohou (Kairat)
11	Patrick Twumasi (Astana)
	Kostyantyn Dudchenko (Irtysh)
10	Mihret Topčagić (Shakhter)
9	Marat Khairullin (Aktobe)
8	Olexiy Antonov (Aktobe)
	Marcos Pizzelli (Aktobe)
	Aslan Darabayev (Kairat)
	Rimo Hunt (Kaysar)

Promoted club

FC Okzhetpes Kokshetau

1957 • Torpedo (10,000) • okzhetpes.kz
Coach: Serik Abdualiyev

Second level final table 2014

		Pld	W	D	L	F	A	Pts
1	FC Okzhetpes Kokshetau	28	21	1	6	59	33	64
2	FC Kyran Shymkent	28	19	3	6	60	30	60
3	FC Astana-64	28	17	4	7	54	29	55
4	FC Kaspiy Aktau	28	17	4	7	44	26	55
5	FC Akzhayik Uralsk	28	16	7	5	46	24	55
6	FC Vostok Oskemen	28	14	5	9	48	31	47
7	FC Ekibastuz	28	11	8	9	40	35	41
8	FC Zhetysu-Sunkar Taldykorgan	28	11	7	10	42	39	40
9	FC Kyzylzhar Petropavlovsk	28	12	1	15	41	45	37
10	FC Bayterek Astana	28	10	2	16	34	52	32
11	FC Lashyn Karatau	28	7	6	15	23	42	27
12	CSKA Almaty	28	6	6	16	32	54	24
13	FC Bolat-AMT Temirtau	28	7	2	19	26	40	23
14	FC Gefest Karagandy	28	6	3	19	16	56	21
15	FC Makhtaaral Zhetysay	28	4	5	19	33	62	17

Promotion/Relegation play-off

(16/11/14)
Taraz 1-1 Kyran *(aet; 3-1 on pens)*

DOMESTIC CUP

Kubok Kazakhstana 2014

FIRST ROUND

(23/04/14)
Astana-64 4-0 Makhtaaral
Bayterek 0-4 Tobol
Bolat-AMT 0-2 Atyrau
CSKA Almaty 0-3 Kyzylzhar
Ekibastuz 0-3 Ordabasy
Gefest 5-1 Zhetysu
Kaspiy 1-4 Vostok
Kyran 3-0 Akzhayik
Lashyn 2-0 Spartak Semey
Okzhetpes 1-3 Kairat
Zhetysu-Sunkar 0-2 Kaysar

Byes – Aktobe, Astana, Irtysh, Shakhter, Taraz

SECOND ROUND

(14/05/14)
Astana 1-0 Astana-64
Irtysh 3-1 Kyzylzhar
Kairat 3-1 Gefest
Kaysar 0-3 Aktobe
Shakhter 3-0 Lashyn
Taraz 3-0 Ordabasy
Tobol 1-0 Kyran
Vostok 1-2 Atyrau *(aet)*

QUARTER-FINALS

(18/06/14)
Aktobe 2-1 Taraz *(Antonov 22, 88; Tleshev 62)*
Astana 4-0 Tobol *(Kojašević 45, 47, Cicero 76, Kéthévoama 87)*
Atyrau 1-3 Kairat *(Trifunović 38; Darabayev 59, Islamkhan 66, Knežević 70)*
Shakhter 1-0 Irtysh *(Murzoev 61)*

SEMI-FINALS

(16/08/14 & 24/09/14)
Aktobe 1-1 Astana *(Pizzelli 63; Kéthévoama 26)*
Astana 1-1 Aktobe *(Nuserbayev 41; Pizzelli 20p)*
(aet)
(2-2; Aktobe 4-3 on pens)
Kairat 2-0 Shakhter *(Sito Riera 20, Darabayev 86)*
Shakhter 0-2 Kairat *(Isael 83, Kislitsyn 87)*
(Kairat 4-0)

FINAL

(22/11/14)
Astana Arena, Astana
FC KAIRAT ALMATY 4 *(Arzumanyan 20og, Gohou 31, 66, Darabayev 86)*
FC AKTOBE 1 *(Logvinenko 27)*
Referee: Duzmambetov
KAIRAT: Tkachuk, Kuantayev, Michalík, Marković, Gurman (Lunin 82), Kuat, Darabayev (Baytana 90+3), Islamkhan, Isael, Sito Riera, Gohou (Rudoselskiy 90+3)
Red card: Sito Riera (89)
AKTOBE: Sidelnikov, Miroshnichenko, Arzumanyan, Logvinenko, Anderson Mineiro, Korobkin, Tsarikayev, Pizzelli (Zhalmukan 90), Khairullin, Tagybergen (Aimbetov 74), Antonov

Cup winners Kairat celebrate with the trophy in Astana

LATVIA
Latvijas Futbola Federācija (LFF)

Address Olympic Sports Centre
Grostonas Street 6b
LV-1013 Rīga
Tel +371 67 292988
Fax +371 67 315604
E-mail futbols@lff.lv
Website lff.lv

President Guntis Indriksons
General secretary Jānis Mežeckis
Media officer Rūdolfs Petrovs
Year of formation 1921
National stadium Skonto, Riga (9,500)

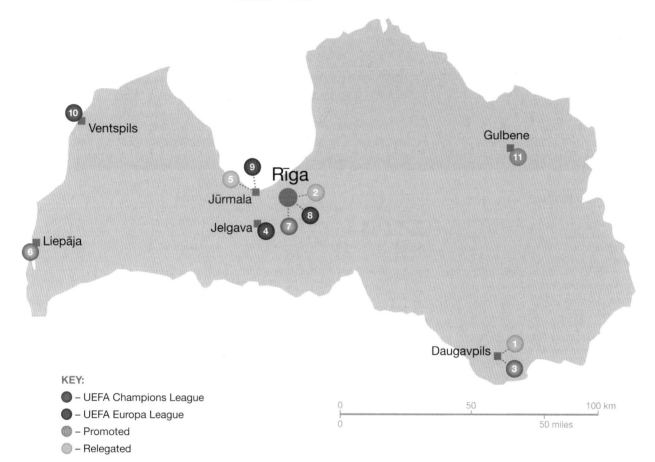

KEY:
● – UEFA Champions League
● – UEFA Europa League
● – Promoted
● – Relegated

VIRSLĪGA CLUBS

  FC Daugava Daugavpils

  FC Daugava Rīga

  BFC Daugavpils

  FK Jelgava

 ⑤ FC Jūrmala

 ⑥ FK Liepāja

 ⑦ FS METTA/LU

 Skonto FC

 ⑨ FK Spartaks Jūrmala

 ⑩ FK Ventspils

PROMOTED CLUB

  FB Gulbene

Ventspils hold on to their crown

FK Ventspils made it three Latvian championship wins in four years as they comfortably shrugged off the challenge of Skonto FC to finish up with a victory margin of 12 points in a Virslīga restored to its longer, more familiar 36-match schedule.

There were fine performances over the campaign from newly-formed FK Liepāja and, especially, FK Jelgava, who, with 167-cap former Latvian international Vitātijs Astafjevs as their new coach, also went on to retain the domestic cup in 2015, beating Ventspils 2-0 in the final.

Third Virslīga title in four years for coastal club

Record champions Skonto run out of gas

Ten-man Jelgava beat Ventspils to retain Latvian Cup

Domestic league

When Ventspils kicked off the season with a club-record run of 12 successive victories, thus stretching an unbeaten sequence carried over from the previous campaign to 34 matches, the Virslīga title race looked over before it had barely begun. However, when Jurģis Pučinskis's side were finally beaten, 2-0 at Liepāja in early June, the shock of defeat appeared to drain the players' confidence, and what followed was an almighty slump that brought just two points in six matches. From being in total command, Ventspils now found themselves five points behind new leaders Skonto.

However, Tamaz Pertia's side soon ran into trouble of their own, and as Ventspils rediscovered the winning habit, a captivating duel at the top of the table ensued. Going into the final quarter of the campaign there was little to choose between the two teams. It was all down to which of them could produce the stronger finish. Ventspils would win that contest hands down, posting seven victories and two draws in their last nine games while Skonto were beaten five times over the same stretch. The summit meeting in Riga two rounds from the end turned out to be the day of deliverance for Ventspils as they ran out handsome 4-2 winners to secure their sixth Virslīga crown.

With final figures of 26 wins, five defeats and a mere 20 goals conceded, Ventspils were more than worthy champions, but such was Skonto's fall from grace in the run-in that they needed to win their last two fixtures simply to grasp on to second place. Jelgava's form in the second half of the season, following the appointment of Astafjevs, Europe's most-capped international, was sublime, and they ended up just one point in arrears of Skonto. Fourth place – but no European spot as they failed to receive a UEFA licence – went to new boys Liepāja, inspired perhaps by the appointment of Latvia's all-time record scorer Māris Verpakovskis as club president (and occasional player).

Domestic cup

Penalty shoot-out winners against Skonto in the 2014 Latvian Cup final, Jelgava won the trophy the hard way again in 2015. There was no post-match drama required this time, but when Jelgava defender Abdoulaye Diallo received a straight red card just three minutes into the final against Ventspils – staged in Ventspils' home stadium – Astafjevs' underdogs faced the steepest of uphill struggles. But Ventspils became complacement and Jelgava made them pay, scoring twice in the first half and improbably holding on to that 2-0 scoreline all the way through to the final whistle.

Europe

The summer of 2014 was an instantly forgettable one for Latvian clubs in Europe as all four fell at the first hurdle without so much as a consolation win between them.

Of the quartet only FC Daugava Daugavpils managed to score, which meant that a solitary goal from Malmö FF was enough to cut short Ventspils' UEFA Champions League adventure in the second qualifying round.

National team

Despite the emergence of 20-year-old ex-Skonto striker Valērijs Šabala as a potential heir to Verpakovskis, the 2014/15 season could not be considered as a positive one for the Latvian national team. Marians Pahars' side failed to win any of their six UEFA EURO 2016 qualifiers and ended the season with only Kazakhstan below them in their group.

In fairness, while three of their qualifying results were bad, the other three (all draws) were reasonably good, and Latvia were desperately unlucky not to claim a famous win against the Czech Republic in Prague, Aleksejs Višņakovs' first-half strike being equalised only moments before the final whistle by a relieved home side.

DOMESTIC SEASON AT A GLANCE

Virslīga 2014 final table

		Pld	Home					Away					Total					Pts
			W	D	L	F	A	W	D	L	F	A	W	D	L	F	A	
1	**FK Ventspils**	36	15	2	1	35	7	11	3	4	40	13	26	5	5	75	20	83
2	Skonto FC	36	13	1	4	38	21	12	0	6	39	13	25	1	10	77	34	71
3	FK Jelgava	36	9	6	3	25	12	11	4	3	32	15	20	10	6	57	27	70
4	FK Liepāja	36	14	1	3	45	14	7	2	9	27	31	21	3	12	72	45	66
5	FC Daugava Daugavpils	36	11	4	3	32	20	8	4	6	21	19	19	8	9	53	39	65
6	FK Spartaks Jūrmala	36	9	5	4	21	10	5	4	9	17	22	14	9	13	38	32	51
7	FC Daugava Rīga	36	8	0	10	26	36	5	4	9	22	28	13	4	19	48	64	43
8	BFC Daugavpils	36	5	3	10	19	30	3	2	13	11	35	8	5	23	30	65	29
9	FS METTA/LU	36	2	4	12	13	35	1	3	14	13	34	3	7	26	26	69	16
10	FC Jūrmala	36	1	3	14	12	54	1	3	14	17	56	2	6	28	29	110	7

NB FC Jūrmala & Skonto FC – 5 pts deducted.

European qualification 2015/16

Champion: FK Ventspils (second qualifying round)

CHAMPIONS LEAGUE

Cup winner: FK Jelgava (first qualifying round)
Skonto FC (first qualifying round)
FK Spartaks Jūrmala (first qualifying round)

EUROPA LEAGUE

Top scorer	Vladislavs Gutkovskis (Skonto), 28 goals
Relegated clubs	FC Jūrmala, FC Daugava Rīga (excluded), FC Daugava Daugavpils (excluded)
Promoted club	FB Gulbene
Cup final	FK Jelgava 2-0 FK Ventspils

Team of the season
(4-4-2)

Coach: Pučinskis *(Ventspils)*

Ikstens *(Jelgava)*

Freimanis *(Jelgava)* Gabovs *(Skonto)* Dubra *(Ventspils)* Kurakins *(Ventspils)*

Rugins *(Skonto)* Paulius *(Ventspils)* V Morozs *(Skonto)* J Ikaunieks *(Liepāja)*

Gutkovskis *(Skonto)* Gauračs *(Spartaks)*

Player of the season

Kaspars Dubra
(FK Ventspils)

The only player to start all 36 matches in Ventspils' 2014 Virslīga title triumph, Dubra was the team's defensive linchpin and leader. While goalkeeper Maksims Livrenko had a fine season, Dubra's consistent ability to get in blocks, tackles and clearing headers was perhaps even more instrumental in giving the champions the league's meanest defence, with 20 clean sheets kept and the same number of goals conceded. The 24-year-old Latvian international moved to Belarusian champions FC BATE Borisov in 2015.

Newcomer of the season

Jānis Ikaunieks
(FK Liepāja)

Playing alongside his older brother Dāvis for Liepāja in 2014, the pair having been transferred from defunct SK Liepājas Metalurgs, Ikaunieks enjoyed a brilliant season, scoring 23 Virslīga goals in 32 matches to become the division's second highest scorer behind Skonto FC's Vladislavs Gutkovskis. His frequent man-of-the-match performances drew interest from abroad, with French club FC Metz eventually signing him up in December 2014, and also earned him regular selection for Latvia.

 **LATVIA**

NATIONAL TEAM

International tournament appearances
UEFA European Championship (1) 2004

Top five all-time caps
Vitālijs Astafjevs (167); Andrejs Rubins (117); Juris Laizāns (113); Imants Bleidelis (106); Mihails Zemļinskis (105)

Top five all-time goals
Māris Verpakovskis (29); Ēriks Pētersons (24); Vitālijs Astafjevs (16); Juris Laizāns & Marians Pahars (15)

Results 2014/15

03/09/14	Armenia	H	Riga	W	2-0	Šabala (16, 74)
09/09/14	Kazakhstan (ECQ)	A	Astana	D	0-0	
10/10/14	Iceland (ECQ)	H	Riga	L	0-3	
13/10/14	Turkey (ECQ)	H	Riga	D	1-1	Šabala (54p)
16/11/14	Netherlands (ECQ)	A	Amsterdam	L	0-6	
28/03/15	Czech Republic (ECQ)	A	Prague	D	1-1	A Višņakovs (30)
31/03/15	Ukraine (ECQ)	A	Lviv	D	1-1	Maksimenko (90+1)
12/06/15	Netherlands (ECQ)	H	Riga	L	0-2	

Appearances 2014/15

Coach: Marians Pahars	05/08/76		Arm	KAZ	ISL	TUR	NED	CZE	Ukr	NED	Caps	Goals
Aleksandrs Koliņko	18/06/75	Baltika (RUS)	G	G	G	G	G		G		94	-
Vladislavs Gabovs	13/07/87	Skonto /Sokol (RUS)	D71	D	D	D38	D		D	s37	16	-
Nauris Bulvītis	15/03/87	Aarau (SUI)	D	D	D						19	2
Kaspars Gorkšs	06/11/81	unattached /Ergotelis (GRE)	D	D	D	D	D	D	D	D	69	5
Vitālijs Maksimenko	08/12/90	VVV (NED)	D46	D				D	s46	D	15	1
Andrejs Kovaļovs	23/03/89	Dacia (MDA)	M	M	M81						10	-
Oļegs Laizāns	28/03/87	Yenisey (RUS)	M46	M			s46	M66	M		25	-
Artūrs Zjuzins	18/06/91	Baltika (RUS)	M75	M		M82	M54	M87	s46	M	22	2
Artis Lazdiņš	03/05/86	Jelgava	M	M27							21	-
Valērijs Šabala	12/10/94	Anorthosis (CYP) /Jablonec (CZE)	A85	A	A81	A	A	A	A68	A62	18	6
Artjoms Rudņevs	13/01/88	Hamburg (GER)	A46	A79	A 55*		s70				31	1
Vitālijs Jagodinskis	28/02/92	Hoverla (UKR)	s46					D	D		3	-
Eduards Višņakovs	10/05/90	Ruch (POL)	s46	s79	s81	A80	A70		s68	s62	11	-
Aleksandrs Fertovs	16/06/87	unattached /Korona (POL)	s46	s27	M	M	M	s82	M46		34	-
Oļegs Timofejevs	28/11/88	Ventspils	s71								3	-
Ritvars Rugins	17/10/89	Skonto	s75		M63						24	-
Jurijs Žigajevs	14/11/85	Ventspils	s85					s87	M46		35	2
Kaspars Dubra	20/12/90	Ventspils /BATE (BLR)			D	D	D	D	s46		7	-
Viktors Morozs	30/07/80	Skonto			M	s82					24	-
Gints Freimanis	09/05/85	Jelgava			s63	s38 91*		D		D37	5	-
Aleksejs Višņakovs	03/02/84	Zimbru (MDA) /Skonto			s81	M	M	M82	s46	M75	59	8
Antons Kurakins	01/01/90	Ventspils				D	D		D46		6	-
Jānis Ikaunieks	16/02/95	Liepāja /Metz (FRA)				M	M46	s66		M	4	-
Deniss Rakels	20/08/92	Cracovia (POL)				s80		M	M	M	9	-
Aleksandrs Cauņa	19/01/88	CSKA Moskva (RUS)					s54				41	11
Andris Vaņins	30/04/80	Sion (SUI)						G		G	65	-
Igors Tarasovs	16/10/88	Jagiellonia (POL)						M	M46	M	7	-
Artūrs Karašausks	29/01/92	Skonto								s75	4	-

EUROPE

FK Ventspils

CHAMPIONS LEAGUE

Second qualifying round - Malmö FF (SWE)
A 0-0
Uvarenko, Dubra, Kurakins, Barinovs, Paulius (Tarkhnishvili 52), Ulimbaševs (Karlsons 64), Mujeci, Abdultaofik (Tidenbergs 64), Freidgeimas, Timofejevs, Rečickis. Coach: Jurģis Pučinskis (LVA)
H 0-1
Uvarenko, Dubra, Kurakins, Barinovs, Tarkhnishvili, Ulimbaševs (Žigajevs 72), Karlsons, Abdultaofik (Tidenbergs 86), Freidgeimas (Mujeci 72), Timofejevs, Rečickis. Coach: Jurģis Pučinskis (LVA)

FK Jelgava

EUROPA LEAGUE

First qualifying round - Rosenborg BK (NOR)
A 0-4
Ikstens, Petrenko, Redjko, Bogdaškins, Žuļevs, Bespalovs (Medeckis 81), Kozlovs (Malašenoks 66), Ošs, Lazdiņš, Daņilovs (Eriba 57), Freimanis. Coach: Vitālijs Astafjevs (LVA)
H 0-2
Ikstens, Petrenko, Redjko, Žuļevs (Eriba 64), Bespalovs, Medeckis (Pētersons 84), Kozlovs, Ošs, Gubins, Freimanis, Malašenoks (Jaudzems 77). Coach: Vitālijs Astafjevs (LVA)

FC Daugava Daugavpils

EUROPA LEAGUE

First qualifying round - Víkingur (FRO)
A 1-2 Kokins (56)
Vlasovs, Chikhradze, Solovjovs, Jaliashvili, Volkovs, Kokins, Ševeļovs, Žatkins (Gryshchenko 18), Kozlov, Kosmačovs, Kuplovs-Oginskis. Coach: Hennadiy Orbu (UKR)
H 1-1 Žatkins (60)
Vlasovs, Chikhradze, Solovjovs, Volkovs, Kokins, Ševeļovs, Žatkins (Sikorskiy 64), Kozlov, Ostrovskis, Kosmačovs, Kuplovs-Oginskis. Coach: Hennadiy Orbu (UKR)
Red card: Solovjovs 90+2

FC Daugava Rīga

EUROPA LEAGUE

First qualifying round - Aberdeen FC (SCO)
A 0-5
Zubas, Ribokas (Blanks 57), Savénas, Kučys, Tomkevičius, Ziļs, Joksts, Mendy, Knapšis, Borovskij (Markevičius 83), Vítor Flora (Abdelaziz 58). Coach: Armands Zeiberliņš (LVA)
Red cards: Ziļs 55, Kučys 81
H 0-3
Krūmiņš, Solovich, Ribokas (Vītolnieks 62), Savénas, Kačanovs, Blanks (Markevičius 66), Tomkevičius, Abdelaziz, Mendy, Knapšis, Vítor Flora (Karkliņš 55). Coach: Armands Zeiberliņš (LVA)

DOMESTIC LEAGUE CLUB-BY-CLUB

FC Daugava Daugavpils

1944 • Celtnieks (1,980) • fcdaugava.lv
Major honours
Latvian League (1) 2012; Latvian Cup (1) 2008
Coach: Viktor Demidov (RUS);
(04/06/14) Hennadiy Orbu (UKR);
(08/08/14) Ivan Tabanov (MDA)

2014

30/03	h	Jelgava	L	1-2	Jaliashvili (p)
09/04	h	Jūrmala	W	2-0	Kosmačovs, Arlashin
13/04	h	Daugava R	W	1-0	Tsintsadze
19/04	h	METTA/LU	W	1-0	Kokins
26/04	a	BFC Daugavpils	W	1-0	Khumarashvili
30/04	h	Liepāja	W	5-3	Hüseynov (p), Kosmačovs, Chikhradze 2 (2p), Bogdanov
06/05	a	Ventspils	L	0-3	
10/05	a	Skonto	L	1-2	Ševeļovs
14/05	h	Spartaks	D	3-3	Arlashin, Solovjovs, Kosmačovs
17/05	h	Jūrmala	W	1-0	Kozlov
21/05	h	Spartaks	W	1-0	Kozlov
24/05	a	Jelgava	D	1-1	Kosmačovs
01/06	a	Daugava R	W	1-0	Kosmačovs
10/06	a	Skonto	L	0-4	
14/06	h	METTA/LU	W	1-0	Kosmačovs
18/06	h	BFC Daugavpils	W	2-1	Kokins, Volkovs
21/06	a	Liepāja	W	3-0	Kozlov, Kosmačovs, Žatkins
25/06	h	Ventspils	D	1-1	Kozlov
29/06	a	Spartaks	D	0-0	
07/07	a	Jūrmala	W	3-2	Volkovs, Kosmačovs, Ševeļovs
13/07	a	Jelgava	L	0-1	
28/07	h	Daugava R	D	2-2	Kosmačovs, Ignatāns
01/08	a	Skonto	L	0-1	
09/08	h	METTA/LU	W	2-1	Kokins, Volkovs
13/08	h	BFC Daugavpils	W	2-0	Kokins 2
16/08	h	Liepāja	W	3-1	Kuplovs-Oginskis (p), Ševeļovs, Arlashin
22/08	h	Ventspils	D	1-1	Žatkins
26/08	a	Spartaks	D	0-0	
12/09	a	Jūrmala	D	1-1	Kosmačovs
20/09	a	Jelgava	W	1-0	Kosmačovs
28/09	a	Daugava R	W	4-1	Kozlov 2, Kosmačovs, Kutsenko
04/10	a	Skonto	L	0-1	
17/10	a	METTA/LU	W	1-0	Ignatāns
26/10	h	BFC Daugavpils	W	5-0	Kozlov, Kutsenko, Ignatāns, Ševeļovs, Žatkins
01/11	a	Liepāja	L	2-3	Ignatāns 2
08/11	a	Ventspils	L	0-4	

Name	Nat	DoB	Pos	Aps	(s)	Gls
Rizvan Ablitarov	UKR	18/04/89	D	9		
Andrei Arlashin	RUS	21/02/90	A	21	(3)	3
Ilya Bogdanov	RUS	08/09/90	M	8	(5)	1
Giorgi Chikhradze	GEO	04/08/87	D	17		2
Ričards Grauze		13/05/96	A	1	(8)	
Rojs Grauze		07/08/96	M	2	(5)	
Pavlo Gryshchenko	UKR	06/07/90	M	3		
Murad Hüseynov	AZE	25/01/89	A	3	(3)	1
Visvaldis Ignatāns		03/08/91	M	8	(4)	5
Aleksandrs Ivanovs		16/11/85	D	7		
Jemal Jaliashvili	GEO	27/10/90	A	11	(3)	1
Giorgi Khumarashvili	GEO	24/08/89	D	17	(1)	1
Ēriks Kokins		11/01/91	A	29	(2)	5
Jevgenijs Kosmačovs		18/02/88	M	30	(1)	12
Dmitri Kozlov	RUS	22/10/84	A	24	(6)	7
Aleksejs Kuplovs-Oginskis		21/01/88	M	15	(5)	1
Dmytro Kushnirov	UKR	01/04/90	D	1		
Valeriy Kutsenko	UKR	02/11/86	M	8	(1)	2
Jurijs Morozs		22/11/87	D		(3)	
Jevģēnijs Nerugals		26/02/89	G	17		
Pāvels Ostrovskis		24/05/94	D	11	(2)	
Deivis Pilacs		08/11/95	D	1		
Sergejs Prokopkins		19/01/94	M	1		
Jans Radevičs		14/03/89	M	24	(5)	
Mārtiņš Rublevskis		19/07/98	D		(1)	
Kirils Ševeļovs		02/06/90	D	33	(2)	4
Ihor Sikorskiy	UKR	29/07/88	M	2	(1)	
Aleksandrs Solovjovs		25/02/88	D	26	(2)	1
Badzina Tsintsadze	GEO	06/04/89	D	15	(1)	1
Edgars Vērdiņš		29/03/93	M	3	(9)	
Aleksandrs Vlasovs		07/05/86	G	19	(1)	
Vladimirs Volkovs		10/08/84	M	12	(18)	3
Oļegs Žatkins		13/04/87	M	18	(1)	3
Žans Zubovs		21/08/94	M		(1)	

FC Daugava Rīga

2003 • Daugava (5,600) • daugavariga.com
Coach: Arvydas Skrupskis (LTU);
(29/05/14) Armands Zeiberliņš

2014

22/03	a	Ventspils	L	0-2
29/03	a	Jūrmala	D	1-1 Markevičius
13/04	a	Daugava D	L	0-1
16/04	a	BFC Daugavpils	L	2-3 Markevičius, Kučys
20/04	a	Liepāja	L	0-1
26/04	h	Spartaks	L	0-2
01/05	a	Jelgava	L	1-4 og (Ošs)
06/05	h	Skonto	L	1-6 Savénas
10/05	a	METTA/LU	W	2-0 Kačanovs, Tomkevičius
14/05	h	BFC Daugavpils	W	1-0 Apiņš
17/05	h	Ventspils	L	0-4
23/05	h	Jūrmala	W	3-0 Borovskij, Savénas 2 (1p)
01/06	h	Daugava D	L	0-1
11/06	h	METTA/LU	W	1-0 Savénas
15/06	h	Liepāja	W	4-0 Tomkevičius, Kučys, Vitolnieks, Ziļs
18/06	a	Spartaks	L	0-1
21/06	a	Jelgava	D	1-1 Kučys
25/06	a	Skonto	L	1-5 Kučys (p)
29/06	a	BFC Daugavpils	L	0-1
13/07	a	Jūrmala	W	6-0 Savénas 3 (2p), Ziļs 2, Blanks
28/07	a	Daugava D	D	2-2 Ziļs, Savénas (p)
01/08	h	METTA/LU	W	2-0 Ziļs, Tomkevičius
09/08	a	Liepāja	W	2-1 Vítor Flora 2
13/08	h	Spartaks	W	2-1 Solovich, Ziļs
17/08	h	Jelgava	L	0-3
22/08	h	Skonto	L	1-2 Regža
28/08	h	BFC Daugavpils	W	4-2 Ziļs, Joksts, Markevičius, Knapšis
13/09	a	Ventspils	D	0-0
19/09	h	Jūrmala	W	3-1 Savénas (p), Ziļs, Regža
24/09	h	Ventspils	L	0-3
28/09	h	Daugava D	L	1-4 Savénas
03/10	a	METTA/LU	W	2-1 Kučys, Savénas (p)
20/10	h	Liepāja	L	2-4 Vítor Flora, Savénas
26/10	a	Spartaks	L	0-1
01/11	h	Jelgava	L	1-3 Kļuškins
08/11	a	Skonto	L	1-4 Knapšis

Name	Nat	DoB	Pos	Aps	(s)	Gls
Verners Apiņš		14/04/92	A	12	(4)	1
Kristaps Blanks		30/01/86	A	21	(2)	1
Valdemar Borovskij	LTU	02/05/84	D	17	(1)	1
Dāvids Čudars		08/08/94	M		(3)	
Edijs Joksts		21/07/92	D	16	(3)	1
Deniss Kačanovs		27/11/79	D	32	(2)	1
Edgars Kārkliņš		21/07/91	M	15	(2)	
Gļebs Kļuškins		01/10/92	M	4	(1)	1
Emīls Knapšis		07/08/95	M	15		2
Kārlis Knūts		18/06/95	D	4	(1)	
Aleksejs Koļesņikovs		05/10/81	A	1	(8)	
Jānis Krūmiņš		09/10/92	G	27		
Aurimas Kučys	LTU	22/02/81	M	24	(3)	6
Tadas Markevičius	LTU	10/04/85	M	12	(18)	3
Emmanuel Mendy	SEN	30/03/90	D	19		
Artis Novickis		09/11/86	D		(4)	
Roberts Ozols		10/09/95	G	9	(2)	
Alekss Regža		16/07/94	D	10	(3)	2
Artjoms Šatskihs		26/03/96	M	2	(6)	
Mantas Savénas	LTU	27/08/82	M	28	(2)	12
Oleh Solovich	UKR	27/09/91	D	25	(4)	1
Giedrius Tomkevičius	LTU	29/02/84	D	34		3
Raivis Vitolnieks		29/07/95	M	28	(4)	1
Vítor Flora	BRA	21/02/90	A	7	(8)	3
Vitālijs Ziļs		19/08/87	A	34	(2)	8

BFC Daugavpils

2009 • Celtnieks (1,980) • bfcdaugava.lv
Coach: Kirils Kurbatovs

2014

23/03	a	Spartaks	W	1-0 Fjodorovs
29/03	h	Liepāja	D	1-1 J Bovins
05/04	a	METTA/LU	L	0-1
16/04	h	Daugava R	W	3-2 Tarasovs, Ryzhevski, Fjodorovs
20/04	a	Skonto	L	1-3 Černomordijs
26/04	h	Daugava D	L	0-1
01/05	h	Ventspils	L	0-3
05/05	a	Jūrmala	W	2-1 Fjodorovs 2
10/05	h	Jelgava	L	2-3 Tarasovs, og (Gubins)
14/05	a	Daugava R	L	0-1
18/05	h	METTA/LU	D	1-1 Ryzhevski
24/05	h	Liepāja	L	0-4
01/06	h	Spartaks	L	1-3 Sokolovs (p)
10/06	a	Jelgava	L	0-1
14/06	h	Skonto	L	0-2
18/06	a	Daugava D	L	1-2 Ryzhevski
22/06	a	Ventspils	W	1-0 Sokolovs
25/06	h	Jūrmala	D	1-1 Fjodorovs (p)
29/06	h	Daugava R	L	0-1
06/07	a	METTA/LU	D	1-1 Tarasovs
12/07	a	Liepāja	L	1-2 Ryotaro
27/07	a	Spartaks	L	0-2
02/08	h	Jelgava	L	0-2
08/08	a	Skonto	L	0-2
13/08	a	Daugava D	L	0-2
17/08	h	Ventspils	L	0-1
21/08	h	Jūrmala	D	1-1 Klimaševičs
28/08	a	Daugava R	L	2-4 Ryotaro, Ryzhevski
13/09	h	METTA/LU	W	4-1 Tarasovs, Lukanyuk, Ryzhevski, Halimons
20/09	a	Liepāja	L	0-5
27/09	h	Spartaks	W	1-0 Catlakšs
04/10	a	Jelgava	L	0-2
19/10	h	Skonto	W	1-0 Ryzhevski
26/10	a	Daugava D	L	0-5
01/11	a	Ventspils	L	0-2
08/11	h	Jūrmala	W	4-2 Ryotaro 3 (1p), Dobratuļins

Name	Nat	DoB	Pos	Aps	(s)	Gls
Vadims Atamaņukovs		12/06/81	M	20	(6)	
Edvīns Bovins		02/10/96	M	1	(2)	
Jānis Bovins		23/06/93	M	14	(9)	1
Jevgenijs Bragins		21/10/95	D	1	(2)	
Aigars Catlakšs		09/02/93	D	11	(6)	1
Antonijs Černomordijs		26/09/96	D	24	(1)	1
Georgijs Čižovs		26/07/92	G	23		
Marks Deružinskis		23/10/97	M		(1)	
Nikita Dobratuļins		20/07/96	A	7	(9)	1
Vladislavs Fjodorovs		27/09/96	A	5	(19)	5
Jurijs Halimons		20/01/92	M	11	(7)	1
Daniels Jakovļevs		06/08/97	A	1	(3)	
Ņikita Kaļiņins		26/11/95	M	1	(2)	
Yuta Kinowaki	JPN	22/01/91	D	21		
Dmitrijs Klimaševičs		16/04/95	D	28	(4)	1
Deniss Komarovs		22/05/95	M		(2)	
Vladislavs Kurakins		09/07/96	G	13	(1)	
Pāvels Liholetovs		04/07/97	M		(1)	
Viktors Litvinskis		07/02/96	D	23		
Ivan Lukanyuk	UKR	05/02/93	A	12		1
Artjoms Murdasovs		24/08/91	D	28	(2)	
Kiyoshi Nakatani	JPN	07/05/91	D	14		
Pāvels Ostrovskis		24/05/94	D	2		
William Pegou	CMR	22/03/91	D	3	(3)	
Nakano Ryotaro	JPN	13/06/88	M	29	(2)	5
Pavel Ryzhevski	BLR	03/03/81	A	23	(4)	6
Jurijs Sokolovs		12/09/83	M	30	(1)	2
Pāvels Tarasovs		16/01/88	M	31	(2)	4
Pāvels Truņins		02/07/95	M	1	(2)	
Sergejs Vasiļjevs		13/06/96	A		(4)	
Taisei Yamazaki	JPN	10/12/91	M	19	(2)	
Verners Zalaks		05/04/97	A		(1)	

FK Jelgava

2004 • Zemgales Olimpiskā centra (1,560);
Olaine (2,500) • fkjelgava.lv
Major honours
Latvian Cup (3) 2010, 2014, 2015
Coach: Vladimirs Beškarevs;
(04/06/14) Vitālijs Astafjevs

2014

22/03	a	Jūrmala	W	3-1 Kozlovs 3
30/03	a	Daugava D	W	2-1 Bespalovs 2 (1p)
09/04	h	Spartaks	D	0-0
13/04	h	Skonto	L	0-3
16/04	a	Liepāja	W	3-2 Petersons, Redjko, Diakvnishvili
20/04	h	Ventspils	L	1-2 Diakvnishvili
01/05	h	Daugava R	W	4-1 Gubins, Ošs 2, Kozlovs
05/05	h	METTA/LU	D	1-1 Petersons
10/05	a	BFC Daugavpils	W	3-2 Bespalovs (p), Freimanis, Žuļevs
14/05	a	Liepāja	L	1-2 Kozlovs
24/05	h	Daugava D	D	1-1 og (Chikhradze)
03/06	a	Skonto	D	1-1 Kozlovs
06/06	a	Spartaks	W	1-0 Malašenoks
10/06	h	BFC Daugavpils	W	1-0 Kozlovs
14/06	a	Ventspils	D	0-0
18/06	h	Jūrmala	W	5-0 Kozlovs 2, Daņilovs 2, Jaudzems
21/06	h	Daugava R	D	1-1 Malašenoks
25/06	a	METTA/LU	D	1-1 Jaudzems
29/06	h	Liepāja	W	3-0 Petersons, Daņilovs 2
06/07	a	Spartaks	D	1-1 Malašenoks
13/07	h	Daugava D	W	1-0 Eriba
28/07	h	Skonto	L	0-1
02/08	a	BFC Daugavpils	W	2-0 Gubins, Ošs
08/08	h	Ventspils	W	1-0 Eriba
13/08	a	Jūrmala	W	2-0 Kozlovs 2 (1p)
17/08	a	Daugava R	W	3-0 Kozlovs, Bogdaškins, Łatka
22/08	h	METTA/LU	D	1-1 Malašenoks
27/08	h	Liepāja	W	1-1 Kozlovs
12/09	h	Spartaks	D	0-0
20/09	a	Daugava D	L	0-1
29/09	a	Skonto	W	3-0 Kozlovs, Malašenoks, Bespalovs
04/10	h	BFC Daugavpils	W	2-0 Freimanis, og (Catlakšs)
18/10	a	Ventspils	L	0-2
25/10	h	Jūrmala	W	2-1 Savčenkovs 2
01/11	a	Daugava R	W	3-1 Ošs, Kozlovs, Malašenoks
08/11	a	METTA/LU	W	3-0 Bogdaškins 2, Jaudzems

Name	Nat	DoB	Pos	Aps	(s)	Gls
Aleksandrs Baturinskis		15/12/91	D	2	(5)	
Romāns Bespalovs		18/10/88	M	27	(4)	4
Boriss Bogdaškins		21/02/90	M	25	(7)	3
Maksim Daņilovs		02/08/86	A	3	(22)	4
Giorgi Diakvnishvili	GEO	21/11/87	M	2	(4)	2
Kennedy Eriba	NGA	05/02/94	M	8	(7)	2
Gints Freimanis		09/05/85	D	34		2
Aleksandrs Gubins		16/05/88	D	27	(1)	2
Pāvels Hohlovs		19/12/89	M		(1)	
Kaspars Ikstens		05/06/88	G	36		
Artis Jaudzems		04/04/95	M		(13)	3
Andrejs Kirilins		01/11/95	M	18	(6)	
Vladislavs Kozlovs		30/11/87	A	34		15
Dariusz Łatka	POL	14/09/78	M	13		1
Artis Lazdiņš		03/05/86	M	18		
Oļegs Malašenoks		27/04/86	A	25	(7)	6
Dmitrijs Medeckis		24/03/95	M	6	(18)	
Mārcis Ošs		25/07/91	D	29		4
Armands Petersons		05/12/90	M	16	(8)	3
Deniss Petrenko		14/03/88	D	14	(1)	
Valerijs Redjko		10/03/83	M	31	(1)	1
Igors Savčenkovs		03/11/82	D	9		2
Andreas Themistocleous	CYP	01/03/94	D	4	(1)	
Vadims Žuļevs		01/03/88	M	15		1

FC Jūrmala

2008 • Sloka (2,500); Kauguru Vidusskola
(2,000) • jurmalafc.lv
**Coach: Mihails Koņevs;
(13/05/14) Gosho Petkov (BUL);
(01/09/14) Andrei Kanchelskis (RUS)**

2014

22/03	h	Jelgava	L	1-3	*Juanma (p)*
29/03	h	Daugava R	D	1-1	*Juanma (p)*
09/04	a	Daugava D	L	0-2	
12/04	a	METTA/LU	W	4-2	*Juanma 2, Loginovs, Trecarichi*
16/04	a	Ventspils	L	1-3	*Juanma*
19/04	a	Spartaks	D	1-1	*Silva*
01/05	a	Skonto	L	0-1	
05/05	h	BFC Daugavpils	L	1-2	*Halvitovs*
10/05	h	Liepāja	L	2-3	*Bordón 2*
14/05	h	Ventspils	L	0-6	
17/05	a	Daugava D	L	0-1	
23/05	a	Daugava R	L	0-3	
01/06	h	METTA/LU	L	0-3	*(w/o)*
11/06	a	Liepāja	L	0-7	
14/06	h	Spartaks	L	0-1	
18/06	a	Jelgava	L	0-5	
22/06	h	Skonto	L	0-5	
25/06	a	BFC Daugavpils	D	1-1	*Ulimbaševs*
29/06	a	Ventspils	L	1-6	*Korban*
07/07	h	Daugava D	L	2-3	*Silva, Montalvo*
13/07	h	Daugava R	L	0-6	
26/07	a	METTA/LU	D	1-1	*Montalvo (p)*
03/08	h	Liepāja	L	0-1	
09/08	a	Spartaks	L	1-4	*Montalvo*
13/08	h	Jelgava	L	0-2	
17/08	a	Skonto	L	3-4	*Silva 2, Kārkliņš*
21/08	h	BFC Daugavpils	D	1-1	*Diakvnishvili*
28/08	h	Ventspils	L	0-7	
12/09	h	Daugava D	D	1-1	*Silva*
19/09	a	Daugava R	L	1-3	*Silva*
27/09	h	METTA/LU	W	1-0	*Montalvo (p)*
04/10	a	Liepāja	L	0-6	
18/10	h	Spartaks	L	1-2	*Tyshchenko*
25/10	a	Jelgava	L	1-2	*Abot*
01/11	h	Skonto	L	1-7	*Abot*
08/11	a	BFC Daugavpils	L	2-4	*Abot, Khardziani*

Name	Nat	DoB	Pos	Aps	(s)	Gls
Nicolás Abot	ARG	28/09/85	A	7	(3)	3
Orlando Bordón	PAR	07/08/86	M	6	(3)	2
Denis Bosnjak	BIH	08/02/91	A	1	(2)	
Ingmars Briškēns		16/06/95	A	11	(2)	
Giorgi Diakvnishvili	GEO	21/11/87	M	18		1
Kristaps Dzelme		30/01/90	G	25		
Romāns Geiko		19/11/93	M	15	(4)	
Kevin Gissi	SUI	10/09/92	A	2		
Ivans Gluško		25/09/84	M	27	(3)	
Kirils Grigorovs		19/10/92	M	15	(2)	
Dmitrijs Halvitovs		03/04/86	D	10		1
Juanma	ESP	22/07/86	M	6	(2)	5
Edgars Kārkliņš		21/03/91	A	14		1
Besarion Khardziani	RUS	06/12/92	M	4	(9)	1
Kirill Korban	RUS	12/06/89	D	5		1
Vjačeslavs Kudrjavcevs		30/03/98	G	2		
Igors Labuts		07/06/90	G	8		
Artjoms Loginovs		20/07/93	A	6	(4)	1
Juris Macuks		01/12/89	M	2	(1)	
Pāvels Mihadjuks		27/05/80	D	8	(2)	
Normunds Miķelsons		31/03/94	D		(2)	
Maksims Miskovs		04/01/97	A	1	(6)	
Benito Montalvo	ARG	19/09/85	M	33	(1)	4
Tauno Mõttus	EST	27/06/95	M		(1)	
Richmond Nketiah	GHA	28/10/94	D	12	(2)	
Andrejs Panasjuks		26/05/87	M	17	(1)	
Sekyi Quaye	GHA	17/06/90	M	2		
Maksims Rafaļskis		14/05/84	M	6	(1)	
Vladas Rimkus		28/05/93	A	22	(1)	
Héctor Romero	ARG	20/04/91	D	6		
Maksims Semakins		06/10/94	M		(3)	
Dmitrijs Šiļuks		21/06/87	D	27	(3)	
Diego Silva	URU	17/05/87	A	26	(1)	6
Rolands Smans		01/02/98	A		(5)	
Deniss Sokoļskis		25/08/81	D	14		
Elvis Studāns		19/12/95	A	3	(2)	
Lucas Trecarichi	ARG	12/02/91	M	4	(3)	1
Olexiy Tyshchenko	UKR	21/07/94	M	9	(2)	1
Daniils Ulimbaševs		12/03/92	M	13		1
Maksims Župerko		24/08/96	D		(1)	

FK Liepāja

2014 • Daugava (5,083); Daugava Artificial
(2,000) • fkliepaja.lv
Coach: Viktors Dobrecovs

2014

21/03	h	METTA/LU	W	2-1	*Grebis, Afanasjevs*
29/03	a	BFC Daugavpils	D	1-1	*Grebis*
09/04	h	Skonto	W	1-0	*J Ikaunieks (p)*
12/04	a	Ventspils	L	2-3	*og (Kiko Insa), J Ikaunieks (p)*
16/04	h	Jelgava	L	2-3	*Grebis, J Ikaunieks*
20/04	h	Daugava R	W	1-0	*Gucs*
26/04	a	METTA/LU	W	4-1	*Afanasjevs, J Ikaunieks, Torres, Verpakovskis*
30/04	a	Daugava D	L	3-5	*D Ikaunieks, J Ikaunieks, Gucs*
05/05	h	Spartaks	W	2-0	*Torres, J Ikaunieks*
10/05	a	Jūrmala	W	3-2	*Torres, J Ikaunieks 2*
14/05	h	Jelgava	W	2-1	*Grebis, J Ikaunieks*
24/04	a	BFC Daugavpils	W	4-0	*Grebis, Afanasjevs, D Ikaunieks, og (Kinowaki)*
03/06	h	Ventspils	W	2-1	*D Ikaunieks, J Ikaunieks*
11/06	h	Jūrmala	W	7-0	*Grebis 2 (1p), J Ikaunieks 4, Šadčins*
15/06	a	Daugava R	L	0-4	
21/06	h	Daugava D	L	0-2	
25/06	a	Spartaks	L	0-2	
29/06	a	Jelgava	L	0-3	
06/07	h	Skonto	W	3-0	*(w/o)*
12/07	h	BFC Daugavpils	W	2-1	*Savaļnieks, og (Litvinskis)*
23/07	a	Skonto	L	0-2	
28/07	a	Ventspils	L	0-1	
03/08	a	Jūrmala	W	1-0	*og (Nketiah)*
09/08	a	Daugava R	L	1-2	*Grebis*
13/08	a	METTA/LU	W	2-0	*Afanasjevs, Gucs*
16/08	a	Daugava D	L	1-3	*Hmizs (p)*
21/08	h	Spartaks	W	3-0	*Afanasjevs, J Ikaunieks, og (Kazačoks)*
27/08	a	Jelgava	L	0-1	
14/09	a	Skonto	W	2-1	*D Ikaunieks 2*
20/09	h	BFC Daugavpils	W	5-0	*J Ikaunieks 3, Gucs, Šadčins*
28/09	h	Ventspils	D	1-1	*J Ikaunieks*
04/10	h	Jūrmala	W	6-0	*J Ikaunieks 2, Šadčins, Grebis 2, Savaļnieks*
20/10	a	Daugava R	W	4-2	*J Ikaunieks 2, Torres, Grebis*
24/10	h	METTA/LU	W	2-0	*D Ikaunieks, Afanasjevs*
01/11	h	Daugava D	W	3-2	*Grebis, Mihadjuks, Hmizs*
08/11	a	Spartaks	D	0-0	

Name	Nat	DoB	Pos	Aps	(s)	Gls
Valerijs Afanasjevs		20/09/82	M	26	(4)	6
Devids Dobrecovs		26/02/97	M		(3)	
Reinis Flaksis		03/04/94	D	25	(4)	
Kristaps Grebis		31/12/80	A	20	(4)	12
Toms Gucs		28/04/92	A	14	(20)	4
Dmitrijs Hmizs		31/07/92	M	16		2
Keisuke Hoshino	JPN	21/08/85	D	13		
Dāvis Ikaunieks		07/01/94	A	25	(7)	6
Jānis Ikaunieks		16/02/95	M	32		23
Deniss Ivanovs		11/01/84	D	11		
Jānis Jēkabsons		20/01/96	D	13	(5)	
Kriss Kārkliņš		31/01/96	M	15	(7)	
Emils Knapšis		07/08/95	M	1	(8)	
Juris Kučma		09/07/93	M	3		
Toms Mežs		07/09/89	D	17		
Pāvels Mihadjuks		27/05/80	D	13		1
Madis Miķelsons		18/01/94	M	5		
Agris Otaņķis		06/10/93	D		(1)	
Ivan Pecha	SVK	23/01/86	D	13	(1)	
Ilja Šadčins		02/07/94	M	12	(16)	3
Roberts Savaļnieks		04/02/93	M	8	(3)	2
Endijs Šlampe		24/07/94	D	32		
Cristián Torres	ARG	18/06/85	M	23	(10)	4
Antons Tumanovs		16/04/97	D	8		
Artūrs Vaičulis		26/02/90	G	14		
Raivo Varažinskis		07/03/93	G	19		
Māris Verpakovskis		15/10/79	A	1	(8)	1
Toms Vīksna		14/01/95	G	2	(1)	
Mareks Zuntners		13/02/83	M	4	(3)	

FS METTA/LU

2006 • Hanzas Vidusskolas (460) • fsmetta.lv
Coach: Andris Riherts

2014

21/03	a	Liepāja	L	1-2	*Kalniņš*
30/03	h	Ventspils	L	0-2	
05/04	h	BFC Daugavpils	W	1-0	*I Stuglis*
12/04	h	Jūrmala	L	2-4	*Kalniņš, Puķītis*
16/04	a	Skonto	L	1-3	*Kalns*
19/04	a	Daugava D	L	0-1	
26/04	h	Liepāja	L	1-4	*og (Mežs)*
01/05	a	Spartaks	L	1-4	*E Stuglis*
05/05	a	Jelgava	D	1-1	*Ostrovskis*
10/05	h	Daugava R	L	0-2	
14/05	h	Skonto	L	1-2	*Pallo*
18/05	a	BFC Daugavpils	D	1-1	*Pallo*
24/05	a	Ventspils	L	0-2	
01/06	a	Jūrmala	W	3-0	*(w/o)*
11/06	a	Daugava R	L	0-1	
14/06	a	Daugava D	L	0-1	
21/06	h	Spartaks	D	2-2	*Kalniņš 2*
25/06	a	Jelgava	D	1-1	*Milaševičs*
28/06	a	Skonto	L	1-3	*Puķītis*
06/07	h	BFC Daugavpils	D	1-1	*E Stuglis*
11/07	h	Ventspils	L	0-3	
26/07	h	Jūrmala	D	1-1	*Kalniņš*
01/08	a	Daugava R	L	0-2	
09/08	a	Daugava D	L	1-2	*Rožkovskis*
13/08	h	Liepāja	L	0-2	
16/08	a	Spartaks	L	0-2	
22/08	a	Jelgava	D	1-1	*og (Freimanis)*
27/08	h	Skonto	L	0-3	
13/09	a	BFC Daugavpils	L	1-4	*Loginovs*
21/09	a	Ventspils	L	1-2	*Putāns*
27/09	a	Jūrmala	L	0-1	
03/10	h	Daugava R	L	1-2	*Puķītis*
17/10	h	Daugava D	L	0-1	
24/10	a	Liepāja	L	0-2	
01/11	h	Spartaks	W	2-1	*Pallo, Milaševičs*
08/11	h	Jelgava	L	0-3	

Name	Nat	DoB	Pos	Aps	(s)	Gls
Tigrans Bagdasarjans		17/05/96	D		(1)	
Artūrs Biezais		08/11/86	G	3		
Oskars Darģis		03/06/93	G	19	(1)	
Dāvis Daugavietis		22/08/96	D	1		
Eduards Emsis		23/03/96	M		(2)	
Konstantīns Fjodorovs		28/04/96	A		(4)	
Raivis Hščanovičs		15/02/87	D	5		
Gatis Kalniņš		12/08/81	A	28	(5)	5
Jurģis Kalns		01/10/82	A	30	(4)	1
Jānis Kauss		11/02/92	D	14	(2)	
Artjoms Loginovs		20/07/93	A	7	(6)	1
Mārtiņš Milaševičs		12/02/92	A	21	(8)	2
Artis Ostrovskis		31/01/93	D	12	(2)	1
Mārtiņš Ozols		17/05/90	A		(1)	
Artūrs Pallo		27/02/89	A	30	(3)	3
Ņikita Parfjonovs		14/03/93	M	8	(8)	
Deniss Petrenko		14/03/88	D	12	(1)	
Kristaps Priedēns		12/01/90	M	24		
Rūdolfs Puķītis		14/02/91	D	32		3
Kārlis Putāns		09/03/90	D	14	(3)	1
Kristers Putniņš		16/07/93	G	13		
Māris Riherts		11/02/92	D	11	(3)	
Romans Rožkovskis		03/12/90	D	23	(5)	1
Elvis Stuglis		04/07/93	A	12	(5)	2
Ingars Stuglis		12/02/96	M	19	(7)	1
Artūrs Švalbe		27/03/95	A	2	(5)	
Deniss Tarasovs		14/10/90	M	1		
Marsels Vapne		02/10/81	M	14	(10)	
Edgars Vardanjans		09/05/93	M	31	(1)	

Skonto FC

1991 • Skonto (9,500); Skonto Hallē (2,000) • skontofc.com
Major honours
Latvian League (15) 1991, 1992, 1993, 1994, 1995, 1996, 1997, 1998, 1999, 2000, 2001, 2002, 2003, 2004, 2010; Latvian Cup (8) 1992, 1995, 1997, 1998, 2000, 2001, 2002, 2012
Coach: Tamaz Pertia (GEO)

2014

30/03	h	Spartaks	W 2-1	Osipovs, Šabala
09/04	a	Liepāja	L 0-1	
13/04	a	Jelgava	W 3-0	Ivanovs 2, Kožans
16/04	a	METTA/LU	W 3-1	Gutkovskis 2, Mingazov
20/04	h	BFC Daugavpils	W 3-1	Mingazov 2, Osipovs
27/04	a	Ventspils	L 0-1	
01/05	h	Jūrmala	W 1-0	Mingazov
06/05	a	Daugava R	W 6-1	Ofosu-Appiah, Šabala 3 (1p), Gutkovskis, Mingazov
10/05	h	Daugava D	W 2-1	Šabala, Gutkovskis
14/05	a	METTA/LU	W 2-1	Gutkovskis 2
25/05	a	Spartaks	W 2-0	Rugins, Gutkovskis
03/06	h	Jelgava	D 1-1	Gutkovskis
10/06	a	Daugava D	W 4-0	Gutkovskis 2, Mingazov, Grīnbergs (p)
14/06	a	BFC Daugavpils	W 2-0	Gabovs, Gutkovskis
18/06	h	Ventspils	W 2-0	Gutkovskis 2 (2p)
22/06	a	Jūrmala	W 5-0	Gutkovskis 2, Mingazov, Ivanovs, Kožans
25/06	h	Daugava R	W 5-1	Mingazov 2, Ivanovs, Rugins 2
28/06	h	METTA/LU	W 3-1	Klimiashvili, Dvali, V Morozs
06/07	a	Liepāja	L 0-3	(w/o)
13/07	h	Spartaks	L 0-1	
23/07	h	Liepāja	W 2-0	Ivanovs, Osipovs
20/07	a	Jelgava	W 1-0	Jermolajevs
01/08	h	Daugava D	W 1-0	Gutkovskis
08/08	h	BFC Daugavpils	W 2-0	V Morozs, Osipovs
13/08	a	Ventspils	L 1-2	J Morozs
17/08	a	Jūrmala	W 4-3	Gutkovskis 2, Osipovs, Dvali
22/08	a	Daugava R	W 2-1	Jermolajevs, Osipovs
27/08	a	METTA/LU	W 3-0	Gutkovskis, Jermolajevs, Dvali
14/09	h	Liepāja	L 1-2	Rugins
21/09	a	Spartaks	L 0-1	
29/09	h	Jelgava	L 0-3	
04/10	a	Daugava D	W 1-0	V Morozs
19/10	a	BFC Daugavpils	L 0-1	
25/10	h	Ventspils	L 2-4	Gutkovskis 2 (1p)
01/11	a	Jūrmala	W 7-1	V Morozs, Gutkovskis 4, J Morozs, Ivanovs
08/11	h	Daugava R	W 4-1	Bērenfelds, Gutkovskis 3

Name	Nat	DoB	Pos	Aps	(s)	Gls
Ņikita Bērenfelds		07/06/95	D	22	(2)	1
Ali Ceesay	GAM	10/10/92	D	2		
Aleksejs Davidenkovs		27/06/98	A		(1)	
Lasha Dvali	GEO	14/05/95	D	32		3
Vladislavs Gabovs		13/07/87	D	27	(2)	1
Dmitrijs Grigorjevs		13/05/92	G	2	(2)	
Jānis Grīnbergs		28/02/99	M	1	(5)	1
Vladislavs Gutkovskis		02/04/95	A	31	(2)	28
Vjačeslavs Isajevs		27/08/93	M	26	(4)	
Ņikita Ivanovs		25/03/96	A	16	(11)	6
Edgars Jermolajevs		16/06/92	M	16	(10)	3
Irakli Klimiashvili	GEO	30/05/88	M	26	(2)	1
Sergejs Kožans		16/02/86	D	12	(1)	2
Juris Laizāns		06/01/79	M	1		
Ruslan Mingazov	TKM	23/11/91	M	15	(1)	9
Jegors Morozs		18/07/98	A		(7)	2
Viktors Morozs		30/07/80	M	30	(2)	4
Mike Ofosu-Appiah	GHA	29/12/89	D	26		1
Artjoms Osipovs		08/01/89	D	24	(2)	6
Andrejs Pavlovs		22/02/79	G	33		
Ritvars Rugins		17/10/89	M	28	(1)	4
Valērijs Šabala		12/10/94	A	9		5
Ēriks Šilings		04/06/97	A		(4)	
Dāvis Strods		24/04/96	D	6	(4)	

FK Spartaks Jūrmala

2007 • Sloka (2,500); Kauguru Vidusskola (2,000) • spartaksjurmala.com
**Coach: Fabio Micarelli (ITA);
(23/05/14) Valeri Semenov;
(02/06/14) Oļegs Blagonadeždins;
(12/06/14) Roman Pylypchuk (UKR)**

2014

23/03	h	BFC Daugavpils	L 0-1	
30/03	a	Skonto	L 1-2	Gauračs
09/04	a	Jelgava	D 0-0	
19/04	h	Jūrmala	D 1-1	Gauračs
26/04	a	Daugava R	W 2-0	Kazačoks, Gauračs (p)
01/05	h	METTA/LU	W 4-1	Gauračs 2, Kazačoks, og (Puķītis)
05/05	a	Liepāja	L 0-2	
10/05	a	Ventspils	L 0-1	
14/05	a	Daugava D	D 3-3	Gauračs, Sapogov, Mena
21/05	a	Daugava D	L 0-1	
25/05	h	Skonto	L 0-2	
01/06	a	BFC Daugavpils	W 3-1	Sapogov 2, Smirnovs
06/06	h	Jelgava	L 0-1	
10/06	h	Ventspils	W 1-0	Gauračs
14/06	a	Jūrmala	W 1-0	Gauračs
18/06	h	Daugava R	W 1-0	Gauračs
21/06	a	METTA/LU	D 2-2	Gauračs 2 (1p)
25/06	h	Liepāja	W 2-0	Gauračs, Mickēvičs
29/06	h	Daugava D	D 0-0	
06/07	h	Jelgava	D 1-1	Gauračs
13/07	a	Skonto	L 0-1	
27/07	h	BFC Daugavpils	W 2-0	Kravchenko 2
03/08	a	Ventspils	L 0-1	
09/08	h	Jūrmala	W 4-1	Punculs 3, Stuglis
13/08	a	Daugava R	L 1-2	Stuglis
16/08	h	METTA/LU	W 2-0	Kravchenko, Punculs
21/08	a	Liepāja	L 0-3	
26/08	h	Daugava D	D 0-0	
12/09	a	Jelgava	D 0-0	
21/09	h	Skonto	W 1-0	Mena
27/09	a	BFC Daugavpils	L 0-1	
04/10	h	Ventspils	L 1-2	Stuglis
18/10	a	Jūrmala	W 2-1	Punculs 2
26/10	h	Daugava R	W 1-0	Yaghoubi
01/11	a	METTA/LU	L 1-2	Mena
08/11	h	Liepāja	D 0-0	

Name	Nat	DoB	Pos	Aps	(s)	Gls
George Arhin	GHA	09/09/95	A	17	(5)	
Davids Bagdasarjans		04/09/94	D	6	(2)	
Nikita Cherepanov	RUS	03/01/96	D	16		
Dmitrijs Daņilovs		25/01/91	D	8		
Pavels Davidovs		30/12/80	G	13		
Peter Domínguez	COL	28/10/90	M	6		
Vitaliy Fedoriv	UKR	21/10/87	D	7		
Edgars Gauračs		10/03/88	A	15	(1)	14
Dmitrijs Hmizs		31/07/92	D	5	(2)	
Jevgeņijs Kazačoks		12/08/95	M	22	(7)	2
Ričards Korzāns		03/05/97	A		(1)	
Igors Kozlovs		26/03/87	M	19	(7)	
Kostyantyn Kravchenko	UKR	24/09/86	M	8		3
Jurijs Krivošeja		14/01/97	A		(6)	
Ritus Krjauklis		23/04/86	D	30		
Issifu Lamptey	GHA	01/06/96	M	17	(9)	
Adi Mehremić	BIH	26/04/92	D	7	(8)	
Vitālijs Meļņičenko		11/11/87	G	23		
Kevin Mena	COL	19/02/93	A	17	(14)	3
Romāns Mickēvičs		23/03/93	M	24	(6)	1
Marko Perišić	BIH	25/01/91	M	15	(1)	
Pāvels Pilāts		04/02/97	M		(1)	
Ēriks Punculs		06/05/93	A	17	(14)	6
Ivan Pylypchuk	UKR	21/05/91	M	1		
Mikheil Rostiashvili	GEO	21/09/90	A	1	(7)	
Aleksei Sapogov	RUS	02/04/88	A	8	(2)	3
Ingus Šlampe		31/01/89	D	33		
Vitālijs Smirnovs		28/06/86	D	34		1
Elvis Stuglis		04/07/93	A	12	(3)	3
Abdallah Suallah	GHA	02/02/96	A	1	(2)	
Eric Tuffor	GHA	25/10/95	M	8	(2)	
Moshtagh Yaghoubi	FIN	08/11/94	A	6		1

FK Ventspils

1997 • OSC Ventspils (3,200) • fkventspils.lv
Major honours
Latvian League (6) 2006, 2007, 2008, 2011, 2013, 2014; Latvian Cup (6) 2003, 2004, 2005, 2007, 2011, 2013
Coach: Jurģis Pučinskis

2014

22/03	h	Daugava R	W 2-0	Abdultaofik 2
30/03	a	METTA/LU	W 2-0	Dubra, Yanchuk
12/04	h	Liepāja	W 3-2	Žigajevs (p), Mujeci, Yanchuk (p)
16/04	h	Jūrmala	W 3-1	Žigajevs 2 (1p), Yanchuk
20/04	a	Jelgava	W 2-1	Žigajevs, Ignatāns
27/04	h	Skonto	W 1-0	og (Dvali)
01/05	a	BFC Daugavpils	W 3-0	Abdultaofik (p), Dubra, Yanchuk
06/05	h	Daugava D	W 3-0	Tidenbergs, Paulius, Mujeci
10/05	h	Spartaks	W 1-0	Tidenbergs
14/05	a	Jūrmala	W 6-0	Abdultaofik, Tarkhnishvili, Ignatāns 2, Paulius, Yanchuk
17/05	a	Daugava R	W 4-0	Yanchuk, Abdultaofik, Tidenbergs, Mujeci
24/05	h	METTA/LU	W 2-0	Dubra, Yanchuk
03/06	a	Liepāja	L 0-2	
10/06	a	Spartaks	L 0-1	
14/06	h	Jelgava	D 0-0	
18/06	a	Skonto	L 0-2	
22/06	h	BFC Daugavpils	L 0-1	
25/06	a	Daugava D	D 1-1	Svārups
29/06	h	Jūrmala	W 6-1	Mujeci 2, Rečickis (p), Abdultaofik, Svārups 2
11/07	a	METTA/LU	W 3-0	Mujeci, Paulius, Abdultaofik
28/07	h	Liepāja	W 1-0	Žigajevs
03/08	h	Spartaks	W 1-0	Diagne
08/08	a	Jelgava	L 0-1	
13/08	h	Skonto	W 2-1	Mujeci, Kurakins
17/08	a	BFC Daugavpils	W 1-0	Rode
22/08	a	Daugava D	D 1-1	Karlsons
28/08	h	Jūrmala	W 7-0	Diagne 2, Kurakins, Karlsons 2, Mujeci 2
13/09	h	Daugava R	D 0-0	
21/09	h	METTA/LU	W 2-1	Mujeci 2
24/09	a	Daugava R	W 3-0	Karlsons, Mujeci, og (Vītolnieks)
28/09	a	Liepāja	D 1-1	Paulius
04/10	a	Spartaks	W 2-1	Abdultaofik 2
18/10	a	Jelgava	W 2-0	Paulius, Diagne
25/10	a	Skonto	W 4-2	Diagne, Paulius, Karlsons, Abdultaofik
01/11	h	BFC Daugavpils	W 2-0	Diagne, Abdultaofik
08/11	h	Daugava D	W 4-0	Diagne, Karlsons 2, Žigajevs

Name	Nat	DoB	Pos	Aps	(s)	Gls
Ahmed Abdultaofik	NGA	25/04/92	A	30	(2)	11
Vitālijs Barinovs		04/05/93	D	4	(1)	
Cheikh Diagne	MTN	20/09/90	A	12	(3)	7
Kaspars Dubra		20/12/90	D	36		3
Robertas Freidgeimas	LTU	21/02/89	D	6	(4)	
Visvaldis Ignatāns		03/08/91	M	15	(2)	3
Dāvis Indrāns		06/06/95	M		(4)	
Ģirts Karlsons		07/06/81	A	14		7
Kiko Insa	ESP	25/01/88	D	15		
Antons Kurakins		01/01/90	D	35	(1)	2
Ndue Mujeci	ALB	24/02/93	A	16	(18)	12
Vladimirs Mukins		28/01/93	M		(7)	
Simonas Paulius	LTU	12/05/91	M	22	(2)	6
Valentīns Raļkevičs		08/03/91	G	2		
Vitālijs Rečickis		08/09/86	M	23		1
Reinis Reinholds		26/09/97	G		(1)	
Renārs Rode		06/04/89	D	14		1
Alans Siņeļnikovs		14/05/90	M		(1)	
Kaspars Svārups		28/01/94	A	3	(12)	3
Tornike Tarkhnishvili	GEO	30/06/90	M	28	(5)	1
Eduards Tidenbergs		18/12/94	M	14	(13)	3
Oļegs Timofejevs		28/11/88	D	34		
Daniils Ulimbaševs		12/03/92	M	6	(5)	
Maksims Uvarenko		17/01/87	G	34		
Edgars Vērdiņš		29/03/93	M		(2)	
Vadim Yanchuk	RUS	16/07/82	A	13		7
Oļegs Žatkins		13/04/87	M		(7)	
Jurijs Žigajevs		14/11/85	M	20	(5)	6

Top goalscorers

28	Vladislavs Gutkovskis (Skonto)
23	Jānis Ikaunieks (Liepāja)
15	Vladislavs Kozlovs (Jelgava)
14	Edgars Gauračs (Spartaks)
12	Jevgenijs Kosmačovs (Daugava D)
	Mantas Savėnas (Daugava R)
	Kristaps Grebis (Liepāja)
	Ndue Mujeci (Ventspils)
11	Ahmed Abdultaofik (Ventspils)
9	Ruslan Mingazov (Skonto)

Promoted club

FB Gulbene

2005 • Gulbenes Sporta Centrs (1,500) •
fbgulbene.lv
Coach: Igors Korabļovs

Second level final table 2014

		Pld	W	D	L	F	A	Pts
1	FB Gulbene	30	27	3	0	128	11	84
2	Rēzeknes BJSS	30	25	2	3	118	27	77
3	Valmiera Glass FK/BSS	30	22	2	6	105	34	68
4	FK 1625 Liepāja	30	21	4	5	87	34	67
5	Rīgas Futbola skola	30	18	4	8	104	39	58
6	FK Auda	30	18	1	11	68	42	55
7	FK Tukums 2000 TSS	30	15	5	10	88	53	50
8	FK Ogre	30	11	4	15	60	50	37
9	FK Jēkabpils/JSC	30	10	7	13	50	71	37
10	Preiļu BJSS	30	10	1	19	60	92	31
11	AFA Olaine	30	8	6	16	51	81	30
12	SFK United	30	7	8	15	38	56	29
13	JFK Saldus	30	8	1	21	37	86	25
14	FK Smiltene/BJSS	30	5	9	16	37	77	24
15	Salaspils	30	2	7	21	24	84	13
16	FK Pļaviņas DM	30	0	2	28	10	228	2

Promotion/Relegation play-offs

(12/11/14 & 16/11/14)
METTA/LU 1-0 Rēzekne
Rēzekne 1-5 METTA/LU
(METTA/LU 6-1)

DOMESTIC CUP

Latvijas Kauss 2014/15

FIFTH ROUND

(19/07/14)
1625 Liepāja 0-6 FK Liepāja
METTA/LU 0-2 Skonto
Smiltene/BJSS 0-2 Daugava Rīga
Tukums 2000 1-4 BFC Daugavpils

(20/07/14)
Jūrmala 1-7 Jelgava
Ogre 1-3 Daugava Daugavpils

(21/07/14)
Rīgas Futbola skola 0-3 Spartaks

(07/10/14)
Gulbene 0-4 Ventspils

QUARTER-FINALS

(04/04/15)
FK Liepāja 2-1 Skonto *(Grebis 29, D Ikaunieks 77; Višņakovs 39p)*

Jelgava w/o Daugava Rīga

(05/04/15)
Ogre 0-5 Spartaks *(Punculs 3, Bulvītis 16, Abdultaofik 51, Mickēvičs 61, Sylyuk 89)*

Ventspils 3-0 BFC Daugavpils *(Karlsons 33, 79, Siņeļņikovs 49)*

NB: NB Ogre received bye to quarter-finals as Daugava Daugavpils were excluded

SEMI-FINALS

(25/04/15)
Jelgava 2-0 Liepāja *(Bogdaškins 76, Musa 87)*

(26/04/15)
Spartaks 1-1 Ventspils *(Abdultaofik 90p; Karlsons 64) (aet; 1-3 on pens)*

FINAL

(20/05/15)
OSC Ventspils, Ventspils
FK JELGAVA 2 *(Eriba 10, Freimanis 31)*
FK VENTSPILS 0
Referee: *Treimanis*
JELGAVA: *Ikstens, Freimanis, Ošs, Diallo, Gubins, Redjko, Bogdaškins, Lazdiņš, Łatka, Eriba (Sosranov 63), Kļuškins (Malašenoks 77)*
Red card: *Diallo (3)*
VENTSPILS: *Meļņičenko, Kurakins, Jemeļins, Krjauklis, Žigajevs, Siņeļņikovs (Tidenbergs 73), Paulius, Rugins, Mordatenko (Ignatāns 32), Karlsons, Diagne (Turkovs 72)*

Jelgava players celebrate the club's successful Latvian Cup defence

LIECHTENSTEIN
Liechtensteiner Fussballverband (FLV)

Address	Landstrasse 149	**President**	Hugo Quaderer
	FL-9494 Schaan	**General secretary**	Roland Ospelt
Tel	+423 237 4747	**Media officer**	Anton Banzer
Fax	+423 237 4748	**Year of formation**	1934
E-mail	info@lfv.li	**National stadium**	Rheinpark, Vaduz
Website	lfv.li		(7,838)

CLUBS

  1 FC Balzers

 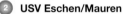 **2** USV Eschen/Mauren

 3 FC Ruggell

 4 FC Schaan

 5 FC Triesen

 6 FC Triesenberg

 7 FC Vaduz

Ruggell

 Mauren

Eschen

Schaan

Vaduz

0   5   10 km

0   10 miles

Triesenberg

Triesen

KEY:

● – UEFA Europa League

Balzers

Vaduz tick all the boxes

It was a case of mission accomplished on all three fronts for Liechtenstein's leading club in 2014/15 as FC Vaduz won the domestic cup for the 43rd time, held on to their place in the Swiss Super League, and also came through their opening tie in Europe.

There were new opponents for Giorgio Contini's team in the final of the Liechtenstein Cup as FC Triesenberg became the last of the country's seven clubs to appear in the end-of-season decider. However, there was a familiar outcome as Vaduz romped to a comprehensive 5-0 victory.

Contini's men stay up and win the cup	First-time finalists Triesenberg defeated 5-0	Impressive showing in EURO qualifiers

A 4-0 aggregate win over Gibraltar's College Europa FC got Vaduz's season off to a decent start, and although they lost narrowly to Poland's Ruch Chorzów in the next round, the European adventure provided useful preparation for the club's campaign in Switzerland's top division. As a newly-promoted club Vaduz were expected to struggle, and struggle they did, winning only seven of their 36 matches, but another side, FC Aarau, fared even worse, so

Liechtenstein's finest avoided relegation by a single point. A particularly poor run-in was interrupted by the club's cup triumph, and there was further cheer for Vaduz's large contingent of Liechtenstein internationals as they helped their country to plunder five points from their opening six UEFA EURO 2016 qualifiers, the highlight a 1-0 win over Moldova in Chisinau secured by a ninth international goal from Vaduz stalwart Franz Burgmeier.

DOMESTIC CUP

FL1 Aktiv Cup 2014/15

FIRST ROUND

(26/08/14)
Balzers II 1-1 Triesen *(aet; 4-1 on pens)*
Triesen II 1-7 Schaan

(27/08/14)
Eschen/Mauren III 1-0 Triesenberg II
Balzers III 0-4 Eschen/Mauren II
Schaan II 0-2 Triesenberg
Vaduz III 0-3 Ruggell II

SECOND ROUND

(30/09/14)
Eschen/Mauren II 0-7 Balzers
Ruggell II 1-3 Balzers II

(01/10/14)
Schaan 1-4 Vaduz U23

(14/10/14)
Eschen/Mauren III 0-1 Triesenberg

QUARTER-FINALS

(04/11/14)
Schaan Azzurri 0-5 Eschen/Mauren

(05/11/14)
Ruggell 1-2 Vaduz *(aet)*

(31/03/15)
Triesenberg 2-0 Balzers II

(07/04/15)
Vaduz U23 3-1 Balzers

SEMI-FINALS

(21/04/15)
Triesenberg 1-0 Vaduz U23 *(J Beck 112) (aet)*
Vaduz 2-0 Eschen/Mauren *(Hasler 28, Sutter 88)*

FINAL

(13/05/15)
Sportpark Eschen-Mauren, Eschen
FC VADUZ 5 *(Abegglen 21, Muntwiler 26, Schürpf 29, Lang 63, Sara 90+1)*
FC TRIESENBERG 0
Referee: *Amhof*
VADUZ: *Klaus, Von Niederhäusern, Kaufmann, Sara, Aliji, Kryeziu (Cecchini 46), Muntwiler, Kuzmanovic, Schürpf (Lang 46), Abegglen, Pak (Sutter 62)*
TRIESENBERG: *Biedermann, Cortese, L Eberle, Barandun (K Beck 68), P Sprenger, N Sprenger, J Sprenger, S Beck, F Eberle, D Schädler (J Beck 58), R Schädler (Kindle 74)*

EUROPE

FC Vaduz

First qualifying round - College Europa FC (GIB)
H 3-0 *Sutter (6), Schürpf (8, 72)*
Jehle, Grippo, Lang (Pak 77), Ciccone, Sutter (Abegglen 57), Burgmeier (Von Niederhäusern 64), Schürpf, Untersee, Stahel, Neumayr, Muntwiler. Coach: Giorgio Contini (SUI)
A 1-0 *Hasler (89)*
Jehle, Grippo, Kaufmann, Schürpf, Abegglen (Sutter 56), Pak (Lang 65), Von Niederhäusern, Kryeziu, Stahel, Neumayr (Hasler 72), Polverino. Coach: Giorgio Contini (SUI)

Second qualifying round - Ruch Chorzów (POL)
A 2-3 *Muntwiler (16), Surma (60og)*
Jehle, Grippo, Ciccone (Polverino 62), Sutter (Lang 70), Burgmeier (Von Niederhäusern 77), Schürpf, Pak, Untersee, Stahel, Neumayr, Muntwiler. Coach: Giorgio Contini (SUI)
H 0-0
Jehle, Grippo, Lang (Schürpf 59), Sutter, Burgmeier (Cecchini 68), Pak, Untersee, Kryeziu (Abegglen 83), Stahel, Neumayr, Muntwiler. Coach: Giorgio Contini (SUI)
Red card: Muntwiler 75

European qualification 2015/16

Cup winner: FC Vaduz (first qualifying round)

NATIONAL TEAM

Top five all-time caps
Mario Frick (121); Martin Stocklasa (113); **Peter Jehle** (112); **Franz Burgmeier** (93); Thomas Beck (92)

Top five all-time goals
Mario Frick (16); **Franz Burgmeier** (9); Thomas Beck, **Michele Polverino** & Martin Stocklasa (5)

Results 2014/15

Date	Opponent		Venue	Result	Score	Scorers
04/09/14	Bosnia & Herzegovina	A	Tuzla	L	0-3	
08/09/14	Russia (ECQ)	A	Khimki	L	0-4	
09/10/14	Montenegro (ECQ)	H	Vaduz	D	0-0	
12/10/14	Sweden (ECQ)	A	Solna	L	0-2	
15/11/14	Moldova (ECQ)	A	Chisinau	W	1-0	*Burgmeier (74)*
27/03/15	Austria (ECQ)	H	Vaduz	L	0-5	
31/03/15	San Marino	H	Eschen	W	1-0	*Kaufmann (29)*
10/06/15	Switzerland	A	Thun	L	0-3	
14/06/15	Moldova (ECQ)	H	Vaduz	D	1-1	*Wieser (20)*

Appearances 2014/15

René Pauritsch (AUT)	04/02/64		Bih	RUS	MNE	SWE	MDA	AUT	Smr	Sui	MDA	Caps	Goals
Peter Jehle	22/01/82	Vaduz	G46	G	G62			G	G46	G46	G	112	-
Ivan Quintans	15/10/89	Balzers	D65	D87	D80	D	D90	D55				21	-
Mario Frick	07/09/74	Balzers	D	D	D	D		D	A73	D	D	121	16
Daniel Kaufmann	22/12/90	Vaduz	D32		D	D	D	D	D	D	D	30	1
Franz Burgmeier	07/04/82	Vaduz	D	D	D	D	D	M	D62	M80	M	93	9
Sandro Wieser	03/02/93	Aarau (SUI)	M	D	M44		D	M	D		M	28	1
Michele Polverino	26/09/84	Vaduz /Ried (AUT)	M	M73	M	M	M	M	M	M	M	48	5
Nicolas Hasler	04/05/91	Vaduz	M	M	M	M	M	A	M	M63		36	1
Martin Büchel	19/02/87	Unterföhring (GER)	M74	M	A	M83	M88	M88	M86	M77	M69	53	2
Andreas Christen	29/08/89	Balzers	M83	M64	s44	M78	M	M83	s78	M	M	21	-
Philippe Erne	14/12/86	Balzers	A62							A83		24	1
Seyhan Yildiz	30/04/89	Balzers	s32	M	M	M27				D	D	15	-
Benjamin Büchel	04/07/89	Bournemouth (ENG)	s46				G		s46			9	-
Dennis Salanovic	26/02/96	Atlético (ESP) /Istra 1961 (CRO)	s62	A	M	A	A	s55	M78	s53		8	-
Simon Kühne	30/04/94	Eschen/Mauren /St Gallen (SUI)	s65		s80	s78	s63	s83	M88	A53	s42	9	-
Robin Gubser	17/04/91	Balzers	s74	s73			s88	s88	s86	s63	s69	14	-
Sandro Wolfinger	24/08/91	Balzers /Heimstetten (GER)	s83	s87		s83			s62	s67		8	-
Daniel Brändle	23/01/92	Münsingen (SUI)		s64		s27	M63		s88	s80	s83	7	-
Cengiz Biçer	11/12/87	Göztepe (TUR)				s62	G			s46		11	-
Niklas Kieber	04/03/93	Eschen/Mauren					s90			s77		5	-
Yves Oehri	15/03/87	YF Juventus (SUI)						D	D	D67	D42	48	-
Armando Heeb	25/09/90	Balzers								s73		1	-

LITHUANIA
Lietuvos futbolo federacija (LFF)

Address	Stadiono g. 2	**President**	Julius Kvedaras
	LT-02106 Vilnius	**General secretary**	Edvinas Eimontas
Tel	+370 5 2638741	**Media officer**	Vaiva Zizaitė
Fax	+370 5 2638740	**Year of formation**	1922
E-mail	v.zizaite@lff.lt	**National stadium**	LFF Stadium, Vilnius
Website	lff.lt		(5,067)

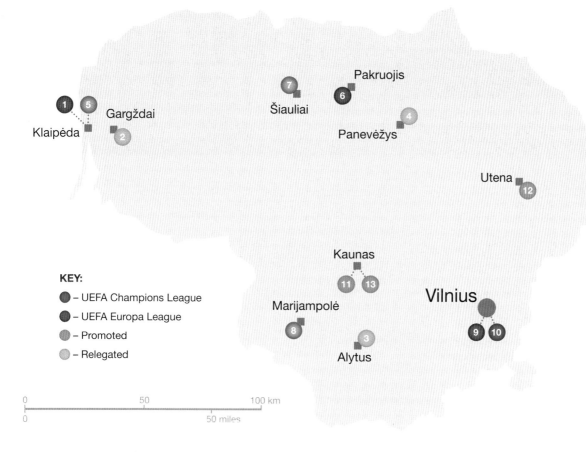

KEY:
- – UEFA Champions League
- – UEFA Europa League
- – Promoted
- – Relegated

A LYGA CLUBS

  FK Atlantas

  FK Banga

  FK Dainava

  FK Ekranas

 FK Klaipėdos granitas

  FK Kruoja

  FC Šiauliai

  FK Sūduva

  FK Trakai

 VMFD Žalgiris

PROMOTED CLUBS

  FC Stumbras

  FK Utenis

  FK Spyris

All too easy for Žalgiris

After winning the Lithuanian A Lyga title on the final day in 2013, VMFD Žalgiris defended it in comparative comfort. There were no rivals to the Vilnius club's supremacy in a 2014 campaign that ended with FK Ekranas, champions five times in a row from 2008-12, being refused a licence to retain their place in the top division.

The Lithuanian Cup remained in Žalgiris's possession for a record fourth straight year as they defeated FK Atlantas 2-0 in the 2015 final under a new coach, Valdas Dambrauskas having replaced the club's two-time title-winning boss Marek Zub.

| Runaway title success for Vilnius club | Calendar-year double followed by fourth straight cup win | False dawn for national team in EURO qualifiers |

Domestic league

Having gone 14 years without a national league title, Žalgiris made it two in a row with ease. Concerted challengers to their crown were non-existent as the Green-and-Whites from the capital cruised to victory unopposed. The final table told the full story of their dominance – an 18-point winning margin, 25 victories in their 36 matches, just two defeats, 92 goals for and only 17 against. Right from early on in proceedings the only burning question circulating among regular A Lyga-goers was which team would finish second.

It was an unexpectedly straightforward success for a side that had undergone several changes in personnel from the previous campaign, with key men such as Pavel Komolov, Luka Perić and top scorer Kamil Biliński all having departed. Most of those who stayed on, though, continued to prosper, and added value was introduced with the return from abroad of experienced Lithuanian internationals Deividas Šemberas and Linas Pilibaitis. Both players excelled, the former as an authoritative captain, the latter as the team's leading marksman with 17 goals.

As Žalgiris sealed the title with four games to spare, the focus shifted to the also-rans battling to qualify for Europe. There were four teams involved, and

ultimately it was FK Sūduva who missed out, finishing in fifth place - a point behind newly promoted FK Trakai, three adrift of Atlantas, and four in arrears of FK Kruoja, who, thanks to the 15 goals and eight assists of evergreen striker Ričardas Beniušis, finished higher than ever before, claiming an unexpected runners-up berth. Ekranas, meanwhile, were way off the pace in sixth, their financial problems eventually sending them down a division along with similarly afflicted FK Banga and rock-bottom FK Dainava.

Domestic cup

Trakai's first ever European qualification was confirmed when Žalgiris and Atlantas coasted through their Lithuanian Cup semi-finals to set up a showdown in Siauliai. Atlantas had beaten Žalgiris in the only previous post-independence final between the two clubs, 1-0 back in 2001, but this time it was the men from Vilnius who prevailed, second-half goals from Šemberas – a penalty – and Pilibaitis – a header – straddling a sending-off for Atlantas midfielder Donatas Navikas. It was Žalgiris's fourth successive victory in the competition, with Atlantas becoming their fourth different final victims – after Ekranas in 2011, FC Šiauliai in 2012 and Banga in 2013 – at four different venues. Dambrauskas was

also the fourth different coach to lead the club to victory during that sequence.

Europe

Žalgiris could not, alas, export their domestic form to the European stage. Handed a tough draw against GNK Dinamo Zagreb in the second qualifying round of the UEFA Champions League, they lost both matches 2-0. Ekranas and Banga both fell at the first hurdle of the UEFA Europa League, with Atlantas going out in the second qualifying round after registering Lithuania's only success with a 3-2 aggregate win over Luxembourg's FC Differdange 03.

National team

Hopes of a decent UEFA EURO 2016 qualifying campaign were high as Lithuania took six points from their first two fixtures, against San Marino and Estonia, but when they came up against superior opposition Igoris Pankratjevas's side were found badly wanting. Beaten 2-0 at home by Slovenia, they then proceeded to lose 4-0 away to both Switzerland and England. The return match against the Swiss in Vilnius offered the promise of a recovery when they took the lead with their first goal in seven internationals, but Lithuania allowed the visitors to come back and win 2-1, effectively extinguishing their hopes of reaching the play-offs.

DOMESTIC SEASON AT A GLANCE

A Lyga 2014 final table

		Pld		Home					Away					Total				Pts
			W	D	L	F	A	W	D	L	F	A	W	D	L	F	A	
1	**VMFD Žalgiris**	36	15	3	0	53	6	10	6	2	39	11	25	9	2	92	17	84
2	FK Kruoja	36	9	6	3	30	15	10	3	5	37	19	19	9	8	67	34	66
3	FK Atlantas	36	12	3	3	45	12	7	5	6	31	24	19	8	9	76	36	65
4	FK Trakai	36	10	4	4	36	20	8	5	5	29	18	18	9	9	65	38	63
5	FK Sūduva	36	6	7	5	25	14	11	4	3	45	24	17	11	8	70	38	62
6	FK Ekranas	36	7	4	7	32	28	5	5	8	19	30	12	9	15	51	58	45
7	FC Šiauliai	36	7	3	8	30	29	5	1	12	20	34	12	4	20	50	63	40
8	FK Klaipėdos granitas	36	5	5	8	23	34	4	5	9	24	33	9	10	17	47	67	37
9	FK Banga	36	3	2	13	17	37	5	4	9	12	28	8	6	22	29	65	30
10	FK Dainava	36	2	2	14	6	67	0	1	17	6	76	2	3	31	12	143	9

European qualification 2015/16

 Champion/Cup winner: VMFD Žalgiris (second qualifying round)

 FK Kruoja (first qualifying round)
FK Atlantas (first qualifying round)
FK Trakai (first qualifying round)

Top scorer Niko Tokić (Šiauliai), 19 goals
Relegated clubs FK Dainava, FK Banga (excluded), FK Ekranas (excluded)
Promoted clubs FC Stumbras, FK Utenis, FK Spyris
Cup final VMFD Žalgiris 2-0 FK Atlantas

Team of the season
(4-4-2)

Coach: Zub (Žalgiris)

Vitkauskas (Žalgiris)

Šemberas (Žalgiris) — Freidgeimas (Žalgiris) — Kerla (Žalgiris) — Vaitkūnas (Žalgiris)

Lukša (Trakai) — Elivelto (Ekranas) — Wilk (Žalgiris) — Pilibaitis (Žalgiris)

Beniušis (Kruoja) — D Kazlauskas (Atlantas)

Player of the season

Deividas Šemberas
(VMFD Žalgiris)

Long-serving former Lithuanian international Šemberas returned to his hometown and boyhood club at the start of the 2014 season after 16 years in Russia, the bulk of it at PFC CSKA Moskva, where he was a frequent trophy-winner. Within 18 months of rejoining Žalgiris he had added three more pieces of silverware to his collection, two Lithuanian Cups and the A Lyga title. His experience, leadership and unquenchable will to win were key factors in all three triumphs.

Newcomer of the season

Edvinas Gertmonas
(FK Atlantas)

Recruited from second division side FK Tauras in mid-season, shortly after his 18th birthday, Gertmonas forced his way into the Atlantas first XI and became something of an overnight sensation, making nine starts and conceding just two goals to help his new club end the season in style with eight wins and a draw. Six months later he was appearing for Atlantas against Žalgiris in the Lithuanian Cup final and, a week after turning 19, making his senior international debut in a friendly against Malta.

LITHUANIA

NATIONAL TEAM

Top five all-time caps
Andrius Skerla (84); Deividas Šemberas (82); **Saulius Mikoliūnas** (73), Tomas Danilevičius (71); Žydrūnas Karčemarskas (66)

Top five all-time goals
Tomas Danilevičius (19); Antanas Lingis (12); Edgaras Jankauskas & Robertas Poškus (10); Virginijus Baltušnikas (9)

Results 2014/15

03/09/14	United Arab Emirates	N	Matrei (AUT)	D	1-1	*Matulevičius (42)*
08/09/14	San Marino (ECQ)	A	Serravalle	W	2-0	*Matulevičius (5), Novikovas (36)*
09/10/14	Estonia (ECQ)	H	Vilnius	W	1-0	*Mikoliūnas (76)*
12/10/14	Slovenia (ECQ)	H	Vilnius	L	0-2	
15/11/14	Switzerland (ECQ)	A	St Gallen	L	0-4	
18/11/14	Ukraine	A	Kyiv	D	0-0	
27/03/15	England (ECQ)	A	London	L	0-4	
05/06/15	Hungary	A	Debrecen	L	0-2	
08/06/15	Malta	A	Ta'Qali	L	0-2	
14/06/15	Switzerland (ECQ)	H	Vilnius	L	1-2	*Černych (64)*

Appearances 2014/15

Coach: Igoris Pankratjevas	09/08/64		Uae	SMR	EST	SVN	SUI	Ukr	ENG	Hun	Mlt	SUI	Caps	Goals
Vytautas Černiauskas	12/03/89	Korona (POL)	G					G					2	-
Georgas Freidgeimas	10/08/87	Žalgiris	D	D	D	D	D	D	D	s46	D		18	-
Tadas Kijanskas	06/09/85	H. Haifa (ISR)	D	D	D	D	D	D	D	s76	s46		43	1
Egidijus Vaitkūnas	08/08/88	Žalgiris	D		D	D	D64	D		D	D	D	19	-
Vaidas Slavickas	26/02/86	Ceahlăul (ROU)	D	D				D	s83				5	-
Karolis Chvedukas	21/04/91	Sūduva	M46	M		M75	M	M	M	M72		s61	13	-
Mindaugas Panka	01/05/84	H. Kiryat Shmona (ISR)	M59	M66	M	M32				M	M	M	36	-
Mindaugas Kalonas	28/02/84	H. Haifa (ISR)	M84	M	M63			s75					49	3
Arvydas Novikovas	18/12/90	Erzgebirge Aue (GER)	M46	M	M	M	M87	M75					23	2
Fedor Černych	21/05/91	Górnik Łęczna (POL)	M46	M90	M	M	M	s58	M			M	17	2
Deivydas Matulevičius	08/04/89	Pandurii (ROU)	A66	A86	A90	A	A	A66	A	A62	A55	A	23	5
Saulius Mikoliūnas	02/05/84	Shakhtyor Soligorsk (BLR)	s46		s63	s75				M88	M		73	5
Gediminas Vičius	05/07/85	Shakhter (KAZ) /Zhetysu (KAZ)	s46	s66	M	s32	M82					s76	18	1
Nerijus Valskis	04/08/87	U Craiova (ROU)	s46										4	-
Artūras Žulpa	10/06/90	Žalgiris /Aktobe (KAZ)	s59			M	M	M		M		M61	10	-
Simonas Stankevičius	03/10/95	Leicester (ENG)	s66	s86				s66	s66		s83		10	-
Mantas Kuklys	10/06/87	Žalgiris	s84	s90			M58			s72	M46		10	-
Giedrius Arlauskis	01/12/87	Steaua (ROU)			G	G	G	G		G			20	-
Marius Žaliūkas	10/11/83	Rangers (SCO)			D					D			26	1
Vytautas Andriuškevičius	08/10/90	Cambuur (NED)				D	D	D	s82	D83	D76	s88	D	20	-
Ričardas Beniušis	23/04/80	Kruoja			s90								30	3
Valdemar Borovskij	02/05/84	Šiauliai					s64						16	-
Tautvydas Eliošius	03/11/91	Kruoja					s82						1	-
Donatas Kazlauskas	31/03/94	Atlantas /Lechia (POL)					s87	M82	s88	M46			4	-
Tomas Mikuckis	13/01/83	Torpedo Moskva (RUS)							M66	D46	D		13	-
Saulius Klevinskas	02/04/84	Žalgiris							G				4	-
Linas Klimavičius	10/04/89	Trakai							D	D46	D		3	-
Deividas Česnauskis	30/06/81	Trakai							M	D88	M86		60	4
Gratas Sirgėdas	17/12/94	Stuttgart (GER)							M58	s46			5	-
Vytautas Lukša	14/08/84	Žalgiris							s46	M83	s86		22	-
Vykintas Slivka	29/04/95	Gorica (SVN)							s58	M73	M76		3	-
Lukas Spalvis	27/07/94	AaB (DEN)							s62	s55			6	1
Edvinas Gertmonas	01/06/96	Atlantas								G			1	-
Rolandas Baravykas	23/08/95	Atlantas								s73			1	-
Emilijus Zubas	10/07/90	Bełchatów (POL)										G	5	-

EUROPE

VMFD Žalgiris

CHAMPIONS LEAGUE

Second qualifying round - GNK Dinamo Zagreb (CRO)

A 0-2

Vitkauskas, Šemberas, Freidgeimas, Žulpa (Janušauskas 67), Adi, Wilk, Švrljuga, Kerla, Nyuiadzi (Šilėnas 85), Vaitkūnas, Kuklys (Pilibaitis 67). Coach: Marek Zub (POL)

H 0-2

Vitkauskas, Šemberas (Janušauskas 76), Freidgeimas, Adi, Wilk (Šilėnas 78), Švrljuga, Kerla, Kamolov, Nyuiadzi, Vaitkūnas, Pilibaitis (Žulpa 65). Coach: Marek Zub (POL)

FK Atlantas

EUROPA LEAGUE

First qualifying round - FC Differdange 03 (LUX)

A 0-1

Galdikas, Bartkus, Razulis, D Kazlauskas, Eliošius (Papšys 67), Navikas (Krušnauskas 90+1), Beneta (Jokšas 25), Gnedojus, Jemeļins, M Kazlauskas, Žukauskas. Coach: Konstantin Sarsania (RUS)

H 3-1 *Gnedojus (10), Papšys (62p), Maksimov (89)*

Galdikas, Bartkus, D Kazlauskas, Papšys, Eliošius (Maksimov 87), Jokšas, Gnedojus (Kruša 65), Jemeļins, M Kazlauskas, Žukauskas, Krušnauskas (Baranauskas 78). Coach: Konstantin Sarsania (RUS)

Second qualifying round - FC Shakhter Karagandy (KAZ)

H 0-0

Galdikas, Bartkus, D Kazlauskas, Papšys, Eliošius (Maksimov 80), Jokšas, Gnedojus, Jemeļins, M Kazlauskas, Žukauskas, Krušnauskas (Baranauskas 70). Coach: Konstantin Sarsania (RUS)

A 0-3

Galdikas, Bartkus, D Kazlauskas, Papšys, Eliošius (Maksimov 62), Jokšas, Gnedojus, Jemeļins, M Kazlauskas, Žukauskas (Rakauskas 80), Krušnauskas (Baranauskas 72). Coach: Konstantin Sarsania (RUS)

FK Ekranas

EUROPA LEAGUE

First qualifying round - Crusaders FC (NIR)

A 1-3 *Šušnjar (88)*

Timofejevas, Meškinis (Tamulevičius 69), Salamanavičius (Stanulevičius 45+2), Šušnjar, Kochanauskas, Norvilas, Džiugas Petrauskas, E Baranauskas (Dapkus 78), Elivelto, Pilotas, Girdvainis. Coach: Valdas Dambrauskas (LTU)

H 1-2 *Kochanauskas (60)*

Žukauskas, Dūda, Donatas Petrauskas, Salamanavičius (Tamulevičius 59), Umeh, Šušnjar, Kochanauskas (Meškinis 65), E Baranauskas (Norvilas 52), Elivelto, Pilotas, Girdvainis. Coach: Valdas Dambrauskas (LTU)

FK Banga

EUROPA LEAGUE

First qualifying round - Sligo Rovers FC (IRL)

H 0-0

Jurevičius, Urbaitis, Grigaitis, Karkusov, Butkus, Shevchuk, Khablov, Epifanov, Arlauskis, Staponka, Zagurskas (Tsalagov 78). Coach: Maksim Tishchenko (RUS)

A 0-4

Jurevičius, Urbaitis, Grigaitis, Karkusov (Stezhka 25), Butkus (Siryk 74), Shevchuk, Khablov (Makiev 71), Epifanov, Arlauskis, Staponka, Zagurskas. Coach: Maksim Tishchenko (RUS)

Red card: Urbaitis 68

DOMESTIC LEAGUE CLUB-BY-CLUB

FK Atlantas

1962 • Centrinis (4,940); Centrinis Artificial (1,500) • atlantas.lt
Major honours
Lithuanian Cup (2) 2001, 2003
Coach: Konstantin Sarsania (RUS)

2014

Date		Opponent	Res	Scorers
08/03	h	Dainava	W 6-0	Razulis 3, og (Stankevičius), Eliošius, Papšys
15/03	a	Klaipėdos granitas	D 2-2	D Kazlauskas, Verbickas
21/03	h	Banga	D 0-0	
25/03	a	Žalgiris	L 0-4	
29/03	h	Sūduva	W 1-0	D Kazlauskas
03/04	a	Trakai	D 0-0	
11/04	h	Šiauliai	W 1-0	Kirilov
16/04	h	Ekranas	D 2-2	Žarskis, Eliošius
21/04	a	Kruoja	D 1-1	Krušnauskas
27/04	a	Dainava	W 7-0	Eliošius 3 (1p), Navikas, og (Ceplinskas), Krušnauskas, Papšys (p)
03/05	h	Klaipėdos granitas	W 2-0	Jokšas, Krušnauskas
07/05	a	Banga	W 2-0	Žarskis, Krušnauskas
10/05	h	Žalgiris	L 0-1	
20/05	a	Sūduva	D 1-1	Papšys (p)
23/05	h	Trakai	L 0-2	
09/06	a	Šiauliai	L 1-3	Papšys
14/06	a	Ekranas	L 1-2	D Kazlauskas
18/06	h	Kruoja	L 1-3	Papšys (p)
21/06	h	Dainava	W 12-0	D Kazlauskas 3, Razulis 3, Eliošius, Papšys, og (Kurneta), Krušnauskas 2, Navikas
28/07	a	Klaipėdos granitas	W 3-0	Papšys, Jemeļins, Razulis
04/08	h	Banga	W 3-1	Razulis, Žarskis, Verbickas
11/08	a	Žalgiris	L 0-3	
16/08	h	Sūduva	D 2-2	Jemeļins, Papšys
22/08	a	Trakai	L 0-3	
30/08	h	Šiauliai	W 4-0	Razulis 2, Verbickas 2
13/09	h	Ekranas	W 4-0	Bartkus, Razulis, Verbickas, Papšys
16/09	a	Kruoja	L 1-4	Maksimov
19/09	a	Dainava	W 4-0	Razulis 2, Virkšas, D Kazlauskas
28/09	h	Klaipėdos granitas	W 3-0	Rakauskas, Verbickas, Eliošius
04/10	a	Banga	W 2-1	Beneta, Baranauskas
18/10	h	Žalgiris	W 2-1	D Kazlauskas 2
25/10	a	Sūduva	D 0-0	
30/10	h	Trakai	W 1-0	D Kazlauskas
09/11	a	Šiauliai	W 3-0	Papšys 2 (1p), og (Raziūnas)
22/11	a	Ekranas	W 3-0	D Kazlauskas 2, Žarskis
29/11	h	Kruoja	W 1-0	Baranauskas

No	Name	Nat	DoB	Pos	Aps	(s)	Gls
21	Lukas Baranauskas		26/11/93	A	5	(4)	2
23	Rolandas Baravykas		23/08/95	D	22	(4)	
6	Andrius Bartkus		21/01/86	M	30	(1)	1
17	Markas Beneta		08/07/93	D	16	(5)	1
45	Edgaras Ditmonas		11/07/95	M	1		
11	Tadas Eliošius		01/03/90	A	17	(8)	7
22	Mantas Galdikas		22/06/89	G	9		
12	Edvinas Gertmonas		01/06/96	G	9		
20	Kazimieras Gnedojus		28/02/86	D	23		
26	Antons Jemeļins	LVA	19/02/84	D	10		2
31	Zigmantas Jesipovas		08/11/94	M	5	(1)	
18	Andrius Jokšas		12/01/79	D	27	(2)	1
15	Justas Kasparavičius		03/04/95	A		(1)	
9	Donatas Kazlauskas		31/03/94	A	21	(2)	12
33	Marius Kazlauskas		01/05/84	D	25		
29	Yuri Kirilov	RUS	19/01/90	M	7	(1)	1
8	Gediminas Kruša		31/10/90	M	2	(7)	
99	Rokas Krušnauskas		04/11/95	A	10	(7)	6
28	Karolis Laukžemis		11/03/92	M	1	(1)	
34	Maksim Maksimov	RUS	04/11/95	A	3	(12)	1
1	Mindaugas Malinauskas		11/08/83	G	9		
13	Donatas Navikas		30/06/83	M	11	(6)	2
10	Marius Papšys		13/05/89	M	18	(6)	11
14	Skirmantas Rakauskas		07/01/96	M	6	(7)	1
7	Evaldas Razulis		03/04/86	A	19	(6)	13
74	Ovidijus Verbickas		04/07/93	M	28	(3)	6
19	Dovydas Virkšas		01/07/97	A	8	(6)	1
35	Edgaras Žarskis		04/05/94	D	25		4
77	Gerardas Žukauskas		07/07/94	M	21	(4)	

FK Banga

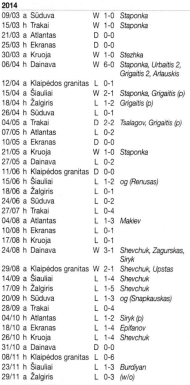

1966 • Gargždai (1,700) • fkbanga.lt

Coach: Maksim Tishchenko (RUS)

2014

09/03	a	Sūduva	W	1-0	*Staponka*
15/03	h	Trakai	W	1-0	*Staponka*
21/03	a	Atlantas	D	0-0	
25/03	h	Ekranas	D	0-0	
30/03	a	Kruoja	W	1-0	*Stezhka*
06/04	h	Dainava	W	6-0	*Staponka, Urbaitis 2, Grigaitis 2, Arlauskis*
12/04	a	Klaipėdos granitas	L	0-1	
15/04	a	Šiauliai	W	2-1	*Staponka, Grigaitis (p)*
18/04	h	Žalgiris	L	1-2	*Grigaitis (p)*
26/04	h	Sūduva	L	0-1	
04/05	a	Trakai	D	2-2	*Tsalagov, Grigaitis (p)*
07/05	h	Atlantas	L	0-2	
10/05	a	Ekranas	D	0-0	
21/05	a	Kruoja	W	1-0	*Staponka*
27/05	a	Dainava	L	0-2	
11/06	h	Klaipėdos granitas	D	0-0	
15/06	h	Šiauliai	L	1-2	*og (Renusas)*
18/06	a	Žalgiris	L	0-1	
24/06	a	Sūduva	L	0-2	
27/07	h	Trakai	L	0-4	
04/08	a	Atlantas	L	1-3	*Makiev*
10/08	h	Ekranas	L	0-1	
17/08	h	Kruoja	L	0-1	
24/08	h	Dainava	W	3-1	*Shevchuk, Zagurskas, Siryk*
29/08	a	Klaipėdos granitas	W	2-1	*Shevchuk, Upstas*
14/09	a	Šiauliai	L	1-4	*Shevchuk*
17/09	h	Žalgiris	L	1-5	*Shevchuk*
20/09	h	Sūduva	L	1-3	*og (Snapkauskas)*
28/09	a	Trakai	L	0-4	
04/10	h	Atlantas	L	1-2	*Siryk (p)*
18/10	a	Ekranas	L	1-4	*Epifanov*
26/10	h	Kruoja	L	1-4	*Shevchuk*
31/10	a	Dainava	D	0-0	
08/11	h	Klaipėdos granitas	L	0-6	
23/11	h	Šiauliai	L	1-3	*Burdiyan*
29/11	a	Žalgiris	L	0-3	*(w/o)*

No	Name	Nat	DoB	Pos	Aps	(s)	Gls
40	Davydas Arlauskis		18/11/86	D	17	(2)	1
1	Soslan Arshiev	RUS	01/01/89	G	10		
2	Mindaugas Bitinas		24/12/92	D	12	(2)	
45	Andriy Burdiyan	UKR	18/01/86	D	6	(1)	1
17	Andrius Butkus		05/04/91	M	27	(1)	
8	Artem Dolzhenko	RUS	12/11/91	M	3	(3)	
44	Edgaras Drąsutis		22/04/96	M	9	(9)	
97	Ignas Driomovas		27/04/97	G	10		
31	Marius Eitutis		03/08/96	D	1	(1)	
25	Aleksei Epifanov	RUS	21/07/83	D	33	(1)	1
11	Evaldas Grigaitis		28/09/87	M	14	(6)	5
13	Mantas Gudauskas		04/01/89	D	7	(2)	
7	Artūr Juchno		17/07/90	M		(3)	
22	Šarūnas Jurevičius		03/05/89	G	15	(1)	
6	Ignas Jurgutis		27/04/97	M		(1)	
74	Zaurbek Karkusov	RUS	09/09/95	M	8	(3)	
20	Maksym Khablov	UKR	08/01/88	M	14	(2)	
10	Mika Kura		01/04/89	M	2	(7)	
23	Paulius Lotužys		15/01/98	M		(3)	
7	Valeri Makiev	RUS	16/06/85	M	10		1
33	Andrius Marcinkevičius		07/01/93	A	4	(6)	
46	Dovydas Pačkauskas		27/08/96	M	6	(7)	
83	Aleksandr Russkikh	RUS	11/09/83	M	17	(1)	
18	Serhiy Shevchuk	UKR	21/09/90	A	29	(1)	5
39	Artur Siryk	UKR	17/02/89	A	12	(1)	2
96	Benas Spietinis		15/02/96	D	7	(4)	
55	Aurelijus Staponka		09/11/83	A	16	(1)	5
74	Artem Stezhka	RUS	06/06/89	D	21	(1)	1
35	Martynas Stirbys		21/11/95	M		(1)	
9	Aslanbek Tsalagov	RUS	11/08/95	A	6	(8)	1
98	Klaudijus Upstas		30/10/94	A	13		1
5	Karolis Urbaitis		12/12/90	D	22	(1)	2
4	Andrei Verbetchi	MDA	21/07/89	D	23	(2)	
99	Eivinas Zagurskas		09/09/89	M	11		1

FK Dainava

1935 • Alytus (3,748); NFA, Kaunas (1,000) • fkdainava.lt

Coach: Sergei Aleinikov (BLR); (27/05/14) Marco Ragini (ITA)

2014

08/03	a	Atlantas	L	0-6	
16/03	h	Ekranas	L	0-3	
23/03	a	Kruoja	L	0-4	
27/03	a	Šiauliai	L	0-5	
30/03	h	Klaipėdos granitas	L	0-5	
06/04	a	Banga	L	0-6	
12/04	h	Žalgiris	L	0-8	
16/04	a	Sūduva	L	0-5	
22/04	h	Trakai	L	1-7	*Kavaliauskas (p)*
27/04	h	Atlantas	L	0-7	
03/05	a	Ekranas	L	0-6	
08/05	h	Kruoja	L	0-5	
13/05	h	Šiauliai	L	0-6	
22/05	a	Klaipėdos granitas	L	0-2	
27/05	h	Banga	W	2-0	*Balčiūnas 2 (1p)*
09/06	a	Žalgiris	L	1-9	*Ivanauskas*
13/06	h	Sūduva	L	0-8	
17/06	a	Trakai	L	0-4	
21/06	a	Atlantas	L	0-12	
27/07	h	Ekranas	L	1-2	*Stankevičius*
01/08	a	Kruoja	L	2-3	*Bellus (p), Kumeta*
07/08	a	Šiauliai	L	1-4	*Sepe*
14/08	h	Klaipėdos granitas	D	0-0	
24/08	a	Banga	L	1-3	*Aniekan*
31/08	h	Žalgiris	L	0-3	
11/09	a	Sūduva	D	0-0	
16/09	h	Trakai	L	0-2	
19/09	h	Atlantas	L	0-4	
25/09	a	Ekranas	L	1-2	*Pintus*
04/10	h	Kruoja	W	2-0	*Mariani, Balčiūnas*
17/10	h	Šiauliai	L	0-1	
26/10	a	Klaipėdos granitas	L	0-2	
31/10	h	Banga	D	0-0	
09/11	a	Žalgiris	L	0-2	
20/11	h	Sūduva	L	0-6	
29/11	a	Trakai	L	0-1	

No	Name	Nat	DoB	Pos	Aps	(s)	Gls
9	Favour Aniekan	NGA	10/04/94	M	8	(5)	1
26	Yanis Bahloul	FRA	12/06/94	A		(1)	
16	Kęstutis Balčiūnas		13/08/90	A	22	(4)	3
6	Ervinas Baranauskas		20/06/97	D	3	(3)	
1	Žygimantas Barauskas		22/07/92	M	3	(2)	
19	Nerijus Bartkevičius		13/11/85	M	6		
92	Christophe Bellus	FRA	13/02/93	D	8	(3)	1
99	Luca Berto	ITA	22/08/90	G	1		
90	Marco Bianchi	ITA	03/08/90	D	13	(1)	
23	Marco Biasini	ITA	26/10/95	M	7	(1)	
99	Mouhamed Camara	SEN	09/01/90	A	10	(2)	
15	Nedas Čeplinskas		15/06/95	M	14	(5)	
18	Ervinas Chvesko		02/02/94	D	14	(3)	
94	Papa Cissé	SEN	10/12/94	M	2		
33	Karolis Čyžius		09/01/97	A	2	(1)	
15	Paulius Drublionis		17/12/91	M		(1)	
31	Fabio Faragalli	ITA	31/05/92	D	7		
25	Kles Galli	ITA	09/07/89	D	1		
19	Edvardas Gaurilovas		10/05/85	D	14		
2	Andrius Genevičius		19/11/95	D	18		
27	Dominykas Grižas		24/04/92	A	2	(1)	
34	Tadas Gustaitis		02/02/97	D	6	(5)	
13	Domas Ivanauskas		20/03/96	M	11	(1)	1
55	Rokas Janilionis		28/08/90	M	10		
5	Povilas Kalimavičius		17/05/97	M	7	(5)	
11	Evgeni Kapitonov	RUS	17/05/91	A		(1)	
14	Nerijus Kavaliauskas		27/10/88	D	26		1
29	Ignas Keldušis		12/02/96	D	6	(2)	
8	Deividas Kumeta		25/04/96	M	20	(4)	1
13	Teisis Leskauskas		05/04/95	M	17	(1)	
26	Kevin Liguori	ITA	26/08/92	M	2	(2)	
27	Luigi Mariani	ITA	27/01/89	A	6		1
95	Martynas Matijoška		22/09/95	G	2		
95	Martynas Matijoška		22/09/95	A		(1)	
91	Donatas Mikučionis		23/04/91	G	17		
91	Donatas Mikučionis		23/04/91	A	1		
33	Sergio Osagho Uyi	NGA	22/06/93	D	10	(2)	
28	Rytis Padegimas		17/05/96	M	13		
32	Marco Pintus	ITA	30/05/96	M	7	2	1
4	Fabio Possagno	ITA	04/12/87	M	6	2	
45	Vaidotas Rutkauskas		09/03/85	D	11	(1)	
17	Vytenis Ruzgas		15/09/97	D	1	(3)	
3	Antonio Sepe	ITA	10/01/92	D	10	(2)	1
7	Skirmantas Šestavickas		23/04/96	D	14	(5)	
12	Renaldas Stankevičius		04/04/91	M	22		1
1	Kornelijus Timofejevas		25/07/92	G	16		

FK Ekranas

1964 • Aukštaitija (4,000); PFA (1,089) • fkekranas.lt

Major honours

Lithuanian League (7) 1993, 2005, 2008, 2009, 2010, 2011, 2012; Lithuanian Cup (4) 1998, 2000, 2010, 2011

Coach: Valdas Dambrauskas; (19/09/14) Marius Skinderis

2014

09/03	h	Kruoja	L	1-2	*Kochanauskas*
16/03	a	Dainava	W	3-0	*Dapkus, Kochanauskas, Salamanavičius*
22/03	h	Klaipėdos granitas	D	1-1	*Elivelto*
25/03	a	Banga	D	0-0	
29/03	h	Žalgiris	D	0-0	
05/04	a	Sūduva	D	2-2	*E Baranauskas, Kochanauskas*
12/04	h	Trakai	D	2-2	*Elivelto 2*
16/04	a	Atlantas	D	2-2	*Elivelto, Dapkus*
19/04	h	Šiauliai	W	3-1	*Elivelto, Kochanauskas, Salamanavičius*
27/04	a	Kruoja	L	0-2	
03/05	h	Dainava	W	6-0	*Šušnjar, Elivelto, Dapkus, Tamulevičius, Kochanauskas 2 (1p)*
06/05	a	Klaipėdos granitas	W	3-1	*Elivelto, Umeh, Kochanauskas*
10/05	h	Banga	D	0-0	
21/05	a	Žalgiris	L	0-1	
24/05	h	Sūduva	L	0-2	
10/06	a	Trakai	L	0-2	
14/06	h	Atlantas	W	2-1	*Kochanauskas, Norvilas*
19/06	a	Šiauliai	L	0-2	
22/06	h	Kruoja	W	3-2	*Salamanavičius, Šušnjar, Elivelto*
27/07	a	Dainava	W	2-1	*Elivelto, Tamulevičius*
03/08	h	Klaipėdos granitas	L	2-3	*Šušnjar (p), Elivelto*
10/08	a	Banga	W	1-0	*Tamulevičius*
16/08	h	Žalgiris	L	1-3	*Salamanavičius*
23/08	a	Sūduva	D	0-0	
30/08	h	Trakai	W	2-1	*Elivelto, Stanulevičius*
13/09	a	Atlantas	L	0-4	
18/09	h	Šiauliai	L	2-3	*Daukša, Elivelto*
21/09	a	Kruoja	L	0-1	
25/09	h	Dainava	W	2-1	*Tamulevičius, Umeh*
05/10	a	Klaipėdos granitas	W	4-2	*Šušnjar (p), Salamanavičius, Tamulevičius, Mandinho*
18/10	h	Banga	W	4-1	*Tamulevičius 2, Elivelto, Filipe*
25/10	a	Žalgiris	L	1-5	*Tamulevičius*
02/11	h	Sūduva	L	1-2	*Tamulevičius*
10/11	a	Trakai	L	1-5	*Stanulevičius*
22/11	h	Atlantas	L	0-3	
29/11	a	Šiauliai	D	0-0	

No	Name	Nat	DoB	Pos	Aps	(s)	Gls
99	Evan Aleksandrov Ridley	AUS	19/06/94	G	4		
77	Edgaras Baranauskas		12/03/93	M	12	(1)	1
27	Lukas Baranauskas		26/11/93	A	4	(6)	
9	Tomas Dapkus		01/04/92	M	13	(11)	3
77	Paulius Daukša		09/09/93	D	12		1
30	Dominykas Donėla		06/06/97	M		(5)	
3	Martynas Dūda		23/01/93	D	25		
36	Elder	BRA	17/02/91	D	6		
80	Elivelto	BRA	02/01/92	M	33	(1)	13
88	Filipe	BRA	21/05/90	M	3	(2)	1
93	Edvinas Girdvainis		17/01/93	D	16		
18	Lukas Kochanauskas		27/02/90	A	16	(3)	8
16	Mandinho	BRA	01/05/84	M	11	(1)	1
5	Aivaras Meškinis		13/11/95	D	5	(6)	
7	Lukas Narbutas		10/05/94	M	1	(1)	
20	Dovydas Norvilas		05/04/93	M	28	(1)	1
6	Donatas Petrauskas		16/03/84	M	22	(2)	
21	Džiugas Petrauskas		21/03/94	D	9	(2)	
88	Rytis Pilotas		17/12/92	D	13	(2)	
10	Tomas Salamanavičius		31/03/93	M	26	(5)	5
17	Jonas Skinderis		04/04/97	M	2	(8)	
14	Rokas Stanulevičius		10/02/94	M	19	(11)	2
15	Aleksandar Šušnjar	SRB	19/08/85	D	17	(5)	4
12	Marius Suvaizdis		22/02/95	G	3		
8	Edvardas Tamulevičius		04/01/94	A	8	(14)	9
99	Kornelijus Timofejevas		25/07/92	G	14		
11	Uchenna Umeh	NGA	10/10/91	M	16	(11)	2
4	Sigitas Urbys		07/11/95	D	26	(1)	
22	Simonas Urbys		07/11/95	M	12	(7)	
2	Gotaras Vasiliauskas		02/03/94	D	5	(1)	
1	Lukas Žukauskas		18/06/93	G	15		

FK Klaipėdos granitas

2012 • Centrinis (4,940); Centrinis Artificial (1,500) • klaipedos-granitas.lt
Coach: Robertas Poškus

2014
10/03	a	Trakai	L	0-2
15/03	h	Atlantas	D	2-2	Poškus, Alaverdashvili
22/03	a	Ekranas	D	1-1	Chargeishvili
26/03	h	Kruoja	D	2-2	Tamošauskas (p), Alaverdashvili
30/03	a	Dainava	W	5-0	Alaverdashvili 2, Chargeishvili 2, Ignatyev
06/04	a	Šiauliai	L	0-1	
12/04	h	Banga	W	1-0	Kurbangalijevas
15/04	a	Žalgiris	D	1-1	Veliulis
19/04	h	Sūduva	L	0-2	
26/04	h	Trakai	D	0-0	
03/05	a	Atlantas	L	0-2	
06/05	h	Ekranas	L	1-3	Veliulis (p)
11/05	a	Kruoja	D	2-2	Jesipovas, Veliulis
22/05	h	Dainava	W	2-0	Veliulis, Adzhiev
25/05	h	Šiauliai	W	3-0	Poškus, Jesipovas, Galkevičius
11/06	a	Banga	D	0-0	
14/06	h	Žalgiris	W	2-1	Jesipovas 2
17/06	a	Sūduva	L	1-5	Moroz
24/06	a	Trakai	L	1-2	Dmytrenko
28/07	h	Atlantas	L	0-3	
03/08	a	Ekranas	W	3-2	Baranauskas, Vilavičius, Galkevičius
08/08	h	Kruoja	L	1-5	Kurbangalijevas
14/08	a	Dainava	D	0-0	
21/08	a	Šiauliai	W	2-1	Borusas, Veliulis (p)
29/08	h	Banga	L	1-2	Galkevičius
12/09	a	Žalgiris	L	0-4	
17/09	h	Sūduva	D	1-1	Ignatyev
20/09	h	Trakai	L	2-3	Veliulis 2
28/09	a	Atlantas	L	0-3	
05/10	h	Ekranas	L	2-4	Poškus 2
19/10	a	Kruoja	L	1-3	Simanavičius
26/10	h	Dainava	W	2-0	Baranauskas, Poškus
31/10	h	Šiauliai	D	0-0	
08/11	h	Banga	W	6-0	Ignatyev, Veliulis 2, og (Špietinis), Kurbangalijevas, Urbelis
23/11	h	Žalgiris	L	1-6	Veliulis
29/11	a	Sūduva	L	1-3	Galkevičius (p)

No	Name	Nat	DoB	Pos	Aps	(s)	Gls
35	Gadzhi Adzhiev	RUS	01/06/94	M	6	(6)	1
10	Giorgi Alaverdashvili	GEO	21/11/87	A	10	(2)	4
22	Edgaras Baranauskas		12/03/93	M	13		2
90	Rokas Borusas		03/01/90	D	26	(4)	1
22	Tamaz Chargeishvili	GEO	12/01/89	M	14	(3)	3
5	Oleh Dmytrenko	UKR	26/11/89	M	27		1
18	Dominykas Galkevičius		16/10/86	M	15	(2)	4
24	Vili Grigaitis		28/09/97	M	1	(2)	
30	Boris Ignatyev	RUS	19/01/91	A	13	(14)	3
77	Zigmantas Jesipovas		08/11/94	M	11	(1)	4
4	Aurimas Jurgelevičius		09/01/97	M	11	(4)	
29	Artūras Kurbangalijevas		29/06/90	M	12	(8)	3
12	Eduardas Kurskis		17/10/76	G	9		
1	Lukas Lidakevičius		29/04/93	G	8		
25	Aivaras Lukošius		16/04/88	D	8	(3)	
35	Aivaras Meškinis		13/11/95	D	8		
99	Jevgenij Moroz		20/01/91	M	10	(2)	1
6	Donatas Nakrošius		17/02/91	D	13		
88	Tadas Norbutas		25/02/94	G	8		
20	Rytis Pilotas		17/12/92	D	10	(1)	
81	Paulius Pocius		09/11/88	G	11		
32	Robertas Poškus		05/05/79	A	8	(7)	5
10	Arnas Ribokas		14/01/93	M	14	(2)	
34	Rokas Simanavičius		20/01/94	D	16	(1)	1
15	Dmitrij Šiškin		17/07/87	D	20		
9	Tomas Tamošauskas		22/05/83	M	9	(3)	1
3	Olexandr Tarasenko	UKR	11/12/78	D	24		
11	Rokas Urbelis		27/01/90	A	8	(12)	1
7	Ernestas Veliulis		22/08/92	M	32		10
9	Justas Vilavičius		20/12/92	M	5	(5)	1
6	Robert Vulpe	ROU	02/07/92	D	3	(2)	
20	Hayato Wakino	JPN	10/04/93	M		(5)	
8	Mihails Zizijevs	LVA	27/12/73	M	13	(12)	

FK Kruoja

2001 • Pakruojis (2,000); PFA, Panevezys (1,089) • fkkruoja.lt
Coach: Vladimir Cheburin (RUS)

2014
09/03	a	Ekranas	W	2-1	Birškys, Beniušis
16/03	a	Šiauliai	D	1-1	Beniušis
23/03	h	Dainava	W	4-0	Nieminen, Bagočius 2, Pilypas
26/03	a	Klaipėdos granitas	D	2-2	Bagočius, Pilypas
30/03	h	Banga	L	0-1	
04/04	a	Žalgiris	L	0-2	
13/04	h	Sūduva	D	1-1	og (Radzinevičius)
17/04	a	Trakai	W	4-1	Beniušis 3 (2p), Thome
21/04	h	Atlantas	D	1-1	Bagočius
27/04	h	Ekranas	W	2-0	Mačiulis, Vėževičius
02/05	a	Šiauliai	W	1-0	Beniušis
08/05	a	Dainava	W	5-0	Beniušis 2 (1p), Bagočius, Nieminen, Bobb
11/05	h	Klaipėdos granitas	D	2-2	og (Poškus), Mačiulis
21/05	h	Banga	L	0-1	
24/05	a	Žalgiris	D	0-0	
10/06	a	Sūduva	W	1-0	Mačiulis
14/06	h	Trakai	L	0-1	
18/06	a	Atlantas	W	3-1	Beniušis, Bobb, Mačiulis
22/06	a	Ekranas	L	2-3	Eliošius, Mačiulis
25/07	a	Šiauliai	W	5-1	Birškys 2, Mačiulis 2, Pocevičius
01/08	h	Dainava	W	3-2	Vėževičius, Jankauskas, Abu Bakr
08/08	a	Klaipėdos granitas	W	5-1	Vėževičius 2, Mačiulis, Birškys, Abu Bakr
17/08	h	Banga	W	1-0	Bagočius
24/08	a	Žalgiris	L	0-1	
28/08	h	Sūduva	W	2-1	Jankauskas, Mačiulis
13/09	a	Trakai	D	0-0	
16/09	h	Atlantas	W	4-1	Bagočius 2, Beniušis, Vėževičius
21/09	h	Ekranas	W	1-0	Vėževičius
27/09	a	Šiauliai	W	4-1	Vėževičius 2, Beniušis, Birškys
04/10	a	Dainava	L	0-2	
19/10	h	Klaipėdos granitas	W	3-1	Beniušis, Vėževičius, Eliošius
26/10	a	Banga	W	4-1	Bagočius, Beniušis 2 (1p), Vėževičius
02/11	h	Žalgiris	D	0-0	
08/11	a	Sūduva	W	2-1	Beniušis, Eliošius
22/11	h	Trakai	D	2-2	Bagočius, og (Lipskis)
29/11	a	Atlantas	L	0-1	

No	Name	Nat	DoB	Pos	Aps	(s)	Gls
6	Radanfah Abu Bakr	TRI	12/02/87	D	23		2
22	Maxym Adamenko	UKR	19/01/91	D	6	(1)	
17	Andrius Arlauskas		16/01/86	M	4	(15)	
18	Aivaras Bagočius		10/10/87	A	30	(4)	10
16	Gediminas Balašauskas		27/01/95	D		(1)	
7	Vazha Bedoidze	GEO	04/02/94	M	3	(2)	
8	Ričardas Beniušis		23/04/80	A	35		15
21	Tomas Birškys		05/11/92	M	8	(14)	5
49	Trayon Bobb	GUY	05/11/93	M	3	(17)	2
10	Tautvydas Eliošius		03/11/91	M	32	(1)	3
99	Haruna Garba	NGA	17/01/94	A		(3)	
27	Darius Jankauskas		27/04/92	M	19	(12)	2
23	Nerijus Mačiulis		01/04/83	M	31	(2)	9
94	Azizbek Madaminov	RUS	26/03/94	G		(2)	
7	Mohamed Mahran	EGY	07/02/87	M		(2)	
1	Martynas Matuzas		28/08/89	G	30		
31	Arnas Mikaitis		21/07/92	D		(1)	
3	Samu Nieminen	FIN	14/01/92	D	22	(3)	2
2	Ernestas Pilypas		17/05/90	D	10	(2)	2
14	Mykola Ploskonos	UKR	14/04/92	D	6	(1)	
4	Valdas Pocevičius		16/05/86	D	33		1
84	Alfredas Skroblas		11/03/84	D	26	(2)	
77	Donatas Strockis		23/03/87	D	25		
5	Jean Thome	CIV	10/10/95	D	13	(2)	1
3	Artūrs Vaičulis	LVA	26/02/92	D	6	(1)	
33	Robertas Vėževičius		05/01/86	M	31	(5)	10

FC Šiauliai

1995 • Savivaldybės (3,000); Gytariai (1,500) • fcsiauliai.lt
Coach: Gedeminas Jarmalavičius

2014
09/03	a	Žalgiris	L	1-3	Tokić
16/03	h	Kruoja	D	1-1	Tokić
22/03	a	Sūduva	L	0-2	
27/03	h	Dainava	W	5-0	Tokić 2, Gašpuitis 2, Keita
30/03	a	Trakai	L	1-2	Juozapaitis
06/04	h	Klaipėdos granitas	W	1-0	Gaurilovas
11/04	a	Atlantas	L	0-1	
15/04	h	Banga	L	1-2	Gedminas
19/04	a	Ekranas	L	1-3	Babić
24/04	h	Žalgiris	D	0-0	
02/05	a	Kruoja	L	0-1	
06/05	h	Sūduva	L	1-4	Renusas
13/05	a	Dainava	W	6-0	Jasaitis, Keita, Tokić, Gedminas, Medžiaušis, Babić (p)
20/05	h	Trakai	L	0-2	
25/05	a	Klaipėdos granitas	L	0-3	
09/06	h	Atlantas	W	3-1	Babić, Tokić, Medžiaušis
15/06	a	Banga	W	2-1	Tokić 2
19/06	h	Ekranas	W	2-0	Tokić, Gašpuitis
22/06	a	Žalgiris	L	0-2	
25/07	h	Kruoja	L	1-5	Tokić
02/08	a	Sūduva	L	0-2	
07/08	h	Dainava	W	4-1	Tokić 2, Gašpuitis, og (Bellus)
15/08	a	Trakai	L	1-3	Jasaitis
21/08	h	Klaipėdos granitas	L	1-2	Strauka
30/08	a	Atlantas	L	0-4	
14/09	h	Banga	W	4-1	Tokić, Moroz, Strauka, Vitukynas
18/09	a	Ekranas	W	3-2	Tokić, Gedminas 2
21/09	h	Žalgiris	L	1-2	Moroz
27/09	a	Kruoja	L	1-4	Moroz
04/10	h	Sūduva	L	2-4	Tokić 2
17/10	a	Dainava	W	1-0	Moroz
24/10	h	Trakai	W	3-1	Strauka, Vitukynas, Tokić (p)
31/10	a	Klaipėdos granitas	D	0-0	
09/11	h	Atlantas	L	0-3	
23/11	a	Banga	W	3-1	Tokić 2, Vitukynas
29/11	h	Ekranas	D	0-0	

No	Name	Nat	DoB	Pos	Aps	(s)	Gls
8	Stjepan Babić	CRO	04/12/88	M	23		3
33	Valdemar Borovskij		02/05/84	D	7		
19	Stefan Caraulan	MDA	02/02/89	D	9	(1)	
22	Elmin Gasanov	RUS	22/02/95	D		(4)	
3	Vytas Gašpuitis		04/03/94	M	27	(2)	4
21	Edvardas Gaurilovas		10/05/85	D	17		
34	Rokas Gedminas		13/04/90	M	24	(9)	4
34	Eligijus Jankauskas		22/06/98	A		(1)	
7	Edvinas Jasaitis		11/04/90	M	32	(1)	2
88	Agnius Juozapaitis		13/11/94	M		(16)	1
16	Yamadou Keita	MLI	16/10/89	A	14	(1)	2
5	Tamirlan Kozubaev	KGZ	01/07/94	D	16	(1)	
18	Rolandas Leščius		05/09/94	A		(8)	
17	Dovydas Medžiaušis		23/01/95	A	6	(15)	2
12	Edgaras Mikšėnas		25/10/97	G	6	(1)	
8	Jevgenij Moroz		20/01/90	M	12	(5)	4
10	Justas Petravičius		10/01/96	M		(6)	
1	Ignas Plukas		08/12/93	G	17		
19	Edvardas Pšelenskis		11/02/88	D	5	(2)	
2	Tomas Rapalavičius		14/04/94	D	3		
23	Justas Raziūnas		23/01/95	D	28	(3)	
27	Aivaras Renusas		27/04/92	M	19	(1)	1
1	Andrei Štinca	MDA	16/06/89	G	11		
14	Mindaugas Strauka		29/06/90	M	23	(2)	3
39	Nerijus Tabokas		14/05/98	G	2		
99	Niko Tokić	CRO	07/06/88	A	35		19
11	Titas Vitukynas		23/10/94	M	22	(6)	3
57	Modestas Vorobjovas		30/12/95	M	15		
33	Filip Žderić	CRO	11/12/91	D	13		

FK Sūduva

1968 • ARVI (6,250); ARVI Arena (2,500) •
fksuduva.lt
Major honours
Lithuanian Cup (2) 2006, 2009
**Coach: Darius Gvildys;
(18/09/14) Audrius Ramonas**

2014

09/03	h	Banga	L 0-1	
16/03	a	Žalgiris	L 1-8	*Baranovskij*
22/03	h	Šiauliai	W 2-0	*Bagdanavičius, Radzinevičius*
26/03	h	Trakai	L 0-1	
29/03	a	Atlantas	L 0-1	
05/04	h	Ekranas	D 2-2	*Grigaravičius 2*
13/04	a	Kruoja	D 1-1	*Brokas*
16/04	h	Dainava	W 5-0	*og 2 (Čeplinskas 2), Andjelković, Radzinevičius (p), Brokas*
19/04	a	Klaipėdos granitas	W 2-0	*Brokas, Radzinevičius*
26/04	a	Banga	W 1-0	*Grigaravičius*
03/05	h	Žalgiris	L 0-3	
06/05	h	Šiauliai	W 4-1	*Brokas, Baranovskij, Radzinevičius, Chvedukas*
11/05	a	Trakai	W 4-3	*Radzinevičius 2 (1p), Andjelković, Grigaravičius*
20/05	h	Atlantas	D 1-1	*Grigaravičius*
24/05	a	Ekranas	W 2-0	*Baranovskij, Šoblinskas*
10/06	h	Kruoja	L 0-1	
13/06	h	Dainava	W 8-0	*Vaskéla 2, Radzinevičius 2, Kadouh 3, Grigaravičius*
17/06	h	Klaipėdos granitas	W 5-1	*Chvedukas 3, Vaskéla, Radzinevičius*
24/06	h	Banga	W 2-0	*Vaskéla, Grigaravičius*
26/07	a	Žalgiris	D 0-0	
02/08	h	Šiauliai	W 2-0	*Vaskéla, Russo*
09/08	h	Trakai	D 0-0	
16/08	a	Atlantas	D 2-2	*og (Jemeļins), Uggè*
23/08	h	Ekranas	D 0-0	
28/08	a	Kruoja	L 1-2	*Vaskéla*
11/09	h	Dainava	D 0-0	
17/09	a	Klaipėdos granitas	D 1-1	*Chvedukas*
20/09	a	Banga	W 3-1	*Uggè (p), Radzinevičius, Kadouh*
27/09	h	Žalgiris	D 1-1	*Radzinevičius*
04/10	a	Šiauliai	W 4-2	*Russo 2, Šoblinskas 2*
16/10	a	Trakai	W 3-1	*Chvedukas, Radzinevičius, Martínez*
25/10	h	Atlantas	D 0-0	
02/11	a	Ekranas	W 2-1	*Martínez 2*
08/11	h	Kruoja	L 1-2	*Russo*
20/11	a	Dainava	W 6-0	*Vaskéla, Radzinevičius, Šoblinskas, Baranovskij 2, Isoda*
29/11	h	Klaipėdos granitas	W 4-1	*Uggè (p), Šoblinskas, Chvedukas, Russo*

No	Name	Nat	DoB	Pos	Aps	(s)	Gls
11	Marko Andjelković	SRB	12/10/84	M	7	(3)	2
24	Vilmantas Bagdanavičius		01/10/92	M	25		1
2	Valentin Baranovskij		15/10/86	M	28	(7)	5
31	Džiugas Bartkus		07/11/89	G	36		
16	Audrius Brokas		20/08/90	A	10	(3)	4
13	Karolis Chvedukas		21/04/91	M	28	(7)	7
3	Marius Činikas		17/05/86	D	27	(3)	
14	Paulius Daukša		09/09/93	D		(1)	
7	Mindaugas Grigaravičius		04/05/93	M	18	(10)	7
5	Darius Isoda		27/07/94	D	16		1
9	Mohammad Kadouh	LIB	04/05/93	A	3	(10)	4
40	Markas Kardokas		19/09/97	M	1	(3)	
94	Povilas Kiselevskis		05/07/94	M	9	(7)	
33	Miloš Kovačević	SRB	31/03/91	D	20	(4)	
4	Carlos Martínez	ESP	29/03/89	M	8	(7)	3
32	Edvinas Puzara		10/01/96	M		(5)	
10	Tomas Radzinevičius		05/06/81	A	36		13
90	Giorgio Russo	ITA	03/02/89	M	16	(18)	5
23	Tomas Snapkauskas		13/06/92	M	12	(7)	
88	Marius Šoblinskas		30/08/87	M	20		5
17	Ilya Tsyvilko	BLR	27/07/92	D	15	(1)	
20	Dovydas Tumosa		02/07/92	D		(2)	
91	Maximiliano Uggè	ITA	24/09/91	D	34		3
22	Gytis Urba		31/03/91	D	1		
21	Arminas Vaskéla		12/08/90	M	26	(7)	7

FK Trakai

2005 • LFF, Vilnius (5,067) • fkt.lt
**Coach: Edgaras Jankauskas;
(30/10/14) Virmantas Lemežis**

2014

10/03	h	Klaipėdos granitas	W 2-0	*Astrauskas, Lukša*
15/03	a	Banga	L 0-1	
21/03	h	Žalgiris	D 1-1	*Mamaev*
26/03	a	Sūduva	W 1-0	*Krasnovskis*
30/03	h	Šiauliai	W 2-1	*Kendysh, Mamaev*
03/04	h	Atlantas	D 0-0	
12/04	a	Ekranas	D 2-2	*Lipskis, Kendysh*
17/04	h	Kruoja	L 1-4	*Labukas*
22/04	a	Dainava	W 7-1	*Labukas 2, Kovb 2, Lukša 2, Klimavičius*
26/04	a	Klaipėdos granitas	D 0-0	
04/05	h	Banga	D 2-2	*Kovb, Krasnovskis*
07/05	a	Žalgiris	D 1-1	*Kovb*
11/05	h	Sūduva	L 3-4	*Kovb, Miceika 2*
20/05	a	Šiauliai	W 2-1	*Mamaev, Krasnovskis*
23/05	a	Atlantas	W 2-0	*Miceika, Labukas*
10/06	h	Ekranas	W 2-0	*Miceika, Labukas (p)*
14/06	a	Kruoja	W 1-0	*Kovb*
17/06	h	Dainava	W 4-0	*Labukas, Kovb 2, Klimavičius*
24/06	h	Klaipėdos granitas	W 2-1	*Mamaev 2*
27/07	a	Banga	W 4-0	*Mamaev, Krasnovskis, Lukša, Lipskis*
03/08	h	Žalgiris	L 0-2	
09/08	a	Sūduva	D 0-0	
15/08	h	Šiauliai	W 3-1	*Kochanauskas 2, Solomin*
22/08	h	Atlantas	W 3-0	*Kendysh, Kochanauskas, Lukša*
30/08	a	Ekranas	L 1-2	*Solomin*
13/09	h	Kruoja	D 0-0	
16/09	a	Dainava	W 2-0	*Labukas, Kovb*
20/09	a	Klaipėdos granitas	W 3-2	*Labukas, Lukša, Mamaev*
28/09	h	Banga	W 4-0	*Klimavičius, Solomin, Kovb, og (Siryk)*
05/10	a	Žalgiris	L 0-3	
16/10	h	Sūduva	L 1-3	*Lukša*
24/10	a	Šiauliai	L 1-3	*Kovb*
30/10	a	Atlantas	L 0-1	
10/11	h	Ekranas	W 5-1	*Mamaev, Kochanauskas 2, Labukas 2 (1p)*
22/11	a	Kruoja	D 2-2	*Kendysh, Kochanauskas*
29/11	h	Dainava	W 1-0	*Kochanauskas*

No	Name	Nat	DoB	Pos	Aps	(s)	Gls
9	Besik Amashukeli	GEO	16/09/92	D	18		
21	Nikoloz Apakidze	GEO	04/04/92	D	6		
20	Nerijus Astrauskas		18/10/80	A	2	(11)	1
28	Deividas Česnauskis		30/06/81	M	8	(1)	
31	Darius Cibulskas		23/05/88	M	5	(5)	
1	Paulius Grybauskas		02/06/84	G	16		
15	Justinas Januševskij		26/03/94	D	35		
12	Tadas Kauneckas		31/03/86	G	19		
77	Yuri Kendysh	BLR	10/06/90	M	34		4
30	Linas Klimavičius		10/04/89	D	34		3
29	Lukas Kochanauskas		27/02/90	A	9	(4)	7
99	Dmitri Kovb	BLR	20/01/87	A	18	(13)	11
8	Povilas Krasnovskis		29/04/89	M	20	(5)	4
14	Tadas Labukas		10/01/84	A	32		10
33	Andrius Lipskis		16/02/88	M	22	(7)	2
5	Vytautas Lukša		14/08/84	M	29	(2)	7
23	Mantas Makutunovič		29/04/91	D	1	(2)	
32	Povilas Malinauskas		20/10/94	M	3	(8)	
79	Yuri Mamaev	RUS	03/02/84	M	29	(2)	8
1	Rokas Masenzovas		02/08/94	M	1	(7)	
6	Darius Miceika		22/02/83	M	25	(3)	4
17	Mantas Rimkus		23/11/93	M		(3)	
93	Jonas Saryčevas		03/01/93	G	1	(1)	
13	Ronald Solomin		23/09/91	A	11	(14)	3
10	Andrius Starta		10/06/90	A	1		
18	Darius Zachaževskij		13/12/91	D	18	(6)	

VMFD Žalgiris

1947 • LFF (5,067) • zalgiris-vilnius.lt
Major honours
*Lithuanian League (5) 1991, 1992, 1999, 2013, 2014;
Lithuanian Cup (9) 1991, 1993, 1994, 1997, 2003
(autumn), 2012, 2013, 2014, 2015*
Coach: Marek Zub (POL)

2014

09/03	h	Šiauliai	W 3-1	*Žulpa, Nyuiadzi, Pilibaitis*
16/03	h	Sūduva	W 8-1	*Nyuiadzi 2, Andreou, Wilk, Pilibaitis, Švrljuga, Janušauskas, Leliūga*
21/03	a	Trakai	D 1-1	*Wilk*
25/03	h	Atlantas	W 4-0	*Wilk, Pilibaitis (p), Andreou 2*
29/03	a	Ekranas	D 0-0	
04/04	h	Kruoja	W 2-0	*Wilk, Andreou*
12/04	a	Dainava	W 8-0	*Leliūga, Velička 2, Nyuiadzi, Jankauskas 2, Fridrikas, Baniulis*
15/04	h	Klaipėdos granitas	D 1-1	*Wilk*
18/04	a	Banga	W 2-0	*Pilibaitis, Andrezinho*
24/04	a	Šiauliai	D 0-0	
03/05	a	Sūduva	W 3-0	*Pilibaitis, Leliūga, Andreou*
07/05	h	Trakai	D 1-1	*Wilk*
10/05	a	Atlantas	W 1-0	*Wilk*
21/05	h	Ekranas	W 1-0	*Šilėnas*
24/05	a	Kruoja	D 0-0	
09/06	h	Dainava	W 9-1	*Andrezinho, Leliūga, Šilėnas 2, Švrljuga, Velička 2, Nyuiadzi (p), og (Genevičius)*
14/06	a	Klaipėdos granitas	L 1-2	*Nyuiadzi*
18/06	h	Banga	W 1-0	*Pilibaitis*
22/06	h	Šiauliai	W 2-0	*Janušauskas, Wilk*
26/07	h	Sūduva	D 0-0	
03/08	a	Trakai	W 2-0	*Adi, Vaitkūnas*
11/08	h	Atlantas	W 3-0	*Pilibaitis 2, Wilk*
16/08	a	Ekranas	W 3-1	*Pilibaitis, Nyuiadzi, Kuklys*
24/08	h	Kruoja	W 1-0	*Velička*
31/08	a	Dainava	W 3-0	*Kerla, Šilėnas, Pilibaitis*
12/09	h	Klaipėdos granitas	W 4-0	*Žulpa, Nyuiadzi 2, Pilibaitis*
17/09	h	Banga	W 5-1	*Šemberas (p), Švrljuga 2, Šilėnas, Kuklys*
21/09	a	Šiauliai	W 2-1	*Šemberas, Kuklys*
27/09	a	Sūduva	D 1-1	*Pilibaitis*
05/10	h	Trakai	W 3-0	*Kerla 2, Vaitkūnas*
18/10	a	Atlantas	L 1-2	*Šemberas (p)*
25/10	h	Ekranas	W 5-1	*Pilibaitis 2, Šemberas, Wilk, Žulpa*
02/11	a	Kruoja	D 0-0	
09/11	h	Dainava	W 2-0	*Nyuiadzi, Pilibaitis*
23/11	a	Klaipėdos granitas	W 6-1	*Nyuiadzi, Pilibaitis 2 (1p), Švrljuga, Adi 2*
29/11	h	Banga	W 3-0	*(w/o)*

No	Name	Nat	DoB	Pos	Aps	(s)	Gls
21	Adi	BRA	15/12/85	A	2	(1)	3
14	Kristis Andreou	CYP	12/08/94	A	11	(6)	5
99	Andrezinho	BRA	12/02/86	M	11	(3)	2
45	Edvinas Baniulis		03/01/97	A	4	(3)	1
12	Aivaras Bražinskas		01/11/90	G	5		
3	Georgas Freidgeimas		10/08/89	D	27	(1)	
25	Mantas Fridrikas		13/09/88	D	3		1
5	Algis Jankauskas		27/09/82	D	16	(1)	2
16	Paulius Janušauskas		28/02/89	M	8	(18)	2
39	Darius Kazubovičius		29/09/95	A		(1)	
15	Semir Kerla	BIH	26/09/87	D	13		3
47	Aldas Korsakas		21/05/96	D	1	(1)	
88	Mantas Kuklys		10/06/87	M	15	(1)	3
81	Justas Lasickas		06/10/97	M	1		
9	Rytis Leliūga		04/01/87	M	5	(7)	4
99	Serge Nyuiadzi	FRA	15/11/94	A	27	(4)	11
77	Linas Pilibaitis		05/04/85	M	32	(1)	17
1	Ramūnas Radavičius		20/01/81	M	16	(2)	
2	Deividas Šemberas		02/08/78	D	28		4
20	Vaidas Šilėnas		16/07/85	M	9	(12)	5
38	Artur Skuratovič		15/01/96	A		(1)	
11	Andro Švrljuga	CRO	24/10/85	M	31	(1)	5
35	Egidijus Vaitkūnas		08/08/88	D	13	(2)	2
7	Andrius Velička		05/04/79	A	14	(14)	5
1	Armantas Vitkauskas		23/03/89	G	30		
10	Jakub Wilk	POL	11/07/85	M	30	(1)	10
21	Artak Yedigaryan	ARM	18/03/90	D	8	(3)	
15	Eivinas Zagurskas		09/09/89	M	3	(13)	
8	Artūras Žulpa		10/06/90	M	28	(2)	3

Top goalscorers

19	Niko Tokić (Šiauliai)

17 Linas Pilibaitis (Žalgiris)

15 Lukas Kochanauskas (Ekranas/Trakai)
Ričardas Beniušis (Kruoja)

13 Evaldas Razulis (Atlantas)
Elivelto (Ekranas)
Tomas Radzinevičius (Sūduva)

12 Donatas Kazlauskas (Atlantas)

11 Marius Papšys (Atlantas)
Dmitri Kovb (Trakai)
Serge Nyuiadzi (Žalgiris)

Promoted clubs

FC Stumbras

2010 • NFA (1,000) • fcstumbras.lt
Coach: Darius Gvildys

FK Utenis

1933 • Utenis (3,000) • utenosutenis.lt
Coach: Mindaugas Čepas

FK Spyris

2005 • S. Dariaus ir S. Girėno SC (8,248) •
no website
Coach: Laimis Bičkauskas

Second level final table 2014

		Pld	W	D	L	F	A	Pts
1	FC Stumbras	31	19	7	5	73	29	64
2	FK MRU	31	18	7	6	67	24	61
3	FK Utenis	31	18	7	6	61	22	61
4	Žalgirietis	31	16	4	11	63	49	52
5	FK Spyris	31	15	6	10	48	36	51
6	FK Šilas	31	14	6	11	58	56	48
7	FK Lietava	31	13	7	11	51	43	46
8	FK Nevėžis	31	12	4	15	62	62	40
9	FK Tauras	28	13	4	11	51	53	43
10	FK Šilutė	28	8	6	14	43	43	30
11	FK Lokomotyvas	20	7	3	18	32	64	24
12	FK Palanga	28	7	1	20	34	76	19
13	FK Baltija	28	2	2	24	24	110	5

*NB League splits into top 8 and bottom 5 after 24
games, after which the clubs play exclusively against
teams in their group; FK Palanga & FK Baltija – 3 pts
deducted; FK Utenis & FK Spyris were subsequently
invited to A Lyga 2015.*

DOMESTIC CUP

LFF Taurė 2014/15

THIRD ROUND

(23/09/14)
Hegelmann Litauen 2-1 Tauras *(aet)*
Mostiškės 1-0 Lietava
Nevėžis 0-3 Klaipėdos granitas
Prelegentai 1-0 Džiugas Telšiai
Šilas 3-2 Trakai *(aet)*
TAIP 2-0 Lokomotyvas
Utenis Utena 1-3 Spyris

(24/09/14)
Šilutė 0-1 MRU

FOURTH ROUND

(30/09/14)
MRU 0-2 Sūduva
Hegelmann Litauen 0-3 Dainava

(01/10/14)
Klaipėdos granitas 2-0 Kruoja
Prelegentai 1-0 Banga
Spyris 0-0 Šiauliai *(aet; 7-6 on pens)*
TAIP 1-3 Atlantas *(aet)*
Žalgiris 3-0 Ekranas

(03/10/14)
Mostiškės 0-4 Šilas

QUARTER-FINALS

(21/10/14 & 29/10/14)
Prelegentai 0-2 Spyris *(Zurza 22og, Bučma 29)*
Spyris 5-0 Prelegentai *(Kšanavičius 30, 88, Bučma
57, Sendžikas 81, Šilkaitis 85)*
(Spyris 7-0)

(22/10/14 & 04/11/14)
Klaipėdos granitas 0-4 Atlantas *(Baranauskas 44,
Verbickas 73, Razulis 90, 90+2)*
Atlantas 3-0 Klaipėdos granitas *(Baravykas 24,
Rakauskas 55, Nakrošius 58og)*
(Atlantas 7-0)

(22/10/14 & 05/11/14)
Šilas 0-2 Dainava *(Stankevičius 21, Gaurilovas 78)*
Dainava 0-3 Šilas *(Sepe 5og, Urba 45,
Veikutis 102) (aet)*
(Šilas 3-2)

Žalgiris 1-0 Sūduva *(Pilibaitis 77)*
Sūduva 2-3 Žalgiris *(Grigaravičius 38,
Radzinevičius 39; Šemberas 52p, Wilk 85,
Pilibaitis 88)*
(Žalgiris 4-2)

SEMI-FINALS

(20/04/15 & 06/05/15)
Šilas 0-1 Atlantas *(Vėževičius 2)*
Atlantas 6-0 Šilas *(Žarskis 21, Maksimov 29, 63p,
Norvilas 69p, Virkšas 74, Vėževičius 89)*
(Atlantas 7-0)

(22/04/15 & 05/05/15)
Žalgiris 4-0 Spyris *(Lukša 17, Wilk 64, Kendysh 64,
Andreou 65)*
Spyris 0-2 Žalgiris *(Pilibaitis 72, Elivelto 76)*
(Žalgiris 6-0)

FINAL

(23/05/15)
Savivaldybės, Siauliai
VMFD ŽALGIRIS 2 *(Šemberas 54p, Pilibaitis 84)*
FK ATLANTAS 0
Referee: *Mažeika*
ŽALGIRIS: Klevinskas, Kerla *(Jankauskas 89)*,
Vaitkūnas, Šemberas, Švrljuga, Kendysh, Kuklys,
Lukša *(Freidgeimas 86)*, Wilk *(Nyuiadzi 67)*,
Pilibaitis, Elivelto
ATLANTAS: Gertmonas, Beneta, Epifanov, Žarskis
(Virkšas 83), Baravykas, Žukauskas *(Norvilas
80)*, Bartkus, Navikas, Vėževičius, Baranauskas
(Panyukov 52), Maksimov
Red card: *Navikas (57)*

A familiar feeling for Žalgiris as they lift the Lithuanian Cup for the fourth successive year

LUXEMBOURG

Fédération Luxembourgeoise de Football (FLF)

Address	BP5, Rue de Limpach	**President**	Paul Philipp
	LU-3901 Mondercange	**General secretary**	Joël Wolff
Tel	+352 488 665 1	**Media officer**	Marc Diederich
Fax	+352 488 665 82	**Year of formation**	1908
E-mail	flf@football.lu	**National stadium**	Josy Barthel,
Website	football.lu		Luxembourg (8,022)

NATIONAL DIVISION CLUBS

 1 FC Differdange 03

 2 F91 Dudelange

 3 FC Etzella Ettelbruck

 4 CS Fola Esch

 5 CS Grevenmacher

 6 US Hostert

 7 FC Jeunesse Canach

 8 AS Jeunesse Esch

 9 UN Käerjéng 97

 10 US Mondorf-les-Bains

 11 FC Progrès Niederkorn

 12 US Rumelange

13 FC Victoria Rosport

14 FC Wiltz 71

PROMOTED CLUBS

 15 FC RM Hamm Benfica

 16 Racing FC Union Lëtzebuerg

 17 FC Una Strassen

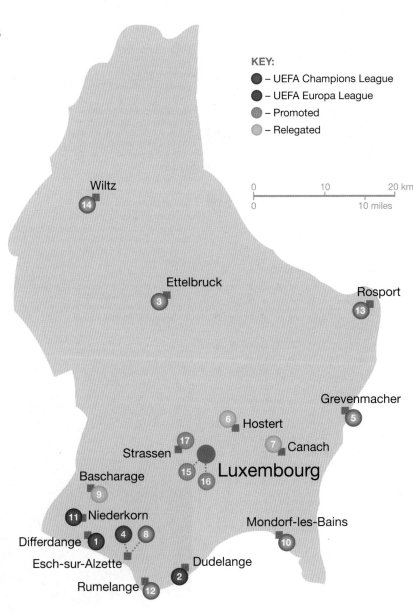

KEY:
- – UEFA Champions League
- – UEFA Europa League
- – Promoted
- – Relegated

Fola reclaim their crown

Beaten to the 2013/14 title by F91 Dudelange in a final-day showdown, CS Fola Esch roared back to regain the title they had won in 2012/13. Former Luxembourg international Jeff Strasser was the team's inspirational coach once again as Fola edged a three-way tussle for the title ahead of the defending champions and FC Differdange 03.

Marc Thomé's Differdange added the Luxembourg Cup to their runners-up spot, defeating Dudelange in the final for the second successive year, this time in a penalty shoot-out after a 1-1 draw at the Stade Josy Barthel.

| Second title in three seasons for Strasser's side | Repeat cup final success for Differdange against Dudelange | National team frustrated by late goal in Skopje |

Domestic league

Fola, Luxembourg's oldest surviving football club, had waited 83 years between their fifth and six league titles, but a 3-0 victory at UN Käerjéng 97 in their penultimate fixture ensured that the gap between the sixth and seventh would be a mere 24 months. It was a well deserved triumph for a team that won 19 of their 26 matches, scored three times as many goals as they conceded, and found the net in every fixture bar the first, which they surprisingly lost 1-0 at FC Progrès Niederkorn.

That defeat, however, was followed by an 18-match unbeaten run that incorporated 14 victories, seven in a row straddling the winter break. While Differdange and Dudelange never allowed Fola to take it easy, Strasser's men always looked in command of their destiny – even when Differdange ended their unbeaten run with a 3-2 win at the Stade Émile Mayrisch, a result that left Fola just one point ahead of Dudelange and two in front of Differdange with six games remaining.

More brittle sides than Strasser's might have cracked at that stage, but Fola proved their toughness by beating local rivals AS Jeunesse Esch next time out and taking maximum points from the next four matches as well to clinch the title with one match remaining. Although

the 3-0 win at Käerjéng wrapped up proceedings, it was the game at home to Dudelange a week earlier that effectively settled the outcome, Fola winning it 1-0 on the pitch but later having the game awarded to them 3-0 after their rivals sent on a late substitute, Frenchman Dylan Deligny, whose name did not appear on the official match sheet.

In the fall-out from that costly defeat, Dudelange coach Sébastien Grandjean was relieved of his duties, with former Luxembourg midfielder and coach Guy Hellers, the club's technical director, drafted in for the remainder of the campaign.

Domestic cup

Hellers' first game in charge was a Luxembourg Cup semi-final against FC Etzella Ettelbruck, which his team won 4-0. He did not have such luck in the final against Differdange, however, as penalties favoured the team that had just finished above them in the league. The two goals in regular time were unconventional, Differdange defender Tom Siebenaler deflecting in an own goal but then, a minute later, sending forward a long-range punt that Dudelange's Jonathan Joubert, the Luxembourg national team goalkeeper, allowed to slip past him into the net. It was Differdange's keeper, Frenchman Julien Weber, who

would ultimately prove to be the match-winner, saving two spot-kicks in the shoot-out to give his club the trophy for the fourth time in six years.

Europe

There was no repeat of Differdange's European heroics from the previous season as all four National Division representatives fell at the first hurdle, Fola failing to build on a first-leg goalless draw at IFK Göteborg and Differdange conceding a late goal in Lithuania to wipe out a 1-0 home win over FK Atlantas provided by their European goal specialist Omar Er Rafik.

National team

Another agonising late goal, scored by FYR Macedonia's Besart Abdurahimi, was to trigger a decline in the fortunes of the Luxembourg national team in their UEFA EURO 2016 qualifying campaign. Having held Belarus 1-1 at home in their opening qualifier, Luc Holtz's side took a 2-1 lead in Skopje with fine goals from Fola's Stefano Bensi and Dudelange's David Turpel, but an equalising penalty and, in the 92nd minute, Abdurahimi's wonder strike left them with nothing to show for their sterling efforts. With confidence duly dented, Luxembourg lost their next four qualifiers without scoring.

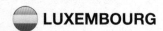
DOMESTIC SEASON AT A GLANCE

National Division 2014/15 final table

		Pld	Home					Away					Total					Pts
			W	D	L	F	A	W	D	L	F	A	W	D	L	F	A	
1	**CS Fola Esch**	26	10	1	2	38	15	9	3	1	25	6	19	4	3	63	21	61
2	FC Differdange 03	26	10	3	0	35	14	8	2	3	26	17	18	5	3	61	31	59
3	F91 Dudelange	26	9	2	2	29	9	7	4	2	26	11	16	6	4	55	20	54
4	FC Progrès Niederkorn	26	9	2	2	28	10	6	3	4	23	19	15	5	6	51	29	50
5	AS Jeunesse Esch	26	8	3	2	29	19	4	5	4	17	15	12	8	6	46	34	44
6	FC Victoria Rosport	26	6	3	4	22	22	2	4	7	14	24	8	7	11	36	46	31
7	FC Etzella Ettelbruck	26	5	2	6	19	21	4	1	8	17	29	9	3	14	36	50	30
8	US Mondorf-les-Bains	26	6	1	6	18	19	2	4	7	12	21	8	5	13	30	40	29
9	CS Grevenmacher	26	3	3	7	8	22	5	2	6	16	26	8	5	13	24	48	29
10	US Rumelange	26	3	5	5	17	18	4	2	7	12	20	7	7	12	29	38	28
11	FC Wiltz 71	26	5	5	3	17	12	2	1	10	12	26	7	6	13	29	38	27
12	UN Käerjéng 97	26	3	2	8	15	26	5	1	7	18	26	8	3	15	33	52	27
13	US Hostert	26	5	4	4	18	17	0	4	9	17	35	5	8	13	35	52	23
14	FC Jeunesse Canach	26	1	3	9	5	22	2	3	8	11	23	3	6	17	16	45	15

European qualification 2015/16

Champion: CS Fola Esch (second qualifying round)

Cup winner: FC Differdange 03 (first qualifying round)
F91 Dudelange (first qualifying round)
FC Progrès Niederkorn (first qualifying round)

Top scorer	Sanel Ibrahimović (Jeunesse Esch), 21 goals
Relegated clubs	FC Jeunesse Canach, US Hostert, UN Käerjéng 97
Promoted clubs	FC RM Hamm Benfica, Racing FC Union Lëtzebuerg, FC Una Strassen
Cup final	FC Differdange 03 1-1 F91 Dudelange (aet; 3-2 on pens)

Team of the season
(4-4-2)

Coach: Strasser (Fola)

Weber (Differdange)

Jans (Fola) Rigo (Progrès) Prempeh (Dudelange) Jänisch (Differdange)

Todorovic (Jeunesse Esch) Ronny (Fola) Peters (Grevenmacher) Cassan (Progrès)

Lascak (Rosport) Ibrahimović (Jeunesse Esch)

Player of the season

Sanel Ibrahimović
(AS Jeunesse Esch)

Jeunesse, the country's 28-time champions, had to bow once again to the superiority of their local rivals CS Fola Esch in 2014/15, but they did boast the National Division's top scorer for the second season running, Ibrahimović repeating his feat of the previous campaign with 21 goals – one fewer than his winning tally in 2013/14 but six more than any other player managed. The 27-year-old Bosnian, who also topped the charts with FC Wiltz 71 in 2010/11, left Jeunesse for F91 Dudelange in the summer.

Newcomer of the season

David Turpel
(F91 Dudelange)

Signed in the summer of 2014 from FC Etzella Ettelbruck, Turpel made a big breakthrough in 2014/15 for both his new club, Dudelange, and the Luxembourg national side. The lively forward scored seven goals in Dudelange's National Division title challenge and another in the cup semi-final against ex-club Etzella. He also appeared in five of his country's opening six UEFA EURO 2016 qualifiers, the highlight of which was an expertly taken goal to give Luxembourg the lead away to FYR Macedonia.

NATIONAL TEAM

Top five all-time caps
Jeff Strasser (98); René Peters (92); Eric Hoffmann & Carlo Weis (88); **Mario Mutsch** (80)

Top five all-time goals
Léon Mart (16); Gusty Kemp (15); Camille Libar (14); Nicolas Kettel (13); François Müller (12)

Results 2014/15

08/09/14	Belarus (ECQ)	H	Luxembourg	D	1-1	*Gerson (42)*
09/10/14	FYR Macedonia (ECQ)	A	Skopje	L	2-3	*Bensi (39), Turpel (44)*
12/10/14	Spain (ECQ)	H	Luxembourg	L	0-4	
15/11/14	Ukraine (ECQ)	H	Luxembourg	L	0-3	
27/03/15	Slovakia (ECQ)	A	Zilina	L	0-3	
31/03/15	Turkey	H	Luxembourg	L	1-2	*Mutsch (31)*
09/06/15	Moldova	H	Luxembourg	D	0-0	
14/06/15	Ukraine (ECQ)	A	Lviv	L	0-3	

Appearances 2014/15

Coach: Luc Holtz	14/06/69		BLR	MKD	ESP	UKR	SVK	Tur	Mda	UKR	Caps	Goals
Jonathan Joubert	12/09/79	Dudelange	G	G	G	G	G	G	G	G	77	-
Laurent Jans	05/08/92	Fola	D	D	D	D	D	D	D	D	22	-
Tom Schnell	08/10/85	Dudelange	D			D	D	D	D	D	45	-
Chris Philipps	08/03/94	Metz (FRA)	D	D	D		D	M74	M63	s77	24	-
Mathias Jänisch	27/08/90	Differdange	D	D	D	D			D27		41	1
Lars Gerson	05/02/90	Norrköping (SWE)/Sundsvall (SWE)	M	M	M	M	M	M	s63	M	45	3
Dwayn Holter	15/06/95	Greuther Fürth (GER)	M77	s63	M	M	M51		M46	M77	9	-
Christopher Martins	19/02/97	Lyon (FRA)	M	M	M61	M53			M46		5	-
Daniel Da Mota	11/09/85	Dudelange	M67	M63	M75	s53	s51	M76	A46	M71	63	4
Stefano Bensi	11/08/88	Fola	M	M75	A	M63	M78		A63	s52	28	4
David Turpel	19/10/92	Dudelange	A63	A70	s61	A76			s46	A52	15	1
Antonio Luisi	07/10/94	Differdange	s63								6	-
Tom Laterza	09/05/92	Fola	s67	s75			s78	s76			32	-
Ben Payal	08/09/88	Fola	s77		s75		s64	M	s46	M	65	-
Maxime Chanot	21/11/89	Kortrijk (BEL)		D		D	D	D	D	D	12	1
Mario Mutsch	03/09/84	St Gallen (SUI)		M	M86	M	M	M	A	M	80	3
Maurice Deville	31/07/92	Kaiserslautern (GER)		s70	s86	s76	M64	s74	s63	s71	22	3
Aurélien Joachim	10/08/86	CSKA Sofia (BUL)				s63	A	A			53	7
Kevin Malget	15/01/91	Dudelange						D	s27	D	6	-
Luca Duriatti	11/02/98	Swift							s46		1	-

LUXEMBOURG

EUROPE

F91 Dudelange

Second qualifying round - PFC Ludogorets Razgrad (BUL)
A 0-4
Joubert, Moreira, Ney, Schnell, Karapetyan (Turpel 78), Benzouien, Pedro, Sylla (Malget 88), Prempeh, Schulz (Stélvio 52), Ben Ajiba. Coach: Sébastian Grandjean (BEL)
H 1-1 *Turpel (81)*
Joubert, Moreira, Ney, Turpel (Schulz 82), Schnell, Benzouien (Malget 68), Pedro, Sylla (Karapetyan 60), Stélvio, Prempeh, Ben Ajiba. Coach: Sébastian Grandjean (BEL)

FC Differdange 03

First qualifying round - FK Atlantas (LTU)
H 1-0 *Er Rafik (87)*
Weber, Martin, May , Pedro Ribeiro (Caron 68), Er Rafik, Bettmer (Kettenmeyer 64), Jänisch, Lebresne, Franzoni, Luisi (Méligner 78), Caillet. Coach: Marc Thomé (LUX)
A 1-3 *Caillet (81)*
Weber, Martin, Rodrigues (Bukvic 21), Pedro Ribeiro (Luisi 70), Er Rafik, Caron, Bettmer, Jänisch, Lebresne (Artur Abreu 90), Franzoni, Caillet. Coach: Marc Thomé (LUX)
Red card: Martin 19

CS Fola Esch

First qualifying round - IFK Göteborg (SWE)
A 0-0
Hym, Keita, Payal, Hornuss (Klapp 83), Hadji, Rani (Skrijelj 88), Jans, Laterza (Lukic 77), Kirch, Ronny, Klein. Coach: Cyril Serredszum (FRA)
H 0-2
Hym, Keita, Payal (Dallevedove 81), Skrijelj (Françoise 64), Hornuss (Lukic 81), Hadji, Rani, Jans, Laterza, Ronny, Klein. Coach: Jeff Strasser (LUX)

AS Jeunesse Esch

First qualifying round - Dundalk FC (IRL)
H 0-2
Oberweis, Kintziger, Vitali, Hoffmann, Portier, Zydko (Albanese 67), Corral, Ibrahimović, Mélisse (De Sousa 81), Dragovic (Todorovic 46), Martins. Coach: Dan Theis (LUX)
A 1-3 *Zydko (55)*
Oberweis, Kintziger, Vitali, Hoffmann, Portier, Zydko (Agovic 78), Corral (Albanese 46), Ibrahimović, Mélisse, Todorovic (Delgado 46), Martins. Coach: Dan Theis (LUX)

DOMESTIC LEAGUE CLUB-BY-CLUB

FC Differdange 03

2003 • Parc des Sports (1,800) • fcd03.lu
Major honours
Luxembourg Cup (4) 2010, 2011, 2014, 2015
Coach: Marc Thomé

2014
03/08	a	Jeunesse Esch	D 3-3	*Franzoni (p), Bettmer 2*
10/08	a	Etzella	W 2-1	*Luisi 2*
17/08	a	Grevenmacher	D 0-0	
24/08	h	Dudelange	D 1-1	*Jänisch*
28/08	a	Käerjéng	W 3-1	*Luisi, Er Rafik 2*
14/09	a	Progrès	W 3-1	*Er Rafik, Pedro Ribeiro, Caron*
21/09	a	Rumelange	W 2-1	*Lebresne, Luisi*
28/09	h	Fola	D 1-1	*Jänisch*
02/10	a	Jeunesse Canach	W 2-1	*Caron (p), Er Rafik*
19/10	h	Wiltz	W 3-0	*(w/o; original result 2-1 Luisi, Er Rafik)*
26/10	a	Hostert	L 1-2	*Caron*
02/11	h	Mondorf-les-Bains	W 3-2	*Rodrigues 2, Franzoni (p)*
23/11	h	Rosport	W 3-2	*Pedro Ribeiro, Er Rafik, Luisi*

2015
22/02	a	Etzella	W 2-1	*Caron, Siebenaler*
01/03	h	Grevenmacher	D 1-1	*Siebenaler*
08/03	a	Dudelange	L 1-2	*Franzoni (p)*
15/03	h	Käerjéng	W 5-0	*Vilmain 2, Er Rafik, Yéyé, Artur Abreu*
18/03	h	Progrès	W 2-1	*og (Rigo), Er Rafik*
08/04	h	Rumelange	W 2-1	*Yéyé, Luisi*
12/04	h	Fola	W 3-2	*Yéyé 2, Er Rafik*
19/04	h	Jeunesse Canach	W 2-1	*Pedro Ribeiro, Caron*
26/04	a	Wiltz	L 1-2	*Franzoni*
03/05	h	Hostert	W 6-1	*Luisi 2, Sinani 2, Bettmer, Caron*
10/05	a	Mondorf-les-Bains	W 2-1	*Caron, Luisi*
17/05	a	Rosport	W 4-0	*Er Rafik, Caron, Luisi, Vilmain*
23/05	h	Jeunesse Esch	W 3-2	*Caron, Sinani, Er Rafik*

Name	Nat	DoB	Pos	Aps	(s)	Gls
Artur Abreu	POR	11/08/94	A	2	(12)	1
Gilles Bettmer		31/03/89	M	16	(5)	3
Ante Bukvic		14/11/87	D	9	(1)	
Jean-Philippe Caillet	FRA	24/06/77	D	12	(1)	
Gauthier Caron	FRA	27/12/89	A	24		9
Omar Er Rafik	FRA	07/01/86	M	25		11
Geoffrey Franzoni	FRA	18/02/91	D	22	(1)	4
Mathias Jänisch		27/08/90	D	21	(1)	2
Michel Kettenmeyer		07/02/89	M	1	(3)	
Philippe Lebresne	FRA	09/07/78	M	13	(10)	1
Antonio Luisi		07/10/94	A	20	(4)	11
Mehdi Martin	FRA	11/01/90	D	14	(1)	
Andy May		02/09/89	M	18	(5)	
Jérémy Méligner	FRA	11/06/91	M	5	(10)	
Pedro Ribeiro	POR	07/01/89	M	17	(2)	3
André Rodrigues		06/12/87	D	12	(4)	2
Tom Siebenaler		28/09/90	D	17	(1)	2
Dejvid Sinani	ALB	02/04/93	M	3	(5)	3
Aldin Skenderovic		28/06/97	M		(1)	
Jérémy Vilmain	FRA	28/08/90	M	3	(3)	3
Julien Weber	FRA	12/10/85	G	26		
Jordan Yéyé	FRA	02/11/88	A	6		4

F91 Dudelange

1991 • Jos Nosbaum (4,500) • f91.lu

Major honours
Luxembourg League (11) 2000, 2001, 2002, 2005, 2006, 2007, 2008, 2009, 2011, 2012, 2014; Luxembourg Cup (5) 2004, 2006, 2007, 2009, 2012

Coach: Sébastien Grandjean (BEL); (11/05/15) (Guy Hellers)

2014

03/08	h	Wiltz	W 3-0	Benzouien 2, Karapetyan
09/08	a	Hostert	W 4-1	Karapetyan 3, Kerić
17/08	h	Mondorf-les-Bains	D 0-0	
24/08	a	Differdange	D 1-1	Karapetyan
28/08	h	Jeunesse Esch	D 2-2	Betorangal, Turpel
14/09	a	Etzella	D 0-0	
21/09	h	Grevenmacher	W 5-0	Karapetyan 2, Laurienté, Turpel 2
28/09	a	Rosport	W 2-1	Karapetyan 2
02/10	a	Käerjéng	W 5-0	Stélvio, Karapetyan, Kerić 3
19/10	h	Progrès	W 1-0	Stélvio
26/10	a	Rumelange	D 1-1	Ben Ajiba (p)
02/11	h	Fola	L 0-2	
23/11	a	Jeunesse Canach	D 0-0	

2015

22/02	h	Hostert	W 3-1	Karapetyan, Idazza, Kerić
01/03	a	Mondorf-les-Bains	W 5-0	Ben Ajiba, Karapetyan, Kerić, Turpel, og (Mutuale)
08/03	h	Differdange	W 2-1	Turpel, Kerić
13/03	a	Jeunesse Esch	W 4-0	Turpel 2, Jahier, Kerić
19/03	h	Etzella	W 2-0	Jahier, De Sousa
08/04	a	Grevenmacher	W 2-0	Karapetyan, Da Mota
12/04	h	Rosport	W 4-0	Da Mota, Deligny, Jahier, Karapetyan
19/04	h	Käerjéng	L 2-3	Benzouien, Ben Ajiba (p)
26/04	a	Progrès	W 2-1	Da Mota, Karapetyan
03/05	h	Rumelange	W 2-0	Da Mota, Stélvio
10/05	a	Fola	L 0-3	(w/o; original result 0-1)
17/05	h	Jeunesse Canach	W 3-0	Pedro, Teixeira Pinto, Ben Ajiba
23/05	a	Wiltz	L 0-3	

Name	Nat	DoB	Pos	Aps	(s)	Gls
Yassine Ben Ajiba	MAR	01/11/84	M	17	(5)	4
Sofian Benzouien	BEL	11/08/86	M	8	(3)	3
Morgan Betorangal	FRA	25/08/88	D	7	(1)	1
Michaël Clepkens	BEL	30/01/86	G	4		
Daniel Da Mota		11/09/85	A	11	(7)	4
Raphaël De Sousa		05/06/93	M	12	(3)	1
Dylan Deligny	FRA	03/04/93	M	5	(2)	1
Saïd Idazza	MAR	25/04/89	A	2	(2)	1
Julien Jahier	FRA	28/11/80	A	5	(2)	3
Jonathan Joubert		12/09/79	G	22		
Alexander Karapetyan	ARM	23/12/87	A	18	(6)	15
Andrej Kerić	CRO	11/02/86	A	10	(9)	8
Alexandre Laurienté	FRA	19/11/89	M	18		1
Filipe Macedo Gonçalves	POR	10/06/95	M		(2)	
Kevin Malget		15/01/91	D	6	(4)	
Tony Mastrangelo		01/09/94	M	1	(1)	
Donovan Maury	BEL	08/05/81	D	16		
Youssef Mokhtari	MAR	05/03/79	M		(3)	
Clayton de Sousa Moreira		24/02/88	D	13	(2)	
Kevin Nakache	FRA	05/04/89	M	7	(1)	
Romain Ney	FRA	06/01/92	D	12	(2)	
Joël Pedro		10/04/92	M	17	(3)	1
Jerry Prempeh	FRA	29/12/88	D	24		
Tom Schnell		08/10/85	D	17		
Gustav Schulz	GER	27/06/85	M	7	(1)	
Stélvio	ANG	24/01/89	M	15	(3)	3
Oumar Sylla	FRA	11/09/88	M		(1)	
Patrik Teixeira Pinto		10/05/96	M	1	(3)	1
David Turpel		19/10/92	A	11	(11)	7
Lehit Zeghdane	FRA	03/10/77	D		(1)	

FC Etzella Ettelbruck

1917 • Stade du Centre Sportif Deich (2,024) • fc-etzella.lu

Major honours
Luxembourg Cup (1) 2001

Coach: Niki Wagner (GER)

2014

03/08	h	Mondorf-les-Bains	W 3-0	Frederico 2, Holtz
10/08	a	Differdange	L 1-2	Jurina
17/08	h	Jeunesse Esch	L 0-3	
24/08	a	Rosport	L 1-4	Mesec
30/08	a	Grevenmacher	W 2-0	Frederico, Augusto
14/09	h	Dudelange	D 0-0	
21/09	a	Käerjéng	W 3-2	Bruno Matias 2, Mesec
28/09	h	Progrès	L 2-3	Mesec, Bruno Matias
02/10	a	Rumelange	D 0-0	
19/10	h	Fola	L 0-3	
26/10	a	Jeunesse Canach	W 4-1	Nîlton (p), Augusto 2, Mesec
02/11	h	Wiltz	W 2-1	Nîlton, Jurina
23/11	a	Hostert	W 2-1	Jurina, Mesec

2015

22/02	h	Differdange	L 1-2	Augusto
01/03	a	Jeunesse Esch	L 1-5	Ožvald
08/03	h	Rosport	D 1-1	Jurina
15/03	h	Grevenmacher	L 2-3	Holtz (p), Agovic
19/03	a	Dudelange	L 0-2	
08/04	h	Käerjéng	L 0-3	
12/04	a	Progrès	L 0-3	
19/04	h	Rumelange	W 1-0	Augusto
25/04	h	Fola	L 1-2	Jurina
03/05	a	Jeunesse Canach	W 4-0	Nîlton, Jurina, Augusto, Frederico
10/05	a	Wiltz	L 1-3	og (Doyennel)
17/05	h	Hostert	W 3-2	Nîlton (p), Augusto, Holtz
23/05	a	Mondorf-les-Bains	L 1-4	Jurina

Name	Nat	DoB	Pos	Aps	(s)	Gls
Alexander Adrian	GER	28/08/84	M	18		
Ernest Agovic		09/02/97	M	1	(6)	1
André Gonçalves	POR	26/09/88	D	12	(6)	
François Augusto		02/06/88	A	19	(5)	7
André Bastos Silva		18/03/91	M	15	(4)	
Felix Börner		14/03/96	D	2	(4)	
Bruno Matias	POR	04/03/89	M	8	(4)	3
Léo Clement		29/11/88	G	22		
David Da Mota		12/05/89	M	18	(3)	
Dany Fernandes	POR	09/05/94	M	6	(10)	
Frederico	POR	28/12/92	M	16	(4)	4
Philippe Hahm		13/01/90	G	3		
Kevin Holtz		06/03/93	M	16	(5)	3
Marin Jurina	CRO	26/11/93	A	24		7
Pol Klopp		18/05/97	G	1		
Johannes Kühne	GER	02/05/88	D	22		
Vedran Mesec	CRO	20/02/88	A	17		5
Killien Neves		01/04/96	M		(1)	
Lex Nicolay		27/03/97	A	10	(3)	
Nîlton	CPV	19/01/79	D	20		4
Dorjan Ožvald	CRO	22/09/87	M	14		1
Bartłomiej Pietrasik	POL	25/05/84	D	12	(1)	
Jader Soares		19/08/96	A	3	(4)	
Frédéric Thill		15/01/96	A	10	(11)	
Nicolas Valletta		28/03/94	D		(4)	

CS Fola Esch

1906 • Emile Mayrisch (6,000) • fola.lu

Major honours
Luxembourg League (7) 1918, 1920, 1922, 1924, 1930, 2013, 2015; Luxembourg Cup (3) 1923, 1924, 1955

Coach: Jeff Strasser

2014

03/08	a	Progrès	L 0-1	
10/08	h	Rumelange	W 7-1	Laterza, Dallevedove 2, Hadji, Françoise, Ronny 2
17/08	h	Rosport	W 4-2	Dallevedove 2, Françoise, Laterza
24/08	a	Jeunesse Canach	W 1-0	Laterza
28/08	h	Wiltz	W 2-1	Hadji, Ronny (p)
14/09	a	Hostert	D 1-1	Dallevedove
21/09	h	Mondorf-les-Bains	W 4-1	Hadji, Bensi, Dallevedove, Laterza
27/09	a	Differdange	D 1-1	Bensi (p)
02/10	a	Jeunesse Esch	D 1-1	Bensi
19/10	a	Etzella	W 3-0	Jans, Bensi, Hornuss
26/10	a	Grevenmacher	W 3-0	Bensi, Hornuss, Lukic
02/11	a	Dudelange	W 2-0	Hornuss, Ronny (p)
23/11	a	Käerjéng	W 4-0	Françoise, Hadji 2, og (Brix)

2015

22/02	a	Rumelange	W 1-0	Françoise
01/03	a	Rosport	W 5-1	Françoise, Hadji 3, Lukic
08/03	h	Jeunesse Canach	W 1-0	Dallevedove
15/03	a	Wiltz	D 1-1	Ronny
19/03	h	Hostert	W 3-1	Ronny, Lukic, Françoise
08/04	a	Mondorf-les-Bains	W 1-0	Hadji
12/04	h	Differdange	L 2-3	Hadji, Lukic
19/04	a	Jeunesse Esch	W 1-0	Dallevedove
25/04	a	Etzella	W 2-1	Hadji, Ronny
03/05	h	Grevenmacher	W 5-1	Kirch 2, Laterza 2, Dallevedove
10/05	h	Dudelange	W 3-0	(w/o; original result 1-0 Hornuss)
17/05	a	Käerjéng	W 3-0	Françoise, Lukic 2
23/05	h	Progrès	L 2-4	Skrijelj, Hadji

Name	Nat	DoB	Pos	Aps	(s)	Gls
Dany Albuquerque		14/10/88	M		(1)	
Stefano Bensi		11/08/88	A	10	(5)	5
Billy Bernard		09/04/91	D	15	(2)	
Carlitos	ESP	11/04/89	A	6	(2)	
Jakob Dallevedove	GER	21/11/87	M	21	(4)	9
Emmanuel Françoise	FRA	07/06/82	M	18	(3)	7
Samir Hadji	FRA	12/09/89	D	24	(2)	12
Julien Hornuss	FRA	01/01/87	A	16	(9)	4
Thomas Hym	FRA	29/08/87	G	24		
Laurent Jans		05/08/92	D	16	(2)	1
Losseni Keita	FRA	01/04/84	D	9	(3)	
Mehdi Kirch	FRA	27/01/90	D	24		2
Ryan Klapp		10/01/93	M	3	(14)	
Julien Klein	FRA	07/04/87	M	20	(2)	
Tom Laterza		09/05/92	M	15	(3)	6
Zarko Lukic		22/05/83	A	3	(15)	6
Enes Mahmutovic		22/05/97	M		(1)	
Erwan Martin	FRA	06/01/93	D	10		
Ben Payal		08/09/88	M	21	(2)	
Christophe Pazos	ESP	19/05/90	M	1	(2)	
Steve Peiffer		01/09/92	G	2	(1)	
Ronny	CPV	07/12/78	M	24	(1)	7
Admir Skrijelj		03/06/92	M	4	(3)	1

LUXEMBOURG

CS Grevenmacher

1909 • Op Flohr (4,000) • csg.lu
Major honours
Luxembourg League (1) 2003; Luxembourg Cup (4) 1995, 1998, 2003, 2008
Coach: Jacques Muller

2014
03/08	h	Hostert	W 2-1	*Kitenge, Almeida*
10/08	a	Mondorf-les-Bains	W 2-1	*Almeida, Feltes*
17/08	h	Differdange	D 0-0	
22/08	a	Jeunesse Esch	L 2-4	*Feltes, Brzyski*
30/08	h	Etzella	L 0-2	
15/09	a	Rosport	L 0-2	
21/09	a	Dudelange	L 0-5	
28/09	h	Käerjéng	L 0-2	
03/10	a	Progrès	L 0-6	
19/10	h	Rumelange	L 0-2	
26/10	a	Fola	L 0-3	
02/11	h	Jeunesse Canach	W 1-0	*Magalhaes*
23/11	a	Wiltz	L 0-1	

2015
22/02	h	Mondorf-les-Bains	D 0-0	
01/03	a	Differdange	D 1-1	*Almeida*
05/03	h	Jeunesse Esch	W 1-0	*Almeida*
15/03	a	Etzella	W 3-2	*Gaspar, Martino, Steinmetz*
19/03	h	Rosport	D 2-2	*Dervisevic, Magalhaes*
08/04	h	Dudelange	L 0-2	
12/04	a	Käerjéng	W 2-1	*Bechtold, Brzyski*
19/04	h	Progrès	L 1-3	*Wang*
26/04	a	Rumelange	W 3-0	*Wang, Peters, Almeida*
03/05	h	Fola	L 1-5	*Wang*
10/05	a	Jeunesse Canach	W 3-0	*Heinz, Steinmetz, Martino*
17/05	h	Wiltz	L 0-3	
23/05	a	Hostert	D 0-0	

Name	Nat	DoB	Pos	Aps	(s)	Gls
Gonçalo Almeida		26/11/90	A	16	(2)	5
Michel Bechtold		01/07/95	M	23		1
Dariusz Brzyski	POL	06/09/86	D	11	(4)	2
Din Dervisevic		19/05/91	M	18	(4)	1
Gilles Feltes		06/12/95	D	18		2
Florian Gaspar	GER	07/07/87	A	13	(3)	1
Keiven Gonçalves Fernandes	CPV	26/08/86	M		(2)	
Ben Guettai		11/05/96	M	6	(8)	
Tim Heinz		05/02/84	D	17		1
Patrick Herres	GER	11/10/89	M	1	(3)	
Joël Kitenge		12/11/87	A	13	(5)	1
Joël Magalhaes		22/04/91	M	17	(6)	2
Massimo Martino		18/09/90	D	15	(6)	2
René Peters		15/06/81	M	21		1
Adrien Pfeiffer		04/02/97	M	1		
David Rowley	AUS	06/02/90	M	2	(4)	
Arnaud Schaab	FRA	03/09/90	G	26		
Inas Sehovic		18/07/94	D	8	(6)	
Vic Speller		03/07/93	D	15	(3)	
Damian Steinmetz		04/02/95	A	5	(14)	2
Mathieu Trierweiler		15/05/96	D	20	(4)	
Juncai Wang		05/04/90	M	20		3

US Hostert

1946 • Jos Becker (1,500) • ushostert.lu
Coach: Manuel Peixoto (FRA);
(28/04/15) Laurent Pellegrino (FRA)

2014
03/08	a	Grevenmacher	L 1-2	*Pereira*
09/08	h	Dudelange	L 1-4	*Battaglia*
17/08	a	Käerjéng	L 0-2	
24/08	h	Progrès	L 1-2	*Sözen*
28/08	a	Rumelange	D 2-2	*Pintar 2*
14/09	h	Fola	D 1-1	*Sözen*
21/09	a	Jeunesse Canach	L 0-1	
28/09	h	Wiltz	W 2-1	*Adler 2 (2p)*
05/10	h	Rosport	W 2-1	*Adler, Dešević*
19/10	a	Mondorf-les-Bains	D 1-1	*Sözen*
26/10	h	Differdange	W 2-1	*Adler, Sözen*
02/11	a	Jeunesse Esch	D 2-2	*Adler 2*
23/11	h	Etzella	L 1-2	*Mura*

2015
22/02	a	Dudelange	L 1-3	*Mura*
01/03	h	Käerjéng	W 3-0	*Battaglia 2, Sözen*
08/03	h	Progrès	L 2-3	*Nomel 2 (1p)*
15/03	h	Rumelange	D 1-1	*Nomel (p)*
19/03	h	Fola	L 1-3	*Adler (p)*
08/04	h	Jeunesse Canach	D 2-2	*Battaglia, Pintar*
12/04	h	Wiltz	D 3-3	*Adler (p), San Andres, Battaglia*
19/04	a	Rosport	L 1-4	*Sözen*
26/04	h	Mondorf-les-Bains	W 2-1	*Nomel, Mura*
03/05	a	Differdange	L 1-6	*Sözen*
10/05	a	Jeunesse Esch	L 0-1	
17/05	a	Etzella	L 2-3	*Sözen, Adler (p)*
23/05	h	Grevenmacher	D 0-0	

Name	Nat	DoB	Pos	Aps	(s)	Gls
Grégory Adler	FRA	27/04/89	M	24		9
Elvir Adrovic		16/11/94	M		(4)	
Thomas Battaglia	FRA	05/08/92	D	25	(1)	5
Tom Birden		26/04/95	D	7	(7)	
Kris D'Exelle		13/07/89	A	1	(3)	
Patrick Da Mota		02/12/86	D	21	(1)	
Admir Dešević	MNE	08/05/92	M	20	(1)	1
Kelvin Fortes		30/09/95	A	1	(11)	
Thomas Fullenwarth	FRA	27/01/87	D	22		
Jonathan Furst	FRA	23/03/87	M	21		
João Freitas	POR	06/07/96	A		(7)	
João Silva	POR	02/12/87	A		(1)	
Demir Koljenovic		09/05/90	D	4	(4)	
Jean-Paul Makasso	CMR	05/11/93	M	16		
Glenn Marques da Costa		10/06/94	G	3		
Stimbol Monteiro		13/03/94	D	9	(2)	
Guillaume Mura	FRA	09/01/86	D	24		3
Jean-Paul Nomel	CIV	23/06/88	A	8	(4)	4
Daniel Pereira		28/12/87	M	6	(4)	1
Johnny Pintar	FRA	22/05/87	A	11	(6)	3
Marc Pleimling		11/06/89	G	23		
Grégory San Andres	FRA	04/01/85	D	23		1
Burak Sözen	GER	05/06/93	A	17	(5)	8

FC Jeunesse Canach

1957 • Stade rue de Lenningen (1,000) • fccanach.lu
Coach: Patrick Maurer

2014
03/08	a	Käerjéng	W 2-1	*Borgniet, Mukendi*
10/08	h	Progrès	L 1-2	*Mukendi*
17/08	a	Rumelange	L 0-1	
24/08	h	Fola	L 0-1	
31/08	h	Rosport	D 0-0	
14/09	a	Wiltz	D 1-1	*Barbosa*
21/09	h	Hostert	W 1-0	*Dimitri*
28/09	a	Mondorf-les-Bains	W 2-1	*Pedro Ferro 2*
02/10	h	Differdange	L 1-2	*Pedro Ferro*
19/10	a	Jeunesse Esch	L 2-4	*Pedro Ferro 2*
26/10	h	Etzella	L 1-4	*Pedro Ferro*
02/11	a	Grevenmacher	L 0-1	
23/11	h	Dudelange	D 0-0	

2015
22/02	a	Progrès	L 0-1	
27/02	h	Rumelange	L 0-1	
08/03	a	Fola	L 0-1	
15/03	a	Rosport	D 1-1	*Selimović*
22/03	h	Wiltz	L 0-3	*(w/o; original result 3-2 Mukendi, Barbosa (p), Selimović)*
08/04	a	Hostert	D 2-2	*Dimitri, Barbosa (p)*
12/04	h	Mondorf-les-Bains	L 0-1	
19/04	a	Differdange	L 1-2	*Mukendi*
25/04	h	Jeunesse Esch	D 0-0	
03/05	a	Etzella	L 0-4	
10/05	h	Grevenmacher	L 0-3	
17/05	a	Dudelange	L 0-3	
23/05	h	Käerjéng	L 1-5	*Pedro Ferro*

Name	Nat	DoB	Pos	Aps	(s)	Gls
George Amartey	GER	22/02/89	A	4		
Augusto Cravo	BRA	06/09/80	M	7	(2)	
Michael Barbosa	POR	31/10/84	M	17	(2)	3
Mehdi Boncoeur	FRA	24/06/90	M	3	(6)	
François Borgniet	FRA	02/08/90	M	23		1
Cadabra	CPV	26/06/84	G	25		
Nedim Cirikovic		13/06/88	A		(5)	
Patricio Da Silva	POR	24/01/93	M		(1)	
Aldi Dervisevic		19/08/89	D	13	(4)	
Dimitri	BRA	18/06/79	D	20		2
Francesco Gagliotti	ITA	16/03/91	M		(1)	
Laurent Hoeser		20/10/86	M	2	(4)	
Eric Indenge	BEL	16/05/93	A	7	(2)	
João Almeida	POR	04/01/80	G	1		
Kalú	CPV	08/09/84	M		(1)	
Giannis Kazoukas	GRE	21/04/91	A	1	(3)	
Thibault Maquart	BEL	31/08/92	D	15	(4)	
Marcão	BRA	19/07/76	M	8		
Marco Semedo	POR	08/10/87	D	21		
Tom Maurer		25/09/97	A	2	(11)	
Olivier Mukendi	BEL	08/06/91	A	16	(1)	4
Mickaël Negi	FRA	22/03/84	D	17	(2)	
Oséias	BRA	13/06/72	A		(2)	
Pedro Ferro	POR	21/07/87	A	21		7
Rodrigão Ribeiro	BRA	18/07/78	D	19		
Christian Rodrigues		17/12/79	M	3		
Fahret Selimović	BIH	26/09/93	A	16	(8)	2
David Teixeira Caçador		17/12/86	D	14	(7)	
Valdino Borges	CPV	01/10/80	M	4	(2)	
Emile Weber		16/05/93	M		(1)	
Pieter Weirig		17/05/91	D	7	(3)	

AS Jeunesse Esch

1907 • Stade de la Frontière (7,000) • jeunesse-esch.lu

Major honours
Luxembourg League (28) 1921, 1937, 1951, 1954, 1958, 1959, 1960, 1963, 1967, 1968, 1970, 1973, 1974, 1975, 1976, 1977, 1980, 1983, 1985, 1987, 1988, 1995, 1996, 1997, 1998, 1999, 2004, 2010; Luxembourg Cup (13) 1935, 1937, 1946, 1954, 1973, 1974, 1976, 1981, 1988, 1997, 1999, 2000, 2013
Coach: Dan Theis

2014

01/08	h	Differdange	D	3-3	Ibrahimović 2, Corral
10/08	a	Rosport	L	1-3	Zydko
17/08	a	Etzella	W	3-0	Todorovic, Ibrahimović, Portier
22/08	h	Grevenmacher	W	4-2	Albanese, Ibrahimović 2, Corral
28/08	a	Dudelange	D	2-2	Delgado, Ibrahimović
14/09	h	Käerjéng	W	2-0	Todorovic, Vitali
19/09	a	Progrès	D	2-2	Ibrahimović 2 (1p)
28/09	a	Rumelange	W	2-1	Vitali, Mélisse
02/10	a	Fola	D	1-1	Ibrahimović
19/10	h	Jeunesse Canach	W	4-2	Deidda, Ibrahimović 2, Albanese
26/10	a	Wiltz	D	0-0	
02/11	h	Hostert	D	2-2	Corral 2
23/11	a	Mondorf-les-Bains	L	1-2	Ibrahimović

2015

22/02	h	Rosport	W	2-1	Ibrahimović (p), Corral
01/03	h	Etzella	W	5-1	Ibrahimović 2, Mélisse, Deidda, Kintziger
05/03	a	Grevenmacher	L	0-1	
13/03	h	Dudelange	L	0-4	
22/03	h	Käerjéng	W	3-1	Deidda, Ibrahimović 2 (1p)
06/04	h	Progrès	D	2-2	og (Rigo), Mélisse
12/04	a	Rumelange	W	1-0	Ibrahimović (p)
19/04	h	Fola	L	0-1	
25/04	a	Jeunesse Canach	D	0-0	
01/05	h	Wiltz	W	2-0	Corral, Ibrahimović
10/05	a	Hostert	W	1-0	Mélisse
17/05	h	Mondorf-les-Bains	W	1-0	Ibrahimović
23/05	a	Differdange	L	2-3	Corral, Ibrahimović

Name	Nat	DoB	Pos	Aps	(s)	Gls
Denis Agović	MNE	12/07/93	M	1	(4)	
Mirko Albanese		04/09/89	M	12	(5)	2
Ken Corral		08/05/92	A	16	(7)	7
Aydine Correia		05/03/92	M	2	(1)	
David De Sousa		15/07/95	M	14	(8)	
Andrea Deidda		15/12/93	A	8	(10)	3
Ricardo Delgado		22/02/94	D	17	(3)	1
Frank Devas		06/03/94	G	1		
Nenad Dragovic		04/06/94	D	21	(2)	
Eric Hoffmann		21/06/84	D	17	(3)	
Sanel Ibrahimović	BIH	24/11/87	A	26		21
Kim Kintziger		02/04/87	D	17	(5)	1
Marvin Martins		17/02/95	D	3	(8)	
Bryan Mélisse	FRA	25/03/89	M	25		4
Hachem Mihoubi	ALG	30/08/86	M	1	(4)	
Marc Oberweis		06/11/82	G	25		
Adrien Portier	FRA	02/02/88	A	21		1
Milos Todorovic		18/08/95	M	23	(3)	2
Fabio Tonini	BEL	30/05/93	A		(5)	
Alexandre Vitali	FRA	17/01/89	D	12	(4)	2
Jonathan Zydko	FRA	12/01/84	M	24		1

UN Käerjéng 97

1997 • Käerjénger Dribbel (2,000) • un-kaerjeng.lu
Coach: Roland Schaack; (10/02/15) Angelo Fiorucci (ITA)

2014

03/08	h	Jeunesse Canach	L	1-2	Terzic
10/08	a	Wiltz	W	2-0	Alunni, Mota
17/08	h	Hostert	W	2-0	Pereira Fereira, Fiorani
24/08	a	Mondorf-les-Bains	L	2-3	N Ewert, Cunha da Fonseca
28/08	h	Differdange	L	1-3	og (Jänisch)
14/09	a	Jeunesse Esch	L	0-2	
21/09	h	Etzella	L	2-3	Alunni, Cunha da Fonseca
28/09	a	Grevenmacher	W	2-0	Marcolino Rodrigues, Cunha da Fonseca
02/10	h	Dudelange	L	0-5	
19/10	a	Rosport	D	0-0	
25/10	a	Progrès	L	0-3	
02/11	h	Rumelange	D	2-2	Alunni, Pereira Fereira
23/11	a	Fola	L	0-4	

2015

22/02	h	Wiltz	D	1-1	Abdullei
01/03	a	Hostert	L	0-3	
08/03	h	Mondorf-les-Bains	W	2-0	D Stumpf, og (Marques)
15/03	a	Differdange	L	0-5	
22/03	h	Jeunesse Esch	L	1-3	Abdullei
08/04	h	Etzella	W	3-0	Pereira Fereira, Abdullei, Alunni
12/04	h	Grevenmacher	L	1-2	Pereira Fereira
19/04	a	Dudelange	W	3-2	Do Rosario (p), T Ewert, Alunni
25/04	h	Rosport	L	0-1	
03/05	h	Progrès	W	2-1	Pereira Fereira, Fiorani
10/05	h	Rumelange	L	1-3	Abdullei
17/05	h	Fola	L	0-3	
23/05	a	Jeunesse Canach	W	5-1	Teixeira Soares, Alunni, Pereira Fereira, Abdullei 2

Name	Nat	DoB	Pos	Aps	(s)	Gls
Amodou Abdullei	NGA	20/12/87	A	8	(3)	6
Alessandro Alunni		19/12/91	A	19	(6)	6
Andrade	BRA	06/03/92	M	4	(7)	
Aleksandar Arsenovic		26/11/92	M		(3)	
Nabil Benhamza	FRA	22/08/88	M	21		
Johann Bernard	FRA	13/03/86	A	1	(6)	
Jérôme Brix		22/09/92	D	19		
Christophe Cunha da Fonseca		08/01/95	A	6	(3)	3
Yannick Dias da Graca		13/07/96	D	2	(1)	
Sébastien Do Rosario	FRA	12/01/84	D	21		1
Noé Ewert		24/02/97	D	18	(5)	1
Tim Ewert		25/10/95	M	1	(5)	1
Alessandro Fiorani		16/02/89	D	23		2
Fabien Heinz		30/07/98	M	3		
Pit Hess		17/01/92	D	16		
Luca Ivesic		07/04/96	G	4		
Sam Loes		25/04/94	M		(3)	
Jérôme Marcolino Rodrigues		27/03/89	D	9	(1)	1
André Mota		02/08/92	M	6	(9)	1
Cristiano Pereira Fereira		21/11/89	A	24	(2)	6
Alex Perrard		12/03/97	M		(3)	
Delvin Skenderovic		23/01/94	M	19	(3)	
Chris Stumpf		28/08/94	M	18	(6)	
Denis Stumpf		09/09/97	A	5	(1)	1
Sergio Teixeira Soares		03/01/92	M	4	(2)	1
Léo Terzic	FRA	24/03/95	A	13	(8)	1
Jérôme Winckel		20/12/85	G	22		

US Mondorf-les-Bains

1915 • John Grün (3,500) • usmondorf.lu
Coach: Arno Bonvini

2014

03/08	a	Etzella	L	0-3	
10/08	h	Grevenmacher	L	1-2	Mutuale
17/08	a	Dudelange	D	0-0	
24/08	h	Käerjéng	W	3-2	Mutuale, Hégué, Medri
29/08	a	Progrès	D	2-2	Nabli, Hégué
14/09	h	Rumelange	L	0-1	
21/09	a	Fola	L	1-4	Nabli
28/09	a	Jeunesse Canach	L	1-2	Mutuale
05/10	a	Wiltz	L	0-2	
19/10	h	Hostert	D	1-1	Di Gregorio
25/10	h	Rosport	W	1-0	Thonon
02/11	a	Differdange	L	2-3	Guerra, Nabli
23/11	h	Jeunesse Esch	W	2-1	Pjanić, Marques

2015

22/02	a	Grevenmacher	D	0-0	
01/03	h	Dudelange	L	0-5	
08/03	a	Käerjéng	L	0-2	
14/03	h	Progrès	W	1-0	Pjanić
22/03	a	Rumelange	D	1-1	Thonon (p)
08/04	h	Fola	L	0-1	
12/04	a	Jeunesse Canach	W	1-0	Thonon
19/04	h	Wiltz	W	3-1	Hégué, Nabli, Hamdi
26/04	a	Hostert	L	1-2	Hégué
03/05	a	Rosport	W	4-1	Pjanić, Mutuale (p), Haddadji, Nabli
10/05	h	Differdange	L	1-2	Mutuale
17/05	a	Jeunesse Esch	L	0-1	
23/05	h	Etzella	W	4-1	Nabli 3, Thonon

Name	Nat	DoB	Pos	Aps	(s)	Gls
Almin Babacic		16/01/84	M	9	(8)	
Suleimane Baio	GNB	12/08/83	A		(1)	
Joris Di Gregorio	FRA	04/09/82	A	4	(4)	1
Papa Aye Dione	SEN	08/03/86	D	16		
Yacine Ettabet	FRA	19/02/88	D	1		
Kevin Feiersinger	GER	02/02/92	A	1	(2)	
Keven Flohr		06/07/92	D	7		
Anthony Guerra	FRA	20/01/90	M	13	(10)	1
Ilies Haddadji	FRA	09/04/90	M	18	(3)	1
Steven Hamdi	FRA	17/02/92	A	1	(10)	1
Benjamin Hégué	FRA	16/03/89	A	15	(2)	4
Hugo Alves	POR	16/02/93	M		(2)	
Olivier Marques		21/03/92	M	14	(9)	1
Anthony Medri	FRA	20/04/89	A	14	(9)	1
Michael Monteiro		11/12/91	D	12	(1)	
Edis Muhić	BIH	10/08/93	D	4		
Yamukile Mutuale	FRA	25/08/87	D	23		5
Mohamed Nabli	TUN	27/05/85	A	21	(4)	8
Christophe Natanelic	FRA	28/05/78	D	8		
Tarek Nouidra	FRA	09/05/87	M	3		
Anel Pjanić	BIH	26/12/83	A	14	(5)	3
Alex Semedo Borges		22/08/89	D	23		
Bryan Simoes		28/09/95	D	7		
Códrio Soares		19/10/95	M	9	(7)	
Thibaut Thonon	FRA	05/02/87	M	23		4
Patrick Worré		01/10/84	G	26		

LUXEMBOURG

FC Progrès Niederkorn

1919 • Jos Haupert (4,000) • progres.lu
Major honours
*Luxembourg League (3) 1953, 1978, 1981;
Luxembourg Cup (4) 1933, 1945, 1977, 1978*
Coach: Olivier Ciancanelli

2014
03/08	h	Fola	W 1-0	*Rigo*
10/08	a	Jeunesse Canach	W 2-1	*Rougeaux, Thill*
17/08	h	Wiltz	W 2-0	*Cassan, Garos*
23/08	a	Hostert	W 2-1	*Rigo, Rougeaux*
29/08	h	Mondorf-les-Bains	D 2-2	*Menaï, Rougeaux*
14/09	a	Differdange	L 1-3	*Zimmer*
19/09	h	Jeunesse Esch	D 2-2	*Garos, Menaï*
28/09	a	Etzella	W 3-2	*Bossi, Cassan, Menaï*
03/10	h	Grevenmacher	W 6-0	*Cassan 2, Menaï 2, Bossi, David Soares*
19/10	a	Dudelange	L 0-1	
25/10	h	Käerjéng	W 3-0	*Menaï, Rougeaux 2*
02/11	a	Rosport	D 1-1	*Rougeaux*
23/11	a	Rumelange	W 4-2	*Garos, Menaï, Thill, Rougeaux*

2015
22/02	h	Jeunesse Canach	W 1-0	*Menaï*
01/03	a	Wiltz	D 0-0	
08/03	h	Hostert	W 3-2	*Bossi, Rougeaux, David Soares*
14/03	a	Mondorf-les-Bains	L 0-1	
18/03	h	Differdange	L 1-2	*Menaï*
06/04	a	Jeunesse Esch	D 2-2	*Bouzid, Rougeaux*
12/04	h	Etzella	W 3-0	*Menaï, Poinsignon, Rougeaux*
19/04	a	Grevenmacher	W 3-1	*Dog, Rigo, Poinsignon*
26/04	h	Dudelange	L 1-2	*Cassan*
03/05	a	Käerjéng	L 1-2	*Poinsignon*
10/05	h	Rosport	W 2-0	*Rougeaux, Ramdedović*
17/05	h	Rumelange	W 1-0	*Menaï*
23/05	a	Fola	W 4-2	*Poinsignon, Bouzid, Thill, Menaï*

Name	Nat	DoB	Pos	Aps	(s)	Gls
Paul Bossi		22/07/91	M	14	(12)	3
Ismaël Bouzid	ALG	21/07/83	D	7		2
Nelson Silva Cabral		24/09/87	D		(1)	
Olivier Cassan	FRA	01/06/84	M	23	(2)	5
Fabiano Castellani		11/05/89	G	23		
Yoann Dargenton	FRA	29/12/89	G	3	(1)	
David Soares	POR	20/02/91	D	21	(3)	2
Marco De Sousa		17/08/86	M	5	(7)	
Samuel Dog	FRA	13/02/85	M	8	(2)	1
Adrien Ferino	FRA	19/06/92	D	18	(1)	
Mickael Garos	FRA	10/05/88	M	25		3
Fabbro Kenzo		23/01/98	M		(1)	
Kevin Lefranc	FRA	01/03/86	A		(2)	
Tim Lehnen		17/06/86	D	21	(5)	
Hakim Menaï	FRA	27/03/86	A	21	(3)	12
Tarek Nouidra	FRA	09/05/87	M	4	(3)	
Valentin Poinsignon	FRA	23/03/94	D	13	(11)	4
Dzenid Ramdedović	MNE	25/02/92	M	19	(3)	1
Jonathan Rigo	FRA	16/09/87	D	25		3
Lévy Rougeaux	FRA	05/05/85	M	17	(7)	11
Anthony Sanches		12/05/94	M		(2)	
Sébastien Thill		29/12/93	M	18	(7)	3
Pierre Zimmer	FRA	12/01/90	D	1		1

US Rumelange

1908 • Stade Municipal (2,950) • usrumelange.lu
Major honours
Luxembourg Cup (2) 1968, 1975
Coach: Carlo Weis

2014
03/08	a	Rosport	L 1-2	*Pupovac*
10/08	a	Fola	L 1-7	*Tino Barbosa*
17/08	h	Jeunesse Canach	W 1-0	*Igor Pereira*
22/08	a	Wiltz	W 1-0	*Cabral*
28/08	h	Hostert	D 2-2	*Cabral, Thior*
14/09	a	Mondorf-les-Bains	W 1-0	*Cabral*
21/09	h	Differdange	L 1-2	*Tino Barbosa*
28/09	a	Jeunesse Esch	L 1-2	*Siebert*
02/10	h	Etzella	D 0-0	
19/10	a	Grevenmacher	W 2-0	*Tino Barbosa, Bryan Gomes*
26/10	h	Dudelange	D 1-1	*José Inácio*
02/11	a	Käerjéng	D 2-2	*Tino Barbosa, Lopes*
23/11	h	Progrès	L 2-4	*Lopes, Thior*

2015
22/02	h	Fola	L 0-1	
27/02	a	Jeunesse Canach	W 1-0	*Lopes*
08/03	h	Wiltz	W 4-0	*Bryan Gomes, Hugo Fernandes, Cabral 2 (1p)*
15/03	a	Hostert	D 1-1	*N'Ganvala*
22/03	h	Mondorf-les-Bains	D 1-1	*Hugo Fernandes*
04/04	a	Differdange	L 1-2	*Cabral*
12/04	h	Jeunesse Esch	L 0-1	
19/04	a	Etzella	L 0-1	
26/04	h	Grevenmacher	L 0-3	
03/05	a	Dudelange	L 0-2	
10/05	h	Käerjéng	W 3-1	*Tino Barbosa, Thior, Lopes*
17/05	a	Progrès	L 0-1	
23/05	h	Rosport	D 2-2	*Zingha, Hugo Fernandes*

Name	Nat	DoB	Pos	Aps	(s)	Gls
Bryan Gomes	POR	05/12/93	M	18	(8)	2
Cabral	POR	30/09/87	A	17	(3)	6
Quentin Depré	FRA	19/11/91	D	10	(1)	
Hugo Fernandes	POR	01/01/90	M	13		3
Igor Pereira	POR	06/07/87	A	24	(1)	1
Johnny Santos	POR	06/06/94	M	2	(4)	
José Inácio	POR	15/11/83	D	21		1
Kim Kleber		24/12/87	M	4	(4)	
Tony Lopes	FRA	04/11/81	A	18	(7)	4
Kevin Majerus		30/09/85	M	7	(5)	
Joël Marques	POR	30/09/85	M	1	(4)	
Grégory Molitor		12/03/80	M		(1)	
Djemel N'Ganvala	BEL	29/01/91	A	1	(4)	1
Romain Ollé-Nicolle	FRA	18/08/87	D	2	(1)	
Mike Post		16/03/93	A	13	(2)	
Nikola Pupovac	FRA	16/02/84	M	15	(6)	1
Rafael Rodrigues		16/02/89	D	21		
Charly Schinker		05/11/87	G	26		
Mateusz Siebert	POL	04/04/89	M	19	(2)	1
François Thior	FRA	11/02/85	D	26		3
Tino Barbosa	POR	06/05/92	A	9	(4)	5
Glodi Zingha		04/11/93	D	19	(1)	1

FC Victoria Rosport

1928 • Stade du Camping (1,500) • fcvictoriarosport.lu
**Coach: Claude Osweiler;
(31/10/14) Guy Reiter;
(25/01/15) Carlos Teixeira (POR)**

2014
03/08	h	Rumelange	W 2-1	*Lascak, Steinbach*
10/08	h	Jeunesse Esch	W 3-1	*Pedro dos Santos 2, Lascak*
17/08	a	Fola	L 2-4	*Lascak (p), Ramiro Valente*
24/08	a	Etzella	W 4-1	*Vogel, Lascak, Förg, Gaspar*
31/08	a	Jeunesse Canach	D 0-0	
15/09	h	Grevenmacher	W 2-0	*Pedro dos Santos, Gaspar*
21/09	a	Wiltz	W 2-1	*Förg, Lascak*
28/09	h	Dudelange	L 1-2	*Lascak*
05/10	a	Hostert	L 1-2	*Lascak*
19/10	h	Käerjéng	D 0-0	
25/10	a	Mondorf-les-Bains	L 0-1	
02/11	h	Progrès	D 1-1	*Adams*
23/11	a	Differdange	L 2-3	*Lascak 2 (1p)*

2015
22/02	a	Jeunesse Esch	L 1-2	*Lascak*
01/03	h	Fola	L 1-5	*Förg*
08/03	a	Etzella	D 1-1	*Steinbach (p)*
15/03	a	Jeunesse Canach	D 1-1	*Lascak (p)*
19/03	a	Grevenmacher	D 2-2	*Jakob, Förg*
08/04	h	Wiltz	W 2-1	*Lascak, Förg*
12/04	a	Dudelange	L 0-4	
19/04	h	Hostert	W 4-1	*Lascak 2, Förg, Freitas*
25/04	a	Käerjéng	W 1-0	*og (Marcolino Rodrigues)*
03/05	h	Mondorf-les-Bains	L 1-4	*Pedro dos Santos*
10/05	a	Progrès	L 0-2	
17/05	a	Differdange	L 0-4	
23/05	a	Rumelange	D 2-2	*og (Igor Pereira), Schmitt*

Name	Nat	DoB	Pos	Aps	(s)	Gls
Christian Adams	GER	22/08/88	M	13	(3)	1
Niklas Bürger	GER	07/10/92	G	24		
Julian Dücker	GER	05/02/90	A	2	(5)	
Nicolas Dücker	GER	05/02/90	D	22		
Sebastian Förg	GER	26/04/88	M	22	(2)	6
Tom Freitas		08/06/95	A		(3)	1
Gabriel Gaspar		20/07/90	M	16	(4)	2
Nicolas Jakob	GER	12/03/93	M	18	(7)	1
Jeff Lascak		13/02/94	A	23	(2)	14
Olivier Lickes		27/06/88	D	22	(1)	
Tim Lieser	GER	03/02/95	D	2		
Steven Machado		24/07/98	D	1		
Philipp Marx	GER	19/07/89	A		(3)	
Thomas Mirkes	GER	25/08/95	M		(1)	
Pedro dos Santos	POR	21/11/90	A	24		4
Lars Peifer	GER	03/07/93	M	2	(7)	
Alex Pott		21/10/08	A	1	(5)	
Kevin Schmitt	GER	23/11/88	A	4	(2)	1
Flavio Schuster	GER	13/02/92	M	25		
Jacques Schwartz		27/07/94	D		(1)	
Johannes Steinbach	GER	02/07/92	D	25		2
Rafael Valente		27/04/87	A	2	(17)	
Ramiro Valente		26/01/89	M	13	(10)	1
Ben Vogel		22/12/94	D	25		1

FC Wiltz 71

1971 • Stade Géitzt (2,000) • fcwiltz.lu
Coach: Claude Ottelé

2014

03/08	a	Dudelange	L	0-3	
10/08	h	Käerjéng	L	0-2	
17/08	a	Progrès	L	0-2	
22/08	h	Rumelange	L	0-1	
28/08	a	Fola	L	1-2	Kalabic
14/09	a	Jeunesse Canach	D	1-1	Admar Moacyr
21/09	h	Rosport	L	1-2	G Mersch
28/09	a	Hostert	L	1-2	Osmanović
05/10	h	Mondorf-les-Bains	W	2-0	G Mersch, Cosic
17/10	a	Differdange	L	0-3	(w/o; original result 1-2 Kalabic)
26/10	h	Jeunesse Esch	D	0-0	
02/11	a	Etzella	L	1-2	Admar Moacyr
23/11	h	Grevenmacher	W	1-0	Faljic

2015

22/02	a	Käerjéng	D	1-1	G Mersch
01/03	h	Progrès	D	0-0	
08/03	h	Rumelange	L	0-4	
15/03	h	Fola	D	1-1	Verbist
22/03	a	Jeunesse Canach	W	3-0	(w/o; original result 2-3 Civic, Verbist)
08/04	a	Rosport	L	1-2	Kouayep
12/04	h	Hostert	D	3-3	Faljic, Doyennel (p), Sené
19/04	a	Mondorf-les-Bains	L	1-3	Verbist
26/04	h	Differdange	W	2-1	Verbist, Osmanović
01/05	a	Jeunesse Esch	L	0-2	
10/05	h	Etzella	W	3-1	Verbist, Kouayep, Osmanović
17/05	a	Grevenmacher	W	3-0	Sené, Osmanović, Sérgio Oliveira
23/05	h	Dudelange	W	3-0	Osmanović 3 (1p)

Name	Nat	DoB	Pos	Aps	(s)	Gls
Admar Moacyr	POR	05/12/87	M	7	(1)	2
Anis Adrović	MNE	15/02/88	M	1	(2)	
Adis Civic		26/11/94	M	11	(9)	1
Jason Conrad	BEL	03/01/90	D	19		
Amel Cosic		19/11/89	A	7	(2)	1
Dennis Souza	BRA	09/01/80	D	24	(1)	
Thomas Doyennel	FRA	14/12/89	D	22		1
Haris Faljic		01/06/91	D	10	(2)	2
Gary Fournier	FRA	09/12/91	M	8	(2)	
Ben Gasper		14/03/95	M		(9)	
Nazif Hajdarović	BIH	22/09/84	A	3		
Emko Kalabic		30/03/89	M	16	(5)	2
Rodrigue Kouayep	CMR	07/12/86	M	21	(1)	2
Etelle Mersch		08/09/96	D		(2)	
Gérard Mersch		08/09/96	M	23		3
Mehmet Mujkic		26/09/83	M	9	(4)	
Edis Osmanović	BIH	30/06/88	A	13	(5)	7
Pol Peiffer		11/08/95	D		(4)	
Romain Ruffier	FRA	04/10/89	G	26		
Pit Scheilz		11/09/96	M		(1)	
Babacar Sené	SEN	01/01/83	D	24		2
Sérgio Oliveira	POR	17/01/94	D	5	(5)	1
Ivan Strkalj	CRO	21/06/92	M	22	(1)	
Amadou Touré	BFA	27/09/82	D	2	(2)	
Christopher Verbist	BEL	08/10/91	A	13		5

Top goalscorers

21	Sanel Ibrahimović (Jeunesse Esch)
15	Alexander Karapetyan (Dudelange)
14	Jeff Lascak (Rosport)
12	Samir Hadji (Fola)
	Hakim Menaï (Progrès)
11	Omar Er Rafik (Differdange)
	Antonio Luisi (Differdange)
	Lévy Rougeaux (Progrès)
9	Gauthier Caron (Differdange)
	Jakob Dallevedove (Fola)
	Grégory Adler (Hostert)

Promoted clubs

FC RM Hamm Benfica

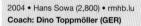

2004 • Hans Sowa (2,800) • rmhb.lu
Coach: Dino Toppmöller (GER)

Racing FC Union Lëtzebuerg

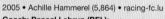

2005 • Achille Hammerel (5,864) • racing-fc.lu
Coach: Pascal Lebrun (BEL);
(04/01/15) Fabien Matagne (FRA)

FC Una Strassen

1922 • Complexe Sportif Jean Wirtz (2,000) • fcuna-strassen.lu
Coach: Patrick Grettnich

Second level final table 2014/15

		Pld	W	D	L	F	A	Pts
1	FC RM Hamm Benfica	26	22	2	2	90	17	68
2	Racing FC Union Lëtzebuerg	26	21	2	3	62	23	65
3	FC Una Strassen	26	18	7	1	72	32	61
4	FC Rodange 91	26	14	4	8	48	40	46
5	FC Mamer 32	26	11	2	13	50	49	35
6	FC Swift Hesperange	26	10	5	11	42	49	35
7	CS Pétange	26	10	5	11	35	45	35
8	Union 05 Kayl-Tétange	26	10	3	13	35	38	33
9	FC 72 Erpeldange	26	9	5	12	45	54	32
10	US Sandweiler	26	9	3	14	37	54	30
11	FC Titus Lamadelaine	26	7	4	15	30	55	25
12	FC Mondercange	26	5	6	15	31	54	21
13	FC Blue Boys Muhlenbach	26	3	7	16	35	60	16
14	FC Minerva Lintgen	26	5	1	20	22	64	16

Promotion/Relegation play-off

(29/05/15)
Käerjéng 0-3 Strassen

DOMESTIC CUP

Coupe de Luxembourg 2014/15

FIFTH ROUND

(28/11/14)
Munsbach 0-2 Mondorf-les-Bains
Schifflange 0-1 Rumelange *(aet)*

(29/11/14)
Berbourg 0-4 Dudelange

(30/11/14)
Beggen 1-1 Jeunesse Canach *(aet; 2-3 on pens)*
Bertrange 1-3 Grevenmacher
Bissen 1-4 Fola
Hamm Benfica 2-1 Jeunesse Esch
Lintgen 1-4 Wiltz
Mersch 2-2 Käerjéng *(aet; 2-4 on pens)*
Muhlenbach 0-4 Rodange
Racing Union 3-0 Rosport
Remich/Bous 1-4 Differdange
Sandweiler 0-5 Hostert
Strassen 4-2 Progrès
Swift 1-0 Lamadelaine

(03/12/14)
Wincrange 1-2 Etzella

SIXTH ROUND

(07/12/14)
Hostert 0-2 Etzella
Jeunesse Canach 3-1 Käerjéng
Mondorf-les-Bains 2-4 Fola *(aet)*
Racing Union 0-2 Hamm Benfica
Rodange 0-3 Differdange
Strassen 0-1 Dudelange
Swift 0-3 Grevenmacher
Wiltz 3-4 Rumelange *(aet)*

QUARTER-FINALS

(04/04/15)
Fola 1-3 Dudelange *(Klein 27; Maury 42, Da Mota 45, 63)*
Grevenmacher 1-2 Etzella *(Gaspar 18; Augusto 61, Jurina 105) (aet)*
Jeunesse Canach 0-0 Hamm Benfica *(aet; 4-2 on pens)*
Rumelange 2-5 Differdange *(Cabral 27, Johnny Santos 74; Caron 22, 40, 44, Franzoni 28, Méligner 78)*

SEMI-FINALS

(14/05/15)
Differdange 3-2 Jeunesse Canach *(Luisi 48, 49, Méligner 89; Pedro Ferro 12, Borgniet 50)*
Dudelange 4-0 Etzella *(Maury 10, Turpel 25, Stélvio 83, 90)*

FINAL

(31/05/15)
Stade Josy Barthel, Luxembourg
FC DIFFERDANGE 03 1 *(Siebenaler 21)*
F91 DUDELANGE 1 *(Siebenaler 20og)*
(aet; 3-2 on pens)
Referee: Krueger
DIFFERDANGE: *Weber, Franzoni, Bukvic, Siebenaler, Rodrigues, Pedro Ribeiro (May 109), Jänisch, Luisi (Méligner 106), Yéyé (Lebresne 78), Er Rafik, Caron*
DUDELANGE: *Joubert, Malget, Maury, Schnell, Ney, Nakache, Stélvio, Laurienté (Jahier 110), Da Mota, Turpel (Pedro 57), Karapetyan (Ben Ajiba 40)*
Red card: *Stélvio (101)*

Former Yugoslav Republic of
MACEDONIA
Fudbalska Federacija na Makedonija (FFM)

Address	Bul. ASNOM bb
	MK-1000 Skopje
Tel	+389 23 129 291
Fax	+389 23 165 448
E-mail	ffm@ffm.com.mk
Website	ffm.mk

President	Ilco Gjorgioski
General secretary	Filip Popovski
(interim)	
Media officer	Zlatko Andonovski
Year of formation	1948
National stadium	Filip II Arena, Skopje
	(32,482)

PRVA LIGA CLUBS

 ① FK Bregalnica Stip

 ② FK Metalurg Skopje

 ③ FK Pelister

 ④ FK Rabotnicki

 ⑤ KF Renova

 ⑥ KF Shkëndija

 ⑦ FK Sileks

 ⑧ FK Teteks

 ⑨ FK Turnovo

 ⑩ FK Vardar

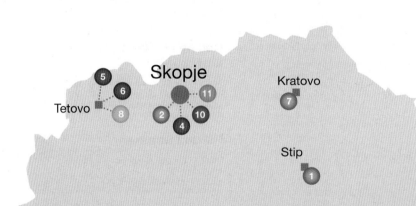

PROMOTED CLUBS

 ⑪ FK Shkupi

 ⑫ FK Mladost Carev Dvor

KEY:

● – UEFA Champions League
● – UEFA Europa League
● – Promoted
● – Relegated

Eighth title for Vardar

FK Vardar, the most popular and decorated club in the Former Yugoslav Republic of Macedonia, made it three Prva Liga titles in four years as they held off the challenge of defending champions FK Rabotnicki with the help of their Russian coach Sergei Andreev.

Rabotnicki surrendered the league title but retained the Macedonian Cup, claiming it for the fifth time thanks to a comeback 2-1 victory over FK Teteks, who managed just three wins in 33 league games and were relegated with FK Pelister.

Russian coach Andreev steers Skopje club to victory	Rabotnicki take runners-up spot and retain the cup	Teteks reach cup final despite propping up Prva Liga

Domestic league

There was a new look to the Prva Liga in 2014/15, with ten teams rather than 12 and a revised structure, in which the top six clubs separated from the bottom four after the regular 27-match season. While the six teams in the championship group played five further matches – three at home for the top three clubs – the four teams in the relegation pool faced each other twice more home and away.

Vardar were in charge from day one, winning their opening three fixtures and adding to their points tally in each of their next dozen encounters to take a commanding lead. Rabotnicki, still led by double-winning boss Igor Angelovski, managed to recover from a shaky start by reeling off eight successive wins, and with Vardar finally falling to defeat, 3-0 at KF Renova in round 16, their deficit on the leaders was down to just three points going into the teams' summit meeting on the eve of the winter break; they had been eight points adrift after Vardar defeated them 2-0 in the first encounter.

A goalless draw left the situation unchanged, but Vardar refused to rest on their laurels, fortifying their squad during the mid-season shutdown with two high-profile players, Bosnia & Herzegovina international Senijad Ibričić

and Dejan Blazevski, the free-scoring midfielder who had topped the 2013/14 Prva Liga scoring charts with 19 goals despite leaving FK Turnovo in mid-season. Both newcomers would make telling contributions as Vardar eventually brushed Rabotnicki off their coat-tails. A 2-0 win over their closest pursuers in the final game of the regular season enabled Andreev's men to enter the play-off series with a six-point advantage. That provided enough of a cushion for them to shrug off a second defeat in three weeks at KF Shkëndija and take the title by a three-point winning margin from Rabotnicki, with Shkëndija seven points further behind in third.

Domestic cup

The 2015 Macedonian Cup final was expected to be a one-sided affair as holders Rabotnicki, making their sixth appearance in eight years, took on a Teteks side who, despite lifting the trophy in 2013 after a penalty shoot-out win over local rivals Shkëndija, were relegated that season and about to drop into the second division again as the Prva Liga's bottom club. Remarkably, though, the rank outsiders took the lead in the Filip II Arena just before half-time and were still in front at the three-quarter mark, only for Rabotnicki to rally and turn the game on its head with two

goals in quick succession from their two most reliable marksmen, Blaze Ilijoski and Marjan Altiparmakovski.

Europe

FK Metalurg Skopje, who had a poor domestic season, were the nation's only success story in Europe, reaching the third qualifying round of the UEFA Europa League thanks to an added-time strike from veteran former FYR Macedonia international Mile Krstev that knocked out fellow Balkans FK Željezničar.

National team

It was another last-gasp goal – a thing of beauty from midfielder Booart Abdurahimi at home to Luxembourg – that gave FYR Macedonia their only win of the UEFA EURO 2016 qualifying campaign. The other five games yielded zero points, with back-to-back home defeats by Slovakia and Belarus prematurely ending the 17-month reign of coach Bosko Djurovski. His place was taken by Ljubinko Drulović, the former FC Porto striker who in 2013 had led his native Serbia to the UEFA European Under-19 Championship title. He was unable to prevent Slovakia from making it six Group C wins out of six in his first game, but a valiant 2-1 defeat in Zilina offered a degree of encouragement for the future.

DOMESTIC SEASON AT A GLANCE

Prva liga 2014/15 final table

		Pld	Home					Away					Total					Pts
			W	D	L	F	A	W	D	L	F	A	W	D	L	F	A	
1	**FK Vardar**	**32**	**12**	**5**	**0**	**32**	**7**	**8**	**4**	**3**	**24**	**14**	**20**	**9**	**3**	**56**	**21**	**69**
2	FK Rabotnicki	32	12	3	2	29	12	8	3	4	26	18	20	6	6	55	30	66
3	KF Shkëndija	32	11	2	4	38	18	7	3	5	20	13	18	5	9	58	31	59
4	KF Renova	32	8	5	3	26	17	5	4	7	15	22	13	9	10	41	39	48
5	FK Sileks	32	6	4	6	17	21	4	7	5	16	21	10	11	11	33	42	41
6	FK Metalurg Skopje	32	4	6	5	17	16	4	3	10	17	26	8	9	15	34	42	33
7	FK Bregalnica Stip	33	7	5	4	19	12	6	4	7	14	17	13	9	11	33	29	48
8	FK Turnovo	33	4	4	8	9	15	5	5	7	17	22	9	9	15	26	37	36
9	FK Pelister	33	3	4	9	11	16	4	5	8	10	19	7	9	17	21	35	30
10	FK Teteks	33	1	3	12	12	35	2	3	12	10	38	3	6	24	22	73	15

NB League splits into top 6 and bottom 4 after 27 games, after which the clubs play exclusively against teams in their group.

European qualification 2015/16

Champion: FK Vardar (second qualifying round)

Cup winner: FK Rabotnicki (first qualifying round)
KF Shkëndija (first qualifying round)
KF Renova (first qualifying round)

Top scorer   Izair Emini (Renova), 20 goals
Relegated clubs   FK Teteks, FK Pelister
Promoted clubs   FK Shkupi, FK Mladost Carev Dvor
Cup final   FK Rabotnicki 2-1 FK Teteks

Team of the season
(4-4-2)

Coach: Angelovski *(Rabotnicki)*

Gacevski
(Bregalnica)

Hambardzumyan   Grncarov   Ilievski   Stojanov
(Vardar)   *(Vardar)*   *(Rabotnicki)*   *(Bregalnica)*

Radeski   Gligorov   Emini   Velkovski
(Metalurg)   *(Vardar)*   *(Renova)*   *(Rabotnicki)*

Altiparmakovski   Vručina
(Rabotnicki)   *(Shkëndija)*

Player of the season

Hovhannes Hambardzumyan
(FK Vardar)

Vardar's successful season in the Prva Liga was underpinned by vital contributions from a number of players with international experience. Hambardzumyan, the Armenia right-back, was arguably the most valuable, providing eight assists, three goals and much more besides in his first campaign abroad. A title-winner in his homeland the previous season with FC Banants, the 24-year-old became a big fan favourite with his technical skills and consistent ability to deliver dangerous crosses into the box.

Newcomer of the season

Filip Gacevski
(FK Bregalnica Stip)

Born in Slovenia of Macedonian stock, goalkeeper Gacevski joined Bregalnica Stip from Austrian club Kapfenberger SV in 2014 and turned out to be the team's star performer, especially in the spring when he set a new Prva Liga record by keeping his goal intact for 912 minutes in the run-up to the league split. He then conceded only once as Bregalnica won all six of their fixtures in the relegation pool, earning himself both an international call-up for FYR Macedonia and a summer transfer to champions Vardar.

NATIONAL TEAM

Top five all-time caps
Goce Sedloski (100); Velice Sumulikoski (84); Goran Pandev (75); Artim Sakiri (72); Igor Mitreski (70)

Top five all-time goals
Goran Pandev (26); Georgi Hristov (16); Artim Sakiri (15); Goran Maznov (10); Ilco Naumoski (9)

Results 2014/15

Date	Opponent		Venue		Res	Scorers
08/09/14	Spain (ECQ)	A	Valencia	L	1-5	Ibraimi (28p)
09/10/14	Luxembourg (ECQ)	H	Skopje	W	3-2	Trajkovski (20), Jahovic (66p), Abdurahimi (90+2)
12/10/14	Ukraine (ECQ)	A	Lviv	L	0-1	
15/11/14	Slovakia (ECQ)	H	Skopje	L	0-2	
27/03/15	Belarus (ECQ)	H	Skopje	L	1-2	Trajkovski (9)
30/03/15	Australia	H	Skopje	D	0-0	
14/06/15	Slovakia (ECQ)	A	Zilina	L	1-2	Ademi (69)

Appearances 2014/15

Coach: Bosko Djurovski 28/12/61 /(28/04/15) Ljubinko Drulović (SRB) 11/09/68

Player / DOB / Club	ESP	LUX	UKR	SVK	BLR	Aus	SVK	Caps	Goals
Tomislav Pacovski — 28/06/82 — Mechelen (BEL)/Vardar	G	G	G	G	G		G	43	-
Stefan Ristovski — 12/02/92 — Parma (ITA)/Latina (ITA)	D	D	D	D	D	s74		17	-
Daniel Mojsov — 25/12/87 — Brann (NOR)/Lierse (BEL)	D	D		D			D	28	-
Vance Sikov — 19/07/85 — Austria Wien (AUT)	D	D	D	D	D	D		39	3
Ardian Cuculi — 19/07/87 — Partizani (ALB)	D	D46						6	-
Ezgjan Alioski — 12/02/92 — Schaffhausen (SUI)	D46	s46		D				6	-
Agim Ibraimi — 29/08/88 — Maribor (SVN)	M	M46			M	M	M89	32	7
Besart Abdurahimi — 31/07/90 — Lokeren (BEL)	M74	s46	M	M	M75	s70	s89	9	1
Stefan Spirovski — 23/08/90 — Beroe (BUL)	M64							8	-
Aleksandar Trajkovski — 05/09/92 — Zulte Waregem (BEL)	M	M	M	M	M	M70	A56	23	4
Adis Jahovic — 18/03/87 — Krylya Sovetov (RUS)	A	s60	A62					12	3
Muhamed Demiri — 20/11/85 — St Gallen (SUI)	s46	M		M74				25	-
Marjan Radeski — 10/02/95 — Metalurg Skopje	s64					A46		4	-
Krste Velkoski — 20/02/88 — Sarajevo (BIH)	s74		s62	A70	A63		s82	8	-
Arijan Ademi — 29/05/91 — Dinamo Zagreb (CRO)		M	M	M			M	4	1
Muarem Muarem — 22/10/88 — Qarabağ (AZE)	M60						M82	7	-
Jovan Kostovski — 19/04/87 — Leuven (BEL)	A	s70		s46				11	2
Aleksandar Damcevski — 21/11/92 — NAC (NED)				D				4	-
Nikola Gligorov — 15/08/83 — Vardar				M86				19	-
Mirko Ivanovski — 31/10/89 — CFR Cluj (ROU)/Videoton (HUN)				M70	s70		s56	24	1
Aco Stojkov — 29/04/83 — Rabotnicki				s86	A46			42	5
David Babunski — 01/03/94 — Barcelona (ESP)				s74				0	-
Bojan Markoski — 08/08/83 — Ayia Napa (CYP)					D			1	-
Daniel Georgievski — 17/02/88 — Melbourne Victory (AUS)					D	D74		22	-
Artim Polozani — 25/06/82 — Shkëndija					M31	M		14	-
Ferhan Hasani — 18/06/90 — Brøndby (DEN)					M	M	M84*	21	1
Enis Bardi — 02/07/95 — Újpest (HUN)					s31	s86		2	-
Blagoja Todorovski — 11/06/85 — Shkëndija					s63	s46		4	-
Dejan Blazevski — 06/12/85 — Vardar					s75	M		4	1
Martin Bogatinov — 26/04/86 — Ermis (CYP)						G46		16	-
Darko Velkovski — 21/06/95 — Rabotnicki						D		3	-
Kire Ristevski — 22/10/90 — Tirana (ALB)						D		4	-
Dusko Trajcevski — 01/11/90 — Rabotnicki						M86	M	2	-
Kristijan Naumovski — 17/09/88 — Dinamo Bucureşti (ROU)						s46		6	-
Aleksandar Todorovski — 26/02/84 — Zagłębie Lubin (POL)							D	16	-
Vladimir Dimitrovski — 30/11/88 — Kerkyra (GRE)							D	4	-
Leonard Zuta — 09/08/92 — Häcken (SWE)							D	1	-

EUROPE

DOMESTIC LEAGUE CLUB-BY-CLUB

FK Rabotnicki

CHAMPIONS LEAGUE

Second qualifying round - HJK Helsinki (FIN)
H 0-0
Siskovski, Najdoski, Vujcic (Bojku 90+2), Anene (Todorovski 52), Sulejmanov, Siljanovski, Markoski, Petrovic, Milusev, Avramovski (Trajcevski 77), Ilievski. Coach: Igor Angelovski (MKD)
A 1-2 Vujcic (47)
Siskovski, Najdoski, Todorovski, Vujcic, Sulejmanov, Siljanovski, Velkovski (Avramovski 59), Markoski (Anene 38), Petrovic, Milusev (Trajcevski 68), Ilievski. Coach: Igor Angelovski (MKD)

FK Turnovo

EUROPA LEAGUE

First qualifying round - FC Chikhura Sachkhere (GEO)
H 0-1
Dimovski, Tasev, Iliev (Kocoski 62) Mutafchiyski, Mecinovic, Dolapchiev (Curlinov 54), Georgiev, Pandev, Varelovski, Najdenov (Stoilov 54), Pandovski. Coach: Goce Sedloski (MKD)
A 1-3 Pandovski (45+1)
Dimovski, Tasev, Harizanov (Kovacev 53), Mutafchiyski, Mavrov (Dolapchiev 60), Georgiev, Curlinov, Pandev, Varelovski, Najdenov, Pandovski (Naumchevski 49). Coach: Goce Sedloski (MKD)

FK Metalurg Skopje

EUROPA LEAGUE

First qualifying round - UE Santa Coloma (AND)
A 3-0 Krstev (3), A Stojanovski (15), Simonovski (83)
Efremov, Ristovski, Gjorgjievski, Leskaroski, Dalceski (Naumoski 77), Simonovski, Mitrev, Radeski (Naumovski 89), Dodevski, Krstev, A Stojanovski (Angelov 68). Coach: Vladimir Kolev (MKD)
H 2-0 Gjorgjievski (19), Simonovski (34)
Efremov, Ristovski (Tanturovski 57), Gjorgjievski, Leskaroski, Naumoski (Georgiev 66), Simonovski, Mitrev (Naumovski 46), Radeski, Dodevski, Angelov, A Stojanovski. Coach: Srgjan Zaharievski (MKD)

Second qualifying round - FK Željezničar (BIH)
H 0-0
Efremov, Ristovski (Tanturovski 86), Gjorgjievski, Leskaroski, Dalceski (Angelov 46), Simonovski, Mitrev (Naumoski 46), Radeski, Dodevski, Krstev, A Stojanovski. Coach: Srgjan Zaharievski (MKD)
A 2-2 Radeski (62), Krstev (90+2)
Efremov, Ristovski (Naumoski 53), Gjorgjievski, Leskaroski, Dalceski, Mitrev, Radeski, Dodevski (Angelov 69), Krstev, A Stojanovski, Tanturovski (Simonovski 32). Coach: Srgjan Zaharievski (MKD)

Third qualifying round - AC Omonia (CYP)
A 0-3
Efremov, Ristovski (Naumoski 58), Gjorgjievski, Leskaroski, Dalceski, Simonovski, Mitrev (Tanturovski 65), Radeski, Krstev, Angelov (Dodevski 29), A Stojanovski. Coach: Srgjan Zaharievski (MKD)
H 0-1
Efremov, Ristovski, Gjorgjievski, Leskaroski, Dalčeski, Mitrev, Dodevski, Angelov (Chavoli 66), A Stojanovski, Tanturovski (Radeski 46), Mitrov (Krstev 46). Coach: Srgjan Zaharievski (MKD)

KF Shkëndija

EUROPA LEAGUE

First qualifying round - FC Zimbru Chisinau (MDA)
H 2-1 Vručina (45+5), Mitrov (47)
Jovanovski, Bejtulai, Selmani (Kurtisi 51), Polozani, Vručina, Murati, Stênio Júnior (Fazliu 81), Mitrov, Huseini, Berisha (Kavdanski 34), Miliev. Coach: Roy Ferenčina (CRO)
A 0-2
Jovanovski, Bejtulai, Polozani, Vručina, Nurishi (Imeri 51), Murati (Kavdanski 86), Stênio Júnior, Mitrov (Selmani 65), Huseini, Berisha, Miliev. Coach: Roy Ferenčina (CRO)
Red card: Huseini 90

FK Bregalnica Stip

1921 • City, Stip (6,000) • no website
Coach: Gjore Jovanovski;
(04/11/14) Nikola Spasov (BUL);
(04/01/15) Vlatko Kostov

2014
03/08	a	Shkëndija	L	1-2 Matić
10/08	a	Teteks	W	1-0 Misev
17/08	h	Vardar	L	1-2 Velkovski
24/08	a	Turnovo	L	1-2 og (Varelovski)
27/08	h	Metalurg	L	0-1
31/08	a	Renova	L	1-2 Misev
14/09	h	Rabotnicki	L	1-2 Zdravkov
21/09	a	Sileks	L	1-1 Velkovski
28/09	h	Pelister	D	0-0
05/10	a	Shkëndija	L	1-3 Zdravkov
19/10	h	Teteks	W	4-1 Markoski 2, Velkovski, Ristovski
26/10	a	Vardar	L	0-1
29/10	h	Turnovo	D	1-1 Markoski
02/11	a	Metalurg	L	0-3
09/11	h	Renova	W	2-0 Stojanov, Nikovski
22/11	a	Rabotnicki	L	0-4
30/11	h	Sileks	D	1-1 Zdravkov (p)

2015
01/03	a	Pelister	W	1-0 Iliev
10/03	a	Renova	L	1-2 Zdravkov
15/03	h	Shkëndija	D	0-0
21/03	a	Rabotnicki	D	0-0
04/04	h	Vardar	D	0-0
07/04	a	Turnovo	W	1-0 Stupić
11/04	h	Pelister	W	1-0 Iliev
19/04	a	Metalurg	D	0-0
22/04	a	Teteks	D	0-0
26/04	h	Sileks	W	2-0 Nacev 2
03/05	h	Teteks	W	1-0 Hristov
06/05	h	Turnovo	W	2-1 Ristovski, Zdravkov
10/05	a	Pelister	W	1-0 Stupić
16/05	a	Teteks	W	4-0 Stupić, og (Stojkovski), Nacev, Hristov
24/05	a	Turnovo	W	1-0 Nacev
27/05	h	Pelister	W	2-0 Misev, Hristov (p)

Name	Nat	DoB	Pos	Aps	(s)	Gls
Oliver Aleksandrov		12/02/94	M	1	(1)	
Dusko Andonov		06/02/87	D	11	(13)	
Tomislav Blazevski		30/08/89	D	25	(3)	
Mario Filipovski		08/08/96	M	3	(4)	
Filip Gacevski		17/08/90	G	33		
Saso Gjoreski		18/09/82	D	24	(3)	
Gligor Gligorov		15/03/87	M	4	(2)	
Nikolay Hristov	BUL	01/08/89	M	29		3
Lazar Iliev		23/05/87	A	3	(10)	2
Milan Jovanović	SRB	14/10/83	A	4	(4)	
Stefan Kocev		23/02/94	D	7		
Stefan Kostov		31/10/96	M	3		
Elmir Mandak		11/11/84	M		(3)	
Riste Markoski		30/04/86	M	11	(4)	3
Zoran Matić	SRB	31/07/89	M	3	(4)	1
Mihajlo Mihailov		29/05/91	M	4	(1)	
Stefan Misev		11/03/96	M	21		3
Dejan Mitrev		20/07/88	D	28	(1)	
Angel Nacev		10/10/89	A	7	(7)	4
Georgi Nikovski		27/08/92	M	8	(12)	1
Sasko Ristov		19/05/83	D	6		
Stefan Ristovski		22/12/92	M	26	(3)	2
Žvonimir Stanković	SRB	22/11/83	D	10		
Darko Stojanov		11/02/90	D	23	(2)	1
Nemanja Stošković	SRB	21/02/90	M	2	(2)	
Boško Stupić	BIH	27/06/84	A	10	(4)	3
Viktor Talevski		03/04/95	D	1		
Nikola Tonev		12/11/85	D	12		
Slavce Velkovski		05/07/87	M	16	(5)	3
Goran Zdravkov		11/11/80	A	28	(1)	5
Miki Zezov		05/03/97	M		(4)	

FK Metalurg Skopje

1964 • FFM (2,500); Gjorce Petrov (2,500); Boris Trajkovski (2,500) • no website
Major honours
Macedonian Cup (1) 2011
Coach: Srgjan Zaharievski

2014
04/08	a	Rabotnicki	W 3-0	Angelov 2, Krstev (p)
10/08	h	Sileks	D 1-1	Leskaroski
17/08	a	Pelister	W 1-0	Tanturovski
23/08	h	Shkëndija	D 1-1	Radeski
27/08	a	Bregalnica	W 1-0	Angelov
31/08	h	Vardar	L 1-4	Krstev
14/09	a	Turnovo	L 0-1	
21/09	a	Teteks	W 1-0	Petrov
28/09	h	Renova	W 3-0	Radeski 2 (1p), A Stojanovski
05/10	h	Rabotnicki	L 1-2	Leskaroski
19/10	a	Sileks	L 1-2	Gjorgjievski
26/10	h	Pelister	D 0-0	
29/10	a	Shkëndija	L 1-2	Radeski
02/11	h	Bregalnica	W 3-0	Krstev (p), Radeski 2 (1p)
09/11	a	Vardar	L 1-3	A Stojanovski (p)
23/11	h	Turnovo	W 2-0	A Stojanovski 2
30/11	h	Teteks	L 0-2	

2015
02/03	a	Renova	L 1-3	Bujcevski
10/03	a	Vardar	L 1-2	Krstev (p)
15/03	a	Sileks	D 1-1	Bakracheski
22/03	h	Turnovo	D 0-0	
04/04	a	Renova	L 0-2	
07/04	h	Pelister	W 3-1	Naumovski, Gjorgjievski, Radeski
14/04	a	Shkëndija	D 2-2	Naumovski, Radeski
19/04	h	Bregalnica	D 0-0	
22/04	a	Rabotnicki	D 2-2	Radeski, A Stojanovski (p)
26/04	h	Teteks	D 0-0	
03/05	a	Vardar	L 0-2	
07/05	h	Renova	L 1-2	Naumovski
12/05	a	Rabotnicki	L 0-2	
18/05	h	Sileks	L 1-3	Radeski
24/05	a	Shkëndija	L 1-2	Angelov

Name	Nat	DoB	Pos	Aps	(s)	Gls
Viktor Angelov		27/03/94	M	26	(2)	4
Naumce Bakracheski		15/11/96	M	11	(10)	1
Lutfi Biljali	SVN	14/04/92	A	4	(4)	
Antonio Bujcevski		24/01/90	A	7	(6)	1
Andrian Chavoli		15/09/96	A		(1)	
Aleksandar Dalceski		18/04/91	M	10	(4)	
Stojan Dimovski		19/09/82	G	3		
Ninoslav Dodevski		29/11/91	D	2		
Andreja Efremov		02/09/92	G	17		
Boban Georgiev		26/01/97	M		(2)	
Bojan Gjorgjievski		25/01/92	D	32		2
Filip Ilic		26/01/97	G	1		
Darko Iloski		14/10/95	D	10		
Mihajlo Jakimoski		16/04/96	M	2	(2)	
Stefan Jevtoski		02/09/97	M	11	(3)	
Besart Krivanjeva		28/02/96	D	9		
Mile Krstev		13/05/79	M	20	(7)	4
Dejan Leskaroski		17/10/85	M	15		2
Vasko Mitrev		23/05/84	M	11	(5)	
Mihailo Mitrov		05/03/95	M	6	(12)	
Angel Nacev		10/10/89	A	1	(2)	
Jordanco Naumoski		15/02/95	M	2	(3)	
Blagoja Naumoski		24/11/93	M	8	(6)	3
Tomica Petrov		16/07/90	D	24	(2)	1
Marjan Radeski		10/02/95	M	31		10
Filip Ristovski		03/01/95	D	25	(3)	
Saso Shoposki		18/06/97	M	2	(5)	
Aleksandar Stojanovski		04/04/84	A	22	(2)	5
Vlatko Stojanovski		23/04/97	M	5	(4)	
Davor Taleski		19/05/95	G	11		
Dejan Tanturovski		12/08/92	M	24	(6)	1

FK Pelister

1945 • Tumbe Kafe (8,000); Goce Delcev, Prilep (15,000) • no website
Major honours
Macedonian Cup (1) 2001
Coach: Marjan Sekulovski;
(24/11/14) Dimitar Kapinkovski;
(04/12/14) Gjoko Hadzievski

2014
03/08	h	Vardar	L 0-1	
10/08	a	Turnovo	W 1-0	Ljamcevski
17/08	h	Metalurg	L 0-1	
24/08	a	Renova	W 2-0	Stupić 2
27/08	h	Rabotnicki	W 1-0	Stupić
31/08	a	Sileks	D 1-1	Markovski
14/09	h	Teteks	W 3-0	Ljamcevski, Stupić, Ristevski
21/09	h	Shkëndija	D 0-0	
28/09	a	Bregalnica	D 0-0	
04/10	a	Vardar	L 0-1	
18/10	h	Turnovo	D 0-0	
26/10	a	Metalurg	D 0-0	
29/10	h	Renova	L 0-1	
01/11	a	Rabotnicki	L 0-1	
09/11	h	Sileks	L 0-1	
23/11	a	Teteks	D 1-1	Stupić
30/11	a	Shkëndija	L 0-5	

2015
01/03	h	Bregalnica	L 0-1	
11/03	a	Shkëndija	L 0-2	
15/03	h	Rabotnicki	L 1-3	Todorovski
22/03	a	Vardar	D 1-1	Todorovski
04/04	h	Turnovo	L 0-1	
07/04	a	Metalurg	L 1-3	Biljali
11/04	a	Bregalnica	L 0-1	
18/04	h	Teteks	W 3-1	Todorovski, M Stepanovski, Mitić
22/04	a	Sileks	L 0-1	
26/04	h	Renova	D 1-1	Ljamcevski
03/05	a	Turnovo	W 1-0	Todorovski
06/05	a	Teteks	W 2-0	Ljamcevski, Stanojević
10/05	h	Bregalnica	L 0-1	
16/05	h	Turnovo	L 0-2	
24/05	h	Teteks	D 2-2	Sulejmani, Trifunovski
27/05	a	Bregalnica	L 0-2	

Name	Nat	DoB	Pos	Aps	(s)	Gls
Aleksandar Anastasov		04/05/93	M	27	(6)	
Kristijan Atanasovski		13/09/95	D	5	(2)	
Dejan Belevski		01/02/97	M	2		
Lutfi Biljali	SVN	14/04/92	A	10	(3)	1
Vladica Brdarovski		07/02/90	D	8	(1)	
Konstantin Cheshmedzhiev		29/01/96	M	13		
Kiril Dinchev	BUL	08/05/89	D	10	(1)	
Miloš Dragojević	MNE	03/02/89	G	14		
Goran Gancev		04/08/83	A	8		
Martin Georgievski		06/03/96	M		(1)	
Blagojce Glavevski		06/04/88	A		(5)	
Hristijan Krklinski		13/09/96	D		(2)	
Aleksandar Krsteski		03/09/83	D	17	(1)	
Hristijan Lavurovski		10/01/96	M		(1)	
Petar Ljamcevski		08/08/91	M	20	(9)	4
Toni Maglovski		14/01/83	D	1	(4)	
Blagojce Markovski		13/10/87	A	3	(3)	1
Stefan Micevski		07/06/97	M	1		
Filip Milenkovski		07/01/90	D	17	(2)	
Martin Mircevski		11/02/97	M	6	(3)	
Nikola Mitić	SRB	27/12/95	M	3	(2)	1
Burhan Mustafov		02/03/94	M	23	(3)	
Aleksandar Nedanoski		12/10/96	A		(1)	
Goran Pasovski		15/02/80	G	19		
Mile Petkovski		19/09/88	D	20		
Vladimir Petreski		08/07/91	M	15	(1)	
Vasko Raspashkovski		10/07/95	A		(2)	
Tome Rechkoski		18/03/91	M		(1)	
Dimce Ristevski		06/11/82	M	13	(2)	1
Milorad Smokovski		15/08/91	D	5	(6)	
Roberto Stajev		29/07/95	A	4	(1)	
Igor Stanojević	SRB	24/10/91	D	9	(4)	1
Kiril Stepanovski		26/05/83	D	3		
Metodija Stepanovski		26/05/83	D	14		1
Boško Stupić	BIH	27/06/84	A	17		5
Ensar Sulejmani		11/09/96	M	2		1
Viktor Sulejmani		03/04/95	D	5		
Goce Todorovski		13/09/82	M	19	(4)	4
Jovanco Trajkovski		18/01/95	M	7	(3)	
Ive Trifunovski		04/07/90	A	2	(4)	1
Georgios Tsirlidis	GRE	15/07/93	M	9	(3)	
Dejan Velevski		22/10/93	M		(1)	
Viktor Velkoski		14/11/95	D	12		

FK Rabotnicki

1937 • Filip II Arena (32,482); FFM (2,500) • fkrabotnicki.com
Major honours
Macedonian League (4) 2005, 2006, 2008, 2014;
Macedonian Cup (4) 2008, 2009, 2014, 2015
Coach: Igor Angelovski

2014
04/08	h	Metalurg	L 0-3	
09/08	a	Renova	L 1-2	Altiparmakovski (p)
16/08	h	Teteks	W 3-1	Altiparmakovski 2, Milusev (p)
23/08	h	Sileks	D 0-0	
27/08	a	Pelister	L 0-1	
30/08	h	Shkëndija	W 3-2	Velkovski 2, Altiparmakovski
14/09	a	Bregalnica	W 2-1	Stojkov, Cikarski
20/09	h	Vardar	L 0-2	
28/09	a	Turnovo	W 1-0	Stojkov
05/10	a	Metalurg	W 2-1	Velkovski, Altiparmakovski
18/10	h	Renova	W 3-0	Altiparmakovski, Stojkov, Churlinov
26/10	a	Teteks	W 5-1	Stojkov, Altiparmakovski 3, Churlinov
29/10	a	Sileks	W 2-0	Cikarski, Todorovski
01/11	h	Pelister	W 1-0	Anene
09/11	a	Shkëndija	W 3-1	Stojkov 2, Altiparmakovski
22/11	h	Bregalnica	W 4-0	Stojkov 3 (1p), Anene
30/11	a	Vardar	D 0-0	

2015
01/03	h	Turnovo	W 1-0	Velkovski
07/03	h	Turnovo	W 2-0	Altiparmakovski, Ilijoski (p)
15/03	a	Pelister	W 3-1	Altiparmakovski, Ilijoski 2 (1p)
21/03	h	Bregalnica	D 0-0	
04/04	a	Teteks	W 2-1	Ilijoski 2
07/04	h	Sileks	W 2-0	Siljanovski, Ilijoski
11/04	a	Renova	L 0-2	
18/04	h	Shkëndija	W 1-0	Altiparmakovski
22/04	h	Metalurg	D 2-2	Ilijoski, Velkovski
28/04	a	Vardar	L 0-2	
02/05	h	Sileks	W 3-1	Markoski, Velkovski, Anene
06/05	a	Vardar	D 2-2	Anene 2
12/05	h	Metalurg	W 2-0	Ilijoski, Anene
16/05	h	Shkëndija	W 2-1	Anene, Markoski
24/05	a	Renova	D 3-3	Markoski, Altiparmakovski 2

Name	Nat	DoB	Pos	Aps	(s)	Gls
Marjan Altiparmakovski		18/07/91	A	31	(1)	15
Chuma Anene	NOR	14/05/93	A	15	(12)	7
Slobodan Bocevski		05/05/97	D	1	(2)	
Besmir Bojku		03/01/95	A	1	(4)	
Daniel Bozinovski		09/07/89	G	14	(3)	
Cvetan Churlinov		24/07/86	A		(10)	2
Mite Cikarski		06/01/93	D	21	(2)	2
Husein Demiri		06/09/95	A		(1)	
Ninoslav Dodevski		29/11/91	D	14	(2)	
Andreja Efremov		02/09/92	G	8		
Teodor Fidanoski		24/10/96	D		(5)	
Tihomir Fidanoski		24/10/96	A	1	(8)	
Igor Gal	CRO	20/01/83	D	5	(2)	
Milan Ilievski		21/07/82	D	28	(2)	
Blaze Ilijoski		09/07/84	A	14		8
Alen Jasarovski		06/11/91	M		(2)	
Darko Jocik		06/03/97	M		(1)	
Kire Markoski		20/05/95	M	6	(6)	3
Aleksandar Milusev		05/04/88	D	5		1
Milovan Petrovic		23/01/90	M	25	(4)	
Milan Ristovski		08/04/98	M	1	(5)	
Nehar Sadiki		16/03/98	M		(5)	
Suad Sahiti	ALB	05/06/95	M	9	(5)	
Ardi Selmani		05/06/95	M	1	(1)	
Goran Siljanovski		01/07/90	D	29	(1)	1
Damjan Siskovski		18/03/95	G	10		
Aco Stojkov		29/04/83	A	11		9
Tauljant Sulejmanov		15/11/96	M	7	(5)	
Blagoja Todorovski		11/06/85	M	16		1
Dusko Trajcevski		01/11/90	D	23	(2)	
Darko Velkovski		21/06/95	M	29		6
Stephan Vujcic	GER	03/01/86	M	27	(1)	

KF Renova

2003 • City, Tetovo (15,000);
Bogovinje (3,500) • kfrenova.com
Major honours
*Macedonian League (1) 2010; Macedonian Cup
(1) 2012*
Coach: Catip Osmani

2014
02/08	h	Teteks	D	0-0
09/08	h	Rabotnicki	W	2-1 *Emini, Bujcevski*
17/08	a	Sileks		0-1
24/08	h	Pelister	L	0-2
27/08	a	Shkëndija	D	1-1 *Emini*
31/08	h	Bregalnica	W	2-1 *Jusufi, Emini*
14/09	a	Vardar	D	1-1 *Emini*
20/09	h	Turnovo	L	2-3 *Bujcevski, Ramadani*
28/09	a	Metalurg	L	0-3
05/10	h	Teteks	W	4-0 *Ramadani 2, Mojsov, Gafuri*
18/10	a	Rabotnicki	L	0-3
25/10	h	Sileks	D	2-2 *Emini, Mojsov*
29/10	a	Pelister	W	1-0 *Čampara*
01/11	a	Shkëndija	W	1-0 *Memedi (p)*
09/11	h	Bregalnica	L	0-2
22/11	h	Vardar	W	3-0 *Emini 2 (1p), Memedi (p)*
30/11	a	Turnovo	D	0-0

2015
02/03	h	Metalurg	W	3-1 *Emini 2 (1p), Musliu*
10/03	h	Bregalnica	W	2-1 *Emini 2*
14/03	a	Teteks	W	2-1 *Gafuri, Skenderi*
21/03	h	Sileks	D	1-1 *Miskovski*
04/04	a	Metalurg	W	2-0 *Emini 2*
08/04	a	Shkëndija	W	1-0 *Ramadani*
11/04	h	Rabotnicki	W	2-0 *Ramadani, Emini*
19/04	a	Vardar	L	0-1
22/04	h	Turnovo	D	1-1 *Emini*
26/04	a	Pelister	D	1-1 *Emini*
03/05	h	Shkëndija	L	1-3 *Redzepi*
07/05	a	Metalurg	W	2-1 *Emini (p), Markovski*
12/05	h	Sileks	L	0-1
16/05	a	Vardar	L	1-4 *Emini*
24/05	h	Rabotnicki	D	3-3 *Emini 2, Selmani*

Name	Nat	DoB	Pos	Aps	(s)	Gls
Ersen Asani		28/05/93	D	10	(3)	
Arlind Bajrami		05/11/95	M	3		
Antonio Bujcevski		24/01/90	A	5	(5)	2
Jasmin Čampara	BIH	08/05/90	A		(3)	1
Erdin Dzheladini		02/06/96	M		(1)	
Izair Emini		04/10/85	M	31		20
Saimir Fetai		04/04/89	M	11	(9)	
Ardjen Gafuri		01/02/89	M	18	(9)	2
Platin Imeri		27/09/94	M	6	(4)	
Fatjon Jusufi		06/03/97	M	5	(2)	1
Blagojce Markovski		13/10/87	A		(6)	1
Jasmin Mecinovic		22/10/90	D	17	(3)	
Agron Memedi		05/12/80	D	29		2
Nenad Miskovski		19/12/86	D	30		1
Gjorgji Mojsov		27/05/85	M	29		2
Visar Musliu		13/11/94	D	12	(1)	1
Saljadin Mustafi		13/04/93	G	27		
Mexhit Neziri		02/09/90	M	22		
Valon Neziri		22/10/93	G	5	(1)	
Fisnik Nuhiu		26/01/83	M	29		
Emran Ramadani		29/01/92	M	19	(8)	5
Elmedin Redzepi		30/09/88	M	9	(5)	1
Burim Sadiki		05/08/89	M	7	(8)	
Remzi Selmani		05/05/97	M	5	(8)	1
Ljavdrim Skenderi		17/01/94	A	13	(7)	1
Flamur Tairi		24/11/90	M	5	(2)	
Bashkim Velija		01/08/93	D	5	(4)	

KF Shkëndija

1979 • City, Tetovo (15,000);
City, Kumanovo (2,000) • kfshkendija.com
Major honours
Macedonian League (1) 2011
Coach: Roy Ferenčina (CRO);
(04/09/14) Ardian Kozniku (CRO);
(27/03/15) Jeton Bekiri

2014
03/08	h	Bregalnica	W	2-1 *Vručina, Kavdanski*
10/08	a	Vardar	L	0-3
17/08	h	Turnovo	W	5-2 *Alimi 2, Imeri 2, Kirovski*
23/08	a	Metalurg	D	1-1 *Vručina (p)*
27/08	h	Renova	D	1-1 *Vručina*
30/08	a	Rabotnicki	L	2-3 *Vručina 2 (1p)*
14/09	h	Sileks	W	3-0 *Mitrov, Kirovski, Vručina*
21/09	a	Pelister	D	0-0
28/09	h	Teteks	W	5-0 *Berisha, Kirovski 2, Vručina 2*
05/10	a	Bregalnica	W	3-1 *Kirovski 2, Vručina*
19/10	h	Vardar	L	1-2 *Imeri*
26/10	a	Turnovo	W	1-0 *Vručina*
29/10	h	Metalurg	W	2-1 *Stênio Júnior, Zeba*
01/11	a	Renova	L	0-1
09/11	h	Rabotnicki	L	1-3 *Kirovski*
23/11	a	Sileks	W	1-0 *Vručina*
30/11	h	Pelister	W	5-0 *Vručina, Zeba, Kirovski, Demiri 2*

2015
01/03	a	Teteks	W	2-1 *Vručina (p), Kirovski*
11/03	h	Pelister	W	2-0 *Kirovski, Stênio Júnior*
15/03	a	Bregalnica	D	0-0
22/03	h	Teteks	L	0-1
04/04	a	Sileks	W	3-0 *Victor Juffo, Selmani, Berisha*
08/04	h	Renova	L	0-1
14/04	h	Metalurg	D	2-2 *Victor Juffo, Kirovski*
18/04	a	Rabotnicki	L	0-1
24/04	h	Vardar	W	3-2 *Stênio Júnior, Vručina (p), Victor Juffo*
28/04	a	Turnovo	W	4-0 *Vručina, Alimi, Kirovski, Victor Juffo*
03/05	h	Renova	W	3-1 *Victor Juffo, Vručina, Stênio Júnior*
06/05	a	Sileks	W	2-0 *Vručina, Kirovski*
12/05	h	Vardar	W	1-0 *Abdula*
16/05	a	Rabotnicki	L	1-2 *Vručina*
24/05	h	Metalurg	W	2-1 *Useini, Kirovski*

Name	Nat	DoB	Pos	Aps	(s)	Gls
Dzhelil Abdula		25/09/91	D	16	(3)	1
Mevlan Adili		30/03/94	D	1		
Armend Alimi		11/12/87	M	25	(1)	3
Shpend Asani		14/11/96	M	1		
Stefan Askovski		24/02/92	M	3	(2)	
Enes Azizi	ALB	09/02/94	G	1		
Egzon Bejtulai		07/01/94	D	10		
Sedat Berisha		23/09/89	A	19	(1)	2
Besmir Bojku		03/01/95	A	11	(6)	
Besir Demiri		01/08/94	M	11		2
Astrit Fazliu		28/09/87	A	1		
Mohammadou Idrissou	CMR	08/03/80	A	4	(1)	
Demir Imeri		27/10/95	A	6	(15)	3
Marko Jovanovski		24/07/88	G	31		
Martin Kavdanski	BUL	13/02/87	D	3	(2)	1
Hristijan Kirovski		12/10/85	A	16	(16)	14
Deni Krleski	SUI	19/01/92	D		(1)	
Yordan Miliev	BUL	05/10/87	D	20		
Ivan Mitrov		24/10/88	M	9	(6)	1
Mevlan Murati		05/03/94	D	13	(1)	
Elvir Nurishi		04/10/92	A		(2)	
Artim Polozani		25/06/82	M	23	(2)	
Jasir Selmani		21/01/91	M	3	(6)	1
Stênio Júnior	BRA	10/06/91	A	22	(5)	4
Blagoja Todorovski		11/06/85	M	12	(1)	
Ennur Totre		29/10/96	M	5	(2)	
Jani Urdinov		28/03/91	D	6	(5)	
Muhamed Useini		21/11/88	M	23	(4)	1
Victor Juffo	BRA	24/02/93	M	11	(1)	5
Bojan Vručina	CRO	08/11/84	A	27	(4)	18
Nikola Vukčević	MNE	23/03/84	D	7		
Zajko Zeba	BIH	22/05/83	M	12	(5)	2

FK Sileks

1965 • Sileks (5,000) • no website
Major honours
*Macedonian League (3) 1996, 1997, 1998;
Macedonian Cup (2) 1994, 1997*
Coach: Zoran Sterjovski

2014
03/08	h	Turnovo	W	2-0 *Panovski, Velinov*
10/08	a	Metalurg	D	1-1 *Georgiev*
17/08	h	Renova	W	1-0 *Janev*
23/08	a	Rabotnicki	D	0-0
27/08	h	Teteks	W	3-1 *Panovski 2, Georgiev*
31/08	h	Pelister	D	1-1 *Janev*
14/09	a	Shkëndija	L	0-3
21/09	h	Bregalnica	D	1-1 *Duranski*
28/09	a	Vardar	L	0-2
05/10	a	Turnovo	D	1-1 *Duranski*
19/10	h	Metalurg	W	2-1 *Nedeljković (p), Duranski*
25/10	a	Renova	D	2-2 *Nedeljković, Georgiev*
29/10	h	Rabotnicki	L	0-2
02/11	a	Teteks	W	3-1 *S Rudan, Velinov, Maric*
09/11	a	Pelister	W	1-0 *Todorov*
23/11	h	Shkëndija	L	0-1
30/11	a	Bregalnica	D	1-1 *Maric*

2015
01/03	h	Vardar	L	0-3
11/03	h	Teteks	W	3-1 *Panovski (p), Timovski, S Rudan*
15/03	h	Metalurg	D	1-1 *M Rudan*
21/03	a	Renova	D	1-1 *Velinov*
04/04	h	Shkëndija	L	0-3
07/04	a	Rabotnicki	L	0-2
11/04	h	Vardar	L	0-2
19/04	a	Turnovo	D	1-1 *Todorov*
22/04	h	Pelister	W	1-0 *Georgiev*
26/04	a	Bregalnica	L	0-2
02/05	a	Rabotnicki	L	1-3 *M Rudan*
06/05	h	Shkëndija	L	0-2
12/05	a	Renova	W	1-0 *Duranski*
18/05	a	Metalurg	W	3-1 *Todorov, Nedeljković, Maric*
24/05	h	Vardar	D	2-2 *Georgiev, og (Despotovski)*

Name	Nat	DoB	Pos	Aps	(s)	Gls
Andrej Acevski		05/06/91	M	7	(7)	
Aleksandar Bagashovski		15/11/93	M	17	(1)	
Filip Duranski		17/07/91	M	29		4
Gjorgje Dzonov		20/09/91	D	13	(1)	
Nikola Georgiev		18/12/83	A	22	(5)	5
Blagojce Glavevski		06/04/88	A	2	(4)	
Ilija Jakov		17/02/89	M	8	(11)	
Tome Janev		02/04/90	D	24	(2)	2
Vlatko Kocev		27/08/86	A	1		
Kristijan Kostovski		15/12/94	A		(11)	
Boban Maric		24/11/88	A	5	(11)	3
Marjan Mickov		10/02/87	M	28	(2)	
Miljan Mijatović	SRB	21/03/89	M	6	(8)	
Slagjan Mitevski		04/05/91	M	1		
Igor Nedeljković	SRB	24/09/91	A	22	(6)	3
Trajce Nikov		20/08/87	G	25	(1)	
Aleksandar Panovski		30/06/88	M	14	(2)	4
Neven Radaković	SRB	12/01/94	A	1	(1)	
Kirce Ristevski		12/06/93	M	10	(1)	
Momčilo Rudan	SRB	09/01/90	D	12	(1)	2
Stefan Rudan	SRB	09/01/90	D	17		2
Mirko Simjanovski		01/01/94	M		(5)	
Goran Simov		31/03/75	G	7		
Roberto Stojkov		04/10/95	M	2	(2)	
Angel Timovski		13/11/94	M	29		1
Krste Todorov		24/12/87	M	25	(5)	3
Stojanco Velinov		03/09/89	A	26	(3)	3

FK Teteks

1953 • City, Tetovo (15,000); Gjorce Petrov, Skopje (2,500); Boris Trajkovski, Skopje (2,500) • no website
Major honours
Macedonian Cup (2) 2010, 2013
Coach: Gjorgi Todorovski;
(19/03/15) Gorazd Mihajlov

2014
02/08	a	Renova	D	0-0	
10/08	h	Bregalnica	L	0-1	
16/08	a	Rabotnicki	L	1-3	Jayme
24/08	h	Vardar	D	2-2	Jayme, Nachevski
27/08	a	Sileks	L	1-3	Bozinovski (p)
01/09	h	Turnovo	L	0-3	
14/09	a	Pelister	L	0-3	
21/09	h	Metalurg	L	0-1	
28/09	a	Shkëndija	L	0-5	
05/10	h	Renova	L	0-4	
19/10	a	Bregalnica	L	1-4	Jayme
26/10	h	Rabotnicki	L	1-5	Bozinovski
29/10	a	Vardar	L	0-5	
02/11	h	Sileks	L	1-3	Nandinho
09/11	a	Turnovo	L	0-2	
23/11	h	Pelister	D	1-1	Nandinho
30/11	a	Metalurg	W	2-0	Nandinho, S Hristov

2015
01/03	h	Shkëndija	L	1-2	Ermadin Adem (p)
11/03	a	Sileks	L	1-3	V Pavlov
14/03	h	Renova	L	1-2	S Hristov
22/03	a	Shkëndija	W	1-0	Oslonovski
04/04	h	Rabotnicki	L	1-2	V Pavlov (p)
08/04	a	Vardar	L	0-2	
11/04	h	Turnovo	L	1-3	Jovanovski
18/04	a	Pelister	L	1-3	Stojkovski
22/04	h	Bregalnica	D	0-0	
26/04	a	Metalurg	D	0-0	
03/05	a	Bregalnica	L	0-1	
06/05	h	Pelister	L	0-2	
10/05	a	Turnovo	L	0-2	
16/05	h	Bregalnica	L	0-4	
24/05	a	Pelister	D	2-2	S Hristov, Atanasovski
27/05	h	Turnovo	W	3-0	Najdoski 2, Bozinovski

Name	Nat	DoB	Pos	Aps	(s)	Gls
Emir Adem		21/10/86	D	5	(2)	
Ermadin Adem		07/07/90	M	17	(6)	1
Muhamet Ajvazi		01/10/94	M		(1)	
David Atanasovski		21/10/96	D	9		1
Martin Blazevski		13/05/92	D	12	(2)	
Goran Bogdanovic		09/06/90	D	9		
Bobi Bozinovski		24/02/81	M	29	(1)	3
Cvetan Churlinov		24/07/86	A	9	(4)	
Dejan Cvetanoski		15/05/90	A	11	(12)	
Vlatko Drobarov		02/11/92	D	20	(1)	
Kristijan Filipovski		02/10/96	M	10	(4)	
Aleksandar Gjorgjievski		24/02/92	M	3	(5)	
Martin Hristov		31/01/97	A	8	(3)	
Simeon Hristov		04/09/92	A	16	(5)	3
Jayme	BRA	20/03/93	A	14	(1)	3
Miroslav Jovanovski		13/05/91	M	19	(4)	1
Tihomir Kostadinov		04/03/96	M	4	(4)	
Igor Kralevski		11/10/78	D	7		
Filip Krstevski		27/07/97	M		(2)	
Zlatan Krstevski		13/10/91	M		(3)	
Arben Ljuma		27/02/96	M	1	(1)	
Vance Mancevski		03/09/82	G	27		
Marcinho	BRA	08/06/87	M	1	(1)	
Nikola Mishovski		22/10/85	D	15	(1)	
Darko Murdzeski		10/03/93	A		(2)	
Dragan Nachevski		27/01/80	M	22	(5)	1
Filip Najdoski		13/09/92	D	9		2
Nandinho	BRA	13/01/92	A	8	(2)	3
Vladislav Oslonovski	RUS	15/01/95	M	10	(3)	1
Ergin Osmanovski		03/06/96	M		(1)	
Dusan Pavlov		12/01/91	G	5		
Vasili Pavlov	RUS	24/07/90	A	7	(3)	2
Anto Pejić	CRO	21/02/89	A		(2)	
Jovan Popzlatanov		06/07/96	D	3	(5)	
Milan Ristovski		01/03/89	A	5	(1)	
Dejan Siljanovski		10/03/94	G	1	(1)	
Zarko Simjanovski		20/01/88	M	4	(4)	
Stojan Stojcevski		30/10/92	D	11		
Trajce Stojkovski		23/02/89	D	20	(2)	1
Kristijan Tosevski		06/05/94	D	5		
Kuzman Zepceski		08/05/96	D		(1)	

FK Turnovo

1950 • Kukus (3,000) • no website
Coach: Goce Sedloski;
(16/07/14) Sefki Arifovski & Ljupco Dimitkovski

2014
03/08	a	Sileks	L	0-2	
10/08	h	Pelister	L	0-1	
17/08	a	Shkëndija	L	2-5	Georgiev, Kocoski
24/08	h	Bregalnica	W	2-1	Georgiev 2
27/08	a	Vardar	D	0-0	
01/09	a	Teteks	W	3-0	Georgiev 2, Pandev (p)
14/09	h	Metalurg	W	1-0	Milusev
20/09	a	Renova	W	3-2	Najdenov, Kocoski, Varelovski
28/09	h	Rabotnicki	L	0-1	
05/10	a	Sileks	D	1-1	Dolapchiev
18/10	a	Pelister	D	0-0	
26/10	h	Shkëndija	L	0-1	
29/10	a	Bregalnica	D	1-1	Pandev
02/11	a	Vardar	D	0-0	
09/11	h	Teteks	W	2-0	Kocoski, Dolapchiev
23/11	a	Metalurg	L	0-2	
30/11	h	Renova	D	0-0	

2015
01/03	h	Rabotnicki	L	0-1	
07/03	a	Rabotnicki	L	0-2	
15/03	a	Vardar	L	0-2	
22/03	h	Metalurg	D	0-0	
04/04	a	Pelister	W	1-0	Najdenov
07/04	h	Bregalnica	L	0-1	
11/04	a	Teteks	W	3-1	Pandev 2, Tanushev
19/04	a	Sileks	D	1-1	Tanushev
22/04	a	Renova	D	1-1	Tanushev
28/04	h	Shkëndija	L	0-4	
03/05	h	Pelister	L	0-1	
06/05	a	Bregalnica	L	1-2	Tanushev
10/05	h	Teteks	W	2-0	Georgiev 2
16/05	h	Pelister	W	2-0	Tasev, Markov
24/05	h	Bregalnica	L	0-1	
27/05	a	Teteks	L	0-3	

Name	Nat	DoB	Pos	Aps	(s)	Gls
Bojan Atanasov		24/07/95	A		(1)	
Nikola Bozinov		15/03/96	M	2	(10)	
Stojan Dimovski		19/09/82	G	14		
Grigor Dolapchiev	BUL	23/02/94	A	7	(9)	2
Ljupce Doriev		13/09/95	D	3	(2)	
Kostadin Dzinov		03/03/94	D	6	(2)	
Dragan Georgiev		16/12/90	A	20	(5)	7
Gjorge Gligorov		13/09/94	M	1	(1)	
Ivo Harizanov	BUL	07/01/87	D	14		
Tome Iliev		02/12/93	D	30	(1)	
Kristijan Ivanov		21/05/95	M	24	(2)	
Atanas Jovanov		06/04/96	G	1		
Valentin Kocoski		01/03/97	A	24	(6)	3
Daniel Kovacev		03/03/90	A	2	(11)	
Mario Krstovski		03/04/98	A	3	(9)	
Gjorgi Markov		22/11/91	M	4	(8)	1
Mitko Mavrov		08/04/91	D	27		
Aleksandar Milusev		05/04/88	D	18	(1)	1
Petar Mitev		06/07/95	D	5	(2)	
Radko Mutafchiyski	BUL	11/05/89	D	21	(2)	
Bojan Najdenov		27/08/91	A	29		2
Sasko Pandev		01/05/87	A	22	(1)	4
Blagoja Spirkoski		13/07/96	M	1		
Gjorgji Stoilov		25/08/95	M	8	(12)	
Stojan Stojcevski		30/10/92	D	11	(1)	
Gjorgi Tanushev		07/01/91	M	15	(1)	4
Marjan Tasev		02/05/85	M	22	(6)	1
Aleksandar Varelovski		08/05/88	M	11		1
Kostadin Zahov		08/11/87	G	18		

FK Vardar

1947 • Filip II Arena (32,482) • fkvardar.mk
Major honours
Macedonian League (8) 1993, 1994, 1995, 2002, 2003, 2012, 2013, 2015 ; Yugoslav Cup (1) 1961; Macedonian Cup (5) 1993, 1995, 1998, 1999, 2007
Coach: Sergei Andreev (RUS)

2014
03/08	a	Pelister	W	1-0	Petrov
10/08	h	Shkëndija	W	3-0	Ivanovski 2, Dashyan
17/08	a	Bregalnica	W	2-1	Hambardzumyan, F Petkovski
24/08	a	Teteks	D	2-2	Ivanovski, Petrov
27/08	h	Turnovo	D	0-0	
31/08	a	Metalurg	W	4-1	Asani, Grncarov, Grozdanoski, Ivanovski
14/09	h	Renova	D	1-1	F Petkovski
20/09	a	Rabotnicki	W	2-0	F Petkovski, Tanevski
28/09	h	Sileks	W	2-0	F Petkovski, Hambardzumyan
04/10	h	Pelister	W	1-0	F Petkovski
19/10	a	Shkëndija	W	2-1	F Petkovski, Grncarov
26/10	h	Bregalnica	W	1-0	Dashyan
29/10	h	Teteks	W	5-0	Petrov, Ivanovski 2, Dashyan, Ivanov
02/11	a	Turnovo	D	0-0	
09/11	h	Metalurg	W	3-1	Dashyan, Asani 2
22/11	a	Renova	L	0-3	
30/11	h	Rabotnicki	D	0-0	

2015
01/03	a	Sileks	W	3-0	Ivanovski, Blazevski 2
10/03	a	Metalurg	W	2-1	Blazevski, Ljamcevski
15/03	a	Turnovo	W	2-0	Ibričić (p), Ivanovski
22/03	h	Pelister	D	1-1	Ibričić
04/04	a	Bregalnica	D	0-0	
08/04	h	Teteks	W	2-0	Ivanovski, Blazevski
11/04	a	Sileks	W	2-0	Ivanovski, Blazevski
19/04	h	Renova	W	1-0	Hambardzumyan
24/04	a	Shkëndija	L	2-3	Ibričić, Gligorov
28/04	h	Rabotnicki	W	2-0	Grozdanoski, Blazevski
03/05	h	Metalurg	W	2-0	Blazevski 2
06/05	h	Rabotnicki	D	2-2	Asani 2
12/05	a	Shkëndija	L	0-1	
16/05	h	Renova	W	4-1	Popov, Ibričić 2 (1p), Spirovski
24/05	a	Sileks	D	2-2	Grozdanoski, Ivanovski

Name	Nat	DoB	Pos	Aps	(s)	Gls
Andrej Acevski		05/06/91	M		(1)	
Jasir Asani		19/05/95	M	20	(6)	5
Dejan Blazevski		06/12/85	M	14		8
Radenko Bojović	SRB	26/12/80	D	8	(2)	
Artak Dashyan	ARM	20/11/89	M	20	(5)	4
Filip Despotovski		18/11/82	M	20	(4)	
Nikola Gligorov		15/08/83	M	28		1
Darko Glishic		23/09/91	D	8	(2)	
Boban Grncarov		12/08/82	D	30		2
Vlatko Grozdanoski		30/01/83	M	20	(2)	3
Hovhannes Hambardzumyan	ARM	04/10/90	D	27		3
Senijad Ibričić	RIH	26/09/86	M	9	(4)	5
Dimitar Ivanov		19/01/95	M	3	(6)	1
Filip Ivanovski		01/05/85	A	17	(6)	11
Matija Kobetić	CRO	08/11/84	G	3		
Blagojce Ljamcevski		07/04/87	M	13	(10)	1
Artur Miranyan	ARM	27/12/95	A	1	(11)	
Dino Najdoski		08/05/92	D	1	(3)	
Tomislav Pacovski		28/06/82	G	12		
Igor Pavlović	MNE	24/02/82	G	17		
Filip Petkovski		24/05/90	A	11	(14)	6
Petar Petkovski		03/01/97	M	8		
Filip Petrov		23/02/89	A	12	(5)	3
Goran Popov		02/10/84	D	9	(1)	1
Viktor Serafimovski		24/10/95	M	5	(2)	
Stefan Spirovski		23/08/90	M	7	(3)	1
Filip Stojanovski		01/12/96	D	5	(2)	
Zlatko Tanevski		03/08/83	D	24		1
Aleksandar Temelkov		06/10/87	M		(2)	

Former Yugoslav Republic of **MACEDONIA**

Top goalscorers

20	Izair Emini (Renova)
18	Bojan Vručina (Shkëndija)
15	Marjan Altiparmakovski (Rabotnicki)
14	Hristijan Kirovski (Shkëndija)
11	Filip Ivanovski (Vardar)
10	Marjan Radeski (Metalurg)
9	Aco Stojkov (Rabotnicki)
8	Boško Stupić (Pelister/Bregalnica)
	Blaze Ilijoski (Rabotnicki)
	Dejan Blazevski (Vardar)

Promoted clubs

FK Shkupi

2012 • Cair (6,000) • fcshkupi.com
Coach: Zekirija Ramadan

FK Mladost Carev Dvor

1930 • Gradski, Resen (6,859); Tumbe Kafe, Bitola (8,000); Atina Bojadji, Ohrid (3,000) • no website
Coach: Kire Sterjov

Second level final table 2014/15

		Pld	W	D	L	F	A	Pts
1	FK Shkupi	27	16	5	6	44	19	53
2	FK Mladost Carev Dvor	27	14	5	8	40	27	47
3	FK Gostivar	27	12	8	7	31	27	44
4	FK Makedonija	27	11	8	8	29	18	41
5	KF Vëllazërimi	27	10	9	8	31	24	39
6	FK Skopje	27	10	9	8	25	19	39
7	FK Kozuv Miravci	27	9	11	7	28	20	38
8	FK Gorno Lisice	27	10	5	12	29	36	35
9	FK Drita	27	8	3	16	26	38	27
10	FK Napredok	27	2	3	22	23	78	9

Promotion/Relegation play-offs

(03/06/15 & 07/06/15)
Turnovo 1-1 Gostivar
Gostivar 0-2 Turnovo
(Turnovo 3-1)

DOMESTIC CUP

Kup na Makedonija 2014/15

FIRST ROUND

(19/08/14)
11 Oktomvri 0-9 Shkupi

(20/08/14)
Belasica 1-1 Napredok *(3-5 on pens)*
Bregalnica Delcevo 1-4 Drita
Fortuna 0-8 Turnovo
Goblen Junior 0-3 Teteks
Kozuv 2-1 Makedonija
Mladost Carev Dvor 0-1 Bregalnica Stip
Novaci 0-5 Gostivar
Pobeda Junior 3-2 Metalurg Skopje
Rabotnik Lozovo 0-3 Sileks *(w/o)*
Sasa 0-2 Renova
Vlaznimi 1-9 Vardar

(21/08/14)
Vulkan 0-2 Pelister

Byes – Gorno Lisice, Rabotnicki, Shkëndija

SECOND ROUND

(24/09/14 & 14/10/14)
Gostivar 1-4, 0-1 Renova *(1-5)*
Kozuv 2-0, 5-1 Napredok *(7-1)*
Pobeda Junior 1-1, 1-1 Drita *(2-2; 1-3 on pens)*
Shkupi 1-1, 0-1 Teteks *(1-2)*
Sileks 1-1, 0-0 Gorno Lisice *(1-1; Gorno Lisice on away goal)*
Turnovo 0-0, 0-0 Bregalnica *(0-0; 4-3 on pens)*

(24/09/14 & 21/10/14)
Pelister 0-0, 1-3 Rabotnicki *(1-3)*

(24/09/14 & 22/10/14)
Shkëndija 2-1, 0-3 Vardar *(2-4)*

QUARTER-FINALS

(18/11/14 & 04/12/14)
Kozuv 1-0 Teteks *(Ilieski 63)*
Teteks 5-0 Kozuv *(Drobarov 21, Nachevski 50, M Hristov 67, 73, S Hristov 68)*
(Teteks 5-1)

Turnovo 5-0 Drita *(Najdenov 43, Dolapchiev 45, 70, 71, Iliev 75)*
Drita 0-1 Turnovo *(Dolapchiev 60)*
(Turnovo 6-0)

(18/11/14 & 06/12/14)
Vardar 3-1 Renova *(Asani 41, Petrov 71, Temelkov 87; Jusufi 29)*
Renova 2-0 Vardar *(Emini 71, Mecinovic 84)*
(3-3; Renova on away goal)

(26/11/14 & 06/12/14)
Gorno Lisice 3-2 Rabotnicki *(Jasarovski 45p, Pandovski 78, Jovanovski 90; Stojkov 6, 37)*
Rabotnicki 3-1 Gorno Lisice *(Todorovski 62, Churlinov 69, Altiparmakovski 78; Mojsovski 76)*
(Rabotnicki 5-4)

SEMI-FINALS

(18/03/15 & 15/04/15)
Rabotnicki 2-1 Renova *(Vujcic 31p, Altiparmakovski 53; Emini 64)*
Renova 1-1 Rabotnicki *(Gafuri 86; Markoski 70)*
(Rabotnicki 3-2)

Teteks 2-1 Turnovo *(Jovanovski 42, 47; Mutafchiyski 67)*
Turnovo 2-1 Teteks *(Georgiev 64, Najdenov 89; Churlinov 10)*
(3-3; Teteks 4-2 on pens)

FINAL

(20/05/15)
Filip II Arena, Skopje
FK RABOTNICKI 2 *(Ilijoski 68, Altiparmakovski 72)*
FK TETEKS 1 *(Churlinov 45)*
Referee: Jakimovski
RABOTNICKI: Efremov, Ilievski, Siljanovski, Trajcevski (Sahiti 58), Cikarski, Petrovic, Vujcic, Velkovski, Altiparmakovski (Markoski 86), Anene, Ilijoski (Dodevski 90+2)
TETEKS: Mancevski, Najdoski, Drobarov, Stojcevski (Stojkovski 66), Ermadin Adem, Kostadinov (Cvetanoski 69), Oslonovski, Nachevski, Bozinovski, Churlinov, S Hristov (Tosevski 74)
Red card: Najdoski (71)

Rabotnicki retained the Macedonian Cup with a 2-1 win over relegated Teteks

MALTA
Malta Football Association (MFA)

Address	Millennium Stand, Floor 2	**President**	Norman
	National Stadium		Darmanin Demajo
	MT-Ta' Qali ATD 4000	**General secretary**	Bjorn Vassallo
Tel	+356 21 232 581	**Media officer**	Mark Attard
Fax	+356 21 245 136	**Year of formation**	1900
E-mail	info@mfa.com.mt	**National stadium**	National, Ta' Qali
Website	mfa.com.mt		(15,914)

KEY:

● – UEFA Champions League
● – UEFA Europa League
● – Promoted
● – Relegated

PREMIER LEAGUE CLUBS

 ① **Balzan FC**

 ② **Birkirkara FC**

 ③ **Floriana FC**

 ④ **Hibernians FC**

 ⑤ **Mosta FC**

 ⑥ **Naxxar Lions FC**

 ⑦ **Pietà Hotspurs FC**

 ⑧ **Qormi FC**

 ⑨ **Sliema Wanderers FC**

 ⑩ **Tarxien Rainbows FC**

 ⑪ **Valletta FC**

 ⑫ **Żebbuġ Rangers FC**

PROMOTED CLUBS

 ⑬ **Pembroke Athleta FC**

 ⑭ **St Andrews FC**

0 — 5 — 10 km
0 — 5 miles

Pembroke ⑬
Naxxar ⑭ St Andrews
Sliema ⑨
Mosta ⑤ ⑥ ⑪
Balzan Birkirkara ⑦
① ② Pietà Valletta
Żebbuġ Floriana ③
⑫ Qormi ④
⑧ Paola
Tarxien ⑩

Hibernians have a ball

Without a Premier League title for six years, Hibernians FC made up for lost time with a spectacular triumph in 2014/15. Powered up front by two Brazilian strikers, Edison and Jorginho, Branko Nišević's side ran in 97 goals to dominate the campaign from start to finish.

The Paola club were poised to claim their first domestic double since 1981/82, but that prize eluded them when they went down 2-0 to Birkirkara FC in the final of the Maltese Trophy. The Stripes had finished third in the league after being overhauled in the second phase by defending champions Valletta FC.

| Brazilian firepower blasts Paola club to Premier League title | First championship triumph in six years achieved in style | Birkirkara deny champions the double with cup final win |

Domestic league

Hibernians never displayed the slightest sign of weakness en route to one of the most comprehensive victories in the history of the Maltese Premier League. Birkirkara, Valletta and the rest were reduced to also-rans as Nišević's stormtroopers swept all before them on a 30-match unbeaten run that contained 26 victories. It was only after the club's 11th title was secure, following a 3-1 win against Floriana FC, that they finally lost – against surprise package Balzan FC, who would go on to finish fourth and qualify for Europe for the first time.

Premier League defences had no answer to the twin threat of Edison and Jorginho, who scored more than half of Hibernians' goals between them, each notching 25 to share the golden boot. Malta international Clayton Failla also found the net 16 times, and although keeping goals out at the other end was rarely a major concern, the team were well served between the posts by Henry Bonello, a replacement for living legend Mario Muscat, who decided to end his 21-year career with the club, making his final appearance in a 2-1 win against Qormi FC in August.

When the league reached the end of its first phase, with 22 matches played,

Hibernians held a 15-point lead over Birkirkara. The competition rules meant they would enter the second phase with just a seven-point advantage, but by the end of term, that had increased to nine, and it was Valletta, not Birkirkara, sitting in second place, the Lilywhites having caught and overtaken the Stripes thanks to a nine-game run in which they dropped just two points.

Unlike previous seasons, there was no split in the league, so all 12 clubs played each other once more. That spelled bad news for Pietà Hotspurs FC, who dropped from tenth to 11th and were relegated with bottom club Żebbuġ Rangers FC. Mosta FC, who fell from seventh to tenth, ultimately saved themselves with a play-off win over Gzira United FC, leaving Pembroke Athleta FC and St Andrews FC as the only two promoted teams.

Domestic cup

Over a month after wrapping up the Premier League title, Hibernians headed to the National Stadium in Ta' Qali in search of a victory in the Maltese Trophy final that would crown a perfect domestic campaign. However, with one of their deadly strike duo, Edison, having departed for South Korea, the Hibs attack was blunted, and instead it was two of

Birkirkara's South American imports, Argentinian defender Mauricio Mazzetti and Brazilian schemer Rafael Ledesma, who scored the goals that won the game and brought the trophy back to Birkirkara for the first time in seven years. The match served as a fitting finale for long-serving Stripes boss Paul Zammit, who left to replace his namesake Ivan at Valletta.

Europe

Another early collective exit of Malta's clubs from European competition was no great surprise, with only Sliema Wanderers FC coming close to making progress in their tie against Ferencvárosi TC. There was certainly no hint of things to come from Hibernians as they were walloped 9-2 on aggregate by FC Spartak Trnava.

National team

Malta made a decent fist of their UEFA EURO 2016 qualifying group, performing creditably in defence to restrict their more illustrious opponents to just ten goals in six games. Their only point came in Sofia, thanks to a penalty convincingly converted by Failla and another blasted over the bar by Bulgaria's Ivelin Popov. That happened to be Malta's only goal, too, but they did add a couple more in a friendly against Lithuania en route to a welcome 2-0 victory.

DOMESTIC SEASON AT A GLANCE

Premier League 2014/15 final tables

First Phase

		Pld	W	D	L	F	A	Pts	
1	Hibernians FC	22	19	3	0	68	13	60	(30)
2	Birkirkara FC	22	14	3	5	41	21	45	(23)
3	Valletta FC	22	14	2	6	51	18	44	(22)
4	Balzan FC	22	9	7	6	35	33	34	(17)
5	Floriana FC	22	7	8	7	38	41	29	(15)
6	Sliema Wanderers FC	22	7	5	10	26	31	26	(13)
7	Mosta FC	22	7	4	11	24	43	25	(13)
8	Naxxar Lions FC	22	5	7	10	26	34	22	(11)
9	Tarxien Rainbows FC	22	4	9	9	22	38	21	(11)
10	Pietà Hotspurs FC	22	5	6	11	19	36	21	(11)
11	Qormi FC	22	4	6	12	22	38	18	(9)
12	Żebbuġ Rangers FC	22	4	6	12	25	51	18	(9)

Second Phase

		Pld	W	D	L	F	A	Pts
1	**Hibernians FC**	33	27	5	1	97	24	56
2	Valletta FC	33	22	3	8	74	30	47
3	Birkirkara FC	33	19	7	7	59	31	43
4	Balzan FC	33	17	8	8	59	45	42
5	Floriana FC	33	13	11	9	58	51	36
6	Sliema Wanderers FC	33	10	9	14	50	56	26
7	Naxxar Lions FC	33	9	9	15	40	51	25
8	Qormi FC	33	8	9	16	40	55	24
9	Tarxien Rainbows FC	33	8	9	16	35	60	23
10	Mosta FC	33	9	6	18	38	72	21
11	Pietà Hotspurs FC	33	6	8	19	30	58	16
12	Żebbuġ Rangers FC	33	5	6	22	37	84	12

NB Figures in brackets indicate points carried forward to the Second Phase

European qualification 2015/16

 Champion: Hibernians FC (second qualifying round)

 Cup winner: Birkirkara FC (first qualifying round)
Valletta FC (first qualifying round)
Balzan FC (first qualifying round)

Top scorer	Edison (Hibernians) & Jorginho (Hibernians), 25 goals
Relegated clubs	Żebbuġ Rangers FC, Pietà Hotspurs FC
Promoted clubs	Pembroke Athleta FC, St Andrews FC
Cup final	Birkirkara FC 2-0 Hibernians FC

Team of the season
(5-3-2)

Coach: Nišević *(Hibernians)*

Bonello *(Hibernians)*

Vukanac *(Birkirkara)* — Rodolfo Soares *(Hibernians)* — Agius *(Hibernians)*

Z Muscat *(Birkirkara)* — Failla *(Hibernians)*

Fenech *(Birkirkara)* — Cohen *(Hibernians)* — Gilmar *(Naxxar)*

Kaljević *(Mosta/Balzan)* — Edison *(Hibernians)*

Player of the season

Clayton Failla
(Hibernians FC)

Voted FA Player of the Year in 2009, when Hibernians last won the title, Failla was an even more prominent figure in the club's 2014/15 Premier League triumph, the 29-year-old Malta international wing-back taking the lead from the team's prolific Brazilian strikers Edison and Jorginho to score 16 goals himself. Just four of those were penalties, the method he used to register Malta's only goal in their opening six UFFA EURO 2016 qualifiers and bring his country an unlikely 1-1 draw in Bulgaria.

Newcomer of the season

Zach Muscat
(Birkirkara FC)

Uncapped at senior level by Malta at the start of the season, Muscat played in all nine of his country's internationals in 2014/15, swiftly establishing himself as the first-choice right-back in Pietro Ghedin's team. The youngster was equally proficient for his club, helping Birkirkara to concede at a rate of less than a goal per game and also playing his part in their FA Trophy triumph, their most important clean sheet of the campaign coming in the 2-0 defeat of champions Hibernians FC in the final.

MALTA

NATIONAL TEAM

Top five all-time caps
David Carabott (121); Gilbert Agius (120); Carmel Busuttil (111); **Michael Mifsud** (110); Joe Brincat (103)

Top five all-time goals
Michael Mifsud (39); Carmel Busuttil (23); David Carabott (12); Gilbert Agius & Hubert Suda (8)

Results 2014/15

04/09/14	Slovakia	A	Zilina	L	0-1	
09/09/14	Croatia (ECQ)	A	Zagreb	L	0-2	
10/10/14	Norway (ECQ)	H	Ta' Qali	L	0-3	
13/10/14	Italy (ECQ)	H	Ta' Qali	L	0-1	
16/11/14	Bulgaria (ECQ)	A	Sofia	D	1-1	Failla (49p)
25/03/15	Georgia	A	Tbilisi	L	0-2	
28/03/15	Azerbaijan (ECQ)	A	Baku	L	0-2	
08/06/15	Lithuania	H	Ta' Qali	W	2-0	P Fenech (62), Effiong (79)
12/06/15	Bulgaria (ECQ)	H	Ta' Qali	L	0-1	

Appearances 2014/15

Coach: Pietro Ghedin (ITA)	21/11/52		Svk	CRO	NOR	ITA	BUL	Geo	AZE	Ltu	BUL	Caps	Goals
Andrew Hogg	02/03/85	Kalloni (GRE)	G	G	G	G	G		G			40	-
Steve Borg	15/05/88	Valletta	D66	D 31*				D89	D			13	-
Ryan Camilleri	22/05/88	Valletta	D	D	D	D	D	D46	D36	D	D	22	-
Jonathan Caruana	24/07/86	Valletta	D			D	D	D	D			35	2
Andrei Agius	12/08/86	Hibernians	D46	D	D	D	D	D	D	D	D	50	1
Clayton Failla	08/01/86	Hibernians	D82	D	D	D93	D81			D82	D	41	2
Ryan Fenech	20/04/86	Valletta	M63	D	M72	s78			s81			42	1
Paul Fenech	20/12/86	Birkirkara	M87	M87	M	M	M		M	M80	M	28	1
Rowen Muscat	05/06/91	Dunaújváros (HUN) /Birkirkara	M	M76	M	M	M	M	M	M89	M	18	-
André Schembri	27/05/86	FSV Frankfurt (GER) /Omonia (CYP)	M78	M	M85	M85	M78	M	M81	s89	s76	66	3
Michael Mifsud	17/04/81	Sliema	A	A33	A	A 27*				A	A84	110	39
Zach Muscat	22/08/93	Birkirkara	s46	M	D	D	D	s46	s36	D	D	9	-
Bjorn Kristensen	05/04/93	Hibernians	s63	s76	s72			M71		s63		7	-
Steve Bezzina	05/01/87	Balzan	s66	s33		s93	s81	D	D46			9	-
Andrew Cohen	13/05/81	Hibernians	s78			s85		M		M60	s84	64	1
Edward Herrera	14/11/86	Birkirkara	s82							s56	s63	19	1
Ryan Scicluna	30/07/93	Birkirkara	s87	s87						s80		3	-
Roderick Briffa	24/08/81	Valletta			D72	M	M		M	M63	M76	84	1
Justin Grioli	20/09/87	Balzan			s72							1	-
Terence Vella	20/04/90	Naxxar			s85		s93					11	-
John Mintoff	23/08/88	Sliema				D72						8	-
Clifford Gatt Baldacchino	09/02/88	Sliema				s72						2	-
Jean-Paul Farrugia	21/03/92	Spartak Trnava (SVK) /Hibernians				A93		A60				3	-
Justin Haber	09/06/81	Birkirkara						G		G	G	54	-
Alfred Effiong	29/11/84	Qormi						s60	A	s60	A	4	1
Mark Scerri	16/01/90	Sliema						s71				3	-
Ryan Camenzuli	08/09/94	Birkirkara						s89				1	-
Steve Pisani	07/08/92	Floriana							s46			1	-
Alex Muscat	14/12/84	Sliema								D56	D63	29	-
Joseph Zerafa	31/05/88	Birkirkara								s82		3	-

EUROPE

Valletta FC

CHAMPIONS LEAGUE

Second qualifying round - Qarabağ FK (AZE)
H 0-1
Vella, J Caruana, Azzopardi, R Camilleri, Fenech, Hugo Faria, Briffa, Elford-Alliyu (Kooh-Sohna 72), Bajada (Arab 90+2), Nafti (Zammit 85), Dimech. Coach: Gilbert Agius (MLT)
Red card: R Camilleri 84
A 0-4
Vella, J Caruana, Azzopardi, Fenech, Hugo Faria, Briffa, Elford-Alliyu (Kooh-Sohna 57), Bajada, Zammit (Montebello 69), Nafti (Al Kamali 85), Dimech. Coach: Gilbert Agius (MLT)
Red cards: J Caruana 19, Fenech 84

Birkirkara FC

EUROPA LEAGUE

First qualifying round - Diósgyőri VTK (HUN)
A 1-2 Matheus Bissi (35)
Murcia, Herrera, Matheus Bissi, Sciberras (Agius 74), Fenech, Camenzuli (Scicluna 59), Vella (Rafael Ledesma 81), Vukanac, Moreno, J Zerafa, Z Muscat. Coach: Paul Zammit (MLT)
Red card: Matheus Bissi 46
H 1-4 Camenzuli (44)
Murcia, Herrera, Fenech, Camenzuli, Vella (Zammit 84), Grech (Omerou 04), Vukanac, Moreno, J Zerafa, Scicluna, Agius (Rafael Ledesma 46). Coach: Paul Zammit (MLT)

Hibernians FC

EUROPA LEAGUE

First qualifying round - FC Spartak Trnava (SVK)
H 2-4 Cohen (49), Failla (50)
Balzan, Tabone Desira, Rui da Gracia, Pearson, Rodolfo Soares, Marcelo Dias (B Muscat 65), Cohen, Kristensen, Failla (Degabriele 81), Bezzina, Farrugia (Mbong 90+3). Coach: Branko Nišević (SRB)
Red card: Pearson 10
A 0-5
Balzan, Tabone Desira, Rui da Gracia, Rodolfo Soares, Marcelo Dias, Cohen, Kristensen, Failla, B Muscat (Degabriele 65), Bezzina, Farrugia. Coach: Branko Nišević (SRB)

Sliema Wanderers FC

EUROPA LEAGUE

First qualifying round - Ferencvárosi TC (HUN)
H 1-1 Ohawuchi (39)
Zammit, A Muscat, Scozzese, Potezica, Mintoff, Scerri, Mifsud, Ohawuchi, Barbetti, G Muscat (Cilia 68), Bianciardi. Coach: Alfonso Greco (ITA)
A 1-2 Scozzese (60)
Zammit, A Muscat, Scozzese, Potezica, Mintoff, Scerri, Mifsud, Ohawuchi, Barbetti, G Muscat (Cilia 80), Bianciardi. Coach: Alfonso Greco (ITA)
Red card: Barbetti 90+3

DOMESTIC LEAGUE CLUB-BY-CLUB

Stadiums

Ta' Qali National Stadium (15,914)
Hibernians Ground (2,000)
Victor Tedesco Stadium (2,000)
MFA Centenary Stadium (2,000)

Balzan FC

1937 • balzanfc.com
Coach: Oliver Spiteri

2014
16/08	Żebbuġ	W 4-2	Piccioni 2, L Micallef, Guerrero
23/08	Naxxar	D 1-1	Piccioni
27/08	Qormi	W 2-1	Guerrero, Darmanin
13/09	Birkirkara	W 3-2	Mifsud Triganza 2, Guerrero
21/09	Mosta	L 0-1	
27/09	Tarxien	W 3-2	Piccioni 2 (1p), Zárate
03/10	Floriana	D 1-1	Serrano
19/10	Pietà	D 1-1	Zárate
26/10	Sliema	D 0-0	
01/11	Valletta	L 0-2	
10/11	Hibernians	L 0-3	
22/11	Żebbuġ	D 1-1	Piccioni
29/11	Naxxar	L 1-3	Piccioni
07/12	Qormi	D 1-1	Guerrero
13/12	Birkirkara	D 0-0	
20/12	Mosta	W 1-0	Zárate
2015			
04/01	Tarxien	W 5-0	Mifsud Triganza 2, Darmanin, Bezzina, Piccioni
11/01	Floriana	W 3-2	Mifsud Triganza, Piccioni (p), Guobadia
18/01	Hibernians	L 0-4	
25/01	Sliema	W 5-3	Piccioni 2, Kaljević 2, Darmanin
01/02	Valletta	W 2-1	Kaljević, Piccioni
07/02	Pietà	L 1-2	Arab
21/02	Mosta	D 1-1	Kaljević
28/02	Naxxar	W 2-1	Kaljević (p), Guerrero
07/03	Floriana	L 0-3	
15/03	Sliema	W 2-1	Kaljević, L Micallef
20/03	Tarxien	W 3-2	Grima, Kaljević 2
06/04	Pietà	W 3-0	Piccioni, L Micallef, Kaljević
13/04	Żebbuġ	W 4-1	Serrano, Kaljević, Grima, Mifsud Triganza
17/04	Qormi	W 5-1	Kaljević 2, Piccioni, Serrano, Arab
26/04	Hibernians	W 3-1	Mifsud Triganza, Piccioni (p), Sciberras
02/05	Valletta	L 0-1	
07/05	Birkirkara	W 1-0	Mifsud Triganza

Name	Nat	DoB	Pos	Aps	(s)	Gls
Terence Agius		15/01/94	M	6	(9)	
Samir Arab		25/03/94	D	17	(5)	2
Steve Bezzina		05/01/87	D	31	(1)	1
Michael Borg		18/10/92	A	1	(9)	
Clive Brincat		31/05/83	M	24		
Christian Cassar		22/03/92	G	10		
Sean Cipriott		10/09/97	D		(2)	
Juan Corbolan		03/03/97	M		(4)	
Ryan Darmanin		12/12/85	M	5	(16)	3
Dylan Grima		18/07/90	M	13	(6)	2
Justin Grioli		20/09/87	M	28	(2)	
Alvarado Guerrero	COL	01/03/85	A	25	(1)	5
Osa Guobadia	NGA	01/06/87	M	28	(2)	1
Bojan Kaljević	MNE	25/01/86	A	10		12
Godwin Mackay		20/06/95	M		(2)	
Gianfranco Micallef		13/02/97	M		(1)	
Lydon Micallef		16/05/92	M	19	(10)	3
Jean Pierre Mifsud Triganza		20/11/81	A	18	(7)	8
Fredrick Odebe	NGA	31/12/88	G	2	(3)	
Gianmarco Piccioni	ITA	18/07/91	A	26	(1)	15
Luke Sciberras		15/09/89	A	18	(6)	1
Elkin Serrano	COL	17/03/84	D	30		3
Mark Spiteri		25/04/92	M		(3)	
Steve Sultana		07/09/90	G	23	(1)	
Edison Zárate	CHI	03/06/87	M	29	(1)	3

Birkirkara FC

1950 • birkirkarafc.com
Major honours
Maltese League (4) 2000, 2006, 2010, 2013;
Maltese Cup (5) 2002, 2003, 2005, 2008, 2015
Coach: Paul Zammit

2014

16/08	Pietà	W 2-1	*Rafael Ledesma, Liliu*
23/08	Żebbuġ	W 4-0	*Grech, Liliu, Eliandro, Rafael Ledesma (p)*
26/08	Naxxar	W 1-0	*Fenech*
13/09	Balzan	L 2-3	*Liliu 2*
20/09	Qormi	W 2-0	*Camenzuli, Rafael Ledesma*
28/09	Mosta	W 2-0	*Liliu, Eliandro*
02/10	Tarxien	L 1-3	*Liliu*
19/10	Valletta	W 2-0	*Rafael Ledesma, Liliu*
25/10	Hibernians	L 0-1	
03/11	Sliema	W 1-0	*Liliu*
10/11	Floriana	L 1-2	*Z Muscat*
22/11	Pietà	L 3-4	*Liliu 2, Rafael Ledesma (p)*
30/11	Żebbuġ	W 3-1	*Rafael Ledesma (p), Liliu, Agius*
07/12	Naxxar	W 3-1	*Scicluna, Rafael Ledesma (p), Matheus Bissi*
13/12	Balzan	D 0-0	
21/12	Qormi	W 2-0	*Shodiya 2*

2015

04/01	Mosta	W 5-1	*Rafael Ledesma, Shodiya 2, Liliu, Fenech*
10/01	Tarxien	W 2-1	*Rafael Ledesma, Shodiya*
18/01	Floriana	W 2-1	*Rafael Ledesma, Scicluna*
24/01	Hibernians	D 1-1	*Vukanac*
01/02	Sliema	D 1-1	*Rafael Ledesma*
08/02	Valletta	D 1-1	*Vukanac*
22/02	Naxxar	W 1-0	*Herrera*
01/03	Mosta	W 3-0	*Camenzuli, Rafael Ledesma, Shodiya*
07/03	Sliema	W 4-2	*Camenzuli 2, Rafael Ledesma, Maachi*
15/03	Floriana	D 0-0	
19/03	Pietà	W 2-1	*Z Muscat, Mazzetti*
04/04	Tarxien	W 2-0	*Vukanac, Shodiya*
10/04	Qormi	D 2-2	*Maachi, Vukanac*
19/04	Żebbuġ	W 3-1	*Matheus Bissi, Camenzuli, Liliu*
25/04	Valletta	L 1-2	*Scicluna*
03/05	Hibernians	D 0-0	
07/05	Balzan	L 0-1	

Name	Nat	DoB	Pos	Aps	(s)	Gls
Edmond Agius		23/02/87	M	9	(14)	1
Dylan Aquilina		12/07/95	A		(1)	
Antoine Borg		04/04/94	M	1	(9)	
Ryan Camenzuli		08/09/94	M	30		5
Andrea Curmi		28/04/96	M		(1)	
Eliandro	BRA	23/04/90	A	12	(4)	2
Paul Fenech		20/12/86	M	29		2
Leighton Grech		23/03/90	A	3	(9)	1
Justin Haber		09/06/81	G	30		
Mirza Hamzabegović	BIH	11/06/90	A	3		
Edward Herrera		14/11/86	D	23	(6)	1
Beppe Jaccarini		01/06/96	D		(1)	
Liliu	BRA	30/03/90	A	18	(3)	13
Nassir Maachi	NED	09/09/85	A	3	(6)	2
Matheus Bissi	BRA	19/03/91	D	20	(8)	2
Mauricio Mazzetti	ARG	18/06/86	D	12		1
Alejandro Moreno	ESP	17/05/86	D	11	(3)	
Rowen Muscat		05/06/91	M	12		
Zach Muscat		22/08/93	D	31		2
Rafael Ledesma	BRA	31/12/82	M	23	(4)	13
Gareth Sciberras		29/03/83	M	9		
Ryan Scicluna		30/07/93	M	26	(1)	3
Vyacheslav Shevchenko	UKR	30/05/85	A	1	(3)	
Shola Shodiya	NGA	17/06/91	A	17	(4)	7
Nikola Vukanac	SRB	14/01/86	D	29	(1)	4
Kurt Zammit		21/01/93	A	2	(19)	
Joseph Zerafa		31/05/88	D	9	(1)	

Floriana FC

1894 • florianafc.com
Major honours
Maltese League (25) 1910, 1912, 1913, 1921, 1922, 1925, 1927, 1928, 1929, 1931, 1935, 1937, 1950, 1951, 1952, 1953, 1955, 1958, 1962, 1968, 1970, 1973, 1975, 1977, 1993; Maltese Cup (19) 1938, 1945, 1947, 1949, 1950, 1953, 1954, 1955, 1957, 1958, 1961, 1966, 1967, 1972, 1976, 1981, 1993, 1994, 2011
Coach: Giovanni Tedesco (ITA)

2014

16/08	Hibernians	L 0-3	
23/08	Sliema	D 1-1	*Piciollo*
26/08	Valletta	L 0-2	
13/09	Pietà	W 3-1	*Piciollo 2, Samb*
20/09	Żebbuġ	D 3-3	*Plut 2, Pisani*
27/09	Naxxar	D 1-1	*Plut*
03/10	Balzan	D 1-1	*Samb*
18/10	Qormi	L 2-4	*I Galea, Plut*
25/10	Mosta	W 3-2	*Plut 2, Farrugia*
02/11	Tarxien	D 1-1	*Samb*
10/11	Birkirkara	W 2-1	*Bonnici, Plut*
22/11	Hibernians	L 0-5	
30/11	Sliema	W 2-1	*Samb, Conor Borg*
06/12	Valletta	L 1-4	*Plut*
13/12	Pietà	D 1-1	*Bonnici*
20/12	Żebbuġ	W 4-1	*Samb 2, Plut, Piciollo*

2015

03/01	Naxxar	W 4-1	*Pisani, Muir (p), Douglas (p), Piciollo*
11/01	Balzan	L 2-3	*Bonnici, G Galea*
18/01	Birkirkara	L 1-2	*Conor Borg*
24/01	Mosta	W 3-1	*Plut, Piciollo, Douglas*
31/01	Tarxien	D 1-1	*Piciollo*
08/02	Qormi	D 2-2	*Muir (p), Piciollo*
21/02	Pietà	W 2-0	*Piciollo, og (K Micallef)*
28/02	Tarxien	W 2-1	*og (Manu Bonaque), Samb*
07/03	Balzan	W 3-0	*Piciollo 2, Conor Borg*
15/03	Birkirkara	D 0-0	
19/03	Qormi	D 0-0	
04/04	Żebbuġ	W 3-1	*Plut, Piciollo, Briffa*
12/04	Valletta	L 0-1	
18/04	Hibernians	L 1-3	*Bonnici*
26/04	Naxxar	W 4-1	*Coronado 3, Piciollo*
03/05	Mosta	D 2-2	*Coronado, Piciollo*
07/05	Sliema	W 3-1	*Coronado, Plut, Piciollo*

Name	Nat	DoB	Pos	Aps	(s)	Gls
Daniel Agius		15/11/96	D		(2)	
Darrell Baldachino		28/02/96	D		(1)	
Steve Bonnici		02/02/89	D	24		4
Clyde Borg		20/03/92	M	23	(2)	
Conor Borg		13/02/94	M	15	(3)	3
Joseph Borg		26/01/87	M	2	(2)	
Sacha Borg		26/04/93	D	13	(4)	
Emanuel Briffa		13/02/94	M	28	(3)	1
Matthew Calleja Cremona		14/09/94	G	11	(1)	
Igor Coronado	BRA	18/08/92	A	3	(8)	5
Douglas	BRA	19/03/87	D	30		2
Emerson	BRA	24/02/91	M	24	(6)	
Brooke Farrugia		17/07/93	M	15	(9)	1
Giovanni Galea		01/04/91	A	5	(14)	1
Isaac Galea		31/08/95	A		(4)	1
Luca Gatt		21/12/99	M		(1)	
Tyrone Gauci		08/11/97	G	8		
Luke Micallef		26/06/96	A	1	(3)	
Manolito Micallef		16/11/83	M	10	(1)	
Sean Mintoff		30/10/85	M	1		
Gary Muir	SCO	15/12/85	M	14	(7)	2
Matteo Piciollo	ITA	15/10/92	A	28	(2)	15
Steve Pisani		07/08/92	M	26	(3)	2
Vito Plut	SVN	08/07/88	A	32		12
Rodrigo Aguiar	BRA	19/05/93	D	3		
Amadou Samb	SEN	22/04/88	A	16	(2)	7
Andre Scicluna		22/09/98	D	13		
Valerio Senatore	ITA	15/11/87	G	13	(1)	
Neil Spiteri		03/06/97	D	5	(4)	
Glenn Tabone		08/02/96	M		(1)	

Hibernians FC

1922 • hiberniansfc.org
Major honours
Maltese League (11) 1961, 1967, 1969, 1979, 1981, 1982, 1994, 1995, 2002, 2009, 2015; Maltese Cup (10) 1962, 1970, 1971, 1980, 1982, 1998, 2006, 2007, 2012, 2013
Coach: Branko Nišević (SRB)

2014

16/08	Floriana	W 3-0	*Jorginho, Failla, Bezzina*
24/08	Qormi	W 2-1	*Edison, Marcelo Dias*
27/08	Sliema	W 3-1	*Edison, Jorginho, Degabriele*
14/09	Valletta	W 2-1	*Jorginho, Edison*
20/09	Pietà	W 3-1	*Jorginho 2, Failla*
27/09	Żebbuġ	W 4-0	*Cohen, Failla, Marcelo Dias, Edison*
03/10	Naxxar	W 5-1	*Cohen, Edison 2, Failla 2 (1p)*
18/10	Tarxien	D 1-1	*Failla*
25/10	Birkirkara	W 1-0	*Edison*
02/11	Mosta	W 5-0	*Edison 4, og (A Borg)*
10/11	Balzan	W 3-0	*Rodolfo Soares 2, Kristensen*
22/11	Floriana	W 5-0	*Edison, Jorginho 2, Failla, Cohen*
29/11	Qormi	W 6-0	*Jorginho 3, Edison 2, Failla*
06/12	Sliema	W 2-1	*Edison 2*
14/12	Valletta	W 3-1	*Cohen, Jorginho 2*
20/12	Pietà	W 3-0	*Edison 2, Failla*

2015

04/01	Żebbuġ	W 5-2	*Jorginho, Rodolfo Soares, Pearson, Edison, Cohen*
11/01	Naxxar	W 2-0	*Failla, Edison*
17/01	Balzan	W 4-0	*Edison, Cohen, Jorginho, Degabriele*
24/01	Birkirkara	D 1-1	*Agius*
31/01	Mosta	D 1-1	*Edison*
07/02	Tarxien	W 4-1	*Jorginho, Luís André, Edison, Failla (p)*
22/02	Qormi	W 2-1	*Edison, Jorginho*
28/02	Żebbuġ	W 5-0	*Jorginho, Failla, Agius, Cohen 2*
07/03	Pietà	W 3-1	*Failla, Agius, Farrugia*
15/03	Tarxien	W 2-0	*Rodolfo Soares, Edison*
19/03	Naxxar	D 2-2	*Jorginho, Jackson*
04/04	Mosta	W 5-0	*Jorginho 2, Farrugia, Luís André, Degabriele*
12/04	Sliema	W 3-2	*Kristensen, Failla (p), Cohen*
18/04	Floriana	W 3-1	*Jorginho 2, Failla (p)*
26/04	Balzan	L 1-3	*Failla*
03/05	Birkirkara	D 0-0	
09/05	Valletta	W 3-1	*Jorginho 3 (1p)*

Name	Nat	DoB	Pos	Aps	(s)	Gls
Andre Agius		12/08/82	D	29		3
Johann Bezzina		30/05/94	A	20	(6)	1
Henry Bonello		13/10/88	G	30		
Jurgen Borg		08/08/94	G	2	(3)	
Andrew Cohen		13/05/81	M	31		9
Jurgen Degabriele		10/10/96	A	1	(21)	3
Edison	BRA	12/08/85	A	25		25
Clayton Failla		08/01/86	D	32		16
Jean-Paul Farrugia		21/03/92	D	4	(3)	2
Jackson	BRA	09/07/82	M	21	(12)	1
Jorginho	BRA	04/12/85	A	33		25
Bjorn Kristensen		05/04/93	M	32		2
Luís André	BRA	29/03/88	A	2	(3)	2
Marcelo Dias	BRA	29/09/85	A	16	(4)	2
Joseph Essien Mbong		15/07/97	A	7	(9)	
Mario Muscat		18/08/76	G	1	(1)	
Jonathan Pearson		13/01/87	D	12	(10)	1
Marko Rajić	SRB	30/07/91	A	4	(2)	
Rodolfo Soares	BRA	25/05/85	D	31		4
Rui da Gracia	EQG	28/05/85	D	21	(1)	
Timothy Tabone Desira		15/07/95	M	4	(6)	
Keith Tanti		11/05/93	D	5	(8)	
Dunstan Vella		27/04/96	D		(3)	

Mosta FC

1935 • no website
Coach: Enrico Piccioni (ITA);
(03/11/14) Peter Smith (ENG)

2014

17/08	Valletta	W 1-0	Kaljević
24/08	Pietà	W 1-0	Daniel Bueno
27/08	Żebbuġ	W 2-0	Kaljević 2 (1p)
13/09	Naxxar	D 1-1	Daniel Bueno
21/09	Balzan	W 1-0	Kaljević
28/09	Birkirkara	L 0-2	
02/10	Qormi	L 0-4	
18/10	Sliema	L 1-4	Kaljević
25/10	Floriana	L 2-3	A Borg, Micallef
02/11	Hibernians	L 0-5	
09/11	Tarxien	W 2-1	Micallef, Kaljević
23/11	Valletta	L 0-5	
29/11	Pietà	W 3-1	Daniel Bueno, Milovanović, Mateus Ribeiro
07/12	Żebbuġ	D 1-1	Mateus Ribeiro
13/12	Naxxar	L 1-2	Kaljević
20/12	Balzan	L 0-1	

2015

04/01	Birkirkara	L 1-5	Jovanović
10/01	Qormi	W 3-1	I Zammit, Diogo, Ekani
17/01	Tarxien	D 1-1	Mateus Ribeiro
24/01	Floriana	L 1-3	I Zammit
31/01	Hibernians	D 1-1	Babangida
07/02	Sliema	L 1-2	Babangida
21/02	Balzan	D 1-1	Niçoise
01/03	Birkirkara	L 0-3	
07/03	Qormi	L 1-3	Roberts
14/03	Żebbuġ	W 3-1	Babangida, I Zammit, Fortune
19/03	Valletta	L 1-3	Roberts
04/04	Hibernians	L 0-5	
10/04	Pietà	W 3-2	I Zammit 2 (1p), Fortune
18/04	Tarxien	L 1-2	Babangida
25/04	Sliema	L 1-5	A Borg
03/05	Floriana	D 2-2	A Borg 2
08/05	Naxxar	L 1-2	Farrugia

Name	Nat	DoB	Pos	Aps	(s)	Gls
Haruna Babangida	NGA	01/10/82	A	9		4
Marcos Bernal	MEX	15/02/93	G	4		
Adrian Borg		20/05/89	D	19	(2)	4
Omar Borg		12/02/81	G	27	(1)	
James Brincat		03/12/96	M	3	(14)	
Mark Brincat		15/06/86	D	15	(3)	
Zachary Brincat		24/06/98	A	2	(5)	
Daniel Bueno	BRA	15/12/83	A	13	(1)	3
Alieu Darbo	GAM	03/08/92	M	1	(3)	
Matteo Di Vita		17/08/97	M	1	(1)	
Diogo	BRA	20/03/90	A	3		1
Jonas Ekani	CMR	13/10/92	D	21	(2)	1
Fábio Paim	POR	15/02/88	A		(2)	
Dyson Falzon		09/03/86	M	22	(2)	
Tyrone Farrugia		22/02/89	D	27		1
Udo Fortune	NGA	02/02/88	A	8	(4)	2
Kyle Frendo		30/06/95	M	5	(5)	
Kyle Gerada		05/01/91	G	2	(1)	
Ismael Grech		26/09/91	D	1	(3)	
Ryan Grech		03/04/85	M	26	(1)	
Saša Jovanović	SRB	12/01/88	A	4	(4)	1
Bojan Kaljević	MNE	25/01/86	A	14	(1)	7
Ousman Koli	GAM	18/10/88	M	8	(1)	
Youssou Lo	SEN	19/03/92	A		(3)	
Kurt Magro		04/06/86	M	31		
Mateus Ribeiro	BRA	16/11/83	M	8	(3)	3
Manolito Micallef		16/11/83	D	12		2
Nemanja Milovanović	SRB	12/06/91	M	17	(1)	1
Michaël Niçoise	FRA	19/09/84	A	9		1
Yannick Ossok	CMR	06/06/86	D	6	(1)	
Pedrinho	BRA	04/08/86	A	7	(3)	
Karl Pulo		30/07/89	M	12	(10)	
Gary Roberts	ENG	02/02/87	M	9		2
Gordon Saliba		07/08/96	M		(1)	
Aaron Sammut		18/06/97	M	1	(3)	
Dexter Xuereb		21/09/97	D		(1)	
Ian Zammit		09/12/86	M	12	(1)	5
Kurt Zammit		01/12/95	M	4	(6)	

Naxxar Lions FC

1920 • no website
Coach: Winston Muscat;
(06/10/14) Jesmond Zerafa

2014

17/08	Qormi	L 0-1	
23/08	Balzan	D 1-1	Gilmar (p)
26/08	Birkirkara	L 0-1	
13/09	Mosta	D 1-1	Vella
20/09	Tarxien	L 1-2	Ibok
27/09	Floriana	D 1-1	Gueye (p)
03/10	Hibernians	L 1-5	Gilmar
18/10	Żebbuġ	D 3-3	Gilmar, Falzon, Gueye (p)
26/10	Valletta	L 0-2	
01/11	Pietà	W 4-0	Falzon, Emenike 2, Vella
08/11	Sliema	W 1-0	og (Mintoff)
23/11	Qormi	D 1-1	Gilmar
29/11	Balzan	W 3-1	Vella 2, Emenike
07/12	Birkirkara	L 1-3	Gilmar
13/12	Mosta	W 2-1	Gilmar, Gueye
20/12	Tarxien	L 0-1	

2015

03/01	Floriana	L 1-4	Emenike
11/01	Hibernians	L 0-2	
17/01	Sliema	D 0-0	
25/01	Valletta	L 0-3	
31/01	Pietà	D 1-1	Buhagiar
07/02	Żebbuġ	W 4-0	Gilmar 2 (1p), Jorge Santos 2
22/02	Birkirkara	L 0-1	
28/02	Balzan	L 1-2	Vella (p)
08/03	Żebbuġ	W 2-1	Gilmar, Jorge Santos
15/03	Qormi	W 2-1	Del Negro, Gilmar
19/03	Hibernians	D 2-2	Jorge Santos, Touré
06/04	Valletta	L 0-1	
13/04	Tarxien	L 0-1	
19/04	Pietà	D 0-0	
26/04	Floriana	L 1-4	Falzon
02/05	Sliema	W 4-3	Scicluna, Touré (p), Jorge Santos, Vella
08/05	Mosta	W 2-1	Vella, Gilmar

Name	Nat	DoB	Pos	Aps	(s)	Gls
Julian Azzopardi		09/10/87	G	31		
Victor Bellia		02/11/79	M	7	(11)	
Duane Bonnici		10/10/95	D		(10)	
Albert Bruce	GHA	30/12/93	M	13	(1)	
Angus Buhagiar		29/04/87	A	28	(1)	1
Gilmour Ryan Cassar		20/11/95	D	19	(5)	
Jurgen Debono		13/12/95	M		(3)	
Mattia Del Negro		07/09/92	M	19	(4)	1
Pablo Doffo	ARG	06/04/83	M	17	(6)	
Mbachu Emenike	NGA	21/05/89	A	12	(5)	4
Darren Falzon		08/05/92	A	27	(5)	3
David Fenech		17/06/88	M	13	(2)	
Gilmar	BRA	26/03/90	M	29	(1)	11
Papé Gueye	SEN	20/07/90	A	12	(4)	3
Emmanuel Ibok	NGA	22/08/89	D	31		1
Jorge Santos	BRA	23/04/87	A	13	(1)	5
Luke Pecorella		04/01/95	G	2	(3)	
David Reano	ARG	20/03/84	D	15		
Terence Scerri		03/04/84	A	1		
Andrew Scicluna		17/06/90	D	32		1
Sidney	BRA	10/02/88	D	3		
Frank Temile	NGA	15/07/90	M	6	(3)	
Demba Touré	SEN	31/12/84	A	5	(4)	2
Edafe Uzeh	NGA	22/03/88	D	4		
Terence Vella		20/04/90	A	24	(9)	7

Pietà Hotspurs FC

1968 • pietahfc.com.mt
Coach: Noel Coleiro

2014

16/08	Birkirkara	L 1-2	Attard
24/08	Mosta	L 0-1	
27/08	Tarxien	D 0-0	
13/09	Floriana	L 1-3	Rafael Xavier
20/09	Hibernians	L 1-3	Rafael Xavier
28/09	Sliema	L 0-2	
02/10	Valletta	W 2-1	Gabriel, Rafael Xavier
19/10	Balzan	D 1-1	L Micallef
25/10	Żebbuġ	W 1-0	Pisani
01/11	Naxxar	L 0-4	
09/11	Qormi	D 0-0	
22/11	Birkirkara	W 4-3	L Micallef, T Agius, Pisani (p), Francés
29/11	Mosta	L 1-3	Francés
07/12	Tarxien	D 0-0	
13/12	Floriana	D 1-1	Pisani (p)
20/12	Hibernians	L 0-3	

2015

04/01	Sliema	L 1-2	L Micallef
10/01	Valletta	L 0-3	
17/01	Qormi	W 1-0	L Micallef
27/01	Żebbuġ	L 1-2	Anonam
31/01	Naxxar	D 1-1	Francés
07/02	Balzan	W 2-1	Grech, Francés
21/02	Floriana	L 0-2	
28/02	Sliema	D 1-1	Léo Fortunato
07/03	Hibernians	L 1-3	Pisani
14/03	Valletta	L 1-3	Francés
19/03	Birkirkara	L 1-2	Léo Fortunato
06/04	Balzan	L 0-3	
10/04	Mosta	L 2-3	Anonam, Francés
19/04	Naxxar	L 0-0	
25/04	Żebbuġ	W 3-1	Cesare, Francés, Gabriel
02/05	Qormi	L 1-2	Newuche
08/05	Tarxien	L 1-3	Francés

Name	Nat	DoB	Pos	Aps	(s)	Gls
Dylan Agius		26/12/96	M	5	(18)	
Terence Agius		15/01/94	M	10	(3)	1
Orosco Anonam		15/06/79	M	18	(6)	2
Cain Attard		10/09/94	M	26	(1)	1
Travis Bartolo		05/04/95	D		(2)	
Cleaven Cassar		02/08/90	D	4	(3)	
David Cassar		24/11/87	G	23		
Kyle Cesare		21/08/95	M	19	(12)	1
Claudio Francés	ARG	26/06/92	M	28	(2)	8
Gabriel	BRA	04/07/84	M	23	(6)	2
Christian Grech		20/02/93	D	30		1
Zsolt Kecskes	HUN	04/10/96	M		(2)	
Léo Fortunato	BRA	14/03/83	D	31		2
Malcolm Licari		18/04/78	A	1	(7)	
Karl Micallef		08/09/96	D	14	(3)	
Luke Micallef		08/11/94	A	20	(9)	4
Ayrton Mizzi		21/02/96	M			
Miguel Montfort		26/08/86	G	10	(1)	
Charles Newuche	NGA	14/03/85	A	10	(2)	1
Neil Pace Cocks		26/04/96	M		(6)	
Jurgen Pisani		03/09/92	D	32		4
Rafael Xavier	BRA	02/06/86	A	12		3
Rafinha	BRA	01/02/86	M	31	(1)	
Quilin Refalo		24/02/88	M	7	(5)	
Ricardo Costa	BRA	17/06/82	A	2	(1)	
Christian Stewart		22/10/95	D		(2)	
Nikola Tasić	SRB	26/01/90	M	7	(2)	

MALTA

Qormi FC

1961 • no website
Coach: Josef Manseuto;
(04/02/15) Mark Miller (ENG)

2014

17/08	Naxxar	W	1-0	Chetcuti
24/08	Hibernians	L	1-2	Effiong (p)
27/08	Balzan	L	1-2	og (Serrano)
13/09	Sliema	D	0-0	
20/09	Birkirkara	L	0-2	
27/09	Valletta	L	0-4	
02/10	Mosta	W	4-0	Vella, Temile 2, Effiong
18/10	Floriana	W	4-2	Anderson Santos, Pisani, Micallef, Effiong
25/10	Tarxien	W	1-0	Effiong (p)
03/11	Żebbuġ	D	1-1	Micallef
09/11	Pietà	D	0-0	
23/11	Naxxar	D	1-1	Pisani
29/11	Hibernians	L	0-6	
07/12	Balzan	D	1-1	Micallef
14/12	Sliema	L	1-3	Temile
21/12	Birkirkara	L	0-2	
2015				
03/01	Valletta	L	2-3	Temile, Levnajić
10/01	Mosta	L	1-3	Mazzetti
17/01	Pietà	L	0-1	
27/01	Tarxien	L	1-2	Effiong
31/01	Żebbuġ	L	0-1	
08/02	Floriana	D	2-2	Marcelinho, Gauci
22/02	Hibernians	L	1-2	Effiong
01/03	Valletta	L	1-3	Effiong (p)
07/03	Mosta	W	3-1	Nilsson, Grech, og (Koli)
15/03	Naxxar	L	1-2	Nilsson
19/03	Floriana	D	0-0	
04/04	Sliema	D	0-0	
10/04	Birkirkara	D	2-2	Effiong 2 (1p)
17/04	Balzan	L	1-5	Effiong (p)
25/04	Tarxien	W	4-0	Marcelinho, Nilsson, Grech, J Bondin
02/05	Pietà	W	2-1	Nilsson, Villalobos
08/05	Żebbuġ	W	3-1	Grech 2, Nilsson

Name	Nat	DoB	Pos	Aps	(s)	Gls
Steve Agius		15/05/93	D	10	(9)	
Anderson Santos	BRA	30/07/84	M	13	(1)	1
Gilmore Azzopardi		09/11/96	M		(1)	
Billy Berntsson	SWE	06/01/84	D	13	(1)	
Bjorn Bondin		25/08/88	M	9	(13)	
Jonathan Bondin		11/10/82	D	31	(1)	1
Albert Bruce	GHA	30/12/93	M	10	(4)	
Alessio Cassar		27/02/92	M	1	(3)	
Joseph Chetcuti		16/08/82	M	17	(4)	1
Jurgen Cilia		13/06/89	G		(1)	
Alfred Effiong		29/11/84	A	31	(1)	10
Carmelo Farrugia		17/06/92	M	1	(6)	
Matthew Farrugia		17/04/81	G	33		
Clifford Gauci		08/04/92	A	16		1
Leighton Grech		23/03/90	A	8	(5)	4
Zoran Levnajić	CRO	04/04/87	M	30		1
Marcelinho	BRA	24/10/86	M	10	(4)	2
Mauricio Mazzetti	ARG	18/06/86	M	15		1
Ryan Micallef		13/10/95	M	10	(16)	3
Alejandro Moreno	ESP	17/05/86	D	7	(4)	
Alexander Nilsson	SWE	23/10/92	A	6	(2)	5
Duncan Pisani		25/05/88	D	30	(1)	2
George Portelli		17/10/96	A		(1)	
Roderick Sammut		07/12/83	D	6	(1)	
Frank Temile	NGA	15/07/90	M	19		4
Edafe Uzeh	NGA	22/03/88	D	6	(1)	
Emerson Vella		09/09/91	D	18	(3)	1
Pietro Viggiani	ITA	29/10/91	A	4	(6)	
Gustavo Villalobos	USA	30/11/91	A	9	(1)	1

Sliema Wanderers FC

1909 • no website
Major honours
*Maltese League (26) 1920, 1923, 1924, 1926, 1930,
1933, 1934, 1936, 1938, 1939, 1940, 1949, 1954,
1956, 1957, 1964, 1965, 1966, 1971, 1972, 1976,
1989, 1996, 2003, 2004, 2005; Maltese Cup (20)
1935, 1936, 1937, 1940, 1946, 1948, 1951, 1952,
1956, 1959, 1963, 1965, 1968, 1969, 1974, 1979,
1990, 2000, 2004, 2009*
Coach: Alfonso Greco (ITA);
(12/10/14) Stephen Azzopardi

2014

16/08	Tarxien	D	1-1	og (Sammut)
23/08	Floriana	D	1-1	Pisanu
27/08	Hibernians	L	1-3	Potezica
13/09	Qormi	D	0-0	
21/09	Valletta	L	0-5	
28/09	Pietà	W	2-0	Mangiacasale, Scerri
02/10	Żebbuġ	W	1-0	Scerri
18/10	Mosta	W	4-1	Gnabouyou 2, Mangiacasale, Pisanu
26/10	Balzan	D	0-0	
03/11	Birkirkara	L	0-1	
08/11	Naxxar	L	0-1	
22/11	Tarxien	D	2-2	Mifsud, Mangiacasale
30/11	Floriana	L	0-2	
06/12	Hibernians	L	1-2	P Xuereb
14/12	Qormi	W	3-1	Bocar Djumo, Scerri, Friggieri
21/12	Valletta	L	1-3	Potezica
2015				
04/01	Pietà	W	2-1	Pisanu, Cilia
10/01	Żebbuġ	L	1-2	Bocar Djumo
17/01	Naxxar	D	0-0	
25/01	Balzan	L	3-5	Pedrinho 2, Bocar Djumo
01/02	Birkirkara	D	1-1	Cilia
07/02	Mosta	W	2-1	Friggieri, Obagbemiro
21/02	Tarxien	W	3-2	Pedrinho, Scerri, Cilia
28/02	Pietà	D	1-1	Bocar Djumo
07/03	Birkirkara	L	2-4	A Muscat, Pisanu
15/03	Balzan	L	1-2	Scerri
20/03	Żebbuġ	W	2-0	Bocar Djumo 2, Scerri
04/04	Qormi	D	0-0	
12/04	Hibernians	L	2-3	Scozzese, Mifsud
17/04	Valletta	D	3-3	Mateus Ribeiro, Potezica, Pedrinho
25/04	Mosta	W	5-1	Pedrinho 2, A Muscat 2 (1p), Mateus Ribeiro
02/05	Naxxar	L	3-4	Pisanu, Pedrinho, Friggieri
07/05	Floriana	L	1-3	Mateus Ribeiro

Name	Nat	DoB	Pos	Aps	(s)	Gls
Paltemio Barbetti	ITA	25/10/89	M	8		
Samuel Bartolo		06/04/92	G	1		
Stefano Bianciardi	ITA	15/03/85	D	19		
Bocar Djumo	POR	21/08/94	A	17	(1)	6
Joseph Borg		23/01/87	M	2	(5)	
Carl Cassar		27/03/97	A		(1)	
Trevor Cilia		01/02/83	A	16	(13)	3
Aldan Jake Friggieri		28/04/98	A	10	(9)	3
Clifford Gatt Baldacchino		09/02/88	D	19	(2)	
Guy Gnabouyou	FRA	01/12/89	A	14	(1)	2
Wisdom Ifeanyi	NGA	10/09/95	A		(1)	
Fabio Mangiacasale	ITA	05/09/87	M	10	(2)	3
Luca Martinelli		03/12/91	D	12	(7)	
Mateus Ribeiro	BRA	08/07/90	M	8	(1)	3
Iousef Meli		07/11/97	D		(3)	
Michael Mifsud		17/04/81	A	18	(2)	2
John Mintoff		23/08/88	M	27	(3)	
Alex Muscat		14/12/84	D	17	(1)	3
Giuseppe Muscat		13/04/89	D	16	(7)	
Junior Obagbemiro	NGA	26/06/85	A	2	(4)	1
Pedrinho	BRA	04/08/86	A	11		7
Andrea Pisanu	ITA	07/01/82	M	23	(2)	5
Marko Potezica	SRB	05/12/85	M	25	(2)	3
Clive Psaila		28/05/96	M	2	(1)	
Mark Scerri		16/01/90	M	27		6
Filippo Scozzese	ITA	08/12/88	D	20		1
Filippo Talato	ITA	24/06/92	A	5	(11)	
Axl Xuereb		02/01/96	A	1	(4)	
Peter Xuereb		07/05/92	M	1	(11)	1
Glenn Zammit		08/05/87	G	32		

Tarxien Rainbows FC

1944 • no website
Coach: Clive Mizzi

2014

16/08	Sliema	D	1-1	T Caruana
23/08	Valletta	D	0-0	
27/08	Pietà	D	0-0	
14/09	Żebbuġ	D	3-3	Pipico, Branquinho, T Caruana
20/09	Naxxar	W	2-1	Branquinho, Pipico
27/09	Balzan	L	2-3	Carlinos, Branquinho
02/10	Birkirkara	W	3-1	Clebinho, Branquinho 2
18/10	Hibernians	D	1-1	Pipico
25/10	Qormi	L	0-1	
02/11	Floriana	D	1-1	Jorge Santos
09/11	Mosta	L	1-2	Clebinho
22/11	Sliema	L	0-2	
29/11	Valletta	L	0-6	
07/12	Pietà	D	0-0	
13/12	Żebbuġ	L	1-2	Carlinos
20/12	Naxxar	W	1-0	Aboulezz
2015				
04/01	Balzan	L	0-5	
10/01	Birkirkara	L	1-2	Aboulezz
17/01	Mosta	D	1-1	Vallecillo
27/01	Qormi	W	2-1	Carlinos, Tabone
31/01	Floriana	D	1-1	Obinna
07/02	Hibernians	L	1-4	Soly
21/02	Sliema	L	2-3	Vallecillo, Aboulezz
28/02	Floriana	L	1-2	T Caruana
08/03	Valletta	L	0-4	
15/03	Hibernians	L	0-5	
20/03	Balzan	L	2-3	og (Grioli), Soly
04/04	Birkirkara	L	0-2	
13/04	Naxxar	W	1-0	Vallecillo
18/04	Mosta	W	2-1	Obinna 2
25/04	Qormi	L	0-4	
02/05	Żebbuġ	W	2-0	Obinna 2
08/05	Pietà	W	3-1	Aboulezz 2, Soly

Name	Nat	DoB	Pos	Aps	(s)	Gls
Firas Aboulezz	LIB	25/07/85	M	14	(7)	5
Alessandro Lopes	BRA	13/02/84	D	16		
Luke Aquilina		14/07/95	M		(4)	
Branquinho	BRA	14/11/89	A	13	(2)	5
Owen Bugeja		20/02/90	D	17		
Carlinos	ESP	17/02/87	A	17	(1)	3
Manuel Caruana		17/02/85	D	26	(3)	
Silas Caruana		21/04/95	M		(1)	
Triston Caruana		15/09/91	M	30	(2)	3
Antonio Chetcuti		14/06/96	D		(2)	
Alexander Cini		28/10/91	M	30	(1)	
Sean Cini		27/07/77	G	6		
Clebinho	BRA	22/06/86	A	10	(5)	2
Jonathan Debono		17/07/85	G	8		
Matthew Degiorgio		16/10/97	M		(1)	
Kane Paul Farrugia		24/03/90	D	18	(10)	
Ismael Grech		26/09/91	D	8	(1)	
Jorge Santos	BRA	23/04/87	A	11	(3)	1
José Ángel	ESP	03/06/90	D	14		
Manu Bonaque	ESP	09/05/89	D	13		
Sean Mintoff		30/10/85	G	19		
Ajoku Obinna	NGA	04/11/84	A	11	(1)	5
Pipico	BRA	07/03/86	A	12		3
Steven Sadowski		21/01/82	D	1	(6)	
Ryan Sammut		06/04/92	M	19	(6)	
Mikhail Schembri		20/03/96	M		(1)	
Mouhamed Soly	SEN	25/11/89	A	7		3
Matthew Tabone		29/04/92	D	20	(7)	1
Eduardo Vallecillo	ESP	14/03/93	A	14		3
Nigel Vella (I)		10/11/94	A	1	(4)	
Nigel Vella (II)		08/02/95	A		(3)	
Manuel Xerri		09/11/92	D	2	(4)	
Jorge Yepes	ESP	25/02/89	M	4	(4)	
Luke Zahra		07/05/95	M	2	(2)	

Valletta FC

1943 • vallettafc.net
Major honours
Maltese League (22) 1915, 1932, 1945, 1946, 1948, 1959, 1960, 1963, 1974, 1978, 1980, 1984, 1990, 1992, 1997, 1998, 1999, 2001, 2008, 2011, 2012, 2014; Maltese Cup (13) 1960, 1964, 1975, 1977, 1978, 1991, 1995, 1996, 1997, 1999, 2001, 2010, 2014
**Coach: Gilbert Agius;
(08/11/14) Ivan Zammit**

2014

17/08	Mosta	L	0-1	
23/08	Tarxien	D	0-0	
26/08	Floriana	W	2-0	*Elford-Alliyu, Nafti*
14/09	Hibernians	L	1-2	*Kooh-Sohna*
21/09	Sliema	W	5-0	*Zahra 2, Alex Terra 2, Fenech*
27/09	Qormi	W	4-0	*Elford-Alliyu, Alex Terra, Azzopardi, Montebello*
02/10	Pietà	L	1-2	*Barry*
19/10	Birkirkara	L	0-2	
26/10	Naxxar	W	2-0	*Kooh-Sohna, Bajada*
01/11	Balzan	W	2-0	*Briffa, Fenech*
08/11	Żebbuġ	W	2-0	*Barry, Nafti*
23/11	Mosta	W	5-0	*Bajada, Briffa, Elford-Alliyu, Nafti, Montebello*
29/11	Tarxien	W	6-0	*Nafti, Barry 2, Elford-Alliyu 2, Kooh-Sohna*
06/12	Floriana	W	4-1	*Elford-Alliyu 3 (1p), Nafti*
14/12	Hibernians	L	1-3	*Elford-Alliyu*
21/12	Sliema	W	3-1	*Cremona, Barry 2*
2015				
03/01	Qormi	W	3-2	*Barry 2, Azzopardi*
10/01	Pietà	W	3-0	*Barry 2, Montebello*
17/01	Żebbuġ	W	2-0	*Nafti, Elford-Alliyu*
25/01	Naxxar	W	3-0	*Leeflang, Elford-Alliyu 2*
01/02	Balzan	L	1-2	*Fenech*
08/02	Birkirkara	D	1-1	*Briffa*
21/02	Żebbuġ	L	2-3	*Fenech, K Borg*
01/03	Qormi	W	3-1	*Briffa 2, S Borg*
08/03	Tarxien	W	4-0	*Cremona, Nafti 2, Azzopardi*
14/03	Pietà	W	2-1	*Nafti 2*
19/03	Mosta	W	3-1	*Hillary, Cremona, Barry*
06/04	Naxxar	W	1-0	*Nafti*
12/04	Floriana	W	1-0	*Dimech*
17/04	Sliema	D	3-3	*Nafti, R Camilleri, Briffa*
25/04	Birkirkara	W	2-1	*S Borg, Barry*
02/05	Balzan	W	1-0	*Elford-Alliyu*
09/05	Hibernians	L	1-3	*Bajada*

Name	Nat	DoB	Pos	Aps	(s)	Gls
Alex Terra	BRA	02/09/82	A	4	(2)	3
Hamdan Al-Kamali	UAE	06/11/92	D		(5)	
Ian Azzopardi		12/08/82	D	30	(1)	3
Shaun Bajada		19/10/83	M	19	(7)	3
Hamza Barry	GAM	15/10/94	M	26	(2)	12
Jean Pierre Borg		08/01/98			(2)	
Kurt Borg		29/08/95	M		(4)	1
Steve Borg		15/05/88	D	27		2
Roderick Briffa		24/08/81	M	27	(1)	6
Daniel Camilleri		13/05/95	D		(2)	
Ryan Camilleri		22/05/88	D	29	(1)	1
Christian Caruana		21/10/86	A	1	(4)	
Jonathan Caruana		24/07/86	D	27		
Luellen Cremona		07/05/95	A	13	(14)	3
Luke Dimech		11/01/77	D	20	(10)	1
Lateef Elford-Alliyu	ENG	01/06/92	A	19	(7)	13
Ryan Fenech		24/08/80	M	28	(1)	4
Ikenna Hillary	NGA	17/04/91	M	6	(4)	1
Hugo Faria	POR	15/02/83	M	9	(3)	
Raphael Kooh-Sohna	CMR	22/04/90	A	6	(4)	3
Djamel Leeflang	NED	15/03/92	A	3	(4)	1
Pietro Marino	ITA	21/11/86	G	9		
Ian Montanaro		09/01/96	A		(1)	
Luke Montebello		13/08/95	A	4	(7)	3
Abdelkarim Nafti	TUN	03/08/81	M	29	(2)	12
Nicholas Pulis		29/01/98	D		(1)	
Vladimir Savićević	MNE	27/11/89	M		(2)	
Jurgen Suda		24/09/96	M		(1)	
Dario Tabone		07/02/96	D		(1)	
Nicholas George Vella		27/08/89	G	24	(2)	
Adrian Zahra	AUS	24/09/90	M	3	(1)	2
Ian Zammit		09/12/86	A		(3)	

Żebbuġ Rangers FC

1943 • no website
**Coach: Jesmond Zammit;
(29/10/14) Alfonso Greco (ITA)**

2014

16/08	Balzan	L	2-4	*Maurício Osmar 2*
23/08	Birkirkara	L	0-4	
27/08	Mosta	L	0-2	
14/09	Tarxien	D	3-3	*Monti 2 (1p), Maurício Osmar*
20/09	Floriana	D	3-3	*Mamić, Monti (p), Maurício Osmar*
27/09	Hibernians	L	0-4	
02/10	Sliema	L	0-1	
18/10	Naxxar	D	3-3	*Maurício Osmar, Monti (p), Mamić*
25/10	Pietà	L	0-1	
03/11	Qormi	D	1-1	*Monti (p)*
08/11	Valletta	L	0-2	
22/11	Balzan	D	1-1	*Mamić*
30/11	Birkirkara	L	1-3	*Maurício Osmar*
07/11	Mosta	D	1-1	*Maurício Osmar*
13/12	Tarxien	W	2-1	*Mamić, Camilleri*
20/12	Floriana	L	1-4	*Maurício Osmar*
2015				
04/01	Hibernians	L	2-5	*Monti 2*
10/01	Sliema	W	2-1	*Monti (p), Maurício Osmar*
17/01	Valletta	L	0-2	
27/01	Pietà	W	2-1	*Muchardi, Galea*
31/01	Qormi	W	1-0	*Yussuff*
07/01	Naxxar	L	0-4	
21/02	Valletta	W	3-2	*Muchardi, Yussuff, Montebello*
28/02	Hibernians	L	0-5	
08/03	Naxxar	L	1-2	*Matthew Bartolo*
14/03	Mosta	L	1-3	*Monti*
20/03	Sliema	L	2-3	*Camilleri, og (Mintoff)*
04/04	Floriana	L	1-3	*Yussuff*
13/04	Balzan	L	1-4	*Muchardi*
19/04	Birkirkara	L	1-3	*Maurício Osmar*
25/04	Pietà	L	1-3	*Montebello*
02/05	Tarxien	L	0-2	
08/05	Qormi	L	1-3	*Maurício Osmar*

Name	Nat	DoB	Pos	Aps	(s)	Gls
Lee James Agius		08/12/90	M	1	(5)	
Anderson Ribeiro	BRA	02/07/81	A		(1)	
Paltemio Barbetti	ITA	25/10/89	M	15		
Manuel Bartolo		26/08/83	G	10		
Matthew Bartolo		14/06/86	D	29	(1)	1
Craig Beattie	SCO	16/01/84	A		(1)	
Jacob Dominic Borg		02/05/91	D	26	(1)	
Shawn Borg		25/01/95	M		(2)	
Miguel Caintar		17/10/90	M	2	(22)	
Yessous Camilleri		27/11/91	D	30		2
Fabrício Rapchan	BRA	29/04/88	G	10		
Jeffrey Farrugia		18/08/88	G	13		
Melvin Farrugia		10/07/80	M	4	(3)	
Lee Galea		14/02/88	D	20	(1)	1
Clifford Gauci		08/04/92	A	10		
Matthew Gauci		02/09/91	M	16	(3)	
Javi Díaz	ESP	01/08/89	D	10		
Bojan Mamić	SRB	13/09/91	A	7	(4)	4
Ratko Mandić	SRB	05/08/91	M	5	(2)	
Maurício Osmar	BRA	22/06/91	A	27	(6)	11
Luke Montebello		13/08/95	A	10	(2)	2
Carlo Monti	SCO	10/07/90	A	25	(2)	9
Matías Muchardi	ARG	09/02/88	M	32		3
John Nwoba	NGA	18/08/89	A	3	(5)	
Thomas Paris		15/11/86	D	22	(2)	
Luis Peña Márquez	MEX	19/07/93	D	1	(2)	
Carlo Polli	SUI	07/02/89	M	1		
David Reano	ARG	20/03/84	D	10	(1)	
Jonathan Xerri		07/01/90	D	1		
Rashid Yussuff	ENG	23/09/89	M	15	(1)	3
Kurt Zammit		01/12/95	A	8	(4)	

Top goalscorers

25	Edison (Hibernians)
	Jorginho (Hibernians)
19	Bojan Kaljević (Mosta/Balzan)
16	Clayton Failla (Hibernians)
15	Gianmarco Piccioni (Balzan)
	Matteo Piciollo (Floriana)
13	Liliu (Birkirkara)
	Rafael Ledesma (Birkirkara)
	Lateef Elford-Alliyu (Valletta)
12	Vito Plut (Floriana)
	Hamza Barry (Valletta)
	Abdelkarim Nafti (Valletta)

Promoted clubs

Pembroke Athleta FC

1962 • no website
Coach: Jacques Scerri

St Andrews FC

1968 • luxolsportsclub.com/fc
Coach: Danilo Dončić (SRB)

Second level final table 2014/15

		Pld	W	D	L	F	A	Pts
1	Pembroke Athleta FC	26	17	4	5	54	22	55
2	St Andrews FC	26	15	6	5	49	32	51
3	Gzira United FC	26	14	3	9	46	31	45
4	Melita FC	26	14	3	9	36	28	45
5	Fgura United FC	26	11	10	5	32	27	43
6	Gudja United FC	26	11	8	7	46	32	41
7	St George's FC	26	11	8	7	43	38	41
8	Lija Athletic FC	26	12	2	12	45	43	38
9	Vittoriosa Stars FC	26	11	5	10	44	43	38
10	Mqabba FC	26	10	6	10	40	36	36
11	Rabat Ajax FC	26	8	5	13	27	37	29
12	Zurrieq FC	26	6	4	16	29	46	22
13	Msida St Joseph FC	26	4	3	19	27	64	15
14	Birzebbugia St Peter's FC	26	3	3	20	25	64	12

Promotion/Relegation play-off

(15/05/15)
Mosta 2-0 Gzira

DOMESTIC CUP

FA Trophy 2014/15

THIRD ROUND

(29/11/14)
Msida 1-2 Zabbar
Nadur 4-1 Gharghur
Swieqi 0-6 Gzira

(30/11/14)
Sirens 1-0 Lija

(02/12/14)
Balzan 2-0 Kirkop
Birzebbuga 1-7 Valletta
Naxxar 1-2 Melita
Pembroke 0-1 Pietà *(aet)*
Siggiewi 5-2 Zurrieq
St George's 0-2 Hibernians

(03/12/14)
Birkirkara 7-1 Hamrun
Floriana 0-0 Sliema *(aet; 5-4 on pens)*
Mosta 6-1 Senglea
Qrendi 0-3 Qormi
Tarxien 0-3 Gudja
Zebbug 0-3 Victoria

FOURTH ROUND

(20/01/15)
Gzira 1-4 Mosta
Melita 0-2 Valletta

(21/01/15)
Balzan 6-0 Zabbar
Floriana 1-3 Qormi
Gudja 0-6 Sirens
Nadur 1-3 Hibernians
Siggiewi 0-3 Birkirkara
Victoria 0-1 Pietà

QUARTER-FINALS

(13/02/15)
Balzan 1-1 Hibernians *(Darmanin 90; Mbong 30)*
(aet; 3-4 on pens)

Mosta 1-3 Valletta *(Roberts 38p; Bajada 30,
Elford-Alliyu 52, 60)*

(14/02/15)
Birkirkara 3-0 Pietà *(Maachi 12, 76, Zammit 83)*

Qormi 7-0 Sirens *(Effiong 16, Nilsson 24,
Marcelinho 30, 82, Levnajić 38, Villalobos 53,
Vella 87)*

SEMI-FINALS

(16/05/15)
Birkirkara 1-0 Valletta *(Fenech 110) (aet)*

(17/05/15)
Qormi 0-2 Hibernians *(Agius 11, Jorginho 65)*

FINAL

(23/05/15)
National Stadium, Ta' Qali
BIRKIRKARA FC 2 *(Mazzetti 29, Rafael Ledesma 69)*
HIBERNIANS FC 0
Referee: *Arciola*
BIRKIRKARA: *Haber, Z Muscat, Mazzetti, Vukanac,
Herrera, Zerafa, Camenzuli (Liliu 64), Rafael
Ledesma (Sciberras 90), Fenech, R Muscat,
Scicluna (Matheus Bissi 73)*
HIBERNIANS: *Bonello, Failla, Agius, Rodolfo
Soares, Rui da Gracia (Rajić 73), Cohen, Jackson,
Kristensen, Marcelo Dias (Mbong 83), Jorginho,
Bezzina*

Jubilation for Birkirkara after their FA Trophy final win against champions Hibernians

MOLDOVA
Federatia Moldoveneasca de Fotbal (FMF)

Address	Str. Tricolorului 39 MD-2012 Chisinau	**President**	Pavel Cebanu
Tel	+373 22 210 413	**General secretary**	Nicolai Cebotari
Fax	+373 22 210 432	**Media officer**	Victor Daghi
E-mail	fmf@fmf.md	**Year of formation**	1990
Website	fmf.md	**National stadium**	Zimbru, Chisinau (10,500)

DIVIZIA NATIONALA CLUBS

 1 **FC Academia Chisinau**

 2 **FC Costuleni**

 3 **FC Dacia Chisinau**

 4 **FC Dinamo-Auto**

 5 **FC Milsami Orhei**

 6 **FC Saxan**

 7 **FC Sheriff**

 8 **FC Tiraspol**

 9 **FC Veris**

 10 **FC Zaria Balti**

 11 **FC Zimbru Chisinau**

PROMOTED CLUBS

 12 **CS Petrocub**

 13 **CSF Speranta**

KEY:
- – UEFA Champions League
- – UEFA Europa League
- – Promoted
- – Relegated

Balti 10

5 9
Orhei

Ghidighici
Nisporeni 13

Vadul lui Voda
2 1 3 Speia
11 **Chisinau**

Sarata-Galbena
12 4 ~Tirnauca

Tiraspol
7 8

0   50   100 km
0   50 miles

Ceadir-Lunga
6

Milsami seize the moment

The battle for the 2014/15 Divizia Nationala title was so keenly contested that three clubs – FC Milsami Orhei, FC Dacia Chisinau and FC Sheriff – ended up with not just the same number of points but identical figures in the won, drawn and lost columns as well.

The head-to-head rule was therefore brought into force and it favoured Milsami, who, thanks to a dramatic last-day 2-1 win at home to Dacia, were crowned Moldovan champions for the first time. There was further agony for Dacia four days later as they lost the cup final 3-2 to Sheriff.

Orhei outfit claim first league title on final day

Head-to-head rule denies Dacia and Sheriff

Cup goes to Sheriff for first time in five years

Domestic league

Recalculations were required when the Divizia Nationala shut down for the winter following the late-autumn withdrawal of two clubs, FC Costuleni and FC Veris. What had started as an 11-club, 30-match division was destined to end as a nine-team event with just the 24 matches between them taken into account, all of the games against Costuleni and Veris having been expunged from the records.

That left Dacia topping the table five points ahead of Milsami and six in front of Sheriff, albeit having played a game more. Everything was to play for in the spring, but while Milsami and Sheriff continued to place faith in their respective coaches, Iurie Osipenco and Zoran Zekić, Dacia hit the panic button, getting rid of first Dejan Vukičević then, after just one game – a defeat at home to FC Tiraspol – Oleg Kubarev. Caretaker boss Veaceslav Semenov steadied the ship, but with Milsami and Sheriff both winning their first five matches following the resumption, the title race could hardly have been tighter.

Eventually, it all came down to a final-day showdown in Orhei between Milsami and Dacia, now under their fourth coach, ex-Moldova boss Igor Dobrovolski. The visitors were three points ahead of their hosts but aware that a defeat would lift Milsami above them on the head-to-head rule. Sheriff, the champions in 13 of the previous 14 seasons, were no longer in contention, having taken a paltry three points from the six meetings with their title rivals.

It was the biggest day in Milsami's short history, and they seized it with impressive conviction, taking the lead through Moldovan international midfielder Gheorghe Andronic just before half-time and doubling it with an own goal seven minutes from the end. Dacia's 95th-minute reply, from in-form striker Petru Leuca, came too late to matter. The title was Milsami's, making them only the fifth club to win the Divizia Nationala.

Domestic cup

Dacia's disappointment at missing out on a second league title deepened when they made it four Moldovan Cup final defeats out of four, losing a five-goal thriller to Sheriff. They did their best to end the hoodoo, with Leuca again striking late to complete a comeback from two goals down and force extra time. But the coup de grace was delivered by Sheriff's Bulgarian striker Ismail Isa after Dacia had been reduced to ten men. It was Sheriff's first cup win in five years and eighth in all.

Europe

Unlike the previous season, Sheriff were unable to extend their European campaign beyond the UEFA Europa League play-offs, where they were well beaten by HNK Rijeka. FC Zimbru Chisinau also exited at the same juncture having come through three qualifying ties, two of them – against PFC CSKA Sofia and SV Grödig – with the aid of the away-goals rule.

National team

Having beaten Montenegro 5-2 in Podgorica in their final 2014 FIFA World Cup qualifier, Moldova were entitled to go into their opening UEFA EURO 2016 engagement, against the same opponents at the same venue, full of confidence. But there would be no repeat performance or result as Ion Caras's team succumbed to a 2-0 defeat. It proved to be the last of the coach's 51 games in charge. He was replaced by Under-21 boss Alexandru Curteian, but by the end of the season the new man was still awaiting a first win. A draw against Russia in Moscow raised spirits but they were quickly dampened by a 1-0 defeat at home to Liechtenstein. A 1-1 draw in the reverse fixture, in Vaduz, kept Moldova glued to the foot of the Group G table.

DOMESTIC SEASON AT A GLANCE

Divizia Nationala 2014/15 final table

		Pld	Home					Away					Total					Pts
			W	D	L	F	A	W	D	L	F	A	W	D	L	F	A	
1	**FC Milsami Orhei**	24	9	2	1	27	5	8	2	2	23	10	17	4	3	50	15	55
2	FC Dacia Chisinau	24	8	3	1	29	7	9	1	2	19	6	17	4	3	48	13	55
3	FC Sheriff	24	9	1	2	38	9	8	3	1	18	7	17	4	3	56	16	55
4	FC Tiraspol	24	8	1	3	34	14	6	1	5	15	14	14	2	8	49	28	44
5	FC Saxan	24	5	3	4	9	8	3	3	6	11	22	8	6	10	20	30	30
6	FC Zimbru Chisinau	24	3	3	6	11	8	4	3	5	12	11	7	6	11	23	19	27
7	FC Academia Chisinau	24	3	1	8	13	22	2	1	9	5	25	5	2	17	18	47	17
8	FC Dinamo-Auto	24	3	1	8	12	21	1	1	10	11	42	4	2	18	23	63	14
9	FC Zaria Balti	24	3	0	9	7	23	1	0	11	3	43	4	0	20	10	66	12
10	FC Costuleni	0	0	0	0	0	0	0	0	0	0	0	0	0	0	0	0	0
11	FC Veris	0	0	0	0	0	0	0	0	0	0	0	0	0	0	0	0	0

NB FC Costuleni withdrew after round 12; FC Veris withdrew after round 14 – all their matches were annulled.

European qualification 2015/16

 Champion: FC Milsami Orhei (second qualifying round)

 Cup winner: FC Sheriff (first qualifying round)
FC Dacia Chisinau (first qualifying round)
FC Saxan (first qualifying round)

Top scorer	Ricardinho (Sheriff), 21 goals
Relegated clubs	FC Veris (withdrew), FC Costuleni (withdrew), FC Tiraspol (withdrew)
Promoted clubs	CS Petrocub, CSF Speranta
Cup final	FC Sheriff 3-2 FC Dacia Chisinau *(aet)*

Team of the season
(4-3-3)

Coach: Osipenco *(Milsami)*

Player of the season

Ricardinho
(FC Sheriff)

Brazilian schemer-cum-striker Ricardinho scored 21 goals in the 2014/15 Divizia Nationala, and although two of those came in matches that were subsequently annulled, he still topped the league's goal charts by a healthy margin. Technically gifted, difficult to dispossess and deadly in front of goal, the 25-year-old was Sheriff's inspiration throughout the campaign, so it was a huge blow to the Tiraspol club when he was suspended for the big game against FC Milsami Orhei in April, which Sheriff lost 3-2.

Newcomer of the season

Radu Mitu
(FC Milsami Orhei)

Just 19 when Milsami's new coach Iurie Osipenco made him the club's No1 goalkeeper at the start of the season, Mitu successfully banished the memories of his debut for the club in May 2013 – when he threw the ball into his net in a 2-1 defeat against FC Rapid Ghidighici – with an outstanding campaign between the posts for the championship winners. He kept clean sheets in 11 of his 24 matches and repeatedly raised his game for the key fixtures against FC Dacia Chisinau and FC Sheriff.

Mitu
(Milsami)

Balima *(Sheriff)* — Posmac *(Dacia)* — Racu *(Veris/ Milsami)* — Gheți *(Milsami)*

Patras *(Milsami)* — Cojocari *(Milsami)* — Cadú *(Sheriff)*

Leuca *(Dacia)* — Boghiu *(Tiraspol)* — Ricardinho *(Sheriff)*

 **MOLDOVA**

NATIONAL TEAM

Top five all-time caps
Radu Rebeja (74); Serghey Clescenco (69); **Alexandru Epureanu** (69); **Victor Golovatenco** (66); Ivan Testimitanu (56)

Top five all-time goals
Serghey Clescenco (11); Serghey Rogaciov (9); Igor Bugaiov, Serghey Dadu & Iurie Miterev (8)

Results 2014/15

03/09/14	Ukraine	A	Kyiv	L	0-1	
08/09/14	Montenegro (ECQ)	A	Podgorica	L	0-2	
09/10/14	Austria (ECQ)	H	Chisinau	L	1-2	Dedov (27p)
12/10/14	Russia (ECQ)	A	Moscow	D	1-1	Epureanu (74)
15/11/14	Liechtenstein (ECQ)	H	Chisinau	L	0-1	
14/02/15	Romania B	N	Antalya (TUR)	L	1-2	Carp (9)
18/02/15	Kazakhstan	N	Antalya (TUR)	D	1-1	Gatcan (54)
27/03/15	Sweden (ECQ)	H	Chisinau	L	0-2	
09/06/15	Luxembourg	A	Luxembourg	D	0-0	
14/06/15	Liechtenstein (ECQ)	A	Vaduz	D	1-1	Boghiu (43)

Appearances 2014/15

Coach: Ion Caras 11/09/50 /(24/09/14) Alexandru Curteian 11/02/74			Ukr	MNE	AUT	RUS	LIE	Rou	Kaz	SWE	Lux	LIE	Caps	Goals
Ilie Cebanu	29/12/86	Mordovia (RUS)	G82	G	G	G	G		G	G	s46	G	15	-
Petru Racu	17/07/87	Veris /Milsami	D84	D		s73	D	D	D	D	D	D	34	-
Victor Golovatenco	28/04/84	Sibir (RUS)	D	D	D	D	D		D	D			66	3
Veaceslav Posmac	07/11/90	Dacia	D	s68				D	D				12	1
Igor Armas	14/07/87	Kuban (RUS)	D	D	D	D	D		D		D	D	42	3
Alexandru Epureanu	27/09/86	İstanbul Başakşehir (TUR)	M	D	D	D	D		D		D60	D46	69	7
Artur Ionita	17/08/90	Verona (ITA)	M	M	M	M	M			M36			19	2
Alexandru Antoniuc	23/05/89	Milsami	M66	M54	s65								18	2
Alexandr Dedov	26/07/89	Zimbru	M79	M	M	M82	M	M46	s57	M	M	M	28	2
Serghei Gheorghiev	20/10/91	Sheriff /unattached /Navbahor (UZB)	M66	M81				s46		s86			18	-
Eugen Sidorenco	19/03/89	H. Nazareth Illit (ISR)	A90	A68	s46	s82			M57				25	7
Maxim Antoniuc	15/01/91	Sheriff	s66	s54				s46			s85	s89	8	-
Evgheny Cebotari	16/10/84	Sibir (RUS)	s66	s81									40	-
Serghei Alexeev	31/05/86	Zimbru	s79	A									25	5
Stanislav Namasco	10/11/86	Olimpik-Şüvälan (AZE)	s82										41	-
Alexandru Vremea	03/11/91	Zimbru	s84										2	-
Denis Calincov	15/09/85	Veris	s90										21	2
Ion Jardan	10/01/90	Zimbru			D	D		D46	D	s60			6	-
Iulian Erhan	01/07/86	Zimbru /Milsami			D87	D		D46	D		D85	D	7	-
Andrei Cojocari	21/01/87	Milsami			M65	M73	M56	M46	s57	s36	M	M	17	1
Alexandru Gatcan	27/03/84	Rostov (RUS)			M	M	M		M84	M		M	46	3
Igor Picusciac	27/03/83	Amkar (RUS)			A46	A46		s46	A46				24	3
Artur Patras	10/01/88	Milsami			s87	s46	M75	s46	s84		M	M89	24	-
Radu Ginsari	10/12/91	Sheriff						A					5	-
Dan Spataru	24/05/94	Zimbru				s56							1	-
Alexandru Suvorov	02/02/87	Mordovia (RUS)					s75						50	5
Nicolae Calancea	29/08/86	Ceahlăul (ROU)						G		G46			17	-
Stefan Burghiu	28/03/91	Zimbru						M					5	-
Vadim Rata	05/05/93	Tiraspol /unattached						M46	s57		s66		3	-
Catalin Carp	20/10/93	CFR Cluj (ROU)						M46			M66	s46	4	1
Gheorghe Boghiu	26/10/81	Tiraspol /unattached						A46	s46	A86	A46	A	6	1
Anatol Cheptine	20/05/90	unattached /Academia						s46	M57		M76	M37	12	-
Alexandru Onica	29/07/84	unattached						s46	M57				20	-
Petru Leuca	19/07/90	Dacia						s46					1	-
Vadim Bolohan	15/08/86	Tiraspol								D			13	-
Gheorghe Andronic	25/09/91	Milsami								M70			5	1
Viorel Frunza	06/12/79	Dacia								s70			37	7
Nicolae Milinceanu	01/08/92	Academia									s46	s37	2	-
Eugeniu Cociuc	11/05/93	Dacia									s76		1	-

EUROPE

FC Sheriff

Second qualifying round - FK Sutjeska (MNE)
H 2-0 *Mureşan (71), Isa (87)*
Degra, Ginsari, Juninho Potiguar (Benson 52), Ricardinho (Isa 61), Metoua, Cadú (Thiago Galvão 75), Blanco, Ernandes, Mureşan, Ligger, Henrique Luvannor. Coach: Veaceslav Rusnac (MDA)
A 3-0 *Benson (5), Henrique Luvannor (35), Isa (54)*
Degra, Ginsari (Leonel Olímpio 46), Metoua, Benson, Cadú, Blanco (Thiago Galvão 85), Ernandes, Isa, Mureşan, Ligger, Henrique Luvannor (Ricardinho 66). Coach: Veaceslav Rusnac (MDA)

Third qualifying round - ŠK Slovan Bratislava (SVK)
A 1-2 *Ricardinho (74)*
Degra, Thiago Galvão (Ginsari 56), Balima, Metoua, Joãozinho, Benson, Cadú, Blanco, Isa (Juninho Potiguar 84), Mureşan, Henrique Luvannor (Ricardinho 72). Coach: Veaceslav Rusnac (MDA)
H 0-0
Degra, Ginsari (Henrique Luvannor 46), Ricardinho (Leonel Olímpio 57), Balima, Metoua, Joãozinho, Benson (Juninho Potiguar 61), Cadú, Blanco, Isa, Mureşan. Coach: Veaceslav Rusnac (MDA)
Red card: *Blanco 56*

Play-offs - HNK Rijeka (CRO)
A 0-1
Degra, Juninho Potiguar (Isa 46), Thiago Galvão (Ricardinho 66), Balima, Metoua, Joãozinho, Leonel Olimpio, Cadú (Ginsari 79), Ernandes, Mureşan, Ligger. Coach: Zoran Zekić (CRO)
H 0-3
Degra, Thiago Galvão, Balima, Metoua (Paireli 18), Joãozinho, Leonel Olímpio (Ricardinho 53), Cadú, Ernandes, Isa (Juninho Potiguar 75), Mureşan, Ligger. Coach: Zoran Zekić (CRO)

FC Zimbru Chisinau

First qualifying round - KF Shkëndija (MKD)
A 1-2 *Grosu (50p)*
Rusu, Erhan, Bogdan, Dedov (Pascenco 53), Klimovich, Pavlyuchek, Amani (Damascan 86), Vremea, Grosu, Cheptine (Anton 73), Jardan. Coach: Oleg Kubarev (BLR)
H 2-0 *Amani (5), Pascenco (87)*
Rusu, Erhan, Bogdan (Burghiu 57), Dedov, Klimovich, Pavlyuchek, Amani (Pascenco 68), Vremea, Grosu, Cheptine (Spataru 46), Jardan. Coach: Oleg Kubarev (BLR)

Second qualifying round - PFC CSKA Sofia (BUL)
A 1-1 *Alexeev (31)*
Rusu, Burghiu, Erhan, Anton (Potirniche 45+2), Dedov, Klimovich, Pavlyuchek, Vremea, Alexeev (Grosu 81), Cheptine (Spataru 60), Jardan. Coach: Oleg Kubarev (BLR)
H 0-0
Rusu, Burghiu, Erhan, Dedov, Klimovich (Potirniche 60), Pavlyuchek, Amani (Alexeev 46), Vremea, Grosu, Cheptine (Spataru 59), Jardan. Coach: Oleg Kubarev (BLR)

Third qualifying round - SV Grödig (AUT)
A 2-1 *Alexeev (35), Handle (59og)*
Rusu, Burghiu, Erhan, Potirniche, Pascenco (Amani 78), Dedov (Grosu 63), Pavlyuchek, Vremea, Alexeev, Cheptine (Spataru 54), Jardan. Coach: Oleg Kubarev (BLR)
H 0-1
Rusu, Burghiu, Erhan, Dedov, Klimovich (Potirniche 76), Pavlyuchek, Amani (Pascenco 66), Vremea, Alexeev, Cheptine (Spataru 60), Jardan. Coach: Oleg Kubarev (BLR)

Play-offs - PAOK FC (GRE)
H 1-0 *Burghiu (80)*
Rusu, Burghiu, Erhan, Klimovich, Pavlyuchek, Amani (Alexeev 69), Vremea, Grosu, Cheptine (Diallo 82), Jardan, Spataru (Višnakovs 61). Coach: Oleg Kubarev (BLR)
A 0-4
Rusu, Burghiu, Erhan, Dedov, Klimovich, Pavlyuchek, Amani, Vremea, Grosu (Alexeev 46), Cheptine (Višnakovs 46), Jardan (Spataru 79). Coach: Oleg Kubarev (BLR)
Red card: *Amani 42*

FC Tiraspol

First qualifying round - İnter Bakı PİK (AZE)
H 2-3 *Novicov (78), Karaneychev (88)*
Georgiev, Eric Barroso, Novicov, Zarichnyuk, Shapoval, Molla, Boghiu (Karaneychev 63), Rata (Bulat 58), Japaridze, Ademar (Ovseannicov 81), Sydorenko. Coach: Vlad Goian (MDA)
A 1-3 *Bulat (6)*
Georgiev, Novicov, Zarichnyuk (Ovseannicov 71), Molla, Hauşi, Karaneychev (Boghiu 56), Japaridze, Vidović, Bulat, Ademar, Sydorenko (Shapoval 46). Coach: Vlad Goian (MDA)
Red cards: Georgiev 76, Japaridze 83

FC Veris

First qualifying round - PFC Litex Lovech (BUL)
H 0-0
Gaiduchevici, Cascaval, Cojocari, Cucerenco, Josan (Zasavitschi 64), Frunza (Cemirtan 53), Ivanov (Turcan 46), Mocanu, Pisla, Racu, Bogdanović. Coach: Lilian Popescu (MDA)
A 0-3
Gaiduchevici, Cascaval, Cojocari, Cucerenco, Josan, Frunza (Milinceanu 59), Mocanu, Zasavitschi (Pisla 49), Racu, Bogdanović (Bugnea 71), Bacal. Coach: Lilian Popescu (MDA)
Red card: Bacal 32

DOMESTIC LEAGUE CLUB-BY-CLUB

FC Academia Chisinau

2006 • CPSN, Vadul lui Voda (1,000); Buiucani (2,000) • academia.md
Coach: Vladimir Vusatii

2014

27/07	a	Dinamo-Auto	L	0-1	
03/08	h	Zimbru	L	0-2	
17/08	a	Veris	L	1-4	*Koné (match annulled)*
24/08	a	Tiraspol	L	0-3	
30/08	a	Saxan	L	0-1	
14/09	h	Dacia	L	0-1	
19/09	a	Costuleni	L	2-4	*Celeadnic, Zlatan (match annulled)*
28/09	h	Milsami	D	1-1	*Matei*
04/10	a	Sheriff	L	0-3	
19/10	h	Dinamo-Auto	W	2-0	*Matei (p), Secrier*
24/10	h	Zaria	W	5-2	*Turcan 2, Koné 2, Bogdan*
02/11	a	Zimbru	W	1-0	*Turcan (p)*
23/11	h	Veris	L	0-3	*(match annulled)*
28/11	a	Tiraspol	L	1-3	*Turcan*
06/12	h	Saxan	L	0-1	
12/12	a	Dacia	L	0-1	

2015

04/03	a	Milsami	L	0-1	
08/03	h	Sheriff	L	0-3	
15/03	a	Dinamo-Auto	L	0-1	
20/03	a	Tiraspol	L	0-5	
04/04	a	Sheriff	L	0-2	
11/04	a	Zimbru	W	1-0	*Cheptine (p)*
25/04	a	Zaria	W	3-0	*Celeadnic, Clonin, Cheptine*
02/05	a	Dinamo-Auto	D	1-1	*Clonin*
10/05	h	Milsami	L	1-3	*Sofroni*
15/05	a	Dacia	L	1-8	*Cheptine*
20/05	h	Saxan	L	1-4	*Matei*

No	Name	Nat	DoB	Pos	Aps	(s)	Gls
27	Mihai Apostol		21/01/97	M	15		
12	Cristian Avram		27/07/94	G	15	(1)	
6	Dumitru Bogdan		04/03/89	D	9		1
22	Maxim Boghiu		24/05/91	D	21		
29	Vasile Caraus		06/08/88	M	3	(1)	
7	Dan Cater		28/02/96	A	4	(2)	
23	Nicolae Cebotari		24/05/97	G	12		
30	Eugen Celeadnic		09/10/90	D	19	(2)	2
11	Alexandru Cheltuiala		05/02/83	D	10		
16	Anatol Cheptine		20/05/90	M	10		3
16	Andrei Ciofu		31/05/94	M	4	(4)	
33	Serghey Ciuico		02/02/83	A	2		
28	Oleg Clonin		04/02/88	M	8	(2)	2
5	Alexandru Costin		21/10/91	D	3	(1)	
29	Maxim Focsa		21/10/91	D	14		
25	Arkadi Galperin	RUS	21/05/92	M	15	(2)	
14	Igor Gritco		22/05/96	M	4	(15)	
2	Petru Hvorosteanov		28/08/86	M	10		
8	Ben Adama Koné	CIV	16/05/92	D	10	(1)	3
32	Alexandru Leu		04/05/91	D	5	(2)	
16	Victor Lisa		10/03/91	A	8	(7)	
4	Oleg Lupusor		14/09/94	M		(6)	
21	Sergiu Matei		23/04/92	A	21	(5)	3
27	Nicolae Milinceanu		01/08/92	A	7	(1)	
31	Vitalie Negru		15/01/87	M	11	(4)	
15	Constantin Sandu		15/09/93	M	1	(1)	
3	Ion Sandu		09/03/93	D	11		
2	Pavel Secrier		11/01/91	M	4	(11)	1
8	Veaceslav Sofroni		30/04/84	A	6	(1)	1
8	Vasile Soltan		09/12/92	M	10		
20	Valeriu Tiron		08/04/93	M	2	(6)	
7	Mihai Turcan		20/08/89	A	6	(1)	4
9	Ion Ursu		19/08/94	A	5	(6)	
26	Vitalie Zlatan		08/04/93	A	12		1

FC Costuleni

1983 • Satesc, Ghidighici (1,500) • no website
Coach: Laurenţiu Tudor (ROU)

2014

27/07	h	Dacia	D	1-1	Soltan
08/08	a	Milsami	L	0-3	
16/08	h	Sheriff	L	0-1	
24/08	a	Dinamo-Auto	W	2-0	Onofrei, Sofroni
29/08	h	Zaria	L	2-3	Onofrei, Sofroni
14/09	a	Zimbru	W	2-1	Sofroni, Carandasov
19/09	h	Academia	W	4-2	Onofrei 2, Truhanov, Ciofu
27/09	a	Veris	L	0-1	
03/10	h	Tiraspol	L	0-3	
18/10	a	Saxan	D	1-1	Muziciuc
24/10	a	Dacia	L	1-3	Cascaval
08/11	h	Milsami	L	0-2	

NB Costuleni withdrew from the league after 12 games; all of their matches were annulled.

No	Name	Nat	DoB	Pos	Aps	(s)	Gls
10	Oleg Andronic		06/02/89	A	2	(4)	
7	Valeriu Andronic		21/12/82	M		(2)	
4	Yevhen Buliy	UKR	18/07/95	D	2		
5	Ionuţ Burnea	ROU	12/08/92	D	5		
21	Ivan Carandasov		21/01/91	M	4	(4)	1
5	Andrian Cascaval		10/06/87	D	3		1
27	Anatol Cebotari		29/03/88	G	2		
19	Andrei Ciofu		31/05/94	M	5	(6)	1
2	Viorel Dinu	ROU	18/09/78	D	12		
16	Marcel Dulghieru		30/06/94	D	1	(3)	
15	Petru Hvorosteanov		28/08/86	M	8	(2)	
22	Nikola Kovačević	SRB	22/08/93	A		(4)	
7	Stanislav Luca		28/08/86	A	2		
18	Alexandr Muziciuc		01/10/95	M	8	(2)	1
17	Petru Ojog		17/07/90	M	1	(6)	
11	Octavian Onofrei		16/05/91	A	12		4
28	Alexandru Oprea	ROU	08/01/89	G	10	(1)	
4	Florian Pîrvu	ROU	30/04/91	M	2	(2)	
26	Alexandru Scripcenco		13/01/91	D	11		
3	Sergiu Sirbu		01/04/86	D	11		
9	Veacaslav Sofroni		30/04/84	A	8	(3)	3
96	Vasile Soltan		09/12/92	M	10	(1)	1
23	Marius Tomozei	ROU	09/09/90	D	8	(1)	
25	Victor Truhanov		30/01/91	M	5	(2)	1

FC Dacia Chisinau

1999 • Moldova, Speia (8,550) • fcdacia.md
Major honours
Moldovan League (1) 2011
**Coach: Dejan Vukićević (MNE);
(20/01/15) Oleg Kubarev (BLR);
(09/03/15) Veaceslav Semenov);
(26/04/15) Igor Dobrovolski (RUS)**

2014

27/07	a	Costuleni	D	1-1	Camara (match annulled)
02/08	h	Milsami	W	2-0	Rosca, og (Rassulov)
10/08	a	Sheriff	W	2-1	Krkotić 2 (1p)
17/08	h	Dinamo-Auto	W	2-0	Golubović, Posmac (p)
23/08	a	Zaria	W	2-0	Posmac, Stjepanović
31/08	h	Zimbru	D	0-0	
14/09	a	Academia	W	1-0	Barakhoev
20/09	h	Veris	L	0-2	(match annulled)
28/09	a	Tiraspol	D	0-0	
04/10	h	Saxan	D	0-0	
24/10	h	Costuleni	W	3-1	Krkotić, Stjepanović, Kovaļovs (match annulled)
02/11	a	Milsami	L	0-3	
09/11	h	Sheriff	W	3-2	Leuca, Zastavniy, Bejan
23/11	a	Dinamo-Auto	W	2-0	Leuca, Krkotić
28/11	h	Zaria	W	3-0	Krkotić, Stjepanović, Leuca
07/12	a	Zimbru	W	1-0	Posmac (p)
12/12	h	Academia	W	1-0	Zastavniy

2015

05/03	h	Tiraspol	L	1-2	Leuca
09/03	a	Saxan	W	1-0	Siradze
20/03	h	Dinamo-Auto	W	6-2	Stoleru 2, V Frunza 3, Rosca
05/04	a	Zaria	W	3-0	Stoleru, Rosca, Leuca 2
17/04	h	Sheriff	D	0-0	
24/04	a	Tiraspol	W	4-0	Posmac (p), Leuca, Rosca, Stjepanović
03/05	h	Saxan	W	3-0	V Frunza, Stjepanović, Bejan
09/05	a	Zimbru	W	1-0	Cociuc
15/05	h	Academia	W	8-1	Barakhoev, Dvali (p), Zaginaylov, Leuca 3, Gavrilenko, Siradze
20/05	a	Milsami	L	1-2	Leuca

No	Name	Nat	DoB	Pos	Aps	(s)	Gls
8	Akhmet Barakhoev	RUS	10/09/84	M	19	(3)	2
10	Alexandru Bejan		07/05/96	M	15	(5)	2
4	Radoš Bulatović	SRB	05/06/84	D	3		
20	Ibrahima Camara	GUI	06/10/92	M	7	(7)	1
12	Dumitru Celeadnic		23/04/92	G	1		
17	Eugeniu Cociuc		11/05/93	M	17	(5)	1
4	Sergiu Cojocari		15/05/88	D	6	(2)	
11	Jaba Dvali	GEO	08/02/85	A	4	(1)	1
12	Maxim Frunza		06/01/96	G		(1)	
21	Viorel Frunza		06/12/79	A	5	(3)	4
1	Artiom Gaiduchevici		22/04/87	G	9		
19	Maxym Gavrilenko	UKR	18/08/91	M	14	(2)	1
23	Radivoje Golubović	MNE	22/04/90	D	1	(4)	1
27	Dan Gustiuc		05/03/97	A		(2)	
3	Vasile Jardan		20/07/93	D	10		
28	Andrejs Kovaļovs	LVA	23/03/89	M	8	(7)	1
7	Miloš Krkotić	MNE	29/09/87	A	14	(3)	5
29	Petru Leuca		19/07/90	A	9	(8)	11
24	Abdul-Gafar Mamah	TOG	24/08/85	D	23		
1	Evgheny Matiughin		31/10/81	G	1		
11	Maxim Mihaliov		22/08/86	M	1		
15	Jude Ogada	NGA	15/12/89	D	8	(3)	
9	Ghenadie Orbu		08/07/82	A	1	(11)	
27	Dumitru Popescu		11/04/95	A		(5)	
5	Veaceslav Posmac		07/11/90	D	25		4
16	Dorian Railean		13/10/93	G	16		
18	Mihai Rosca		26/02/95	D	21	(2)	4
13	Ruslan Shauhvalov	RUS	31/12/96	M		(2)	
21	David Siradze	GEO	21/10/81	A	5	(4)	2
6	Alphonse Soppo	CMR	15/05/85	M	8	(2)	
18	Slaven Stjepanović	MNE	02/11/87	A	18	(4)	5
30	Marian Stoleru		20/11/88	M	7	(13)	3
22	Serhiy Zaginaylov	UKR	03/01/91	M	1	(5)	1
26	Volodymyr Zastavniy	UKR	02/09/90	D	20	(2)	2

FC Dinamo-Auto

2009 • Dinamo-Auto, Tirnauca (1,300);
Teren Sintetic, Tirnauca (1,000) • dinamo-auto.com
**Coach: Dmitri Arabadji;
(03/09/14) Igor Negrescu**

2014

27/07	h	Veris	L	0-5	(match annulled)
02/08	a	Tiraspol	L	1-8	Volosin
08/08	h	Saxan	L	0-2	
17/08	h	Dacia	L	0-2	
24/08	h	Costuleni	L	0-2	(match annulled)
29/08	a	Milsami	L	0-6	
13/09	h	Sheriff	L	1-2	Mandricenco
28/09	a	Zaria	L	0-2	
03/10	h	Zimbru	L	0-3	
19/10	a	Academia	L	0-2	
24/10	a	Veris	L	0-5	(match annulled)
01/11	h	Tiraspol	L	0-1	
09/11	a	Saxan	L	1-2	Mihaliov
23/11	h	Dacia	L	0-2	
07/12	h	Milsami	L	0-5	
13/12	a	Sheriff	L	2-7	Mihaliov, Iularji

2015

04/03	a	Zaria	W	4-0	og (Orlovschi), Cemirtan 2, Mihaliov
08/03	a	Zimbru	L	0-2	
15/03	h	Academia	W	1-0	Mudrac
20/03	a	Dacia	L	2-6	Iularji 2
05/04	h	Milsami	L	1-2	Cemirtan
10/04	a	Tiraspol	L	0-4	
18/04	h	Saxan	W	4-1	Ilescu, Mihaliov, Mudrac (p), Cemirtan
25/04	a	Zimbru	D	0-0	
02/05	h	Academia	D	1-1	Orbu
10/05	a	Zaria	W	5-1	Cemirtan 2, Mihaliov, Apostol, Orbu
20/05	h	Sheriff	L	0-1	

No	Name	Nat	DoB	Pos	Aps	(s)	Gls
7	Andrian Apostol		19/01/92	M	10	(5)	1
17	Alexandru Arabadji		15/04/94	A	6		
18	Denis Bazarov		19/01/93	D		(1)	
25	Dumitru Bivol		22/01/93	D	8	(1)	
13	Alexandr Bolsacov		19/11/94	D	8	(2)	
20	Ibrahima Camara	GUI	06/10/92	M	1		
16	Evgheni Ceaban		07/07/94	D	4	(2)	
11	Vadim Cemirtan		21/07/87	A	6	(2)	6
14	Chirill Coval		18/08/89	A	3	(1)	
3	Serghey Diulgher		21/03/91	D	15	(1)	
20	Vladimir Dragovozov		01/01/84	A	18	(1)	
2	Maxim Focsa		21/04/92	D	6	(1)	
10	Evgheny Gorodetschi		24/09/85	M	6		
15	Roman Grancear		06/03/94	D	3		
11	Serghei Iarovoi		12/03/94	M		(8)	
2	Oleg Iastrebov		30/10/90	D	1		
3	Denis Ilescu		20/01/87	D	10		1
21	Alexei Iularji		03/12/92	M	2	(19)	3
12	Stanislav Ivanov		22/04/96	D	6	(2)	
14	Vitaly Jancov		26/05/94	M	11	(4)	
17	Artiom Litviacov		23/10/96	A		(3)	
19	Constantin Mandricenco		19/02/91	A	11		1
1	Evgheny Matiughin		31/10/81	G	12		
10	Maxim Mihaliov		22/08/86	M	21		5
9	Alexandru Mironet		12/11/95	A		(7)	
4	Victor Mudrac		03/03/94	M	24		2
6	Alexandru Namasco		09/10/81	M		(2)	
13	Jude Ogada	NGA	15/12/89	D	6		
22	Vadim Oleinic		10/11/92	M	11	(5)	
9	Ghenadie Orbu		08/07/82	A	11		2
1	Mihai Paius		06/02/83	G	2		
17	Mihail Paseciniuc		09/03/91	M		(2)	
18	Andrei Petuhov		12/04/94	D	5		
7	Igor Picus		07/05/90	M	6		
15	Dumitru Popescu		11/04/95	A	2	(5)	
8	Petru Postoronca		09/12/91	M	8	(1)	
15	Vladislav Salogub		04/08/95	D	3		
5	Cornel Schiopu		31/07/94	D	9		
6	Alexandru Scripcenco		13/01/91	D	6	(2)	
24	Stanislav Sincovschi		16/04/94	M		(2)	
5	Alphonse Soppo	CMR	15/05/85	M	11		
12	Dmitri Stajila		02/08/91	G	1		
19	Alexandr Tofan		19/08/87	M	3	(4)	
5	Constantin Turcan		03/06/93	D	6		
3	Nicolai Volcov		29/04/95	D	1		
7	Dmitri Volosin		26/07/94	M	11	(5)	1
1	Alexandr Zveagintsev		26/07/87	G	6		

FC Milsami Orhei

2005 • Municipal (3,000) • milsami.md
Major honours
Moldovan League (1) 2015; Moldovan Cup (1) 2012
Coach: Iurie Osipenco

2014

26/07	h	Saxan	D	1-1	Bud
02/08	a	Dacia	L	0-2	
08/08	h	Costuleni	W	3-0	Surdu, Andronic, Belak (match annulled)
24/08	a	Sheriff	D	0-0	
29/08	h	Dinamo-Auto	W	6-0	Andronic, Surdu 3 (1p), Rhaili, Iavorschi
13/09	a	Zaria	W	3-1	Surdu 2, Iavorschi
20/09	h	Zimbru	W	1-0	Patras
28/09	a	Academia	D	1-1	Antoniuc
04/10	a	Veris	L	0-1	(match annulled)
19/10	a	Tiraspol	W	2-1	og (Smirnov), Surdu
25/10	h	Saxan	W	2-0	Belak, og (Kouadja)
02/11	h	Dacia	W	3-0	Monday, Bud, Gheţi
08/11	a	Costuleni	W	2-0	Bud 2 (match annulled)
29/11	h	Sheriff	D	0-0	
07/12	a	Dinamo-Auto	W	5-0	Iavorschi, Surdu 2, Andronic, Belak (p),
13/12	h	Zaria	W	4-0	Diulghier, Rhaili, Belak, Bud

2015

28/02	a	Zimbru	W	2-0	Bud 2
04/03	h	Academia	W	1-0	Monday
15/03	h	Tiraspol	W	1-0	Bud
05/04	a	Dinamo-Auto	W	2-1	Bud (p), Racu
11/04	a	Sheriff	W	3-2	Racu, Rhaili, Cojocari
18/04	a	Tiraspol	L	1-2	Surdu
24/04	a	Saxan	L	0-1	
03/05	h	Zimbru	W	2-1	Surdu 2
10/05	a	Academia	W	3-1	Patras 2, Antoniuc
15/05	h	Zaria	W	5-0	Andronic, Patras, Bud 2, Suvorov
20/05	h	Dacia	W	2-1	Andronic, og (Mamah)

No	Name	Nat	DoB	Pos	Aps	(s)	Gls
4	Octavian Abrudan	ROU	16/03/84	D	4	(2)	
22	Gheorghe Andronic		25/09/91	M	22	(2)	5
9	Alexandru Antoniuc		23/05/89	M	17	(7)	2
21	Gheorghe Bantis		19/06/89	G	1	(1)	
14	Karlo Belak	CRO	22/04/91	D	20	(3)	4
26	Cristian Bud	ROU	26/06/86	A	3	(20)	11
23	Dumitru Calaras		13/10/95	A		(5)	
18	Vadim Calugher		07/09/94	M	3	(3)	
20	Andrei Cojocari		21/01/87	M	25	(1)	1
16	Alexandru Diulghier		03/01/95	D	6	(7)	1
4	Iulian Erhan		01/07/86	D	7	(2)	
24	Victor Gheorghiu		24/06/92	D	5	(1)	
3	Cornel Gheţi	ROU	20/03/82	D	15	(9)	1
10	Constantin Iavorschi		16/03/90	A	7	(10)	3
7	Ovidiu Mendizov	ROU	09/08/86	M	6	(7)	
1	Radu Mitu		04/11/94	G	24		
6	Ovye Monday	NGA	14/08/92	D	19	(3)	2
12	Andrian Negai		28/01/85	G	2		
8	Artur Patras		10/01/88	M	22	(2)	4
5	Petru Racu		17/07/87	D	11		2
24	Alexandru Railean		04/10/90	A	1	(1)	
15	Denis Rassulov		02/01/90	A	21	(3)	
2	Adil Rhaili	MAR	25/04/91	D	22	(1)	3
17	Eugen Slivca		13/07/89	M	8	(4)	
19	Romeo Surdu	ROU	12/01/84	A	25	(1)	12
87	Alexandr Suvorov		02/02/87	M	4	(6)	1

FC Saxan

2010 • Ceadir-Lunga municipal (2,000) • fc-saxan.com
Coach: Volodymyr Lyutiy (UKR); (19/04/15) Ivan Burduniuc

2014

26/07	a	Milsami	D	1-1	Sebai
02/08	h	Sheriff	D	1-1	A Popovici
08/08	a	Dinamo-Auto	W	3-0	Sebai 2, Nicologlo
17/08	h	Zaria	W	1-0	Ouédraogo
24/08	a	Zimbru	W	1-0	
30/08	h	Academia	W	1-0	Aliyu
14/09	a	Veris	D	0-0	(match annulled)
19/09	h	Tiraspol	W	2-0	Demerji, Fofana
04/10	a	Dacia	D	0-0	
18/10	h	Costuleni	D	1-1	Goginashvili (match annulled)
25/10	h	Milsami	L	0-2	
02/11	a	Sheriff	L	0-4	
09/11	h	Dinamo-Autio	W	2-1	Afolabi, A Popovici
22/11	a	Zaria	L	0-2	
29/11	h	Zimbru	D	0-0	
06/12	a	Academia	W	1-0	Sebai

2015

01/03	a	Tiraspol	L	0-4	
09/03	h	Dacia	L	0-1	
20/03	h	Zimbru	D	1-1	Bamba (p)
10/04	h	Zaria	L	0-1	
18/04	a	Dinamo.Auto	L	1-4	Dima
24/04	h	Milsami	W	1-0	D Popovici
03/05	a	Dacia	L	0-3	
09/05	h	Sheriff	L	0-1	
15/05	a	Tiraspol	L	1-3	Truhanov
20/05	a	Academia	W	4-1	Goginashvili 3, Dao

No	Name	Nat	DoB	Pos	Aps	(s)	Gls
18	Abdulwaheed Afolabi	NGA	08/12/91	A	16	(1)	1
24	Mohammed Aliyu	NGA	12/02/93	D	23		1
24	Yao Konan Allou	CIV	10/11/95	D	1	(2)	
15	Ion Arabadji		31/07/84	D	5	(2)	
3	Dumitru Bacal		28/11/85	D	4	(1)	
10	Yacouba Bamba	CIV	30/11/91	M	16		1
99	Maxim Bogacic		05/04/86	D		(6)	
12	Vasilii Buza		01/03/92	G	1		
16	Constantin Calmis		19/08/95	D	15	(4)	
23	Igor Cebotari		23/03/97	M	1	(5)	
28	Alexei Coselev		19/11/93	G	12		
88	Vadim Cravcescu		07/03/85	M	12	(2)	
3	Lassina Dao	CIV	20/12/96	A	4	(2)	1
9	Ion Demerji		28/04/89	A	8	(3)	1
13	Igor Dima		11/02/93	M	6	(13)	1
11	Sekou Doumbia	CIV	11/02/94	M	7	(3)	
8	Mamadou Fofana	CIV	21/05/95	M	4	(8)	1
29	Irakli Goginashvili	GEO	29/03/94	M	21	(4)	4
19	Vladimir Haritov		05/01/95	M		(3)	
14	Sani Kaita	NGA	02/05/86	M	10	(1)	
18	Mohamed Koné	CIV	12/12/93	M	9		
15	Kouassi Kouadja	CIV	22/06/95	D	15		
93	Veaceslav Lisa		24/03/93	A	2	(2)	
22	Nikita Lorne	CIV	09/06/95	A		(1)	
41	Catalin Lungu		22/03/94	M	6	(1)	
22	Iurie Mirza		05/03/93	A	6	(5)	
93	Eric Né	CIV	22/01/96	M		(1)	
10	Gheorghe Nicologlo		02/01/91	M		(5)	1
20	Boubacar Ouédraogo	BFA	11/01/92	A	13	(7)	1
11	Mihail Paseciniuc		09/03/91	M		(2)	
17	Alexandru Popovici		09/04/77	A	13	(1)	2
17	Dumitru Popovici		05/08/83	D	9		1
2	Ion Prodan		21/03/92	D	10	(3)	
1	Dmitri Radu		03/03/88	G	12		
19	Senin Sebai	CIV	18/12/93	A	10	(4)	4
12	Andrei Stinca		16/06/89	G	1		
88	Victor Truhanov		30/01/91	M	9	(1)	1
9	Valeri Zgibarta	RUS	20/04/95	M	5	(2)	

FC Sheriff

1997 • Sheriff Main (13,300); Sheriff Small (8,000); Sheriff Indoor Arena (3,570) • fc-sheriff.com
Major honours
Moldovan League (13) 2001, 2002, 2003, 2004, 2005, 2006, 2007, 2008, 2009, 2010, 2012, 2013, 2014; Moldovan Cup (8) 1999, 2001, 2002, 2006, 2008, 2009, 2010, 2015
Coach: Veaceslav Rusnac; (14/08/14) Zoran Zekić (CRO)

2014

25/07	h	Tiraspol	W	2-1	Juninho Potiguar, Thiago Galvão
02/08	a	Saxan	D	1-1	Balima
10/08	h	Dacia	L	1-2	Metoua
16/08	a	Costuleni	W	1-0	Ricardinho (match annulled)
24/08	h	Milsami	D	0-0	
13/09	a	Dinamo-Auto	W	2-1	Juninho Potiguar 2
20/09	h	Zaria	W	4-0	Ricardinho 2, Paireli 2
27/09	a	Zimbru	W	1-0	Mureşan
04/10	h	Academia	W	3-0	Ginsari, Balima, Benson
18/10	a	Veris	W	3-0	Juninho Potiguar, Cadú, Ricardinho (match annulled)
25/10	a	Tiraspol	W	4-2	Ricardinho 3, Juninho Potiguar
02/11	h	Saxan	W	4-0	Paireli, Ricardinho, Ginsari, Juninho Potiguar
09/11	a	Dacia	L	2-3	Ginsari, Ricardinho
29/11	a	Milsami	D	0-0	
13/12	h	Dinamo-Auto	W	7-2	Juninho Potiguar, Isa, Ricardinho 4, Antoniuc

2015

28/02	a	Zaria	W	1-0	Ricardinho
04/03	h	Zimbru	W	3-0	Cadú, Ricardinho (p), Dupovac
08/03	a	Academia	W	3-0	og (I Sandu), Ricardinho, Ernandes
21/03	h	Zaria	W	6-0	Ricardinho 2, Cadú, Ginsari, Juninho Potiguar 2
04/04	a	Academia	W	2-0	Iurcu 2
11/04	h	Milsami	L	2-3	Ginsari, Leonel Olímpio (p)
17/04	a	Dacia	D	0-0	
03/05	h	Tiraspol	W	4-0	Ricardinho 2 , Leonel Olímpio, Antoniuc
09/05	a	Saxan	W	1-0	Rebenja
15/05	h	Zimbru	W	2-1	Paireli, Cadú
20/05	a	Dinamo-Auto	W	1-0	Ricardinho

No	Name	Nat	DoB	Pos	Aps	(s)	Gls
26	Aitor Monroy	ESP	18/10/87	M	8	(3)	
7	Maxim Antoniuc		15/01/91	A	10	(3)	2
14	Wilfried Balima	BFA	20/03/85	D	13	(5)	2
19	Fred Benson	NED	10/04/84	A	2	(4)	1
21	Elkin Blanco	COL	09/05/89	M	4	(3)	
21	Igor Bondarenco		28/06/95	D	1		
20	Cadú	BRA	31/08/86	M	14	(4)	4
32	Matías Degra	ARG	18/06/83	G	4		
22	Amer Dupovac	BIH	30/11/90	D	9	(1)	1
23	Ernandes	BRA	11/11/87	D	14	(2)	1
91	Serghei Gheorghiev		20/10/91	M	6	(3)	
8	Radu Ginsari		10/12/91	M	11	(6)	5
90	Henrique Luvannor	BRA	19/05/90	M		(1)	
29	Ismail Isa	BUL	26/06/89	A	9	(10)	1
89	Maxim Iurcu		01/02/93	A	8	(2)	2
17	Joãozinho	BRA	02/07/89	D	3	(1)	
9	Juninho Potiguar	BRA	22/02/90	A	15	(7)	9
25	Serghei Juric		03/03/84	G	4		
19	Petar Lela	CRO	17/03/94	D		(1)	
18	Leonel Olímpio	BRA	07/07/82	M	20		2
88	Ligger	BRA	18/05/88	D	4	(4)	
33	Valeriu Macritschi		20/10/92	D	21	(2)	
15	Marcel Metoua	CIV	15/11/88	D	6	(1)	1
30	Andrei Mureşan	ROU	01/08/85	D	15	(3)	1
16	Vadim Paireli		08/11/95	A	15	(8)	4
1	Serghei Pascenco		18/12/82	G	18		
21	Maxim Potirniche		13/06/89	D	5		
17	Artiom Razginiuc		01/10/95	D	1		
88	Eugeniu Rebenja		05/03/95	A	3	(5)	1
11	Ricardinho	BRA	04/09/89	A	23	(2)	21
24	Dmitri Semirov		27/12/95	M		(7)	
55	Mateo Sušić	BIH	18/11/90	D	10	(1)	
19	Serghei Svinarenco		18/09/96	D	1	(1)	
10	Thiago Galvão	BRA	24/08/89	M	9	(14)	1

MOLDOVA

FC Tiraspol

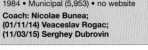

2001 • Sheriff Small (8,000); Sheriff Indoor Arena (3,570) • fc-tiraspol.com
Major honours
Moldovan Cup (1) 2013
Coach: Vlad Goian;
(15/12/14) Lilian Popescu

2014
25/07	a	Sheriff	L 1-2	*Ovsiannicov*
02/08	h	Dinamo-Auto	W 8-1	*Sydorenko, Molla 2, Karaneychev, Boghiu 2, Ovsiannicov, Smirnov*
08/08	a	Zaria	W 1-0	*Grosu*
16/08	h	Zimbru	W 2-1	*Birdan, Ovsiannicov*
24/08	a	Academia	W 3-0	*Ovsiannicov 2, Boghiu*
29/08	a	Veris	D 1-1	*Molla (match annulled)*
19/09	a	Saxan	L 0-2	
28/09	h	Dacia	D 0-0	
03/10	a	Costuleni	W 3-0	*Bulat, Molla, Karaneychev (match annulled)*
19/10	h	Milsami	L 1-2	*Karaneychev*
25/10	h	Sheriff	L 2-4	*Poiarcov, Boghiu*
01/11	a	Dinamo-Auto	W 1-0	*Smirnov*
08/11	h	Zaria	W 2-0	*Khachaturov, Boghiu*
23/11	a	Zimbru	L 1-3	*Molla*
28/11	h	Academia	W 3-1	*Boghiu, Karaneychev (p), Zarichnyuk*

2015
01/03	h	Saxan	W 4-0	*Shapoval, Ermak (p), Molla, Boghiu*
05/03	a	Dacia	W 2-1	*Zarichnyuk, Alexeev*
15/03	a	Milsami	L 0-1	
20/03	a	Academia	W 5-0	*Bolohan, Boghiu 3 (1p), Puntus*
04/04	a	Zimbru	D 0-0	
10/04	h	Dinamo-Auto	W 4-0	*Boghiu 2, Bulat, Alexeev*
18/04	a	Milsami	W 2-1	*Eric Barroso, Boghiu*
24/04	h	Dacia	L 0-4	
03/05	a	Sheriff	L 0-4	
15/05	h	Saxan	W 3-1	*Shapoval 2 (1p), Mocanu*
20/05	a	Zaria	W 4-0	*Shapoval 2 (1p), Alexeev, Calincov*

No	Name	Nat	DoB	Pos	Aps	(s)	Gls
27	Ademar	BRA	08/01/85	M	2	(4)	
21	Serghei Alexeev		31/05/86	A	3	(8)	3
17	Valentin Birdan		13/05/95	M	9	(5)	1
19	Anatol Boestean		26/03/85	D	6		
11	Gheorghe Boghiu		26/10/81	A	20	(6)	13
27	Vadim Bolohan		15/08/86	D	5	(6)	1
23	Victor Bulat		05/01/85	M	16	(3)	2
4	Mihajlo Cakić	SRB	27/05/90	M	10		
24	Denis Calincov		15/09/85	A		(7)	1
25	Alexei Coselev		19/11/93	G	10		
3	Eric Barroso	ESP	15/10/90	D	15		1
16	Oleh Ermak	UKR	09/03/86	D	16		1
25	Georgi Georgiev	BUL	12/10/88	G	14		
20	Alexandru A Grosu		18/04/88	M	10	(6)	1
13	Bogdan Hauşi	ROU	29/09/85	D	4	(3)	
15	Georgi Karaneychev	BUL	09/06/88	M	7	(11)	4
26	Artem Khachaturov	ARM	18/06/92	D	8		1
12	Vladimir Livsit		23/03/84	G	2		
22	Andrei Macritschi		13/02/96	A	13	(4)	
4	Dmytro Matvienko	UKR	25/05/92	D	6		
19	Sergiu Mocanu		24/10/87	M	9	(1)	1
10	Oleg Molla		22/02/86	A	14	(4)	6
5	Andrei Novicov		24/04/86	D	12	(4)	
9	Gheorghii Ovsiannicov		12/10/85	A	5	(5)	5
24	Igor Poiarcov		26/07/94	D	4	(2)	1
28	Artiom Puntus		31/01/96	A		(6)	1
14	Vadim Rata		05/05/93	M	11	(5)	
6	Eugeniu Rebenja		05/03/95	A	1	(3)	
8	Serhiy Shapoval	UKR	07/02/90	M	11	(2)	5
6	Yevhen Smirnov	UKR	16/04/93	M	13		2
77	Kyrylo Sydorenko	UKR	25/07/85	D	18		1
7	Yevhen Zarichnyuk	UKR	03/02/89	M	12	(5)	2

FC Veris

2011 • Municipal, Orhei (3,000); Satesc, Ghidighici (1,500) • fcveris.md
Coach: Lilian Popescu

2014
27/07	a	Dinamo-Auto	W 5-0	*Pisla, Frunza 3, Calincov*
03/08	h	Zaria	W 2-1	*Cascaval, Josan*
10/08	a	Zimbru	L 0-1	
17/08	h	Academia	W 4-1	*Calincov 2, Bacal, Cascaval*
29/08	a	Tiraspol	D 1-1	*Racu*
14/09	a	Saxan	D 0-0	
20/09	a	Dacia	W 2-0	*Mocanu, Racu*
27/09	h	Costuleni	W 1-0	*Racu*
04/10	a	Milsami	W 1-0	*Racu*
18/10	h	Sheriff	L 0-3	
24/10	h	Dinamo-Auto	W 5-0	*Cucerenco 2, Akimov, Racu, Frunza*
01/11	a	Zaria	W 2-1	*Frunza 2*
08/11	h	Zimbru	W 1-0	*Racu*
23/11	a	Academia	W 3-0	*Calincov, Frunza, Racu*

NB Veris withdrew from the league after 14 games; all of their matches were annulled.

No	Name	Nat	DoB	Pos	Aps	(s)	Gls
11	Vyacheslav Akimov	UKR	17/10/89	A	3	(2)	1
4	David Andronic		09/07/95	M		(2)	
17	Dumitru Bacal		28/11/85	D	1		1
32	Vladimir Bogdanović	SRB	05/10/86	M	10	(1)	
9	Vitalie Bordian		11/08/84	D	3		
9	Andrei Bugneac		30/03/88	A	6	(6)	
9	Denis Calincov		15/09/85	A	10	(2)	4
2	Vasile Caraus		06/08/88	M	3	(1)	
4	Andrian Cascaval		10/06/87	D	5		2
28	Vadim Cemirtan		21/07/87	A	1	(3)	
8	Cristian Cirlan		09/01/95	M		(1)	
5	Sergiu Cojocari		15/05/88	D	12		
16	Igor Costrov		03/08/87	A	11		
5	Alexandr Cucerenco		01/10/91	D	14		2
10	Viorel Frunza		06/12/79	A	13	(1)	7
12	Artiom Gaiduchevici		22/04/87	G	14		
4	Anton Grigoryev	RUS	13/12/85	D	7		
21	Denis Ilescu		20/01/87	D		(1)	
17	Vladislav Ivanov		07/05/90	A	1	(9)	
11	Nicolae Josan		18/09/83	M	7	(5)	1
11	Nicolae Milinceanu		01/08/92	A		(1)	
2	Sergiu Mocanu		24/10/87	M	14		1
21	Daniel Pisla		14/06/86	M	4	(5)	1
25	Petru Racu		17/07/87	D	13		7
9	Mihai Turcan		20/08/89	A	1	(2)	
15	Ion Ursu		19/08/94	A	1	(8)	
22	Evgheny Zasavitschi		24/11/92	M		(3)	

FC Zaria Balti

1984 • Municipal (5,953) • no website
Coach: Nicolae Bunea;
(01/11/14) Veaceslav Rogac;
(11/03/15) Serghey Dubrovin

2014
27/07	h	Academia	W 1-0	*Bezimov*
03/08	a	Veris	L 1-2	*Lacusta (match annulled)*
08/08	h	Tiraspol	L 0-1	
17/08	a	Saxan	L 0-1	
23/08	h	Dacia	L 0-2	
29/08	a	Costuleni	W 3-2	*Marina, Bojii, Chemschi (match annulled)*
13/09	h	Milsami	L 1-3	*Bojii*
20/09	h	Sheriff	L 0-4	
28/09	h	Dinamo-Auto	W 2-0	*Marina, Kokhia*
19/10	a	Zimbru	L 0-6	
24/10	h	Academia	L 2-5	*Marina, Lacusta*
01/11	h	Veris	L 1-2	*Lacusta (match annulled)*
08/11	a	Tiraspol	L 0-2	
22/11	h	Saxan	W 2-0	*Hovanschi, Bojii*
28/11	a	Dacia	L 0-3	
13/12	h	Milsami	L 0-4	

2015
28/02	h	Sheriff	L 0-1	
04/03	a	Dinamo-Auto	L 0-4	
14/03	h	Zimbru	L 0-1	
21/03	a	Sheriff	L 0-6	
05/04	h	Dacia	L 0-4	
10/04	a	Saxan	W 1-0	*Bezimov*
17/04	h	Zimbru	L 0-2	
25/04	a	Academia	L 0-3	
10/05	h	Dinamo-Auto	L 1-5	*Dobrovinschi*
15/05	a	Milsami	L 0-5	
20/05	h	Tiraspol	L 0-4	

No	Name	Nat	DoB	Pos	Aps	(s)	Gls
19	Olexandr Bezimov	UKR	08/02/84	M	26		2
7	Danu Bojii		29/08/96	M	20	(3)	3
8	Ivan Carandasov		21/01/91	M	10	(1)	
16	David Chemschi		12/05/95	D	14	(10)	1
20	Vladimir Cheptenari		26/09/89	D	23	(1)	
1	Andrei Chilari		15/05/94	G	1		
15	Raveliu Chiorescu		06/11/98	M		(2)	
17	Artur Dobrovinschi		17/08/97	A	2	(3)	1
8	Ion Dombrovschi		03/05/95	D	1	(14)	
4	Cristian Dros		15/04/98	M	3	(5)	
17	Alexandr Dubinschi		17/03/96	M		(8)	
21	Vladimir Ghinaitis		30/03/95	D	15	(2)	
3	Vitalie Grijuc		11/01/94	M	26		
22	Vadim Gulceac		06/08/98	A	3	(12)	
9	Mihail Hovanschi		24/02/90	D	15		1
18	David Kokhia	GEO	22/04/93	M	13		1
9	Ivan Lacusta		24/01/95	A	16	(9)	3
15	Maxim Latisov		05/08/98	M		(2)	
10	Andrei Marina		21/02/90	M	27		3
12	Ghenadie Mosneaga		25/04/85	G	15		
12	Dmitry Oleinic		12/03/91	G	11		
19	Octavian Onofrei		16/05/91	A	5	(2)	
2	Nicolai Orlovschi		01/04/85	D	10		
22	Sergiu Patic		23/06/93	M	6	(3)	
18	Corneliu Pavalachi		15/05/94	M	7	(2)	
14	Radu Rogac		07/06/95	D	27		
13	Vladimir Senegur		05/09/95	M	1	(5)	
15	Serghei Trofan		08/11/97	M		(1)	

FC Zimbru Chisinau

1947 • Zimbru (10,500); Baza Zimbru (2,142) • zimbru.md

Major honours
Moldovan League (8) 1992, 1993, 1994, 1995, 1996, 1998, 1999, 2000; Moldovan Cup (6) 1997, 1998, 2003, 2004, 2007, 2014

Coach: Oleg Kubarev (BLR); (17/12/14) Veaceslav Rusnac

2014

03/08	a	Academia	W	2-0	Grosu, Damascan
10/08	h	Veris	W	1-0	Spataru (match annulled)
16/08	a	Tiraspol	L	1-2	Amani
24/08	h	Saxan	D	0-0	
31/08	a	Dacia	D	0-0	
14/09	h	Costuleni	L	1-2	Cheptine (match annulled)
20/09	a	Milsami	L	0-1	
27/09	h	Sheriff	L	0-1	
03/10	a	Dinamo-Auto	W	3-0	Spataru, og (Bivol), Alexeev
19/10	h	Zaria	W	6-0	Spataru, Pavlyuchek, Platica 2, Cheptine, Dedov
02/11	h	Academia	L	0-1	
08/11	a	Veris	L	0-1	(match annulled)
23/11	h	Tiraspol	W	3-1	Platica, Višņakovs, Dedov
29/11	a	Saxan	D	0-0	
07/12	h	Dacia	L	0-1	

2015

28/02	h	Milsami	L	0-2	
04/03	a	Sheriff	L	0-3	
08/03	h	Dinamo-Auto	W	2-0	Khachaturov, Dedov
14/03	a	Zaria	W	1-0	Damascan
20/03	a	Saxan	D	1-1	Amani
04/04	h	Tiraspol	D	0-0	
11/04	h	Academia	L	0-1	
17/04	a	Zaria	W	2-0	Furdui, Dedov (p)
25/04	a	Dinamo-Auto	D	0-0	
03/05	h	Milsami	L	1-2	Anton
09/05	h	Dacia	L	0-1	
15/05	a	Sheriff	L	1-2	Vremea

No	Name	Nat	DoB	Pos	Aps	(s)	Gls
10	Serghei Alexeev		31/05/86	A	3	(9)	1
25	Jean-Marie Amani	FRA	15/04/89	M	22	(3)	2
7	Gheorghe Anton		27/01/93	M	15	(7)	1
13	Alexandru Belevschi		21/03/95	D	5	(2)	
94	Sergiu Berestean		01/02/96	M		(1)	
4	Anatol Boestean		26/03/85	D	3	(1)	
5	Constantin Bogdan		29/12/93	D	3		
8	Andrei Bugneac		30/03/88	A	4	(3)	
3	Stefan Burghiu		28/03/91	D	21	(1)	
23	Radu Catan		30/05/88	A		(5)	
77	Anatol Cheptine		20/05/90	M	3	(4)	2
89	Anatol Chiriniciuc		04/02/89	G	5		
95	Ilie Damascan		12/10/95	A	7	(5)	2
11	Alexandr Dedov		26/07/89	M	21	(3)	4
18	Mamadou Diallo	GUI	17/03/95	A		(1)	
4	Iulian Erhan		01/07/86	D	12		
27	Valentin Furdui		01/07/87	M	8	(1)	1
44	Dinu Graur		27/01/94	D	6	(5)	
21	Alexandru S Grosu		16/05/86	A	7	(7)	1
90	Ion Jardan		10/01/90	D	23	(2)	
16	Artem Khachaturov	ARM	18/06/92	D	8		1
18	Dmitri Klimovich	BLR	09/02/84	D	4	(4)	
10	Gheorghe Nicologlo		02/01/91	M	1		
77	Alexandru Onica		29/07/84	M	7	(1)	
10	Alexandr Pascenco		28/05/89	M	2	(8)	
96	Corneliu Pavalachi		15/05/94	M	2		
21	Kirill Pavlyuchek	BLR	27/06/84	D	12		1
31	Daniel Pisla		14/06/86	M	8	(2)	
13	Mihai Platica		15/03/90	M	10		3
18	Maxim Potirniche		13/06/89	D	11	(1)	
55	Vladimir Rassulov		11/11/92	M		(8)	
12	Denis Rusu		02/08/90	G	22		
94	Dan Spataru		24/05/94	A	14	(1)	3
95	Alexandru Staris		04/01/95	M	2	(1)	
13	Andrei Trifan		11/02/96	M		(2)	
18	Andrei Verbetschi		21/07/89	M	1		
30	Aleksejs Višņakovs	LVA	03/02/84	M	6	(6)	1
26	Alexandru Vremea		03/11/91	M	19	(6)	1

NB Appearances and goals for all clubs include those from the annulled matches against FC Costuleni & FC Veris.

Top goalscorers

21	Ricardinho (Sheriff)
13	Gheorghe Boghiu (Tiraspol)
12	Romeo Surdu (Milsami)
11	Petru Leuca (Dacia)
	Cristian Bud (Milsami)
	Viorel Frunza (Veris/Dacia)
9	Juninho Potiguar (Sheriff)
	Petru Racu (Veris/Milsami)
6	Vadim Cemirtan (Dinamo-Auto)
	Oleg Molla (Tiraspol)

Promoted clubs

CS Petrocub

1994 • Sarata-Galbena (1,500) • no website
Coach: Eduard Blanuta

CSF Speranta

1991 • Orasenesc (8,000) • fcsperanta.com
Coach: Cristian Efros

Second level final table 2014/15

		Pld	W	D	L	F	A	Pts
1	FC Sheriff-2	22	15	4	3	53	14	49
2	CS Petrocub	22	13	6	3	55	21	45
3	CSF Speranta	22	14	2	6	33	16	44
4	FC Budai	22	10	5	7	31	23	35
5	FC Zimbru-2 Chisinau	22	9	7	6	36	29	34
6	FC Sfintul Gheorghe	22	10	3	9	41	34	33
7	FC Victoria Bardar	22	9	4	9	34	27	31
8	FC Edinet	22	8	3	11	30	35	27
9	CF Intersport-Aroma	22	6	5	11	13	37	23
10	FC Dacia-2 Buiucani	22	4	6	12	18	32	18
11	Real Succes Lilcora FC	22	3	6	13	19	46	15
12	CF Gagauziya Comrat	22	3	5	14	19	68	14

NB FC Sheriff-2 ineligible for promotion.

Cupa Moldovei 2014/15

1/16 FINALS

(23/09/14)
Speranta 1-0 Saxan
Victoria 0-2 Academia *(aet)*

(24/09/14)
Sfintul Gheorghe 0-3 Zaria
Spicul 1-2 Singerei

1/8 ROUND

(28/10/14)
Costuleni 6-1 Edinet
Dinamo-Auto 4-0 Zaria
Intersport-Aroma 0-1 Milsami *(aet)*
Speranta 0-2 Tiraspol

(29/10/14)
Academia 0-4 Sheriff
Dacia 3-1 Petrocub
Gagauziya 0-10 Zimbru
Singerei 1-4 Veris

QUARTER-FINALS

(02/12/14)
Dinamo-Auto 0-3 Dacia *(Leuca 8, Krkotić 61, Popescu 76)*

(03/12/14)
Tiraspol 0-0 Zimbru *(aet; 4-3 on pens)*
Veris 0-1 Sheriff *(Benson 117) (aet)*
Milsami w/o Costuleni

SEMI-FINALS

(29/04/15)
Dacia 1-1 Tiraspol *(V Frunza 41; Cakić 57) (aet; 6-5 on pens)*

Sheriff 3-0 Milsami *(Isa 24, Ricardinho 70, Leonel Olímpio 79)*

FINAL

(24/05/15)
Zimbru, Chisinau
FC SHERIFF 3 *(Juninho Potiguar 9, Iurcu 52, Isa 110)*
FC DACIA CHISINAU 2 *(Juric 66og, Leuca 90+4)*
(aet)
Referee: Drachta *(AUT)*
SHERIFF: *Juric, Sušić, Metoua, Potirniche, Svinarenco, Leonel Olímpio, Thiago Galvão, Cadú (Dupovac 70), Ricardinho (Isa 90), Juninho Potiguar (Ernandes 75), Iurcu (Paireli 88)*
DACIA: *Gaiduchevici, Mamah, Posmac, Rosca (Stoleru 62), Zastavniy, Cociuc, Bejan (Leuca 64), Barakhoev, Zaginaylov (Jardan 23), V Frunza, Stjepanović (Gavrilenko 38)*
Red card: *Barakhoev (94)*

Sheriff defeated Dacia to win the Moldovan Cup

MONTENEGRO
Futbalski savez Crne Gore (FSCG)

Address	Ulica "19. decembra" 13 ME-81000 Podgorica	**President**	Dejan Savićević
Tel	+382 20 445 600	**General secretary**	Momir Djurdjevac
Fax	+382 20 445 660	**Media officer**	Ivan Radović
E-mail	info@fscg.me	**Year of formation**	1931
Website	fscg.me	**National stadium**	Pod Goricom, Podgorica (12,508)

PRVA LIGA CLUBS

 ① **FK Berane**

 ② **FK Bokelj**

 ③ **FK Budućnost Podgorica**

 ④ **OFK Grbalj**

 ⑤ **FK Lovćen**

 ⑥ **FK Mladost Podgorica**

 ⑦ **FK Mogren**

 ⑧ **FK Mornar**

 ⑨ **OFK Petrovac**

 ⑩ **FK Rudar Pljevlja**

 ⑪ **FK Sutjeska**

 ⑫ **FK Zeta**

PROMOTED CLUBS

 ⑬ **FK Iskra**

 ⑭ **FK Dečić**

KEY:

● – UEFA Champions League
● – UEFA Europa League
● – Promoted
● – Relegated

0		40		80 km
0			40 miles	

Rudar stand firm to regain title

FK Rudar Pljevlja became the fourth club to win the Montenegrin Prva Liga twice, clinching the title on the final day to deny defending champions FK Sutjeska a hat-trick. Although they faded towards the finish, Mirko Marić's unfancied side led throughout and were worthy champions.

The Montenegrin Cup went to FK Mladost Podgorica as they claimed their first major trophy thanks to an extra-time 2-1 win over OFK Petrovac. There was little to celebrate in international competition, with serious crowd disorder forcing the abandonment of Montenegro's home UEFA EURO 2016 qualifier against Russia.

Pljevlja club claim second Prva Liga crown

Mladost edge Petrovac after extra time in cup final

EURO qualifying campaign scarred by crowd trouble

Domestic league

A mere sixth in 2013/14 – the club's lowest final placing in the first eight seasons of the Prva Liga – Rudar were not among the clubs tipped to challenge Sutjeska for the title at the start of the campaign. However, the decision to keep faith with coach Marić was to bear juicy fruit as the club from Pljevlja in the far north reclaimed the title they had won in 2009/10, thus joining three other clubs – FK Budućnost Podgorica, FK Mogren and Sutjeska – as two-time champions.

Rudar made a wonderful start, beating Sutjeska 3-1 in Niksic on the opening day – thanks to a double from Japanese midfielder Kohei Kato – and taking maximum points from eight of their first nine matches. Another impressive burst in mid-season, which yielded 25 points from a possible 27, meant that with two thirds of the campaign completed Rudar held a ten-point lead. It looked to be an invincible position, but as they began to drop points in unlikely places, Sutjeska, who lost their Montenegro midfielder Goran Jovović to a six-month suspension after he assaulted the referee in a 3-0 defeat by Budućnost, suddenly hit top form under their new coach Brajan Nenezić, with the league's leading marksman Goran Vujović also rediscovering his scoring touch.

It was Vujović who struck the winner when Sutjeska beat Rudar 1-0 in Pljevlja in round 30 to fling the title race wide open. Now Rudar's lead was down to just three points. A week later, after a goalless draw at Budućnost, there was just a single point in it. Sutjeska could scent a third successive title, but Rudar had two home games left and, with the pressure on, duly delivered the two wins they needed to keep the defending champions at bay, beating Mladost 3-1 and, a week later, bottom club FK Berane 4-1.

While Berane filled the one automatic relegation spot, Mogren accompanied them down after a heavy play-off defeat by FK Dečić, with FK Mornar only just avoiding the same fate after a marathon penalty shoot-out against OFK Igalo. FK Iskra took the direct route to promotion as they ascended to the top flight for the first time.

Domestic cup

There was also a first for Mladost, the club that produced the country's two most illustrious players, Dejan Savićević and Predrag Mijatović, as they made up for a disappointing second half of the season in the league by narrowly defeating Petrovac in the cup final. Mladost were helped by two costly faux pas from their opponents, who had goalkeeper Nemanja Popović sent off just before the interval and then conceded an own goal in extra time.

Europe

It was a desperately poor summer for Montenegrin clubs in Europe, with the quartet's only wins and – worse still – only goals coming in Budućnost's UEFA Europa League first qualifying round tie against SS Folgore of San Marino.

National team

Montenegro made a bright start to the UEFA EURO 2016 campaign with a 2-0 home win over Moldova, but that would be the only three-pointer they could muster in their opening six games. An entertaining 1-1 draw at home to Sweden in November raised spirits, but when the team returned to Podgorica to face Russia in the spring, the on-field endeavours of Branko Brnović's side were immediately overshadowed when a flare thrown from the crowd struck and injured opposition goalkeeper Igor Akinfeev. After a lengthy stoppage the match resumed, but the unruly behaviour in the stands later spilled over on to the pitch, and the match was abandoned at 0-0 on 67 minutes, with the points subsequently awarded to Russia.

DOMESTIC SEASON AT A GLANCE

Prva Liga 2014/15 final table

		Pld	Home W	D	L	F	A	Away W	D	L	F	A	Total W	D	L	F	A	Pts
1	**FK Rudar Pljevlja**	33	13	3	1	31	9	9	3	4	27	9	22	6	5	58	18	72
2	FK Sutjeska	33	10	4	3	31	12	10	5	1	27	11	20	9	4	58	23	69
3	FK Budućnost Podgorica	33	9	5	3	27	11	9	4	3	19	9	18	9	6	46	20	63
4	FK Mladost Podgorica	33	11	3	3	30	13	5	6	5	23	23	16	9	8	53	36	57
5	OFK Grbalj	33	10	4	3	31	26	5	3	8	21	18	15	7	11	52	44	52
6	FK Lovćen	33	9	3	5	22	13	6	2	8	20	19	15	5	13	42	32	50
7	OFK Petrovac	33	7	2	7	17	17	5	5	7	13	18	12	7	14	30	35	43
8	FK Bokelj	33	5	5	6	16	17	6	3	8	22	28	11	8	14	38	45	41
9	FK Zeta	33	8	3	5	34	19	3	4	10	14	25	11	7	15	48	44	40
10	FK Mornar	33	6	1	9	18	27	3	4	10	14	36	9	5	19	32	63	32
11	FK Mogren	33	2	6	8	11	26	3	0	14	15	44	5	6	22	26	70	21
12	FK Berane	33	3	2	11	16	34	0	2	15	9	44	3	4	26	25	78	13

European qualification 2015/16

Champion: FK Rudar Pljevlja (second qualifying round)

Cup winner: FK Mladost Podgorica (first qualifying round)
FK Sutjeska (first qualifying round)
FK Budućnost Podgorica (first qualifying round)

Top scorer	Goran Vujović (Sutjeska), 21 goals
Relegated clubs	FK Berane, FK Mogren
Promoted clubs	FK Iskra, FK Dečić
Cup final	FK Mladost Podgorica 2-1 OFK Petrovac *(aet)*

Team of the season
(4-4-2)

Coach: Marić *(Rudar)*

Player of the season

Nedjeljko Vlahović
(FK Rudar Velenje)

A Rudar player since 2009 and a double-winner in his debut season, Vlahović skippered the club to a second Prva Liga triumph in 2014/15. The 31-year-old playmaker was the champions' second top scorer – after 13-goal Igor Ivanović – with eight goals, and he also supplied ten assists in what was unquestionably his most productive season in Rudar colours. Capped once by his country, back in 2007, his claims for a belated recall went unheeded by Montenegro boss Branko Brnović.

Newcomer of the season

Ilija Tučević
(OFK Grbalj)

Grbalj exceeded most pre-season expectations by finishing fifth in the Prva Liga, and one of the key factors in their success was the emergence of 19-year-old Tučević, a fast-raiding left-back with an eye for goal who enjoyed a fabulous first season in the country's top division, earning himself a call-up to Montenegro's Under-21 team. He was not the only youngster in the Grbalj squad to make a huge impression, with 16-year-old Lazar Carević keeping goal for the club in the last six games of the season.

Mileta Radulović
(Mladost)

Pejović *(Mladost)*   Simović *(Budućnost)*   Mijušković *(Rudar)*   Nestorović *(Rudar)*

Igor Ivanović *(Rudar)*   Božović *(Lovćen/Sutjeska)*   Vlahović *(Rudar)*   Jablan *(Grbalj)*

G Vujović *(Sutjeska)*   B Milić *(Mladost)*

NATIONAL TEAM

Top five all-time caps
Elsad Zverotić (53); **Simon Vukčević** (45); **Vladimir Božović** (42); **Mirko Vučinić** (41); **Savo Pavićević** (39)

Top five all-time goals
Mirko Vučinić (16); **Stevan Jovetić** (14); **Dejan Damjanović** (8); Radomir Djalović (7); Andrija Delibašić (6)

Results 2014/15

08/09/14	Moldova (ECQ)	H	Podgorica	W	2-0	*Vučinić (45+2), Tomašević (73)*
09/10/14	Liechtenstein (ECQ)	A	Vaduz	D	0-0	
12/10/14	Austria (ECQ)	A	Vienna	L	0-1	
15/11/14	Sweden (ECQ)	H	Podgorica	D	1-1	*Jovetić (80p)*
27/03/15	Russia (ECQ)	H	Podgorica	L	0-3	*(w/o; original match abandoned after 67 mins at 0-0)*
08/06/15	Denmark	A	Viborg	L	1-2	*Jovetić (17)*
14/06/15	Sweden (ECQ)	A	Solna	L	1-3	*Damjanović (64p)*

Appearances 2014/15

Coach: Branko Brnović	08/08/67		MDA	LIE	AUT	SWE	RUS	Den	SWE	Caps	Goals
Vukašin Poleksić	30/08/82	Pécs (HUN)	G	G	G		G		G	32	-
Stefan Savić	08/01/91	Fiorentina (ITA)	D		D	D		D	D	31	2
Marko Simić	16/06/87	Kayserispor (TUR)	D	D	D		D	D	D74	10	-
Žarko Tomašević	22/02/90	Kortrijk (BEL)	D	D		D77		D	D	10	1
Vladimir Volkov	06/06/86	Partizan (SRB)	D46		D	D	D			16	-
Elsad Zverotić	31/10/86	Fulham (ENG) /Sion (SUI)	M	M	M70	M		M	D58	53	5
Nemanja Nikolić	01/01/88	Dinamo Minsk (BLR)	M	s57	M			s43		8	-
Vladimir Božović	13/11/81	Mordovia (RUS)	M		M76	M46				42	-
Fatos Bećiraj	05/05/88	Changchun Yatai (CHN) /Dinamo Minsk (BLR)	M66	M46	M	s67		s63	M	32	3
Dejan Damjanović	27/07/81	Beijing Guoan (CHN)	A81	A	s76	A67			A	28	8
Mirko Vučinić	01/10/83	Al-Jazira (UAE)	A	s46	A		A			41	16
Saša Balić	29/01/90	Metalurh Zaporizhya (UKR)	s46				D46		s74	9	-
Vladimir Jovović	26/10/94	Sutjeska	s66	M	s70	M				5	-
Nikola Vukčević	13/12/91	Braga (POR)	s81			M	M	M59	M	8	-
Milan Jovanović	21/07/83	Padideh (IRN)	D							36	-
Savo Pavićević	11/12/80	Crvena zvezda (SRB)	D							39	-
Simon Vukčević	29/01/86	Levadiakos (GRE)	M57	M46						45	2
Stevan Jovetić	02/11/89	Man. City (ENG)	A74	s46	A	A	A	A43		37	14
Petar Grbić	07/08/88	Partizan (SRB)	s74					s65		5	-
Marko Baša	29/12/82	LOSC (FRA)			D	D	D	D46		33	2
Mladen Božović	01/08/84	Khimik Dzerzhinsk (RUS) /Tom (RUS)					G		G	37	-
Marko Bakić	01/11/93	Spezia (ITA)				s46	s46	M75		7	-
Branislav Janković	13/06/92	Grbalj				s77				3	-
Mladen Kašćelan	13/02/83	Arsenal Tula (RUS)					M	M	M46	21	-
Adam Marušić	17/10/92	Kortrijk (BEL)					M		M	2	-
Marko Vešović	28/08/91	Rijeka (CRO)						M63		6	-
Stefan Mugoša	26/02/92	Erzgebirge Aue (GER)						A65	M	2	-
Esteban Saveljić	20/05/91	Defensa y Justicia (ARG)						s46	s58	2	-
Vladimir Boljević	17/01/88	AEK Larnaca (CYP)						s59	s46	2	-
Marko Vukčević	07/06/93	Olimpija Ljubljana (SVN)						s75		1	-

EUROPE

FK Sutjeska

CHAMPIONS LEAGUE

Second qualifying round - FC Sheriff (MDA)
A 0-2
Janjušević, Ognjanović, Stefanović, Jovović, Nikolić, Stijepović, G Vujović, Pejović (Kovačević 63), Ćuković, Igumanović (Fukui 76), Lukić (Krivokapić 39). Coach: Mile Tomić (SRB)
H 0-3
Janjušević, Ognjanović, Stefanović, Jovović (Djajić 90), Nikolić, Stijepović (J Vujović 81), G Vujović, Ćuković, Igumanović, Lukić, Fukui (Kovačević 66). Coach: Mile Tomić (SRB)
Red card: G Vujović 10

FK Lovćen

EUROPA LEAGUE

First qualifying round - FK Željezničar (BIH)
A 0-0
Perović, Radunović, V Martinović (Djurović 65), Tatar, Simović, Radović, Merdović (N Draganić 67), Bogdanović, Brnović, Kosović, Božović. Coach: Mojaš Radonjić (MNE)
H 0-1
Perović, Radunović, V Martinović, Tatar, Simović, Radović, Bogdanović, Brnović, Kosović (Djurović 73), Božović, N Draganić (Vujanović 66). Coach: Mojaš Radonjić (MNE)
Red card: Bogdanović 11

FK Čelik Nikšić

EUROPA LEAGUE

First qualifying round - FC Koper (SVN)
H 0-5
Giljen, Vuković, Adrović, Ivanović (Nikolić 79), Djalac, Prtenjak, Bubanja (Bulatović 52), Vidakanić, Jovović, Kalezić (Božović 83), Brnović. Coach: Željko Ćeha (MNE)
Red card: Jovović 74
A 0-4
Giljen, Vuković, Adrović, Ivanović (Vujović 89), Djalac, Prtenjak, Bubanja (Nikolić 81), Bulatović (Delibašić 16), Vidakanić, Kalezić, Brnović. Coach: Željko Ćeha (MNE)
Red card: Giljen 13

FK Budućnost Podgorica

EUROPA LEAGUE

First qualifying round - SS Folgore (SMR)
A 2-1 *Raspopović (30), Raičković (36)*
Ljuljanović, Tomković, Kopitović, Ilinčić (Burzanović 81), Vujačić (Milošević 90+1), Vukčević, Rogošić, Raičković, Raspopović, Raičević, Hočko. Coach: Goran Perišić (MNE)
H 3-0 *Tomković (14), Raičević (58), Vujačić (72)*
Ljuljanović, Tomković, Kopitović, Ilinčić (Burzanović 69), Vujačić, Rogošić (Vukčević 73), Raičković, Raspopović, Raičević (Milošević 84), Banović, Hočko. Coach: Goran Perišić (MNE)

Second qualifying round - AC Omonia (CYP)
H 0-2
Ljuljanović, Tomković, Kopitović, Ilinčić (Burzanović 72), Vujačić, Vukčević, Rogošić (Ćetković 46), Raičković, Raspopović, Raičević, Hočko. Coach: Goran Perišić (MNE)
A 0-0
Ljuljanović, Tomković, Kopitović, Ilinčić (Burzanović 86), Vujačić, Ćetković, Vukčević, Rogošić, Raspopović, Raičević, Hočko. Coach: Goran Perišić (MNE)

DOMESTIC LEAGUE CLUB-BY-CLUB

FK Berane

1920 • Gradski (10,000) • no website
Coach: Ratko Stevović;
(14/10/14) Rade Vešović

2014
09/08	a	Mornar	L	1-5	*Toyoshima*
16/08	h	Zeta	D	1-1	*Vukićević*
22/08	a	Mladost	L	1-2	*Djalović*
27/08	h	Mogren	L	0-2	
30/08	a	Sutjeska	L	0-4	
13/09	h	Grbalj	L	2-3	*Toyoshima, Djalović*
18/09	a	Petrovac	L	0-1	
21/09	h	Rudar	L	0-4	
27/09	a	Budućnost	L	0-1	
04/10	h	Lovćen	L	0-5	
18/10	a	Bokelj	D	1-1	*Nerić*
25/10	a	Mornar	L	2-3	*Nerić, Tomović*
01/11	a	Zeta	L	0-3	
08/11	h	Mladost	L	1-3	*Djalović*
22/11	a	Mogren	D	2-2	*Djukanović, Vukićević*
29/11	h	Sutjeska	L	0-2	
06/12	a	Grbalj	L	0-1	

2015
24/02	h	Petrovac	L	0-1	
28/02	a	Rudar	L	0-3	
11/03	a	Lovćen	L	0-2	
14/03	h	Bokelj	L	0-2	
18/03	h	Budućnost	L	1-2	*Zejnilović*
21/03	a	Grbalj	L	1-2	*Dulović*
31/03	h	Mogren	W	2-1	*Stavrić, Tomović*
04/04	a	Lovćen	L	0-2	
11/04	h	Zeta	W	2-1	*Krušćić, Djalović*
18/04	a	Sutjeska	L	1-3	*Zejnilović*
25/04	h	Bokelj	L	0-1	
02/05	a	Budućnost	L	0-4	
09/05	h	Mornar	D	2-2	*Vučetić, Tomović*
16/05	a	Mladost	L	1-4	*Krušćić*
23/05	h	Petrovac	W	3-1	*Tmušić 2, A Huremović*
30/05	a	Rudar	L	1-4	*Nišavić*

Name	Nat	DoB	Pos	Aps	(s)	Gls
Ibrahim Arifović	BIH	24/02/90	D	13		
Eldin Bećić		05/03/96	G	2	(1)	
Igor Bjelanović		30/06/94	M	1		
Nemanja Bulatović		13/08/91	A		(6)	
Boris Cimbaljević		27/07/88	D	19	(4)	
Arslan Dacić		25/08/82	G	5		
Nebojša Djalović		27/03/94	A	28	(2)	4
Nenad Djukanović		08/12/92	M	5	(4)	1
Zoran Djurić	SRB	22/10/93	D	6	(1)	
Zoran Djurišić		28/05/96	M	1		
Momčilo Dulović		25/05/92	D	22	(2)	1
Arijan Efović		22/02/93	M	3	(6)	
Danilo Golubović		28/06/97	M	1		
Almedin Huremović		10/12/92	M	11	(16)	1
Omar Huremović		12/01/95	M		(1)	
Stefan Kastratović		04/01/94	G	17		
Kristijan Krstović		09/07/89	M		(1)	
Nikola Krušćić		03/08/95	M	9	(1)	2
Gavrilo Lekić		18/02/96	M	2		
Stefan Lutovac		02/06/86	D	12		
Anes Mećikukić		16/10/96	D		(1)	
Bajram Mećikukić		15/05/98	M		(2)	
Milenko Nerić		11/03/88	A	11	(4)	2
Milovan Nikolić		27/11/93	D	7	(1)	
Zoran Nišavić		22/08/97	M	1	(1)	1
Shimora Noboru	JPN	11/03/93	M	11		
Soma Otani	JPN	25/07/90	M	6	(2)	
Stefan Pandrc	SRB	19/10/93	D	3	(3)	
Gavrilo Petrović		21/05/84	D	9		
Igor Poček		23/12/94	A	13		
Vladan Radović		09/03/91	M	1	(1)	
Mihailo Radulović		08/03/87	G	9		
Novak Rajković		05/10/89	M	7	(1)	
Milan Stavrić	SRB	21/05/87	A	4		1
Admir Šabotić		09/01/92	M	3	(4)	
Nemanja Tmušić		20/05/96	M	11	(8)	2
Nikola Tomović		25/07/89	M	26	(1)	3
Yusaku Toyoshima	JPN	06/07/91	M	18	(4)	1
Darko Vučetić		23/03/85	D	16	(7)	1
Nikola Vukadinović		28/07/92	M	1		
Dragoslav Vukićević		10/10/90	A	24	(3)	2
Takuto Yasuoka	JPN	29/10/96	M	1	(1)	
Admir Zejnilović		20/08/86	M	24	(5)	2

FK Bokelj

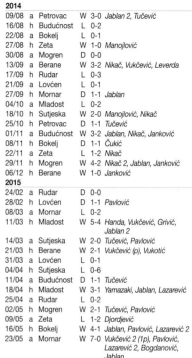

1922 • pod Vrmcem (5,000) • no website
Coach: Slobodan Drašković

2014

09/08	h	Zeta	D	1-1	*Lazarević*
16/08	a	Mogren	W	2-0	*Lazarević, A Mikijelj*
23/08	h	Grbalj	W	1-0	*Nikezić*
27/08	a	Rudar	L	0-2	
30/08	h	Lovćen	L	0-1	
13/09	a	Mornar	L	0-1	
17/09	h	Mladost	L	0-2	
21/09	a	Sutjeska	L	0-2	
27/09	h	Petrovac	W	2-1	*Šćekić 2*
04/10	a	Budućnost	D	2-2	*L Maraš, Ikeda*
18/10	h	Berane	D	1-1	*Vujović*
25/10	a	Zeta	L	1-3	*L Maraš*
01/11	h	Mogren	W	5-0	*Ikeda, Šćekić, A Mikijelj, Kotorac, Nikezić*
08/11	a	Grbalj	D	1-1	*Nikezić*
22/11	h	Rudar	L	1-5	*L Maraš*
29/11	a	Lovćen	L	1-4	*Pržica*
06/12	h	Mornar	L	0-1	

2015

24/02	a	Mladost	L	2-4	*L Maraš, Macanović*
28/02	h	Sutjeska	D	0-0	
08/03	a	Petrovac	W	3-0	*L Maraš, Nikezić 2 (1p)*
11/03	h	Budućnost	L	0-1	
14/03	a	Berane	W	2-0	*Nikezić, Zorica*
21/03	h	Budućnost	W	1-0	*Zorica*
31/03	a	Mladost	L	0-3	
04/04	a	Rudar	W	1-0	*Zorica*
11/04	a	Mogren	W	3-0	*L Maraš, Macanović 2*
18/04	h	Zeta	L	1-2	*Todorović*
25/04	a	Berane	W	1-0	*Macanović*
02/05	a	Mornar	W	2-1	*Zorica, Macanović*
09/05	h	Petrovac	D	0-0	
16/05	a	Grbalj	L	1-4	*Pajović*
23/05	h	Lovćen	D	1-1	*Zorica*
30/05	a	Sutjeska	D	1-1	*Macanović*

Name	Nat	DoB	Pos	Aps	(s)	Gls
Nikola Bogdanović		22/03/87	M	16		
Nikola Braunović		21/07/97	M		(1)	
Nikola Čelebić		04/07/89	D	12	(1)	
Takuo Ikeda	JPN	22/12/92	M	15		2
Dejan Kotorac		31/05/96	M	11	(11)	1
Egzon Krasnići		17/07/95	M		(1)	
Bojan Lazarević		09/09/93	M	13	(3)	2
Aleksandar Macanović		16/04/93	M	10	(4)	6
Luka Maraš		24/05/96	M	19	(9)	6
Milo Maraš		24/11/94	M		(4)	
Milan Mijatović		26/07/87	G	32		
Aleksandar Mikijelj		05/02/79	D	18		2
Zoran Mikijelj		13/12/91	D	16		
Filip Mitrović		17/11/93	D		(2)	
Siniša Mladenović	SRB	05/01/91	D	32		
Milenko Nerić		11/03/88	A	5	(1)	
Miloš Nikezić		02/03/87	A	23	(4)	6
Lazar Pajović		10/11/95	M	2	(20)	1
Ivan Pavićević		28/06/89	A		(3)	
Petar Perošević		14/01/89	D	8	(3)	
Mihailo Petrović		12/12/89	D	12	(2)	
Dejan Pržica		19/01/91	M	4	(16)	1
Aleksandar Šćekić		12/12/91	M	30		3
Ilija Todorović		29/02/92	G	1	(1)	
Mirko Todorović	SRB	22/08/85	D	32		1
Marko Vujović		23/07/85	M	22	(2)	1
Damir Vuković		16/05/97	M		(1)	
Miroslav Zlatičanin	SRB	26/05/85	M	15		1
Milan Zorica	SRB	07/01/92	M	15		5

FK Budućnost Podgorica

1925 • Pod Goricom (12,508) • no website
Major honours
Montenegrin League (2) 2008, 2012; Montenegrin Cup (1) 2013
Coach: Goran Perišić;
(30/07/14) Dragan Radojičić

2014

09/08	h	Mogren	W	3-0	*Raspopović, Adrović 2 (1p)*
16/08	a	Grbalj	W	2-0	*Adrović 2 (1p)*
23/08	h	Rudar	W	1-0	*Adrović (p)*
27/08	a	Lovćen	L	2-3	*Adrović, Raičković*
30/08	a	Mornar	W	2-0	*Adrović (p), Vujačić*
13/09	a	Mladost	W	1-0	
18/09	h	Sutjeska	L	1-2	*Raičević*
21/09	a	Petrovac	W	1-0	*Tomković*
27/09	h	Berane	W	1-0	*S Gazivoda*
04/10	h	Bokelj	D	2-2	*Adrović, Pavićević*
19/10	a	Zeta	W	2-1	*Bakrač, Vujačić*
25/10	a	Mogren	W	2-0	*Vujačić 2*
01/11	h	Grbalj	L	2-3	*Adrović 2*
09/11	a	Rudar	L	0-1	
22/11	h	Lovćen	W	2-0	*Raičević, Hočko*
29/11	a	Mornar	W	1-0	*Adrović*
06/12	h	Mladost	D	0-0	

2015

24/02	a	Sutjeska	W	3-0	*Ilinčić 2, Raspopović*
28/02	h	Petrovac	L	0-1	
11/03	a	Bokelj	W	1-0	*Raičević*
14/03	h	Zeta	W	1-0	*Vujačić*
18/03	a	Berane	W	2-1	*Vukčević, Ilinčić*
21/03	h	Bokelj	L	0-1	
31/03	h	Mornar	W	3-1	*Tomković, Simović, Bakrač*
04/04	a	Petrovac	D	0-0	
11/04	h	Grbalj	D	1-1	*Raspopović*
18/04	a	Lovćen	D	0-0	
26/04	h	Sutjeska	D	1-1	*Ilinčić*
02/05	h	Berane	W	4-0	*Simović (p), Raičević (p), Burzanović, og (Tomović)*
09/05	a	Mladost	W	2-1	*Simović (p), Raičević*
16/05	h	Rudar	D	0-0	
23/05	a	Mogren	D	1-1	*Tomković*
30/05	h	Zeta	W	3-0	*Milošević, Kopitović, Camaj*

Name	Nat	DoB	Pos	Aps	(s)	Gls
Admir Adrović		08/05/88	A	17		11
Jasmin Agović		13/02/91	M	30		
Miloš Bakrač		25/02/92	D	21		2
Balša Banović		26/01/98	D		(1)	
Marko Banović		28/04/96	D	4	(5)	
Luka Bojić		09/04/92	M	1	(1)	
Blažo Bulatović	SRB	19/11/91	M		(1)	
Marko Burzanović		13/01/98	M	2	(9)	1
Driton Camaj		07/03/97	A		(1)	1
Andjelo Drobnjak		31/07/95	A		(1)	
Flávio Beck	BRA	14/03/87	M	25	(5)	
Miloš Gazivoda		29/04/96	A	1		
Savo Gazivoda		18/07/94	M	1	(7)	1
Deni Hočko		22/04/94	M	30		1
Marko Ilinčić		06/11/95	M	12	(7)	4
Marko Kažić		16/11/95	M	1	(1)	
Boris Kopitović		17/05/94	D	23	(2)	1
Damir Ljuljanović		23/02/92	G	3		
Stefan Milošević		23/06/96	M	1	(8)	1
Miloš Pavićević		09/02/94	M	15	(8)	1
Milivoje Raičević		21/07/93	M	25	(4)	5
Miloš Raičković		02/12/93	M	18	(9)	1
Momčilo Raspopović		18/03/94	D	28		3
Marko Rogošić		21/06/96	D	1	(1)	
Vladislav Rogošić		21/05/94	M	9	(12)	
Janko Simović		02/04/87	D	28	(1)	3
Uroš Smolović		28/09/92	M		(1)	
Mihailo Tomković		10/06/91	D	27		3
Aleksandar Vujačić		19/03/90	A	16	(7)	5
Andrija Vukčević		11/10/96	D	24	(1)	1

OFK Grbalj

1970 • Pod Sutvarom (1,500) • no website
Coach: Marko Vidojević;
(05/03/15) Ilija Radović

2014

09/08	a	Petrovac	W	3-0	*Jablan 2, Tučević*
16/08	h	Budućnost	L	0-2	
22/08	a	Bokelj	L	0-1	
27/08	h	Zeta	W	1-0	*Manojlović*
30/08	a	Mogren	D	0-0	
13/09	h	Berane	W	3-2	*Nikač, Vukčević, Leverda*
17/09	h	Rudar	L	0-3	
21/09	a	Lovćen	L	0-1	
27/09	h	Mornar	D	1-1	*Jablan*
04/10	a	Mladost	L	0-2	
18/10	h	Sutjeska	W	2-0	*Manojlović, Nikač*
25/10	h	Petrovac	D	1-1	*Tučević*
01/11	a	Budućnost	W	3-2	*Jablan, Nikač, Janković*
08/11	h	Bokelj	D	1-1	*Čukić*
22/11	a	Zeta	L	1-2	*Nikač*
29/11	h	Mogren	W	4-2	*Nikač 2, Jablan, Janković*
06/12	h	Berane	W	1-0	*Janković*

2015

24/02	a	Rudar	D	0-0	
28/02	h	Lovćen	D	1-1	*Pavlović*
08/03	a	Mornar	L	0-2	
11/03	h	Mladost	W	5-4	*Handa, Vukčević, Grivić, Jablan 2*
14/03	a	Sutjeska	W	2-0	*Tučević, Pavlović*
21/03	h	Berane	W	2-1	*Vukčević (p), Vukotić*
31/03	a	Lovćen	L	0-1	
04/04	h	Sutjeska	L	0-6	
11/04	a	Budućnost	D	1-1	*Tučević*
18/04	h	Mladost	W	3-1	*Yamazaki, Jablan, Lazarević*
25/04	a	Rudar	L	0-2	
02/05	h	Mogren	W	2-1	*Tučević, Pavlović*
09/05	a	Zeta	L	1-2	*Djordjević*
16/05	h	Bokelj	W	4-1	*Jablan, Pavlović, Lazarević 2*
23/05	a	Mornar	W	7-0	*Vukčević 2 (1p), Pavlović, Lazarević 2, Bogdanović, Jablan*
30/05	h	Petrovac	W	3-1	*Jablan 2, Vukčević*

Name	Nat	DoB	Pos	Aps	(s)	Gls
Ilija Bogdanović		14/03/92	M	31		1
Ognjen Bogićević		14/09/93	G	3		
Boris Bulajić		27/04/88	M		(4)	
Lazar Carević		16/03/99	G	6		
Milan Carević		05/10/93	D	16		
Bojan Čukić	SRB	05/02/88	M	1	(5)	1
Stefan Djordjević		16/11/90	M		(3)	1
Spasoje Djuričanin		09/06/94	G		(1)	
Ljubomir Djurović	SRB	06/01/92	G	4	(1)	
Ilija Glavan	BIH	03/07/90	D	25	(1)	
Dragan Grivić		22/06/92	D	6	(1)	1
Yuki Handa	JPN	10/01/96	A	5	(4)	1
Ivan Jablan		18/07/79	A	26	(1)	12
Branislav Janković		13/06/92	M	11	(6)	3
Miloš Kalezić		09/08/93	M	2	(1)	
Vladan Kordić		22/06/98	M		(1)	
Nemanja Kosović		15/05/93	D	12	(3)	
Miroslav Kovačević		03/05/94	M	2	(2)	
Bojan Lazarević		09/09/93	A	6	(8)	5
Nemanja Leverda		07/06/92	M	2	(10)	1
Aleksandar Macanović		16/04/93	M		(1)	
Bojan Magud		10/12/97	M	1	(7)	
Ćetko Manojlović		03/01/91	D	22	(3)	2
Mirko Marković		26/12/88	D	1	(1)	
Goran Milojko		05/01/94	D	30		
Darko Nikač		15/09/90	A	9	(2)	6
Stevan Pavićević		07/11/86	A	8	(18)	
Vojin Pavlović		09/11/93	M	29	(2)	5
Dejan Pepić		27/07/93	A	4	(4)	
Gorčin Todorović		28/05/94	A		(2)	
Ilija Tučević		18/10/95	D	18	(5)	5
Petar Vukčević		15/08/87	M	30	(1)	6
Goran Vukliš	BIH	24/09/89	G	20		
Ilija Vukotić		07/01/99	M	1	(1)	1
Kenta Yamazaki	JPN	19/05/87	D	32		1
Danijel Zindović		18/03/96	D		(1)	

FK Lovćen

1913 • Obilića Poljana (5,000) • fklovcen.me
Major honours
Montenegrin Cup (1) 2014
Coach: Mojaš Radonjić;
(17/11/14) (Djuro Mijušković);
(07/01/15) Radovan Kavaja

2014
09/08	a	Mladost	L	0-1
16/08	h	Sutjeska	L	1-2 *Djurović*
22/08	a	Petrovac	L	0-1
27/08	h	Budućnost	W	3-2 *Božović, Vušurović, Djurišić*
30/08	a	Bokelj	W	1-0 *Vukčević*
13/09	h	Zeta	D	1-1 *Kosović*
17/09	a	Mogren	W	2-1 *Tatar (p), Vučić*
21/09	h	Grbalj	W	1-0 *Djurović*
28/09	a	Rudar	L	0-1
04/10	a	Berane	W	5-0 *Božović 3 (1p), Djurović, Bogdanović*
18/10	h	Mornar	W	3-1 *Božović, Vukčević, Vušurović*
25/10	h	Mladost	L	0-1
01/11	a	Sutjeska	L	0-2
08/11	h	Petrovac	L	0-1
22/11	a	Budućnost	L	0-2
29/11	h	Bokelj	W	4-1 *Tatar, Vujanović 2, og (Bogdanović)*
06/12	a	Zeta	W	3-2 *Vušurović, Bogdanović, Vujović*

2015
24/02	h	Mogren	W	1-0 *Vujanović*
28/02	a	Grbalj	D	1-1 *Vujanović*
08/03	h	Rudar	L	0-2
11/03	h	Berane	W	2-0 *Vušurović 2*
14/03	a	Mornar	W	5-1 *Djurović 2 (1p), V Martinović, Vujović, og (Graovac)*
21/03	a	Petrovac	L	0-2
31/03	h	Grbalj	W	1-0 *Djurović*
04/04	h	Berane	W	2-0 *Djurović, Vušurović*
11/04	a	Sutjeska	L	0-3
18/04	h	Budućnost	D	0-0
25/04	a	Mladost	L	0-1
02/05	h	Rudar	D	0-0
09/05	h	Mogren	W	2-0 *V Martinović, Vujanović*
16/05	h	Zeta	L	1-2 *Perutović*
23/05	a	Bokelj	D	1-1 *M Draganić*
30/05	h	Mornar	W	2-0 *N Draganić, V Radunović*

Name	Nat	DoB	Pos	Aps	(s)	Gls
Draško Adžić		22/08/96	M	2	(2)	
Ivan Batrićević		23/06/97	M		(1)	
Dejan Bogdanović		08/08/90	M	17	(1)	2
Filip Borozan		05/04/95	A	1	(2)	
Draško Božović		30/06/88	M	15		5
Nenad Brnović		18/01/80	M	25	(2)	
Ivan Delić		15/02/86	M	11	(1)	
Milan Djurišić		18/04/87	A	10	(2)	1
Marko Djurović		08/05/88	A	18	(8)	7
Marko Draganić		19/09/94	M	6	(5)	1
Nikola Draganić		19/09/94	M	5	(3)	1
Jovan Jablan		13/02/99	D		(1)	
Joko Jabučanin		16/07/97	M		(1)	
Srdja Kosović		02/05/92	M	19	(7)	1
Željko Marković		25/02/96	M	5	(4)	
Ilija Martinović		31/01/94	D	19	(5)	
Vuk Martinović		19/09/89	D	29		2
Jovan Perović		28/12/89	G	29		
Mićo Perović		04/07/93	G	4		
Blažo Perutović		08/12/83	M	5	(8)	1
Miloš Radunović		07/07/90	D	26	(1)	
Vladan Radunović		02/01/89	A	3	(12)	1
Vladimir Sjekloća		11/02/95	A	5	(1)	
Vladan Tatar		23/01/84	D	30	(1)	2
Hirofumi Ueda	JPN	13/10/94	A	6	(3)	
Darko Vučić		28/08/91	A	8	(1)	1
Luka Vujanović		17/07/94	M	20	(4)	5
Nikola Vujović		23/06/81	M	11	(11)	2
Nikola Vukčević		22/03/84	D	12		1
Milan Vušurović		18/04/95	M	22	(7)	6

FK Mladost Podgorica

1950 • Stari Aerodrom (1,000) •
fkmladost.c-g.me
Major honours
Montenegrin Cup (1) 2015
Coach: Aleksandar Nedović

2014
10/08	h	Lovćen	W	1-0 *Jovanović*
16/08	a	Mornar	W	2-1 *Milić, Knežević*
22/08	h	Berane	W	2-1 *Knežević (p), Šćepanović*
27/08	h	Sutjeska	L	1-3 *Krstović*
30/08	a	Petrovac	L	2-4 *Milić 2 (1p)*
13/09	h	Budućnost	D	0-0
17/09	a	Bokelj	W	2-0 *og (M Todorović), Novović*
21/09	h	Zeta	W	3-1 *Milić 2 (1p), Jovanović*
27/09	a	Mogren	W	3-1 *Mirković, Milić, Knežević*
04/10	h	Grbalj	W	2-0 *Djalac, Šćepanović*
18/10	a	Rudar	D	0-0
25/10	a	Lovćen	W	1-0 *Jovanović*
01/11	h	Mornar	W	3-0 *Milić, Šćepanović 2*
08/11	a	Berane	W	3-1 *Knežević 2, Djalac*
22/11	a	Sutjeska	D	0-0
29/11	h	Petrovac	W	2-0 *Djalac, Knežević*
06/12	a	Budućnost	D	0-0

2015
24/02	h	Bokelj	W	4-2 *Jovanović, Djalac 2, Vuković*
28/02	a	Zeta	D	1-1 *Djurišić*
08/03	h	Mogren	W	3-0 *Vuković, Jovanović 2*
11/03	h	Grbalj	L	4-5 *Djalac, Vuković, Milić 2 (2p)*
14/03	h	Rudar	D	0-0
21/03	a	Zeta	D	2-2 *Vuković, Šćepanović*
31/03	h	Bokelj	W	3-0 *Djalac, Milić, Djurišić*
04/04	a	Mornar	L	0-1
11/04	h	Petrovac	L	0-1
18/04	a	Grbalj	L	1-3 *Vuković*
25/04	h	Lovćen	W	1-0 *Djurišić*
02/05	a	Sutjeska	D	1-1 *Vuković*
09/05	h	Budućnost	L	1-2 *Milić*
16/05	h	Berane	W	4-1 *Osmajlić 2, Djalac (p), Milić*
23/05	a	Rudar	L	1-3 *Vuković*
30/05	h	Mogren	L	0-3

Name	Nat	DoB	Pos	Aps	(s)	Gls
Goran Adamović	SRB	24/04/87	D	8		
Bojan Oliver Babović		02/04/94	M	1	(2)	
Balša Boričić		07/01/97	M	1	(1)	
Matija Božanović		13/04/94	M	2		
Miloš Djalac		17/10/82	A	28	(2)	8
Milan Djurišić		11/04/87	A	6	(8)	3
Miroje Jovanović		10/03/87	M	27	(4)	6
Stefan Jovović		02/03/96	M		(1)	
Darko Karadžić		17/04/89	A	5	(7)	
Ivan Knežević		22/02/86	A	3	(11)	6
Koča Krstović		27/03/95	A	1	(5)	1
Dušan Lagator		29/03/94	D	29	(1)	
Miloš Lakić		21/12/85	D	30		
Vojin Manojlović		14/09/98	M		(1)	
Aleksandar Milić		24/08/98	A	1	(2)	
Bogdan Milić		24/11/87	A	24	(9)	12
Luka Mirković		01/11/90	D	17	(2)	1
Admir Musić		15/08/98	M		(1)	
Ivan Novović		26/04/89	D	26	(2)	1
Dragan Obradović		28/02/95	A	6	(6)	
Božo Osmajlić		01/02/94	M	1	(1)	2
Luka Pejović		31/07/85	D	30		
Zoran Petrović		14/07/97	A	1	(1)	
Mileta Radulović		29/01/81	G	33		
Miloš Radulović		19/10/92	M	11	(3)	
Igor Radusinović		15/03/84	D	16		
Vladimir Savićević		27/11/89	M	2	(12)	
Marko Šćepanović		08/08/82	M	17	(9)	5
Miloš Vukčević		26/01/97	A		(1)	
Ivan Vuković		09/02/87	A	13	(2)	7
Radule Živković		20/10/90	D	24		

FK Mogren

1920 • Lugovi (4,000) • no website
Major honours
Montenegrin League (2) 2009, 2011; Montenegrin Cup (1) 2008
Coach: Branislav Milačić

2014
09/08	a	Budućnost	L	0-3
16/08	h	Bokelj	L	0-2
23/08	a	Zeta	L	0-5
27/08	a	Berane	W	2-0 *V Vujačić 2*
30/08	h	Grbalj	D	0-0
13/09	a	Rudar	L	1-2 *Marković*
17/09	h	Lovćen	L	1-2 *Grbović*
21/09	a	Mornar	W	3-1 *Grbović 2, V Vujačić*
27/09	h	Mladost	L	1-3 *Mugoša*
04/10	a	Sutjeska	L	0-4
18/10	h	Petrovac	L	1-3 *Zec (p)*
25/10	h	Budućnost	L	0-2
01/11	h	Bokelj	L	0-5
08/11	h	Zeta	W	2-1 *Zec, Grbović*
22/11	h	Berane	D	2-2 *Grbović 2*
29/11	a	Grbalj	L	2-4 *Grbović, Petričević*
06/12	h	Rudar	L	0-3

2015
24/02	a	Lovćen	L	0-1
28/02	h	Mornar	D	1-1 *Inuma*
08/03	a	Mladost	L	0-3
11/03	h	Sutjeska	D	0-0
14/03	a	Petrovac	L	0-2
21/03	h	Rudar	W	1-0 *Delić*
31/03	a	Berane	L	1-2 *Delić*
04/04	a	Zeta	L	0-5
11/04	h	Bokelj	L	0-2
18/04	a	Mornar	L	2-3 *Adrović (p), Grbović*
25/04	a	Petrovac	D	1-1 *Poček*
02/05	a	Grbalj	L	1-2 *Jovović*
09/05	h	Lovćen	L	0-2
16/05	a	Sutjeska	L	0-3
23/05	h	Budućnost	D	1-1 *Goto*
30/05	a	Mladost	W	3-0 *Jovović 2, Karadžić*

Name	Nat	DoB	Pos	Aps	(s)	Gls
Zijad Adrović		17/02/86	M	21	(4)	1
Danilo Bakić		28/10/95	M	10	(2)	
Jovan Baošić		07/07/95	D	17	(1)	
Ivan Butorović		23/11/92	G	12		
Marko Ćosić		18/02/95	M	26	(4)	
Nemanja Ćosović		07/05/92	M		(2)	
Ivan Delić		15/02/86	M	9	(2)	2
Ilija Djurović		25/12/94	G	7	(2)	
Ivan Dragićević	SRB	21/10/81	D	8		
Kyosuke Goto	JPN	29/07/92	M	10	(2)	1
Žarko Grbović		20/05/95	M	19	(5)	8
Goran Grujić	SRB	27/11/82	D	8		
Masaki Inuma	JPN	27/11/92	M	10	(2)	1
Petar Jovović		31/01/91	A	5	(8)	3
Aleksandar Kapisoda	CRO	17/09/89	D	13	(1)	
Vladan Karadžić		04/02/95	M	2	(8)	1
Nemanja Krstić	SRB	23/04/85	M	9	(4)	
Stefan Kruščić		20/11/93	A		(1)	
Nikola Marčelja		30/11/85	G	13		
Darko Marković		15/05/87	M	12	(2)	1
Zoran Mikijelj		13/12/91	D	16		
Drago Milović		23/05/94	M	1	(4)	
Filip Mitrović		17/11/93	D	13	(3)	
Marko Mugoša		04/04/84	M	13	(2)	1
Stefan Nedović		24/02/95	M	7	(9)	
Balša Pelićić		05/08/95	A		(1)	
Petar Perošević		14/01/89	D	6		
Luka Petričević		06/07/92	D	10		1
Igor Poček		23/12/94	A	8	(4)	1
Marko Popović		18/08/84	M	11	(3)	
Dragiša Prelević		08/06/93	G	1		
Ivan Racković		13/09/94	D	15	(2)	
Marko Radulović		17/06/85	D	9	(2)	
Nikola Šćepanović		08/01/93	M	1		
Igor Vujačić		08/08/94	D	11	(1)	
Vule Vujačić		20/03/88	A	13	(4)	3
Nikola Vujošević		07/03/96	M	1	(2)	
Filip Vukićević		24/01/95	M	1	(1)	
Miodrag Zec		14/10/82	A	12	(6)	2
Krsto Zvicer		10/06/87	A	3	(5)	

FK Mornar

1923 • Topolica (2,500) • no website
Coach: Mladen Vukićević

2014
09/08	h	Berane	W	5-1	Bubanja 2, Lalošević, Jovančov (p), Darmanović
16/08	h	Mladost	L	1-2	Radulović
23/08	a	Sutjeska	L	0-3	
27/08	h	Petrovac	L	0-1	
30/08	a	Budućnost	L	0-2	
13/09	h	Bokelj	W	1-0	Rotković (p)
17/09	a	Zeta	D	0-0	
21/09	h	Mogren	L	1-3	Rotković
27/09	a	Grbalj	D	1-1	Kalezić
04/10	h	Rudar	W	2-1	Graovac, Rotković
18/10	a	Lovćen	L	1-3	Rotković
25/10	a	Berane	W	3-2	Rotković 3
01/11	a	Mladost	L	0-3	
08/11	h	Sutjeska	L	0-3	
22/11	a	Petrovac	W	1-0	Rotković
29/11	h	Budućnost	L	0-1	
10/12	a	Bokelj	W	1-0	Rotković

2015
24/02	h	Zeta	D	0-0	
28/02	a	Mogren	L	1-1	Kalezić
08/03	h	Grbalj	W	2-0	Lalošević, Jovančov
11/03	a	Rudar	L	0-3	
14/03	h	Lovćen	L	1-5	B Ivanović
21/03	h	Sutjeska	L	0-1	
31/03	a	Budućnost	L	1-3	B Ivanović
04/04	h	Mladost	W	1-0	Karadžić
11/04	a	Rudar	L	3-4	Lalošević, Kim, Pejović
18/04	a	Mogren	W	3-2	Vojvodić, Jovančov (p), Leković
25/04	a	Zeta	L	0-4	
02/05	h	Bokelj	L	1-2	Vojvodić
09/05	a	Berane	D	2-2	Kim, Vojvodić (p)
16/05	a	Petrovac	L	0-3	
23/05	h	Grbalj	L	0-7	
30/05	a	Lovćen	L	0-2	

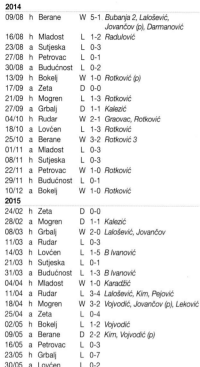

Name	Nat	DoB	Pos	Aps	(s)	Gls
Igor Arsenijević	SRB	29/05/86	D	9	(2)	
Ramazan Biševič		11/02/92	M		(4)	
Bogdan Bogdanović		05/03/89	A	14	(1)	
Balša Božović		01/05/87	M	17		
Danko Bubanja		12/09/88	D	19	(1)	2
Arsenije Darmanović		29/03/97	A		(1)	1
Nemanja Djurković		03/05/95	M	1		
Irfan Duraković		13/07/95	G	4	(1)	
Denis Džanović		03/06/93	M		(6)	
Siniša Graovac	BIH	01/09/84	D	24	(3)	1
Bojan Ivanović		03/12/81	D	14		2
Saša Ivanović		26/06/84	G	25		
Dejan Jovančov	SRB	28/09/87	A	27	(2)	3
Vuk Jovović		06/04/91	A		(1)	
Bojan Kalezić		11/03/88	M	24		2
Darko Karadžić		17/04/89	M	10	(1)	1
Kim Young-seop	KOR	10/08/91	M	6	(4)	2
Edi Kujović		29/04/90	M	2	(10)	
Lazar Lalošević		07/05/95	A	10	(12)	3
Marko Leković		07/05/96	M	1	(10)	1
Stevan Marković		31/01/88	D	14		
Boris Merdović		08/12/89	M	23	(5)	
Luka Merdović		06/10/97	M	7	(12)	
Željko Mrvaljević		25/06/79	D	25		
Sava Mugoša		10/08/93	G	1	(1)	
Vuk Orlandić		05/01/97	M	1	(6)	
Nikola Pejanović		26/02/97	M	1		
Andrija Pejović		16/09/91	M	10	(1)	1
Nemanja Perunović		16/11/92	M		(2)	
Miloš M Radulović		23/02/90	D	12	(1)	1
Luka Raičević		02/12/94	G	3	(1)	
Luka Rotković		05/06/88	A	11		9
Semir Seratlić		30/05/95	A			
Djordje Vojvodić		31/05/86	M	24	(2)	3
Nino Vukmarković		17/12/94	M	24	(2)	

OFK Petrovac

1969 • Pod Malim brdom (1,630) • no website
Major honours
Montenegrin Cup (1) 2009
Coach: Milorad Malovrazić

2014
09/08	h	Grbalj	L	0-3	
16/08	a	Rudar	L	0-1	
23/08	h	Lovćen	W	1-0	Kacić
27/08	a	Mornar	W	1-0	Muhović
30/08	h	Mladost	W	4-2	Grbović, Tomić 2, Golubović
13/09	a	Sutjeska	D	1-1	Kacić
17/09	h	Berane	W	1-0	Radišić (p)
21/09	h	Budućnost	L	0-1	
27/09	a	Bokelj	L	1-2	Kacić (p)
04/10	h	Zeta	W	1-0	Kacić
18/10	a	Mogren	W	3-1	Ivanović, Marković, Tomić
25/10	a	Grbalj	D	1-1	Kacić
01/11	h	Rudar	L	0-1	
08/11	a	Lovćen	W	1-0	Tomić
22/11	h	Mornar	L	0-1	
29/11	a	Mladost	L	0-2	
06/12	h	Sutjeska	D	1-1	Muhović

2015
24/02	a	Berane	W	1-0	Knežević
28/02	a	Budućnost	W	1-0	Knežević
08/03	h	Bokelj	L	0-3	
11/03	a	Zeta	L	0-2	
14/03	h	Mogren	W	2-0	Muhović, Stevović
21/03	h	Lovćen	W	2-0	Muhović, Pejaković
31/03	a	Sutjeska	L	0-1	
04/04	h	Budućnost	D	0-0	
11/04	a	Mladost	D	0-0	
18/04	h	Rudar	L	1-3	Radišić
25/04	a	Mogren	D	1-1	Pejaković
02/05	h	Zeta	L	1-2	Kopitović
09/05	a	Bokelj	D	0-0	
16/05	h	Mornar	W	3-0	Pepić 2, Kopitović
23/05	a	Berane	L	1-3	Grbović
30/05	a	Grbalj	L	1-3	Pejaković

Name	Nat	DoB	Pos	Aps	(s)	Gls
Bogdan Bogdanović		05/03/89	A	1	(6)	
Mehmed Divanović		12/12/84	M	4	(6)	
Bojan Golubović		28/11/86	M	31	(1)	1
Boris Grbović		31/01/80	D	32		2
Bojan Ivanović		03/12/81	D	16	1	
Benjamin Kacić		28/06/91	M	28	(4)	5
Demir Kajević		20/04/89	M	21		
Ivan Knežević		22/02/86	A	12	(2)	2
Boris Kopitović		27/04/95	A	4	(10)	2
Aleksandar Leposavić	SRB	03/11/87	A	5	(11)	
Marko Marković		05/09/87	M	22	(6)	1
Lazar Martinović		03/07/89	M	20	(8)	
Luka Medigović		03/04/95	M	3		
Marko Memedović	SRB	18/01/91	M		(11)	
Jasmin Muhović		02/04/89	A	22	(3)	4
Ivan Pejaković		22/08/92	M	29	(2)	3
Dejan Pepić		27/07/93	A	7	(9)	2
Nemanja Popović		20/05/84	G	30		
Stefan Popović		11/01/93	G	3		
Dragoljub Radišević		07/12/96	A		(1)	
Mirko Radišić		01/09/90	A	25	(1)	2
Nikola Savović		30/09/94	M	7	(3)	
Nemanja Sekulić		29/03/94	M		(1)	
Miloš Stevović		14/09/89	M	4	(1)	
Danilo Tomić		23/06/86	M	27	(1)	4
Nenad Vujović		02/01/89	D	14	(6)	

FK Rudar Pljevlja

1920 • Pod Golubinjom (8,500) • no website
Major honours
Montenegrin League (2) 2010, 2015; Montenegrin Cup (3) 2007, 2010, 2011
Coach: Mirko Marić

2014
10/08	a	Sutjeska	W	3-1	Kato 2, Igor Ivanović
16/08	h	Petrovac	W	1-0	Vlahović
23/08	a	Budućnost	L	0-1	
27/08	h	Bokelj	W	2-0	Gačević, Ivan Ivanović
30/08	a	Zeta	W	2-1	Kato, Igor Ivanović
13/09	h	Mogren	W	2-1	Brnović, Mrdak
17/09	a	Grbalj	W	3-0	Jovović, Vlahović 2
21/09	a	Berane	W	4-0	Mijušković, Gačević, Mrdak, Vlahović
27/09	h	Lovćen	W	1-0	Damjanović
04/10	a	Mornar	L	1-2	Vlahović
18/10	h	Mladost	D	0-0	
26/10	h	Sutjeska	D	0-0	
01/11	a	Petrovac	W	1-0	Brnović
08/11	h	Budućnost	W	1-0	Djurić (p)
22/11	h	Bokelj	W	5-1	Noma 2, Kato, Mijušković, Jovović
29/11	h	Zeta	W	2-1	Ivan Ivanović, Igor Ivanović
10/12	a	Mogren	W	3-0	Djurić, Igor Ivanović, Kato

2015
24/02	h	Grbalj	D	0-0	
28/02	h	Berane	W	3-0	Igor Ivanović , Jovović, Vujačić
08/03	a	Lovćen	W	2-0	Vlahović (p), Noma
11/03	h	Mornar	W	3-0	Igor Ivanović 2, Vujačić
14/03	a	Mladost	D	0-0	
21/03	a	Mogren	L	0-1	
31/03	h	Zeta	W	3-1	Kato, Igor Ivanović 2
04/04	a	Bokelj	L	0-1	
11/04	a	Mornar	W	4-3	Mijušković, Jovović, Igor Ivanović 2
18/04	a	Petrovac	W	3-1	Igor Ivanović, Vlahović, Brnović
25/04	h	Grbalj	W	2-0	Vlahović (p), Kato
02/05	a	Lovćen	D	0-0	
09/05	h	Sutjeska	L	0-1	
16/05	a	Budućnost	D	0-0	
23/05	h	Mladost	W	3-1	Vujačić 2, Igor Ivanović
30/05	h	Berane	W	4-1	Nestorović, Mijušković, Radanović (p), Brnović

Name	Nat	DoB	Pos	Aps	(s)	Gls
Andrey Atanasov	BUL	09/04/87	M		(3)	
Adi Bambur		14/09/92	M		(1)	
Predrag Brnović		22/10/86	M	30	(1)	4
Boris Bulajić		27/04/88	M		(1)	
Dejan Damjanović		08/07/86	D	17	(8)	1
Djordje Djurić	SRB	10/08/91	D	20	(4)	2
Aleksandar Dubljević		09/03/85	D	1	(3)	
Nikola Gačević		14/05/87	M	18	(8)	2
Milija Golubović		25/04/86	D		(5)	
Vladan Gordić		27/07/90	D	1	(3)	
Igor Ivanović		09/09/90	M	20		13
Ivan Ivanović		14/09/89	M	16		2
Milan Jelovac		06/08/93	G		(1)	
Vasilije Jovović		12/05/86	A	12	(10)	4
Kohei Kato	JPN	14/06/89	M	31		7
Nemanja Mijušković		04/03/92	D	29		4
Milivoje Mrdak		17/02/93	A		(10)	2
Dušan Nestorović	SRB	26/06/86	D	31	1	
Ryota Noma	JPN	15/11/92	M	20	(2)	3
Yoshiki Otsuki	JPN	05/06/91	M	2	(4)	
Miloš Radanović		05/11/80	G	33		1
Stevan Reljić		31/03/86	D	8	(1)	
Nikola Sekulić		10/04/81	M		(4)	
Danin Talović		08/03/95	M	2	(4)	
Željko Tomašević		05/04/88	D	26	(2)	
Nedjeljko Vlahović		15/01/84	M	28		8
Vule Vujačić		20/03/88	A	3	(10)	4
Marko Vuković		20/03/96	A	9	(9)	

FK Sutjeska

1927 • Kraj Bistrice (10,800) • fksutjeska.me
Major honours
Montenegrin League (2) 2013, 2014
Coach: Mile Tomić (SRB);
(18/03/15) Brajan Nenezić

2014

10/08	h	Rudar	L	1-3	G Vujović
16/08	a	Lovćen	W	2-1	Fukui, Kovačević
23/08	h	Mornar	W	3-0	G Vujović 3 (1p)
27/08	a	Mladost	W	3-1	Kovačević 3
30/08	h	Berane	W	4-0	G Vujović 2, Kovačević, Pejović
13/09	h	Petrovac	D	1-1	G Vujović
17/09	a	Budućnost	W	2-1	Jovović, G Vujović
21/09	h	Bokelj	W	2-0	Fukui, G Vujović
27/09	a	Zeta	W	3-2	Jovović 2, Lončar
04/10	h	Mogren	W	4-0	Jovović, G Vujović 2, Igumanović
18/10	a	Grbalj	L	0-2	
26/10	a	Rudar	D	0-0	
01/11	h	Lovćen	W	2-0	Fukui, G Vujović
08/11	a	Mornar	W	1-0	Kovačević
22/11	h	Mladost	D	0-0	
29/11	a	Berane	W	2-0	Kovačević, M Vujović
06/12	a	Petrovac	D	1-1	Kovačević

2015

24/02	h	Budućnost	L	0-3	
28/02	a	Bokelj	D	1-1	Lukić
08/03	h	Zeta	W	1-0	G Vujović (p)
11/03	a	Mogren	D	0-0	
14/03	h	Grbalj	L	0-2	
21/03	a	Mornar	W	1-0	Lukić
31/03	h	Petrovac	W	1-0	G Vujović
04/04	a	Grbalj	W	6-0	G Vujović 2, Božović, J Nikolić, Miloš Vučić, Kovačević
11/04	h	Lovćen	W	3-0	Božović, Fukui 2
18/04	h	Berane	W	3-1	Božović, Kovačević, Igumanović
26/04	a	Budućnost	D	1-1	G Vujović
02/05	h	Mladost	D	1-1	Božović
09/05	a	Rudar	W	1-0	G Vujović
16/05	h	Mogren	W	4-0	G Vujović 2, M Vujović, Kovačević
23/05	a	Zeta	W	3-1	Božović, Miloš Vučić, G Vujović (p)
30/05	h	Bokelj	D	1-1	Kovačević

Name	Nat	DoB	Pos	Aps	(s)	Gls
Draško Božović		30/06/88	M	15		5
Petar Čolaković		13/09/93	M		(1)	
Igor Čuković		06/06/93	D	2	(3)	
Andrija Delibašić		24/04/81	A	2		
Stefan Djajić		24/12/94	A		(1)	
Masato Fukui	JPN	14/11/88	A	27	(3)	5
Blažo Igumanović		19/01/86	M	15	(6)	2
Ivan Janjušević		11/07/87	G	30		
Vlado Jeknić		14/08/83	D	9		
Vladimir Jovović		26/10/94	M	13	(1)	4
Stevan Kovačević	SRB	09/01/88	M	33		12
Stefan Lončar		19/02/96	M	1	(16)	1
Slavko Lukić	SRB	14/03/89	D	31		2
Mileta Nikčević		02/09/96	M		(1)	
Jovan Nikolić		21/07/91	M	28	(1)	1
Nemanja Nikolić		18/05/97	M		(1)	
Dejan Ognjanović		21/06/78	D	25		
Andrija Pejović		21/11/91	M	2	(7)	1
Nikola Popović		13/09/97	D	6	(3)	
Marko Radović		26/06/93	G	3	(1)	
Stefan Stefanović	SRB	22/08/91	M	31	(1)	
Nikola Stijepović		02/11/93	D	33		
Aleksandar Šofranac		21/10/90	D	6	(2)	
Filip Vorotović		08/03/98	A		(2)	
Marko Vučić		30/12/96	M			
Miloš Vučić		26/08/95	M	11	(5)	2
Mladen Vučić		23/09/96	M	1		
Goran Vujović		03/05/87	A	32		21
Jovan Vujović		20/01/96	M		(3)	
Matija Vujović		09/06/95	M	7	(20)	2

FK Zeta

1927 • Trešnjica (5,000) • fkzeta.me
Major honours
Montenegrin League (1) 2007
Coach: Rade Vešović;
(18/09/14) Mladen Lambulić;
(15/04/15) Dušan Vlaisavljević

2014

09/08	a	Bokelj	D	1-1	Orlandić
16/08	a	Berane	D	1-1	Rajović
23/08	h	Mogren	W	3-0	Burzanović, Orlandić, Kukuličić
27/08	a	Grbalj	L	0-1	
31/08	h	Rudar	L	1-2	og (Mijušković)
13/09	a	Lovćen	L	1-1	Kukuličić
17/09	h	Mornar	D	0-0	
21/09	a	Mladost	L	1-3	Dujković
27/09	h	Sutjeska	L	2-3	Burzanović (p), Orlandić
04/10	a	Petrovac	L	0-1	
19/10	h	Budućnost	L	1-2	Vlaisavljević
25/10	h	Bokelj	W	3-1	Burzanović, Orlandić, Kopitović
01/11	h	Berane	W	3-0	Orlandić 3
08/11	a	Mogren	L	1-2	Orlandić
22/11	h	Grbalj	W	2-1	Dujković, Kopitović
29/11	a	Rudar	L	1-2	Orlandić
06/12	a	Lovćen	L	2-3	og (M Radunović), Šofranac

2015

24/02	a	Mornar	D	0-0	
28/02	h	Mladost	D	1-1	Kukuličić
08/03	a	Sutjeska	L	0-1	
11/03	h	Petrovac	W	2-0	Vlaisavljević (p), Kukuličić
14/03	a	Budućnost	L	0-1	
21/03	h	Mladost	D	2-2	Klikovac, Vujačić
31/03	a	Rudar	L	1-3	Vlaisavljević
04/04	h	Mogren	W	5-0	Vlaisavljević 4 (1p), S Vukčević
11/04	a	Berane	L	1-2	og (Arifović)
18/04	a	Bokelj	W	2-1	Burzanović, Dujković
25/04	h	Mornar	W	4-0	Klikovac, Kukuličić 2, Vlaisavljević
02/05	a	Petrovac	W	2-1	Klikovac, Dujković
09/05	h	Grbalj	W	2-1	Damjanović, Dujković
16/05	a	Lovćen	W	2-1	Vlaisavljević, Vujačić
23/05	h	Sutjeska	L	1-3	Sekulić
30/05	a	Budućnost	L	0-3	

Name	Nat	DoB	Pos	Aps	(s)	Gls
Bojan Aligrudić		08/02/95	D	17	(1)	
Goran Burzanović		04/08/84	M	30		5
Nemanja Cavnic		05/09/95	D	29	(2)	
Marko Čolaković		20/06/80	D	11	(1)	
Aleksandar Dabetić		08/07/94	A	3	(2)	
Vuk Damjanović		20/06/96	A	4	(4)	1
Miloš Dujković	BIH	09/10/90	M	27	(1)	4
Rodolfo Miguel Durand	PER	14/06/96	A	1	(4)	
Nemanja Jakšić	SRB	11/07/95	D	24		
Camilo Jimenez	PER	02/07/96	D	1	(5)	
Luka Klikovac		01/06/93	M	14		3
Stefan Knežević		07/05/97	M		(1)	
Bojan Kopitović		12/10/93	M	6	(15)	2
Pavle Krstović		18/04/99	M		(1)	
Željko Krstović	SRB	19/10/89	M	4	(4)	
Filip Kukuličić		13/02/91	M	18	(6)	6
Marko Novović		24/11/96	G	3	(1)	
Petar Orlandić		06/08/90	A	16		9
Periša Pešukić		07/12/97	M	1	(2)	
Danijel Petković		25/05/93	G	26		
Jovan Popović		08/02/96	M	2	(1)	
Miloš Popović		05/09/96	M		(1)	
Filip Radonjić		20/05/96	M	1	(2)	
Miloš Radulović		23/02/90	D	19	(8)	
Blažo Rajović		26/03/86	D	5		1
Filip Rosandić		27/03/97	G	1	(1)	
Onimisi Segun	NGA	29/11/93	M	4	(2)	
Marko Sekulić		03/02/96	M		(4)	1
Demir Škrijelj		10/07/97	M	2	(9)	
Nenad Šofranac		20/04/83	M	32		1
Djordje Trifković	SRB	12/07/94	M		(6)	
Pavle Velimirović		11/04/90	G	3		
Predrag Videkanić		23/08/86	D	3		
Miljan Vlaisavljević		16/04/91	A	30	(1)	9
Igor Vujačić		08/08/94	D	14		2
Stefan Vukčević		11/04/97	M	16	(8)	1
Velimir Vukčević		17/05/95	M		(3)	

Top goalscorers

21	Goran Vujović (Sutjeska)
13	Igor Ivanović (Rudar)
12	Ivan Jablan (Grbalj)
	Bogdan Milić (Mladost)
	Stevan Kovačević (Sutjeska)
11	Admir Adrović (Budućnost)
10	Draško Božović (Lovćen/Sutjeska)
9	Luka Rotković (Mornar)
	Petar Orlandić (Zeta)
	Miljan Vlaisavljević (Zeta)

Promoted clubs

FK Iskra

1919 • Braće Velašević (1,500) • no website
Coach: Dejan Mrvaljević

FK Dečić

1926 • Tuško polje (3,000) • no website
Coach: Fuad Krkanović

Second level final table 2014/15

		Pld	W	D	L	F	A	Pts
1	FK Iskra	33	20	7	6	55	26	67
2	FK Dečić	33	20	6	7	58	28	65
3	OFK Igalo	33	16	12	5	42	24	60
4	FK Jedinstvo Bijelo Polje	33	12	12	9	28	29	48
5	FK Radnički	33	13	6	14	50	39	45
6	FK Kom	33	9	13	11	35	38	40
7	FK Cetinje	33	11	6	16	36	54	39
8	FK Ibar	33	9	10	14	31	41	37
9	FK Jezero	33	9	10	14	34	45	37
10	FK Bratstvo	33	10	6	17	38	58	36
11	FK Zabjelo	33	10	7	16	38	46	36
12	FK Arsenal Tivat	33	9	5	19	30	47	32

NB FK Ibar – 1 pt deducted.

Promotion/Relegation play-offs

(03/06/15 & 07/06/15)
Mogren 0-5 Dečić
Dečić 2-1 Mogren
(Dečić 7-1)

Mornar 2-0 Igalo
Igalo 2-0 Mornar
(2-2; Mornar 9-8 on pens)

DOMESTIC CUP

Kup Crne Gore 2014/15

FIRST ROUND

(24/09/14)
Bratstvo 2-0 Radnički
Čelik 0-1 Petrovac
Cetinje 1-3 Zeta
Hajduk 0-2 Mornar
Ibar 3-0 Bokelj
Igalo 3-1 Arsenal
Jezero 1-2 Budućnost
Kom 1-4 Mogren
Polimlje 0-2 Grbalj
Rudar 5-0 Jedinstvo
Sloga 0-1 Berane
Sutjeska 2-0 Iskra
Zabjelo 2-4 Dečić

(25/09/14)
Grafičar 0-1 Pljevlja

Byes – Lovćen, Mladost

SECOND ROUND

(01/10/14 & 22/10/14)
Berane 3-2, 0-2 Sutjeska *(3-4)*
Grbalj 2-0, 3-2 Igalo *(5-2)*
Ibar 1-1, 0-2 Petrovac *(1-3)*
Lovćen 0-0, 1-0 Rudar *(1-0)*
Mogren 1-5, 2-1 Mladost *(3-6)*
Mornar 3-2, 3-0 Bratstvo *(6-2)*
Pljevlja 0-4, 0-9 Budućnost *(0-13)*
Zeta 6-0, 3-1 Dečić *(9-1)*

QUARTER-FINALS

(05/11/14 & 26/11/14)
Grbalj 0-0 Budućnost
Budućnost 1-0 Grbalj *(Pavićević 47)*
(Budućnost 1-0)

Petrovac 1-0 Lovćen *(Kacić 55)*
Lovćen 1-1 Petrovac *(Božović 24; Pejaković 68)*
(Petrovac 2-1)

Sutjeska 3-0 Mornar *(Lukić 59, G Vujović 78, Igumanović 90)*
Mornar 2-0 Sutjeska *(Jovančov 68, Božović 72)*
(Sutjeska 3-2)

Zeta 0-0 Mladost
Mladost 0-0 Zeta
(0-0; Mladost 4-3 on pens)

SEMI-FINALS

(08/04/15 & 22/04/15)
Petrovac 0-0 Budućnost
Budućnost 0-1 Petrovac *(Kacić 43)*
(Petrovac 1-0)

Sutjeska 0-2 Mladost *(Šćepanović 24, Djurišić 75)*
Mladost 2-0 Sutjeska *(Šćepanović 26, Djurišić 86)*
(Mladost 4-0)

FINAL

(20/05/15)
Pod Goricom, Podgorica
FK MLADOST PODGORICA 2 *(Šćepanović 19, Marković 106og)*
OFK PETROVAC 1 *(Knežević 27)*
(aet)
Referee: Savović
MLADOST: *Mileta Radulović, Pejović, Lakić, Adamović (Mirković 91), Novović, Šćepanović, Jovanović, Miloš Radulović (Milić 74), Obradović (Djalac 60), Vuković, Djurišić*
PETROVAC: *N Popović, Vujović, Radišić, Grbović, Kacić (Pepić 66), Tomić, Marković, Golubović, Pejaković (Martinović 106), Knežević, Muhović (S Popović 44)*
Red card: *N Popović (44)*

The players of Mladost Podgorica take to the victory podium after their cup final win against Petrovac

NETHERLANDS
Koninklijke Nederlandse Voetbalbond (KNVB)

Address	Woudenbergseweg 56-58	**President**	Michael van Praag
	Postbus 515	**General secretary**	Bert van Oostveen
	NL-3700 AM Zeist	**Media officer**	Bas Ticheler
Tel	+31 343 499 201	**Year of formation**	1889
Fax	+31 343 499 189		
E-mail	concern@knvb.nl		
Website	knvb.nl		

EREDIVISIE CLUBS

 1 **ADO Den Haag**

 2 **AFC Ajax**

 3 **AZ Alkmaar**

 4 **SC Cambuur**

 5 **FC Dordrecht**

 6 **SBV Excelsior**

 7 **Feyenoord**

 8 **Go Ahead Eagles**

 9 **FC Groningen**

 10 **sc Heerenveen**

 11 **Heracles Almelo**

 12 **NAC Breda**

 13 **PEC Zwolle**

 14 **PSV Eindhoven**

 15 **FC Twente**

 16 **FC Utrecht**

 17 **Vitesse**

 18 **Willem II**

PROMOTED CLUBS

 19 **NEC Nijmegen**

 20 **Roda JC**

 21 **De Graafschap**

KEY:
● – UEFA Champions League
● – UEFA Europa League
● – Promoted
● – Relegated
● – Relegated club in UEFA Europa League

Runaway triumph for revitalised PSV

PSV Eindhoven finally returned to the pinnacle of Dutch football in 2014/15 as they brought a seven-year wait for the Eredivsie title to an end with one of the most comprehensive of their 22 championship triumphs.

Phillip Cocu's team were head and shoulders above the rest, with AFC Ajax, the champions of the previous four seasons, finishing 17 points adrift as runners-up. The other domestic honour went to FC Groningen, who claimed a first major trophy by lifting the Dutch Cup. It was a season short of success for Dutch teams on the international front, especially Guus Hiddink's struggling Oranje.

Eindhoven club storm to first Eredivisie title since 2008

Goals aplenty as Groningen grab the Dutch Cup

Hiddink's second coming with Oranje ends early

Domestic league

PSV began the season with a spring in their step. Not only had coach Cocu recovered fully from an operation to have a tumour removed from his back, but Dutch internationals Memphis Depay and Georginio Wijnaldum had both agreed to stay on in Eindhoven for another season. With Ajax and, especially, 2013/14 runners-up Feyenoord weakened by summer departures, a season of promise beckoned for PSV. They would go on to fulfil it with emphatic conviction.

A 3-1 win at newly-promoted Willem II got the show on the road, and when PSV won by the same score in their second away fixture, at the Amsterdam ArenA, the tone was set. Cocu's men were on top of the Eredivisie table and would remain there as an all-powerful force for the next nine months, beating every one of their 17 opponents at least once, most of them twice, to post a record final tally of 88 points.

For most of the autumn PSV were closely pressed by Ajax, but whereas Frank de Boer's side had taken charge post-Christmas in each of the previous three seasons, this time they wilted under the pressure imposed by their southern rivals, who broke clear during the winter months, winning all ten league games in December, January and February – the highlight a thrilling 4-3 victory at home to Feyenoord a week before Christmas – while racking up 31 goals in the process. Ajax ended that run with a 3-1 win in Eindhoven on 1 March, but by then PSV were out of reach with an 11-point cushion. Although that advantage was further reduced when PSV lost again, 2-1 at Feyenoord, the title was wrapped up in mid-April with a 4-1 home win over sc Heerenveen

Always a joy to watch, PSV attacked in every game and were rewarded for their enterprise with 29 wins and 92 goals. Winger Depay scored 22 times to scoop the Eredivisie golden boot, having been pushed hard by centre-forward Luuk de Jong, who put his disappointing experience at Newcastle United FC behind him to hit 20 goals. Skipper Wijnaldum also chipped in with 14 from midfield, while elsewhere there were decisive contributions from Mexican winger Andrés Guardado, left-back Jetro Willems and central defensive duo Karim Rekik and Jeffrey Bruma.

Ajax's concession of the title was a disappointment, especially as they were seeking to become the first club ever to win five successive Dutch titles, but having lost stalwarts Daley Blind and Siem de Jong, they did well to accumulate the same number of points (71) that had won them the championship 12 months earlier. On this occasion, however, that tally merited only a runners-up spot and a place in the third qualifying round of the UEFA Champions League. While coach De Boer sampled Eredivisie failure for the first time since he arrived in November 2010, on the positive side there were strong performances from debutant winger Anwar El Ghazi and on-loan striker Arkadiusz Milik in attack, with Netherlands No1 Jasper Cillessen continuing to impress between the posts.

AZ Alkmaar jumped five places from the previous season to finish third and return to European competition after a first absence for six years in 2014/15. Marco van Basten started the season as head coach but stood down almost immediately due to a stress-related condition and eventually settled in a role as assistant to John van den Brom. The ex-RSC Anderlecht boss steered the Alkmaar club up the table and, eventually, above Feyenoord, who endured a dreadful run-in, picking up just two points in their last five matches to drop into the UEFA Europa League qualification bracket.

NETHERLANDS

Having lost coach Ronald Koeman as well as four key players – Dutch internationals Daryl Janmaat, Bruno Martins Indi and Stefan de Vrij plus free-scoring Italian spearhead Graziano Pellè – the previous summer, the Rotterdam club were not expected to repeat their 2013/14 runners-up placing. But they recovered from a bad start and appeared to be on the up again until that late stumble, which cost new boss Fred Rutten his job. Giovanni van Bronckhorst was handed the responsibility of leading Feyenoord back into Europe via the play-offs, but they were defeated on entry by Heerenveen, who went on to lose the final 7-4 on aggregate to Vitesse.

There was a fourth UEFA Europa League place open to Dutch clubs with the award of a Fair Play berth, but FC Twente, who had been docked six points for financial reasons and finished tenth, declined the opportunity and passed it on to relegated Go Ahead Eagles. The Deventer club were one of three teams to go down. They and NAC Breda both failed to negotiate the promotion/relegation play-offs, enabling De Graafschap and – after just one season away – Roda JC to come up in their stead. FC Dordrecht were relegated directly and replaced by NEC Nijmegen, who stormed to victory in the Eerste Divisie, racking up 100 goals and 101 points.

Domestic cup

The big guns were spiked early in the 2014/15 KNVB-Beker, with PSV, Ajax and Feyenoord all exiting before the quarter-finals. PEC Zwolle, the improbable 2013/14 winners, took advantage by reaching the final again, but at De Kuip they were defeated 2-0 by Groningen. Two second-half goals from young Slovakian midfielder Albert Rusnák ensured a triumphant conclusion to a brilliant cup campaign from Erwin van de Looi's side, in which they posted high-scoring victories in every round. In total they found the net 24 times in their six matches, conceding just twice.

Europe

It was a familiar story for Ajax in Europe as the Amsterdammers finished third in their UEFA Champions League group for the fifth season running. Unlike the three previous years, though, De Boer's men

Albert Rusnák is full of joy after scoring for Groningen in the Dutch Cup final

survived their round of 32 tie in the UEFA Europa League as Milik scored three times against his Polish compatriots of Legia Warszawa. In the next round, though, Ajax lost after extra time in the Amsterdam ArenA to an FC Dnipro Dnipropetrovsk away goal, and with their elimination Dutch interest in Europe ended for another year.

While Groningen, Zwolle and Twente all lasted just one round in the UEFA Europa League, Feyenoord and PSV made it through to the last 32, the former after an early UEFA Champions League exit at the hands of Beşiktaş JK. Three home wins in the group stage gave Feyenoord fans genuine hope of further progress when they entertained AS Roma after a 1-1 draw in the Stadio Olimpico, but a night of drama scarred by a lengthy stoppage and two red cards ended in a 2-1 defeat. PSV's departure was considerably less eventful as they surrendered meekly to FC Zenit, the second Russian side to beat them home and away after FC Dinamo Moskva in the group stage.

National team

After the euphoria of finishing third at the FIFA World Cup in Brazil, the 2014/15 season was one of deflation and concern for the Dutch national team. The return of Hiddink to the role of Bondscoach after a

16-year gap turned out to be an ill-fated move, and by the end of the season the 68-year-old successor to Louis van Gaal had stepped down, to be replaced by his assistant Danny Blind.

The reason for Hiddink's early departure was a season of struggle in which the Oranje lost five of their ten matches, two of them in the UEFA EURO 2016 qualifying campaign. Defeats against the Czech Republic in Prague and Iceland in Reykjavik, coupled with a 1-1 home draw against Turkey salvaged only with a stoppage-time equaliser, left the Netherlands in a precarious position. While an autumn recovery under Blind would still make automatic qualification for France possible, the team's sharp decline since the World Cup was a shock to all concerned.

Memories of Brazil were briefly revived with another win against Spain, 2-0 in Amsterdam, and there was positive news also for a couple of Oranje stalwarts as Wesley Sneijder became the Netherlands' most-capped outfield player, passing De Boer's 112 appearances in that friendly against Spain, and Klaas-Jan Huntelaar overtook Ruud van Nistelrooy, Dennis Bergkamp and Patrick Kluivert to become his country's second highest scorer – with only 49-goal team-mate Robin van Persie ahead of him.

DOMESTIC SEASON AT A GLANCE

Eredivisie 2014/15 final table

		Pld	Home					Away					Total					Pts
			W	D	L	F	A	W	D	L	F	A	W	D	L	F	A	
1	**PSV Eindhoven**	**34**	**16**	**0**	**1**	**50**	**12**	**13**	**1**	**3**	**42**	**19**	**29**	**1**	**4**	**92**	**31**	**88**
2	AFC Ajax	34	12	3	2	37	11	9	5	3	32	18	21	8	5	69	29	71
3	AZ Alkmaar	34	9	3	5	30	27	10	2	5	33	29	19	5	10	63	56	62
4	Feyenoord	34	10	2	5	31	20	7	6	4	25	19	17	8	9	56	39	59
5	Vitesse	34	8	8	1	36	18	8	2	7	30	25	16	10	8	66	43	58
6	PEC Zwolle	34	11	4	2	40	15	5	1	11	19	28	16	5	13	59	43	53
7	sc Heerenveen	34	8	5	4	33	21	5	6	6	20	25	13	11	10	53	46	50
8	FC Groningen	34	7	8	2	26	18	4	5	8	23	35	11	13	10	49	53	46
9	Willem II	34	8	5	4	25	22	5	2	10	21	28	13	7	14	46	50	46
10	FC Twente	34	8	4	5	26	23	5	6	6	30	28	13	10	11	56	51	43
11	FC Utrecht	34	6	4	7	32	31	5	4	8	28	31	11	8	15	60	62	41
12	SC Cambuur	34	8	2	7	25	22	3	6	8	21	34	11	8	15	46	56	41
13	ADO Den Haag	34	8	4	5	30	23	1	6	10	14	30	9	10	15	44	53	37
14	Heracles Almelo	34	5	4	8	23	29	6	0	11	24	35	11	4	19	47	64	37
15	SBV Excelsior	34	4	5	8	26	37	2	9	6	21	26	6	14	14	47	63	32
16	NAC Breda	34	3	5	9	19	32	3	5	9	17	36	6	10	18	36	68	28
17	Go Ahead Eagles	34	4	3	10	14	29	3	3	11	15	30	7	6	21	29	59	27
18	FC Dordrecht	34	3	4	10	15	34	1	4	12	9	42	4	8	22	24	76	20

NB FC Twente – 6 pts deducted. UEFA Europa League qualification play-offs are on page 536.

European qualification 2015/16

Champion: PSV Eindhoven (group stage)
AFC Ajax (third qualifying round)

Cup winner: FC Groningen (group stage)
AZ Alkmaar (third qualifying round)
Vitesse (third qualifying round)
Go Ahead Eagles (first qualifying round)

Top scorer   Memphis Depay (PSV), 22 goals
Relegated clubs   FC Dordrecht, Go Ahead Eagles, NAC Breda
Promoted clubs   NEC Nijmegen, Roda JC, De Graafschap
Cup final   FC Groningen 2-0 PEC Zwolle

Team of the season
(4-3-3)

Coach: Cocu *(PSV)*

Player of the season

Memphis Depay
(PSV Eindhoven)

Having impressed for his country at the FIFA World Cup in Brazil, Dutch international Depay delivered for his club with a brilliant 2014/15 campaign that inspired PSV to an easy victory in the Eredivisie. The multi-talented 21-year-old scored 22 times to top the league's goal charts – the first PSV player to do so since Mateja Kežman in 2003/04 and the youngest since Ronaldo in 1994/95 – before moving abroad at the end of term to rejoin his ex-Oranje boss Louis van Gaal at Manchester United FC.

Newcomer of the season

Anwar El Ghazi
(AFC Ajax)

A shining light in a generally gloomy season for Ajax was the emergence of explosive winger El Ghazi. Having impressed coach Frank de Boer during pre-season, the untried youngster quickly established himself as a key member of the side. Tall, pacy and full of tricks, he turned many an Eredivisie defence inside out, registering nine league goals and eight assists. The undoubted highlight of his season, though, was the goal he scored at the Camp Nou against FC Barcelona in the UEFA Champions League.

NATIONAL TEAM

International honours
UEFA European Championship (1) 1988

International tournament appearances
FIFA World Cup (10) 1934, 1938, 1974 (runners-up), 1978 (runners-up), 1990 (2nd round), 1994 (qtr-finals), 1998 (4th), 2006 (2nd round), 2010 (runners-up), 2014 (3rd)
UEFA European Championship (9) 1976 (3rd), 1980, 1988 (Winners), 1992 (semi-finals), 1996 (qtr-finals), 2000 (semi-finals), 2004 (semi-finals), 2008 (qtr-finals), 2012

Top five all-time caps
Edwin van der Sar (130); **Wesley Sneijder** (115); Frank de Boer (112); Rafael van der Vaart (109); Giovanni van Bronckhorst (106)

Top five all-time goals
Robin van Persie (49); **Klaas-Jan Huntelaar** (41); Patrick Kluivert (40); Dennis Bergkamp (37); Ruud van Nistelrooy & Faas Wilkes (35)

Results 2014/15

Date	Opponent		Venue		Score	Scorers
04/09/14	Italy	A	Bari	L	0-2	
09/09/14	Czech Republic (ECQ)	A	Prague	L	1-2	De Vrij (55)
10/10/14	Kazakhstan (ECQ)	H	Amsterdam	W	3-1	Huntelaar (62), Afellay (82), Van Persie (89p)
13/10/14	Iceland (ECQ)	A	Reykjavik	L	0-2	
12/11/14	Mexico	H	Amsterdam	L	2-3	Sneijder (49), Blind (74)
16/11/14	Latvia (ECQ)	H	Amsterdam	W	6-0	Van Persie (6), Robben (35, 82), Huntelaar (42, 89), Bruma (78)
28/03/15	Turkey (ECQ)	H	Amsterdam	D	1-1	Huntelaar (90+2)
31/03/15	Spain	H	Amsterdam	W	2-0	De Vrij (13), Klaassen (16)
05/06/15	United States	H	Amsterdam	L	3-4	Huntelaar (27, 49), Depay (53)
12/06/15	Latvia (ECQ)	A	Riga	W	2-0	Wijnaldum (67), Narsingh (71)

Appearances 2014/15

Coach: Guus Hiddink	08/11/46		Ita	CZE	KAZ	ISL	Mex	LVA	TUR	Esp	Usa	LVA	Caps	Goals
Jasper Cillessen	22/04/89	Ajax	G	G	G	G		G	G		G	G	23	-
Daryl Janmaat	22/07/89	Newcastle (ENG)	D72	D						D	D46	s77	26	-
Stefan de Vrij	05/02/92	Lazio (ITA)	D	D	D	D	s24	D	D	D		D	28	3
Bruno Martins Indi	08/02/92	Porto (POR)	D 9*	D	D81	D			D77	D	D	D	30	2
Daley Blind	09/03/90	Man. United (ENG)	D	D	D	D	M	M20	D	M73	D	M	29	2
Georginio Wijnaldum	11/11/90	PSV	M85	M			s68	s79	M46	s62	M	s63	20	3
Nigel de Jong	30/11/84	Milan (ITA)	M63	M	M56	M			M63				81	1
Wesley Sneijder	09/06/84	Galatasaray (TUR)	M	M	M	M46	M81	M	M	M62	s78	M	115	28
Dirk Kuyt	22/07/80	Fenerbahçe (TUR)	A										104	24
Robin van Persie	06/08/83	Man. United (ENG)	A80	A	A	A		A79			M57	M63	98	49
Jeremain Lens	24/11/87	Dynamo Kyiv (UKR)	A12		A	A68						s87	30	8
Joël Veltman	15/01/92	Ajax	s12	D39			D						7	-
Erik Pieters	07/08/88	Stoke (ENG)	s63										18	-
Gregory van der Wiel	03/02/88	Paris (FRA)	s72		D	D		D	D		s46	D	44	-
Luciano Narsingh	13/09/90	PSV	s80	s39					s46	A	s46	A	13	3
Leroy Fer	05/01/90	QPR (ENG)	s85		s81	s78	s81						11	1
Memphis Depay	13/02/94	PSV		A			A60	s69	A	A84	A	A87	17	3
Ibrahim Afellay	02/04/86	Olympiacos (GRE)			M	M78	M68	M69	A	s84			50	6
Arjen Robben	23/01/84	Bayern (GER)			A	A	A	A					86	28
Klaas-Jan Huntelaar	12/08/83	Schalke (GER)			s56	s46	A	A	A	A79	A78	A	73	41
Quincy Promes	04/01/92	Spartak Moskva (RUS)				s68	s60				A46		4	-
Tim Krul	03/04/88	Newcastle (ENG)					G						7	-
Ricardo van Rhijn	13/06/91	Ajax					D						8	-
Ron Vlaar	16/02/85	Aston Villa (ENG)					D24						32	1
Jetro Willems	30/03/94	PSV					D	D	s77	D		D77	16	-
Jeffrey Bruma	13/11/91	PSV						D		D			9	1
Jordy Clasie	27/06/91	Feyenoord						s20		M78			12	-
Bas Dost	31/05/89	Wolfsburg (GER)						s63	s79				2	-
Kenneth Vermeer	10/01/86	Feyenoord								G			5	-
Davy Klaassen	21/02/93	Ajax								M			2	1
Jonathan de Guzmán	13/09/87	Napoli (ITA)								s73			14	-
Davy Pröpper	02/09/91	Vitesse									s57		1	-
Luuk de Jong	27/08/90	PSV									s78		8	1

EUROPE

AFC Ajax

Group F
Match 1 - Paris Saint-Germain (FRA)
H 1-1 *Schöne (74)*
Cillessen, Van Rhijn, Veltman, Moisander, Boilesen, Sigthórsson (El Ghazi 61), Klaassen, Andersen, Schöne (Milik 82), Serero, Viergever (Zimling 46). Coach: Frank de Boer (NED)
Match 2 - APOEL FC (CYP)
A 1-1 *Andersen (28)*
Cillessen, Van Rhijn, Veltman, Moisander, Boilesen, Sigthórsson, Klaassen, Andersen (Kishna 74), Schöne (El Ghazi 74), Serero, Viergever. Coach: Frank de Boer (NED)
Match 3 - FC Barcelona (ESP)
A 1-3 *El Ghazi (88)*
Cillessen, Van Rhijn, Veltman, Moisander, Sigthórsson (El Ghazi 73), Klaassen, Kishna (Milik 46), Andersen, Schöne, Viergever, Zimling (Riedewald 56). Coach: Frank de Boer (NED)
Match 4 - FC Barcelona (ESP)
H 0-2
Cillessen, Van Rhijn, Veltman, Moisander, Boilesen, Sigthórsson (Milik 62), Klaassen, Andersen (Riedewald 72), Schöne, El Ghazi, Serero (Denswil 80). Coach: Frank de Boer (NED)
Red card: Veltman 71
Match 5 - Paris Saint-Germain (FRA)
A 1-3 *Klaassen (67)*
Cillessen, Van Rhijn, Boilesen (Viergever 10), Van Der Hoorn, Klaassen, Kishna, Andersen, Milik, Schöne, Denswil, Serero (Zimling 69). Coach: Frank de Boer (NED)
Match 6 - APOEL FC (CYP)
H 4-0 *Schöne (45+1p, 50), Klaassen (53), Milik (74)*
Cillessen, Van Rhijn, Veltman, Moisander, Klaassen, Kishna, Andersen (Riedewald 68), Milik (Zivkovic 85), Schöne (El Ghazi 75), Serero, Viergever. Coach: Frank de Boer (NED)

Round of 32 - Legia Warszawa (POL)
H 1-0 *Milik (35)*
Cillessen, Van Rhijn, Boilesen, Van der Hoorn, Klaassen (Sinkgraven 82), Kishna (Schöne 74), Milik, El Ghazi, Serero (Riedewald 71), Viergever, Bazoer. Coach: Frank de Boer (NED)
A 3-0 *Milik (11, 43), Viergever (13)*
Cillessen, Van Rhijn, Veltman, Van der Hoorn 72), Boilesen, Klaassen (Sinkgraven 46), Kishna (Andersen 79), Milik, El Ghazi, Serero, Bazoer. Coach: Frank de Boer (NED)

Round of 16 - FC Dnipro Dnipropetrovsk (UKR)
A 0-1
Cillessen, Van Rhijn, Veltman, Boilesen, Klaassen, Milik (Zivkovic 77), Schöne (Kishna 61), El Ghazi, Serero (Sinkgraven 60), Viergever, Bazoer. Coach: Frank de Boer (NED)
H 2-1 *Bazoer (60), Van der Hoorn (117)* **(aet)**
Cillessen, Van Rhijn, Veltman, Boilesen (Van der Hoorn 100), Sinkgraven (Serero 87), Klaassen, Kishna (Sigthórsson 78), Milik, El Ghazi, Viergever, Bazoer. Coach: Frank de Boer (NED)
Red card: Van der Hoorn 120+4

Feyenoord

Third qualifying round - Beşiktaş JK (TUR)
H 1-2 *Te Vrede (90+5p)*
Mulder, Mathijsen, Kongolo, Clasie, Boëtius, Immers, Verhoek (Manu 65), Te Vrede, Trindade de Vilhena, Van Beek, Schaken (Boulahrouz 61). Coach: Fred Rutten (NED)
A 1-3 *Manu (74)*
Mulder, Mathijsen, Kongolo, Clasie (Karsdorp 69), Boëtius, Immers, Nelom (Vormer 57), Te Vrede (Manu 57), Trindade de Vilhena, Van Beek, Schaken. Coach: Fred Rutten (NED)

Play-offs - FC Zorya Luhansk (UKR)
A 1-1 *Te Vrede (38)*
Mulder, Wilkshire (Karsdorp 82), Mathijsen, Kongolo, Clasie (Vormer 72), Boëtius (Bilal Başaçıkoğlu 62), Immers, Te Vrede, Trindade de Vilhena, Van Beek, Schaken. Coach: Fred Rutten (NED)
H 4-3 *Te Vrede (18), Schaken (26), Biliy (48og), Manu (90+2)*
Mulder, Wilkshire, Mathijsen (Manu 84), Kongolo, Clasie (Achahbar 84), Immers, Bilal Başaçıkoğlu (Nelom 78), Te Vrede, Trindade de Vilhena, Van Beek, Schaken. Coach: Fred Rutten (NED)

Group G
Match 1 - Sevilla FC (ESP)
A 0-2
Vermeer, Wilkshire, Mathijsen, Clasie (Te Vrede 73), El Ahmadi, Manu (Boëtius 82), Nelom, Trindade de Vilhena, Van Beek, Schaken (Bilal Başaçıkoğlu 64), Toornstra. Coach: Fred Rutten (NED)
Match 2 - R Standard de Liège (BEL)
H 2-1 *Van Beek (47), Manu (84)*
Vermeer, Wilkshire, Kongolo, Clasie, El Ahmadi, Immers (Bilal Başaçıkoğlu 77), Kazim-Richards, Manu (Trindade de Vilhena 90+1), Nelom, Van Beek, Toornstra. Coach: Fred Rutten (NED)
Match 3 - HNK Rijeka (CRO)
A 1-3 *Toornstra (66)*
Vermeer, Wilkshire (Karsdorp 46), Kongolo, Clasie, El Ahmadi, Immers, Kazim-Richards (Te Vrede 80), Manu (Boëtius 80), Nelom, Steenvoorden, Toornstra. Coach: Fred Rutten (NED)
Match 4 - HNK Rijeka (CRO)
H 2-0 *El Ahmadi (8), Immers (20)*
Vermeer, Wilkshire (Boulahrouz 73), Kongolo, Clasie, El Ahmadi, Immers, Kazim-Richards, Manu (Boëtius 62), Nelom, Van Beek, Toornstra. Coach: Fred Rutten (NED)
Match 5 - Sevilla FC (ESP)
H 2-0 *Toornstra (56), El Ahmadi (83)*
Vermeer, Kongolo, Clasie, Boëtius, El Ahmadi, Immers, Kazim-Richards, Nelom, Van Beek, Boulahrouz, Toornstra. Coach: Fred Rutten (NED)
Match 6 - R Standard de Liège (BEL)
A 3-0 *Toornstra (16), Boëtius (60), Manu (88)*
Vermeer, Kongolo (Dammers 67), Clasie, Boëtius (Manu 82), Immers, Kazim-Richards, Trindade de Vilhena, Van Beek, Boulahrouz (Wilkshire 26), Woudenberg, Toornstra. Coach: Fred Rutten (NED)

Round of 32 - AS Roma (ITA)
A 1-1 *Kazım-Richards (55)*
Vermeer, Wilkshire (Karsdorp 30), Kongolo, Clasie, El Ahmadi, Immers, Kazım-Richards, Nelom, Trindade de Vilhena, Boulahrouz, Toornstra. Coach: Fred Rutten (NED)
H 1-2 *Manu (57)*
Vermeer, Kongolo, Clasie, El Ahmadi, Kazım-Richards (Te Vrede 30), Nelom, Trindade de Vilhena (Achahbar 83), Van Beek, Boulahrouz (Manu 54), Karsdorp, Toornstra. Coach: Fred Rutten (NED)
Red cards: Te Vrede 54, Mulder 57

PEC Zwolle

Play-offs - AC Sparta Praha (CZE)
H 1-1 *Lukoki (77)*
Boer, van Polen, Sainsbury, van der Werff, van Hintum, Saymak, Ioannidis (Lukoki 46), Drost, Necid, Rienstra, Thomas (Nijland 65). Coach: Ron Jans (NED)
A 1-3 *Nijland (83p)*
Boer, van Polen, Sainsbury, van der Werff, van Hintum, Saymak, Lukoki (Dekker 77), Drost, Nocid (Nijland 54), Rienstra, Thomas (Moro 69). Coach: Ron Jans (NED)

FC Twente

Play-offs - Qarabağ FK (AZE)
A 0-0
Marsman, Martina, Lachman, Schilder, Mokhtar, Ebecilio, Ziyech (Eghan 77), Bengtsson, Mokotjo, Castaignos (Børven 90+3), Kusk (Hölscher 69). Coach: Alfred Schreuder (NED)
H 1-1 *Castaignos (37)*
Marsman, Martina, Bjelland, Lachman, Schilder, Mokhtar (Ould-Chikh 90+4), Ebecilio (Eghan 64), Ziyech (Børven 79), Mokotjo, Castaignos, Kusk. Coach: Alfred Schreuder (NED)

PSV Eindhoven

Third qualifying round - SKN St Pölten (AUT)
H 1-0 *De Jong (56)*
Zoet, Bruma, Maher, De Jong, Narsingh (Jozefzoon 72), Locadia, Brenet, Ritzmaier (Vloet 78), Hiljemark, Tamata, Hendrix. Coach: Phillip Cocu (NED)
Red card: Jozefzoon 90+2
A 3-2 *Locadia (28), Depay (69), De Jong (70)*
Zoet, Bruma, Maher, De Jong, Narsingh (Depay 62), Locadia (Arias 74), Brenet, Ritzmaier (Vloet 81), Hiljemark, Tamata, Hendrix. Coach: Phillip Cocu (NED)

Play-offs - FC Shakhtyor Soligorsk (BLR)
H 1-0 *Maher (59)*
Pasveer, Rekik, Bruma, Maher (Ritzmaier 89), Depay, De Jong, Wijnaldum, Locadia (Narsingh 63), Brenet, Hiljemark (Hendrix 51), Tamata. Coach: Phillip Cocu (NED)
A 2-0 *Depay (89, 90+3)*
Zoet, Rekik, Bruma, Maher (Ritzmaier 78), Depay, De Jong, Locadia (Narsingh 66), Brenet, Hiljemark, Tamata, Hendrix. Coach: Phillip Cocu (NED)

Group E
Match 1 - Estoril Praia (POR)
H 1-0 *De Jong (26p)*
Zoet, Rekik, Bruma, Maher (Ritzmaier 74), De Jong, Wijnaldum, Narsingh, Willems, Locadia (Jozefzoon 65), Brenet, Hendrix. Coach: Phillip Cocu (NED)
Match 2 - FC Dinamo Moskva (RUS)
A 0-1
Zoet, Rekik, Arias, Bruma, Maher (Ritzmaier 86), Wijnaldum, Narsingh, Jozefzoon (Vloet 84), Willems, Locadia, Hendrix. Coach: Phillip Cocu (NED)
Match 3 - Panathinaikos FC (GRE)
H 1-1 *Depay (44)*
Pasveer, Rekik, Bruma, Maher, Depay (Jozefzoon 67), De Jong, Narsingh (Ritzmaier 75), Willems, Guardado, Brenet, Hendrix (Isimat-Mirin 90). Coach: Phillip Cocu (NED)
Red card: Bruma 89
Match 4 - Panathinaikos FC (GRE)
A 3-2 *Depay (27), De Jong (65), Wijnaldum (78)*
Zoet, Isimat-Mirin, Rekik, Arias, Maher, Depay, De Jong, Wijnaldum, Narsingh (Jozefzoon 90+6), Willems (Hendrix 90+2), Guardado. Coach: Phillip Cocu (NED)
Match 5 - Estoril Praia (POR)
A 3-3 *Depay (6), Narsingh (14), Wijnaldum (82)*
Zoet, Rekik, Arias, Bruma, Maher (Hendrix 78), Depay, De Jong (Isimat-Mirin 88), Wijnaldum, Narsingh (Locadia 83), Willems, Guardado. Coach: Phillip Cocu (NED)
Match 6 - FC Dinamo Moskva (RUS)
H 0-1
Pasveer, Isimat-Mirin, Rekik, Maher (Wijnaldum 81), Depay (De Jong 67), Jozefzoon, Willems, Locadia, Guardado, Brenet, Hendrix (Ritzmaier 67). Coach: Phillip Cocu (NED)

Round of 32 - FC Zenit (RUS)
H 0-1
Zoet, Isimat-Mirin, Arias (Brenet 74), Bruma, Depay, De Jong, Wijnaldum, Narsingh (Locadia 74), Willems, Guardado, Hiljemark (Maher 86). Coach: Phillip Cocu (NED)
A 0-3
Zoet, Isimat-Mirin, Bruma, Maher, Depay, De Jong, Wijnaldum, Narsingh (Locadia 63), Willems, Guardado (Hendrix 80), Brenet (Tamata 69). Coach: Phillip Cocu (NED)

FC Groningen

Second qualifying round - Aberdeen FC (SCO)
A 0-0
Padt, Kappelhof, Botteghin, Burnet, Kieftenbeld, Hoesen (Antonia 65), Chery, Kostić, Lindgren, Van der Velden (Islamovic 82), Hateboer. Coach: Erwin van de Looi (NED)
H 1-2 *Kieftenbeld (44)*
Padt, Kappelhof, Botteghin, Burnet (Van Nieff 62), Kieftenbeld (Antonia 46), Hoesen (De Leeuw 46), Chery, Kostić, Lindgren, Van der Velden, Hateboer. Coach: Erwin van de Looi (NED)

DOMESTIC LEAGUE CLUB-BY-CLUB

ADO Den Haag
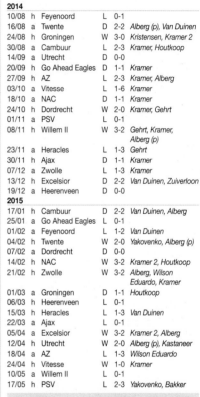

1971 • ADO Den Haag (15,000) • adodenhaag.nl
Major honours
Dutch Cup (2) 1968, 1975
Coach: Henk Fräser

2014

Date		Opponent	Res	Score	Scorers
10/08	h	Feyenoord	L	0-1	
16/08	a	Twente	D	2-2	Alberg (p), Van Duinen
24/08	a	Groningen	W	3-0	Kristensen, Kramer 2
30/08	a	Cambuur	L	2-3	Kramer, Houtkoop
14/09	a	Utrecht	D	0-0	
20/09	h	Go Ahead Eagles	D	1-1	Kramer
27/09	h	AZ	L	2-3	Kramer, Alberg
03/10	a	Vitesse	L	1-6	Kramer
18/10	a	NAC	D	1-1	Kramer
24/10	h	Dordrecht	W	2-0	Kramer, Gehrt
01/11	a	PSV	L	0-1	
08/11	h	Willem II	W	3-2	Gehrt, Kramer, Alberg (p)
23/11	a	Heracles	L	1-3	Gehrt
30/11	h	Ajax	D	1-1	Kramer
07/12	a	Zwolle	L	1-3	Kramer
13/12	h	Excelsior	D	2-2	Van Duinen, Zuiverloon
19/12	a	Heerenveen	D	0-0	
2015					
17/01	h	Cambuur	D	2-2	Van Duinen, Alberg
25/01	a	Go Ahead Eagles	L	0-1	
01/02	h	Feyenoord	L	1-2	Van Duinen
04/02	h	Twente	W	2-0	Yakovenko, Alberg (p)
07/02	a	Dordrecht	D	0-0	
14/02	h	NAC	W	3-2	Kramer 2, Houtkoop
21/02	h	Zwolle	W	3-2	Alberg, Wilson Eduardo, Kramer
01/03	a	Groningen	D	1-1	Houtkoop
06/03	h	Heerenveen	L	0-1	
15/03	h	Heracles	L	1-3	Van Duinen
22/03	a	Ajax	L	0-1	
05/04	a	Excelsior	W	3-2	Kramer 2, Alberg
12/04	h	Utrecht	W	2-0	Alberg (p), Kastaneer
18/04	a	AZ	L	1-3	Wilson Eduardo
24/04	a	Vitesse	W	1-0	Kramer
10/05	a	Willem II	L	0-1	
17/05	h	PSV	L	2-3	Yakovenko, Bakker

No	Name	Nat	DoB	Pos	Aps	(s)	Gls
23	Roland Alberg		06/08/90	M	29	(3)	8
17	Danny Bakker		16/01/95	M	12	(8)	1
25	Mitchell de Vlugt		11/02/94	M		(1)	
4	Timothy Derijck	BEL	25/05/87	D	17	(5)	
28	Tyronne Ebuehi		16/12/95	D	2	(5)	
10	Mathias Gehrt	DEN	07/06/92	M	9	(3)	3
1	Martin Hansen	DEN	15/06/90	G	32		
31	Hector Hevel		15/05/96	M		(1)	
26	Xander Houtkoop		26/03/89	A	4	(19)	3
7	Kevin Jansen		08/04/92	M	18	(7)	
5	Wilfried Kanon	CIV	06/07/93	D	14	(1)	
33	Gervane Kastaneer		09/06/96	A		(7)	1
29	Michiel Kramer		03/12/88	A	31	(1)	17
6	Thomas Kristensen	DEN	17/04/83	M	28	(2)	1
2	Dion Malone		13/02/89	D	33		
8	Aaron Meijers		28/10/87	D	33		
38	Papito Merencia	CUW	04/03/94	M		(2)	
30	Segun Owobowale		22/03/97	M		(2)	
19	Mitchell Schet		28/01/88	A	6	(6)	
32	Guy Smith		08/03/96	M		(1)	
9	Mike van Duinen		06/11/91	A	31	(2)	5
11	Wilson Eduardo	POR	08/07/90	A	9	(5)	2
3	Vito Wormgoor		16/11/88	D	26		
21	Olexandr Yakovenko	UKR	23/07/87	M	8	(3)	2
51	Gianni Zuiverloon		30/12/86	D	30	(2)	1
22	Robert Zwinkels		04/05/83	G	2		

AFC Ajax

1900 • Amsterdam ArenA (51,638) • ajax.nl

Major honours
European Champion Clubs' Cup/UEFA Champions League (4) 1971, 1972, 1973, 1995; UEFA Cup Winners' Cup (1) 1987; UEFA Cup (1) 1992; UEFA Super Cup (3) 1972, 1974, 1995; European/ South American Cup (2) 1972, 1995; Dutch League (33) 1918, 1919, 1931, 1932, 1934, 1937, 1939, 1947, 1957, 1960, 1966, 1967, 1968, 1970, 1972, 1973, 1977, 1979, 1980, 1982, 1983, 1985, 1990, 1994, 1995, 1996, 1998, 2002, 2004, 2011, 2012, 2013, 2014; Dutch Cup (18) 1917, 1943, 1961, 1967, 1970, 1971, 1972, 1979, 1983, 1986, 1987, 1993, 1998, 1999, 2002, 2006, 2007, 2010

Coach: Frank de Boer

2014
10/08	h	Vitesse	W	4-1	Viergever, Schöne 2, Van der Hoorn
17/08	a	AZ	W	3-1	Klaassen, Schöne, El Ghazi
24/08	h	PSV	L	1-3	El Ghazi
31/08	a	Groningen	L	0-2	
13/09	h	Heracles	W	2-1	Milik 2
21/09	a	Feyenoord	W	1-0	Van Rhijn
27/09	a	NAC	W	5-2	Van Rhijn, Sigthórsson 3, Veltman
05/10	h	Zwolle	D	0-0	
18/10	a	Twente	D	1-1	Sigthórsson
25/10	h	Go Ahead Eagles	W	3-1	El Ghazi, Milik, Schöne
01/11	h	Dordrecht	W	4-0	Schöne 2, Veltman, Andersen
09/11	a	Cambuur	W	4-2	Milik 2, Klaassen, El Ghazi
22/11	h	Heerenveen	W	4-1	og (Sinkgraven), El Ghazi, Kishna, Milik (p)
30/11	a	Den Haag	D	1-1	Klaassen
06/12	h	Willem II	W	5-0	Sigthórsson, Milik 2, Veltman, Klaassen
14/12	h	Utrecht	W	3-1	Serero, Klaassen, El Ghazi
21/12	h	Excelsior	W	2-0	Van der Hoorn, Zivkovic
2015					
16/01	h	Groningen	W	2-0	Kishna, og (Kappelhof)
25/01	h	Feyenoord	D	0-0	
01/02	a	Vitesse	L	0-1	
05/02	h	AZ	L	0-1	
08/02	a	Go Ahead Eagles	W	2-1	El Ghazi, og (Verhoek)
15/02	h	Twente	W	4-2	Viergever, Bazoer, Kishna 2
22/02	a	Willem II	D	1-1	Milik
01/03	a	PSV	W	3-1	Kishna, Schöne, El Ghazi
08/03	h	Excelsior	W	1-0	El Ghazi
15/03	a	Heerenveen	W	4-1	Milik 2, Klaassen, Veltman
22/03	h	Den Haag	W	1-0	og (Houtkoop)
05/04	a	Utrecht	D	1-1	og (Leeuwin)
11/04	a	Heracles	W	2-0	Sigthórsson, Andersen
19/04	h	NAC	D	0-0	
26/04	a	Zwolle	D	1-1	Sigthórsson
10/05	h	Cambuur	W	3-0	Fischer 2, Schöne
17/05	a	Dordrecht	L	1-2	Fischer

No	Name	Nat	DoB	Pos	Aps	(s)	Gls
16	Lucas Andersen	DEN	13/09/94	M	19	(8)	2
27	Riechedly Bazoer		12/10/96	M	14	(3)	1
17	Daley Blind		09/03/90	D	2	(1)	
33	Diederik Boer		24/09/80	G	1		
5	Nicolai Boilesen	DEN	16/02/92	D	22		
1	Jasper Cillessen		22/04/89	G	32		
24	Stefano Denswil		07/05/93	D	1		
8	Lerin Duarte		11/08/90	M		(4)	
21	Anwar El Ghazi		03/05/95	A	23	(8)	9
7	Viktor Fischer	DEN	09/06/94	A	3	(1)	3
11	Ricardo Kishna		04/01/95	A	18	(8)	5
10	Davy Klaassen		21/02/93	M	30		6
29	Ruben Ligeon		24/05/92	D	2	(1)	
34	Queensy Menig		19/08/95	A		(3)	
19	Arkadiusz Milik	POL	28/02/94	A	14	(7)	11
4	Niklas Moisander	FIN	29/09/85	D	25		
12	Jaïro Riedewald		09/09/96	D	10	(9)	
20	Lasse Schöne	DEN	27/05/86	M	26	(3)	8
25	Thulani Serero	RSA	11/04/90	M	21	(8)	1
9	Kolbeinn Sigthórsson	ISL	14/03/90	A	13	(8)	7
8	Daley Sinkgraven		04/07/95	M	9	(1)	
23	Kenny Tete		09/10/95	D	4	(1)	
6	Mike van der Hoorn		15/10/92	D	9	(6)	2
2	Ricardo van Rhijn		13/06/91	D	28		2
3	Joël Veltman		15/01/92	D	25		4
1	Kenneth Vermeer		10/01/86	G	1		
26	Nick Viergever		03/08/89	D	20	(6)	2
32	Niki Zimling	DEN	19/04/85	M	2	(7)	
30	Richairo Zivkovic		05/09/96	A		(7)	1

AZ Alkmaar

1967 • DSB (17,150) • az.nl

Major honours
Dutch League (2) 1981, 2009; Dutch Cup (4) 1978, 1981, 1982, 2013

Coach: Marco van Basten; (28/08/14) (Alex Pastoor); (18/09/14) (Dennis Haar); (30/09/14) John van den Brom

2014
09/08	a	Heracles	W	3-0	Berghuis, Hufperts, Tankovic
17/08	h	Ajax	L	1-3	Berghuis
23/08	a	Willem II	L	0-3	
30/08	h	Dordrecht	W	3-1	Hufperts, Tankovic, Berghuis
13/09	h	Heerenveen	L	0-1	
21/09	h	Zwolle	W	1-0	Henriksen
27/09	a	Den Haag	W	3-2	Poulsen, Johansson, Gudelj
05/10	h	Twente	D	2-2	Mühren, Tankovic
18/10	a	PSV	L	0-3	
25/10	h	Groningen	D	2-2	Rosheuvel, Gudelj
02/11	h	Excelsior	D	3-3	Gudelj, og (Van Diermen), Tankovic
08/11	a	NAC	W	1-0	Gudelj
22/11	h	Vitesse	W	1-0	Jóhannsson
29/11	a	Cambuur	W	2-0	Gudelj 2 (1p)
06/12	h	Go Ahead Eagles	W	2-0	Jóhannsson, Dos Santos
14/12	a	Feyenoord	D	2-2	Hoedt, Tankovic
20/12	h	Utrecht	L	0-3	
2015					
17/01	h	Dordrecht	W	2-0	Poulsen, Gudelj
24/01	a	Zwolle	D	1-1	Gudelj
01/02	h	Heracles	W	3-1	Jóhannsson, Berghuis, Henriksen
05/02	a	Ajax	W	1-0	Jóhannsson
08/02	a	Groningen	W	4-2	Berghuis, Gouweleeuw, Henriksen 2
13/02	h	PSV	L	2-4	Henriksen, Mühren
21/02	a	Go Ahead Eagles	W	2-0	Poulsen, Mühren
28/02	h	Willem II	W	2-0	Berghuis, Dos Santos
08/03	a	Utrecht	L	2-6	Jóhannsson, og (Markiet)
13/03	a	Vitesse	L	1-3	Berghuis
21/03	h	Cambuur	W	2-1	Gudelj (p), Henriksen
05/04	a	Feyenoord	L	1-4	og (Van Beek)
11/04	a	Heerenveen	L	2-5	Berghuis 2
18/04	h	Den Haag	W	3-1	Gudelj 2, Luckassen
26/04	a	Twente	W	2-0	Hoedt, Jóhannsson
10/05	h	NAC	W	3-2	Berghuis, Mühren, Jóhannsson
17/05	a	Excelsior	W	4-1	Jóhannsson 2, Berghuis, Henriksen

No	Name	Nat	DoB	Pos	Aps	(s)	Gls
1	Esteban Alvarado	CRC	28/04/89	G	26		
17	Djavan Anderson		21/04/95	M		(1)	
22	Steven Berghuis		19/12/91	M	19	(3)	11
36	Dabney dos Santos		31/07/96	M	17	(6)	2
12	Viktor Elm	SWE	13/11/85	M	6	(14)	
3	Jeffrey Gouweleeuw		10/07/91	D	34		1
8	Nemanja Gudelj	SRB	16/11/91	M	32		11
24	Ridgeciano Haps		12/06/93	D	2	(16)	
20	Thom Haye		09/02/95	M	22	(6)	
10	Markus Henriksen	NOR	25/07/92	M	22		7
14	Wesley Hoedt		06/03/94	D	24		2
7	Guus Hufperts		25/04/92	A	13	(15)	2
9	Aron Jóhannsson	USA	10/11/90	A	17	(4)	9
2	Mattias Johansson	SWE	16/02/92	D	27	(4)	1
23	Derrick Luckassen		03/07/95	D	12	(1)	1
5	Dirk Marcellis		13/04/88	D		(1)	
21	Robert Mühren		18/05/89	M	11	(6)	4
6	Celso Ortíz	PAR	26/01/89	M	24		
15	Simon Busk Poulsen	DEN	10/10/84	D	32		3
25	Sergio Rochet	URU	23/03/93	G	8		
18	Mikhail Rosheuvel		10/08/90	A	4	(5)	1
40	Stijn Spierings		12/03/96	M		(2)	
11	Muamer Tankovic	SWE	22/02/95	A	17	(9)	5
4	Jan Wuytens	BEL	09/06/85	D	5		

SC Cambuur

1964 • Cambuurstadion (10,000) • cambuur.nl

Coach: Henk de Jong

2014
09/08	h	Twente	D	1-1	Rusnák
16/08	a	Vitesse	D	2-2	Hemmen, Ogbeche
22/08	a	Heracles	W	1-0	Hemmen
30/08	h	Den Haag	W	3-2	Bakker 2 (1p), Hemmen
14/09	h	Groningen	W	3-0	Rusnák, Ogbeche, Van de Streek
21/09	a	PSV	L	0-4	
28/09	a	Excelsior	D	1-1	Ogbeche
04/10	a	Dordrecht	W	4-1	De Ridder, Ogbeche 2, Van de Streek
19/10	a	Heerenveen	D	2-2	Ogbeche, Reijnen
26/10	h	Feyenoord	L	0-1	
02/11	a	Willem II	D	1-1	Rusnák
09/11	h	Ajax	L	2-4	Steblecki, Ogbeche (p)
23/11	a	Utrecht	W	3-1	Barto, Ogbeche, Meleg
29/11	h	AZ	L	0-2	
06/12	h	NAC	L	0-1	
13/12	a	Go Ahead Eagles	W	2-1	Barto, Rusnák
20/12	h	Zwolle	W	2-1	Van de Streek, Bakker (p)
2015					
17/01	h	Den Haag	D	2-2	Ogbeche 2
24/01	h	PSV	L	1-2	De Ridder
31/01	a	Twente	L	1-2	Barto
04/02	h	Vitesse	L	0-2	
08/02	a	Feyenoord	L	1-2	Barto
15/02	h	Heerenveen	W	2-1	Van de Streek 2
20/02	a	NAC	L	1-2	Ogbeche
28/02	h	Heracles	W	1-0	Van de Streek
07/03	a	Zwolle	L	1-6	Rosheuvel
14/03	h	Utrecht	W	3-1	Bakker (p), Van de Streek, Rosheuvel
21/03	a	AZ	L	1-2	Ogbeche
05/04	h	Go Ahead Eagles	W	1-0	Steblecki
12/04	a	Groningen	L	2-3	Rosheuvel, og (Botteghin)
17/04	h	Excelsior	D	1-1	Ogbeche
26/04	a	Dordrecht	D	0-0	
10/05	a	Ajax	L	0-3	
17/05	h	Willem II	L	1-2	Bakker (p)

No	Name	Nat	DoB	Pos	Aps	(s)	Gls
4	Vytautas Andriuškevičius	LTU	08/10/90	D	26	(1)	
6	Erik Bakker		21/03/90	M	22	(5)	5
9	Martijn Barto		23/08/84	A	12	(17)	4
17	Lucas Bijker		04/03/93	D	28	(2)	
11	Sinan Bytyqi	AUT	15/01/95	M	4	(4)	
8	Daniël de Ridder		06/03/84	M	15	(6)	2
15	Mart Dijkstra		10/08/90	D	3	(8)	
2	Wout Droste		20/05/89	D	15	(1)	
21	Mohamed El Makrini		06/07/87	M	32		
12	Michiel Hemmen		28/06/87	A	6	(6)	3
30	Calvin Mac-Intosch		06/03/92	D	13	(7)	
10	Dejan Meleg	SRB	01/10/94	M	5	(5)	1
7	Furdjel Narsingh		13/03/88	A	19	(4)	
22	Leonard Nienhuis		16/03/90	G	34		
18	Bartholomew Ogbeche	NGA	01/10/84	A	30	(1)	13
5	Marlon Pereira		26/03/87	D	17	(4)	
3	Etiënne Reijnen		05/04/87	D	33		1
14	Mikhail Rosheuvel		10/08/90	A	11	(3)	3
11	Albert Rusnák	SVK	07/07/94	M	17		4
27	Bob Schepers		30/03/92	A		(6)	
19	Damiano Schet		08/04/90	A	2	(1)	
31	Donovan Slijngard		28/08/97	D	1	(1)	
24	Sebastian Steblecki	POL	16/01/92	M	4	(7)	2
20	Sander van de Streek		24/03/93	M	25	(4)	7
26	Harm Zeinstra		21/07/89	G		(2)	

FC Dordrecht

1883 • Riwal Hoogwerkers Stadion (4,100) • fcdordrecht.nl

Major honours
Dutch Cup (2) 1914, 1932

Coach: Ernie Brandts;
(19/02/15) Gérard de Nooijer;
(10/03/15) Jan Everse

2014

09/08	a	Heerenveen	W	2-1	Korte, Van Overeem
16/08	h	Zwolle	L	1-2	Korte
23/08	a	Go Ahead Eagles	D	0-0	
30/08	h	AZ	L	1-3	Lieder
14/09	h	NAC	L	0-1	
20/09	a	Excelsior	D	1-1	Gosens
27/09	a	Vitesse	L	2-6	Jeffrey Fortes, Koolwijk
04/10	a	Cambuur	L	1-4	Meulens
19/10	h	Utrecht	L	1-3	Ten Voorde
24/10	a	Den Haag	L	0-2	
01/11	a	Ajax	L	0-4	
09/11	h	Twente	L	0-4	
22/11	a	Feyenoord	L	0-2	
28/11	h	Willem II	L	0-4	
06/12	h	PSV	L	1-3	Lieder
12/12	a	Heracles	D	1-1	Koolwijk
20/12	h	Groningen	D	1-1	Gosens

2015

17/01	a	AZ	L	0-2	
24/01	h	Excelsior	W	1-0	Lieder
30/01	h	Heerenveen	D	0-0	
04/02	a	Zwolle	L	0-4	
07/02	h	Den Haag	D	0-0	
15/02	a	Utrecht	L	1-6	Josimar Lima
22/02	h	PSV	L	0-3	
27/02	h	Go Ahead Eagles	W	2-1	Jeffrey Fortes, Klaiber
08/03	a	Groningen	L	0-2	
15/03	h	Feyenoord	L	1-2	Jeffrey Fortes
21/03	a	Willem II	L	1-2	Biekman
04/04	h	Heracles	L	2-3	Pisas, Van Overeem
11/04	a	NAC	D	2-2	Korte, Pisas
18/04	a	Vitesse	L	0-3	
26/04	h	Cambuur	D	0-0	
10/05	a	Twente	L	0-3	
17/05	h	Ajax	W	2-1	Klaiber, Van Haaren

No	Name	Nat	DoB	Pos	Aps	(s)	Gls
10	Adnan Alisic		10/02/84	M	2	(3)	
25	Anthony Biekman		16/05/94	A	6	(4)	1
16	Quincy Boogers		28/12/95	M			
16	Erixon Danso		22/07/89	A	3	(1)	
15	Noël Goossens		17/06/94	M		(4)	
8	Robin Gosens	GER	05/07/94	M	27	(4)	2
3	Ilias Haddad		01/03/89	D	23	(2)	
18	Mohamed Hamdaoui		10/06/93	A	1	(2)	
2	Jeffrey Fortes	CPV	22/03/89	D	30	(1)	3
23	Josimar Lima	CPV	02/08/89	D	19	(1)	1
17	Sean Klaiber		31/07/94	M	10	(2)	2
22	Ryan Koolwijk		08/08/85	M	5	(4)	2
11	Giovanni Korte		01/08/93	A	16	(1)	3
1	Filip Kurto	POL	14/06/91	G	32		
16	Fernando Lewis		31/01/93	A	7		
9	Mart Lieder		01/05/90	A	20	(3)	3
7	Rihairo Meulens		05/08/88	A	5	(8)	1
6	Funso Ojo	BEL	28/08/91	M	19		
5	Marvin Peersman	BEL	10/02/91	D	24	(2)	
20	Everon Pisas		13/10/94	A	16	(9)	2
18	Andwélé Slory		27/09/82	A	1	(4)	
22	Matthew Steenvoorden		09/01/93	M	13		
13	Robbert te Loeke		01/12/88	G	2	(1)	
12	Rick ten Voorde		20/06/91	A	11	(14)	1
24	Ibrahima Toure		01/01/95	A	4	(3)	
4	William Troost-Ekong		01/09/93	D	17	(5)	
19	Jordy van Deelen		29/06/93	M	10	(4)	
21	Ricky van Haaren		21/06/91	M	17	(4)	1
14	Joris van Overeem		01/06/94	M	33	(1)	2
19	Sai van Wermeskerken		28/06/94	A	1		
15	Javier Vet		09/09/93	M		(1)	

SBV Excelsior

1902 • Stadion Woudestein (3,531) • sbvexcelsior.nl

Coach: Marinus Dijkhuizen

2014

09/08	h	NAC	D	1-1	Stans (p)
17/08	h	Go Ahead Eagles	W	3-2	Botaka, Van Weert, Fischer (p)
23/08	a	Heerenveen	L	0-2	
30/08	h	Heracles	W	3-1	Stans 2 (1p), Van Mieghem
14/09	a	Vitesse	L	1-3	Stans (p)
20/09	h	Dordrecht	D	1-1	Auassar
28/09	h	Cambuur	D	1-1	Van Weert
05/10	a	PSV	L	0-3	
19/10	a	Groningen	D	1-1	og (Kieftenbeld)
26/10	h	Twente	W	2-1	Van Weert, Stans
02/11	a	AZ	D	3-3	Auassar, Karami, De Reuver
07/11	a	Utrecht	D	2-2	Van Weert, De Reuver
22/11	a	Willem II	D	1-1	Van Weert
30/11	h	Zwolle	L	0-5	
06/12	h	Feyenoord	L	2-5	Stans, og (Van Beek)
13/12	a	Den Haag	D	2-2	Bruins, Gouriye
21/12	h	Ajax	L	0-2	

2015

18/01	a	Heracles	W	3-0	Van Weert, Van Mieghem, De Reuver
24/01	a	Dordrecht	L	0-1	
31/01	h	NAC	D	0-0	
03/02	a	Go Ahead Eagles	D	0-0	
07/02	a	Twente	W	3-1	Stans, Bovenberg, Vermeulen
14/02	h	Groningen	D	1-1	Bovenberg
22/02	a	Feyenoord	L	2-3	Van Weert 2
01/03	a	Heerenveen	W	3-0	Bruins, Van Weert, Vermeulen
08/03	a	Ajax	L	0-1	
14/03	h	Willem II	L	2-3	Van Weert, Stans
22/03	h	Zwolle	D	1-1	Stans
05/04	h	Den Haag	L	2-3	Auassar, Gouriye
11/04	h	Vitesse	L	1-3	Van Weert
17/04	a	Cambuur	D	1-1	Auassar
25/04	h	PSV	L	2-3	og (De Jong), Stans (p)
10/05	a	Utrecht	D	2-2	Van Weert 2
17/05	h	AZ	L	1-4	og (Gouweleeuw)

No	Name	Nat	DoB	Pos	Aps	(s)	Gls
8	Adil Auassar		06/10/86	M	29	(2)	4
14	Cedric Badjeck	CMR	25/01/95	A		(2)	
7	Jordan Botaka	COD	24/06/93	A	26	(7)	1
24	Daan Bovenberg		25/10/88	D	18	(1)	2
20	Elso Brito		02/04/94	M	6		
23	Luigi Bruins		09/03/87	M	20	(2)	2
26	Gino Coutinho		05/08/82	G	19		
16	Alessandro Damen		17/05/90	G	11		
21	Carlo de Reuver		29/01/95	A		(9)	3
1	Jordy Deckers		20/06/89	G	4		
17	Sander Fischer		03/09/88	D	34		1
17	Ninos Gouriye		14/01/91	A	10	(13)	2
25	Lars Hutten		18/03/90	A		(1)	
2	Khalid Karami		29/12/89	D	16	(2)	1
4	Rick Kruys		09/05/85	M	28		
5	Bas Kuipers		17/08/94	D	28	(2)	
25	Marko Maletić	BIH	25/10/93	A		(5)	
2	Jurgen Mattheij		01/04/93	D	18	(2)	
10	Jeff Stans		20/03/90	M	32	(2)	10
22	Toni Varela	CPV	13/06/86	M	4	(12)	
3	Kevin van Diermen		03/07/89	D	17	(2)	
11	Daryl van Mieghem		05/12/89	A	20	(5)	2
9	Tom van Weert		07/06/90	A	32		13
18	Kevin Vermeulen		20/11/94	A	2	(22)	2

Feyenoord

1908 • De Kuip (51,137) • feyenoord.nl

Major honours
European Champion Clubs' Cup (1) 1970; UEFA Cup (2) 1974, 2002; European/South American Cup (1) 1970; Dutch League (14) 1924, 1928, 1936, 1938, 1940, 1961, 1962, 1965, 1969, 1971, 1974, 1984, 1993, 1999; Dutch Cup (11) 1930, 1935, 1965, 1969, 1980, 1984, 1991, 1992, 1994, 1995, 2008

Coach: Fred Rutten;
(18/05/15) Giovanni van Bronckhorst

2014

10/08	a	Den Haag	W	1-0	Te Vrede
15/08	h	Heerenveen	D	1-1	Te Vrede
24/08	h	Utrecht	L	1-2	Te Vrede
31/08	a	Twente	D	0-0	
13/09	h	Willem II	L	1-2	Kazim-Richards
21/09	h	Ajax	L	0-1	
27/09	a	Go Ahead Eagles	W	4-0	og (Wijnaldum), Toornstra, Kazim-Richards, Te Vrede
05/10	h	Groningen	W	4-0	Kazim-Richards, Immers, Boëtius, Te Vrede
18/10	h	Heracles	W	2-1	Manu 2
26/10	a	Cambuur	W	1-0	Toornstra
01/11	h	Zwolle	W	2-0	Van Beek, Boëtius
09/11	a	Vitesse	D	0-0	
22/11	h	Dordrecht	W	2-0	Toornstra, Schaken
06/12	a	Excelsior	W	5-2	Kazim-Richards, Boëtius, Immers 2, Toornstra
14/12	h	AZ	D	2-2	Kazim-Richards, Clasie
17/12	h	PSV	L	3-4	Manu, El Ahmadi, Kazim-Richards
21/12	a	NAC	W	1-0	Kazim-Richards

2015

18/01	h	Twente	W	3-1	Immers, Toornstra, Boëtius
25/01	a	Ajax	D	0-0	
01/02	h	Den Haag	W	2-1	Immers, og (Derijck)
04/02	a	Heerenveen	L	1-3	Kazim-Richards
08/02	h	Cambuur	W	2-1	El Ahmadi, Kazim-Richards
14/02	a	Heracles	L	0-2	
22/02	h	Excelsior	W	3-2	Kazim-Richards (p), Toornstra, Immers
01/03	a	Utrecht	D	0-0	
08/03	h	NAC	W	3-0	Immers, Te Vrede 2
15/03	a	Dordrecht	W	2-1	Manu, Achahbar
22/03	h	PSV	W	2-1	Achahbar 2
05/04	a	AZ	W	4-1	og (Luckassen), Achahbar, Manu 2
12/04	a	Willem II	D	2-2	Manu, Kazim-Richards
19/04	h	Go Ahead Eagles	L	0-1	
26/04	a	Groningen	D	1-1	Clasie
11/05	h	Vitesse	L	1-4	Toornstra
17/05	a	Zwolle	L	0-3	

No	Name	Nat	DoB	Pos	Aps	(s)	Gls
29	Anass Achahbar		13/01/94	A	4	(8)	4
14	Bilal Başaçıkoğlu	TUR	26/03/95	A	2	(9)	
7	Jean-Paul Boëtius		22/03/94	A	20	(11)	4
23	Khalid Boulahrouz		28/12/81	D	8	(4)	
6	Jordy Clasie		27/06/91	M	31		2
8	Karim El Ahmadi	MAR	27/01/85	M	29		2
10	Lex Immers		08/06/86	M	30		7
26	Rick Karsdorp		11/02/95	M	14	(5)	
15	Colin Kazim-Richards	TUR	26/08/86	A	25	(2)	11
5	Terence Kongolo		14/02/94	D	30	(1)	
17	Elvis Manu		13/08/93	A	15	(11)	7
4	Joris Mathijsen		05/04/80	D	8		
1	Erwin Mulder		03/03/89	G	4		
18	Miguel Nelom		22/09/90	D	30		
27	Ruben Schaken		03/04/82	A	4	(3)	1
24	Matthew Steenvoorden		09/01/93	M		(1)	
19	Mitchell te Vrede		07/08/91	A	7	(13)	7
28	Jens Toornstra		04/04/89	M	24	(5)	7
21	Tonny Trindade de Vilhena		03/01/95	M	10	(11)	
22	Sven van Beek		28/07/94	D	31		1
34	Calvin Verdonk		26/04/97	D		(1)	
16	Kenneth Vermeer		10/01/86	G	30		
8	Ruud Vormer		11/05/88	M	1	(1)	
2	Luke Wilkshire	AUS	02/10/81	D	16		
25	Lucas Woudenberg		25/04/94	D	1	(1)	

Go Ahead Eagles

1902 • De Adelaarshorst (6,750) •
ga-eagles.nl
Major honours
Dutch League (4) 1917, 1922, 1930, 1933
Coach: Foeke Booy;
(22/03/15) Dennis Demmers

2014

10/08	h	Groningen	L	2-3	Schalk, De Sa
17/08	a	Excelsior	L	2-3	Cummins, Nieuwpoort
23/08	h	Dordrecht	D	0-0	
29/08	h	Willem II	W	1-0	Vriends
13/09	a	Twente	L	1-2	Kolder
20/09	a	Den Haag	D	1-1	og (Derijck)
27/09	a	Feyenoord	L	0-4	
04/10	h	Utrecht	W	3-2	Turuc, Vriends, Rijsdijk
19/10	h	Zwolle	W	3-2	Rijsdijk, Lewis, Vriends
25/10	a	Ajax	L	1-3	Lewis
02/11	h	Heracles	L	1-3	Kolder
08/11	a	Heerenveen	D	2-2	Kolder, Schalk
22/11	h	NAC	W	2-0	Reimerink, Schalk
29/11	a	Vitesse	D	2-2	Schalk, Amevor
06/12	h	AZ	L	0-2	
13/12	h	Cambuur	L	1-2	Turuc
20/12	a	PSV	L	0-5	

2015

18/01	a	Willem II	L	0-1	
25/01	h	Den Haag	W	1-0	Van der Linden (p)
31/01	a	Groningen	L	0-2	
03/02	h	Excelsior	D	0-0	
08/02	h	Ajax	L	1-2	Overgoor
15/02	a	Zwolle	W	1-0	Rijsdijk
21/02	h	AZ	L	0-2	
27/02	a	Dordrecht	L	1-2	Plet
07/03	h	PSV	L	0-3	
14/03	a	NAC	L	0-1	
21/03	h	Vitesse	L	0-2	
05/04	a	Cambuur	L	0-1	
12/04	h	Twente	L	1-3	Verhoek
19/04	a	Feyenoord	W	1-0	Reimerink
25/04	h	Utrecht	L	0-2	
10/05	h	Heerenveen	D	1-1	Verhoek
17/05	a	Heracles	L	0-1	

No	Name	Nat	DoB	Pos	Aps	(s)	Gls
14	Mawouna Amevor	TOG	16/12/91	D	7	(6)	1
16	Erik Cummins		10/08/88	G	12		1
21	Nick de Bondt		21/04/94	A		(3)	
11	Lesley de Sa		02/04/93	A	11	(5)	1
15	Sander Duits		29/08/83	M	20	(3)	
9	Marnix Kolder		31/01/81	A	20	(8)	3
18	Lars Lambooij		16/04/88	M	8	(10)	
19	Fernando Lewis		31/01/93	A	11	(6)	2
17	Sven Nieuwpoort		13/04/93	D	26	(1)	1
6	Sjoerd Overgoor		06/09/88	M	31		1
29	Glynor Plet		30/01/87	A	9	(4)	1
22	Jules Reimerink		30/09/89	M	11	(17)	2
10	Jeffrey Rijsdijk		12/09/87	M	18	(7)	3
7	Alex Schalk		07/08/92	A	12	(8)	4
5	Xandro Schenk		28/04/93	D	21	(5)	
26	Teije ten Den		29/04/93	M		(8)	
8	Deniz Turuc		29/01/93	M	28	(1)	2
1	Mickey van der Hart		13/06/94	G	22		
4	Jop van der Linden		17/07/90	D	32		1
20	Peter van Ooijen		16/02/92	M	12	(3)	
28	Wesley Verhoek		25/09/86	A	15		2
3	Bart Vriends		09/05/91	D	31		3
25	Giliano Wijnaldum		31/08/92	D	17	(2)	

FC Groningen

1926 • Euroborg (22,329) • fcgroningen.nl
Major honours
Dutch Cup (1) 2015
Coach: Erwin van de Looi

2014

10/08	a	Go Ahead Eagles	W	3-2	Chery, De Leeuw, Antonia
17/08	h	Heracles	W	3-1	Chery, De Leeuw, Van Nieff
24/08	a	Den Haag	L	0-3	
31/08	h	Ajax	W	2-0	Botteghin, De Leeuw
14/09	a	Cambuur	L	0-3	
21/09	a	Utrecht	L	0-1	
28/09	h	Willem II	W	1-0	De Leeuw (p)
05/10	a	Feyenoord	L	0-4	
19/10	h	Excelsior	D	1-1	Botteghin
25/10	a	AZ	D	2-2	De Leeuw, Hoesen
02/11	h	NAC	W	1-0	Chery
08/11	a	Zwolle	L	0-2	
23/11	h	PSV	L	0-2	
30/11	a	Twente	W	2-1	De Leeuw, Chery
07/12	h	Heerenveen	D	1-1	De Leeuw
14/12	h	Vitesse	D	1-1	Chery
20/12	a	Dordrecht	D	1-1	De Leeuw

2015

16/01	a	Ajax	L	0-2	
25/01	h	Utrecht	D	2-2	Chery, De Leeuw
31/01	h	Go Ahead Eagles	W	2-0	Rusnák, Chery
05/02	a	Heracles	D	2-2	De Leeuw, Chery
08/02	h	AZ	L	2-4	og (Berghuis), De Leeuw
14/02	a	Excelsior	D	1-1	Rusnák
22/02	a	Heerenveen	L	1-3	De Leeuw
01/03	h	Den Haag	D	1-1	Chery (p)
08/03	h	Dordrecht	W	2-0	Rusnák, Chery
15/03	h	PSV	L	1-2	Botteghin
22/03	h	Twente	D	2-2	Burnet, Mahi
04/04	a	Vitesse	D	1-1	Lindgren
12/04	h	Cambuur	W	3-2	Chery, Tibbling, Van der Velden
18/04	a	Willem II	W	4-1	Antonia, Chery 2, De Leeuw
26/04	h	Feyenoord	D	1-1	Chery
10/05	h	Zwolle	L	0-1	
17/05	a	NAC	W	5-4	De Leeuw 3, Chery, Hoesen

No	Name	Nat	DoB	Pos	Aps	(s)	Gls
7	Jarchinio Antonia		27/12/90	A	22	(5)	2
39	Jafar Arias		16/06/95	A	1	(1)	
34	Roland Baas		02/03/96	D		(1)	
38	Juninho Bacuna		07/08/97	A		(12)	
18	Henk Bos		12/11/92	M		(2)	
3	Eric Botteghin	BRA	31/08/87	D	34		3
5	Lorenzo Burnet		11/01/91	D	9		1
10	Tjaronn Chery		04/06/88	M	34		15
8	Michael de Leeuw		07/10/86	A	23	(5)	17
31	Arjen Hagenauw		08/11/94	A		(3)	
33	Hans Hateboer		09/01/94	D	18	(5)	
24	Tom Hiariej		25/07/88	M	16		
9	Danny Hoesen		15/01/91	A	16	(5)	2
19	Dino Islamovic	SWE	17/01/94	A	1	(10)	
2	Johan Kappelhof		05/08/90	D	29		
6	Maikel Kieftenbeld		26/06/90	M	33		
21	Rasmus Lindgren	SWE	29/11/84	D	20	(3)	1
14	Mimoun Mahi		13/03/94	M	13	(13)	1
1	Sergio Padt		06/06/90	G	32		
37	Desevio Payne	USA	30/11/95	D	2		
11	Albert Rusnák	SVK	07/07/94	M	16		3
22	Simon Tibbling	SWE	07/09/94	M	17		1
4	Martijn van der Laan		29/07/88	D	6	(6)	
23	Nick van der Velden		16/12/81	M	11	(12)	1
26	Peter van der Vlag		05/12/77	G	2		
20	Yoëll van Nieff		17/06/93	M	19	(5)	1

sc Heerenveen

1920 • Abe Lenstra (26,100) •
sc-heerenveen.nl
Major honours
Dutch Cup (1) 2009
Coach: Dwight Lodeweges

2014

09/08	h	Dordrecht	L	1-2	Ziyech
15/08	a	Feyenoord	D	1-1	Ziyech
23/08	h	Excelsior	W	2-0	De Roon (p), Larsson
30/08	a	Utrecht	W	3-1	Uth 3
13/09	a	AZ	W	1-0	Sinkgraven
20/09	a	Vitesse	D	1-1	Uth
28/09	h	PSV	W	1-0	Sinkgraven
04/10	a	Willem II	L	1-2	Uth
19/10	h	Cambuur	D	2-2	Uth (p), og (Pereira)
26/10	a	Zwolle	D	2-2	Uth 2 (1p)
01/11	a	Twente	L	0-2	
08/11	h	Go Ahead Eagles	D	2-2	Sinkgraven, Raitala
22/11	a	Ajax	L	1-4	Slagveer
29/11	h	Heracles	L	0-1	
07/12	a	Groningen	D	1-1	Uth
13/12	a	NAC	W	2-0	Uth 2
19/12	h	Den Haag	D	0-0	

2015

18/01	a	Utrecht	W	2-1	Slagveer, Larsson
24/01	h	Vitesse	W	4-1	Slagveer 2, Uth, Sinkgraven
30/01	a	Dordrecht	D	0-0	
04/02	h	Feyenoord	W	3-1	Thern, Larsson 2
07/02	h	Zwolle	W	4-0	Slagveer, Larsson, Uth (p), Veerman
15/02	a	Cambuur	L	1-2	Slagveer
22/02	h	Groningen	W	3-1	Thern, og (Hateboer), Veerman
01/03	a	Excelsior	L	0-3	
07/03	h	Den Haag	W	1-0	Slagveer
15/03	h	Ajax	L	1-4	og (Veltman)
21/03	a	Heracles	W	4-1	Slagveer 2, Larsson, Uth
04/04	h	NAC	D	0-0	
11/04	h	AZ	W	5-2	Thern, Slagveer, Larsson 2, Van den Berg
18/04	a	PSV	L	1-4	Van den Berg
25/04	h	Willem II	D	1-1	Uth
10/05	a	Go Ahead Eagles	D	1-1	Duarte
17/05	h	Twente	L	1-3	Slagveer

No	Name	Nat	DoB	Pos	Aps	(s)	Gls
23	Jordy Buijs		28/12/88	M	12		
9	Thomas Dalgaard	DEN	13/04/84	A		(10)	
15	Marten de Roon		29/03/91	M	32		1
10	Lerin Duarte		11/08/90	M	2	(6)	1
26	Janio Bikel	POR	28/06/95	M	3	(3)	
36	Tarik Kada		26/05/96	A		(1)	
11	Sam Larsson	SWE	10/04/93	A	21		8
37	Jeroen Lumu		27/05/95	A		(1)	
6	Stefano Marzo	BEL	22/03/91	D	31		
29	Younes Namli	DEN	20/06/94	M	2	(9)	
1	Kristoffer Nordfeldt	SWE	23/06/89	G	34		
2	Kenny Otigba	HUN	29/08/92	D	17	(7)	
20	Jukka Raitala	FIN	15/09/88	D	2	(4)	1
12	Doke Schmidt		07/04/92	D	8	(14)	
16	Daley Sinkgraven		04/07/95	M	20		4
17	Luciano Slagveer		05/10/93	A	33		11
39	Jerry St Juste		19/10/96	D	5	(4)	
7	Simon Thern	SWE	18/09/92	M	14	(1)	3
8	Morten Thorsby	NOR	05/05/96	M	10	(6)	
19	Mark Uth	GER	24/08/91	A	32		15
14	Joost van Aken		13/05/94	D	30		
40	Pelle van Amersfoort		01/04/96	A	2	(8)	
5	Pele van Anholt		23/04/91	D	32		
21	Joey van den Berg		13/02/86	M	29		2
20	Henk Veerman		30/06/93	A	1	(13)	2
33	Yanic Wildschut		01/11/91	A		(4)	
22	Hakim Ziyech		19/03/93	A	2		2

NETHERLANDS

Heracles Almelo

1903 • Polman (8,500) • heracles.nl
Major honours
Dutch League (2) 1927, 1941
Coach: Jan de Jonge;
(01/09/14) John Stegeman

2014
09/08	h	AZ	L	0-3	
17/08	a	Groningen	L	1-3	*Bel Hassani*
22/08	h	Cambuur	L	0-1	
30/08	a	Excelsior	L	1-3	*Avdic*
13/09	a	Ajax	L	1-2	*Weghorst*
21/09	h	Twente	L	1-4	*Weghorst*
27/09	a	Zwolle	L	2-4	*Bruns, Tannane*
04/10	h	NAC	W	6-1	*Veldmate (p), Bruns, Weghorst, Pelupessy, Bel Hassani, Navrátil*
18/10	a	Feyenoord	L	1-2	*Veldmate (p)*
25/10	h	Willem II	L	1-3	*Tannane*
02/11	a	Go Ahead Eagles	W	3-1	*Linssen 3*
09/11	h	PSV	L	1-2	*Linssen*
23/11	h	Den Haag	W	3-1	*Tannane 2, Bruns*
29/11	a	Heerenveen	W	1-0	*Weghorst*
07/12	a	Utrecht	W	4-2	*Bruns, Fledderus, Weghorst, Bel Hassani*
12/12	h	Dordrecht	D	1-1	*Tannane (p)*
21/12	a	Vitesse	L	0-3	

2015
18/01	h	Excelsior	L	0-3	
23/01	a	Twente	L	0-2	
01/02	a	AZ	L	1-3	*Darri*
05/02	h	Groningen	D	2-2	*Darri, Weghorst*
08/02	h	Willem II	L	0-3	
14/02	a	Feyenoord	W	2-0	*Linssen, Bruns*
21/02	h	Utrecht	D	1-1	*Avdic*
28/02	a	Cambuur	L	0-1	
07/03	a	Vitesse	D	1-1	*Avdic*
15/03	a	Den Haag	W	3-1	*Weghorst, Avdic, Bel Hassani*
21/03	h	Heerenveen	L	1-4	*Bruns*
04/04	a	Dordrecht	W	3-2	*Linssen 2, Weghorst*
11/04	h	Ajax	L	0-2	
19/04	h	Zwolle	W	2-0	*Bruns, Linssen*
25/04	a	NAC	W	3-1	*Linssen, Zomer, Navrátil*
10/05	a	PSV	L	0-3	
17/05	h	Go Ahead Eagles	W	1-0	*Linssen*

No	Name	Nat	DoB	Pos	Aps	(s)	Gls
5	Fahd Aktaou		13/01/93	D	19	(2)	
9	Denni Avdic	SWE	05/09/88	A	13	(9)	4
8	Iliass Bel Hassani		19/09/92	M	16	(15)	4
20	Tim Breukers		04/11/87	D	15		
10	Thomas Bruns		07/01/92	M	29	(3)	7
16	Bram Castro	BEL	30/09/82	G	12		
21	Simon Cziommer	GER	06/11/80	M	14	(12)	
7	Brahim Darri		14/09/94	A	13	(2)	2
30	Mark Engberink		22/07/82	D	3		
23	Mark-Jan Fledderus		14/12/82	M	31	(2)	1
20	Edwin Gyasi		01/07/91	A		(3)	
2	Milano Koenders		31/07/86	D	11	(4)	
11	Bryan Linssen		08/10/90	A	31	(2)	10
15	Jaroslav Navrátil	CZE	30/12/91	A	1	(14)	2
13	Dragan Paljic	GER	08/04/83	A		(1)	
14	Joey Pelupessy		15/05/93	M	10	(7)	1
31	Daan Rienstra		06/10/92	M		(1)	
3	Bart Schenkeveld		28/08/91	D	15	(3)	
6	Bas Sibum		26/12/82	M	2	(6)	
22	Oussama Tannane		23/03/94	A	19		5
32	Mike te Wierik		08/06/92	D	24		
1	Dennis Telgenkamp		09/05/87	G	22		
4	Jeroen Veldmate		08/11/88	D	21		2
17	Dario Vujičević	CRO	04/04/90	M	12	(2)	
19	Wout Weghorst		07/08/92	A	27	(4)	8
18	Ramon Zomer		13/04/83	D	14	(1)	1

NAC Breda

1912 • Rat Verlegh (17,254) • nac.nl
Major honours
Dutch League (1) 1921; Dutch Cup (1) 1973
Coach: Nebojša Gudelj (SRB);
(13/10/14) Eric Hellemons;
(02/01/15) Robert Maaskant

2014
09/08	h	Excelsior	D	1-1	*Tighadouini*
16/08	a	PSV	L	1-6	*Tighadouini*
24/08	h	Twente	D	1-1	*Tighadouini (p)*
31/08	a	Zwolle	W	3-1	*Perica, Falkenburg (p), Hooi*
14/09	a	Dordrecht	W	1-0	*Boateng*
19/09	h	Willem II	L	1-2	*Matic*
27/09	a	Ajax	L	2-5	*Perica 2*
04/10	a	Heracles	L	1-6	*Seuntjens*
18/10	h	Den Haag	D	1-1	*Seuntjens*
25/10	a	Vitesse	D	2-2	*Tighadouini 2*
02/11	a	Groningen	L	0-1	
08/11	h	AZ	L	0-1	
22/11	a	Go Ahead Eagles	L	0-2	
29/11	h	Utrecht	L	1-5	*Sarpong*
06/12	a	Cambuur	W	1-0	*Falkenburg*
13/12	h	Heerenveen	L	0-2	
21/12	h	Feyenoord	L	0-1	

2015
17/01	a	Zwolle	L	1-4	*Tighadouini*
25/01	h	Willem II	D	0-0	
31/01	a	Excelsior	D	0-0	
03/02	h	PSV	L	0-2	
07/02	a	Vitesse	L	0-1	
14/02	a	Den Haag	L	2-3	*De Zeeuw 2*
20/02	h	Cambuur	W	2-1	*Tighadouini 2*
28/02	a	Twente	D	1-1	*Falkenburg*
08/03	a	Feyenoord	L	0-2	
14/03	h	Go Ahead Eagles	W	1-0	*Tighadouini*
20/03	a	Utrecht	W	4-3	*Falkenburg 2, Van der Weg, Seuntjens*
04/04	a	Heerenveen	D	0-0	
11/04	h	Dordrecht	D	2-2	*Tighadouini 2*
19/04	a	Ajax	D	0-0	
25/04	h	Heracles	L	1-3	*Seuntjens*
10/05	a	AZ	L	2-3	*Sarpong, Tighadouini*
17/05	h	Groningen	L	4-5	*Fernandez 2, Tighadouini 2*

No	Name	Nat	DoB	Pos	Aps	(s)	Gls
5	Rémy Amieux	FRA	05/09/86	D	20	(1)	
9	Kingsley Boateng	ITA	07/04/94	A	10	(4)	1
7	Hakim Borahsasar	BEL	14/01/95	A	1	(6)	
4	Aleksandar Damcevski	MKD	21/11/92	D	8	(3)	
6	Joeri de Kamps		10/02/92	M	27	(2)	
18	Sepp De Roover	BEL	12/11/84	D	8	(2)	
16	Demy de Zeeuw		26/05/83	M	12		2
3	Henrico Drost		21/01/87	D	18		
19	Mounir El Allouchi		27/09/94	M		(2)	
17	Erik Falkenburg		05/05/88	A	24	(3)	5
9	Guyon Fernandez		18/04/86	A	9	(6)	2
7	Elson Hooi	CUW	01/10/91	A	5	(2)	1
25	Menno Koch		02/07/94	D	9		
16	Ruben Ligeon		24/05/92	D	14		
24	Dirk Marcellis		13/04/88	D	17		
23	Uros Matic	MKD	23/05/90	M	23	(5)	1
23	Divine Naah	GHA	04/04/96	M	8	(1)	
18	Stipe Perica	CRO	07/07/95	A	9	(1)	3
27	Brandon Robinson		25/02/95	M		(1)	
8	Jeffrey Sarpong		03/08/88	M	19	(9)	2
20	Mats Seuntjens		17/05/92	M	14	(17)	4
16	Isak Ssewankambo	SWE	27/02/96	D	12	(1)	
16	Joey Suk		08/07/89	M	3	(5)	
22	Gill Swerts	BEL	23/09/82	D	12	(4)	
1	Jelle ten Rouwelaar		24/12/80	G	34		
21	Adnane Tighadouini	MAR	30/11/92	A	31	(2)	14
15	Jesse van Bezooijen		28/04/94	D	4		
28	Kenny van der Weg		19/02/91	D	22	(2)	1
19	Feliciano Zschusschen	CUW	24/01/92	A	1	(8)	
18	Miloš Zukanović	SRB	08/02/96	A		(3)	

PEC Zwolle

1990 • FC Zwolle Stadion (12,500) • peczwolle.nl
Major honours
Dutch Cup (1) 2014
Coach: Ron Jans

2014
08/08	h	Utrecht	W	2-0	*Drost, Moro*
16/08	a	Dordrecht	W	2-1	*Thomas, Saymak*
24/08	h	Vitesse	W	2-1	*Van der Werff, Nijland*
31/08	a	NAC	L	1-3	*Necid*
13/09	h	PSV	W	3-1	*Drost, Broerse, Rienstra*
21/09	a	AZ	L	0-1	
27/09	h	Heracles	W	4-2	*Saymak, Necid (p), Nijland, Drost*
05/10	a	Ajax	D	0-0	
19/10	a	Go Ahead Eagles	L	2-3	*Nijland, Necid*
26/10	h	Heerenveen	D	2-2	*Necid, Van der Werff*
01/11	a	Feyenoord	L	0-2	
08/11	h	Groningen	W	2-0	*og (Kappelhof), Necid*
23/11	h	Twente	L	1-2	*Thomas*
30/11	a	Excelsior	W	5-0	*Nijland 2, Saymak 2, Drost*
07/12	h	Den Haag	W	3-1	*Necid 2 (1p), Drost*
13/12	h	Willem II	W	1-0	*Necid*
20/12	a	Cambuur	L	1-2	*Lam*

2015
17/01	h	NAC	W	4-1	*Van Hintum, Drost, Lukoki, Rienstra*
24/01	a	AZ	D	1-1	*Lukoki*
01/02	h	Utrecht	W	2-0	*Lam, Nijland*
04/02	a	Dordrecht	W	4-0	*Nijland 2, Becker, Rienstra*
07/02	a	Heerenveen	L	0-4	
15/02	h	Go Ahead Eagles	L	0-1	
21/02	a	Den Haag	L	2-3	*Rienstra, Saymak*
28/02	a	Vitesse	L	1-2	*Saymak*
07/03	h	Cambuur	W	6-1	*Drost, Van der Werff, Thomas, Nijland 3 (1p)*
14/03	a	Twente	L	0-2	
22/03	h	Excelsior	D	1-1	*og (Fischer)*
04/04	h	Willem II	W	1-0	*Van Polen*
10/04	a	PSV	L	1-3	*Van der Werff*
19/04	a	Heracles	L	0-2	
26/04	h	Ajax	D	1-1	*Drost*
10/05	a	Groningen	W	1-0	*Necid*
17/05	h	Feyenoord	W	3-0	*Rienstra, Necid 2 (1p)*

No	Name	Nat	DoB	Pos	Aps	(s)	Gls
9	Eli Babalj	AUS	21/02/92	A	1	(3)	
17	Sheraldo Becker		09/02/95	A	4	(5)	1
22	Aleksandar Bjelica		07/01/94	D	2	(1)	
1	Diederik Boer		24/09/80	G	4		
11	Wout Brama		21/08/86	M	15	(5)	
14	Joost Broerse		08/05/79	D	14	(6)	1
39	Max de Boom		17/02/96	M		(1)	
19	Rick Dekker		15/03/95	D		(4)	
11	Jesper Drost		11/01/93	M	32	(1)	8
26	Kingsley Ehizibue		25/05/95	M		(2)	
44	Dimitrios Ferfelis	GER	05/04/93	A		(5)	
30	Warner Hahn		15/06/92	G	30		
9	Nikolaos Ioannidis	GRE	26/04/94	A		(4)	
8	Athanasios Karagounis	GRE	25/09/91	M		(3)	
28	Thomas Lam	FIN	18/12/93	D	22	(6)	2
7	Jody Lukoki	COD	15/11/92	A	28	(3)	2
20	Soufian Moro		21/02/93	M	1	(8)	1
10	Tomáš Necid	CZE	13/08/89	A	19	(5)	11
10	Stefan Nijland		10/08/88	A	15	(14)	11
24	Steven Pereira		13/04/94	D		(2)	
23	Ben Rienstra		05/06/90	M	32		5
13	Trent Sainsbury	AUS	05/01/92	D	14	(3)	
6	Mustafa Saymak		11/02/93	M	21	(5)	6
30	Ryan Thomas	NZL	20/12/94	M	26	(4)	3
4	Maikel van der Werff		22/04/89	D	29	(4)	4
4	Bart van Hintum		16/01/87	D	33		1
2	Bram van Polen		11/10/85	D	32		1

PSV Eindhoven

1913 • Philips (35,000) • psv.nl
Major honours
European Champion Clubs' Cup (1) 1988;
UEFA Cup (1) 1978; Dutch League (22) 1929, 1935,
1951, 1963, 1975, 1976, 1978, 1986, 1987, 1988,
1989, 1991, 1992, 1997, 2000, 2001, 2003, 2005,
2006, 2007, 2008, 2015; Dutch Cup (9) 1950, 1974,
1976, 1988, 1989, 1990, 1996, 2005, 2012
Coach: Phillip Cocu

2014
10/08	a	Willem II	W	3-1	Locadia, Depay 2 (1p)
16/08	h	NAC	W	6-1	Wijnaldum 2, og (Damcevski), Depay 2, Locadia
24/08	a	Ajax	W	3-1	Depay, Narsingh, Jozefzoon
31/08	h	Vitesse	W	2-0	De Jong, Maher
13/09	a	Zwolle	L	1-3	De Jong (p)
21/09	h	Cambuur	W	4-0	De Jong, Willems, Bruma, Maher
28/09	a	Heerenveen	L	0-1	
05/10	h	Excelsior	W	3-0	Maher, Narsingh, Locadia
18/10	h	AZ	W	3-0	Narsingh, Maher 2
26/10	a	Utrecht	W	5-1	Maher, Depay (p), Hendrix, og (Kum), Wijnaldum
01/11	h	Den Haag	W	1-0	Depay
09/11	h	Heracles	W	2-1	De Jong, Rekik
23/11	a	Groningen	D	1-1	De Jong
06/12	a	Dordrecht	W	3-1	Wijnaldum 2, De Jong
14/12	h	Twente	W	2-0	De Jong, Wijnaldum
17/12	h	Feyenoord	W	4-3	De Jong 3, Depay
20/12	h	Go Ahead Eagles	W	5-0	Arias, Depay 2, Locadia, Jozefzoon

2015
17/01	a	Vitesse	W	1-0	Maher
24/01	a	Cambuur	W	2-1	Wijnaldum, Depay
31/01	h	Willem II	W	2-1	Locadia, Depay
03/02	a	NAC	W	2-0	Depay, Wijnaldum
07/02	h	Utrecht	W	3-1	Narsingh, Depay 2
13/02	a	AZ	W	4-2	De Jong 3, Wijnaldum
22/02	h	Dordrecht	W	3-0	og (Jeffrey Fortes), De Jong (p), Bruma
01/03	h	Ajax	L	1-3	De Jong
07/03	h	Go Ahead Eagles	W	3-0	Depay, og (Van der Linden), Guardado
15/03	h	Groningen	W	2-1	Wijnaldum, Isimat-Mirin
22/03	a	Feyenoord	L	1-2	Depay
04/04	a	Twente	W	5-0	De Jong, Bruma, Wijnaldum, Depay 2
10/04	h	Zwolle	W	3-1	Wijnaldum, Brenet, De Jong
18/04	a	Heerenveen	W	4-1	De Jong 2, Depay, Narsingh
25/04	a	Excelsior	W	3-2	Wijnaldum, Depay, Locadia
10/05	h	Heracles	W	2-0	Depay, Willems
17/05	a	Den Haag	W	3-2	Narsingh, De Jong, Wijnaldum

No	Name	Nat	DoB	Pos	Aps	(s)	Gls
48	Suently Alberto		09/06/96	D		(1)	
4	Santiago Arias	COL	13/01/92	D	19	(2)	1
49	Steven Bergwijn		08/10/97	M		(1)	
20	Joshua Brenet		20/03/94	D	13	(5)	1
5	Jeffrey Bruma		13/11/91	D	29	(2)	3
9	Luuk de Jong		27/08/90	A	32		20
7	Memphis Depay		13/02/94	A	30		22
18	Andrés Guardado	MEX	28/09/86	M	27	(1)	1
29	Jorrit Hendrix		06/02/95	M	12	(8)	1
27	Oscar Hiljemark	SWE	28/06/92	M	2	(9)	
2	Nicolas Isimat-Mirin	FRA	15/11/91	D	10	(5)	1
14	Florian Jozefzoon		09/02/91	A	4	(11)	2
25	Menno Koch		02/07/94	D		(1)	
17	Jürgen Locadia		07/11/93	A	5	(18)	6
6	Adam Maher		20/07/93	M	30	(1)	7
11	Luciano Narsingh		13/09/90	A	31	(1)	6
22	Remko Pasveer		08/11/83	G	2		
3	Karim Rekik		02/12/94	D	29		1
24	Marcel Ritzmaier	AUT	22/04/93	M		(4)	
8	Stijn Schaars		11/01/84	M		(2)	
28	Abel Tamata	COD	05/12/90	D	5	(3)	
23	Rai Vloet		08/05/95	A		(7)	
10	Georginio Wijnaldum		11/11/90	M	32	(1)	14
15	Jetro Willems		30/03/94	D	30		2
1	Jeroen Zoet		06/01/91	G	32		

FC Twente

1965 • De Grolsch Veste (24,244) •
fctwente.nl
Major honours
Dutch League (1) 2010; Dutch Cup (3) 1977, 2001, 2011
Coach: Alfred Schreuder

2014
09/08	a	Cambuur	D	1-1	Mokhtar
16/08	h	Den Haag	D	2-2	Mokotjo, Eghan
24/08	a	NAC	D	1-1	Castaignos
31/08	h	Feyenoord	D	0-0	
13/09	a	Go Ahead Eagles	W	2-1	Castaignos, Corona
21/09	a	Heracles	W	4-1	Castaignos 2, Ziyech, Mokhtar
28/09	h	Utrecht	W	3-1	Ebecilio, og (Kum), Castaignos
05/10	a	AZ	D	2-2	Ebecilio, Ziyech
18/10	h	Ajax	D	1-1	Corona
26/10	a	Excelsior	L	1-2	Castaignos
01/11	h	Heerenveen	W	2-0	Bengtsson, Mokhtar
09/11	a	Dordrecht	W	4-0	Ziyech, Bjelland, og (Ojo), Mokhtar
23/11	a	Zwolle	W	2-1	Castaignos 2
30/11	h	Groningen	L	1-2	Castaignos
07/12	a	Vitesse	D	2-2	Corona, Ziyech (p)
14/12	a	PSV	L	0-2	
21/12	h	Willem II	W	3-2	Mokhtar, Bjelland, Børven

2015
18/01	a	Feyenoord	L	1-3	Engelaar
23/01	h	Heracles	W	2-0	Corona, Ould-Chikh
31/01	h	Cambuur	W	2-1	Tapia, Ebecilio
04/02	a	Den Haag	L	0-2	
07/02	h	Excelsior	L	1-3	Corona
15/02	a	Ajax	L	2-4	Corona, Ziyech
22/02	h	Vitesse	L	1-2	Corona
28/02	h	NAC	D	1-1	Castaignos
06/03	a	Willem II	D	2-2	Ziyech 2
14/03	h	Zwolle	W	2-0	Tapia, Ziyech
22/03	a	Groningen	D	2-2	Tapia, Andersen
04/04	h	PSV	L	0-5	
12/04	a	Go Ahead Eagles	W	3-1	Ziyech (p), Tapia 2
19/04	a	Utrecht	L	0-1	
26/04	h	AZ	L	0-2	
10/05	h	Dordrecht	W	3-0	Corona 2, Bjelland
17/05	h	Heerenveen	W	3-1	Ziyech 2, Engelaar

No	Name	Nat	DoB	Pos	Aps	(s)	Gls
23	Joachim Andersen	DEN	31/05/96	D	5	(2)	1
17	Rasmus Bengtsson	SWE	26/06/86	D	15	(2)	1
31	Peet Bijen		28/01/95	D	1		
3	Andreas Bjelland	DEN	11/07/88	D	26		3
9	Torgeir Børven	NOR	03/12/91	A	4	(18)	1
16	Tim Breukers		04/11/87	D	2	(3)	
30	Luc Castaignos		27/09/92	A	27	(2)	10
11	Jesús Corona	MEX	06/01/93	M	27		9
16	Chris David		06/03/93	M		(2)	
8	Kyle Ebecilio		17/04/94	M	21	(5)	3
19	Shadrach Eghan	GHA	04/07/94	M	2	(9)	1
24	Orlando Engelaar		24/08/79	M	4	(7)	2
6	Felipe Gutiérrez	CHI	08/10/90	M	2	(3)	
37	Tim Hölscher	GER	01/01/92	M	1		
15	Dico Koppers		31/01/92	D	6	(3)	
33	Kasper Kusk	DEN	10/11/91	M	5	(5)	
4	Darryl Lachman		11/11/89	D	13	(2)	
1	Nick Marsman		01/10/90	G	21		
2	Cuco Martina	CUW	25/09/89	D	31	(1)	
14	Ryo Miyaichi	JPN	14/12/92	M	6	(4)	
7	Youness Mokhtar		04/09/90	A	24	(8)	5
22	Kamohelo Mokotjo	RSA	11/03/91	M	32	(1)	1
29	Jari Oosterwijk		03/03/95	A		(1)	
25	Bilal Ould-Chikh		28/07/97	A	4	(11)	1
5	Robbert Schilder		18/04/86	D	29	(1)	
20	Sonny Stevens		22/06/92	G	13		
26	Renato Tapia	PER	28/07/95	D	12	(5)	5
18	Hidde ter Avest		20/05/97	D	10		
28	Jelle van der Heyden		28/08/95	M	1		
10	Hakim Ziyech		19/03/93	M	31		11

FC Utrecht

1970 • Galgenwaard (24,500) • fcutrecht.nl
Major honours
Dutch Cup (3) 1985, 2003, 2004
Coach: Rob Alflen

2014
08/08	a	Zwolle	L	0-2	
17/08	h	Willem II	W	2-1	Toornstra, De Kogel
24/08	a	Feyenoord	W	2-1	Barazite, Antwi
30/08	a	Heerenveen	L	1-3	Janssen
14/09	a	Den Haag	D	0-0	
21/09	h	Groningen	W	1-0	Boymans
28/09	a	Twente	L	1-3	Ayoub
04/10	a	Go Ahead Eagles	L	2-3	Kerk, Boymans
19/10	a	Dordrecht	W	3-1	Boymans, og (Josimar Lima), Ayoub
26/10	h	PSV	L	1-5	Boymans
02/11	h	Vitesse	W	3-1	Kum, Boymans 2 (1p)
07/11	a	Excelsior	D	2-2	Van der Maarel, Kum
23/11	h	Cambuur	L	1-3	Boymans (p)
29/11	h	NAC	W	5-1	Boymans 2, Duplan, Rubin, Barazite
07/12	h	Heracles	L	2-4	Peterson, Markiet
14/12	a	Ajax	L	1-3	Rubin
20/12	a	AZ	W	3-0	Duplan 2, Diemers

2015
18/01	h	Heerenveen	L	1-2	Janssen (p)
25/01	a	Groningen	D	2-2	Duplan, Ayoub
01/02	h	Zwolle	L	0-1	
04/02	a	Willem II	L	0-1	
07/02	a	PSV	L	1-3	Ayoub
15/02	h	Dordrecht	W	6-1	Haller 4 (1p), Kum, Hardeveld
21/02	a	Heracles	D	1-1	Haller
01/03	h	Feyenoord	D	0-0	
08/03	h	AZ	W	6-2	Janssen, Diemers, Haller 2 (2p), Peterson, Duplan
14/03	a	Cambuur	L	1-3	Duplan
20/03	h	NAC	L	3-4	Duplan, Markiet, Rubin
05/04	h	Ajax	D	1-1	Markiet
12/04	h	Den Haag	L	0-1	
19/04	h	Twente	W	1-0	Haller
25/04	a	Go Ahead Eagles	W	2-0	Haller 2
10/05	h	Excelsior	D	2-2	Haller (p), Verbeek
17/05	a	Vitesse	D	3-3	Ayoub, Ramselaar, Verbeek

No	Name	Nat	DoB	Pos	Aps	(s)	Gls
44	Sofyan Amrabat	MAR	21/08/96	M	2	(2)	
47	Rodney Antwi		03/11/95	A	1	(3)	1
16	Yassine Ayoub		06/03/94	M	31		5
39	Cedric Badjeck	CMR	25/01/95	A	1		
10	Nacer Barazite		27/05/90	A	5	(11)	2
9	Ruud Boymans		28/04/89	A	8	(1)	9
24	Yannick Cortie		07/05/93	D	2		
12	Leon de Kogel		13/11/91	A	1	(1)	1
50	Jelle de Lange		30/01/98	D	1		
15	Mark Diemers		11/10/93	M	17	(4)	2
7	Édouard Duplan	FRA	13/05/83	A	16		7
22	Sébastien Haller	FRA	22/06/94	A	14	(3)	11
34	Jeff Hardeveld		27/02/95	D	15		1
14	Kai Heerings		12/01/90	D	4	(10)	
8	Willem Janssen		04/07/86	M	30		3
49	Issa Kallon		03/01/96	A	1	(4)	
37	Gyrano Kerk		02/12/95	A	2	(2)	1
42	Sean Klaiber		31/07/94	M		(1)	
5	Christian Kum		13/09/85	D	26	(3)	4
3	Ramon Leeuwin		01/09/87	D	27		
25	Timo Letschert		25/05/93	D	19	(4)	
13	Gévero Markiet		04/04/91	D	21	(8)	3
11	Tommy Oar	AUS	10/12/91	M		(1)	
21	Kristoffer Peterson	SWE	28/11/94	M	14	(6)	2
48	Bart Ramselaar		29/06/96	M	4	(1)	1
38	Darren Rosheuvel		15/05/94	M		(1)	
45	Rubio Rubin	USA	01/03/96	A	21	(7)	3
1	Robbin Ruiter		25/03/87	G	31		
19	Adam Sarota	AUS	28/12/88	M		(1)	
28	Jens Toornstra		04/04/89	M	2		1
51	Giovanni Troupée		20/03/98	D		(1)	
2	Mark van der Maarel		12/08/89	D	21	(3)	1
27	Gyliano van Velzen		14/04/94	M	1	(1)	
20	Danny Verbeek		15/08/90	A	3	(10)	2
30	Jeroen Verhoeven		30/04/80	G	3	(2)	

Vitesse

1892 • Gelredome (26,600) • vitesse.nl
Coach: Peter Bosz

2014

10/08	a	Ajax	L	1-4	Vejinovic
16/08	h	Cambuur	D	2-2	Labyad 2 (1p)
24/08	a	Zwolle	L	1-2	Pröpper
31/08	a	PSV	L	0-2	
14/09	h	Excelsior	W	3-1	Dauda 3
20/09	h	Heerenveen	D	1-1	Pröpper
27/09	a	Dordrecht	W	6-2	Dauda, Oliynyk, Kazaishvili 3, Wallace
03/10	h	Den Haag	W	6-1	Leerdam 2, og (Derijck), Vejinovic 3 (2p)
18/10	a	Willem II	W	4-1	Pröpper, Traoré, Oliynyk, Dauda
25/10	h	NAC	D	2-2	Vejinovic 2 (1p)
02/11	a	Utrecht	L	1-3	Pröpper
09/11	h	Feyenoord	D	0-0	
22/11	a	AZ	L	0-1	
29/11	h	Go Ahead Eagles	D	2-2	Vejinovic, Dauda
07/12	a	Twente	D	2-2	Vejinovic, Van der Heijden
14/12	a	Groningen	D	1-1	Traoré
21/12	h	Heracles	W	3-0	Traoré 2, Labyad

2015

17/01	h	PSV	L	0-1	
24/01	a	Heerenveen	L	1-4	Kashia
01/02	h	Ajax	W	1-0	Djurdjević
04/02	a	Cambuur	W	2-0	Kazaishvili, Oliynyk
07/02	a	NAC	W	1-0	Traoré
14/02	h	Willem II	W	2-0	Labyad, Traoré
22/02	a	Twente	W	2-1	Labyad, Kazaishvili
28/02	h	Zwolle	W	2-1	Traoré, Pröpper
07/03	a	Heracles	D	1-1	Traoré
13/03	a	AZ	W	3-1	Traoré, Vejinovic (p), Kazaishvili
21/03	a	Go Ahead Eagles	W	2-0	Labyad, Vejinovic
04/04	h	Groningen	D	1-1	og (Padt)
11/04	a	Excelsior	W	3-1	Traoré 2, Ibarra
18/04	a	Dordrecht	W	3-0	Kazaishvili 2, Ibarra
24/04	a	Den Haag	L	0-1	
11/05	a	Feyenoord	W	4-1	Kazaishvili, Van der Heijden, Achenteh, Labyad
17/05	h	Utrecht	D	3-3	Traoré 2, Labyad

No	Name	Nat	DoB	Pos	Aps	(s)	Gls
35	Rochdi Achenteh	MAR	07/03/88	D	30	(3)	1
25	Gino Bosz		23/04/93	M		(1)	
14	Abiola Dauda	NGA	03/02/88	A	11	(5)	6
40	Kevin Diks		06/10/96	D	20	(2)	
9	Uroš Djurdjević	SRB	02/03/94	A	1	(16)	1
30	Renato Ibarra	ECU	20/01/91	A	11	(12)	2
37	Guram Kashia	GEO	04/07/87	D	24	(2)	1
8	Valeri Kazaishvili	GEO	29/01/93	A	27	(6)	9
15	Arnold Kruiswijk		02/11/84	D	13	(3)	
20	Zakaria Labyad	MAR	09/03/93	M	24	(5)	8
5	Kelvin Leerdam		24/06/90	D	14	(6)	2
6	Josh McEachran	ENG	01/03/93	M	7	(8)	
3	Dan Mori	ISR	08/11/88	D	3	(3)	
18	Marvelous Nakamba	ZIM	19/01/94	M		(6)	
11	Denys Oliynyk	UKR	16/06/87	M	22	(8)	3
10	Davy Pröpper		02/09/91	M	30		5
1	Eloy Room	CUW	06/02/89	G	23		
27	Bertrand Traoré	BFA	06/09/95	M	27	(2)	13
23	Jan-Arie van der Heijden		03/03/88	D	32		2
7	Marko Vejinovic		03/02/90	M	31		10
22	Piet Velthuizen		03/11/86	G	11		
2	Wallace	BRA	01/05/94	D	13	(5)	1

Willem II

1896 • Koning Willem II stadion (14,700) • willem-ii.nl
Major honours
Dutch League (3) 1916, 1952, 1955; Dutch Cup (2) 1944, 1963
Coach: Jürgen Streppel

2014

10/08	h	PSV	L	1-3	Bruno Andrade
17/08	a	Utrecht	L	1-2	Haemhouts
23/08	h	AZ	W	3-0	Bruno Andrade, Messaoud, Vicento
29/08	a	Go Ahead Eagles	L	0-1	
13/09	h	Feyenoord	W	2-1	Van der Struijk, Armenteros
19/09	h	NAC	W	2-1	Sahar, Braber
28/09	a	Groningen	L	0-1	
04/10	a	Heerenveen	W	2-1	D Wuytens, Ondaan
18/10	h	Vitesse	L	1-4	Sahar
25/10	a	Heracles	W	3-1	S Wuytens, Armenteros 2
02/11	h	Cambuur	D	1-1	Armenteros
08/11	a	Den Haag	L	2-3	og (Hansen), Armenteros
22/11	h	Excelsior	D	1-1	Armenteros (p)
28/11	a	Dordrecht	W	4-0	Armenteros 2, Sahar, Ondaan
06/12	a	Ajax	L	0-5	
13/12	h	Zwolle	L	0-1	
21/12	a	Twente	L	2-3	Messaoud, Haemhouts

2015

18/01	h	Go Ahead Eagles	W	1-0	Braber
25/01	a	NAC	D	0-0	
31/01	a	PSV	L	1-2	Braber
04/02	h	Utrecht	W	1-0	Haemhouts
08/02	h	Heracles	W	3-0	Armenteros, Haemhouts, og (Veldmate)
14/02	a	Vitesse	L	0-2	
22/02	h	Ajax	D	1-1	Messaoud
28/02	a	AZ	L	0-2	
06/03	h	Twente	D	2-2	Cabral 2
14/03	a	Excelsior	W	3-2	Haemhouts, Messaoud, Sahar
21/03	h	Dordrecht	W	2-1	Sahar 2
04/04	a	Zwolle	L	0-1	
12/04	h	Feyenoord	D	2-2	Heerkens, Bruno Andrade
18/04	h	Groningen	L	1-4	Messaoud
25/04	a	Heerenveen	D	1-1	Bruno Andrade
10/05	h	Den Haag	W	1-0	Armenteros
17/05	a	Cambuur	W	2-1	Sahar, Armenteros (p)

No	Name	Nat	DoB	Pos	Aps	(s)	Gls
9	Samuel Armenteros	SWE	27/05/90	A	29		11
17	Robert Braber		09/11/82	M	11	(17)	3
11	Bruno Andrade	BRA	02/03/89	A	18	(9)	4
20	Jerson Cabral		03/01/91	A	8	(9)	2
28	Tim Cornelisse		03/04/78	D	4	(1)	
24	Frenkie de Jong		12/05/97	M		(1)	
35	Mitchell Dijks		09/02/93	D	28		
8	Robbie Haemhouts	BEL	09/12/83	M	31		5
3	Freek Heerkens		13/09/89	D	8	(6)	1
19	Jonas Heymans	BEL	06/02/93	D	6	(1)	
12	Ricardo Ippel		31/08/90	M		(8)	
1	Kostas Lamprou	GRE	18/09/91	G	33		
10	Ali Messaoud		13/04/91	M	23	(4)	5
21	David Meul	BEL	03/07/81	G	1	(1)	
7	Terell Ondaan		09/09/93	A	20	(13)	2
4	Jordens Peters		03/05/87	D	34		
23	Wiljan Pluim		04/01/89	M	3	(5)	
24	Renan Zanelli	BRA	18/05/92	M		(1)	
14	Ben Sahar	ISR	10/08/89	A	26	(7)	7
6	Fabian Sporkslede		03/08/93	M		(1)	
5	Frank van der Struijk		28/03/85	D	25	(4)	1
36	Charlton Vicento	CUW	19/01/91	A	1	(10)	1
15	Dries Wuytens	BEL	03/03/91	D	31	(1)	1
29	Stijn Wuytens	BEL	08/10/89	M	34		1

Top goalscorers

22	Memphis Depay (PSV)
20	Luuk de Jong (PSV)
17	Michiel Kramer (Den Haag)
	Michael de Leeuw (Groningen)
15	Tjaronn Chery (Groningen)
	Mark Uth (Heerenveen)
14	Adnane Tighadouini (NAC)
	Georginio Wijnaldum (PSV)
13	Bartholomew Ogbeche (Cambuur)
	Tom van Weert (Excelsior)
	Hakim Ziyech (Heerenveen/Twente)
	Bertrand Traoré (Vitesse)

UEFA Europa League qualification play-offs

FIRST ROUND

(21/05/15 & 24/05/15)
Heerenveen 1-0 Feyenoord *(Thern 83)*
Feyenoord 2-2 Heerenveen *(Achahbar 41, Kazim-Richards 110; Uth 100, 105) (aet)*
(Heerenveen 3-2)

Zwolle 1-2 Vitesse *(Van der Werff 31; Vejinovic 68, Kazaishvili 74)*
Vitesse 1-1 Zwolle *(Traoré 18; Necid 56)*
(Vitesse 3-2)

SECOND ROUND

(28/05/15 & 31/05/15)
Heerenveen 2–2 Vitesse *(Slagveer 32, Uth 75; Kazaishvili 21, Pröpper 66)*
Vitesse 5-2 Heerenveen *(Kashia 11, Vejinovic 56p, Pröpper 77, Labyad 82, Van der Heijden 86; Uth 4, 24)*
(Vitesse 7-4)

Promoted clubs

NEC Nijmegen

1900 • Goffert (12,500) • nec-nijmegen.nl
Coach: Ruud Brood

Roda JC

1962 • Parkstad Limburg (19,979) • rodajc.nl
Major honours
Dutch Cup (2) 1997, 2000
Coach: René Trost;
(07/04/15) (Rick Plum & Regillio Vrede)

De Graafschap

1954 • De Vijverberg (12,600) • degraafschap.nl
Coach: Jan Vreman

Second level final table 2014/15

		Pld	W	D	L	F	A	Pts
1	NEC Nijmegen (*1)	38	33	2	3	100	32	101
2	FC Eindhoven (*4)	38	26	2	10	70	39	80
3	Roda JC	38	21	6	11	69	58	69
4	FC Emmen	38	19	10	9	88	57	67
5	FC Volendam	38	18	8	12	83	68	62
6	De Graafschap	38	18	7	13	73	49	61
7	VVV-Venlo	38	16	12	10	48	43	60
8	Sparta Rotterdam	38	16	10	12	72	46	58
9	FC Oss (*3)	38	17	5	16	73	67	56
10	Almere City FC (*2)	38	13	9	16	64	63	48
11	MVV Maastricht	38	14	6	18	51	70	48
12	Jong Ajax	38	12	11	15	64	67	47
13	Jong FC Twente	38	12	11	15	49	64	47
14	Jong PSV	38	11	13	14	50	56	46
15	Telstar	38	12	6	20	53	68	42
16	FC Den Bosch	38	10	9	19	46	61	39
17	Helmond Sport	38	10	8	20	52	85	38
18	Achilles '29	38	8	9	21	44	71	33
19	Fortuna Sittard	38	7	8	23	30	72	29
20	RKC Waalwijk	38	7	8	23	39	82	29

N.B. (*) period champions

Promotion/Relegation play-offs

FIRST ROUND

(11/05/15 & 15/05/15)
Almere 1-1 De Graafschap
De Graafschap 2-1 Almere (aet)
(Graafschap 3-2)

Oss 1-2 VVV
VVV 0-0 Oss
(VVV 2-1)

SECOND ROUND

(22/05/15 & 25/05/15)
De Graafschap 1-0 Go Ahead Eagles
Go Ahead Eagles 0-1 De Graafschap
(De Graafschap 2-0)

Emmen 0-1 Roda
Roda 2-2 Emmen
(Roda 3-2)

Volendam 2-1 Eindhoven
Eindhoven 1-1 Volendam
(Volendam 3-2)

VVV 0-1 NAC
NAC 3-0 VVV
(NAC 4-0)

THIRD ROUND

(28/05/15 & 31/05/15)
De Graafschap 0-0 Volendam
Volendam 0-1 De Graafschap
(De Graafschap 1-0)

Roda 0-1 NAC
NAC 1-2 Roda (aet)
(2-2; Roda on away goals)

DOMESTIC CUP

KNVB-Beker 2014/15

SECOND ROUND

(23/09/14)
Ajax (amateurs) 2-2 NEC (aet; 3-5 on pens)
Almere City 2-2 Den Haag (aet; 2-0 on pens)
Capelle 0-1 Volendam
Deltasport 2-1 Willem II
Excelsior Maassluis 1-4 Emmen
Flevo Boys 1-0 DOS 37
HHC 1-0 RKC
Kozakken Boys 1-2 Sportlust 46 (aet)
ONS 0-3 Dordrecht
Rijnsburgse Boys 0-3 Sparta Rotterdam
Roda 2-1 Heerenveen
Scheveningen 4-1 Lisse
Spakenburg 3-4 NAC
VVSB 1-2 Vitesse
VVV 0-0 Eindhoven (aet; 4-2 on pens)

(24/09/14)
AFC 0-2 Excelsior
ASWH 2-3 WKE
Barendrecht 1-4 Groningen
De Dijk 4-7 Fortuna Sittard (aet)
De Treffers 2-1 Telstar (aet)
Den Bosch 0-4 Cambuur
DOSKO 0-1 De Graafschap
EVV 0-1 AZ
Go Ahead Eagles 2-0 Feyenoord
HBS 1-2 Heracles
JOS 0-9 Ajax
JVC 1-2 GVVV
MVV 4-3 Helmond Sport (aet)
Urk 2-1 UNA
Zwolle 3-2 Oss

(25/09/14)
Achilles 29 1-3 Twente
PSV 2-0 Utrecht

THIRD ROUND

(28/10/14)
De Graafschap 4-1 Deltasport
Fortuna Sittard 2-3 NAC (aet)
Heracles 6-2 Emmen
Urk 0-4 Ajax
Vitesse 2-1 Dordrecht
VVV 2-0 MVV

(29/10/14)
Almere City 1-5 PSV
Cambuur 2-0 Scheveningen (aet)
Flevo Boys 1-8 Groningen
Go Ahead Eagles 0-0 Twente (aet; 4-5 on pens)
GVVV 0-5 AZ
Volendam 3-0 Sportlust 46
Zwolle 6-1 HHC

(30/10/14)
De Treffers 1-3 NEC
Roda 4-2 Sparta (aet)
WKE 0-3 Excelsior

FOURTH ROUND

(16/12/14)
Heracles 0-3 Cambuur
VVV 0-1 Zwolle

(17/12/14)
AZ 2-1 NEC
De Graafschap 2-4 Twente
Groningen 3-0 Volendam

(18/12/14)
Ajax 0-4 Vitesse
Excelsior 6-0 NAC

(20/01/15)
Roda 3-2 PSV (aet)

QUARTER-FINALS

(27/01/15)
Cambuur 2-3 Zwolle (Narsingh 55, 60; Lam 24, Thomas 50, Lukoki 108) (aet)
Twente 3-0 AZ (Castaignos 24, Ziyech 44, 62)

(28/01/15)
Groningen 4-0 Vitesse (Chery 63, De Leeuw 66, Van Nieff 76, Kieftenbeld 78)
Roda 1-4 Excelsior (Jansen 77; Gouriye 16, Mattheij 30, Van Weert 34, 84)

SEMI-FINALS

(07/04/15)
Twente 1-1 Zwolle (Mokhtar 87; Brama 82) (aet; 2-4 on pens)

(08/04/15)
Groningen 3-0 Excelsior (Hateboer 40, Rusnák 53, Chery 88)

FINAL

(03/05/15)
De Kuip, Rotterdam
FC GRONINGEN 2 (Rusnák 64, 75)
PEC ZWOLLE 0
Referee: Liesveld
GRONINGEN: Padt, Kappelhof, Botteghin, Lindgren, Burnet (Hateboer 46), Tibbling, Chery, Kieftenbeld, Mahi (Antonia 62), De Leeuw (Bacuna 86), Rusnák
ZWOLLE: Hahn, Van Polen, Lam (Becker 81), Broerse (Sainsbury 65), Van Hintum, Rienstra, Drost, Saymak, Lukoki, Necid, Thomas (Nijland 81)

First-time Dutch Cup winners Groningen enjoy the spoils of victory

NORTHERN IRELAND

Irish Football Association (IFA)

Address	20 Windsor Avenue	**President**	Jim Shaw
	GB-Belfast BT9 6EG	**Chief executive**	Patrick Nelson
Tel	+44 2890 669 458	**Media officer**	Sueann Harrison
Fax	+44 2890 667 620	**Year of formation**	1880
E-mail	info@irishfa.com	**National stadium**	Windsor Park, Belfast
Website	irishfa.com		(15,602)

Coleraine 4

Drumahoe 9

Ballymena 2

Carrickfergus 13

Belfast

3 10

5 8

Dungannon 6

Lurgan 7

Ballinamallard 1

11 Portadown

Warrenpoint 12

0 — 50 — 100 km
0 — 50 miles

PREMIERSHIP CLUBS

 1 Ballinamallard United FC

 2 Ballymena United FC

 3 Cliftonville FC

 4 Coleraine FC

 5 Crusaders FC

 6 Dungannon Swifts FC

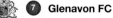 **7 Glenavon FC**

 8 Glentoran FC

 9 Institute FC

 10 Linfield FC

 11 Portadown FC

 12 Warrenpoint Town FC

PROMOTED CLUB

 **13 Carrick Rangers FC**

KEY:

● – UEFA Champions League

● – UEFA Europa League

● – Promoted

● – Relegated

Crusaders end 18-year wait

A brilliant second half to the 2014/15 Premiership season brought the Irish League title back to Crusaders FC after an 18-year wait. The high-scoring north Belfast outfit were steered to success by former striker Stephen Baxter in his tenth full season as manager.

While deposed champions Cliftonville FC won the League Cup, the Irish Cup, the country's principal knockout trophy, was collected for the 23rd time by Glentoran FC. Meanwhile, great excitement was generated nationwide by Northern Ireland's exceptional efforts in the UEFA EURO 2016 qualifying campaign.

Manager Baxter completes decade in charge with title

Glentoran lift Irish Cup for 23rd time

Lafferty goals boost national team's EURO hopes

Domestic league

A prominent member of Crusaders' playing staff when they were crowned champions of Northern Ireland twice in three seasons during the mid-1990s, Baxter completed a personal hat-trick in leading his team to glory. Appointed manager in February 2005, the 49-year-old was able to celebrate his tenth anniversary with the team in prime form. While they had been just one of several title candidates in the autumn, alongside Linfield FC, Portadown FC and local rivals Cliftonville, a run of relentlessly impressive results after Christmas carried them clear.

Fuelled by goals from their prolific strike duo of Jordan Owens and Paul Heatley, Crusaders took maximum points from 15 of their last 18 matches to propel themselves into an unassailable position. Thanks to their massively superior goal difference over Linfield, a 1-0 win at Cliftonville on 11 April effectively secured the club's fifth title, but it was another victory a week later, 2-0 at home to Glentoran FC, that settled the matter mathematically, leading to emotional scenes at the club's Seaview ground. With 25 wins, 93 goals and a final ten-point victory margin, the Crues were worthy champions in every respect

Linfield, the country's 51-time champions, were thus unable to adorn manager Warren Feeney's first season at the helm with a major trophy, a lack of goals hampering the efforts of David Jeffrey's successor. Glenavon, who finished one place behind the Belfast Blues in third, had the league's second most prolific attack, while Cliftonville, who dropped to a disappointing fifth after a laboured run-in, still managed to supply the Premier Division's top marksman as 31-goal Joe Gormley topped the charts for the second season running.

Newly-promoted Institute FC, who failed to register a single win after October, suffered immediate relegation, but 11th-placed Warrenpoint Town FC rescued their Premier Division status in extremis thanks to a penalty shoot-out win in the play-off against Bangor FC, who were narrowly beaten to the one automatic promotion place by Carrick Rangers FC.

Domestic cup

Glentoran, who finished sixth in the league, needed to regain the Irish Cup they had last won in 2013 to qualify for the UEFA Europa League at the expense of their opponents in the final, fourth-placed Portadown. They had the advantage of playing the fixture on home turf at The Oval because of major reconstruction work at Windsor Park, and they made it count, striker David Scullion scoring the only goal of the game just after half-time.

Europe

Linfield and Crusaders won their opening UEFA Europa League qualifying ties, against B36 Tórshavn and FK Ekranas respectively, but that was as far as they went, Swedish opposition blocking both teams' path to further progress.

National team

Northern Ireland went into their opening UEFA EURO 2016 qualifying fixture, away to Hungary, low on confidence after failing to win any of their previous eight matches, but a remarkable comeback win in Budapest, sealed by Kyle Lafferty's late strike, utterly transformed the team's fortunes. The following month Michael O'Neill's side grabbed two more wins, with Lafferty on target again as the Faroe Islands were defeated 2-0 in Belfast and, remarkably, group seeds Greece by the same margin in Piraeus.

The run ended with defeat in Romania but the following spring O'Neill's men were back to winning ways – and Lafferty back in the goals – as Finland were beaten 2-1 at Windsor Park. A 0-0 draw against Romania at the same venue left Northern Ireland in a strong position to qualify for the UEFA European Championship finals for the first time – and reach their first major tournament since the 1986 FIFA World Cup.

DOMESTIC SEASON AT A GLANCE

Premiership 2014/15 final table

		Pld	Home					Away					Total					Pts
			W	D	L	F	A	W	D	L	F	A	W	D	L	F	A	
1	**Crusaders FC**	**38**	**14**	**2**	**3**	**49**	**19**	**11**	**5**	**3**	**44**	**24**	**25**	**7**	**6**	**93**	**43**	**82**
2	Linfield FC	38	11	3	5	37	24	10	6	3	30	22	21	9	8	67	46	72
3	Glenavon FC	38	9	3	7	38	35	11	3	5	44	30	20	6	12	82	65	66
4	Portadown FC	38	10	6	3	38	25	7	5	7	27	31	17	11	10	65	56	62
5	Cliftonville FC	38	8	7	4	42	21	8	6	5	29	26	16	13	9	71	47	61
6	Glentoran FC	38	11	2	6	37	22	5	8	6	30	29	16	10	12	67	51	58
7	Ballymena United FC	38	9	3	7	35	35	6	3	10	27	40	15	6	17	62	75	51
8	Coleraine FC	38	5	6	10	21	32	8	1	8	27	23	13	7	18	48	55	46
9	Ballinamallard United FC	38	8	7	4	29	29	2	2	13	11	42	10	9	19	40	71	39
10	Dungannon Swifts FC	38	4	6	8	19	28	4	7	9	19	28	8	13	17	38	56	37
11	Warrenpoint Town FC	38	5	5	8	29	35	1	7	12	21	41	6	12	20	50	76	30
12	Institute FC	38	2	6	9	15	28	2	3	16	21	56	4	9	25	36	84	21

NB League splits into top and bottom halves after 33 games, after which the clubs play exclusively against teams in their group.

European qualification 2015/16

Champion: Crusaders FC (first qualifying round)

Cup winner: Glentoran FC (first qualifying round)
Linfield FC (first qualifying round)
Glenavon FC (first qualifying round)

Top scorer Joe Gormley (Cliftonville), 31 goals
Relegated club Institute FC
Promoted club Carrick Rangers FC
Cup final Glentoran FC 1-0 Portadown FC

Team of the season
(4-4-2)

Coach: Baxter (Crusaders)

Player of the season

Paul Heatley
(Crusaders FC)

Two goals in Crusaders' final game of the season – a 4-0 win against Glenavon FC – enabled Heatley to lift his final tally of Premier Division goals for the season to 27, one more than his equally prolific team-mate, Jordan Owens. The winger was particularly productive in the games against the other top-six teams during the run-in, with opposition defences struggling to tame his deadly left foot, and he was duly voted both Ulster Player of the Year and Northern Ireland Football Writers' Player of the Year.

Newcomer of the season

Gavin Whyte
(Crusaders FC)

While Paul Heatley took the plaudits thanks to his goalscoring prowess, Crusaders were also well served on the other wing by 19-year-old Whyte, whose rapid rise to prominence attracted the scouts of several English Premier League clubs. With just one Premiership appearance to his name before the 2014/15 kick-off, he quickly bedded himself into Stephen Baxter's team and soon became one of its principal assets, setting up a number of goals for Heatley and Jordan Owens and scoring nine himself.

O'Neill
(Crusaders)

Marshall (Glenavon) · Haughey (Linfield) · Coates (Crusaders) · McClean (Crusaders)

Whyte (Crusaders) · Clarke (Crusaders) · Caddell (Crusaders) · Heatley (Crusaders)

Gormley (Cliftonville) · Owens (Crusaders)

NATIONAL TEAM

International tournament appearances

FIFA World Cup (3) 1958 (qtr-finals), 1982 (2nd phase), 1986

Top five all-time caps

Pat Jennings (119); **Aaron Hughes** (96); David Healy (95); Mal Donaghy (91); Sammy McIlroy & Maik Taylor (88)

Top five all-time goals

David Healy (36); **Kyle Lafferty** (14); Colin Clarke & Billy Gillespie (13); Gerry Armstrong, Joe Bambrick, Iain Dowie & Jimmy Quinn (12)

Results 2014/15

07/09/14	Hungary (ECQ)	A	Budapest	W	2-1	*McGinn (81), K Lafferty (88)*
11/10/14	Faroe Islands (ECQ)	H	Belfast	W	2-0	*McAuley (6), K Lafferty (20)*
14/10/14	Greece (ECQ)	A	Piraeus	W	2-0	*Ward (9), K Lafferty (51)*
14/11/14	Romania (ECQ)	A	Bucharest	L	0-2	
25/03/15	Scotland	A	Glasgow	L	0-1	
29/03/15	Finland (ECQ)	H	Belfast	W	2-1	*K Lafferty (33, 38)*
31/05/15	Qatar	N	Crewe (ENG)	D	1-1	*Dallas (46)*
13/06/15	Romania (ECQ)	H	Belfast	D	0-0	

Appearances 2014/15

Coach: Michael O'Neill	05/07/69		HUN	FRO	GRE	ROU	Sco	FIN	Qat	ROU	Caps	Goals
Roy Carroll	30/09/77	Notts County (ENG)	G	G	G	G		G	G46		41	-
Conor McLaughlin	26/07/91	Fleetwood (ENG)	D	D	D	D		D	D	D	10	-
Aaron Hughes	08/11/79	Brighton (ENG)	D	D	D	D	D		D61		96	1
Gareth McAuley	05/12/79	West Brom (ENG)	D72	D56	D	D		D		D	53	5
Chris Brunt	14/12/84	West Brom (ENG)	D					D		D	50	1
Corry Evans	30/07/90	Blackburn (ENG)	M		M	M78	s46	M	s79		29	1
Oliver Norwood	12/04/91	Reading (ENG)	M79	M	M	M	M69	M	M	M	25	-
Steven Davis	01/01/85	Southampton (ENG)	M	M	M		s69	M46		M	74	5
Chris Baird	25/02/82	West Brom (ENG)	M	M	M	M	M58	M		M	72	-
Jamie Ward	12/05/86	Derby (ENG)	M66	M	M59			M	s61	M79	16	2
Kyle Lafferty	16/09/87	Norwich (ENG) /Rizespor (TUR)	A	A84	A72	A		A79		A	43	14
Niall McGinn	20/07/87	Aberdeen (SCO)	s66	M67		M63		M64	M61		36	2
Craig Cathcart	06/02/89	Watford (ENG)	s72						D	s79	21	-
Billy McKay	22/10/88	Inverness (SCO) /Wigan (ENG)	s79			s78	s75				10	-
Shane Ferguson	12/07/91	Newcastle (ENG)		D	D78						18	1
Luke McCullough	15/02/94	Doncaster (ENG)		s56			s81				4	-
Paddy McCourt	16/12/83	Brighton (ENG) /Notts County (ENG)		s67			s58		s74		17	2
Josh Magennis	15/08/90	Kilmarnock (SCO)		s84	s72		M75	s79	s81		12	-
Ryan McGivern	08/01/90	Port Vale (ENG)			s59	D					23	-
Ben Reeves	19/11/91	MK Dons (ENG)			s78		M69				2	-
Sammy Clingan	13/01/84	Kilmarnock (SCO)					s63				39	-
Michael McGovern	12/07/84	Hamilton (SCO)					G		s46	G	4	-
Paddy McNair	27/04/95	Man. United (ENG)					D		M81		2	-
Jonny Evans	03/01/88	Man. United (ENG)					D81	D	s61	D79	42	1
Daniel Lafferty	18/05/89	Rotherham (ENG) /Burnley (ENG)					D		D		12	-
Stuart Dallas	19/04/91	Brentford (ENG)					M	s64	M74	M	5	1
Will Grigg	03/07/91	MK Dons (ENG) /Brentford (ENG)					A58		A74		7	-
Lee Hodson	02/10/91	MK Dons (ENG)					s58				15	-
Ryan McLaughlin	30/09/94	Liverpool (ENG)					s69				3	-
Liam Boyce	08/04/91	Ross County (SCO)							s74		5	-

EUROPE

Cliftonville FC

Second qualifying round - Debreceni VSC (HUN)
H 0-0
Devlin, McGovern, Scannell, Johnston, Flynn, Curran, M Donnelly (Garrett 63), Seydak (McMullan 83), Catney, Gormley (Murray 90+2), Cosgrove. Manager: Tommy Breslin (NIR)
A 0-2
Devlin, McGovern, Scannell, Johnston, Flynn, Curran, Garrett (Winchester 62), M Donnelly, Seydak, Catney (Caldwell 81), Cosgrove (Smyth 56). Manager: Tommy Breslin (NIR)
Red card: McGovern 54

Glenavon FC

First qualifying round - FH Hafnarfjördur (ISL)
A 0-3
McGrath, Neill, Lindsay, Bates (Rainey 86), Bradley, Dillon, McIlveen, McGrory, Marshall, Braniff (Hamilton 86), McCabe. Manager: Gary Hamilton (NIR)
H 2-3 *Braniff (58), Bradley (60)*
Blayney, Neill, Lindsay (McKeown 55), Hamilton (Rainey 78), Bates, Bradley, Dillon, Marshall, Braniff, McCabe, Martyn (Sykes 83). Manager: Gary Hamilton (NIR)

Linfield FC

First qualifying round - B36 Tórshavn (FRO)
A 2-1 *Mulgrew (38), Carvill (88)*
Tuffey, Richards, Hegarty, Haughey (Callacher 30), Waterworth (Thompson 74), Lowry, Carvill (Morrow 90+2), Burns, M Clarke, Mulgrew, Sproule. Manager: Warren Feeney (NIR)
H 1-1 *Carvill (17)*
Tuffey, Richards, Hegarty, Haughey, Waterworth (Thompson 68), Lowry, Carvill (Callacher 86), Burns (R Clarke 72), M Clarke, Mulgrew, Sproule. Manager: Warren Feeney (NIR)

Second qualifying round - AIK Solna (SWE)
H 1-0 *Waterworth (87)*
Tuffey, Richards, Hegarty, Lowry, Thompson (Waterworth 74), Carvill, Burns, M Clarke, Mulgrew (Ward 21), Reece Glendinning (Callacher 80), Sproule. Manager: Warren Feeney (NIR)
A 0-2
Tuffey, Richards, Hegarty, Waterworth, Lowry, Carvill (Thompson 75), Burns, Ward, M Clarke, Reece Glendinning (Mulgrew 58), Sproule (R Clarke 62). Manager: Warren Feeney (NIR)

Crusaders FC

First qualifying round - FK Ekranas (LTU)
H 3-1 *Cockcroft (23), Owens (43), Coates (58)*
O'Neill, Burns, Coates, Morrow, Robinson, Caddell, McClean, Owens (Adamson 85), Clarke, Cockcroft, O'Carroll 78), Heatley. Manager: Jeff Spiers (NIR)
A 2-1 *Heatley (56, 71)*
O'Neill, Burns, Leeman, Morrow (Magowan 90), Robinson, Caddell, McClean, Owens, Clarke, Cockcroft (O'Carroll 55), Heatley (Snoddy 73). Manager: Stephen Baxter (NIR)

Second qualifying round - IF Brommapojkarna (SWE)
A 0-4
O'Neill, Burns, Coates, Morrow, O'Carroll (Cockcroft 58), Robinson, Caddell, McClean, Owens (Adamson 82), Clarke (Leeman 76), Heatley. Manager: Stephen Baxter (NIR)
H 1-1 *Coates (17)*
O'Neill, Burns, Leeman, Coates (Magowan 81), Morrow (Snoddy 57), O'Carroll, McClean, Owens, Clarke, Cockcroft (McCutcheon 63), Heatley. Manager: Stephen Baxter (NIR)

DOMESTIC LEAGUE CLUB-BY-CLUB

Ballinamallard United FC

1975 • Ferney Park (2,000) • no website
Manager: Whitey Anderson

2014
09/08	a	Coleraine	D	1-1	*McCartney*
13/08	h	Dungannon	D	1-1	*McMenamin*
16/08	h	Crusaders	L	1-3	*Lafferty*
23/08	h	Glentoran	D	2-2	*Elding, Stafford*
30/08	h	Cliftonville	L	0-4	
02/09	a	Glenavon	L	0-1	
06/09	h	Ballymena	W	3-0	*Elding, Martin 2*
13/09	h	Institute	L	2-3	*Elding, Carters*
20/09	a	Portadown	L	0-3	
27/09	h	Linfield	L	1-3	*Currie*
03/10	a	Warrenpoint	L	0-2	
10/10	h	Coleraine	W	1-0	*Campbell*
18/10	h	Dungannon	W	2-0	*McCartney (p), Martin*
25/10	a	Cliftonville	L	2-3	*McCartney, Lafferty*
01/11	h	Portadown	L	0-2	
08/11	h	Crusaders	D	1-1	*Currie*
15/11	h	Institute	W	2-0	*McCartney (p), Kee*
22/11	h	Ballymena	L	0-3	
28/11	h	Warrenpoint	W	3-1	*og (McVeigh), Currie, Campbell*
06/12	a	Glentoran	L	1-3	*Kee*
13/12	a	Linfield	L	0-3	
20/12	h	Glenavon	W	1-0	*Campbell*
26/12	h	Dungannon	L	0-2	
30/12	h	Cliftonville	D	1-1	*Stafford*

2015
03/01	a	Crusaders	L	0-3	
23/01	a	Warrenpoint	L	0-7	
27/01	h	Linfield	D	1-1	*McLaughlin*
31/01	h	Portadown	D	0-0	
14/02	h	Coleraine	W	2-1	*Feeney, McCartney (p)*
21/02	a	Institute	D	1-1	*Martin*
07/03	h	Glenavon	L	1-3	*Martin*
13/03	a	Glentoran	L	0-4	
28/03	h	Ballymena	L	1-3	*Martin*
04/04	h	Dungannon	W	1-0	*C Beacom*
07/04	h	Institute	W	2-0	*McCartney 2*
11/04	a	Coleraine	W	2-1	*Campbell 2*
18/04	a	Ballymena	L	1-2	*C Beacom*
25/04	h	Warrenpoint	D	3-3	*Martin, Campbell, Feeney*

No	Name	Nat	DoB	Pos	Aps	(s)	Gls
16	Cathal Beacom		01/08/88	M	10	(7)	2
19	Nigel Beacom		12/12/89	M	3	(1)	
22	Ben Brown		31/10/93	A		(1)	
20	Ryan Campbell		08/07/81	A	21	(15)	6
4	Leon Carters		23/07/84	D	6	(1)	1
22	Kane Connor		25/09/92	M		(3)	
23	Jonathan Courtney		09/03/95	A	4	(6)	
21	Christopher Crilly		03/03/84	D	21	(3)	
12	John Currie		10/09/93	M	28	(5)	3
3	Jake Dykes		30/06/95	D	9	(5)	
9	Anthony Elding	ENG	16/04/82	A	13	(4)	3
24	David Elliott		08/09/95	D		(2)	
15	Steve Feeney	IRL	16/05/84	D	13	(5)	2
17	Raymond Foy	IRL	10/03/93	M	11	(10)	
8	Stuart Hutchinson		10/05/91	M	21	(7)	
6	David Kee		09/08/88	D	27	(2)	2
10	Johnny Lafferty		02/01/87	A	26	(7)	2
7	Liam Martin		23/01/94	M	30	(5)	7
11	Jason McCartney	IRL	06/09/86	M	28	(5)	7
13	Stefan McCusker		01/12/89	G	20		
14	James McKenna		20/07/84	M	13	(2)	
24	Colm McLaughlin		01/08/93	D	28	(2)	1
2	Liam McMenamin		10/04/89	D	30	(1)	1
1	Adam Murphy	IRL	20/11/95	G	2		
1	Fergal Murphy		30/06/87	G	16	(1)	
18	Dale Noble		29/06/92	A		(4)	
18	Gary Phair		24/01/94	D	2	(1)	
14	Ciaran Smith		16/01/97	A		(3)	
5	Mark Stafford		20/08/87	D	36		2

Ballymena United FC

1928 • The Showgrounds (4,390) • ballymenaunitedfc.com

Major honours
Irish Cup (6) 1929, 1940, 1958, 1981, 1984, 1989

Manager: Glenn Ferguson

2014

09/08	h	Warrenpoint	W	2-0	*Cushley, Gawley*
13/08	a	Crusaders	D	2-2	*Taggart, Taylor*
16/08	h	Portadown	W	3-2	*McVey, Jenkins, Boyce*
23/08	a	Dungannon	W	3-0	*Tipton 2, Cushley*
29/08	a	Glenavon	L	1-2	*Cushley*
02/09	h	Institute	W	2-1	*Teggart 2 (1p)*
06/09	a	Ballinamallard	L	0-3	
13/09	h	Glentoran	D	2-2	*Boyce, Thompson*
20/09	a	Coleraine	W	2-1	*Thompson, Ruddy*
27/09	h	Cliftonville	D	2-2	*Tipton, Jenkins*
04/10	a	Linfield	L	2-3	*Taylor 2*
11/10	h	Dungannon	D	2-2	*Jenkins, Teggart*
18/10	a	Portadown	L	1-2	*McVey*
25/10	h	Glenavon	L	1-4	*Jenkins*
01/11	a	Glentoran	L	0-4	
08/11	h	Coleraine	L	0-2	
15/11	a	Warrenpoint	D	2-2	*Tipton 2*
22/11	h	Ballinamallard	W	3-0	*Surgenor 2, Shevlin*
29/11	a	Cliftonville	L	0-7	
06/12	h	Linfield	L	2-3	*Jenkins, Tipton (p)*
13/12	h	Crusaders	L	0-2	
20/12	a	Institute	W	2-1	*Munster, Teggart (p)*
26/12	h	Coleraine	W	4-3	*Boyce, Tipton 2, Jenkins*

2015

01/01	a	Warrenpoint	L	0-2	
03/01	h	Glenavon	L	2-4	*Boyce, McCutcheon*
17/01	a	Portadown	D	5-5	*Tipton 2, Boyce, Taylor, Jenkins*
31/01	a	Linfield	L	1-2	*Cushley*
10/02	h	Glentoran	L	1-3	*T Kane*
14/02	h	Institute	W	3-0	*McCutcheon (p), Jenkins, McAllister*
21/02	a	Cliftonville	L	0-1	
06/03	a	Dungannon	L	0-1	
14/03	h	Crusaders	L	1-3	*Jenkins*
28/03	a	Ballinamallard	W	3-1	*Surgenor, Gawley, Tipton*
04/04	a	Coleraine	W	1-0	*Boyce*
07/04	h	Warrenpoint	W	2-1	*Tipton, Boyce*
11/04	a	Institute	W	2-1	*Teggart (p), og (Forker)*
18/04	h	Ballinamallard	W	2-1	*Gawley, McAllister*
25/04	h	Dungannon	W	1-0	*Jenkins*

No	Name	Nat	DoB	Pos	Aps	(s)	Gls
18	Stuart Addis		05/07/79	G	7		
20	Tim Allen	AUS	05/04/92	G	10		
9	Darren Boyce		25/01/86	A	22	(14)	7
11	David Cushley		22/07/89	M	23	(3)	4
4	Alan Davidson	SCO	19/03/88	M	3	(2)	
21	Jim Ervin		05/06/85	D	12		
28	Matthew Ferguson		21/11/95	M	2	(3)	
28	Craig Gardiner		02/08/96	D		(1)	
27	Neal Gawley		20/02/86	M	24	(7)	3
10	Allan Jenkins	SCO	07/10/81	M	30	(4)	10
21	Eoin Kane		10/01/96	M	1	(3)	
2	Tony Kane		29/08/87	D	26	(5)	1
29	Eamon McAllister		19/11/87	A	6	(4)	2
3	Stephen McBride		06/04/83	D	31	(1)	
19	Brian McCaul		06/08/90	M	5	(7)	
20	Mark McCullagh		10/05/87	D	16	(4)	
30	Gary McCutcheon	SCO	08/10/78	A	5		2
4	Paddy McNally		20/08/94	D	6		
25	Jake McNeill		09/01/97	A		(2)	
22	Kyle McVey		07/07/86	D	7	(1)	2
16	David Munster		24/02/79	M	16	(2)	1
1	Dwayne Nelson		05/09/84	G	21		
30	Stewart Nixon		08/05/97	A		(1)	
17	Michael Ruddy		05/08/93	D	9	(6)	1
25	Matthew Shevlin		07/12/98	A		(4)	1
6	Aaron Stewart		03/12/89	D	7	(1)	
15	Mark Surgenor		19/12/85	D	14	(10)	3
8	Gavin Taggart		15/11/84	M	10	(3)	1
5	Johnny Taylor		30/06/88	D	30		4
12	Alan Teggart		24/11/86	A	23	(8)	5
7	Gary Thompson		26/05/90	A	19	(5)	2
14	Matthew Tipton	WAL	29/06/80	A	33	(2)	12

Cliftonville FC

1879 • Solitude (5,442) • cliftonvillefc.net

Major honours
Irish League (5) 1906 (shared), 1910, 1998, 2013, 2014; Irish Cup (8) 1883, 1888, 1897, 1900, 1901, 1907, 1909, 1979

Manager: Tommy Breslin

2014

09/08	h	Glentoran	D	0-0	
13/08	a	Portadown	W	1-0	*Gormley*
16/08	a	Institute	W	3-2	*McDaid, Curran, Garrett*
23/08	h	Glenavon	D	3-3	*Gormley 2, McDaid*
30/08	a	Ballinamallard	W	4-0	*McMullan (p), Curran, Gormley, McDaid*
02/09	h	Linfield	D	0-0	
06/09	a	Warrenpoint	D	1-1	*Gormley*
13/09	h	Coleraine	L	2-3	*Flynn, M Donnelly*
20/09	h	Dungannon	D	1-1	*Gormley*
27/09	a	Ballymena	D	2-2	*Curran, Winchester*
04/10	a	Crusaders	W	1-0	*Gormley*
11/10	h	Portadown	W	2-0	*M Donnelly, McDaid*
18/10	a	Linfield	W	3-1	*Winchester, McDaid, Seydak*
25/10	h	Ballinamallard	W	3-2	*M Donnelly, Gormley, McDaid*
01/11	a	Dungannon	W	3-1	*Gormley 2 (1p), Cosgrove*
07/11	h	Warrenpoint	W	3-1	*Gormley 3*
15/11	a	Crusaders	L	1-4	*Flynn*
22/11	a	Glenavon	W	3-1	*Gormley, Garrett 2*
29/11	h	Ballymena	W	7-0	*M Donnelly, Gormley 3, McDaid 2, J Donnelly*
06/12	a	Coleraine	L	0-2	
13/12	h	Institute	W	4-0	*J Donnelly, Gormley 3*
20/12	a	Glentoran	L	1-2	*McDaid*
26/12	h	Crusaders	L	0-1	
30/12	a	Ballinamallard	D	1-1	*J Donnelly*

2015

03/01	a	Dungannon	D	1-1	*Cosgrove*
17/01	h	Warrenpoint	D	2-2	*J Donnelly, Gormley*
31/01	h	Glentoran	D	1-1	*Gormley*
10/02	a	Linfield	D	2-2	*Murray 2*
14/02	a	Portadown	W	2-0	*McMullan (p), Gormley*
21/02	h	Ballymena	W	1-0	*Winchester*
07/03	a	Coleraine	D	0-0	
14/03	h	Glenavon	L	2-3	*M Donnelly, Knowles*
28/03	h	Institute	W	5-1	*M Donnelly, Gormley 3 (1p), J Donnelly*
04/04	h	Portadown	W	4-0	*Gormley 3 (1p), M Donnelly*
07/04	a	Glenavon	L	0-5	
11/04	h	Crusaders	L	0-1	
18/04	h	Linfield	D	2-2	*Gormley 2 (1p)*
25/04	a	Glentoran	L	0-1	

No	Name	Nat	DoB	Pos	Aps	(s)	Gls
6	Robert Bayly	IRL	28/02/88	D	5	(1)	
24	Caoimhin Bonner		15/01/93	D	10		
1	Ryan Brown		27/11/80	G	4		
17	Ryan Catney		17/02/87	M	32		
28	Peter Cherrie	SCO	01/10/83	G	13		
23	Tomas Cosgrove		11/12/92	M	27	(1)	2
7	Chris Curran		05/01/91	M	17	(1)	3
12	Conor Devlin		23/09/91	G	21		
21	Jay Donnelly		10/04/95	A	9	(9)	5
11	Martin Donnelly		28/08/88	M	33	(4)	7
5	Johnny Flynn		18/11/89	D	22		2
10	Stephen Garrett		13/04/87	A	6	(12)	3
19	Joe Gormley		26/11/89	A	35	(2)	31
4	Barry Johnston		28/10/79	M	12	(7)	
26	Guillaume Keke	FRA	13/03/91	A	1	(3)	
14	James Knowles		06/04/93	M	12	(11)	1
27	Sean McCarron		08/08/91	A		(4)	
9	David McDaid		03/12/90	A	27	(4)	9
2	Jamie McGovern		29/05/89	D	28	(2)	
8	George McMullan		04/08/81	D	16	(4)	2
25	Jonathan McMurray		19/09/94	A	3	(7)	
22	Andrew Mooney		08/02/97	A		(1)	
30	Conor Morgan		07/02/97	M	1		
88	Tiarnan Mulvenna	IRL	10/12/88	A	1	(15)	
20	Martin Murray		18/08/93	M	5	(11)	2
3	Ronan Scannell		11/05/79	D	21	(2)	
15	Eamon Seydak		25/02/86	D	18	(2)	1
16	Marc Smyth	SCO	27/12/82	D	16		
18	Jude Winchester		13/04/93	M	23	(8)	3

Coleraine FC

1927 • The Showgrounds (3,960) • colerainefc.com

Major honours
Irish League (1) 1974; Irish Cup (5) 1965, 1972, 1975, 1977, 2003

Manager: Oran Kearney

2014

09/08	h	Ballinamallard	D	1-1	*McDaid*
13/08	a	Institute	L	0-2	
16/08	h	Linfield	L	1-2	*McCafferty*
23/08	a	Warrenpoint	W	3-1	*Harkin, Browne, Ogilby*
29/08	h	Portadown	D	0-0	
02/09	h	Crusaders	L	2-6	*Parkhill, Ogilby*
06/09	a	Glentoran	L	0-2	
13/09	a	Cliftonville	W	3-2	*McCafferty 2 (1p), Parkhill*
20/09	h	Ballymena	L	1-2	*Browne*
27/09	h	Glenavon	W	2-1	*McCafferty 2 (1p)*
04/10	a	Dungannon	W	1-0	*Ogilby*
10/10	a	Ballinamallard	L	0-1	
18/10	h	Glentoran	W	1-0	*Parkhill*
25/10	a	Portadown	W	2-0	*Miskimmin, Harkin*
01/11	h	Institute	L	0-3	*(w/o; original result 4-0 Ogilby, Miskimmin 3 (1p))*
08/11	a	Ballymena	W	2-0	*McCafferty, Harkin*
15/11	h	Dungannon	L	1-2	*Browne*
21/11	a	Crusaders	L	0-3	
29/11	a	Linfield	L	1-2	*McCafferty*
06/12	h	Cliftonville	W	2-0	*McGinty, Beverland*
13/12	a	Glenavon	W	3-2	*McCafferty, McGinty, Parkhill*
20/12	h	Warrenpoint	D	0-0	
26/12	a	Ballymena	L	3-4	*Browne, Parkhill, Ogilby*

2015

01/01	h	Portadown	L	0-1	
03/01	a	Linfield	D	1-1	*McCafferty*
23/01	h	Dungannon	L	1-2	*Browne*
27/01	h	Glenavon	D	1-1	*McCafferty (p)*
31/01	a	Institute	W	2-0	*Parkhill, Snoddy*
14/02	a	Ballinamallard	L	1-2	*Snoddy*
21/02	h	Glentoran	D	1-1	*McCauley*
07/03	h	Cliftonville	D	0-0	
14/03	a	Warrenpoint	W	5-0	*Lyons 2, Canning, McCafferty (p), Browne*
28/03	h	Crusaders	L	1-5	*McCafferty (p)*
04/04	h	Ballymena	L	0-1	
07/04	a	Dungannon	L	0-1	
11/04	h	Ballinamallard	L	1-2	*McGonigle*
18/04	h	Warrenpoint	W	2-1	*Parkhill 2*
25/04	h	Institute	W	3-1	*Parkhill, McGonigle 2*

No	Name	Nat	DoB	Pos	Aps	(s)	Gls
27	Oran Barton		01/08/97	D	1		
2	Howard Beverland		30/03/90	D	23		1
9	Gary Browne		17/01/83	A	12	(14)	6
12	Aaron Canning		07/03/92	D	30	(1)	1
1	Michael Doherty		19/10/83	G	29		
5	Stephen Douglas		27/09/77	D	24	(1)	
1	Eugene Ferry		20/01/92	G	4		
20	Andy Findlay		01/02/95	G	5		
10	Ruairi Harkin	IRL	11/10/89	M	17	(2)	3
4	Michael Hegarty		09/12/83	M	9	(10)	
4	Ruaidhri Higgins		23/10/84	M	12		
24	Lyndon Kane		15/02/97	D	15	(4)	
26	Bradley Lyons		26/05/97	A	6	(5)	2
8	Neil McCafferty	IRL	19/07/84	M	36		12
22	Darren McCauley		21/02/91	M	19	(1)	1
19	David McDaid		03/12/90	A	1		1
11	Shane McGinty	IRL	14/04/94	M	27	(7)	2
27	Jamie McGonigle		05/03/96	A	5	(2)	3
3	Ryan McIlmoyle		12/12/84	M		(1)	
23	Joseph McNeill		23/08/88	M	21	(5)	
19	Mark Miskimmin		11/06/88	A	12	(12)	4
18	Craig Moore		28/12/84	M		(3)	
15	Adam Mullan		24/10/95	A	31		
6	David Ogilby		02/06/84	D	26	(1)	5
16	Ian Parkhill		07/04/90	A	34	(3)	9
7	Matthew Snoddy		02/06/93	M	9	(1)	2
26	Cameron Stewart		11/03/97	M	1		
14	John Watt		20/03/86	D	9	(7)	

Crusaders FC

1898 • Seaview (3,330) • crusadersfc.com

Major honours
Irish League (5) 1973, 1976, 1995, 1997, 2015;
Irish Cup (3) 1967, 1968, 2009

Manager: Stephen Baxter

2014

09/08	a	Glenavon	D	2-2	O'Carroll, Owens
13/08	h	Ballymena	D	2-2	Owens, Adamson
16/08	h	Ballinamallard	W	3-1	Heatley, Robinson 2
23/08	a	Portadown	L	1-3	Owens
30/08	h	Glentoran	W	1-0	Coates
02/09	a	Coleraine	W	6-2	Heatley 2, Whyte, McCutcheon (p), Owens, O'Carroll
13/09	a	Dungannon	D	2-2	Owens, O'Carroll (p)
20/09	a	Warrenpoint	W	3-0	Owens, Adamson, O'Carroll
26/09	h	Institute	W	3-2	Heatley 2, Owens
29/09	h	Linfield	D	2-2	Heatley, Whyte
04/10	h	Cliftonville	L	0-1	
11/10	a	Glentoran	W	3-1	Owens, O'Carroll (p), McCutcheon
18/10	h	Glenavon	L	1-4	Caddell
25/10	a	Linfield	W	2-1	Coates, Heatley
01/11	h	Warrenpoint	W	3-0	Owens 2, O'Carroll
08/11	a	Ballinamallard	D	1-1	Heatley
15/11	h	Cliftonville	W	4-1	Owens 2, Coates, Hanley
21/11	h	Coleraine	W	3-0	Whyte, Heatley, Owens
29/11	a	Institute	D	1-1	og (A Walsh)
06/12	h	Portadown	L	2-3	Burns, Owens
13/12	a	Ballymena	W	2-0	Robinson, Whyte
19/12	a	Dungannon	W	1-0	Adamson
26/12	a	Cliftonville	W	1-0	Heatley

2015

01/01	h	Linfield	W	2-1	Owens, Heatley
03/01	h	Ballinamallard	W	3-0	Whyte, Owens, Burns
17/01	a	Glentoran	W	2-1	Adamson, Heatley
23/01	h	Portadown	W	6-0	Owens 3, Heatley 2, O'Carroll (p)
31/01	a	Dungannon	D	1-1	Heatley
14/02	h	Warrenpoint	W	4-1	Heatley 2, Owens, Whyte
21/02	a	Glenavon	W	7-3	Heatley 2, Whyte 3, O'Carroll (p), Owens
07/03	h	Institute	W	3-1	Owens 2, O'Carroll (p)
14/03	a	Ballymena	W	3-1	Heatley, Adamson, Owens
28/03	a	Coleraine	W	5-1	Burns, Owens 2, Heatley 2
07/04	a	Portadown	L	0-1	
11/04	h	Cliftonville	W	1-0	Heatley
18/04	h	Glentoran	W	2-0	Caddell, Heatley
21/04	a	Linfield	L	1-3	Heatley
25/04	a	Glenavon	W	4-0	Caddell, Heatley 2, Burns

No	Name	Nat	DoB	Pos	Aps	(s)	Gls
9	Timmy Adamson		05/01/83	A	20	(11)	5
2	Billy Joe Burns		28/04/89	D	36		4
12	Declan Caddell		13/04/88	M	29		3
20	Richard Clarke		28/11/85	M	32	(3)	
6	Colin Coates		26/10/85	D	30		3
21	Stephen Cockcroft		01/02/94	D	4	(3)	
24	Kyle Dillon		03/05/95	M		(1)	
7	Emmett Friars		14/09/85	D	4	(2)	
3	Nathan Hanley		18/07/90	M	5	(12)	1
22	Paul Heatley		30/06/87	A	32		27
4	Paul Leeman		21/01/78	D	1	(4)	
5	David Magowan		04/10/83	D	26	(1)	
17	Craig McClean		06/07/85	D	31	(2)	
30	Gary McCutcheon	SCO	08/10/78	A	7	(7)	2
16	Barry Molloy		28/11/83	M	3	(3)	
8	Chris Morrow		20/09/85	M	4	(2)	
10	Diarmuid O'Carroll	IRL	16/03/97	A	19	(12)	9
15	Stephen O'Flynn	IRL	27/04/82	A	1	(11)	
1	Sean O'Neill		11/04/88	G	38		
26	Jordan Owens		09/07/89	A	34	(3)	26
11	Joshua Robinson		30/06/93	D	26	(2)	3
19	Matthew Snoddy		02/06/93	M	3	(9)	
23	Gavin Whyte		31/01/96	A	33	(1)	9

Dungannon Swifts FC

1949 • Stangmore Park (2,154) •
dungannonswifts.co.uk

Manager: Darren Murphy

2014

09/08	h	Institute	D	2-2	Liggett, Harpur (p)
13/08	a	Ballinamallard	D	1-1	McCaffrey
16/08	a	Glenavon	W	2-0	Liggett, Harpur
23/08	h	Ballymena	L	0-3	
30/08	h	Linfield	L	0-1	
02/09	h	Warrenpoint	L	0-2	
06/09	a	Portadown	L	0-1	
13/09	h	Crusaders	D	2-2	Douglas 2
20/09	a	Cliftonville	D	1-1	og (Brown)
27/09	a	Glentoran	L	0-1	
04/10	h	Coleraine	L	0-1	
11/10	a	Ballymena	D	2-2	Sanusi, Liggett
18/10	a	Ballinamallard	L	0-2	
25/10	a	Institute	D	1-1	Harpur
01/11	h	Cliftonville	L	1-3	Hazley
08/11	a	Linfield	L	0-4	
15/11	a	Coleraine	W	2-1	Harpur, Mitchell
22/11	h	Portadown	L	2-3	Wilson, Tomelty
28/11	h	Glenavon	W	2-1	Tomelty, Hazley
06/12	a	Warrenpoint	D	3-3	Mitchell 2, Harpur (p)
13/12	h	Glentoran	L	2-3	McCullough, Mitchell
19/12	a	Crusaders	L	0-1	
26/12	h	Ballinamallard	W	2-0	Burns 2

2015

03/01	h	Cliftonville	D	1-1	Mitchell
06/01	a	Glenavon	L	1-2	Harpur
23/01	a	Coleraine	W	2-1	Mitchell, Mullen
27/01	a	Institute	W	2-1	Liggett, Harpur
31/01	h	Crusaders	D	1-1	Harpur
14/02	h	Linfield	L	0-3	
21/02	a	Warrenpoint	D	1-1	Mitchell
06/03	h	Ballymena	W	1-0	Fitzpatrick
14/03	a	Portadown	D	1-1	Liggett
28/03	a	Glentoran	L	0-2	
04/04	a	Ballinamallard	L	0-1	
07/04	h	Coleraine	W	1-0	Mitchell
11/04	a	Warrenpoint	D	1-1	Glackin
18/04	h	Institute	D	1-1	og (Wilson)
25/04	a	Ballymena	L	0-1	

No	Name	Nat	DoB	Pos	Aps	(s)	Gls
5	David Armstrong		23/01/87	D	30	(1)	
24	Joshua Barton		23/03/94	M	8	(2)	
22	Francis Brennan		11/09/91	D	22	(3)	
14	Andrew Burns		29/05/92	D	26	(2)	2
1	Andy Coleman		13/06/85	G	33		
7	Jamie Douglas		04/07/92	A	15	(7)	2
6	Terry Fitzpatrick		23/03/82	M	19	(4)	1
17	Jamie Glackin		16/02/95	M	29	(6)	1
3	Cameron Grieve		22/12/81	A	15	(3)	
10	Ryan Harpur		01/12/88	M	28		7
8	Matt Hazley		25/02/87	M	22	(5)	2
18	Grant Hutchinson		11/11/89	M	20	(1)	
20	Stefan Lavery		20/07/93	A	5	(11)	
9	Gary Liggett		28/09/87	A	20	(15)	6
15	Kris Lowe		06/01/96	M	11	(1)	
4	Dermot McCaffrey		29/03/86	D	15		1
12	Sean McCashin		29/09/90	D	2	(1)	
2	David McCullough		24/04/87	D	20	(10)	1
26	Stefan McMaster		11/10/96	D	1	(1)	
16	Andrew Mitchell		25/01/94	A	19	(11)	8
26	Conor Mullen		19/10/96	A	1	(2)	1
27	Jarlath O'Rourke		13/02/95	D	9	(2)	
21	Alvin Rouse	BRB	17/01/80	G	5		
23	Abiola Sanusi	NGA	20/02/92	A	14	(6)	1
11	Jamie Tomelty		16/09/83	M	5	(5)	2
25	Douglas Wilson		03/03/93	A	24	(3)	1

Glenavon FC

1889 • Mourneview Park (4,160) •
glenavonfc.com

Major honours
Irish League (3) 1952, 1957, 1960; Irish Cup (6)
1957, 1959, 1961, 1992, 1997, 2014

Manager: Gary Hamilton

2014

09/08	h	Crusaders	D	2-2	Bradley, Lindsay
13/08	a	Warrenpoint	W	2-0	Marshall, Mulvenna (p)
16/08	h	Dungannon	L	0-2	
23/08	a	Cliftonville	D	3-3	Martyn 3
29/08	a	Ballymena	W	2-1	Lindsay, Marshall
02/09	a	Ballinamallard	W	1-0	Braniff
06/09	h	Institute	W	4-1	Bradley 2, McKeown, Martyn
13/09	h	Portadown	L	2-4	McKeown, Martyn
20/09	a	Linfield	W	1-0	Braniff
27/09	a	Coleraine	L	1-2	McGrory
04/10	h	Glentoran	L	1-2	Dillon
10/10	h	Warrenpoint	W	3-2	Hamilton, Braniff, Singleton
18/10	a	Crusaders	W	4-1	Braniff 2, Bradley, Caldwell
25/10	a	Ballymena	W	4-1	Neill, Bradley, Marshall, Hamilton
01/11	h	Linfield	L	1-2	Braniff
08/11	h	Glentoran	W	4-2	Hamilton 2, Marshall, Neill
15/11	a	Portadown	L	2-3	Marshall, Bradley
22/11	h	Cliftonville	L	1-3	Hamilton
28/11	h	Dungannon	L	1-2	Martyn
05/12	h	Institute	D	1-1	Hamilton
13/12	h	Coleraine	L	2-3	Martyn, Bradley
20/12	a	Ballinamallard	L	0-1	
26/12	a	Portadown	D	3-3	Bradley 2 (1p), Caldwell

2015

03/01	a	Ballymena	W	4-2	Martyn, O'Brien 3
06/01	h	Dungannon	W	2-1	Marshall, Braniff
23/01	h	Institute	W	2-1	Caldwell, Martyn
27/01	a	Coleraine	D	1-1	Braniff
31/01	h	Warrenpoint	D	2-2	Braniff, McCabe
14/02	a	Glentoran	W	2-1	Singleton, Hamilton
21/02	h	Crusaders	L	3-7	Marshall, Martyn, Braniff (p)
07/03	a	Ballinamallard	W	3-1	Patton, Martyn, Braniff (p)
14/03	a	Cliftonville	W	3-2	Braniff 2 (1p), Bradley
28/03	h	Linfield	W	1-0	Bradley
04/04	a	Glentoran	W	4-0	Singleton 2, Patton, McGrory
07/04	h	Cliftonville	W	5-0	Braniff 2, Bradley, Elebert, Patton
11/04	a	Linfield	W	2-0	Braniff, Martyn
18/04	h	Portadown	W	3-2	Singleton, Bradley, McGrory (p)
25/04	a	Crusaders	L	0-4	

No	Name	Nat	DoB	Pos	Aps	(s)	Gls
9	Guy Bates	ENG	31/10/85	A	4	(1)	
1	Alan Blayney		13/06/85	G	19		
10	Eoin Bradley		30/12/83	M	31	(2)	13
22	Kevin Braniff		04/03/83	A	33		16
16	Ciaran Caldwell		10/10/89	M	26	(3)	3
15	Conor Dillon	IRL	07/12/88	D	20		1
14	Andrew Drylie		26/09/97	A		(1)	
25	David Elebert	IRL	21/03/96	D	3	(2)	1
26	Adam Foley	IRL	11/12/89	M		(2)	
28	Darren Forsyth	IRL	21/02/88	A	3	(3)	
8	Gary Hamilton		06/10/80	A	4	(21)	7
28	Andrew Hoey		07/03/97	A		(1)	
11	Simon Kelly		04/07/84	M	7	(1)	
7	Andy Kilmartin		08/01/83	M	16	(4)	
6	Kris Lindsay		05/02/84	D	17	(3)	2
14	Matthew Lynch		07/03/99	M		(2)	
20	Rhys Marshall	IRL	16/01/95	D	34	(1)	7
24	Ciaran Martyn		25/03/80	M	25	(7)	12
23	Shane McCabe		21/12/81	M	25	(1)	1
4	Eddie McCallion		25/01/79	D	1	(2)	
33	James McGrath		19/04/88	G	19		
17	Andrew McGrory		15/12/91	M	22	(9)	3
30	Conor McKendry		21/10/98	A		(2)	
2	Gareth McKeown		14/07/83	D	20		2
21	Paddy McNally		20/08/94	D	7	(3)	
30	Tony McNamee	IRL	16/08/93	M	1	(3)	
88	Tiarnan Mulvenna	IRL	10/12/88	A	1	(2)	1
5	William Murphy		29/01/74	D	14	(3)	
3	Kyle Neill		30/03/78	D	23	(7)	2
19	Declan O'Brien		16/06/79	A	5	(3)	3
12	Mark Patton		21/06/89	M	9	(5)	3
10	Jamie Rea		23/05/97	D	1		
27	James Singleton		22/08/95	D	28	(2)	5
14	Mark Sykes		04/08/97	M		(2)	

Glentoran FC

1882 • The Oval (9,400) • glentoran.com

Major honours

Irish League (23) 1894, 1897, 1905, 1912, 1913, 1921, 1925, 1931, 1951, 1953, 1964, 1967, 1968, 1970, 1972, 1977, 1981, 1988, 1992, 1999, 2003, 2005, 2009; Irish Cup (22) 1914, 1917, 1921, 1932, 1933, 1935, 1951, 1966, 1973, 1983, 1985, 1986, 1987, 1988, 1990, 1996, 1998, 2000, 2001, 2004, 2013, 2015

Manager: Eddie Patterson

2014

09/08	a	Cliftonville	D	0-0	
13/08	h	Linfield	L	2-3	*Scullion 2*
16/08	h	Warrenpoint	W	3-1	*Allen 2, McCaffrey*
23/08	a	Ballinamallard	D	2-2	*Magee, Allen*
30/08	a	Crusaders	L	0-1	
02/09	h	Portadown	D	1-1	*Scullion*
06/09	h	Coleraine	W	2-0	*og (Beverland), Scullion*
13/09	a	Ballymena	D	2-2	*McCaffrey (p), Stewart*
20/09	a	Institute	D	1-1	*Allen*
27/09	h	Dungannon	W	1-0	*McAlorum*
04/10	a	Glenavon	W	2-1	*Stewart, Scullion*
11/10	h	Crusaders	L	1-3	*Kane*
18/10	a	Coleraine	L	0-1	
25/10	a	Warrenpoint	W	5-2	*Allen 3, Kane, Nelson*
01/11	h	Ballymena	W	4-0	*O'Hanlon, Allen, Stewart 2*
08/11	h	Glenavon	L	2-4	*Allen, Stewart*
15/11	a	Linfield	D	2-2	*McCaffrey, Addis*
22/11	h	Institute	W	2-1	*Magee, Gordon*
29/11	a	Portadown	L	1-3	*Scullion*
06/12	h	Ballinamallard	W	3-1	*Gordon 2, Allen*
13/12	a	Dungannon	W	3-2	*Allen, Stewart, Henderson*
20/12	h	Cliftonville	W	2-1	*Scullion, McKee*
26/12	a	Linfield	L	1-2	*Gordon*

2015

01/01	h	Institute	W	4-1	*Scullion 2, McKee, Stewart*
03/01	a	Warrenpoint	W	5-0	*Stewart 3 (1p), McKee, Gordon*
17/01	h	Crusaders	L	1-2	*Stewart*
31/01	a	Cliftonville	D	1-1	*Stewart*
10/02	a	Ballymena	W	3-1	*Gordon, Scullion, Allen*
14/02	h	Glenavon	L	1-2	*Gordon*
21/02	a	Coleraine	D	1-1	*Gordon*
07/03	a	Portadown	D	1-1	*Stewart*
13/03	h	Ballinamallard	W	4-0	*Allen 2, Gordon, McCaffrey*
28/03	h	Dungannon	W	2-0	*Allen, McAlorum*
04/04	a	Glenavon	L	0-4	
07/04	h	Linfield	L	1-2	*McCaffrey*
11/04	h	Portadown	D	0-0	
18/04	a	Crusaders	L	0-2	
25/04	h	Cliftonville	W	1-0	*McCaffrey*

No	Name	Nat	DoB	Pos	Aps	(s)	Gls
19	Jonny Addis		27/09/92	M	26	(8)	1
9	Curtis Allen		22/02/88	A	29	(3)	15
5	Calum Birney		19/04/93	D	20	(2)	
2	William Garrett		31/08/91	D	20	(3)	
22	Steven Gordon		27/07/93	D	21	(7)	9
27	George Gray		20/03/96	D	1		
14	Niall Henderson		07/02/88	M	28	(3)	1
18	Aaron Hogg		14/01/88	G	5		
25	Barry Holland		10/05/84	D	26	(1)	
8	David Howland		17/09/86	M	8	(2)	
3	Marcus Kane		08/12/91	M	31	(1)	2
18	Chris Keenan		27/01/87	G	2		
6	Jay Magee		04/05/88	D	10	(1)	2
16	Stephen McAlorum		11/06/86	M	31	(3)	2
4	Francis McCaffrey		22/04/93	M	21	(10)	6
26	Stephen McCullough		30/08/94	D	12	(4)	
27	Sandy McDermott		03/11/94	M		(1)	
19	John McGuigan		26/08/93	M		(2)	
24	Danny McKee		10/06/95	A	7	(22)	3
19	Mark Miskimmin		11/06/88	A	2		
1	Elliott Morris		04/05/81	G	31		
21	Kym Nelson		18/07/95	M	20	(7)	1
20	Jim O'Hanlon		14/03/93	M	3	(7)	1
7	David Scullion		27/04/84	A	33	(3)	10
27	Colin Smith		02/05/94	D		(1)	
11	Jordan Stewart		31/03/95	A	31	(5)	13

Institute FC

1905 • Riverside (1,570) • stutefc.co.uk

Manager: Paul Kee

2014

09/08	a	Dungannon	D	2-2	*O'Flynn 2*
13/08	h	Coleraine	W	2-0	*S Curry, McCauley*
16/08	h	Cliftonville	L	2-3	*McKeever, S Curry*
23/08	h	Linfield	D	1-1	*P McLaughlin*
30/08	h	Warrenpoint	W	1-0	*O'Flynn*
02/09	a	Ballymena	L	1-2	*O'Flynn*
06/09	h	Glenavon	L	1-4	*Armstrong*
13/09	a	Ballinamallard	W	3-2	*McFadden, O'Flynn, McCrudden*
20/09	h	Glentoran	D	1-1	*McBride*
26/09	a	Crusaders	L	2-3	*O'Flynn 2*
04/10	h	Portadown	L	0-4	
13/10	a	Linfield	L	1-3	*O'Flynn*
17/10	a	Warrenpoint	W	1-0	*McVeigh*
25/10	h	Dungannon	D	1-1	*O'Flynn*
01/11	a	Coleraine	L	0-3	*(w/o; original result 0-4)*
08/11	a	Portadown	L	1-4	*McKeever*
15/11	h	Ballinamallard	L	0-2	
22/11	a	Glentoran	L	1-2	*Hume*
29/11	h	Crusaders	D	1-1	*A Walsh (p)*
05/12	a	Glenavon	D	1-1	*O'Flynn*
13/12	a	Cliftonville	L	0-4	
20/12	h	Ballymena	L	1-2	*Hume*
26/12	h	Warrenpoint	D	1-1	*Hume*

2015

01/01	a	Glentoran	L	1-4	*Hume*
05/01	a	Portadown	L	1-2	*S Curry*
23/01	a	Glenavon	L	1-2	*Hume*
27/01	h	Dungannon	L	1-2	*Hume*
31/01	h	Coleraine	L	0-2	
14/02	a	Ballymena	L	0-3	
21/02	h	Ballinamallard	D	1-1	*McCrudden*
07/03	a	Crusaders	L	1-3	*Hume*
14/03	h	Linfield	L	0-1	
28/03	a	Cliftonville	L	1-5	*D Curry*
04/04	a	Warrenpoint	L	1-5	*D Walsh*
07/04	a	Ballinamallard	L	0-2	
11/04	h	Ballymena	L	1-2	*S Curry*
18/04	a	Dungannon	D	1-1	*Burke*
25/04	a	Coleraine	L	1-3	*McIntyre*

No	Name	Nat	DoB	Pos	Aps	(s)	Gls
38	Jordan Armstrong		21/11/96	A	3	(4)	1
16	Jude Ballard		25/11/94	A	1	(5)	
3	Peter Bradley		26/05/91	D	6	(1)	
28	Cormac Burke		11/08/93	M	12	(7)	1
2	Graham Crown		02/03/92	D	35	(1)	
4	John Curran		17/05/82	M	1		
20	Dean Curry		11/11/94	D	20	(3)	1
12	Stephen Curry		05/11/90	A	25	(2)	4
1	Saul Deeney	IRL	23/03/83	G	3		
26	Ben Doherty		24/03/97	M	4	(8)	
1	Michael Doherty		19/10/83	G	4		
27	Ronan Doherty	IRL	10/01/96	M	2	(4)	
41	James Dunne		02/07/97	A	1	(1)	
1	Eugene Ferry		26/08/88	G	13	(1)	
24	Mark Forker		03/04/88	A	19	(2)	
30	Martin Gallagher		26/10/90	G	13		
19	David Healy		17/05/94	A		(1)	
32	Gary Henderson		02/07/95	D	4		
35	Robbie Hume		02/02/92	M	25	(2)	7
34	Rory Kelly		07/08/91	G	1		
39	Dylan King		27/08/98	D	1		
19	Thomas McBride		30/05/92	M	5	(1)	1
7	Darren McCauley		21/02/91	M	5		1
10	Michael McCrudden		31/07/91	A	10	(5)	2
11	Darren McFadden		21/01/93	M	6	(3)	1
21	Jamie McIntyre		01/12/96	A	2	(8)	1
6	Declan McKeever		20/10/86	M	24	(5)	2
3	Colm McLaughlin	IRL	01/08/93	M		(1)	
5	Paddy McLaughlin		10/10/79	D	29	(1)	1
8	Duwayne McManus		20/01/87	M	26		
31	Paul McVeigh	IRL	25/05/92	D	6	(7)	1
15	Stephen O'Donnell		01/09/92	D	18	(4)	
9	Stephen O'Flynn	IRL	27/04/82	A	18	(1)	10
23	Sean Roddy	IRL	02/10/85	D	1		
29	Mark Scoltock		26/03/85	D	21	(1)	
36	Graeme Taylor		14/06/91	D	1		
31	Jordan Thompson		18/09/96	M		(2)	
18	Lee Toland		02/10/93	D	3	(4)	
17	Ryan Varma		31/08/96	M	1	(1)	
14	Aaron Walsh		06/08/82	A	32		1
7	Davitt Walsh		25/07/86	A	3	(2)	1
25	Corey Wilson		07/11/93	G	4		
22	Matthew Young		17/03/96	M	10	(6)	

Linfield FC

1886 • Windsor Park (15,602) • linfieldfc.com

Major honours

Irish League (51) 1891, 1892, 1893, 1895, 1898, 1902, 1904, 1907, 1908, 1909, 1911, 1914, 1922, 1923, 1930, 1932, 1934, 1935, 1949, 1950, 1954, 1955, 1956, 1959, 1961, 1962, 1966, 1969, 1971, 1975, 1978, 1979, 1980, 1982, 1983, 1984, 1985, 1986, 1987, 1989, 1993, 1994, 2000, 2001, 2004, 2006, 2007, 2008, 2010, 2011, 2012; Irish Cup (42) 1891, 1892, 1893, 1895, 1898, 1899, 1902, 1904, 1912, 1913, 1915, 1916, 1919, 1922, 1923, 1930, 1931, 1934, 1936, 1939, 1942, 1945, 1946, 1948, 1950, 1953, 1960, 1962, 1963, 1970, 1978, 1980, 1982, 1994, 1995, 2002, 2006, 2007, 2008, 2010, 2011, 2012

Manager: Warren Feeney

2014

09/08	a	Portadown	L	0-3	
13/08	a	Glentoran	W	3-2	*Burns 2, Thompson*
16/08	a	Coleraine	W	2-1	*M Clarke 2*
23/08	a	Institute	D	1-1	*Sproule*
30/08	a	Dungannon	W	1-0	*Sproule*
02/09	a	Cliftonville	D	0-0	
13/09	h	Warrenpoint	W	1-0	*Haughey*
20/09	h	Glenavon	L	0-1	
27/09	a	Ballinamallard	W	3-1	*Lowry, Burns 2*
29/09	a	Crusaders	D	2-2	*Waterworth, Carvill*
04/10	h	Ballymena	W	3-2	*Hegarty 2, Burns*
13/10	h	Institute	W	3-1	*Hegarty, Waterworth, Lowry*
18/10	h	Cliftonville	L	1-3	*Waterworth*
25/10	h	Crusaders	L	1-2	*Waterworth*
01/11	a	Glenavon	W	2-1	*Waterworth, Callacher*
08/11	h	Dungannon	W	4-0	*Burns 2, Waterworth, Sproule*
15/11	h	Glentoran	D	2-2	*Morrow, Lowry*
22/11	a	Warrenpoint	W	2-1	*Waterworth, Haughey*
29/11	h	Coleraine	W	2-1	*Waterworth, Burns*
06/12	a	Ballymena	W	3-2	*Lowry, Morrow, Waterworth*
13/12	h	Ballinamallard	W	3-0	*Burns 2, Waterworth*
20/12	h	Portadown	W	3-2	*Callacher, Burns (p), Morrow*
26/12	h	Glentoran	W	2-1	*Morrow, Sproule*

2015

01/01	a	Crusaders	L	1-2	*Waterworth*
03/01	h	Coleraine	D	1-1	*Waterworth*
27/01	a	Ballinamallard	D	1-1	*Waterworth*
31/01	h	Ballymena	W	2-1	*McCann, R Clarke*
10/02	h	Cliftonville	D	2-2	*Burns (p), Mulgrew*
14/02	a	Dungannon	W	3-0	*Burns, Callacher, Waterworth*
20/02	h	Portadown	L	1-2	*Feeney*
07/03	h	Warrenpoint	W	3-0	*R Clarke, Morrow, og (Boyle)*
14/03	a	Institute	W	1-0	*Burns*
28/03	a	Glenavon	L	0-1	
07/04	a	Glentoran	W	2-1	*Burns (p), Haughey*
11/04	h	Glenavon	L	0-2	
18/04	a	Cliftonville	D	2-2	*Carvill, Burns (p)*
21/04	h	Crusaders	W	3-1	*Sproule, Carvill, Waterworth*
25/04	a	Portadown	D	1-1	*Burns*

No	Name	Nat	DoB	Pos	Aps	(s)	Gls
2	Glenn Belezika	ENG	24/12/94	D	10		
27	Rodney Brown		13/08/95	M	1	(5)	
14	Aaron Burns		29/05/92	M	36		17
6	Jimmy Callacher		11/06/91	M	25	(5)	3
10	Michael Carvill		03/04/88	M	12	(17)	3
16	Matthew Clarke		03/03/94	D	17	(1)	2
32	Ross Clarke		17/05/93	A	18	(6)	2
28	Seanan Clucas		08/11/92	M	3	(8)	
35	Gareth Deane		14/06/94	G	1		
21	Warren Feeney		17/01/81	A	5	(3)	1
23	Reece Glendinning		09/06/95	D	4	(3)	
19	Ross Glendinning		18/05/93	G	16		
5	Mark Haughey		23/01/91	D	29		3
4	Chris Hegarty		13/08/92	D	14		3
8	Stephen Lowry		14/10/86	M	33	(3)	4
18	Grant McCann		14/04/80	M	5		1
12	Kirk Millar		07/07/92	A	7	(14)	
17	Sammy Morrow		03/03/85	A	17	(6)	5
22	Jamie Mulgrew		05/06/86	M	22	(6)	1
36	Dale Patton		21/09/96	A		(1)	
31	Niall Quinn		02/08/93	D	24	(1)	
3	Jamie Richards	ENG	24/06/94	D	14	(1)	
26	Ivan Sproule		18/02/81	A	23	(4)	5
9	Peter Thompson		02/05/84	A	8	(6)	1
33	Jonathan Tuffey		20/01/87	G	21		
15	Sean Ward		12/01/84	D	22	(1)	
7	Andrew Waterworth		11/04/86	A	31	(3)	15

NORTHERN IRELAND

Portadown FC

1924 • Shamrock Park (15,800) •
portadownfc.co.uk
Major honours
*Irish League (4) 1990, 1991, 1996, 2002; Irish Cup (3)
1991, 1999, 2005*
Manager: Ronnie McFall

2014
09/08	h	Linfield	W	3-0	*Twigg 2, og (Ward)*
13/08	h	Cliftonville	L	0-1	
16/08	a	Ballymena	L	2-3	*Garrett, Murray (p)*
23/08	h	Crusaders	W	3-1	*Murray, McAllister 2*
29/08	a	Coleraine	D	0-0	
02/09	a	Glentoran	D	1-1	*Murray (p)*
06/09	h	Dungannon	W	1-0	*Murray*
13/09	a	Glenavon	W	4-2	*Mackle, Casement, Murray (p), P McMahon*
20/09	h	Ballinamallard	W	3-0	*Mackle, Murray 2*
27/09	h	Warrenpoint	D	2-2	*McAllister, Twigg*
04/10	a	Institute	W	4-0	*Mouncey, P McMahon 2, Twigg*
11/10	a	Cliftonville	L	0-2	
18/10	h	Ballymena	W	2-1	*P McMahon, Twigg*
25/10	h	Coleraine	L	0-2	
01/11	a	Ballinamallard	W	2-0	*Casement (p), Twigg*
08/11	h	Institute	W	4-1	*Murray, Twigg, Casement, O'Hara*
15/11	h	Glenavon	W	3-2	*Casement (p), Mackle, McAllister*
22/11	a	Dungannon	W	3-2	*Murray, Twigg, Mouncey*
29/11	a	Glentoran	W	3-1	*McAllister, Twigg, Casement (p)*
06/12	a	Crusaders	W	3-2	*Gault, McAllister, Murray*
12/12	a	Warrenpoint	L	1-2	*Breen*
20/12	a	Linfield	L	2-3	*Mackle, McAllister*
26/12	h	Glenavon	D	3-3	*Murray, McAllister 2*

2015
01/01	a	Coleraine	W	1-0	*McAllister*
05/01	h	Institute	W	2-1	*Mackle, Gault*
17/01	h	Ballymena	D	5-5	*Twigg 3, P McMahon, Murray*
23/01	a	Crusaders	L	0-6	
31/01	a	Ballinamallard	D	0-0	
14/02	h	Cliftonville	L	0-2	
20/02	a	Linfield	W	2-1	*og (Callacher), Mackle*
07/03	h	Glentoran	D	1-1	*P McMahon*
14/03	h	Dungannon	D	1-1	*Casement*
28/03	a	Warrenpoint	D	0-0	
04/04	a	Cliftonville	L	0-4	
07/04	h	Crusaders	W	1-0	*Mouncey*
11/04	a	Glentoran	D	0-0	
18/04	a	Glentoran	L	2-3	*P McMahon, Twigg*
25/04	h	Linfield	D	1-1	*Murray*

No	Name	Nat	DoB	Pos	Aps	(s)	Gls
15	James Begley		02/07/92	A		(1)	
6	Gary Breen	IRL	17/03/89	D	29		1
13	Billy Brennan	IRL	06/03/85	G	4	(2)	
2	Chris Casement		12/01/88	D	33		6
19	Shea Conaty		19/01/98	A	9	(10)	
17	Chris Ferguson		01/09/97	A		(1)	
20	Robert Garrett		05/05/88	M	33		1
16	Michael Gault		15/04/83	M	26	(1)	2
15	Padraig Judge		13/03/96	M		(2)	
23	Jordan Lyttle		14/05/96	D	7	(2)	
8	Sean Mackle	SCO	10/04/88	M	33	(3)	6
26	Márcio Soares	POR	07/04/96	A	1	(2)	
10	Mark McAllister		26/04/88	A	27	(3)	10
14	Paul McElroy		07/07/94	A	1	(3)	
12	Matthew McMahon		23/01/95	M		(2)	
7	Pete McMahon	IRL	20/04/89	M	36	(1)	7
1	David Miskelly		03/09/79	G	34		
11	Tim Mouncey		27/04/82	M	17	(11)	3
9	Darren Murray		24/10/91	A	21	(7)	13
4	Keith O'Hara		03/02/81	D	23		1
12	Ken Oman	IRL	29/07/82	D	6	(3)	
5	Chris Ramsey		24/05/90	D	16	(5)	
3	Ross Redman		23/11/89	D	36		
24	Jake Richardson		18/08/96	D	4		
25	Christian Stewart		13/02/96	D	1	(2)	
18	Gary Twigg	SCO	19/03/84	A	21	(9)	13

Warrenpoint Town FC

1987 • Milltown (1,280) •
warrenpointtownfc.co.uk
Manager: Barry Gray

2014
09/08	a	Ballymena	L	0-2	
13/08	h	Glenavon	L	0-2	
16/08	a	Glentoran	L	1-3	*S Hughes*
23/08	h	Coleraine	L	1-3	*McVeigh*
30/08	a	Institute	L	0-1	
02/09	a	Dungannon	W	2-0	*S Hughes (p), O'Connor*
06/09	h	Cliftonville	D	1-1	*S Hughes*
13/09	a	Linfield	L	0-1	
20/09	h	Crusaders	L	0-3	
27/09	a	Portadown	D	2-2	*McCabe, Breen*
03/10	h	Ballinamallard	W	2-0	*D Hughes (p), Cowan*
10/10	a	Glenavon	L	2-3	*Devlin, Breen*
17/10	h	Institute	L	0-1	
25/10	h	Glentoran	L	2-5	*D Hughes, M Hughes*
01/11	a	Crusaders	L	0-3	
07/11	a	Cliftonville	L	1-3	*O'Connor*
15/11	h	Ballymena	D	2-2	*D Hughes 2*
22/11	h	Linfield	L	1-2	*D Hughes*
28/11	a	Ballinamallard	L	1-3	*D Hughes*
06/12	h	Dungannon	D	3-3	*O'Connor, D Hughes 2 (1p)*
12/12	h	Portadown	W	2-1	*O'Connor 2*
20/12	a	Coleraine	D	0-0	
26/12	a	Institute	D	1-1	*S Hughes*

2015
01/01	h	Ballymena	W	2-0	*D Hughes 2 (1p)*
03/01	h	Glentoran	L	0-5	
17/01	a	Cliftonville	D	2-2	*S Hughes, M Hughes*
23/01	h	Ballinamallard	W	7-0	*Bagnall, McGuigan, S Hughes 3, D Hughes, Forsyth*
31/01	a	Glenavon	D	2-2	*McDonald, og (McGrath)*
14/02	a	Crusaders	L	1-4	*McCabe (p)*
21/02	h	Dungannon	D	1-1	*McGuigan*
07/03	a	Linfield	L	0-3	
14/03	a	Coleraine	L	0-5	
28/03	h	Portadown	D	0-0	
04/04	h	Institute	W	5-1	*D Hughes 3 (2p), Forsyth, S Hughes*
07/04	a	Ballymena	L	1-2	*D Hughes*
11/04	a	Dungannon	D	1-1	*King*
18/04	a	Coleraine	L	1-2	*S Hughes*
25/04	a	Ballinamallard	D	3-3	*D Hughes 2 (1p), Frazer*

No	Name	Nat	DoB	Pos	Aps	(s)	Gls
16	Liam Bagnall		17/05/92	D	29	(2)	1
21	John Boyle		01/03/96	D	30	(3)	
27	Jonathan Breen		25/02/91	A	10	(7)	2
4	John Cowan		07/07/81	D	20	(5)	1
22	Ruairi Devlin		02/05/90	M	21	(11)	1
28	Darren Forsyth	IRL	21/02/88	A	5	(6)	2
20	Jonathan Frazer		30/05/96	A	4	(3)	1
7	Ciaran Gargan		09/02/86	M	3	(1)	
23	Timmy Grant		15/05/83	A	5	(19)	
25	Marty Havern		25/02/87	A	1	(7)	
9	Daniel Hughes		03/05/92	A	25	(3)	17
17	Mark Hughes		23/03/85	M	31	(2)	2
10	Stephen Hughes		18/11/86	A	28	(4)	10
2	Darren King		16/10/85	D	31	(2)	1
24	Martin Marron		24/01/96	G	13		
11	Stephen McCabe		03/07/84	M	17	(9)	2
19	Jack McCreanor		01/07/94	M		(1)	
3	Conor McDonald	IRL	14/06/95	M	12	(1)	1
3	Stephen McDonnell		28/03/92	D	4		
19	John McGuigan		26/08/93	M	11		2
5	Dermot McVeigh		24/07/90	D	37		1
18	Stephen Moan		04/09/90	D	25	(1)	
20	Ciaran O'Connor	IRL	04/07/96	M	13	(4)	5
1	Jonny Parr		26/11/85	G	15		
12	Padraig Smith		30/09/82	M	18	(5)	

Top goalscorers

31	Joe Gormley (Cliftonville)
27	Paul Heatley (Crusaders)
26	Jordan Owens (Crusaders)
17	Aaron Burns (Linfield) Daniel Hughes (Warrenpoint)
16	Kevin Braniff (Glenavon)
15	Curtis Allen (Glentoran) Andrew Waterworth (Linfield)
13	Eoin Bradley (Glenavon) Jordan Stewart (Glentoran) Darren Murray (Portadown) Gary Twigg (Portadown)

Promoted club

Carrick Rangers FC

1939 • Taylors Avenue (6,000) •
carrickrangers.co.uk
Manager: Glenn Taggart

Second level final table 2014/15
		Pld	W	D	L	F	A	Pts
1	Carrick Rangers FC	26	19	5	2	54	22	62
2	Bangor FC	26	18	6	2	71	32	60
3	Ards FC	26	16	8	2	61	30	56
4	Harland & Wolff Welders FC	26	15	5	6	59	37	50
5	Larne FC	26	13	3	10	52	36	42
6	Dergview FC	26	8	9	9	40	43	33
7	Armagh City FC	26	9	5	12	38	48	32
8	Knockbreda FC	26	9	3	14	31	43	30
9	Ballyclare Comrades FC	26	8	4	14	46	48	28
10	Lisburn Distillery FC	26	8	4	14	38	58	28
11	Loughgall FC	26	7	6	13	36	54	27
12	Donegal Celtic FC	26	5	9	12	35	42	24
13	PSNI FC	26	6	5	15	27	64	23
14	Dundela FC	26	3	4	19	34	65	13

Promotion/Relegation play-offs
(28/04/15 & 01/05/15)
Bangor 2-0 Warrenpoint
Warrenpoint 2-0 Bangor *(aet)*
(2-2; Warrenpoint 3-1 on pens)

DOMESTIC CUP

Irish Cup 2014/15

FIFTH ROUND

(10/01/15)
Annagh United 1-3 Ballyclare
Armagh City 3-0 Newtowne
Ballymena 4-0 Crumlin Star
Bangor 4-0 Brantwood
Cliftonville 6-0 Ards Rangers
Coleraine 1-3 Warrenpoint
Crusaders 6-0 Newington YC
Dungannon 4-2 Ballinamallard *(aet)*
Glentoran 2-0 Ards
Harland & Wolff Welders 2-0 Derriaghy CC
Institute 5-1 Loughgall
Moyola Park 2-3 Glenavon
Portstewart 3-2 Dundela
PSNI 1-2 Portadown *(aet)*
Tobermore United 0-2 Linfield

(20/01/15)
Larne 1-2 Carrick Rangers

SIXTH ROUND

(07/02/15)
Ballyclare 0-0 Dungannon *(aet; 4-5 on pens)*
Bangor 0-2 Crusaders
Carrick Rangers 3-1 Institute *(aet)*
Cliftonville 1-2 Ballymena
Glentoran 4-1 Armagh City
Harland & Wolff Welders 2-0 Glenavon
Linfield 5-0 Warrenpoint
Portstewart 0-2 Portadown

QUARTER-FINALS

(28/02/15)
Crusaders 4-1 Carrick Rangers *(Clarke 55, 85, O'Carroll 65, Whyte 86; McClean 42og)*

Glentoran 3-0 Dungannon *(Allen 14, Kane 67, Henderson 85p)*

Harland & Wolff Welders 2-3 Ballymena *(McLellan 35p, 51; Boyce 79, Tipton 85, Thompson 90)*

Portadown 3-2 Linfield *(Casement 7p, Twigg 21, 42; Lowry 73, 84)*

SEMI-FINALS

(21/03/15)
Ballymena 1-3 Portadown *(Boyce 70; McAllister 4, Gault 15, P McMahon 27)*

Crusaders 0-1 Glentoran *(Allen 39)*

FINAL

(02/05/15)
The Oval, Belfast
GLENTORAN FC 1 *(Scullion 54)*
PORTADOWN FC 0
Referee: *Dunlop*
GLENTORAN: *Morris, Garrett, Birney, Holland, Gordon, Kane, Henderson (Addis 89), McAlorum, Scullion (McCaffrey 89), Allen, Stewart (Nelson 90+3)*
PORTADOWN: *Miskelly, Casement, Redman, O'Hara, Breen, P McMahon, Gault, Mackle, Garrett, Twigg, McAllister (Murray 72)*

Glentoran players parade the trophy after their Irish Cup final win against Portadown at The Oval

NORWAY
Norges Fotballforbund (NFF)

Address	Serviceboks 1	**President**	Yngve Hallén
	Ullevaal stadion	**General secretary**	Kjetil P Siem
	NO-0840 Oslo	**Media officer**	Yngve Haavik
Tel	+47 210 29300	**Year of formation**	1902
Fax	+47 210 29301	**National stadium**	Ullevaal, Oslo
E-mail	nff@fotball.no		(27,182)
Website	fotball.no		

TIPPELIGAEN CLUBS

 1 **Aalesunds FK**

 2 **FK Bodø/Glimt**

 3 **SK Brann**

 4 **FK Haugesund**

 5 **Lillestrøm SK**

 6 **Molde FK**

 7 **Odds BK**

 8 **Rosenborg BK**

 9 **Sandnes Ulf**

 10 **Sarpsborg 08 FF**

 11 **Sogndal Fotball**

 12 **Stabæk Fotball**

 13 **IK Start**

 14 **Strømsgodset IF**

 15 **Viking FK**

 16 **Vålerenga Fotball**

PROMOTED CLUBS

 17 **Sandefjord Fotball**

 18 **Tromsø IL**

 19 **Mjøndalen IF**

Tromsø 18

2 Bodø

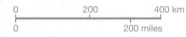

8 Trondheim

6 Molde

1 Aalesund

11 Sogndal

Bergen

3

14 ~Drammen

Oslo~ 12 16

Haugesund

4

19 ~Mjøndalen

10

Lillestrøm~ 5

15 ~Stavanger

7 ~Skien

Sarpsborg

Sandefjord~ 17

9 ~Sandnes

13 Kristiansand

KEY:
- – UEFA Champions League
- – UEFA Europa League
- – Promoted
- – Relegated

Historic double for Molde

Molde FK were the toast of Norwegian football in 2014 as they reaffirmed their status as the country's team of the decade by regaining the Tippeligaen title and retaining the Norwegian Cup. Furthermore, their first domestic double was achieved with a new, unheralded coach, Tor Ole Skullerud proving to be the perfect replacement for the departed Ole Gunnar Solskjær.

Odds BK exceeded expectations in the league and also reached the cup final, while fallen giants Rosenborg BK completed a fourth straight season without silverware. Meanwhile, deposed champions Strømsgodet IF unearthed a gem in 15-year-old Martin Ødegaard.

SERIEMESTER 2014

| Blues bag third Tippeligaen title in four years | Odd defeated in Oslo as Norwegian Cup retained | Wonderkid Ødegaard joins Real Madrid |

Domestic league

With Solskjær, the man who led Molde to two league titles and one cup, lured away to the English Premier League, there was understandable concern among the locals that the club's treasure hunt might be over. Skullerud's only previous claim to fame had been as the coach of Norway's Under-21 team. But if his appointment was a gamble, it certainly paid off.

Unlike in 2013, Molde got off to a great start. Although they lost their opening away fixture against Odd, there was no stopping them thereafter. Five straight victories followed, including one at previously unbeaten Rosenborg, and once at the top of the table, Skullerud's side would not be dislodged. Indeed, they became invincible, putting together a 24-match unbeaten run that only ended once the championship title was safely under lock and key, a 2-1 win at Viking FK sealing the deal with four fixtures still to complete.

No other team could live with Molde's consistency. Their defence, containing Norwegian internationals Ørjan Håskjold Nyland, Martin Linnes, Vegard Forren and Per-Egil Flo, was rock-solid, conceding only 24 goals, while there was variety and efficiency in attack, where 20-year-old winger Mohamed Elyounoussi, who struck 13 goals,

enjoyed an outstanding debut season. Although Molde lost two of those last four games, they still ended up with a league-best tally of 71 points.

Record champions Rosenborg finished powerfully under new coach Kåre Ingebrigtsen to snatch second place from Odd and suggest that better times might soon be around the corner after four barren years. Optimism about the future was rather less forthcoming at another major club, SK Brann, who, despite the recruitment of esteemed Swedish coach Rikard Norling, allowed the unthinkable to happen and were relegated, their play-off defeat by Mjøndalen IF ending an unbroken 27-year run among the elite.

Domestic cup

Belatedly edged out of the league runners-up spot, Odd had the opportunity to erase that disappointment in the Norwegian Cup – a competition they had won 11 times during the early years of the 20th century and again in 2000. But Dag-Eilev Fagermo's side were out of sorts going into the final with Molde. Indeed, they had lost their last league game 2-0 to the champions, and history was to repeat itself in the Ullevaal as late goals from Fredrik Gulbrandsen and Elyounoussi enabled Molde to retain the trophy and complete their historic double.

Europe

Given their fabulous domestic form, Molde might have expected to make waves in Europe, but they were dumped out of the UEFA Europa League in the third qualifying round following a painful 2-1 home defeat by FC Zorya Luhansk. That was the furthest any of the five Norwegian sides managed to get, Rosenborg matching them after reversing a first-leg deficit against Sligo Rovers FC (the 2-1 defeat in Trondheim cost coach Per Joar Hansen his job) but then going out on the away-goals rule to Kardemir Karabükspor.

National team

Norway began the 2014/15 international season with the headline-making debut of 15-year-old Martin Ødegaard. The precocious young midfielder would later become a household name across planet football after agreeing to leave Strømsgodset IF for the mighty Real Madrid CF, but although he became a regular in Per-Mathias Høgmo's side as the UEFA EURO 2016 qualifying campaign progressed, there was not too much else for Norwegian fans to get excited about. They effectively surrendered hope of challenging Croatia and Italy for automatic qualification by losing to both teams and then drawing 0-0 at home to Azerbaijan – a result that, with Bulgaria breathing down their neck, also placed their play-off prospects in jeopardy.

DOMESTIC SEASON AT A GLANCE

Tippeligaen 2014 final table

		Pld	Home					Away					Total					Pts
			W	D	L	F	A	W	D	L	F	A	W	D	L	F	A	
1	**Molde FK**	**30**	**12**	**2**	**1**	**40**	**14**	**10**	**3**	**2**	**22**	**10**	**22**	**5**	**3**	**62**	**24**	**71**
2	Rosenborg BK	30	12	1	2	40	20	6	5	4	24	23	18	6	6	64	43	60
3	Odds BK	30	10	3	2	30	14	7	4	4	22	18	17	7	6	52	32	58
4	Strømsgodset IF	30	10	2	3	28	18	5	3	7	20	24	15	5	10	48	42	50
5	Lillestrøm SK	30	10	2	3	33	12	3	5	7	16	23	13	7	10	49	35	46
6	Vålerenga Fotball	30	8	5	2	33	19	3	4	8	26	34	11	9	10	59	53	42
7	Aalesunds FK	30	6	5	4	25	14	5	3	7	15	25	11	8	11	40	39	41
8	Sarpsborg 08 FF	30	7	6	2	25	17	3	4	8	16	31	10	10	10	41	48	40
9	Stabæk Fotball	30	6	3	6	21	21	5	3	7	23	31	11	6	13	44	52	39
10	Viking FK	30	4	5	6	24	23	4	7	4	18	19	8	12	10	42	42	36
11	FK Haugesund	30	6	4	5	27	20	4	2	9	16	29	10	6	14	43	49	36
12	IK Start	30	5	4	6	28	28	5	1	9	19	32	10	5	15	47	60	35
13	FK Bodø/Glimt	30	6	5	4	27	29	4	0	11	18	31	10	5	15	45	60	35
14	SK Brann	30	4	1	10	16	21	4	4	7	25	33	8	5	17	41	54	29
15	Sogndal Fotball	30	5	3	7	16	18	1	3	11	15	31	6	6	18	31	49	24
16	Sandnes Ulf	30	4	5	6	14	20	0	5	10	13	33	4	10	16	27	53	22

European qualification 2015/16

Champion/Cup winner: Molde FK (second qualifying round)

Rosenborg BK (first qualifying round)
Odds BK (first qualifying round)
Strømsgodset IF (first qualifying round)

Top scorer	Vidar Örn Kjartansson (Vålerenga), 25 goals
Relegated clubs	Sandnes Ulf, Sogndal Fotball, SK Brann
Promoted clubs	Sandefjord Fotball, Tromsø IL, Mjøndalen IF
Cup final	Molde FK 2-0 Odds BK

Team of the season
(4-4-2)

Coach: Skullerud (Molde)

Grytebust (Aalesund)

Linnes (Molde) — Hagen (Odd) — Forren (Molde) — Flo (Molde)

Samuelsen (Odd) — Jensen (Rosenborg)
Ødegaard (Strømsgodset) — Elyounoussi (Molde)

Kjartansson (Vålerenga) — Gulbrandsen (Molde)

Player of the season

Jone Samuelsen
(Odds BK)

A Tippeligaen stalwart for several years, first with Viking FK then, since 2010, with Odd, Samuelsen suddenly raised his game to a new level in 2014, the year he turned 30. Previously famous for scoring a header from his own half – in a September 2011 fixture for Odd against Tromsø IL – the all-purpose midfielder was in the news for more conventional reasons as he inspired his side to a third-place finish in the league, in which he scored a personal-best tally of nine goals, and a runners-up spot in the cup.

Newcomer of the season

Martin Ødegaard
(Strømsgodset IF)

Strømsgodset were unable to defend their Tippeligaen title in 2014, finishing a disappointing fourth following the departure of their championship-winning coach Ronny Deila to Celtic FC, but the emergence of the multi-talented Ødegaard, aged 15 throughout the season, placated most of their fans. Having set all sorts of 'youngest-ever' records in the Tippeligaen, he then repeated the feat with Norway at international level before Real Madrid CF, ever-alert to special talent, whisked him away to Spain.

NATIONAL TEAM

International tournament appearances

FIFA World Cup (3) 1938, 1994, 1998 (2nd round)
UEFA European Championship (1) 2000

Top five all-time caps

John Arne Riise (110); Thorbjørn Svenssen (104); Henning Berg (100); Erik Thorstvedt (97); John Carew & Brede Hangeland (91)

Top five all-time goals

Jørgen Juve (33); Einar Gundersen (26); Harald Hennum (25); John Carew (24); Tore André Flo & Ole Gunnar Solskjær (23)

Results 2014/15

Date	Opponent		Venue	Result		Scorers
27/08/14	United Arab Emirates	H	Stavanger	D	0-0	
03/09/14	England	A	London	L	0-1	
09/09/14	Italy (ECQ)	H	Oslo	L	0-2	
10/10/14	Malta (ECQ)	A	Ta' Qali	W	3-0	Dæhli (22), King (26, 49)
13/10/14	Bulgaria (ECQ)	H	Oslo	W	2-1	T Elyounoussi (13), Nielsen (72)
12/11/14	Estonia	H	Oslo	L	0-1	
16/11/14	Azerbaijan (ECQ)	A	Baku	W	1-0	Nordtveit (25)
28/03/15	Croatia (ECQ)	A	Zagreb	L	1-5	Tettey (80)
08/06/15	Sweden	H	Oslo	D	0-0	
12/06/15	Azerbaijan (ECQ)	H	Oslo	D	0-0	

Appearances 2014/15

Coach: Per-Mathias Høgmo	01/12/59		Uae	Eng	ITA	MLT	BUL	Est	AZE	CRO	Swe	AZE	Caps	Goals
Rune Almenning Jarstein	29/09/84	Hertha (GER)	G										38	-
Martin Linnes	20/09/91	Molde	D	D36		D	D	s46		D	s46		12	-
Steffen Hagen	08/03/86	Odd	D										3	-
Vegard Forren	16/02/88	Molde	D	D	D	D	D	D	D	D	D	D	23	-
Per-Egil Flo	18/01/89	Molde	D58	s36	D			s46					4	-
Yann-Erik de Lanlay	14/05/92	Viking	M15										5	1
Jone Samuelsen	06/07/84	Odd	M46		s62	s83	s68	s57	s19				8	-
Martin Ødegaard	17/12/98	Strømsgodset /Real Madrid (ESP)	M				s63	s57		A	M	M	6	-
Mohamed Elyounoussi	04/08/94	Molde	M	s69									3	-
Marcus Pedersen	08/06/90	Brann	A66										7	1
Fredrik Gulbrandsen	10/09/92	Molde	A46						s91				2	-
Christian Grindheim	17/07/83	Vålerenga	s15 /74										54	2
Morten Gamst Pedersen	08/09/81	Rosenborg	s46	s87	s75								83	17
Fredrik Ulvestad	17/06/92	Aalesund	s46										1	-
Thomas Grøgaard	08/02/94	Odd	s58										1	-
Fredrik Brustad	22/06/89	Stabæk	s66										1	-
André Danielsen	20/01/85	Viking	s74										2	-
Ørjan Håskjold Nyland	10/09/90	Molde		G	G	G	G	G	G	G	G	G	13	-
Omar Elabdellaoui	05/12/91	Olympiacos (GRE)		D	D	D	D	D46	D		D46		15	-
Håvard Nordtveit	21/06/90	Mönchengladbach (GER)		D	D	D	D	D	D	D	D	M	24	2
Mats Møller Dæhli	02/03/95	Cardiff (ENG) /Freiburg (GER)		M56	M	M	M63	M57	M57	M61			12	1
Per Ciljan Skjelbred	16/06/87	Hertha (GER)		M69	M75	M62	M	M68	M	M19	M58	M52	32	1
Stefan Johansen	08/01/91	Celtic (SCO)		M	M	M	M	M75	M	M	M86	M	18	1
Ruben Yttergård Jenssen	04/05/88	Kaiserslautern (GER)		M87	M70								34	-
Tarik Elyounoussi	23/02/88	Hoffenheim (GER)		M78	s50	A	A83	A	A91	A79	s58		39	9
Joshua King	15/01/92	Blackburn (ENG)		A76	A	A75	A58				A46	A79	17	4
Anders Konradsen	18/07/90	Rennes (FRA)		s56				M			s86		8	1
Håvard Nielsen	15/07/93	Braunschweig (GER)		s76	M50	s75	s58	A46	A72	s61	A69		13	2
Ola Kamara	15/10/89	Austria Wien (AUT)		s78									7	1
Alexander Tettey	04/04/86	Norwich (ENG)			s70	M78	M		M	M	M46		24	1
Harmeet Singh	12/11/90	Molde					s78	s75					7	-
Tom Høgli	24/02/84	København (DEN)					D46	D	D	D	D		46	2
Alexander Søderlund	03/08/87	Rosenborg					s46	s72			s46	A68	19	-
Mohammed Abdellaoue	23/10/85	Stuttgart (GER)								s79			33	7
Even Hovland	14/02/89	Nürnberg (GER)									s46	D	6	-
Pål André Helland	04/01/90	Rosenborg									s69	s52	2	-
Magnus Wolff Eikrem	08/08/90	Malmö (SWE)									s68		16	-
Adama Diomandé	14/02/90	Stabæk										s79	1	-

EUROPE

Strømsgodset IF

Second qualifying round - FC Steaua Bucureşti (ROU)
H 0-1
Kwarasey, Hamoud, Francisco Júnior, Storflor, Fossum, Kastrati (Wikheim 69), Abu, L Vilsvik (Ødegaard 85), Storbæk, Høibråten, Ogunjimi (Sørum 61). Coach: David Nielsen (DEN)
A 0-2
Kwarasey, Hamoud, Francisco Júnior (Sørum 75), Storflor (Kovács 75), Fossum, Kastrati, Abu, L Vilsvik (Wikheim 61), Storbæk, Høibråten, Ogunjimi. Coach: David Nielsen (DEN)

Molde FK

Second qualifying round - ND Gorica (SVN)
H 4-1 Toivio (16), Forren (37, 41p), Hoseth (88)
Nyland, Toivio, Singh, Moström (Hoseth 57), Linnes (K Rindarøy 70), Flo, Hussain (Berg Hestad 80), Agnaldo, Elyounoussi, Forren, Chima. Coach: Tor Ole Skullerud (NOR)
A 1-1 Agnaldo (49)
Nyland, Toivio, Singh (Hestad 60), Hoseth, Linnes, Flo (O Rindarøy 82), Hussain, Høiland, Agnaldo (Svendsen 66), Forren, Diouf. Coach: Tor Ole Skullerud (NOR)

Third qualifying round - FC Zorya Luhansk (UKR)
A 1-1 Svendsen (88)
Nyland, Gabrielsen, Toivio, Berg Hestad, Singh, Flo, Agnaldo (Linnes 84), Elyounoussi, Forren, Chima (Høiland 75), Diouf (Svendsen 68). Coach: Tor Ole Skullerud (NOR)
H 1-2 Gulbrandsen (43)
Nyland, Toivio, Berg Hestad, Singh, Gulbrandsen (Høiland 73), Moström (Agnaldo 90), Linnes, Flo, Forren, Chima, Diouf (Elyounoussi 63). Coach: Tor Ole Skullerud (NOR)

Rosenborg BK

First qualifying round - FK Jelgava (LVA)
H 4-0 Gamst Pedersen (23), Søderlund (44, 54p), Jensen (73)
Lund Hansen, Dorsin (Skjelvik 71), Reginiussen, Jensen, Gamst Pedersen (Berntsen 80), Riski, Søderlund, Selnæs, Svensson, Helland (Sørmo 88), Strandberg. Coach: Per Joar Hansen (NOR)
A 2-0 Jensen (30), Diskerud (73)
Örlund, Reginiussen (Svensson 70), Rønning, Jensen (Selnæs 46), Riski, Mikkelsen, Søderlund (Gamst Pedersen 57), Skjelvik, Berntsen, Strandberg, Diskerud. Coach: Per Joar Hansen (NOR)

Second qualifying round - Sligo Rovers FC (IRL)
H 1-2 Rogers (81og)
Lund Hansen, Dorsin, Reginiussen, Jensen (Diskerud 71), Gamst Pedersen, Riski, Mikkelsen, Søderlund, Skjelvik, Berntsen (Selnæs 57), Helland (Sørloth 82). Coach: Per Joar Hansen (NOR)
A 3-1 Helland (16), Jensen (48, 64)
Lund Hansen, Dorsin, Reginiussen, Jensen, Gamst Pedersen, Riski, Mikkelsen, Søderlund (Sørloth 78), Selnæs, Helland (Diskerud 27), Strandberg. Coach: Kåre Ingebrigtsen (NOR)

Third qualifying round - Kardemir Karabükspor (TUR)
A 0-0
Lund Hansen, Dorsin, Reginiussen, Jensen, Gamst Pedersen, Riski, Mikkelsen, Skjelvik, Selnæs, Strandberg (Rønning 84), Diskerud (Berntsen 84). Coach: Kåre Ingebrigtsen (NOR)
H 1-1 Helland (8)
Lund Hansen, Dorsin, Reginiussen, Jensen, Riski (Søderlund 60), Skjelvik (Sørloth 89), Selnæs, Svensson, Helland, Strandberg, Diskerud (Gamst Pedersen 75). Coach: Kåre Ingebrigtsen (NOR)
Red card: Reginiussen 90+6

FK Haugesund

First qualifying round - AUK Broughton FC (WAL)
A 1-1 Daniel Bamberg (43)
Bråtveit, Myrestam, Elsner, Gytkjær, Nielsen, Andreassen, Fevang, Skjerve, Sema (Haraldseid 72), Stølås, Daniel Bamberg. Coach: Jostein Grindhaug (NOR)
H 2-1 Agdestein (7), Sema (56)
Bråtveit, Myrestam, Mawejje, Andreassen, Agdestein, Anyora, Haraldseid, Sema (Fevang 87), Daniel Bamberg (Nielsen 71), Aasheim (Stølås 46), Cvetinović. Coach: Jostein Grindhaug (NOR)

Second qualifying round - FK Sarajevo (BIH)
A 1-0 Daniel Bamberg (85)
Bråtveit, Myrestam, Elsner, Ekpo (Fevang 68), Andreassen, Agdestein (Nielsen 84), Bjørnbak, Anyora, Haraldseid, Aasheim (Daniel Bamberg 64), Cvetinović. Coach: Jostein Grindhaug (NOR)
H 1-3 Sema (47p)
Kristiansen, Myrestam, Ekpo (Nielsen 46), Agdestein, Bjørnbak (Andreassen 56), Anyora, Haraldseid, Sema, Stølås (Gytkjær 49), Daniel Bamberg, Cvetinović. Coach: Jostein Grindhaug (NOR)

Tromsø IL

First qualifying round - FC Santos Tartu (EST)
A 7-0 Andersen (14, 44), J Johansen (22), Moldskred (24), Drage (56), Norbye (75), L Johnsen (79)
Lekström (Herlofsen 46), Moldskred, Koppinen, Bendiksen, Drage, J Johansen (Nilsen 77), Norbye, Andersen, R Johansen (L Johnsen 62), Frantzen, Wangberg. Coach: Bård Flovik (NOR)
H 6-1 Espejord (13), Drage (23), Andersen (28, 57), Wangberg (54, 79)
Herlofsen, Moldskred, Bendiksen (L Johnsen 46), Drage, Norbye, Andersen (Andreassen 76), R Johansen (Ingebrigtsen 61), Frantzen, Wangberg, Nilsen, Espejord. Coach: Steinar Nilsen (NOR)

Second qualifying round - Víkingur (FRO)
A 0-0
Lekström, Moldskred, Bendiksen, Drage (L Johnsen 83), J Johansen (Espejord 71), Norbye, Andersen, R Johansen, Frantzen, Wangberg, Nilsen. Coach: Steinar Nilsen (NOR)
H 1-2 Wangberg (51)
Lekström, Moldskred (Espejord 76), Koppinen, Drage, J Johansen, Andersen, L Johnsen (Bendiksen 46), R Johansen, Frantzen, Wangberg, Nilsen (Norbye 46). Coach: Steinar Nilsen (NOR)
Red card: J Johansen 41

DOMESTIC LEAGUE CLUB-BY-CLUB

Aalesunds FK

1914 • Color Line (10,778) • aafk.no
Major honours
Norwegian Cup (2) 2009, 2011
Coach: Jan Jönsson (SWE)

2014

30/03	a	Bodø/Glimt	D	1-1	*Phillips*
05/04	h	Rosenborg	D	1-1	*Larsen*
13/04	a	Strømsgodset	L	0-2	
21/04	h	Start	L	1-2	*Arnefjord*
28/04	a	Lillestrøm	D	0-0	
01/05	h	Viking	L	1-2	*Grytten*
04/05	a	Haugesund	W	2-1	*Mattila, Grytten*
10/05	h	Brann	L	0-1	
16/05	h	Sogndal	D	2-2	*Arnefjord, Barrantes*
20/05	a	Odd	L	1-2	*Tollås*
25/05	h	Sarpsborg	D	0-0	
09/06	a	Vålerenga	L	0-3	
12/06	h	Sandnes Ulf	W	3-0	*Aarøy, Ulvestad, James*
06/07	a	Stabæk	W	2-0	*Larsen, James*
11/07	h	Molde	L	0-1	
22/07	a	Sarpsborg	L	2-3	*Larsen, Abdellaoue*
26/07	h	Lillestrøm	D	1-1	*Mattila*
03/08	h	Bodø/Glimt	W	2-1	*Barrantes, James*
08/08	a	Brann	L	0-1	
16/08	h	Haugesund	W	3-0	*James, Ulvestad (p), Larsen*
24/08	a	Molde	L	0-5	
30/08	a	Strømsgodset	W	2-0	*Mattila 2 (2p)*
14/09	a	Sogndal	D	1-1	*James*
21/09	h	Stabæk	W	3-0	*Mattila, James, Ulvestad*
28/09	a	Rosenborg	L	0-3	
04/10	h	Odd	D	2-2	*Barrantes, Latifu*
18/10	a	Start	W	2-1	*James, Larsen*
26/10	a	Viking	W	2-1	*James 2*
02/11	h	Vålerenga	W	4-1	*James, Barrantes 2, Abdellaoue*
09/11	a	Sandnes Ulf	W	2-1	*Barrantes, Mattila*

No	Name	Nat	DoB	Pos	Aps	(s)	Gls
19	Tor Hogne Aarøy		20/03/77	A	5	(14)	1
30	Mustafa Abdellaoue		01/08/88	A	6	(7)	2
15	Daniel Arnefjord	SWE	21/03/79	D	26	(2)	2
31	Michael Barrantes	CRC	04/10/83	M	18	(2)	6
35	Henrik Bjørdal		04/02/97	M	14	(8)	
8	Fredrik Carlsen		01/12/89	M	7	(3)	
6	Mikael Dyrestam	SWE	10/12/91	D	9	(3)	
40	Sondre Fet		20/01/97	M		(1)	
13	Sten Grytebust		25/10/89	G	30		
37	Torbjørn Grytten		06/04/95	M	10	(8)	2
39	Vebjørn Hoff		13/02/96	M		(2)	
14	Leke James	NGA	01/11/92	A	23		10
24	El Mehdi Karnass	MAR	12/03/90	M	8	(5)	
10	Peter Orry Larsen		25/02/89	M	23	(3)	5
2	Akeem Latifu	NGA	16/11/89	D	29		1
5	Oddbjørn Lie		31/08/87	D	24	(1)	
20	Thomas Martinussen		05/02/95	M		(3)	
22	Jo Nymo Matland		21/04/87	D	11	(10)	
7	Sakari Mattila	FIN	14/07/89	M	18	(7)	6
17	Demar Phillips	JAM	23/09/83	M	23	(2)	1
11	Tremaine Stewart	JAM	01/05/88	A	3	(2)	
4	Jonatan Tollås		01/07/90	D	12		1
23	Fredrik Ulvestad		17/06/92	M	29		3
16	Hugues Wembangomo		10/05/92	D	2	(2)	

FK Bodø/Glimt

1916 • Aspmyra (7,354) • glimt.no
Major honours
Norwegian Cup (2) 1975, 1993
Coach: Jan Halvor Halvorsen

2014

30/03	h	Aalesund	D	1-1	*Richards*
06/04	a	Vålerenga	L	1-3	*Olsen*
13/04	h	Sogndal	W	4-2	*Sané, Richards, P Ndiaye, M Ndiaye*
21/04	h	Rosenborg	D	2-2	*Laajab, Olsen*
27/04	a	Stabæk	L	1-2	*M Ndiaye*
01/05	h	Lillestrøm	L	1-2	*Chatto*
04/05	a	Strømsgodset	L	0-2	
10/05	h	Haugesund	W	2-1	*Laajab, P Ndiaye*
16/05	h	Brann	W	2-1	*Olsen, P Ndiaye*
20/05	h	Start	W	3-1	*Laajab 2*
25/05	a	Viking	W	3-2	*M Ndiaye, Karlsen 2*
09/06	a	Sandnes Ulf	L	0-1	
12/06	h	Molde	D	1-1	*og (O Rindarøy)*
06/07	a	Sarpsborg	L	1-2	*P Ndiaye*
12/07	h	Odd	L	0-3	
19/07	a	Start	L	1-2	*Laajab*
27/07	h	Sarpsborg	L	3-4	*Laajab 2 (1p), P Ndiaye*
03/08	a	Aalesund	L	1-2	*og (Grytebust)*
10/08	a	Sogndal	W	1-0	*Chatto*
17/08	h	Sandnes Ulf	D	1-1	*P Ndiaye*
24/08	a	Haugesund	W	2-1	*P Ndiaye, Olsen*
30/08	h	Vålerenga	W	4-3	*M Ndiaye, Olsen, Laajab 2 (1p)*
12/09	a	Rosenborg	L	1-3	*Olsen*
20/09	h	Strømsgodset	L	0-4	
27/09	a	Molde	L	1-2	*Laajab*
05/10	h	Stabæk	D	1-1	*Moe*
19/10	a	Odd	L	3-4	*Richards, P Ndiaye 2*
26/10	h	Brann	W	2-1	*Laajab 2 (1p)*
02/11	a	Lillestrøm	L	0-4	
09/11	h	Viking	W	3-2	*Moe, Konradsen, Laajab*

No	Name	Nat	DoB	Pos	Aps	(s)	Gls
27	Patrick Berg		24/11/97	M		(1)	
20	Ulrik Berglann		31/05/92	A	2	(6)	
8	Daniel Berntsen		04/04/93	M	10		
4	Thomas Braaten		30/06/87	D	18	(2)	
24	Kristian Brix		13/06/90	D	25	(3)	
15	Dominic Chatto	NGA	12/07/85	M	25		2
2	Ruben Imingen		04/12/86	D	17	(1)	
5	Thomas Jacobsen		16/09/83	M	21	(6)	
9	Jim Johansen		06/02/87	A	1	(5)	
6	Anders Karlsen		15/02/90	M	6	(14)	2
16	Morten Konradsen		03/05/96	M	5	(11)	1
10	Abdurahim Laajab		21/05/85	A	30		13
1	Pavel Londak	EST	14/05/80	G	18		
18	Brede Moe		15/12/91	D	25	(1)	2
19	Mouhamadou Ndiaye	SEN	24/08/94	M	12	(15)	4
7	Papa Alioune Ndiaye	SEN	27/10/90	M	30		9
30	Trond Olsen		05/02/84	A	28		6
28	Dane Richards	JAM	14/12/83	A	14	(8)	3
14	Ulrik Saltnes		10/11/92	M	2	(5)	
23	Vieux Sané	SEN	04/08/89	D	27		1
25	Lasse Staw		01/01/88	G	12	(2)	
3	Zarek Valentin	USA	06/08/91	D	2	(1)	

SK Brann

1908 • Brann (17,686) • brann.no
Major honours
Norwegian League (3) 1962, 1963, 2007; Norwegian Cup (6) 1923, 1925, 1972, 1976, 1982, 2004
Coach: Rikard Norling (SWE)

2014

30/03	a	Sarpsborg	L	0-3	
06/04	h	Stabæk	L	1-2	*Orlov*
11/04	a	Sandnes Ulf	D	1-1	*Larsen*
21/04	h	Lillestrøm	W	2-0	*Orlov 2*
27/04	a	Rosenborg	L	2-5	*Skaanes 2*
30/04	h	Haugesund	L	1-3	*Orlov*
04/05	a	Start	D	1-1	*og (Berger)*
10/05	a	Aalesund	W	1-0	*Vindheim*
16/05	a	Bodø/Glimt	L	1-2	*Lorentzen*
20/05	a	Sogndal	L	0-1	
25/05	a	Vålerenga	L	2-3	*Grønner, Lorentzen*
09/06	a	Molde	L	2-4	*Askar 2*
12/06	h	Odd	L	0-1	
06/07	a	Viking	W	2-0	*Grønner, Orlov*
12/07	h	Strømsgodset	L	0-1	
18/07	a	Stabæk	D	1-1	*Skaanes*
27/07	h	Viking	L	0-1	
01/08	a	Lillestrøm	L	3-4	*Huseklepp, Barmen, Orlov*
08/08	h	Aalesund	W	1-0	*Orlov*
17/08	h	Rosenborg	W	3-1	*Mojsov, Skaanes, Pedersen*
23/08	a	Vålerenga	D	3-3	*Haugen, Hanstveit, Sævarsson*
31/08	h	Molde	L	0-1	
13/09	a	Strømsgodset	W	4-1	*Pedersen, Skaanes, Askar, Huseklepp*
19/09	h	Sandnes Ulf	D	1-1	*Askar*
28/09	a	Odd	L	0-1	
05/10	h	Start	L	1-2	*Pedersen*
17/10	a	Sarpsborg	L	1-2	*Haugen*
26/10	a	Bodø/Glimt	L	1-2	*Mojsov*
02/11	h	Sogndal	W	2-1	*Grønner, Karadas*
09/11	a	Haugesund	W	3-2	*Huseklepp, Orlov, Vindheim*

No	Name	Nat	DoB	Pos	Aps	(s)	Gls
22	Amin Askar		01/10/85	M	18	(10)	4
17	Stéphane Badji	SEN	29/05/90	M	17	(4)	
29	Kristoffer Barmen		19/08/83	A	19	(6)	1
4	Eirik Birkelund		13/01/94	M		(2)	
6	Vadim Demidov		10/10/86	D	5		
27	Erdin Demir	SWE	27/03/90	D	13	(4)	
15	Ibrahima Dramé	SEN	23/09/95	A		(5)	
7	Hassan El Fakiri		18/04/77	M	11	(5)	
30	Jonas Grønner		11/04/94	D	19	(4)	3
3	Erlend Hanstveit		28/01/81	D	20	(2)	1
8	Fredrik Haugen		13/06/92	M	28	(1)	2
23	Erik Huseklepp		05/09/84	A	22	(8)	3
18	Markus Jonsson	SWE	09/03/81	D	7		
9	Azar Karadas		09/08/81	D	9	(1)	1
19	Kristoffer Larsen		19/01/92	M	2	(10)	1
24	Piotr Leciejewski	POL	23/03/85	G	27		
20	Håkon Lorentzen		02/08/97	A	1	(7)	2
5	Daniel Mojsov	MKD	25/12/87	D	16	(1)	2
1	Ådne Nissestad		18/11/95	G	1		
10	Jakob Orlov	SWE	15/03/86	A	25	(4)	9
19	Marcus Pedersen		08/06/90	A	10		3
26	Kasper Skaanes		19/03/95	M	24	(4)	5
2	Birkir Már Sævarsson	ISL	11/11/84	D	13	(7)	1
21	Andreas Vindheim		04/08/95	D	21	(1)	2
12	Øystein Øvretveit		25/06/94	G	2		

NORWAY

FK Haugesund

1993 • Haugesund (8,096) • fkh.no
Coach: Jostein Grindhaug

2014

29/03	h	Lillestrøm	D	1-1	Gytkjær
06/04	a	Start	L	1-3	Engblom
12/04	h	Vålerenga	D	1-1	Fevang
21/04	a	Viking	L	0-2	
27/04	h	Sogndal	L	0-3	
30/04	a	Brann	W	3-1	Gytkjær 3 (1p)
04/05	a	Aalesund	L	1-2	Daniel Bamberg
10/05	a	Bodø/Glimt	L	1-2	Stølås
16/05	h	Odd	L	1-2	Fevang
20/05	a	Sandnes Ulf	D	0-0	
23/05	h	Molde	D	1-1	Stølås
09/06	a	Strømsgodset	L	1-2	Stølås
12/06	h	Sarpsborg	W	4-0	Sema 2, Gytkjær, Fevang
06/07	a	Rosenborg	L	3-5	Gytkjær 2, Sema
13/07	h	Stabæk	W	2-0	Fevang, Sema
20/07	a	Odd	D	0-0	
27/07	h	Start	W	5-1	Gytkjær 2, Daniel Bamberg, Sema 2
03/08	a	Sarpsborg	W	2-0	Andreassen, Gytkjær
10/08	h	Viking	D	1-1	Gytkjær
16/08	a	Aalesund	L	0-3	
24/08	h	Bodø/Glimt	L	1-2	Gytkjær
31/08	a	Lillestrøm	L	0-2	
14/09	a	Vålerenga	L	1-4	Cvetinović
21/09	h	Rosenborg	W	2-1	Daniel Bamberg, Sema
27/09	a	Sogndal	L	1-4	Sema
05/10	h	Sandnes Ulf	W	2-0	Sema, Daniel Bamberg
18/10	a	Molde	W	2-1	Stølås, Sema
25/10	h	Strømsgodset	W	3-2	Gytkjær, Cvetinović, Daniel Bamberg
02/11	a	Stabæk	W	1-0	Gytkjær (p)
09/11	h	Brann	L	2-3	Gytkjær, Haraldseid

No	Name	Nat	DoB	Pos	Aps	(s)	Gls
27	Tor André Aasheim		06/03/96	A		(4)	
14	Torbjørn Agdestein		18/09/91	A	1	(12)	
11	Tor Arne Andreassen		03/03/83	M	28		1
16	Ugonna Anyora	NGA	29/04/91	M	13	(4)	
15	Martin Bjørnbak		22/03/92	D	11	(1)	
24	Per Kristian Bråtveit		15/02/96	G	5		
50	Dušan Cvetinović	SRB	24/12/88	D	26		2
12	Olav Dalen		06/03/85	G	6	(1)	
23	Daniel Bamberg	BRA	23/04/84	M	27	(3)	5
6	Emmanuel Ekpo	NGA	20/12/87	M	1		
5	Rok Elsner	SVN	25/01/86	D	9		
21	Pontus Engblom	SWE	03/11/91	A	3	(4)	1
17	Geir Ludvig Fevang		17/11/80	M	24	(3)	4
7	Christian Gytkjær	DEN	06/05/90	A	23	(3)	15
19	Kristoffer Haraldseid		17/01/94	M	22	(5)	1
9	Nikola Komazec	SRB	15/11/87	A		(3)	
4	Mirko Kramarić	CRO	27/01/89	M	1	(3)	
1	Per Morten Kristiansen		14/07/81	G	19		
3	David Myrestam	SWE	04/04/87	D	14	(9)	
13	Eirik Mæland		15/02/89	M	7		
10	Joakim Våge Nilsen		24/04/91	M	30		
20	Maic Sema	SWE	02/12/88	M	21	(5)	10
18	Vegard Skjerve		22/05/88	D	24		
22	Alexander Stølås		30/04/89	A	15	(13)	4

Lillestrøm SK

1917 • Åråsen (11,637) • lsk.no
Major honours
Norwegian League (5) 1959, 1976, 1977, 1986, 1989;
Norwegian Cup (5) 1977, 1978, 1981, 1985, 2007
Coach: Magnus Haglund (SWE)

2014

29/03	a	Haugesund	D	1-1	Ringstad
06/04	h	Sandnes Ulf	W	4-1	Vaagan Moen (p), Pálmason, og (Halldórsson), Omoijuanfo
12/04	h	Viking	L	0-1	
21/04	a	Brann	L	0-2	
28/04	h	Aalesund	D	0-0	
01/05	a	Bodø/Glimt	W	2-1	Knudtzon, Fofana
04/05	h	Sogndal	W	2-0	Pálmason, Knudtzon
11/05	a	Odd	W	2-0	Ringstad, Lundemo
16/05	h	Molde	L	1-2	Gabrielsen
19/05	a	Vålerenga	D	2-2	Kippe, Fofana
24/05	h	Stabæk	W	5-1	Gabrielsen, Knudtzon, Fofana, Høiland 2
09/06	a	Rosenborg	L	1-3	Kippe
12/06	h	Strømsgodset	W	3-0	Fofana, Knudtzon, Høiland
06/07	a	Start	L	1-3	Mjelde
12/07	h	Sarpsborg	D	0-0	
20/07	a	Viking	D	0-0	
26/07	a	Aalesund	D	1-1	Pálmason
01/08	h	Brann	W	4-3	Vaagan Moen 2 (1p), Lundemo, Friday
10/08	a	Sandnes Ulf	D	0-0	
17/08	h	Vålerenga	W	2-1	Vaagan Moen, Knudtzon
24/08	a	Sogndal	W	1-0	Amundsen
31/08	h	Haugesund	W	2-0	Fofana, Vaagan Moen
14/09	a	Molde	L	2-3	Pálmason, Vaagan Moen
21/09	h	Odd	W	2-0	Vaagan Moen, Ringstad
28/09	a	Stabæk	L	0-2	
03/10	a	Rosenborg	L	0-2	
19/10	a	Strømsgodset	L	1-2	Kippe
26/10	h	Start	W	4-1	Pálmason 3, Knudtzon
02/11	h	Bodø/Glimt	W	4-0	Friday 2, Fofana, Pálmason
09/11	a	Sarpsborg	L	2-3	Mjelde, Pálmason

No	Name	Nat	DoB	Pos	Aps	(s)	Gls
4	Marius Amundsen		30/11/91	D	14		1
7	Johan Andersson	SWE	22/08/83	M	26		
21	Moryké Fofana	CIV	23/11/91	M	24	(5)	6
23	Fred Friday	NGA	22/05/95	A	2	(14)	3
4	Ruben Gabrielsen		10/03/92	D	14		2
9	Tommy Høiland		11/04/89	A	2	(11)	3
18	Bonke Innocent	NGA	20/01/96	M		(1)	
13	Frode Kippe		17/01/78	D	19		3
11	Erling Knudtzon		15/12/88	A	26	(1)	6
32	Jørgen Kolstad		31/08/95	M		(1)	
15	Marius Lundemo		11/04/94	M	24	(2)	2
3	Simen Kind Mikalsen		04/05/93	D	7	(9)	
17	Erik Mjelde		06/03/84	M	2	(17)	2
16	Ohi Omoijuanfo		30/11/93	M	11	(13)	1
77	Arnold Origi	KEN	15/11/83	G	30		
14	Pálmi Rafn Pálmason	ISL	09/11/84	A	24	(3)	9
9	Amahl Pellegrino		18/06/90	A	2	(5)	
8	Bjørn Helge Riise		21/06/83	M	27		
20	Stian Ringstad		29/08/91	D	23		3
10	Petter Vaagan Moen		05/02/84	A	22	(5)	7
5	Magnar Ødegaard		11/05/93	D	21		
2	Anders Østli		08/01/83	D	10		

Molde FK

1911 • Aker (11,800) • moldefk.no
Major honours
Norwegian League (3) 2011, 2012, 2014;
Norwegian Cup (4) 1994, 2005, 2013, 2014
Coach: Tor Ole Skullerud

2014

28/03	h	Vålerenga	W	2-0	Forren, Sigurdarson
05/04	a	Odd	L	1-2	Berg Hestad
13/04	a	Stabæk	W	2-0	Sigurdarson, Chima
21/04	h	Sarpsborg	W	5-1	Gulbrandsen 2, Elyounoussi 2, Svendsen
27/04	a	Sandnes Ulf	W	3-1	Moström, Gulbrandsen, Elyounoussi
01/05	h	Start	W	2-0	Gulbrandsen, og (Acosta)
04/05	a	Rosenborg	W	2-0	Gulbrandsen, Flo
11/05	h	Strømsgodset	D	2-2	Elyounoussi 2
16/05	a	Lillestrøm	W	2-1	Chima, Hovland
20/05	h	Viking	W	1-0	Elyounoussi
23/05	a	Haugesund	D	1-1	Linnes
09/06	h	Brann	W	4-2	Elyounoussi 3 (1p), Gulbrandsen
12/06	a	Bodø/Glimt	D	1-1	Toivio
05/07	h	Sogndal	W	3-0	Chima, og (Valsvik), Linnes
11/07	h	Aalesund	W	1-0	Forren
20/07	h	Sandnes Ulf	W	3-1	Høiland 3
27/07	h	Rosenborg	W	3-1	Moström, Chima, Singh
03/08	a	Start	D	1-1	Chima
10/08	h	Stabæk	D	2-2	Høiland, Elyounoussi
17/08	a	Sarpsborg	W	2-0	Forren, Høiland
24/08	a	Aalesund	W	5-0	Gulbrandsen, Linnes 2, Chima 2
31/08	a	Brann	W	1-0	Forren
14/09	h	Lillestrøm	W	3-2	Gulbrandsen, Elyounoussi 2
20/09	a	Vålerenga	W	2-0	Chima, Gulbrandsen
27/09	h	Bodø/Glimt	W	2-1	Gulbrandsen, Singh (p)
04/10	a	Viking	W	2-1	Singh (p), Sigurdarson
18/10	h	Haugesund	L	1-2	Chima
26/10	a	Sogndal	W	1-0	Elyounoussi
02/11	a	Strømsgodset	L	0-2	
09/11	h	Odd	W	2-0	Hussain, Chima

No	Name	Nat	DoB	Pos	Aps	(s)	Gls
21	Agnaldo	BRA	11/03/94	M	6	(10)	
6	Daniel Berg Hestad		30/07/75	M	14	(11)	1
27	Daniel Chima	NGA	04/04/91	A	24	(3)	10
3	Amidou Diop	SEN	25/02/92	M		(1)	
30	Pape Paté Diouf	SEN	04/04/86	A	1	(6)	
29	Emmanuel Ekpo	NGA	20/12/87	M	1	(1)	
24	Mohamed Elyounoussi		04/08/94	A	28	(2)	13
15	Per-Egil Flo		18/01/89	D	20	(4)	1
25	Vegard Forren		16/02/88	D	28		4
4	Ruben Gabrielsen		10/03/92	D	7	(3)	
8	Fredrik Gulbrandsen		10/09/92	A	19	(4)	10
19	Eirik Hestad		26/06/95	M	6	(2)	
10	Magne Hoseth		13/10/80	M	1	(4)	
9	Even Hovland		14/02/89	D	9		1
16	Etzaz Hussain		27/01/93	M	14	(5)	1
20	Tommy Høiland		11/04/89	A	2	(7)	5
14	Martin Linnes		20/09/91	D	28		4
9	Mattias Moström	SWE	25/02/83	M	26	(2)	2
12	Ørjan Håskjold Nyland		10/09/90	G	28		
1	Espen Bugge Pettersen		10/05/80	G	2	(1)	
23	Knut Olav Rindarøy		17/07/85	D	6	(1)	
37	Ole Martin Rindarøy		16/05/95	D	2		
11	Björn Bergmann Sigurdarson	ISL	26/02/91	A	9	(6)	3
18	Magne Simonsen		13/07/88	D	2	(1)	
7	Harmeet Singh		12/11/90	M	27	(1)	3
32	Sander Svendsen		06/08/97	A	1	(11)	1
5	Joona Toivio	FIN	10/03/88	D	19	(3)	1

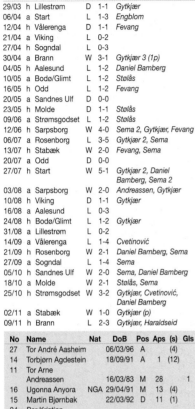

Odds BK

1894 • Skagerak Arena (13,500) • odd.no

Major honours
Norwegian Cup (12) 1903, 1904, 1905, 1906, 1913, 1915, 1919, 1922, 1924, 1926, 1931, 2000

Coach: Dag-Eilev Fagermo

2014

30/03	a	Sandnes Ulf	D	1-1	Johnsen
05/04	h	Molde	W	2-1	Rashani, Samuelsen
13/04	a	Rosenborg	L	0-2	
21/04	h	Stabæk	W	2-1	og (Fontanello), Rashani
27/04	a	Strømsgodset	L	1-2	Samuelsen
01/05	h	Sarpsborg	W	2-0	Samuelsen, Johnsen
05/05	a	Viking	D	1-1	Rashani
11/05	h	Lillestrøm	L	0-2	
16/05	a	Haugesund	W	2-1	Shala, Storbæk
20/05	h	Aalesund	W	2-1	Samuelsen 2
25/05	a	Start	W	1-0	og (Owello)
09/06	h	Sogndal	D	0-0	
12/06	h	Brann	W	1-0	Hurme
07/07	h	Vålerenga	D	2-2	Hagen, og (Gunnarsson)
12/07	a	Bodø/Glimt	W	3-0	Samuelsen, Rashani, Halvorsen
20/07	h	Haugesund	D	0-0	
27/07	a	Sogndal	W	3-1	Samuelsen, Nordkvelle, Storbæk
03/08	h	Sandnes Ulf	W	3-1	Johnsen, Jensen, Shala
09/08	h	Strømsgodset	W	1-0	Shala
17/08	a	Stabæk	W	3-1	Shala, Halvorsen, og (Mandé)
24/08	h	Start	W	4-1	Akabueze, Storbæk, Johnsen 2
30/08	a	Sarpsborg	D	2-2	Samuelsen, Shala
13/09	a	Viking	W	4-1	Samuelsen, Akabueze, Johnsen, Shala
21/09	a	Lillestrøm	L	0-2	
28/09	h	Brann	W	4-0	Akabueze, Johnsen, Shala (p), og (Mojsov)
04/10	a	Aalesund	D	2-2	Akabueze, Johnsen 2
19/10	h	Bodø/Glimt	W	4-3	Akabueze, Shala, Johnsen 2
24/10	a	Vålerenga	W	2-1	Shala, Storbæk
02/11	h	Rosenborg	L	0-1	
09/11	h	Molde	L	0-2	

No	Name	Nat	DoB	Pos	Aps	(s)	Gls
26	Chukwuma Akabueze	NGA	06/05/89	A	18	(11)	4
4	Vegard Bergan		20/02/95	D	4	(1)	
23	Lars-Kristian Eriksen		28/06/83	D	25		
3	Ardian Gashi		20/06/81	M	4	(7)	
5	Thomas Grøgaard		08/02/94	D	30		
21	Steffen Hagen		08/03/86	D	30		1
7	Ole Jørgen Halvorsen		02/10/87	A	16	(10)	2
1	André Hansen		17/12/89	G	29		
18	Jarkko Hurme	FIN	04/06/86	D	11	(2)	1
20	Fredrik Oldrup Jensen		18/05/93	M	27	(2)	1
9	Henrik Kjelsrud Johansen		22/03/93	A		(8)	
11	Frode Johnsen		17/03/74	A	28	(2)	11
2	Emil Jonassen		17/02/93	D	2	(1)	
19	Snorre Krogsgård		25/05/91	A		(6)	
14	Fredrik Nordkvelle		13/09/85	M	13	(13)	1
15	Elba Rashani		09/05/93	A	14	(1)	4
12	Sondre Rossbach		02/07/93	G	1	(2)	
8	Jone Samuelsen		06/07/84	M	28		9
3	Fredrik Semb Berge		06/02/90	D	11		
10	Herolind Shala	ALB	01/02/92	A	24	(6)	9
22	Håvard Storbæk		25/05/86	M	15	(12)	4

Rosenborg BK

1917 • Lerkendal (21,166) • rbk.no

Major honours
Norwegian League (22) 1967, 1969, 1971, 1985, 1988, 1990, 1992, 1993, 1994, 1995, 1996, 1997, 1998, 1999, 2000, 2001, 2002, 2003, 2004, 2006, 2009, 2010; Norwegian Cup (9) 1960, 1964, 1971, 1988, 1990, 1992, 1995, 1999, 2003

Coach: Per Joar Hansen;
(21/07/14) Kåre Ingebrigtsen

2014

29/03	h	Viking	D	2-2	Diskerud, Dorsin
05/04	a	Aalesund	D	1-1	Riski
13/04	h	Odd	W	2-0	Strandberg, Nielsen
21/04	a	Bodø/Glimt	D	2-2	Gamst Pedersen, Søderlund
27/04	h	Brann	W	5-2	Reginiussen, Svensson, Jensen, Søderlund (p), Nielsen (p)
01/05	a	Sogndal	W	2-1	Reginiussen, Søderlund
04/05	h	Molde	L	0-2	
12/05	a	Sandnes Ulf	W	2-0	og (Halldórsson), Mikkelsen
16/05	h	Stabæk	L	1-3	Reginiussen
19/05	a	Sarpsborg	D	1-1	Svensson
24/05	a	Strømsgodset	D	1-1	Nielsen
09/06	h	Lillestrøm	W	3-1	Selnæs, Mikkelsen, Riski
12/06	a	Start	W	4-2	Søderlund 2, Riski 2
06/07	h	Haugesund	W	5-3	Jensen 2, Søderlund, Riski, Gamst Pedersen
13/07	a	Vålerenga	D	2-2	Søderlund, Reginiussen
20/07	h	Sogndal	W	1-0	Søderlund (p)
27/07	a	Molde	L	1-3	Gamst Pedersen
03/08	a	Stabæk	L	1-4	Riski
10/08	h	Start	W	3-2	Diskerud, Søderlund 2
17/08	a	Brann	L	1-3	Søderlund
24/08	h	Sarpsborg	W	2-0	Søderlund 2
31/08	a	Viking	W	2-1	Skjelvik, Jensen
12/09	h	Bodø/Glimt	W	3-1	Riski, Helland (p), Malec
21/09	a	Haugesund	L	1-2	Malec
28/09	h	Aalesund	W	3-0	Jensen, Eyjólfsson, Malec
03/10	a	Lillestrøm	W	2-0	Helland, Jensen
19/10	h	Vålerenga	W	3-2	Helland, Dorsin, Malec
26/10	h	Sandnes Ulf	W	3-1	Jensen, Helland, Mikkelsen
02/11	a	Odd	W	1-0	Skjelvik
09/11	h	Strømsgodset	W	4-1	Dorsin, Jensen 2, Riski

No	Name	Nat	DoB	Pos	Aps	(s)	Gls
18	Daniel Berntsen		04/04/93	M	8	(2)	
10	John Chibuike	NGA	10/10/88	A	3	(5)	
42	Mikkel Diskerud	USA	02/10/90	M	19	(3)	2
3	Mikael Dorsin	SWE	06/10/81	D	23	(2)	3
25	Hólmar Örn Eyjólfsson	ISL	06/08/90	D	8	(2)	1
2	Cristian Gamboa	CRC	24/10/89	D	2		
8	Morten Gamst Pedersen		08/09/81	M	19	(5)	3
23	Pål André Helland		04/01/90	A	11	(10)	4
7	Mike Jensen	DEN	19/02/88	M	29		9
12	Alexander Lund Hansen		06/10/82	G	17		
10	Tomáš Malec	SVK	05/01/93	A	5	(5)	4
11	Tobias Mikkelsen	DEN	18/09/86	A	14	(12)	3
14	Nicki Bille Nielsen	DEN	07/02/88	A	6	(5)	3
4	Tore Reginiussen		10/04/86	D	24		4
9	Riku Riski	FIN	16/08/89	A	25	(4)	8
5	Per Verner Rønning		09/01/83	D	3	(1)	
20	Ole Kristian Selnæs		07/07/94	M	20	(1)	1
16	Jørgen Skjelvik		05/07/91	D	21	(7)	2
24	Stefan Strandberg		25/07/90	D	18	(2)	1
22	Jonas Svensson		06/03/93	D	23		2
32	John Hou Sæter		13/01/98	M		(1)	
15	Alexander Søderlund		03/08/87	A	17	(6)	13
37	Alexander Sørloth		05/12/95	A	2	(4)	
31	Bent Sørmo		22/09/96	M		(1)	
1	Daniel Örlund	SWE	23/06/80	G	13	(1)	

Sandnes Ulf

1911 • Sandnes Idrettspark (4,969) • sandnesulf.no

Coach: Asle Andersen;
(16/07/14) (Bjarte Lunde Aarsheim);
(23/07/14) Tom Nordlie

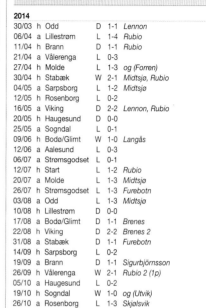

2014

30/03	h	Odd	D	1-1	Lennon
06/04	a	Lillestrøm	L	1-4	Rubio
11/04	h	Brann	D	1-1	Rubio
21/04	a	Vålerenga	L	0-3	
27/04	h	Molde	L	1-3	og (Forren)
30/04	h	Stabæk	W	2-1	Midtsjø, Rubio
04/05	a	Sarpsborg	L	1-2	Midtsjø
12/05	h	Rosenborg	L	0-2	
16/05	h	Viking	D	2-2	Lennon, Rubio
20/05	h	Haugesund	D	0-0	
25/05	a	Sogndal	L	0-1	
09/06	h	Bodø/Glimt	W	1-0	Langås
12/06	a	Aalesund	L	0-3	
06/07	a	Strømsgodset	L	0-1	
12/07	h	Start	L	1-2	Rubio
20/07	a	Molde	L	1-3	Midtsjø
26/07	h	Strømsgodset	L	1-3	Furebotn
03/08	a	Odd	L	1-3	Midtsjø
10/08	h	Lillestrøm	D	0-0	
17/08	a	Bodø/Glimt	D	1-1	Brenes
22/08	h	Viking	D	2-2	Brenes 2
31/08	a	Stabæk	D	1-1	Furebotn
14/09	h	Sarpsborg	L	0-2	
19/09	a	Brann	D	1-1	Sigurbjörnsson
26/09	h	Vålerenga	W	2-1	Rubio 2 (1p)
05/10	a	Haugesund	L	0-2	
19/10	h	Sogndal	W	1-0	og (Utvik)
26/10	a	Rosenborg	L	1-3	Skjølsvik
02/11	a	Start	D	3-3	Frejd, Midtsjø, Brenes
09/11	a	Aalesund	L	1-2	Rubio

No	Name	Nat	DoB	Pos	Aps	(s)	Gls
19	Vegard Aanestad		12/06/87	D	18	(4)	
10	Randall Brenes	CRC	13/08/83	A	11		4
27	Zymer Bytyqi		14/09/96	A		(7)	
28	Derek Decamps	FRA	02/05/85	D	27		
30	Kent Håvard Eriksen		29/05/91	A	2	(8)	
5	Edier Frejd	SWE	16/12/79	D	21	(1)	1
7	Henrik Furebotn		11/02/86	M	24		2
1	Hannes Thór Halldórsson	ISL	27/04/84	G	30		
9	Marius Helle		11/08/83	A	11	(13)	
20	Tijan Jaiteh	GAM	31/12/88	M	19	(5)	
17	Ole Kristian Langås		07/05/93	A	8	(7)	1
10	Steven Lennon	SCO	20/01/88	M	15		2
4	Malaury Martin	FRA	25/08/88	M	5		
24	Fredrik Midtsjø		11/08/93	A	18	(10)	5
6	Avni Pepa		14/11/92	D	8	(3)	
21	Anel Raskaj	ALB	19/08/89	M	21	(5)	
11	Diego Rubio	CHI	15/05/93	A	19	(7)	8
16	Niklas Sandberg		18/05/95	M	1	(3)	
2	Eidur Aron Sigurbjörnsson	ISL	26/02/90	D	8		1
15	Hannes Sigurdsson	ISL	10/04/83	A	9	(1)	
8	Aksel Berget Skjølsvik		15/05/87	A	18	(5)	1
25	Vegard Skjørestad		30/08/95	D	1	(1)	
26	Kenneth Sola		25/08/85	D	14	(2)	
23	Erik Tønne		03/07/91	A	22	(3)	

Sarpsborg 08 FF

2000 • Sarpsborg (4,700) • sarpsborg08.no
Coach: Brian Deane (ENG)

2014

30/03	h	Brann	W	3-0	Zajić, Samuel 2 (2p)
06/04	a	Sogndal	D	1-1	Dja Djédjé
13/04	h	Start	D	1-1	Ernemann
21/04	a	Molde	L	1-5	Samuel
28/04	h	Vålerenga	W	3-0	Dja Djédjé, Samuel, Zajić
01/05	a	Odd	L	0-2	
04/05	h	Sandnes Ulf	W	2-1	Berthod, Samuel
11/05	a	Stabæk	L	2-3	Thórarinsson, Wiig
16/05	a	Strømsgodset	L	1-4	Kronberg
19/05	h	Rosenborg	D	1-1	Tokstad
25/05	a	Aalesund	D	0-0	
09/06	h	Viking	D	1-1	Ernemann
12/06	a	Haugesund	L	0-4	
06/07	h	Bodø/Glimt	W	2-1	Zajić, Wiig
12/07	a	Lillestrøm	D	0-0	
22/07	h	Aalesund	W	3-2	Jensen, Kronberg 2
27/07	a	Bodø/Glimt	W	4-3	Zajić, Jensen, Kronberg (p), Thórarinsson
03/08	h	Haugesund	L	0-2	
09/08	a	Vålerenga	D	2-2	Breive, Tokstad
17/08	h	Molde	L	0-2	
24/08	a	Rosenborg	L	0-2	
30/08	h	Odd	D	2-2	Berge, Castro
14/09	a	Sandnes Ulf	W	2-0	Thórarinsson, Tokstad
21/09	h	Sogndal	W	3-1	Castro, Feldballe, Zajić
28/09	a	Start	L	1-3	Wiig
05/10	h	Strømsgodset	D	0-0	
17/10	a	Brann	W	2-1	Nordvik, Thórarinsson
26/10	a	Stabæk	D	1-1	Tokstad
02/11	a	Viking	L	0-1	
09/11	h	Lillestrøm	W	3-2	Kronberg (p), Zajić, Thomassen

No	Name	Nat	DoB	Pos	Aps	(s)	Gls
4	Kjetil Berge		05/06/81	D	22	(2)	1
69	Jérémy Berthod	FRA	24/04/84	D	15	(1)	1
23	Tom Erik Breive		18/04/80	M	13	(10)	1
6	Christian Brink		17/03/83	D	1		
10	Alejandro Castro	CRC	11/09/90	A	9	(5)	2
19	Franck Dja Djédjé	CIV	02/06/86	A	13	(1)	2
17	Steffen Ernemann	DEN	26/04/82	M	23	(1)	2
21	Oliver Feldballe	DEN	03/04/90	M	6	(3)	1
13	Ole Christoffer Heieren Hansen		26/02/87	D	26		
26	Martin Thømt Jensen		08/07/90	D	21		2
27	Duwayne Kerr	JAM	16/01/87	G	20		
1	Gudmund Kongshavn		23/01/91	G	7		
22	Claes Kronberg	DEN	19/04/87	M	28		5
41	Gagandeep Singh Lally		08/07/95	M		(1)	
3	Andreas Nordvik		18/03/87	D	6	(4)	1
6	Jérome Polenz	GER	07/11/86	D	1	(1)	
99	Aaron Samuel	NGA	30/11/93	A	11	(2)	5
31	Christian Sukke		21/01/93	G	3	(1)	
16	Joachim Thomassen		04/05/88	D	18	(1)	1
8	Gudmundur Thórarinsson	ISL	15/04/92	M	29		4
11	Kristoffer Tokstad		05/07/91	M	12	(15)	4
5	Thórarinn Ingi Valdimarsson	ISL	04/11/90	M	8	(5)	
43	Brice Wembangomo		18/12/96	D		(1)	
7	Martin Wiig		22/08/83	A	13	(9)	3
36	Bojan Zajić	SRB	17/06/80	M	22	(6)	6
12	Olav Øby		13/10/94	M	3	(14)	

Sogndal Fotball

1926 • Fosshaugane Campus (5,523) • sogndalfotball.no
Coach: Jonas Olsson (SWE)

2014

30/03	a	Stabæk	L	0-3	
06/04	h	Sarpsborg	D	1-1	Flo
13/04	a	Bodø/Glimt	L	2-4	Flo 2
21/04	h	Strømsgodset	L	1-3	Hopen
27/04	a	Haugesund	W	3-0	Otoo, Valgardsson, Utvik
01/05	h	Rosenborg	L	1-2	Otoo
04/05	a	Lillestrøm	L	0-2	
11/05	h	Start	W	2-1	Otoo, Valsvik
16/05	a	Aalesund	D	2-2	Otoo, Nilsen
20/05	h	Brann	W	2-1	Otoo, Strand
25/05	h	Sandnes Ulf	W	1-0	Nilsen
09/06	a	Odd	D	0-0	
12/06	h	Vålerenga	W	2-0	Flo, Holsæter
05/07	a	Molde	L	0-3	
12/07	h	Viking	D	0-0	
20/07	a	Rosenborg	L	0-1	
27/07	h	Odd	L	1-3	Psyché
02/08	a	Strømsgodset	D	1-1	Söderberg
10/08	h	Bodø/Glimt	L	0-1	
16/08	a	Viking	L	2-4	Flo, Brochmann
24/08	h	Lillestrøm	L	0-1	
31/08	a	Start	L	2-3	Otoo 2
14/09	h	Aalesund	D	1-1	Psyché
21/09	a	Sarpsborg	L	1-3	Otoo
27/09	h	Haugesund	W	4-1	Flo, Nilsen 2, Otoo
05/10	a	Vålerenga	L	1-2	Nilsen
19/10	a	Sandnes Ulf	L	0-1	
26/10	h	Molde	L	0-1	
02/11	a	Brann	L	1-2	Flo
09/11	h	Stabæk	L	0-2	

No	Name	Nat	DoB	Pos	Aps	(s)	Gls
7	Rune Bolseth		14/07/80	M	25	(2)	
23	Tonny Brochmann	DEN	27/11/90	M	5	(12)	1
26	Erik Dahlin	SWE	28/04/89	G	5		
1	Mathias Dyngeland		07/10/95	G	19		
8	Ulrik Flo		06/10/88	A	23	(3)	7
6	Helge Haugen		15/02/82	M	25	(2)	
25	Ruben Holsæter		20/04/91	M	6	(11)	1
10	Ørjan Hopen		19/03/92	M	2	(4)	1
35	Truls Hovland		20/12/95	M		(1)	
9	Azar Karadas		09/08/81	D	10		
22	Tim Nilsen		07/10/92	A	10	(16)	5
19	Edward Ofere	NGA	28/03/86	A	3	(5)	
20	Kristian Opseth		06/01/90	A	2	(8)	
18	Mahatma Otoo	GHA	06/02/92	A	26	(1)	9
4	Hannu Patronen	FIN	23/05/84	D	21	(1)	
17	Christophe Psyché	FRA	28/07/88	D	5	(5)	2
16	Babacar Sarr	SEN	15/02/91	M	10	(1)	
24	Eirik Skaasheim		22/01/93	D	7	(2)	
27	Kristoffer Stephensen		01/06/91	D	3	(1)	
15	Petter Strand		24/08/94	M	27	(2)	1
14	Tom Söderberg	SWE	25/08/87	D	7		1
2	Taijo Teniste	EST	31/01/88	D	25		
28	Joar Tryti		12/01/97	D		(1)	
12	Kenneth Udjus		02/07/83	G	6		
3	Bjørn Inge Utvik		28/02/96	D	22	(2)	1
5	Hjörtur Logi Valgardsson	ISL	27/09/88	D	26		1
17	Gustav Valsvik		26/05/93	D	10		1

Stabæk Fotball

1912 • Nadderud (7,000) • stabak.no
Major honours
Norwegian League (1) 2008; Norwegian Cup (1) 1998
Coach: Bob Bradley (USA)

2014

30/03	h	Sogndal	W	3-0	Henderson, Næss, Brustad
06/04	a	Brann	W	2-1	Boli 2
13/04	h	Molde	L	0-2	
21/04	a	Odd	L	1-2	Boli
27/04	a	Bodø/Glimt	W	2-1	Høiland (p), Fontanello
30/04	a	Sandnes Ulf	L	1-2	Boli
05/05	h	Vålerenga	L	0-3	
11/05	h	Sarpsborg	W	3-2	Kassi, Adu (p), Brustad
16/05	h	Rosenborg	W	3-1	Brustad, Kassi, Boli
20/05	h	Strømsgodset	W	2-1	Brustad, Boli
24/05	a	Lillestrøm	L	1-5	Kassi
09/06	h	Start	L	1-2	Trondsen
12/06	a	Viking	L	1-4	Thorsby
06/07	h	Aalesund	L	0-2	
13/07	a	Haugesund	L	0-2	
18/07	h	Brann	D	1-1	Høiland
29/07	a	Vålerenga	L	2-3	Brustad 2
03/08	h	Rosenborg	W	4-1	Boli, Brustad 2, og (Rønning)
10/08	a	Molde	D	2-2	Stephens, Boli
17/08	h	Odd	L	1-3	Boli
23/08	a	Strømsgodset	W	3-2	Hoseth, Boli, Jalasto
31/08	h	Sandnes Ulf	D	1-1	Sortevik
14/09	a	Start	W	3-2	Brustad, Jacobson, Boli
21/09	a	Aalesund	L	0-3	
28/09	h	Lillestrøm	W	2-0	Brustad, Kassi
05/10	a	Bodø/Glimt	D	1-1	Jalasto
19/10	h	Viking	D	1-1	Høiland (p)
26/10	a	Sogndal	D	1-1	Boli
02/11	h	Haugesund	L	0-1	
09/11	a	Sogndal	W	2-0	Kassi, Boli

No	Name	Nat	DoB	Pos	Aps	(s)	Gls
7	Enoch Adu	GHA	14/09/90	M	16		1
11	Franck Boli	CIV	07/12/93	A	28		13
6	Fredrik Brustad		22/06/89	A	24	(6)	10
10	Emil Dahle		30/10/90	A		(4)	
29	Pablo Fontanello	ARG	26/09/84	D	9	(1)	1
9	Giorgi Gorozia	GEO	26/03/95	M	2	(2)	
21	Daniel Granli		01/05/94	D	18	(3)	
5	Jørgen Hammer		02/04/91	D		(2)	
13	Eirik Haugstad		17/01/94	G	1		
13	Eirik Haugstad		17/01/94	M		(9)	
18	Craig Henderson	NZL	24/06/87	M	4	(2)	1
16	Magne Hoseth		13/10/80	M	8	(1)	1
14	Jon Inge Høiland		20/09/77	M	22	(1)	3
22	Espen Isaksen		16/01/79	G	1		
7	Andrew Jacobson	USA	25/09/85	M	12		1
15	Ville Jalasto	FIN	19/04/86	D	21		2
2	Timmi Johansen	DEN	06/05/87	D	3	(4)	
28	Luc Kassi	CIV	20/08/94	M	20	(9)	5
1	Sayouba Mandé	CIV	15/06/93	G	27		
25	Birger Meling		30/11/93	M	1	(1)	
4	Nicolai Næss		18/01/93	D	17	(7)	1
42	Simen Omholt-Jensen		05/05/95	G		(1)	
3	Morten Morisbak Skjønsberg		12/02/83	D	14	(1)	
32	Tomasz Sokolowski		25/06/85	M	19	(6)	
8	Stian Sortevik		17/07/88	A	2	(19)	1
30	Michael Stephens	USA	03/04/89	M	29	(1)	1
12	Borger Thomas		15/02/95	G	2		
16	Morten Thorsby		05/05/96	M	6	(4)	1
81	Anders Trondsen		30/03/95	M	25	(1)	1

IK Start

1905 • Sør Arena (11,700) • ikstart.no
Major honours
Norwegian League (2) 1978, 1980
Coach: Mons Ivar Mjelde

2014

Date		Opponent		Score	Scorers
30/03	a	Strømsgodset	L	2-4	Asante 2
06/04	h	Haugesund	W	3-1	Sarr, Berger, Kristjánsson
13/04	a	Sarpsborg	D	1-1	Vikstøl
21/04	a	Aalesund	W	2-1	Tripic, Asante
27/04	a	Viking	L	0-2	
01/05	a	Molde	L	0-2	
04/05	h	Brann	D	1-1	Hoff
11/05	a	Sogndal	L	1-2	Andersen
16/05	h	Vålerenga	D	2-2	Hoff, Tripic
20/05	a	Bodø/Glimt	L	1-2	Andersen
25/05	h	Odd	L	0-1	
09/06	a	Stabæk	W	2-1	Nouri, Castro
12/06	h	Rosenborg	L	2-4	Castro, Hoff
06/07	a	Lillestrøm	W	3-1	Tripic (p), Børufsen, Hoff
12/07	a	Sandnes Ulf	W	2-1	Vilhjálmsson 2
19/07	h	Bodø/Glimt	W	2-1	og (Sané), Asante
27/07	a	Haugesund	L	1-5	Hoff
03/08	h	Molde	D	1-1	Hoff
10/08	a	Rosenborg	L	2-3	Asante, Børufsen
15/08	h	Strømsgodset	L	2-3	Acosta, Asante
24/08	a	Odd	L	1-4	Børufsen
31/08	h	Sogndal	W	3-2	Tripic, Vikstøl, Asante (p)
14/09	h	Stabæk	L	2-3	Vilhjálmsson, Asante
21/09	a	Viking	W	1-0	Vilhjálmsson
28/09	h	Sarpsborg	W	3-1	Ajer, Tripic 2
05/10	a	Brann	W	2-1	Vilhjálmsson, og (Karadas)
18/10	h	Aalesund	L	1-2	Owello
26/10	a	Lillestrøm	L	1-4	og (Mikalsen)
02/11	h	Sandnes Ulf	D	3-3	Kristjánsson, Acosta, Salvesen
09/11	a	Vålerenga	L	0-1	

No	Name	Nat	DoB	Pos	Aps	(s)	Gls
15	Bismark Acosta	CRC	19/12/86	D	25		2
19	Kristoffer Ajer		17/04/98	M	7	(6)	1
2	Glenn Andersen		05/04/80	D	25	(2)	2
9	Ernest Asante	GHA	06/11/88	M	21	(8)	8
4	Markus Berger	AUT	21/01/85	D	11		1
14	Espen Børufsen		04/03/88	M	21	(2)	3
11	Alejandro Castro	CRC	11/09/90	A	2	(5)	2
24	Pål Vestly Heigre		15/03/95	G	1		
21	Jon Hodnemyr		04/12/95	D	1		
8	Espen Hoff		20/11/81	A	22	(6)	6
17	Gudmundur Kristjánsson	ISL	01/03/89	M	23	(6)	2
16	Alexander Lind		23/03/89	A	2	(10)	
26	Jesper Mathisen		17/03/87	D	4		
33	Amin Nouri		10/01/90	D	16	(6)	1
4	Seyi Olofinjana	NGA	30/06/80	M	4	(3)	
1	Håkon André Opdal		11/06/82	G	20		
10	Solomon Owello	NGA	25/12/88	M	24	(4)	1
99	Fernando Paniagua	CRC	09/09/88	M	12	(3)	
32	Mathias Rasmussen		25/11/97	M		(1)	
30	Terje Reinertsen		14/09/87	G	9		
22	Lars-Jørgen Salvesen		19/02/96	A	1	(2)	1
5	Robert Sandnes		29/12/91	D	4	(11)	
6	Babacar Sarr	SEN	15/02/91	M	4	(9)	1
13	Zlatko Tripic		02/12/92	A	26	(2)	6
28	Rolf Daniel Vikstøl		22/02/89	D	26	(1)	2
18	Matthías Vilhjálmsson	ISL	30/01/87	A	19	(3)	5

Strømsgodset IF

1907 • Marienlyst (8,935) • godset.no
Major honours
Norwegian League (2) 1970, 2013; Norwegian Cup (5) 1969, 1970, 1973, 1991, 2010
Coach: Ronny Deila;
(07/06/14) (David Nielsen) (DEN);
(06/08/14) David Nielsen (DEN)

2014

Date		Opponent		Score	Scorers
30/03	h	Start	W	4-2	Wikheim 2, Francisco Júnior, Sørum
04/04	a	Viking	D	0-0	
13/04	h	Aalesund	W	2-0	Storflor, Sørum
21/04	a	Sogndal	W	3-1	Høibråten, Wikheim, Kovács
27/04	h	Odd	W	2-1	Kovács, Sætra
01/05	a	Vålerenga	L	0-3	
04/05	h	Bodø/Glimt	W	2-0	Fossum, Hamoud
11/05	a	Molde	D	2-2	Kovács 2
16/05	h	Sarpsborg	W	4-1	Hamoud, Kovács, Vilsvik (p), Ødegaard
20/05	a	Stabæk	L	1-2	Kovács
24/05	h	Rosenborg	D	1-1	Sørum
09/06	h	Haugesund	W	2-1	Fossum, Ødegaard
12/06	a	Lillestrøm	L	0-3	
06/07	h	Sandnes Ulf	W	1-0	Hamoud
12/07	a	Brann	W	1-0	Kovács
19/07	h	Vålerenga	L	0-2	
26/07	a	Sandnes Ulf	W	3-1	Ødegaard, Wikheim, Sørum
02/08	h	Sogndal	D	1-1	Ogunjimi
09/08	a	Odd	L	0-1	
15/08	a	Start	W	3-2	Adjei-Boateng, Ogunjimi 2
23/08	h	Stabæk	L	2-3	Vilsvik, Ogunjimi
30/08	a	Aalesund	L	0-1	
13/09	h	Brann	L	1-4	Kastrati
20/09	a	Bodø/Glimt	W	4-0	Sørum 2 (1p), Fossum, Kastrati
27/09	h	Viking	W	2-1	Adjei-Boateng, Storflor
05/10	a	Sarpsborg	D	0-0	
19/10	h	Lillestrøm	W	2-1	Ødegaard 2
25/10	h	Haugesund	L	2-3	Kovács 2
02/11	h	Molde	W	2-0	Storflor 2
09/11	a	Rosenborg	L	1-4	Kovács

No	Name	Nat	DoB	Pos	Aps	(s)	Gls
20	Mohammed Abu	GHA	14/11/91	M	28		
22	Bismark Adjei-Boateng	GHA	10/05/94	M	10	(1)	2
6	Simen Brenne		17/03/81	M		(1)	
3	Jeb Brovsky	USA	03/12/88	D	1	(2)	
14	Iver Fossum		15/07/96	M	23	(3)	3
8	Francisco Júnior	POR	18/01/92	M	10	(2)	1
21	Mathias Gjerstrøm		30/06/97	M		(1)	
13	Anders Gundersen		10/04/94	G	4		
2	Mounir Hamoud		01/02/85	D	24		3
5	Jørgen Horn		07/06/87	D	5	(1)	
25	Marius Høibråten		23/01/95	D	16		1
7	Bassel Jradi	DEN	06/08/93	M		(8)	
15	Flamur Kastrati		14/11/91	A	7	(11)	2
7	Muhamed Keita		02/09/90	A	4	(2)	
10	Péter Kovács	HUN	07/02/78	A	15	(9)	10
12	Adam Larsen Kwarasey	GHA	12/12/87	G	26		
4	Kim André Madsen		12/03/89	D	6	(1)	
18	Divine Naah	GHA	20/04/96	M		(1)	
25	Tokmac Nguen		20/10/93	A		(3)	
75	Marvin Ogunjimi	BEL	12/10/87	A	10	(1)	4
90	Patrick Olsen	DEN	23/04/94	M	2	(3)	
17	Thomas Lehne Olsen		29/06/91	A	1	(3)	
11	Martin Rønning Ovenstad		18/04/94	M	10	(3)	
27	Jarl-André Storbæk		21/09/78	D	19	(4)	
9	Øyvind Storflor		18/12/79	A	23	(3)	4
3	Lars Sætra		24/07/91	D	9		1
23	Thomas Sørum		17/11/92	A	6	(8)	6
71	Gustav Valsvik		26/05/93	D	13		
26	Lars Christopher Vilsvik		18/10/88	D	25		2
19	Gustav Wikheim		18/03/93	A	17	(10)	4
16	Martin Ødegaard		17/12/98	M	15	(8)	5

Viking FK

1899 • Viking (16,300) • viking-fk.no
Major honours
Norwegian League (8) 1958, 1972, 1973, 1974, 1975, 1979, 1982, 1991; Norwegian Cup (5) 1953, 1959, 1979, 1989, 2001
Coach: Kjell Jonevret (SWE)

2014

Date		Opponent		Score	Scorers
29/03	a	Rosenborg	D	2-2	Bödvarsson 2
04/04	h	Strømsgodset	D	0-0	
12/04	a	Lillestrøm	W	1-0	Bödvarsson
21/04	h	Haugesund	W	2-0	Ingason, Thorsteinsson
27/04	a	Start	W	2-0	Lanlay, Thorsteinsson
01/05	a	Aalesund	W	2-1	og (Tollås), Sverrisson
05/05	h	Odd	D	1-1	Ingason
11/05	a	Vålerenga	D	1-1	Sigurdsson
16/05	h	Sandnes Ulf	D	2-2	Nisja 2
20/05	a	Molde	L	0-1	
25/05	h	Bodø/Glimt	L	2-3	Sverrisson, Nisja
09/06	a	Sarpsborg	D	1-1	Bödvarsson
12/06	h	Stabæk	W	4-1	Danielsen, Bödvarsson, Sverrisson, Thorsteinsson
06/07	h	Brann	L	0-2	
12/07	a	Sogndal	D	0-0	
20/07	h	Lillestrøm	D	0-0	
27/07	a	Brann	W	1-0	Sverrisson
02/08	a	Vålerenga	D	5-5	Sigurdsson, Thioune, Nisja 2, Sverrisson
10/08	a	Haugesund	D	1-1	Chikere
16/08	h	Sogndal	W	4-2	Sigurdsson, Haugen, Nisja, Lanlay
22/08	a	Sandnes Ulf	D	2-2	Thorsteinsson, Sverrisson
31/08	h	Rosenborg	L	1-2	Skogseid
13/09	a	Odd	L	1-4	og (Grøgaard)
21/09	h	Start	L	0-1	
27/09	a	Strømsgodset	L	1-2	Landu Landu
04/10	h	Molde	L	1-2	Nisja
19/10	a	Stabæk	L	1-2	Berisha
26/10	h	Aalesund	L	1-2	Ingason
02/11	a	Sarpsborg	W	1-0	Nisja
09/11	a	Bodø/Glimt	L	2-3	Nisja, og (Sané)

No	Name	Nat	DoB	Pos	Aps	(s)	Gls
30	Iven Austbø		22/02/85	G	12	(1)	
10	Veton Berisha		13/04/94	A	10	(15)	1
2	Trond Erik Bertelsen		05/06/84	D	12		
17	Jón Dadi Bödvarsson	ISL	25/05/92	A	24	(5)	5
18	Osita Chikere	NGA	03/02/91	A	3	(10)	1
14	André Danielsen		20/01/85	D	28		1
26	Pål Fjelde		26/07/94	D		(1)	
28	Kristoffer Haugen		21/02/94	D	18	(4)	1
27	Martin Hummervoll		13/03/96	M	1		
5	Sverrir Ingi Ingason	ISL	05/08/93	D	29		3
4	Joackim Jørgensen		20/09/88	M	25	(2)	
13	Christian Landu Landu		25/01/92	D	7	(10)	1
16	Yann-Erik de Lanlay		14/05/92	A	26		2
25	Rasmus Martinsen		14/04/96	D		(1)	
8	Vidar Nisja		21/08/86	M	20	(8)	9
29	Carl-Henrik Refvik			A		(1)	
20	Indridi Sigurdsson	ISL	12/10/81	D	26		3
6	Håkon Skogseid		14/01/88	D	8	(5)	1
7	Björn Daniel Sverrisson	ISL	29/05/90	M	27	(2)	6
11	El Hadji Makhtar Thioune	SEN	05/08/84	M	12	(12)	1
23	Steinthór Thorsteinsson	ISL	29/07/85	A	24	(5)	4
21	Julian Veen Uldal		11/06/97	A		(1)	
1	Arild Østbø		19/04/91	G	18		

NORWAY

Vålerenga Fotball

1913 • Ullevaal (27,182) • vif-fotball.no
Major honours
*Norwegian League (5) 1965, 1981, 1983, 1984,
2005; Norwegian Cup (4) 1980, 1997, 2002, 2008*
Coach: Kjetil Rekdal

2014

28/03	a	Molde	L	0-2	
06/04	h	Bodø/Glimt	W	3-1	Kjartansson 2 (1p), Lindkvist
12/04	a	Haugesund	D	1-1	Kjartansson (p)
21/04	h	Sandnes Ulf	W	3-0	Kjartansson, Lindkvist, Gunnarsson
28/04	a	Sarpsborg	L	0-3	
01/05	h	Strømsgodset	W	3-0	Kjartansson 2 (1p), Lindkvist
05/05	a	Stabæk	W	3-0	og (Fontanello), Larsen, Kjartansson
11/05	h	Viking	D	1-1	Kjartansson
16/05	a	Start	D	2-2	Kjartansson 2 (1p)
19/05	h	Lillestrøm	D	2-2	Lindkvist, og (Kippe)
25/05	a	Brann	W	3-2	Høgh, Kjartansson, Stengel
09/06	h	Aalesund	W	3-0	Kjartansson 2, Holm
12/06	a	Sogndal	L	0-2	
07/07	a	Odd	D	2-2	Mathisen, Larsen
13/07	h	Rosenborg	D	2-2	Berre, Grindheim
19/07	a	Strømsgodset	W	2-0	Zahid, Kjartansson
29/07	h	Stabæk	W	3-2	Zahid 2, Kjartansson
02/08	a	Viking	D	5-5	Larsen, Kjartansson 3, Zahid
09/08	h	Sarpsborg	D	2-2	Kjartansson (p), Zahid
17/08	a	Lillestrøm	L	1-2	Berre
23/08	h	Brann	D	3-3	Zahid, Kjartansson 2
30/08	a	Bodø/Glimt	L	3-4	Larsen, Grindheim 2
14/09	h	Haugesund	W	4-1	Kjartansson 3, Zahid
20/09	a	Molde	L	0-2	
26/09	a	Sandnes Ulf	L	1-2	Grindheim
05/10	h	Sogndal	W	2-1	Zahid, og (Patronen)
19/10	a	Rosenborg	L	2-3	Kjartansson, Gunnarsson
24/10	h	Odd	L	1-2	Zahid
02/11	a	Aalesund	L	1-4	Larsen
09/11	h	Start	W	1-0	Stengel

No	Name	Nat	DoB	Pos	Aps	(s)	Gls
11	Morten Berre		10/08/75	A	11	(18)	2
15	Max Bjørsvik		07/06/89	D	2	(4)	
36	Mathias Blårud		06/06/95	M	1	(11)	
25	Markus Brændsrød		09/06/95	M	0	(6)	
22	Diego Calvo	CRC	25/03/91	A	7	(3)	
19	Christian Grindheim		17/07/83	M	28	(1)	4
2	Niklas Gunnarsson		27/04/91	D	29		2
7	Daniel Fredheim Holm		30/07/85	A	14	(6)	1
24	Nicolai Høgh	DEN	09/11/83	D	14		1
35	Ali Iqbal		20/02/95	D	4	(6)	
38	Fitim Kastrati		08/10/94	A		(1)	
10	Vidar Örn Kjartansson	ISL	11/03/90	A	29		25
34	Gudmund Kongshavn		23/01/91	G	2		
3	Ruben Kristiansen		20/02/88	D	26		
30	Michael Langer	AUT	06/01/85	G	28		
6	Simon Larsen		01/06/88	D	30		5
5	Rasmus Lindkvist	SWE	16/05/90	A	19	(3)	4
21	Alexander Mathisen		24/11/86	M	17	(7)	1
4	André Muri		22/04/81	D	4		
39	Moussa Nije		02/10/95	A		(2)	
8	Sivert Heltne Nilsen		02/10/91	M	28		
37	Ivan Näsberg		22/04/96	D	3	(1)	
26	Simen Olafsen		26/05/96	D		(1)	
14	Herman Stengel		26/08/95	M	8	(16)	2
17	Ghayas Zahid		18/11/94	M	26	(3)	9

Top goalscorers

25	Vidar Örn Kjartansson (Vålerenga)
15	Christian Gytkjær (Haugesund)
13	Abdurahim Laajab (Bodø/Glimt)
	Mohamed Elyounoussi (Molde)
	Alexander Søderlund (Rosenborg)
	Franck Boli (Stabæk)
11	Frode Johnsen (Odd)
10	Leke James (Aalesund)
	Maic Sema (Haugesund)
	Daniel Chima (Molde)
	Fredrik Gulbrandsen (Molde)
	Fredrik Brustad (Stabæk)
	Péter Kovács (Strømsgodset)

Promoted clubs

Sandefjord Fotball

1998 • Komplett.no Arena (6,000) •
sandefjordfotball.no
Coach: Lars Bohinen

Tromsø IL

1920 • Alfheim (6,859) • til.no
Major honours
Norwegian Cup (2) 1986, 1996
Coach: Steinar Nilsen

Mjøndalen IF

1910 • Mjøndalen (2,500) • mif.no
Coach: Vegard Hansen

Second level final table 2014

		Pld	W	D	L	F	A	Pts
1	Sandefjord Fotball	30	20	9	1	62	24	69
2	Tromsø IL	30	18	5	7	67	27	59
3	Mjøndalen IF	30	14	9	7	57	36	51
4	Kristiansund BK	30	13	10	7	53	39	49
5	Bærum SK	30	15	4	11	51	52	49
6	Fredrikstad FK	30	14	6	10	35	26	48
7	Ranheim IL	30	13	7	10	45	34	46
8	IL Hødd Fotball	30	12	7	11	48	49	43
9	Bryne FK	30	13	3	14	48	55	42
10	Strømmen IF	30	11	8	11	59	54	41
11	Hønefoss BK	30	12	4	14	39	55	40
12	IL Nest-Sotra	30	10	7	13	49	51	37
13	Alta IF	30	9	7	14	33	51	34
14	Tromsdalen UIL	30	8	7	15	44	56	31
15	Ullensaker/Kisa IL	30	6	5	19	26	51	23
16	HamKam Fotball	30	1	4	25	22	78	7

Promotion/Relegation play-offs

(09/11/14)
Kristiansund 0-2 Bærum
Mjøndalen 2-0 Fredrikstad

(15/11/14)
Mjøndalen 4-1 Bærum *(aet)*

(23/11/14 & 26/11/14)
Brann 1-1 Mjøndalen
Mjøndalen 3-0 Brann
(Mjøndalen 4-1)

DOMESTIC CUP

Norgesmesterskapet 2014

FIRST ROUND

(24/04/14)
Asker 3-1 Kvik Halden *(aet)*
Aurskog-Høland 0-5 Ullensaker/Kisa
Bergsøy 0-5 Aalesund
Bjarg 2-2 Åsane *(aet; 0-3 on pens)*
Bossekop 1-4 Alta
Brattvåg 0-3 Kristiansund
Brodd 0-3 Viking
Brumunddal 1-2 Nybergsund
Drammen 2-10 Strømsgodset
Drøbak-Frogn 1-4 Pors Grenland
Fana 1-2 Stord
Fet 0-7 Lillestrøm
Florø 2-0 Førde
Fløya 0-3 Ranheim
Fram Larvik 6-1 Larvik Turn
Frigg Oslo 1-4 Sandefjord
Gjøvik-Lyn 5-1 Eidsvold Turn
Grorud 7-0 Lokomotiv Oslo
Grue 0-1 Kongsvinger
Harstad 2-1 Medkila
Hasle-Løren 0-2 Bærum
Hauerseter 1-2 Strømmen
Høllen 0-4 Start
Jevnaker 0-8 Stabæk
Jerv 3-0 Fløy
KFUM Oslo 0-4 Notodden
Kirkenes 0-4 Tromsdalen
Kjapp 0-4 Odd
Klepp 1-4 Bryne
Kolstad 3-1 Rødde
Kråkerøy 0-5 Moss
Larsnes/Gursken 2-5 Hødd
Lommedalen 0-6 Mjøndalen
Lyn 4-0 Skeid
Lyngbø 1-1 Nest-Sotra *(aet; 1-4 on pens)*
Lyngdal 1-2 Egersund
Lørenskog 3-2 Birkebeineren
Mjølner 0-0 Tromsø *(aet; 7-8 on pens)*
Mo 2-1 Sandnessjøen
Modum 0-3 Hønefoss
Nordstrand 0-5 Vålerenga
Orkla 0-3 Rosenborg
Os 1-2 Vard Haugesund
Oslojuvelene 1-5 Fredrikstad
Ottestad 2-4 HamKam *(aet)*
Raufoss 2-1 Holmen
Sarpsborg FK 0-11 Sarpsborg 08
Senja 1-3 Finnsnes
Sola 1-0 Sandnes Ulf
Strindheim 2-0 Nardo
Surnadal 0-9 Molde
Tynset 0-1 Elverum
Tverlandet 0-5 Bodø/Glimt
Vadmyra 0-2 Fyllingsdalen
Valdres 0-8 Follo
Varegg 2-3 Brann
Verdal 1-5 Byåsen
Ørn-Horten 2-1 Kjelsås
Åkra 1-2 Haugesund
Årdal 0-4 Sogndal

(25/04/14)
Arendal 4-2 Vindbjart
Herd 2-3 Træff *(aet)*
Steinkjer 3-4 Levanger
Ålgård 2-4 Vidar

SECOND ROUND

(07/05/14)
Byåsen 1-3 Kristiansund
Bærum 3-4 Lyn *(aet)*
Egersund 3-2 Arendal *(aet)*
Finnsnes 2-2 Tromsø *(aet; 2-4 on pens)*
Follo 1-0 Fredrikstad
Hødd 1-5 Florø
Hønefoss 1-2 Grorud
Jerv 1-2 Start
Kolstad 2-10 Rosenborg
Kongsvinger 5-3 Alta *(aet)*
Lørenskog 0-1 Sarpsborg 08
Mo 1-3 Bodø/Glimt
Moss 0-5 Lillestrøm
Nest-Sotra 1-2 Fyllingsdalen *(aet)*
Notodden 3-2 Sandefjord
Nybergsund 0-0 HamKam *(aet; 3-4 on pens)*
Pors Grenland 0-1 Mjøndalen
Stord 1-2 Brann
Strindheim 0-1 Molde
Strømmen 3-0 Asker
Tromsdalen 1-1 Harstad *(aet; 6-5 on pens)*
Træff 0-3 Aalesund
Ullensaker/Kisa 2-1 Gjøvik-Lyn
Vard Haugesund 1-0 Bryne
Vidar 2-3 Haugesund
Ørn-Horten 1-2 Strømsgodset *(aet)*
Åsane 0-2 Sogndal

(08/05/14)
Elverum 2-3 Vålerenga
Fram Larvik 2-4 Odd *(aet)*
Ranheim 6-2 Levanger
Raufoss 1-2 Stabæk
Sola 1-7 Viking

THIRD ROUND

(28/05/14)
Grorud 0-3 Stabæk *(aet)*

(04/06/14)
Egersund 0-3 Viking
Florø 1-2 Molde
Fyllingsdalen 1-3 Brann
Kristiansund 0-1 Aalesund
Lillestrøm 4-1 Kongsvinger
Mjøndalen 1-0 Ullensaker/Kisa
Notodden 0-4 Odd
Rosenborg 3-4 Ranheim *(aet)*
Sarpsborg 08 2-0 Follo
Sogndal 3-0 Strømmen

Start 4-0 Vard Haugesund
Tromsdalen 4-2 Strømsgodset *(aet)*
Vålerenga 5-2 Lyn

(05/06/14)
HamKam 0-1 Haugesund
Tromsø 1-2 Bodø/Glimt

FOURTH ROUND

(27/06/14)
Aalesund 1-3 Lillestrøm *(aet)*
Brann 4-2 Ranheim
Haugesund 5-0 Tromsdalen
Molde 4-1 Mjøndalen
Odd 3-2 Vålerenga
Sarpsborg 08 3-2 Start
Viking 4-1 Sogndal

(23/07/14)
Bodø/Glimt 0-2 Stabæk

QUARTER-FINALS

(13/08/14)
Molde 5-1 Viking *(Chima 14, Elyounoussi 40, Moström 50, Flo 58, Gulbrandsen 68; Lanlay 32)*
Stabæk 1-0 Haugesund *(Hoseth 1)*

(14/08/14)
Lillestrøm 0-2 Sarpsborg 08 *(Zajić 15, Wiig 80)*
Odd 3-1 Brann *(Shala 66p, 87, Johnsen 78; Huseklepp 24)*

SEMI-FINALS

(24/09/14)
Stabæk 0-1 Molde *(Elyounoussi 86)*

(25/09/14)
Odd 5-2 Sarpsborg 08 *(Shala 49p, 71, Halvorsen 58, 90+3, Johnsen 66; Zajić 38, Thórarinsson 77)*

FINAL

(23/11/14)
Ullevaal stadion, Oslo
MOLDE FK 2 *(Gulbrandsen 73, Elyounoussi 88)*
ODDS BK 0
Referee: *Hafsås*
MOLDE: *Nyland, Linnes, Toivio, Forren, Flo, Moström (Berg Hestad 90), Hussain, Singh, Elyounoussi, Gulbrandsen (Høiland 80), Chima (Sigurdarson 70)*
ODD: *Hansen, Hurme, Eriksen, Hagen, Grøgaard, Samuelsen, Jensen (Gashi 82), Nordkvelle (Storbæk 84), Akabueze, Johnsen, Shala (Halvorsen 66)*

The celebrations continue for Molde as they add the Norwegian Cup to their league title

POLAND

Polski Związek Piłki Nożnej (PZPN)

Address	Bitwy Warszawskiej 1920 r.7 PL-02 366 Warszawa
Tel	+48 22 551 2300
Fax	+48 22 551 2240
E-mail	pzpn@pzpn.pl
Website	pzpn.pl

President	Zbigniew Boniek
General secretary	Maciej Sawicki
Media officer	Janusz Basałaj
Year of formation	1919
National stadium	National Stadium, Warsaw (53,224)

EKSTRAKLASA CLUBS

 1 **GKS Bełchatów**

 2 **MKS Cracovia Kraków**

 3 **GKS Górnik Łęczna**

 4 **Górnik Zabrze**

 5 **Jagiellonia Białystok**

 6 **Korona Kielce**

 7 **KKS Lech Poznań**

 8 **KS Lechia Gdańsk**

 9 **Legia Warszawa**

 10 **GKS Piast Gliwice**

 11 **TS Podbeskidzie Bielsko-Biała**

 12 **MKS Pogoń Szczecin**

 13 **Ruch Chorzów**

 14 **WKS Śląsk Wrocław**

 15 **Wisła Kraków**

 16 **Zawisza Bydgoszcz**

PROMOTED CLUBS

 17 **Zagłębie Lubin**

 18 **KS Nieciecza**

0 200 400 km	
0 200 miles	

KEY:

● – UEFA Champions League

● – UEFA Europa League

● – Promoted

● – Relegated

Late show from Lech

Poland's Ekstraklasa was the last of Europe's top divisions to provide a champion in 2014/15. The marathon campaign, which kicked off in July 2014, finally delivered a winner on 7 June 2015 when KKS Lech Poznań drew 0-0 at home to Wisła Kraków to take the title by a point from defending champions Legia Warszawa.

A month earlier the roles were reversed as Legia defeated Lech 2-1 in a Polish Cup final played to a packed house at the Stadion Narodowy in Warsaw, home also of the Polish national team, whose excellent season was highlighted by a historic 2-0 win over Germany.

LECH POZNAŃ
MISTRZ POLSKI 2014/2015

| Poznan club dethrone Legia in marathon title race | Roles reversed in cup final as Warsaw club prevail | Historic victory over Germany sparks EURO charge |

Domestic league

Legia, led again by 2013/14 title-winning coach Henning Berg, were bidding to claim a hat-trick of league titles for the first time, and although they started hesitantly, a strong surge of form took them into the winter break as leaders with a three-point buffer ahead of WKS Śląsk Wrocław, with three other teams – Lech, Wisła and Jagiellonia Białystok – all three further points in arrears.

When the 30-match first phase ended in late April, Legia still led, but Lech, now under Maciej Skorża, a double Polish championship-winning coach with Wisła, had closed the gap to just one point. Legia had been table-toppers for several months, but when Lech beat them 2-1 in Warsaw in the first play-off fixture, the challengers from Poznan leapfrogged the champions to the summit.

Lech lost the following week, 3-1 at home to Jagiellonia, who in turn went down 1-0 at Legia. The team from Bialystok would finish with four straight wins, but Michał Probierz's brave battlers came up just short. So, too, did Legia, whose goalless draw at KS Lechia Gdańsk enabled Lech to go into round 37 with a three-point lead. Had the two clubs finished level on points, Legia would have been champions by virtue of their first place at the end of

the regular 30-match season, but Lech duly held out for the goalless draw they needed against Wisła to clinch their first title in five years.

Lech's chief asset was being hard to beat, but they were also the league's top-scoring team, with 13-goal Finnish midfielder Kasper Hämäläinen their sole marksman in double figures. The only Ekstraklasa player to score 20 goals was GKS Piast Gliwice's Kamil Wilczek, his final four coming in a 6-3 win over newly promoted GKS Bełchatów, who were relegated alongside 2013/14 Polish Cup winners Zawisza Bydgoszcz.

Domestic cup

Zawisza's trophy defence ended early, and it was the league's leading duo, Legia and Lech, who contested the final. A sell-out crowd gathered at the national stadium in early May and, unlike in the clubs' pivotal Ekstraklasa fixture a week later, it was the Legia fans celebrating at the end, a 2-1 comeback win sealed by 36-year-old Marek Saganowski delivering the Warsaw club's fourth Polish Cup victory in five years and record 17th in all.

Europe

Legia's hopes of participating in the UEFA Champions League group stage were

destroyed by an administrative error. Comprehensive victors over Celtic FC in the third qualifying round, they had to forfeit the second leg 3-0 after sending on an ineligible player, Bartosz Bereszyński, in the closing minutes. Honour was restored in the UEFA Europa League, where they won five group games, but the dream of reaching the final in their home city was dashed by AFC Ajax – and in particular Polish striker Arkadiusz Milik, who scored three times in the Amsterdam club's round of 32 success.

National team

Milik was a key contributor to Poland's unbeaten run in the first six games of their UEFA EURO 2016 qualifying campaign. He scored in four of those matches, starting with a fine header in the 2-0 home win over the world champions that brought Poland their first victory in 19 attempts against (West) Germany. Dropped points against Scotland and the Republic of Ireland could not dislodge Adam Nawałka's impressive side from the Group D summit, and although a third successive EURO participation was far from guaranteed, a 4-0 win over Georgia in June, capped by a late quickfire hat-trick from star striker Robert Lewandowski, suggested that Poland were more than capable of sustaining their ebullient form all the way to France.

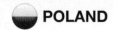
DOMESTIC SEASON AT A GLANCE

Ekstraklasa 2014/15 final table

		Pld	Home					Away					Total					Pts
			W	D	L	F	A	W	D	L	F	A	W	D	L	F	A	
1	**KKS Lech Poznań**	37	12	5	2	39	14	7	8	3	28	19	19	13	5	67	33	43
2	Legia Warszawa	37	13	3	3	36	16	8	4	6	28	17	21	7	9	64	33	42
3	Jagiellonia Białystok	37	11	4	4	35	24	8	4	6	24	20	19	8	10	59	44	41
4	WKS Śląsk Wrocław	37	11	6	2	26	12	4	7	7	24	31	15	13	9	50	43	35
5	KS Lechia Gdańsk	37	8	5	5	21	18	5	5	9	24	29	13	10	14	45	47	29
6	Wisła Kraków	37	7	6	5	26	22	5	7	7	30	26	12	13	12	56	48	28
7	Górnik Zabrze	37	6	7	5	28	32	6	4	9	22	28	12	11	14	50	60	26
8	MKS Pogoń Szczecin	37	8	3	7	26	20	3	6	10	19	32	11	9	17	45	52	22
9	MKS Cracovia Kraków	37	10	5	4	27	20	5	4	9	23	24	15	9	13	50	44	36
10	Ruch Chorzów	37	7	4	7	26	21	5	6	8	18	25	12	10	15	44	46	30
11	Korona Kielce	37	8	6	5	28	28	4	5	9	16	27	12	11	14	44	55	28
12	GKS Piast Gliwice	37	10	3	6	36	26	3	5	10	14	30	13	8	16	50	56	28
13	TS Podbeskidzie Bielsko-Biała	37	7	6	6	25	29	5	4	9	22	31	12	10	15	47	60	27
14	GKS Górnik Łęczna	37	7	7	4	25	18	4	4	11	14	28	11	11	15	39	46	27
15	Zawisza Bydgoszcz	37	6	4	8	20	24	4	4	11	25	39	10	8	19	45	63	24
16	GKS Bełchatów	37	5	6	7	18	24	4	3	12	17	36	9	9	19	35	60	21

NB League splits into top and bottom halves after 30 games, after which the clubs play exclusively against teams in their group. Points obtained during the regular season are halved (and rounded upwards).

European qualification 2015/16

Champion: KKS Lech Poznań (second qualifying round)

Cup winner: Legia Warszawa (second qualifying round)
Jagiellonia Białystok (first qualifying round)
WKS Śląsk Wrocław (first qualifying round)

Top scorer	Kamil Wilczek (Piast), 20 goals
Relegated clubs	GKS Bełchatów, Zawisza Bydgoszcz
Promoted clubs	Zagłębie Lubin, KS Nieciecza
Cup final	Legia Warszawa 2-1 KKS Lech Poznań

Team of the season
(4-2-3-1)

Coach: Probierz (Jagiellonia)

Drągowski (Jagiellonia)
Wójcicki (Zawisza) · Pazdan (Jagiellonia) · Arajuuri (Lech) · Brzyski (Legia)
Linetty (Lech) · R Murawski (Pogoń)
Rakels (Cracovia) · Štilić (Wisła) · Pawłowski (Lech)
Wilczek (Piast)

Player of the season

Karol Linetty
(KKS Lech Poznań)

Lech's Ekstraklasa triumph was very much a collective effort, with organisation, discipline and resilience at the heart of their success. The turning point of the title race, however, was provided by a moment of individual magic as Lech defeated long-time leaders Legia Warszawa 2-1 in Warsaw, the winning goal coming from Linetty as he raced from halfway before curling in an unstoppable right-foot shot. The 20-year-old midfielder's excellent season was rewarded with a couple of caps for Poland.

Newcomer of the season

Bartłomiej Drągowski
(Jagiellonia Białystok)

Poland has produced many top-class goalkeepers down the years, and on the evidence of the 2014/15 season another has been unearthed in Drągowski. A mere 17 years of age during a debut top-flight campaign in which his sustained excellence helped Jagiellonia to the brink of a first ever league title, he was voted the Ekstraklasa's goalkeeper and discovery of the season by his fellow top-flight players. With foreign scouts monitoring his progress, a lengthy stay in his home town of Bialystok appears unlikely.

POLAND

NATIONAL TEAM

International tournament appearances

FIFA World Cup (7) 1938, 1974 (3rd), 1978 (2nd phase), 1982 (3rd), 1986 (2nd round), 2002, 2006
UEFA European Championship (2) 2008, 2012

Top five all-time caps

Michał Żewłakow (102); Grzegorz Lato (100); Kazimierz Deyna (97); Jacek Bąk & Jacek Krzynówek (96)

Top five all-time goals

Włodzimierz Lubański (48); Grzegorz Lato (45); Kazimierz Deyna (41); Ernest Pol (39); Andrzej Szarmach (32)

Results 2014/15

07/09/14	Gibraltar (ECQ)	A	Faro (POR)	W	7-0	Grosicki (11, 48), Lewandowski (50, 53, 86, 90+2), Szukała (58)
11/10/14	Germany (ECQ)	H	Warsaw	W	2-0	Milik (51), Mila (88)
14/10/14	Scotland (ECQ)	H	Warsaw	D	2-2	Mączyński (11), Milik (76)
14/11/14	Georgia (ECQ)	A	Tbilisi	W	4-0	Glik (51), Krychowiak (71), Mila (73), Milik (90+2)
18/11/14	Switzerland	H	Wroclaw	D	2-2	Jędrzejczyk (45), Milik (61)
29/03/15	Republic of Ireland (ECQ)	A	Dublin	D	1-1	Peszko (26)
13/06/15	Georgia (ECQ)	H	Warsaw	W	4-0	Milik (62), Lewandowski (89, 90+2, 90+3)
16/06/15	Greece	H	Gdansk	D	0-0	

Appearances 2014/15

Coach: Adam Nawałka	23/10/57		GIB	GER	SCO	GEO	Sui	IRL	GEO	Gre	Caps	Goals
Wojciech Szczęsny	18/04/90	Arsenal (ENG)	G	G	G	G				s46	23	-
Paweł Olkowski	13/02/90	Köln (GER)	D				D	D			9	-
Łukasz Szukała	26/05/84	Steaua (ROU) /Al-Ittihad (KSA)	D	D	D	D		D	D	s86	13	1
Kamil Glik	03/02/88	Torino (ITA)	D	D	D	D	D	D		D	31	3
Jakub Wawrzyniak	07/07/83	Amkar (RUS) /Lechia	D	D84				D			44	1
Kamil Grosicki	08/06/88	Rennes (FRA)	M78	M71	M89	M69			M80	M	29	2
Mateusz Klich	13/06/90	Wolfsburg (GER)	M71								10	1
Grzegorz Krychowiak	29/01/90	Sevilla (ESP)	M	M	M	M	M68	M	M		26	1
Arkadiusz Milik	28/02/94	Ajax (NED)	M71	M77	M	M	s46	M84	M	A78	17	7
Maciej Rybus	19/08/89	Terek (RUS)	M	M		s69	M	M	D	s78	35	2
Robert Lewandowski	21/08/88	Bayern (GER)	A	A	A	A	A63	A	A		68	26
Krzysztof Mączyński	23/05/87	Guizhou Renhe (CHN)	s71		M	M66			M	s60	8	1
Waldemar Sobota	19/05/87	Club Brugge (BEL)	s71	s71	M63						17	4
Filip Starzyński	27/05/91	Ruch	s78								1	-
Łukasz Piszczek	03/06/85	Dortmund (GER)		D	D	D			D		40	2
Tomasz Jodłowiec	08/09/85	Legia		M		s66	M	M	s80		37	-
Sebastian Mila	10/07/82	Śląsk /Lechia		s77	s63	M86	s63	s84		s60	36	8
Artur Jędrzejczyk	04/11/87	Krasnodar (RUS)		s84	D	D	D52				15	2
Michał Żyro	20/09/92	Legia			s89		s53 83*				4	-
Karol Linetty	02/02/95	Lech					s86			M60	6	1
Artur Boruc	20/02/80	Bournemouth (ENG)					G46		G46		60	-
Thiago Cionek	21/04/86	Modena (ITA)					D		D		3	-
Michał Kucharczyk	20/03/91	Legia					M53	s88			9	1
Piotr Zieliński	20/05/94	Empoli (ITA)					M46		M60		9	3
Łukasz Fabiański	18/04/85	Swansea (ENG)					s46	G	G		24	-
Łukasz Broź	17/12/85	Legia					s52				3	-
Łukasz Teodorczyk	03/06/91	Dynamo Kyiv (UKR)					s68				7	3
Sławomir Peszko	19/02/85	Köln (GER)						M88	M64	s60	32	2
Michał Pazdan	21/09/87	Jagiellonia						D90	D		11	-
Jakub Błaszczykowski	14/12/85	Dortmund (GER)							s64	M60	70	14
Marcin Komorowski	17/04/84	Terek (RUS)							s90	D	13	1
Ariel Borysiuk	29/07/91	Lechia								M86	10	-

Legia Warszawa

CHAMPIONS LEAGUE

Second qualifying round - Saint Patrick's Athletic FC (IRL)
H 1-1 *Radović (90+1)*
Kuciak, Jodłowiec, Iñaki Astiz, Brzyski, Kosecki (Duda 77), Hélio Pinto (Vrdoljak 66), Rzeźniczak, Broź, Radović, Żyro, Orlando Sá (Saganowski 16). Coach: Henning Berg (NOR)
A 5-0 *Radović (25, 82), Żyro (69), Saganowski (87), Byrne (90+2og)*
Kuciak, Jodłowiec, Duda (Saganowski 84), Iñaki Astiz, Brzyski, Kucharczyk (Kosecki 85), Vrdoljak, Rzeźniczak, Broź, Radović (Piech 88), Żyro. Coach: Henning Berg (NOR)

Third qualifying round - Celtic FC (SCO)
H 4-1 *Radović (10, 36), Żyro (84), Kosecki (90+1)*
Kuciak, Jodłowiec, Duda, Iñaki Astiz, Brzyski, Kucharczyk (Kosecki 75), Vrdoljak, Rzeźniczak, Broź, Radović, Żyro (Saganowski 88). Coach: Henning Berg (NOR)
A 0-3 (w/o) original result 2-0 *(Żyro (36), Kucharczyk (61))*
Kuciak, Jodłowiec, Duda (Hélio Pinto 86), Iñaki Astiz, Brzyski, Kucharczyk (Kosecki 74), Vrdoljak, Rzeźniczak, Broź, Radović, Żyro (Bereszyński 86). Coach: Henning Berg (NOR)

EUROPA LEAGUE

Play-offs - FC Aktobe (KAZ)
A 1-0 *Duda (48)*
Kuciak, Dossa Júnior, Jodłowiec, Duda, Brzyski, Kucharczyk, Vrdoljak, Rzeźniczak, Broź, Radović, Żyro. Coach: Henning Berg (NOR)
H 2-0 *Kucharczyk (26), Vrdoljak (66p)*
Kuciak, Dossa Júnior, Jodłowiec, Duda (Saganowski 88), Brzyski, Kucharczyk (Kosecki 66), Vrdoljak, Rzeźniczak, Broź, Radović, Żyro. Coach: Henning Berg (NOR)

Group L
Match 1 - KSC Lokeren OV (BEL)
H 1-0 *Radović (58)*
Kuciak, Dossa Júnior, Jodłowiec, Duda (Saganowski 90+2), Brzyski, Kucharczyk, Vrdoljak, Rzeźniczak, Broź, Radović, Żyro. Coach: Henning Berg (NOR)
Match 2 - Trabzonspor AŞ (TUR)
A 1-0 *Kucharczyk (16)*
Kuciak, Dossa Júnior, Jodłowiec, Duda, Brzyski, Kucharczyk (Kosecki 90+5), Vrdoljak, Rzeźniczak, Broź, Radović (Saganowski 90+1), Żyro. Coach: Henning Berg (NOR)
Red card: Żyro 88
Match 3 - FC Metalist Kharkiv (UKR)
A 1-0 *Duda (28)*
Kuciak, Jodłowiec, Guilherme, Duda, Iñaki Astiz, Kucharczyk, Kosecki, Vrdoljak, Rzeźniczak, Broź, Orlando Sá (Saganowski 81). Coach: Henning Berg (NOR)
Match 4 - FC Metalist Kharkiv (UKR)
H 2-1 *Saganowski (29), Duda (84)*
Kuciak, Jodłowiec, Guilherme, Duda, Saganowski (Orlando Sá 75), Iñaki Astiz, Kucharczyk (Kosecki 81), Vrdoljak, Rzeźniczak, Broź, Żyro. Coach: Henning Berg (NOR)

Match 5 - KSC Lokeren OV (BEL)
A 0-1
Kuciak, Jodłowiec, Guilherme, Duda, Iñaki Astiz, Kucharczyk, Kosecki (Żyro 46), Vrdoljak, Rzeźniczak, Broź, Orlando Sá (Saganowski 63). Coach: Henning Berg (NOR)
Match 6 - Trabzonspor AŞ (TUR)
H 2-0 *Fatih Öztürk (22og), Orlando Sá (56)*
Kuciak, Jodłowiec, Lewczuk, Guilherme, Duda (Bielik 88), Iñaki Astiz, Kucharczyk (Saganowski 86), Vrdoljak, Broź, Żyro (Kosecki 34), Orlando Sá. Coach: Henning Berg (NOR)

Round of 32 - AFC Ajax (NED)
A 0-1
Kuciak, Dossa Júnior, Jodłowiec, Guilherme, Masłowski, Kucharczyk, Vrdoljak, Rzeźniczak, Broź, Żyro, Orlando Sá. Coach: Henning Berg (NOR)
H 0-3
Kuciak, Dossa Júnior, Jodłowiec, Guilherme, Masłowski (Hélio Pinto 72), Kucharczyk, Vrdoljak, Rzeźniczak, Broź, Żyro (Kosecki 60), Orlando Sá (Saganowski 60). Coach: Henning Berg (NOR)

Zawisza Bydgoszcz

EUROPA LEAGUE

Second qualifying round - SV Zulte Waregem (BEL)
A 1-2 *Drygas (15)*
Sandomierski, Joshua Silva (Petasz 46), André Micael, Bernardo Vasconcelos, Wójcicki (Jorge Kadú 56), Ziajka, Drygas, Luís Carlos, Sochań (Gevorgyan 76), Wagner, Nawotczyński. Coach: Jorge Paixão (POR)
H 1-3 *Petasz (52)*
Sandomierski, Petasz, Bernardo Vasconcelos, Alvarinho, Ziajka, Drygas (Wójcicki 73), Strąk, Luís Carlos, Wagner (Jorge Kadú 58), Nawotczyński (André Micael 53), Samuel Araújo. Coach: Jorge Paixão (POR)
Red card: Bernardo Vasconcelos 68

KKS Lech Poznań

EUROPA LEAGUE

Second qualifying round - Nõmme Kalju FC (EST)
A 0-1
Burić, Kędziora, Trałka, Linetty (Kownacki 60), Pawłowski, Lovrencsics, Jevtic, Hämäläinen, Wołąkiewicz, Henríquez, Wilusz. Coach: Mariusz Rumak (POL)
H 3-0 *Kędziora (33), Hämäläinen (43), Kownacki (90+3)*
Burić, Kędziora, Trałka, Pawłowski (Keita 74), Lovrencsics, Ubiparip (Teodorczyk 85), Jevtic, Hämäläinen (Kownacki 68), Wołąkiewicz, Henríquez, Kamiński. Coach: Mariusz Rumak (POL)

Third qualifying round - Stjarnan (ISL)
A 0-1
Burić, Kędziora, Trałka, Pawłowski, Lovrencsics (Douglas 87), Ubiparip, Jevtic, Hämäläinen (Keita 70), Wołąkiewicz, Henríquez, Kamiński. Coach: Mariusz Rumak (POL)
H 0-0
Kotorowski, Kędziora (Kownacki 76), Trałka, Pawłowski, Ubiparip, Jevtic, Hämäläinen (Teodorczyk 54), Wołąkiewicz, Henríquez, Kamiński, Keita (Lovrencsics 59). Coach: Mariusz Rumak (POL)

Ruch Chorzów

EUROPA LEAGUE

Second qualifying round - FC Vaduz (LIE)
H 3-2 *Zieńczuk (19), Stawarczyk (21, 74)*
Kamiński, Stawarczyk, Dziwniel, Surma, Zieńczuk, Kowalski, Kuświk, Starzyński (Efir 69), Konczkowski, Babiarz, Malinowski. Coach: Ján Kocian (SVK)
A 0-0
Kamiński, Stawarczyk, Dziwniel (Konczkowski 90), Surma, Szewczyk (Efir 66), Kowalski (Włodyka 89), Kuświk, Starzyński, Babiarz, Malinowski, Helik. Coach: Ján Kocian (SVK)

Third qualifying round - Esbjerg fB (DEN)
H 0-0
Kamiński, Stawarczyk, Dziwniel, Surma, Zieńczuk, Kowalski (Efir 83), Kuświk (Szewczyk 75), Starzyński, Babiarz, Malinowski, Helik. Coach: Ján Kocian (SVK)
A 2-2 *Starzyński (13p), Surma (90+5)*
Kamiński, Stawarczyk, Dziwniel (Kuś 88), Surma, Zieńczuk (Włodyka 69), Kowalski, Kuświk (Efir 69), Starzyński, Babiarz, Malinowski, Helik. Coach: Ján Kocian (SVK)

Play-offs - FC Metalist Kharkiv (UKR)
H 0-0
Kamiński, Stawarczyk, Dziwniel, Surma, Zieńczuk (Gigolaev 74), Kowalski, Kuświk (Efir 76), Starzyński, Babiarz, Kuś (Helik 90+3), Malinowski. Coach: Ján Kocian (SVK)
A 0-1 (aet)
Kamiński, Stawarczyk, Dziwniel (Gigolaev 83), Surma, Zieńczuk (Lech 105), Kowalski (Włodyka 81), Kuświk, Starzyński, Babiarz, Kuś, Malinowski. Coach: Ján Kocian (SVK)
Red card: Kamiński 103

POLAND

DOMESTIC LEAGUE CLUB-BY-CLUB

GKS Bełchatów

1977 • GIEKSA Arena (5,238) •
gksbelchatow.com
Coach: Kamil Kiereś;
(25/03/15) Marek Zub;
(21/05/15) Kamil Kiereś

2014
19/07	a	Legia	W	1-0	Ślusarski
25/07	h	Korona	W	2-0	Ślusarski (p), Mateusz Mak
04/08	a	Górnik Łęczna	D	1-1	Michał Mak
09/08	h	Śląsk	W	2-0	Michał Mak (p), Poźniak
18/08	a	Podbeskidzie	D	1-1	Komolov
25/08	h	Piast	D	0-0	
29/08	a	Wisła	L	0-1	
14/09	h	Lechia	D	1-1	Ślusarski
21/09	a	Ruch	W	1-0	Basta
27/09	h	Pogoń	W	1-0	Komolov
05/10	a	Lech	L	0-5	
20/10	a	Zawisza	L	1-2	Mójta (p)
24/10	h	Górnik Zabrze	W	1-0	Prokić
03/11	a	Jagiellonia	W	1-0	Ślusarski
08/11	h	Cracovia	D	1-1	Mójta (p)
21/11	a	Legia	L	0-3	
29/11	a	Korona	L	0-2	
06/12	h	Górnik Łęczna	D	1-1	Basta
12/12	a	Śląsk	L	1-2	Ślusarski

2015
14/02	h	Podbeskidzie	L	1-2	Piech
23/02	a	Piast	L	1-3	Piech
28/02	h	Wisła	W	3-1	Piech 2, og (Głowacki)
07/03	a	Lechia	L	0-1	
16/03	h	Ruch	L	0-1	
20/03	a	Pogoń	L	0-3	
04/04	h	Lech	L	1-2	Wroński
12/04	a	Zawisza	L	1-4	Piech
20/04	a	Górnik Zabrze	L	0-2	
25/04	h	Jagiellonia	D	0-0	
29/04	a	Cracovia	L	1-3	Olszar
10/05	a	Cracovia	D	1-1	Piech
16/05	h	Podbeskidzie	L	0-1	
19/05	a	Piast	L	3-6	Piech (p), Wroński, Zbozień
25/05	a	Ruch	W	4-2	Piech 4
30/05	h	Zawisza	L	1-4	Małkowski
02/06	h	Korona	D	2-2	Wacławczyk, Baranowski
05/06	a	Górnik Łęczna	L	0-1	

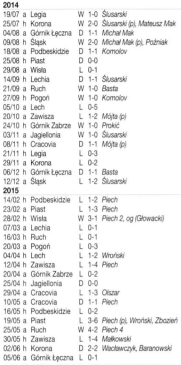

No	Name	Nat	DoB	Pos	Aps	(s)	Gls
3	Grzegorz Baran		23/12/82	M	25	(3)	
5	Paweł Baranowski		11/10/90	D	33	(1)	1
45	Bartłomiej Bartosiak		26/02/91	A	4	(2)	
17	Adrian Basta		01/12/88	D	28		2
96	Dawid Flaszka		31/07/96	M	1		
94	Marcin Flis		10/02/94	D	9	(2)	
10	Pavel Komolov	RUS	10/03/89	M	15	(16)	2
16	Mateusz Mak		14/11/91	M	3		1
9	Michał Mak		14/11/91	A	33	(1)	2
1	Arkadiusz Malarz		19/06/80	G	19		
88	Maciej Małkowski		19/03/85	M	13	(2)	1
42	Seweryn Michalski		12/09/94	D		(1)	
15	Adam Mójta		30/06/86	D	26	(3)	2
21	Alexis Norambuena	PLE	31/03/84	D	6		
33	Sebastian Olszar		16/12/81	A	6	(7)	1
7	Arkadiusz Piech		07/06/85	A	15		11
19	Kamil Poźniak		11/12/89	M	17	(3)	1
8	Andreja Prokić	SRB	09/04/89	M	2	(18)	1
20	Patryk Rachwał		27/01/81	M	25	(1)	
6	Szymon Sawala		25/09/82	M	5	(7)	
4	Damian Szymański		16/06/95	M	14	(5)	
46	Mateusz Szymorek		04/11/93	D	3		
18	Bartosz Ślusarski		11/12/81	A	19	(3)	5
66	Błażej Telichowski		06/06/84	D	27	(1)	
44	Dariusz Trela		05/12/89	G	10		
7	Danils Turkovs	LVA	17/02/88	A		(6)	
30	Kamil Wacławczyk		29/03/87	M	11	(6)	1
25	Piotr Witasik		04/12/92	D	4	(4)	
11	Łukasz Wroński		13/01/94	M	13	(11)	2
24	Damian Zbozień		25/04/89	D	12	(1)	1
69	Paweł Zięba		05/02/94	M	1	(1)	
22	Emilijus Zubas	LTU	10/07/90	G	8	(1)	

MKS Cracovia Kraków

1906 • im. Józefa Piłsudskiego (15,016) •
cracovia.pl
Major honours
Polish League (5) 1921, 1930, 1932, 1937, 1948
Coach: Robert Podoliński;
(20/04/15) Jacek Zieliński

2014
21/07	a	Górnik Zabrze	L	0-2	
26/07	h	Legia	L	1-3	Nowak
01/08	a	Jagiellonia	L	1-2	Rakels
08/08	h	Korona	W	2-1	Diabang, Budziński
17/08	a	Śląsk	D	0-0	
23/08	h	Podbeskidzie	L	1-3	Deleu
31/08	a	Lech	D	1-1	Budziński
13/09	h	Górnik Łęczna	W	2-1	Čovilo, Rakels
20/09	a	Piast	L	2-4	Żytko (p), Čovilo
28/09	h	Wisła	W	1-0	Čovilo
04/10	a	Lechia	L	0-1	
17/10	h	Ruch	W	1-0	Marciniak
25/10	a	Pogoń	L	1-2	Budziński
02/11	h	Zawisza	W	1-0	Rakels
08/11	a	Bełchatów	D	1-1	Kapustka
24/11	h	Górnik Zabrze	W	1-0	Rakels
01/12	a	Legia	L	0-2	
08/12	a	Jagiellonia	D	1-1	Rakels
12/12	h	Korona	W	2-1	Budziński, Rakels

2015
15/02	h	Śląsk	D	1-1	Budziński
20/02	a	Podbeskidzie	D	1-1	Čovilo
27/02	h	Lech	D	0-0	
09/03	a	Górnik Łęczna	L	1-2	Čovilo
13/03	h	Piast	W	3-1	og (Hebert), Rakels, Jendrišek
21/03	a	Wisła	L	1-2	Budziński
04/04	h	Lechia	W	3-2	Budziński, Rakels (p), Polczak
10/04	a	Ruch	L	0-3	
18/04	h	Pogoń	L	0-1	
24/04	a	Zawisza	W	3-0	Čovilo, Diabang, Dąbrowski
29/04	h	Bełchatów	W	3-0	Čovilo, Rakels, Zjawiński
10/05	h	Bełchatów	D	1-1	Jendrišek
16/05	a	Górnik Łęczna	W	3-0	Cetnarski 2, Budziński
19/05	h	Zawisza	W	3-1	Jendrišek, Rakels, Budziński
22/05	h	Korona	D	1-1	Rakels (p)
29/05	a	Podbeskidzie	W	3-0	Diabang 3
02/06	h	Ruch	W	1-0	Polczak
05/06	a	Piast	W	3-0	Kapustka, Jendrišek, Zjawiński

No	Name	Nat	DoB	Pos	Aps	(s)	Gls
20	Armiche	ESP	12/06/88	M	2	(4)	
27	Marcin Budziński		06/07/90	M	35	(1)	9
10	Mateusz Cetnarski		06/07/88	M	9	(7)	2
5	Miroslav Čovilo	SRB	06/05/86	M	25	(1)	7
14	Damian Dąbrowski		27/08/92	M	32	(4)	1
26	Deleu	BRA	01/03/84	D	21	(1)	1
7	Boubacar Diabang	BIH	13/07/88	A	22	(6)	5
37	Bartłomiej Dudzic		18/08/98	M		(6)	
44	Paweł Jaroszyński		02/10/94	D	9	(6)	
62	Erik Jendrišek	SVK	26/10/86	A	9	(5)	4
67	Bartosz Kapustka		23/12/96	M	11	(12)	2
18	Przemysław Kita		19/10/93	A	3	(8)	
4	Adam Marciniak		07/08/87	D	34		1
15	Tomislav Mikulić	CRO	04/01/82	D	1		
70	Jakub Mrozik		21/06/93	M		(2)	
11	Dawid Nowak		30/11/84	A	6	(3)	1
8	Krzysztof Nykiel		08/08/82	D	12	(5)	
80	Krzysztof Pilarz		09/11/80	G	36		
24	Piotr Polczak		25/08/86	M	17		2
92	Deniss Rakels	LVA	20/08/92	A	31	(2)	11
25	Bartosz Rymaniak		13/11/89	D	24	(2)	
3	Sreten Sretenović	SRB	12/01/85	D	17		
17	Sebastian Steblecki		16/01/92	M		(6)	
19	Krystian Stępniowski		05/12/92	G	1		
21	Sławomir Szeliga		17/07/82	M	6	(4)	
32	Krzysztof Szewczyk		06/03/96	A		(1)	
96	Mateusz Wdowiak		28/08/96	A	5	(7)	
23	Łukasz Zejdler		22/03/92	M	4	(3)	
9	Dariusz Zjawiński		19/08/86	A	10	(15)	2
4	Mateusz Żytko		27/11/82	D	21		1

GKS Górnik Łęczna

1979 • GKS Górnik Łęczna (7,496) •
gornik.leczna.pl
Coach: Yuriy Shatalov (UKR)

2014
18/07	h	Wisła	D	1-1	Nowak
27/07	a	Ruch	W	2-1	Bielák, Božok
04/08	h	Bełchatów	D	1-1	Mierzejewski
09/08	a	Legia	L	0-5	
16/08	h	Zawisza	W	5-2	Bonin 2, Černych 2, Szałachowski
23/08	a	Górnik Zabrze	L	0-2	
30/08	h	Pogoń	W	4-2	Hasani 2, Bonin, Černych
13/09	a	Cracovia	L	1-2	Černych
22/09	h	Jagiellonia	D	0-0	
26/09	a	Śląsk	L	1-2	Božok
04/10	h	Korona	W	1-0	Černych
18/10	a	Podbeskidzie	L	0-1	
26/10	a	Lech	L	0-1	
31/10	h	Lechia	D	1-1	Mráz
07/11	a	Piast	D	0-0	
22/11	h	Wisła	L	0-2	
28/11	h	Ruch	W	3-0	Mierzejewski, Černych, Nowak (p)
06/12	a	Bełchatów	D	1-1	Černych
14/12	h	Legia	W	3-1	Černych 2, Mráz

2015
13/02	h	Zawisza	D	0-0	
21/02	a	Górnik Zabrze	L	0-1	
02/03	a	Pogoń	W	1-0	Bonin
09/03	h	Cracovia	W	2-1	Mráz, Božok
14/03	a	Jagiellonia	L	1-2	Bonin
20/03	h	Śląsk	D	1-1	Nowak
06/04	a	Korona	D	0-2	
13/04	h	Podbeskidzie	D	0-0	
19/04	h	Lech	D	1-1	Rudik
26/04	a	Lechia	L	0-2	
29/04	a	Piast	L	1-2	Bonin
11/05	h	Piast	W	3-2	Černych, Božok, Hasani
16/05	a	Cracovia	L	0-3	
19/05	a	Korona	W	3-1	Hasani, Nikitović, Černych
22/05	a	Zawisza	D	1-1	Nikitović
30/05	h	Ruch	L	0-1	
02/06	a	Podbeskidzie	L	0-1	
05/06	h	Bełchatów	W	1-0	Hasani

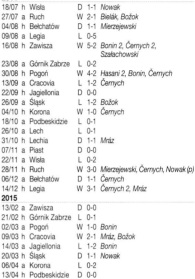

No	Name	Nat	DoB	Pos	Aps	(s)	Gls
20	Lukáš Bielák	SVK	14/12/86	D	28	(4)	1
15	Grzegorz Bonin		02/12/83	M	34		6
26	Tomislav Božić	CRO	01/11/87	D	27		
19	Miroslav Božok	SVK	19/10/84	M	28	(4)	4
87	Filip Burkhardt		23/03/87	M	12	(5)	
10	Paweł Buzała		27/12/85	A	2	(5)	
11	Fedor Černych	LTU	21/05/91	A	30	(2)	11
14	Shpëtim Hasani	ALB	10/08/82	A	13	(16)	5
99	Josué	ESP	27/02/93	M	2	(6)	
16	Wojciech Kalinowski		09/09/93	M	1	(4)	
25	Marcin Kalkowski		06/11/89	M	8	(1)	
18	Przemysław Kaźmierczak		05/05/82	M	8		
22	Łukasz Mierzejewski		31/08/82	D	31	(2)	2
2	Patrik Mráz	SVK	01/02/87	D	32	(1)	3
4	Veljko Nikitović	SRB	03/10/80	M	18	(7)	2
7	Tomasz Nowak		30/10/85	M	36		3
93	Piotr Okuniewicz		09/08/93	A		(1)	
17	Radosław Pruchnik		11/10/86	M	7	(5)	
79	Sergiusz Prusak		05/05/79	G	31		
90	Evaldas Razulis	LTU	03/04/86	A	5	(5)	
1	Silvio Rodić	CRO	25/07/87	G	6		
8	Filipp Rudik	BLR	22/03/87	M	8	(7)	1
7	Paweł Sasin		02/10/83	D	8	(5)	
13	Paweł Socha		13/08/91	G		(1)	
9	Sebastian Szałachowski		21/01/84	M		(20)	1
23	Maciej Szmatiuk		09/05/80	D	32	(1)	
34	Volodymyr Tanchyk	UKR	17/10/91	M		(5)	

POLAND

Górnik Zabrze

1948 • im. Ernesta Pohla (3,500) • gornikzabrze.pl
Major honours
Polish League (14) 1957, 1959, 1961, 1963, 1964, 1965, 1966, 1967, 1971, 1972, 1985, 1986, 1987, 1988; Polish Cup (6) 1965, 1968, 1969, 1970, 1971, 1972
Coach: Józef Dankowski

2014
21/07	h	Cracovia	W	2-0	Augustyn, Zachara
27/07	h	Lech	D	1-1	Zachara
02/08	a	Legia	D	1-1	og (Lewczuk)
08/08	a	Jagiellonia	W	3-0	Jeż 2 (1p), Zachara
15/08	a	Korona	W	3-0	Kosznik, Jeż, Gergel
23/08	h	Górnik Łęczna	W	2-0	Madej 2
30/08	a	Śląsk	L	0-2	
14/09	h	Piast	L	1-2	Danch
20/09	a	Podbeskidzie	W	3-0	Shevelyukhin, Zachara 2
28/09	h	Lechia	D	2-2	Magiera, Łuczak
04/10	a	Ruch	W	2-1	Łuczak, Madej
19/10	h	Wisła	L	0-5	
24/10	a	Bełchatów	L	0-1	
02/11	h	Pogoń	D	1-1	Zachara
09/11	a	Zawisza	W	2-1	Iwan, Gergel
24/11	a	Cracovia	W	2-1	Zachara 2
30/11	a	Lech	L	0-3	
05/12	h	Legia	L	0-4	
13/12	h	Jagiellonia	L	0-1	

2015
16/02	h	Korona	D	1-1	Skrzypczak
21/02	a	Górnik Łęczna	W	1-0	Kosznik
28/02	h	Śląsk	D	3-3	Gergel, Madej, Magiera (p)
07/03	a	Piast	D	2-2	Kosznik, og (Brożek)
14/03	h	Podbeskidzie	D	3-3	Kosznik, Magiera 2 (2p)
21/03	a	Lechia	L	0-1	
06/04	h	Ruch	D	2-2	Augustyn, Gergel
10/04	a	Wisła	W	1-0	Grendel
20/04	h	Bełchatów	W	2-0	Kosznik, Shevelyukhin
25/04	a	Pogoń	L	1-3	Magiera
29/04	h	Zawisza	W	2-1	Jeż 2
09/05	h	Wisła	L	1-4	Gergel
17/05	h	Pogoń	W	2-0	Gergel, Madej
20/05	h	Lechia	L	0-1	
23/05	a	Śląsk	D	1-1	Iwan
31/05	a	Jagiellonia	L	2-3	og (Pazdan), Skrzypczak
03/06	h	Lech	L	1-6	Nowak
07/06	a	Legia	L	0-2	

No	Name	Nat	DoB	Pos	Aps	(s)	Gls
2	Błażej Augustyn		26/01/88	D	17		2
14	Armin Ćerimagić	BIH	14/01/94	M	2	(2)	
24	Adam Danch		15/12/87	D	36		1
16	Szymon Drewniak		11/07/93	M		(1)	
22	Seweryn Gancarczyk		22/11/81	D	17	(2)	
11	Roman Gergel	SVK	22/02/88	M	35		6
20	Erik Grendel	SVK	13/10/88	M	17		1
25	Dzikamai Gwaze	ZIM	22/04/89	M	3	(9)	
38	Bartosz Iwan		18/04/84	M	14	(4)	2
81	Róbert Jeż	SVK	10/07/81	M	22	(10)	5
99	Grzegorz Kasprzik		20/09/83	G	1		
4	Rafał Kosznik		17/12/83	D	35		5
7	Rafał Kurzawa		29/01/93	M	6	(6)	
89	Wojciech Łuczak		28/07/89	M	10	(9)	2
18	Łukasz Madej		14/04/82	M	34	(2)	5
21	Mariusz Magiera		25/08/84	D	20	(5)	5
15	Maciej Małkowski		19/03/85	M		(1)	
13	Maciej Mańka		30/06/89	D	1	(7)	
10	Konrad Nowak		07/11/94	M	5	(7)	1
8	Przemysław Ożiębała		24/08/86	A		(4)	
35	Fabian Piasecki		04/05/95	A	1	(2)	
9	Dawid Plizga		17/11/85	M		(8)	
19	Mariusz Przybylski		19/01/82	M	2	(5)	
17	Dominik Sadzawicki		19/04/94	D	17	(4)	
5	Olexandr Shevelyukhin	UKR	27/08/82	D	20	(10)	2
23	Szymon Skrzypczak		14/03/90	A	7	(8)	2
3	Mateusz Słodowy		08/08/91	D	1		
6	Radosław Sobolewski		13/12/76	M	30		
1	Pāvels Šteinbors	LVA	21/09/85	G	32		
20	Mateusz Zachara		27/03/90	A	18		8

Jagiellonia Białystok

1932 • Miejski (22,432) • jagiellonia.pl
Major honours
Polish Cup (1) 2010
Coach: Michał Probierz

2014
19/07	h	Lechia	D	2-2	Tuszyński 2
27/07	a	Zawisza	W	3-1	Dani Quintana, Piątkowski 2
01/08	h	Cracovia	W	2-1	Gajos, Pazdan
08/08	a	Górnik Zabrze	L	0-3	
15/08	h	Legia	L	0-3	
23/08	h	Śląsk	L	1-3	Piątkowski
30/08	a	Korona	W	3-0	Piątkowski 2, Pawłowski
13/09	h	Lech	W	1-0	Piątkowski
22/09	a	Górnik Łęczna	D	0-0	
29/09	h	Podbeskidzie	W	4-2	Piątkowski 2, Gajos, Dzalamidze
03/10	a	Wisła	W	2-0	Pazdan, Piątkowski
18/10	h	Pogoń	W	5-0	Gajos, Piątkowski 2, Dzalamidze 2
25/10	a	Piast	W	2-0	Gajos, Tuszyński
03/11	h	Bełchatów	L	0-1	
09/11	a	Ruch	L	2-5	Romanchuk, Tuszyński
23/11	a	Lechia	D	1-1	Tymiński
29/11	h	Zawisza	D	0-0	
06/12	a	Cracovia	D	1-1	Piątkowski
13/12	h	Górnik Zabrze	W	1-0	Frankowski

2015
15/02	a	Legia	W	3-1	Gajos 2, Tuszyński
21/02	h	Śląsk	W	1-0	Mackiewicz
01/03	h	Korona	L	1-2	Tuszyński (p)
06/03	a	Lech	L	0-2	
14/03	h	Górnik Łęczna	W	2-1	Piątkowski 2
22/03	a	Podbeskidzie	L	0-1	
06/04	h	Wisła	D	2-2	Tuszyński 2
11/04	a	Pogoń	L	0-2	
18/04	h	Piast	W	2-1	Tymiński, Romanchuk
25/04	a	Bełchatów	D	0-0	
29/04	h	Ruch	W	2-0	Frankowski, Tuszyński
08/05	h	Śląsk	D	1-1	Frankowski
17/05	a	Lech	W	3-1	Tuszyński 2, Gajos
20/05	a	Legia	L	0-1	
23/05	h	Wisła	W	2-1	Tuszyński, Pawłowski
31/05	h	Górnik Zabrze	W	3-2	og (Grendel), Tuszyński, Romanchuk
03/06	a	Pogoń	W	3-1	Tarasovs, Tuszyński, Świderski
07/06	h	Lechia	W	4-2	Tuszyński (p), Modelski, Romanchuk, Gajos (p)

No	Name	Nat	DoB	Pos	Aps	(s)	Gls
25	Rafał Augustyniak		14/10/93	D		(1)	
33	Krzysztof Baran		12/02/90	G	6		
18	Martin Baran	SVK	03/01/88	D	11	(2)	
99	Dani Quintana	ESP	08/03/87	M	6		1
69	Bartłomiej Drągowski		19/08/97	G	28	(1)	
10	Nika Dzalamidze	GEO	06/01/92	M	23	(10)	3
21	Przemysław Frankowski		12/04/95	M	15	(13)	3
20	Maciej Gajos		19/03/91	M	35	(1)	8
22	Rafał Grzyb		16/01/83	M	36		
11	Radosław Jasiński		09/04/90	D	5	(1)	
11	Damian Kądzior		16/06/92	M		(1)	
12	Povilas Leimonas	LTU	16/11/87	M	3	(1)	
1	Karol Mackiewicz		01/06/92	A	14	(3)	1
7	Sebastian Madera		30/05/85	D	31		
2	Filip Modelski		28/09/92	D	24	(2)	1
13	Przemysław Mystkowski		25/04/98	A	2	(5)	
23	Michał Pawlik		08/05/95	M	1	(1)	
9	Jan Pawłowski		18/11/92	A	4	(17)	2
4	Michał Pazdan		21/09/87	D	25	(2)	2
27	Mateusz Piątkowski		22/11/84	A	19	(5)	14
77	Giorgi Popkhadze	GEO	25/09/86	D	5	(1)	
24	Tomasz Porębski		12/01/92	D	1		
6	Taras Romanchuk	UKR	14/11/91	M	15	(12)	4
88	Pavel Savitsky	BLR	31/07/94	A	2	(3)	
1	Jakub Słowik		31/08/91	G	3		
3	Jonatan Straus		30/06/94	D	16		
8	Karol Świderski		23/01/97	A	2	(5)	1
19	Igors Tarasovs	LVA	16/10/88	M	12	(3)	1
8	Patryk Tuszyński		13/12/89	A	33	(4)	15
8	Łukasz Tymiński		18/11/90	M	8	(12)	2
14	Marek Wasiluk		03/06/87	D	19	(1)	
25	Adam Waszkiewicz		06/12/93	D	3		

Korona Kielce

1973 • Kolporter Arena (15,550) • korona-kielce.pl
Coach: Ryszard Tarasiewicz

2014
20/07	h	Zawisza	L	0-2	
25/07	a	Bełchatów	L	0-2	
02/08	h	Pogoń	D	2-2	Kiełb, Golański
08/08	a	Cracovia	L	1-2	Trytko (p)
15/08	h	Górnik Zabrze	L	0-3	
24/08	a	Legia	L	0-3	
30/08	h	Jagiellonia	L	0-3	
15/09	h	Podbeskidzie	W	2-1	Sylwestrzak, Kiełb
19/09	a	Śląsk	L	0-1	
26/09	h	Piast	W	1-0	Trytko
04/10	a	Górnik Łęczna	L	0-1	
19/10	h	Lech	L	1-2	Kapo, Sylwestrzak
27/10	a	Ruch	W	1-0	Dejmek
31/10	h	Wisła	W	3-2	Petrov, og (Guzmics), Kapo
08/11	h	Lechia	W	2-1	Kapo, Jovanović
22/11	h	Zawisza	W	2-1	Malarczyk, Kapo
29/11	h	Bełchatów	W	2-0	Sylwestrzak, Trytko
06/12	a	Pogoń	L	0-2	
12/12	h	Cracovia	L	1-2	Trytko

2015
16/02	a	Górnik Zabrze	D	1-1	Dejmek
22/02	h	Legia	D	0-0	
01/03	a	Jagiellonia	L	1-2	Kapo, Dejmek
08/03	a	Podbeskidzie	D	2-2	Rafael Porcelis, Luís Carlos
15/03	h	Śląsk	D	2-2	Kiełb 2
22/03	a	Piast	W	2-1	Kiełb (p), Leandro
06/04	h	Górnik Łęczna	W	2-0	Kiełb, Sylwestrzak
12/04	a	Lech	D	1-1	Luís Carlos
17/04	h	Ruch	D	0-0	
26/04	a	Wisła	L	0-2	
29/04	h	Lechia	W	3-2	Kapo, Luís Carlos, Rafael Porcellis
08/05	h	Ruch	L	0-2	
15/05	a	Zawisza	L	1-3	Malarczyk
19/05	a	Górnik Łęczna	L	1-3	Kiełb
22/05	a	Cracovia	D	1-1	Sylwestrzak
29/05	h	Piast	W	2-1	Trytko, Rafael Porcellis
02/06	a	Bełchatów	W	2-1	Kiełb, Kapo
05/06	h	Podbeskidzie	W	3-1	Luís Carlos 2, Kiełb (p)

No	Name	Nat	DoB	Pos	Aps	(s)	Gls
19	Nabil Aankour	MAR	09/08/93	M	7	(11)	
7	Marcin Cebula		06/12/95	M	3	(10)	
22	Vytautas Černiauskas	LTU	12/03/89	G	35		
32	Radek Dejmek	CZE	02/02/88	D	24		3
87	Aleksandrs Fertovs	LVA	16/06/87	M	16	(2)	
44	Paweł Golański		12/10/82	D	31		1
10	Michał Janota		29/07/90	M	12	(5)	
8	Vlastimir Jovanović	BIH	03/04/85	M	31		1
11	Olivier Kapo	FRA	27/09/80	A	23	(4)	7
27	Sergei Khizhnichenko	KAZ	17/07/91	A	3	(10)	
27	Jacek Kiełb		10/01/88	M	26	(8)	9
13	Krzysztof Kiercz		16/02/89	D		(1)	
6	Lukas Klemenz		24/09/95	M	8	(2)	
20	Maciej Korzym		02/05/88	A	1		
21	Jakub Kotarzewski		22/01/94	M		(1)	
3	Kamil Kuzera		11/03/83	D	1	(2)	
39	Bartosz Kwiecień		07/05/94	M		(1)	
28	Leandro	BRA	29/12/83	D	21	(2)	1
10	Luís Carlos	BRA	15/06/87	A	14	(1)	5
4	Piotr Malarczyk		01/08/91	D	34	(1)	2
90	Wojciech Małecki		11/10/90	G	2		
23	Vanja Marković	SRB	26/06/94	M	10	(1)	
14	Bouliguiba Ouattara	CIV	02/07/88	D	8	(1)	
26	Kyrylo Petrov	UKR	22/06/90	D	12		1
17	Serhiy Pylypchuk	UKR	26/11/84	M	16	(8)	
18	Rafael Porcellis	BRA	19/01/87	A	8	(7)	3
29	Paweł Sobolewski		20/06/79	M	9	(3)	
2	Kamil Sylwestrzak		16/07/88	D	27	(1)	4
9	Przemysław Trytko		26/08/87	A	25	(6)	5

KKS Lech Poznań

1922 • INEA (42,837) • lechpoznan.pl

Major honours
Polish League (7) 1983, 1984, 1990, 1992, 1993, 2010, 2015; Polish Cup (5) 1982, 1984, 1988, 2004, 2009

Coach: Mariusz Rumak;
(12/08/14) (Krzysztof Chrobak);
(01/09/14) Maciej Skorża

2014

20/07	h	Piast	W	4-0	*Ubiparip 3, Kownacki*
27/07	a	Górnik Zabrze	D	1-1	*Teodorczyk*
03/08	h	Wisła	L	2-3	*Wołąkiewicz (p), Douglas*
10/08	a	Lechia	W	2-1	*Teodorczyk 2*
16/08	h	Pogoń	D	1-1	*Pawłowski*
24/08	a	Ruch	D	0-0	
31/08	h	Cracovia	D	1-1	*Hämäläinen*
13/09	a	Jagiellonia	L	0-1	
20/09	h	Zawisza	W	6-2	*Sadayev, Lovrencsics, Hämäläinen, Jevtic 2 (1p), Pawłowski*
27/09	a	Legia	D	2-2	*Kamiński, Formella*
05/10	h	Bełchatów	W	5-0	*Hämäläinen 2, og (Malarz), Lovrencsics, Jevtic*
19/10	a	Korona	D	2-2	*Hämäläinen, Pawłowski*
26/10	h	Górnik Łęczna	W	1-0	*Keita*
02/11	a	Śląsk	D	1-1	*Jevtic*
07/11	h	Podbeskidzie	D	1-1	*Kownacki*
23/11	a	Piast	L	2-3	*Pawłowski, Kamiński*
30/11	h	Górnik Zabrze	W	3-0	*Hämäläinen, Pawłowski, Kędziora*
07/12	a	Wisła	W	2-1	*Kędziora, Sadayev*
13/12	h	Lechia	W	1-0	*Formella*

2015

14/02	a	Pogoń	D	1-1	*Arajuuri*
22/02	h	Ruch	W	2-1	*Sadayev, Hämäläinen*
27/02	a	Cracovia	D	0-0	
06/03	h	Jagiellonia	W	2-0	*Douglas, Kędziora (p)*
14/03	a	Zawisza	L	0-1	
22/03	h	Legia	W	2-1	*Douglas, Hämäläinen*
04/04	a	Bełchatów	W	2-1	*Keita, Arajuuri*
12/04	h	Korona	D	1-1	*Lovrencsics*
19/04	a	Górnik Łęczna	D	1-1	*Sadayev*
25/04	h	Śląsk	W	2-0	*Hämäläinen, Arajuuri*
29/04	a	Podbeskidzie	W	2-0	*Formella, Hämäläinen*
09/05	a	Legia	W	2-1	*Jevtic, Linetty*
17/05	h	Jagiellonia	L	1-3	*Kownacki*
20/05	h	Śląsk	W	3-0	*Kownacki, Pawłowski 2*
24/05	a	Lechia	W	2-1	*Hämäläinen, Pawłowski*
31/05	h	Pogoń	W	1-0	*Linetty*
03/06	a	Górnik Zabrze	W	6-1	*Pawłowski, Hämäläinen 2, Sadayev, Jevtic 2*
07/06	h	Wisła	D	0-0	

No	Name	Nat	DoB	Pos	Aps	(s)	Gls
23	Paulus Arajuuri	FIN	15/06/88	D	24	(1)	3
40	Jan Bednarek		12/04/96	D	1	(1)	
1	Jasmin Burić	BIH	18/02/87	G	11		
21	Kebba Ceesay	GAM	14/11/87	D		(2)	
3	Barry Douglas	SCO	04/09/89	D	21	(6)	3
17	Szymon Drewniak		11/07/93	M	1	(4)	
28	Dariusz Formella		21/10/95	A	8	(20)	3
33	Maciej Gostomski		27/09/88	G	20	(1)	
19	Kasper Hämäläinen	FIN	08/08/86	M	33	(3)	13
25	Luis Henríquez	PAN	23/11/81	D	14	(2)	
20	Dávid Holman	HUN	17/03/93	M		(1)	
16	Darko Jevtic	SUI	08/02/93	M	22	(7)	7
5	Tamás Kádár	HUN	14/03/90	D	3	(6)	
35	Marcin Kamiński		15/01/92	D	35	(1)	2
4	Tomasz Kędziora		11/06/94	D	35		3
77	Muhamed Keita	NOR	02/09/90	A	6	(13)	2
27	Krzysztof Kotorowski		12/09/76	G	6		
24	Dawid Kownacki		14/03/97	M	17	(13)	4
7	Karol Linetty		02/02/95	M	22	(1)	2
11	Gergő Lovrencsics	HUN	01/09/88	A	20	(5)	3
8	Szymon Pawłowski		04/11/86	M	27	(6)	9
95	Zaur Sadayev	RUS	06/11/89	A	20	(5)	5
22	Jakub Serafin		25/05/96	M	2		
88	Arnaud Sutchuin	BEL	02/05/89	M	3		
10	Łukasz Teodorczyk		03/06/91	A	3	(1)	3
6	Łukasz Trałka		11/05/84	M	32		
14	Vojo Ubiparip	SRB	10/05/88	A	5	(2)	3
26	Maciej Wilusz		25/09/88	D	7	(1)	
20	Hubert Wołąkiewicz		21/10/85	D	9	(4)	1
37	Niklas Zulciak	GER	03/02/94	M		(2)	

KS Lechia Gdańsk

1945 • PGE Arena Gdańsk (43,165) • lechia.pl

Major honours
Polish Cup (1) 1983

Coach: Quim Machado (POR);
(21/09/14) Tomasz Unton & Maciej Kalkowski;
(17/11/14) Jerzy Brzęczek

2014

19/07	a	Jagiellonia	D	2-2	*Wiśniewski, og (Wasiluk)*
25/07	h	Podbeskidzie	W	1-0	*Makuszewski*
01/08	a	Piast	W	3-1	*Wiśniewski 2, Vranješ (p)*
10/08	h	Lech	L	1-2	*Vranješ (p)*
17/08	a	Wisła	L	1-3	*Vranješ (p)*
22/08	a	Zawisza	W	2-0	*Čolak, Makuszewski*
31/08	h	Ruch	D	3-3	*Vranješ, Čolak, Friesenbichler*
14/09	a	Bełchatów	D	1-1	*Grzelczak*
19/09	h	Pogoń	L	0-1	
28/09	a	Górnik Zabrze	D	2-2	*Čolak 2*
04/10	h	Cracovia	W	1-0	*Makuszewski*
17/10	a	Legia	L	0-1	
25/10	h	Śląsk	L	1-4	*Friesenbichler*
31/10	a	Górnik Łęczna	D	1-1	*Čolak*
08/11	h	Korona	L	1-2	*Čolak*
23/11	h	Jagiellonia	D	1-1	*og (Madera)*
29/11	a	Podbeskidzie	L	0-1	
07/12	h	Piast	W	3-1	*Wiśniewski 3*
13/12	a	Lech	L	0-1	

2015

13/02	h	Wisła	W	1-0	*Grzelczak*
21/02	h	Zawisza	D	0-0	
27/02	a	Ruch	D	1-1	*Friesenbichler (p)*
07/03	h	Bełchatów	W	1-0	*Čolak*
13/03	a	Pogoń	W	1-0	*Mila*
21/03	h	Górnik Zabrze	W	1-0	*Čolak*
04/04	a	Cracovia	L	2-3	*Grzelczak, Vranješ*
11/04	h	Legia	W	1-0	*Makuszewski*
18/04	a	Śląsk	L	0-3	
26/04	h	Górnik Łęczna	W	2-0	*Vranješ, Bruno Nazário*
29/04	a	Korona	L	2-3	*Friesenbichler, Makuszewski*
09/05	a	Pogoń	W	3-1	*Čolak, Vranješ (p), Gérson*
15/05	h	Wisła	D	2-2	*Makuszewski, Friesenbichler*
20/05	a	Górnik Zabrze	W	1-0	*Mila*
24/05	h	Lech	L	1-2	*Vranješ (p)*
30/05	a	Śląsk	L	0-1	
03/06	h	Legia	D	0-0	
07/06	a	Jagiellonia	L	2-4	*Leković, Čolak*

No	Name	Nat	DoB	Pos	Aps	(s)	Gls
7	Danijel Aleksić	SRB	30/04/91	A	1	(2)	
24	Mateusz Bąk		24/02/83	G	21		
16	Ariel Borysiuk		29/07/91	M	33	(1)	
13	Mavroudis Bougaidis	GRE	01/06/93	D	10	(2)	
10	Bruno Nazário	BRA	09/02/95	M	19	(8)	1
1	Łukasz Budziłek		19/03/91	G	7		
18	Adam Buksa		12/07/96	A	1	(7)	
20	Antonio Čolak	CRO	17/09/93	A	26	(4)	10
28	Paweł Czychowski		19/07/93	A		(1)	
15	Adam Dźwigała		25/09/95	D	4	(6)	
29	Kevin Friesenbichler	AUT	06/05/94	A	8	(9)	5
4	Damian Garbacik		30/01/96	D	2		
35	Gérson	BRA	07/01/92	D	13	(1)	1
9	Piotr Grzelczak		02/03/88	A	11	(18)	3
26	Henrique Miranda	BRA	10/05/93	D	1		
2	Rafał Janicki		05/07/92	D	34		
7	Donatas Kazlauskas	LTU	31/03/94	M		(1)	
33	Nikola Leković	SRB	19/12/89	D	16	(2)	1
8	Daniel Łukasik		28/04/91	M	19	(8)	
27	Przemysław Macierzyński		11/02/99	A		(1)	
11	Maciej Makuszewski		29/09/89	M	34		6
22	Filip Malbašić	SRB	18/11/92	M	2	(1)	
6	Sebastian Mila		10/07/82	M	15	(1)	2
32	Mateusz Możdżeń		14/03/91	D	13	(11)	
19	Bartłomiej Pawłowski		13/11/92	M	7	(5)	
17	Marcin Pietrowski		01/03/88	M	15	(4)	
5	Rudinilson	POR	20/08/94	D	2	(2)	
95	Zaur Sadayev	RUS	06/11/89	A	4		
6	Tiago Valente	POR	24/04/85	D	12		
12	Dariusz Trela		05/12/89	G	9		
21	Stojan Vranješ	BIH	11/10/86	M	32	(1)	8
3	Jakub Wawrzyniak		07/07/83	D	11		
14	Piotr Wiśniewski		11/08/82	M	9	(14)	6
23	Grzegorz Wojtkowiak		26/01/84	D	16		

Legia Warszawa

1916 • Wojska Polskiego im. Marszałka Józefa Piłsudskiego (31,284) • legia.com

Major honours
Polish League (10) 1955, 1956, 1969, 1970, 1994, 1995, 2002, 2006, 2013, 2014; Polish Cup (17) 1955, 1956, 1964, 1966, 1973, 1980, 1981, 1989, 1990, 1994, 1995, 1997, 2008, 2011, 2012, 2013, 2015

Coach: Henning Berg (NOR)

2014

19/07	h	Bełchatów	L	0-1	
26/07	a	Cracovia	W	3-1	*Kosecki, Jodłowiec, Vrdoljak (p)*
02/08	h	Górnik Zabrze	D	1-1	*Saganowski*
09/08	h	Górnik Łęczna	W	5-0	*Vrdoljak 2 (1p), Kosecki, Orlando Sá 2*
15/08	a	Jagiellonia	W	3-0	*Żyro, Radović, Kucharczyk*
24/08	h	Korona	W	2-0	*Orlando Sá, Saganowski*
31/08	a	Podbeskidzie	L	1-2	*Orlando Sá*
13/09	h	Śląsk	W	4-3	*Radović 2, Dossa Júnior 2*
21/09	a	Wisła	W	3-0	*Orlando Sá, Duda, Radović*
27/09	h	Lech	D	2-2	*Brzyski, Dossa Júnior*
05/10	a	Piast	L	1-3	*Duda*
17/10	h	Lechia	W	1-0	*Orlando Sá*
26/10	a	Zawisza	W	2-1	*Rzeźniczak, Żyro*
02/11	h	Ruch	W	2-1	*Orlando Sá (p), Ryczkowski*
09/11	a	Pogoń	L	1-2	*Rzeźniczak*
21/11	a	Bełchatów	W	3-0	*Kosecki, Duda, Rzeźniczak*
01/12	h	Cracovia	W	2-0	*og (Marciniak), Orlando Sá*
05/12	a	Górnik Zabrze	W	4-0	*Iñaki Astiz, Żyro, Radović, Orlando Sá*
14/12	a	Górnik Łęczna	L	1-3	*Duda*

2015

15/02	h	Jagiellonia	L	1-3	*Hélio Pinto*
22/02	a	Korona	D	0-0	
01/03	h	Podbeskidzie	W	3-0	*Ryczkowski, Duda (p), Orlando Sá*
08/03	a	Śląsk	W	3-1	*Rzeźniczak, Jodłowiec, Kucharczyk*
15/03	h	Wisła	D	2-2	*Żyro, og (Jovič)*
22/03	a	Lech	L	1-2	*Kucharczyk*
04/04	h	Piast	W	2-0	*Kucharczyk, Orlando Sá*
11/04	a	Lechia	L	0-1	
19/04	a	Zawisza	W	2-0	*Żyro, Kucharczyk*
24/04	a	Ruch	D	0-0	
29/04	h	Pogoń	W	2-1	*Guilherme, Lewczuk*
09/05	h	Lech	L	1-2	*Vrdoljak*
17/05	a	Śląsk	D	1-1	*Jodłowiec*
20/05	h	Jagiellonia	W	1-0	*Orlando Sá (p)*
23/05	a	Pogoń	W	1-0	*Orlando Sá*
31/05	h	Wisła	W	1-0	*Rzeźniczak*
03/06	a	Lechia	D	0-0	
07/06	h	Górnik Zabrze	W	2-0	*Kucharczyk, og (Magiera)*

No	Name	Nat	DoB	Pos	Aps	(s)	Gls
27	Robert Bartczak		12/03/96	M	1		
19	Bartosz Bereszyński		12/07/92	D	14	(2)	
31	Krystian Bielik		04/01/98	M	2	(3)	
28	Łukasz Broź		17/12/85	D	21	(1)	
17	Tomasz Brzyski		10/01/82	D	24	(1)	1
2	Dossa Júnior	CYP	28/07/86	D	8	(1)	3
8	Ondrej Duda	SVK	05/12/94	M	14	(13)	5
13	Vladimer Dvalishvili	GEO	20/04/86	A	1		
37	Dominik Furman		06/07/92	M	8	(2)	
6	Guilherme	BRA	21/05/91	M	13	(5)	1
23	Hélio Pinto	POR	29/02/84	M	16	(2)	1
15	Iñaki Astiz	ESP	05/11/83	D	19		1
91	Konrad Jałocha		09/05/91	G	2	(1)	
3	Tomasz Jodłowiec		08/09/85	D	27	(4)	3
76	Bartłomiej Kalinkowski		11/07/94	M	2	(1)	
20	Jakub Kosecki		29/08/90	M	17	(3)	3
18	Michał Kucharczyk		20/03/91	A	18	(9)	6
12	Dušan Kuciak	SVK	21/05/85	G	30	(1)	
4	Igor Lewczuk		30/05/85	D	20	(2)	1
34	Arkadiusz Malarz		19/06/80	G	5		
16	Michał Masłowski		19/12/89	M	5	(7)	
52	Norbert Misiak		25/06/94	M	1		
73	Łukasz Moneta		13/05/94	M	1	(1)	
7	Henrik Ojamaa	EST	20/05/91	M	1		
70	Orlando Sá	POR	26/05/88	A	15	(11)	13
11	Arkadiusz Piech		07/06/85	A	4		
32	Miroslav Radović	SRB	16/01/84	M	8	(2)	5
45	Adam Ryczkowski		30/04/97	A	6	(2)	2
25	Jakub Rzeźniczak		26/10/86	D	30	(1)	5
9	Marek Saganowski		31/10/78	A	18	(13)	2
14	Mateusz Szwoch		19/03/93	M	6	(2)	
21	Ivica Vrdoljak	CRO	19/09/83	M	25	(3)	4
5	Mateusz Wieteska		11/02/97	D	2		
33	Michał Żyro		20/09/92	M	23	(4)	5

POLAND

GKS Piast Gliwice

1945 • Miejski (10,037) • piast.gliwice.pl
Coach: Ángel Pérez García (ESP);
(20/03/15) Radoslav Látal (CZE)

2014
20/07	a	Lech	L	0-4
28/07	a	Wisła	D	1-1 *Polák*
01/08	h	Lechia	L	1-3 *Rubén Jurado*
11/08	a	Pogoń	D	0-0
16/08	h	Ruch	L	0-1
25/08	a	Bełchatów	L	0-1
29/08	h	Zawisza	W	3-0 *Rubén Jurado 2, Wilczek*
14/09	a	Górnik Zabrze	W	2-1 *Gerard Badía, Szeliga*
20/09	h	Cracovia	W	4-2 *Szeliga, Gerard Badía, Rubén Jurado, Wilczek*
26/09	a	Korona	L	0-1
05/10	h	Legia	W	3-1 *Wilczek 3*
18/10	a	Śląsk	L	0-3
25/10	h	Jagiellonia	L	0-2
03/11	a	Podbeskidzie	W	4-2 *Wilczek, Vassiljev, Hebert, Szeliga*
07/11	h	Górnik Łęczna	D	0-0
23/11	h	Lech	W	3-2 *Wilczek, Szeliga, Podgórski*
28/11	h	Wisła	D	0-0
07/12	a	Lechia	L	1-3 *Wilczek*
15/12	h	Pogoń	W	1-0 *Wilczek*

2015
14/02	a	Ruch	L	0-2
23/02	h	Bełchatów	W	3-1 *Wilczek, Gerard Badía, Podgórski*
28/02	a	Zawisza	L	0-2
07/03	h	Górnik Zabrze	D	2-2 *Gerard Badía, Szeliga*
13/03	a	Cracovia	L	1-3 *Wilczek*
22/03	h	Korona	L	1-2 *Wilczek*
04/04	a	Legia	L	0-2
11/04	h	Śląsk	W	2-0 *Hanzel, og (Juanito)*
18/04	a	Jagiellonia	L	1-2 *Moskwik*
26/04	h	Podbeskidzie	W	3-0 *Hebert, Osyra, Wilczek*
29/04	a	Górnik Łęczna	W	2-1 *Wilczek 2*
11/05	a	Górnik Łęczna	L	2-3 *Horváth, Wilczek (p)*
16/05	a	Ruch	D	1-1 *Vassiljev*
19/05	h	Bełchatów	W	6-3 *Vassiljev 2, Wilczek 4 (1p)*
24/05	h	Podbeskidzie	W	2-1 *Hebert, Vassiljev*
29/05	a	Korona	L	1-2 *Moskwik*
02/06	a	Zawisza	D	0-0
05/06	a	Cracovia	L	0-3

No	Name	Nat	DoB	Pos	Aps	(s)	Gls
91	Alberto	ESP	29/05/79	G	15		
19	Piotr Brożek		21/04/83	D	23		
23	Tomáš Dočekal	CZE	24/05/89	A		(1)	
7	Patrick Dytko		28/03/94	M		(2)	
27	Patryk Dziczek		25/03/98	M	1		
21	Gerard Badía	ESP	18/10/89	M	26	(5)	4
16	Amine Hadj Saïd	TUN	17/02/87	M	2	(2)	
20	Łukasz Hanzel		16/09/86	M	17	(10)	1
33	Hebert	BRA	23/05/91	D	25		3
3	Csaba Horváth	SVK	02/05/82	D	25	(3)	1
18	Matej Ižvolt	SVK	06/06/86	M	2	(6)	
15	Dawid Janczyk		23/09/87	A		(3)	
24	Wojciech Kędziora		20/12/80	A	1	(10)	
14	Adrian Klepczyński		01/04/81	D	30	(1)	
4	Carles Martínez	ESP	03/01/88	M	23	(1)	
22	Tomasz Mokwa		10/02/93	D	12	(1)	
11	Paweł Moskwik		08/06/92	D	11	(2)	2
9	Radosław Murawski		22/04/94	M	22	(7)	
28	Kornel Osyra		07/02/93	D	29	(4)	1
17	Tomasz Podgórski		30/12/85	M	20	(11)	2
5	Jan Polák	CZE	26/03/89	D	3	(1)	1
77	Rubén Jurado	ESP	25/04/86	M	17	(7)	4
31	Dobrivoj Rusov	SVK	13/01/93	G	5		
26	Bartosz Szeliga		10/01/93	M	17	(14)	5
1	Jakub Szmatuła		22/03/81	G	17	(1)	
84	Konstantin Vassiljev	EST	16/08/84	M	19	(6)	5
10	Kamil Wilczek		14/01/88	M	33	(2)	20
12	Saša Živec	SVN	02/04/91	M	12	(7)	

TS Podbeskidzie Bielsko-Biała

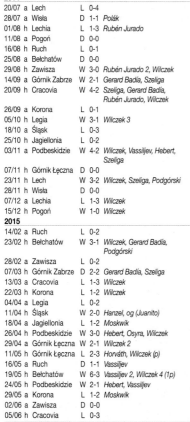

1995 • Miejski (6,962) • tspodbeskidzie.pl
Coach: Leszek Ojrzyński;
(04/05/15) Dariusz Kubicki

2014
18/07	h	Pogoń	L	2-3 *Konieczny, Sokołowski*
25/07	a	Lechia	L	0-1
03/08	h	Ruch	W	3-0 *Korzym, Górkiewicz, Chmiel*
10/08	a	Zawisza	W	2-1 *Kołodziej, Chmiel*
18/08	h	Bełchatów	D	1-1 *Patejuk*
23/08	a	Cracovia	W	3-1 *Korzym, Chmiel 2*
31/08	h	Legia	W	2-1 *Sloboda, Korzym*
15/09	h	Korona	L	1-2 *Staňo*
20/09	h	Górnik Zabrze	D	0-3
29/09	a	Jagiellonia	L	2-4 *Demjan 2*
03/10	a	Śląsk	D	2-2 *Chmiel, Chrapek*
18/10	h	Górnik Łęczna	W	1-0 *Demjan*
24/10	a	Wisła	L	2-3 *Iwański 2 (1p)*
03/11	h	Piast	L	2-4 *Sokołowski 2 (1p)*
07/11	a	Lech	D	1-1 *Śpiączka*
22/11	a	Pogoń	W	2-1 *Chmiel, Iwański (p)*
29/11	h	Lechia	W	1-0 *Staňo*
08/12	a	Ruch	L	0-2
14/12	a	Zawisza	W	2-1 *Malinowski, Śpiączka*

2015
14/02	a	Bełchatów	W	2-1 *Iwański 2 (1p)*
20/02	h	Cracovia	D	1-1 *Iwański (p)*
01/03	a	Legia	L	0-3
08/03	h	Korona	D	2-2 *Sokołowski, Korzym*
14/03	a	Górnik Zabrze	D	3-3 *Chmiel 2, Śpiączka*
22/03	h	Jagiellonia	W	1-0 *Demjan*
04/04	a	Śląsk	D	0-0
13/04	a	Górnik Łęczna	D	0-0
17/04	h	Wisła	D	2-2 *Iwański (p), Górkiewicz*
26/04	a	Piast	L	0-3
29/04	h	Lech	L	0-2
10/05	h	Zawisza	D	2-2 *Chmiel, Iwański (p)*
16/05	a	Bełchatów	W	2-0 *Śpiączka, Kołodziej*
19/05	h	Ruch	L	0-2
24/05	a	Piast	L	1-2 *Cissé*
29/05	h	Cracovia	L	0-3
02/06	h	Górnik Łęczna	W	1-0 *Konieczny*
05/06	a	Korona	L	1-3 *Kołodziej*

No	Name	Nat	DoB	Pos	Aps	(s)	Gls
5	Frank Adu Kwame	GHA	16/05/85	D	13	(5)	
29	Sebastian Bartlewski		13/06/94	A		(2)	
14	Damian Chmiel		06/05/87	M	34		9
15	Krzysztof Chrapek		07/10/85	A	2	(12)	1
99	Idrissa Cissé	SEN	01/01/90	A		(9)	1
23	Adam Deja		24/06/93	M	20	(1)	
23	Róbert Demjan	SVK	26/10/82	A	22	(10)	4
21	Tomasz Górkiewicz		28/01/82	D	27	(2)	2
4	Grzegorz Horoszkiewicz		18/03/95	D	1		
7	Maciej Iwański		07/05/81	M	32		8
90	Kristián Kolčák	SVK	30/01/90	D	12	(1)	
9	Dariusz Kołodziej		17/04/82	M	6	(8)	3
26	Bartłomiej Konieczny		09/06/81	D	30		2
77	Maciej Korzym		02/05/88	A	14	(6)	4
8	Artur Lenartowski		17/03/88	M	5	(4)	
8	Piotr Malinowski		24/03/84	M	5	(18)	1
37	Róbert Mazáň	SVK	09/02/94	D	1	(1)	
28	Wojciech Okińczyc		15/02/86	A		(1)	
13	Sylwester Patejuk		30/11/82	M	13	(5)	1
32	Adam Pazio		27/09/92	D	13	(7)	
33	Michal Peškovič	SVK	08/02/82	G	21		
17	Dariusz Pietrasiak		12/02/80	D	14		
17	Anton Sloboda	SVK	10/07/87	M	17	(3)	1
10	Marek Sokołowski		11/03/78	D	31		4
16	Pavol Staňo	SVK	29/09/77	D	26		2
18	Bartosz Śpiączka		19/08/91	A	12	(11)	4
30	Piotr Tomasik		31/10/87	M	19	(1)	
20	Wojciech Trochim		31/03/89	M	1	(2)	
1	Richard Zajac	SVK	16/08/76	G	16		

MKS Pogoń Szczecin

1948 • im. Floriana Krygiera (15,717) • pogonszczecin.pl
Coach: Dariusz Wdowczyk;
(22/10/14) Ján Kocian (SVK);
(09/04/15) Czesław Michniewicz

2014
18/07	a	Podbeskidzie	W	3-2 *Zwoliński, Dąbrowski, Frączczak*
26/07	h	Śląsk	W	4-1 *Frączczak, Zwoliński, Murayama, Golla*
02/08	a	Korona	D	2-2 *Hernâni, Rogalski*
11/08	h	Piast	D	0-0
16/08	a	Lech	D	1-1 *Robak*
22/08	h	Wisła	L	0-3
30/08	a	Górnik Łęczna	L	2-4 *Robak 2*
12/09	h	Ruch	D	1-1 *Dąbrowski*
19/09	a	Lechia	W	1-0 *Robak*
27/09	a	Bełchatów	L	0-1
05/10	h	Zawisza	W	3-0 *Frączczak, Zwoliński 2*
18/10	a	Jagiellonia	L	0-5
25/10	h	Cracovia	W	2-1 *Murayama 2*
02/11	a	Górnik Zabrze	D	1-1 *Matras*
09/11	h	Legia	W	2-1 *R Murawski, Frączczak*
22/11	h	Podbeskidzie	L	1-2 *Zwoliński*
30/11	a	Śląsk	D	1-1 *Murayama*
06/12	h	Korona	W	2-0 *Zwoliński, Murayama*
15/12	a	Piast	L	0-1

2015
14/02	h	Lech	D	1-1 *Robak*
20/02	a	Wisła	D	1-1 *Robak (p)*
02/03	h	Górnik Łęczna	L	0-1
06/03	a	Ruch	L	1-2 *Robak*
13/03	h	Lechia	L	0-1
20/03	h	Bełchatów	W	3-0 *Robak 3 (2p)*
07/04	a	Zawisza	L	1-2 *Robak*
11/04	h	Jagiellonia	W	2-0 *Zwoliński 2*
18/04	a	Cracovia	W	1-0 *Zwoliński*
25/04	h	Górnik Zabrze	W	3-1 *og (Kosznik), Zwoliński, Rogalski*
29/04	a	Legia	L	1-2 *Zwoliński*
09/05	h	Lechia	L	1-3 *Zwoliński*
17/05	a	Górnik Zabrze	L	0-1
20/05	a	Wisła	D	2-2 *Frączczak, R Murawski*
23/05	h	Legia	L	0-1
31/05	a	Lech	L	0-1
03/06	h	Jagiellonia	L	1-3 *Kun*
07/06	a	Śląsk	L	1-2 *R Murawski*

No	Name	Nat	DoB	Pos	Aps	(s)	Gls
27	Takafumi Akahoshi	JPN	27/05/86	M	7	(5)	
3	Jakub Bąk		28/05/93	M	2	(12)	
20	Karol Danielak		29/09/91	M	7	(8)	
3	Maciej Dąbrowski		20/04/87	D	6	(8)	2
9	Adam Frączczak		07/08/87	M	33	(1)	5
14	Wojciech Golla		12/01/92	M	34		1
44	Hernâni	BRA	03/02/84	D	21	(1)	1
8	Michał Janota		29/07/90	M	5	(4)	
84	Radosław Janukiewicz		05/05/84	G	32		
99	Vladimirs Kamešs	LVA	28/10/88	A	4	(2)	
4	Michał Koj		28/07/93	D	2		
18	Filip Kozłowski		11/07/95	A	1	(1)	
66	Dawid Kudła		21/03/92	G	5		
7	Dominik Kun		22/06/93	M	15	(9)	1
28	Mateusz Lewandowski		18/03/93	M	5		
26	Tomasz Lisowski		04/04/85	D	1	(1)	
29	Marcin Listkowski		10/02/98	A		(2)	
11	Patryk Małecki		01/08/88	M	7	(4)	
23	Mateusz Matras		23/01/91	M	26	(5)	1
15	Hubert Matynia		04/11/95	D	21	(2)	
4	Rafał Murawski		09/10/81	M	36		3
26	Sebastian Murawski		03/03/94	D	4		
13	Takuya Murayama	JPN	08/08/89	A	14	(3)	5
32	Robert Obst		06/07/95	M	1	(1)	
20	Shohei Okuno	JPN	18/08/90	M	2	(3)	
77	Ricardo Nunes	RSA	18/06/86	D	18	(4)	
11	Marcin Robak		29/11/82	A	15	(2)	11
24	Maksymilian Rogalski		24/06/83	M	21	(7)	2
21	Sebastian Rudol		21/02/95	D	33	(1)	
16	Michał Walski		27/02/97	M	5	(1)	
98	Kamil Wojtkowski		26/02/98	M	2	(6)	
93	Łukasz Zwoliński		24/02/93	A	26	(7)	12

Ruch Chorzów

1920 • Miejski (9,300) • ruchchorzow.com.pl

Major honours
Polish League (14) 1933, 1934, 1935, 1936, 1938,
1951, 1952, 1953, 1960, 1968, 1974, 1975, 1979,
1989, Polish Cup (3) 1951, 1974, 1996

Coach: Ján Kocian (SVK);
(07/10/14) Waldemar Fornalik

2014
20/07	a	Śląsk	L 0-2	
27/07	h	Górnik Łęczna	L 1-2	Stawarczyk
03/08	a	Podbeskidzie	L 0-3	
10/08	a	Wisła	D 2-2	Dziwniel, Efir
16/08	a	Piast	W 1-0	Kuświk
24/08	h	Lech	D 0-0	
31/08	a	Lechia	D 3-3	Starzyński, Kowalski, Višņakovs
12/09	a	Pogoń	D 1-1	Kuświk
21/09	h	Bełchatów	L 0-1	
27/09	a	Zawisza	D 1-1	Starzyński (p)
04/10	a	Górnik Zabrze	L 1-2	Kuświk
17/10	a	Cracovia	L 0-1	
27/10	h	Korona	L 0-1	
02/11	a	Legia	L 1-2	Kuświk
09/11	h	Jagiellonia	W 5-2	Starzyński (p), Kowalski, Kuświk 2, Efir
21/11	h	Śląsk	W 1-0	Kuświk
28/11	a	Górnik Łęczna	L 0-3	
08/12	h	Podbeskidzie	W 2-0	Gigolaev, Kuświk
13/12	h	Wisła	L 1-2	Surma

2015
14/02	h	Piast	W 2-0	Kuświk, Kowalski
22/02	a	Lech	L 1-2	Starzyński (p)
27/02	h	Lechia	D 1-1	Starzyński (p)
06/03	h	Pogoń	W 2-1	Babiarz, Kuświk
16/03	a	Bełchatów	W 1-0	Višņakovs
21/03	h	Zawisza	L 0-1	Konczkowski
06/04	a	Górnik Zabrze	D 2-2	Kuświk 2
10/04	h	Cracovia	W 3-0	Kuświk, Gigolaev, Starzyński
17/04	a	Korona	D 0-0	
24/04	h	Legia	D 0-0	
29/04	a	Jagiellonia	L 0-2	
08/05	a	Korona	W 2-0	Starzyński, Zieńczuk
16/05	h	Piast	D 1-1	Efir
19/05	h	Podbeskidzie	W 2-0	Grodzicki, Gigolaev
25/05	a	Bełchatów	L 2-4	Helik, og (Baranowski)
30/05	a	Górnik Łęczna	W 1-0	Kuświk
02/06	a	Cracovia	L 0-1	
05/06	h	Zawisza	W 3-2	Gigolaev, Starzyński (p), Višņakovs

No	Name	Nat	DoB	Pos	Aps	(s)	Gls
16	Bartłomiej Babiarz		03/02/89	M	34	(2)	1
33	Ján Chovanec	SVK	22/03/84	M	2	(7)	
3	Daniel Dziwniel		19/08/92	D	16	(1)	1
11	Michał Efir		14/04/92	A	1	(27)	3
13	Roland Gigolaev	RUS	04/01/90	M	21	(6)	4
51	Rafał Grodzicki		28/10/83	D	14		1
39	Michał Helik		09/09/95	D	17	(1)	1
14	Sebastian Janik		18/04/89	M		(2)	
21	Krzysztof Kamiński		26/11/90	G	19		
15	Martin Konczkowski		14/09/93	D	29	(1)	1
7	Jakub Kowalski		09/10/87	M	24	(9)	3
22	Marcin Kuś		02/09/81	D	7	(2)	
9	Grzegorz Kuświk		23/05/87	A	31	(4)	14
92	Mateusz Kwiatkowski		23/11/92	A		(2)	
10	Patryk Lipski		12/06/94	M		(1)	
32	Marcin Malinowski		06/11/75	M	22		
23	Paweł Oleksy		01/04/91	D	13	(1)	
30	Matúš Putnocký	SVK	01/11/84	G	18		
10	Filip Starzyński		27/05/91	M	36		8
2	Piotr Stawarczyk		29/09/83	D	19	(1)	1
4	Łukasz Surma		28/06/77	M	37		1
6	Michał Szewczyk		17/10/92	M	2	(3)	
20	Marek Szyndrowski		30/10/80	D	7	(2)	
34	Volodymyr Tanchyk	UKR	17/10/91	M	1	(2)	
17	Maciej Urbańczyk		02/04/95	M		(2)	
90	Eduards Višņakovs	LVA	10/05/90	A	10	(17)	3
29	Kamil Włodyka		11/10/94	M		(3)	
5	Marek Zieńczuk		24/09/78	M	27	(9)	1

WKS Śląsk Wrocław

1947 • Miejski (42,771) • slaskwroclaw.pl

Major honours
Polish League (2) 1977, 2012; Polish Cup (2) 1976, 1987

Coach: Tadeusz Pawłowski

2014
20/07	h	Ruch	W 2-0	Mila, Pich
26/07	a	Pogoń	L 1-4	Pich
03/08	h	Zawisza	W 2-1	Pich 2
09/08	a	Bełchatów	L 0-2	
17/08	h	Cracovia	D 0-0	
23/08	a	Jagiellonia	W 3-1	Mila (p), Droppa, Ostrowski
30/08	h	Górnik Zabrze	W 1-0	Flávio Paixão 2
13/09	a	Legia	L 3-4	Mila, Pich, Flávio Paixão
19/09	h	Korona	W 1-0	Flávio Paixão
26/09	a	Górnik Łęczna	W 2-1	Ostrowski, Mila
03/10	a	Podbeskidzie	D 2-2	Celeban, Flávio Paixão
18/10	h	Piast	W 3-0	Flávio Paixão 2, Pich
25/10	a	Lechia	W 4-1	og (Tiago Valente), Flávio Paixão 3 (1p)
02/11	h	Lech	D 1-1	Machaj
08/11	a	Wisła	D 1-1	Flávio Paixão (p)
21/11	a	Ruch	L 0-1	
30/11	h	Pogoń	D 1-1	Zieliński
05/12	a	Zawisza	W 1-0	Mila
12/12	h	Bełchatów	W 2-1	Marco Paixão, Flávio Paixão (p)

2015
15/02	h	Cracovia	D 1-1	Grajciar
21/02	h	Jagiellonia	L 0-1	
28/02	h	Górnik Zabrze	D 3-3	Marco Paixão, Machaj, Flávio Paixão
08/03	h	Legia	L 1-3	Marco Paixão
15/03	h	Korona	D 2-2	Marco Paixão, Pich
20/03	a	Górnik Łęczna	D 1-1	Flávio Paixão
04/04	h	Podbeskidzie	D 0-0	
11/04	a	Piast	D 1-1	Flávio Paixão
18/04	a	Lechia	W 3-0	Machaj (p), Celeban, Marco Paixão
25/04	a	Lech	L 0-2	
29/04	h	Wisła	W 1-0	Pich
08/05	a	Jagiellonia	D 1-1	Pich
17/05	h	Legia	D 1-1	Flávio Paixão
20/05	a	Lech	L 0-3	
23/05	a	Górnik Zabrze	D 1-1	Marco Paixão
30/05	h	Lechia	W 1-0	Flávio Paixão
03/06	a	Wisła	W 1-0	Pich
07/06	h	Pogoń	W 2-1	Flávio Paixão 2 (1p)

No	Name	Nat	DoB	Pos	Aps	(s)	Gls
14	Karol Angielski		20/03/96	A	1	(7)	
25	Michał Bartkowiak		03/02/97	M		(2)	
3	Piotr Celeban		25/06/85	D	36	(1)	2
5	Krzysztof Danielewicz		26/07/91	M	23	(7)	
30	Kamil Dankowski		22/07/96	M	5	(5)	
20	Lukáš Droppa	CZE	22/04/89	M	19	(3)	1
12	Dudu Paraíba	BRA	11/03/85	D	27	(2)	
28	Flávio Paixão	POR	19/09/84	A	36	(1)	18
29	Peter Grajciar	SVK	17/09/83	M	9	(7)	1
51	Rafał Grodzicki		28/10/83	D	4		
4	Tom Hateley	ENG	12/09/89	M	23	(7)	
6	Tomasz Hołota		27/01/91	M	33	(1)	
21	Juanito	ESP	12/05/88	D	2	(9)	
18	Konrad Kaczmarek		01/03/91	M	2	(5)	
15	Miloš Lačný	SVK	08/03/88	A	1	(5)	
8	Mateusz Machaj		28/06/89	M	19	(11)	3
19	Marco Paixão	POR	19/09/84	A	18	(2)	6
11	Sebastian Mila		10/07/82	M	19		5
2	Krzysztof Ostrowski		03/05/82	M	6	(18)	2
17	Mariusz Pawelec		14/04/86	D	17	(2)	
33	Mariusz Pawełek		17/03/81	G	28	(1)	
1	Wojciech Pawłowski		18/01/93	G	2		
10	Róbert Pich	SVK	12/11/88	M	35	(2)	10
7	Sebino Plaku	ALB	20/05/85	A		(3)	
22	Jakub Wrąbel		08/06/96	G	7		
23	Paweł Zieliński		17/07/90	D	35		1

Wisła Kraków

1906 • im. Henryka Reymana (33,326) • wisla.krakow.pl

Major honours
Polish League (13) 1927, 1928, 1949, 1950, 1978,
1999, 2001, 2003, 2004, 2005, 2008, 2009, 2011;
Polish Cup (4) 1926, 1967, 2002, 2003

Coach: Franciszek Smuda;
(10/03/15) Kazimierz Moskal

2014
18/07	a	Górnik Łęczna	D 1-1	Sadlok
28/07	h	Piast	D 1-1	Jankowski
03/08	a	Lech	W 3-2	Garguła 2, Guerrier
10/08	h	Ruch	D 2-2	Boguski (p), Brożek
17/08	h	Lechia	W 3-1	Sadlok, Štilić 2
22/08	a	Pogoń	W 3-0	Štilić, Brożek 2
29/08	h	Bełchatów	W 1-0	Boguski
12/09	a	Zawisza	W 4-2	og (Wójcicki), Brożek, Stępiński, Štilić (p)
21/09	h	Legia	L 0-3	
28/09	a	Cracovia	L 0-1	
03/10	h	Jagiellonia	L 0-1	
19/10	h	Górnik Zabrze	W 5-0	Štilić 2, Brożek 3
24/10	a	Podbeskidzie	W 3-2	og (Pietrasiak), Burliga, Štilić (p)
31/10	a	Korona	L 2-3	Burliga, og (Dejmek)
08/11	h	Śląsk	D 1-1	Brożek
22/11	h	Górnik Łęczna	W 2-0	Boguski, Sarki
28/11	a	Piast	D 0-0	
07/12	h	Lech	L 1-2	Burliga
13/12	a	Ruch	W 2-1	Brożek 2

2015
13/02	a	Lechia	L 0-1	
20/02	a	Pogoń	D 1-1	Brożek
28/02	a	Bełchatów	L 1-3	Głowacki
07/03	h	Zawisza	L 0-1	
15/03	a	Legia	D 2-2	Burliga, Brożek (p)
21/03	h	Cracovia	W 2-1	Štilić, Brożek
06/04	a	Jagiellonia	D 2-2	Brożek, Guerrier
10/04	a	Górnik Zabrze	D 1-1	Guerrier
17/04	a	Podbeskidzie	D 2-2	Guerrier 2
26/04	h	Korona	W 2-0	Guerrier, Jankowski
29/04	a	Śląsk	L 0-1	
09/05	h	Górnik Zabrze	W 4-1	Boguski, Garguła, Burliga, Brożek
15/05	a	Lechia	D 2-2	Boguski, Barrientos
20/05	h	Pogoń	D 2-2	Štilić, Stępiński
23/05	a	Jagiellonia	L 1-2	Jankowski
31/05	a	Legia	L 0-1	
03/06	h	Śląsk	L 0-1	
07/06	a	Lech	D 0-0	

No	Name	Nat	DoB	Pos	Aps	(s)	Gls
8	Jean Barrientos	URU	16/09/90	A	7	(9)	1
9	Rafał Boguski		09/06/84	A	30	(6)	5
23	Paweł Brożek		21/04/83	A	32	(3)	15
22	Michał Buchalik		03/02/89	G	36		
21	Łukasz Burliga		10/05/88	D	33		5
3	Michał Czekaj		13/02/92	D	1		
2	Dariusz Dudka		09/12/83	D	33	(1)	
10	Łukasz Garguła		25/02/81	M	23	(7)	3
6	Arkadiusz Głowacki		13/03/79	D	34		1
77	Wilde-Donald Guerrier	HAI	31/03/89	M	14	(9)	6
26	Richárd Guzmics	HUN	16/04/87	D	20	(1)	
7	Maciej Jankowski		04/01/90	M	22	(4)	3
20	Boban Jović	SVN	25/06/91	D	16		
32	Przemysław Lech		05/07/95	M	1		
1	Michał Miśkiewicz		20/01/89	G	1		
4	Maciej Sadlok		29/06/89	D	29	(2)	2
11	Emmanuel Sarki	HAI	26/12/87	M	5	(16)	1
14	Mariusz Stępiński		12/05/95	A	7	(18)	2
18	Semir Štilić	BIH	08/10/87	M	33	(3)	9
17	Ostoja Stjepanovic	MKD	17/01/85	M	1	(2)	
34	Alan Uryga		19/02/94	M	29	(2)	
29	Tomasz Zając		14/07/95	A		(9)	
43	Piotr Żemło		10/07/95	D	1	(2)	

Zawisza Bydgoszcz

1946 • im. Zdzisława Krzyszkowiaka
(20,247) • wkszawisza.pl
Major honours
Polish Cup (1) 2014
Coach: Jorge Paixão (POR);
(01/09/14) Mariusz Rumak

2014
20/07	h	Korona	W	2-0	Jorge Kadú, Luís Carlos
27/07	h	Jagiellonia	L	1-3	Bernardo Vasconcelos
03/08	a	Śląsk	L	1-2	Drygas
10/08	h	Podbeskidzie	L	1-2	Jorge Kadú
16/08	a	Górnik Łęczna	L	2-5	Wójcicki, Drygas
22/08	h	Lechia	L	0-2	
29/08	a	Piast	L	0-3	
12/09	h	Wisła	L	2-4	Luís Carlos, Wagner
20/09	a	Lech	L	2-6	André Micael, Wagner
27/09	h	Ruch	D	1-1	Alvarinho
05/10	a	Pogoń	L	0-3	
20/10	h	Bełchatów	W	2-1	Petasz, Masłowski
26/10	h	Legia	L	1-2	Wagner
02/11	a	Cracovia	L	0-1	
09/11	h	Górnik Zabrze	L	1-2	Drygas
22/11	a	Korona	D	2-2	Masłowski, og (Dejmek)
29/11	a	Jagiellonia	D	0-0	
05/12	h	Śląsk	L	0-1	
14/12	a	Podbeskidzie	L	1-2	Alvarinho

2015
13/02	h	Górnik Łęczna	D	0-0	
21/02	a	Lechia	L	0-0	
28/02	h	Piast	W	2-0	Predescu, Mica
07/03	a	Wisła	W	1-0	Alvarinho
14/03	h	Lech	W	1-0	Barišić
21/03	a	Ruch	W	2-1	André Micael, Barišić
07/04	h	Pogoń	W	2-1	Alvarinho, Barišić
12/04	a	Bełchatów	W	4-1	Alvarinho, Mica 2, Świerczok
19/04	a	Legia	L	0-2	
24/04	a	Cracovia	L	0-3	
29/04	a	Górnik Zabrze	L	1-2	Barišić
10/05	a	Podbeskidzie	D	2-2	Mayevski, Barišić
15/05	h	Korona	W	3-1	Alvarinho 2 (1p), Barišić
19/05	a	Cracovia	L	1-3	Świerczok
22/05	h	Górnik Łęczna	L	0-1	
30/05	a	Bełchatów	W	4-1	Mica, Barišić 2, Świerczok
02/06	h	Piast	D	0-0	
05/06	a	Ruch	L	2-3	Barišić, Drygas

No	Name	Nat	DoB	Pos	Aps	(s)	Gls
6	Giorgi Alaverdashvili	GEO	21/11/87	A		(4)	
8	Alvarinho	POR	03/09/90	A	23	(9)	8
4	André Micael	POR	04/02/89	D	33		2
27	Anestis Argyriou	GRE	04/01/88	D	8		
90	Josip Barišić	CRO	14/11/86	A	15	(3)	8
5	Bernardo Vasconcelos	POR	10/06/79	A	3	(5)	1
18	Damian Ciechanowski		03/04/96	D	1	(3)	
19	Stefan Denković	MNE	16/06/91	M		(3)	
14	Kamil Drygas		07/09/91	M	32	(1)	4
7	David Fleurival	FRA	19/02/84	M	5		
19	Vahan Gevorgyan		19/12/81	M	3	(4)	
16	Hérold Goulon	FRA	12/06/88	M	7	(1)	
23	Jorge Kadú	CPV	10/04/91	A	11	(5)	2
3	Joshua Silva	POR	21/08/90	D	1	(1)	
15	Sebastian Kamiński		15/08/92	M	4	(12)	
22	Luís Carlos	BRA	15/06/87	A	16	(2)	2
21	Jakub Łukowski		25/05/96	M	1	(9)	
5	Luka Marić	CRO	25/04/87	D	17		
6	Michał Masłowski		19/12/89	M	6	(2)	2
27	Ivan Mayevski	BLR	05/05/88	M	18		1
77	Mica	POR	16/03/93	M	16	(5)	4
32	Łukasz Nawotczyński		30/03/82	D	2	(1)	
16	Bartłomiej Pawłowski		13/11/92	M	13	(2)	
2	Piotr Petasz		27/06/84	D	5	(2)	1
23	Cornel Predescu	ROU	21/12/87	M	5	(2)	1
3	Cristian Pulhac	ROU	17/08/84	D	4	(3)	
9	Rafael Porcellis	BRA	19/01/87	A	7	(1)	
44	Samuel Araújo	BRA	28/03/88	D	10	(1)	
12	Grzegorz Sandomierski		05/09/89	G	28		
7	Jakub Smektała		26/08/87	M	3	(4)	
26	Korneliusz Sochań		22/01/96	M	1		
15	Paweł Strąk		24/03/83	D	14	(4)	
40	Jakub Świerczok		28/12/92	A	5	(10)	4
28	Wagner	BRA	03/04/87	M	14	(4)	3
1	Andrzej Witan		22/02/90	G	9		
10	Jakub Wójcicki		09/07/88	D	35	(1)	1
11	Sebastian Ziajka		15/12/82	M	32		

Top goalscorers

20	Kamil Wilczek (Piast)
18	Flávio Paixão (Śląsk)
15	Patryk Tuszyński (Jagiellonia)
	Paweł Brożek (Wisła)
14	Mateusz Piątkowski (Jagiellonia)
	Grzegorz Kuświk (Ruch)
13	Kasper Hämäläinen (Lech)
	Orlando Sá (Legia)
12	Łukasz Zwoliński (Pogoń)
11	Arkadiusz Piech (Bełchatów)
	Deniss Rakels (Cracovia)
	Fedor Černych (Górnik Łęczna)
	Marcin Robak (Pogoń)

Promoted clubs

Zagłębie Lubin

1945 • Zagłębia (16,100) • zaglebie.com
Major honours
Polish League (2) 1991, 2007
Coach: Piotr Stokowiec

KS Nieciecza

1922 • KS Nieciecza (2,262) •
termalica.brukbet.com
Coach: Piotr Mandrysz

Second level final table 2014/15

		Pld	W	D	L	F	A	Pts
1	Zagłębie Lubin	34	23	8	3	57	20	77
2	KS Nieciecza	34	22	7	5	60	26	73
3	Wisła Płock	34	20	9	5	50	25	69
4	GKS Olimpia Grudziądz	34	15	8	11	46	37	53
5	Chojniczanka Chojnice	34	13	11	10	50	37	50
6	MKS Dolcan Ząbki	34	12	14	8	43	39	50
7	Stomil Olsztyn	34	12	13	9	47	47	49
8	GKS Katowice	34	14	6	14	44	41	48
9	Wigry Suwałki	34	12	11	11	36	37	47
10	Arka Gdynia	34	10	13	11	38	39	43
11	Chrobry Głogów	34	10	11	13	41	45	41
12	Miedź Legnica	34	11	7	16	44	45	40
13	MKS Bytovia Bytów	34	10	10	14	39	45	40
14	MKS Sandecja Nowy Sącz	34	9	8	17	40	55	35
15	MKP Pogoń Siedlce	34	7	9	18	34	53	30
16	GKS Tychy	34	6	10	18	31	56	28
17	RTS Widzew Łódź	34	4	10	20	25	58	22
18	MKS Flota Świnoujście	34	9	9	16	26	46	36

NB MKS Flota Świnoujście withdrew after round 28 and were placed last; their remaining matches were awarded as 0-3 defeats.

DOMESTIC CUP

Puchar Polski 2014/15

FIRST ROUND

(12/08/14)
Energetyk ROW Rybnik 2-1 Siarka Tarnobrzeg
Stal Stalowa Wola 2-0 Olimpia Grudziądz
Znicz Pruszków 2-1 Nieciecza

(13/08/14)
Błękitni Stargard Szczeciński 1-0 Chojniczanka
Chojnice
Flota Świnoujście 2-0 Wigry Suwałki
GKS Katowice 1-2 Chrobry Głogów
Gryf Wejherowo 1-0 Arka Gdynia
Okocimski KS Brzesko 2-1 Stomil Olsztyn
Ostrovia Ostrów 2-1 Puszcza Niepołomice *(aet)*
Polonia Bytom 1-3 Wisła Płock
Radomiak Radom 1-2 Dolcan Ząbki *(aet)*
Rozwój Katowice 0-1 GKS Tychy
Sandecja Nowy Sącz 0-1 GKS Bełchatów
Sokół Kleczew 1-4 Miedź Legnica
Stal Rzeszów 2-1 Górnik Łęczna

Kolejarz Stróże 0-3 Wisła Puławy *(w/o)*

SECOND ROUND

(23/09/14)
Górnik Zabrze 2-1 Korona Kielce
Widzew Łódź 1-2 Śląsk Wrocław
Wisła Puławy 1-1 Piast Gliwice *(aet; 3-4 on pens)*

(24/09/14)
Dolcan Ząbki 2-3 Pogoń Szczecin *(aet)*
Energetyk ROW Rybnik 0-4 Zagłębie Lubin
Flota Świnoujście 1-2 GKS Bełchatów
Gryf Wejherowo 1-2 Błękitni Stargard Szczeciński
Lech Poznań 2-0 Wisła Kraków
Miedź Legnica 0-4 Legia Warszawa
Okocimski KS Brzesko 1-2 Cracovia Kraków
Ostrovia Ostrów 2-1 Ruch Chorzów
Stal Stalowa Wola 2-1 Lechia Gdańsk
Stal Rzeszów 1-3 Znicz Pruszków
Wisła Płock 2-2 GKS Tychy *(aet; 3-4 on pens)*
Zawisza Bydgoszcz 0-2 Podbeskidzie
Bielsko-Biała

(25/09/14)
Chrobry Głogów 1-3 Jagiellonia Białystok

THIRD ROUND

(15/10/14)
Błękitni Stargard Szczeciński 3-2 GKS Tychy
Znicz Pruszków 2-1 Zagłębie Lubin

(28/10/14)
Górnik Zabrze 2-4 Podbeskidzie Bielsko-Biała
Stal Stalowa Wola 0-1 Śląsk Wrocław

(29/10/14)
Ostrovia Ostrów 1-2 Cracovia Kraków *(aet)*
Piast Gliwice 5-0 GKS Bełchatów

(30/10/14)
Lech Poznań 4-2 Jagiellonia Białystok *(aet)*
Legia Warszawa 3-1 Pogoń Szczecin *(aet)*

QUARTER-FINALS

(12/02/15 & 05/03/15)
Śląsk Wrocław 1-1 Legia Warszawa *(Marco Paixão
85; Żyro 45)*
Legia Warszawa 1-1 Śląsk Wrocław *(Żyro 53;
Grajciar 12) (aet)*
(2-2; Legia Warszawa 3-1 on pens)

(03/03/15 & 18/03/15)
Znicz Pruszków 1-5 Lech Poznań *(Jędrych 50;
Linetty 17, Formella 62, Sadayev 65, 67, Keita 90)*
Lech Poznań 1-0 Znicz Pruszków *(Formella 89)*
(Lech Poznań 6-1)

(04/03/15 & 17/03/15)
Błękitni Stargard Szczeciński 2-0 Cracovia Kraków
(Wiśniewski 88, Sretenović 90og)
Cracovia Kraków 0-2 Błękitni Stargard Szczeciński
(Wiśniewski 30, Flis 83)
(Błękitni Stargard Szczeciński 4-0)

(04/03/15 & 19/03/15)
Piast Gliwice 1-2 Podbeskidzie Bielsko-Biała
(Ciechański 85; Kołodziej 64p, Malinowski 67)
Podbeskidzie Bielsko-Biała 1-0 Piast Gliwice
(Kołodziej 45)
(Podbeskidzie Bielsko-Biała 3-1)

SEMI-FINALS

(01/04/15 & 08/04/15)
Podbeskidzie Bielsko-Biała 1-4 Legia Warszawa
*(Korzym 84; Masłowski 24, Vrdoljak 30, Kucharczyk
71, Kosecki 87)*
Legia Warszawa 2-0 Podbeskidzie Bielsko-Biała
(Saganowski 19, 46)
(Legia Warszawa 6-1)

(01/04/15 & 09/04/15)
Błękitni Stargard Szczeciński 3-1 Lech Poznań
(Pustelnik 54, 64, Kosakiewicz 84; Sadayev 9)
Lech Poznań 5-1 Błękitni Stargard Szczeciński
*(Arajuuri 34, Formella 44, Kownacki 74, 106,
Hämäläinen 100; Wojtasiak 19) (aet)*
(Lech Poznań 6-4)

FINAL

(02/05/15)
Stadion Narodowy, Warsaw
LEGIA WARSZAWA 2 *(Jodłowiec 30, Saganowski
55)*
KKS LECH POZNAŃ 1 *(Jodłowiec 20og)*
Referee: Stefański
LEGIA: Kuciak, Broź, Rzeźniczak, Iñaki Astiz,
Brzyski, Guilherme (Żyro 37; Kosecki 89), Vrdoljak,
Jodłowiec, Duda (Masłowski 79), Kucharczyk,
Saganowski
LECH: Gostomski, Kędziora, Arajuuri, Kamiński,
Douglas, Kownacki, Trałka, Linetty (Jevtic 68),
Hämäläinen, Pawłowski (Keita 79), Sadayev
(Formella 72)
Red card: Douglas (88)

Legia lift the Polish Cup for the fourth time in five years

PORTUGAL
Federação Portuguesa de Futebol (FPF)

Address	Rua Alexandre Herculano 58	**President**	Fernando Gomes
	Apartado 24013	**General secretary**	Paulo Manuel
	PT-1250-012 Lisboa		Lourenço
Tel	+351 21 325 2700	**Media officer**	Onofre Costa
Fax	+351 21 325 2780	**Year of formation**	1914
E-mail	ceo@fpf.pt		
Website	fpf.pt		

PRIMEIRA LIGA CLUBS

 1 A. Académica de Coimbra

 2 FC Arouca

 3 CF Os Belenenses

 4 SL Benfica

 5 Boavista FC

 6 SC Braga

 7 Estoril Praia

 8 Gil Vicente FC

 9 CS Marítimo

 10 Moreirense FC

 11 CD Nacional

 12 FC Paços de Ferreira

 13 Penafiel FC

 14 FC Porto

 15 Rio Ave FC

 16 Sporting Clube de Portugal

 17 Vitória FC

 18 Vitória SC

PROMOTED CLUBS

 19 CD Tondela

 20 CF União da Madeira

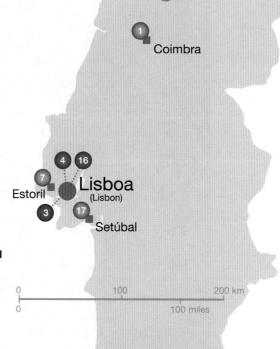

KEY:
- UEFA Champions League
- UEFA Europa League
- Promoted
- Relegated

Back-to-back titles for Benfica

SL Benfica, Portugal's most decorated club, made a successful defence of the Primeira Liga title for the first time in 31 years, resolutely holding on to their crown despite a major exodus of key players and a persistent challenge from FC Porto.

Benfica were succeeded as Portuguese Cup winners, however, by Lisbon rivals Sporting Clube de Portugal, who claimed the trophy for the first time in seven years after a dramatic ten-man comeback in the final against SC Braga. Porto were Portugal's standout performers in European club competition, while captain Cristiano Ronaldo's goals boosted the national team's bid to qualify for UEFA EURO 2016.

| Eagles hold off Porto to keep Liga crown in Lisbon | Sporting end trophy drought with Portuguese Cup win | Ronaldo drives national team towards EURO finals |

Domestic league

It was a Benfica depleted by summer transfer activity that set about defending their Primeira Liga title. While coach Jorge Jesus remained to start his sixth season at the helm, the club lost a plethora of players who had been key to their domestic treble-winning success of the previous campaign. Among the notable departures were centre-back Ezequiel Garay (to FC Zenit), striker Óscar Cardozo (Trabzonspor AŞ), goalkeeper Jan Oblak (Club Atlético de Madrid) and winger Lazar Marković (Liverpool FC), but as Benfica did their best to replace them while also holding on to other important individuals such as Uruguayan full-back Maxi Pereira and Argentinian wingers Nicolás Gaitán and Eduardo Salvio, the general consensus was that eternal rivals Porto and Sporting were equally, if not better, equipped to take the title.

Benfica needed a good start, and they got one. The only points shed in their opening seven matches came in a 1-1 draw at home to Sporting, and with new Brazilian recruit Talisca having hit the ground running, the Eagles quickly soared to the top of the table. Their first defeat, 2-1 at Braga, did not dislodge them – indeed it inspired them to a nine-match winning run, featuring eight

clean sheets, that hoisted them into a six-point lead. At the heart of that victory sequence was a crucial 2-0 win at Porto, a goal in each half from Brazilian striker Lima silencing the Estádio do Dragão.

Having constructed a decent lead at halfway, Benfica spent the second half of the season protecting it. With another Brazilian striker, Jonas, now coming into his own, the goals and points continued to accumulate. Although fortunate to get another draw against in-form Sporting with a last-gasp equaliser from defender Jardel, that goal symbolised the team's never-say-die resolve. It was displayed time and again in victories and also, just as importantly, in a goalless draw at home to Porto that preserved Benfica's three-point – and head-to-head – advantage with four games remaining.

It was the first time in six years that Benfica had failed to score in a home league game, but the vast bulk of the 63,534 spectators in the Estádio da Luz were quite content with the outcome. They were even happier with another goalless draw three weeks later, against Vitória SC in Guimaraes, which, accompanied by a late equaliser from CF Os Belenenses at home to Porto, put the seal on the club's 34th league title.

There was a painful sting in the tail to the Benfica fans' celebrations, however, when it was revealed that coach Jesus had not only failed to agree terms on a new contract but had left to take up the reins at Sporting, who had just sacked Marco Silva after a solitary season at the helm. The former Estoril Praia boss was entitled to feel hard done by after a productive campaign on all fronts, in which Sporting, commanded once again in midfield by William Carvalho, lost fewer league games than Benfica and none in the Estádio José Alvalade. An inability to turn draws into victories, however, proved to be the Lions' downfall, with both Lisbon derbies and the home game against Porto notable cases in point.

Sporting finished six points behind Porto, who also lost just two league fixtures under their new coach, Julen Lopetegui. Unfortunately, one of them was that 2-0 home loss to Benfica, which effectively cost them the title. A final tally of 82 points from their 34 games compared favourably with the 61 from 30 in 2013/14, when they finished third, so Lopetegui, the former Spain Under-21 team coach, emerged with his reputation enhanced. He was well served on the field by compatriots Cristian Tello – who scored a brilliant hat-trick at home to Sporting – and

20-year-old playmaker Óliver Torres, while the team's defence, marshalled with authority by Maicon, was the best in the league, conceding just 13 goals. Algerian international Yacine Brahimi and Brazilian right-back Danilo also enjoyed excellent campaigns, while up front the ever-reliable Jackson Martínez won the Primeira Liga golden boot for the third season in a row.

Braga, Guimarães and Belenenses finished well adrift of the big three, but top-six placings earned all three clubs qualification for the UEFA Europa League – although Guimarães's progressive coach Rui Vitória would subsequently move south to become Jorge Jesus's replacement at Benfica, where he had previously worked as youth coach. Only one of the three newly-promoted teams, Penafiel FC, suffered immediate relegation. They were escorted down by Gil Vicente FC, whose fate was prematurely sealed by a failure to win any of their first 15 matches. An intense battle for promotion ended with CD Tondela topping the Segunda Liga and ascending to the top flight for the first time, with CF União da Madeira's runners-up spot giving the mainland clubs of the Primeira Liga three flights to the Atlantic holiday island, rather than two, in 2015/16.

Domestic cup

Without a major trophy for seven years, Sporting finally gave their fans something to shout about as they closed the season by lifting the Taça de Portugal. There was more suffering first, however, as Braga, cup winners once before, in 1966, took an early 2-0 lead and held on to it, with a one-man advantage, until six minutes from time. They could not see the job through, and after Sporting's two top marksmen, Islam Slimani and Fredy Montero, had struck late to prolong the contest, the Portuguese Cup final's first penalty shoot-out was won by the club from the capital, who scored all three of their spot-kicks – through Adrien Silva, Nani and Slimani – while Braga missed three of theirs. It was Sporting's 16th cup triumph, putting them level on the all-time honours board with Porto.

Europe

There were differing fortunes for Portugal's three UEFA Champions League challengers in 2014/15, with Benfica ending up bottom of their group, Porto topping theirs and Sporting crossing over to the UEFA Europa League after finishing third. Having reached each of the previous two season's UEFA Europa League finals,

Benfica's early exit from Europe was a shock, but it may have had benefits on the domestic front, where in addition to defending the league title they also retained the League Cup.

Despite home and away defeats by Chelsea FC, Sporting were slightly unfortunate not to reach the knockout phase of the UEFA Champions League at the expense of FC Schalke 04. Porto, though, enjoyed a fabulous run, remaining undefeated for 11 matches, play-offs included, until FC Bayern München smashed their previously rock-solid defence to smithereens in the second leg of the quarter-final, overturning a 3-1 deficit at the Estádio do Dragão, in which two-goal Ricardo Quaresma was back to his ingenious best, with a 6-1 battering in Bavaria.

National team

Portugal's UEFA EURO 2016 qualifying campaign began with a shock 1-0 home defeat by Albania and a consequent change of coach, with Fernando Santos, a 2014 FIFA World Cup success with Greece, replacing Paulo Bento, a failure in Brazil with Portugal. Things improved dramatically thereafter, with Cristiano Ronaldo, as ever, galloping to his country's rescue. Absent through injury for the Albania game, the country's all-time top goalscorer returned with a vengeance, netting winning goals against Denmark – in the 95th minute – and Armenia, inspiring the side to a 2-1 victory against Serbia and, to cap it all, bagging a brilliant hat-trick in a thrilling end-of-season 3-2 victory in Yerevan.

Four successive wins – all by a one-goal margin – placed Portugal at the top of their group, and although Denmark and Albania remained in close proximity, those 12 points already guaranteed Portugal a play-off place – the team's qualifying route to each of the previous three major tournaments. As Ronaldo continued to set new records, including the most goals scored in the UEFA European Championship (26 and counting), a new wave of bright young Portuguese talent revealed itself at the UEFA European Under-21 Championship in the Czech Republic, where Rui Jorge's gifted side, including several players already capped at senior level, destroyed Germany 5-0 in the semi-final before losing on penalties in the final to Sweden.

Sporting goalkeeper Rui Patrício is mobbed by his team-mates at the end of the Portuguese Cup final penalty shoot-out

DOMESTIC SEASON AT A GLANCE

Primeira Liga 2014/15 final table

		Pld	Home					Away					Total					Pts
			W	D	L	F	A	W	D	L	F	A	W	D	L	F	A	
1	**SL Benfica**	34	15	2	0	48	5	12	2	3	38	11	27	4	3	86	16	85
2	FC Porto	34	15	1	1	41	3	10	6	1	33	10	25	7	2	74	13	82
3	Sporting Clube de Portugal	34	12	5	0	38	14	10	5	2	29	15	22	10	2	67	29	76
4	SC Braga	34	11	3	3	32	9	6	4	7	23	19	17	7	10	55	28	58
5	Vitória SC	34	10	5	2	28	7	5	5	7	22	28	15	10	9	50	35	55
6	CF Os Belenenses	34	5	7	5	17	17	7	5	5	17	18	12	12	10	34	35	48
7	CD Nacional	34	10	4	3	27	12	3	4	10	18	34	13	8	13	45	46	47
8	FC Paços de Ferreira	34	8	6	3	28	20	4	5	8	12	25	12	11	11	40	45	47
9	CS Marítimo	34	8	4	5	27	17	4	4	9	19	28	12	8	14	46	45	44
10	Rio Ave FC	34	6	7	4	21	15	4	6	7	17	27	10	13	11	38	42	43
11	Moreirense FC	34	6	5	6	18	20	5	5	7	15	22	11	10	13	33	42	43
12	Estoril Praia	34	6	6	5	22	24	3	7	7	16	32	9	13	12	38	56	40
13	Boavista FC	34	8	2	7	20	19	1	5	11	7	31	9	7	18	27	50	34
14	Vitória FC	34	6	3	8	17	21	1	5	11	7	35	7	8	19	24	56	29
15	A. Académica de Coimbra	34	1	12	4	16	23	3	5	9	10	23	4	17	13	26	46	29
16	FC Arouca	34	5	3	9	16	26	2	4	11	10	24	7	7	20	26	50	28
17	Gil Vicente FC	34	2	7	8	11	30	2	4	11	14	30	4	11	19	25	60	23
18	Penafiel FC	34	3	3	11	17	37	2	4	11	12	32	5	7	22	29	69	22

European qualification 2015/16

Champion: SL Benfica (group stage)
FC Porto (group stage)
Cup winner: Sporting Clube de Portugal (play-offs)

SC Braga (group stage)
Vitória SC (third qualifying round)
CF Os Belenenses (third qualifying round)

Top scorer	Jackson Martínez (Porto), 21 goals
Relegated clubs	Penafiel FC, Gil Vicente FC
Promoted clubs	CD Tondela, CF União da Madeira
Cup final	Sporting Clube de Portugal 2-2 SC Braga *(aet; 3-1 on pens)*

Team of the season
(4-3-3)

Coach: Jorge Jesus *(Benfica)*

Player of the season

Jonas
(SL Benfica)

Signed in September as a free agent following a three-year spell with Valencia CF, Jonas took a while to adapt in Lisbon, but once he got in the groove, there was no stopping him. The 31-year-old Brazilian struck 18 goals in the Primeira Liga after Christmas to fire Benfica to the title. Adored by the Eagles fans, he was also recognised for his efforts with the official Primeira Liga Player of the Year award, becoming the third successive recipient from Benfica after Nemanja Matić and Enzo Pérez.

Newcomer of the season

João Mário
(Sporting Clube de Portugal)

Having distinguished himself repeatedly in the Sporting B team, João Mário was drafted into the first XI by Marco Silva at the start of the 2014/15 season. It proved to be a smart move as the young, do-it-all midfielder enhanced his profile with every game. He established himself as a useful ally to William Carvalho both with Sporting and the Portuguese Under-21 team, helping the latter to a runners-up spot at the 2015 European finals, not least with the winning goal in a group game against England.

NATIONAL TEAM

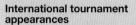

International tournament appearances

FIFA World Cup (6) 1966 (3rd), 1986, 2002, 2006 (4th), 2010 (2nd round), 2014
UEFA European Championship (6) 1984 (semifinals), 1996 (qtr-finals), 2000 (semi-finals), 2004 (runners-up), 2008 (qtr-finals), 2012 (semi-finals)

Top five all-time caps

Luís Figo (127); **Cristiano Ronaldo** (120); Fernando Couto (110); Rui Costa (95); Pauleta (88)

Top five all-time goals

Cristiano Ronaldo (55); Pauleta (47); Eusébio (41); Luís Figo (32); Nuno Gomes (29)

Results 2014/15

Date	Opponent		Venue		Score	Scorers
07/09/14	Albania (ECQ)	H	Aveiro	L	0-1	
11/10/14	France	A	Saint-Denis	L	1-2	Ricardo Quaresma (77p)
14/10/14	Denmark (ECQ)	A	Copenhagen	W	1-0	Cristiano Ronaldo (90+5)
14/11/14	Armenia (ECQ)	H	Faro	W	1-0	Cristiano Ronaldo (72)
18/11/14	Argentina	N	Manchester (ENG)	W	1-0	Raphael Guerreiro (90+1)
29/03/15	Serbia (ECQ)	H	Lisbon	W	2-1	Ricardo Carvalho (10), Fábio Coentrão (63)
31/03/15	Cape Verde	H	Estoril	L	0-2	
13/06/15	Armenia (ECQ)	A	Yerevan	W	3-2	Cristiano Ronaldo (29p, 55, 58)
16/06/15	Italy	N	Geneva (SUI)	W	1-0	Éder (52)

Appearances 2014/15

Coach: Paulo Bento 20/06/69 / (23/09/14) Fernando Santos 10/10/54 (Ilídio Vale) 13/12/57

Player	DOB	Club	ALB	Fra	DEN	ARM	Arg	SRB	Cpv	ARM	Ita	Caps	Goals
Rui Patrício	15/02/88	Sporting	G	G	G	G		G		G		37	-
João Pereira	25/02/84	Valencia (ESP)	D									40	-
Pepe	26/02/83	Real Madrid (ESP)	D	D	D	D	D46					65	3
Ricardo Costa	16/05/81	Al-Sailiya (QAT)	D73									22	1
Fábio Coentrão	11/03/88	Real Madrid (ESP)	D					M78		M72	D24	50	5
João Moutinho	08/09/86	Monaco (FRA)	M	M	M	M	M	M		M	M	79	2
William Carvalho	07/04/92	Sporting	M56	s46	M	s88	s78	s86		s63		13	-
André Gomes	30/07/93	Valencia (ESP)	M	M46			M66		M80			4	-
Vieirinha	24/01/86	Wolfsburg (GER)	A46	s85					A	D	D46	15	1
Éder	22/12/87	Braga	A	s68	s77	s56	s46		s65		A	18	1
Nani	17/11/86	Sporting	A	A68	A68	M88	A	A		A	s75	86	15
Ivan Cavaleiro	18/10/93	Deportivo (ESP)	s46									2	-
Ricardo Horta	15/09/94	Málaga (ESP)	s56									1	-
Miguel Veloso	11/05/86	Dynamo Kyiv (UKR)	s73									53	2
Cédric	31/08/91	Sporting		D	D				D66		s46	4	-
Bruno Alves	27/11/81	Fenerbahçe (TUR)		D46			D	D		D	D59	80	10
Eliseu	01/10/83	Benfica		D	D			D		D	s24	9	1
Tiago	02/05/81	Atlético (ESP)		M68	M84	M	M78	M		M62*	M46	65	3
Danny	07/08/83	Zenit (RUS)		A85	A77	A70	A46	A86		A63		32	4
Cristiano Ronaldo	05/02/85	Real Madrid (ESP)		A76	A	M	A46	A		A		120	55
Ricardo Carvalho	18/05/78	Monaco (FRA)		s46	D	D		D17		D78		80	5
Ricardo Quaresma	26/09/83	Porto		s68	s84	s70	s46	s78			A87	41	4
João Mário	19/01/93	Sporting		s76	s68				M46			3	-
José Bosingwa	24/08/82	Trabzonspor (TUR)					D	D	D			27	-
Raphael Guerreiro	22/12/93	Lorient (FRA)					D	s51				2	1
Hélder Postiga	02/08/82	Deportivo (ESP)				A56						71	27
Beto	01/05/82	Sevilla (ESP)						G			G	11	-
Tiago Gomes	29/07/86	Braga					D51					1	-
José Fonte	22/12/86	Southampton (ENG)						s46	s17	s78	D	4	-
Adrien Silva	15/03/89	Sporting						s66	M66	s72	s46	4	-
Anthony Lopes	01/10/90	Lyon (FRA)							G			1	-
André Pinto	05/10/89	Braga							D60*			1	-
Paulo Oliveira	08/01/92	Sporting							D			1	-
Antunes	01/04/87	Dynamo Kyiv (UKR)							D			9	-
Bernardo Silva	10/08/94	Monaco (FRA)							A61			1	-
Hugo Almeida	23/05/84	Kuban (RUS)							A65			57	19
Ukra	16/03/88	Rio Ave							s46			1	-
Danilo Pereira	09/09/91	Marítimo							s61		M	2	-
André André	26/08/89	Guimarães							s66			1	-
Pizzi	06/10/89	Benfica							s66	s87		4	1
André Almeida	10/09/90	Benfica							s80			8	-
Silvestre Varela	02/02/85	Parma (ITA)									A75	27	5
Daniel Carriço	04/08/88	Sevilla (ESP)									s59	1	-

EUROPE

SL Benfica

Group C
Match 1 - FC Zenit (RUS)
H 0-2
Artur, Luisão, Samaris (André Almeida 74), Gaitán, Lima (Derley 74), Maxi Pereira, Salvio, Eliseu, Talisca (Paulo Lopes 20), Jardel, Pérez. Coach: Jorge Jesus (POR)
Red card: Artur 18
Match 2 - Bayer 04 Leverkusen (GER)
A 1-3 *Salvio (62)*
Júlio César, Luisão, Derley, Gaitán, Salvio, Eliseu, Cristante (Maxi Pereira 46), Talisca (Lima 46), Jardel, André Almeida, Pérez (Samaris 77). Coach: Jorge Jesus (POR)
Match 3 - AS Monaco FC (FRA)
A 0-0
Artur, López, Luisão, Gaitán (César 78), Lima, Maxi Pereira, Salvio, Eliseu, Talisca (Tiago 68), André Almeida, Pérez (Samaris 87). Coach: Jorge Jesus (POR)
Red card: López 76
Match 4 - AS Monaco FC (FRA)
H 1-0 *Talisca (82)*
Júlio César, Luisão, Samaris (Lima 62), Derley (Cristante 86), Gaitán (Tiago 90+1), Maxi Pereira, Salvio, Talisca, Jardel, André Almeida, Pérez. Coach: Jorge Jesus (POR)
Match 5 - FC Zenit (RUS)
A 0-1
Júlio César, Luisão, Samaris (John 82), Gaitán, Lima, Maxi Pereira, Salvio, Talisca (Derley 70), Jardel, André Almeida, Pérez. Coach: Jorge Jesus (POR)
Red card: Luisão 90+2
Match 6 - Bayer 04 Leverkusen (GER)
H 0-0
Artur, López, Derley (Nélson Oliveira 76), Lima (Talisca 62), John, Pizzi, Benito, Cristante, Tiago (João Teixeira 87), André Almeida, César. Coach: Jorge Jesus (POR)

Sporting Clube de Portugal

Group G
Match 1 - NK Maribor (SVN)
A 1-1 *Nani (80)*
Rui Patrício, Maurício, Jefferson, André Martins (João Mário 46), Slimani (Montero 90+2), William Carvalho, Carrillo (Carlos Mané 66), Adrien Silva, Sarr, Cédric, Nani. Coach: Marco Silva (POR)
Match 2 - Chelsea FC (ENG)
H 0-1
Rui Patrício, Maurício (Paulo Oliveira 64), Slimani, William Carvalho, João Mário, Carrillo (Diego Capel 81), Adrien Silva (Montero 81), Sarr, Silva, Cédric, Nani. Coach: Marco Silva (POR)
Match 3 - FC Schalke 04 (GER)
A 3-4 *Nani (16), Adrien Silva (64p, 78)*
Rui Patrício, Maurício, Slimani (Montero 25), William Carvalho, João Mário (Sarr 38), Carrillo (Diego Capel 89), Adrien Silva, Paulo Oliveira, Silva, Cédric, Nani. Coach: Marco Silva (POR)
Red card: Maurício 33
Match 4 - FC Schalke 04 (GER)
H 4-2 *Sarr (26), Jefferson (52), Nani (72), Slimani (90+1)*
Rui Patrício, Jefferson, Slimani, William Carvalho, João Mário (Oriol Rosell 82), Adrien Silva, Paulo Oliveira, Sarr, Carlos Mané (Carrillo 68), Cédric, Nani (Diego Capel 89). Coach: Marco Silva (POR)
Match 5 - NK Maribor (SVN)
H 3-1 *Carlos Mané (10), Nani (35), Slimani (65)*
Rui Patrício, Maurício, Jefferson, Slimani (Montero 75), William Carvalho, João Mário (André Martins 82), Adrien Silva, Paulo Oliveira, Carlos Mané (Carrillo 66), Cédric, Nani. Coach: Marco Silva (POR)
Match 6 - Chelsea FC (ENG)
A 1-3 *Silva (50)*
Rui Patrício, Maurício, Slimani, Diego Capel (Carlos Mané 61), William Carvalho (Montero 61), João Mário (André Martins 70), Carrillo, Adrien Silva, Paulo Oliveira, Silva, Ricardo Esgaio. Coach: Marco Silva (POR)

Round of 32 - VfL Wolfsburg (GER)
A 0-2
Rui Patrício, Jefferson, Montero (Tanaka 80), João Mário, Carrillo (Carlos Mané 70), Adrien Silva, Oriol Rosell (André Martins 80), Paulo Oliveira, Cédric, Tobias Figueiredo, Nani. Coach: Marco Silva (POR)
H 0-0
Rui Patrício, William Carvalho, João Mário, Carrillo (Carlos Mané 77), Tanaka (Montero 77), Adrien Silva (Slimani 64), Paulo Oliveira, Silva, Cédric, Tobias Figueiredo, Nani. Coach: Marco Silva (POR)

FC Porto

Play-offs - LOSC Lille (FRA)
A 1-0 *Herrera (61)*
Fabiano, Danilo, Martins Indi, Maicon, Casemiro, Brahimi (Tello 60), Martínez, Herrera, Alex Sandro, Óliver Torres (Ricardo Quaresma 89), Rúben Neves (Evandro 74). Coach: Julen Lopetegui (ESP)
H 2-0 *Brahimi (49), Martínez (69)*
Fabiano, Danilo, Martins Indi, Maicon, Casemiro (Ricardo 84), Brahimi, Martínez, Herrera, Alex Sandro (Reyes 39), Óliver Torres, Rúben Neves (Evandro 62). Coach: Julen Lopetegui (ESP)

Group H
Match 1 - FC BATE Borisov (BLR)
H 6-0 *Brahimi (5, 32, 57), Martínez (37), Adrián (61), Aboubakar (76)*
Fabiano, Danilo, Martins Indi, Maicon, Casemiro, Ricardo Quaresma, Brahimi (Evandro 59), Martínez (Aboubakar 64), Herrera (Tello 69), Adrián, Alex Sandro. Coach: Julen Lopetegui (ESP)
Match 2 - FC Shakhtar Donetsk (UKR)
A 2-2 *Martínez (89p, 90+4)*
Fabiano, Danilo, Martins Indi, Maicon, Marcano (Quintero 65), Brahimi (Adrián 78), Tello, Herrera, Alex Sandro, Óliver Torres, Aboubakar (Martínez 65). Coach: Julen Lopetegui (ESP)
Match 3 - Athletic Club (ESP)
H 2-1 *Herrera (45), Ricardo Quaresma (75)*
Fabiano, Danilo, Martins Indi, Maicon, Casemiro (Ricardo Quaresma 71), Brahimi, Martínez, Quintero (Rúben Neves 64), Tello (Óliver Torres 82), Herrera, Alex Sandro. Coach: Julen Lopetegui (ESP)
Match 4 - Athletic Club (ESP)
A 2-0 *Martínez (56), Brahimi (73)*
Fabiano, Danilo, Martins Indi, Maicon, Casemiro, Brahimi (Adrián 90+1), Martínez, Tello (Ricardo Quaresma 60), Herrera, Alex Sandro, Óliver Torres (Rúben Neves 82). Coach: Julen Lopetegui (ESP)
Match 5 - FC BATE Borisov (BLR)
A 3-0 *Herrera (56), Martínez (65), Tello (89)*
Fabiano, Danilo, Martins Indi, Marcano, Casemiro, Ricardo Quaresma (Tello 71), Brahimi (Adrián 83), Martínez (Quintero 90), Herrera, Alex Sandro, Óliver Torres. Coach: Julen Lopetegui (ESP)
Match 6 - FC Shakhtar Donetsk (UKR)
H 1-1 *Aboubakar (87)*
Andrés Fernández, Maicon, Marcano, Ricardo Quaresma, Quintero (Óliver Torres 69), Evandro, Adrián (Kelvin 53), Ricardo, Alex Sandro, Rúben Neves (Martins Indi 41), Aboubakar. Coach: Julen Lopetegui (ESP)

Round of 16 - FC Basel 1893 (SUI)
A 1-1 *Danilo (79p)*
Fabiano, Danilo, Maicon, Marcano, Casemiro, Brahimi (Ricardo Quaresma 61), Martínez, Tello (Quintero 81), Herrera, Alex Sandro, Óliver Torres (Rúben Neves 68). Coach: Julen Lopetegui (ESP)
H 4-0 *Brahimi (14), Herrera (47), Casemiro (56), Aboubakar (76)*
Fabiano, Danilo (Martins Indi 22), Maicon, Marcano, Casemiro, Brahimi (Rúben Neves 74), Tello, Evandro (Ricardo Quaresma 79), Herrera, Alex Sandro, Aboubakar. Coach: Julen Lopetegui (ESP)

Quarter-finals - FC Bayern München (GER)
H 3-1 *Ricardo Quaresma (3p,10), Martínez (65)*
Fabiano, Danilo, Martins Indi, Maicon, Casemiro, Ricardo Quaresma (Evandro 84), Brahimi (Hernâni 80), Martínez, Herrera, Alex Sandro, Óliver Torres (Rúben Neves 75). Coach: Julen Lopetegui (ESP)
A 1-6 *Martínez (73)*
Fabiano, Martins Indi, Maicon, Marcano, Casemiro, Ricardo Quaresma (Rúben Neves 46), Brahimi (Evandro 67), Martínez, Reyes (Ricardo 33), Herrera, Óliver Torres. Coach: Julen Lopetegui (ESP)
Red card: Marcano 87

Estoril Praia

Group E
Match 1 - PSV Eindhoven (NED)
A 0-1
Kieszek, Yohan Tavares, Bruno Miguel, Filipe Gonçalves, Bruno Lopes (Arturo 73), Mano, Sebá (Ricardo Vaz 88), Kuca, Emídio Rafael, Diogo Amado, Tozé (Babanco 73). Coach: José Couceiro (POR)
Match 2 - Panathinaikos FC (GRE)
H 2-0 *Kléber (52), Diogo Amado (66)*
Vagner, Yohan Tavares, Anderson Luiz, Bruno Lopes (Kléber 46), Esiti, Cabrera, Sebá, Emídio Rafael, Diogo Amado (Filipe Gonçalves 78), Bruno Nascimento, Tozé (Kuca 62). Coach: José Couceiro (POR)
Match 3 - FC Dinamo Moskva (RUS)
H 1-2 *Yohan Tavares (90+5)*
Vagner, Yohan Tavares, Bruno Miguel, Anderson Luiz, Kléber (Cabrera 81), Esiti, Sebá (Ricardo Vaz 85), Kuca, Diogo Amado, Rúben Fernandes, Tozé (Arturo 77). Coach: José Couceiro (POR)
Match 4 - FC Dinamo Moskva (RUS)
A 0-1
Kieszek, Yohan Tavares, Anderson Luiz (Filipe Gonçalves 87), Kléber (Bruno Lopes 73), Esiti, Sebá, Kuca, Emídio Rafael, Diogo Amado (Ricardo Vaz 87), Rúben Fernandes, Tozé. Coach: José Couceiro (POR)
Match 5 - PSV Eindhoven (NED)
H 3-3 *Tozé (12), Kuca (30), Diogo Amado (39)*
Kieszek, Yohan Tavares, Anderson Luiz, Kléber, Esiti, Sebá, Kuca, Emídio Rafael, Diogo Amado, Rúben Fernandes (Arturo 86), Tozé. Coach: José Couceiro (POR)
Match 6 - Panathinaikos FC (GRE)
A 1-1 *Kléber (87)*
Vagner, Yohan Tavares, Arthuro (Kléber 61), Mano, Esiti, Cabrera, Sebá, Kuca (Balboa 68), Emídio Rafael, Bruno Nascimento, Babanco (Diogo Amado 73). Coach: José Couceiro (POR)

CD Nacional

Play-offs - FC Dinamo Minsk (BLR)
A 0-2
Gottardi, Zainaidine Júnior (Lucas João 60), Miguel Rodrigues, Ezzat, Marçal, João Aurélio, Suk (Reginaldo 57), Gomaa, Rondón, Ghazal, Marco Matias. Coach: Manuel Machado (POR)
H 2-3 *Marco Matias (30p), Ghazal (53)*
Gottardi, Zainaidine Júnior, Miguel Rodrigues, Marçal, João Aurélio (Fofana 67), Ayala (Suk 45+3), Gomaa (Reginaldo 67), Rondón, Rui Correia, Ghazal, Marco Matias. Coach: Manuel Machado (POR)

Rio Ave FC

Third qualifying round - IFK Göteborg (SWE)
A 1-0 *Hassan (22)*
Cássio, Gouano, Filipe Augusto (Diego Lopes 75), Tarantini, Hassan, Lionn, Tiago Pinto, Ukra (André Vilas Boas 88), Pedro Moreira, Del Valle (Boateng 64), Marcelo. Coach: Pedro Martins (POR)
H 0-0
Cássio, Gouano, Filipe Augusto (Wakaso 87), Tarantini, Hassan (Boateng 79), Lionn, Tiago Pinto, Ukra (Roderick 90+2), Pedro Moreira, Del Valle, Marcelo. Coach: Pedro Martins (POR)

Play-offs - IF Elfsborg (SWE)
A 1-2 *Marcelo (65)*
Cássio, Gouano, Filipe Augusto, Tarantini, Lionn, Boateng (Hassan 81), Tiago Pinto, Ukra, Pedro Moreira (Renan Bressan 46), Del Valle (Diego Lopes 46), Marcelo. Coach: Pedro Martins (POR)
H 1-0 *Esmaël Gonçalves (90+2)*
Cássio, Gouano, Filipe Augusto, Tarantini, Hassan, Diego Lopes (Jebor 70), Renan Bressan (Boateng 57), Lionn (Esmaël Gonçalves 79), Tiago Pinto, Ukra, Marcelo. Coach: Pedro Martins (POR)

Group J
Match 1 - FC Dynamo Kyiv (UKR)
H 0-3
Cássio, Gouano, Tarantini, Diego Lopes (Wakaso 77), Renan Bressan (Jebor 64), Lionn, Boateng, Tiago Pinto, Ukra (Esmaël Gonçalves 81), Pedro Moreira, Marcelo. Coach: Pedro Martins (POR)

Match 2 - Aalborg BK (DEN)
A 0-1
Cássio, Gouano (André Vilas Boas 43), Tarantini, Diego Lopes, Boateng (Renan Bressan 74), Tiago Pinto, Nuno Lopes, Ukra, Pedro Moreira (Hassan 63), Wakaso, Marcelo. Coach: Pedro Martins (POR)
Match 3 - FC Steaua Bucureşti (ROU)
A 1-2 *Del Valle (48)*
Cássio, Gouano, Tarantini, Diego Lopes, Tiago Pinto, Nuno Lopes, Ukra (Boateng 69), Del Valle (Renan Bressan 81), Wakaso, Marcelo, Esmaël Gonçalves (Hassan 75). Coach: Pedro Martins (POR)
Match 4 - FC Steaua Bucureşti (ROU)
H 2-2 *Diego Lopes (35, 77p)*
Ederson, Tarantini, Diego Lopes (André Vilas Boas 80), Tiago Pinto, Nuno Lopes, Ukra, Del Valle (Renan Bressan 59), Wakaso, Marcelo, Esmaël Gonçalves (Hassan 68). Coach: Pedro Martins (POR)
Red card: Gouano 90+2
Match 5 - FC Dynamo Kyiv (UKR)
A 0-2
Ederson, Luís Gustavo, Hassan, Renan Bressan (Diego Lopes 62), Lionn (Marcelo 81), Boateng (Ukra 61), André Vilas Boas, Tiago Pinto, Pedro Moreira, Roderick, Del Valle. Coach: Pedro Martins (POR)
Match 6 - Aalborg BK (DEN)
H 2-0 *Del Valle (59, 79)*
Cássio, Luís Gustavo (Wakaso 77), Hassan, Renan Bressan (Tarantini 75), Lionn, Boateng (Ukra 68), André Vilas Boas, Tiago Pinto, Pedro Moreira, Roderick, Del Valle. Coach: Pedro Martins (POR)

DOMESTIC LEAGUE CLUB-BY-CLUB

A. Académica de Coimbra

1876 • Cidade de Coimbra (30,075) •
academica-oaf.pt
Major honours
Portuguese Cup (2) 1939, 2012
Coach: Paulo Sérgio;
(15/02/15) José Viterbo

2014
16/08	h	Sporting	D	1-1 *Rafael Lopes*
23/08	a	Marítimo	L	1-2 *Rui Pedro*
29/08	h	Setúbal	D	1-1 *og (Raeder)*
14/09	a	Boavista	L	0-1
22/09	h	Estoril	D	2-2 *Schumacher (p), Marinho*
28/09	a	Arouca	W	1-0 *Rui Pedro*
05/10	h	Moreirense	D	0-0
26/10	a	Nacional	L	0-1
02/11	h	Braga	D	1-1 *Aderlan*
10/11	a	Rio Ave	L	0-3
30/11	h	Benfica	L	0-2
06/12	h	Porto	L	0-3
13/12	a	Gil Vicente	D	1-1 *Rafael Lopes*
21/12	h	Penafiel	D	1-1 *Ivanildo*
2015				
02/01	a	Belenenses	D	0-0
10/01	h	Paços Ferreira	D	2-2 *Marcos Paulo (p), Lucas Mineiro*
17/01	a	Guimarães	L	0-4
25/01	a	Sporting	L	0-1
01/02	h	Marítimo	D	1-1 *Aderlan*
08/02	a	Setúbal	D	0-0
15/02	h	Boavista	D	0-0
22/02	a	Estoril	W	2-1 *Marinho, Rui Pedro*
01/03	h	Arouca	D	1-1 *Marinho*
08/03	h	Moreirense	W	2-0 *Rui Pedro 2*
15/03	a	Nacional	W	2-1 *Marcos Paulo, Lucas Mineiro*
20/03	a	Braga	D	0-0
03/04	h	Rio Ave	D	0-0
11/04	a	Benfica	L	1-5 *Rafael Lopes*
18/04	h	Porto	L	0-1
25/04	h	Gil Vicente	L	1-2 *Rui Pedro (p)*
03/05	a	Penafiel	D	0-0
09/05	h	Belenenses	D	1-1 *Rafael Lopes*
17/05	a	Paços Ferreira	L	2-3 *Aderlan, João Real*
23/05	h	Guimarães	L	2-4 *Pedro Nuno, Ivanildo*

No	Name	Nat	DoB	Pos	Aps	(s)	Gls
29	Aderlan	BRA	18/08/90	D	10	(5)	3
3	Aníbal Capela		08/05/91	D	13	(2)	
12	Salim Cissé	GUI	24/12/92	A	4	(5)	
1	Cristiano		29/11/90	G	25	(1)	
19	Ulysse Diallo	MLI	26/10/92	D		(5)	
65	Fernando Alexandre		02/08/85	M	21	(4)	
77	Hugo Seco		17/06/88	M	9	(7)	
14	Iago	BRA	22/05/92	D	22	(6)	
10	Ivanildo	GNB	09/01/86	M	13	(4)	2
8	Jimmy	CPV	13/07/94	M		(1)	
13	João Real		13/05/83	D	19		1
32	Lee	BRA	09/03/88	G	9		
16	Lino	BRA	01/06/77	D	3	(1)	
92	Lucas Mineiro	BRA	16/06/92	A	4	(7)	2
11	Goualy Magique	CIV	21/01/93	M	10	(10)	
6	Tripy Makonda	FRA	24/01/90	D	2		
21	Marcos Paulo	BRA	13/07/88	M	19	(4)	2
7	Marinho		26/04/83	A	7	(6)	3
28	Nuno Piloto		19/02/82	M	23		
4	Nwankwo Obiora	NGA	12/07/91	M	25	(2)	
37	Richard Ofori	GHA	24/04/93	D	11	(4)	
17	Carlos Olascuaga	PER	22/07/92	A	3	(1)	
22	Christopher Oualembo	COD	31/01/87	D	18		
27	Pedro Nuno		13/01/95	D	1	(2)	1
30	Rafael Lopes		28/07/91	A	25	(3)	4
47	Ricardo Esgaio		16/05/93	D	15		
5	Ricardo Nascimento	BRA	07/02/87	D	30	(1)	
20	Rui Pedro		02/07/88	M	20	(9)	6
23	Edgar Salli	CMR	17/08/92	M	6	(3)	
9	Schumacher	BRA	31/08/96	A	7	(8)	1

FC Arouca

1951 • Municipal de Arouca (5,100) •
fcarouca.eu
Coach: Pedro Emanuel

2014
18/08	h	Estoril	D	1-1 *Pintassilgo*
23/08	a	Sporting	L	0-1
31/08	a	Nacional	L	0-2
13/09	h	Braga	W	1-0 *André Claro*
21/09	a	Rio Ave	W	2-1 *Nildo, David Simão*
28/09	h	Académica	L	0-1
05/10	a	Benfica	L	0-4
25/10	h	Porto	L	0-5
02/11	a	Gil Vicente	D	1-1 *Diallo*
07/11	h	Guimarães	L	1-2 *Diego Galo*
29/11	a	Belenenses	D	0-0
07/12	h	Penafiel	L	0-1
13/12	a	Paços Ferreira	L	1-2 *Pintassilgo*
21/12	h	Marítimo	W	1-0 *Roberto*
2015				
04/01	a	Boavista	L	1-3 *Roberto*
11/01	h	Setúbal	W	1-0 *Nuno Coelho*
18/01	a	Moreirense	L	0-1
25/01	a	Estoril	L	0-1
01/02	h	Sporting	L	1-3 *David Simão (p)*
08/02	h	Nacional	D	3-3 *Rui Sampaio, Roberto 2*
15/02	a	Braga	L	0-2
22/02	h	Rio Ave	W	1-0 *Vuletich*
01/03	a	Académica	D	1-1 *David Simão*
08/03	h	Benfica	L	1-3 *Iuri Medeiros*
15/03	a	Porto	L	0-1
22/03	h	Gil Vicente	W	3-1 *Iuri Medeiros, Kayembe, Roberto*
03/04	a	Guimarães	L	0-1
10/04	h	Belenenses	L	0-1
19/04	a	Penafiel	W	2-0 *Hugo Basto, Roberto*
26/04	h	Paços Ferreira	L	1-3 *Rui Sampaio*
03/05	a	Marítimo	D	1-1 *Iuri Medeiros*
10/05	h	Boavista	D	0-0
17/05	a	Setúbal	L	1-2 *Nildo*
23/05	h	Moreirense	L	1-2 *Vuletich*

No	Name	Nat	DoB	Pos	Aps	(s)	Gls
8	André Claro		31/03/91	M	17	(9)	1
7	Artur		18/02/84	M	17	(11)	
9	Bruno Amaro		17/02/83	M	12	(3)	
11	Lucas Colitto	ARG	01/06/94	M		(6)	
6	David Simão		15/05/90	M	31	(1)	3
17	Ulysse Diallo	MLI	26/10/92	A	1	(3)	1
14	Diego Galo	BRA	14/01/84	M	30	(3)	1
25	Fabrice Fokobo	CMR	25/01/94	D	1	(5)	
1	Mauro Goicoechea	URU	27/03/88	G	33		
3	Hugo Basto		14/05/93	D	12		1
23	Hugo Monteiro		09/05/83	A		(5)	
45	Iuri Medeiros		10/07/94	A	12	(5)	3
25	Iván Balliu	ESP	01/01/92	D	32		
28	Joris Kayembe	BEL	08/08/94	M	12	(3)	1
22	Luís Tinoco		17/10/86	D	13	(2)	
4	Miguel Oliveira		18/08/83	D	17	(1)	
55	Nelsinho	BRA	01/01/88	D	22	(3)	
30	Nildo	BRA	01/05/86	A	10	(3)	2
66	Nuno Coelho		23/11/87	M	26	(3)	1
10	Pintassilgo		30/06/85	M	24	(3)	2
71	Roberto		28/11/88	A	23	(6)	6
13	Rui Sacramento		31/01/85	G	1		
35	Rui Sampaio		29/05/78	M	23	(5)	2
77	Serginho		21/02/91	A		(2)	
16	Tomás Dabó	GNB	20/10/93	D	3	(3)	
5	Tucka		13/02/96	M		(1)	
5	Ustaritz	ESP	16/02/83	D		(1)	
91	Agustín Vuletich	ARG	03/11/91	A	2	(8)	2

CF Os Belenenses

1919 • Restelo (19,856) • osbelenenses.com
Major honours
Portuguese League (1) 1946; Portuguese Cup (3) 1942, 1960, 1989
Coach: Lito Vidigal (ANG);
(17/03/05) Jorge Simão

2014
17/08	a	Penafiel	W	3-1 *Fábio Sturgeon, Deyverson, Miguel Rosa*
24/08	h	Nacional	W	3-1 *Deyverson, Rodrigo Dantas, Fredy*
30/08	h	Guimarães	L	0-3
13/09	a	Sporting	D	1-1 *Deyverson*
21/09	h	Marítimo	W	1-0 *Miguel Rosa*
29/09	a	Paços Ferreira	L	0-2
05/10	h	Setúbal	D	1-1 *Deyverson*
26/10	a	Estoril	W	2-1 *Miguel Rosa, Deyverson*
03/11	a	Boavista	W	3-1 *Deyverson 2, Miguel Rosa*
09/11	a	Moreirense	W	1-0 *Tiago Silva (p)*
29/11	h	Arouca	D	0-0
06/12	a	Benfica	L	0-3
13/12	h	Braga	L	0-1
22/12	a	Rio Ave	D	0-0
2015				
02/01	h	Académica	D	0-0
10/01	a	Porto	L	0-3
18/01	h	Gil Vicente	W	2-0 *Pelé, Deyverson*
25/01	h	Penafiel	D	0-0
31/01	a	Nacional	L	1-2 *Miguel Rosa*
08/02	a	Guimarães	W	1-0 *Carlos Martins*
14/02	h	Sporting	D	1-1 *Rui Fonte*
22/02	h	Marítimo	W	2-1 *Abel Camará, Pelé (p)*
02/03	a	Paços Ferreira	L	0-1
07/03	h	Setúbal	D	1-1 *Pelé (p)*
14/03	a	Estoril	D	2-2 *Ricardo Dias, Pelé (p)*
22/03	h	Boavista	L	0-1
04/04	a	Moreirense	W	2-0 *Fábio Sturgeon, og (Danielson)*
10/04	a	Arouca	W	1-0 *Pelé (p)*
18/04	h	Benfica	L	0-2
24/04	a	Braga	D	1-1 *Pelé*
04/05	h	Rio Ave	L	1-3 *Rui Fonte*
09/05	a	Académica	D	1-1 *Fábio Nunes*
17/05	h	Porto	D	1-1 *Tiago Caeiro*
23/05	a	Gil Vicente	W	2-0 *Fábio Nunes, Tiago Caeiro*

No	Name	Nat	DoB	Pos	Aps	(s)	Gls
30	Abel Camará	GNB	06/01/90	A	15	(10)	1
15	Adilson	CPV	25/11/87	D		(1)	
16	Bruno China		05/08/82	M	19	(4)	
12	Carlos Martins		29/04/82	M	13	(1)	1
14	Dálcio		22/04/94	A	7	(9)	
55	Daniel Martins		20/07/93	M			
8	Helgi Valur Danielsson	ISL	13/07/81	M	1	(1)	
66	Deyverson	BRA	08/05/91	A	15	(1)	8
91	Diogo Ribeiro		14/01/91	M		(1)	
92	Fábio Nunes		24/07/92	M	5	(12)	2
17	Fábio Sturgeon		04/02/94	A	27	(4)	2
20	Filipe Ferreira		20/07/90	M	22	(2)	
11	Fredy		27/03/90	M	10	(4)	1
28	Gonçalo Brandão		09/10/86	D	28	(1)	
13	João Afonso		11/02/82	D	12	(1)	
83	João Meira		30/04/87	D	16	(2)	
1	Matt Jones	ENG	11/05/86	G	15		
25	Mailo	CPV	10/01/92	M		(3)	
7	Miguel Rosa		13/01/89	M	25		5
22	Nélson		10/06/83	D	28		
47	Palmeira		24/09/89	D	24	(1)	
5	Pelé		29/09/91	M	24	(6)	6
18	Ricardo Dias		25/02/91	M	13	(1)	1
35	Rodrigo Dantas	BRA	20/10/89	M	7	(4)	1
83	Rui Fonte		23/04/90	A	13		2
23	Steven Thicot	FRA	14/02/87	D	9		
9	Tiago Caeiro		29/03/84	A	2	(14)	2
10	Tiago Silva		02/06/93	M	5	(16)	1
24	Ventura		14/02/88	G	19		

SL Benfica

1904 • Sport Lisboa e Benfica (65,647) • slbenfica.pt

Major honours
*European Champion Clubs' Cup (2) 1961, 1962;
Portuguese League (34) 1936, 1937, 1938, 1942,
1943, 1945, 1950, 1955, 1957, 1960, 1961, 1963,
1964, 1965, 1967, 1968, 1969, 1971, 1972, 1973,
1975, 1976, 1977, 1981, 1983, 1984, 1987, 1989,
1991, 1994, 2005, 2010, 2014, 2015; Portuguese
Cup (25) 1940, 1943, 1944, 1949, 1951, 1952, 1953,
1955, 1957, 1959, 1962, 1964, 1969, 1970, 1972,
1980, 1981, 1983, 1985, 1986, 1987, 1993, 1996,
2004, 2014*

Coach: Jorge Jesus

2014

17/08	h	Paços Ferreira	W 2-0	Maxi Pereira, Salvio
24/08	a	Boavista	W 1-0	Eliseu
31/08	h	Sporting	D 1-1	Gaitán
12/09	h	Setúbal	W 5-0	Salvio, Talisca 3, John
21/09	h	Moreirense	W 3-1	Eliseu, Maxi Pereira, Lima (p)
27/09	a	Estoril	W 3-2	Talisca 2, Lima
05/10	h	Arouca	W 4-0	Talisca, Derley, Salvio, Jonas
26/10	a	Braga	L 1-2	Talisca
31/10	h	Rio Ave	W 1-0	Talisca
09/11	h	Nacional	W 2-1	Salvio, Jonas
30/11	a	Académica	W 2-0	Gaitán, Luisão
06/12	h	Belenenses	W 3-0	Lima, Pérez (p), Salvio
14/12	a	Porto	W 2-0	Lima 2
21/12	h	Gil Vicente	W 1-0	Gaitán

2015

04/01	a	Penafiel	W 3-0	Talisca, Jonas, Jardel
10/01	h	Guimarães	W 3-0	Jonas, John, Gaitán
18/01	a	Marítimo	W 4-0	Salvio 2, John, Lima
26/01	a	Paços Ferreira	L 0-1	
31/01	h	Boavista	W 3-0	Lima, Maxi Pereira, Jonas (p)
08/02	a	Sporting	D 1-1	Jardel
15/02	h	Setúbal	W 3-0	Jardel, Lima 2
21/02	a	Moreirense	W 3-1	Luisão, Eliseu, Jonas
28/02	h	Estoril	W 6-0	Luisão, Salvio, Pizzi, Jonas 2, Lima
08/03	a	Arouca	W 3-1	Jonas, Lima 2
14/03	h	Braga	W 2-0	Jonas, Eliseu
21/03	a	Rio Ave	L 1-2	Salvio
04/04	a	Nacional	W 2-0	Jonas 2, Lima
11/04	h	Académica	W 5-1	Jardel, Jonas 2, Lima, Fejsa
18/04	a	Belenenses	W 2-0	Jonas 2
26/04	h	Porto	D 0-0	
02/05	a	Gil Vicente	W 5-0	Maxi Pereira 2, Jonas, Luisão, Lima
09/05	h	Penafiel	W 4-0	Lima 2, Jonas, Pizzi
17/05	a	Guimarães	D 0-0	
23/05	h	Marítimo	W 4-1	Lima 2, Jonas 2

No	Name	Nat	DoB	Pos	Aps	(s)	Gls
34	André Almeida		10/09/90	M	12	(8)	
1	Artur	BRA	25/01/81	G	11	(1)	
32	Bebé		12/07/90	A		(1)	
23	Loris Benito	SUI	07/01/92	D	1	(1)	
37	César	BRA	28/12/92	D	2	(1)	
24	Bryan Cristante	ITA	03/03/95	M	1	(4)	
9	Derley	BRA	29/12/87	A	1	(14)	1
19	Eliseu		01/10/83	D	26		4
5	Ljubomir Fejsa	SRB	14/08/88	M	1	(4)	1
10	Nicolás Gaitán	ARG	23/02/88	M	26	(1)	4
78	Gonçalo Guedes		29/11/96	M		(5)	
22	Franco Jara	ARG	15/07/88	A	1	(1)	
33	Jardel	BRA	29/03/86	D	31		4
15	Ola John	NED	19/05/92	A	9	(17)	3
17	Jonas	BRA	01/04/84	A	25	(2)	20
20	Júlio César	BRA	03/09/79	G	23		
11	Lima	BRA	11/08/83	A	32	(2)	19
2	Lisandro López	ARG	01/09/89	D	5	(1)	
4	Luisão	BRA	13/02/81	D	30		4
14	Maxi Pereira	URU	08/06/84	D	32		5
27	Hany Mukhtar	GER	21/03/95	M		(1)	
35	Enzo Pérez	ARG	22/02/86	M	11	1	1
21	Pizzi		06/10/89	M	15	(8)	2
25	Jonathan Rodríguez	URU	06/07/93	A		(1)	
6	Rúben Amorim		27/01/85	M	2	(8)	
18	Eduardo Salvio	ARG	13/07/90	M	28	(1)	9
7	Andreas Samaris	GRE	13/06/89	M	27	(1)	
28	Sílvio		28/09/87	D		(1)	
8	Miralem Sulejmani	SRB	05/12/88	M	2	(2)	
30	Talisca	BRA	01/02/94	M	20	(12)	9

Boavista FC

1903 • Bessa (30,000) • boavistafc.pt

Major honours
*Portuguese League (1) 2001; Portuguese Cup (5)
1975, 1976, 1979, 1992, 1997*

Coach: Petit

2014

17/08	a	Braga	L 0-3	
24/08	h	Benfica	L 0-1	
01/09	a	Rio Ave	L 0-4	
14/09	h	Académica	W 1-0	og (Ofori)
21/09	a	Porto	D 0-0	
28/09	h	Gil Vicente	W 3-2	Philipe Sampaio, Anderson Carvalho 2
03/10	a	Guimarães	L 0-3	
25/10	h	Paços Ferreira	L 1-2	Uchebo
03/11	a	Belenenses	L 1-3	Brito
09/11	h	Penafiel	W 1-0	Carlos Santos
30/11	a	Marítimo	L 0-4	
05/12	h	Sporting	L 1-3	og (Silva)
12/12	a	Setúbal	W 1-0	José Manuel
21/12	a	Moreirense	L 0-1	

2015

04/01	h	Arouca	W 3-1	José Manuel, Uchebo, Brito
11/01	a	Nacional	L 1-2	Leozinho
18/01	h	Estoril	L 1-2	Mandiang
25/01	h	Braga	W 1-0	Uchebo
31/01	a	Benfica	L 0-3	
09/02	h	Rio Ave	D 1-1	Tengarrinha (p)
15/02	a	Académica	D 0-0	
23/02	h	Porto	L 0-2	
28/02	a	Gil Vicente	D 1-1	Brito
08/03	h	Guimarães	W 3-1	Čech, Uchebo, José Manuel
13/03	a	Paços Ferreira	L 0-1	
22/03	h	Belenenses	W 1-0	Brito
04/04	a	Penafiel	D 2-2	Carlos Santos, José Manuel
11/04	h	Marítimo	L 0-2	
19/04	a	Sporting	L 1-2	José Manuel
26/04	h	Setúbal	L 0-2	
03/05	h	Moreirense	W 3-1	og (André Simões), Mandiang, José Manuel
10/05	a	Arouca	D 0-0	
18/05	h	Nacional	L 0-1	
23/05	a	Estoril	L 0-2	

No	Name	Nat	DoB	Pos	Aps	(s)	Gls
25	Afonso Figueiredo		06/01/93	D	20		
80	Ancelmo Júnior	BRA	03/04/90	A		(1)	
27	Anderson Carvalho	BRA	20/05/90	M	14	(6)	2
91	Anderson Correia	BRA	06/05/91	A	9	(2)	
32	Aaron Appindangoye	GAB	29/02/92	D	8	(1)	
5	Mamadou Ba	SEN	08/05/85	G	1	(1)	
55	Brayan Beckeles	HON	28/11/85	D	24	(2)	
10	Bobô	BRA	20/03/82	A	4	(7)	
7	Brito	CPV	16/11/87	A	21	(8)	4
22	Carlos Santos		31/03/89	D	25		2
16	Marek Čech	SVK	26/01/83	D	7	(8)	1
20	Diego Lima	BRA	30/08/88	M	11	(4)	
66	Diogo Gouveia		25/01/95	M	1	(1)	
4	Fábio Ervões		26/02/87	D	5	(2)	
9	Fary Faye	SEN	24/12/74	A	1	(1)	
24	Reuben Gabriel	NGA	25/09/90	M	15	(2)	
23	João Dias		23/12/86	D	20	(2)	
70	José Manuel		23/10/90	A	27	(4)	6
8	Leozinho	BRA	07/06/88	A	8	(15)	1
3	Lucas	BRA	14/07/91	D	8		
35	Yoro Lamien Ly	SEN	27/08/88	M		(6)	
42	Idrissa Mandiang	SEN	27/12/84	M	28	(1)	2
30	Miguel Cid		21/05/92	M	1	(2)	
1	Mika		08/03/91	G	29		
21	Daniel Monllor	ARG	20/07/84	G	4		
14	Julián Montenegro	ARG	23/03/88	D	11	(2)	
17	Quincy Owusu-Abeyie	GHA	15/04/86	A	5	(2)	
94	Philipe Sampaio	BRA	11/11/84	D	21	(2)	1
11	Christian Pouga	CMR	19/06/86	A	4	(4)	
6	Tengarrinha		27/03/89	M	25	(2)	1
75	Michael Uchebo	NGA	03/02/90	A	17	(8)	4
77	Wei Shihao	CHN	08/04/95	A		(4)	

SC Braga

1921 • Municipal de Braga (30,286) • scbraga.pt

Major honours
Portuguese Cup (1) 1966

Coach: Sérgio Conceição

2014

17/08	h	Boavista	W 3-0	Pedro Tiba, Rúben Micael, Éder (p)
25/08	a	Moreirense	D 0-0	
30/08	h	Estoril	W 2-1	Pedro Santos , Éder
13/09	a	Arouca	L 0-1	
20/09	a	Nacional	D 1-1	Zé Luís
27/09	h	Rio Ave	W 3-0	Zé Luís, Rúben Micael, Pardo
05/10	a	Porto	L 1-2	Zé Luís
26/10	h	Benfica	W 2-1	Éder, Salvador Agra
02/11	a	Académica	D 1-1	Éder
08/11	h	Gil Vicente	W 2-0	Pardo, Pedro Santos
29/11	a	Penafiel	W 6-1	Rafa, Aderlan Santos, Pardo, André Pinto, Luiz Carlos, Sami
07/12	h	Guimarães	D 0-0	
13/12	a	Belenenses	W 1-0	Aderlan Santos
22/12	h	Paços Ferreira	W 3-0	Pardo, Éder, Rafa

2015

03/01	a	Marítimo	L 1-2	Danilo
11/01	h	Sporting	L 0-1	
18/01	a	Setúbal	W 3-1	Danilo, og (Venâncio), Zé Luís
25/01	h	Boavista	L 0-1	
30/01	h	Moreirense	W 1-0	Pedro Santos
08/02	a	Estoril	W 2-0	Rúben Micael, Pedro Santos
15/02	h	Arouca	W 2-0	Zé Luís, Éder
21/02	h	Nacional	W 3-1	Pedro Santos, Rúben Micael, Salvador Agra
28/02	a	Rio Ave	W 2-0	Zé Luís, Salvador Agra
06/03	h	Porto	L 0-1	
14/03	a	Benfica	L 0-2	
20/03	a	Académica	D 0-0	
03/04	h	Gil Vicente	W 2-0	Zé Luís 2 (1p)
12/04	h	Penafiel	W 4-0	Rúben Micael 2, Pardo 2
17/04	a	Guimarães	L 0-1	
24/04	h	Belenenses	D 1-1	Pedro Tiba
29/04	a	Paços Ferreira	D 2-2	Aderlan Santos, Éder
09/05	h	Marítimo	L 1-3	Éder (p)
17/05	a	Sporting	L 1-4	Pardo (p)
23/05	h	Setúbal	W 5-0	og (João Schmidt), Éder 2, Pedro Tiba, Salvador Agra

No	Name	Nat	DoB	Pos	Aps	(s)	Gls
33	Aderlan Santos	BRA	09/04/89	D	31		3
30	Alan	BRA	19/09/79	A	8	(15)	
6	André Pinto		05/10/89	D	33		1
15	Baiano	BRA	23/02/87	D	29		
27	Custódio		24/05/83	M	5	(3)	
19	Danilo	BRA	28/02/96	M	23		2
16	Djavan	BRA	31/12/87	D	17		
9	Dolly Menga	ANG	02/05/93	A	1		
17	Éder		22/12/87	A	19	(10)	10
26	Fábio Martins		24/07/93	A		(1)	
84	Gamboa		31/08/96	M		(1)	
1	Stanislav Kritsyuk	RUS	01/12/90	G	11		
5	Luís Carlos	BRA	05/07/85	M	9	(7)	1
87	Marcelo Goiano	BRA	13/10/87	D	5		
92	Matheus	BRA	29/03/92	G	23		
63	Mauro	BRA	30/10/90	M	5		
55	Núrio Fortuna	ANG	24/03/95	D	1		
90	Felipe Pardo	COL	17/08/90	A	21	(5)	7
4	Pedro Monteiro		30/01/94	D	1		
23	Pedro Santos		22/04/88	M	10	(16)	5
25	Pedro Tiba		31/08/88	M	29	(3)	3
18	Rafa		17/05/93	M	33	(1)	2
14	Rúben Micael		19/08/86	M	24	(1)	6
7	Salvador Agra		11/11/91	A	2	(23)	4
10	Sami	GNB	18/12/88	A	1	(8)	1
2	Vincent Sasso	FRA	16/02/91	D	3	(2)	
3	Tiago Gomes		29/07/86	D	16		
20	Zé Luís	CPV	24/01/91	A	14	(6)	8

Estoril Praia

1939 • António Coimbra da Mota (5,015) •
estorilpraia.pt
Coach: José Couceiro;
(03/04/15) Hugo Leal

2014
18/08	a	Arouca	D	1-1	*Kuca*
24/08	h	Rio Ave	L	1-5	*João Pedro Galvão*
30/08	a	Braga	L	1-2	*Emídio Rafael*
14/09	h	Nacional	W	2-1	*Bruno Miguel 2*
22/09	a	Académica	D	2-2	*Kuca 2*
27/09	h	Benfica	L	2-3	*Diogo Amado, Kléber*
05/10	a	Gil Vicente	D	1-1	*Kléber*
26/10	h	Belenenses	L	1-2	*Kléber*
01/11	a	Penafiel	W	2-1	*Emídio Rafael, Tozé*
09/11	h	Porto	D	2-2	*Kuca, Tozé (p)*
01/12	a	Paços Ferreira	D	1-1	*Rúben Fernandes*
06/12	h	Setúbal	W	1-0	*Kuca*
14/12	a	Marítimo	D	0-0	
20/12	h	Guimarães	W	1-0	*Kléber*

2015
03/01	a	Sporting	L	0-3	
09/01	h	Moreirense	D	1-1	*Rúben Fernandes*
18/01	a	Boavista	W	2-1	*Kléber 2*
25/01	a	Arouca	W	1-0	*Léo Bonatini*
01/02	a	Rio Ave	L	1-2	*Sebá*
08/02	h	Braga	L	0-2	
16/02	a	Nacional	L	0-1	
22/02	h	Académica	L	1-2	*Léo Bonatini*
28/02	a	Benfica	L	0-6	
08/03	h	Gil Vicente	D	1-1	*Sebá*
14/03	a	Belenenses	D	2-2	*Balboa (p), Tozé*
21/03	h	Penafiel	D	3-3	*Tozé (p), Léo Bonatini, Rúben Fernandes*
06/04	a	Porto	L	0-5	
13/04	h	Paços Ferreira	W	1-0	*Tozé*
19/04	a	Setúbal	W	2-1	*Kléber, Sebá*
25/04	h	Marítimo	D	1-1	*Fernandinho*
01/05	a	Guimarães	L	0-2	
10/05	h	Sporting	D	1-1	*Sebá*
17/05	a	Moreirense	D	1-1	*Kléber*
23/05	h	Boavista	W	2-0	*Léo Bonatini, Rúben Fernandes*

No	Name	Nat	DoB	Pos	Aps	(s)	Gls
6	Afonso Taira		17/06/92	M	8	(5)	
5	Anderson Luiz	BRA	31/07/88	D	20		
11	Arthuro	BRA	27/08/82	A	2	(12)	
55	Babanco	CPV	27/07/85	D	14	(7)	
7	Javier Balboa	EQG	13/05/85	A	4	(10)	1
9	Bruno Lopes	BRA	19/08/86	A	3	(6)	
4	Bruno Miguel		24/09/82	D	7	(1)	2
30	Bruno Nascimento		30/05/91	D	5	(4)	
16	Matías Cabrera	URU	16/05/86	M	8	(12)	
25	Diogo Amado		21/01/90	M	31	(1)	1
22	Emídio Rafael		29/04/89	D	16		2
15	Anderson Esiti	NGA	24/05/94	M	13	(4)	
93	Fernandinho	BRA	16/03/93	A	7	(12)	1
8	Filipe Gonçalves		12/08/84	M	14	(4)	
10	João Pedro Galvão	BRA	09/03/92	A	2	(1)	1
31	Paweł Kieszek	POL	16/04/84	G	24		
13	Kléber	BRA	02/05/90	A	19	(2)	8
20	Kuca	CPV	02/08/89	A	15		5
3	Alex Kukuba	UGA	12/06/91	D	8		
94	Léo Bonatini	BRA	28/03/94	A	11	(4)	4
12	Mano		09/04/87	D	15	(2)	
27	Matheus	BRA	07/06/84	M	2	(1)	
32	Ricardo Vaz		26/11/94	A		(2)	
37	Rúben Dionísio		07/07/95	G		(1)	
26	Rúben Fernandes		06/05/86	D	31		4
19	Sebá	BRA	08/06/92	A	32	(1)	4
17	Tijane		28/06/91	A	1	(2)	
20	Tozé		14/01/93	A	22	(6)	5
1	Vagner	BRA	06/06/86	G	10		
2	Yohan		02/03/88	D	30		

Gil Vicente FC

1924 • Cidade Barcelos (13,350) •
gilvicentefc.pt
Coach: João de Deus;
(10/09/14) José Mota

2014
16/08	h	Guimarães	L	1-3	*Evaldo*
24/08	a	Setúbal	L	0-2	
31/08	h	Marítimo	L	1-2	*Diogo Valente*
14/09	a	Paços Ferreira	D	1-1	*Pecks*
21/09	h	Sporting	L	0-4	
28/09	a	Boavista	L	2-3	*Simy 2*
05/10	h	Estoril	D	1-1	*Simy*
25/10	a	Moreirense	L	0-1	
02/11	a	Arouca	D	1-1	*Rui Caetano*
08/11	a	Braga	L	0-2	
30/11	h	Nacional	D	0-0	
06/12	a	Rio Ave	D	0-0	
13/12	h	Académica	D	1-1	*Paulinho*
21/12	a	Benfica	L	0-1	

2015
03/01	h	Porto	L	1-5	*Vítor Gonçalves*
11/01	h	Penafiel	W	2-1	*João Vilela (p), Simy*
18/01	a	Belenenses	L	0-2	
24/01	a	Guimarães	D	2-2	*Simy, Evaldo*
01/02	h	Setúbal	D	1-1	*João Vilela*
08/02	a	Marítimo	W	2-1	*João Vilela (p), Simy*
14/02	h	Paços Ferreira	W	1-0	*Simy*
22/02	a	Sporting	L	0-2	
28/02	h	Boavista	D	1-1	*Berger*
08/03	a	Estoril	D	1-1	*Yazalde*
15/03	h	Moreirense	L	0-1	
22/03	a	Arouca	L	1-3	*Rúben Ribeiro*
03/04	h	Braga	L	0-2	
12/04	a	Nacional	L	2-3	*Simy 2*
19/04	h	Rio Ave	D	0-0	
25/04	a	Académica	W	2-1	*Rúben Ribeiro, Cadú (p)*
02/05	h	Benfica	L	0-5	
10/05	a	Porto	L	0-2	
17/05	a	Penafiel	L	1-2	*João Vilela*
23/05	h	Belenenses	L	0-2	

No	Name	Nat	DoB	Pos	Aps	(s)	Gls
1	Adriano	BRA	12/03/83	G	34		
44	Markus Berger	AUT	22/01/85	D	11		1
12	Cadú		21/12/81	D	17		1
25	César Peixoto		12/05/80	M	3	(2)	
89	David Batista	BRA	13/04/89	M	1	(4)	
21	Diogo Valente		23/09/84	A	4	(6)	1
7	Diogo Viana		22/02/90	M	25	(7)	
11	Avtandil Ebralidze	GEO	03/10/91	A	11	(4)	
3	Manassé Enza-Yamissi	CTA	29/09/89	D	17	(2)	
6	Evaldo	BRA	18/03/82	D	29		2
2	Gabriel	BRA	18/06/88	D	30		
4	Gladstone	BRA	29/01/85	D	3	(1)	
14	Hossam Hassan	EGY	30/04/89	M	1		
13	Jander	BRA	08/07/88	M	18	(3)	
77	João Vilela		09/09/85	A	25	(2)	4
19	Alphousseyni Keita	MLI	13/11/85	M	1		
17	Leandro Pimenta		07/09/90	M		(1)	
26	Luan	BRA	30/12/88	M	10	(1)	
8	Luís Silva		29/09/92	M	13	(5)	
9	Marwan Mohsen	EGY	26/02/89	A	8	(12)	
45	Paulinho		09/11/92	A	4	(10)	1
23	Pecks	CPV	10/04/93	D	18	(2)	1
30	Piquetti		12/02/93	M		(3)	
24	Ricardinho		24/03/94	D	4	(2)	
70	Rúben Ribeiro		01/08/87	M	15	(2)	2
10	Rui Caetano		20/04/91	A	11	(9)	1
65	Semedo	CPV	23/08/82	M	14		
99	Simy	NGA	07/05/92	A	23	(7)	9
20	Vítor Gonçalves		29/03/92	M	14	(11)	1
15	Yazalde		10/09/88	A	10	(4)	1

CS Marítimo

1910 • Barreiros (8,922) • csmaritimo.pt
Coach: Leonel Pontes;
(02/03/15) Ivo Vieira

2014
15/08	a	Porto	L	0-2	
23/08	h	Académica	W	2-1	*Fransérgio, Maâzou*
31/08	a	Gil Vicente	W	2-1	*Bauer, Maâzou*
14/09	h	Penafiel	W	2-0	*Fransérgio, Weeks*
21/09	a	Belenenses	L	0-1	
28/09	h	Guimarães	W	4-0	*Edgar Costa, Fransérgio 2, Maâzou*
05/10	a	Paços Ferreira	L	2-3	*Maâzou 2*
26/10	h	Sporting	L	2-4	*Maâzou 2*
02/11	h	Moreirense	L	1-2	*Danilo Pereira*
09/11	a	Setúbal	L	0-1	
30/11	h	Boavista	W	4-0	*og (Mandiang), Bruno Gallo (p), Maâzou (p), Dyego Souza*
08/12	a	Nacional	L	0-3	
14/12	h	Estoril	D	0-0	
21/12	a	Arouca	L	0-1	

2015
03/01	h	Braga	W	2-1	*Maâzou, Bruno Gallo*
11/01	h	Rio Ave	D	0-0	
18/01	h	Benfica	L	0-4	
25/01	h	Porto	W	1-0	*Bruno Gallo*
01/02	a	Académica	D	1-1	*Edgar Costa*
08/02	h	Gil Vicente	L	1-2	*Ebinho*
15/02	a	Penafiel	W	4-3	*António Xavier (p), Ebinho, Raúl Silva, Marega*
22/02	h	Belenenses	L	1-2	*Edgar Costa*
27/02	a	Guimarães	L	0-1	
08/03	h	Paços Ferreira	W	2-1	*António Xavier, Weeks*
15/03	h	Sporting	L	0-1	
22/03	a	Moreirense	D	1-1	*Edgar Costa*
06/04	h	Setúbal	D	1-1	*Bauer*
11/04	a	Boavista	W	2-0	*Éber Bessa, Alex Soares*
20/04	h	Nacional	D	1-1	*Bruno Gallo (p)*
25/04	a	Estoril	D	1-1	*Marega*
03/05	h	Arouca	D	1-1	*Marega*
09/05	a	Braga	W	3-1	*João Diogo, Danilo Pereira, Marega*
17/05	h	Rio Ave	W	4-0	*Raúl Silva, Marega 2, Danilo Pereira*
23/05	a	Benfica	L	1-4	*Marega*

No	Name	Nat	DoB	Pos	Aps	(s)	Gls
7	Alex Soares	BRA	01/03/91	M	20	(7)	1
50	António Xavier		06/07/92	A	18	(3)	2
5	Patrick Bauer	GER	28/10/92	D	29		2
21	Briguel		08/03/79	D	10	(1)	
20	Bruno Gallo	BRA	07/05/88	M	23	(2)	4
37	Christian	BRA	01/12/93	M	1	(2)	
8	Danilo Pereira		09/09/91	M	29		3
9	Dyego Sousa	BRA	14/09/89	A	11	(7)	1
92	Éber Bessa	BRA	23/03/92	M	3	(7)	1
57	Ebinho	BRA	18/01/88	A	6	(5)	2
12	Edgar Costa		14/04/87	A	23	(7)	4
93	Fábio Abreu		29/01/93	A		(7)	
26	Fernando Ferreira		20/11/86	M	11	(6)	
35	Fransérgio	BRA	18/10/90	A	16	(12)	4
14	Gégé	CPV	24/02/88	D	19	(1)	
98	Mohamed Ibrahim	EGY	01/03/92	M	4	(3)	
4	Igor Rossi	BRA	01/03/89	D		(2)	
2	João Diogo		28/02/88	D	30		1
91	José Sá		17/01/93	G	3		
17	Kukula	CPV	22/01/93	A		(2)	
18	Luís Olim		22/08/81	M	1	(1)	
31	Moussa Maâzou	NIG	25/08/88	A	13	(5)	9
32	Moussa Marega	MLI	14/04/91	M	12	(2)	7
33	Félix Micolta	COL	30/11/89	M		(2)	
3	Kaj Ramsteijn	NED	17/01/90	D	7	(3)	
34	Raúl Silva	BRA	04/11/89	D	15		2
41	Rúben Ferreira		17/02/90	D	28		
78	Romain Salin	FRA	29/07/84	G	27		
16	Jhony Vidales	PER	21/04/92	M	2	(7)	
10	Theo Weeks	LBR	19/01/90	M	9	(7)	2
1	Wellington	BRA	21/04/90	G	4		

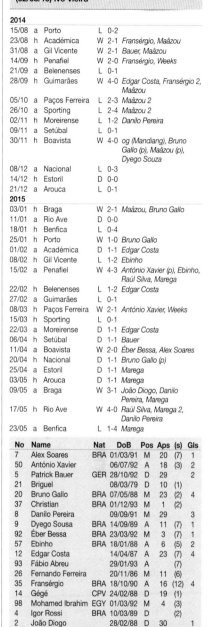

PORTUGAL

Moreirense FC

1938 • Comendador Joaquim Almeida
Freitas (6,151) • moreirensefc.pt
Coach: Miguel Leal

2014

17/08	a	Nacional	W 1-0	Cardozo
25/08	h	Braga	D 0-0	
31/08	a	Porto	L 0-3	
13/09	h	Rio Ave	D 1-1	Vítor Gomes
21/09	a	Benfica	L 1-3	João Pedro
28/09	h	Penafiel	D 0-0	
05/10	a	Académica	D 0-0	
25/10	h	Gil Vicente	W 2-0	Gerso, Arsénio
02/11	h	Marítimo	W 2-1	João Pedro, André Simões
09/11	h	Belenenses	L 0-1	
28/11	h	Guimarães	L 1-2	Elízio
07/12	a	Paços de Ferreira	W 2-0	André Simões (p), Battaglia
14/12	a	Sporting	D 1-1	Cardozo
21/12	h	Boavista	W 1-0	André Simões

2015

04/01	a	Setúbal	L 1-2	og (Dani)
09/01	a	Estoril	D 1-1	Vítor Gomes
18/01	h	Arouca	W 1-0	Vítor Gomes
25/01	h	Nacional	L 2-3	Battaglia, Gerso
30/01	a	Braga	L 0-1	
07/02	h	Porto	L 0-2	
15/02	a	Rio Ave	D 1-1	André Simões
21/02	h	Benfica	L 1-3	João Pedro
01/03	a	Penafiel	W 2-1	Diogo Cunha, og (Bura)
08/03	a	Académica	L 0-2	
15/03	h	Gil Vicente	W 1-0	Gerso
22/03	h	Marítimo	D 1-1	André Simões
04/04	a	Belenenses	L 0-2	
11/04	h	Guimarães	W 2-1	André Simões, João Pedro
19/04	a	Paços de Ferreira	D 0-0	
27/04	h	Sporting	L 1-4	Leandro Sousa
03/05	a	Boavista	L 1-3	Bolívia
10/05	h	Setúbal	W 3-1	Arsénio 2, Alex
17/05	h	Estoril	D 1-1	Danielson
23/05	a	Arouca	W 2-1	Gerso 2

No	Name	Nat	DoB	Pos	Aps	(s)	Gls
9	Alex	BRA	20/05/90	A	14	(12)	1
5	André Marques		01/08/87	D	12		
8	André Simões		16/12/89	M	32		6
3	Anílton	BRA	10/07/80	D	6	(4)	
77	Arsénio		30/08/89	A	29	(2)	3
16	Rodrigo Battaglia	ARG	12/07/91	M	19	(6)	2
11	Bolívia	BOL	17/11/85	M	7	(6)	1
20	Ramón Cardozo	PAR	21/04/86	A	13	(7)	2
4	Danielson	BRA	09/01/81	D	34		1
7	Diogo Cunha		10/02/86	A	10	(2)	1
22	Elízio	BRA	22/02/88	D	21	(1)	1
17	Ença Fati		11/08/93	M	1	(1)	
6	Filipe Melo		03/11/89	M	17		
70	Gerso	GNB	23/02/91	A	5	(20)	5
14	Caleb Gomina	GHA	24/09/96	A	1		
10	João Pedro		04/05/86	M	32	(1)	4
21	João Pedro Silva		29/12/87	D	1	(4)	
13	João Sousa		13/05/94	D		(1)	
17	Jorge Monteiro		15/08/88	M		(1)	
19	Leandro Sousa	BRA	14/09/82	M	6	(9)	1
33	Lucas Souza	BRA	04/06/90	A	2	(4)	
30	Luís Aurélio		17/08/88	M		(1)	
87	Marafona		08/05/87	G	34		
26	Marcelo Oliveira	BRA	05/09/81	D	27		
27	Patrick	CPV	09/02/93	M	1	(4)	
2	Paulinho		13/07/91	D	30		
18	Pedro Coronas		19/09/90	M	6	(7)	
72	Ricardo Almeida		09/05/97	A		(1)	
23	Vítor Gomes		25/12/87	M	13	(3)	3
15	Djibril Zidnaba	BFA	20/02/94	M	1	(2)	

CD Nacional

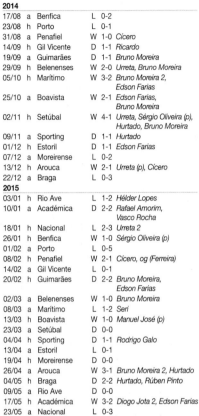

1910 • Madeira (5,132) • cdnacional.pt
Coach: Manuel Machado

2014

17/08	h	Moreirense	L 0-1	
24/08	a	Belenenses	L 1-3	Marco Matias (p)
31/08	h	Arouca	W 2-0	Rondón, Suk
14/09	a	Estoril	L 1-2	Marco Matias
20/09	h	Braga	D 1-1	Gomaa
28/09	h	Setúbal	L 0-2	
05/10	h	Rio Ave	D 0-0	
26/10	h	Académica	W 1-0	Marco Matias
01/11	a	Porto	L 0-2	
09/11	h	Benfica	L 1-2	Edgar Abreu
30/11	a	Gil Vicente	D 0-0	
08/12	h	Marítimo	W 3-0	Willyan, Marco Matias 2 (1p)
13/12	a	Penafiel	L 1-2	Suk
21/12	h	Sporting	L 0-1	

2015

04/01	a	Guimarães	L 0-4	
11/01	h	Boavista	W 2-1	Lucas João 2
18/01	a	Paços de Ferreira	W 3-2	Lucas João, Marco Matias, Luís Aurélio
25/01	a	Moreirense	W 3-2	Marco Matias, Rondón, Lucas João
31/01	h	Belenenses	W 2-1	Tiago Rodrigues, Marco Matias
08/02	a	Arouca	D 3-3	Rondón 3
15/02	h	Estoril	W 1-0	Lucas João
21/02	a	Braga	L 1-3	Tiago Rodrigues
01/03	h	Setúbal	W 3-0	Luís Aurélio, Marco Matias, Lucas João
09/03	a	Rio Ave	D 1-1	Marco Matias
15/03	a	Académica	L 1-2	Marco Matias (p)
21/03	h	Porto	D 1-1	Wagner
04/04	a	Benfica	L 1-3	Tiago Rodrigues
12/04	h	Gil Vicente	W 3-2	Marco Matias 2, Ghazal
20/04	a	Marítimo	D 1-1	Soares
26/04	h	Penafiel	W 2-0	Zainadine Júnior, Soares
02/05	a	Sporting	L 0-2	
11/05	h	Guimarães	D 2-2	Marco Matias 2
18/05	a	Boavista	W 1-0	
23/05	h	Paços de Ferreira	W 3-0	og (Fábio Cardoso), Marco Matias, Tiago Rodrigues

No	Name	Nat	DoB	Pos	Aps	(s)	Gls
8	Jhoan Ayala	COL	14/09/95	M	3	(3)	
11	Camacho		23/06/94	M	1	(8)	
20	Christian	BRA	14/06/89	M	7	(5)	
68	Edgar Abreu		16/02/94	M	3	(4)	1
4	Mahmoud Ezzat	EGY	05/02/92	D	4		
88	Ali Fathy	EGY	02/01/92	D		(2)	
17	Boubacar Fofana	GUI	06/11/89	M	15	(6)	
66	Ali Ghazal	EGY	01/02/92	M	28	(1)	1
10	Saleh Gomaa	EGY	01/08/93	M	21	(2)	1
1	Gottardi	BRA	18/10/85	G	25		
43	João Aurélio		17/08/88	A	32	(2)	
43	Leandro Freire	BRA	21/08/89	D	7	(1)	
18	Lucas João	ANG	04/09/93	A	24	(6)	6
30	Luís Aurélio		17/08/88	M	15	(2)	2
5	Marçal	BRA	19/02/89	D	28	(1)	
77	Marco Matias		10/05/89	A	32	(1)	17
3	Miguel Rodrigues		16/03/93	D	16		
22	Nuno Campos		13/06/93	D	1		
55	Nuno Sequeira		19/08/90	M	6	(2)	
19	Reginaldo	MOZ	14/06/90	A	2	(3)	
21	Mario Rondón	VEN	26/03/86	A	17	(4)	5
33	Rui Correia		23/08/90	D	15	(1)	
12	Rui Silva		07/02/94	G	9		
38	Dejan Školnik	CRO	01/01/89	M		(1)	
99	Soares	BRA	17/01/91	A		(12)	2
9	Suk Hyun-jun	KOR	29/06/91	A	10	(3)	2
42	Tiago Rodrigues		29/01/92	M	17	(1)	4
87	Wagner	BRA	03/04/87	A	2	(9)	1
28	Willyan	BRA	17/02/84	A	1	(21)	1
70	Witi	MOZ	26/08/96	M	1		
2	Zainadine Júnior	MOZ	24/06/88	D	32		1

FC Paços de Ferreira

1950 • Mata Real (5,172) • fcpf.pt
Coach: Paulo Fonseca

2014

17/08	a	Benfica	L 0-2	
23/08	h	Porto	L 0-1	
31/08	a	Penafiel	W 1-0	Cícero
14/09	h	Gil Vicente	D 1-1	Ricardo
19/09	a	Guimarães	D 1-1	Bruno Moreira
29/09	h	Belenenses	W 2-0	Urreta, Bruno Moreira
05/10	h	Marítimo	W 3-2	Bruno Moreira 2, Edson Farias
25/10	a	Boavista	W 2-1	Edson Farias, Bruno Moreira
02/11	h	Setúbal	W 4-1	Urreta, Sérgio Oliveira (p), Hurtado, Bruno Moreira
09/11	a	Sporting	D 1-1	Hurtado
01/12	h	Estoril	D 1-1	Edson Farias
07/12	h	Moreirense	L 0-2	
13/12	a	Arouca	W 2-1	Urreta (p), Cícero
22/12	h	Braga	L 0-3	

2015

03/01	a	Rio Ave	L 1-2	Hélder Lopes
10/01	a	Académica	D 2-2	Rafael Amorim, Vasco Rocha
18/01	h	Nacional	L 2-3	Urreta 2
26/01	h	Benfica	W 1-0	Sérgio Oliveira (p)
01/02	a	Porto	L 0-5	
08/02	h	Penafiel	W 2-1	Cícero, og (Ferreira)
14/02	a	Gil Vicente	L 0-1	
20/02	h	Guimarães	D 2-2	Bruno Moreira, Edson Farias
02/03	a	Belenenses	W 1-0	Bruno Moreira
08/03	a	Marítimo	L 1-2	Seri
13/03	h	Boavista	W 1-0	Manuel José (p)
23/03	a	Setúbal	D 0-0	
04/04	h	Sporting	D 1-1	Rodrigo Galo
13/04	a	Estoril	L 0-1	
19/04	h	Moreirense	D 0-0	
26/04	a	Arouca	W 3-1	Bruno Moreira 2, Hurtado
04/05	h	Braga	D 2-2	Hurtado, Rúben Pinto
09/05	a	Rio Ave	D 0-0	
17/05	h	Académica	W 3-2	Diogo Jota 2, Edson Farias
23/05	a	Nacional	L 0-3	

No	Name	Nat	DoB	Pos	Aps	(s)	Gls
25	Andrézinho		06/08/95	A	5		
45	António Filipe		14/04/85	G	12		
11	Bruno Moreira		06/09/87	A	24	(4)	10
26	Bruno Sousa		15/05/96	D	3		
9	Cícero	GNB	08/05/86	A	11	(14)	3
18	Diogo Jota		04/12/96	A	8	(2)	2
31	Diogo Rosado		21/02/90	M	3	(2)	
12	Edson Farias	BRA	12/01/92	A	6	(21)	5
65	Fábio Cardoso		19/04/94	D	15	(1)	
3	Flávio Boaventura	BRA	12/07/87	D		(2)	
5	Hélder Lopes		04/01/89	M	30		1
16	Paolo Hurtado	PER	27/07/90	A	15	(6)	4
13	Jailson	BRA	21/01/91	D	22	(1)	
14	Jaime Poulson		22/06/89	M	1		
81	Manuel José		04/02/81	M	14	(2)	1
7	Minhoca		29/04/89	A	19	(8)	
15	Nélson Pedroso		18/06/85	D	4	(7)	
30	Barnes Osei	GHA	08/01/95	A		(3)	
44	Rafael Amorim	BRA	30/07/87	D	17	(2)	1
1	Rafael Defendi	BRA	22/12/83	G	22		
19	Ricardo	CPV	19/08/80	D	27		1
6	Ricardo Ferreira		25/11/92	D	8	(2)	
22	Rodrigo Galo	BRA	19/09/86	D	9	(1)	1
4	Romeu		17/02/86	M	4	(4)	
77	Rúben Pinto		24/04/92	M	15		1
7	Rúben Ribeiro		01/08/87	D		(3)	
10	Sérgio Oliveira		02/06/92	M	22	(4)	2
88	Jean Michaël Seri	CIV	19/07/91	M	32	(1)	1
21	Jonathan Urreta	URU	19/03/90	A	13	(1)	5
17	Vasco Rocha		29/01/89	M	13	(8)	1

FC Penafiel

1951 • Municipal 25 de Abril (5,087) • fcpenafiel.pt

Coach: Ricardo Chéu;
(10/09/14) Rui Quinta;
(19/03/15) Carlos Brito

2014

17/08	h	Belenenses	L	1-3	*João Martins (p)*
22/08	a	Guimarães	L	0-3	
31/08	h	Paços Ferreira	L	0-1	
14/09	a	Marítimo	L	0-2	
20/09	h	Setúbal	W	2-0	*Hélder Guedes,*
					André Fontes
28/09	a	Moreirense	D	0-0	
04/10	h	Sporting	L	0-4	
27/10	a	Rio Ave	L	2-3	*Ferreira, Hélder Guedes (p)*
01/11	h	Estoril	L	1-2	*Rabiola (p)*
09/11	a	Boavista	L	0-1	
29/11	h	Braga	L	1-6	*Rabiola (p)*
07/12	a	Arouca	W	1-0	*Capela*
13/12	h	Nacional	W	2-1	*Quiñones, Rabiola*
21/12	a	Académica	D	1-1	*Quiñones*

2015

04/01	h	Benfica	L	0-3	
11/01	a	Gil Vicente	L	1-2	*Rabiola*
17/01	h	Porto	L	1-3	*Rabiola*
25/01	a	Belenenses	D	0-0	
31/01	h	Guimarães	D	1-1	*João Martins*
08/02	a	Paços Ferreira	L	1-2	*João Martins*
15/02	h	Marítimo	L	3-4	*Rabiola, André Fontes,*
					Hélder Guedes
21/02	a	Setúbal	W	1-0	*Hélder Guedes*
01/03	h	Moreirense	L	1-2	*Hélder Guedes*
09/03	a	Sporting	L	2-3	*Braga, Vítor Bruno*
15/03	h	Rio Ave	L	0-2	
21/03	a	Estoril	D	3-3	*Hélder Guedes 2 (2p),*
					Quiñones
04/04	h	Boavista	D	2-2	*og (Appindangoye),*
					João Martins
12/04	a	Braga	L	0-4	
19/04	h	Arouca	L	0-2	
26/04	a	Nacional	L	0-2	
03/05	h	Académica	D	0-0	
09/05	a	Benfica	L	0-4	
17/05	h	Gil Vicente	W	2-1	*Hélder Guedes, Mbala*
22/05	a	Porto	L	0-2	

No	Name	Nat	DoB	Pos	Aps	(s)	Gls
7	Aldair	GNB	31/01/92	M	15	(12)	
27	André Fontes		27/05/85	M	25	(4)	2
25	Braga		17/03/83	A	9	(3)	1
17	Bruninho		30/09/88	A		(5)	
3	Bura		17/12/88	D	10	(2)	
26	Capela		28/01/86	D	2	(1)	1
1	Coelho		18/07/84	G	11	(2)	
20	Dani		17/01/90	D	24	(2)	
24	Ezequiel	ESP	12/01/91	M	3	(3)	
6	Ferreira		13/06/80	M	22	(2)	1
88	Alireza Haghighi	IRN	02/05/88	G	22		
11	Hélder Guedes		05/07/87	A	17	(14)	8
10	João Martins		30/06/88	M	25	(5)	4
4	João Pedro		29/12/87	D	9		
28	David Mbala	COD	19/04/93	A	11	(15)	1
70	Michel	BRA	22/08/86	A		(1)	
21	Nélson Lenho		22/03/84	D	12		
23	Nuno Henrique		19/10/86	D		(1)	
21	Paulo Grilo		19/08/91	D	3		
19	Pedro Ribeiro		25/01/83	D	26		
92	Héctor Quiñones	COL	17/03/92	A	21	(3)	3
29	Rabiola		25/07/89	A	18	(8)	6
30	Rafa		25/08/88	M	21	(1)	
32	Romeu Ribeiro		13/01/89	M	13	(4)	
9	Rui Miguel		30/01/84	A	5	(3)	
37	Tiago Rocha		04/09/90	G	1	(1)	
2	Tiago Valente		24/04/85	D	12	(1)	
16	Tony		20/12/80	D	10	(1)	
29	Ustaritz	ESP	16/02/83	D	7		
5	Vítor Bruno		13/01/90	A	20	(6)	1

FC Porto

1893 • Dragão (50,476) • fcporto.pt

Major honours
European Champion Clubs' Cup/UEFA Champions League (2) 1987, 2004; UEFA Cup (1) 2003; UEFA Europa League (1) 2011; UEFA Super Cup (1) 1987; European/South American Cup (2) 1987, 2004; Portuguese League (27) 1935, 1939, 1940, 1956, 1959, 1978, 1979, 1985, 1986, 1988, 1990, 1992, 1993, 1995, 1996, 1997, 1998, 1999, 2003, 2004, 2006, 2007, 2008, 2009, 2011, 2012, 2013; Portuguese Cup (16) 1956, 1958, 1968, 1977, 1984, 1988, 1991, 1994, 1998, 2000, 2001, 2003, 2006, 2009, 2010, 2011

Coach: Julen Lopetegui (ESP)

2014

15/08	h	Marítimo	W	2-0	*Rúben Neves, Martínez*
23/08	a	Paços Ferreira	W	1-0	*Martínez*
31/08	h	Moreirense	W	3-0	*Óliver Torres, Martínez 2*
14/09	a	Guimarães	D	1-1	*Martínez (p)*
21/09	h	Boavista	D	0-0	
26/09	a	Sporting	D	1-1	*og (Sarr)*
05/10	h	Braga	W	2-1	*Martins Indi, Quintero*
25/10	a	Arouca	W	5-0	*Quintero, Martínez 2,*
					Casemiro, Aboubakar
01/11	h	Nacional	W	2-0	*Danilo, Brahimi*
09/11	h	Estoril	D	2-2	*Brahimi, Óliver Torres*
30/11	h	Rio Ave	W	5-0	*Tello, Martínez,*
					Alex Sandro, Óliver Torres,
					Danilo
06/12	a	Académica	W	3-0	*Martínez 2, Herrera*
14/12	h	Benfica	L	0-2	
19/12	h	Setúbal	W	4-0	*Ricardo Quaresma (p),*
					Martínez, Brahimi,
					Danilo (p)

2015

03/01	a	Gil Vicente	W	5-1	*Casemiro, Martins Indi,*
					Brahimi, Óliver Torres,
					Martínez
10/01	h	Belenenses	W	3-0	*Martínez, Óliver Torres,*
					Evandro
17/01	h	Penafiel	W	3-1	*Herrera, Martínez,*
					Óliver Torres
25/01	a	Marítimo	L	0-1	
01/02	h	Paços Ferreira	W	5-0	*Martínez,*
					Ricardo Quaresma 2 (1p),
					Herrera, Tello
07/02	a	Moreirense	W	2-0	*Martínez, Casemiro*
13/02	h	Guimarães	W	1-0	*Brahimi*
23/02	a	Boavista	W	2-0	*Martínez, Brahimi*
01/03	h	Sporting	W	3-0	*Tello 3*
06/03	a	Braga	W	1-0	*Tello*
15/03	h	Arouca	W	1-0	*Aboubakar*
21/03	a	Nacional	D	1-1	*Tello*
06/04	h	Estoril	W	5-0	*Óliver Torres, Aboubakar,*
					Ricardo Quaresma 2 (1p),
					Danilo
11/04	a	Rio Ave	W	3-1	*Ricardo Quaresma (p),*
					Danilo, Hernâni
18/04	a	Académica	W	1-0	*Hernâni*
26/04	a	Benfica	D	0-0	
03/05	a	Setúbal	W	2-0	*Brahimi, Martínez*
10/05	h	Gil Vicente	W	2-0	*Martínez 2*
17/05	a	Belenenses	D	1-1	*Martínez*
22/05	h	Penafiel	W	2-0	*Aboubakar, Danilo*

No	Name	Nat	DoB	Pos	Aps	(s)	Gls
99	Vincent Aboubakar	CMR	22/01/92	A	5	(9)	4
18	Adrián López	ESP	08/01/88	A	3	(6)	
26	Alex Sandro	BRA	26/01/91	D	28		1
25	Andrés Fernández	ESP	16/12/86	G	1		
8	Yacine Brahimi	ALG	08/02/90	M	25	(3)	7
22	José Campaña	ESP	31/05/93	M	2		
6	Casemiro	BRA	23/02/92	M	27	(1)	3
2	Danilo	BRA	15/07/91	D	29		6
15	Evandro	BRA	23/08/86	M	7	(14)	1
12	Fabiano	BRA	29/02/88	G	27		
39	Gonçalo Paciência		01/08/94			(1)	
1	Helton	BRA	18/05/78	G	6	(1)	
17	Hernâni		20/08/91	A	2	(6)	2
16	Héctor Herrera	MEX	19/04/90	M	28	(5)	3
14	José Angel	ESP	05/09/89	D	6		
4	Maicon	BRA	14/09/88	D	26		
5	Iván Marcano	ESP	23/06/87	D	18	(2)	
9	Jackson Martínez	COL	03/10/86	A	29	(1)	21
3	Bruno Martins Indi	NED	08/02/92	D	22	(2)	2
30	Óliver Torres	ESP	10/11/94	M	22	(4)	7
10	Juan Quintero	COL	18/01/93	M	7	(13)	2
13	Diego Reyes	MEX	19/09/92	D	2	(1)	
21	Ricardo		06/10/93	A	5		
7	Ricardo Quaresma		26/09/83	A	20	(10)	6
36	Rúben Neves		13/03/97	M	11	(13)	1
11	Cristian Tello	ESP	11/08/91	A	16	(9)	7

Rio Ave FC

1939 • Rio Ave (12,815) • rioave-fc.pt

Coach: Pedro Martins

2014

17/08	h	Setúbal	W	2-0	*Diego Lopes, Marcelo*
24/08	a	Estoril	W	5-1	*Hassan 3,*
					Pedro Moreira 2
01/09	h	Boavista	W	4-0	*Renan Bressan,*
					Diego Lopes,
					Esmaël Gonçalves,
					Boateng
13/09	a	Moreirense	D	1-1	*Diego Lopes*
21/09	h	Arouca	L	1-2	*Tarantini*
27/09	a	Braga	L	0-3	
05/10	a	Nacional	D	0-0	
27/10	h	Penafiel	W	3-2	*Ukra, Diego Lopes,*
					Hassan
31/10	a	Benfica	L	0-1	
10/11	h	Académica	W	3-0	*Hassan 2, Ukra*
30/11	a	Porto	L	0-5	
06/12	h	Gil Vicente	D	0-0	
14/12	a	Guimarães	D	0-0	
22/12	h	Belenenses	D	0-0	

2015

03/01	a	Paços Ferreira	W	2-1	*Hassan, Pedro Moreira*
11/01	h	Marítimo	D	0-0	
18/01	a	Sporting	L	2-4	*Del Valle, Hassan*
25/01	a	Setúbal	L	1-4	*Ukra*
01/02	a	Estoril	W	2-1	*Del Valle (p), Hassan*
09/02	a	Boavista	D	1-1	*Hassan (p)*
15/02	h	Moreirense	D	1-1	*Hassan*
22/02	a	Arouca	L	0-1	
28/02	h	Braga	L	0-2	
09/03	h	Nacional	D	1-1	*Zegelaar*
15/03	a	Penafiel	W	2-0	*Del Valle, Hassan*
21/03	h	Benfica	W	2-1	*Ukra (p), Del Valle*
03/04	a	Académica	D	0-0	
11/04	h	Porto	L	1-3	*Tarantini*
19/04	a	Gil Vicente	D	0-0	
25/04	h	Guimarães	D	1-1	*Renan Bressan*
04/05	a	Belenenses	W	3-1	*Diego Lopes, Tiago Pinto,*
					Del Valle
09/05	h	Paços Ferreira	D	0-0	
17/05	a	Marítimo	L	0-4	
23/05	h	Sporting	L	0-1	

No	Name	Nat	DoB	Pos	Aps	(s)	Gls
22	Sunday Abalo	NGA	14/05/95	M	3	(4)	
14	André Vilas Boas		04/06/83	M	19	(2)	
13	Emmanuel Boateng	GHA	23/05/96	A	4	(9)	1
1	Cássio	BRA	12/09/90	G	17		
28	Yonathan Del Valle	VEN	28/05/90	A	22	(6)	5
10	Diego Lopes	BRA	03/05/94	A	25	(7)	5
93	Ederson	BRA	17/08/93	G	17		
77	Esmaël Gonçalves		25/06/91	A	7	(5)	1
7	Filipe Augusto	BRA	12/08/93	M	1		
3	Prince-Désir Gouano	FRA	24/12/93	D	26	(1)	
9	Ahmed Hassan	EGY	05/03/93	A	17	(5)	12
33	William Jebor	LBR	10/11/91	A	7		
5	Jony	ESP	02/04/85	M		(1)	
12	Lionn	BRA	29/01/89	D	26		
6	Luís Gustavo		28/09/92	M	1	(9)	
46	Marcelo	BRA	27/07/89	D	14		1
44	Nélson Monte		30/07/95	D	5	(1)	
16	Nuno Lopes		19/12/86	D	6	(1)	
20	Pedro Moreira		15/03/89	M	17	(9)	3
11	Renan Bressan	BLR	03/11/88	M	10	(10)	2
25	Roderick		30/03/91	D	2	(1)	
4	Pape Sow	SEN	02/12/85	M	4	(2)	
8	Tarantini		07/10/83	M	28	(1)	2
15	Tiago Pinto		01/02/88	D	26	(1)	1
17	Ukra		18/08/88	A	28	(5)	4
30	Alhassan Wakaso	GHA	07/01/92	M	26	(3)	
21	Marvin Zegelaar	NED	12/08/90	M	16	(9)	1

PORTUGAL

Sporting Clube de Portugal

1906 • José Alvalade (50,466) • sporting.pt

Major honours
UEFA Cup Winners' Cup (1) 1964; Portuguese League (18) 1941, 1944, 1947, 1948, 1949, 1951, 1952, 1953, 1954, 1958, 1962, 1966, 1970, 1974, 1980, 1982, 2000, 2002; Portuguese Cup (16) 1941, 1945, 1946, 1948, 1954, 1963, 1971, 1973, 1974, 1978, 1982, 1995, 2002, 2007, 2008, 2015
Coach: Marco Silva

2014
16/08	a	Académica	D	1-1	Carrillo
23/08	h	Arouca	W	1-0	Carlos Mané
31/08	a	Benfica	D	1-1	Slimani
13/09	h	Belenenses	D	1-1	Carrillo
21/09	a	Gil Vicente	W	4-0	Adrien Silva, Nani, Slimani, Carrillo
26/09	h	Porto	D	1-1	Silva
04/10	a	Penafiel	W	4-0	Slimani 2, Montero, Nani
26/10	h	Marítimo	W	4-2	og (Bauer), João Mário, Paulo Oliveira, Montero
01/11	a	Guimarães	L	0-3	
09/11	h	Paços Ferreira	D	1-1	Montero
29/11	h	Setúbal	W	3-0	Slimani 2, Montero
05/12	a	Boavista	W	3-1	Carrillo, Carlos Mané, João Mário
14/12	h	Moreirense	D	1-1	Montero
21/12	a	Nacional	W	1-0	Carlos Mané

2015
03/01	h	Estoril	W	3-0	Adrien Silva 2 (1p), Slimani
11/01	a	Braga	W	1-0	Tanaka
18/01	h	Rio Ave	W	4-2	Nani (p), Montero, João Mário, Tanaka
25/01	h	Académica	W	1-0	João Mário
01/02	a	Arouca	W	3-1	Montero, Carrillo, Tobias Figueiredo
08/02	h	Benfica	D	1-1	Jefferson
14/02	h	Belenenses	D	1-1	Carlos Mané
22/02	h	Gil Vicente	W	2-0	Tanaka, Nani
01/03	a	Porto	L	0-3	
09/03	h	Penafiel	W	3-2	William Carvalho, Slimani, Nani
15/03	a	Marítimo	W	1-0	Adrien Silva (p)
22/03	h	Guimarães	W	4-1	João Mário, Adrien Silva (p), Slimani, Nani (p)
04/04	a	Paços Ferreira	D	1-1	Slimani
12/04	a	Setúbal	W	2-1	Carlos Mané, Tanaka
19/04	h	Boavista	W	2-1	Adrien Silva, Slimani
27/04	a	Moreirense	W	4-1	Carlos Mané, Montero 2, Tanaka
02/05	h	Nacional	W	2-0	Montero 2
10/05	a	Estoril	D	1-1	Ewerton
17/05	h	Braga	W	4-1	Adrien Silva 2 (1p), Tobias Figueiredo, Slimani
23/05	a	Rio Ave	W	1-0	Nani

No	Name	Nat	DoB	Pos	Aps	(s)	Gls
23	Adrien Silva		15/03/89	M	27	(3)	8
8	André Martins		21/01/90	M	12	(5)	
36	Carlos Mané		11/03/94	A	13	(16)	6
18	André Carrillo	PER	14/06/91	A	26	(6)	5
41	Cédric		31/08/91	D	23	(1)	
11	Diego Capel	ESP	16/02/88	M	2	(19)	
5	Ewerton	BRA	23/03/89	D	8	(1)	1
27	Ryan Gauld	SCO	16/12/95	M		(2)	
20	Héldon	CPV	14/11/88	A	1	(1)	
4	Jefferson	BRA	05/07/88	D	23		1
17	João Mário		19/01/93	M	23	(7)	5
22	Marcelo	BRA	28/11/84	G	1		
3	Maurício	BRA	20/09/88	D	14		
13	Miguel Lopes		19/12/86	D	8	(2)	
10	Fredy Montero	COL	26/07/87	A	18	(8)	11
77	Nani		17/11/86	A	27		7
24	Oriol Rosell	ESP	07/07/92	M	6	(6)	
26	Paulo Oliveira		08/01/92	D	26	(1)	1
47	Ricardo Esgaio		16/05/93	M	3		
1	Rui Patrício		15/02/88	G	33		
29	Naby Sarr	FRA	13/08/93	D	8		
33	Jonathan Silva	ARG	29/06/94	D	11		1
9	Islam Slimani	ALG	18/06/88	A	16	(5)	12
19	Junya Tanaka	JPN	15/07/87	A	5	(12)	5
55	Tobias Figueiredo		02/02/94	D	12	(2)	2
42	Wallyson	BRA	16/02/94	M		(1)	
14	William Carvalho		07/04/92	M	28	(2)	1

Vitória FC (Setúbal)

1910 • Bonfim (18,694) • vfc.pt

Major honours
Portuguese Cup (3) 1965, 1967, 2005
Coach: Domingos Paciência; (21/01/15) Bruno Ribeiro

2014
17/08	a	Rio Ave	L	0-2	
24/08	h	Gil Vicente	W	2-0	Miguel Pedro, João Schmidt
29/08	a	Académica	D	1-1	Venâncio
12/09	h	Benfica	L	0-5	
20/09	a	Penafiel	L	0-2	
28/09	h	Nacional	W	2-0	Lupeta, Miguel Pedro
05/10	a	Belenenses	D	1-1	João Schmidt (p)
24/10	h	Guimarães	L	0-1	
02/11	a	Paços Ferreira	L	1-4	Paulo Tavares
09/11	h	Marítimo	W	1-0	Giovani Rosa
29/11	a	Sporting	L	0-3	
06/12	h	Estoril	L	0-1	
12/12	h	Boavista	L	0-1	
19/12	a	Porto	L	0-4	

2015
04/01	h	Moreirense	W	2-1	og (Marcelo Oliveira), Pelkas
11/01	a	Arouca	L	0-1	
18/01	a	Braga	L	1-3	Zéquinha
25/01	h	Rio Ave	W	4-1	Suk, Zéquinha (p), Pelkas, João Schmidt
01/02	a	Gil Vicente	D	1-1	Zéquinha
08/02	a	Académica	D	0-0	
15/02	a	Benfica	L	0-3	
21/02	h	Penafiel	L	0-1	
01/03	a	Nacional	L	0-3	
07/03	h	Belenenses	D	1-1	João Schmidt
14/03	a	Guimarães	W	1-0	Rambé
23/03	h	Paços Ferreira	D	0-0	
06/04	h	Marítimo	D	1-1	Zéquinha
12/04	h	Sporting	L	1-2	Suk
19/04	h	Estoril	L	1-2	Suk
26/04	a	Boavista	D	0-0	
03/05	h	Porto	L	0-2	
10/05	h	Moreirense	L	1-3	João Schmidt
17/05	a	Arouca	W	2-1	Suk, João Schmidt
23/05	a	Braga	L	0-5	

No	Name	Nat	DoB	Pos	Aps	(s)	Gls
82	Luís Advíncula	PER	02/03/90	D	20	(6)	
90	André Horta		07/11/96	A	4	(2)	
66	Dani		30/01/82	M	29		
14	Ulises Dávila	MEX	13/04/91	A	4	(7)	
11	Diego Maurício	BRA	25/06/91	A	1	(3)	
4	Ericson	BRA	25/11/87	M	4	(4)	
91	Forbes	GNB	20/06/89	A	4	(3)	
9	Giovani Rosa	BRA	07/01/92	A	3	(4)	1
55	Hélder Cabral		07/05/84	M	17		
8	João Schmidt	BRA	19/05/93	M	25	(3)	6
20	Kiko		20/01/93	A	10	(1)	
45	Lupeta		24/03/93	A	6	(6)	1
7	Manu		28/08/82	A	10	(1)	
21	Marcos Vinícius	BRA	27/06/91	D	2	(2)	
44	Miguel Lourenço		27/05/92	M	10	(1)	
10	Miguel Pedro		06/11/83	A	21	(7)	2
68	Ney Santos	BRA	23/02/81	D	1	(6)	
8	Paulo Tavares		09/12/85	M	26		1
24	Pedro Queirós		08/08/84	D	28	(1)	
22	Dimitrios Pelkas	GRE	26/10/93	M	8	(16)	2
17	Júnior Ponce	PER	16/02/94	A	4	(3)	
1	Lukas Raeder	GER	30/12/93	G	17		
23	Rambé	CPV	04/10/89	A	4	(6)	1
33	Ricardo Batista		19/11/86	G	17		
48	Adama Sene	SEN	30/11/89	D	25		
39	Suk Hyun-jun	KOR	29/06/91	A	14	(3)	4
16	Tiago Terroso		13/01/88	M		(1)	
3	Venâncio		23/10/92	D	31		1
28	Yann Rolim	BRA	15/03/95	M	1	(9)	
87	Zéquinha		07/01/87	A	28	(3)	4

Vitória SC (Guimarães)

1922 • D. Afonso Henriques (30,146) • vitoriasc.pt

Major honours
Portuguese Cup (1) 2013
Coach: Rui Vitória

2014
16/08	a	Gil Vicente	W	3-1	Hernâni 2, Mensah
22/08	h	Penafiel	W	3-0	Mensah 2, Tómané
30/08	a	Belenenses	W	3-0	André André, Tómané, Alex
14/09	h	Porto	D	1-1	Mensah (p)
19/09	h	Paços Ferreira	D	1-1	Álvez
28/09	a	Marítimo	L	0-4	
03/10	h	Boavista	W	3-0	Álvez 2, André André (p)
24/10	a	Setúbal	W	1-0	João Afonso
01/11	h	Sporting	W	3-0	Saré, og (Maurício), André André (p)
07/11	a	Arouca	W	2-1	Josué Sá, Hernâni
28/11	h	Moreirense	W	2-1	André André (p), Álvez
07/12	a	Braga	D	0-0	
14/12	h	Rio Ave	D	0-0	
20/12	a	Estoril	L	0-1	

2015
04/01	h	Nacional	W	4-0	Ricardo, André André 3 (1p)
10/01	a	Benfica	L	0-3	
17/01	h	Académica	W	4-0	Ricardo Valente, André André (p), Tómané, Hernâni
24/01	a	Gil Vicente	D	2-2	Ricardo Valente, André André (p)
31/01	a	Penafiel	D	1-1	André André (p)
08/02	h	Belenenses	L	0-1	
13/02	a	Porto	L	0-1	
20/02	a	Paços Ferreira	D	2-2	Saré, André André
27/02	h	Marítimo	W	1-0	Josué Sá
08/03	a	Boavista	L	1-3	Alex (p)
14/03	h	Setúbal	L	0-1	
22/03	a	Sporting	L	1-4	Kanu
03/04	h	Arouca	W	1-0	Moreno
11/04	a	Moreirense	L	1-2	Alex
17/04	h	Braga	W	1-0	Ricardo Valente
25/04	a	Rio Ave	D	1-1	Álvez
01/05	h	Estoril	W	2-0	Ricardo Valente 2
11/05	a	Nacional	D	2-2	Ricardo Valente, Mensah
17/05	h	Benfica	D	0-0	
23/05	a	Académica	W	4-2	Ricardo Valente 2, Otávio, Tomané

No	Name	Nat	DoB	Pos	Aps	(s)	Gls
14	Alex		27/08/91	A	20		3
45	Alex Silva		16/03/97	A		(1)	
10	Jonatan Álvez	URU	30/05/87	A	7	(11)	5
55	Joseph Amoah	GHA	26/06/94	M		(1)	
11	André André		26/08/89	M	31		11
13	Assis	BRA	14/10/89	G	15	(1)	
66	Breno	BRA	09/03/95	D	5		
48	Bruno Alves		09/06/90	D	2	(6)	
76	Bruno Gaspar		21/04/93	D	24		
26	Cafú		26/02/93	M	22	(7)	
28	Khalil Chemmam	TUN	24/07/87	D	4		
50	Crivellaro	BRA	18/02/89	A	1	(4)	
88	David Caiado		02/05/87	A	2	(4)	
1	Douglas	BRA	09/03/83	G	19		
80	Inters Gui	CIV	08/08/93	A	1	(12)	
7	Hernâni		20/08/91	A	17	(1)	4
37	Ivo Rodrigues		30/03/95	M	2	(1)	
15	João Afonso		28/05/90	D	22	(1)	1
58	João Pedro		03/04/93	M		(1)	
3	Josué Sá		17/06/92	D	25	(1)	2
25	Kanu	BRA	03/05/84	D	5		1
5	Luís Rocha		27/06/93	D	7		
43	Bernard Mensah	GHA	17/10/94	A	29	(1)	5
6	Moreno		19/08/81	D	10	(2)	1
52	Otávio	BRA	09/02/95	M	7	(3)	1
40	Nii Plange	BFA	26/06/89	A	12	(5)	
18	Ricardo	CPV	18/12/91	M	3	(7)	1
91	Ricardo Valente		03/04/91	M	11	(4)	8
2	Rodrigo Defendi	BRA	17/06/86	D	7		
49	Rui Areias		22/11/93	A		(2)	
34	Sami	GNB	18/12/88	A	10	(4)	
99	Bakary Saré	CIV	05/04/90	M	12	(10)	2
7	Tómané		23/10/92	A	27	(5)	4
32	Adama Traoré	CIV	03/02/90	D	15		
8	Nassim Zitouni	ALG	31/03/94	M		(4)	

Top goalscorers

21	Jackson Martínez (Porto)
20	Jonas (Benfica)
19	Lima (Benfica)
17	Maroo Matias (Nacional)
12	Ahmed Hassan (Rio Ave)
	Islam Slimani (Sporting)
11	Fredy Montero (Sporting)
	André André (Guimarães)
10	Éder (Braga)
	Bruno Moreira (Paços Ferreira)

Promoted clubs

CD Tondela

1933 • João Cardoso (2,674) • cdtondela.pt
Coach: Carlos Pinto;
(07/10/14) Quim Machado

CF União da Madeira

1913 • Complexo Desportivo da Madeira
(2,500) • uniaodamadeira.com
Coach: Vítor Oliveira

Second level final table 2014/15

		Pld	W	D	L	F	A	Pts
1	CD Tondela	46	21	18	7	67	51	81
2	CF União da Madeira	46	22	14	10	69	39	80
3	GD Chaves	46	20	20	6	68	45	80
4	SC Covilhã	46	23	11	12	78	46	80
5	Sporting Clube de Portugal B	46	22	12	12	66	57	78
6	SL Benfica B	46	22	11	13	81	60	77
7	CD Feirense	46	21	12	13	61	51	75
8	SC Freamunde	46	18	17	11	48	32	71
9	Vitória SC B	46	19	8	19	71	57	65
10	SC Beira-Mar	46	16	15	15	52	48	63
11	SC Farense	46	16	14	16	51	54	62
12	Académico de Viseu FC	46	17	11	18	55	56	62
13	FC Porto B	46	17	10	19	66	64	61
14	Portimonense SC	46	15	15	16	56	62	60
15	Clube Oriental de Lisboa	46	15	13	18	47	59	58
16	SC Olhanense	46	13	16	17	51	56	55
17	UD Oliveirense	46	14	13	19	50	67	55
18	CD Aves	46	12	17	17	52	58	53
19	CD Santa Clara	46	10	21	15	33	42	51
20	Leixões SC	46	13	11	22	53	67	50
21	SC Braga B	46	12	15	19	48	62	49
22	Atlético CP	46	11	14	21	56	70	47
23	CS Marítimo B	46	10	11	25	37	67	41
24	CD Trofense	46	9	9	28	35	81	36

NB SC Braga B – 2 pts deducted.

DOMESTIC CUP

Taça de Portugal 2014/15

THIRD ROUND

(17/10/14)
Atlético CP 3-0 Beira-Mar

(18/10/14)
Aves 4-1 Boavista
Covilhã 2-3 Benfica
Famalicão 2-1 Pombal
Feirense 5-1 Amora
Olhanense 2-4 Oriental
Pedras Salgadas 1-3 Trofense *(aet)*
Porto 1-3 Sporting
Varzim 2-1 Estoril

(19/10/14)
AD Oliveirense 2-3 Belenenses *(aet)*
Braga 4-1 Alcains
Casa Pia 1-4 Vizela *(aet)*
Chaves 7-0 Cova Piedade
Coimbrões 0-1 Rio Ave
Freamunde 3-2 Felgueiras 1932
Gil Vicente 2-1 Real
Marítimo 4-0 Gondomar
Moreirense 2-1 Pedras Rubras
Mortágua 1-3 Fafe
Moura 0-2 Guimarães
Nacional 6-1 Alcananense
Operário 3-1 Tirsense
Paços Ferreira 4-0 Reguengos
Penafiel 2-2 Tondela *(aet; 4-3 on pens)*
Riachense 2-1 Benfica Castelo Branco
Ribeirão 2-0 Torreense *(aet)*
Salgueiros 08 1-3 UD Oliveirense
Santa Maria 1-0 Académica
Serzedo 1-1 Espinho *(aet; 7-8 on pens)*
Setúbal 1-0 Arouca
Sourense 0-1 Santa Eulália
Vitória Sernache 1-1 Vieira *(aet; 1-4 on pens)*

FOURTH ROUND

(21/11/14)
Espinho 0-5 Sporting

(22/11/14)
Atlético CP 0-2 Marítimo
Benfica 4-1 Moreirense
Famalicão 4-0 Fafe
Rio Ave 2-0 UD Oliveirense
Trofense 0-5 Belenenses

(23/11/14)
Feirense 0-2 Chaves
Gil Vicente 1-1 Varzim *(aet; 3-1 on pens)*
Guimarães 1-2 Braga
Nacional 2-0 Ribeirão
Oriental 1-0 Setúbal
Paços Ferreira 9-0 Riachense
Penafiel 1-0 Aves
Santa Maria 2-1 Santa Eulália
Vieira 0-1 Freamunde
Vizela 2-2 Operário *(aet; 4-2 on pens)*

FIFTH ROUND

(16/12/14)
Belenenses 2-0 Freamunde

(17/12/14)
Gil Vicente 2-1 Penafiel
Marítimo 1-1 Oriental *(aet; 9-8 on pens)*
Nacional 2-1 Santa Maria
Paços Ferreira 1-2 Famalicão
Rio Ave 2-0 Chaves
Vizela 2-3 Sporting

(18/12/14)
Benfica 1-2 Braga

QUARTER-FINALS

(06/01/15)
Rio Ave 5-2 Gil Vicente *(Diego Lopes 6, Ukra 54p, Pedro Moreira 76, Lionn 78, Hassan 89; João Vilela 65, Simy 72)*

(07/01/15)
Braga 7-1 Belenenses *(Aderlan Santos 16, Rafa 21, Rúben Micael 42, Pardo 48, Éder 68, Alan 77, Pedro Tiba 88; Fábio Nunes 57)*
Sporting 4-0 Famalicão *(Carrillo 34, João Mário 48, Paulo Oliveira 69, Montero 75)*

(08/01/15)
Marítimo 1-1 Nacional *(Bruno Gallo 19p; Marco Matias 47p) (aet; 5-6 on pens)*

SEMI-FINALS

(05/03/15 & 08/04/15)
Nacional 2-2 Sporting *(Luís Aurélio 50, Lucas João 59; Tobias Figueiredo 55, Carlos Mané 83)*
Sporting 1-0 Nacional *(Ewerton 85)*
(Sporting 3-2)

(07/04/15 & 30/04/15)
Braga 3-0 Rio Ave *(Zé Luís 16, 27, 51)*
Rio Ave 1-1 Braga *(Jebor 48; Éder 43)*
(Braga 4-1)

FINAL

(31/05/15)
Estádio Nacional, Lisbon
SPORTING CLUBE DE PORTUGAL 2 *(Slimani 84, Montero 90+3)*
SC BRAGA 2 *(Éder 16p, Rafa 25)*
(aet; 3-1 on pens)
Referee: *Marco Ferreira*
SPORTING: *Rui Patrício, Cédric, Paulo Oliveira, Ewerton, Jefferson, João Mário (Miguel Lopes 21; Montero 74), William Carvalho, Adrien Silva, Carrillo (Carlos Mané 54), Slimani, Nani*
Red card: *Cédric (15)*
BRAGA: *Kritsyuk, Baiano, Aderlan Santos, André Pinto, Djavan (Sasso 82), Mauro, Luiz Carlos, Rúben Micael (Alan 61), Pardo (Salvador Agra 75), Rafa, Éder*
Red card: *Mauro (115)*

REPUBLIC OF IRELAND
Cumann Peile na héireann/Football Association of Ireland (FAI)

Address	National Sports Campus	**President**	Tony Fitzgerald
	Abbotstown	**Chief executive**	John Delaney
	IE-Dublin 15	**Media officer**	Peter Sherrard
Tel	+353 1 8999500	**Year of formation**	1921
Fax	+353 1 8999501	**National stadium**	Dublin Arena, Dublin
E-mail	info@fai.ie		(51,700)
Website	fai.ie		

PREMIER DIVISION CLUBS

 1 **Athlone Town FC**

 2 **Bohemian FC**

 3 **Bray Wanderers FC**

 4 **Cork City FC**

 5 **Derry City FC**

 6 **Drogheda United FC**

 7 **Dundalk FC**

 8 **Limerick FC**

 9 **Saint Patrick's Athletic FC**

 10 **Shamrock Rovers FC**

 11 **Sligo Rovers FC**

 12 **University College Dublin AFC**

PROMOTED CLUBS

 13 **Longford Town FC**

 14 **Galway FC**

NB Renamed Galway United FC for 2015 season

KEY:
- – UEFA Champions League
- – UEFA Europa League
- – Promoted
- – Relegated
- – Relegated club in UEFA Europa League

Dundalk deliver tenth title

On the brink of relegation in 2012, Dundalk FC's rapid revival under manager Stephen Kenny resulted in a remarkable Premier Division triumph in 2014. Out in front for most of the campaign, the County Louth side almost let the title slip, only to leapfrog Cork City FC back to the top of the table with a memorable 2-0 win over their rivals on the final day.

Saint Patrick's Athletic FC were unable to defend their league crown, but the Dublin side won the FAI Cup for the first time in over half a century, defeating Derry City FC in the final.

| Rivals Cork defeated in last-day showdown | St Patrick's end 53-year wait with FAI Cup triumph | Late goals keep hopes alive in EURO qualifiers |

Domestic league

Only a play-off win had spared Dundalk relegation at the end of a fraught 2012 campaign, but Kenny's appointment transformed the club's fortunes and they came a close second to St Patrick's in 2013. Eager to go one better and return the title to Oriel Park for the first time in 19 years, Dundalk shrugged off a heavy opening-day derby defeat at Drogheda United FC to soar to the Premier Division summit.

A 25-match unbeaten run kept them there, and although that included two wins over closest challengers Cork, the team from Turner's Cross refused to throw in the towel. Indeed, after losing at home to the leaders in early August, John Caulfield's side found their best form. With four games to go Dundalk's lead was down to three points, but as Cork continued to win, the long-time leaders dropped four points in as many days with damaging draws against Shamrock Rovers FC and Bray Wanderers AFC and all of a sudden Cork were in the driving seat.

Fortunately, Dundalk's destiny was still in their own hands as their final game was at home to Cork. Over 5,000 spectators packed into Oriel Park to witness the title showdown. Goalless at half-time, it was

looking good for the visitors, but three minutes after the interval Dundalk went ahead, with a goal from captain Stephen O'Donnell, starting his first game for six months after a knee injury, and the three points – and title – were duly sealed six minutes from time with a raucously-greeted second from defender Brian Gartland.

With 73 goals scored to Cork's 51, and three wins out of three against their rivals, Dundalk's triumph brooked no argument. It was their their tenth title – the most of any non-Dublin club. The relegation of University College Dublin AFC meant that there would be only three clubs from the capital in the 2015 Premier Division – the smallest number for 30 years.

Domestic cup

A generally poor season for Dublin clubs in the league was partially remedied by the long-awaited FAI Cup success of St Pat's. Since winning the trophy in 1961 the club had been to seven finals and lost them all. The two most recent had been against Derry, in 2006 and 2012, but the Saints finally ended their jinx against the same opposition thanks to a brace of goals from Christy Fagan, the Premier Division's joint top scorer with Dundalk's Patrick Hoban.

Europe

Irish interest in Europe ended with early elimination across the board and was characterised by poor results on home soil. Dundalk and Sligo Rovers FC both posted impressive away wins – at HNK Hajduk Split and Rosenborg BK, respectively – only to have them rendered inconsequential by defeats at home, while the high hopes that St Pat's carried into the second leg of their UEFA Champions League qualifier following a 1-1 draw at Legia Warszawa were dashed by a 5-0 drubbing in Dublin.

National team

Ending the season fourth in UEFA EURO 2016 Qualifying Group D was not what the Republic of Ireland's new manager Martin O'Neill would have anticipated after an encouraging start that included a 1-1 draw away to world champions Germany. But one point from a possible six against Scotland plus an equally disappointing draw at home to Poland left Irish hopes of reaching France via the automatic route dangling by a thread. Indeed, but for the team's consistent ability to rescue themselves with late goals – which were responsible for half of their eight points – their chances of even reaching the play-offs might have all but disappeared with four matches still to play.

REPUBLIC OF IRELAND

DOMESTIC SEASON AT A GLANCE

Premier Division 2014 final table

		Pld	Home					Away					Total					Pts
			W	D	L	F	A	W	D	L	F	A	W	D	L	F	A	
1	**Dundalk FC**	**33**	**12**	**4**	**0**	**45**	**9**	**10**	**4**	**3**	**28**	**15**	**22**	**8**	**3**	**73**	**24**	**74**
2	Cork City FC	33	12	4	1	29	11	10	2	4	22	14	22	6	5	51	25	72
3	Saint Patrick's Athletic FC	33	12	2	3	39	21	7	6	3	27	16	19	8	6	66	37	65
4	Shamrock Rovers FC	33	10	3	3	18	8	8	5	4	25	18	18	8	7	43	26	62
5	Sligo Rovers FC	33	7	5	4	29	18	5	2	10	15	18	12	7	14	44	36	43
6	Limerick FC	33	7	1	8	22	24	5	4	8	15	21	12	5	16	37	45	41
7	Bohemian FC	33	5	8	4	21	21	4	5	7	21	22	9	13	11	42	43	40
8	Derry City FC	33	6	5	6	22	14	3	6	7	20	27	9	11	13	42	41	38
9	Drogheda United FC	33	5	4	8	23	28	5	2	9	17	35	10	6	17	40	63	36
10	Bray Wanderers FC	33	4	4	8	15	29	1	7	9	13	32	5	11	17	28	61	26
11	University College Dublin AFC	33	4	5	8	12	30	2	2	12	15	41	6	7	20	27	71	25
12	Athlone Town FC	33	3	5	8	17	23	1	5	11	18	33	4	10	19	35	56	22

European qualification 2015/16

Champion: Dundalk FC (second qualifying round)

Cup winner: Saint Patrick's Athletic FC (first qualifying round)

Cork City FC (first qualifying round)
Shamrock Rovers FC (first qualifying round)
University College Dublin AFC (first qualifying round)

Top scorers Patrick Hoban (Dundalk) & Christy Fagan (St Patrick's), 20 goals
Relegated clubs Athlone Town FC, University College Dublin AFC
Promoted clubs Longford Town FC, Galway FC
Cup final Saint Patrick's Athletic FC 2-0 Derry City FC

Team of the season
(4-3-3)

Coach: Kenny (Dundalk)

Player of the season

Christy Fagan
*(Saint Patrick's
Athletic FC)*

A former Manchester United FC apprentice who played in the English Football League at Lincoln City FC, Fagan's third season with St Patrick's was far and away his best as he scored 27 goals in all competitions, including two in the FAI Cup final against Derry City FC and another in a UEFA Champions League qualifier away to Legia Warszawa. His league haul of 20 was enough to put him joint top of the scorers' charts and also helped him to scoop the PFAI Player of the Year title.

Newcomer of the season

Sean Hoare
*(Saint Patrick's
Athletic FC)*

An unused member of the St Patrick's squad when they won the 2013 Premier Division title, Hoare established himself in Liam Buckley's side during the 2014 campaign, showing real class and composure in central defence and swiftly becoming a fans' favourite at Richmond Park. He was a starter in the team's historic FAI Cup final victory and later that month received his first cap for the Republic of Ireland Under-21 side, his rapid development inevitably attracting interest from across the Irish Sea.

McNulty *(Cork)*

Gannon *(Dundalk)* Gartland *(Dundalk)* Boyle *(Dundalk)* Bermingham *(St Patrick's)*

Healy *(Cork)* Towell *(Dundalk)* Horgan *(Dundalk)*

O'Sullivan *(Cork)* Hoban *(Dundalk)* Fagan *(St Patrick's)*

NATIONAL TEAM

International tournament appearances

FIFA World Cup (3) 1990 (qtr-finals), 1994 (2nd round), 2002 (2nd round)
UEFA European Championship (2) 1988, 2012

Top five all-time caps

Robbie Keane (140); **Shay Given** (130); Kevin Kilbane (110); **John O'Shea** (104); Stephen Staunton (102)

Top five all-time goals

Robbie Keane (65); Niall Quinn (21); Frank Stapleton (20); John Aldridge, Tony Cascarino & Don Givens (19)

Results 2014/15

03/09/14	Oman	H	Dublin	W	2-0	Doyle (20), Pearce (81)
07/09/14	Georgia (ECQ)	A	Tbilisi	W	2-1	McGeady (24, 90)
11/10/14	Gibraltar (ECQ)	H	Dublin	W	7-0	Keane (6, 14, 18p), McClean (46, 53), J Perez (52og), Hoolahan (56)
14/10/14	Germany (ECQ)	A	Gelsenkirchen	D	1-1	O'Shea (90+4)
14/11/14	Scotland (ECQ)	A	Glasgow	L	0-1	
18/11/14	United States	H	Dublin	W	4-1	Pilkington (7), Brady (55, 86), McClean (82)
29/03/15	Poland (ECQ)	H	Dublin	D	1-1	Long (90+1)
07/06/15	England	H	Dublin	D	0-0	
13/06/15	Scotland (ECQ)	H	Dublin	D	1-1	Walters (38)

Appearances 2014/15

Coach: Martin O'Neill (NIR)	01/03/52		Oma	GEO	GIB	GER	SCO	Usa	POL	Eng	SCO	Caps	Goals
Shay Given	20/04/76	Aston Villa (ENG)	G46					G84	G	s61	G	130	-
David Meyler	29/05/89	Hull (ENG)	D85	s91	D	D		M				13	-
Richard Keogh	11/08/86	Derby (ENG)	D				D					7	1
Alex Pearce	09/11/88	Reading (ENG)	D					D				6	2
Stephen Ward	20/08/85	Burnley (ENG)	D	D	D70	D	D					29	2
Anthony Pilkington	06/06/88	Cardiff (ENG)	M59					M64				8	1
Stephen Quinn	01/04/86	Hull (ENG)	M	M76		M76	s68	M				12	-
Darron Gibson	25/10/87	Everton (ENG)	M70		M	s63	M68					25	1
Robbie Brady	14/01/92	Hull (ENG)	M	s76	s70		s68	D	D	D	D	14	3
Wes Hoolahan	20/05/82	Norwich (ENG)	A59		A63	s76		A		A73		20	2
Kevin Doyle	18/09/83	Crystal Palace (ENG)	A59		s63							61	14
Rob Elliot	30/04/86	Newcastle (ENG)	s46					s84				3	-
Aiden McGeady	04/04/86	Everton (ENG)	s59	M	M	M	M	s59	M68	M		76	5
Robbie Keane	08/07/80	LA Galaxy (USA)	s59	A76	A63	A63	s78		A		s73	140	65
Shane Long	22/01/87	Southampton (ENG)	s59	s76			A68	s77	s84	s46	s80	54	12
Glenn Whelan	13/01/84	Stoke (ENG)	s70	M		M53			M84	M63	M68	64	2
Daryl Murphy	15/03/83	Ipswich (ENG)	s85		s63			A77		A56	A80	15	-
David Forde	20/12/79	Millwall (ENG)		G	G	G	G					23	-
Séamus Coleman	11/10/88	Everton (ENG)		D			D		D	D	D	28	-
Marc Wilson	17/08/87	Stoke (ENG)		D	D	D			D	D	D	23	1
John O'Shea	30/04/81	Sunderland (ENG)		D	D	D	D		D	D72	D	104	3
James McCarthy	12/11/90	Everton (ENG)		M91				M	M46	M		27	-
Jonathan Walters	20/09/83	Stoke (ENG)		M		M	M		M	s56	M	33	6
James McClean	22/04/89	Wigan (ENG)			M	M	M	s64	s68	s46	s68	30	4
Jeff Hendrick	31/01/92	Derby (ENG)			M	s53	M78	s77		M	M	13	-
Cyrus Christie	30/09/92	Derby (ENG)						D				1	-
Ciaran Clark	26/09/89	Aston Villa (ENG)						D				11	1
Anthony Stokes	25/07/88	Celtic (SCO)						M59				9	-
David McGoldrick	29/11/87	Ipswich (ENG)						A77		A46		2	-
Keiren Westwood	23/10/84	Sheffield Wednesday (ENG)								G61		18	-
Harry Arter	28/12/89	Bournemouth (ENG)								s63		1	-
Paul McShane	06/01/86	Hull (ENG)								s72		32	-

EUROPE

Saint Patrick's Athletic FC

Second qualifying round - Legia Warszawa (POL)
A 1-1 *Fagan (38)*
Clarke, O'Brien, Bermingham, Oman, Bolger, Byrne, Fahey, Fagan (Lynch 85), Brennan (Chambers 76), Browne, Forrester (Quigley 49). Coach: Liam Buckley (IRL)
H 0-5
Clarke, O'Brien (Hoare 62), Bermingham, Foran, Bolger, Byrne, Fahey, Fagan, Brennan, Browne (Lynch 74), Forrester (Quigley 46). Coach: Liam Buckley (IRL)

Sligo Rovers FC

First qualifying round - FK Banga (LTU)
A 0-0
Rogers, Keane (Ledwith 89), McMillan, North, Cawley, Cretaro (Greene 74), Gaynor, O'Conor, Russell, Djilali, Conneely. Coach: John Coleman (ENG)
H 4-0 *Keane (45+1), Greene (72), North (83), Cawley (89)*
Rogers (Brush 84), Keane (Peers 87), McMillan, North, Cawley, Cretaro, Spillane (Gaynor 23), Russell, Greene, Djilali, Conneely. Coach: John Coleman (ENG)

Second qualifying round - Rosenborg BK (NOR)
A 2-1 *Keane (56), North (70)*
Rogers, Keane, Ledwith (O'Conor 27), McMillan, North (Keating 82), Cawley, Gaynor, Spillane, Russell, Djilali (Maguire 85), Conneely. Coach: John Coleman (ENG)
H 1-3 *North (13)*
Rogers, Keane, McMillan, North, Cawley, Gaynor (Maguire 70), O'Conor (Keating 70), Spillane, Russell, Djilali (Ledwith 84), Conneely. Coach: John Coleman (ENG)

Dundalk FC

First qualifying round - AS Jeunesse Esch (LUX)
A 2-0 *Towell (59p, 71)*
Cherrie, Gannon, Gartland, Boyle, Shields, Horgan (Mountney 85), Byrne (Higgins 70), Massey, McMillan (Hoban 79), Towell, Meenan. Coach: Stephen Kenny (IRL)
H 3-1 *Gartland (8), Byrne (37), Mountney (45+1)*
Cherrie, Gannon, Gartland (Kelly 80), Boyle, Horgan (Griffin 46), Mountney, Byrne (Hoban 62), Higgins, Massey, McMillan, Towell. Coach: Stephen Kenny (IRL)

Second qualifying round - HNK Hajduk Split (CRO)
H 0-2
Cherrie, Gannon, Gartland, Boyle, Shields (Higgins 73), Horgan (McMillan 82), Mountney (McDermott 57), Hoban, Massey, Towell, Meenan. Coach: Stephen Kenny (IRL)
A 2-1 *Hoban (66), Byrne (74)*
Sava, Gannon, Gartland, Boyle, Shields, Mountney, Higgins (Meenan 87), Massey, McMillan (Byrne 68), Towell, McDermott (Hoban 57). Coach: Stephen Kenny (IRL)

Derry City FC

First qualifying round - Aberystwyth Town FC (WAL)
H 4-0 *P McEleney (15), Patterson (25p), Timlin (47), B McNamee (86)*
Doherty, Jarvis, Molloy, McBride, B McNamee, P McEleney (Lowry 76), Patterson (Boyle 82), Duffy, Timlin (Tracey 68), Byrne, Barry. Coach: Peter Hutton (IRL)
A 5-0 *Duffy (11), B McNamee (14), Patterson (60, 84, 86p)*
Doherty, Jarvis, Molloy (S McEleney 69), McBride, B McNamee, P McEleney (Lowry 61), Patterson, Duffy, Timlin, Byrne, Barry (Ventre 46). Coach: Peter Hutton (IRL)

Second qualifying round - FC Shakhtyor Soligorsk (BLR)
H 0-1
Doherty, Molloy, McBride, S McEleney, B McNamee, P McEleney (Boyle 86), Patterson, Duffy (Dooley 63), Timlin, Byrne, Barry. Coach: Peter Hutton (IRL)
A 1-5 *Duffy (6)*
Doherty, Molloy, McBride, B McNamee, Ventre, P McEleney, Patterson (Boyle 79), Duffy (Lowry 73), Dooley (Timlin 61), Byrne, Barry. Coach: Peter Hutton (IRL)

DOMESTIC LEAGUE CLUB-BY-CLUB

Athlone Town FC

1887 • Athlone Town Stadium (4,000) • athlonetownfc.ie
Major honours
League of Ireland (2) 1981, 1983; FAI Cup (1) 1924
Manager: Mick Cooke;
(28/04/14) Keith Long

2014

Date		Opponent	Res	Score	Scorers
08/03	a	Sligo	L	1-2	Gorman (p)
14/03	h	Shamrock Rovers	L	1-4	A Byrne
21/03	a	UCD	L	1-2	Gorman
28/03	h	Cork	L	0-3	
04/04	a	Drogheda	L	2-3	Gorman 2
07/04	h	Bohemians	L	1-3	Rusk
11/04	a	Derry	L	2-3	O'Brien, Marks
18/04	a	Limerick	L	1-2	Dillon
21/04	h	Dundalk	L	0-1	
25/04	a	St Patrick's	L	0-4	
02/05	h	Bray	D	0-0	
17/05	a	Shamrock Rovers	L	0-1	
20/05	a	Sligo	L	0-2	
23/05	h	UCD	W	2-0	Dillon, S Brennan
30/05	a	Cork	L	0-1	
13/06	a	Drogheda	W	6-0	Gorman 2, Prendergast, O'Brien, S Brennan, Sweeney
27/06	a	Bohemians	D	2-2	O'Brien 2
06/07	h	Derry	L	0-1	
11/07	a	Limerick	W	3-0	Gorman 2, Dillon
20/07	a	Dundalk	L	0-2	
26/07	h	St Patrick's	L	0-2	
01/08	a	Bray	D	1-1	A Byrne
09/08	a	Sligo	L	1-3	O'Connor
15/08	h	Shamrock Rovers	D	1-1	Sweeney
18/08	a	UCD	D	1-1	Mulroy
29/08	h	Cork	D	2-2	Mulroy, O'Brien
05/09	a	Drogheda	D	1-1	Sweeney
19/09	h	Bohemians	D	0-0	
26/09	a	Bray	D	1-1	Doyle
03/10	a	Limerick	L	2-4	Doyle, A Byrne
10/10	h	Dundalk	L	0-3	
17/10	a	St Patrick's	W	2-0	Gorman, Dillon
24/10	h	Bray	D	1-1	Gorman (p)

No	Name	Nat	DoB	Pos	Aps	(s)	Gls
18	Declan Brennan		29/10/91	D	7	(4)	
10	Seán Brennan		01/01/86	D	27	(4)	2
6	Alan Byrne		21/07/83	D	27		3
3	Sean Byrne		13/07/89	D	15	(1)	
14	Barry Clancy		20/04/85	M	13	(5)	
5	Aidan Collins		22/03/84	D	4	(2)	
21	Ryan Coulter		08/02/89	G	14	(1)	
7	Kealan Dillon		21/02/94	M	32		4
25	Derek Doyle		30/04/86	M	11	(1)	2
29	Stephen Dunne		12/09/95	D	1	(1)	
26	Dean Ebbe		16/07/94	A		(3)	
23	Eric Foley		30/01/90	M	9	(3)	
9	Philip Gorman		07/08/81	A	27	(3)	10
12	Neil Harney		20/02/91	D	3	(3)	
2	Dylan Hayes		09/04/95	D	8	(1)	
8	Mark Hughes		28/04/93	M	22	(4)	
28	Kevin Knight		13/02/93	M	10		
23	Jason Marks		02/05/89	M	9	(6)	1
2	Conor McMahon		04/12/86	D	8	(3)	
19	Michael Monaghan		22/07/95	D		(1)	
17	Thomas Mulroney		24/03/95	M		(3)	
22	John Mulroy		23/04/94	A	7	(2)	2
16	James O'Brien		08/06/90	M	25	(5)	5
19	Sam O'Connor		22/12/95	A		(2)	1
4	Derek Prendergast		17/10/84	D	28		1
24	Stephen Quigley		13/01/85	D	11	(1)	
15	Graham Rusk		13/12/89	A	15	(6)	1
20	Craig Sexton		23/01/92	G	3		
28	Brian Shortall		28/05/85	D	6		
1	Paul Skinner		03/02/89	G	16		
11	Ian Sweeney		20/03/94	M	5	(25)	3

Bohemian FC

1890 • Dalymount Park (4,500) •
bohemianfc.com
Major honours
*League of Ireland (11) 1924, 1928, 1930, 1934,
1936, 1975, 1978, 2001, 2003 (spring), 2008, 2009;
Irish Cup (1) 1908; FAI Cup (7) 1928, 1935, 1970,
1976, 1992, 2001, 2008*
Manager: Owen Heary

2014

07/03	a	UCD	W	3-0	Kavanagh, Corcoran, J Byrne
14/03	h	Drogheda	D	2-2	Corcoran 2 (1p)
21/03	h	Shamrock Rovers	L	1-3	og (Kenna)
28/03	a	Dundalk	D	1-1	Price
04/04	h	Bray	D	1-1	Corcoran
07/04	a	Athlone	W	3-1	D Byrne, og (O'Brien), J Byrne
11/04	h	Limerick	L	0-1	
18/04	h	St Patrick's	L	1-3	J Byrne
21/04	h	Sligo	L	0-2	
25/04	a	Cork	D	1-1	J Byrne
02/05	h	Derry	D	1-1	J Byrne
09/05	h	UCD	D	0-0	
16/05	a	Drogheda	L	0-1	
23/05	a	Shamrock Rovers	D	0-0	
30/05	h	Dundalk	L	0-2	
13/06	a	Bray	W	5-0	Corcoran 3 (2p), og (Maloney), Buckley
27/06	a	Athlone	D	2-2	Devaney, Corcoran
04/07	a	Limerick	W	2-1	Kavanagh, Wearen
11/07	h	St Patrick's	D	1-1	Wearen
25/07	a	Cork	W	2-0	Beattie, Wearen
01/08	a	Derry	L	0-4	
08/08	a	UCD	D	0-0	
15/08	h	Drogheda	W	2-1	Moore, J Byrne
29/08	a	Dundalk	L	2-3	Moore, Corcoran
05/09	h	Bray	W	2-1	Corcoran, J Byrne
08/09	a	Sligo	L	2-3	Hyland, Corcoran
19/09	a	Athlone	D	0-0	
23/09	h	Shamrock Rovers	D	1-1	Pender
26/09	h	Limerick	W	2-0	J Byrne, Mulcahy
30/09	a	St Patrick's	L	1-3	A Murphy
10/10	h	Sligo	D	2-2	Corcoran, Beattie
17/10	a	Cork	L	0-1	
24/10	h	Derry	W	2-1	J Byrne, Corcoran

No	Name	Nat	DoB	Pos	Aps	(s)	Gls
22	Steven Beattie		20/08/88	M	26	(3)	2
19	Stephen Best		15/03/97	M		(1)	
20	Keith Buckley		17/06/92	M	10	(6)	1
15	Daniel Byrne		07/05/93	D	16	(1)	1
10	Jason Byrne		23/03/78	A	16	(13)	9
11	Daniel Corcoran		13/02/89	A	23	(4)	13
1	Dean Delany		15/09/80	G	26		
16	Kevin Devaney		26/09/90	M	16	(10)	1
18	Adam Evans		03/05/94	M	1	(6)	
12	Jake Hyland		10/08/95	M	2	(3)	1
14	Patrick Kavanagh		29/12/85	M	23	(6)	2
4	Roberto Lopes		17/06/92	D	29	(1)	
23	Philip McCabe		04/08/93	D	1		
9	Ryan McEvoy		19/07/90	M	8	(3)	
3	Jack Memery		05/03/93	D	16		
7	Karl Moore		09/11/88	M	20	(9)	2
5	Dave Mulcahy		28/01/78	M	15	(2)	1
18	Andy Mulligan		07/07/93	M	1		
17	Anthony Murphy		01/08/82	M	12	(2)	1
25	Lee Murphy		09/04/85	M	6	(1)	
2	Derek Pender		02/10/84	D	28		1
6	Aidan Price		08/12/81	D	30		1
19	Darragh Reynor		14/02/93	M	5	(1)	
25	Aaron Shanahan		20/04/84	D	1		
8	Stephen Traynor		25/10/91	M	2	(3)	
21	Craig Walsh		27/01/92	M	16	(6)	
13	Eoin Wearen		02/10/92	M	14	(1)	3

Bray Wanderers FC

1942 • Carlisle Grounds (3,000) •
braywanderers.ie
Major honours
FAI Cup (2) 1990, 1999
Manager: Alan Mathews

2014

07/03	a	Limerick	D	0-0	
14/03	h	Sligo	W	1-0	C Byrne
21/03	a	Cork	L	1-3	Scully
28/03	h	UCD	L	3-5	S O'Connor, Cassidy 2
04/04	a	Bohemians	D	1-1	G Kelly (p)
07/04	h	St Patrick's	L	1-3	Cassidy
11/04	a	Drogheda	W	2-0	Scully, O'Neill
18/04	h	Derry	D	0-0	
21/04	a	Shamrock Rovers	L	1-2	Scully (p)
25/04	h	Dundalk	W	1-0	Scully
02/05	a	Athlone	D	0-0	
09/05	h	Limerick	W	1-0	Hanlon
17/05	a	Sligo	L	0-3	
23/05	h	Cork	L	0-2	
30/05	a	UCD	D	0-0	
13/06	h	Bohemians	L	0-5	
27/06	a	St Patrick's	L	2-3	J Kelly 2
04/07	h	Drogheda	L	1-3	J Kelly
13/07	a	Derry	L	0-5	
18/07	h	Shamrock Rovers	L	0-3	
27/07	a	Dundalk	L	1-5	Akinade
01/08	h	Athlone	D	1-1	Barker
07/08	a	Limerick	L	1-4	Zambra
15/08	h	Sligo	L	0-1	
18/08	a	Cork	D	1-1	McDonagh
29/08	h	UCD	W	2-0	Akinade, J Kelly
05/09	a	Bohemians	L	1-2	og (Mulcahy)
19/09	h	St Patrick's	L	2-4	J Kelly (p), Hanlon
26/09	a	Drogheda	D	1-1	Hanlon
30/09	h	Derry	D	1-1	Mitchell
10/10	a	Shamrock Rovers	L	0-1	
17/10	h	Dundalk	D	1-1	Cassidy
24/10	a	Athlone	D	1-1	Zambra

No	Name	Nat	DoB	Pos	Aps	(s)	Gls
9	Ismahil Akinade	NGA	17/06/92	A	24	(4)	2
14	Michael Barker		16/08/93	D	10		1
17	Michael Brown		21/02/96	D		(4)	
18	Ciarán Byrne		06/07/93	A	4	(3)	1
23	Shane Byrne		25/04/93	M	6	(4)	
8	David Cassidy		23/05/85	M	29	(1)	4
13	Ryan Coombes		19/07/90	M		(3)	
12	Niall Cooney		09/11/88	D	22	(1)	
21	Gary Curran		22/09/87	M	2	(3)	
4	Joe Gorman		01/09/94	D	9		
11	Adam Hanlon		03/06/92	M	19	(4)	3
20	Philip Hughes		12/09/81	A	2	(8)	
33	Sean Hurley		30/08/93	M		(1)	
24	Graham Kelly		31/10/91	M	29	(1)	1
10	Jake Kelly		18/06/90	A	18	(4)	5
22	Robert Maloney		06/06/93	D	17	(4)	
23	Gareth McDonagh		27/02/96	M	3	(3)	1
6	Eric McGill		16/10/87	M	13	(1)	
3	Jamie McGlynn		07/06/94	D	3	(1)	
32	Stephen McGuinness		10/03/95	G	26	(1)	
5	Adam Mitchell		02/10/84	D	23		1
18	Sean Noble		20/03/96	M	1		
4	Danny O'Connor		10/11/93	M	2		
15	Shane O'Connor		14/06/87	D	10	(2)	1
7	Shane O'Neill		09/01/89	M	11	(7)	1
1	Shane Redmond		23/03/89	G	7		
19	Dave Scully		20/01/85	A	19	(8)	4
32	Gavin Sheridan		03/01/96	G		(1)	
13	Ryan Swan		13/04/96	A		(2)	
2	David Webster		08/09/89	D	21		
16	Dean Zambra		30/07/88	M	33		2

Cork City FC

1984 • Turner's Cross (7,365) • corkcityfc.ie
Major honours
*League of Ireland (2) 1993, 2005; FAI Cup (2) 1998,
2007*
Manager: John Caulfield

2014

07/03	h	St Patrick's	D	1-1	Buckley
16/03	a	Derry	W	1-0	D Dennehy
21/03	h	Bray	W	3-1	J Kavanagh, B Dennehy (p), Buckley
28/03	a	Athlone	W	3-0	O'Sullivan, B Dennehy, Kearney
04/04	h	Shamrock Rovers	W	3-0	B Dennehy, O'Sullivan, D Dennehy
11/04	h	Sligo	D	1-1	B Dennehy (p)
18/04	h	Drogheda	W	3-1	Kearney, Buckley, B Dennehy
21/04	a	UCD	W	1-0	B Dennehy
25/04	h	Bohemians	D	1-1	B Dennehy (p)
02/05	a	Dundalk	L	0-4	
09/05	h	St Patrick's	L	2-3	O'Sullivan, Lehane
16/05	h	Derry	W	2-0	B Dennehy (p), G Morrissey
20/05	a	Limerick	W	2-1	Buckley, B Dennehy
23/05	a	Bray	W	2-0	og (McGuinness), Healy (p)
30/05	a	Athlone	W	1-0	O'Sullivan
13/06	a	Shamrock Rovers	W	2-0	O'Sullivan, G Morrissey
27/06	h	Limerick	W	3-0	O'Sullivan 2, Buckley
06/07	a	Sligo	D	0-0	
11/07	a	Drogheda	W	1-0	Buckley
18/07	h	UCD	W	2-1	B Dennehy (p), O'Sullivan
25/07	a	Bohemians	L	0-2	
01/08	h	Dundalk	L	1-2	D Dennehy
08/08	h	St Patrick's	W	1-0	Healy
15/08	a	Derry	W	1-0	O'Flynn
18/08	h	Bray	D	1-1	Buckley
29/08	a	Athlone	D	2-2	D Dennehy, O'Sullivan
05/09	a	Shamrock Rovers	W	1-0	Murray
21/09	a	Limerick	W	1-0	Lehane
26/09	h	Sligo	W	2-1	O'Sullivan, B Dennehy
03/10	h	Drogheda	W	2-1	Dunleavy, O'Sullivan
10/10	a	UCD	W	4-0	Gaynor, B Dennehy (p), Buckley 2
17/10	h	Bohemians	W	1-0	B Dennehy
24/10	a	Dundalk	L	0-2	

No	Name	Nat	DoB	Pos	Aps	(s)	Gls
26	Garry Buckley		19/08/93	M	28	(1)	9
28	Iarflaith Davoren		12/05/86	D	7	(3)	
20	Billy Dennehy		17/02/87	M	30		13
5	Darren Dennehy		21/09/88	D	29		4
4	John Dunleavy		03/07/91	D	31		1
9	Anthony Elding	ENG	16/04/82	A	2		
11	Ross Gaynor		09/09/87	D	9		1
7	Colin Healy		14/03/80	M	27		2
16	Gavin Kavanagh		22/11/87	D	1		
3	John Kavanagh		19/07/94	D	9	(9)	1
30	Liam Kearney		10/01/83	M	18	(10)	2
24	Robert Lehane		19/02/94	A		(15)	2
19	Brian Lenihan		08/06/94	M	21		
1	Mark McNulty		13/10/80	G	33		
18	Michael McSweeney		17/06/88	D	4	(3)	
10	Cillian Morrison		25/07/91	A	3	(2)	
15	Danny Morrissey		13/12/93	A		(7)	
6	Gearóid Morrissey		17/11/91	M	26		2
18	Kevin Mulcahy		02/03/86	D		(1)	
8	Darren Murphy		04/04/95	M	3	(1)	
17	Dan Murray	ENG	16/05/82	D	32		1
9	John O'Flynn		11/07/82	M	9	(5)	1
21	David O'Leary		17/07/92	M	3	(15)	
29	Josh O'Shea		20/01/92	A	6	(9)	
23	Mark O'Sullivan		01/02/83	A	32	(1)	11
11	Ian Turner		19/04/89	M		(2)	

Derry City FC

1928 • The Brandywell (8,200) • derrycityfc.net

Major honours
Irish League (1) 1965; League of Ireland (2) 1989, 1997; Irish Cup (3) 1949, 1954, 1964; FAI Cup (5) 1989, 1995, 2002 (autumn), 2006, 2012

Manager: Roddy Collins;
(13/05/14) Peter Hutton

2014

09/03	a	Shamrock Rovers	D	1-1	Stewart
16/03	h	Cork	L	0-1	
21/03	a	Drogheda	D	1-1	Byrne
28/03	h	St Patrick's	D	0-0	
04/04	h	Sligo	W	1-0	E Curran
07/04	a	Dundalk	L	0-3	
11/04	h	Athlone	W	3-2	E Curran, Patterson, Duffy
18/04	a	Bray	D	0-0	
21/04	h	Limerick	D	0-0	
25/04	h	UCD	D	1-1	Duffy
02/05	a	Bohemians	D	1-1	P McEleney
09/05	h	Shamrock Rovers	L	0-1	
16/05	a	Cork	L	0-2	
23/05	h	Drogheda	W	2-0	Duffy, Patterson
30/05	a	St Patrick's	L	2-5	Duffy, Patterson
13/06	a	Sligo	D	2-2	McBride 2
27/06	h	Dundalk	D	2-2	B McNamee, Duffy
06/07	a	Athlone	W	1-0	P McEleney
13/07	h	Bray	W	5-0	P McEleney 2, Patterson 2, Dooley
27/07	a	UCD	W	6-1	Duffy 3, Patterson 2, Molloy
01/08	h	Bohemians	W	4-0	Patterson 2, Duffy 2
08/08	a	Shamrock Rovers	L	0-2	
15/08	h	Cork	L	0-1	
18/08	a	Drogheda	L	0-1	
25/08	a	Limerick	W	4-0	P McEleney, Duffy, Lowry, R Curran
29/08	h	St Patrick's	L	0-1	
05/09	h	Sligo	W	2-1	McBride, Barry
08/09	h	Dundalk	L	0-5	
26/09	h	Athlone	D	1-1	Patterson
30/09	a	Bray	D	1-1	Patterson (p)
10/10	h	Limerick	L	1-2	B McNamee
17/10	h	UCD	L	0-1	
24/10	a	Bohemians	L	1-2	Timlin

No	Name	Nat	DoB	Pos	Aps	(s)	Gls
30	Aaron Barry		24/11/94	D	25	(2)	1
9	Nathan Boyle		14/04/94	A	5	(8)	
32	Cormac Burke		11/08/93	M	1		
26	Cliff Byrne		26/04/82	D	17		1
2	Roddy Collins		06/08/94	D	12		
9	Enda Curran		11/06/92	A	11	(1)	2
23	Ryan Curran		13/10/93	A	5	(16)	1
12	Joshua Daniels	NIR	22/02/96	M	5	(5)	
1	Gerard Doherty		24/08/81	G	30		
22	Stephen Dooley		19/10/91	M	9	(5)	1
14	Michael Duffy	NIR	28/07/94	A	24	(5)	11
15	Shay Dunlop	NIR	07/04/96	D	1		
25	David Elebert		21/03/86	D	2	(1)	
17	Raymond Foy		10/03/93	M	1	(3)	
20	Ciaran Gallagher		01/04/92	G	3		
16	Sean Houston		29/10/89	M	5	(2)	
3	Dean Jarvis	NIR	01/06/92	D	20	(5)	
2	Shaun Kelly		15/10/89	D	8		
18	Philip Lowry	NIR	15/07/89	M	12	(3)	1
5	Ryan McBride		15/12/89	D	19	(3)	3
10	Patrick McEleney		26/09/92	A	21	(6)	5
6	Shane McEleney		31/01/91	D	13	(3)	
15	Jon-Paul McGovern	SCO	03/10/80	M	6	(2)	
7	Barry McNamee		17/02/92	M	18	(3)	2
36	Tony McNamee		16/08/93	M	2	(2)	
4	Barry Molloy	NIR	28/11/83	D	24	(1)	1
11	Rory Patterson	NIR	16/07/84	A	20	(3)	11
16	Mark Stewart	SCO	22/06/88	A	8	(4)	1
19	Mark Timlin		07/11/94	M	15	(3)	1
8	Danny Ventre	ENG	23/01/86	M	21	(1)	

Drogheda United FC

1919 • Hunky Dorys Park (2,500) • droghedaunited.ie

Major honours
League of Ireland (1) 2007; FAI Cup (1) 2005

Manager: Robbie Horgan;
(17/06/14) (Darius Kierans);
(26/07/14) Damien Richardson

2014

07/03	h	Dundalk	W	4-1	Foley, Brennan, O'Brien 2
14/03	a	Bohemians	D	2-2	O'Neill 2
21/03	h	Derry	D	1-1	Daly
28/03	a	Limerick	W	1-0	O'Brien
04/04	h	Athlone	W	3-2	O'Brien 3
07/04	a	Sligo	D	1-1	O'Brien
11/04	h	Bray	L	0-2	
18/04	a	Cork	L	1-3	Walshe
21/04	h	St Patrick's	L	0-4	
25/04	a	Shamrock Rovers	L	2-3	Brennan, Hughes
02/05	a	UCD	L	1-2	O'Neill
16/05	h	Bohemians	W	1-0	Walshe
20/05	a	Dundalk	L	0-7	
23/05	a	Derry	L	0-2	
30/05	h	Limerick	L	1-4	O'Brien
02/06	a	St Patrick's	L	0-6	
13/06	a	Athlone	L	0-6	
27/06	h	Sligo	L	1-2	Brennan (p)
04/07	a	Bray	W	3-1	Brennan, Holohan, C Brady
11/07	h	Cork	L	0-1	
25/07	a	Shamrock Rovers	W	1-0	Holohan
01/08	h	UCD	W	4-0	Brennan, O'Neill 2, C Brady
08/08	h	Dundalk	D	1-1	O'Neill
15/08	a	Bohemians	L	1-2	Brennan
18/08	h	Bray	W	1-0	C Brady
29/08	a	Limerick	W	3-0	Daly, Holohan, C Brady
05/09	a	Athlone	D	1-1	Holohan
20/09	a	Sligo	W	2-0	O'Brien, Maher
26/09	h	Bray	D	1-1	Andrews
03/10	a	Cork	L	1-2	O'Brien
10/10	h	St Patrick's	L	2-3	Holohan, McGlynn
17/10	h	Shamrock Rovers	L	0-2	
24/10	a	UCD	L	0-1	

No	Name	Nat	DoB	Pos	Aps	(s)	Gls
4	Paul Andrews		22/03/90	D	10	(5)	1
7	Cathal Brady		24/03/85	M	22	(2)	4
26	Gareth Brady		24/02/94	M	3	(3)	
11	Gavin Brennan		23/01/88	M	21		6
40	Dylan Connolly		02/05/95	G	2	(1)	
6	Paul Crowley		13/08/80	M	5	(9)	
2	Michael Daly		10/01/89	M	28	(1)	2
18	Daire Doyle		07/07/93	M	26	(3)	
22	Eric Foley		30/01/90	M	11	(2)	1
3	Shane Grimes		09/03/87	D	31		
8	Gavan Holohan		15/12/91	M	24	(3)	5
9	Philip Hughes		12/09/81	A	1	(7)	1
24	Roy Kierans		10/02/95	D	1		
13	Stephen Maher		03/03/88	M	13	(7)	1
8	Austin McCann		20/12/84	D		(4)	
45	Peter McGlynn		02/05/89	D	7	(2)	1
12	Ciarán McGuigan	NIR	08/12/89	D	26		
5	Alan McNally		15/09/82	D	30		
19	Declan O'Brien		16/06/79	A	15	(16)	10
22	Ciaran O'Connor		04/05/95	D		(1)	
17	Sean O'Connor		04/05/95	M	3	(5)	
10	Gary O'Neill		30/01/82	A	28	(1)	6
1	Dave Ryan		10/05/88	G	15	(1)	
16	Michael Schlingermann		23/06/91	G	16		
14	Carl Walshe		07/10/92	M	23	(8)	2
27	Adam Wixted		03/08/95	A	2	(4)	

Dundalk FC

1903 • Oriel Park (4,000) • dundalkfc.com

Major honours
League of Ireland (10) 1933, 1963, 1967, 1976, 1979, 1982, 1988, 1991, 1995, 2014; FAI Cup (9) 1942, 1949, 1952, 1958, 1977, 1979, 1981, 1988, 2002 (spring)

Manager: Stephen Kenny

2014

07/03	a	Drogheda	L	1-4	Hoban
14/03	h	Limerick	W	2-1	Hoban, Byrne
22/03	a	Sligo	W	1-0	Massey
28/03	h	Bohemians	D	1-1	Gartland
04/04	a	St Patrick's	W	4-1	Mountney, Horgan, McMillan, Gannon
07/04	h	Derry	W	3-0	Gartland, Towell, McMillan
11/04	h	UCD	W	4-1	Hoban 2, O'Donnell, og (Langtry)
18/04	a	Shamrock Rovers	D	2-2	Towell (p), Meenan
21/04	a	Athlone	W	1-0	Towell (p)
25/04	a	Bray	L	0-1	
02/05	h	Cork	W	4-0	Mountney, Hoban 2, Towell
16/05	a	Limerick	W	2-1	Gartland, Meenan
20/05	h	Drogheda	W	7-0	Gannon, Horgan, og (Crowley), Boyle, McMillan 2, Towell
23/05	a	Sligo	W	3-0	Horgan, Byrne, Hoban
30/05	a	Bohemians	W	2-0	Horgan, Towell
02/06	h	UCD	W	5-2	Hoban 2 (1p), Byrne, Horgan, Gartland
13/06	h	St Patrick's	D	0-0	
27/06	a	Derry	D	2-2	Byrne, Towell
13/07	a	Shamrock Rovers	W	1-0	Hoban
20/07	a	Athlone	W	2-0	Hoban, Gartland
27/07	h	Bray	W	5-1	Towell, Byrne 2, Hoban 2
01/08	a	Cork	W	2-1	Towell, Gartland
08/08	a	Drogheda	D	1-1	Hoban
15/08	h	Limerick	W	1-0	Hoban
18/08	a	Sligo	D	1-1	McMillan
29/08	h	Bohemians	W	3-2	Boyle, McMillan 2
05/09	a	St Patrick's	L	0-1	
08/09	h	Derry	W	5-0	Meenan, Byrne, Massey, Hoban, Gartland
26/09	a	UCD	W	2-0	Towell, Hoban
10/10	a	Athlone	W	3-0	Hoban 2, Towell
13/10	h	Shamrock Rovers	D	0-0	
17/10	h	Bray	D	1-1	Hoban
24/10	h	Cork	W	2-0	O'Donnell, Gartland

No	Name	Nat	DoB	Pos	Aps	(s)	Gls
4	Andy Boyle		07/03/91	D	32		2
11	Kurtis Byrne		09/04/90	A	25	(6)	7
1	Peter Cherrie	SCO	01/10/83	G	33		
2	Sean Gannon		11/07/91	D	32	(1)	2
3	Brian Gartland		04/11/86	D	30		8
15	Mark Griffin		16/06/91	A		(10)	
12	Ruaidhri Higgins	NIR	23/10/84	M	6	(17)	
9	Patrick Hoban		28/07/91	A	30	(2)	20
7	Daryl Horgan		10/08/92	M	33		5
14	Dane Massey		17/04/88	D	33		2
20	Donal McDermott		19/10/89	M		(11)	
16	David McMillan		14/12/88	A	3	(21)	7
21	Darren Meenan	NIR	16/11/86	M	26	(6)	3
8	John Mountney		22/02/93	M	7	(14)	2
6	Stephen O'Donnell		15/01/86	M	9	(3)	2
18	Mark Rossiter		27/05/83	D	4	(2)	
5	Chris Shields		27/12/90	M	27	(1)	
17	Richie Towell		17/09/91	M	33		11
10	Keith Ward		12/10/90	M		(1)	

Limerick FC

1937 • Thomond Park (26,500) • limerickfc.ie

Major honours
League of Ireland (2) 1960, 1980; FAI Cup (2) 1971, 1982

Manager: Stuart Taylor (SCO);
(08/07/14) (Tommy Barrett);
(14/07/14) Martin Russell

2014

07/03	h Bray	D	0-0	
14/03	a Dundalk	L	1-2	Tracy
22/03	a St Patrick's	D	1-1	McGrath
28/03	h Drogheda	L	0-1	
04/04	a UCD	D	1-1	Hughes
11/04	a Bohemians	W	1-0	Gaffney
18/04	h Athlone	W	2-1	Williams, McManus
21/04	a Derry	D	0-0	
25/04	h Sligo	L	0-3	
02/05	a Shamrock Rovers	D	1-1	Gaffney
09/05	a Bray	L	0-1	
16/05	h Dundalk	L	1-2	Tracy (p)
20/05	h Cork	L	1-2	Gaffney
23/05	h St Patrick's	W	2-0	Galbraith, Hughes
30/05	a Drogheda	W	4-1	Galbraith, McManus, Duggan, Tracy
13/06	h UCD	W	2-1	McManus, Duggan
27/06	a Cork	L	0-3	
04/07	h Bohemians	L	1-2	Folan
11/07	a Athlone	L	0-3	
27/07	a Sligo	L	0-2	
01/08	h Shamrock Rovers	W	4-1	Gaffney, Turner, og (Kenna), Folan
07/08	h Bray	W	4-1	Gaffney 3, Lynch
15/08	a Dundalk	L	0-1	
18/08	a St Patrick's	W	1-0	Gaffney
25/08	h Derry	L	0-4	
29/08	h Drogheda	L	0-3	
05/09	a UCD	W	3-1	Gaffney 2, Turner
21/09	h Cork	L	0-1	
26/09	a Bohemians	L	0-2	
03/10	h Athlone	W	4-2	Gaffney 2, Djilali 2
10/10	a Derry	W	2-1	Duggan, Gaffney
17/10	h Sligo	W	1-0	Gaffney
24/10	a Shamrock Rovers	L	0-1	

No	Name	Nat	DoB	Pos	Aps	(s)	Gls
34	Ali Abass	GHA	15/02/95	G	4		
16	Prince Agyemang	GHA	25/12/94	M	23	(2)	
17	Shane Costelloe		03/08/95	D	2		
26	Garbhan Coughlan		24/01/93	A	1	(1)	
10	Craig Curran	ENG	23/08/89	A	2	(2)	
1	Shane Cusack		24/06/92	G	7		
10	Kieran Djilali	ENG	01/01/91	A	10	(3)	2
35	Jack Doherty		03/08/94	M	5	(1)	
8	Shane Duggan		11/03/89	M	30		3
21	Val Feeney		12/01/96	M		(2)	
5	Stephen Folan		14/01/92	D	29		2
9	Rory Gaffney		23/10/89	A	31		14
7	Danny Galbraith	SCO	19/08/90	M	6	(2)	2
29	Jason Hughes		09/04/91	M	24	(1)	2
2	Shaun Kelly		15/10/89	D	14		
15	Michael Leahy		30/04/89	D	6	(2)	
7	Lee Lynch		27/11/91	M	12		1
30	Ross Mann		09/01/96	A	4	(13)	
22	James McGrath		09/02/95	M	6	(5)	1
18	Tam McManus	SCO	28/02/81	A	6	(11)	3
23	Colm Murphy		28/11/95	M	2		
4	Joseph Ndo	CMR	28/04/76	D		(3)	
12	Patrick Nzuzi	COD	24/10/92	D	26	(2)	
19	Shane O'Connor		14/04/90	M	8	(3)	
24	Sam Oji	ENG	09/10/85	D	26	(2)	
20	Daragh Rainsford		15/11/94	A	3	(9)	
14	Barry Ryan		29/08/78	G	22		
11	Shane Tracy		14/09/88	M	18	(5)	3
6	Ian Turner		19/04/89	M	14	(1)	2
25	Tony Whitehead		22/12/94	M	4	(4)	
3	Robbie Williams	ENG	02/10/84	D	18	(2)	1

Saint Patrick's Athletic FC

1929 • Richmond Park (4,000) • stpatsfc.com

Major honours
League of Ireland (8) 1952, 1955, 1956, 1990, 1990, 1998, 1999, 2013; FAI Cup (3) 1959, 1961, 2014

Manager: Liam Buckley

2014

07/03	a Cork	D	1-1	Fagan
14/03	h UCD	W	3-2	Byrne 2, Fagan
22/03	h Limerick	D	1-1	Fagan
28/03	a Derry	D	0-0	
04/04	a Dundalk	L	1-4	Forrester
07/04	a Bray	W	3-1	Fagan, Lynch, Forrester
11/04	h Shamrock Rovers	W	1-0	Brennan (p)
18/04	h Bohemians	W	3-1	Fagan 2, Forrester
21/04	a Drogheda	W	4-0	Lynch, Forrester 2, Byrne
25/04	h Athlone	W	4-0	Chambers, Fagan 2, Lynch
03/05	a Sligo	D	2-2	Bermingham, Byrne (p)
09/05	h Cork	W	3-2	Byrne 2 (1p), Browne
16/05	a UCD	D	1-1	Fagan
23/05	a Limerick	L	0-2	
30/05	h Derry	W	5-2	Fagan 3, Byrne, Hoare
02/06	h Drogheda	W	6-0	Forrester 2, Fagan, Byrne 3
13/06	h Dundalk	D	0-0	
27/06	h Bray	W	3-2	Forrester, Fagan 2
05/07	a Shamrock Rovers	L	1-2	Fagan
11/07	a Bohemians	D	1-1	Quigley
26/07	a Athlone	W	2-0	Forrester, Hoare
01/08	h Sligo	W	1-0	Forrester
08/08	a Cork	L	0-1	
15/08	h UCD	W	3-2	Fahey, Byrne, Bermingham
18/08	h Limerick	L	0-1	
29/08	a Derry	W	1-0	Greene
05/09	h Dundalk	W	1-0	Fagan
19/09	a Bray	W	4-2	Forrester, Fahey, Byrne 2
26/09	h Shamrock Rovers	D	1-1	Byrne
30/09	h Bohemians	W	3-1	Fagan, Greene, Byrne
10/10	a Drogheda	W	3-2	Byrne, og (Doyle), Fagan
17/10	h Athlone	L	0-2	
24/10	a Sligo	W	4-1	Byrne 2, og (Brush), Fagan

No	Name	Nat	DoB	Pos	Aps	(s)	Gls
26	Jack Bayly		18/06/96	M		(1)	
3	Ian Bermingham		16/06/89	D	30		2
6	Greg Bolger		09/09/88	M	19	(5)	
11	Killian Brennan		31/01/84	M	17	(7)	1
15	Kenny Browne		07/08/86	D	27		1
7	Conán Byrne		10/07/85	M	33		18
14	James Chambers		14/02/87	M	19	(6)	1
1	Brendan Clarke		17/09/85	G	33		
23	Peter Durrad		16/12/94	A		(2)	
9	Christy Fagan		11/05/89	A	31	(1)	20
8	Keith Fahey		15/01/83	M	24	(2)	2
21	Rory Feely		03/01/97	M		(1)	
12	Lorcan Fitzgerald		03/01/89	D	2	(4)	
4	Derek Foran		09/10/89	D	9	(2)	
17	Chris Forrester		17/12/92	M	28	(2)	11
16	Rene Gilmartin		31/05/87	G		(1)	
21	Aaron Greene		02/01/90	M	5	(4)	2
20	Sean Hoare		15/03/94	D	20	(2)	2
21	Daryl Kavanagh		11/08/86	A	1	(12)	
18	Lee Lynch		27/11/91	M	10	(7)	3
22	Conor McCormack		18/05/90	M	17	(8)	
19	Jamie McGrath		30/09/96	M	1		
2	Ger O'Brien		02/07/84	D	22	(2)	
5	Ken Oman		29/07/82	D	7	(2)	
10	Mark Quigley		27/10/85	A	8	(11)	1
24	Sam Verdon		03/09/95	M		(1)	

Shamrock Rovers FC

1901 • Tallaght Stadium (6,500) • shamrockrovers.ie

Major honours
League of Ireland (17) 1923, 1925, 1927, 1932, 1938, 1939, 1954, 1957, 1959, 1964, 1984, 1985, 1986, 1987, 1994, 2010, 2011; FAI Cup (24) 1925, 1929, 1930, 1931, 1932, 1933, 1936, 1940, 1944, 1945, 1948, 1955, 1956, 1962, 1964, 1965, 1966, 1967, 1968, 1969, 1978, 1985, 1986, 1987

Manager: Trevor Croly;
(06/08/14) Pat Fenlon

2014

09/03	h Derry	D	1-1	Kilduff
14/03	a Athlone	W	4-1	Kilduff 2, McCabe, Zayed
21/03	a Bohemians	W	3-1	McCabe (p), Finn, Waters
28/03	h Sligo	W	1-0	Brennan
04/04	a Cork	L	0-3	
07/04	h UCD	W	2-0	Finn, Brennan
11/04	a St Patrick's	L	0-1	
18/04	a Dundalk	D	2-2	Kilduff, Finn
21/04	h Bray	W	2-1	McCabe (p), Heaney
25/04	a Drogheda	W	3-2	Finn, Zayed, Kilduff
02/05	h Limerick	D	1-1	McGuinness
09/05	a Derry	W	1-0	McCabe
17/05	h Athlone	W	1-0	Zayed
23/05	h Bohemians	D	0-0	
01/06	a Sligo	W	1-0	og (Keane)
13/06	h Cork	L	0-2	
27/06	a UCD	W	2-0	Finn, Kelly
05/07	h St Patrick's	W	2-1	Kelly, McCabe
13/07	h Dundalk	L	0-1	
18/07	a Bray	W	3-0	Kelly, McGuinness, Robinson
25/07	a Drogheda	L	0-1	
01/08	a Limerick	L	1-4	S O'Connor
08/08	h Derry	W	2-0	Finn, Kelly
15/08	a Athlone	D	1-1	Sheppard
29/08	h Sligo	W	1-0	Madden
05/09	a Cork	L	0-1	
23/09	a Bohemians	D	1-1	Robinson
26/09	a St Patrick's	D	1-1	McCabe
30/09	h UCD	W	3-0	Brennan, S O'Connor, McCabe (p)
10/10	h Bray	W	1-0	S O'Connor
13/10	a Dundalk	D	0-0	
17/10	a Drogheda	W	2-0	Kilduff, S O'Connor
24/10	h Limerick	W	1-0	McCabe (p)

No	Name	Nat	DoB	Pos	Aps	(s)	Gls
15	Robert Bayly		22/02/88	M	8	(13)	
8	Ryan Brennan		11/11/91	M	19	(5)	3
3	Luke Byrne		08/07/93	D	20	(2)	
2	Robert Cornwall		16/10/94	D	11	(3)	
6	Patrick Cregg		21/02/86	M	6	(1)	
21	Ronan Finn		21/12/87	M	25	(3)	6
23	Sean Heaney		27/01/96	D	3	(1)	1
25	Craig Hyland		08/09/90	G	3		
26	Cian Kavanagh		16/09/96	M		(1)	
24	Dean Kelly		18/09/85	A	8	(7)	4
4	Conor Kenna		21/11/84	D	28		
31	Ciaran Kilduff		29/09/88	A	22	(7)	6
17	Simon Madden		01/05/88	D	32		1
7	Gary McCabe		01/08/88	M	30	(1)	8
5	Jason McGuinness		08/08/82	D	29	(1)	2
37	Stephen McPhail		09/12/79	M	16	(3)	
1	Barry Murphy		08/06/85	G	30		
14	David O'Connor		24/08/91	D	6		
10	Sean O'Connor		21/10/83	M	17	(8)	4
26	Evan Osam		17/08/97	D	3		
18	Shane Robinson		17/12/80	M	20	(4)	2
9	Karl Sheppard		14/02/91	A	6	(13)	1
11	Kieran Waters		05/05/90	A	14	(11)	1
19	Eamon Zayed	LBY	04/10/83	A	7	(7)	3

Sligo Rovers FC

1928 • The Showgrounds (5,500) • sligorovers.com

Major honours
League of Ireland (3) 1937, 1977, 2012; FAI Cup (5) 1983, 1994, 2010, 2011, 2013

Manager: Ian Baraclough (ENG); (21/06/14) John Coleman (ENG); (14/09/14) (Gavin Dykes)

2014

08/03	h Athlone	W	2-1	Russell, McMillan
14/03	a Bray	L	0-1	
22/03	h Dundalk	L	0-1	
28/03	a Shamrock Rovers	L	0-1	
04/04	a Derry	L	0-1	
07/04	h Drogheda	D	1-1	Keane
11/04	a Cork	D	1-1	Djilali
18/04	h UCD	W	5-0	Keane (p), O'Conor, Greene, Ledwith, Odhiambo
21/04	a Bohemians	W	2-0	McMillan, North
25/04	a Limerick	W	3-0	O'Conor, Greene, Conneely
03/05	h St Patrick's	D	2-2	Russell, North (p)
17/05	h Bray	W	3-0	O'Conor, Russell, Odhiambo
20/05	a Athlone	W	2-0	Ledwith, North
23/05	a Dundalk	L	0-3	
01/06	h Shamrock Rovers	L	0-1	
13/06	a Derry	D	2-2	Russell, Ledwith
27/06	a Drogheda	W	2-1	North, Djalili
06/07	h Cork	D	0-0	
13/07	a UCD	L	0-1	
27/07	a Limerick	W	2-0	Maguire, North
01/08	a St Patrick's	L	0-1	
09/08	a Athlone	W	3-1	Russell, McMillan 2
15/08	a Bray	W	1-0	Zayed
18/08	h Dundalk	D	1-1	North (p)
29/08	a Shamrock Rovers	L	0-1	
05/09	a Derry	L	1-2	Zayed
08/09	h Bohemians	W	3-2	Cawley, Zayed, North
20/09	a Drogheda	L	0-2	
26/09	a Cork	L	1-2	Ledwith
04/10	h UCD	W	4-0	Zayed, Armstrong, O'Conor, Ledwith
10/10	a Bohemians	D	2-2	O'Conor, Zayed
17/10	a Limerick	L	0-1	
24/10	h St Patrick's	L	1-4	Armstrong

No	Name	Nat	DoB	Pos	Aps	(s)	Gls
20	Gary Armstrong		28/01/96	M	3	(4)	2
25	Gary Boylan		24/04/96	D	6	(2)	
12	Richard Brush	ENG	26/11/84	G	6		
8	David Cawley		17/09/91	M	31	(1)	1
29	Seamus Conneely		09/07/88	M	20	(5)	1
10	Raffaele Cretaro		15/10/81	M	11	(2)	
23	Iarfhlaith Davoren		12/05/86	D	5		
21	Kieran Djilali	ENG	01/01/91	A	10	(1)	2
27	Regan Donelon		17/04/96	D	3	(5)	
11	Ross Gaynor		09/09/87	D	16		
20	Aaron Greene		02/01/90	M	15	(2)	2
6	Jeff Henderson	ENG	19/12/91	A	15		
11	Daryl Kavanagh		11/08/86	A	2		
2	Alan Keane		23/09/84	D	19		2
26	Ruairi Keating		16/07/95	D	3	(11)	
3	Danny Ledwith		17/08/91	M	22	(4)	5
35	Jordan Loftus		26/04/95	A		(1)	
9	Sean Maguire		01/05/94	A	11	(7)	1
35	Ryan McManus		15/06/96	M		(2)	
5	Evan McMillan		20/11/86	A	27	(3)	4
15	Joseph Ndo	CMR	28/04/76	D	6	(1)	
7	Danny North	ENG	07/09/87	M	22	(5)	7
14	Paul O'Conor		10/08/87	A	21	(7)	5
22	Eric Odhiambo	ENG	12/05/89	M	6	(8)	2
4	Gavin Peers		10/11/85	D	11		
1	Gary Rogers		25/09/81	G	27		
18	John Russell		18/05/85	M	18	(3)	5
16	Kalen Spillane		19/08/91	D	16	(4)	
17	Eamon Zayed	LBY	04/10/83	A	11	(1)	5

University College Dublin AFC

1895 • UCD Bowl (2,500) • ucdsoccer.com

Major honours
FAI Cup (1) 1984

Manager: Aaron Callaghan

2014

07/03	h Bohemians	L	0-3	
14/03	a St Patrick's	L	2-3	Mulhall 2
21/03	h Athlone	W	2-1	Creevy, Ben Mohamed
28/03	a Bray	W	5-3	Morrison 3, Langtry, Clarke
04/04	h Limerick	D	1-1	Boyle
07/04	a Shamrock Rovers	L	0-2	
11/04	h Dundalk	L	1-4	Burke
18/04	a Sligo	L	0-5	
21/04	h Cork	L	0-1	
25/04	a Derry	D	1-1	Benson
02/05	h Drogheda	W	2-1	Benson, Morrisson
09/05	a Bohemians	D	0-0	
16/05	h St Patrick's	D	1-1	Belhout
23/05	a Athlone	L	0-2	
30/05	h Bray	D	0-0	
02/06	a Dundalk	L	2-5	Mulhall, Benson (p)
13/06	a Limerick	L	1-2	Belhout
27/06	h Shamrock Rovers	L	0-2	
13/07	h Sligo	W	1-0	Belhout
18/07	a Cork	L	1-2	Creevy
27/07	h Derry	L	1-6	Benson
01/08	a Drogheda	L	0-4	
08/08	h Bohemians	D	0-0	
15/08	a St Patrick's	L	2-3	Douglas, Benson
18/08	h Athlone	D	1-1	Cannon
29/08	a Bray	L	0-2	
05/09	h Limerick	L	1-3	Cannon
26/09	h Dundalk	L	0-2	
30/09	a Shamrock Rovers	L	0-3	
04/10	a Sligo	L	0-4	
10/10	h Cork	L	0-4	
17/10	a Derry	W	1-0	Langtry
24/10	h Drogheda	W	1-0	Cannon

No	Name	Nat	DoB	Pos	Aps	(s)	Gls
12	Michael Barker		16/08/93	D	8	(3)	
22	Samir Belhout		15/07/91	A	21	(8)	3
19	Ayman Ben Mohamed	TUN	08/12/94	M	14	(3)	1
10	Robbie Benson		07/05/92	A	33		5
5	Tomas Boyle		10/08/91	D	12		1
7	Gary Burke		27/03/91	M	9	(11)	1
24	Conor Cannon		23/08/94	M	12	(2)	3
9	Dean Clarke		29/03/93	A	6		1
16	Niall Corbet		13/11/94	G	2		
15	Sean Coyne		23/05/95	D	5	(2)	
8	Robbie Creevy		24/08/89	M	31		2
17	Colm Crowe		12/04/95	M	16	(6)	
14	Hugh Douglas		22/06/93	M	24	(2)	1
18	Adam Harney		12/06/96	D		(1)	
6	James Kavanagh		12/01/93	M	22	(6)	
3	Mark Langtry		09/12/87	D	19		2
2	Gareth Matthews		13/02/90	D	26	(2)	
18	Barry McCabe		12/01/92	M	2	(2)	
12	Timmy Molloy		07/04/94	A	9	(5)	
24	Cillian Morrison		25/07/91	A	12	(2)	4
11	Chris Mulhall		09/11/88	M	25	(5)	3
1	Conor O'Donnell		17/01/94	G	31		
21	Tom O'Halloran		05/11/92	M	4	(7)	
4	Ian Ryan		09/06/87	D	18	(1)	
13	Michael Scott		23/04/94	D		(1)	
23	Kaleem Simon		08/07/96	M		(3)	
25	Greg Sloggett		03/07/96	M	1	(3)	
13	Daniel Tobin		27/02/97	D	1	(4)	
23	Dwayne Wilson		14/06/87	M		(6)	

Top goalscorers

Patrick Hoban   Christy Fagan

20	Patrick Hoban (Dundalk)
	Christy Fagan (St Patrick's)
18	Conán Byrne (St Patrick's)
14	Rory Gaffney (Limerick)
13	Daniel Corcoran (Bohemians)
	Billy Dennehy (Cork)
11	Mark O'Sullivan (Cork)
	Michael Duffy (Derry)
	Rory Patterson (Derry)
	Richie Towell (Dundalk)
	Chris Forrester (St Patrick's)

Promoted clubs

Longford Town FC

1924 • City Calling Stadium (4,500) • ltfc.ie

Major honours
FAI Cup (2) 2003, 2004

Manager: Tony Cousins

Galway FC

2013 • Eamonn Deacy Park (5,000) • galwayunitedfc.ie

Manager: Tommy Dunne

Second level final table 2014

		Pld	W	D	L	F	A	Pts
1	Longford Town FC	28	18	6	4	56	19	60
2	Shelbourne FC	28	14	10	4	46	30	52
3	Galway FC	28	13	10	5	47	23	49
4	Wexford Youths FC	28	13	7	8	45	35	46
5	Finn Harps FC	28	7	11	10	26	28	32
6	Shamrock Rovers FC B	28	7	5	16	25	50	26
7	Waterford United FC	28	6	7	15	25	43	25
8	Cobh Ramblers FC	28	2	8	18	24	66	14

Promotion/Relegation play-offs

(17/10/14 & 24/10/14)
Galway 2-0 Shelbourne
Shelbourne 1-2 Galway
(Galway 4-1)

(27/10/14 & 31/10/14)
UCD 1-2 Galway
Galway 3-0 UCD
(Galway 5-1)

DOMESTIC CUP

FAI Cup 2014

SECOND ROUND

(01/06/14)
Collinstown 0-2 Avondale
Mayfield 1-3 Malahide

(06/06/14)
Athlone 0-2 Longford
Belgrove 0-1 Finn Harps
Cork 6-0 St Mochta's
Drogheda 4-2 Cockhill
Dundalk 3-0 Sligo
Shelbourne 1-0 Waterford
St Patrick's CY 0-3 St Patrick's Athletic
UCD 1-3 Galway
Wexford 1-0 Bray

(07/06/14)
Cobh 0-2 Derry
Limerick 1-2 Bohemians
Sheriff 0-4 Shamrock Rovers

(08/06/14)
Ballynanty 2-1 Phoenix
UCC 0-0 St Michael's

Replay

(15/06/14)
St Michael's 4-2 UCC

THIRD ROUND

(22/08/14)
Cork 2-2 Bohemians
Derry 3-0 Malahide
Dundalk 2-1 Galway
Shamrock Rovers 3-0 Longford
St Patrick's Athletic 1-1 Shelbourne
Wexford 1-2 Finn Harps

(23/08/14)
Ballynanty 0-4 Drogheda
St Michael's 0-0 Avondale

Replays

(25/08/14)
Bohemians 1-0 Cork

(30/08/14)
Avondale 2-0 St Michael's

(01/09/14)
Shelbourne 0-1 St Patrick's Athletic

QUARTER-FINALS

(12/09/14)
Drogheda 2-2 Derry *(McNally 23, 53; McBride 13, Lowry 84)*
Shamrock Rovers 0-0 Dundalk
St Patrick's Athletic 3-2 Bohemians *(Fagan 23, 59, Brennan 49; Pender 20, Price 82)*

(14/09/14)
Avondale 1-1 Finn Harps *(D Long 77; Funston 52)*

Replays

(15/09/14)
Dundalk 1-2 Shamrock Rovers *(Hoban 41; Sheppard 81, 88)*

(16/09/14)
Derry 5-0 Drogheda *(P McEleney 6, Patterson 60, 81, 90+1, Duffy 72)*

(17/09/14)
Finn Harps 4-1 Avondale *(Harkin 11, McNulty 38, McHugh 60, 66p; R Long 85)*

SEMI-FINALS

(05/10/14)
Shamrock Rovers 1-1 Derry *(Kelly 78; Patterson 87)*
St Patrick's Athletic 6-1 Finn Harps *(Brennan 20, 65, Hoare 37, Byrne 44, 78, Fagan 70; Mailey 29)*

Replay

(07/10/14)
Derry 2-0 Shamrock Rovers *(Duffy 88, Patterson 90)*

FINAL

(02/11/14)
Aviva Stadium, Dublin
ST PATRICK'S ATHLETIC FC 2 *(Fagan 51, 90+3)*
DERRY CITY FC 0
Referee: Sutton
ST PATRICK'S: *Clarke, O'Brien (McCormack 80), Hoare, Browne, Bermingham, Fahey (Chambers 90+4), Bolger, Brennan, Byrne, Forrester (Fitzgerald 90+1), Fagan*
DERRY: *Doherty, Barry, McBride (B McNamee 65), Jarvis, Molloy, Dooley, Ventre, Lowry, Duffy, P McEleney (Houston 90+1), Patterson*

Joy and relief for St Patrick's as they break their long FAI Cup final hoodoo with victory over Derry

ROMANIA
Federaţia Română de Fotbal (FRF)

Address	Casa Fotbalului	**President**	Răzvan Burleanu
	Str. Serg. Serbanica	**General secretary**	Gheorghe
	Vasile 12		Chivorchian
	RO-022186 Bucureşti	**Media officer**	Paul-Daniel Zaharia
Tel	+40 21 325 0678	**Year of formation**	1909
Fax	+40 21 325 0679	**National stadium**	Arena Naţională,
E-mail	frf@frf.ro		Bucharest (55,611)
Website	frf.ro		

KEY:

● – UEFA Champions League
● – UEFA Europa League
● – Promoted
● – Relegated

LIGA I CLUBS

 1 FC Astra Giurgiu

 2 FC Botoşani

 3 FC Braşov

 4 FC Ceahlăul Piatra Neamţ

 5 CFR 1907 Cluj

 6 CS Concordia Chiajna

 7 FC Dinamo Bucureşti

 8 CS Gaz Metan Mediaş

 9 CSMS Iaşi

 10 FC Oţelul Galaţi

 11 CS Pandurii Târgu Jiu

 12 FC Petrolul Ploieşti

 13 FC Rapid Bucureşti

 14 FC Steaua Bucureşti

 15 ASA Tîrgu Mureş

 16 FC Universitatea Cluj

 17 CS Universitatea Craiova

 18 FC Viitorul

PROMOTED CLUBS

 19 FC Voluntari

 20 ACS Poli Timişoara

Staying power steers Steaua home

FC Steaua Bucureşti made it three Liga I titles in a row in 2014/15, with inexperienced new coach Constantin Gâlcă also taking the club to their first league and cup double for 18 years.

It was not all plain sailing for Steaua, however, as they blew a big halfway lead in the league, returning to the top of the table only at the finish as surprise challengers ASA Tîrgu Mureş, outstanding in the spring, lost their last two matches. The double was completed with an easy 3-0 win over FC Universitatea Cluj in the final of the Romanian Cup.

New boss Gâlcă delivers domestic double

Tîrgu Mureş falter at finish in Liga I title race

Iordănescu back in charge of national team

Domestic league

Champions in each of the previous two seasons under Laurenţiu Reghecampf, Steaua's bid for a first hat-trick of Liga I titles since they won six in a row during the 1990s looked to be well on track under new boss Gâlcă as their opening 17 fixtures yielded 14 wins, giving them a huge lead at the winter break, with newly-promoted Tîrgu Mureş 13 points adrift and seemingly out of contention.

Steaua, however, were to have their squad picked apart in January, with three key players – Claudiu Keşerü, Lucian Sânmărtean and Łukasz Szukała – all departing. Keşerü was the league's leading marksman at the time, six of his 12 goals having come in one game, against CS Pandurii Târgu Jiu, which surpassed the club record of five set 20 years earlier by Gâlcă. Steaua looked half a team without those three internationals, and as they shipped points with alarming regularity, Tîrgu Mureş, under newly appointed coach Liviu Ciobotariu, went into overdrive, gradually eroding Steaua's lead to the point where they actually surrendered it, Tîrgu Mureş defeating the leaders 1-0 in Bucharest to take over at the top with a two-point advantage.

Whereas Ciobotariu's team were confident chasers, they proved to be fragile front-runners, and when they lost their next two away games while Steaua won theirs, it left Gâlcă's men two points ahead going into the final day.

With Tîrgu Mureş benefiting from the head-to-head advantage, Steaua had to win at CSMS Iaşi to be sure of finishing first. They only drew 0-0, but Tîrgu Mureş could not take advantage, their dream of a first championship win turning to dust as they conceded a late goal to lose 2-1 at home to FC Oţelul Galaţi – one of six clubs relegated as the Liga I reduced its number to 14 in 2014/15.

Domestic cup

Three days after snatching a 26th league title, Steaua added a 23rd Romanian Cup. Their opponents were relegated Universitatea Cluj and, as in the team's two league meetings, it was a one-sided affair, Steaua midfielder Adrian Popa scoring two goals and assisting another for Raul Rusescu. That result should have enabled CFR 1907 Cluj, fourth in the league, to take Romania's third UEFA Europa League spot, but they and the three teams below them were all denied a European licence, so eighth-placed FC Botoşani – the only Liga I team other than Steaua to employ just one coach (Leo Grozavu) in 2014/15 – claimed it instead.

Europe

Steaua missed out on the UEFA Champions League group stage on penalties but then marked their entry into the UEFA Europa League with a record 6-0 win against Aalborg BK, only to be ultimately denied further progress by the Danish champions. FC Astra Giurgiu also reached the group stage but won only once, at home to GNK Dinamo Zagreb, the club that had ousted FC Petrolul Ploieşti – surprisingly convincing conquerors of FC Viktoria Plzeň – in the play-offs.

National team

Victor Piţurcă's third stint as Romania coach ended in October when he left for Saudi Arabia. The man who replaced him was Anghel Iordănescu, another embarking on a third spell in charge, the first of those having incorporated Romania's memorable run to the 1994 FIFA World Cup quarter-finals. The 'General' had been out of the game for several years, having taken up politics, but he carried on where Piţurcă had left off, matching his predecessor's record of two wins and a draw in three UEFA EURO 2016 qualifiers to give Romania – the team with the best defensive record in the competition – an excellent chance of going through to France as Group F winners.

DOMESTIC SEASON AT A GLANCE

Liga I 2014/15 final table

		Pld	Home					Away					Total					Pts
			W	D	L	F	A	W	D	L	F	A	W	D	L	F	A	
1	**FC Steaua Bucureşti**	34	10	2	5	32	12	12	3	2	27	11	22	5	7	59	23	71
2	ASA Tîrgu Mureş	34	14	2	1	29	7	6	6	5	22	18	20	8	6	51	25	68
3	FC Astra Giurgiu	34	10	4	3	37	13	5	8	4	16	14	15	12	7	53	27	57
4	CFR 1907 Cluj	34	10	2	5	32	17	6	7	4	14	12	16	9	9	46	29	57
5	CS Universitatea Craiova	34	7	7	3	19	10	7	4	6	21	24	14	11	9	40	34	53
6	FC Petrolul Ploieşti	34	6	3	8	19	20	8	7	2	23	10	14	10	10	42	30	52
7	FC Dinamo Bucureşti	34	7	6	4	25	19	6	3	8	22	25	13	9	12	47	44	48
8	FC Botoşani	34	7	5	5	22	17	5	6	6	18	26	12	11	11	40	43	47
9	CS Pandurii Târgu Jiu	34	6	6	5	25	16	6	3	8	22	26	12	9	13	47	42	45
10	CSMS Iaşi	34	7	6	4	18	17	4	4	9	13	22	11	10	13	31	39	43
11	FC Viitorul	34	5	4	8	19	21	6	6	5	25	33	11	10	13	44	54	43
12	CS Concordia Chiajna	34	6	7	4	20	16	3	7	7	19	28	9	14	11	39	44	41
13	CS Gaz Metan Mediaş	34	5	8	4	16	14	3	7	7	13	20	8	15	11	29	34	39
14	FC Braşov	34	5	4	8	20	24	4	5	8	13	22	9	9	16	33	46	36
15	FC Universitatea Cluj	34	5	7	5	14	18	4	10	15	15	23	8	11	15	29	41	35
16	FC Rapid Bucureşti	34	3	6	8	13	23	5	3	9	8	19	8	9	17	21	42	33
17	FC Oţelul Galaţi	34	4	5	8	16	19	3	6	8	8	26	7	11	16	24	45	32
18	FC Ceahlăul Piatra Neamţ	34	2	7	8	14	27	4	2	11	11	31	6	9	19	25	58	27

European qualification 2015/16

Champion/Cup winner: FC Steaua Bucureşti (second qualifying round)

ASA Tîrgu Mureş (third qualifying round)
FC Astra Giurgiu (second qualifying round)
FC Botoşani (first qualifying round)

Top scorer Grégory Tadé (CFR Cluj), 18 goals
Relegated clubs FC Ceahlăul Piatra Neamţ, FC Oţelul Galaţi, FC Rapid Bucureşti, FC Universitatea Cluj, FC Braşov, CS Gaz Metan Mediaş
Promoted clubs FC Voluntari, ACS Poli Timişoara
Cup final FC Steaua Bucureşti 3-0 FC Universitatea Cluj

Team of the season
(4-2-3-1)

Coach: Ciobotariu (Tîrgu Mureş)

Player of the season

Alexandru Chipciu
(FC Steaua Bucureşti)

Having joined Steaua from FC Braşov in January 2012, Chipciu celebrated his third successive Liga I title in 2014/15. It was unquestionably the best of his three championship-winning campaigns, although, like many of his team-mates, his finest form came when the club were flying high in the first half of the season. As several team-mates left in the winter, the do-it-all Romania midfielder stayed on to see the job through, completing the double-winning campaign with 45 games in all competitions and eight goals.

Newcomer of the season

Claudiu Bumba
(ASA Tîrgu Mureş)

While his FC Steaua Bucureşti rival Nicolae Stanciu proved to be a decisive figure during the Liga I run-in, Bumba grabbed the headlines more frequently during the season as a whole, the young Tîrgu Mureş playmaker impressing in particular during the club's spring surge after a proposed mid-season transfer to FC Astra Giurgiu had fallen through. The 21-year-old was a frustrated runner-up at the end of the season, but he had done enough to earn a summer transfer to Israeli club Hapoel Tel-Aviv FC.

Stăncioiu (Tîrgu Mureş)
Alcénat (Petrolui) — Varela (Steaua) — Constantin (Tîrgu Mureş) — Vătăjelu (U Craiova)
N'Doye (Tîrgu Mureş) — Brandán (U Craiova)
Budescu (Astra) — Chipciu (Steaua) — Bawab (U Craiova)
Tadé (CFR Cluj)

NATIONAL TEAM

International tournament appearances

FIFA World Cup (7) 1930, 1934, 1938, 1970, 1990 (2nd round), 1994 (qtr-finals), 1998 (2nd round)
UEFA European Championship (4) 1984, 1996, 2000 (qtr-finals), 2008

Top five all-time caps

Dorinel Munteanu (134); Gheorghe Hagi (124); Gheorghe Popescu (115); **Răzvan Raț** (103); László Bölöni (102)

Top five all-time goals

Gheorghe Hagi & Adrian Mutu (35); Iuliu Bodola (30); **Ciprian Marica** & Viorel Moldovan (25)

Results 2014/15

Date	Opponent		Venue	Result		Scorers
07/09/14	Greece (ECQ)	A	Piraeus	W	1-0	*Marica (10p)*
11/10/14	Hungary (ECQ)	H	Bucharest	D	1-1	*Rusescu (45)*
14/10/14	Finland (ECQ)	A	Helsinki	W	2-0	*Stancu (54, 83)*
14/11/14	Northern Ireland (ECQ)	H	Bucharest	W	2-0	*Papp (74, 79)*
18/11/14	Denmark (ECQ)	H	Bucharest	W	2-0	*Keșerü (53, 58)*
29/03/15	Faroe Islands (ECQ)	H	Ploiesti	W	1-0	*Keșerü (21)*
13/06/15	Northern Ireland (ECQ)	A	Belfast	D	0-0	

Appearances 2014/15

Coach: Victor Pițurcă /(27/10/14) Anghel Iordănescu	08/05/56 04/05/50		GRE	HUN	FIN	NIR	Den	FRO	NIR	Caps	Goals
Ciprian Tătărușanu	09/02/86	Fiorentina (ITA)	G	G	G	G			G	29	-
Gabriel Tamaș	09/11/83	Watford (ENG) /Steaua	D						s90	65	3
Vlad Chiricheș	14/11/89	Tottenham (ENG)	D	D	D	D	D70	D	D	32	-
Dragoș Grigore	07/09/86	Toulouse (FRA)	D	D	D	D		D	D	12	-
Răzvan Raț	26/05/81	PAOK (GRE)	D	D	D	D	D	D		103	2
Ovidiu Hoban	27/12/82	H. Beer Sheva (ISR)	M84	M	M	s80	M			11	-
Alexandru Chipciu	18/05/89	Steaua	M90	M	M49	M	s46		M61	18	3
Mihai Pintilii	09/11/84	Al-Hilal (KSA) /Pandurii	M	M	M	M	s84	M	M	24	1
Alexandru Maxim	08/07/90	Stuttgart (GER)	M68	M84		s58	M64	M	M90	21	2
Bogdan Stancu	28/06/87	Gençlerbirliği (TUR)	M	s84	A86	A46			s61	34	8
Ciprian Marica	02/10/85	Konyaspor (TUR)	A 53*							72	25
Gabriel Enache	18/08/90	Astra	s68		s84		M46			3	-
Andrei Prepeliță	08/12/85	Steaua	s84				M84	s86	M	4	-
Gabriel Torje	22/11/89	Konyaspor (TUR)	s90		M	M80		s71	M	41	10
Dorin Goian	12/12/80	Asteras (GRE)		D5						60	5
Lucian Sânmărtean	13/03/80	Steaua /Al-Ittihad (KSA)		M67	s49	M	M46	M86		12	-
Raul Rusescu	09/07/88	Steaua		A	s86		M60			8	1
Florin Gardoș	29/10/88	Southampton (ENG)		s5			D			14	-
Cristian Tănase	18/02/87	Steaua		s67	M84	M58		s60		41	6
Srdjan Luchin	04/03/86	Steaua			D		s79			11	1
Paul Papp	11/11/89	Steaua				D	D79	D	D	15	3
Claudiu Keșerü	02/12/86	Steaua /Al-Gharafa (QAT)				s46	A	A	A72	5	4
Costel Pantilimon	01/02/87	Sunderland (ENG)					G	G		20	-
Adrian Popa	24/07/88	Steaua					s46	M71		6	-
Eric Bicfalvi	05/02/88	Volyn (UKR)					s64			1	-
Cosmin Moți	03/12/84	Ludogorets (BUL)					s70			6	-
Laszlo Sepsi	07/06/87	Tirgu Mureș							D	4	-
Florin Andone	11/04/93	Córdoba (ESP)							s72	1	-

EUROPE

FC Steaua Bucureşti

CHAMPIONS LEAGUE

Second qualifying round - Strømsgodset IF (NOR)
A 1-0 *Iancu (49)*
Arlauskis, Râpă, Szukała, Chipciu, Iancu (Filip 75), Tănase, Prepeliță, Latovlevici, Sânmărtean (Vâlceanu 90), Pârvulescu (Stanciu 58), Varela. Coach: Constantin Gâlcă (ROU)
H 2-0 *Râpă (72), Stanciu (84)*
Arlauskis, Râpă, Szukała, Chipciu (Vâlceanu 87), Filip, Tănase, Prepeliță, Latovlevici, Sânmărtean (Stanciu 60), Varela, Popa (Grădinaru 71). Coach: Constantin Gâlcă (ROU)

Third qualifying round - FC Aktobe (KAZ)
A 2-2 *Keşerü (44), Prepeliță (78)*
Arlauskis, Râpă, Szukała, Chipciu (Iancu 88), Filip, Tănase, Prepeliță, Latovlevici, Keşerü (Lemnaru 71), Varela, Popa (Stanciu 84). Coach: Constantin Gâlcă (ROU)
H 2-1 *Chipciu (3), Stanciu (39)*
Arlauskis, Râpă, Szukała, Chipciu, Tănase (Pîrvulescu 82), Prepeliță, Stanciu (Iancu 48), Latovlevici, Sânmărtean (Filip 12), Varela, Popa. Coach: Constantin Gâlcă (ROU)

Play-offs - PFC Ludogorets Razgrad (BUL)
H 1-0 *Chipciu (88)*
Arlauskis, Râpă, Szukała, Chipciu, Prepeliță, Stanciu (Keşerü 57), Latovlevici, Sânmărtean (Filip 90+2), Breeveld, Varela, Popa (Iancu 83). Coach: Constantin Gâlcă (ROU)
A 0-1 (aet; 5-6 on pens)
Arlauskis, Râpă, Szukała, Tănase (Stanciu 5), Prepeliță, Latovlevici (Pârvulescu 67), Sânmărtean (Filip 83), Breeveld, Keşerü, Varela, Popa. Coach: Constantin Gâlcă (ROU)

EUROPA LEAGUE

Group J
Match 1 - Aalborg BK (DEN)
H 6-0 *Sânmărtean (51), Rusescu (59p, 73), Keşerü (61, 65, 72)*
Arlauskis, Râpă (Rusescu 49), Szukała, Chipciu, Prepeliță, Latovlevici, Sânmărtean (Breeveld (Papp 67), Keşerü (Iancu 74), Varela, Popa. Coach: Constantin Gâlcă (ROU)
Match 2 - FC Dynamo Kyiv (UKR)
A 1-3 *Rusescu (89)*
Arlauskis, Szukała, Papp, Chipciu, Iancu (Stanciu 57; Rusescu 82), Tănase, Prepeliță, Latovlevici, Sânmărtean, Keşerü, Varela. Coach: Constantin Gâlcă (ROU)
Match 3 - Rio Ave FC (POR)
H 2-1 *Rusescu (17, 45)*
Arlauskis, Râpă, Szukała, Papp, Tănase, Prepeliță, Latovlevici, Sânmărtean (Filip 89), Rusescu (Stanciu 69), Keşerü, Popa (Breeveld 66). Coach: Constantin Gâlcă (ROU)
Match 4 - Rio Ave FC (POR)
A 2-2 *Keşerü (61), Filip (90+4)*
Arlauskis, Szukała, Papp, Chipciu, Filip, Tănase, Prepeliță, Sânmărtean, Keşerü, Varela, Popa (Bourceanu 75). Coach: Constantin Gâlcă (ROU)
Match 5 - Aalborg BK (DEN)
A 0-1
Arlauskis, Luchin, Papp, Chipciu, Filip, Tănase (Stanciu 77), Sânmărtean, Keşerü, Varela, Bourceanu (Breeveld 65), Popa. Coach: Constantin Gâlcă (ROU)
Match 6 - FC Dynamo Kyiv (UKR)
H 0-2
Arlauskis, Szukała, Papp, Chipciu, Filip (Latovlevici 78), Tănase (Popa 78), Prepeliță, Sânmărtean, Keşerü, Varela, Bourceanu (Rusescu 61). Coach: Constantin Gâlcă (ROU)

FC Astra Giurgiu

EUROPA LEAGUE

Third qualifying round - FC Slovan Liberec (CZE)
H 3-0 *Fatai (4, 74, 81)*
Lung, Ben Youssef, Yahaya, Enache (Rus 85), Budescu, Júnior Morais, Laban, Fatai (Bukari 82), Pliatsikas, Găman, William (Cristescu 87). Coach: Daniel Isăilă (ROU)
A 3-2 *Enache (37), Rus (83), Bukari (89)*
Lung, Yahaya, Enache (Rus 74), Budescu, Júnior Morais, Laban (Seto 37), Oros, Fatai (Bukari 78), Pliatsikas, Găman, William. Coach: Daniel Isăilă (ROU)

Play-offs - Olympique Lyonnais (FRA)
A 2-1 *Fatai (72), Budescu (81p)*
Lung, Ben Youssef, Yahaya, Seto (William 46), Enache, Budescu, Júnior Morais, Laban (Rus 86), Oros, Fatai (Bukari 82), Pliatsikas. Coach: Daniel Isăilă (ROU)
H 0-1
Lung, Ben Youssef, Yahaya, Enache, Budescu (Rus 89), Júnior Morais, Laban (Seto 85), Oros, Bukari (Grandin 90+2), Pliatsikas, William. Coach: Daniel Isăilă (ROU)

Group D
Match 1 - GNK Dinamo Zagreb (CRO)
A 1-5 *Chiţu (82)*
Lung, Ben Youssef, Yahaya (Florescu 74), Enache (Chiţu 57), Budescu, Júnior Morais, Laban, Oros, Fatai (Bukari 65), Pliatsikas, William. Coach: Daniel Isăilă (ROU)
Match 2 - FC Salzburg (AUT)
H 1-2 *Seto (15)*
Lung, Ben Youssef, Seto, Enache, Budescu, Júnior Morais, Laban (Florescu 73), Oros, Bukari, Pliatsikas, William. Coach: Daniel Isăilă (ROU)
Match 3 - Celtic FC (SCO)
A 1-2 *Enache (81)*
Lung, Ben Youssef, Yahaya, Seto (Fatai 78), Enache, Budescu, Júnior Morais, Laban (Florescu 88), Oros, Pliatsikas, William (Rus 87). Coach: Oleh Protasov (UKR)
Match 4 - Celtic FC (SCO)
H 1-1 *William (79)*
Lung, Ben Youssef, Yahaya (Seto 81), Enache, Budescu (Florescu 62), Júnior Morais, Laban, Oros, Bukari, Pliatsikas, Joãozinho (William 46). Coach: Oleh Protasov (UKR)
Red card: Laban 90+2
Match 5 - GNK Dinamo Zagreb (CRO)
H 1-0 *Bukari (50)*
Lung, Florescu, Ben Youssef, Yahaya, Seto, Enache, Budescu (William 76), Júnior Morais, Oros, Bukari (Chiţu 90+2), Rus. Coach: Oleh Protasov (UKR)
Match 6 - FC Salzburg (AUT)
A 1-5 *Florescu (51)*
Lung, Florescu, Ben Youssef, Seto, Budescu (Fatai 90), Júnior Morais, Oros, Chiţu (Yahaya 57), Pliatsikas, Rus, William (Grandin 78). Coach: Oleh Protasov (UKR)

FC Petrolul Ploieşti

EUROPA LEAGUE

Second qualifying round - KS Flamurtari (ALB)
H 2-0 *Nepomuceno (77), Tamuz (84)*
Peçanha, Alcénat, Geraldo Alves, Mutu, Albín (Nepomuceno 46), Hoban, Marinescu (Nkoyi 72), Fanchone, Filipe Teixeira, De Lucas, Tamuz (Morar 85). Coach: Răzvan Lucescu (ROU)
A 3-1 *Filipe Teixeira (39), De Lucas (83), Priso (90)*
Peçanha, Alcénat, Geraldo Alves, Nepomuceno (Priso 59), Mutu, Hoban, Gerson, Fanchone (Beţa 76), Filipe Teixeira, De Lucas, Tamuz (Albín 72). Coach: Răzvan Lucescu (ROU)

Third qualifying round - FC Viktoria Plzeň (CZE)
H 1-1 *Mutu (76)*
Peçanha, Alcénat, Geraldo Alves, Nepomuceno (Priso 72), Albín (Mutu 56), Hoban, Gerson, Fanchone, Filipe Teixeira, De Lucas, Tamuz (Nkoyi 87). Coach: Răzvan Lucescu (ROU)
A 4-1 *Filipe Teixeira (20), Mutu (38), De Lucas (43), Tamuz (69)*
Peçanha, Alcénat, Geraldo Alves, Nepomuceno (Mustivar 64), Mutu (Albín 73), Hoban, Gerson, Fanchone, Filipe Teixeira (Marinescu 83), De Lucas, Tamuz. Coach: Răzvan Lucescu (ROU)

Play-offs - GNK Dinamo Zagreb (CRO)
H 1-3 *Tamuz (45)*
Peçanha, Alcénat, Geraldo Alves, Mutu (Nepomuceno 83), Hoban (Mustivar 50), Priso (Albín 62), Gerson, Fanchone, Filipe Teixeira, De Lucas, Tamuz. Coach: Răzvan Lucescu (ROU)
Red card: Geraldo Alves 90+5
A 1-2 *Albín (59)*
Cobrea, Alcénat, Mustivar (Marinescu 79), Satli, Mutu (Nepomuceno 67), Albín, Hoban, Gerson, Filipe Teixeira, De Lucas (Nkoyi 74), Tamuz. Coach: Răzvan Lucescu (ROU)

CFR 1907 Cluj

EUROPA LEAGUE

Second qualifying round - FK Jagodina (SRB)
H 0-0
Mário Felgueiras, Sušić, Larie, Deac, Muniru, Costea (Jakoliš 58), Ogbu, Negruţ (Christian 75), Tiago Lopes, Rada, Aitor Monroy (Păun 88). Coach: Vasile Miriuţă (HUN)
A 1-0 *Guima (81)*
Mário Felgueiras, Sušić, Larie, Deac (Jakoliš 90+2), Muniru, Costea (Guima 69), Tadé, Negruţ (Christian 85), Rada, Aitor Monroy, Camora. Coach: Vasile Miriuţă (HUN)

Third qualifying round - FC Dinamo Minsk (BLR)
A 0-1
Mário Felgueiras, Sušić, Larie, Deac (Christian 76), Muniru, Costea (Jakoliš 55), Tadé, Negruţ (Guima 59), Rada, Aitor Monroy, Camora. Coach: Vasile Miriuţă (HUN)
H 0-2
Mário Felgueiras, Sušić, Larie, Deac, Muniru, Costea (Jazvić 46), Tadé (Ivanovski 67), Negruţ (Guima 46), Rada, Aitor Monroy, Camora. Coach: Vasile Miriuţă (HUN)
Red card: Rada 26

DOMESTIC LEAGUE CLUB-BY-CLUB

FC Astra Giurgiu

1937 • Marin Anastasovici (7,000) •
afcastragiurgiu.ro
Major honours
Romanian Cup (1) 2014
Coach: Daniel Isăilă;
(10/10/14) Oleh Protasov (UKR);
(04/03/15) Dorinel Munteanu;
(28/04/15) Marius Șumudică

2014
25/07	a Concordia	W	2-0	*Fatai, Budescu*	
03/08	h Brașov	W	5-0	*Seto, Gâman 2 (1p), Enache, Bukari*	
10/08	a Botoșani	L	0-1		
16/08	h Iași	W	2-1	*Seto, Fatai*	
24/08	a Rapid	W	2-0	*William, Grandin*	
31/08	a U Craiova	W	5-0	*Budescu 3 (1p), Bukari, Enache*	
13/09	a CFR Cluj	L	1-4	*William*	
21/09	h Pandurii	W	2-1	*Joãozinho, Bukari*	
28/09	a Steaua	D	0-0		
05/10	h Viitorul	D	0-0		
19/10	a Gaz Metan	D	1-1	*Enache (p)*	
27/10	h Petrolul	D	0-0		
01/11	h Ceahlăul	W	2-1	*Budescu (p), Bukari*	
09/11	a Oțelul	D	1-1	*Alibec*	
22/11	h U Cluj	D	1-1	*Bukari*	
30/11	a Tirgu Mureș	W	1-0		
06/12	h Dinamo	W	6-1	*Budescu, Seto, William, Oros, Alibec, Ben Youssef (p)*	

2015
22/02	h Concordia	D	2-2	*Fatai 2*	
01/03	a Brașov	D	1-1	*Tembo*	
07/03	h Botoșani	W	2-0	*Gâman, Fatai*	
15/03	a Iași	L	0-1		
18/03	h Rapid	W	2-1	*William, Budescu*	
21/03	a U Craiova	D	0-0		
04/04	h CFR Cluj	L	0-1		
09/04	a Pandurii	D	1-1	*Seto*	
12/04	h Steaua	D	0-0		
18/04	a Viitorul	L	0-2		
26/04	h Gaz Metan	L	1-2	*Alibec*	
30/04	a Petrolul	W	2-1	*Seto, Alibec*	
03/05	a Ceahlăul	W	3-1	*og (Ichim), Budescu, Fatai*	
11/05	h Oțelul	W	4-1	*Budescu, Alibec, Seto, William*	
18/05	a U Cluj	D	0-0		
24/05	h Tirgu Mureș	W	3-1	*Alibec 2, Fatai*	
29/05	a Dinamo	W	2-0	*Alibec, Budescu (p)*	

No	Name	Nat	DoB	Pos	Aps	(s)	Gls
7	Denis Alibec		05/01/91	M	9	(7)	8
5	Syam Ben Youssef	TUN	31/03/89	D	21	(2)	1
10	Constantin Budescu		19/02/89	A	26	(2)	10
19	Sadat Bukari	GHA	12/04/89	A	6	(4)	5
20	Aurelian Chițu		25/03/91	A	3	(8)	
18	Marian Cristescu		17/03/85	M	4	(8)	
9	Gabriel Enache		18/08/90	M	30	(1)	3
21	Kehinde Fatai	NGA	19/02/90	A	15	(6)	7
4	George Florescu		21/05/84	M	11	(7)	
25	Valerică Gâman		25/02/89	D	17		3
2	George Gavrilaș		15/12/90	G	3		
22	Toni Gorupec	CRO	04/07/93	D	11		
16	Elliot Grandin	FRA	17/10/87	M		(2)	1
11	Alexandru Ioniță		14/12/94	M		(9)	
23	Joãozinho	POR	02/07/87	D	4		1
13	Júnior Morais	BRA	22/07/86	M	29		
18	Kouassi Kouadja	CIV	22/06/95	D		(1)	
14	Vincent Laban	CYP	09/09/84	M	20	(2)	
1	Silviu Lung		04/06/89	G	31		
28	Nuno Pinto	POR	06/08/86	D	3	(4)	
15	Cristian Oros		15/10/84	D	26	(1)	1
22	Vasilios Pliatsikas	GRE	14/04/88	M	9	(2)	
24	Iulian Roșu		30/05/94	M	1	(4)	
26	Laurențiu Rus		07/05/85	D	10	(5)	
11	Senin Sebai	CIV	18/12/93	A		(4)	
8	Takayuki Seto	JPN	05/02/86	M	29	(3)	6
94	Dan Spătaru		24/05/94	M	3	(3)	
30	Fwayo Tembo	ZAM	09/02/89	M	4	(9)	1
89	Alassane Touré	FRA	09/02/89	D	2		
91	William	BRA	15/12/91	M	30	(1)	5
3	Hubert Wołąkiewicz	POL	21/10/85	D	1		
6	Seidu Yahaya	GHA	31/12/89	M	17	(3)	

FC Botoșani

2001 • Municipal (12,000) • fcbotosani.ro
Coach: Leo Grozavu

2014
27/07	h Gaz Metan	L	0-3		
03/08	a Petrolul	L	1-4	*Batin*	
10/08	h Astra	W	1-0	*Batin*	
17/08	a Oțelul	W	1-0	*Martinus*	
24/08	h U Cluj	W	1-0	*Vașvari (p)*	
31/08	a Tirgu Mureș	L	1-2	*Hadnagy*	
14/09	h Dinamo	W	3-2	*Fülöp, Ngadeu, Ngankam*	
20/09	a Concordia	D	3-3	*Vașvari (p), Fülöp 2*	
27/09	h Brașov	D	0-0		
04/10	a Ceahlăul	W	1-0	*Hadnagy*	
17/10	a Iași	D	2-2	*Martinus, Codoban*	
25/10	h Rapid	W	3-0	*Martinus, Ngankam, Vașvari (p)*	
01/11	a U Craiova	L	1-2	*Vașvari (p)*	
08/11	h CFR Cluj	L	0-1		
23/11	a Pandurii	W	2-1	*Batin, Vașvari (p)*	
01/12	h Steaua	L	0-2		
05/12	a Viitorul	W	2-1	*Hadnagy, Batin*	

2015
21/02	a Gaz Metan	D	1-1	*Hadnagy*	
27/02	h Petrolul	L	0-1		
07/03	a Astra	L	0-2		
14/03	a Oțelul	D	1-1	*Croitoru*	
17/03	a U Cluj	D	0-0		
20/03	h Tirgu Mureș	L	1-2	*Acsinte*	
03/04	a Dinamo	D	0-0		
08/04	h Concordia	W	3-0	*Vașvari, Roșu, Hadnagy*	
12/04	a Brașov	W	1-0	*Hadnagy*	
18/04	h Ceahlăul	W	2-0	*Hadnagy, Ivanovici*	
25/04	h Iași	D	0-0		
28/04	a Rapid	D	2-2	*Ivanovici, Vașvari (p)*	
02/05	h U Craiova	W	2-0	*Acsinte, Batin*	
10/05	a CFR Cluj	L	0-4		
15/05	h Pandurii	D	1-1	*Acsinte*	
24/05	a Steaua	L	0-2		
29/05	h Viitorul	D	4-4	*Croitoru 2, Hadnagy 2 (1p)*	

No	Name	Nat	DoB	Pos	Aps	(s)	Gls
20	Florin Acsinte		10/04/87	D	30		3
25	Marian Anghelina		02/05/91	D		(2)	
29	Paul Batin		29/06/87	A	21	(6)	5
18	Cătălin Bordeianu		18/11/91	M	6	(3)	
23	Rashid Browne	NED	28/09/93	A	2	(3)	
17	Claudiu Codoban		08/04/88	M	3	(6)	1
8	Marius Croitoru		02/10/80	M	26	(5)	3
12	Vasile Curileac		18/02/84	G	24		
28	Cristian Danci		15/07/88	M	17	(9)	
27	Jérémy Faug-Porret	FRA	04/02/87	D	6		
24	Istvan Fülöp		18/05/90	A	16	(1)	3
80	Attila Hadnagy		08/09/80	A	21	(8)	9
30	Sergiu Homei		06/07/87	D	5	(3)	
7	Sebastian Ianc		06/12/86	M	3	(9)	
10	Petre Ivanovici		02/03/90	A	10	(12)	2
1	David Lazar		08/08/91	G	10		
11	Quenten Martinus	CUW	07/03/91	A	24	(6)	3
13	Michael Ngadeu	CMR	23/11/90	D	28		1
21	Roussel Ngankam	CMR	15/09/93	A	15	(10)	2
4	Sergiu Oltean		24/07/87	D	10	(2)	
19	Andrei Patache		29/10/87	D	28		
9	Neluț Roșu		05/07/87	M	6	(7)	1
5	Armand Șvichi		19/04/96	A	2	(4)	
6	Răzvan Tincu		15/07/87	D	30	(1)	
14	Valeriu Tiron	MDA	08/04/93	M		(1)	
22	Călin Tiuț		02/01/92	G		(1)	
10	Gabriel Vașvari		13/11/86	M	31	(2)	7

FC Brașov

1937 • Tineretului (12,670) • no website
Coach: Cornel Țălnar;
(16/08/14) Adrian Szabo;
(11/01/15) Vjekoslav Lokica (CRO);
(19/04/15) Adrian Szabo

2014
27/07	h Petrolul	L	0-1		
03/08	a Astra	L	0-5		
11/08	h Oțelul	D	1-1	*Constantinescu*	
18/08	a U Cluj	D	1-1	*Aganović*	
22/08	h Tirgu Mureș	W	2-1	*Grigorie, Constantinescu*	
30/08	a Dinamo	L	1-2	*Aganović*	
12/09	h Concordia	W	4-1	*Constantinescu 2, Grigorie (p), Leko*	
21/09	a Ceahlăul	D	2-2	*Serginho, L Ganea*	
27/09	a Botoșani	D	0-0		
03/10	h Iași	W	2-0	*Ricardo Machado, Constantinescu*	
17/10	a Rapid	W	1-0	*Aganović*	
24/10	h U Craiova	L	2-3	*Constantinescu (p), L Ganea*	
03/11	a CFR Cluj	W	2-1	*Constantinescu 2 (1p)*	
08/11	h Pandurii	L	0-3		
22/11	a Steaua	L	0-2		
30/11	h Viitorul	L	1-3	*Aganović*	
05/12	a Gaz Metan	L	1-2	*Constantinescu*	

2015
20/02	a Petrolul	L	0-1		
01/03	h Astra	D	1-1	*C Ganea*	
07/03	a Oțelul	D	1-1	*Constantinescu*	
13/03	h U Cluj	W	1-0	*Leko*	
16/03	a Tirgu Mureș	D	0-0		
21/03	h Dinamo	W	1-0	*C Ganea*	
05/04	a Concordia	D	1-1	*Leko*	
09/04	h Ceahlăul	L	0-2		
12/04	h Botoșani	L	0-1		
17/04	a Iași	L	0-1		
24/04	h Rapid	L	1-2	*Novaković*	
29/04	a U Craiova	W	1-0	*Bencun*	
02/05	h CFR Cluj	D	2-2	*Constantinescu, Bencun*	
08/05	a Pandurii	L	0-2		
16/05	h Steaua	L	2-3	*Jurić, Țîră*	
23/05	a Viitorul	W	2-0	*Țîră, Moraru*	
27/05	h Gaz Metan	D	0-0		

No	Name	Nat	DoB	Pos	Aps	(s)	Gls
19	Adnan Aganović	CRO	03/10/87	M	30	(3)	4
3	Artjom Artjunin	EST	24/01/90	D	3		
77	Daniel Barna		22/09/86	D	4	(2)	
21	Marko Bencun	CRO	09/11/92	M	11	(2)	2
24	Vlad Botia		14/09/95	M		(1)	
26	Bruno Madeira	POR	17/09/84	M	11	(1)	
29	Mugurel Buga		16/12/77	A	4	(10)	
7	Alexandru Ciocâlteu		16/04/90	M	2	(14)	
20	Marian Constantinescu		08/08/81	A	33	(1)	11
12	Călin Cristea		06/05/88	M	2		
5	Diogo Santos	POR	13/11/84	M	11		
94	Rareș Enceanu		05/08/94	M	6	(9)	
25	Cristian Ganea		24/05/92	M	15	(1)	2
89	Liviu Ganea		23/02/88	A	12	(11)	2
6	Lucian Goian		10/02/83	D	13	(2)	
6	Alexandru Grigoraș		05/07/89	A		(1)	
31	Ștefan Grigorie		31/01/82	M	14	(1)	2
30	Florin Iacob		16/08/93	G	25	(1)	
8	Tomislav Jurić	CRO	08/04/90	M	14		1
28	Mislav Leko	CRO	10/12/87	D	24	(6)	3
1	Andrei Marinescu		11/02/85	G	5		
16	Gabriel Matei		26/02/90	D	10		
5	Șerban Moraru		09/02/86	D	6	(6)	1
7	Cătălin Munteanu		26/01/79	M	9	(5)	
13	Daniel Mutu		11/09/87	G	4	(1)	
22	Leopold Novak	CRO	03/12/90	D	11	(2)	
47	Saša Novaković	CRO	27/05/91	D	15	(1)	1
10	Georgian Păun		24/10/85	A	1	(1)	
11	Tiberiu Petriș		20/06/94	M		(1)	
23	Ricardo Machado	POR	13/09/88	D	13		1
22	Serginho	POR	13/09/92	D	17		1
32	Bogdan Strǎuț		28/04/86	D	16	(4)	
9	Cătălin Țîră		18/06/94	A	11	(8)	2
25	Alexandru Vagner		19/08/89	D	9	(2)	
4	Damir Zlomislić	BIH	20/07/91	D	13	(1)	

FC Ceahlăul Piatra Neamț

1919 • Ceahlăul (18,000) • fcceahlaul.ro

Coach: Marin Barbu;
(02/08/14) Florin Marin;
(11/01/15) Zé María (BRA);
(20/04/15) Vanja Radinović (SRB)

2014
27/07	a	CFR Cluj	L	0-4	
01/08	h	Tirgu Mureş	L	1-4	Cârjan
09/08	a	Pandurii	W	1-0	Dumitraş
17/08	h	Dinamo	D	1-1	Achim (p)
23/08	a	Steaua	W	1-0	Achim
29/08	h	Concordia	W	2-0	Achim 2 (1p)
13/09	a	Viitorul	L	0-2	
21/09	h	Braşov	D	2-2	Cârjan, Ştefănescu
27/09	a	Gaz Metan	D	2-2	Dumitraş, Marginã
04/10	h	Botoşani	L	0-1	
20/10	a	Petrolul	L	0-2	
25/10	h	Iaşi	D	2-2	Cârjan, Mândruşcă
01/11	a	Astra	L	1-2	Pavel
10/11	a	Rapid	D	1-1	Ştefănescu
22/11	h	Oţelul	L	0-1	
29/11	a	U Craiova	L	0-2	
06/12	h	U Cluj	L	0-6	

2015
23/02	h	CFR Cluj	D	0-0	
02/03	a	Tirgu Mureş	L	0-3	
06/03	h	Pandurii	D	1-1	Sialmas
14/03	a	Dinamo	L	1-3	Marković
18/03	h	Steaua	L	0-1	
23/03	a	Concordia	W	1-0	Francisco Torres
05/04	h	Viitorul	L	1-2	Achim (p)
09/04	a	Braşov	W	2-0	Achim (p), Popadiuc
13/04	h	Gaz Metan	L	0-2	
18/04	a	Botoşani	L	0-2	
27/04	h	Petrolul	D	1-1	Stana
30/04	a	Iaşi	L	0-2	
03/05	h	Astra	L	1-3	Sialmas
11/05	h	Rapid	L	0-2	
17/05	a	Oţelul	L	1-4	Balint
24/05	h	U Craiova	W	2-1	Sialmas, Buden
27/05	a	U Cluj	L	0-2	

No	Name	Nat	DoB	Pos	Aps	(s)	Gls
10	Alexandru Achim		07/04/89	M	19	(1)	6
8	Alexandru Aldea		05/03/95	M	2	(3)	
9	Valentin Balint		07/02/94	A	7	(5)	1
12	Alexandru Barna		06/07/93	G	2		
6	Vinko Buden	CRO	18/01/86	D	11		1
22	Nicolae Calancea	MDA	29/08/86	G	24		
3	Cristian Călin		29/04/94	M		(2)	
7	George Cârjan		07/11/88	A	14	(8)	3
8	Robert Căruţă		14/01/96	M	2	(2)	
4	Lucian Cazan		25/12/89	D	9		
20	Christian Chirieletti	ITA	02/03/88	D	3	(1)	
17	Sebastian Chitoşcă		02/10/92	M	21	(9)	
28	Oleg Clonin	MDA	04/02/88	M	6		
35	Marian Drăghiceanu		07/07/99	A		(1)	
23	Andrei Dumitraş		23/01/88	D	12		2
1	Francisco Torres	BRA	03/09/89	A	5	(2)	1
30	Lucas García	ARG	13/01/88	M	1	(3)	
25	Adrian Gheorghiu		30/11/81	M	13	(9)	
2	Răzvan Gorea		14/01/92	D	9	(3)	
5	Alexandru Ichim		16/01/89	D	19	(1)	
1	Bojan Jović	SRB	01/04/82	G	8	(1)	
8	Tudor Mândruşcă		04/02/89	A	2	(7)	1
3	Andrei Marc		24/04/93	D	15		
32	Alexandru Marginã		08/03/93	A	10	(7)	1
86	Miloš Marković	SRB	10/12/86	D	15		1
2	Dragoş Mateciuc		06/03/93	D		(1)	
15	Oliver Nagy		30/01/89	M	2	(1)	
18	Marius Onciu		23/04/87	M	12	(1)	
19	Andrei Pavel		29/07/92	A	9	(1)	1
27	Doru Popadiuc		18/02/95	M	18	(7)	1
18	Rafael Knief	BRA	24/04/92	M	13	(1)	
13	Marius Rusu		22/02/90	D		(1)	
11	Dimitrios Sialmas	GRE	19/06/86	A	7	(2)	3
21	Vaidas Slavickas	LTU	06/01/86	D	18		
30	Ionel Stana		02/12/82	M	3		1
31	Cătălin Ştefănescu		30/11/94	M	26	(3)	2
16	Sorin Tăbăcariu		23/07/94	M	21	(3)	
33	Andrei Ţepeş		23/02/91	D	4	(6)	
23	Wellyson	BRA	06/03/94	D	12	(1)	

CFR 1907 Cluj

1907 • Dr Constantin Rădulescu (23,500) • cfr1907.ro

Major honours
Romanian League (3) 2008, 2010, 2012; Romanian
Cup (3) 2008, 2009, 2010

Coach: Vasile Miriuţă (HUN);
(24/11/14) (Francisc Dican);
(06/01/15) Eugen Trică;
(03/04/15) (Francisc Dican)

2014
27/07	h	Ceahlăul	W	4-0	Tadé 2, Costea, Negruţ
03/08	a	Pandurii	D	0-0	
10/08	h	Steaua	L	0-1	
18/08	a	Viitorul	W	2-0	Deac, Tadé
25/08	h	Gaz Metan	W	4-1	Guima, Larie, Tadé 2 (1p)
31/08	a	Petrolul	W	2-1	Jakoliš, Tadé
13/09	h	Astra	W	4-1	Deac, Tadé 2 (1p), Guima
20/09	a	Oţelul	W	1-0	Tadé
29/09	h	U Cluj	W	1-0	Tiago Lopes
06/10	a	Tirgu Mureş	L	0-2	
18/10	h	Dinamo	W	2-1	Chanturia (p), Guima
26/10	a	Concordia	D	1-1	og (Dragarski)
03/11	h	Braşov	L	1-2	Chanturia (p)
08/11	a	Botoşani	W	1-0	Jazvić
23/11	h	Iaşi	W	4-0	Ivanovski 2, Tadé, Jazvić
29/11	a	Rapid	D	0-0	
07/12	h	U Craiova	D	0-0	

2015
23/02	a	Ceahlăul	D	0-0	
01/03	h	Pandurii	L	0-4	
08/03	a	Steaua	L	0-1	
15/03	h	Viitorul	L	1-2	Chanturia
19/03	a	Gaz Metan	D	0-0	
22/03	h	Petrolul	L	0-1	
04/04	a	Astra	W	1-0	Larie
07/04	a	Oţelul	W	1-0	Tadé
10/04	a	U Cluj	L	0-1	
17/04	h	Tirgu Mureş	D	2-2	Doré, Tadé
24/04	a	Dinamo	D	1-1	Camora
28/04	h	Concordia	W	2-1	Păun, Tiago Lopes
02/05	a	Braşov	D	2-2	Negruţ, Tadé (p)
10/05	h	Botoşani	W	4-0	Tadé 2, Guima, Chanturia
16/05	a	Iaşi	W	3-0	Tadé 2 (2p), Jakoliš
23/05	h	Rapid	W	2-1	Petrucci, Tadé (p)
30/05	a	U Craiova	L	0-3	

No	Name	Nat	DoB	Pos	Aps	(s)	Gls
44	Aitor Monroy	ESP	18/10/87	M	15		
28	Remo Amadio	ITA	24/11/87	G	4		
45	Camora	POR	10/11/86	D	33		1
93	Catalin Carp	MDA	20/09/93	D	15		
23	Anthony Carter	AUS	31/08/94	A		(3)	
11	Giorgi Chanturia	GEO	11/04/93	A	13	(9)	4
25	Christian	BRA	14/06/89	M	7	(8)	
7	Florin Costea		16/05/85	A	5	(7)	1
7	Ciprian Deac		16/02/86	M	18		2
18	Férébory Doré	CGO	21/01/89	A	9	(5)	1
2	Cornel Ene		21/07/93	D	5	(1)	
9	Guima	POR	11/03/86	A	13	(5)	4
99	Mirko Ivanovski	MKD	31/10/89	A	9	(5)	2
17	Antonio Jakoliš	CRO	28/02/92	A	22	(7)	2
12	Filip Jazvić	CRO	22/10/90	A	11	(7)	2
12	Ionuţ Larie		16/01/87	D	32		2
1	Mário Felgueiras	POR	12/12/86	G	17		
32	Mihai Mincă		08/10/84	G	13		
4	Sulley Muniru	GHA	25/09/92	M	22	(4)	
21	Sergiu Negruţ		01/04/93	A	5	(7)	2
95	Alexandru Păun		01/04/95	M	14	(6)	1
4	Davide Petrucci	ITA	05/10/91	M	12	(2)	1
14	Ionuţ Rada		06/07/82	D	17		
5	Mateo Sušić	BIH	18/11/90	D	16		
16	Veres Szilard		27/01/96	M	7	(6)	
15	Grégory Tadé	FRA	02/09/86	A	26	(1)	18
23	Andrei Tânc		03/10/85	D	3		
22	Tiago Lopes	POR	04/01/89	M	11	(9)	2

CS Concordia Chiajna

1957 • Concordia (5,123) • csconcordia.ro

Coach: Marius Şumudică;
(06/04/15) Marius Baciu

2014
25/07	h	Astra	L	0-2	
02/08	a	Oţelul	W	2-1	Purece 2
11/08	h	U Cluj	L	0-2	
17/08	a	Tirgu Mureş	L	0-2	
22/08	h	Dinamo	D	0-0	
29/08	a	Ceahlăul	L	0-2	
12/09	h	Braşov	L	1-4	Fernando Henrique
20/09	h	Botoşani	D	3-3	Purece, Maftei, Fernando Henrique (p)
26/09	a	Iaşi	W	2-1	Pena, Wellington
03/10	h	Rapid	D	0-0	
19/10	a	U Craiova	D	1-1	Wellington (p)
26/10	h	CFR Cluj	D	1-1	Bagarić
04/11	a	Pandurii	D	1-1	Serediuc
09/11	h	Steaua	L	0-1	
21/11	a	Viitorul	D	2-2	Dina, Florea
28/11	h	Gaz Metan	D	1-1	Dina 2
08/12	a	Petrolul	D	2-2	Dina, Florea (p)

2015
22/02	a	Astra	D	2-2	Wellington 2
27/02	h	Oţelul	W	3-0	Dina 2, Purece
08/03	a	U Cluj	D	0-0	
13/03	h	Tirgu Mureş	D	0-0	
17/03	a	Dinamo	W	3-0	Ricardo Alves, og (Elhamed), Dina
23/03	h	Ceahlăul	L	0-1	
05/04	h	Braşov	D	1-1	Bucurică
08/04	a	Botoşani	L	0-3	
11/04	h	Iaşi	W	2-1	Fernando Henrique, Grigorie
20/04	a	Rapid	L	0-1	
24/04	h	U Craiova	D	2-2	Maftei, Dina
28/04	a	CFR Cluj	L	1-2	Serediuc
01/05	h	Pandurii	W	1-0	Dina
10/05	a	Steaua	D	2-2	Fernando Henrique 2 (1p)
17/05	h	Viitorul	W	2-0	Maftei, Fernando Henrique
22/05	a	Gaz Metan	L	0-2	
27/05	h	Petrolul	W	3-2	Cristea, Purece, Pena

No	Name	Nat	DoB	Pos	Aps	(s)	Gls
27	Cristian Albu		17/08/93	D		(1)	
17	Matej Bagarić	CRO	16/01/89	D	14		1
30	Liviu Băjenaru		06/05/83	M	4	(2)	
16	Mario Brlečić	CRO	01/01/89	M	7		
6	Bruno Madeira	POR	17/09/84	M	12	(1)	
11	Bogdan Bucurică		11/02/86	D	29		1
11	Cristian Ciobanu		03/07/94	M	1		
14	Adrian Cristea		30/11/83	M	7	(6)	1
88	Donovan Deekman	NED	23/06/88	A		(3)	
15	Leoh Digbeu	CIV	25/06/90	M	2	(1)	
9	Mihai Dina		15/09/85	A	16	(12)	9
27	Hristijan Dragarski	MKD	16/04/92	D	8	(4)	
5	Alexander Dyulgerov	BUL	19/04/90	D	7	(2)	
23	Fernando Henrique	BRA	23/02/89	M	30	(2)	6
11	Daniel Florea		17/04/88	A	11	(10)	2
30	Ştefan Grigorie		30/01/82	M	4	(4)	1
20	Florin Ilie		18/06/92	D		(1)	
15	Florin Lovin		11/02/82	M	19	(1)	
15	Daniel Lung		02/03/87	D	3		
24	Vasile Maftei		01/01/81	D	25		3
2	Florin Matache		03/08/82	G	19		
16	Nicolae Muşat		04/12/86	D	4	(3)	
6	Olberdam	BRA	06/02/85	M	3		
26	Marius Pena		02/05/85	A	15	(7)	2
10	Florin Purece		06/11/91	M	19	(10)	5
5	Robert Răducanu		05/09/96	M		(1)	
77	Cristian Raiciu		03/07/96	M		(2)	
18	Victor Râmniceanu		30/11/89	G	15		
18	Stevan Reljić	MNE	31/08/86	D	4		
25	Ricardo Alves	POR	09/05/91	D	28		1
93	Neluţ Roşu		05/07/93	M	4	(8)	
7	Tiberiu Serediuc		02/07/92	A	17	(11)	2
77	Alexandru Stan		07/02/89	M	19	(5)	
20	Filip Timov	MKD	22/05/92	M	2	(1)	
2	Alexandru Vagner		19/08/89	D	11	(1)	
99	Wellington	BRA	05/10/87	A	12	(2)	4

FC Dinamo Bucureşti

1948 • Dinamo (15,032) • fcdinamo.ro

Major honours
Romanian League (18) 1955, 1962, 1963, 1964,
1965, 1971, 1973, 1975, 1977, 1982, 1983, 1984,
1990, 1992, 2000 ,2002, 2004, 2007; Romanian
Cup (13) 1959, 1964, 1968, 1982, 1984, 1986, 1990,
2000, 2001, 2003, 2004, 2005, 2012

Coach: Flavius Stoican;
(13/11/14) Ion Dănciulescu;
(07/01/15) Mihai Teja;
(12/03/15) Flavius Stoican;
(06/05/15) Mircea Rednic

2014

28/07	h	Oţelul	W 4-0	Elton Figueiredo, Biliński 3 (1p)
04/08	a	U Cluj	W 3-2	Matei (p), Lazăr, Biliński
09/08	h	Tîrgu Mureş	D 1-1	og (Balaur)
17/08	a	Ceahlăul	D 1-1	Matei
22/08	a	Concordia	D 0-0	
30/08	h	Braşov	W 2-1	Cordoş, Matei
14/09	a	Botoşani	L 2-3	Alexe (p), Gavrilă
20/09	h	Iaşi	W 1-0	Alexe
27/09	a	Rapid	W 3-0	Cordoş, Alexe, Bărboianu
05/10	h	U Craiova	L 0-1	Biliński (p)
18/10	a	CFR Cluj	L 1-2	Lazăr
26/10	h	Pandurii	W 3-2	Alexe, Rotariu, Biliński
31/10	a	Steaua	L 0-3	
07/11	h	Viitorul	L 2-3	Gavrilă, Petre
21/11	a	Gaz Metan	W 2-1	Mansaly, Biliński
30/11	h	Petrolul	D 0-0	
06/12	a	Astra	L 1-6	Biliński

2015

21/02	h	Oţelul	W 1-0	Niculae
28/02	a	U Cluj	W 3-0	Biliński 2, Lazăr
06/03	h	Tîrgu Mureş	L 1-2	Biliński
14/03	h	Ceahlăul	W 3-1	Grozav 2, Niculae
17/03	h	Concordia	L 0-3	
21/03	a	Braşov	L 0-1	
03/04	a	Botoşani	D 0-0	
07/04	a	Iaşi	L 0-1	
11/04	h	Rapid	W 2-0	og (Čmovš), Gavrilă
19/04	a	U Craiova	D 0-0	
24/04	h	CFR Cluj	D 1-1	Elhamed
28/04	a	Pandurii	L 2-3	Niculae, Alexe
03/05	h	Steaua	L 1-3	Elhamed
08/05	a	Viitorul	W 2-0	Alexe, Bunoza
15/05	h	Gaz Metan	D 1-1	og (Pleşca)
22/05	a	Petrolul	W 3-0	Gavrilă, Elhamed, Grozav
29/05	h	Astra	L 0-2	

No	Name	Nat	DoB	Pos	Aps	(s)	Gls
55	Marius Alexe		22/02/90	M	20	(6)	6
20	Ştefan Bărboianu		24/01/88	D	26		1
9	Kamil Biliński	POL	23/01/88	A	24	(9)	11
6	Gordan Bunoza	BIH	05/02/88	D	16		1
6	Andrei Cordoş		06/06/88	D	13		2
18	Marian Cristescu		17/03/85	M	8	(6)	
16	Alexandre Durimel	FRA	16/03/90	D	9	(1)	
4	Hatem Elhamed	ISR	18/03/91	D	11	(2)	3
17	Elton Figueiredo	BRA	12/02/86	M	12		1
14	Collins Fai	CMR	13/08/92	D	24		
7	Steliano Filip		15/05/94	D	20	(3)	
70	Dragoş Fîrţulescu		15/05/89	M		(1)	
77	Bogdan Gavrilă		06/02/92	M	4	(20)	4
88	Constantin Grecu		08/06/88	D	11	(1)	
5	Nicolae Grigore		19/07/83	M	12		
7	Gheorghe Grozav		29/09/90	A	8	(3)	3
93	Valentin Lazăr		21/08/89	M	20	(4)	3
22	Denis Lemac		24/07/94	A		(1)	
19	Boubacar Mansaly	SEN	04/02/88	M	16	(2)	1
1	Alexandru Marc		16/01/83	G	23		
21	Andrei Marc		29/04/93	D	10	(1)	
10	Cosmin Matei		30/09/91	M	24	(2)	3
34	Kristijan Naumovski	MKD	17/09/88	G	8		
27	Ionuţ Nedelcearu		25/04/96	D	12	(1)	
29	Marius Niculae		16/05/81	A	7	(6)	3
15	Patrick Petre		09/05/97	M		(2)	1
24	Adrian Popa		07/04/90	D	4		
3	Ricardo Machado	POR	13/09/88	D	5	(1)	
8	Dorin Rotariu		29/07/95	M	14	(17)	1
12	Cătălin Samoilă		12/01/90	G	3		
8	Ionuţ Şerban		07/08/95	D	2	(9)	
11	Serginho	POR	12/10/85	D	5		
16	Kevin Trabalka		28/11/96	A		(1)	
26	Robert Văduva		05/09/92	M		(1)	
30	Wanderson	BRA	08/02/90	M	3	(2)	

CS Gaz Metan Mediaş

1945 • Municipal (7,814) •
gaz-metan-medias.ro

Coach: Cristian Dulca;
(29/11/14) Dan Matei;
(16/04/15) (Ion Balaur)

2014

27/07	a	Botoşani	W 3-0	Todea, Tahar (p), Figliomeni
04/08	h	Iaşi	D 0-0	
08/08	a	Rapid	D 1-1	Llullaku
15/08	h	U Craiova	W 1-0	Figliomeni
25/08	a	CFR Cluj	L 1-4	Petre
29/08	h	Pandurii	L 0-2	
12/09	a	Steaua	L 1-3	Llullaku
19/09	h	Viitorul	W 3-1	Roman, Figliomeni, Petre
27/09	h	Ceahlăul	D 2-2	Tahar, Roman
04/10	a	Petrolul	L 0-1	
19/10	h	Astra	D 1-1	Petre (p)
24/10	a	Oţelul	D 1-1	Roman
01/11	h	U Cluj	D 1-1	Llullaku
07/11	a	Tîrgu Mureş	L 0-2	
21/11	h	Dinamo	L 1-2	Tahar
28/11	a	Concordia	L 0-2	
05/12	h	Braşov	W 2-1	Llullaku 2

2015

21/02	a	Botoşani	D 1-1	Curtean
28/02	a	Iaşi	L 0-1	
09/03	h	Rapid	L 0-1	
14/03	a	U Craiova	D 1-1	Llullaku
19/03	h	CFR Cluj	D 0-0	
22/03	a	Pandurii	W 1-0	Roman
05/04	h	Steaua	L 1-2	Roman
08/04	a	Viitorul	L 0-1	
13/04	a	Ceahlăul	D 0-0	
18/04	h	Petrolul	D 0-0	
26/04	a	Astra	W 2-1	Roman, Curtean (p)
30/04	h	Oţelul	D 0-0	
03/05	a	U Cluj	D 1-1	Llullaku (p)
10/05	h	Tîrgu Mureş	W 1-0	Bâjenaru
15/05	a	Dinamo	D 1-1	Zaharia
22/05	h	Concordia	W 2-0	Muntean, Llullaku
27/05	a	Braşov	D 0-0	

No	Name	Nat	DoB	Pos	Aps	(s)	Gls
4	Octavian Abrudan		16/03/84	D	8		
10	Răzvan Avram		12/10/86	M	2	(9)	
19	Liviu Bâjenaru		06/05/83	M	2	(2)	1
9	Godfred Bekoé	GHA	12/11/92	A		(6)	
30	Miloš Buchta	SVK	19/07/80	G	7		
8	Ionuţ Buzean		18/09/82	D	18	(2)	
9	Alexandru Buziuc		15/03/94	A	7	(2)	
89	Valentin Creţu		02/01/89	D	26		
11	Iulian Cristea		17/07/94	M	11	(4)	
27	Alexandru Curtean		27/03/87	M	15	(4)	2
19	Florin Dan		01/04/79	M	1	(4)	
26	Elton Lexandro	BRA	25/08/85	M	9	(3)	
85	Andrei Enescu		12/10/87	M	1	(2)	
17	Cosimo Figliomeni	ITA	07/10/92	A	16	(11)	3
6	Costin Gheorghe		08/01/89	M		(2)	
7	Azdren Llullaku	ALB	15/02/88	A	16	(14)	8
28	Ahmed Mujdragić	SRB	13/03/86	D	14		
5	Alex Muntean		31/07/90	M	10	(3)	1
23	Sergiu Muth		24/07/90	D	29	(1)	
2	Ciprian Petre		10/12/80	M	22	(5)	3
12	Răzvan Pleşca		25/11/82	G	27		
20	Dan Roman		22/12/85	A	24	(6)	6
80	Roberto Romeo	ITA	27/04/90	M	8	(6)	
24	Loránd Szilagyi		21/09/85	D	14	(1)	
22	Aymen Tahar	ALG	02/10/89	M	30		3
25	Alexandru Târnovan		27/07/95	M	2	(5)	
21	Cristian Todea		18/10/78	M	14	(2)	1
3	Jasmin Trtovac	SRB	28/02/93	D	6	(1)	
18	Julián Velázquez	ARG	23/10/90	D	13	(1)	
85	Bogdan Vişa		27/05/86	D	3		
11	Vitinho	BRA	20/02/89	A	4	(5)	
16	Radu Zaharia		25/01/89	D	15		1

CSMS Iaşi

2010 • Emil Alexandrescu (12,500) •
csmsiasi.ro

Coach: Marius Lăcătuş;
(28/08/14) Ionuţ Chirilă;
(13/10/14) Nicolò Napoli (ITA)

2014

28/07	h	Viitorul	D 0-0	
04/08	a	Gaz Metan	D 0-0	
10/08	h	Petrolul	L 1-5	Wesley
16/08	a	Astra	L 1-2	Munteanu
25/08	h	Oţelul	D 0-0	
01/09	a	U Cluj	L 0-2	
14/09	h	Tîrgu Mureş	D 2-2	Creţu, og (Hora)
20/09	a	Dinamo	L 0-1	
26/09	h	Concordia	L 1-2	Creţu
03/10	a	Braşov	L 0-2	
17/10	h	Botoşani	D 2-2	Coşereanu, Onduku
25/10	a	Ceahlăul	D 2-2	Novac, Wesley
04/11	a	Rapid	W 1-0	Wesley (p)
09/11	h	U Craiova	L 1-3	Bôle
23/11	a	CFR Cluj	L 0-4	
28/11	h	Pandurii	W 3-0	og (Matulevičius), Bôle, Bosoi
07/12	a	Steaua	L 0-1	

2015

20/02	a	Viitorul	W 3-0	Ciucur 2, Plămadă
28/02	h	Gaz Metan	W 1-0	Golubović
09/03	a	Petrolul	W 2-0	Ciucur, Fábio Braga
15/03	h	Astra	W 1-0	Bădic
18/03	a	Oţelul	D 0-0	
23/03	h	U Cluj	W 2-0	Mihalache, Golubović
03/04	a	Tîrgu Mureş	L 0-1	
07/04	h	Dinamo	W 1-0	Bôle
11/04	a	Concordia	L 1-2	Golubović
17/04	h	Braşov	W 1-0	Mihalache
25/04	a	Botoşani	D 0-0	
30/04	h	Ceahlăul	W 2-0	Golubović, Bădic
04/05	h	Rapid	D 0-0	
09/05	a	U Craiova	W 1-0	Creţu
16/05	h	CFR Cluj	L 0-3	
24/05	a	Pandurii	L 2-5	Boiciuc, Enescu
28/05	h	Steaua	D 0-0	

No	Name	Nat	DoB	Pos	Aps	(s)	Gls
9	Kabiru Akinsola	NGA	21/01/91	A		(2)	
5	Narcis Bădic		01/07/91	M	13	(6)	2
9	Alexandru Boiciuc	MDA	21/08/97	A		(5)	1
21	Lukács Bôle	HUN	21/08/90	M	15	(4)	3
8	Gabriel Bosoi		11/08/87	M	15	(12)	1
77	Marius Călugăru		10/05/90	M		(6)	
1	Alessandro Caparco	ITA	07/09/83	G	13	(2)	
19	Marius Ciucă		04/11/82	D	4	(7)	
11	Alexandru Ciucur		01/03/90	A	31		3
20	Valentin Coşereanu		17/07/91	A	3	(4)	1
18	Mădălin Crengăniş		08/01/95	A		(3)	
6	Alexandru Creţu		24/04/92	M	23	(5)	3
25	Mugurel Dedu		01/03/85	M	4	(4)	
22	Valentin Dima		25/06/89	D	1	(2)	
17	Leonard Dobre		16/06/92	A	7	(2)	
13	Andrei Enescu		12/10/87	M	16		1
23	Fábio Braga	BRA	06/09/92	M	1	(9)	1
14	Bojan Golubović	BIH	22/08/83	A	17		4
12	Branko Grahovac	BIH	08/07/83	G	21	(1)	
9	Dulee Johnson	LBR	07/11/84	M	1		
17	Bojan Marković	BIH	12/11/85	D		(3)	
41	Cristian Melinte		09/05/88	D	3		
10	Liviu Mihai		12/03/88	M	3	(2)	
4	Marius Mihalache		14/12/84	D	24		2
22	Milan Mitić	SRB	22/01/84	D	18	(2)	
77	Andu Moisii		12/08/96	D		(1)	
28	Cristian Munteanu		17/10/80	D	17		1
13	Daniel Novac		26/09/87	M	9	(5)	1
7	Adrian Olah		30/04/81	M	14	(3)	
16	Gomo Onduku	NGA	17/11/93	A	16		1
19	Clement Pălimaru		24/02/86	A	5	(1)	
29	Florin Plămadă		30/04/92	D	22	(2)	1
30	Alexandru Ţigănaşu		12/06/90	D	19		
14	Bogdan Visa		27/05/86	D		(2)	
20	Iulian Vladu		02/02/82	D	3	(1)	
26	Ionuţ Voicu		02/08/84	D	28		
80	Wesley	BRA	11/10/80	A	8		3

ROMANIA

FC Oțelul Galați

1937 • Oțelul (13,500) • otelul-galati.ro
Major honours
Romanian League (1) 2011
**Coach: Michael Weiss (GER);
(16/09/14) (Daniel Florea);
(22/09/14) Tibor Selymes;
(02/03/15) Florin Marin**

2014
28/07	a	Dinamo	L	0-4
02/08	h	Concordia	L	1-2 Tudorie
11/08	a	Brașov	D	1-1 Zaharia (p)
17/08	h	Botoșani	L	0-1
25/08	a	Iași	L	0-1
01/09	h	Rapid	W	2-0 Cristea 2
15/09	a	U Craiova	L	0-1
20/09	h	CFR Cluj	L	0-1
29/09	a	Pandurii	L	0-4
05/10	h	Steaua	L	0-3
18/10	a	Viitorul	L	0-3
24/10	h	Gaz Metan	D	1-1 Cristea
03/11	a	Petrolul	D	0-0
09/11	h	Astra	D	1-1 Tudorie
22/11	a	Ceahlăul	W	1-0 Cristea
29/11	h	U Cluj	D	0-0
07/12	h	Tîrgu Mureș	L	0-2

2015
21/02	h	Dinamo	L	0-1
27/02	a	Concordia	L	0-3
07/03	h	Brașov	D	1-1 Iorga
14/03	a	Botoșani	D	1-1 Hamroun
18/03	h	Iași	D	0-0
21/03	h	Rapid	L	0-2
04/04	h	U Craiova	L	0-1
07/04	a	CFR Cluj	L	0-1
13/04	h	Pandurii	L	0-2
19/04	a	Steaua	W	2-1 og (Latovlevici), Hamroun
26/04	h	Viitorul	W	3-0 Miron, Cernat 2
30/04	a	Gaz Metan	D	0-0
04/05	h	Petrolul	D	1-1 Cernat
11/05	a	Astra	L	1-4 Popa
17/05	h	Ceahlăul	W	4-1 Cernat 3 (1p), Hamroun
23/05	h	U Cluj	W	2-1 Hamroun, Tudorie
28/05	a	Tîrgu Mureș	W	2-1 Tudorie, Hélder

No	Name	Nat	DoB	Pos	Aps	(s)	Gls
22	Gabriel Abraham		22/03/91	G	11		
19	Mihai Adăscăliței		01/11/94	M		(3)	
14	Sanaa Altama	FRA	23/07/90	M	4	(1)	
7	Marcel Avdic	GER	28/02/91	M	7	(1)	
10	Florin Cernat		10/03/80	M	25	(1)	6
1	Serkan Ciftci	AUT	03/08/89	A		(7)	
40	Samoel Cojoc		08/07/87	D	8	(1)	
9	Cristian Cristea		31/05/88	A	10	(3)	4
17	Stelian Cucu		15/09/89	M	22	(4)	
80	Emil Dică		17/07/82	M	5	(1)	
8	Vasile Gheorghe		05/09/85	M	4	(1)	
21	Răzvan Grădinaru		23/08/95	M	10	(8)	
11	Jugurtha Hamroun	ALG	27/01/89	M	10	(1)	4
18	Hélder	POR	26/12/89	M	25		1
1	Dumitru Hotoboc		23/12/78	G	14		
7	Cătălin Iorga		17/03/88	M	15	(2)	1
27	Emil Jula		03/01/80	A	3	(6)	
16	Karol Karlík	SVK	29/06/86	D	13		
6	Mihai Leca		14/04/92	D	9	(2)	
77	Yves Ma-Kalambay	BEL	31/01/86	G	2		
26	Andrei Măruș		16/04/92	D	2	(2)	
29	Ciprian Milea		12/07/84	M	8	(4)	
13	George Miron		28/05/94	D	20	(2)	1
5	Constantin Mișelăricu		25/09/89	D	11	(2)	
72	Robert Moglan		05/07/90	D		(1)	
23	Lucian Murgoci		25/03/92	D	16	(3)	
21	Benjamin Onwuachi	NGA	09/04/84	A	1		
7	Paulinho	POR	30/01/85	M		(1)	
38	Ivan Pecha	SVK	23/01/86	D	2		
88	Mihai Plopeanu		09/11/88	G	6		
20	Iulian Popa		07/07/84	M	18	(2)	1
24	Daniel Popescu		20/02/88	D	27	(2)	
77	Rúben Brigido	POR	23/06/91	M	5	(5)	
4	Enes Šipović	BIH	11/09/90	D	10		
4	Mahamadou Sissoko	FRA	08/08/88	D	10		
88	Athos Solomou	CYP	30/11/85	D	15	(1)	
8	Cosmin Stoian		08/01/95	M	1	(9)	
30	Robert Tătar		10/07/93	M		(8)	
96	Alexandru Tudorie		19/03/96	A	15	(9)	4
28	Alexandru Vlăsie		28/02/90	G	1	(1)	
34	Jeanvion Yulu-Matondo	BEL	05/01/86	A	2	(4)	
90	Alexandru Zaharia		25/05/90	M	7	(2)	1

CS Pandurii Târgu Jiu

1962 • Tudor Vladimirescu (9,200) •
panduriics.ro
**Coach: Petre Grigoraș;
(16/12/14) Edward Iordănescu**

2014
25/07	a	U Craiova	D	1-1 Shalaj
03/08	h	CFR Cluj	D	0-0
09/08	h	Ceahlăul	L	0-1
15/08	a	Steaua	L	0-6
23/08	h	Viitorul	D	1-1 Roman
29/08	a	Gaz Metan	W	2-0 Buleică, Matulevičius (p)
15/09	h	Petrolul	D	1-1 Roman
21/09	a	Astra	L	1-2 Momčilović
29/09	h	Oțelul	W	4-0 Roman 2, Matulevičius 2
04/10	a	U Cluj	L	0-2
18/10	h	Tîrgu Mureș	L	1-1 Momčilović
26/10	a	Dinamo	L	2-3 Roman 2
04/11	h	Concordia	D	1-1 Shamsin
08/11	a	Brașov	W	3-0 Buleică 2, Roman
23/11	h	Botoșani	L	1-2 Erico
28/11	a	Iași	L	0-3
06/12	h	Rapid	W	2-0 Roman, Matulevičius

2015
23/02	h	U Craiova	L	0-1
01/03	a	CFR Cluj	W	4-0 Roman, og (Amadio), Eric, Shalaj
06/03	a	Ceahlăul	D	1-1 Matulevičius
15/03	h	Steaua	W	3-1 Roman, Shalaj, Eric (p)
19/03	a	Viitorul	L	0-4
22/03	h	Gaz Metan	L	0-1
06/04	a	Petrolul	W	1-0 Momčilović
09/04	h	Astra	D	1-1 Cordoș
13/04	a	Oțelul	W	2-0 Momčilović, Roman (p)
20/04	h	U Cluj	L	0-1
25/04	a	Tîrgu Mureș	L	1-2 Roman (p)
28/04	h	Dinamo	W	3-2 Nicoară, Șandru, Nistor
01/05	a	Concordia	L	0-1
08/05	h	Brașov	W	2-0 Anton, Roman
15/05	a	Botoșani	D	1-1 Cordoș
24/05	h	Iași	W	5-2 Mrzljak, Pintilii, Roman 3 (2p)
27/05	a	Rapid	W	3-0 Mrzljak, og (Čmovš), Răduț (p)

No	Name	Nat	DoB	Pos	Aps	(s)	Gls
19	Paul Anton		10/05/91	D	27	(1)	1
91	Ciprian Brata		24/03/91	M	1	(1)	
8	Nicandro Breeveld	NED	07/10/86	M	2		
7	Florian Buleică		12/09/91	M	14	(13)	3
5	Paraskevas Christou	CYP	02/02/84	D	7		
8	Andrei Cordoș		06/06/88	D	15		2
27	Elton	BRA	20/07/89	M	19	(7)	
11	Eric	BRA	05/12/85	M	1	(12)	2
8	Erico	BRA	20/07/89	M	11	(1)	1
1	Michał Gliwa	POL	08/04/88	G	15		
23	Constantin Grecu		08/06/88	D	1	(2)	
77	Laurențiu Iorga		17/03/88	M	6	(2)	
99	Deivydas Matulevičius	LTU	08/04/89	A	11	(9)	5
3	Nejc Mevlja	SVN	12/06/90	D	1	(1)	
4	Marko Momčilović	SRB	11/06/87	M	33		4
24	Filip Mrzljak	CRO	04/04/93	D	7	(1)	2
26	Viorel Nicoară		27/09/87	M	17	(11)	1
10	Dan Nistor		05/06/88	M	31		1
6	Cătălin Pârvulescu		11/06/91	D	1		
80	Pedro Mingote	POR	02/08/80	G	4		
14	Mihai Pintilii		09/11/84	M	10		1
90	Andrei Pițian		16/11/95	M		(1)	
25	Marian Pleașcă		06/02/90	D	12	(4)	
21	Cornel Predescu		21/12/87	M	3	(8)	
20	Mihai Răduț		18/03/90	M	24	(2)	1
9	Mihai Roman		31/05/92	A	27	(5)	16
20	Bogdan Șandru		04/07/89	D	4		1
52	Gezim Shalaj	SUI	28/07/90	M	16	(11)	3
17	Faiz Shamsin	LIB	12/07/92	A		(5)	1
89	Matija Smrekar	CRO	08/04/89	A		(1)	
33	Răzvan Stanca		18/01/80	G	15		
2	Rodemis Trifu		08/10/95	M		(2)	
18	Bogdan Unguruşan		20/02/83	D	23	(2)	
6	Nikola Vasiljević	SRB	30/06/91	D	16		

FC Petrolul Ploiești

1952 • Ilie Oană (15,500) • fcpetrolul.ro
Major honours
Romanian League (3) 1958, 1959, 1966; Romanian
Cup (3) 1963, 1995, 2013
**Coach: Răzvan Lucescu;
(17/09/14) Gheorghe Mulțescu;
(10/01/15) Mircea Rednic;
(05/05/15) (Valentin Sinescu)**

2014
27/07	a	Brașov	W	1-0 Filipe Teixeira
03/08	h	Botoșani	W	4-1 Mutu, Albín, Tamuz 2
10/08	a	Iași	W	5-1 Filipe Teixeira, Mutu, Tamuz 2, Albín
16/08	h	Rapid	D	0-0
24/08	a	U Craiova	W	2-0 Albín, Tamuz
31/08	h	CFR Cluj	L	1-2 Filipe Teixeira
15/09	a	Pandurii	D	1-1 De Lucas
21/09	h	Steaua	L	2-3 Tamuz 2
28/09	a	Viitorul	W	3-1 Tamuz (p), Astafei 2
04/10	h	Gaz Metan	W	1-0 Astafei
20/10	h	Ceahlăul	W	2-0 Geraldo Alves, Tamuz
27/10	a	Astra	D	0-0
03/11	h	Oțelul	D	0-0
08/11	a	U Cluj	W	3-0 Tamuz, Alcénat, Albín
23/11	h	Tîrgu Mureș	W	2-0 Albín, Geraldo Alves
30/11	a	Dinamo	W	1-0
08/12	h	Concordia	D	2-2 Astafei, Filipe Teixeira

2015
20/02	h	Brașov	W	1-0 Filipe Teixeira
27/02	a	Botoșani	W	1-0 Filipe Teixeira (p)
09/03	h	Iași	L	0-2
13/03	a	Rapid	D	1-1 Filipe Teixeira
17/03	h	U Craiova	L	1-2 Astafei
22/03	a	CFR Cluj	W	1-0 Filipe Teixeira (p)
06/04	h	Pandurii	L	0-1
09/04	a	Steaua	W	1-0 Nepomuceno
13/04	h	Viitorul	L	1-2 Vasilache
18/04	a	Gaz Metan	W	1-0
27/04	a	Ceahlăul	D	1-1 og (Marković)
30/04	h	Astra	L	1-2 Tamuz (p)
04/05	a	Oțelul	D	1-1 Kronaveter
09/05	h	U Cluj	W	1-0 Ipša
16/05	a	Tîrgu Mureș	L	0-1
22/05	h	Dinamo	L	0-3
27/05	a	Concordia	L	2-3 Nkoyi, Kronaveter

No	Name	Nat	DoB	Pos	Aps	(s)	Gls
11	Juan Albín	URU	17/07/86	M	9	(5)	5
2	Jean Sony Alcénat	HAI	23/01/86	D	31		1
21	Victoraș Astafei		06/07/87	M	23	(6)	5
6	Marian Beța		11/05/91	D	5		
93	Alexandru Chiriță		24/06/96	A		(1)	
12	Alberto Cobrea		01/11/90	G	3		
20	Alexandru Coman		16/10/91	M	2	(5)	
91	Pablo De Lucas	ESP	20/09/86	M	25		1
39	Jean-Alain Fanchone	FRA	02/09/88	D	12	(4)	
4	Ioan Filip		20/05/89	M	21	(3)	
80	Filipe Teixeira	POR	02/09/80	M	19	(1)	8
13	Sebastián Gallegos	URU	18/01/92	M		(2)	
3	Geraldo Alves	POR	08/11/80	D	21		2
35	Gerson	BRA	07/01/92	D	7		
15	Shai Haddad	ISR	02/07/87	M	1		
15	Ovidiu Hoban		27/12/82	A	3	(1)	
86	Kristijan Ipša	CRO	04/04/88	D	18	(3)	1
11	Rok Kronaveter	SVN	07/12/86	M	8	(4)	2
18	George Mareș		16/05/96	A	3	(3)	
35	Marian Marin		11/09/87	D	3		
30	Laurențiu Marinescu		25/08/84	M	18	(4)	
5	Sony Mustivar	HAI	12/02/90	M	7	(4)	
10	Adrian Mutu		08/01/79	A	5	(1)	2
7	Gevaro Nepomuceno	CUW	10/11/92	M	10	(15)	1
99	Patrick Nkoyi	NED	04/11/93	A	6	(11)	1
23	Rodrigo Pastorini	URU	04/03/90	A	8	(8)	
1	Peçanha	BRA	11/01/80	G	31		
77	Andrei Peteleu		20/08/92	D	12	(5)	
8	Njongo Priso	CMR	24/12/88	M	9	(2)	
8	Mourad Satli	FRA	29/01/90	D	22	(3)	
99	Toto Tamuz	ISR	01/04/88	A	22		11
10	Mohammed Tchité	COD	31/01/84	A	5	(6)	
5	Ciprian Vasilache		14/09/83	M	5	(3)	1

FC Rapid Bucureşti

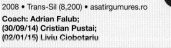

1923 • Valentin Stănescu (19,100) • fcrapid.ro

Major honours
Romanian League (3) 1967, 1999, 2003; Romanian Cup (13) 1935, 1937, 1938, 1939, 1940, 1941, 1942, 1972, 1975, 1998, 2002, 2000, 2007

Coach: Ionel Ganea;
(30/09/14) Marian Rada;
(08/01/15) Cristian Pustai;
(14/04/15) Cristiano Bergodi (ITA)

2014					
26/07	h	Steaua	L	1-3	*Pancu*
01/08	a	Viitorul	W	2-1	*Dică (p), Ciolacu*
08/08	h	Gaz Metan	D	1-1	*Pancu*
16/08	a	Petrolul	D	0-0	
24/08	h	Astra	L	0-2	
01/09	a	Oţelul	L	0-2	
14/09	h	U Cluj	W	2-1	*Buş, Călin*
19/09	a	Tîrgu Mureş	L	0-1	
27/09	h	Dinamo	L	0-3	
03/10	a	Concordia	D	0-0	
17/10	h	Braşov	L	0-1	
25/10	a	Botoşani	L	0-3	
04/11	h	Iaşi	L	0-1	
10/11	h	Ceahlăul	D	1-1	*Martin*
24/11	a	U Craiova	L	0-2	
29/11	h	CFR Cluj	D	0-0	
06/12	a	Pandurii	L	0-2	
2015					
22/02	a	Steaua	W	1-0	*Gecov*
02/03	h	Viitorul	D	0-0	
09/03	a	Gaz Metan	W	1-0	*Gecov*
13/03	h	Petrolul	D	1-1	*Săpunaru*
18/03	a	Astra	L	0-2	
21/03	h	Oţelul	W	2-0	Meulens, Niculae
04/04	a	U Cluj	L	0-1	
08/04	h	Tîrgu Mureş	L	1-2	*Săpunaru*
11/04	a	Dinamo	L	0-2	
20/04	h	Concordia	W	1-0	*Gecov*
24/04	a	Braşov	W	2-1	*Meulens, Săpunaru (p)*
28/04	h	Botoşani	D	2-2	*Edu Oriol, Săpunaru (p)*
04/05	a	Iaşi	D	0-0	
11/05	a	Ceahlăul	W	1-0	*Edu Oriol*
17/05	h	U Craiova	L	1-2	*Niculae*
23/05	a	CFR Cluj	L	1-2	*Niculae*
27/05	h	Pandurii	L	0-3	

No	Name	Nat	DoB	Pos	Aps	(s)	Gls
18	Aritz Borda	ESP	03/01/85	D	7		
25	Valentin Balint		07/02/94	A	3	(2)	
9	Fred Benson	NED	10/04/84	A	9	(4)	
23	Mircea Bornescu		03/05/80	G	14		
27	Jean Boukaka	FRA	12/03/92	A		(1)	
30	Miloš Buchta	SVK	19/07/80	G	16		
26	Laurenţiu Buş		27/08/87	M	8	(4)	1
14	Florin Călin		16/08/93	M	3	(5)	1
14	Andrei Cerlincă		06/08/95	M	1	(8)	
9	Andrei Ciolacu		09/08/92	A	9	(6)	1
27	Pavel Čmovš	CZE	29/06/90	D	17		
20	Sebastian Cojocnean		11/07/89	M	6	(2)	
10	Alexandru Coman		16/10/91	M	15	(1)	
8	Alexandru Dan		30/01/94	M	4	(6)	
7	Emil Dică		17/07/82	M	10	(1)	1
90	Virgil Drăghia		31/07/90	G	4		
2	Edu Oriol	ESP	05/11/86	A	10	(4)	2
15	Marcel Gecov	CZE	01/01/88	M	17		3
6	Alexandru Iacob		14/04/89	D	15		
3	Joan Oriol	ESP	05/11/86	D	13		
28	João Coimbra	POR	24/05/86	M	8	(4)	
6	Tomáš Josl	CZE	12/11/84	D	7	(2)	
70	Kikas	POR	12/01/91	M	4	(2)	
29	Aritz López Garay	ESP	06/11/80	D	17		
5	Daniel Lung		02/03/87	D	6		
80	Mădălin Martin		21/06/92	A	7	(8)	1
3	Gaston Mendy	SEN	22/11/85	M	7	(1)	
24	Ioan Mera		05/01/87	D	10		
7	Rihairo Meulens	CUW	03/06/88	M	11	(3)	2
22	Nicolae Milinceanu	MDA	01/08/92	A		(1)	
11	Valentin Negru		04/09/82	M	12	(2)	
21	Daniel Niculae		06/10/82	A	13	(1)	3
10	Daniel Pancu		17/08/77	A	12	(6)	2
33	Cătălin Păun		03/01/88	D		(1)	
16	Ricardo Alves	POR	25/03/93	M	3	(4)	
28	Iulian Roşu		30/05/94	M	9	(4)	
18	Rui Miguel	POR	15/11/83	M	7	(4)	
15	Dan Săndulescu		01/04/85	M	5	(3)	
4	Jérémy Sapina	FRA	01/02/85	D	11		
22	Cristian Săpunaru		05/04/84	D	13		4
2	Cătălin Savin		08/11/90	D	6		
20	Ciprian Selagea		21/01/90	M	1	(1)	
21	Marian Stoica		26/08/89	D	7	(1)	
4	Andrei Tânc		03/10/85	D	13	(1)	
19	Nicolae Vasile		29/12/95	D	4	(2)	

FC Steaua Bucureşti

1947 • Steaua (27,557);
Arena Naţională (55,611) • steauafc.ro

Major honours
European Champion Clubs' Cup (1) 1986; UEFA Super Cup (1) 1986; Romanian League (26) 1951, 1952, 1953, 1956, 1960, 1961, 1968, 1976, 1978, 1985, 1986, 1987, 1988, 1989, 1993, 1994, 1995, 1996, 1997, 1998, 2001, 2005, 2006, 2013, 2014, 2015; Romanian Cup (23) 1949, 1950, 1951, 1952, 1955, 1962, 1966, 1967, 1969, 1970, 1971, 1976, 1979, 1985, 1987, 1988, 1989, 1992, 1996, 1997, 1999, 2011, 2015

Coach: Constantin Gâlcă

2014					
26/07	a	Rapid	W	3-1	*Keşerü, Popa, Chipciu*
02/08	h	U Craiova	W	3-1	*Popa, Sânmărtean, Varela*
10/08	a	CFR Cluj	W	1-0	*Tănase*
15/08	h	Pandurii	W	6-0	*Keşerü 6 (1p)*
23/08	h	Ceahlăul	L	0-1	
30/08	a	Viitorul	W	1-0	*Iancu (p)*
12/09	h	Gaz Metan	W	3-1	*Keşerü 2, Sânmărtean*
21/09	a	Petrolul	W	3-2	*Chipciu, Keşerü, Varela*
28/09	h	Astra	D	0-0	
05/10	a	Oţelul	W	3-0	*Latovlevici, Sânmărtean, Szukała*
19/10	h	U Cluj	W	4-1	*Papp, Szukała, Popa, Keşerü*
26/10	a	Tîrgu Mureş	L	0-1	
31/10	h	Dinamo	W	3-0	*Szukała, Papp, Keşerü*
09/11	a	Concordia	W	1-0	*Tănase*
22/11	h	Braşov	W	2-0	*Popa, Chipciu*
01/12	a	Botoşani	W	2-0	*Prepeliţă 2*
07/12	h	Iaşi	W	1-0	*Szukała*
2015					
22/02	h	Rapid	L	0-1	
01/03	a	U Craiova	D	0-0	
08/03	h	CFR Cluj	W	1-0	*Ţucudean*
15/03	a	Pandurii	L	1-3	*Iancu*
18/03	a	Ceahlăul	W	1-0	*Rusescu*
22/03	h	Viitorul	W	4-1	*Tănase 2, Rusescu, Ţucudean*
05/04	a	Gaz Metan	W	2-1	*Prepeliţă, Popa*
09/04	h	Petrolul	L	0-1	
12/04	a	Astra	D	0-0	
19/04	h	Oţelul	L	1-2	*Ţucudean*
25/04	a	U Cluj	W	3-0	*Stanciu 2, Prepeliţă*
29/04	h	Tîrgu Mureş	L	0-1	
03/05	a	Dinamo	W	3-1	*Stanciu 2 (1p), Prepeliţă*
10/05	h	Concordia	D	2-2	*Stanciu (p), Iancu*
16/05	a	Braşov	W	3-2	*Tănase, Rusescu 2*
24/05	h	Botoşani	W	2-0	*Varela, Stanciu*
28/05	a	Iaşi	D	0-0	

No	Name	Nat	DoB	Pos	Aps	(s)	Gls
24	Giedrius Arlauskis	LTU	01/12/87	G	25		
55	Alexandru Bourceanu		24/04/85	M	5	(6)	
21	Nicandro Breeveld	NED	07/10/86	M	14	(9)	
7	Alexandru Chipciu		18/05/89	M	23	(3)	3
95	Valentin Cojocaru		01/10/95	G	7		
94	Rareş Enceanu		05/08/94	M		(1)	
8	Lucian Filip		25/09/90	D	14	(2)	
27	Răzvan Grădinaru		23/08/95	M		(2)	
16	Guilherme	BRA	01/04/90	D	13	(2)	
9	Gabriel Iancu		15/04/94	A	5	(15)	3
28	Claudiu Keşerü		02/12/86	A	15	(2)	12
14	Iasmin Latovlevici		11/05/86	D	9	(3)	1
5	Srdjan Luchin		04/03/86	D	7	(2)	
26	Ionuţ Neagu		26/10/89	M	5	(5)	
1	Florin Niţă		03/07/87	G	2	(1)	
6	Paul Papp		11/11/89	D	18	(2)	2
22	Paul Pârvulescu		11/08/88	D	5	(1)	
77	Adrian Popa		24/07/88	M	27	(1)	5
11	Andrei Prepeliţă		08/12/85	M	27		5
2	Cornel Râpă		16/01/90	D	14	(2)	
25	Raul Rusescu		09/07/88	A	12	(9)	4
18	Lucian Sânmărtean		13/03/80	M	13	(1)	3
12	Nicolae Stanciu		07/05/93	M	15	(13)	6
4	Łukasz Szukała	POL	26/05/84	D	15	(1)	4
30	Gabriel Tamaş		09/11/83	D	8	(2)	
10	Cristian Tănase		18/02/87	M	20	(3)	5
13	Alin Toşca		14/03/92	D	14	(1)	
29	George Ţucudean		30/04/91	A	11	(6)	3
33	Fernando Varela	CPV	26/11/87	D	30		3
97	Robert Vâlceanu		29/03/97	M	1	(4)	

ASA Tîrgu Mureş

2008 • Trans-Sil (8,200) • asatirgumures.ro

Coach: Adrian Falub;
(30/09/14) Cristian Pustai;
(02/01/15) Liviu Ciobotariu

2014					
26/07	h	U Cluj	D	0-0	
01/08	a	Ceahlăul	W	4-1	*N'Doye 2, Henrique, Hora*
09/08	a	Dinamo	D	1-1	*Mureşan*
17/08	h	Concordia	W	2-0	*Bruno Martins, Amauri*
22/08	a	Braşov	L	1-2	*Bumba*
31/08	h	Botoşani	W	2-1	*N'Doye 2*
14/09	a	Iaşi	D	2-2	*N'Doye, Goga*
19/09	h	Rapid	W	1-0	*Goga*
28/09	a	U Craiova	L	0-1	
06/10	h	CFR Cluj	W	2-0	*Hora, N'Doye*
18/10	a	Pandurii	D	1-1	*og (Elton)*
26/10	h	Steaua	W	1-0	*Axente*
03/11	a	Viitorul	D	0-0	
07/11	h	Gaz Metan	W	2-0	*Bumba, Hora*
23/11	a	Petrolul	L	0-2	
30/11	h	Astra	D	0-0	
07/12	a	Oţelul	W	2-0	*Mureşan, Hora*
2015					
22/02	a	U Cluj	W	3-0	*N'Doye (p), Bumba, Hora (p)*
02/03	h	Ceahlăul	W	3-0	*Bumba, Zicu, N'Doye*
06/03	h	Dinamo	W	2-1	*Mureşan 2*
13/03	a	Concordia	D	0-0	
16/03	h	Braşov	W	1-0	*Zicu*
20/03	a	Botoşani	W	2-1	*Zicu, Constantin*
03/04	h	Iaşi	W	1-0	*Bumba*
08/04	a	Rapid	W	2-1	*Hora, Manolov*
11/04	h	U Craiova	W	2-1	*Zicu, N'Doye*
17/04	a	CFR Cluj	D	2-2	*N'Doye 2*
25/04	h	Pandurii	W	2-1	*Bumba, Axente*
29/04	a	Steaua	W	1-0	*Zicu*
02/05	h	Viitorul	W	6-1	*Hora 3, N'Doye, Axente, Goga*
10/05	a	Gaz Metan	L	0-1	
16/05	h	Petrolul	W	1-0	*Voiculeţ*
24/05	a	Astra	L	1-3	*Bumba*
28/05	h	Oţelul	L	1-2	*Mureşan (p)*

No	Name	Nat	DoB	Pos	Aps	(s)	Gls
11	Amauri	BRA	01/02/82	A	1	(8)	1
20	Mircea Axente		14/03/87	A	12	(11)	3
21	Ionuţ Balaur		06/06/89	D	8	(1)	
5	Florin Bejan		28/03/91	D	31		
77	Bruno Martins	BRA	21/07/86	M	3	(6)	1
8	Claudiu Bumba		05/01/94	M	19	(10)	7
23	Marius Constantin		25/10/84	D	26		1
26	Patrice Feussi	CMR	03/10/86	D	23	(1)	
18	Dorin Goga		02/07/84	A	18	(8)	3
25	Nicolás Gorobsov	ARG	25/11/89	M	18	(10)	
3	Costinel Gugu		20/05/92	D		(1)	
44	Sergiu Hanca		04/04/92	M	5	(2)	
70	Hélder Castro	POR	24/01/86	M		(1)	
9	Henrique	BRA	19/01/87	A	3	(5)	1
88	Ioan Hora		21/08/88	M	25	(5)	9
14	Silviu Ilie		27/06/88	D	2	(1)	
4	Iván Gonzalez	ESP	15/02/88	D	4	(7)	
2	Javier Velayos	ESP	06/04/87	D	6		
31	Miroslav Manolov	BUL	20/05/85	A	12	(5)	1
6	Gabriel Mureşan		13/02/82	M	24	(1)	5
78	Ousmane N'Doye	SEN	21/03/78	M	20	(3)	12
47	Adrian Sălăgeanu		09/04/83	D	1	(1)	
19	Laszlo Sepsi		07/06/87	D	30		
33	Eduard Stăncioiu		03/03/81	G	31		
7	János Székely		13/05/83	M	3	(4)	
30	Adrian Viciu		14/01/91	G	3		
20	Claudiu Voiculeţ		08/08/85	M	22	(5)	1
83	Ianis Zicu		23/10/83	M	24	(6)	5

ROMANIA

FC Universitatea Cluj

1919 • Cluj Arena (32,000) •
universitateacluj.ro
Major honours
Romanian Cup (1) 1965
**Coach: Mihai Teja;
(05/09/14) George Ogăraru;
(02/03/15) Adrian Falub**

2014
26/07	a	Tîrgu Mureş	D	0-0	
04/08	h	Dinamo	L	2-3	Ninu, Boutadjine
11/08	a	Concordia	W	2-0	Nuno Viveiros, Costin
18/08	a	Braşov	D	1-1	Nuno Viveiros
24/08	a	Botoşani	L	0-1	
01/09	h	Iaşi	W	2-0	Nuno Viveiros, Muşat (p)
14/09	a	Rapid	L	1-2	Muşat (p)
22/09	h	U Craiova	L	0-2	
29/09	a	CFR Cluj	L	0-1	
04/10	h	Pandurii	W	2-0	Cristocea, Kovacs
19/10	a	Steaua	L	1-4	Bucşă
25/10	h	Viitorul	D	2-2	Ceppelini, Gravenberch
01/11	a	Gaz Metan	D	1-1	og (Creţu)
08/11	h	Petrolul	L	0-1	
22/11	h	Astra	D	1-1	Lemnaru (p)
29/11	h	Oţelul	D	0-0	
06/12	h	Ceahlăul	W	6-0	Lemnaru 2 (2p), Mengolo 3, Paulinho

2015
22/02	h	Tîrgu Mureş	L	0-3	
28/02	a	Dinamo	L	0-3	
08/03	h	Concordia	D	0-0	
13/03	a	Braşov	D	0-1	
17/03	h	Botoşani	D	0-0	
23/03	a	Iaşi	L	0-2	
04/04	h	Rapid	W	1-0	Castillion
07/04	a	U Craiova	L	0-3	
10/04	h	CFR Cluj	W	1-0	Morar
20/04	a	Pandurii	W	1-0	Nuno Viveiros
25/04	h	Steaua	L	0-3	
09/04	a	Viitorul	D	1-1	Mengolo
03/05	h	Gaz Metan	D	1-1	Morar
09/05	a	Petrolul	L	0-1	
18/05	h	Astra	D	0-0	
23/05	a	Oţelul	L	1-2	Mengolo
27/05	h	Ceahlăul	W	2-0	Ceppelini, Morar

No	Name	Nat	DoB	Pos	Aps	(s)	Gls
20	Florin Achim		16/07/91	M	1	(3)	
31	Narcisse Bambara	BFA	23/06/89	D	15		
19	Karim Boutadjine	FRA	23/03/89	M	7	(1)	1
3	Doru Bratu		27/05/89	D	1		
5	Dan Bucşă		23/06/88	M	12	(2)	1
11	Andreas Calcan		09/04/94	M	1	(8)	
29	Geoffrey Castillion	NED	25/05/91	A	8	(3)	1
11	Pablo Ceppelini	URU	11/09/91	M	16	(6)	2
13	Raul Ciupe		24/11/83	D	23		
23	Raul Costin		29/01/85	M	20	(6)	1
10	Vasilică Cristocea		27/09/80	M	15	(4)	1
5	Daniel Martins	POR	20/07/93	D	1		
30	Emilian Dolha		03/11/79	G	1	(1)	
26	Danzell Gravenberch	NED	13/02/94	A	14	(3)	1
17	Petar Jovanović	BIH	12/07/82	D	15	(3)	
26	Emil Jula		03/01/80	A	2	(3)	
27	Lorant Kovacs		06/06/93	M	9	(8)	1
9	Valentin Lemnaru		24/06/84	A	9	(10)	3
30	Andrei Lungu		29/01/89	M	18	(2)	
28	Justin Mengolo	CMR	24/06/93	A	23	(5)	5
7	Vlad Morar		01/08/93	A	8	(6)	3
24	Cristian Munteanu		17/10/80	D	9	(2)	
14	Nicolae Muşat		04/12/86	D	15		2
8	Ioan Neag		18/02/94	D	21	(1)	
1	Vladimir Niculescu		26/09/87	G	2		
29	Emil Ninu		28/08/86	D	15	(1)	1
16	Nuno Viveiros	POR	22/06/83	M	24	(2)	4
87	Leonidas Panagopoulos	GRE	03/01/87	G	6	(1)	
22	Paulinho	BRA	23/04/92	M	2	(6)	1
8	Patrick Popescu		19/12/96	M		(1)	
21	Florent Sauvadet	FRA	31/01/89	M		(1)	
4	Dino Škvorc	CRO	02/02/90	D	26		
8	Saša Stojanović	SRB	21/01/83	M	5	(5)	
7	Ionuţ Târnăcop		22/04/87	M	1	(2)	
8	Benjamin van den Broek	NZL	21/09/87	M	2	(3)	
33	Róbert Veselovský	SVK	02/09/85	G	25		
14	Sergio Zijler	NED	08/07/87	M	2		

CS Universitatea Craiova

2013 • Ion Oblemenco (22,252);
Extensiv (6,000) • csuc.ro
**Coach: Ionel Gane;
(03/09/14) Emil Săndoi**

2014
25/07	h	Pandurii	D	1-1	Curelea
02/08	a	Steaua	L	1-3	Ivan
08/08	h	Viitorul	D	2-2	Curelea 2
15/08	a	Gaz Metan	L	0-1	
24/08	h	Petrolul	L	0-2	
31/08	a	Astra	L	0-5	
15/09	h	Oţelul	W	1-0	Mádson
22/09	a	U Cluj	W	2-0	og (Muşat), Bancu
28/09	h	Tîrgu Mureş	W	1-0	Brandán (p)
05/10	a	Dinamo	D	1-1	og (Filip)
19/10	h	Concordia	D	1-1	Ferfelea (p)
24/10	a	Braşov	W	3-2	Vătăjelu, Bawab, Nuno Rocha
01/11	h	Botoşani	W	2-1	Băluţă, Brandán
09/11	a	Iaşi	W	3-1	Nuno Rocha 2, Târnăcop
24/11	h	Rapid	W	2-0	Brandán, Bawab
29/11	h	Ceahlăul	W	2-0	Bawab, Herghelegiu
07/12	a	CFR Cluj	D	0-0	

2015
23/02	a	Pandurii	W	1-0	Bawab
01/03	h	Steaua	D	0-0	
08/03	a	Viitorul	D	1-1	Nuno Rocha
14/03	h	Gaz Metan	D	1-1	Târnăcop
17/03	a	Petrolul	W	2-1	Nuno Rocha, Brandán (p)
21/03	h	Astra	D	0-0	
04/04	a	Oţelul	W	1-0	Bawab
07/04	h	U Cluj	W	3-0	Bawab, Nuno Rocha 2
11/04	a	Tîrgu Mureş	L	1-2	Herghelegiu
19/04	h	Dinamo	D	0-0	
24/04	a	Concordia	D	2-2	Târnăcop, Bawab
29/04	h	Braşov	D	0-0	
02/05	a	Botoşani	L	0-2	
09/05	h	Iaşi	L	0-1	
17/05	a	Rapid	W	2-1	Mateiu, Nuno Rocha
24/05	a	Ceahlăul	L	1-2	Herghelegiu
30/05	h	CFR Cluj	W	3-0	Bawab 2, Băluţă

No	Name	Nat	DoB	Pos	Aps	(s)	Gls
2	Sebastian Achim		02/06/86	D	26		
3	Stephane Acka	CIV	11/10/90	D	26	(1)	
26	Adrian Avrămia		31/01/92	D		(1)	
27	Nicuşor Bancu		18/09/92	M	11	(2)	1
34	Cristian Bălgrădean		21/03/88	G	27		
13	Alexandru Băluţă		13/09/93	M	25	(5)	2
11	Thaer Bawab	JOR	01/03/85	A	25		9
1	Bojan Brać	SRB	28/02/89	G	4		
14	Pablo Brandán	ARG	05/03/83	M	20	(2)	4
7	Marius Briceag		06/04/92	M	2	(6)	
21	Adrian Cârstea		27/03/95	M	1	(6)	
9	Costin Curelea		11/07/84	A	10	(5)	3
18	Ovidiu Dănănae		26/08/85	D	1		
19	Andrei Dumitraş		23/01/88	D	4	(4)	
10	Viorel Ferfelea		26/04/85	A	6	(6)	1
4	Cosmin Frăsinescu		10/02/85	D	27	(1)	
17	Andrei Herghelegiu		21/03/92	A	6	(14)	3
22	Ionuţ Irimia		17/05/79	G	1		
16	Andrei Ivan		04/01/97	A	3	(14)	1
30	Silviu Izvoranu		03/12/82	M	7	(2)	
8	Kay	CPV	05/01/88	D	10	(5)	
28	Mádson	BRA	09/05/91	M	26	(1)	1
8	Alexandru Mateiu		10/12/89	M	18	(4)	1
11	Sergiu Neacşa		03/09/91	M	1	(2)	
5	Nuno Rocha	CPV	25/03/92	M	27	(3)	8
19	Mihăiţă Pleşan		19/02/83	M	1	(8)	
12	Cătălin Straton		09/10/89	G	2		
24	Ionuţ Târnăcop		24/04/87	M	23	(2)	3
20	Nerijus Valskis	LTU	04/08/87	A		(1)	
20	Dacian Varga		15/10/84	M	1	(3)	
5	Bogdan Vătăjelu		24/04/93	D	33		1
7	Gabriel Velcovici		02/10/84	D		(3)	

FC Viitorul

2009 • Concordia (5,123) • academiahagi.tv
**Coach: Bogdan Stelea;
(21/08/14) Bogdan Vintilă;
(13/10/14) Gheorghe Hagi**

2014
28/07	a	Iaşi	D	0-0	
01/08	h	Rapid	L	1-2	Mitrea (p)
08/08	a	U Craiova	D	2-2	Mitrea 2 (1p)
18/08	h	CFR Cluj	L	0-2	
23/08	a	Pandurii	D	1-1	Nikolov
30/08	h	Steaua	L	0-1	
13/09	h	Ceahlăul	W	2-0	Tănase, Mitriţă
19/09	a	Gaz Metan	L	1-3	Mitrea
28/09	h	Petrolul	L	1-3	Daminuţă
05/10	a	Astra	W	1-0	Bonilla
18/10	h	Oţelul	W	3-0	Mitrea (p), Bonilla 2
25/10	a	U Cluj	D	2-2	Mitriţă, Mitrea (p)
03/11	h	Tîrgu Mureş	W	1-0	
07/11	a	Dinamo	W	3-2	Mitrea 2 (1p), Bonilla
21/11	h	Concordia	D	2-2	Tănase, Mitrea (p)
30/11	a	Braşov	W	3-1	Mitriţă, Bonilla, Mitrea (p)
05/12	h	Botoşani	L	1-2	Tănase

2015
20/02	h	Iaşi	L	0-3	
02/03	a	Rapid	D	0-0	
08/03	h	U Craiova	D	1-1	Mitriţă
15/03	a	CFR Cluj	W	2-1	Henrique, Marin
19/03	h	Pandurii	W	4-0	Mitrea (p), Benzar 2, Ţiru
22/03	a	Steaua	L	1-4	Bonilla
05/04	a	Ceahlăul	W	2-1	Mitrea 2 (2p)
08/04	h	Gaz Metan	W	1-0	Bonilla
13/04	a	Petrolul	W	2-1	Mitrea, Manea
18/04	h	Astra	W	2-0	Mitriţă, Nicoliţă
26/04	a	Oţelul	L	0-3	
29/04	h	U Cluj	D	1-1	Tănase
02/05	a	Tîrgu Mureş	L	1-6	Nicoliţă
08/05	h	Dinamo	L	0-3	
17/05	a	Concordia	L	0-2	
23/05	h	Braşov	L	0-2	
29/05	a	Botoşani	D	4-4	Manea, Ţiru, Hagi, Casap

No	Name	Nat	DoB	Pos	Aps	(s)	Gls
1	Călin Albuţ		23/05/81	G	13		
47	Marko Andjelković	SRB	12/10/84	M	9	(3)	
33	Dragoş Balauru		11/11/89	G	6		
30	Romario Benzar		26/03/92	M	27	(2)	2
17	Nelson Bonilla	SLV	11/09/90	A	20	(5)	7
31	Alexandru Buzbuchi		31/01/93	G	15		
92	Alin Cârstocea		16/01/92	M	3	(3)	
8	Roberto Carlos Casap		29/12/98	M		(1)	1
27	Florin Cioablă		23/04/96	M		(3)	
98	Florinel Coman		10/04/98	A		(1)	
23	Cristian Daminuţă		15/02/90	M	28	(1)	1
9	Cristian Gavra		03/04/93	A	4	(4)	
20	Ianis Hagi		22/10/98	M	1	(6)	1
99	Henrique	BRA	19/01/87	A	5	(4)	1
2	Robert Hodorogea		23/04/95	D	11	(4)	
14	Iulian Mamele		17/02/85	D	26		
4	Cristian Manea		09/08/97	D	25	(1)	2
33	Răzvan Marin		23/05/96	M	7	(10)	1
21	Adrian Mărkuş		10/04/92	A	1	(3)	
3	Bogdan Mitrea		29/09/87	D	30		14
24	Alexandru Mitriţă		08/02/95	M	23	(4)	5
7	Cătălin Munteanu		26/01/79	M	2	(3)	
11	Ionuţ Năstăsie		07/01/92	M	2	(3)	
91	Sergiu Neacşa		03/09/91	M	1	(4)	
16	Dragoş Nedelcu		16/02/97	D	9	(6)	
19	Bănel Nicoliţă		07/01/85	M	13	(2)	2
34	Boban Nikolov	MKD	28/07/94	M	9	(6)	1
7	Silviu Pană		24/09/91	M	16	(8)	
22	Ciprian Perju		18/03/96	M		(4)	
16	Adrian Piţ		16/07/83	D	1		
22	Paul Pîrvulescu		11/08/88	D		(1)	
5	Adrian Puţanu		09/01/94	D	5		
19	Vlad Rusu		22/06/90	A	2	(1)	
13	Andrei Sava		07/05/91	M	1		
55	Alin Şeroni		26/03/87	D		(2)	
10	Florin Tănase		30/12/94	M	27	(5)	4
15	Bogdan Ţiru		15/03/94	D	30	(1)	2
95	Ionuţ Vînă		20/02/95	A	2	(3)	

Top goalscorers

18	Grégory Tadé (CFR Cluj)
16	Mihai Roman (Pandurii)
14	Bogdan Mitrea (Viitorul)
12	Claudiu Keşerü (Steaua)
	Ousmane N'Doye (Tîrgu Mureş)
11	Marian Constantinescu (Braşov)
	Kamil Biliński (Dinamo)
	Toto Tamuz (Petrolul)
10	Constantin Budescu (Astra)
9	Attila Hadnagy (Botoşani)
	Mihai Dina (Concordia)
	Ioan Hora (Tîrgu Mureş)
	Thaer Bawab (U Craiova)

Promoted clubs

FC Voluntari

2010 • Niţă Pintea (1,000) • fcvoluntari.ro
Coach: Ilie Poenaru

ACS Poli Timişoara

2012 • Dan Păltinişanu (22,019) • acspoli.ro
Coach: Dan Alexa

Second level final tables 2014/15

Seria 1

Promotion pool	Pld	W	D	L	F	A	Pts
1 FC Voluntari	32	25	4	3	81	28	79
2 FC Academica Argeş Piteşti	32	20	7	5	67	21	67
3 FC Gloria Buzău	32	15	4	13	55	55	49
4 SC Bacău	32	13	7	12	53	43	46
5 ACS Rapid CFR Suceava	32	11	9	12	50	53	42
6 CF Brăila	32	8	12	12	39	45	36

Relegation pool	Pld	W	D	L	F	A	Pts
7 FCM Dorohoi	28	9	8	11	42	47	35
8 CS Baloteşti	28	9	7	12	39	43	34
9 ACS Berceni	28	8	9	11	38	51	33
10 FC Farul Constanţa	28	5	8	15	36	59	23
11 CSM Unirea 04 Slobozia	21	3	4	14	14	42	13
12 AFC Săgeata Năvodari	21	6	3	12	14	41	-37

Seria 2

Promotion pool	Pld	W	D	L	F	A	Pts
1 ACS Poli Timişoara	30	19	9	2	52	11	66
2 CS Mioveni	30	15	9	6	38	20	54
3 CSM Metalul Reşiţa	30	14	9	7	40	30	51
4 CS Unirea Tărlungeni	30	12	7	11	34	31	43
5 FC Olimpia Satu Mare	30	10	7	13	33	34	37
6 FC Olt Slatina	30	9	7	14	28	49	32

Relegation pool	Pld	W	D	L	F	A	Pts
7 CSM Râmnicu Vâlcea	26	7	11	8	24	25	32
8 FC Caransebeş	26	8	7	11	30	32	31
9 CS Şoimii Pâncota	26	5	9	12	22	32	24
10 FC Bihor Oradea	26	4	10	12	17	28	22
11 AFC Fortuna Poiana Câmpina	20	5	3	12	16	42	8

NB Leagues split into two halves after 22 and 20 matches respectively, after which the clubs play exclusively against teams in their group. AFC Săgeata Năvodari – 58 pts deducted; AFC Fortuna Poiana Câmpina – 10 pts deducted; FC Olt Slatina – 2 pts deducted. AFC Săgeata Năvodari, CSM Unirea 04 Slobozia & AFC Fortuna Poiana Câmpina withdrew during first phase; FC Olt Slatina withdrew during second phase – their remaining matches were awarded as 0-3 defeats.

DOMESTIC CUP

Cupa României 2014/15

FIRST ROUND

(23/09/14)
Brăila 0-1 Oţelul
Râmnicu Vâlcea 0-1 Iaşi
Rapid Bucureşti 0-0 Botoşani *(aet; 5-4 on pens)*
Rapid Suceava 1-0 Gaz Metan *(aet)*
Şoimii Pâncota 1-2 Pandurii
Tîrgu Mureş 4-1 Concordia

(24/09/14)
Bacău 1-5 Ceahlăul *(aet)*
Chindia 1-3 Braşov
Fortuna Poiana 2-5 Dinamo Bucureşti *(aet)*
Unirea Jucu 0-3 Petrolul
Viitorul Axintele 0-2 CFR Cluj

(25/09/14)
Berceni 0-3 Steaua
Bihor 1-1 U Cluj *(aet; 4-5 on pens)*
Caransebeş 1-2 U Craiova
Mioveni 3-1 Astra
Săgeata 0-3 Viitorul

SECOND ROUND

(28/10/14)
Iaşi 0-1 Steaua
Mioveni 1-0 Dinamo Bucureşti

(29/10/14)
Braşov 1-3 U Cluj
Tîrgu Mureş 4-0 Ceahlăul
U Craiova 2-1 Viitorul *(aet)*

(30/10/14)
Oţelul 2-3 Pandurii *(aet)*
Rapid Bucureşti 1-2 CFR Cluj
Rapid Suceava 2-3 Petrolul

QUARTER-FINALS

(02/12/14)
Mioveni 3-4 CFR Cluj *(Stoica 36, Nilă 52, Galan 59; Tadé 62p, 88, Chanturia 68, Ivanovski 90)*

(03/12/14)
U Cluj 1-0 Pandurii *(Ceppelini 55)*

(04/12/14)
Tîrgu Mureş 0-1 Petrolul *(Albín 88)*
U Craiova 0-1 Steaua *(Rusescu 69p)*

SEMI-FINALS

(04/03/15 & 01/04/15)
CFR Cluj 0-0 U Cluj
U Cluj 0-0 CFR Cluj *(aet)*
(0-0; U Cluj 4-2 on pens)

(05/03/15 & 02/04/15)
Petrolul 1-1 Steaua *(Tchité 21; Chipciu 90+4)*
Steaua 3-1 Petrolul *(Popa 20, Iancu 33, Tănase 68; Ipša 70)*
(Steaua 4-2)

FINAL

(31/05/15)
Arena Naţională, Bucharest
FC STEAUA BUCUREŞTI 3 *(Popa 9, 53, Rusescu 48)*
FC UNIVERSITATEA CLUJ 0
Referee: *Tudor*
STEAUA: *Niţă, Papp (Râpă 68), Luchin, Varela (Tamaş 77), Guilherme, Breeveld, Neagu (Iancu 65), Popa, Stanciu, Chipciu, Rusescu*
U CLUJ: *Veselovský, Jovanović (Bambara 56), Neag, Škvorc, Munteanu, Ciupe, Lungu, Ceppelini (Nuno Viveiros 46), Kovacs (Cristocea 68), Mengolo, Morar*

Silverware and a big cheque for Romanian Cup winners Steaua

RUSSIA
Russian Football Union (RFS)

Address	Ulitsa Narodnaya 7	**President (interim)**	Nikita Simonyan
	RU-115172 Moskva	**General secretary**	Anatoli Vorobyev
Tel	+7 495 926 1300	**Media officer**	Igor Vladimirov
Fax	+7 495 201 1303	**Year of formation**	1912
E-mail	info@rfs.ru		
Website	rfs.ru		

0   2000 km
0   1000 miles

KEY:
- – UEFA Champions League
- – UEFA Europa League
- – Promoted
- – Relegated

St Peterburg
(St Petersburg)

16

7 11 13

4

3   Moskva (Moscow)

Tula

2

Saransk

10

8   Kazan   1   Perm

Rostov-na-Donu

Samara   14   Yekaterinburg

5   9   17   15

Ufa

6   Krasnodar

12

Grozny

18   Makhachkala

0   1000   2000 km
0   1000 miles

PREMIER-LIGA CLUBS

 ① FC Amkar Perm

 ② PFC Arsenal Tula

 ③ PFC CSKA Moskva

 ④ FC Dinamo Moskva

 ⑤ FC Krasnodar

 ⑥ FC Kuban Krasnodar

 ⑦ FC Lokomotiv Moskva

 ⑧ FC Mordovia Saransk

 ⑨ FC Rostov

 ⑩ FC Rubin Kazan

 ⑪ FC Spartak Moskva

 ⑫ FC Terek Grozny

 ⑬ FC Torpedo Moskva

 ⑭ FC Ufa

 ⑮ FC Ural Sverdlovsk Oblast

 ⑯ FC Zenit

PROMOTED CLUBS

 ⑰ PFC Krylya Sovetov Samara

 ⑱ FC Anji Makhachkala

Zenit all the way

Astutely led by Portuguese coach André Villas-Boas, FC Zenit regained the Russian Premier-Liga title in 2014/15. The St Petersburg club made up for their agonising near-miss of the previous season by dominating from the start and finishing seven points clear of defending champions PFC CSKA Moskva.

Up-and-coming FC Krasnodar were narrowly edged out of second place by CSKA, while city rivals FC Kuban Krasnodar finished runners-up in the Russian Cup to another club from the capital, FC Lokomotiv Moskva. On the international front there was more woe for Fabio Capello's 2014 FIFA World Cup flops, with the Italian coach departing in the summer.

Wire-to-wire triumph for Villas-Boas's team	Sixth Russian Cup win for Lokomotiv	Capello sacked as national team struggle

Domestic league

Villas-Boas, the former FC Porto, Chelsea FC and Tottenham Hotspur FC coach, made it a successful first full season in St Petersburg as he steered Russia's richest club to their fourth Premier-Liga title since 2007. Runners-up to CSKA in each of the previous two seasons, Zenit were on a mission right from the outset. Fortified by new signings Ezequiel Garay and Javi García, they made the perfect start with victories in each of their first eight fixtures, including a record-equalling 8-1 win over newly-promoted FC Torpedo Moskva in their opening home game.

Zenit's winning run finally came to a halt at the end of September when they were held 0-0 at home by FC Spartak Moskva, and it was also in the Petrovski stadium that they fell to their first defeat, 3-1 to FC Terek Grozny.

A month later, however, with three more wins under their belt, the last of them a 4-0 demolition of Krasnodar, Villas-Boas's troops headed into the winter recess armed with a seven-point lead. It was an advantage they would protect with assurance in the spring, avoiding further defeat all the way through to the 1-1 draw away to FC Ufa on 17 May that wrapped up the title.

It was a powerful and commanding triumph, with the club's investment in top-class foreign imports paying off in all departments of the team. Argentinian international centre-back Garay, recruited from SL Benfica, acclimatised brilliantly to the unfamiliar surroundings and, in tandem with long-serving Nicolas Lombaerts, brought security to a defence that conceded just 17 goals all season – 15 fewer than in 2013/14. Midfielder Axel Witsel and left-back Domenico Criscito were also the best in their positions in the league, while in attack the South American pairing of Hulk and José Salomón Rondón scored 28 goals between them, with the Brazilian's tally of 15 proving sufficient to top the scoring charts.

Goals were not exactly in plentiful supply throughout the Premier-Liga, with only CSKA averaging more than two per game and six teams less than one – a reason perhaps for the drop in the league's average attendance to below five figures for the first time in a decade. CSKA's goal ratio was boosted by a burst of five successive victories in the run-in during which they found the net 15 times. That came too late to threaten Zenit, but it did enable them to re-qualify for the UEFA Champions League as runners-up, Leonid Slutski's side finishing level on points with Krasnodar

but above them by virtue of the local rule prioritising the number of victories.

Although second place would have disappointed CSKA at the start of the campaign as they sought a Premier-Liga hat-trick, it was ultimately greeted with relief and pleasure. The club were grateful for the outstanding contributions of two newcomers, ex-FC Rubin Kazan duo Roman Eremenko and Bebras Natcho, who not only outshone local hero Alan Dzagoev in midfield but also shared 25 goals – a tally much needed following the mid-season sale of 2013/14 Premier-Liga top scorer Seydou Doumbia to AS Roma.

Krasnodar had second place snatched away from them despite avoiding defeat during their 13 spring fixtures – an impressive response to that 4-0 drubbing by Zenit in December. Brilliantly led by Belarusian coach Oleg Kononov, who had taken the club to fifth place and the Russian Cup final the previous season (his first in charge), Krasnodar kicked on in 2014/15 and were not just difficult to beat but entertaining with it. Their Brazilian strike force of Ari and Wanderson were deprived of their injured compatriot Joãozinho in the spring, but against that the team benefited enormously from the mid-season arrival from Spartak of Russia captain Roman Shirokov.

Fallen giants Spartak endured another poor campaign, which proved to be the first and last under Swiss coach Murat Yakin. They finished sixth, outside the European places, and there would be no UEFA Europa League return either for their fourth-placed city rivals FC Dinamo Moskva, whose failure to meet financial fair play requirements resulted in their exclusion, enabling fifth-placed Rubin to enter the competition instead.

Unlike the previous season, there were only two clubs, rather than four, promoted and relegated to and from the Premier-Liga because the two play-offs went the way of the top-flight teams. Furthermore, as two of the sides promoted 12 months before – Torpedo and PFC Arsenal Tula – dropped back down again, so two of the teams that had ceded their top-flight membership a year earlier – PFC Krylya Sovetov Samara and FC Anji Makhachkala – reclaimed it at the first attempt.

Domestic cup

A lowly seventh in the league – after finishing third in 2013/14 – Lokomotiv salvaged their season by winning the Russian Cup. A couple of penalty shoot-out wins carried them through to the final against Kuban, but the man who had navigated them through those spot-kick successes, Montenegrin coach Miodrag Božović, was not around

to see the job through – or to repeat his 2013/14 success in the competition with FC Rostov. He had been jettisoned following a wretched run in the league and replaced by interim boss Igor Cherevchenko, and the former Lokomotiv defender would make history as the first man to win the trophy as both player and coach when his team came from behind to defeat the semi-final conquerors of CSKA 3-1 in Astrakhan. Once again Lokomotiv were taken to extra time, but on this occasion they were spared penalties as goals from Mbark Boussoufa and Aleksei Miranchuk secured the club's sixth victory in the competition – one behind CSKA's record tally.

Europe

Neither CSKA nor Zenit made it beyond the group stage of the UEFA Champions League. CSKA finished bottom of their section despite registering four points against English champions Manchester City FC, who had defeated them home and away the previous season, while Zenit, who had come through two qualifying rounds, failed to build on a confidence-boosting opening 2-0 win at Benfica and ended up third. Villas-Boas's men extended their European adventure to 16 matches by reaching the quarter-finals of the UEFA Europa League, but when their 100% home record in that competition was brought

to an end by a late equaliser from Sevilla FC, it proved fatal.

Zenit were the last Russian club standing in Europe. Rostov and Lokomotiv both went out in the UEFA Europa League play-offs, the latter's calamitous 4-1 home defeat to Apollon Limassol FC costing coach Leonid Kuchuk his job. Stanislav Cherchesov's Dinamo were seconds away from falling at the same hurdle to another Cypriot club, AC Omonia, but they survived and went on to win all six group games – in each case by a single-goal margin – and eliminate RSC Anderlecht before bowing out against SSC Napoli in the round of 16. Krasnodar also exceeded expectations when they defeated Real Sociedad de Fútbol 3-0 at home to join Dinamo in the group stage, but heavy back-to-back defeats by VfL Wolfsburg killed their chances of further progress.

National team

A weak effort from Capello's Russia at the World Cup in Brazil was followed by another poor showing in the UEFA EURO 2016 qualifying campaign that left the 2018 World Cup hosts some way adrift of the top two teams in their group, Austria and Sweden, with four matches left to play. Those remaining fixtures would be overseen by a new coach, Capello having been relieved of his duties on 14 July 2015 – three years before the end of his contract.

As in his previous job as manager of England, the Italian struggled to make his experience and expertise count on the international stage. Although Russia began their quest for a place in France with a 4-0 win against Liechtenstein, their only other three-pointer over the next nine months would come via a 3-0 forfeit victory following an abandoned match against Montenegro in Podgorica. A 1-1 draw in Sweden would have been considered a positive outcome had it not been for a repeat result at home to Moldova three days later. That was followed by further dismay as Russia were defeated by Austria in Vienna and, seven months later, by the same opponents in Moscow, going down 1-0 on both occasions. Comprehensively outplayed in that home defeat in June, Russia's prospects of qualification looked grim indeed, and a month to the day later Capello's three-year reign was over.

Seydou Doumbia (left) scores the first of his two goals in CSKA Moskva's 2-1 win at Manchester City in the UEFA Champions League group stage

DOMESTIC SEASON AT A GLANCE

Premier-Liga 2014/15 final table

		Pld	Home					Away					Total					Pts
			W	D	L	F	A	W	D	L	F	A	W	D	L	F	A	
1	**FC Zenit**	**30**	**12**	**2**	**1**	**36**	**8**	**8**	**5**	**2**	**22**	**9**	**20**	**7**	**3**	**58**	**17**	**67**
2	PFC CSKA Moskva	30	11	1	3	39	9	8	2	5	28	18	19	3	8	67	27	60
3	FC Krasnodar	30	9	4	2	29	14	8	5	2	23	13	17	9	4	52	27	60
4	FC Dinamo Moskva	30	7	5	3	31	17	7	3	5	22	19	14	8	8	53	36	50
5	FC Rubin Kazan	30	8	4	3	22	15	5	5	5	17	18	13	9	8	39	33	48
6	FC Spartak Moskva	30	6	6	3	23	20	6	2	7	19	22	12	8	10	42	42	44
7	FC Lokomotiv Moskva	30	8	4	3	21	12	3	6	6	10	13	11	10	9	31	25	43
8	FC Mordovia Saransk	30	7	3	5	10	10	4	2	9	12	33	11	5	14	22	43	38
9	FC Terek Grozny	30	6	4	5	19	13	4	3	8	11	17	10	7	13	30	30	37
10	FC Kuban Krasnodar	30	6	6	3	21	15	2	6	7	11	21	8	12	10	32	36	36
11	FC Amkar Perm	30	8	2	5	15	11	0	6	9	10	31	8	8	14	25	42	32
12	FC Ufa	30	2	6	7	13	20	5	4	6	13	19	7	10	13	26	39	31
13	FC Ural Sverdlovsk Oblast	30	5	2	8	17	20	4	1	10	14	24	9	3	18	31	44	30
14	FC Rostov	30	6	3	6	15	19	1	5	9	12	32	7	8	15	27	51	29
15	FC Torpedo Moskva	30	3	6	6	14	19	3	5	7	14	26	6	11	13	28	45	29
16	PFC Arsenal Tula	30	2	3	10	11	25	5	1	9	9	21	7	4	19	20	46	25

European qualification 2015/16

Champion: FC Zenit (group stage)
PFC CSKA Moskva (third qualifying round)

Cup winner: FC Lokomotiv Moskva (group stage)
FC Krasnodar (third qualifying round)
FC Rubin Kazan (third qualifying round)

Top scorer   Hulk (Zenit), 15 goals
Relegated clubs   PFC Arsenal Tula, FC Torpedo Moskva
Promoted clubs   PFC Krylya Sovetov Samara, FC Anji Makhachkala
Cup final   FC Lokomotiv Moskva 3-1 FC Kuban Krasnodar (aet)

Team of the season
(4-3-3)

Coach: Villas-Boas (Zenit)

Player of the season

Hulk
(FC Zenit)

Brazilian international Hulk scored fewer goals in the 2014/15 Premier-Liga than the season before, but while there might have been a slight reduction in the quantity – which still earned him the golden boot – the quality of his strikes was every bit as good and the importance of them even greater. The 15th and last of his tally, a blistering free-kick against FC Ufa, clinched the title for the St Petersburg club, and he also scored both of Zenit's goals in a vital 2-1 win at home to PFC CSKA Moskva.

Newcomer of the season

Denis Davydov
(FC Spartak Moskva)

Spartak's first season in their splendid new Otkrytie-Arena was largely one of underachievement as they failed to qualify for Europe. Countering the disappointment, however, was the exciting emergence of academy graduate Davydov, a stocky, skilful, 20-year-old striker dubbed 'our Messi' by club owner Leonid Fedun. The Russian Under-21 international made his senior bow in March and looks likely to be heavily involved in Russia's three-year countdown to the 2018 FIFA World Cup.

NATIONAL TEAM

International honours*
UEFA European Championship (1) 1960

International tournament appearances*
FIFA World Cup (10) 1958 (qtr-finals), 1962 (qtr-finals), 1966 (4th), 1970 (qtr-finals), 1982 (2nd phase), 1986 (2nd round), 1990, 1994, 2002, 2014
UEFA European Championship (10) 1960 (Winners), 1964 (runners-up), 1968 (4th), 1972 (runners-up), 1988 (runners-up), 1992, 1996, 2004, 2008 (semi-finals), 2012

Top five all-time caps
Viktor Onopko (113); Oleh Blokhin (112); **Sergei Ignashevich** (108); Rinat Dasaev (91); **Vasili Berezutski, Aleksandr Kerzhakov** & Albert Shesternyov (90)

Top five all-time goals
Oleh Blokhin (42); **Aleksandr Kerzhakov** (30); Oleh Protasov (29); Vladimir Beschastnykh & Valentin Ivanov (26)

(* before 1992 as USSR; 1992 as CIS)

Results 2014/15

Date	Opponent		Venue	Res	Score	Scorers
03/09/14	Azerbaijan	H	Khimki	W	4-0	Kerzhakov (6, 12), Ignashevich (41), Granat (81)
08/09/14	Liechtenstein (ECQ)	H	Khimki	W	4-0	M Büchel (4og), Burgmeier (50og), Kombarov (54p), Dzyuba (65)
09/10/14	Sweden (ECQ)	A	Solna	D	1-1	Kokorin (10)
12/10/14	Moldova (ECQ)	H	Moscow	D	1-1	Dzyuba (73p)
15/11/14	Austria (ECQ)	A	Vienna	L	0-1	
18/11/14	Hungary	A	Budapest	W	2-1	Ignashevich (49), Kerzhakov (80)
27/03/15	Montenegro (ECQ)	A	Podgorica	W	3-0	(w/o; original match abandoned after 67 mins at 0-0)
31/03/15	Kazakhstan	H	Khimki	D	0-0	
07/06/15	Belarus	H	Khimki	W	4-2	Kokorin (20), Golovin (77), Miranchuk (83), Kerzhakov (90+1)
14/06/15	Austria (ECQ)	H	Moscow	L	0-1	

Appearances 2014/15

Coach: Fabio Capello (ITA)	18/06/46		Aze	LIE	SWE	MDA	AUT	Hun	MNE	Kaz	Blr	AUT	Caps	Goals
Igor Akinfeev	08/04/86	CSKA Moskva	G46	G72	G	G	G		G2		G	G	80	-
Igor Smolnikov	08/08/88	Zenit	D	D	D				D		D	D	7	-
Vasili Berezutski	20/06/82	CSKA Moskva	D	D	D	D	D	D46	D	D22		D12	90	4
Sergei Ignashevich	14/07/79	CSKA Moskva	D46	D	D	D	D	s46	D		D	D71	108	7
Dmitri Kombarov	22/01/87	Spartak Moskva	D68	D	D88		D		D		D	D71	33	2
Denis Glushakov	27/01/87	Spartak Moskva	M	M	M	M	M	M77			M75	M	37	3
Alan Dzagoev	17/06/90	CSKA Moskva	M	M64	s87	M	s81	M	M46		M46		44	8
Oleg Shatov	29/07/90	Zenit	M46		M		M81		M		M	M	16	2
Denis Cheryshev	26/12/90	Villarreal (ESP)	M83	M		M62	M56	s46					7	-
Dmitri Poloz	12/07/91	Rostov	A75			s62							2	-
Aleksandr Kerzhakov	27/11/82	Zenit	A	A46		A46		s62			s61	s71	90	30
Yuri Lodygin	26/05/90	Zenit	s46	s72				G	s2	G			8	-
Vladimir Granat	22/05/87	Dinamo Moskva	s46		s88	D	D70						9	1
Magomed Ozdoev	05/11/92	Rubin	s46	s64	s46		s77			s46	s75		6	-
Sergei Parshivlyuk	18/03/89	Spartak Moskva	s68			D	D						3	-
Aleksandr Samedov	19/07/84	Lokomotiv Moskva	s75	M	M73			M		M			25	3
Aleksei Ionov	18/02/89	Dinamo Moskva	s83			M75	s56						8	-
Aleksandr Kokorin	19/03/91	Dinamo Moskva		A	A	A	A	s46	A		A61	A	32	8
Artem Dzyuba	22/08/88	Spartak Moskva /Rostov		s46	A	A	s75	A62			A46		9	2
Viktor Fayzulin	22/04/86	Zenit			M87	M75							24	4
Maksim Grigoryev	06/07/90	Rostov			s73								4	-
Georgi Schennikov	27/04/91	CSKA Moskva			s75		D			D71			7	-
Roman Shirokov	06/07/81	Spartak Moskva /Krasnodar				M	M46		M		M62	M	46	12
Evgeni Makeev	24/07/89	Spartak Moskva						D			s78		3	-
Maksim Kanunnikov	14/07/91	Rubin						M46		M80			6	-
Andrei Semyonov	24/03/89	Terek						s70					2	-
Yuri Zhirkov	20/08/83	Dinamo Moskva							M		M71	M	65	1
Igor Denisov	17/05/84	Dinamo Moskva							M				47	-
Dmitri Torbinski	28/04/84	Rostov							s46	M63			28	2
Aleksei Kozlov	25/12/86	Dinamo Moskva									D		14	-
Ivan Novoseltsev	25/08/91	Rostov									D	D	2	-
Ruslan Kambolov	01/01/90	Rubin									M		1	-
Aleksandr Ryazantsev	05/09/86	Zenit								M46			5	-
Roman Zobnin	11/02/94	Dinamo Moskva								s22			1	-
Igor Portnyagin	07/01/89	Rubin								s46			1	-
Denis Davydov	22/03/95	Spartak Moskva								s63			1	-
Elmir Nabiullin	08/03/95	Rubin								s71			1	-
Dmitri Yefremov	01/04/95	CSKA Moskva								s80			1	-
Nikita Chernov	14/01/96	CSKA Moskva									D78	s12	2	-
Oleg Ivanov	04/08/86	Terek									s46	M46	2	-
Aleksandr Golovin	30/05/96	CSKA Moskva									s62		1	1
Aleksei Miranchuk	17/10/95	Lokomotiv Moskva									s71	s46	2	-

EUROPE

PFC CSKA Moskva

CHAMPIONS LEAGUE

Group E
Match 1 - AS Roma (ITA)
A 1-5 *Musa (82)*
Akinfeev, Mário Fernandes, Ignashevich, Tošić (Efremov 53), Nababkin (Schennikov 46), Musa, Milanov, V Berezutski, Eremenko (Panchenko 66), Natcho, Doumbia. Coach: Leonid Slutski (RUS)
Match 2 - FC Bayern München (GER)
H 0-1
Akinfeev, Mário Fernandes, Ignashevich, A Berezutski, Tošić (Efremov 78), Musa, Milanov, V Berezutski, Eremenko, Schennikov, Natcho (Doumbia 66). Coach: Leonid Slutski (RUS)
Match 3 - Manchester City FC (ENG)
H 2-2 *Doumbia (65), Natcho (86p)*
Akinfeev, Mário Fernandes, Ignashevich, A Berezutski (Doumbia 46; Cauņa 90), Tošić (Efremov 69), Musa, Milanov, V Berezutski, Eremenko, Schennikov, Natcho. Coach: Leonid Slutski (RUS)
Match 4 - Manchester City FC (ENG)
A 2-1 *Doumbia (2, 34)*
Akinfeev, Mário Fernandes, Wernbloom, Ignashevich, Dzagoev (Efremov 86), Musa, V Berezutski, Eremenko, Schennikov, Natcho, Doumbia (Milanov 46). Coach: Leonid Slutski (RUS)
Match 5 - AS Roma (ITA)
H 1-1 *V Berezutski (90+3)*
Akinfeev, Mário Fernandes, Ignashevich, Dzagoev, Musa (Tošić 81), Cauņa (Milanov 64), V Berezutski, Eremenko, Schennikov, Natcho, Doumbia. Coach: Leonid Slutski (RUS)
Match 6 - FC Bayern München (GER)
A 0-3
Akinfeev, Mário Fernandes, Wernbloom, Ignashevich, Dzagoev, Musa (Efremov 90), V Berezutski, Eremenko (Milanov 82), Natcho (Tošić 66), Doumbia. Coach: Leonid Slutski (RUS)

FC Zenit

CHAMPIONS LEAGUE

Third qualifying round - AEL Limassol FC (CYP)
A 0-1
Lodygin, Anyukov (Smolnikov 73), Criscito, Hulk, Kerzhakov (Rondón 60), Luís Neto, Fayzulin, Garay, Witsel, Danny (Shatov 69), Tymoshchuk. Coach: André Villas-Boas (POR)
Red card: Witsel 67
H 3-0 *Rondón (55), Danny (88), Kerzhakov (90p)*
Lodygin, Criscito, Lombaerts, Hulk, Shatov (Solovyev 85), Smolnikov (Kerzhakov 46), Fayzulin, Rondón, Garay, Danny, Tymoshchuk (Ryazantsev 75). Coach: André Villas-Boas (POR)

Play-offs - R Standard de Liège (BEL)
A 1-0 *Shatov (16)*
Lodygin, Criscito, Lombaerts, Hulk (Solovyev 90+1), Shatov (Ryazantsev 82), Smolnikov, Fayzulin, Rondón, Garay, Danny, Tymoshchuk. Coach: André Villas-Boas (POR)
H 3-0 *Rondón (30), Hulk (54p, 58)*
Lodygin, Criscito, Lombaerts, Hulk (Arshavin 90), Shatov (Anyukov 83), Smolnikov, Fayzulin, Rondón (Tymoshchuk 46), Garay, Witsel, Danny. Coach: André Villas-Boas (POR)
Red card: Fayzulin 44

Group C
Match 1 - SL Benfica (POR)
A 2-0 *Hulk (5), Witsel (22)*
Lodygin, Criscito, Lombaerts, Hulk (Arshavin 85), Shatov, Smolnikov (Anyukov 46), Javi García, Rondón (Mogilevets 76), Garay, Witsel, Danny. Coach: André Villas-Boas (POR)
Match 2 - AS Monaco FC (FRA)
H 0-0
Lodygin, Anyukov (Arshavin 88), Criscito, Lombaerts, Hulk, Shatov (Smolnikov 66), Fayzulin, Javi García, Rondón (Kerzhakov 75), Garay, Danny. Coach: André Villas-Boas (POR)
Match 3 - Bayer 04 Leverkusen (GER)
A 0-2
Lodygin, Anyukov, Criscito, Lombaerts, Hulk, Fayzulin (Shatov 62), Javi García, Rondón, Garay, Witsel (Kerzhakov 82), Danny. Coach: André Villas-Boas (POR)
Match 4 - Bayer 04 Leverkusen (GER)
H 1-2 *Rondón (89)*
Lodygin, Anyukov, Criscito, Lombaerts, Hulk, Kerzhakov (Rondón 79), Shatov (Arshavin 87), Javi García, Garay, Witsel, Danny (Ryazantsev 79). Coach: André Villas-Boas (POR)
Match 5 - SL Benfica (POR)
H 1-0 *Danny (79)*
Lodygin, Anyukov, Criscito, Ryazantsev (Shatov 65), Lombaerts (Luís Neto 23), Hulk, Javi García (Fayzulin 58), Rondón, Garay, Witsel, Danny. Coach: André Villas-Boas (POR)
Match 6 - AS Monaco FC (FRA)
A 0-2
Lodygin, Criscito, Lombaerts, Hulk, Smolnikov (Ryazantsev 79), Fayzulin (Shatov 68), Javi García, Rondón, Garay, Witsel, Danny. Coach: André Villas-Boas (POR)

EUROPA LEAGUE

Round of 32 - PSV Eindhoven (NED)
A 1-0 *Hulk (64)*
Lodygin, Criscito, Hulk (Arshavin 90+2), Luís Neto, Shatov, Smolnikov, Javi García, Rondón (Ryazantsev 76), Garay, Witsel (Tymoshchuk 86), Danny. Coach: André Villas-Boas (POR)
H 3-0 *Rondón (28, 67), Hulk (48)*
Lodygin, Anyukov, Hulk (Mogilevets 85), Luís Neto, Shatov, Smolnikov, Javi García, Rondón, Garay, Witsel (Tymoshchuk 72), Danny (Ryazantsev 81). Coach: Luís Martins (POR)

Round of 16 - Torino FC (ITA)
H 2-0 *Witsel (38), Criscito (53)*
Lodygin, Criscito, Hulk, Luís Neto, Shatov (Ryazantsev 81), Smolnikov, Javi García, Rondón, Garay, Witsel (Tymoshchuk 90), Danny. Coach: André Villas-Boas (POR)
A 0-1
Lodygin, Criscito, Hulk, Luís Neto, Shatov (Ryazantsev 81), Smolnikov, Rondón, Garay, Witsel, Danny (Lombaerts 87), Tymoshchuk. Coach: André Villas-Boas (POR)

Quarter-finals - Sevilla FC (ESP)
A 1-2 *Ryazantsev (29)*
Lodygin, Anyukov, Ryazantsev (Tymoshchuk 82), Lombaerts, Luís Neto, Shatov (Khodzhaniyazov 75), Javi García, Rondón, Garay, Witsel, Rodić (Mogilevets 65). Coach: André Villas-Boas (POR)
H 2-2 *Rondón (48), Hulk (72)*
Lodygin, Criscito, Lombaerts, Hulk, Luís Neto, Shatov, Smolnikov, Javi García, Rondón (Kerzhakov 83), Witsel, Danny. Coach: André Villas-Boas (POR)

FC Rostov

EUROPA LEAGUE

Play-offs - Trabzonspor AŞ (TUR)
A 0-2
Pletikosa, Kalachev, Torbinski, Dyakov, Grigoryev (Bukharov 64), Kanga, Poloz (Doumbia 68), Milić, Goreux, Bastos, Gatcan. Coach: Miodrag Božović (MNE)
H 0-0
Pletikosa, Kalachev, Torbinski (Bukharov 68), Dyakov, Grigoryev (Yoo 77), Kanga, Poloz (Doumbia 60), Milić, Goreux, Bastos, Gatcan. Coach: Miodrag Božović (MNE)

FC Lokomotiv Moskva

EUROPA LEAGUE

Play-offs - Apollon Limassol FC (CYP)
A 1-1 *Kasaev (39)*
Guilherme, Kasaev (Maicon 62), Manuel Fernandes, Ćorluka, Samedov, Niasse (N'Doye 46), Tarasov (Mikhalik 65), Tigorev, Ďurica, Denisov, Shishkin. Coach: Leonid Kuchuk (BLR)
Red cards: Tigorev 76, Denisov 87
H 1-4 *Pavlyuchenko (85)*
Guilherme, Kasaev (Samedov 67), Manuel Fernandes (Miranchuk 53), Pejčinović, Maicon, Ćorluka, Niasse (Pavlyuchenko 53), Tarasov, Ďurica, Shishkin, Seraskhov. Coach: Leonid Kuchuk (BLR)

FC Dinamo Moskva

EUROPA LEAGUE

Third qualifying round - Hapoel Kiryat Shmona FC (ISR)
H 1-1 *Kuranyi (71)*
Gabulov, Büttner, Samba, Vainqueur, Dzsudzsák, Ionov, Granat, Noboa (Kokorin 54), Kuranyi, Manolev, Denisov. Coach: Stanislav Cherchesov (RUS)
A 2-1 *Kuranyi (22p), Ionov (30)*
Berezovski, Büttner, Samba, Vainqueur, Dzsudzsák (Zhirkov 68), Kokorin, Ionov (Smolov 62), Granat, Kuranyi (Noboa 58), Kozlov, Denisov. Coach: Stanislav Cherchesov (RUS)

Play-offs - AC Omonia (CYP)
H 2-2 *Samba (33), Büttner (72)*
Berezovski, Samba, Douglas, Vainqueur, Dzsudzsák, Kokorin, Ionov (Büttner 36), Granat, Valbuena (Manolev 90), Kuranyi, Denisov. Coach: Stanislav Cherchesov (RUS)
Red card: Kokorin 62
A 2-1 *Stepanov (11og), Samba (90+3)*
Berezovski, Büttner (Prudnikov 83), Samba, Douglas, Vainqueur, Dzsudzsák (Noboa 75), Ionov (Zhirkov 68), Valbuena, Kuranyi, Manolev, Denisov. Coach: Stanislav Cherchesov (RUS)
Red card: Vainqueur 73

Group E
Match 1 - Panathinaikos FC (GRE)
A 2-1 *Kokorin (40), Ionov (49)*
Gabulov, Büttner (Granat 69), Samba, Douglas, Dzsudzsák, Yusupov, Kokorin (Hubočan 89), Ionov, Noboa, Kuranyi (Prudnikov 90+3), Manolev. Coach: Stanislav Cherchesov (RUS)
Match 2 - PSV Eindhoven (NED)
H 1-0 *Zhirkov (90+3)*
Gabulov, Büttner, Samba, Douglas, Vainqueur, Dzsudzsák (Zhirkov 61), Yusupov, Kokorin, Ionov (Valbuena 73), Hubočan, Noboa (Kuranyi 68). Coach: Stanislav Cherchesov (RUS)
Match 3 - Estoril Praia (POR)
A 2-1 *Kokorin (52), Zhirkov (80)*
Gabulov, Büttner, Samba, Douglas, Vainqueur, Kokorin (Kuranyi 75), Ionov (Zhirkov 56), Valbuena (Rotenberg 90+2), Noboa, Kozlov, Denisov. Coach: Stanislav Cherchesov (RUS)
Match 4 - Estoril Praia (POR)
H 1-0 *Kuranyi (77)*
Gabulov, Büttner, Samba, Douglas, Vainqueur, Dzsudzsák (Zhirkov 76), Kokorin (Kuranyi 74), Ionov, Valbuena (Yusupov 86), Hubočan, Denisov. Coach: Stanislav Cherchesov (RUS)
Match 5 - Panathinaikos FC (GRE)
H 2-1 *Triantafyllopoulos (55og), Ionov (61)*
Gabulov, Büttner, Samba, Douglas, Vainqueur, Ionov (Dzsudzsák 81), Valbuena, Noboa, Zhirkov (Yusupov 73), Kuranyi (Prudnikov 88), Rotenberg. Coach: Stanislav Cherchesov (RUS)
Match 6 - PSV Eindhoven (NED)
A 1-0 *Ionov (90)*
Shunin, Douglas, Vainqueur (Ionov 59), Dzsudzsák (Tashaev 90+3), Yusupov, Valbuena, Hubočan, Noboa, Kuranyi (Prudnikov 68), Manolev, Kozlov. Coach: Stanislav Cherchesov (RUS)

Round of 32 - RSC Anderlecht (BEL)
A 0-0
Gabulov, Büttner, Samba, Vainqueur, Dzsudzsák (Zhirkov 69), Yusupov, Kokorin, Valbuena (Ionov 80), Hubočan, Kuranyi (Denisov 51), Kozlov. Coach: Stanislav Cherchesov (RUS)
Red card: Büttner 75
H 3-1 *Kozlov (47), Yusupov (64), Kuranyi (90+5)*
Gabulov, Samba, Douglas, Vainqueur, Dzsudzsák (Ionov 68), Yusupov, Kokorin, Valbuena (Kuranyi 84), Hubočan, Zhirkov, Kozlov (Douglas 53), Denisov. Coach: Stanislav Cherchesov (RUS)

Round of 16 - SSC Napoli (ITA)
A 1-3 *Kuranyi (2)*
Gabulov, Samba, Vainqueur, Dzsudzsák (Tashaev 90+2), Kokorin, Valbuena (Ionov 72), Hubočan, Zhirkov, Kuranyi (Büttner 62), Kozlov, Zobnin. Coach: Stanislav Cherchesov (RUS)
Red card: Zobnin 46
H 0-0
Gabulov, Büttner (Ionov 85), Samba, Vainqueur, Dzsudzsák, Kokorin, Valbuena, Hubočan, Zhirkov, Kuranyi, Kozlov. Coach: Stanislav Cherchesov (RUS)

FC Krasnodar

Second qualifying round - JK Sillamäe Kalev (EST)
A 4-0 *Ari (9), Gazinski (39), Wanderson (68), Bystrov (86)*
Sinitsin, Jędrzejczyk, Granqvist, Gazinski, Ari (Wanderson 56), Ahmedov, Kaleshin, Laborde (Bystrov 46), Joãozinho, Sigurdsson, Pereyra (Pomerko 69). Coach: Oleg Kononov (BLR)
H 5-0 *Joãozinho (28), Laborde (65), Wanderson (67, 74p), Burmistrov (76)*
Dykan, Martynovich, Gazinski (Ahmedov 46), Wanderson, Pomerko, Bystrov (Markov 68), Burmistrov, Joãozinho (Laborde 57), Sigurdsson, Pereyra, Petrov. Coach: Oleg Kononov (BLR)

Third qualifying round - Diósgyőri VTK (HUN)
A 5-1 *Ari (28), Ahmedov(40), Pereyra (51), Joãozinho (88p), Bystrov (90)*
Sinitsin, Martynovich, Jędrzejczyk, Gazinski, Ari (Wanderson 58), Ahmedov, Kaleshin, Laborde (Bystrov 58), Joãozinho, Sigurdsson, Pereyra (Pomerko 81). Coach: Oleg Kononov (BLR)
H 3-0 *Konaté (30, 55), Ari (86)*
Sinitsin, Markov, Martynovich, Granqvist, Izmailov, Wanderson (Ari 61), Pomerko, Burmistrov, Laborde (Joãozinho 61), Konaté (Ageev 76), Petrov. Coach: Oleg Kononov (BLR)

Play-offs - Real Sociedad de Fútbol (ESP)
A 0-1
Dykan, Jędrzejczyk, Granqvist, Gazinski, Ari (Wanderson 59), Ahmedov, Izmailov, Joãozinho (Bystrov 81), Sigurdsson, Pereyra (Laborde 81), Petrov. Coach: Oleg Kononov (BLR)
H 3-0 *Joãozinho (71p), Pereyra (88), Ari (90)*
Dykan, Jędrzejczyk, Granqvist, Gazinski (Laborde 64), Ari, Ahmedov, Izmailov (Wanderson 53), Kaleshin, Joãozinho, Sigurdsson, Pereyra (Adzhindzhal 90+3). Coach: Oleg Kononov (BLR)
Red card: Joãozinho 90+2

Group H
Match 1 - LOSC Lille (FRA)
A 1-1 *Laborde (35)*
Dykan, Jędrzejczyk, Granqvist, Gazinski, Ari, Ahmedov, Izmailov (Bystrov 69; Burmistrov 86), Kaleshin, Laborde (Wanderson 70), Sigurdsson, Pereyra. Coach: Oleg Kononov (BLR)
Match 2 - Everton FC (ENG)
H 1-1 *Ari (43)*
Dykan, Jędrzejczyk, Granqvist, Gazinski, Ari, Ahmedov, Izmailov (Wanderson 64), Kaleshin, Laborde (Mamaev 70), Sigurdsson, Pereyra (Petrov 84). Coach: Oleg Kononov (BLR)
Match 3 - VfL Wolfsburg (GER)
H 2-4 *Granqvist (51p), Wanderson (86)*
Dykan, Jędrzejczyk, Granqvist, Mamaev (Adzhindzhal 68), Gazinski (Petrov 80), Ari, Ahmedov, Kaleshin, Laborde, Sigurdsson, Pereyra (Wanderson 68). Coach: Oleg Kononov (BLR)
Match 4 - VfL Wolfsburg (GER)
A 1-5 *Wanderson (72)*
Dykan, Jędrzejczyk, Granqvist, Gazinski, Ari (Izmailov 71), Ahmedov, Wanderson (Mamaev 80), Kaleshin (Petrov 30), Laborde, Sigurdsson, Pereyra. Coach: Oleg Kononov (BLR)
Match 5 - LOSC Lille (FRA)
H 1-1 *Ari (35)*
Dykan, Jędrzejczyk (Martynovich 45+2), Mamaev (Wanderson 82), Gazinski, Ari, Izmailov (Laborde 46), Kaleshin, Joãozinho, Sigurdsson, Pereyra, Petrov. Coach: Oleg Kononov (BLR)
Match 6 - Everton FC (ENG)
A 1-0 *Laborde (30)*
Sinitsin, Granqvist, Gazinski, Izmailov, Wanderson, Kaleshin, Laborde (Burmistrov 73), Joãozinho (Ageev 90+1), Sigurdsson, Pereyra, Petrov. Coach: Oleg Kononov (BLR)

FC Amkar Perm

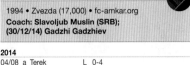

1994 • Zvezda (17,000) • fc-amkar.org
Coach: Slavoljub Muslin (SRB);
(30/12/14) Gadzhi Gadzhiev

2014
04/08	a	Terek	L	0-4
08/08	h	Ufa	L	0-1
12/08	a	Torpedo	D	1-1 *Picusciac*
18/08	a	Kuban	L	0-1
23/08	a	Zenit	L	0-2
30/08	h	Spartak	W	2-0 *Kireev, Peev*
15/09	h	Ural	W	2-1 *Dzasokhov, Peev*
22/09	h	Krasnodar	L	1-2 *Kireev*
28/09	a	Lokomotiv	L	1-3 *Jovičić*
25/10	h	Rostov	W	2-0 *Ogude, Kolomeitsev*
03/11	a	Rubin	D	1-1 *Jovičić*
08/11	h	Mordovia	L	0-1
23/11	a	Arsenal	L	0-4
28/11	a	Rostov	D	1-1 *Gol*
02/12	a	CSKA	L	1-2 *Takazov*
07/12	a	Dinamo	L	0-5

2015
09/03	h	Torpedo	D	0-0
14/03	h	Ufa	D	1-1 *Prudnikov*
21/03	a	Ural	L	0-1
04/04	h	Rubin	L	0-3
07/04	a	Mordovia	L	0-1
13/04	h	CSKA	W	1-0 *Kireev*
20/04	a	Arsenal	L	0-1
25/04	h	Terek	W	2-1 *Prudnikov, Jovičić*
30/04	h	Dinamo	W	2-0 *Peev (p), Kolomeitsev*
03/05	h	Lokomotiv	D	1-1 *Peev (p)*
11/05	a	Krasnodar	D	1-1 *Gol*
16/05	h	Kuban	W	1-0 *Prudnikov*
23/05	h	Zenit	W	1-0 *Kolomeitsev*
30/05	a	Spartak	D	3-3 *Prudnikov, Peev, Budko*

No	Name	Nat	DoB	Pos	Aps	(s)	Gls
50	Robert Arzumanyan	ARM	24/07/85	D	8		
13	Sergei Balanovich	BLR	29/08/87	M	24		
4	Maksim Batov		05/06/92	M	3	(7)	
21	Dmitri Belorukov		24/03/83	D	15		
91	Bohdan Budko	UKR	13/01/91	D	11	(1)	1
23	Ivan Cherenchikov		25/08/84	D	22	(4)	
17	David Dzasokhov		18/01/89	M	13	(2)	1
77	Blagoy Georgiev	BUL	21/12/81	M	3		
1	Roman Gerus		14/09/80	G	27		
5	Janusz Gol	POL	11/11/85	M	17	(6)	2
16	Brian Oladapo Idowu		18/05/92	D	2	(9)	
26	Martin Jakubko	SVK	26/02/80	A	2	(12)	
33	Branko Jovičić	SRB	18/03/93	M	16	(5)	3
15	Dmitri Khomich		14/09/84	G	1		
8	Igor Kireev		17/02/92	M	14	(4)	3
19	Aleksandr Kolomeitsev		21/02/89	M	26	(2)	3
18	Aleksei Kurzenyov		09/01/95	A	1		
42	Sergei Narubin		05/12/81	G	2		
6	Aleksei Nikitin		27/01/92	D	9	(1)	
87	Fegor Ogude	NGA	29/07/87	M	24		1
7	Georgi Peev	BUL	11/03/79	M	9	(6)	5
10	Thomas Phibel	FRA	21/05/86	D	11		
10	Igor Picusciac	MDA	27/03/83	A	5	(6)	1
9	Aleksandr Prudnikov		26/02/89	A	13		4
22	Alikhan Shavaev		05/01/93	M	2	(3)	
11	Marko Simonovski	MKD	02/01/92	A		(4)	
14	Zahari Sirakov	BUL	08/10/77	D	8	(2)	
88	Pavel Solomatin		04/04/93	A	4	(3)	
99	Aleksandr Subbotin		20/10/91	A	1		
30	Soslan Takazov		28/02/93	D	9	(1)	1
43	Evgeni Tyukalov		07/08/92	A		(1)	
31	Jakub Wawrzyniak	POL	07/07/83	D	4	(2)	
3	Petar Zanev	BUL	18/10/85	D	23	(1)	
25	Damian Zbozień	POL	25/04/89	D	2		

PFC Arsenal Tula

1946 • Arsenal (20,048) • arsenaltula.ru
Coach: Dmitri Alenichev

2014

02/08	h	Zenit	L	0-4
10/08	h	Lokomotiv	L	0-2
13/08	h	Rubin	D	0-0
17/08	h	Dinamo	L	1-2 *Yershov*
22/08	a	Terek	L	0-3
30/08	h	Kuban	L	0-1
13/09	a	CSKA	L	1-2 *Zotov*
19/09	h	Mordovia	L	0-1
28/09	a	Krasnodar	L	0-3
19/10	h	Rostov	D	1-1 *Maloyan*
24/10	a	Ural	L	0-1
03/11	a	Torpedo	W	1-0 *Maloyan*
09/11	a	Spartak	L	0-2
23/11	h	Amkar	W	4-0 *Kuznetsov 2, Osipov, Kutyin*
29/11	h	Ural	L	1-2 *Maslov*
02/12	h	Ufa	L	0-1
08/12	a	Rostov	W	1-0 *Kaščelan*

2015

09/03	a	Rubin	L	0-1
14/03	a	Lokomotiv	W	1-0 *Zotov*
21/03	h	CSKA	L	1-4 *Timokhin*
05/04	h	Torpedo	L	1-3 *Maloyan*
09/04	h	Spartak	W	1-0 *Smirnov*
12/04	a	Ufa	L	0-2
20/04	a	Amkar	W	1-0 *Smirnov*
26/04	a	Zenit	L	0-1
04/05	h	Krasnodar	L	0-3
11/05	a	Mordovia	L	0-1
16/05	h	Terek	D	1-1 *Kutyin*
24/05	a	Dinamo	D	2-2 *Osipov, Hagush*
30/05	a	Kuban	L	1-5 *Kuznetsov*

No	Name	Nat	DoB	Pos	Aps	(s)	Gls
75	Evgeni Alfyorov		31/01/95	D	1		
24	Aleksei Bazanov		24/01/86	A	2	(6)	
86	Leonid Boyev		19/01/86	A	1		
63	Aleksandr Chibirov		28/02/92	D	1		
11	Florin Costea	ROU	16/05/85	A	3	(4)	
55	Artur Farion		27/01/95	D	1		
1	Aleksandr Filimonov		15/10/73	G	17		
14	Anri Hagush		23/09/86	D	11		1
27	Sergei Ignatyev		09/12/86	M	4	(4)	
23	Igor Kaleshin		29/05/83	D	17		
18	Mladen Kaščelan	MNE	13/02/83	M	25	(1)	1
9	Vladimir Korytko	BLR	06/07/79	M	7	(1)	1
16	Sergei Kotov		17/03/82	G	1		
85	Aleksandr Kryuchkov		20/07/85	M	1		
48	Aleksandr Kutyin		13/02/86	A	13	(3)	2
10	Sergei Kuznetsov		07/05/86	M	21	(6)	3
77	Maksim Lepskiy		07/12/85	M	2	(1)	
3	Ivan Lozenkov		14/04/84	D	12	(1)	
90	Andrei Lyakh		24/09/90	M	15	(7)	
18	Aleksandr Makarenko		04/02/86	M	1	(3)	
38	Artur Maloyan		04/02/89	A	15	(7)	3
14	Sergei Maslov		03/09/90	M	11	(2)	1
4	Yuri Medvedev		17/03/90	D		(1)	
99	Ján Mucha	SVK	05/12/82	G	12		
92	Andrei Naletov		31/03/95	D	1		
19	Evgeni Osipov		29/10/86	D	24		2
28	Vladislav Ryzhkov		28/07/90	M	18	(8)	
81	Roman Salimov		24/03/95	M	1		
21	Pavel Sergeev		20/06/93	M		(1)	
24	Dmitri Smirnov		13/08/80	M	7	(9)	2
89	Dmitri Starodub		19/05/95	M	1		
8	Sergei Sukharev		29/01/87	D	14	(2)	
22	Lukáš Tesák	SVK	08/03/85	D	22	(1)	
45	Rinat Timokhin		28/02/88	A		(1)	1
4	Andrei Vasilyev		11/02/92	D	14	(1)	
98	Maksim Votinov		29/08/88	A	3	(6)	
2	Ivan Yershov		22/05/79	D	11	(4)	1
82	Evgeni Yezhov		11/02/92	D	1		
54	Aleksandr Zakarlyuka		24/06/95	A	1		
7	Aleksandr Zotov		27/08/90	M	18	(3)	2

PFC CSKA Moskva

1911 • Arena Khimki (18,636); Eduard Streltsov (13,450) • pfc-cska.com

Major honours
UEFA Cup (1) 2005; USSR League (7) 1946, 1947, 1948, 1950, 1951, 1970, 1991; Russian League (5) 2003, 2005, 2006, 2013, 2014; USSR Cup (5) 1945, 1948, 1951, 1955, 1991; Russian Cup (7) 2002, 2005, 2006, 2008, 2009, 2011, 2013
Coach: Leonid Slutski

2014

02/08	h	Torpedo	W	4-1 *Doumbia (p), Panchenko, og (Aidov), Vitinho*
09/08	a	Mordovia	W	1-0 *Doumbia (p)*
13/08	h	Terek	W	1-0 *Tošić*
17/08	h	Spartak	L	0-1
23/08	a	Rubin	L	1-2 *Natcho (p)*
31/08	h	Rostov	W	6-0 *Natcho 3 (1p), Musa 2, Eremenko*
13/09	h	Arsenal	W	2-1 *Natcho (p), Eremenko*
21/09	h	Lokomotiv	W	1-0 *Musa*
27/09	a	Ural	W	4-3 *Dzagoev, Eremenko, Doumbia 2*
18/10	h	Kuban	W	6-0 *Musa 2, Eremenko, og (Armas), Doumbia 2*
26/10	a	Ufa	D	3-3 *V Berezutski, Natcho 2 (2p)*
01/11	h	Zenit	L	0-1
09/11	a	Dinamo	L	0-1
22/11	a	Krasnodar	L	1-2 *Eremenko*
29/11	h	Ufa	W	5-0 *Natcho, Tošić 2, Doumbia, Musa*
02/12	h	Amkar	W	2-1 *Eremenko 2*
06/12	h	Kuban	W	1-0 *Musa*

2015

07/03	a	Terek	W	2-1 *Musa 2*
14/03	h	Mordovia	W	4-0 *Dzagoev, Eremenko 2, Nababkin*
21/03	a	Arsenal	W	4-1 *Dzagoev, Natcho, Eremenko, Strandberg*
05/04	a	Zenit	L	1-2 *Strandberg*
08/04	h	Dinamo	L	1-2 *Milanov*
13/04	a	Amkar	L	0-1
19/04	h	Krasnodar	D	1-1 *Wernbloom*
25/04	a	Torpedo	W	2-0 *Strandberg, Natcho*
04/05	h	Ural	W	3-1 *Natcho (p), Milanov, Dzagoev*
10/05	a	Lokomotiv	W	3-1 *Dzagoev, Tošić, Natcho (p)*
17/05	a	Spartak	W	4-0 *Eremenko 2, Tošić, Musa*
25/05	h	Rubin	W	3-0 *Tošić 2, Eremenko*
30/05	a	Rostov	D	1-1 *Wernbloom*

No	Name	Nat	DoB	Pos	Aps	(s)	Gls
35	Igor Akinfeev		08/04/86	G	30		
71	Konstantin Bazelyuk		12/04/93	A		(1)	
6	Aleksei Berezutski		20/06/82	D	1	(6)	
24	Vasili Berezutski		20/06/82	D	30		1
19	Aleksandrs Cauņa	LVA	19/01/88	M		(5)	
88	Seydou Doumbia	CIV	31/12/87	A	8	(5)	7
4	Alan Dzagoev		17/06/90	M	18	(3)	5
25	Roman Eremenko	FIN	19/03/87	M	25		13
60	Aleksandr Golovin		30/05/96	M		(7)	
4	Sergei Ignashevich		14/07/79	D	30		
2	Mário Fernandes	BRA	19/09/90	D	29		
23	Georgi Milanov	BUL	19/02/92	M	24	(4)	2
18	Ahmed Musa	NGA	14/10/92	A	28	(2)	10
14	Kirill Nababkin		08/09/86	D	18	(3)	1
66	Bebras Natcho	ISR	18/02/88	M	24	(2)	12
8	Kirill Panchenko		16/10/89	A	4	(11)	1
42	Georgi Schennikov		27/04/91	D	12		
97	Carlos Strandberg	SWE	14/04/96	A	3	(7)	3
7	Zoran Tošić	SRB	28/04/87	M	22	(5)	7
31	Vitinho	BRA	09/10/93	A		(5)	1
3	Pontus Wernbloom	SWE	25/06/86	M	24	(1)	2
15	Dmitri Yefremov		01/04/95	M		(10)	
17	Steven Zuber	SUI	17/08/91	M		(2)	

FC Dinamo Moskva

1923 • Arena Khimki (18,636) • fcdynamo.ru

Major honours
USSR League (11) 1936 (spring), 1937, 1940, 1945, 1949, 1954, 1955, 1957, 1959, 1963, 1976 (spring); USSR Cup (6) 1937, 1953, 1967, 1970, 1977, 1984; Russian Cup (1) 1995
Coach: Stanislav Cherchesov

2014

03/08	h	Rostov	W	7-3 *Kuranyi 2 (1p), Samba, Dzsudzsák, Kokorin 3 (1p)*
10/08	h	Spartak	L	1-2 *Kokorin*
13/08	a	Ufa	W	2-0 *Samba, Kuranyi*
17/08	a	Arsenal	W	2-1 *Douglas, Kuranyi*
24/08	a	Ural	W	2-0 *Ionov 2*
31/08	a	Krasnodar	W	2-0 *Valbuena, Noboa*
13/09	a	Zenit	L	2-3 *Valbuena, Samba*
22/09	a	Torpedo	W	3-1 *Ionov 2, Dzsudzsák*
28/09	h	Kuban	D	2-2 *Kokorin, Manolev*
27/10	h	Rubin	L	0-2
02/11	a	Lokomotiv	L	2-4 *Ionov, Dzsudzsák*
09/11	h	CSKA	W	1-0 *Kokorin*
23/11	h	Terek	W	3-0 *Kokorin, Kuranyi 2 (1p)*
30/11	a	Rubin	D	1-1 *Dzsudzsák*
04/11	a	Mordovia	W	1-0 *Hubočan*
07/12	h	Amkar	W	5-0 *Kuranyi, Valbuena, Dzsudzsák, Ionov, Yusupov*

2015

08/03	h	Ufa	W	3-1 *Ionov, Valbuena, Kuranyi*
15/03	h	Spartak	L	0-1
22/03	h	Zenit	L	0-1
04/04	h	Lokomotiv	D	2-2 *Vainqueur, Kuranyi (p)*
08/04	a	CSKA	W	2-1 *Ionov, Dzsudzsák*
12/04	h	Mordovia	W	2-1 *Douglas, Kuranyi*
19/04	a	Terek	D	0-0
26/04	a	Rostov	D	2-2 *Kokorin, Samba*
30/04	a	Amkar	L	0-2
03/05	a	Kuban	W	2-1 *Douglas, og (Xandão)*
10/05	h	Torpedo	D	0-0
18/05	a	Ural	L	1-2 *Zobnin*
24/05	h	Arsenal	D	2-2 *Ionov, Vainqueur*
30/05	h	Krasnodar	D	1-1 *Dzsudzsák*

No	Name	Nat	DoB	Pos	Aps	(s)	Gls
21	Roman Berezovski	ARM	05/08/74	G	6		
3	Alexander Büttner	NED	11/02/89	D	18	(1)	
81	Egor Danilkin		01/08/95	D		(1)	
27	Igor Denisov		17/05/84	M	13		
8	Douglas	BRA	12/01/88	D	19	(3)	3
7	Balázs Dzsudzsák	HUN	23/12/86	M	19	(10)	7
30	Vladimir Gabulov		19/10/83	G	22		
3	Vladimir Granat		22/05/87	D	9		
15	Tomáš Hubočan	SVK	17/09/85	D	17	(1)	1
11	Aleksei Ionov		18/02/89	M	25	(5)	9
74	Anatoli Katrich		09/07/94	M		(4)	
9	Aleksandr Kokorin		19/03/91	A	18	(9)	8
25	Aleksei Kozlov		25/12/86	D	7	(5)	
22	Kevin Kuranyi	GER	02/03/82	A	18	(6)	10
96	Maksim Kuzmin		01/06/96	M		(1)	
29	Stanislav Manolev	BUL	16/12/85	D	5	(3)	1
16	Christian Noboa	ECU	08/04/85	M	7	(4)	1
9	Aleksandr Prudnikov		26/02/89	A	2	(4)	
28	Boris Rotenberg	FIN	19/05/86	D	8	(1)	
4	Christopher Samba	CGO	28/03/84	D	24		4
1	Anton Shunin		27/01/87	G	2		
90	Fedor Smolov		09/02/90	A	1	(1)	
88	Aleksandr Tashaev		23/06/94	M		(1)	
6	William Vainqueur	FRA	19/11/88	M	23	(4)	2
14	Mathieu Valbuena	FRA	28/09/84	M	24	(1)	4
8	Artur Yusupov		01/09/89	M	17	(4)	1
18	Yuri Zhirkov		20/08/83	M	21	(3)	
47	Roman Zobnin		11/02/94	M	5	(10)	1

RUSSIA

FC Krasnodar

2008 • Kuban (35,200) • fckrasnodar.ru
Coach: Oleg Kononov (BLR)

2014
03/08	a	Lokomotiv	D	0-0
10/08	a	Ural	D	1-1 Joãozinho (p)
14/08	h	Spartak	W	4-0 Izmailov, Ari, Bystrov, Joãozinho (p)
17/08	a	Rostov	W	2-0 Joãozinho, Ahmedov
24/08	a	Torpedo	W	3-0 Bystrov, Wanderson, Pereyra
31/08	h	Dinamo	L	0-2
14/09	h	Ufa	L	0-2
22/09	a	Amkar	W	2-1 Wanderson, Joãozinho (p)
28/09	a	Arsenal	W	3-0 Wanderson, Pereyra, Ari
18/10	h	Zenit	D	2-2 Sigurdsson, Mamaev
27/10	h	Terek	W	2-0 Joãozinho (p), Laborde
02/11	a	Mordovia	L	1-2 Joãozinho
09/11	h	Rubin	W	2-0 Petrov, Laborde
22/11	h	CSKA	W	2-1 Ari 2
30/11	a	Terek	W	1-0 Wanderson
03/12	a	Kuban	D	1-1 Pereyra
06/12	a	Zenit	L	0-4

2015
08/03	a	Spartak	W	3-1 Pereyra, Ari, Ahmedov
13/03	h	Ural	D	1-1 Mamaev
20/03	a	Ufa	W	2-0 Kaleshin, Ari
04/04	h	Mordovia	W	4-0 Mamaev 2, Laborde, Bystrov
07/04	a	Rubin	W	2-1 Pereyra 2
11/04	h	Kuban	W	3-2 Pereyra, Shirokov, Kaleshin
19/04	a	CSKA	D	1-1 Wanderson
25/04	h	Lokomotiv	W	1-0 Pereyra (p)
05/05	a	Arsenal	W	3-0 Shirokov, Ari, Laborde
11/05	h	Amkar	D	1-1 Pereyra
17/05	h	Torpedo	D	2-2 Wanderson (p), Laborde
24/05	h	Rostov	W	2-1 Shirokov, Wanderson
30/05	a	Dinamo	D	1-1 Shirokov

No	Name	Nat	DoB	Pos	Aps	(s)	Gls
20	Ruslan Adzhindzhal		22/06/74	M	1	(8)	
10	Odil Ahmedov	UZB	25/11/87	M	26		2
9	Ari	BRA	11/12/85	A	18	(8)	7
19	Nikita Burmistrov		06/07/89	A	2	(3)	
18	Vladimir Bystrov		31/01/84	M	5	(14)	3
31	Andriy Dykan	UKR	16/07/77	G	25		
8	Yuri Gazinski		20/07/89	M	19	(2)	
6	Andreas Granqvist	SWE	16/04/85	D	27		
11	Marat Izmailov		21/09/82	M	15	(7)	1
5	Artur Jedrzejczyk	POL	04/11/87	D	14		
22	Joãozinho	BRA	25/12/88	M	18	(1)	6
2	Vitali Kaleshin		03/10/80	D	24		2
21	Ricardo Laborde	COL	16/02/88	M	5	(20)	5
7	Pavel Mamaev		17/09/88	M	20	(1)	4
4	Aleksandr Martynovich	BLR	26/08/87	D	10	(1)	
33	Mauricio Pereyra	URU	15/03/90	M	26	(1)	9
98	Sergei Petrov		02/01/91	D	18	(4)	1
20	Aleksei Pomerko		03/05/90	M	1		
15	Roman Shirokov		06/07/81	M	13		4
27	Ragnar Sigurdsson	ISL	19/06/86	D	24	(2)	1
88	Andrei Sinitsin		23/06/88	G	5	(1)	
14	Wanderson	BRA	18/02/86	A	14	(16)	7

FC Kuban Krasnodar

1928 • Kuban (35,200) • fckuban.ru
Coach: Viktor Goncharenko (BLR);
(17/11/14) Leonid Kuchuk (BLR);
(25/05/15) (Andrei Sosnitski (BLR))

2014
03/08	h	Ufa	W	2-0 Ignatyev, Popov
08/08	h	Rostov	D	2-2 Popov 2 (1p)
15/08	a	Mordovia	D	0-0
18/08	h	Amkar	W	1-0 Bucur
24/08	h	Lokomotiv	W	2-1 Melgarejo, Šunjić
30/08	a	Arsenal	W	1-0 Bucur
15/09	a	Terek	D	0-0
20/09	h	Rubin	W	2-1 Danilo, Oliseh
28/09	a	Dinamo	D	2-2 Ignatyev, Oliseh
18/10	a	CSKA	L	0-6
25/10	a	Torpedo	D	0-0
02/11	h	Spartak	D	3-3 Oliseh 2, Popov (p)
07/11	a	Ural	W	1-0 Danilo (p)
22/11	a	Zenit	L	0-1
29/11	h	Torpedo	D	1-1 Baldé
03/12	h	Krasnodar	D	1-1 Bucur
06/12	h	CSKA	L	0-1

2015
09/03	h	Mordovia	D	0-0
16/03	a	Rostov	L	1-2 Hugo Almeida
22/03	h	Terek	W	1-0 Tkachyov
04/04	a	Spartak	D	1-1 Tkachyov
08/04	h	Ural	L	0-2
11/04	a	Krasnodar	L	2-3 Sosnin, Ignatyev
19/04	h	Zenit	D	0-0
24/04	a	Ufa	L	2-3 Ignatyev, Baldé
03/05	h	Dinamo	L	1-2 Hugo Almeida
08/05	a	Rubin	L	0-1
16/05	a	Amkar	L	0-1
25/05	a	Lokomotiv	D	1-1 Baldé
30/05	h	Arsenal	W	5-1 Baldé 2, Tkachyov 2, og (Kaleshin)

No	Name	Nat	DoB	Pos	Aps	(s)	Gls
2	Igor Armas	MDA	14/07/87	D	12	(3)	
99	Ibrahima Baldé	SEN	01/09/90	A	14	(5)	5
23	Aleksandr Belenov		13/09/86	G	30		
11	Gheorghe Bucur	ROU	08/04/80	A	5	(19)	3
43	Roman Bugaev		11/02/89	D	10	(1)	
19	Danilo	BRA	12/11/86	A	11	(3)	2
38	Andrei Eschenko		09/02/84	D	20	(1)	
27	Hugo Almeida	POR	23/05/84	A	6	(4)	2
18	Vladislav Ignatyev		20/01/87	M	19	(8)	4
10	Charles Kaboré	BFA	09/02/88	M	25	(1)	
42	Sergei Karetnik		14/02/95	M		(1)	
9	Arsen Khubulov		13/12/90	M	6	(9)	
7	Vladislav Kulik		27/02/85	M	19	(6)	
29	Stanislav Manolev	BUL	16/12/85	D	5	(1)	
25	Lorenzo Melgarejo	PAR	10/08/90	D	11	(3)	1
26	Sekou Oliseh	LBR	05/06/90	A	9	(3)	4
21	Ivelin Popov	BUL	26/10/87	M	24	(3)	4
71	Mohammed Rabiu	GHA	31/12/89	M	17	(4)	
22	Anton Sosnin		27/01/90	M	23	(1)	1
14	Toni Šunjić	BIH	15/12/88	D	22		1
57	Sergei Tkachyov		19/05/89	M	9	(2)	4
8	Artur Tlisov		10/06/82	M	4	(7)	
4	Xandão	BRA	23/02/88	D	27	(1)	
15	Maksim Zhavnerchik	BLR	09/02/85	D	2		

FC Lokomotiv Moskva

1923 • Lokomotiv (28,800) • fclm.ru
Major honours
Russian League (2) 2002, 2004; USSR Cup (2) 1936, 1957; Russian Cup (6) 1996, 1997, 2000, 2001, 2007, 2015

Coach: Leonid Kuchuk (BLR);
(17/09/14) (Igor Cherevchenko);
(04/10/14) Miodrag Božović (MNE);
(11/05/15) (Igor Cherevchenko)

2014
03/08	h	Krasnodar	D	0-0
10/08	a	Arsenal	W	2-0 Manuel Fernandes, N'Doye
14/08	h	Rostov	W	2-1 Kasaev, Samedov
17/08	a	Rubin	D	1-1 Miranchuk
24/08	a	Kuban	L	1-2 Manuel Fernandes (p)
31/08	h	Zenit	L	0-1
13/09	a	Mordovia	D	1-1 Niasse
21/09	a	CSKA	D	0-0
28/09	h	Amkar	W	3-1 Ćorluka 2, Niasse
18/10	h	Terek	W	2-1 Niasse, Pavlyuchenko (p)
26/10	a	Spartak	D	1-1 Manuel Fernandes
02/11	h	Dinamo	W	4-2 N'Doye, Samedov, Kasaev, Pavlyuchenko
08/11	a	Torpedo	W	1-0 N'Doye
24/11	h	Ufa	D	0-0
30/11	h	Spartak	W	1-0 Kasaev
03/12	h	Ural	W	1-0 N'Doye
07/12	a	Terek	D	0-0

2015
08/03	a	Rostov	W	1-0 Škuletić
14/03	h	Arsenal	L	0-1
22/03	a	Mordovia	D	0-0
04/04	a	Dinamo	D	2-2 Škuletić, Manuel Fernandes (p)
08/04	h	Torpedo	W	2-0 Manuel Fernandes 2 (1p)
13/04	a	Ural	L	0-2
18/04	a	Ufa	L	0-1
25/04	a	Krasnodar	L	0-1
03/05	a	Amkar	D	1-1 Samedov
10/05	h	CSKA	L	1-3 Niasse
16/05	h	Rubin	W	3-0 og (Ozdoev), Pavlyuchenko, Samedov (p)
25/05	h	Kuban	D	1-1 Manuel Fernandes
30/05	a	Zenit	L	0-1

No	Name	Nat	DoB	Pos	Aps	(s)	Gls
81	Ilya Abayev		02/08/81	G	11		
36	Dmitri Barinov		11/09/96	M		(2)	
11	Mbark Boussoufa	MAR	15/08/84	M	15	(2)	
4	Vedran Ćorluka	CRO	05/02/86	D	26		2
29	Vitali Denisov	UZB	23/02/87	D	26		
28	Ján Ďurica	SVK	10/12/81	D	21		
1	Guilherme	BRA	12/12/85	G	19		
7	Alan Kasaev		08/04/86	M	18	(8)	4
15	Arseni Logashov		20/08/91	D	7		
7	Maicon	BRA	18/02/90	A	13	(11)	
4	Manuel Fernandes	POR	05/02/86	M	20	(8)	7
17	Taras Mikhalik	UKR	28/10/83	D	12	(4)	
59	Aleksei Miranchuk		17/10/95	M	10	(7)	1
28	Dame N'Doye	SEN	21/02/85	A	9	(5)	4
9	Oumar Niasse	SEN	18/04/90	A	8	(5)	4
9	Roman Pavlyuchenko		15/12/81	A	5	(15)	3
5	Nemanja Pejčinović	SRB	04/11/86	D	10	(4)	
19	Aleksandr Samedov		19/07/84	M	29		4
8	Aleksandr Sheshukov		15/04/83	M	12	(3)	
49	Roman Shishkin		27/01/87	D	20	(3)	
25	Petar Škuletić	SRB	29/06/90	A	7	(4)	2
23	Dmitri Tarasov		18/03/87	M	13	(1)	
26	Yan Tigorev	BLR	10/03/84	M	3	(2)	
77	Sergei Tkachyov		19/05/89	M	1	(3)	
55	Renat Yanbaev		07/04/84	M	15	(1)	

FC Mordovia Saransk

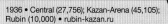

1961 • Start (11,613) • fc-mordovia.ru
Coach: Yuri Semin

2014

02/08	a	Ural	W	3-2	Donald, Vlasov, Lutsenko
09/08	h	CSKA	L	0-1	
15/08	h	Kuban	D	0-0	
18/08	a	Terek	L	0-1	
24/08	a	Rostov	L	1-2	Donald
30/08	h	Torpedo	W	1-0	Lutsenko
13/09	a	Lokomotiv	D	1-1	Vasin
19/09	h	Arsenal	W	1-0	Ruslan Mukhametshin
27/09	h	Ufa	L	0-2	
20/10	a	Rubin	L	0-5	
26/10	h	Zenit	L	0-5	
02/11	h	Krasnodar	W	2-1	Lomić 2 (1p)
08/11	a	Amkar	W	1-0	Vasin
23/11	a	Spartak	L	2-4	Lomić (p), Ruslan Mukhametshin
29/11	h	Zenit	W	1-0	Vlasov
04/12	h	Dinamo	L	0-1	
08/12	h	Rubin	L	0-1	
2015					
09/03	a	Kuban	D	0-0	
14/03	a	CSKA	L	0-4	
22/03	h	Lokomotiv	D	0-0	
04/04	a	Krasnodar	L	0-4	
07/04	h	Amkar	W	1-0	Yannick Djaló (p)
12/04	a	Dinamo	L	1-2	Danilo
18/04	h	Spartak	L	1-3	Niasse
24/04	h	Ural	W	2-1	Dudiev, Ruslan Mukhametshin
04/05	a	Ufa	W	2-1	Perendija, Ebecilio
11/05	h	Arsenal	W	1-0	og (Hagush)
15/05	h	Rostov	D	0-0	
24/05	h	Terek	W	1-0	Ebecilio
30/05	a	Torpedo	L	0-2	

No	Name	Nat	DoB	Pos	Aps	(s)	Gls
7	Anton Bober		28/09/82	M		(11)	
12	Vladimir Božović	MNE	13/11/81	M	11	(2)	
10	Danilo	BRA	13/01/90	M	6	(10)	1
6	Mitchell Donald	NED	10/12/88	M	11	(1)	2
17	Aslan Dudiev		15/06/90	D	13	(9)	1
91	Lorenzo Ebecilio	NED	24/09/91	M	7	(3)	2
3	Evgeni Gapon		20/04/91	D	8	(1)	
99	Pavel Ignatovich		24/05/89	M		(5)	
88	Aleksei Ivanov		01/09/81	M	2	(2)	
1	Anton Kochenkov		02/04/87	G	30		
7	Damien Le Tallec	FRA	14/10/90	A	29		
32	Marko Lomić	SRB	13/09/83	D	17		3
48	Evgeni Lutsenko		25/02/87	A	16	(6)	2
13	Mikhail Markin		21/11/93	A		(2)	
23	Ruslan Mukhametshin		29/10/81	A	9	(8)	3
9	Rustem Mukhametshin		02/04/84	M		(3)	
55	Ruslan Nakhushev		05/09/84	D	20	(4)	
18	Ibrahima Niasse	SEN	18/04/88	D	22	(4)	1
40	Milan Perendija	SRB	05/01/86	D	19	(3)	1
22	Sergei Samodin		14/02/85	A	3	(4)	
4	Igor Shitov	BLR	24/10/86	D	21	(1)	
11	Dmitri Sysuev		13/01/88	M	9	(1)	
5	Viktor Vasin		06/10/88	D	30		2
84	Oleg Vlasov		10/12/84	M	29		2
14	Pavel Yakovlev		07/04/91	A	10	(1)	
16	Yannick Djaló	POR	05/05/86	A	8	(1)	1

FC Rostov

1958 • Olimp 2 (17,023) • fc-rostov.ru
Major honours
Russian Cup (1) 2014
Coach: Miodrag Božović (MNE);
(25/09/14) Igor Gamula;
(18/12/14) Kurban Berdyev

2014

03/08	a	Dinamo	L	3-7	Poloz 2, Gatcan
08/08	a	Kuban	D	2-2	Kalachev, Dyakov
14/08	a	Lokomotiv	L	1-2	Poloz (p)
17/08	h	Krasnodar	L	0-2	
24/08	h	Mordovia	W	2-1	Grigoryev, Kanga
31/08	a	CSKA	L	0-6	
13/09	h	Rubin	L	1-2	Grigoryev
20/09	h	Zenit	L	0-5	
28/09	a	Terek	L	1-2	Grigoryev
19/10	a	Arsenal	D	1-1	Bukharov
25/10	a	Amkar	L	0-2	
31/10	h	Ural	W	1-0	Poloz
09/11	a	Ufa	D	0-0	
22/11	a	Torpedo	L	1-2	Torbinski
28/11	h	Amkar	D	1-1	Bukharov (p)
04/12	a	Spartak	D	1-1	Torbinski
08/12	h	Arsenal	L	0-1	
2015					
08/03	h	Lokomotiv	L	0-1	
16/03	h	Kuban	W	2-1	Bukharov, Azmoun
21/03	a	Rubin	L	0-2	
05/04	a	Ural	W	1-0	Dzyuba
09/04	h	Ufa	W	2-0	Azmoun, Bukharov
13/04	h	Spartak	W	2-1	Grigoryev 2
20/04	h	Torpedo	W	1-0	Dyakov (p)
26/04	h	Dinamo	D	2-2	Azmoun, Bastos
02/05	h	Terek	L	0-1	
10/05	a	Zenit	L	0-3	
15/05	a	Mordovia	D	0-0	
24/05	a	Krasnodar	L	1-2	Dyakov
30/05	h	CSKA	D	1-1	Dyakov (p)

No	Name	Nat	DoB	Pos	Aps	(s)	Gls
3	Ruslan Abazov		25/05/93	D	3		
20	Sardar Azmoun	IRN	01/01/95	A	4	(7)	3
77	Bastos	ANG	27/03/91	D	26	(1)	1
15	Maksim Bordachev	BLR	18/06/86	D	16	(3)	
11	Aleksandr Bukharov		12/03/85	A	18	(8)	4
17	Nika Chkhapelia		26/04/94	M		(4)	
8	Moussa Doumbia	MLI	15/08/94	M	8	(11)	
5	Vitali Dyakov		31/01/89	D	29		4
22	Artem Dzyuba		22/08/88	A	5	(6)	1
26	Azim Fatulaev		07/05/86	M	7	(4)	
84	Alexandru Gatcan	MDA	27/03/84	M	25	(1)	1
20	Réginal Goreux	HAI	31/12/87	D	13	(1)	
7	Maksim Grigoryev		06/07/90	M	16	(6)	5
2	Timofei Kalachev	BLR	01/05/81	M	25		1
9	Guélor Kanga	GAB	01/09/90	M	17	(2)	1
27	Igor Lolo	CIV	22/07/82	D	8		
19	Hrvoje Milić	CRO	10/05/89	D	18	(2)	
99	Nemanja Nikolić	MNE	19/10/92	A		(1)	
25	Ivan Novoseltsev		25/08/91	D	11		
13	Mihai Platica	MDA	15/03/90	M	1		
1	Stipe Pletikosa	CRO	08/01/79	G	30		
14	Dmitri Poloz		12/07/91	A	14	(6)	4
6	Aleksei Rebko		23/04/86	M	5	(12)	
4	Dmitri Torbinski		28/04/84	M	27		2
23	Aleksandr Troshechkin		23/04/96	M	1	(2)	
55	Siyanda Xulu	RSA	30/12/91	D	3	(1)	
10	Yoo Byung-soo	KOR	26/03/88	A		(4)	

FC Rubin Kazan

1936 • Central (27,756); Kazan-Arena (45,105);
Rubin (10,000) • rubin-kazan.ru
Major honours
Russian League (2) 2008, 2009; Russian Cup (1) 2012
Coach: Rinat Bilyaletdinov

2014

01/08	h	Spartak	L	0-4	
09/08	a	Terek	D	1-1	Azmoun
13/08	a	Arsenal	D	0-0	
17/08	h	Lokomotiv	D	1-1	Gökdeniz (p)
23/08	h	CSKA	W	2-1	Portnyagin, Gökdeniz
31/08	h	Ufa	D	1-1	Kanunnikov
13/09	a	Rostov	W	2-1	Portnyagin 2
20/09	a	Kuban	L	1-2	Kanunnikov
29/09	h	Torpedo	W	2-1	Carlos Eduardo, Georgiev
20/10	h	Mordovia	W	5-0	Portnyagin, Kanunnikov, Gökdeniz 2 (1p), Carlos Eduardo
27/10	a	Dinamo	W	2-0	Ozdoev, Kanunnikov
03/11	h	Amkar	D	1-1	Gökdeniz
09/11	a	Krasnodar	L	0-2	
22/11	a	Ural	W	3-1	Gökdeniz, Portnyagin, Ozdoev
30/11	h	Dinamo	D	1-1	Portnyagin
03/12	h	Zenit	L	0-1	
08/12	a	Mordovia	W	1-0	Carlos Eduardo
2015					
09/03	h	Arsenal	W	1-0	Portnyagin
15/03	h	Terek	W	2-1	Kanunnikov, Portnyagin
21/03	h	Rostov	W	2-0	Portnyagin, Ozdoev
04/04	a	Amkar	W	3-0	Portnyagin 2, og (Jovičić)
07/04	h	Krasnodar	L	1-2	Dyadyun
12/04	a	Zenit	D	1-1	Nabiullin
18/04	a	Ural	W	2-1	Dyadyun, Ozdoev
26/04	a	Spartak	L	0-1	
03/05	a	Torpedo	D	2-2	Kverkvelia, Ozdoev
08/05	h	Kuban	W	1-0	Ozdoev
16/05	a	Lokomotiv	L	0-3	
25/05	a	CSKA	L	0-3	
30/05	a	Ufa	D	1-1	Gökdeniz

No	Name	Nat	DoB	Pos	Aps	(s)	Gls
85	Ilzat Akhmetov		31/12/97	M		(9)	
69	Sardar Azmoun	IRN	01/01/95	A	4	(9)	1
4	Taras Burlak		22/02/90	D	2		
87	Carlos Eduardo	BRA	18/07/87	M	19	(3)	3
44	César Navas	ESP	14/02/80	D	21	(1)	
4	Guillermo Cotugno	URU	17/03/95	D	9	(1)	
11	Marko Dević	UKR	21/10/83	A		(3)	
8	Vladimir Dyadyun		12/07/88	A	14	(8)	2
77	Blagoy Georgiev	BUL	21/12/81	M	22		1
61	Gökdeniz Karadeniz	TUR	11/01/80	M	20	(5)	7
88	Ruslan Kambolov		01/01/90	M	14	(5)	
99	Maksim Kanunnikov		14/07/91	A	22	(4)	5
15	Sergei Kislyak	BLR	06/08/87	M	7	(8)	
23	Mamuka Kobakhidze	GEO	23/08/92	D	3	(1)	
2	Oleg Kuzmin		09/05/81	D	27		
5	Solomon Kverkvelia	GEO	06/02/92	D	29		1
10	Marko Livaja	CRO	26/08/93	A	5	(6)	
8	Pavel Mogilevits		25/01/93	M	5		
3	Elmir Nabiullin		08/03/95	D	24	(1)	1
91	Yuri Nesterenko		12/06/91	G	3		
14	Dmitri Otstavnov		04/06/93	A	1		
27	Magomed Ozdoev		05/11/92	M	27	(2)	6
7	Igor Portnyagin		07/01/89	A	24	(2)	11
1	Sergei Ryzhikov		19/09/80	G	27		
80	Egor Sorokin		04/11/95	D		(1)	
49	Vitali Ustinov		03/05/91	D		(1)	
32	Wakaso Mubarak	GHA	25/07/90	M	1	(1)	

FC Spartak Moskva

1922 • Otkrytie-Arena (44,929) • spartak.com

Major honours
USSR League (12) 1936 (autumn), 1938, 1939, 1952, 1953, 1956, 1958, 1962, 1969, 1979, 1987, 1989; Russian League (9) 1992, 1993, 1994, 1996, 1997, 1998, 1999, 2000, 2001; USSR Cup (10) 1938, 1939, 1946, 1947, 1950, 1958, 1963, 1965, 1971, 1992; Russian Cup (3) 1994, 1998, 2003
Coach: Murat Yakın (SUI)

2014
01/08	a	Rubin	W 4-0	Dzyuba 2, Glushakov, Barrios
10/08	a	Dinamo	W 2-1	Dzyuba 2
14/08	a	Krasnodar	L 0-4	
17/08	a	CSKA	W 1-0	Kombarov (p)
23/08	a	Ufa	W 2-1	Dzyuba 2
30/08	a	Amkar	L 0-2	
14/09	h	Torpedo	W 3-1	Promes 2, Jurado
20/09	h	Terek	D 1-1	Jurado
27/09	a	Zenit	D 0-0	
19/10	a	Ural	L 0-2	
26/10	h	Lokomotiv	D 1-1	Shirokov
02/11	a	Kuban	D 3-3	Taşçı, Källström 2
09/11	h	Arsenal	W 2-0	Movsisyan, Promes
23/11	h	Mordovia	W 4-2	Promes 2, João Carlos, Dzyuba
30/11	a	Lokomotiv	L 0-1	
04/12	h	Rostov	D 1-1	Glushakov
08/12	h	Ural	W 2-0	Jurado, Rômulo

2015
08/03	h	Krasnodar	L 1-3	Promes
15/03	h	Dinamo	W 1-0	og (Douglas)
21/03	a	Torpedo	W 1-0	Promes
04/04	h	Kuban	D 1-1	Kombarov (p)
09/04	a	Arsenal	L 0-1	
13/04	h	Rostov	L 1-2	Insaurralde
18/04	a	Mordovia	W 3-1	Promes 2, Movsisyan
26/04	h	Rubin	W 1-0	Promes
02/05	h	Zenit	D 1-1	Rômulo
11/05	a	Terek	L 2-4	Promes, Krotov
17/05	h	CSKA	L 0-4	
23/05	h	Ufa	L 1-2	Krotov
30/05	h	Amkar	D 3-3	Promes 2, Krotov

No	Name	Nat	DoB	Pos	Aps	(s)	Gls
7	Jano Ananidze	GEO	10/10/92	A	7	(8)	
10	Lucas Barrios	PAR	13/11/84	A		(1)	1
19	Salvatore Bocchetti	ITA	30/11/86	D	3		
3	Sergei Bryzgalov		15/11/92	D	6	(2)	
69	Denis Davydov		22/03/95	A	7	(12)	
22	Artem Dzyuba		22/08/88	A	10	(3)	7
20	Patrick Ebert	GER	17/03/87	M	15	(2)	
8	Denis Glushakov		27/01/87	M	24	(3)	2
2	Juan Insaurralde	ARG	03/10/84	D	17	(3)	1
55	João Carlos	BRA	01/01/82	D	10	(5)	1
19	José Manuel Jurado	ESP	29/06/86	M	10	(8)	3
21	Kim Källström	SWE	24/08/82	M	26	(2)	2
23	Dmitri Kombarov		22/01/87	D	24	(1)	2
57	Vyacheslav Krotov		14/02/93	A	7	(3)	3
64	Denis Kutin		05/10/93	D	1		
34	Evgeni Makeev		24/07/89	D	23	(2)	
37	Georgi Melkadze		04/04/97	M		(2)	
1	Anton Mitryushkin		08/02/96	G	1		
10	Yura Movsisyan	ARM	02/08/87	A	9	(7)	2
11	Aras Özbiliz	ARM	09/03/90	M		(1)	
4	Sergei Parshivlyuk		18/03/89	D	26		
30	Sergei Pesyakov		16/12/88	G	1		
24	Quincy Promes	NED	04/01/92	A	27	(1)	13
6	Rafael Carioca	BRA	18/06/89	M		(1)	
32	Artem Rebrov		04/03/84	G	28		
15	Rômulo	BRA	19/09/90	M	16	(3)	2
15	Roman Shirokov		06/07/81	M	3	(2)	1
35	Serdar Taşçı	GER	24/04/87	D	20	(2)	1
40	Artyom Timofeev		12/01/94	M		(3)	
20	Tino Costa	ARG	09/01/83	M	4	(3)	
28	Abdul Majeed Waris	GHA	19/09/91	A	1	(3)	
14	Pavel Yakovlev		07/04/91	A	4	(4)	
87	Aleksandr Zuev		26/06/96	M		(2)	

FC Terek Grozny

1946 • Ahmat-Arena (30,597) • fc-terek.ru

Major honours
Russian Cup (1) 2004
Coach: Rashid Rakhimov

2014
04/08	h	Amkar	W 4-0	Rybus 2, Lebedenko, Maurício
09/08	h	Rubin	D 1-1	Aîlton
13/08	a	CSKA	L 0-1	
18/08	h	Mordovia	W 1-0	Utsiyev
22/08	h	Arsenal	W 3-0	Lebedenko, Maurício, Komorowski
29/08	a	Ural	W 1-0	Ivanov
15/09	h	Kuban	D 0-0	
20/09	a	Spartak	D 1-1	Maurício
28/09	h	Rostov	W 2-1	Rybus, Utsiyev
18/10	a	Lokomotiv	L 1-2	og (Niasse)
27/10	a	Krasnodar	L 0-2	
03/11	h	Ufa	W 1-0	Bokila
08/11	a	Zenit	W 3-1	Aîlton 2, Lebedenko
23/11	a	Dinamo	L 0-3	
30/11	h	Krasnodar	L 0-1	
03/12	h	Torpedo	L 0-1	
07/12	h	Lokomotiv	D 0-0	

2015
07/03	h	CSKA	L 1-2	Lebedenko
15/03	a	Rubin	L 1-2	Komorowski
22/03	a	Kuban	L 0-1	
05/04	a	Ufa	W 1-0	Komorowski
08/04	h	Zenit	L 1-2	Semyonov
13/04	a	Torpedo	D 0-0	
19/04	h	Dinamo	D 0-0	
25/04	a	Amkar	L 1-2	Maurício
02/05	a	Rostov	W 1-0	Mbengue
11/05	h	Spartak	W 4-2	Mbengue 2, Aîlton 2
16/05	a	Arsenal	D 1-1	Mbengue
24/05	a	Mordovia	L 0-1	
30/05	h	Ural	L 1-3	og (Yemelianov)

No	Name	Nat	DoB	Pos	Aps	(s)	Gls
6	Adílson	BRA	16/01/87	M	22	(2)	
9	Aîlton	BRA	20/08/84	A	25	(5)	5
14	Ismail Aissati	MAR	16/08/88	M	7	(17)	
18	Jeremy Bokila	COD	14/11/88	A	3	(14)	1
5	António Ferreira	BRA	24/08/84	D	2		
16	Evgeni Gorodov		13/12/85	G	2		
1	Yaroslav Hodzyur	UKR	06/03/85	G	28		
19	Oleg Ivanov		04/08/86	M	25	(2)	1
7	Khalid Kadyrov		19/04/94	A	2	(2)	
10	Kanu	BRA	23/09/87	M	6	(12)	
24	Marcin Komorowski	POL	17/04/84	D	25	(1)	3
17	Fedor Kudryashov		05/04/87	D	27		
21	Daler Kuzyaev		15/01/93	M	13	(8)	
55	Igor Lebedenko		27/05/83	A	26	(3)	4
8	Maurício	BRA	21/10/88	M	27	(1)	4
17	Ablaye Mbengue	SEN	19/05/92	A	4	(1)	4
4	Juhani Ojala	FIN	19/06/89	D		(1)	
23	Facundo Píriz	URU	27/03/90	M	3	(8)	
2	Rodolfo	BRA	23/10/82	M	4	(2)	
31	Maciej Rybus	POL	19/08/89	M	26	(1)	3
10	Marko Šćepović	SRB	23/05/91	A		(1)	
15	Andrei Semyonov		24/03/89	D	29		1
3	Adolphe Teikeu	CMR	23/06/90	D		(1)	
40	Rizvan Utsiyev		07/02/88	D	24		2

FC Torpedo Moskva

1924 • Eduard Streltsov (13,450); Saturn, Ramenskoe (14,685) • fc-tm.ru

Major honours
USSR League (3) 1960, 1965, 1976 (autumn); USSR Cup (6) 1949, 1952, 1960, 1968, 1972, 1986; Russian Cup (1) 1993
Coach: Nikolai Savichev; (04/11/14) Valeri Petrakov

2014
02/08	a	CSKA	L 1-4	Fomin
09/08	a	Zenit	L 1-8	Aidov
12/08	h	Amkar	D 1-1	Rykov
16/08	a	Ural	W 2-0	Pugin, og (Ottesen)
24/08	h	Krasnodar	L 0-3	
30/08	a	Mordovia	L 0-1	
14/09	a	Spartak	L 1-3	Hugo Vieira
22/09	h	Dinamo	L 1-3	Katsalapov
29/09	a	Rubin	L 1-2	Stevanović (p)
20/10	a	Ufa	D 1-1	Bilyaletdinov
25/10	h	Kuban	D 0-0	
03/11	h	Arsenal	L 0-1	
08/11	h	Lokomotiv	L 0-1	
22/11	h	Rostov	W 2-1	Stevanović, Salugin
29/11	a	Kuban	D 1-1	Bilyaletdinov
03/12	a	Terek	W 1-0	Putilo
08/12	h	Ufa	D 2-2	Putilo, Mirzov

2015
09/03	a	Amkar	D 0-0	
15/03	h	Zenit	D 1-1	Smárason
21/03	h	Spartak	L 0-1	
05/04	a	Arsenal	W 3-1	Pugin, Kombarov, Putilo
08/04	a	Lokomotiv	L 0-2	
13/04	h	Terek	D 0-0	
20/04	a	Rostov	L 0-1	
25/04	h	CSKA	L 0-2	
03/05	h	Rubin	D 2-2	Kombarov, Smárason
10/05	a	Dinamo	D 0-0	
17/05	a	Krasnodar	D 2-2	Putilo, Kombarov
23/05	h	Ural	W 3-1	Hugo Vieira 2 (2p), Stevanović
30/05	h	Mordovia	W 2-0	Rykov, Pugin

No	Name	Nat	DoB	Pos	Aps	(s)	Gls
3	Dmitri Aidov		10/04/82	D	5		1
17	Mikhail Bagaev		28/02/85	M	3	(3)	
71	Konstantin Bazelyuk		12/04/93	A		(1)	
23	Diniyar Bilyaletdinov		27/02/85	M	14	(3)	2
98	Aleksandr Budakov		10/02/85	G	1		
10	Sergei Davydov		22/07/85	A	3	(4)	
7	Semyon Fomin		10/01/89	M	7	(8)	1
8	Ivan Franjic	AUS	10/07/87	D	3	(1)	
27	Hugo Vieira	POR	25/07/88	A	14	(6)	3
34	Aleksandr Katsalapov		05/04/86	D	18	(2)	1
5	Ivan Knyazev		05/11/92	D		(1)	
3	Adam Kokoszka	POL	06/10/86	D	20	(2)	
9	Kirill Kombarov		22/01/87	D	23		3
40	Yuri Kuleshov		12/04/81	M	2	(2)	
6	Tomas Mikuckis	LTU	13/01/83	D	8	(2)	
11	Reziuan Mirzov		22/06/93	M	20	(6)	1
25	Ivan Novoseltsev		25/08/91	D	12	(3)	
18	Aleksei Pugin		07/03/87	M	8	(11)	3
14	Anton Putilo	BLR	10/06/87	M	17	(3)	4
33	Vladimir Rykov		13/11/87	D	28		2
77	Aleksandr Salugin		23/10/88	M	10	(8)	1
88	Igor Shevchenko		02/02/85	A	13	(1)	
4	Arnór Smárason	ISL	07/09/88	M	3	(8)	2
20	Vadim Steklov		24/03/87	M	20	(1)	
16	Dalibor Stevanović	SVN	27/09/84	M	26		3
15	Egor Tarakanov		17/04/87	D	5		
22	Lukáš Tesák	SVK	08/03/85	D	6		
67	Georgi Tigiev		20/06/95	D	4	(1)	
19	Sergei Zenev	EST	20/04/89	A	8	(2)	
30	Yuri Zhevnov	BLR	17/04/81	G	29		

FC Ufa

2010 • Dinamo (6,000); Start, Saransk (11,613); Zvezda, Perm (17,000) • fcufa.pro
Coach: Igor Kolyvanov

2014
03/08	a	Kuban	L	0-2
08/08	a	Amkar	W	1-0 Marcinho (p)
13/08	h	Dinamo	L	0-2
16/08	a	Zenit	L	0-1
23/08	h	Spartak	L	1-2 Diego Carlos
31/08	a	Rubin	D	1-1 Marcinho
14/09	a	Krasnodar	W	2-0 Marcinho, Alikin
20/09	h	Ural	L	0-1
27/09	a	Mordovia	W	2-0 Semakin, Handžić (p)
20/10	h	Torpedo	D	1-1 Handžić
26/10	a	CSKA	D	3-3 Brown Forbes, Semakin, Safronidi
03/11	a	Terek	L	0-1
09/11	h	Rostov	D	0-0
24/11	a	Lokomotiv	D	0-0
29/11	h	CSKA	L	0-5
02/12	a	Arsenal	W	1-0 Handžić
08/12	a	Torpedo	D	2-2 Diego Carlos, Tumasyan

2015
08/03	a	Dinamo	L	1-3 Marcinho (p)
14/03	h	Amkar	D	1-1 Shevchenko
20/03	h	Krasnodar	L	0-2
05/04	h	Terek	L	0-1
09/04	a	Rostov	L	0-2
12/04	h	Arsenal	L	0-1
18/04	h	Lokomotiv	W	1-0 Paurević
24/04	h	Kuban	W	3-2 Tumasyan, Marcinho (p), Alikin
04/05	h	Mordovia	L	1-2 Marcinho
08/05	a	Ural	D	1-1 Alikin
17/05	h	Zenit	D	1-1 Handžić
23/05	a	Spartak	W	2-1 Paurević, Stotski
30/05	h	Rubin	D	1-1 Stotski

No	Name	Nat	DoB	Pos	Aps	(s)	Gls
27	Takafumi Akahoshi	JPN	27/05/86	M	1	(1)	
3	Pavel Alikin		06/03/84	D	21		3
87	Igor Bezdenezhnykh		08/08/96	M			
77	Nikita Bezlikhotnov		19/08/90	M		(4)	
28	Felicio Brown Forbes	CRC	28/08/91	D	7	(2)	1
11	Diego Carlos	BRA	15/05/88	A	13	(7)	2
5	Emmanuel Frimpong	GHA	10/01/92	M	13	(4)	
22	Vagiz Galiulin	UZB	03/04/84	M	19	(4)	
18	Dmitri Golubov		24/06/85	A	4	(4)	
9	Haris Handžić	BIH	20/06/90	A	21	(8)	4
23	Anton Kilin		14/11/90	M	1	(5)	
10	Marcinho	BRA	14/05/86	M	27	(1)	6
19	Ivan Paurević	CRO	01/07/91	M	28	(1)	2
70	Nikolai Safronidi		10/09/83	M	10	(13)	1
14	Maksim Semakin		26/10/83	M	18	(3)	2
88	Igor Shevchenko		02/02/85	A	2	(9)	1
4	Pavlo Stepanets	UKR	26/05/87	M	8	(2)	
89	Dmitri Stotski		01/12/89	M	10		2
15	Aleksandr Sukhov		03/01/86	D	20	(1)	
31	Maksim Tishkin		11/11/89	D	19		
20	Denis Tumasyan		24/04/85	D	20	(1)	2
49	Aleksandr Vasilyev		23/12/84	M		(4)	
16	Sergei Veremko	BLR	16/10/82	G	5		
81	Dmitri Verkhovtsov	BLR	10/10/86	D	7	(4)	
6	William	BRA	20/10/82	D	1		
1	David Yurchenko		27/03/86	G	25		
13	Azamat Zaseev		29/04/88	M	28		
17	Olexandr Zinchenko	UKR	15/12/96	M	2	(5)	

FC Ural Sverdlovsk Oblast

1930 • Central (27,500); Manezh Ural (3,000); Geolog, Tyumen (13,057) • fc-ural.ru
Coach: Aleksandr Tarkhanov

2014
02/08	h	Mordovia	L	2-3 Manucharyan (p), Yaroshenko
10/08	h	Krasnodar	D	1-1 Lungu
13/08	h	Zenit	L	1-2 Acevedo
16/08	h	Torpedo	L	0-2
24/08	a	Dinamo	L	0-2
29/08	h	Terek	L	0-1
15/09	a	Amkar	L	1-2 Smolov
20/09	a	Ufa	W	1-0 Yerokhin
27/09	h	CSKA	L	3-4 Manucharyan, Smolov, Yerokhin
19/10	h	Spartak	W	2-0 Yerokhin, Fontanello
24/10	a	Arsenal	W	1-0 Yerokhin
31/10	a	Rostov	L	0-1
07/11	h	Kuban	L	0-1
22/11	h	Rubin	L	1-3 Gogniev
29/11	a	Arsenal	W	2-1 Khozin, Smolov
03/12	a	Lokomotiv	L	0-1
08/12	h	Spartak	L	0-2

2015
07/03	a	Zenit	L	0-3
13/03	h	Krasnodar	D	1-1 Smolov
21/03	h	Amkar	W	1-0 Acevedo
05/04	h	Rostov	L	0-1
08/04	h	Kuban	W	2-0 Smolov 2
13/04	h	Lokomotiv	W	2-0 og (Mikhalik), Smolov
18/04	a	Rubin	L	1-2 Yerokhin
24/04	a	Mordovia	L	1-2 Yerokhin
04/05	a	CSKA	L	1-3 Sapeta
08/05	h	Ufa	D	1-1 Khozin
18/05	h	Dinamo	W	2-1 Acevedo, Smolov
23/05	a	Torpedo	L	1-3 Fontanello
30/05	a	Terek	W	3-1 Gogniev, Khozin, Serchenkov

No	Name	Nat	DoB	Pos	Aps	(s)	Gls
21	Gerson Acevedo	CHI	05/04/88	M	14	(9)	3
35	Dmitri Arapov		16/04/90	G	1	(1)	
63	Aleksandr Belozyorov		27/10/81	D	5	(1)	
4	Markus Berger	AUT	21/01/85	D	3		
7	Aleksandr Dantsev		14/10/84	D	20	(6)	
34	Denis Dorozhkin		08/06/87	A		(10)	
57	Artem Fidler		14/07/83	M	16	(2)	
17	Denis Fomin		03/05/96	D		(2)	
29	Pablo Fontanello	ARG	26/09/84	D	25		2
9	Spartak Gogniev		19/01/81	A	3	(11)	2
2	Vladimir Khozin		03/07/89	D	29		3
3	Chisamba Lungu	ZAM	02/10/91	A	19	(5)	1
10	Edgar Manucharyan	ARM	19/01/87	A	16	(2)	2
50	Nikolai Markov		20/04/85	D	12		
2	Andrei Novikov		12/10/84	M	11	(1)	
18	Georgi Nurov		08/06/92	A		(2)	
28	Arsen Oganesyan		17/06/90	M	1	(4)	
6	Sölvi Geir Ottesen	ISL	18/02/84	D	15		
14	Vyacheslav Podberyozkin		21/06/92	M	15	(5)	
41	Aleksandr Sapeta		28/06/89	M	13	(5)	1
13	Aleksandr Schanitsin		02/12/84	M	1	(1)	
85	Sergei Serchenkov		01/01/97	M		(2)	1
90	Fedor Smolov		09/02/90	A	21	(1)	8
25	Aleksandr Stavpets		04/07/89	A	8	(10)	
99	Kostyantyn Yaroshenko	UKR	12/09/86	M	15	(4)	1
92	Roman Yemelianov		08/05/92	M	13	(1)	
89	Aleksandr Yerokhin		13/10/89	M	25		6
28	Nikolai Zabolotnyi		16/04/90	G	29		

FC Zenit

1925 • Petrovski (21,405) • fc-zenit.ru
Major honours
UEFA Cup (1) 2008; UEFA Supor Cup (1) 2000; USSR League (1) 1984; Russian League (4) 2007, 2010, 2012, 2015; USSR Cup (1) 1944; Russian Cup (2) 1999, 2010
Coach: André Villas-Boas (POR)

2014
02/08	a	Arsenal	W	4-0 Criscito 2, Rondón, Hulk
09/08	h	Torpedo	W	8-1 Smolnikov, Rondón 2, Hulk 2 (1p), Shatov, Kerzhakov 2 (1p)
13/08	a	Ural	W	2-1 Danny, Rondón
16/08	h	Ufa	W	1-0 Hulk (p)
23/08	h	Amkar	W	2-0 Shatov, Hulk
31/08	a	Lokomotiv	W	1-0 Javi García
13/09	h	Dinamo	W	3-2 og (Douglas), Arshavin, Smolnikov
20/09	a	Rostov	W	5-0 Rondón 3, og (Xulu), og (Dyakov)
27/09	h	Spartak	D	0-0
18/10	a	Krasnodar	D	2-2 Javi García, Hulk
26/10	h	Mordovia	W	5-0 Hulk, Kerzhakov, og (Nakhushev), Witsel, Danny
01/11	a	CSKA	W	1-0 Javi García
08/11	h	Terek	L	1-3 Ryazantsev
22/11	h	Kuban	W	1-0 Hulk
29/11	a	Mordovia	L	0-1
03/12	a	Rubin	W	1-0 Witsel
06/12	h	Krasnodar	W	4-0 Garay, Witsel, Danny, Smolnikov

2015
07/03	h	Ural	W	3-0 Rondón 3
15/03	a	Torpedo	D	1-1 Hulk
22/03	a	Dinamo	W	1-0 Smolnikov
05/04	h	CSKA	W	2-1 Hulk 2
08/04	a	Terek	W	2-1 Shatov, Rondón
12/04	h	Rubin	D	1-1 Hulk (p)
19/04	a	Kuban	D	0-0
26/04	h	Arsenal	W	1-0 Witsel
02/05	a	Spartak	D	1-1 Hulk
10/05	h	Rostov	W	3-0 Shatov, Hulk, Rondón
17/05	a	Ufa	D	1-1 Hulk
23/05	a	Amkar	L	0-1
30/05	h	Lokomotiv	W	1-0 Rondón

No	Name	Nat	DoB	Pos	Aps	(s)	Gls
2	Aleksandr Anyukov		28/09/82	D	14	(3)	
10	Andrey Arshavin		29/05/81	M	4	(10)	1
71	Egor Baburin		09/08/90	G		(1)	
4	Domenico Criscito	ITA	30/12/86	D	25		2
35	Danny	POR	07/08/83	A	26	(2)	3
94	Aleksei Evseev		30/03/94	M		(1)	
20	Viktor Fayzulin		22/04/86	M	11	(3)	
24	Ezequiel Garay	ARG	10/10/86	D	25	(1)	1
7	Hulk	BRA	25/07/86	A	27	(1)	15
21	Javi García	ESP	08/02/87	M	21	(3)	3
11	Aleksandr Kerzhakov		27/11/82	A	5	(9)	3
1	Yuri Lodygin		26/05/90	G	28		
6	Nicolas Lombaerts	BEL	20/03/85	D	21	(3)	
13	Luís Neto	POR	26/05/88	D	15	(5)	
16	Vyacheslav Malafeev		04/03/79	G	2		
8	Pavel Mogilevets		25/01/93	M		(9)	
33	Milan Rodić	SRB	02/04/91	D		(1)	
23	José Salomón Rondón	VEN	16/09/89	A	17	(9)	13
5	Aleksandr Ryazantsev		05/09/86	M	12	(8)	1
17	Oleg Shatov		29/07/90	A	24	(4)	4
90	Ramil Sheydaev		15/03/96	A		(5)	
19	Igor Smolnikov		08/08/88	D	23		4
99	Ivan Solovyev		29/03/93	M		(1)	
44	Anatoliy Tymoshchuk	UKR	30/03/79	M	4	(7)	
28	Axel Witsel	BEL	12/01/89	M	26	(2)	4

Top goalscorers

15	Hulk (Zenit)
13	Roman Eremenko (CSKA Moskva)
	Quincy Promes (Spartak Moskva)
	José Salomón Rondón (Zenit)
12	Bebras Natcho (CSKA Moskva)
11	Igor Portnyagin (Rubin)
10	Kevin Kuranyi (Dinamo Moskva)
	Ahmed Musa (CSKA Moskva)
9	Aleksei Ionov (Dinamo Moskva)
	Mauricio Pereyra (Krasnodar)

Promoted clubs

PFC Krylya Sovetov Samara

1942 • Metallurg (33,001) • kc-camapa.ru
Coach: Frank Vercauteren (BEL)

FC Anji Makhachkala

1991 • Anji-Arena (30,000) • fc-anji.ru
Coach: Sergei Tashuyev

Second level final table 2014/15

		Pld	W	D	L	F	A	Pts
1	PFC Krylya Sovetov Samara	34	22	7	5	53	19	73
2	FC Anji Makhachkala	34	22	5	7	60	22	71
3	FC Tosno	34	18	10	6	57	34	64
4	FC Tom Tomsk	34	19	6	9	47	36	63
5	FC Gazovik Orenburg	34	15	13	6	52	31	58
6	FC Shinnik Yaroslavl	34	12	17	5	44	33	53
7	FC Volgar Astrakhan	34	13	13	8	48	39	52
8	FC Yenisey Krasnoyarsk	34	11	9	14	39	42	42
9	FC Tyumen	34	11	9	14	41	38	42
10	FC Luch-Energia Vladivostok	34	11	9	14	40	46	42
11	FC Sibir Novosibirsk	34	11	9	14	35	46	42
12	PFC Sokol Saratov	34	10	11	13	38	41	41
13	FC Volga Nizhny Novgorod	34	12	4	18	44	57	40
14	FC SKA-Energia Khabarovsk	34	8	13	13	32	46	37
15	FC Baltika Kaliningrad	34	8	13	13	25	37	37
16	FC Sakhalin Yuzhno-Sakhalinsk	34	9	9	16	28	47	36
17	FC Khimik Dzerzhinsk	34	7	6	21	35	59	27
18	FC Dinamo St Petersburg	34	2	7	25	18	63	13

Promotion/Relegation play-offs

(03/06/15 & 07/06/15)
Tom 0-1 Ural
Ural 0-0 Tom
(Ural 1-0)

Tosno 0-1 Rostov
Rostov 4-1 Tosno
(Rostov 5-1)

DOMESTIC CUP

Kubok Rossii 2014/15

1/16 FINALS

(23/09/14)
Smena Komsomolsk-na-Amure 0-1 Spartak Moskva

(24/09/14)
Anji 1-2 Zenit
Baltika Kaliningrad 1-2 Kuban
Gazovik Orenburg 2-1 Terek
Khimik Dzerzhinsk 1-2 CSKA Moskva
Krylya Sovetov 3-1 Ural
Luch-Energia 0-2 Rubin
Ryazan 1-2 Mordovia
Sibir Novosibirsk 1-3 Lokomotiv Moskva
Syzran-2003 3-0 Rostov
Volgar Astrakhan 0-1 Arsenal Tula
Yenisey Krasnoyarsk 2-3 Ufa *(aet)*

(25/09/14)
Fakel Voronezh 1-2 Torpedo Moskva *(aet)*
Shinnik Yaroslavl 2-0 Dinamo Moskva
Sokol Saratov 0-5 Krasnodar
Tosno 0-0 Amkar *(aet; 4-2 on pens)*

1/8 FINALS

(29/10/14)
CSKA Moskva 2-0 Torpedo Moskva
Ufa 0-1 Lokomotiv Moskva
Kuban 3-0 Tosno
Syzran-2003 0-1 Gazovik Orenburg
Zenit 2-3 Arsenal Tula *(aet)*

(30/10/14)
Krasnodar 1-3 Krylya Sovetov
Mordovia 5-1 Shinnik Yaroslavl
Rubin 2-0 Spartak Moskva *(aet)*

QUARTER-FINALS

(02/03/15)
CSKA Moskva 1-0 Krylya Sovetov *(Natcho 51)*
Kuban 1-0 Mordovia *(Šunjić 34)*

(03/03/15)
Arsenal Tula 0-1 Gazovik Orenburg *(Koronov 112) (aet)*
Lokomotiv Moskva 0-0 Rubin *(aet; 4-2 on pens)*

SEMI-FINALS

(29/04/15)
Gazovik Orenburg 1-1 Lokomotiv Moskva *(Vasiev 50; Škuletić 87) (aet; 3-4 on pens)*
Kuban 1-0 CSKA Moskva *(Hugo Almeida 71)*

FINAL

(21/05/15)
Central, Astrakhan
FC LOKOMOTIV MOSKVA 3 *(Niasse 73, Boussoufa 104, Miranchuk 111)*
FC KUBAN KRASNODAR 1 *(Ignatyev 28)*
(aet)
Referee: Bezborodov
LOKOMOTIV MOSKVA: *Guilherme, Logashov, Ćorluka, Pejčinović, Denisov, Shishkin, Manuel Fernandes (Miranchuk 71), Samedov, Boussoufa, Kasaev (Maicon 108), Pavlyuchenko (Niasse 64)*
KUBAN: *Belenov, Sosnin, Armas, Šunjić, Bugaev, Rabiu, Kaboré, Tkachyov (Bucur 80), Popov, Ignatyev (Kulik 105), Hugo Almeida (Baldé 69)*

SAN MARINO
Federazione Sammarinese Giuoco Calcio (FSGC)

Address	Strada di Montecchio 17 SM-47890 San Marino	**President**	Giorgio Crescentini
Tel	+378 0549 990 515	**General secretary**	Luciano Casadei
Fax	+378 0549 992 348	**Media officer**	Matteo Rossi
E-mail	fsgc@omniway.sm	**Year of formation**	1931
Website	fsgc.sm	**National stadium**	San Marino Stadium, Serravalle (4,801)

CAMPIONATO SAMMARINESE CLUBS

 ① **SP Cailungo**

 ② **SS Cosmos**

 ③ **FC Domagnano**

 ④ **SC Faetano**

 ⑤ **FC Fiorentino**

 ⑥ **SS Folgore**

 ⑦ **AC Juvenes/Dogana**

 ⑧ **SP La Fiorita**

 ⑨ **AC Libertas**

 ⑩ **SS Murata**

 ⑪ **SS Pennarossa**

 ⑫ **SS San Giovanni**

 ⑬ **SP Tre Fiori**

 ⑭ **SP Tre Penne**

 ⑮ **Virtus FC**

KEY:

● – UEFA Champions League

● – UEFA Europa League

0		5		10 km

0		5 miles	

Folgore hold firm for first double

Runners-up to SP La Fiorita in the 2013/14 Campionato Sammarinese, SS Folgore went one better in 2014/15 to recapture a league crown they had not won since their halcyon days around the turn of the century, when they were champions three times in four seasons.

Local rivals AC Juvenes/Dogana were Folgore's victims in the championship play-off decider, with SS Murata having been outclassed a month earlier in the final of the Coppa Titano, coach Nicola Berardi leading his team to the first part of the double with a comprehensive 5-0 victory.

Berardi's side end 15-year wait for league title

Coppa Titano captured for first time with 5-0 win

New ground broken in EURO qualifying campaign

Domestic league

Although the winners of San Marino's domestic league are determined by a convoluted knockout system, which can often reward teams that hold back their best form until the business end of the season, Folgore proved that they were worthy champions by playing the best football throughout the two phases of the campaign. Not only did they finish on top of their group, with 44 points from their 21 matches; they also won all three of their play-off fixtures.

While Folgore ran away with Group B, finishing six points clear of La Fiorita and eight ahead of third-placed FC Domagnano, Juvenes/Dogana just edged out SP Tre Fiori by two points to take top spot in Group A. SC Faetano completed the six-team play-off contingent thanks to a staggering revival in the second half of the campaign. Having lost five of their first eight matches, they won six of the last eight, drawing the other two, to overtake Virtus FC and SP Cailungo.

Folgore's form was of a far more consistent standard, 13 wins, three defeats and 41 goals enabling them to top all three of those categories. As group winners, they were spared the first two rounds of the play-offs, but when they opened their post-season campaign, their fine form continued, a 2-1 win over Juvenes/Dogana

– a team they had already overcome 2-0 in the first phase – taking them through to the next round, where a dramatic 2-1 revenge win over La Fiorita, secured by a 91st-minute equaliser and extra-time winner, booked their place in the final.

The play-off rules decree that defeated teams have a second chance to remain in the competition, which allowed Juvenes/Dogana and La Fiorita to meet in the semi-final to determine Folgore's opposition in the San Marino Stadium. Two hours of football produced no goals, so it went down to penalties, with Juvenes/Dogana, who had never won the league title, prevailing 4-2 to knock out the defending champions. The final was equally tight but much more exciting. Juvenes/Dogana took the lead before Folgore's leading marksman Francesco Perrotta made it 1-1 at half-time. Then, with extra-time looming and Juvenes/Dogana a man down, Berardi's battlers struck twice in the last three minutes, through Manuel Muccini's free-kick and Perrotta's deft chip, to crown a magnificent season in fanfare style.

Domestic cup

Four weeks before the championship climax, the Folgore players had their hands on another piece of silverware. The club had never made an appearance in the final of the Coppa Titano, but they

certainly made the most of their debut, taking three-time winners Murata to the cleaners in a match adorned by five goals from Folgore but marred by two red cards for Murata. Berardi's side had been much harder pressed in the semi-finals, when it took a 118th-minute winner from Fabio Ceschi to knock out the holders and record 11-time winners AC Libertas.

Europe

Although Folgore predictably joined La Fiorita and Libertas on the first qualifying round scrapheap, unlike the other two of San Marino's 2014/15 European representatives they did manage to score a goal, through Perrotta, in their elimination by Montenegro's FK Budućnost Podgorica.

National team

With Giampaolo Mazza gone after 15 years in charge, San Marino entered a new era under his replacement coach Pierangelo Manzaroli, but while the team failed to mark his arrival by scoring a goal in their first six UEFA EURO 2016 qualifiers, they did win a rare point. Indeed, the 0-0 draw at home to Estonia was the first time San Marino had ever avoided defeat in a UEFA European Championship qualifier – at the 60th attempt.

DOMESTIC SEASON AT A GLANCE

Campionato Sammarinese 2014/15 final tables

FIRST PHASE

Group A

		Pld	W	D	L	F	A	Pts
1	AC Juvenes/Dogana	20	12	4	4	35	15	40
2	SP Tre Fiori	20	12	2	6	36	17	38
3	SC Faetano	20	9	5	6	26	21	32
4	Virtus FC	20	8	4	8	27	28	28
5	SP Cailungo	20	8	4	8	28	29	28
6	SS Murata	20	5	5	10	26	34	20
7	SS Cosmos	20	0	5	15	13	48	5

Group B

		Pld	W	D	L	F	A	Pts
1	SS Folgore	21	13	5	3	41	19	44
2	SP La Fiorita	21	11	5	5	37	25	38
3	FC Domagnano	21	11	3	7	28	23	36
4	AC Libertas	21	8	8	5	23	16	32
5	FC Fiorentino	21	9	5	7	24	22	32
6	SS Pennarossa	21	9	3	9	33	26	30
7	SP Tre Penne	21	5	3	13	24	43	18
8	SS San Giovanni	21	2	3	16	21	56	9

CHAMPIONSHIP PLAY-OFFS

FIRST ROUND

(04/05/15)
La Fiorita 3-1 Faetano *(Petráš 19, Selva 51, 83; Stefanelli 43)*
Tre Fiori 1-0 Domagnano *(Lini 55)*

SECOND ROUND

(08/05/15)
Domagnano 0-2 Faetano *(A Moroni 27, Stefanelli 70)*
(Domagnano eliminated)

(09/05/15)
Tre Fiori 0-1 La Fiorita *(Marino 66)*

THIRD ROUND

(11/05/15)
Folgore 2-1 Juvenes/Dogana *(Hirsch 11, 35; Maccagno 66p)*

(14/05/15)
Faetano 3-5 Tre Fiori *(A Moroni 7, Valentini 61, Cavoli 63; O'Neil 26, 38, 99, Andreini 32, Succi 101) (aet)*
(Faetano eliminated)

FOURTH ROUND

(16/05/15)
Folgore 2-1 La Fiorita *(Magnani 90+1, Della Valle 101; Rinaldi 56) (aet)*

(18/05/15)
Tre Fiori 0-3 Juvenes/Dogana *(Mantovani 33, Mariotti 78p, Ugolini 90+1)*
(Tre Fiori eliminated)

SEMI-FINAL

(23/05/15)
Juvenes/Dogana 0-0 La Fiorita *(aet; 4-2 on pens)*
(La Fiorita eliminated)

FINAL

(26/05/15)
San Marino Stadium, Serravalle
SS FOLGORE 3 *(Perrotta 43, 90, Muccini 87)*
AC JUVENES/DOGANA 1 *(Gasperoni 24)*
Referee: *Casanova*
FOLGORE: *Bicchiarelli, Rossi, Berardi, Magnani, Genestreti, Bollini, Pacini (Casadei 74), Muccini, Hirsch, Ceschi, Perrotta (Righi 90)*
JUVENES/DOGANA: *Manzaroli, Mantovani, Merlini, Villa, Gasperoni, Bagli, Maccagno, Canini, Santini, Ugolini, Mariotti*
Red card: *Canini (85)*

European qualification 2015/16

 Champion/Cup winner: SS Folgore (first qualifying round)

 AC Juvenes/Dogana (first qualifying round)
SP La Fiorita (first qualifying round)

Top scorer   Daniele Frigugljetti (San Giovanni), 16 goals
Cup final   SS Folgore 5-0 SS Murata

Player of the season

Adolfo Hirsch
(SS Folgore)

As his name suggests, Hirsch was not born in San Marino but emigrated there from Argentina in 2009. Two years later he was a San Marino international, but not until the 2014/15 season, with new coach Pierangelo Manzaroli on board, did he become a national team regular. The 29-year-old's consistent selection was down to an excellent season of domestic football with Folgore, which ended with a league and cup double. Although used in midfield by Manzaroli, he predominantly played in attack for his club.

Newcomer of the season

Armando Aruci
(SS Pennarossa)

Pennarossa failed to make the championship play-offs but they unveiled an exciting new addition to the Campionato Sammarinese in Aruci. Recruited from nearby Italian amateur club ASD Asca Borghi, the 25-year-old striker with Albanian roots struck 15 goals in the league – just one behind leading marksman Daniele Frigugljetti, who, remarkably, scored all but five of Group B basement club SS San Giovanni's 21 goals – and another ten in the Coppa Titano, which was the highest tally in the competition.

Team of the season
(3-4-3)

Coach: Berardi *(Folgore)*

Manzaroli *(Juvenes/Dogana)*

Genestreti *(Folgore)* — Petráš *(La Fiorita)* — Mantovani *(Juvenes/Dogana)*

Stradaioli *(Cailungo)* — Cuttone *(Murata)* — Santini *(Juvenes/Dogana)* — M Giardi *(Faetano)*

Frigugljetti *(San Giovanni)* — Perrotta *(Folgore)* — Hirsch *(Tre Fiori)*

NATIONAL TEAM

Top five all-time caps
Andy Selva (69); Damiano Vannucci (68); Simone Bacciocchi (60); **Alessandro Della Valle** (54); Mirco Gennari (48)

Top five all-time goals
Andy Selva (8); Manuel Marani (2)

NB No other player has scored more than one goal.

Results 2014/15

08/09/14	Lithuania (ECQ)	H	Serravalle	L	0-2
09/10/14	England (ECQ)	A	London	L	0-5
14/10/14	Switzerland (ECQ)	H	Serravalle	L	0-4
15/11/14	Estonia (ECQ)	H	Serravalle	D	0-0
27/03/15	Slovenia (ECQ)	A	Ljubljana	L	0-6
31/03/15	Liechtenstein (ECQ)	A	Eschen	L	0-1
14/06/15	Estonia (ECQ)	A	Tallinn	L	0-2

Appearances 2014/15

Coach: Pierangelo Manzaroli	25/03/69		LTU	ENG	SUI	EST	SVN	Lie	EST	Caps	Goals
Aldo Simoncini	30/08/86	Libertas	G	G	G	G		G	G	44	-
Giovanni Bonini	05/09/86	Tre Penne & Torconca (ITA)	D87		D	D	D		D	22	-
Davide Simoncini	30/08/86	Libertas	D			D	D	D		37	-
Cristian Brolli	28/02/92	Sammaurese (ITA)	D	D	D	D	D		D	10	-
Fabio Vitaioli	05/04/84	Tropical Coriano (ITA)	D	D	D17	D	s78	D82		39	-
Manuel Battistini	22/07/94	Juvenes/Dogana	D	D	D	s60	s56	D	D	10	-
Luca Tosi	04/11/92	Sant'Ermete (ITA)	M55	M63		M	M56	M46	M71	7	-
Adolfo Hirsch	31/01/86	Folgore	M75	M	s61	M60	M84	s82	M	8	-
Matteo Vitaioli	27/10/89	Tropical Coriano (ITA)	M	M	M61	M77	M	s46	M89	38	-
Alex Gasperoni	30/06/84	Tre Penne	M		M69					35	1
Andy Selva	23/05/76	La Fiorita	A	A87		A83	A	A57		69	8
Michele Cervellini	14/04/88	Pennarossa	s55		s17				s71	27	-
Mattia Stefanelli	12/03/93	San Marino (ITA)	s75		A			s57	s79	4	-
Lorenzo Buscarini	27/05/91	Murata	s87	s74						10	-
Mirko Palazzi	24/03/87	San Marino (ITA)		D74	M	D	D	D69	D	21	-
Alessandro Della Valle	08/06/82	Sant'Ermete (ITA)		D	D		D78	D	D	54	1
Nicola Chiaruzzi	25/12/87	Tre Penne		M	M	M				5	-
Lorenzo Gasperoni	03/01/90	Juvenes/Dogana & Pietracuta (ITA)		s63	s69			M	M	6	-
Danilo Rinaldi	18/04/86	La Fiorita		s87		s83		A69	A79	20	1
Enrico Golinucci	16/07/91	Libertas				s77		s75		2	-
Elia Benedettini	22/06/95	Pianese (ITA)					G			1	-
Pier Filippo Mazza	20/08/88	Sant'Ermete (ITA)					M			11	-
Alessandro Golinucci	10/10/94	Tropical Coriano (ITA)					s84	M75		2	-
Davide Cesarini	16/02/95	Ribelle (ITA)						s69		1	-
Fabio Tomassini	05/02/96	Bellaria (ITA)						s69		1	-
Alessandro Bianchi	19/07/89	Pietracuta (ITA)							s89	5	-

NB The San Marino amateur players are permitted to appear for more than one club at the same time.

EUROPE

DOMESTIC LEAGUE CLUB-BY-CLUB

Stadiums

Stadio di Domagnano, Domagnano (200)
Serravalle B, Serravalle (350)
Stadio Federico Crescentini, Fiorentino (1,500)

Montecchio, Città di San Marino (500)
Stadio Ezio Conti, Dogana (350)
San Marino Stadium, Serravalle (4,801)

SP La Fiorita

First qualifying round - FC Levadia Tallinn (EST)
H 0-1
Montanari, Angeletti, Bugli, Mazzola, Rinaldi, Pensalfini, Cangini, Bollini, Ceci, Selva (Gualtieri 35; Scarponi 87), Calzolari (Confalone 53). Coach: Alberto Manca (ITA)
A 0-7
Montanari, Angeletti, Confalone, Bugli, Mazzola, Rinaldi, Pensalfini, Cangini (Cavalli 55), Bollini (Scarponi 75), Ceci (Forcellini 64), Selva. Coach: Alberto Manca (ITA)

AC Libertas

First qualifying round - PFC Botev Plovdiv (BUL)
A 0-4
A Simoncini, Molinari, A Benvenuti, Rocchetti, Facondini (Zavoli 88), Rosti (Angeli 74), Morelli, Antonelli, Zennaro (Golinucci 61), Righi, Torelli. Coach: Roberto Marcucci (SMR)
H 0-2
A Simoncini, Molinari (Angeli 79), Rocchetti, Facondini, D Simoncini (Rossi 70), Rosti (Zennaro 72), Golinucci, Morelli, Antonelli, Righi, Rocchi. Coach: Roberto Marcucci (SMR)

SS Folgore

First qualifying round - FK Budućnost Podgorica (MNE)
H 1-2 Perrotta (55)
Bicchiarelli, Nucci, Muraccini, Pacini, Ceschi, Perrotta (Berardi 88), Della Valle (Vagnetti 84), Loiodice (Berretti 81), Paglialonga, Muccini, Sartori. Coach: Nicola Berardi (SMR)
A 0-3
Bicchiarelli, Nucci, Muraccini, Pacini (Casadei 72), Ceschi, Perrotta, Loiodice, Paglialonga, Muccini (A Ottaviani 88), Sartori, Magnani (Della Valle 49). Coach: Nicola Berardi (SMR)

SP Cailungo

1974 • no website
Coach: Sereno Uraldi

2014

14/09	Virtus	L	1-4	Cannini
28/09	Juvenes/Dogana	L	0-3	
05/10	Cosmos	D	1-1	Polidori
18/10	Murata	W	5-1	Cannini 2, Bartoli 2, Polidori
25/10	Tre Fiori	L	1-3	Stradaioli (p)
02/11	Faetano	L	1-2	Troiano
09/11	Tre Penne	W	2-1	Stradaioli, L Boschi
22/11	Pennarossa	L	0-2	
29/11	Libertas	D	0-0	
07/12	Fiorentino	D	1-1	Cannini
13/12	Folgore	W	2-0	Tomassoni, Stradaioli
2015				
31/01	La Fiorita	L	2-3	Conti, Stradaioli (p)
11/02	Domagnano	W	2-1	Polidori, Santarini
14/02	San Giovanni	W	1-0	Polidori
21/02	Virtus	L	2-3	Stradaioli (p), Brighi
04/03	Juvenes/Dogana	D	1-1	Stradaioli
14/03	Cosmos	W	1-0	L Boschi
22/03	Murata	W	3-0	Bartoli 2, Conti
12/04	Tre Fiori	W	1-0	Stradaioli
18/04	Faetano	L	1-3	Stradaioli

Name	Nat	DoB	Pos	Aps	(s)	Gls
Michele Andreini		15/04/90	D	10	(3)	
Andrea Bartoli	ITA	20/09/76	A	15		4
Adonay Bonfini		23/06/96	A		(5)	
Lorenzo Boschi		30/04/86	A	19	(1)	2
Michele Boschi		19/08/90	D	4	(2)	
Denny Bozzi		06/06/89	D	19		
Ivan Brighi	ITA	20/12/82	M	16		1
Alberto Cannini	ITA	13/01/81	A	9	(1)	4
Massimiliano Casali		02/02/96	M	5	(7)	
Simone Ciavatta		18/09/81	M	5	(7)	
Michele Conti		26/04/91	A	8	(1)	2
Davide Errani	ITA	09/11/82	M	9		
Nicolas Lazzaro	ITA	20/07/93	G	1	(1)	
Gabriele Lotti	ITA	09/07/74	D	2	(1)	
Gianluca Micheloni		21/03/90	M	10	(2)	
Nicola Polidori		12/03/91	M	13	(2)	4
Andrea Sammaritani		14/05/79	D	6	(3)	
Simone Santarini		17/10/91	M	7	(13)	1
Nicholas Stradaioli	ITA	21/01/85	M	18		8
Nicolò Tamagnini		07/02/88	G	19		
Omar Tomassoni	ITA	06/12/88	D	16	(1)	1
Antonello Troiano	ITA	24/09/84	M	9		1

SS Cosmos

1979 • no website
Major honours
San Marino League (1) 2001; San Marino Cup (4) 1980, 1981, 1995, 1999
Coach: Roberto Sarti; (31/01/15) Francesco Donnini

2014

21/09	Juvenes/Dogana	L	0-3	
26/09	Murata	L	2-5	Bugli (p), Negri
05/10	Cailungo	D	1-1	Baldiserra
18/10	Virtus	L	2-3	Negri, Parma
25/10	Faetano	D	1-1	Parma
02/11	Tre Fiori	D	0-0	
09/11	San Giovanni	D	1-1	Pasolini
22/11	Tre Penne	L	0-1	
29/11	Fiorentino	L	0-1	
07/12	Folgore	L	0-2	
13/12	Pennarossa	L	0-4	
2015				
31/01	Libertas	L	0-3	
08/02	La Fiorita	D	1-1	Negri
14/02	Domagnano	L	0-3	
28/02	Juvenes/Dogana	L	2-3	Negri, Moretti
07/03	Murata	L	1-3	Di Paolo
14/03	Cailungo	L	0-1	
22/03	Virtus	L	0-3	
12/04	Faetano	L	1-4	Negri
18/04	Tre Fiori	L	1-5	Negri

Name	Nat	DoB	Pos	Aps	(s)	Gls
Matteo Albani		10/10/77	M	7	(3)	
Riccardo Aluigi		29/03/94	A	14	(2)	
Alessandro Baldiserra	ITA	15/02/80	D	19		1
Marco Borgelli	ITA	19/01/81	D	16	(1)	
Matteo Bugli		03/03/83	M	15	(1)	1
Andrea Busignani		28/06/78	D	3	(2)	
Marco Casalboni	ITA	04/12/82	G	18		
Alex Cavalli		26/02/92	D	16	(1)	
Marco De Luigi		21/03/78	A	6	(5)	
Domenico Di Paolo	ITA	25/08/81	A	7	(9)	1
Rabi El Haloui	ITA	08/01/92	D	11		
Alessandro Esposito	ITA	06/08/93	A	2	(3)	
Marco Fantini	ITA	28/08/78	A		(2)	
Nicola Giorgini		03/04/93	A		(1)	
Filippo Lualdi	ITA	09/05/82	D	14	(1)	
Bartolo Maggiore	ITA	18/10/75	A	4	(1)	
Luca Mondardini	ITA	16/09/86	A	6		
Nicola Moretti		20/04/84	M	12	(2)	1
Cristian Negri	ITA	16/01/85	A	18		6
Stefano Pari		13/12/93	A	6	(8)	
Simon Parma	ITA	20/03/83	A	9	(2)	2
Simon Parma	ITA	20/03/83	G	1		
Davide Pasolini	ITA	13/10/89	M	10		1
Christian Stilli	ITA	19/09/83	D	1	(4)	
Denis Veronesi		17/07/88	M	4		

FC Domagnano

1966 • no website

Major honours
San Marino League (4) 1989, 2002, 2003, 2005;
San Marino Cup (8) 1972, 1988, 1990, 1992, 1996,
2001, 2002, 2003

Coach: Cristian Protti (ITA)

2014
12/09	Folgore	L	1-3	*Chiarabini*
21/09	Fiorentino	W	2-1	*Porchia, Chiarabini (p)*
27/09	Tre Penne	D	1-1	*Chiarabini*
03/10	La Fiorita	L	0-1	
18/10	Pennarossa	W	1-0	*Mami*
26/10	San Giovanni	W	2-1	*Chiarabini 2 (1p)*
02/11	Libertas	D	0-0	
22/11	Tre Fiori	W	1-0	*Chiarabini*
30/11	Virtus	D	1-1	*Chiarabini*
06/12	Faetano	L	0-2	
13/12	Murata	W	1-0	*Aissaoui*

2015
01/02	Juvenes/Dogana	L	0-1	
11/02	Cailungo	L	1-2	*Aissaoui*
14/02	Cosmos	W	3-0	*Mami, Chiarabini, Venerucci*
22/02	Folgore	L	1-2	*Chiarabini*
28/02	Fiorentino	W	1-0	*Lusini*
08/03	Tre Penne	W	4-0	*Aissaoui, Mami 2, L Ceccaroli*
14/03	La Fiorita	L	2-5	*L Ceccaroli, Chiarabini*
22/03	Pennarossa	W	2-1	*Aissaoui, Chiarabini*
11/04	San Giovanni	W	3-2	*L Ceccaroli, Bucci, Mami*
19/04	Libertas	W	1-0	*Bucci*

Name	Nat	DoB	Pos	Aps	(s)	Gls
Amir Aissaoui	ITA	30/12/90	A	14		4
Marco Bucci	ITA	04/03/75	M	20		2
Federico Buldrini	ITA	19/08/83	D	18	(1)	
Luca Ceccaroli		05/07/95	M	18	(1)	3
Marco Ceccaroli		09/03/92	M		(9)	
Mattia Censoni		31/03/96	D	3		
Carlo Chiarabini	ITA	27/04/76	A	21		11
Davide Dolcini		30/01/91	A	9	(5)	
Alessio Faetanini		15/03/90	M	5	(6)	
Matteo Ferrini	ITA	24/07/84	M	3	(8)	
Denis Iencinella	ITA	10/01/84	A	4	(3)	
Daniele Lusini	ITA	10/03/82	M	16		1
Alessandro Mami	ITA	24/07/92	A	16	(3)	5
Alberto Menghi		17/10/90	D		(2)	
Alessandro Moraccini		30/04/96	M	1	(2)	
Lorenzo Moretti		20/08/79	M		(1)	
Michele Moretti		26/10/81	M	20		
Giacomo Muraccini		15/09/90	G	21		
Mirko Piscaglia		29/09/90	M	15	(2)	
Sandro Porchia	ITA	14/06/77	D	8		1
Nicola Ranocchini		01/04/85	D	4	(2)	
Giovanni Righi		05/07/94	D		(1)	
Luca Sensoli		07/03/91	A	1	(3)	
Alex Stefanelli		26/11/89	A		(3)	
Andrea Venerucci		21/11/89	M	14	(1)	1

SC Faetano

1962 • faetanocalcio.sm

Major honours
San Marino League (3) 1986, 1991, 1999;
San Marino Cup (3) 1993, 1994, 1998

Coach: Ligor Cobo (ALB)

2014
13/09	Juvenes/Dogana	D	0-0	
21/09	Murata	L	0-2	
28/09	Tre Fiori	L	0-2	
04/10	Virtus	L	1-2	*A Moroni (p)*
25/10	Cosmos	D	1-1	*M Giardi*
02/11	Cailungo	W	2-1	*Lonardo, Mazza*
09/11	Libertas	L	0-1	
22/11	San Giovanni	L	1-2	*Cavoli (p)*
29/11	Tre Penne	D	1-1	*A Moroni (p)*
06/12	Domagnano	W	2-0	*M Giardi, Cavoli*
14/12	La Fiorita	W	1-0	*A Moroni*

2015
31/01	Folgore	L	0-2	
08/02	Pennarossa	W	3-2	*A Moroni 2 (1p), Stefanelli*
14/02	Fiorentino	D	1-1	*Merendino*
21/02	Juvenes/Dogana	W	1-0	*M Giardi*
28/02	Murata	W	3-1	*A Moroni (p), M Giardi, Stefanelli*
07/03	Tre Fiori	W	2-1	*Stefanelli, Cavoli*
15/03	Virtus	D	0-0	
12/04	Cosmos	W	4-1	*A Moroni 2, Stefanelli, M Giardi*
18/04	Cailungo	W	3-1	*Marcatilli 2, M Giardi*

Name	Nat	DoB	Pos	Aps	(s)	Gls
Mattia Casali		06/05/97	M	4	(4)	
Francesco Cavoli	ITA	20/03/87	M	17		3
Alex Della Valle		13/06/90	D	18		
Rabi El Haloui	ITA	08/01/92	D	8		
Mattia Giardi		15/12/91	M	17	(2)	6
Nicola Giardi		18/07/82	G	1		
Simone Lamantia	ITA	08/02/79	G	19		
Omar Lepri	ITA	10/05/77	D	4	(1)	
Gaetano Lonardo	ITA	15/01/78	D	9		1
Lorenzo Marcatilli	ITA	20/09/93	M	18		2
Mattia Mazza		03/05/89	D	6	(4)	1
Dario Merendino	ITA	14/11/83	D	9		1
Andrea Moroni		10/10/85	A	16	(1)	8
Marco Moroni		30/12/85	D		(1)	
Luca Patregnani	ITA	08/04/85	M	16		
Maurizio Pedrelli	ITA	26/02/68	D	3	(5)	
Simone Quadrelli		28/12/95	D	2		
Enrico Raggini		30/07/90	M	6	(1)	
Giacomo Rinaldi		23/03/90	D	13	(4)	
Stefano Stefanelli		05/10/79	A	12		4
Simone Ugolini	ITA	28/02/91	A	15	(4)	
Vittorio Valentini		09/10/73	D	9	(7)	

FC Fiorentino

1974 • no website

Major honours
San Marino League (1) 1992

Coach: Ermanno Zonzini

2014
13/09	San Giovanni	W	2-1	*Lipen, Iencinella*
21/09	Domagnano	L	1-2	*Iencinella*
27/09	La Fiorita	W	2-1	*Zenunay, Pratelli*
04/10	Libertas	D	0-0	
19/10	Tre Penne	W	2-0	*Andruccioli, Palanghi*
25/10	Folgore	W	3-2	*Jaupi 3*
01/11	Pennarossa	L	1-2	*Lazzarini*
08/11	Murata	D	1-1	*Jaupi*
23/11	Juvenes/Dogana	L	1-2	*Molinari (p)*
29/11	Cosmos	W	1-0	*Lazzarini (p)*
07/12	Cailungo	D	1-1	*Lazzarini*

2015
01/02	Virtus	W	1-0	*Baizan*
07/02	Tre Fiori	L	0-1	
14/02	Faetano	D	1-1	*Jaupi*
22/02	San Giovanni	W	2-0	*Paglialonga, Stefanelli*
28/02	Domagnano	L	0-1	
08/03	La Fiorita	L	0-2	
15/03	Libertas	D	1-1	*Lazzarini*
21/03	Tre Penne	W	1-0	*Jaupi*
11/04	Folgore	L	1-3	*Jaupi*
18/04	Pennarossa	W	2-1	*Evandro, Baizan*

Name	Nat	DoB	Pos	Aps	(s)	Gls
Mattia Andruccioli	ITA	07/02/92	A	9		1
Maximiliano Baizan		23/03/93	M	15	(1)	2
Giacomo Bartoli		30/01/93	M	4	(1)	
Michele Berardi		07/04/92	G	1		
Andrea Bernardi		08/11/88	D	16	(1)	
Manuel Carlini		26/05/93	D	2	(3)	
Andrea Ceccoli		22/09/93	M	7	(3)	
Evandro	BRA	04/02/87	M	9	(1)	1
Genghini Gabriele		07/10/90	D	7	(1)	
Federico Gennari		28/08/92	M	5	(9)	
Denis Iencinella	ITA	10/01/84	A	4	(4)	2
Enea Jaupi	ALB	06/10/93	A	11	(6)	7
Andrea Lazzarini	ITA	08/04/86	M	12	(5)	4
Luca Lelli	ITA	25/09/79	G	20		
Evgeni Lipen	BLR	15/12/92	D	12	(1)	1
Daniele Maiani		04/08/93	D	4	(3)	
Elia Marchetti		26/01/95	M	1		
Alessandro Molinari	ITA	14/05/89	M	18	(1)	1
Mirko Paglialonga	ITA	19/09/83	D	9		1
Daniele Palanghi	ITA	24/12/81	M	16	(2)	1
Andrea Paoletti		26/02/92	A	4	(5)	
Massimiliano Pratelli	ITA	14/04/83	D	21		1
Matteo Scarponi		28/09/91	D	4		
Lorenzo Scianella		17/04/90	M		(1)	
Alex Stefanelli		26/11/89	A	4	(3)	1
Adriano Zanotti		15/07/86	M		(2)	
Gerhard Zenunay	ALB	12/06/89	M	3	(3)	1
Davide Zonzini		01/04/84	D	13	(2)	

SS Folgore

1972 • folgorecalcio.com

Major honours
San Marino League (4) 1997, 1998, 2000, 2015;
San Marino Cup (1) 2015

Coach: Nicola Berardi

2014

12/09	Domagnano	W	3-1	Muccini, Hirsch, Nucci
20/09	Libertas	W	4-1	Perrotta, Hirsch 3
28/09	Pennarossa	W	3-1	Genestreti, Ceschi, Casadei
05/10	Tre Penne	W	1-0	Hirsch
19/10	San Giovanni	D	0-0	
25/10	Fiorentino	L	2-3	Ceschi, Perrotta
01/11	La Fiorita	D	2-2	Perrotta, Hirsch
07/11	Tre Fiori	W	4-2	Della Valle 2, Hirsch, Perrotta
23/11	Murata	D	1-1	Bollini
07/12	Cosmos	W	2-0	Casadei, Perrotta
13/12	Cailungo	L	0-2	

2015

31/01	Faetano	W	2-0	Rossi, Perrotta
07/02	Juvenes/Dogana	W	2-0	Genestreti, Muccini
15/02	Virtus	W	2-1	Magnani, Della Valle
22/02	Domagnano	W	2-1	Ceschi, Perrotta
01/03	Libertas	D	0-0	
07/03	Pennarossa	L	0-1	
14/03	Tre Penne	W	3-1	Bollini, Perrotta 2
21/03	San Giovanni	W	4-0	Bollini, Della Valle 2, Hirsch
11/04	Fiorentino	W	3-1	Genestreti, Della Valle, Ceschi
19/04	La Fiorita	D	1-1	Contato

Name	Nat	DoB	Pos	Aps	(s)	Gls
Emanuel Amici		21/05/86	M	2	(5)	
Mirko Bartoli		18/05/89	D		(1)	
Marco Berardi		12/02/93	D	19		
Davide Bicchiarelli	ITA	19/05/89	G	19		
Fabio Bollini		19/09/83	M	13	(4)	3
Michele Casadei		24/01/92	M	13	(8)	2
Fabio Ceschi	ITA	19/01/82	A	20		4
Andrea Contato	ITA	21/02/98	D	1		1
Umberto Del Core	ITA	30/11/79	A		(2)	
Achille Della Valle		31/01/89	A	9	(10)	6
Christofer Genestreti	ITA	30/05/84	D	18	(2)	3
Tomas Guidi		04/09/92	D	1	(1)	
Adolfo Hirsch		31/01/86	M	15	(3)	8
Davide Magnani	ITA	19/02/80	D	8		1
Gianluca Martinini	ITA	19/02/80	M	1	(1)	
Manuel Muccini		24/11/89	M	5	(3)	2
Marco Muraccini		25/02/91	D	11		
Andrea Nucci	ITA	06/09/86	M	16	(2)	1
Andrea Ottaviani		16/06/85	D	4	(3)	
Mirko Ottaviani		09/02/95	G	2	(1)	
Simone Pacini	ITA	08/01/81	M	3	(2)	
Mirko Paglialonga	ITA	19/09/83	D	10		
Francesco Perrotta	ITA	27/08/81	A	19		9
Marco Rattini		31/12/84	M	2	(1)	
Luca Righi		01/04/95	D	6	(1)	
Luca Rossi	ITA	14/04/93	D	11	(2)	1
Francesco Sartori	ITA	07/03/93	D		(1)	
Davide Vagnetti		19/07/83	M	1	(2)	
Nicolò Venerucci		27/08/95	A	2	(2)	

AC Juvenes/Dogana

2000 • no website

Major honours
San Marino Cup (2) 2009, 2011

Coach: Fabrizio Costantini

2014

13/09	Faetano	D	0-0	
21/09	Cosmos	W	3-0	Santini, Canini, Ugolini
28/09	Cailungo	W	3-0	Santini, Mantovani, Bagli (p)
05/10	Murata	D	2-2	Santini, Mariotti
19/10	Tre Fiori	W	1-0	Ugolini
01/11	Virtus	W	3-0	Mariotti 3
08/11	La Fiorita	L	1-2	og (Calzolari)
23/11	Fiorentino	W	2-1	Ugolini, Mariotti
30/11	Pennarossa	D	1-1	Mariotti
06/12	San Giovanni	W	6-0	Zafferani, Maccagno 2, E Casadei, Mantovani, Mariotti (p)
13/12	Tre Penne	W	3-1	Mantovani, Zafferani, Ugolini

2015

01/02	Domagnano	W	1-0	Santini
07/02	Folgore	L	0-2	
15/02	Libertas	W	2-0	Mariotti, Canini
21/02	Faetano	L	0-1	
28/02	Cosmos	W	3-2	Santini, Gasperoni, N Cavalli
07/03	Cailungo	D	1-1	Mariotti
14/03	Murata	W	1-0	Mantovani
21/03	Tre Fiori	L	0-1	
18/04	Virtus	W	2-1	Gasperoni, Canini

Name	Nat	DoB	Pos	Aps	(s)	Gls
Giordo Bagli	ITA	15/01/81	M	11	(1)	1
Manuel Battistini		22/07/94	M	2		
Nicola Canini		14/08/88	M	18		3
Andrea Casadei		16/04/77	D		(1)	
Enrico Casadei		18/02/96	M		(1)	1
Nicolas Cavalli	ITA	22/04/94	D		(3)	1
Thomas Cavalli	ITA	17/01/88	D	14	(1)	
Alberto Colombini		12/08/88	M	1	(1)	
Eugenio Colombini		16/01/92	M	7	(4)	
Mattia Dominici	ITA	29/07/94	D	6	(4)	
Lorenzo Francini		11/04/95	M	2	(10)	
Lorenzo Gasperoni		03/01/90	M	8	(1)	2
Eros Gobbi		16/10/89	G	3	(1)	
Tommaso Guerra		22/08/90	M		(3)	
Cristian Maccagno	ITA	05/06/83	M	15	(1)	2
Mirko Mantovani	ITA	14/11/86	D	19		4
Mattia Manzaroli		03/10/91	G	17		
Giorgio Mariotti	ITA	06/05/86	A	15	(1)	9
Mattia Merlini		23/12/93	D	19		
Riccardo Santini	ITA	18/10/86	M	18		5
Marco Ugolini	ITA	23/12/86	A	12	(2)	4
Daniele Villa	ITA	24/05/82	D	14		
Nicola Zafferani		06/11/91	D	12	(6)	2
Alessandro Zonzini		11/10/94	D	7	(7)	

SP La Fiorita

1933 • lafiorita.sm

Major honours
San Marino League (3) 1987, 1990, 2014;
San Marino Cup (3) 1986, 2012, 2013

Coach: Alberto Manca (ITA);
(20/12/14) Paolo Bertaccini (ITA)

2014

14/09	Tre Penne	D	3-3	Rinaldi 2, Casadei
20/09	San Giovanni	W	4-1	og 2 (Mosconi 2), Cavalli 2
27/09	Fiorentino	L	1-2	Cavalli
03/10	Domagnano	W	1-0	Cavalli
17/10	Libertas	L	0-1	
26/10	Pennarossa	L	0-2	
01/11	Folgore	D	2-2	Selva, Cavalli
08/11	Juvenes/Dogana	W	2-1	Selva 2
23/11	Virtus	W	1-0	Cangini
30/11	Tre Fiori	L	1-2	Selva
14/12	Faetano	L	0-1	

2015

31/01	Cailungo	W	3-2	Selva 2 (1p), Bollini
08/02	Cosmos	D	1-1	Bollini
14/02	Murata	W	1-0	Selva
21/02	Tre Penne	W	3-1	Rinaldi 2, Marino
01/03	San Giovanni	W	3-1	Bollini, Selva 2 (1p)
08/03	Fiorentino	W	2-0	Selva, Marino
14/03	Domagnano	W	5-2	Bollini, Ceci, Petráš, Rinaldi 2
21/03	Libertas	D	1-1	Selva
11/04	Pennarossa	W	2-1	Rinaldi, Selva
19/04	Folgore	D	1-1	og (Magnani)

Name	Nat	DoB	Pos	Aps	(s)	Gls
Gian Luca Bollini		24/03/80	D	18		4
Davide Bugli		23/12/84	D	19	(1)	
Pietro Calzolari		28/10/91	M	16	(2)	
Alessio Cangini	ITA	05/01/91	M	20		1
Nicola Casadei		24/01/89	D	3	(9)	1
Nicola Cavalli		15/02/86	M	11	(4)	5
Francesco Ceci	ITA	28/12/84	M	19		1
Thomas De Biagi		03/11/90	M	1	(6)	
Lorenzo Forcellini		21/10/84	M	3	(5)	
Alessandro Guidi		14/12/86	A	8	(6)	
Antonio Marino	ITA	08/06/74	A	7	(2)	2
Andrea Martini	ITA	24/12/81	D	8		
Alberto Mazzola	ITA	21/07/84	D	2		
Simone Montanari	ITA	11/03/80	G	19		
Tiziano Mottola	ITA	06/07/86	A	1		
Filippo Pensalfini	ITA	08/02/77	M	9	(1)	
Martin Petráš	SVK	02/11/79	D	18		1
Emanuele Quadrelli		12/10/81	G	2		
Andrea Righi		10/07/97	M	4	(5)	
Danilo Rinaldi		18/04/86	A	16	(1)	7
Matteo Scarponi		28/09/91	D	3	(1)	
Andy Selva		23/05/76	A	17	(1)	12
Samuel Toccaceli		09/11/96	M	3	(5)	
Massimo Vagnetti		25/06/79	D	4	(4)	

AC Libertas

1928 • polisportivalibertas.com

Major honours
San Marino League (1) 1996; San Marino Cup (11)
1937, 1950, 1954, 1958, 1959, 1961, 1987, 1989,
1991, 2006, 2014
Coach: Roberto Marcucci

2014
14/09	Pennarossa	D	1-1	*Golinucci*
20/09	Folgore	L	1-4	*Antonelli*
27/09	San Giovanni	W	4-2	*Giardi, Antonelli 2 (1p), Rossi*
04/10	Fiorentino	D	0-0	
17/10	La Fiorita	W	1-0	*Morelli*
25/10	Tre Penne	W	1-0	*Morelli*
02/11	Domagnano	D	0-0	
09/11	Faetano	W	1-0	*D Simoncini*
29/11	Cailungo	D	0-0	
06/12	Virtus	L	0-1	
14/12	Tre Fiori	L	0-2	

2015
31/01	Cosmos	W	3-0	*Nanni, Golinucci, Giunta*
07/02	Murata	W	1-0	*og (Valentini)*
15/02	Juvenes/Dogana	L	0-2	
21/02	Pennarossa	D	1-1	*Golinucci*
01/03	Folgore	D	0-0	
08/03	San Giovanni	W	4-0	*Giunta 2, Antonelli, Morelli*
15/03	Fiorentino	D	1-1	*Golinucci*
21/03	La Fiorita	D	1-1	*D Simoncini*
11/04	Tre Penne	W	3-0	*Morelli, D Simoncini, Rosti*
19/04	Domagnano	L	0-1	

Name	Nat	DoB	Pos	Aps	(s)	Gls
Daniele Angeli		29/07/92	D	7	(6)	
Filippo Antonelli	ITA	28/01/83	M	18		4
Lorenzo Bacciocchi		18/11/93	M		(6)	
Andrea Benvenuti		24/07/90	D	7	(5)	
Marco Benvenuti		09/12/95	M		(2)	
Francesco Cherubini		14/12/95	M		(3)	
Mirco Facondini	ITA	30/09/82	M	19		
Mirko Giardi		11/05/95	M	4	(9)	1
Alessandro Giunta	ITA	22/01/77	A	10		3
Enrico Golinucci		16/07/91	M	21		4
Manuel Molinari		08/08/86	D	12	(5)	
Gian Luca Morelli	ITA	12/02/85	A	16		4
Federico Nanni		22/09/81	M	9		1
Paolo Rocchetti	ITA	21/04/86	D	19		
Daniele Rocchi	ITA	23/06/82	D	18		
Michele Rossi		26/01/95	D	10	(2)	1
Marco Rosti		21/10/88	A	14	(5)	1
Aldo Simoncini		30/08/86	G	21		
Davide Simoncini		30/08/86	D	14		3
Andrea Zavoli		04/07/94	M	10	(5)	
Nicolò Zennaro	ITA	29/07/85	A	2		

SS Murata

1966 • no website

Major honours
San Marino League (3) 2006, 2007, 2008;
San Marino Cup (3) 1997, 2007, 2008
Coach: Paolo Tarini (ITA);
(24/03/15) Fabio Baschetti (ITA)

2014
13/09	Tre Fiori	L	1-3	*Marco Casadei*
21/09	Faetano	W	2-0	*Sternini, Marco Casadei*
26/09	Cosmos	W	5-2	*Sternini (p), Marco Casadei 4*
05/10	Juvenes/Dogana	D	2-2	*Marco Casadei, Faetanini*
18/10	Cailungo	L	1-5	*Cuttone (p)*
26/10	Virtus	D	0-0	
08/11	Fiorentino	D	1-1	*Mattia Angelini*
23/11	Folgore	D	1-1	*Vannoni*
29/11	San Giovanni	D	1-1	*Mastronicola*
07/12	Tre Penne	W	3-1	*Cuttone 3*
13/12	Domagnano	L	0-1	

2015
01/02	Pennarossa	L	1-2	*Cuttone (p)*
07/02	Libertas	L	0-1	
14/02	La Fiorita	L	0-1	
22/02	Tre Fiori	L	1-4	*N Angelini*
28/02	Faetano	L	1-3	*Marco Casadei*
07/03	Cosmos	W	3-1	*Mastronicola, Cuttone (p), Marco Casadei*
14/03	Juvenes/Dogana	L	0-1	
22/03	Cailungo	L	0-3	
12/04	Virtus	W	3-1	*Brandino 2, Michael Angelini*

Name	Nat	DoB	Pos	Aps	(s)	Gls
Mattia Angelini	ITA	14/01/90	D	9		1
Michael Angelini	ITA	25/11/83	M	7		1
Nicolò Angelini		15/03/92	A	5	(2)	1
Francesco Baldinini	ITA	27/11/82	A	8	(1)	
Gian Marco Baschetti	ITA	29/11/91	A	1	(2)	
Davide Bellucci	ITA	03/10/79	D	9		
Christopher Brandino	ITA	20/09/87	A	3	(1)	2
Lorenzo Buscarini		27/05/91	M	14		
Marco Casadei		20/09/85	A	15		9
Matteo Casadei		01/08/84	D		(1)	
Mattia Casadei		26/01/89	D	1		
Giuseppe Casali		08/07/73	G	2		
Alberto Celli		24/06/85	A	12	(1)	
Alessandro Cuttone	ITA	24/03/84	M	17		6
Angelo Faetanini		17/01/93	D	13	(1)	1
Michael Giovagnoli		19/06/90	G	2	(1)	
Marco Graziosi		26/08/89	G	16		
Filippo Mainardi		16/12/90	M	9		
Jacopo Manzari		06/03/88	A	1	(5)	
Manuel Marani		07/06/84	A	1	(2)	
Alessandro Mastronicola	ITA	29/11/74	D	19		2
Alex Mattioli		14/06/95	M	2	(3)	
Alessandro Protti		28/07/81	M		(3)	
Michael Simoncini		01/02/87	A	11	(1)	
Francesco Sternini	ITA	29/06/87	M	16	(1)	2
Luca Tomassoni		21/11/94	M	6	(6)	
Carlo Valentini		15/03/82	D	4	(1)	
Fabio Vannoni	ITA	07/10/77	M	13	(2)	1
Giacomo Zonzini		20/09/90	A	4	(2)	

SS Pennarossa

1968 • pennarossa.com

Major honours
San Marino League (1) 2004; San Marino Cup (2)
2004, 2005
Coach: Davide Nicolini (ITA);
(26/10/14) Alessandro Carta (ITA)

2014
14/09	Libertas	D	1-1	*N Ciacci*
19/09	Tre Penne	L	1-2	*Aruci*
28/09	Folgore	L	1-3	*Bonifazi*
04/10	San Giovanni	W	3-1	*Berretti, Aruci 2*
18/10	Domagnano	L	0-1	
26/10	La Fiorita	W	2-0	*Fabbri, Aruci*
01/11	Fiorentino	W	2-1	*Aruci 2*
08/11	Virtus	L	1-2	*Fabbri (p)*
22/11	Cailungo	W	2-0	*Aruci 2*
30/11	Juvenes/Dogana	D	1-1	*Bonifazi*
06/12	Tre Fiori	L	0-1	
13/12	Cosmos	W	4-0	*Aruci 3, Cervellini*

2015
01/02	Murata	W	2-1	*Bernabucci, Del Pivo*
08/02	Faetano	L	2-3	*Aruci 2 (1p)*
21/02	Libertas	D	1-1	*Del Pivo*
01/03	Tre Penne	W	3-1	*Capozzi, Del Pivo, Aruci*
07/03	Folgore	W	1-0	*Capozzi*
15/03	San Giovanni	W	3-1	*Brici, Bernabucci, A Ciacci*
22/03	Domagnano	L	1-2	*Bernabucci*
11/04	La Fiorita	L	1-2	*Aruci (p)*
18/04	Fiorentino	L	1-2	*M Broccoli*

Name	Nat	DoB	Pos	Aps	(s)	Gls
Nicola Albani		15/04/81	D	18		
Armando Aruci	ITA	10/07/89	A	18	(1)	15
Davide Bernabucci	ITA	27/04/85	A	11	(4)	3
Maicol Berretti		01/05/89	M	16	(1)	1
Luca Bonifazi		12/11/82	M	20	(1)	2
Emanuele Brici		16/02/87	D	16	(1)	1
Denis Broccoli		10/08/88	G	3		
Massimo Broccoli		22/09/83	A	1	(3)	1
Nicholas Capozzi	ITA	12/12/87	A	6	(6)	2
Michele Cervellini		14/04/88	M	20		1
Alessandro Ciacci		15/07/96	A	1	(9)	1
Nicola Ciacci		07/07/82	A	9	(3)	1
Fabio Colonna	ITA	07/01/84	G	2		
Daniele Conti	ITA	06/06/90	M	7	(4)	
Nicola Del Pivo	ITA	10/04/92	M	7		3
Enrico Esposito		13/11/76	M		(1)	
Stefano Fabbri	ITA	27/09/82	M	14	(3)	2
Andrea Giovannini		03/04/92	A		(5)	
Antonino Guidi		23/12/72	G	2		
Luca Lazzarini		08/04/86	D	15	(1)	
Paolo Mariotti		05/11/79	M	9	(6)	
Michele Rastelli		23/11/88	D	12	(2)	
Glori Taraj	ALB	21/09/90	D	10		
Kengie Valentini	ITA	05/06/90	G	16		

SS San Giovanni

1948 • no website

Coach: Andrea Lani (ITA);
(06/10/14) Gabriele Rossi;
(15/12/14) Federico Pastori (ITA)

2014

13/09	Fiorentino	L	1-2	Cecchetti
20/09	La Fiorita	L	1-4	Friguglietti (p)
27/09	Libertas	L	2-4	Friguglietti 2 (1p)
04/10	Pennarossa	L	1-3	Friguglietti
19/10	Folgore	D	0-0	
26/10	Domagnano	L	1-2	Friguglietti (p)
31/10	Tre Penne	L	1-3	Friguglietti
09/11	Cosmos	D	1-1	Friguglietti
22/11	Faetano	W	2-1	Friguglietti 2
29/11	Murata	D	1-1	Friguglietti
06/12	Juvenes/Dogana	L	0-6	
14/12	Virtus	L	0-4	
2015				
31/01	Tre Fiori	L	1-3	Moroni (p)
14/02	Cailungo	L	0-1	
22/02	Fiorentino	L	0-2	
01/03	La Fiorita	L	1-3	Friguglietti
08/03	Libertas	L	0-4	
15/03	Pennarossa	L	1-3	Friguglietti
21/03	Folgore	L	0-4	
11/04	Domagnano	L	2-3	Friguglietti, Magnani
19/04	Tre Penne	W	5-2	Magnani, Friguglietti 3 (1p), A Valentini

Name	Nat	DoB	Pos	Aps	(s)	Gls
Giacomo Bacciocchi		24/09/84	D	7	(1)	
Marco Balducci		07/01/77	M		(5)	
Adonay Bonfini		23/06/96	D		(5)	
Andrea Borgagni		21/10/93	M	3	(4)	
Alessandro Casadei	ITA	18/03/92	M	12		
Edoardo Cecchetti		14/07/93	M	18		1
Valentino Chiaravallotti	ITA	14/02/89	M	7		
Francesco Colonna		15/02/84	M	6	(1)	
Sam Fantini		17/09/92	M	5	(1)	
Thomas Felici		26/11/95	D	6	(1)	
Daniele Friguglietti	ITA	21/11/79	A	19	(1)	16
Fabio Giardi		15/03/71	D	3	(1)	
Mirco Giorgi	ITA	10/01/79	D	16		
Gianni Magnani	ITA	06/03/81	M	19	(1)	2
Micheal Mercatelli	ITA	27/04/94	A		(6)	
Andrea Molari	ITA	25/04/89	A	1	(1)	
Nicola Montanari	ITA	30/05/82	G	17		
Massimo Moroni		17/02/90	A	14		1
Luca Mosconi		28/06/82	D	19		
Federico Nanni		22/09/81	M	7	(2)	
Juan Carlos Pasquali		18/03/84	D	2	(5)	
Nicola Raschi		22/01/81	D	2		
Andrea Valentini		04/11/98	A	4	(8)	1
Stefano Valentini		17/04/82	M	9		
Fabio Vecchiola	ITA	23/02/82	M	11	(4)	
Matteo Venerucci		16/12/80	G	4	(1)	
Elia Zafferani		25/06/92	M	2	(5)	
Loris Zafferani		14/08/83	D	18		

SP Tre Fiori

1949 • no website

Major honours
San Marino League (7) 1988, 1993, 1994, 1995, 2009, 2010, 2011; San Marino Cup (6) 1966, 1971, 1974, 1975, 1985, 2010

Coach: Floriano Sperindio

2014

13/09	Murata	W	3-1	Lago, Valle, Macerata
20/09	Virtus	D	0-0	
28/09	Faetano	W	2-0	Colonna, Lago
19/10	Juvenes/Dogana	L	0-1	
25/10	Cailungo	W	3-1	Lago (p), Amici, Balducci
02/11	Cosmos	D	0-0	
07/11	Folgore	L	2-4	Lago, Teodorani (p)
22/11	Domagnano	L	0-1	
30/11	La Fiorita	W	2-1	Lago 2
06/12	Pennarossa	W	1-0	Lago
14/12	Libertas	W	2-0	Maiani, Canarezza
2015				
31/01	San Giovanni	W	3-1	Lisi, Teodorani, O'Neil (p)
07/02	Fiorentino	W	1-0	Maiani
15/02	Tre Penne	L	1-2	O'Neil
22/02	Murata	W	4-1	Lini, O'Neil 2, Teodorani
28/02	Virtus	W	5-0	Semprini 2, O'Neil (p), Valle, Andreini
07/03	Faetano	L	1-2	O'Neil
21/03	Juvenes/Dogana	W	1-0	O'Neil
12/04	Cailungo	L	0-1	
18/04	Cosmos	W	5-1	Teodorani 3, Valle, O'Neil

Name	Nat	DoB	Pos	Aps	(s)	Gls
Federico Amici		27/03/82	A	7	(1)	1
Matteo Andreini		10/10/81	D	14		1
Alberto Balducci	ITA	16/08/93	M	7	2	1
Domenico Bartolomeo	ITA	27/06/93	D		(1)	
Davide Bellucci	ITA	03/10/79	D	7		
Giacomo Benedettini		07/10/82	D	5	(2)	
Nicola Canarezza	ITA	16/08/78	M	8		1
Michele Ceccoli		04/12/73	G	19		
Francesco Colonna	ITA	15/02/84	M	6		1
Stefano Conti		18/07/70	D	7	(2)	
Nicola Della Valle		19/05/97	D	1	(3)	
Nicolò Grini		14/02/92	D	1	(1)	
Luca Guerra		25/06/96	D	1	(9)	
Ramiro Martin Lago	ARG	14/10/87	A	10		7
Nicolò Lini	ITA	13/04/93	D	5	1	
Altin Lisi	ALB	09/03/74	M	17		1
Lorenzo Liverani		13/05/93	M	4	(10)	
Sandro Macerata	ITA	08/10/69	D	14	(1)	1
Federico Macina		22/02/81	M		(3)	
Federico Maiani		25/12/95	A	11	(5)	2
Eugenio Marconi	ITA	22/10/98	G	1		
Filippo Matteoni		27/05/96	D		(1)	
Simone Matteoni		26/04/92	M	4	(5)	
Alex Mattioli		14/11/95	M	4	(4)	
Oscar Muratori	ITA	20/02/84	D	5		
Ephraim O'Neil	GHA	14/01/93	A	8		8
Pietro Semprini		27/01/93	M	7		2
Davide Succi	ITA	07/06/90	D	5		
Alessandro Teodorani	ITA	09/12/71	M	18		6
Luca Valle	ITA	25/01/81	M	7		3
Matteo Vendemini		18/01/82	D	17	(1)	

SP Tre Penne

1956 • trepenne.sm

Major honours
San Marino League (2) 2012, 2013; San Marino Cup (5) 1967, 1970, 1982, 1993, 2000

Coach: Marco Protti

2014

14/09	La Fiorita	D	3-3	Palazzi, Baschetti, Chiaruzzi
19/09	Pennarossa	W	2-1	Valentini, Pignieri
27/09	Domagnano	D	1-1	Chiaretti
05/10	Folgore	L	0-1	
19/10	Fiorentino	L	0-2	
25/10	Libertas	L	0-1	
31/10	San Giovanni	W	3-1	Pignieri 2 (1p), Chiaretti
09/11	Cailungo	L	1-2	Pignieri
22/11	Cosmos	W	1-0	M Rossi
29/11	Faetano	D	1-1	Fattori
07/12	Murata	L	1-3	Fattori
13/12	Juvenes/Dogana	L	1-3	Zanotti
2015				
07/02	Virtus	W	3-1	Chiaruzzi, Pignieri 2
15/02	Tre Fiori	W	2-1	Berardi, og (Ceccoli)
21/02	La Fiorita	L	1-3	Fucili
01/03	Pennarossa	L	1-3	Fucili
08/03	Domagnano	L	0-4	
14/03	Folgore	L	1-3	og (Muccini)
21/03	Fiorentino	L	0-1	
11/04	Libertas	L	0-3	
19/04	San Giovanni	L	2-5	Giuliani, G Zafferani

Name	Nat	DoB	Pos	Aps	(s)	Gls
Francesco Baschetti	ITA	08/01/86	D	19		1
Mattia Bellardita		05/04/93	M		(2)	
Federico Berardi	ITA	14/12/78	M	17		1
Giovanni Bonini		05/09/86	M	7		
Lorenzo Canini		31/03/84	D	2	(3)	
Lorenzo Capicchioni		27/01/89	D	13	(2)	
Emanuele Chiaretti	ITA	20/04/78	A	7		2
Nicola Chiaruzzi		25/12/87	M	15	(1)	2
Alfredo Chierighini	ITA	07/02/66	G	8		
Matteo Colonna		10/05/90	D	1	(1)	
Thomas De Marini		02/11/98	M		(1)	
Sam Fantini		17/09/92	M		(3)	
Enrico Fattori	ITA	12/06/78	D	17		2
Mario Fucili	ITA	04/03/78	A	7	(1)	2
Alex Gasperoni		30/06/84	M	10	(2)	
Michele Giuliani		26/08/93	M	11	(3)	1
Tommaso Guidi		21/10/98	M	1	(1)	
Fabio Macaluso		05/08/86	G	13	(1)	
Federico Muccioli		20/06/96	D	10	(3)	
Mirko Palazzi		21/03/87	D	2		1
Daniele Pignieri	ITA	14/05/75	A	13	(3)	6
Davide Ranocchini		29/04/86	D	3	(3)	
Nicola Raschi		22/01/81	D	4	(1)	
Andrea Rossi	ITA	20/07/87	D	12	(1)	
Matteo Rossi		09/07/86	M	6	(4)	1
Moris Tamburini	ITA	20/03/78	D	1		
Simone Valentini		24/11/84	D	10	(3)	1
Matteo Valli		11/09/86	A	8	(1)	
Andrea Zafferani		24/03/90	A	1	(3)	
Giacomo Zafferani		16/07/96	M	5	(7)	1
Andrea Zanotti		05/05/92	M	8	(8)	1

Virtus FC

1964 • no website
Coach: Matteo Cecchetti (ITA);
(08/03/15) Maurizio Gasperoni

2014

14/09	Cailungo	W	4-1	Franklin 2, Sacco, Innocenti
20/09	Tre Fiori	D	0-0	
04/10	Faetano	W	2-1	Franklin 2
18/10	Cosmos	W	3-2	Innocenti, Semprini, Henrique António
26/10	Murata	D	0-0	
01/11	Juvenes/Dogana	L	0-3	
08/11	Pennarossa	W	2-1	Innocenti, Marigliano
23/11	La Fiorita	L	0-1	
30/11	Domagnano	D	1-1	Franklin
06/12	Libertas	W	1-0	Franklin
14/12	San Giovanni	W	4-0	Innocenti (p), Henrique António (p), Sacco, Franklin

2015

01/02	Fiorentino	L	0-1	
07/02	Tre Penne	L	1-3	Tosi
15/02	Folgore	L	1-2	Esposito
21/02	Cailungo	W	3-2	Innocenti, Righetti, Franklin
28/02	Tre Fiori	L	0-5	
15/03	Faetano	D	0-0	
22/03	Cosmos	W	3-0	Marigliano 2, Innocenti (p)
12/04	Murata	L	1-3	Sacco
18/04	Juvenes/Dogana	L	1-2	L Nanni

Name	Nat	DoB	Pos	Aps	(s)	Gls
Luca Bianchi	ITA	27/02/90	G	15		
Francesco Bonfé	ITA	27/05/94	D	4	(6)	
Vittorio Cesari	ITA	11/01/92	M	12		
Alessandro Esposito	ITA	06/08/93	A	4	(2)	1
Franklin	BRA	13/03/84	A	17	(2)	8
Michele Giacobbi		29/11/79	D	1		
Emanuele Giglietti		06/10/93	M	1	(5)	
Mattia Gualandi		08/04/94	D	7	(1)	
Henrique António	BRA	19/05/82	M	13	(1)	2
William Innocenti	ITA	30/04/87	A	17	(2)	6
Massimiliano La Monaca		26/04/95	G	4		
Jacopo Manzari		06/03/88	A		(1)	
Kevin Marigliano	ITA	10/05/93	A	19	(1)	3
Luca Nanni		30/01/95	M	17		1
Matteo Nanni		07/03/93	M	2	(9)	
Dalibor Riccardi		04/09/83	D	3	(2)	
Manuel Ricci	ITA	19/05/88	D	8		
Enea Righetti	ITA	08/10/86	M	16		1
Stefano Sacco		10/02/91	M	17		3
Stefano Semprini		12/09/85	A	5	(7)	1
Luca Tosi	ITA	23/07/94	M	3	(6)	1
Davide Vagnetti		19/07/83	D	5	(1)	
Denis Veronesi		17/07/88	M	6	(3)	
Alex Zanotti		23/01/79	G	1		
Michele Zanotti		05/11/88	D	9		
Evert Zavoli		10/08/69	M	3	(3)	
Donald Zenunay	ALB	11/01/91	M	11	(4)	

Top goalscorers

(excluding Play-offs)

16 Daniele Friguglietti (San Giovanni)

15 Armando Aruci (Pennarossa)

12 Andy Selva (La Fiorita)

11 Carlo Chiarabini (Domagnano)

9 Francesco Perrotta (Folgore)
Giorgio Mariotti (Juvenes/Dogana)
Marco Casadei (Murata)

8 Nicholas Stradaioli (Cailungo)
Andrea Moroni (Faetano)
Adolfo Hirsch (Folgore)
Ephraim O'Neil (Tre Fiori)
Franklin (Virtus)

DOMESTIC CUP

Coppa Titano 2014/15

FIRST PHASE

(Played in Groups)

Group A

(27/08/14)
Domagnano 0-0 Libertas
Tre Penne 1-2 La Fiorita

(01/09/14)
Tre Penne 2-1 Domagnano

(11/09/14)
La Fiorita 1-2 Cosmos

(22/10/14)
Cosmos 1-1 Tre Penne
La Fiorita 4-0 Libertas

(19/11/14)
Cosmos 1-1 Domagnano
Libertas 3-1 Tre Penne

(26/11/14)
Domagnano 1-2 La Fiorita
Libertas 0-0 Cosmos

(18/01/15)
La Fiorita 0-1 Tre Penne
Libertas 1-0 Domagnano

(24/01/15)
Domagnano 0-3 Tre Penne

(25/01/15)
Cosmos 0-0 La Fiorita

(18/02/15)
Libertas 1-1 La Fiorita
Tre Penne 2-0 Cosmos

(04/03/15)
Tre Penne 4-6 Libertas

(11/03/15)
Domagnano 1-2 Cosmos

(18/03/15)
Cosmos 0-1 Libertas
La Fiorita 4-0 Domagnano

Final standings

Libertas 15 pts *(qualified)*
La Fiorita 14 pts *(qualified)*
Tre Penne 13 pts *(play-offs)*
Cosmos 10 pts
Domagnano 2 pts

Group B

(27/08/14)
Cailungo 0-3 Folgore
Pennarossa 2-1 Virtus

(01/09/14)
Pennarossa 1-2 Juvenes/Dogana
Virtus 0-1 Cailungo

(22/10/14)
Folgore 2-0 Pennarossa
Virtus 0-1 Juvenes/Dogana

(19/11/14)
Folgore 2-0 Virtus
Juvenes/Dogana 2-0 Cailungo

(26/11/14)
Cailungo 0-2 Pennarossa
Juvenes/Dogana 0-1 Folgore

(17/01/15)
Folgore 5-0 Cailungo
Virtus 0-4 Pennarossa

(24/01/15)
Cailungo 2-2 Virtus

(25/01/15)
Juvenes/Dogana 0-0 Pennarossa

(18/02/15)
Juvenes/Dogana 2-2 Virtus
Pennarossa 1-2 Folgore

(04/03/15)
Cailungo 1-5 Juvenes/Dogana
Virtus 1-1 Folgore

(11/03/15)
Folgore 1-2 Juvenes/Dogana
Pennarossa 5-0 Cailungo

Final standings

Folgore 19 pts *(qualified)*
Juvenes/Dogana 17 pts *(qualified)*
Pennarossa 13 pts *(play-offs)*
Cailungo 4 pts
Virtus 3 pts

Group C

(27/08/14)
Fiorentino 1-4 San Giovanni
Murata 1-1 Faetano

(01/09/14)
Fiorentino 3-2 Tre Fiori
San Giovanni 2-3 Murata

(22/10/14)
Faetano 1-0 Fiorentino
San Giovanni 1-0 Tre Fiori

(19/11/14)
Faetano 1-3 San Giovanni
Tre Fiori 1-3 Murata

(26/11/14)
Murata 3-2 Fiorentino
Tre Fiori 0-1 Faetano

(17/01/15)
San Giovanni 0-1 Fiorentino

(18/01/15)
Faetano 3-0 Murata

(24/01/15)
Murata 4-1 San Giovanni

(25/01/15)
Tre Fiori 1-3 Fiorentino

(18/02/15)
Fiorentino 3-2 Faetano
Tre Fiori 1-3 San Giovanni

(04/03/15)
Murata 2-1 Tre Fiori
San Giovanni 3-0 Faetano

(11/03/15)
Faetano 0-2 Tre Fiori
Fiorentino 4-1 Murata

Final standings

Murata 16 pts *(qualified)*
San Giovanni 15 pts *(qualified)*
Fiorentino 15 pts *(play-offs)*
Faetano 10 pts
Tre Fiori 3 pts

Play-offs

(24/03/15)
Tre Penne 1-1 Pennarossa

(31/03/15)
Pennarossa 1-0 Fiorentino

(07/04/15)
Fiorentino 1-1 Tre Penne

Final standings

Pennarossa 4 pts *(qualified)*
Tre Penne 2 pts *(qualified)*
Fiorentino 1 pt *(eliminated)*

QUARTER-FINALS

(22/04/15)
Folgore 4-1 La Fiorita *(Ceschi 26, Hirsch 40, 48, Rossi 68; Bollini 10)*

Libertas 2-1 Pennarossa *(Morelli 28, Giunta 56; Aruci 6)*

Murata 3-1 Tre Penne *(Cuttone 72, Sternini 77, Michael Angelini 90+3; Fucili 5)*

San Giovanni 1-1 Juvenes/Dogana *(Mosconi 18; Villa 90+2) (aet; 4-5 on pens)*

SEMI-FINALS

(27/04/15)
Libertas 0-1 Folgore *(Ceschi 118) (aet)*

Murata 2-1 Juvenes/Dogana *(Cuttone 71p, Gasperoni 116og; Mantovani 85)*

FINAL

(30/04/15)
San Marino Stadium, Serravalle
SS FOLGORE 5 *(Bellucci 22og, Genestreti 53, Casadei 54, 66, Rossi 86)*
SS MURATA 0
Referee: *Guidi*
FOLGORE: *Bicchiarelli, Sartori, Berardi, Genestreti, Bollini, Muccini, Pacini (Della Valle 64), Casadei, Ceschi, Perrotta (Rossi 58), Hirsch (Rattini 74)*
MURATA: *Graziosi, Buscarini, Mattia Casadei, Bellucci, Mastronicola, Simoncini, Vannoni, Sternini, Brandino (Celli 46; Tomassoni 62), Michael Angelini, Marco Casadei (N Angelini 68)*
Red cards: *Mattia Casadei (42), Michael Angelini (56)*

SCOTLAND
Scottish Football Association (SFA)

Address	Hampden Park	**President**	Alan McRae
	GB-Glasgow G42 9AY	**Chief executive**	Stewart Regan
Tel	+44 141 616 6000	**Media officer**	Darryl Broadfoot
Fax	+44 141 616 6001	**Year of formation**	1873
E-mail	info@scottishfa.co.uk	**National stadium**	Hampden Park,
Website	scottishfa.co.uk		Glasgow (52,063)

PREMIERSHIP CLUBS

 1 **Aberdeen FC**

 2 **Celtic FC**

 3 **Dundee FC**

 4 **Dundee United FC**

 5 **Hamilton Academical FC**

 6 **Inverness Caledonian Thistle FC**

 7 **Kilmarnock FC**

 8 **Motherwell FC**

 9 **Partick Thistle FC**

 10 **Ross County FC**

 11 **Saint Johnstone FC**

 12 **Saint Mirren FC**

PROMOTED CLUB

 13 **Heart of Midlothian FC**

KEY:

● – UEFA Champions League

● – UEFA Europa League

● – Promoted

● – Relegated

Easy in the end for Celtic

Celtic FC got off to a rocky start under their new, relatively unknown Norwegian manager Ronny Deila, but despite a gallant effort from Aberdeen FC to dethrone them, the Scottish Premiership trophy ended up at Celtic Park for the fourth season in a row.

Celtic also won the League Cup – after defeating Rangers FC in the last four – but hopes of a domestic treble were dashed in the semi-finals of the Scottish Cup with an extra-time defeat by Inverness Caledonian Thistle FC, who went on to lift the trophy and earn a first qualification for Europe.

| Bhoys fend off Aberdeen to claim 46th league title | Inverness end Celtic's treble dream and win Scottish Cup | UEFA EURO 2016 qualifying hopes alive and kicking |

Domestic league

The final Premiership table may have suggested that the title race was another joyride for Celtic, but for several months their 46th triumph was far from secure. Indeed, Aberdeen actually topped the table in January, when there was still an element of dissent among the Celtic rank and file following the club's poor start under Deila, which bottomed out with a home defeat by Hamilton Academical FC.

With 38 fixtures to fulfil, however, it was always likely that Celtic, with their vastly superior resources, would reign supreme once again. It took a couple of mid-season signings from Dundee United FC – Stuart Armstrong and Gary Mackay-Steven – to give them the push they needed, but once they had defeated Aberdeen 4-0 at home in early March, the rest of the campaign became a breeze. With Leigh Griffiths scoring freely in attack, Stefan Johansen and Scott Brown dovetailing impressively in midfield, Virgil van Dijk and Jason Denayer keeping things tight at the back and Craig Gordon back to his best in goal, Celtic suddenly resembled the dominant force of old under Neil Lennon.

Celtic still had three games to play when Aberdeen's 1-0 defeat at Dundee United FC concluded the title race. The following weekend the new champions made it four wins out of four against the Dons with a 1-0 success at Pittodrie. As a consolation, Derek McInnes's plucky challengers had already secured second place, and they also boasted the Premiership's most potent striker in 18-goal Adam Rooney.

There would be a quick return to the top flight for Heart of Midlothian FC, who romped to victory in the Championship (second tier), but Rangers' three-year plan to climb back to the top rung of the league ladder hit the buffers when they lost their play-off to Motherwell FC, runners-up to Celtic in each of the previous two Premiership campaigns, going down 6-1 on aggregate.

Domestic cups

The first Old Firm derby in three years – and 400th in all – was won by Celtic as they defeated Rangers 2-0 at Hampden Park to reach the League Cup final at the same venue, where they beat Dundee United by the same score.

The Bhoys' next trip to the national stadium, however, ended in a shock 3-2 extra-time defeat by Inverness – a result that sent John Hughes' Highlanders through to the Scottish Cup final against Championship side Falkirk FC, which they won 2-1 to claim their first major trophy.

Europe

Much of the early criticism directed towards Deila was sourced by Celtic's failure in the UEFA Champions League. Despite the helping hand of an administrative aberration from Legia Warszawa that allowed them to progress, sheepishly, into the play-offs, they failed to make their good fortune count against NK Maribor, losing the second leg at home and switching instead to the UEFA Europa League, where they reached the round of 32, losing narrowly to 1967 European Cup final victims FC Internazionale Milano.

National team

Drawn in a tough UEFA EURO 2016 qualifying group, Scotland enjoyed their best season for years and, notwithstanding a painful friendly defeat at home to England, were entitled to feel confident about qualifying for France – the country that last welcomed the Tartan Army to a major tournament, in 1998. Unlucky losers away to world champions Germany, Gordon Strachan's spirited side ticked all the boxes in their next five qualifiers, drawing in Poland, taking four points off the Republic of Ireland and beating Georgia and Gibraltar at home. As an added bonus, striker Steven Fletcher became the first Scotland player to score a hat-trick for 45 years when he found the net three times in the 6-1 romp against Gibraltar.

DOMESTIC SEASON AT A GLANCE

Premiership 2014/15 final table

		Pld	Home					Away					Total					Pts
			W	D	L	F	A	W	D	L	F	A	W	D	L	F	A	
1	**Celtic FC**	**38**	**15**	**2**	**2**	**50**	**8**	**14**	**3**	**2**	**34**	**9**	**29**	**5**	**4**	**84**	**17**	**92**
2	Aberdeen FC	38	12	3	4	32	15	11	3	5	25	18	23	6	9	57	33	75
3	Inverness Caledonian Thistle FC	38	10	6	3	29	19	9	2	8	23	23	19	8	11	52	42	65
4	Saint Johnstone FC	38	8	5	6	19	17	8	4	7	15	17	16	9	13	34	34	57
5	Dundee United FC	38	12	2	5	32	20	5	3	11	26	36	17	5	16	58	56	56
6	Dundee FC	38	5	8	7	25	27	6	4	8	21	30	11	12	15	46	57	45
7	Hamilton Academical FC	38	8	6	5	30	20	7	2	10	20	33	15	8	15	50	53	53
8	Partick Thistle FC	38	8	4	7	32	22	4	6	9	16	22	12	10	16	48	44	46
9	Ross County FC	38	7	0	12	21	31	5	8	6	25	32	12	8	18	46	63	44
10	Kilmarnock FC	38	7	1	10	23	27	4	7	9	21	32	11	8	19	44	59	41
11	Motherwell FC	38	7	5	7	23	21	3	1	15	15	42	10	6	22	38	63	36
12	Saint Mirren FC	38	3	2	14	14	30	6	1	12	16	36	9	3	26	30	66	30

NB League splits into top and bottom halves after 33 games, with each team playing a further five matches exclusively against clubs from its half of the table

European qualification 2015/16

Champion: Celtic FC (second qualifying round)

Cup winner: Inverness Caledonian Thistle FC (second qualifying round)

Aberdeen FC (first qualifying round)
Saint Johnstone FC (first qualifying round)

Top scorer	Adam Rooney (Aberdeen), 18 goals
Relegated club	Saint Mirren FC
Promoted club	Heart of Midlothian FC
Scottish Cup final	Inverness Caledonian Thistle FC 2-1 Falkirk FC
League Cup final	Celtic FC 2-0 Dundee United FC

Player of the season

Craig Gordon
(Celtic FC)

Seemingly lost to the game after two inactive years as a free agent, Gordon returned to top-level football with a bang in 2014/15. Signed by Celtic as the replacement for Fraser Forster, the former Heart of Midlothian FC and Sunderland AFC goalkeeper showed no signs of the terrible injury problems that appeared to have foreshortened his career and was a leading figure in Celtic's Premiership triumph – a fact recognised with a recall for Scotland and, at the season's end, the Scottish Football Writers' Player of the Year award.

Newcomer of the season

Ryan Christie
(Inverness Caledonian Thistle FC)

Twenty-year-old Christie showed no signs of being burdened by the feats of his father, former Inverness midfield stalwart Charlie, as he helped the Highlanders to third place in the Premiership, victory in the Scottish Cup and a debut appearance in Europe. A crafty young midfielder with good balance and vision, he proved himself to be an invaluable member of John Hughes' history-making team and won his first Scotland Under-21 cap at the start of the season. Senior recognition seems sure to follow.

Team of the season
(4-3-3)

Manager: Deila *(Celtic)*

Gordon *(Celtic)*

Logan *(Aberdeen)* — Denayer *(Celtic)* — Van Dijk *(Celtic)* — Shinnie *(Inverness)*

Brown *(Celtic)* — Johansen *(Celtic)* — Armstrong *(Dundee United/Celtic)*

Nadir *(Dundee United)* — Rooney *(Aberdeen)* — Stewart *(Dundee)*

SCOTLAND

NATIONAL TEAM

International tournament appearances

FIFA World Cup (8) 1954, 1958, 1974, 1978, 1982, 1986, 1990, 1998
UEFA European Championship (2) 1992, 1996

Top five all-time caps

Kenny Dalglish (102); Jim Leighton (91); Alex McLeish (77); Paul McStay (76); Tommy Boyd (72)

Top five all-time goals

Kenny Dalglish & Denis Law (30); Hughie Gallacher (23); Lawrie Reilly (22), Ally McCoist (19)

Results 2014/15

07/09/14	Germany (ECQ)	A	Dortmund	L	1-2	Anya (66)
11/10/14	Georgia (ECQ)	H	Glasgow	W	1-0	Khubutia (28og)
14/10/14	Poland (ECQ)	A	Warsaw	D	2-2	Maloney (18), Naismith (57)
14/11/14	Republic of Ireland (ECQ)	H	Glasgow	W	1-0	Maloney (75)
18/11/14	England	H	Glasgow	L	1-3	Robertson (83)
25/03/15	Northern Ireland	H	Glasgow	W	1-0	Berra (86)
29/03/15	Gibraltar (ECQ)	H	Glasgow	W	6-1	Maloney (18p, 34p), S Fletcher (29, 77, 90), Naismith (39)
05/06/15	Qatar	H	Edinburgh	W	1-0	Ritchie (41)
13/06/15	Republic of Ireland (ECQ)	A	Dublin	D	1-1	O'Shea (47og)

Appearances 2014/15

Coach: Gordon Strachan	09/02/57		GER	GEO	POL	IRL	Eng	Nir	GIB	Qat	IRL	Caps	Goals
David Marshall	05/03/85	Cardiff (ENG)	G	G	G	G	G46		G	G46	G	19	-
Alan Hutton	30/11/84	Aston Villa (ENG)	D	D	D				D		D	45	-
Russell Martin	04/01/86	Norwich (ENG)	D	D	D	D	D	D46	D		D	19	-
Grant Hanley	20/11/91	Blackburn (ENG)	D	D		D	D67					17	1
Steven Whittaker	16/06/84	Norwich (ENG)	D		D	D	D	D79				29	-
Barry Bannan	01/12/89	Crystal Palace (ENG) /Bolton (ENG)	M58				s61			s74		20	-
Charlie Mulgrew	06/03/86	Celtic	M 94*			M	M			D	D	18	2
James Morrison	25/05/86	West Brom (ENG)	M	M	M		s46	s63	M	s46	M	39	3
Darren Fletcher	01/02/84	Man. United (ENG) /West Brom (ENG)	M58		s71	s88	s46	M		s59		68	5
Ikechi Anya	03/01/88	Watford (ENG)	M	M	M	M88	M61	M	M74	D	s46	15	2
Steven Naismith	14/09/86	Everton (ENG)	A82	A80	A71	M	M	s46	A67	A59	M92	38	5
Steven Fletcher	26/03/87	Sunderland (ENG)	s58	A90	A71	A56		A63	A		A	21	4
James McArthur	07/10/87	Crystal Palace (ENG)	s58	s80				M63		M46	s85	20	1
Shaun Maloney	24/01/83	Wigan (ENG) /Chicago Fire (USA)	s82	M	M	M	M81	M46	M	M59	M	41	6
Andrew Robertson	11/03/94	Hull (ENG)		D		D	D		D			6	1
Scott Brown	25/06/85	Celtic		M	M	M	M46		M	M59	M85	45	4
Chris Martin	04/11/88	Derby (ENG)		s90	s71	s56	A46					5	-
Gordon Greer	14/12/80	Brighton (ENG)			D			D	s46	D		8	-
Craig Gordon	31/12/82	Celtic					s46	G46		s46		43	-
Stevie May	03/11/92	Sheffield Wednesday (ENG)					s67					1	-
Johnny Russell	08/04/90	Derby (ENG)					s81	s79		s74		3	-
Craig Forsyth	24/02/89	Derby (ENG)						D		D	D	4	-
Matt Ritchie	10/09/89	Bournemouth (ENG)						M	M46	M	M46	4	1
Allan McGregor	31/01/82	Hull (ENG)						s46				33	-
Christophe Berra	31/01/85	Ipswich (ENG)						s46			s92	30	3
Jordan Rhodes	05/02/90	Blackburn (ENG)						s63	s67			13	3
James Forrest	07/07/91	Celtic								M74		10	-
Charlie Adam	10/12/85	Stoke (ENG)								s59		26	-
Leigh Griffiths	20/08/90	Celtic								s59		5	-

EUROPE

Celtic FC

CHAMPIONS LEAGUE

Second qualifying round - KR Reykjavík (ISL)
A 1-0 *McGregor (84)*
Forster, Izaguirre, Ambrose, Van Dijk, Stokes (Pukki 74), Commons, Mulgrew, Lustig, Johansen, Griffiths (Boerrigter 74), McGregor. Coach: Ronny Deila (NOR)
H 4-0 *Van Dijk (13, 20), Pukki (27, 71)*
Forster, Izaguirre (Matthews 62), Ambrose, Van Dijk, Commons, Pukki (Henderson 72), Mulgrew, Lustig, Johansen, Griffiths (Kayal 61), McGregor. Coach: Ronny Deila (NOR)

Third qualifying round - Legia Warszawa (POL)
A 1-4 *McGregor (8)*
Forster, Matthews, Ambrose, Van Dijk, Commons (Griffiths 75), Berget (Izaguirre 63), Pukki (Kayal 46), Mulgrew, Lustig, Johansen, McGregor. Coach: Ronny Deila (NOR)
Red card: Ambrose 44
H 3-0 (w/o) original result 0-2
Forster, Matthews, Izaguirre, Van Dijk, Biton, Stokes (Forrest 70), Commons (Pukki 71), Mulgrew, Lustig (Griffiths 57), Johansen, McGregor. Coach: Ronny Deila (NOR)

Play-offs - NK Maribor (SVN)
A 1-1 *McGregor (6)*
Gordon, Izaguirre, Van Dijk, Stokes (Griffiths 80), Berget (Ambrose 73), Mulgrew, Denayer, Lustig, Johansen, Kayal (Biton 87), McGregor. Coach: Ronny Deila (NOR)
H 0-1
Gordon, Izaguirre, Ambrose, Van Dijk, Stokes, Berget (Matthews 66), Mulgrew, Lustig (Boerrigter 72), Johansen, Kayal (Commons 46), McGregor. Coach: Ronny Deila (NOR)

EUROPA LEAGUE

Group D
Match 1 - FC Salzburg (AUT)
A 2-2 *Wakaso (14), Brown (60)*
Gordon, Izaguirre, Ambrose, Van Dijk, Brown, Šćepović (Stokes 68), Commons (Tonev 75), Denayer, Johansen (Kayal 90+2), Wakaso, McGregor. Coach: Ronny Deila (NOR)
Match 2 - GNK Dinamo Zagreb (CRO)
H 1-0 *Commons (6)*
Gordon, Izaguirre, Ambrose, Van Dijk, Brown, Stokes, Commons (Kayal 69), Denayer, Johansen, Tonev (Berget 88), Wakaso (Griffiths 78). Coach: Ronny Deila (NOR)
Match 3 - FC Astra Giurgiu (ROU)
H 2-1 *Šćepović (73), Johansen (79)*
Gordon, Izaguirre, Van Dijk, Brown, Stokes (Kayal 77), Šćepović, Mulgrew (Wakaso 66), Denayer, Lustig, Johansen, McGregor (Tonev 57). Coach: Ronny Deila (NOR)
Match 4 - FC Astra Giurgiu (ROU)
A 1-1 *Johansen (32)*
Gordon, Izaguirre, Van Dijk, Brown, Šćepović (Griffiths 72), Mulgrew, Denayer, Lustig, Johansen, Wakaso (Matthews 80), McGregor. Coach: Ronny Deila (NOR)

Match 5 - FC Salzburg (AUT)
H 1-3 *Johansen (30)*
Gordon, Matthews, Izaguirre, Ambrose, Van Dijk, Brown, Stokes (Commons 67), Mulgrew (Tonev 74), Johansen, Griffiths, McGregor (Forrest 67). Coach: Ronny Deila (NOR)
Match 6 - GNK Dinamo Zagreb (CRO)
A 3-4 *Commons (23), Šćepović (30), Pivarić (82og)*
Gordon, Matthews (Fisher 56), Izaguirre, Ambrose, Van Dijk, Biton, Šćepović, Commons, Johansen, Wakaso (Stokes 76), McGregor (Henderson 63). Coach: Ronny Deila (NOR)

Round of 32 - FC Internazionale Milano (ITA)
H 3-3 *Armstrong (24), Campagnaro (26og), Guidetti (90+3)*
Gordon, Matthews (Ambrose 81), Izaguirre, Van Dijk, Biton, Brown, Armstrong (Henderson 75), Mackay-Steven, Denayer, Johansen, Griffiths (Guidetti 75). Coach: Ronny Deila (NOR)
A 0-1
Gordon, Matthews, Izaguirre, Van Dijk, Biton, Brown, Guidetti (Forrest 58), Armstrong (Commons 78), Mackay-Steven (Ambrose 41), Denayer, Johansen. Coach: Ronny Deila (NOR)
Red card: Van Dijk 37

Saint Johnstone FC

EUROPA LEAGUE

Second qualifying round - FC Luzern (SUI)
A 1-1 *MacLean (47)*
Mannus, Mackay, Wright, Millar, MacLean, Wotherspoon, Caddis (O'Halloran 76), Miller, Brown, Croft (Scobbie 90), Easton. Coach: Tommy Wright (NIR)
H 1-1 *May (22p) (aet; 5-4 on pens)*
Mannus, Mackay, Wright, Millar, MacLean, Wotherspoon (Caddis 97), May, Miller (Scobbie 114), Brown, Easton, O'Halloran (Croft 74). Coach: Tommy Wright (NIR)

Third qualifying round - FC Spartak Trnava (SVK)
H 1-2 *Mackay (90+3)*
Mannus, Mackay, Wright, Millar (McDonald 29), MacLean, Wotherspoon, Miller, Brown, Croft, Easton, O'Halloran (Kane 76). Coach: Tommy Wright (NIR)
A 1-1 *May (42)*
Mannus, Mackay, Scobbie, Millar, McDonald (O'Halloran 79), MacLean, Wotherspoon, Caddis (Croft 64), May, Miller, Easton. Coach: Tommy Wright (NIR)

Motherwell FC

EUROPA LEAGUE

Second qualifying round - Stjarnan (ISL)
H 2-2 *Law (9, 19)*
Twardzik, Reid, Hammell, Carswell, Ramsden, McManus, Ainsworth (Erwin 70), Sutton, Vigurs, Lasley, Law (Kerr 70). Coach: Stuart McCall (SCO)
A 2-3 *Hammell (11), Ainsworth (66)* **(aet)**
Twardzik, Reid, Hammell, Carswell (Leitch 95), Ramsden, McManus, Ainsworth (Francis-Angol 77), Sutton, Vigurs, Lasley, Law (Kerr 77). Coach: Stuart McCall (SCO)

Aberdeen FC

EUROPA LEAGUE

First qualifying round - FC Daugava Riga (LVA)
H 5-0 *Logan (33), McGinn (49), Rooney (52p, 90+2), Hayes (75)*
Langfield, Logan, Anderson, Reynolds, Flood, Rooney, McGinn (McManus 89), Hayes, Robson (Wright 78), Pawlett (Smith 50), Jack. Coach: Derek McInnes (SCO)
A 3-0 *Rooney (22, 40, 45)*
Langfield, Logan, Considine, Taylor, Reynolds, Flood, Rooney, McGinn (Wright 80), Hayes (Smith 62), Robson (Low 80), Jack. Coach: Derek McInnes (SCO)

Second qualifying round - FC Groningen (NED)
H 0-0
Langfield, Logan, Anderson, Reynolds, Flood, Rooney (Goodwillie 76), McGinn, Hayes, Robson, Pawlett (Low 89), Jack. Coach: Derek McInnes (SCO)
A 2-1 *Rooney (26p), McGinn (33)*
Langfield, Logan, Considine, Anderson, Reynolds, Flood (Low 90+2), Rooney (Goodwillie 73), McGinn, Hayes, Pawlett (Robson 66), Jack. Coach: Derek McInnes (SCO)

Third qualifying round - Real Sociedad de Fútbol (ESP)
A 0-2
Langfield, Logan, Anderson, Reynolds, Flood, Rooney (Goodwillie 71), McGinn, Hayes, Robson (Low 71), Pawlett (Considine 62), Jack. Coach: Derek McInnes (SCO)
H 2-3 *Pawlett (44), Reynolds (57)*
Langfield, Logan, Considine (Low 73), Anderson, Reynolds, Flood, McGinn, Hayes, Pawlett (Rooney 65), Goodwillie (Taylor 82), Jack. Coach: Derek McInnes (SCO)

DOMESTIC LEAGUE CLUB-BY-CLUB

Aberdeen FC

1903 • Pittodrie (20,897) • afc.co.uk

Major honours
UEFA Cup Winners' Cup (1) 1983; UEFA Super Cup (1) 1983; Scottish League (4) 1955, 1980, 1984, 1985; Scottish Cup (7) 1947, 1970, 1982, 1983, 1984, 1986, 1990; Scottish League Cup (6) 1956, 1977, 1986, 1990, 1996, 2014

Manager: Derek McInnes

2014
10/08	h	Dundee United	L	0-3	
13/08	a	Kilmarnock	W	2-0	*Pawlett, Jack*
23/08	a	St Johnstone	L	0-1	
30/08	h	Partick	W	2-0	*Low, McGinn*
13/09	a	Celtic	L	1-2	*Goodwillie*
20/09	a	Ross County	W	3-0	*Rooney, Goodwillie, Pawlett*
27/09	a	Inverness	W	3-2	*Rooney, Logan, Hayes*
30/09	h	St Mirren	D	2-2	*Reynolds, Pawlett*
04/10	a	Dundee	W	3-2	*Considine, og (McPake), Goodwillie*
17/10	a	Hamilton	L	0-3	
24/10	h	Motherwell	W	1-0	*Hayes*
03/11	a	Ross County	W	1-0	*og (P Quinn)*
09/11	h	Celtic	L	1-2	*Rooney*
23/11	a	Partick	W	1-0	*Rooney (p)*
06/12	h	Hamilton	W	3-0	*Taylor, McGinn, Rooney (p)*
13/12	a	Dundee United	W	2-0	*Rooney 2*
20/12	a	Kilmarnock	W	1-0	*Pawlett*
28/12	a	Inverness	W	1-0	*Pawlett*

2015
01/01	h	St Johnstone	W	2-0	*Goodwillie, Smith*
04/01	a	Motherwell	W	2-0	*Rooney 2 (1p)*
10/01	a	St Mirren	W	2-0	*McGinn, Logan*
17/01	a	Dundee	D	3-3	*Goodwillie, Hayes (p), Jack*
23/01	a	St Johnstone	D	1-1	*Rooney*
07/02	h	Ross County	W	4-0	*Rooney, Pawlett, Logan, Goodwillie*
15/02	a	Hamilton	W	3-0	*Considine, Jack, McGinn*
21/02	h	St Mirren	W	3-0	*Rooney 2, Reynolds*
01/03	a	Celtic	L	0-4	
13/03	h	Motherwell	W	2-1	*Taylor, Rooney*
21/03	a	Dundee	D	1-1	*Rooney*
04/04	h	Partick	D	0-0	
08/04	h	Inverness	W	1-0	*Taylor*
12/04	a	Kilmarnock	W	2-1	*Rooney, Smith*
18/04	h	Dundee United	W	1-0	*Rooney*
25/04	a	Inverness	W	2-1	*og (Raven), McGinn*
02/05	a	Dundee United	L	0-1	
10/05	h	Celtic	L	0-1	
16/05	a	Dundee	D	1-1	*Rooney*
24/05	h	St Johnstone	L	0-1	

No	Name	Nat	DoB	Pos	Aps	(s)	Gls
4	Russell Anderson		25/10/78	D	2		
20	Scott Brown	ENG	26/04/85	G	25		
3	Andrew Considine		01/04/87	D	36	(1)	2
28	Donervon Daniels	MSR	24/11/93	D	7	(2)	
29	Andrew Driver	ENG	20/11/87	M	1		
8	Willo Flood	IRL	10/04/85	M	22	(3)	
32	Kieran Gibbons		06/02/95	M		(1)	
17	David Goodwillie		28/03/89	A	21	(10)	6
11	Jonny Hayes	IRL	09/07/87	M	32		3
22	Ryan Jack		27/02/92	M	30	(2)	3
1	Jamie Langfield		22/12/79	G	13		
2	Shay Logan	ENG	29/01/88	D	35		3
18	Nicky Low		06/01/92	M	3	(4)	1
10	Niall McGinn	NIR	20/07/87	A	34	(2)	5
7	Kenny McLean		08/01/92	M	11	(2)	
7	Jeffrey Monakana	ENG	05/11/93	M		(10)	
27	Craig Murray		17/04/94	M	1	(1)	
16	Peter Pawlett		18/06/91	M	28	(8)	6
6	Mark Reynolds		07/05/87	D	37		2
19	Clark Robertson		05/09/93	D		(1)	
15	Barry Robson		07/11/78	M	9	(11)	
9	Adam Rooney	IRL	21/04/88	A	32	(5)	18
38	Frank Ross		18/02/98	M		(2)	
25	Lawrence Shankland		10/08/95	A	2	(15)	
21	Joe Shaughnessy	IRL	06/07/92	D	1	(2)	
14	Cameron Smith		24/08/95	M	5	(19)	2
5	Ash Taylor	WAL	02/09/90	D	31	(1)	3
39	Scott Wright		08/08/97	A		(1)	

Celtic FC

1888 • Celtic Park (60,355) • celticfc.net

Major honours
European Champion Clubs' Cup (1) 1967; Scottish League (46) 1893, 1894, 1896, 1898, 1905, 1906, 1907, 1908, 1909, 1910, 1914, 1915, 1916, 1917, 1919, 1922, 1926, 1936, 1938, 1954, 1966, 1967, 1968, 1969, 1970, 1971, 1972, 1973, 1974, 1977, 1979, 1981, 1982, 1986, 1988, 1998, 2001, 2002, 2004, 2006, 2007, 2008, 2012, 2013, 2014, 2015; Scottish Cup (36) 1892, 1899, 1900, 1904, 1907, 1908, 1911, 1912, 1914, 1923, 1925, 1927, 1931, 1933, 1937, 1951, 1954, 1965, 1967, 1969, 1971, 1972, 1974, 1975, 1977, 1980, 1985, 1988, 1989, 1995, 2001, 2004, 2005, 2007, 2011, 2013; Scottish League Cup (15) 1957, 1958, 1966, 1967, 1968, 1969, 1970, 1975, 1983, 1998, 2000, 2001, 2006, 2009, 2015

Manager: Ronny Deila (NOR)

2014
13/08	a	St Johnstone	W	3-0	*Stokes, Biton (p), McGregor*
16/08	h	Dundee United	W	6-1	*Denayer, Commons, Johansen, Stokes, Berget 2*
23/08	a	Inverness	L	0-1	
31/08	a	Dundee	D	1-1	*Griffiths*
13/09	h	Aberdeen	W	2-1	*Denayer, Commons*
21/09	h	Motherwell	D	1-1	*Commons (p)*
27/09	a	St Mirren	W	2-1	*Guidetti 2*
05/10	h	Hamilton	L	0-1	
18/10	a	Ross County	W	5-0	*Guidetti, McGregor, Stokes 2, Denayer*
26/10	h	Kilmarnock	W	2-0	*Guidetti, Šćepović*
01/11	h	Inverness	W	1-0	*Guidetti*
09/11	a	Aberdeen	W	2-1	*Johansen, Van Dijk*
22/11	h	Dundee	W	2-1	*Stokes, Guidetti*
03/12	h	Partick	W	1-0	*Van Dijk*
06/12	a	Motherwell	W	1-0	*Stokes*
14/12	h	St Mirren	W	4-1	*Brown 2, Forrest, Stokes*
21/12	a	Dundee United	L	1-2	*Griffiths*
27/12	h	Ross County	D	0-0	

2015
05/01	a	Kilmarnock	W	2-0	*Izaguirre, Šćepović*
17/01	a	Hamilton	W	2-0	*Matthews, Henderson*
21/01	h	Motherwell	W	4-0	*Van Dijk, Griffiths, Lustig 2*
24/01	a	Ross County	W	1-0	*Commons*
11/02	a	Partick	W	3-0	*Mackay-Steven, Armstrong, Johansen*
14/02	a	St Johnstone	W	2-1	*Griffiths, Johansen*
22/02	h	Hamilton	W	4-0	*Commons 2, Johansen, Guidetti*
01/03	h	Aberdeen	W	4-0	*Denayer, Griffiths (p), Mackay-Steven, Johansen*
04/03	h	St Johnstone	L	0-1	
21/03	a	Dundee United	W	3-0	*Mackay-Steven, Guidetti, Denayer*
03/04	a	St Mirren	W	2-0	*Forrest, Johansen (p)*
08/04	h	Partick	W	2-0	*Commons (p), Johansen*
11/04	a	Inverness	D	1-1	*Griffiths*
15/04	h	Kilmarnock	W	4-1	*Commons, Griffiths 3*
22/04	h	Dundee	W	2-1	*Mackay-Steven, Van Dijk*
26/04	a	Dundee United	W	3-0	*Griffiths 3 (1p)*
01/05	h	Dundee	W	5-0	*Griffiths, Brown, Commons (p), Forrest, Biton*
10/05	a	Aberdeen	W	1-0	*Brown*
15/05	a	St Johnstone	D	0-0	
24/05	h	Inverness	W	5-0	*Šćepović 2, Johansen, Griffiths, Commons*

No	Name	Nat	DoB	Pos	Aps	(s)	Gls
4	Efe Ambrose	NGA	18/10/88	D	21	(6)	
14	Stuart Armstrong		30/03/92	M	12	(3)	1
16	Jo Inge Berget	NOR	11/09/90	M	2	(2)	2
6	Nir Biton	ISR	30/10/91	M	24	(7)	2
11	Derk Boerrigter	NED	16/10/86	M		(1)	
8	Scott Brown		25/06/85	M	31	(1)	4
15	Kris Commons		30/08/83	M	20	(9)	10
22	Jason Denayer	BEL	28/06/95	D	29		5
41	Darnell Fisher	ENG	04/04/94	D	1	(4)	
49	James Forrest		07/07/91	M	12	(7)	3
26	Craig Gordon		31/12/82	G	33		
28	Leigh Griffiths		20/08/90	A	14	(10)	14
9	John Guidetti	SWE	15/04/92	A	19	(5)	8
53	Liam Henderson		25/04/96	M	4	(5)	1
3	Emilio Izaguirre	HON	10/05/86	D	34	(1)	1
25	Stefan Johansen	NOR	08/01/91	M	33	(1)	9
33	Beram Kayal	ISR	02/05/88	M	2	(4)	
23	Mikael Lustig	SWE	13/12/86	D	3	(2)	2
16	Gary Mackay-Steven		31/08/90	M	10	(3)	4
2	Adam Matthews	WAL	13/01/92	D	24	(5)	1
46	Dylan McGeouch		15/01/93	M	1		
42	Callum McGregor		14/06/93	M	8	(10)	2
21	Charlie Mulgrew		06/03/86	D	7	(3)	
34	Eoghan O'Connell	IRL	13/08/95	D	2	(1)	
20	Teemu Pukki	FIN	29/03/90	A	1		
12	Stefan Šćepović	SRB	10/01/90	A	4	(14)	4
10	Anthony Stokes	IRL	25/07/88	A	18	(3)	7
63	Kieran Tierney		05/06/97	D	1	(1)	
27	Alexandar Tonev	BUL	03/02/90	M	3	(3)	
56	Filip Twardzik	CZE	10/02/93	M	1		
5	Virgil van Dijk	NED	08/07/91	D	35		4
32	Wakaso Mubarak	GHA	25/07/90	M	4	(1)	
24	Łukasz Załuska	POL	16/06/82	G	5		

Dundee FC

1893 • Dens Park (11,506) • dundeefc.co.uk

Major honours
Scottish League (1) 1962; Scottish Cup (1) 1910;
Scottish League Cup (3) 1952, 1953, 1974

Manager: Paul Hartley

2014
09/08	h	Kilmarnock	D	1-1	*Harkins (p)*
13/08	a	Inverness	D	0-0	
16/08	h	Partick	D	1-1	*Wighton*
23/08	a	St Mirren	W	1-0	*MacDonald*
31/08	h	Celtic	D	1-1	*McPake*
13/09	a	St Johnstone	W	1-0	*Konrad*
21/09	h	Dundee United	L	1-4	*Stewart*
27/09	a	Ross County	L	1-2	*Clarkson*
04/10	a	Aberdeen	L	2-3	*Harkins, Clarkson (p)*
18/10	a	Motherwell	W	3-1	*Clarkson, Harkins, Stewart*
25/10	h	Hamilton	W	2-0	*Clarkson, Stewart*
01/11	a	Kilmarnock	W	3-1	*Stewart 2, Clarkson*
08/11	h	St Johnstone	D	1-1	*Clarkson*
22/11	h	Celtic	L	1-2	*Clarkson*
06/12	h	Inverness	L	1-2	*Stewart*
13/12	a	Hamilton	L	1-2	*Stewart*
20/12	h	Partick	D	1-1	*og (Balatoni)*
27/12	h	St Mirren	L	1-3	*Irvine*

2015
01/01	a	Dundee United	L	2-6	*Stewart, Tankulic*
04/01	h	Ross County	D	1-1	*McAlister*
10/01	h	Motherwell	W	4-1	*Harris, Stewart, Irvine, og (O'Brien)*
17/01	a	Aberdeen	D	3-3	*Irvine, Stewart, Harkins*
21/01	h	Kilmarnock	W	1-0	*Stewart (p)*
24/01	a	St Mirren	L	2-3	*Irvine, Davidson*
31/01	h	Hamilton	D	1-1	*Stewart*
14/02	h	Partick	W	1-0	*McGowan*
21/02	a	Motherwell	W	1-0	*P McGinn*
28/02	a	Ross County	L	0-1	
21/03	h	Aberdeen	D	1-1	*S McGinn*
04/04	a	Inverness	D	1-1	*Clarkson*
08/04	h	Dundee United	W	3-1	*Stewart, McPake, Heffernan*
11/04	a	St Johnstone	L	0-1	
22/04	h	Celtic	L	1-2	*McAlister*
25/04	h	St Johnstone	L	0-2	
01/05	a	Celtic	L	0-5	
09/05	h	Inverness	L	0-1	
16/05	h	Aberdeen	D	1-1	*Tankulic*
24/05	a	Dundee United	L	0-3	

No	Name	Nat	DoB	Pos	Aps	(s)	Gls
12	Scott Bain		22/11/91	G	22		
24	Andrew Black		20/09/95	M		(1)	
23	Martin Boyle		25/04/93	A	6	(12)	
28	Dylan Carreiro	CAN	20/01/95	M		(1)	
16	David Clarkson		10/10/85	A	18	(5)	8
35	Calvin Colquhoun		25/07/96	M	1	(1)	
6	Iain Davidson	ENG	14/01/84	M	8	(5)	1
3	Willie Dyer		25/02/87	D	18	(3)	
11	Simon Ferry		11/01/88	M	14	(5)	
26	Kostadin Gadzhalov	BUL	20/07/89	D	6	(2)	
29	Gary Harkins		02/01/85	M	21	(7)	4
47	Alex Harris		31/08/94	M	11	(5)	1
49	Paul Heffernan	IRL	29/12/81	A	4	(3)	1
2	Gary Irvine		17/03/85	D	25	(1)	4
30	Cameron Kerr		10/09/95	D		(2)	
4	Thomas Konrad	GER	05/11/89	D	30	(3)	1
1	Kyle Letheren	WAL	26/12/87	G	15		
9	Peter MacDonald		17/11/80	A	2	(5)	1
20	Jim McAlister		02/11/85	M	34	(3)	2
8	Kevin McBride		14/06/81	M	4	(2)	
19	Paul McGinn		22/10/90	D	34		1
48	Stephen McGinn		02/12/88	M	11	(2)	1
17	Paul McGowan		07/10/87	M	30		1
5	James McPake	NIR	24/06/84	D	34		2
14	Phil Roberts	IRL	07/04/94	A	4	(4)	
25	Arvid Schenk	GER	12/03/90	G	1		
15	Greg Stewart		17/03/90	A	32	(2)	13
21	Luka Tankulic	GER	21/06/91	A	12	(14)	2
10	Kevin Thomson		14/10/84	M	20	(4)	
33	Craig Wighton		27/07/97	A	1	(15)	1

Dundee United FC

1909 • Tannadice (14,229) • dufc.co

Major honours
Scottish League (1) 1983; Scottish Cup (2) 1994,
2010; Scottish League Cup (2) 1980, 1981

Manager: Jackie McNamara

2014
10/08	a	Aberdeen	W	3-0	*Dow, Mackay-Steven, Erskine*
13/08	h	Motherwell	W	1-0	*Bilate*
16/08	a	Celtic	L	1-6	*Rankin*
23/08	h	Ross County	W	2-1	*Nadir, Erskine*
30/08	a	St Mirren	W	3-0	*Erskine, Fojut, Spittal*
13/09	h	Hamilton	D	2-2	*Nadir, Fojut*
21/09	a	Dundee	W	4-1	*Bilate (p), Dow, Morris, Watson*
27/09	h	St Johnstone	W	2-0	*Erskine, Paton*
03/10	a	Kilmarnock	L	0-2	
18/10	h	Partick	W	1-0	*Nadir (p)*
25/10	a	Inverness	L	0-1	
01/11	h	St Mirren	W	3-0	*Paton, Nadir, Telfer*
07/11	a	Motherwell	L	0-1	
22/11	a	Kilmarnock	W	3-1	*Nadir, Armstrong, Connolly*
05/12	a	Ross County	W	3-2	*Nadir 2, Armstrong*
13/12	a	Aberdeen	L	0-2	
21/12	h	Celtic	W	2-1	*Nadir, Armstrong*
27/12	a	St Johnstone	L	1-2	*Butcher*

2015
01/01	h	Dundee	W	6-2	*Armstrong, Mackay-Steven 2, Erskine, Fojut, Telfer*
04/01	a	Partick	D	2-2	*Mackay-Steven, Nadir*
12/01	a	Hamilton	W	3-2	*Armstrong, Mackay-Steven, Dillon*
21/01	a	St Mirren	D	1-1	*Armstrong*
24/01	h	Motherwell	W	3-1	*Telfer 2, Fojut*
14/02	a	Kilmarnock	L	2-3	*Nadir (p), Anier*
21/02	h	St Johnstone	L	0-2	
24/02	h	Inverness	D	1-1	*McGowan*
28/02	h	Partick	L	0-2	
21/03	a	Celtic	L	0-3	
04/04	a	Ross County	L	1-2	*Nadir (p)*
08/04	a	Dundee	L	1-3	*Nadir (p)*
11/04	h	Hamilton	W	1-0	*Erskine*
18/04	a	Aberdeen	L	0-1	
26/04	h	Celtic	L	0-3	
02/05	a	Aberdeen	W	1-0	*Muirhead*
05/05	a	Inverness	L	1-2	*Muirhead*
09/05	a	St Johnstone	D	1-1	*Rankin*
16/05	a	Inverness	L	0-3	
24/05	h	Dundee	W	3-0	*Nadir 2 (1p), Spittal*

No	Name	Nat	DoB	Pos	Aps	(s)	Gls
49	Ola Adeyemo	NGA	15/01/95	A		(1)	
30	Henri Anier	EST	17/12/90	A	4	(8)	1
10	Stuart Armstrong		30/03/92	M	17	(3)	6
19	Mario Bilate	NED	16/07/91	A	6	(8)	2
20	Calum Butcher	ENG	26/02/91	M	15		1
1	Radosław Cierzniak	POL	24/04/83	G	36	(1)	
22	Aidan Connolly		15/08/95	A	8	(10)	1
43	Ali Coote		11/06/98	M		(3)	
2	Seán Dillon	IRL	30/07/83	D	26	(1)	1
3	Paul Dixon		22/11/86	D	15		
9	Ryan Dow		07/06/91	A	17	(7)	2
17	Chris Erskine		08/02/87	M	27	(7)	6
5	Jarosław Fojut	POL	17/10/87	D	36		4
8	Brian Graham		27/11/87	A		(1)	
53	Justin Johnson	NED	27/08/96	A		(1)	
11	Gary Mackay-Steven		31/08/90	A	14	(7)	5
16	Ryan McGowan	AUS	15/08/89	D	12		1
14	Callum Morris	NIR	03/02/90	D	23	(2)	1
10	Robbie Muirhead		08/03/96	A	6	(7)	2
7	Nadir Çiftçi	TUR	12/02/92	A	34	(2)	14
6	Paul Paton		18/04/87	M	22	(2)	2
8	John Rankin		27/06/83	M	29	(1)	2
23	Scott Smith		21/07/95	M		(3)	
4	Jon Souttar		25/09/96	D	13		
33	Euan Spark		29/11/96	D		(2)	
24	Blair Spittal		19/12/95	M	13	(12)	2
26	Michał Szromnik	POL	04/03/93	G	2	(2)	
21	Charlie Telfer		04/07/95	M	13	(8)	4
3	Conor Townsend	ENG	04/03/93	D	16	(1)	
12	Keith Watson		14/11/89	D	14		1

Hamilton Academical FC

1874 • New Douglas Park (6,078) •
acciesfc.co.uk

**Manager: Alex Neil;
(09/01/15) Martin Canning**

2014
09/08	h	Inverness	L	0-2	
13/08	a	St Mirren	W	2-0	*Crawford 2*
16/08	h	St Johnstone	W	1-0	*MacKinnon*
23/08	a	Partick	W	2-1	*Andreu, Scotland*
30/08	h	Ross County	W	4-0	*Canning, Antoine-Curier 2 (2p), Scotland*
13/09	a	Dundee United	D	2-2	*Antoine-Curier, Andreu*
20/09	h	Kilmarnock	D	0-0	
27/09	a	Motherwell	W	4-0	*Andreu, Crawford 2, Antoine-Curier (p)*
05/10	a	Celtic	W	1-0	*Crawford*
17/10	a	Aberdeen	W	3-0	*Andreu 2, Antoine-Curier*
25/10	a	Dundee	L	0-2	
01/11	h	Partick	D	3-3	*MacKinnon, Redmond, Andreu*
08/11	a	Inverness	L	2-4	*Andreu 2*
22/11	h	St Mirren	W	3-0	*Andreu, Antoine-Curier, Crawford*
06/12	a	Aberdeen	L	0-3	
13/12	h	Dundee	W	2-1	*Andreu, Antoine-Curier*
20/12	a	Ross County	W	1-0	*Canning*
27/12	a	Kilmarnock	L	0-1	

2015
01/01	h	Motherwell	W	5-0	*Imrie, Crawford, Antoine-Curier, Andreu, Redmond*
04/01	a	St Johnstone	W	1-0	*Andreu*
12/01	h	Dundee United	L	2-3	*García Tena, Crawford*
17/01	h	Celtic	L	0-2	
21/01	a	Partick	L	0-5	
24/01	h	Inverness	L	0-2	
31/01	a	Dundee	D	1-1	*Canning*
07/02	h	Kilmarnock	D	0-0	
15/02	h	Aberdeen	L	0-3	
22/02	a	Celtic	L	0-4	
28/02	a	St Mirren	L	0-1	
14/03	h	Ross County	D	2-2	*Scotland, Imrie*
20/03	a	Motherwell	L	0-4	
04/04	h	St Johnstone	D	1-1	*Crawford*
11/04	a	Dundee United	L	0-1	
24/04	h	Motherwell	W	2-0	*Scotland, Crawford*
02/05	a	Kilmarnock	W	3-2	*Scotland, MacKinnon, Hasselbaink*
09/05	h	Partick	D	1-1	*Docherty*
16/05	a	Ross County	L	1-2	*Lucas*
23/05	h	St Mirren	W	1-0	*Crawford*

No	Name	Nat	DoB	Pos	Aps	(s)	Gls
22	Anthony Andreu	FRA	22/05/88	M	21	(2)	12
99	Mickaël Antoine-Curier	FRA	05/03/83	A	20	(2)	8
42	Steven Boyd		12/04/97			(1)	
20	Eamonn Brophy		10/03/96	A	2	(14)	
5	Martin Canning		03/12/81	D	22	(1)	3
11	Ali Crawford		03/12/91	M	37	(1)	11
4	Michael Devlin		03/10/93	D	25	(3)	
21	Greg Docherty		10/09/96	M	1	(6)	1
24	Jesús García Tena	ESP	07/06/90	D	25	(1)	1
6	Grant Gillespie		02/07/91	M	36		
2	Ziggy Gordon		23/04/93	D	24		
14	Nigel Hasselbaink	NED	21/11/90	A	4	(6)	1
3	Stephen Hendrie		08/01/95	D	26	(4)	
7	Dougie Imrie		03/08/83	M	33	(1)	2
17	Louis Longridge		05/07/91	A	9	(23)	
44	Lucas	BRA	05/11/90	D	2	(4)	1
23	Darren Lyon		08/06/95	M	8	(6)	
15	Kieran MacDonald		21/07/93	M	1	(1)	
18	Darian MacKinnon		09/10/85	M	27	(3)	3
1	Michael McGovern	NIR	12/07/84	G	38		
23	Scott McMann		09/07/96	D		(1)	
10	Alex Neil		09/06/81	M	7		
28	Daniel Redmond	ENG	24/03/96	M	20	(3)	2
8	Jon Routledge	ENG	23/11/89	M	12	(3)	
32	Andy Ryan		29/09/94	M		(7)	
9	Jason Scotland	TRI	18/02/79	A	12	(12)	5
45	Nicolas Šumský	CZE	13/11/93	M		(1)	
16	Craig Watson		13/02/95	M		(2)	

 **SCOTLAND**

Inverness Caledonian Thistle FC

1994 • Caledonian Stadium (7,800) • ictfc.com
Major honours
Scottish Cup (1) 2015
Manager: John Hughes

2014
09/08	a	Hamilton	W 2-0	McKay, Christie
13/08	h	Dundee	D 0-0	
16/08	a	Motherwell	W 2-0	Tansey, Doran
23/08	h	Celtic	W 1-0	og (O'Connell)
30/08	h	Kilmarnock	W 2-0	Doran, og (Samson)
13/09	a	Partick	L 1-3	Doran
20/09	h	St Johnstone	W 2-1	Watkins, Christie
27/09	a	Aberdeen	L 2-3	Meekings, Watkins
05/10	h	Ross County	D 1-1	Watkins
18/10	a	St Mirren	W 1-0	Tansey (p)
25/10	h	Dundee United	W 1-0	Watkins
01/11	a	Celtic	L 0-1	
08/11	h	Hamilton	W 4-2	McKay 2, Warren, Vincent
22/11	h	Motherwell	W 3-1	McKay, Watkins, Meekings
06/12	a	Dundee	W 2-1	McKay, Christie
13/12	h	Partick	L 0-4	
20/12	a	St Johnstone	L 0-1	
28/12	h	Aberdeen	L 0-1	

2015
01/01	a	Ross County	W 3-1	Doran 2, McKay
04/01	h	St Mirren	W 1-0	McKay
10/01	a	Kilmarnock	W 2-1	McKay 2
20/01	h	St Johnstone	W 2-0	McKay, Watkins
24/01	a	Hamilton	W 2-0	og (Gillespie), Ross
31/01	h	Ross County	D 1-1	Watkins
14/02	a	St Mirren	W 2-1	Tansey, Christie
21/02	h	Kilmarnock	D 3-3	Shinnie, Ross, Williams
24/02	a	Dundee United	L 1-1	Tansey (p)
28/02	a	Motherwell	L 1-2	Ofere
21/03	a	Partick	L 0-1	
04/04	h	Dundee	D 1-1	Shinnie
08/04	h	Aberdeen	L 0-1	
11/04	h	Celtic	D 1-1	Ofere
25/04	a	Aberdeen	L 1-2	Ofere
02/05	a	St Johnstone	D 1-1	Doran
05/05	h	Dundee United	W 2-1	Ofere, Williams
09/05	a	Dundee	W 1-0	Ofere
16/05	h	Dundee United	W 3-0	Meekings, Ross, Warren
24/05	a	Celtic	L 0-5	

No	Name	Nat	DoB	Pos	Aps	(s)	Gls
12	Dean Brill	ENG	02/12/85	G	24		
22	Ryan Christie		28/04/95	M	26	(9)	4
14	Daniel Devine	NIR	07/09/92	D	6	(2)	
10	Aaron Doran	IRL	13/05/91	A	15	(18)	6
8	Ross Draper	ENG	20/10/88	M	31	(1)	
1	Ryan Esson		19/03/80	G	14	(2)	
39	Calum Ferguson	CAN	12/02/95	A		(2)	
17	Lewis Horner	ENG	01/02/92	M	1	(1)	
25	Tarmo Kink	EST	06/10/85	M	1	(4)	
31	Cameron Mackay		09/12/96	G		(1)	
7	Billy McKay	NIR	22/12/88	A	22	(1)	10
6	Josh Meekings	ENG	02/09/92	D	37		3
7	Edward Ofere	NGA	28/03/86	A	7	(3)	5
20	Liam Polworth		12/10/94	M	1	(4)	
2	David Raven	ENG	10/03/85	D	33		
11	Nick Ross		11/11/91	M	13	(13)	3
13	Ibra Sekajja	ENG	31/10/92	A		(4)	
3	Graeme Shinnie		04/08/91	D	37		2
37	Alisdair Sutherland		19/09/96	A		(2)	
16	Greg Tansey	ENG	21/11/88	M	36		4
18	Carl Tremarco	ENG	11/10/85	D	9	(2)	
4	James Vincent	ENG	27/09/89	M	13	(7)	1
5	Gary Warren	ENG	16/08/84	D	36		2
15	Marley Watkins	ENG	17/10/90	M	29	(4)	7
19	Danny Williams	ENG	25/01/88	M	27	(7)	2

Kilmarnock FC

1869 • Rugby Park (18,128) •
kilmarnockfc.co.uk
Major honours
Scottish League (1) 1965; Scottish Cup (3) 1920, 1929, 1997; Scottish League Cup (1) 2012
**Manager: Allan Johnston;
(06/02/15) (Gary Locke)**

2014
09/08	a	Dundee	D 1-1	Slater
13/08	a	Ross County	W 2-1	Magennis, Obadeyi
16/08	h	Aberdeen	L 0-2	
23/08	h	Motherwell	W 2-0	Muirhead, Clingan
30/08	a	Inverness	L 0-2	
13/09	h	St Mirren	W 2-1	Muirhead, Connolly
20/09	a	Hamilton	D 0-0	
27/09	h	Partick	W 3-0	Obadeyi 2, Pascali
03/10	h	Dundee United	W 2-0	Obadeyi, Connolly
18/10	a	St Johnstone	W 2-1	Magennis 2
26/10	h	Celtic	L 0-2	
01/11	h	Dundee	L 1-3	Eremenko
08/11	h	Ross County	L 0-3	
22/11	a	Dundee United	L 1-3	Pascali
06/12	a	Aberdeen	D 1-1	Obadeyi
13/12	h	St Johnstone	L 0-1	
20/12	a	Aberdeen	L 0-1	
27/12	h	Hamilton	W 1-0	Eremenko

2015
01/01	a	St Mirren	W 2-1	Eremenko (p), Slater (p)
05/01	h	Celtic	L 0-2	
10/01	h	Inverness	L 1-2	Eremenko (p)
21/01	a	Dundee	L 0-1	
24/01	a	Partick	D 2-2	Magennis, Pascali
07/02	a	Hamilton	D 0-0	
14/02	h	Dundee United	W 3-2	Magennis, Johnston, Clingan
21/02	a	Inverness	D 3-3	Eccleston, Slater, Obadeyi
28/02	h	St Johnstone	D 0-0	
07/03	h	Motherwell	D 1-1	Obadeyi
14/03	h	St Mirren	W 1-0	Miller
21/03	a	Ross County	L 1-2	Ashcroft
04/04	h	Motherwell	L 1-2	og (Straker)
12/04	h	Aberdeen	L 1-2	Slater
15/04	a	Celtic	L 1-4	Westlake
25/04	a	St Mirren	L 1-4	Magennis
02/05	h	Hamilton	L 2-3	Ashcroft, Kiltie
08/05	a	Motherwell	L 1-3	Magennis
16/05	a	Partick	W 4-1	Hamill, Obadeyi 2, Magennis
23/05	h	Ross County	L 1-2	Kiltie

No	Name	Nat	DoB	Pos	Aps	(s)	Gls
18	Lee Ashcroft		29/08/93	D	20	(2)	2
2	Ross Barbour		01/02/93	D	28	(2)	
13	Conor Brennan	NIR	30/03/94	G	3	(1)	
11	Paul Cairney		29/08/87	M	3	(13)	
23	Chris Chantler	ENG	16/12/90	D	26		
8	Sammy Clingan	NIR	13/01/84	M	22	(2)	2
6	Mark Connolly	IRL	16/12/91	D	25	(1)	2
14	Nathan Eccleston	ENG	30/12/90	A	6	(4)	1
20	Aleksei Eremenko	FIN	24/03/83	M	17	(10)	4
3	Jamie Hamill		29/07/86	M	20	(1)	1
10	Chris Johnston		03/09/94	M	19	(11)	1
30	Greg Kiltie		18/01/97	M	2	(6)	2
28	Josh Magennis	NIR	15/08/90	A	38		8
7	Rory McKenzie		07/10/93	M	21	(7)	
9	Lee Miller		18/03/83	A	9	(10)	1
33	Robbie Muirhead		08/03/96	A	7	(13)	2
17	Michael Ngoo	ENG	22/10/92	A	3	(3)	
26	Mark O'Hara		12/12/95	M	14	(4)	
16	Tope Obadeyi	ENG	29/10/89	A	28	(1)	9
29	Manuel Pascali	ITA	09/09/81	D	29	(2)	3
1	Craig Samson		01/04/84	G	35		
19	Craig Slater		26/04/94	M	23	(3)	4
37	Aaron Splaine		13/10/96	M	1		
36	David Syme		23/06/97	D	3	(2)	
22	Darryl Westlake	ENG	01/03/91	D	16	(1)	1

Motherwell FC

1886 • Fir Park (13,677) • motherwellfc.co.uk
Major honours
Scottish League (1) 1932; Scottish Cup (2) 1952, 1991; Scottish League Cup (1) 1951
**Manager: Stuart McCall;
(02/11/14) (Kenny Black);
(13/12/14) Ian Baraclough (ENG)**

2014
09/08	h	St Mirren	W 1-0	Erwin
13/08	a	Dundee United	L 0-1	
16/08	h	Inverness	L 0-2	
23/08	h	Kilmarnock	L 0-2	
30/08	h	St Johnstone	L 0-1	
13/09	a	Ross County	W 2-1	Vigurs, Sutton
21/09	a	Celtic	D 1-1	Sutton
27/09	h	Hamilton	L 0-4	
04/10	a	Partick	L 1-3	Ainsworth
18/10	h	Dundee	L 1-3	Ojamaa
24/10	a	Aberdeen	L 0-1	
31/10	a	St Johnstone	L 1-2	Ainsworth
07/11	h	Dundee United	W 1-0	Vigurs
22/11	a	Inverness	L 1-3	Ojamaa
06/12	h	Celtic	L 0-1	
13/12	a	Ross County	D 2-2	Sutton, Ojamaa
20/12	a	St Mirren	W 1-0	Sutton
27/12	a	Partick	W 1-0	Sutton (p)

2015
01/01	a	Hamilton	L 0-5	
04/01	a	Aberdeen	L 0-2	
10/01	a	Dundee	L 1-4	Sutton
21/01	a	Celtic	L 0-4	
24/01	a	Dundee United	L 1-3	Ramsden
31/01	h	St Johnstone	D 1-1	Sutton
14/02	a	Ross County	L 2-3	Grant, Kerr
21/02	h	Dundee	L 0-1	
28/02	h	Inverness	W 2-1	Laing, Ainsworth
07/03	h	Kilmarnock	D 1-1	McDonald
13/03	a	Aberdeen	L 1-2	McDonald
20/03	h	Hamilton	W 4-0	Ainsworth 2, Sutton 2 (1p)
04/04	a	Kilmarnock	W 2-1	Pearson, Erwin
07/04	h	St Mirren	W 5-0	Erwin 2, McDonald, Sutton 2
11/04	a	Partick	L 0-2	
24/04	a	Hamilton	L 0-2	
02/05	h	Ross County	D 1-1	McDonald
08/05	h	Kilmarnock	W 3-1	McDonald, Erwin, Ainsworth
16/05	a	St Mirren	L 1-2	Sutton (p)
23/05	h	Partick	D 0-0	

No	Name	Nat	DoB	Pos	Aps	(s)	Gls
7	Lionel Ainsworth	ENG	01/10/87	M	19	(15)	6
29	Chris Cadden		19/09/96	M		(3)	
4	Stewart Carswell		09/09/92	M	14	(5)	
19	Lee Erwin		19/03/94	A	20	(14)	5
30	David Ferguson		24/03/96	M	3	(3)	
17	Zaine Francis-Angol	ATG	30/06/93	D	10	(1)	
47	Conor Grant	ENG	18/04/95	M	10	(1)	1
3	Steven Hammell		18/02/82	D	8		
24	Marvin Johnson	ENG	01/12/90	M	10	(1)	
20	Fraser Kerr		17/01/93	D	16	(5)	1
45	Louis Laing	ENG	06/03/93	D	11		1
14	Keith Lasley		21/09/79	M	33		
18	Josh Law	ENG	20/07/89	M	28	(6)	
8	Paul Lawson		15/05/84	M	3		
21	Jack Leitch		17/07/85	M	4	(3)	
1	George Long	ENG	05/11/93	G	13		
39	Ross MacLean		13/03/97	M		(1)	
77	Scott McDonald	AUS	21/08/83	A	11		5
16	Robert McHugh		16/07/91	A	1	(3)	
6	Stephen McManus		10/09/82	D	36		
22	Craig Moore		16/08/94	A	2	(7)	
15	Mark O'Brien	IRL	20/11/92	D	17	(2)	
24	Henrik Ojamaa	EST	20/05/91	A	16	(2)	3
48	Stephen Pearson		02/10/82	M	13		1
5	Simon Ramsden	ENG	17/12/81	D	20	(2)	1
2	Craig Reid		26/02/86	D	19	(1)	
44	Anthony Straker	GRN	23/09/88	D	11	(1)	
9	John Sutton	ENG	26/12/83	A	27	(11)	12
26	Dom Thomas		14/02/96	M	2	(13)	
46	Nathan Thomas	ENG	27/09/94	M	1	(1)	
12	Daniel Twardzik	GER	13/04/91	G	25		
5	Iain Vigurs		07/05/88	M	10	(1)	2
38	Luke Watt		20/06/97	D	5		

Partick Thistle FC

1876 • Firhill (10,102) • ptfc.co.uk
Major honours
Scottish Cup (1) 1921; Scottish League Cup (1) 1972
Manager: Alan Archibald

2014

13/08	h	Ross County	W	4-0	*Bannigan, og (Frempah), Fraser, O'Donnell*
16/08	a	Dundee	D	1-1	*Fraser*
23/08	h	Hamilton	L	1-2	*Higginbotham*
30/08	a	Aberdeen	L	0-2	
13/09	h	Inverness	W	3-1	*Lawless, Osman, Higginbotham*
19/09	h	St Mirren	L	1-2	*Doolan*
27/09	a	Kilmarnock	L	0-3	
04/10	h	Motherwell	W	3-1	*Bannigan, Doolan, O'Donnell*
18/10	a	Dundee United	L	0-1	
25/10	h	St Johnstone	D	0-0	
01/11	a	Hamilton	D	3-3	*McMillan, Craigen, Elliott*
08/11	a	St Mirren	W	1-0	*Elliott*
23/11	h	Aberdeen	L	0-1	
03/12	a	Celtic	L	0-1	
06/12	h	Kilmarnock	D	1-1	*Seaborne*
13/12	a	Inverness	W	4-0	*Stevenson 2, Fraser, Balatoni*
20/12	h	Dundee	D	1-1	*Craigen*
27/12	a	Motherwell	L	0-1	

2015

04/01	h	Dundee United	D	2-2	*Stevenson, Doolan*
17/01	a	St Johnstone	L	0-2	
21/01	h	Hamilton	W	5-0	*Doolan 4, Eccleston*
24/01	a	Kilmarnock	D	2-2	*Stevenson, Frans*
30/01	h	St Mirren	L	0-1	
11/02	h	Celtic	L	0-3	
14/02	a	Dundee	L	0-1	
21/02	h	Ross County	L	1-3	*Taylor*
28/02	a	Dundee United	W	2-0	*O'Donnell, og (McGowan)*
07/03	a	Ross County	L	0-1	
14/03	h	St Johnstone	W	3-0	*Doolan, Balatoni, Bannigan*
21/03	h	Inverness	W	1-0	*Lawless*
04/04	a	Aberdeen	D	0-0	
08/04	a	Celtic	L	0-2	
11/04	h	Motherwell	W	2-0	*Taylor 2*
25/04	a	Ross County	W	2-1	*Frans, O'Donnell*
02/05	h	St Mirren	W	3-0	*Stevenson, Doolan, Lawless*
09/05	a	Hamilton	D	1-1	*O'Donnell*
16/05	h	Kilmarnock	L	1-4	*Balatoni*
23/05	a	Motherwell	D	0-0	

No	Name	Nat	DoB	Pos	Aps	(s)	Gls
6	Conrad Balatoni	ENG	27/01/91	D	32		3
8	Stuart Bannigan		17/09/92	M	34	(2)	3
5	Callum Booth		30/05/91	D	14		
17	Jake Carroll	IRL	11/08/91	D	8	(2)	
7	James Craigen	ENG	28/03/91	M	19	(7)	2
9	Kris Doolan		14/09/86	A	18	(17)	9
19	Nathan Eccleston	ENG	30/12/90	A		(9)	1
14	Christie Elliott	ENG	26/05/91	M	18	(8)	2
1	Scott Fox		28/06/87	G	22		
13	Frédéric Frans	BEL	03/07/89	D	20		2
22	Gary Fraser		20/06/83	M	13	(10)	3
12	Paul Gallacher		16/08/79	G	16	(2)	
24	Jack Hendry		07/05/95	D	1		
15	Kallum Higginbotham	ENG	15/06/89	M	24	(6)	2
30	Dale Keenan		27/06/94	M	4	(1)	
11	Steven Lawless		12/04/91	M	28	(5)	3
26	Liam Lindsay		12/10/85	D	1		
28	Declan McDaid		22/11/95	M	5	(11)	
33	Neil McLaughlin		06/11/98	A		(1)	
16	Jordan McMillan		16/10/88	M	11		1
5	Aaron Muirhead		30/08/90	D	3	(2)	
2	Stephen O'Donnell		11/05/92	D	34		5
18	Abdul Osman	GHA	27/02/87	M	34		1
21	Ben Richards-Everton	ENG	17/10/92	D	1	(1)	
3	Danny Seaborne	ENG	05/03/87	D	18		1
10	Ryan Stevenson		24/08/84	M	28	(4)	5
29	Lyle Taylor	ENG	29/03/90	A	10	(5)	3
4	Sean Welsh		15/03/90	M	1	(2)	
23	David Wilson		06/09/94	M	1	(5)	

Ross County FC

1929 • Global Energy Stadium (6,541) • rosscountyfootballclub.co.uk
Manager: Derek Adams;
(28/08/14) (Steve Ferguson);
(09/09/14) Jim McIntyre

2014

10/08	h	St Johnstone	L	1-2	*Jervis*
13/08	a	Partick	L	0-4	
16/08	h	Kilmarnock	L	1-2	*Boyce*
23/08	a	Dundee United	L	1-2	*Jervis*
30/08	a	Hamilton	L	0-4	
13/09	h	Motherwell	L	1-2	*Boyce*
20/09	a	Aberdeen	L	0-3	
27/09	a	Dundee	W	2-1	*Gardyne, Maatsen*
05/10	a	Inverness	D	1-1	*Arquin*
18/10	h	Celtic	L	0-5	
25/10	a	St Mirren	D	2-2	*P Quinn, Carey*
03/11	h	Aberdeen	L	0-1	
08/11	a	Kilmarnock	W	3-0	*Carey, Gardyne, P Quinn*
22/11	a	St Johnstone	L	1-2	*Jervis*
05/12	h	Dundee United	L	2-3	*Arquin, Maatsen*
13/12	a	Motherwell	D	2-2	*Dingwall 2*
20/12	h	Hamilton	L	0-1	
27/12	a	Celtic	D	0-0	

2015

01/01	h	Inverness	L	1-3	*Irvine*
03/01	a	Dundee	D	1-1	*Curran*
17/01	h	St Mirren	L	1-2	*Boyce*
24/01	h	Celtic	L	0-1	
31/01	a	Inverness	D	1-1	*Jervis*
07/02	a	Aberdeen	L	0-4	
14/02	h	Motherwell	W	3-2	*Woods, P Quinn, De Vita*
21/02	a	Partick	W	3-1	*Curran, De Vita, Fraser*
28/02	h	Dundee	W	1-0	*Reckord*
07/03	h	Partick	W	1-0	*Curran*
14/03	a	Hamilton	D	2-2	*Curran, Gardyne*
21/03	h	Kilmarnock	W	2-1	*Gardyne, Curran*
04/04	a	Dundee United	W	2-1	*Irvine, De Vita*
07/04	h	St Johnstone	W	1-0	*Boyce*
13/04	a	St Mirren	W	3-0	*Boyce 3*
25/04	a	Partick	L	1-2	*Gardyne*
02/05	a	Motherwell	D	1-1	*Boyce*
09/05	h	St Mirren	L	1-2	*Woods (p)*
16/05	h	Hamilton	W	2-1	*Gardyne, Boyce*
23/05	a	Kilmarnock	W	2-1	*Boyce, R Quinn*

No	Name	Nat	DoB	Pos	Aps	(s)	Gls
15	Yoann Arquin	MTQ	15/04/88	A	14	(3)	2
20	Jordi Balk	NED	26/04/94	D	4		
13	Darren Barr		17/03/85	D	5	(1)	
16	Liam Boyce	NIR	08/04/91	A	17	(13)	10
5	Scott Boyd		06/04/86	D	31	(1)	
8	Richard Brittain		24/09/83	M	18	(3)	
21	Mark Brown		22/01/81	G	22		
7	Joe Cardle	ENG	07/02/87	M	11	(11)	
23	Graham Carey	IRL	20/05/89	M	17	(5)	2
3	Uroš Celcer	SVN	07/04/89	D	5		
11	Craig Curran	ENG	23/08/89	A	17	(2)	5
11	Melvin de Leeuw	NED	25/04/88	A	3	(3)	
24	Raffaele De Vita	ITA	23/09/87	M	13	(1)	3
30	Tony Dingwall		25/07/94	M	10	(9)	2
2	Timothy Dreesen	BEL	30/01/87	D	3		
31	Terry Dunfield	CAN	20/02/82	M	4		
19	Jim Fenlon	ENG	03/03/94	D	4		
44	Marcus Fraser		23/06/94	D	16		1
18	Ben Frempah	ENG	03/04/95	D	4	(2)	
40	Michael Gardyne		12/09/86	M	22	(2)	6
36	Jackson Irvine	AUS	07/03/93	M	27	(1)	2
9	Jake Jervis	ENG	17/09/91	A	10	(17)	4
11	Filip Kiss	SVK	13/10/90	M	21	(10)	
14	Darren Maatsen	NED	30/01/91	A		(8)	2
22	Rubén Palazuelos	ESP	11/04/83	M	1	(4)	
43	Paul Quinn		21/07/85	D	28	(1)	3
4	Rocco Quinn		07/09/86	M	8	(5)	1
12	Jamie Reckord	ENG	09/03/92	D	26		1
1	Antonio Reguero	ESP	04/07/82	G	16		
17	Steven Ross		29/08/93	M	2	(3)	
6	Steven Saunders		30/03/91	D	6	(1)	
20	Darvydas Šernas	LTU	22/07/84	M		(5)	
25	Lewis Toshney		26/04/92	D	7	(2)	
26	Martin Woods		01/01/86	M	26	(1)	2

Saint Johnstone FC

1884 • McDiarmid Park (10,696) • perthstjohnstonefc.co.uk
Major honours
Scottish Cup (1) 2014
Manager: Tommy Wright (NIR)

2014

10/08	a	Ross County	W	2-1	*O'Halloran, MacLean*
13/08	h	Celtic	L	0-3	
16/08	a	Hamilton	L	0-1	
23/08	a	Aberdeen	W	1-0	*MacLean*
30/08	a	Motherwell	W	1-0	*Graham*
13/09	h	Dundee	L	0-1	
20/09	a	Inverness	L	1-2	*Graham*
27/09	a	Dundee United	L	0-2	
04/10	a	St Mirren	L	1-2	*Anderson*
18/10	h	Kilmarnock	L	1-2	*Davidson*
25/10	a	Partick	D	0-0	
31/10	h	Motherwell	W	2-1	*O'Halloran 2*
08/11	a	Dundee	D	1-1	*Graham (p)*
22/11	h	Ross County	W	2-1	*McFadden, O'Halloran*
06/12	a	St Mirren	W	1-0	*O'Halloran*
13/12	a	Kilmarnock	W	1-0	*Graham (p)*
20/12	h	Inverness	W	1-0	*Graham (p)*
27/12	h	Dundee United	W	2-1	*O'Halloran, Millar*

2015

01/01	a	Aberdeen	L	0-2	
04/01	h	Hamilton	L	0-1	
17/01	h	Partick	W	2-0	*Mackay, Anderson*
20/01	a	Inverness	L	0-2	
23/01	a	Aberdeen	D	1-1	*Lappin*
31/01	a	Motherwell	D	1-1	*Davidson*
14/02	h	Celtic	L	0-1	*O'Halloran*
21/02	a	Dundee United	W	2-0	*O'Halloran 2*
28/02	h	Kilmarnock	D	0-0	
04/03	a	Celtic	W	1-0	*Swanson*
14/03	a	Partick	L	0-3	
21/03	h	St Mirren	W	2-0	*Graham, Anderson*
04/04	a	Hamilton	D	1-1	*Graham*
07/04	h	Ross County	L	0-1	
11/04	h	Dundee	W	1-0	*Graham*
25/04	a	Dundee	W	2-0	*Swanson, Wotherspoon*
02/05	h	Inverness	D	1-1	*Graham*
09/05	h	Dundee United	D	1-1	*Davidson*
15/05	h	Celtic	D	0-0	
24/05	a	Aberdeen	W	1-0	*Kane*

No	Name	Nat	DoB	Pos	Aps	(s)	Gls
6	Steven Anderson		19/12/85	D	37		3
20	Scott Brown		25/11/94	M	8	(2)	
16	Liam Caddis		20/09/93	M	6	(9)	
21	Lee Croft	ENG	21/06/85	M	17	(10)	
18	Murray Davidson		07/03/88	M	17	(6)	3
24	Brian Easton		05/03/88	D	31		
14	Brian Graham		23/11/87	A	17	(7)	9
25	Chris Kane		05/09/94	A	4	(11)	1
4	Simon Lappin		25/01/83	M	19	(8)	1
2	David Mackay		02/05/80	D	34		1
9	Steven MacLean		23/08/82	A	23	(4)	2
1	Alan Mannus	NIR	19/05/82	G	38		
8	Gary McDonald		10/04/82	M	10	(6)	
17	James McFadden		14/04/83	A	8	(9)	1
7	Chris Millar		30/03/83	M	32		1
19	Gary Miller		15/04/87	D	8	(12)	
11	Adam Morgan	ENG	21/04/94	A	1	(4)	
29	Michael O'Halloran		06/01/91	A	30	(8)	9
3	Tam Scobbie		31/03/88	D	17	(3)	
11	Danny Swanson		28/12/86	M	8	(3)	2
10	David Wotherspoon		16/01/90	M	30	(5)	1
5	Frazer Wright		23/12/79	D	23	(1)	

Saint Mirren FC

1877 • Saint Mirren Park (8,023) • saintmirren.net

Major honours
Scottish Cup (3), 1926, 1959, 1987; Scottish League Cup (1) 2013

Manager: Tommy Craig; (09/12/14) Gary Teale

2014
09/08	a	Motherwell	L	0-1	
13/08	h	Hamilton	L	0-2	
23/08	h	Dundee	L	0-1	
30/08	h	Dundee United	L	0-3	
13/09	a	Kilmarnock	L	1-2	Drury
19/09	a	Partick	W	2-1	Ball, McLean (p)
27/09	h	Celtic	L	1-2	McLean
30/09	a	Aberdeen	D	2-2	Ball, McLean (p)
04/10	a	St Johnstone	W	2-1	Naismith, Drury
18/10	h	Inverness	L	0-1	
25/10	h	Ross County	D	2-2	Drury,Tesselaar
01/11	a	Dundee United	L	0-3	
08/11	h	Partick	L	0-1	
22/11	a	Hamilton	L	0-3	
06/12	h	St Johnstone	L	0-1	
14/12	a	Celtic	L	1-4	Kelly
20/12	a	Motherwell	L	0-1	
27/12	a	Dundee	W	3-1	McLean 2 (1p), Mallan

2015
01/01	h	Kilmarnock	L	1-2	Wylde (p)
04/01	a	Inverness	L	0-1	
10/01	h	Aberdeen	L	0-2	
17/01	a	Ross County	W	2-1	Kelly, Mallan
21/01	h	Dundee United	D	1-1	McLean
24/01	h	Dundee	L	1-2	McLean
30/01	a	Partick	W	1-0	Dayton
14/02	h	Inverness	L	1-2	Goodwin
21/02	a	Aberdeen	L	0-3	
28/02	h	Hamilton	W	1-0	Thompson
14/03	a	Kilmarnock	L	0-1	
21/03	a	St Johnstone	L	0-2	
03/04	h	Celtic	L	0-2	
07/04	a	Motherwell	L	0-5	
13/04	h	Ross County	L	0-3	
25/04	h	Kilmarnock	W	4-1	Kelly, Sadlier, Thompson 2 (2p)
02/05	a	Partick	L	0-3	
09/05	a	Ross County	W	2-1	Mallan, Thompson (p)
16/05	h	Motherwell	W	2-1	Naismith, Mallan
23/05	a	Hamilton	L	0-1	

No	Name	Nat	DoB	Pos	Aps	(s)	Gls
15	Yoann Arquin	MTQ	15/04/88	A	8	(4)	
30	Jack Baird		07/02/97	D	7	(1)	
16	Callum Ball	ENG	08/10/92	A	11	(9)	2
19	Adam Brown		09/06/95	M	1	(6)	
29	Ross Caldwell		26/10/93	A	2	(11)	
36	Barry Cuddihy		19/12/96	M		(3)	
17	James Dayton	ENG	12/12/88	M	13		1
17	Adam Drury	ENG	09/09/93	M	10	(2)	3
52	Viktor Genev	BUL	27/10/88	D	6		
6	Jim Goodwin	IRL	20/11/81	M	28		1
8	Alan Gow		09/10/82	M	5	(3)	
28	Marián Kello	SVK	05/09/82	G	15		
3	Sean Kelly		01/11/93	D	28	(3)	3
31	Stephen Mallan		25/03/96	M	24	(1)	4
10	James Marwood	ENG	21/05/90	A	10	(3)	
4	Marc McAusland		13/08/88	D	28	(1)	
7	John McGinn		18/10/94	M	30		
8	Kenny McLean		08/01/92	M	25		7
32	Lewis McLear		26/05/96	M	6	(5)	
34	Lewis Morgan		30/09/96	M	1	(7)	
2	Jason Naismith		25/06/94	D	38		2
13	Isaac Osbourne	ENG	22/06/86	M	13	(1)	
5	Ellis Plummer	ENG	02/09/94	D	6		
14	Thomas Reilly		15/09/94	A	14	(6)	
12	Marc Ridgers		09/08/90	G	23		
10	Kieran Sadlier	IRL	14/09/94	A	5	(6)	1
23	Emmanuel Sonupe	ENG	21/03/96	M		(4)	
45	Jordan Stewart		05/03/96	M		(1)	
21	Gary Teale		21/07/78	M	3	(2)	
22	Jeroen Tesselaar	NED	16/01/89	D	32		1
9	Steven Thompson		14/10/78	A	15	(3)	4
11	Greg Wylde		23/03/91	M	11	(16)	

Top goalscorers

18	Adam Rooney (Aberdeen)
14	Leigh Griffiths (Celtic)
	Nadir Çiftçi (Dundee United)
13	Greg Stewart (Dundee)
12	Anthony Andreu (Hamilton)
	John Sutton (Motherwell)
11	Ali Crawford (Hamilton)
10	Kris Commons (Celtic)
	Billy McKay (Inverness)
	Liam Boyce (Ross County)

Promoted club

Heart of Midlothian FC

1874 • Tynecastle (17,529) • heartsfc.co.uk

Major honours
Scottish League (4) 1895, 1897, 1958, 1960; Scottish Cup (8) 1891, 1896, 1901, 1906, 1956, 1998, 2006, 2012; Scottish League Cup (4) 1955, 1959, 1960, 1963

Manager: Robbie Neilson

Second level final table 2014/15

		Pld	W	D	L	F	A	Pts
1	Heart of Midlothian FC	36	29	4	3	96	26	91
2	Hibernian FC	36	21	7	8	70	32	70
3	Rangers FC	36	19	10	7	69	39	67
4	Queen of the South FC	36	17	9	10	58	41	60
5	Falkirk FC	36	14	11	11	48	48	53
6	Raith Rovers FC	36	12	7	17	42	65	43
7	Dumbarton FC	36	9	7	20	36	79	34
8	Livingston FC	36	8	8	20	41	53	27
9	Alloa Athletic FC	36	6	9	21	34	56	27
10	Cowdenbeath FC	36	7	4	25	31	86	25

NB Livingston FC – 5 pts deducted.

Promotion/Relegation play-offs

(09/05/15 & 17/05/15)
Queen of the South 1-2 Rangers
Rangers 1-1 Queen of the South
(Rangers 3-2)

(20/05/15 & 23/05/15)
Rangers 2-0 Hibernian
Hibernian 1-0 Rangers
(Rangers 2-1)

(28/05/15 & 31/05/15)
Rangers 1-3 Motherwell
Motherwell 3-0 Rangers
(Motherwell 6-1)

DOMESTIC CUPS

Scottish Cup 2014/15

FOURTH ROUND

(29/11/14)
Alloa 1-2 Hibernian
Annan 1-1 Brechin
Berwick 1-1 Albion Rovers
Bo'ness United 0-5 Arbroath
Dundee 2-1 Aberdeen
Falkirk 1-0 Cowdenbeath
Motherwell 1-2 Dundee United
Partick 2-0 Hamilton
Queen of the South 4-1 Brora
Spartans 2-1 Greenock Morton
St Johnstone 2-1 Ross County
St Mirren 1-1 Inverness
Stirling 0-2 Raith Rovers
Stranraer 2-2 Dunfermline

(30/11/14)
Hearts 0-4 Celtic
Rangers 3-0 Kilmarnock

Replays
(02/12/14)
Inverness 4-0 St Mirren

(09/12/14)
Dunfermline 1-3 Stranraer
Albion Rovers 0-1 Berwick
Brechin 4-2 Annan

FIFTH ROUND

(07/02/15)
Dundee 0-2 Celtic
Falkirk 2-1 Brechin
Hibernian 3-1 Arbroath
Partick 1-2 Inverness
Queen of the South 2-0 St Johnstone
Spartans 1-1 Berwick

(08/02/15)
Rangers 1-2 Raith Rovers
Stranraer 0-3 Dundee United

Replay
(17/02/15)
Berwick 1-0 Spartans

QUARTER-FINALS

(06/03/15)
Queen of the South 0-1 Falkirk *(Sibbald 34)*

(08/03/15)
Dundee United 1-1 Celtic *(Nadir 45p; Griffiths 71)*

Hibernian 4-0 Berwick *(Cummings 26, Stevenson 28, Stanton 66, Fontaine 82)*

(10/03/15)
Inverness 1-0 Raith Rovers *(Devine 63)*

Replay
(18/03/15)
Celtic 4-0 Dundee United *(Denayer 17, Griffiths 57, Commons 79, Van Dijk 90)*

SEMI-FINALS

(18/04/15)
Falkirk 1-0 Hibernian *(Sibbald 75)*

(19/04/15)
Inverness 3-2 Celtic *(Tansey 58p, Ofere 96, Raven 117; Van Dijk 18, Guidetti 103) (aet)*

FINAL

(30/05/15)
Hampden Park, Glasgow
INVERNESS CALEDONIAN THISTLE FC 2 *(Watkins 38, Vincent 86)*
FALKIRK FC 1 *(Grant 80)*
Referee: *Collum*
INVERNESS: *Esson, Shinnie, Devine, Meekings, Tremarco, Tansey, Draper, Watkins (Ross 90+2), Doran (Williams 78), Christie (Vincent 72), Ofere*
Red card: *Tremarco (75)*
FALKIRK: *MacDonald, Duffie, McCracken, Grant, Leahy, Alston, Vaulks, Taiwo, Sibbald, Smith (Bia-Bi 63), Loy (Morgan 90+5)*

Celebration time for first-time Scottish Cup winners Inverness

League Cup 2014/15

QUARTER-FINALS

(28/10/14)
Rangers 1-0 St Johnstone *(Macleod 86)*

(29/10/14)
Aberdeen 1-0 Hamilton *(Rooney 24)*

Celtic 6-0 Partick *(Guidetti 31, 52, 56p, Izaguirre 48, Griffiths 62, 68)*

Hibernian 3-3 Dundee United *(Malonga 16, Cummings 57, Kennedy 78; Erskine 12, Connolly 19, Dow 61) (aet; 6-7 on pens)*

SEMI-FINALS

(31/01/15)
Aberdeen 1-2 Dundee United *(Daniels 49; Morris 60, Nadir 84)*

(01/02/15)
Celtic 2-0 Rangers *(Griffiths 10, Commons 31)*

FINAL

(15/03/15)
Hampden Park, Glasgow
CELTIC FC 2 *(Commons 28, Forrest 79)*
DUNDEE UNITED FC 0
Referee: *Madden*
CELTIC: *Gordon, Ambrose, Denayer, Van Dijk, Izaguirre, Brown, Biton (Henderson 82), Commons (Forrest 69), Johansen, Stokes, Griffiths (Guidetti 69)*
DUNDEE UNITED: *Cierzniak, Dillon, Morris, Fojut, Dixon, McGowan, Butcher, Paton (Erskine 72), Rankin, Dow, Bilate (Anier 59)*
Red card: *Dillon (56)*

SERBIA
Fudbalski savez Srbije (FSS)

Address	Terazije 35, CP 263
	RS-11000 Beograd
Tel	+381 11 323 4253
Fax	+381 11 323 3433
E-mail	office@fss.rs
Website	fss.rs

President	Tomislav Karadžić
General secretary	Zoran Laković
Media officer	Aleksandar
	Bošković
Year of formation	1919

SUPERLIGA CLUBS

 1 FK Borac Čačak

 2 FK Crvena zvezda

 3 FK Čukarički

 4 FK Donji Srem

 5 FK Jagodina

 6 FK Mladost Lučani

 7 FK Napredak

 8 FK Novi Pazar

 9 OFK Beograd

 10 FK Partizan

 11 FK Rad

 12 FK Radnički 1923

 13 FK Radnički Niš

 14 FK Spartak Subotica

 15 FK Vojvodina

 16 FK Voždovac

PROMOTED CLUBS

 17 FK Radnik Surdulica

 18 FK Javor

 19 FK Metalac

KEY:
- – UEFA Champions League
- – UEFA Europa League
- – Promoted
- – Relegated

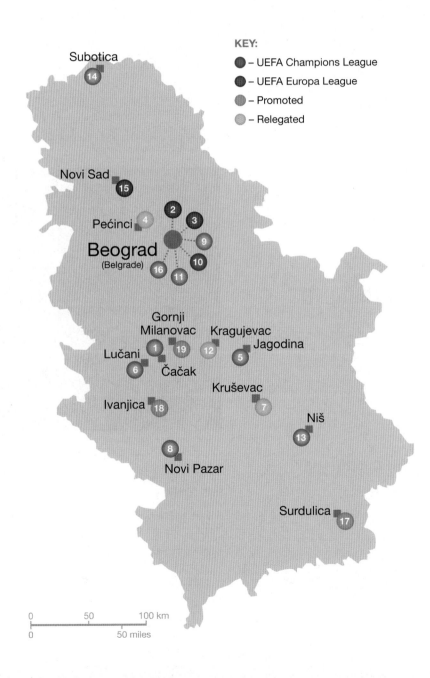

Partizan back in business

After ceding the Superliga crown to FK Crvena zvezda in 2013/14, FK Partizan won it back 12 months later to rejoin their Belgrade rivals at the top of the Yugoslav/Serbian league's victory roll of honour with a record-equalling 26th title.

Partizan lost only once in the Superliga but they were defeated again in the final of the Serbian Cup as FK Čukarički denied them the double with a shock 1-0 win. On the international front, Serbia's youth teams upstaged the senior national side, who endured a nightmare season in the European qualifiers.

| Black-and-Whites dethrone arch-rivals Crvena zvezda | Čukarički deny champions the double in cup final | U-20 World Cup win soothes pain of EURO campaign |

Domestic league

Partizan's seventh Superliga title in eight seasons was built on an excellent start, with free-scoring strikers Danko Lazović and Petar Škuletić spearheading Marko Nikolić's side to eight successive wins, the last of them 1-0 at home to a Crvena zvezda side hitherto unbeaten under their new coach Nenad Lalatović. Although Partizan's 100% record went up in smoke the following week when they lost 1-0 away to FK Jagodina, they regrouped and reached the winter break six points clear of the defending champions, with Škuletić topping the league's scoring charts on 14 goals.

Everything looked rosy in the Black-and-White camp at that stage, but the Partizan fans' optimism turned to concern when Škuletić and Lazović were both sold in the mid-season transfer window, the former to FC Lokomotiv Moskva, the latter to Chinese club Beijing BG. When Partizan dropped four points in their first two games after the resumption, both at home, the alarm bells started to clang, and after another draw, 2-2 at Čukarički in which Partizan avoided defeat only with a last-minute equaliser, the gap at the top was down to just two points.

That would be coach Nikolić's last game in charge, Partizan surprisingly replacing him with Zoran Miliniković, who was also going through a rough patch with FK Voždovac. The move worked, though, as the new man quickly returned the team, inspired by highly talented youngster Andrija Živković, to winning ways. A goalless draw in a typically volatile Eternal Derby at Crvena zvezda was the only interruption to a victory charge that eventually saw Partizan home with two games to spare.

Domestic cup

Vladan Milojević's impressive Čukarički side took third place in the Superliga on the back of a remarkable 15-match unbeaten run, and they qualified for the UEFA Europa League twice over by causing a massive upset against Partizan in the cup final. Promoted to the top flight only two years previously, the unsung Belgrade club became the fifth different Serbian Cup winners in as many seasons thanks to Slavoljub Srnić's 39th-minute strike. It brought Čukarički the first major trophy in their 89-year history while also denying their opponents a sixth domestic double.

Europe

Čukarički's first European campaign proper ended, alongside those of FK Vojvodina and FK Jagodina, in the second qualifying round of the UEFA Europa League, whereas FK Partizan reached the group stage of the competition – albeit after a disappointing away-goals exit in the third qualifying round of the UEFA Champions League, where they were representing Serbia in place of the banned Crvena zvezda.

National team

Fancied at the outset to make a strong impression in their UEFA EURO 2016 qualifying group under new coach Dick Advocaat, Serbia's campaign could hardly have gone worse. Two defeats against Denmark and one to Portugal were bad enough, but all hope of qualifying for France was extinguished when a decision in July by the Court of Arbitration for Sport overturned the result of their abandoned qualifier at home to Albania, handing them a 3-0 forfeit defeat to go with their three-point penalty.

By then Advocaat was long gone, with Under-21 boss Radovan Ćurčić having stepped up to replace him. Ćurčić had earned his spurs by qualifying the U21 side for the 2015 European finals with a sensational play-off win against Spain, but while his successor Mladen Dodić struggled in the Czech Republic, over in New Zealand another group of Serbian youngsters were making the nation proud by winning the FIFA U-20 World Cup, a 2-1 victory over Brazil in the final crowning a glorious effort from Veljko Paunović's young braves.

SERBIA

DOMESTIC SEASON AT A GLANCE

Superliga 2014/15 final table

		Pld	Home W	D	L	F	A	Away W	D	L	F	A	Total W	D	L	F	A	Pts
1	**FK Partizan**	30	11	4	0	31	10	10	4	1	36	12	21	8	1	67	22	71
2	FK Crvena zvezda	30	11	3	1	26	7	8	4	3	20	13	19	7	4	46	20	64
3	FK Čukarički	30	8	5	2	26	11	8	4	3	22	13	16	9	5	48	24	57
4	FK Vojvodina	30	8	0	7	27	22	8	4	3	17	14	16	4	10	44	36	52
5	FK Novi Pazar	30	9	3	3	24	12	4	5	6	15	16	13	8	9	39	28	47
6	FK Rad	30	8	2	5	16	14	5	2	8	17	24	13	4	13	33	38	43
7	FK Mladost Lučani	30	7	4	4	25	22	4	3	8	16	25	11	7	12	41	47	40
8	OFK Beograd	30	8	4	3	19	15	2	5	8	16	28	10	9	11	35	43	39
9	FK Radnicki Niš	30	8	5	2	18	10	1	5	9	7	21	9	10	11	25	31	37
10	FK Jagodina	30	5	3	7	22	24	5	2	8	16	21	10	5	15	38	45	35
11	FK Spartak Subotica	30	7	3	5	13	14	2	4	9	10	19	9	7	14	23	33	34
12	FK Voždovac	30	6	3	6	11	16	3	4	8	13	21	9	7	14	24	37	34
13	FK Borac Čačak	30	5	6	4	14	10	3	3	9	15	25	8	9	13	29	35	33
14	FK Napredak	30	4	3	8	14	20	4	4	7	9	14	8	7	15	23	34	31
15	FK Donji Srem	30	3	4	8	16	19	3	4	8	9	23	6	8	16	25	42	26
16	FK Radnički 1923	30	2	6	7	10	19	2	1	12	7	23	4	7	19	17	42	19

European qualification 2015/16

Champion: FK Partizan (second qualifying round)

Cup winner: FK Čukarički (first qualifying round)
FK Crvena zvezda (first qualifying round)
FK Vojvodina (first qualifying round)

Top scorer Patrick Eze Friday (Mladost), 15 goals
Relegated clubs FK Radnički 1923, FK Donji Srem, FK Napredak
Promoted clubs FK Radnik Surdulica, FK Javor, FK Metalac
Cup final FK Čukarički 1-0 FK Partizan

Team of the season
(4-4-2)

Coach: Milojević (Čukarički)

Rajković (Crvena zvezda)

Stojković (Čukarički) — Rendulić (Čukarički) — Pavićević (Crvena zvezda) — Brežančić (Čukarički)

A Živković (Partizan) — Matić (Čukarički) — Drinčić (Partizan) — Gaćinović (Vojvodina)

Stojiljković (Čukarički) — Friday (Mladost Lučani)

Player of the season

Andrija Živković
(FK Partizan)

Having become Serbia's youngest senior international at 17, Živković confirmed his potential at 18 with a brilliant performance for his country at the 2015 FIFA U-20 World Cup, where he scored the goal of the tournament – a free-kick against Mexico – and set up Nemanja Maksimović's extra-time winner in the final against Brazil. Prior to becoming a national hero in New Zealand the gifted young winger enjoyed a splendid domestic campaign for Partizan, which ended with his first Superliga title.

Newcomer of the season

Predrag Rajković
(FK Crvena zvezda)

The 2014/15 season brought no trophies for Crvena zvezda but it made a star of their brilliant 19-year-old goalkeeper, who ended the campaign by helping Serbia to victory at the FIFA U-20 World Cup, where he was awarded the Golden Glove as the tournament's best goalkeeper. He was sensational also in the Superliga, keeping 16 clean sheets in his 28 appearances to give Crvena zvezda the best defensive figures in the league. Furthermore, despite his youth, he was appointed as the new club captain in February.

NATIONAL TEAM

International tournament appearances*

FIFA World Cup (11) 1930 (semi-finals), 1950, 1954 (qtr-finals), 1958 (qtr-finals), 1962 (4th), 1974 (2nd phase), 1982, 1990 (qtr-finals), 1998 (2nd round), 2006, 2010
UEFA European Championship (5) 1960 (runners-up), 1968 (runners-up), 1976 (4th), 1984, 2000 (qtr-finals)

Top five all-time caps
Dejan Stanković (103); Savo Milošević (102); Dragan Džajić (85); Dragan Stojković (84); **Branislav Ivanović (79)**

Top five all-time goals
Stjepan Bobek (38); Milan Galić & Savo Milošević (37); Blagoje Marjanović (36); Rajko Mitić (32)

(* before 2006 as Yugoslavia; 2006 as Serbia & Montenegro.)

Results 2014/15

Date	Opponent		Venue		Result	Scorers
07/09/14	France	H	Belgrade	D	1-1	*Kolarov (80)*
11/10/14	Armenia (ECQ)	A	Yerevan	D	1-1	*Z Tošić (89)*
14/10/14	Albania (ECQ)	H	Belgrade	L	0-3	*(w/o; original match abandoned after 42 mins at 0-0)*
14/11/14	Denmark (ECQ)	H	Belgrade	L	1-3	*Z Tošić (4)*
18/11/14	Greece	A	Chania	W	2-0	*Petrović (60), Gudelj (90+2)*
29/03/15	Portugal (ECQ)	A	Lisbon	L	1-2	*Matić (61)*
07/06/15	Azerbaijan	N	St Polten (AUT)	W	4-1	*Ivanović (10, 63), Ljajić (55), Marković (89)*
13/06/15	Denmark (ECQ)	A	Copenhagen	L	0-2	

Appearances 2014/15

Coach: Dick Advocaat (NED) /(16/11/14) Radovan Ćurčić	27/09/47 10/01/72		Fra	ARM	ALB	DEN	Gre	POR	Aze	DEN	Caps	Goals
Vladimir Stojković	28/07/83	M. Haifa (ISR)	G	G	G	G	G	G		G	61	-
Branislav Ivanović	22/02/84	Chelsea (ENG)	D	D	D	D	D		D76	D	79	10
Stefan Mitrović	22/05/90	Freiburg (GER)	D	D	D	D	s88				6	-
Matija Nastasić	28/03/93	Man. City (ENG) /Schalke (GER)	D	D	D		D	D		D	19	-
Aleksandar Kolarov	10/11/85	Man. City (ENG)	D	D	D		D	D		D	55	6
Nemanja Gudelj	16/11/91	AZ (NED)	M60	M74	M	M66	s82				9	1
Nemanja Matić	01/08/88	Chelsea (ENG)	M	M	M	M	M	M	M60	M	21	1
Dušan Tadić	20/11/88	Southampton (ENG)	M60	M	M	M71		M78			30	6
Zoran Tošić	28/04/87	CSKA Moskva (RUS)	M	M	M	M	M89	s78	M	M65	65	10
Lazar Marković	02/03/94	Liverpool (ENG)	M86	M26		s71	M66	M65	s56	M	20	3
Filip Djordjević	28/09/87	Lazio (ITA)	A75	A69							14	4
Zdravko Kuzmanović	22/09/87	Internazionale (ITA)	s60	s26		s46					50	6
Filip Djuričić	30/01/92	Mainz (GER) /Southampton (ENG)	s60		M	M46	s66	s65	s56	s81	22	4
Aleksandar Mitrović	16/09/94	Anderlecht (BEL)	s75	s74		s66	A	A	A73	A90	13	1
Adem Ljajić	29/09/91	Roma (ITA)	s86					M85	M56	M81	12	1
Danko Lazović	17/05/83	Partizan		s69	A	A	s66				47	11
Milan Biševac	31/08/83	Lyon (FRA)					D				19	-
Duško Tošić	19/01/85	Gençlerbirliği (TUR)					D	D			14	1
Nenad Tomović	30/08/87	Fiorentina (ITA)					D		s76		17	-
Nikola Maksimović	25/11/91	Torino (ITA)					D88		D	D	7	-
Radosav Petrović	08/03/89	Gençlerbirliği (TUR)					M82	M	s60		42	2
Miloš Jojić	19/03/92	Dortmund (GER)					M66				5	1
Antonio Rukavina	26/01/84	Villarreal (ESP)					s89				30	-
Dušan Basta	18/08/84	Lazio (ITA)						D			17	2
Petar Škuletić	29/06/90	Lokomotiv Moskva (RUS)						s85	s73	s90	3	-
Željko Brkić	09/07/86	Cagliari (ITA)							G		11	-
Luka Milivojević	07/04/91	Olympiacos (GRE)							M83		8	-
Filip Kostić	01/11/92	Stuttgart (GER)							M56	s65	2	-
Ljubomir Fejsa	14/08/88	Benfica (POR)							s83	M	19	-

EUROPE

FK Partizan

CHAMPIONS LEAGUE

Second qualifying round - HB Tórshavn (FRO)
H 3-0 *Lazović (14, 64), Škuletić (71)*
Lukač, Vulićević, Petrović, Stanković, Brašanac, Grbić
(A Živković 54), Trajković, Drinčić, Lazović (Ninković 83),
Škuletić, Pantić (Ilić 72). Coach: Marko Nikolić (SRB)
A 3-1 *Ninković (49), Lazović (75), Grbić (90+1)*
Lukač, Volkov, Stanković, Luka (Grbić 66), Brašanac,
Ninković, Drinčić, Lazović (Fofana 78), Ilić, Škuletić (Ilić 73),
Ostojić. Coach: Marko Nikolić (SRB)

Third qualifying round - PFC Ludogorets Razgrad (BUL)
A 0-0
Lukač, Volkov, Vulićević, Stanković, Brašanac, Trajković, A
Živković (Grbić 67), Drinčić, Ilić (Luka 81), Lazović (Ninković
54), Škuletić. Coach: Marko Nikolić (SRB)
H 2-2 *Škuletić (30, 35)*
Lukač, Volkov, Vulićević, Stanković, Brašanac (Ninković 83),
Trajković, A Živković (Luka 70), Drinčić, Ilić (Ilić 46), Lazović,
Škuletić. Coach: Marko Nikolić (SRB)
Red card: Trajković 41

EUROPA LEAGUE

Play-offs - Neftçi PFK (AZE)
H 3-2 *Dénis Silva (29og), Grbić (32), Yunuszadä (69og)*
Lukač, Vulićević, Petrović, Stanković, Brašanac, Ninković
(A Živković 61), Grbić (Ilić 70), Drinčić, Lazović, Ilić, Škuletić
(Fofana 79). Coach: Marko Nikolić (SRB)
A 2-1 *Škuletić (24, 90+2)*
Lukač, Vulićević, Petrović, Stanković, Brašanac, Grbić (Ilić
59), A Živković (Ostojić 90+5), Drinčić, Lazović (Pantić 84),
Ilič, Škuletić. Coach: Marko Nikolić (SRB)
Red card: Škuletić 90+4

Group C
Match 1 - Tottenham Hotspur FC (ENG)
H 0-0
Lukač, Volkov (Petrović 54), Vulićević, Stanković, Ćirković
(Marković 68), Grbić (Luka 85), Drinčić, Ilić, Lazović, Ilič,
Pantić. Coach: Marko Nikolić (SRB)
Match 2 - Asteras Tripolis FC (GRE)
A 0-2
Lukač, Volkov, Vulićević, Stanković, Ćirković, Grbić (Ninković
63), A Živković (Fofana 46), Ilić (Kojić 78), Lazović, Ilič, Pantić.
Coach: Marko Nikolić (SRB)
Match 3 - Beşiktaş JK (TUR)
H 0-4
Lukač, Volkov, Stanković, Ćirković, A Živković (Grbić 67),
Drinčić (Marković 61), Lazović (Ninković 61), Ilič, Škuletić,
Stevanović, Pantić. Coach: Marko Nikolić (SRB)
Match 4 - Beşiktaş JK (TUR)
A 1-2 *Marković (78)*
Lukač, Volkov, Stanković, Ninković, Ćirković, Grbić (A
Živković 67), Drinčić, Marković, Škuletić (Lazović 67),
Stevanović, Pantić (Ilić 65). Coach: Marko Nikolić (SRB)

Match 5 - Tottenham Hotspur FC (ENG)
A 0-1
Lukač, Volkov, Stanković, Ninković (A Živković 62), Ćirković,
Grbić, Marković, Ilić (Marinković 74), Lazović, Ilič, Škuletić
(Kojić 78). Coach: Marko Nikolić (SRB)
Match 6 - Asteras Tripolis FC (GRE)
H 0-0
Lukač, Volkov, Petrović, Stanković, Ninković (Luka 81), Grbić
(Ilić 74), A Živković, Drinčić, Marković, Ilič, Škuletić (Kojić 89).
Coach: Marko Nikolić (SRB)

FK Vojvodina

EUROPA LEAGUE

Second qualifying round – FK AS Trenčín (SVK)
A 0-4
Jovanov, Radoja, Ivanić, Makarić (Stojanović 57), Pekarić,
Alivodić, Puškarić (Živković 58), Veselinović (Popara 80),
Nastić, Poletanović, Babić. Coach: Zoran Marić (SRB)
Red card: Živković 66
H 3-0 *Ivanić (17), Alivodić (52), Stojanović (68)*
Jovanov, Radoja, Ivanić, Makarić (Grgić 66), Pekarić, Alivodić,
Puškarić, Pankov, Nastić, Poletanović, Stojanović. Coach:
Zoran Marić (SRB)

FK Jagodina

EUROPA LEAGUE

Second qualifying round - CFR 1907 Cluj (ROU)
A 0-0
Djuričić, Šimac, Filipović, Djurić (Martinović 77), Šušnjar,
Mihajlović (Gašić 54), Mitošević, I Cvetković, Milinković,
Jakimovski (Lepović 84), F Arsenijević. Coach: Mladen Dodić
(SRB)
H 0-1
Djuričić, Šimac, Gašić, Filipović, Djurić (Martinović 85),
Šušnjar (Stoičev 85), Mitošević, I Cvetković, Milinković,
Jakimovski (Lepović 62), F Arsenijević. Coach: Mladen Dodić
(SRB)

FK Čukarički

EUROPA LEAGUE

First qualifying round - UE Sant Julià (AND)
H 4-0 *Mirosavljević (8), Bojić (49), S Srnić (89), Stoiljković
(90+1p)*
Ristić, Piasentin, Todorović, Stoiljković, Matić, S Srnić
(Mandić 90), Stojković, Ostojić, Bojić (D Srnić 58),
Mirosavljević (A Pavlović 77), Brežančić. Coach: Vladan
Milojević (SRB)
A 0-0
Ristić, Piasentin, Todorović, Stoiljković (A Pavlović 81), Matić,
S Srnić, Stojković, Ostojić, Bojić (D Srnić 72), Mirosavljević,
Brežančić (Boljević 86). Coach: Vladan Milojević (SRB)

Second qualifying round - SV Grödig (AUT)
H 0-4
Ristić, Piasentin, D Srnić, Todorović, Stoiljković, Matić
(A Pavlović 80), S Srnić, Janković (Bojić 62), Ostojić,
Mirosavljević (Boljević 46), Brežančić. Coach: Vladan
Milojević (SRB)
Red card: Piasentin 25
A 2-1 *Bojić (61), Stoiljković (65)*
Ristić, D Srnić (Radovanović 89), Todorović, Stoiljković,
A Pavlović (Matić 85), S Srnić, D Pavlović (Janković 79),
Stojković, Bojić, Boljević, Brežančić. Coach: Vladan Milojević
(SRB)

DOMESTIC LEAGUE CLUB-BY-CLUB

FK Borac Čačak

1928 • Gradski stadion (8,000) • boracfk.com
Coach: Bogić Bogićević

2014
09/08	h	Donji Srem	W 2-0	Mutavdžić, Djenić
16/08	a	Rad	L 1-2	S Živković
23/08	a	Čukarički	D 0-0	
30/08	a	Radnički 1923	W 1-0	Milojević
13/09	h	OFK Beograd	D 1-1	Djenić
20/09	a	Mladost	L 1-2	Djenić
29/09	h	Crvena zvezda	L 0-1	
04/10	a	Jagodina	L 0-2	
19/10	h	Vojvodina	L 0-1	Božić (p)
25/10	h	Spartak	D 2-2	Mutavdžić, Mašović
01/11	h	Napredak	L 0-1	
08/11	h	Novi Pazar	D 2-2	Stojanović 2
22/11	h	Radnički Niš	D 0-0	
29/11	h	Voždovac	D 0-0	
07/12	a	Partizan	L 1-5	Djoković

2015
21/02	a	Donji Srem	W 1-0	Ožegović
28/02	h	Rad	L 0-1	
07/03	h	Čukarički	D 1-1	Djerić
14/03	h	Radnički 1923	W 2-0	Ožegović, Zec
21/03	a	OFK Beograd	L 0-1	
04/04	h	Mladost	L 0-1	
09/04	a	Crvena zvezda	L 1-3	Krunić
18/04	h	Jagodina	W 3-1	Ožegović 2, Stojanović
25/04	a	Vojvodina	W 3-1	Mutavdžić, Jevtović, Krunić
29/04	h	Spartak	W 1-0	Ožegović
03/05	a	Napredak	L 1-2	Zec
09/05	h	Novi Pazar	W 1-0	S Živković (p)
13/05	h	Radnički Niš	L 0-1	
16/05	a	Voždovac	L 0-1	
24/05	h	Partizan	D 3-3	Ožegović, Zec, Mutavdžić

No	Name	Nat	DoB	Pos	Aps	(s)	Gls
8	Dejan Babić		20/04/89	M	8	(1)	
30	Vladimir Bajić		28/11/87	G	15		
2	Nikola Boranijaševic		19/05/92	D	16	(1)	
25	Mario Božić	BIH	25/05/83	M	14	(1)	1
6	Javier Cohene	PLE	03/05/87	D	6		
9	Dejan Djenić		02/06/86	A	11		3
18	Uroš Djerić		28/05/92	A	8	(16)	1
27	Ivan Djoković		20/12/82	D	4	(3)	1
19	Stefan Drašković		27/07/89	D	1	(3)	
12	Marko Drobnjak		17/05/95	G		(1)	
15	Aleksandar Gojković		18/08/88	D	25		
11	Milan Jevtović		13/06/93	A	13	(9)	1
22	Ivan Josović		27/12/89	D	3	(1)	
29	Dušan Jovančić		19/10/90	M	27		
20	Rade Krunić	BIH	10/07/93	M	13		2
17	Mario Maslać		09/09/90	D	15		
24	Alen Mašović		07/08/94	M	6	(10)	1
33	Nemanja Miletić		16/01/91	D	11	(5)	
26	Stefan Milojević		29/01/89	M	10	(14)	1
32	Miljan Mutavdžić		03/02/86	M	18	(6)	4
16	Nikola Nešović		17/10/93	A		(5)	
20	Baćo Nikolić	MNE	19/01/86	M	4		
4	Lazar Obradović		05/12/92	D	11	(4)	
51	Ognjen Ožegović		06/09/94	A	13		6
1	Nikola Petrić		11/05/91	G	15		
3	Risto Radunović	MNE	04/05/92	D	5		
7	Slaviša Stojanović		27/01/89	A	12	(7)	3
14	Radan Šunjevarić		10/02/83	M	1		
36	Michael Tawiah	GHA	12/01/90	M	2		
77	Djuro Zec		03/06/90	A	15		3
10	Marko Zoćević		19/05/93	D	2	(2)	
13	Dejan Živković		28/04/82	D	2		
28	Stefan Živković		01/06/90	M	24		2

FK Crvena zvezda

1945 • Rajko Mitić (51,328) • crvenazvezdafk.com

Major honours
European Champion Clubs' Cup (1) 1991;
European/South American Cup (1) 1991;
Yugoslav/Serbian League (26) 1951, 1953, 1956,
1957, 1959, 1960, 1964, 1968, 1969, 1970, 1973,
1977, 1980, 1981, 1984, 1988, 1990, 1991, 1992,
1995, 2000, 2001, 2004, 2006, 2007, 2014;
Yugoslav/Serbian Cup (24) 1948, 1949, 1950, 1958,
1959, 1964, 1968, 1970, 1971, 1982, 1985, 1990,
1993, 1995, 1996, 1997, 1999, 2000, 2002, 2004,
2006, 2007, 2010, 2012
Coach: Nenad Lalatović

2014
09/08	h	Radnički Niš	W 2-0	Milijaš 2
16/08	a	Jagodina	W 3-0	Milijaš, Rakić, Lazović
23/08	a	Vojvodina	W 1-0	Rakić
30/08	h	Spartak	W 1-0	Avramovski
13/09	a	Napredak	D 0-0	
20/09	h	Novi Pazar	W 2-0	Rakić 2
29/09	a	Borac	W 1-0	Gavrić
04/10	h	Voždovac	D 2-2	Gavrić, Mijailović
18/10	a	Partizan	L 0-1	
25/10	h	Donji Srem	W 1-0	Pečnik (p)
02/11	a	Rad	W 2-1	Lazović, Pavićević
08/11	h	Čukarički	D 0-0	
22/11	a	Radnički 1923	D 0-0	
29/11	h	OFK Beograd	W 2-1	Katai, Despotović
07/12	a	Mladost	D 1-1	Pečnik

2015
22/02	a	Radnički Niš	D 0-0	
01/03	h	Jagodina	W 3-2	Lazović 2, Katai
07/03	h	Vojvodina	W 3-0	Parker 2, Jović
14/03	a	Spartak	W 3-1	Lazić, Ristić (p), Jović
21/03	h	Napredak	W 1-0	Lazović
04/04	a	Novi Pazar	L 1-2	Cvetković
09/04	h	Borac	W 3-1	Jović 2, Lazović (p)
18/04	a	Voždovac	W 1-0	Jović
25/04	h	Partizan	D 0-0	
29/04	a	Donji Srem	W 2-0	Orlandić, Lazović 2
03/05	h	Rad	W 2-0	Orlandić, Jović
10/05	a	Čukarički	L 0-2	
13/05	h	Radnički 1923	L 1-2	Ristić (p)
16/05	a	OFK Beograd	W 4-2	Lazović 2, Orlandić, Savićević
24/05	h	Mladost	W 3-1	Orlandić 2, S Stojanović

No	Name	Nat	DoB	Pos	Aps	(s)	Gls
33	Dušan Andjelković		15/06/82	D	14		
15	Nikola Antić		04/01/94	D	3		
10	Daniel Avramovski	MKD	20/02/95	M	1	(11)	1
20	Miloš Bosančić		22/05/88	M	11	(8)	
19	Miloš Cvetković		01/06/90	D	13	(1)	1
84	Djordje Despotović		04/03/92	A	3	(7)	1
17	Stefan Djordjević		13/03/91	D	3		
44	Nenad Gavrić		12/12/91	M	9	(6)	2
25	Goran Gogić		24/04/86	M		(4)	
35	Marko Grujić		13/04/96	M	6	(3)	
30	Vukašin Jovanović		17/05/96	D	11	(2)	
9	Luka Jović		23/12/97	A	11	(11)	6
1	Damir Kahriman		19/11/84	G	2	(1)	
27	Aleksandar Katai		06/02/91	A	14	(6)	2
55	Aleksandar Kovačević		09/01/92	M	18	(3)	
4	Darko Lazić		19/07/94	D	21		1
8	Darko Lazović		15/09/90	M	28		10
16	Mamadou Mbodj	SEN	12/03/93	D	1	(2)	
5	Nikola Mijailović		15/02/82	D	13		1
10	Nenad Milijaš		30/04/83	M	3		3
99	Petar Orlandić	MNE	08/06/90	A	8	(5)	5
23	Josh Parker	ATG	01/12/90	A	9		2
14	Savo Pavićević	MNE	11/12/80	D	27		1
11	Nejc Pečnik	SVN	03/01/86	M	15		2
2	Marko Petković		03/09/92	D	10	(3)	
6	Bogdan Planić		19/01/92	D	5		
95	Predrag Rajković		31/10/95	G	28		
7	Djordje Rakić		31/10/85	A	11	(1)	4
24	Mihailo Ristić		31/10/95	D	14	(9)	2
28	Vukan Savićević		29/01/94	M	8	(2)	1
34	Miloš Stojanović		18/01/97	D		(1)	
7	Saša Stojanović		21/01/83	M	12	(2)	1

FK Čukarički

1926 • FK Čukarički (4,070) • fkcukaricki.rs
Major honours
Serbian Cup (1) 2015
Coach: Vladan Milojević

2014
09/08	a	Napredak	W 2-0	A Pavlović, Mirosavljević
16/08	h	Novi Pazar	D 1-1	Bojić
23/08	a	Borac	D 0-0	
30/08	h	Voždovac	W 2-0	S Srnić, Matić
13/09	a	Partizan	L 2-4	Stojiljković, S Srnić
20/09	h	Donji Srem	D 1-1	Mirosavljević
29/09	h	Rad	W 3-1	Matić 2, Mirosavljević
04/10	a	Radnički Niš	L 1-2	Mandić
18/10	h	Radnički 1923	W 4-1	Regan 2, og (Terzić), S Srnić
25/10	a	OFK Beograd	W 4-0	Matić 2, S Srnić, Bojić
01/11	h	Mladost	W 1-0	Matić (p)
08/11	h	Crvena zvezda	D 0-0	
23/11	a	Jagodina	L 0-3	
29/11	a	Vojvodina	W 2-1	Todorović, Stojiljković
07/12	h	Spartak	W 2-0	Todorović, Stojiljković (p)

2015
21/02	h	Napredak	W 1-0	Todorović
28/02	a	Novi Pazar	W 2-1	Matić, S Srnić
07/03	h	Borac	D 1-1	Matić
14/03	a	Voždovac	D 0-0	
22/03	h	Partizan	D 2-2	Bojić, Stojiljković
04/04	a	Donji Srem	W 1-0	S Srnić, Stojiljković
13/04	h	Rad	W 7-0	Rendulić, Stojiljković 2, Matić, og (Gnjatić), S Srnić, Todorović
18/04	h	Radnički Niš	D 1-1	Brežančić
25/04	a	Radnički 1923	D 0-0	
29/04	a	OFK Beograd	W 1-0	S Srnić
03/05	h	Mladost	D 2-2	Regan, Lucas
10/05	h	Crvena zvezda	W 2-0	Stojiljković, Matić
13/05	a	Jagodina	W 1-0	Stojiljković
16/05	h	Vojvodina	L 0-1	
24/05	a	Spartak	L 0-1	

No	Name	Nat	DoB	Pos	Aps	(s)	Gls
21	Aleksandar Alempijević		25/07/88	M		(1)	
3	Djordje Bašanović		31/07/96	D	1		
24	Petar Bojić		04/09/91	M	24	(5)	3
25	Dejan Boljević	MNE	30/05/90	D		(3)	
31	Rajko Brežančić		21/08/89	D	29		1
15	Stefan Dimić		01/05/93	M		(1)	
17	Nikola Janković		07/06/93	D	4	(7)	
4	Lucas	BRA	17/03/86	D	20		1
7	Staniša Mandić		27/01/95	A	4	(13)	1
10	Igor Matić		22/07/81	M	20	(5)	10
30	Nenad Mirosavljević		04/09/77	A	8	(17)	3
23	Bojan Ostojić		12/02/84	D	16	(5)	
14	Andrija Pavlović		16/11/93	M	11	(10)	1
19	Deni Pavlović		01/09/93	D	1		
20	Obeng Regan	GHA	15/08/84	M	23	(2)	3
77	Zoran Rendulić		22/05/84	D	11	(1)	2
6	Dragoljub Srnić		12/01/92	M	12	(9)	
14	Slavoljub Srnić		12/01/92	A	27	(2)	8
12	Nemanja Stevanović		08/05/92	G	24		
9	Nikola Stojiljković		17/08/92	A	26	(2)	9
22	Filip Stojković		22/01/93	D	25	(2)	
8	Ivan Todorović		29/07/83	M	26	(2)	4
5	Ugochukwu Ukah	NGA	18/01/84	D	12	(1)	

SERBIA

FK Donji Srem

1927 • Kutpoint arena (3,500) • fkdonjisrem.com

Coach: Nenad Vanić;
(19/10/14) Zlatomir Zagorčić (BUL);
(17/03/15) Nebojša Vučković;
(05/04/15) (Dragan Despotović);
(14/04/15) Zoran Govedarica

2014
09/08 a Borac	L 0-2	
16/08 h Voždovac	W 1-0	Stanisavljevic
24/08 a Partizan	L 0-3	
30/08 a Radnički Niš	W 1-0	Beljić
13/09 h Rad	D 1-1	Zec
20/09 a Čukarički	D 1-1	Beljić (p)
29/09 h Radnički 1923	W 1-0	Stanisavljevic
04/10 a OFK Beograd	L 0-4	
18/10 h Mladost	L 1-2	Spalević (p)
25/10 a Crvena zvezda	L 0-1	
02/11 h Jagodina	L 2-3	Krunić, Zec
08/11 a Vojvodina	W 3-2	Šarac, Stanisavljevic, Zec
22/11 h Spartak	D 1-1	Spalević (p)
29/11 a Napredak	L 1-3	Stanisavljevic
07/12 h Novi Pazar	D 0-0	

2015
21/02 h Borac	L 0-1	
28/02 a Voždovac	W 1-0	Spalević
07/03 h Partizan	L 1-2	Spalević
14/03 h Radnički Niš	D 0-0	
21/03 a Rad	L 0-2	
04/04 h Čukarički	L 1-2	Spalević (p)
09/04 a Radnički 1923	D 0-0	
18/04 h OFK Beograd	W 4-0	og (Antonov), Mirković, Lakićević, Bogunović
25/04 a Mladost	D 0-0	
29/04 h Crvena zvezda	L 1-3	Mitrevski
03/05 a Jagodina	D 0-0	
09/05 h Vojvodina	L 1-2	Lakićević
13/05 a Spartak	L 2-3	Mirković, Prljević
16/05 h Napredak	L 1-2	Stanisavljevic (p)
24/05 a Novi Pazar	L 0-2	

No	Name	Nat	DoB	Pos	Aps	(s)	Gls
38	Nemanja Belić		24/04/87	G	20		
21	Bojan Beljić		08/05/85	M	13	(1)	2
22	Miloš Bogunović		06/10/85	A	13	(1)	1
20	Dario Božičić		30/08/89	D	1		
8	Stefan Bukorac		15/02/91	M	5		
88	Djordje Crnomarković		10/09/93	D	12	(5)	
44	Srdjan Grujičić		19/07/87	M	7	(4)	
9	Martin Hristov	MKD	31/01/97	A		(8)	
15	Dušan Ivanov		17/02/91	D	1		
19	Goran Janković		10/12/78	M	1	(8)	
10	Igor Jelić		28/12/89	M	9	(4)	
3	Miloš Josimov		27/09/84	D	13		
4	Uroš Košutić		11/11/91	M	5	(5)	
10	Rade Krunić	BIH	07/10/93	M	7	(4)	1
14	Nemanja Lakić Pešić		22/09/91	D	14		
24	Ivan Lakićević		27/07/93	D	29		2
9	Damjan Marčeta		11/05/94	A	2	(10)	
1	Miloš Milinović		12/07/84	G	9		
23	Uroš Mirković		08/08/90	M	8	(3)	2
19	Risto Mitrevski	MKD	10/05/91	D	5	(5)	1
5	Aboubakar Moro	GHA	17/08/91	M	19		
25	Sladjan Nikodijević		01/05/90	A		(1)	
7	Abdul Rashid Obuobi	GHA	18/12/94	A	5	(5)	
6	Marko Prljević		02/08/88	D	26		1
3	Dušan Punoševac		28/07/91	D	9	(1)	
8	Luka Sindjić		19/09/93	M	4	(8)	
18	Darko Spalević		24/03/77	A	21	(1)	5
11	Aleksandar Stanisavljevic	AUT	11/06/89	M	18	(2)	5
55	Nemanja Stanković		08/08/97	M		(4)	
33	Dino Šarac		06/09/90	M	19	(4)	1
12	Matija Šegavac		02/01/95	G	1		
21	Zoran Švonja		10/04/95	M	7	(1)	
99	Vladimir Tufegdžić		12/06/91	A		(1)	
14	Djordje Vukobrat		05/05/84	D	13	(1)	
22	Djuro Zec		06/03/90	A	14		3

FK Jagodina

1918 • Pod Djurdjevim brdom (15,000) • fkjagodina.org.rs

Major honours
Serbian Cup (1) 2013

Coach: Mladen Dodić;
(18/09/14) Simo Krunić (BIH)

2014
09/08 h Mladost	D 1-1	Šušnjar
16/08 a Crvena zvezda	L 0-3	
23/08 h Radnički Niš	W 3-1	Savković, Lepović, Djurić
31/08 h Vojvodina	L 2-3	N Arsenijević, Lepović
14/09 a Spartak	W 1-0	
20/09 h Napredak	D 1-1	Lepović
29/09 a Novi Pazar	L 0-3	
04/10 h Borac	W 2-0	Šušnjar, Djurić
18/10 a Voždovac	L 0-1	
26/10 h Partizan	W 1-0	Jovančić
02/11 a Donji Srem	W 3-2	Filipović, F Arsenijević, Šušnjar
08/11 h Rad	L 0-2	
23/11 a Čukarički	W 3-0	Jovančić, Šušnjar, Djurić
29/11 a Radnički 1923	W 2-1	Martinović, Šušnjar
07/12 h OFK Beograd	D 1-1	Šušnjar

2015
21/02 a Mladost	W 3-2	Savković, Mihajlović, Lepović
01/03 h Crvena zvezda	L 2-3	Šušnjar, Jovančić
07/03 a Radnički Niš	L 0-1	
14/03 h Vojvodina	W 4-1	Gašić, Savković, Lepović, Martinović
22/03 h Spartak	L 1-3	Jovančić
04/04 a Napredak	W 1-0	Savković
13/04 h Novi Pazar	L 1-3	Djurić (p)
18/04 a Borac	L 1-3	Djurić (p)
25/04 h Voždovac	L 1-2	N Arsenijević
29/04 a Partizan	L 0-1	
03/05 h Donji Srem	D 0-0	
10/05 a Rad	L 0-1	
13/05 h Čukarički	L 0-1	
16/05 a Radnički 1923	D 0-0	
24/05 h OFK Beograd	W 5-3	Martinović, Savković 2, Djurić (p), Antonijević

No	Name	Nat	DoB	Pos	Aps	(s)	Gls
17	Nikola Antić		01/04/94	D	7	(1)	
14	Veljko Antonijević		28/05/92	D		(2)	1
77	Filip Arsenijević		02/09/83	A	10	(1)	1
99	Nemanja Arsenijević		29/03/86	A	12	(10)	2
6	Aleksandar Cvetković		04/06/95	D	1		
31	Ivan Cvetković		12/02/81	M	13		
31	Nemanja Djekić		13/05/97	M	4	(3)	
7	Milan Djurić		03/10/87	A	24	(1)	6
44	Andjelko Djuričić		21/11/80	G	11		
15	Aleksandar Filipović		20/12/94	D	23		1
5	Danijel Gašić		19/01/87	D	18	(1)	1
26	Vladimir Ilić		23/03/82	D	13	(1)	
36	Igor Ivanović		28/07/97	A		(2)	
50	Nikola Jakimovski	MKD	26/02/90	M	1		
91	Vladimir Jovančić		31/05/87	A	8	(4)	4
23	Miloš Lepović		03/10/87	M	24	(4)	5
8	Dušan Martinović		22/12/87	M	15	(9)	3
32	Zoran Mihailović		02/06/96	M	1	(5)	
10	Danijel Mihajlović		02/06/85	D	21		1
20	Sladjan Mijatović		23/05/94	D	2		
33	Milan Milinković		04/05/85	D	21	(3)	
77	Nemanja Milošević		18/08/96	M		(1)	
29	Vuk Mitošević		12/02/91	M	16	(1)	
11	Uroš Nikolić		14/12/93	M		(6)	
50	Samuel Nnamani	NGA	03/06/95	A		(1)	
14	Ognjen Ožegović		09/06/94	A		(4)	
1	Nikola Perić		04/02/92	G	19		
4	Nikola Popara	BIH	03/08/92	M	8	(3)	
21	Mile Savković		03/11/92	M	19	(7)	6
35	Mladen Stoicev		21/10/95	A	4	(4)	
4	Dajan Šimac	GER	04/01/82	A	4	(1)	
9	Djordje Šušnjar		18/02/92	A	21	(6)	7
3	Aleksandar Varjačić		23/05/91	D	2	(3)	
19	Aleksandar Živanović		04/08/87	D	8		

FK Mladost Lučani

1952 • SC Mladost (8,050) • fkmladostlucani.com

Coach: Nenad Milovanović

2014
09/08 a Jagodina	D 1-1	Adamović (p)
16/08 h Vojvodina	L 1-2	Adamović
23/08 a Spartak	L 0-1	
30/08 h Napredak	W 2-1	S Jovanović, Milosavljević
13/09 a Novi Pazar	W 2-1	Friday 2
20/09 h Borac	W 2-1	Friday, Zonjić
29/09 a Voždovac	L 0-2	
05/10 h Partizan	L 1-2	Friday
18/10 a Donji Srem	W 2-1	Milunović, Zonjić
25/10 h Rad	W 2-1	Friday, Milunović
01/11 a Čukarički	L 0-1	
08/11 h Radnički 1923	D 0-0	
23/11 a OFK Beograd	L 1-2	Živadinović
29/11 a Radnički Niš	D 2-2	Živadinović, Friday
07/12 h Crvena zvezda	D 1-1	S Jovanović

2015
21/02 h Jagodina	L 2-3	Friday (p), Milosavljević
28/02 a Vojvodina	L 1-2	Golemić (p)
07/03 h Spartak	W 3-2	Friday 3 (2p)
14/03 a Napredak	D 1-1	Pavlov
21/03 h Novi Pazar	L 1-3	Živadinović
04/04 a Borac	W 1-0	S Jovanović
13/04 h Voždovac	W 3-2	S Jovanović, Gavrić, Friday
19/04 a Partizan	L 0-3	
25/04 h Donji Srem	D 0-0	
29/04 a Rad	L 1-3	Friday
03/05 h Čukarički	D 2-2	L Jovanović, Friday
09/05 a Radnički 1923	W 3-2	Friday (p), L Jovanović, Živadinović
13/05 h OFK Beograd	W 4-2	Tešić, Friday, L Jovanović, S Jovanović
16/05 h Radnički Niš	W 1-0	Gavrić
24/05 a Crvena zvezda	L 1-3	Pavlov

No	Name	Nat	DoB	Pos	Aps	(s)	Gls
4	Miloš Adamović		19/06/88	M	24	(2)	2
28	Nemanja Ahčin		07/04/94	M	9	(7)	
58	Stefan Cicmil	MNE	16/08/90	D	5	(1)	
33	Miloš Crnomarković		15/09/93	M	4	(5)	
13	Predrag Djordjević		30/06/90	D	2	(3)	
45	Patrick Eze Friday	NGA	22/12/92	A	24	(2)	15
93	Milan Gašić		13/11/93	D	2	(3)	
11	Nebojša Gavrić		27/08/91	M	24	(3)	2
5	Vladimir Golemić		28/06/91	D	22	(4)	1
14	Gradimir Grujičić		22/03/90	A		(4)	
14	Milan Jagodić		03/11/91	D	2		
32	Lazar Jovanović		13/07/93	A	6	(3)	3
7	Saša Jovanović		15/12/91	A	22	(3)	5
1	Nemanja Krznarić		29/05/84	G	30		
27	Matija Ljujić		28/01/93	M	1		
15	Marko Marković		12/01/93	D	2		
10	Radomir Milosavljević		30/07/92	A	20	(8)	2
27	Nikola Milošević		06/08/93	M	1		
19	Nemanja Milunović		31/05/89	D	15		2
31	Ljubo Nenadić		19/04/86	D	4		
58	Vladimir Otašević		06/08/86	D	12	(1)	
8	Yevhen Pavlov	UKR	12/03/91	A	3	(7)	2
17	Ivan Pešić		07/07/89	M	18	(8)	
32	Igor Petrović		18/03/87	D	11	(1)	
20	Ivan Plazinić		14/02/98	M		(1)	
6	Milan Radin		25/06/91	M	20	(1)	
8	Nemanja Stojanović		09/04/87	M	3	(5)	
30	Dušan Tešić		16/07/88	A	13	(4)	1
69	Igor Zonjić	MNE	16/10/91	D	21		2
21	Predrag Živadinović		07/07/83	A	10	(14)	4

FK Napredak

1946 • Mladost (10,331) • fknapredak.rs
Coach: Siniša Gogić (CYP);
(25/08/14) Branko Smiljanić;
(01/10/14) Saša Štrbac;
(15/01/15) Slavko Matić

2014
09/08	h	Čukarički	L 0-2
17/08	a	Radnički 1923	D 0-0
23/08	h	OFK Beograd	L 2-4 *Mićić 2*
30/08	a	Mladost	L 1-2 *Bajić*
13/09	h	Crvena zvezda	D 0-0
20/09	a	Jagodina	D 1-1 *Janičić*
29/09	h	Vojvodina	L 0-1
04/10	a	Spartak	D 0-0
19/10	h	Radnički Niš	W 3-1 *Janičić (p), Božović, Trujić*
25/10	h	Novi Pazar	L 0-1
01/11	a	Borac	W 1-0 *Božović*
08/11	h	Voždovac	L 0-2
23/11	a	Partizan	L 1-3 *N'Diaye*
29/11	h	Donji Srem	W 3-1 *Božović 2, N'Diaye*
07/12	a	Rad	W 1-0 *N'Diaye*

2015
21/02	a	Čukarički	L 0-1
28/02	h	Radnički 1923	W 1-0 *Ivičić*
08/03	a	OFK Beograd	L 0-1
14/03	h	Mladost	D 1-1 *Dimitrov*
21/03	a	Crvena zvezda	L 0-1
04/04	a	Jagodina	L 0-1
09/04	a	Vojvodina	W 1-0 *Gobeljić*
18/04	h	Spartak	D 0-0
25/04	a	Radnički Niš	L 0-2
29/04	a	Novi Pazar	D 1-1 *Lemajić*
03/05	h	Borac	W 2-1 *Dimitrov, Trujić*
09/05	a	Voždovac	L 0-1
13/05	h	Partizan	L 0-2
16/05	a	Donji Srem	W 2-1 *Urošević, Lemajić (p)*
24/05	h	Rad	L 2-3 *N'Diaye, Paunović*

No	Name	Nat	DoB	Pos	Aps	(s)	Gls
99	Miloš Bajić		27/04/94	A	13	(11)	1
33	Zoran Belošević		20/06/83	D		(2)	
19	Bojan Božović		03/02/85	A	11	(1)	4
90	Miloš Cvetković		06/01/90	D	10		
30	Srdjan Dimitrov		28/07/92	M	14	(6)	2
29	Aleksandar Djoković		16/12/91	M	2	(3)	
6	Abraham Frimpong	GHA	06/04/93	M	16	(1)	
77	Marko Gobeljić		13/09/92	M	24	(2)	1
10	Predrag Govedarica		21/10/84	M	7		
24	Tomislav Ivičić	CRO	27/10/87	A	4	(3)	1
23	Nemanja Janičić	BIH	13/07/86	D	10		2
32	Slobodan Janković		29/08/81	G	11		
20	Predrag Lazić		15/01/82	M	5	(5)	
21	Darko Lemajić		20/08/93	A	5	(8)	2
18	Stevan Luković		16/03/93	D	21	(2)	
79	Andrija Majdevac		08/07/97	A		(5)	
34	Mamadou Mbodj	SEN	12/03/93	D		(7)	
21	Dušan Mićić		29/11/84	M	4		2
0	Ibrahima N'Diaye	SEN	15/04/93	A	26	(3)	4
10	Dušan Pantelić		15/04/93	M	1	(4)	
28	Marko Paunović		28/01/88	D	23		1
13	Strahinja Petrović		14/06/92	A		(3)	
11	Nikola Popović		31/05/94	A	1	(2)	
1	Zoran Popović		28/05/88	G	19		
3	Dušan Punoševac		28/07/91	D	3		
5	Ilija Radović	MNE	05/09/85	D	4	(1)	
22	Miloš Radulović	MNE	23/02/90	D	9		
20	Obeng Regan	GHA	15/08/84	M	1		
17	Marko Ristić		30/03/97	M		(1)	
69	Miloš Stanojević		20/11/93	M	14	(3)	
87	Tai	BRA	13/03/87	M	2	(2)	
5	Vukašin Tomić		08/04/87	D	4		
31	Nemanja Trajković		13/06/91	D	1	(2)	
14	Nikola Trujić		14/04/92	A	28		2
27	Slobodan Urošević		15/04/94	D	26		1
3	Aleksandar Vasiljević		19/08/82	D	3		
80	Marko Vučetić		24/06/86	M	8	(4)	
7	Miloš Vulić		19/08/96	M		(2)	

FK Novi Pazar

1928 • Gradski stadion – Abdulah Gegić
Duce (6,500) • fknovipazar.rs
Coach: Dragi Kanatlarovski (MKD);
(20/09/14) Milorad Kosanović

2014
09/08	h	Rad	W 1-0 *Kecap*
16/08	a	Čukarički	D 1-1 *Mijić*
23/08	h	Radnički 1923	W 2-0 *Hadžibulić, Djordjević*
31/08	a	OFK Beograd	L 2-3 *Rusmir (p), Vidaković*
13/09	h	Mladost	L 1-2 *Tintor*
20/09	a	Crvena zvezda	L 0-2
29/09	h	Jagodina	W 3-0 *Kecap, Radivojević, Jevtović*
04/10	a	Vojvodina	L 0-1
18/10	h	Spartak	W 1-0 *Kecap*
25/10	a	Napredak	L 0-1 *og (Paunović)*
01/11	h	Radnički Niš	W 3-1 *Bruno, Rusmir (p), Kecap*
08/11	h	Borac	D 2-2 *Tintor, Kecap*
30/11	a	Partizan	D 1-1 *Bruno*
07/12	a	Donji Srem	D 0-0
10/12	a	Voždovac	D 0-0

2015
21/02	h	Rad	L 0-1
28/02	h	Čukarički	L 1-2 *Radivojević*
07/03	a	Radnički 1923	W 1-0 *Radivojević*
14/03	h	OFK Beograd	W 3-1 *Kostić, Pavlović, Radivojević*
21/03	a	Mladost	W 3-1 *Bruno, Radivojević, Pavlović (p)*
04/04	h	Crvena zvezda	W 2-1 *Pavlović, Jevtović (p)*
13/04	a	Jagodina	W 3-1 *Radivojević, og (Mihajlović), Kecap*
18/04	h	Vojvodina	L 0-1
25/04	a	Spartak	W 2-0 *Mijić 2*
29/04	h	Napredak	D 1-1 *Bruno*
03/05	a	Radnički Niš	L 1-3 *og (Ćulum)*
09/05	a	Borac	L 0-1
13/05	h	Voždovac	W 1-0 *Jevtović (p)*
16/05	a	Partizan	D 1-1 *Pavlović*
24/05	h	Donji Srem	W 2-0 *Rusmir, Kostić*

No	Name	Nat	DoB	Pos	Aps	(s)	Gls
23	Ibrahim Arifović		22/03/90	M		(2)	
11	Filip Arsenijević		09/02/83	A	5	(6)	
17	Bruno	BRA	05/06/90	M	22		4
91	Miloš Budaković		10/07/91	G	5		
4	Željko Djokić		05/10/82	D	6	(2)	
2	Bojan Djordjević		05/04/84	D	24	(1)	1
18	José Luis Gutiérrez	ECU	03/03/93	A		(2)	
10	Sead Hadžibulić	BIH	30/01/83	A	6	(5)	1
30	Marko Jevtović		24/07/93	M	28		3
14	Admir Kecap		25/11/87	A	27	(1)	6
9	Miroljub Kostić		06/05/88	M	14		2
9	Miloš Mijić		01/11/89	M	24	(6)	3
6	José Mina	ECU	03/04/93	M	1	(1)	
8	Ivan Obrovac		08/12/86	M	3	(10)	
4	Vladimir Otašević		08/06/86	D	2		
21	Lazar Pajović		26/08/91	D	1	(1)	
77	Predrag Pavlović		19/06/86	M	20	(9)	4
27	Vladimir Radivojević		04/02/86	M	18	(5)	6
28	Kenan Ragipović		24/11/90	M	7	(1)	
10	Richard Falcão	BRA	29/06/87	A		(3)	
20	Dejan Rusmir		28/01/80	A	15	(9)	3
45	Anes Rušević		12/02/96	A		(2)	
69	Stefan Savić		10/01/94	D	2	(1)	
80	Edin Selimović		28/01/91	M		(4)	
46	Vuk Sotirović		13/07/82	A		(6)	
7	Siniša Stevanović		12/01/89	D	8	(3)	
99	Miloš Tintor		21/08/86	D	20	(1)	2
31	Žarko Udovičić		31/08/87	D	14		
11	Nemanja Vidaković		29/09/85	A	3	(5)	1
26	Marko Vuković		23/01/86	D	26		
1	Zlatko Zečević		10/08/83	G	24		
5	Miloš Živković		01/12/84	D	4	(2)	
23	Mladen Živković		26/08/89	G	1		

OFK Beograd

1911 • Omladinski stadion (13,900) •
ofkbeograd.co.rs
Major honours
Yugoslav League (5) 1931, 1933, 1935, 1936, 1939;
Yugoslav Cup (5) 1934, 1953, 1955, 1962, 1966
Coach: Dejan Djurdjević

2014
10/08	a	Vojvodina	L 0-3
16/08	h	Spartak	W 0-0
23/08	a	Napredak	W 4-2 *Paločević, Čavrić 2, Gajić*
31/08	h	Novi Pazar	W 3-2 *Jovanović, Čavrić, M Janković*
13/09	a	Borac	D 1-1 *Vuković*
20/09	h	Voždovac	W 1-0 *Vuković (p)*
04/10	h	Donji Srem	W 4-0 *Dražić 2, Jovanović, Paločević*
19/10	a	Rad	D 1-1 *Micevski*
25/10	h	Čukarički	L 0-4
29/10	a	Partizan	D 1-1 *Dražić*
02/11	a	Radnički 1923	D 0-0
08/11	a	Radnički Niš	D 0-0
23/11	h	Mladost	W 2-1 *Jovanović, M Janković*
29/11	a	Crvena zvezda	L 1-2 *Duronjić*
07/12	h	Jagodina	D 1-1 *Gajić*

2015
21/02	a	Vojvodina	D 0-0
28/02	a	Spartak	L 0-1
08/03	h	Napredak	W 1-0 *Jovanović*
14/03	a	Novi Pazar	L 1-3 *Jovanović (p)*
21/03	h	Borac	W 1-0 *Liščević*
04/04	a	Voždovac	W 2-0 *M Janković, Dražić*
13/04	h	Partizan	L 1-3 *Zarubica*
18/04	a	Donji Srem	L 0-4
26/04	h	Rad	W 1-0 *Jovanović (p)*
29/04	a	Čukarički	L 0-1
03/05	h	Radnički 1923	W 2-0 *Micevski, M Janković*
09/05	h	Radnički Niš	L 0-1
13/05	a	Mladost	L 2-4 *Jovanović 2 (1p)*
16/05	h	Crvena zvezda	L 2-4 *Zarubica, Cuckić*
24/05	a	Jagodina	L 3-5 *Gojkov, Zarubica, Matović*

No	Name	Nat	DoB	Pos	Aps	(s)	Gls
16	Nikola Aksentijević		09/03/93	D	14	(1)	
27	Aleksandar Alempijević		25/07/88	M	1	(7)	
36	Komnen Andrić		01/07/95	A	9	(4)	
11	Miloš Antić		28/10/94	M	6	(3)	
3	Nemanja Antonov		06/05/95	D	24		
33	Nemanja Belaković		01/08/97	M	1	(2)	
14	Luka Belić		18/04/96	A	1	(2)	
32	Mihajlo Cakić		27/05/90	M	1	(1)	
28	Nikola Cuckić		04/11/97	M	1	(1)	1
12	Ognjen Čančarević		25/09/89	G	1		
11	Aleksandar Čavrić		18/05/94	A	4		3
13	Stefan Čolović		16/04/94	M		(1)	
1	Stefan Čupić		07/05/94	G	28		
15	Emir Dautović	SVN	02/05/95	D	10	(3)	
10	Dejan Dražić		26/09/95	A	25	(1)	4
17	Borko Duronjić		24/09/97	A	3	(6)	1
20	Milan Gajić		28/01/96	D	23	(1)	2
90	Petar Gigić		03/07/97	A	1	(1)	
30	Damjan Gojkov		01/02/88	M		(1)	1
9	Marko Janković	MNE	09/07/95	A	12	(7)	4
37	Stefan Janković		25/06/97	M	2	(7)	
7	Aleksandar Ješić		13/09/94	M	5	(10)	
22	Ivica Jovanović	MNE	04/12/87	A	22	(5)	8
26	Zlatko Liščević		03/08/91	D	13	(1)	1
27	Filip Matović		02/06/95	D	7	(1)	1
23	Darko Micevski	MKD	12/04/92	M	15	(2)	2
21	Petar Milić		03/12/98	A	1		
26	Milan Obradović		03/08/77	D	4	(1)	
8	Aleksandar Paločević		22/08/93	M	17	(7)	2
6	Bogdan Planić		19/01/92	D	6		
5	Milan Savić		04/04/94	D	17	(1)	
32	Milan Sekulić		26/01/95	M		(1)	
29	Alexander Spoljaric	CYP	28/11/95	G	1		
2	Jovica Vasilić		08/07/90	D	11		
6	Nikola Vasiljević		30/06/91	D	15		
11	Ivan Vuković	MNE	09/02/87	A	7	(1)	2
19	Dejan Zarubica	MNE	11/04/93	A	4	(7)	3
4	Saša Zdjelar		20/03/95	M	18	(1)	
24	Miloš Zlatković		01/01/97	D	1	(1)	

FK Partizan

1945 • FK Partizan (30,900) • partizan.rs
Major honours
Yugoslav/Serbian League (26) 1947, 1949, 1961, 1962, 1963, 1965, 1976, 1978, 1983, 1986, 1987, 1993, 1994, 1996, 1997, 1999, 2002, 2003, 2005, 2008, 2009, 2010, 2011, 2012, 2013, 2015; Yugoslav/Serbian Cup (12) 1947, 1952, 1954, 1957, 1989, 1992, 1994, 1998, 2001, 2008, 2009, 2011
**Coach: Marko Nikolić;
(25/03/15) Zoran Milinković**

2014
10/08	a	Voždovac	W 3-1	og (Stojković), Volkov, Fofana
16/08	a	Radnički Niš	W 4-1	Grbić, Lazović, og (Djordjević), Škuletić
24/08	h	Donji Srem	W 3-0	Škuletić (p), Lazović, Marković
31/08	a	Rad	W 4-0	Škuletić, Lazović 2, Fofana
13/09	h	Čukarički	W 4-2	Pantić, Lazović, Škuletić, Luka
21/09	a	Radnički 1923	W 3-0	Škuletić 2 (1p), Ilić
05/10	a	Mladost	W 2-1	Škuletić, Lazović
18/10	h	Crvena zvezda	W 1-0	Drinčić
26/10	a	Jagodina	L 0-1	
29/10	h	OFK Beograd	D 1-1	Lazović
02/11	h	Vojvodina	W 1-0	Škuletić
09/11	a	Spartak	W 3-0	Škuletić 3
23/11	h	Napredak	W 3-1	Lazović, Ilić, Škuletić
30/11	a	Novi Pazar	D 1-1	Lazović
07/12	h	Borac	W 5-1	Volkov, Škuletić 2, A Živković, Ilić

2015
21/02	h	Voždovac	D 3-3	Ninković, Ilić, Šaponjić
28/02	h	Radnički Niš	D 0-0	
07/03	a	Donji Srem	W 2-1	Kojić 2
14/03	h	Rad	W 2-0	Drinčić, Ninković
22/03	a	Čukarički	D 2-2	Babović, Ilić
04/04	a	Radnički 1923	W 2-1	Babović, Ilić
13/04	h	OFK Beograd	W 3-1	A Živković 2, Šaponjić
19/04	h	Mladost	W 3-0	Marković, Šaponjić, A Živković
25/04	a	Crvena zvezda	D 0-0	
29/04	a	Jagodina	W 1-0	Šaponjić
03/05	a	Vojvodina	W 4-0	Volkov 2, Ninković, Brašanac
09/05	h	Spartak	W 1-0	Ninković
13/05	a	Napredak	W 2-0	Ilić, A Živković
16/05	h	Novi Pazar	D 1-1	Šaponjić
24/05	a	Borac	D 3-3	Luka, Marinković, Grbić (p)

No	Name	Nat	DoB	Pos	Aps	(s)	Gls
10	Stefan Babović		01/07/87	M	12		2
6	Gregor Balažič	SVN	12/02/88	D	13		
2	Ivan Bandalovski	BUL	23/11/86	D	14	(1)	
8	Darko Brašanac		12/02/92	M	13	(4)	1
13	Lazar Ćirković		22/08/92	D	12	(1)	
18	Nikola Drinčić	MNE	07/09/84	M	23		2
10	Ismaël Fofana	CIV	08/09/88	A		(5)	2
14	Petar Grbić	MNE	07/08/88	M	18	(7)	2
36	Nikola Gulan		23/03/89	M	1	(1)	
30	Branko Ilić	SVN	06/02/83	D	27		4
22	Saša Ilić		30/12/77	M	15	(12)	3
9	Nemanja Kojić		03/02/90	A	5	(8)	2
37	Miloš Kukolj		12/01/98	A		(1)	
27	Danko Lazović		17/05/83	A	13	(2)	9
7	Predrag Luka		11/05/88	M	1	(7)	2
25	Milan Lukač		04/10/85	G	16		
20	Saša Lukić		13/08/96	M	2		
29	Nenad Marinković		28/09/88	A	2	(6)	1
21	Saša Marković		13/03/91	M	14	(3)	2
11	Nikola Ninković		19/12/94	M	15	(8)	4
40	Miloš Ostojić		29/12/89	D		(1)	
55	Danilo Pantić		26/10/96	M	3	(4)	1
28	Ivan Petrović		03/07/93	M		(1)	
5	Nemanja Petrović		17/04/92	D	14	(1)	
99	Vojislav Stanković		22/09/87	D	15		
35	Miladin Stevanović		11/02/96	D	3		
33	Ivan Šaponjić		08/02/97	A	8	(6)	5
32	Petar Škuletić		29/06/90	A	15		14
3	Vladimir Volkov	MNE	06/06/86	D	17	(1)	4
4	Miroslav Vulićević		29/05/85	D	9	(1)	
17	Andrija Živković		11/07/96	M	16	(8)	5
1	Živko Živković		14/04/89	G	14		

FK Rad

1958 • Kralj Petar I (6,000); Stadion na Vračaru (4,506) • fkrad.rs
Coach: Milan Milanović

2014
09/08	a	Novi Pazar	L 0-1	
16/08	h	Borac	W 2-1	N Mihajlović, Maraš
23/08	a	Voždovac	W 6-1	Jelić 5, Perović
31/08	h	Partizan	L 0-4	
13/09	a	Donji Srem	D 1-1	Jelić
20/09	a	Radnički Niš	L 0-3	
29/09	h	Čukarički	L 1-3	Perović
04/10	a	Radnički 1923	W 3-0	Simić, Rodić, Jelić
19/10	h	OFK Beograd	D 1-1	Veselinović
25/10	a	Mladost	L 1-2	Rodić
02/11	h	Crvena zvezda	L 1-2	Jelić
08/11	h	Jagodina	W 2-0	Raspopović, Perović
22/11	h	Vojvodina	D 0-0	
29/11	a	Spartak	D 0-0	
07/12	h	Napredak	L 0-1	

2015
21/02	h	Novi Pazar	W 1-0	I Djuric
28/02	a	Borac	W 1-0	N Mihajlović
07/03	h	Voždovac	W 2-0	Veselinović, Simić
14/03	a	Partizan	L 0-2	
21/03	h	Donji Srem	W 2-0	Milošević (p), Rodić
04/04	h	Radnički Niš	W 1-0	Nenadović
13/04	a	Čukarički	L 0-7	
18/04	h	Radnički 1923	W 1-0	Milošević (p)
26/04	a	OFK Beograd	L 0-1	
29/04	h	Mladost	W 3-1	Veselinović, I Djuric, Milošević
03/05	a	Crvena zvezda	L 0-2	
10/05	h	Jagodina	W 1-0	Mladenović
13/05	a	Vojvodina	L 0-2	
16/05	h	Spartak	L 0-1	
24/05	a	Napredak	W 3-2	og (Vučetić), Rodić, Ljujić

No	Name	Nat	DoB	Pos	Aps	(s)	Gls
55	Delimir Bajić	BIH	28/03/83	D	6	(3)	
99	Miloš Čudić		21/08/96	M		(2)	
12	Darko Dejanović		17/03/95	G	2		
35	Djordje Denić		01/04/96	M	4	(4)	
23	Igor Djuric		22/02/85	D	12		2
4	Nikola Djuric		06/11/89	D	20	(1)	
19	Ognjen Gnjatić	BIH	16/10/91	M	22	(1)	
11	Petar Jelić	BIH	18/01/86	A	21	(2)	8
92	Aleksandar Jovanović		06/12/92	G	7		
22	Matija Ljujić		28/01/93	M	4	(3)	1
25	Nikola Maraš		19/12/95	D	23		1
9	Ivan Marković		23/12/91	A	4	(10)	
86	Miloš Marković		10/12/86	D	12		
7	Nemanja Mihajlović		19/01/96	M	16	(8)	2
8	Stefan Milisavljević		24/06/94	A	1	(3)	
8	Miloš Milisavljević		26/10/92	M	5	(8)	
29	Branislav Milošević		13/05/88	D	28		3
33	Bogdan Mladenović		04/04/96	M	2	(9)	1
70	Uroš Nenadović		28/01/94	A	4	(9)	1
5	Miloš Obradović		30/03/87	D	12		
51	Slavko Perović		09/06/89	A	13		3
1	Boris Radunović		26/05/96	G	21		
21	Nikola Raspopović		18/10/89	D	21		1
30	Vladimir Rodić		07/09/93	D	28	(2)	4
37	Aleksandar Simić		31/01/80	M	10	(16)	2
22	Perica Stanceski	MKD	29/01/85	D		(4)	
5	Miloš Stanojević		20/11/93	M	3		
55	Aleksandar Trninić		23/03/87	D	2	(1)	
77	Borko Veselinović		06/01/86	A	23		3
24	Stefan Vico		28/02/95	D	4	(1)	
18	Nikola Vujnović	MNE	11/01/97	A		(1)	

FK Radnički 1923

1923 • Čika Dača (22,100) • fkradnicki.com
**Coach: Dragoljub Bekvalac;
(07/10/14) Vlado Čapljić;
(26/10/14) Neško Milovanović**

2014
09/08	a	Spartak	L 0-1	
17/08	h	Napredak	D 0-0	
23/08	a	Novi Pazar	L 0-2	
30/08	h	Borac	L 0-2	
13/09	a	Voždovac	W 1-0	Sotirović
21/09	h	Partizan	L 0-3	
29/09	a	Donji Srem	L 0-5	
04/10	h	Rad	L 0-3	
18/10	a	Čukarički	L 1-4	N Kovačević
25/10	a	Radnički Niš	L 0-1	
02/11	h	OFK Beograd	D 0-0	
08/11	h	Mladost	D 0-0	
22/11	h	Crvena zvezda	D 0-0	
29/11	a	Jagodina	L 1-2	D Milovanović
07/12	h	Vojvodina	L 3-4	Arsić, D Milovanović, Tiodorović

2015
21/02	h	Spartak	W 1-0	N Kovačević
28/02	a	Napredak	L 0-1	
07/03	h	Novi Pazar	D 1-1	D Milovanović
14/03	a	Borac	L 0-2	
21/03	h	Voždovac	W 2-1	D Miljuš, D Milovanović
04/04	a	Partizan	L 1-2	Rosić
09/04	h	Donji Srem	D 0-0	
18/04	a	Rad	L 0-1	
25/04	h	Čukarički	L 0-1	
29/04	h	Radnički Niš	L 1-2	Goljović
03/05	a	OFK Beograd	L 0-2	
09/05	h	Mladost	L 2-3	N Kovačević (p), Jović
13/05	a	Crvena zvezda	W 2-1	Goljović, Stević
16/05	h	Jagodina	D 0-0	
24/05	a	Vojvodina	L 1-3	Stević

No	Name	Nat	DoB	Pos	Aps	(s)	Gls
10	Lazar Arsić		24/09/91	M	13		1
19	Vladimir Bubanja		02/08/89	D	17	(4)	
28	Joseph Cudjoe	GHA	17/10/95	M	2	(1)	
61	Milan Ćulum		28/10/84	M	10	(1)	
9	Branislav Čonka		29/01/89	A	4	(4)	
82	Filip Djurović		19/11/96	D		(1)	
3	Darko Fejsa		27/08/87	D	1		
22	Željko Goljović		04/03/98	A	2	(1)	2
6	Georgije Ilić		13/05/95	A	1	(1)	
6	Aleksandar Janković		16/09/95	M		(1)	
13	Vladimir Jašić		04/01/84	D	17	(1)	
55	Predrag Jović		29/05/87	D	8	(6)	1
21	Aleksandar Keljević		14/06/89	M	8	(4)	
95	Marko Kostić		10/10/95	G	1		
15	Nikola Kovačević		14/04/94	M	17	(2)	3
32	Savo Kovačević		15/08/88	A		(8)	
88	Radovan Krivokapić		14/08/78	M		(1)	
2	Jovan Krneta		04/05/92	D	9		
24	Jovan Lukić		22/09/97	M	3	(2)	
42	Aleksandar Miletić		04/01/96	D	4	(2)	
41	Bojan Miljuš		24/10/94	D	9		
27	Dejan Miljuš		24/10/94	A	13	(4)	1
7	Dragan Milovanović		03/01/86	A	14	(3)	4
84	Vasilije Milovanović		30/12/98	M		(2)	
81	Lazar Milutinović		30/09/98	A		(1)	
83	Nikola Nedeljković		24/12/96	M	1		
33	David Nikolić		09/02/96	D	1		
23	Godwin Osei Bonsu	GHA	03/03/89	D	16		
29	Marko Perović		11/01/84	M	8	(1)	
99	David Poljanec	SVN	27/11/86	A	4	(3)	
47	Lazar Popović		04/11/93	A	1	(4)	
30	Miloš Rnić		24/01/89	D	5		
5	Lazar Rosić		29/06/93	D	19		1
46	Vuk Sotirović		13/07/82	A	8		1
25	Dušan Stević		17/06/95	A	3	(3)	2
18	Stefan Stojanović		12/01/88	A	2		
85	Miloš Tatović		09/05/98	M		(1)	
44	Borislav Terzić		01/11/91	D	18	(1)	
4	Luka Tiodorović	MNE	21/01/86	M	14	(4)	1
49	Dragan Trajković		22/07/97	M		(4)	
50	Žarko Trifunović		20/09/89	G	27		
45	Strahinja Uroševič		03/04/96	M	10	(1)	
1	Miloš Vesić		23/07/89	G	2		
26	Nemanja Vidić		06/08/89	M	5	(4)	
16	Uroš Vidović		09/06/94	M	15	(2)	
77	Irfan Vušljanin		07/01/86	M	11	(7)	
43	Ivan Živanović		21/08/95	D	3		
11	Stefan Živković		18/01/89	A	4	(3)	

FK Radnički Niš

1923 • Čair (18,151) • fkradnickinis.rs
Coach: Dragoslav Stepanović;
(07/09/14) Saša Mrkić;
(26/12/14) Miodrag Ješić;
(01/01/15) Milan Rastavac

2014
09/08 a	Crvena zvezda	L	0-2	
16/08 h	Partizan	L	1-4	Djordjević
23/08 a	Jagodina	L	1-3	Batioja
30/08 h	Donji Srem	L	0-1	
14/09 a	Vojvodina	L	0-3	
20/09 h	Rad	W	3-0	Djilas, Djordjević, Popara
29/09 a	Spartak	L	0-1	
04/10 h	Čukarički	W	2-1	Pavlović, Djilas
19/10 a	Napredak	L	1-3	Pavlović
25/10 h	Radnički 1923	W	1-0	Djilas
01/11 a	Novi Pazar	L	1-3	Punoševac
08/11 h	OFK Beograd	D	0-0	
22/11 a	Borac	D	0-0	
29/11 h	Mladost	D	2-2	Djordjević, Marjanović (p)
07/12 h	Voždovac	L	1-2	Marjanović

2015
22/02 h	Crvena zvezda	D	0-0	
28/02 h	Partizan	D	0-0	
07/03 h	Jagodina	W	1-0	Popara
14/03 h	Donji Srem	D	0-0	
21/03 h	Vojvodina	D	1-1	Marjanović
04/04 a	Rad	L	0-1	
09/04 h	Spartak	W	1-0	Djuričković
18/04 a	Čukarički	D	1-1	Marjanović
25/04 a	Napredak	W	2-0	R Bulatović, Pejčić
29/04 h	Radnički 1923	W	2-1	og (D Miljuš), Popara
03/05 h	Novi Pazar	W	3-1	Pejčić, Marjanović, Ašćerić
09/05 a	OFK Beograd	D	0-0	
13/05 h	Borac	W	1-0	Zemlyanukhin
16/05 a	Mladost	L	0-1	
24/05 h	Voždovac	D	0-0	

No	Name	Nat	DoB	Pos	Aps	(s)	Gls
91	Nikola Ašćerić		19/04/91	A	10	(4)	1
88	Augusto Batioja	ECU	04/05/90	A	11	(1)	1
18	Milan Borjan	CAN	23/10/87	G	15		
89	Darko Bulatović	MNE	05/09/89	D	12		
4	Radoš Bulatović		06/05/84	D	13	1	
61	Milan Ćulum		28/10/84	M	13		
91	Vladimir Djilas		03/03/83	A	5	(3)	3
28	Vladimir Djordjević		25/12/82	M	16	(1)	3
7	Petar Djuričković		20/06/91	M	25	(1)	1
1	Nenad Filipović		24/04/87	G	5		
24	Aleksandar Jovanović		17/12/84	M	27		
23	Aleksandar Kesić		18/08/87	G	10	(1)	
8	Dušan Kolarević		19/04/87	M	14	(9)	
44	Nemanja Lakić Pešić		22/09/91	D	12		
4	Vlade Lazarevski	MKD	09/06/83	D	1	(2)	
15	Zoran Ljubinković		07/12/81	D	9	(2)	
21	Saša Marjanović		13/11/87	M	27		5
9	Vladimir Milenković		22/06/82	A	4	(6)	
19	Marko Mrkić		20/08/96	A		(7)	
49	Branko Pauljević		01/05/87	D	11		
13	Vladan Pavlović		24/02/84	D	19	(6)	2
11	Ivan Pejčić		11/09/82	A	13	(7)	2
14	Miloš Petrović		05/05/90	D	24		
20	Petar Petrovic	SWE	15/09/95	M	4	(7)	
5	Pavle Popara		20/05/87	M	9	(6)	3
30	Bratislav Punoševac		09/07/87	A	6	(3)	1
44	Miodrag Todorović		10/09/95	A		(2)	
6	Marko Tomić		28/10/91	D	3	(4)	
55	Aleksandar Trninić		23/03/87	D	1		
44	Baurzhan Turysbek	KAZ	15/10/91	A		(4)	
3	Nikola Valentić		09/06/83	D	2	(4)	
20	Anton Zemlyanukhin	KGZ	11/12/88	A	9	(2)	1

FK Spartak Subotica

1945 • Gradski stadion (25,000) • fkspartak.com
Coach: Petar Kurćubić;
(10/04/15) Stevan Mojsilović

2014
09/08 h	Radnički 1923	W	1-0	Balabanović
16/08 a	OFK Beograd	D	0-0	
23/08 h	Mladost	W	1-0	Milić
30/08 a	Crvena zvezda	L	0-1	
14/09 h	Jagodina	W	2-0	Milić, Torbica
20/09 a	Vojvodina	L	2-5	Torbica, Maksimović
29/09 h	Radnički Niš	W	1-0	Milić
04/10 h	Napredak	D	0-0	
18/10 h	Novi Pazar	L	0-1	
25/10 h	Borac	D	2-2	Torbica (p), Milić
02/11 a	Voždovac	D	1-1	Georgijević
09/11 h	Partizan	L	0-3	
22/11 a	Donji Srem	D	1-1	Georgijević
29/11 h	Rad	D	0-0	
07/12 a	Čukarički	L	0-2	

2015
21/02 a	Radnički 1923	L	0-1	
28/02 h	OFK Beograd	W	1-0	Ivanović
07/03 a	Mladost	L	2-3	Ivanović 2
14/03 h	Crvena zvezda	L	1-3	Georgijević
22/03 a	Jagodina	W	3-1	Plavšić, Milić 2
04/04 h	Vojvodina	L	0-1	
09/04 a	Radnički Niš	L	0-1	
18/04 a	Napredak	D	0-0	
25/04 h	Novi Pazar	L	0-2	
29/04 a	Borac	L	0-1	
03/05 a	Voždovac	L	0-1	
09/05 a	Partizan	L	0-1	
13/05 h	Donji Srem	W	3-2	Maksimović, Torbica (p), Lazarević (p)
16/05 a	Rad	W	1-0	Milić
24/05 h	Čukarički	W	1-0	Mrkela

No	Name	Nat	DoB	Pos	Aps	(s)	Gls
17	Goran Antonić		05/11/90	D	29		
10	Milorad Balabanović		18/01/90	M	10	(7)	1
22	Nikola Banjac		18/09/96	D		(1)	
11	Duško Dukić		21/06/86	D	15	(4)	
20	Danijel Farkaš		13/01/93	D	14	(11)	
20	Dejan Georgijević		19/01/94	A	3	(11)	3
19	Stefan Ilić		07/04/95	A	9	(10)	
28	Djordje Ivanović		20/11/95	A	10	(5)	3
24	Slobodan Jakovljević		26/05/89	D	7	(2)	
1	Budimir Janosević		21/10/89	G	15		
4	Branimir Jočić		30/11/94	D	12	(1)	
26	Marko Jondić		03/05/95	D	5	(5)	
6	Vladimir Kovačević		11/11/92	D	22		
23	Mladen Lazarević		16/01/84	D	2	(2)	1
5	Nenad Lukić		02/09/92	M	2	(17)	
18	Novica Maksimović		04/04/88	M	24	(2)	2
14	Nebojša Mezei		15/02/91	M	4	(3)	
16	Nemanja Milić		25/05/90	A	26		7
15	Stefan Milošević		07/04/95	D	26		
12	Nikola Mirković		26/07/91	G	15		
27	Andrej Mrkela		09/04/92	M	18	(5)	1
2	Srdjan Plavšić		03/11/95	M	21		1
24	Ilija Radović	MNE	09/05/85	D	13		
8	Vladimir Torbica		20/09/80	M	28		4
13	Danijel Zlatković		29/03/96	M		(1)	

FK Vojvodina

1914 • Karadjordje (15,754) • fkvojvodina.rs
Major honours
Yugoslav League (2) 1966, 1989; Serbian Cup (1) 2014
Coach: Zoran Marić;
(16/03/15) Zlatomir Zagorčić (BUL)

2014
10/08 h	OFK Beograd	W	3-0	Gaćinović, Ivanić, Alivodić
16/08 a	Mladost	W	2-1	Veselinović 2
23/08 h	Crvena zvezda	L	0-1	
31/08 a	Jagodina	W	3-2	Veselinović 2 (1p), Pekarić
14/09 h	Radnički Niš	W	3-0	Ivanić, Pekarić, Alivodić
20/09 h	Spartak	W	5-2	Alivodić, Gaćinović, Poletanović, Veselinović 2 (1p)
29/09 a	Napredak	W	1-0	Gaćinović
04/10 h	Novi Pazar	W	1-0	S Novaković
19/10 a	Borac	D	1-1	Gaćinović
25/10 h	Voždovac	W	3-0	Veselinović (p), Gaćinović, Luković
02/11 a	Partizan	L	0-1	
08/11 h	Donji Srem	L	2-3	Gaćinović, Veselinović (p)
22/11 a	Rad	D	0-0	
29/11 h	Čukarički	L	1-2	Tumbasević
07/12 a	Radnički 1923	W	4-3	Gaćinović 2, Ivanić 2

2015
21/02 a	OFK Beograd	D	0-0	
28/02 h	Mladost	W	2-1	Gaćinović, Ivanić
07/03 a	Crvena zvezda	L	0-3	
14/03 h	Jagodina	L	1-4	Stojanović
21/03 h	Radnički Niš	D	1-1	Gaćinović
04/04 a	Spartak	W	1-0	Ivanić (p)
09/04 h	Napredak	L	0-1	
18/04 a	Novi Pazar	W	1-0	Ivanić
25/04 h	Borac	L	1-3	Makarić
29/04 a	Voždovac	L	0-1	
03/05 h	Partizan	L	0-4	
09/05 h	Donji Srem	W	2-1	Asani, Ivanić
13/05 h	Rad	W	2-0	Ivanić, Makarić
16/05 a	Čukarički	W	1-0	Gaćinović
24/05 h	Radnički 1923	W	3-1	M Novaković, Ivanić, Stojanović

No	Name	Nat	DoB	Pos	Aps	(s)	Gls
7	Enver Alivodić		27/12/84	M	12		3
20	Elmir Asani		15/09/95	M	7	(3)	1
33	Srdjan Babić		22/04/96	D	24		
29	Saša Ćurko		07/12/96	D	9	(5)	
11	Mijat Gaćinović		08/02/95	M	23	(2)	11
22	Luka Grgić		07/06/96	A		(2)	
4	Mirko Ivanić		13/09/93	M	26		10
17	Dragan Karanov		04/10/95	D		(4)	
25	Marko Kordić	MNE	22/02/95	G	3		
10	Luka Luković		11/10/96	M	9	(9)	1
16	Milan Makarić		04/10/95	M	5	(10)	2
30	Vanja Milinković-Savić		20/02/97	G	17		
15	Bojan Nastić		06/07/94	D	28		
19	Stefan Nikolić		14/03/94	D		(1)	
5	Milko Novaković	MNE	21/01/88	D	1	(3)	1
35	Slobodan Novaković		15/10/86	M	10	(11)	1
13	Radovan Pankov		08/08/95	D	10	(4)	
6	Nino Pekarić		16/08/82	D	28		2
18	Marko Poletanović		20/07/93	M	15		1
8	Darko Puškarić		13/07/85	M	13		
2	Nemanja Radoja		06/02/93	M	1		
23	Slaviša Radović	BIH	10/08/93	M	2	(1)	
7	Ivan Rogač		18/06/92	M	6	(4)	
24	Danilo Sekulić		18/04/90	M	12	(5)	
22	Jovan Stojanović		21/04/92	A	10	(14)	2
32	Janko Tumbasević	MNE	14/01/85	M	21	(2)	1
2	Jovica Vasilić		07/08/90	D	12	(1)	
9	Lazar Veselinović		04/08/86	A	14		8
1	Srdjan Žakula		22/03/79	G	10		
17	Marko Živković		17/05/94	D	2	(1)	

FK Voždovac

1912 • Bojan Majić (5,172) •
fkvozdovac.rs
**Coach: Zoran Milinković;
(25/03/15) Bratislav Živković**

2014

10/08	h	Partizan	L	1-3	Tripković
16/08	a	Donji Srem	L	0-1	
23/08	h	Rad	L	1-6	Andjelković
30/08	h	Čukarički	L	0-2	
13/09	h	Radnički 1923	L	0-1	
20/09	a	OFK Beograd	L	0-1	
29/09	h	Mladost	W	2-0	Odita, Babović
04/10	a	Crvena zvezda	D	2-2	Injac, Beljić
18/10	h	Jagodina	W	1-0	Babović
25/10	a	Vojvodina	L	0-3	
02/11	h	Spartak	D	1-1	Babović
08/11	a	Napredak	W	2-0	Džugurdić, Škerjanc
29/11	a	Borac	W		
07/12	h	Radnički Niš	W	2-1	Nikolić, Babović (p)
10/12	h	Novi Pazar	D	0-0	

2015

21/02	a	Partizan	D	3-3	Škerjanc, Odita, Džugurdić
28/02	h	Donji Srem	L	0-1	
07/03	a	Rad	L	0-2	
14/03	h	Čukarički	D	0-0	
21/03	a	Radnički 1923	L	1-2	Karaklajić
04/04	h	OFK Beograd	L	0-2	
13/04	a	Mladost	L	2-3	Odita 2
18/04	h	Crvena zvezda	L	0-1	
25/04	a	Jagodina	W	2-1	Škerjanc, Sikimić
29/04	h	Vojvodina	W	1-0	Sindjić
03/05	a	Spartak	W	1-0	Odita
09/05	h	Napredak	W	1-0	M Pavlović
13/05	a	Novi Pazar	L	0-1	
16/05	h	Borac	W	1-0	Adamović
24/05	a	Radnički Niš	D	0-0	

No	Name	Nat	DoB	Pos	Aps	(s)	Gls
71	Marko Adamović		11/03/91	M	11	(8)	1
99	Dragoljub Andjelković		14/04/93	A	1	(2)	1
8	Stefan Babović		07/01/87	M	10		4
7	Nikola Beljić		14/05/83	M	11		1
1	Darko Božović	MNE	09/08/78	G	1	(1)	
9	Ognjan Damnjanović		20/04/85	A	3	(1)	
7	Dejan Djermanovič	SVN	17/06/88	A	1	(6)	
50	Miloš Džugurdić		02/12/92	A	7	(12)	2
11	Nenad Injac		04/09/85	A	7	(1)	1
41	Saša Ivković		13/05/93	D	8		
8	Milan Jokić		21/03/95	M	6	(3)	
11	Nikola Karaklajić		02/05/95	M	6		1
3	Tome Kitanovski	MKD	21/05/92	D	20	(1)	
20	Anej Lovrečič	SVN	10/05/87	M	6	(5)	
52	Zoran Marušić		29/11/83	D	1	(1)	
21	Miloš Mihajlov		15/12/82	D	13		
22	Marko Milošević		02/07/91	G	2		
29	Danilo Nikolić		29/07/83	D	16	(4)	1
23	Miloš Obradović		30/03/87	D	4		
18	Obiora Odita	NGA	14/05/83	A	19	(2)	5
55	Dušan Pantelić		15/04/93	M	3	(1)	
21	Deni Pavlović		09/01/93	D	9		
25	Miloš Pavlović		27/11/83	M	23		1
22	Aleksandar Petrović		01/02/85	M	3	(2)	
6	Todor Petrović		18/08/94	M	20	(1)	
5	Miloš Radivojević		04/05/90	D	12		
16	Nenad Radonjić		19/03/96	A		(1)	
24	Danilo Sekulić		18/04/90	M	1	(2)	
9	Predrag Sikimić		29/08/82	A	8	(2)	1
4	Uroš Sindjić		19/01/86	M	12	(3)	1
2	Predrag Stanimirović		09/09/95	D	8	(2)	
15	Danijel Stojković		14/08/90	D	13	(3)	
5	Miodrag Stošić		25/02/81	D	4		
27	Nemanja Supić	BIH	12/01/82	G	27		
14	Davor Škerjanc	SVN	07/01/86	A	20	(4)	3
10	Stefan Tripković		19/09/94	M	2	(4)	1
77	Nemanja Zlatković		21/08/88	M	12		

Top goalscorers

15	Patrick Eze Friday (Mladost)	
14	Petar Škuletić (Partizan)	
11	Mijat Gaćinović (Vojvodina)	
10	Darko Lazović (Crvena zvezda)	
	Igor Matić (Čukarički)	
	Mirko Ivanić (Vojvodina)	
9	Nikola Stojiljković (Čukarički)	
	Danko Lazović (Partizan)	
8	Slavoljub Srnić (Čukarički)	
	Ivica Jovanović (OFK Beograd)	
	Petar Jelić (Rad)	
	Lazar Veselinović (Vojvodina)	

Promoted clubs

FK Radnik Surdulica

1926 • Gradski stadion (3,500) • fkradnik.org
Coach: Mladen Milinković

FK Javor

1912 • Kraj Moravice (4,000) • fkjavor.com
**Coach: Slavenko Kuzeljević;
(27/04/15) Aleksandar Janjić**

FK Metalac

1961 • Gradski stadion kraj Despotovice (4,500)
• fkmetalac.rs
**Coach: Vladica Petrović;
(14/05/15) Nenad Vanić**

Second level final table 2014/15

		Pld	W	D	L	F	A	Pts
1	FK Radnik Surdulica	30	19	7	4	41	14	64
2	FK Javor	30	17	10	3	47	19	61
3	FK Metalac	30	16	7	7	43	29	55
4	FK Bačka	30	14	6	10	37	30	48
5	FK Indjija	30	14	4	12	39	31	46
6	FK Sindjelić	30	12	4	14	40	39	40
7	FK Proleter Novi Sad	30	11	7	12	33	32	40
8	FK Sloga Petrovac	30	10	10	10	37	37	40
9	FK Bežanija	30	11	7	12	25	27	40
10	FK BSK Borča	30	8	12	31	34	38	
11	FK Kolubara	30	9	11	10	34	43	38
12	FK Sloboda Užice	30	8	12	10	24	28	36
13	FK Moravac Orion	30	10	5	15	32	41	35
14	FK Jedinstvo Putevi	30	7	8	15	24	35	29
15	FK Sloga Kraljevo	30	8	2	20	21	56	26
16	FK Mačva	30	6	10	15	23	36	25

Promotion/Relegation play-offs

(30/05/15 & 03/06/15)
Metalac 3-1 Napredak
Napredak 1-1 Metalac
(Metalac 4-2)

DOMESTIC CUP

Kup Srbije 2014/15

FIRST ROUND

(24/09/14)
Bežanija 0-1 Partizan
Crvena zvezda 1-0 Borac
Čukarički 3-2 Mladost
Dorćol 0-1 Radnički 1923
Indjija 2-1 Javor
Jagodina 4-0 BSK Borča
Jedinstvo Putevi 0-3 Rad
Moravac Orion 0-1 Radnički Niš
Napredak 0-0 Metalac (2-4 on pens)
Proleter 0-0 Donji Srem (4-3 on pens)
Semendria 1924 0-2 OFK Beograd
Sloboda 1-1 Sindjelić Beograd (4-3 on pens)
Sloga Petrovac 1-0 Novi Pazar
Spartak 1-0 Radnik
Trepča 0-1 Vojvodina
Voždovac 3-2 Sloga Kraljevo

SECOND ROUND

(29/10/14)
Metalac 0-0 Voždovac (4-5 on pens)
Rad 1-0 Crvena zvezda
Radnički 1923 0-3 Jagodina
Radnički Niš 0-0 Indjija (4-1 on pens)
Spartak 2-0 Proleter
Vojvodina 1-0 Sloboda

(19/11/14)
OFK Beograd 1-2 Čukarički
Partizan 3-0 Sloga Petrovac

QUARTER-FINALS

(03/12/14)
Čukarički 2-1 Vojvodina (Regan 10, Bojić 47;
Poletanović 13)

Rad 0-1 Partizan (Škuletić 45p)

Radnički Niš 0-1 Jagodina (Djurić 31)

Voždovac 2-1 Spartak (Babović 15, Škerjanc 90;
Ilić 90)

SEMI-FINALS

(18/03/15 & 08/04/15)
Čukarički 2-0 Voždovac (Mirosavljević 15, 39)
Voždovac 1-4 Čukarički (Zlatković 13p; Ostojić 6,
S Srnić 64, Stojiljković 74, Mandić 90)
(Čukarički 6-1)

Partizan 3-0 Jagodina (Grbić 3, A Živković 44,
Brašanac 90)
Jagodina 0-2 Partizan (Šaponjić 3, A Živković 27)
(Partizan 5-0)

FINAL

(20/05/15)
Rajko Mitić, Belgrade
FK ČUKARIČKI 1 (S Srnić 39)
FK PARTIZAN 0
Referee: Glodjović
ČUKARIČKI: Stevanović, Stojković, Rendulić,
Ostojić, Brežančić, Regan (Todorović 65), D Srnić,
Matić (A Pavlović 83), Bojić, S Srnić (Mandić 90),
Stojiljković
PARTIZAN: Ž Živković, Bandalovski, Balažič, Ilić,
Volkov (Vulićević 67), Brašanac, Drinčić, Babović,
A Živković, Ilić (Kojić 59), Grbić (Ninković 70)

SLOVAKIA
Slovenský futbalový zväz (SFZ)

Address	Trnavská 100/II	**President**	Ján Kováčik
	SK-821 01 Bratislava	**General secretary**	Jozef Kliment
Tel	+421 2 4820 6000	**Media officer**	Juraj Čurný
Fax	+421 2 4820 6099	**Year of formation**	1938
E-mail	office@futbalsfz.sk		
Website	futbalsfz.sk		

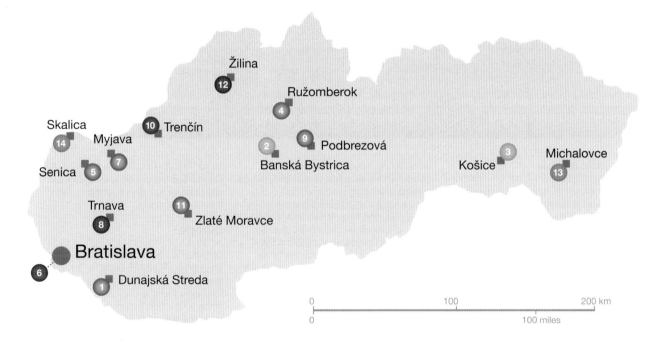

1. LIGA CLUBS

 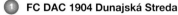 **1** FC DAC 1904 Dunajská Streda

  **2** FK Dukla Banská Bystrica

 3 MFK Košice

 4 MFK Ružomberok

 5 FK Senica

 6 ŠK Slovan Bratislava

 7 TJ Spartak Myjava

 8 FC Spartak Trnava

 9 ŽP Šport Podbrezová

 10 FK AS Trenčín

 11 FC ViOn Zlaté Moravce

 12 MŠK Žilina

PROMOTED CLUBS

  **13** MFK Zemplín Michalovce

  14 MFK Skalica

KEY:

● – UEFA Champions League

● – UEFA Europa League

● – Promoted

● – Relegated

Two trophies for Trenčín

MAJSTER FORTUNA LIGY

Without a trophy to their name going into the 2014/15 season, FK AS Trenčín ended it with not one but two, lifting the Slovakian Cup after a penalty shoot-out victory over FK Senica and then the 1. Liga title following a season-long duel with MŠK Žilina.

While Martin Ševela's attack-minded team took the domestic plaudits and prizes, Ján Kozák's Slovakia side were the talk of the nation with their extraordinary success on the international front, their first six UEFA EURO 2016 qualifiers yielding a maximum 18 points, three of them from a famous win against Spain.

| Glorious double success for unheralded provincials | Mid-season league leaders Žilina overhauled in spring | Season of perfection for Kozák's national team |

Domestic league

It was widely anticipated that defending champions ŠK Slovan Bratislava would complete a 1. Liga hat-trick in 2014/15, but after kicking off with four straight wins under their illustrious new coach, ex-Czech Republic boss František Straka, they went to pieces. Before long, Straka was gone, replaced by another former Czech Republic coach Jozef Chovanec, but it was not until late in the season, under Dušan Tittel, that Slovan found any consistent form, six successive victories enabling them to close the campaign in third place.

With Slovan out of the way, FC Spartak Trnava struggling for points and 2013/14 cup winners MFK Košice ailing financially, the title race developed into a two-way tussle between Trenčín, runners-up under Ševela in 2013/14, and their local rivals Žilina, who had finished an ugly ninth the previous season under Ševela's predecessor, Adrian Guľa, but decided to stick with him for the new campaign. It was a show of faith that looked set to be rewarded when, after a 13-match unbeaten run, the six-time champions entered the winter break with a three-point lead, Trenčín having surrendered their early advantage by picking up just one point in five away fixtures.

In the spring, however, Ševela's men cured their travel sickness and became an irresistible winning machine. Ten three-pointers on the trot powered them past Žilina, and when their rivals lost 2-1 at home to Slovan in round 31, the race was over. A home defeat by Žilina three days later was a disappointing way for Trenčín to toast the club's first league title, but it could not spoil the celebration party.

Trenčín played an enticing brand of football but they were short of stars. While 19 of their players scored at least once, none reached double figures, although winger Gino van Kessel poached six very handy goals after returning to the club in mid-season. The 1. Liga's golden boot was shared by Žilina's Croatian striker Matej Jelić and Senica's Czech hitman Jan Kalabiška, who both finished with 19 goals.

Domestic cup

Van Kessel and Kalabiška were both on target in extra time of the Slovakian Cup final as Trenčín and Senica matched each other in a May Day spectacular that ended 2-2 after 120 minutes. Both clubs were seeking a first victory in the competition, and it was a contest that did not deserve a loser, but penalty shoot-outs offer no sympathy and it was Trenčín, dramatic quarter-final conquerors of Slovan, who

came through to claim the trophy, Milan Rundić scoring the decisive spot-kick after keeper Igor Šemrinec had made three crucial saves.

Europe

Defeated in the UEFA Champions League play-offs by FC BATE Borisov, Slovan switched to the UEFA Europa League, but they were found badly wanting in the group stage, their poor domestic form mirrored by a total eclipse in Europe as they lost all six games, conceding a record 20 goals and scoring just once themselves.

National team

A first ever qualification for the UEFA European Championship appeared to be Slovakia's prize-in-waiting as they stormed to victory in each of their opening six qualifiers. It was an astonishing performance by Kozák and his widely-scattered band of expatriates, the highlights coming at the start with a brilliant 1-0 win in Ukraine and an even more majestic 2-1 triumph in Zilina against holders Spain. As if any further proof were needed of Slovakia's sudden resurgence, they also won all three of their friendly fixtures, including one in March against their Czech Republic neighbours in which 20-year-old rising star Ondrej Duda scored the only goal on his first start.

DOMESTIC SEASON AT A GLANCE

1. Liga 2014/15 final table

		Pld	Home					Away					Total					Pts
			W	D	L	F	A	W	D	L	F	A	W	D	L	F	A	
1	**FK AS Trenčín**	**33**	**15**	**1**	**1**	**41**	**12**	**8**	**4**	**4**	**26**	**16**	**23**	**5**	**5**	**67**	**28**	**74**
2	MŠK Žilina	33	11	3	2	38	11	9	6	2	30	14	20	9	4	68	25	69
3	ŠK Slovan Bratislava	33	11	1	5	27	17	7	2	7	22	25	18	3	12	49	42	57
4	FC Spartak Trnava	33	14	2	1	44	13	2	6	8	9	18	16	8	9	53	31	56
5	FK Senica	33	10	5	2	31	18	2	6	8	21	32	12	11	10	52	50	47
6	MFK Košice	33	9	4	4	28	15	2	4	10	15	33	11	8	14	43	48	41
7	MFK Ružomberok	33	7	7	3	22	14	3	3	10	19	31	10	10	13	41	45	40
8	FC DAC 1904 Dunajská Streda	33	6	7	3	18	14	3	5	9	14	30	9	12	12	32	44	39
9	TJ Spartak Myjava	33	8	3	5	26	27	3	3	11	12	26	11	6	16	38	53	39
10	FC ViOn Zlaté Moravce	33	5	5	6	15	21	3	3	11	12	33	8	8	17	27	54	32
11	ŽP Šport Podbrezová	33	6	5	5	23	19	1	3	13	9	35	7	8	18	32	54	29
12	FK Dukla Banská Bystrica	33	2	6	8	13	24	2	4	11	16	33	4	10	19	29	57	22

European qualification 2015/16

Champion/Cup winner: FK AS Trenčín (second qualifying round)

MŠK Žilina (first qualifying round)
ŠK Slovan Bratislava (first qualifying round)
FC Spartak Trnava (first qualifying round)

Top scorer   Ján Kalabiška (Senica) & Matej Jelič (Žilina), 19 goals
Relegated clubs   FK Dukla Banská Bystrica, MFK Košice (excluded)
Promoted clubs   MFK Zemplín Michalovce, MFK Skalica
Cup final   FK AS Trenčín 2-2 FK Senica *(aet; 3-2 on pens)*

Team of the season
(3-5-2)

Coach: Ševela *(Trenčín)*

Player of the season

Igor Šemrinec
(FK AS Trenčín)

Singled out by Trenčín boss Martin Ševela as one of his key players, goalkeeper Šemrinec was indeed pivotal to the club's double-winning triumph. Like the team, he was at his best in the spring, conceding just four goals in the 12-match unbeaten run that catapulted Trenčín to the league title and also saving three spot-kicks in the cup final penalty shoot-out success against FK Senica. The 27-year-old earned himself a long-awaited shave at the end of the season after vowing not to touch a razor until the title was won.

Newcomer of the season

Matúš Bero
(FK AS Trenčín)

A graduate of Trenčín's academy, Bero was kept on the bench for much of the first part of the season, but the 19-year-old midfielder emerged in the spring to become a major contributor to the club's league and cup triumphs. Sharp and intuitive, he scored five goals in the 1. Liga, including two in a 3-1 win at defending champions ŠK Slovan Bratislava, and also provoked a couple of penalties. He also started the cup final against FK Senica and became a member of Pavel Hapal's Slovakian Under-21 side.

Šemrinec *(Trenčín)*

Škriniar *(Žilina)* — Saláta *(Dunajská Streda/Slovan)* — Čonka *(Trnava)*

Čmelík *(Žilina)* — Pečovský *(Žilina)* — Vlasko *(Trnava)* — Lobotka *(Trenčín)* — Mihalík *(Žilina)*

Jelič *(Žilina)* — Kalabiška *(Senica)*

SLOVAKIA

NATIONAL TEAM

International tournament appearances

FIFA World Cup (1) 2010 (2nd round)

Top five all-time caps

Miroslav Karhan (107); Róbert Vittek (80); **Marek Hamšík** (78); **Ján Ďurica** (74); **Martin Škrtel** (73)

Top five all-time goals

Róbert Vittek (23); Szilárd Németh (22); **Marek Hamšík** (15); Miroslav Karhan & Marek Mintál (14)

Results 2014/15

04/09/14	Malta	H	Zilina	W	1-0	Nemec (43)
08/09/14	Ukraine (ECQ)	A	Kyiv	W	1-0	Mak (17)
09/10/14	Spain (ECQ)	H	Zilina	W	2-1	Kucka (17), Stoch (87)
12/10/14	Belarus (ECQ)	A	Borisov	W	3-1	Hamšík (65, 84), Šesták (90+1)
15/11/14	FYR Macedonia (ECQ)	A	Skopje	W	2-0	Kucka (25), Nemec (38)
18/11/14	Finland	H	Zilina	W	2-1	Hološko (1), Hamšík (7)
27/03/15	Luxembourg (ECQ)	H	Zilina	W	3-0	Nemec (10), Weiss (21), Pekarík (40)
31/03/15	Czech Republic	H	Zilina	W	1-0	Duda (49)
14/06/15	FYR Macedonia (ECQ)	H	Zilina	W	2-1	Saláta (8), Hamšík (38)

Appearances 2014/15

Coach: Ján Kozák	17/04/54		Mlt	UKR	ESP	BLR	MKD	Fin	LUX	Cze	MKD	Caps	Goals
Matúš Kozáčik	27/12/83	Plzeň (CZE)	G	G	G	G	G		G		G	10	-
Peter Pekarík	30/10/86	Hertha (GER)	D	D	D	D	D46		D	D	D	61	2
Norbert Gyömbér	03/07/92	Catania (ITA)	D	D	M	D						7	-
Ján Ďurica	10/12/81	Lokomotiv Moskva (RUS)	D	D	D	D	D	D	D	s46		74	4
Tomáš Hubočan	17/09/85	Dinamo Moskva (RUS)	D73	D	D		D	D	D	D	D	38	-
Viktor Pečovský	24/05/83	Žilina	M	M	M	M	M	M	M	s82	M	25	1
Filip Kiss	13/10/90	Ross County (SCO)	M85	s63	s83	s86	s55	s59				8	-
Vladimír Weiss	30/11/89	Lekhwiya (QAT)	M62	M67	M54	M80	M78	s25	M71	M60	M	44	4
Marek Hamšík	27/07/87	Napoli (ITA)	M73	M	A	M	M	M59	M	A46	M80	78	15
Miroslav Stoch	19/10/89	Al-Ain (UAE)	M62	s67	s61	s80	M	s80	M80			49	5
Adam Nemec	02/09/85	Union Berlin (GER)/New York City (USA)	A62	A63		A	A		A		A84	16	3
Róbert Mak	08/03/91	PAOK (GRE)	s62	M92	M61	M62		M25	s71	M60	M	18	3
Stanislav Šesták	16/12/82	Bochum (GER)	s62		s62			M80	s80	s60		60	13
Jakub Sylvestr	02/02/89	Nürnberg (GER)	s62									6	-
Michal Breznaník	16/12/85	Sparta Praha (CZE)	s73									10	-
Michal Ďuriš	01/06/88	Mladá Boleslav (CZE)	s73	s92	s54		s78	s59		s60		17	-
Karim Guédé	07/01/85	Freiburg (GER)	s85									14	-
Juraj Kucka	26/02/87	Genoa (ITA)		M	M83	M86	M55	M59			M73	41	4
Martin Škrtel	15/12/84	Liverpool (ENG)			D	D	D	D	D	D46	D	73	5
Dušan Švento	01/08/85	Köln (GER)				s46	D					31	1
Ján Mucha	05/12/82	Krylya Sovetov (RUS)/Arsenal Tula (RUS)						G		G		43	-
Patrik Hrošovský	22/04/92	Plzeň (CZE)						M59	s59	M	s73	4	-
Filip Hološko	17/01/84	Rizespor (TUR)						A59			s84	65	8
Ondrej Duda	05/12/94	Legia (POL)						s59	M82	s80		3	1
Kornel Saláta	24/01/85	Slovan Bratislava								D46	D	31	2
Ján Greguš	29/01/91	Jablonec (CZE)								M		1	-
Martin Jakubko	26/02/80	Amkar (RUS)								s46		37	9
Ľubomír Michalík	13/08/83	Dunajská Streda								s46		8	2

EUROPE

ŠK Slovan Bratislava

CHAMPIONS LEAGUE

Second qualifying round - The New Saints FC (WAL)
H 1-0 *Čikoš (52)*
Perniš, Niňaj, Čikoš, Fořt, Halenár (Grendel 89), Žofčák (Peltier 70), Milinković, Jablonský, Soumah, Hudák, Lásik. Coach: František Straka (CZE)
A 2-0 *Milinković (74, 89)*
Perniš, Niňaj, Čikoš, Fořt, Grendel (Jakúbek 90), Žofčák (Mészáros 66), Milinković, Jablonský, Soumah (Halenár 69), Hudák, Lásik. Coach: František Straka (CZE)

Third qualifying round - FC Sheriff (MDA)
H 2-1 *Žofčák (42p), Mészáros (85)*
Perniš, Niňaj, Čikoš, Fořt (Peltier 80), Grendel, Žofčák (Mészáros 58), Milinković, Jablonský, Soumah (Halenár 65), Hudák, Lásik. Coach: František Straka (CZE)
Red card: Lásik 61
A 0-0
Perniš, Niňaj, Čikoš, Fořt (Vittek 59), Grendel, Žofčák, Milinković, Jablonský, Soumah (Jakúbek 90+2), Kolčák (Halenár 85), Hudák. Coach: František Straka (CZE)

Play-offs - FC BATE Borisov (BLR)
H 1-1 *Vittek (80)*
Perniš, Čikoš, Fořt (Vittek 72), Grendel, Žofčák (Halenár 59), Milinković, Jablonský, Gorosito, Štefánik (Lásik 46), Soumah, Hudák. Coach: František Straka (CZE)
A 0-3
Perniš, Čikoš, Fořt (Vittek 62), Grendel (Peltier 83), Halenár, Žofčák (Štefánik 46), Jablonský, Gorosito, Soumah, Kolčák, Hudák. Coach: František Straka (CZE)
Red card: Soumah 79

EUROPA LEAGUE

Group I
Match 1 - BSC Young Boys (SUI)
A 0-5
Perniš, Čikoš, Kubík, Grendel (Milinković 63), Halenár (Jakúbek 76), Mészáros (Žofčák 71), Gorosito, Kolčák, Hudák, Peltier, Lásik. Coach: František Straka (CZE)
Match 2 - SSC Napoli (ITA)
H 0-2
Perniš, Ninaj, Čikoš, Kubík (Žofčák 71), Grendel (Milinković 46), Halenár, Jablonský, Gorosito, Soumah, Peltier, Lásik (Kolčák 85). Coach: František Straka (CZE)
Match 3 - AC Sparta Praha (CZE)
H 0-3
Perniš, Čikoš, Grendel (Hudák 76), Halenár (Fořt 79), Žofčák, Jablonský (Kubík 59), Gorosito, Bagayoko, Soumah, Kolčák, Lásik. Coach: Jozef Chovanec (CZE)
Match 4 - AC Sparta Praha (CZE)
A 0-4
Perniš, Ninaj, Čikoš, Kubík (Vittek 73), Grendel (Štefánik 82), Žofčák, Milinković, Bagayoko, Kolčák, Peltier (Soumah 46), Lásik. Coach: Jozef Chovanec (CZE)

Match 5 - BSC Young Boys (SUI)
H 1-3 *Soumah (11)*
Perniš, Čikoš, Kubík (Milinković 82), Grendel (Žofčák 80), Halenár, Gorosito, Štefánik, Soumah, Kolčák, Hudák, Peltier. Coach: Jozef Chovanec (CZE)
Match 6 - SSC Napoli (ITA)
A 0-3
Perniš, Čikoš, Kubík (Gašparovič 87), Žofčák (Duriš 62), Milinković (Halenár 72), Jablonský, Gorosito, Štefánik, Kolčák, Hudák, Peltier. Coach: Jozef Chovanec (CZE)

MFK Košice

EUROPA LEAGUE

Second qualifying round - FC Slovan Liberec (CZE)
H 0-1
Tofiloski, Sekulič, Pačinda (Diaby 80), Šinglár (Skvašík 90), Korijkov, Kavka, Viazanko (Ostojić 85), Redžič, Bukata, Novák, Bašista. Coach: Radoslav Látal (CZE)
A 0-3
Tofiloski, Sekulič, Ostojić, Skvašík (Haskić 68), Šinglár (Novák 77), Diaby, Korijkov, Kavka, Viazanko (Pačinda 67), Bukata, Bašista. Coach: Radoslav Látal (CZE)

FK AS Trenčín

EUROPA LEAGUE

Second qualifying round - FK Vojvodina (SRB)
H 4-0 *Simon (20, 53, 60), Jairo (72)*
Volešák, Mišák (Hajradinović 69), Baéz (Rundić 85), Kubík, Jairo (Mondek 79), Holúbek, Čögley, Ramón, Simon, Lobotka, Kleščík. Coach: Martin Ševela (SVK)
A 0-3
Volešák, Rundić, Mišák (Madu 46), Kubík (Mondek 55), Jairo (Hajradinović 80), Holúbek, Čögley, Ramón, Simon, Lobotka, Kleščík. Coach: Martin Ševela (SVK)

Third qualifying round - Hull City AFC (ENG)
H 0-0
Volešák, Rundić, Mišák (Mondek 83), Kubík (Malec 67), Holúbek, Čögley, Ramón, Hajradinović (Opatovský 87), Simon, Lobotka, Kleščík. Coach: Martin Ševela (SVK)
A 1-2 *Malec (2)*
Volešák, Malec, Mišák (Mondek 82), Kubík, Holúbek, Čögley, Ramón, Hajradinović (Opatovský 74), Simon (Rundić 90+1), Lobotka, Kleščík. Coach: Martin Ševela (SVK)

FC Spartak Trnava

EUROPA LEAGUE

First qualifying round - Hibernians FC (MLT)
A 4-2 *Sabo (11p, 13), Vlasko (36), Mikinič (88)*
Strapák, Siva (Bortel 58), Janečka, Mikovič (Mikinič 74), Vlasko, Chovanec, Tóth, Čonka, Sabo, Kuzma, Špalek (Schranz 55). Coach: Juraj Jarábek (SVK)
H 5-0 *Mikovič (12), Sabo (21, 90+2), Vlasko (28), Mikinič (85)*
Strapák, Janečka, Mikovič (Mikinič 64), Vlasko, Chovanec, Bortel, Tóth (Banovič 46), Čonka, Sabo, Schranz (Špalek 59), Kuzma. Coach: Juraj Jarábek (SVK)

Second qualifying round - FC Zestafoni (GEO)
A 0-0
Rusov, Janečka, Mikovič, Vlasko (Špalek 78), Chovanec (Siva 87), Bortel, Tóth, Čonka, Sabo, Schranz (Casado 73), Kuzma. Coach: Juraj Jarábek (SVK)
H 3-0 *Janečka (4, 43), Sabo (60p)*
Rusov, Siva, Janečka (Chovanec 84), Mikovič (Mikinič 80), Vlasko, Bortel, Casado, Tóth, Čonka, Sabo, Schranz (Špalek 76). Coach: Juraj Jarábek (SVK)

Third qualifying round - Saint Johnstone FC (SCO)
A 2-1 *Schranz (34, 63)*
Rusov, Siva, Janečka, Mikovič (Vyskočil 61), Vlasko (Chovanec 78), Bortel, Casado, Tóth, Čonka, Sabo, Schranz (Mikinič 89). Coach: Juraj Jarábek (SVK)
H 1-1 *Mikovič (82)*
Rusov, Siva, Janečka, Mikovič (Špalek 90+3), Vlasko (Vyskočil 59), Bortel, Casado, Tóth, Čonka, Sabo, Schranz (Grabež 86). Coach: Juraj Jarábek (SVK)

Play-offs - FC Zürich (SUI)
H 1-3 *Vlasko (14p)*
Rusov, Janečka, Vlasko (Vyskočil 85), Bortel, Casado, Tóth, Čonka, Jendrišek, Schranz (Špalek 72), Kuzma, Cléber (Chovanec 76). Coach: Juraj Jarábek (SVK)
A 1-1 *Špalek (90+2)*
Rusov, Siva, Janečka, Mikovič, Bortel (Soungole 74), Casado, Tóth, Čonka, Jendrišek, Schranz (Kuzma 51), Cléber (Špalek 56). Coach: Juraj Jarábek (SVK)

DOMESTIC LEAGUE CLUB-BY-CLUB

FC DAC 1904 Dunajská Streda

1904 • DAC (6,100) • fcdac.sk
Major honours
Czechoslovakian Cup (1) 1987
Coach: Mikuláš Radványi;
(17/01/15) Tomislav Marić (CRO)

2014

12/07	a Trenčín	L 1-2	Brašeň
20/07	h Spartak Trnava	D 0-0	
26/07	a Ružomberok	D 1-1	Sabler
02/08	h Košice	W 3-1	Ujlaky, Sabler, Jurčo
09/08	a Senica	L 1-2	Jurčo
16/08	h Spartak Myjava	W 1-0	Černák
23/08	a Banská Bystrica	D 0-0	
29/08	h Žilina	D 2-2	Jurčo, Krišto
13/09	a Zlaté Moravce	D 1-1	Saláta
16/09	a Podbrezová	L 0-3	
21/09	h Slovan	D 1-1	Szabó (p)
27/09	h Trenčín	W 3-2	Szabó 2 (1p), Saláta
04/10	a Spartak Trnava	L 1-3	Štepanovský
18/10	h Ružomberok	L 1-2	Szarka
25/10	a Košice	D 1-1	Sabler
01/11	h Senica	W 3-0	og (Pavlík), Štepanovský, Černák
07/11	a Spartak Myjava	L 1-3	Jurčo
22/11	h Banská Bystrica	D 0-0	
30/11	a Žilina	L 1-3	Szarka

2015

01/03	h Zlaté Moravce	D 1-1	Ljubičić
07/03	h Podbrezová	W 1-0	Michalík
15/03	a Slovan	W 1-0	Štepanovský
21/03	a Trenčín	L 0-3	
03/04	h Spartak Trnava	L 0-1	
11/04	a Ružomberok	L 1-2	Černák
18/04	h Košice	D 1-1	Horváth
25/04	a Senica	L 0-4	
05/05	h Spartak Myjava	L 1-4	Štepanovský
08/05	a Banská Bystrica	W 1-0	Szarka
15/05	h Žilina	L 0-1	
19/05	a Zlaté Moravce	D 0-0	
23/05	a Podbrezová	W 3-2	Szarka 2, Brašeň
30/05	h Slovan	L 0-3	

No	Name	Nat	DoB	Pos	Aps	(s)	Gls
15	Goran Antunović	SRB	02/03/89	M	1	(6)	
38	Jean Paul Boya	CMR	23/09/84	M		(1)	
21	Jakub Brašeň		02/05/89	M	29	(3)	2
23	Roland Černák		22/07/97	M	6	(14)	3
11	Vojtech Horváth		28/06/94	M	12	(7)	1
29	Pavol Jurčo		12/02/86	A	14	(7)	4
6	Alan Kováč		22/05/93	A	1	(1)	
10	Dario Krišto	CRO	05/03/89	M	23	(1)	1
14	Achile Kwin	CMR	14/01/90	M	14	(4)	
4	Marin Ljubičić	CRO	15/06/88	M	13		1
9	Branislav Ľupták		05/06/91	M	6	(2)	
25	Peter Majerník		31/12/78	D	8	(3)	
5	Ľubomír Michalík		13/08/83	D	13		1
17	Franky Nguekam	CMR	29/06/89	A		(3)	
1	Pavol Penksa		07/12/85	G	14		
22	Andrej Pernecký		16/03/91	G	6		
30	Martin Poláček		02/04/90	G	13		
20	Roman Sabler		04/09/95	A	7	(19)	3
16	Kornel Saláta		24/01/85	D	10		2
8	Pape Sarr	SEN	25/07/91	M	5	(8)	
17	Ivan Sesar	BIH	29/08/89	M	7	(1)	
6	Miroslav Stanić	SRB	11/12/93	M		(2)	
7	Gábor Straka		18/12/81	M	19	(1)	
13	Peter Struhár		17/01/84	D	8	(1)	
28	Otto Szabó		01/03/81	D	25		3
27	Ákos Szarka		24/11/90	A	18	(1)	5
21	Ivan Šnirc		11/06/93	D	5	(1)	
24	Peter Štepanovský		12/01/88	M	21		4
3	Mário Tóth		06/04/95	D	13	(2)	
19	Matúš Turňa		11/05/86	D	30		
12	Erik Ujlaky		13/02/92	M	22	(5)	1

FK Dukla Banská Bystrica

1965 • Na Štiavničkách (7,380) • fkdukla.sk
Major honours
Slovakian Cup (1) 2005
Coach: Norbert Hrnčár;
(09/10/14) Štefan Rusnák

2014

12/07	a Košice	W 2-1	Vajda, Střihavka
19/07	h Senica	D 2-2	Dolný, Rejdovian
26/07	h Spartak Myjava	D 0-0	
02/08	a Podbrezová	L 0-3	
09/08	h Žilina	D 0-0	
15/08	a Zlaté Moravce	D 1-1	Střihavka
23/08	h Dunajská Streda	D 0-0	
31/08	a Slovan	L 1-3	Střihavka
30/09	h Trenčín	L 1-3	Vajda (p)
16/09	a Spartak Trnava	L 2-5	Mazan 2
20/09	h Ružomberok	W 3-1	Šovčík, Mazan, Střihavka
27/09	h Košice	D 0-0	
03/10	a Senica	L 2-3	Peňaška, Ľupták
18/10	a Spartak Myjava	L 1-3	Mazan
24/10	h Podbrezová	D 3-3	og (Minčič), Polievka, Vajda
02/11	a Žilina	L 0-2	
08/11	h Zlaté Moravce	W 2-0	Vajda (p), Dolný
22/11	a Dunajská Streda	D 0-0	
30/11	h Slovan	L 0-1	

2015

28/02	a Trenčín	L 0-2	
06/03	h Spartak Trnava	D 1-1	Vajda (p)
14/03	a Ružomberok	D 1-1	Kapor
21/03	a Košice	L 1-2	Vajda
04/04	h Senica	L 0-4	
12/04	a Spartak Myjava	L 2-3	Vajda, Marinkovic
18/04	a Podbrezová	L 1-3	Vajda (p)
24/04	h Žilina	L 0-3	
05/05	a Zlaté Moravce	W 1-0	Rejdovian
08/05	h Dunajská Streda	L 0-1	
16/05	a Slovan	L 0-1	
19/05	h Trenčín	L 0-1	
23/05	a Spartak Trnava	L 1-3	Rejdovian
30/05	h Ružomberok	L 1-2	Šovčík

No	Name	Nat	DoB	Pos	Aps	(s)	Gls
15	Jozef Adámik		10/04/85	D	8		
7	Maroš Balko		16/09/95	A	1	(10)	
2	Patrik Banovič		13/11/91	D	6		
13	Peter Boroš		17/02/80	G	29		
77	Viktor Budinský		09/05/93	G	4		
14	Marco De Vito	CRO	14/01/91	D	21	(6)	
8	Jozef Dolný		13/05/92	A	14	(3)	2
1	Ján Ďurčo		25/02/88	G		(1)	
29	Tomáš Fajčík		21/05/95	M		(1)	
23	Michal Faško		24/08/94	M	17	(5)	
3	Miroslav Gálik		24/07/90	D	8	(6)	
28	Marián Had		16/09/82	D	14		
26	Erik Hric		24/09/97	M	2	(3)	
18	Milovan Kapor	CAN	05/08/91	D	13		1
3	Šimon Kupec		11/02/96	D	14	(6)	
22	Peter Lipták		07/09/89	M	10	(1)	
30	Branislav Ľupták		05/06/91	D	19		1
19	Stefan Marinkovic	SUI	20/02/94	D		(4)	1
11	Peter Mazan		13/05/90	M	11		4
12	Miroslav Neušel		05/02/96	D	3		
16	Michal Peňaška		30/08/86	M	14	(2)	1
17	Róbert Polievka		09/06/96	A	16	(8)	1
24	Jozef Rejdovian		18/03/91	M	12	(2)	3
11	Saša Savić	SRB	05/02/84	D	28	(2)	
29	Mouhamadou Seye	SEN	10/10/88	A	1	(5)	
21	Gabriel Snitka		14/08/85	M	8	(5)	
15	David Střihavka	CZE	04/03/83	A	12	(1)	4
9	Marek Šovčík		08/01/93	A	17	(15)	2
10	Nicolas Šumský	CZE	13/12/93	M	10	(5)	
27	Patrik Vajda		20/03/89	D	30		8
33	Ľubomír Wilwéber		11/09/92	M	14		
9	Petr Wojnar	CZE	12/01/89	M	7	(4)	

MFK Košice

2005 • Lokomotívy v Čermeli (4,817) • mfkkosice.sk
Major honours
Slovakian League (2) 1997, 1998 (as 1. FC Košice);
Slovakian Cup (2) 2009, 2014
Coach: Radoslav Látal (CZE);
(30/11/14) Marek Fabuľa

2014

12/07	h Banská Bystrica	L 1-2	Skvašík
20/07	a Žilina	L 1-4	Diaby
27/07	h Zlaté Moravce	L 1-3	Haskić
02/08	a Dunajská Streda	L 1-3	Pačinda
10/08	h Slovan	L 1-2	Viazanko
17/08	a Trenčín	L 2-4	Haskić 2
24/08	h Spartak Trnava	W 2-0	Sekulić, Skvašík
30/08	a Ružomberok	D 1-1	Novák
13/09	h Podbrezová	W 3-0	Viazanko, Škutka, Novák
16/09	h Senica	D 0-0	
20/09	a Spartak Myjava	W 2-0	Haskić 2
27/09	a Banská Bystrica	W 2-0	Haskić, Škutka
04/10	h Žilina	D 1-1	Škutka
18/10	a Zlaté Moravce	L 0-3	
25/10	h Dunajská Streda	D 1-1	Novák
02/11	a Slovan	L 0-3	
08/11	h Trenčín	W 2-0	Sekulić, Novák (p)
22/11	h Spartak Trnava	L 1-3	Diaby
29/11	a Ružomberok	W 2-1	Diaby, Haskić

2015

28/02	a Podbrezová	D 1-1	Pačinda
06/03	a Senica	L 1-3	Novák
14/03	h Spartak Myjava	W 2-0	Huk, Dimun
21/03	h Banská Bystrica	D 1-1	Diaby, Viazanko
28/03	a Ružomberok	L 0-1	
04/04	a Žilina	L 1-4	Pačinda
11/04	h Zlaté Moravce	L 1-2	Haskić
18/04	a Dunajská Streda	D 1-1	Haskić
25/04	h Slovan	W 2-1	Huk, og (Simović)
05/05	a Trenčín	L 0-1	
08/05	h Spartak Trnava	W 1-0	Viazanko
19/05	h Podbrezová	W 5-0	Huk, Diaby, Haskić, Djordjević, Pačinda
23/05	a Senica	D 1-1	Žebík
30/05	a Spartak Myjava	D 1-1	Viazanko

No	Name	Nat	DoB	Pos	Aps	(s)	Gls
38	Peter Bašista		06/04/85	D	12	(1)	
28	Martin Bukata		02/10/93	M	18	(1)	
11	Oumar Diaby	FRA	07/02/90	A	15	(10)	5
8	Milan Dimun		19/09/96	M	11	(4)	1
24	Lazar Djordjević	SRB	14/07/92	D	12	(2)	1
17	Boris Gáll		27/04/94	M		(11)	
7	Nermin Haskić	BIH	27/06/89	A	28	(2)	10
7	Ladislav Hirjak		16/10/95	D		(1)	
29	Michal Horodník		29/10/96	M		(4)	
9	Tomáš Huk		22/12/94	D	21	(4)	3
31	Michal Jonec		30/07/96	D		(2)	
16	Peter Kavka		20/11/90	M	20		
12	Ľubomír Korijkov		12/01/93	D	18	(3)	
7	Tomáš Kubík		18/03/92	A	2	(3)	
26	Lamine Ndiaye	FRA	19/06/95	D		(1)	
18	Ján Novák		06/03/85	A	12	(8)	5
4	Ivan Ostojić	SRB	26/06/89	D	21	(3)	
9	Erik Pačinda		09/05/89	A	17	(4)	4
22	František Pavúk		21/07/93	D	4	(7)	
22	Ajdin Redžič	SVN	05/12/89	A	2		
1	Matúš Ružinský		15/01/92	G	2	(1)	
2	Boris Sekulić	SRB	21/10/91	D	25		2
2	Jozef Skvašík		08/09/91	M	6	(2)	2
21	Nikola Stijaković	SRB	03/03/89	G	14	(1)	
10	Peter Šinglár		24/07/79	M	24	(3)	
33	Dávid Škutka		25/05/88	A	11	(4)	3
25	Darko Tofiloski	MKD	13/01/86	M	17		
15	Mikuláš Tóth		15/03/88	D	15	(1)	
14	František Vančák		19/07/94	M	1	(3)	
14	Miroslav Viazanko		27/10/81	M	28		5
13	Zoltán Žebík		03/08/92	D	7		1

MFK Ružomberok

1906 • Mestský štadión (4,817) •
mfkruzomberok.sk
Major honours
Slovakian League (1) 2006; Slovakian Cup (1) 2006
Coach: Ladislav Šimčo;
(16/11/14) Ivan Galád

2014

12/07	h	Žilina	L	0-1
19/07	a	Zlaté Moravce	D	1-1 *Turčák*
26/07	h	Dunajská Streda	D	1-1 *Turčák*
01/08	a	Slovan	L	1-2 *Gerát*
10/08	h	Trenčín	D	1-1 *Lupták*
16/08	a	Spartak Trnava	L	0-2
23/08	h	Podbrezová	W	2-0 *Zrelák, Kružliak*
30/08	h	Košice	D	1-1 *Mário Almaský*
13/09	a	Senica	L	0-1
16/09	h	Spartak Myjava	D	2-2 *Nagy, Zrelák*
20/09	a	Banská Bystrica	L	1-3 *og (De Vito)*
28/09	a	Žilina	L	1-5 *Lupták*
04/10	a	Zlaté Moravce	W	3-0 *Janič, Zrelák, Turčák*
18/10	a	Dunajská Streda	D	1-1 *Zrelák*
26/10	h	Slovan	L	1-2 *Vavrík*
30/10	h	Trenčín	L	3-4 *Zrelák 2, Práznovský*
08/11	h	Spartak Trnava	D	0-0
22/11	a	Podbrezová	W	2-1 *Mário Almaský, Nagy*
29/11	a	Košice	L	1-2 *Vavrík*

2015

28/02	h	Senica	W	2-1 *Masaryk 2*
07/03	h	Spartak Myjava	W	2-1 *Rosa, Maslo*
14/03	h	Banská Bystrica	W	1-0 *Masaryk (p)*
22/03	h	Žilina	D	1-1 *Rosa*
28/03	h	Košice	W	1-0 *Lovás*
04/04	a	Zlaté Moravce	W	2-0 *Maslo, Gerát*
11/04	h	Dunajská Streda	W	2-1 *Masaryk, Janič*
18/04	a	Slovan	L	0-1
25/04	a	Trenčín	L	0-1
04/05	h	Spartak Trnava	L	1-2 *Masaryk*
08/05	h	Podbrezová	W	2-0 *Masaryk, og (Podio)*
20/05	a	Senica	L	2-4 *Masaryk 2*
23/05	a	Spartak Myjava	D	1-1 *Boszorád*
30/05	a	Banská Bystrica	W	2-1 *Masaryk, Nagy*

No	Name	Nat	DoB	Pos	Aps	(s)	Gls
7	Mário Almaský		25/06/91	M	20	(8)	2
15	Miroslav Almaský		08/07/94	M		(1)	
20	Richard Bartoš		28/06/92	M	5	(1)	
24	Martin Boszorád		13/11/89	D	14		1
19	Gagik Daghbashyan	ARM	19/10/90	D	4		
4	Milan Ferenčík		02/02/95	M	1	(4)	
8	Tomáš Gerát		15/06/93	M	17	(9)	2
15	Štefan Gerec		10/11/92	M		(3)	
6	Lukáš Greššák		23/01/89	D	2	(1)	
18	Michal Habánek		12/04/94	D	4	(4)	
28	Lukáš Janič		30/12/86	A	17	(6)	2
23	Ivan Kotora		27/06/91	M		(2)	
2	Dominik Kružliak		10/07/96	D	26		1
30	Tomáš Lešňovský		07/10/93	G	4		
22	Erik Liener		02/10/94	M	3	(3)	
12	Andrej Lovás		28/05/91	A	28	(2)	1
14	Lukáš Lupták		28/07/90	M	15	(13)	2
3	Armando Mance	CRO	07/01/92	A	2	(2)	
20	Pavol Masaryk		11/02/80	A	11	(3)	9
3	Ján Maslo		05/02/86	D	12		2
6	Martin Mečiar		23/07/93	M		(1)	
10	Martin Nagy		05/09/90	M	33		3
33	Milorad Nikolić	SRB	06/02/84	G	9		
12	Martin Nosek		26/01/87	D	3	(1)	
16	Lukáš Ondrek		11/07/93	D	9	(2)	
21	Oliver Práznovský		15/02/91	D	24		1
1	Matúš Putnocký		01/11/84	G	6		
22	Antonín Rosa	CZE	12/11/86	D	13		
27	Marek Sapara		31/07/82	M	6		
34	Štefan Senecký		06/01/80	G	1		
35	Matej Šavol		14/04/84	G	13	(1)	
17	Boris Turčák		21/02/93	M	22	(4)	3
25	Róbert Vaniš		29/09/92	D		(2)	
13	Juraj Vavrík		09/02/91	M	11	(13)	2
18	Štefan Zošák		03/04/84	M	10		
9	Adam Zrelák		05/05/94	A	18		6

FK Senica

1921 • Mastský štadión (4,500) • fksenica.eu
Coach: Pavel Hapal (CZE);
(04/01/15) Jozef Kostelník;
(16/05/15) Eduard Pagáč

2014

12/07	h	Spartak Myjava	W	1-0 *J Kosorín*
19/07	a	Banská Bystrica	D	2-2 *J Kosorín, Hlohovský*
25/07	h	Žilina	D	1-1 *Kalabiška*
02/08	a	Zlaté Moravce	D	0-0
09/08	h	Dunajská Streda	W	2-1 *Piroska, Hlohovský*
15/08	a	Slovan	L	1-4 *Kalabiška*
22/08	h	Trenčín	D	1-1 *Kalabiška*
31/08	a	Spartak Trnava	D	2-2 *Pillár 2*
13/09	h	Ružomberok	W	1-0 *Majtán*
16/09	a	Košice	D	0-0
20/09	h	Podbrezová	D	1-1 *Pillár*
26/09	a	Spartak Myjava	W	2-1 *Piroska 2*
03/10	h	Banská Bystrica	W	3-2 *Kalabiška 2, Piroska*
18/10	a	Žilina	D	1-1 *Kalabiška*
25/10	h	Zlaté Moravce	W	2-0 *Kalabiška 2*
01/11	a	Dunajská Streda	L	0-3
09/11	h	Slovan	W	2-1 *Piroska, Kalabiška*
22/11	a	Trenčín	L	1-3 *Piroska*
28/11	h	Spartak Trnava	D	1-1 *Mráz*

2015

28/02	a	Ružomberok	L	1-2 *Dolný*
06/03	h	Košice	W	3-1 *Majtán 2, Hlohovský*
14/03	a	Podbrezová	L	1-2 *Kalabiška*
20/03	h	Spartak Myjava	D	1-1 *J Kosorín*
04/04	a	Banská Bystrica	W	4-0 *Kalabiška 3, Opiela*
10/04	h	Žilina	L	1-2 *Kóňa*
18/04	a	Zlaté Moravce	L	2-3 *og (Chren), og (Charizopulos)*
25/04	h	Dunajská Streda	W	4-0 *Majtán, Hlohovský, Kalabiška 2*
04/05	a	Slovan	L	1-4 *Pillár*
08/05	h	Trenčín	L	0-4
17/05	a	Spartak Trnava	L	2-4 *Kalabiška, Pillár*
20/05	h	Ružomberok	W	4-2 *Pillár, Kalabiška, Hlohovský, Komara*
23/05	a	Košice	D	1-1 *Pillár*
30/05	h	Podbrezová	W	3-0 *Pillár, Kalabiška 2*

No	Name	Nat	DoB	Pos	Aps	(s)	Gls
2	Juraj Chvátal		13/07/96	M	17		
8	Pavel Čermák	CZE	14/05/89	D	4		
28	Jakub Čunta		28/08/96	A	1		
10	Jozef Dolný		13/05/92	M	11	(2)	1
8	Zdenko Filipek		24/04/95	D	2	(1)	
26	Július Gombala		09/11/93	D		(3)	
13	Filip Hlohovský		13/06/88	M	31		5
20	Luboš Hušek	CZE	26/03/84	M	29		
39	Martin Junas		09/03/96	G		(1)	
19	Jan Kalabiška	CZE	22/12/86	A	30		19
7	Tomáš Komara		23/05/94	M	4	(16)	1
6	Tomáš Kóňa		01/03/84	M	19	(4)	1
10	Jakub Kosorín		27/04/95	A	15	(13)	3
12	Matej Kosorín		03/04/97	M		(2)	
27	Timotej Královič		26/10/96	A		(2)	
5	Jakub Krč		02/09/97	M	3	(3)	
9	Tomáš Majtán		30/03/87	A	19	(1)	4
15	Dominik Malý		24/01/96	M	2	(1)	
21	Róbert Mazáň		09/02/94	D	18		
15	Samuel Mráz		13/05/97	A	1	(14)	1
22	Mulumba Mukendi	COD	27/05/85	A	3	(1)	
23	Lukáš Opiela		13/01/86	D	20	(3)	1
4	Petr Pavlík	CZE	22/02/87	D	33		
17	Róbert Pillár		27/05/91	D	32		8
33	Juraj Piroska		27/02/87	A	19		6
14	Marek Pittner		14/02/97	M	7	(3)	
2	Martin Prível		11/04/96	D	2		
1	Michal Šulla		15/07/91	G	33		
24	Denis Ventúra		01/08/95	M	2	(9)	
22	Vítor Gava	BRA	20/05/91	D	2	(2)	

ŠK Slovan Bratislava

1919 • Pasienky (11,907) • skslovan.com
Major honours
UEFA Cup Winners' Cup (1) 1969; Czechoslovakian League (8) 1949, 1950, 1951, 1955, 1970, 1974, 1975, 1992; Slovakian League (12) 1940, 1941, 1942, 1944, 1994, 1995, 1996, 1999, 2009, 2011, 2013, 2014; Czechoslovakian Cup (5) 1962, 1963, 1968, 1974, 1982; Slovakian Cup (6) 1994, 1997, 1999, 2010, 2011, 2013
Coach: František Straka (CZE);
(16/10/14) Jozef Chovanec (CZE);
(07/04/15) Dušan Tittel

2014

11/07	h	Podbrezová	W	2-1 *Milinković 2*
01/08	h	Ružomberok	W	2-1 *Soumah, Kolčák*
10/08	a	Košice	W	4-1 *Halenár 2*
15/08	h	Senica	W	4-1 *Soumah 2, Meszáros, Fořt*
23/08	a	Spartak Myjava	L	1-2 *Halenár*
31/08	h	Banská Bystrica	W	3-1 *Soumah, Štefánik, Halenár*
14/09	a	Žilina	L	0-3
21/09	a	Dunajská Streda	D	1-1 *Soumah*
24/09	h	Trenčín	L	0-2
28/09	a	Podbrezová	W	1-0
05/10	a	Trenčín	L	0-4
26/10	a	Ružomberok	W	2-1 *og (Práznovský), Peltier*
30/10	a	Spartak Trnava	L	0-4
02/11	h	Košice	W	3-0 *Kolčák, Kubík, Halenár*
09/11	a	Senica	L	1-2 *Čikoš*
23/11	a	Spartak Myjava	W	1-0
30/11	a	Banská Bystrica	W	1-0 *Peltier*
03/12	h	Zlaté Moravce	W	2-1 *Milinković 2 (1p)*

2015

27/02	h	Žilina	L	0-2
07/03	a	Zlaté Moravce	W	2-0 *Peltier, Zrelák*
10/03	h	Spartak Trnava	D	1-1 *Kubík*
15/03	h	Dunajská Streda	L	0-1
21/03	h	Podbrezová	W	2-1 *Milinković (p), Meszáros*
05/04	h	Trenčín	L	1-3 *Meszáros*
11/04	a	Spartak Trnava	D	0-0
18/04	h	Ružomberok	W	1-0 *Saláta*
25/04	a	Košice	L	1-2 *Milinković*
04/05	h	Senica	W	4-1 *Meszáros, Zrelák 2, Soumah*
08/05	a	Spartak Myjava	W	6-3 *Soumah, Simović, Zrelák, Niňaj, Oršula, Meszáros*
16/05	h	Banská Bystrica	W	1-0 *Soumah*
20/05	a	Žilina	W	2-1 *og (Škriniar), Milinković*
23/05	a	Zlaté Moravce	W	1-0 *Meszáros*
30/05	a	Dunajská Streda	W	3-0 *Kubík 2, Meszáros*

No	Name	Nat	DoB	Pos	Aps	(s)	Gls
18	Mamadou Bagayoko	CIV	31/12/89	D	6	(1)	
19	Adrián Čermák		01/07/93	M		(2)	
4	Erik Čikoš		31/07/88	D	25	(1)	1
6	Martin Dobrotka		22/01/85	D	4		
27	Filip Ďuriš		28/03/95	A		(11)	
6	Pavel Fořt	CZE	26/06/83	A	7	(2)	1
23	Lukáš Gašparovič		17/02/93	M		(2)	
16	Nicolás Gorosito	ARG	17/08/88	D	23	(1)	
8	Erik Grendel		13/10/88	M	9	(2)	
9	Juraj Halenár		28/06/83	A	9	(5)	5
26	Dávid Hudák		21/03/93	D	11	(1)	
14	Tomáš Jablonský	CZE	21/08/87	D	20	(1)	
2	Miloš Josimov	SRB	27/09/84	D	2		
21	Kristián Kolčák		30/01/90	D	11	(2)	2
28	Juraj Kotula		30/09/95	D	4		
30	Martin Krnáč		30/01/85	G	8		
7	František Kubík		14/03/89	A	14	(3)	4
81	Richard Lásik		18/08/92	M	12	(10)	
12	Karol Mészáros		25/07/93	M	16	(9)	7
11	Marko Milinković	SRB	16/04/88	M	20	(4)	7
3	Branislav Niňaj		17/05/94	D	17	(5)	1
11	Filip Oršula		25/02/93	M	3	(6)	1
77	Lester Peltier	TRI	13/09/88	A	20	(9)	3
1	Dušan Perniš		28/11/84	G	25		
19	Kornel Saláta		24/01/85	D	15		1
27	Slobodan Simović	SRB	22/05/89	M	14		1
25	Michal Siplak		20/02/93	D	1		
20	Seydouba Soumah	GUI	11/06/91	M	19	(3)	8
17	Samuel Štefánik		16/11/91	M	23	(3)	1
33	Róbert Vittek		01/04/82	A	1	(4)	
28	Martin Vrablec		13/01/92	M		(1)	
15	Timotej Záhumenský		17/07/95	M	1	(2)	
9	Adam Zrelák		05/05/94	A	13		4
10	Igor Žofčák		04/03/84	M	10	(4)	

TJ Spartak Myjava

1920 • Štadión Spartaka (2,728) •
spartakmyjava.sk
Coach: Peter Gergely

2014
12/07	a	Senica	L	0-1
19/07	a	Podbrezová	W	2-1 Sládek 2
26/07	a	Banská Bystrica	D	0-0
03/08	a	Žilina	L	1-2 Daniel
09/08	a	Zlaté Moravce	L	0-1
16/08	a	Dunajská Streda	L	0-1
23/08	h	Slovan	W	2-1 Kuzma, Pekár
30/08	h	Trenčín	L	0-2
12/09	h	Spartak Trnava	W	2-0 Pekár, Jánošík
16/09	a	Ružomberok	D	2-2 Ciprys, Sládek
20/09	h	Košice	L	0-2
26/09	h	Senica	L	1-2 Pekár
04/10	h	Podbrezová	W	1-0 Pekár
18/10	h	Banská Bystrica	W	2-1 Sládek (p), Pekár
25/10	h	Žilina	L	1-4 Duga
01/11	h	Zlaté Moravce	W	2-0 Kuzma 2
07/11	h	Dunajská Streda	W	3-1 Kuzma, Pekár, Daniel
23/11	a	Slovan	W	1-0 Oršula
29/11	h	Trenčín	W	2-1 Oršula, Pekár (p)

2015
28/02	a	Spartak Trnava	L	1-5 Pekár
07/03	a	Ružomberok	L	1-2 Pekár
14/03	a	Košice	L	0-2
20/03	a	Senica	L	1-2 Kuzma
12/04	a	Banská Bystrica	W	3-2 Duga, Černáček, Daniel
19/04	a	Žilina	W	1-0 Duga
25/04	a	Zlaté Moravce	D	2-2 Duga, og (Pintér)
29/04	a	Podbrezová	L	1-2 Daniel
05/05	a	Dunajská Streda	L	0-1
08/05	h	Slovan	L	3-6 Pekár (p), Kuzma, og (Saláta)
16/05	a	Trenčín	L	1-3 Marček
20/05	h	Spartak Trnava	L	0-3
23/05	h	Ružomberok	D	1-1 Daniel
30/05	h	Košice	D	1-1 Pekár

No	Name	Nat	DoB	Pos	Aps	(s)	Gls
28	Tomáš Belic		02/07/78	G	1		
8	Lukáš Beňo		07/11/89	D	11		
19	Frederik Bilovský		03/03/92	M	19	(6)	
21	Tomáš Bruško		21/02/83	M		(9)	
17	Radoslav Ciprys		24/06/87	D	25	(4)	1
15	Roman Častulín		03/04/85	D	17	(3)	
10	Martin Černáček		09/11/79	D	27		1
23	Erik Daniel	CZE	04/02/92	M	33		5
18	Denis Duga		05/09/94	M	15	(10)	4
11	Dominik Ferenčič		29/05/96	A		(1)	
28	Matúš Hruška		17/09/94	G	3		
12	Martin Janco		25/01/95	A		(5)	
3	Peter Jánošík		02/01/88	D	31		1
2	Marek Jastráb		16/07/93	M	2	(13)	
6	Jakub Kastelovič		14/06/95	D	6	(1)	
14	Ľuboš Kolár		01/09/89	M	12	(2)	
7	Pavol Kosík		02/07/80	A	1	(2)	
16	Marek Kuzma		22/06/88	A	20	(8)	6
20	Tomáš Marček		10/03/87	M	31		1
5	Ivan Múdry		03/08/92	D	1		
11	Filip Oršula		25/02/93	A	12	(6)	2
9	Štefan Pekár		03/12/88	M	32		11
24	Michal Peňaška		30/08/85	M	2	(9)	
26	Peter Sládek		07/07/89	A	15	(2)	4
1	Peter Solnička		14/06/82	G	27	(1)	
24	Arnold Šimonek		19/09/90	A	5	(1)	
14	Peter Šulek		21/09/88	M	1		
25	Denis Švec		16/03/96	D	12	(2)	
30	Lukáš Urminský		23/07/92	G	2		

FC Spartak Trnava

1923 • Antona Malatinského (3,500) •
spartak.sk
Major honours
Czechoslovakian League (5) 1968, 1969, 1971,
1972, 1973; Czechoslovakian Cup (4) 1967, 1971,
1975, 1986; Slovakian Cup (1) 1998
Coach: Juraj Jarábek

2014
13/07	h	Zlaté Moravce	W	3-0 Mikovič, Vlasko 2 (1p)
20/07	a	Dunajská Streda	D	0-0
03/08	a	Trenčín	L	0-2
10/08	h	Podbrezová	L	0-1
16/08	h	Ružomberok	W	2-0 Vlasko 2 (1p)
24/08	a	Košice	L	0-2
31/08	h	Senica	D	2-2 Vlasko, Mikovič
12/09	a	Spartak Myjava	L	0-2
16/09	h	Banská Bystrica	W	5-2 Sabo, Schranz, Bortel, Jendrišek, Mikovič
20/09	a	Žilina	L	0-1
27/09	h	Zlaté Moravce	L	1-2 Sabo (p)
04/10	h	Dunajská Streda	W	3-1 Vyskočil 2, Jendrišek
25/10	h	Trenčín	W	1-0 Sabo (p)
30/10	h	Slovan	W	4-0 Vlasko, Sabo (p), Jendrišek, Casado
02/11	a	Podbrezová	D	1-1 Jendrišek
08/11	a	Ružomberok	D	0-0
22/11	h	Košice	W	3-1 Mikovič, Schranz, Jendrišek
28/11	a	Senica	W	1-0 Mikovič

2015
28/02	h	Spartak Myjava	W	5-1 Vlasko, Cléber, Mikovič, Sabo 2
06/03	a	Banská Bystrica	D	1-1 Mikovič
10/03	a	Slovan	D	1-1 Nikolić
14/03	h	Žilina	W	1-0 og (Piaček)
21/03	h	Zlaté Moravce	W	3-0 Sabo, Cléber 2
03/04	a	Dunajská Streda	W	1-0 Vlasko
11/04	a	Slovan	D	0-0
17/04	a	Trenčín	L	0-1
26/04	h	Podbrezová	W	3-1 Kuzma, Sabo (p), Sládek
04/05	h	Ružomberok	W	2-1 Vlasko, Sabo
08/05	a	Košice	L	0-1
17/05	h	Senica	W	4-2 Cléber 2, Mikovič 2
20/05	a	Spartak Myjava	W	3-0 Sabo (p), Vlasko (p), Vojtuš
23/05	h	Banská Bystrica	W	3-1 Vlasko, Sabo (p), Mikovič
30/05	a	Žilina	L	0-3

No	Name	Nat	DoB	Pos	Aps	(s)	Gls
7	Boris Bališ		23/11/93	M		(1)	
5	Patrik Banovič		13/11/91	D		(3)	
13	Milan Bortel		07/04/87	D	24	(2)	1
17	José David Casado	ESP	14/01/88	M	25	(4)	1
11	Ján Chovanec		22/03/84	M	2	(2)	
30	Cléber	BRA	03/06/86	M	16	(4)	5
16	Patrik Čarnota		10/10/86	D		(1)	
20	Matúš Čonka		15/10/90	D	33		
24	Stefan Djurić	SRB	22/05/95	M		(1)	
35	Jean-Paul Farrugia	MLT	21/03/93	A		(2)	
5	Srdjan Grabež	SRB	02/04/91	D	2		
34	Lukáš Greššák		23/01/89	D	14	(5)	
33	Marek Hlinka		04/10/90	M	7	(6)	
22	Adam Jakubech		02/01/97	G	1		
6	Marek Janečka		09/06/83	D	27	(5)	
21	Erik Jendrišek		26/10/86	A	10	(3)	5
36	Erik Jirka		10/09/97	M		(2)	
31	Miroslav Kasaj		11/03/88	A		(1)	
18	Ivan Kelava	CRO	20/02/88	G	14		
27	Kamil Kuzma		28/08/88	M	11	(3)	1
32	Tomáš Mikinič		22/11/92	M	1	(2)	
8	Martin Mikovič		12/09/90	M	24	(3)	10
15	Miloš Nikolić	SRB	21/02/89	D	13		1
12	Róbert Richnák		03/05/92	M		(2)	
31	Dobrivoj Rusov		13/01/93	G	18		
25	Erik Sabo		22/11/91	M	28		11
26	Ivan Schranz		13/09/93	M	8	(1)	2
2	Matej Siva		10/10/84	D	9	(3)	
29	Peter Sládek		07/07/89	A	8	(4)	1
28	Soune Soungole	CIV	26/02/95	M		(1)	
29	Nikolas Špalek		12/02/97	M	6	(8)	
19	Martin Tóth		13/10/86	D	25		
16	Ján Vlasko		11/01/90	M	27	(3)	11
28	Jakub Vojtuš		22/10/93	A	4	(10)	1
7	Martin Vyskočil	CZE	15/09/82	A	6	(14)	2

ŽP Šport Podbrezová

1920 • Kolkáreň (1,950) • zpfutbal.sk
Coach: Jaroslav Kentoš;
(16/02/15) Branislav Benko

2014
11/07	a	Slovan	L	1-2 Hovančík
19/07	h	Spartak Myjava	L	1-2 Podio
27/07	h	Trenčín	L	0-2
02/08	h	Banská Bystrica	W	3-0 Kupčík, Harvilko, Nworah
10/08	a	Spartak Trnava	W	1-0 Gál-Andrezly
16/08	h	Žilina	W	1-0 Gál-Andrezly
23/08	h	Ružomberok	L	0-1
30/08	h	Zlaté Moravce	D	0-0
13/09	a	Košice	L	0-3
16/09	h	Dunajská Streda	W	3-0 Vaščák 2, Kochan (p)
20/09	a	Senica	D	1-1 M Pančík
28/09	h	Slovan	W	1-0 Podio
04/10	a	Spartak Myjava	L	0-1
18/10	h	Trenčín	D	2-2 Vaščák, Minčič
24/10	a	Banská Bystrica	D	3-3 M Pančík, J Pančík, Minčič
02/11	h	Spartak Trnava	D	1-1 Vaščák
05/11	a	Žilina	D	0-0
22/11	h	Ružomberok	L	1-2 Vaščák
29/11	a	Zlaté Moravce	L	0-1

2015
28/02	h	Košice	D	1-1 Škutka (p)
07/03	a	Dunajská Streda	L	0-1
14/03	h	Senica	W	2-1 Nworah, Vaščák
21/03	a	Slovan	L	1-2 Migala
12/04	a	Trenčín	L	1-4 Škutka
18/04	h	Banská Bystrica	D	1-1 Škutka
26/04	a	Spartak Trnava	L	1-3 Škutka
29/04	h	Spartak Myjava	W	2-1 Kupčík, Škutka (p)
05/05	h	Žilina	L	2-3 Vaščák, Škutka (p)
08/05	a	Ružomberok	L	0-2
16/05	h	Zlaté Moravce	L	0-2
19/05	a	Košice	L	0-5
23/05	h	Dunajská Streda	L	2-3 Kupčík, Nworah
30/05	a	Senica	L	0-3

No	Name	Nat	DoB	Pos	Aps	(s)	Gls
10	Nikola Andrić	SRB	23/05/92	A	18	(1)	
27	Juraj Baláž		12/06/80	G	10		
3	Peter Gál-Andrezly		03/05/90	M	16	(8)	2
4	Tomáš Galo		06/12/96	M		(6)	
7	Štefan Gerec		10/11/92	A		(5)	
13	Vratislav Greško		24/07/77	D	22	(1)	
1	Jozef Hanák		08/08/76	G	2		
2	Milan Harvilko		17/08/88	D	15	(11)	1
22	Juraj Hovančík		22/11/90	D	12	(1)	1
15	Kamil Karaš		01/03/91	M	4	(5)	
11	Matej Kochan		21/11/92	M	25	(3)	1
14	Lukáš Kožička		15/10/87	M		(4)	
23	Dominik Kunca		04/03/92	A	1	(1)	
12	Ľuboš Kupčík		03/03/89	D	32		3
30	Andrej Maťašovský		20/08/88	G	13		
7	Lukáš Migala		04/07/94	D	12		1
5	Ivan Minčič		18/08/82	D	28		2
20	Ján Nosko		25/05/88	D	7	(3)	
18	Peter Nworah	NGA	15/12/90	A	22	(9)	3
19	Juraj Pančík		11/05/90	M	16	(13)	1
19	Michal Pančík		18/08/82	M	22	(3)	2
30	Pavol Penksa		07/12/85	G	8		
9	Pablo Podio	ARG	07/08/89	M	30		2
14	Róbert Richnák		03/05/92	M	1	(2)	
21	Gabriel Snitka		14/08/85	D	5	(7)	
6	Dávid Škutka		25/05/88	A	12	(1)	6
21	Martin Šlapák	CZE	25/03/87	M	2	(3)	
8	Blažej Vaščák		21/11/83	A	28	(3)	7

FK AS Trenčín

1992 • Na Sihoti (4,300) • astrencin.sk
Major honours
Slovakian League (1) 2015; Slovakian Cup (1) 2015
Coach: Martin Ševela

2014
12/07	h	Dunajská Streda	W	2-1	Simon, og (Szabó)
27/07	h	Podbrezová	W	2-0	Hajradinović, Malec
03/08	h	Spartak Trnava	W	2-0	Holúbek, Simon
10/08	a	Ružomberok	D	1-1	Hajradinović
17/08	h	Košice	W	4-2	Holúbek, Kubík 3
22/08	a	Senica	D	1-1	Ramón
30/08	h	Spartak Myjava	W	2-0	Simon, Opatovský
30/09	a	Banská Bystrica	W	3-1	Guba, Simon, Jairo
17/09	h	Žilina	D	2-2	Edmond 2
20/09	a	Zlaté Moravce	W	1-0	Mišák
24/09	a	Slovan	W	2-0	Mišák, Jairo
27/09	a	Dunajská Streda	L	2-3	Holúbek, og (Tóth)
05/10	h	Slovan	W	4-0	Madu, Simon, Hajradinović 2 (1p)
18/10	a	Podbrezová	D	2-2	Mišák, Simon
25/10	a	Spartak Trnava	L	0-1	
30/10	h	Ružomberok	W	4-3	Hajradinović (p), Holúbek, Guba, Jairo
08/11	a	Košice	L	0-2	
22/11	h	Senica	W	3-1	Guba, Hajradinović, Jairo
29/11	a	Spartak Myjava	L	1-2	Hajradinović

2015
28/02	h	Banská Bystrica	W	2-0	Holúbek, Ibrahim
08/03	a	Žilina	D	1-1	Holúbek
13/03	h	Zlaté Moravce	W	2-0	Jairo, Bero
21/03	h	Dunajská Streda	W	3-0	Van Kessel, Ibrahim, Edmond
05/04	a	Slovan	W	3-1	Van Kessel, Bero 2
12/04	h	Podbrezová	W	4-1	Ibrahim, Bero, Jairo, Van Kessel
17/04	h	Spartak Trnava	W	1-0	Ibrahim
25/04	a	Ružomberok	W	1-0	Van Kessel (p)
05/05	h	Košice	W	1-0	Bero
08/05	a	Senica	W	4-0	Jairo, Van Kessel, Guba, Lobotka
16/05	h	Spartak Myjava	W	3-1	Rundić (p), Jairo, Koolwijk
19/05	a	Banská Bystrica	W	1-0	Van Kessel
23/05	h	Žilina	L	0-1	
30/05	a	Zlaté Moravce	W	3-1	Jairo, Madu, Skovajsa

No	Name	Nat	DoB	Pos	Aps	(s)	Gls
8	Aldo Baéz	ARG	05/09/88	M	1		
5	Damián Bariš		09/12/94	M		(1)	
21	Matúš Bero		06/09/95	M	14	(4)	5
17	Peter Čögley		11/08/88	D	29		
28	Emmanuel Edmond	NGA	13/06/96	A	3	(6)	3
19	Dávid Guba		29/06/91	M	15	(10)	4
23	Haris Hajradinović	BIH	18/02/94	M	19		7
14	Jakub Holúbek		12/01/91	M	21	(2)	6
10	Rabiu Ibrahim	NGA	15/03/91	M	12	(5)	4
11	Jairo	BRA	06/05/92	A	26	(1)	9
27	Denis Jančo		01/08/97	M		(1)	
19	Peter Kleščík		18/09/88	D	22	(6)	
8	Ryan Koolwijk	NED	08/08/85	M	5	(8)	1
9	František Kubík		14/03/89	A	7		3
18	Jamie Lawrence	ENG	22/08/92	D	10	(8)	
29	Stanislav Lobotka		25/11/94	M	31	(1)	1
15	Kingsley Madu	NGA	12/12/95	D	15		2
6	Tomáš Malec		05/01/93	A	1	(2)	1
7	Patrik Mišák	CZE	29/03/91	M	14	(3)	3
16	Karol Mondek		02/06/91	M	5	(23)	
20	Matúš Opatovský		22/07/94	D	1	(7)	1
22	Ramón	BRA	22/08/90	D	24	(1)	1
3	Milan Rundić	SRB	29/03/92	D	21	(1)	1
27	Moses Simon	NGA	12/07/95	A	18	(1)	6
2	Lukáš Skovajsa		27/03/94	D	2	(2)	1
24	Igor Šemrinec		22/11/87	G	26		
9	Gino van Kessel	CUW	09/03/93	A	14		6
26	Martin Vlček		05/02/96	A		(1)	
1	Miloš Volešák		20/04/84	G	7		

FC ViOn Zlaté Moravce

1995 • ViOn (3,300) • fcvion.sk
Major honours
Slovakian Cup (1) 2007
Coach: Branislav Mráz;
(12/01/15) Ladislav Totkovič;
(20/02/15) Branislav Mráz

2014
13/07	a	Spartak Trnava	L	0-3	
19/07	h	Ružomberok	D	1-1	Sabo
27/07	a	Košice	W	3-1	Štrbák, Charizopulos, Ďurica (p)
02/08	h	Senica	D	0-0	
09/08	h	Spartak Myjava	W	1-0	Pavlenda
15/08	h	Banská Bystrica	D	1-1	Orávik (p)
23/08	a	Žilina	L	0-4	
30/08	a	Podbrezová	D	0-0	
13/09	h	Dunajská Streda	D	1-1	Djuričić
20/09	h	Trenčín	L	0-1	
27/09	h	Spartak Trnava	W	2-1	Sabo, Nikolić
04/10	a	Ružomberok	L	0-3	
18/10	h	Košice	W	3-0	Pavelka, Charizopulos 2
25/10	a	Senica	L	0-2	
01/11	a	Spartak Myjava	L	0-2	
08/11	a	Banská Bystrica	L	0-2	
21/11	h	Žilina	L	1-6	Pavelka
29/11	h	Podbrezová	W	1-0	Pavelka
03/12	a	Slovan	L	1-2	Charizopulos

2015
01/03	a	Dunajská Streda	D	1-1	Mazan
07/03	h	Slovan	L	0-2	
13/03	a	Trenčín	L	0-2	
21/03	a	Spartak Trnava	L	0-3	
04/04	h	Ružomberok	L	0-2	
11/04	a	Košice	W	2-1	Karaš, Juhar
18/04	h	Senica	W	3-2	Juhar 3 (1p)
25/04	a	Spartak Myjava	D	2-2	Karaš, Mikinič
05/05	h	Banská Bystrica	L	0-1	
09/05	a	Žilina	L	1-4	Mikinič
16/05	h	Podbrezová	W	2-0	Pintér, Mance
19/05	h	Dunajská Streda	D	0-0	
23/05	a	Slovan	L	0-1	
30/05	h	Trenčín	L	1-3	Orávik

No	Name	Nat	DoB	Pos	Aps	(s)	Gls
7	Stefan Cebara	CAN	12/04/91	D	2	(3)	
6	Márius Charizopulos		09/11/90	M	26	(6)	4
12	Martin Chren		02/01/84	D	31		
19	Dušan Djuričić	SRB	11/03/90	M	17	(1)	1
10	Peter Ďurica		05/03/86	M	16	(3)	1
25	Martin Juhar		09/03/88	M	6	(3)	4
11	Kamil Karaš		29/06/91	M	10	(3)	2
16	Andrejs Kiriļins	LVA	03/11/95	M	2	(2)	
25	Lukáš Kováč		21/06/87	M	2		
30	Pavol Kováč		12/08/74	G	31		
17	Marko Kovjenić	SVN	02/02/93	M	1	(3)	
9	Armando Mance	CRO	27/10/92	A	2	(10)	1
8	Peter Mazan		13/05/90	M	6	(6)	1
32	Tomáš Mikinič		22/11/92	M	23	(2)	2
11	Milan Mujkoš		28/05/86	D	5	(8)	
15	Miloš Nikolić	SRB	21/02/89	D	18		1
24	Jozef Novota		24/01/86	G	2	(1)	
10	Peter Orávik		18/12/88	M	33		2
31	Karol Pavelka		31/07/83	A	9	(6)	3
5	Patrik Pavlenda		03/05/82	D	29		1
4	Juraj Pilát		02/02/92	D	3	(6)	
11	Michal Pintér		04/02/94	D	20		1
17	Patrik Sabo		09/03/93	M	23	(3)	2
25	Branislav Stanič	SRB	30/07/88	M		(2)	
27	Elvis Mashike Sukisa	CGO	06/06/94	A		(8)	
21	Július Szöke		18/08/95	M	13	(8)	
23	Marián Štrbák		13/02/86	D	5		1
4	Toni Tipuric	AUT	10/09/90	D	13		
3	Filip Ungar	SRB	14/01/95	D	2		
37	Róbert Valenta		01/01/90	M	9	(7)	
28	Martin Vrablec		19/01/92	M	4	(4)	

MŠK Žilina

1908 • Pod Dubňom (10,770) • mskzilina.sk
Major honours
Slovakian League (6) 2002, 2003, 2004, 2007, 2010, 2012; Slovakian Cup (1) 2012
Coach: Adrián Guľa

2014
12/07	a	Ružomberok	W	1-0	Jelić
20/07	h	Košice	W	4-1	Jelić, Paur, Ľupčo, Škriniar
25/07	a	Senica	D	1-1	Jelić
03/08	h	Spartak Myjava	W	2-1	Čmelík, Mihalík
09/08	a	Banská Bystrica	D	0-0	
16/08	h	Podbrezová	L	0-1	
23/08	h	Zlaté Moravce	W	4-0	Škriniar (p), Ľupčo, Škvarka, Pečovský
29/08	a	Dunajská Streda	D	2-2	Čmelík, Mihalík
14/09	h	Slovan	W	3-0	Mihalík, Káčer, Jelić
17/09	a	Trenčín	D	2-2	Jelić, Piaček
20/09	h	Spartak Trnava	W	1-0	Škriniar (p)
28/09	h	Ružomberok	W	5-1	Čmelík, Škriniar, Mihalík, Škvarka 2
04/10	a	Košice	D	1-1	Willian
18/10	a	Senica	D	1-1	Škvarka
25/10	a	Spartak Myjava	W	4-1	Čmelík, Škvarka, Pečovský, Mihalík
02/11	h	Banská Bystrica	W	2-0	Káčer, Jelić
05/11	h	Podbrezová	D	0-0	
21/11	a	Zlaté Moravce	W	6-1	Paur, Jelić 3, Mihalík 2
30/11	h	Dunajská Streda	W	3-1	Čmelík, Jelić, Škriniar

2015
27/02	a	Slovan	W	2-0	Čmelík, Mihalík
08/03	h	Trenčín	D	1-1	Mihalík
14/03	a	Spartak Trnava	L	0-1	
22/03	a	Ružomberok	D	1-1	Čmelík
04/04	h	Košice	W	4-1	Jelić 3, Čmelík
10/04	a	Senica	W	2-1	Škvarka, Čmelík (p)
19/04	h	Spartak Myjava	W	3-0	Čmelík
24/04	a	Banská Bystrica	W	3-0	Jelić, Mihalík 2
05/05	a	Podbrezová	W	3-2	Škriniar (p), Jelić 2
09/05	h	Zlaté Moravce	W	4-1	Ľupčo, Mihalík, Káčer 2
15/05	a	Dunajská Streda	W	1-0	Čmelík
20/05	h	Slovan	L	1-2	Káčer
23/05	a	Trenčín	W	1-0	Jelić
30/05	h	Spartak Trnava	W	2-0	Jelić 2, Mihalík

No	Name	Nat	DoB	Pos	Aps	(s)	Gls
22	László Bénes		09/09/97	M	2	(6)	
16	Lukáš Čmelík		13/04/96	M	29	(2)	10
28	Ľubomír Gorelčík		13/03/97	A		(1)	
11	Dávid Guba		29/06/91	A		(3)	
3	Tomáš Hučko		03/10/85	D	5	(6)	
35	Matej Jelić	CRO	05/11/90	A	27	(2)	19
6	Miroslav Káčer		02/02/96	M	28	(3)	5
27	Andrej Kadlec		02/02/96	D	3	(1)	
33	Michal Klec		05/12/95	M	1	(5)	
24	Martin Králik		03/04/95	D	2	(2)	
22	Martin Krnáč		30/01/85	G	8		
21	Bojan Letić	BIH	21/12/92	D	28	(1)	
4	Peter Ľupčo		21/04/95	M	13	(5)	3
45	Ernest Mabouka	CMR	16/06/88	D	29	(1)	
23	Jaroslav Mihalík		27/07/94	A	32		13
29	Jakub Paur		04/07/92	M	8	(14)	2
12	Viktor Pečovský		24/05/83	M	32		2
15	Jozef Piaček		20/06/83	D	26	(1)	1
3	Milan Škriniar		11/02/95	D	32		6
20	Michal Škvarka		19/08/92	M	16	(11)	6
11	Nikolas Špalek		12/02/97	A	1	(7)	
19	Denis Vavro		10/04/96	D	6		
1	Miloš Volešák		20/04/84	G	25		
10	Willian	BRA	07/12/91	A	10	(19)	1
26	Marek Zuziak		11/01/95	A		(2)	

Top goalscorers

Ján Kalabiška   Matej Jelić

19 Ján Kalabiška (Senica)
Matej Jelić (Žilina)

13 Jaroslav Mihalík (Žilina)

11 Štefan Pekár (Spartak Myjava)
Erik Sabo (Spartak Trnava)
Ján Vlasko (Spartak Trnava)

10 Nermin Haskić (Košice)
Adam Zreľák (Ružomberok/Slovan)
Martin Mikovič (Spartak Trnava)
Lukáš Čmelík (Žilina)

Promoted clubs

MFK Zemplín Michalovce

1912 • Zemplín štadión (4,400) •
mfkzemplin.sk
Coach: František Šturma

MFK Skalica

1920 • Mestský štadión (2,500) •
mfkskalica.sk
Coach: Štefan Horný

Second level final tables 2014/15

First stage

West	Pld	W	D	L	F	A	Pts
1 MFK Skalica	22	15	4	3	40	16	49
2 MŠK Žilina II	22	13	2	7	43	33	41
3 FC Nitra	22	12	4	6	39	22	40
4 ŠKF Sereď	22	11	6	5	39	22	39
5 FK Slovan Duslo Šaľa	22	10	7	5	33	24	37
6 ŠK Senec	22	9	7	6	28	21	34
7 FK Pohronie	22	10	3	9	32	35	33
8 ŠK Slovan Bratislava II	22	7	5	10	18	30	26
9 FC Spartak Trnava II	22	5	5	12	20	35	20
10 FC ŠTK 1914 Šamorín	22	4	7	11	21	34	19
11 MFK Dubnica	22	3	6	13	25	42	15
12 AFC Nové Mesto nad Váhom	22	3	4	15	15	39	13

East	Pld	W	D	L	F	A	Pts
1 MFK Zemplín Michalovce	22	16	3	3	46	11	51
2 MFK Lokomotíva Zvolen	22	10	9	3	35	14	39
3 Partizán Bardejov	22	10	9	3	36	17	39
4 1. FC Tatran Prešov	22	11	5	6	39	22	38
5 MFK Tatran Liptovský Mikuláš	22	11	4	7	31	18	37
6 FK Poprad	22	8	4	10	31	37	28
7 MFK Rimavská Sobota	22	7	7	8	21	28	28
8 FC Lokomotíva Košice	22	6	6	10	30	36	24
9 MFK Dolný Kubín	22	7	2	13	21	40	23
10 MFK Košice II	22	5	6	11	30	40	21
11 FK Bodva Moldava nad Bodvou	22	4	7	11	18	37	19
12 FK Slavoj Trebišov	22	4	4	14	13	51	16

Promotion play-offs final table

	Pld	W	D	L	F	A	Pts
1 MFK Zemplín Michalovce	22	15	6	1	40	11	51
2 MFK Skalica	22	15	3	4	32	15	48
3 1. FC Tatran Prešov	22	10	6	6	32	24	36
4 MFK Tatran Liptovský Mikuláš	22	9	6	7	29	23	33
5 FC Nitra	22	8	7	7	26	25	31
6 Partizán Bardejov	22	7	7	8	27	24	28
7 MFK Lokomotíva Zvolen	22	7	7	8	23	20	28
8 MŠK Žilina II	22	8	2	12	26	36	26
9 ŠK Senec	22	6	7	9	18	28	25
10 ŠKF Sereď	22	6	4	12	27	38	22
11 FK Slovan Duslo Šaľa	22	4	8	10	27	40	20
12 FK Poprad	22	5	1	16	26	49	16

NB The top six clubs from each regional group progress to the promotion play-offs, carrying forward their records from the ten matches against the other five qualified teams. In the play-offs they play a further 12 matches (home and away) against the six teams from the other regional group.

DOMESTIC CUP

Slovenský pohár 2014/15

SECOND ROUND

(12/08/14)
Futura Humenné 0-3 Lokomotíva Zvolen
Gabčíkovo 1-4 Senica
Karpaty Limbach 1-2 Skalica
Kinex Bytča 2-2 Dolný Kubín *(3-0 on pens)*
Lamač Bratislava 0-6 Slovan Duslo Šaľa
Rovinka 1-1 Nové Mesto nad Váhom *(5-4 on pens)*
Slovan Poproč 1-0 Slavoj Trebišov
Slovan Šimonovany 0-3 Zlaté Moravce
Tatran Bytčica 0-6 Dukla Banská Bystrica
Tatran Stupava 0-4 Senec
Tisovec 0-5 Partizán Bardejov

(13/08/14)
Báhoň 2-0 Bernolákovo
Baník Horná Nitra 2-0 Šurany
Brusno Ondrej 1-2 Spartak Trnava
Čaňa 1-3 Lokomotíva Košice
Častkovce 3-1 Palárikovo
ČFK Nitra 1-6 Nové Zámky
Danubia Bratislava 1-4 Lozorno
Detva 0-4 Teplička nad Váhom
Družstevník Liptovská Štiavnica 1-3 Rakytovce 85
Družstevník Velké Ludince 3-0 Spartak Vráble
Družstevník Velký Horeš 1-5 Tatran Liptovský Mikuláš
Jednota Málinec 2-4 Tatran Oravské Veselé
Jednota Sokol Chocholná Velčice 0-6 Slovan Nemšová
Kalná nad Hronom 1-1 Slovan Čeľadice *(5-3 on pens)*
Kráľová pri Senci 1-7 Žilina
Kremnička 1-0 Ružomberok
Kysucké Nové Mesto 1-5 Tvrdošín
Lokomotíva Devínska Nová Ves 1-3 Slovan Most pri Bratislave
Lokomotíva Michaľany 2-10 Tatran Prešov
Lučenec 2-0 Liptovský Hrádok
Máj Ružomberok Černová 1-1 Stráža *(3-2 on pens)*
Močenok 0-0 Crystal Lednické Rovne *(5-4 on pens)*
Námestovo 0-4 MFK Košice
Nová Dubnica 5-1 Kolárovo
Partizán Domaniža 0-3 Dunajská Streda
Pezinok 1-3 Dubnica
Pokrok Krompachy 2-2 Poprad *(3-5 on pens)*
Prenaks Jablonec 0-3 Dunajská Lužná
Raslavice 0-1 Tatran Spišské Vlachy
Rožňava 3-1 Fiľakovo
Šenkvice 1-3 Rača
Slavoj Boleráz 0-4 Pohronie
Slovan Ivanka pri Dunaji 1-6 Šamorín
Slovan Trenčianske Teplice 3-0 Ružinov Bratislava
Slovenské Ďarmoty 0-2 Fomat Martin
Slovenský Grob 0-1 Inter Bratislava
Spartak Hriňová 1-3 Nová Baňa
Spartak Medzev 2-1 Spišská Nová Ves
Strážske 0-4 Trenčín
Svätý Jur 1-2 Rohožník
Tatran Zámutov 5-0 Slavoj Kráľovský Chlmec
Topvar Topoľčany 2-0 Thermál Velký Meder
Vajnory 1-12 Sereď
Vrakuňa Bratislava 2-9 Spartak Myjava
Vrbové 0-3 FC Nitra
Vyšné Opátske 0-1 Podbrezová
Žarnovica 2-1 Tatran Krásno nad Kysucou
Závažná Poruba 1-3 Čadca

(20/08/14)
Podlavice Badín 2-1 Javorník Makov
Velke Kapušany 0-3 Bodva Moldava nad Bodvou

(27/08/14)
Baník Stráňavy 1-1 Rimavská Sobota *(3-4 on pens)*
Štrba 0-5 Zemplín Michalovce

(10/09/14)
Modranka 1-5 Slovan Bratislava

Continued over the page

THIRD ROUND

(02/09/14)
Bodva Moldava nad Bodvou 0-2 Partizán Bardejov
Poprad 2-2 Tatran Prešov *(4-2 on pens)*
Rovinka 1-3 Slovan Duslo Šaľa
Skalica 4-0 Senec

(03/09/14)
Baník Horná Nitra 0-1 Senica
Dunajská Lužná 4-0 Lozorno
Lokomotíva Košice 1-2 Trenčín
Máj Ružomberok-Černová 1-4 Dukla Banská Bystrica
Močenok 0-2 Dunajská Streda
Podlavice Badín 6-2 Žarnovica
Rohožník 1-1 Dubnica *(3-1 on pens)*
Sereď 1-0 Spartak Myjava
Slovan Trenčianske Teplice 2-0 Nová Dubnica
Spartak Medzev 0-1 Tatran Liptovský Mikuláš
Tatran Spišské Vlachy 0-1 Lokomotíva Zvolen
Tvrdošín 0-4 MFK Košice

(09/09/14)
Kalná nad Hronom 1-4 Zlaté Moravce

(10/09/14)
Kinex Bytča 2-2 Kremnička *(2-3 on pens)*
Nová Baňa 4-1 Rakytovce 85
Rača 2-0 Šamorín
Rožňava 3-1 Lučenec
Slovan Poproč 2-0 Tatran Zámutov

(23/09/14)
Báhoň 0-3 Žilina
Nové Zámky 1-0 Družstevník Veľké Ludince
Teplička nad Váhom 0-3 Spartak Trnava
Zemplín Michalovce 1-1 Podbrezová *(4-2 on pens)*

(24/09/14)
Častkovce 1-2 Slovan Nemšová
Inter Bratislava 1-0 Slovan Most pri Bratislave
Topvar Topoľčany 0-2 FC Nitra

(01/10/14)
Fomat Martin 2-0 Rimavská Sobota
Tatran Oravské Veselé 2-2 Čadca *(6-7 on pens)*

(12/11/14)
Pohronie 0-4 Slovan Bratislava

FOURTH ROUND

(08/10/14)
Slovan Nemšová 1-4 MFK Košice

(14/10/14)
Nové Zámky 1-3 Dunajská Streda
Zemplín Michalovce 0-3 Zlaté Moravce

(15/10/14)
Čadca 1-3 Slovan Duslo Šaľa
Dunajská Lužná 1-0 Tatran Liptovský Mikuláš
Kremnička 0-2 Poprad
Lokomotíva Zvolen 0-2 Trenčín
FC Nitra 2-1 Sereď
Nová Baňa 0-2 Senica
Podlavice Badín 2-1 Inter Bratislava
Rožňava 1-1 Fomat Martin *(5-4 on pens)*
Slovan Poproč 1-2 Rohožník
Slovan Trenčianske Teplice 0-7 Spartak Trnava

(21/10/14)
Partizán Bardejov 0-1 Dukla Banská Bystrica

(22/10/14)
Rača 0-6 Žilina

(19/11/14)
Skalica 3-5 Slovan Bratislava

FIFTH ROUND

(12/11/14)
Dunajská Lužná 1-2 Dukla Banská Bystrica
Podlavice Badín 0-1 MFK Košice
Rožňava 0-2 Dunajská Streda
Slovan Duslo Šaľa 0-0 Poprad *(5-3 on pens)*
Zlaté Moravce 1-3 Trenčín

(15/11/14)
Rohožník 1-4 Senica

(25/11/14)
Žilina 1-1 Spartak Trnava *(3-4 on pens)*

(03/03/15)
Slovan Bratislava 5-2 FC Nitra

QUARTER-FINALS

(17/03/15)
Dukla Banská Bystrica 4-1 Slovan Duslo Šaľa *(Faško 11, 13, 70, Balko 59; Nurkovic 90)*
Spartak Trnava 1-2 Senica *(Sabo 45; Majtán 40, J Kosorín 75)*

(18/03/15)
MFK Košice 1-1 Dunajská Streda *(Viazanko 64; Ljubičić) (2-3 on pens)*
Trenčín 2-1 Slovan Bratislava *(Jairo 75, Van Kessel 80; Mészáros 56)*

SEMI-FINALS

(07/04/15 & 21/04/15)
Dunajská Streda 1-0 Senica *(Štepanovský 13)*
Senica 1-0 Dunajská Streda *(Kóňa 66)*
(1-1; Senica 6-5 on pens)
(08/04/15 & 21/04/15)
Trenčín 2-0 Dukla Banská Bystrica *(Koolwijk 9, Ramón 85)*
Dukla Banská Bystrica 0-1 Trenčín *(Jairo 30)*
(Trenčín 3-0)

FINAL

(01/05/15)
NTC, Poprad
FK AS TRENČÍN 2 *(Ibrahim 36, Van Kessel 110)*
FK SENICA 2 *(Čögley 4og, Kalabiška 114)*
(aet; 3-2 on pens)
Referee: *Trutz*
TRENČÍN: *Šemrinec, Čögley, Ramón, Rundić, Madu (Lawrence 72), Lobotka, Bero (Koolwijk 64), Van Kessel, Ibrahim, Guba (Mondek 55), Jairo*
SENICA: *Šulla, Opiela, Pavlík, Pillár, Čermák, Kóňa, Hušek (Pittner 113), Dolný (J Kosorín 89), Hlohovský, Kalabiška, Majtán*

May Day joy for Slovakian Cup final winners Trenčín after their penalty shoot-out triumph against Senica

SLOVENIA

Nogometna zveza Slovenije (NZS)

Address	Brnčičeva 41g	**President**	Aleksander Čeferin
	SI-1231 Ljubljana-Črnuče	**General secretary**	Aleš Zavrl
Tel	+386 1 530 0400	**Media officer**	Matjaž Krajnik
Fax	+386 1 530 0410	**Year of formation**	1920
E-mail	nzs@nzs.si		
Website	nzs.si		

KEY:

- ● – UEFA Champions League
- ● – UEFA Europa League
- ● – Promoted
- ● – Relegated

PRVA LIGA CLUBS

 1 NK Celje

 2 NK Domžale

 3 ND Gorica

 4 FC Koper

 5 NK Krka

 6 NK Maribor

 7 NK Olimpija Ljubljana

 8 NK Radomlje

 9 NK Rudar Velenje

 10 NK Zavrč

PROMOTED CLUB

 11 NK Krško

Maribor reel in their rivals

NK Maribor successfully warded off the unexpected challenge of twin title rivals NK Celje and NK Domžale to claim the Slovenian Prva Liga for the fifth year in a row.

It was a positive season also for Ante Šimundza's team on the European front as they qualified for the group stage of the UEFA Champions League, but domestic double dreams were dashed when they fell at the semi-final stage of the Slovenian Cup to Celje, who then lost the final against league strugglers FC Koper to finish second in both domestic competitions.

Fifth straight title for perennial champions

Challengers Domžale and Cejle fade after fast start

Koper claim Slovenian Cup for third time

Domestic league

Although there was a familiar name at the top of the Prva Liga in the final 2014/15 standings, with Maribor capturing a record 13th national title, the rest of the table had a topsy-turvy look to it in comparison to the previous season. While Celje leapt six places to the runners-up berth and Domžale moved up from sixth to third, on the flip side Koper dropped from second to eighth and ND Gorica from fourth to ninth, putting the four-time champions into a relegation play-off, which they narrowly survived against NK Aluminij.

For much of the season it looked as if Maribor might drop a place or two as well. Domžale, champions in 2006/07 and 2007/08, got off to a magical start, keeping clean sheets in their opening ten fixtures, nine of which were victories, while Celje, seeking a first league title, recovered from defeats in their opening two games by going unbeaten for the next 19. Furthermore, Maribor lost all four pre-Christmas games against their two rivals, away from home in August and at their Ljudski vrt stadium in October.

Luka Elsner's Domžale were still out in front at the winter break, but while their defence, shored up by goalkeeper extraordinaire Nejc Vidmar, remained rock-solid after the resumption, the goals

dried up at the other end. Simon Rožman's Celje were more consistent than Domžale during the spring, but Maribor, now freed of European commitments, gathered momentum and charged back to the Prva Liga summit. Crucially, Simundža's side found the measure of their rivals as they pocketed six points from Celje and four from Domžale, a 1-0 win at home to the latter, courtesy of long-serving skipper Marcos Tavares's 73rd-minute strike – his 17th goal of the season, the highest in the division – securing the title with two matches remaining.

Domestic cup

Four days after Maribor won the league, Koper lifted a third Slovenian Cup. The seaside club endured a dreadful season in the league, but they beat Domžale in the cup semi-finals to earn a final date with Celje, who had also caused something of a surprise by knocking out Maribor. Having taken just one point from their four league meetings with Celje, Koper, with Italian boss Rodolfo Vanoli back at the helm, would have been rank outsiders under normal circumstances, but they had the advantage of playing the final in their home stadium – and that proved to be telling as goals from defender Denis Halilović and striker Jaka Štromajer returned the trophy to the club

for the first time since 2007 while also sentencing Celje to their seventh defeat in eight finals.

Europe

After three successive seasons in the UEFA Europa League group stage, Maribor reached the UEFA Champions League equivalent in 2014/15, two goals in Israel from Macedonian midfielder Agim Ibraimi accounting for Maccabi Tel-Aviv FC, and a late Tavares strike in Glasgow dumping out Celtic FC. As expected, the Slovenian champions found the going tough, but they did at least manage a draw against all three of their group opponents – Sporting Clube de Portugal, FC Schalke 04 and Chelsea FC.

National team

There was a mixed bag of results for Slovenia as they sought a first UEFA European Championship qualification in 16 years. Japan-based stalwart Milivoje Novakovič was among the goals as Srečko Katanec's team recovered from an opening defeat in Estonia by defeating both Switzerland in Maribor and Lithuania in Vilnius and moving into second place, but two defeats against England – after having led 1-0 in both – suggested that the team's more realistic route into France would be via the play-offs.

DOMESTIC SEASON AT A GLANCE

Prva liga 2014/15 final table

			Home					Away					Total					
		Pld	W	D	L	F	A	W	D	L	F	A	W	D	L	F	A	Pts
1	**NK Maribor**	**36**	**13**	**3**	**2**	**44**	**18**	**11**	**4**	**3**	**30**	**14**	**24**	**7**	**5**	**74**	**32**	**79**
2	NK Celje	36	9	5	4	29	17	11	5	2	29	14	20	10	6	58	31	70
3	NK Domžale	36	11	3	4	33	11	10	2	6	19	11	21	5	10	52	22	68
4	NK Olimpija Ljubljana	36	9	4	5	29	15	8	6	4	26	17	17	10	9	55	32	61
5	NK Zavrč	36	7	4	7	13	15	8	0	10	25	37	15	4	17	38	52	49
6	NK Rudar Velenje	36	7	5	6	26	19	5	5	8	18	24	12	10	14	44	43	46
7	NK Krka	36	6	5	7	23	26	5	2	11	15	28	11	7	18	38	54	40
8	FC Koper	36	7	0	11	17	26	5	4	9	18	32	12	4	20	35	58	40
9	ND Gorica	36	6	4	8	25	20	4	3	11	15	26	10	7	19	40	46	37
10	NK Radomlje	36	3	1	14	9	40	1	3	14	12	45	4	4	28	21	85	16

European qualification 2015/16

 Champion: NK Maribor (second qualifying round)

 Cup winner: FC Koper (first qualifying round)
NK Celje (first qualifying round)
NK Domžale (first qualifying round)

Top scorer	Marcos Tavares (Maribor), 17 goals
Relegated club	NK Radomlje
Promoted club	NK Krško
Cup final	FC Koper 2-0 NK Celje

Team of the season
(4-3-3)

Coach: Rožman (Celje)

Vidmar (Domžale)

Stojanovič (Maribor) — Rajčevič (Maribor) — Korun (Domžale) — Viler (Maribor)

Vrhovec (Celje) — Zajc (Olimpija) — Ibraimi (Maribor)

Šporar (Olimpija) — Marcos Tavares (Maribor) — Verbič (Celje)

Player of the season

Benjamin Verbič
(NK Celje)

Celje ended the 2014/15 season empty-handed, but that was not for the want of trying on the part of 21-year-old local lad Verbič, who registered 15 goals and ten assists in his 32 league outings to earn the club a runners-up placing behind champions NK Maribor. The pacy winger with an eye for goal was handed a first senior cap for Slovenia against Qatar in March and the following month agreed terms on a four-year contract to join top Danish club FC København for the 2015/16 season.

Newcomer of the season

Luka Zahovič
(NK Maribor)

The son of arguably Slovenia's greatest ever player, Zlatko Zahovič, enjoyed a fabulous first full season in the purple and gold of Maribor, prompting early comparisons with his father by scoring a dozen goals in the club's Prva Liga title triumph and also netting a last-gasp equaliser at home to Sporting Clube de Portugal on his UEFA Champions League debut. The 19-year-old has a tough act to follow but appears ready, willing and – with his pace and trickery – able to give it his best shot.

SLOVENIA

NATIONAL TEAM

International tournament appearances
FIFA World Cup (2) 2002, 2010
UEFA European Championship (1) 2000

Top five all-time caps
Boštjan Cesar (83); Zlatko Zahovič (80);
Samir Handanovič (76); **Mišo Brečko** (75);
Milenko Ačimovič & Aleš Čeh (74)

Top five all-time goals
Zlatko Zahovič (35); **Milivoje Novaković** (30);
Sašo Udovič (16); Ermin Šiljak (14); Milenko
Ačimovič (13)

Results 2014/15

08/09/14	Estonia (ECQ)	A	Tallinn	L	0-1	
09/10/14	Switzerland (ECQ)	H	Maribor	W	1-0	Novakovič (79p)
12/10/14	Lithuania (ECQ)	A	Vilnius	W	2-0	Novakovič (33, 37)
15/11/14	England (ECQ)	A	London	L	1-3	Henderson (58og)
18/11/14	Colombia	H	Ljubljana	L	0-1	
27/03/15	San Marino (ECQ)	H	Ljubljana	W	6-0	Iličič (10), Kampl (49), Struna (50), Novakovič (52), Lazarevič (73), Ilič (88)
30/03/15	Qatar	A	Doha	L	0-1	
14/06/15	England (ECQ)	H	Ljubljana	L	2-3	Novakovič (37), Pečnik (84)

Appearances 2014/15

Coach: Srečko Katanec	16/07/63		EST	SUI	LTU	ENG	Col	SMR	Qat	ENG	Caps	Goals
Samir Handanovič	14/07/84	Internazionale (ITA)	G	G	G	G		G		G	76	-
Mišo Brečko	01/05/84	Köln (GER)	D	D	D	D		D76	s77	D	75	-
Miral Samardžič	17/02/87	Rijeka (CRO)	D				D				5	-
Boštjan Cesar	09/07/82	Chievo (ITA)	D	D	D	D		D		D	83	6
Andraž Struna	23/04/89	Giannina (GRE)	D	D	D	D	s46	D	D77		19	1
Rajko Rotman	19/03/89	İstanbul Başakşehir (TUR)	M89			s75	M		M55		6	-
Kevin Kampl	09/10/90	Salzburg (AUT) /Dortmund (GER)	M	M	M	M		M	M	M	17	2
Dalibor Stevanovič	27/09/84	Torpedo Moskva (RUS)	M79*		M46						21	1
Josip Iličič	29/01/88	Fiorentina (ITA)	M62					M72		M61	29	2
Jasmin Kurtič	10/01/89	Fiorentina (ITA)	M	s46	M	M75	s46	M		M79	25	1
Milivoje Novaković	18/05/79	Shimizu S-Pulse (JPN) /Nagoya Grampus (JPN)	A	A	A	A		A		A	69	30
Valter Birsa	07/08/86	Chievo (ITA)	s62	M55	s66	M63		M		s61	72	5
Dejan Lazarevič	15/02/90	Chievo (ITA) /Sassuolo (ITA)	s89	s55	s86	s63	M59	s60	M59	s79	16	1
Branko Ilič	06/02/83	Partizan (SRB)		D	D	D		D		D	58	1
Andraž Kirm	06/09/84	Omonia (CYP)		M72	M86	M78		M60	s77	M72	68	6
Aleš Mertelj	22/03/87	Maribor		M	s46	M			M	M	16	-
Zlatan Ljubijankič	15/12/83	Omiya Ardija (JPN)		A46		s78					44	6
Nejc Pečnik	03/01/86	Crvena zvezda (SRB) /JEF United (JPN)		s72	M66		M			s72	27	5
Jan Oblak	07/01/93	Atlético (ESP)					G		G		5	-
Martin Milec	20/09/91	Standard Liège (BEL)					D46				4	-
Dominic Maroh	04/03/87	Köln (GER)					D46		D65		7	-
Erik Janža	21/06/93	Domžale					D46				1	-
Željko Filipovič	03/10/88	Maribor					M				4	-
Goran Cvijanovič	09/09/86	Rijeka (CRO)					M46				4	-
Robert Berič	17/06/91	Rapid Wien (AUT)					A68	s72	s46		6	-
Petar Stojanovič	07/10/95	Maribor					s46	s76	D		3	-
Siniša Andjelkovič	13/02/86	Palermo (ITA)					s46		D		5	-
Damjan Bohar	18/10/91	Maribor					s59				1	-
Džengis Čavuševič	26/11/87	St Gallen (SUI)					s68				2	-
Benjamin Verbič	27/11/93	Celje							M77		1	-
Tim Matavž	13/01/89	Augsburg (GER)							A46		29	10
Roman Bezjak	21/02/89	Ludogorets (BUL)							s55		6	-
Nik Omladič	21/08/89	Braunschweig (GER)							s59		1	-
Luka Krajnc	19/09/94	Cesena (ITA)							s65		1	-
Bojan Jokič	17/05/86	Villarreal (ESP)								D	69	1

NK Maribor

Second qualifying round - HŠK Zrinjski (BIH)
A 0-0
Handanovič, Šuler, Filipovič, Ibraimi (Bohar 81), Mendy (Marcos Tavares 67), Fajić, Derviševič, Vršič, Rajčevič, Viler, Stojanovič. Coach: Ante Šimundža (SVN)
H 2-0 Vršič (45), Ibraimi (57p)
Handanovič, Šuler, Filipovic, Marcos Tavares (Bohar 72), Ibraimi, Mendy (Fajić 87), Derviševič (Mertelj 81), Vršič, Rajčevič, Viler, Stojanovič. Coach: Ante Šimundža (SVN)

Third qualifying round - Maccabi Tel-Aviv FC (ISR)
H 1-0 Bohar (90+4)
Handanovič, Šuler, Filipovič, Ibraimi (Sallalich 78), Mendy (Marcos Tavares 62), Derviševič, Vršič, Rajčevič, Viler, Stojanovič, Bohar. Coach: Ante Šimundža (SVN)
A 2-2 Ibraimi (36, 55)
Handanovič, Šuler, Filipovič, Marcos Tavares (Mendy 67), Ibraimi, Derviševič (Mertelj 73), Vršič (Sallalich 85), Rajčevič, Viler, Stojanovič, Bohar. Coach: Ante Šimundža (SVN)

Play-offs - Celtic FC (SCO)
H 1-1 Bohar (14)
Handanovič, Šuler, Filipovič, Marcos Tavares, Ibraimi, Derviševič (Mertelj 81), Vršič (Mendy 73), Rajčevič, Viler, Stojanovič, Bohar (Sallalich 79). Coach: Ante Šimundža (SVN)
A 1-0 Marcos Tavares (75)
Handanovič, Šuler, Filipovič, Marcos Tavares (Derviševič 90+2), Ibraimi, Mendy, Vršič (Bohar 83), Rajčevič, Viler, Stojanovič, Mertelj. Coach: Ante Šimundža (SVN)

Group G
Match 1 - Sporting Clube de Portugal (POR)
H 1-1 Zahovič (90+2)
Handanovič, Filipovič, Sallalich (Bohar 58), Marcos Tavares (Mendy 84), Ibraimi, Vršič (Zahovič 81), Rajčevič, Viler, Stojanovič, Arghus, Mertelj. Coach: Ante Šimundža (SVN)
Match 2 - FC Schalke 04 (GER)
A 1-1 Bohar (37)
Handanovič, Šuler, Filipovič, Mejač, Marcos Tavares, Ibraimi, Vršič (Mendy 67), Rajčevič, Viler, Bohar (Sallalich 82), Mertelj (N'Diaye 80). Coach: Ante Šimundža (SVN)
Match 3 - Chelsea FC (ENG)
A 0-6
Handanovič, Šuler, Filipovič, Mejač, Marcos Tavares (Mendy 72), Ibraimi (Zahovič 68), Rajčevič, Viler (Vršič 57), Stojanovič, Bohar, Mertelj. Coach: Ante Šimundža (SVN)
Match 4 - Chelsea FC (ENG)
H 1-1 Ibraimi (50)
Handanovič, Filipovič, Sallalich (N'Diaye 90+2), Marcos Tavares, Ibraimi (Bohar 90), Zahovič (Mendy 73), Rajčevič, Viler, Stojanovič, Arghus, Mertelj. Coach: Ante Šimundža (SVN)
Match 5 - Sporting Clube de Portugal (POR)
A 1-3 Jefferson (42og)
Handanovič, Filipovič, Mejač, Sallalich (Bohar 69), Marcos Tavares, Zahovič (Mendy 76), Vršič (Ibraimi 46), Rajčevič, Stojanovič, Arghus, Mertelj. Coach: Ante Šimundža (SVN)

Match 6 - FC Schalke 04 (GER)
H 0-1
Handanovič, Filipovič, Sallalich (Mendy 65), Marcos Tavares, Ibraimi (Zahovič 83), Rajčevič, Viler, Stojanovič (Vršič 76), Bohar, Arghus, Mertelj. Coach: Ante Šimundža (SVN)

ND Gorica

Second qualifying round - Molde FK (NOR)
A 1-4 Majcen (70p)
Simčič, Modolo, Vetrih, Širok, Majcen, Žigon (Džuzdanovič 66), Arčon, Kolenc (Enow 46), Jogan, Vanin, Johnson. Coach: Luigi Apolloni (ITA)
H 1-1 Jogan (63)
Simčič, Enow, Modolo (Kavčič 58), Vetrih, Širok, Majcen (Nagode 75), Žigon, Arčon, Osuji (Džuzdanovič 42), Jogan, Johnson. Coach: Luigi Apolloni (ITA)
Red card: Vetrih 79

FC Koper

First qualifying round - FK Čelik Nikšić (MNE)
A 5-0 Palčič (21), Halilovič (37), Čovilo (49, 85), Guberac (87)
Radošević, Blažič, Guberac, Ivetić, Galešić (Lotrič 68), Halilovič, Črnigoj (Žibert 80), Hadžič, Palčič, Štromajer (Pučko 61), Čovilo. Coach: Rodolfo Vanoli (ITA)
H 4-0 Štromajer (10), Galešić (16p, 90+4), Pučko (90)
Radošević, Gregorič, Blažič, Guberac, Ivetić, Galešić, Halilovič, Črnigoj, Palčič (Pučko 52), Štromajer (Žibert 89), Čovilo (Štulac 52). Coach: Rodolfo Vanoli (ITA)

Second qualifying round - Neftçi PFK (AZE)
A 2-1 Galešić (24), Palčič (41)
Radošević, Blažič, Guberac, Ivetić, Galešić (Lotrič 83), Halilovič, Črnigoj, Hadžič, Palčič (Gregorič 87), Štromajer (Pučko 66), Čovilo. Coach: Rodolfo Vanoli (ITA)
H 0-2
Radošević, Blažič (Pučko 63), Guberac, Ivetić, Galešić, Halilovič, Črnigoj (Gregorič 70), Hadžič (Lotrič 89), Palčič, Štromajer, Čovilo. Coach: Rodolfo Vanoli (ITA)
Red card: Štromajer 51

NK Rudar Velenje

First qualifying round - KF Laçi (ALB)
H 1-1 Klinar (17)
Rozman, Bukšek, Stjepanović, Kocič (45+1), Rošer (Bolha 75), Firer, Krefl (Jahič 60), Črnčič, Tolimir, Klinar, Knezović, Eterović. Coach: Jernej Javornik (SVN)
A 1-1 Eterović (90+3) **(aet; 2-3 on pens)**
Rozman, Rošer, Firer (Kocič 32), Črnčič, Jahič (Krefl 58), Tolimir, Klinar, Dedič (Plesec 82), Radujko, Knezović, Eterović. Coach: Jernej Javornik (SVN)

DOMESTIC LEAGUE CLUB-BY-CLUB

NK Celje

1919 • Petrol Arena (13,400) • nk-celje.si
Major honours
Slovenian Cup (1) 2005
Coach: Simon Rožman

2014

18/07	h	Zavrč	L	0-1	
27/07	a	Domžale	L	0-1	
01/08	h	Krka	W	3-0	Verbič, Ahmedi, Vrhovec
09/08	a	Koper	W	2-0	Omoregie, Bajde
16/08	h	Maribor	W	3-1	T Klemenčič, Omoregie, Bajde
24/08	a	Radomlje	W	3-0	Verbič 2, Ahmedi
30/08	h	Olimpija	D	0-0	
13/09	a	Gorica	D	1-1	Ahmedi (p)
20/09	h	Rudar	W	1-0	Omoregie
24/09	a	Zavrč	D	0-0	
27/09	h	Domžale	W	2-0	Oršić, Omoregie
05/10	a	Krka	D	1-1	Ahmedi
15/10	h	Koper	D	1-1	Miškić
18/10	a	Maribor	W	2-1	og (Rajčevič), Omoregie
25/10	h	Radomlje	W	5-0	Miškić 3, Ahmedi, Vrhovec, Omoregie (p)
02/11	a	Olimpija	W	3-1	Miškić, Omoregie, Oršić
08/11	h	Gorica	W	2-0	Lovrečič 2
22/11	a	Rudar	D	0-0	
29/11	h	Zavrč	W	3-0	Verbič 2, Miškić
06/12	a	Domžale	W	1-0	Verbič

2015

04/03	h	Krka	W	2-1	Bajde, Omoregie
07/03	h	Maribor	L	0-2	
11/03	a	Koper	W	1-0	Lendrić
15/03	a	Radomlje	W	1-0	Miškić
21/03	h	Olimpija	D	0-0	
04/04	a	Gorica	D	2-2	Verbič 2
10/04	h	Rudar	L	1-3	Verbič
18/04	a	Zavrč	W	2-1	Jeslínek, Omoregie
25/04	h	Domžale	D	0-0	
29/04	a	Krka	W	4-0	Miškić 2, Omoregie, Bajde
02/05	h	Koper	W	3-2	Šporn, Omoregie, Gobec
06/05	a	Maribor	L	1-4	Lendrić (p)
09/05	h	Radomlje	W	2-0	Verbič 2, Miškić
16/05	a	Olimpija	W	2-1	Bajde, Verbič
23/05	h	Gorica	L	0-3	
30/05	a	Rudar	W	3-1	Jugović, Omoregie 2

No	Name	Nat	DoB	Pos	Aps	(s)	Gls
10	Valon Ahmedi	ALB	07/10/94	M	20		5
9	Gregor Bajde		29/04/94	A	19	(3)	5
23	Adnan Bašić	BIH	13/12/96	A		(2)	
21	Dejan Djermanovič		17/06/88	A		(10)	
18	Sebastjan Gobec		06/12/79	M	5	(11)	1
20	Marko Jakolič		16/04/91	D	16	(7)	
21	Jiři Jeslínek	CZE	30/09/87	A	6	(8)	1
8	Igor Jugović	CRO	23/01/89	M	14	(7)	1
31	Metod Jurhar		07/12/97	G	1		
3	Marko Klemenčič		09/03/97	D	2	(1)	
6	Tilen Klemenčič		21/08/95	D	31	(1)	1
12	Matic Kotnik		23/07/90	G	32		
5	Marko Krajcer		06/06/85	D	24		
25	Yuto Kubo	JPN	07/08/92	M	5	(3)	
33	Ivan Lendrić	CRO	08/08/91	A	8	(8)	2
25	Anej Lovrečič		10/05/87	M	3	(11)	2
19	Danijel Miškić	CRO	11/10/93	M	27	(3)	7
1	Amel Mujčinovič		20/11/73	G	3	(1)	
11	Sunny Omoregie	NGA	02/01/89	A	30	(5)	12
28	Mislav Oršić	CRO	29/12/92	A	13		2
32	Janez Pišek		04/05/98	D		(1)	
32	Nicolas Rajsel	FRA	31/05/93	A		(3)	
27	Ramón Soria	ESP	07/03/89	D	15		
13	Jon Šporn		22/05/97	M	6	(4)	1
7	Benjamin Verbič		27/11/93	M	31	(1)	15
30	Tadej Vidmajer		10/03/92	D	33		
4	Blaž Vrhovec		20/02/92	M	25		2
6	Miha Zajc		01/07/94	M	3		
16	Blaž Zbičajnik		24/07/95	M		(2)	
24	Matic Žitko		21/02/90	D	20	(3)	
29	Andraž Žurej		17/05/93	A	4	(7)	

NK Domžale

1921 • Športni park (3,212) • nkdomzale.si
Major honours
Slovenian League (2) 2007, 2008; Slovenian Cup (1) 2011
Coach: Luka Elsner

2014

20/07	a	Gorica	W	1-0	Ožbolt
27/07	h	Celje	W	1-0	Požeg Vancaš
01/08	a	Zavrč	W	2-0	Morel, Šišić
09/08	a	Rudar	W	1-0	og (Knezović)
16/08	h	Krka	W	2-0	Aneff, Korun
24/08	a	Koper	W	1-0	Živec
30/08	h	Maribor	W	2-0	Šišić, Kous
13/09	a	Radomlje	W	2-0	Parker, Aneff
20/09	h	Olimpija	D	0-0	
24/09	a	Gorica	W	3-0	Aneff, Horić, Parker
27/09	a	Celje	L	0-2	
04/10	h	Zavrč	L	1-3	Maksimović
15/10	h	Rudar	D	1-1	Korun (p)
19/10	a	Krka	W	1-0	Morel
25/10	h	Koper	W	2-0	Morel, og (Delić)
31/10	a	Maribor	W	1-0	Aneff
09/11	h	Radomlje	W	3-0	Morel, Aneff, Maksimović
22/11	a	Olimpija	L	1-2	Maksimović
29/11	a	Gorica	W	2-1	Korun, Parker
06/12	h	Celje	L	0-1	

2015

28/02	a	Rudar	D	0-0	
04/03	a	Zavrč	D	0-0	
07/03	h	Krka	W	2-1	Črnic 2 (2p)
15/03	a	Koper	L	0-1	
22/03	h	Maribor	D	0-0	
03/04	a	Radomlje	W	3-0	Črnic (p), Juninho, Morel
11/04	h	Olimpija	L	0-1	
18/04	a	Gorica	W	3-1	Vuk 2, Podlogar
25/04	a	Celje	D	0-0	
29/04	a	Zavrč	L	2-3	Morel, Podlogar
02/05	h	Rudar	W	4-0	Požeg Vancaš, Zec, Morel, Ožbolt
06/05	a	Krka	L	2-3	Podlogar, Zec
12/05	h	Koper	W	3-0	Podlogar 2, Juninho
16/05	a	Maribor	L	0-1	
23/05	h	Radomlje	W	4-0	Vuk 2, Podlogar, Ožbolt
30/05	a	Olimpija	W	2-0	Vuk 2

No	Name	Nat	DoB	Pos	Aps	(s)	Gls
26	Sasha Aneff	URU	26/06/91	A	11	(5)	5
11	Matic Črnic		12/06/92	M	10	(4)	3
27	Gaber Dobrovoljc		27/01/93	D	4	(1)	
32	Mate Eterović	CRO	13/07/84	A	3	(4)	
21	Ernest Grvala		11/10/96	M		(2)	
6	Kenan Horić	BIH	13/07/90	D	29		1
23	Lucas Horvat	ARG	13/10/85	A	4	(4)	
90	Zeni Husmani	MKD	28/11/90	M	9	(2)	
64	Erik Janža		21/06/93	D	19		
8	Anže Jelar		18/08/91	A	3	(10)	
9	Jorrin John	ATG	06/11/91	A		(2)	
84	Juninho	BRA	13/03/84	D	7	(2)	2
88	Uroš Korun		25/05/87	D	34		3
92	Žiga Kous		27/10/92	D	4	(7)	1
37	Žan Majer		25/07/92	M	32		
19	Nemanja Maksimović	SRB	26/01/95	M	14	(2)	3
87	Benjamin Morel	FRA	10/06/87	A	24	(8)	7
31	Alen Ožbolt		24/06/96	A	4	(15)	3
23	Josh Parker	ATG	01/12/90	A	16	(1)	3
17	Matej Podlogar		23/02/91	A	5	(11)	6
7	Rudi Požeg Vancaš		15/03/94	M	19	(7)	2
30	Veljko Simić	SRB	17/02/95	M	12	(5)	
2	Nejc Skubic		13/06/89	D	34		
20	Aladin Šišić	BIH	28/09/91	A	11	(4)	2
24	Dejan Trajkovski		20/07/92	D	15		
12	Antonin Trilles	FRA	20/07/83	G	1		
41	Nejc Vidmar		31/03/89	G	35		
10	Slobodan Vuk		15/09/89	A	11	(10)	6
5	Darko Zec		21/02/89	D	20	(1)	2
11	Saša Aleksander Živec		02/04/91	A	6		1

ND Gorica

1947 • Športni park (5,000) • nd-gorica.com
Major honours
Slovenian League (4) 1996, 2004, 2005, 2006; Slovenian Cup (3) 2001, 2002, 2014
**Coach: Luigi Apolloni (ITA);
(06/10/14) Miran Srebrnič;
(11/11/14) Iztok Kavčič;
(20/01/15) Miran Srebrnič**

2014

20/07	h	Domžale	L	0-1	
27/07	a	Krka	L	1-2	Arčon
03/08	h	Koper	L	0-1	
09/08	a	Maribor	L	1-5	Makinwa
17/08	h	Radomlje	W	4-0	Majcen 2, Vetrih, Širok
23/08	a	Olimpija	D	0-0	
31/08	h	Rudar	L	1-2	Žigon (p)
13/09	h	Celje	D	1-1	Žigon
21/09	a	Zavrč	D	0-0	
24/09	a	Domžale	L	0-3	
29/09	h	Krka	W	2-1	Henty, Majcen (p)
04/10	a	Koper	L	0-1	
15/10	h	Maribor	L	0-2	
19/10	a	Radomlje	W	3-0	og (Zavrl), Majcen, Henty
25/10	h	Olimpija	L	0-3	
02/11	a	Rudar	L	0-1	
08/11	a	Celje	L	0-2	
22/11	h	Zavrč	W	1-0	Johnson
29/11	h	Domžale	L	1-2	Majcen
07/12	a	Krka	W	2-0	Napoli, Majcen

2015

28/02	a	Maribor	L	1-5	Eleke
04/03	a	Koper	L	1-2	Taïder
08/03	h	Radomlje	D	0-0	
14/03	a	Olimpija	L	1-3	Taïder
21/03	h	Rudar	W	3-0	Žigon 2, Širok
04/04	h	Celje	D	2-2	Martinović, Vetrih
10/04	a	Zavrč	D	0-0	
18/04	a	Domžale	L	1-3	Žigon
25/04	h	Krka	W	3-0	Slivka, Majcen, Ruggiero
29/04	a	Koper	L	0-2	
02/05	h	Maribor	D	1-1	Eleke
06/05	a	Radomlje	L	0-1	
09/05	h	Olimpija	L	1-2	Žigon
16/05	a	Rudar	W	2-1	Vetrih, Žigon
23/05	a	Celje	W	3-0	Johnson, Eleke, Vetrih (p)
30/05	h	Zavrč	W	4-0	Džuzdanović 2, Johnson, Vetrih

No	Name	Nat	DoB	Pos	Aps	(s)	Gls
11	Sandi Arčon		06/01/91	A	11	(8)	1
4	Matteo Boccaccini	ITA	08/02/93	D	5	(2)	
93	Alexander Caputo	ITA	12/01/93	D	7		
26	Amel Džuzdanović		26/08/94	M	18	(18)	2
19	Blessing Eleke	NGA	05/03/96	A	14	(4)	3
3	Solomon Enow	CMR	18/03/87	D	11	(4)	
37	Daniele Ferri	ITA	07/03/92	A		(1)	
92	Alberto Gallinetta	ITA	16/04/92	G	8		
15	Daniele Gragnoli	ITA	03/01/94	A		(1)	
30	Ezekiel Henty	NGA	13/05/93	A	9	(1)	2
16	Tine Hlede		22/04/96	D	1		
32	Alessio Innocenti	ITA	04/02/93	M	6	(11)	
13	Sead Jakupović	BIH	17/11/92	D	2		
27	Alen Jogan		24/08/85	D	23		
90	Marshal Johnson	NGA	12/12/89	M	20	(3)	3
42	Juninho	BRA	25/03/91	M	7	(1)	
23	Tine Kavčič		16/02/94	D	6	(3)	
2	Miha Kokol		23/11/89	D	1	(1)	
14	Jaka Kolenc		23/02/94	M		(1)	
9	Luka Majcen		25/07/89	A	20	(9)	7
20	Stephen Makinwa	NGA	26/07/83	A	4	(11)	1
15	Dino Martinović		20/07/90	A	9	(4)	1
6	Marco Modolo	ITA	23/03/89	D	10		
96	Tilen Nagode		21/03/96	A		(5)	
21	Simone Napoli	ITA	10/07/94	D	14		1
17	Bede Osuji	NGA	21/01/96	A	1	(11)	
14	Luigi Palumbo	ITA	30/05/91	D	9		
29	Lorenzo Pasqualini	ITA	19/08/89	M	28		
31	Ronaldo Vanin	BRA	31/01/83	D	13		
28	Giuseppe Ruggiero	ITA	28/10/93	M	6	(4)	1
12	Vasja Simčič		01/07/83	G	20		
95	Vykintas Slivka	LTU	29/04/95	M	12		1
1	Gregor Sorčan		05/03/96	G	8		
8	Matija Širok		31/05/91	D	26	(4)	2
18	Nabil Taïder	TUN	26/05/83	M	10	(1)	2
7	Amedej Vetrih		16/09/90	M	31		5
10	Dejan Žigon		30/03/89	A	25	(4)	7

 **SLOVENIA**

FC Koper

1920 • Bonifika (5,000) • fckoper.si

Major honours
Slovenian League (1) 2010; Slovenian Cup (3) 2006, 2007, 2015

Coach: Rodolfo Vanoli (ITA);
(28/08/14) Alen Ščulac;
(12/04/15) Rodolfo Vanoli (ITA)

2014

20/07	a	Radomlje	W	2-1	Ivetić, Štromajer
03/08	a	Gorica	W	1-0	Lotrič
09/08	h	Celje	L	0-2	
15/08	a	Zavrč	L	0-1	
24/08	h	Domžale	L	0-1	
27/08	h	Olimpija	L	1-2	Lotrič
31/08	a	Krka	W	3-1	Žibert, Hadžić, Pučko
13/09	a	Rudar	W	3-2	og (Knezović), Hadžić, Štromajer
20/09	h	Maribor	L	1-2	Žibert
24/09	h	Radomlje	L	0-1	Pučko
27/09	a	Olimpija	L	0-4	
04/10	h	Gorica	W	1-0	Guberac
15/10	a	Celje	D	1-1	Pučko
18/10	h	Zavrč	W	2-1	Delić, Lotrič
25/10	a	Domžale	L	0-2	
02/11	h	Krka	W	1-0	Pučko
08/11	h	Rudar	L	1-3	Hadžić
22/11	a	Maribor	L	0-4	
30/11	a	Radomlje	L	1-2	Guberac
06/12	h	Olimpija	W	2-1	Gregorič, Lotrič

2015

04/03	a	Gorica	W	2-1	og (Enow), Črnigoj
11/03	h	Celje	L	0-1	
07/03	a	Zavrč	L	1-2	Hadžibulić
15/03	h	Domžale	W	1-0	Hadžič (p)
22/03	a	Krka	L	0-3	
04/04	a	Rudar	D	2-2	Lotrič 2
11/04	h	Maribor	L	1-4	Blažič
18/04	h	Radomlje	W	2-0	Lotrič 2
25/04	a	Olimpija	D	0-0	
29/04	h	Gorica	W	2-0	Štromajer, Hadžič
02/05	a	Celje	L	2-3	Galešić, Rahmanović
06/05	h	Zavrč	L	1-2	Halilović
12/05	h	Domžale	L	0-3	
16/05	h	Krka	L	0-2	
23/05	h	Rudar	L	0-3	
30/05	a	Maribor	D	0-0	

No	Name	Nat	DoB	Pos	Aps	(s)	Gls
12	David Adam		15/11/93	G	3	(1)	
2	Jan Andrejašič		16/09/95	D	5	(2)	
5	Miha Blažič		08/05/93	D	16		1
9	Daniel Bradaschia	ITA	02/03/89	A	1	(3)	
33	Miroslav Čovilo	SRB	06/05/86	M	2	(1)	
20	Domen Črnigoj		18/11/95	M	24	(4)	1
14	Uroš Delić	SRB	10/08/87	M	3	(2)	1
14	Goran Galešić	BIH	11/03/89	M	5	(2)	1
3	Miha Gregorič		22/08/89	D	25	(3)	1
7	Ivica Guberac		05/07/88	M	26	(1)	2
11	Sead Hadžibulić	BIH	30/01/83	A	2	(3)	1
27	Damir Hadžič		01/10/84	D	28	(1)	5
16	Denis Halilovič		02/03/86	D	22	(1)	1
1	Ermin Hasić		19/05/75	G	10		
11	Perica Ivetić	BIH	28/11/86	M	14		1
24	Miha Kokol		23/11/89	D	2	(1)	
23	Marko Krivičić		01/02/96	M	6	(4)	
10	Mitja Lotrič		03/09/94	A	18	(8)	8
9	Timotej Mate		30/08/96	D	1	(1)	
88	Ante Mitrović	CRO	04/04/89	M	1	(9)	
6	Nik Mršić		07/03/96	M		(2)	
45	Žan Nikolič		06/07/96	M		(3)	
29	Matej Palčič		21/06/93	M	15	(2)	
99	Dejan Pesevski	MKD	05/08/93	M	5	(6)	
22	Patrik Posavac		14/03/95	M	7	(3)	
49	Matej Pučko		06/10/93	A	26	(8)	4
25	Božidar Radošević	CRO	04/04/89	G	10		
8	Amar Rahmanović	BIH	13/05/94	M	8	(1)	1
83	Vasja Simčič		01/07/83	G	13	(1)	
19	Žiga Smrtnik		01/02/94	A	4	(4)	
21	Nenad Srečković	SRB	11/04/88	A	10	(5)	
4	Denis Šme		22/03/94	D	18	(4)	
30	Jaka Štromajer		27/07/83	A	26	(4)	3
18	Leo Štulac		26/09/94	M	25	(3)	
28	Ante Tomić	CRO	23/05/83	M	4		
8	Urban Žibert		08/05/92	M	11	(8)	2

NK Krka

1922 • Portoval (1,500) • nkkrka.com

Coach: Miloš Rus;
(04/11/14) Andrej Kastrevec

2014

19/07	a	Olimpija	L	1-3	Šaban
27/07	h	Gorica	W	2-1	Ihbeisheh, Kramarič
01/08	a	Celje	L	0-3	
10/08	h	Zavrč	L	2-3	Kastrevec 2
16/08	a	Domžale	L	0-2	
23/08	a	Rudar	L	1-3	Kramarič
31/08	h	Koper	L	1-3	Mojstrović
13/09	a	Maribor	L	0-2	
21/09	h	Radomlje	D	0-0	
24/09	h	Olimpija	W	2-1	Fuček, Dežmar
29/09	a	Gorica	L	1-2	Fuček
05/10	h	Celje	D	1-1	Jurić
15/10	a	Zavrč	L	0-1	
19/10	h	Domžale	L	0-1	
26/10	h	Rudar	D	1-1	Perić
02/11	a	Koper	L	0-1	
09/11	h	Maribor	L	1-3	Palić (p)
23/11	a	Radomlje	W	2-0	Welbeck, Perić
29/11	a	Olimpija	W	2-1	Perić, og (Matič)
07/12	a	Gorica	L	0-2	

2015

01/03	h	Zavrč	W	3-0	Perić, Ejup, Kramar
04/03	a	Celje	L	1-2	Fuček
07/03	h	Domžale	L	1-2	Ejup
14/03	a	Rudar	D	0-0	
22/03	h	Koper	W	3-0	Welbeck, Novinić, Kauber
04/04	a	Maribor	D	2-2	Kastrevec, Palić (p)
12/04	h	Radomlje	D	1-1	Kastrevec
19/04	a	Olimpija	D	0-0	
25/04	a	Gorica	L	0-3	
29/04	h	Celje	L	0-4	
02/05	a	Zavrč	W	1-0	Ihbeisheh
06/05	h	Domžale	W	3-2	Danijel Rašić, Fuček, Perić
10/05	h	Rudar	W	2-0	Novinić, Kastrevec
16/05	a	Koper	W	2-0	Kastrevec, Fuček (p)
23/05	h	Maribor	L	1-3	Aniekan
30/05	a	Radomlje	W	1-0	Žižić

No	Name	Nat	DoB	Pos	Aps	(s)	Gls
8	Favour Aniekan	NGA	10/04/94	M	3	(6)	1
23	Luka Bele		25/02/94	D		(2)	
6	Vinko Buden	CRO	18/01/86	D	12		
47	Mario Carević	CRO	29/03/82	M	4	(2)	
17	Danijel Dežmar		31/03/88	D	22	(7)	1
13	Lamin Diallo		31/08/91	D	5	(1)	
15	Leo Ejup		09/09/94	D	10	(1)	2
7	Josip Fuček	CRO	26/02/85	A	32		5
11	Jaka Ihbeishen	PLE	03/08/86	M	19	(8)	2
8	Tomislav Jurić	CRO	09/04/90	M	12	(4)	1
77	Žiga Kastrevec		25/02/94	M	28	(3)	6
28	Kevin Kauber	EST	23/03/95	A	1	(10)	1
19	Urban Kramar		03/10/90	M	2	(17)	1
97	Martin Kramarič		14/11/97	A	3	(4)	2
90	Nikola Maksimović	SRB	01/07/95	M		(1)	
31	Miodrag Mitrovic	SUI	14/07/91	G	13	(1)	
17	Denis Mojstrović		17/10/86	M	17	(6)	1
44	Jan Novak		04/10/97	M		(2)	
9	Enes Novinić	CRO	18/07/85	A	10	(6)	2
14	Andrija Novosel	CRO	12/08/93	M	1	(5)	
69	Matko Obradović	CRO	11/05/91	G	7		
16	Antun Palić	CRO	25/06/88	M	21	(1)	2
12	Tomislav Pelin	CRO	26/03/81	G	16		
12	Marin Perić	CRO	17/10/90	A	29	(3)	6
55	Matej Potokar		19/10/96	M	2		
33	Damir Rašić	CRO	05/10/88	D	11		
21	Danijel Rašić	CRO	05/10/88	D	28	(2)	1
8	Martin Šaban	CRO	26/12/87	A	6	(7)	1
5	Alen Vučkič		01/02/90	D	23	(2)	
24	Nana Welbeck	GHA	24/11/94	M	27		2
4	Nikola Žižić	CRO	23/01/88	D	28	(1)	1
3	Gregor Žugelj		02/09/91	M	4	(1)	

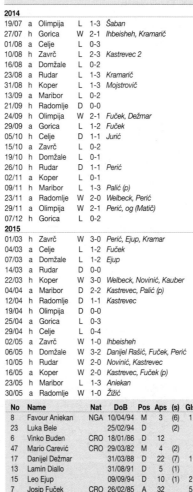

NK Maribor

1960 • Ljudski vrt (12,432) • nkmaribor.com

Major honours
Slovenian League (13) 1997, 1998, 1999, 2000, 2001, 2002, 2003, 2009, 2011, 2012, 2013, 2014, 2015; Slovenian Cup (8) 1992, 1994, 1997, 1999, 2004, 2010, 2012, 2013

Coach: Ante Šimundža

2014

19/07	h	Rudar	W	1-0	Viler
26/07	h	Radomlje	W	3-2	og (Balkovec), Zahovič 2
09/08	h	Gorica	W	2-1	Marcos Tavares, Bohar
16/08	a	Celje	L	1-3	og (Vrhovec)
23/08	h	Zavrč	W	3-0	Bohar, Zahovič, Mendy
30/08	a	Domžale	L	0-2	
13/09	h	Krka	W	2-0	Zahovič 2
20/09	a	Koper	W	2-1	Dervišević, Marcos Tavares
24/09	a	Rudar	W	1-0	Marcos Tavares
27/09	a	Radomlje	D	0-0	
04/10	h	Olimpija	D	3-3	Mendy, Šuler, Marcos Tavares
15/10	a	Gorica	W	2-0	Zahovič 2
18/10	h	Celje	L	1-2	Zahovič
25/10	a	Zavrč	W	2-0	Marcos Tavares (p)
31/10	h	Domžale	L	0-1	
09/11	a	Krka	W	3-1	Marcos Tavares, Sallalich, Mendy
22/11	h	Koper	W	4-0	Marcos Tavares, Mendy, Arghus, Biton
29/11	h	Rudar	W	3-2	Marcos Tavares 2, Zahovič
06/12	h	Radomlje	W	4-1	Bohar 2, Marcos Tavares, Sallalich

2015

28/02	h	Gorica	W	5-1	Volaš 3, Zahovič, Marcos Tavares
04/03	a	Olimpija	W	1-0	N'Diaye
07/03	h	Celje	W	2-0	Mendy, N'Diaye
14/03	a	Zavrč	W	2-1	Ibraimi (p), Marcos Tavares
22/03	a	Domžale	D	0-0	
04/04	h	Krka	D	2-2	Šuler, Marcos Tavares
08/04	a	Olimpija	D	0-0	
11/04	a	Koper	W	4-1	Volaš 2 (2p), Bohar, Zahovič
18/04	a	Rudar	L	0-2	
24/04	a	Radomlje	W	6-1	Zahovič, Marcos Tavares 2, Viler, Volaš 2
29/04	h	Olimpija	W	4-1	Bohar 2, Vršič, Rajčević
02/05	a	Gorica	D	1-1	Mertelj
06/05	h	Celje	W	4-1	Šuler, Volaš 2, Ibraimi
09/05	a	Zavrč	W	3-1	Sallalich, Volaš, Marcos Tavares
16/05	h	Domžale	W	1-0	Marcos Tavares
23/05	a	Krka	W	3-1	Sallalich 2, Mendy
30/05	h	Koper	D	0-0	

No	Name	Nat	DoB	Pos	Aps	(s)	Gls
44	Arghus	BRA	19/01/88	D	15		1
20	Dudu Biton	ISR	01/03/88	A	3	(8)	1
39	Damjan Bohar		18/10/91	M	24	(9)	7
1	Aljaž Cotman		26/04/94	G			
21	Amir Dervišević		04/07/92	M	14	(2)	1
17	Nusmir Fajić	BIH	12/01/87	A	2	(2)	
5	Željko Filipović		03/10/88	M	14		
33	Jasmin Handanović		28/01/78	G	34		
23	Dino Hotić		26/07/95	M		(4)	
10	Agim Ibraimi	MKD	29/08/88	M	20	(4)	2
3	Erik Janža		21/06/93	D	5	(1)	
97	Martin Kramarič		14/11/97	A		(1)	
9	Marcos Tavares	BRA	30/03/84	A	26	(8)	17
7	Aleš Mejač		18/03/83	D	15	(6)	
14	Jean-Philippe Mendy	FRA	04/03/87	A	12	(14)	6
70	Aleš Mertelj		22/03/87	M	22	(6)	1
6	Welle N'Diaye	SEN	05/04/90	M	12	(3)	2
69	Matko Obradović	CRO	11/05/91	G	1		
45	Robert Pušaver			D		(1)	
26	Aleksander Rajčević		17/11/86	D	30	(1)	1
8	Sintayehu Sallalich	ISR	20/06/91	M	17	(10)	5
30	Petar Stojanovič		07/10/95	D	22	(1)	
4	Marko Šuler		09/03/83	D	24		3
24	Dejan Trajkovski		14/04/92	D	1		
24	Mitja Viler		01/09/86	D	26	(2)	2
24	Dejan Vokić		12/06/96	M	1	(1)	
17	Dalibor Volaš		27/02/87	A	10	(4)	10
13	Dare Vršič		26/09/84	M	18	(8)	1
31	Daniel Vujčič		12/04/95	M	2		
16	Damjan Vuklišević		28/06/95	D	2		
2	Luka Zahovič		15/11/95	A	22	(8)	12
36	Žiga Živko		21/07/95	D		(1)	

NK Olimpija Ljubljana

2005 • Stožice (16,038) • nkolimpija.si
Coach: Darko Karapetrovič;
(17/05/15) Aleksandar Radosavljevič

2014
19/07	h	Krka	W	3-1	Šporar, Omladič, Rodič
10/08	a	Radomlje	W	4-1	Rodič, Omladič, Bajrič, Vukčevič
16/08	h	Rudar	W	2-0	Rodič, Omladič
23/08	h	Gorica	D	0-0	
27/08	a	Koper	W	2-1	Omladič, Šporar
30/08	h	Celje	D	0-0	
13/09	h	Zavrč	W	2-0	Kapun, og (Datkovič)
20/09	a	Domžale	D	0-0	
24/09	a	Krka	L	1-2	Vukčevič
27/09	h	Koper	W	4-0	Zajc, Šporar, Zarifovič, Omladič (p)
04/10	a	Maribor	D	3-3	Vukčevič, Šporar, Kapun
15/10	h	Radomlje	W	4-0	Rodič, Vukčevič, Djurkovič, Šporar
18/10	a	Rudar	D	0-0	
25/10	a	Gorica	W	3-0	Zajc, Valenčič, Burgič
02/11	h	Celje	L	1-3	Mitrovič
08/11	h	Zavrč	W	2-0	Šporar, Škarabot
22/11	h	Domžale	W	2-1	Matič, Vukčevič
29/11	h	Krka	L	1-2	Šporar
06/12	a	Koper	L	1-2	Rodič

2015
28/02	a	Radomlje	W	4-0	Šporar 2, og (Cankar), Ivančič
04/03	h	Maribor	L	0-1	
07/03	h	Rudar	D	0-0	
14/03	h	Gorica	W	3-1	Mitrovič 2, Henty
21/03	a	Celje	D	0-0	
04/04	h	Zavrč	W	3-1	Henty, Zajc, Kapun
08/04	h	Maribor	D	0-0	
11/04	a	Domžale	W	1-0	Zajc
19/04	a	Krka	D	0-0	
25/04	h	Koper	D	0-0	
29/04	a	Maribor	L	1-4	Bajrič
02/05	h	Radomlje	W	3-1	Šporar 2 (1p), Henty
06/05	a	Rudar	L	0-2	
09/05	a	Gorica	W	2-1	Henty, Vukčevič
16/05	h	Celje	L	1-2	Šporar
23/05	a	Zavrč	W	2-1	Mitrovič, Šporar
30/05	h	Domžale	L	0-2	

No	Name	Nat	DoB	Pos	Aps	(s)	Gls
88	Stjepan Babić	CRO	04/12/88	M	5	(6)	
24	Kenan Bajrič		20/12/94	D	31	(2)	2
29	Rok Baskera		26/05/93	M	8	(7)	
16	Blaž Božič		23/10/90	M	2	(4)	
21	Darko Brljak		23/12/84	G	14		
30	Miran Burgič		25/09/84	A	7	(14)	1
26	Jaka Corn		14/04/95	M		(2)	
20	Antonio Delamea Mlinar		10/06/91	D	23		
9	Enis Djurkovič		24/05/89	A		(10)	1
17	Matic Fink		27/02/90	D	16	(3)	
11	Luka Gajič		06/05/96	A		(4)	
25	Josip Golubar	CRO	04/03/85	A	4	(4)	
55	Ezekiel Henty	NGA	13/05/93	A	13	(1)	4
1	Aljaž Ivačič		29/12/93	G	2		
19	Kruno Ivančič	CRO	04/03/85	A	2	(7)	1
5	Boban Jovič		25/06/91	D	18		
19	Mario Jurčevič		01/06/95	M	1	(2)	
23	Nik Kapun		09/01/94	M	26	(2)	3
18	Aleksandar Lazevski	MKD	21/01/88	D	7		
8	Darijan Matič		28/05/83	M	35		1
32	Nemanja Mitrovič		15/10/92	D	34		4
21	Nik Omladič		21/08/89	M	16		5
7	Aleksandar Rodič		26/12/79	A	16	(9)	5
44	Hrvoje Spahija	CRO	23/03/88	D	4	(3)	
1	Aleksander Šeliga		01/02/80	G	20	(1)	
4	Matija Škarabot		04/02/88	D	1	(2)	1
10	Andraž Šporar		27/02/94	A	31	(1)	13
11	Filip Valenčič		07/01/92	A	9	(3)	1
15	Marko Vukčevič	MNE	07/06/93	M	21	(8)	6
6	Miha Zajc		01/07/94	M	16	(3)	4
27	Aris Zarifovič		02/06/88	D	8	(3)	1
5	Luka Žinko		23/03/83	M	6	(4)	

NK Radomlje

1972 • Športni park, Domžale (3,212) • nk-radomlje.si
Coach: Dejan Djuranovič

2014
20/07	h	Koper	L	1-2	og (Gregorič)
26/07	a	Maribor	L	2-3	Zavrl, Stoiljkovič
02/08	h	Rudar	L	1-2	Zavrl
10/08	h	Olimpija	L	1-4	Avbelj
17/08	a	Gorica	L	0-4	
24/08	h	Celje	L	0-3	
29/08	a	Zavrč	L	1-2	Snoj
13/09	h	Domžale	L	0-2	
21/09	a	Krka	D	0-0	
24/09	h	Koper	W	2-1	Snoj, Zavrl
27/09	h	Maribor	D	0-0	
04/10	a	Rudar	L	0-2	
15/10	a	Olimpija	L	0-4	
19/10	h	Gorica	L	0-3	
25/10	a	Celje	L	0-5	
02/11	h	Zavrč	L	1-2	Zavrl (p)
09/11	a	Domžale	L	0-3	
23/11	h	Krka	L	0-2	
30/11	a	Koper	W	2-1	Stoiljkovič 2
06/12	a	Maribor	L	1-4	Zavrl

2015
28/02	h	Olimpija	L	0-4	
04/03	h	Rudar	W	1-0	Djurkovič (p)
08/03	a	Gorica	D	0-0	
15/03	h	Celje	L	0-1	
20/03	a	Zavrč	L	0-1	
04/04	h	Domžale	L	0-3	
12/04	a	Krka	D	1-1	Djurkovič (p)
18/04	a	Koper	L	0-2	
24/04	h	Maribor	L	1-6	Vuk
29/04	a	Rudar	L	2-3	Vrhunc, og (Krefl)
02/05	a	Olimpija	L	1-3	Barukčič
06/05	h	Gorica	W	1-0	Zorc
09/05	h	Celje	L	2-3	Barukčič 2
17/05	h	Zavrč	L	0-4	
23/05	a	Domžale	L	0-1	
30/05	h	Krka	L	0-1	

No	Name	Nat	DoB	Pos	Aps	(s)	Gls
25	Vjekoslav Andrič		05/08/92	G	23		
8	Tomaž Avbelj		26/08/91	M	19	(7)	1
55	Denis Bajalica	CRO	31/01/91	D	10	(1)	
1	Izidor Balažič		13/05/91	G	3		
29	Jure Balkovec		09/09/94	D	28	(1)	
6	Igor Barukčič		12/11/90	M	8		3
24	Deni Blaževič		13/02/93	G	2		
14	Žan Cankar		13/11/90	D	16	(4)	
26	Matej Centrih		05/09/88	D	13		
20	Luka Cerar		26/05/92	M	25	(5)	
16	Martin Cesar		27/10/95	M		(2)	
89	Enis Djurkovič		24/05/89	A	13	(1)	2
12	Filip Drakovič		31/03/91	D	2	(1)	
18	Eito Furuyama	JPN	08/11/93	D	4	(1)	
18	Luka Gajič		06/05/96	A	3	(10)	
1	Aljaž Ivačič		29/12/93	G	2		
19	Robi Jakovljevič		07/05/93	M	10	(9)	
44	Rok Jazbec		23/09/95	D	13		
23	Mario Jurčevič		01/06/95	M	1	(2)	
32	Alen Koprivec		19/04/93	G	1		
5	Gregor Kosec		02/07/87	D	6		
42	Denis Lidjan		24/09/93	D	14	(4)	
27	Marko Perkovič	CRO	30/08/91	D	13		
39	Tadej Rems		31/07/93	D	13	(2)	
11	Matic Seferovič		22/12/86	M	8	(2)	
33	Žiga Smrtnik		01/02/94	A	8	(7)	
17	Niko Snoj		13/07/90	M	14	(4)	2
12	Kris Stergulc		10/03/92	G	3		
21	Dušan Stoiljkovič	SRB	05/09/94	M	22	(10)	3
3	Dalibor Teinovič	BIH	22/03/77	M	12		
7	Luka Vrhunc		11/03/91	A	17	(9)	1
9	Goran Vuk	CRO	11/10/87	A	18	(8)	1
10	Janez Zavrl		25/12/82	M	24	(7)	5
22	Anže Zorc		06/02/94	M	12	(6)	1
4	Aleksander Zukič		05/01/91	D	15	(1)	
15	Gregor Želko		06/01/94	D		(1)	

NK Rudar Velenje

1948 • Ob jezeru (7,000) • nkrudarvelenje.com
Major honours
Slovenian Cup (1) 1998
Coach: Jernej Javornik

2014
19/07	a	Maribor	L	0-1	
26/07	h	Zavrč	L	0-2	
02/08	a	Radomlje	W	2-1	Radujko, Firer
09/08	h	Domžale	L	0-1	
16/08	a	Olimpija	L	0-2	
23/08	h	Krka	W	3-1	Firer, Bolha, Klinar
31/08	a	Gorica	W	2-1	Jelič, Firer (p)
13/09	h	Koper	L	2-3	Jahič, Džinič
20/09	a	Celje	D	1-1	Jelič
24/09	h	Maribor	D	0-0	
28/09	a	Zavrč	L	0-1	
04/10	h	Radomlje	W	2-0	Džinič, Jelič
15/10	a	Domžale	D	1-1	Jahič
18/10	h	Olimpija	D	0-0	
26/10	a	Krka	D	1-1	Džinič
02/11	h	Gorica	W	1-0	Jelič
08/11	a	Koper	W	3-1	Bolha, Krefl, Trifkovič
22/11	h	Celje	D	0-0	
29/11	a	Maribor	L	2-3	Jelič 2
06/12	h	Zavrč	W	7-2	Jelič, Radujko, Džinič 2, Firer 2, Klinar

2015
28/02	h	Domžale	D	0-0	
04/03	a	Radomlje	L	0-1	
07/03	a	Olimpija	D	0-0	
14/03	h	Krka	D	0-0	
21/03	a	Gorica	L	0-3	
04/04	h	Koper	D	2-2	Firer, Jelič
10/04	a	Celje	W	3-1	Bolha, Babič 2
18/04	h	Maribor	W	2-0	Babič, Knezovič
24/04	a	Zavrč	D	0-0	
29/04	h	Radomlje	W	3-2	Firer, Jelič, Kocič
02/05	a	Domžale	L	0-4	
06/05	h	Olimpija	W	2-0	Firer 2
10/05	a	Krka	L	0-2	
16/05	h	Gorica	L	1-2	Radujko
23/05	a	Koper	W	3-0	Bolha, Tolimir, Radujko
30/05	h	Celje	L	1-3	Jahič

No	Name	Nat	DoB	Pos	Aps	(s)	Gls
33	Mario Babić	CRO	03/07/92	M	27	(6)	3
25	Klemen Bolha		19/03/93	D	19	(8)	4
2	Alen Bukšek		25/07/95	D	1		
1	Matic Čretnik		02/03/91	G	1		
10	Leon Črnčič		02/03/90	M	17		
27	Rusmin Dedič		11/09/82	M	7	(5)	
3	Elvedin Džinič		25/08/85	D	25	(1)	5
32	Mate Eterovič	CRO	13/07/84	A	1		
7	Ivan Firer		19/11/84	A	36		9
19	Senad Jahič		13/05/87	D	19	(12)	3
15	Dragan Jelič		27/02/86	A	25	(4)	9
4	David Kašnik		16/01/87	D	8	(4)	
23	Denis Klinar		21/02/92	M	27		2
29	Ivan Knezovič	CRO	25/09/82	D	32		1
14	Milan Kocič		16/02/90	M	14	(18)	1
8	Aljaž Krefl		20/02/94	M	18	(3)	1
6	Semin Omerovič		06/08/97	A		(1)	
11	Nejc Plesec		13/03/94	M	5	(13)	
28	Dalibor Radujko		17/06/85	M	29	(1)	4
6	Uroš Rošer		27/06/86	M	1	(7)	
22	Matjaž Rozman		03/01/87	G	35		
24	Enis Saramati		19/04/94	A	1	(10)	
5	Nemanja Stjepanovič	BIH	07/02/84	M	21	(3)	
21	Nikola Tolimir		01/04/89	M	8	(5)	1
9	Damjan Trifkovič		22/07/87	M	19	(4)	1

SLOVENIA

NK Zavrč

1998 • Športni park (962); Mestni stadion,
Ptuj (1,700) • nkzavrc.si

**Coach: Željko Orehovec;
(22/12/14) Ivica Solomun (CRO)**

2014

18/07	a	Celje	W	1-0	Šafarić
26/07	a	Rudar	W	2-0	Smrekar, Datković
01/08	h	Domžale	L	0-2	
10/08	a	Krka	W	3-2	Kelenc 2 (1p), Kresinger
15/08	h	Koper	W	1-0	Šafarić (p)
23/08	a	Maribor	L	0-3	
29/08	h	Radomlje	W	2-1	Težak, Datković
13/09	a	Olimpija	L	0-2	
21/09	h	Gorica	D	0-0	
24/09	h	Celje	D	0-0	
28/09	h	Rudar	W	1-0	Brdar
04/10	a	Domžale	W	3-1	Šafarić (p), Kresinger 2
15/10	h	Krka	W	2-0	Jertec, Kresinger
18/10	a	Koper	L	1-2	Cvek
25/10	h	Maribor	L	0-1	
02/11	a	Radomlje	W	2-1	Antolek, Kresinger
08/11	h	Olimpija	L	0-2	
22/11	a	Gorica	L	0-1	
29/11	h	Celje	L	0-3	
06/12	a	Rudar	L	2-7	Kelenc, Antolek

2015

01/03	a	Krka	L	0-3	
04/03	h	Domžale	W	1-0	Cvek
07/03	h	Koper	W	2-1	Kiš, Datković
14/03	a	Maribor	L	1-2	Muminović
20/03	h	Radomlje	W	1-0	Kiš
04/04	a	Olimpija	L	1-3	og (Delamea Mlinar)
10/04	h	Gorica	D	0-0	
18/04	h	Celje	L	1-2	Novoselec
24/04	h	Rudar	D	0-0	
29/04	a	Domžale	W	3-2	og (Dobrovoljc), Kelenc 2
02/05	h	Krka	L	0-1	
06/05	a	Koper	W	2-1	Zorko, Kiš
09/05	h	Maribor	L	1-3	Zorko
17/05	a	Radomlje	W	4-0	Kelenc, Zorko, Kiš 2 (1p)
23/05	h	Olimpija	L	1-2	Kiš
30/05	a	Gorica	L	0-4	

No	Name	Nat	DoB	Pos	Aps	(s)	Gls
13	Sebastijan Antić	CRO	05/11/91	D	14	(2)	
23	Ivan Antolek	CRO	27/01/93	A	7	(8)	2
19	Josip Balić	CRO	08/07/93	M		(3)	
16	Lovro Benić		08/10/94	M		(2)	
3	Luka Bogdan		26/03/96	D	8	(1)	
29	Robert Brdar	CRO	03/04/95	M	4	(11)	1
32	Antonio Brzoja	CRO	05/04/94	D		(2)	
4	Lovro Cvek		06/07/95	M	28	(1)	2
11	Sandi Čeh		06/04/83	D	4	(5)	
25	Hrvoje Čubić	CRO	31/03/92	G	1		
18	Toni Datković	CRO	06/11/93	D	31		3
15	Nenad Dedić	CRO	02/02/90	D	12	(2)	
20	Bojan Djukič		06/11/86	D	11	(1)	
44	Blaž Dobaj		28/01/96	A	2	(1)	
19	Andrej Dugolin		19/09/86	M	10	(6)	
7	Eros Grezda	ALB	15/04/95	M	2	(9)	
6	Alan Hočevar		03/09/92	D	1		
9	Dario Jertec	CRO	05/09/85	M	6	(1)	1
10	Doris Kelenc		08/02/86	A	23	(6)	6
5	Tomislav Kiš	CRO	04/04/94	A	11	(3)	6
9	Nikola Kolarek	CRO	29/01/96	M		(1)	
14	Miha Korošec		11/08/91	D	6	(4)	
7	Dino Kresinger	CRO	20/03/82	A	16	(2)	5
21	Matija Kristić	CRO	10/10/78	D	16		
15	Dejan Kurbus		16/01/93	D	2	(1)	
16	David Magdić	CRO	13/01/96	A		(2)	
22	Jure Matjašič		31/05/92	M	28	(4)	
11	Ante Mitrović	CRO	01/04/88	A	5	(1)	
9	Mateo Monjac		20/06/96	M	1	(5)	
1	Ante Mrmić		06/08/92	G	2		
6	Sanin Muminović	CRO	02/11/90	M	14		1
33	Ivan Novoselec	CRO	19/06/95	D	11	(1)	1
26	Filip Petanjek	CRO	02/06/94	D	2	(2)	
50	Nikola Petrović	SRB	10/04/88	G	8		
16	Patrick Petrovič		07/10/97	M		(1)	
8	Dejan Polić	CRO	21/04/93	D	26	(1)	
1	Marko Pridigar		18/05/85	G	7		
25	Marko Ranilović		25/11/86	G	18	(1)	
5	Marko Roškar		21/10/92	D	7	(4)	
14	Boris Sambolec		25/08/80	D	12		
9	Matija Smrekar	CRO	08/04/89	A	4		1
2	Jure Srnec		30/07/90	D	1	(1)	
8	Nikola Šafarić	CRO	11/03/81	M	17		3
28	Karlo Težak	CRO	30/10/93	M	12	7	1
17	Rok Zorko		20/10/93	A	6	(3)	3

Top goalscorers

17	Marcos Tavares	(Maribor)
15	Benjamin Verbič	(Celje)
13	Andraž Šporar	(Olimpija)
12	Sunny Omoregie	(Celje)
	Luka Zahovič	(Maribor)
10	Dalibor Volaš	(Maribor)
9	Ivan Firer	(Rudar)
	Dragan Jelič	(Rudar)
8	Mitja Lotrič	(Koper)
7	Danijel Miškić	(Celje)
	Benjamin Morel	(Domžale)
	Luka Majcen	(Gorica)
	Dejan Žigon	(Gorica)
	Damjan Bohar	(Maribor)

Promoted club

NK Krško

1922 • Matije Gubca (1,728) • nkkrsko.com
Coach: Tomaž Petrovič

Second level final table 2014/15

		Pld	W	D	L	F	A	Pts
1	NK Krško	27	15	6	6	48	28	51
2	NK Aluminij	27	15	5	7	49	21	50
3	NK Dob	27	15	4	8	52	26	49
4	NK Ankaran Hrvatini	27	12	6	9	45	37	42
5	NK Tolmin	27	13	2	12	49	42	41
6	NK Triglav	27	11	6	10	45	41	39
7	NK Veržej	27	11	5	11	37	45	38
8	NK Šenčur	27	9	5	13	34	48	32
9	ND Dravinja	27	7	8	12	45	47	29
10	NK Šmartno 1928	27	1	5	21	19	88	8

Promotion/Relegation play-offs

(03/06/15 & 07/06/15)
Gorica 0-0 Aluminij
Aluminij 1-2 Gorica
(Gorica 2-1)

DOMESTIC CUP

Pokal NZS 2014/15

FIRST ROUND

(19/08/14)
Tabor Sežana 2-0 Aluminij

(20/08/14)
Adria 1-6 Radomlje
Dob 1-6 Celje
Drava 2-3 Veržej *(aet)*
Jadran 0-2 Zavrč
Korotan 2-0 Brda *(aet)*
Lenart 0-5 Triglav
Nafta 1903 0-1 Šenčur *(aet)*
Odranci 0-4 Zarica Kranj
Šmarje pri Jelšah 2-4 Krka
Šmartno 1928 0-5 Domžale
Tromejnik 0-4 Olimpija

Byes - Gorica, Koper, Maribor, Rudar

SECOND ROUND

(16/09/14)
Korotan 0-4 Olimpija
Zarica Kranj 1-2 Celje

(17/09/14)
Rudar 0-1 Krka
Šenčur 0-2 Zavrč
Tabor Sežana 0-1 Koper
Triglav 3-3 Domžale *(aet; 3-4 on pens)*

(08/10/14)
Veržej 0-2 Gorica

(28/10/14)
Maribor 1-0 Radomlje

QUARTER-FINALS

(22/10/14 & 28/10/14)
Domžale 0-1 Olimpija *(Zarifovič 34)*
Olimpija 1-3 Domžale *(Burgič 82; Korun 8, Maksimovič 18, Zec 41)*
(Domžale 3-2)

(22/10/14 & 29/10/14)
Gorica 3-1 Koper *(Majcen 37, Napoli 47, Innocenti 56; Lotrič 63)*
Koper 4-1 Gorica *(Štromajer 30, Gregorič 57, Štulac 90+2, Pučko 98; Henty 45p) (aet)*
(Koper 5-4)

Zavrč 2-3 Celje *(Datković 43, Matjašič 78; Žurej 17, Ahmedi 56, Omoregie 75)*
Celje 2-1 Zavrč *(Verbič 47, Omoregie 70; Matjašič 39)*
(Celje 5-3)

(19/11/14 & 03/12/14)
Krka 1-2 Maribor *(Fuček 24; Mendy 35, Mejač 65)*
Maribor 4-2 Krka *(Bohar 23, 68, Zahovič 66, Biton 72; Kastrevec 4, Fuček 63)*
(Maribor 6-3)

SEMI-FINALS

(14/04/15 & 22/04/15)
Koper 1-0 Domžale *(Guberac 5)*
Domžale 1-1 Koper *(Črnic 69; Halilovič 61)*
(Koper 2-1)

(15/04/15 & 21/04/15)
Maribor 2-3 Celje *(Marcos Tavares 53, Volaš 66; Omoregie 11, Vrhovec 88, Lendrić 90+3)*
Celje 0-0 Maribor
(Celje 3-2)

FINAL

(20/05/15)
Bonifika, Koper
FC KOPER 2 *(Halilovič 6, Štromajer 87)*
NK CELJE 0
Referee: *Vinčič*
KOPER: *Simčič, Halilovič, Hadžič, Šme, Palčič, Rahmanovič (Štromajer 84), Krivičič, Črnigoj, Guberac, Galešić (Gregorič 88), Lotrič (Pučko 65)*
Red card: *Palčič (85)*
CELJE: *Mujčinovič, Jakolič, T Klemenčič, Soria, Vidmajer, Miškić, Jugovič (Jeslínek 73), Šporn (Ahmedi 46), Verbič, Bajde (Lendrić 46), Omoregie*

SPAIN

Real Federación Española de Fútbol (RFEF)

Address	Ramón y Cajal s/n	**President**	Ángel María Villar Llona
	Apartado postal 385		
	ES-28230 Las Rozas	**General secretary**	Jorge Juan Pérez Arias
	(Madrid)		
Tel	+34 91 495 9800	**Media officer**	Antonio Bustillo Abella
Fax	+34 91 495 9801		
E-mail	rfef@rfef.es	**Year of formation**	1909
Website	rfef.es		

LIGA CLUBS

1. UD Almería
2. Athletic Club
3. Club Atlético de Madrid
4. FC Barcelona
5. RC Celta de Vigo
6. Córdoba CF
7. RC Deportivo La Coruña
8. SD Eibar
9. Elche CF
10. RCD Espanyol
11. Getafe CF
12. Granada CF
13. Levante UD
14. Málaga CF
15. Rayo Vallecano de Madrid
16. Real Madrid CF
17. Real Sociedad de Fútbol
18. Sevilla FC
19. Valencia CF
20. Villarreal CF

PROMOTED CLUBS

21. Real Betis Balompié
22. Real Sporting de Gijón
23. UD Las Palmas

KEY:

- – UEFA Champions League
- – UEFA Europa League
- – Promoted
- – Relegated

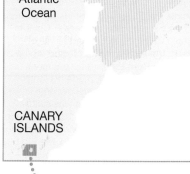

Historic treble for brilliant Barcelona

Having finished the 2013/14 season empty-handed, FC Barcelona bounced back brilliantly to win the Spanish Liga, Copa del Rey and UEFA Champions League, enabling new coach Luis Enrique to end his first season at the Camp Nou, like Josep Guardiola before him, with a historic treble.

Inspired by a scintillating South American strike force of Lionel Messi, Luis Suárez and Neymar, Barça swept the board in thrilling style. Real Madrid CF had been the Catalans' superiors during the autumn, but despite the best efforts of Cristiano Ronaldo, they missed out on all the big prizes. Spain's other major trophy winners were Sevilla FC, who retained the UEFA Europa League.

Luis Enrique cleans up in first season at Camp Nou

Ronaldo goals fail to save Ancelotti's job at Madrid

Emery's Sevilla retain UEFA Europa League

Domestic league

Pipped at the post by Club Atlético de Madrid in the previous season's Liga climax, Barcelona bade farewell to coach Gerardo 'Tata' Martino after just one year and brought in from RC Celta de Vigo the former Barça (and Real Madrid) midfielder who had succeeded Guardiola as the club's B team coach back in 2008.

Luis Enrique's first few months as the main man at the Camp Nou were not wholly convincing. Although his team got off to a positive start, picking up 22 points from the first eight league games, with newly-signed goalkeeper Claudio Bravo keeping clean sheets in all of them, the season's first clásico, at the Santiago Bernabéu – where Suárez, another new signing, made his long-awaited Liga debut – resulted in a sobering 3-1 defeat. That was swiftly followed by another loss, 1-0 at home to Celta, which meant Barcelona not only surrendered top spot to Real Madrid but had to field an increasing number of questions about whether the club had appointed the right man as coach.

With Carlo Ancelotti's high-flying Madrid posting 12 successive victories, Barcelona found themselves four points behind their rivals, who also had a game

in hand, as the Liga closed down for the end-of-year festivities. A drama became a full-blown crisis in the first game of the new year as Barcelona lost 1-0 at Real Sociedad de Fútbol, Enrique's decision to leave Messi on the bench exposing him to a tidal wave of criticism amidst claims of a fall-out between the two. But while sporting director Andoni Zubizarreta was dismissed and president Josep Bartomeu pressed into calling for a summer election, the defeat in San Sebastian would prove to be the catalyst for an astonishing upturn in the fortunes of Enrique, Messi and the team.

Fortunately for Barça, as they lost to Real Sociedad, Madrid did likewise at Valencia CF so they ceded no further ground. An excellent 3-1 win at home to Atlético the following weekend, in which Neymar, Suárez and a fired-up Messi all scored in a match for the first time, provided the spur for a brilliant run that would enable them to catch and overtake Madrid. With the exception of a freak 1-0 home defeat by Málaga CF, Barça became an irresistible force, not just beating teams but beating them easily, with the South American trident, led by the incomparable Messi, scoring goals galore on a regular weekly basis. Madrid made them work harder for their three points when they visited the Camp Nou in March, but an excellent Suárez

goal decided an even contest and doubled Barcelona's lead to six points.

From that point on, it was just a matter of avoiding pitfalls as Barcelona homed in on a 23rd Spanish title. With the exception of a 2-2 draw at Sevilla, Enrique's men never looked likely to surrender their position – despite Madrid's tenacious pursuit. A record-equalling 8-0 away win at bottom club Córdoba CF and a revenge 2-0 home win over Real Sociedad on the same day that Madrid drew 2-2 at home to Valencia gave them a four-point cushion with two games remaining. The first of those was away at Atlético, and it was there, against the team that had snatched the league from them at the Camp Nou a year earlier, that Barça duly secured the title, a typically clinical 65th-minute finish from Messi giving his team a precious 1-0 win.

Eighteen wins in 20 games – garnished by 67 goals, 52 of them from the team's magical attacking trio – had completed an incredible title-winning turnaround since the San Sebastian debacle. While Messi, who found the net 43 times, Neymar (22 goals) and Suárez (16) were all hugely influential, Enrique's exciting team contained heroes in all parts of the field, from Bravo in goal and the reinvigorated Dani Alves and Gerard Piqué in defence to midfield anchorman

Sergio Busquets and newly-recruited playmaker Ivan Rakitić. The elegant Croatian did a fine job as the heir apparent to the great Xavi Hernández, who, like his long-time midfield partner Andrés Iniesta, started only half of the 38 Liga fixtures in what would be a fittingly triumphant swansong campaign.

The 2014/15 season would also be the last at Real Madrid for another living legend of Spanish football, Iker Casillas, who, as Xavi set off for an end-of-career wind-down in Qatar with Al Sadd SC, left for FC Porto. The 34-year-old goalkeeper would have hoped for a happier ending to his 16 years as a Madrid first-teamer, but the only two winner's medals he added to his vast collection came in the pre-season UEFA Super Cup and the mid-term FIFA Club World Cup, both claimed with 2-0 victories – against Sevilla and CA San Lorenzo, respectively.

Madrid actually improved on their 2013/14 Liga showing, finishing one place higher and with five more points. They also outscored Barcelona, registering 118 goals in their 38 matches, with the ever-prolific Ronaldo bagging 48 of those to retain the Pichichi award. They also won as many games as the champions, 30 apiece, but, critically, lost two games more, including both derbies against Atlético – 2-1 at home in September and 4-0 away in February. On fire during the autumn, with post-FIFA World Cup marquee signings Toni Kroos and James Rodríguez both adding to the team's creative riches, Madrid were comparatively burnt out during the spring. Granted, they continued to beat the Liga's rank and file with ease, even banging in nine in one game against Granada CF (including five from Ronaldo), but in the more taxing encounters they sorely missed the midfield control of the injured Luka Modrić, while Casillas and his defenders looked increasingly ill at ease and Ronaldo's illustrious attacking accomplices Gareth Bale and Karim Benzema both struggled to deliver.

Consequently, just 12 months after he had returned Madrid to the pinnacle of European football, Ancelotti was sacked by club president Florentino Pérez and replaced by locally-born Rafael Benítez, a man who, prior to winning a cluster of trophies abroad, had been active at Real

Madrid as a B and youth team coach. Whether the policy of re-hiring a man who had served his coaching apprenticeship at the club would work quite so successfully at the Bernabéu as it had done (twice) at the Camp Nou, only time would tell.

Diego Simeone's Atlético were never serious challengers to the Barça-Madrid duopoly as they sought to defend their Liga title. The loss of goalscorer Diego Costa and goalkeeper Thibaut Courtois to Chelsea FC reduced the team's capabilities in key areas, and although Antoine Griezmann, a new signing from Real Sociedad, enjoyed a fruitful debut campaign, scoring 22 league goals, third place was always the best the Colchoneros could realistically hope for. That is what they got – albeit by just a point from Valencia, who, free from European involvement and under new ownership, enjoyed a fine first season under Portuguese coach Nuno Espírito Santo, with several players, such as goalkeeper Diego Alves, midfielder Daniel Parejo and young left-back José Gayá, all emerging with considerable credit.

The battle to avoid relegation was lost early by Córdoba but it stretched to the final day and beyond for other teams.

Four sides went into their last fixture still under threat, but while Granada and RC Deportivo La Coruña – with an unlikely 2-2 draw at the Camp Nou – saved themselves, UD Almería and SD Eibar went down. Or so it seemed at the time. A subsequent decision by the league authorities restored Eibar to the top flight and instead relegated Elche CF on the grounds of unpaid fiscal debts. The promotion issue was more clear-cut, with Real Betis Balompié winning the Segunda División to make an immediate return to the top flight and Real Sporting de Gijón going up too as runners-up. The third spot, decided by the post-season play-offs, was claimed by UD Las Palmas of the Canary Islands, who won both ties, against Real Valladolid CF and Real Zaragoza, on the away goals rule.

Domestic cup

The second part of Barcelona's trophy-winning trilogy was a Copa del Rey triumph in which they won all nine of their matches, including home and away wins in the quarter-finals over Atlético, the earlier conquerors of holders Real Madrid, and a 3-1 victory against Athletic Club in the final. It was of considerable advantage to the champions to have the decider staged in their own Camp Nou,

Cristiano Ronaldo (centre) gets the approval of team-mates Marcelo and Gareth Bale after scoring one of his 48 Pichichi-winning goals in the Liga campaign

and although Athletic filled half of the stadium with their noisy and colourful fans, it was an illustrious local who, not for the first time, illuminated the arena. Messi scored two goals, the first one of the very best of his 400-plus in a Barça shirt as he somehow worked his way infield from the right touchline, bamboozling several defenders with his incredible footwork and balance before drilling in an unstoppable shot at the near post with that magic wand of a left foot. It was Barcelona's record-extending 27th win in the competition, which completed a half-century of major domestic honours.

Europe

A week after lifting the Copa del Rey, Barcelona and their departing skipper Xavi were at it again, hoisting the UEFA Champions League trophy into the Berlin sky after a wonderfully entertaining 3-1 victory over Juventus. It was Barça's fourth European Cup triumph in a decade and fifth in all. Having won 11 of their 13 matches, including nine in succession, scored 31 goals, including ten apiece for Messi and Neymar, and eliminated the champions of the Netherlands, England, France, Germany and Italy en route, it was a triumph of incontestable merit and magnitude.

Real Madrid became the latest team to suffer the curse of the UEFA Champions League holders, ceding the trophy in the semi-finals after a 2-1 aggregate defeat to Juventus. They had only just scraped through the previous two knockout rounds, against FC Schalke 04 and Atlético, finally beating their city rivals for the first time in eight meetings since the 2014 final with a late Javier Hernández strike set up by Ronaldo, who scored ten goals in the competition to match Messi and Neymar as its top marksman. Five of those came in the group stage, where Madrid won all six matches.

Whereas Ancelotti's side failed to defend their European crown, Unai Emery's Sevilla claimed back-to-back UEFA Europa League triumphs, two goals from Colombian striker Carlos Bacca and one from Polish midfielder Grzegorz Krychowiak defeating FC Dnipro Dnipropetrovsk 3-2 in Warsaw after the Andalusian side had won seven and drawn one of their eight previous knockout fixtures. In addition to the

National team newcomer Paco Alcácer scores for Spain in a friendly win against Costa Rica

trophy and a place in history as the first club to lift it four times (twice as UEFA Cup winners), Sevilla were also rewarded with a place in the UEFA Champions League, giving Spain a fifth participant – and fourth guaranteed group stage starter – in 2015/16.

National team

After their disastrous World Cup defence in Brazil, Spain needed an immediate pick-me-up in the UEFA EURO 2016 qualifying tournament. But after opening their campaign with a welcome 5-1 victory over FYR Macedonia in Valencia, Vicente del Bosque's team re-descended into ignominy with a shock 2-1 defeat in Slovakia. They won their next four qualifiers, including an important 1-0 success at home to Ukraine, but friendly defeats against France, Germany and World Cup conquerors the Netherlands – all without scoring – confirmed that Spain still had a long way to go before

they could be confident of completing a UEFA European Championship hat-trick in France, where Del Bosque's reign will come to an end.

The Brazilian misadventure marked the end of an era for La Roja, not just in terms of their sequence of successes but with the retirement from the team of long-serving mainstays such as Xavi, David Villa and Xabi Alonso. David Silva, not always a first choice in the past, was the side's standout performer in 2014/15, but there were discreet contributions elsewhere from several of his long-time associates. Of the 14 players handed first caps during the season, Valencia striker Paco Alcácer was arguably the most impressive, with FC Bayern München's Juan Bernat and Sevilla's Vitolo also staking decent claims for regular inclusion in the future, both under Del Bosque – who took charge of his 100th international in the June qualifier against Belarus – and the man appointed to the difficult task of replacing him.

DOMESTIC SEASON AT A GLANCE

Liga 2014/15 final table

		Pld	Home					Away					Total					Pts
			W	D	L	F	A	W	D	L	F	A	W	D	L	F	A	
1	**FC Barcelona**	38	16	1	2	64	11	14	3	2	46	10	30	4	4	110	21	94
2	Real Madrid CF	38	16	2	1	65	15	14	0	5	53	23	30	2	6	118	38	92
3	Club Atlético de Madrid	38	14	3	2	42	11	9	6	4	25	18	23	9	6	67	29	78
4	Valencia CF	38	15	3	1	42	10	7	8	4	28	22	22	11	5	70	32	77
5	Sevilla FC	38	13	5	1	38	13	10	2	7	33	32	23	7	8	71	45	76
6	Villarreal CF	38	12	1	6	29	17	4	11	4	19	20	16	12	10	48	37	60
7	Athletic Club	38	8	6	5	28	20	7	4	8	14	21	15	10	13	42	41	55
8	RC Celta de Vigo	38	8	5	6	30	22	5	7	7	17	22	13	12	13	47	44	51
9	Málaga CF	38	8	6	5	26	20	6	2	11	16	28	14	8	16	42	48	50
10	RCD Espanyol	38	8	6	5	23	19	5	4	10	24	32	13	10	15	47	51	49
11	Rayo Vallecano de Madrid	38	8	2	9	26	26	7	2	10	20	42	15	4	19	46	68	49
12	Real Sociedad de Fútbol	38	9	5	5	29	21	2	8	9	15	30	11	13	14	44	51	46
13	Elche CF	38	6	3	10	19	31	5	5	9	16	31	11	8	19	35	62	41
14	Levante UD	38	6	6	7	20	30	3	4	12	14	37	9	10	19	34	67	37
15	Getafe CF	38	6	5	8	16	22	4	2	13	17	42	10	7	21	33	64	37
16	RC Deportivo La Coruña	38	5	6	8	22	30	2	8	9	13	30	7	14	17	35	60	35
17	Granada CF	38	4	10	5	13	17	3	4	12	16	47	7	14	17	29	64	35
18	SD Eibar	38	5	3	11	20	29	4	5	10	14	26	9	8	21	34	55	35
19	UD Almería	38	3	7	9	20	28	5	1	13	15	36	8	8	22	35	64	32
20	Córdoba CF	38	1	6	12	12	33	2	5	12	10	35	3	11	24	22	68	20

NB Elche CF excluded from 2015/16 Liga.

European qualification 2015/16

Champion/Cup winner: FC Barcelona (group stage)
Real Madrid CF (group stage)
Club Atlético de Madrid (group stage)
Sevilla FC (group stage)
Valencia CF (play-offs)

Villarreal CF (group stage)
Athletic Club (third qualifying round)

Top scorer   Cristiano Ronaldo (Real Madrid), 48 goals
Relegated clubs   Córdoba CF, UD Almería, Elche CF (excluded)
Promoted clubs   Real Betis Balompié, Real Sporting de Gijón, UD Las Palmas
Cup final   FC Barcelona 3-1 Athletic Club

Team of the season
(4-3-3)

Coach: Luis Enrique *(Barcelona)*

Player of the season

Lionel Messi
(FC Barcelona)

Barcelona's all-South American forward line registered 122 goals during the club's treble-winning season. Messi's contribution was 58, including ten in the UEFA Champions League and 43 in the Liga. His scoring statistics continue to beggar belief – he reached 400 goals for Barça in April and his now the Liga's all-time leading marksman – but that is only part of his game. The Argentinian's all-round genius has been on display for many years now, but in 2014/15, aged 27, he was as good as he has ever been, perhaps even better.

Newcomer of the season

Luciano Vietto
(Villarreal CF)

Little known to Spanish football followers when he arrived at Villarreal from Argentinian club Racing Club de Avellaneda in August 2014, the versatile young forward took the Liga by storm, racking up 18 goals and seven assists in his first 22 appearances. His form, and that of his club, tapered off in the spring, but the 21-year-old's reputation was made, and although he was overlooked for Argentina's Copa América squad, his career took another upward turn when he was signed in June by Club Atlético de Madrid.

NATIONAL TEAM

International honours
FIFA World Cup (1) 2010
UEFA European Championship (3) 1964, 2008, 2012

International tournament appearances
FIFA World Cup (14) 1934, 1950 (4th), 1962, 1966, 1978, 1982 (2nd phase), 1986 (qtr-finals), 1990 (2nd round), 1994 (qtr-finals), 1998, 2002 (qtr-finals), 2006 (2nd round), 2010 (Winners), 2014
UEFA European Championship (9) 1964 (Winners), 1980, 1984 (runners-up), 1988, 1996 (qtr-finals), 2000 (qtr-finals), 2004, 2008 (Winners), 2012 (Winners)

Top five all-time caps
Iker Casillas (162); Xavi Hernández (133); **Sergio Ramos** (128); Andoni Zubizarreta (126); Xabi Alonso (114)

Top five all-time goals
David Villa (59); Raúl González (44); Fernando Torres (38); Fernando Hierro (29); Fernando Morientes (27)

Results 2014/15

04/09/14	France	A	Saint-Denis	L	0-1	
08/09/14	FYR Macedonia (ECQ)	H	Valencia	W	5-1	*Sergio Ramos (16p), Paco Alcácer (17), Busquets (45+3), Silva (50), Pedro (90+1)*
09/10/14	Slovakia (ECQ)	A	Zilina	L	1-2	*Paco Alcácer (82)*
12/10/14	Luxembourg (ECQ)	A	Luxembourg	W	4-0	*Silva (27), Paco Alcácer (42), Diego Costa (69), Bernat (88)*
15/11/14	Belarus (ECQ)	H	Huelva	W	3-0	*Isco (18), Busquets (19), Pedro (55)*
18/11/14	Germany	H	Vigo	L	0-1	
27/03/15	Ukraine (ECQ)	H	Seville	W	1-0	*Morata (28)*
31/03/15	Netherlands	A	Amsterdam	L	0-2	
11/06/15	Costa Rica	H	Leon	W	2-1	*Paco Alcácer (8), Fàbregas (30)*
14/06/15	Belarus (ECQ)	A	Borisov	W	1-0	*Silva (45)*

Appearances 2014/15

Coach: Vicente del Bosque 23/12/50			Fra	MKD	SVK	LUX	BLR	Ger	UKR	Ned	Crc	BLR	Caps	Goals
David de Gea	07/11/90	Man. United (ENG)	G			G				G	G		5	-
Daniel Carvajal	11/01/92	Real Madrid	D			D				D	D		4	-
Mikel San José	30/05/89	Athletic	D							s69	M73		3	-
Sergio Ramos	30/03/86	Real Madrid	D	D68			D	D46	D	s69	D57	D	128	10
César Azpilicueta	28/08/89	Chelsea (ENG)	D					D					10	-
Koke	08/01/92	Atlético	M	M77	M	M	M		M		M58		17	-
Sergio Busquets	16/07/88	Barcelona	M46	M	M	M	M46	M46	M		s73	M	77	2
Cesc Fàbregas	04/05/87	Chelsea (ENG)	M68	M	M					M	M82	M75	97	14
Raúl García	11/07/86	Atlético	A58					M70					2	-
Diego Costa	07/10/88	Chelsea (ENG)	A67		A	A82							7	1
Santi Cazorla	13/12/84	Arsenal (ENG)	A78		s81		M69		s74	M76	s58	M	73	11
Ander Iturraspe	08/03/89	Athletic	s46										2	-
David Silva	08/01/86	Man. City (ENG)	s58	A	M71	M70			A	s46	s58	A85	91	23
Paco Alcácer	30/08/93	Valencia	s67	A57	s71	A	A				A		6	4
Pedro Rodríguez	28/07/87	Barcelona	s68	A	s58	s70	A	s77	s65	M46		A65	51	16
Isco	21/04/92	Real Madrid	s78	s57			M80	M	A	M46	s82	s75	10	1
Iker Casillas	20/05/81	Real Madrid		G	G		G	G77	G			G	162	-
Juanfran	09/01/85	Atlético		D	D81		D		D			D	14	1
Raúl Albiol	04/09/85	Napoli (ITA)		D	D58			s46		D			51	-
Jordi Alba	21/03/89	Barcelona		D	D	D	D		D78			D	35	5
Marc Bartra	15/01/91	Barcelona			s68	D		s46			D		5	-
Munir El Haddadi	01/09/95	Barcelona			s77								1	-
Gerard Piqué	02/02/87	Barcelona			D	D	D	D46	D	D69	s57	D	69	4
Andrés Iniesta	11/05/84	Barcelona			M	M70			M74	s76			104	11
Juan Bernat	01/03/93	Bayern (GER)				s70		D	s78	D	D	s85	6	1
Rodrigo	06/03/91	Valencia				s82							1	-
Bruno Soriano	12/06/84	Villarreal					s46	M					6	-
José Callejón	11/02/87	Napoli (ITA)					s69	s70					2	-
Álvaro Morata	23/10/92	Juventus (ITA)					s80	A	A65	s62		A	5	1
Nolito	15/10/86	Celta						M77			M58		2	-
Ignacio Camacho	04/05/90	Málaga						s46					1	-
Kiko Casilla	02/10/86	Espanyol						s77					1	-
Mario Suárez	24/02/87	Atlético								M69			3	-
Juanmi	20/05/93	Málaga							A62				1	- .
Vitolo	02/11/89	Sevilla								s46	s46	s65	3	-
Aleix Vidal	21/08/89	Sevilla									M46		1	-

EUROPE

Real Madrid CF

Group B
Match 1 - FC Basel 1893 (SUI)
H 5-1 *Suchý (14og), Bale (30), Cristiano Ronaldo (31), James Rodríguez (37), Benzema (79)*
Casillas, Pepe, Sergio Ramos (Varane 66), Cristiano Ronaldo, Kroos, Benzema (Hernández 82), James Rodríguez, Bale, Marcelo, Nacho, Modrić (Illarramendi 74). Coach: Carlo Ancelotti (ITA)
Match 2 - PFC Ludogorets Razgrad (BUL)
A 2-1 *Cristiano Ronaldo (24p), Benzema (77)*
Casillas, Varane, Sergio Ramos, Cristiano Ronaldo, Bale, Marcelo, Hernández (Benzema 67), Arbeloa, Modrić (Kroos 73), Isco (James Rodríguez 76), Illarramendi. Coach: Carlo Ancelotti (ITA)
Match 3 - Liverpool FC (ENG)
A 3-0 *Cristiano Ronaldo (23), Benzema (30, 41)*
Casillas, Varane, Pepe, Cristiano Ronaldo (Khedira 75), Kroos (Illarramendi 81), Benzema, James Rodríguez, Marcelo (Nacho 85), Arbeloa, Modrić, Isco. Coach: Carlo Ancelotti (ITA)
Match 4 - Liverpool FC (ENG)
H 1-0 *Benzema (27)*
Casillas, Varane, Sergio Ramos, Cristiano Ronaldo, Kroos, Benzema (Hernández 87), James Rodríguez (Bale 62), Marcelo, Arbeloa (Nacho 83), Modrić, Isco. Coach: Carlo Ancelotti (ITA)
Match 5 - FC Basel 1893 (SUI)
A 1-0 *Cristiano Ronaldo (35)*
Navas, Varane, Sergio Ramos, Fábio Coentrão, Cristiano Ronaldo, Kroos, Benzema (Illarramendi 71), James Rodríguez (Marcelo 89), Bale, Arbeloa, Isco (Nacho 90+3). Coach: Carlo Ancelotti (ITA)
Match 6 - PFC Ludogorets Razgrad (BUL)
H 4-0 *Cristiano Ronaldo (20p), Bale (38), Arbeloa (80), Medrán (88)*
Navas, Varane, Fábio Coentrão (Marcelo 60), Cristiano Ronaldo, Kroos (Jesé 60), Bale (Medrán 83), Hernández, Arbeloa, Nacho, Isco, Illarramendi. Coach: Carlo Ancelotti (ITA)

Round of 16 - FC Schalke 04 (GER)
A 2-0 *Cristiano Ronaldo (26), Marcelo (79)*
Casillas, Varane, Pepe, Cristiano Ronaldo, Kroos, Benzema (Hernández 78), Bale, Marcelo, Carvajal (Arbeloa 82), Lucas Silva, Isco (Illarramendi 85). Coach: Carlo Ancelotti (ITA)
H 3-4 *Cristiano Ronaldo (25, 45), Benzema (53)*
Casillas, Varane, Pepe, Fábio Coentrão (Marcelo 58), Khedira (Modrić 58), Cristiano Ronaldo, Kroos, Benzema, Bale, Arbeloa (Nacho 83), Isco. Coach: Carlo Ancelotti (ITA)

Quarter-finals - Club Atlético de Madrid (ESP)
A 0-0
Casillas, Varane, Sergio Ramos, Cristiano Ronaldo, Kroos, Benzema (Isco 76), James Rodríguez, Bale, Marcelo, Carvajal (Arbeloa 85), Modrić. Coach: Carlo Ancelotti (ITA)
H 1-0 *Hernández (88)*
Casillas, Varane, Pepe, Sergio Ramos, Fábio Coentrão (Arbeloa 90+1), Cristiano Ronaldo, Kroos, James Rodríguez, Hernández (Jesé 90+2), Carvajal, Isco (Illarramendi 90+3). Coach: Carlo Ancelotti (ITA)

Semi-finals - Juventus (ITA)
A 1-2 *Cristiano Ronaldo (27)*
Casillas, Varane, Pepe, Sergio Ramos, Cristiano Ronaldo, Kroos, James Rodríguez, Bale (Jesé 86), Marcelo, Carvajal, Isco (Hernández 63). Coach: Carlo Ancelotti (ITA)
H 1-1 *Cristiano Ronaldo (23p)*
Casillas, Varane, Sergio Ramos, Cristiano Ronaldo, Kroos, Benzema (Hernández 67), James Rodríguez, Bale, Marcelo, Carvajal, Isco. Coach: Carlo Ancelotti (ITA)

Club Atlético de Madrid

Group A
Match 1 - Olympiacos FC (GRE)
A 2-3 *Mandžukić (38), Griezmann (86)*
Oblak, Godín, Mario Suárez (Saúl Ñíguez 75), Koke, Raúl García (Cerci 66), Mandžukić, Arda Turan, Gabi (Griezmann 56), Ansaldi, Juanfran, Miranda. Coach: Germán Burgos (ESP)
Match 2 - Juventus (ITA)
H 1-0 *Arda Turan (75)*
Moyá, Godín, Tiago, Koke, Raúl García, Mandžukić (Mario Suárez 84), Arda Turan (Siqueira 90), Ansaldi, Saúl Ñíguez (Griezmann 53), Juanfran, Miranda. Coach: Diego Simeone (ARG)
Match 3 - Malmö FF (SWE)
H 5-0 *Koke (48), Mandžukić (61), Griezmann (63), Godín (87), Cerci (90+3)*
Moyá, Godín, Siqueira, Mario Suárez, Koke, Griezmann (Rodríguez 72), Mandžukić (Cerci 77), Arda Turan (Raúl García 68), Saúl Ñíguez, Juanfran, Miranda. Coach: Diego Simeone (ARG)
Match 4 - Malmö FF (SWE)
A 2-0 *Koke (30), Raúl García (78)*
Moyá, Godín, Siqueira, Mario Suárez, Koke, Raúl García, Mandžukić (Griezmann 69), Arda Turan (Rodríguez 76), Gabi, Juanfran, Miranda. Coach: Diego Simeone (ARG)
Match 5 - Olympiacos FC (GRE)
H 4-0 *Raúl García (9), Mandžukić (38, 62, 65)*
Moyá, Godín, Tiago (Mario Suárez 46), Koke, Raúl García, Mandžukić (Griezmann 69), Arda Turan (Jiménez 66), Gabi, Ansaldi, Juanfran, Giménez. Coach: Diego Simeone (ARG)
Match 6 - Juventus (ITA)
A 0-0
Moyá, Godín, Siqueira, Mario Suárez, Koke, Raúl García, Mandžukić, Arda Turan, Gabi, Juanfran, Giménez. Coach: Diego Simeone (ARG)

Round of 16 - Bayer 04 Leverkusen (GER)
A 0-1
Moyá, Godín, Siqueira (Jesús Gámez 38), Tiago, Griezmann, Mandžukić, Arda Turan (Fernando Torres 64), Gabi, Saúl Ñíguez (Raúl García 42), Juanfran, Miranda. Coach: Diego Simeone (ARG)
Red card: Tiago 76
H 1-0 *Mario Suárez (27)* **(aet; 3-2 on pens)**
Moyá (Oblak 23), Mario Suárez, Koke, Griezmann, Mandžukić (Fernando Torres 83), Arda Turan, Jesús Gámez, Juanfran, Cani (Raúl García 46), Miranda, Giménez. Coach: Diego Simeone (ARG)

Quarter-finals - Real Madrid CF (ESP)
H 0-0
Oblak, Godín, Siqueira, Mario Suárez, Koke (Fernando Torres 83), Griezmann (Raúl García 77), Mandžukić, Arda Turan, Gabi, Juanfran, Miranda. Coach: Diego Simeone (ARG)
A 0-1
Oblak, Godín, Tiago (Giménez 86), Koke, Griezmann (Raúl García 65), Mandžukić, Arda Turan, Saúl Ñíguez (Gabi 46), Jesús Gámez, Juanfran, Miranda. Coach: Diego Simeone (ARG)
Red card: Arda Turan 76

FC Barcelona

Group F
Match 1 - APOEL FC (CYP)
H 1-0 *Piqué (28)*
Ter Stegen, Piqué, Xavi (Iniesta 61), Messi, Neymar, Bartra, Sergi Roberto (Rafinha 79), Adriano, Dani Alves, Samper, Munir (Sandro Ramírez 68). Coach: Luis Enrique (ESP)
Match 2 - Paris Saint-Germain (FRA)
A 2-3 *Messi (12), Neymar (56)*
Ter Stegen, Rakitic (Xavi 69), Busquets, Pedro (Munir 62), Iniesta, Messi, Neymar, Mascherano, Jordi Alba, Dani Alves (Sandro Ramírez 83), Mathieu. Coach: Luis Enrique (ESP)
Match 3 - AFC Ajax (NED)
H 3-1 *Neymar (7), Messi (24), Sandro Ramírez (90+4)*
Ter Stegen, Piqué, Rakitic, Pedro, Iniesta (Rafinha 76), Messi (Munir 67), Neymar (Sandro Ramírez 62), Mascherano, Bartra, Jordi Alba, Dani Alves. Coach: Luis Enrique (ESP)
Match 4 - AFC Ajax (NED)
A 2-0 *Messi (36, 76)*
Ter Stegen, Rakitic (Rafinha 80), Busquets, Xavi, Suárez, Messi, Neymar (Pedro 74), Mascherano, Bartra, Jordi Alba (Adriano 83). Coach: Luis Enrique (ESP)
Match 5 - APOEL FC (CYP)
A 4-0 *Suárez (27), Messi (38, 58, 87)*
Ter Stegen, Piqué, Rakitic (Xavi 82), Pedro, Suárez (Busquets 77), Messi, Rafinha, Mascherano, Bartra, Jordi Alba (Adriano 62), Dani Alves. Coach: Luis Enrique (ESP)
Red card: Rafinha 70
Match 6 - Paris Saint-Germain (FRA)
H 3-1 *Messi (19), Neymar (42), Suárez (77)*
Ter Stegen, Piqué, Busquets, Pedro (Rafinha 68), Iniesta (Xavi 73), Suárez, Messi, Neymar, Mascherano, Bartra (Adriano 90+2), Mathieu. Coach: Luis Enrique (ESP)

Round of 16 - Manchester City FC (ENG)
A 2-1 *Suárez (16,30)*
Ter Stegen, Piqué, Rakitic (Mathieu 71), Busquets, Iniesta, Suárez, Messi, Neymar (Pedro 80), Mascherano, Jordi Alba, Dani Alves (Adriano 75). Coach: Luis Enrique (ESP)
H 1-0 *Rakitic (31)*
Ter Stegen, Piqué, Rakitic (Rafinha 84), Iniesta, Suárez, Messi, Neymar, Mascherano, Jordi Alba, Dani Alves (Adriano 90+1), Mathieu. Coach: Luis Enrique (ESP)

Quarter-finals - Paris Saint-Germain (FRA)
A 3-1 *Neymar (18), Suárez (67, 79)*
Ter Stegen, Montoya (Adriano 80), Piqué, Rakitic (Mathieu 74), Busquets, Iniesta (Xavi 53), Suárez, Messi, Neymar, Mascherano, Jordi Alba. Coach: Luis Enrique (ESP)
H 2-0 *Neymar (14, 34)*
Ter Stegen, Piqué, Rakitic, Busquets (Sergi Roberto 55), Iniesta (Xavi 46), Suárez (Pedro 75), Messi, Neymar, Mascherano, Jordi Alba, Dani Alves. Coach: Luis Enrique (ESP)

Semi-finals - FC Bayern München (GER)
H 3-0 *Messi (77, 80), Neymar (90+4)*
Ter Stegen, Piqué, Rakitic (Xavi 82), Busquets, Iniesta (Rafinha 87), Suárez, Messi, Neymar, Mascherano (Bartra 89), Jordi Alba, Dani Alves. Coach: Luis Enrique (ESP)
A 2-3 *Neymar (15, 29)*
Ter Stegen, Piqué, Rakitic (Mathieu 72), Busquets, Iniesta (Xavi 75), Suárez (Pedro 46), Messi, Neymar, Mascherano, Jordi Alba, Dani Alves. Coach: Luis Enrique (ESP)

Final - Juventus (ITA)
N 3-1 *Rakitic (4), Suárez (68), Neymar (90+7)*
Ter Stegen, Piqué, Rakitic (Mathieu 90+1), Busquets, Iniesta (Xavi 78), Suárez (Pedro 90+6), Messi, Neymar, Mascherano, Jordi Alba, Dani Alves. Coach: Luis Enrique (ESP)

Athletic Club

Play-offs - SSC Napoli (ITA)
A 1-1 *Muniain (41)*
Iraizoz, Laporte, Beñat (San José 75), Iturraspe (Morán 89), De Marcos, Susaeta (Ibai Gómez 80), Mikel Rico, Gurpegui, Muniain, Aduriz, Balenziaga. Coach: Ernesto Valverde (ESP)
H 3-1 *Aduriz (61, 69), Ibai Gómez (74)*
Iraizoz, Laporte, Beñat (Ibai Gómez 58), Iturraspe, De Marcos, Susaeta (Unai López 72), Mikel Rico, Gurpegui, Muniain (San José 85), Aduriz, Balenziaga. Coach: Ernesto Valverde (ESP)

Group H
Match 1 - FC Shakhtar Donetsk (UKR)
H 0-0
Iraizoz, Laporte, Beñat (Susaeta 64), Iturraspe, De Marcos, Ibai Gómez, Mikel Rico, Gurpegui, Muniain (Aketxe 75), Aduriz (Guillermo Fernández 77), Balenziaga. Coach: Ernesto Valverde (ESP)
Match 2 - FC BATE Borisov (BLR)
A 1-2 *Aduriz (45)*
Iraizoz, Laporte, San José, Beñat, Iturraspe, Ibai Gómez (De Marcos 46), Iraola (Toquero 77), Mikel Rico (Susaeta 46), Muniain, Aduriz, Balenziaga. Coach: Ernesto Valverde (ESP)
Match 3 - FC Porto (POR)
A 1-2 *Guillermo Fernández (58)*
Iraizoz, Laporte, Beñat (Muniain 46), Iturraspe, De Marcos, Susaeta, Etxeita, Mikel Rico (Gurpegui 73), Aduriz (Beñat 46), Guillermo Fernández, Balenziaga. Coach: Ernesto Valverde (ESP)
Match 4 - FC Porto (POR)
H 0-2
Iraizoz, Laporte, San José, Beñat (Iraola 46), De Marcos, Ibai Gómez (Viguera 73), Susaeta (Muniain 46), Mikel Rico, Gurpegui, Guillermo Fernández, Balenziaga. Coach: Ernesto Valverde (ESP)
Match 5 - FC Shakhtar Donetsk (UKR)
A 1-0 *San José (68)*
Iraizoz, San José, Beñat, Iturraspe, De Marcos, Susaeta (Aduriz 65), Etxeita (Gurpegui 32), Mikel Rico, Muniain (Unai López 88), Viguera, Balenziaga. Coach: Ernesto Valverde (ESP)
Match 6 - FC BATE Borisov (BLR)
H 2-0 *San José (47), Susaeta (88)*
Iraizoz, Laporte, San José, Iturraspe, De Marcos, Ibai Gómez (Viguera 87), Susaeta, Iraola (Unai López 76), Mikel Rico, Guillermo Fernández (Aduriz 78), Balenziaga. Coach: Ernesto Valverde (ESP)

Round of 32 - Torino FC (ITA)
A 2-2 *Iñaki Williams (9), Gurpegi (73)*
Iago Herrerín, Aurtenetxe (Iraola 57), Laporte, San José, Beñat, De Marcos, Etxeita, Mikel Rico, Muniain, Viguera (Gurpegui 57), Iñaki Williams (Kike Sola 72). Coach: Ernesto Valverde (ESP)
H 2-3 *Iraola (44), De Marcos (61)*
Iago Herrerín, Laporte, San José, Beñat (Susaeta 70), De Marcos, Etxeita, Mikel Rico (Unai López 79), Gurpegui (Iñaki Williams 42), Muniain, Aduriz. Coach: Ernesto Valverde (ESP)

Sevilla FC

Group G
Match 1 - Feyenoord (NED)
H 2-0 *Krychowiak (8), Mbia (31)*
Sergio Rico, Fernando Navarro, Krychowiak (Denis Suárez 60), Diogo Figueiras, Daniel Carriço, Bacca (Iago Aspas 60), Reyes, Kolodziejczak, Deulofeu, Éver Banega, Mbia. Coach: Unai Emery (ESP)
Match 2 - HNK Rijeka (CRO)
A 2-2 *Iago Aspas (26), Mbia (90+1)*
Beto, Fernando Navarro, Krychowiak, Daniel Carriço, Reyes (Trémoulinas 57), Iborra, Iago Aspas (Bacca 72), Kolodziejczak, Éver Banega (Mbia 57), Aleix Vidal, Coke. Coach: Unai Emery (ESP)
Red card: Kolodziejczak 52
Match 3 - R Standard de Liège (BEL)
A 0-0
Beto, Fernando Navarro, Krychowiak, Diogo Figueiras, Daniel Carriço, Gameiro (Bacca 63), Reyes (Denis Suárez 64), Iborra, Éver Banega, Aleix Vidal (Deulofeu 78), Arribas. Coach: Unai Emery (ESP)
Match 4 - R Standard de Liège (BEL)
H 3-1 *Gameiro (19), Reyes (41), Bacca (90)*
Beto (Sergio Rico 46), Trémoulinas, Krychowiak, Diogo Figueiras, Daniel Carriço, Gameiro, Reyes (Vitolo 57), Denis Suárez, Deulofeu (Bacca 71), Pareja, Mbia. Coach: Unai Emery (ESP)
Match 5 - Feyenoord (NED)
A 0-2
Sergio Rico, Krychowiak, Daniel Carriço, Gameiro, Reyes (Vitolo 80), Iago Aspas (Bacca 60), Kolodziejczak, Denis Suárez (Deulofeu 60), Coke, Arribas, Mbia. Coach: Unai Emery (ESP)
Match 6 - HNK Rijeka (CRO)
H 1-0 *Denis Suárez (20)*
Beto, Fernando Navarro, Daniel Carriço, Bacca (Gameiro 66), Reyes, Denis Suárez (Arribas 60), Éver Banega, Vitolo, Pareja, Coke (Diogo Figueiras 77), Mbia. Coach: Unai Emery (ESP)

Round of 32 - VfL Borussia Mönchengladbach (GER)
H 1-0 *Iborra (70)*
Sergio Rico, Fernando Navarro, Krychowiak, Daniel Carriço, Bacca, Reyes (Diogo Figueiras 55), Iborra, Éver Banega (Denis Suárez 88), Vitolo, Pareja, Aleix Vidal (Deulofeu 90+2). Coach: Unai Emery (ESP)
A 3-2 *Bacca (8), Vitolo (26,79)*
Sergio Rico, Trémoulinas (Fernando Navarro 82), Krychowiak, Diogo Figueiras, Daniel Carriço, Bacca (Gameiro 77), Iborra, Kolodziejczak, Éver Banega (Mbia 65), Vitolo, Aleix Vidal. Coach: Unai Emery (ESP)

Round of 16 - Villarreal CF (ESP)
A 3-1 *Vitolo (1), Mbia (26), Gameiro (50)*
Sergio Rico, Trémoulinas, Krychowiak, Diogo Figueiras, Daniel Carriço, Gameiro (Bacca 64), Iborra (Éver Banega 75), Vitolo (Reyes 78), Pareja, Aleix Vidal, Mbia. Coach: Unai Emery (ESP)
H 2-1 *Iborra (69), Denis Suárez (83)*
Sergio Rico, Trémoulinas, Diogo Figueiras, Daniel Carriço, Gameiro (Bacca 65), Iborra (Denis Suárez 80), Kolodziejczak, Vitolo, Pareja, Aleix Vidal (Reyes 75), Mbia. Coach: Unai Emery (ESP)

Quarter-finals - FC Zenit (RUS)
H 2-1 *Bacca (73), Denis Suárez (88)*
Sergio Rico, Trémoulinas, Krychowiak, Gameiro (Bacca 64), Reyes, Iborra (Mbia 46), Kolodziejczak, Éver Banega, Aleix Vidal, Coke (Denis Suárez 46). Coach: Unai Emery (ESP)
A 2-2 *Bacca (6p), Gameiro (85)*
Beto, Trémoulinas, Krychowiak, Daniel Carriço, Bacca (Gameiro 75), Banega, Vitolo (Denis Suárez 90+2), Pareja (Iborra 21), Aleix Vidal, Coke, Mbia. Coach: Unai Emery (ESP)

Semi-finals - ACF Fiorentina (ITA)
H 3-0 *Aleix Vidal (17, 52), Gameiro (75)*
Sergio Rico, Trémoulinas, Krychowiak, Daniel Carriço, Bacca (Gameiro 74), Reyes (Coke 58), Kolodziejczak, Éver Banega, Vitolo, Aleix Vidal, Mbia (Iborra 73). Coach: Unai Emery (ESP)
A 2-0 *Bacca (22), Daniel Carriço (27)*
Sergio Rico, Trémoulinas, Krychowiak, Daniel Carriço, Bacca (Gameiro 70), Kolodziejczak, Éver Banega (Iborra 55), Vitolo (Reyes 74), Aleix Vidal, Coke, Mbia. Coach: Unai Emery (ESP)

Final - FC Dnipro Dnipropetrovsk (UKR)
N 3-2 *Krychowiak (28), Bacca (31, 73)*
Sergio Rico, Trémoulinas, Krychowiak, Daniel Carriço, Bacca (Gameiro 82), Reyes (Coke 58), Kolodziejczak, Éver Banega (Iborra 89), Vitolo, Aleix Vidal, Mbia. Coach: Unai Emery (ESP)

Villarreal CF

Play-offs - FC Astana (KAZ)
A 3-0 *Cani (33), Giovani dos Santos (48), Mario (84)*
Asenjo, Mario, Musacchio, Uche (Vietto 63), Giovani dos Santos, Cani, Trigueros, Cheryshev (Espinosa 74), Jaume Costa, Gabriel (Víctor Ruiz 32), Bruno Soriano. Coach: Marcelino (ESP)
H 4-0 *Vietto (21, 54), Bruno Soriano (61p), Leiva (67)*
Juan Carlos, Mario, Pina, Musacchio, Vietto, Trigueros (Bruno Soriano 46), Jaume Costa (Marín 56), Moi Gómez (Leiva 64), Gabriel, Gerard Moreno, Espinosa. Coach: Marcelino (ESP)

Group A
Match 1 - VfL Borussia Mönchengladbach (GER)
A 1-1 *Uche (68)*
Asenjo, Mario, Pina (Trigueros 60), Musacchio, Vietto (Uche 67; Jonathan dos Santos 73), Cani, Víctor Ruiz, Cheryshev, Moi Gómez, Gabriel, Bruno Soriano. Coach: Marcelino (ESP)
Match 2 - Apollon Limassol FC (CYP)
H 4-0 *Gerard Moreno (9, 82), Espinosa (44, 51)*
Juan Carlos, Mario, Pina, Jonathan dos Santos (Trigueros 63), Vietto (Giovani dos Santos 72), Cani, Víctor Ruiz, Gabriel, Bruno Soriano, Rukavina (Mario 15), Gerard Moreno, Espinosa, Marín. Coach: Juan Corral (ESP)
Match 3 - FC Zürich (SUI)
H 4-1 *Cani (6), Vietto (57), Bruno Soriano (60), Giovani dos Santos (78)*
Juan Carlos, Mario, Jonathan dos Santos, Vietto (Giovani dos Santos 66), Cani (Cheryshev 74), Víctor Ruiz, Gabriel, Bruno Soriano (Pina 69), Gerard Moreno, Espinosa, Marín. Coach: Marcelino (ESP)
Match 4 - FC Zürich (SUI)
A 2-3 *Pina (19), Gerard Moreno (23)*
Juan Carlos, Pina (Bruno Soriano 65), Jonathan dos Santos, Giovani dos Santos, Víctor Ruiz, Moi Gómez (Vietto 59), Gabriel, Rukavina, Gerard Moreno, Espinosa (Cheryshev 68), Marín. Coach: Marcelino (ESP)

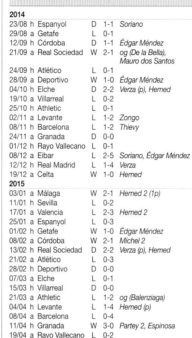

DOMESTIC LEAGUE CLUB-BY-CLUB

Match 5 - VfL Borussia Mönchengladbach (GER)
H 2-2 *Vietto (26), Cheryshev (63)*
Asenjo, Mario, Vietto, Uche (Pina 71), Cani (Jonathan dos Santos 56), Trigueros (Espinosa 87), Víctor Ruiz, Cheryshev, Jaume Costa, Gabriel, Bruno Soriano. Coach: Marcelino (ESP)

Match 6 - Apollon Limassol FC (CYP)
A 2-0 *Gerard Moreno (35), Vietto (40)*
Asenjo, Mario (Espinosa 46), Pina, Vietto (Uche 60), Dorado, Jaume Costa, Moi Gómez , Gabriel, Bruno Soriano (Trigueros 46), Rukavina, Gerard Moreno. Coach: Marcelino (ESP)

Round of 32 - FC Salzburg (AUT)
H 2-1 *Uche (32), Cheryshev (54)*
Asenjo, Mario, Pina, Musacchio, Jonathan dos Santos (Campbell 67), Vietto, Uche (Giovani dos Santos 70), Trigueros, Víctor Ruiz, Cheryshev, Jaume Costa. Coach: Marcelino (ESP)

A 3-1 *Vietto (33, 76), Giovani dos Santos (79)*
Asenjo, Mario, Pina (Campbell 86), Musacchio, Jonathan dos Santos, Vietto (Moi Gómez 81), Uche (Giovani dos Santos 68), Trigueros, Víctor Ruiz, Cheryshev, Jaume Costa. Coach: Marcelino (ESP)

Round of 16 - Sevilla FC (ESP)
H 1-3 *Vietto (48)*
Asenjo, Mario, Musacchio (Dorado 84), Jonathan dos Santos, Vietto, Uche (Gerard Moreno 68), Trigueros, Cheryshev, Jaume Costa, Moi Gómez (Campbell 45), Bailly. Coach: Marcelino (ESP)

A 1-2 *Giovani dos Santos (73)*
Asenjo, Mario, Pina, Musacchio, Jonathan dos Santos, Vietto (Dorado 85), Uche (Giovani dos Santos 46), Trigueros, Rukavina, Campbell (Gerard Moreno 70), Bailly. Coach: Juan Corral (ESP)
Red card: Bailly 77

Real Sociedad de Fútbol

EUROPA LEAGUE

Third qualifying round - Aberdeen FC (SCO)
H 2-0 *Zurutuza (53), Canales (68)*
Zubikarai, Aritz Elustondo, Markel Bergara, Íñigo Martínez, Finnbogason, Xabi Prieto (Agirretxe 75), Pardo (Granero 83), Zurutuza, Castro (Canales 64), Zaldúa, De la Bella. Coach: Jagoba Arrasate (ESP)

A 3-2 *Xabi Prieto (28, 86p), Markel Bergara (90+1)*
Zubikarai, Aritz Elustondo, Markel Bergara, Íñigo Martínez, Finnbogason (Agirretxe 58), Xabi Prieto, Pardo, Zurutuza (Granero 43), Castro (Canales 64), Zaldúa, De la Bella. Coach: Jagoba Arrasate (ESP)

Play-offs - FC Krasnodar (RUS)
H 1-0 *Xabi Prieto (71)*
Zubikarai, Aritz Elustondo, Markel Bergara, Íñigo Martínez, Agirretxe (Vela 76), Xabi Prieto, Pardo (Granero 67), Canales, Castro (Zurutuza 67), Zaldúa, De la Bella. Coach: Jagoba Arrasate (ESP)

A 0-3
Rulli (Zubikarai 85), Aritz Elustondo, Markel Bergara, Íñigo Martínez, Agirretxe, Xabi Prieto, Pardo (Granero 63), Canales, Zurutuza (Vela 79), Zaldúa, De la Bella. Coach: Jagoba Arrasate (ESP)
Red card: Markel Bergara 90+1

UD Almería

1989 • Juegos Mediterráneos (15,000) • udalmeriasad.com
Coach: Francisco Javier Rodríguez;
(09/12/14) (Miguel Rivera);
(13/12/14) Juan Ignacio Martínez;
(06/04/15) Sergi Barjuán

2014
23/08	h	Espanyol	D	1-1	*Soriano*
29/08	a	Getafe	L	0-1	
12/09	h	Córdoba	D	1-1	*Édgar Méndez*
21/09	a	Real Sociedad	W	2-1	*og (De la Bella), Mauro dos Santos*
24/09	h	Atlético	L	0-1	
28/09	a	Deportivo	W	1-0	*Édgar Méndez*
04/10	h	Elche	D	2-2	*Verza (p), Hemed*
19/10	a	Villarreal	L	0-2	
25/10	h	Athletic	L	0-1	
02/11	a	Levante	L	1-2	*Zongo*
08/11	h	Barcelona	L	1-2	*Thievy*
24/11	a	Granada	D	0-0	
01/12	h	Rayo Vallecano	L	0-1	
08/12	a	Eibar	L	2-5	*Soriano, Édgar Méndez*
12/12	h	Real Madrid	L	1-4	*Verza*
19/12	a	Celta	W	1-0	*Hemed*

2015
03/01	h	Málaga	W	2-1	*Hemed 2 (1p)*
11/01	h	Sevilla	L	0-2	
17/01	a	Valencia	L	2-3	*Hemed 2*
25/01	a	Espanyol	L	0-3	
01/02	h	Getafe	W	1-0	*Édgar Méndez*
08/02	a	Córdoba	W	2-1	*Míchel 2*
13/02	h	Real Sociedad	D	2-2	*Verza (p), Hemed*
21/02	a	Atlético	L	0-3	
28/02	h	Deportivo	D	0-0	
07/03	a	Elche	L	0-1	
15/03	h	Villarreal	D	0-0	
21/03	a	Athletic	L	1-2	*og (Balenziaga)*
04/04	h	Levante	L	1-4	*Hemed (p)*
08/04	a	Barcelona	L	0-4	
11/04	h	Granada	W	3-0	*Partey 2, Espinosa*
19/04	a	Rayo Vallecano	L	0-2	
26/04	h	Eibar	W	2-0	*Thievy, Verza (p)*
29/04	a	Real Madrid	L	0-3	
04/05	h	Celta	D	2-2	*Thievy, Zongo*
10/05	h	Málaga	L	1-2	*Partey*
17/05	a	Sevilla	L	0-2	
23/05	h	Valencia	L	2-3	*Partey, Soriano*

No	Name	Nat	DoB	Pos	Aps	(s)	Gls
28	Antonio Marín		17/06/96	D	1	(1)	
31	Ramon Azeez	NGA	12/12/92	M	10	(4)	
35	Carlos Selfa		25/04/92	M		(1)	
14	José Manuel Casado		09/08/86	D	5	(3)	
15	Corona		12/02/81	M	23	(8)	
18	Teerasil Dangda	THA	06/06/88	A		(6)	
16	Sebastián Dubarbier	ARG	02/02/86	D	32		
17	Édgar Méndez		30/04/91	M	21	(9)	4
24	Javier Espinosa		19/09/92	M	8	(7)	1
3	Fran Vélez		19/09/91	D	14	(3)	
10	Tomer Hemed	ISR	02/05/87	A	26	(9)	8
1	Julián		28/03/91	G	15		
21	Mané		21/12/81	D	3	(2)	
6	Mauro dos Santos	ARG	07/07/89	D	27	(2)	1
2	Míchel	BRA	15/02/90	D	13	(1)	2
33	Gaspar Panadero		12/12/97	M		(1)	
22	Thomas Partey	GHA	13/06/93	M	28	(3)	4
11	Quique		16/05/90	A		(3)	
32	Daniel Romera		23/08/95	A		(5)	
25	Rubén		22/06/84	G	23		
23	Fernando Soriano		24/09/79	M	13	(15)	3
9	Thievy Bifouma	CGO	13/05/92	A	21	(8)	4
5	Ángel Trujillo		08/09/87	D	35	(1)	
7	Verza		29/09/86	M	33		4
8	Wellington Silva	BRA	06/01/93	A	23	(8)	
4	Ximo Navarro		23/01/90	D	28		
19	Jonathan Zongo	BFA	06/04/89	A	16	(11)	2

Athletic Club

1898 • Nuevo San Mamés (53,289) • athletic-club.net
Major honours
Spanish League (8) 1930, 1931, 1934, 1936, 1943, 1956, 1983, 1984; Spanish Cup (23) 1903, 1904, 1910, 1911, 1914, 1915, 1916, 1921, 1923, 1930, 1931, 1932, 1933, 1943, 1944, 1945, 1950, 1955, 1956, 1958, 1969, 1973, 1984
Coach: Ernesto Valverde

2014
23/08	a	Málaga	L	0-1	
30/08	h	Levante	W	3-0	*Aduriz, Iturraspe, Muniain*
13/09	a	Barcelona	L	0-2	
20/09	h	Granada	L	0-1	
24/09	a	Rayo Vallecano	L	1-2	*Aduriz*
27/09	h	Eibar	D	0-0	
05/10	a	Real Madrid	L	0-5	
18/10	h	Celta	D	1-1	*Aduriz (p)*
25/10	a	Almería	W	1-0	*Etxeita*
02/11	h	Sevilla	W	1-0	*Aduriz*
09/11	a	Valencia	D	0-0	
21/11	h	Espanyol	W	3-1	*Aduriz, Viguera, Iturraspe*
29/11	a	Getafe	W	2-1	*San José, Beñat*
06/12	h	Córdoba	L	0-1	
14/12	a	Real Sociedad	D	1-1	*De Marcos*
21/12	a	Atlético	L	1-4	*Mikel Rico*

2015
03/01	a	Deportivo	L	0-1	
11/01	h	Elche	L	1-2	*San José*
17/01	a	Villarreal	L	0-2	
25/01	h	Málaga	D	1-1	*San José*
01/02	a	Levante	W	2-0	*Aduriz 2*
08/02	h	Barcelona	L	2-5	*Mikel Rico, Aduriz*
14/02	a	Granada	D	0-0	
22/02	h	Rayo Vallecano	W	1-0	*Aduriz*
01/03	a	Eibar	W	1-0	*Gurpegui*
07/03	h	Real Madrid	W	1-0	*Aduriz*
14/03	a	Celta	W	2-1	*Aduriz (p), San José*
21/03	h	Almería	W	2-1	*Etxeita, Mikel Rico*
04/04	a	Sevilla	L	0-2	
09/04	h	Valencia	D	1-1	*Aduriz*
12/04	a	Espanyol	L	0-1	
18/04	h	Getafe	W	4-0	*Aduriz 2 (1p), Ibai Gómez, Susaeta*
24/04	a	Córdoba	W	1-0	*og (Deivid)*
28/04	h	Real Sociedad	D	1-1	*Aduriz (p)*
02/05	a	Atlético	D	0-0	
09/05	h	Deportivo	D	1-1	*Aduriz*
17/05	h	Elche	W	3-2	*Aketxe, San José, Iñaki Williams*
23/05	h	Villarreal	W	4-0	*Aduriz 2 (1p), Iraola, Beñat*

No	Name	Nat	DoB	Pos	Aps	(s)	Gls
20	Aritz Aduriz		11/02/81	A	30	(1)	18
23	Ager Aketxe		30/12/93	M	3	(5)	1
3	Jon Aurtenetxe		03/01/92	D	3	(1)	
24	Mikel Balenziaga		29/02/88	D	33		
7	Beñat Etxebarria		19/02/87	M	20	(8)	2
12	Unai Bustinza		02/02/92	D	1	(1)	
10	Óscar De Marcos		14/04/89	M	32	(3)	1
16	Xabier Etxeita		31/10/87	D	22	(2)	2
22	Guillermo Fernández		23/05/93	A	5	(9)	
18	Carlos Gurpegui		19/08/80	M	15	(8)	1
13	Iago Herrerín		25/01/88	G	4		
11	Ibai Gómez		11/11/89	A	9	(12)	1
30	Iñaki Williams		15/06/94	A	15	(4)	1
1	Gorka Iraizoz		06/03/81	G	34		
15	Andoni Iraola		22/06/82	D	16	(6)	1
8	Ander Iturraspe		08/03/89	M	20	(5)	2
9	Kike Sola		25/02/86	A	1	(4)	
4	Aymeric Laporte	FRA	27/05/94	D	33		
17	Mikel Rico		04/11/84	M	32	(4)	3
5	Erik Morán		25/05/91	M	1	(1)	
19	Iker Muniain		19/12/92	M	25		1
6	Mikel San José		30/05/89	D	23	(5)	5
14	Markel Susaeta		14/12/87	M	20	(11)	1
2	Gaizka Toquero		09/08/84	M		(4)	
29	Unai López		30/10/95	M	11	(8)	
21	Borja Viguera		26/03/87	A	10	(10)	1

SPAIN

Club Atlético de Madrid

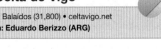

1903 • Vicente Calderón (54,851) • clubatleticodemadrid.com

Major honours
UEFA Cup Winners' Cup (1) 1962; UEFA Europa League (2) 2010, 2012; UEFA Super Cup (2) 2010, 2012; European/South American Cup (1) 1974; Spanish League (10) 1940, 1941, 1950, 1951, 1966, 1970, 1973, 1977, 1996, 2014; Spanish Cup (10) 1960, 1961, 1965, 1972, 1976, 1985, 1991, 1992, 1996, 2013

Coach: Diego Simeone (ARG)

2014

25/08	a	Rayo Vallecano	D	0-0	
30/08	h	Eibar	W	2-1	Miranda, Mandžukić
13/09	a	Real Madrid	W	2-1	Tiago, Arda
20/09	a	Celta	D	2-2	Miranda, Godín
24/09	a	Almería	W	1-0	Miranda
27/09	h	Sevilla	W	4-0	Koke, Saúl, Raúl García (p), Jiménez
04/10	a	Valencia	L	1-3	Mandžukić
19/10	a	Espanyol	W	2-0	Tiago, Mario Suárez
26/10	a	Getafe	W	1-0	Mandžukić
01/11	h	Córdoba	W	4-2	Griezmann 2, Mandžukić, Raúl García
09/11	a	Real Sociedad	L	1-2	Mandžukić
22/11	h	Málaga	W	3-1	Tiago, Griezmann, Godín
30/11	h	Deportivo	W	2-0	Saúl, Arda
06/12	a	Elche	W	2-0	Giménez, Mandžukić
14/12	h	Villarreal	L	0-1	
21/12	a	Athletic	W	4-1	Griezmann 3, Raúl García (p)

2015

03/01	h	Levante	W	3-1	Griezmann 2, Godín
11/01	a	Barcelona	L	1-3	Mandžukić (p)
18/01	h	Granada	W	2-0	Mandžukić (p), Raúl García
24/01	a	Rayo Vallecano	W	3-1	Griezmann 2, og (Manucho)
31/01	a	Eibar	W	3-1	Greizmann, Mandžukić 2
07/02	h	Real Madrid	W	4-0	Tiago, Saúl, Griezmann, Mandžukić
15/02	a	Celta	L	0-2	
21/02	h	Almería	W	3-0	Mandžukić (p), Griezmann 2
01/03	a	Sevilla	D	0-0	
08/03	h	Valencia	D	1-1	Koke
14/03	a	Espanyol	D	0-0	
21/03	h	Getafe	W	2-0	Fernando Torres, Tiago
04/04	a	Córdoba	W	2-0	Griezmann, Saúl
07/04	h	Real Sociedad	W	2-0	og (Mikel González), Griezmann
11/04	a	Málaga	D	2-2	Griezmann 2
18/04	a	Deportivo	W	2-1	Griezmann 2
25/04	h	Elche	W	3-0	Griezmann 2, Raúl García
29/04	a	Villarreal	W	1-0	Fernando Torres
02/05	h	Athletic	D	0-0	
10/05	a	Levante	D	2-2	Siqueira, Fernando Torres
17/05	h	Barcelona	L	0-1	
23/05	a	Granada	D	0-0	

No	Name	Nat	DoB	Pos	Aps	(s)	Gls
15	Cristian Ansaldi	ARG	20/09/86	D	6	(1)	
10	Arda Turan	TUR	30/01/87	M	28	(4)	2
22	Cani		03/08/81	M		(4)	
22	Alessio Cerci	ITA	23/07/87	A		(6)	
19	Fernando Torres		20/03/84	A	10	(9)	3
14	Gabi		10/07/83	M	32	(2)	
24	José María Giménez	URU	20/01/95	D	19	(1)	1
2	Diego Godín	URU	16/02/86	D	34		3
7	Antoine Griezmann	FRA	21/03/91	A	29	(8)	22
27	Héctor Hernández		14/09/95	M		(1)	
28	Lucas Hernández	FRA	14/02/96	D		(1)	
18	Jesús Gámez		10/04/85	D	12	(2)	
11	Raúl Jiménez	MEX	05/05/91	A	4	(17)	1
20	Juanfran		09/01/85	D	34	(1)	
6	Koke		08/01/92	M	33	(1)	2
9	Mario Mandžukić	CRO	21/05/86	A	24	(4)	12
4	Mario Suárez		24/02/87	M	11	(9)	1
23	Miranda	BRA	07/09/84	D	23		3
1	Miguel Ángel Moyá		02/04/84	G	27		
13	Jan Oblak	SVN	07/01/93	G	11		
8	Raúl García		11/07/86	M	17	(14)	4
21	Cristian Rodríguez	URU	30/09/85	M		(6)	
17	Saúl Ñíguez		21/11/94	M	9	(15)	4
3	Guilherme Siqueira	BRA	28/04/86	D	24	(1)	1
5	Tiago	POR	02/05/81	M	31		5

FC Barcelona

1899 • Camp Nou (98,772) • fcbarcelona.com

Major honours
European Champion Clubs' Cup/UEFA Champions League (5) 1992, 2006, 2009, 2011, 2015; UEFA Cup Winners' Cup (4) 1979, 1982, 1989, 1997; Inter Cities Fairs Cup (3) 1958, 1960, 1966; UEFA Super Cup (4) 1992, 1997, 2009, 2011; FIFA Club World Cup (2) 2009, 2011; Spanish League (23) 1929, 1945, 1948, 1949, 1952, 1953, 1959, 1960, 1974, 1985, 1991, 1992, 1993, 1994, 1998, 1999, 2005, 2006, 2009, 2010, 2011, 2013, 2015; Spanish Cup (27) 1910, 1912, 1913, 1920, 1922, 1925, 1926, 1928, 1942, 1951, 1952, 1953, 1957, 1959, 1963, 1968, 1971, 1978, 1981, 1983, 1988, 1990, 1997, 1998, 2009, 2012, 2015

Coach: Luis Enrique

2014

24/08	h	Elche	W	3-0	Messi 2, Munir
31/08	a	Villarreal	W	1-0	Sandro Ramírez
13/09	h	Athletic	W	2-0	Neymar 2
21/09	a	Levante	W	5-0	Neymar, Rakitić, Sandro Ramírez, Pedro, Messi
24/09	a	Málaga	D	0-0	
27/09	h	Granada	W	6-0	Neymar 3, Rakitić, Messi 2
04/10	a	Rayo Vallecano	W	2-0	Messi, Neymar
18/10	h	Eibar	W	3-0	Xavi, Neymar, Messi
25/10	a	Real Madrid	L	1-3	Neymar
01/11	h	Celta	L	0-1	
08/11	h	Almería	W	2-1	Neymar, Jordi Alba
22/11	h	Sevilla	W	5-1	Messi 3, Neymar, Rakitić
30/11	a	Valencia	W	1-0	Busquets
07/12	h	Espanyol	W	5-1	Messi 3, Piqué, Pedro
13/12	a	Getafe	D	0-0	
20/12	h	Córdoba	W	5-0	Pedro, Suárez, Piqué, Messi 2

2015

04/01	a	Real Sociedad	L	0-1	
11/01	h	Atlético	W	3-1	Neymar, Suárez, Messi
18/01	a	Deportivo	W	4-0	Messi 3, og (Sidnei)
24/01	a	Elche	W	6-0	Piqué, Messi 2 (1p), Neymar 2, Pedro
01/02	h	Villarreal	W	3-2	Neymar, Rafinha, Messi
08/02	a	Athletic	W	5-2	Messi, Suárez, og (De Marcos), Neymar, Pedro
15/02	h	Levante	W	5-0	Neymar, Messi 3 (1p), Suárez
21/02	h	Málaga	L	0-1	
28/02	a	Granada	W	3-1	Rakitić, Suárez, Messi
08/03	h	Rayo Vallecano	W	6-1	Suárez 2, Piqué, Messi 3 (1p)
14/03	a	Eibar	W	2-0	Messi 2 (1p)
22/03	h	Real Madrid	W	2-1	Mathieu, Suárez
05/04	a	Celta	W	1-0	Mathieu
08/04	h	Almería	W	4-0	Messi, Suárez 2, Bartra
11/04	a	Sevilla	D	2-2	Messi, Neymar
18/04	h	Valencia	W	2-0	Suárez, Messi
25/04	a	Espanyol	W	2-0	Neymar, Messi
28/04	h	Getafe	W	6-0	Messi 2 (1p), Suárez 2, Neymar, Xavi
02/05	a	Córdoba	W	8-0	Rakitić, Suárez 3, Messi 2, Piqué, Neymar (p)
09/05	h	Real Sociedad	W	2-0	Neymar, Pedro
17/05	a	Atlético	W	1-0	Messi
23/05	h	Deportivo	D	2-2	Messi 2

No	Name	Nat	DoB	Pos	Aps	(s)	Gls
21	Adriano	BRA	26/10/84	D	10	(6)	
3	Marc Bartra		15/01/91	D	11	(3)	1
13	Claudio Bravo	CHI	13/04/83	G	37		
5	Sergio Busquets		16/07/88	M	29	(4)	1
22	Dani Alves	BRA	06/05/83	D	29	(1)	
16	Douglas	BRA	06/08/90	D	1	(1)	
8	Andrés Iniesta		11/05/84	M	19	(5)	
18	Jordi Alba		21/03/89	D	27		1
25	Jordi Masip		03/01/89	G	1		
14	Javier Mascherano	ARG	08/06/84	D	26	(2)	
24	Jérémy Mathieu	FRA	29/10/83	D	23	(5)	2
10	Lionel Messi	ARG	24/06/87	A	37	(1)	43
2	Martín Montoya		14/04/91	D	6	(2)	
31	Munir El Haddadi		01/09/95	A	7	(3)	1
11	Neymar	BRA	05/02/92	A	29	(4)	22
7	Pedro Rodríguez		28/07/87	A	15	(20)	6
3	Gerard Piqué		02/02/87	D	26	(1)	5
12	Rafinha	BRA	12/02/93	A	13	(11)	1
4	Ivan Rakitić	CRO	10/03/88	M	23	(9)	5
29	Sandro Ramírez		09/07/95	M		(7)	2
20	Sergi Roberto		07/02/92	M	4	(8)	
9	Luis Suárez	URU	24/01/87	A	25	(2)	16
23	Thomas Vermaelen	BEL	14/11/85	D	1		
6	Xavi Hernández		25/01/80	M	19	(12)	1

RC Celta de Vigo

1923 • Balaídos (31,800) • celtavigo.net

Coach: Eduardo Berizzo (ARG)

2014

24/08	h	Getafe	W	3-1	Nolito, Orellana, Larrivey
30/08	a	Córdoba	D	1-1	Orellana
13/09	h	Real Sociedad	D	2-2	Orellana, Larrivey
20/09	a	Atlético	D	2-2	Hernández, Nolito (p)
23/09	h	Deportivo	W	2-1	Nolito, Larrivey
26/09	a	Elche	W	1-0	Nolito
05/10	h	Villarreal	L	1-3	Larrivey
18/10	a	Athletic	D	1-1	Nolito
24/10	h	Levante	W	3-0	Larrivey 2, Álex López
01/11	a	Barcelona	W	1-0	Larrivey
08/11	h	Granada	D	0-0	
23/11	a	Rayo Vallecano	L	0-1	
29/11	h	Eibar	L	0-1	
06/12	a	Real Madrid	L	0-3	
13/12	h	Málaga	L	0-1	
19/12	a	Almería	L	0-1	

2015

03/01	a	Sevilla	L	0-1	
10/01	h	Valencia	D	1-1	Orellana
17/01	a	Espanyol	L	0-1	
26/01	a	Getafe	L	1-2	Charles
31/01	h	Córdoba	W	1-0	Nolito
07/02	a	Real Sociedad	D	1-1	Nolito
15/02	h	Atlético	W	2-0	Nolito (p), Orellana
21/02	a	Deportivo	W	2-0	Charles, Larrivey
02/03	h	Elche	D	1-1	Krohn-Dehli
08/03	h	Villarreal	L	1-4	Fernández
14/03	h	Athletic	L	1-2	Larrivey
21/03	a	Levante	W	1-0	Charles
05/04	h	Barcelona	L	0-1	
08/04	a	Granada	D	1-1	Bongonda
11/04	h	Rayo Vallecano	W	6-1	Larrivey 2, Santi Mina 4
19/04	a	Eibar	W	1-0	Nolito (p)
26/04	h	Real Madrid	L	2-4	Nolito, Santi Mina
29/04	h	Málaga	W	1-0	Nolito
04/05	a	Almería	D	2-2	Nolito, Santi Mina
10/05	h	Sevilla	D	1-1	Santi Mina (p)
17/05	a	Valencia	D	1-1	Hernández
23/05	h	Espanyol	W	3-2	Hugo Mallo, Cabral, Nolito

No	Name	Nat	DoB	Pos	Aps	(s)	Gls
8	Álex López		11/01/88	M	12	(13)	1
18	Theo Bongonda	BEL	20/11/95	A		(8)	1
28	Borja Fernández		16/08/95	M	1	(5)	
34	Borja Iglesias		17/01/93	A		(1)	
22	Gustavo Cabral	ARG	14/10/85	D	35		1
9	Charles	BRA	04/04/84	A	12	(16)	3
15	David Costas		26/03/95	D	1		
24	Augusto Fernández	ARG	10/04/86	M	24	(6)	1
3	Andreu Fontàs		14/11/89	D	33	(1)	
5	Pablo Hernández	ARG	24/10/86	D	15	(14)	2
2	Hugo Mallo		22/06/91	D	27	(1)	1
19	Jonny		03/03/94	D	32	(4)	
23	Michael Krohn-Dehli	DEN	06/06/83	M	35	(1)	1
11	Joaquín Larrivey	ARG	20/08/84	A	26	(9)	11
17	Levy Madinda	GAB	22/06/92	M		(5)	
10	Nolito		15/10/86	M	32	(4)	13
14	Fabián Orellana	CHI	27/01/86	A	34	(1)	5
21	Carlos Planas		04/03/91	D	10	(1)	
6	Nemanja Radoja	SRB	06/02/93	M	23	(5)	
13	Rubén Blanco		25/07/95	G		(1)	
7	Santi Mina		07/12/95	A	14	(6)	7
20	Sergi Gómez		28/07/92	D	14	(8)	
1	Sergio Álvarez		03/08/86	G	38		

Córdoba CF

1954 • Nuevo El Arcángel (20,989) • cordobacf.com
Coach: Albert Ferrer;
(21/10/14) Miroslav Djukić (SRB);
(16/03/15) José Antonio Romero

2014

25/08	a	Real Madrid	L	0-2	
30/08	h	Celta	D	1-1	Fede Cartabia
12/09	a	Almería	D	1-1	Fede Cartabia
21/09	h	Sevilla	L	1-3	Borja García
25/09	a	Valencia	L	0-3	
28/09	h	Espanyol	D	0-0	
03/10	a	Getafe	D	1-1	Ekeng
18/10	h	Málaga	L	1-2	Ghilas
25/10	h	Real Sociedad	D	1-1	Xisco
01/11	a	Atlético	L	2-4	Ghilas 2
07/11	h	Deportivo	D	0-0	
23/11	a	Elche	D	2-2	Fidel, Fede Cartabia
30/11	h	Villarreal	L	0-2	
06/12	h	Athletic	W	1-0	Ghilas
13/12	a	Levante	D	0-0	
20/12	a	Barcelona	L	0-5	

2015

05/01	h	Granada	W	2-0	Ghilas, Andone
12/01	a	Rayo Vallecano	W	1-0	og (Ba)
16/01	h	Eibar	D	1-1	Andone
24/01	h	Real Madrid	L	1-2	Ghilas (p)
31/01	a	Celta	L	0-1	
08/02	h	Almería	L	1-2	Fede Cartabia
14/02	a	Sevilla	L	0-3	
21/02	a	Valencia	L	1-2	Ghilas (p)
27/02	a	Espanyol	L	0-1	
09/03	h	Getafe	L	1-2	Andone
15/03	a	Málaga	L	0-2	
22/03	a	Real Sociedad	L	1-3	Andone
04/04	h	Atlético	L	0-2	
08/04	h	Deportivo	D	1-1	Andone
12/04	h	Elche	L	0-2	
19/04	a	Villarreal	D	0-0	
24/04	h	Athletic	L	0-1	
28/04	a	Levante	L	0-1	
02/05	h	Barcelona	L	0-8	
09/05	a	Granada	L	0-2	
17/05	h	Rayo Vallecano	L	1-2	Luso
23/05	a	Eibar	L	0-3	

No	Name	Nat	DoB	Pos	Aps	(s)	Gls
23	Abel Gómez		20/02/82	M	14	(8)	
28	Florin Andone	ROU	11/04/93	A	17	(3)	5
24	Bebé	POR	12/07/90	A	16	(2)	
36	Jonathan Bijimine	COD	09/07/94	M		(1)	
18	Borja García		02/11/90	M	22	(6)	1
4	Iago Bouzón		17/03/83	D	3		
21	Carlos Caballero		05/10/84	M		(2)	
33	Eduardo Campabadal		26/01/93	D	12	(2)	
3	José Ángel Crespo		09/02/87	D	26	(1)	
15	Deivid		27/01/89	D	21		
11	Edimar	BRA	21/05/86	D	17		
5	Patrick Ekeng	CMR	26/03/90	M	8	(6)	1
10	Fede Cartabia	ARG	20/01/93	M	24	(6)	4
35	Fede Vico		07/04/94	M	8	(12)	
16	Fidel		27/10/89	M	17	(8)	1
38	Fran Serrano		20/04/95	D	1	(1)	
14	Nabil Ghilas	ALG	20/04/90	A	23	(4)	7
17	Adrián Gunino	URU	03/02/89	D	21	(2)	
24	Mike Havenaar	JPN	20/05/87	A	4	(1)	
9	Héldon	CPV	14/11/88	A	6	(8)	
12	Íñigo López		23/07/82	D	21		
11	José Carlos		17/07/87	M		(1)	
1	Juan Carlos		20/01/88	G	32		
21	Rene Krhin	SVN	21/05/90	M	14		
22	Aritz López Garay		06/11/80	M	5	(2)	
19	José López Silva		02/02/83	M	4	(4)	
6	Luso		04/12/84	D	16	(2)	1
2	Aleksandar Pantić	SRB	11/04/92	D	27	(2)	
29	Daniel Pinillos		22/10/92	D	9	(3)	
7	Fausto Rossi	ITA	03/12/90	M	16	(8)	
20	Ryder Matos	BRA	02/02/93	M	2	(1)	
13	Mikel Saizar		18/01/83	G	6		
40	Sergio García		27/12/96	A		(1)	
9	Xisco		26/06/86	M	1	(8)	1
20	Bruno Zuculini	ARG	02/04/93	A	5	(3)	

RC Deportivo La Coruña

1906 • Riazor (34,600) • canaldeportivo.com
Major honours
Spanish League (1) 2000; Spanish Cup (2) 1995, 2002
Coach: Víctor Fernández;
(08/04/15) Víctor Sánchez

2014

23/08	a	Granada	L	1-2	Ivan Cavaleiro
31/08	h	Rayo Vallecano	D	2-2	José Rodríguez, Cuenca (p)
15/09	a	Eibar	W	1-0	Juan Domínguez
20/09	h	Real Madrid	L	2-8	Medunjanin (p), Toché
23/09	a	Celta	L	1-2	Cuenca
28/09	h	Almería	L	0-1	
05/10	a	Sevilla	L	1-4	Medunjanin
19/10	h	Valencia	W	3-0	og (Mustafi), Lucas Pérez, Toché
26/10	h	Espanyol	D	0-0	
31/10	h	Getafe	L	1-2	Hélder Postiga
07/11	a	Córdoba	D	0-0	
22/11	h	Real Sociedad	D	0-0	
30/11	a	Atlético	L	0-2	
06/12	h	Málaga	L	0-1	
15/12	h	Elche	W	1-0	Fariña
21/12	a	Villarreal	L	0-3	

2015

03/01	h	Athletic	W	1-0	Ivan Cavaleiro
09/01	a	Levante	D	0-0	
18/01	h	Barcelona	L	0-4	
25/01	h	Granada	D	2-2	José Rodríguez, Lucas Pérez
30/01	a	Rayo Vallecano	W	2-1	Borges 2 (1p)
06/02	h	Eibar	W	2-0	Lucas Pérez, Ivan Cavaleiro
14/02	a	Real Madrid	L	0-2	
21/02	h	Celta	L	0-2	
28/02	a	Almería	D	0-0	
07/03	h	Sevilla	L	3-4	Oriol Riera 2, Lucas Pérez (p)
13/03	a	Valencia	L	0-2	
22/03	h	Espanyol	D	0-0	
05/04	a	Getafe	L	1-2	Toché
08/04	h	Córdoba	D	1-1	og (Andone)
12/04	a	Real Sociedad	D	2-2	Lucas Pérez, Toché
18/04	a	Atlético	L	1-2	Oriol Riera
26/04	a	Málaga	D	1-1	Oriol Riera
29/04	a	Elche	L	0-4	
02/05	h	Villarreal	D	1-1	Borges
09/05	a	Athletic	D	1-1	Lopo
17/05	h	Levante	W	2-0	Lopo, Juanfran
23/05	a	Barcelona	D	2-2	Lucas Pérez, Diogo Salomão

No	Name	Nat	DoB	Pos	Aps	(s)	Gls
4	Alex Bergantiños		07/06/85	M	29	(4)	
22	Celso Borges	CRC	27/05/88	M	17		3
3	Roberto Canella		07/02/88	D	5	(4)	
14	Isaac Cuenca		27/04/91	M	14	(13)	2
21	Modibo Diakité	FRA	02/03/87	D	2		
32	Diogo Salomão	POR	14/09/88	M	2	(4)	1
13	Fabricio		31/12/87	G	31		
24	Luis Fariña	ARG	12/03/91	M	15	(6)	1
32	Hélder Costa	ANG	12/01/94	M		(6)	
9	Hélder Postiga	POR	02/08/82	A	8	(6)	1
5	Pablo Insúa		09/09/93	D	14	(3)	
19	Ivan Cavaleiro	POR	18/10/93	M	27	(7)	3
6	José Rodríguez		16/12/94	M	17	(8)	2
25	Juan Carlos		15/03/91	D		(2)	
19	Juan Domínguez		08/01/90	M	13	(9)	1
11	Juanfran		11/09/88	D	33	(1)	1
15	Laure		22/03/85	D	14	(5)	
23	Alberto Lopo		05/05/80	D	30		2
7	Lucas Pérez		10/09/88	A	20	(1)	6
16	Luisinho	POR	05/05/85	D	34	(1)	
1	Germán Lux	ARG	07/06/82	G	7		
2	Manuel Pablo		25/01/76	D	5		
8	Haris Medunjanin	BIH	08/03/85	M	16	(8)	2
21	Oriol Riera		03/07/86	A	18	(3)	4
21	Sidnei	BRA	23/06/89	D	32		
18	Toché		01/01/83	A	9	(16)	4
20	Cezary Wilk	POL	12/02/86	M	6	(5)	

SD Eibar

1940 • Ipurúa (5,250) • sdeibar.com
Coach: Gaizka Garitano

2014

24/08	h	Real Sociedad	W	1-0	Lara
30/08	a	Atlético	L	1-2	Abraham
15/09	h	Deportivo	L	0-1	
19/09	a	Elche	W	2-0	Dani García, Albentosa
24/09	h	Villarreal	D	1-1	Arruabarrena
27/09	a	Athletic	D	0-0	
04/10	h	Levante	D	3-3	og (Pedro López), Saúl Berjón, Piovaccari
18/10	a	Barcelona	L	0-3	
25/10	h	Granada	D	1-1	Bóveda
03/11	a	Rayo Vallecano	W	3-2	Arruabarrena 2 (1p), Piovaccari
08/11	h	Málaga	L	1-2	Arruabarrena
22/11	h	Real Madrid	L	0-4	
29/11	a	Celta	W	1-0	Manu del Moral
08/12	h	Almería	W	5-2	Piovaccari, Saúl Berjón, Albentosa, Raúl Navas, Capa
14/12	a	Sevilla	D	0-0	
20/12	h	Valencia	L	0-1	

2015

04/01	a	Espanyol	W	2-1	Manu del Moral, Bóveda
10/01	h	Getafe	W	2-1	Manu del Moral, Capa
16/01	a	Córdoba	D	1-1	Arruabarrena
24/01	a	Real Sociedad	L	0-1	
31/01	h	Atlético	L	1-3	Piovaccari
06/02	a	Deportivo	L	0-2	
16/02	h	Elche	L	0-1	
22/02	a	Villarreal	L	0-1	
01/03	h	Athletic	L	0-1	
06/03	a	Levante	L	1-2	Saúl Berjón
14/03	h	Barcelona	L	0-2	
21/03	a	Granada	D	0-0	
03/04	h	Rayo Vallecano	L	1-2	Arruabarrena (p)
07/04	h	Málaga	W	1-0	Arruabarrena
11/04	a	Real Madrid	L	0-3	
19/04	h	Celta	L	0-1	
26/04	a	Almería	L	0-2	
29/04	h	Sevilla	L	1-3	Piovaccari
03/05	a	Valencia	L	1-3	Arruabarrena
08/05	h	Espanyol	L	0-2	
17/05	a	Getafe	D	1-1	Borja Fernández
23/05	h	Córdoba	W	3-0	Arruabarrena, Raúl Navas, Capa

No	Name	Nat	DoB	Pos	Aps	(s)	Gls
24	Abraham		22/02/86	D	14	(8)	1
6	Raúl Albentosa		07/09/88	D	17		2
9	Ángel		26/04/87	A	6	(9)	
4	Txema Añibarro		26/07/79	M	12	(3)	
10	Mikel Arruabarrena		09/02/83	A	29	(5)	9
18	Derek Boateng	GHA	02/05/83	M	8	(5)	
12	Borja Fernández		14/01/81	M	14	(2)	1
7	Eneko Bóveda		08/02/92	M	27	(7)	3
14	Dani García		24/05/90	M	34		1
17	Dídac Vilà		09/06/89	D	11	(3)	
5	Borja Ekiza		06/03/88	D	12		
8	Jon Errasti		06/06/88	M	19	(6)	
25	Jaime		10/12/80	G	1		
23	Javier Lara		04/12/86	M	16	(15)	1
15	Dejan Lekić	SRB	07/06/85	A	1	(17)	
16	Lillo		27/03/89	D	28	(3)	
20	Manu del Moral		25/02/84	A	21	(7)	3
11	Daniel Nieto		04/05/91	M	1	(8)	
19	Federico Piovaccari	ITA	01/09/84	A	17	(11)	5
22	Raúl Navas		11/06/88	D	28	(1)	2
21	Saúl Berjón		24/05/86	M	30	(4)	3
1	Xabi Irureta		21/03/86	G	33		

Elche CF

1923 • Martínez Valero (36,017) • elchecf.es
Coach: Fran Escribá

2014
24/08	a Barcelona	L	0-3	
31/08	h Granada	D	1-1	*Lombán*
14/09	a Rayo Vallecano	W	3-2	*Albácar, Jonathas, Mosquera*
19/09	h Eibar	L	0-2	
23/09	a Real Madrid	L	1-5	*Albácar (p)*
26/09	h Celta	L	0-1	
04/10	a Almería	D	2-2	*Víctor Rodríguez, Jonathas*
19/10	h Sevilla	L	0-2	
25/10	a Valencia	L	1-3	*Jonathas*
02/11	h Espanyol	W	2-0	*Jonathas 2*
08/11	a Getafe	D	0-0	
23/11	h Córdoba	D	2-2	*Lombán (p), Jonathas*
28/11	a Real Sociedad	L	0-3	
06/12	h Atlético	L	0-0	
15/12	h Deportivo	L	0-1	
21/12	a Málaga	L	1-2	*Lombán*
2015				
03/01	h Villarreal	D	2-2	*Jonathas, Víctor Rodríguez*
11/01	a Athletic	W	2-1	*Víctor Rodríguez, Fajr*
18/01	h Levante	W	1-0	*Jonathas*
24/01	a Barcelona	L	0-6	
31/01	a Granada	L	0-1	
09/02	h Rayo Vallecano	W	2-0	*Suárez, Mendes Rodrigues*
16/02	a Eibar	L	0-2	
22/02	h Real Madrid	L	0-2	
02/03	a Celta	D	1-1	*Lombán (p)*
07/03	h Almería	W	1-0	*Víctor Rodríguez*
15/03	a Sevilla	L	0-3	
20/03	h Valencia	L	0-4	
06/04	a Espanyol	D	1-1	*Cristian Herrera*
09/04	h Getafe	L	0-1	
12/04	a Córdoba	W	2-0	*Albácar, Pašalić*
20/04	h Real Sociedad	W	1-0	*Jonathas*
25/04	a Atlético	L	0-3	
29/04	h Deportivo	W	4-0	*Jonathas, Lombán (p), Pašalić, Mendes Rodrigues*
03/05	a Málaga	W	2-1	*Jonathas, Pašalić*
10/05	a Villarreal	L	0-1	
17/05	h Athletic	L	2-3	*Jonathas 2*
23/05	a Levante	D	0-0	

No	Name	Nat	DoB	Pos	Aps	(s)	Gls
7	Aarón Ñíguez		26/04/89	M	15	(6)	
8	Adrián		25/05/88	M	23	(6)	
21	Edu Albácar		16/11/79	D	16	(2)	3
28	Mario Arqués		19/01/92	M		(1)	
5	Domingo Cisma		09/02/82	D	24	(1)	
10	Ferran Corominas		05/01/83	A	14	(20)	
9	Cristian Herrera		13/03/91	A	7	(19)	1
20	Fayçal Fajr	MAR	01/08/88	M	29	(5)	1
34	Franco Fragapane	ARG	06/02/93	A		(1)	
35	Rafael Gálvez		20/05/93	M	1	(3)	
19	Álvaro Giménez		19/05/91	A	2	(15)	
1	Manu Herrera		29/09/82	G	6	(1)	
22	Jonathas	BRA	06/03/89	A	34		14
14	José Angel		02/03/89	D	8	(5)	
4	David Lombán		05/06/87	D	33	(1)	5
11	Garry Mendes Rodrigues	CPV	27/11/90	M	16	(15)	2
6	Pedro Mosquera		21/04/88	M	24	(1)	1
24	Mario Pašalić	CRO	09/02/95	M	26	(5)	3
18	Sergio Pelegrín		18/04/79	D	8	(2)	
31	Pol Freixanet		22/08/91	G		(1)	
3	Enzo Roco	CHI	16/08/92	D	32		
32	Samu Martínez		15/04/94	M	2		
2	Damián Suárez	URU	27/04/88	D	34		1
25	Przemysław Tytoń	POL	04/01/87	G	32		
17	Víctor Rodríguez		23/07/89	A	32	(3)	4

RCD Espanyol

1900 • Power8 (40,500) • rcdespanyol.com

Major honours
Spanish Cup (4) 1929, 1940, 2000, 2006
Coach: Sergio González

2014
23/08	a Almería	D	1-1	*Sergio García*
30/08	h Sevilla	L	1-2	*Stuani*
14/09	a Valencia	L	1-3	*Sergio García (p)*
20/09	h Málaga	D	2-2	*Caicedo, Stuani*
25/09	h Getafe	W	2-0	*Sergio García, Stuani*
28/09	a Córdoba	D	0-0	
05/10	h Real Sociedad	W	2-0	*Lucas Vázquez, Stuani*
19/10	a Atlético	L	0-2	
26/10	h Deportivo	D	0-0	
02/11	h Elche	L	1-2	*Stuani (p)*
09/11	h Villarreal	D	1-1	*Colotto*
21/11	a Athletic	L	0-3	*Víctor Sánchez*
29/11	h Levante	W	2-1	*Caicedo, Sergio García*
07/12	a Barcelona	L	1-5	*Sergio García*
14/12	h Granada	D	2-2	*Caicedo, Stuani*
20/12	a Rayo Vallecano	W	3-1	*Sergio García 2, Lucas Vázquez*
2015				
04/01	h Eibar	L	1-2	*Caicedo*
10/01	a Real Madrid	L	0-3	
17/01	h Celta	W	1-0	*Caicedo*
25/01	h Almería	W	3-0	*Stuani 2, Caicedo*
01/02	a Sevilla	L	2-3	*Stuani (p), Víctor Sánchez*
08/02	h Valencia	L	1-2	*Sergio García*
14/02	a Málaga	W	2-0	*Álvaro, Sergio García*
20/02	a Getafe	L	1-2	*Arbilla*
27/02	h Córdoba	W	1-0	*Abraham*
08/03	a Real Sociedad	L	0-1	
14/03	h Atlético	D	0-0	
22/03	a Deportivo	D	0-0	
06/04	h Elche	D	1-1	*Sergio García*
09/04	a Villarreal	W	3-0	*Caicedo 2, Víctor Sánchez*
12/04	h Athletic	W	1-0	*Sergio García*
17/04	a Levante	D	2-2	*Lucas Vázquez, Caicedo*
25/04	h Barcelona	L	0-2	
30/04	a Granada	W	2-1	*Sergio García, Paco Montañés*
03/05	h Rayo Vallecano	D	1-1	*Moreno*
08/05	a Eibar	W	2-0	*Sergio García, Stuani*
17/05	h Real Madrid	L	1-4	*Stuani*
23/05	a Celta	L	2-3	*Sergio García (p), Stuani*

No	Name	Nat	DoB	Pos	Aps	(s)	Gls
10	Abraham		16/07/85	M	16	(6)	1
22	Alex Fernández		15/10/92	M	2	(3)	
22	Álvaro González		08/01/90	D	34	(2)	1
23	Anaitz Arbilla		15/05/87	D	25	(3)	1
30	Eric Bailly	CIV	12/04/94	D	4	(1)	
20	Felipe Caicedo	ECU	05/09/88	A	25	(10)	9
14	José Cañas		27/05/87	M	24	(5)	
13	Kiko Casilla		02/10/86	G	37		
19	Diego Colotto	ARG	10/03/81	D	22	(1)	1
14	David López		09/10/89	M	1		
27	Rubén Duarte		18/10/95	M	11		
2	Felipe Mattioni	BRA	15/10/88	D		(1)	
18	Juan Fuentes		05/01/90	D	21	(1)	
29	Jairo Morilla		02/07/93	A		(3)	
16	Javi López		21/01/86	M	25	(3)	
28	Joan Jordán		06/07/94	M	1	(2)	
17	Lucas Vázquez		01/07/91	M	30	(3)	3
32	Julián Luque		27/02/92	A		(1)	
15	Héctor Moreno	MEX	17/01/88	D	18	(1)	1
24	Paco Montañés		08/10/86	M	11	(14)	1
25	Pau López		13/12/94	G	1	(1)	
3	Raúl Rodríguez		22/09/87	D		(1)	
6	Salva Sevilla		18/03/84	M	17	(9)	
9	Sergio García		09/06/83	A	34	(1)	14
8	Christian Stuani	URU	12/10/86	A	15	(21)	12
5	Víctor Álvarez		14/03/93	D	15	(3)	
4	Víctor Sánchez		08/09/87	D	29	(5)	3

Getafe CF

1983 • Coliseum Alfonso Pérez (17,000) • getafecf.com

Coach: Cosmin Contra (ROU); (05/01/15) Quique Sánchez Flores; (26/02/15) Pablo Franco

2014
24/08	a Celta	L	1-3	*Sammir*
29/08	h Almería	W	1-0	*Álvaro Vázquez*
14/09	a Sevilla	L	0-2	
22/09	h Valencia	L	0-3	
25/09	a Espanyol	L	0-2	
28/09	h Málaga	W	1-0	*Míchel*
03/10	h Córdoba	D	1-1	*Baba Diawara*
20/10	a Real Sociedad	W	2-1	*Yoda 2*
26/10	h Atlético	L	0-1	
31/10	a Deportivo	W	2-1	*Yoda, Lafita*
08/11	h Elche	D	0-0	
23/11	a Villarreal	L	1-2	*Lacen*
29/11	h Athletic	L	1-2	*Lafita*
08/12	a Levante	D	1-1	*Yoda*
13/12	a Barcelona	D	0-0	
21/12	h Granada	D	1-1	*Velázquez*
2015				
04/01	h Rayo Vallecano	L	1-2	*Álvaro Vázquez*
10/01	a Eibar	L	1-2	*Diego Castro*
18/01	h Real Madrid	L	0-3	
26/01	h Celta	W	2-1	*Álvaro Vázquez, Sarabia*
01/02	a Almería	L	0-1	
08/02	h Sevilla	W	2-1	*Álvaro Vázquez (p), Pedro León*
15/02	a Valencia	L	0-1	
20/02	h Espanyol	W	2-1	*Sarabia, Álvaro Vázquez*
28/02	a Málaga	L	2-3	*Álvaro Vázquez 2*
09/03	a Córdoba	W	2-1	*og (Fede Vico), Juan Rodríguez*
16/03	h Real Sociedad	L	0-1	
21/03	h Atlético	L	0-2	
05/04	h Deportivo	W	2-1	*Alexis, Sergio Escudero*
09/04	a Elche	W	1-0	*Hinestroza*
12/04	h Villarreal	D	1-1	*Diego Castro*
18/04	a Athletic	L	0-4	
25/04	h Levante	L	0-1	
28/04	a Barcelona	L	0-6	
03/05	h Granada	L	1-2	*Pedro León*
11/05	a Rayo Vallecano	L	0-2	
17/05	h Eibar	D	1-1	*Hinestroza*
23/05	a Real Madrid	L	3-7	*Sergio Escudero, Diego Castro, Lacen*

No	Name	Nat	DoB	Pos	Aps	(s)	Gls
36	Álex Felip		03/04/92	M		(10)	
2	Alexis		04/08/85	D	28	(1)	1
9	Álvaro Vázquez		27/04/91	A	19	(2)	7
12	Álvaro Arroyo		20/07/88	D	10	(2)	
15	Baba Diawara	SEN	05/01/88	A	5	(16)	1
13	Jordi Codina		27/04/82	G	5		
17	Diego Castro		02/07/82	A	25	(7)	3
32	Emi Buendía	ARG	25/12/96	A	1	(5)	
25	Vicente Guaita		18/02/87	G	29		
23	Fredy Hinestroza	COL	05/04/90	M	21	(12)	2
26	Ivi López		29/06/94	A		(8)	
1	Jonathan López		16/04/81	G	4		
22	Juan Rodríguez		01/04/82	M	32	(2)	1
8	Medhi Lacen	ALG	15/05/84	M	29	(1)	2
7	Ángel Lafita		07/08/84	M	12	(3)	2
21	Míchel		29/07/88	A	8	(4)	1
5	Naldo	BRA	25/08/88	D	28	(2)	
14	Pedro León		24/11/86	M	16	(9)	2
15	Rafa López		09/04/85	M	1		
3	Roberto Lago		30/08/85	D	11	(5)	
6	Sammir	CRO	23/04/87	M	16	(7)	1
10	Pablo Sarabia		11/05/92	M	31	(4)	2
18	Sergio Escudero		02/09/89	D	26	(4)	2
20	Juan Valera		21/12/84	D	12		
4	Dani Velázquez	URU	30/04/94	D	27		1
27	Carlos Vigaray		07/09/94	D	10	(3)	
11	Abdoul Yoda	FRA	25/10/88	M	12	(6)	4

Granada CF

1931 • Nuevo Los Cármenes (16,200) • granadacf.es
Coach: Joaquín Caparrós;
(16/01/15) (Joseba Aguado);
(19/01/15) Abel Resino;
(01/05/15) José Ramón Sandoval

2014

23/08	h	Deportivo	W	2-1	Rubén Rochina, Babin
31/08	a	Elche	D	1-1	Fran Rico
14/09	h	Villarreal	D	0-0	
20/09	a	Athletic	W	1-0	Córdoba
24/09	h	Levante	L	0-1	
27/09	a	Barcelona	L	0-6	
04/10	a	Málaga	L	1-2	El-Arabi
17/10	h	Rayo Vallecano	L	0-1	
25/10	a	Eibar	D	1-1	Nyom
01/11	h	Real Madrid	L	0-4	
08/11	a	Celta	D	0-0	
24/11	h	Almería	D	0-0	
30/11	a	Sevilla	L	1-5	El-Arabi (p)
07/12	h	Valencia	D	1-1	Success
14/12	a	Espanyol	L	1-2	El-Arabi
21/12	h	Getafe	D	1-1	Córdoba

2015

05/01	a	Córdoba	L	0-2	
11/01	h	Real Sociedad	D	1-1	Fran Rico (p)
18/01	a	Atlético	L	0-2	
25/01	a	Deportivo	D	2-2	Piti, Ibáñez
31/01	h	Elche	W	1-0	Córdoba
07/02	a	Villarreal	L	0-1	
14/02	h	Athletic	D	0-0	
23/02	a	Levante	L	1-2	El-Arabi (p)
28/02	h	Barcelona	L	1-3	Fran Rico (p)
07/03	h	Málaga	W	1-0	Ibáñez
14/03	a	Rayo Vallecano	L	1-3	Córdoba
21/03	h	Eibar	D	0-0	
05/04	a	Real Madrid	L	1-9	Ibáñez
08/04	h	Celta	D	1-1	Ibáñez
11/04	a	Almería	L	0-3	
19/04	h	Sevilla	D	1-1	Mainz
27/04	a	Valencia	L	0-4	
30/04	h	Espanyol	L	1-2	Mainz
03/05	a	Getafe	W	2-1	El-Arabi 2 (1p)
09/05	h	Córdoba	W	2-0	Mainz, El-Arabi (p)
17/05	a	Real Sociedad	W	3-0	El-Arabi, Ibáñez, Rubén Rochina
23/05	h	Atlético	D	0-0	

No	Name	Nat	DoB	Pos	Aps	(s)	Gls
17	Adrián Colunga		17/11/84	A	3	(1)	
6	Jean-Sylvain Babin	MTQ	14/10/86	D	34		1
15	Alhassane "Lass" Bangoura	GUI	30/03/92	A	12	(2)	
19	Cala		26/11/89	D	6	(1)	
18	John Córdoba	COL	10/05/93	A	16	(10)	4
7	Daniel Candeias	POR	25/02/88	A	5	(6)	
35	Stole Dimitrievski	MKD	25/12/93	G	1		
9	Youssef El-Arabi	MAR	03/02/87	A	24	(4)	8
22	Dimitri Foulquier	FRA	23/03/93	D	18	(7)	
4	Fran Rico		03/08/87	M	28	(3)	3
21	Robert Ibáñez		22/03/93	A	12	(5)	5
25	Emanuel Insúa	ARG	10/04/91	D	12		
14	Eddy Ísrafilov	AZE	02/08/92	M	1	(4)	
16	Manuel Iturra	CHI	23/06/84	M	27	(3)	
20	Juan Carlos		20/03/90	D	15	(6)	
19	Daniel Larsson	SWE	25/01/87	M		(1)	
3	Luís Martins	POR	10/06/92	D	1	(2)	
27	Darwin Machis	VEN	07/02/93	A	2	(1)	
5	Diego Mainz		29/12/82	D	18	(5)	3
8	Javi Márquez		11/05/86	M	15	(10)	
26	Sulayman Marreh	GAM	18/07/94	M	1		
24	Jeison Murillo	COL	27/05/92	M	18	(1)	
2	Allan Nyom	CMR	10/05/88	D	34		1
1	Oier Olazábal		14/09/89	G	14		
21	Alfredo Ortuño		21/01/91	M	2	(3)	
10	Piti		26/05/81	A	28	(5)	1
11	Riki		11/08/80	A		(9)	
13	Roberto		25/01/79	G	23		
12	Rubén Pérez		26/04/89	M	13	(1)	
23	Rubén Rochina		23/03/91	A	12	(7)	2
17	Abdoul Sissoko	FRA	20/03/90	M	10	(1)	
29	Isaac Success	NGA	07/01/96	A	9	(10)	1
36	Uche Agbo	NGA	04/12/95	M		(1)	
7	Héctor Yuste		12/01/88	M	4	(2)	

Levante UD

1939 • Ciutat de València (25,354) • levanteud.com
Coach: José Luis Mendilíbar;
(22/10/14) Lucas Alcaraz

2014

24/08	h	Villarreal	L	0-2	
30/08	a	Athletic	L	0-3	
13/09	a	Málaga	D	0-0	
21/09	h	Barcelona	L	0-5	
24/09	a	Granada	W	1-0	Rubén García
27/09	h	Rayo Vallecano	L	0-2	
04/10	a	Eibar	D	3-3	Morales, Camarasa, Víctor Casadesús
18/10	h	Real Madrid	L	0-5	
24/10	a	Celta	L	0-3	
02/11	h	Almería	W	2-1	Barral, Víctor Casadesús
09/11	a	Sevilla	D	1-1	Víctor Casadesús
23/11	h	Valencia	W	2-1	Víctor Casadesús, Morales
29/11	a	Espanyol	L	1-2	Morales
08/12	h	Getafe	D	1-1	Rafael Martins
13/12	a	Córdoba	D	0-0	
20/12	h	Real Sociedad	D	1-1	Ivanschitz (p)

2015

03/01	a	Atlético	L	1-3	El Zhar
09/01	h	Deportivo	D	0-0	
18/01	a	Elche	L	0-1	
24/01	h	Villarreal	L	0-1	
01/02	a	Athletic	L	0-2	
07/02	h	Málaga	W	4-1	Barral 3 (2p), Uche
15/02	a	Barcelona	L	0-5	
23/02	h	Granada	W	2-1	Camarasa, Barral
28/02	a	Rayo Vallecano	L	2-4	Víctor Casadesús, Uche
06/03	h	Eibar	W	2-1	Barral, Uche
15/03	a	Real Madrid	L	0-2	
21/03	h	Celta	L	0-1	
04/04	a	Almería	W	4-1	Barral 3, Víctor Casadesús
07/04	h	Sevilla	L	1-2	Uche
13/04	a	Valencia	L	0-3	
17/04	h	Espanyol	D	2-2	Simão, Víctor Casadesús
25/04	a	Getafe	W	1-0	Víctor Casadesús
28/04	h	Córdoba	W	1-0	Barral
01/05	a	Real Sociedad	L	0-3	
10/05	h	Atlético	D	2-2	Barral, Uche
17/05	a	Deportivo	L	0-2	
23/05	h	Elche	D	0-0	

No	Name	Nat	DoB	Pos	Aps	(s)	Gls
7	David Barral		10/05/83	A	32	(3)	11
26	Víctor Camarasa		28/05/94	D	20	(4)	2
4	David Navarro		25/05/80	D	21		
23	Pape Diop	SEN	19/03/86	M	18	(1)	
16	Issam El Adoua	MAR	09/12/86	M	3	(1)	
8	Nabil El Zhar	MAR	27/08/86	M	5	(12)	1
14	Jaime Gavilán		12/05/85	M	1	(1)	
5	Héctor Rodas		07/03/88	D	6	(1)	
2	Iván López		23/08/93	D	23	(3)	
21	Andreas Ivanschitz	AUT	15/10/83	M	16	(4)	1
30	Jason Remeseiro		06/07/94	A		(2)	
1	Jesús Fernández		11/06/88	G	6		
25	José Mari		06/12/87	M	6	(8)	
12	Juanfran		15/07/76	D	16	(1)	
15	Nikolaos Karabelas	GRE	20/12/84	D	12	(2)	
13	Diego Mariño		09/05/90	G	32		
23	José Luis Morales		23/07/87	A	33	(3)	3
19	Pedro López		01/11/83	D	10		
9	Rafael Martins	BRA	17/03/89	A	2	(11)	1
14	Iván Ramis		25/10/84	D	13		
10	Rubén García		14/07/93	A	13	(14)	1
24	Simão	MOZ	23/07/88	M	24	(3)	1
22	Mohamed Sissoko	MLI	22/01/85	M	12	(9)	
3	Toño		11/07/89	D	20	(2)	
5	Kalu Uche	NGA	15/11/82	A	9	(7)	5
18	Víctor Casadesús		28/02/85	A	26	(9)	8
20	Víctor Pérez		12/01/88	M	2	(3)	
6	Loukas Vyntra	GRE	05/02/81	D	26	(1)	
17	Jordi Xumetra		24/10/85	M	11	(7)	

Málaga CF

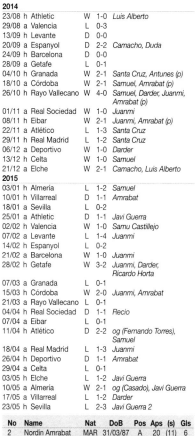

1994 • La Rosaleda (28,963) • malagacf.com
Coach: Javier Gracia

2014

23/08	h	Athletic	W	1-0	Luis Alberto
29/08	a	Valencia	L	0-3	
13/09	h	Levante	D	0-0	
20/09	a	Espanyol	D	2-2	Camacho, Duda
24/09	h	Barcelona	D	0-0	
28/09	a	Getafe	L	0-1	
04/10	h	Granada	W	2-1	Santa Cruz, Antunes (p)
18/10	a	Córdoba	W	2-1	Samuel, Amrabat (p)
26/10	h	Rayo Vallecano	W	4-0	Samuel, Darder, Juanmi, Amrabat (p)
01/11	a	Real Sociedad	W	1-0	Juanmi
08/11	h	Eibar	W	2-1	Juanmi, Amrabat (p)
22/11	a	Atlético	L	1-3	Santa Cruz
29/11	h	Real Madrid	L	1-2	Santa Cruz
06/12	a	Deportivo	W	1-0	Darder
13/12	a	Celta	W	1-0	Samuel
21/12	a	Elche	W	2-1	Camacho, Luis Alberto

2015

03/01	h	Almería	L	1-2	Samuel
10/01	h	Villarreal	D	1-1	Amrabat
18/01	a	Sevilla	L	0-2	
25/01	a	Athletic	D	1-1	Javi Guerra
02/02	h	Valencia	W	1-0	Samu Castillejo
07/02	a	Levante	L	1-4	Juanmi
14/02	h	Espanyol	L	0-2	
21/02	a	Barcelona	W	1-0	Juanmi
28/02	h	Getafe	W	3-2	Juanmi, Darder, Ricardo Horta
07/03	a	Granada	L	0-1	
15/03	h	Córdoba	W	2-0	Juanmi, Amrabat
21/03	a	Rayo Vallecano	L	0-1	
04/04	h	Real Sociedad	D	1-1	Recio
07/04	a	Eibar	L	0-1	
11/04	h	Atlético	D	2-2	og (Fernando Torres), Samuel
18/04	a	Real Madrid	L	1-3	Juanmi
26/04	h	Deportivo	D	1-1	Amrabat
29/04	a	Celta	L	0-1	
03/05	h	Elche	L	1-2	Javi Guerra
10/05	a	Almería	W	2-1	og (Casado), Javi Guerra
17/05	a	Villarreal	L	1-2	Darder
23/05	h	Sevilla	L	2-3	Javi Guerra 2

No	Name	Nat	DoB	Pos	Aps	(s)	Gls
2	Nordin Amrabat	MAR	31/03/87	A	20	(11)	6
15	Marcos Angeleri	ARG	07/04/83	D	21	(1)	
5	Antunes	POR	01/04/87	D	15		1
19	Arthur Boka	CIV	02/04/83	D	18	(5)	
6	Ignacio Camacho		04/05/90	M	25		2
30	Sergi Darder		22/12/93	M	33	(1)	4
17	Duda	POR	27/06/80	M	9	(16)	1
9	Javi Guerra		15/03/82	A	7	(6)	5
11	Juanmi		20/05/93	A	26	(8)	8
28	Juanpi	VEN	24/01/94	M	2	(3)	
1	Carlos Kameni	CMR	18/02/84	G	38		
22	Luis Alberto		28/09/92	M	6	(9)	2
23	Miguel Torres		28/01/86	D	13	(3)	
16	Recio		11/09/91	M	15	(15)	1
16	Ezequiel Rescaldini	ARG	11/06/92	A		(1)	
10	Ricardo Horta	POR	15/09/94	A	16	(15)	1
11	Roberto Rosales	VEN	20/11/88	D	34		
29	Samu Castillejo		18/01/95	A	28	(6)	1
7	Samuel		13/07/90	A	27	(5)	5
9	Roque Santa Cruz	PAR	16/08/81	A	11	(1)	3
21	Sergio Sánchez		03/04/86	D	19	(2)	
12	Fernando Tissone	ARG	24/07/86	D	3	(4)	
3	Weligton	BRA	26/08/79	D	32		

SPAIN

Rayo Vallecano de Madrid

1924 • Vallecas (15,500) • rayovallecano.es
Coach: Paco Jémez

2014

25/08	h	Atlético	D	0-0	
31/08	a	Deportivo	D	2-2	Bueno 2
14/09	h	Elche	L	2-3	Kakuta, Bueno (p)
21/09	a	Villarreal	L	2-4	Kakuta, Bueno
24/09	h	Athletic	W	2-1	Léo Baptistão 2
27/09	a	Levante	W	2-0	Léo Baptistão 2
04/10	h	Barcelona	L	0-2	
17/10	a	Granada	W	1-0	Manucho
26/10	a	Málaga	L	0-4	
03/11	h	Eibar	L	2-3	Léo Baptistão 2
08/11	a	Real Madrid	L	1-5	Bueno
23/11	h	Celta	W	1-0	Bueno
01/12	a	Almería	W	1-0	Kakuta
07/12	h	Sevilla	L	0-1	
13/12	a	Valencia	L	0-3	
20/12	h	Espanyol	L	1-3	Léo Baptistão

2015

04/01	a	Getafe	W	2-1	Jozabed, Baena
12/01	h	Córdoba	L	0-1	
17/01	a	Real Sociedad	W	1-0	Manucho
24/01	a	Atlético	L	1-3	Trashorras
30/01	h	Deportivo	L	1-2	Bueno
09/02	a	Elche	L	0-2	
15/02	h	Villarreal	W	2-0	Bueno, Kakuta
22/02	a	Athletic	L	0-1	
28/02	h	Levante	W	4-2	Bueno 4
08/03	a	Barcelona	L	1-6	Bueno (p)
14/03	h	Granada	W	3-1	Bueno 2, Embarba
21/03	h	Málaga	W	1-0	Kakuta
03/04	a	Eibar	W	2-1	Bueno, Manucho
08/04	h	Real Madrid	L	0-2	
11/04	a	Celta	L	1-6	Manucho
19/04	h	Almería	W	2-0	Amaya, Miku
26/04	a	Sevilla	L	0-2	
30/04	h	Valencia	D	1-1	Embarba
03/05	a	Espanyol	D	1-1	Insúa
11/05	h	Getafe	W	2-0	Manucho, Miku
17/05	a	Córdoba	W	2-1	Baena, Embarba
23/05	h	Real Sociedad	L	2-4	Bueno, Morcillo

No	Name	Nat	DoB	Pos	Aps	(s)	Gls
27	Álex Moreno		08/06/93	A	4	(7)	
4	Antonio Amaya		31/05/83	D	19		1
16	Javier Aquino	MEX	11/02/90	M	13	(11)	
15	Abdoulaye Ba	SEN	01/01/91	D	20		
8	Raúl Baena		02/03/89	M	28		2
7	Alhassane "Lass" Bangoura	GUI	30/03/92	A		(1)	
23	Alberto Bueno		20/03/88	A	35	(1)	17
34	Pablo Clavería		01/04/96	M		(1)	
1	David Cobeño		06/04/82	G	2	(1)	
13	Cristian Álvarez	ARG	13/11/85	G	16	(1)	
29	Adrián Embarba		07/05/92	M	9	(5)	3
6	Mohammed Fatau	GHA	24/12/92	M	9	(1)	
14	Emiliano Insúa	ARG	07/01/89	D	21	(3)	1
11	Jonathan Pereira		12/05/87	A	1	(2)	
21	Jozabed		08/03/91	M	10	(13)	1
12	Gaël Kakuta	FRA	21/06/91	M	35		5
19	Léo Baptistão	BRA	26/08/92	A	22	(3)	7
22	Licá	POR	08/09/88	A	17	(4)	
9	Manucho	ANG	07/03/83	A	12	(25)	5
7	Miku	VEN	19/08/85	A	2	(5)	2
20	Jorge Morcillo		11/03/86	D	7	(6)	1
3	Nacho		07/03/89	D	11	(2)	
24	Alejandro Pozuelo		20/09/91	M	3	(8)	
17	Quini		01/01/90	D	10	(7)	
2	Tito		11/07/85	D	31	(2)	
25	Toño		17/12/79	G	20	(1)	
10	Roberto Trashorras		28/02/81	M	33		1
18	Zé Castro	POR	13/01/83	D	28		

Real Madrid CF

1902 • Santiago Bernabéu (80,354) • realmadrid.com
Major honours
European Champion Clubs' Cup/UEFA Champions League (10) 1956, 1957, 1958, 1959, 1960, 1966, 1998, 2000, 2002, 2014; UEFA Cup (2) 1985, 1986; UEFA Super Cup (2) 2002, 2014; European/South American Cup (3) 1960, 1998, 2002; FIFA Club World Cup (1) 2014; Spanish League (32) 1932, 1933, 1954, 1955, 1957, 1958, 1961, 1962, 1963, 1964, 1965, 1967, 1968, 1969, 1972, 1975, 1976, 1978, 1979, 1980, 1986, 1987, 1988, 1989, 1990, 1995, 1997, 2001, 2003, 2007, 2008, 2012; Spanish Cup (19) 1905, 1906, 1907, 1908, 1917, 1934, 1936, 1946, 1947, 1962, 1970, 1974, 1975, 1980, 1982, 1989, 1993, 2011, 2014
Coach: Carlo Ancelotti (ITA)

2014

25/08	h	Córdoba	W	2-0	Benzema, Cristiano Ronaldo
31/08	a	Real Sociedad	L	2-4	Sergio Ramos, Bale
13/09	h	Atlético	L	1-2	Cristiano Ronaldo (p)
20/09	a	Deportivo	W	8-2	Cristiano Ronaldo 3, James Rodríguez, Bale 2, Hernández 2
23/09	h	Elche	W	5-1	Bale, Cristiano Ronaldo 4 (2p)
27/09	a	Villarreal	W	2-0	Modrić, Cristiano Ronaldo
05/10	h	Athletic	W	5-0	Cristiano Ronaldo 3, Benzema 2
18/10	a	Levante	W	5-0	Cristiano Ronaldo 2 (1p), Hernández, James Rodríguez, Isco
25/10	h	Barcelona	W	3-1	Cristiano Ronaldo (p), Pepe, Benzema
01/11	a	Granada	W	4-0	Cristiano Ronaldo, James Rodríguez 2, Benzema
08/11	h	Rayo Vallecano	W	5-1	Bale, Sergio Ramos, Kroos, Benzema, Cristiano Ronaldo
22/11	a	Eibar	W	4-0	James Rodríguez, Cristiano Ronaldo 2 (1p), Benzema
29/11	a	Málaga	W	2-1	Benzema, Bale
06/12	h	Celta	W	3-0	Cristiano Ronaldo 3 (1p)
12/12	a	Almería	W	4-1	Isco, Bale, Cristiano Ronaldo 2

2015

04/01	a	Valencia	L	1-2	Cristiano Ronaldo (p)
10/01	h	Espanyol	W	3-0	James Rodríguez, Bale, Nacho
18/01	a	Getafe	W	3-0	Cristiano Ronaldo 2, Bale
24/01	a	Córdoba	W	2-1	Benzema, Bale (p)
31/01	h	Real Sociedad	W	4-1	James Rodríguez, Sergio Ramos, Benzema 2
04/02	h	Sevilla	W	2-1	James Rodríguez, Jesé
07/02	a	Atlético	L	0-4	
14/02	h	Deportivo	W	2-0	Isco, Benzema
22/02	a	Elche	W	2-0	Benzema, Cristiano Ronaldo
01/03	a	Villarreal	D	1-1	Cristiano Ronaldo (p)
07/03	a	Athletic	L	0-1	
15/03	h	Levante	W	2-0	Bale 2
22/03	a	Barcelona	L	1-2	Cristiano Ronaldo
05/04	h	Granada	W	9-1	Bale, Cristiano Ronaldo 5, Benzema 2, og (Mainz)
08/04	a	Rayo Vallecano	W	2-0	Cristiano Ronaldo, James Rodríguez
11/04	h	Eibar	W	3-0	Cristiano Ronaldo, Hernández, Jesé
18/04	h	Málaga	W	3-1	Sergio Ramos, James Rodríguez, Cristiano Ronaldo
26/04	a	Celta	W	4-2	Kroos, Hernández 2, James Rodríguez
29/04	h	Almería	W	3-0	James Rodríguez, og (Mauro dos Santos), Arbeloa
02/05	a	Sevilla	W	3-2	Cristiano Ronaldo 3
09/05	h	Valencia	D	2-2	Pepe, Isco
17/05	a	Espanyol	W	4-1	Cristiano Ronaldo 3, Marcelo
23/05	h	Getafe	W	7-3	Cristiano Ronaldo 3 (1p), Hernández, James Rodríguez, Jesé, Marcelo

No	Name	Nat	DoB	Pos	Aps	(s)	Gls
17	Álvaro Arbeloa		17/01/83	D	12	(10)	1
11	Gareth Bale	WAL	16/07/89	A	30	(1)	13
9	Karim Benzema	FRA	19/12/87	A	29		15
15	Daniel Carvajal		11/01/92	D	25	(5)	
1	Iker Casillas		20/05/81	G	32		
7	Cristiano Ronaldo	POR	05/02/85	A	35		48
5	Fábio Coentrão	POR	11/03/88	D	5	(4)	
14	Javier Hernández	MEX	01/06/88	A	7	(16)	7
24	Asier Illarramendi		08/03/90	M	10	(20)	
23	Isco		21/04/92	M	26	(8)	4
10	James Rodríguez	COL	12/07/91	M	29		13
20	Jesé		26/02/93	A	3	(13)	3
6	Sami Khedira	GER	04/04/87	M	3	(8)	
8	Toni Kroos	GER	04/01/90	M	36		2
16	Lucas Silva	BRA	16/02/93	M	3	(5)	
12	Marcelo	BRA	12/05/88	D	33	(1)	2
26	Álvaro Medrán		15/03/94	M		(2)	
19	Luka Modrić	CRO	09/09/85	M	16		1
18	Nacho		18/01/90	D	5	(9)	1
13	Keylor Navas	CRC	15/12/86	G	6		
41	Martin Ødegaard	NOR	17/12/98	M		(1)	
3	Pepe	POR	26/02/83	D	25	(2)	2
4	Sergio Ramos		30/03/86	D	27		4
2	Raphaël Varane	FRA	25/04/93	D	21	(6)	

Real Sociedad de Fútbol

1909 • Anoeta (32,000) • realsociedad.com
Major honours
Spanish League (2) 1981, 1982; Spanish Cup (2) 1909, 1987
Coach: Jagoba Arrasate;
(03/11/14) (Asier Santana);
(11/11/14) David Moyes (SCO)

2014
24/08	a	Eibar	L	0-1	
31/08	h	Real Madrid	W	4-2	Íñigo Martínez, Zurutuza 2, Vela
13/09	a	Celta	D	2-2	Agirretxe, og (Jonny)
21/09	a	Almería	L	1-2	Castro
24/09	a	Sevilla	L	0-1	
28/09	h	Valencia	D	1-1	Canales
05/10	a	Espanyol	L	0-2	
20/10	a	Getafe	L	1-2	Hervías
25/10	a	Córdoba	D	1-1	Íñigo Martínez
01/11	h	Málaga	L	0-1	
09/11	h	Atlético	W	2-1	Vela, Agirretxe
22/11	a	Deportivo	D	0-0	
28/11	h	Elche	W	3-0	Vela 3
07/12	a	Villarreal	L	0-4	
14/12	h	Athletic	D	1-1	Vela
20/12	a	Levante	D	1-1	Canales

2015
04/01	h	Barcelona	W	1-0	og (Jordi Alba)
11/01	a	Granada	W	2-1	Vela (p)
17/01	h	Rayo Vallecano	L	0-1	
24/01	a	Eibar	W	1-0	Xabi Prieto
31/01	a	Real Madrid	L	1-4	Aritz Elustondo
07/02	h	Celta	D	1-1	Agirretxe
13/02	a	Almería	D	2-2	Agirretxe, Canales
22/02	h	Sevilla	W	4-3	Agirretxe, Xabi Prieto 2 (1p), og (Arribas)
01/03	a	Valencia	L	0-2	
08/03	h	Espanyol	W	1-0	Canales
16/03	a	Getafe	W	1-0	og (Guaita)
22/03	h	Córdoba	W	3-1	Agirretxe, Castro, Finnbogason
04/04	a	Málaga	D	1-1	Rubén Pardo
07/04	a	Atlético	L	0-2	
12/04	h	Deportivo	D	2-2	Xabi Prieto (p), Castro
20/04	a	Elche	L	0-1	
25/04	a	Villarreal	D	0-0	
28/04	a	Athletic	D	1-1	De la Bella
01/05	h	Levante	W	3-0	Finnbogason, Markel Bergara, Vela
09/05	a	Barcelona	L	0-2	
17/05	h	Granada	L	0-3	
23/05	a	Rayo Vallecano	W	4-2	Vela, Castro, Agirretxe, Elustondo

No	Name	Nat	DoB	Pos	Aps	(s)	Gls
9	Imanol Agirretxe		24/02/87	A	21	(10)	7
15	Ion Ansotegi		13/07/82	D	19		
34	Aritz Elustondo		28/03/94	M	4		1
16	Sergio Canales		16/02/91	M	31	(5)	4
36	Eneko Capilla		13/06/95	M		(2)	
2	Carlos Martínez		09/04/86	D	13	(2)	
18	Gonzalo Castro	URU	14/09/84	M	22	(10)	4
24	Alberto de la Bella		02/12/85	D	21	(2)	1
4	Gorka Elustondo		18/03/87	M	12	(7)	1
7	Alfred Finnbogason	ISL	01/02/89	A	6	(19)	2
23	Jon Gaztañaga		28/06/91	M	1	(2)	
8	Esteban Granero		02/07/87	M	29	(4)	
32	Iker Hernández		08/04/94	A		(1)	
29	Pablo Hervías		08/03/93	M	2	(13)	1
6	Íñigo Martínez		17/05/91	D	34		2
5	Markel Bergara		05/05/86	M	24	(6)	1
3	Mikel González		24/09/85	D	14	(2)	
14	Rubén Pardo		22/10/92	M	21	(7)	1
1	Gerónimo Rulli	ARG	20/05/92	G	22		
11	Carlos Vela	MEX	01/03/89	A	23	(6)	9
10	Xabi Prieto		29/08/83	M	33	(2)	4
19	Yuri Berchiche		10/02/90	D	17	(4)	
20	Joseba Zaldúa		24/06/92	D	21	(2)	
13	Eñaut Zubikarai		26/02/84	G	16		
17	David Zurutuza		19/07/86	M	12	(4)	2

Sevilla FC

1905 • Ramón Sánchez Pizjuán (45,500) • sevillafc.es ¨
Major honours
UEFA Cup (2) 2006, 2007; UEFA Europa League (2) 2014, 2015; UEFA Super Cup (1) 2006; Spanish League (1) 1946; Spanish Cup (5) 1935, 1939, 1948, 2007, 2010
Coach: Unai Emery

2014
24/08	h	Valencia	D	1-1	Aleix Vidal
30/08	a	Espanyol	W	2-1	Bacca, Iborra
14/09	a	Getafe	W	2-0	Bacca (p), Aleix Vidal
21/09	a	Córdoba	W	3-1	Bacca 2 (1p), Mbia
24/09	h	Real Sociedad	W	1-0	Deulofeu
27/09	a	Atlético	L	0-4	
05/10	h	Deportivo	W	4-1	Mbia 2, Bacca, Vitolo
19/10	a	Elche	W	2-0	Bacca, Gameiro
26/10	h	Villarreal	W	2-1	Denis Suárez, Bacca (p).
02/11	a	Athletic	L	0-1	
09/11	h	Levante	D	1-1	Vitolo
22/11	a	Barcelona	L	1-5	og (Jordi Alba)
30/11	h	Granada	W	5-1	Bacca 2, Éver Banega, Mbia, Gameiro
07/12	a	Rayo Vallecano	W	1-0	Bacca
14/12	h	Eibar	D	0-0	

2015
03/01	h	Celta	W	1-0	Pareja
11/01	a	Almería	W	2-0	Iborra, Coke
18/01	h	Málaga	W	2-0	Bacca, Denis Suárez
25/01	a	Valencia	L	1-3	Bacca (p)
01/02	h	Espanyol	W	3-2	Diogo Figueiras, Vitolo, Iago Aspas
04/02	a	Real Madrid	L	1-2	Iago Aspas
08/02	a	Getafe	L	1-2	Krychowiak
14/02	h	Córdoba	W	3-0	Krychowiak, Bacca, Iborra
22/02	a	Real Sociedad	L	3-4	Kolodziejczak, Bacca, Gameiro (p)
01/03	h	Atlético	D	0-0	
07/03	a	Deportivo	W	4-3	Vitolo 2, Gameiro (p), og (Sidnei)
15/03	h	Elche	W	3-0	Bacca 2 (1p), Gameiro
22/03	a	Villarreal	W	2-0	Coke, Vitolo
04/04	h	Athletic	W	2-0	Aleix Vidal, Bacca
07/04	a	Levante	W	2-1	Gameiro, Reyes
11/04	h	Barcelona	D	2-2	Éver Banega, Gameiro
19/04	a	Granada	D	1-1	og (Mainz)
26/04	h	Rayo Vallecano	W	2-0	Iborra, Daniel Carriço
29/04	a	Eibar	W	3-1	Bacca 2, Reyes
02/05	h	Real Madrid	L	2-3	Bacca (p), Iborra
10/05	a	Celta	D	1-1	Gameiro
17/05	h	Almería	W	2-1	Iborra 2
23/05	a	Málaga	W	3-2	Reyes, Éver Banega, Aleix Vidal

No	Name	Nat	DoB	Pos	Aps	(s)	Gls
22	Aleix Vidal		21/08/89	M	22	(9)	4
24	Alejandro Arribas		01/05/89	D	10	(1)	
9	Carlos Bacca	COL	08/09/86	A	31	(6)	20
1	Mariano Barbosa	ARG	27/07/84	G	1	(1)	
13	Beto	POR	01/05/82	G	18		
28	Carlos Fernández		22/05/96	A		(1)	
23	Coke		26/04/87	D	21	(1)	2
6	Daniel Carriço	POR	04/08/88	D	28		1
18	Denis Suárez		06/01/94	M	16	(15)	2
18	Gerard Deulofeu		13/03/94	M	10	(7)	1
5	Diogo Figueiras	POR	01/07/91	D	19	(5)	1
19	Éver Banega	ARG	29/06/88	M	23	(11)	3
3	Fernando Navarro		25/06/82	D	15	(4)	
7	Kevin Gameiro	FRA	09/05/87	A	7	(19)	8
18	Iago Aspas		01/08/87	A	4	(12)	2
12	Vicente Iborra		16/01/88	M	24	(2)	7
30	Juan Muñoz		12/11/95	M		(1)	
15	Timothée Kolodziejczak	FRA	01/10/91	D	18		1
4	Grzegorz Krychowiak	POL	29/01/90	M	31	(1)	2
26	Luismi		05/05/92	M		(1)	
25	Stéphane Mbia	CMR	20/05/86	M	17	(6)	4
2	Nicolás Pareja	ARG	19/01/84	D	26		1
10	José Antonio Reyes		01/09/83	M	15	(4)	3
29	Sergio Rico		01/09/93	G	19	(2)	
2	Benoît Trémoulinas	FRA	28/12/85	D	18	(2)	
20	Vitolo		02/11/89	M	25	(3)	6

Valencia CF

1919 • Mestalla (52,000) • valenciacf.com
Major honours
UEFA Cup Winners' Cup (1) 1980; UEFA Cup (1) 2004; Inter Cities Fairs Cup (2) 1962, 1963; UEFA Super Cup (2) 1980, 2004; Spanish League (6) 1942, 1944, 1947, 1971, 2002, 2004; Spanish Cup (7) 1941, 1949, 1954, 1967, 1979, 1999, 2008
Coach: Nuno Espírito Santo (POR)

2014
23/08	a	Sevilla	D	1-1	Orbán
29/08	h	Málaga	W	3-0	Paco Alcácer, Parejo, Piatti
14/09	a	Espanyol	W	3-1	Piatti, Parejo, Paco Alcácer
22/09	a	Getafe	W	3-0	Paco Alcácer, André Gomes, Rodrigo (p)
25/09	h	Córdoba	W	3-0	Paco Alcácer, Gayá, Feghouli
28/09	a	Real Sociedad	D	1-1	Gil
04/10	h	Atlético	W	3-1	og (Miranda), André Gomes, Otamendi
19/10	a	Deportivo	L	0-3	
25/10	h	Elche	W	3-1	Mustafi, Parejo, og (Lombán)
02/11	a	Villarreal	W	3-1	og (Trigueros), Mustafi 2
09/11	h	Athletic	D	0-0	
23/11	a	Levante	L	1-2	Parejo
30/11	h	Barcelona	L	0-1	
07/12	a	Granada	D	1-1	Negredo
13/12	h	Rayo Vallecano	W	3-0	Feghouli 2, Piatti
20/12	a	Eibar	W	1-0	Paco Alcácer

2015
04/01	h	Real Madrid	W	2-1	Barragán, Otamendi
10/01	a	Celta	D	1-1	Rodrigo
17/01	h	Almería	W	3-2	Parejo, Rodrigo, Negredo
25/01	h	Sevilla	W	3-1	Parejo 2 (1p), Javi Fuego
02/02	a	Málaga	L	0-1	
08/02	h	Espanyol	W	2-1	Piatti, og (Pau López)
15/02	h	Getafe	W	1-0	Negredo
21/02	a	Córdoba	W	2-1	André Gomes, Piatti
01/03	h	Real Madrid	W	2-1	Piatti 2
08/03	a	Atlético	D	1-1	Mustafi
13/03	h	Deportivo	W	2-0	Parejo (p), Paco Alcácer
20/03	a	Elche	W	4-0	André Gomes, Paco Alcácer, og (Roco), Otamendi
05/04	h	Villarreal	D	0-0	
09/04	h	Athletic	D	1-1	De Paul
13/04	h	Levante	W	3-0	Paco Alcácer, Feghouli, Negredo
18/04	a	Barcelona	L	0-2	
27/04	h	Granada	W	4-0	Javi Fuego, Parejo (p), Feghouli, Negredo
30/04	a	Rayo Vallecano	D	1-1	Parejo
03/05	h	Eibar	W	3-1	Otamendi, Parejo, Paco Alcácer
09/05	a	Real Madrid	D	2-2	Paco Alcácer, Javi Fuego
17/05	a	Celta	D	1-1	Otamendi
23/05	a	Almería	W	3-2	Otamendi, Feghouli, Paco Alcácer

No	Name	Nat	DoB	Pos	Aps	(s)	Gls
21	André Gomes	POR	30/07/93	M	31	(2)	4
19	Antonio Barragán		12/06/87	D	32	(2)	1
20	Rodrigo de Paul	ARG	24/05/94	D	6	(19)	1
2	Diego Alves	BRA	24/06/85	G	37		
8	Sofiane Feghouli	ALG	26/12/89	M	20	(13)	6
4	Filipe Augusto	BRA	12/08/93	M	1	(5)	
31	José Gayá		25/05/95	D	32	(3)	1
22	Carles Gil		22/11/92	M	2	(6)	1
27	Robert Ibáñez		22/03/93	A		(4)	
18	Javi Fuego		04/01/84	M	34	(1)	3
2	João Cancelo	POR	27/05/94	D	5	(5)	
5	Shkodran Mustafi	GER	17/04/92	D	33		4
7	Álvaro Negredo		20/08/85	A	14	(16)	5
6	Lucas Orbán	ARG	03/02/89	D	8	(14)	1
23	Nicolás Otamendi	ARG	12/02/88	D	35		6
9	Paco Alcácer		30/08/93	A	26	(6)	11
10	Daniel Parejo		16/04/89	M	33	(1)	11
15	Enzo Pérez	ARG	22/02/86	M	12	(2)	
11	Pablo Piatti	ARG	31/03/89	A	26	(2)	7
17	Rodrigo		06/03/91	A	24	(7)	3
3	Rúben Vezo	POR	25/04/94	D	6	(1)	
28	Tropi		12/05/95	M		(1)	
9	Yoel		28/08/88	G	1	(1)	
16	Bruno Zuculini	ARG	02/04/93	A		(1)	

SPAIN

Villarreal CF

1923 • El Madrigal (24,400) • villarrealcf.es
Coach: Marcelino

2014

24/08	a	Levante	W	2-0	Uche, Cheryshev
31/08	h	Barcelona	L	0-1	
14/09	a	Granada	D	0-0	
21/09	h	Rayo Vallecano	W	4-2	Espinosa, Musacchio, Vietto 2
24/09	a	Eibar	D	1-1	Gerard Moreno
27/09	h	Real Madrid	L	0-2	
05/10	a	Celta	W	3-1	Moi Gómez 2, Mario
19/10	h	Almería	W	2-0	Uche 2
26/10	a	Sevilla	L	1-2	Vietto
02/11	h	Valencia	L	1-3	Trigueros
09/11	a	Espanyol	D	1-1	Mario
23/11	h	Getafe	W	2-1	Mario, Gerard Moreno
30/11	a	Córdoba	W	2-0	Vietto, Uche
07/12	h	Real Sociedad	W	4-0	Bruno Soriano, Cheryshev, Moi Gómez 2
14/12	a	Atlético	W	1-0	Vietto
21/12	h	Deportivo	W	3-0	Jonathan dos Santos, Vietto 2

2015

03/01	a	Elche	D	2-2	Vietto, Uche
10/01	a	Málaga	D	1-1	Jonathan dos Santos
17/01	h	Athletic	W	2-0	Cheryshev, Bruno Soriano (p)
24/01	h	Levante	W	1-0	Vietto
01/02	a	Barcelona	L	2-3	Cheryshev, Vietto
07/02	h	Granada	W	2-0	Musacchio, Gerard Moreno
15/02	a	Rayo Vallecano	L	0-2	
22/02	h	Eibar	W	1-0	Vietto
01/03	a	Real Madrid	D	1-1	Gerard Moreno
08/03	h	Celta	W	4-1	Giovani dos Santos, Musacchio, Vietto, Gerard Moreno
15/03	a	Almería	D	0-0	
22/03	h	Sevilla	L	0-2	
05/04	h	Valencia	D	0-0	
09/04	h	Espanyol	L	0-3	
12/04	a	Getafe	D	1-1	Uche (p)
19/04	h	Córdoba	D	0-0	
25/04	a	Real Sociedad	D	0-0	
29/04	h	Atlético	L	0-1	
02/05	a	Deportivo	D	1-1	Jaume Costa
10/05	h	Elche	W	1-0	Campbell
17/05	h	Málaga	W	2-1	Gerard Moreno 2
23/05	a	Athletic	L	0-4	

No	Name	Nat	DoB	Pos	Aps	(s)	Gls
60	Aleix García		28/06/97	M		(1)	
61	Alfonso Pedraza		09/04/96	M		(2)	
1	Sergio Asenjo		28/06/89	G	34		
24	Eric Bailly	CIV	12/04/94	D	10		
21	Bruno Soriano		12/06/84	M	23	(1)	2
10	Joel Campbell	CRC	26/06/92	A	16		1
10	Cani		03/08/81	M	5	(4)	
17	Denis Cheryshev	RUS	26/12/90	M	18	(8)	4
16	José Antonio Dorado		10/07/82	D	13	(2)	
24	Javier Espinosa		19/09/92	M	3	(3)	1
43	Fran Sol		13/03/92	A		(2)	
20	Gabriel	BRA	26/11/90	D	18	(1)	
23	Gerard Moreno		07/04/92	A	19	(7)	7
9	Giovani dos Santos	MEX	11/05/89	A	15	(11)	1
18	Jaume Costa		18/03/88	D	28	(1)	1
3	Bojan Jokič	SVN	17/05/86	D	6	(1)	
6	Jonathan dos Santos	MEX	26/04/90	M	17	(11)	2
25	Juan Carlos		27/07/87	G	4	(1)	
28	Adrian Marín		09/01/97	D	4		
2	Mario Gaspar		24/11/90	D	31	(3)	3
19	Moi Gómez		23/06/94	M	17	(14)	4
5	Mateo Musacchio	ARG	26/08/90	D	12	(2)	3
4	Tomás Pina		14/10/87	M	17	(5)	
22	Antonio Rukavina	SRB	26/01/84	D	15	(6)	
26	Sergio Marcos		03/02/92	M	5	(2)	
14	Manu Trigueros		17/10/91	M	28	(5)	1
8	Ikechukwu Uche	NGA	05/01/84	A	19	(4)	6
15	Víctor Ruiz		25/01/89	D	24	(1)	
7	Luciano Vietto	ARG	05/12/93	A	17	(15)	12

Top goalscorers

48	Cristiano Ronaldo (Real Madrid)
43	Lionel Messi (Barcelona)
22	Antoine Griezmann (Atlético)
	Neymar (Barcelona)
20	Carlos Bacca (Sevilla)
18	Aritz Aduriz (Athletic)
17	Alberto Bueno (Rayo Vallecano)
16	Luis Suárez (Barcelona)
15	Karim Benzema (Real Madrid)
14	Jonathas (Elche)
	Sergio García (Espanyol)

Promoted clubs

Real Betis Balompié

1907 • Benito Villamarín (51,700) • realbetisbalompie.es
Major honours
Spanish League (1) 1935; Spanish Cup (2) 1977, 2005
Coach: Julio Velázquez; (25/11/14) (Juan Merino); (22/12/14) Pepe Mel

Real Sporting de Gijón

1905 • El Molinón (29,600) • realsporting.com
Coach: Abelardo Fernández

UD Las Palmas

1949 • Gran Canaria (31,250) • udlaspalmas.es
Coach: Paco Herrera

Second level final table 2014/15

		Pld	W	D	L	F	A	Pts
1	Real Betis Balompié	42	25	9	8	73	40	84
2	Real Sporting de Gijón	42	21	19	2	57	27	82
3	Girona FC	42	24	10	8	63	35	82
4	UD Las Palmas	42	22	12	8	73	47	78
5	Real Valladolid CF	42	21	9	12	65	40	72
6	Real Zaragoza	42	15	16	11	61	58	61
7	SD Ponferradina	42	16	12	14	55	51	60
8	CD Mirandés	42	16	11	15	42	44	59
9	UE Llagostera	42	15	12	15	41	41	57
10	CD Leganés	42	15	11	16	48	42	56
11	AD Alcorcón	42	12	18	12	44	49	54
12	CD Numancia de Soria	42	12	17	13	54	55	53
13	Deportivo Alavés	42	14	11	17	49	53	53
14	Albacete Balompié	42	14	9	19	55	65	51
15	CD Lugo	42	11	16	15	48	56	49
16	RCD Mallorca	42	13	9	20	51	64	48
17	CD Tenerife	42	11	15	16	41	48	48
18	CA Osasuna	42	11	12	19	41	60	45
19	Real Racing Club de Santander	42	12	8	22	42	53	44
20	RC Recreativo de Huelva	42	10	11	21	37	59	41
21	CE Sabadell FC	42	8	14	20	41	66	38
22	FC Barcelona B	42	9	9	24	55	83	36

Promotion/Relegation play-offs

(10/06/15 & 13/06/15)
Valladolid 1-1 Las Palmas
Las Palmas 0-0 Valladolid
(1-1; Las Palmas on away goal)

(11/06/15 & 14/06/15)
Zaragoza 0-3 Girona
Girona 1-4 Zaragoza
(4-4; Zaragoza on away goals)

(17/06/15 & 21/06/15)
Zaragoza 3-1 Las Palmas
Las Palmas 2-0 Zaragoza
(3-3; Las Palmas on away goal)

DOMESTIC CUP

Copa del Rey 2014/15

FOURTH ROUND

(29/10/14 & 02/12/14)
Cornella 1-4, 0-5 Real Madrid *(1-9)*

(29/10/14 & 03/12/14)
Sabadell 1-6, 1-5 Sevilla *(2-11)*

(02/12/14 & 16/12/14)
Las Palmas 2-1, 1-3 Celta *(3-4)*

(02/12/14 & 17/12/14)
Alavés 0-2, 0-1 Espanyol *(0-3)*

(02/12/14 & 18/12/14)
Alcoyano 1-1, 0-1 Athletic *(1-2)*
Valladolid 0-0, 0-1 Elche *(0-1)*

(03/12/14 & 16/12/14)
Huesca 0-4, 1-8 Barcelona *(1-12)*

(03/12/14 & 17/12/14)
Granada 1-0, 1-1 Córdoba *(2-1)*

(03/12/14 & 18/12/14)
Deportivo 1-1, 1-4 Málaga *(2-5)*
Hospitalet 0-3, 2-2 Atlético *(2-5)*

(04/12/14 & 16/12/14)
Rayo Vallecano 1-2, 4-4 Valencia *(5-6)*

(04/12/14 & 17/12/14)
Cádiz 1-2, 0-3 Villarreal *(1-5)*
Oviedo 0-0, 0-2 Real Sociedad *(0-2)*

(05/12/14 & 16/12/14)
Betis 3-4, 1-2 Almería *(4-6)*

(05/12/14 & 17/12/14)
Albacete 1-1, 0-0 Levante *(1-1; Levante on away goal)*
Getafe 3-0, 2-1 Éibar *(5-1)*

FIFTH ROUND

(06/01/15 & 13/01/15)
Málaga 2-0, 2-3 Levante *(4-3)*

(06/01/15 & 14/01/15)
Celta 2-4, 2-0 Athletic *(4-4; Athletic on away goals)*

(07/01/15 & 13/01/15)
Valencia 2-1, 0-2 Espanyol *(2-3)*

(07/01/15 & 14/01/15)
Almería 1-1, 0-1 Getafe *(1-2)*
Villarreal 1-0, 2-2 Real Sociedad *(3-2)*

(07/01/15 & 15/01/15)
Atlético 2-0, 2-2 Real Madrid *(4-2)*

(08/01/15 & 14/01/15)
Granada 1-2, 0-4 Sevilla *(1-6)*

(08/01/15 & 15/01/15)
Barcelona 5-0, 4-0 Elche *(9-0)*

QUARTER-FINALS

(21/01/15 & 28/01/15)
Barcelona 1-0 Atlético *(Messi 84)*
Atlético 2-3 Barcelona *(Fernando Torres 1, Raúl García 28p; Neymar 10, 41, Miranda 37og)*
(Barcelona 4-2)

(21/01/15 & 29/01/15)
Villarreal 1-0 Getafe *(Bruno Soriano 85)*
Getafe 0-1 Villarreal *(Gerard Moreno 78)*
(Villarreal 2-0)

Málaga 0-0 Athletic
Athletic 1-0 Málaga *(Aduriz 48)*
(Athletic 1-0)

(22/01/15 & 29/01/15)
Espanyol 3-1 Sevilla *(Caicedo 18, Sergio García 73p, Lucas Vázquez 80; Bacca 89)*
Sevilla 1-0 Espanyol *(Diogo Figueiras 88)*
(Espanyol 3-2)

SEMI-FINALS

(11/02/15 & 04/03/15)
Athletic 1-1 Espanyol *(Aduriz 10; Víctor Sánchez 35)*
Espanyol 0-2 Athletic *(Aduriz 13, Etxeita 42)*
(Athletic 3-1)

Barcelona 3-1 Villarreal *(Messi 41, Iniesta 49, Piqué 64; Trigueros 47)*
Villarreal 1-3 Barcelona *(Jonathan dos Santos 39; Neymar 3, 88, Suárez 73)*
(Barcelona 6-2)

FINAL

(30/05/15)
Camp Nou, Barcelona
FC BARCELONA 3 *(Messi 20, 73, Neymar 36)*
ATHLETIC CLUB 1 *(Iñaki Williams 79)*
Referee: *Velasco*
BARCELONA: Ter Stegen, Dani Alves, Piqué, Mascherano, Jordi Alba (Mathieu 76), Rakitić, Busquets, Iniesta (Xavi 55), Messi, Suárez (Pedro 77), Neymar
ATHLETIC: Iago Herrerín, Bustinza, Etxeita, Laporte, Balenziaga, Iraola (Susaeta 58), San José, Mikel Rico (Iturraspe 74), Beñat (Ibai Gómez 74), Iñaki Williams, Aduriz

Celebration time for Barcelona after their Copa del Rey triumph

SWEDEN
Svenska Fotbollförbundet (SvFF)

Address	Evenemangsgatan 31	**President**	Karl-Erik Nilsson
	SE-171 23 Solna	**General secretary**	Håkan Sjöstrand
Tel	+46 8 7350900	**Media officer**	Camilla Hagman
Fax	+46 8 7350901	**Year of formation**	1904
E-Mail	svff@svenskfotboll.se	**National stadium**	Friends Arena, Solna
Website	svenskfotboll.se		(54,329)

ALLSVENSKAN CLUBS

 ① AIK Solna

 ② IF Brommapojkarna

 ③ Djurgårdens IF

 ④ IF Elfsborg

 ⑤ Falkenbergs FF

⑥ Gefle IF

 ⑦ IFK Göteborg

 ⑧ Halmstads BK

 ⑨ Helsingborgs IF

 ⑩ BK Häcken

 ⑪ Kalmar FF

 ⑫ Malmö FF

 ⑬ Mjällby AIF

 ⑭ IFK Norrköping

 ⑮ Åtvidabergs FF

 ⑯ Örebro SK

PROMOTED CLUBS

 ⑰ Hammarby Fotboll

 ⑱ GIF Sundsvall

KEY:
- – UEFA Champions League
- – UEFA Europa League
- – Promoted
- – Relegated

0 ———— 400 km
0 — 200 — 200 miles

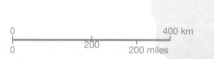

Sundsvall ⑱

Gävle ⑥

Stockholm

Örebro ⑯

Norrköping
Åtvidaberg ④ ⑭

Göteborg (Gothenburg) ⑦ ⑩

Borås ⑮

① ② ③ ⑰

Falkenberg ⑤

Halmstad ⑧

Kalmar ⑪

Helsingborg ⑨ ⑬ Mjällby

⑫ Malmö

Malmö make their mark

Malmö FF did what no team had managed since Djurgårdens IF in 2003 and successfully defended the Allsvenskan title. Leaders from start to finish, they benefited from the experience of new coach Åge Hareide and returning striker Markus Rosenberg to join IFK Göteborg as Sweden's joint record champions with an 18th league title. For good measure they also reached the group stage of the UEFA Champions League.

Göteborg, the Allsvenskan runners-up, also had a trophy to lift, winning the Swedish Cup for the second time in three years thanks to a 2-1 win in the final against Örebro SK.

SVENSKA MÄSTARE 2014

First successful Allsvenskan defence in 11 years

Gun-to-tape triumph for Hareide's side

Historic season for Under-21s and Ibrahimović

Domestic league

Rocked by the unexpected departure of 2013 title-winning coach Rikard Norling, Malmö found the perfect replacement in Hareide, although they had to lure him out of retirement first. The Norwegian had a long track record of success in Scandinavian football, having won the Allsvenskan with Helsingborgs IF in 1999 as well as the national titles of Denmark (with Brøndby IF) and Norway (with Rosenborg BK). Any doubts about his durability were dispelled as he led his new team to victories in their opening four fixtures and kept them at the top of the table from March through to November, the title being sewn up three matches before the end with a 3-2 victory in the Friends Arena against AIK Solna.

AIK were Malmö's closest pursuers for much of the campaign but, like the other teams in the division, they lacked the resilience and stamina of the defending champions, beaten only twice by the time they clinched the title. Rosenberg, back at his hometown club after almost a decade abroad, was hugely influential, scoring 15 goals, one more than Emil Forsberg, who, like Magnus Eriksson, goalkeeper Robin Olsen and a number of other youngsters, maintained or improved on their championship-winning form from the previous campaign.

Malmö's squad strength was the envy of the Allsvenskan, but by the end of term Göteborg were the champions' equal, winning nine of their last 11 games to overtake AIK and IF Elfsborg and finish second. Elfsborg's end to the campaign was filled with sadness as their coach at the start of the season, ex-Sweden international midfielder Klas Ingesson, passed away after a lengthy battle with cancer.

Domestic cup

Despite their strong finish to the Allsvenskan, Göteborg parted company with coach Mikael Stahre, so it was a new man, ex-Elfsborg boss Jörgen Lennartsson, who led them into the Svenska Cupen final, staged in their Nya Gamla Ullevi home. Up against them were Örebro SK, the team responsible for knocking out champions Malmö and cup holders Elfsborg but who had never won a major trophy. Göteborg fell behind before their Danish duo of Lasse Vibe – the Allsvenskan's leading marksman in 2014 – and Søren Rieks turned the match in their favour.

Europe

For the first time in 14 years Sweden had a representative in the UEFA Champions League group stage as Malmö eliminated AC Sparta Praha and FC Salzburg with memorable Rosenberg-inspired second-leg comebacks. Predictably they found the going tough in a group containing Juventus and Club Atlético de Madrid, but they did beat Olympiacos FC at home, with Rosenberg grabbing another double. Elfsborg were the best of the rest, but, like Göteborg a round earlier, their UEFA Europa League campaign was halted by European debutants Rio Ave FC.

National team

Sweden's Under-21 side became European champions for the first time in June, with Zlatan Ibrahimović starring again for the senior side. He won the race to reach 50 international goals before claiming his 100th cap, a double in a friendly against Estonia taking him to the top of his country's all-time goalscoring list. His 100th appearance came four days later as Sweden opened their UEFA EURO 2016 qualifying campaign with a 1-1 draw in Austria. That would be the only qualifier in which Ibrahimović played but did not score. He missed the next two with injury before keeping his country on track for automatic qualification with five goals in the next three, closing the season with another brace in a 3-1 win at home to Montenegro as Erik Hamrén's side maintained their unbeaten run on the road to France.

DOMESTIC SEASON AT A GLANCE

Allsvenskan 2014 final table

		Pld	Home					Away					Total					Pts
			W	D	L	F	A	W	D	L	F	A	W	D	L	F	A	
1	**Malmö FF**	30	9	4	2	34	16	9	4	2	25	15	18	8	4	59	31	62
2	IFK Göteborg	30	11	2	2	38	15	4	9	2	20	19	15	11	4	58	34	56
3	AIK Solna	30	9	2	4	29	17	6	5	4	30	25	15	7	8	59	42	52
4	IF Elfsborg	30	10	3	2	23	8	5	4	6	17	23	15	7	8	40	31	52
5	BK Häcken	30	7	5	3	30	19	6	2	7	28	26	13	7	10	58	45	46
6	Örebro SK	30	7	4	4	33	22	6	3	6	21	22	13	7	10	54	44	46
7	Djurgårdens IF	30	5	5	5	21	17	6	5	4	26	16	11	10	9	47	33	43
8	Åtvidabergs FF	30	8	4	3	24	19	4	3	8	15	27	12	7	11	39	46	43
9	Helsingborgs IF	30	7	5	3	26	18	3	4	8	15	26	10	9	11	41	44	39
10	Halmstads BK	30	5	5	5	24	22	6	1	8	20	28	11	6	13	44	50	39
11	Kalmar FF	30	6	6	3	22	19	4	3	8	14	26	10	9	11	36	45	39
12	IFK Norrköping	30	7	3	5	25	21	2	6	7	14	29	9	9	12	39	50	36
13	Falkenbergs FF	30	6	4	5	26	23	3	2	10	11	26	9	6	15	37	49	33
14	Gefle IF	30	6	3	6	17	14	2	5	8	17	28	8	8	14	34	42	32
15	Mjällby AIF	30	6	2	7	16	18	2	3	10	13	29	8	5	17	29	47	29
16	IF Brommapojkarna	30	1	4	10	14	32	1	2	12	14	37	2	6	22	28	69	12

European qualification 2015/16

 Champion: Malmö FF (second qualifying round)

 Cup winner: IFK Göteborg (second qualifying round)
AIK Solna (first qualifying round)
IF Elfsborg (first qualifying round)

Top scorer   Lasse Vibe (Göteborg), 23 goals
Relegated clubs   IF Brommapojkarna, Mjällby AIF
Promoted clubs   Hammarby Fotboll, GIF Sundsvall
Cup final   IFK Göteborg 2-1 Örebro SK

Team of the season
(4-4-2)

Coach: Hareide (Malmö)

Stuhr Ellegaard (Kalmar)

Larsson (Elfsborg)   Helander (Malmö)   Karlsson (AIK)   Augustinsson (Göteborg)

Simon Gustafsson (Häcken)   Forsberg (Malmö)   Bahoui (AIK)   Accam (Helsingborg)

Rosenberg (Malmö)   Vibe (Göteborg)

Player of the season

Markus Rosenberg
(Malmö FF)

After nine years plying his trade on foreign fields – in the Netherlands, Germany, Spain and England – Rosenberg came back home to Malmö and inspired the club not only to a successful defence of their Allsvenskan title but into the group stage of the UEFA Champions League. He supplied 15 goals and the same number of assists in the league and found the net seven times in Europe, sending the locals wild with doubles in three successive home games. At the age of 32 he had never played better.

Newcomer of the season

Lasse Vibe
(IFK Göteborg)

A relatively discreet run in his homeland with FC Vestsjælland and SønderjyskE was followed by an uneventful debut season with Göteborg, but at the age of 27 the breakthrough finally arrived for Vibe as he fired 23 goals to finish top of the 2014 Allsvenskan scoring charts and help Göteborg finish second to Malmö FF. The winger's belated coming-of-age was rewarded with regular selection for Denmark, and he also scored in the 2015 Swedish Cup final to collect the first major silverware of his career.

NATIONAL TEAM

International tournament appearances

FIFA World Cup (11) 1934 (2nd round), 1938 (4th), 1950 (3rd), 1958 (runners-up), 1970, 1974 (2nd phase), 1978, 1990, 1994 (3rd), 2002 (2nd round), 2006 (2nd round) UEFA European Championship (5) 1992 (semi-finals), 2000, 2004 (qtr-finals), 2008, 2012

Top five all-time caps

Anders Svensson (148); Thomas Ravelli (143); **Andreas Isaksson** (121); **Kim Källström** (120); Olof Mellberg (117)

Top five all-time goals

Zlatan Ibrahimović (56); Sven Rydell (49); Gunnar Nordahl (43); Henrik Larsson (37); Gunnar Gren (32)

Results 2014/15

04/09/14	Estonia	H	Solna	W	2-0	*Ibrahimović (3, 24)*
08/09/14	Austria (ECQ)	A	Vienna	D	1-1	*Zengin (12)*
09/10/14	Russia (ECQ)	H	Solna	D	1-1	*Toivonen (49)*
12/10/14	Liechtenstein (ECQ)	H	Solna	W	2-0	*Zengin (34), Durmaz (46)*
15/11/14	Montenegro (ECQ)	A	Podgorica	D	1-1	*Ibrahimović (9)*
18/11/14	France	A	Marseille	L	0-1	
15/01/15	Ivory Coast	N	Abu Dhabi (UAE)	W	2-0	*Mårtensson (65), Rohdén (87)*
19/01/15	Finland	N	Abu Dhabi (UAE)	L	0-1	
27/03/15	Moldova (ECQ)	A	Chisinau	W	2-0	*Ibrahimović (46, 84p)*
31/03/15	Iran	H	Solna	W	3-1	*Ibrahimović (11), Berg (21), Toivonen (89)*
08/06/15	Norway	A	Oslo	D	0-0	
14/06/15	Montenegro (ECQ)	H	Solna	W	3-1	*Berg (37), Ibrahimović (40, 44)*

Appearances 2014/15

Coach: Erik Hamrén	27/06/57		Est	AUT	RUS	LIE	MNE	Fra	Civ	Fin	MDA	Irn	Nor	MNE	Caps	Goals
Kristoffer Nordfeldt	23/06/89	Heerenveen (NED)	G										s75		5	-
Pierre Bengtsson	12/04/88	København (DEN) /Mainz (GER)	D	D	D	D	D	D46			D	D	D	D	22	-
Andreas Granqvist	16/04/85	Krasnodar (RUS)	D	D	D	D	D	D			D 93*	D			42	2
Mikael Antonsson	31/05/81	København (DEN)	D	D	D	D	D								23	-
Martin Olsson	17/05/88	Norwich (ENG)	D77	D	D	D					D				27	5
Sebastian Larsson	06/06/85	Sunderland (ENG)	M	M	M		s63	M			M80	s43	M75	M	74	6
Kim Källström	24/08/82	Spartak Moskva (RUS)	M64	M85	M86	M	M	M46			M	M74	M62	M72	120	16
Albin Ekdal	28/07/89	Cagliari (ITA)	M46	M		M74	M	s46			M	M92	M	M	17	-
Nabil Bahoui	05/02/91	AIK	A64		A79	s74		A46	A86	s64					8	-
Zlatan Ibrahimović	03/10/81	Paris (FRA)	A64	A			A				A	A46	A62	A90	105	56
Emil Forsberg	23/10/91	Malmö /RB Leipzig (GER)	A46			A66	A63	s86			s80	M43	s63	s64	9	-
Branimir Hrgota	12/01/93	Mönchengladbach (GER)	s46			s66		s67							3	-
Ola Toivonen	03/07/86	Rennes (FRA)	s46		A57						s46	s62	s90		43	9
Jimmy Durmaz	22/03/89	Olympiacos (GRE)	s64	A72	M	M	M	s46				s75			24	2
Tobias Hysén	09/03/82	Shanghai East Asia (CHN)	s64												34	10
Erkan Zengin	05/08/85	Eskişehirspor (TUR) /Trabzonspor (TUR)	s64	A	A	A	A86	A67			M85	M66	M63	M64	15	2
Mattias Johansson	16/02/92	AZ (NED)	s77												3	-
Andreas Isaksson	03/10/81	Kasımpaşa (TUR)		G	G	G	G	G			G		G75	G	121	-
Johan Elmander	27/05/81	Brøndby (DEN)		s72	s57	A79			A64	A46		s65			85	20
Pontus Wernbloom	25/06/86	CSKA Moskva (RUS)		s85	s86	s79					s85	s74	s62	s72	47	2
Alex Kacaniklic	13/08/91	København (DEN)			s79		M86								19	3
Mikael Lustig	13/12/86	Celtic (SCO)					D46								44	2
Oscar Wendt	24/10/85	Mönchengladbach (GER)					s46	s46					D	D	25	-
Isaac Kiese Thelin	24/06/92	Malmö /Bordeaux (FRA)					s86	A67	A82	s59	A70				5	-
Emil Krafth	02/08/94	Helsingborg						D	D56						4	-
Pontus Jansson	13/02/91	Torino (ITA)						D							7	-
John Guidetti	15/04/92	Celtic (SCO)						s67							2	-
Robin Olsen	08/01/90	Malmö							G			G			2	-
Per Karlsson	02/01/86	AIK							D						2	-
Erik Johansson	30/12/88	Malmö							D	D46	D	D		D	6	-
Ludwig Augustinsson	21/04/94	København (DEN)							D74	D46					2	-
Marcus Rohdén	11/05/91	Elfsborg							M	M		s92			3	1
Oscar Lewicki	14/07/92	Häcken							M	M					4	-
Johan Mårtensson	16/02/89	Helsingborg							M89	s75					2	1
Johan Larsson	05/05/90	Elfsborg							s56	D					3	-
Anton Tinnerholm	26/02/91	Malmö							s64	s46	D				3	-
Simon Gustafsson	11/01/95	Häcken							s74	M					2	-
Mikael Ishak	31/03/93	Randers (DEN)							s82	A64					2	-
Nicklas Bärkroth	19/01/92	Brommapojkarna							s86	A59					2	-
Sebastian Holmén	29/04/92	Elfsborg							s89	D75					2	-
Karl-Johan Johnsson	28/01/90	Randers (DEN)								G					2	-
Emil Bergström	19/05/93	Djurgården								s46					1	-
Simon Lundevall	23/09/88	Gefle								s46					1	-
Marcus Berg	17/08/86	Panathinaikos (GRE)									s70	A65	A	A	30	8
Robin Quaison	09/10/93	Palermo (ITA)										s66			5	2
Alexander Milosevic	30/01/92	Beşiktaş (TUR)											D	D	4	-
Jonas Olsson	10/03/83	West Brom (ENG)											D		25	1

EUROPE

Malmö FF

Second qualifying round - FK Ventspils (LVA)
H 0-0
Olsen, Concha, Halsti, Eriksson, Rosenberg, Hammar, Ricardinho, E Johansson, Nazari (Rakip 85), Kiese Thelin (Cibicki 69), Forsberg. Coach: Åge Hareide (NOR)
A 1-0 *Kiese Thelin (19)*
Olsen, Concha, Halsti, Rosenberg (P Johansson 90+3), Kroon (Cibicki 83), Hammar, Ricardinho, E Johansson, Nazari, Kiese Thelin (Eriksson 62), Forsberg. Coach: Åge Hareide (NOR)

Third qualifying round - AC Sparta Praha (CZE)
A 2-4 *Forsberg (17), Kiese Thelin (27)*
Olsen, Concha (Nazari 53), Tinnerholm, Helander, Halsti (Kroon 85), Adu, Rosenberg, Hammar, Ricardinho, Kiese Thelin (Mehmeti 75), Forsberg. Coach: Åge Hareide (NOR)
H 2-0 *Rosenberg (35, 55)*
Olsen, Tinnerholm, Helander, Halsti, Adu, Rosenberg (Cibicki 90+5), Kroon (Mehmeti 65), Ricardinho, E Johansson, Kiese Thelin (Eriksson 83), Forsberg. Coach: Åge Hareide (NOR)

Play-offs - FC Salzburg (AUT)
A 1-2 *Forsberg (90)*
Olsen, Tinnerholm, Helander, Halsti, Adu, Rosenberg, Kroon (Cibicki 87), Ricardinho, E Johansson, Kiese Thelin (Eriksson 61), Forsberg. Coach: Åge Hareide (NOR)
H 3-0 *Rosenberg (11p, 84), Eriksson (19)*
Olsen, Tinnerholm, Helander, Halsti, Eriksson (Kroon 73), Adu, Rosenberg, E Johansson, Kiese Thelin (Mehmeti 72), Konate, Forsberg. Coach: Åge Hareide (NOR)

Group A
Match 1 - Juventus (ITA)
A 0-2
Olsen, Tinnerholm, Helander, Halsti, Eriksson (Rakip 81), Adu, Rosenberg (Mehmeti 53), Ricardinho, E Johansson, Kiese Thelin (Kroon 73), Konate, Forsberg. Coach: Åge Hareide (NOR)
Match 2 - Olympiacos FC (GRE)
H 2-0 *Rosenberg (42, 82)*
Olsen, Tinnerholm, Helander, Halsti, Eriksson (Cibicki 75), Adu, Rosenberg, Ricardinho, E Johansson, Kiese Thelin, Forsberg (Rakip 90+2). Coach: Åge Hareide (NOR)
Match 3 - Club Atlético de Madrid (ESP)
A 0-5
Olsen, Tinnerholm, Helander, Halsti, Eriksson (Thern 87), Adu, Rosenberg, Ricardinho (Konate 90+1), E Johansson, Kiese Thelin, Forsberg (Kroon 66). Coach: Åge Hareide (NOR)
Match 4 - Club Atlético de Madrid (ESP)
H 0-2
Olsen, Tinnerholm, Helander, Halsti, Eriksson, Adu, Rosenberg, Ricardinho, E Johansson (Kroon 64), Kiese Thelin, Forsberg (Thern 86). Coach: Åge Hareide (NOR)
Match 5 - Juventus (ITA)
H 0-2
Olsen, Tinnerholm (Rakip 85), Helander, Halsti, Eriksson, Adu, Rosenberg, Ricardinho, E Johansson, Kiese Thelin (Cibicki 70), Forsberg. Coach: Åge Hareide (NOR)
Red card: E Johansson 89

Match 6 - Olympiacos FC (GRE)
A 2-4 *Kroon (59), Rosenberg (81)*
Olsen, Tinnerholm, Helander, Halsti, Eriksson (Thern 75), Adu, Rosenberg, Ricardinho, Kiese Thelin (Cibicki 80), Konate (Kroon 57), Forsberg. Coach: Åge Hareide (NOR)
Red card: Adu 90+3

IF Elfsborg

Second qualifying round - İnter Bakı PİK (AZE)
H 0-1
Hassan, Jönsson, Larsson, Svensson, Beckmann, Holmén, Klarström (Lundqvist 62), Claesson (Hedlund 86), Frick (Nilsson 69), Prodell, Rohdén. Coach: Janne Mian (SWE)
A 1-0 *Holmén (45+1)* **(aet; 4-3 on pens)**
Stuhr Ellegaard, Larsson (Klarström 71), Svensson, Nilsson, Mobaeck, Holmén, Claesson (Beckmann 16), Frick (Prodell 110), Lundqvist, Hauger, Rohdén. Coach: Janne Mian (SWE)

Third qualifying round - FH Hafnarfjördur (ISL)
H 4-1 *Holmén (55p), Frick (70), Rohdén (81), Hedlund (89p)*
Stuhr Ellegaard, Larsson, Svensson, Nilsson, Beckmann (Hedlund 36), Mobaeck, Holmén, Claesson, Lundqvist, Prodell (Frick 68), Rohdén. Coach: Janne Mian (SWE)
A 1-2 *Beckmann (90+4)*
Stuhr Ellegaard, Jönsson (Mobaeck 25), Beckmann, Holmén, Klarström, Claesson, Frick (Larsson 85), Hedlund (Zeneli 61), Lundqvist, Hauger, Rohdén. Coach: Janne Mian (SWE)

Play-offs - Rio Ave FC (POR)
H 2-1 *Prodell (27), Mobaeck (38)*
Stuhr Ellegaard, Larsson, Svensson, Beckmann (Hedlund 75), Mobaeck, Holmén, Claesson, Lundqvist, Hauger, Prodell (Frick 79), Rohdén. Coach: Janne Mian (SWE)
A 0-1
Stuhr Ellegaard, Larsson, Svensson, Beckmann (Klarström 75), Holmén, Claesson (Frick 90), Lundqvist, Hauger, Lans, Prodell, Rohdén. Coach: Janne Mian (SWE)

AIK Solna

Second qualifying round - Linfield FC (NIR)
A 0-1
Carlgren, Karlsson, Johansson, Borges, Bahoui, Pavey (Ofori 70), Lorentzson, Sonko Sundberg, Igboananike (Moro 86), Salétros, Goitom. Coach: Andreas Alm (SWE)

H 2-0 *Igboananike (55), Goitom (72)*
Carlgren, Karlsson, Johansson, Milosevic, Borges, Bahoui, Lorentzson, Ofori (Salétros 75), Moro, Igboananike (Pavey 84), Goitom. Coach: Andreas Alm (SWE)

Third qualifying round - FC Astana (KAZ)
A 1-1 *Bahoui (9)*
Carlgren, Karlsson, Johansson, Milosevic, Bahoui, Pavey, Lorentzson, Moro, Karikari, Salétros, Goitom. Coach: Andreas Alm (SWE)
H 0-3
Carlgren, Karlsson, Johansson, Milosevic, Borges, Lorentzson (Atakora 75), Moro, Karikari, Lundholm, Salétros (Igboananike 46), Goitom (Nikolic 75). Coach: Andreas Alm (SWE)
Red card: Borges 84

IFK Göteborg

First qualifying round - CS Fola Esch (LUX)
H 0-0
Sandberg, Salomonsson, Wæhler (Jónsson 17), Svensson, J Johansson, Larsson, Mané (Söder 56), A Johansson (Allansson 60), Mahlangu, Vibe, Bjärsmyr. Coach: Mikael Stahre (SWE)
A 2-0 *Vibe (76), Mahlangu (81)*
Sandberg, Salomonsson, Augustinsson (A Johansson 79), Smedberg-Dalance (Svensson 62), Söder, Jónsson (Engvall 85), J Johansson, Larsson, Mahlangu, Vibe, Bjärsmyr. Coach: Mikael Stahre (SWE)

Second qualifying round - Győri ETO FC (HUN)
A 3-0 *Vibe (8), J Johansson (56), Mahlangu (83)*
Sandberg, Augustinsson, Smedberg-Dalance (Daniel Sobralense 80), Svensson, Jónsson, J Johansson, Larsson, A Johansson, Mahlangu (Allansson 87), Vibe (Söder 70), Bjärsmyr. Coach: Mikael Stahre (SWE)
H 0-1
Sandberg, Augustinsson, Smedberg-Dalance (Söder 79), Jónsson, J Johansson, Larsson (Daniel Sobralense 69), A Johansson, Mahlangu, Allansson, Vibe, Bjärsmyr. Coach: Mikael Stahre (SWE)

Third qualifying round - Rio Ave FC (POR)
H 0-1
Alvbåge, Augustinsson, Smedberg-Dalance (Daniel Sobralense 66), Svensson, Jónsson, J Johansson (Engvall 66), Larsson, A Johansson (Salomonsson 80), Mahlangu, Vibe, Bjärsmyr. Coach: Mikael Stahre (SWE)
A 0-0
Alvbåge, Wæhler, Augustinsson, Söder (Daniel Sobralense 61), Svensson, J Johansson, Larsson, A Johansson (Allansson 76), Mahlangu, Vibe, Bjärsmyr. Coach: Mikael Stahre (SWE)

DOMESTIC LEAGUE CLUB-BY-CLUB

IF Brommapojkarna

First qualifying round - VPS Vaasa (FIN)
A 1-2 *Kouakou (33)*
Blazevic, Segerström, Jónsson, Karlström, Rexhepi (Söderström 75), Kouakou, Björkström, Bärkroth, Starfelt (Özkan 73), Sandberg Magnusson, Une Larsson. Coach: Stefan Billborn (SWE)
H 2-0 *Une Larsson (64), Petrovic (78)*
Blazevic, Segerström, Jónsson, Karlström (Söderström 90), Petrovic, Martinsson Ngouali, Björkström, Bärkroth, Sandberg Magnusson, Une Larsson, Falkeborn (Åsbrink 63). Coach: Stefan Billborn (SWE)

Second qualifying round - Crusaders FC (NIR)
H 4-0 *Rexhepi (9), Albornoz (27), Une Larsson (62), Bärkroth (65p)*
Blazevic, Segerström (Starfelt 46), Albornoz (Karlström 46), Jónsson, Petrovic, Martinsson Ngouali, Rexhepi (Sandberg Magnusson 50), Kouakou, Björkström, Bärkroth, Une Larsson. Coach: Stefan Billborn (SWE)
A 1-1 *Rexhepi (27)*
Blazevic, Jónsson, Karlström (Albornoz 68), Petrovic, Martinsson Ngouali, Rexhepi, Björkström, Starfelt, Åsbrink (Vecchia 64), Sandberg Magnusson (Söderström 79), Une Larsson. Coach: Stefan Billborn (SWE)

Third qualifying round - Torino FC (ITA)
H 0-3
Blazevic, Segerström, Jónsson, Karlström, Petrovic (Albornoz 63), Martinsson Ngouali (Åsbrink 76), Rexhepi (Sandberg Magnusson 63), Björkström, Bärkroth, Une Larsson, Falkeborn. Coach: Stefan Billborn (SWE)
Red card: Segerström 44
A 0-4
Blazevic, Albornoz (Petrovic 46), Jónsson, Karlström, Martinsson Ngouali, Rexhepi (Sandberg Magnusson 61), Björkström, Bärkroth, Starfelt (Söderström 77), Åsbrink, Falkeborn. Coach: Stefan Billborn (SWE)

AIK Solna

1891 • Friends Arena (54,329) • aikfotboll.se
Major honours
Swedish League (11) 1900, 1901, 1911, 1914, 1916, 1923, 1932, 1937, 1992, 1998, 2009; Swedish Cup (8) 1949, 1950, 1976, 1985, 1996, 1997, 1999, 2009
Coach: Andreas Alm

2014
31/03	h	Göteborg	L	0-2
06/04	h	Gefle	W	2-1	*Milosevic, Igboananike*
13/04	a	Örebro	D	1-1	*Markkanen*
16/04	a	Djurgården	W	3-2	*Lorentzson, Bahoui, Markkanen*
20/04	h	Norrköping	L	1-2	*Markkanen*
27/04	a	Häcken	D	2-2	*Borges 2*
05/05	h	Helsingborg	W	2-1	*Borges, Goitom*
08/05	a	Halmstad	D	2-2	*Goitom, Igboananike*
11/05	h	Mjällby	W	2-1	*Johansson, Borges (p)*
15/05	h	Elfsborg	W	2-1	*Bahoui, Pavey*
27/05	a	Malmö	D	2-2	*Markkanen, Quaison*
02/06	h	Brommapojkarna	W	4-2	*Bahoui 2, Markkanen 2*
07/07	a	Åtvidaberg	W	3-0	*Lorentzson, Bahoui, Goitom*
12/07	h	Kalmar	W	3-0	*Bahoui, Milosevic, Moro*
20/07	a	Falkenberg	L	1-4	*Sonko Sundberg*
28/07	h	Falkenberg	W	3-0	*Lorentzson, Johansson, Moro*
04/08	a	Göteborg	W	2-0	*Igboananike, Bahoui*
10/08	h	Gefle	W	3-1	*Goitom 3*
13/08	a	Djurgården	D	1-1	*Bahoui*
17/08	a	Örebro	L	2-4	*Goitom, Igboananike*
24/08	h	Häcken	W	1-0	*Goitom*
31/08	a	Norrköping	W	4-2	*Goitom 2, Lundholm, Eliasson*
15/09	a	Helsingborg	L	1-3	*Igboananike*
21/09	h	Halmstad	L	0-1	
25/09	h	Mjällby	L	0-1	
28/09	a	Elfsborg	D	1-1	*Bahoui*
05/10	h	Malmö	L	2-3	*Bahoui 2*
19/10	a	Brommapojkarna	W	4-0	*Bahoui, Goitom 2, Borges*
26/10	h	Åtvidaberg	W	4-1	*Ofori, Bahoui 2, Milosevic*
01/11	a	Kalmar	D	1-1	*Borges*

No	Name	Nat	DoB	Pos	Aps	(s)	Gls
30	Lalawélé Atakora	TOG	09/11/90	M	1	(1)	
11	Nabil Bahoui		05/02/91	M	26		14
10	Celso Borges	CRC	27/05/88	A	26		6
35	Patrik Carlgren		08/01/92	G	22		
5	Panajotis Dimitriadis		12/08/86	M	5	(1)	
28	Niclas Eliasson		07/12/95	M	6	(10)	1
15	Gabriel Ferreyra	ARG	03/02/94	M	1	(1)	
36	Henok Goitom		22/09/84	A	27	(1)	12
21	Kennedy Igboananike	NGA	26/02/89	A	17	(9)	5
4	Nils-Eric Johansson		13/01/80	D	27		2
22	Kwame Karikari	GHA	21/01/92	A		(4)	
3	Per Karlsson		02/01/86	D	26	(1)	
16	Martin Lorentzson		21/07/84	D	28		3
25	Sam Lundholm		01/07/94	M	5	(7)	1
7	Eero Markkanen	FIN	03/07/91	A	9	(5)	6
6	Alexander Milosevic		30/01/92	D	27		3
20	Ibrahim Moro	GHA	10/11/93	M	22	(1)	2
24	Marko Nikolic		17/09/97	M		(9)	
17	Ebenezer Ofori	GHA	01/07/95	D	22	(1)	1
14	Kenny Pavey	ENG	23/08/79	M	6	(13)	1
15	Robin Quaison		09/10/93	M	8	(2)	1
29	Anton Salétros		12/04/96	M	3	(12)	
18	Noah Sonko Sundberg		06/06/96	D	4	(1)	1
13	Kenny Stamatopoulos	CAN	28/08/79	G	8		
2	Sauli Väisänen	FIN	05/06/94	D	4	(2)	

IF Brommapojkarna

1942 • Grimsta IP (8,000) • brommapojkarna.se
Coach: Stefan Billborn

2014
30/03	h	Kalmar	L	1-2	*Petrovic*
05/04	a	Falkenberg	L	0-1	
14/04	h	Göteborg	D	1-1	*Segerström*
17/04	a	Gefle	L	0-3	
21/04	h	Örebro	D	2-2	*Petrovic, Rexhepi (p)*
27/04	a	Djurgården	L	2-3	*Petrovic, Une Larsson*
03/05	h	Norrköping	W	3-0	*Karlström, Bärkroth, Rexhepi*
07/05	h	Häcken	L	1-3	*Rexhepi*
12/05	h	Helsingborg	L	0-1	
15/05	h	Mjällby	L	0-1	
19/05	h	Halmstad	L	0-3	
02/06	h	AIK	L	2-4	*Petrovic, Rexhepi*
06/07	h	Malmö	D	1-1	*Karlström*
13/07	a	Elfsborg	D	2-2	*og (Hauger), Une Larsson*
20/07	a	Åtvidaberg	L	2-3	*Åsbrink, Kouakou*
27/07	h	Åtvidaberg	D	2-2	*Rexhepi, Petrovic*
03/08	a	Kalmar	D	1-1	*Sandberg Magnusson*
10/08	h	Falkenberg	L	2-3	*Sandberg Magnusson 2*
13/08	h	Gefle	L	1-2	*Albornoz*
17/08	a	Göteborg	L	0-3	
25/08	h	Djurgården	L	0-4	
29/08	h	Örebro	L	1-3	*Sandberg Magnusson*
15/09	h	Norrköping	L	1-3	*Albornoz*
20/09	h	Häcken	L	1-5	*Martinsson Ngouali*
24/09	h	Helsingborg	L	1-3	*Karlström*
29/09	h	Halmstad	L	0-3	
04/10	a	Mjällby	W	1-0	*Björkström*
19/10	h	AIK	L	0-4	
26/10	a	Malmö	L	0-2	
01/11	h	Elfsborg	L	0-1	

No	Name	Nat	DoB	Pos	Aps	(s)	Gls
4	Mauricio Albornoz		10/03/88	M	14	(7)	2
13	Tim Björkström		08/01/91	D	29		1
1	Davor Blazevic		07/02/93	G	18		
14	Nicklas Bärkroth		19/01/92	A	26	(2)	1
21	Andreas Eriksson		03/11/81	M	1	(10)	
22	Martin Falkeborn		08/01/93	D	6	(3)	
24	Seth Hellberg		19/08/95	M	1	(8)	
3	Fredric Jonson		15/07/87	D	1		
5	Kristinn Jónsson	ISL	04/08/90	D	22		
6	Jesper Karlström		21/06/95	M	27		3
12	Christian Kouakou		20/04/95	A		(4)	1
8	Serge-Junior Martinsson Ngouali		23/01/92	M	24	(4)	1
11	Jacob Ortmark		29/08/97	M		(1)	
7	Gabriel Petrovic		25/05/84	M	25	(2)	5
9	Dardan Rexhepi		16/01/92	A	24	(3)	5
17	Gustav Sandberg Magnusson		03/02/92	M	25	(3)	4
2	Pontus Segerström		17/02/81	D	14		1
15	Carl Starfelt		01/06/95	D	14	(6)	
23	Victor Söderström		17/01/94	A	3	(10)	
11	Filip Tronét		11/05/93	A	1	(3)	
18	Jacob Une Larsson		08/04/94	D	27		2
30	Ivo Vazgec		06/02/86	G	12		
19	Stefano Vecchia Holmquist		23/01/95	M	2	(3)	
10	Gabriel Özkan		23/05/86	M		(7)	
16	Pontus Åsbrink		27/06/92	M	14	(8)	1

Djurgårdens IF

1891 • Tele2Arena (33,000) • dif.se
Major honours
Swedish League (11) 1912, 1915, 1917, 1920, 1955,
1959, 1964, 1966, 2002, 2003, 2005; Swedish
Cup (4) 1990, 2002, 2004, 2005
Coach: Per Olsson

2014

30/03	a	Helsingborg	D	1-1	Prijovic
06/04	h	Halmstad	W	3-0	Broberg, Prijovic, Jawo
11/04	a	Mjällby	W	2-0	Jawo, Fejzullahu
16/04	h	AIK	L	2-3	Fejzullahu (p), Radetinac
21/04	a	Malmö	D	2-2	Radetinac, Fejzullahu
27/04	h	Brommapojkarna	W	3-2	Fejzullahu 2, Prijovic
04/05	a	Åtvidaberg	D	1-1	Broberg
07/05	h	Kalmar	D	0-0	
12/05	a	Falkenberg	L	0-1	
21/05	h	Göteborg	D	0-0	
26/05	a	Gefle	D	1-1	Jawo
30/05	a	Örebro	W	1-0	Bergström
07/07	h	Elfsborg	D	1-1	Fejzullahu (p)
14/07	a	Norrköping	W	5-3	Fejzullahu 2, Jawo, Radetinac, Prijovic
21/07	h	Häcken	L	1-2	Fejzullahu
28/07	a	Häcken	L	1-2	Hellquist
04/08	h	Helsingborg	D	2-2	Faltsetas, Prijovic
10/08	a	Halmstad	L	1-2	Broberg
13/08	a	AIK	D	1-1	og (Karlsson)
18/08	h	Mjällby	W	4-0	Faltsetas, Jawo, Radetinac, Bergström
25/08	a	Brommapojkarna	W	4-0	Andersson 3, Jawo
31/08	h	Malmö	W	2-0	Radetinac, Andersson
14/09	h	Åtvidaberg	L	0-1	
21/09	a	Kalmar	W	4-0	Arvidsson, Johansson, Andersson, Hellquist
24/09	h	Falkenberg	W	1-0	Mayambela
29/09	a	Göteborg	L	1-2	Andersson
04/10	h	Gefle	L	1-2	Tibbling
20/10	h	Örebro	L	0-3	
26/10	a	Elfsborg	W	1-0	Radetinac
01/11	h	Norrköping	D	1-1	Broberg

No	Name	Nat	DoB	Pos	Aps	(s)	Gls
18	Daniel Amartey	GHA	21/12/94	D	11		
16	Sebastian Andersson		15/07/91	A	11	(2)	6
27	Vytautas Andriuškevičius	LTU	08/01/90	D	14	(1)	
2	Jesper Arvidsson		01/01/85	D	19	(1)	1
13	Emil Bergström		19/05/93	D	30		2
7	Martin Broberg		24/09/90	M	21	(6)	4
17	Yussif Chibsah	GHA	30/12/83	M	5	(5)	
6	Alexander Faltsetas		04/07/87	M	26		2
10	Erton Fejzullahu		09/04/88	A	11	(2)	9
22	Philip Hellquist		12/05/91	M	3	(15)	2
12	Kenneth Høie	NOR	11/09/79	G	30		
11	Amadou Jawo		26/09/84	A	27	(2)	6
8	Andreas Johansson		05/07/78	M	14	(7)	1
5	Stefan Karlsson		15/12/88	D	30		
15	Mark Mayambela	RSA	09/09/87	A	2	(13)	1
28	Aleksandar Prijovic	SUI	21/04/90	A	9	(8)	5
9	Haris Radetinac	SRB	28/10/85	M	21	(2)	6
35	Christian Sivodedov		07/01/97	M		(6)	
3	Fredrik Stenman		02/06/83	D	13		
20	Simon Tibbling		07/09/94	M	30		1
14	Mattias Östberg		24/08/77	D	3	(1)	

IF Elfsborg

1904 • Borås Arena (16,284) • elfsborg.se
Major honours
Swedish League (6) 1936, 1939, 1940, 1961, 2006,
2012; Swedish Cup (3) 2001, 2003, 2014
**Coach: Klas Ingesson;
(06/05/14) Janne Mian**

2014

31/03	a	Åtvidaberg	L	1-2	Frick
04/04	h	Häcken	W	3-1	Svensson, Larsson, Nilsson (p)
14/04	a	Kalmar	D	0-0	
17/04	h	Helsingborg	W	1-0	Larsson
21/04	a	Falkenberg	W	3-2	og (T Karlsson), Rohdén 2
28/04	h	Halmstad	W	4-1	Nilsson 2, og (Liverstam), Prodell
04/05	a	Göteborg	D	0-0	
07/05	h	Mjällby	W	3-1	Claesson 2, Nilsson
11/05	a	Gefle	W	1-0	Prodell
15/05	a	AIK	L	1-2	Rohdén
24/05	h	Örebro	W	1-0	Larsson
01/06	h	Malmö	L	0-1	
07/07	a	Djurgården	D	1-1	Claesson
13/07	h	Brommapojkarna	D	2-2	Holmén, Rohdén
20/07	a	Norrköping	L	2-4	Beckmann, Prodell
27/07	h	Norrköping	W	3-0	Rohdén, Larsson, Mobaeck
03/08	a	Åtvidaberg	W	1-0	Claesson
11/08	a	Häcken	W	2-0	Prodell, Claesson
14/08	a	Helsingborg	L	1-4	Prodell
17/08	h	Kalmar	W	2-0	Larsson, Lundqvist
24/08	a	Halmstad	D	1-1	Beckmann
31/08	h	Falkenberg	W	1-0	Prodell
14/09	h	Göteborg	D	0-0	
21/09	a	Mjällby	L	0-1	
24/09	h	Gefle	W	1-0	Larsson
28/09	h	AIK	D	1-1	Hedlund
05/10	a	Örebro	L	1-5	Svensson
20/10	a	Malmö	W	2-1	Larsson 2 (1p)
26/10	h	Djurgården	L	0-1	
01/11	a	Brommapojkarna	W	1-0	Zeneli

No	Name	Nat	DoB	Pos	Aps	(s)	Gls
14	Anton Andreasson		26/07/93	M		(4)	
10	Mikkel Beckmann	DEN	24/10/83	A	11	(8)	2
16	Viktor Claesson		02/01/92	A	23	(3)	5
17	Per Frick		14/04/92	A	11	(12)	1
30	Abbas Hassan	LIB	10/05/85	G	2	(1)	
21	Henning Hauger	NOR	17/07/85	M	24		
19	Simon Hedlund		11/03/93	M	19	(8)	1
12	Sebastian Holmén		29/04/92	D	25	(1)	1
23	Niklas Hult		13/02/90	M	10	(1)	
6	Jon Jönsson		08/07/83	D	11	(1)	
15	Andreas Klarström		23/12/77	D	14	(4)	
22	Anton Lans		17/04/91	D	8	(2)	
7	Johan Larsson		05/05/90	D	29		8
20	Adam Lundqvist		20/03/94	M	13	(7)	1
11	Daniel Mobaeck		22/05/80	M	16	(2)	1
9	Lasse Nilsson		03/01/82	A	11	(6)	4
24	Viktor Prodell		29/02/88	M	22	(5)	6
25	Marcus Rohdén		11/05/91	M	25	(3)	5
1	Kevin Stuhr Ellegaard	DEN	23/05/86	G	28		
8	Anders Svensson		17/07/76	M	23	(2)	2
13	Arber Zeneli		25/02/95	M	5	(11)	1

Falkenbergs FF

1928 • Falkenbergs IP (6,000) •
falkenbergsff.se
Coach: Henrik Larsson

2014

30/03	a	Malmö	L	0-3	
05/04	h	Brommapojkarna	W	1-0	Keat
12/04	a	Åtvidaberg	L	0-2	
17/04	h	Kalmar	L	1-3	Vall
21/04	h	Elfsborg	L	2-3	A Wede, Rodevåg
25/04	a	Göteborg	L	0-1	
05/05	h	Gefle	D	1-1	C-O Andersson
08/05	a	Örebro	D	0-0	
12/05	h	Djurgården	W	1-0	Donyoh
15/05	h	Norrköping	W	3-0	Rodevåg (p), Svensson, Donyoh
24/05	h	Häcken	D	1-1	A Wede
01/06	h	Helsingborg	L	0-1	
07/06	h	Halmstad	D	1-1	C Wede
12/07	h	Mjällby	D	1-1	T Karlsson
20/07	h	AIK	W	4-1	Ingelsten, Rodevåg, Vall, Nilsson
27/07	a	AIK	L	0-3	
02/08	h	Malmö	L	2-5	Donyoh, Vall
10/08	a	Brommapojkarna	W	3-2	Rodevåg, Ingelsten, Vall
14/08	a	Kalmar	L	1-3	Keat
17/08	h	Åtvidaberg	W	3-0	Rodevåg, Ingelsten, A Wede
24/08	h	Göteborg	L	1-2	A Wede (p)
31/08	a	Elfsborg	L	0-1	
14/09	a	Gefle	L	1-3	Rodevåg
20/09	h	Örebro	L	1-3	Donyoh
24/09	a	Djurgården	L	0-1	
28/09	a	Norrköping	W	4-2	Johansson, Ingelsten, C-O Andersson, A Wede
05/10	a	Häcken	W	2-1	Ingelsten, Keat
20/10	h	Helsingborg	W	2-0	T Karlsson, Rodevåg
26/10	a	Halmstad	L	0-4	
01/11	h	Mjällby	D	1-1	Keat

No	Name	Nat	DoB	Pos	Aps	(s)	Gls
5	Carl-Oscar Andersson		02/04/92	M		(13)	2
6	Rasmus Andersson		17/04/93	M		(1)	
25	Halldór Orri Björnsson	ISL	02/03/87	M	7	(4)	
12	Christoffer Carlsson		15/01/89	M	16	(5)	
22	Godsway Donyoh	GHA	14/10/94	A	11	(5)	4
13	Adam Eriksson		02/02/88	D	27		
23	Patrik Ingelsten		25/01/82	A	14	(1)	5
4	Daniel Johansson		28/07/87	D	30		1
33	Tibor Joza		10/08/86	D	5	(1)	
14	Per Karlsson		20/04/89	D	3	(4)	
8	Tobias Karlsson		25/02/75	D	30		2
21	Dan Keat	NZL	28/09/87	M	20	(6)	4
1	Otto Martler		14/04/87	G	30		
9	Gustaf Nilsson		23/05/97	A		(5)	1
15	Stefan Rodevåg		11/06/80	A	27	(3)	7
2	Rasmus Sjöstedt		28/02/92	D	25	(1)	
7	David Svensson		09/04/84	M	23	(3)	1
9	Andrés Thorleifsson		19/07/88	A	3	(4)	
11	Johannes Vall		19/10/92	M	3	(19)	4
10	Anton Wede		20/04/90	M	29	(1)	5
20	Carl Wede		20/04/90	M	27	(2)	1

Gefle IF

1882 • Strömvallen (7,302) • gefleiffotboll.se
Coach: Roger Sandberg

2014

30/03	a	Mjällby	D	2-2	Lantto, Williams
06/04	h	AIK	L	1-2	Williams
12/04	a	Malmö	L	0-1	
17/04	h	Brommapojkarna	W	3-0	Portin, Hansson 2
21/04	a	Åtvidaberg	D	2-2	Oremo, Williams
28/04	a	Kalmar	L	0-2	
05/05	a	Falkenberg	D	1-1	Oremo (p)
08/05	h	Göteborg	D	1-1	Lundevall
11/05	h	Elfsborg	L	0-1	
19/05	a	Örebro	D	2-2	Lantto, Oremo (p)
26/05	h	Djurgården	D	1-1	Hansson
02/06	a	Norrköping	L	0-1	
05/07	h	Häcken	W	1-0	Lundevall
13/07	a	Helsingborg	D	1-1	Williams
19/07	h	Halmstad	W	2-0	Lundevall, Oremo
26/07	a	Halmstad	L	2-3	Lundevall, Fridgeirsson
04/08	h	Mjällby	W	1-0	Bååth
10/08	a	AIK	L	1-3	Hansson
13/08	a	Brommapojkarna	W	2-1	Williams, Lundevall
16/08	h	Malmö	D	0-0	
25/08	a	Kalmar	L	1-2	Oremo
30/08	a	Åtvidaberg	L	0-1	
14/09	h	Falkenberg	W	3-1	Bååth, Bertilsson 2
19/09	a	Göteborg	L	0-4	
24/09	a	Elfsborg	L	0-1	
29/09	h	Örebro	L	1-2	Lantto
04/10	a	Djurgården	W	2-1	Bellander, Lundevall (p)
19/10	h	Norrköping	L	1-2	Mustafa
26/10	a	Häcken	L	1-3	Oremo
01/11	h	Helsingborg	W	2-1	Oremo 2

No	Name	Nat	DoB	Pos	Aps	(s)	Gls
20	Emil Bellander		05/01/94	A	2	(12)	1
13	Johan Bertilsson		15/02/88	M	1	(10)	2
12	Anders Bååth		13/04/91	M	20	(5)	2
16	David Fällman		04/02/90	D	29		
6	Jesper Florén		11/09/90	D	21	(3)	
15	Skúli Jón Fridgeirsson	ISL	30/07/88	D	7	(3)	1
19	Marcus Hansson		12/02/90	M	29		4
1	Emil Hedvall		09/06/83	G	26		
23	Oskar Karlsson		16/11/92	M		(3)	
17	Jonas Lantto		22/05/87	M	27	(1)	3
8	Simon Lundevall		23/09/88	M	29		6
18	Dardan Mustafa		05/02/92	A	2	(14)	1
2	Olof Mård		31/01/89	D	5		
7	Robin Nilsson		15/09/88	M	27	(3)	
24	Erik Olsson		22/09/95	M		(3)	
3	Jonas Olsson		21/03/90	D	10	(1)	
9	Johan Oremo		24/10/86	A	21	(5)	8
14	Jens Portin	FIN	13/12/84	D	29		1
22	Sasa Sjanic		18/02/86	G	4	(1)	
4	Anders Wikström		14/12/81	D	19		
10	Dioh Williams	LBR	08/01/84	A	22	(5)	5

IFK Göteborg

1904 • Nya Gamla Ullevi (19,000) • ifkgoteborg.se
Major honours
UEFA Cup (2) 1982, 1987; Swedish League (18) 1908, 1910, 1918, 1935, 1942, 1958, 1969, 1982, 1983, 1984, 1987, 1990, 1991, 1993, 1994, 1995, 1996, 2007; Swedish Cup (7) 1979, 1982, 1983, 1991 (autumn), 2008, 2013, 2015
Coach: Mikael Stahre

2014

31/03	a	AIK	W	2-0	Vibe, Mané
07/04	h	Malmö	L	0-3	
14/04	a	Brommapojkarna	D	1-1	Söder
17/04	h	Åtvidaberg	W	5-0	Vibe 3, Larsson, Bojanic
20/04	a	Kalmar	D	1-1	Smedberg-Dalance
25/04	h	Falkenberg	W	1-0	Larsson (p)
04/05	h	Elfsborg	D	0-0	
08/05	a	Gefle	D	1-1	J Johansson
11/05	h	Örebro	W	2-1	Mahlangu, J Johansson
21/05	a	Djurgården	D	0-0	
25/05	h	Norrköping	D	2-2	Vibe, J Johansson
02/06	a	Häcken	D	1-1	og (Zuta)
07/06	h	Helsingborg	W	6-2	Vibe 2, J Johansson, Salomonsson, Söder, Mahlangu
13/07	a	Halmstad	D	2-2	Vibe 2
20/07	h	Mjällby	W	3-1	Vibe 3
27/07	a	Mjällby	L	0-3	
04/08	h	AIK	L	0-2	
10/08	a	Malmö	D	2-2	Vibe, Engvall
13/08	a	Åtvidaberg	D	1-1	Engvall
17/08	h	Brommapojkarna	W	3-0	Engvall, Vibe, Zohore
24/08	a	Falkenberg	W	2-1	Rieks, Mahlangu
31/08	h	Kalmar	W	2-0	Engvall, Mahlangu (p)
14/09	a	Elfsborg	D	0-0	
19/09	h	Gefle	W	4-0	Wæhler, Vibe 2, Salomonsson
24/09	a	Örebro	W	4-3	Vibe 3, Augustinsson
29/09	h	Djurgården	W	2-1	Vibe, Smedberg-Dalance
05/10	a	Norrköping	L	0-3	
19/10	h	Häcken	W	3-2	Vibe, Engvall, Zohore
26/10	a	Helsingborg	W	3-0	Mahlangu, Vibe, Rieks
01/11	h	Halmstad	W	5-1	Engvall 3, Vibe, Salomonsson

No	Name	Nat	DoB	Pos	Aps	(s)	Gls
27	Joel Allansson		03/11/92	M	5	(16)	
1	John Alvbåge		10/08/82	G	19		
6	Ludwig Augustinsson		21/04/94	D	28		1
30	Mattias Bjärsmyr		03/01/86	D	30		
32	Karl Bohm		24/08/95	M		(1)	
18	Darijan Bojanic		28/12/94	M		(3)	1
24	Diego Calvo	CRC	25/03/91	M		(3)	
10	Daniel Sobralense	BRA	11/02/83	M	2	(6)	
19	Gustav Engvall		29/04/96	A	13	(7)	8
5	Philip Haglund		22/03/87	M	3	(4)	
22	Adam Johansson		21/02/83	D	15	(1)	
15	Jakob Johansson		21/06/90	M	28		4
14	Hjálmar Jónsson	ISL	29/07/80	D	7	(1)	
17	Sam Larsson		10/04/93	M	18		2
26	May Mahlangu	RSA	01/05/89	A	19	(5)	5
21	Malick Mané	SEN	14/10/88	A	6	(5)	1
8	Søren Rieks	DEN	07/04/87	M	11	(1)	2
2	Emil Salomonsson		28/04/89	D	22	(2)	3
12	Markus Sandberg		07/11/90	G	11		
9	Martin Smedberg-Dalance	BOL	10/05/84	M	17	(5)	2
13	Gustav Svensson		07/02/87	M	17	(7)	
11	Robin Söder		01/04/91	A	15	(4)	2
29	Lasse Vibe	DEN	22/02/87	M	25	(1)	23
4	Kjetil Wæhler	NOR	16/03/76	D	19		1
3	Hampus Zackrisson		24/08/94	M		(2)	
16	Kenneth Zohore	DEN	31/01/94	A		(5)	2

Halmstads BK

1914 • Örjans Vall (15,500) • hbk.se
Major honours
Swedish League (4) 1976, 1979, 1997, 2000; Swedish Cup (1) 1995
Coach: Jens Gustafsson

2014

30/03	h	Örebro	L	1-2	Steindórsson
06/04	a	Djurgården	L	0-3	
13/04	h	Norrköping	D	0-0	
16/04	a	Häcken	L	0-3	
20/04	h	Helsingborg	W	2-1	Blomberg, Steindórsson
28/04	a	Elfsborg	L	1-4	Boman
03/05	a	Mjällby	L	1-2	Steindórsson (p)
08/05	h	AIK	D	2-2	Baldvinsson, Steindórsson (p)
12/05	a	Malmö	L	1-3	Magyar
19/05	h	Brommapojkarna	W	3-0	Baldvinsson 2, Liverstam
24/05	a	Åtvidaberg	L	0-1	
31/05	h	Kalmar	D	1-1	Steindórsson
05/07	a	Falkenberg	D	1-1	Blomberg
13/07	h	Göteborg	D	2-2	Boman, Baldvinsson
19/07	a	Gefle	L	0-2	
26/07	h	Gefle	W	3-2	Boman, Rojas, Fagercrantz
02/08	a	Örebro	W	2-1	Boman, Smith
10/08	h	Djurgården	W	2-1	Blomberg, Steindórsson
14/08	h	Häcken	L	1-4	S Silverholt
18/08	a	Norrköping	W	2-1	Baffo, Boman
24/08	h	Elfsborg	D	1-1	Blomberg
29/08	h	Helsingborg	W	4-1	Steindórsson, Boman 2, Rojas
14/09	h	Mjällby	L	1-2	Boman
21/09	a	AIK	W	1-0	Blomberg
24/09	h	Malmö	L	0-1	
29/09	a	Brommapojkarna	W	3-0	Antonsson, Blomberg, Ljung
05/10	a	Åtvidaberg	L	1-3	Antonsson
18/10	a	Kalmar	W	3-1	Boman, Antonsson 2
26/10	h	Falkenberg	W	4-0	Boman, Antonsson 2, Steindórsson
01/11	a	Göteborg	L	1-5	Blomberg

No	Name	Nat	DoB	Pos	Aps	(s)	Gls
23	Marcus Antonsson		08/05/91	A	13	(13)	6
4	Joseph Baffo		07/11/92	D	27		1
9	Gudjón Baldvinsson		15/02/86	A	17	(6)	4
15	Preparim Beqaj		03/08/95	A		(2)	
26	Alexander Berntsson		30/03/96	D		(1)	
6	Johan Blomberg		14/06/87	M	30		7
14	Mikael Boman		14/07/88	A	27	(2)	10
8	Kristoffer Fagercrantz		09/10/86	M	2	(14)	1
11	King Osei Gyan	GHA	22/12/88	M	28		
3	Fredrik Liverstam		04/03/88	D	25		1
2	Viktor Ljung		19/04/91	D	18	(6)	1
1	Stojan Lukic		28/12/79	G	30		
25	Richard Magyar		03/05/91	D	24	(1)	1
10	Antonio Rojas	PAR	27/03/84	M	28	(1)	2
17	Oliver Silverholt		22/06/94	D	3	(14)	
24	Simon Silverholt		17/06/93	M		(9)	1
16	Eric Smith		08/01/97	M		(9)	1
7	Kristinn Steindórsson	ISL	29/04/90	M	29		8
13	Kristoffer Thydell		17/03/93	M	1	(2)	
28	Jesper Westerberg		01/02/86	D	28	(1)	

SWEDEN

Helsingborgs IF

1907 • Olympia (17,200) • hif.se
Major honours
Swedish League (5) 1933, 1934, 1941, 1999, 2011;
Swedish Cup (5) 1941, 1998, 2006, 2010, 2011
Coach: Roar Hansen

2014

Date		Opponent	Res		Scorers
30/03	h	Djurgården	D	1-1	Accam
06/04	a	Norrköping	L	0-2	
13/04	h	Häcken	W	4-2	Sadiku, Smárason 2, Accam
17/04	a	Elfsborg	L	0-1	
20/04	a	Halmstad	L	1-2	Lindström
27/04	h	Mjällby	W	3-1	Accam 2, Khalili
05/05	a	AIK	L	1-2	Accam
08/05	h	Malmö	L	0-1	
13/05	a	Brommapojkarna	W	1-0	Accam
21/05	h	Åtvidaberg	D	0-0	
25/05	a	Kalmar	L	0-2	
01/06	h	Falkenberg	W	1-0	Accam
06/07	a	Göteborg	L	2-6	Lindström, Nordmark
13/07	h	Gefle	D	1-1	Lindström
20/07	a	Örebro	D	1-1	Accam
27/07	a	Örebro	D	1-1	Dahlberg
04/08	a	Djurgården	D	2-2	Bojanic, Accam
10/08	h	Norrköping	D	0-0	
14/08	h	Elfsborg	W	4-1	Dahlberg 2, Accam, Bojanic
18/08	a	Häcken	D	1-1	Dahlberg
22/08	a	Mjällby	W	2-1	Accam 2
29/08	h	Halmstad	L	1-4	Dahlberg
15/09	h	AIK	W	3-1	C Andersson, Accam 2
21/09	a	Malmö	D	1-1	Dahlberg
24/09	h	Brommapojkarna	W	3-1	Accam 2 (1p), Smárason
29/09	a	Åtvidaberg	W	2-1	Accam, Pálsson
03/10	h	Kalmar	W	4-1	Krafth, Dahlberg, Pálsson, Smárason
20/10	a	Falkenberg	L	0-2	
26/10	a	Göteborg	L	0-3	
01/11	a	Gefle	L	1-2	Lindström

No	Name	Nat	DoB	Pos	Aps	(s)	Gls
25	David Accam	GHA	28/09/90	M	23	(2)	17
13	Alexander Achinioti-Jönsson		17/04/96	M	5	(2)	
10	Álvaro	BRA	30/01/80	A	5	(10)	
21	Christoffer Andersson		22/10/78	D	21	(3)	1
31	Elias Andersson		31/01/96	M	4	(5)	
29	Jesper Björkman		29/04/93	D	15	(2)	
20	Emmanuel Boateng	GHA	17/01/94	M	3	(9)	
19	Darijan Bojanic		28/12/94	M	10	(1)	2
16	Mikael Dahlberg		16/03/85	A	16		7
27	Måns Ekvall		04/01/95	M		(2)	
8	Ardian Gashi	NOR	20/06/81	M	13		
30	Pär Hansson		22/06/86	G	28		
14	Marcus Holgersson		16/04/85	D	4		
32	Gustav Jarl		28/05/95	M	1		
2	Carl Johansson		23/05/94	D	8	(3)	
55	Abdul Khalili		07/06/92	M	12		1
24	Anton Kinnander		23/02/96	A		(6)	
15	Emil Krafth		02/08/94	D	28		1
18	Jordan Larsson		27/06/97	A		(9)	
26	Peter Larsson		30/04/84	D	29		
22	Andreas Linde		24/07/93	G	2		
7	Mattias Lindström		18/04/80	M	18	(6)	4
5	Johan Mårtensson		16/02/89	M	13		
23	Daniel Nordmark		04/01/88	M		(1)	1
8	Gudlaugur Victor Pálsson	ISL	30/04/91	M	11	(1)	2
3	Loret Sadiku	ALB	28/07/91	D	12		1
9	Robin Simovic		29/05/91	A	7	(4)	
11	Arnór Smárason	ISL	07/09/88	M	17	(9)	4
33	David Svensson		04/08/93	M	2	(1)	
28	Jere Uronen	FIN	13/07/94	D	23	(1)	

BK Häcken

1940 • Nya Gamla Ullevi (19,000) •
bkhacken.se
Coach: Peter Gerhardsson

2014

Date		Opponent	Res		Scorers
31/03	h	Norrköping	W	2-0	Ericsson, El Kabir
04/04	a	Elfsborg	L	1-3	Makondele
13/04	a	Helsingborg	L	2-4	El Kabir, Ericsson (p)
16/04	h	Halmstad	W	3-0	El Kabir, Simon Gustafsson, Mohammed
20/04	a	Mjällby	W	4-1	Simon Gustafsson 2, Strandberg, Makondele
27/04	h	AIK	D	2-2	El Kabir, Strandberg
04/05	a	Malmö	W	2-1	El Kabir 2
07/05	h	Brommapojkarna	W	3-1	Simon Gustafsson, Strandberg, Anklev
12/05	a	Åtvidaberg	L	0-1	
20/05	h	Kalmar	W	4-1	El Kabir, Mohammed, Ericsson, Strandberg
24/05	a	Falkenberg	D	1-1	Makondele
02/06	h	Göteborg	D	1-1	Simon Gustafsson
05/07	h	Gefle	L	0-1	
13/07	h	Örebro	W	4-1	Ericsson, Jeremejeff, Makondele, Anklev
21/07	a	Djurgården	W	2-1	Strandberg, Ericsson
28/07	h	Djurgården	W	2-1	Makondele 2
02/08	a	Norrköping	D	0-0	
11/08	h	Elfsborg	L	0-2	
14/08	a	Halmstad	W	4-1	Samuel Gustafsson 2, Mohammed 2
18/08	h	Helsingborg	D	1-1	Simon Gustafsson
24/08	a	AIK	L	0-1	
30/08	h	Mjällby	D	1-1	Makondele
14/09	h	Malmö	D	3-3	Simon Gustafsson, Thorvaldsson, Samuel Gustafsson
20/09	a	Brommapojkarna	W	5-1	Mohammed 3, Ericsson (p), Anklev
25/09	a	Åtvidaberg	L	0-2	
28/09	h	Kalmar	W	3-2	Simon Gustafsson 2, Jeremejeff
05/10	h	Falkenberg	L	1-2	Frölund
19/10	a	Göteborg	L	2-3	Jeremejeff, Arkivuo
26/10	h	Gefle	W	3-1	Simon Gustafsson, Ericsson, Strandberg
01/11	a	Örebro	L	2-5	Thorvaldsson, Mohammed

No	Name	Nat	DoB	Pos	Aps	(s)	Gls
25	Hosam Aiesh		14/04/95	A		(1)	
17	Björn Anklev		13/04/79	D	14	(11)	3
15	Kari Arkivuo	FIN	23/06/83	D	24	(1)	1
4	Walid Atta	ETH	28/08/86	D	26		
3	Fredrik Björck		22/10/79	D		(5)	
10	Moestafa El Kabir	NED	05/10/88	A	10	(1)	7
14	Martin Ericsson		04/09/80	M	25	(1)	7
6	David Frölund		04/06/79	M	22	(1)	1
28	Samuel Gustafsson		11/01/95	M	12	(10)	3
7	Simon Gustafsson		11/01/95	M	26	(2)	10
18	Alexander Jeremejeff		12/10/93	A	8	(9)	3
1	Christoffer Källqvist		26/08/83	G	30		
12	Oscar Lewicki		14/07/92	M	27		
24	René Makondele	COD	20/04/82	M	24	(2)	7
21	Nasiru Mohammed	GHA	06/06/94	M	16	(8)	8
20	Ronald Mukibi		16/09/91	D		(1)	
13	Sebastian Ohlsson		31/12/92	M		(2)	
9	Augustine Okrah	GHA	14/09/93	A		(1)	
8	Ivo Pekalski		03/11/90	M	7	(6)	
23	Simon Sandberg		25/03/94	D	13	(2)	
42	Carlos Strandberg		14/04/96	A	4	(15)	6
11	Gunnar Heidar Thorvaldsson	ISL	01/04/82	A	9	(4)	2
5	Emil Wahlström		02/03/87	D	20		
19	Leonard Zuta	MKD	09/08/92	D	13	(4)	

Kalmar FF

1910 • Guldfågeln Arena (12,105) •
kalmarff.se
Major honours
Swedish League (1) 2008; Swedish Cup (3) 1981, 1987, 2007
Coach: Hans Eklund

2014

Date		Opponent	Res		Scorers
30/03	a	Brommapojkarna	W	2-1	Söderqvist 2
07/04	h	Åtvidaberg	D	2-2	Söderqvist 2
14/04	h	Elfsborg	D	0-0	
17/04	a	Falkenberg	W	3-1	Elm 2, Diouf
20/04	h	Göteborg	D	1-1	Hallberg
28/04	a	Gefle	W	2-0	Andersson, Söderqvist
04/05	a	Örebro	W	2-0	Söderqvist, Solheim
07/05	a	Djurgården	D	0-0	
10/05	h	Norrköping	W	2-0	Eriksson 2
20/05	a	Häcken	L	1-4	Ring
25/05	h	Helsingborg	W	2-0	Elm, Söderqvist
31/05	h	Halmstad	D	1-1	Djordjević
05/07	h	Mjällby	W	2-1	Elm, Söderqvist
12/07	a	AIK	L	0-3	
19/07	a	Malmö	D	1-1	Söderqvist
26/07	a	Malmö	L	1-3	Andersson
03/08	h	Brommapojkarna	D	1-1	Elm
09/08	a	Åtvidaberg	L	1-3	Söderqvist
14/08	h	Falkenberg	W	3-1	Elm, Eriksson, Nouri
17/08	a	Elfsborg	L	0-2	
25/08	h	Gefle	W	2-1	Diouf 2
31/08	a	Göteborg	L	0-2	
15/09	a	Örebro	L	0-2	
21/09	h	Djurgården	L	0-4	
25/09	a	Norrköping	D	0-0	
28/09	h	Häcken	L	2-3	Romarinho, Diouf
03/10	a	Helsingborg	L	1-4	Ericsson
18/10	h	Halmstad	L	1-3	Ericsson
26/10	a	Mjällby	W	2-0	Hovda, Nilsson
01/11	h	AIK	D	1-1	Solheim

No	Name	Nat	DoB	Pos	Aps	(s)	Gls
9	Sebastian Andersson		15/07/91	A	6	(6)	2
30	César Santin	BRA	24/02/81	A	2	(9)	
77	Lars Cramer	NOR	25/05/91	G	21	(1)	
27	Pape Alioune Diouf	SEN	22/06/89	A	15	(9)	4
80	Nenad Djordjević	SRB	07/08/79	D	14	(2)	1
16	David Elm		10/01/83	A	15	(6)	6
26	Pär Ericsson		21/07/88	A	8	(7)	2
10	Tobias Eriksson		19/03/85	M	26	(3)	3
22	Melker Hallberg		20/10/95	M	12	(2)	1
18	Tor Øyvind Hovda	NOR	24/09/89	M	15	(4)	1
1	John Håkansson		28/03/98	G	1		
21	Ismael	BRA	01/12/94	M	17	(2)	
14	Stefan Larsson		21/01/83	D	2		
6	Marcus Nilsson		26/02/88	D	25		1
10	Emin Nouri	AZE	22/07/85	D	19		1
19	Melvin Platje	NED	16/12/88	M		(4)	
33	Johan Ramhorn		03/05/96	M		(1)	
31	Sebastian Ramhorn		03/05/96	D	8	(2)	
11	Jonathan Ring		05/12/91	M	21	(2)	1
29	Romarinho	BRA	10/08/85	M	16	(10)	1
24	Filip Sachpekidis		03/07/97	M	1	(4)	
7	Mats Solheim	NOR	03/12/87	D	26		2
1	Ole Söderberg		20/07/90	G	8		
34	Måns Söderqvist		08/02/93	M	24	(3)	10
2	Markus Thorbjörnsson		01/10/87	D	25		
5	Peter Westberg		22/09/95	M		(1)	
4	Ludvig Öhman		09/10/91	D	3	(3)	

Malmö FF

1910 • Swedbank Stadion (24,000) • mff.se

Major honours
Swedish League (18) 1944, 1949, 1950, 1951, 1953, 1965, 1967, 1970, 1971, 1974, 1975, 1977, 1986, 1988, 2004, 2010, 2013, 2014; Swedish Cup (14) 1944, 1946, 1947, 1951, 1953, 1967, 1973, 1974, 1975, 1978, 1980, 1984, 1986, 1989

Coach: Åge Hareide (NOR)

2014

Date		Opp	Res	Scorers
30/03	h	Falkenberg	W 3-0	Eriksson, Thern 2
07/04	a	Göteborg	W 3-0	Molins 2, Rosenberg
12/04	h	Gefle	W 1-0	Rosenberg
16/04	a	Örebro	W 2-1	Molins, Jansson
21/04	h	Djurgården	D 2-2	Molins, Eriksson
28/04	a	Norrköping	W 2-1	Eriksson, Forsberg
04/05	h	Häcken	L 1-4	Halsti
08/05	a	Helsingborg	W 1-0	Molins (p)
12/05	h	Halmstad	W 3-1	Rosenberg, Cibicki, Molins
22/05	a	Mjällby	W 1-0	Molins
26/05	h	AIK	D 2-2	Molins, Cibicki
01/06	a	Elfsborg	W 1-0	Rosenberg
06/07	a	Brommapojkarna	D 1-1	Rosenberg
12/07	h	Åtvidaberg	W 3-0	Forsberg 3
19/07	a	Kalmar	D 1-1	Kiese Thelin
26/07	h	Kalmar	W 3-1	Forsberg, og (Solheim), Rosenberg
02/08	a	Falkenberg	W 5-2	Mehmeti 2, Rosenberg, Forsberg, Eriksson
10/08	h	Göteborg	D 2-2	Rosenberg, Forsberg
13/08	h	Örebro	W 3-2	Rosenberg 2 (1p), Kiese Thelin
16/08	a	Gefle	D 0-0	
23/08	h	Norrköping	W 3-0	Forsberg, Kiese Thelin, Helander
31/08	a	Djurgården	L 0-2	
14/09	a	Häcken	D 3-3	Forsberg 2, Kiese Thelin
21/09	h	Helsingborg	D 1-1	Rosenberg
24/09	a	Halmstad	W 1-0	Cibicki
28/09	h	Mjällby	W 4-1	Forsberg 3, Rosenberg
05/10	a	AIK	W 3-2	Kiese Thelin, Eriksson, Rosenberg
20/10	h	Elfsborg	L 1-2	Rosenberg
26/10	h	Brommapojkarna	W 2-0	Forsberg, Rosenberg
01/11	a	Åtvidaberg	L 1-2	Tinnerholm

No	Name	Nat	DoB	Pos	Aps	(s)	Gls
8	Enoch Adu	GHA	14/09/90	M	14	(1)	
3	Miiko Albornoz	CHI	30/11/90	D	9		
27	Zlatan Azinovic		31/01/88	G	1	(1)	
35	Paweł Cibicki	POL	09/01/94	M	6	(14)	3
2	Mattias Concha		31/03/80	D	7	(1)	
7	Magnus Eriksson		08/04/90	A	28	(2)	5
33	Emil Forsberg		23/10/91	M	26	(3)	14
6	Markus Halsti	FIN	19/03/84	M	21	(5)	1
18	Johan Hammar		22/02/94	D	5	(2)	
15	Filip Helander		22/04/93	D	27	(1)	1
5	Pontus Jansson		13/02/91	D	7	(2)	1
21	Erik Johansson		30/12/88	D	23	(2)	
35	Piotr Johansson		28/02/95	M	1	(1)	
24	Isaac Kiese Thelin		24/06/92	A	9	(5)	5
32	Pa Konate		25/04/94	D	9	(2)	
14	Simon Kroon		16/06/93	M	9	(9)	
26	Agon Mehmeti	ALB	20/11/89	A	5	(5)	2
10	Guillermo Molins		26/09/88	M	10	(2)	8
22	Amin Nazari		26/04/93	M	5	(5)	
25	Robin Olsen		08/01/90	G	29		
31	Erdal Rakip		13/02/96	M	7	(8)	
20	Ricardinho	BRA	09/09/84	D	22	(1)	
9	Markus Rosenberg		27/09/82	A	25	(3)	15
11	Simon Thern		18/09/92	M	10	(4)	2
3	Anton Tinnerholm		26/02/91	D	14		1
24	Mahmut Özen		01/09/88	D	1		

Mjällby AIF

1939 • Strandvallen (7,000) • maif.se

Coach: Lars Jacobsson;
(19/07/14) (Jonas Andersson);
(21/07/14) Anders Linderoth

2014

Date		Opp	Res	Scorers
30/03	h	Gefle	D 2-2	Håkansson, Blomqvist
08/04	a	Örebro	L 0-1	
11/04	h	Djurgården	L 0-2	
16/04	a	Norrköping	D 1-1	Blomqvist
20/04	h	Häcken	L 1-4	Håkansson
27/04	a	Helsingborg	L 1-3	Haynes (p)
03/05	h	Halmstad	W 2-1	Haynes, Ekenberg
07/05	a	Elfsborg	L 1-3	Håkansson
11/05	a	AIK	L 1-2	Blomqvist
15/05	a	Brommapojkarna	W 1-0	Ekenberg
22/05	h	Malmö	L 0-1	
31/05	h	Åtvidaberg	W 1-0	Strömberg
05/07	a	Kalmar	L 1-2	Håkansson
12/07	h	Falkenberg	D 1-1	Blomqvist
20/07	a	Göteborg	L 1-3	Haynes (p)
27/07	h	Göteborg	W 3-0	og (Sandberg), Strömberg, Blomqvist
04/08	a	Gefle	L 0-1	
09/08	h	Örebro	L 0-1	
14/08	h	Norrköping	W 3-1	Wilhelmsson 2 (1p), Haynes
18/08	a	Djurgården	L 0-4	
22/08	h	Helsingborg	L 1-2	Wilhelmsson
30/08	a	Häcken	D 1-1	Enarsson
14/09	a	Halmstad	W 2-1	Löfquist, Wilhelmsson (p)
21/09	h	Elfsborg	W 1-0	Löfquist
25/09	a	AIK	W 1-0	Wilhelmsson
28/09	a	Malmö	L 1-4	Blomqvist
04/10	h	Brommapojkarna	L 0-1	
18/10	a	Åtvidaberg	L 1-2	Blomqvist
26/10	h	Kalmar	L 0-2	
01/11	a	Falkenberg	D 1-1	Enarsson

No	Name	Nat	DoB	Pos	Aps	(s)	Gls
2	Victor Agardius		23/10/89	D	28		
3	Gbenga Arokoyo	NGA	01/11/92	D	12		
1	Mattias Asper		20/03/74	G	30		
18	Hampus Bergdahl		05/02/95	A		(1)	
5	Eric Björkander		11/06/96	D	2		
75	Andreas Blomqvist		05/05/92	M	28	(1)	7
20	Kwame Bonsu	GHA	25/09/94	A	17	(7)	
25	Anton Dahlström		27/08/90	D	5	(7)	
10	Marcus Ekenberg		16/06/80	A	9	(5)	2
11	Joel Enarsson		27/06/93	A	2	(5)	2
29	Danny Ervik		24/02/89	D	28		
17	Lucas Grill	GER	09/02/93	D	13	(1)	
21	Viktor Götesson		14/07/95	A		(5)	
7	Kristian Haynes		20/12/80	A	22	(3)	4
24	Mattias Håkansson		20/02/93	A	21	(6)	4
11	Patrik Ingelsten		25/01/82	A	6	(6)	
4	Daniel Ivanovski	MKD	27/06/83	D	8	(5)	
12	David Löfquist		06/08/86	M	16	(6)	2
13	Daniel Nilsson		21/09/82	M	24	(2)	
21	Simon Nilsson		01/07/92	M		(2)	
15	Viktor Nilsson		14/07/93	A	11	(8)	
25	Rasmus Persson		25/05/96	M		(2)	
8	Robin Strömberg		23/01/92	A	13	(11)	2
21,3	Jasmin Sudic		24/11/90	D	13		
6	Gudmann Thórisson	ISL	30/01/87	D	8	(3)	
10	Christian Wilhelmsson		08/12/79	M	11	(1)	5
5	Rickard Östlin		16/01/94	D	3	(1)	

IFK Norrköping

1897• Nya Parken (17,234) • ifknorrkoping.se

Major honours
Swedish League (12) 1943, 1045, 1940, 1947, 1948, 1952, 1956, 1957, 1960, 1962, 1963, 1989; Swedish Cup (6) 1943, 1945, 1969, 1988, 1991 (spring), 1994

Coach: Jan Andersson

2014

Date		Opp	Res	Scorers
31/03	a	Häcken	L 0-2	
06/04	h	Helsingborg	W 2-0	Nyman, Lawan
13/04	a	Halmstad	D 0-0	
16/04	h	Mjällby	D 1-1	Lawan
20/04	a	AIK	W 2-1	Falk-Olander, og (Lorentzson)
28/04	h	Malmö	L 1-2	Kamara
03/05	a	Brommapojkarna	L 0-3	
07/05	h	Åtvidaberg	W 2-1	Gerson (p), Kamara
10/05	a	Kalmar	L 0-2	
15/05	h	Falkenberg	L 0-3	
25/05	a	Göteborg	D 2-2	Meneses, Kamara
02/06	h	Gefle	W 1-0	Kamara
06/07	a	Örebro	D 2-2	Nyman, Kamara
14/07	a	Djurgården	L 3-5	Traustason, Nyman, Kujovic
20/07	h	Elfsborg	W 4-2	Kujovic 2, Traustason, Kamara
27/07	a	Elfsborg	L 0-3	
02/08	h	Häcken	D 0-0	
10/08	a	Helsingborg	D 0-0	
14/08	a	Mjällby	L 1-3	Fransson
18/08	h	Halmstad	L 1-2	Kujovic
23/08	a	Malmö	L 0-3	
31/08	h	AIK	L 2-4	Skagestad, Kamara
15/09	h	Brommapojkarna	W 3-1	Kamara, Kujovic, Traustason
22/09	a	Åtvidaberg	D 2-2	Skagestad, Gerson
25/09	h	Kalmar	D 0-0	
28/09	a	Falkenberg	L 2-4	Kujovic 2
05/10	h	Göteborg	W 3-0	Gerson, Fransson, Kujovic
19/10	a	Gefle	W 2-1	Kamara, Kujovic
26/10	h	Örebro	W 2-0	Nyman, Kujovic
01/11	a	Djurgården	D 1-1	Kamara

No	Name	Nat	DoB	Pos	Aps	(s)	Gls
25	Filip Dagerstål		01/02/97	M		(2)	
15	Marcus Falk-Olander		21/05/87	D	19	(3)	1
26	Alexander Fransson		02/04/94	M	19	(7)	2
14	James Frempong		11/01/89	M	3	(5)	
7	Lars Gerson	LUX	05/02/90	M	6	(13)	3
21	Andreas Hadenius		18/03/91	D	3		
19	Mirza Halvadzic		15/02/96	M		(2)	
4	Andreas Johansson		10/03/82	M	29		
17	Al-Hadji Kamara	SLE	16/04/94	A	18	(8)	10
20	Isaac Kiese Thelin		24/06/92	A	9	(3)	
10	Emir Kujovic		22/06/88	A	17	(2)	10
8	Rawez Lawan		04/10/87	A	23	(1)	2
1	Andreas Lindberg		14/12/80	G	1		
22	Cristopher Meneses	CRC	02/05/90	D	20	(1)	1
91	David Mitov Nilsson		12/01/91	G	21		
5	Christoffer Nyman		05/10/92	A	22	(7)	4
29	Marcus Sahlman		02/01/85	G	7		
29	Edvard Setterberg		26/01/95	G	1		
2	Edvard Skagestad	NOR	06/07/88	D	17	(1)	2
3	Morten Morisbak Skjønsberg	NOR	12/02/83	D	9		
11	Christopher Telo		04/11/89	M	25	(4)	
13	Nikola Tkalčić	CRO	03/12/89	D	12	(8)	
9	Arnór Ingvi Traustason	ISL	30/04/93	M	14	(4)	3
28	Linus Wahlquist		11/11/96	D	20	(4)	
23	David Boo Wiklander		03/10/84	D	15	(3)	

Åtvidabergs FF

1907 • Kopparvallen (8,600) •
atvidabergsff.se
Major honours
Swedish League (2) 1972, 1973; Swedish Cup (2) 1970, 1971
Coach: Peter Swärdh

2014

31/03	h	Elfsborg	W 2-1	*Ricardo Santos, Abubakari*
07/04	a	Kalmar	D 2-2	*Abubakari, Ricardo Santos*
12/04	h	Falkenberg	W 2-0	*Owoeri, Zatara*
17/04	a	Göteborg	L 0-5	
21/04	h	Gefle	D 2-2	*Karlsson, Sköld*
25/04	a	Örebro	L 2-3	*Owoeri 2*
04/05	h	Djurgården	D 1-1	*Ricardo Santos*
07/05	a	Norrköping	L 1-2	*Sköld*
12/05	h	Häcken	W 1-0	*Owoeri*
21/05	a	Helsingborg	D 0-0	
24/05	h	Halmstad	W 1-0	*Sköld*
31/05	a	Mjällby	L 0-1	
07/07	a	AIK	L 0-3	
12/07	a	Malmö	L 0-3	
20/07	h	Brommapojkarna	W 3-2	*Ricardo Santos 3*
27/07	a	Brommapojkarna	D 2-2	*Hallingström, Ricardo Santos*
03/08	a	Elfsborg	L 0-1	
09/08	h	Kalmar	W 3-1	*Christensen 2, og (Solheim)*
13/08	h	Göteborg	D 1-1	*Ricardo Santos*
17/08	a	Falkenberg	L 0-3	
25/08	h	Örebro	L 1-2	*Ricardo Santos*
30/08	a	Gefle	W 1-0	*Sköld*
14/09	a	Djurgården	W 1-0	*Ricardo Santos*
22/09	h	Norrköping	D 2-2	*Ricardo Santos 2*
25/09	a	Häcken	W 2-0	*Owoeri 2*
29/09	h	Helsingborg	L 1-2	*Pettersson*
05/10	a	Halmstad	W 3-1	*Ricardo Santos (p), Owoeri 2*
18/10	h	Mjällby	W 2-1	*Ricardo Santos 2*
26/10	a	AIK	L 1-4	*Ricardo Santos*
01/11	h	Malmö	W 2-1	*Ricardo Santos, Bergström*

No	Name	Nat	DoB	Pos	Aps	(s)	Gls
6	Mohammed Abubakari	GHA	15/02/86	M	26		2
13	Álberis Silva	BRA	02/12/84	D	9	(4)	
7	Kristian Bergström		08/01/74	M	30		1
23	Emmanuel Boakye	GHA	25/03/85	D	1		
12	Bruno Marinho	BRA	05/07/84	M		(2)	
32	Martin Christensen	DEN	23/12/87	M	25	(2)	2
4	Andreás Dahlén		11/12/82	D	17	(1)	
21	Emmanuel Dogbe	GHA	06/06/92	M	1	(1)	
1	Henrik Gustafsson		21/10/76	G	30		
8	Petter Gustafsson		16/09/85	M	2	(3)	
5	Daniel Hallingström		10/02/81	D	28		1
3	Månz Karlsson		04/04/89	D	23	(4)	1
16	Pontus Nordenberg		16/02/95	D	10	(2)	
2	Allan Olesen	DEN	20/05/82	D	14	(4)	
19	John Owoeri	NGA	13/01/87	A	23	(4)	8
24	Tom Pettersson		25/03/90	D	15		1
18	Joel Rajalakso		02/04/93	A		(4)	
11	Ricardo Santos	BRA	13/02/87	A	25	(4)	17
10	Daniel Sjölund	FIN	22/04/83	M	19	(4)	
14	Simon Skrabb	FIN	19/01/95	M	2	(16)	
9	Victor Sköld		31/07/89	A	10	(20)	4
23	Anton Tinnerholm		26/02/91	D	12		
25	Imad Zatara	PLE	01/10/84	A	8	(4)	1

Örebro SK

1908 • Behrn Arena (12,674) • oskfotboll.se
**Coach: Per-Ola Ljung;
(13/06/14) Alexander Axén**

2014

30/03	a	Halmstad	W 2-1	*Hasani, Saeid*
08/04	h	Mjällby	W 1-0	*Hasani*
13/04	a	AIK	D 1-1	*Hasani*
16/04	h	Malmö	L 1-2	*Yasin*
21/04	a	Brommapojkarna	D 2-2	*Hasani, Holmberg*
25/04	h	Åtvidaberg	W 3-2	*Holmberg 2, Gustavsson*
04/05	a	Kalmar	L 0-2	
08/05	h	Falkenberg	D 0-0	
11/05	a	Göteborg	L 1-2	*Moberg*
19/05	h	Gefle	D 2-2	*Hasani, Gerzic*
24/05	a	Elfsborg	L 0-1	
30/05	a	Djurgården	L 0-1	
06/07	h	Norrköping	D 2-2	*Pode, Åhman Persson*
13/07	a	Häcken	L 1-4	*Pode*
20/07	h	Helsingborg	D 1-1	*Pode*
27/07	a	Helsingborg	D 1-1	*Gustavsson*
02/08	h	Halmstad	L 1-2	*og (Magyar)*
09/08	a	Mjällby	W 1-0	*Kamara*
13/08	a	Malmö	L 2-3	*Kamara 2*
17/08	h	AIK	W 4-2	*Kamara, Pode 2, Yasin*
25/08	a	Åtvidaberg	W 2-1	*Kamara 2*
29/08	h	Brommapojkarna	W 3-1	*Daniel Sobralense 2, Gustavsson*
15/09	h	Kalmar	W 2-0	*Haginge, Kamara (p)*
20/09	a	Falkenberg	W 3-1	*Kamara, Haginge, Nordmark*
24/09	h	Göteborg	L 3-4	*Moberg, Pode, Kamara (p)*
29/09	a	Gefle	W 2-1	*Kamara, Pode*
05/10	h	Elfsborg	W 5-1	*Pode 2, Holmberg, Gustavsson, Saeid*
20/10	a	Djurgården	W 3-0	*Kamara, Pode, Holmberg*
26/10	a	Norrköping	L 0-2	
01/11	h	Häcken	W 5-2	*Kamara 3, Gerzic, Daniel Sobralense*

No	Name	Nat	DoB	Pos	Aps	(s)	Gls
5	Ilir Berisha	ALB	25/06/91	D	2	(3)	
12	Daniel Björnkvist		08/01/89	D	29		
14	Daniel Sobralense	BRA	11/02/83	M	10	(1)	3
25	Nordin Gerzic		09/11/83	M	28		2
90	Daniel Gustavsson		29/08/90	M	19	(10)	4
2	Patrik Haginge		02/04/85	D	28		2
16	Shpëtim Hasani	ALB	10/08/82	A	12	(1)	5
17	Karl Holmberg		03/03/93	A	7	(14)	5
1	Oscar Jansson		23/12/90	G	21		
10	Alhassan Kamara	SLE	13/01/93	A	14	(5)	14
32	Christer Lipovac		07/03/96	A		(3)	
27	Boris Lumbana		19/06/91	D		(1)	
23	Samuel Mensah	GHA	19/05/89	D	5	(2)	
20	Erik Moberg		05/07/86	D	25		2
3	Ayanda Nkili	RSA	11/09/90	D	7	(11)	
16	Daniel Nordmark		04/01/88	M	3	(7)	1
11	Marcus Pode		27/03/86	A	20	(6)	10
30	Jakob Rinne		20/06/93	G	9	(2)	
8	Mohammed Saeid		24/12/90	M	18	(2)	2
4	Magnus Wikström		07/12/77	D	26	(1)	
21	Christoffer Wiktorsson		22/03/89	D	4	(6)	
9	Ahmed Yasin	IRQ	21/04/91	M	26	(3)	2
15	Robert Åhman Persson		26/03/87	M	17	(2)	1

Top goalscorers

23	Lasse Vibe (Göteborg)
17	David Accam (Helsingborg) Ricardo Santos (Åtvidaberg)
15	Markus Rosenberg (Malmö)
14	Nabil Bahoui (AIK) Emil Forsberg (Malmö) Alhassan Kamara (Örebro)
12	Henok Goitom (AIK)
10	Mikael Boman (Halmstad) Simon Gustafsson (Häcken) Måns Söderqvist (Kalmar) Al-Hadji Kamara (Norrköping) Emir Kujovic (Norrköping) Markus Pode (Örebro)

Promoted clubs

Hammarby Fotboll

1915 • Tele2Arena (33,000) •
hammarbyfotboll.se
Major honours
Swedish League (1) 2001
Coach: Nanne Bergstrand

GIF Sundsvall

1903 • Norrporten Arena (8,500) •
gifsundsvall.se
Coach: Joel Cedergren & Roger Franzén

Second level final table 2014

		Pld	W	D	L	F	A	Pts
1	Hammarby Fotboll	30	18	7	5	68	27	61
2	GIF Sundsvall	30	19	4	7	55	34	61
3	Ljungskile SK	30	16	12	2	60	25	60
4	Jönköpings Södra IF	30	16	4	10	60	42	52
5	Östersunds FK	30	12	9	9	40	40	45
6	IK Sirius FK	30	11	10	9	47	36	43
7	Degerfors IF	30	10	10	10	47	46	40
8	Varbergs BoIS FC	30	10	9	11	38	43	39
9	IFK Värnamo	30	10	9	11	43	52	39
10	Syrianska FC	30	11	4	15	37	55	37
11	GAIS Göteborg	30	9	8	13	31	38	35
12	Ängelholms FF	30	9	8	13	30	51	35
13	Östers IF	30	7	11	12	39	48	32
14	Assyriska FF	30	5	12	13	28	44	27
15	Landskrona BoIS	30	6	8	16	35	55	26
16	Husqvarna FF	30	5	7	18	27	49	22

Promotion/Relegation play-offs

(06/11/14 & 09/11/14)
Ljungskile 1-3 Gefle
Gefle 1-0 Ljungskile
(Gefle 4-1)

DOMESTIC CUP

Svenska Cupen 2014/15

SECOND ROUND

(20/08/14)
Assyriska Jönköping 0-5 Göteborg
BW 90 0-5 Öster
Dalkurd 4-1 Sundsvall
Eskilstuna City 0-2 Örebro
Frej 1-5 Brommapojkarna
Huddinge 2-2 Åtvidaberg *(aet; 5-4 on pens)*
Hudiksvall 2-0 Husqvarna
Kristianstad 2-1 Kalmar
Luleå 0-2 AIK
Lödde 0-1 Ljungskile
Nyköping 1-3 Syrianska
Skövde 4-5 Varberg
Sävedalen 2-5 Ängelholm
Trollhättan 2-1 Falkenberg *(aet)*
Valsta Syrianska 2-3 Gefle
Vasalund 2-5 Sirius
Västerås 3-1 Östersund

(21/08/14)
Athletic United 2-1 Degerfors *(aet)*
Myresjö/Vetlanda 2-1 Värnamo *(aet)*
Oskarshamn 0-4 Häcken
Sollefteå 0-1 Assyriska
Torn 1-1 Landskrona *(aet; 3-4 on pens)*
Värmdö 0-2 Jönköpings Södra
Örgryte 1-2 Halmstad *(aet)*

(26/08/14)
Torslanda 1-4 Helsingborg

(03/09/14)
Motala 0-4 Djurgården

(04/09/14)
Norrby 3-2 GAIS *(aet)*

(07/09/14)
Utsikten 0-2 Mjällby

(11/09/14)
Carlstad United 1-3 Norrköping

(17/09/14)
Karlstad 1-2 Hammarby

(22/10/14)
Eskilsminne 1-6 Elfsborg

(15/11/14)
Halmia 1-2 Malmö *(aet)*

THIRD ROUND

Group 1

(21/02/15)
Hudiksvall 1-4 Jönköping

(22/02/15)
Malmö 3-0 Assyriska

(28/02/15)
Hudiksvall 0-5 Malmö
Jönköping 2-0 Assyriska

(07/03/15)
Assyriska 3-1 Hudiksvall
Malmö 4-0 Jönköping

Final standings
1 Malmö 9 pts *(qualified)*
2 Jönköpings Södra 6 pts; 3 Assyriska 3 pts;
4 Hudiksvall 0 pts *(eliminated)*

Group 2

(21/02/15)
Trollhättan 2-2 Göteborg

(22/02/15)
Myresjö/Vetlanda 0-5 Ljungskile

(28/02/15)
Ljungskile 1-1 Trollhättan
Myresjö/Vetlanda 0-6 Göteborg
(08/03/15)
Göteborg 5-0 Ljungskile
Trollhättan 2-1 Myresjö/Vetlanda

Final standings
1 Göteborg 7 pts *(qualified)*
2 Trollhättan 5 pts; 3 Ljungskile 4 pts; 4 Myresjö/
Vetlanda 0 pts *(eliminated)*

Group 3

(21/02/15)
AIK 4-0 Landskrona
Kristianstad 0-1 Hammarby

(28/02/15)
Kristianstad 0-3 AIK

(01/03/15)
Hammarby 1-1 Landskrona

(07/03/15)
AIK 1-2 Hammarby
Landskrona 2-1 Kristianstad

Final standings
1 Hammarby 7 pts *(qualified)*
2 AIK 6 pts; 3 Landskrona 4 pts;
4 Kristianstad 0 pts *(eliminated)*

Group 4

(21/02/15)
Elfsborg 4-0 Sirius

(22/02/15)
Athletic United 1-0 Brommapojkarna

(28/02/15)
Brommapojkarna 1-3 Sirius

(01/03/15)
Athletic United 1-5 Elfsborg

(08/03/15)
Elfsborg 1-0 Brommapojkarna
Sirius 3-1 Athletic United

Final standings
1 Elfsborg 9 pts *(qualified)*
2 Sirius 6 pts; 3 Athletic United 3 pts;
4 Brommapojkarna 0 pts *(eliminated)*

Group 5

(21/02/15)
Huddinge 0-4 Mjällby

(25/02/15)
Häcken 2-0 Öster

(28/02/15)
Huddinge 1-3 Häcken

(01/03/15)
Mjällby 2-0 Öster

(07/03/15)
Häcken 4-2 Mjällby
Öster 3-0 Huddinge

Final standings
1 Häcken 9 pts *(qualified)*
2 Mjällby 6 pts; 3 Öster 3 pts; 4 Huddinge 0 pts
(eliminated)

Group 6

(21/02/15)
Örebro 3-3 Varberg

(22/02/15)
Dalkurd 1-2 Gefle

(01/03/15)
Dalkurd 0-1 Örebro
Gefle 2-1 Varberg

(08/03/15)
Varberg 2-0 Dalkurd
Örebro 2-1 Gefle

Final standings
1 Örebro 7 pts *(qualified)*
2 Gefle 6 pts; 3 Varberg 4 pts; 4 Dalkurd 0 pts
(eliminated)

Group 7

(22/02/15)
Djurgården 0-0 Ängelholm
Norrby 0-4 Norrköping

(01/03/15)
Norrby 4-2 Djurgården
Norrköping 2-0 Ängelholm

(05/03/15)
Djurgården 3-1 Norrköping
Ängelholm 0-5 Norrby

Final standings
1 Norrköping 6 pts *(qualified)*
2 Norrby 6 pts; 3 Djurgården 4 pts;
4 Ängelholm 1 pt *(eliminated)*

Group 8

(21/02/15)
Västerås 2-2 Halmstad

(28/02/15)
Halmstad 3-0 Syrianska

(01/03/15)
Västerås 0-4 Helsingborg

(04/03/15)
Helsingborg 2-2 Syrianska

(08/03/15)
Helsingborg 1-1 Halmstad
Syrianska 3-1 Västerås

Final standings
1 Helsingborg 5 pts *(qualified)*
2 Halmstad 5 pts; 3 Syrianska 4 pts;
4 Västerås 1 pt *(eliminated)*

QUARTER-FINALS

(14/03/15)
Göteborg 2-0 Helsingborg *(Engvall 2, Ankersen 80)*
Malmö 0-1 Örebro *(Valgardsson 22)*

(15/03/15)
Elfsborg 3-0 Hammarby *(Hedlund 4, Svensson 63, Frick 72)*
Häcken 3-1 Norrköping *(Thorvaldsson 36, 46, Simon Gustafsson 57; Traustason 27)*

SEMI-FINALS

(21/03/15)
Göteborg 3-1 Häcken *(Ankersen 22, 51, Vibe 66; Rexhepi 82)*

(22/03/15)
Örebro 2-0 Elfsborg *(Gustavsson 13, Holmberg 73)*

FINAL

(17/05/15)
Nya Gamla Ullevi, Göteborg
IFK GÖTEBORG 2 *(Vibe 67, Rieks 76)*
ÖREBRO SK 1 *(Nkili 23)*
Referee: Strömbergsson
GÖTEBORG: Alvbåge, Aleesami, Rogne, Bjärsmyr, Salomonsson, Rieks, Eriksson, Svensson, Ankersen (Pettersson 82), Vibe, Boman (Engvall 69)
ÖREBRO: Jansson, Haginge, Sigurbjörnsson, Moberg, Björnkvist, Gustavsson (Seaton 82), Åhman Persson, Nkili (Nordmark 79), Yasin, Gerzic, Holmberg (Pode 79)

SWITZERLAND

Schweizerischer Fussballverband/Association Suisse de Football (SFV/ASF)

Address	Worbstrasse 48, Postfach
	CH-3000 Bern 15
Tel	+41 31 950 8111
Fax	+41 31 950 8181
E-mail	sfv.asf@football.ch
Website	football.ch

President	Peter Gilliéron
General secretary	Alex Miescher
Media officer	Marco von Ah
Year of formation	1895

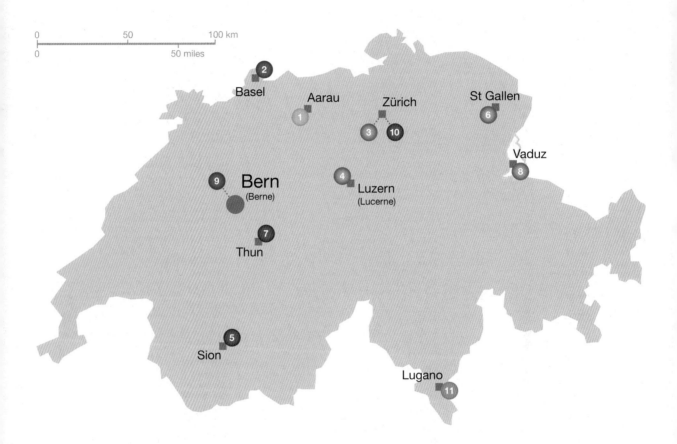

SUPER LEAGUE CLUBS

  FC Aarau

  FC Basel 1893

 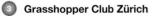 Grasshopper Club Zürich

  FC Luzern

 FC Sion

  FC St Gallen

  FC Thun

  FC Vaduz

 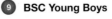 BSC Young Boys

 FC Zürich

PROMOTED CLUB

  FC Lugano

KEY:

● – UEFA Champions League
● – UEFA Europa League
● – Promoted
● – Relegated

Basel push the boundaries

FC Basel 1893's monopoly of the Swiss Super League title in the second decade of the 21st century continued in 2014/15 as they were crowned champions for the sixth season in succession, new coach Paulo Sousa steering the club to another straightforward triumph with three matches to spare.

There was a third successive defeat for Basel, however, in the Swiss Cup final, where FC Sion maintained their incredible 100% win ratio in the fixture with a handsome 3-0 victory at their opponents' St Jakob-Park home.

Sixth successive title for St Jakob-Park club

Sion maintain remarkable cup final record

National team recover after poor EURO start

Domestic league

With Murat Yakin departed for FC Spartak Moskva, Basel brought in Sousa to plug the gap. Twice a UEFA Champions League winner as a player, the ex-Portugal midfielder had just upgraded his coaching CV by leading Maccabi Tel-Aviv FC to the 2013/14 Israeli league title. His methods, which emphasised the importance of pressing the opposition and getting the ball wide at every opportunity, were unfamiliar to the Basel players at first, but once the defending champions got into their stride, no other team could live with their consistency. FC Zürich made a bright start, and BSC Young Boys raised their game in mid-season, but Basel's 18th title was never under serious threat.

Buoyed by the 22 goals of new signing from Grasshopper Club Zürich, Shkëlzen Gashi, who topped the Super League scoring charts for the second season running, Basel boasted by far the strongest attack in the league. Retiring captain Marco Streller signed off with a dozen goals, while 18-year-old prodigy Breel Embolo hit ten.

There were impressive contributions elsewhere from newly-signed Czech goalkeeper Tomáš Vaclík, his compatriot Marek Suchý and Swiss internationals Fabian Schär and Fabian Frei. Basel's final points tally of 78 was six more than in each of the two previous seasons, with their final margin of victory up to 12.

The gap between second-placed Young Boys and third-placed Zürich was even greater, with the Berne club, led by Swiss-Italian coach Uli Forte, sharing the same European prize as the champions – a place in the 2015/16 UEFA Champions League third qualifying round – thanks to an impressive run from November to early May, during which they lost only once. That concluded with a goalless draw at Basel, which clinched the title for their hosts. FC Thun finished a point behind Zürich to qualify for the UEFA Europa League, a performance that prompted Basel to sign up their coach Urs Fischer when Sousa left for ACF Fiorentina in the summer.

Domestic cup

The last Basel game for both Sousa and Streller would not be a memorable one. Despite benefiting from home advantage in the Swiss Cup final, the newly-crowned champions were denied the double for the third successive season as FC Sion romped to a 3-0 win, Sousa's Portuguese compatriot Carlitos stealing the show with a goal and two assists. The result prolonged one of European football's most extraordinary sequences as, exactly 50 years after their first Swiss Cup triumph, Sion made it 13 wins in 13 final appearances.

Europe

After two lengthy adventures in the UEFA Europa League, Basel reached the last 16 of the UEFA Champions League. In doing so they maintained their excellent record against English clubs by beating Liverpool FC 1-0 at home and drawing the all-important final group fixture 1-1 at Anfield.

But as Basel eventually fell in the first knockout round, to FC Porto, another Merseyside club, Everton FC, emphatically ended the UEFA Europa League involvement of Young Boys, Switzerland's only other post-Christmas European survivor.

National team

Vladimir Petković, the successor to Ottmar Hitzfeld as Switzerland head coach, got his reign off to an inauspicious start when the team lost their opening two UEFA EURO 2016 qualifiers without scoring, against England in Basel and Slovenia in Maribor. Those two defeats, however, were followed by four straight wins – with a goal aggregate of 13-1 – to leave Switzerland as strong favourites for automatic qualification as Group E runners-up. As at the FIFA World Cup in Brazil, their most potent attacking threat came from Xherdan Shaqiri, who scored four goals, the last of them a vital late winner in Lithuania.

DOMESTIC SEASON AT A GLANCE

Super League 2014/15 final table

		Pld	Home					Away					Total					Pts
			W	D	L	F	A	W	D	L	F	A	W	D	L	F	A	
1	**FC Basel 1893**	36	12	4	2	43	15	12	2	4	41	26	24	6	6	84	41	78
2	BSC Young Boys	36	12	3	3	42	21	7	6	5	22	24	19	9	8	64	45	66
3	FC Zürich	36	6	4	8	24	22	9	4	5	31	26	15	8	13	55	48	53
4	FC Thun	36	10	6	2	34	20	3	7	8	13	25	13	13	10	47	45	52
5	FC Luzern	36	5	8	5	25	19	7	3	8	29	27	12	11	13	54	46	47
6	FC St Gallen	36	8	6	4	32	24	5	2	11	25	41	13	8	15	57	65	47
7	FC Sion	36	8	4	6	33	25	4	5	9	14	23	12	9	15	47	48	45
8	Grasshopper Club Zürich	36	7	5	6	25	22	4	5	9	25	34	11	10	15	50	56	43
9	FC Vaduz	36	3	5	10	14	30	4	5	9	14	29	7	10	19	28	59	31
10	FC Aarau	36	5	3	10	17	30	1	9	8	14	34	6	12	18	31	64	30

European qualification 2015/16

Champion: FC Basel 1893 (third qualifying round)
BSC Young Boys (third qualifying round)

Cup winner: FC Sion (group stage)
FC Zürich (third qualifying round)
FC Thun (second qualifying round)

Top scorer	Shkëlzen Gashi (Basel), 22 goals
Relegated club	FC Aarau
Promoted club	FC Lugano
Cup final	FC Sion 3-0 FC Basel 1893

Team of the season
(4-4-2)

Coach: Fischer (Thun)

Vaclík (Basel)
Lang (Grasshoppers) Suchý (Basel) Schär (Basel) Xhaka (Basel)
Steffen (Young Boys) Frei (Basel) Chikhaoui (Zürich) Schönbächler (Zürich)
Streller (Basel) Gashi (Basel)

Player of the season

Fabian Frei
(FC Basel 1893)

There were several notable contributors to Basel's Super League triumph, but Frei was arguably the most consistent performer in Paulo Sousa's side. Conducting the play from the centre of midfield, he scored only once in the league but his was the vital strike away to Liverpool FC that enabled Basel to reach the last 16 of the UEFA Champions League. After winning his fifth Swiss title, the 26-year-old decided to move to pastures new in the summer, joining German Bundesliga club 1. FSV Mainz 05.

Newcomer of the season

Breel Embolo
(FC Basel 1893)

Introduced to the Basel first XI at 17 in the closing weeks of the 2013/14 season, Embolo made rapid progress in his first full season, scoring ten goals in the club's title triumph, including a hat-trick in a 5-1 home win against FC Zürich. He also found the net in the UEFA Champions League at home to PFC Ludogorets Razgrad. Born in Cameroon and raised in Basel, the pacy young striker acquired Swiss citizenship in December 2014 and became a senior Swiss international the following spring.

NATIONAL TEAM

SWITZERLAND

International tournament appearances

FIFA World Cup (10) 1934, 1938 (qtr-finals), 1950, 1954 (qtr-finals), 1962, 1966, 1994 (2nd round), 2006 (2nd round), 2010, 2014 (2nd round)
UEFA European Championship (3) 1996, 2004, 2008

Top five all-time caps

Heinz Hermann (118); Alain Geiger (112); Stéphane Chapuisat (103); Johann Vogel (94); Hakan Yakin (87)

Top five all-time goals

Alexander Frei (42); Xam Abegglen & Kubilay Türkyilmaz (34); André Abegglen & Jacky Fatton (29)

Results 2014/15

Date	Opponent		Venue	Result	Score	Scorers
08/09/14	England (ECQ)	H	Basel	L	0-2	
09/10/14	Slovenia (ECQ)	A	Maribor	L	0-1	
14/10/14	San Marino (ECQ)	A	Serravalle	W	4-0	Seferovic (10, 23), Dzemaili (30), Shaqiri (79)
15/11/14	Lithuania (ECQ)	H	St Gallen	W	4-0	Arlauskis (66og), Schär (68), Shaqiri (80, 90)
18/11/14	Poland	A	Wroclaw	D	2-2	Drmic (4), Frei (88)
27/03/15	Estonia (ECQ)	H	Lucerne	W	3-0	Schär (17), Xhaka (27), Seferovic (80)
31/03/15	United States	H	Zurich	D	1-1	Stocker (80)
10/06/15	Liechtenstein	H	Thun	W	3-0	Dzemaili (29, 68), Shaqiri (60)
14/06/15	Lithuania (ECQ)	A	Vilnius	W	2-1	Drmic (69), Shaqiri (84)

Appearances 2014/15

Coach: Vladimir Petković	15/08/63		ENG	SVN	SMR	LTU	Pol	EST	Usa	Lie	LTU	Caps	Goals
Yann Sommer	17/12/88	Mönchengladbach (GER)	G	G	G	G		G			G	12	-
Stephan Lichtsteiner	16/01/84	Juventus (ITA)	D	D	D59	D		D78	D46	D46	D	75	5
Johan Djourou	18/01/87	Hamburg (GER)	D	D	D	D		D		s46	D	55	1
Steve von Bergen	10/06/83	Young Boys	D	s70	D		D		D	D46		49	-
Ricardo Rodriguez	25/08/92	Wolfsburg (GER)	D	D	D			D			D	30	-
Valon Behrami	19/04/85	Hamburg (GER)	M	M		M	s46	M		M46	M	59	2
Gökhan Inler	27/06/84	Napoli (ITA)	M	M82		M	M46	M	M46		M57	84	6
Granit Xhaka	27/09/92	Mönchengladbach (GER)	M74	M	M			M87	s46		M	36	6
Xherdan Shaqiri	10/10/91	Bayern (GER) /Internazionale (ITA)	M	M	M	M	M	M	M	M63	M	46	17
Admir Mehmedi	16/03/91	Freiburg (GER)	A64	s74	s46	A63	s63		A46	M	s57	33	2
Haris Seferovic	22/02/92	Eintracht Frankfurt (GER)	A	A	A	A83	s68	A	s73		A57	24	5
Josip Drmic	08/08/92	Leverkusen (GER)	s64	A74	A46	s63	A77	A62	A56	A46	A81	20	5
Blerim Dzemaili	12/04/86	Galatasaray (TUR)	s74		M					M74	s57	42	5
Philippe Senderos	14/02/85	Aston Villa (ENG)		D70								55	5
Pajtim Kasami	02/06/92	Olympiacos (GRE)		s82	M71		M68		s46	M		7	1
Silvan Widmer	05/03/93	Udinese (ITA)			s59			s78	s46	s46		4	-
Tranquillo Barnetta	22/05/85	Schalke (GER)			s71							75	10
François Moubandje	21/06/90	Toulouse (FRA)				D75	D		D	D		4	-
Fabian Schär	20/12/91	Basel				D	D	D	D		D	13	5
Gelson Fernandes	02/09/86	Rennes (FRA)				s75	M63		M73	s46		52	2
Marco Schönbächler	11/01/90	Zürich				s83	s77					2	-
Roman Bürki	14/11/90	Freiburg (GER)					G		G			2	-
Michael Lang	08/02/91	Grasshoppers					D			s74		9	1
Valentin Stocker	12/04/89	Hertha (GER)					M63	s62	s46	s46		29	4
Fabian Frei	08/01/89	Basel					s63	s87	M46			7	1
Breel Embolo	14/02/97	Basel						s56	s63	s81		3	-
Marwin Hitz	18/09/87	Augsburg (GER)								G		1	-
Timm Klose	09/05/88	Wolfsburg (GER)								D		9	-

EUROPE

FC Basel 1893

Group B
Match 1 - Real Madrid CF (ESP)
A 1-5 González (38)
Vaclík, Samuel (Kakitani 64), Zuffi, Streller (Embolo 73), Schär, Suchý, Safari, Frei (Delgado 83), González, Elneny, Xhaka. Coach: Paulo Sousa (POR)
Match 2 - Liverpool FC (ENG)
H 1-0 Streller (52)
Vaclík, Serey Die, Streller, Schär, Suchý, Safari (González 9), Frei, Hamoudi (Zuffi 90+2), Elneny, Xhaka, Embolo (Callà 81). Coach: Paulo Sousa (POR)
Match 3 - PFC Ludogorets Razgrad (BUL)
A 0-1
Vaclík, Serey Die, Schär, Suchý, Frei, González (Sio 87), Aliji (Arlind Ajeti 75), Elneny, Xhaka, Embolo, Callà (Hamoudi 84). Coach: Paulo Sousa (POR)
Red card: Serey Die 18
Match 4 - PFC Ludogorets Razgrad (BUL)
H 4-0 Embolo (34), González (41), Gashi (59), Suchý (65)
Vaclík, Zuffi, Gashi (Delgado 74), Schär, Suchý, Safari, Frei (Díaz 81), González (Callà 69), Elneny, Xhaka, Embolo. Coach: Paulo Sousa (POR)
Match 5 - Real Madrid CF (ESP)
H 0-1
Vaclík, P Degen (Hamoudi 76), Zuffi (Kakitani 87), Gashi, Schär, Suchý, Safari, Frei (Díaz 83), González, Elneny, Embolo. Coach: Paulo Sousa (POR)
Match 6 - Liverpool FC (ENG)
A 1-1 Frei (25)
Vaclík, Zuffi (Samuel 88), Streller (Embolo 74), Gashi, Schär, Suchý, Safari, Frei, González, Elneny (Díaz 83), Xhaka. Coach: Paulo Sousa (POR)

Round of 16 - FC Porto (POR)
H 1-1 González (11)
Vaclík, Samuel, Zuffi, Streller (Embolo 63), Gashi (Hamoudi 83), Suchý, Safari, Frei, González (Callà 25), Elneny, Xhaka. Coach: Paulo Sousa (POR)
A 0-4
Vaclík, Samuel, Zuffi, Streller, Gashi (Callà 77), Schär (Embolo 57), Safari, Frei (Kakitani 63), González, Elneny, Xhaka. Coach: Paulo Sousa (POR)
Red card: Samuel 90+1

Grasshopper Club Zürich

Third qualifying round - LOSC Lille (FRA)
H 0-2
Davari, Grichting (Kahraba 46), Jahić, Lang, Salatic, Abrashi, Dabbur, Ravet (Tarashaj 74), Pavlovic, Sinkala (Merkel 61), Dingsdag. Coach: Michael Skibbe (GER)
A 1-1 Abrashi (33)
Vasić, Grichting, Jahić, Lang, Salatic, Kahraba (Bauer 75), Abrashi, Dabbur, Ravet (Tarashaj 68), Pavlovic, Sinkala. Coach: Michael Skibbe (GER)
Red card: Pavlovic 68

Play-offs - Club Brugge KV (BEL)
H 1-2 Lang (8)
Vasić, Grichting, Jahić, Lang, Salatic, Kahraba, Abrashi, Dabbur, Ravet (Merkel 73), Ngamukol (Tarashaj 62), Garcia. Coach: Michael Skibbe (GER)
A 0-1
Davari, Grichting, Jahić, Lang, Abrashi, Dabbur, Ravet (Kahraba 67), Ngamukol, Sinkala (Merkel 67), Gülen, Tarashaj (Al Abbadie 83). Coach: Michael Skibbe (GER)

FC Zürich

Play-offs - FC Spartak Trnava (SVK)
A 3-1 Chermiti (4, 45+2, 58)
Da Costa, Djimsiti, Chermiti (Etoundi 73), Chiumiento, Buff, Koch, Chikhaoui, Rikan (Rossini 83), Kecojević, Schönbächler, Yapi Yapo. Coach: Urs Meier (SUI)
H 1-1 Chikhaoui (48)
Da Costa, Djimsiti, Chermiti, Chiumiento, Buff (Rodriguez 78), Koch, Chikhaoui (Etoundi 69), Rikan, Kecojević, Schönbächler (M Brunner 82), Yapi Yapo. Coach: Urs Meier (SUI)

Group A
Match 1 - Apollon Limassol FC (CYP)
A 2-3 Rikan (50), Yapi Yapo (53)
Da Costa, Djimsiti, Chermiti (Etoundi 68), Chiumiento (Rossini 90+1), Koch, Chikhaoui, Rikan, Kukeli, Kecojević, Schönbächler (Buff 73), Yapi Yapo. Coach: Urs Meier (SUI)
Red card: Chikhaoui 90
Match 2 - VfL Borussia Mönchengladbach (GER)
H 1-1 Etoundi (23)
Da Costa, Djimsiti, Chermiti (Rossini 90+1), Chiumiento, Nef, Etoundi, Rikan (Rodriguez 20), Kukeli, Kecojević, Schönbächler (Koch 84), Yapi Yapo. Coach: Urs Meier (SUI)
Match 3 - Villarreal CF (ESP)
A 1-4 Schönbächler (43)
Da Costa, Djimsiti (Elvedi 84), Chermiti (Etoundi 75), Chiumiento, Nef, Buff, Koch, Chikhaoui, Kukeli, Schönbächler (Rodriguez 74), Yapi Yapo. Coach: Urs Meier (SUI)
Match 4 - Villarreal CF (ESP)
H 3-2 Etoundi (21), Buff (26), Chikhaoui (29)
Da Costa, Djimsiti, Nef, Etoundi (Chermiti 54), Buff (Rossini 71), Chikhaoui, Kukeli, Schönbächler, Elvedi, Rodriguez (M Brunner 82), Yapi Yapo. Coach: Urs Meier (SUI)
Match 5 - Apollon Limassol FC (CYP)
H 3-1 Djimsiti (32), Chikhaoui (39p, 59p)
Da Costa, Djimsiti (Elvedi 80), Chiumiento, Nef, Etoundi (Chermiti 76), Buff, Chikhaoui, Kajević, Kecojević, Schönbächler, Rodriguez (Koch 72). Coach: Urs Meier (SUI)
Match 6 - VfL Borussia Mönchengladbach (GER)
A 0-3
Da Costa, Chiumiento, Etoundi (Chermiti 69), Buff, Koch, Chikhaoui, Kukeli, Kecojević (C Brunner 25), Schönbächler, Elvedi, Rodriguez (M Brunner 69). Coach: Urs Meier (SUI)

BSC Young Boys

Third qualifying round - Ermis Aradippou FC (CYP)
H 1-0 Nuzzolo (58)
Mvogo, Lecjaks, Costanzo, Steffen (Zárate 69), Gajić, Frey (Nikci 78), Rochat, Wüthrich, Sutter, Nuzzolo, Kubo (Afum 22). Coach: Uli Forte (SUI)
A 2-0 Steffen (36), Frey (66)
Mvogo, Lecjaks, Costanzo, Steffen (Nikci 58), Gajić (Bertone 60), Frey, Rochat, Wüthrich, Sutter (Afum 66), Nuzzolo, Sanogo. Coach: Uli Forte (SUI)

Play-offs - Debreceni VSC (HUN)
H 3-1 Nuzzolo (26), Steffen (67), Frey (87)
Mvogo, Hadergjonaj, Von Bergen, Bertone, Lecjaks, Costanzo (Kubo 77), Steffen (Nikci 86), Frey (Afum 90), Rochat, Nuzzolo, Sanogo. Coach: Uli Forte (SUI)
A 0-0
Mvogo, Hadergjonaj, Von Bergen, Bertone, Lecjaks, Costanzo (Wüthrich 67), Steffen, Frey (Kubo 81), Rochat, Nuzzolo (Sutter 90+1), Sanogo. Coach: Uli Forte (SUI)

Group I
Match 1 - ŠK Slovan Bratislava (SVK)
H 5-0 Lecjaks (5), Steffen (29), Nuzzolo (63), Nikci (80), Hoarau (90+2)
Mvogo, Hadergjonaj, Von Bergen, Bertone, Afum (Hoarau 70), Lecjaks, Costanzo (Kubo 64), Steffen (Nikci 79), Rochat, Nuzzolo, Sanogo. Coach: Uli Forte (SUI)
Match 2 - AC Sparta Praha (CZE)
A 1-3 Hoarau (52)
Mvogo, Von Bergen, Lecjaks, Steffen (Nikci 89), Gajić, Rochat, Wüthrich (Afum 69), Sutter (Hadergjonaj 66), Nuzzolo, Sanogo, Hoarau. Coach: Uli Forte (SUI)
Match 3 - SSC Napoli (ITA)
H 2-0 Hoarau (52), Bertone (90+2)
Mvogo, Vilotić, Von Bergen, Lecjaks, Steffen (Nikci 90+3), Gajić, Sutter, Nuzzolo (Rochat 86), Kubo (Bertone 71), Sanogo, Hoarau. Coach: Uli Forte (SUI)

DOMESTIC LEAGUE CLUB-BY-CLUB

Match 4 - SSC Napoli (ITA)
A 0-3
Mvogo, Hadergjonaj, Vilotić, Von Bergen, Bertone, Steffen, Gajić (Kubo 60), Rochat, Nuzzolo (Nikci 60), Sanogo, Hoarau (Afum 68). Coach: Uli Forte (SUI)

Match 5 - ŠK Slovan Bratislava (SVK)
A 3-1 *Hoarau (9p), Kubo (18, 63)*
Mvogo, Vilotić, Von Bergen, Bertone, Lecjaks, Steffen (Nuzzolo 71), Zárate (Hadergjonaj 80), Sutter, Kubo, Sanogo, Hoarau (Afum 67). Coach: Uli Forte (SUI)

Match 6 - AC Sparta Praha (CZE)
H 2-0 *Hoarau (75p), Steffen (90+4)*
Mvogo, Hadergjonaj, Vilotić, Von Bergen, Lecjaks, Steffen, Gajić (Rochat 89), Nuzzolo (Zárate 63), Kubo (Bertone 82), Sanogo, Hoarau. Coach: Uli Forte (SUI)

Round of 32 - Everton FC (ENG)
H 1-4 *Hoarau (10)*
Mvogo, Hadergjonaj, Vilotić, Von Bergen, Lecjaks, Steffen (Sulejmanov 79), Gajić (Gerndt 70), Nuzzolo, Kubo, Sanogo (Bertone 90), Hoarau. Coach: Uli Forte (SUI)
A 1-3 *Sanogo (13)*
Wölfli, Vilotić, Bertone, Lecjaks (Bürki 57), Zárate, Rochat, Sutter, Nuzzolo (Gerndt 68), Kubo (Afum 76), Sanogo, Hoarau. Coach: Uli Forte (SUI)

FC Luzern

EUROPA
LEAGUE

Second qualifying round - Saint Johnstone FC (SCO)
H 1-1 *Schneuwly (68)*
Zibung, Rogulj, Doubai (Sava Bento 60), Lustenberger, Hyka (Bozanic 75), Thiesson, Schneuwly, Affolter, Winter, Wiss (Lezcano 61), Freuler. Coach: Carlos Bernegger (ARG)
A 1-1 *Schneuwly (60)* (aet; 4-5 on pens)
Zibung, Bozanic (Wiss 15), Rogulj, Lustenberger, Hyka (Thiesson 91), Affolter, Winter, Hochstrasser (Schneuwly 54), Lezcano, Sarr, Freuler. Coach: Carlos Bernegger (ARG)

FC Aarau

1914 • Brügglifeld (8,000) • fcaarau.ch
Major honours
Swiss League (3) 1912, 1914, 1993; Swiss Cup (1) 1985
Coach: Sven Christ;
(22/03/15) Raimondo Ponte

2014

19/07	h	Basel	L	1-2	*Schultz*
23/07	h	Sion	W	1-0	*Gauracs*
27/07	a	Young Boys	D	1-1	*Senger*
06/08	h	Vaduz	D	1-1	*Senger*
09/08	a	St Gallen	D	2-2	*Radice, Garat*
16/08	h	Grasshoppers	L	1-2	*Garat*
30/08	a	Luzern	D	1-1	*Djuric*
13/09	h	Thun	W	2-1	*Radice, Wieser*
24/09	a	Zürich	D	0-0	
27/09	h	Grasshoppers	L	1-2	*Nganga*
05/10	h	Young Boys	W	3-2	*Nganga, Andrist 2*
18/10	h	Sion	L	0-3	
25/10	a	Thun	D	0-0	
02/11	a	Sion	D	2-2	*Lüscher, Wieser*
09/11	h	Zürich	L	0-1	
23/11	a	Basel	L	0-3	
29/11	h	Luzern	L	0-3	
07/12	a	Vaduz	L	0-1	

2015

08/02	a	Thun	D	1-1	*Costanzo*
15/02	h	Vaduz	L	0-1	
22/02	a	Luzern	L	0-4	
28/02	a	Zürich	D	0-0	
08/03	h	St Gallen	L	0-2	
15/03	h	Young Boys	D	1-1	*Sliškovic*
21/03	a	Grasshoppers	L	1-3	*Sliškovic*
04/04	a	Basel	L	0-6	
12/04	h	Sion	L	0-1	
19/04	a	Vaduz	W	2-0	*Senger, Costanzo*
25/04	a	Zürich	D	0-0	
29/04	a	Young Boys	D	2-2	*Radice 2*
03/05	h	Luzern	L	2-6	*Andrist, Feltscher*
09/05	h	Grasshoppers	L	0-1	
16/05	a	Sion	L	0-1	
20/05	h	Basel	W	2-1	*og (Elneny), Djuric*
25/05	a	St Gallen	L	1-5	*Sliškovic*
29/05	h	Thun	W	3-2	*Senger 2, Radice*

No	Name	Nat	DoB	Pos	Aps	(s)	Gls
7	Stephan Andrist		12/12/87	A	30	(3)	3
3	Nauris Bulvītis	LVA	15/03/87	D	2	(2)	
6	Sandro Burki		06/10/85	M	34		
29	Moreno Costanzo		20/02/88	M	11	(3)	2
9	Dusan Djuric	SWE	16/09/84	M	14	(7)	2
88	Frank Feltscher	VEN	17/05/88	M	7	(14)	1
24	Sandro Foschini		07/02/88	A		(1)	
19	Juan Pablo Garat	ARG	19/04/83	D	20	(6)	2
23	Edgars Gauracs	LVA	10/03/88	A		(2)	1
11	Daniel Gygax		28/08/81	M	10	(12)	
4	Kim Jaggy	HAI	14/11/82	D	35		
16	Olivier Jäckle		07/01/93	M	25	(3)	
14	Sven Lüscher		05/03/84	M	30	(4)	1
15	Richard Magyar	SWE	03/05/91	M	5	(2)	
1	Joël Mall		05/04/91	G	34		
13	Bruno Martignoni		13/12/92	M	4	(1)	
20	Joy-Slayd Mickels	GER	29/03/94	A		(2)	
21	Frano Mlinar	CRO	30/03/92	M	12	(2)	
91	Ognjen Mudrinski	SRB	15/11/91	A	4	(8)	
22	Igor Nganga	COD	14/04/87	D	30	(2)	2
18	Ulisse Pelloni		07/02/94	G	2		
5	Luca Radice	ITA	09/04/87	M	30	(4)	5
10	Alain Schultz		17/02/83	M	2	(4)	1
27	Dante Senger	ARG	04/03/83	A	17	(7)	5
10	Petar Sliškovic	CRO	21/02/91	A	10	(5)	3
2	Marco Thaler		28/06/94	D	22	(3)	
8	Sandro Wieser	LIE	03/02/93	M	6	(8)	2

FC Basel 1893

1893 • St Jakob-Park (39,107) • fcb.ch
Major honours
Swiss League (18) 1953, 1967, 1969, 1970, 1972, 1973, 1977, 1980, 2002, 2004, 2005, 2008, 2010, 2011, 2012, 2013, 2014, 2015; Swiss Cup (11) 1933, 1947, 1963, 1967, 1975, 2002, 2003, 2007, 2008, 2010, 2012
Coach: Paulo Sousa (POR)

2014

19/07	a	Aarau	W	2-1	*Embolo, Aliji*
27/07	h	Luzern	W	3-0	*Streller, Gashi, Callà*
02/08	a	Thun	W	3-2	*Streller, Gashi, Schär*
09/08	h	Zürich	W	4-1	*Gashi, Zuffi, Kakitani, Delgado*
14/08	h	St Gallen	L	0-2	
17/08	a	Sion	W	3-2	*Gashi, Streller, og (Vanins)*
31/08	h	Young Boys	W	3-1	*González, Streller, Kakitani*
13/09	a	Grasshoppers	L	1-3	*Zuffi*
23/09	h	Vaduz	W	3-1	*Zuffi, Streller, Hamoudi*
27/09	h	Thun	D	1-1	*Xhaka*
04/10	a	St Gallen	L	1-2	*Callà*
18/10	a	Young Boys	W	1-0	*Gashi*
25/10	a	Sion	D	1-1	*Sio*
01/11	h	Grasshoppers	W	2-0	*Gashi, González*
09/11	a	Vaduz	W	4-0	*Díaz, Embolo 2, Gashi*
23/11	a	Aarau	W	3-0	*Gashi 2, Embolo*
30/11	a	Zürich	W	2-1	*Gashi 2*
06/12	a	Luzern	W	3-0	*Delgado 2, Embolo*

2015

08/02	a	Grasshoppers	W	4-2	*Elneny, Gashi, Streller, Callà*
14/02	h	Sion	D	1-1	*Gashi*
22/02	a	Young Boys	L	2-4	*Gashi, Streller*
28/02	h	Vaduz	W	1-0	*Frei*
07/03	h	Thun	W	3-0	*Gashi 2, Streller*
15/03	a	St Gallen	D	2-2	*Delgado, Callà*
21/03	h	Luzern	W	4-1	*Gashi 2, Delgado (p), Callà*
04/04	h	Aarau	W	6-0	*Delgado 2 (1p), Streller 2, Gashi 2*
12/04	h	Zürich	W	5-1	*Gashi, Embolo 3, og (Djimsiti)*
18/04	a	Sion	W	1-0	*Embolo*
26/04	h	Luzern	L	1-2	*Delgado*
29/04	a	Vaduz	W	3-1	*Streller, González, Zuffi*
02/05	h	Grasshoppers	W	2-1	*Elneny, Callà*
10/05	a	Zürich	W	2-1	*Callà, Suchý*
17/05	h	Young Boys	D	0-0	
20/05	a	Aarau	L	1-2	*Embolo*
25/05	a	Thun	D	2-2	*Gashi (p), Kakitani*
29/05	h	St Gallen	W	4-3	*Streller, Samuel, Zuffi, Albian Ajeti*

No	Name	Nat	DoB	Pos	Aps	(s)	Gls
38	Albian Ajeti		26/02/97	A	1	(3)	1
5	Arlind Ajeti	ALB	25/09/93	D	2	(1)	
27	Naser Aliji	ALB	27/12/93	D	5		1
39	Davide Callà		06/10/84	M	15	(8)	7
4	Philipp Degen		15/02/83	D	15	(3)	
10	Matías Delgado	ARG	15/12/82	M	19	(7)	8
21	Marcelo Díaz	CHI	30/12/86	M	10	(3)	1
33	Mohamed Elneny	EGY	11/07/92	M	17	(11)	2
36	Breel Embolo		14/02/97	A	18	(9)	10
20	Fabian Frei		08/01/89	M	25	(6)	1
11	Shkëlzen Gashi	ALB	15/07/88	A	26	(5)	22
25	Derlis González	PAR	20/03/94	A	20	(6)	3
24	Ahmed Hamoudi	EGY	30/07/90	M	4	(8)	1
28	Robin Huser		24/01/98	M	2		
14	Yōichirō Kakitani	JPN	03/01/90	A	5	(9)	3
19	Behrang Safari	SWE	09/02/85	D	23	(1)	
6	Walter Samuel	ARG	23/03/78	D	8	(4)	1
16	Fabian Schär		20/12/91	D	30		1
8	Serey Die	CIV	07/11/84	M	5	(2)	
30	Giovanni Sio	CIV	31/03/89	A	1	(6)	1
9	Marco Streller		18/06/81	A	20	(4)	12
17	Marek Suchý	CZE	29/03/88	D	29	(1)	1
3	Adama Traoré	CIV	03/02/90	D	8	(4)	
1	Tomáš Vaclík	CZE	29/03/89	G	32		
18	Germano Vailati		30/08/80	G	4	(1)	
34	Taulant Xhaka	ALB	28/03/91	D	27	(2)	1
7	Luca Zuffi		27/03/90	M	25	(4)	5

SWITZERLAND

Grasshopper Club Zürich

1886 • Letzigrund (26,104) • gcz.ch

Major honours
Swiss League (27) 1898, 1900, 1901, 1905, 1921, 1927, 1928, 1931, 1937, 1939, 1942, 1943, 1945, 1952, 1956, 1971, 1978, 1982, 1983, 1984, 1990, 1991, 1995, 1996, 1998, 2001, 2003; Swiss Cup (19) 1926, 1927, 1932, 1934, 1937, 1938, 1940, 1941, 1942, 1943, 1946, 1952, 1956, 1983, 1988, 1989, 1990, 1994, 2013

Coach: Michael Skibbe (GER);
(14/01/15) Pierluigi Tami

2014
20/07	a	Zürich	L 0-1	
26/07	h	Thun	L 2-3	Dabbur 2
02/08	h	Sion	D 0-0	
10/08	a	Luzern	D 1-1	Lang
13/08	a	Young Boys	L 0-4	
16/08	a	Aarau	W 2-1	Kahraba, Ngamukol
31/08	h	Vaduz	L 0-1	
13/09	h	Basel	W 3-1	Ngamukol, Dingsdag, Lang
24/09	a	St Gallen	L 0-3	
27/09	h	Aarau	W 2-1	Ravet, Abrashi
04/10	a	Thun	L 2-3	Kahraba, Lang
19/10	h	Zürich	L 1-3	Caio
26/10	a	Vaduz	D 1-1	Ngamukol
01/11	a	Basel	L 0-2	
08/11	h	St Gallen	W 3-0	Salatic, Dabbur 2
22/11	h	Luzern	W 3-2	Dabbur, Ravet, Caio
29/11	a	Sion	D 3-3	Ravet, Dabbur, Caio (p)
06/12	h	Young Boys	L 0-1	

2015
08/02	h	Basel	L 2-4	Dabbur, Lang
14/02	a	Young Boys	L 2-4	Dabbur, Ben Khalifa
21/02	h	Zürich	L 0-2	
01/03	a	St Gallen	D 1-1	Lang
07/03	h	Luzern	W 1-0	Caio
14/03	a	Thun	D 2-2	Dabbur, Tarashaj
21/03	h	Aarau	W 3-1	Ravet, Caio, Dabbur
03/04	a	Sion	W 5-0	Vadócz 2, Abrashi, Dabbur, Caio
12/04	h	Vaduz	D 1-1	Caio
19/04	a	Luzern	L 0-2	
26/04	h	Young Boys	D 2-2	Ravet, Caio
29/04	h	Thun	D 0-0	
02/05	h	Basel	L 1-2	Ravet
09/05	a	Aarau	W 1-0	Dabbur
17/05	h	St Gallen	W 2-0	Dabbur, Caio
20/05	h	Sion	D 0-0	
25/05	a	Vaduz	W 1-0	Caio
29/05	a	Zürich	L 3-4	Ravet 2, Caio

No	Name	Nat	DoB	Pos	Aps	(s)	Gls
8	Amir Abrashi	ALB	27/03/90	M	25	(1)	2
34	Moritz Bauer		25/01/92	D	8	(8)	
15	Nassim Ben Khalifa		13/01/92	A	8	(17)	1
2	Jordan Brown	GER	12/11/91	M		(2)	
21	Caio	BRA	29/05/86	A	26	(3)	11
9	Munas Dabbur	ISR	14/05/92	A	32		13
1	Daniel Davari	IRN	06/01/88	G	9		
23	Michael Dingsdag	NED	18/10/82	D	26	(2)	1
16	Matteo Fedele		20/07/92	M	11	(1)	
35	Nikola Gjorgjev		22/08/97	M		(2)	
3	Stéphane Grichting		30/03/79	D	28		
29	Levent Gülen		24/02/94	D	23		
2	Gianluca Hossmann		25/03/91	D	1	(3)	
4	Sanel Jahić	BIH	10/12/81	D	13	(1)	
	Mahmoud Kahraba	EGY	13/04/94	A	5	(6)	2
5	Michael Lang		08/02/91	D	35		5
22	Benjamin Lüthi		30/11/88	D	10	(1)	
10	Aleksandr Merkel	KAZ	22/02/92	M	3	(3)	
17	Anatole Ngamukol	FRA	15/01/88	A	16	(14)	3
20	Daniel Pavlovic		22/04/88	D	25		
14	Yoric Ravet	FRA	12/09/89	A	29	(6)	8
6	Veroljub Salatic		14/11/85	M	10		1
22	Nathan Sinkala	ZAM	22/11/90	M	4	(3)	
30	Shani Tarashaj		07/02/95	A	2	(17)	1
6	Krisztián Vadócz	HUN	30/05/85	M	12	(3)	2
18	Vaso Vasić	SRB	26/04/90	G	27	(1)	
19	Grégory Wüthrich		04/12/94	D	8		

FC Luzern

1901 • swissporarena (16,520) • fcl.ch

Major honours
Swiss League (1) 1989; Swiss Cup (2) 1960, 1992

Coach: Carlos Bernegger (ARG);
(12/10/14) Markus Babbel (GER)

2014
20/07	h	Sion	D 1-1	Schneuwly
27/07	a	Basel	L 0-3	
03/08	a	St Gallen	L 1-2	Freuler
10/08	h	Grasshoppers	D 1-1	Schneuwly
13/08	a	Vaduz	D 1-1	Mobulu
16/08	h	Zürich	D 1-1	Schneuwly
30/08	h	Aarau	D 1-1	Lezcano
14/09	a	Young Boys	L 2-3	Schneuwly, Jantscher
23/09	a	Thun	L 2-3	Schneuwly, Jantscher
28/09	h	St Gallen	L 1-2	Lezcano
05/10	a	Sion	L 1-3	Schneuwly
19/10	h	Vaduz	D 0-0	
01/11	a	Zürich	W 3-2	Freuler (p), Lezcano, og (Koch)
08/11	h	Thun	D 0-0	
22/11	a	Grasshoppers	L 2-3	Freuler, Doubai
29/11	a	Aarau	W 3-0	Schneuwly, Lezcano, Mobulu
03/12	h	Young Boys	L 1-2	Bozanic
06/12	h	Basel	L 0-3	

2015
07/02	h	Young Boys	D 1-1	Puljić
15/02	a	St Gallen	D 0-0	
22/02	h	Aarau	W 4-0	Freuler (p), Lezcano, Schneuwly 2
01/03	a	Sion	D 2-2	Lezcano, Freuler
07/03	a	Grasshoppers	L 0-1	
14/03	h	Vaduz	D 2-0	Schneuwly, Jantscher
21/03	h	Basel	L 1-4	Puljić
04/04	a	Zürich	W 1-0	Puljić
11/04	a	Thun	L 0-1	
19/04	h	Grasshoppers	W 2-0	Schneuwly 2
26/04	a	Basel	W 2-1	Lezcano, Schneuwly
30/04	h	St Gallen	W 6-2	Jantscher 2 (1p), Sarr, Schneuwly, Affolter, Lezcano
03/05	a	Aarau	W 6-2	Jantscher, Schneuwly 2, Winter, Lezcano, Freuler
10/05	h	Thun	D 0-0	
16/05	a	Vaduz	W 2-0	Lezcano, Schneuwly
21/05	a	Young Boys	W 1-0	Freuler
25/05	h	Zürich	L 0-1	
29/05	h	Sion	W 3-0	Lezcano 2, Lustenberger

No	Name	Nat	DoB	Pos	Aps	(s)	Gls
16	François Affolter		13/03/91	D	27	(4)	1
33	Fidan Aliti	ALB	03/10/93	D	7	(3)	
4	Oliver Bozanic	AUS	08/01/89	M	21	(2)	1
10	Lorenzo Bucchi	ITA	21/11/83	G	2		
6	Thierry Doubai	CIV	01/07/88	M	22	(5)	1
26	Remo Freuler		15/04/92	M	33		7
26	Nicolas Haas		23/01/96	M	2	(6)	
17	Claudio Holenstein		10/09/90	M		(2)	
8	Jahmir Hyka	ALB	08/03/88	M	8	(14)	
20	Cristian Ianu	ROU	16/10/83	A		(7)	
10	Jakob Jantscher	AUT	08/01/89	M	28	(5)	6
2	Andrés Lamas	URU	16/01/84	D	4		
17	Darío Lezcano	PAR	30/06/90	A	28	(5)	12
7	Claudio Lustenberger		06/01/87	D	33		1
3	Ferid Matri		16/01/94	D		(1)	
11	Ridge Mobulu	COD	29/06/91	M	1	(11)	2
22	Haxhi Neziraj	ALB	16/03/93	M		(1)	
30	Jonas Omlin		10/01/94	G	1		
17	Tomislav Puljić	CRO	21/03/83	D	9		3
9	Bryan Rabello	CHI	16/05/94	M	4	(5)	
5	Kaja Rogulj	CRO	15/06/86	D	19		
23	Sally Sarr	FRA	06/05/86	D	19	(1)	1
28	Sava Bento	POR	02/01/91	M		(2)	
15	Marco Schneuwly		27/03/85	A	33	(3)	17
14	Jérôme Thiesson		06/08/87	D	24	(4)	
19	Adrian Winter		08/07/86	M	16	(15)	1
24	Alain Wiss		21/08/90	M	22	(5)	
1	David Zibung		10/01/84	G	33		

FC Sion

1909 • Tourbillon (14,283) • fc-sion.ch

Major honours
Swiss League (2) 1992, 1997; Swiss Cup (13) 1965, 1974, 1980, 1982, 1986, 1991, 1995, 1996, 1997, 2006, 2009, 2011, 2015

Coach: Frédéric Chassot;
(06/08/14) Jochen Dries (GER) & Frédéric Chassot;
(29/09/14) Jochen Dries (GER) & Admir Smajić (BIH);
(17/12/14) Didier Tholot (FRA)

2014
20/07	a	Luzern	D 1-1	Vanczák
23/07	a	Aarau	L 0-1	
26/07	h	St Gallen	W 1-0	Christofi
02/08	a	Grasshoppers	D 0-0	
10/08	h	Vaduz	W 1-0	Vanczák
17/08	h	Basel	L 2-3	Herea, Carlitos (p)
30/08	a	Thun	L 1-2	Herea
14/09	a	Zürich	L 1-4	Vidosic
24/09	h	Young Boys	L 0-1	
28/09	a	Vaduz	L 0-1	
05/10	h	Luzern	W 3-1	Konaté, Carlitos, Perrier
19/10	h	Thun	D 0-0	
25/10	a	Basel	D 1-1	Konaté
02/11	h	Aarau	D 2-2	N'Doye, Modou
09/11	a	Young Boys	L 1-2	Konaté
22/11	h	Zürich	L 1-3	Vidosic
29/11	h	Grasshoppers	D 3-3	Christofi, Modou 2 (1p)
07/12	a	St Gallen	L 0-2	

2015
14/02	a	Basel	D 1-1	Modou (p)
25/02	a	Vaduz	W 2-0	Konaté 2
01/03	h	Luzern	D 2-2	Fernandes, Herea
08/03	a	Young Boys	L 2-3	Konaté, Carlitos
15/03	a	Zürich	W 1-0	Follonier
18/03	h	St Gallen	W 3-0	Konaté 3
22/03	h	Thun	W 3-0	Konaté 2, Ziegler
03/04	h	Grasshoppers	L 0-5	
12/04	a	Aarau	W 1-0	Follonier
18/04	a	Basel	L 0-1	
25/04	a	Thun	L 1-2	Follonier
28/04	h	Zürich	L 1-2	Follonier
03/05	a	St Gallen	W 1-0	Konaté
09/05	h	Vaduz	W 4-0	Vanczák, Konaté 3
16/05	h	Aarau	W 1-0	Konaté
20/05	a	Grasshoppers	D 0-0	
25/05	h	Young Boys	W 6-2	Carlitos 2, Follonier 2, Herea (p), Perrier
29/05	a	Luzern	L 0-3	

No	Name	Nat	DoB	Pos	Aps	(s)	Gls
13	Chadrac Akolo	CGO	01/04/95	A	3	(13)	
21	Ebenezer Assifuah	GHA	03/07/93	A	8	(8)	
30	Carlitos	POR	06/09/82	M	29	(3)	5
7	Dimitris Christofi	CYP	28/09/88	A	13	(3)	2
35	Fousseyni Cissé	FRA	17/07/89	A	1	(3)	
35	Dany Da Silva		02/03/93	G	2		
18	Steven Deana		04/03/90	G	11		
16	Matteo Fedele	ITA	20/07/92	M	4	(7)	
32	Edmilson Fernandes		15/04/96	M	14	(2)	1
12	Daniel Follonier		18/01/94	M	15	(4)	6
19	Ovidiu Herea	ROU	26/03/85	M	7	(10)	4
19	Gaëtan Karlen		07/06/93	A	1	(7)	
14	Moussa Konaté	SEN	03/04/93	A	26	(1)	16
6	Xavier Kouassi	CIV	28/12/89	M	32		
27	Léo Lacroix		27/02/92	D	26	(2)	
11	Léo Itaperuna	BRA	12/04/89	A	6	(6)	
34	Pa Modou	GAM	26/12/89	D	28	(4)	
34	Birama N'Doye	SEN	23/03/94	M	26	(1)	1
26	Michael Perrier		01/03/89	M	8	(11)	2
26	Pedro Ramírez	VEN	24/08/92	M	3	(4)	
27	Steve Rouiller		10/07/90	D	6		
22	Vincent Rüfli		22/01/88	D	25	(2)	
6	Veroljub Salatic		14/11/85	M	16		
36	Vincent Sierro		08/10/95	M		(1)	
20	Vilmos Vanczák	HUN	20/06/83	D	18	(1)	3
2	Andris Vaņins	LVA	30/04/80	G	23		
23	Dario Vidosic	AUS	08/04/87	A	12	(5)	2
29	Sébastien Wüthrich		29/05/90	M	1	(6)	
15	Ishmael Yartey	GHA	11/01/90	M	2	(3)	
3	Reto Ziegler		16/01/86	D	17		1
31	Elsad Zverotić	MNE	31/10/86	D	13		

FC St Gallen

1879 • AFG Arena (19,456) • fcsg.ch
Major honours
Swiss League (2) 1904, 2000; Swiss Cup (1) 1969
Coach: Jeff Saibene (LUX)

2014
19/07	h	Young Boys	D	2-2	Čavušević, og (Gajić)
26/07	a	Sion	L	0-1	
03/08	h	Luzern	W	2-1	Mathys, Čavušević
09/08	a	Aarau	D	2-2	Čavušević, Bunjaku
14/08	a	Basel	W	2-0	Bunjaku 2
17/08	a	Thun	L	1-3	Rodriguez
31/08	h	Zürich	L	0-2	
14/09	a	Vaduz	D	2-2	Tafer, Russo
24/09	h	Grasshoppers	W	3-0	Tréand, Tafer, Rodriguez (p)
28/09	a	Luzern	W	2-1	Russo, Besle
04/10	h	Basel	W	2-1	Čavušević, Bunjaku
18/10	a	Aarau	W	3-0	Besle, Tafer, Tréand
26/10	a	Zürich	D	1-1	Karanovic
02/11	h	Thun	W	1-0	Rodriguez (p)
08/11	h	Grasshoppers	L	0-3	
23/11	h	Vaduz	D	3-3	Tafer, Rodriguez (p), Russo
30/11	a	Young Boys	L	2-4	Aratore, Tafer
07/12	h	Sion	W	2-0	Mathys, Tafer

2015
07/02	h	Zürich	L	1-4	Čavušević
15/02	h	Luzern	D	0-0	
01/03	h	Grasshoppers	D	1-1	Rodriguez (p)
08/03	a	Aarau	W	2-0	Bunjaku, Rodriguez
15/03	h	Basel	D	2-2	Sikorski, Tréand
18/03	a	Sion	L	0-3	
22/03	a	Vaduz	L	1-3	Mathys
04/04	a	Thun	L	1-4	Lässer
11/04	h	Young Boys	W	3-1	Rodriguez, Tafer (p), Karanovic
18/04	a	Zürich	W	2-1	Karanovic 2
26/04	a	Vaduz	L	1-2	Mathys
30/04	a	Luzern	L	2-6	Čavušević, Karanovic
03/05	h	Sion	L	0-1	
10/05	a	Young Boys	L	1-3	Čavušević
17/05	a	Grasshoppers	L	0-2	
20/05	h	Thun	W	2-1	Tafer (p), Janjatovic
25/05	a	Aarau	W	5-1	Karanovic 4, Čavušević
29/05	a	Basel	L	3-4	Mathys, Aleksić, Aratore

No	Name	Nat	DoB	Pos	Aps	(s)	Gls
23	Danijel Aleksić	SRB	30/04/91	A	3	(1)	1
22	Marco Aratore		04/06/91	M	8	(16)	2
15	Stéphane Besle	FRA	23/01/84	D	28		2
10	Albert Bunjaku		29/11/83	A	24	(5)	6
20	Džengis Čavušević	SVN	26/11/87	A	22	(14)	8
8	Muhamed Demiri	MKD	20/11/85	M	8	(1)	
2	Daniel Dziwniel	POL	19/08/92	D	3		
25	Michael Eisenring		29/03/93	D	1		
5	Everton Luiz	BRA	24/05/88	M	24		
3	Mickaël Facchinetti		15/02/91	D	23		
14	Roy Gelmi		01/03/95	D	4		
18	Marcel Herzog		28/06/80	G	19		
31	Dejan Janjatovic	GER	25/02/92	M	26	(1)	1
55	Nisso Kapiloto	ISR	01/10/89	D	11	(2)	
11	Goran Karanovic		13/10/87	A	8	(18)	9
24	Daniel Lässer		17/03/95	M		(1)	1
28	Ermir Lenjani	ALB	05/08/89	D	10	(2)	
1	Daniel Lopar		19/04/85	G	17		
27	Marco Mathys		05/07/87	M	19	(13)	5
6	Philippe Montandon		15/07/82	D	3		
19	Mario Mutsch	LUX	03/09/84	D	24	(3)	
34	Roberto Rodriguez		28/07/90	M	14	(14)	7
33	Daniele Russo		03/11/85	D	18		3
26	Daniel Sikorski	AUT	02/11/87	A	5	(3)	1
9	Yannis Tafer	FRA	11/02/91	A	27	(2)	8
16	Pascal Thrier		04/11/84	M	24	(1)	
7	Geoffrey Tréand	FRA	16/01/86	M	23	(10)	

FC Thun

1898 • Stockhorn Arena (9,752) • fcthun.ch
Coach: Urs Fischer

2014
20/07	h	Vaduz	W	1-0	Sadik (p)
23/07	a	Zürich	L	1-2	Kaludjerović
26/07	a	Grasshoppers	W	3-2	Schneuwly 3
02/08	h	Basel	L	2-3	Kaludjerović, Sadik
10/08	a	Young Boys	D	1-1	Sadik
17/08	h	St Gallen	W	3-1	Siegfried, Reinmann, og (Besle)
30/08	h	Sion	W	2-1	Sadik (p), Frontino
13/09	a	Aarau	L	1-2	Sadik
23/09	h	Luzern	W	3-2	Sadik (p), Nélson Ferreira, Sulmoni
27/09	a	Basel	D	1-1	Sadik
04/10	h	Grasshoppers	W	3-2	Sadik (p), Schirinzi, Frontino
19/10	a	Sion	D	0-0	
25/10	h	Aarau	D	0-0	
02/11	a	St Gallen	L	0-1	
08/11	a	Luzern	L	0-1	
23/11	h	Young Boys	L	0-1	
30/11	a	Vaduz	W	1-0	og (Grippo)
07/12	h	Zürich	W	2-1	Nélson Ferreira, Schneuwly

2015
08/02	a	Aarau	D	1-1	Rojas
15/02	a	Zürich	W	1-0	González
22/02	a	Vaduz	D	1-1	Sadik
01/03	h	Young Boys	D	0-0	
07/03	a	Basel	L	0-3	
14/03	h	Grasshoppers	D	2-2	Frontino, Wittwer
22/03	a	Sion	L	0-3	
04/04	h	St Gallen	W	4-1	Frontino, Wittwer, González, Hediger
11/04	h	Luzern	W	1-0	González
19/04	a	Young Boys	L	0-4	
25/04	h	Sion	W	2-1	González, Nélson Ferreira
29/04	a	Grasshoppers	D	0-0	
02/05	h	Vaduz	W	4-0	Sadik, Reinmann, Sulmoni 2
10/05	a	Luzern	D	0-0	
17/05	h	Zürich	D	2-2	Sulmoni, Siegfried
20/05	a	St Gallen	L	1-2	Rojas
25/05	h	Basel	D	2-2	Sadik 2
29/05	a	Aarau	L	2-3	Karlen 2

No	Name	Nat	DoB	Pos	Aps	(s)	Gls
25	Kevin Bigler		05/10/92	M	3	(1)	
16	Cássio	BRA	20/08/90	A		(9)	
1	Guillaume Faivre		20/02/87	G	32		
7	Gianluca Frontino		29/11/89	M	14	(12)	4
31	Stefan Glarner		21/11/87	D	34		
30	Alexander González	VEN	13/09/92	M	24	(7)	4
17	Dennis Hediger		22/09/86	M	33		1
29	Andrija Kaludjerović	SRB	05/07/87	A	2	(10)	2
19	Gaëtan Karlen		07/06/93	A	8	(8)	2
22	Christian Leite	BRA	09/11/85	G	4		
23	Marco Mangold		07/04/87	M	1	(4)	
42	Ivan Markovic		15/06/97	A		(2)	
20	Ridge Munsy	COD	09/07/89	A	3	(15)	
21	Nélson Ferreira	POR	26/05/82	M	32	(2)	3
40	Adrien Rawyler		13/06/93	M	1	(1)	
26	Thomas Reinmann		09/04/83	D	25		2
10	Marco Rojas	NZL	05/11/91	M	13	(4)	2
9	Berat Sadik	FIN	14/09/86	A	34	(1)	12
3	Lukas Schenkel		01/04/84	D	4		
14	Nicolas Schindelholz		12/02/88	D	9	(3)	
27	Enrico Schirinzi	ITA	14/11/84	D	12	(1)	1
19	Christian Schneuwly		07/02/88	M	17		4
8	Michael Siegfried		18/02/88	D	24	(2)	2
5	Fulvio Sulmoni		04/01/86	D	28		4
34	Nicola Sutter		08/05/95	M	14	(4)	
28	Andreas Wittwer		05/10/90	M	25	(7)	2

FC Vaduz

1932 • Rheinpark (7,838) • fcvaduz.li
Major honours
Liechtenstein Cup (43) 1949, 1952, 1953, 1954, 1956, 1957, 1958, 1959, 1960, 1961, 1962, 1966, 1967, 1968, 1969, 1970, 1971, 1974, 1980, 1985, 1986, 1988, 1990, 1992, 1995, 1996, 1998, 1999, 2000, 2001, 2002, 2003, 2004, 2005, 2006, 2007, 2008, 2009, 2010, 2011, 2013, 2014, 2015
Coach: Giorgio Contini

2014
20/07	a	Thun	L	0-1	
27/07	h	Zürich	L	1-4	Cecchini
06/08	a	Aarau	D	1-1	Schürpf
10/08	a	Sion	L	0-1	
13/08	h	Luzern	D	1-1	Schürpf
17/08	h	Young Boys	L	0-2	
31/08	a	Grasshoppers	W	1-0	Muntwiler
14/09	h	St Gallen	D	2-2	Grippo, Lang
23/09	a	Basel	L	1-3	Lang (p)
28/09	a	Sion	W	1-0	Burgmeier
05/10	a	Zürich	L	0-3	
19/10	a	Luzern	D	0-0	
26/10	h	Grasshoppers	D	1-1	Schürpf
02/11	a	Young Boys	W	1-0	Neumayr (p)
09/11	h	Basel	L	0-4	
23/11	a	St Gallen	D	3-3	Sutter, Neumayr 2 (1p)
30/11	h	Thun	L	0-1	
07/12	h	Aarau	W	1-0	Neumayr

2015
15/02	a	Aarau	W	1-0	Schürpf
22/02	h	Thun	D	1-1	Burgmeier
25/02	a	Sion	L	0-2	
28/02	a	Basel	L	0-1	
08/03	a	Zürich	D	2-2	Schürpf, Sutter
14/03	a	Luzern	L	0-2	
22/03	h	St Gallen	W	3-1	Burgmeier 2, Stahel
03/04	h	Young Boys	L	0-2	
12/04	a	Grasshoppers	D	1-1	Neumayr
19/04	a	Aarau	L	0-2	
26/04	a	St Gallen	W	2-1	og (Facchinetti), Schürpf
29/04	h	Basel	L	1-3	Pak
02/05	a	Thun	L	0-4	
09/05	a	Sion	L	0-4	
16/05	h	Luzern	L	0-2	
21/05	a	Zürich	D	2-2	Sutter, Schürpf
25/05	h	Grasshoppers	L	0-1	
29/05	a	Young Boys	L	1-2	Hasler

No	Name	Nat	DoB	Pos	Aps	(s)	Gls
15	Nicola Abegglen		16/02/90	A	2	(10)	
30	Naser Aliji	ALB	27/12/93	D	17		
11	Franz Burgmeier	LIE	07/04/82	M	23	(7)	4
12	Ramon Cecchini		30/08/90	M	5	(6)	1
8	Diego Ciccone		21/07/87	M	22	(4)	
3	Simone Grippo		12/12/88	D	24		1
20	Nicolas Hasler	LIE	04/05/91	M	24	(1)	1
18	Andreas Hirzel		25/03/93	G	1		
1	Peter Jehle	LIE	22/01/82	G	28		
4	Daniel Kaufmann	LIE	22/12/90	D	16	(3)	
35	Oliver Klaus		04/05/90	G	7		
21	Hekuran Kryeziu		12/02/93	M	15	(10)	
28	Kristian Kuzmanovic	NED	06/05/88	M	2	(5)	
7	Steven Lang		03/09/87	M	21	(11)	2
27	Philipp Muntwiler		25/02/87	M	33		1
23	Markus Neumayr	GER	26/03/86	M	30	(2)	5
16	Pak Kwang-ryong	PRK	27/09/92	A	11	(8)	1
5	Pavel Pergl	CZE	14/11/77	D	1	(1)	
24	Michele Polverino	LIE	26/09/84	M	3	(1)	
6	Mario Sara	AUT	21/02/82	D	5	(3)	
13	Pascal Schürpf		15/07/89	M	21	(13)	7
22	Florian Stahel		10/03/85	D	32		1
9	Manuel Sutter	AUT	08/03/91	A	13	(13)	3
17	Joel Unterneger		11/02/94	D	16	(5)	
19	Nick von Niederhäusern		28/09/89	D	24	(4)	

BSC Young Boys

1898 • Stade de Suisse (31,789) • bscyb.ch
Major honours
Swiss League (11) 1903, 1909, 1910, 1911, 1920, 1929, 1957, 1958, 1959, 1960, 1986; Swiss Cup (6) 1930, 1945, 1953, 1958, 1977, 1987
Coach: Uli Forte

2014
19/07	a	St Gallen	D	2-2	Kubo, Afum
27/07	h	Aarau	D	1-1	Kubo
03/08	a	Zürich	L	1-2	Gajić (p)
10/08	h	Thun	D	1-1	Frey
13/08	h	Grasshoppers	W	4-0	Nuzzolo 2, Wüthrich, Frey
17/08	a	Vaduz	W	2-0	Frey, Steffen
31/08	a	Basel	L	1-3	Nuzzolo
14/09	h	Luzern	W	3-2	Nuzzolo, Afum, Rochat
24/09	a	Sion	W	1-0	Nuzzolo (p)
28/09	h	Zürich	W	2-1	Steffen, Hoarau
05/10	a	Aarau	L	2-3	Bertone, Steffen
18/10	h	Basel	L	0-1	
02/11	h	Vaduz	L	0-1	
09/11	h	Sion	W	2-1	Gajić, Vilotić
23/11	a	Thun	W	1-0	Hoarau
30/11	h	St Gallen	W	4-2	Hoarau 2 (1p), Vilotić, Steffen
03/12	a	Luzern	W	2-1	Kubo, Steffen
06/12	a	Grasshoppers	W	1-0	Vilotić

2015
07/02	a	Luzern	D	1-1	Vilotić
14/02	h	Grasshoppers	W	4-2	Kubo, Hoarau 2, Steffen
22/02	h	Basel	W	4-2	Gerndt 2, Gajić, Hoarau
01/03	a	Thun	D	0-0	
08/03	h	Sion	W	3-2	Gerndt, Hoarau 2
15/03	a	Aarau	D	1-1	Hoarau
22/03	h	Zürich	W	3-0	Hoarau 2 (1p), Bertone
04/04	a	Vaduz	W	1-0	Hoarau (p)
11/04	a	St Gallen	L	1-3	Gerndt
19/04	h	Thun	W	4-0	Bertone, Steffen 2, Hoarau
26/04	a	Grasshoppers	D	2-2	Kubo, Hoarau
29/04	a	Aarau	D	2-2	Sanogo, Zárate
03/05	a	Zürich	W	1-0	Hoarau (p)
10/05	h	St Gallen	W	3-1	Hoarau (p), Zárate, Nuzzolo
17/05	a	Basel	D	0-0	
21/05	h	Luzern	L	0-1	
25/05	a	Sion	L	2-6	og (Carlitos), Gerndt
29/05	h	Vaduz	W	2-1	Gajić (p), Steffen

No	Name	Nat	DoB	Pos	Aps	(s)	Gls
7	Samuel Afum	GHA	24/12/90	A	9	(10)	2
6	Leonardo Bertone		14/03/94	M	19	(6)	3
93	Marco Bürki		10/07/93	D	2	(3)	
10	Moreno Costanzo		20/02/88	M	6	(6)	
20	Michael Frey		19/07/94	A	5	(2)	3
14	Milan Gajić	SRB	17/11/86	M	29	(4)	4
9	Alexander Gerndt	SWE	14/07/86	A	15	(3)	5
3	Florent Hadergjonaj		31/07/94	D	23	(3)	
99	Guillaume Hoarau	FRA	05/03/84	A	22	(6)	17
24	Yuya Kubo	JPN	24/12/93	A	14	(13)	5
8	Jan Lecjaks	CZE	09/08/90	D	30	(3)	
18	Yvon Mvogo		06/06/94	G	35		
30	Adrian Nikci		10/11/89	M	3	(5)	
29	Raphael Nuzzolo		05/07/83	M	27	(8)	6
21	Alain Rochat		01/02/83	D	17	(5)	1
35	Sekou Sanogo	CIV	05/05/89	M	22	(3)	1
11	Renato Steffen		03/11/91	M	33	(1)	9
16	Tauljant Sulejmanov	MKD	15/11/96	M		(1)	
23	Scott Sutter		13/05/86	D	20	(4)	
4	Milan Vilotić	SRB	21/10/86	D	20		4
17	Matias Vitkieviez		16/05/85	M	1	(2)	
5	Steve von Bergen		10/06/83	D	32		
1	Marco Wölfli		22/08/82	G	1		
22	Gregory Wüthrich		04/12/94	D	5	(4)	1
19	Gonzalo Zárate	ARG	06/08/84	A	6	(15)	2

FC Zürich

1896 • Letzigrund (26,104) • fcz.ch
Major honours
Swiss League (12) 1902, 1924, 1963, 1966, 1968, 1974, 1975, 1976, 1981, 2006, 2007, 2009; Swiss Cup (8) 1966, 1970, 1972, 1973, 1976, 2000, 2005, 2014
Coach: Urs Meier

2014
20/07	h	Grasshoppers	W	1-0	Chiumiento
23/07	h	Thun	W	2-1	Chikhaoui 2
27/07	a	Vaduz	W	4-1	Chiumiento, Rodriguez, Chikhaoui, Chermiti (p)
03/08	h	Young Boys	W	2-1	Chiumiento, Chermiti (p)
09/08	a	Basel	L	1-4	Chermiti
16/08	a	Luzern	D	1-1	Kecojević
31/08	h	St Gallen	W	2-0	Rikan, Etoundi
14/09	h	Sion	W	4-1	Chiumiento 2, Djimsiti, Chermiti
24/09	h	Aarau	D	0-0	
28/09	a	Young Boys	L	1-2	Chikhaoui
05/10	h	Vaduz	W	3-0	Kukeli, Schönbächler 2
19/10	a	Grasshoppers	W	3-1	Etoundi 2, Rodriguez
26/10	h	St Gallen	D	1-1	Chikhaoui (p)
01/11	h	Luzern	L	2-3	Chikhaoui (p), Chermiti
09/11	a	Aarau	W	1-0	Elvedi
22/11	a	Sion	W	3-1	Chiumiento, Etoundi 2
30/11	h	Basel	L	1-2	Chikhaoui (p)
07/12	a	Thun	L	1-2	Etoundi

2015
07/02	a	St Gallen	W	4-1	Etoundi, Schönbächler, Rikan, Sadiku
15/02	h	Thun	L	0-1	
21/02	a	Grasshoppers	W	2-0	Kajević, Chermiti
28/02	h	Aarau	D	0-0	
08/03	a	Vaduz	D	2-2	Nef, Gavranovic
15/03	h	Sion	L	0-1	
22/03	a	Young Boys	L	0-3	
04/04	h	Luzern	L	0-1	
12/04	h	Basel	L	1-5	Etoundi
18/04	h	St Gallen	L	1-2	Etoundi
25/04	a	Aarau	D	0-0	
28/04	a	Sion	W	2-1	Rikan 2 (2p)
03/05	h	Young Boys	L	0-1	
10/05	h	Basel	L	1-2	Kecojević
17/05	a	Thun	D	2-2	Nef, Chikhaoui
21/05	h	Vaduz	D	2-2	Schneuwly, Djimsiti
25/05	a	Luzern	W	1-0	Sadiku
29/05	h	Grasshoppers	W	4-3	Schneuwly, Chermiti 2, Sadiku

No	Name	Nat	DoB	Pos	Aps	(s)	Gls
19	Armin Alesevic		06/03/94	D		(1)	
28	Yanick Brecher		25/05/93	G	11		
26	Cédric Brunner		17/02/94	M	3	(2)	
24	Maurice Brunner		29/01/91	M	1	(6)	
15	Oliver Buff		03/08/92	M	17	(13)	
9	Amine Chermiti	TUN	26/12/87	A	17	(9)	8
17	Yassine Chikhaoui	TUN	22/09/86	M	29	(2)	8
10	Davide Chiumiento		22/11/84	M	27	(4)	6
1	David Da Costa		19/04/86	G	25		
5	Berat Djimsiti		19/02/93	D	31	(2)	2
30	Nico Elvedi		30/09/96	D	12	(4)	1
14	Franck Etoundi	CMR	30/08/90	A	18	(8)	9
7	Mario Gavranovic		24/11/89	A	6	(5)	1
22	Asmir Kajević	MNE	15/02/90	M	14	(2)	1
25	Ivan Kecojević	MNE	10/04/88	D	27		2
21	Mike Kleiber		04/02/93	M	2	(2)	
16	Philippe Koch		08/02/91	D	27	(2)	
20	Burim Kukeli	ALB	16/01/84	M	20	(1)	1
13	Alain Nef		06/02/82	D	27		2
18	Avi Rikan	ISR	10/09/88	M	13	(8)	4
34	Francisco Rodriguez		14/09/95	M	14	(14)	2
23	Patrick Rossini		02/04/88	A		(6)	
11	Armando Sadiku	ALB	27/05/91	A	3	(11)	3
29	Sangoné Sarr	SEN	07/07/92	M	2	(1)	
8	Christian Schneuwly		07/02/88	M	17	(1)	2
27	Marco Schönbächler		11/01/90	M	19		3
37	Gilles Yapi Yapo	CIV	30/01/82	M	14		

Top goalscorers

22	Shkëlzen Gashi (Basel)
17	Marco Schneuwly (Luzern)
	Guillaume Hoarau (Young Boys)
16	Moussa Konaté (Sion)
13	Munas Dabbur (Grasshoppers)
12	Marco Streller (Basel)
	Darío Lezcano (Luzern)
	Berat Sadik (Thun)
11	Caio (Grasshoppers)
10	Breel Embolo (Basel)

Promoted club

FC Lugano

1908 • Cornaredo (10,500) • fclugano.com
Major honours
Swiss League (3) 1938, 1941, 1949; Swiss Cup (3) 1931, 1968, 1993
Coach: Livio Bordoli

Second level final table 2014/15

		Pld	W	D	L	F	A	Pts
1	FC Lugano	36	22	8	6	64	31	74
2	FC Wohlen	36	20	4	12	57	43	64
3	FC Winterthur	36	15	8	13	65	49	53
4	FC Schaffhausen	36	13	8	15	55	54	47
5	FC Lausanne-Sport	36	12	8	16	47	57	44
6	FC Le Mont	36	10	9	17	39	56	39
7	FC Chiasso	36	9	12	15	30	49	39
8	FC Wil 1900	36	9	10	17	47	63	37
9	FC Biel-Bienne	36	7	12	17	39	52	33
10	Servette FC	36	20	7	9	51	40	67

NB Servette FC did not receive licence for 2015/16 and were therefore placed last.

DOMESTIC CUP

Schweizer Cup/Coupe de Suisse 2014/15

FIRST ROUND

(23/08/14)
Baden 0-3 St Gallen
Breitenrain 2-3 Thun
Buochs 1-0 Frauenfeld
Cham 2-1 Düdingen
CS Italien 0-4 Basel
Dietikon 0-4 Wil
Eschenbach 1-3 Winterthur
Hergiswil 2-1 Tuggen
Mendrisio 0-2 Chiasso
Muri 0-3 Wohlen
Neuchâtel Xamax 1-1 Étoile Carouge *(aet; 4-2 on pens)*
Old Boys Basel 1-2 Lugano
Pratteln 0-8 Black Stars
Rothrist 0-1 Le Mont
Stade Lausanne-Ouchy 0-1 Münsingen
Stade Payerne 1-4 Schötz
Terre Sainte 0-1 Biel-Bienne
Vedeggio Calcio 0-2 Grasshoppers
Veltheim 2-3 Herisau *(aet)*
YF Juventus 1-3 Lausanne-Sport

(24/08/14)
ASI Audax-Friul 0-2 Locarno
Bavois 0-1 Young Boys
Greifensee 2-1 Subingen
Konolfingen 0-9 Luzern
La Chaux-de-Fonds 1-3 Sion
Murten 0-4 Stade Nyonnais
Nottwil 0-5 Köniz
Perly-Certoux 2-4 Schaffhausen
Schönbühl 0-7 Zürich
Sirnach 0-8 Servette
Taverne 1-7 Aarau
Tägerwilen 4-1 Visp

SECOND ROUND

(19/09/14)
Lausanne-Sport 0-1 Thun

(20/09/14)
Biel-Bienne 0-1 Sion
Buochs 1-0 Young Boys
Chiasso 0-1 Aarau
Henau 2-3 Wil *(aet)*
Hergiswil 1-3 Schötz
Münsingen 1-0 Locarno
Schaffhausen 3-5 Luzern *(aet)*
Tägerwilen 3-9 Lugano

(21/09/14)
Black Stars 1-2 Zürich *(aet)*
Greifensee 2-3 Cham
Le Mont 1-2 St Gallen
Neuchâtel Xamax 3-5 Grasshoppers
Servette 1-2 Wohlen
Stade Nyonnais 1-2 Köniz
Winterthur 0-4 Basel

THIRD ROUND

(29/10/14)
Lugano 0-1 Grasshoppers *(aet)*
Luzern 1-2 Aarau
St Gallen 2-1 Thun *(aet)*
Wohlen 1-3 Basel

(30/10/14)
Buochs 2-0 Schötz
Köniz 0-3 Sion
Münsingen 3-2 Wil

(03/12/14)
Cham 0-5 Zürich

QUARTER-FINALS

(04/03/15)
Münsingen 1-6 Basel *(Plüss 81; Hamoudi 7, Kakitani 24, 43, 59, Embolo 34, Delgado 41)*
Zürich 1-0 Grasshoppers *(Rodriguez 96) (aet)*

(05/03/15)
Sion 2-1 Aarau *(Konaté 3, Fernandes 27; Senger 90+4)*

(11/03/15)
Buochs 0-5 St Gallen *(Sikorski 27, 54, Rodriguez 44, Aratore 57, Tafer 88)*

SEMI-FINALS

(07/04/15)
Zürich 0-1 Sion *(Konaté 49)*

(08/04/15)
St Gallen 1-3 Basel *(Čavuševič 86; Gashi 14, 60, Mutsch 45og)*

FINAL

(07/06/15)
St Jakob-Park, Basel
FC SION 3 *(Konaté 18, Fernandes 50, Carlitos 60)*
FC BASEL 0
Referee: *Hänni*
SION: *Vanins, Zverotić, Lacroix, Modou, Ziegler, Salatic, Carlitos, Kouassi, Fernandes (Perrier 73), Assifuah (Follonier 75), Konaté (Christofi 85)*
BASEL: *Vailati, Xhaka (Delgado 74), Schär, Suchý, Traoré, Frei, Zuffi, Callà (Hamoudi 53), Elneny, Gashi, Streller (Albian Ajeti 74)*
Red cards: *Sauro (66), Sio (99)*

Cup final specialists Sion celebrate their 3-0 win against champions Basel at St Jakob-Park

TURKEY
Türkiye Futbol Federasyönü (TFF)

Address	Hasan Doğan Milli Takımlar Kamp ve Eğitim Tesisleri Riva, Beykoz TR-İstanbul	**President**	Yıldırım Demirören
		General secretary	Kadir Kardaş
		Media officer	İlker Uğur
		Year of formation	1923
Tel	+90 216 554 5100		
Fax	+90 216 319 1945		
E-mail	iletisim@tff.org		
Website	tff.org		

SÜPER LIG CLUBS

 1 Akhisar Belediyespor

 2 Balıkesirspor

 3 Beşiktaş JK

 4 Bursaspor

 5 Eskişehirspor

 6 Fenerbahçe SK

 7 Galatasaray AŞ

 8 Gaziantepspor

 9 Gençlerbirliği SK

 10 İstanbul Başakşehir

 11 Kardemir Karabükspor

 12 Kasımpaşa SK

 13 Kayseri Erciyesspor

 14 Konyaspor

 15 Mersin İdman Yurdu

 16 Rizespor

 17 Sivasspor

 18 Trabzonspor AŞ

PROMOTED CLUBS

 19 Kayserispor

 20 Osmanlıspor

 21 Antalyaspor

KEY:

 – UEFA Champions League

– UEFA Europa League

– Promoted

– Relegated

Double glory for Galatasaray

One of the most exciting Süper Lig title races for years ended in triumph for Galatasaray AŞ, who, thanks to a burst of six successive victories in the run-in, became the first club to win 20 Turkish titles, moving one ahead of arch-rivals and runners-up Fenerbahçe SK.

The other member of Istanbul's Big Three, Beşiktaş JK, also challenged strongly in the league, but the domestic honours belonged exclusively to Galatasaray, who capped a memorable campaign with a 3-2 victory over Bursaspor, in Bursa, to retain the Turkish Cup and complete their first double for 15 years.

Cim Bom beat Fenerbahçe to record 20th title

Beşiktaş also miss out in thrilling three-horse race

Free-scoring Bursaspor defeated in Turkish Cup final

Domestic league

There was little to choose between Galatasaray, Fenerbahçe and Beşiktaş in a riveting three-horse race for the Süper Lig crown. The Istanbul giants were neck-and-neck virtually throughout, with Beşiktaş, led by Slaven Bilić, front-running for several weeks and Fenerbahçe, under little-known coach İsmail Kartal, taking the lead intermittently before, in the final furlong, Galatasaray galloped clear.

The Red-and-Yellows had replaced Roberto Mancini with another Italian coach, Cesare Prandelli, in the summer, but after a poor showing in Europe, the club made another change in late autumn, appointing ex-midfielder Hamza Hamzaoğlu. It worked a treat as the team put together a lengthy unbeaten run that lifted them to the Süper Lig summit in February. Although that lead was subsequently relinquished, they came good again when it mattered most, winning six successive matches without conceding to claim that coveted 20th title. The crowning moment was something of an anti-climax, however, as victory was sealed when Fenerbahçe drew 2-2 with fourth-placed İstanbul Başakşehir – a day after Galatasaray had beaten Beşiktaş 2-0 at home.

While Galatasaray and Fenerbahçe shared home wins, Beşiktaş lost all four matches against their two rivals. In fairness, Bilić's side, spearheaded by the prolific Demba Ba, did well to challenge for so long given that they spent all season playing away from home while awaiting the construction of their new stadium. Fenerbahçe also deserved credit for sticking to their task after bullets were fired at their team bus, injuring the driver, following a 5-1 win at Rizespor in early April – a shocking incident that led to a one-week postponement of the Süper Lig.

Domestic cup

Trabzonspor AŞ, under ex-Fenerbahçe coach Ersun Yanal, finished fifth in the league on the head-to-head rule above high-scoring Bursaspor, but the latter, led by ex-Trabzonspor boss Şenol Güneş and featuring the Süper Lig's leading marksman in 22-goal Fernandão, had the chance to snatch back the UEFA Europa League place by defeating Galatasaray in the Turkish Cup final. Bursaspor had spectacularly eliminated holders Fenerbahçe with a 3-0 away win in the semi-finals, but on home turf in the final they could not serve up an encore. Fernandão put them 1-0 up, but the match would belong to Galatasaray's Turkish international Burak Yılmaz, who, not for the first time, raised his game for the big occasion, scoring a hat-trick in a 3-2 win that completed Cim Bom's first double since their famous treble-winning season (UEFA Cup included) of 1999/2000.

Europe

For all their domestic success, Galatasaray endured a miserable time abroad. Handed automatic entry to the UEFA Champions League group stage because of Fenerbahçe's European ban, they registered just one point – thanks to a late Burak strike at RSC Anderlecht – and conceded 19 goals. Beşiktaş lost out narrowly to Arsenal FC in the UEFA Champions League play-offs, but they got the better of two other English clubs, Tottenham Hotspur FC and Liverpool FC, en route to the UEFA Europa League round of 16, where they fell to Club Brugge KV. The Black Eagles were Turkey's last survivors, Trabzonspor having been trounced by SSC Napoli a round earlier.

National team

A terrible start to Turkey's UEFA EURO 2016 qualifying campaign, which began with an error-strewn 3-0 defeat in Reykjavik, left Fatih Terim's side with a mountain to climb. A recovery of sorts was staged as home and away wins against Kazakhstan sandwiched a 1-1 draw against the Netherlands in Amsterdam – with Burak (again) supplying the crucial goal – but despite the exciting emergence of playmaker Hakan Çalhanoğlu and a favourable closing fixture schedule, Turkey still had their work cut out simply to reach the play-offs.

DOMESTIC SEASON AT A GLANCE

Süper Lig 2014/15 final table

		Pld	Home					Away					Total					Pts
			W	D	L	F	A	W	D	L	F	A	W	D	L	F	A	
1	**Galatasaray AŞ**	**34**	**13**	**3**	**1**	**32**	**17**	**11**	**2**	**4**	**28**	**18**	**24**	**5**	**5**	**60**	**35**	**77**
2	Fenerbahçe SK	34	13	3	1	30	14	9	5	3	30	15	22	8	4	60	29	74
3	Beşiktaş JK	34	9	5	3	30	19	12	1	4	25	13	21	6	7	55	32	69
4	İstanbul Başakşehir	34	8	8	1	31	15	7	6	4	18	15	15	14	5	49	30	59
5	Trabzonspor AŞ	34	12	3	2	38	26	3	9	5	20	22	15	12	7	58	48	57
6	Bursaspor	34	10	5	2	43	18	6	4	7	26	26	16	9	9	69	44	57
7	Mersin İdman Yurdu	34	8	4	5	29	22	5	4	8	25	26	13	8	13	54	48	47
8	Konyaspor	34	9	4	4	20	16	3	6	8	10	23	12	10	12	30	39	46
9	Gençlerbirliği SK	34	6	6	5	25	18	4	4	9	21	26	10	10	14	46	44	40
10	Gaziantepspor	34	6	3	8	15	24	5	4	8	16	24	11	7	16	31	48	40
11	Eskişehirspor	34	6	4	7	22	23	3	8	6	23	29	9	12	13	45	52	39
12	Akhisar Belediyespor	34	5	8	4	23	20	4	3	10	18	31	9	11	14	41	51	38
13	Kasımpaşa SK	34	6	5	5	32	32	3	4	10	24	41	9	10	15	56	73	37
14	Sivasspor	34	4	6	7	20	20	5	3	9	23	30	9	9	16	43	50	36
15	Rizespor	34	3	5	9	17	31	6	4	7	24	24	9	9	16	41	55	36
16	Kardemir Karabükspor	34	6	4	7	20	19	1	3	13	24	45	7	7	20	44	64	28
17	Kayseri Erciyesspor	34	4	3	10	25	31	1	9	7	18	31	5	12	17	43	62	27
18	Balıkesirspor	34	4	4	9	25	31	2	5	10	23	38	6	9	19	48	69	27

European qualification 2015/16

Champion/Cup winner: Galatasaray AŞ (group stage)
Fenerbahçe SK (third qualifying round)

Beşiktaş JK (group stage)
İstanbul Başakşehir (third qualifying round)
Trabzonspor AŞ (second qualifying round)

Top scorer Fernandão (Bursaspor), 22 goals
Relegated clubs Balıkesirspor, Kayseri Erciyesspor, Kardemir Karabükspor
Promoted clubs Kayserispor, Osmanlıspor, Antalyaspor
Cup final Galatasaray AŞ 3-2 Bursaspor

Player of the season

Fernando Muslera
(Galatasaray AŞ)

Galatasaray were well served by several stalwarts in their Süper Lig triumph, with Selçuk İnan, Burak Yılmaz, Hakan Balta and Wesley Sneijder all doing their bit. But it was the heroics of goalkeeper Muslera during the six-match winning streak at the end of the campaign, in which he kept his goal intact throughout to secure 18 crucial points, that tipped the balance of the title race in Galatasaray's favour. The Uruguay international had to miss the Turkish Cup final, however, due to Copa América commitments.

Newcomer of the season

Oğulcan Çağlayan
(Kayseri Erciyesspor)

Erciyesspor were unable to retain their Süper Lig status in 2014/15, going down with Balıkesirspor and Kardemir Karabükspor, but they did make some waves during the final weeks of the campaign when new boss Fatih Tekke handed an opportunity to tall, 19-year-old striker Oğulcan. A prolific marksman with Turkey's junior selections while on the books of Gaziantepspor, the 'next Ibrahimović' seized his opportunity with aplomb, demonstrating rare skill and enterprise and scoring three Süper Lig goals.

Team of the season
(4-5-1)

Coach: Hamza Hamzaoğlu (Galatasaray)

Muslera (Galatasaray)

Gökhan (Fenerbahçe) **Serdar** (Bursaspor) **Hakan** (Galatasaray) **Caner Erkin** (Fenerbahçe)

Mehmet Topal (Fenerbahçe) **Mehmet** (Trabzonspor) **Sneijder** (Galatasaray)

Volkan (Bursaspor) **Gökhan** (Beşiktaş)

Fernandão (Bursaspor)

NATIONAL TEAM

International tournament appearances
FIFA World Cup (2) 1954, 2002 (3rd)
UEFA European Championship (3) 1996, 2000 (qtr-finals), 2008 (semi-finals)

Top five all-time caps
Rüştü Reçber (120); Hakan Şükür (112); Bülent Korkmaz (102); Tugay Kerimoğlu (94); **Emre Belözoğlu** (93)

Top five all-time goals
Hakan Şükür (51); Tuncay Şanlı (22); Lefter Küçükandonyadis (21); Cemil Turan, Metin Oktay & Nihat Kahveci (19)

Results 2014/15

03/09/14	Denmark	A	Odense	W	2-1	Olcay (54), Ozan (90+2)
09/09/14	Iceland (ECQ)	A	Reykjavik	L	0-3	
10/10/14	Czech Republic (ECQ)	H	Istanbul	L	1-2	Umut (8)
13/10/14	Latvia (ECQ)	A	Riga	D	1-1	Bilal (47)
12/11/14	Brazil	H	Istanbul	L	0-4	
16/11/14	Kazakhstan (ECQ)	H	Istanbul	W	3-1	Burak (26p, 29), Serdar (83)
28/03/15	Netherlands (ECQ)	A	Amsterdam	D	1-1	Burak (37)
31/03/15	Luxembourg	A	Luxembourg	W	2-1	Mevlüt (4), Hakan Çalhanoğlu (87)
08/06/15	Bulgaria	H	Istanbul	W	4-0	Hakan Çalhanoğlu (49, 54), Burak (56, 80)
12/06/15	Kazakhstan (ECQ)	A	Almaty	W	1-0	Arda (83)

Appearances 2014/15

Coach: Fatih Terim	04/09/53		Den	ISL	CZE	LVA	Bra	KAZ	NED	Lux	Bul	KAZ	Caps	Goals
Onur Kıvrak	01/01/88	Trabzonspor	G	G									12	-
Gökhan Gönül	04/01/85	Fenerbahçe	D	D	D	D			D		D	D	51	1
Ömer Toprak	21/07/89	Leverkusen (GER)	D	D 59*									23	2
Ersan Gülüm	17/05/87	Beşiktaş	D	D					s69				7	-
Caner Erkin	04/10/88	Fenerbahçe	D89	D	D	D	s46	D	D	D			38	2
Oğuzhan Özyakup	23/09/92	Beşiktaş	M46		s79	M40							10	-
Mehmet Topal	03/03/86	Fenerbahçe	M	M76	D	D	M78	s74	M		s46	M46	49	-
Selçuk İnan	10/02/85	Galatasaray	M76	M65	M79		s46	M	M	s70	s46	M	44	5
Olcay Şahan	26/05/87	Beşiktaş	M68		M66	M59		M85		M58	s69		18	2
Ahmet İlhan Özek	01/01/88	Karabükspor	M46										5	1
Burak Yılmaz	15/07/85	Galatasaray	A71	A				A	A79		s46	A	40	18
Emre Belözoğlu	07/09/80	Fenerbahçe	s46	M									93	9
Olcan Adın	30/09/85	Galatasaray	s46	M65	s68								10	1
Arda Turan	30/01/87	Atlético (ESP)	s68	M	M	M	M	M		M88	M69	M	81	14
Mustafa Pektemek	11/08/88	Beşiktaş	s71	s65									12	1
Ozan Tufan	23/03/95	Bursaspor	s76	s65	M	M	M	D	M	D	M84	M64	13	1
İsmail Köybaşı	10/07/89	Beşiktaş	s89				D						13	-
Hakan Çalhanoğlu	08/02/94	Leverkusen (GER)		s76					s61	M	M78	M	9	3
Tolga Zengin	10/10/83	Beşiktaş			G								9	-
Semih Kaya	24/02/91	Galatasaray			D	D	D	D			D	D75	23	-
Gökhan Töre	20/01/92	Beşiktaş			M68	M70		s81	M				23	-
Umut Bulut	15/03/83	Galatasaray			A	A	A85	A74		s46		s64	36	10
Muhammet Demir	10/01/92	Gaziantepspor			s66						s84		2	-
Volkan Babacan	11/08/88	İstanbul Başakşehir				G	s46	G	G		G	G	6	-
Bilal Kısa	22/06/83	Akhisar				s40	M46						7	1
Adem Büyük	30/08/87	Kasımpaşa				s59							4	-
Hamit Altıntop	08/12/82	Galatasaray				s70	D46						82	7
Volkan Demirel	27/10/81	Fenerbahçe					G46						63	-
Bekir İrtegün	20/04/84	Fenerbahçe					D						10	-
Mevlüt Erdinç	25/02/87	St-Étienne (FRA)					A46			A46	A46		33	8
Volkan Şen	07/07/87	Bursaspor					s46	M81	M61	s46 /75	M46	s46	8	-
Tarık Çamdal	24/03/91	Galatasaray					s78						6	1
Alper Potuk	08/04/91	Fenerbahçe					s85						11	-
Serdar Aziz	23/10/90	Bursaspor						D	D69		D	D	4	1
Mehmet Ekici	25/03/90	Trabzonspor						s85		M70	s78		12	-
Hakan Balta	23/03/83	Galatasaray							D			D	39	2
Colin Kazim-Richards	26/08/86	Feyenoord (NED)							s79	M46			37	2
Mert Günok	01/03/89	Fenerbahçe								G			6	-
Mahmut Tekdemir	20/01/88	İstanbul Başakşehir								D			1	-
Şener Özbayraklı	23/01/90	Bursaspor								D			1	-
Enes Ünal	10/05/97	Bursaspor								s58			1	-
Eren Albayrak	23/04/91	Rizespor								s75			1	-
Ümit Kurt	02/05/91	Sivasspor								s88			1	-
Emre Taşdemir	08/08/95	Bursaspor									D	s75	2	-
Yasin Öztekin	19/03/87	Galatasaray									M46			-

EUROPE

Galatasaray AŞ

Group D

Match 1 - RSC Anderlecht (BEL)
H 1-1 *Burak Yılmaz (90+1)*
Muslera, Felipe Melo, Dzemaili, Selçuk İnan (Umut Bulut 72), Sneijder, Alex Telles (Tarık Çamdal 79), Burak Yılmaz, Pandev (Bruma 57), Chedjou, Semih Kaya, Veysel Sarı. Coach: Cesare Prandelli (ITA)
Match 2 - Arsenal FC (ENG)
A 1-4 *Burak Yılmaz (63p)*
Muslera, Felipe Melo, Dzemaili, Sneijder, Alex Telles, Burak Yılmaz, Pandev (Bruma 68), Chedjou, Semih Kaya, Yekta Kurtuluş (Hamit Altıntop 46), Veysel Sarı (Umut Bulut 68). Coach: Cesare Prandelli (ITA)
Match 3 - Borussia Dortmund (GER)
H 0-4
Muslera, Felipe Melo, Hamit Altıntop (Dzemaili 61), Selçuk İnan, Sneijder, Alex Telles (Yasin Öztekin 62), Burak Yılmaz, Pandev (Emre Çolak 78), Chedjou, Semih Kaya, Tarık Çamdal. Coach: Cesare Prandelli (ITA)
Match 4 - Borussia Dortmund (GER)
A 1-4 *Hakan Balta (70)*
Muslera, Felipe Melo, Hamit Altıntop (Yasin Öztekin 82), Dzemaili, Selçuk İnan, Umut Bulut (Burak Yılmaz 85), Sneijder, Chedjou, Hakan Balta, Semih Kaya, Tarık Çamdal. Coach: Cesare Prandelli (ITA)
Match 5 - RSC Anderlecht (BEL)
A 0-2
Muslera, Felipe Melo, Hamit Altıntop (Furkan Özçal 90), Selçuk İnan, Sneijder, Bruma (Umut Bulut 75), Alex Telles, Burak Yılmaz, Chedjou, Semih Kaya, Tarık Çamdal. Coach: Cesare Prandelli (ITA)
Red card: Selçuk İnan 83
Match 6 - Arsenal FC (ENG)
H 1-4 *Sneijder (88)*
Sinan Bolat, Felipe Melo, Umut Bulut, Sneijder, Bruma (Olcan Adın 77), Alex Telles, Burak Yılmaz (Yasin Öztekin 46), Hakan Balta, Semih Kaya, Emre Çolak, Tarık Çamdal (Hamit Altıntop 46). Coach: Hamza Hamzaoğlu (TUR)

Beşiktaş JK

Third qualifying round - Feyenoord (NED)
A 2-1 *Mustafa Pektemek (13), Kerim Koyunlu (71)*
Tolga Zengin, Serdar Kurtuluş, Olcay Şahan (İsmail Köybaşı 75), Mustafa Pektemek, Hutchinson, Oğuzhan Özyakup (Ba 59), Franco, Necip Uysal, Kerim Koyunlu (Cenk Tosun 89), Ersan Gülüm, Ramon. Coach: Slaven Bilić (CRO)
H 3-1 *Ba (28, 80, 86)*
Tolga Zengin, Kavlak, Ba (Cenk Tosun 87), Olcay Şahan, Mustafa Pektemek (Oğuzhan Özyakup 85), Hutchinson, Franco, Necip Uysal, Kerim Koyunlu (İsmail Köybaşı 74), Ersan Gülüm, Ramon. Coach: Slaven Bilić (CRO)

Play-offs - Arsenal FC (ENG)
H 0-0
Tolga Zengin, İsmail Köybaşı, Kavlak, Ba, Olcay Şahan (Gökhan Töre 73), Mustafa Pektemek (Cenk Tosun 88), Oğuzhan Özyakup (Kerim Koyunlu 81), Franco, Necip Uysal, Ersan Gülüm, Ramon. Coach: Slaven Bilić (CRO)
A 0-1
Tolga Zengin, İsmail Köybaşı, Kavlak (Necip Uysal 77), Ba, Olcay Şahan (Gökhan Töre 63), Mustafa Pektemek (Cenk Tosun 87), Hutchinson, Oğuzhan Özyakup, Franco, Ersan Gülüm, Ramon. Coach: Slaven Bilić (CRO)

Group C

Match 1 - Asteras Tripolis FC (GRE)
H 1-1 *Gökhan Töre (33)*
Tolga Zengin, Sivok, Gökhan Töre, Kavlak, Olcay Şahan (Kerim Koyunlu 85), Mustafa Pektemek (Cenk Tosun 30), Hutchinson, Oğuzhan Özyakup (Sosa 69), Franco, Necip Uysal, Ramon. Coach: Slaven Bilić (CRO)
Match 2 - Tottenham Hotspur FC (ENG)
A 1-1 *Ba (89p)*
Tolga Zengin, Serdar Kurtuluş, Sosa, Sivok, Gökhan Töre (Kerim Koyunlu 82), Kavlak (Oğuzhan Özyakup 65), Ba, Olcay Şahan (Mustafa Pektemek 72), Hutchinson, Franco, Ramon. Coach: Slaven Bilić (CRO)
Match 3 - FK Partizan (SRB)
A 4-0 *Kavlak (18), Ba (45), Oğuzhan Özyakup (52), Gökhan Töre (54)*
Tolga Zengin, Sivok, Gökhan Töre (Kerim Koyunlu 64), Kavlak, Ba (Cenk Tosun 69), Olcay Şahan, Hutchinson, Oğuzhan Özyakup (İsmail Köybaşı 78), Franco, Necip Uysal, Ramon. Coach: Slaven Bilić (CRO)
Match 4 - FK Partizan (SRB)
H 2-1 *Ba (57p, 62)*
Cenk Gönen, İsmail Köybaşı, Sivok, Gökhan Töre (Necip Uysal 90), Kavlak, Ba, Olcay Şahan (Mustafa Pektemek 58), Hutchinson, Oğuzhan Özyakup (Sosa 70), Franco, Ramon. Coach: Slaven Bilić (CRO)
Match 5 - Asteras Tripolis FC (GRE)
A 2-2 *Ba (15), Gökhan Töre (61p)*
Cenk Gönen, Serdar Kurtuluş, Sosa (Oğuzhan Özyakup 72), Gökhan Töre (Necip Uysal 86), Kavlak, Ba, Olcay Şahan (Kerim Koyunlu 64), Hutchinson, Franco, Ersan Gülüm, Ramon. Coach: Slaven Bilić (CRO)
Red card: Hutchinson 72
Match 6 - Tottenham Hotspur FC (ENG)
H 1-0 *Cenk Tosun (59)*
Tolga Zengin, Serdar Kurtuluş, Sosa, Gökhan Töre (İsmail Köybaşı 84), Olcay Şahan, Franco, Necip Uysal, Kerim Koyunlu (Furkan Yaman 90+3), Ersan Gülüm (Atınç Nukan 46), Cenk Tosun, Ramon. Coach: Slaven Bilić (CRO)

Round of 32 - Liverpool FC (ENG)
A 0-1
Cenk Gönen, Serdar Kurtuluş, Sosa (Oğuzhan Özyakup 60), Gökhan Töre, Kavlak, Ba, Olcay Şahan (Kerim Koyunlu 72), Hutchinson, Franco, Ersan Gülüm, Ramon. Coach: Slaven Bilić (CRO)
H 1-0 *Arslan (72) (aet; 5-4 on pens)*
Cenk Gönen, Serdar Kurtuluş, Sosa (Arslan 61), Gökhan Töre, Kavlak, Ba, Olcay Şahan (Kerim Koyunlu 106), Hutchinson, Franco, Necip Uysal, Opare. Coach: Slaven Bilić (CRO)

Round of 16 - Club Brugge KV (BEL)
A 1-2 *Gökhan Töre (46)*
Cenk Gönen, Serdar Kurtuluş, Gökhan Töre, Kavlak, Ba, Olcay Şahan (Mustafa Pektemek 83), Oğuzhan Özyakup (Kerim Koyunlu73), Arslan, Necip Uysal, Ersan Gülüm, Opare. Coach: Slaven Bilić (CRO)
H 1-3 *Ramon (48)*
Tolga Zengin, Gökhan Töre, Kavlak, Ba, Olcay Şahan, Mustafa Pektemek (Cenk Tosun 74), Arslan, Franco, Necip Uysal, Ramon, Opare (Kerim Koyunlu71). Coach: Slaven Bilić (CRO)
Red card: Olcay Şahan 90+2

Trabzonspor AŞ

Play-offs - FC Rostov (RUS)
H 2-0 *Medjani (37), Cardozo (73)*
Onur Kıvrak, Bosingwa, Medjani, Cardozo (Deniz Yılmaz 84), Soner Aydoğdu, Sefa Yılmaz, Constant (Salih Dursun 77), Belkalem, Mustafa Yumlu, Yusuf Erdoğan (Fatih Atik 67), Musa Nizam. Coach: Vahid Halilhodžić (BIH)
A 0-0
Onur Kıvrak, Aykut Demir (Mustafa Yumlu 19), Medjani, Soner Aydoğdu (Batuhan Artarslan 80), Sefa Yılmaz (Cardozo 70), Deniz Yılmaz, Belkalem, Salih Dursun, Zeki Yavru, Fatih Atik, Musa Nizam. Coach: Vahid Halilhodžić (BIH)

Group L

Match 1 - FC Metalist Kharkiv (UKR)
A 2-1 *Constant (25), Papadopoulos (90+4)*
Onur Kıvrak, Medjani, Cardozo (Yatabaré 58), Sefa Yılmaz, Constant, Belkalem, Waris (Yusuf Erdoğan 82), Papadopoulos, Salih Dursun (Mehmet Ekici 71), Zeki Yavru, Musa Nizam. Coach: Vahid Halilhodžić (BIH)
Match 2 - Legia Warszawa (POL)
H 0-1
Onur Kıvrak (Fatih Öztürk 64), Bosingwa, Mehmet Ekici (Yatabaré 76), Medjani, Cardozo, Constant, Belkalem, Waris, Papadopoulos, Fatih Atik (Sefa Yılmaz 46), Musa Nizam. Coach: Vahid Halilhodžić (BIH)
Match 3 - KSC Lokeren OV (BEL)
H 2-0 *Yatabaré (54), Constant (87)*
Fatih Öztürk, Bosingwa, Mehmet Ekici (Salih Dursun 73), Medjani, Cardozo (Sefa Yılmaz 82), Constant (Soner Aydoğdu 88), Belkalem, Waris, Papadopoulos, Zeki Yavru, Yatabaré. Coach: Jacky Bonnevay (BIH)
Match 4 - KSC Lokeren OV (BEL)
A 1-1 *Waris (45+2)*
Fatih Öztürk, Bosingwa, Mehmet Ekici (Salih Dursun 76), Medjani, Constant, Belkalem, Waris, Papadopoulos, Fatih Atik (Sefa Yılmaz 86), Musa Nizam, Yatabaré (Cardozo 90+3). Coach: Vahid Halilhodžić (BIH)
Match 5 - FC Metalist Kharkiv (UKR)
H 3-1 *Belkalem (36), Mehmet Ekici (86), Goryainov (90+5og)*
Fatih Öztürk, Bosingwa, Mehmet Ekici, Medjani, Cardozo (Sefa Yılmaz 59), Soner Aydoğdu (Fatih Atik 59), Belkalem, Waris (Musa Nizam 88), Papadopoulos, Yusuf Erdoğan, Yatabaré. Coach: Ersun Yanal (TUR)
Red card: Medjani 77
Match 6 - Legia Warszawa (POL)
A 0-2
Fatih Öztürk, Bosingwa, Aykut Demir, Mehmet Ekici, Cardozo, Sefa Yılmaz (İshak Doğan 86), Constant, Belkalem, Salih Dursun (Fatih Atik 46), Musa Nizam, Yatabaré. Coach: Ersun Yanal (TUR)
Red card: Mehmet Ekici 90+1

Round of 32 - SSC Napoli (ITA)
H 0-4
Hakan Arıkan, Bosingwa, Aykut Demir, Medjani, Cardozo, Soner Aydoğdu (Zeki Yavru 85), Sefa Yılmaz, Özer Hurmacı (Musa Nizam 90+2), Fatih Atik (Salih Dursun 90+2), İshak Doğan, Erkan Zengin. Coach: Ersun Yanal (TUR)
A 0-1
Hakan Arıkan, Bosingwa, Aykut Demir, Mehmet Ekici, Medjani, Cardozo, Özer Hurmacı, Salih Dursun (Zeki Yavru 88), Fatih Atik (Soner Aydoğdu 77), İshak Doğan, Erkan Zengin (Sefa Yılmaz 84). Coach: Ersun Yanal (TUR)

DOMESTIC LEAGUE CLUB-BY-CLUB

Kardemir Karabükspor

EUROPA
LEAGUE

Third qualifying round - Rosenborg BK (NOR)
H 0-0
Waterman, Emre Güngör, Yiğit İncedemir, Mabiala, Traoré (Hakan Özmert 69), Ahmet İlhan Özek, Kumbela (Onur Ayık 76), Sow, Erdem Özgenç, Kayhan, Erkan Kaş. Coach: Tolunay Kafkas (TUR)
A 1-1 Hakan Özmert (35)
Waterman, Emre Güngör, Yiğit İncedemir, Mabiala, Traoré (Erkan Kaş 66), Hakan Özmert (Onur Ayık 81), Ahmet İlhan Özek, Kumbela (Murat Akça 86), Sow, Erdem Özgenç, Kayhan. Coach: Tolunay Kafkas (TUR)

Play-offs - AS Saint-Étienne (FRA)
H 1-0 Kumbela (60)
Waterman, Emre Güngör, Yiğit İncedemir, Mabiala, Traoré (Hakan Özmert 79), Ahmet İlhan Özek (Viola 73), Kumbela (Akpala 89), Sow, Erdem Özgenç, Kayhan, Erkan Kaş. Coach: Tolunay Kafkas (TUR)
A 0-1 (aet; 3-4 on pens)
Waterman, Emre Güngör, Yiğit İncedemir, Mabiala, Traoré (Aykut Akgün 105), Ahmet İlhan Özek, Kumbela (Akpala 46), Sow, Erdem Özgenç, Kayhan, Erkan Kaş (Hakan Özmert 46). Coach: Tolunay Kafkas (TUR)

Bursaspor

EUROPA
LEAGUE

Second qualifying round - FC Chikhura Sachkhere (GEO)
H 0-0
Harun Tekin, Civelli, Belluschi, Traoré, Fernandão (Enes Ünal 56), Volkan Şen, Şener Özbayraklı, Behich, İbrahim Öztürk, Bekir Yılmaz (Ozan Tufan 82), Aydın Karabulut (Ferhat Kiraz 46). Coach: Şenol Güneş (TUR)
A 0-0 (aet; 1-4 on pens)
Harun Tekin, Civelli, Şamil Çinaz, Traoré, Enes Ünal (Mustafa Altıntaş 80), Volkan Şen, Şener Özbayraklı, Behich, İbrahim Öztürk, Ferhat Kiraz, Bekir Yılmaz (Ozan Tufan 53). Coach: Şenol Güneş (TUR)
Red card: Şener Özbayraklı 94

Akhisar Belediyespor

1970 • 19 Mayıs, Manisa (16,597) •
akhisarbelediyespor.com
Coach: Mustafa Akçay;
(29/12/14) (Feridun Yarkın);
(11/01/15) Roberto Carlos (BRA)

2014
29/08	a	Balıkesirspor	W 2-1	Ntibazonkiza, Mehmet
15/09	h	Sivasspor	D 2-2	Gekas 2
20/09	a	Erciyesspor	W 2-1	Gekas 2
28/09	h	Fenerbahçe	W 2-0	Gekas 2
05/10	a	İstanbul Başakşehir	L 0-4	
19/10	h	Kasımpaşa	W 2-0	Uğur (p), Gekas
24/10	a	Karabükspor	L 1-2	Gekas
01/11	h	Trabzonspor	D 1-1	Gekas
07/11	a	Gaziantepspor	L 0-1	
22/11	h	Mersin	D 1-1	Bilal
28/11	h	Konyaspor	D 0-0	
06/12	a	Galatasaray	L 1-2	Gekas
13/12	h	Gençlerbirliği	D 1-1	Gekas
21/12	a	Beşiktaş	L 1-3	Bilal
28/12	h	Rizespor	L 0-4	

2015
03/01	a	Bursaspor	L 1-3	İsmail
24/01	h	Eskişehirspor	D 2-2	Bilal, Bruno Mezenga
20/01	h	Balıkesirspor	D 2-2	Bilal, Güray
07/02	a	Sivasspor	L 0-2	
14/02	h	Erciyesspor	W 1-0	Douglão
23/02	a	Fenerbahçe	W 2-1	Güray, Vaz Té
01/03	h	İstanbul Başakşehir	L 0-2	
06/03	a	Kasımpaşa	D 2-2	og (Dvali), Bruno Mezenga
14/03	h	Karabükspor	W 5-1	LuaLua, Güray, Vaz Té 2, Gekas
22/03	a	Trabzonspor	L 0-2	
05/04	h	Gaziantepspor	W 3-0	Vaz Té 2, Bilal
20/04	a	Mersin	D 1-1	Bilal
26/04	a	Konyaspor	L 1-2	Custódio
04/05	h	Galatasaray	L 0-2	
09/05	a	Gençlerbirliği	D 0-0	
14/05	h	Beşiktaş	D 1-1	Mehmet
18/05	a	Rizespor	L 1-3	Kadir
25/05	h	Bursaspor	L 0-1	
29/05	a	Eskişehirspor	W 3-1	Custódio, Bruno Mezenga, Mehmet

No	Name	Nat	DoB	Pos	Aps	(s)	Gls
20	Ahmet Cebe		02/03/83	M	17	(3)	
5	Bilal Kısa		22/06/83	M	31		6
80	Bruno Mezenga	BRA	08/08/88	A	24	(7)	3
27	Custódio	POR	24/05/83	M	15		2
61	Çağlar Birinci		02/10/85	D	3		
40	Douglão	BRA	15/08/96	D	29		1
44	Emrah Tuncel		14/09/87	G	6		
11	Theofanis Gekas	GRE	23/05/80	A	22	(2)	12
22	Güray Vural		11/06/88	M	31		3
4	İsmail Konuk		16/01/88	D	19	(5)	1
89	Kadir Keleş		01/01/88	D	16	(4)	1
10	Kenan Özer		16/08/87	M	6	(2)	
29	Kerim Zengin		13/04/87	D	5	(7)	
51	Koray Arslan		01/10/83	D	1	(1)	
9	Bahattin Köse	GER	26/08/90	A		(2)	
32	Lomana LuaLua	COD	28/12/80	A	10	(4)	1
23	Luan	BRA	30/12/88	M	3	(5)	
17	Mehmet Akyüz		02/01/86	A	8	(16)	3
6	Merter Yüce		18/02/87	M	18	(1)	
26	Saïdi Ntibazonkiza	BDI	01/05/87	M	9	(4)	1
18	Oğuz Dağlaroğlu		18/08/79	G	27		
2	Orhan Taşdelen		06/02/87	D	9		
58	Pekin Köşnek		18/09/91	M	4	(5)	
77	Sertan Vardar		13/03/82	M	4	(2)	
8	Arnaud Sutchuin	BEL	02/05/89	M	9	(4)	
7	Taşkın Çalış		25/07/93	M		(1)	
24	Tolga Ünlü		10/09/89	D	12		
15	Uğur Demirok		08/07/88	D	13		1
14	Ricardo Vaz Té	POR	01/10/86	A	5	(9)	5
39	Yiğit Gökoğlan		05/06/89	M		(2)	
1	Zeki Ayvaz		01/10/89	G	1		
45	Didier Zokora	CIV	14/12/80	M	17	(8)	

Balıkesirspor

1966 • Atatürk (15,800) • balikesirspor.org.tr
Coach: İsmail Ertekin;
(24/11/14) (Muhammet Yılmaz);
(30/11/14) Kemal Özdeş;
(27/04/15) Cihat Arslan

2014
29/08	h	Akhisar	L 1-2	Alanzinho
13/09	a	Konyaspor	L 0-2	
20/09	h	Galatasaray	W 2-0	Sercan, Gökhan
28/09	a	Gençlerbirliği	L 1-3	Sercan
05/10	h	Beşiktaş	L 0-1	
20/10	a	Rizespor	D 2-2	André Santos, Jabbie
25/10	h	Bursaspor	L 0-5	
03/11	a	Eskişehirspor	D 2-2	Sercan, Nuno André Coelho
08/11	a	Mersin	L 1-2	Sercan
24/11	a	Sivasspor	L 1-3	Vargas (p)
29/11	a	Erciyesspor	L 0-4	
06/12	h	Fenerbahçe	L 0-4	
13/12	a	İstanbul Başakşehir	L 0-1	
21/12	h	Kasımpaşa	W 5-3	Gökhan, Burak, Sercan, Ali, Muğdat
27/12	a	Karabükspor	W 1-0	Gökhan

2015
05/01	h	Trabzonspor	D 2-2	Vargas 2 (1p)
24/01	a	Gaziantepspor	L 0-1	
30/01	a	Akhisar	D 2-2	og (Douglão), Kulušić
08/02	h	Konyaspor	L 0-1	
16/02	a	Galatasaray	L 1-3	Zec
22/02	h	Gençlerbirliği	L 0-1	
01/03	h	Beşiktaş	D 2-2	Zec, Vargas (p)
07/03	h	Rizespor	D 2-2	Zec, Kulušić
13/03	a	Bursaspor	L 2-4	Gökhan 2
20/03	h	Eskişehirspor	W 4-1	Promise 2, Vargas 2
04/04	h	Mersin	L 1-3	Kulušić
19/04	a	Sivasspor	D 1-1	Berkan
26/04	h	Erciyesspor	D 1-1	Sercan
02/05	a	Fenerbahçe	L 3-4	Promise, Kulušić, Berkan
09/05	h	İstanbul Başakşehir	L 1-2	Zec
12/05	h	Kasımpaşa	W 3-2	Muğdat, Zec 2
16/05	h	Karabükspor	W 4-2	Sercan 2 (1p), Zec, Burak
23/05	a	Trabzonspor	L 2-3	Aykut, Eray
29/05	a	Gaziantepspor	D 1-1	Glumac

No	Name	Nat	DoB	Pos	Aps	(s)	Gls
23	Abdülhamit Yıldız		07/06/87	D	6	(2)	
25	Alanzinho	BRA	22/02/83	M	7	(7)	1
10	Ali Öztürk		12/04/87	A	1	(16)	1
13	André Santos	POR	02/03/89	M	11		1
6	Aykut Çeviker		03/01/90	M	26	(4)	1
3	Berkan Emir		06/02/88	D	13	(1)	2
61	Bülent Cevahir		13/02/92	M	21	(1)	
24	Burak Çalık		05/02/89	A	3	(9)	2
15	Emrullah Şalk		28/07/87	D	22		
5	Eray Ataseven		29/06/93	M	22	(1)	1
89	Ertuğrul Furkan		29/04/89	G	1		
44	Tomislav Glumac	CRO	14/05/91	D	13		1
9	Gökhan Ünal		23/07/82	A	19	(4)	5
45	Hasan Hatipoğlu		19/07/89	D	19	(1)	
11	İlhan Depe		10/09/92	M	6	(18)	
14	Khalifa Jabbie	SLE	20/01/93	M	8	(2)	1
39	Kerem Akyüz		01/07/89	D	2		
20	Ante Kulušić	CRO	06/06/86	D	28	(1)	4
88	Muğdat Çelik		03/01/90	A	13	(8)	2
7	Murat Gürbüzerol		01/02/88	A	1	(1)	
4	Nuno André Coelho	POR	07/01/86	D	9	(1)	1
17	Okan Alkan		08/09/90	D	14	(2)	
30	Isaac Promise	NGA	02/12/87	A	11	(2)	3
19	Sercan Yıldırım		05/04/90	A	28	(3)	8
77	Uğur Akdemir		22/09/88	D	18	(2)	
8	Ronald Vargas	VEN	02/12/86	M	17	(7)	6
12	Vítor Gomes	POR	08/01/89	M	12	(1)	
99	Andrija Vuković	CRO	03/08/83	G	10		
50	Ermin Zec	BIH	18/02/88	A	12	(4)	7
1	Zeki Ayvaz		01/10/89	G	1		

TURKEY

Beşiktaş JK

1903 • Atatürk Olimpiyat (76,092); Recep
Tayyip Erdoğan (14,234); Osmanlı, Ankara (19,626)
• bjk.com.tr

Major honours
*Turkish League (13) 1957, 1958, 1960, 1966, 1967,
1982, 1986, 1990, 1991, 1992, 1995, 2003, 2009;
Turkish Cup (9) 1975, 1989, 1990, 1994, 1998, 2006,
2007, 2009, 2011*

Coach: Slaven Bilić (CRO)

2014
30/08	a Mersin	W	1-0	*Cenk Tosun*
15/09	h Rizespor	D	1-1	*Olcay*
22/09	a Bursaspor	W	1-0	*Olcay*
27/09	h Eskişehirspor	D	1-1	*Olcay*
05/10	a Balıkesirspor	W	1-0	*Mustafa*
19/10	h Sivasspor	W	3-2	*Ba 2, Olcay*
27/10	a Erciyesspor	L	2-3	*Kerim 2*
02/11	h Fenerbahçe	L	0-2	
09/11	a İstanbul Başakşehir	W	2-1	*Ba, Kerim*
23/11	h Kasımpaşa	W	2-0	*Ba 2 (1p)*
01/12	a Karabükspor	W	2-1	*Ba 2*
07/12	h Trabzonspor	W	3-0	*Kavlak, Ba, Cenk Tosun*
14/12	a Gaziantepspor	W	1-0	*Oğuzhan*
21/12	h Akhisar	W	3-1	*Cenk Tosun, Sosa, Gökhan*
28/12	a Konyaspor	W	2-1	*Gökhan, Sosa*

2015
04/01	h Galatasaray	L	0-2	
26/01	a Gençlerbirliği	W	2-0	*Ba, Olcay*
01/02	h Mersin	W	2-1	*Olcay, Ba*
08/02	a Rizespor	W	2-1	*Sosa, Ba (p)*
15/02	h Bursaspor	W	3-2	*Ba 2 (1p), Gökhan*
22/02	a Eskişehirspor	L	0-1	
01/03	h Balıkesirspor	D	2-2	*Ba (p), Opare*
08/03	a Sivasspor	W	1-0	*Hutchinson*
15/03	h Erciyesspor	W	5-1	*Gökhan, Ba (p), Olcay, Mustafa, Ramon*
22/03	a Fenerbahçe	L	1-1	
06/04	h İstanbul Başakşehir	D	0-0	
18/04	a Kasımpaşa	W	5-1	*Mustafa, Ba, Ramon, Olcay, Sosa*
27/04	h Karabükspor	W	2-1	*Hutchinson, Cenk Tosun*
03/05	a Trabzonspor	W	2-0	*Ba, Mustafa*
10/05	h Gaziantepspor	D	1-1	*Sosa*
14/05	a Akhisar	W	1-1	*Ba*
18/05	h Konyaspor	L	0-1	
24/05	a Galatasaray	L	0-2	
29/05	h Gençlerbirliği	W	2-1	*Cenk Tosun, Oğuzhan*

No	Name	Nat	DoB	Pos	Aps	(s)	Gls
18	Tolgay Arslan	GER	16/08/90	M	11	(5)	
33	Atınç Nukan		20/07/93	D	5	(4)	
9	Demba Ba	SEN	25/05/85	A	27	(2)	18
1	Cenk Gönen		21/02/88	G	8	(1)	
23	Cenk Tosun		07/06/91	A	6	(12)	6
22	Ersan Gülüm		17/05/87	D	26	(1)	
19	Pedro Franco	COL	23/04/91	D	18	(3)	
7	Gökhan Töre		20/01/92	M	26	(2)	4
27	Günay Güvenç		25/06/91	G	9	(1)	
13	Atiba Hutchinson	CAN	08/02/83	M	27	(3)	2
3	İsmail Köybaşı		10/07/89	D	8	(4)	
8	Veli Kavlak	AUT	03/11/88	M	21	(1)	1
21	Kerim Koyunlu		19/11/93	M	10	(19)	3
4	Alexander Milosevic	SWE	30/01/92	D		(1)	
1	Mustafa Pektemek		11/08/88	A	9	(10)	4
20	Necip Uysal		24/01/91	M	12	(6)	
15	Oğuzhan Özyakup		23/09/92	M	13	(12)	2
10	Olcay Şahan		26/05/87	M	27	(3)	8
44	Daniel Opare	GHA	18/10/90	D	6		1
31	Ramon	BRA	06/05/88	D	24	(2)	2
2	Serdar Kurtuluş		23/07/87	D	25	(2)	
6	Tomáš Sivok	CZE	15/09/83	D	15	(2)	
5	José Sosa	ARG	19/06/85	M	24	(3)	5
29	Tolga Zengin		10/10/83	G	17		
25	Uğur Boral		14/04/82	D		(1)	

Bursaspor

1963 • Atatürk (25,661) • bursaspor.org.tr

Major honours
Turkish League (1) 2010; Turkish Cup (1) 1986

Coach: Şenol Güneş

2014
30/08	h Galatasaray	L	0-2	
13/09	a Gençlerbirliği	W	2-1	*Volkan, Fernandão*
22/09	h Beşiktaş	L	0-1	
28/09	a Rizespor	W	1-0	*Fernandão*
03/10	a Mersin	L	1-2	*Serdar*
19/10	h Eskişehirspor	D	2-2	*Bakambu 2*
25/10	a Balıkesirspor	W	5-0	*Belluschi 2, Bakambu 3*
01/11	h Sivasspor	W	3-0	*Josué, Volkan, Fernandão*
09/11	a Erciyesspor	D	1-1	*Fernandão*
24/11	h Fenerbahçe	D	1-1	*Volkan*
28/11	a İstanbul Başakşehir	D	0-0	
07/12	h Kasımpaşa	W	5-1	*Fernandão 2, Josué (p), Ozan Tufan, Volkan*
14/12	a Karabükspor	L	2-3	*Bakambu, Fernandão*
21/12	h Trabzonspor	D	3-3	*Fernandão (p), Ozan Tufan, Volkan (p)*
28/12	a Gaziantepspor	W	2-1	*Fernandão, Belluschi*

2015
03/01	h Akhisar	W	3-1	*Josué, Civelli, Fernandão*
23/01	h Konyaspor	W	3-2	*Volkan, Civelli, Fernandão*
01/02	a Galatasaray	D	2-2	*Volkan, Fernandão*
06/02	h Gençlerbirliği	W	3-1	*Josué, Holmén, Fernandão*
15/02	a Beşiktaş	L	2-3	*Bakambu, Ozan Tufan*
21/02	h Rizespor	D	1-1	*Bakambu*
01/03	h Mersin	W	2-1	*Fernandão (p), Civelli*
07/03	a Eskişehirspor	D	0-0	
13/03	h Balıkesirspor	W	4-2	*Josué, Holmén, Fernandão (p), Enes*
21/03	a Sivasspor	L	1-4	*Volkan*
05/04	a Erciyesspor	W	3-0	*Fernandão 2, Volkan*
20/04	a Fenerbahçe	L	0-1	
25/04	h İstanbul Başakşehir	W	4-1	*Bakambu 2, Fernandão (p), Holmén*
03/05	h Kasımpaşa	L	3-5	*Bakambu, Volkan 2*
09/05	h Karabükspor	W	7-1	*Holmén, Fernandão 4 (2p), Volkan, Bakambu*
13/05	a Trabzonspor	L	0-1	
17/05	h Gaziantepspor	W	2-0	*Bakambu, Josué*
25/05	a Akhisar	W	1-0	*Josué (p)*
30/05	h Konyaspor	D	0-0	

No	Name	Nat	DoB	Pos	Aps	(s)	Gls
94	Cédric Bakambu	COD	11/04/91	A	23	(4)	13
23	Aziz Behich	AUS	16/12/90	D	27	(2)	
88	Bekir Yılmaz		06/03/88	M	14	(11)	
5	Fernando Belluschi	ARG	10/09/83	M	30	(2)	3
2	Renato Civelli	ARG	14/10/83	D	24		3
19	Emre Taşdemir		08/08/95	D	9	(4)	
10	Enes Ünal		10/05/97	A		(19)	1
24	Ertuğrul Ersoy		13/02/97	D	1	(7)	
50	Ethem Pülgir		02/04/93	D	1		
9	Ferhat Kiraz		02/01/89	A	1	(4)	
9	Fernandão	BRA	27/03/87	A	33		22
12	Harun Tekin		17/06/89	G	34		
20	Samuel Holmén	SWE	28/06/84	M	10	(17)	4
38	İbrahim Öztürk		21/06/81	D	1	(1)	
30	Josué	POR	17/09/90	M	28	(1)	7
25	Okan Kocuk		27/07/95	G		(1)	
33	Ozan İpek		10/10/86	M	2	(10)	
7	Ozan Tufan		23/03/95	M	32		3
4	Serdar Aziz		23/10/90	D	27		1
6	Şamil Çinaz		08/03/86	M	16	(5)	
22	Şener Özbayraklı		23/01/90	D	31		
8	Bakaye Traoré	MLI	06/03/85	M	2	(8)	
16	Volkan Şen		07/07/87	M	28	(2)	12

Eskişehirspor

1965 • Atatürk (13,520) • eskisehirspor.org.tr

Major honours
Turkish Cup (1) 1971

**Coach: Ertuğrul Sağlam;
(12/01/15) Michael Skibbe (GER)**

2014
30/08	h Konyaspor	W	2-1	*Hürriyet, Zengin (p)*
13/09	a Galatasaray	D	0-0	
19/09	h Gençlerbirliği	L	0-2	
27/09	a Beşiktaş	D	1-1	*Berkay*
05/10	h Rizespor	L	1-2	*Čaušić*
19/10	a Bursaspor	D	2-2	*Hürriyet, Funes Mori*
26/10	a Mersin	L	2-4	*Ömer, Zengin (p)*
03/11	h Balıkesirspor	D	2-2	*Lawal, Funes Mori*
07/11	a Sivasspor	D	1-1	*Ömer*
23/11	h Erciyesspor	W	2-1	*Čaušić, Lawal*
30/11	h Fenerbahçe	D	2-2	*Zengin, Funes Mori*
07/12	h İstanbul Başakşehir	L	0-1	
13/12	a Kasımpaşa	L	0-1	
20/12	h Karabükspor	D	1-1	*Čaušić*
29/12	a Trabzonspor	W	4-1	*Funes Mori, Ömer 2, Andaç*

2015
04/01	h Gaziantepspor	L	1-3	*Mirkan*
24/01	a Akhisar	D	2-2	*Sezgin, Onur*
01/02	a Konyaspor	L	0-1	
09/02	h Galatasaray	L	1-2	*Sissoko*
16/02	a Gençlerbirliği	W	2-1	*Toko, Funes Mori*
22/02	h Beşiktaş	W	1-0	*Kaan*
28/02	a Rizespor	L	0-3	
07/03	h Bursaspor	D	0-0	
15/03	h Mersin	W	2-0	*Sezer, Ömer*
20/03	a Balıkesirspor	L	1-4	*og (Glumac)*
04/04	h Sivasspor	L	1-3	*Sezer (p)*
19/04	a Erciyesspor	W	1-0	*Sezgin*
25/04	h Fenerbahçe	W	1-0	*Emre*
02/05	a İstanbul Başakşehir	D	1-1	*Funes Mori*
08/05	h Kasımpaşa	W	4-1	*Kaan, Funes Mori, Ömer, Diego Ângelo*
12/05	a Karabükspor	D	2-2	*Ömer, Emre*
17/05	h Trabzonspor	W	2-0	*Ömer, Funes Mori*
24/05	a Gaziantepspor	L	2-3	*Sezer (p), Erkut*
29/05	h Akhisar	L	1-3	*Ömer*

No	Name	Nat	DoB	Pos	Aps	(s)	Gls
1	Ali Şaşal Vural		10/07/90	G	8	(1)	
99	Andaç Güleryüz		31/07/93	A	3	(7)	1
35	Aytaç Kara		28/03/93	M	2	(1)	
6	Berkay Dabanlı		27/06/95	D	16	(4)	1
53	Birol Parlak		01/03/90	D	11	(5)	
25	Ruud Boffin	BEL	05/11/87	G	25		
92	Goran Čaušić	SRB	05/05/92	M	22	(5)	3
3	Diego Ângelo	BRA	17/02/86	D	17	(3)	1
19	Emre Güral		05/04/89	A		(8)	2
7	Ergün Teber		01/09/85	D	11	(8)	
20	Erkut Şentürk		06/05/94	M	1	(3)	1
11	Erman Kılıç		20/09/83	M	1		
18	Rogelio Funes Mori	ARG	05/03/91	A	28	(1)	8
50	Hürriyet Güçer		25/10/81	M	18	(3)	2
17	Kaan Kanak		06/10/90	D	22	(2)	2
65	Kamil Çörekçi		01/02/92	D	30		
4	Raheem Lawal	NGA	04/05/90	M	22	(6)	2
96	Mehmet Feyzi Yıldırım		23/01/96	M		(2)	
9	Mirkan Aydın		08/07/87	A	4	(9)	1
22	Mustafa Yumlu		25/09/87	D	13		
8	Onur Bayramoğlu		04/01/90	M	4	(1)	1
7	Ömer Şişmanoğlu		01/08/89	A	18	(4)	9
60	Özgür Çek		03/01/91	M	11	(4)	
55	Semih Güleryüz		30/11/94	D	1		
54	Serdar Özkan		01/01/87	M	8	(14)	
13	Sezer Öztürk		03/11/85	M	10	(1)	3
5	Sezgin Coşkun		23/08/84	D	18	(2)	
87	Sinan Ören		21/11/87	G	1		
32	Ibrahim Sissoko	CIV	29/11/91	A	21	(5)	1
38	Tarık Çamdal		24/03/91	D	1		
28	Nzuzi Toko	COD	20/12/90	M	13		1
10	Erkan Zengin	SWE	05/08/85	M	14	(1)	3

Fenerbahçe SK

1907 • Şükrü Saraçoğlu (50,509) •
fenerbahce.org

Major honours
*Turkish League (19) 1959, 1961, 1964, 1965, 1968,
1970, 1974, 1975, 1978, 1983, 1985, 1989, 1996,
2001, 2004, 2005, 2007, 2011, 2014; Turkish Cup (6)
1968, 1974, 1979, 1983, 2012, 2013*

Coach: İsmail Kartal

2014
31/08	h	Karabükspor	W 3-2	Emenike, Sow, Webó
14/09	a	Trabzonspor	D 0-0	
21/09	h	Gaziantepspor	W 1-0	Emre (p)
28/09	a	Akhisar	L 0-2	
04/10	h	Konyaspor	W 2-1	Webó, Sow
18/10	a	Galatasaray	L 1-2	Alper
25/10	h	Gençlerbirliği	W 2-1	Emre (p), Kuyt (p)
02/11	a	Beşiktaş	W 2-0	Emenike, Sow
08/11	h	Rizespor	W 2-1	Kadlec, Webó
24/11	a	Bursaspor	D 1-1	Kuyt
30/11	h	Eskişehirspor	D 2-2	Webó, Sow (p)
06/12	a	Balıkesirspor	W 1-0	Raul Meireles
12/12	h	Sivasspor	W 4-1	Bekir, Sow 2, Kuyt
19/12	a	Erciyesspor	W 1-0	Emre (p)
27/12	h	Mersin	W 1-0	Mehmet Topal

2015
03/01	h	İstanbul Başakşehir	W 2-0	Kuyt, Alper
24/01	a	Kasımpaşa	W 3-0	Kuyt 2, Caner Erkin
31/01	a	Karabükspor	W 2-1	Selçuk, Emenike
07/02	h	Trabzonspor	D 0-0	
14/02	a	Gaziantepspor	W 5-0	Emenike, Kuyt, Sow 2, Emre (p)
23/02	h	Akhisar	L 1-2	Raul Meireles
28/02	a	Konyaspor	D 1-1	Egemen
08/03	h	Galatasaray	W 1-0	Kuyt
15/03	a	Gençlerbirliği	L 1-2	Mehmet Topal
22/03	h	Beşiktaş	W 1-0	Sow
04/04	a	Rizespor	W 5-1	Mehmet Topuz, Sow 2, Webó, Caner Erkin
20/04	a	Bursaspor	W 1-0	Webó
25/04	a	Eskişehirspor	D 1-1	og (Mustafa)
02/05	h	Balıkesirspor	W 4-3	Caner Erkin, Diego, Sow 2
09/05	h	Sivasspor	W 3-2	Diego, Webó, Sow
13/05	h	Erciyesspor	D 1-1	Egemen
17/05	a	Mersin	W 1-0	Emre
25/05	a	İstanbul Başakşehir	D 2-2	Diego, Webó
30/05	h	Kasımpaşa	W 2-0	Emre, Alper

No	Name	Nat	DoB	Pos	Aps	(s)	Gls
26	Alper Potuk		08/04/81	M	21	(9)	3
4	Bekir Irtegün		20/04/84	D	18	(2)	1
22	Bruno Alves	POR	27/11/81	D	23	(1)	
88	Caner Erkin		04/10/88	D	30	(1)	3
41	Caner Koca		14/04/96	M		(1)	
10	Diego	BRA	28/02/85	M	18	(7)	3
2	Egemen Korkmaz		03/11/82	D	17		2
29	Emmanuel Emenike	NGA	10/05/87	A	21	(6)	4
20	Emre Belözoğlu		07/09/80	M	23	(3)	6
77	Gökhan Gönül		04/01/85	D	32		
3	Hasan Ali Kaldırım		09/12/89	D	5	(8)	
24	Michal Kadlec	CZE	13/12/84	D	10	(2)	1
11	Dirk Kuyt	NED	22/07/80	A	30	(2)	8
5	Mehmet Topal		03/03/86	M	32		2
38	Mehmet Topuz		07/09/83	M	3	(6)	1
23	Mert Günok		01/03/89	G	8	(1)	
14	Raul Meireles	POR	17/03/83	M	17	(6)	2
21	Selçuk Şahin		31/01/81	M	5	(18)	1
53	Serdar Kesimal		24/01/89	D		(1)	
7	Moussa Sow	SEN	19/01/86	A	26	(7)	14
15	Uygar Mert Zeybek		04/06/96	M		(1)	
1	Volkan Demirel		27/10/81	G	26		
9	Pierre Webó	CMR	20/01/82	A	9	(17)	8

Galatasaray AŞ

1905 • Türk Telekom Arena (52,600) •
galatasaray.org

Major honours
*UEFA Cup (1) 2000; UEFA Super Cup (1) 2000; Turkish
League (20) 1962, 1963, 1969, 1971, 1972, 1973,
1987, 1988, 1993, 1994, 1997, 1998, 1999, 2000,
2002, 2006, 2008, 2012, 2013, 2015; Turkish Cup (16)
1963, 1964, 1965, 1966, 1973, 1976, 1982, 1985,
1991, 1993, 1996, 1999, 2000, 2005, 2014, 2015*

**Coach: Cesare Prandelli (ITA);
(27/11/14) (Cláudio Taffarel (BRA));
(01/12/14) Hamza Hamzaoğlu**

2014
30/08	a	Bursaspor	W 2-0	Burak, Olcan
13/09	h	Eskişehirspor	D 0-0	
20/09	a	Balıkesirspor	L 0-2	
26/09	h	Sivasspor	W 2-1	Chedjou, Burak
04/10	a	Erciyesspor	W 2-1	Burak, Sneijder
18/10	a	Fenerbahçe	W 2-1	Sneijder 2
26/10	a	İstanbul Başakşehir	L 0-4	
31/10	h	Kasımpaşa	W 2-1	Burak, Umut
08/11	a	Karabükspor	W 2-1	Chedjou, Umut
22/11	h	Trabzonspor	L 0-3	
29/11	a	Gaziantepspor	W 1-0	Burak
06/12	h	Akhisar	W 2-1	Burak 2
13/12	h	Konyaspor	W 5-0	Umut, Emre, Burak 2, Hamit
20/12	h	Mersin	W 3-2	og (Güven Varol), Burak (p), Umut
26/12	h	Gençlerbirliği	D 1-1	Emre

2015
04/01	a	Beşiktaş	W 2-0	Felipe Melo, Burak
25/01	h	Rizespor	W 2-0	Sneijder, Bruma
01/02	h	Bursaspor	D 2-2	Umut, Emre (p)
09/02	a	Eskişehirspor	W 2-1	Umut, Selçuk
16/02	h	Balıkesirspor	W 3-1	Chedjou, Sneijder, Burak
21/02	a	Sivasspor	W 3-2	Yasin, Burak, Alex Telles
27/02	a	Erciyesspor	W 3-1	Umut, Chedjou, Sneijder
08/03	a	Fenerbahçe	L 0-1	
14/03	h	İstanbul Başakşehir	D 2-2	Selçuk, Umut
21/03	a	Kasımpaşa	W 3-2	Selçuk, Umut, Burak
05/04	h	Karabükspor	W 4-2	Yasin, Sneijder 2, Umut
19/04	a	Trabzonspor	L 1-2	Emre
26/04	a	Gaziantepspor	W 1-0	Hakan
04/05	a	Akhisar	W 2-0	Burak 2
08/05	h	Konyaspor	W 1-0	Selçuk
12/05	a	Mersin	W 1-0	Yasin
16/05	h	Gençlerbirliği	W 1-0	Sneijder
24/05	a	Beşiktaş	W 2-0	Yasin, Sneijder
30/05	a	Rizespor	D 1-1	Umut

No	Name	Nat	DoB	Pos	Aps	(s)	Gls
13	Alex Telles	BRA	15/12/92	D	19	(3)	1
7	Aydın Yılmaz		29/01/88	A	1		
11	Bruma	POR	24/10/94	M	14	(6)	1
17	Burak Yılmaz		15/07/85	A	26	(2)	16
21	Aurélien Chedjou	CMR	20/06/85	D	26		4
6	Blerim Dzemaili	SUI	12/04/86	M	7	(4)	
52	Emre Çolak		20/05/91	M	14	(11)	4
3	Felipe Melo	BRA	26/06/83	M	20		1
28	Koray Günter	GER	16/08/94	D	10	(1)	
22	Hakan Balta		23/03/83	D	18	(4)	1
4	Hamit Altıntop		08/12/82	M	12	(10)	1
1	Fernando Muslera	URU	16/06/86	G	32		
29	Olcan Adın		30/09/85	M	16	(12)	1
19	Goran Pandev	MKD	27/07/83	A	1	(3)	
55	Sabri Sarıoğlu		26/07/84	D	25		
8	Selçuk İnan		10/02/85	M	32		4
26	Semih Kaya		24/02/91	D	19		
38	Sinan Bolat		03/09/88	G	2		
18	Sinan Gümüş		15/01/94	M	6	(1)	
10	Wesley Sneijder	NED	09/06/84	M	29	(2)	10
77	Tank Çamdal		24/03/91	D	10	(2)	
9	Umut Bulut		15/03/83	A	16	(16)	11
88	Veysel Sarı		25/07/88	D	5	(1)	
23	Yasin Öztekin		19/03/87	M	14	(7)	4
35	Yekta Kurtuluş		11/12/85	M	6	(9)	

Gaziantepspor

1969 • Kamil Ocak (16,981) •
gaziantepspor.org.tr

Coach: Okan Buruk

2014
31/08	a	Sivasspor	W 2-1	Muhammet 2
14/09	h	Erciyesspor	D 2-2	Oğulcan, Chico
21/09	a	Fenerbahçe	L 0-1	
29/09	h	İstanbul Başakşehir	D 0-0	
04/10	a	Kasımpaşa	L 2-4	Chibuike, Oğulcan
18/10	h	Karabükspor	W 1-0	Chico
26/10	a	Trabzonspor	D 4-4	Muhammet 2, Erdem, Chibuike
02/11	h	Mersin	W 1-0	Chibuike
07/11	h	Akhisar	W 1-0	Muhammet
23/11	a	Konyaspor	L 0-2	
29/11	h	Galatasaray	L 0-1	
06/12	a	Gençlerbirliği	L 0-2	
14/12	h	Beşiktaş	L 0-1	
22/12	a	Rizespor	W 1-0	Mustafa
28/12	h	Bursaspor	L 1-2	Muhammet

2015
04/01	a	Eskişehirspor	W 3-1	Erdem 2, Mustafa
24/01	h	Balıkesirspor	W 1-0	Muhammet
31/01	h	Sivasspor	L 1-3	Muhammet
07/02	a	Erciyesspor	W 1-0	Chico
14/02	h	Fenerbahçe	L 0-5	
21/02	a	İstanbul Başakşehir	L 0-1	
01/03	h	Kasımpaşa	D 0-0	
08/03	h	Karabükspor	D 0-0	
16/03	h	Trabzonspor	W 2-0	Chibuike, Muhammet
21/03	a	Mersin	W 1-0	Erdem
05/04	a	Akhisar	L 0-3	
17/04	h	Konyaspor	D 1-1	Chico
26/04	a	Galatasaray	L 0-1	
03/05	h	Gençlerbirliği	L 0-3	
10/05	a	Beşiktaş	D 1-1	Chibuike
13/05	h	Rizespor	L 1-2	Muhammet
17/05	a	Bursaspor	L 0-2	
24/05	h	Eskişehirspor	W 3-2	Camara 2, Chibuike
29/05	h	Balıkesirspor	D 1-1	Chico

No	Name	Nat	DoB	Pos	Aps	(s)	Gls
20	Abdülkadir Kayalı		30/01/91	M	2	(7)	
15	Gbenga Arokoyo	NGA	01/11/92	D	18	(2)	
26	Barış Yardımcı		16/08/92	D	29		
28	Gilles Binya	CMR	29/08/84	D	8	(2)	
35	Bora Sevim		17/02/84	G		(1)	
9	Aboubacar Camara	GUI	07/11/94	A	7	(4)	2
4	John Chibuike	NGA	10/10/88	D	22	(5)	6
25	Chico	BRA	02/02/87	D	33		5
13	Carlo Costly	HON	18/07/82	A		(7)	
3	Elyasa Süme		13/08/83	D	26		
7	Emre Nefiz		24/11/94	M	16	(4)	
34	Eray Birniçan		20/07/88	G	8	(1)	
6	Erdem Şen		05/01/89	M	25		4
17	Ferhat Ayaz		10/10/94	M	3	(6)	
22	Gökhan Süzen		12/07/87	D	11	(7)	
11	İbrahim Akın		04/01/84	M	5	(6)	
66	Muhammet Ildız	AUT	14/05/91	M	4	(10)	
88	João Vítor	BRA	01/06/88	M	7	(1)	
1	Žydrūnas Karčemarskas	LTU	24/05/83	G	26		
51	Koray Arslan		01/10/83	D	5	(4)	
87	Luís Leal	STP	29/05/87	A	5	(6)	
10	Muhammet Demir		10/01/92	A	29		10
21	Mustafa Durak		13/08/88	A	21	(7)	2
96	Müslüm Talşik		20/04/96	M		(1)	
19	Oğulcan Çağlayan		22/03/96	A	6	(7)	2
8	Oğuzhan Türk		17/05/86	M	13	(5)	
14	Orkan Çınar		29/01/96	M	1	(2)	
94	Lucas Ontivero	ARG	09/09/94	A		(1)	
27	Serhan Yılmaz		20/02/85	A		(6)	
5	Şenol Can		03/04/83	D	33		
41	Ognjen Vranješ	BIH	24/10/89	D	11		

TURKEY

Gençlerbirliği SK

1923 • 19 Mayıs (19,209) • genclerbirligi.org.tr
Major honours
Turkish Cup (2) 1987, 2001
Coach: Mustafa Kaplan;
(13/09/14) (Osman Işılar);
(24/09/14) İrfan Buz;
(17/02/15) Mesut Bakkal;
(23/05/15) (Mustafa Kaplan)

2014
29/08	a	Rizespor	D 1-1	Guido
13/09	h	Bursaspor	L 1-2	Stancu
19/09	a	Eskişehirspor	W 2-0	Uğur, Stancu
28/09	h	Balıkesirspor	W 3-1	Berat 2, Uğur
04/10	a	Sivasspor	L 0-1	
20/10	h	Erciyesspor	D 0-0	
25/10	a	Fenerbahçe	L 1-2	Antal
01/11	h	İstanbul Başakşehir	W 1-0	Tomić
09/11	a	Kasımpaşa	D 2-2	Tomić, İrfan Can
23/11	h	Karabükspor	D 2-2	Stancu 2
01/12	a	Trabzonspor	L 1-4	Çelik
06/12	h	Gaziantepspor	W 2-0	og (Arokoyo), İrfan Can
13/12	a	Akhisar	D 1-1	Tomić
20/12	h	Konyaspor	W 5-0	Stancu, Guido, Petrović, İrfan Can, Artun
26/12	h	Galatasaray	D 1-1	Stancu

2015
05/01	a	Mersin	D 1-1	Berat
26/01	h	Beşiktaş	L 0-2	
01/02	h	Rizespor	L 1-2	
08/02	a	Bursaspor	L 1-3	Stancu
26/02	h	Eskişehirspor	L 1-2	Stancu
22/02	a	Balıkesirspor	W 1-0	og (Berkan)
28/02	h	Sivasspor	D 0-0	
07/03	a	Erciyesspor	W 4-2	Hleb, Landel, Çelik
15/03	h	Fenerbahçe	W 2-1	Petrović, El Kabir
22/03	a	İstanbul Başakşehir	L 1-3	Tošić
04/04	h	Kasımpaşa	W 5-2	Çelik, El Kabir 3, İrfan Can
18/04	a	Karabükspor	L 1-2	Çelik
26/04	h	Trabzonspor	D 1-1	Tomić
03/05	a	Gaziantepspor	W 3-0	Çelik, Hleb, Stancu
09/05	h	Akhisar	D 0-0	
12/05	a	Konyaspor	L 0-1	
16/05	a	Galatasaray	L 0-1	
22/05	h	Mersin	L 1-2	İrfan Can
29/05	a	Beşiktaş	L 1-2	Çağrı

No	Name	Nat	DoB	Pos	Aps	(s)	Gls
4	Ahmet Çalık		26/02/94	D	29		
2	Ahmet Oğuz		16/01/93	D	3	(2)	
18	Liviu Antal	ROU	02/06/89	M	3	(6)	1
9	Artun Akçakın		06/05/93	A		(5)	1
99	Berat Tosun		01/01/94	A	9	(10)	3
6	Çağrı Bülbül		01/02/92	M		(5)	1
11	Mervan Çelik	SWE	28/05/90	M	19	(8)	5
27	Johan Dahlin	SWE	08/09/86	G	10		
20	Doğa Kaya		30/06/84	M	21	(1)	
22	Moestafa El Kabir	NED	05/10/88	A	13	(2)	4
14	Ferhat Görgülü		28/10/91	D	6	(1)	
35	Ferhat Kaplan		07/01/89	G	10	(2)	
19	Jean-Jacques Gosso	CIV	15/03/83	M	22	(5)	
25	Guido Koçer		15/09/88	M	15	(5)	2
42	Hakan Aslantaş		26/08/85	D	31	(2)	
33	Halil Pehlivan		21/08/93	D	11	(1)	
45	Hikmet Balıoğlu		04/08/90	D	6	(1)	
13	Aleksandr Hleb	BLR	01/05/81	M	8	(7)	2
17	İrfan Can Kahveci		15/07/95	M	16	(8)	5
16	Guy-Michel Landel	GUI	07/07/90	M	12	(2)	2
62	Deniz Naki	GER	09/07/89	M		(5)	
5	Nizamettin Çalışkan		20/03/87	M	5	(2)	
24	Özgür İleri		17/11/87	M	1		
8	Radosav Petrović	SRB	08/03/89	M	23	(5)	2
1	Ramazan Köse		12/05/88	G	14		
61	Sedat Bayrak		10/04/81	D	12	(2)	
10	Bogdan Stancu	ROU	28/06/87	A	24		9
48	Taylan Antalyalı		08/01/95	M		(2)	
7	Nemanja Tomić	SRB	21/01/88	M	9	(6)	4
3	Duško Tošić	SRB	19/01/85	D	27	(1)	1
58	Uğur Çiftçi		04/05/92	D	15	(4)	2

İstanbul Başakşehir

2014 • Başakşehir Fatih Terim (17,310) • ibfk.com.tr
Coach: Abdullah Avcı

2014
30/08	h	Kasımpaşa	D 1-1	Perbet
13/09	a	Karabükspor	D 0-0	
22/09	h	Trabzonspor	D 1-1	Višća
29/09	a	Gaziantepspor	D 0-0	
05/10	h	Akhisar	W 4-0	Epureanu, Semih 3 (1p)
18/10	a	Konyaspor	D 0-0	
26/10	h	Galatasaray	W 4-0	Mossoró 2, Semih, Doka Madureira
01/11	a	Gençlerbirliği	L 0-1	
09/11	h	Beşiktaş	L 1-2	Epureanu
22/11	a	Rizespor	W 2-0	Mossoró, Semih
28/11	h	Bursaspor	D 0-0	
07/12	a	Eskişehirspor	W 1-0	Semih
13/12	h	Balıkesirspor	W 1-0	Semih
20/12	a	Sivasspor	W 2-0	Epureanu, Perbet
27/12	h	Erciyesspor	W 3-1	Epureanu, Doka Madureira, Perbet

2015
03/01	a	Fenerbahçe	L 0-2	
24/01	h	Mersin	D 2-2	Višća, Perbet
31/01	a	Kasımpaşa	W 1-0	Semih (p)
06/02	h	Karabükspor	D 2-2	Višća, Yalçın
15/02	a	Trabzonspor	L 2-3	Mahmut, Višća
21/02	h	Gaziantepspor	W 1-0	Mahmut
01/03	a	Akhisar	W 2-0	Semih, og (Merter)
08/03	h	Konyaspor	D 0-0	
14/03	a	Galatasaray	D 2-2	Mehmet, Cenk
22/03	h	Gençlerbirliği	W 3-1	Višća, Doka Madureira 2
06/04	a	Beşiktaş	D 0-0	
19/04	h	Rizespor	W 3-1	Mahmut, Višća, Sedat
25/04	a	Bursaspor	L 1-4	Mossoró
02/05	h	Eskişehirspor	D 1-1	Doka Madureira
09/05	a	Balıkesirspor	W 2-1	Mehmet (p), Semih
12/05	h	Sivasspor	W 2-1	Višća, Semih
17/05	a	Erciyesspor	W 1-0	Mahmut
25/05	h	Fenerbahçe	D 2-2	Mehmet 2
30/05	a	Mersin	D 2-2	Doka Madureira, Višća

No	Name	Nat	DoB	Pos	Aps	(s)	Gls
39	Alparslan Erdem		11/12/88	D	11	(9)	
96	Altuğ Taş		10/01/96	A		(2)	
77	Stéphane Badji	SEN	29/05/90	M	14	(1)	
67	Cenk Şahin		22/09/94	M	2	(16)	1
10	Doka Madureira	BRA	11/02/84	A	26	(3)	6
99	Michael Eneramo	NGA	26/11/85	A		(3)	
6	Alexandru Epureanu	MDA	27/09/86	D	32		4
87	Ferhat Öztorun		08/05/87	D	29		
66	Gençer Cansev		04/01/89	D	4	(1)	
5	Mahmut Tekdemir		20/01/88	D	29		4
9	Mehmet Batdal		24/02/86	A	7	(10)	4
29	Mossoró	BRA	04/07/83	M	26	(2)	4
17	Murat Akın		22/10/86	M	1		
14	Ömer Sokullu		14/08/88	M		(2)	
24	Jérémy Perbet	FRA	12/12/84	A	9	(13)	4
53	Rızvan Şahin		30/10/81	D	1		
40	Rajko Rotman	SVN	19/03/89	M	16	(5)	
3	Sedat Ağçay		22/09/81	M	15	(10)	1
23	Semih Şentürk		29/04/83	A	18	(5)	11
20	Sezer Öztürk		03/11/85	M	1	(7)	
11	Tayfun Pektürk		13/05/88	M	2	(11)	
26	Tom	BRA	23/07/85	A		(1)	
7	Uğur Uçar		02/04/87	D	30		
7	Edin Višća	BIH	17/02/90	M	34		8
1	Volkan Babacan		11/06/88	G	34		
22	Yalçın Ayhan		01/05/82	D	31		1

Kardemir Karabükspor

1969 • Dr Necmettin Şeyhoğlu (12,400) • kardemirkarabukspor.org.tr
Coach: Tolunay Kafkas;
(24/02/15) Yılmaz Vural

2014
31/08	a	Fenerbahçe	L 2-3	Kumbela, og (Kadlec)
13/09	h	İstanbul Başakşehir	D 0-0	
21/09	a	Kasımpaşa	L 1-2	Kumbela
29/09	h	Mersin	L 0-2	
05/10	a	Trabzonspor	W 3-0	Traoré 2, og (Zeki)
18/10	a	Gaziantepspor	L 0-1	
24/10	h	Akhisar	W 2-1	Traoré (p), Turgay
03/11	a	Konyaspor	L 0-1	
08/11	h	Galatasaray	L 1-2	Emre Güngör
23/11	a	Gençlerbirliği	D 2-2	Traoré (p), Viola
01/12	h	Beşiktaş	L 1-2	Musa
07/12	a	Rizespor	W 3-0	Onur Ayık, Akpala 2
14/12	h	Bursaspor	W 3-2	Viola 2 (1p), Traoré
20/12	a	Eskişehirspor	D 1-1	Kumbela
27/12	h	Balıkesirspor	L 0-1	

2015
04/01	a	Sivasspor	L 0-2	
25/01	h	Erciyesspor	L 1-2	Erkan
31/01	h	Fenerbahçe	L 1-2	Traoré
06/02	a	İstanbul Başakşehir	D 2-2	Akpala, Traoré
14/02	h	Kasımpaşa	D 0-0	
22/02	a	Mersin	L 1-2	Musa
02/03	h	Trabzonspor	L 2-3	Traoré, Onur Ayık
08/03	a	Gaziantepspor	D 0-0	
14/03	a	Akhisar	L 1-5	Traoré (p)
20/03	h	Konyaspor	L 0-1	
05/04	a	Galatasaray	L 2-4	og (Hakan), Furkan
18/04	h	Gençlerbirliği	W 2-1	Fatih, Furkan (p)
27/04	a	Beşiktaş	L 1-2	Musa
02/05	h	Rizespor	L 2-3	Ahmet İlhan, Erkan
09/05	a	Bursaspor	L 1-7	Akpala
12/05	h	Eskişehirspor	D 2-2	Traoré, Ahmet İlhan
16/05	a	Balıkesirspor	L 2-4	Musa, Murat
24/05	h	Sivasspor	L	Ahmet İlhan, Sow
29/05	a	Erciyesspor	L 3-4	Ahmet İlhan, Erdem 2 (2p)

No	Name	Nat	DoB	Pos	Aps	(s)	Gls
21	Abdülaziz Demircan		05/02/91	G	13	(1)	
9	Ahmet İlhan Özek		01/01/88	M	17	(1)	4
25	Joseph Akpala	NGA	24/08/86	A	20	(5)	4
78	Alpay Koçaklı		19/09/98	M		(1)	
18	Aykut Akgün		18/09/87	M	7	(10)	
1	Aykut Özer		01/01/93	G		(1)	
13	Bertul Kocabaş		15/02/92	A	5	(3)	
2	Emre Güngör		01/08/84	D	11	(1)	1
5	Emre Özkan		24/12/88	D	10	(1)	
22	Erdem Özgenç		22/08/84	D	27		2
39	Erkan Kaş		10/09/91	M	7	(15)	2
33	Fatih Candan		30/12/89	A	5	(1)	1
20	Furkan Özçal		05/09/90	M	11	(2)	2
8	Hakan Özmert		03/06/85	M	22	(4)	
23	Tanju Kayhan	AUT	22/07/89	D	25	(2)	
90	Kuca	CPV	02/08/89	A	1	(1)	
12	Domi Kumbela	COD	20/04/84	A	17	(6)	3
6	Larrys Mabiala	COD	08/10/87	D	31		
3	Murat Akça		13/07/90	D	17	(6)	1
35	Musa Çağıran		17/11/92	M	23	(5)	4
66	Onur Ayık		28/01/90	M	15	(5)	2
66	Onur Cenik		24/09/92	D	2	(3)	
34	Serdar Aydın		19/07/96	M		(1)	
7	Samba Sow	MLI	25/04/89	M	14	(4)	1
7	Abdou Traoré	BFA	28/12/88	M	21	(4)	10
11	Turgay Bahadır		15/01/84	A		(9)	1
10	Valentín Viola	ARG	28/08/91	A	17	(4)	3
99	Boy Waterman	NED	24/01/84	G	21		
4	Yiğit İncedemir		09/03/85	M	15	(3)	

Kasımpaşa SK

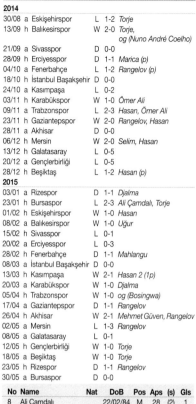

1921 • Recep Tayyip Erdoğan (14,234) •
kasimpasaspor.org.tr
Coach: Shota Arveladze (GEO);
(24/03/15) (Jan Wouters (NED));
(14/04/15) Önder Özen

2014

30/08	a	İstanbul Başakşehir	D 1-1	Adem
14/09	h	Mersin	D 2-2	Malki, Adem
21/09	h	Karabükspor	W 2-1	Viudez (p), Halil
27/09	a	Trabzonspor	D 1-1	Scarione
04/10	h	Gaziantepspor	W 4-2	Adem 2, Malki, Tunay
19/10	a	Akhisar	L 0-2	
24/10	h	Konyaspor	W 2-0	Scarione, Babel
31/10	a	Galatasaray	L 1-2	Adem
09/11	h	Gençlerbirliği	D 2-2	Adem, André Castro
23/11	a	Beşiktaş	L 0-2	
29/11	h	Rizespor	W 3-1	Babel 2, Halil
07/12	a	Bursaspor	L 1-5	Babel
13/12	h	Eskişehirspor	W 1-0	André Castro
21/12	h	Balıkesirspor	L 3-5	Scarione, Tunay, Donk
28/12	h	Sivasspor	D 0-0	

2015

04/01	a	Erciyesspor	W 5-2	Scarione 2 (1p), İlhan, Babel, og (Özen)
24/01	h	Fenerbahçe	L 0-3	
31/01	h	İstanbul Başakşehir	L 0-1	
08/02	a	Mersin	L 2-6	Veysel, Babel
22/02	h	Trabzonspor	D 1-1	Donk
14/02	a	Karabükspor	D 0-0	
01/03	a	Gaziantepspor	W 2-0	Scarione, André Castro
06/03	h	Akhisar	D 2-2	Adem, Scarione
13/03	a	Konyaspor	L 1-2	Donk
21/03	h	Galatasaray	L 2-3	André Castro, Tunay
04/04	a	Gençlerbirliği	L 2-5	Babel, Scarione
18/04	a	Beşiktaş	L 1-5	Tunay
25/04	h	Rizespor	W 3-1	Scarione 2, Babel
03/05	h	Bursaspor	W 5-3	Scarione, İlhan, André Castro, Malki, Derdiyok
08/05	a	Eskişehirspor	L 1-4	Scarione
12/05	h	Balıkesirspor	L 2-3	Scarione (p), Babel
16/05	a	Sivasspor	D 1-1	Derdiyok
23/05	h	Erciyesspor	D 3-3	Tunay, Donk, Malki
30/05	a	Fenerbahçe	L 0-2	

No	Name	Nat	DoB	Pos	Aps	(s)	Gls
10	Adem Büyük		30/08/87	A	21	(2)	7
23	Alpaslan Öztürk		16/07/93	M	22	(1)	
88	André Castro	POR	02/04/88	M	32		5
89	Atila Turan		10/04/92	D	1	(5)	
8	Ryan Babel	NED	19/12/86	A	28	(1)	9
22	Barış Başdaş		17/01/90	D	20	(2)	
73	Barış Kurtuldu		23/06/96	D		(2)	
9	Eren Derdiyok	SUI	12/06/88	A	2	(5)	2
6	Ryan Donk	NED	20/03/86	D	32		4
29	Lasha Dvali	GEO	14/05/95	D	9	(1)	
48	Erhan Kartal		01/03/93	D	4	(2)	
1	Ertaç Özbir		25/10/89	G	9		
39	Ferhat Kiraz		02/01/89	A	3	(8)	
33	Matías Fritzler	ARG	23/08/86	M		(3)	
7	Halil Çolak		29/01/88	M	8	(8)	2
15	Andreas Isaksson	SWE	03/10/81	G	25		
77	İdris Cengiz		01/01/95	D		(1)	
4	İlhan Eker		01/01/83	D	19	(3)	2
27	İsmail Ayaz		04/01/95	M	2	(7)	
20	Kerem Şeras		01/01/84	M	6	(4)	
36	Kubilay Aktaş		29/01/95	M	2	(3)	
16	Sanharib Malki	SYR	01/03/84	A	11	(14)	4
34	Mert Kula		01/01/95	D	1	(1)	
67	Orhan Şam		01/06/86	D	13	(1)	
5	Sancak Kaplan		25/05/82	D	31	(1)	
11	Ezequiel Scarione	ARG	14/07/85	A	28	(4)	13
55	Tunay Torun		21/04/90	M	26	(5)	5
18	Veysel Sarı		25/07/88	D	14	(1)	1
19	Tabaré Viudez	URU	08/09/89	A	5	(10)	1

Kayseri Erciyesspor

1966 • Kadir Has (32,864) • erciyesspor.org
Coach: Bülent Korkmaz;
(25/11/14) (Mustafa Imşek Ökkeş);
(07/12/14) Uğur Tütüneker;
(10/01/15) Mehmet Özdilekı
(29/03/15) Fatih Tekke

2014

31/08	h	Trabzonspor	D 0-0	
14/09	a	Gaziantepspor	D 2-2	Zoua, og (Elyasa)
20/09	h	Akhisar	L 1-2	Cenk
28/09	a	Konyaspor	D 1-1	Necati
04/10	h	Galatasaray	L 1-2	Caner
20/10	a	Gençlerbirliği	D 0-0	
27/10	h	Beşiktaş	W 3-2	Boye, Edinho, Cenk
02/11	a	Rizespor	D 1-1	Edinho
09/11	h	Bursaspor	D 1-1	Zoua
23/11	a	Eskişehirspor	L 1-2	Murat
29/11	h	Balıkesirspor	W 4-0	Mangane, Zoua, Edinho, Cenk
09/12	a	Sivasspor	D 1-1	Edinho
14/12	a	Mersin	D 1-1	Anıl
19/12	h	Fenerbahçe	L 0-1	
27/12	a	İstanbul Başakşehir	L 1-3	Edinho

2015

04/01	h	Kasımpaşa	L 2-5	Necati, Edinho
25/01	a	Karabükspor	W 2-1	Drenthe, Edinho
30/01	a	Trabzonspor	L 1-2	Anıl
07/02	a	Gaziantepspor	L 0-1	
20/02	h	Konyaspor	W 3-0	Boye, Drenthe, Vleminckx (p)
14/02	a	Akhisar	L 0-1	
27/02	a	Galatasaray	L 1-3	Vleminckx
07/03	h	Gençlerbirliği	L 2-4	Sylla, Serdar
15/03	a	Beşiktaş	L 1-5	Drenthe
21/03	h	Rizespor	L 0-3	
05/04	a	Bursaspor	L 0-3	
19/04	h	Eskişehirspor	L 0-1	
26/04	a	Balıkesirspor	D 1-1	Zoua
04/05	h	Sivasspor	L 2-3	Oğulcan, Vleminckx (p)
08/05	h	Mersin	D 2-2	Oğulcan, Zoua
13/05	a	Fenerbahçe	D 1-1	Zoua
17/05	h	İstanbul Başakşehir	L 0-1	
23/05	a	Kasımpaşa	D 3-3	Zoua, Edinho, Oğulcan
29/05	h	Karabükspor	W 4-3	Mehmet Seçme, Edinho 2, Orhan

No	Name	Nat	DoB	Pos	Aps	(s)	Gls
3	Anıl Karaer		04/07/88	D	29	(1)	2
61	Barış Memiş		05/01/90	M	10	(13)	
21	John Boye	GHA	23/04/87	D	22	(1)	2
88	Caner Osmanpaşa		15/01/88	D	26		1
40	Cem Can		01/04/81	M	2	(4)	
99	Cenk Alkılıç		09/12/87	M	25	(1)	3
15	Pape Diakhaté	SEN	21/06/84	D	6	(1)	
36	Royston Drenthe	NED	08/04/87	M	8	(3)	3
36	Edinho	POR	07/07/82	A	15	(11)	10
42	Emre Öztürk		26/08/92	D	9	(4)	
55	Ethem Pülgir		02/04/93	D	6	(1)	
35	Gökhan Değirmenci		21/03/89	G	25	(1)	
8	Senijad Ibričić	BIH	26/09/85	M	10		
38	İlhan Parlak		18/01/87	A	7	(1)	
7	Kerim Avcı		14/12/89	M	1	(1)	
14	Georges Mandjeck	CMR	09/12/88	M	7	(5)	
5	Kader Mangane	SEN	23/03/83	D	8	(1)	1
56	Mehmet Akgün		06/08/86	M	13	(4)	
56	Mehmet Seçme		24/10/96	A	1	(2)	1
15	Murat Yıldırım		18/05/87	M	30	(2)	1
19	Necati Ateş		03/01/80	A	15	(7)	2
23	Oğulcan Çağlayan		22/03/96	A	6	(5)	3
4	Orhan Gülle		15/01/92	M	1	(2)	1
2	Mahmut Özen	SWE	01/09/88	D	5	(7)	
27	Yasin Pehlivan	AUT	05/01/89	M	15		
67	Serdar Gürler		14/09/91	M	8	(2)	1
70	Serkan Demirezen		23/02/96	M		(2)	
95	Yacouba Sylla	MLI	29/11/90	M	24	(3)	1
32	Uğur Demirkol		16/01/90	D	1		
19	Björn Vleminckx	BEL	01/12/85	A	10	(11)	3
93	Yusuf Balcıoğlu		01/01/93	G	1		
9	Jacques Zoua	CMR	06/09/91	A	20	(3)	6
22	Zülküf Özer		10/05/88	G	8		

Konyaspor

1981 • Büyükşehir (42,144) • konyaspor.org.tr
Coach: Mesut Bakkal;
(28/10/14) Aykut Kocaman

2014

30/08	a	Eskişehirspor	L 1-2	Torje
13/09	h	Balıkesirspor	W 2-0	Torje, og (Nuno André Coelho)
21/09	a	Sivasspor	D 0-0	
28/09	h	Erciyesspor	D 1-1	Marica (p)
04/10	a	Fenerbahçe	L 1-2	Rangelov (p)
18/10	h	İstanbul Başakşehir	D 0-0	
24/10	a	Kasımpaşa	L 0-2	
03/11	h	Karabükspor	W 1-0	Ömer Ali
09/11	a	Trabzonspor	L 2-3	Hasan, Ömer Ali
23/11	h	Gaziantepspor	W 2-0	Rangelov, Hasan
28/11	a	Akhisar	D 0-0	
06/12	h	Mersin	W 2-0	Selim, Hasan
13/12	h	Galatasaray	L 0-5	
20/12	a	Gençlerbirliği	L 0-5	
28/12	h	Beşiktaş	L 1-2	Hasan (p)

2015

03/01	a	Rizespor	D 1-1	Djalma
23/01	h	Bursaspor	L 2-3	Ali Çamdalı, Torje
01/02	a	Eskişehirspor	W 1-0	Hasan
08/02	a	Balıkesirspor	W 1-0	Uğur
15/02	h	Sivasspor	L 0-1	
20/02	a	Erciyesspor	L 0-3	
28/02	h	Fenerbahçe	D 1-1	Mahlangu
08/03	a	İstanbul Başakşehir	D 0-0	
13/03	h	Kasımpaşa	W 2-1	Hasan 2 (1p)
20/03	a	Karabükspor	W 1-0	Djalma
05/04	h	Trabzonspor	W 1-0	og (Bosingwa)
17/04	a	Gaziantepspor	D 1-1	Rangelov
26/04	h	Akhisar	W 2-1	Mehmet Güven, Rangelov
02/05	a	Mersin	L 1-3	Rangelov
08/05	a	Galatasaray	L 0-1	
12/05	h	Gençlerbirliği	W 1-0	Torje
18/05	a	Beşiktaş	W 1-0	Torje
23/05	h	Rizespor	D 1-1	Rangelov
30/05	a	Bursaspor	D 0-0	

No	Name	Nat	DoB	Pos	Aps	(s)	Gls
8	Ali Çamdalı		22/02/84	M	28	(2)	1
4	Ali Turan		06/09/83	D	20	(2)	
52	Barış Örücü		10/05/92	D		(6)	
27	Vid Belec	SVN	06/06/90	G	13	(1)	
30	Djalma	ANG	30/05/87	A	16	(8)	2
18	Benjamin Fuchs	AUT	20/10/83	D	11	(10)	
99	Hasan Kabze		26/05/82	A	23	(5)	7
10	Aleksandr Hleb	BLR	01/05/81	M	13	(1)	
1	Kaya Tarakçı		23/04/81	G	21		
20	Kenan Özer		16/08/87	M	6	(6)	
44	Elvis Kokalović	CRO	17/07/88	D	20	(5)	
12	May Mahlangu	RSA	01/05/89	M	5	(3)	1
6	Ciprian Marica	ROU	02/10/85	A	4	(2)	1
6	Mehmet Güven		30/07/87	M	28	(1)	1
54	Mehmet Uslu		25/02/88	D	28	(1)	
7	Ömer Ali Şahiner		02/01/92	M	29	(1)	2
88	Özgür Özkaya		08/02/88	D	1		
9	Dimitar Rangelov	BUL	09/02/83	A	16	(7)	6
17	Recep Aydın		27/01/90	M	1	(16)	
5	Selim Ay		31/07/91	D	19		1
14	Tolga Ünlü		10/09/89	D	5	(2)	
11	Gabriel Torje	ROU	22/11/89	M	22	(5)	5
80	Uğur İnceman		25/05/81	M	22	(3)	1
20	Vedat Bora		27/01/95	M		(8)	
2	Volkan Fındıklı		13/10/90	D	3	(4)	
26	Jagoš Vuković	SRB	10/06/88	D	20	(1)	

TURKEY

Mersin İdman Yurdu

1925 • Tevfik Sırrı Gür (17,500); Mersin Arena (25,497) • mersinidmanyurdu.org.tr
Coach: Rıza Çalımbay

2014
30/08	h	Beşiktaş	L	0-1
14/09	a	Kasımpaşa	D	2-2 *Tita 2*
20/09	h	Rizespor	W	2-0 *Servet, Sinan*
29/09	a	Karabükspor	W	2-0 *Sadiku, Efe*
03/10	h	Bursaspor	W	2-1 *Servet, Sinan*
19/10	a	Trabzonspor	L	1-3 *Oktay*
26/10	h	Eskişehirspor	W	4-2 *Oktay 2, og (Berkay), Sinan*
02/11	a	Gaziantepspor	L	0-1
08/11	h	Balıkesirspor	W	2-1 *Welliton, Oktay*
22/11	a	Akhisar	D	1-1 *Welliton*
30/11	h	Sivasspor	W	2-0 *Nakoulma, Sinan*
06/12	a	Konyaspor	L	0-2
14/12	h	Erciyesspor	D	1-1 *Futács*
20/12	a	Galatasaray	L	2-3 *Güven Varol, Mitrović (p)*
27/12	a	Fenerbahçe	L	0-1

2015
05/01	h	Gençlerbirliği	D	1-1 *Welliton*
24/01	a	İstanbul Başakşehir	D	2-2 *Sinan, Mehmet*
01/02	a	Beşiktaş	L	1-2 *Sinan*
08/02	h	Kasımpaşa	W	6-2 *Welliton 3, Khalili, Mitrović (p), Pedriel*
15/02	a	Rizespor	W	4-0 *Futács 2, Nakoulma 2*
22/02	h	Karabükspor	W	2-1 *Servet, Mitrović (p)*
01/03	h	Bursaspor	L	1-2 *Mitrović (p)*
09/03	h	Trabzonspor	L	1-5 *Sinan*
15/03	h	Eskişehirspor	L	0-2
21/03	h	Gaziantepspor	L	0-1
04/04	a	Balıkesirspor	W	3-1 *Khalili, Welliton, Nakoulma*
20/04	h	Akhisar	D	1-1 *Gökçek Vederson (p)*
24/04	a	Sivasspor	W	2-1 *Sinan, Futács*
02/05	h	Konyaspor	W	3-1 *Welliton, Nakoulma, Gökçek Vederson*
08/05	a	Erciyesspor	D	2-2 *Gökçek Vederson (p), Sadiku*
12/05	h	Galatasaray	L	0-1
17/05	h	Fenerbahçe	L	0-1
22/05	a	Gençlerbirliği	W	2-1 *Welliton, Nakoulma*
30/05	h	İstanbul Başakşehir	D	2-2 *Welliton, Oktay*

No	Name	Nat	DoB	Pos	Aps	(s)	Gls
33	Efe Özarslan		29/03/90	D	9	(6)	1
44	Enes Sığırcı		24/02/93	D	1		
28	Eren Tozlu		27/12/90	A		(1)	
9	Márkó Futács	HUN	22/02/90	A	12	(14)	4
6	Gökçek Vederson		22/07/81	D	32		3
17	Adem Güven	NOR	11/10/85	M	1		
7	Güven Varol		02/06/81	M	17	(11)	1
55	Abdul Khalili	SWE	07/06/92	M	28	(2)	2
91	Mehmet Taş		20/03/91	M	2	(6)	1
31	Nikolay Mihaylov	BUL	28/06/88	G	6		
51	Milan Mitrović	SRB	02/07/88	D	21	(3)	4
21	Muammer Yıldırım		14/09/90	G	7		
5	Murat Ceylan		02/03/88	M	29	(2)	
22	Prejuce Nakoulma	BFA	21/04/87	A	31		6
1	Nihat Şahin		15/09/89	G	21	(1)	
72	Nurullah Kaya		20/07/86	A	2	(1)	
13	Oktay Delibalta		27/10/85	M	17	(2)	5
68	Ricardo Pedriel	BOL	19/01/87	A	9	(15)	1
3	Loret Sadiku	ALB	28/07/91	D	26		2
30	Serkan Balcı		22/08/83	D	26		
77	Serkan Yanık		02/04/87	D	2	(1)	
88	Serol Demirhan		05/12/88	M	1		
76	Servet Çetin		17/03/81	D	33		3
11	Sinan Kaloğlu		10/06/81	A	2	(22)	8
10	Tita	BRA	20/07/81	A	16	(8)	2
73	Welliton	BRA	22/10/86	A	23	(7)	10

Rizespor

1953 • Yeni Şehir (15,558) • caykurrizespor.org.tr
Coach: Mehmet Özdilek; (11/12/14) Hikmet Karaman

2014
29/08	h	Gençlerbirliği	D	1-1 *Korkmaz*
15/09	a	Beşiktaş	D	1-1 *Korkmaz*
20/09	a	Mersin	L	0-2
28/09	h	Bursaspor	L	0-1
05/10	a	Eskişehirspor	W	2-1 *Murat, Kweuke*
20/10	a	Balıkesirspor	D	2-2 *Giray, Hološko*
25/10	a	Sivasspor	W	1-0 *Kweuke*
02/11	h	Erciyesspor	D	1-1 *Oboabona*
08/11	h	Fenerbahçe	L	1-2 *og (Kadlec)*
22/11	h	İstanbul Başakşehir	L	0-2
29/11	a	Kasımpaşa	L	1-3 *Deniz*
07/12	h	Karabükspor	L	0-3
15/12	a	Trabzonspor	L	2-3 *Deniz, Kweuke*
22/12	h	Gaziantepspor	L	0-1
28/12	a	Akhisar	W	4-0 *Deniz 2, Viera, Hološko*

2015
03/01	h	Konyaspor	D	1-1 *Deniz*
25/01	a	Galatasaray	D	1-1
01/02	a	Gençlerbirliği	W	2-0 *Sercan, Obraniak*
08/02	h	Beşiktaş	L	1-2 *Sercan*
21/02	a	Bursaspor	D	1-1 *Kweuke*
15/02	h	Mersin	L	0-4
28/02	h	Eskişehirspor	W	3-0 *Deniz, Eren, Lafferty*
07/03	a	Balıkesirspor	D	2-2 *Kıvanç, Kweuke*
14/03	h	Sivasspor	W	2-1 *Kweuke 2*
21/03	a	Erciyesspor	W	3-0 *Kweuke, Obraniak (p), Sercan*
04/04	h	Fenerbahçe	L	1-5 *Deniz*
19/04	a	İstanbul Başakşehir	L	1-3 *Kweuke*
25/04	h	Kasımpaşa	L	1-3 *Kweuke*
02/05	h	Karabükspor	L	0-2
10/05	h	Trabzonspor	L	0-2
13/05	a	Gaziantepspor	W	2-1 *Deniz (p), Lafferty*
18/05	h	Akhisar	W	3-1 *Kweuke, Deniz, Sercan*
23/05	a	Konyaspor	D	1-1 *Kweuke*
30/05	h	Galatasaray	D	1-1 *Eren*

No	Name	Nat	DoB	Pos	Aps	(s)	Gls
10	Liban Abdi	NOR	05/10/88	M	3	(4)	
53	Ali Adnan	IRQ	19/12/93	D	7	(3)	
15	Aykut Erçetin		14/09/92	G	1		
63	Deniz Kadah		02/03/86	A	18	(11)	9
28	Engin Bekdemir		07/02/92	M	10	(2)	
11	Eren Albayrak		23/04/91	M	30	(1)	2
23	Giray Kaçar		15/03/85	D	28		1
51	Filip Hološko	SVK	17/01/84	A	19	(6)	2
66	Kıvanç Karakaş		03/03/85	M	29		1
4	Koray Altınay		11/10/91	D	18	(4)	
55	Ümit Korkmaz	AUT	17/09/85	M	9	(12)	2
9	Leonard Kweuke	CMR	12/07/87	A	27	(2)	12
16	Kyle Lafferty	NIR	16/09/87	A	4	(10)	2
32	Lomana LuaLua	COD	28/12/80	A	4	(4)	
19	Muhammed Emin Balcılar		15/04/96	A	1		
20	Murat Duruer		15/01/88	M	9	(6)	1
2	Godfrey Oboabona	NGA	16/08/90	D	17	(2)	1
8	Ludovic Obraniak	POL	10/11/84	M	14	(2)	2
12	Oğuzhan Berber		10/04/92	D		(3)	
17	Orhan Ovacıklı		23/11/88	D	25	(1)	
7	Sercan Kaya		15/03/88	M	13	(6)	4
1	Serkan Kırıntılı		15/02/85	G	33		
5	Sezer Özmen		07/07/92	D	1		
14	Ludovic Sylvestre	FRA	05/02/84	M	24	(5)	
88	Tevfik Köse		12/07/88	A	1	(12)	
3	Ousmane Viera	CIV	21/12/86	D	26		1

Sivasspor

1967 • 4 Eylül (14,998) • sivasspor.org.tr
Coach: Roberto Carlos (BRA); (23/12/14) Sergen Yalçın

2014
31/08	h	Gaziantepspor	L	1-2 *Utaka*
15/09	a	Akhisar	D	2-2 *Chahéchouche 2*
21/09	h	Konyaspor	D	0-0
26/09	a	Galatasaray	L	1-2 *Chrisantus*
04/10	h	Gençlerbirliği	W	1-0 *Manuel da Costa*
19/10	a	Beşiktaş	L	2-3 *Manuel da Costa, Hakan*
25/10	h	Rizespor	L	0-1
01/11	a	Bursaspor	L	0-3
07/11	h	Eskişehirspor	D	1-1 *Utaka*
24/11	a	Balıkesirspor	W	3-1 *Batuhan, Chahéchouche (p), Ahmet Aras*
30/11	a	Mersin	L	0-2
09/12	h	Erciyesspor	D	1-1 *Burhan*
12/12	a	Fenerbahçe	L	1-4 *Chahéchouche*
20/12	h	İstanbul Başakşehir	L	0-2
28/12	h	Kasımpaşa	D	0-0

2015
04/01	h	Karabükspor	W	2-0 *Batuhan, Ahmet Aras*
23/01	a	Trabzonspor	L	1-3 *Taouil*
31/01	h	Gaziantepspor	W	3-1 *Chahéchouche (p), İbrahim Akın, Kadir*
07/02	h	Akhisar	W	2-0 *Chahéchouche 2 (1p)*
15/02	a	Konyaspor	W	1-0 *Taouil*
21/02	h	Galatasaray	L	2-3 *Chahéchouche, İbrahim Akın*
28/02	a	Gençlerbirliği	D	0-0
08/03	h	Beşiktaş	L	0-1
14/03	a	Rizespor	L	1-2 *Burhan*
21/03	h	Bursaspor	W	4-1 *Batuhan 2, Burhan, Chahéchouche*
04/04	a	Eskişehirspor	W	3-1 *Chahéchouche 2, Utaka*
19/04	a	Balıkesirspor	D	1-1 *Batuhan*
24/04	h	Mersin	L	1-2 *Chahéchouche (p)*
04/05	h	Erciyesspor	W	3-2 *İbrahim Öztürk, Burhan 2*
09/05	h	Fenerbahçe	L	2-3 *Taouil, Cicinho*
12/05	a	İstanbul Başakşehir	L	1-2 *Burhan*
16/05	h	Kasımpaşa	L	1-2 *Chahéchouche*
24/05	a	Karabükspor	L	1-2 *Sinan*
30/05	h	Trabzonspor	D	1-1 *Batuhan*

No	Name	Nat	DoB	Pos	Aps	(s)	Gls
2	Abdurrahman Dereli		15/02/81	D	2	(1)	
66	Adem Koçak		01/09/83	M	29	(1)	
39	Ahmet Aras		13/12/87	A	3	(8)	2
46	Ahmet Şahbaz		12/03/91	M	1	(2)	
23	Aydın Karabulut		25/01/88	M	1		
35	Batuhan Karadeniz		24/04/91	A	19	(12)	6
5	Berk Neziroğluları		01/02/91	D	2	(1)	
21	Burhan Eşer		01/01/85	M	31		6
92	Aatif Chahéchouche	MAR	02/07/86	M	33		13
9	Macauley Chrisantus	NGA	20/08/90	A	3	(4)	1
12	Cicinho	BRA	24/06/80	D	32		1
10	Michael Eneramo	NGA	26/11/85	A	1	(2)	
16	Ertuğrul Taşkıran		05/11/89	G	20		
25	Fatih Çıplak		01/05/87	D	8	(1)	
37	Hakan Arslan		18/07/88	D	10	(10)	1
55	İbrahim Akın		04/01/84	M	5	(10)	2
3	İbrahim Öztürk		21/06/81	D	13		1
4	İbrahim Toraman		20/11/81	D	9	(1)	
8	Kadir Bekmezci		05/07/85	M	25	(1)	1
1	Korcan Çelikay		31/12/87	G	14		
22	Manuel da Costa	MAR	06/05/86	D	22	(2)	2
17	Cihan Özkara	AZE	14/07/91	A		(1)	
11	Sinan Yılmazer		31/01/87	M	3	(18)	1
91	Mehdi Taouil	MAR	20/05/83	M	22	(7)	3
7	John Utaka	NGA	08/01/82	A	16	(9)	3
80	Ümit Kurt		02/05/91	M	30		
58	Ziya Erdal		05/01/88	D	21		

Trabzonspor AŞ

1967 • Hüseyin Avni Aker (24,169) •
trabzonspor.org.tr
Major honours
*Turkish League (6) 1976, 1977, 1979, 1980, 1981,
1984, Turkish Cup (0) 1977, 1970, 1904, 1992, 1995,
2003, 2004, 2010*
**Coach: Vahid Halilhodžić (BIH);
(08/11/14) (Jacky Bonnevay (FRA));
(12/11/14) Ersun Yanal**

2014

31/08	a	Erciyesspor	D	0-0	
14/09	h	Fenerbahçe	D	0-0	
22/09	a	İstanbul Başakşehir	D	1-1	*Cardozo (p)*
27/09	h	Kasımpaşa	D	1-1	*Yusuf*
05/10	a	Karabükspor	L	0-3	
19/10	h	Mersin	W	3-1	*Belkalem, Medjani, Cardozo*
26/10	h	Gaziantepspor	D	4-4	*Belkalem, Yatabaré, Sefa, Cardozo*
01/11	a	Akhisar	D	1-1	*Mehmet*
09/11	h	Konyaspor	W	3-2	*Cardozo 2 (1p), Yusuf*
22/11	a	Galatasaray	W	3-0	*Medjani 2, Yusuf*
01/12	h	Gençlerbirliği	W	4-1	*Cardozo 3, Özer*
07/12	a	Beşiktaş	L	0-3	
15/12	h	Rizespor	W	3-2	*Medjani, Sefa 2*
21/12	a	Bursaspor	D	3-3	*Özer, Yusuf, Mustafa Akbaş*
29/12	a	Eskişehirspor	L	1-4	*Özer*

2015

05/01	a	Balıkesirspor	D	2-2	*Mehmet, Cardozo*
23/01	h	Sivasspor	W	3-1	*Cardozo 2 (1p), Mehmet*
30/01	h	Erciyesspor	W	2-1	*Mehmet, Cardozo*
07/02	a	Fenerbahçe	D	0-0	
15/02	h	İstanbul Başakşehir	W	3-2	*Mehmet, Sefa, Özer*
22/02	a	Kasımpaşa	D	1-1	*Mehmet*
02/03	h	Karabükspor	W	3-2	*Mehmet 2, Cardozo*
09/03	a	Mersin	W	5-1	*Mehmet, Sefa 2, og (Serol), Cardozo*
16/03	a	Gaziantepspor	L	0-2	
22/03	h	Akhisar	W	2-0	*Cardozo, Deniz*
05/04	a	Konyaspor	L	0-1	
19/04	h	Galatasaray	W	2-1	*Özer, Medjani*
26/04	a	Gençlerbirliği	D	1-1	*Medjani*
03/05	h	Beşiktaş	L	0-2	
10/05	a	Rizespor	W	2-0	*Salih, Deniz*
13/05	h	Bursaspor	W	1-0	*Özer*
17/05	a	Eskişehirspor	L	0-2	
23/05	h	Balıkesirspor	W	3-2	*Medjani, Cardozo 2*
30/05	a	Sivasspor	D	1-1	*Özer*

No	Name	Nat	DoB	Pos	Aps	(s)	Gls
4	Aykut Demir		22/10/88	D	10	(3)	
35	Aytaç Kara		28/03/93	M	4		
21	Essaïd Belkalem	ALG	01/01/89	D	13	(3)	2
3	José Bosingwa	POR	24/08/82	D	24		
7	Óscar Cardozo	PAR	20/05/83	A	23	(6)	17
11	Kévin Constant	GUI	10/05/87	M	12	(2)	
16	Deniz Yılmaz		26/02/88	A	10	(3)	2
66	Fatih Atik		25/06/84	M	16	(9)	
26	Fatih Öztürk		22/12/86	G	10	(1)	
50	Ferhat Yazgan		20/10/93	M	1	(3)	
17	Gökhan Karadeniz		02/05/90	A		(1)	
12	Hakan Arıkan		17/08/82	G	17		
13	İbrahim Demir		02/09/95	G	3		
68	İshak Doğan		09/08/90	D	6	(5)	
6	Carl Medjani	ALG	15/05/85	M	30		7
8	Mehmet Ekici		25/03/90	M	28	(1)	9
23	Mertcan Çam		16/11/95	M		(1)	
77	Musa Nizam		08/09/90	D	11	(1)	
14	Mustafa Akbaş		30/05/90	D	16	(5)	1
22	Mustafa Yumlu		25/09/87	D	2	(1)	
1	Onur Kıvrak		01/01/88	G	4		
10	Özer Hurmacı		20/11/86	M	22	(3)	7
30	Avraam Papadopoulos	GRE	03/12/84	D	5		
38	Salih Dursun		12/07/91	M	18	(4)	1
9	Sefa Yılmaz		14/02/90	M	16	(5)	6
67	Serdar Gürler		14/09/91	M	3	(4)	
20	Soner Aydoğdu		05/01/91	M	7	(7)	
15	Uğur Demirok		08/07/88	D	12	(2)	
28	Majeed Waris	GHA	19/09/91	A	9	(9)	
86	Mustapha Yatabaré	MLI	26/01/86	A	6	(8)	1
32	Yusuf Erdoğan		07/08/92	M	17	(5)	4
61	Zeki Yavru		05/09/91	D	7	(3)	
99	Erkan Zengin	SWE	05/08/85	M	12	(3)	

Top goalscorers

22	Fernandão (Bursaspor)
18	Demba Ba (Beşiktaş)
17	Óscar Cardozo (Trabzonspor)
16	Burak Yılmaz (Galatasaray)
14	Moussa Sow (Fenerbahçe)
13	Cédric Bakambu (Bursaspor)
	Ezequiel Scarione (Kasımpaşa)
	Aatif Chahéchouche (Sivasspor)
12	Theofanis Gekas (Akhisar)
	Volkan Şen (Bursaspor)
	Leonard Kweuke (Rizespor)

Promoted clubs

Kayserispor

1966 • Kadir Has (32,864) • kayserispor.org.tr
Major honours
Turkish Cup (1) 2008
**Coach: Mutlu Topçu;
(29/09/14) Cüneyt Dumlupınar**

Osmanlıspor

1978 • Osmanlı (19,626) • no website
**Coach: Osman Özköylü;
(25/12/14) Yılmaz Vural;
(21/01/15) Uğur Tütüneker**

Antalyaspor

1966 • Akdeniz Üniversitesi (7,083) •
antalyaspor.com.tr
**Coach: Engin Korukır;
(11/11/14) Hami Mandıralı;
(27/02/15) Yusuf Şimşek**

Second level final table 2014/15

		Pld	W	D	L	F	A	Pts
1	Kayserispor	34	21	9	4	61	24	72
2	Osmanlıspor	34	18	12	4	64	29	66
3	Alanyaspor	34	17	6	11	55	40	57
4	Adana Demirspor	34	16	8	10	57	48	56
5	Antalyaspor	34	15	10	9	56	43	55
6	Samsunspor	34	15	13	6	48	30	55
7	Altınordu	34	15	9	10	60	39	54
8	Şanlıurfaspor	34	13	13	8	41	29	52
9	Karşıyaka SK	34	13	6	15	49	57	45
10	Boluspor	34	11	11	12	47	40	44
11	Giresunspor	34	9	17	8	31	36	44
12	Elazığspor	34	11	9	14	42	45	42
13	Gaziantep BB	34	10	11	13	38	47	41
14	Adanaspor	34	10	9	15	42	54	39
15	Denizlispor	34	8	9	17	38	51	33
16	Manisaspor	34	10	3	21	42	60	33
17	Bucaspor	34	7	11	16	39	67	32
18	Orduspor	34	3	2	29	19	90	11

NB Samsunspor – 3 pts deducted.

Promotion play-offs
(28/05/15 & 01/06/15)
Antalyaspor 3-0 Adana Demirspor
Adana Demirspor 2-0 Antalyaspor
(Antalyaspor 3-2)

Samsunspor 5-1 Alanyaspor
Alanyaspor 0-4 Samsunspor
(Samsunspor 9-1)

(05/06/15)
Samsunspor 2-2 Antalyaspor *(aet; 1-4 on pens)*

DOMESTIC CUP

Türkiye Kupası 2014/15

SECOND ROUND

(23/09/14)
Akçaabat 0-0 Denizlispor *(aet; 4-2 pens)*
Anadolu Selçuk 1-2 Gaziantep BB
Bayrampaşaspor 1-1 Adanaspor *(aet; 5-4 pens)*
Bucaspor 2-1 Batman Petrolspor
Çorum Belediyespor 2-2 Manisaspor *(aet; 3-4 pens)*
Göztepe 2-1 Bursa Nilüferspor
Kayserispor 7-0 Kahramanmaraş BB
Osmanlıspor 0-2 Kırıkhanspor
Tarsus İdman Yurdu 1-6 Eskişehirspor
Tekirdağspor 1-5 Rizespor
Yeni Diyarbakırspor 1-2 Samsunspor

(24/09/14)
Adana Demirspor 4-1 Güngörenspor
Altınordu 2-0 Menemen Belediyespor
Ankaragücü 2-0 Gölcükspor
Balçova Yaşamspor 1-1 Balıkesirspor *(aet; 3-1 pens)*
Bayburt GÖİ 1-1 Pendikspor *(aet; 4-2 pens)*
BUGSAŞ 0-1 68 Yeni Aksarayspor *(aet)*
Cizrespor 3-1 Aydınspor 1923
Çankırıspor 2-1 Nazilli Belediyespor *(aet)*
Diyarbakır BB 4-2 Adliyespor *(aet)*
Erciyesspor 0-1 Etimesgut Belediyespor
Fethiyespor 1-0 Derincespor
Gölbaşıspor 1-1 Kırklarelispor *(aet; 4-3 pens)*
Hacettepe 0-0 Konyaspor *(aet; 2-4 pens)*
Hatayspor 3-1 Gaziosmanpaşaspor
İnegölspor 2-0 Niğde Belediyespor
Kahramanmaraşspor 4-2 12 Bingölspor *(aet)*
Karagümrük 3-2 Bandırmaspor *(aet)*
Karşıyaka 1-1 Altay *(aet; 3-4 pens)*
Keçiörengücü 2-1 Boluspor
Körfez İskenderunspor 0-1 Alanyaspor
Mersin 3-0 Kemer Tekirovaspor
Ofspor 1-0 Tirespor 1922
Orduspor 2-1 Düzyurtspor *(aet)*
Sakaryaspor 2-2 Giresunspor *(aet; 6-7 pens)*
Sandıklıspor 1-0 Kocaeli Birlik
Sarıyer 3-0 Turgutluspor
Tavşanlı Linyitspor 1-1 Denizli BB *(aet; 6-5 pens)*
Tepecikspor 2-0 Anadolu Üsküdar 1908
Tuzlaspor 2-0 Kartalspor
Ümraniyespor 2-1 Pazarspor
Yeni Malatyaspor 1-0 Eyüpspor
Yeşil Bursa 1-3 1461 Trabzon
Zonguldak Kömürspor 4-2 Gümüşhanespor

(25/09/14)
Antalyaspor 1-3 BB Erzurumspor
İstanbul Başakşehir 1-0 Tokatspor
Elazığspor 3-2 Ayvalıkgücü Belediyespor
Erzin Belediyespor 0-5 Gaziantepspor
Şanlıurfaspor 3-3 Sivas 4 Eylül Belediyespor *(aet; 1-3 pens)*

THIRD ROUND

(28/10/14)
Akhisar 2-1 BB Erzurumspor *(aet)*
Cizrespor 2-0 Göztepe
Gençlerbirliği 6-0 Etimesgut Belediyespor
Tuzlaspor 3-1 Kasımpaşa

(29/10/14)
1461 Trabzon 0-1 Sivas 4 Eylül Belediyespor
Altınordu 1-0 Ofspor
Bayrampaşaspor 0-1 Giresunspor
Bursaspor 2-0 Tepecikspor
Çankırıspor 2-3 Gaziantepspor
Diyarbakır BB 3-2 Alanyaspor *(aet)*
Gaziantep BB 1-0 68 Yeni Aksarayspor
Kahramanmaraşspor 1-3 Karagümrük

Keçiörengücü 1-0 Fethiyespor *(aet)*
Kırıkhanspor 0-4 Eskişehirspor
Rizespor 4-1 Akçaabat
Samsunspor 0-0 Yeni Malatyaspor *(aet; 4-1 pens)*
Tavşanlı Linyitspor 0-2 Ankaragücü

(30/10/14)
Altay 1-2 Konyaspor
Gölbaşıspor 0-0 Kayserispor *(aet; 3-4 pens)*
İnegölspor 2-2 Karabükspor *(aet; 2-4 pens)*
Mersin 2-0 Hatayspor
Sarıyer 1-0 Orduspor

(05/11/14)
Adana Demirspor 2-0 Sandıklıspor
Balçova Yaşamspor 1-0 Elazığspor *(aet)*
Bayburt GÖİ 2-2 Bucaspor *(aet; 5-4 pens)*
İstanbul Başakşehir 3-1 Ümraniyespor *(aet)*
Manisaspor 2-1 Zonguldak Kömürspor

GROUP STAGE

Group A

(02/12/14)
Gaziantep BB 2-3 Tuzlaspor

(03/12/14)
Sivasspor 1-2 Gaziantepspor

(16/12/14)
Tuzlaspor 3-1 Sivasspor

(17/12/14)
Gaziantepspor 0-0 Gaziantep BB

(24/12/14)
Sivasspor 4-0 Gaziantep BB

(25/12/14)
Gaziantepspor 2-2 Tuzlaspor

(31/12/14)
Gaziantep BB 1-2 Sivasspor
Tuzlaspor 2-1 Gaziantepspor

(28/01/15)
Gaziantepspor 0-2 Sivasspor
Tuzlaspor 3-1 Gaziantep BB

(04/02/15)
Gaziantep BB 1-3 Gaziantepspor
Sivasspor 3-0 Tuzlaspor

Final standings
1 Tuzlaspor 13 pts; 2 Sivasspor 12 pts *(qualified)*
3 Gaziantepspor 8 pts; 4 Gaziantep BB 1 pt *(eliminated)*

Group B

(02/12/14)
Akhisar 3-2 Manisaspor

(04/12/14)
Keçiörengücü 1-1 Trabzonspor

(17/12/14)
Manisaspor 1-0 Keçiörengücü

(18/12/14)
Trabzonspor 0-0 Akhisar

(25/12/14)
Keçiörengücü 1-1 Akhisar
Trabzonspor 9-0 Manisaspor

(31/12/14)
Akhisar 1-2 Keçiörengücü

(01/01/15)
Manisaspor 0-2 Trabzonspor

(27/01/15)
Manisaspor 1-1 Akhisar
Trabzonspor 0-0 Keçiörengücü

(03/02/15)
Akhisar 0-2 Trabzonspor

(04/02/15)
Keçiörengücü 1-2 Manisaspor

Final standings
1 Trabzonspor 12 pts; 2 Manisaspor 7 pts *(qualified)*
3 Keçiörengücü 6 pts; 4 Akhisar 6 pts *(eliminated)*

Group C

(03/12/14)
Samsunspor 0-1 Karagümrük

(10/12/14)
Bursaspor 1-1 Mersin

(17/12/14)
Karagümrük 1-1 Bursaspor
Mersin 3-1 Samsunspor

(23/12/14)
Karagümrük 1-0 Mersin

(24/12/14)
Samsunspor 2-3 Bursaspor

(31/12/14)
Bursaspor 1-1 Samsunspor

(01/01/15)
Mersin 3-0 Karagümrük

(27/01/15)
Mersin 0-5 Bursaspor

(28/01/15)
Karagümrük 0-3 Samsunspor

(04/02/15)
Samsunspor 1-1 Mersin

(05/02/15)
Bursaspor 3-0 Karagümrük

Final standings
1 Bursaspor 12 pts; 2 Mersin 8 pts *(qualified)*
3 Karagümrük 7 pts; 4 Samsunspor 5 pts *(eliminated)*

Group D

(02/12/14)
İstanbul Başakşehir 3-2 Ankaragücü

(04/12/14)
Sivas 4 Eylül Belediyespor 2-1 Karabükspor

(17/12/14)
Karabükspor 2-2 İstanbul Başakşehir

(18/12/14)
Ankaragücü 1-1 Sivas 4 Eylül Belediyespor

(23/12/14)
Ankaragücü 0-3 Karabükspor

(24/12/14)
İstanbul Başakşehir 0-0 Sivas 4 Eylül Belediyespor

(30/12/14)
Karabükspor 2-0 Ankaragücü
Sivas 4 Eylül Belediyespor 1-2 İstanbul Başakşehir

(27/01/15)
Ankaragücü 1-1 İstanbul Başakşehir

(28/01/15)
Karabükspor 2-1 Sivas 4 Eylül Belediyespor

(03/02/15)
İstanbul Başakşehir 1-2 Karabükspor

(05/02/15)
Sivas 4 Eylül Belediyespor 1-2 Ankaragücü

Final standings
1 Karabükspor 13 pts; 2 İstanbul Başakşehir 9 pts *(qualified)*
3 Ankaragücü 5 pts; 4 Sivas 4 Eylül Belediyespor 5 pts *(eliminated)*

Group E

(02/12/14)
Fenerbahçe 1-2 Kayserispor

(03/12/14)
Altınordu 1-0 Bayburt GÖİ

(16/12/14)
Bayburt GÖİ 1-3 Fenerbahçe
Kayserispor 3-0 Altınordu

(23/12/14)
Fenerbahçe 1-1 Altınordu

(24/12/14)
Kayserispor 2-2 Bayburt GÖİ

(31/12/14)
Bayburt GÖİ 3-0 Kayserispor

(20/01/15)
Altınordu 0-1 Fenerbahçe

(27/01/15)
Kayserispor 1-1 Fenerbahçe

(28/01/15)
Bayburt GÖİ 3-1 Altınordu

(03/02/15)
Fenerbahçe 5-0 Bayburt GÖİ

(04/02/15)
Altınordu 0-3 Kayserispor

Final standings
1 Kayserispor 11 pts; 2 Fenerbahçe 11 pts *(qualified)*;
3 Bayburt GÖİ 7 pts; 4 Altınordu 4 pts *(eliminated)*

Group F

(03/12/14)
Rizespor 2-1 Adana Demirspor

(04/12/14)
Sarıyer 0-4 Beşiktaş

(18/12/14)
Adana Demirspor 1-0 Sarıyer
Beşiktaş 0-1 Rizespor

(24/12/14)
Beşiktaş 1-2 Adana Demirspor

(25/12/14)
Sarıyer 0-2 Rizespor

(31/12/14)
Rizespor 1-0 Sarıyer

(21/01/15)
Adana Demirspor 1-4 Beşiktaş

(28/01/15)
Adana Demirspor 1-1 Rizespor

(29/01/15)
Beşiktaş 3-1 Sarıyer

(05/02/15)
Rizespor 0-0 Beşiktaş
Sarıyer 3-2 Adana Demirspor

Final standings
1 Rizespor 14 pts; 2 Beşiktaş 10 pts *(qualified)*;
3 Adana Demirspor 7 pts; 4 Sarıyer 3 pts *(eliminated)*

Group G

(03/12/14)
Diyarbakır BB 2-2 Balçova Yaşamspor
Galatasaray 4-2 Eskişehirspor

(16/12/14)
Balçova Yaşamspor 1-9 Galatasaray

(17/12/14)
Eskişehirspor 3-0 Diyarbakır BB

(23/12/14)
Diyarbakır BB 1-4 Galatasaray

(24/12/14)
Balçova Yaşamspor 1-2 Eskişehirspor

(16/01/15)
Eskişehirspor 3-0 Balçova Yaşamspor

(22/01/15)
Galatasaray 0-2 Diyarbakır BB

(28/01/15)
Balçova Yaşamspor 1-1 Diyarbakır BB
Eskişehirspor 1-0 Galatasaray

(04/02/15)
Diyarbakır BB 1-0 Eskişehirspor
Galatasaray 3-1 Balçova Yaşamspor

Final standings
1 Galatasaray 12 pts; 2 Eskişehirspor 12 pts
(qualified);
3 Diyarbakır BB 8 pts; 4 Balçova Yaşamspor 2 pts
(eliminated)

Group H

(02/12/14)
Konyaspor 1-2 Giresunspor

(09/12/14)
Cizrespor 1-2 Gençlerbirliği

(16/12/14)
Gençlerbirliği 2-0 Konyaspor

(17/12/14)
Giresunspor 1-2 Cizrespor

(23/12/14)
Giresunspor 2-2 Gençlerbirliği

(24/12/14)
Konyaspor 7-1 Cizrespor

(30/12/14)
Gençlerbirliği 0-0 Giresunspor

(31/12/14)
Cizrespor 2-0 Konyaspor

(27/01/15)
Giresunspor 0-2 Konyaspor

(29/01/15)
Gençlerbirliği 4-0 Cizrespor

(04/02/15)
Cizrespor 0-0 Giresunspor
Konyaspor 0-0 Gençlerbirliği

Final standings
1 Gençlerbirliği 12 pts; Konyaspor 7 pts *(qualified)*;
3 Cizrespor 7 pts; Giresunspor 6 pts *(eliminated)*

1/8 FINALS

(10/02/15)
Trabzonspor 2-3 Sivasspor *(aet)*

(11/02/15)
Bursaspor 1-1 Başakşehir *(aet; 3-2 pens)*
Karabükspor 2-4 Mersin *(aet)*
Kayserispor 1-0 Beşiktaş
Rizespor 1-4 Fenerbahçe

(12/02/15)
Galatasaray 4-1 Konyaspor
Gençlerbirliği 3-0 Eskişehirspor
Tuzlaspor 1-3 Manisaspor

QUARTER-FINALS

(03/03/15 & 15/04/15)
Galatasaray 4-0 Manisaspor *(Dzemaili 34, Emre
40p, Pandev 68, 87)*
Manisaspor 1-1 Galatasaray *(Hakan 70; Yekta 1)*
(Galatasaray 5-1)

(04/03/15 & 14/04/15)
Bursaspor 1-1 Gençlerbirliği *(Serdar 59; Çelik 49)*
Gençlerbirliği 2-3 Bursaspor *(Petrović 15, El Kabir
38; Volkan 59, 73, Fernandão 90)*
(Bursaspor 4-3)

(04/03/15 & 16/04/15)
Mersin 1-2 Fenerbahçe *(Welliton 74; Diego 44,
Sow 45)*
Fenerbahçe 4-1 Mersin *(Kuyt 6, 31p, Hasan Ali 49,
Caner Erkin 61; Futács 72)*
(Fenerbahçe 6-2)

(05/03/15 & 07/04/15)
Kayserispor 1-1 Sivasspor *(Çağlar 48; Batuhan 20)*
Sivasspor 1-1 Kayserispor *(Chahéchouche 45;
Bobô 90p) (aet)*
(2-2; Sivasspor 3-1 on pens)

SEMI-FINALS

(28/04/15 & 21/05/15)
Bursaspor 1-2 Fenerbahçe *(Belluschi 33; Emenike
26, Bruno Alves 36)*
Fenerbahçe 0-3 Bursaspor *(Volkan 33, Fernandão
76, Şamil 84)*
(Bursaspor 4-2)

(30/04/15 & 19/05/15)
Galatasaray 4-1 Sivasspor *(Sabri 32, Felipe Melo
35, Sneijder 65, Selçuk 77p; Utaka 9)*
Sivasspor 2-1 Galatasaray *(Batuhan 69, 74; Emre 82p)*
(Galatasaray 5-3)

FINAL

(03/06/15)
Atatürk, Bursa
GALATASARAY AŞ 3 *(Burak 40, 48, 60)*
BURSASPOR 2 *(Fernandão 27p, Volkan 58)*
Referee: Bülent Yıldırım
GALATASARAY: Sinan Bolat, Sabri, Semih, Hakan,
Alex Telles, Hamit *(Emre 79)*, Felipe Melo, Selçuk
(Umut 89), Yasin, Sneijder, Burak *(Olcan 90)*
BURSASPOR: Harun, Şener, Ertuğrul, Şamil,
Behich *(Emre 64)*, Ozan Tufan *(Bekir 86)*, Belluschi,
Volkan, Josué, Bakambu *(Enes 90)*, Fernandão

Victorious Galatasaray players pose with the Turkish Cup

UKRAINE
Federatsiya Futbola Ukrainy (FFU)

Address	Provulok Laboratorniy 7-A	**President**	Andriy Pavelko
	PO Box 55	**General secretary**	Volodymyr Geninson
	UA-01133 Kyiv	**Media officer**	Olexandr Hlyvynskiy
Tel	+380 44 521 0521	**Year of formation**	1989
Fax	+380 44 521 0550	**National stadium**	NSK Olimpiyskiy,
E-mail	info@ffu.org.ua		Kyiv (70,050)
Website	ffu.org.ua		

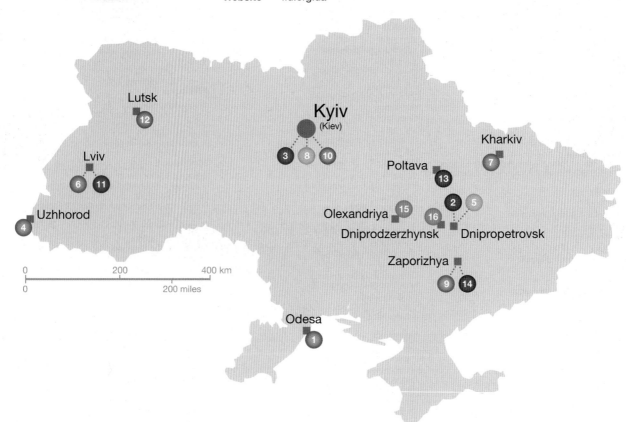

PREMIER LEAGUE CLUBS

 1 FC Chornomorets Odesa

 2 FC Dnipro Dnipropetrovsk

 3 FC Dynamo Kyiv

 4 FC Hoverla Uzhhorod

 5 FC Illychivets Mariupil

 6 FC Karpaty Lviv

 7 FC Metalist Kharkiv

 8 FC Metalurh Donetsk

 9 FC Metalurh Zaporizhya

 10 FC Olimpik Donetsk

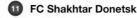 11 FC Shakhtar Donetsk

 12 FC Volyn Lutsk

 13 FC Vorskla Poltava

 14 FC Zorya Luhansk

PROMOTED CLUBS

 15 FC Olexandriya

 16 FC Stal Dniprodzerzhynsk

KEY:
● – UEFA Champions League
● – UEFA Europa League
● – Promoted
● – Relegated

Dynamo Kyiv back in charge

FC Dynamo Kyiv, the traditional powerhouse of Ukrainian football, reasserted their authority in 2014/15 as former striker Serhiy Rebrov led the club to an impressive domestic double in his first full season as head coach.

Unbeaten in their 26 Premier League fixtures, Dynamo also avoided defeat in their eight Ukrainian Cup outings, the last of them a 0-0 draw against deposed champions FC Shakhtar Donetsk, which they won in an extended penalty shoot-out. FC Dnipro Dnipropetrovsk, meanwhile, thrilled the nation by finishing runners-up in the UEFA Europa League.

Rebrov leads record champions to domestic double

Shakhtar's five-year reign ended by unbeaten champions

Dnipro defy odds to reach UEFA Europa League final

Domestic league

There was an unfamiliar look and feel to the 2014/15 Ukrainian Premier League, with its number reduced to 14 clubs and those from the unsettled south-east, including Shakhtar, having to re-locate to other parts of the country. The champions of the previous five seasons opted to play their home games approximately 1,000 km away in Lviv. It was a handicap that Mircea Lucescu's Brazilian-heavy side failed to overcome as they ended the campaign ten points adrift of their rivals from the capital.

Shakhtar and Dnipro were the league's early pacesetters, but once Dynamo had defeated the latter 3-0 to go top, they were never unseated. Comprehensive victories became commonplace, and on the rare days that Rebrov's men were not in prime form, they either won narrowly or drew. The concession of just 12 goals all season told its own story, with Austrian international Aleksandar Dragovic the standout figure in a watertight defence as homegrown pair Andriy Yarmolenko and Artem Kravets ensured a regular supply of goals at the other end.

The main plaudits, however, belonged to rookie coach Rebrov, appointed as an interim replacement for Oleh Blokhin in April 2014 before securing the job full-time in the summer. Dynamo had

finished fourth in 2013/14 – their lowest-ever placing – so the turnaround was rapid. The club's 27th national title – and 14th in Ukraine – was cemented with a 1-0 home win over Dnipro, who then beat Shakhtar 3-2 but had to cede the second UEFA Champions League spot to their Lviv-based rivals on the final day. Joining Dnipro in the UEFA Europa League were FC Zorya Luhansk and FC Vorskla Poltava as FC Metalist Kharkiv, top-three residents for eight straight seasons, dropped to sixth.

Domestic cup

The eighth Ukrainian Cup final between Dynamo and Shakhtar ended in a fifth victory for the former and a second in as many years as Rebrov's team emerged victorious on penalties in their own NSK Olimpiyskiy stadium following a 0-0 stalemate. Shakhtar led 3-1 in the shoot-out, but Dynamo turned things around thanks to their 40-year-old goalkeeper Olexandr Shovkovskiy. Not content with having collected his 13th league title with the club, he made sure of a tenth cup winner's medal by saving twice, from Taison and – with the 14th and last kick of the contest – Olexandr Gladkiy, to help Dynamo to a 5-4 victory.

Europe

While Shakhtar and Dynamo performed creditably in Europe, both were upstaged

by Myron Markevych's Dnipro, who clocked up the air miles in a 19-game journey that began in the third qualifying round of the UEFA Champions League and ended in the final of the UEFA Europa League.

Yevhen Konoplyanka and co were masters of pragmatism, scoring a maximum two goals per game and keeping nine clean sheets. Having knocked out the champions of Greece and the Netherlands, they edged past Club Brugge KV and SSC Napoli with 1-0 second-leg wins in Kyiv before playing their part in an excellent final against Sevilla FC, which they lost 3-2 in Warsaw.

National team

Rocked by a 1-0 defeat at home to Slovakia in their opening UEFA EURO 2016 fixture, Mykhailo Fomenko's Ukraine – still an all-home-based outfit apart from 140-cap skipper Anatoliy Tymoshchuk - did their best to rectify the situation with four wins in their next five qualifiers and a gallant 1-0 defeat in Spain.

However, that lifted them no higher than third place and the likelihood was that, barring revenge wins against the two teams above them, they would have to prevail in the play-offs to achieve a first qualification for a tournament they co-hosted in 2012.

DOMESTIC SEASON AT A GLANCE

Premier League 2014/15 final table

			Home				Away					Total					
		Pld	W	D	L	F	A	W	D	L	F	A	W	D	L	F	A	Pts
1	**FC Dynamo Kyiv**	**26**	**9**	**4**	**0**	**30**	**5**	**11**	**2**	**0**	**35**	**7**	**20**	**6**	**0**	**65**	**12**	**66**
2	FC Shakhtar Donetsk	26	9	3	1	34	6	8	2	3	37	15	17	5	4	71	21	56
3	FC Dnipro Dnipropetrovsk	26	7	4	2	24	11	9	2	2	23	6	16	6	4	47	17	54
4	FC Zorya Luhansk	26	7	3	3	25	17	6	3	4	15	14	13	6	7	40	31	45
5	FC Vorskla Poltava	26	8	2	3	22	10	3	7	3	13	12	11	9	6	35	22	42
6	FC Metalist Kharkiv	25	5	5	3	19	18	3	6	3	15	14	8	11	6	34	32	35
7	FC Metalurh Zaporizhya	26	3	4	6	11	19	3	4	6	9	21	6	8	12	20	40	26
8	FC Olimpik Donetsk	26	6	2	5	15	23	1	3	9	9	41	7	5	14	24	64	26
9	FC Volyn Lutsk	26	4	4	5	20	18	5	3	5	18	26	9	7	10	38	44	25
10	FC Metalurh Donetsk	26	4	6	3	15	17	2	4	7	12	21	6	10	10	27	38	22
11	FC Chornomorets Odesa	25	3	6	3	9	10	0	5	8	6	21	3	11	11	15	31	20
12	FC Hoverla Uzhhorod	26	2	6	5	11	20	1	4	8	11	27	3	10	13	22	47	19
13	FC Karpaty Lviv	26	4	2	7	13	15	1	7	5	9	16	5	9	12	22	31	15
14	FC Illychivets Mariupil	26	3	3	7	20	28	0	2	11	5	27	3	5	18	25	55	14

NB FC Karpaty Lviv & FC Volyn Lutsk – 9 pts deducted; FC Metalurh Donetsk – 6 pts deducted; match between FC Chornomorets and FC Metalist Kharkiv was not played.

European qualification 2015/16

Champion/Cup winner: FC Dynamo Kyiv (group stage)
FC Shakhtar Donetsk (third qualifying round)

FC Dnipro Dnipropetrovsk (group stage)
FC Zorya Luhansk (third qualifying round)
FC Vorskla Poltava (third qualifying round)

Top scorer   Alex Teixeira (Shakhtar) & Eric Bicfalvi (Volyn), 17 goals
Relegated clubs   FC Illychivets Mariupil, FC Metalurh Donetsk (withdrew)
Promoted clubs   FC Olexandriya, FC Stal Dniprodzerzhynsk
Cup final   FC Dynamo Kyiv 0-0 FC Shakhtar Donetsk *(aet; 5-4 on pens)*

Team of the season
(4-1-3-2)

Coach: Rebrov *(Dynamo)*

Shovkovskiy *(Dynamo)*

Srna *(Shakhtar)*   Dragovic *(Dynamo)*   Vida *(Dynamo)*   Shevchuk *(Shakhtar)*

Rybalka *(Dynamo)*

Yarmolenko *(Dynamo)*   Alex Teixeira *(Shakhtar)*   Konoplyanka *(Dnipro)*

Bicfalvi *(Volyn)*   Kravets *(Dynamo)*

Player of the season

Andriy Yarmolenko
(FC Dynamo Kyiv)

The heir to Andriy Shevchenko as Ukrainian football's golden boy, Yarmolenko enjoyed his finest season yet, inspiring Dynamo to a domestic double and into the quarter-finals of the UEFA Europa League. On top form throughout, the dynamic left-footed winger registered 14 league goals and 12 assists while consistently outfoxing defenders with his strength and technique. He also became Ukraine's second highest goalscorer, overtaking his club coach Serhiy Rebrov with a hat-trick against Luxembourg.

Newcomer of the season

Valeriy Luchkevych
(FC Dnipro Dnipropetrovsk)

A pacy, explosive right-back who can also operate with equal effectiveness in midfield, Luchkevych did not break into the Dnipro first team until several months after his arrival from FC Metalurh Zaporizhya in December 2013. However, once he had finally made his debut, the talented teenager became an important asset to Myron Markevych's side, both in domestic competition and in the UEFA Europa League, where he started all four quarter-final and semi-final ties only to be left out for the final.

NATIONAL TEAM

International tournament appearances
FIFA World Cup (1) 2006 (qtr-finals)
UEFA European Championship (1) 2012

Top five all-time caps
Anatoliy Tymoshchuk (140); Andriy Shevchenko (111); **Oleh Gusev** (96); Olexandr Shovkovskiy (92); **Ruslan Rotan** (80)

Top five all-time goals
Andriy Shevchenko (48); **Andriy Yarmolenko** (19); Serhiy Rebrov (15); **Oleh Gusev** (13); Serhiy Nazarenko (12)

Results 2014/15

03/09/14	Moldova	H	Kyiv	W	1-0	*Bezus (63)*
08/09/14	Slovakia (ECQ)	H	Kyiv	L	0-1	
09/10/14	Belarus (ECQ)	A	Borisov	W	2-0	*Martynovich (82og), Sydorchuk (90+3)*
12/10/14	FYR Macedonia (ECQ)	H	Lviv	W	1-0	*Sydorchuk (45+2)*
15/11/14	Luxembourg (ECQ)	A	Luxembourg	W	3-0	*Yarmolenko (33, 53, 56)*
18/11/14	Lithuania	H	Kyiv	D	0-0	
27/03/15	Spain (ECQ)	A	Seville	L	0-1	
31/03/15	Latvia	H	Lviv	D	1-1	*Yarmolenko (35)*
09/06/15	Georgia	N	Linz (AUT)	W	2-1	*Kravets (57), Konoplyanka (67)*
14/06/15	Luxembourg (ECQ)	H	Lviv	W	3-0	*Kravets (48), Garmash (57), Konoplyanka (86)*

Appearances 2014/15

Coach: Mykhailo Fomenko	19/09/48		Mda	SVK	BLR	MKD	LUX	Ltu	ESP	Lva	Geo	LUX	Caps	Goals
Andriy Pyatov	28/06/84	Shakhtar Donetsk	G	G	G	G	G		G			G	55	-
Artem Fedetskiy	26/04/85	Dnipro	D	D	D	D	D	s67	D	D			39	2
Olexandr Kucher	22/10/82	Shakhtar Donetsk	D	D	D	D			D	D		s77	46	2
Yaroslav Rakitskiy	03/08/89	Shakhtar Donetsk	D	D			D			D	D	D77	32	4
Vyacheslav Shevchuk	13/05/79	Shakhtar Donetsk	D46	D	D	D	D		D	D	s46	D	44	-
Anatoliy Tymoshchuk	30/03/79	Zenit (RUS)	M27		s91	s92	M	s77	M	M	s46		140	4
Taras Stepanenko	08/08/89	Shakhtar Donetsk	M	M	M	M			M76		M46	M	21	1
Oleh Gusev	25/04/83	Dynamo Kyiv	M75	M81				D		M59	D46		96	13
Edmar	16/06/80	Metalist	M46	M	M79	s95							15	1
Andriy Yarmolenko	23/10/89	Dynamo Kyiv	M46	M	M	M	M	s46	M	M		M	49	19
Roman Zozulya	17/11/89	Dnipro	A64	A	A91	A77	A72		A32				22	3
Kyrylo Kovalchuk	11/06/86	Chornomorets Odesa	s27	M66			s85	s46					4	-
Artem Gromov	14/01/90	Vorskla	s46	s81									2	-
Yevhen Makarenko	21/05/91	Dynamo Kyiv	s46										3	-
Roman Bezus	26/09/90	Dynamo Kyiv /Dnipro	s46	s66				M77		M85			19	4
Olexandr Gladkiy	24/08/87	Shakhtar Donetsk	s64										9	1
Mykola Morozyuk	17/01/88	Metalurh Donetsk	s75				s76	D67			D	D	13	1
Yevhen Khacheridi	28/07/87	Dynamo Kyiv			D	D	D		D		D	D	34	3
Yevhen Konoplyanka	29/09/89	Dnipro			M	M	M76	s46	M	s59	M76	M	45	10
Ruslan Rotan	29/10/81	Dnipro			M64	M92		M77	M		M46	M46	80	7
Serhiy Sydorchuk	02/05/91	Dynamo Kyiv			s64	M95	M	s77			s46	M	6	2
Pylyp Budkivskiy	10/03/92	Zorya			s79	s77	s72	A	s91	s75			6	-
Denys Oliynyk	16/06/87	Vitesse (NED)				M85	M46			s76			12	-
Denys Boyko	29/01/88	Dnipro					G		G	G	G		3	-
Ivan Ordets	08/07/92	Shakhtar Donetsk					D						2	1
Vitaliy Vernydub	17/10/87	Zorya					D46						1	-
Andriy Pylyavskiy	04/12/88	Zorya					M						1	-
Dmytro Khomchenovskiy	16/04/90	Zorya					M46						4	-
Artem Kravets	03/06/89	Dynamo Kyiv						s32 /91	A75	s46	A69		6	2
Denys Garmash	19/04/90	Dynamo Kyiv						s76	M46	M46	s46		20	2
Serhiy Rybalka	01/04/90	Dynamo Kyiv							s46	s46			2	-
Ruslan Malinovskiy	04/05/93	Zorya							s85				1	-
Pavlo Ksionz	02/01/87	Dnipro								M			1	-
Yevhen Seleznyov	20/07/85	Dnipro								A46	s69		44	9

EUROPE

FC Shakhtar Donetsk

Group H
Match 1 - Athletic Club (ESP)
A 0-0
Pyatov, Kucher, Stepanenko, Luiz Adriano (Gladkiy 89), Fernando (Fred 73), Douglas Costa, Taison (Marlos 80), Alex Teixeira, Srna, Rakitskiy, Azevedo. Coach: Mircea Lucescu (ROU)
Match 2 - FC Porto (POR)
H 2-2 *Alex Teixeira (52), Luiz Adriano (85)*
Pyatov, Kucher, Stepanenko, Luiz Adriano, Fernando, Douglas Costa (Bernard 79), Taison (Ilsinho 75), Alex Teixeira, Srna, Rakitskiy, Azevedo. Coach: Mircea Lucescu (ROU)
Match 3 - FC BATE Borisov (BLR)
A 7-0 *Alex Teixeira (11), Luiz Adriano (28p, 36, 40, 44, 82p), Douglas Costa (35)*
Pyatov, Kucher, Stepanenko, Luiz Adriano, Shevchuk, Fernando (Fred 46), Douglas Costa (Marlos 46), Taison (Bernard 46), Alex Teixeira, Srna, Rakitskiy. Coach: Mircea Lucescu (ROU)
Match 4 - FC BATE Borisov (BLR)
H 5-0 *Srna (19), Alex Teixeira (48), Luiz Adriano (58p, 83, 90+3)*
Pyatov, Stepanenko, Luiz Adriano, Shevchuk (Marlos 64), Fernando (Fred 66), Ordets, Douglas Costa, Taison (Bernard 73), Alex Teixeira, Srna, Rakitskiy. Coach: Mircea Lucescu (ROU)
Match 5 - Athletic Club (ESP)
H 0-1
Pyatov, Kucher, Stepanenko, Luiz Adriano, Shevchuk, Fernando (Fred 77), Douglas Costa (Marlos 68), Taison (Bernard 71), Alex Teixeira, Srna, Rakitskiy. Coach: Mircea Lucescu (ROU)
Match 6 - FC Porto (POR)
A 1-1 *Stepanenko (50)*
Pyatov, Stepanenko (Fernando 86), Fred, Bernard (Taison 66), Shevchuk, Douglas Costa (Marlos 66), Gladkiy, Alex Teixeira, Kryvtsov, Rakitskiy, Ilsinho. Coach: Mircea Lucescu (ROU)

Round of 16 - FC Bayern München (GER)
H 0-0
Pyatov, Kucher, Fred, Luiz Adriano (Gladkiy 89), Shevchuk, Fernando, Douglas Costa (Marlos 78), Taison (Wellington Nem 84), Alex Teixeira, Srna, Rakitskiy. Coach: Mircea Lucescu (ROU)
A 0-7
Pyatov, Kucher, Stepanenko, Fred, Luiz Adriano, Shevchuk, Douglas Costa (Wellington Nem 79), Taison (Kryvtsov 9), Alex Teixeira (Ilsinho 70), Srna, Rakitskiy. Coach: Mircea Lucescu (ROU)
Red card: Kucher 3

FC Dnipro Dnipropetrovsk

Third qualifying round - FC København (DEN)
H 0-0
Boyko, Mazuch, Kankava (Kravchenko 54), Kalinić, Konoplyanka, Seleznyov (Bruno Gama 63), Léo Matos, Douglas, Fedetskiy, Politylo, Matheus. Coach: Myron Markevych (UKR)
A 0-2
Boyko, Mazuch, Kankava, Polyoviy, Konoplyanka, Léo Matos, Bartulović (Seleznyov 46), Douglas, Fedetskiy (Bruno Gama 75), Politylo, Matheus (Kalinić 54). Coach: Myron Markevych (UKR)

Play-offs - HNK Hajduk Split (CRO)
H 2-1 *Kalinić (50), Shakhov (88)*
Boyko, Mazuch, Kravchenko, Kalinić, Seleznyov (Bartulović 78), Strinić, Zozulya, Bruno Gama (Shakhov 59), Douglas, Rotan, Fedetskiy (Léo Matos 70). Coach: Myron Markevych (UKR)
A 0-0
Boyko, Mazuch, Kankava, Léo Matos, Strinić, Zozulya, Bruno Gama (Bartulović 90+1), Douglas, Shakhov (Kalinić 72), Rotan (Kravchenko 40), Fedetskiy. Coach: Myron Markevych (UKR)

Group F
Match 1 - FC Internazionale Milano (ITA)
H 0-1
Boyko, Mazuch, Kravchenko (Shakhov 67; Luchkevych 74), Kankava, Konoplyanka, Strinić, Zozulya (Kalinić 79), Bruno Gama, Douglas, Rotan, Fedetskiy. Coach: Myron Markevych (UKR)
Red card: Rotan 68
Match 2 - AS Saint-Étienne (FRA)
A 0-0
Boyko, Mazuch, Kravchenko, Kankava (Shakhov 80), Kalinić (Konoplyanka 56), Strinić, Zozulya (Seleznyov 73), Bruno Gama, Douglas, Fedetskiy, Politylo. Coach: Myron Markevych (UKR)
Match 3 - Qarabağ FK (AZE)
H 0-1
Boyko, Mazuch, Kravchenko, Kalinić, Konoplyanka, Strinić, Bruno Gama, Douglas, Shakhov (Seleznyov 46), Rotan, Fedetskiy. Coach: Myron Markevych (UKR)
Match 4 - Qarabağ FK (AZE)
A 2-1 *Kalinić (15, 73)*
Boyko, Mazuch, Kalinić, Konoplyanka, Cheberyachko, Strinić (Kankava 46), Zozulya, Bruno Gama (Shakhov 85), Douglas, Rotan (Kravchenko 90), Fedetskiy. Coach: Myron Markevych (UKR)
Match 5 - FC Internazionale Milano (ITA)
A 1-2 *Rotan (16)*
Boyko, Vlad, Mazuch (Seleznyov 82), Kravchenko (Bruno Gama 73), Kalinić, Konoplyanka, Cheberyachko, Douglas, Luchkevych, Rotan, Fedetskiy (Matheus 70). Coach: Myron Markevych (UKR)

Match 6 - AS Saint-Étienne (FRA)
H 1-0 *Fedetskiy (66)*
Boyko, Vlad, Kravchenko, Kalinić, Konoplyanka, Cheberyachko, Zozulya (Bruno Gama 67), Douglas, Shakhov (Matheus 67), Rotan (Politylo 88), Fedetskiy. Coach: Myron Markevych (UKR)

Round of 32 - Olympiacos FC (GRE)
H 2-0 *Kankava (50), Rotan (54)*
Boyko, Egídio, Kankava, Konoplyanka, Cheberyachko, Zozulya (Fedorchuk 70), Bezus (Kalinić 46), Douglas, Luchkevych, Rotan, Matheus (Bruno Gama 89). Coach: Myron Markevych (UKR)
A 2-2 *Fedetskiy (22), Kalinić (90+2)*
Boyko, Egídio, Kankava, Konoplyanka, Cheberyachko, Zozulya (Kalinić 62), Douglas, Fedorchuk (Bezus 84), Rotan, Fedetskiy, Matheus (Bruno Gama 76). Coach: Myron Markevych (UKR)

Round of 16 - AFC Ajax (NED)
H 1-0 *Zozulya (30)*
Boyko, Egídio, Konoplyanka (Shakhov 82), Seleznyov (Kalinić 76), Cheberyachko, Zozulya, Bezus (Bruno Gama 58), Douglas, Fedorchuk, Rotan, Fedetskiy. Coach: Myron Markevych (UKR)
A 1-2 *Konoplyanka (97)* **(aet)**
Boyko, Egídio, Kankava, Kalinić, Konoplyanka (Seleznyov 108), Léo Matos, Cheberyachko, Bezus (Shakhov 85), Douglas, Luchkevych (Bruno Gama 90+1), Fedorchuk. Coach: Olexandr Ivanov (UKR)

Quarter-finals - Club Brugge KV (BEL)
A 0-0
Boyko, Kankava, Kalinić (Seleznyov 78), Konoplyanka, Léo Matos, Cheberyachko, Douglas, Luchkevych (Bruno Gama 80), Fedorchuk, Rotan (Bezus 89), Fedetskiy. Coach: Myron Markevych (UKR)
H 1-0 *Shakhov (82)*
Boyko, Kankava, Konoplyanka, Seleznyov (Kalinić 73), Léo Matos, Cheberyachko, Bezus (Shakhov 46), Douglas, Luchkevych (Bruno Gama 90+1), Rotan, Fedetskiy. Coach: Myron Markevych (UKR)

Semi-finals - SSC Napoli (ITA)
A 1-1 *Seleznyov (81)*
Boyko, Kankava (Bezus 69), Kalinić (Seleznyov 80), Konoplyanka, Léo Matos, Cheberyachko, Douglas, Luchkevych (Bruno Gama 57), Fedorchuk, Rotan, Fedetskiy. Coach: Myron Markevych (UKR)
H 1-0 *Seleznyov (58)*
Boyko, Kankava, Konoplyanka (Bruno Gama 86), Seleznyov (Kalinić 75), Léo Matos, Cheberyachko, Douglas, Luchkevych (Matheus 67), Fedorchuk, Rotan, Fedetskiy. Coach: Myron Markevych (UKR)

Final - Sevilla FC (ESP)
N 2-3 *Kalinić (7), Rotan (44)*
Boyko, Kankava (Shakhov 85), Kalinić (Seleznyov 78), Konoplyanka, Léo Matos, Cheberyachko, Douglas, Fedorchuk (Bezus 68), Rotan, Fedetskiy, Matheus. Coach: Myron Markevych (UKR)

FC Dynamo Kyiv

Group J

Match 1 - Rio Ave FC (POR)
A 3-0 *Yarmolenko (20), Belhanda (25), Kravets (70)*
Rybka, Dragovic, Lens (Kalitvintsev 79), Yarmolenko, Sydorchuk (Miguel Veloso 67), Rybalka, Kravets, Vida, Burda (Selin 86), Makarenko, Belhanda. Coach: Serhiy Rebrov (UKR)

Match 2 - FC Steaua Bucureşti (ROU)
H 3-1 *Yarmolenko (40), Kravets (66), Teodorczyk (90+1)*
Rybka, Danilo Silva, Dragovic, Lens (Kalitvintsev 83), Yarmolenko, Sydorchuk (Buyalskiy 75), Rybalka, Kravets (Teodorczyk 90), Vida, Burda, Belhanda. Coach: Serhiy Rebrov (UKR)

Match 3 - Aalborg BK (DEN)
A 0-3
Rybka, Danilo Silva, Dragovic, Lens (Gusev 77), Yarmolenko, Sydorchuk, Rybalka (Miguel Veloso 46), Kravets, Vida, Burda, Belhanda (Teodorczyk 67). Coach: Serhiy Rebrov (UKR)

Match 4 - Aalborg BK (DEN)
H 2-0 *Vida (70), Gusev (90+3)*
Shovkovskiy, Danilo Silva, Dragovic, Lens (Burda 72), Yarmolenko (Gusev 84), Sydorchuk (Miguel Veloso 77), Rybalka, Kravets, Vida, Khacheridi, Belhanda. Coach: Serhiy Rebrov (UKR)
Red card: Dragovic 68

Match 5 - Rio Ave FC (POR)
H 2-0 *Lens (53), Miguel Veloso (78)*
Shovkovskiy, Danilo Silva, Lens (Gusev 81), Yarmolenko, Sydorchuk (Miguel Veloso 62), Rybalka, Kravets (Mbokani 69), Vida, Burda, Khacheridi, Belhanda. Coach: Serhiy Rebrov (UKR)

Match 6 - FC Steaua Bucureşti (ROU)
A 2-0 *Yarmolenko (71), Lens (90+4)*
Shovkovskiy, Miguel Veloso (Sydorchuk 65), Dragovic, Lens, Yarmolenko, Rybalka, Gusev, Kravets (Mbokani 79), Burda, Khacheridi, Belhanda (Buyalskiy 81). Coach: Serhiy Rebrov (UKR)

Round of 32 - EA Guingamp (FRA)
A 1-2 *Miguel Veloso (19)*
Shovkovskiy, Danilo Silva, Miguel Veloso, Antunes, Dragovic, Lens (Gusev 7; Khacheridi 76), Yarmolenko, Sydorchuk (Belhanda 41), Rybalka, Kravets, Vida. Coach: Serhiy Rebrov (UKR)
Red cards: Yarmolenko 39, Belhanda 45
H 3-1 *Teodorczyk (31), Buyalskiy (46), Gusev (75p)*
Shovkovskiy, Danilo Silva, Miguel Veloso (Teodorczyk 9), Antunes, Dragovic, Lens, Rybalka, Gusev (Kalitvintsev 90+2), Kravets, Vida, Buyalskiy (Chumak 72). Coach: Serhiy Rebrov (UKR)

Round of 16 - Everton FC (ENG)
A 1-2 *Gusev (14)*
Shovkovskiy, Danilo Silva, Miguel Veloso (Chumak 84), Antunes, Dragovic, Yarmolenko, Sydorchuk, Gusev (Kravets 76), Vida, Buyalskiy (Garmash 67), Mbokani. Coach: Serhiy Rebrov (UKR)
H 5-2 *Yarmolenko (21), Teodorczyk (35), Miguel Veloso (37), Gusev (56), Antunes (76)*
Shovkovskiy, Danilo Silva, Miguel Veloso, Antunes, Dragovic, Yarmolenko, Sydorchuk (Buyalskiy 64), Rybalka, Gusev (Kalitvintsev 90), Khacheridi, Teodorczyk (Kravets 75). Coach: Serhiy Rebrov (UKR)

Quarter-finals - ACF Fiorentina (ITA)
H 1-1 *Lens (36)*
Shovkovskiy, Danilo Silva, Antunes (Vida 24), Dragovic, Lens, Yarmolenko, Sydorchuk (Belhanda 68), Rybalka, Buyalskiy (Chumak 80), Khacheridi, Teodorczyk. Coach: Serhiy Rebrov (UKR)
A 0-2
Shovkovskiy, Danilo Silva, Antunes, Lens, Yarmolenko, Rybalka, Vida, Buyalskiy (Sydorchuk 69), Khacheridi, Belhanda (Kalitvintsev 63), Teodorczyk (Gusev 45+2). Coach: Serhiy Rebrov (UKR)
Red card: Lens 40

FC Metalist Kharkiv

Play-offs - Ruch Chorzów (POL)
A 0-0
Shust, Villagra, Edmar, Cleiton Xavier, Chaco Torres (Krasnopyorov 53), Kulakov, Yussuf, Gueye, Osman, Jajá (Homenyuk 64), Rebenok. Coach: Ihor Rakhayev (UKR)
H 1-0 *Cleiton Xavier (105+1p)*
Shust, Edmar, Cleiton Xavier, Homenyuk, Pshenychnykh, Kulakov, Yussuf, Gueye, Krasnopyorov, Jajá (Villagra 62), Rebenok (Radchenko 68). Coach: Ihor Rakhayev (UKR)

Group L

Match 1 - Trabzonspor AŞ (TUR)
H 1-2 *Homenyuk (61)*
Goryainov, Villagra, Torsiglieri, Bolbat (Radchenko 80), Cleiton Xavier (Kulakov 90+3), Homenyuk, Pshenychnykh, Gueye, Krasnopyorov, Jajá (Rebenok 82), Kobin. Coach: Ihor Rakhayev (UKR)

Match 2 - KSC Lokeren OV (BEL)
A 0-1
Dišljenković, Villagra, Bolbat (Kulakov 68), Edmar, Cleiton Xavier, Homenyuk, Pshenychnykh (Berezovchuk 85), Yussuf, Gueye, Krasnopyorov, Kobin (Radchenko 61). Coach: Ihor Rakhayev (UKR)

Match 3 - Legia Warszawa (POL)
H 0-1
Goryainov, Villagra, Torsiglieri, Bolbat, Edmar, Homenyuk, Pshenychnykh (Kulakov 61), Chaco Torres, Yussuf (Berezovchuk 75), Krasnopyorov (Kobin 57), Jajá. Coach: Ihor Rakhayev (UKR)

Match 4 - Legia Warszawa (POL)
A 1-2 *Kobin (22)*
Dišljenković, Villagra, Berezovchuk, Torsiglieri, Cleiton Xavier, Chaco Torres (Homenyuk 90+2), Krasnopyorov (Edmar 80), Radchenko (Kulakov 51), Jajá, Kobin, Rebenok. Coach: Ihor Rakhayev (UKR)

Match 5 - Trabzonspor AŞ (TUR)
A 1-3 *Homenyuk (68)*
Goryainov, Villagra (Bolbat 84), Torsiglieri, Homenyuk, Pshenychnykh, Gueye, Krasnopyorov, Tkachuk, Jajá, Kobin (Kulakov 70), Rebenok (Osman 88). Coach: Ihor Rakhayev (UKR)

Match 6 - KSC Lokeren OV (BEL)
H 0-1
Goryainov, Berezovchuk, Bolbat, Homenyuk, Pshenychnykh, Krasnopyorov, Tkachuk, Osman, Radchenko (Kostyuk 88), Kobin, Rebenok. Coach: Ihor Rakhayev (UKR)

FC Chornomorets Odesa

Third qualifying round - RNK Split (CRO)
A 0-2
Bezotosniy, Kovalchuk (Grechyshkin 76), Gai, Arzhanov, Fomin, Shinder (Didenko 41), Balashov (Danchenko 37), Sivakov, Opanasenko, Teikeu, Kutas. Coach: Roman Hryhorchuk (UKR)
H 0-0
Bezotosniy, Kovalchuk (Grechyshkin 89), Didenko (Nazarenko 83), Gai, Arzhanov, Fomin, Shinder, Sivakov, Slinkin, Zubeiko (Kabayev 89), Teikeu. Coach: Roman Hryhorchuk (UKR)

FC Zorya Luhansk

Second qualifying round - KF Laçi (ALB)
A 3-0 *Sheta (23og), Ljubenović (47), Boli (75)*
Shevchenko, Chaykovskiy, Kamenyuka, Vernydub, Ignjatijević (Yarmash 46), Karavayev, Ljubenović (Lipartia 60), Biliy, Hrytsai (Borodai 75), Khomchenovskiy, Boli. Coach: Yuriy Vernydub (UKR)
H 2-1 *Ignjatijević (74), Budkivskiy (87)*
Shevchenko, Chaykovskiy, Kamenyuka, Lipartia (Ljubenović 46), Vernydub, Yarmash, Ignjatijević, Budkivskiy, Petryak (Karavayev 61), Hrytsai (Biliy 65), Khomchenovskiy. Coach: Yuriy Vernydub (UKR)

DOMESTIC LEAGUE CLUB-BY-CLUB

Third qualifying round - Molde FK (NOR)

H 1-1 *Kamenyuka (62)*
Santini, Chaykovskiy, Kamenyuka, Khudzik (Malinovskiy 59), Vernydub, Ignjatijević, Karavayev (Pysko 75), Biliy, Budkivskiy (Ljubenović 46), Hrytsai, Khomchenovskiy. Coach: Yuriy Vernydub (UKR)
A 2-1 *Kamenyuka (2), Forren (89og)*
Shevchenko, Kamenyuka, Malyshev (Malinovskiy 46), Vernydub, Ignjatijević, Karavayev, Ljubenović (Lipartia 90+2), Biliy, Budkivskiy (Khudzik 60), Hrytsai, Khomchenovskiy. Coach: Yuriy Vernydub (UKR)

Play-offs - Feyenoord (NED)
H 1-1 *Biliy (27)*
Shevchenko, Pysko, Chaykovskiy, Kamenyuka, Malyshev (Hrytsai 46), Segbefia (Malinovskiy 56), Ignjatijević, Karavayev, Biliy, Budkivskiy, Khomchenovskiy. Coach: Yuriy Vernydub (UKR)
A 3-4 *Malinovskiy (56, 80), Biliy (71)*
Shevchenko, Chaykovskiy (Hrytsai 79), Kamenyuka, Segbefia (Ljubenović 66), Ignjatijević (Pysko 72), Malinovskiy, Karavayev, Biliy, Budkivskiy, Khomchenovskiy, Pylyavskyi. Coach: Yuriy Vernydub (UKR)

FC Chornomorets Odesa

1936 • Chornomorets (34,164); Meteor, Dnipropetrovsk (24,381); Dynamo V. Lobanovskiy, Kyiv (16,873) • chernomorets.odessa.ua
Major honours
Ukrainian Cup (2) 1992, 1994
Coach: Roman Hryhorchuk;
(16/12/14) (Olexandr Babych)

2014
26/07	h	Olimpik	W	4-0	*Balashov 2 (1p), Gai 2*
04/08	a	Illychivets	D	3-3	*Fomin, Didenko, Gai*
11/08	h	Volyn	W	1-0	*Sivakov*
16/08	h	Zorya	D	0-0	
30/08	a	Dynamo	L	0-2	
13/09	h	Shakhtar	L	0-2	
21/09	a	Hoverla	D	0-0	
04/10	h	Metalurh Donetsk	D	2-2	*Gai (p), Fomin*
19/10	a	Dnipro	L	1-2	*Bobko*
01/11	a	Metalurh Zaporizhya	D	0-0	
08/11	h	Vorskla	W	1-0	*Fomin*
29/11	a	Olimpik	L	1-2	*Nazarenko*
07/12	h	Karpaty	D	0-0	

2015
27/02	h	Illychivets	D	0-0	
08/03	a	Volyn	D	1-1	*og (Žunić)*
15/03	a	Zorya	L	0-1	
04/04	h	Dynamo	L	0-2	
11/04	a	Shakhtar	L	0-5	
19/04	h	Hoverla	D	1-1	*Didenko (p)*
24/04	a	Metalurh Donetsk	L	0-1	
03/05	h	Dnipro	L	0-3	
10/05	a	Karpaty	L	0-2	
15/05	h	Metalurh Zaporizhya	D	0-0	
20/05	a	Metalist	D	0-0	
25/05	a	Vorskla	L	0-2	
31/05	h	Metalist			*match not played*

No	Name	Nat	DoB	Pos	Aps	(s)	Gls
17	Volodymyr Arzhanov		29/11/85	M	13		
27	Vitaliy Balashov		07/02/91	A	12	(3)	2
12	Dmytro Bezotosniy		15/11/83	G	7		
11	Ivan Bobko		10/12/90	M	8		1
94	Oleh Danchenko		01/08/94	M	12	(3)	
9	Anatoliy Didenko		09/06/82	A	14	(6)	2
16	Artem Filimonov		21/02/94	M	11		
19	Ruslan Fomin		02/03/86	A	12	(1)	3
15	Giorgi Gadrani	GEO	30/09/94	D	2	(2)	
10	Olexiy Gai		06/11/82	M	13		4
24	Dmytro Grechyshkin		22/09/91	M	10	(6)	
22	Vladyslav Kabayev		01/09/95	A	5	(4)	
19	Olexandr Kalitov		29/09/93	D		(3)	
8	Anton Kicha		01/05/90	D	1	(2)	
8	Kyrylo Kovalchuk		11/06/86	M	11	(1)	
42	Jovan Krneta	SRB	04/05/92	D	11		
77	Pavlo Kutas		03/09/82	D	14	(1)	
88	Oleh Lutsenko		14/02/93	D		(2)	
25	Yevheniy Martynenko		25/06/93	D	9		
13	Yuriy Martyshchuk		22/04/86	G	9		
14	Yevhen Murashov		09/05/95	A	1	(4)	
28	Serhiy Nazarenko		16/02/80	M	6	(4)	1
2	Yaroslav Oliynyk		14/03/91	D	4		
39	Yevhen Opanasenko		25/08/90	M	6	(4)	
44	Yevhen Past		16/03/88	G	9		
21	Petro Pereverza		10/07/94	A		(1)	
32	Serhiy Petko		23/01/94	M	9		
4	Yuriy Putrash		29/01/90	D	4	(2)	
51	Vladyslav Shchetinin		29/08/97	D	3		
26	Anton Shinder		13/06/87	M	2	(5)	
32	Mikhail Sivakov	BLR	16/01/88	M	10		1
33	Andriy Slinkin		19/02/91	D	7	(5)	
11	Yevhen Smirnov		16/04/93	M	5	(3)	
52	Adolphe Teikeu	CMR	23/06/90	D	11		
39	Denys Vasin		04/03/89	A	9	(2)	
99	Vadym Yavorskiy		26/06/94	A	2	(4)	
42	Yevhen Zubeiko		30/09/89	M	13		

FC Dnipro Dnipropetrovsk

1918 • Dnipro-Arena (31,003) • fcdnipro.ua
Major honours
USSR League (2) 1983, 1988; USSR Cup (1) 1989
Coach: Myron Markevych

2014
25/07	a	Metalurh Donetsk	W	2-0	*Konoplyanka, Matheus (p)*
02/08	a	Volyn	W	1-0	*Shakhov*
10/08	h	Karpaty	W	4-0	*Bruno Gama, Shakhov 2, Kalinić*
15/08	a	Metalurh Zaporizhya	W	1-0	*Fedetskiy*
31/08	h	Vorskla	D	1-1	*Kalinić (p)*
13/09	a	Metalist	W	5-2	*Bruno Gama 3, Seleznyov, Konoplyanka*
22/09	h	Olimpik	W	5-0	*Seleznyov, Bruno Gama, og (Sytnyk), Kalinić 2*
05/10	a	Illychivets	W	1-0	*Seleznyov*
19/10	h	Chornomorets	W	2-1	*Kalinić 2*
02/11	h	Dynamo	L	0-3	
09/11	a	Shakhtar	D	0-0	
22/11	h	Hoverla	D	1-1	*Kalinić*
01/12	h	Metalurh Donetsk	D	1-1	*Konoplyanka*
06/12	a	Zorya	L	1-2	*Konoplyanka*

2015
01/03	h	Volyn	W	5-0	*Konoplyanka, Ksionz, Kalinić, Blyznychenko, Zozulya*
08/03	a	Karpaty	W	1-0	*Kalinić*
15/03	h	Metalurh Zaporizhya	W	1-0	*Luchkevych*
04/04	a	Vorskla	W	3-1	*Seleznyov 2, Konoplyanka*
11/04	h	Metalist	D	0-0	
19/04	h	Olimpik	W	5-0	*Blyznychenko, Seleznyov 2 (1p), Konoplyanka, Kalinić*
26/04	h	Illychivets	W	1-0	*Blyznychenko*
03/05	a	Chornomorets	W	3-0	*Kalinić 2 (1p), Seleznyov*
10/05	a	Zorya	L	0-2	
17/05	a	Dynamo	L	0-1	
23/05	h	Shakhtar	W	3-2	*Matheus, Bezus, Luchkevych*
30/05	a	Hoverla	D	0-0	

No	Name	Nat	DoB	Pos	Aps	(s)	Gls
17	Denys Balanyuk		16/01/97	M		(2)	
21	Mladen Bartulović	CRO	05/10/86	M		(3)	
19	Roman Bezus		26/09/90	M	10	(1)	1
97	Andriy Blyznychenko		24/07/94	M	6	(2)	3
22	Yevhen Bokhashvili		05/01/93	A	1		
71	Denys Boyko		29/01/88	G	21		
20	Bruno Gama	POR	15/11/87	M	19	(4)	5
14	Yevhen Cheberyachko		19/06/83	D	8	(3)	
15	Dmytro Chygrynskiy		07/11/86	D	2		
23	Douglas	BRA	04/04/90	D	17		
6	Egídio	BRA	18/06/86	D	1		
44	Artem Fedetskiy		26/04/85	D	14	(2)	1
25	Valeriy Fedorchuk		05/10/88	M	7	(3)	
47	Serhiy Gorbunov		14/03/94	M	1		
30	Papa Gueye	SEN	07/07/84	D	10		
9	Nikola Kalinić	CRO	05/01/88	A	12	(11)	12
7	Jaba Kankava	GEO	18/03/86	M	14	(1)	
10	Yevhen Konoplyanka		29/09/89	M	14	(7)	7
4	Serhiy Kravchenko		24/04/83	M	9	(3)	
8	Pavlo Ksionz		02/01/87	M	12		1
16	Jan Laštůvka	CZE	07/07/82	G	5		
12	Léo Matos	BRA	02/04/86	D	5	(2)	
24	Valeriy Luchkevych		11/01/96	D	11	(2)	2
99	Matheus	BRA	15/01/83	A	4	(4)	2
3	Ondřej Mazuch	CZE	15/03/89	D	10		
90	Olexandr Mihunov		13/04/94	M	1	(2)	
89	Serhiy Politylo		09/01/89	M	1	(3)	
8	Volodymyr Polyoviy		28/07/85	D	1		
29	Ruslan Rotan		29/10/81	M	13	(3)	
11	Yevhen Seleznyov		20/07/85	A	12	(9)	8
28	Yevhen Shakhov		30/11/90	M	10	(7)	3
17	Ivan Strinić	CRO	17/07/87	D	8		
39	Olexandr Svatok		27/09/94	D	5		
27	Olexandr Vasiliyev		27/04/94	M	1	(1)	
2	Alexandru Vlad	ROU	06/12/89	D	1		
18	Roman Zozulya		17/11/89	A	11	(2)	1

FC Dynamo Kyiv

1927 • NSK Olimpiyskiy (70,050) •
fcdynamo.kiev.ua
Major honours
UEFA Cup Winners' Cup (2) 1975, 1986; UEFA
Super Cup (1) 1975; USSR League (13) 1961, 1966,
1967, 1968, 1971, 1974, 1975, 1977, 1980, 1981,
1985, 1986, 1990; Ukrainian League (14) 1993,
1994, 1995, 1996, 1997, 1998, 1999, 2000, 2001,
2003, 2004, 2007, 2009, 2015; USSR Cup (9) 1954,
1964, 1966, 1974, 1978, 1982, 1985, 1987, 1990;
Ukrainian Cup (11) 1993, 1996, 1998, 1999, 2000,
2003, 2005, 2006, 2007, 2014, 2015
Coach: Serhiy Rebrov

2014

27/07	h	Vorskla	W 1-0	Bezus
02/08	a	Metalist	W 2-1	Kravets, Yarmolenko (p)
09/08	h	Olimpik	D 0-0	
17/08	h	Illychivets	W 4-1	Kravets 3, Gusev
30/08	h	Chornomorets	W 2-0	Yarmolenko 2
13/09	a	Zorya	D 2-2	Teodorczyk, Kravets
22/09	h	Volyn	W 4-1	Yarmolenko 2, Lens, Kalitvintsev
05/10	h	Shakhtar	W 1-0	Vida
18/10	a	Hoverla	W 4-0	Kravets, Sydorchuk, Lens, Gusev (p)
02/11	a	Dnipro	W 3-0	Lens, Yarmolenko, Kravets
09/11	h	Karpaty	D 0-0	
23/11	a	Metalurh Zaporizhya	W 4-2	Yarmolenko, Lens 2, Miguel Veloso
30/11	a	Vorskla	W 3-0	Yarmolenko, Mbokani 2
05/12	h	Metalurh Donetsk	W 3-0	Mbokani, Yarmolenko, Kravets

2015

01/03	h	Metalist	W 3-0	Belhanda, Buyalskiy, Chumak
08/03	a	Olimpik	W 1-0	Burda
15/03	h	Illychivets	W 5-0	Yarmolenko 2 (1p), og (Zubkov), Teodorczyk, Antunes
04/04	a	Chornomorets	W 2-0	Gusev, Teodorczyk
12/04	h	Zorya	D 2-2	Kravets, Rybalka
19/04	a	Volyn	W 3-1	Kravets 2, Buyalskiy
26/04	a	Shakhtar	D 0-0	
04/05	h	Hoverla	W 6-0	Kravets 2, og (Hlushytskiy), Yarmolenko (p), Sydorchuk, Teodorczyk
10/05	a	Metalurh Donetsk	W 6-0	Yarmolenko 2, Khacheridi, Kravets, Belhanda, Teodorczyk
17/05	h	Dnipro	W 1-0	Vida
24/05	a	Karpaty	W 1-0	Kravets
30/05	h	Metalurh Zaporizhya	D 2-2	Sydorchuk, og (Rudyka)

No	Name	Nat	DoB	Pos	Aps	(s)	Gls
37	Bohdan Andriyevskiy		21/03/97	M		(1)	
5	Antunes	POR	01/04/87	D	8		1
90	Younes Belhanda	MAR	25/02/90	M	22	(2)	2
9	Roman Bezus		26/09/90	M	2	(7)	1
26	Mykyta Burda		24/03/95	D	3	(1)	1
29	Vitaliy Buyalskiy		06/01/93	M	5	(6)	2
28	Yevhen Chumak		25/08/95	M		(2)	1
2	Danilo Silva	BRA	24/11/86	D	25		
6	Aleksandar Dragovic	AUT	06/03/91	D	24		
19	Denys Garmash		19/04/90	M	3	(3)	
20	Oleh Gusev		25/04/83	M	8	(9)	3
45	Vladyslav Kalitvintsev		04/01/93	M	4	(2)	1
34	Yevhen Khacheridi		28/07/87	D	13		1
22	Artem Kravets		03/06/89	A	19	(5)	15
7	Jeremain Lens	NED	24/11/87	A	18	(3)	5
27	Yevhen Makarenko		21/05/91	D	7		
85	Dieumerci Mbokani	COD	22/11/85	A	5	(3)	3
4	Miguel Veloso	POR	11/05/86	M	9	(5)	1
14	Bohdan Mykhaylichenko		21/03/97	M		(1)	
17	Serhiy Rybalka		01/04/90	M	19	(3)	1
23	Olexandr Rybka		10/04/87	G	8		
3	Yevhen Selin		09/05/88	D		(2)	
1	Olexandr Shovkovskiy		02/01/75	G	18		
16	Serhiy Sydorchuk		02/05/91	M	18	(4)	3
91	Łukasz Teodorczyk	POL	03/06/91	A	2	(11)	5
28	Benoît Trémoulinas	FRA	28/12/85	D	2	(1)	
24	Domagoj Vida	CRO	29/04/89	D	20		2
10	Andriy Yarmolenko		23/10/89	M	24	(2)	14

FC Hoverla Uzhhorod

1925 • Avanhard (12,000) • fcgoverla.uz.ua
Coach: Vyacheslav Hrozniy

2014

27/07	h	Karpaty	D 2-2	Shatskikh, Tudose
02/08	a	Metalurh Zaporizhya	L 1-2	Shatskikh
08/08	h	Vorskla	D 0-0	
16/08	a	Metalist	L 0-1	
30/08	h	Olimpik	L 0-1	
14/09	a	Illychivets	D 2-2	Kaverin, Kacharaba
21/09	h	Chornomorets	D 0-0	
04/10	a	Zorya	L 1-2	Shatskikh
18/10	h	Dynamo	L 0-4	
03/11	h	Volyn	D 0-0	
08/11	h	Metalurh Donetsk	W 1-0	Myakushko
22/11	a	Dnipro	D 1-1	Kaverin
30/11	a	Karpaty	L 0-1	
05/12	a	Shakhtar	L 1-4	Myakushko

2015

01/03	h	Metalurh Zaporizhya	L 0-1	
08/03	a	Vorskla	L 0-2	
14/03	h	Metalist	D 2-2	Jagodinskis, Feshchuk
03/04	h	Olimpik	W 2-1	Khlebas, Feshchuk
10/04	h	Illychivets	W 2-1	Grishin, Feshchuk
19/04	a	Chornomorets	D 1-1	Khlebas
25/04	h	Zorya	L 1-2	Myakushko
04/05	a	Dynamo	L 0-6	
09/05	h	Shakhtar	L 3-7	Khlebas 2, Myakushko
17/05	a	Volyn	L 2-4	Feshchuk, Khlebas
23/05	a	Metalurh Donetsk	D 0-0	
30/05	h	Dnipro	D 0-0	

No	Name	Nat	DoB	Pos	Aps	(s)	Gls
5	Serge Akakpo	TOG	15/10/87	D	19	(1)	
88	Vyacheslav Akimov		17/10/89	M	1	(3)	
22	Dmytro Babenko		28/06/78	G	2	(1)	
7	Lucian Burdujan	ROU	18/02/84	A	5	(1)	
3	Éverson	BRA	01/07/86	D	1		
42	Vitaliy Fedoriv		21/10/87	D	1		
10	Maxym Feshchuk		25/11/85	A	22	(1)	4
77	Valeriy Grishin		12/06/94	A	8	(2)	1
25	Lukman Haruna	NGA	04/12/90	M	5		
9	Oleh Herasymyuk		25/09/86	M	15	(2)	
29	Illya Hlushytskiy		02/08/93	D	8	(2)	
20	Vitālijs Jagodinskis	LVA	28/02/92	D	22		1
14	Taras Kacharaba		07/01/95	D	9	(5)	1
24	Vitaliy Kaverin		04/09/90	M	1	(12)	2
99	Dmytro Khlebas		09/05/94	A	5	(6)	5
4	Andriy Khomyn		02/01/82	D	15	(1)	
23	Ihor Korotetskiy		13/09/87	D	2		
21	Maxym Koval		09/12/92	G	21		
11	Serhiy Kuznetsov		31/08/82	A	2		
95	Vyacheslav Lukhtanov		12/02/95	D		(1)	
23	Serhiy Lyulka		22/02/90	D	21		
8	Serhiy Myakushko		15/04/93	M	19		4
1	Olexandr Nagy		02/09/85	G	3		
17	Vyacheslav Panfilov		24/06/93	A		(4)	
26	Vladyslav Pavlenko		05/04/94	M	4		
2	Olexiy Polyanskiy		02/04/86	M	9	(1)	
7	Mirko Raičević	MNE	22/03/82	D	9	(6)	
28	Ivan Rodić	CRO	11/11/85	A	2	(2)	
16	Maksim Shatskikh	UZB	30/08/78	A	17	(1)	3
44	Lorenco Šimić	CRO	15/07/96	D	3		
25	Ruslan Stepanyuk		16/01/92	A	5	(8)	
96	Yuriy Toma		27/04/96	M		(1)	
15	Dmytro Trukhin		29/06/83	M	7	(8)	
6	Alexandru Tudose	ROU	03/04/87	M	23		1
18	Mykola Vechurko		06/06/92	D		(2)	

FC Illychivets Mariupil

2003 • Avanhard, Lutsk (10,792);
Chornomorets, Odesa (34,164); NSK Olimpiyskiy,
Kyiv (70,050); Meteor, Dnipropetrovsk (24,381) •
fcilich.com
Coach: Mykola Pavlov

2014

26/07	h	Volyn	L 1-2	Kulach (p)
04/08	h	Chornomorets	D 3-3	Dovhiy, og (Sivakov), Churko
11/08	a	Zorya	L 0-1	
17/08	h	Dynamo	L 1-4	Yavorskiy
29/08	a	Shakhtar	L 0-3	
14/09	h	Hoverla	D 2-2	Totovytskiy 2
20/09	a	Metalurh Donetsk	L 0-3	
05/10	h	Dnipro	L 0-1	
19/10	a	Karpaty	L 0-1	
01/11	a	Vorskla	D 0-0	
09/11	h	Metalist	L 1-3	Hryn
22/11	a	Olimpik	L 2-3	Totovytskiy, Yavorskiy
30/11	a	Volyn	L 1-3	Yavorskiy
07/12	h	Metalurh Zaporizhya	L 1-2	Kulach (p)

2015

27/02	a	Chornomorets	D 0-0	
07/03	h	Zorya	W 2-1	Zubkov, Hryn
15/03	a	Dynamo	L 0-5	
05/04	h	Shakhtar	L 2-6	Shevchuk, Hryn
10/04	a	Hoverla	L 1-2	Churko (p)
18/04	h	Metalurh Donetsk	D 1-1	og (Checher)
26/04	a	Dnipro	L 0-1	
02/05	h	Karpaty	W 1-0	Hryn
10/05	a	Metalurh Zaporizhya	L 0-2	
16/05	h	Vorskla	L 1-2	Churko
24/05	a	Metalist	L 1-3	Churko (p)
30/05	h	Olimpik	W 4-1	Hryn 3, Shaparenko

No	Name	Nat	DoB	Pos	Aps	(s)	Gls
5	Olexandr Aksyonov		07/01/94	D	3		
91	Bohdan Butko		13/01/91	D	8		
96	Ihor Bykovskiy		05/09/96	D		(1)	
3	Olexandr Chizhov		10/08/86	D	5		
33	Olexandr Churilov		06/06/84	G	5		
20	Vyacheslav Churko		10/05/93	M	12		4
17	Semen Datsenko		10/05/94	D	3		
50	Olexandr Dekhtyarenko		13/02/96	D		(1)	
4	Olexiy Dovhiy		02/11/89	M	4		1
17	Vitaliy Fedotov		16/07/91	M	1	(4)	
18	Serhiy Garashchenkov		16/05/90	D	3		
1	Yevhen Halchuk		05/03/92	G	20		
11	Serhiy Hryn		06/06/94	M	25		7
45	Maxim Ilyuk		10/11/90	A	3	(2)	
32	Mykola Ishchenko		09/03/83	D	3		
95	Ihor Kalinin		11/11/96	M	2	(1)	
14	Ruslan Kisil		23/10/91	A		(1)	
99	Mykyta Kravchenko		14/06/97	M		(2)	
32	Mykyta Kryukov		30/04/91	G	1		
39	Vladyslav Kulach		07/05/93	A	12		2
80	Olexandr Luchyk		30/03/94	A		(3)	
16	Olexandr Mandzyuk		10/01/83	A	2	(6)	
23	Olexandr Matveyev		11/02/89	D	10		
15	Ivan Matyash		15/02/88	A	9		
51	Dmytro Mishnyov		26/01/94	M	16	(1)	
65	Yevheniy Nemtinov		03/10/95	M	1	(5)	
9	Andriy Oberemko		18/03/84	M	10	(4)	
19	Zurab Ochigava		18/05/95	D	4	(3)	
94	Serhiy Prykhodko		21/01/94	M	1	(3)	
77	Artem Putivtsev		29/08/88	D	5		
98	Mykola Shaparenko		04/10/98	M		(2)	1
7	Serhiy Shevchuk		18/06/85	D	18	(2)	1
21	Dmytro Skoblov		30/11/89	M	8	(3)	
30	Bohdan Sukhodub		09/02/94	D	4		
99	David Targamadze	GEO	22/08/89	M	2	(1)	
8	Andriy Totovytskiy		20/01/93	M	14		3
93	Ivan Tsyupa		25/06/93	D	16	(1)	
79	Serhiy Vakulenko		07/09/93	D	11		
88	Rinar Valeyev		22/08/87	M	9		
5	Denys Vasin		04/03/89	A	2	(1)	
8	Serhiy Vovkodav		02/07/88	D	8		
31	Ivan Yanakov		07/07/94	M		(2)	
13	Serhiy Yavorskiy		05/07/89	M	16	(4)	3
12	Maxym Zhichikov		07/11/92	D	2		
24	Ruslan Zubkov		24/11/91	M	8	(1)	1

UKRAINE

FC Karpaty Lviv

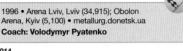

1963 • Ukraina (27,925) • fckarpaty.lviv.ua
Major honours
USSR Cup (1) 1969
Coach: Igor Jovićević (CRO)

2014
27/07	a	Hoverla	D	2-2	Puchkovskiy, Balažič
03/08	h	Metalurh Donetsk	L	0-1	
10/08	a	Dnipro	L	0-4	
17/08	a	Volyn	W	2-0	Kozhanov, Balažič
31/08	h	Metalurh Zaporizhya	L	1-2	Hitchenko
14/09	a	Vorskla	L	0-2	
21/09	h	Metalist	D	3-3	Holodyuk, Kozhanov, Balažič
04/10	a	Olimpik	L	0-1	
19/10	h	Illychivets	W	1-0	Balažič
02/11	a	Zorya	L	1-2	Serhiychuk
09/11	a	Dynamo	D	0-0	
21/11	h	Shakhtar	L	0-2	
30/11	h	Hoverla	W	1-0	Kostevych
07/12	a	Chornomorets	D	0-0	

2015
01/03	a	Metalurh Donetsk	D	1-1	Plastun
08/03	h	Dnipro	L	0-2	
13/03	h	Volyn	L	0-1	
05/04	a	Metalurh Zaporizhya	L	1-2	Strashkevych
13/04	h	Vorskla	D	0-0	
18/04	h	Metalist	D	0-0	
26/04	h	Olimpik	W	4-1	Khudobyak 2, Shved 2
02/05	a	Illychivets	L	0-1	
10/05	h	Chornomorets	W	2-0	Kostevych, Strashkevych
16/05	a	Zorya	D	1-1	Plastun
24/05	h	Dynamo	L	0-1	
30/05	a	Shakhtar	D	2-2	Karnoza, Khudobyak

No	Name	Nat	DoB	Pos	Aps	(s)	Gls
4	Gregor Balažič	SVN	12/02/88	M	12	(1)	4
92	Ambrosiy Chachua		02/04/94	D	16	(4)	
38	Murtaz Daushvili	GEO	01/05/89	M	12	(5)	
5	Andriy Hitchenko		02/10/84	D	21		1
17	Oleh Holodyuk		02/01/88	M	22	(3)	1
76	Oleksiy Hutsulyak		25/12/97	A	1	(6)	
29	Olexandr Ilyushchenkov		23/03/90	G	6		
10	Artur Karnoza		02/08/90	M	5	(9)	1
16	Ihor Khudobyak		20/02/85	M	17	(6)	3
48	Dmytro Klots		15/04/96	M	10		
18	Mykhailo Kopolovets		29/01/84	M		(7)	
8	Volodymyr Kostevych		23/10/92	D	23		2
9	Denys Kozhanov		13/06/87	M	19	(5)	2
86	Vasyl Kravets		20/08/97	D		(2)	
7	Pavlo Ksionz		02/01/87	M	14		
70	Ivan Lobai		21/05/96	D	2		
19	Yaroslav Martynyuk		20/02/89	M	4	(3)	
41	Maxym Marusych		17/07/93	M		(2)	
94	Denys Miroshnychenko		11/10/94	D	26		
23	Roman Mysak		09/09/91	G	20		
26	Artur Novotryasov		19/07/92	D	6		
2	Ihor Plastun		20/08/90	M	21		2
22	Taras Puchkovskiy		23/08/94	M	2	(6)	1
14	Mykhailo Serhiychuk		29/07/91	A	13	(8)	1
35	Maryan Shved		16/07/97	A	8	(2)	2
27	Vadym Strashkevych		21/04/94	M	6	(7)	2
45	Yuriy Zakharkiv		21/03/96	M		(1)	

FC Metalist Kharkiv

1925 • Metalist Stadium (41,307); Arena Lviv, Lviv (34,915) • metalist.ua
Major honours
USSR Cup (1) 1988
Coach: Ihor Rakhayev

2014
27/07	a	Zorya	W	2-1	Kulakov, Villagra
02/08	h	Dynamo	L	1-2	Cleiton Xavier (p)
09/08	a	Shakhtar	L	0-1	
16/08	h	Hoverla	W	1-0	Homenyuk
31/08	a	Metalurh Donetsk	D	1-1	Cleiton Xavier
13/09	h	Dnipro	L	2-5	Bolbat, Cleiton Xavier
21/09	a	Karpaty	D	3-3	Bolbat, Cleiton Xavier (p), Jajá
05/10	h	Metalurh Zaporizhya	W	2-1	Cleiton Xavier, Yussuf
18/10	a	Vorskla	D	0-0	
02/11	h	Olimpik	D	0-0	
09/11	a	Illychivets	W	3-1	Cleiton Xavier 3 (1p)
30/11	h	Zorya	W	4-2	Jajá 3 (1p), Bolbat
07/12	a	Volyn	W	3-0	(w/o; match abandoned after 88 mins at 2-1 Edmar, Jajá (p))

2015
01/03	a	Dynamo	L	0-3	
07/03	h	Shakhtar	D	2-2	Dovhiy, Priyomov
14/03	a	Hoverla	D	2-2	David Caiado, Priyomov (p)
04/04	h	Metalurh Donetsk	W	1-0	Nazarenko
11/04	a	Dnipro	D	0-0	
18/04	h	Karpaty	D	0-0	
26/04	a	Metalurh Zaporizhya	D	0-0	
03/05	h	Vorskla	L	0-2	
11/05	h	Volyn	D	3-3	Priyomov 2, Besedin
17/05	a	Olimpik	L	1-2	David Caiado
20/05	h	Chornomorets	D	0-0	
24/05	h	Illychivets	W	3-1	Bolbat (p), Priyomov 2 (1p)
31/05	a	Chornomorets			match not played

No	Name	Nat	DoB	Pos	Aps	(s)	Gls
52	Dmytro Antonov		28/08/96	D		(1)	
56	Maxym Averyanov		22/07/97	D	1		
11	Serhiy Barylko		05/01/87	M	1	(4)	
86	Volodymyr Barylko		29/01/94	M		(1)	
4	Andriy Berezovchuk		16/04/81	D	4	(1)	
21	Artem Besedin		31/03/96	A	4	(4)	1
9	Ivan Bobko		10/12/90	M	10	(1)	
47	Bohdan Boichuk		30/05/96	A	2	(2)	
7	Serhiy Bolbat		13/06/93	M	11	(6)	4
30	Jurica Buljat	CRO	12/09/86	D	10		
19	Chaco Torres	ARG	20/06/85	M	6	(3)	
42	Yehor Chehurko		27/01/95	D	1		
10	Cleiton Xavier	BRA	23/03/83	M	9		8
3	David Caiado	POR	02/05/87	A	8	(3)	2
25	Serhiy Davydov		16/12/84	A		(2)	
81	Vladimir Dišljenković	SRB	02/07/81	G	5		
2	Oleksiy Dovhiy		02/11/89	M	10		1
8	Edmar		16/06/80	M	10		1
29	Olexandr Goryainov		29/06/75	G	5		
30	Papa Gueye	SEN	07/06/84	D	6		
14	Volodymyr Homenyuk		19/07/85	A	8	(2)	1
3	Mykola Ishchenko		09/03/83	D	10		
50	Jajá	BRA	28/02/86	A	9	(1)	5
77	Vasyl Kobin		24/05/85	M	9		
5	Kyrylo Kovalchuk		11/06/86	M	12		
54	Olexiy Kovtun		05/02/95	D	1		
32	Oleh Krasnopyorov		25/07/80	M	8		
22	Denys Kulakov		01/05/86	M	13	(3)	1
20	Márcio Azevedo	BRA	16/02/86	D	3		
28	Serhiy Nazarenko		16/02/80	M	4	(4)	1
45	Olexandr Osman		18/04/96	D	1	(2)	
23	Serhiy Pohorily		28/07/86	G	10		
80	Volodymyr Priyomov		02/01/86	A	12		6
17	Serhiy Pshenychnykh		19/11/81	D	10	(1)	
46	Artem Radchenko		02/01/95	M	2	(6)	
82	Pavlo Rebenok		23/07/85	M	7	(5)	
15	Dmytro Ryzhuk		05/04/92	D	10		
19	Yevhen Selin		09/05/88	D	11		
35	Bohdan Shust		04/03/86	G	3	(1)	
55	Daniil Solomakha		12/06/96	A		(2)	
1	Denys Sydorenko		18/04/89	G	2		
53	Serhiy Syziy		01/09/95	M		(1)	
43	Yuriy Tkachuk		18/04/95	M	1	(2)	
6	Marco Torsiglieri	ARG	12/01/88	D	8	(2)	
3	Cristian Villagra	ARG	27/12/85	D	12		1
24	Ayila Yussuf	NGA	04/11/84	D	6		1

FC Metalurh Donetsk

1996 • Arena Lviv, Lviv (34,915); Obolon Arena, Kyiv (5,100) • metallurg.donetsk.ua
Coach: Volodymyr Pyatenko

2014
25/07	h	Dnipro	L	0-2	
03/08	a	Karpaty	W	1-0	Lazić
09/08	h	Metalurh Zaporizhya	D	1-1	Alexandre
16/08	a	Vorskla	L	1-2	Nelson
31/08	h	Metalist	D	1-1	Postupalenko
13/09	a	Olimpik	L	2-3	Lazić 2 (1p)
20/09	h	Illychivets	W	3-0	Adorno, Morozyuk, Lazić (p)
04/10	a	Chornomorets	D	2-2	Makrides, Morozyuk
19/10	h	Zorya	D	0-0	
31/10	h	Shakhtar	W	2-1	Morozyuk, Lazić
08/11	a	Hoverla	W	1-0	
23/11	h	Volyn	L	1-2	Júnior Moraes
01/12	a	Dnipro	D	1-1	Júnior Moraes
05/12	a	Dynamo	L	0-3	

2015
01/03	h	Karpaty	D	1-1	Morozyuk
07/03	a	Metalurh Zaporizhya	W	1-0	Lazić
14/03	h	Vorskla	D	1-1	Lazić
04/04	a	Metalist	L	0-1	
11/04	h	Olimpik	W	4-2	Júnior Moraes 2 (1p), Checher, Makrides
18/04	a	Illychivets	D	1-1	Checher
25/04	h	Chornomorets	W	1-0	Lazić
02/05	a	Zorya	L	2-4	Júnior Moraes (p), Lazić
10/05	h	Dynamo	L	0-6	
16/05	h	Shakhtar	L	0-2	
23/05	h	Hoverla	D	0-0	
29/05	a	Volyn	D	1-1	Postupalenko

No	Name	Nat	DoB	Pos	Aps	(s)	Gls
21	Aldo Adorno	PAR	08/04/82	A	4		1
11	Olexandr Akymenko		05/09/85	A		(1)	
14	Alexandre	BRA	15/08/83	M	15	(3)	1
12	Olexandr Bandura		30/05/86	G	17		
2	Artem Baranovskiy		17/03/90	D	6	(8)	
4	Vyacheslav Checher		15/12/80	D	23		2
77	Maxym Degtyarev		30/05/93	A	1	(2)	
20	Vitaliy Fedotov		16/07/91	M	4	(12)	
37	Gabriel	BRA	29/01/92	M	8	(6)	
84	Denys Holaido		03/06/84	M		(1)	
9	Rumyan Hovsepyan	ARM	13/11/91	M	8	(3)	
10	Júnior Moraes	BRA	04/04/87	A	12	(1)	5
24	Ihor Koshman		07/03/95	M		(1)	
25	Olexandr Kozak		25/07/94	M	1	(1)	
9	Djordje Lazić	SRB	18/06/83	M	22		9
13	Konstantinos Makrides	CYP	13/01/82	M	19	(1)	2
7	Mykola Morozyuk		17/01/88	M	22		4
87	Bohdan Myshenko		29/12/94	M	2	(7)	
40	Maryan Mysyk		02/10/96	M		(1)	
23	Olexandr Nasonov		28/04/92	D	12	(3)	
8	Gregory Nelson	NED	31/01/88	M	23	(2)	1
18	Olexandr Noyok		15/05/92	M	16	(6)	
79	Yuriy Pankiv		03/11/84	G	9		
22	Vasilios Pliatsikas	GRE	14/04/88	M	3		
21	Anton Postupalenko		28/08/88	M	1	(7)	2
44	Vasyl Pryima		10/06/91	D	20	(2)	
5	Artem Putivtsev		29/08/88	D	17		
15	Vyacheslav Sharpar		02/06/87	M	6	(1)	
55	Eduard Sobol		20/04/95	D	15		
94	Maxym Zaderaka		07/09/94	M		(5)	

FC Metalurh Zaporizhya

1935 • Slavutych Arena (11,756) •
fcmetalurg.com
**Coach: Oleh Taran;
(07/11/14) (Olexandr Tomakh);
(24/02/15) (Anatoliy Chantsev)**

2014

27/07	a	Shakhtar	L	0-2
02/08	h	Hoverla	W	2-1 *og (Lyulka), Léo*
09/08	a	Metalurh Donetsk	D	1-1 *Kapliyenko*
15/08	h	Dnipro	L	0-1
31/08	a	Karpaty	W	2-1 *Tatarkov, Liopa*
14/09	a	Volyn	L	0-3
20/09	a	Vorskla	L	0-3
05/10	a	Metalist	L	1-2 *Platon*
18/10	h	Olimpik	D	2-2 *Shturko 2*
01/11	h	Chornomorets	D	0-0
08/11	a	Zorya	L	0-3
23/11	h	Dynamo	L	2-4 *Platon, Orelesi*
30/11	h	Shakhtar	L	0-4
07/12	h	Illychivets	W	2-1 *Havrysh, Lysytskiy*

2015

01/03	a	Hoverla	W	1-0 *Lysytskiy (p)*
07/03	h	Metalurh Donetsk	L	0-1
15/03	a	Dnipro	L	0-1
05/04	h	Karpaty	W	2-1 *Lysytskiy (p), Kapliyenko*
10/04	h	Volyn	D	1-1 *Platon*
19/04	a	Vorskla	L	0-5
26/04	h	Metalist	D	0-0
04/05	a	Olimpik	D	0-0
10/05	h	Illychivets	W	2-0 *Platon, Tsurikov*
15/05	a	Chornomorets	D	0-0
24/05	h	Zorya	L	0-1
30/05	a	Dynamo	D	2-2 *Platon, Kapliyenko*

No	Name	Nat	DoB	Pos	Aps	(s)	Gls
3	Saša Balić	MNE	29/01/90	D	20		
32	Yevhen Borovyk		02/03/85	G	10		
80	Valeriane Gviliya		24/05/94	M	8	(4)	
9	Vitaliy Havrysh		18/03/86	M	4	(6)	1
12	Libor Hrdlička	SVK	02/01/86	G	1		
97	Danylo Ihnatenko		13/03/97	M		(1)	
18	Olexandr Kapliyenko		07/03/96	D	14	(5)	3
60	Yehor Klymenchuk		11/11/97	M		(1)	
13	Ihor Korotetskiy		13/09/87	D	4		
7	Vladyslav Kulach		07/05/93	A	9		
27	Serhiy Kulinich		09/01/95	D	2		
8	Olexiy Kurilov		24/04/88	D	10		
15	Artur Kuznetsov		09/03/95	D	6	(1)	
30	Léo	BRA	29/11/89	A		(3)	1
39	Dmytro Liopa		23/11/88	M	15		1
22	Vitaliy Lysytskiy		16/04/82	D	20	(2)	3
7	Ivan Matyazh		15/02/88	M		(5)	
5	Andriy Nesterov		02/07/90	D	5	(2)	
88	Nurudeen Orelesi	NGA	10/04/89	M	18	(1)	1
20	Pavlo Pashayev		04/01/88	D	22		
24	Ruslan Platon		12/01/82	A	13	(3)	5
6	Roman Pomazan		05/09/94	D	2	(1)	
95	Roman Popov		29/06/95	M	1		
10	Volodymyr Priyornov		02/01/86	A	13		
19	Serhiy Rudyka		14/06/88	M	9	(9)	
2	Andriy Sakhnevych		17/04/89	D	2	(1)	
77	Serginho	POR	16/06/85	M	11	(1)	
16	Tymofiy Sheremeta		06/10/95	G	1		
21	Yuriy Shturko		08/10/84	M	6	(6)	2
1	Maxym Startsev		20/01/80	G	13		
4	Mykyta Tatarkov		04/01/95	A	4	(5)	1
17	Andriy Tsurikov		05/10/92	M	6	(1)	1
33	Dmytro Ulyanov		01/12/93	D	4	(1)	
23	Valeriy Yurchuk		12/04/90	G	1		
44	Dmytro Yusov		11/05/93	M	18	(5)	
25	Ihor Zhurakhovskiy		19/09/94	M	14	(8)	

FC Olimpik Donetsk

2001 • NTK FFU im. V. Bannikov, Kyiv (1,678);
NSK Olimpiyskiy, Kyiv (70,050) • olimpik.com.ua
Coach: Roman Sanzhar

2014

26/07	a	Chornomorets	L	0-4
03/08	h	Zorya	W	1-0 *Lysenko*
09/08	a	Dynamo	D	0-0
15/08	h	Shakhtar	L	0-5
30/08	h	Hoverla	W	1-0 *Hryshko*
13/09	h	Metalurh Donetsk	W	3-2 *Doroshenko, Sytnyk, Semenyna*
22/09	a	Dnipro	L	0-5
04/10	h	Karpaty	W	1-0 *Doroshenko*
18/10	a	Metalurh Zaporizhya	D	2-2 *Isa, Rhasalla*
02/11	a	Metalist	D	0-0
09/11	h	Volyn	L	0-4
22/11	h	Illychivets	W	3-2 *Kadymyan, Gelzin, Tyshchenko*
29/11	h	Chornomorets	W	2-1 *Semenyna, Rhasalla*
06/12	h	Vorskla	D	1-1 *Semenyna*

2015

28/02	a	Zorya	L	1-5 *Kadymyan*
08/03	h	Dynamo	L	0-1
15/03	a	Shakhtar	L	0-6
03/04	h	Hoverla	L	1-2 *Doroshenko (p)*
11/04	a	Metalurh Donetsk	L	2-4 *Doroshenko, Isa*
19/04	h	Dnipro	L	0-5
26/04	a	Karpaty	L	1-4 *Kadymyan*
04/05	h	Metalurh Zaporizhya	D	0-0
09/05	a	Vorskla	L	1-3 *Kadymyan*
17/05	h	Metalist	W	2-1 *Tyshchenko, Lysenko*
23/05	h	Volyn	L	1-3 *Lysenko*
30/05	a	Illychivets	L	1-4 *Sytnyk*

No	Name	Nat	DoB	Pos	Aps	(s)	Gls
33	Yuriy Brovchenko		25/01/88	M	3	(1)	
34	Olexiy Dityatyev		07/11/88	D	21	(1)	
8	Volodymyr Doronin		15/01/93	M	11	(1)	
5	Kyrylo Doroshenko		17/11/89	M	18	(1)	4
7	Maxym Drachenko		28/01/90	M	20	(5)	
6	Denys Galenkov		13/10/95	A	1		
10	Vladyslav Gelzin		27/08/73	A	1	(5)	1
99	Vitaliy Hoshkoderya		08/01/88	D	4	(2)	
4	Dmytro Hryshko		02/12/85	D	21	(1)	1
23	Sheriff Isa	NGA	10/11/90	M	21		2
3	Pavlo Ivanov		28/09/84	D	20		
77	Gegam Kadymyan	ARM	19/10/92	A	17	(4)	4
55	Valeriy Lebed		05/01/88	M	10	(2)	
21	Volodymyr Lysenko		20/04/88	A	9	(9)	3
72	Ihor Lytovka		05/06/88	G	13		
1	Zauri Makharadze		24/03/93	G	13		
22	Andriy Mishchenko		07/04/91	D	11	(4)	
17	Artem Nedolya		20/10/93	M		(1)	
30	Yevhen Odintsov		23/08/88	D	1	(1)	
13	Vladyslav Ohyrya		03/04/90	M	21	(1)	
2	Yaroslav Oliynyk		14/03/91	D	2	(1)	
11	Mohammed Rhasalla	MAR	15/09/93	A	13	(5)	2
18	Ihor Semenyna		01/01/89	A	4	(11)	3
9	Olexandr Sytnyk		07/07/84	A	8	(12)	2
2	Yevheniy Tsymbalyuk		19/06/96	D	1		
19	Ihor Tyshchenko		11/05/89	M	17	(4)	2
6	Dmytro Yeremenko		20/06/90	M	5	(3)	

FC Shakhtar Donetsk

1936 • Arena Lviv, Lviv (34,915); NTK FFU
im. V. Bannikov, Kyiv (1,678); Obolon Arena, Kyiv
(5,100) • shakhtar.com
Major honours
*UEFA Cup (1) 2009; Ukrainian League (9) 2002, 2005,
2006, 2008, 2010, 2011, 2012, 2013, 2014; USSR Cup
(4) 1961, 1962, 1980, 1983; Ukrainian Cup (1) 1995,
1997, 2001, 2002, 2004, 2008, 2011, 2012, 2013*
Coach: Mircea Lucescu (ROU)

2014

27/07	h	Metalurh Zaporizhya	W	2-0 *Luiz Adriano, Gladkiy*
01/08	a	Vorskla	W	2-1 *Gladkiy, Stepanenko*
09/08	h	Metalist	W	1-0 *Rakitskiy*
15/08	a	Olimpik	W	5-0 *Kryvtsov, Taison, Gladkiy, Wellington Nem, Stepanenko*
29/08	h	Illychivets	W	3-0 *Gladkiy, Alex Teixeira, Taison*
13/09	a	Chornomorets	W	2-0 *Fernando, Gladkiy*
21/09	h	Zorya	L	0-1
05/10	a	Dynamo	L	0-1
17/10	h	Volyn	W	6-2 *Dentinho, Luiz Adriano 2, Alex Teixeira, Douglas Costa*
31/10	a	Metalurh Donetsk	L	1-2 *Srna*
09/11	h	Dnipro	D	0-0
21/11	a	Karpaty	W	2-0 *Alex Teixeira, Luiz Adriano*
30/11	a	Metalurh Zaporizhya	W	4-0 *Marlos, Alex Teixeira 2, Wellington Nem*
05/12	h	Hoverla	W	4-1 *Gladkiy 2, og (Khomyn), Fred*

2015

28/02	h	Vorskla	W	3-0 *Shevchuk, Douglas Costa, Alex Teixeira*
07/03	a	Metalist	D	2-2 *Srna (p), Luiz Adriano*
15/03	h	Olimpik	W	6-0 *Srna (p), Marlos 2, Gladkiy, Taison, Alex Teixeira*
05/04	a	Illychivets	W	6-2 *Gladkiy, og (Zubkov), Alex Teixeira 2, Marlos, Wellington Nem*
11/04	h	Chornomorets	W	5-0 *Douglas Costa, Luiz Adriano 2, Stepanenko, Taison*
18/04	a	Zorya	W	4-1 *Kryvtsov, Alex Teixeira 2, Luiz Adriano (p)*
26/04	h	Dynamo	D	0-0
04/05	a	Volyn	D	0-0
09/05	h	Hoverla	W	7-3 *Gladkiy 2, Douglas Costa, Rakitskiy, Luiz Adriano, Stepanenko, Alex Teixeira (p)*
16/05	h	Metalurh Donetsk	W	2-0 *Alex Teixeira 2*
23/05	a	Dnipro	L	2-3 *Alex Teixeira 2*
30/05	h	Karpaty	D	2-2 *Kryvtsov, Alex Teixeira*

No	Name	Nat	DoB	Pos	Aps	(s)	Gls
29	Alex Teixeira	BRA	06/01/90	M	18	(4)	17
10	Bernard	BRA	08/09/92	M	6	(8)	
50	Serhiy Bolbat		13/06/93	M		(1)	
27	Dmytro Chygrynskiy		07/11/86	D	1		
89	Dentinho	BRA	19/01/89	M	1	(10)	1
20	Douglas Costa	BRA	14/09/90	M	14	(6)	4
17	Fernando	BRA	03/03/92	M	11	(2)	1
8	Fred	BRA	05/03/93	M	14	(8)	1
21	Olexandr Gladkiy		24/08/87	A	14	(5)	11
77	Ilsinho	BRA	12/10/85	M	11	(3)	
31	Ismaily	BRA	11/01/90	D	8		
32	Anton Kanibolotskiy		16/05/88	G	11		
74	Viktor Kovalenko		14/02/96	M		(2)	
5	Olexandr Kucher		22/10/82	D	9	(2)	
38	Serhiy Kryvtsov		15/03/91	D	16	(1)	3
9	Luiz Adriano	BRA	12/04/87	A	19	(2)	9
66	Márcio Azevedo	BRA	05/02/86	D	1	(1)	
11	Marlos	BRA	07/06/88	M	12	(9)	4
18	Ivan Ordets		08/07/92	D	9		
30	Andriy Pyatov		28/06/84	G	15		
44	Yaroslav Rakitskiy		03/08/89	D	17	(1)	2
13	Vyacheslav Shevchuk		13/05/79	D	16		1
33	Darijo Srna	CRO	01/05/82	D	23		4
6	Taras Stepanenko		08/08/89	D	22		4
28	Taison	BRA	13/01/88	A	18	(3)	4
7	Wellington Nem	BRA	06/02/92	A		(8)	3

UKRAINE

FC Volyn Lutsk

1960 • Avanhard (10,792) • fcvolyn.net
Coach: Vitaliy Kvartsyaniy

2014
26/07	a	Illychivets	W	2-1	*Bicfalvi, Babenko*
02/08	h	Dnipro	L	0-1	
11/08	a	Chornomorets	L	0-1	
17/08	h	Karpaty	L	0-2	
31/08	a	Zorya	W	2-1	*Bicfalvi, Memeshev*
14/09	h	Metalurh Zaporizhya	W	3-0	*Memeshev, Žunić, Matei*
22/09	a	Dynamo	L	1-4	*Žunić*
03/10	h	Vorskla	D	2-2	*Bicfalvi, Danilo Mariotto (p)*
17/10	a	Hoverla	L	2-6	*Bicfalvi, Celin*
03/11	a	Shakhtar	D	0-0	
09/11	h	Olimpik	W	4-0	*Matei, Bicfalvi 2, Kobakhidze*
23/11	a	Metalurh Donetsk	W	2-1	*Siminin, Bicfalvi*
30/11	h	Illychivets	W	3-1	*Shabanov, Bicfalvi 2*
07/12	h	Metalist	L	0-3	*(w/o; match abandoned after 88 mins at 1-2 Kobakhidze)*

2015
01/03	a	Dnipro	L	0-5	
08/03	h	Chornomorets	D	1-1	*Žunić*
13/03	a	Karpaty	W	2-0	*Kobakhidze, Bicfalvi*
05/04	h	Zorya	L	1-2	*Sharpar*
10/04	a	Metalurh Zaporizhya	D	1-1	*Bicfalvi (p)*
19/04	h	Dynamo	L	1-3	*Bicfalvi (p)*
25/04	a	Vorskla	L	0-2	
04/05	h	Shakhtar	D	0-0	
11/05	a	Metalist	D	3-3	*Kobakhidze, Bicfalvi 2*
17/05	h	Hoverla	W	4-2	*Kobakhidze, Babatunde, Bicfalvi, Kozban*
23/05	a	Olimpik	W	3-1	*Bicfalvi, Babatunde, Kobakhidze*
29/05	h	Metalurh Donetsk	D	1-1	*Bicfalvi*

No	Name	Nat	DoB	Pos	Aps	(s)	Gls
79	Michel Babatunde	NGA	24/12/92	M	11	(2)	2
6	Ruslan Babenko		08/07/92	M	16	(1)	1
10	Eric Bicfalvi	ROU	05/02/88	M	26		17
77	Yevheniy Bokhashvili		05/01/93	A	1		
11	Celin	BRA	11/09/89	A	2	(5)	1
17	Danilo Mariotto	BRA	15/01/96	A	5	(4)	1
7	Valeriy Fedorchuk		05/10/88	M	11		
36	Roman Hodovaniy		04/10/90	D	4	(1)	
30	Oleh Humenyuk		03/05/83	D	5	(11)	
94	Viktor Khomchenko		11/11/94	A	1	(3)	
19	Aleksandr Kobakhidze	GEO	11/02/87	M	21	(2)	6
89	Dmytro Kozban		27/04/89	A	1	(9)	1
74	Artem Kychak		16/05/89	G	6	(3)	
93	Florentin Matei	ROU	15/04/93	M	20	(1)	2
9	Redvan Memeshev		15/08/93	A	15	(4)	2
42	Vitaliy Nedilko		21/08/82	G	10		
23	Dmytro Nemchaninov		27/01/90	D	6		
33	Yevheniy Novak		01/02/89	D	3	(4)	
26	Roman Nykytyuk		09/09/93	D		(2)	
91	Temur Partsvaniya		06/07/91	M	8	(2)	
38	Serhiy Petrov		21/05/97	A	1	(2)	
8	Serhiy Politylo		09/01/89	M	9	(2)	
14	Volodymyr Polyoviy		28/07/85	D	9	(2)	
4	Vitaliy Pryndeta		02/02/93	D	5		
13	Artem Shabanov		07/03/92	D	20	(2)	1
11	Vyacheslav Sharpar		02/06/87	M	11		1
16	Gal Shish	ISR	28/01/89	D	5	(4)	
1	Bohdan Shust		04/03/86	G	10		
3	Serhiy Siminin		09/10/87	M	13		1
39	Olexandr Svatok		27/09/94	D	1	(3)	
5	Serhiy Voronin		24/03/87	D	4	(1)	
20	Dmytro Zaderetskiy		03/08/94	D		(3)	
98	Olexiy Zinkevych		12/05/97	M		(1)	
15	Ivica Žunić	CRO	11/09/88	D	26		3

FC Vorskla Poltava

1955 • Vorskla im. Olexiy Butovskiy (24,795) • vorskla.com.ua
Major honours
Ukrainian Cup (1) 2009
Coach: Vasyl Sachko

2014
27/07	a	Dynamo	L	0-1	
01/08	h	Shakhtar	L	1-2	*Gromov*
08/08	a	Hoverla	D	0-0	
16/08	h	Metalurh Donetsk	W	2-1	*Gromov 2*
31/08	a	Dnipro	D	1-1	*Barannyk*
14/09	h	Karpaty	W	2-0	*Dedechko, Kovpak*
20/09	a	Metalurh Zaporizhya	W	3-0	*Januzi, Tursunov, A Tkachuk*
03/10	a	Volyn	D	2-2	*Tursunov, Dedechko*
18/10	h	Metalist	D	0-0	
01/11	h	Illychivets	D	0-0	
08/11	a	Chornomorets	L	0-1	
23/11	h	Zorya	W	2-0	*og (Hordiyenko), Kovpak*
30/11	h	Dynamo	L	0-3	
06/12	a	Olimpik	D	1-1	*Dedechko*

2015
28/02	a	Shakhtar	L	0-3	
08/03	h	Hoverla	W	2-0	*og (Lyulka), Gromov*
14/03	a	Metalurh Donetsk	D	1-1	*Shinder*
04/04	h	Dnipro	L	1-3	*Tursunov*
13/04	a	Karpaty	D	0-0	
19/04	h	Metalurh Zaporizhya	W	5-0	*Kovpak 2, Tursunov, Shinder, Gromov*
25/04	a	Volyn	W	2-0	*Tursunov, Sapai*
03/05	a	Metalist	W	2-0	*Gromov, Kovpak*
09/05	h	Olimpik	W	3-1	*Kovpak, Sklyar, Shinder*
16/05	a	Illychivets	W	2-1	*Kovpak, Mishchenko*
24/05	h	Chornomorets	W	2-0	*Gromov, Kovpak*
29/05	a	Zorya	D	1-1	*Shinder*

No	Name	Nat	DoB	Pos	Aps	(s)	Gls
24	Oleh Barannyk		20/03/92	A	8	(7)	1
31	Stanislav Bohush		25/10/83	G	23		
22	Yevhen Budnyk		04/09/90	M	1	(1)	
17	Volodymyr Chesnakov		12/02/88	D	23		
4	Armend Dallku	ALB	16/06/83	D	22		
15	Denys Dedechko		02/07/87	M	19	(1)	3
7	Artem Gromov		14/01/90	M	24		7
9	Ahmed Januzi	ALB	08/07/88	A	8	(6)	1
39	Olexandr Kovpak		02/02/83	A	18	(6)	8
11	Ivan Kryvosheyenko		11/05/84	A	2	(5)	
14	Dzhemal Kyzylatesh		14/09/94	M		(1)	
10	Jovan Markoski	SRB	23/06/80	M	5	(9)	
99	Oleh Mishchenko		10/10/89	A		(12)	1
12	Dmytro Nepogodov		17/02/88	G	3		
40	Ihor Preduta		15/11/90	D	7	(8)	
84	Olexandr Romanchuk		21/10/84	D		(1)	
23	Vadym Sapai		07/02/86	D	23		1
1	Anton Shinder		13/06/87	A	11		4
47	Bohdan Sichkaruk		01/08/94	A		(2)	
3	Serhiy Siminin		09/10/87	D	11		
6	Olexandr Sklyar		26/02/91	M	17	(2)	1
8	Andriy Tkachuk		18/11/87	M	13	(5)	1
34	Yevhen Tkachuk		27/06/91	D	22		
77	Sanzhar Tursunov	UZB	29/12/86	M	26		5

FC Zorya Luhansk

1923 • Slavutych Arena, Zaporizhya (11,756) • zarya-lugansk.com
Major honours
USSR League (1) 1972
Coach: Yuriy Vernydub

2014
27/07	h	Metalist	L	1-2	*Ljubenović*
03/08	a	Olimpik	L	0-1	
11/08	h	Illychivets	W	1-0	*Budkivskiy*
16/08	a	Chornomorets	D	0-0	
31/08	h	Volyn	L	1-2	*Karavayev*
13/09	h	Dynamo	D	2-2	*Khomchenovskiy, Ljubenović*
21/09	a	Shakhtar	W	1-0	*Malyshev*
04/10	h	Hoverla	W	2-1	*Malyshev, Ljubenović*
19/10	a	Metalurh Donetsk	D	0-0	
02/11	a	Karpaty	W	2-1	*Vernydub, Khomchenovskiy*
08/11	h	Metalurh Zaporizhya	W	3-0	*Vernydub, Budkivskiy 2*
23/11	h	Vorskla	L	0-2	
30/11	a	Metalist	L	2-4	*Pylyavskiy, Petryak*
06/12	h	Dnipro	W	2-1	*Budkivskiy, Segbefia*

2015
28/02	h	Olimpik	W	5-1	*Malyshev, og (Drachenko), Malinovskiy, Kamenyuka, Pylyavskiy*
07/03	h	Illychivets	L	1-2	*Lipartia*
15/03	h	Chornomorets	W	1-0	*Lipartia*
05/04	a	Volyn	W	2-1	*Khomchenovskiy, Budkivskiy*
12/04	a	Dynamo	D	2-2	*Pylyavskiy (p), Ljubenović*
18/04	h	Shakhtar	L	1-4	*Ljubenović (p)*
25/04	a	Hoverla	W	2-1	*Ljubenović, Lipartia*
02/05	h	Metalurh Donetsk	W	4-2	*Khomchenovskiy, Karavayev, Biliy, Totovytskiy*
10/05	a	Dnipro	W	2-0	*Khomchenovskiy, Budkivskiy*
16/05	h	Karpaty	D	1-1	*Ljubenović*
24/05	a	Metalurh Zaporizhya	W	1-0	*Ljubenović*
29/05	h	Vorskla	D	1-1	*Budkivskiy*

No	Name	Nat	DoB	Pos	Aps	(s)	Gls
25	Maxym Biliy		21/06/90	D	10	(6)	1
28	Pylyp Budkivskiy		10/03/92	A	25		8
4	Ihor Chaykovskiy		07/10/91	M	9	(5)	
45	Artem Hordiyenko		04/03/91	D	5	(1)	
35	Olexandr Hrytsai		30/09/77	M	14	(2)	
17	Nikola Ignjatijević	SRB	12/12/83	D	10	(1)	
6	Mykyta Kamenyuka		03/06/85	M	23		1
20	Olexandr Karavayev		02/06/92	M	22	(2)	2
37	Dmytro Khomchenovskiy		16/04/90	M	22	(1)	4
12	Ruslan Khudzhamov		05/10/82	G	1		
7	Pavlo Khudzik		29/04/85	M		(2)	
91	Ihor Levchenko		23/02/91	G	1		
10	Jaba Lipartia	GEO	16/11/87	A	6	(10)	3
22	Željko Ljubenović	SRB	09/07/81	M	11	(13)	8
49	Dmytro Lukano		02/03/95	A		(1)	
18	Ruslan Malinovskiy		04/05/93	M	16	(7)	1
8	Maxym Malyshev		24/12/92	D	16		3
21	Yevhen Opanasenko		25/08/90	D	6	(2)	
34	Ivan Petryak		13/03/94	M	3	(7)	1
36	Andriy Poltavtsev		07/12/91	G	1	(1)	
99	Andriy Pylyavskiy		04/12/88	D	19		3
3	Mykhailo Pysko		19/03/93	D	1	(3)	
1	Krševan Santini	CRO	11/04/87	G	8		
9	Prince Segbefia	TOG	11/03/91	M	7	(2)	1
30	Mykyta Shevchenko		26/01/93	G	15		
29	Andriy Totovytskiy		20/01/93	M	3	(6)	1
15	Vitaliy Vernydub		17/10/87	D	23		2
16	Hryhoriy Yarmash		04/01/85	M	9	(3)	

Top goalscorers

17	Alex Teixeira (Shakhtar)
	Eric Bicfalvi (Volyn)
15	Artem Kravets (Dynamo)
14	Andriy Yarmolenko (Dynamo)
12	Nikola Kalinić (Dnipro)
11	Olexandr Gladkiy (Shakhtar)
9	Djordje Lazić (Metalurh Donetsk)
	Luiz Adriano (Shakhtar)
8	Yevhen Seleznyov (Dnipro)
	Cleiton Xavier (Metalist)
	Olexandr Kovpak (Vorskla)
	Pylyp Budkivskiy (Zorya)
	Željko Ljubenović (Zorya)

Promoted clubs

FC Olexandriya

1948 • KSK Nika (7,000) • fco.com.ua
Coach: Volodymyr Sharan

FC Stal Dniprodzerzhynsk

1926 • Metalurh (2,900) • fcstal.com.ua
Coach: Volodymyr Mazyar

Second level final table 2014/15

		Pld	W	D	L	F	A	Pts
1	FC Olexandriya	30	22	6	2	53	15	72
2	FC Stal Dniprodzerzhynsk	30	17	9	4	45	21	60
3	FC Hirnyk-Sport Komsomolsk	30	16	9	5	44	24	57
4	FC Zirka Kirovohrad	30	14	7	9	42	27	49
5	FC Desna Chernihiv	30	12	11	7	44	27	47
6	FC Dynamo-2 Kyiv	30	12	8	10	35	29	44
7	FC Helios Kharkiv	30	12	8	10	30	25	44
8	FC Sumy	30	12	7	11	35	41	43
9	FC Hirnyk Kryvyi Rih	30	10	12	8	32	26	42
10	FC Poltava	30	11	9	10	29	27	42
11	FC Ternopil	30	11	8	11	33	49	41
12	FC Naftovyk-Ukrnafta Okhtyrka	30	10	10	10	32	34	40
13	FC Nyva Ternopil	30	8	3	19	25	52	27
14	MFC Mykolaiv	30	6	6	18	34	67	24
15	FC Stal Alchevsk	30	5	0	25	16	28	15
16	FC Bukovyna Chernivtsi	30	4	3	23	24	61	15

NB FC Stal Alchevsk withdrew after round 17 - their remaining matches were awarded as goalless defeats.

DOMESTIC CUP

Kubok Ukraïny 2014/15

SECOND ROUND

(22/08/14)
FC Ternopil 1-1 Olexandriya *(aet; 3-4 on pens)*

(23/08/14)
Bukovyna Chernivtsi 0-4 Chornomorets Odesa
Chaika Chaiky 0-4 Karpaty Lviv
Cherkaskiy Dnipro Cherkasy 1-2 Hoverla Uzhhorod
Desna Chernihiv 0-1 Dnipro Dnipropetrovsk
Helios Kharkiv 0-1 Metalurh Zaporizhya
Mykolaiv 0-1 Illychivets Mariupil
Naftovyk-Ukrnafta Okhtyrka 0-1 Volyn Lutsk
Nyva Ternopil 1-5 Vorskla Poltava
Obolon-Brovar Kyiv 0-1 Shakhtar Donetsk
Poltava 2-1 Metalurh Donetsk
Real Farma Ovidiopil 0-1 Olimpik Donetsk
Stal Alchevsk 0-3 *(w/o)* Stal Dniprodzerzhynsk
Zirka Kirovohrad 1-3 Dynamo Kyiv

(24/08/14)
Kremin Kremenchuk 0-2 Zorya Luhansk
Sumy 0-1 Metalist Kharkiv *(aet)*

THIRD ROUND

(25/09/14 & 27/10/14)
Poltava 1-5, 1-4 Shakhtar Donetsk *(2-9)*

(26/09/14 & 30/10/14)
Olexandriya 0-1, 1-1 Zorya Luhansk *(1-2)*

(27/09/14 & 27/10/14)
Volyn Lutsk 1-0, 0-4 Dnipro Dnipropetrovsk *(1-4)*

(27/09/14 & 28/10/14)
Karpaty Lviv 0-1, 0-1 Dynamo Kyiv *(0-2)*

(27/09/14 & 29/10/14)
Hoverla Uzhhorod 2-2, 1-1 Metalist Kharkiv *(3-3; Metalist Kharkiv on away goals)*
Illychivets Mariupil 0-1, 2-3 Vorskla Poltava *(2-4)*

(28/09/14 & 28/10/14)
Olimpik Donetsk 2-0, 4-0 Metalurh Zaporizhya *(6-0)*

(28/09/14 & 29/10/14)
Stal Dniprodzerzhynsk 2-1, 1-2 Chornomorets Odesa *(aet; 3-3, 2-4 on pens)*

QUARTER-FINALS

(04/03/15 & 08/04/15)
Metalist Kharkiv 0-2 Shakhtar Donetsk *(Kucher 4, Gladkiy 54)*
Shakhtar Donetsk 1-0 Metalist Kharkiv *(Luiz Adriano 49)*
(Shakhtar Donetsk 3-0)

Vorskla Poltava 0-0 Olimpik Donetsk
Olimpik Donetsk 1-0 Vorskla Poltava *(Sytnyk 57)*
(Olimpik Donetsk 1-0)

Zorya Luhansk 1-2 Dynamo Kyiv *(Kamenyuka 50; Gusev 12p, Kravets 33)*
Dynamo Kyiv 2-0 Zorya Luhansk *(Belhanda 32, Teodorczyk 41)*
(Dynamo Kyiv 4-1)

(01/04/15 & 08/04/15)
Chornomorets Odesa 0-4 Dnipro Dnipropetrovsk *(Rotan 52, Seleznyov 56p, 86, Bezus 90+2)*
Dnipro Dnipropetrovsk 1-0 Chornomorets Odesa *(Shakhov 28)*
(Dnipro Dnipropetrovsk 5-0)

SEMI-FINALS

(29/04/15 & 20/05/15)
Dnipro Dnipropetrovsk 0-1 Shakhtar Donetsk *(Gladkiy 45+1)*
Shakhtar Donetsk 1-1 Dnipro Dnipropetrovsk *(Luiz Adriano 77p; Kalinić 30)*
(Shakhtar Donetsk 2-1)

Olimpik Donetsk 0-0 Dynamo Kyiv
Dynamo Kyiv 4-1 Olimpik Donetsk *(Miguel Veloso 3, 53, Yarmolenko 37, Lens 90+2; Dityatyev 76)*
(Dynamo Kyiv 4-1)

FINAL

(04/06/15)
NSK Olimpiyskiy, Kyiv
FC DYNAMO KYIV 0
FC SHAKHTAR DONETSK 0
(aet; 5-4 on pens)
Referee: *Mozharovskiy*
DYNAMO KYIV: *Shovkovskiy, Danilo Silva (Antunes 46), Khacheridi, Dragovic, Vida, Rybalka, Miguel Veloso, Yarmolenko, Sydorchuk (Belhanda 102), Lens, Kravets (Gusev 76)*
Red card: *Rybalka (115)*
SHAKHTAR DONETSK: *Pyatov, Srna, Kucher (Kryvtsov 45+2), Rakitskiy, Shevchuk, Stepanenko, Ilsinho (Gladkiy 91), Douglas Costa, Alex Teixeira, Bernard (Taison 69), Luiz Adriano*

Dynamo Kyiv captain Olexandr Shovkovskiy lifts the Ukrainian Cup after his team's penalty shoot-out triumph against Shakhtar

WALES

Cymdeithas Bêl-droed Cymru / Football Association of Wales (FAW)

Address	11/12 Neptune Court, Vanguard Way GB-Cardiff CF24 5PJ	**President**	Trefor Hughes
		General secretary	Jonathan Ford
		Media officer	Ian Gwyn Hughes
Tel	+44 29 2043 5830	**Year of formation**	1876
Fax	+44 29 2049 6953	**National stadium**	Cardiff City Stadium (28,018)
E-mail	info@faw.co.uk		
Website	faw.org.uk		

PREMIER LEAGUE CLUBS

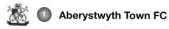 **1** Aberystwyth Town FC

2 AUK Broughton FC

 **3** Bala Town FC

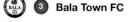 **4** Bangor City FC

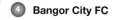 **5** Carmarthen Town AFC

 **6** Cefn Druids AFC

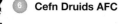 **7** Connah's Quay FC

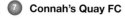 **8** Newtown AFC

 **9** Port Talbot Town FC

10 Prestatyn Town FC

11 Rhyl FC

12 The New Saints FC

PROMOTED CLUBS

13 Llandudno FC

14 Haverfordwest County AFC

KEY:

- – UEFA Champions League
- – UEFA Europa League
- – Promoted
- – Relegated

The New Saints go marching on

The New Saints FC were more dominant than ever in 2014/15 as they romped unopposed to a fourth successive Welsh Premier League title while also collecting silverware in the two domestic knockout competitions to secure an unprecedented trophy treble.

While TNS hogged the headlines domestically, Welsh football followers were gripped by the exploits of Chris Coleman's national team as, inspired by the brilliant Gareth Bale, they took a giant leap towards the UEFA EURO 2016 finals in France and a first major tournament qualification for 58 years.

Clean sweep of domestic honours for border club

Bala, Broughton and Newtown qualify for Europe

Brilliant Bale leads national team towards dreamland

Domestic league

As the only fully-professional club in the Welsh Premier League, TNS are expected to win it every season, but such was the Oswestry-based club's omnipotence in 2014/15 that they ended the 32-match campaign with a mammoth 18-point victory margin. Indeed, Craig Harrison's winning machine did not lose a game until the club's record-extending ninth national title was safe and secure. They racked up 90 goals and were Europe's first domestic champions of 2015, concluding proceedings in mid-March, six weeks before the end of term.

TNS were largely unchanged in personnel from the previous campaign, the only significant differences being that Harrison held the managerial reins alone – rather than in tandem with Carl Darlington – and that the team boasted an exotic new foreigner in Polish winger Adrian Cieślewicz, recruited from B36 Tórshavn. He chalked up ten goals, the last of them to open the scoring in the 3-0 win over Bala Town FC that clinched the title, but, as in the previous campaign, the bulk of the side's goalscoring duties were carried out by Englishman Michael Wilde and his Kiwi strike partner Greg Draper.

While TNS repeatedly mowed down the opposition to turn the title race into a

victory parade, interest switched to the battle for the runners-up spot. Fuelled by the goals of the prolific Chris Venables, Aberystwyth Town FC were favourites until they hit the wall in February and failed to win any of their next eight matches.

Their demise let in Bala and AUK Broughton FC, but although the latter denied TNS a defeat-free season in the penultimate round, Bala's 1-1 draw against the champions the following week secured second place by a point, giving the team from the Gwynedd market town their highest-ever finish. Broughton joined Bala in the UEFA Europa League, but there was no place for Aberystwyth, defeated in the post-season play-off final by Newtown AFC.

Domestic cup

Newtown could have secured their European ticket a fortnight earlier had they won the Welsh Cup. Manager Chris Hughes had taken the club to their first final since 1897, but despite holding their own – on their home ground – in the first half, the underdogs were eventually worn down by TNS, who claimed a 2-0 win with a double from one-time Manchester United FC reserve-teamer Matty Williams. The victory completed TNS's first ever clean sweep of the three domestic trophies following a 3-0 win against Bala in the League Cup final.

Europe

There was no joy for Welsh teams in Europe, although TNS's veteran midfielder Scott Ruscoe set a record for a Welsh Premier League player with his 30th European appearance in the club's 1-0 defeat away to ŠK Slovan Bratislava in the UEFA Champions League second qualifying round.

National team

Encouraged to end their long major tournament absence by the provision of 23 qualifying places at UEFA EURO 2016, Wales set about their task with gusto and fortitude, but not even the team's most ardent followers could have imagined that after six of their ten fixtures Coleman's charges would be sitting undefeated on top of the Group B table having taken four points from 2014 FIFA World Cup quarter-finalists Belgium.

Bale's contribution to that position of strength was immense. The Real Madrid CF superstar was on fire in every game, scoring five of Wales's eight goals, including a brilliant double in Israel and the winner at home to Belgium. Those vital strikes made him the country's all-time leading marksman in UEFA EURO qualifiers, but more importantly they served to carry his country to within touching distance of a tournament for which they had never qualified.

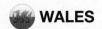

DOMESTIC SEASON AT A GLANCE

Premier League 2014/15 final table

		Pld	Home					Away					Total					Pts
			W	D	L	F	A	W	D	L	F	A	W	D	L	F	A	
1	**The New Saints FC**	32	12	4	0	46	10	11	4	1	44	14	23	8	1	90	24	77
2	Bala Town FC	32	9	3	4	42	19	9	2	5	25	23	18	5	9	67	42	59
3	AUK Broughton FC	32	12	1	3	44	16	6	3	7	18	18	18	4	10	62	34	58
4	Aberystwyth Town FC	32	8	4	4	33	28	6	6	4	36	33	14	10	8	69	61	52
5	Port Talbot Town FC	32	10	1	5	33	20	3	3	10	21	39	13	4	15	54	59	43
6	Newtown AFC	32	6	4	6	30	29	4	4	8	22	36	10	8	14	52	65	38
7	Connah's Quay FC	32	4	6	6	20	27	7	4	5	24	26	11	10	11	44	53	43
8	Rhyl FC	32	4	7	5	20	23	7	2	7	21	26	11	9	12	41	49	42
9	Carmarthen Town AFC	32	7	3	6	29	27	5	3	8	19	30	12	6	14	48	57	42
10	Bangor City FC	32	5	3	8	25	32	4	5	7	23	30	9	8	15	48	62	35
11	Cefn Druids AFC	32	4	2	10	15	29	3	4	9	23	35	7	6	19	38	64	27
12	Prestatyn Town FC	32	3	4	9	23	36	1	2	13	20	50	4	6	22	43	86	18

NB League splits into top and bottom halves after First Phase of 22 games, with each team playing a further ten matches (home and away) exclusively against clubs from its half of the table.

European qualification 2015/16

 Champion/Cup winner: The New Saints FC (first qualifying round)

 Bala Town FC (first qualifying round)
AUK Broughton FC (first qualifying round)
Newtown AFC (first qualifying round)

Top scorer   Chris Venables (Aberystwyth), 28 goals
Relegated clubs   Prestatyn Town FC, Cefn Druids AFC
Promoted clubs   Llandudno FC, Haverfordwest County AFC
Cup final   The New Saints FC 2-0 Newtown AFC

Team of the season
(4-3-1-2)

Coach: Harrison *(TNS)*

Morris *(Bala)*
Spender *(TNS)* — Baker *(TNS)* — Pearson *(Broughton)* — Marriott *(TNS)*
Cieślewicz *(TNS)* — Field *(Broughton)* — A Edwards *(TNS)*
Venables *(Aberystwyth)*
Oswell *(Newtown)* — Hunt *(Bala)*

Player of the season

Chris Venables
(Aberystwyth Town FC)

Having become the first midfielder to top the Welsh Premier League's scoring charts with his 24 goals in 2013/14, Venables repeated the trick in 2014/15, increasing his golden boot-winning tally to 28 – in 27 matches – to help the seaside club to a fourth-place finish. The 29-year-old started as he meant to go on with four goals against Cefn Druids AFC on the opening day, and he had already bagged 20 goals by Christmas. The season ended in frustration, however, as Aberystwyth failed to qualify for Europe.

Newcomer of the season

Sean Miller
(Connah's Quay FC)

A lowly tenth in the 2013/14 Welsh Premier League, Connah's Quay topped the relegation pool, in seventh, 12 months later, and much of the team's improvement was down to the efforts of Miller, their newly-recruited 19-year-old winger, who ended the campaign as the Nomads' top scorer with nine goals. The pacy Englishman, previously on the books of nearby Chester FC, was rewarded with a mid-season contract extension and, in June, with the Welsh Premier League young player of the year award.

NATIONAL TEAM

International tournament appearances
FIFA World Cup (1) 1958 (qtr-finals)

Top five all-time caps
Neville Southall (92); Gary Speed (85); Craig Bellamy (78); Dean Saunders (75); Peter Nicholas & Ian Rush (73)

Top five all-time goals
Ian Rush (28); Ivor Allchurch & Trevor Ford (23); Dean Saunders (22); Craig Bellamy (19)

Results 2014/15

09/09/14	Andorra (ECQ)	A	Andorra la Vella	W	2-1	Bale (22, 81)	
10/10/14	Bosnia & Herzegovina (ECQ)	H	Cardiff	D	0-0		
13/10/14	Cyprus (ECQ)	H	Cardiff	W	2-1	Cotterill (13), Robson-Kanu (23)	
16/11/14	Belgium (ECQ)	A	Brussels	D	0-0		
28/03/15	Israel (ECQ)	A	Haifa	W	3-0	Ramsey (45+1), Bale (50, 77)	
12/06/15	Belgium (ECQ)	H	Cardiff	W	1-0	Bale (25)	

Appearances 2014/15

Coach: Chris Coleman	10/06/70		AND	BIH	CYP	BEL	ISR	BEL	Caps	Goals
Wayne Hennessey	24/01/87	Crystal Palace (ENG)	G	G	G	G	G	G	49	-
Chris Gunter	21/07/89	Reading (ENG)	D	D	D	D	D	D	59	-
Ashley Williams	23/08/84	Swansea (ENG)	D	D	D	D	D	D	51	1
James Chester	23/01/89	Hull (ENG)	D	D	D	D		D	6	-
Ben Davies	24/04/93	Tottenham (ENG)	D	D			D		13	-
Joe Allen	14/03/90	Liverpool (ENG)	M			M	M	M	21	-
Andy King	29/10/88	Leicester (ENG)	M77	M	M 47*			s93	29	2
Aaron Ramsey	26/12/90	Arsenal (ENG)	M94			M	M85	M	34	9
Neil Taylor	07/02/89	Swansea (ENG)	M	D	D	D	D	D	22	-
Gareth Bale	16/07/89	Real Madrid (ESP)	M	M	M	M	M	M87	50	17
Simon Church	10/12/88	Charlton (ENG)	A62	A65	A6				29	2
Joe Ledley	23/01/87	Crystal Palace (ENG)	s62	M	M	M	M47	M	57	3
George Williams	07/09/95	Fulham (ENG)	s77	s83	M58	s46			5	-
Emyr Huws	30/09/93	Wigan (ENG)	s94			s95			4	-
Jonathan Williams	09/10/93	Ipswich (ENG)		M83					7	-
Hal Robson-Kanu	21/05/89	Reading (ENG)		s65	M84	A95	A68	A93	26	2
David Cotterill	04/12/87	Birmingham (ENG)			s6	M46			22	2
David Edwards	03/02/86	Wolves (ENG)			s58				27	3
Jake Taylor	01/12/91	Reading (ENG)			s84				1	-
James Collins	23/08/83	West Ham (ENG)					D		45	3
David Vaughan	18/02/83	Nottingham Forest (ENG)					s47		39	1
Sam Vokes	21/10/89	Burnley (ENG)					s68	s87	33	6
Shaun MacDonald	17/06/88	Bournemouth (ENG)					s85		2	-
Ashley Richards	12/04/91	Swansea (ENG)						D	5	-

WALES

EUROPE

DOMESTIC LEAGUE CLUB-BY-CLUB

The New Saints FC

Second qualifying round - ŠK Slovan Bratislava (SVK)
A 0-1
Harrison, Spender, Marriott, K Edwards, Finley (Ruscoe 89), Williams, Fraughan (Darlington 46), Seargeant, Rawlinson, Wilde, A Edwards (Draper 84). Coach: Craig Harrison (ENG)
H 0-2
Harrison, Spender, Marriott, Baker, K Edwards, Finley, Draper, Williams (Darlington 59), Seargeant (Quigley 75), Wilde (Evans 80), A Edwards. Coach: Craig Harrison (ENG)

Bangor City FC

First qualifying round - Stjarnan (ISL)
A 0-4
Cudworth, Walker, Chris Roberts, Johnston, Miley, Chris Jones (McDaid 70), Davies, S Edwards (R Jones 80), Hart, Allen, R Edwards (Culshaw 90). Coach: Nev Powell (WAL)
Red card: Hart 77
H 0-4
Cudworth, Walker, Chris Roberts, Johnston (Hughes 56), Miley, Chris Jones (Culshaw 71), Davies, S Edwards, McDaid, Allen, R Edwards (Corey Jones 82). Coach: Nev Powell (WAL)

AUK Broughton FC

First qualifying round - FK Haugesund (NOR)
H 1-1 *Johnson (29)*
Coates, Short, Pearson, Kearney, Field (Barrow 90+1), Jones, Rule, Budrys, Johnson, Wignall (Wade 59), Owens. Coach: Andy Preece (ENG)
A 1-2 *Pearson (14)*
Coates, Short, Pearson, Kearney, Field (Roddy 80), Jones, Rule, Budrys (Barrow 52), Johnson (Hassall 61), Wade, Owens. Coach: Andy Preece (ENG)
Red card: Barrow 72

Aberystwyth Town FC

First qualifying round - Derry City FC (IRL)
A 0-4
Lewis, Chris Davies (Morgan 66), Cledan Davies, Corbisiero, S Jones, Kellaway, Sherbon, M Jones, Venables, C Williams (Draper 25), Thomas. Coach: Ian Hughes (WAL)
Red card: Lewis 23
H 0-5
Draper, Cledan Davies (James 87), Corbisiero, S Jones, Atyeo, Kellaway, Sherbon (R Davies 87), M Jones, Venables, C Williams, Morgan (Chris Davies 61). Coach: Ian Hughes (WAL)

Aberystwyth Town FC

1884 • Park Avenue (3,000) • atfc.org.uk
Major honours
Welsh Cup (1) 1900
Manager: Ian Hughes

2014
22/08	a	Cefn Druids	W 5-0	*Venables 4, Sherbon*
25/08	h	TNS	D 1-1	*M Jones*
29/08	h	Bangor	D 3-3	*Venables 2 (1p), og (Cudworth)*
07/09	a	Rhyl	W 1-0	*Venables*
12/09	h	Connah's Quay	D 1-1	*Venables*
19/09	a	Port Talbot	W 2-1	*Venables, M Jones*
26/09	h	Bala	W 4-0	*M Jones 2, Kellaway, Venables (p)*
04/10	a	Newtown	L 3-6	*Venables 2 (1p), M Jones*
11/10	h	Broughton	W 2-1	*Kellaway, Venables*
18/10	a	Prestatyn	L 1-2	*Venables*
24/10	a	Bala	L 0-4	
31/10	h	Newtown	W 1-0	*Venables (p)*
07/11	a	Cefn Druids	W 4-2	*Venables 2, M Jones, S Williams*
14/11	a	TNS	D 1-1	*Venables*
21/11	a	Bangor	D 2-2	*Kellaway, og (Davies)*
07/12	a	Rhyl	W 2-0	*C Williams, Venables*
12/12	a	Connah's Quay	W 4-2	*Venables 2, M Jones, S Jones*
20/12	h	Port Talbot	L 0-3	
26/12	a	Carmarthen	W 3-1	*Venables 2, Kellaway*
2015				
01/01	h	Carmarthen	W 5-3	*Sherbon 2, C Williams, Kellaway, Cledan Davies*
09/01	a	Broughton	D 1-1	*M Jones*
17/01	h	Prestatyn	W 3-1	*Venables, C Williams, Kellaway*
31/01	h	Newtown	W 3-2	*M Jones, Stephens, James*
14/02	a	Broughton	L 2-3	*Venables (p), S Jones*
22/02	h	TNS	L 0-4	
27/02	a	Bala	D 3-3	*Kellaway 3*
13/03	h	Port Talbot	D 2-2	*C Williams 2 (1p)*
21/03	a	Newtown	D 3-3	*Sherbon, Venables, Stephens*
29/03	h	Broughton	L 1-3	*Venables*
10/04	a	TNS	D 3-3	*M Jones 2, S Jones*
17/04	h	Bala	L 1-2	*Venables*
26/04	a	Port Talbot	W 2-1	*Kellaway, C Williams*

No	Name	Nat	DoB	Pos	Aps	(s)	Gls
6	Thomas Atyeo		22/05/96	D		(1)	
19	Ryan Batley		17/11/91	D	11	(6)	
4	Antonio Corbisiero	ENG	17/11/84	D	23	(2)	
2	Chris Davies		21/10/90	M	27	(2)	
3	Cledan Davies		10/03/90	D	22	(9)	1
15	Rhydian Davies		05/10/95	M		(4)	
13	Philip Draper	ENG	05/07/91	G	2	(2)	
12	Sion James		03/02/80	D	26	(3)	1
9	Mark Jones		01/05/89	A	29	(2)	11
5	Stuart Jones		14/03/84	D	30		3
7	Geoff Kellaway		07/04/86	A	29	(1)	10
1	Mike Lewis		04/04/89	G	30		
14	Bari Morgan		13/08/80	M		(1)	
18	Tom Shaw		12/09/89	M	8	(4)	
8	Luke Sherbon		06/06/86	M	28		4
20	Ross Stephens		28/05/85	M	7		2
16	Wyn Thomas		11/01/79	D	4	(3)	
10	Chris Venables		23/07/85	M	27		28
11	Craig Williams		28/01/83	M	31		6
17	Steffan Williams		08/06/92	M	4	(7)	1
6	Stephen Wright	ENG	08/02/80	D	14	(1)	

AUK Broughton FC

1946 • The Airfield (4,000) • airbusfc.com
Manager: Andy Preece (ENG)

2014

25/08	a	Bala	D 0-0	
29/08	h	Newtown	W 3-0	Wignall, Williams, McGinn
05/09	a	Bangor	W 2-1	Field, McGinn (p)
13/09	a	Prestatyn	W 2-0	Field (p), Rule
21/09	h	Carmarthen	W 2-0	McGinn, Field (p)
27/09	a	Cefn Druids	L 2-3	Jones, Wade
04/10	a	TNS	L 2-3	McGinn (p), Kearney
08/10	h	Port Talbot	W 3-0	Budrys, Wignall 2
11/10	a	Aberystwyth	L 1-2	Field (p)
18/10	h	Rhyl	W 2-1	Kearney, Wade
26/10	a	Cefn Druids	D 1-1	Healing
02/11	a	TNS	D 1-1	Rule
08/11	a	Port Talbot	L 0-2	
15/11	h	Bala	W 2-1	Budrys 2
22/11	a	Newtown	L 0-1	
06/12	h	Bangor	W 5-1	Field 2 (2p), Healing, Wignall 2
13/12	h	Prestatyn	W 2-1	Jones, Budrys
20/12	a	Carmarthen	L 1-2	Field (p)
26/12	h	Connah's Quay	W 4-0	Rule, Field (p), Jones, Barrow

2015

01/01	a	Connah's Quay	W 3-0	Rule, McGinn, Field
09/01	a	Aberystwyth	D 1-1	Jones
24/01	a	Rhyl	W 2-1	Wignall, Pearson
01/02	h	Bala	L 1-2	Field
14/02	h	Aberystwyth	W 3-2	Field 3 (2p)
21/02	h	Port Talbot	W 5-0	Wade, Wignall, Budrys, Riley, Healing
01/03	a	TNS	L 0-2	
14/03	a	Newtown	W 2-0	Field 2 (1p)
22/03	a	Bala	L 0-3	
29/03	a	Aberystwyth	W 3-1	Wignall, Field, Wade
11/04	a	Port Talbot	L 0-1	
18/04	h	TNS	W 1-0	Rule
26/04	h	Newtown	W 6-1	Evans 2, Williams, Wade, Riley, McGinn

No	Name	Nat	DoB	Pos	Aps	(s)	Gls
12	Jordan Barrow	ENG	18/10/93	D	12	(18)	1
9	Chris Budrys	SCO	13/08/85	A	27	(3)	5
21	James Coates	ENG	27/02/85	G	32		
24	Ricky Evans		24/09/76	M	5	(5)	2
20	Jake Eyre	ENG	02/11/95	M		(6)	
6	Tom Field	ENG	02/08/85	M	26	(1)	16
15	Ellis Healing	ENG	11/05/94	M	13	(11)	3
7	Andy Jones	ENG	23/03/85	A	23	(7)	4
5	Ian Kearney	ENG	15/06/87	D	10		2
22	Matty McGinn	ENG	27/06/83	D	21	(6)	6
18	James Owen		14/01/91	M	16	(2)	
26	Lee Owens	ENG	29/06/86	D	22	(2)	
4	Mike Pearson		19/01/88	D	32		1
10	Wayne Riley	ENG	26/09/89	M	5	(5)	2
14	Michael Roddy	ENG	22/09/88	M	1	(1)	
8	Glenn Rule	ENG	30/11/89	M	30	(1)	5
3	Lewis Short	ENG	11/06/90	D	22	(1)	
19	Jonny Spittle	ENG	13/08/94	D	1	(1)	
11	Ryan Wade	ENG	22/01/88	A	13	(8)	5
21	Ryan Wignall	ENG	28/03/89	M	19		8
17	Ashley Williams	ENG	08/10/87	M	22	(3)	2

Bala Town FC

1880 • Maes Tegid (2,000) •
balatownfc.co.uk
Manager: Colin Caton

2014

23/08	a	Newtown	W 2-1	Valentine, Hayes
25/08	h	Broughton	D 0-0	
30/08	a	Prestatyn	D 3-3	K Smith, Connolly 2
07/09	a	Carmarthen	W 8-1	Sheridan, Kelly, Valentine, Hayes 2, Connolly 3
12/09	a	Cefn Druids	W 1-0	Connolly
19/09	h	TNS	L 0-3	
26/09	a	Aberystwyth	L 0-4	
03/10	h	Rhyl	L 1-2	Sheridan
11/10	a	Connah's Quay	W 1-0	Brown
19/10	h	Port Talbot	W 4-1	Sheridan 2, Connolly 2
24/10	a	Aberystwyth	W 4-0	Sheridan 2, K Smith, M Jones
01/11	h	Rhyl	W 1-0	K Smith
15/11	a	Broughton	L 1-2	Murtagh
21/11	h	Prestatyn	W 4-2	Lunt, Hunt 2, Connolly
06/12	a	Carmarthen	W 2-1	Sheridan, Hunt
13/12	h	Cefn Druids	W 3-1	Hunt, K Smith 2
20/12	a	TNS	L 0-1	

2015

02/01	a	Bangor	W 3-0	Hunt 2, Lunt
05/01	h	Newtown	W 3-1	Sheridan, Connolly, Artell
14/01	h	Bangor	W 3-0	Hunt 2, Sheridan
18/01	a	Port Talbot	L 3-4	Hunt, Connolly, M Jones
28/01	h	Connah's Quay	L 0-1	
01/02	a	Broughton	W 2-1	Hunt, K Smith
14/02	a	Port Talbot	W 3-1	Sheridan, Valentine, Murtagh (p)
21/02	a	Newtown	D 1-1	Connolly
27/02	h	Aberystwyth	D 3-3	Hunt, M Jones, Bell
14/03	a	TNS	L 0-3	
22/03	h	Broughton	W 3-0	M Jones, Connolly, Hunt
28/03	h	Port Talbot	W 4-1	Sheridan, Murtagh, M Jones 2
11/04	h	Newtown	L 1-2	Hunt
17/04	a	Aberystwyth	W 2-1	Hunt, Sheridan
26/04	h	TNS	D 1-1	Sheridan

No	Name	Nat	DoB	Pos	Aps	(s)	Gls
5	David Artell	GIB	22/11/80	D	21	(1)	1
15	Will Bell	ENG	29/09/94	M	30		1
17	Stephen Brown	ENG	11/08/84	M	10	(10)	1
7	Mark Connolly	ENG	02/07/84	M	30		13
16	Tony Davies	ENG	23/11/84	D		(2)	
21	Stephen Fisher	ENG	19/06/73	D		(1)	
9	Mike Hayes	ENG	21/11/87	A	10	(12)	3
18	Lee Hunt	ENG	05/06/82	A	15	(2)	14
8	Mark Jones	ENG	21/08/84	M	21	(7)	6
22	Ryan Jones		17/01/96	M		(3)	
4	Stuart Jones	ENG	28/08/86	D	8		
12	James Kelly	ENG	18/08/94	M	6	(6)	1
20	Kenny Lunt	ENG	20/11/79	M	5	(18)	2
1	Ashley Morris		31/03/84	G	32		
6	Conall Murtagh	NIR	29/06/85	M	29		3
28	Wade Muscat	ENG	15/10/95	A		(2)	
24	Kyle Parle	ENG	24/02/95	M		(2)	
19	Cai Parry		04/11/97	A		(1)	
14	Rob Pearson	ENG	16/11/90	M	31		
10	Ian Sheridan	ENG	12/03/89	A	24	(2)	13
11	Kieran Smith	ENG	06/03/92	A	23	(2)	6
3	Sean Smith	ENG	12/12/94	D	31		
2	Ryan Valentine		19/08/82	D	26	(1)	3
23	Craig Vernon	ENG	07/02/89	G		(1)	

Bangor City FC

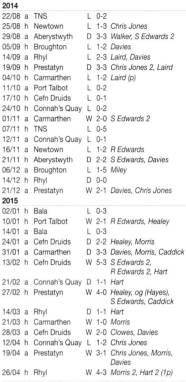

1876 • Nantporth (1,800) • bangorcityfc.com
Major honours
Welsh League (3) 1994, 1995, 2011; Welsh Cup (8) 1889, 1896, 1962, 1998, 2000, 2008, 2009, 2010
Manager: Nev Powell

2014

22/08	a	TNS	L 0-2	
25/08	h	Newtown	L 1-3	Chris Jones
29/08	a	Aberystwyth	D 3-3	Walker, S Edwards 2
05/09	h	Broughton	L 1-2	Davies
14/09	h	Rhyl	L 2-3	Laird, Davies
19/09	h	Prestatyn	D 3-3	Chris Jones 2, Laird
04/10	h	Carmarthen	L 1-2	Laird (p)
11/10	a	Port Talbot	L 0-2	
17/10	h	Cefn Druids	L 0-1	
24/10	h	Connah's Quay	L 0-2	
01/11	a	Carmarthen	W 2-0	S Edwards 2
07/11	h	TNS	L 0-5	
12/11	h	Connah's Quay	L 0-1	
16/11	h	Newtown	L 1-2	R Edwards
21/11	a	Aberystwyth	D 2-2	S Edwards, Davies
06/12	a	Broughton	L 1-5	Miley
14/12	h	Rhyl	D 0-0	
21/12	a	Prestatyn	W 2-1	Davies, Chris Jones

2015

02/01	h	Bala	L 0-3	
10/01	h	Port Talbot	W 2-1	R Edwards, Healey
14/01	a	Bala	L 0-3	
24/01	a	Cefn Druids	D 2-2	Healey, Morris
31/01	a	Carmarthen	D 3-3	Davies, Morris, Caddick
13/02	h	Cefn Druids	W 5-3	S Edwards 2, R Edwards 2, Hart
21/02	a	Connah's Quay	D 1-1	Hart
27/02	h	Prestatyn	W 4-0	Healey, og (Hayes), S Edwards, Caddick
14/03	a	Rhyl	D 1-1	Hart
21/03	h	Carmarthen	W 1-0	Morris
28/03	a	Cefn Druids	W 2-0	Clowes, Davies
12/04	h	Connah's Quay	L 1-2	Chris Jones
19/04	a	Prestatyn	W 3-1	Chris Jones, Morris, Davies
26/04	h	Rhyl	W 4-3	Morris 2, Hart 2 (1p)

No	Name	Nat	DoB	Pos	Aps	(s)	Gls
19	Damien Allen	ENG	01/08/86	M	28		
8	Liam Caddick		01/06/89	A	3	(6)	2
25	Shaun Cavanagh		18/12/97	A		(4)	
26	Leon Clowes	ENG	27/02/92	D	22		1
1	Jack Cudworth	ENG	11/09/90	G	19		
14	Joe Culshaw		03/07/93	D	2	(2)	
9	Les Davies		29/10/84	A	28		7
20	Ryan Edwards		22/06/88	D	32		4
11	Sion Edwards		01/08/87	M	30		8
14	Sam Faulkener		25/09/96	M		(2)	
17	Sam Hart	ENG	29/11/91	D	26		5
18	Lee Healey	ENG	13/08/84	A	11		3
16	Iolo Hughes		12/10/95	D	6		
4	Michael Johnston		16/12/87	D	22	(4)	
7	Chris Jones		09/10/85	M	18	(12)	6
22	Corey Jones		28/11/94	M		(7)	
8	Robert Jones	ENG	23/06/89	M	3	(7)	
18	Jack Laird	ENG	11/11/93	A	5	(7)	3
15	Jamie McDaid		29/03/94	M		(1)	
6	Anthony Miley	ENG	30/08/92	D	21	(6)	1
15	Callum Morris	ENG	12/09/92	M	13		6
10	Jamie Petrie	ENG	15/05/86	A	4	(10)	
3	Chris Roberts		14/08/85	D	20	(1)	
27	Connor Roberts		08/12/92	G	13		
2	Declan Walker	IRL	01/03/92	D	26		1
24	Phil Warrington		21/12/95	M		(6)	

WALES

Carmarthen Town AFC

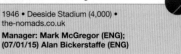

1896 • Richmond Park (3,000) •
carmarthentownafc.com
Major honours
Welsh Cup (1) 2007
Manager: Mark Aizlewood

2014
23/08	h	Rhyl	W	1-0	*Cummings*
25/08	a	Connah's Quay	D	1-1	*Brooks*
29/08	h	Port Talbot	W	2-1	*Harling, L Thomas*
07/09	a	Bala	L	1-8	*Bassett*
13/09	h	Newtown	D	1-1	*Morgan*
21/09	a	Broughton	L	0-2	
27/09	h	Prestatyn	W	3-1	*Prosser 2, Belle (p)*
04/10	a	Bangor	W	2-1	*Prosser, L Thomas*
11/10	h	Cefn Druids	W	3-1	*Brooks, Prosser, Walters*
17/10	h	TNS	L	1-2	*L Thomas*
25/10	a	Prestatyn	W	3-1	*Belle 2 (1p), Brooks*
01/11	h	Bangor	L	0-2	
15/11	h	Connah's Quay	D	1-1	*L Thomas*
23/11	a	Port Talbot	L	0-2	
06/12	h	Bala	L	1-2	*White*
13/12	h	Newtown	W	2-0	*L Thomas, Brooks*
20/12	a	Broughton	W	2-1	*Belle 2*
26/12	h	Aberystwyth	L	1-3	*Prosser*
2015					
01/01	a	Aberystwyth	L	3-5	*Bassett, L Thomas, Prosser*
06/01	a	Rhyl	D	1-1	*Cummings*
10/01	h	Cefn Druids	W	2-1	*Prosser, Hartland*
28/01	a	TNS	L	0-3	
31/01	h	Bangor	D	3-3	*Hartland 3*
14/02	a	Prestatyn	D	1-1	*Belle*
21/02	a	Rhyl	L	0-1	
28/02	h	Connah's Quay	L	2-3	*Fowler, Walters*
14/03	h	Cefn Druids	W	3-1	*Ham, L Thomas, Bassett*
21/03	a	Bangor	L	0-1	
28/03	h	Prestatyn	W	5-2	*L Thomas 2 (1p), Wells, Morgan, Prosser*
11/04	h	Rhyl	L	1-3	*White*
18/04	a	Connah's Quay	L	1-2	*White*
26/04	a	Cefn Druids	W	1-0	*Cummings*

No	Name	Nat	DoB	Pos	Aps	(s)	Gls
11	Kyle Bassett		10/09/88	A	26	(1)	3
4	Cortez Belle	ENG	27/08/83	D	21		6
39	David Brooks		19/05/89	M	12	(5)	4
2	Luke Cummings		25/10/91	D	28	(1)	3
5	Ibrahim Farah		24/01/92	M	1	(1)	
8	Paul Fowler		02/08/85	M	28	(1)	1
16	Clayton Greene		27/02/94	M		(1)	
16	Chris Ham		06/09/92	M	5	(3)	1
3	Craig Hanford		08/07/84	D	28	(3)	
12	Taylor Harding		16/11/92	D	3	(4)	
10	Lewis Harling		11/06/92	M	25	(3)	1
7	Chris Hartland		20/06/90	M	16	(12)	4
1	Lee Idzi		08/02/88	G	32		
15	Jordan Knott		13/09/93	D	13		
19	Hywel Llyr		07/09/95	M		(1)	
14	Ceri Morgan		22/01/91	M	16	(11)	2
9	Luke Prosser		08/01/91	A	11	(9)	8
6	Chris Thomas		16/01/83	D	24		
20	Danny Thomas		13/05/85	M	2	(3)	
18	Liam Thomas		06/11/91	M	27	(1)	9
22	Sacha Walters		20/06/84	A	14	(17)	2
5	Jordan Wells	ENG	18/10/96	D	4	(1)	1
17	Jeff White		18/01/86	A	16	(11)	3

Cefn Druids AFC

1869 • The Rock (2,000) • cefndruidsafc.co.uk
Major honours
Welsh Cup (8) 1880, 1881, 1882, 1885, 1886, 1898, 1899, 1904
**Manager: John Keegan;
(11/04/15) Mark Roberts**

2014
22/08	h	Aberystwyth	L	0-5	
25/08	a	Rhyl	D	1-1	*Taylor*
29/08	h	Connah's Quay	W	3-2	*Donegan, Taylor, Griffiths*
06/09	a	Port Talbot	L	1-4	*Healey*
12/09	h	Bala	L	0-1	
20/09	a	Newtown	L	1-4	*Rimmer*
27/09	a	Broughton	W	3-2	*Donegan, Taylor 2*
04/10	a	Prestatyn	W	4-0	*Noon (p), Edwards 2, Healey*
11/10	h	Carmarthen	L	1-3	*Healey*
17/10	a	Bangor	W	1-0	*Taylor*
26/10	h	Broughton	D	1-1	*Healey*
31/10	h	Prestatyn	W	3-1	*Healey 3*
07/11	a	Aberystwyth	L	2-4	*Donegan, Cadwallader*
14/11	h	Rhyl	L	0-1	
21/11	a	Connah's Quay	D	1-1	*Healey*
06/12	h	Port Talbot	W	2-1	*Healey (p), Kershaw*
13/12	a	Bala	L	1-3	*Taylor*
19/12	h	Newtown	L	0-2	
2015					
01/01	h	TNS	L	0-4	
06/01	a	TNS	L	1-3	*Taylor*
10/01	a	Carmarthen	L	1-2	*Marsh*
24/01	h	Bangor	D	2-2	*Harvey, Marsh*
03/02	a	Connah's Quay	D	0-0	
13/02	a	Bangor	L	3-5	*Marsh, Taylor 2*
20/02	a	Prestatyn	D	1-1	*Donegan*
27/02	h	Rhyl	L	1-2	*Donegan*
14/03	a	Carmarthen	L	1-3	*Culshaw*
21/03	h	Connah's Quay	W	2-0	*Laird, Harvey*
28/03	h	Bangor	L	0-1	
10/04	h	Prestatyn	L	0-1	
18/04	a	Rhyl	L	1-2	*Taylor*
26/04	h	Carmarthen	L	0-1	

No	Name	Nat	DoB	Pos	Aps	(s)	Gls
3	Moses Barnett	SLE	13/12/90	D	7	(2)	
14	Mark Beech	ENG	02/11/94	M	6	(11)	
26	Anthonie Bollan		30/12/94	D	21		6
7	Jonathan Breeze	NIR	22/10/91	M	23	(5)	
5	Bruno Fernandes	GNB	06/11/78	D	28	(1)	
9	Alan Bull		25/11/87	A	9	(7)	
12	Gavin Cadwallader	ENG	18/04/86	D	8	(1)	1
12	Sam Cook	ENG	08/05/95	M		(2)	
16	Joe Culshaw		03/07/93	D	13		1
18	Thomas Donegan	ENG	15/09/92	M	27		5
8	Peter Doran	ENG	30/11/88	M	3	(1)	
3	Phil Doran	ENG	30/11/88	D	6		
11	Oscar Durnin	ENG	16/06/94	A		(3)	
11	Ryan Edwards		25/05/94	M	18	(2)	2
13	Callum Glover		04/02/96	G	1		
32	Louis Gray		11/08/95	G	13		
16	Dan Griffiths	ENG	25/10/94	A	2	(1)	1
8	Neil Harvey	BRB	05/12/94	A	12		2
10	Lee Healey	ENG	13/11/86	A	10	(5)	9
15	Adam Hesp		30/08/91	D	13	(5)	
2	Peter Hoy	ENG	06/05/82	D	11	(2)	
28	Craig Jones		07/11/84	M	18	(4)	
22	Ryan Kershaw	ENG	21/09/95	M	4		1
20	Chris King	ENG	14/11/80	D	5		
9	Jack Laird	ENG	11/11/93	M	3	(6)	1
21	Chris Lynskey	ENG	10/11/94	D	6	(1)	
22	Phil Marsh	ENG	15/11/86	A	9		3
33	Jamie Matthews	ENG	18/06/93	A	4	(3)	
6	Mark McGregor	ENG	16/02/77	D	11	(1)	
34	Joshua Millington		17/04/95	M		(1)	
35	Karl Noon	ENG	15/09/86	A	8	(3)	1
25	Greg Patrick-Mills		17/01/95	D	1	(2)	
23	Liam Randles	ENG	04/11/97	M	1	(7)	
4	Chris Rimmer	ENG	02/07/92	D	25		1
1	David Roberts	ENG	10/12/88	G	18		
17	Derek Taylor	ENG	29/06/92	M	29	(1)	10
26	Chris Whittaker	ENG	08/01/96	A		(1)	

Connah's Quay FC

1946 • Deeside Stadium (4,000) •
the-nomads.co.uk
**Manager: Mark McGregor (ENG);
(07/01/15) Alan Bickerstaffe (ENG)**

2014
22/08	a	Prestatyn	L	2-3	*O'Toole, Holden*
25/08	h	Carmarthen	D	1-1	*Rowntree*
29/08	a	Cefn Druids	L	2-3	*og (Peter Doran), Rainford*
05/09	h	TNS	L	1-5	*Rowlands*
12/09	a	Aberystwyth	D	1-1	*Miller*
19/09	h	Rhyl	L	1-3	*Miller*
05/10	a	Port Talbot	D	1-1	*Miller*
11/10	h	Bala	L	0-1	
18/10	a	Newtown	W	2-1	*Miller, O'Toole*
24/10	a	Bangor	W	2-0	*R Evans, Miller*
01/11	h	Port Talbot	D	1-1	*Horan*
09/11	h	Prestatyn	W	3-1	*R Evans, O'Toole 2*
12/11	h	Bangor	W	1-0	*Miller*
15/11	a	Carmarthen	D	1-1	*S Evans*
21/11	h	Cefn Druids	D	1-1	*O'Toole*
05/12	h	TNS	L	0-2	
12/12	a	Aberystwyth	L	2-4	*S Evans, R Evans (p)*
20/12	a	Rhyl	D	1-1	*Rowntree*
26/12	a	Broughton	L	0-4	
2015					
01/01	h	Broughton	L	0-3	
24/01	h	Newtown	L	2-3	*Fraughan, Rowlands*
28/01	a	Bala	W	1-0	*og (Morris)*
03/02	h	Cefn Druids	D	0-0	
14/02	h	Rhyl	D	1-1	*Ukuno*
21/02	h	Bangor	D	1-1	*R Jones*
28/02	a	Carmarthen	W	3-2	*Courtney 2, og (Hanford)*
13/03	a	Prestatyn	W	4-3	*Ukuno 2, Miller, Crowther*
21/03	a	Cefn Druids	L	0-2	
28/03	a	Rhyl	W	2-1	*S Evans, Miller*
12/04	a	Bangor	W	2-1	*Fraughan (p), Miller*
18/04	a	Carmarthen	W	2-1	*Forbes, Horan*
26/04	h	Prestatyn	W	3-1	*Bull 2, Fraughan*

No	Name	Nat	DoB	Pos	Aps	(s)	Gls
10	Cortez Belle	ENG	27/08/83	D	3		
40	Thomas Bibby		17/03/98	M		(4)	
11	Alan Bull	ENG	25/11/87	A	8	(3)	2
15	Niki-Lee Bulmer		06/09/91	G	1		
31	Jack Chambers		31/10/97	D		(6)	
33	Jack Cheetham		18/11/94	D		(1)	
7	James Colbeck	ENG	05/08/93	A	3		
18	Jack Cookson	ENG	08/10/94	G		(1)	
46	Sean Cookson	ENG	12/12/94	M	1	(2)	
6	Russell Courtney	ENG	10/11/85	D	9	(1)	2
4	Jamie Crowther		10/02/92	M	9		1
20	John Dillon	ENG	02/08/88	M	15	(1)	
10	Ricky Evans		24/09/76	M	16	(2)	3
4	Steve Evans		26/02/79	D	22	(1)	3
7	David Forbes	ENG	07/08/84	A	6	(3)	1
16	Ryan Fraughan	ENG	11/02/91	A	10	(1)	3
39	Kieron Gaul	ENG	30/06/97	M		(1)	
3	Marcus Giglio		01/09/92	D	8	(12)	
21	Danny Harrison	ENG	04/11/82	D	11		
11	Luke Holden	ENG	24/11/88	A	5	(1)	1
5	George Horan	ENG	19/02/82	D	27		2
6	Craig Jones	ENG	07/11/84	M	1	(1)	
8	Robert Jones		23/09/89	M	9	(2)	1
25	Terry McCormick	ENG	25/08/83	G	31		
4	Mark McGregor	ENG	16/02/77	D	17	(1)	
28	Kevin McIntyre	ENG	23/12/77	D	30		
17	Sean Miller	ENG	09/05/95	M	30	(1)	9
53	Ben Nash	ENG	23/07/98	D	1	(1)	
9	Gary O'Toole	ENG	29/01/87	A	15	(2)	5
16	Kyle Parle	ENG	24/02/95	M		(1)	
8	Jamie Rainford	ENG	21/02/88	A	2	(2)	1
47	Jack Riley		06/03/97	M	12		
24	Gary Roberts	ENG	04/02/87	M	13		
12	Jack Rowlands	ENG	11/09/89	D	10	(7)	2
2	Chris Rowntree		14/04/88	D	15	(2)	2
38	Anthony Stanton	ENG	21/08/96	M	7	(6)	
27	Apai Ukuno	LBY	31/08/91	M	5		3

Newtown AFC

1875 • Latham Park (6,000) •
newtownafc.co.uk
Major honours
Welsh Cup (2) 1879, 1895
Manager: Chris Hughes

2014
23/08	h	Bala	L	1-2	Oswell
25/08	a	Bangor	W	3-1	Boundford, Price, Oswell
29/08	a	Broughton	L	0-3	
06/09	h	Prestatyn	W	4-3	Oswell 2, og (Hayes), Boundford
13/09	a	Carmarthen	D	1-1	Mitchell
20/09	h	Cefn Druids	W	4-1	Oswell, Williams, Hearsey, og (Rimmer)
28/09	a	TNS	D	1-1	Sutton
04/10	h	Aberystwyth	W	6-3	Oswell 2, Boundford 3, Hearsey
12/10	a	Rhyl	D	2-2	Mitchell, Oswell
18/10	h	Connah's Quay	L	1-2	og (McCormick)
25/10	h	TNS	L	2-3	Oswell, Hearsey
31/10	a	Aberystwyth	L	0-1	
16/11	h	Bangor	W	2-1	Boundford, Oswell
22/11	h	Broughton	W	1-0	Williams (p)
06/12	a	Prestatyn	D	2-2	Oswell, Sutton
13/12	a	Carmarthen	L	0-2	
19/12	a	Cefn Druids	W	2-0	Hearsey, Oswell
26/12	a	Port Talbot	L	0-2	

2015
01/01	h	Port Talbot	D	3-3	Mitchell, Owen, Boundford
05/01	a	Bala	L	1-3	Evans
11/01	h	Rhyl	W	1-0	Mitchell
24/01	a	Connah's Quay	W	3-2	Oswell, Boundford, Goodwin
31/01	a	Aberystwyth	L	2-3	Boundford, Price (p)
14/02	h	TNS	D	0-0	
21/02	h	Bala	D	1-1	Oswell
28/02	a	Port Talbot	L	0-4	
14/03	h	Broughton	L	0-2	
21/03	a	Aberystwyth	D	3-3	Williams, Oswell, Hearsey
27/03	a	TNS	L	2-4	Oswell, Owen (p)
11/04	a	Bala	W	2-1	Boundford, Oswell
18/04	h	Port Talbot	L	1-3	Oswell
26/04	a	Broughton	L	1-6	Hearsey

No	Name	Nat	DoB	Pos	Aps	(s)	Gls
9	Luke Boundford		30/01/88	D	29	(2)	10
16	Gavin Cadwallader	ENG	18/04/86	D	6		
8	Matthew Cook	ENG	07/09/85	M	15	(4)	
17	David Easthope	ENG	27/12/95	M		(4)	
3	Stefan Edwards		10/10/89	D	31		
18	Sean Evans		25/09/87	M	9	(11)	1
20	Tom Goodwin		12/01/90	M	25	(2)	1
24	Craig Peter Harris	ENG	15/04/96	M		(3)	
7	Matthew Hearsey	ENG	25/02/91	A	28	(3)	6
16	Alex Hughes	ENG	25/03/94	A		(9)	
1	David Jones		03/02/92	G	31		
5	Kieran Mills-Evans	ENG	11/10/92	D	13	(1)	
11	Neil Mitchell	ENG	01/04/88	A	26	(1)	4
10	Jason Oswell	ENG	07/10/92	A	29	(2)	18
4	Matty Owen	ENG	23/06/94	M	28	(3)	2
14	Gareth Partridge		26/09/91	M	4	(5)	
12	Max Penk		17/02/93	D	5	(5)	
13	Jack Perry	ENG	31/10/97	G	1	(1)	
26	Jamie Petrie	ENG	15/05/86	A	6	(3)	
15	Jamie Price	ENG	22/07/88	M	8	(13)	2
6	Shane Sutton		31/01/89	D	26		2
2	Ashley Wells	ENG	26/01/93	D	3	(2)	
19	Craig Williams		21/12/87	M	29	(1)	3

Port Talbot Town FC

1901 • GenQuip stadium (3,000) •
porttalbottown.co.uk
**Manager: Jarred Harvey;
(26/02/15) Bernard McNally (ENG);
(10/03/15) Andy Dyer**

2014
25/08	h	Prestatyn	W	3-0	Rose, Lewis, McCreesh
29/08	a	Carmarthen	L	1-2	Sheehan
06/09	h	Cefn Druids	W	4-1	Rose 2 (1p), Bowen 2
13/09	a	TNS	L	0-2	
19/09	a	Aberystwyth	L	1-2	Rose
27/09	a	Rhyl	W	3-0	Lewis 2, C Evans
05/10	a	Connah's Quay	D	1-1	Griffiths
08/10	a	Broughton	L	0-3	
11/10	h	Bangor	W	2-0	Rose 2 (1p)
19/10	a	Bala	L	1-4	Bond
25/10	a	Rhyl	W	3-0	Bowen 2, Griffiths
01/11	a	Connah's Quay	D	1-1	Rose
08/11	a	Broughton	W	2-0	Griffiths (p), Corey Thomas
15/11	a	Prestatyn	L	1-2	Rose
23/11	a	Carmarthen	W	2-0	McCreesh, Bowen
06/12	a	Cefn Druids	L	1-2	Bowen
12/12	h	TNS	L	1-5	Corey Thomas
20/12	a	Aberystwyth	W	3-0	Rose 3 (1p)
26/12	h	Newtown	W	2-0	Lewis, Bowen

2015
01/01	a	Newtown	D	3-3	Bowen 2, Rose
10/01	a	Bangor	L	1-2	Bowen
18/01	a	Bala	W	4-3	Rose 2, Bond, Corey Thomas
31/01	a	TNS	L	0-6	
14/02	h	Bala	L	1-3	Bowen
21/02	a	Broughton	L	0-5	
28/02	h	Newtown	W	4-0	Surman, McCreesh, Rose 2
13/03	a	Aberystwyth	D	2-2	Bowen, Bond
21/03	h	TNS	L	1-3	McCreesh
28/03	a	Bala	L	1-4	Bowen
11/04	a	Broughton	W	1-0	McCreesh
18/04	a	Newtown	W	3-1	Rose 2, McCreesh
26/04	h	Aberystwyth	L	1-2	Bowen

No	Name	Nat	DoB	Pos	Aps	(s)	Gls
11	Jason Bertorelli		04/03/86	A	2	(8)	
25	Matthew Birdsley		05/11/95	D		(3)	
18	Chad Bond		20/04/87	M	20	(4)	3
17	Luke Borrelli		28/03/91	A		(2)	
10	Luke Bowen		07/03/88	A	31		14
13	Steve Cann		20/01/88	G	29		
12	Leigh De-Vulgt		10/03/81	D	13	(2)	
4	Ashley Evans		18/07/89	M	27		
5	Carl Evans		13/06/86	D	9	(1)	1
17	Kostya Georgievsky	NIR	28/06/96	A		(3)	
26	Rhys Griffiths		01/03/80	A	11	(7)	3
15	Lendl Guest	ZIM	12/09/89	M		(2)	
7	Chris Jones		02/09/89	M	12		
14	Kieron Lewis		26/06/93	M	24	(5)	4
8	Liam McCreesh		09/09/85	M	26		6
1	Conah McFenton		18/05/96	G	3		
19	Laurent Mondo		18/09/94	M		(2)	
3	James Parry		27/05/95	D	17	(5)	
19	Nikki Parvin		08/05/95	M	1	(2)	
15	Keyon Reffel		06/10/90	M	13	(1)	
9	Martin Rose	ENG	29/02/84	A	29	(1)	18
16	Duane Saunders	ENG	22/09/86	M		(3)	
22	Dan Sheehan		22/12/90	D	20	(2)	1
6	Lee Surman		03/04/86	D	30		1
16	Casey Thomas		14/11/90	A	5	(6)	
2	Corey Thomas		30/11/89	D	22		3
20	Kieran Williams		08/10/96	M	8	(4)	

Prestatyn Town FC

1910 • Bastion Gardens (3,000) •
ptfconline.co.uk
Major honours
Welsh Cup (1) 2013
Manager: Neil Gibson

2014
22/08	h	Connah's Quay	W	3-2	J Lewis, Parker, Parkinson
25/08	a	Port Talbot	L	0-3	
30/08	a	Bala	D	3-3	Stephens, J Lewis, Parkinson
06/09	a	Newtown	L	3-4	Hunt 2, Stead
13/09	h	Broughton	L	0-2	
19/09	a	Bangor	D	3-3	Hunt, Pritchard, J Lewis
27/09	a	Carmarthen	L	1-3	Parkinson
04/10	a	Cefn Druids	L	0-4	
11/10	a	TNS	L	0-6	
18/10	a	Aberystwyth	W	2-1	Parker, Hayes
25/10	a	Carmarthen	L	1-3	og (Belle)
31/10	a	Cefn Druids	L	1-3	Parkinson
09/11	a	Connah's Quay	L	1-3	J Lewis
15/11	h	Port Talbot	W	2-1	Pritchard, Davies
21/11	a	Bala	L	2-4	Weaver, J Lewis
06/12	h	Newtown	D	2-2	Pritchard, Davies
13/12	a	Broughton	L	1-2	Parkinson
21/12	a	Bangor	L	1-2	Davies
27/12	a	Rhyl	D	2-2	Z Edwards, og (Benson)

2015
02/01	h	Rhyl	L	1-2	Weaver
10/01	h	TNS	L	1-3	Davies
17/01	a	Aberystwyth	L	1-3	Pritchard
30/01	a	Rhyl	L	1-2	Parker
14/02	a	Carmarthen	D	1-1	Parker
20/02	a	Cefn Druids	D	1-1	Jones
27/02	a	Bangor	L	0-4	
13/03	h	Connah's Quay	L	3-4	Parker 2 (1p), Beattie
20/03	a	Rhyl	L	1-2	Parker
28/03	a	Carmarthen	L	2-5	J Lewis, Parker
10/04	a	Cefn Druids	W	1-0	Parker (p)
19/04	a	Bangor	L	1-3	Beattie
26/04	a	Connah's Quay	L	1-3	Parkinson

No	Name	Nat	DoB	Pos	Aps	(s)	Gls
10	Lee Beattie		18/08/88	M	4	(4)	2
21	Ben Cawley	ENG	11/09/93	M		(3)	
18	Jordan Davies		16/11/95	M	23	(6)	4
24	Ryan Dean		08/07/95	D	5	(3)	
28	Noah Edwards		30/05/97	M	1	(4)	
19	Zyaac Edwards		30/05/97	M	15	(5)	1
27	Jon Fisher-Cooke		13/05/82	M		(4)	
8	Neil Gibson		11/10/79	M		(1)	
21	Steve Harris	NIR	05/02/86	A		(3)	
4	David Hayes		15/01/82	D	30		1
10	Lee Hunt	ENG	06/06/82	A	5	(1)	4
11	Alex Jones		04/08/94	M	8		1
2	Tom Kemp		30/12/94	D	7	(4)	
14	Dale Lee		23/12/92	M	16	(3)	
3	Jack Lewis		18/05/88	D	32		6
15	Rhys Lewis		21/04/94	M	4	(3)	
27	Ben Maher		28/09/95	D	13	(2)	
20	Joe Newell		17/04/98	A		(1)	
20	Rhys Owen		10/06/93	M	4	(1)	
7	Michael Parker		31/10/87	M	31		9
9	Andy Parkinson	ENG	27/05/79	M	28	(2)	6
16	Michael Pritchard		10/12/91	A	16	(5)	4
23	Connor Shackleton		17/02/96	M		(2)	
12	James Stead		18/05/94	D	20	(5)	1
11	Ross Stephens		28/05/85	M	19	(1)	1
23	Greg Stones	ENG	04/05/82	D	4	(1)	
17	Liam Walsh		28/07/96	M	5	(1)	
22	Ross Weaver		31/01/96	M	18	(4)	2
26	Scott Williams		02/12/94	G	25		
6	Gareth Wilson		23/05/78	M	12	(4)	
1	Kieran Wolland	ENG	02/01/96	G	7	(1)	

Rhyl FC

1879 • Belle Vue Stadium (3,000) • rhylfc.co.uk
Major honours
Welsh League (2) 2004, 2009; Welsh Cup (4) 1952, 1953, 2004, 2006
Manager: Greg Strong (ENG)

2014

23/08	a	Carmarthen	L	0-1	
25/08	h	Cefn Druids	D	1-1	Dawson
29/08	a	TNS	L	1-6	Forbes
07/09	h	Aberystwyth	L	0-1	
14/09	h	Bangor	W	3-2	Bowen 3
19/09	a	Connah's Quay	W	3-1	Dawson, Walsh, Makin
27/09	a	Port Talbot	L	0-3	
03/10	a	Bala	W	2-1	Bowen, Astles
12/10	h	Newtown	D	2-2	Bowen, Dawson
18/10	a	Broughton	L	1-2	Bowen
25/10	h	Port Talbot	L	0-3	
01/11	h	Bala	L	0-1	
14/11	a	Cefn Druids	W	1-0	Cadwallader
22/11	h	TNS	D	2-2	Halewood, Stott
07/12	a	Aberystwyth	L	0-2	
14/12	a	Bangor	D	0-0	
20/12	h	Connah's Quay	D	1-1	og (McGregor)
27/12	h	Prestatyn	D	2-2	Astles, Stott

2015

02/01	a	Prestatyn	W	2-1	Kenny, og (Hayes)
06/01	h	Carmarthen	D	1-1	Astles
11/01	a	Newtown	L	0-1	
24/01	h	Broughton	L	1-2	Hughes
30/01	h	Prestatyn	W	2-1	Astles, Kenny
14/02	a	Connah's Quay	D	1-1	Cadwallader (p)
21/02	h	Carmarthen	W	1-0	Ruane
27/02	a	Cefn Druids	W	2-1	Cadwallader, Ruane
14/03	h	Bangor	D	1-1	Gossett
20/03	a	Prestatyn	W	2-1	Lamb, Walsh
28/03	a	Connah's Quay	L	1-2	Ruane
11/04	a	Carmarthen	W	3-1	Ruane, Astles, Hughes
18/04	a	Cefn Druids	W	2-1	Kenny, McManus (p)
26/04	a	Bangor	L	3-4	Ruane, Kenny, McManus (p)

No	Name	Nat	DoB	Pos	Aps	(s)	Gls
40	Michael Askew	ENG	15/08/96	G	3		
14	Ryan Astles	ENG	01/07/94	D	28		5
3	Liam Benson	ENG	25/02/92	D	14		
9	Aaron Bowen	ENG	30/03/91	A	19	(1)	6
5	Jamie Brewerton		17/11/79	D	9		
25	Mark Cadwallader	ENG	08/07/88	M	14	(6)	3
17	Regan Carthey		01/09/95	A		(1)	
7	Liam Dawson	ENG	12/01/91	A	16	(8)	3
10	Lloyd Ellams	ENG	11/01/91	A	1	(2)	
17	David Forbes	ENG	07/08/88	A	7	(7)	1
18	Danny Gossett		30/09/94	A	13	(2)	1
5	Stefan Halewood	ENG	19/05/98	D	13		1
22	Robert Hughes		22/04/92	M	13	(5)	2
15	Gerwyn Jones		18/01/91	D	1	(2)	
32	Jack Kenny	ENG	14/10/91	A	6	(13)	4
41	Carl Lamb	ENG	10/11/84	A	7	(4)	1
16	Levi Makin	ENG	04/04/86	A	26		1
24	John McKenna	ENG	15/05/90	A	13		
8	Paul McManus	ENG	22/04/90	M	16		2
4	Paul O'Neill	ENG	17/06/82	D		(1)	
6	Mark Powell	ENG	08/05/75	D		(1)	
1	Alex Ramsay		15/07/93	G	29		
11	Tom Rowlands	ENG	28/10/85	A	7	(6)	
12	Ashley Ruane	ENG	26/06/85	A	9	(1)	5
10	Greg Stones	ENG	04/05/82	D	15	(3)	
19	Ashley Stott	ENG	14/06/88	A	11	(9)	2
27	Dave Thompson	ENG	27/02/91	M	21	(5)	
34	Michael Walsh	ENG	30/05/86	M	16	(6)	2
17	Julian Williams		03/04/95	A	1		
2	Matty Woodward	ENG	14/06/83	D	24		

The New Saints FC

1959 • The Venue (3,000) • tnsfc.co.uk
Major honours
Welsh League (9) 2000, 2005, 2006, 2007, 2010, 2012, 2013, 2014, 2015; Welsh Cup (5) 1996, 2005, 2012, 2014, 2015
Manager: Craig Harrison (ENG)

2014

22/08	h	Bangor	W	2-0	Draper, Finley
25/08	a	Aberystwyth	D	1-1	Finley
29/08	h	Rhyl	W	6-1	Draper 2, Finley, Darlington, Cieślewicz, A Edwards
05/09	a	Connah's Quay	W	5-1	Cieślewicz, Darlington, Draper 2, Seargeant
13/09	h	Port Talbot	W	2-0	Darlington (p), Draper
19/09	a	Bala	W	3-0	Fraughan, Finley, A Edwards
28/09	h	Newtown	D	1-1	A Edwards
04/10	a	Broughton	W	3-2	Cieślewicz, Wilde 2
11/10	h	Prestatyn	W	6-0	Williams, Wilde 2, Cieślewicz, Darlington, og (Weaver)
17/10	a	Carmarthen	W	2-1	Wilde, A Edwards
25/10	a	Newtown	W	3-2	A Edwards, Wilde, Seargeant
02/11	h	Broughton	D	1-1	Wilde
07/11	a	Bangor	W	5-0	A Edwards, Quigley, K Edwards, Wilde, Cieślewicz
14/11	h	Aberystwyth	D	1-1	Draper
22/11	h	Rhyl	D	2-2	Draper, Seargeant
05/12	a	Connah's Quay	W	2-0	Seargeant (p), Wilde
12/12	a	Port Talbot	W	5-1	Mullan 2, Marriott, Wilde, K Edwards
20/12	a	Bala	W	1-0	Darlington

2015

01/01	a	Cefn Druids	W	4-0	Draper 2, Rawlinson, Cieślewicz
06/01	h	Cefn Druids	W	3-1	Wilde, Cieślewicz, K Edwards
10/01	a	Prestatyn	W	3-1	Quigley, Reed, Williams
28/01	h	Carmarthen	W	3-0	Quigley, Reed, Draper
31/01	h	Port Talbot	W	6-0	Draper 2, Quigley 2, Rawlinson, Mullan
14/02	a	Newtown	D	0-0	
22/02	a	Aberystwyth	W	4-0	Cieślewicz, Wilde 2, Williams
01/03	h	Broughton	W	2-0	Williams, Cieślewicz
14/03	h	Bala	W	3-0	Cieślewicz, Williams 2
21/03	a	Port Talbot	W	3-1	Wilde 2, Rawlinson
27/03	h	Newtown	W	4-2	Draper 4
10/04	h	Aberystwyth	D	3-3	Reed, Quigley, Wilde
18/04	a	Broughton	L	0-1	
26/04	a	Bala	D	1-1	Reed

No	Name	Nat	DoB	Pos	Aps	(s)	Gls
4	Phil Baker	ENG	04/11/82	D	22	(1)	
21	Adrian Cieślewicz	POL	16/11/90	M	26	(2)	10
20	Alex Darlington		26/12/88	A	10	(8)	5
9	Greg Draper	NZL	13/08/89	A	17	(7)	17
23	Aeron Edwards		16/02/88	M	29	(1)	6
6	Kai Edwards		29/01/91	D	30		3
17	Ryan Edwards		25/05/94	M	3	(2)	
8	Sam Finley	ENG	04/08/92	M	8	(2)	4
11	Ryan Fraughan	ENG	11/02/91	M	8	(1)	1
1	Paul Harrison	ENG	18/12/84	G	29		
24	Ryan Kershaw	ENG	21/09/95	M		(1)	
3	Chris Marriott	ENG	24/09/89	D	30		1
14	Jamie Mullan	ENG	10/02/88	A	11	(8)	3
25	Chris Mullock		16/09/88	G	3	(1)	
32	Ryan Pryce	ENG	30/06/97	D	5	(1)	
22	Scott Quigley	ENG	02/09/92	A	14	(14)	6
16	Connell Rawlinson		22/09/91	D	26	(3)	3
19	Jamie Reed		13/08/87	A	5	(4)	4
7	Scott Ruscoe	ENG	15/12/77	M	1	(1)	
12	Christian Seargeant	ENG	13/09/86	M	15	(9)	4
2	Simon Spender		15/11/85	D	29		
18	Michael Wilde	ENG	27/08/83	A	18	(6)	16
10	Matty Williams		05/11/82	A	13	(9)	6

Top goalscorers

28	Chris Venables (Aberystwyth)
18	Jason Oswell (Newtown)
	Martin Rose (Port Talbot)
17	Lee Hunt (Prestatyn/Bala)
	Greg Draper (TNS)
16	Tom Field (Broughton)
	Michael Wilde (TNS)
14	Luke Bowen (Port Talbot)
13	Mark Connolly (Bala)
	Ian Sheridan (Bala)

UEFA Europa League qualification play-offs

SEMI-FINALS

(09/05/15)
Port Talbot 0-1 Newtown *(Boundford 120) (aet)*

(10/05/15)
Aberystwyth 3-2 Connah's Quay *(Venables 19p, S Evans 84og, M Jones 90; Miller 15, S Evans 69)*

FINAL

(17/05/15)
Aberystwyth 1-2 Newtown *(Venables 28p; Goodwin 9, Hearsey 43)*

Promoted clubs

Llandudno FC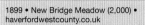

1878 • Maesdu Park (1,013) •
pitchero.com/clubs/llandudno
Manager: Alan Morgan

Haverfordwest County AFC

1899 • New Bridge Meadow (2,000) •
haverfordwestcounty.co.uk
Manager: Wayne Jones

Second level final tables 2014/15

North		Pld	W	D	L	F	A	Pts
1	Llandudno FC	30	22	5	3	96	27	71
2	Caernarfon Town FC	30	20	6	4	82	25	66
3	Guilsfield FC	30	19	6	5	68	33	63
4	Buckley Town FC	30	15	7	8	69	47	52
5	Holyhead Hotspur FC	30	15	6	9	49	38	51
6	CPD Porthmadog FC	30	15	5	10	63	35	50
7	Denbigh Town FC	30	14	6	10	54	51	48
8	Caersws FC	30	13	8	9	61	47	47
9	Mold Alexandra FC	30	13	5	12	58	49	44
10	Flint Town United FC	30	13	5	12	39	45	44
11	Conwy Borough FC	30	12	5	13	52	46	41
12	Rhayader Town FC	30	8	6	16	42	53	30
13	Llanidloes Town FC	30	8	5	17	55	78	29
14	Penycae FC	30	6	4	20	46	78	22
15	Llandrindod Wells FC	30	5	3	22	32	103	18
16	Rhydymwyn FC	30	1	0	29	21	132	0

NB Rhydymwyn FC – 3 pts deducted.

South		Pld	W	D	L	F	A	Pts
1	Caerau (Ely) FC	30	21	5	4	75	39	68
2	Haverfordwest County AFC	30	19	6	5	69	32	63
3	Cardiff Metropolitan University FC	30	19	6	5	57	20	63
4	Goytre United AFC	30	16	8	6	74	41	56
5	Penybont FC	30	17	5	8	73	52	56
6	Monmouth Town FC	30	16	3	11	57	35	51
7	Briton Ferry Llansawel AFC	30	13	9	8	52	37	48
8	Taffs Well AFC	30	15	2	13	61	45	47
9	Ton Pentre AFC	30	12	4	14	44	54	40
10	Goytre AFC	30	11	3	16	46	47	36
11	Aberdare Town FC	30	10	5	15	48	68	35
12	Garden Village AFC	30	8	10	12	49	61	34
13	Afan Lido FC	30	9	6	15	40	60	33
14	Cambrian & Clydach Vale BGC	30	7	7	16	45	46	28
15	Pontardawe Town FC	30	4	6	20	28	66	18
16	AFC Porth	30	0	1	29	16	131	1

NB Caerau (Ely) FC did not obtain licence for Premier League; Haverfordwest County AFC promoted instead.

DOMESTIC CUP

Welsh Cup 2014/15

THIRD ROUND

(29/11/14)
Afan Lido 0-3 Llanrhaeadr
Bala 2-1 Port Talbot
Bangor 1-0 Garden Village
Broughton 5-0 Haverfordwest
Buckley 0-1 Holywell
Cardiff Metropolitan 4-1 Prestatyn
Cefn Druids 1-5 Aberystwyth
Conwy 4-3 Briton Ferry Llansawel
Connah's Quay 5-3 Monmouth
Gresford 5-0 St Asaph
Newtown 2-0 Nomads
Penrhyncoch 0-5 Caerau (Ely)
Rhyl 2-1 Goytre United
Tiger Bay 0-4 Caersws

(30/11/14)
Caernarfon 2-3 TNS
Undy 2-4 Carmarthen

FOURTH ROUND

(07/02/15)
Bangor 3-0 Conwy
Caerau (Ely) 0-4 Carmarthen *(aet)*
Cardiff Metropolitan 1-4 Broughton
Connah's Quay 2-2 Bala *(aet; 4-2 on pens)*
Holywell 0-0 Aberystwyth *(aet; 2-3 on pens)*
Llanrhaeadr 2-4 Rhyl

(08/02/15)
TNS 3-0 Gresford

(10/02/15)
Caersws 2-3 Newtown

QUARTER-FINALS

(07/03/15)
Aberystwyth 1-1 Broughton *(C Williams 93; Wignall 96) (aet; 2-4 on pens)*

Bangor 1-2 Newtown *(Morris 45; Owen 49, 67)*

Connah's Quay 0-1 TNS *(Quigley 29)*

(08/03/15)
Carmarthen 1-2 Rhyl *(Belle 67p; Cadwallader 4, Ruane 30)*

SEMI-FINALS

(04/04/15)
Newtown 2-1 Rhyl *(Oswell 54, Owen 71; Astles 3)*

(05/04/15)
TNS 4-2 Broughton *(Cieślewicz 43, Wilde 63, 90, Quigley 90+2; Barrow 47, Riley 87)*

FINAL

(02/05/15)
Latham Park, Newtown
THE NEW SAINTS FC 2 *(Williams 53, 84p)*
NEWTOWN AFC 0
Referee: *John*
TNS: *Harrison, Spender, Marriott, Baker, Rawlinson (Seargeant 10), K Edwards, Williams, Cieślewicz (Quigley 71), A Edwards, Mullan, Wilde (Draper 87)*
NEWTOWN: *Jones, Edwards, Mills-Evans, Sutton, Boundford, Owen, Cook (Hearsey 88), Williams, Goodwin, Oswell, Mitchell (Evans 78)*

TNS lift the Welsh Cup after defeating Newtown 2-0 in the final

National team

UEFA EURO 2016

03-08/09/2015	Qualifying round matches
08-13/10/2015	Qualifying round matches
18/10/2015	Play-off draw (Nyon, Switzerland)
12-17/11/2015	Play-off round matches
12/12/2015	Final tournament draw (Paris, France)
10/06-10/07/2016	Final tournament (France)

2017 UEFA European Under-21 Championship

31/08-08/09/2015	Qualifying round matches
05-13/10/2015	Qualifying round matches
09-17/11/2015	Qualifying round matches
21-29/03/2016	Qualifying round matches

Club

2015/16 UEFA Champions League

27/08/2015	Group stage draw (Monaco)
15-16/09/2015	Group stage, Matchday 1
29-30/09/2015	Group stage, Matchday 2
20-21/10/2015	Group stage, Matchday 3
03-04/11/2015	Group stage, Matchday 4
24-25/11/2015	Group stage, Matchday 5
08-09/12/2015	Group stage, Matchday 6
14/12/2015	Round of 16 draw (Nyon, Switzerland)
16-17/02/2016	Round of 16, first leg
23-24/02/2016	Round of 16, first leg
08-09/03/2016	Round of 16, second leg
15-16/03/2016	Round of 16, second leg
18/03/2016	Quarter-final draw (Nyon, Switzerland)
05-06/04/2016	Quarter-finals, first leg
12-13/04/2016	Quarter-finals, second leg
15/04/2016	Semi-final and Final draw (Nyon, Switzerland)
26-27/04/2016	Semi-final, first leg
03-04/05/2016	Semi-final, second leg
28/05/2016	Final (Milan, Italy)

28/08/2015	Group stage draw (Monaco)
17/09/2015	Group stage, Matchday 1
01/10/2015	Group stage, Matchday 2
22/10/2015	Group stage, Matchday 3
05/11/2015	Group stage, Matchday 4
26/11/2015	Group stage, Matchday 5
10/12/2015	Group stage, Matchday 6
14/12/2015	Round of 32 draw (Nyon, Switzerland)
18/02/2016	Round of 32, first leg
25/02/2016	Round of 32, second leg
26/02/2016	Round of 16 draw (Nyon, Switzerland)
10/03/2016	Round of 16, first leg
17/03/2016	Round of 16, second leg
18/03/2016	Quarter-final draw (Nyon, Switzerland)
07/04/2016	Quarter-finals, first leg
14/04/2016	Quarter-finals, second leg
15/04/2016	Semi-final and Final draw (Nyon, Switzerland)
28/04/2016	Semi-final, first leg
05/05/2016	Semi-final, second leg
18/05/2016	Final (Basel, Switzerland)

2015/16 UEFA Youth League

27/08/2015	Group stage draw (Monaco)
01/09/2015	Domestic champions path draw (Nyon)
15-16/09/2015	Group stage, Matchday 1
29-30/09/2015	Group stage, Matchday 2
30/09/2015	Round 1, Domestic champions path, first leg matches
20-21/10/2015	Group stage, Matchday 3
21/10/2015	Round 1, Domestic champions path, second leg matches
03-04/11/2015	Group stage, Matchday 4
25/11/2015	Round 2, Domestic champions path, first leg matches
24-25/11/2015	Group stage, Matchday 5
04/11/2015	Round 2, Domestic champions path, second leg matches
08-09/12/2015	Group stage, Matchday 6
14/12/2015	Knockout play-off round draw (Nyon, Switzerland)
08-09/02/2016	Knockout play-off round matches
15/02/2016	Knockout round draw (Nyon, Switzerland)
23-24/02/2016	Round of 16 matches
08-09/03/2016	Quarter-final matches
15-18/04/2016	Final Four (Nyon, Switzerland)

2015 FIFA Club World Cup

10-20/12/2015	Final tournament (Morocco)

Youth & Amateur

2015/16 UEFA European Under-19 Championship

18/09-18/11/2015	Qualifying round matches
03/12/2015	Elite round draw (Nyon, Switzerland)
01/03-31/05/2016	Elite round matches
tbd	Final tournament draw (Stuttgart, Germany)
11-24/07/2016	Final tournament (Germany)

2016/17 UEFA European Under-19 Championship

03/12/2015	Qualifying round draw (Nyon, Switzerland)

2015/16 UEFA European Under-17 Championship

22/09-31/10/2015	Qualifying round matches
03/12/2015	Elite round draw (Nyon, Switzerland)
01-31/03/2016	Elite round matches
06/04/2016	Final tournament draw (Baku, Azerbaijan)
05-21/05/2016	Final tournament (Azerbaijan)

2016/17 UEFA European Under-17 Championship

03/12/2015	Qualifying round draw (Nyon, Switzerland)

03/12/2015	Preliminary and Intermediary round draw (Nyon, Switzerland)